Hôtels de France

THE ROUGH GUIDE

le guide du ROUTARD

Rough Guides and France

In addition to this guide to French hotels and restaurants, Rough Guides publish five guidebooks on France:

France • Brittany & Normandy
Provence & the Côte d'Azur • Paris
The Pyrenees (French and Spanish)

There is also a
Rough Guide French phrasebook

Credits

Routard
Directeur de collection: Philippe Gloaguen
Rédacteur: Amanda Gaumont

Rough Guides
Managing editor: Jonathan Buckley
Series editor: Mark Ellingham
Typesetting: Link Hall, Helen Ostick
Production: Susanne Hillen, Maxine Burke, Judy Pang
Design: Henry Iles

Lexus
Editor-in-chief: Jane Goldie
Editors: Céline Reynaud, Peter Terrell, Sophie Curien, Alice Grandison
Translators: Jane Goldie, Lesley Harkins, Sarah Cartwright, David Alun Jones, Anita Leyerzapf

---

Distributed by the Penguin Group:
Penguin Books Ltd, 27 Wrights Lane, London W8 5TZ
Penguin Books USA Inc., 375 Hudson Street, New York 10014, USA
Penguin Books Australia Ltd, 487 Maroondah Highway, PO Box 257, Ringwood, Victoria 3134, Australia
Penguin Books Canada Ltd, 10 Alcorn Avenue, Toronto, Ontario, Canada M4V 1E4
Penguin Books (NZ) Ltd, 182–190 Wairau Road, Auckland 10, New Zealand

880pp, includes index
A catalogue record for this book is available from the British Library.
ISBN 1-85828-306-X

Printed in England by Clays Ltd, St Ives PLC

Hôtels & Restos de France

THE ROUGH GUIDE

le guide du ROUTARD

ENGLISH EDITION
1998–99

LE GUIDE DU ROUTARD
EDITOR: PHILIPPE GLOAGUEN

Translated by LEXUS

Contents

NORD-
PAS-DE-CALAIS
HAUTE-
NORMANDIE
PICARDIE
BASSE-
NORMANDIE
ILE DE
FRANCE
LORRAINE
CHAMPAGNE-
ARDENNE
ALSACE
BRETAGNE
PAYS DE
LA LOIRE
CENTRE
BOURGOGNE
FRANCHE-
COMTÉ
POITOU-
CHARENTES
LIMOUSIN
AUVERGNE
RHÔNE-ALPES
AQUITAINE
MIDI-
PYRÉNÉES
LANGUEDOC-
ROUSSILLON
PROVENCE-
ALPES-CÔTE-D'AZUR
CORSE

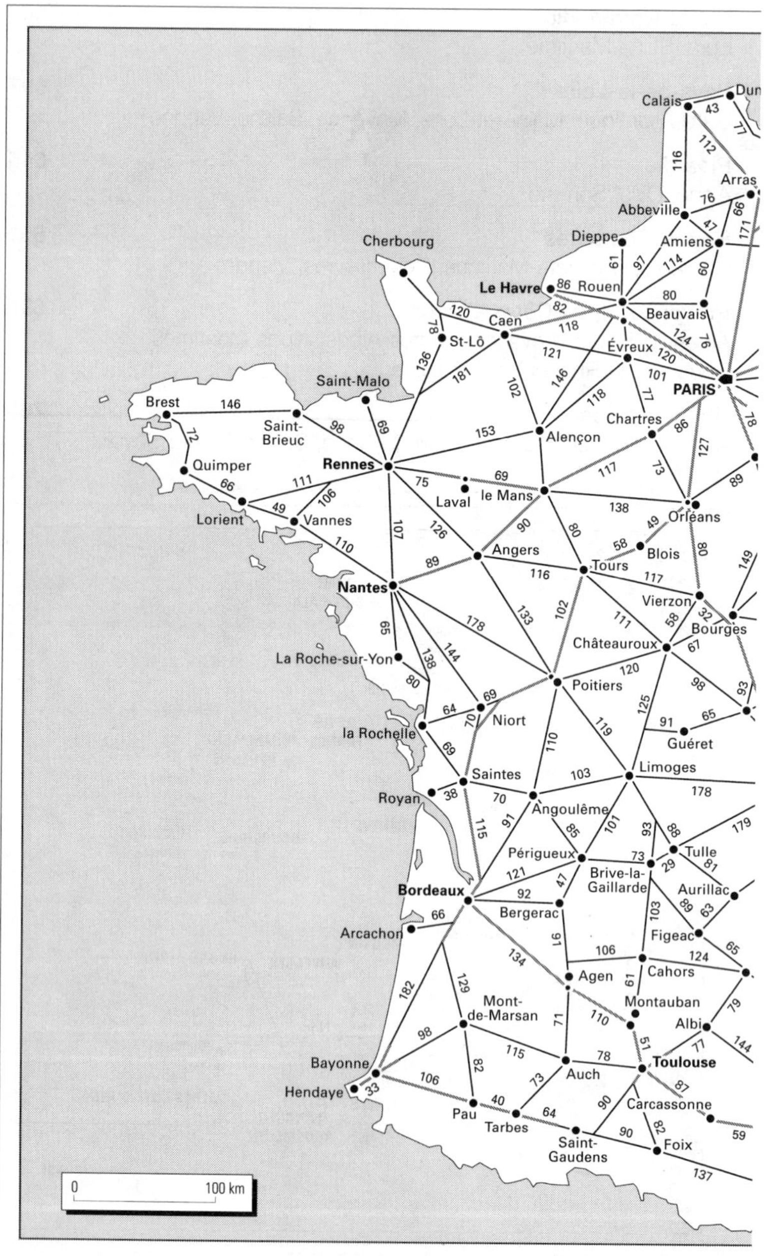
Calais
Dun
Arras
Abbeville
Dieppe
Amiens
Cherbourg
Le Havre
Rouen
Beauvais
Caen
St-Lô
Évreux
PARIS
Saint-Malo
Brest
Saint-Brieuc
Chartres
Alençon
Rennes
Quimper
Laval
le Mans
Orléans
Lorient
Vannes
Angers
Blois
Tours
Nantes
Vierzon
Bourges
Châteauroux
La Roche-sur-Yon
Poitiers
Niort
la Rochelle
Guéret
Limoges
Saintes
Royan
Angoulême
Périgueux
Tulle
Brive-la-Gaillarde
Aurillac
Bordeaux
Bergerac
Arcachon
Figeac
Agen
Cahors
Mont-de-Marsan
Montauban
Albi
Bayonne
Auch
Toulouse
Hendaye
Carcassonne
Pau
Tarbes
Saint-Gaudens
Foix
0
100 km

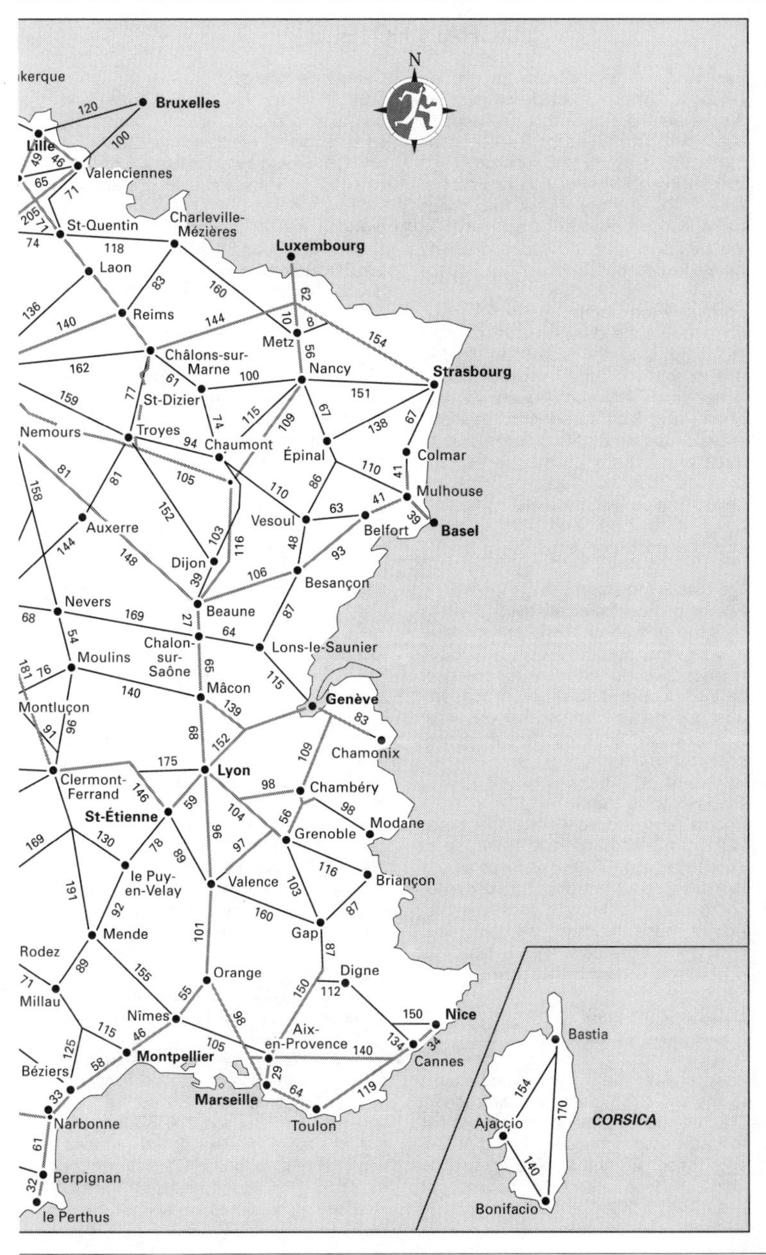
Bruxelles
Lille
Valenciennes
St-Quentin
Charleville-Mézières
Luxembourg
Laon
Reims
Metz
Châlons-sur-Marne
Nancy
Strasbourg
St-Dizier
Nemours
Troyes
Chaumont
Épinal
Colmar
Mulhouse
Vesoul
Belfort
Basel
Auxerre
Dijon
Besançon
Nevers
Beaune
Chalon-sur-Saône
Lons-le-Saunier
Moulins
Mâcon
Montluçon
Genève
Chamonix
Clermont-Ferrand
Lyon
Chambéry
St-Étienne
Grenoble
Modane
le Puy-en-Velay
Valence
Briançon
Mende
Gap
Rodez
Orange
Digne
Millau
Nîmes
Nice
Aix-en-Provence
Cannes
Montpellier
Béziers
Marseille
Toulon
Narbonne
Perpignan
le Perthus
Bastia
Ajaccio
Bonifacio
CORSICA

CHAIN HOTELS

Few of the hotels listed in this guide belong to any chain, but chain hotels are so prevalent in France that it's handy to keep them in mind as back-up. In most cases they are new and functional, and their settings fairly uninspiring, having been chosen because they're close to business parks, industrial estates or major roads. On the plus side, they're cheap, and usually have a free car park.

Formule 1 (no stars)
Formule 1 is the cheapest hotel chain, a fact which it flaunts. Prices start at 119F and for that you get a room with both a double and single bed, basin, TV and alarm clock. There's a self-cleaning shower/wc on the landing. Rooms sleep up to three at no extra charge. Self-service breakfast 22F. No restaurant. Free car parks. There's an automatic system of payment by bank card if reception is closed when you arrive.

1re Classe (no stars)
Rooms with contemporary décor sleeping one, two or three for 155F. All rooms have a work area, colour TV, shower cubicle, basin and wc. No restaurant, but breakfast for 22F. Reception closed noon–5pm and after 9pm but you can use their electronic reservation system if you have an appropriate bank card.

Etap Hôtel (no stars)
Rooms have a double bed, bunk beds, bathroom facilities, TV and alarm clock. Prices start at 150F. "Eat as much as you like" buffet breakfast 24F. No charge for under-12s sharing with their parents. Access round the clock, with automatic payment by bank card when reception is closed. Free parking in most towns.

Balladins (one-star)
Rooms have TV with Canal+, direct-dial telephone and private bathroom with basin, shower and wc. Single and double rooms 195–275F, cheaper at weekends. Children under 12 free. If you want to eat there are several *formules* starting at 59F and dinner, bed and breakfast packages from 275F. Free parking. Also a number of rooms with facilities for the disabled.

Campanile (two-star)
This "environmentally friendly" hotel chain boasts an extra star and more comfortable en suite rooms, with telephone, colour TV with Canal+ and a welcome tray. Expect to pay 320–420F for a double in Paris and 280F in the rest of France. Extra bed(s) provided free of charge for under 12s sharing. Set meals 84–107F. Buffet breakfast 34F. Some rooms suitable for disabled guests. Car parks sometimes charged.

Climat de France (two-star)
Attractive, well-designed rooms with the choice of a double bed, twin beds or three beds. Doubles 270F. Three people sharing pay a 40F supplement. All rooms have a bathroom, private wc, colour TV with Canal+, direct-dial telephone and radio alarm. Under 13s sharing with parents stay for free. Healthy 34F buffet breakfast. Set meals from 75F. Also has rooms with facilities for disabled guests, conference rooms and free supervised parking. Electronic reception facilities after 11pm using Visa or Carte Bleue.

Ibis (two-star)
Ibis hotels are to be found in town centres as well as the outskirts. Rooms are comfortable and have TV with Canal+, telephone and bathroom. Extra bed provided free of charge for under 12s sharing. A number of rooms have facilities for disabled guests. All Ibis hotels provide bar snacks and most have restaurants. Car park or garage. Rooms run from 300–450F, with breakfast 35F. Special 160F (220F in Paris) rate for anyone under-26 booking in after 9pm (no reservations). Special weekend rates Oct–May.

Clarine (two-star)
This chain has 60 quality two-star hotels, all decorated in an individual, regional style. Comfortable double or twin rooms with bathroom, direct-dial telephone, colour TV with Canal+ or satellite channels and a welcome tray. Expect to pay 400–500F in Paris and 270–320F in the rest of France. Additional bed provided free of charge for under 12s sharing. Set meals 58–110F. Buffet breakfast 30–40F. Free parking subject to availability.

About this book

This is the first appearance in English of Guide du Routard's ***Hôtels et Restos de France***, France's best-selling guide to good-value restaurants and accommodation. Thoroughly revised each year, *Hôtels et Restos* is up-to-date, comprehensive, and opens up the country in a way that no other guide does. Its critical listings include everything from simple hostels and family-run bistros to high-comfort rural retreats and city-centre three-stars, all selected and reviewed by Routard's team of locally based writers, who re-assess every single entry for each edition.

The hotels (and restaurants) we've selected tend to be small, independent establishments. You'll soon become accustomed to noticing the Routard stickers on their front doors. You'll sometimes see a *Logis de France* sticker, too – a fireplace symbol (one to three fires according to facilities provided). This shows membership of a scheme that promotes family-run hotels, often in rural locations well away from major towns.

The guide's lay-out

The guide is divided into 22 **chapter regions**, each preceded by a map on which are shown all locations where we have included a hotel or restaurant listing.

The regions are listed alphabetically, and the **main towns** are listed in alphabetical order within each chapter, their names appearing in a black box that also shows the post code (eg Quiberon 56170). **Small towns and villages** within a radius of 30km of a larger town are included under the entries for that town; for each, we've indicated how far in a given direction (N, S, E, W) they are from the major town.

Within each town entry, **hotels** are listed before **restaurants**, and both are listed in **ascending order of price.** Stars indicated are the official ratings of the French hotel industry and not of this guide.

After the address of the establishments we give tips on how to get there (where they are needed), plus phone number, fax number, details of opening hours and a summary of facilities.

Symbols

The following symbols have been used:

🏠	hotel
I●I	restaurant
10%	10% discount offer

The **hotel discount offer** has been negotiated by Routard on behalf of readers of both the French and English editions (you may need to point this out to some hoteliers, as this is the first ever English edition). The offer applies to the price of a **room only** (not meals) and to benefit, you must stay a minimum of **two consecutive nights**.

French idiosyncracies

It pays to know what's what in French hotels and restaurants. Here, then, is a brief introduction to some of their idiosyncracies – and to a few of your rights as a consumer.

• Hotels and restaurants are required by law to **display their prices**. The cheapest **set meals** are often served on weekdays only – this should be clearly marked on the board outside.

• **Wine lists** aren't always very clear. For example, you may order a bottle of Burgundy at 50F a bottle and be charged 100F. When you check the list again, you find (maybe in small print) that the price was for a half-bottle. A bottle of wine must be opened in front of the customer – otherwise you've no way of knowing that you're getting what you ordered. A jug of tap water is free if you're ordering a meal.

• Restaurants occasionally **refuse to serve** customers if they feel they haven't ordered enough. This practice is technically against the law.

• When you're **reserving a room** (by phone or in writing), it's not unusual for the hotel to ask for a **deposit** by way of guarantee. There's no law to say how much this deposit should be, but they shouldn't ask for more than 25–30 percent of the total. The French have two words for deposit – ***arrhes*** and ***acompte***. The first is refundable, the second is not. So in the event of cancellation your *arrhes* can be returned in full if you give the hotel reasonable notice. If it's the hotel that cancels the booking, then under Article 1590 of the Civil Code (which dates back to 1804) you're entitled to double the amount of the *arrhes* you paid. So if you do make a deposit, be specific in your letter as to whether it's *arrhes* or *acompte*.

• Hotels aren't allowed to try to sell you something you haven't asked for – for example, they can't **force you to book for several nights** if you only want to stay for one. Similarly, they can't force you to have breakfast or any other meal at the hotel unless it's clearly stated that **half-board or full board** is compulsory. Find out if this is the case before you book into a hotel with a restaurant and bear in mind that half-board prices often apply to a minimum stay of three nights. This is permitted by law.

Alsace

67 Bas-Rhin

68 Haut-Rhin

ALTKIRCH 68130

AUBERGE SUNDGOVIENNE**

route de Belfort (West); coming from Mulhouse, don't go into Altkirch, keep going for about 3km on the road to Belfort.

☎ 03.89.40.97.18 F 03.89.40.67.73

Closed Mondays, Tuesday lunchtimes, and Dec 23–Feb 1.

Secure parking. TV. Disabled access.

This inn has all the characteristics of a Swiss chalet (and in fact we're not that far from Switzerland here). Even though it's beside the road it's still very pleasant. Ask for a room at the back – numbers.18 and 19 are really nice. Avoid number 16, though, as it's right above the kitchen. All the rooms (270–310F) are pretty, clean and comfortable, and a few of them have a balcony. Weekday set meals 68F (starter, main course and dessert), 100F, 150F and 230F. À la carte you'll find some specialities from the Alsace region: monkfish with Riesling and baby vegetables, trout with almonds, and game (in season). Half-board 290F and full board 360F per person. Sit and have a drink on the terrace and take in the lovely countryside scenery of Sundgau, the southern region of Alsace at the gates of Jura.

RESTAURANT DE LA VICTOIRE

10 rue des Alliés (North-East); it's just as you come into the town.

☎ 03.89.40.90.65

Closed Wednesdays and Saturday lunchtimes.

If you like little pigs then this is the place for you, since there are lots of them in the dining room, mainly in the form of piggy banks. This has to be one of the most individual restaurants in Alsace since the other dining room houses a collection of local dolls (and we don't mean of the 'Miss Alsace' kind!). But it's the wine collection of the owner, Monsieur Miesch, that's even more impressive. Wine connoisseurs will be in seventh heaven in the bar with its row upon row of bottles covered in dust (well, you need to protect them!). He must have every single vintage under the sun. And as for the food, you've got a choice of seven set meals (60–250F) with specialities such as stuffed char, rabbit in Pinot Noir, and the local dish, fried carp. Not to mention chicken in beer flambéd in Gewurtztraminer, and snail pie.Well, it's all good, hearty stuff as well it should be in Sundgau, a region which can get quite chilly in the winter. Well done and thank you Monsieur Miesch for your gourmet knowledge, your words of wisdom and your warm welcome.

HIRTZBACH 68118 (4KM S)

10% OTTIÉ-BAUR

17 rue de Lattre-de-Tassigny; it's just as you come into the village in the direction of Ferrette.

☎ 03.89.40.93.22 F 03.89.08.85.19

Closed Monday evenings, Tuesdays, 2 weeks in June–July and Christmas.

Secure parking.

A lovely little blue inn right in the heart of Sundgau run by Monsieur and Madame Laperrière. Doubles with washing facilities 150F, with shower 160F and with bath 200F. Half-board 196–240F. Creative cooking. We opted for the 88F set meal and enjoyed a gazpacho of summer vegetables, braised pork cheeks and a dessert. Zander, trout and salmon were also on the menu. Try the *terrine* of artichokes and *foie gras* and the dan-

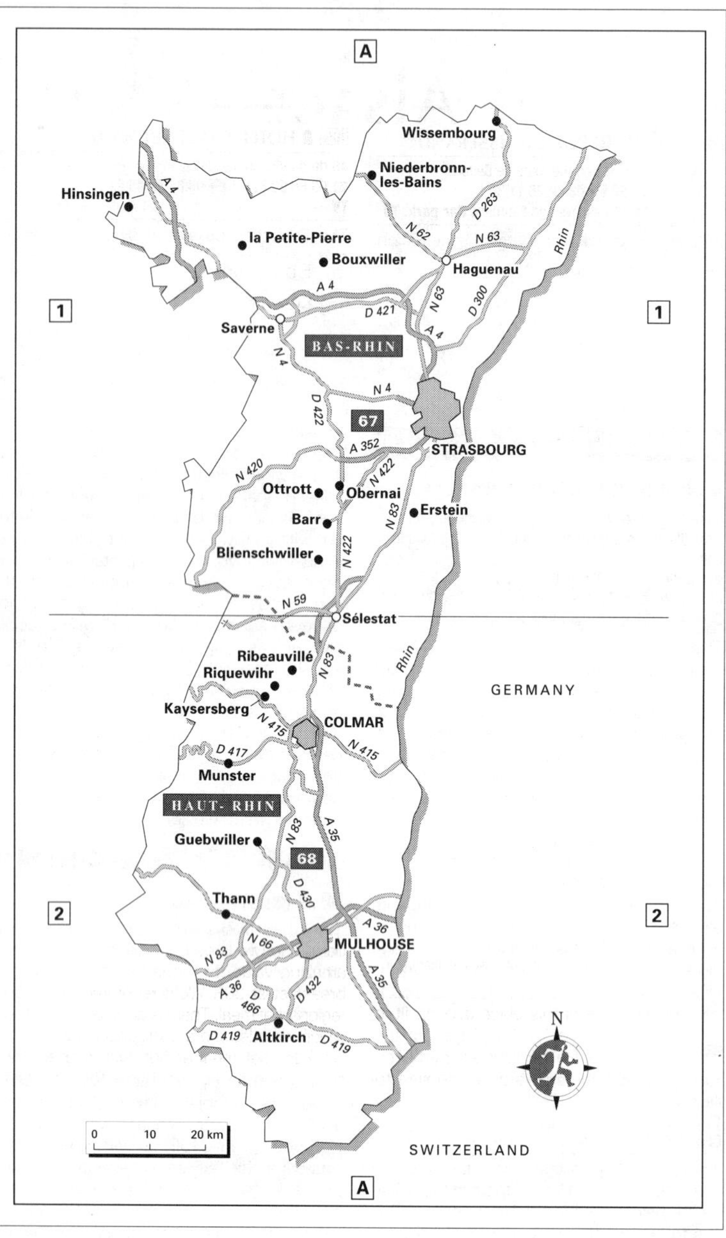
A
Wissembourg
Niederbronn-les-Bains
Hinsingen
A 4
D 263
N 62
N 63
la Petite-Pierre
Bouxwiller
Haguenau
Rhin
A 4
1
D 421
N 63
D 300
1
Saverne
A 4
BAS-RHIN
N 4
N 4
D 422
67
STRASBOURG
A 352
N 420
N 422
Ottrott
Obernai
Erstein
N 83
Barr
N 422
Blienschwiller
N 59
Sélestat
Rhin
Ribeauvillé
N 83
Riquewihr
GERMANY
Kaysersberg
N 415
COLMAR
N 415
D 417
Munster
HAUT-RHIN
N 83
A 35
Guebwiller
68
D 430
Thann
2
2
A 36
N 66
MULHOUSE
N 83
A 35
A 36
D 466
D 432
D 419
Altkirch
D 419
N
0
10
20 km
SWITZERLAND
A

delion salad. Other set meals 120–210F. Terrace and garden. The level of reception and service was not always consistent.

GOMMERSDORF 68210 (12KM W)

10% ☗ |●| L'AUBERGE DU TISSERAND**

28 rue de Cernay; it's on the route de Belfort.
☎ 03.89.07.21.80 F 03.89.25.11.34
Closed Mondays, Tuesdays and February. **Car park. TV.**

This inn, which is typical of the Alsace region has got a bit of history attached to it. It belonged to a weaver in the 17th century but parts of it go back even further. On the 1st floor (the smoking area) the floor has buckled with age. The owners, Édouard and Doris Guldenfels, will offer you reasonable prices and enormous portions of food. There's a 45F set meal (weekday lunchtimes) or you can pay about 62F for a main course on its own (*choucroute, pot-au-feu*). Flambéd tarts every night. A really delightful place with a few rooms (200–280F). For reservations phone 03.89.07.26.26

BARR 67140

10% ☗ |●| HÔTEL MAISON ROUGE**

1 av. de la Gare (South); it's near the post office.
☎ 03.88.08.90.40 F 03.88.08.90.85
Closed Mondays and 3 weeks in Feb. **Secure parking.**

It's far enough away from the centre not to attract too many tourists. Set meal 55F (weekdays) or expect to pay about 95F or 150F. Good choice of beers. Pleasant rooms 220F–300F (with bath). Terrace.

HEILIGENSTEIN 67140 (1.5KM N)

☗ |●| RELAIS DU KLEVENER**

51 rue Principale; on the D35, direction Ottrott.
☎ 03.88.08.05.98 F 03.88.08.40.83
Closed Mondays, Tuesday lunchtimes and January.
Car park. TV.

The architechture of this place doesn't fit in too well with the rest of the village but the panoramic view you get from it is superb! The hotel overlooks the vineyards so be sure to ask for a room with a view. Rooms 210–260F. Number 30 is specially laid out for disabled access. Brasserie and restaurant. Generous set meal 95F. Reckon on 125–180F à la carte. Half-board 230F and 240F. Sit out on the terrace and have a drink of...klevener, for example. Remember that klevener here in Heiligenstein is an old wine which is pretty rare in Alsace now; don't confuse it with the Pinot Blanc klevner.

BLIENSCHWILLER 67650

10% ☗ HÔTEL WINZENBERG**

46 rte du Vin; on the N422.
☎ 03.88.92.62.77 F 03.88.42.45.22
TV.

The Dresches believe in division of labour and keeping things in the family, so mother and daughter look after the hotel while father and son take charge of the vineyard. They've got the place running like clockwork. Unfortunately we didn't get a chance to taste any of their wine, but we did have the time to appreciate Madame Dresch's welcome and see just how comfortable the rooms are. The pretty Alsace furniture, the bed linen and the bright and cheery curtains really make you feel at home. It's all good value for money too; with doubles 265–290F. There's secure parking about 100m away. You can of course visit their cellars (which date back to 1508) and do some wine-tasting. Cheers!

BOUXWILLER 67330

☗ |●| HÔTEL-RESTAURANT HEINTZ**

84 Grande rue; it's just as you get to the town coming from Ingwiller.
☎ 03.88.70.72.57
Closed 3 weeks in January; restaurant closed Sun evening and Mon. **TV.**

This is a well-looked after property where you'll get a warm welcome. The rooms, without being the height of luxury, are pretty comfortable. Ask for one which looks out onto the garden as they're quieter and have a more relaxing atmosphere. Prices are reasonable – 210–230F with shower/wc, 260–280F with bath. The two large rooms that sleep four are amazing value for money at 370F, as is the breakfast at 30F. We'd recommend the 80F regional set meal. There is another one at 140F which includes more traditional dishes, and a weekday set meal at 50F with starter, main course, and dessert or coffee. There's a small terrace and a swimming pool in the garden.

COLMAR 68000

☗ AUBERGE DE JEUNESSE

2 rue Pasteur; from the station take bus no.4 and get off at the Lycée technique stop. If you want to walk (it'll

take 15 minutes), cross the bridge at the back of the station and head for Ingersheim. It's well sign-posted.
☎ 03.89.80.57.39 F➜ 03.89.80.76.16
Doors open 7am–10am and 5pm–midnight. **Closed** mid Dec–mid Jan. **Car park**.

This big modern building is very clean, well looked after and (very important) quiet. There are 11 rooms with 8 beds in each and 3 rooms for 4. Expect to pay 68F for one night, breakfast included. There are also a few double rooms at 160F with supplement. No meals (except for large groups and on request). Visitor tax: 1F. No sports facilities. Very busy in May. It's probably best to make a reservation, and you should have an hostelling card.

LA CHAUMIÈRE

74 av. de la République; it's opposite the post office, not very far from the station.
☎ 03.89.41.08.99

It's small, it's pink, and it's simple in the way hotels used to be. It may not be that modern or luxurious but who cares? What's nice about it is the fact that the owners are really friendly and the prices are pretty good. You get to the hotel through the bar. On the left there's a wooden staircase that leads up to the bedrooms which are all very clean. There are no airs and graces about this place, it's just nice and simple. You'll pay 180F for a room at the front without a shower and 220F for one at the back with shower. We'd say take one of the cheaper rooms because they're just as nice as the others and there's not much noise from the street.

10% HÔTEL COLBERT**

2 rue des Trois-Épis (West); it's near the station and a stone's throw from place de Lattre.
☎ 03.89.41.31.05 F➜ 03.89.23.66.75
Secure parking. **TV**. **Canal+**.

The rooms here are comfortable, clean and have double-glazing to keep out any noise. Doubles with bath 260–300F. A small detail that will keep the beer drinkers among you happy: there's a bottle-opener on the bathroom wall. Friendly atmosphere guaranteed. 20% reduction for sales reps. There's a disco disco in the hotel basement but don't worry, it's not that loud!

HÔTEL BEAU SÉJOUR**

25 rue du Ladhof (East); it's about a 10 minute walk from the town centre.
☎ 03.89.41.37.16 F➜ 03.89.41.43.07
Car park. **TV**. **Canal+**. **Disabled access**.

This hotel has belonged to the Keller family since 1913 and a family photo dating from around that time takes pride of place in the reception area. It has lots of rooms at prices ranging from 280F to 520F. A number of discounts are available depending on how busy the hotel is. Breakfast buffet 45F. There's a sauna and a gym and a little garden to sit in when the sun's out. They've maybe rushed the job of modernizing the place, judging by the state of the chairs and the wiring in a few rooms. Even so, the rooms are pleasant, but don't hesitate about asking to see them before taking one. The restaurant is nicely decorated and the cooking is stylish and imaginative. Set meals 80F (weekdays), 98F, 115F, 150F, 160F and 280F. This is a comfortable and elegant place that's getting better.

WISTUB BRENNER

1 rue de Turenne; it's just beside little Venice.
☎ 03.89.41.42.33
Closed Tuesday evenings, Wednesdays, the second fortnight in January, the third week in June, and the third week in November. **Car park**.

The owner of this place, Gilbert Brenner, is a real character, like something out of a musical comedy.. He's small, stocky, rosy-cheeked and absolutely hilarious. He's also glad to be alive and it shows. He does the cooking and the serving, helped by his wife Christine who's always laughing at one of Gilbert's jokes. They keep things simple here, with hearty dishes like *pâté en croûte, bibbelskäse* (fresh cheese flavoured with horseradish and herbs), knuckle of ham with potatoes, and onion tart, all of them 30–65F. The beer always flows well into the small hours and you can sit and have a laugh with the Brenners every night. Students, regulars, wine-growers, tourists, they all come and have a great time. This is the kind of place we love.

LE PETIT GOURMAND

9 quai de la Poissonnerie; follow the little river.
☎ 03.89.41.09.32
Closed Tuesdays and Monday evenings out of season, two weeks in November, and two weeks in January.

This pretty little restaurant is right in the heart of the area known as little Venice and offers you things like extremely good *tartiflettes* of Munster cheese with salad and *charcuterie* for the modest sum of 65F. You get good, hearty portions here. Inside the décor is low-key, with just a few photos of old Colmar on the white walls. In summer sit outside on the waterside terrace. You always get a warm welcome and the owner makes a nice fuss over you. If you're struck by the quality of the *tartiflettes*, it's because they're left to simmer for 3 days before they're served. A real treat.

|●| RESTAURANT GARBO

15 rue Berthe-Molly; it's in the centre.
☎ 03.89.24.48.55
Closed Saturday lunchtimes, Sundays, the first two weeks in August, and public holidays.

Given the name, you won't be surprised by all the pictures of Greta Garbo in this restaurant in one of the town's old shopping streets. The salmon-pink dining room is huge and has a rather hushed atmosphere. Lunchtime set meal 75F (starter, main course and dessert) or 61F for 2 courses. In the evenings there are set meals at 145, 180F and 280F Good regional cooking which changes with the seasons. Ideal for a reasonably priced lunch or dinner on the spur of the moment. Aperitif on the house on presentation of this guide.

|●| LE CAVEAU SAINT-PIERRE

24 rue de la Herse (Centre).
☎ 03.89.41.99.33
Closed Sunday evenings, Mondays, two weeks in January, one week in March, and 10 days in June–July.

Elegant but affordable, this is undoubtedly the nicest restaurant in the most romantic part of town. You can only get to it on foot (all the better!) by a sort of wooden footbridge which crosses an adorable little canal lined with half-timbered houses and beautiful gardens. When it's sunny the tables are put outside beside the water. The prices are reasonable for a place in such lovely surrroundings, the service is polite without being fussy, and you feel relaxed and comfortable. There are a few mouth-watering specialities like smoked pork with potatoes and bacon or potato salad, oxtail with shallots in Pinot Noir and, of course, *choucroute*, not to mention the salad *vosgienne*. Set meals from 76F. À la carte, expect to pay about 100F and possibly much more for a hearty meal. They have *baeckoffa* (a stew of beef, mutton and pork marinated in local wine) every Saturday and Sunday in winter.

|●| RESTAURANT LES TANNEURS

12 rue des Tanneurs (Centre); it's in the heart of the old part of town, two minutes from little Venice.
☎ 03.89.23.72.12
Closed Wednesdays, Thursday lunchtimes and Dec 15–Jan 15.

This is a lovely little spot with a terrace.where you can sit outside in the summer and have a meal or even just a drink. Set meals at 89F (with things like *choucroute* and an excellent Munster cheese flavoured with cumin) and 99F (with trout in Riesling). Usually quite popular with German tourists. Attentive service.

WETTOLSHEIM 68920 (6KM SW)

☗ HÔTEL "AU SOLEIL"**

20 rue Sainte-Gertrude.
☎ 03.89.80.62.66 F➔ 03.89.79.84.45
Closed Thursdays, mid June 17–early July, and Dec 19–Jan 5. **Car park**. **TV**.

This is a great little place just outside Colmar in a tiny and fairly unknown village on the route des vins. It's simple and welcoming and the prices are still pretty reasonable unlike many other hotels in the area. You go into an old half-timbered building which has been renovated but you actually stay in a quiet annexe where all the rooms look out either onto a little car park or acres of vines. Rooms are 215F a night for 2. If you're staying in the hotel, you can have an evening meal if you order it in advance. There's a small set meal available at 55F. So, it's a good place to stay if you want to be quite near the town but not actually in it. However, be warned – half-board is compulsory in July, August and September (230F).

AMMERSCHWIHR 68770 (7KM NW)

☗ |●| L'ARBRE VERT**

7 rue des Cigognes (North-West); N415.
☎ 03.89.47.12.23 F➔ 03.89.78.27.21
Closed beginning of Feb–end of March and the last two weeks in November. **TV**.

This is a large, pleasant building which dates back to the post-war period. Both the management and the chef are very experienced and it shows. There are a few good specialities on the menu, like escalope of goose liver in Pinot Noir or peach soufflé, not to mention the *croustillant* of salmon with leeks which is a real treat. Set meals 80F–230F. Children's set meal 45F. It's a good place if you're looking for gourmet food – a bit more chic than the type of establishment we usually include in the guidebook. The rooms are gradually being refurbished and are really nice. The owners have Celtic blood, which explains the Breton sideboard in the corridor. Expect to pay 290F for one night (big double bed with bath or shower/wc, telephone, mini-bar) or if you prefer twin beds like a great deal of Germans seem to (which explains the increase in the number of twin rooms in a few hotels in the region), you'll need to pay 10F extra. A piece of advice: the rooms in the annexe are slightly more expensive (350F) but not necessarily any nicer than the perfectly delightful ones in the hotel.

TURCKHEIM 68230 (7KM W)

10% ☗ |●| AUBERGE DU BRAND**

8 Grand-Rue
☎ 03.89.27.06.10 ⮕ 03.89.27.55.51
Closed Tuesday evenings, Wednesdays, early Jan to early March and June 26–July 5. **TV**.

Service noon–1.45pm and 7pm–10.30pm. This half-timbered building is a superb example of a traditional Alsatian house and a great place if you're looking for a meal or accommodation. The forest provides lots of food in the autumn, and the chef here takes button mushrooms, chanterelles, ceps, boletus, oyster mushrooms, horns of plenty and varieties that you've probably never even heard of, fries them up, and produces a dish that just bursts with flavour. If you fancy something else why not try the ham in beer with leeks, or the succulent fillets of hare? The warm décor of the dining room really complements the food and makes you feel nice and relaxed. You could never get bored with the menu because it changes with the seasons. Set meals 86–270F. The stylish and cosy rooms ,come with shower/wc and cost 220–340F, breakfast included. It's worth your while taking half-board if you want to spend a few days in this beautiful wine-growing region of the Rhine.

☗ |●| HÔTEL DES DEUX CLEFS**

3 rue du Conseil; it's in place de l'hôtel de ville.
☎ 03.89.27.06.01 ⮕ 03.89.27.18.07
TV. Disabled access.

Is this place an inn or a palace? Well, it's a bit of both really. A number of famous people have been in this wonderful half-timbered house which dates back to 1540 (it was renovated in 1620), including General de Gaulle and General Leclerc after the liberation of Alsace, Dr. Albert Schweitzer (a friend of relatives of the current owners), and the American actor James Stewart. The huge front door creaks open to reveal a thick curtain, the colour of wine (a good sign!) and it's like walking into a palace as you see the superb wood panelling, antique carpets, and the romantic dining room. It's lit like a Rembrandt painting, with the light filtering through the "stained glass" windows (actually, they're made from the bottoms of bottles). There is even a little conservatory full of house plants and a garden at the back. Funnily enough, although the rooms are very comfortable, they're not the height of luxury. You won't pay luxury prices either. Doubles range from 310F with shower/wc to 450F with twin beds, bath and TV. The cheaper ones are tucked away in the attic and look out onto the town hall. You'll get a 50% discount on breakfast on presentation of this guide. The restaurant has good food and a set meal at 135F. À la carte also available. Basically this is a super place with lots of character – there are not many like it.

|●| À L'HOMME SAUVAGE

19 Grand-Rue.
☎ 03.89.27.56.15
Closed Tuesday evenings, Wednesdays, Sunday evenings (except in summer and on public holidays), the last week in June and one week at Christmas.

What a town! What an adorable little street! What a pretty place! This restaurant is as simple as it is elegant and is also very reasonable. Look at all the imaginative dishes you can get in the brightly coloured dining room: knuckle of beef *pot-au-feu* in a creamy cheese sauce, braised knuckle of veal in lager, and pot-roasted leg of duck in Pinot Noir. Hmmm! And what about the pan-fried skate with clams in parsley and the mashed potatoes with saffron? All these cost less than 100F à la carte and there are also set meals 120F–295F. Very good value for money for the area. Such a place really does deserve a round of applause!

NIEDERMORSCHWIHR 68230 (10KM W)

|●| RESTAURANT CAVEAU MORAKOPF

7 rue des Trois-Épis (South); N415 and the D11.
☎ 03.89.27.05.10
Closed Sundays and lunchtimes out of season.

This big green and pink house can be found tucked away in the middle of the vineyards. Adorable garden in the summer. Terrace at the back. Meticulously prepared food and generous portions. Excellent home-made *presskopf* (brawn) and *baeckeoffa* (stew of different meats and potatoes marinated for 12 hours) for 4 people minimum (you'll have to order ahead of time). Their *confit* of *choucroute* is not to be missed! Attentive, friendly service. Unpretentious décor. Expect to pay about 100F for a meal.

TROIS ÉPIS (LES) 68410 (15.5KM W)

10% ☗ |●| HÔTEL-RESTAURANT VILLA ROSA**

route de Turckheim; it's about 400m from the village

overlooking the valley of Munster.
☎ 03.89.49.81.19 ⊳ 03.89.78.90.45
Closed Thursdays and Jan 1–Feb 15.

This place is owned by a lovely couple, Anne-Rose and Alain, who are outdoor types themselves and make their guests feel really at home here – they really sum up the whole spirit of travelling! The rooms are delightful and some have a view of the garden and swimming pool – ask for one of those. We've got a bit of a soft spot for number 3 with its litle balcony and its heart-shaped bath. Numbers 4 and 5 are also nice. For couples who want somewhere cosy, rooms 7, 8 and 9 are tucked away in the attic. A charming hotel which is quite reasonable, from 280F for 2. Hearty buffet breakfast 48F. The special 28F breakfast for readers of this guide – snack, coffee and orange juice – will set you up for the day. There is a restaurant but it's only open for evening meals. Aperitif on the house on presentation of this guide. Good deals for families and couples if you're staying for 2 nights or one week. You can hire mountain bikes and snowshoes in winter.

ERSTEIN 67150

L'ESTAMINET DES BORDS DE L'ILL

9 rue du gal-de-Gaulle (Centre).
☎ 03.88.98.03.70

What we like about this place is the fact that the owners make such an effort to preserve the traditional local recipes. There's smoked eel (supplied by one of the last remaining professional fishermen in Alsace), served with toast, horseradish and compote of red onions in sherry (75F), trout (66F), and *choucroute* with seven accompaniments (90F). There's also a fish stew of five types of fish, and you can have it with either fish steaks (85F) or fillets (105F). The fact that you can choose a wonderful bottle of wine from Alsace or elsewhere, from a lengthy wine-list that features every region in France (except Jura) makes the food even better. There are set meals to suit all budgets: 42F (*menu du jour*), 50F (lunchtimes only), 56F (Saturday lunchtimes), 80F and 100F (both come with regional specialities) and 140F. Children's set meal 55F.

HAGUENAU 67500

RESTAURANT AU TIGRE

4 place d'Armes (Centre); it's very near the pedestrian precinct.
☎ 03.88.93.93.79

This is a classic brasserie and the handsome dining room has high ceilings, wood panelling and lots of wrought iron. The dish of the day on weekdays costs 42F. The food is a mixture of typical brasserie dishes and more exotic things like ostrich and kangaroo steak. Set meal 98F. Large terrace for when the sun's out.

S'BUEREHIESEL – CHEZ MONIQUE

13 rue Meyer; it's next to the theatre.
☎ 03.88.93.30.90
Closed Sundays, Mondays, the first week in May and the second fortnight in December.

A *winstub* wine bar serves nothing but wine from the region (as opposed to a *bierstub* or beer cellar, which only serves beer). This one is popular with all the stars from the theatre nearby and photos of them, with broad smiles and red eyes (from the flash!) adorn one of the walls in the main dining room. They do a set meal at lunchtime for 45F. Expect to pay about 60F for a main course in the evening. They concentrate on regional dishes including *choucroute* (of course), braised knuckle of pork in a cheese sauce (they use *Munster*, a rather strong local variety), *quenelles* of liver, house *spaetzle* (a type of noodle), and snails *à l'alsacienne* (stuffed with spiced butter and herbs and cooked in local wine). Friendly welcome and warm, pleasant surroundings.

HINSINGEN 67260

LA GRANGE DU PAYSAN

rue Principale
☎ 03.88.00.91.83
Closed Mondays.

This little restaurant 500m from the border with Lorraine is something of local institution. You can't miss it – it's the one with all the French electricity board vans and sales reps' cars parked outside. (They know where to come alright!) Considering the size of the place it probably used to belong to a pretty well-off farmer. Conventional rustic décor (of course). You'll get an excellent welcome from the professional staff and the service is particularly efficient. You've got to admire the way they prepare the steak tartare in full view of the customer,which is a bit of a spectacle in itself. Country-style food served in hearty portions which really fill you up. Everyone always looks really satisfied and, dare we say, flushed, when they've finished, which is a real testament to the consistently good quality of food here: home-made black pudding with sautéd apples and home-grown horse-radish (delicious), chargrilled suckling pig, braised ox cheek, ham cooked in a hay box, stuffed pig's stomach. Good set meals from 65F (*choucroute* and Munster cheese). Main courses around 50F. Other set meals 98F, 125F, 145F, 150F and 265F.

KAYSERSBERG 68240

AUBERGE DE LA CIGOGNE

73 route de Lapoutroie; leave the old village in the direction of Lapoutroie.
☎ 03.89.47.30.33
Closed Friday evenings and Sunday evenings. **Car park**.

This place is just outside the village where Dr. Schweitzer (1875–1965) was born. He was famous for the humanitarian work he carried out in Africa and was awarded the Nobel Peace Prize in 1953. Anyway, after that brief history lesson, let's take a look at the restaurant, which is popular with long distance lorry drivers and workers from the nearby factory. This is the type of roadside establishment where you can get a good, hearty meal without forking out a lot of money. Dish of the day 35F, set meals 68F–160F. The food you get ranges from the old brasserie classics to a few house specialities like fillet of zander, trout in Riesling and *choucroute*. A good place to stop.

RESTAURANT DU COUVENT

1 rue du couvent; it's a stone's throw from the tourist office.
☎ 03.89.78.23.29
Closed Tuesdays. **Disabled access**.

This is a little blue building decorated with vine leaves on the walls. The interior is spick and span. Set meals 120–240F. For 60F you can have the "chef's suggestion", which is always the kind of dish that's been lovingly prepared using fresh vegetables, meat or fish. A little tip from us: if you happen to be there when salmon and baby vegetables are on the menu then go for it – it's divine.The prices are not bad considering the surroundings and the mouth-watering à la carte menu, which offers fillet steak with morels (115F), *millefeuille* of Roquefort (34F) and, one of chef's specialities, *baekoffa* (beef, mutton and pork stew) with snails. A real treat. The service is a bit formal.

LAPOUTROIE 68650 (9KM W)

L'ORÉE DU BOIS**

6 rue Faudé (South); on the N415 – you'll see the arrows once you get to within 3km of Lapoutroie.
☎ 03.89.47.50.30 ➡ 03.89.47.24.02
Closed Monday lunchtimes and mid Nov–mid Dec.
Car park. **TV**. **Disabled access**.

To get up to the inn, you'll take a lovely little road that winds up the mountain past fields with cows and pine forests. The view is nothing short of superb. The very modern-looking inn, first a farmhouse and then a holiday camp is an ideal retreat for outdoor types who want to have a nice quiet break with plenty of beautiful countryside. and walking. Each room has its own cooking area. The one called *"Pâturages"* has a lovely view. Expect to pay 230–250F for a double room, 330F for one that sleeps four. Half-board 235F per person. As for the food, it's mostly traditional dishes like warm Munster cheese with almonds, fish *choucroute*, and frog's legs in Gewurtztraminer. Cheapest set meal 90F. The view from the large terrace is stunning. Good place to stay for a week, and very good for a couple with children.

MULHOUSE 68100

10% AUBERGE DE JEUNESSE

37 rue de l'Illberg (South-West); take bus no.2 or 8 from the station and get off at the Salle des sports stop.
☎ 03.89.42.63.28 ➡ 03.89.59.74.95
Doors open 8am–noon and 5pm–11pm (midnight in summer). **Closed** Christmas and New Year's Day.
Car park. **Disabled access**.

This pink house with a very pleasant large garden is in the university area of Mulhouse, which is in the process of being developed. You can stay in a small, bright and cheery dorm or in a double room for a good price. 47F per night. Meal 35F. Sheets 16F. Camp site: 26F. Membership card: 100F (70F if you're under 26).

10% HÔTEL SCHOENBERG*

14 rue Schoenberg (South-West); it's about 10 minutes from the centre; rue Schoenberg runs at right angles to avenue d'Altkirch which is behind the station.
☎ 03.89.44.19.41 ➡ 03.89.44.49.80
TV.

This is a good little hotel with clean, well-kept rooms where you'll get a good night's sleep. They seem to have forgotten to put the prices up. Expect to pay 140–160F for a double room with basin and 220F with shower/wc. The toilet and the shower are behind a sliding door. There's a little garden at the back where you can laze about in the sun and have your breakfast.

10% HÔTEL SAINT-BERNARD**

3 rue des Fleurs (Centre).
☎ 03.89.45.82.32 F 03.89.45.26.32
Secure parking 300m from hotel. **TV**. **Canal+**.

This is the nicest hotel in Mulhouse, a status which isn't that difficult to achieve when you consider how dead the town can be. It's run by someone who prefers reading (look at all the books in reception) to watching TV. Don't worry if you ARE a fan of the small screen, you can get lots of cable channels. You'll get a nice welcome from the St Bernard dog sprawled by the entrance and then you can repair to the white bar and put the world to rights under a picture of General de Gaulle. The rooms are impeccable and have high ceilings. We fell in love with number 16 with its hundred year old fresco of the four seasons on the ceiling. You could spend a whole day just admiring it! The prices of the rooms vary according to size: 200–270F with bathroom/wc, but also according to what floor they're on. If you're a bit broke then go for the ones on the third floor. There's no lift but it's cheaper and the rooms are just as big. Bicycles available free of charge.

WINSTUB HENRIETTE

9 rue Henriette (Centre); it's in a pedestrian area off place de la Réunion.
☎ 03.89.46.27.83
Closed Sundays.

This place is named after Henriette, the first girl in the town to officially become a French citizen in 1798. The inside is decorated in typical Alsace style and has seen many a year go by. As for the food here, most of it is regional, like *choucroute* (87F). The chef's specialities include fillet of trout with *choucroute* or fillet of beef with Munster cheese (125F). At lunchtime, there's a 60F *formule* of starter and main course. Expect to pay about 90F in the evening for a hearty main course. Terrace for the summer. The service, welcome, food and surroundings are all good. And it's a nice place to be when it's a bit chilly outside.

SOULTZ 68360 (21KM NW)

METZGERSTUWA

69 rue du Maréchal-de-Lattre-de-Tassigny; it's in the main street.
☎ 03.89.74.89.77
Closed weekends, three weeks in July, and Christmas–Jan 1.

This little restaurant has a *menu du jour* at 42F – who could ask for more? Meat dishes 60F, platter of house *charcuterie* 48F. The locals in particular seem to like it. You can also buy home-made produce here to take away.

MUNSTER 68140

10% HÔTEL-RESTAURANT LE CHALET*

col de la Schlucht (West); from the centre take the D417 to col de la Schlucht on the border between Alsace and the Vosges.
☎ 03.89.77.38.33 F 03.89.77.15.65
Closed Wednesday afternoons, two weeks in June, and three weeks in Nov–Dec. **Secure parking**. **TV**.

Warm welcome. The rooms aren't fancy but they're quite charming. Doubles with basin 180F, with shower/wc 250F. The big dining room. serves good food, including *choucroute* (82F) and chicken with a creamy white wine sauce (69F). It's a brasserie too. Half-board with evening meal (250F) is compulsory in peak season. It's just at the foot of the ski slopes and a great place to have some wonderful walks.

10% HÔTEL AUX DEUX SAPINS**

49 rue du 9e-Zouaves (South-West).
☎ 03.89.77.33.96 F 03.89.77.03.90
Closed Sunday evenings, Mondays out of season, and mid Nov–mid Dec. **Car park**. **TV**. **Disabled access**.

You're best to make a reservation here as early as possible. This is a very good place where the emphasis is on great quality at reasonable prices. The 70F *menu du jour* comes with an excellent trout with almonds in Riesling. Other set meals up to 200F. The rooms are very pleasant but the décor's slightly too rustic. Double rooms from 240F. There's a lot of traffic noise from outside so try and reserve a room at the back.

RESTAURANT À L'ALSACIENNE

1 rue du Dôme (South-East); it's behind the Protestant church (temple).
☎ 03.89.77.43.49
Closed Tuesday afternoons and Wednesdays.
Disabled access.

Locals and tourists both come here , and they all sit side by side quite happily at tables on the pavement alongside the church. The décor is typical of the Alsace region but it lacks a bit of old-fashioned character. The set meals in the 62–80F price range include *choucroute garnie.* Other set meals (105F and 150F) offer things like escalope of veal Munster cheese (a must!), wild boar, and the local Munster cheese, served with a glass of Gewurztraminer. Delightful welcome.

SOULTZEREN 68140 (4KM E)

10% ⌂ |●| VILLA CANAAN-LÉOPOLDINE

8 chem. du Buchteren; take the D47 in the direction of col de la Schlucht; once you're past the village it's sign-posted on the right.
☎ 03.89.77.05.64. ➡ same.
Car park.

This huge yellow house looks right over the wonderful valley of Munster. Prices are reasonable. Rooms are 260F with basin, 320F with bath, and half-board is 250F per person. Léopoldine, the owner, really takes care of everything. The bathrooms have just been refurbished, each one in a slightly different style, and the rooms have all got a nice personal touch about them. You'll get a good night's sleep here, and then in the morning it's lovely to open the shutters and be greeted with such an amazing view. The cooking is organic and be warned – Léopoldine doesn't stint on the portions, so you'd better prepare yourself! This place is perfect for ramblers, the col of the Schlucht is barely an hour's walk away and there's some incredible scenery on the doorstep (ask Léopoldine which routes to take, she'll be only to happy to help).

STOSSWIHR-AMPFERBACH 68140 (6KM W)

|●| AUBERGE DES CASCADES

How to get there: leave Stosswihr by the route des Crêtes and take a left turn before the church.
☎ 03.89.77.44.74
Closed Mondays and Tuesdays out of season, Mondays after 14th July, the last two weeks in January, and the first two weeks in February.

Service up to 11pm. A very good inn that doesn't get many tourists (yet). It's pretty and has lots of flowers and you can hear the lovely sound of a little waterfall just nearby. There's a hearty set meal at 48F or, à la carte, rather strange specialities such as flambéd tart of frogs' legs which you can enjoy watched over by the attentive Madame Decker (and her rows of china ducks on the window sills!). If you'd rather have something more classic, the rib steak with ceps is a real treat. As for wine, treat your friends to the house Edelzwicker. It isn't expensive and it's the best we've had in the region. The flambéd tart is baked in a wood-fired stove.

STOSSWIHR 68140 (8KM W)

|●| AUBERGE DU SCHUPFEREN

Centre; leave Munster by the D417 going towards col de la Schlucht and turn right towards Le Tanet ski resort. When you see the sign on a tree about 4km down the road, take the dirt track (it's OK in a car) and it's about 3km away. Keep the Sarrois refuge on the left and continue along the road on your right (there is a sign).
☎ 03.89.77.31.23
Closed Mondays and Tuesdays.

Service 9am–7pm. This place is really off the beaten track but it's definitely worth the effort to get there. It's popular with skiers in winter and walkers in summer. Christophe Kuhlman, the nice easy-going owner, will give you a warm welcome. He cooks great little dishes like *Fleischsnecke* (pastry with a filling of mince) or can make you a salad with produce from the garden. The menu is written on a blackboard. Main courses 40F, starters 20–25F. Don't forget to order a small jug of house Edelzwicker (a white wine made from a blend of grapes). And what a wonderful view you get here right over the forest and valleys! A real favourite of ours that you just won't want to leave!

NIEDERBRONN-LES-BAINS 67110

10% ⌂ |●| HÔTEL-RESTAURANT CULLY**

33-37 rue de la République (West); it's near the station.
☎ 03.88.09.01.42 ➡ 03.88.09.05.80
Restaurant closed Tuesday evenings and Wednesdays Nov–March, and during the February school holidays.
Secure parking. TV. Disabled access.

Book well in advance because it tends to get busy around the times when people traditionally come to take the waters. The hotel is low-key and comfortable. Rooms are big and the majority of them have a balcony. Doubles 270 and 290F with shower/wc or bath. Half-board 270F. Good set meals 58F (weekday lunchtimes), 140F, 165F and 230F. There's a shady arbour where you can sit and have a drink or a quiet meal. The hotel is right beside a park with golfing facilities and games for the kids.

|●| RESTAURANT LES ACACIAS**

35 rue des Acacias (North-West); leave the main street, go past the station and take rue des Acacias — watch out, it's steep.

☎ 03.88.09.00.47
Closed Fridays and Saturday lunchtimes out of season, and Feb 1–15. **Car park**. **Disabled access**.

This is a very classy place on the edge of the forest. Terrace for the summer. Stylish service. Expect to pay about 200F à la carte but they also do a nice set meals for 65F (weekday lunchtimes); others 85F, 115F, 140F and 215F. Traditional Alsace cooking. Pretty view of the valley and the factory.

OBERNAI 67210

10% HÔTEL LA CLOCHE

90 rue du Général-Gouraud
☎ 03.88.95.52.89 F 03.88.95.07.63
TV.

The rooms are modern and cosy, and prices are reasonable: from 200F for a double with shower and a private wc outside the room, up to 395F for a split-level room in the attic that sleeps 4. There are three single rooms at 160F with shower and private wc on the landing (with own key). The rooms that look out onto the square are bathed in sunlight and come with an enormous bathroom (290F). The restaurant next door (which we haven't tried) has original paintings and beautiful stained glass windows. It also, rather incongruously, lists a fair number of *nems* (spring rolls) among the starters on offer.

10% HOSTELLERIE LA DILIGENCE**

23 place de la Mairie (Centre).
☎ 03.88.95.55.69 F 03.88.95.42.46
TV.

It would be difficult to find anywhere more central – the rooms at the front look out onto place de l'Hôtel de ville, the heart of the town. With such a great location, you'd think the owners would just sit back and watch the customers roll in, but fortunately that isn't the case. The rooms have nearly all been renovated and are now of an excellent standard. There is a lovely breakfast room with bay windows overlooking the square. Rooms 410F with bath.

L'AGNEAU D'OR

99 rue du Général-Gouraud; it's on the main road.
☎ 03.88.95.28.22
Closed Mondays.

This is an authentic *winstub* (inn which only serves wine of the region). The painted ceiling, cuckoo clock, prints and decorated plates all make for a cosy atmosphere. Tasty local dishes are served up in generous portions. Good *menu du jour* at 55F (weekday lunchtimes only). Other set meals 110F, 140F and 180F. Children's set meal 45F. À la carte, there's fritters of Munster cheese flavoured with cumin, mixed salad and potatoes for 60F and braised stuffed zander served with *choucroute*, cumin sauce and *lardons* for 85F.

KLINGENTHAL 67530 (6KM W)

10% HÔTEL-RESTAURANT AU CYGNE

23 route du Mont-Sainte-Odile (South-West); D426.
☎ 03.88.95.82.94
Closed two weeks in June and two weeks in November. Restaurant closed Tuesday evenings and Wednesdays. **Car park**.

This is a nice little place in a good location on the Mont-Sainte-Odile road. Traditional atmosphere. The rooms are simple and clean: expect to pay 130–200F for a double. Half-board is 180F. Set meals at 85F, 100F, 110F and 145F with all the delights of home-cooking. Generous portions. Delicious fruit tarts made in the family bakery nextdoor. Children's meal 25F.

OTTROTT 67530

10% À L'AMI FRITZ***

8 rue des Châteaux
☎ 03.88.95.80.81 F 03.88.95.84.85
Closed Wednesdays. **Car park**. **TV**. **Canal+**.

This house is quite impressive from both the outside (it dates back to the 17th century) and the inside. The rooms are all beautifully decorated and you're guaranteed a good night's sleep. The bathrooms are fitted with all mod cons and are just as pretty as the bedrooms. The ones overlooking the street have air-conditioning. Make sure you ask for a room in the main hotel because there's also an annexe about 600m away. The prices are decent (from 380F for a double in the hotel and 260F in the annexe). Pleasant dining room with rustic décor and efficient, attentive service. Patrick Fritz, the owner, prepares inventive fresh-tasting dishes with regional overtones. His strudel of black pudding with horseradish (in season), his soup of split peas and smoked duck, or his warm salad of suckling pig make incredibly good starters. To follow, try the fillet of zander with beer-flavoured butter served with *choucroute*, the *choucroute* with duck, the *choucroute royale*, or the gratinéd tripe braised in Sylvaner. Dishes also reflect what the market has to offer. When we were there, for example, there was pigeon salad with truffle shavings and poached John Dory with *mousserons* (a kind of mushroom). Expect to pay about 200F à la carte. Set meals at 125, 198, 255F. Children's meal 45F.

PETITE-PIERRE (LA) 67290

10% HÔTEL-RESTAURANT AU LION D'OR**

15 rue Principale
☎ 03.88.70.45.06 F 03.88.70.45.56
Closed in January. **Car park. TV. Disabled access.**

This rather chic little village right in the centre of the regional park of Vosges is a favourite with German holiday-makers. All of the hotels and restaurants qualify as top of the range and the *Lion d'Or* is no exception. In summer, you can have something from the grill and eat in the garden or there's a *winstub* (wine bar) with affordable prices. Come in the autumn or spring, when it's not too hot. The restaurant is quite expensive. Set meals 120F, 175F, 190F and 260F. The hotel has two rooms at 200F with washing facilities. Expect to pay 380– 440F for the others. Indoor swimming pool and sauna. Courteous welcome, wonderful view of the forest. An ideal spot for a romantic weekend for two.

WINGEN-SUR-MODER 67290 (10KM N)

RELAIS NATURE

7 rue de Zittersheim (Centre).
☎ 03.88.89.80.07 F 03.88.89.82.85
Car park.

We really like this lovely country inn that stands in a little village in the middle of the Vosges regional park. Owners Linda and Jacky Bergmann have seven pleasant and well-equipped rooms (but no TV!). Bright, fresh décor (white walls and pine furniture). Warm welcome. 300F for 2 (breakfast included). Evening meals on request. Jacky, who loves the forest of Vosges, is a real fountain of knowledge when it comes to what you can do in the area and he can give you pointers about walks, mountain biking, and the local wildlife. Bicycle hire available. Small swimming pool. One of our favourite places.

À LA PETITE GROTTE

Lieu-dit "Huhnerscher"
How to get there: D256.
☎ 03.88.89.83.55
Closed Monday–Saturday lunchtime (out of season), two weeks end of Oct–beginning of Nov, and Feb 15–28. Open weekdays by reservation only (10 people minimum). **Car park.**

A nice little inn offering good food at very low prices in a tiny village deep in the forest. The young German owner has been in France for a while now and she'll give you a really warm welcome. The décor is lovely and fresh (pine furniture, big traditional stove). Hearty set meal 70F. Excellent couscous and fondue (these have to be ordered in advance). Also a small selection of salads, soup etc.

RIBEAUVILLÉ 68150

HÔTEL DE LA TOUR**

1 rue de la Mairie (Centre); it's in place de la Mairie.
☎ 03.89.73.72.73 F 03.89.73.38.74
Closed Jan to mid-March. **Secure parking. TV.**

The hotel is right in the heart of this little medieval town. Pleasant rooms 340F with shower/wc, 420F with bath. Free facilities for hotel guests (sauna, Turkish baths, jacuzzi, and tennis courts outside the village). No restaurant but there is a *winstub* (a little bistro where you can taste local wines). Very pleasant, quite stylish place.

CAVEAU DE L'AMI FRITZ

place de l'Ancien Hôpital.
☎ 03.89.73.68.11 F 03.89.73.30.63

You'll need to book a long time in advance for this place – as its name implies, it's very popular with German tourists. It's always lively and full of bustle with the smiling waitresses running upstairs and down to take orders. Germans and French people mingle together in this friendly atmosphere. The meals are a bit dear, expect to pay 100–150F. As for the rooms, they're divine. You get to them by a series of staircases and doors and soon lose your bearings. But the walk is worth it – the rooms are absolutely huge. For 350F (which is well worth it) you get a beautiful half-timbered room with shower and a little sitting room. It's almost like a two-roomed flat!

L'AUBERGE AU ZAHNACKER

8 rue du Général-de-Gaulle (Centre).
☎ 03.89.73.60.77
Closed mid Jan–beginning of March.

Service 9am–10pm. This inn, owned by the local wine co-operative, is a little oasis just off the main street where all the tourists seem to flock together like sheep. It's wonderful in summer to sit out on the terrace when the sweet-smelling wisteria is in full bloom and have a glass of Pinot Blanc while you wait for your *presskopf* (brawn) or onion tart. In winter the *winstub* (wine bar) is warm and pleasant and you can squeeze up next to your neighbour on a wooden bench and have a drop of Edelzwicker (a white wine made from a blend of grapes). Expect to pay 110–180F for a meal, but if you're not that peckish you can always settle for a quiche at 37F. Specialities are game in season, calf's head *vinaigrette,* and smoked tongue with Madeira sauce.

ILLHAEUSERN 68970 (11KM E)

À LA TRUITE

17 rue du 25-Janvier; coming from Ribeauville on the D106, it's on the left before the bridge just as you come into the village.
☎ 03.89.71.83.51
Closed Tuesday evenings, Wednesdays, two weeks in February and one week in June.

A nice country inn with a terrace which looks out onto the river and the weeping willows. The simple and relaxed dining room is full of office workers, factory workers, farmers, long distance lorry drivers and anyone else on the road looking for an inexpensive meal. They serve the best fish stew in the whole of Alsace here (made to order) which they call Marie-Louise. The chef's speciality, it's served with noodles and costs 132F. If you don't fancy that, then try the trout with boiled potatoes or the fried carp, a real delicacy! The bill will never come as a shock. Set meals 89–130F plus dishes à la carte. They have oysters too.

RIQUEWIHR 68340

HÔTEL DE LA COURONNE

5 rue de la Couronne; it's just next to rue du Général de Gaulle.
☎ 03.89.49.03.03 F➜ 03.89.49.01.01
Car park.

This attractive hotel, which dates back to the 16th century, is simply perfect. There's a welcoming atmosphere about the place and, unusually for Riquewihr. the owners' only concern is to ensure you have a pleasant stay. When you see the little wooden benches and tables outside you'll want just one thing: a glass of Gewurztraminer before going off to explore the forests nearby. Inside, all the rooms have been refurbished and, a playful touch, the plain walls have been stencilled with a flower here and a tree there — all in good taste. In fact, everything about this hotel is pleasing and the prices are pretty decent for where it is. Doubles with bath 320F–600F. We've been to just about everywhere in Riquewihr and this is the nicest place in the area.

RESTAURANT ST-ALEXIS

lieu-dit Kaysersberg; leave Riquewihr by place des Charpentiers and follow the pretty road which goes up to the left. It's not well sign-posted so just stay in the outside lane when you come to a junction. It's about ten minutes by car.
☎ 03.89.73.90.38
Closed Fridays.

Service noon–8pm. We thought it was impossible to find a good and not too expensive place to eat in Roquewihr — well, we were wrong! Mind you, this pretty converted farmhouse, covered in ivy, is tucked away in the middle of the forest and only the locals seem to find their way there. Inside, there's a tantalizing smell of soup and *choucroute*. Set meals 60F, 82F and 98F. The 82F one is very filling. Good home-made soup and a large and succulent ham omelette and *crudités* tickle your taste buds in preparation for a delicious free-range chicken which has been simmering in the pan for hours. And then, after all that, a lovely *tarte alsacienne* (a kind of jam tart) which finishes everything off nicely. If you're not that hungry, share —- the portions are enormous. If the weather's nice you can sit and eat outside.

HUNAWIHR 68150 (4KM N)

WINSTUB SUZEL

2 rue de l'Église; it's very near the village church.
☎ 03.89.73.30.85
Closed Mondays. **Disabled access**.

You'll get a warm welcome from the Mittnacht family. In summer the shady terrace is covered with flowers and has a view of the pretty church tower. You can also visit the cellars and do a bit of wine-tasting. But the main reason to come here is the fine food. Whatever you have it'll be good. An onion tart with salad may be enough for some, while the 89F set meal will be just the thing if you're famished, since it consists of onion tart, *roulades farcies* (rolled meat or fish with stuffing), sauté potatoes, green salad and dessert. The 85F set meal comes with home-made *choucroute*. They also have *kougel-*

hopfs (a ring cake with dried fruit and almonds) and *bretzels* (pretzels) and, on Sunday evenings, flambéd tarts.

SAVERNE 67700

10% AUBERGE DE JEUNESSE

château des Rohan (Centre).
☎ 03.88.91.14.84 F 03.88.71.15.97
Closed Dec 15–Jan 15. **Car park**.

Doors open 8–10am and 5–10pm. The hostel is housed in the right wing of his superb château, above a school. 65F per person in a dorm with 6 beds, and 85F for a single or double room. Sheets: 16F. Meal: 49F.

HÔTEL EUROPE**

7 rue de la Gare; it's 5 minutes from the station and the château.
☎ 03.88.71.12.07 F 03.88.71.11.43
TV.

This is without a doubt the best hotel in town. It has 29 rooms in all. Doubles 330–350F with shower/wc, 410F with bath. The latter are more spacious and have cable TV. The ritzy atmosphere, the first-rate service, and the excellent buffet breakfast all keep the customers coming back, including a large number of people who work at the European Parliament in Strasbourg. For families there's a flat (700F) in an adjoining house.

CAVEAU DE L'ESCALE

10 quai du Canal; it's a stone's throw from the centre – quai du Canal runs parallel to the main street.
☎ 03.88.91.12.23
Closed Wednesdays, Saturday lunchtimes and Christmas–Jan 1.

The dining room, which has a vaulted ceiling, is in the basement. Nice welcome. The meticulously prepared classic regional dishes include *waedele* served with horseradish sauce or on a bed of *choucroute,* roast beef *à l'alsacienne*, and *quenelles* of liver with sauté potatoes, and are served up in generous portions. Dish of the day 40F. Cheapest set meal 52F, others 96F and 155F. Flambéd tarts in the evening. The terrace faces the marina. Good wine list. House wine 65F (weekday lunchtimes only).

TAVERNE KATZ

80 Grand-Rue (Centre); it's not far from the château des Rohan.
☎ 03.88.71.16.56
Closed Tuesday evenings and Wednesdays Oct–April.

The building, one of the most beautiful in Alsace, was originally erected in 1605 as a residence for a man called Katz, who was a kind of tax collector. You can read all about the history of the place on a board outside just above the menu. Beautiful dining room with wood veneer.The cooking is first-rate. Cheapest set meal 89F. Specialities include *timbale* of chicken in pastry served with *spaetzles* (noodles), marinated *baeckeoffa* (stew of beef, mutton and pork), *rognons blancs* (testicles), braised ham, and *choucroute à l'alsacienne.* Traditional dishes and excellent desserts. The terrace looks out onto the pedestrian precinct. As in most *winstubs,* the food doesn't vary much, and you can be pretty sure of finding the same menu year in year out. Suzie and Jos are the friendly owners and it's always a pleasure to be here.

SÉLESTAT 67600

10% HÔTEL VAILLANT**

place de la République (Centre); it's halfway between the town centre and the station.
☎ 03.88.92.09.46 F 03.88.82.95.01
Restaurant closed Saturday and Sunday lunchtimes out of season. **Secure parking**. **TV**. **Canal+**. **Disabled access**.

This is a large modern hotel which dates back to 1967 and it'll be a hit with those who love contemporary-style bedrooms. The rooms, individually furnished with pieces that are brightly coloured without being overpowering, all have their own personality. Choose the one that matches yours. Double rooms 250–310F with shower/wc, 290–380F with bath. Small gym with sauna and jacuzzi. Set meals in the restaurant start at 88F. À la carte also available.

AUBERGE DES ALLIÉS**

39 rue des Chevaliers (Centre); it's between tour des Chevaliers and the churches of Saint-Foy and Saint-George.
☎ 03.88.92.09.34 F 03.88.92.12.88
Closed Sunday evenings, Jan 15–30, and June 27–July 10. **TV**.

The building has a long history. It dates back to at least 1372, was a bakery in the first half of the 19th century when Louis-Philippe ruled France, and became a restaurant in 1918. In the middle of the dining room there's an impressive old stove, typical of the Alsace region. There's also a beautiful fresco from the first half of the 19th century, which is interesting for its depiction of what local life was like back in the olden days. The à la carte menu is typical of this type of restaurant, offering dishes along the lines of ham with *choucroute*. Set meals 98, 138 and 185F. Double rooms with bath 330F. Ask to have a look at the rooms before you decide which one you want. Half-board from 300F per person.

RATHSAMHAUSEN 67600 (3KM E)

10% HÔTEL-RESTAURANT À L'ÉTOILE**

Grande-Rue; on the D21 in the direction of Muttersholtz.
☎ 03.88.92.35.79 F 03.88.82.91.66
Closed three weeks in November. **Car park**. **TV**.

A young couple have cleverly modernized this old house by adding an extension with a bright foyer and stairway in wood and glass. Pleasant rooms 250F for 2 and 340F for 4. The dining room is warm and intimate in the evening and there's a little Christmas crèche in one corner. We had excellent fried fillets of carp from the small à la carte menu. Set meals 38 and 85F. In summer the terrace is covered with flowers and there's a swimming pool. A really nice little place.

EBERSMUNSTER 67600 (9KM NE)

LES DEUX CLEFS

How to get there: take the N83, then the D210.
☎ 03.88.85.71.55
Closed Thursdays, end of Dec–end of Jan, and 10 days in July.

This friendly little place opposite the most beautiful baroque church in Bas-Rhin is well known for the quality of its regional cooking. Madame Baur and her daughter are really nice and make you feel at home. The old clock that's 10 minutes fast, the gleaming copperware and the wooden bench that runs along the wall all make for a cosy atmosphere. The famous fish stew, which has to be the one of the main reasons for coming here, is the house speciality and it really does fill you up (which is a shame – the desserts are delicious). It's always made with three or four kinds of river fish (eel, tench, pike, perch and so on, depending on availability) in a smooth white sauce that's full of flavour and served with home-made pasta. It costs 130F and is well worth it!

DAMBACH-LA-VILLE 67650 (10KM N)

HÔTEL-RESTAURANT À LA COURONNE*

13 place du Marché
☎ 03.88.92.40.85 F 03.88.92.63.63
Closed Thursdays, the last three weeks in February, and the second fortnight in November.

The building that houses this little hotel and restaurant in the centre of a delightful village dates back to 1569. The architecture is superb. There are only three bedrooms unfortunately but they're pleasant and have got character (the furniture is in the style typical of the region). Doubles with shower/basin (wc on the landing) are 180F. Set meals in the restaurant at 50F, 75F, 105F and 110F. There's a nice *winstub* on the ground floor.

HÔTEL LE VIGNOBLE**

1 rue de l'Église; it's beside the church.
☎ 03.88.92.43.75
Closed Sundays and Mondays out of season, two weeks in mid Nov, and mid Dec–mid March. **Car park**. **TV**. **Disabled access**.

This charming hotel has been converted very tastefully from an old 18th century gabled barn. Stylish, comfortable rooms, with doubles at 275 and 300F. Extra bed 80F. Traditional or "vigneron" breakfast 35F.

THANNENKIRCH 68590 (15.5KM SW)

AUBERGE LA MEUNIÈRE**

30 rue Sainte-Anne; there are only two ways you can get to this village (which is 510m up) – the more scenic route comes via the château of Haut-Koenigsbourg.
☎ 03.89.73.10.47 F 03.89.73.12.31
Closed Nov 15–March 30. **Car park**. **TV**.

This is a friendly and delightful inn with a pretty round tower. It' s ideally located and looks right over the valley, conjuring up images of deepest Switzerland. The carved shutters and the whole atmosphere of the place makes you want to write poetry! You'll get a very warm welcome and a wonderful view wherever you are. All the rooms have their own name – 'Lucie' is a family room with a mezzanine floor which looks out onto the meadows and the mountains, while 'Barbe' and 'Octave' both have big wooden balconies, and the wood panelling in 'Bernardine' is 150 years old. Fine, inventive cuisine in the restaurant. Prices are reasonable, with a set meal at 95F (not available Sunday lunchtimes). À la carte, you can choose from succulent dishes like *baeckoffa* of snails in Riesling, oven-baked pike, wild boar with juniper berries, andl ox tongue with a horseradish sauce. Bed and breakfast from 310F for two. Good deal for half-board. If you're romantically inclined then this is the place for you, if you can afford it. But the prices are justified given the quality of the place.

STRASBOURG 67000

SEE MAP ON PAGE 18

AUBERGE DE JEUNESSE RENÉ-CASSIN

9 rue de l'Auberge-de-Jeunesse – La Montagne Verte (South-West); take bus no.3 or 23 in the direction of Lingolsheim and get off at the "Auberge de jeunesse" stop.
☎ 03.88.30.26.46 F 03.88.30.35.16
Closed Jan 1–Feb 10. **Car park. Disabled access.**

It's advisable to book in advance here. It has a total of 286 beds and you'll pay 69F a night in a room for 5–6 people (breakfast included). Sheets 17F. Doubles 99F per person, singles 149F. Campsite 42F. You can pitch your own tent. Packed lunch or evening meal 30–49F. Equipped kitchen for own use. Evening entertainment.

AUBERGE DE JEUNESSE DU PARC DU RHIN

rue des Cavaliers (West); it's near the border, in the direction of Kehl – from the station take the tram to place Homme de Fer, then a no. 2 bus, direction Pont du Rhin.
☎ 03.88.45.54.20 F 03.88.45.54.21
Closed December. **Car park. Disabled access.**

This hostel has 221 beds. 98F per person in a room for 3 or 4, 138F per person for a double, 184F for a single room. Prices include sheet hire and breakfast. Four of the four-bedded rooms have been adapted for disabled access and come with bathroom. Meal with drink 54F. Prices reduced in Jan–Feb, July–August and November.

HÔTEL SCHUTZENBOCK

81 av. Jean-Jaurès – Neudorf (South-East); start from place de l'Étoile and it's about 2km from the town centre.
☎ 03.88.34.04.19
Closed Saturday lunchtimes, Sundays, in July, and during the Christmas holidays.

An inexpensive, clean, and friendly hotel. Rooms with basin 140F (for a double), 170F (with twin beds), 190F (for 3). Set meals 49F (lunchtimes) and 90F (evenings). Simple, regional cooking. Half-board 170F, full board 210F. Who could say fairer than that?

10% HÔTEL LE GRILLON**

2 rue Thiergarten. **MAP A3-4**
☎ 03.88.32.71.88 F 03.88.32.22.01
TV.

The cheaper rooms, at 160F for a single and from 200F for a double (shower/wc on the landing), are in the fourth-floor attic. Unfortunately there's no lift but they do have a lovely view over the rooftops. There's a lovely family room (double bed and two singles) for 390F, where the sun comes pouring in through three windows (it's on a corner). Number 307 also gets a lot of light though it isn't on the corner. Rooms at the back are a bit smaller and number 112 just above the bar should be avoided because it's very noisy.

HÔTEL DE L'ILL**

8 rue des Bateliers – Krutenau. **MAP D3-7**
☎ 03.88.36.20.01 F 03.88.35.30.03
Closed Christmas–Jan 1. **TV. Disabled access.**

This is a good place with good prices in a quiet street and you really should book in advance. Doubles with shower 230F, with shower/wc or bath 270–350F. There are about 10 non-smoking rooms which is a good idea for those of you who can't stand the lingering smell of tobacco. There's a lovely terrace (to which two rooms have direct access) on the first floor, and from 11am to 5pm you can lounge about in the sun with a view of the nearby church of Saint-Madeleine. Generous breakfast and new, comfy bedding. Friendly welcome from the Ehrhardt family.

HÔTEL COUVENT DU FRANCISCAIN**

18 rue du Faubourg-de-Pierre. **MAP B1-5**
☎ 03.88.32.93.93 x03.88.75.68.46
Closed at Christmas and on New Year's Day.
Car park. TV. Disabled access.

A centrally located and carefully renovated hotel with lots of rooms to suit all pockets. Double rooms 230F with basin/wc and 320F with shower/wc or bath. Warm welcome.

HÔTEL GUTENBERG**

31 rue des Serruriers. **MAP C3-8**
☎ 03.88.32.17.15 F 03.88.75.76.67
Closed the first week in January. **TV.**

The owner here is mad about military engravings from the Napoleonic period (his great-grandfather was an officer in the Grande Armée) and you can see some of them on the walls of each floor. A few are quite pretty. This passion for the Empire can be seen in the décor of the rooms but it's not oppressive thanks to the old pieces of family furniture that the owner had the good sense to hang on to. Depending on which room you're in, you'll be sharing it with grandmother's wardrobe or uncle's old writing desk or possibly even pieces of an old church altar found by chance in an antique shop. The rooms on the fifth floor (three of which have a mezzanine floor) have a delightful view out over the rooftops (you'll get more or less the same view on the fourth floor). It's an attractive hotel but there are still a few things that could be improved – for example, the rooms on the first floor haven't been refurbished yet (they'll be done in the year 2000 apparently) so give these a miss if you can, and the breakfast on offer is pretty bland and too expensive. Double rooms 245F with basin/wc, 320F with shower/wc, and 350–450F with bath/wc. Warm welcome.

LE PETIT TRIANON**

8 Petite-Rue-de-la-Course. **MAP A3-6**
☎ 03.88.32.63.97 F→ 03.88.32.94.92
Car park. TV. Canal+.

The rooms here vary in price according to their size. Odd-numbered rooms are bigger and the ones that look out onto the street are brighter. All 25 rooms come with shower/wc and Canal+. Doubles 250–340F. It certainly isn't Versailles, and Marie-Antoinette would undoubtedly have turned her nose up at the place. But we have simpler tastes and this hotel will do us nicely for a short stay in the town. Obviously if you're planning to stay longer then go for something a bit nicer, but there aren't many places in Strasbourg with prices like these. Be warned – they don't accept cheques.

10% HÔTEL SAINT-CHRISTOPHE**

2 pl. de la gare. **MAP A3-9**
☎ 03.88.22.30.30
TV. Canal+.

This well-kept hotel called after the patron saint of travellers is useful both for businessmen coming from the station opposite and holiday-makers travelling by car (it's difficult to get into the centre by car). It's really comfortable and you'll get a good night's sleep. Double rooms 300–380F. The most expensive, which are at the back, are bigger and quieter. The pleasant little inner courtyard is bathed in sunlight nearly all day and is a nice place for breakfast or a late-afternoon refreshment.

HÔTEL DE L'EUROPE***

38-40 rue du Fossé-des-Tanneurs. **MAP B3-10**
☎ 03.88.32.17.88 F→ 03.88.75.65.45
Closed Dec 22–29.**Secure parking. TV. Canal+. Disabled access.**

Ideally located for exploring the city. Some rooms are non-smoking and all have spacious bathrooms – 370–420F with shower/wc and 480–550F with bath. Use of garage 60F. In the hall ther'es an amazing sandstone reproduction of the cathedral which is 2.82m high and nearly touches the ceiling. It weighs a ton and a half!

10% SUISSE HÔTEL**

24 rue de la Rape. **MAP C3-12**
☎ 03.88.35.22.11 F→ 03.88.25.74.23
TV.

This wonderful azure blue building dates back to 1763, but it only recently became a hotel. Inside, there's a handful of rooms, all different, decorated in lovely warm colours. Number 21 is the nicest —- it has a huge bathroom, it looks out onto the cathedral and is ideal for families. Doubles 430–530F.

ROMANTIK HÔTEL BEAUCOUR***

5 rue des Bouchers. **MAP C4-11**
☎ 03.88.76.72.00 F→ 03.88.76.72.60
TV. Canal+.

This hotel is housed in five half-timbered listed buildings from the 18th century. There's been so much renovation that they don't look altogether authentic but the place does have a certain charm. It's comfortable, there's no other place like it, and you'll have a great time staying here. Honestly, we liked every single room here, whatever the style – attic, Italian, regional. Suite number 103 (950F) which looks out onto the cathedral and has a small office area, bathroom and jacuzzi, is first-class, and number 404 in the attic, pleasant, bright and spacious, would suit a businessman who wanted to do some work. Prices vary from 550F for a single to 780F for a double with bath. Suites are 950F. Use of garage 55F. Buffet breakfast 65F.

AU PONT CORBEAU

21 quai Saint-Nicolas. **MAP C4-21**
☎ 03.88.35.60.68
Closed Saturdays, Sunday lunchtimes, and July 12–Aug 10.

In our opinion, this place has got quite a few qualities which are worthy of mention. First, the owner will always give you a warm, friendly welcome. Secondly the food here is great, and lastly it's one of the few *winstubs* in the town centre (in fact it's a stone's throw from the cathedral) which opens on Sunday nights. And – though these may be minor details – the mineral water is from the Bas-Rhin, which

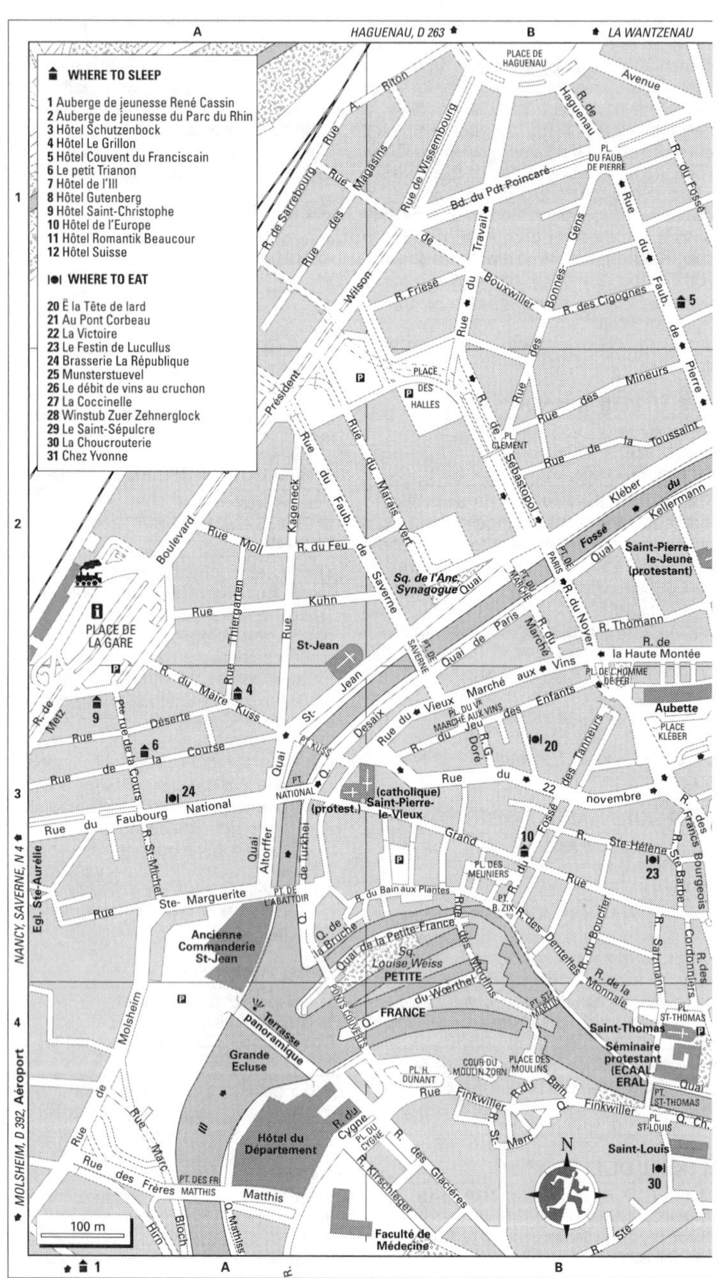
WHERE TO SLEEP
1 Auberge de jeunesse René Cassin
2 Auberge de jeunesse du Parc du Rhin
3 Hôtel Schutzenbock
4 Hôtel Le Grillon
5 Hôtel Couvent du Franciscain
6 Le petit Trianon
7 Hôtel de l'Ill
8 Hôtel Gutenberg
9 Hôtel Saint-Christophe
10 Hôtel de l'Europe
11 Hôtel Romantik Beaucour
12 Hôtel Suisse
WHERE TO EAT
20 Ë la Tête de lard
21 Au Pont Corbeau
22 La Victoire
23 Le Festin de Lucullus
24 Brasserie La République
25 Munsterstuevel
26 Le débit de vins au cruchon
27 La Coccinelle
28 Winstub Zuer Zehnerglock
29 Le Saint-Sépulcre
30 La Choucrouterie
31 Chez Yvonne
HAGUENAU, D 263
LA WANTZENAU
NANCY, SAVERNE, N 4
MOLSHEIM, D 392, Aéroport
PLACE DE HAGUENAU
PLACE DE LA GARE
PLACE DES HALLES
PLACE KLÉBER
Sq. de l'Anc. Synagogue
St-Jean
Saint-Pierre-le-Jeune (protestant)
Saint-Pierre-le-Vieux
Aubette
Ancienne Commanderie St-Jean
Terrasse panoramique
Grande Ecluse
Hôtel du Département
Faculté de Médecine
PETITE FRANCE
Sq. Louise Weiss
Saint-Thomas
Séminaire protestant (ECAAL, ERAL)
Saint-Louis
Egl. Ste-Aurélie
100 m

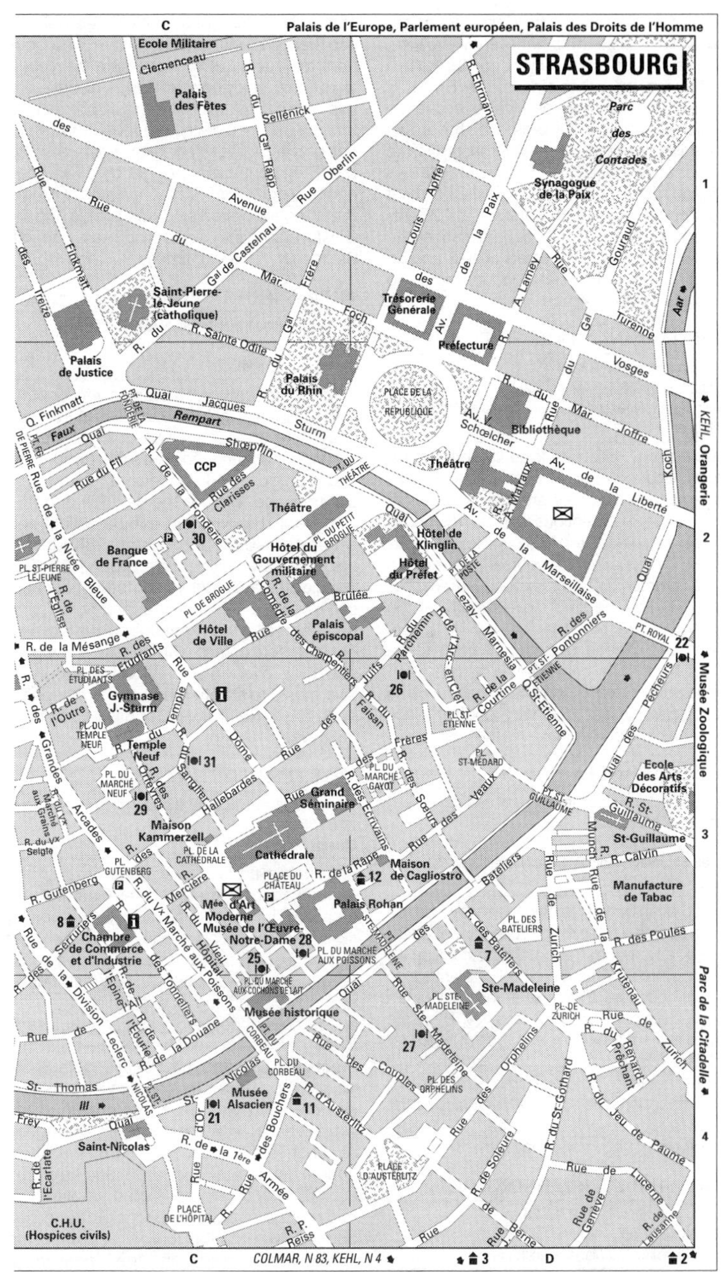
STRASBOURG
Palais de l'Europe, Parlement européen, Palais des Droits de l'Homme
KEHL, Orangerie
Musée Zoologique
Parc de la Citadelle
COLMAR, N 83, KEHL, N 4
Ecole Militaire
Palais des Fêtes
Parc des Contades
Synagogue de la Paix
Saint-Pierre-le-Jeune (catholique)
Palais de Justice
Trésorerie Générale
Préfecture
Palais du Rhin
PLACE DE LA RÉPUBLIQUE
Bibliothèque
Théâtre
CCP
Hôtel de Klinglin
Hôtel du Préfet
Hôtel du Gouvernement militaire
Banque de France
Hôtel de Ville
Palais épiscopal
Gymnase J.-Sturm
Temple Neuf
Maison Kammerzell
Cathédrale
Maison de Cagliostro
Palais Rohan
Mée d'Art Moderne
Musée de l'Œuvre-Notre-Dame
Chambre de Commerce et d'Industrie
Musée historique
Musée Alsacien
Saint-Nicolas
C.H.U. (Hospices civils)
Ste-Madeleine
Ecole des Arts Décoratifs
St-Guillaume
Manufacture de Tabac
PLACE D'AUSTERLITZ
PLACE DE L'HÔPITAL

is a nice change from the Carola (from the Haut-Rhin) you seem to get everywhere else, and the draught beer which comes from a brewery on the other side of the Rhine, is excellent (Kronenbourg and Heineken are the usuals elsewhere). You see, it's these little things which make all the difference. On the menu there's grilled ham with sauté potatoes at 75F (a must), salad with a selection of meat and *crudités*, and sauté potatoes at 72F, fritters of calf's brains in a *remoulade* sauce with steamed potatoes and salad at 82F and so on. This place really does sum up everything that's great about Alsace.

|●| RESTAURANT À LA TÊTE DE LARD

3 rue Hannomg. **MAP B3-20**
☎ 03.88.32.13.56
Closed Saturday lunchtimes, Sundays, and Monday lunchtimes

Flambéd tart, grilled knuckle of pork, house salads, *choucroutes*, Munster, Riesling... All the regional specialities are here and they're served in an unpretentious fashion. The prices are easy on the pocket. You can expect to pay 40–80F for a hearty main course. You've got to try the *flammenküche* (or flambéd tart) which is cooked in a wood-fired stove directly on top of the logs so that the topping of bacon, onions and cheese is slightly charred. Originally the tart was cooked in a baker's oven alongside the bread. Don't be shy about using your fingers to eat it! A very popular place which has stayed special over the years.

|●| RESTAURANT LA VICTOIRE

2 bd de la Victoire; it's on the corner of quai des Pêcheurs. **MAP D2-22**
☎ 03.88.35.39.35
Closed Saturday evenings, Sundays, and 3 weeks in August.

Service until 1am. This place is always full, so either reserve a table or get here early! It doesn't look much from the outside, but inside it's pretty impressive and you're guaranteed a great atmosphere. It's where all the intellectuals come — the university isn't far away. There are quite a few set meals for less than 50F (starter and the day's special). Very conventional regional cooking, but you come here more for the atmosphere than for the originality of the food! *Menu complet* around 100–120F. Philosophy evenings every Monday 6pm–8pm.

|●| WINSTUB ZUER ZEHNERGLOCK

4 rue du Vieil-Hôpital. **MAP C3-28**
☎ 03.88.32.87.09
Closed Sundays and Monday lunchtimes.

The cosy interior, beautiful painted dresser, checked napkins, and an owner who goes from table to table to make sure everyone's alright and enjoying themselves all have you hoping for great things from this place in the touristy part of the city. However, it's nothing out of the ordinary, and like most *winstubs* today, this one seems to get by on its good name alone. On Friday evenings, Roger Krautt gets a bit of a sing-song going and the *winstub* turns into something like a cabaret. Set meals 49F (lunchtimes), 90F and 125F.

|●| BRASSERIE LA RÉPUBLIQUE

40 rue du Faubourg-National. **MAP A3-24**
☎ 03.88.32.07.86
Closes at midnight.

This big brasserie-restaurant is very popular with the locals, including families in from the country to do their shopping. It has a reputation for serving consistently good food and is a godsend if you're on a budget. Efficient service. Dish of the day 40F and 45F with hors d'œuvre (unbeatable value) and set meals at 52F, 72F, 88F and 98F. Most of the à la carte dishes are around 60–75F. Specialities are kidneys flambéd in cognac, calf's head, house steak tartare, horse meat (foal, actually) with garlic, and pizzas. The 68F set meal comes with *choucroute*. Flambéd tarts every night. Wine by the glass. Live music to create a bit of an atmosphere on Fridays, Saturdays, Sundays and public holidays.

|●| LE FESTIN DE LUCULLUS

18 rue sainte-Hélène. **MAP B3-23**
☎ 03.88.22.40.78
Closed Sundays.

Four years under the watchful eye of the famous French chef, Michel Guérard, will definitely influence you and your cooking skills! All the good ideas which the chef picked up from his time at Eugénie-les-Bains can now be seen here. Fresh herbs, seasoning, cooking – everything the chef learned about cooking times and the use of fresh herbs and seasonings he puts into practice here and he always gets great results. The cheerful, friendly welcome and service along with the great prices means you'll want to come back again and again. At lunchtime there's a 56F *formule* (main course and starter or dessert) and an amazing 70F *menu complet* When we went we had muzzle of ox in herb vinaigrette, grilled poussin with onion *confit* and *mesclun* (mixed green salad), and fresh pear tart *à l'alsacienne* with soft fruit *coulis*. An imaginative menu which we'd like to see in a lot more places for those prices. Evening set meals 150F and 170F. Expect to pay about 200F à la carte.

|●| LA CHOUCROUTERIE

20 rue Saint-Louis. **MAP B4-31**
☎ 03.88.36.52.87
Closed Sundays.

Service 7pm–1am. Proprietor Roger Siffer was a folk-singer before he went into the restaurant business and he does still break into song from time to time here, sometimes with a little help from friends who happen to be passing through town. The restaurant has been a post house (in the 18th century) and the head-quarters of the last *choucroute* maker in Strasbourg (where you apparently got the best *choucroute* in town). Today it attracts a lot of politicians of the New Left and it's become the headquarters for the Greens of the European Parliament. It's got a cheery, fun atmosphere, music (there's a very beautiful collection of musical instruments on the walls) and a few erotic engravings here and there if you look hard enough. If you like gipsy music then come along to Roger's place and listen to one of great bands who often come to entertain the customers. And as for food, there are seven varieties of *choucroute* and rissoles of Munster with salad. Set meals at 78F, 113F and 178F. Children's set meal 50F.

|●| LA COCCINELLE

22 rue Sainte-Madeleine. **MAP D4-27**
☎ 03.88.36.19.27
Closed Saturday lunchtimes, Sundays, and the first three weeks of August.

A team of two sisters run this place, with one doing the cooking and the other looking after the dining room. The dish of the day at 49F fills the place at lunchtimes (usually with regulars). It quietens down a bit in the evenings. On the menu are regional specialities like *quenelles* of liver, salad of *pot-au-feu*, and *vigneronne* pie. On Saturday evenings in winter they have that great Alsace classic *baeckeoffa* (a stew of beef, mutton and pork). Expect to pay about 110F for the latter; the other dishes are about 79F. Set meals 110F and 175F. Friendly welcome and service.

|●| LE SAINT-SÉPULCRE

15 rue des Orfèvres. **MAP C3-29**
☎ 03.88.32.39.97
Closed Sundays, Mondays, and July 1–15.

This is one of the most extraordinary places in Alsace. It's run by Robert Lauck, a real character who'll welcome you to his *winstub* by playing one of his little jokes on you – he'll accost you at the door and demand to know your business. After this little prank, he'll show you to a table (telling off one of the regulars on his way for spilling crumbs on the table) and while you're cursing him under your breath, he'll be away, laughing his head off! He really is a lovely man, a real joker. His little "show" is legendary now but you expect it every time you go there. The food is excellent – there's *confit* of pork tongue, potato salad, ham *choucroute*, and a fabulous ham *en croûte* which is sliced in front of the customer. The typical little bistro glasses, carafes of wine, checked napkins, little curtains, polished floors, and the wooden stove in the middle of the room create the right kind of atmosphere for an unforgettable meal in this fantastic place. It'll cost you about 130F per person.

|●| CHEZ YVONNE

10 rue du Sanglier. **MAP C3-32**
☎ 03.88.32.84.15
Closed Sundays, Monday lunchtimes, and mid July–mid August.

Yvonne Haller owns this great little *winstub* which is a bit of an institution in Strasbourg. Politicians and show-biz celebs will come here if they happen to be in town. It's also very popular with locals who all come to pay their respects to this great lady's cooking. *Fleischschnakke*, calf's head and *choucroute* tart are all first-class. Expect to pay about 170F. The impressive *stammtisch*, the regulars' table, is a tradition! Yvonne will greet you with a smile whether you're a regular or a new-comer.

|●| WINSTUB MUNSTERSTUEVEL

8 pl. du Marché aux cochons de lait. **MAP C3-25**
☎ 03.88.32.17.63
Closed Sundays and Mondays.

Patrick Klipfel, a professional through and through, has a solid fan club who come here almost with their eyes closed! Along with his wife Marlène he works hard to keep his customers satisfied. Of course, the prices are slightly higher than in a traditional *winstub* but as long as the quality's there people won't complain. Ox tail *pot au feu* with vegetables, marrowbone and crudités with horseradish sauce (110F), cheek of pork with *choucroute* and jacket potatoes (79F), and *choucroute* (138F) are just a few of the hearty dishes à la carte. Good selection of wines, spirits and draught Météor. For dessert we recommend the *kougelhopf glacé* with Gewurztraminer. Be warned – as soon as the sun's out there's always a fight to get the best spot on the terrace in the square.

HANDSCHUHEIM 67117 (13KM W)

L'AUBERGE À L'ESPÉRANCE

5 rue Principale.
☎ 03.88.69.00.52
Closed Mondays, Tuesdays (except in July–Aug), and Aug 16–Sep 2. **Car park**.

This half-timbered house looks really inviting. Climb a few stairs and you've got a choice of five little rooms. It's a real favourite with *flammenküche* lovers (flambéd tart), cooked here in the old-fashioned way on wood ashes, which gives it its unique flavour and texture. With tables full of families and groups of friends the atmosphere is warm and friendly. They have some good wines, and they don't push the local vintages too hard. Expect to pay 75–120F à la carte, depending on how hungry you are.

THANN 68800

10% HÔTEL-RESTAURANT KLÉBER**

39 rue Kléber (Centre).
☎ 03.89.37.13.66 F 03.89.37.39.67
Restaurant closed Saturday lunchtimes, Sunday evenings and February. **Car park**. **TV**. **Canal+**. **Disabled access**.

This hotel is in a residential area away from the hustle and bustle of the town. It's quite new and stylish, but the prices aren't too over the top. Ask for rooms 24 or 26 in the annexe as they've both got balconies which look out over the orchards. Doubles with shower/wc 245–300F. The restaurant has a good reputation and does set meals from 90F. Good value for money for a 2-star. Pleasant welcome.

MOOSCH 68690 (7KM NW)

FERME AUBERGE DU GSANG

How to get there: from Moosch, head for the Mine d'Argent campsite, follow the forest road for 7km, and leave your car in the Gsang **Car park**; it's about 10–20 minutes walk from there.
☎ 03.89.38.96.85
Closed Fridays except July and August.

This place is really worth a visit, but remember to bring your candles! After a nice walk make for this delightful farmhouse where electricity has still to be discovered. They do sandwiches, smoked scrag of mutton, roasts, *fleischschnaka*, and the most wonderful thick soup. You can arrive at almost any time and Josiane will always be happy to put together a little something for you. For 60F per person you get a darn good meal. On Sundays the two dining rooms are bursting at the seams – the Germans and the locals have known about this place for a long time! If you need somewhere to stay, Josiane has dormitories which are clean and basic (half-board 135F). If you plan on spending a few days here then bring your guitar or your harmonica, for the Bleus, who own the place, love to hear music and singing in their restaurant. Great atmosphere. You'll have a memorable stay here. The view is fabulous and you have to walk everywhere.

HÔTEL AUX TROIS ROIS – RESTAURANT GULLY***

35 rue du Général-de-Gaulle; on the N66 in the direction of col de Bussang; it's opposite the church.
☎ 03.89.82.34.66 F 03.89.82.39.27
Restaurant closed Tuesday evenings and Wednesdays. **Secure parking**. **TV**.

People stop at this roadside hotel to eat rather than to stay, since the road gets very busy. The dining room itself is quite attractive with exposed beams and lanterns. Good welcome. Set meals at 60F, 70F, 85F, 95F, 110F and 150F with game in season. Not bad at all and the portions are enormous! On public holidays they don't do meals à la carte. The hotel has seven comfortable but extremely noisy bedrooms at 325F. A good place to stop for something to fill you up before tackling the route des Crêtes!

SAINT-AMARIN 68550 (8KM NW)

10% AUBERGE DU MEHRBÄCHEL*

route de Geishouse; be warned — this isn't easy! Leave the N66 at Saint-Amarin. Go in the direction of Geishouse but don't go as far as the village. About 3km along the main road turn off to your left and keep going (where all the pine trees are) until you come to the inn (the road doesn't go any further).
☎ 03.89.82.60.68 F 03.89.82.66.05
Closed Fridays and in January. **Car park**.

The chalet, which clings to the side of the mountain with woods on one side and pastures on the other, overhangs the valley of Thur. The bedrooms are in a modern annexe and the view is better than TV any day (which is why there's no TV here). The restaurant is really worth the effort of getting here. The cooking is traditional but the chef has added his own personal touches and there are specialities such as trout stuffed with mushrooms, lamb and lamb's brains with thyme, salmon in herbs and Tokay, and superb duck with juniper berries and ginger. The Munster cheese coated with breadcrumbs and served with salad and cumin is also a treat. A veritable feast indeed, and all at reasonable prices. Set meals 75–160F. Generous breakfast buffet (now that we like!), with smoked bacon, ham, cereal, yoghurt and so on. And outside there's the comforting sound of cowbells. Pleasant double rooms without much character 270–300F.

WISSEMBOURG 67160

HÔTEL-RESTAURANT WALK**

2 rue de la Walk (North-West); follow boulevard Clemenceau as far as the swimming pool; it's next to the hospital on the edge of the forest.
☎ 03.88.94.06.44 F 03.88.54.38.03
Closed Friday lunchtimes, Sunday evenings, Mondays, Feb 8–28 and June 15–30. **Car park**. **TV**. **Disabled access**.

It's on the outskirts of the town and there's lots of greenery around. Relaxing atmosphere. Comfortable, cheery rooms 260–360F. There are 10 rooms in an annexe which is in an old mill and a few of them have a lovely view of the park. There's also a restaurant in another building separate from the hotel. The food's all pretty up-market. Cheapest set meal 180F.

CLIMBACH 67510 (9KM SW)

RESTAURANT AU COL DE PFAFFENSCHLICK

How to get there: take the D3 to Climbach and turn left – keep going until you reach the pass.
☎ 03.88.54.28.84
Closed Tuesdays, Saturdays and mid Jan–mid Feb. **Car park**.

The Séraphin family will give you a genuinely warm welcome to their little inn in the heart of the forest. The dining room has lots of wood and a friendly atmosphere. Terrace for the summer. They have ham, snails, salads, cheeses, quiches, onion tarts and so on. Expect to pay about 40F for a generous plateful. Regional specialities around 75F, like free-range chicken in Riesling, wild boar or *baeckeoffe* (a stew of beef, mutton and pork) have to be ordered in advance. You'll pay 110F for a main course and a 1/4 litre of wine. Madame Séraphin will do everything she can to make your meal as pleasant as possible. A good place only a few kilometres from Four à Chaud, an important part of the Maginot Line.

AQUITAINE

24 Dordogne

33 Gironde

40 Landes

47 Lot-et-Garonne

64 Pyrénées-Atlantiques

AGEN 47000

AUBERGE DE JEUNESSE

17 rue Léo-Lagrange, cité Léon-Blum; follow the directions to Cahors; by bus take the Lalande line and get off at the Léon-Blum stop.
☎ 05.53.66.18.98 F 05.53.47.78.81

40F a night for dormitory accommodation. Facilities for preparing meals (for groups) and breakfast. Cafeteria and hypermarket 600m away.

HÔTEL DES AMBANS*

59 rue des Ambans (Centre).
☎ 05.53.66.28.60 F 05.53.87.94.01
TV.

This simple little hotel which is clean and well looked after is situated in a quite street in the old part of town. There's not much in the way of décor in the 9 rooms but at prices like these we owed it to you to include this place. Doubles without shower 130F, with shower 160F and with shower/wc 190F. Really nice proprietor who'll welcome you like a friend.

HÔTEL DES ISLES

25 rue Baudin (Centre).
☎ 05.53.47.11.33
TV.

There's a good chance of its being the proprietor who welcomes you, his ever-present cigarillo wedged in the corner of his mouth, when you arrive at this lovely hotel. Behind the white stone façade, despite the nonchalant atmosphere, you'll quickly notice that everything is well organized. The 10 rooms are clean and well looked after and you'll have peace and quiet in this residential area. Doubles with shower 140F and with shower/wc 210F. A hotel without any stars which deserves at least one.

10% ROYAL HÔTEL*

129 bd de la République (Centre).
☎ 05.53.47.28.84 F 05.53.47.79.04
TV.

This hotel may not look very welcoming from the outside, but appearances can be deceptive. Once you reach the inner courtyard you'll be charmed by this very well looked after little hotel which offers excellent value for money. Doubles with shower 170F, with shower/wc 200F and with bath 230F. Obviously you should go for the rooms looking out onto the courtyard for preference; the street is rather noisy, especially if you like a lie-in in the morning.

HÔTEL-RESTAURANT LE BORDEAUX**

8 place Jasmin (Centre).
☎ 05.53.47.25.66 F 05.53.66.85.99
Restaurant closed Sundays. **TV**.

Don't be put off by the exterior which has no character at all – it conceals a lovely little establishment. Very friendly welcome. Rooms basic but clean. Doubles with shower 180F, with shower or bath and wc 210F. Very acceptable food at the kind of prices you would have expected to pay years ago. Daily special 45F. Set meals at 57F, 60F, 78F and 110F.

10% ATLANTIC HÔTEL**

133 av. Jean-Jaurès (South-East); take the N113 in the Toulouse/Montauban direction.

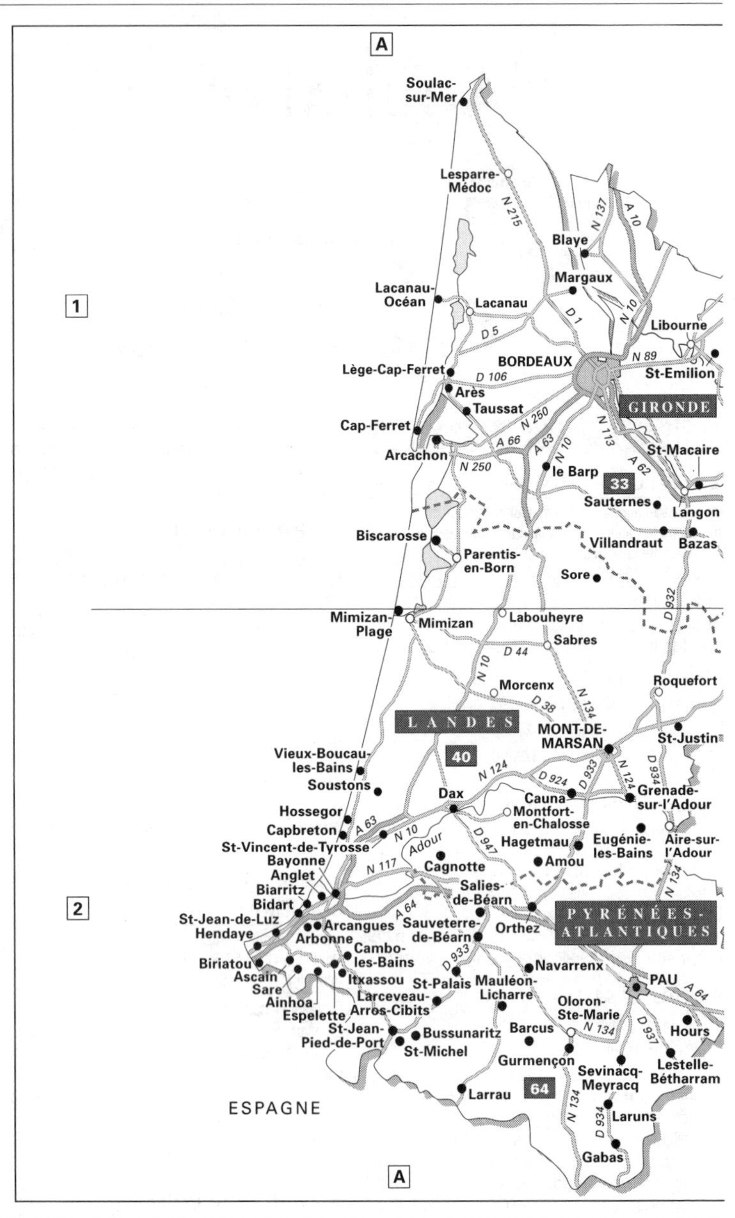
A
1
2
Soulac-sur-Mer
Lesparre-Médoc
N 215
Blaye
N 137
A 10
Margaux
Lacanau-Océan
Lacanau
D 1
N 10
Libourne
D 5
N 89
BORDEAUX
St-Emilion
Lège-Cap-Ferret
D 106
Arès
GIRONDE
Taussat
N 250
Cap-Ferret
N 113
A 66
A 63
N 10
St-Macaire
Arcachon
N 250
le Barp
A 62
33
Sauternes
Langon
Biscarosse
Villandraut
Bazas
Parentis-en-Born
Sore
D 932
Mimizan-Plage
Mimizan
Labouheyre
Sabres
D 44
N 10
Roquefort
Morcenx
D 38
N 134
LANDES
MONT-DE-MARSAN
St-Justin
40
Vieux-Boucau-les-Bains
N 124
D 924
D 933
N 124
D 934
Soustons
Dax
Cauna
Grenade-sur-l'Adour
Hossegor
Montfort-en-Chalosse
Capbreton
A 63
N 10
D 947
Hagetmau
Eugénie-les-Bains
Aire-sur-l'Adour
St-Vincent-de-Tyrosse
Adour
Bayonne
N 117
Cagnotte
Amou
Anglet
Salies-de-Béarn
N 134
Biarritz
Bidart
A 64
PYRÉNÉES-ATLANTIQUES
St-Jean-de-Luz
Arcangues
Sauveterre-de-Béarn
Orthez
Hendaye
Arbonne
Cambo-les-Bains
D 933
Navarrenx
Biriatou
Ascain
PAU
A 64
Sare
Itxassou
St-Palais
Mauléon-Licharre
Ainhoa
Larceveau-Arros-Cibits
Oloron-Ste-Marie
Espelette
D 937
N 134
Hours
St-Jean-Pied-de-Port
Bussunaritz
Barcus
St-Michel
Gurmençon
Sevinacq-Meyracq
Lestelle-Bétharram
Larrau
64
ESPAGNE
N 134
D 934
Laruns
Gabas

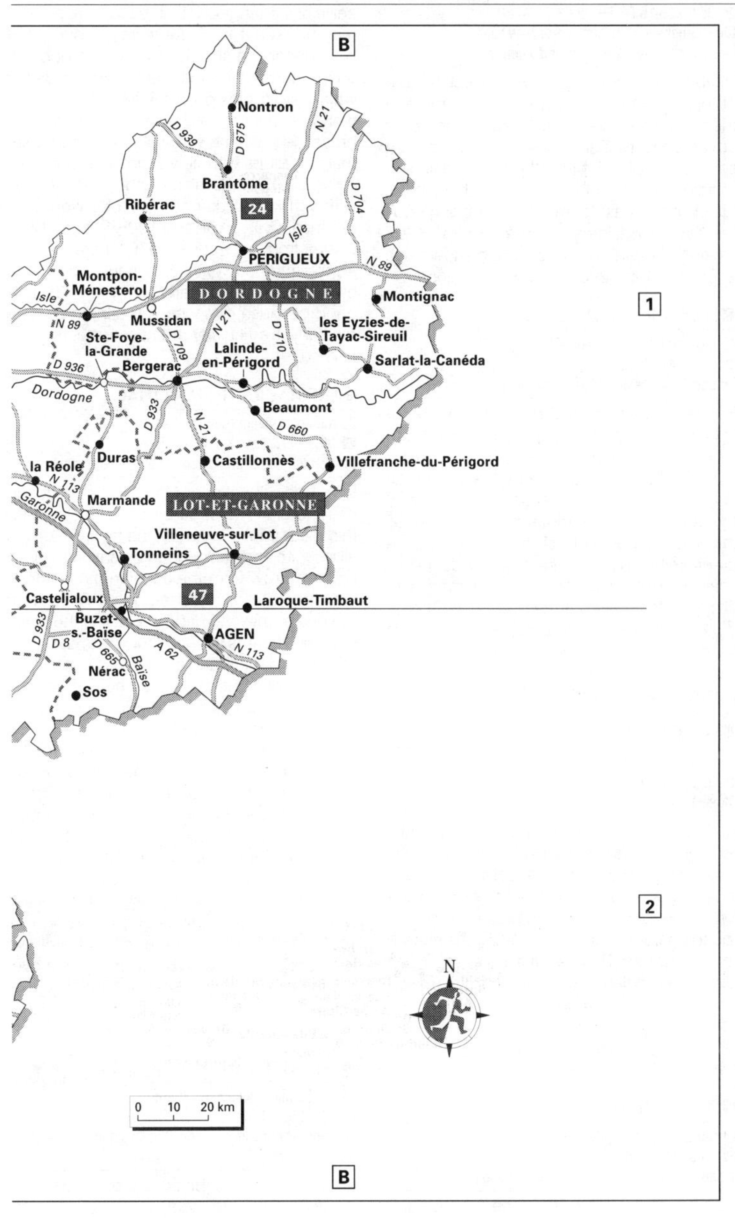
B
Nontron
D 939
D 675
N 21
Brantôme
D 704
Ribérac
24
Isle
PÉRIGUEUX
N 89
Montpon-
Ménesterol
DORDOGNE
Montignac
1
Isle
N 89
Mussidan
N 21
D 710
les Eyzies-de-
Tayac-Sireuil
Ste-Foye-
la-Grande
D 709
Lalinde-
en-Périgord
Sarlat-la-Canéda
D 936
Bergerac
Dordogne
Beaumont
D 933
N 21
D 660
Duras
Castillonnès
Villefranche-du-Périgord
la Réole
N 113
Marmande
LOT-ET-GARONNE
Garonne
Villeneuve-sur-Lot
Tonneins
47
Casteljaloux
Laroque-Timbaut
D 933
Buzet-
s.-Baïse
D 8
D 665
AGEN
A 62
N 113
Nérac
Baïse
Sos
2
N
0 10 20 km
B

☎ 05.53.96.16.56 ➡ 05.53.98.34.80
Closed between Christmas and New Year.
Secure parking. **TV**. **Disabled access**.

Neither the surroundings nor the architecture of this building have anything to recommend them, but there are nevertheless a number of advantages to being here. The rooms are spacious and quiet and the air-conditioning enables you to ignore the scorching heat. Last but not least there's the swimming pool! We have a weakness for the 6 rooms overlooking the garden. Doubles with shower/wc 270F, with bath 290F. Very warm welcome.

LES MIGNARDISES

40 rue Camille Desmoulins (Centre).
☎ 05.53.47.18.62
Closed Sundays and Monday evenings.

Before discovering this place we thought it was no longer possible to get a set meal with soup, starter, main course and dessert for 50F. We have to admit we were wrong. Of course the food isn't the gourmet cuisine of this restaurant's illustrious neighbour but all the same it's good to sit down on the olive green imitation leather seats and indulge in a veal stew which brings back memories of childhood, a fine trout *meunière* or a smooth *crème caramel*. Be warned – the place is always packed at lunchtime (is it any wonder?). Other set meals at 70F, 90F and 150F. Generous seafood platter 100F.

LA GRILLÉE

14 rue des Cornières (Centre).
☎ 05.53.66.60.24
Closed Sundays.

At lunchtime the locals meet in this little restaurant under arcades with a large terrace which is always cool. The set meal at 63F including wine (weekday lunchtimes) is excellent value for money. If you prefer cosier surroundings, you can dine beneath the restaurant's age-old beams. We enjoyed a fine gizzard salad flambéd in sherry, fillets of souffléd trout with almonds and an excellent salmon *à l'unilatéral* (grilled on side only but don't worry – it's cooked through!). Set meals 90F and 150F.

LA BOHÊME

14 rue Émile Sentini (Centre).
☎ 05.53.68.31.00.
Closed Sundays and Wednesday evenings in winter.

As soon as you enter *La Bohême* you can't help but think to yourself, "My, that period which is a mystery to the under-twenties has certainly changed". But even though you may not see it from the warm-coloured but plain décor, the proprietor remains a bohemian at heart. He invites you to join him as the whim takes him on his wanderings in the world of flavours. Dishes include spicy duck breast, leg of lamb with mild garlic and rosemary, scallops with new vegetables and pork *colombo*. If you finish with the *crème brûlée* with vanilla and saffron, you'll be won over. Set meals 69F, 110F and 130F. Set meal with dishes from La Réunion 97F. There are also regular theme evenings, concentrating on a given country, local area or wine, which is good because it means you can come here regularly. Particularly attentive welcome and service.

RESTAURANT MARIOTTAT

25 rue Louis Vivent (Centre).
☎ 05.53.77.99.77
Closed Sunday evenings and Mondays. **Car park**.

Éric and Christiane Mariottat abandoned their hotel in the suburbs of Agen to set up this restaurant – in a very fine family mansion all in white and surrounded by parkland just a stone's throw from the Jacobin monastery – but fortunately it's just as good. Right from the outset they've made it a bit like the place of their dreams with a good atmosphere, attention to detail and elaborate décor worthy of the chef's cooking. The chef, of course, still makes full use of all a duck has to offer, from the liver to the breast (his duck pâté *en croûte* is a real delight!). Alain is still one for local produce, bought at the market. Every morning he invents and modifies his dishes to suit his purchases. His cooking is a permanent and self-renewing festival of food. From the potato *millefeuille* with warm *foie gras* and truffle gravy to the suckling lamb medley with basil and to finish prune ravioli in wine and orange, this is about as good as you can get. What's more, the prices have remained very reasonable despite the move. Set meals at 95F (weekdays), 155F, 200F (all fish) and 265F (surprise). With prices like that you won't get tired of coming here.

MICHEL LATRILLE

66 rue Camille Desmoulins (Centre).
☎ 05.53.66.24.35
Closed Saturday lunchtimes, Sundays and the first 2 weeks in June.

An unpretentious brick façade and, once across the threshold, one of Lot-et-Garonne's finest restaurants. Décor entirely redone and a mixture of out-and-out modern and refined rustic. Michel Latrille has been delighting his guests' taste buds for over a decade. He makes no apology for favouring local produce and experiments with flavour combinations that never strike a false note. Dishes include roast pigeon casserole, warm monkfish and sliced tomato salad in parsley oil, crispy veal sweetbreads and duck *foie gras* with truffles and zander in chicken gravy with garden beans. An outward appearance of simplicity which overlies great know-how. Perhaps that's what you call great cuisine! Attentive service and a wine list as long as your arm. What's more, the cheapest set meals are reasonably priced at 105F (weekdays) and 155F, then 205F and 310F.

LE CAUQUIL

9 av. du Gal de Gaulle.
☎ 05.53.48.02.34
Closed Sundays.

This is the ideal restaurant for lovers of fine food who, just for once, don't want a huge meal. Not that the portions are stingy, quite the contrary, but there's no menu – everything is on the blackboard so you can have a salad or a single course without being looked at suspiciously. The atmosphere is informal and the food fresh and well prepared. Just one little quibble – a little more care could be taken with how things are cooked. The establishment is a new one though so no doubt these little adjustments will have been made by the time you're reading this. Dishes include cuttlefish salad with tons of garlic, fillet of zander in herb butter, *filet mignon* of pork with roquefort and crispy duck preserve. Reckon on paying about 40F for the starters and 60F for a main course. Daily lunchtime special 45F. Pleasant staff who like to smile.

AIGUILLON 47190

10% LE JARDIN DES CYGNES**

rte de Villeneuve.
☎ 05.53.79.60.02 Fax 05.53.88.10.22
Closed Saturdays (out of season) and Dec 15–Jan 15. **Car park**.

Pleasant roadside hotel. Given its position, go for the rooms overlooking the garden and the swimming pool for preference. Décor a bit flashy for our taste but you quickly forget that once you're sitting in front of dishes such as gizzard casserole with ceps, wild boar stew in armagnac, duck preserve, escalope of zander in shallot vinegar or pork spare ribs with prunes – mainly local dishes. Decent set meals at reasonable prices (71–152F). Reckon on paying 185–280F for a double room.

AUBERGE DES 4 VENTS

Lagarrigue; take the N113 towards Agen then the C22.
☎ 05.53.79.62.18
Closed Sunday evenings and Mondays (except in July/August) and during the February school holidays.

At the end of a little road which doesn't lead anywhere. You realize very quickly why the name of this old 18th century farm translates as "Inn of the 4 Winds". North, south, east or west, when the wind gets up it blows, it roars, it caterwauls and it moans, making you glad to take refuge inside with one eye riveted to the horizon and the other to your plate. There are plenty of superbly prepared Basque dishes in Bruno Fava's à la carte menu. Guess why! The three set meals pay tribute to the provinces of the French Basque country with Labourd at 100F, Basse Navarre at 156F and Soule at 198F. All the classics are there, including *axoa d'espelette* and *pimientos del piquillos* (peppers). There's also warm oysters with saffron, roast pigeon with garlic, duck preserve in a salad with *foie gras* and sole with ceps. The décor, which is also Basque in style, is chic and sophisticated. For dessert we have a weakness for the gingerbread-flavoured *millfeuille*.

AMOU 40330

10% HÔTEL-RESTAURANT LES VOYAGEURS**

pl. de Latécoère.
☎ 05.58.89.02.31 Fax 05.58.89.25.12
Closed Fridays and in November. **Car park**. **TV**.

A square with plane trees, an exterior covered in Virginia creeper. All that's missing are the pétanque players. No, they're there too! If you had chosen a room overlooking the square, you could have shouted encouragement from your window. Doubles with bath 230F. Travellers in a hurry should stop off to discover the good food here. Set meals at 105F, 125F, 145F and 195F, each with soup, starter, fish course, meat course and dessert. The food is simple with dishes such as duck breast, (cep) mushroom omelette, trout, vol-au-vent and woodpigeon stew. Indulge yourself and rediscover the joys of good, uncomplicated dishes. That's what a peaceful village like this is begging you to do.

ARCACHON 33120

🏨 |●| HÔTEL-RESTAURANT SAINT-CHRISTAUD

8 allée de la Chapelle (West).
☎ 05.56.83.38.53 📠 05.56.83.38.53
Closed Nov 1–Feb 31.

Just a stone's throw from the beach and yet one of the cheapest places in town. It may not be particularly luxurious but it's a very well looked after little family hotel. It also has its regulars – both young backpackers and pensioners – who are delighted at their good fortune in having found this place in a town as expensive as this. What's more, the hotel is not lacking in charm. This part of town has retained its authenticity and you get a warm welcome. Rooms from 120F (with basin). Reckon on paying at least 180F for a double with shower/wc. Half-board is compulsory in July/August (from 250F per person – again one of the cheapest in Arcachon). Snack-type meals available. Set meal 65F, daily special 39.50F. Discount in April and September.

10% 🏨 HÔTEL LES MIMOSAS**

77 [bis] av. de la République (Centre); it's near place de Verdun.
☎ 05.56.83.45.86 📠 05.56.22.53.40
Car park. **TV**. **Disabled access**.

In a fine and large Arcachon house in the "summer town", so the ocean isn't very far away. Warm welcome. Rooms decorated in an impersonal style but clean and tidy. Doubles with shower 350F, with bath 380F. If you want a bit of space choose number 3, 4, 5, 9 or 10.

10% 🏨 |●| HÔTEL-RESTAURANT SÉMIRAMIS***

villa Térésa, 4 allée Rebsomen (Centre).
☎ 05.56.83.25.87 📠 05.57.52.22.41
Closed in January. **Car park**. **TV**.

Situated in the "winter town", a wonderful mixture of architectural styles (neo-Gothic, Swiss, colonial etc), this 19th century villa is Hispano-Moorish in style (maybe to please the Sultan of Morocco who stayed here in the 20s). By the 70s, having been looted and squatted in, villa Térésa was only a shadow of its former self. It was nearly demolished but that proposal was met with anger by the locals and a residents' committee was set up. The house was saved and listed as a historic monument. The owners rolled up their sleeves and renovated it from top to bottom as a family (the mother painted the ceilings – what talent!). Today you can come and see (for free) the ceramic panels in the entrance hall and the staircase with its superb carved banisters. You can also stay here (but not for free). The attractive rooms are very different from one other even though they all reflect a certain classicism. Doubles 495F (with shower) to 630F (with bath) in high season. Some have a terrace, others are in a little red and white pavilion next to the pleasant swimming pool. The restaurant serves fish (Biscay sea bream, bass caught on the line) and seafood specialities. One set meal only at 138F (180F on Sundays). Half-board 445–555F per person per night.

|●| RESTAURANT LA TAVERNE DU PÊCHEUR

84 [bis] bd de la Plage (Centre).
☎ 05.56.83.78.33
Closed Sunday evenings and Wednesdays out of season.

The name (literally The Fisherman's Tavern Restaurant) sounds a little too "typical" and the area is awfully touristy; yet this is a restaurant which year after year offers food of consistently high quality. The welcome remains friendly, the surroundings pleasant and the prices reasonable! Decent set meal at 58F. Others at 78F and 158F. It goes without saying that fish and seafood predominate. Dishes include home-smoked salmon, fisherman's hot pot, squid fricassee, fish and shellfish platter and *bouillabaisse* (to order).

|●| RESTAURANT LE CHIPIRON

69 bd Chanzy (East); it's near the marina.
☎ 05.57.52.06.33
Closed Wednesdays.

Spanish bistro a little away from the hoards of tourists. This little restaurant's standard décor includes a rather old-fashioned poster advertising a bullfight and a few hams hanging from the ceiling for local colour. Standard fare too, with dishes such as tapas, grilled fish and meat and, of course (given the restaurant's name), "*chipirons à la plancha*" (baby squid). Generous servings of good authentic and tasty little dishes. Reckon on paying 100–120F à la carte. Set meal at 65F (weekday lunchtimes). Friendly welcome, pleasant service, clientele of regulars – in short, the type of little place where you feel at ease (and eat well). Here simplicity is the name of the game.

|●| RESTAURANT LE DAUPHIN DE L'AVENUE

196 bd de la Plage; it's opposite the casino.
☎ 05.56.83.43.98

Strange – this very well-situated restaurant (albeit without a terrace) on a street which is going to be visited by any tourist worthy of the name could have contented itself with being a success thanks to the passing trade, attracting customers with fishing nets and stuffed crabs galore. But no – here the décor is on the plain side (almost like a cafeteria) and the proprietors make an effort to keep quality standards high throughout the year (even in July you are guaranteed a large, fresh seafood platter). The house *bouillabaisse*, the paella (rich and aromatic) and the *zarzuela* (stew) are good. Efficient service. Set meals 75F (except Sundays), then 90–220F. There's also an à la carte menu.

|●| LA MARÉE

21 rue de Lattre-de-Tassigny (Centre).
☎ 05.56.83.24.05
Closed Tuesdays (out of season) and December–January inclusive.

Where better to eat fish and seafood than at a fishmonger's? Here the fish are served whole or in portions, the menu varies according to what has been caught and the prices fluctuate with those of the day's catch. Dishes include fish soup, eels in parsley vinaigrette, grilled bass in pesto, mullet and sole. Good choice of seafood (à la carte), including stuffed oysters, fried scallops and shellfish platter. Seafood platter 125F, royal platter (with half a fresh Breton lobster) 180F. Set meals 50F (weekday lunchtimes) and 99F (including a 1/4 litre of wine). A few tables above the shop or on the balcony (when the sun cooperates). A terrace in season when the street is pedestrianized. Unfortunately, especially in high season, the food can sometimes be prepared in a bit of a slapdash fashion.

PYLA-SUR-MER 33115 (5KM SW)

☗ |●| HÔTEL-RESTAURANT CÔTÉ SUD*

4 av. du Figuier.
☎ 05.56.83.25.00 ➡ 05.56.83.24.13
Closed mid November–beginning of February. **TV**.

Thanks to its position (south-facing as indicated by the name) and wonderful yellow and blue exterior, you feel like you're on holiday as soon as you see this unpretentious hotel (just one floor) by the beach! Wonderful welcome. Comfortable rooms at 195–250F (in low season). The prices go up in high season (370–450F). Highly rated restaurant. Follow the example of the people from Bordeaux and the villas in the area (often one and the same) and sit on the terrace (also south-facing but in the shade) to try the famous house specialities such as mussels ("Côté Sud" with tomato, with Bayonne ham which is smoked and cured, in cream sauce etc), seafood platter or lobster fricassee in Sauternes with vanilla and spices. Set meals at 98F and 150F. 68–95F à la carte.

☗ HÔTEL MAMINOTTE**

allée des Acacias; take the D217 or the D218 and it's 200m from the beach.
☎ 05.56.54.55.73 ➡ 05.57.52.24.30
Disabled access.

A small hotel (just 12 rooms) which looks just like the other houses in this peaceful part of town, lost amongst the pine trees and 100m from the ocean. Friendly welcome. Rooms nothing out of the ordinary but comfortable and not unpleasant. Some have little balconies. Very reasonable out of season (210F for a double with shower, 310F with bath) but a bit pricey in high season (460–510F). No restaurant.

PILAT-PLAGE 33115 (8KM SW)

☗ |●| HÔTEL-RESTAURANT LA CORNICHE**

46 bd Louis-Gaume.
☎ 05.56.22.72.11 ➡ 05.56.22.70.21
Closed from All Saints' Day to end March; restaurant closed Wednesdays (except in July/August). **Car park**. **TV**.

Nestling between pine trees and clumps of flowers at the foot of a large dune on a little coastal road overlooking the beach. A few steps down and you can take a quick dip. Well integrated into the surroundings (in a style typical of a resort in the Landes region). Very warm welcome. Rooms to suit every pocket. Double with basin 200F, with shower/wc 380F and with bath from 400F. Rooms 12, 23, 24 and 25 have a terrace looking out onto the ocean. If they're already taken, console yourself on the large communal terrace with deckchairs and hammocks. The panoramic restaurant (overlooking, you've guessed it, the ocean!) offers set meals at 95F, 149F and 180F. Fish and seafood predominate with dishes such as creole-style stuffed crab, Spanish-style sea bream and fresh cod with pickled onions and *piquillos*. More expensive à la carte (reckon on paying an average of 170F). Dishes include Arachon-style mussels, escalope of meagre (fish similar to sea bass) with sorrel and fillet of beef with *gigas*. Half-board compulsory in July/August (250–500F per person). All in all (and compared to many other establishments) very good value for money.

ARES 33740

RESTAURANT LA POISSONNIÈRE

2 rue des P∏cheurs; go along the bassin d'Arcachon – it's on the seafront, 10m past the tower.
☎ 05.56.60.05.77
Closed September–end June, except Saturdays and Sundays from May 1 or 15.

A little restaurant which only opens in season. The proprietor's oilskins and fishing nets give the place an authentic atmosphere. Terrace (with entertainment in summer) and barbecue. Set meals start at 60F (available every day) and don't go beyond 100F. The à la carte menu (which won't break the bank either – reckon on paying 70F for a meal excluding wine) is made up exclusively of fish and seafood dishes such as mussels with bacon cubes, "fishmonger's"clams, surprise platter and *églades*.

BARCUS 64130

RESTAURANT CHEZ SYLVAIN

place du Fronton.
☎ 05.59.28.92.11
Closed Thursdays and May 7–15.

Charming welcome in a nice little Soule village. The pleasant surroundings are those of a country inn. Local clientele and a few brave lost souls like ourselves. Country-style cooking prepared with a great deal of care and taste. Dishes include lamb in wine, lamb sweetbreads with parsley (December–May) and delicious omelettes. Excellent home-made Béarnaise vegetable broth. Daily set meals 60F, 70F, 90F and 130F (the latter two have to be ordered in advance). Really worth going out of your way for.

BARP (LE) 33114

10% LE RÉSINIER

route de Bayonne (N10); 36km south of Bordeaux.
☎ 05.56.88.60.07 Fax 05.56.88.67.37
Car park. **TV**.

Past the "border" of the Landes regional park, this is a good place to stop on the dusty and often congested N10. Small hotel and restaurant in the heart of a village. A small number of rooms (doubles with shower or bath 225F) and good plain local cooking. Dishes include *grenier médocain* (combination of sliced cold meats), Bordeaux-style sturgeon, lamb and the trilogy of duck *foie gras*, *confit* and breast. Set meals 75F (weekdays) 105F, 130F and 180F. House wine 37F. Other wines from 75F.

BAYONNE 64100

HÔTEL PORT NEUF

44 rue du Port-Neuf.
☎ 05.59.25.65.83
Closed Sundays. **TV**.

Rooms only. 160–230F with shower or bath. In the heart of the old town. Pleasant breakfast terrace. Reservation strongly recommended.

10% HÔTEL DES BASSES-PYRÉNÉES**

1 place des Victoires and 14 rue Tour-de-Sault (Centre).
☎ 05.59.59.00.29 Fax 05.59.59.42.02
Restaurant closed Sundays and Monday lunchtimes (except in July/August), and Dec 15–Jan 15.
Secure parking. **TV**.

Rooms 200–320F. Out of season prices start at 170F for a double with shower/wc. Strategically situated in Grand Bayonne by the walls. The rooms overlooking the square are quieter but the view of the walls compensates for a little more noise. Extremely well looked after family hotel.

10% HÔTEL FRANTOUR***

1, pl. de la République (Centre); it's near pont Saint-Esprit.
☎ 05.59.55.08.08 Fax 05.59.55.69.36
Car park. **TV**. **Disabled access**.

On the River Adour with an uninterrupted view of old Bayonne and the Pyrenees, this 200 year old hotel offers clean, well sound-proofed rooms which are excellent value for money. Doubles with bath or shower from 360F. The restaurant offers the same quality of service with specialities such as *favouille* soup or Basque-style *piperade* (made with egg and tomatoes). Set meals 90–240F.

LE BISTROT SAINTE-CLUQUE

9 rue Hughes.
☎ 05.59.55.82.43
Closed Mondays October–July.

The place to eat in Bayonne and the kind of restaurant you'd like to find in all the towns along the coast. David is an English chef – and what a chef! He invents and mixes flavours using simple produce at very reasonable prices. Try, for example, his house paella or his duck with honey and lemon. Éric and Tracy welcome you with a big smile even if you're late. Basic set meal 55F and a menu which allows you to dine for under 100F including wine. It goes without saying that you are strongly advised to book; the place is always full both inside and out on the terrace.

|●| RESTAURANT LE TRINQUET MODERNE

60 av. Dubrocq (West); follow the Adour, turn left into avenue Dubrocq and it's the first on the left after avenue de la Légion-Tchèque.
☎ 05.59.59.05.22
Closed Sunday evenings and at Christmas. **Car park**.

Despite the run-of-the-mill décor, you get more of the feeling of the Basque country here than in the taverns of Petit Bayonne. Jean-Marie Mailharro is mad on pelota and has succeeded in attracting all the region's pelota and *mus* players to this part of town away from the centre. These folk have healthy appetites and he serves them good, solid, simple regional dishes such as ham omelette, Béguios sausages, veal sweetbreads with ceps, Spanish-style hake caught on the line and cod and crab lasagnes. Set meal prices range from 60F (not Sundays) to 160F. You always get a plateful and there's always a good atmosphere. If they like you they'll put you on the big main table where you can nonchalantly rub shoulders with the top pelota champions and magistrates from the neighbouring law courts.

|●| CHEZ JACQUES

17, quai Jauréguiberry (Centre); it's on the banks of the Nive.
☎ 05.59.25.66.33

Family establishment specializing in fish and shellfish. Seafood platter 90F, grilled prawns and sole with ceps. Set meals 85F, 105F and 158F. Warm welcome. Riverside terrace. You can even finish off the evening in the adjoining wine bar El rio which is run by the same family.

|●| LE CHISTERA

42 rue Port-Neuf.
☎ 05.59.59.25.93
Closed Monday to Wednesday evenings except in season and during the Easter holidays.

The name, the décor – everything tells you that these are pelota fans. Jean-Pierre Marmouyet has taken over the restaurant originally opened by his father, a former *cestapunta* champion and a great coach. He manages to combine his profession of restaurateur and his activities as a professional pelota player. The food is typical of Bayonne (with fabulous tripe) and the daily specials (mainly fish) can be found chalked up on the blackboard. If there's pigs' or *louvines'* trotters, look no further. Given that the prices are reasonable (reckon on paying 100–120F), the service is friendly and the menu (done by one of the last French illuminators) is superb, a large number of people in Bayonne use this restaurant as their "canteen".

|●| RESTAURANT FRANÇOIS MIURA

24 rue Marengo.
☎ 05.59.59.49.89
Closed Sunday evenings, Wednesdays, mid July–beginning of August and Dec 15–31.

He has set up here in ultramodern surroundings but François Miura hasn't lost the touch which gained him his reputation. A great chef when it comes to fish (in particular flat fish such as sole and turbot), he's also good with meat. Set meals 105F and 180F. A fine wine list with relatively affordable regional wines. Reckon on paying 200–250F à la carte, including a good little Bordeaux. Booking recommended as it's a very popular place.

BAZAS 33430

10% ⌂ HOSTELLERIE SAINT-SAUVEUR**

14 rue du Gal-de-Gaulle (Centre).
☎ 05.56.25.12.18
Closed Sundays in winter and the first fortnight in October. **Secure parking**. **TV**. **Disabled access**.

"You can stay here whether you arrive on foot, by bike or by car," the answering machine tells you (with a strong accent!). And they've been going since 1886! For five generations the business has been passed on from mother to daughter. The exterior isn't really worth looking at (it's hard to imagine that Grégoire de Saint-Sauveur, the last bishop of Bazas, lived here). The (heavy) décor mixes house plants and 70s seating with cheerful kitsch. The rooms though are good value for money, given the region, coming in at 200F for a double with shower/wc. No restaurant but a local bistro on the ground floor, the "Saint-Sô".

|●| RESTAURANT DES REMPARTS

espace Mauvezin.
☎ 05.56.25.95.24
Closed Sunday evenings and Mondays (out of season).

Superbly situated on the *brèche de Bazas*, overlooking the Sultan's garden. Quite exceptional surroundings (if you followed our advice on how to get here you'll already know) which you can enjoy from the terrace when the weather is fine. The very classic décor is on the plain side. Don't let anything disturb your tête-à-tête with this very inspired local cuisine. Quality produce (Bazas beef of course or Grignol capon but to order) well prepared by the Decaux brothers. Excellent set meal at 68F (weekdays only). The one at 90F offers dishes such as smoked salmon in a herb vinaigrette dressing, boned quail fried in armagnac, roast rabbit's legs with prunes in Madeira and prune mousse in armagnac. Other set meals at 115F, 145F and 188F. Examples from the à la carte menu include shellfish *millefeuille* in creamy port sauce and veal sweetbreads in Sauternes with mushrooms.

GOUALADE 33840 (16.5KM SE)

|●| RESTAURANT L'AUBERGE GASCONNE

How to get there: it's on the main road opposite the church.
☎ 05.56.65.81.77
Closed Mondays, Sunday evenings and Aug 16–Sept 3.

An inn out in the middle of nowhere between the Gironde and Landes regions. In this woodland tundra you would expect a rather rustic inn where electricity had only just been installed (opposite the old village church, of course). Although the church is indeed there (and very nice it is too with its turret), the inn has a certain smartness about it and is comfortable and (would you believe it?) air-conditioned. A lucky group of regulars including lorry drivers and workmen from the electricity board have made this place their own with its good local cooking and the kind of prices you would have expected to pay years ago. Here no one would dream of "reinventing" the local dishes. The simple country cooking comes from good old recipes and is substantial and filling, unpretentious and unaffected. Large slices of Bayonne (smoked and cured) ham, woodpigeon stew, turkey preserve, duck, pork, wild boar casserole, stuffed chicken and vegetable stew every Sunday – all served on tablecloths decorated with fresh flowers. As many crispy chips as you can eat. Set meal at 55F (including wine and coffee). Under 100F à la carte. A bottle of cheap wine (10% vol.) costs 12F (unbeatable!). And a warm welcome into the bargain.

CAPTIEUX 33840 (19.5KM S)

⌂ |●| HÔTEL-RESTAURANT CAP DES LANDES*

rue Principale.
☎ 05.56.65.64.93

In the middle of a small market town but on a road where numerous lorries pass at night – so try to get one of the (simple but acceptable) rooms at the back. Double with shower from 160F (wc on the landing). Nice family atmosphere. The hotel may be a bit on the noisy side but there are no complaints about the restaurant. Set meal at 60F (weekday lunchtimes only) served in a little room not far from the bar. For 100F you eat in surroundings which are a little more sophisticated. The menu and set meals offer regional duck specialities, various gourmet salads, escalope of *foie gras* with apples and fresh grapes, duck breast with morels in armagnac and grilled Bazas beef.

BERGERAC 24100

10% ⌂ |●| FAMILY HÔTEL**

place du Marché-Couvert (Centre).
☎ 05.53.57.80.90
Secure parking. **TV**.

A hotel which has lots going for it. First of all it's in a great location in the old centre; secondly it's one of the cheapest places in town; and finally it has a pretty relaxed youthful atmosphere. No complaints about the rooms, they're good value for money (180F for a double with shower/wc to 240F with bath). If you like a bit of space go for room number 1, 4, 7 or 10. Also a number of self-catering apartments. Bistro which is lively on market days and restaurant. Very traditional cooking with permanent fixtures such as *coq au vin* and a number of standard regional dishes such as duck breast preserve, pork, sausage and bean casserole and *enchaud*). Daily special 44F (lunchtimes and evenings). Large range of set meals at 72–145F.

10% ⌂ |●| HÔTEL-RESTAURANT LA FLAMBÉE***

av. Marceau-Feyry; 2km north of Bergerac on the N21 towards Périgueux.

☎ 05.53.57.52.33 ➡ 05.53.61.07.57
Restaurant closed Sunday evenings and Mondays out of season. **Car park**. **TV**.

Not far from the main road and surrounded by a trading estate but quiet as anything behind its thick curtain of trees. Park with swimming pool and tennis courts. Twenty or so standard rooms split between a large, fine Périgord residence and a summer house. Doubles 350F with shower/wc, 10F extra for a bath. Some rooms have a small terrace. One of the Bergerac social circle's preferred places to eat thanks to its opulent-looking restaurant and its reliable cuisine (local dishes and good plain home cooking). Set meals 100F, 150F, 200F and 350F. À la carte dishes include scallop *marguerite* in champagne, escalope of salmon in Monbazillac wine, *croustade* of sliced duck with apples and strawberries *au gratin* in a Monbazillac sabayon. Pleasant terrace when the weather is fine.

LA BLANCHE HERMINE

place du Marché-Couvert (Centre).
☎ 05.53.57.63.42
Closed Sundays, Mondays and Aug 20–Sept 20.
Car park.

A pancake house named after a song by a well-known Breton songwriter. It's popular with young people in the area, this nice cool little place, even if the music is more blues and jazz than folk and the names of the excellent buckwheat pancakes (Cap Vert, Si bémol, Provençale etc) are rather exotic-sounding. The rest of the food is also very cosmopolitan with numerous salads, tzaziki, houmus, stuffed grapefruit, *mafé* and even a pork chop Gothic-style (leaf spinnach with apricot and mustard sauce). Very reasonable prices. Reckon on paying 60F for a full meal, served with a smile, in an atmosphere which is definitely very friendly.

RESTAURANT LA SAUVAGINE

18-20 rue Eugène-Leroy.
☎ 05.53.57.06.97
Closed Mondays and the first 2 weeks in June.

This restaurant is air-conditioned and its modern décor is quite well done. Traditional, well-prepared cuisine which doesn't systematically conform to Périgord norms (and for those staying in the area for some time that's good news!). Fish (lamprey for example – the Bordeaux region isn't far away), seafood, game in season and delicious desserts. Great little set meal at 75F after which prices climb to 120–300F. Clientele a bit on the posh side but the welcome remains unaffected.

RESTAURANT L'ENFANCE DE LARD

rue Pélissière (Centre).
☎ 05.53.57.52.88
Closed Tuesdays and Wednesday lunchtimes.

On the first floor of a 12th century house on one of Bergerac's finest squares, this charming little restaurant soon fills up (it's essential to book a table!). Warm, intimate atmosphere. A sophisticated selection of operatic arias plays in the background. Remarkable regional cuisine. Tradition rules but there's still a certain subtlety in the way dishes are prepared. Quality meats are grilled over vine stock in the superb fireplace and dishes include Sarlat-style apples which melt in the mouth, rack of lamb with mint, warm *foie gras* with peaches and ceps in parsley vinaigrette. Generous helpings. No set meals. Reckon on paying 200–300F à la carte for a full meal, but it's worth it.

SAINT-JULIEN-DE-CREMPSE 24140 (12KM N)

10% LE MANOIR DU GRAND VIGNOBLE***

How to get there: take the N21 then the D107.
☎ 05.53.24.23.18 ➡ 05.53.24.20.89
Closed Nov 15–Feb 28. **Car park**. **TV**.

A very fine 17th century manor house in beautiful countryside (it's also an equestrian centre so you'll see horses frolicking about there too). Luxury establishment for the better-off amongst you. Enormous, rustic rooms with a great deal of charm, all very well appointed. From 380F (in low season) to 680F for a double with bath. Huge gardens, tennis, heated swimming pool and fitness centre. The restaurant has set meals at 150–290F with dishes such as poached foie gras with grapes, duck breast roll with morels and zander demi-deuil.

ISSIGEAC 24560 (19KM SE)

10% HÔTEL-RESTAURANT LA BRUCELLÈRE**

place Capelle; take the N21 then the D14.
☎ 05.53.58.72.28
Closed Sunday evenings and Mondays in low season and in February and November. **Car park**. **TV**.

A small hotel on the edge of this medieval market town where time sometimes seems to have stood still since the fifties. Rooms not always very large but pleasant enough. 200F for a double with shower, 270F with bath. Rather elegant restaurant for those who like a quiet atmosphere. As soon as there's a hint of sunshine everyone heads for the terrace! Very very traditional, sometimes regional cooking (dishes include home-smoked salmon, Béarnaise vegetable broth, snails with ceps and lamb steaks in a creamy garlic sauce). The portions are large and the produce carefully selected. Small set meal 65F (weekday lunchtimes). Otherwise the range starts at 80F.

RAZAC-D'EYMET 24500 (20KM S)

LA PETITE AUBERGE**

☎ 05.53.24.69.27 ➡ 05.53.61.02.63
Restaurant closed Sundays, Mondays and lunchtimes from April to October (except for residents). Only open for hotel guests the rest of the year. **Car park. Disabled access.**

Peace and quiet is guaranteed in this tiny village. Two tractors, a lost sales rep and the canary-yellow post office van (plus you perhaps) pass in the course of the day and that's it. This former farm on the edge of the village has been transformed into a charming hotel by an English couple. Only 7 rooms, all of them pleasant, and something for every pocket. From 180F for a double with basin (shower/wc outside) to 250F (shower/wc in the room this time), 300F (bath) and 375F (en suite). The lounge has a high ceiling and the restaurant is welcoming. No set meals but it shouldn't cost much more than 100F to eat à la carte. Dishes include soup, poached salmon in butter sauce and nut tart. Half board 180–265F per person per night. Delightful swimming pool. Possibility of renting adjacent self-catering houses. The "Poulailler" (henhouse) sleeps 4 and the "Ferme" (farm) 6. Prices vary according to season.

BIARRITZ 64200

HÔTEL DE LA MARINE

1 rue des Goélands (Centre).
☎ 05.59.24.34.09

Hotel where backpackers will feel totally at home in a town which is a bit on the posh side. Very friendly atmosphere and warm welcome. Clean and very well kept rooms. Doubles with shower 160F. The bar downstairs done out in blue and white isn't part of the hotel but we're including it in our recommendation, in particular for the *Txirrisklas*. It's amazing and it brightens up your evenings.

HÔTEL PALYM*

7 rue du Port-Vieux; 100m from the sea.
☎ 05.59.24.16.56

Old-fashioned but well-kept hotel with old-world charm. The little winding staircase takes you past cork oak panels decorated with exotic landscapes, numerous plants and an overwhelming array of bric-à-brac on your way to the old-fashioned, neat and tidy rooms. Well worth the price (from 200F; 210F with shower/wc and 320F with bath). We have a big weakness for the bed in room 16. Ask for a room at the rear (quieter). Friendly staff. The restaurant below the hotel belongs to the owner's son.

HÔTEL LA ROMANCE**

6 allée des Acacias (South); it's near the racecourse.
☎ 05.59.41.25.65

In a residential area not that easy to find. The wonderful proprietor for whom nothing is too much trouble has decorated the 10 rooms using flowers as the theme. We liked room 5 which is called Hortensia. Doubles with shower/wc or bath 350–400F (180–280F in low season).

10% HÔTEL MAÏTAGARIA**

34 av. Carnot; 500m from the sea.
☎ 05.59.24.26.65
TV.

It's not a bad idea to reserve here because the regulars have known for a very long time that this is a good place to stay. You can't help becoming addicted to this charming little private hotel with its warm welcome. Quiet, comfortable rooms. Doubles from 265F (with shower/wc) to 290F (with bath). A very pleasant garden with flowers.

HÔTEL LE SAINT-CHARLES**

47 av. Reine-Victoria (North).
☎ 05.59.24.10.54 ➡ 05.59.24.56.74
Closed from end November to the February holidays. **Secure parking. TV.**

A real haven of peace and very pretty it is, all done out in pink. Annie goes out of her way to be pleasant to her guests. If you like peace and quiet, greenery and flowers you'll find it as hard as we did to leave this cocoon, especially after breakfasting in the garden. Clean rooms furnished and decorated with a great deal of taste 290–390F. Half-board available. A little out of the centre but *Le Saint-Charles* is well worth going out of your way for.

10% HÔTEL-RESTAURANT WINDSOR***

av. Édouard-VII (North-East); it's a stone's throw from place Clemenceau.

☎ 05.59.24.08.52 F➜ 05.59.24.98.90
Closed in January/February. **TV**. **Disabled access**.

For those who like a bit of luxury but don't want to pay a fortune for it! Wonderful welcome. Double rooms with every comfort (direct-dial telephone, cable TV, mini-bar etc) and a view of the open sea 350F. Avoid the rooms looking out onto the street, which are rather depressing. Good restaurant where set meals start at 100F. Direct access to the main beach and near the superb casino. Reservation essential in summer.

10% ⌂ LE CHÂTEAU DU CLAIR DE LUNE

48 av. Alan-Seeger (South-East); it's near the station on the Arbonne road.
☎ 05.59.41.53.20 F➜ 05.59.41.53.29
Car park. **TV**.

This secluded 19th century residence, situated in wonderful grounds full of flowers with formal and landscaped gardens, is delightfully decorated in art deco style. Doubles from 450F – you buy yourself a slice of the good life here, far from the cares of the outside world. The rooms are enormous and furnished to a high standard. A dream of a place in which to relax away from the hectic life on the coast. Advance reservation advisable!

I●I BAR JEAN

5 rue des Halles (Centre); it's opposite the indoor market.
☎ 05.59.24.80.38
Closed Tuesday evenings and Wednesdays.
Disabled access.

This charming tapas bar is a Biarritz and bullfighting mecca. The pictures and engravings decorating the entire bar portray the area's bull-running and bullfighting events. Lots of regulars meet at the bar and nibble at tapas. Generous daily specials such as baby squid cooked in their own ink, garlic prawns and battered squid at around 50F. Nice terrace with service until 11pm.

I●I RESTAURANT LE BISTROT DES HALLES

1 rue du Centre (Centre); it's near the covered market.
☎ 05.59.24.21.22
Open until 11pm (11.30pm in summer). **Closed** Sunday evenings out of season and Mondays.

We really liked the jovial proprietor here who has brought his talkative nature from Lot to Biarritz – a breath of fresh air. The place itself is friendly (good bistro atmosphere) and the food is good. If any proof were needed, the number of regulars speaks for itself. The dishes up on the blackboard can include salmon with leeks, mussels in white wine and T-bone steak. Reckon on paying around 110F for a full meal. Dinner reservations strongly recommended, even if you eat late.

ANGLET 64600 (3KM E)

10% ⌂ I●I AUBERGE DE JEUNESSE

19 route des Vignes (North-East); from the station take blue line 2 and change at "Biarritz-Hôtel-de-Ville" to line 4 – there's a stop in front of the youth hostel.
☎ 05.59.58.70.00 F➜ 05.59.58.70.07
Access 8.30am–10pm in summer, 8.30–10am and 6–10pm out of season. **Closed** Dec 15–Jan 15.

It's advisable to reserve by phone or fax for courses/accommodation. Near the ocean in pleasant surroundings, this is a large, comfortable and really welcoming youth hostel. Impeccable dormitories. 80F per night including breakfast. Offers surfing (in which it specializes), sailing and diving courses – just so you won't get bored in Anglet! Cafeteria open 7–9pm in high season. Main courses 33F, meals 51F.

ARCANGUES 64200 (4KM SE)

I●I L'AUBERGE DU CHAPELET

East; take the D255 – it's at the top of the hill.
☎ 05.59.23.54.63
Closed Sunday evenings and Wednesdays in winter.
Secure parking.

Typical setting. Garden. Warm welcome. To pronounce the owner's name – Iñaki Oxandaburu – you either need to come from around here or to take a deep breath. Typical Basque cuisine – surprise, surprise! Elaborate and nicely presented little dishes. Try the Spanish-style hake, the mussels with leeks *au gratin*, the fresh cod steak with lentils and (smoked and cured) Bayonne ham, the fricassee of local lamb or the duck breast with *foie gras*. Set meals 85F, 130Fand 165F. Reasonable à la carte prices.

ARBONNE 64210 (5KM SE)

I●I ESKUALDUNA

How to get there: take the D255.
☎ 05.59.41.95.41
Closed Sunday evenings in winter. **Car park**.

Jacky is the head of the family and runs this place with them. He's one of the region's life and soul types without knowing it. Between 2 courses he'll jolly along the conversation at the bar with talk of the next rugby world cup

– they're all rugby fanatics here. He welcomes people, largely factory workers, into his big dining room, chatting up away nineteen to the dozen as he makes up his sauces. He also used to cook for children from the local school. Jacky is as generous as his set meals (60F, 80F and 120F).

BIDART 64200

BLUE CARGO

plage d'Ibarritz; it's by the beach.
☎ 05.59.23.54.87
Car park.

Facing the beach (but with its feet in the sand, not the water) and spread between two white tents and a protected terrace for those who feel the cold, this restaurant is a very nice place to come just before you take a dip or if you're returning from the beach. Fish (Spanish-style sea bream, fried pirates' baby squid) and seafood (gambas in all kind of sauces) specialities. Set meal 120F. Around 150F à la carte.

BISCARROSSE 40600

10% HÔTEL LA CARAVELLE**

5314 route des lacs, quartier ISPE, lac nord.
☎ 05.58.09.82.67 F➔ 05.58.09.82.18
Restaurant closed Monday lunchtimes and Nov 15–Feb 15. **Car park**.

Very well situated right by the lac de Cazaux. A fine, large building in a pleasant setting. Nearly all the rooms have a little balcony and look out onto the lake. Doubles from 290F (with shower/wc) to 390F (with bath). A lovely tranquil place (even though in spring the frogs may disturb some guests at night). We really like room 24. The restaurant serves good local food. Dishes include Landes-style salad with *foie gras*, conserve of duck breast, shin of lamb in a creamy garlic sauce, monkfish kebabs, veal sweetbreads in Jurançon wine, eel fricassee and fillet of zander with leek fondue. Set meals 90F, 138F and 240F. Half-board (compulsory in summer) good value for money at 300F per person.

RESTAURANT CHEZ CAMETTE

532 av. Latécoère (South).
☎ 05.58.78.12.78
Closed Friday evenings out of season.

Just the kind of popular and quaint little inn we like with its white exterior and red blinds. People come here from work, as do sales reps and people passing through, for the little set meal at 58F. Wonderful welcome and generous helpings from the proprietor who loves her country and doesn't mind letting you know it. The food is simple and unpretentious, even if it's not what you fancy. The day we went there we got soup, mussels in white wine, escalope in cream sauce and a dessert. Great for 58F. Other set meals at 88F and 138F.

BLAYE 33390

L'AUBERGE DU PORCHE**

5 rue Ernest-Régnier (South-West).
☎ 05.57.42.22.69 F➔ 05.57.42.82.83
Restaurant closed Mondays, 1 week in February, end September and beginning of October. **Secure parking**. **TV**.

Very pretty little stone house behind a tiny park. Only 8 rooms and they're named after flowers. Doubles 275–335F. An effort has made with the décor (athough you may not share the proprietor's tastes). Particularly warm welcome and no fuss. The restaurant is good whether you go for a pancake or simple little dishes such as *coq au vin* or veal stew. The menu also includes local dishes such as pork, sausage and bean casserole, Landes-style salad, escalope of duck liver and rib of beef with ceps. *Formule* at 58F (lunchtimes and evenings) and set meals at 98F, 145F and 248F. Reckon on paying 130F à la carte. The wine cellar has a number of very nice little Côtes de blaye. Terrace and small patio.

HÔTEL-RESTAURANT LA CITADELLE**

place d'Armes.
☎ 05.57.42.17.10 F➔ 05.57.42.10.34
Car park. **TV** with **Canal+**.

This fine 17th century house is superbly situated overlooking the walls. We find it a shame that the décor of the hotel in general and the bedrooms in particular is ordinary in the extreme. From the great majority of the rooms you can console yourself with the superb view of the Gironde which here starts to spread out in all its glory. If you don't want to bathe in the estuary, the swimming pool overlooking it is really lovely. Doubles looking out onto the water 360F and onto the place d'armes 340F (the view isn't half as impressive but the rooms are larger). Good restaurant where set meals start at 130F. Others at 220F and 300F. The house specialities include sturgeon in Côtes de blaye, snail profiteroles in Côtes de blaye (the vineyard is nearby) and lamb chop cooked on a piece of slate.

BORDEAUX 33000

SEE MAP ON PAGE 40

10% HÔTEL STUDIO*

26 rue Huguerie. **MAP B2-2**
☎ 05.56.48.00.14 F 05.56.81.25.71
Secure parking. TV. Disabled access.

A dozen or so rooms in the hotel itself and thirty or so spread between other small hotels nearby. Try to see several before choosing one. In view of the prices and the plethora of rooms, don't expect luxurious comfort. Sometimes the rooms look like victims of amateurish DIY, but the entire team running this handful of hotels is very friendly and the level of comfort is improved on a reasonably regular basis, for example with double-glazing on the side looking out onto the street or new bedding. Rooms, all with shower/wc and (cable) TV, 120–135F depending on size. Half-board available. Garage.

10% HÔTEL BOULAN

28 rue Boulan. **MAP B3-4**
☎ 05.56.52.23.62 F 05.56.52.23.62
TV.

A simple little hotel with no stars but the cleanness of the place, the obliging proprietors and the peaceful atmosphere (despite the hotel's prime location) win you over. Doubles with basin 120F, with shower (wc on the landing) 140F. Breakfast served in your room as a matter of course.

10% HÔTEL DAUPHIN*

82 rue du Palais Gallien. **MAP B2-3**
☎ 05.56.52.24.62 F 05.56.01.10.91
Closed the final 3 weeks in August.

Right in the city centre in a quiet part of a street which is rather busy in the evening. A little hotel straight out of the thirties/forties but given a new lease of life and renovated from top to bottom by a new owner. The comfortable rooms are all different. Only a tiny bit more expensive than the other 1-star rooms in the area but well worth the few extra francs. Rooms with shower (wc on the landing) 129F, with shower/wc and on the quiet side of the hotel round a little patio 139F (159F with TV).

10% HÔTEL DE LYON

31 rue des Remparts. **MAP B3-5**
☎ 05.56.81.34.38 F 05.56.52.92.82
TV.

This small hotel in a pedestrianized street doesn't have any stars but is well run by an unassuming little old lady. Very central but quiet, even the rooms on the side looking out onto the street (except when the people of Bordeaux decide to party – which doesn't happen often). Rooms which come close to having a certain charm at very reasonable prices. Singles 125F, doubles 135F. All rooms with shower/wc.

10% HÔTEL D'AMBOISE

22 rue de la Vieille-Tour. **MAP B2-6**
☎ 05.56.81.62.67 F 05.56.52.92.82
TV. Disabled access.

Small, old-fashioned looking hotel in a charming pedestrianized street. Well run by a young couple (same owners as the *Hôtel de Lyon*) who do their best to keep prices down. Simple but acceptable. Fully renovated double rooms 137F with shower/wc. Make sure you don't get one looking out onto the street. We like this hotel and on a value for money basis it's one of the best in this category.

HÔTEL DU VIEUX BORDEAUX**

22 rue du Cancéra. **MAP C3-8**
☎ 05.56.48.07.27 F 05.56.51.93.13
Closed Sunday afternoons until 6pm.

Pleasant little hotel hidden away in a picturesque street in the old town (as you'd probably have guessed if we told you its name literally means Hotel of Old Bordeaux). Just on the edge of the Saint-Pierre district with its animated nightlife. Some rooms have a certain charm and they are all excellent value for money. Doubles with shower/wc 202–210F.

10% HÔTEL BLAYAIS**

17 rue Mautrec. **MAP C2-7**
☎ 05.56.48.17.87 F 05.56.79.38.34
TV.

Tiny hotel in a tiny street (not too noisy but you're still in the city centre). Rooms renovated with verve. Doubles with shower/wc excellent value for money at 170F. Warm welcome (access until 10.30pm).

10% HÔTEL DE LA TOUR INTENDANCE**

16 rue de la Vieille-Tour. **MAP B2-10**
☎ 05.56.81.46.27 F 05.56.81.60.90
TV with **Canal+. Car park.**

Two sisters take turns on reception at this charming establishment so that their guests

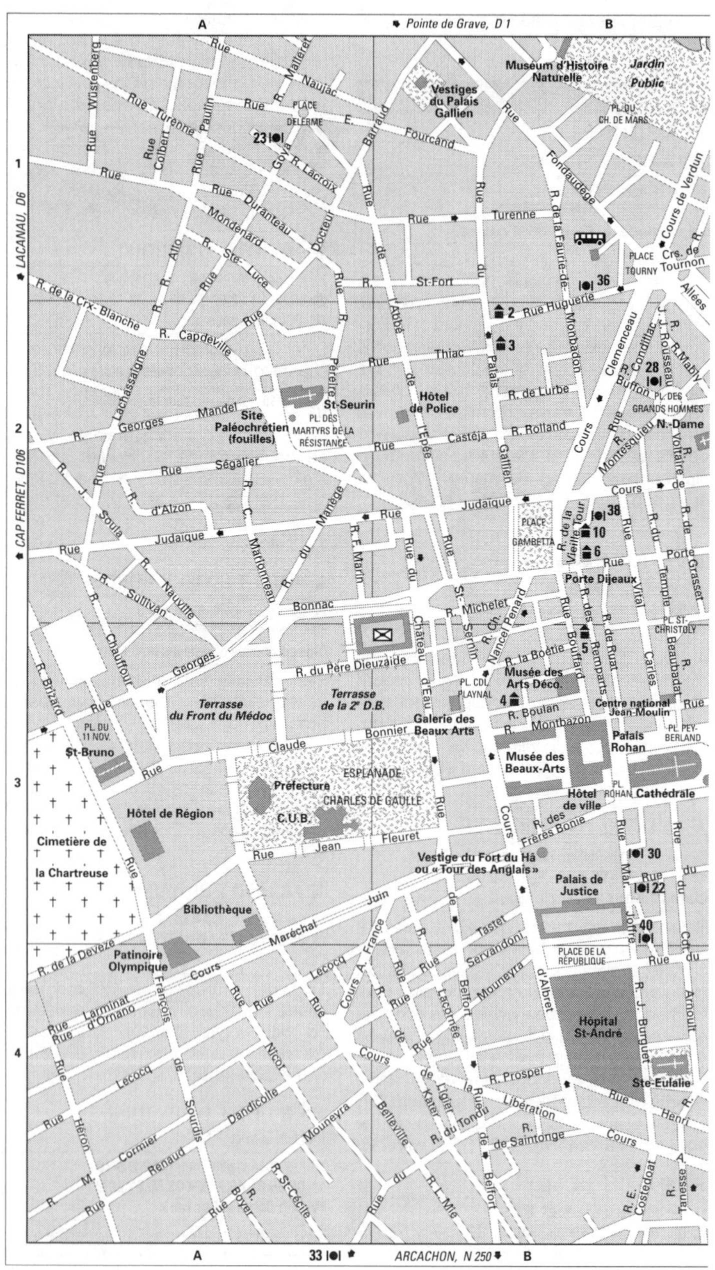
A
Pointe de Grave, D 1
B
Muséum d'Histoire Naturelle
Jardin Public
Vestiges du Palais Gallien
PL. DU CH. DE MARS
PLACE DELERME
23
1
LACANAU, D6
PLACE TOURNY
36
Crs. de Tournon
Cours de Verdun
Allées
2
3
28
PL. DES GRANDS HOMMES
N.-Dame
St-Seurin
Site Paléochrétien (fouilles)
PL. DES MARTYRS DE LA RÉSISTANCE
Hôtel de Police
2
CAP FERRET, D106
PLACE GAMBETTA
38
10
6
Porte Dijeaux
PL. ST-CHRISTOLY
5
Musée des Arts Déco.
PL. CDL PLAYNAL
4
Terrasse du Front du Médoc
Terrasse de la 2e D.B.
Galerie des Beaux Arts
Centre national Jean-Moulin
PL. PEY-BERLAND
Palais Rohan
PL. DU 11 NOV.
St-Bruno
Musée des Beaux-Arts
ESPLANADE CHARLES DE GAULLE
Préfecture
C.U.B.
3
PL. ROHAN
Cathédrale
Hôtel de ville
Hôtel de Région
Cimetière de la Chartreuse
Vestige du Fort du Hâ ou « Tour des Anglais »
30
Palais de Justice
22
40
Bibliothèque
Patinoire Olympique
PLACE DE LA RÉPUBLIQUE
Hôpital St-André
4
Ste-Eulalie
A
33
ARCACHON, N 250
B

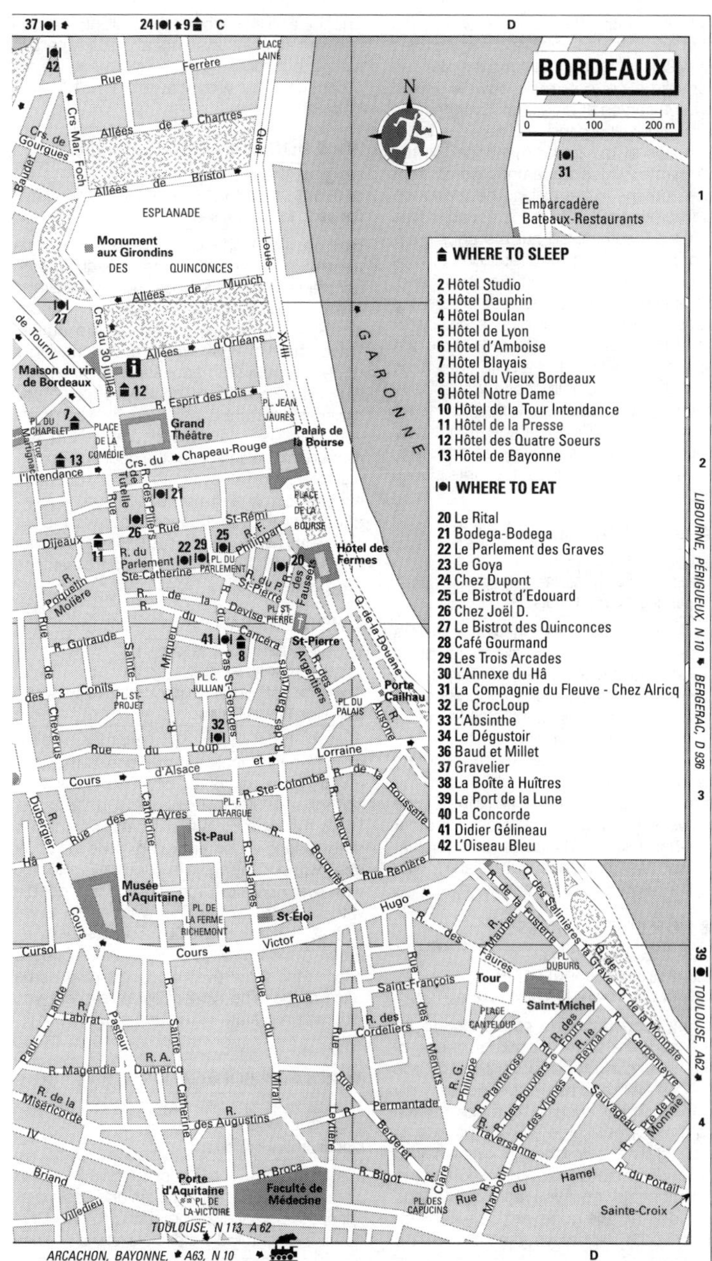
BORDEAUX
0 100 200 m
N
WHERE TO SLEEP
2 Hôtel Studio
3 Hôtel Dauphin
4 Hôtel Boulan
5 Hôtel de Lyon
6 Hôtel d'Amboise
7 Hôtel Blayais
8 Hôtel du Vieux Bordeaux
9 Hôtel Notre Dame
10 Hôtel de la Tour Intendance
11 Hôtel de la Presse
12 Hôtel des Quatre Soeurs
13 Hôtel de Bayonne
WHERE TO EAT
20 Le Rital
21 Bodega-Bodega
22 Le Parlement des Graves
23 Le Goya
24 Chez Dupont
25 Le Bistrot d'Edouard
26 Chez Joël D.
27 Le Bistrot des Quinconces
28 Café Gourmand
29 Les Trois Arcades
30 L'Annexe du Hâ
31 La Compagnie du Fleuve - Chez Alricq
32 Le CrocLoup
33 L'Absinthe
34 Le Dégustoir
36 Baud et Millet
37 Gravelier
38 La Boîte à Huîtres
39 Le Port de la Lune
40 La Concorde
41 Didier Gélineau
42 L'Oiseau Bleu
Embarcadère
Bateaux-Restaurants
ESPLANADE DES QUINCONCES
Monument aux Girondins
Maison du vin de Bordeaux
Grand Théâtre
Palais de la Bourse
Hôtel des Fermes
St-Pierre
Porte Cailhau
St-Paul
Musée d'Aquitaine
St-Éloi
Tour
Saint-Michel
Porte d'Aquitaine
Faculté de Médecine
Sainte-Croix
GARONNE
LIBOURNE, PÉRIGUEUX, N 10 BERGERAC, D 936
TOULOUSE, A62
TOULOUSE, N 113, A 62
ARCACHON, BAYONNE, A63, N 10

always encounter the same friendly and obliging service. Here the welcome includes numerous little thoughtful touches like the real orange juice (not a vile powder mixed with water) served at breakfast. Everything is efficient and well organized. There are still a few remains of the tower mentioned in the hotel's name (which apparently dates from the 3rd century) in the cellar. The rooms on the side looking out onto the street are a little noisy (it's pedestrianized but the people sitting on the restaurant terraces don't always keep their voices down). On the other hand, it's completely quiet at the rear where the cheapest rooms (singles) offer a nice view over the city's rooftops. On the whole the rooms aren't very large but an effort has been made with the décor in those which have been renovated. Doubles with shower/wc 250F, with bath 270F. Garage (night-time parking only, 7.30pm–9am). Cars 40F, motorcycles free. One of our favourite places in Bordeaux.

10% HÔTEL NOTRE-DAME**

36 rue Notre-Dame. **MAP C1-9**
☎ 05.56.52.88.24 F 05.56.79.12.67
Secure parking. TV with **Canal+**.

At the heart of the Les Chartrons district which used to be full of wine merchants but is now on the quiet side. A 19th century house with a stone façade cleaned to good effect in the shadow of the monumental Cité Mondiale du vin where you can find anything and everything related to wine. To compensate for the décor of the rooms which is rather too modern and neutral, the rue Notre-Dame overflows with antique dealers and other second-hand shops. Doubles with shower from 255F (less spacious but quieter), with bath 280F. (Pay) car park nearby.

10% HÔTEL DE LA PRESSE***

6 rue Porte-Dijeaux. **MAP C2-11**
☎ 05.56.48.53.88 F 05.56.01.05.82
Car park. TV with **Canal+. Disabled access.**

Ideally situated a couple of feet (or to be more accurate a dozen or so!) from one of the city's major crossroads, that of rue Sainte-Catherine and rue Porte-Dijeaux. Only pedestrians have access to these streets during the day but some cars do go past in the evening. The rooms though, which have a high level of comfort, are soundproofed (and air-conditioned). And if you really can't stand any noise at all, the courtyard side is quiet. But then you'd deprive yourself of the view from rooms 207 and 320 of the Grand Théâtre and a little bit of the Garonne. A certain degree of luxury (if not absolutely certain luxury) but more than acceptable value for money. Doubles with shower from 310F, with bath 385F.

10% HÔTEL DES QUATRE SŒURS**

6 cours du 30-Juillet. **MAP C2-12**
☎ 05.57.81.19.20 F 05.56.01.04.28
Car park. TV with **Canal+**.

Built in the 18th century when Bordeaux aspired to being a city of grand architecture. Located between allées de Tourny, the Grand Théâtre and place des Quinconces, this hotel is steeped in history. Wagner, for example, stayed here in 1850 when he was having a rather eventful (and adulterous) affair with a lady from Bordeaux. The type of place you expect to be rather posh but which surprises you with its relaxed welcome. Attractive rooms overlooking either the cours de Tourny and allées de Tourny (more elegant but more expensive too and noisier although there's double glazing) or the inner courtyard. Doubles with every comfort 350F with shower and from 400F with bath. Buffet breakfast. Car park.

HÔTEL DE BAYONNE***

15 cours de l'Intendance. **MAP C2-13**
☎ 05.56.48.00.88 F 05.56.52.03.79
Closed the first week in January and the last week in December. **TV** with **Canal+**.

A large hotel in an 18th century building which doesn't look out of place in this very middle-class part of the city. Courteous staff. Attractive 1930s style lounge. On the upper floors the rooms have just been completely renovated in a contemporary style which, it goes without saying, is in good taste. Rooms with every comfort from 430F (for a double with shower/wc) to 505F (with bath). Suite also available at 800–900F. The nearby *hôtel Etche-Onna* in rue Mautrec forms an annexe offering the same level of comfort in the same price range. The type of establishment you wouldn't hesitate to recommend to your in-laws.

BODEGA-BODEGA

4 rue des Piliers-de-Tutelle. **MAP C2-21**
☎ 05.56.01.24.24
Closed Sunday lunchtimes.

Just think of it – a Spanish-style wine bar which was an instant success and has maintained its popularity. Something to give Bordeaux's quiet middle-class citizens sleepless nights. Large premises where the traditional separation between bar and restaurant (here on the mezzanine floor) has been respected. The atmosphere is like down in Andalusia or the Lavapiès area of Madrid though the place still lacks real characters (the pleb complete with repartee, the epicurean pensioner, the ascetic student desperate to meet someone etc) – yuppies still predominate. In short, although the atmosphere is often friendly here, it still lacks a little soul. Beneath the dozens of hams hanging above the bar, decent tapas such as *boquerones* (anchovies marinated in vinegar), *tortilla, mejillones à la rocca* (grilled Spanish mussels), *bacalao* (sautéd cod) with salad, grilled sardines, squid rings fried in batter, grilled gambas and lamb chops are served at very affordable prices (25–35F), all washed down with a Spanish rosé such as Gran Corpas at 50F a bottle.

I●I RESTAURANT LE RITAL

3 rue des Faussets. **MAP C2-20**
☎ 05.56.48.16.69
Closed weekends, public holidays and between mid August and the beginning of September.

In a part of the city where numerous restaurants appear only to disappear again after a few months, this little Italian place has been here for 15 years – which must be a good sign. The food is very good here and it's the type of place where friends meet. Warm welcome. Series of linked rooms with a view of the kitchen which produces remarkable specialities, including fresh pasta (fettucine with gorgonzola and basil, pasta with *foie gras*, spaghetti "di baggio" and cannelloni), but also the traditional Italian stew, aubergine *au gratin*, etc. The house desserts are good too. Small lunchtime set meal 50F (the 58F set meal is served at lunchtime and in the evening). Two other set meals at 75F and 98F in the evening. You'll get away with under 100F à la carte.

I●I LE PARLEMENT DES GRAVES

9 rue du Parlement Sainte-Catherine. **MAP C2-22**
☎ 05.56.51.68.54

We were a bit doubtful about the décor though the terrace is very comfortable. Staff young but pretty efficient. Decent set meals 55F (if you're in a hurry) and 66F (a more substantial meal) at lunchtime during the week. Evening set meals 89F, 98F and 138F. Good produce from the local land and the sea prepared simply and skillfully. Dishes include duck breast, a duo of fish of the day and *carpaccio* of salmon and tuna. The wine list has an exceptionally good selection of Graves wines (logical given the place's name) but not all the bottles are in stock in the cellar – the only negative point at this good little establishment. Surprising value for money in this area, which is starting to get too touristy.

I●I RESTAURANT LE PÈRE OUVRARD

12 rue du Maréchal-Joffre. **MAP B3-30**
☎ 05.56.44.11.58
Closed Saturday lunchtimes and Sundays.

When the sun makes an appearance a few tables are set up outside opposite the école nationale de la magistrature, where you study to become a judge. Given the location, it will come as no surprise to find judges and lawyers in a hurry in this bistro with its fresh and colourful décor. Nor will it come as a surprise to find good little bistro dishes such as grilled sardines *fleur de sel*, mussels in white wine and devilled chicken on the large blackboard. There are though also more sophisticated dishes such as caramelized pigeon with pepper and olives, salad of caramelized veal sweetbreads with almonds and fine *couscous* of cod flavoured with harissa and cumin. The prices are reasonable too. Lunchtime *formule* at 55F and set meals at 80F (starter, main course, glass of wine and coffee) and 130F (also includes a dessert, a 1/2 litre of wine and coffee). The set meals are the same in the evening (but the wine isn't included).

I●I RESTAURANT LE GOYA

89 rue Goya. **MAP A1-23**
☎ 05.56.48.29.19
Closed Saturdays, Sundays, public holidays and in August.

In this old part of Bordeaux not far from the palais Gallien where things move at a sluggish pace, this is the kind of little place we like. Away from the crowds of tourists, simple and friendly – particularly on fine days when the deliciously shady rear courtyard becomes just like a Greek taverna. The little set meal for 58F at lunchtimes enjoyed by locals and people who work in the area is fine. The cooking is more elaborate in the evening and the set meal goes up to 120F. Dishes include marbled mussels, bread rolls filled with cold ratatouille, cod with spinach, Spanish-style pig's cheeks, mullet in *sauce vierge*, rabbit black pudding with sage, upside-down apricot tart and iced melon soup with verbena-flavoured liqueur. Wonderful welcome. If we didn't know you except no less from this guide, we would almost be reluctant to tell you about such a good place! But we've done it now and with this in mind you are advised to book.

|●| LE BISTROT D'ÉDOUARD

16 place du Parlement. **MAP C2-25**
☎ 05.56.81.48.87
Closed 1 May and 25 December.

A mini-brasserie without any nasty surprises. Quite elegant traditional bistro décor. Efficient service. The little lunchtime set meal at 59.50F isn't bad at all. The same goes for its evening counterpart at 69.50F (no excessive marking up here!). Brasserie menu (calf's head and tongue, fried kidneys in port) and specialities of the south-west such as eels stewed in white wine and Bordeaux-style rib steak. Also a set meal devoted to the duck at 135F. Varied clientele (white-collar workers, groups of students, tourists, families who don't want to eat at home, etc). On fine days there are also seats out on the very touristy place du Parlement.

|●| LES TROIS ARCADES

10 place du Parlement. **MAP C2-29**
☎ 05.56.81.21.68
Closed Sundays and in February.

On one of our favourite squares. A bit on the touristy side at the weekend. During the week it's a meeting place for people working in the area. Given that you're not always particularly hungry at lunchtime, you can have a generous salad or go for one of the set meals (which are fine) at 60–100F.

|●| CHEZ JOËL D.

13 rue des Piliers-de-Tutelle. **MAP C2-26**
☎ 05.56.52.68.31

This oyster bar has made a (first) name for itself. Well done Joël! The man also has taste! Rather than giving us a fake bistro which pretends to be established of old with re-issues of advertisements, this former oyster farmer (you can trust him as regards the supplies) has created a modern establishment with simple but carefully thought-out décor which takes the sea as its theme. Staff are young and relaxed but professional and efficient. Freshness guaranteed and quality produce. By the dozen or half-dozen, the oysters are reasonably priced and the little white wines accompanying them are well chosen. Incidentally, in Bordeaux and around Arcachon, oysters are also eaten with a little grilled sausage (the *crépinette*). Reckon on paying 60–140F depending on whether it's early in the evening and you're not particularly hungry or you're set on satisfying a mad craving for oysters. Food served until midnight.

|●| CHEZ DUPONT

45 rue Notre-Dame. Off the map **C1-24**
☎ 05.56.81.49.59
Closed Sundays in summer.

About the best value for money you'll get in the Les Chartrons district. Attractive bistro-style surroundings, waiters wearing aprons and traditional dishes on the blackboard such as grandma's *pot au feu*. The *formule* at 62F (lunchtimes and weekday evenings) changes every day and includes a starter and main course or a main course and dessert. More substantial set meal (starter, main course and dessert) at 129F. The à la carte menu is also updated regularly (reckon on paying 120–150F for a meal). Dishes include fricassee of scallops with morels, veal sweetbreads in champagne and good fish in summer. Friendly welcome. Here everyone is in a good mood (and for humour pay a visit to the toilets!). Sometimes in the evening (generally Thursdays), a pianist and guitarist come to play jazz together.

|●| RESTAURANT LE BISTROT DES QUINCONCES

4 place des Quinconces. **MAP C2-27**
☎ 05.56.52.84.56

The "in" bistro in Bordeaux. It's located opposite the square with its famous monument to the people of Gironde. We prefer to sit on the terrace, weather permitting. Efficient service. The dishes are mainly bistro ones (steak and roast leg of mutton for example) but they are varied (with *carpaccio* of scallops, fisherman's grill and duck breast with honey) and the prices are reasonable. Small lunch *formules* 70F (weekdays) and 115F; reckon on paying around 150F à la carte in the evening. *Tapas* are also served in the evening.

|●| LE CROC LOUP

35 rue du Loup. **MAP C3-32**
☎ 05.56.44.21.19
Closed Sundays and Mondays.

The name of this place makes it sound a bit like a snack-bar or a fast-food joint but in fact it's a lovely little place with a certain refinement about it. Warm welcome. The set meal at 67F (lunch only) isn't elaborate (duck pâté with green pepper, grilled beef with shallots and chocolate *millefeuille* with coffee sauce) but offers amazing value for money. Other set meals at 115F (2 courses) and 145F (3 courses) with dishes such as cuttlefish salad *à la provençale*, cuttlefish ravioli with coriander, fresh sea trout *julienne* in saffron sauce, chicken drumstick with ceps and *foie gras* and stuffed rabbit with mushrooms – food which may appear relatively simple but which is not without a degree of sophistication.

RESTAURANT CAFÉ GOURMAND

3 rue Buffon. **MAP B2-28**
☎ 05.56.79.23.85
Closed Sundays.

Popular in certain Bordeaux social circles. A few tables are set up outside as soon as the sun makes an appearance and there are soft velvet seats for chillier days. The Olivers are a well-known family of chefs and photographs of them adorn the walls. Set meals at 70F and 85F (except evenings and Sundays), 110F and 120F (Monday to Saturday evenings). Excellent brasserie menu at affordable prices (reckon on paying 120–150F). Dishes include crunchy salad with mussels and chives, knuckle of ham with sage caramel, Louis Oliver fried eggs, fish stew flavoured with tarragon, artichoke stuffed with brie de Meaux and almond and lime tart.

RESTAURANT LA COMPAGNIE DU FLEUVE - CHEZ ALRIQ

quai des Queyries. **MAP D1-31**
☎ 05.56.86.58.49
Closed Mondays and lunchtimes (except Sundays and public holidays) and in January/February.

Food served until 2am. At the heart of a harbour and industrial area which has seen better days. Right next to it, the station ruins of the old gare d'Orléans look like something from a former war zone (but redevelopment of the area is on the cards). An unusual restaurant in an unusual setting – a cross between a squat canteen and an alternative self-service restaurant. Extremely cool welcome. The restaurant is large (still a bit of a building site) and sometimes puts on plays or concerts. It has an "unstructured" garden running down to the river with chairs from which you can admire the view over Bordeaux, although this is spoilt somewhat by a cruiser called the Colbert. The restaurant is now a bit of an "in" place to come which may explain why the prices are rather on the high side given the location. Set meals 140F (including wine and coffee). Otherwise reckon on paying at least 100F à la carte. The dishes available vary according to season – mussels in summer and Béarnaise vegetable broth in winter; shad, very young eels and lampreys when they're available. More regular features include fish soup, rabbit with onions and Portuguese-style cod. Wines from 55F a bottle.

RESTAURANT L'ABSINTHE

137 rue du Tondu. Off the map **A4-33**
☎ 05.56.96.72.73
Closed Saturday lunchtimes and Sundays.

This bistro restaurant with genuine period décor (as its name would suggest, the Toulouse-Lautrec and absinthe period) is worth going out of your way for, for one simple and obvious reason – the food is good! Lunchtime *formule* 50F and set meals 92–117F. Wide-ranging menu with Landes-style salad next to escalope of veal with cheese *au gratin*, fricassee of scallops with oyster mushrooms and veal sweetbreads in port. The sweets (chocolate gâteau for example) are real home-made ones.

LA BOÎTE À HUÎTRES

8 rue de la Vieille-Tour. **MAP B2-38**
☎ 05.56.81.64.97

A restaurant specializing in oysters which has soon established itself. It may be a little on the small side but it's pleasant and colourful and on fine days tables and chairs spill out onto the pedestrianized street, which is rather nice. Here the oysters are wonderfully fresh and it's always a case of the best at their best, for example if the Marennes special is a little fatty they'll only serve you the Quiberon from the open sea (and vice versa). There's also a small menu to complement the oysters which includes fish soup, smoked salmon, *foie gras* and home-made desserts. Wine by the glass. Post-theatre set meal 98F for 9 Quiberon number 3, a Landes-style meat pie and a glass of white wine. Oysters to take away (opened for free).

RESTAURANT LE PORT DE LA LUNE

59 quai de Paludate. Off the map **D4-39**
☎ 05.56.49.15.55

Opposite the abattoirs in a part of Bordeaux which has recently acquired a nightlife, this is the place to run aground. Listen out for the jazz music and make for it. They like their jazz here. That's actually a bit of an understatement – in fact they're absolutely mad about it and the house slogan is "Jazz abuse is good for you." Bistro-style surroundings with a friendly atmosphere. On the walls there are all the greats, the golden oldies, the handless pianists playing with their teeth – all the jazz legends, their trademark mannerisms immortalized by the camera or peering out from behind the smoke which is destined one day to ruin their lungs or voices. A lively, "lived in" place with a personal touch where it doesn't matter how much money you've got. You eat very well here with little bistro dishes – as choice a selection as the music – at very reasonable prices. À la carte dishes at 58–96F include harbour salad, mussels and oysters, whole duck breast and traditional-style veal kidneys. Reckon on paying 150F for a meal. Wines from 58F. For 100F you get a good harbour snack consisting of 6 oysters, main course, dessert, wine and coffee. Baby eels *à l'espagnole*, shad in pesto, lamprey, etc. In season Michel, the cheerful and chatty proprietor with his large Dali-style moustache wanders around making sure that everyone is happy. No worries on that score – here you've always come to the right place. Food served until 2am, 7 days a week, including public holidays, which in Bordeaux is something of a record.

|●| RESTAURANT LA CONCORDE

50 rue du Maréchal-Joffre. **MAP B3-40**
☎ 05.56.44.68.97
Closed Sundays and public holidays.

Both In this attractive brasserie (dating from the early part of the century –some restoration work has been done) and in the pleasant winter garden the food here varies according to season. Fresh produce (of course) and varied dishes such as sole with crab, veal kidneys, Bordeaux-style sturgeon, rib of beef, salmon with sorrel and home-made cakes served in generous portions at reasonable prices. Daily special 55F; reckon on paying 100–130F à la carte (170–180F if you succumb to the wine list). The set meal at 100F (which includes a starter, a choice of 3 main courses, a dessert, coffee and a glass of wine) is a good compromise. Lawyers come here to eat – hardly surprising given the location – but (quite unconnected) people also come here to play draughts and billiards. Jazz groups also sometimes play here.

|●| RESTAURANT BAUD ET MILLET

19 rue Huguerie. **MAP B1-36**
☎ 05.56.79.05.77
Closed Sundays.

Our specialist cheese restaurant in Bordeaux. Over 200 kinds of cheese available, selected by M. Baud who has a great passion for his work and applies strict criteria. The cheeses are of course eaten in their natural state but they are also used in numerous specialities, from the real classics like *raclette* and *tartiflette* to more daring concoctions. At Baud et Millet, for example, the "cheese and dessert" *formule* may just be one dish, a surprising but tasty combination of sweet and savoury ingredients! Impressive and well chosen selection of wines from all over the world (nearly a thousand different wines), arranged on shelves around the very pleasant, air-conditioned restaurant. Friendly staff. Set meals 105F, 135F and 155F.

|●| RESTAURANT GRAVELIER

114 cours de Verdun. Off the map **C1-37**
☎ 05.56.48.17.15
Closed Saturday lunchtimes, Sundays, during the February holidays and Aug 3–23.

Restaurant Gravelier has quickly established itself as part of the new wave of restaurants in Bordeaux. We're tempted to say this is understandable given that it's run by the daughter of one of the famous Troisgros brothers and we still believe in such talents being handed down. Her husband, Yves Gravelier, is an original and creative chef. The surroundings are modern but not flashy and the prices amazingly reasonable. Who says you can't get a good cheap meal in Bordeaux? Set meal at 105F (lunchtimes only). Others at 150F and 195F. Dishes include pollock in butter with shallots, *foie gras* in red wine and grilled rabbit with garlic, duckling cooked in the oven and stewed leg of duck with dried apricots, etc. Reckon on paying 200–220F à la carte. The menu is on the short side but the advantage of this is that it changes frequently. Dishes include "exotic" ravioli soup, mussels and cod in white wine with celery and a pinch of curry powder, mullet cooked in a charcoal pan with vine shoots, fried liver and toasted French bread and saddle of rabbit in creamy truffle sauce.

|●| RESTAURANT L'OISEAU BLEU

65 cours de Verdun. **MAP C1-42**
☎ 05.56.81.09.39
Closed Saturday lunchtimes and 3 weeks in August.

Vincent Poussard who is in charge at this restaurant was François Mitterand's private chef at the Elysée. We know that the former French president liked traditional cuisine and the simplest and best produce when in season (including the famous ortolans). *L'Oiseau Bleu* is quite prepared, for example, to fly off to Laguiole to bring back dried sausage, to Landes for the black pudding combined with its traditional "Lulu" purée or to Laruns to find the best cheese in the Pyrenees. The set menu at 157F (lunchtimes and evenings) is absolutely ideal to discover this cuisine which brings out all the flavours and colours of the great south. Dishes include Gascony-style *macaronade* with fried *foie gras*, rosette of fillets of mullet with tagliatelle in pesto and Mediterranean sardine tart. There are also fine desserts such as strawberry slice and sugared brioche with blue poppy seeds. À la carte reckon on paying between 200F and 250F. It's worth it. Comfortable restaurant and friendly welcome to make things perfect.

DIDIER GÉLINEAU

26 rue du Pas-Saint-Georges. **MAP C3-41**
☎ 05.56.52.84.25
Closed Saturday lunchtimes and Sundays.

In just a few short years this restaurant has become one of the city's musts thanks to cooking which subtly blends traditional and modern. This success hasn't gone to their heads though and the prices are still unbelievably reasonable. Take, for example, the wonderful set meal of the day at 120F which immediately makes you want to try the one at 190F too, especially when the line-up is iced gazpacho with smoked salmon and marinated scampi, young rabbit with goat's cheese and prunes (cooked for 3 hours!), cheeses (from M. Baud!) and two-chocolate royale. Another set meal at 270F and a menu which, like the set meals, varies according to season. À la carte dishes include flakes of cod *au gratin* with *piquillos* in onion, pepper and tomato fondue, roast pigeon with chestnut blossom or herbs, duck *foie gras* with morels, Bordeaux-style braised sturgeon and roast rack of suckling lamb. As for the desserts (such as pyramid of caramelized gingerbread and apple ice-cream with bourbon sauce), we prefer not to go into too much detail. You see, Didier Gélineau was once the French dessert champion and if we do we'll be straight back to keep the promise we made ourselves to return to this lovely little restaurant.

BOULIAC 33270 (5KM SE)

RESTAURANT LE BISTROY

3 place Camille-Hostein.
☎ 05.57.97.06.06
Car park.

A surprising place to find on this peaceful village square. To tell the truth, we thought we were entering a night club given the long bar, neon lights and high-tech metal chairs, but the napkins are made of fine white cotton and there's nothing way out about the food. Dishes include aubergine chutney, aubergines in caviar, ox cheek with grapes, fillet of cod roasted in spices and simple but tasty apple tart. The *"Bistroy"* forms an annexe to the *Saint-James de Jean-Marie Amat*, one of the south-west's top restaurants, and the dishes (served in generous helpings) come from its kitchens. This means you get the same culinary skill but at more affordable prices. Reckon on paying around 150F for a meal. In summer the wine list is quite varied but a little on the short side. Try the Basque cider for something different! The service is on the slow side, leaving you time to try out your amateur ethno-sociology on the clientele who arrive on their Harley Davidsons. To sum up, it's good, friendly, not too upmarket and above all it really buzzes!

GRADIGNAN 33170 (6KM SW)

HÔTEL-RESTAURANT LE CHALET LYRIQUE**

169 cours du Général-de-Gaulle (Centre); take exit 16 off the outer ring road; just after place de l'Église.
☎ 05.56.89.11.59 F 05.56.89.53.37
Restaurant closed Sundays and in August.
Secure parking. TV with **Canal+. Disabled access.**

Less than 15 minutes from Bordeaux-Mérignac airport. In the centre of either a large village or a suburb of Bordeaux – it can't seem to make up its mind. Thoroughly modern building arranged around a patio with one hundred year old olive trees. In the middle there's a fountain gurgling out of a giant clay urn. 40 very comfortable rooms (some with sloping roofs and a balcony). Doubles with bath 345F. In the restaurant (closed Sundays and in August) set meals start at 65F (weekday lunchtimes). The meats (steak, mutton steak, rib steak, stew, etc) are wonderful (the proprietor used to work at a butcher's) but à la carte you don't half pay for it (the menu is translated into 7 languages, including Chinese).

CAMBES 33880 (15KM SE)

RESTAURANT LA GUINGUETTE DE LA VARENNE

How to get there: it's on the right bank of the Garonne heading up towards Cadillac.
☎ 05.56.21.85.69
Closed Mondays and November–Easter. **Car park.**

Old riverside country inn transformed into a trendy café-type establishment (for want of a better description). Varied clientele including middle-class people from Bordeaux, young people and local families. The food covers the basics such as whelks, mussels and chips, grilled fish and meats. Charming service and relaxed atmosphere (the weekend accordionist adds a touch of old-time authenticity). The deckchairs are very tempting when it's time for the aperitif and the terrace on the bank of the Garonne is very pleasant. The only problem is that you don't get great value for money. Set meal at 130F. Reckon on paying 150F à la carte. Be warned: credit cards not taken.

BRANTÔME 24310

HOSTELLERIE DU PÉRIGORD VERT**

av. de Thiviers.
☎ 05.53.05.70.58
Restaurant closed Fridays and Sunday evenings in winter and in January/February. **Secure parking**. **TV**. **Disabled access**.

You could almost miss this ivy-swathed bungalow. Its situation at the bottom of a garden means that it's quiet despite the central location. Comfortable rooms 260–305F for a double – good value for money. Set meals a bit expensive from 95F (not available Sunday lunchtimes and public holidays) to 250F. Half-board 260F. You don't get a particularly warm welcome.

RESTAURANT AU FIL DE L'EAU

21 quai Bertin (Centre).
☎ 05.53.05.73.65
Closed on Tuesdays except June 15–Sept 15.

This used to be a bistro for anglers. You no longer find fishing permits on sale behind the bar or hear endless discussions on the size of the latest catches but the décor of this adorable little restaurant still has fishing very much as its theme. There's even a boat anchored next to the lovely little terrace on the banks of the Dronne. It comes as no surprise then to find a number of freshwater fish (trout, fillets of perch, etc) and local dishes on the menu. This is short and relatively expensive (reckon on paying at least 150F), so you might want to settle for the only set meal at 95F to get an idea of the relatively uncomplicated but well presented cuisine. Friendly welcome and efficient service.

MONSEC 24340 (12KM NW)

HÔTEL-RESTAURANT BEAUSÉJOUR

rue Principale; take the D939.
☎ 05.53.60.92.45 Fax 05.53.56.39.88
Closed Friday evenings and Saturdays (in low season), and during the Christmas week. **Car park**. **TV**.

An excellent place to stop off in this area. Really friendly welcome and quality food served in a pleasant restaurant (with a panoramic view of the garden). Fine range of set meals often celebrating local cuisine. Dishes include duck sausage, (oyster) mushroom omelette, *foie gras*, preserve and duck breast kebab. The cheapest set meal at 75F (including a 1/4 litre of wine) is more than acceptable and we couldn't fault those at 100F, 110F and 150F. Rooms simple but impeccable from 150F for a double with basin.

SAINT-JEAN-DE-CÔLE 24800 (20KM NE)

10% HÔTEL SAINT-JEAN**

route de Nontron; take the D78.
☎ 05.53.52.23.20
Closed January. **Car park**. **TV**.

Nice little place, one of those which, thanks to professional and conscientious proprietors, contribute to safeguarding the good reputation of country hotels. It's on a main road but not too busy at night. Traditional, comfortable and meticulously kept rooms. 200F for a double with shower/wc. The proprietor concocts quality regional dishes such as home-made duck *foie gras* pâté, monkfish in batter and duck breast *à l'orange* in parsley vinaigrette with slivers of truffle. Set meals start at 65F (weekdays). Others at 88F, 120F and 140F.

BUZET SUR BAÏZE 47690

AUBEGE DU GOUJON QUI FRÉTILLE

rue Gambetta.
☎ 05.53.84.26.51
Closed Tuesday evenings and Wednesdays, Nov 1–15 and March 15–31.

The village is quiet and pretty – and so is this inn. Despite its mischievous name (literally The Inn of the Wriggling Gudgeon), you sit down to generous helpings of fine food in calm surroundings. The daily set meal offered us pig's tongue in aspic, roast veal and pear tart – all for 55F. Set meals at 90F, 115F and 140F in the evening when dishes include freshwater crayfish soup with scallops, potatoes in garlic mayonnaise, duck breast in parsley gravy, shin of veal and Landes-style fattened chicken in Buzet white wine – a choice to satisfy the healthiest appetites.

CAGNOTTE 40300

HÔTEL BONI-RESTAURANT LE FOURNIL**.

☎ 05.58.73.03.78 F➔ 05.58.73.13.48
Closed Sunday evenings and Mondays.

As soon as you see this place's name you know it used to be a baker's. You won't find a working kneading trough here any more but it is a nice country inn where you'll enjoy stopping off for a good meal. The menu is geared towards the sea and offers fish specialities. The proprietor regularly goes up to Brittany for his supplies. There's a wonderful sole with fresh pasta, a warm scallop and gizzard salad on a bed of endives, a turnip and gizzard tart, a cod steak with smoked bacon and then duck stew and potato ravioli, veal sweetbreads with ceps and a whole host of specialities cooked in duck fat. Set meals of the day at 80F and 100F and three set menus at 130F, 150F and 190F. If you take to the place you may decide to spend the night here. There are a few simple rooms at 180F with shower and 220F or 240F with shower/wc.

CAMBO-LES-BAINS 64250

10% L'AUBERGE DE TANTE URSULE**

fronton du Bas-Cambo; it's by the pelota court.
☎ 05.59.29.78.23 F➔ 05.59.29.28.57
Closed Tuesdays out of season and mid January–mid February. **Car park**. **TV**. **Disabled access**.

Old farm painted all in white and rather sweet. Decent rooms 165F (with basin) to 280F (with bath). Good food. Set meals start at 80F (weekdays). Others at 120F, 150F and 200F (dishes include gourmet salad, monkfish with green pepper, woodpigeon stew and duck breast *à l'orange*). Specialities include braised lamb sweetbreads with ceps and mild peppers and home-made grilled black pudding with apples. The welcome could be warmer but it's good value for money.

ESPELETTE 64250 (5KM W)

HÔTEL-RESTAURANT EUZKADI**

rue Principale (Centre); take the D918 towards Saint-Jean-de-Luz.
☎ 05.59.93.91.88 F➔ 05.59.93.90.19
Closed Mondays, Tuesdays out of season and Nov 5–Dec 15. **Car park**.

This is one of the country hotel and restaurants most typical of the Basque country and it may be a good idea to reserve quite a bit in advance. Michèle and André Darraïdou are completely mad about Basque cooking and make it a point of honour to dig out old country-style recipes (often on the verge of oblivion) and revamp them for today's tastes. In their enormous restaurant you'll discover dishes you would have very little chance of finding elsewhere. For example, *tripoxa*, a black pudding made from veal or mutton and served with a tomato sauce with capsicums (a delicious delicacy!), *axoa* (cubed veal browned with onions), *merluza salsa verde* (poached hake with peas, asparagus, cockles and hard-boiled eggs in a sauce made with Jurançon wine and fish stock – yum!) and *elzekaria* (vegetable soup). Set meals 95–175F. If you want to stay the night or have a nice siesta after all that, there are lovely little rooms at 270F for a double with bath. To the rear there's a pleasant garden, tennis court and swimming pool.

ITXASSOU 64250 (5KM S)

HÔTEL-RESTAURANT DU CHÊNE**

How to get there: take the D918 towards Saint-Jean-Pied-de-Port then the D349 as you enter the Nive valley.
☎ 05.59.29.75.01 F➔ 05.59.29.27.39
Closed Mondays and Tuesdays out of season and in January/February. **Car park**.

This establishment is superbly situated. Doubles 235F (with bath). Unpretentious but delicious local cuisine. Set meals 80–180F. Specialities include Biscay-style cod, escalopes of *foie gras* in cherry vinegar and tuna with capsicums.

10% HÔTEL DU FRONTON - RESTAURANT BONNET**

La Place; it's on the D249.
☎ 05.59.29.75.10 F➔ 05.59.29.23.50
Closed Wednesdays out of season and Jan 1–Feb 15. **Car park**. **TV**.

The *Hôtel du Fronton* is a fine establishment hidden beneath the square's plane trees. Lovely swimming pool which is very pleasant in summer. People sit at the bar and invariably order the Bayonne ham, one of the best in the Basque country. It's matured and cured up under the roof. Jean-Paul Bonnet knows good produce when he sees it. *Chichons* (potted mince) and black pudding are eaten early in the morning here. You can also try a glass of Jurançon wine and a piece of *ardi-gasna* (ewe's milk cheese) which you eat with cherry jam. The bill won't come as a nasty shock either. Set meals start at 84F. Others at 98F and 135F. Rooms with shower/wc 238F.

AINHOA 64250 (12KM SW)

☗ |●| PENSION ETCHARTENEA

Dancharia (South-West); take the D918 then turn onto the D20 near the Spanish border; when you get to Ainhoa turn left 100m before the border point.
☎ 05.59.29.90.26 F➜ 05.59.29.73.82
Secure parking.

The lovely *Pension Etchartenea* has 8 little double rooms with basin and bidet at 160F. Set meals start at 85F. A real find by the fast-flowing Pitxuri. Cross the bridge which spans it and you're in Spain. Further up the road are the famous *ventas* where you can get alcoholic drinks, jams, garlic etc at Spanish prices. You return the same way loaded up and with no problems about getting through Customs.

10% ☗ |●| ITHURRIA***

rue principale (Centre).
☎ 05.59.29.92.11 F➜ 05.59.29.81.28
Closed Tuesday evenings and Wednesdays out of season and mid November–end March. **Car park**. **TV**.

One of the finest inns we know of. Large 17th century house and former coaching inn of Saint-Jacques-de-Compostelle. Very attractively furnished rooms 450–600F. Food not cheap but it has a good reputation. Set meals 170F and 250F with *foie gras*, hake steak, duck breast and iced nougat. Fine garden and swimming pool to the rear. A pity the welcome is a bit on the brusque side!

CAPBRETON 40130

|●| RESTAURANT LA PÊCHERIE DUCAMP

rue du Port-d'Albret.
☎ 05.58.72.11.33
Closed Mondays in winter, during the February school holidays and end October.

Direct from the fishmonger to the consumer – the tables are arranged around the fishmonger's counter and the waitresses wear boots and plastic aprons. Set meals start at 120F for a seafood platter, main course and dessert. Small fish and seafood platter 130F and gourmet set meal with platter and grilled fish 220F.

|●| LES COPAINS D'ABORD

Port des Mille Sabords.
☎ 05.58.72.22.80
Closed Sunday evenings and Mondays (out of season) and the last 2 weeks in November and January.

Capbreton's classiest restaurant. The elegant mahogany décor conjures up a strong flavour of the sea, the surroundings are comfortable and the polite welcome is just right. No possibility of an unpleasant surprise. There's just one set menu at 150F, almost all of which is connected somehow to the sea – not surprising given the location. Dishes include Basque-style browned sardine *tian*, seafood stew, bass caught on the line with fennel, mullet or sole *meunière* and for very healthy appetites Landes-style *macarronnade,* a simple little dish with grilled truffles, ceps and *foie gras* – delicious! Lovely terrace which, paradoxically, is more pleasant in the evening in summer. At lunchtime the heat is a little too much.

CAPDROT 24540

10% ☗ |●| HOSTELLERIE LE SAINT-HUBERT**

le bourg.
☎ 05.53.23.44.91 F➜ 05.53.36.66.90
Closed Wednesdays (except June 15–Sept 15).
Secure parking.

In the centre of a peaceful little village. Even though this place was only built recently and there's a tennis court and a swimming pool, it's a typical example of a country hotel. There's even a little grocer's – just like the old days! Wonderful welcome. 11 pleasant rooms some of which (numbers 6, 7, 9 and 11) look out onto the surrounding countryside. Doubles with shower 240F, with bath 260F. A couple owns the place and you'll find the "man of the house" in the kitchen and the "lady of the house" in the restaurant – hard work! The daily special at 35F and the basic set meal at 75F (weekday lunchtimes) are served in a little room which is a bit on the gloomy side. For a few extra francs you're allowed to eat in the large dining room with its nice quiet atmosphere where you'll be reacquainted with the good old traditional flavours. You'll (re)discover skillfully prepared regional dishes such as goose soup, warm *foie gras* with asparagus spears, calf's mesentery cooked in the traditional style, home-made grilled black pudding with chestnut purée and game in season. Set meals 95F, 110F and 135F. Good place to stop in the heart of a region with a rich architectural heritage. Notable buildings include the collégiale de Capdrot, the bastide de Montpazier and the château de Biron.

CAP-FERRET 33970

10% HÔTEL DES PINS**

10 rue des Rossignols (Centre).
☎ 05.56.60.60.11 Fax 05.56.60.67.41
Closed Nov 10–Easter. **TV**.

Quietly situated between the bassin d'Arcachon and the ocean. Delightful house dating from the early part of the century with a front garden full of flowers. Time seems to have had no effect on what must once have been a family guest house but in actual fact the hotel's décor has been redone with manic attention to detail – old advertisements, billiards tables etc – to create this impression. If there weren't people about, we'd almost think we were on a film set. The place is also sometimes adorned with fashion photographs. Warm welcome. The rooms are all pretty much identical and all have a shower or bath. 245–335F in low season, 319–435F in high season. The restaurant is only open when the weather is at its best (that's to say in the evenings from mid June to the beginning of September) because you eat on a veranda adjacent to the garden or on the actual lawn. Set meals 90–120F. Fish and local produce are used in dishes such as fresh cod steak with garlic mayonnaise, Bordeaux-style grilled tuna and Pauillac lamb.

PINASSE CAFÉ

2 bis av. de l'Océan (Centre).
☎ 05.56.03.77.87

Near the landing stage. In an attractive house from the early part of the century, painted blue and white. The type of restaurant where friends come to eat. This is where a certain section of Cap-Ferret's youths hang out. Young staff offering wonderfully laid-back (yet efficient) service. The terrace, ideally situated looking out onto the ocean (and its oyster beds) and the dune du pyla, sometimes resounds to the beat of house and techno music. Set meals 75F (lunchtimes only) and 110F. Good little simple fish (grilled mullet in pesto), seafood (whelks, winkles and mussels with pine needles) and grilled meat dishes (we enjoyed their pork spare ribs).

10% LA FRÉGATE**

34 av. de l'Océan (Centre).
☎ 05.56.60.41.62 Fax 05.56.03.76.18
Closed in November. **Car park. TV. Disabled access.**

Ideally situated (between the bassin d'Arcachon and the ocean, 300m from where the boat from Arcachon arrives), *La Frégate* has obliging proprietors at the helm, "steering" it simply but well. A sizeable asset is the swimming pool which is as ultraclean as the rooms. Doubles with shower 220F out of season (260F in season), with bath from 300F (out of season) to 550F for the best rooms (numbers 23–29 with a large balcony/terrace overlooking the swimming pool).

RESTAURANT MOULES AND BLUES

How to get there: it's by the landing stage.
☎ 05.56.60.41.85
Closed lunchtimes (except Saturdays, Sundays and public holidays) and end September to the first weekend in May.

You've heard of rhythm and blues but here, literally, we have mussels and blues! It's an unusual name for this little seasonal restaurant which specializes in mussels and plays blues in the background. Dishes include mussels with ham, with basil and with ginger, pasty with mussels and cognac and profiteroles with mussels and saffron. Generous portions of tasty food. Set meal 65F at lunchtime and 120F in the evening. À la carte (reckon on paying 100F) there are other specialities from the sea such as fish soup, paella and fisherman's platter. In summer, of course, you can eat on the terrace in the shade, but there's no sea view.

CANON (LE) 33950 (6KM N)

HÔTEL-RESTAURANT DE LA PLAGE.

L'Herbe, 1 rue des Marins.
☎ 05.56.60.50.15
Closed Mondays out of season and in December.

A little hotel and restaurant which has survived modernism (each year we ask ourselves how it does it). Typical wooden house just by the water with a small grocer's, an old-fashioned telephone and large, traditional-style mattresses airing on the balconies during the day. You feel like you're in a film with Gabin and Arletty. The prices too are from a different age. Doubles with basin 180F (the shower is on the landing). The 7 rooms are of course basic but they're nice and 6 of them look out onto the water. Restaurant nothing special. Although it's quite classy, you'll find tourists and ordinary working folk there on Sundays on the little terrace tucking into mussels in white wine or grilled sea bream. You eat what there is and as the proprietors do exactly what they feel like you don't complain. If it's full, wait your turn with your elbows on the old bar like the regulars. Set meals 90F with meat and 150F with meat and fish.

|●| RESTAURANT ARKÉSEON

1 rue du Débarcadère.
☎ 05.56.60.80.95
Closed Wednesdays out of season, 2 weeks in February and 2 in October.

The little villages around Cap-Ferret still have some picturesque and authentic places hidden away to be discovered on foot, like this one in a lane which forms part of an oyster-farming harbour. Unpretentious little bistro with a warm welcome and simple cooking. Produce of the sea which goes to make dishes such as fresh prawn fricassee, cod *accras*, fresh cod steak in garlic mayonnaise, cuttlefish stew and fried eel with parsley. Inexpensive wines – the house wine costs just 25F and other bottles start at 45F. Set meal 65F (lunchtimes) and generally reckon on paying 120F à la carte although, unfortunately, the bill can sometimes mount up with all kinds of little extras.

CASTELJALOUX 47700

|●| LA VIEILLE AUBERGE

11 rue Posterne.
☎ 05.53.93.01.36
Closed Sunday evenings, Wednesdays (out of season) and Nov 15–30.

In one of the oldest streets in town, this inn has a thoroughly local flavour. Enjoy all the tastes Gascony has to offer with produce skillfully selected according to the season. Just to whet your appetite, there are goujons of sole and boiled cabbage with butter, bass with endives, local lamb stew, grenadine of veal with kidneys and morels and monkfish fricassee with salad. The prices of the set meals may seem high (120–230F) but they're pretty good value for money – and it does you good to treat yourself from time to time, all the more so at a nice place like this.

CASTILLONNÈS 47330

⌂ |●| HÔTEL DES REMPARTS

26 rue de la Paix.
☎ 05.53.36.80.97 F 05.53.36.93.87
Closed Sunday evenings, Mondays and in January/February.

In a really quiet part of town you'll find this superb, characterful establishment with its lovely shaded garden. The owner welcomes you as though you were a a friends. The way she's decorated and furnished the rooms shows exquisite taste. It's hard to leave again once you've had a taste of what it's like here. Doubles 295–395F. The restaurant is just as good as the rest of the place. Set meals 95F (weekdays) and 150F. High-quality traditional cooking. Dishes include skate pâté with herbs, roast suckling lamb in rosemary gravy, strawberry slice with whipped cream and ice-cream with vervein on a bed of strawberries.

CAUNA 40500

⌂ |●| LE RELAIS DE LA CHALOSSE*

Centre.
☎ 05.58.76.10.47 F 05.58.76.32.84
Closed Sunday evenings out of season. **TV**.

Local cooking has ruled here for generations. Tradition is upheld, as is quality, and all kinds of lovers of fine food happily recommend this place to one another. Dishes such as *foie gras* with apple, pigeon breast in sherry, goose stew with morels and roast zander in wine will please the most delicate of stomachs. You sit in the fine rustic restaurant typical of the region, put on your serviette and wait for the food to arrive. Set meals at reasonable prices (75–130F). A number of rooms at 160F (with shower/wc) and 180F (with bath). Cheap but don't expect any great luxury.

DAX 40100

10% ⌂ |●| HÔTEL-RESTAURANT BEAUSOLEIL**

38 rue du Tuc-d'Eauze (Centre).
☎ 05.58.74.18.32 F 05.58.56.03.81
Restaurant closed Monday and Thursday evenings.
Secure parking. **TV**. **Disabled access**.

Definitely comes out top for charm and friendliness. Near the centre but quietly situated, this pretty little white house with a terrace has 32 comfortable family rooms with shower/wc. Doubles 250–360F. Set meals 65F (weekdays), 75F, 100F, 130F, 180F and 220F. The food is conventional but good and prepared with quality produce. This is the type of place where your bottle awaits you on the table with your serviette ring. Excellent value for money and, as an added extra, free breakfast on presentation of this guide.

|●| LA TABLE DE PASCAL

4 rue de la Fontaine Chaude.
☎ 05.58.74.89.00
Closed Saturday lunchtimes and Sundays.

A genuine little bistro with attractive bistro-style décor serving, you've guessed it, good bistro food. A good place to come for a tuck-in at lunchtime with a client or in the evening with a friend. Examples include leeks in mustard, Béarnaise vegetable broth, salmon steak, calf's liver with parsley, salted belly pork and beef and vegetable stew. No set meal but you'll get away with around 80F.

|●| L'AMPHYTRION

38 quai Galliéni.
☎ 05.58.74.58.05
Closed Sunday evenings, Mondays, a fortnight at the beginning of January and the last 2 weeks in August.

The word *amphytrion* means host and Eric Pujos has chosen to be one. He'll delight you with produce from the Landes region and the Basque country in a little restaurant with plain but bright and modern décor. A place which all Dax's lovers of good food have in their address books. They come here for the rustic-style *foie gras*, the lamb stuffed with *axoa* (cubed veal browned with onions), with *pimientos del piquillos (*peppers*)* and with traditional-style boned pigeon and, to finish, a delicious pastis from the Landes region. Set meals very reasonable at 80–200F. Prompt and pleasant service under the watchful eye of Mme Pujos. Just one little quibble – the seasoning could do with a touch less salt.

DURAS 47120

10% ⌂ |●| L'HOSTELLERIE DES DUCS**

bd Jean-Brisseau; it's near the castle.
☎ 05.53.83.74.58 F 05.53.83.75.03
Closed Sunday evenings and Mondays except in July, August and September. **Secure parking**. **TV**.

Quietly situated, these 2 fine semi-detached houses which used to be a convent now house the region's most prestigious hotel and restaurant. Pleasant terrace, lovely swimming pool and a large garden full of flowers outside and a friendly atmosphere inside. The food enjoys an excellent reputation – only fresh produce is used. Set meals 80F, 120F, 170F and 250F. Dishes include soup with garlic, traditional-style Tonneins ham, bass with a Sauvignon sauce, escalope of duck *foie gras*, fillet of beef with morels and strawberry and chocolate tart. The chef puts quality regional produce before originality and the result is good, simple cooking. Comfortable rooms at 275–490F for a double. Our favourites are rooms 15, 16 and 17. Attentive staff. Apparently, it's pretty much essential to book in season.

EUGÉNIE-LES-BAINS 40320

|●| LA FERME AUX GRIVES

Centre.
☎ 05.58.51.19.08
Closed Monday evenings, Tuesdays and in January.
Car park.

Everyone has heard of Eugénie-les-Bains and Michel Guérard. He invented lean cuisine and here his "domain" extends to two hotels, a spa and two restaurants. *Près d'Eugénie* (tel: 05-58-05-06-07), the flagship restaurant, spearheads things of course. Of course talent comes at a price and set meals start at 590F, but it is worth making a few sacrifices just to be able to eat there once in your life. You will, however, be overjoyed to hear that Guérard has decided to have a little fun and make his guests happy by refurbishing the old farm to create an inn at the other end of his domain. Here you'll enter a veritable theatre where you'll be the actors in the play they perform twice daily – the meal. If the word "eating" no longer means anything to you, then this is the place to come. Rediscover the tastes of yesteryear, relearn what simple produce can do, let old memories flood back or new ones be stored up. This place is nothing less than a vast library of culinary flavours, as rich and as genuine as the solid old farmhouse table on which lines of fresh vegetables lie waiting for the chef to come and fetch them, soon to reappear upon your plate. Hams are cured hanging from the ceiling, the suckling pig turns slowly on the spit in the fireplace and the casks around it smell of the good old days. You feel good just as soon as you've sat down and you cannot help but take up the challenge. What challenge? To find the time to take your time – here at this festive table, in the company of friends, with simple cooking (at this level the word simple takes on a whole new meaning!). Dishes include boiled beef and pork salad in a herb and shallot dressing, coconut and cod salad with fresh marinated anchovies, smooth calf's head pâté with mayonnaise, Castile-style suckling pig, tripe cooked in armagnac and Landes-style grilled chicken. You won't have tasted better! For dessert there's Paris-Brest (a large choux pastry ring) with praline-flavoured cream, *crème brûlée* with grilled oats and fruit tart (the fruits used depend on the season). It's a wonderful celebration, a dream come true. And the price? 175F. Nothing more to be said, except make sure you try the toilets!

EYZIES-DE-TAYAC (LES) 24620

HÔTEL DE FRANCE - AUBERGE DU MUSÉE**

rue du Moulin.
☎ 05.53.06.97.23 F 05.53.06.90.97
Closed November–Easter. **Car park. Disabled access.**

Two establishments opposite each other at the foot of the cliff (complete with museum of course given its mention in the name of one of them). The inn serves traditional and regional food, both in the two rooms inside and outside under the wisteria arbour. Dishes include sliced duck with morels, snail casserole in Sauvignon and goose and duck *foie gras*. Set meals at 70F, 80F and 90F then 140–208F. There are a few rooms within the solid stone walls of the *Hôtel de France*. More rooms a few hundred metres away in an annexe by the Vézève which has a garden and a swimming pool (for the use of all customers!). Doubles with shower/wc 230–290F and with bath 250–320F. Half-board 250–330F per person (compulsory 1–20 August).

10% HÔTEL-RESTAURANT DU CENTRE**

Centre; it's opposite the museum.
☎ 05.53.06.97.13 F 05.53.06.91.63
Closed November–March. **Car park. TV.**

On a little pedestrianized square by the river (so it's quiet). The white of the shutters adds a touch of charm to the old ivy-covered walls. Very attractively decorated rooms. Doubles with bath 250F and 300F. Beautifully restored "bourgeois" rustic restaurant. Traditional cuisine, well prepared with regional dishes. The cheapest set meal at 95F (available every day) offers good value for money with dishes such as Périgord delight with *foie gras*, chicken breast with nuts and chicken preserve. Other set meals at 150F, 190F and 220F. Reckon on paying 175F à la carte – dishes include a *foie gras* platter, veal sweetbreads with morels, fried scallops with ceps, conserve of rabbit in truffle gravy, chocolate rissoles with pine kernels and almonds and hot nut soufflé. Children's set meal 56F.

LE MOULIN DE LA BEUNE**

Centre.
☎ 05.53.06.94.33 F 05.53.06.98.06
Closed Tuesday lunchtimes and Nov 1–April 1; restaurant closed Jan 3–Feb 15. **Car park.**

This place takes its name from the part of it which used to be a mill and it is of course by the water, at the bottom end of the village in a part where the tourist coaches don't venture. Courteous staff. The décor of the rooms is exceptionally low-key (some may find it a little austere) but they're comfortable and are good value for money (from 260F for a double). The restaurant, *Le Vieux Moulin*, offers tasty and well-prepared food, served in a room where you can see the original mill machinery. The cheapest set menu at 95F has dishes such as country-style Périgord medallion, chicken roll and trout supreme with almonds. Other set meals at 140F (chicken pâté in aspic and duck preserve with Périgord *mojettes*), 175F, 195F and 250F. In summer you eat in the garden on an adorable terrace, lulled by the gentle murmur of the river.

10% HÔTEL-RESTAURANT LE CENTENAIRE

rocher de la Penne; it's in the main street.
☎ 05.53.06.68.68 F 05.53.06.92.41
Restaurant closed Tuesday lunchtimes in low season; hotel closed start Nov–start April. **Secure parking. TV.**

This type of place doesn't often appear in our guides, but we have to acknowledge in all humility that it's an exceptional establishment. Not to beat about the bush, this is the best restaurant in Périgord, yet it's able to offer a set meal at 165F (weekday lunchtimes). It's a better bet though to wait until the evening when there's a remarkable set meal at 295F. It would be a real shame not to let your taste buds enjoy this true feast at least once. And what a feast of aromas, of creativity, of imagination and of inspired madness – imagine combining chestnut purée with chopped oysters! But also a rediscovery of traditional local dishes using the best regional produce. The restaurant gets you completely under its spell, awe-struck at rediscovering a genuine feeling of pleasure which you never thought you'd experience again. What's more, the atmosphere has none of the affectedness you usually find in such places. Roland Mazère, the youngest centenarian in the world if the place is named after him, and Alain Scholly, his "accomplice" in the actual restaurant, have managed to create a marvellously convivial and low-key, relaxed atmosphere in these elegant surroundings which reflect good taste but avoid ostentatious luxury. The wine waiter isn't outdone with his calm professionalism and a wine list featuring the finest Bergeracs. After an introduction like that, how could you be anything other than happy and relaxed, waiting to try the superb set meals. Let's start with the one at 295F for which you get tender vegetables with *foie gras* and goose preserve, poached hake and a crispy tart with pigs' trotters and goose preserve. Wonderful dessert trolley – but we'll stop here otherwise our readers will think we've been on the bottle. When our next royalty cheque comes in we're going to fast for three days and then have the set meal at 550F, a 6-course marathon plus a few desserts. The rooms are expensive, but you won't need to have a siesta after your meal. Everything you're served is lovely and light and well balanced.

TURSAC 24620 (6KM N)

RESTAURANT LA SOURCE

Centre.
☎ 05.53.06.98.00
Closed Wednesdays (in low season) and Nov 15–Feb 15.

Decent little village inn run by a friendly young couple. Rustic-style restaurant and when the weather is fine you can also eat out on the terrace and enjoy the garden with the spring mentioned in the name. Plain food (it could do with a bit more personality). The cheapest set meal at 68F concentrates on local produce as do two others at 90F and 135F. Dishes include semi-cooked *foie gras*, mushroom (cep) omelette, rack of lamb with mild garlic and preserve. Staff unobtrusive but pleasant.

BUGUE (LE) 24260 (11KM SW)

10% L'AUBERGE DU NOYER

Le Reclaud de Bouny Bas; it's 5km from Le Bugue – take the D706 to Campagne then the D703.
☎ 05.53.07.11.73 Fax 05.53.54.57.44
Closed from All Saints' Day to Palm Sunday.
Secure parking.

This splendid 18th century building is right out in the country and used to be a farm. Turned into an inn by an English couple who, like many of their compatriots, fell in love with the area. We can understand why! The place certainly has a great deal of charm. Warm welcome and relaxed atmosphere. Reckon on paying 360F for a double room with bath but the nicest rooms, tastefully furnished and decorated, will cost you at least 440F. 5 of them look out onto a very pleasant terrace. Good breakfast. Half-board compulsory in July/August (from 360F per person per night). The food on offer in the equally charming restaurant varies according to the season and to what is available at the market. Set meals 80F, 120F and 160F. Swimming pool and garden to the rear. Guaranteed peace and relaxation.

TAMNIÈS 24620 (14KM NE)

HÔTEL-RESTAURANT LABORDERIE**

Centre; take the D47 and the D48 – it's between Sarlat and Montignac.
☎ 05.53.29.68.59 Fax 05.53.29.65.31
Closed Nov–April. **Car park**. **TV**.

On the peaceful central square of a little market town perched on a hillside, so the surroundings are something special. This place used to be a farm, then a country café and restaurant and it has now become a rather chic although (relatively) inexpensive establishment. Lovely rooms at reasonable prices. Doubles with shower/wc 140–290F; 470F for the most comfortable rooms (with bath). Some rooms are in the main building which has a great deal of charm with its pinnacle turret; others are in an annexe in the middle of a garden which gives way to open countryside. Our favourites, on the ground floor, look out onto the swimming pool. The restaurant has become one of the musts in Périgord, despite the abundance of fine places to eat. The chef skillfully prepares generous helpings of Périgord classics such as *mique* (maize flour dumplings – to order), Périgord platter, semi-cooked *foie gras* and duck with peaches. Set meals start at 100F. Others at 140F, 160F and 250F. Large, bright restaurant with a terrace.

SIORAC-EN-PÉRIGORD 24170 (19KM SW)

10% HÔTEL-RESTAURANT LE TRÈFLE À QUATRE FEUILLES

rue de la Gare.
☎ 05.53.31.60.26
Closed Sunday evenings and Mondays out of season (Monday lunchtimes only in season).

In the centre of a little town overloooked by mass tourism. Wonderfully cosy little hotel. Some people may find the décor a bit over the top (there's an amazing number of ornaments) but the place has a certain charm about it. Pleasant, quiet rooms around an inner courtyard with arbour (where you can eat when the weather is fine). Doubles with shower/wc 210F for 2 (230F if you want twin beds). There's also a studio (sleeping 3) with a living room and kitchenette which is rented out on a nightly (250F) or weekly basis (from 1100F out of season to 1900F in August) and an apartment sleeping 4, which makes it ideal for families. The place is very much family-orientated. The father and his daughter cook the food and the son lends a hand with the desserts before going into the restaurant to help his mother. Set meals start at 52F (available every day or the regulars complain). Others at 89F, 135F and 145F. The dishes are prepared using quality local produce (the vegetables come from the garden) and include home-made semi-cooked *foie gras* and salad of dried duck breast on hot apples.

GABAS 64440

10% ☗ |●| HÔTEL-RESTAURANT VIGNAU*

☎ 05.59.05.34.06
Closed for 10 days in both April and November.
Car park.

This is a good place to stop off on the magnificent road which climbs up to the col du Pourtalet – hard work for amateur cyclists. The hotel is on one side of the road with the restaurant on the other. Clean, simple rooms 140F (with basin), 190F (with shower) and 210F (with shower/wc). Tasty food at the kind of prices you used to see years ago. Set meals 50–120F. Friendly welcome from the young proprietor. What's more, watching the sun rise on the mountain shrouded in mist is a wonderful experience.

GRENADE SUR ADOUR 40270

☗ |●| PAIN, ADOUR ET FANTAISIE***

14-16 pl. des Tilleuls.
☎ 05.58.45.18.60 F➔ 05.58.45.16.57
Closed Sunday evenings and Mondays (Monday lunchtimes only in summer). **Car park**. **TV**.

This is one of our favourite places in the region. The old village dwelling situated between the main square and the Adour can't help but go down well – even the most miserable of souls will leave here happy. If you're intending to stop off in the area, stay in one of the 11 rooms. They're comfortable, tastefully decorated and have a great deal of charm regardless of whether you get one overlooking the river or the square. The rooms called *"Retour du Nil"*, *"ronds dans l'eau"* and *"Au bois dormant"* will leave you with happy memories. You won't be able to forget the taste of the food either, whatever walk of life you're from. Philippe Garret is an artist. If he were a painter he'd be an impressionist. He works in little touches and invents like someone in love writing poetry. The result is a veritable symphony for the tastebuds, performed on your plate. And whether you eat inside in the restaurant with its sophisticated décor or out on the terrace by the Adour, you'll enjoy the experience from start to finish. Do you need any more convincing? How about glazed risotto with prawns, potatoes stuffed with ribbons of pork, fried mullet in lavender vinegar and braised rabbit with ceps in braised chestnut gravy? The entire menu is this good. The service is unobstrusive and refined without being over-formal. Everything is so good it almost seems out of place to talk about prices. Rooms cost 380–700F and set meals 150F (weekdays), 210F, 280F and 350F, offering unbeatable charm and value for money.

GURMENÇON 64400

10% |●| ☗ RELAIS ASPOIS

route du col du Somport.
☎ 05.59.39.09.50
Closed Monday lunchtimes and the first fortnight in November.

The restaurant has a good reputation and real character with its slate tiles, bare stone and beams. Once autumn arrives the fire crackles in the hearth. Set meals start at 55F. Daily set meal at 70F and "house" set meals at 100F (Béarnaise vegetable broth, *foie gras*, duck in preserve or rib steak *béarnaise*). À la carte dishes include ceps in parsley vinaigrette, Basque-style tripe pâté, *piperade* (a Basque dish with egg and tomatoes) and very good desserts. Garden.

HAGETMAU 40700

☗ |●| LE JAMBON**

27 rue Carnot.
☎ 05.58.79.32.02. F➔ 05.58.79.34.78
Closed Sunday evenings and Mondays. **TV**.

We admit the name of this place makes it sound rather like a sandwich bar, but don't be taken in. Behind the freshly painted pink and white exterior you'll find the "respectable" place to eat in the area. It's famous for dishes such as home-made *foie gras,* which appears on the menu beside lobster with tarragon *au gratin,* and saddle of stuffed hare *à la royale* which goes with scrambled eggs and truffles. Set meals for all pockets and appetites 98–240F. Both the food and the rooms are recommended. Doubles 220–260F with shower/wc and 280–450F with bath. What's more, a proprietor as nice as this with his cap wedged on his head has to inspire confidence.

HENDAYE 64700

10% HÔTEL LES BUISSONNETS**

29 rue des Seringas.
☎ 05.59.20.04.75 F 05.59.20.79.72
Closed 3 weeks in December. **Secure parking**. **TV**.

A fine, large town house with the added attraction of a swimming pool and a pleasant garden. Friendly staff. Doubles 240–360F with shower/wc. The upper floors offer a superb view over Hendaye and the ocean but don't bring too much luggage – it's quite a climb.

BIRIATOU 64700 (4KM S)

10% HÔTEL-RESTAURANT BAKEA**

How to get there: take the D258 and follow the signs.
☎ 05.59.20.76.36 F 05.59.20.58.21
Closed Sun evening and Mon (except April–Sept), and Jan 26–Feb 13. **Car park**. **TV**. **Disabled access**.

A real little corner of paradise in the Bidassoa valley which the well-known French author Pierre Loti loved so much. You'll find complete rest and relaxation in this isolated location. 7 clean rooms with flowery décor and bath/TV at 260F and 370F. Half-board compulsory in July/August; reckon on paying 390–420F per person. Excellent restaurant with a wonderful terrace. Unfortunately, it's rather expensive. Set meals 155–205F. Attentive and refined staff and service.

HOSSEGOR 40150

10% HÔTEL LES HÉLIANTHES**

av. de la Côte-d'Argent (West); 10min on foot from the beaches and 300m from the centre.
☎ 05.58.43.52.19 F 05.58.43.95.19
Closed mid Oct–start April.

This sweet little hotel is the best place in the area if you're after value for money, a warm welcome and peace and quiet. We developed a weakness for the place as soon as we saw the little white building with its red shutters. It's an unpretentious family establishment surrounded by pine trees with a small swimming pool. The wonderful proprietor gives his hotel a lovely family guest house feel. Doubles from 220F (with shower/wc) and 290F (with bath). Evening meal on request (out of season only). Brunch *formule* 60F per person in high season. If you want a TV ask when you book.

10% HÔTEL-RESTAURANT LES HUÎTRIÈRES DU LAC**

av. du Touring-Club.
☎ 05.58.43.51.48 F 05.58.41.73.11
Closed in January; restaurant closed Mondays.
Car park. **TV**.

Reserve sufficiently in advance to be sure of getting a room overlooking the lake. To give you a brief idea of what to expect, it's a bit "bourgeois" but very well kept and a bit expensive for the area, but the food is excellent. The atmosphere is essentially a family one. Doubles 300–350F. We have a weakness for rooms 1, 2, 3, 4, 12 and 14 which have just been redecorated and look out onto the lake. Half-board rather expensive at 450F per person but fortunately it's not compulsory at any time of year. Whether or not you spend the night here, it's worth stopping off to eat for dishes like *foie gras* with peach, pigeon with honey and bass with fennel. Set meals 95F and 145F.

LACANAU-OCÉAN 33680

HÔTEL-RESTAURANT L'ÉTOILE D'ARGENT**

place de l'Europe (Centre).
☎ 05.56.03.21.07 F 05.56.03.25.29
Closed Mondays out of season and Dec–mid Jan inclusive. **Car park**. **TV**.

Solid-looking building, one of the last in Lacanau (where the developers have had a field day) to retain a certain degree of authenticity. Doubles with shower 350F and with bath 400F. Rooms 5, 6, 10, 11 and 12 are the most spacious. Half-board compulsory in July/August (from 350F per person per night). The restaurant offers set meals at 70F (available every day), 95F, 115F and 160F. The food does the south-west proud. The menu includes fish (fisherman's casserole and fish stew for example), *foie gras*, preserve, duck breast and fatted duck. Wonderful wines. Good prices out of season, as is the case throughout the area. Unfortunately, the welcome sometimes leaves something to be desired.

LALINDE-EN-PÉRIGORD 24150

10% HÔTEL-RESTAURANT LE CHÂTEAU***

rue de la Tour; Centre.
☎ 05.53.61.01.82 F 05.53.24.74.60
Closed Sunday evenings and Mondays in winter, just Mondays in autumn and spring and just Monday lunchtimes in July/August; also closed in January and the 3rd week in September. **TV**.

This is a proper little castle with its corbelled turret, pepper-box towers and a balcony overlooking the sleepy Dordogne. Guy Gensou, who has redecorated the entire place, is in charge in the kitchen and gives you a very warm welcome. His enthusiasm (which sometimes wanes a little) for taking local dishes and complementing them with his own personal touch is combined with superb fresh produce. The rooms in the restaurant are peaceful and the staff pleasant. Set meal at 110F (lunchtimes) which includes a free aperitif, traditional pâté with truffle pieces, stuffed trout in white Bergerac or black pudding with apples and Périgord *milla* (maize flour porridge) or *fromage frais* with melon jam. For 165F you still get the free aperitif along with fillet of smoked goose with onion preserve, knuckle of lamb with vegetables or pigs' trotter stew in red wine, roast *Rocamadour* (a type of cheese) with nut salad and a dessert. Set meals at 225F and 295F good value for money. Rooms comfortable and expensive (410–820F for a double – well this is a castle!), but the reasonable restaurant prices are within everyone's reach. Sometimes you see motorcycle helmets in the doorway, which you may find strange, but Guy Gensou rides a motorbike himself and welcomes fellow bikers with open arms. Small swimming pool overlooking the Dordogne.

MONTFERRAND-DU-PÉRIGORD 24440 (23KM SE)

10% HÔTEL-RESTAURANT LOU PEYROL

La Barrière; it's below Montferrand on the D26.
☎ 05.53.63.24.45 F 05.53.63.24.45
Closed Tuesday lunchtimes (in April, May, June and September) and Oct 1–Easter. **Car park**.

Pretty little country hotel and restaurant on a relatively quiet road. Run by Sarah and Thierry, a very welcoming Anglo-French couple (so the clientele includes a number of Brits). Rooms basic but clean. Doubles from 175F with basin to 240F with shower or bath. Numbers 5 and 6 stay nice and cool even in summer. Ideal base for exploring this sunny region, all the more so since the food is good. Dishes include country mushroom (cep, morrel or chanterelle) omelette, roast Barbary duckling, freshwater crayfish with parsley and, for dessert, a chocolate and nut gâteau. Set meals 75F (available every day, lunchtimes and evenings), 105F, 135F and 200F.

LARCEVEAU-ARROS-CIBITS 64120

10% HÔTEL-RESTAURANT ESPELLET**

☎ 05.59.37.81.91 F 05.59.37.86.09
Closed Tuesdays (except public holidays and July–Oct) and in December. **Secure parking. TV**.

For over 30 years Pierre Espellet has been serving generous portions of excellent traditional, hearty Basque food at his inn. Dishes include woodpigeon stew, home-made duck *foie gras*, mushroom (cep) omelette and a Béarnaise vegetable broth to remember. What's more, in all this time the prices have hardly gone up at all. Set meals 55F, 75F, 90F, 100F and 140F. You'll need to be a big eater to finish the latter. If you can manage to, get a room quick! They're simple and clean and you'll get a good night's sleep. Doubles 180F (with shower/wc) and 220F (with bath and TV). Dinner is compulsory, mind, if you stay the night!

LAROQUE TIMBAUT 47340

LE ROQUENTIN

Centre.
☎ 05.53.77.99.77
Closed Sunday evenings, Mondays and the evenings of public holidays.

Recently built establishment, very Provençal in style, with spring-like décor which appears to be almost impulsive. The chef's cooking has acquired a good reputation in the region. He starts with quality produce and prepares it using traditional methods of the south-west. Dishes include duck preserve, sautéd chicken with ceps, zander in a butter sauce, frogs' legs in parsley vinaigrette and scrambled eggs with truffles. Set meals 58–190F; the one at 160F deserves a special mention. Fine wine list with a good Cahors La Coutale 92 at 80F and a Madiran 91 from Bouscassé at 82F. A place for those who know it to appreciate and those who don't to discover.

LARRAU 64560

HÔTEL-RESTAURANT ETCHEMAÏTE**

☎ 05.59.28.61.45 ➡ 05.59.28.72.71
Closed Sunday evenings and Mondays out of season plus Jan 15–30. **Car park.**

Pierre Loti's famous lines "Mountains which stand out clearly against the sky and yet are bathed in some diaphanous and golden quality" could have been written about Larrau and we can understand how someone could fall in love with this wonderfully inspirational spot. The welcome and kindness of the Etchemaïte family also contributes a great deal. Here Larrau becomes magical. The rooms may be simple but it's so wonderful to sleep under a duvet. Doubles from 160F (with basin) to 210F (with shower/wc) or 250F with bath. And then there's Pierre's cooking. He sets out to delight you with dishes which combine tradition and originality including salad *souletine*, Bordeaux-style oxtail, duo of duckling and a quite simply exceptional calf's head. Great art! Set meals 95–150F. It's all eaten in a rustic restaurant with refined décor and a view over the mountains. Wine list full of pleasant surprises at reasonable prices. As you'll have gathered, we were really taken by this place.

LARUNS 64400

AUBERGE BELLEVUE

55 rue Bourguet (Centre).
☎ 05.59.05.31.58
Closed Tuesday evenings and Wednesdays.

A really attractive and friendly place offering 5 set meals from 75F to 140F. In a chalet with an abundance of flowers and an uninterrupted view of the mountains. We enjoyed the fresh monkfish with scampi and the chicken fricassee with freshwater crayfish.

LESTELLE-BETHARRAM 64800

LE VIEUX LOGIS**

rte des Crottes (South-East); it's as you leave the village heading towards the caves.
☎ 05.59.71.94.87 ➡ 05.59.71.96.75
Car park. TV. Disabled access.

Very large modern hotel at the foot of the mountains with a swimming pool and extensive grounds. An ideal place to relax which offers excellent value for money. Impeccable double rooms from 270F. The real must though are the 5 wooden chalets in the grounds with their little balconies at 250F. The restaurant offers gourmet food with set meals at 90F, 150F and 210F. Base for watersports such as canoeing and rafting nearby on the fast-flowing gave de Pau.

MARGAUX 33460

RESTAURANT LE SAVOIE

rue de la Poste (North).
☎ 05.57.88.31.76
Closed Sundays and public holidays all year and during the February school holidays.

In a fine, solidly built town house next to the big wine store. The restaurant is made up of several quite intimate little rooms but the atmosphere is a bit formal - and that's a shame, because if the service and the welcome were a bit more relaxed you could appreciate the food properly. This deliberately avoids the local dishes (done to death) and shows real originality. Dishes include capuccino of lobster and vegetable spaghetti. Set meals 80F (except Saturday evenings) and 130F. Wines rather expensive.

MAULÉON-LICHARRE 64130

10% HÔTEL-RESTAURANT BIDEGAIN**

Centre.
☎ 05.59.28.16.05 ➡ 05.59.28.09.96
Closed Dec 15–Jan 15; restaurant closed Friday–Sunday evenings (out of season).
Secure parking.

This former coaching inn has now belonged to the same family for 7 generations. The reading room is superb, as is the carved wooden reception desk. The rooms are just as good as the rest of the place, offering stylish furniture, ornaments, comfort and peace and quiet. From 180F (with washing facilities) to 300F (with bath and TV). Ask for a room looking out onto the courtyard. To the rear there's a romantic garden full of trees and flowers which dates from the early part of the century and provides a pleasant route from the hotel to the restaurant. Set meals 70F and 140F. Dishes include duck breast with two kinds of apple, stuffed aubergines, little *croustades* and chocolate delights. We're still under the spell of the old-fashioned atmosphere.

MIMIZAN-PLAGE 40200

☗ |●| HÔTEL-RESTAURANT ATLANTIQUE

38 av. de la Côte-d'Argent.
☎ 05.58.09.09.42 F➔ 05.58.82.42.63
Closed Wednesdays (except during the school holidays) and in January.
Car park. **TV**. **Disabled access**.

On the seafront but with a limited sea view. Incredible little simple family establishment which is really friendly. 40 rooms in all, in a big old wooden building behind which a new hotel has appeared. Pleasant garden. Conventional comfort of a little family guest house to which regulars return year after year. Only 16 rooms with shower/wc. The others only have a shower or basin. You'll be amazed at the prices – double with basin 130F, with shower 165F and with shower/wc 200–260F. Half board compulsory in July/August (from 165F per person). Personally we prefer the rooms in the main house (4 of which have a sea view), but it's a matter of taste. Nice place to eat. Set meals 75F (weekday lunchtimes), 99F and 139F. Dishes include *coq au vin*, grilled bass in garlic butter, vol au vent with mussels in a rich white sauce, Bordeaux-style lamprey and pigeon roll stuffed with *foie gras*. Simple and nourishing.

10% ☗ |●| HÔTEL-RESTAURANT L'ÉMERAUDE DES BOIS**

66-68 av. du Courant; take the D626; 10 minutes on foot from the centre.
☎ 05.58.09.05.28
Closed Oct–Easter.
Car park.

This hotel and restaurant is another good little family establishment in a charming house surrounded by large trees and decorated in traditional style. Very warm welcome. Double rooms 220F (with shower) and 310–360F (with shower/wc). Half board (compulsory in July/August) 290–320F per person. If you're staying for a number of days we would strongly recommend half-board given the quality of the cooking. Delightful set meals at 98F, 120F and 160F. Dishes include cream of courgette soup, poached fillet of gilthead and roast rabbit in mustard sauce, monkfish *à la provençale*, home-made *foie gras*, duck breast with honey and nut gâteau. Not really inventive but a great deal of care goes into the preparation.

|●| RESTAURANT LA GOÉLETTE

30 av. de la Côte-d'Argent; head for plage nord.
☎ 05.58.09.05.25
Closed Monday lunchtimes (except in season) and Sept 30–April 1.

Typical little restaurant which hasn't let the tourists and their money change it one iota. Our favourite place to eat in Mimizan. Overlit with very 70s décor, plastic flowers and little tables packed tightly together. The food includes produce from both the sea (fish soup and American-style squid for example) and the land (such as the delicious sliced duck). The paella also goes down a treat. Set meals 55F, 89F and 130F.

LÜE 40210 (22KM E)

|●| RESTAURANT L'AUBERGE LANDAISE

How to get there: take the D626.
☎ 05.58.07.06.13
Closed Sunday evenings, Mondays and in October.
Car park.

Jolly little Landes inn. A string of set meals to suit every pocket, from 56F up to 190F. It's impossible not to find something you fancy with dishes such as woodpigeon stew, baby squid cooked in their own ink, Bordeaux-style lamprey and Armorican-style monkfish steak. It's no doubt thanks to the range of prices that people from all walks of life meet at Monsieur Berthet's – from the local worthies to sales reps, working men and women and tourists – to enjoy the mussels in white wine, delicious preserve or duck breast.

MONT-DE-MARSAN 40000

☗ |●| HÔTEL-RESTAURANT LE MIDOU

place Porte-Campet (Centre).
☎ 05.58.75.24.26
Closed Sunday evenings.

Friendly, popular and unpretentious traditional little hotel. The rooms offer a basic but adequate level of comfort. Doubles 130F (with shower) and 180F (with shower/wc). If you want to indulge yourself, set meals start at 68F (weekdays). Those at 120F and 180F may seem a little expensive but they're very substantial. Everything is as it should be. Book well in advance.

☗ |●| HÔTEL-RESTAURANT DES PYRÉNÉES

4 rue du 34ème R.I.
☎ 05.58.46.49.46 F➔ 05.58.06.43.57
TV.

It's hard to miss this wonderful old pink house which all the locals know. At lunchtimes it's used rather like a canteen and we bet you'll be back once you've tried the 65F set meal (which includes soup, starter, main course and dessert), not only because of the quality of the food but also because it's rather a nice place. The decoration of the 3 public rooms, which have been left in their original style, almost allows you to relive the house's history. Large bay windows look out onto a terrace surrounded by trees and flowers for use in fine weather. Indulge yourself with duck breast, *foie gras* and chicken, pork or mutton preserve. With each of the set meals (65F, 105F, 145F and 190F) you'll rediscover food which is simple, hearty and awfully good. There are some pleasant little rooms, in particular those looking out onto the greenery. It's a lot noisier on the side looking out onto the crossroads. Doubles 145F with shower and 210F with shower/wc. It's a good idea to book to get one of the better rooms. Polite service worthy of a hotel and catering college, with all that implies.

HÔTEL-RESTAURANT ZANCHETTIN**

1565 av. de Villeneuve; it's next to the campsite in the Saint-Médard district.
☎ 05.58.75.19.52 F 05.58.85.92.04
Closed Mondays and Aug 15–Sept 15. **Car park**. **TV**.

Relatively quiet hotel and restaurant with a bar plus a family tobacconist's and 9 good rooms at 170–260F. You can eat here for 100–150F (on a terrace under the plane trees or in a sweet little restaurant with tables all in a line). Weekday daily set meal 60F including wine and coffee. A well-run establishment which is worth going a little bit out of your way for.

10% HÔTEL-RESTAURANT RICHELIEU**

rue Wlérick (Centre); it's just behind the theatre.
☎ 05.58.06.10.20 F 05.58.06.00.68
Secure parking. **TV** with **Canal+**. **Disabled access**.

The only "bourgeois" hotel in the centre. It's a family establishment with a rather formal atmosphere but perfectly fine, just very provincial. Doubles with wc and shower or bath 260F. Good value for money. At the *Richelieu* you also get some of the best cooking in town. Excellent traditional food. No surprises but it's tasty and the portions are generous. Set meals 86F, 112F, 142F and 180F. Dishes include the inevitable warm liver salad in shallot vinaigrette, sole fricassee with asparagus tips, roast suckling lamb with wild mushrooms and strawberry *millefeuille*. We had no complaints. This is where all the local worthies come for their business lunches.

RESTAURANT L'AFICION

4 rue Molière; it's just behind the theatre.
☎ 05.58.75.12.81
Closed Sundays.

You enter this restaurant by way of a nice and pretty lively tapas bar frequented by several generations of locals. On the first floor you plunge into an atmosphere which couldn't be more Spanish. Attractive, brightly coloured décor (the proprietor is a fan of bullfighting) and warm welcome. Quality produce direct from Spain such as *callos* (tripe), *boquerones* (anchovies), *tortillas* and paella (at weekends to order). Reckon on paying between 50F and 75F for really wonderful dishes such as stuffed baby squid, grilled sole, roast suckling pig and rabbit braised in garlic mayonnaise.

RESTAURANT LE PALOUMET

50 rue Armand Dulamon.
☎ 05.58.46.30.60
Closed Saturday lunchtimes, Sundays and public holidays.

As you enter you may think the same thing we did. Why have an aluminium bar ceiling when you've got old stonework, traditional floor tiles and old wooden beams? But the peacefulness of the place, a bit like the stream which runs just next to it, will make you forget such metaphysical problems. The atmosphere is calm and the welcome warm – the proprietor will treat you like a friend. You'll enjoy studying the menu to work up an appetite. The two set meals (65F and 89F) offer the kind of simple dishes which could have been taken from our grandmothers' cookery books – fried snails, salmon crêpes, kidney casserole and veal sweetbreads with mushrooms, braised quail and fried monkfish medallions with leek fondue. You'll leave with a full stomach, pleased to have had some fine traditional cooking, without any eccentricities, prepared with great care by someone who appreciates fine produce.

MONTIGNAC 24290

10% HÔTEL-RESTAURANT DE LA GROTTE

65 rue du 4-Septembre (Centre); it's opposite the Lascaux road.

☎ 05.53.51.80.48 ➧ 05.53.51.84.16
Closed the first fortnight in January.
Secure parking. TV.

In an old building (a former coaching inn which became a hotel when the grotte de Lascaux was discovered). Right in the centre so make sure you ask for a room looking out onto the garden. Rooms simple but competitively priced for the area at 165F (for a double with basin), 205F (with shower/wc) and 285F (with bath). In the restaurant, the food – which had experienced some problems – seems to have picked up to a certain extent. Dishes include zander pie with snails in a creamy garlic sauce and risotto with scallops, ceps and truffles. Small set meal 60F (weekdays). Others 79F, 90F and 115F. Two terraces for when the weather is fine. We prefer the one in the garden by the water. Half-board compulsory in August (285F per person per night).

RESTAURANT BELLEVUE

Regourdou.
☎ 05.53.51.81.29
Closed evenings, Saturday lunchtimes and in January.
Car park.

Surrounded by greenery and right next to the grotte de Lascaux (so look out for the coachloads of tourists who can sometimes descend on the place). As its name indicates, the restaurant has a superb view from its bay windows and terrace. Decent food with a hint of regional flavour at reasonable prices. Daily special 38F. You can get chicken preserve and *enchaud* (baked loin of pork and pigs' trotters with garlic and truffles), gizzard salad and mushroom (cep) omelette for about the same price. Set meals at 68F, 98F and 138F. A number of rooms from 190F with shower/wc. It's advisable to reserve for Sunday lunch.

10% HOSTELLERIE LA ROSERAIE***

pl. d'Armes (Centre).
☎ 05.53.50.53.92 ➧ 05.53.51.02.23
Closed from All Saints' Day to Easter.
TV.

Solidly built, elegant 19th century town house on place d'Armes. Very courteous staff. Jérôme Guimbaud is a charming young man (but don't insist on knowing what goes into the famous Périgueux sauce which his family has been producing and selling since 1927!). Fourteen exquisite rooms, all of them different and all with bath. Doubles from 395F either side of high season to 450F in high season. Half-board (compulsory in August) from 370F per person per night (rates go down if you stay for more than 3 nights). With its wooden staircase and cosy little lounges, the place really does have a great deal of charm. What's more you feel much more as if you're in a B&B or even a good old family guest house (where they'll keep your bottle of wine for you if you don't finish it) than in a classy 3-star establishment. There's a small park surrounded by high walls in which you instantly forget you're in a town and hidden behind the swimming pool is the little rose garden referred to in the place's name. Sweet little restaurant with a delightful terrace in the garden for when the sun is shining. Skillfully prepared, sophisticated local cuisine (dishes include escalope of *foie gras* with strawberries, fillet steak "rossini" in Périgueux sauce with truffles and strawberry delight) at very reasonable prices. The cheapest set meal (a bit limited) is 80F at lunchtimes (except Sundays). Other set meals at 100F (recommended), 160F, 190F and 250F.

SAINT-AMAND-DE-COLY 24290 (8KM E)

10% HÔTEL-RESTAURANT GARDETTE

Centre.
☎ 05.53.51.68.50 ➧ 05.53.51.68.50
Closed November–Easter.

Two little pale stone houses dominated by one of the finest churches in Périgord, the pride of this tiny (and charming) village. Rooms basic but recently renovated, quiet and reasonably priced. 170F with shower (wc on the landing), 220F with bath. The restaurant is on the other side of the lane and consists of a few tiny little tables in one corner because during the school year the proprietor cooks the school meals! If your schooldays are behind you, there are set meals at 65F (except Sundays), 95F and 120F. Various salads and regional dishes from the south-west such as mushroom (cep) or truffle omelette, preserve and duck breast. In summer during the classical music festival (when it's advisable to book) there's a special platter to mark the event – at 50F – including home-made pâté, *crudités* and smoked duck breast.

SERGEAC 24290 (8.5KM S)

RESTAURANT L'AUBERGE DU PEYROL

How to get there: it's on the D65, half way between Montignac and Les Eyzies.
☎ 05.53.50.72.91
Closed Mondays (except in July/August) and November–Easter.
Car park.

Traditional inn in fine local stone out on its own just outside a quaint little village. A large bay window offers a wonderful panorama over the lovely Vézère valley. The fine rustic restaurant has a large fireplace where fillets of duck breast are smoked. Excellent welcome and when you've tasted the food you'll be won over for good! Jeanine concocts country dishes the likes of which we're sure you'll never have tasted before – goose liver and *enchaud* (baked loin of pork and pigs' trotters with garlic and truffles). Set meal at 70F (with mushroom omelette). Sample *formule* 100F (including truffle omelette, fromage frais with home-made jam and a glass of Bergerac). Unbeatable set meal at 115F with duck liver, duck preserve, Sarlat-style apples, nut salad, cheeses and dessert. There's another set meal at 150F and for 200F you get the lot – goose liver, truffle omelette, duck breast in Périgueux sauce, salad, cheeses and dessert. It goes without saying that this place is starting to make a name for itself, so you're advised to book.

CHAPELLE-AUBAREIL (LA) 24290 (12KM S)

10% HÔTEL-RESTAURANT LA TABLE DU TERROIR**

"Fougeras"; from Montignac or Les Eyzies take the road to Lascaux II from where it's sign-posted.
☎ 05.53.50.72.14 F→ 05.53.51.16.23
Closed Dec–March except weekends.
Car park. TV. Disabled access.

The Gibertie family have created a real little tourist complex around a farm right out in the country. The restaurant is on a hill 100m from the hotel. Between the two there's a swimming pool with views over the countryside. The buildings are new but in traditional Périgord style, so they blend in well with their surroundings. Pleasant rooms at all prices (including breakfast), 200F (with basin), 280F (with shower/wc) and 300F (with bath). A little less expensive in May/June and September/October. Half-board compulsory July 15–Sept 1 (from 250F per person per night). Set meals 65–215F. Regional dishes based on farm produce such as sliced duck, preserve, stuffed chicken, country salad, panfried *foie gras* and truffles cooked in hot ashes. Packed lunches and tours of the farm available.

MONTPON-MÉNESTÉROL 24700

AUBERGE DE L'ÉCLADE

Centre; take the D708 from Ribérac, turn right at the crossroads before reaching the town and it's signposted.
☎ 05.53.80.28.64
Closed Tuesday evenings, Wednesdays and the first two weeks in March and October.

This inn, although rather out of the way (it can't count much on passing trade!), has quickly made a name for itself thanks to the enthusiasm by which its reputation has been spread by word of mouth. The restaurant's décor is rustic and flowery in style, using bold colours. Warm welcome and good atmosphere. The food is creative without ignoring tradition. Dishes include escalope of roast salmon in coconut suace with arabica, scallops on a bed of endives with a vanilla dressing, potted crab with ginger and chervil and fillet of lamb in a butter and basil sauce. Fine produce chosen from the best the area has to offer (in particular the *foie gras*). Small set meal 70F (weekday lunchtimes) but given their excellent value for money, the set meals at 120F and 170F are worth a try. There's also a set meal at 220F.

NAVARRENX 64190

10% HÔTEL-RESTAURANT DU COMMERCE CAMDEBORDE**

place des Casernes (Centre).
☎ 05.59.66.50.16 F→ 05.59.66.52.67
Closed Saturdays and Sunday evenings (out of season) and also 3 weeks in January.
TV.

One of the oldest Béarn houses in Navarrenx, a town from another age where time seems to have stood still. The large fireplace in the foyer starts to crackle at the first sign of wintry weather. Pleasant rooms (the nicest have sloping roofs) 215–225F (with shower or bath). The food is full of wonderful Béarn flavours and is served in rather plush surroundings but the prices are still very reasonable. Set meals from 60F (except Sunday lunchtimes) to 150F and the wonderful proprietor can only add to your enjoyment of the occasion.

NÉRAC 47600

10% AUBERGE DU PONT VIEUX**

19 rue Séderie; it's by the river.
☎ 05.53.97.13.22

This place has just opened in a very old building in the old part of Nérac. Plush surroundings and friendly and attentive staff. You really feel at ease in the 3 rooms (270–460F) which have been attractively furnished and decorated. If you're not convinced (which would be amazing), the chef will see to it that you soon are thanks to food prepared using fine produce and a few little touches of his own. Dishes include *foie gras* in a bread roll with armagnac, medallion of veal in a creamy sesame sauce, fillet of bass in a creamy sauce with beans and fried frogs *à la provençale*. Set meals 120F, 160F and 210F.

|●| LES DÉLICES DU ROY

7 rue du Château.
☎ 05.53.65.81.12
Closed Wednesdays.

Although there's hardly anything to speak of in the way of décor (admittedly the place had only just opened when we were there), we were very impressed by the food. We can still taste the winning combination of tradition, subtle mixtures and high-quality produce. Daily set meal 68F, including wine, and two fine set meals at 95F and 145F. Dishes include raw salmon canelloni, *foie gras* with spinach shoots, cockles in butter with a salad of lamb's lettuce, grilled mullet with olive paste and braised ox cheek with vegetables. A shark steak in parsley vinaigrette provides a little touch of the exotic and there's a remarkable *crème brûlée* for dessert. Young and attentive staff.

FRANCESCAS 46600 (13KM SE)

|●| LE RELAIS DE LA HIRE

7 rue du Château; take the D930 for 9km towards Condom, then left onto the D112..
☎ 05.53.65.41.59
Closed Sunday evenings and Mondays.

This 18th century manor house wins you over even as you walk by. The subtle aromas from the garden and the peaceful atmosphere are a good sign of the gastronomical feast in store. After working with Robuchon, Roger Verger, in the kitchens at the Ritz, and running the kitchens at the Carlton, Jean-Noël Prabonne has settled down in his native Gascony. He takes a particular pride in choosing produce from local suppliers. Talented, subtle flavours and some magnificent creations – you'll soon be under his spell! Choose from dishes such as local ceps *en cocotte*, Albret artichokes with a soufflé of *foie gras*, red sea bream poached with herbs, young farm-bred pigeon with *foie gras*, rack of roast lamb with cloves of garlic and thyme, and leg of braised yellow chicken. A festival of tastes and aromas in charming, stylish surroundings. Pleasant reception from Mme Prabonne and attentive service. Good 125F set meal weekdays. Otherwise, 175F, 225F and 265F for an unforgettable experience.

NONTRON 24300

10% 🏠 |●| HÔTEL-RESTAURANT PELISSON**

place Alfred-Agard.
☎ 05.53.56.11.22 📠 05.53.56.59.94 **Car park. TV. Disabled access.**

This "grand hotel" right in the centre has an elegant but rather austere exterior. Hidden behind it though you're surprised to find a pleasant garden and a lovely swimming pool. Traditional rooms, quiet at the rear, and reasonable prices. Doubles 190F with washing facilities, 220F with shower and 270F with bath. Family atmosphere (the Pélissons have been here for several generations) but a bit on the formal side. Huge rustic yet plush restaurant with attractive tableware (made locally) and a terrace looking out onto the garden. Traditional local food which has a good reputation. Dishes include asparagus pasty, calf's head in a dressing with herbs and shallots, sliced beef in red wine and sole casserole with ceps. Reasonable prices. Set meals start at 82F. Others at 110–250F. Good wine list.

ORTHEZ 64300

🏠 |●| HÔTEL-RESTAURANT AU TEMPS DE LA REINE JEANNE**

44 rue du Bourg-Vieux (Centre); it's opposite the tourist office.
☎ 05.59.67.00.76 📠 05.59.69.09.63
Closed 1 week in March. **Car park. TV** with **Canal+. Disabled access.**

This is an historic place in Orthez because the mother of Henri IV, Jeanne d'Albret, extolled the virtues of Protestantism here despite all the obstacles (it wasn't a good idea to go against the Catholic norm at the time). Peace and quiet have, however, long since returned to the hotel. Lovely rooms furnished and decorated with a great deal of taste. Doubles with shower or bath 265–295F. The restaurant is a bit like a canteen at lunchtimes but the food is decent and conventional. Set meals 70–180F.

PAU 64000

🏠 HÔTEL D'ALBRET*

11 rue Jeanne-d'Albret (Centre); it's near the château d'Henri IV.
☎ 05.59.27.81.58

In a pretty little house dating from the previous century. Very warm welcome. Rooms 90–145F. Old-fashioned with flowery paper but quite large and very well kept.

HÔTEL BEAU SOLEIL**

81 av. des Lauriers; 200m from the supermarket on the Tarbes road.
☎ 05.59.02.40.29
Secure parking. TV.

In the fashionable part of town (understandable given that the English have long since "colonized" the area). It's hard not to like this superb characterful pebble-dash hotel. The surrounding garden is luxurious. It's really worth venturing out of the centre for. Doubles from 175F (with basin) to 225F (with shower, wc and TV). Simple and very well kept. Genuine family welcome. You'll really feel good staying here.

10% LE POSTILLON**

10 cours Camou (Centre).
☎ 05.59.72.83.00 F 05.59.72.83.13
TV with **Canal+. Disabled access.**

Just by place de Verdun. Hotel in neo-romantic style. Sweet little rooms with shower or bath 220F (180F at weekends). In the courtyard there's a little garden with flowers and a fountain. One of our favourites places in Pau. Excellent value for money.

10% HÔTEL MONTPENSIER***

36 rue Montpensier.
☎ 05.59.27.42.72 F 05.59.27.70.95
Secure parking. TV with **Canal+.**

Attractive 3-star hotel which is rather like an old English house – understandable given that we're in Pau! What's more, everything is candy pink and full of very olde-worlde charm. Very good level of comfort at reasonable prices (230–350F). Meals on trays are served in the evening to order. Warm welcome which goes well with the rest of the place.

10% HÔTEL-RESTAURANT LE COMMERCE**

9 rue du Maréchal-Joffre (Centre).
☎ 05.59.27.24.40 F 05.59.83.81.74
Restaurant closed Sundays.
Car park. TV.

Traditional hotel with a certain amount of charm and a warm welcome. Comfortable, soundproofed rooms with direct-dial telephone 255–320F. Bar. Fine restaurant with rustic décor including a pebble-dash wall. Set meals 90F and 150F. Specialities include fresh liver with caramelized apples, sole with ceps and *filet mignon* of veal with morels. Courtyard terrace as pleasant as the staff.

RESTAURANT LA BROCHETTERIE

16 rue Henri-IV (Centre); it's near the château d'Henri IV.
☎ 05.59.27.40.33
Food served until 11pm. **Closed** Saturday lunchtimes.

Attractive restaurant all in stone with, as its centrepiece, the grill where fillets of duck breast and meats are roasted. The lunchtime clientele consists primarily of people working in the area and white-collar workers. Set meals 59F and 78F (79F and 98F in the evening; 85F, 95F and 105F at the weekend). Attentive staff. À la carte dishes include grilled gilthead flambéd in aniseed, rib of wild boar (in season) and various fresh salads. Very well known in Pau. On Thursday evening don't miss the spit-roast pig or the suckling lamb – a real treat! Book in advance.

RESTAURANT LA TABLE D'HÔTE

1 rue du Hedas.
☎ 05.59.27.56.06
Closed Saturday lunchtimes and Sundays.

In one of the oldest parts of Pau. Pierre will welcome you like a regular to his large restaurant full of stained-glass windows and beams. The food is spot on with lots of quality produce. Dishes include quail salad in sherry, duck pie with truffle flavouring, braised sole in Jurançon wine and fricassee of lamb sweetbreads with ceps and peppers. Set meals 60F (lunchtimes), 118F and 149F. A place people come back to.

RESTAURANT LA MICHODIÈRE

34 rue Pasteur.
☎ 05.59.27.53.85
Closed Sundays and the first fortnight in August.

Superb building with blue blinds and if we tell you the chef is responsible for the interior decoration you'll expect nothing but good things of his cooking. Set meals 68F (lunchtimes), 85F (evenings), 95F and 130F. Dishes include lobster in coral sauce, fresh duck's liver and paper-thin slices of apple in calvados. A lot of imagination produces a tasty, tempting result. A treat for the eyes – and the tastebuds.

LE PALMARIUM

10 rue des Cordelins (Centre).
☎ 05.59.27.41.40
Closed Saturday lunchtimes and Sundays.

Attractive restaurant in pastel shades with a terrace which couldn't be quieter. Daily special 42F. Set meals 77F (lunchtimes) and 97F. Lots of fish dishes, including grilled salmon, sole and scallops, prepared using produce which is always excellent. Courteous and unobtrusive staff. Hardly surprising that you find quite a few regulars here.

LA TAVERNE DU ROY

7 rue de la Fontaine (Centre).
☎ 05.59.27.01.11
Closed Sundays and Monday lunchtimes. **Car park**.

Really nice surroundings with exposed beams and an old fireplace. Warm welcome. Go for the specialities such as *parrillada* (seafood platter) at 115F or fillet of beef in cream sauce – a real treat! Numerous other dishes which are also very tempting. More than decent set meal at 85F.

AU FIN GOURMET

24 av. Gaston Lacoste (Centre).
☎ 05.59.27.47.71
Closed Mondays. **Car park**. **Disabled access**.

One of the best restaurants in town according to many locals. As soon as you read the menu you realize that this place lives up to its name. Very reasonable set meal at 90F and a very good one at 165F. À la carte dishes include fried crayfish tails with orange and a delicious fresh fruit *craquant*.

SÉVIGNACQ-MEYRACQ 64260 (21KM S)

10% HÔTEL-RESTAURANT LES BAINS DE SECOURS**

☎ 05.59.05.62.11 F 05.59.05.76.56
Closed Sunday evenings and Mondays. **Car park**. **TV**.

A scenic road leads to this inn in a old restored Béarn farm with flower-filled balconies and an inner courtyard. Only 7 rooms. Well appointed and very quiet, being right out in the country. From 280F (with shower/wc) to 360F (with bath) depending on the season. Delicious food by the fireplace in winter and on the terrace in summer. Set meals 80F and 148F. Try the fillet of sole salad with ceps, the 3 little fillets of beef in 3 sauces, the squid stuffed with foie gras and ceps and the lamb sweetbread fricassee. A very good place to eat, close to a very old spa.

HOURS 64420 (25KM SE)

LE FIGUIER

How to get there: from Pau take the N117 towards Soumoulou then the D940 towards Lourdes; turn right towards Nay and it's the first street on the left after the church.
☎ 05.59.04.67.70
Closed Tuesdays, Wednesdays, 1 week in October and 1 week in February. **Car park**.

Totally lost out in the country on a former farm. Thierry is in charge in the kitchen and his attentive fiancée will look after you in the restaurant. Thierry prepares very tasty dishes such as fresh duck's liver with apples, veal sweetbreads with ceps and stuffed pigs' trotters. Set meals 85–195F. You'll leave here full and happy!

PÉRIGUEUX 24000

10% HÔTEL-RESTAURANT DU MIDI**

18 rue Denis-Papin (North-West).
☎ 05.53.53.41.06 F 05.53.08.19.32
Closed Saturdays, Oct 20–April 15 and Dec 21–Jan 2. **Secure parking**. **TV** with **Canal+**.

Typical little station hotel. Friendly welcome from the young couple who have renovated the entire place. Nice family atmosphere. Very clean, modern rooms. 140–220F for a double. The restaurant is fairly quiet. Set meals 74–195F. Traditional cooking with local dishes such as truffle omelette, rib steak with ceps and duck breast in a creamy sauce with *foie gras*. Free parking for (motor)bikes.

HÔTEL-RESTAURANT PÉRIGORD**

74 rue Victor-Hugo (North).
☎ 05.53.53.33.63 F 05.53.08.19.74
Restaurant closed Saturday and Sunday evenings, 1 week in February and Oct 20–Nov 3. **TV**.

This elegant establishment boasting a large flower-filled garden is situated just out of the centre. Not short on charm and the staff have a ready smile. Double rooms (some at the bottom of the garden) 235–270F, representing superb value for money. The restaurant enjoys a good repuation. Set meals 75F (weekday lunchtimes), 100F, 128F and 165F. À la carte dishes include Périgord salad with *foie gras*, veal sweetbreads with tomatoes, garlic and herbs and preserve with *pommes noisettes*. Lots of types of meat and fish including hake, trout, sole and grilled salmon with anchovy paste. Restaurant pleasantly reminiscent of the France of days gone by.

RESTAURANT HERCULE POIREAU

2 rue de la Nation (Centre); it's opposite the main door of the cathedral.
☎ 05.53.08.90.76

Closed Saturday lunchtimes and Sundays, over New Year and end July–mid August.

Warm welcome. Food pretty good, as is the play on words in the place's name which corrupts Agatha Christie's spelling of Poirot to give the French word for leek! Traditional home-made, brasserie (*andouillette*, stew) and local (duck "rossini") dishes are all at home in these splendid yet cosily laid-out surroundings (a 16th century vaulted cellar). Small set meal 65F (nut salad and rib steak for example). Other at 85F and 160F. Hercule Poireau got it right!

RESTAURANT LE 8

8 rue de la Clarté (Centre); it's next to the cathedral.
☎ 05.53.35.15.15
Closed Saturday lunchtimes, Sundays and in July.

This little restaurant (reservation advisable) decorated all in yellow and blue and recently opened in the old town by young proprietors is a ray of sunshine, as is the food which is both regional and creative. The cheapest set meal at 100F (weekday lunchtimes), for example, offers stuffed neck of duck, preserve with potatoes and a dessert. The home-made *foie gras* has already made quite a name for itself. Other set meals 150–400F.

CHANCELADE 24650 (3KM W)

LE PONT DE LA BEAURONNE**

4 route de Ribérac; it's where the D710 and the D939 cross.
☎ 05.53.08.42.91 Fax 05.53.03.97.69
Closed Sunday evenings, Monday lunchtimes and Sept 20–Oct 20. **TV**. **Disabled access**.

Food served until 9.30pm. We have known better locations and the place doesn't possess a great deal of charm but the rooms are reasonable, well kept and are good value for money for the area. 140F (with basin) to 250F (with shower or bath) and you can try to get one at the rear looking out onto the garden. Family atmosphere. The restaurant which is "neo-rustic" in style offers simple food with a regional flavour. Dishes include veal sweetbreads with morels, crayfish stew and scallops with ceps. Set meals 72F, 100F, 120F, 140F and 200F.

MANZAC-SUR-VERN 24110 (20KM SW)

10% HÔTEL-RESTAURANT LE LION D'OR**

Centre; take the D43 and the D4.
☎ 05.53.54.28.09 Fax 05.53.54.25.50
Closed Sunday evenings and Mondays (just Mondays in July/August) plus mid Jan–mid Feb. **Car park**.

In the heart of a region which isn't too touristy. In the centre of a small village where everything goes quiet after 7pm, including this hotel's very typical rooms. Doubles with shower or bath 200F. Numbers 4 and 5 look out onto the garden. The restaurant successfully mixes modern décor with old-style touches. Traditional cooking. Set meal at 70F (except Sundays and public holidays). Other well thought out set meals at 100F, 125F, 155F and 200F. The chef's specialities include warm *foie gras*, salmon with mead, veal sweetbreads in Monbazillac, *millas* (maize flour porridge) with apples and cinnamon ice-cream. You can eat outside in summer. Half board 250F per person.

SORGES 24420 (23KM NE)

10% AUBERGE DE LA TRUFFE**

N21 (Centre).
☎ 05.53.05.02.05 Fax 05.53.05.39.27
Closed Sunday evenings in winter and the first fortnight in January. **Car park**. **TV** with **Canal+**.

Good traditional food (a good idea in the self-proclaimed capital of the truffle) which local people and tourists still like and always will. The proprietor oversees both the kitchen and the restaurant with a watchful eye. She's quite a character and always has a little word for customers but sometimes it seems a little put on. The small set meals at 80F and 100F (not Saturday evenings or Sundays) are wonderful. For 120F (2 courses) or 165F (3 courses) you get duck with *foie gras*, traditional style stuffed carp or mushroom (cep) omelette and beef with *foie gras* or sliced duck. Other set meals at 150F, 200F, 230F, 260F and 330F – phew! À la carte dishes include lentil salad with *foie gras*, rosette of scallops in sabayon sauce, trio of duck in Périgeux sauce and, in season, a number of truffle-based dishes (of course!) which really make the bill shoot up. Even though the inn is a roadside inn, the rooms are pleasant, in particular those on the ground floor looking out onto the garden (numbers 25–29). Good breakfast buffet. Swimming pool and sauna. Annexe in the centre of the village called "*hôtel de la Mairie*". Only open in summer. Pleasant rooms looking out onto the open countryside (300F for a double). Set meals 80F and 100F.

RÉOLE (LA) 33190

RESTAURANT LES FONTAINES

24 rue A.-Bénac.
☎ 05.56.61.15.25

Closed Sunday evenings, Mondays (except public holidays), 1 week in March and Nov 13–20.

This restaurant on a sloping pedestrianized street enjoys unanimous approval throughout the region – understandable given that it's one of the best! Some people may not be sure about the décor (overdone or elegant and comfortable), others may go into raptures over the spring (a real one) running through the first room you come to, but they'll all agree on the excellent value for money of the set meals. The cheapest one won't break the bank at 75F and (we're stressing this because it's becoming ever rarer) it's available every day. Dishes include French bean mousse with warm chicken livers, stuffed trout with mushroom purée and herb gravy and strawberry jelly with candied orange. Two other set meals at 105F and 150F depending on the number of courses you want. One final set meal at 240F. We can't resist telling you some of the specialities appearing on these set meals and the menu which changes every month. They include Les Fontaines salad (conserve of gizzards, home-made pâté, filllets of 3 different meats and *foie gras*), a trio of duck preparations (sliced, fillet and preserve), beef marrow rib steak, glazed zander sprinkled with *foie gras* and braised lettuce with mullet and potatoes mashed together.

RIBÉRAC 24600

10% 🏠 |●| HÔTEL-RESTAURANT DE FRANCE**

3 rue Marc-Dufraisse (Centre); it's at the top end of the market place.
☎ 05.53.90.00.61 F→ 05.53.91.06.05
TV.

Very central. A former coaching inn covered in ivy and with the guaranteed charm of old stonework. There's also a small garden with flowers. Warm welcome. The rooms are old-fashioned but they're redecorated regularly and very well kept. 205F for a double with shower, 225F with bath. Fireplace in the restaurant. Set meals start at 70F (served every day). Other set meals at 100–150F and à la carte menu. Substantial local dishes which never go out of fashion (for example, thinly sliced duck breast with chanterelles, *croustade* of chicken livers and gizzards and baked apples). And they show imagination. As witnessed by theme menus built around herbs, spices, desserts etc.

|●| RESTAURANT LE CHEVILLARD

Gayet; 2km from Ribérac, on the Montpon-Bordeaux road (D708).
☎ 05.53.90.16.50
Closed Mondays (except July/August) and the second fortnight in September. **Secure parking**.

Welcoming restaurant in a former farm. Decorated with good taste in rustic style and surrounded by a huge garden. The proprietor (who used to be a sales rep) gives you a very warm welcome. Large portions of quality food. Good meats (the place's name literally means Restaurant of the Wholesale Butcher) which are grilled over an open fire. The set meal at 105F offers you a choice of three meats after a buffet of hors d'œuvres which we couldn't fault. This same buffet is on the decent little set meal at 60F (weekday lunchtimes). Two other set meals at 120F and 165F. Seafood at reasonable prices. Good little selection of wines.

SABRES 40630

🏠 |●| L'AUBERGE DES PINS***

Quartier Barthes.
☎ 05.58.07.50.47 F→ 05.58.07.56.74
Closed Sunday evenings and Mondays out of season, and also in January. **Car park. TV**.

Large house typical of the Landes region with timber frame, a balcony with flowers and a wide roof. Here the word tradition really means something. The Lesclauze family are only happy when you're happy. They'll pull out all the stops to leave you with fond memories of the place and make you want to return. They have several trump cards to play. First of all there are the rooms with some fine pieces of furniture, pretty little ornaments and comfortable beds whether you're in the main building or in the annexe. Doubles with shower or bath 280–600F. The surroundings are at the same time rustic and rather classy and the food is just as good as the rest of the place. With dishes including roast pigeon with truffles tucked under the skin, local lamb with garlic, Landes-style casserole, crayfish ravioli with ceps and hot or cold *foie gras*, you're faced with a bit of a dilemma; everything on this menu full of traditional local produce enhanced with subtle and tasty little touches by the chef, who you feel genuinely loves cooking, is tempting. Set meals 90F (weekdays) and 200–350F. It's really a pity that there isn't a set meal in between the two price extremes.

SAINT-ÉMILION 33330

L'AUBERGE DE LA COMMANDERIE**

rue des Cordeliers (Centre).
☎ 05.57.24.70.19 F 05.57.74.44.53
Closed Jan 15–Feb 15. **Car park. TV. Disabled access.**

A senior officer of the Order of the Knights Templar used to live here and during the French Revolution it was used as a hiding place by the disgraced Girondins. Very little of its rich past is visible today however and it's now a conventional family hotel with rather modern rooms. Doubles 280–450F with shower and up to 550F with bath.

HÔTEL-RESTAURANT PALAIS-CARDINAL***

place du 11-Novembre-1918 (North).
☎ 05.57.24.72.39 F 05.57.74.47.54
Closed Dec–March. Restaurant closed Wednesdays. **Secure parking. TV**

The promotional leaflet for the hotel says that it stands in the grounds of the former residence of the first dean of the collegiate church. That implies it must be quite something, even though there's nothing historical about the rooms. It's a middle class type of place. You must ask for one of the rooms – number 20, 21, 25, 27 or 29 – that look out onto the tiny garden. In theory, half-board is compulsory Easter–mid Oct but check the exact dates with the hotel. You'll pay 383F per day per person. Otherwise, doubles are 345F with shower and 390F with bath. Set meals in the restaurant 79–199F. Little heated swimming pool surrounded by a pleasant terrace.

HÔTEL AU LOGIS DES REMPARTS***

rue Guadet.
☎ 05.57.24.70.43 F 05.57.74.47.44
Closed Dec 15–Jan 15. **Car park. TV.**

A pleasant hotel in a very old building that still has a few features – a stone staircase and a garden bordering the ramparts – that point to just how old it is. The recently renovated rooms have now got a bit of character. Doubles 350–420F with shower, 450–550F with bath. A few of them can sleep up to five people. When the weather's nice you can have breakfast (which is substantial and very good – just try the fruit cake) on the elegantly paved terrace or in the garden. Plans to build a swimming pool are in the pipeline (but it's a listed site so planning permission could take some time).

RESTAURANT FRANCIS GOULLÉE

27 rue Guadet (Centre).
☎ 05.57.24.70.49
Closed Nov 25–Dec 10.

Hidden away in a narrow old street, this is the least touristy restaurant in Saint-Émilion – and it also just happens to be the best! Francis Goulé, ably assisted by his chatty wife, carries on the tradition of local cooking. Warm, comfortable dining room and very reasonable prices. On weekdays, there's a fast *formule* for 90F (main course plus dessert and a glass of wine). If you have the 125F set mea, you'll get a glass of white wine and appetizers, puff pastry filled with chicory and gravadlax of salmon, breast of duck *en aiguillettes*, roast potatoes with onion fondue and dried figs with spices, and pear *dacquoise*. We recommend you splash out a bit and have the 190F set meal (230F with two main courses), which offers marvellous *foie gras* and a choice of pigeon *en croûte* with mild spices and Szechuan pepper accompanied by preserve of turnips and baby vegetables or casserole of *brandade de morue* (creamed salt cod) with morels. Good produce, traditional recipes of the South-West reworked with surprising results, and new flavours. Enough to help you forget the occasional slip-ups in the service.

SAINT-JEAN-DE-LUZ 64500

MARIA CHRISTINA**

13 rue Paul-Gelos (North-East); it's beside the sea, a little further along from the beach.
☎ 05.59.26.81.70 F 05.59.26.36.04
TV.

This big pink house with green shutters is swathed in wisteria and looks superb in springtime. Friendly owner, cosy refined décor. Very quiet. Rooms 225–310F with shower or bath. One of our favourite places.

HÔTEL DE LA PLAGE**

33 rue Garat (Centre).
☎ 05.59.51.03.44 F 05.59.51.03.48
Closed Feb–March. **TV.**

As its name implies, this charming white hotel with red shutters is opposite the beach. Bright, clean well-equipped rooms. Ask for one with a sea view and if you want to give yourself a bit of a treat go for one with a private terrace. Doubles range in price from 370F for one overlooking the courtyard to 490F for one with a sea view out of season (the out of season price range is 310–410F). The brasserie is quite lively in the evenings and you get a perfect view of the sea.

10% ☗ LA MARISA**

16 rue Sopite (Centre).
☎ 05.59.26.95.46 ➡ 05.59.51.17.06
TV.

A charming hotel ideally located in a very quiet street between the town centre and the beach. We take our hats off to the owner who keeps things running marvellously in his hotel even though he's also mayor of a nearby village. Beautiful half-timbered façade covered in flowers. The rooms, which have been entirely refurbished, are well-equipped but quite expensive at 400F Oct–June, 480F June–Sept.

I●I RESTAURANT RAMUNTCHO

24 rue Garat; it's in the old town, between the church and the beach.
☎ 05.59.26.03.89
Closed Mondays out of season and Nov 11–Feb school holidays

A pretty ordinary name (well, it is in this area!) for a place that's anything but. Rather pleasant rustic décor. Good welcome. Set meals 88F, 120F and 160F. À la carte there's smoked salmon and avocado mousse, *piperade* (omelette with peppers and tomatoes), pan-fried squid with garlic and chillis, *confit* of chicken with mushrooms, monkfish with a creamy leek sauce, *aiguillettes* of duck breast, and *paella* (which has to be ordered ahead of time). Children's meal 42F. It's best to reserve in peak-season.

I●I RESTAURANT CHEZ MATTIN

place de la Croix-Rouge-Ciboure (South-West); it's in Ciboure, about 1km from the centre of Saint-Jean-de-Luz.
☎ 05.59.47.19.52
Closed Mondays and Jan–Feb.

Be warned, this place gets busy in summer. One of the best known fish restaurants in the area. The décor is very ordinary but that fades into insignificance when you see the exceptional quality of the food. Expect to pay about 120F for specialities like *ttoro* (fish stew with onions, tomatoes and garlic), which is deservedly famous. You can have something chargrilled too.

I●I RESTAURANT CHEZ PABLO

5 rue Mademoiselle-Etcheto; it's behind the market.
☎ 05.59.26.37.81
Closed Wednesdays, June and in October.

A big Basque house, white with red shutters, in a quiet little street. Cosy décor and atmosphere. This bistro-style restaurant gets lots of regulars and offers good home cooking. Expect to pay about 130F for a meal.

I●I LE KAIKU

17 rue de la République (Centre).
☎ 05.59.26.13.20
Closed Wednesdays (out of season), Monday lunchtimes and mid Nov–mid Dec

Superb medieval house with elegant mullion windows. Lovely décor of old ceiling, exposed stonework and pastel shades. The restaurant specializes in fish and seafood and, though it's quite expensive and touristy, the cooking is of a very high standard. Set meals 145–250F. Try the exquisite gratinéd oysters, the ravioli stuffed with langoustines or the sole with ceps.

ASCAIN 64310 (7KM SE)

☗ I●I L'AUBERGE ACHAFLA-BAÏTA*

How to get there: take the D918 – it's about 2km from Ascain on the Olhette-Urrugne road (D4).
☎ 05.59.54.00.30
Closed Monday evenings out of season and Nov 15–30. **Car park.**

You can enjoy both the countryside and the seaside at this lovely inn that's only 7km from the coast and far far away from the hustle and bustle of Saint-Jean. You'll get peace and quiet on the beautiful terrace or in the flower-filled garden. Rooms from 180F with basin. Homy atmosphere and home cooking. Set meals 80–155F with an excellent *piperade* (omelette with peppers and tomatoes), breast of duck in Muscat and salt cod *a donostiara*. Excellent welcome. It's a pretty popular place so it's a good idea to book.

SARE 64310 (13.5KM SE)

☗ I●I HÔTEL-RESTAURANT BARATCHARTEA

How to get there: it's in the part of town known as Ihalar.
☎ 05.59.54.20.48 ➡ 05.59.47.50.84
Closed Jan 1–beginning of March. **Secure parking**

A superb Basque house in a typically Basque neighbourhood. The beautiful rustic dining room offers regional cooking and generous portions – the Basques are big eaters! Set meals 85–160F. Pleasant rooms, all with a magnificent view of the mountain. You'll pay 220F for one with shower and 230F with bath. A room that sleeps four is 330F, which is a pretty good price.

SAINT-JEAN-PIED-DE-PORT 64220

10% ITZALPEA**

5 pl. du Trinquet (Centre).
☎ 05.59.37.03.66 F 05.59.37.33.18
Closed Saturdays out of season. **TV**.

Professional management. The rooms are comfortable, and have been fully renovated. You'll pay 150F with basin, 200F with shower and 220F with bath. The 85F set meal in the restaurant is very generous. Other set meals 58F, 95F and 160F.

CENTRAL HÔTEL**

1 pl. du Gal-de-Gaulle (Centre).
☎ 05.59.37.00.22 F 05.59.37.27.79
Closed Dec 22–Feb 10. **Car park**. **TV**. Canal +

Superb hand-carved staircase. Luxurious and impeccably clean rooms 320F with shower – 390F with bath. Ask for one with a view of the Nive. Top-quality restaurant with set meals 100–200F. The dining room is slightly dated but has a certain charm. Lamb's sweetbreads with *piquillos*, wild salmon, and soufflé with Izarra (a liqueur similar to Chartreuse). Good welcome and attentive service.

LES PYRÉNÉES***

19 pl. du Gal de Gaulle (Centre).
☎ 05.59.37.01.01 F 05.59.37.18.97
Closed Tuesdays Sept 20–June 30. **Secure parking**. **TV**. **Canal+**.

The rooms are very expensive (550–900F) but they're impeccable. Very pleasant indoor swimming pool. The restaurant is said to be one of the best in Basque country. Fine cuisine and skilfully prepared dishes. Try the delicious *garbure* (vegetable soup served with a piece of preserved goose or duck), the equally good *foie gras* of duck, the roast pigeon with cep-filled ravioli or the freshly caught salmon. Remarkable sorbets. Set meals 230–500F.

RESTAURANT ARBILLAGA

8 rue de l'Église.
☎ 05.59.37.06.44
Closed Wednesdays out of season and 2 weeks in Oct.

A restaurant full of pleasant surprises that's squeezed in between the ramparts and the nearby houses. The little dining room is straight out of an Italian opera. Good food served in generous portions. Set meals 78F, 110F and 210F with dishes like scrambled eggs with *foie gras* and roast lamb with garlic. Great welcome and service. Intimate atmosphere.

SAINT-MICHEL 64220 (4KM S)

HÔTEL-RESTAURANT XOKO-GOXOA**

How to get there: on the D301.
☎ 05.59.37.06.34 F 05.59.37.34.63
Closed Tuesdays out of season and Jan 1–March 15. **Car park**.

This is a large traditional house surrounded with greenery. Most of the rooms look straight out onto the countryside. Comfortable double rooms 200–240F. Cosy rustic-style dining room and unpretentious cooking. The set meals at 65F, 85F, 100F and 150F feature trout *etxekoa*, rib steak *à la navarraise* (with sweet peppers, onions, and garlic), salad *gourmande* and so on. The à la carte prices are very reasonable. Large terrace with a wonderful panoramic view.

BUSSUNARITZ 64220 (7KM E)

HÔTEL-RESTAURANT DU COL DE GAMIA**

col de Gamia.
☎ 05.59.37.13.48
Closed Jan–mid March. **Car park**.

The little road which leads you to this place is one of the loveliest in the region. When you get to the top, the view is tremendous. Clean comfortable rooms 200F with bath. Excellent Basque cuisine. Delicious stew of wild boar in the hunting season. Set meals 65–180F. Charming owners

SAINT-JUSTIN 40240

10% HÔTEL DE FRANCE*.

☎ 05.58.44.83.61 F 05.58.44.83.89
Car park

It's got the kind of name hotels in small French towns had in the 50s, inside it looks like a set for a 1930s detective film, and it's located in the middle of a 13th century fortified town. It's quite a mixture, and that's what makes it so attractive. You'll get peace and quiet in a traditional family atmosphere. Lovely rooms 230F with shower/wc and 280F with bath. The restaurant, which is at the back, serves traditional cooking and fine dishes bursting with flavour and made from fresh produce. There's steamed red mullet fillets in salad with lemon and orange peel, roast rack of lamb coated with crushed pine nuts and, the speciality, goose simmered in red wine. Delicious! Set meals 100F, 140F and 190F. Friendly welcome and laid-back atmosphere.

SAINT-MACAIRE 33490

L'ABRICOTIER

☎ 05.56.76.83.63
Closed Tuesdays and Nov 12–Dec 5. **Car park**.

By rights, it should be in one of the traditional houses in this beautiful village (one of the nicest in the region). Instead it's more or less at the side of the main road. But we really did like the cute little dining room that looks out onto the back and the terrace with its apricot tree (*abricotier* in French) that's lovely when the sun's out. Pleasant décor. The kitchen turns out some great imaginative dishes including gazpacho of scallops with Jerusalem artichokes, roast sea bass with asparagus, braised shoulder of lamb, *cassolette* of snails with *confit* of pig's trotters, salad of duck's neck with artichokes, fillet of bream with mixed vegetable *confit*, vegetables with *foie gras* and, for dessert, roast pineapple with vanilla. Set meals 70F (weekday lunchtimes), 105F, 155F and 210F. Very good wine list – nothing but Bordeaux. Go on, treat yourself!

SAINT-PALAIS 64120

10% HÔTEL-RESTAURANT DE LA PAIX**

33 rue du Jeu-de-Paume (Centre).
☎ 05.59.65.73.15 Fax 05.59.65.63.83
Closed the first fortnight in January. **Car park**. **TV**. **Disabled access**.

You'd never think from the outside that the hotel's been around for 200 years. And you'll get an even bigger shock inside – it's just been entirely rebuilt and is now a practical, pleasant place to stay with modern facilities. Rooms 270–290F with bath. Good regional cooking with set meals 65–135F and dishes like lamb's sweetbreads with ham and ceps, bream *oyarsun*, monkfish, *ttoro* (fish stew), and game in season. Charming welcome. It'll be some time before it gets back all its old character – it's still too new!

SAINT-VINCENT-DE-TYROSSE 40230

LES GOURMETS

av. Nationale.
☎ 05.58.77.16.97
Closed Tuesday evenings, Wednesdays (out of season) and during the Christmas holidays.

You can't walk past this restaurant – the large terrace acts like a magnet and feels like the kind of place where you'll enjoy taking your time over things. At lunchtimes, a lot of reps stop off for the 55F *formule* of dish of the day plus dessert and coffee. Or you could spend a bit more – 65F, 89F, 130F or 165F – and get something a bit more substantial. The honey-glazed breast of duck with *grelot* onions (which come from the South of France) wins the flavour stakes, the monkfish kebab with *beurre blanc* comes a close second, and the house *foie gras* deserves an honourable mention. A solid dependable restaurant serving classic dishes.

SARLAT-LA-CANÉDA 24200

AUBERGE DE JEUNESSE

77 av. de Selves (North).
☎ 05.53.59.47.59 Fax 05.53.30.21.27
Closed Nov 15–March 15.

Open to individuals July 1–Oct 15. It's often full at other times of the year because of group bookings. Doors open 6pm–10pm. No curfew. It has a total of 32 beds in three dormitories. and you'll pay 45F a night. Occupants are responsible for the upkeep of the place. You can pitch a tent for 25F a night. You really must book – it attracts travellers from about 24 different countries.

10% HÔTEL LES RÉCOLLETS**

4 rue Jean-Jacques-Rousseau (Centre).
☎ 05.53.31.36.00 Fax 05.53.30.32.62
Car park. **TV**.

In a quiet, picturesque little pedestrian street away from the streams of cars and tourists who seem to descend on Sarlat as soon as the sun comes out. And since this is a historic town, it would be a shame not to stay in a hotel with a bit of history behind it. This one is housed in what used to be the cloisters of a 17th century convent. Great welcome, homely atmosphere (a father and son team manage the place). The rooms have all been tastefully renovated. There's one room with basin (soon to go) for 180F for 2, doubles with shower/wc 200–280F, with bath 350F. A few of them look out onto a little courtyard where you have breakfast. We particularly liked number 15,which gets lots of light and has a lovely view of the tiled rooftops in the old town, and number 8 with its elegant stone archways. We might even go so far as to say that this is our favourite hotel in Sarlat.

HÔTEL LE MAS DE CASTEL**

Sudalissant (South); it's 3km from the town – take the D704 in the direction of Souillac, then La Canéda, and after that it's sign-posted.
☎ 05.53.59.02.59 F 05.53.28.25.62
Closed Nov 11–Easter. **Car park. Disabled access.**

Charming hotel on one level, in the local style (beautiful white stonework in the traditional fashion) surrounded with greenery. Excellent welcome. The rooms, decorated in soft pastel shades, are comfortable, pleasant and restful. Expect to pay 230F minimum for a double with shower, 250F with bath. Numbers 2, 3, 4, 5 and 14 are larger than the others. Beautiful swimming pool where you can cool off in summer. No restaurant. The ideal spot for a stay in the country, but still just a stone's throw from Sarlat.

HÔTEL-RESTAURANT SAINT-ALBERT ET HÔTEL MONTAIGNE**

pl. Pasteur et 11 rue Émile Faure (South).
☎ 05.53.31.55.55 F 05.53.59.19.99
Closed Sunday evenings and Mondays (out of season). **TV. Disabled access.**

Two hotels and a restaurant only just outside the centre of the old town. Behind the tasteful bourgeois façade of Hotel Montaigne you'll find pretty rooms (we've got a soft spot for the ones on the top floor that have exposed beams) that are well equipped and decorated in a modern style that that no-one could possibly dislike. Doubles with shower or bath 250–320F. They also have suites (480–520F). There's a glassed-in terrace where you have breakfast. On the other side of the street is Hotel Saint Albert. The rooms there are more old-fashioned and the ones that look onto the street are a teeny bit noisy (so of course you should ask for one at the back). Doubles with shower or bath 250–290F. In the huge dining room you'll rub shoulders with the (very) old regulars and local worthies, people who like the old classics (calf's head, pig's trotters) and swear by regional food (salad *périgourdine*, mushroom omelette, *confit aux noix*). The house motto seems to be that if you want gourmet meals you have to start off with good food. We couldn't agree more! At lunchtime on weekdays, the bistro has a dish of the day for 45F and a set meal for 65F. Other set meals 97–170F.

HÔTEL DE COMPOSTELLE**

av. de Selves (Centre).
☎ 05.53.59.08.53 F 05.53.30.31.65
Closed Nov 11–Easter. **TV. Disabled access.**

Friendly welcome, and large pleasant rooms that are impeccably clean. Two will pay 280F for a room with shower/wc, 300F with bath. A few have a glassed-in balcony but they look out onto the street. The quieter rooms overlook a tiny little garden at the back. For families, small suites with two bedrooms and bath are 400–450F a night.

RESTAURANT LES 4 SAISONS

2 Côte de Toulouse (Centre).
☎ 05.53.29.48.59
Closed Wednesdays (out of season).

A restaurant that has only recently opened in a steep, narrow street and is miles away (metaphorically speaking) from the flashy kind of place selling cheap and nasty foie gras, of which there are so many in Sarlat. This particular restaurant without any fuss is slowly building a reputation for itself, and the set meals at 65F and 85F offer some of the best value for money in town. Other set meals at 110F and 130F offer dishes like salad of scrambled eggs with morels, and breast of duck with juniper berry sauce. Imaginative desserts include *gratin* of seasonal fruit and a great chocolate pudding with a saffron sauce. It has two little dining rooms and, like the regulars, we've got a bit of a weakness for the one on the first floor. A good little restauant.

RESTAURANT CHEZ MARC

4 rue Tourny (Centre).
☎ 05.53.59.02.71
Closed Sundays and Mondays out of season.

This is a tiny little bistro, so take our advice and book. Two or threetables make up the terrace on a busy old street in the centre. It's ideal for lunch. and has a 48F lunchtime *formule* (except Sundays) of main course plus dessert and coffee. There's a better choice on the 75F set meal. À la carte there's *andouillette* in Cahors wine, breast of duck with soft fruit, a fair amount of fish, and apple *fondant*. Jug of wine 26F. Cheapest bottle 57F. Children's set meal 35F.

RESTAURANT LE BOUFFON

11 rue Albéric-Cahuet (Centre).
☎ 05.53.31.03.36

Closed Wednesdays out of school holidays, in January and in December.

The young chef, who hasn't been here for long, has quickly made a name for himself and gained a loyal following, which is only natural since the restaurant is in the most touristy part of the town and is an excellent place to try out regional gourmet dishes. Pleasant décor and friendly welcome. Traditional Périgord cuisine based on well chosen ingredients like a superb *foie gras* that is full of flavour. They have set meals at 75F (starter, main course, and dessert), 98F (good value for money this one) and 128F (the regional set meal and it's excellent). The chef's signature dishes are medallions of zander with chanterelle mushrooms, veal kidneys and sweetbread with fresh pasta, and the house *terrine* of *foie gras*. Pretty good desserts like walnut cake. Long may it continue!

|●| LE RELAIS DE LA POSTE

Impasse de la Vieille Poste.
☎ 05.53.59.63.13
Closed Mondays.

A former coaching inn with an impressive fireplace. The atmosphere is warm and relaxed but the service is very stylish – the food comes under dome-shaped covers! The prices stay much the same from year to year, the food is good, and they use fresh produce. They have a 55F lunchtime *formule* of starter or soup plus the dish of the day (breast of goose with soft fruit, for example), a 95F *menu du marché* (the market's just nearby) that changes often of course, and two other set meals at 115F and 135F featuring local dishes like gizzard salad, *confit*, and duck or goose breast. Good desserts. Affordable wine. All in all, a pleasant surprise in a town where some restaurants don't seem to realise that a good meal does not necessarily mean an expensive meal! It's best to book in advance of course.

ROQUE-GAGEAC (LA) 24250 (9KM S)

⌂ |●| HÔTEL-RESTAURANT LA BELLE ÉTOILE**

rue Principale (Centre).
☎ 05.53.29.51.44 ➡ 05.53.29.45.63
Closed Mondays (out of season) and mid Oct–Easter.
Secure parking. **TV**.

A charming hotel that blends in perfectly with what is one of the most beautiful villages in France. Inevitably there's quite a stylish feel to the place. The rooms have been individually decorated and furnished with taste. A few – numbers 1 to 11 – have a nice view of the slow-moving Dordogne. Doubles 300F with shower or bath. There's an elegant dining room decorated in shades of pink and a terrace swathed in vines overhanging the river. The food is excellent and the kitchen concentrates on the classics (adding a few modern touches here and there) such as *millefeuille* of *foie gras* with asparagus, pigeon, and potatoes with *foie gras*. Set meals 120F and 175F.

MONTFORT-CAUDON 24200 (11KM S)

|●| RESTAURANT DE LA FERME – CHEZ LACOUR ESCALIER

How to get there: on the D46 coming from the north and the D46E coming from the south; it's on the north bank of the Dordogne.
☎ 05.53.28.33.35
Closed Sunday evenings and Mondays in winter, Mondays only in summer, Oct 1–31, and Dec 20–Jan 28.

This inn has long had a solid reputation thanks to the hard work of its owner, Maurice Escalier. His talented daughter Arlette is now carrying on the family tradition and all of Périgord flocks to this friendly place for the fresh fried fish from the Dordogne in season, the truffle omelette, the chicken in verjuice with potatoes and truffles, duck liver, rib of beef with shallots, *confit*, and walnut cake. Set meals range in price from 85F (farmhouse soup and country ham) to 165F. The restaurant has moved with the times and is now air-conditioned. And though you may see the occasional TV personality, the hens and ducks still wander around the courtyard and the Dordogne flows peacefully by. A place where time stands still.

MEYRALS 24220 (12KM NW)

10% ⌂ HÔTEL DE LA FERME LAMY***

How to get there: on the D47 in the direction of Les Eyzies/Périgeux, then turn left at Benive.
☎ 05.53.29.62.46 ➡ 05.53.59.61.41
Car park. **TV**. **Canal+**. **Disabled access**

We lost track of Nelly and Michel Bougon after they sold their place in Porto Vecchio. Well thankfully we've caught up with them at last in this old Perigord farmhouse – parts of which date back to the 17th century – in the depths of the country. In three years they've almost single-handedly turned it into a charming hotel. They have delightful rooms with bathrooms, all decorated with great care. It's the height of luxury, but the owners also wanted to keep it affordable and doubles with shower/wc start at 310F. You'll pay about 800F for the most expensive room. That happens to be number 1 and, with its massive fireplace and a bathroom (complete with jacuzzi) right in the middle of the room, it's like something you'd find in a Hollywood mansion. Breakfast comes with walnut bread, *brioche* and home-made jam and in fine weather can be eaten outside under the lime trees in the very well kept garden. Superb swimming pool overlooks a gentle landscape of fields and hills. Moreover, you'll get a simple, genuine welcome. There's no restaurant but you'll find a good farmhouse inn a short distance away.

DOMME 24250 (12KM S)

NOUVEL HÔTEL*

rue Maleville and Grande rue (opposite place de la Halle).
☎ 05.53.28.38.67 F 05.53.28.27.13
Closed Nov 1–Easter.

A pretty stone house ideally situated in the centre of the old fortified town. The second good thing about it is that the prices are good for the area. Doubles 210F with shower/wc, 280F with bath. The rooms are rather pleasant on the whole. The restaurant has set meals at 70F and 80–240F. Regional cuisine with a few specialities like snails and ceps in puff pastry, *confit,* breast of duck, and stuffed quail.

MARQUAY 24620 (12KM NW)

HÔTEL-RESTAURANT DES BORIES**

☎ 05.53.29.67.02 F 05.53.29.64.15
Closed Nov 2–end of March; restaurant closed Monday lunchtimes. **Car park. Disabled access.**

A delightful hotel in a very good location in a nice village off the beaten track. It has a big garden, a swimming pool and a superb view. Bright clean rooms 160–295F. Friendly welcome. The restaurant next door has a good reputation and for 80F you can have *tourin blanchi* (onion and milk soup poured over slices of bread), house *pâté* with shallots, breast of duck with *guinettes*, cheese and dessert. Other set meals 100F, 120F and 150F (*farandole périgourdine*, fillet of monkfish with ceps, beef with morels and so on). Gourmet set meal 240F. Children's set meal: 50F. One of our favourite places in this part of the world.

PAULIN 24590 (24KM NE)

LA MEYNARDIE

How to get there: from Sarlat, go in the direction of Salignac-Eyvignes, then Archignac.
☎ 05.53.28.85.98
Closed Wednesdays Oct–May. **Car park.**

An old farmhouse deep in the country. Even though it's been restored the dining room still has a certain cachet with its paved floor and massive fireplace that dates back to 1603. Courteous welcome. The atmosphere's a little on the chic side but it's not over the top. There's a wide range of set meals starting at 72F (weekday lunchtimes) and 98F – these are good value for money – and going up to 220F. The dishes are of the traditional local variety but show lots of imagination with things like *carpaccio* of duck breast, and pan-fried duck livers with truffles. Good desserts include an iced soufflé with walnuts. Sit out on the terrace in summer and stroll through the chestnut tree forest after your meal. One for the address book.

LAVAL-DE-JAYAC 24590 (25KM NE)

10% HÔTEL-RESTAURANT COULIER**

Centre; take the D60.
☎ 05.53.28.86.46 F 05.53.28.26.33
Closed Saturdays (out of season), and mid Dec–2nd week in Jan. **Car park. TV. Canal+. Disabled access.**

A hamlet – it's not big enough to be called a village – in deepest, darkest Périgord. The U-shaped hotel, a prettily converted farmhouse, stands on a hillock at a reasonable distance from the road. It has 15 fairly small but pretty rooms dotted all over the building. Doubles 260F with shower/wc, 270F with bath. Friendly welcome. The restaurant serves traditional and regional dishes like warm semi-cooked *foie gras*, *confit*, veal sweetbreads, duck stew with blackcurrants, and breast of duck with mustard. Set meals 75F, 125F, 160F and 240F. Children's set meal 40F. If you don't want to spend all day by the pool, you can always go for a walk on one of the several trails in the surrounding area (they won't take you long, but they are lovely). The owners know the area very well so don't hesitate to ask them for advice.

SAUTERNES 33210

AUBERGE LES VIGNES

place de l'Église.
☎ 05.56.76.60.06
Closed Mondays and end of Jan–end of Feb. **Disabled access.**

You're guaranteed to find checked tablecloths

and log fires in this lovely little country inn. Friendly welcome from the American owner. Warm homely atmosphere. The kitchen uses local and seasonal produce and though the food falls into the gourmet category it's not at all pretentious. Set meals start at 60F (except on Saturday evenings and Sundays) and for that you'll get steak grilled over vine shoots. The 105F set meal consists of country ham followed by a stew of lamb's brains or duck drumstick *confit*, while if you take the 135F set meal, you'll have a choice of quail in Sauternes or rib steak grilled over vine shoots for your main course. The puff pastry fruit tart comes straight from the oven to your plate and the mushrooms in the omelette will have been picked that morning. Superb selection of wines in the cellar. The restaurant's been going for a good 30 years now – let's hope for at least another 30!

RESTAURANT LE SAPRIEN

11 rue Principale.
☎ 05.56.76.60.87
Closed Sunday evenings (and Mondays out of season), during the February school holidays, and Nov 15–Dec 15.

A little house with thick stone walls on the outskirts of the village. It's ever so slightly chic and the elegant interior is a successful blend of old and new. It has a delightful little reading room and also a huge terrace that opens out onto the vineyard – so naturally they grill food over vine shoots and offer Sauternes by the glass. But primarily, they offer dishes that reflect the changing seasons and what the market has to offer. If it's available, try the warm salad of *foie gras* (expensive but absolutely delicious), the lamprey in Sauternes, or the roasted veal sweetbreads in a Sauternes and curry sauce. Expect to pay about 200F à la carte. Set meals 109–199F. For 119F, you'll get *terrine* of young rabbit with onion marmalade followed by pan-fried trout with five kinds of pepper and for 169F, *tartare* of salmon with oysters and shallots, asparagus flan with shellfish sauce, and roast pork fillet with mango and ginger.

SAUVETERRE-DE-BÉARN 64390

10% L'HOSTELLERIE DU CHÂTEAU*

Centre.
☎ 05.59.38.52.10
Closed Jan 10–Feb 15.**Car park**. **TV**.

A superb house in peaceful surroundings. It has a magnificent view of the Pyrenees and a large terrace that looks over the valley. Lunch is served under an ancient copper beech. The restaurant offers set meals ranging in price from 90F to 170F and delicious *béarnaise* specialities like braised trout in Jurançon, squid *à la basquaise* (with tomatoes, peppers, and rice), and ovenbaked black pudding and sausage. Good prices considering the quality. The rooms, some of them more than 20 metres square(!) are furnished with antiques. Ask for one with a view of the garden. Doubles 110F with basin, 180F with shower and 230F with bath.

SORE 40430

LE RELAIS DES CHASSEURS

quartier Barthes; it's on the road from Sore to Pissos.
☎ 05.58.07.62.36
Closed Mondays–Wednesdays, in January and in February.

If anyone out there ever said that there was nothing but pine trees in Landes, well, it's time to eat your words. This inn in the middle of the forest, a traditional farmhouse made of brick and half timbering, is very popular with the locals. It has charming rustic décor and a little terrace sheltered by huge plane trees. As you may have guessed from its name, this is where the hunters come during the season. And like you, they come for the duck breast, the *ceps à la bordelaise* (sautéd in oil with shallots and parsley), the duckling with prunes flambéd in Armagnac, the roast quail, and the *confits fondants* – all of it the kind of food that sticks to your ribs at prices that stick in the mind. Set meals 100–165F. And you'll get a genuinely friendly welcome too.

SOS 47170

LE POSTILLON

pl. Édouard Delbousquet.
☎ 05.53.65.60.27

This grey building isn't aesthetically pleasing. Don't be put off though, for it's an exceptional place. Here's what you'll get if you take the 85F set meal: crayfish, *daube de bœuf* (a kind of beef stew) with prunes, cheese, and dessert. We opted for the 120F one and had soup, salad *landaise*, *daube de bœuf*, duck breast, cheese and dessert. A food lover's dream!

SOULAC-SUR-MER 33780

10% HÔTEL MICHELET**

1 rue Baguenard (Centre).
☎ 05.56.09.82.69 F→ 05.56.09.86.20

Closed one week at the end of October and the last three weeks in January. **TV.Disabled access**.

A typical seaside villa. The staff are above criticism and there are lots of thoughtful gestures like little presents for kids. The rooms, in mint condition, are pleasant and comfortable. Eight of them have a balcony and four lead out into a little gravel garden. There are three price ranges. Doubles 180–300F out of season (Nov–March), 220–320F mid-season, and 320–420F in July and August. And we almost forgot the most important thing – it's just a stone's throw from the ocean.

SOUSTONS 40140

10% LE PAVILLON LANDAIS***

26 av. du Lac.
☎ 05.58.41.14.49 F 05.58.41.26.03
Closed Sunday evenings and Mondays (out of season) and in January.**Secure parking**. **TV**.

The kind of place where you can feel yourself unwind. It's very, very quiet – hardly surprising since you've got the lake right beneath your window and the forest nearby. If you're suffering from writer's block, come here and you might well end up winning the Booker prize! And it's easy to see why the late François Mitterand, gourmet and adopted citizen of Landes, was a regular. The pleasant and very comfortable rooms are prettily furnished and prices start at 315F. The *menu-carte* is an original idea – you can have one course for 85F, two for 125F, three for 180F, and a dessert for 40F. Take your pick –they're all great. We particularly liked the lightly cooked semi-salt cod, the pigeon with Brussels sprouts and smoked breast of pork, the stew of white fish with saffron, and the *aiguillettes* of duck in breadcrumbs. Whatever you do, don't pass on the hot *foie gras* with rhubarb, a subtle combination in which the slightly sour rhubarb contrasts with the smoothness of the liver and brings out the flavour of the duck. A special moment!

TAUSSAT 33148

RESTAURANT LES FONTAINES

port de plaisance de Taussat.
☎ 05.56.82.13.86
Closed Sunday evenings and Mondays (except in summer), and two weeks in November. **Car park**.

A modern building near the marina. To be honest, it doesn't exactly ooze charm but it doesn't fit in too badly with the surrounding area. And it's very pleasant to sit on the terrace on a lovely spring or summer evening and enjoy the wonderfully fresh cooking of Jean-Pascal Paubert who is an inspired chef. Just try his *tartare* of salmon with chives! The cheapest set meal is 95F (served every day), and there are *menus-carte* at 155F and 210F. As in a few other restaurants in the wine growing area, you can bring your own wine which will be served "with all the attention it deserves" (J-P. Paubert is also chairman of the local wine waiters'association).

TONNEINS 47400

10% CÔTÉ GARONNE

36 cours de l'Yser.
☎ 05.53.84.34.34 F 05.53.84.31.31
Closed Mondays and Aug 15–31.

The street doesn't look particularly appealing (and neither does the town for that matter) so this beautiful building really stands out. It's like entering a different world when you step inside this tastefully decorated hotel with its almost magical atmosphere. Jean-Luc Rabanel took a bit of a gamble settling in what was virgin territory and he had to gain acceptance for a style of cooking that was surprising and sometimes disconcerting. You're taken aback at first by his combinations of local produce and spices, then delighted with the meticulous presentation of his dishes and in the end won over by his sea bass with caramelized asparagus tips sprinkled with parmesan, his roast zander served with risotto (he uses spelter, a type of wheat, rather than rice), and his smoked duck with oriental spices. A typical set meal might consist of grilled veal with baby vegetables and fresh herbs followed by blancmange with almonds, barley water and wild strawberries. Set meals 85F (weekday lunchtimes), 115F, 155F, 195F and 250F. If you want to stay the night, they have five rooms but these are pretty luxurious and, at 650–850F, way out of our price range.

VIEUX-BOUCAU-LES-BAINS 40480

HÔTEL-RESTAURANT LE MOÏSAN**

av. de Moïsan.
☎ 05.58.48.10.32 F 05.58.48.37.84
Closed Sept 20–April 1.**Car park**. **TV**.

A good family hotel with rustic décor in a

rather peaceful area. Doubles 200–400F depending on the facilities, which range from basin to shower/wc or bath. The restaurant is fairly decent and has set meals at 90F (served every day), 110F (this is the regional one), and 155F (fish). The cooking shows strong Basque influences with dishes like *piquillos* of salt cod with a chilli sauce and squid. Simple and very acceptable.

HÔTEL-RESTAURANT DE LA CÔTE D'ARGENT**

4 Grand Rue.
☎ 05.58.48.13.17 F 05.58.48.01.15
Closed Mondays Oct–June. **Car park**. **TV**.

A building with orange shutters that seems always to have been part of the main street of the old village. It has about 40 well-kept, comfortable rooms, a few of which have a terrace. Doubles 220F with washing facilities, 280F with shower/wc or bath. A triple with bath, shower/wc and TV is 340F. A word of warning: the rooms overlooking the pedestrian street are noisy. The restaurant offers very traditional food with no surprises and simple but effective dishes like *confit* of duck, *salmis de palombes* (pigeon in red wine sauce), hake, *blanquette* of scallops, pan-fried prawns with garlic, and sole with ceps. Set meals 89–149F.

VILLANDRAUT 33730

HÔTEL-RESTAURANT DE GOTH**

place Principale (Centre).
☎ 05.56.25.31.25 F same
Closed Mondays out of season and mid Nov–mid Jan. **Car park**.

A pretty building with stone walls that seem to hold the light. This is the way you imagine a village inn. The rooms are clean and well cared for. Doubles from 220F. Decent traditional local dishes like chicken *confit*, *assiette landaise*, whole breast of duck with peaches, duck *foie gras* with apples, and lamb medallions *persillé*. Set meals 70F, 98F and 149F. In fine weather, sit on the sheltered terrace on the square.

VILLEFRANCHE-DU-PÉRIGORD 24550

HÔTEL-RESTAURANT LA PETITE AUBERGE**

How to get there: it's 800m from the village and well sign-posted.
☎ 05.53.29.91.01 F 05.53.28.88.10
Closed the first fortnight in November and the first fortnight in February. **Car park**. **TV**.

A large house built in the depths of the country in a style typical of the region. It's got an enormous garden and very inviting sun-loungers The rooms are tastefully decorated. Double 240F with shower/wc, 260F with bath. As for the restaurant, the meals are based on regional produce and whatever's in season. Cheapest set meal 65F (weekdays), others 79–145F. Terrace for the summer. A haven of peace and serenity.

VILLENEUVE DE MARSAN 40190

57 GRANDE RUE

☎ 05.58.45.29.92
Closed Sunday evenings, Mondays out of season, and in January.

Hélène Darroze, who has no equal when it comes to cooking, gained a loyal following for her main restaurant. Cooking runs in her family, a tradition that's passed on from generation to generation, and now that she's taken over from her father, Hélène has opened this homely bistro. Country-style décor and meticulous service. For 140F you'll be presented with 12 savoury dishes and 6 desserts. Yes, you're right, that's a total of 18 courses! The portions are small of course but you won't leave hungry and you'll enjoy the simple tasty dishes – the kind that are left to simmer for a long time – made from local produce. Try the warm scallop salad followed by *confit* of milk-fed lamb and *tian provençale*, and *clafoutis* with prunes. If you're worried about not finishing one of the set meals then why not go for something à la carte? Starters 45F, main courses 65F and desserts 25F.

VILLENEUVE-SUR-LOT 47300

10% HÔTEL LA RÉSIDENCE**

17 av. Lazare Carnot (Centre)
☎ 05.53.40.17.03 F 05.53.01.57.34

A pretty little hotel with a pink façade, green shutters, and lots of character in a very quiet neighbourhood near the old station. As soon as you set foot inside, you're drawn to the garden you can see at the end of the corridor. It has quite a few rooms at various prices. Doubles 125–165F with washing facilities, 189–239F with shower/wc and 230–285F with bath. Ideal if you like things simple and if you're looking for peace and quiet.

|●| CHEZ CALINE

2 rue Notre-Dame (Centre).
☎ 05.53.70.42.08

Let's get things clear from the start. Mushroom picking is forbidden in the restaurant. Well, at least you're warned before you go in!. There's a bit of a Lewis Carrol in the owner. He's got a sense of humour and that's reflected in the restaurant. By the way, Calîne is the cocker spaniel and the flowers are artificial (which means they don't need to be picked or changed). Anyway, for those of you who are interested in the food, here goes: breast of duck stuffed with *foie gras*, fillet of salmon with sorrel, eggs *vignerons* (fried in walnut oil, with white wine, shallot and garlic sauce) and cherry soup with mint. One set meal only, 75F, smile included.

|●| RESTAURANT AUX BERGES DU LOT

3 rue de l'Hôtel-de-Ville.
☎ 05.53.70.84.81
Closed Sunday evenings, Mondays, and two weeks in November.

A nice restaurant which has become a bit of an institution in a town that's a bit short of good places to eat. Sheltered terrace and a view of the Lot. The chef sticks to the tried and true and dishes like young rabbit with broad beans and tarragon or scallops in puff pastry with fennel-flavoured butter make an excellent curtain raiser for the duck leg *confit* served with pan-fried fresh liver or the veal *paupiette* with a lobster and star anis mousse. Set meals 75F (weekday lunchtimes), 115F, 165F and 210F.

PUJOLS 47300 (3KM S)

|●| LE FIGUIER

Passage du Pont du Castel; take the D118 in the direction of Prayrass.
☎ 05.53.36.72.12

The décor is fairly restrained and stylish, and the atmosphere restful. You feel yourself slipping into a dreamy and contemplative mood as if you were sitting under a tree with the contents of a picnic hamper spread out before you on a checked tablecloth.. The food definitely awakens memories of Provence with dishes like stuffed baby vegetables, *pissaladière* (a kind of onion tart), quail with olives, and garlic chicken. There are no set meals but the à la carte menu offers lots of tasty dishes. Expect to pay about 40–60F for a starters and 60–70F for a main course. Very reasonable.

MONCLAR 47380 (18KM E)

|●| LE RELAIS

How to get there: take the D911 to Sainte Livrade, then the D667 for 5km, then the D113.
☎ 05.53.49.44.74

The locals come here in droves on Sundays and public holidays to enjoy the simple dishes that are served up in generous portions. Make yourself comfortable in the rustic dining room with its beautiful terrace overlooking the valley – lunch could well last for some time. If you take the 100F set meal you'll get country ham, tuna flan on a bed of courgettes, lightly salted roast duck, cheese and a good dessert. The 140F set meal is more substantial. Attentive service.

AUVERGNE

03 Allier

15 Cantal

43 Haute-Loire

63 Puy-de-Dôme

AMBERT 63600

10% HÔTEL-RESTAURANT LES COPAINS**

42 bd Henri-IV.
☎ 04.73.82.01.02 F 04.73.82.67.34
Closed Saturdays, Sunday evenings, and September.

Service noon–1.30pm and 7.30–8.30pm. Neither the façade nor the name of this place is particularly inspiring but it would be a great pity to miss out on the cooking of Thierry Chelle, the fourth generation of his family to be in charge of the kitchen here. It's simple, traditional and based largely on local produce but he's also picked up some tricks from the time he spent in the Robuchon kitchens, which give it that bit extra. Try for yourself dishes such as boned quail stuffed with *foie gras*, salad of boned frog's legs with chopped parsley and garlic, duck leg with *fourme d'Ambert* (a local cheese) and *terrine* of pig's trotters with port. Set meals 70–220F. Completely refurbished bedrooms 250F with shower/wc and 340F with bath.

10% HÔTEL-RESTAURANT LA CHAUMIÈRE**

41 av. Foch; from the town centre go towards Puy-en Velay.
☎ 04.73.82.14.94 F 04.73.82.33.52
Closed Saturdays Oct–May; restaurant closed Friday evenings Nov–March, Sunday evenings (except public holidays and beginning of July–end of Sept). Also closed Dec 26–Jan 31. **Secure parking**. **TV**. **Canal+**. **Disabled access**.

Service noon–2pm and 7–9pm. *La Chaumière* is a hangover from the days when you could eat well at reasonable prices. There's nothing fancy here, just good plain cooking and substantial set meals ranging in price from 92F to 200F. The restaurant has been renovated throughout and is decorated in a very classical style, a description that could also apply to the cooking which sticks to old faithfuls like *croustillant* of frog's legs with fennel, snails in *beurre marin*, *coq au vin*, mutton tripe, and casseroled pigeon. The bedrooms are as good as any you'll find in one of the big hotel chains and cost 310–320F

RESTAURANT BALI

37 av. du 11-Novembre.
☎ 04.73.82.23.10
Closed Mondays out of season and Sundays.

The *Bali*, open in the evenings, is just across from the station – ideal for keeping up to date with the various comings and goings. This is an exceptionally good Indonesian restaurant in a part of France better known for its thick soups. It's essential to book since very often there's not a table to be had in the beautifully decorated little dining room. There are two *formules*, the first offering an *assiette balinaise* and dessert for 95F, and the other a magnificent 175F *rijsttafel* of more than ten very refined dishes. You'll have to order that ahead of time since it takes five hours to prepare. At lunchtime there's a *formule brasserie* for 50F which includes the day's special. Chef Armand van Poppel is Dutch in origin and all his family lived in Indonesia before independence. He's a fervent admirer of Indonesian cooking and keen to share that enthusiasm with his customers.

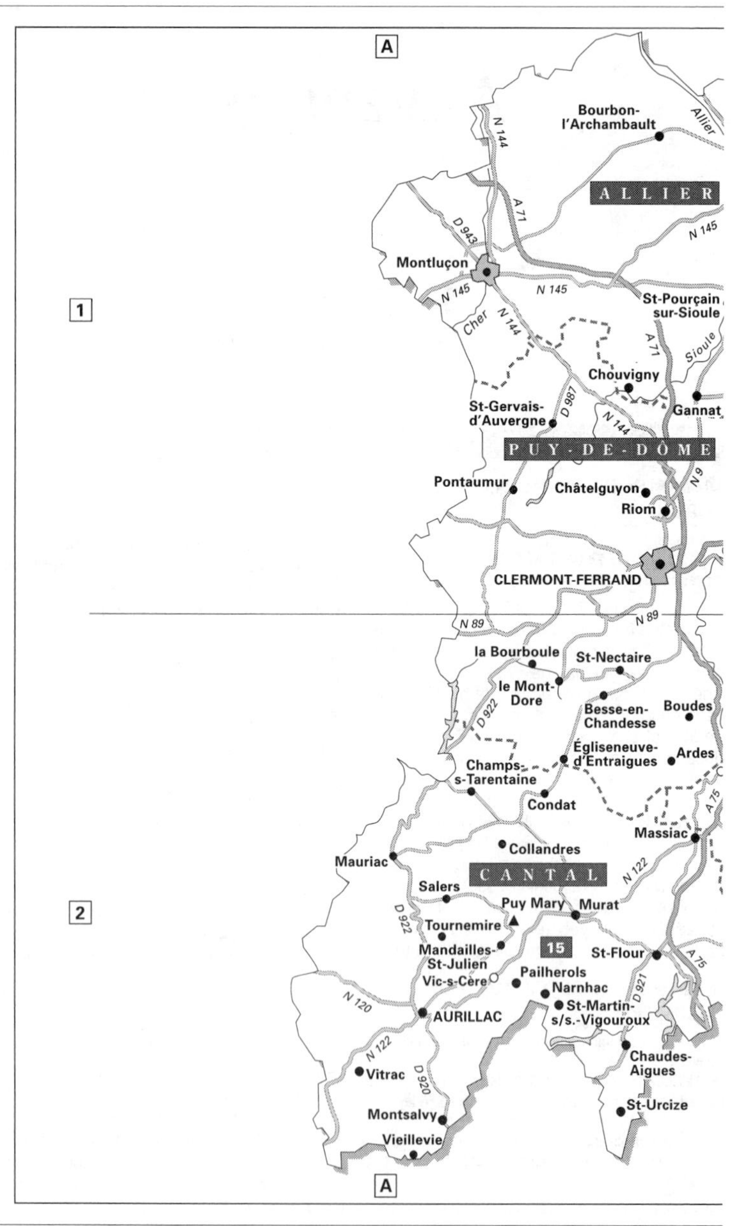
A
1
2
Bourbon-
l'Archambault
Allier
N 144
ALLIER
A 71
D 943
N 145
Montluçon
N 145
N 145
St-Pourçain
sur-Sioule
Cher
N 144
A 71
Sioule
Chouvigny
Gannat
St-Gervais-
d'Auvergne
D 987
N 144
PUY-DE-DÔME
N 9
Pontaumur
Châtelguyon
Riom
CLERMONT-FERRAND
N 89
N 89
la Bourboule
St-Nectaire
le Mont-
Dore
D 922
Besse-en-
Chandesse
Boudes
Égliseneuve-
d'Entraigues
Ardes
Champs-
s-Tarentaine
Condat
A 75
Massiac
Collandres
Mauriac
CANTAL
N 122
Salers
Puy Mary
Murat
D 922
Tournemire
Mandailles-
St-Julien
15
St-Flour
A 75
Vic-s-Cère
Pailherols
Narnhac
D 921
N 120
AURILLAC
St-Martin-
s/s.-Vigouroux
N 122
Chaudes-
Aigues
Vitrac
D 920
St-Urcize
Montsalvy
Vieillevie
A

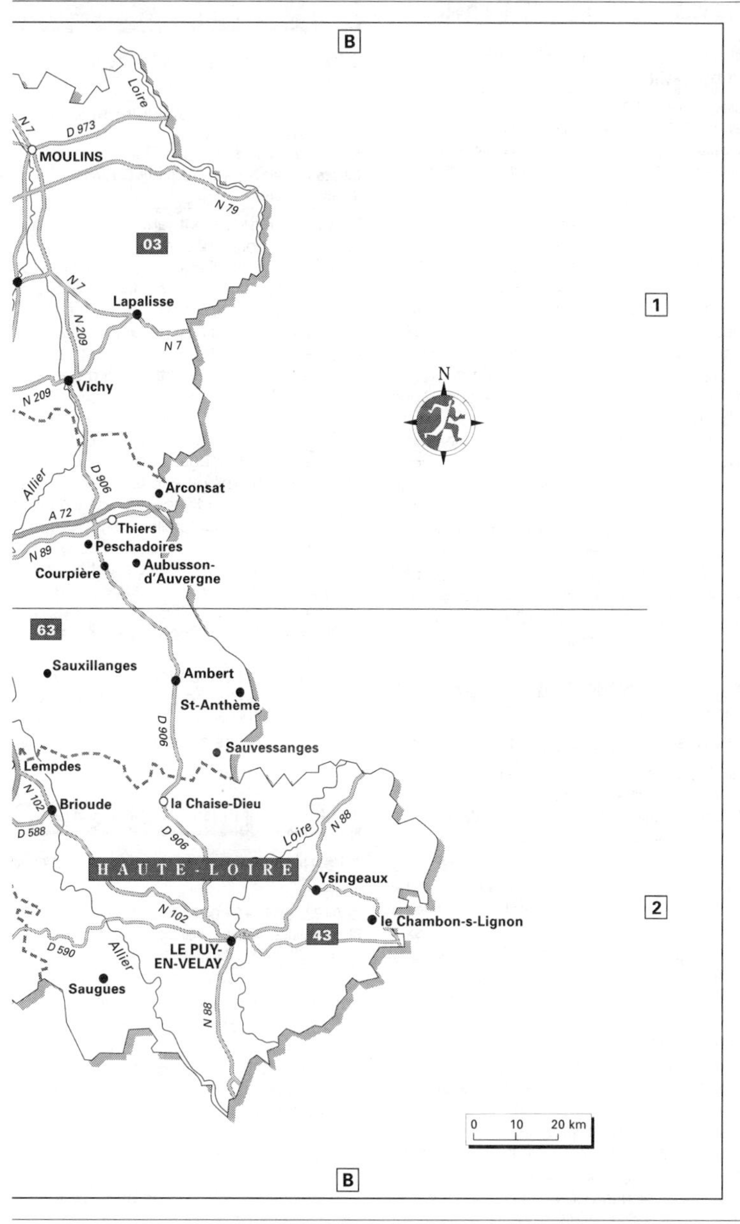
B
Loire
N 7
D 973
MOULINS
N 79
03
N 7
Lapalisse
N 209
N 7
1
N
Vichy
N 209
Allier
D 906
Arconsat
A 72
Thiers
N 89
Peschadoires
Courpière
Aubusson-d'Auvergne
63
Sauxillanges
Ambert
St-Anthème
D 906
Sauvessanges
Lempdes
N 102
Brioude
la Chaise-Dieu
D 588
D 906
Loire
N 88
HAUTE-LOIRE
Ysingeaux
N 102
le Chambon-s-Lignon
2
43
D 590
Allier
LE PUY-EN-VELAY
Saugues
N 88
0 10 20 km
B

VERTOLAYE 63480 (14KM NW)

HÔTEL-RESTAURANT DES VOYAGEURS**

Centre; take the D906.
☎ 04.73.95.20.16 F 04.75.95.23.85
Closed Friday evenings and Saturdays Nov–April, Saturday evenings May–June, and the first three weeks in October. **Secure parking. TV**.

Service noon–2pm and 7–9pm. You'll find this roadside hotel opposite the old railway station. It makes a pleasant stopping place, standing in its own grounds and with a swimming pool. The dining room is decorated with beautiful murals and painted in shades of dark green that echo the many trees on the mountains round about. In summer you've the choice of sitting out in the garden. Since it's well-known locally, we'd advise you to book in the high season and at the weekend. The good 115F set meal – warm *fourme d'Ambert* (a local cheese) with toast and salad, mutton tripe, cheese, and home-made dessert – offers a taste of traditional dishes. Classic dishes, served up in large portions feature in the gourmet set meals (150F and 200F). Clean comfortable bedrooms with shower/wc or bath 260–320F. Go for one overlooking the garden.

ARCONSAT 63250

10% L'AUBERGE DE MONTONCEL**

Les Cros d'Arconsat; take the N89 then the D86.
☎ 04.73.94.20.96 F 04.73.94.28.33
Closed Mondays Oct–May and Jan 1–30. **Car park. TV. Disabled access**.

Service noon–2.30pm and 7.30–9pm. This old building can be found in the heart of the forest just north of Chabreloche. The hotel's just alongside in the recently built annexe. The old-style dining room does a very substantial 60F *menu du jour* – the restaurant's own raw ham, lamb stew, a fine platter of mature cheese, and fresh fruit. Other set meals at 80F, 90F, 115F and 125F offer dishes like frog's legs, grilled crayfish, sirloin steak with *bleu d'Auvergne* (a local blue cheese), and fillet of duck flavoured with brandy and served with ceps. Your mouth waters just thinking about it! The hotel is simple, quiet and clean with bedrooms from 200F. Ask for number 4, 6 or 7, all of which have a balcony overlooking the pleasant garden.

ARDES-SUR-COUZE 63420

L'AUBERGE DE LA BARAQUE D'AUBIAT**

How to get there: D23 from Ardes in the direction of Anzat and drive for 11km.
☎ 04.73.71.74.33 F 04.73.71.74.99
Closed Wednesdays and in January. **Car park. Disabled access**.

Service noon–1.15pm and 7.30–8.30pm. You have to book out of season. This place is sheer heaven for hikers and people who love peace and quiet – it's an old farm, now completely refurbished, that stands on the Cézalier plateau south of Puy-de-Dôme. The owners, who have made the most of the restaurant's rustic style, offer their guests two set meals. The 68F one (not available Sunday lunchtimes) consists of generous portions of simple traditional dishes – good house *terrines*, stuffed cabbage, cheese and home-made fruit tart. The other one, at 95F, is a bit more elaborate and includes an excellent guinea fowl with chanterelle mushrooms. The comfortable bedrooms are both cosy – the beds come with duvets – and practical (some have a mezzanine, which is ideal if you have children). Doubles 175F with shower/wc, 220F with bath. Good-sized breakfasts including a selection of wonderful home-made jams cost 30F and 32F. You'll receive a very friendly welcome and good advice on day trips. Basic hostel-type accommodation available for hikers at a cost of 45F per person.

AUBUSSON-D'AUVERGNE 63120

HÔTEL-RESTAURANT AU BON COIN

Centre.
☎ 04.73.53.55.78 F 04.73.53.56.29
Closed Sunday evenings and Mondays out of season, and Dec 20–Jan 20. **Car park**.

This little inn with its pleasant country style décor can get a bit noisy when the big dining room's opened up to accommodate coach parties. The proprietor/chef uses quality ingredients in his cooking and serves up generous portions of things like poached trout with a crayfish sauce, duck breast with calvados (yummy!), *entre-deux* of veal with a cream sauce, and fillets of zander with Cahors wine (yummy again!) You should also try the house *terrines* and, for afters, the delicious pear in puff pastry with raspberry *coulis* – and don't miss out on the crayfish season on any account. There are a few rooms available – 100F with basin and 200F with shower/wc. You'll feel quite at home here. And far away from the madding crowd.

AURILLAC 15000

10% HÔTEL-RESTAURANT LES JARDINS DU PALAIS**

4-6 rue Beauclair (Centre); behind the Palais de Justice
☎ 04.71.48.24.86 F 04.71.64.97.92
Closed Sundays and Christmas/New Year holidays.
Secure parking. **TV**. **Canal+**.

A simple quiet hotel that has conventional bedrooms with bath, TV and phone. Number 8 sleeps four people and looks onto the patio. Half-board 270F a day per person. As far as food is concerned, the restaurant offers a fairly substantial "taste of Auvergne" set meal for 100F and another set meal at 120F. If you'd rather go à la carte, the restaurant's specialities are calf's head, veal sweetbreads with ceps, and a duo of scallops and salmon.

10% HÔTEL-RESTAURANT DELCHER**

20 rue des Carmes (West).
☎ 04.71.48.01.69 F 04.71.48.86.66
Closed Sunday evenings, the second fortnight in July, and between Christmas and New Year's Day.
Secure parking. **TV**. **Canal+**.

Service noon–2pm and 7–9pm. This friendly family hotel, centrally located in a busy street, is very well looked after and has an efficient professional staff. Doubles 250F, 280F for three. There are two adjoining rooms (390F), which families will probably find useful but you'll have to book these ahead of time. There are paintings by Danish artist Gorn Hansen, in one of the bedrooms and in the lounge – he often paid his bills with a picture. Regional specialities take centre stage in the restaurant – *truffade* (potato cake with *Cantal* cheese), rib steak with *bleu d'Auvergne* cheese (the meat is from the famous Salers breed), *pounti* (a mixture of bacon and Swiss chard), mutton tripe, *Cantal* (yet another local cheese) in puff pastry, salmon with pink peppercorns, and monkfish *osso bucco*. Set meals 75F, 93F and 135F.

10% GRAND HÔTEL DE BORDEAUX***

2 av. de la République.
☎ 04.71.48.01.84 F 04.71.48.49.93
Closed Dec 20–Jan 7. **Car park**. **TV**. **Canal+**.

A charming hotel with lots of character located in the centre of town. You'll be welcomed with great courtesy and in a very professional manner. Bedrooms are exceptionally comfortable and cost 395F with shower/wc and 445F with bath. You'll get a good view of the Palais de Justice garden from number 234. Stylish bar and lounges and a good breakfast.

LE BISTRO – CABARET LICENCE IV;

Corner of avenue Gambetta and rue Paul-Doumer (Centre).
☎ 04.71.48.01.04 F 04.71.48.92.08

Here's a find – a bistro that's open every day until 11pm! The décor is modern, vaguely hi-tech, and the lighting, thankfully, is dim. You'll get non-stop service here, and very decent classic cooking served up in generous portions. Good choice of meat. The day's special plus dessert costs 55F. Some days they have a lively cabaret in the basement.

L'ARSÈNE

24 rue Arsène-Vermenouze (Centre).
☎ 04.71.48.48.97
Closed lunchtimes, Mondays, and two weeks in July.

Service 7–10.30pm. The warm and cosy dining room, with its exposed stonework and modern paintings which go so well together, is very popular with the local youngsters, who flock here for the cheap hearty dishes on offer. The restaurant specializes in *fondue*, top rump of beef, *tartiflette*, and either pork fillet or breast of duck for cooking yourself on a hot stone. Unfortunately, all of these goodies are for two people but if you're on your own, you can vent your frustration on the wonderful onion soup (it's the genuine article) and traditional grills. Mixed salads (they're pretty big) and savoury tarts are also available. Set meals 68F (except Saturday evenings and public holidays) and 110F. Wines are reasonably priced – the house wine, for example, is 45F and Côte-d'Auvergne 59F.

LE TERROIR DU CANTAL-AUBERGE FROMAGÈRE AUVERGNATE

rue du Buis – place des Docks.
☎ 04.71.64.31.26
Closed Sundays and Mondays (not the Bouchon Fromager).

Service noon–2.30pm and 7–10pm. This delightful restaurant, which specializes in local cooking, has just opened up in the old part of town known as Saint-Géraud – an area that's starting to become popular again – on the street famous for its cheese. It's decorated in conventional country style but there's a good atmosphere and a large choice à la carte – *pavé du Cantal* (breaded Cantal cheese with local ham), salad of *cabecou* (goat's cheese) and honey, *pounti*, (a mixture of bacon and Swiss chard) Cantal cheese tart, *truffade* (that's potato cake with *Cantal* cheese and very tasty it was too!), stuffed cabbage, and *gâteau à la tomme* (a mild cheese). Prices are moderate. Wine by the glass is 10–40F and they even had a Saint-Pourçain at 45.50F. If you're in a bit of a rush or not very hungry, try the wine and cheese place next door, "Le Bouchon fromager", owned by the same people – top quality cheese and very drinkable wines from some tiny vineyards. There's also a pleasant terrace. Expect to spend a maximum of 70F for a full meal.

LE POTAGER D'AURINQUES

24 rue Arsène-Vermenouze.
☎ 04.71.48.17.18
Closed Sundays and Monday lunchtimes.

You'll receive a friendly welcome here. The décor is low-key and they serve traditional dishes re-interpreted in a slightly more refined vein. The à la carte dishes reflect the changing seasons – there's cod with *lardons*, thin slivers of duck with cider and honey vinegar, calf's head, kidneys with mustard seeds, and lightly salted leg of duck with lentils. Set meals 95–160F. The wine list is fairly limited. Wine is also available by the glass.

SANSAC DE MARMIESSE 15130 (8KM)

LA BELLE ÉPOQUE

Les Fargues; take the RN122 – it's well signposted
☎ 04.71.62.87.87
Closed Sunday evenings and Mondays (except in July and August), and in January.

The restaurant is a restored farmhouse deep in the country near the tiny villages of Haut-Cros and Labattude. The large dining room is decorated in the style of the Belle Époque (as you'd probably guessed from the name) – a welcome change from the country look. Its reputation has grown by word of mouth and it's almost always full, even on a weekday evening out of season. It has a lively atmosphere, very friendly staff and great local cooking. Prices are very reasonable, with set meals at 65F (weekdays), 95F, 120F, and 150F. They use fresh produce and soft fruit and vegetables from the garden depending on the season. À la carte, there are classic dishes like roast farm-bred veal with garlic and sherry vinegar, *cassoulet*, mutton tripe, duck breast with green peppercorns, cep omelette, and *coq au vin* (the wine here being from Cahors). The terrace is very pleasant in fine weather.

POLMINHAC 15800 (14KM E)

LE BERGANTY

place de l'Église; take the N122.
☎ 04.71.47.47.47
Closed Saturdays and Sundays, reservations only summer weekends.

The square is superb with its church and houses with their roofs of "lauzes" (flat stones). And the dining room's absolutely wonderful! It has an old polished sideboard, a massive table positioned in front of the fireplace, and large bouquets of flowers from the garden. You can have trout with bacon, *truffade* (potato cake with *Cantal* cheese) or ham at any time but if you take the trouble to order ahead you can have stuffed cabbage, *pounti* (a mixture of bacon and Swiss chard) or *potée auvergnate* (the hearty local soup). There are some rather nice house specialities such as rabbit with prunes and carrots, and shoulder of beef. The young owner has a natural flair for making people feel welcome and the quality of the ingredients is high. The meat, for example, comes from the local butcher who makes trips into the countryside to choose his animals on the hoof. *Menu du jour* 75F.

BESSE-EN-CHANDESSE 63610

HÔTEL-RESTAURANT LE CLOS**

La Villetour.
☎ 04.73.79.52.77 F→ 04.73.79.56.67
Closed Oct 1–Dec 19, and March 23–April 10.
Car park. TV.

This modern establishment, a bit out of the town centre, offers a wide range of facilities – indoor pool, well-equipped gym, Turkish bath, and games room. Bedrooms are pleasant and very clean. Doubles 230F with shower/wc and 240F with bath. The owners want to make sure guests get the most out of their stay and can provide lots of suggestions for excursions and walks. Set meals cost 88F, 98F, 135F and 140F. The food is decent enough but there are no surprises.

SUPER-BESSE 63610 (7KM W)

RESTAURANT LA BERGERIE

route de Vassivières (West); take the D149.

☎ 04.73.79.61.06
Closed Sept 15–Dec 15 (except during the November school holidays). Open Easter weekend–mid-June and every day the rest of the year.

If you come here and don't try the *truffade* (potato cake with *Cantal* cheese), you'll be committing a crime in the eyes of the average native of Auvergne. The young owner will serve you a hearty portion straight from the frying pan, together with some of the local ham, for 68F. And this most traditional of dishes, which is satisfying to say the least, is such a delight that it's well worth the 30-minute wait. And what's more, we're sure it's made to order – not surprising then that it's one of the very best we've tried in the region. You'll find everything you want in the set meals at 90F, 125F and 155F – pig's trotters in puff pastry, *croustillant* of veal sweetbreads, *chausson* of frog's legs, Salers (the local beef) with *tomme* (a mild cheese), duck breast with honey, and fantastic cabbage stuffed with trout. What's more, you'll feel quite at home in this country inn with its delightful décor and atmosphere. It's becoming more and more popular, in winter as well as in summer, when you can eat on the terrace overlooking the lake.

BOUDES 63340

10% 🏠 🍽 LE BOUDES LA VIGNE**

place de la Mairie.
☎ 04.73.96.55.66 📠 04.73.96.55.55
Closed Sunday evenings, Mondays, Jan 2–24, and one week late Aug–early Sept. **TV**.

Service noon–2pm and 7.30–10pm. This little hotel-cum-restaurant in the centre of a small wine-growing village south of Puy-de-Dôme was our all-time favourite in the area. The building has been pleasantly renovated, we got a nice welcome, and the cooking was quite delightful. The cheapest set meal of the day (served lunchtimes) costs 70F; others 105–230F. However, you'll have a hard time choosing between *ravioles* of snail with a garlic sauce, *blanquette* of chicken with honey, *croustillant* of *rascasse* with herb butter, and quail wrapped in vine leaves with rosemary. But we had no trouble when it came to dessert – we just couldn't resist the peach soup with fresh mint. And, since we're right in the midst of the best vineyards of the Auvergne, you can imagine the kind of wine list they have. Wine's also served by the glass. The hotel was built only recently and is very quiet. Doubles 180F with shower/wc.

BOURBON-L'ARCHAMBAULT 03160

🏠 🍽 LES TROIS PUITS*

rue des Trois-Puits (Centre).
☎ 04.70.67.08.35 📠 04.70.67.06.05
Closed Dec–end Feb; restaurant closed Sunday evenings and Mondays. **Secure parking. Disabled access.**

The village well was where people bumped into their neighbours and caught up with all the news and this inn is aptly named ("puits" means "well") since you'll get a cordial welcome and find a convivial atmosphere. Rooms are comfortable and bathrooms are large. Doubles 110F with basin/wc and 140F with bath. You might think you're in one of Simenon's novels when you walk into the restaurant – it's so very like the kind of thing he describes that he must surely have written bits of his *Maigret* stories here. They do good plain traditional cooking with dishes like *confit* of duck, veal kidneys with port, trout with bacon, and duck breast with bilberries. Set meals 55F (weekdays), 85F and 110F.

10% 🏠 🍽 GRAND HÔTEL MONTESPAN-TALLEYRAND**

1-3 place des Thermes (Centre).
☎ 04.70.67.00.24 📠 04.70.67.12.00
Closed late Oct–early April. **Secure parking**. **TV**. **Disabled access**

A superb hotel housed in a fine building and full of old-fashioned charm. It's an oasis of peace and quiet – there are reading rooms and card rooms with lots of velvet and tapestries, a bright flower-filled dining room, and a pool amongst the greenery of the French-style garden. You'll also be delighted by the bedrooms – tastefully and stylishly decorated – some of which are more like suites. Doubles 190F with basin/wc, 294F with shower/wc, and 360F with bath. Very reasonable, given the standard of accommodation. Although the restaurant sticks to the old favourites – calf's head *gribiche*, fillet of *charolais*, rabbit in mustard sauce, and *coq au vin* (the wine in this case being Saint-Pourçain) – the cooking is still worth the trip. Set meals 95F (weekdays), 110F, 130F and 160F. Half-board 237–310F per day per person. Add to that the friendly staff and the excellent service and you'll see why we're so fond of the *Grand Hôtel*.

SAINT-BONNET-TRONÇAIS 03360 (23KM NW)

🏠 🍽 LE TRONÇAIS**

Rond de Tronçais; take the N144, then the D978 in the

direction of the forest of Tronçais as far as the Rond de Tronçais, and it's 3km south of Saint-Bonnet-Tronçais.
☎ 04.70.06.11.95 F➜ 04.70.06.16.15
Closed Sunday evenings, Mondays out of season, and mid-Nov–mid-March. **Car park**. **TV**.

Service noon–1.30pm and 7.30–9pm. Peace and quiet are the ideal words to describe what you'll get in this lakeside hotel. But it's so pleasant that you'll have to add charm and comfort too if you're going to give the full picture. Mind you, the setting has a lot to do with it. The forest of Tronçais, one of the oldest and most beautiful in France, turns every shade of green in spring and every shade of yellow, red and brown in autumn. Spacious bedrooms, with doubles 273–361F. The restaurant is strong on traditional local dishes like snails with walnuts, chicken *à la bourbonnaise*, terrine of eel with blackberries, pike with Saint-Pourçain, and veal cutlet with ceps. Set meals 100F, 140F and 180F. The two dining rooms are very elegantly and tastefully decorated, and the staff are delightful. Pleasant view of the grounds and surrounding countryside.

TRONGET 03240 (23KM S)

HÔTEL DU COMMERCE**

D945; take the D1 towards Montet.
☎ 04.70.47.12.95 F➜ 04.70.47.32.53 **Car park**. **TV**.

Here's a hotel that's full of contrasts. On the one hand, it's practically brand new and has comfortable, modern, and well-equipped bedrooms. Doubles 250–290F with shower/wc and TV. It still feels pretty new and the rooms are a bit lacking in character, but the restaurant more than makes up for that. Monsieur Auberger serves traditional local dishes, including lamb *au Bourbonnais* with thyme, frog's legs, duck *confit* with ceps and *coq au vin*. Set meals 70F, 95F, 110F, 140F and 170F.

BOURBOULE (LA) 63150

10% AVIATION HÔTEL**

rue de Metz.
☎ 04.73.65.50.50 F➜ 04.73.81.02.85
Closed Oct 1–Dec 20. **TV**. Private garage, for which there's a 25F charge.

This hotel with its all-white rather retro-style façade has been welcoming holidaymakers from all walks of life and people here to take the waters since 1935 – perhaps that explains the slight air of nostalgia. It's still doing things right though and has 51 very pleasant rooms – some of them pretty plush – to suit all budgets. Doubles 140F with washing facilities, 160F with shower, and 270–400F with shower/wc or bath. Don't forget there's also an annexe! There's a beautiful swimming pool, a gym and if you want to make up for any weight you lose in there, try out the food in the restaurant – a bit pedestrian but good enough. Set meals 69–99F.

10% HÔTEL-RESTAURANT LES FLEURS**

av. Gueneau-de-Mussy.
☎ 04.73.81.09.44 F➜ 04.73.65.52.03
Closed Oct 10–Feb 1 (except Christmas holidays). **Secure parking**. **TV**.

Service 12.15–1.15pm and 7.15–8.30pm. It's in a quiet area but it IS by the road. It looks like a chalet and every bedroom has a balcony with a magnificent view of the valley and plateau of Charlanne. Rooms are clean and very well looked after. Doubles 170F with basin, 210–280F with shower/wc and 260–320F with bath. Service with a smile here. There's also a restaurant providing meals from 90F. Good cooking, lots of *terrines* – try the salt pork and lentil one with basil sauce. Duck wings with sweet peppers also available.

10% HÔTEL LE CHARLET**

94 bd Louis-Chousy.
☎ 04.73.81.33.00 F➜ 04.73.65.50.82
Closed mid-Oct–end Dec. **Secure parking**. **TV**.

Service noon–2pm and 7–9pm. *Le Charlet* is situated in a quiet residential area – but then the whole town is quiet and residential! We rather liked this family-run hotel, maybe because they don't play up the health farm side too much. The décor in the 38 pleasant bedrooms is a bit bland but they come equipped with modern facilities. Doubles with shower/wc overlooking the street 220F, with bath and a mountain view 340F. There's a very nice pool (we've heard it's got a wave machine!) with a Turkish bath and a gym. The cooking tends to be traditional and local, with dishes like *coq au vin*, stuffed trout and rabbit *terrine* with hazelnuts. Set meals 95–165F.

BRIOUDE 43100

10% HÔTEL DE LA POSTE ET CHAMPANNE*

1 bd du Docteur-Devins (Ouest).
☎ 04.71.50.14.62 F➜ 04.71.50.10.55
Closed Sunday evenings Oct–June, also Jan 2–31. **Secure parking**. **TV**.

Service noon–2pm and 7.30–9pm. This is an old country hotel that's been updated to suit modern tastes. The bar's still there on the ground floor. The bedrooms facing the street are rather noisy, while those in the annexe at the back are very quiet. Expect to spend 240F for a double with shower/wc (or bath) and balcony, and 160F for one with shower (wc on the landing) overlooking the street. The restaurant on the first floor has long had a reputation for good food and does a number of set meals (72–190F) and also à la carte. The 72F one (not available Sundays) offers traditional unpretentious and good food and dessert is followed by a large platter of local cheese and a basket of fruit, something that's becoming increasingly rare. But the star attraction around here is the owner – he's a jolly, chubby guy with a ruddy face and a glint in his eye. Followed by the waitresses, he serves up the food himself in the same simple yet imaginative way that innkeepers used to. If you want bigger helpings all you have to do is ask! It's because he's so natural that the restaurant still has a soul and hasn't turned into one of those chic formal places.

HÔTEL LE BAUDIÈRE – RESTAURANT LE VIEUX FOUR**

Saint-Bauzire; it's 8km west of Brioude before Saint-Bauzire, at the D588 and D17 junction.
☎ 04.71.76.81.70 F 04.71.76.80.66
Closed Dec 26–Jan 26; restaurant closed Mondays. **Secure parking**. **TV**. **Canal+**. **Disabled access**.

A pleasant modern hotel with sauna, indoor and outdoor swimming pools, and very comfy bedrooms. Doubles with bath, TV and satellite channels 270F. Right next door is the restaurant, which has a handsome stone oven in the main dining room. We really liked the grilled meat, the escalope of veal sweetbreads with mushrooms, the seafood *choucroute*, the lentils with morels, the *crépinette* of pig's trotters and the *crème brûlée*. Set meals 90F, 130F and 170F. It's quite well-known since some of the better-off customers arrive by helicopter. There's a landing strip nearby.

LAVAUDIEU 43100 (9KM SE)

AUBERGE DE L'ABBAYE

Centre.
☎ 04.71.76.44.44
Closed Sunday evenings, and Monday evenings July 15–Aug 31. **Car park**.

Service noon–1.30pm and 7.30–9pm. This charming village inn is in the little street facing the church. It has a country-style interior (complete with log fires in winter) and has been very nicely renovated and decorated. The carefully prepared traditional dishes, based on local produce, include zander with thyme, monkfish with raw ham, and ling with sorrel. Set meals 95F, 135F and 180F. In summer, there's also one at 75F but it's only available at lunchtime. And here's something new – a *menu forfait* at 110F which includes a visit to the cloister and museum.

VILLENEUVE-D'ALLIER 43380 (14KM S)

10% HOSTELLERIE SAINT-VERNY*

Route D585; from Brioude go towards the gorges of Allier and Lavoute-Chilhac.
☎ 04.71.74.73.77 F 04.71.74.74.20
Closed Dec 1–April 1. **Secure parking**.

Located a few kilometres from the wonderful village of Lavoute-Chilhac, here's a genuine country inn that's simple and very well-kept. It stands on the south bank of the Allier across from the romantic ruin of the château of Saint-Ilpize. Bedrooms look onto the street (250F) or have a wonderful view of the valley. They're small and well laid out and there are bunkbeds for people with children. To make the most of the views, ask for a room with a balcony like no.7 (300F for two). The food in the restaurant is cooked the way it should be and dishes are based largely on local produce. Set meals 80F, 100F and 120F; à la carte also available. The house speciality is the 50F *plateau du vigneron* – grilled Cantal cheese, local ham and a salad with walnut oil. There's a bar on the ground floor and a quiet terrace at the back. It faces the garden and you can enjoy your meals there in the summer. We'd advise you to take half-board at 250–280F per person per day. Lots of things to do.

CHAVANIAC-LAFAYETTE 43230 (27KM SE)

10% HÔTEL-RESTAURANT LAFAYETTE*

Centre; take the N102 after Saint-Georges-d'Aurac, turn left onto the D513 then continue ahead for 2km.
☎ 04.71.77.50.38 F 04.71.77.54.90
Closed Jan–Feb. **Secure parking**.

This very nice family hotel is in the village where General Lafayette, one of the heroes of the American War of Independence, was born. In the ground-floor bar there's a sprightly old lady pouring drinks for the regulars, and you'll find the adjoining restaurant, which is simple and impeccably clean, quite inviting. The bedrooms too are simple, unpretentious and very well kept. Numbers 10 and 11 overlook the Lafayette château. Doubles range in price from 160F (bathroom on the landing) to 225F (with shower/wc or bath). The restaurant does set meals at 55F (not available Sundays), 85F and 130F. The chef's specialities are veal kidneys and veal sweetbreads with mushrooms. Prices very reasonable and staff very friendly.

CHAISE-DIEU (LA) 43160

HÔTEL LE LION D'OR**

av. de la Gare.
☎ 04.71.00.01.58 F 04.71.00.08.84
Closed Mondays end Sept–Easter and two weeks in January. **TV**.

Service noon–2pm and 7–9.30pm. This place, which is very central, being opposite the tourist information office and the abbey, is better known as a restaurant, though it's a hotel too. The chef uses regional produce including wild mushrooms and serves up large portions of hearty dishes like lentil and cep soup, ceps in puff pastry and fried wild mushrooms. Tasty satisfying meals. Judging by the glowing reports from various foreign singers and musicians who've called in during the festival, it seems there are no cultural barriers when it comes to good food. It has 15 impeccably clean rooms with shower/wc or bath and telephone. Doubles 200–260F. Set meals 65–175F.

10% HÔTEL DE LA CASADEÏ**

place de l'Abbaye (Centre); it's near the stairs to the abbey.
☎ 04.71.00.00.58 F 04.71.00.01.67
Closed Nov–April. **TV**.

Service noon–2.30pm and 7–9pm. It's only open in summer because heavy snowfalls make the roads impassable in winter. It has twelve nicely furnished rooms at prices ranging from 210F to 280F for a double(200F in May, June and Oct) and 190F for a single. The most attractive ones have a view of the abbey but they're also the most expensive. A little terrace at the back. There's also a restaurant serving *potée auvergnate* (a thick local soup), omelette of chanterelle mushrooms, mutton tripe, and *truffade* (potato cake with *Cantal* cheese). Three set meals – 75F, 90F and 110F. Staff are friendly. All those photos, by the way, are of artists who've stayed at the hotel during the town's festival of sacred music.

10% HÔTEL-RESTAURANT DE L'ÉCHO ET DE L'ABBAYE**

place de l'Écho (Centre).
☎ 04.71.00.00.45 F 04.71.00.00.22
Closed Oct 13–May 1; restaurant closed lunchtimes.
Car park. **TV**.

This delightful inn will be fully booked during the festival. We would need about ten pages to list all the famous people who stay here when the festival's on but if you want to know who they are, ask the owner – she's well up on the subject. The very handsome dining room with its antiques and Louis XIII décor is housed in the former monastery kitchens. Eleven bedrooms available, with doubles costing 300–360F. Number 7 (310F) has a wonderful view of the abbey but numbers. 9, 11 and 15 aren't too bad either. Set meals (95–170F) include dishes such as fillet steak with *fourme d'Ambert* (a type of blue cheese), mutton tripe, Puy lentils and verbena icecream.

CHOMELIX 43500 (15KM SE)

10% AUBERGE DE L'ARZON**

How to get there: take the D906 then the D135.
☎ 04.71.03.62.35 F 04.71.03.61.62 **Closed** Monday evenings and Tuesdays out of season, and Nov 11–Easter (beginning of April). **TV**. **Disabled access**.

Service noon–1.45pm and 7.30–9.15pm. This is a good village inn and the restaurant is extremely popular in the area. You'd be wise to book ahead in summer, especially during the music festival in La Chaise. The bedrooms are impeccable and situated in a quiet modern annexe with shower/wc upstairs and bathroom downstairs. Expect to pay 245–300F for a double. Set meals 98–230F. The restaurant uses local produce in carefully prepared local dishes of the kind that need long slow cooking. It also has some excellent fish and a good selection of home-made desserts. Decent service.

PONTEMPEYRAT 43500 (25KM E)

HÔTEL-RESTAURANT MISTOU***

take the D498.
☎ 04.77.50.62.46 F 04.77.50.66.70
Restaurant closed lunchtimes (except weekends), public holidays, and July 1–Aug 31.
Car park. **TV**. **Disabled access**.

The surroundings, deep in the beautiful valley of the Ance, are as bucolic as you could hope for. The river runs past fir trees at the bottom of the garden, which is a delight in springtime. There used to be a watermill down there, built around 1730, and an old turbine was recovered and nowadays still produces enough electricity for the hotel lighting. From the outside the hotel looks a bit new and functional but it's very well laid out inside. The rooms are enormous, quiet and perfectly decorated. The ones with a view of the garden were our favourites. There are seventeen rooms in all, ranging in price from 280F for one in the annexe to 540F. The stylish dining room has set meals 125–315F. Trout features in quite a few dishes, including a thick fish soup, and you should also try the *craquelin* of salmon with bacon and the *tournedos* of milk-fed veal with crayfish.

CHAMBON-SUR-LIGNON (LE) 43400

10% ☗ |●| HÔTEL LE BOIS VIALOTTE**

Le Bois Vialotte; from Chambon take the D151 going towards Le Mazet, then turn left on to the route de la Suchère and left again onto a smaller road (there will be a signpost).
☎ 04.71.59.74.03
Closed Sept 30–May 1. **Car park.**

It's surrounded by pine woods and meadows and stands in 15 acres of beautiful grounds but it's more like a family guest house out in the country than a country house hotel or a country inn. The proprietress – an attentive but unobtrusive hostess – takes great pride in looking after this recently built house. The décor of the simple bedrooms is a bit old-fashioned but they're comfortable and very clean. Expect to spend 190–320F for a double where you can be sure of peace and quiet with a view out over the fields and the trees. The restaurant offers home cooking and simple traditional dishes. Meals 75–100F. We'd advise you to take half-board (particularly with an evening meal) since the hotel is rather isolated, but it's not compulsory. A good place with reasonable prices if you're planning on spending some time in the area.

10% ☗ |●| HÔTEL-RESTAURANT LA PLAGE*

rue de la Grande-Fontaine (Centre).
☎ 04.71.59.70.56
Closed Oct–end April. **Car park.**

Despite the name, it's peace and quiet you'll find here, not a beach. Big smiles from the staff when you arrive and you'll find the other guests – most of them boarders – don't disturb you at all. Everything's been well thought out. Doubles 270F with shower/wc, 240F with bath. It's a teeny bit kitschy (the bed covers!) but apart from that it's a very nice place with genuine people.. Set meals (75–110F) offer honest provincial dishes such as mousse of chicken livers and port, frog's legs in a saffron sauce, and trout with almonds.There are two terraces that give you a view of the river.

TENCE 43190 (8.5KM N)

☗ |●| CAFÉ-RESTAURANT BROLLES

Mas-de-Tence.
☎ 04.71.65.42.91

It'd be a good idea to book in advance. The flower-filled restaurant has been tastefully decorated and the stone floor makes the place feel nice and cool. Sit at the round table beside the fireplace and enjoy home-made *saucisson* and an omelette made from eggs laid by their own hens. Everything's good, from the sautéd baby potatoes to the lentils, and the snails are absolute perfection. People come from miles around for the oven-cooked dishes and the ewe's milk cheese, which is eaten warm. Set meals 60–150F. Simple but clean rooms 110F a night for two people; breakfast 20F.

CHAMPS-SUR-TARENTAINE 15270

10% ☗ |●| L'AUBERGE DU VIEUX CHÊNE**

34 route des Lacs.
☎ 04.71.78.71.64 Fax 04.71.78.70.88
Closed Sunday evenings and Mondays (except in July and August), also Nov 15–March 15. **Car park. TV.**

Service noon–1.30pm and 7–8.30pm. *L'Auberge du Vieux Chêne* is a haven of peace and warmth in an old renovated farm in northern Cantal. Bedrooms have been nicely done up in bright cheerful colours and they all come with bath. Doubles cost 330F. There's a wonderful and enormous fireplace on the back wall of the restaurant, and though the dining room's on the large side it feels intimate because of the way it's laid out. Set meals cost 90F (available Sundays), 140F, 170F and 250F and feature regional specialities alongside more classical dishes. Try the delicious snails in puff pastry, the equally tasty veal sweetbreads with morels, or the trout with local ham. It's a pity the vegetables aren't presented quite as nicely as the dishes they come with. Attentive and courteous service. There's also a very pleasant garden.

MARCHAL 15270 (5KM NE)

HÔTEL-RESTAURANT L'AUBERGE DE L'EAU VERTE

Centre; take the D679 then the D22.
☎ 04.71.78.71.48
Closed for a fortnight in February. **Car park**.

The village is near Champs and this traditional little inn stands on a small hill beside the church. You'll get a super friendly welcome. The *menu du jour* costs 60F (120F on Sundays) and "taste of Auvergne" set meals (which you'll have to order ahead of time) offer a delicious plate of cold meat, *truffade*, (potato cake with Cantal cheese), salad, cheese and dessert. The 100F regional set meal offers substantial portions of well prepared dishes. There are a few bedrooms (some were refurbished in 1996) and prices start at 170F. Full board 220F, half-board 170F. A good place to indulge in traditional Auvergne cuisine.

CHÂTELGUYON 63140

10% HÔTEL-RESTAURANT CASTEL RÉGINA**

rue de Brocqueville.
☎ 04.73.86.00.15 ➡ 04.73.86.19.44
Closed end Sept–May.

Service 12.15pm and 7.15pm. This is a beautiful stylish spa hotel. The Belle Époque décor gives it a delightful old-fashioned charm, and it has the relaxed atmosphere of a place where time seems to stand still. You'll receive a charming welcome with a personal touch. The guests seem to have come out of the same mould as the hotel – mind you, people don't come to Châtelguyon for the nightlife! Clean well-kept bedrooms 130F with washing facilities, 160F with shower/wc, 185F with bath. Full board 300–400F per person. The 72F *menu du jour* features the type of dishes you'd find at a health farm.

10% LES CHÊNES**

15 rue Guy-de-Maupassant; take the D985.
☎ 04.73.86.02.88 ➡ 04.73.86.46.60
Closed Jan 1–March 15. **Car park. TV**.

Service 12.30–2pm and 7.30–10pm. This is a good restaurant a bit out of the way in the old village of Châtelguyon. It's lovely in fine weather when you can eat on the terrace. Refined classic cooking with a *menu du jour* at 60F, and three gourmet ones at 97F, 120F and 145F. The rooms are quiet and pleasant but there aren't many of them so it's a good idea to book ahead. Doubles 180F with basin/wc, 220F with shower/wc. The owner's charming and full of life – she's quite a tonic.

LE CANTALOU*

17 rue du Lac-Saint-Hippolyte; on the D985 – leave Châtelguyon and head for Saint-Hippolyte.
☎ 04.73.86.04.67 ➡ 04.73.86.24.36
Closed Oct 15–Easter; restaurant closed Monday lunchtimes (except for guests). **Car park**.

This little family guest house, a bit off the beaten track, is well-known for its welcome and value for money. Bedrooms are clean and well-kept although the décor is a bit old-fashioned. Doubles 190F with shower/wc, 210F with bath. The restaurant serves generous helpings of simple food. Set meals 65–96F. The chicken *à l'auvergnate* (stewed in white wine) is excellent.

RESTAURANT LA POTÉE

34 av. Baraduc.
☎ 04.73.86.06.60
Closed Oct–end March.

This is the great kind of little restaurant you only seem to find in the deepest darkest part of the provinces nowadays. The owner, who's larger than life, tends to the needs of her guests from her position behind the bar. You can sit at the bistro style tables, covered with red and white checked tablecloths, and sample classic dishes such as *andouillettes* (a type of sausage), mutton tripe, *truffade* (a kind of potato cake with Cantal cheese), pork knuckle and trout with bacon – the kind of thing that does the waistline no good at all. Expect to spend about 70F.

CHAUDES-AIGUES 15110

10% HÔTEL LA RÉSIDENCE*

16 av. Georges-Pompidou (Centre).
☎ 04.71.23.51.89 ➡ 04.71.23.92.81
Closed Tuesdays Feb 15–April 30, and Nov 15–Feb 15. **TV**.

Located in the main street, this friendly hotel provides comfortable and attractive rooms – 170F with basin/wc, 220F with shower/wc and direct phone, 230F with bath and direct phone. Light sleepers are advised to take a room at the back. Delightful welcome. The restaurant offers set meals at 65F, 110F, 120F, 150F and 180F and dishes like *coq au vin*, duck breast with cider, trout with bacon, pig's trotters *à l'auvergnate* and snails with ceps.

HÔTEL AUX BOUILLONS D'OR**

10 quai du Remontalou (Centre).
☎ 04.71.23.51.42
Closed Sunday evenings, Wednesdays, and Jan 1–March 1. **TV**.

Service noon–2pm and 7–9.30pm. This is a conventional well-kept hotel, set back from the main street. You'll get a courteous welcome. Bedrooms (180–270F) are comfortable and come with TV and telephone. Set meals 65F, 85F, 95F, 130F and 160F. The restaurant offers classical cooking that's in keeping with the style of hotel and dishes like *briochin* with Cantal cheese, *aligot saucisse* (mashed potatoes and cheese with sausage), local mutton tripe, *paupiettes* of chicken and green cabbage, and *quenelles* of pike with a prawn sauce.

VENTUEJOLS 15110 (5KM N)

10% AU RENDEZ-VOUS DES PÊCHEURS

Pont-de-Lanau; take the D921.
☎ 04.71.23.51.68

An unobtrusive little inn at the side of the road, this is the place for you if you like home cooking, set meals at set prices, regular customers and slightly worn oilcloth. The hands of the clock are stuck at 1pm – perhaps to indicate that lunch is served pretty early. The owner's son is carrying on the lovely tradition of friendly and unpretentious service. On the walls you'll see various pictures and caricatures of musicians and famous local characters, which is only to be expected since he's a big music fan. For 67F you can have two starters, a substantial main course, cheese and dessert. And bottle after bottle of cheap red wine! There are a few basic but clean rooms for 160F – a bargain these days.

CHOUVIGNY 03450

HÔTEL DES GORGES DE CHOUVIGNY**

How to get there: it's on the banks of the Sioule.
☎ 04.70.90.42.11 F 04.70.90.91.54
Closed Tuesday evenings, Wednesdays out of season, and mid-Dec–end Feb. **Car park**. **Disabled access**.

It's quite magical here when the sun comes out (it's another story when it doesn't). The area surrounding the gorges of Sioule merits the description – it's a dark mysterious place and you can quite easily lose your way along the winding road that takes you there. But it's definitely worth the trouble, for the view as much as for the building – or buildings rather, since you eat on one side of the road and sleep on the other. The very pretty bedrooms are in an old building covered with Virginia creeper. Doubles 200–300F. Sit by the river and sample the low-key cooking of Eric Fleury, who uses seasonal produce to make dishes like frog's legs, American-style crayfish (in season), duck breast with green peppercorns, and *confit* of duck *à l'auvergnate*. Set meals 95F, 145F and 185F.

CLERMONT-FERRAND 63000

SEE MAP OVERLEAF

AUBERGE DE JEUNESSE

55 av. de l'Union-Soviétique. **MAP D2-1**
☎ 04.73.92.26.39 F 04.73.92.99.96
Open 7–9.30am and 5–10pm. **Closed** Nov 1–March 1.

It may not be jumping with life but the owner's very nice and there are sometimes quite lively parties in the little inner courtyard. Rooms with two, four, six or eight beds cost 60F per night and that includes breakfast. Half-board, which is compulsory for groups April–end June, is 110F.

HÔTEL LE FOCH*

22 rue du Maréchal-Foch. **MAP B3-8**
☎ 04.73.93.48.40 F 04.73.35.47.41
TV.

The entrance is so unobtrusive you could quite easily pass it by if you weren't looking out for it. And it would certainly be a shame to miss out on this pretty little hotel with its candy-pink English-style façade. The corridors are full of artificial flowers, which gives the place its own particular character. Rooms are adequate and clean and very reasonably priced. Doubles 140F with washing facilities (no TV), 180F with shower, 185F with shower/wc (no TV) and 195F. Pleasant, unobtrusive staff.

10% HÔTEL DE BORDEAUX**

39 av. Franklin-Roosevelt. **MAP A3-3**
☎ 04.73.37.32.32 F 04.73.31.40.56
Secure parking. **TV**. **Canal+**.

This hotel is a bit away from the centre – a distinct advantage, since it means the area is

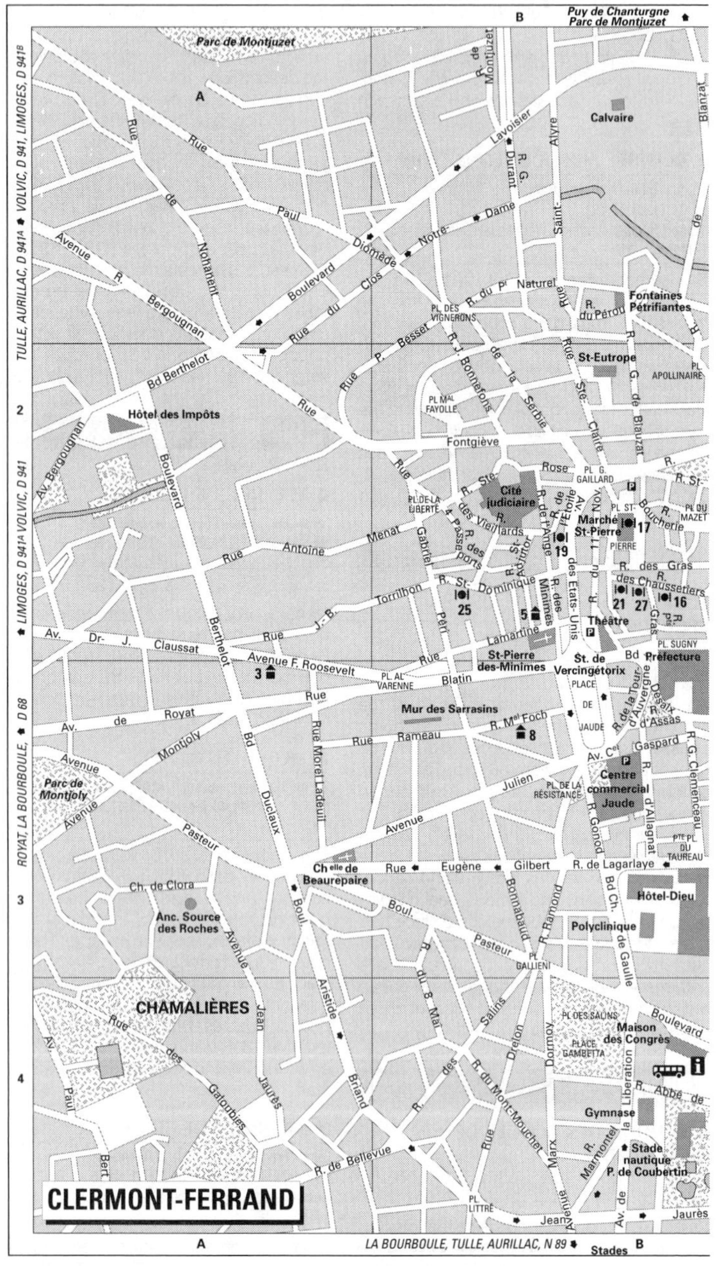
CLERMONT-FERRAND
Puy de Chanturgne
Parc de Montjuzet
Parc de Montjuzet
Calvaire
Fontaines Pétrifiantes
St-Eutrope
Hôtel des Impôts
Cité judiciaire
Marché St-Pierre
Théâtre
Préfecture
St-Pierre des-Minimes
St. de Vercingétorix
Mur des Sarrasins
Centre commercial Jaude
Parc de Montjoly
Anc. Source des Roches
CHAMALIÈRES
Hôtel-Dieu
Polyclinique
Maison des Congrès
Gymnase
Stade nautique P. de Coubertin
Boulevard Lavoisier
Rue Bergougnan
Avenue F. Roosevelt
Avenue Julien
Boul. Pasteur
Rue Eugène Gilbert
R. de Lagarlaye
Place de Jaude
Av. Dr. J. Claussat
Av. de Royat
Avenue Jean Jaurès
R. de Bellevue
TULLE, AURILLAC, D 941A VOLVIC, D 941, LIMOGES, D 941B
ROYAT, LA BOURBOULE, D 68
LIMOGES, D 941A VOLVIC, D 941
LA BOURBOULE, TULLE, AURILLAC, N 89
Stades
A
B
2
3
4

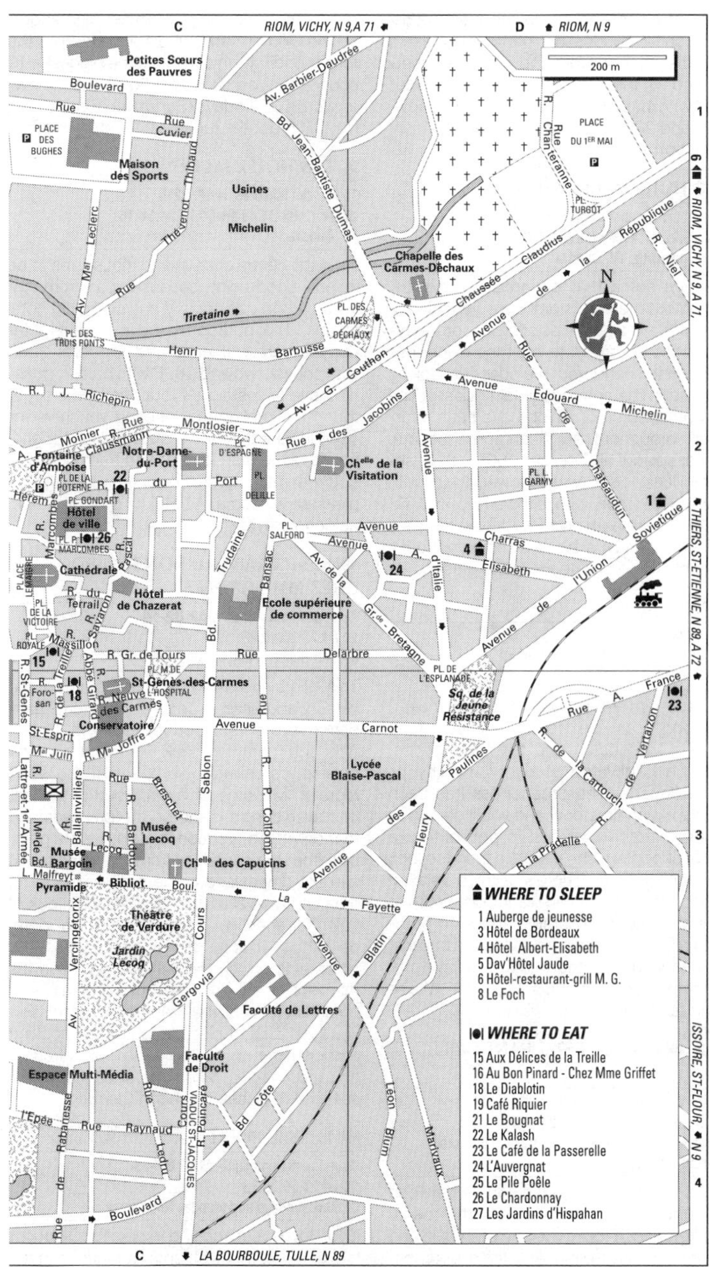
RIOM, VICHY, N 9, A 71
RIOM, N 9
200 m
Petites Sœurs des Pauvres
PLACE DES BUGHES
Maison des Sports
Usines Michelin
Chapelle des Carmes-Déchaux
PLACE DU 1ER MAI
Notre-Dame-du-Port
Ch^elle de la Visitation
Hôtel de ville
Cathédrale
Hôtel de Chazerat
Ecole supérieure de commerce
St-Genès-des-Carmes
Conservatoire
Sq. de la Jeune Résistance
Lycée Blaise-Pascal
Musée Lecoq
Musée Bargoin
Ch^elle des Capucins
Bibliot.
Pyramide
Théâtre de Verdure
Jardin Lecoq
Faculté de Lettres
Faculté de Droit
Espace Multi-Média
THIERS, ST-ETIENNE, N 89, A 72
ISSOIRE, ST-FLOUR, N 9
LA BOURBOULE, TULLE, N 89
WHERE TO SLEEP
1 Auberge de jeunesse
3 Hôtel de Bordeaux
4 Hôtel Albert-Elisabeth
5 Dav'Hôtel Jaude
6 Hôtel-restaurant-grill M. G.
8 Le Foch
WHERE TO EAT
15 Aux Délices de la Treille
16 Au Bon Pinard - Chez Mme Griffet
18 Le Diablotin
19 Café Riquier
21 Le Bougnat
22 Le Kalash
23 Le Café de la Passerelle
24 L'Auvergnat
25 Le Pile Poêle
26 Le Chardonnay
27 Les Jardins d'Hispahan

quiet yet close enough to the main tourist attractions. The pleasant bedrooms make a welcome change from the soulless variety you find in the big hotel chains. Doubles 150F with basin/wc, 200–245F with shower/wc and 280F with bath. Staff are pleasant and unobtrusive.

10% HÔTEL ALBERT-ÉLISABETH**

37 av. Albert-Élisabeth. **MAP D2-4**
☎ 04.73.92.47.41 Fax 04.73.90.78.32
Secure parking. **TV**. **Canal+**.

Okay, we admit that the area's not terribly exciting but the hotel's definitely worth a visit. Since it's a bit noisy, ask for a room overlooking the courtyard (even if the owner has promised to soundproof the ones overlooking the street!) The entrance is fairly classy. The bedrooms, some of which have been refurbished throughout, are clean and adequate, but that's about all. Doubles 160F with washing facilities, 180F with shower, 210F with shower/wc, 240F with shower/wc and TV, and 275F with bath and TV. At least there's a choice! Parking's a bit of a problem, so it's advisable to book a space in the garage.

HÔTEL RAVEL

8 rue de Maringues.
☎ 04.73.91.51.33 Fax 04.73.92.28.48
TV.

This little family-run hotel in a quiet neighbourhood can be found tucked away between the station and the town centre. You'll be captivated straight away by its mosaic façade. The proprietress has been here for a long time now and you'll get a nice welcome. If she ever has to pop out for a spot of shopping, she'll leave a friend to look after the guests. There's a nice relaxed atmosphere here – if you want more bread at breakfast time, for example, that's no problem at all, she'll just nip across to the baker's. The décor in the bedrooms is simple but rather charming. Doubles 170–220F. We're still under its spell!

10% HÔTEL-RESTAURANT-GRILL M.G.**

18 place de la Rodade (North-East).
☎ 04.73.23.10.61 Fax 04.73.24.75.58
Restaurant closed Sundays. **Car park**. **TV**. **Canal+**.
Disabled access.

You'll find it in a lovely little square between Clermont and Montferrand near the town's old fairground. It looks like one of a chain and is quiet and well-kept. Ask for a bedroom overlooking the range of mountains known as the Dômes. And here's a good tip – the rooms ending in a seven are the biggest – 17 square metres! Doubles 250F with shower/wc (200F Fridays–Sundays). Evening set meal 70F but the food's rather uninteresting.

DAV'HÔTEL JAUDE**

10 rue des Minimes. **MAP B2-5**
☎ 04.73.93.31.49 Fax 04.73.34.38.16
TV. **Canal+**.

It's in the centre of town and that seems to be its only good point, because apart from that it's a carbon copy of any one of the big hotel chains. The bedrooms, have no character but they are well-equipped. Doubles 250F with shower/wc and 280F with bath. It doesn't have a restaurant but the owners get round the problem by offering vouchers for eight local eateries – a pizza parlour, a grill-house, a German tavern, and traditional and gourmet restaurants. Fortunately, you'll get a pleasant welcome. A hotel for business trips, not long stays.

RESTAURANT AU BON PINARD – CHEZ MME GRIFFET

7 rue des Petits-Gras. **MAP B2-16**
☎ 04.73.36.40.95
Closed Sundays and in August.

This little bistro dates back to the turn of the century and used to be called *Au Bon Pinard* before being renamed *Chez Mme Griffet.* Although it may not look like much from the outside, it's definitely worth a visit. You won't regret it. Madame Griffet is proud of the fact that everything's made on the premises and that only fresh produce is used, be it vegetables from the garden or from the market. You can eat downstairs in the bar's small dining area and marvel at the never-ending stock of colourful apéritifs. The upstairs dining room, delightfully kitschy, is for latecomers. The ornaments on the Henri II sideboard and the mantelpiece are of the "A souvenir from Blackpool variety" – or the French equivalent. But you'll get a lot of pleasure out of the cooking and dishes such as *coq au vin*, pig's trotters and *andouillettes*. *Menu du jour* 65–69F. You'll see a lot of places like this in Clermont.

LE PILE POÊLE

9 rue Saint-Dominique. **MAP B2-25**
☎ 04.73.36.08.88
Closed Sundays and Monday lunchtimes.

If you love meat and find yourself in Clermont late at night, try this friendly restaurant in the town's liveliest street, a few steps from place de Jaude. There are some thick juicy cuts of meat available à la carte until one in the morning. Or you might be tempted by one of the set meals at 58F (lunchtimes only), 85F, 120F and 150F. Whatever you decide on, you won't leave feeling hungry!

|●| LE CHARDONNAY

1 place Philippe-Marcombes. **MAP C2-26**
☎ 04.73.90.18.28
Closed Sundays.

It's the wine that matters here – and that's made perfectly clear from the start as you'll see from the shelves of bottles proudly displayed behind the bar. So raise your wine glasses and bend your elbow (easy does it though!) The owner's a wine waiter by profession and will produce some delightful little bottles for you. He also does a fairly brisk trade in wine by the glass. As for food, there's a lovely *formule* at 60F or if you'd rather go à la carte reckon on 110F for earthy and robust dishes *andouillette* with green lentils, calf's head *gribiche* (with a sauce of mayonnaise, capers, gherkins and herbs), and boned and stuffed pig's trotters. For afters how about jam waffles (one is never enough!) Friendly but unobtrusive staff. There's even a piano to add a bit of atmosphere.

|●| RESTAURANT LE DIABLOTIN

8 rue de l'Abbé-Girard. **MAP C3-18**
☎ 04.73.92.85.20
Closed Saturday lunchtimes and Sundays.

This tiny restaurant can be found on a little street in the pedestrian area but a bit away from the touristy parts of town. To look at it, you would never guess there was a restaurant here. The *menu du jour* at lunchtime costs 60F and there are set meals at 100F, 155F and 205F. They have a few good dishes that might sometimes surprise you, such as scrambled eggs Scandinavian-style, frog's legs with seafood, lamb's tongue with a lentil sauce, and tuna Stroganoff. The wine cellar is fully stocked. Service is courteous if not very outgoing.

|●| RESTAURANT CAFÉ RIQUIER

11 rue de l'Étoile. **MAP B2-19**
☎ 04.73.36.67.25

This delightful brasserie, with its dark and stylish décor, offers some of the best value for money around at the moment. There's a good *formule* at 69F which could almost be something you've ordered à la carte, and the owner gives a 50% reductions if you're under 13 or over 90. There's an interesting choice of traditional and earthy dishes like veal kidney kebabs, *andouillette* and an excellent steak tartare. The portions are always very generous. Lovely terrace in summer. Staff provide a courteous and efficient service until 11pm every day.

|●| RESTAURANT LE CAFÉ DE LA PASSERELLE

22 rue Anatole-France. **MAP D3-23**
☎ 04.73.91.62.12
Closed Sundays and July 13–Aug 21.

This is one of Clermont's most picturesque spots, thanks in large part to its extrovert owner. Alain Aumaly may come from the south but his cooking's typical of the Auvergne region; portions are extremely generous, and the locals seem to approve. You must try the pig's trotters, the *potée* (a thick soup) and stuffed cabbage (all à la carte) and the thick juicy steaks are very satisfying. There's only one set meal – and for 75F you'll get a starter, main course, cheese and dessert. This is a good restaurant but on the small side so it's a good idea to book in advance.

|●| RESTAURANT LE KALASH

8-10 rue du Port. **MAP C2-22**
☎ 04.73.90.19.22
Closed Sundays.

This Pakistani restaurant offers quality cooking. It's unusual for a restaurant to do a vegetarian set meal but this one does for 75F. Two other set meals (97F and 130F) offer a wide range of dishes from all over Pakistan. We would list the house specialities, but we don't have the waiter's extraordinary talent for rhyming off a long list. Pleasant décor. Staff are efficient and very friendly and only too happy to advise you in your choice. Last orders 11.30pm.

|●| RESTAURANT LE BOUGNAT

29 rue des Chaussetiers. **MAP B2-21**
☎ 04.73.36.36.98
Closed Sundays, Monday lunchtimes, and July.

Here's a restaurant that offers a wonderful selection of skilfully prepared regional dishes, including mutton tripe, *pounti* (a mixture of bacon and Swiss chard) pig's trotters with white beans and *potée auvergnate* (the thick local soup), which strangely is becoming harder and harder to find in Clermont. Decorated in traditional Auvergne style, it has a wood burning stove in the foyer where the chef prepares the local pancakes (sorry, no pizzas here!) The 76F set meal is very decent. The wine list contains some fine examples from the Auvergne. If you're on your own, try to get one of the stools at the counter where the regulars sit. Lots of atmosphere.

L'AUVERGNAT

50 av. Albert-Élisabeth. **MAP D2-24**
☎ 04.73.92.20.91
Closed Sunday evenings.

You might think this was just another tourist trap when you hear that people scramble to get in here because it's "so typically Auvergne". Admittedly, the owner hasn't skimped on the décor – large fireplace, boar's head and farming tools – but it all hangs together and the cooking is in keeping. The dishes are classics and there's nothing on the menu but well-known dishes like *potée* (the thick local soup), mutton tripe, *coq au vin*, potato pie, veal chop with *mousserons* (a type of mushroom), and fillet of perch with tarragon. Generous portions. Set meals 87F and 110F.

LES JARDINS D'HISPAHAN

11ter rue des Chaussetiers. **MAP B2-27**
☎ 04.73.90.23.07.
Closed lunchtimes and Sundays.

Persian cooking is all about subtle flavours and flowery combinations rather than spices, so if you like strong flavours this is not the place for you. The décor's not particularly exciting but that's all to the good since it means you can concentrate on the food. The *kebab bargue* (grilled veal kebabs that have been marinated in lemon) is absolutely delightful as are the dishes that come with sauce. Lovely set meal at 90F. And if you and rice parted company some time ago, the way they cook basmati here will make you change your mind.

CHAMALIÈRE S 63400 (3KM W)

10% HÔTEL RADIO***

43 av. Pierre-Curie; take the D941b in the direction of Pontgibaud.
☎ 04.73.30.87.83 Fax 04.76.36.42.44
Closed Sunday evenings, Monday lunchtimes, January, and July 19–24. **Secure parking. TV.**

Service noon–1.30pm and 7–9.30pm. Built in the 1930s as a radio station, this place was run for many happy years by Michel Mioche. Now his daughter has abandoned her career as a journalist in Paris and taken over the reins, although Michel still helps out in the kitchen. Together, she and her young chef and a head waiter who's hardly out of his teens form a trio which we hope will be successful. It certainly seems to be looking that way! Only top-quality produce is used and dishes are skilfully prepared and imaginative – even a bit crazy sometimes. But Monsieur Mioche is there to keep their enthusiasm in check and the end result is absolutely perfect. What you experience here is a revival of French cooking. Set meals 160F, 270F, and 330F. The latter features fish, with four main courses that vary depending on deliveries. The rabbit *tartare*, the roast casseroled pigeon and the John Dory are unforgettable. Your taste buds are in for a treat here! Beautiful bedrooms with lots of style. Doubles 350–450F with shower/wc, 490–750F with bath.

ORCINES 63870 (5KM W)

10% LE RELAIS DES PUYS**

La Baraque; take the D941a towards Pontgibaud.
☎ 04.73.62.10.51 Fax 04.73.62.22.09
Closed Sunday evenings, Monday lunchtimes, and Dec-Jan. **Car park. TV.**

Service noon–2pm and 7.30–9pm. Situated beside the Puy de Dôme, this is the place to visit if you're looking for a hearty meal after climbing the mountain. Try the salad of pig's trotters, trout with lentils, roast fillet of perch or panfried veal with chanterelle mushrooms – all very satisfying. Set meals 78–175F. It's warm and cosy, especially when the owner lights a roaring fire. The inn has been in the Esbelin family for seven generations now so they know what tradition, quality and hospitality mean. The bedrooms are very pleasant, especially the ones that don't overlook the street. Prices range from 210F with shower/wc to 225F with bath.

PONTGIBAUD 63230 (23KM NW)

HÔTEL-RESTAURANT DE L'UNIVERS

How to get there: take the D941 and you'll find it opposite the station.
☎ 04.73.88.70.09.
Car park.

This little family guest house looks just like something you'd see on a postcard. Charlot grows the vegetables and milks the cows, while Marie-Antoinette (her brother's a chef at the *Ritz*) does the cooking. The dining room with its flowery wallpaper is clean and bright. As long as you've ordered in advance, you can have a memorable calf's head, a terrific grilled *andouillette* or good pig's trotters. whenever you want. There's no rush to leave when you've finished your meal – sit a while before heading off to play cards – and if you're missing a player Charlot or Marie-Antoinette will happily make up the numbers. Set meals 60F, 75F and 130F. Doubles cost 150F (shower on the landing) or 200F for ones that sleep three or four.

HÔTEL DE LA POSTE*

place de la République.
☎ 04.73.88.70.02 ➡ 04.73.88.79.74
Closed Sunday evenings and Mondays (except July-Aug), January, and the first fortnight in October.

People come here mainly to try out the restaurant since the owner has such a good reputation and his customers don't have to take out a bank loan in order to eat well. Delicious local and seasonal dishes – don't miss the game in autumn. Apart from that there's roasted local rabbit with honey, thin slivers of duck breast with orange sauce, chicken stuffed with morels, and char with *mousserons* (small white or yellow mushrooms). Set meals start at 80F (except Sundays) and go up to 190F. The hotel's fairly average. Bedrooms 165–195F.

COLLANDRES 15400

HÔTEL-RESTAURANT DES TILLEULS

place de l'Église (South); take the D63.
☎ 04.71.78.06.54
Closed two weeks in May.

Madame Duval is a very capable woman who sees to everything in this lovely old-fashioned café-cum-hotel. Both the building and the cooking ooze rustic simplicity and authentic local style, and there are even chickens, ducks and geese scratching about outside. The hotel's closed in May, which is when Madame Duval tends to her garden, digging and planting so she'll have fresh vegetables to simmer on her old cooker (or her "wooden microwave" as she likes to call it!). The 55F set meal has the natural charm that goes hand in hand with home cooking, but don't forget you'll have to order the *potée* (thick local soup) 24 hours in advance and the stuffed cabbage 48 hours. The house *terrines* are excellent and whatever you do, don't miss out when she serves stuffed rabbit and prune tart. Bedrooms are simple and well-kept – you'll find a shower in the basement and toilets on the landing. Doubles with full board cost 180F per person, and 150F with half-board. If you're here in winter and can show them a copy of this guidebook you'll get a 10% reduction if you stay at least four nights full or half-board. Madame Duval is extremely nice though you might find her a bit curt to start with.

CONDAT-EN-FENIERS 15190

HÔTEL-RESTAURANT CHÉ MARISSOU

Le Veysset, it's 3km from Condat on the D62.
☎ 04.71.78.55.45
Open during all school holidays and weekends Feb–Nov 11. **Car park. Disabled access.**

Non-stop service. This hotel, the smallest in the world, was born out of the seemingly genuine passion of a Laval industrialist – a local boy made good – and an elaborate though sometimes heavy-handed marketing campaign. He had a holiday home in Veyssat, between Condat and Montboudif (where the late President Pompidou came from) and turned it into an inn, one that is not without charm. You'll be welcomed by the owner himself in a dining room that looks as much like a living museum as it does a restaurant. The aim here is to send you away full, no matter how hungry you were when you arrived. You can go back as often as you like to the table of traditional cold meat and *crudités*. That will be followed by the day's special – *potée* (the thick local soup) or mutton tripe – a table displaying a selection of mature regional cheeses, and dessert. With the cheese you'll get a chance to sample, on the house, a glass of wine made from late-harvested grapes. How much you pay depends on how old you are! You eat for free if you're under 7 or over 100; 60F for 7-10s; 120F for 10-65s and 100F 65-99. The one and only bedroom is as traditional as it can be and is a good choice if you're looking for somewhere special – 500F including champagne.

COURPIÈRE 63120

RESTAURANT L'AIR DU TEMPS

38 av. de la Gare.
☎ 04.73.51.25.91
Closed Sunday evenings and Mondays in summer, and Sunday evening–Wednesday in winter (except by reservation).

Service noon–2.15pm and 7–9.15pm. Here's a delightful restaurant in an area that doesn't have all that many. It's decorated very simply in shades of cream and pale green and the furniture is modern and minimalist. But it's the cooking that will grab your attention. If you enjoy traditional local cooking, then the 89F set meal's right up your street – we had *pounti* (a mixture of bacon and Swiss chard), leg of lamb, baked potatoes, cheese and *millard* (a kind of cherry cake). The other set meals (100–136F) are worthy of a high-class restaurant and feature dishes like sardine ravioli with prawns, panfried red mullet with dill, veal with spinach and, the house speciality, seafood *choucroute*. And for dessert the *crème catalane* is out of this world! A pleasant welcome.

ÉGLISENEUVE-D'ENTRAIGUES 63850

HÔTEL DU NORD*

rue principale.
☎ 04.73.71.90.28.
Closed Sept 1–15. **Car park**.

This pretty little country inn is a lovely place to stop whether you just want a snack or something a bit more substantial after a day's walking in the Cézallier. They do classic dishes like stuffed cabbage, *truffade* (potato cake with *Cantal* cheese), local *charcuterie* and mutton tripe. Snacks 59F and set meals 75F, 130F, 150F and 180F. The last three have to be ordered ahead of time but you won't regret it. Accommodation available. Doubles 130F.

GANNAT 03800

HÔTEL DU CHÂTEAU

9 place Rantian; it's across from the château.
☎ 04.70.90.00.88 F➔ 04.70.90.30.79
Closed Fridays out of season, and mid-Dec–Jan 5.
Secure parking. **TV**. **Canal+**.

Nineteenth century bourgeois buildings in provincial towns have their own special charm and this hotel, which is almost perfectly square, is no exception – the old folks playing cards in the middle of the afternoon look as if they haven't moved for years. The kitchen provides earthy traditional dishes of the kind our grandmothers made – *andouillette bonne femme*, for example, sautéd veal, and chicken with garlic sauce. They also do a wonderful *pâté bourbonnais* (potato and bacon pie) and a very good delicious walnut cake. Set meals 66F, 87F, 100F, and 120F. Clean simple bedrooms 200F with shower/wc and TV.

CHARROUX 03140 (10KM NW)

LA FERME DE SAINT-SÉBASTIEN

chemin de Bourion; take the N9, then turn right onto the D42.
☎ 04.70.56.88.83
Closed Jan 5–20, June 15–25, Sept 20–Oct 5, Monday evenings and Tuesdays (except July-Aug). **Car park**. **Disabled access**.

Service noon–1.30pm and 7.30–9pm. This delightful restaurant was opened in 1994 in one of France's most beautiful villages and has very quickly become one of the locals' favourite places. An old farm building, it's been well renovated and the intercommunicating little rooms provide an intimate atmosphere in which to enjoy Valérie Saignie's fresh and creative cooking. The 120F set meal offers local dishes such as courgette fritters with a chive sauce, chicken in a mustard sauce, and artichokes with bacon, local cheeses, and a lovely choice of desserts. Set meals 90F (except Sundays), 120F, 180F and 240F. The staff are warm and attentive. You'll definitely have to book in advance as it's a very popular place.

LAPALISSE 03120

HÔTEL DU BOURBONNAIS*

1 place du 14-Juillet.
☎ 04.70.99.04.11
Closed Mondays out of season, Sunday evenings, and January. **Car park**. **TV**.

A comfortable and efficiently run hotel. Hungry travellers will greatly appreciate the thick steaks. The *pavé* of Charolais beef with chanterelle mushrooms is superb and the veal kidneys with raspberry vinegar are excellent. Set meals 75F (a bit of a disappointment), 95F and 195F. Gourmet set meals go up to 220F. Rooms are simple and well equipped. Doubles with shower/wc start at 245F.

HÔTEL-RESTAURANT GALLAND**

20 place de la République.
☎ 04.70.99.07.21 F➔ 04.70.99.34.64
Closed Wednesdays, during the February school holidays, and late November. **Secure parking**. **TV**.

Service noon–2pm and 7–9pm. Here's another of the places we fell in love with in the département. To say that you can eat rather well in this part of the country is a bit of an understatement! The green salad with chicken livers and poached egg, stew of duck breast with *foie gras*, fillet of scorpion fish on a bed of green cabbage, and escalope of fried *foie gras* are a sheer delight. The cooking is fresh, imaginative and full of subtle flavours and the dishes are skilfully prepared. What more can we say to convince the disbelievers? Well, the delightful owner is lively, good-humoured, and very stylish, and the staff are keen and attentive. To sum things up, we'd say that we feel quite at home in these rather elegant modern surroundings. Set meals 125–270F. There are a few pleasant spic-and-span bedrooms costing 250F for a double with shower/wc. Ask for one overlooking the interior courtyard. A very good establishment with absolutely wonderful breakfasts!

MANDAILLES-SAINT-JULIEN 15590

10% HÔTEL-RESTAURANT AU BOUT DU MONDE

Centre.
☎ 04.71.47.92.47.

A nice place in the Jordanne valley, where hillwalkers start their climb on the Puy-Mary. The hotel is quiet, simple, and well-kept. Doubles 135–200F. The restaurant, with its traditional *cantou* (inglenook fireplace), two armchairs and gleaming copperware is as cosy as you could hope for. The cooking will satisfy the hungriest hiker – the portions served in the 80F set meal are generous beyond belief – and everything's delicious, from the selection of cold meats, to the vegetable soup and regional specialities such as *potée* (thick soup), *truffade* (potato cake with *Cantal* cheese), *aligot* and mutton tripe. Day's special 40F. Stuffed cabbage made to order. You'll get a pleasant smiling welcome, even at the height of the rush hour.

10% HÔTEL-RESTAURANT AUX GENÊTS D'OR*

Centre.
☎ 04.71.47.96.45 F 04.71.47.93.65
TV.

This is a little hotel with a homy atmosphere. You'll find it in the centre of the village, 50m down a cul-de-sac, so you'll definitely get peace and quiet. Bedrooms are comfortable and spruce, and doubles cost 170F. Good cooking, with a set meal at 85F. It has a few specialities on offer such as tournedos in a gentian flavoured sauce, cep omelette, cabbage stuffed with salmon in a red wine sauce, and duck breast with honey. You can have half-board if you like. There are a few duplex rooms with small kitchens.

SAINT-CIRGUES-DE-JORDANNE 15590 (8KM SE)

10% HÔTEL-RESTAURANT LES TILLEULS**

Centre; take the D17.
☎ 04.71.47.92.19 F 04.71.47.91.06
Closed Sunday evenings and the holiday Monday marking All Saints Day. **Secure parking. TV**.

Service noon–1.30pm and 7–8.30pm. This is a beautiful building that overlooks the road and the valley of the Jordanne. You can relax in the garden, swimming pool or sauna when you come back from a walk on the nearby Puy-Mary. The quiet pleasant bedrooms all come with bath and numbers 15 and16 also have a terrace. Doubles 250–270F. The dining room is equally pleasant and the fireplace is a welcome sight in winter. Generous portions and a style of cooking that can be quite sophisticated. You'll get a nice welcome from Yvette Fritsch who develops her own special recipes with some wonderful end results. Set meals featuring regional specialities are 70F and 85F, while for 90F you can have duck leg with wild mushrooms, bacon and potatoes, and for 115F snails in puff pastry and duck with dandelion honey. If you'd rather go à la carte, there's goat's cheese and spinach in puff pastry, pork chop with Cantal cheese and morels or capon with raspberry vinegar. Half-board 240–265F per person.

MASSIAC 15500

10% GRAND HÔTEL DE LA POSTE**

26 av. du Général-de-Gaulle (Centre); via the N9; on the A75 motorway, take exit 23 if you're coming from the direction of Paris or exit 24 from Montpellier.
☎ 04.71.23.02.01 F 04.71.23.09.23
Car park. TV. Disabled access.

Service noon–2pm and 7.30–9pm. There are thirty-two bedrooms, many of which have been renovated in trendy elegant neo-classical style. All mod cons. Doubles 235–335F. Number 11 (420F) has two double beds. There's not much more to add, except perhaps that if you want a change from swimming or something relaxing to do after a workout, how about examining the collection of keyrings at the reception desk. There's a pleasant restaurant at the back that does set meals at 70F (except Sundays and public holidays), 100F, 160F and 180F. A la carte also available. It has a few specialities, including cheese tart (made with the firm yellow cheese known as *Cantal*), potato pie, two types of fish in *beurre blanc*, pig's trotters with lentils, and warm apple tart.

MONT-DORE (LE) 63240

AUBERGE DE JEUNESSE

route de Sancy (South-East); it's 3km from the station.
☎ 04.73.65.03.53 F 04.73.65.26.39
Car park.

Two-, three- and four-bedded rooms available at 50F. You can stay for as long as you want provided there's room. Meals 50F.

10% HÔTEL LE CASTELET**

av. Michel-Bertrand (North-West); it's near the town centre.
☎ 04.73.65.05.29 F 04.73.65.27.95
Closed March 31–May 15 and Oct 1–Dec 23. **Car park**. **TV**.

Service 12.15–1.30pm and 7.15–8.30pm. This establishment is less obsessed with healthy living than other hotels in town. It has a swimming pool, garden and terrace and is a bit on the expensive side. There are thirty-seven rooms in the hotel. Doubles 323F with bath. The cooking is fairly sophisticated, with dishes like smoked duck breast and mango with walnut oil, trout and pike in a gentian flavoured sauce, white pudding and potatoes with honey, and salmon escalope with green lentils. Set meals 69–192F.

RESTAURANT LE BOUGNAT

23 av. Georges-Clemenceau.
☎ 04.73.65.28.19
Closed Tuesdays (except during school holidays), and Nov 15–Dec 15. **Car park**.

If you want traditional cooking that has been updated to suit modern tastes then this is the place for you – nobody in Mont-Dore does it better. A former stable has been very nicely transformed into a delightful dining area with little tables and tiny sideboards. The *pounti* (a mixture of bacon and Swiss chard) was one of the best we've ever tasted, the *truffade* (potato cake with *Cantal* cheese) was excellent, and they also do garlic soup, sautéd rabbit *à la gentiane* and stuffed cabbage. Set meals 79F, 99F and 129F. This is the type of place people like to visit on cold winter evenings after a good day's skiing. Guaranteed to lift your spirits! Just make sure you book ahead as it's very popular.

MONTLUÇON 03100

10% HÔTEL DES BOURBONS – RESTAURANT AUX DUCS DE BOURBON**

47 av. Marx-Dormoy (South-West); it's near the station.
☎ 04.70.05.28.93 F 04.70.05.16.92
Closed Sunday evenings and Mondays, public holidays excepted. **Secure parking**. **TV**. **Canal+**.

Service noon–2.30pm and 7–11pm. This beautiful 18th century town house has been renovated recently and is very stylish indeed. The bedrooms are modern and comfortable but the décor is practically non-existent, which is a great shame. Doubles 250F with shower/wc or bath. When it comes to eating, you might prefer the brasserie (tel 04.70.05.22.79) to the restaurant since it's cosier. The set meals (76–200F) offer things like braised sole with prawns, tasty grilled meat and delicious tarts made from seasonal fruits. Very professional staff.

10% HÔTEL DE LA GARE**

42 av. Marx-Dormoy (South-West).
☎ 04.70.05.44.22 F 04.70.05.90.89
Closed Dec 23–Jan 3. **Secure parking**. **TV**. **Canal+**.

This little hotel, the headquarters of the *Contact-hôtel* chain, is a typical traditional family-run establishment. It's pleasant, quiet, and very handy for the station. Bedrooms are simple and well-kept and staff are always helpful. Hearty breakfasts 30F. Doubles – most of them have been redecorated recently – 205F with shower/wc and 255F with bath.

LE SAFRAN D'OR

12 place des Toiles.
☎ 04.70.05.09.18
Closed Sunday evenings and Mondays.

This is one of our favourite places in the area. With its yellow frontage painted to resemble marble, it looks like a Paris brasserie and the cooking tastes like the kind you'd get in a bistro with a high-class chef. You'll get a warm welcome from the owner, who'll do all she can for you. The service is quick and efficient, but don't worry – you'll have all the time in the world to enjoy the chef's excellent cooking. He uses fresh seasonal produce and the end result is simple traditional dishes like sirloin steak in an Armagnac-based sauce, breast of duck with a fricassee of ceps, sole *meunière* with lemon, and a delicious *crème brûlée.* And it won't cost you a fortune either, with set meals at 85F, 115F and 148F.

🍴 LA VIE EN ROSE

7 rue de la Fontaine; it's beside the church of Notre-Dame, in the old part of town.
☎ 04.70.03.88.79

Unwind here in the relaxed atmosphere created by the friendly, rather trendy owner, the walls decorated with old photos of the town and adverts from the 50s and 60s, and the background music – no Muzak here, just a collection of the best French songs which changes at the dessert stage to standards by American crooners. We don't have any criticisms of the cooking either. Cuts of meat like flank and rib steak are thick and tasty and the salads are fresh and come in generous portions. The potato pie is excellent. Expect to pay 100F à la carte. *Menu du jour* 85F.

NÉRIS-LES-BAINS 03310 (8KM SE)

🍴 LE RELAIS DU VIEUX MOULIN

take the N144.
☎ 04.70.03.24.88
Closed Nov 15–March 1. **Car park**.

Service noon–2pm and 7–11.30pm. It's lovely to come out here, especially in summer when you can sit on the delightful terrace below the viaduct. You won't find typical regional cooking since it's really a crêperie. But we fell for it because, even though you're in Charolais beef country, this is the only place for 30km around where you can have a superb chargrilled rib of beef that's both tender and tasty. The rib of beef is sold by weight, with a kilo – enough for 2-3 people – going for 180F. You'll find a wide variety of sweet pancakes (costing around 25F), savoury ones (16–54F) and salads (16–34F).

ESTIVAREILLES 03190 (10KM N)

10% 🏠 🍴 HOSTELLERIE DU LION D'OR**

23 rue de Paris; take the N144 in the direction of Bourges.
☎ 04.70.06.00.35 Fax 00.70.06.09.78
Closed Sunday evenings, Mondays, during the February school holidays, and in August. **Secure parking**.

Service from noon and 7pm. This former coaching inn is surrounded by greenery and has a terrace and a veranda. The foyer and the restaurant are superb and the staff pleasant and efficient. The owner doubles as the chef – you'll find him in the kitchen preparing the prawn salad with sea urchins, guinea fowl with honey, and chocolate fondant with candied orange. Set meals 75F (weekdays) and 140–260F. Bedrooms are comfy and pretty. Prices start at 170F for a double with shower/wc. There's a beautiful view over the neighbouring lake.

COURÇAIS 03370 (21KM NW)

🏠 🍴 BAR-HÔTEL-RESTAURANT JOSETTE LAUMONIER

take the D943.
☎ 04.70.07.11.13
Closed Mondays and the first three weeks in September.

Situated in a peaceful village, this is a simple, pleasant and relaxing place – ideal for families. There's a cosy atmosphere in the rustic restaurant – the fireplace has a lot to do with that – or you might prefer the terrace if the sun comes out. There are two set meals, 70F and 120F, for those with big appetites. The free-range poultry from the neighbouring farm is excellent and, if you order ahead, they can provide snails and veal sweetbreads. There are four country-style bedrooms with shower (130–150F). Half-board at 190F per person is compulsory from April to the end of August.

MONTSALVY 15120

🏠 🍴 L'AUBERGE FLEURIE*

place du Barry (Centre).
☎ 04.71.49.20.02
Restaurant closed Jan 15 -Feb 15.

Service noon–2pm and 7.30–9.30pm. Everything's well-kept and has a rustic feel about it – from the ivy and the fireplace to the exposed beams and century-old doors. There's always a good crowd in the bar and restaurant, and you'll find the staff very friendly. The owner's other passions are travel and reading. We like the kind of prices he charges for the rooms (about a quarter of which have phone and TV) – 120F with basin, 140F and 145F with basin/wc, and 160F and 170F with shower/wc. There's a good choice of set meals in the cosy restaurant – 55F (except Sundays), 95F (regional specialities), 120F (fricassee of veal knuckle, breast of duck, and leg of chicken with mushrooms), and 185F. Wines are reasonably priced, with a Saint-Pourçain for 55F and the house wine for 50F. Half-board available (265–305F for two).

10% ☗ |●| HÔTEL DU NORD**

Centre.
☎ 04.71.49.20.03 F→ 04.71.49.29.00
Closed Jan 1–March 31. **Car park**. **TV**. **Canal+**.

The *Hôtel du Nord*, situated right in the heart of the Châtaigneraie, is geared more towards the beautiful people living locally than the man in the street. Staff are very amiable and facilities include a bar, lounge and garden. Colourful and comfortable rooms with telephone, Minitel and mini-bar cost 250F and 280F. The quiet, rather plush restaurant has an excellent reputation for its traditional local dishes. This is one of the few places in the Auvergne to have a woman chef (her husband looks after the dining room). They do set meals at 85F (which comes with *crépinette* of pig's trotters), 120F (trout soufflée with lentil sauce, *falette* – stuffed breast of mutton – and stew of suckling pig), 160F (three courses) and 240F. Dishes served à la carte vary depending on the time of year. There might be snails panfried with ceps and walnuts, medallions of milk-fed veal, *fondant* of Scottish salmon, an upside down cake of ceps in a vinegar, marinade and pepper sauce and, for dessert, mousse *glacé* flavoured with gentian liqueur. The classics are also available, including *aligot*, duck breast, and *confit*.

CALVINET 15340 (17.5KM W)

☗ |●| HÔTEL DE LA TERRASSE*

place Jean-de-Bonnefon (Centre); take the D19.
☎ 04.71.49.91.59
Closed Saturdays out of season and Oct 15–April 30. **Car park**.

The very chatty old lady who's been running the *Hôtel de la Terrasse* since 1936 likes to spoil her guests and has a talent for creating a wonderful homy atmosphere. All the things you'd expect to see in the country are there, including copper pans, an old clock, and a sideboard. Her specialities are pear tart and stuffed pig's trotters and she has set meals at 55F, 80F, 100F and 120F (two starters included in this last one). The bedrooms, ten in all, are furnished with antiques and range in price from 145F with basin to 200F with bath. Numbers 1, 2, 10 and 11 have just been done up. Half-board comes in at 180F per person.

☗ |●| HÔTEL BEAUSÉJOUR**

route de Maurs; get there by the D66, the D45 and the D51.
☎ 04.71.49.91.68 F→ 04.71.49.98.63
Closed Sunday evenings and Mondays out of season, and mid-Jan–mid-Feb. **TV**.

Michelin gave it a star recently – an honour it shares with only one other place in the Cantal region – and everyone's talking about it. People come from far and near for Louis-Bernard Puech's cooking and the traditional local dishes that vary according to what the market has to offer. However, Louis remains remarkably down-to-earth despite all this success and the place is as friendly, good-natured and simple as ever. And the regulars – notaries, sales reps, and farming families – still come and make a day of it. Staff are particularly friendly and offer efficient service. You will be astonished at the quality of the good, very reasonably-priced set meals served in the fairly conventional dining room. Prices start at 95F (weekday lunchtimes) rising to 140F (*tarte briochée* with mussels and a stew of shoulder of milk-fed veal), 205F (*fondant* of duck liver, roast red mullet, medallions of lamb spiked with anchovies or fricassee of free-range chicken with chanterelle mushrooms), and 300F. À la carte there's a succulent *marbré* of duck liver and oxtail, stuffed pig's trotters, neck of goose with *foie gras*, and delicious Salers beef. Good range of wines at reasonable prices. Comfortable and pretty bedrooms cost 260F.

MOULINS 03000

10% ☗ |●| LE GRAND HÔTEL DU DAUPHIN**

59 place d'Allier (Centre).
☎ 04.70.44.33.05 F→ 04.70.34.05.75
Secure parking. **TV**. **Canal+**. **Disabled access**.

It used to be a coaching inn and there's a slight air of romance about it. The tables are nicely laid out and the cooking's classical and sophisticated. Regional specialities on offer include *salmi* of duck with Saint-Pourçain, frog's legs with garlic sauce and duck leg *confit*. Set meals 70F (except Sundays) and 115–185F. *Coq au vin* (they use Saint-Pourçain) and *cassoulet* with *confit* (for four people) must be ordered ahead of time. Delightful comfortable bedrooms 165F with washing facilities and doubles with bath 275F.

10% ☗ |●| LE PARC**

31 av. du Général-Leclerc (East).
☎ 04.70.44.12.25 F→ 04.70.46.79.35
Restaurant closed Saturdays, July 4–18, Sept 27–Oct 4, and Dec 23–Jan 4. **Car park**. **TV**. **Canal+**.

This hotel has been in the hands of the Barret family since 1956 and they continue to welcome their guests in the same friendly fashion. It's a beautiful building, classic in style and exceptionally comfortable. You can relax in the bright dining room, where the furniture, fabrics and colours are simple and go well together. The restaurant serves local dishes that are a combination of tradition and imagination. Rabbit stew, roast fillet of zander with mustard, panfried fillet of Charolais beef with *fourme d'Ambert* (a local blue cheese) and duck breast with Sancerre are some of the dishes to be found in the set meals at 90F (weekdays), 130F, 145F and 210F. Soundproofed double rooms cost 200–260F with shower/wc and 330F with bath. Some of the rooms are in an annexe.

|●| LE GRAND CAFÉ

49 place d'Allier (Centre).
☎ 04.70.44.00.05
Car park.

Service 11.30–2pm and 7–11.30pm. This superb 1900s brasserie is a listed building. If you're at all self-conscious you might well feel uncomfortable because there are lots of large mirrors dotted about. Even so, it's still the most popular place in the area with young and old alike. They come for the atmosphere more than the food and if you want to eat it's probably best to go for the *menu du jour* (41F), the veal kidneys (65F), the grilled pig's trotters (58F) or the *andouillette* (58F).

|●| RESTAURANT LA PETITE AUBERGE

7 rue des Bouchers (Centre).
☎ 04.70.44.11.68 F➔ 04.70.44.82.04
Closed Monday evenings, Sundays, and July 27–Aug 17.

Service noon–1.30pm and 7.15–9.30pm. You'll feel quite at home here in this long narrow room decorated in traditional local style. The cooking too is traditional and the chef's expertise combines with first-rate ingredients to produce dishes that are full of flavour – classics such as scallops on a bed of leeks, breast of duck with a lentil *coulis* and mussels with chanterelle mushrooms. Set meals 80F, 110F, 135F and 160F. The delightful welcome is a good indication of what's in store.

COULANDON 03000 (6KM W)

⌂ |●| HÔTEL LE CHALET -RESTAURANT LE MONTÉGUT***

☎ 04.70.44.50.08 F➔ 04.70.44.07.09
Closed Dec 16–Jan 31. **Car park**. **TV**. **Canal+**. **Disabled access**.

If you're on the lookout for a peaceful relaxing break in a hotel where service always comes with a smile, this late 19th century chalet – rather plush and middle-class – nestling in the depths of the countryside is the ideal solution. Bedrooms have been tastefully decorated and they're all different. Doubles 380F with shower/wc, 440F with bath. Depending on which way your room faces, you'll have a view of the countryside or of a 100 year old park with a beautiful lake. The restaurant is in a separate building and as soon as summer arrives, you can eat beside the swimming pool. The 120F weekday set meal, based on fresh market produce, is good and the ones at 185F and 230F offer bigger portions and even fancier dishes. Some of the dishes that caught our eye were cucumber with cream and fresh mint, fillet of lamb *en croûte,* sautéd veal with fresh pasta, mousse *glacé* with Chivas Regal, and panfried peaches with verbena flavoured liqueur and peach icecream. Everything was well thought out. Good service.

SOUVIGNY 03210 (11KM W)

|●| AUBERGE LES TILLEULS

place Saint-Éloi.
☎ 04.70.43.60.70
Closed Sunday evenings (except July-Aug) and Mondays.

This is a welcoming inn in a delightful village that has a magnificent church and basilica built between the 10th and 15th centuries. It's very fresh and spruce inside and on the walls there are naive paintings of village life in the 40s and 50s. Set meals 69F (available weekday lunchtimes but not public holidays) and 92–230F. Some of the specialities to try are panfried duck *foie gras* with fruit purée and an infusion of cider, red mullet with fresh pasta, *grenadins* of veal and veal kidneys with Saint-Pourçain, and local venison steak with ceps and sautéd potatoes. The local cheeses, whether of cow's milk or goat's, were perfect.

CHAPELLE-AUX-CHASSES (LA) 03230 (22KM NE)

|●| L'AUBERGE DE LA CHAPELLE-AUX-CHASSES

Centre; take the N79 towards Bourbon-Lancy, then the D30 as far as the village; the restaurant is beside the church.
☎ 04.70.43.44.71

Closed Tuesday evenings, Wednesdays, and the second fortnight in September.

There's not much to distinguish this building from the others in the village, except that it radiates an indefinable charm. It looks very like a child's picture of a house and you walk through the garden to find yourself in a pretty little dining room. From then on, the only things that might rouse you from your reverie are the chirping of the birds and the delicious smells coming from the kitchen. The cooking is classical, imaginative and full of freshness; dishes include fricassee of farmed rabbit with rosemary and lime, "fisherman's stew" with a mandarin and almond sauce, stew of *rascasse* (type of fish) with saffron, and iced soufflé flavoured with verbena liqueur. The prices make it one of the more popular places in the area. Set meals 60F (weekdays), 92F, 112F and 142F.

DOMPIERRE-SUR-BESBRE 03290 (30KM E)

AUBERGE DE L'OLIVE**

129 av. de la Gare; take the D12.
☎ 04.70.34.51.87 F→ 04.70.34.61.68
Closed Fridays (except July–Aug), ten days during the February school holidays, and Nov 15–Dec 8.
Secure parking. TV.

This handsome and well looked after building covered in Virginia creeper makes a delightful place to stop. Care is taken with the cooking and the service is faultless. Set meals range in price from 60F (except Sundays and public holidays) to 235F. Comfortable bedrooms 190F with shower/wc and TV and 230F with bath and TV. The street's very noisy so if you want some peace and quiet make sure you book well in advance so as to get one of the six quiet rooms at the back. Half-board from 270F is compulsory in July and August.

MURAT 15300

10% AUX GLOBE-TROTTERS**

22 av. du Docteur-Mallet (South).
☎ 04.71.20.07.22 F→ 04.71.20.16.88
Closed Sundays, the last week in September and during the November school holidays. **Car park. TV. Canal+.**

Service noon–2pm and 1.30–9pm. There are twenty modern and very clean rooms. Doubles 170–220F. The attic rooms on the second floor are absolutely delightful – very tall people might be of a slightly different opinion! – and inexpensive. Very laid-back atmosphere in the downstairs bar which is popular with young people. The young owners are maybe a bit too casual. The cooking's OK. Set meals 65F, 85F, 110F and 140F..

10% HÔTEL-RESTAURANT LES MESSAGERIES**

18 av. du Docteur-Louis-Mallet.
☎ 04.71.20.04.04 F→ 04.71.20.02.81
Closed beginning of Nov–Dec 24. **Secure parking. TV. Canal+. Disabled access.**

Service noon–2pm and 7.30–9pm. This is a good 2-star provincial hotel. Staff are courteous and attentive, the bedrooms are pleasant and well-kept, and there are numerous facilities. Rooms with shower/wc 260F based on two people sharing, 310F for three and 360F for four. There's also a nice swimming pool, sauna and fitness studio. Good place for a short stay or as a base for hiking. Try to get one of the rooms at the back, as they're quieter. The restaurant offers classic cooking and set meals at 75F, 95F (local specialities), and 150F (offering two starters and scallops with saffron or fillet of zander with fresh pasta).

RESTAURANT LE JARROUSSET

RN122; it's 4km from Murat heading in the direction of Massiac.
☎ 04.71.20.10.69 F→ 04.71.20.15.26
Closed Monday evenings, Wednesdays, and in January (except weekends).

Service 12.15–1.30pm and 5.15–9.30pm. You'll find the setting particularly elegant and the service faultless. Eliane Andrieu runs this place with exceptional know-how and is always courteous and attentive to her guests. Only the best local produce is used in the cooking and the result is clever combinations of flavours and subtle aromas. Nothing clashes. The fish dishes are particularly well cooked and everything's wonderfully fresh. The cheeses and desserts are incredibly good – we had one of the best *crème brûlées* we've ever tasted and the chocolate tart's not bad either. Now here's the cherry on the cake – they have the best 135F set meal we've had in a very long time in France, a veritable feast (not available Saturday evenings or Sunday lunchtimes). Other set meals 190F (two starters, leg of duck *au sel*, braised cabbage with a *coulis* of peppers, or quail stuffed with *foie gras*), 270F and 360F. A la carte there's escalope of *foie gras* with caramelized apples, *blanquette* (a kind of stew) of veal sweetbreads, cabbage stuffed with truffles, and fillet of sea bass with *fondue* of fennel. Expect to spend 300–400F. Good choice of wines.

DIENNE 15300 (11KM NW)

|●| RESTAURANT DU LAC SAUVAGE

take the D3 from Murat then the D23.
☎ 04.71.20.82.65
Closed beginning of Oct to mid-June. **Car park.**

This little restaurant is the place to be when summer comes to Dienne. Run by the head of the Super-Lioran ski school, it stands by a private lake at an altitude of 1,230m – heaven on earth for hikers and fishermen! The setting is magnificent, you'll get a nice welcome, and the kitchen uses local produce to prepare tasty regional specialities that are served up in generous portions. The trout with bacon, the *truffade* (potato cake with *Cantal* cheese), the *pounti* (a mixture of bacon and Swiss chard), and the mutton tripe are especially good. You've the choice of the 75F set meal or à la carte. You can even fish for your own trout – no permit needed and there's equipment for hire.

SUPER-LIORAN 15300 (12KM SW)

10% ⌂ |●| HÔTEL-RESTAURANT LE ROCHER DU CERF**

How to get there: take the N122 from Murat then the D67.
☎ 04.71.49.50.14 F 04.71.49.54.07
Closed second half of April–end of June and second half of Sept–Dec 19. **Car park. TV.**

This is a typical family hotel in a ski resort. Located near the slopes, it's the nicest place in the area and the staff are always friendly and helpful. Bedrooms are simple and well-kept – the ones overlooking the valley are especially nice. Doubles 150F with basin, 190F with shower/wc and 230F with bath. The restaurant has the same kind of homy atmosphere and the set meals for guests taking board are planned over a two week period so you won't get the same thing day after day. Set meals 49F, 72F and up to 170F. Specialities include stuffed cauliflower, trout with bacon, *truffade* (potato cake with *Cantal* cheese), *pounti* (bacon and Swiss chard), rib steak with *bleu d'Auvergne* (a local blue cheese), escalope *cantalienne* and bilberry fruit tart. Children's menu also available. A friendly hotel, ideal for skiing in winter and walking in summer.

LAVIGERIE 15300 (15KM W)

|●| AUBERGE ADRIENNE NIOCEL

route de Dienne; take the D680 – it's just after Dienne.
☎ 04.71.20.82.25
By reservation only in the evenings and in the low season.

If you want to experience regional cooking at its best then head for this lovely inn – an authentic Cantal house – on the road that plunges from Puy-Mary to Dienne. This is where gifted Adrienne Niocel prepares her dishes with loving care. You'll have to go through the pantry to get to the delightful dining room that's full of hikers and locals. It's very colourful, with large stone slabs on the floor and box beds lining the walls. For 80F you'll get good country ham, one of the tastiest *truffades* (potato cake with *Cantal* cheese) in the region, cheese, and homemade fruit tart. You'll get a warm and unpretentious welcome.

ALLANCHE 15160 (23KM NE)

⌂ |●| HÔTEL-RESTAURANT AU FOIRAIL

Maillargues; take the N122 from Murat, then the D679.
☎ 04.71.20.41.15
Closed Jan 1–10 and evenings Oct–June. **Car park.**

Service noon–2pm and, in the summer, 7–8pm. *Au Foirail* can be found on a little hill 1km outside Allanche right in the middle of the summer pasture near one of the Auvergne's biggest cattle markets. It's a simple place, the staff are friendly and the meat is excellent, of course. The restaurant serves Salers beef, although other kinds are starting to invade the market. Hearty *menu du jour* 60F. On Sundays, try the *repas amélioré* for 90F. There are panoramic views from the dining-room windows. Bedrooms are simple and well-kept.

NARNHAC 15230

10% ⌂ |●| L'AUBERGE DE PONT LA VIEILLE**

Pont-la-Vieille.
☎ 04.71.73.42.60 F 04.71.73.42.20
Closed in November. **Car park. TV.**

Service noon–2pm and 7–9pm. This is a welcoming little hotel housed in a well restored building. It's set back a little from the D990 and has a pretty garden in front. Rooms are quiet and pleasant. Doubles 190–250F. Half-board – from 190F per person – is compulsory in July and August. Set meals feature regional specialities and for 59F you'll get trout with bacon *à l'ancienne*, for 78F guinea fowl with ceps, and for 100F *rissole Saint-Flour* (a sort of fritter with a cabbage and bacon filling) and stuffed cabbage. The 130F set meal comes with two starters. A good place if you want to do some fishing or just relax.

PAILHEROLS 15800

10% ☗ |●| L'AUBERGE DES MONTAGNES**

Centre; take the D154 then the D54; it's east of Vic-sur-Cère.
☎ 04.71.47.57.01 ➡ 04.71.49.63.83
Closed Oct 15–Dec 20 (except during the November school holidays). **Car park**. **TV**. **Disabled access**.

This is the kind of good family hotel you dream of. A pretty little winding road from Vic-sur-Cère will lead you up to a friendly old farmhouse on the outskirts of the village that's been nicely renovated and has a terrace and, in the old barn on the other side of the road, an indoor swimming pool and a games room. It also has an outdoor pool and recently added a couple of new attractions – rides in a horse-drawn carriage and a climbing wall. The bedrooms might be on the small side but they're cosy and well decorated. Doubles 215F with shower/wc. There are bigger rooms at 280F in another building a few hundred metres away. The restaurant has two very bright dining areas (one of which is the lounge with the traditional *cantou,* or inglenook fireplace) and you'll find the set meals excellent value for money. The *menus du jour* at 72F and 95F offer *pounti* (bacon and Swiss chard) with prunes, meat or mutton tripe and *truffade* (potato cake with *Cantal* cheese). For 122F you can have the special fish dish or medallions of lamb with pink peppercorns. The 150F gourmet set meal has to be ordered in advance. Some of the specialities are salmon trout in puff pastry, goose tart, duck with apples and bilberries, and *croustine* with praline. Half-board and children's set meal available. A two-star hotel that definitely deserves to be upgraded to three! Although it's fairly new, it's in keeping with the traditional style of building and the beautiful turret, tiny pond and wonderful view just set it off nicely. It's popular, so it would be a good idea to book ahead.

PLEAUX 15700

☗ |●| HÔTEL-RESTAURANT DU COMMERCE

Centre.
☎ 04.71.40.41.11
Closed Dec 20–Jan 10. **Car park**. **TV**.

Located 20km south-west of Mauriac, this is your classic country hotel – small, very simple and welcoming. Bedrooms are clean and well-kept. Doubles 180–220F. The restaurant serves up generous portions of local dishes. The 70F *menu du jour* comes with a good selection of cold meats, a roast, *truffade* (potato cake with *Cantal* cheese), cheese, and dessert. Half-board is possible (200F per person). Staff are friendly and attentive.

PONTAUMUR 63380

10% ☗ |●| HÔTEL-RESTAURANT DE LA POSTE**

av. du Marronnier.
☎ 04.73.79.90.15 ➡ 04.73.79.73.17
Closed Sunday evenings and Mondays (except in July and August) and Dec 15–Feb 1. **Secure parking**. **TV**.

Service noon–2pm and 7.30–9.30pm. Jean-Paul Quinty is a wonderful chef who knows the region like the back of his hand and is equally knowledgeable about its produce. He matures his cheese himself and in winter produces wonderful brawn and very tasty *saucissons.* You'll find the regulars at the counter reading the local newspaper and commenting on the news. The wine here is marvellous – Quinty has one of the best cellars in the Auvergne – and it comes in carafes. The restaurant offers gourmet cooking and set meals ranging in price from 90F to 250F. There's a great *grenadin* of veal with *bleu d'Auvergne* (a local blue cheese), excellent fish and various types of home-made bread to suit the different dishes. A few very pretty rooms are available if you want to sleep off all that delicious food – 210F with shower/wc and 230F with bath.

PUY-EN-VELAY (LE) 43000

10% ☗ HÔTEL LE RÉGIONAL*

36 bd Maréchal-Fayolle (Centre).
☎ 04.71.09.37.74
Closed Sunday afternoons. **TV**.

This little hotel in the centre of town may not look like much from the outside but the inside's been renovated. Bedrooms are ordinary but they're cheap. The ones at the back are quieter. The reception area is rather simple but still has a certain style. Good place if you're doing some hillwalking or you're on a tight budget. Doubles 120F with washing facilities and 160F with bath/wc.

10% ☗ |●| HÔTEL BRISTOL**

7 and 9 av. Maréchal-Foch.
☎ 04.71.09.13.38 ➡ 04.71.09.51.70
Closed Mondays out of season. **Secure parking**. **TV**. **Canal+**. **Disabled access**.

Service noon–2pm and 7.30–10pm. A very British hotel as you might expect from the name. It's a tall old building, the kind of place you'd find in a spa town in the Auvergne, with an entirely renovated and modernized interior. The staff are friendly and professional. Round the back there's a brand new building overlooking the garden – this is where you'll find the bedrooms, which are impeccable, very bright and very quiet. All come with bath and direct-dial phone and cost 215–290F. Some of the bathrooms are really big. It may look chic but *Le Bristol* will give you a warm welcome whether you happen to be a sales rep with a mobile phone or a tourist caught in the rain while out cycling – a good sign. Try the carefully prepared traditional dishes in the restaurant, which has set meals from 88F.

☗ |●| HÔTEL-RESTAURANT LE VAL VERT**

6 av. Baptiste-Marcet; it's at the side of the road near the Puy south exit heading for Aubenas.
☎ 04.71.09.09.30 ➡ 04.71.09.36.49 **Car park**. **TV**. **Canal+**. **Disabled access**.

Service noon–2pm and 7–10pm. This little hotel, renovated very recently, looks like one of a chain from the outside. Once you're inside though, you'll find a friendly, homy atmosphere. The staff are always smiling and provide an excellent service. The comfortable and modern rooms come with phone and are nicely decorated and very well looked after. The ones overlooking the road are soundproofed, but if it's absolute peace and quiet you're after try for one at the back with a view of the shopping and residential area. Bedrooms with shower/wc 290F. Good cooking and carefully prepared meals in the classical restaurant. Set meals 72–160F.

☗ DYKE HÔTEL**

37 bd Maréchal-Fayolle (Centre).
☎ 04.71.09.05.30 ➡ 04.71.02.58.66
Closed Christmas–New Year's Day. **Secure parking**. **TV**. **Canal+**.

The *Dyke Hôtel* has all the advantages of a chain hotel plus it's centrally located and has secure parking. Everything's clean and brand-new, the décor's low-key, and the service is efficient. Bedrooms are identical and the mattresses very firm. Doubles 230F with shower/wc and 250F with bath. "Dyke", by the way, refers to the sugar loaf type of rock formation they get around here.

☗ |●| HÔTEL LE RÉGINA***

34 bd Maréchal-Fayolle (Centre).
☎ 04.71.09.14.71 ➡ 04.71.09.18.57
Secure parking. **TV**. **Canal+**. **Disabled access**.

Service noon–2.30pm and 7–11pm.This centrally located hotel, housed in a beautiful old building, is something of an institution in Puy. Although it has three stars, the prices are very reasonable considering the high standard of comfort and service provided. Doubles with shower/wc or bath cost 250–350F depending on the season. Staff are courteous and friendly. If you want peace and quiet ask for a room at the back rather than one overlooking the street. The ground-floor restaurant offers incredible value for money and some of the best cooking in Puy. For less than 100F (well, 78F to be exact), you can have the set meal of regional specialities. And the fine Auvergne cooking is set off by the elegant tableware. A meal of the same quality in Paris would cost at least 200F!

|●| RESTAURANT L'OLYMPE

8 rue du Collège (Centre).
☎ 04.71.05.90.59 ➡ same.
Closed Sunday evenings and Mondays.

You'll get a jovial friendly welcome in this delightful little pastel green restaurant that's only a stone's throw from the town hall in a cobbled alleyway in the conservation area. Thanks to the young chef, it's become one of the best eating places in Puy in the space of a few years. He's very keen on sticking as much as possible to local dishes while at the same time giving them his own touch – sometimes bordering on the exotic. The result is a style of cooking that's faithful to its roots but that has been made considerably lighter. The food is presented very artistically on large plates, with lentils, trout, bilberries and verbena playing star roles. A 72F *menu du jour* is served weekday lunchtimes. Other set meals, equally delightful, range in price from 87F to 272F.

|●| RESTAURANT MARC ET ÉRIC TOURNAYRE

12 rue Chênebouterie (Centre); it's behind the town hall.
☎ 04.71.09.58.94 ➡ 04.71.02.68.38
Closed Sunday evenings and Mondays.

With its beautiful façade and its superb vaulted dining room that dates from the 16th century and has some beautiful murals, this is the most delightful restaurant in Puy, as far as we're concerned. The service is pleasant and unobtrusive and the Tournayre brothers are first-rate chefs. The two cheapest set meals (105F and 150F) are just perfect – try the knuckle of veal and *croustillant* of pig's trotters, the *truffade* (potato cake with *Cantal* cheese) with a Saint-Agur sauce or the *galette* of veal sweetbreads and panfried *foie gras* with ceps. There's a good range of desserts and they're served up in generous helpings. That also applies to the children's 70F set meal.

LE PETIT PRINCE

26 rue Vibert.
☎ 04.71.02.95.91
Closed Sunday evenings and Mondays.

A pretty little restaurant in a quiet street. The young chef may not have travelled to India or the Middle East but he certainly knows a lot about spices and their subtle flavours. Coriander, cinnamon, curry powder and lemon grass give his regional specialities an imaginative and exotic touch and prices are reasonable considering the quality of the food. Set meals are 89F, 125F and 150F and à la carte is also available. Specialities include pork with lemon grass, sea bream with aniseed and curry powder, lentils with dill and, for dessert, kiwi fruit with cinammon. The wine comes from vintages specially chosen by the restaurant and offer very good value for money. So even if you have some wine the bill will be reasonable. Courteous welcome and service. There you have it – a *Petit Prince* with his head in the clouds but his feet planted firmly on the ground.

SAINT-VINCENT 43800 (18KM N)

RESTAURANT LA RENOUÉE

Cheyrac; take the D103 that follows the gorges of the Loire.
☎ 04.71.08.55.94
Closed Mondays and Sunday evenings (except in July and August), and beginning of Jan–end of Feb.

The most delightful place in the area with its tiny garden, romantic looking building, warm welcome, and fine imaginative cooking. Try the zander with crispy onions, the morels stuffed with duck *foie gras* or the fricassee of pike with green lentil sauce. Set meals 98–230F and children's menu 55F. Nice afternoon tea *formule* available Sunday afternoons.

SAINT-JULIEN-CHAPTEUIL 43260 (20KM E)

RESTAURANT VIDAL

place du Marché; take the D15.
☎ 04.71.08.70.50 F 04.71.08.40.14
Closed Monday evenings and Tuesdays out of season and mid-Jan–end Feb. **Car park**.

Service noon–2pm and 7.30–9pm. Jean-Pierre Vidal is one of the most brilliant and creative chefs – and consequently one of the most important – in the Haute-Loire. He describes himself as "a country cook" and is modest about his talent. The 95F set meal (not available Sundays) sums up to perfection what it is he does. The 140F set meal gives green Puy lentils pride of place (and in fact is called Esau – who, you will remember, gave up his birthright for a dish of lentils) and they make an appearance in every course. There's terrine of lentils, zander or met with lentils, *gratiné* of *fourme d'Ambert* (a blue cheese) with lentils, and even a warm soufflé with green lentils and honey. A virtuoso performance and enough to make even the most confirmed lentil-hater think again. The cooking is superb and the kitchen uses nothing but the freshest of local produce. You'll get courteous and attentive service in the quiet, pleasant dining room. It's next to the bar belonging to Jean-Pierre's father, who keeps a quizzical eye on his brilliant son. A place it's worth travelling at least 20km for. They're planning on adding a few bedrooms some time in the future.

SAINT-HAON 43340 (29KM SW)

10% AUBERGE DE LA VALLÉE**

Centre; take the N88 in the direction of Pradelles/Langogne, then the D33 as far as Cayres (7km away) and the D31.
☎ 04.71.08.20.73 F 04.71.08.29.21
Closed Mondays out of season, January, and February.

The village is at an altitude of 970m and the inn stands in the square dominated by an unusual church tower. Just 3km away the Allier cascades between the rock faces of a deep valley. The inn has ten comfortable and well laid out bedrooms, some of which have the heavy solid kind of furniture you associate with your grandparents' day. Expect to pay 210F for a double with shower/wc and telephone. Revel in the peace and quiet you'll find out here in the wilds. The restaurant offers regional set meals at 70F, 110F, 135F and 150F. The chef's specialities include veal sweetbreads with morels, salad of smoked goose fillets, and escalope with a cream and *mousseron* (a type of mushroom) sauce. You'll receive a nice welcome. A good place to stay between Le Puy and Langogne in Lozère.

RIOM 63200

|●| RESTAURANT L'ÂNE GRIS

13 rue Gomot (Centre).
☎ 04.73.38.25.10
Closed Sundays, Monday lunchtimes and August.

Crazy? Dreadful? Heaven on earth? We're not too sure what you'll think of the restaurant and its owner. Casimir's slightly mad but ever so nice, even if he does spend his time making jokes at his customers' expense. Born and brought up in the Auvergne, he's a bit of a chauvinist, a bit of a complainer, and a bit of a tease, but he's generous too. His pet nickname for people is "baboon" (he started off using it on his chef and now that's what his favourite customers get called too). As soon as you step inside you'll hear a very loud, cheerful voice asking "What do you want?" Play along with him – give as good as you get! Casimir says people are so fed up sometimes that coming here to get teased is more fun than the cinema! Sometimes he's just not in the mood to act as waiter and a customer will have to do it for him. And whatever you do, don't compliment him about the collection on display in the pretty and rather rustic dining room. He'll come back with a retort to the effect that collections are made up of dead things and he's much more interested in living! To hear him talk, you wouldn't think the food was up to much, but don't believe a word of it. The kitchen produces traditional local dishes such as *truffade* (potato cake with *Cantal* cheese) with ham (74F), *aligot* (fried potato cakes made with *Aligot* cheese) and sausage (58F), and salt pork with lentils (64F). There are also good Charolais grills and a brilliant list of local wines. Casimir lovingly chooses these and is only too pleased to tell you all about them. No set meals so expect to pay about 110F à la carte. We love this place, in fact we're crazy about it and just can't get enough. Give it a try!

VOLVIC 63530 (7KM W)

⌂ |●| HÔTEL-RESTAURANT DU COMMERCE**

3 place de l'Église (West); take the D986.
☎ 04.73.33.60.64 📠 04.73.33.56.94
Closed end Jan–end Feb. **Car park**.

The name might sound pretty ordinary but it's synonymous with the traditional kind of hotel that this is. The cooking is traditional and there's a wide choice of set meals 80–330F. Specialities include zander with a cep sauce, calf's head *terrine*, frog's legs with Chanturgue wine, panfried veal sweetbreads with langoustines, and sautéd fillet of veal. Doubles with shower/wc 200F. Friendly, genuine welcome.

BLOT L'ÉGLISE 63440 (29KM NW)

|●| AUBERGE LES PEYTOUX

lieu-dit Les Peytoux; it's between Chardonnières-les-Vieilles and Blot-l'Eglise.
☎ 04.73.97.44.17
Closed Mondays–Thursdays. **Car park**.

A word of warning: a meal here doesn't come easy. They don't advertise but its reputation has grown by word of mouth and you have to book about a month in advance! Located in a remote valley near the Morge, the inn is the creation of Adrian, a rugged kind-hearted man with something of the Viking about him. He arrived here from Alsace about fifteen years ago with great hopes of sailing off on a barge into the unknown. But that's looking increasingly remote – this is such a magical little place! Ingrid's in charge of the kitchen and everything she uses comes from the farm. The goat's cheese for the salad is excellent, as are the salads, and the poultry and kid are both first rate. All those plus *potée* (thick soup) feature in the set meals which range from 60F to 130F and include coffee and liqueur.

SAIGNES 15240

⌂ |●| HÔTEL RELAIS ARVERNE*

Centre.
☎ 04.71.40.62.64 📠 04.71.40.61.14
Closed during the February school holidays and the first two weeks in October; restaurant closed Friday and Sunday evenings out of season. **Car park**. **TV**.

A renovated stone building with a huge corner watchtower where everything points to there being a skilled handyman around – for example, the tables on the terrace are made from very old stone wheels, and in some rooms the wcs are concealed behind an old wardrobe door. The bedrooms are comfortable and they can all be reached from the outside terrace, which means you can come and go as you please. Doubles 220–250F with bath. The hotel's full of nooks and crannies – no long monotonous corridors here! In the dining room with its big clock and even bigger fireplace, you'll be served dishes that are influenced by the nearby Dordogne. Set meals 70F, 95F (a choice of fricassee of rabbit *provençale* or trout with bacon), 170F and 210F. Some of the other dishes on offer are monkfish with bilberries, escalope of *foie gras* with cider sauce, mutton tripe *bonne femme*, veal sweetbreads in puff pastry with morels, and grilled steak *au bleu*. There's a garden too.

SAINT-ANTHÈME 63660

10% HÔTEL-RESTAURANT AU PONT DE RAFFINY**

Saint-Romain; take the D261 for 5km in the direction of Viverols.
☎ 04.73.95.49.10 F 04.73.95.80.21
Closed Sunday evenings and Mondays out of season and beginning of Jan–mid-Feb. **Car park**.

If you're looking for a gourmet meal, head for this place. It stands on the banks of a little river near Saint-Anthème and has recently been renovated. But the main attraction is Alain Beaudoux's light creative cooking and dishes like the superb *andouillette* of fish, the young rabbit *en crépine*, and the verbena *parfait*. Set meals 85F (weekdays), 120F and 160F. There are some wonderful finds on the wine list and prices are reasonable. The hotel is quiet and comfortable and rooms with shower/wc or bath cost 210–240F.

SAINT-FLOUR 15100

HÔTEL DU NORD*

18 rue des Lacs (Centre).
☎ 04.71.60.28.00 F 04.71.60.07.33
Secure parking. **TV**.

Service noon–1.30pm and 7.30–9pm. Known locally primarily for its restaurant. The dining room's a bit showy and provincial but the prices are very good, with the daily special at 40F and set meals at 65F, 85F, 90F, 100F and 140F. Portions are generous, and there are at least four main courses to choose from including quail and grapes in puff pastry, and beef with a mushroom sauce. Expect to spend 180F for a double with shower/wc. Everything's very well kept and it's refurbished every few years. If you stay for at least three days you can get half-board at 200F.

HÔTEL-RESTAURANT DES ROCHES**

place d'Armes; it's opposite the museum, a stone's throw from the cathedral.
☎ 04.71.60.09.70. F 04.71.60.45.21
Closed Sundays out of season. **TV**. **Canal+**.

It's very central and was renovated throughout in 1993. It has bright pleasant bedrooms and you'll get a very nice welcome. Doubles 230–260F. The restaurant has set meals at 69F, 95F, 125F and 165F and you can choose between regional specialities or classics like fricassee of scallops, veal sweetbreads with morels and duck breast with raspberry vinegar. It's worth noting that they aren't as strict here when it comes to mealtimes – you can still order at 9pm.

10% AUBERGE DE LA PROVIDENCE**

1 rue du Château-d'Alleuze (South).
☎ 04.71.60.12.05 F 04.71.60.33.94
Closed Monday lunchtimes in season, Sunday evenings and Mondays out of season, and Oct 15–Nov 15.
Secure parking. **TV**. **Canal+**.

This very old inn has been completely refurbished and the bedrooms decorated in pastel shades of pink, blue, green and yellow. The décor generally is fairly low-key. There are about 10 rooms in all, ranging in price from 270F to 300F. The bathrooms are well designed. The set meals offer some of the best value for money in town. For 100F you can have morels (in season). There's storage for motorbikes.

RESTAURANT CHEZ GENEVIÈVE

25 rue des Lacs (Centre).
☎ 04.71.60.17.97
Closed Sundays except in July and August.

We'll have to rename this place *Chez Valérie* after the new owner, who's carrying on where Geneviève left off. This used to be a shop but is now a simple, tastefully decorated restaurant. Valérie serves hearty meals at very good prices (48–95F) and the cooking of Auvergne has pride of place. The red meat comes from Aubrac and is tasty and tender. Choose from dishes such as leg of lamb with garlic sauce, country-style *aligot* (fried potato cakes made with *aligot* cheese), *potée* (thick soup), thick steak with pepper sauce and hazelnut salad *au bleu*. The kitchen is upstairs beside a little dining room that's popular with the regulars. This is one of our favourite places in Saint-Flour.

SAINT-GEORGES 15100 (4KM SE)

10% 🏠 🍽 L'AUBERGE DU BOUT DU MONDE

Le Bout du Monde Saint-Georges.
☎ 04.71.60.15.84 F 04.71.73.05.10
Car park. TV. Disabled access.

Service noon–1.30pm and 7.30–9pm. No, it's not quite at the end of the world but the road doesn't go any further. This traditional little hotel cum restaurant is situated right in the heart of the valley very close to Saint-Flour – an ideal place for anglers and walkers – and serves the best regional specialities in the area, including *pounti* (bacon and Swiss chard), stuffed rabbit, *truffade* (potato cake with *Cantal* cheese), and *aligot* (potato cakes made with *aligot* cheese and fried). There's a *menu du jour* at 60F and a wide range of set meals. The 70F one comes with the restaurant's own ham, while 90F gets you *tourte de caillé* (curds), *pounti*, and stuffed rabbit with cabbage, and 110F salad of black pudding with walnuts, trout with bacon or a dozen snails and *coq au vin* (110F). The most expensive set mea, at 140F, consists of young goat *à la cantalienne*, snails in puff pastry and asparagus with garlic sauce, and frog's legs *à la lozérienne*. You'll get the kind of welcome that makes you feel like one of the family. Simple well-kept bedrooms – 120F with shower/wc on the landing or 230F with bath.

GARABIT 15320 (12KM SE)

10% 🏠 🍽 HÔTEL-RESTAURANT BEAU SITE**

☎ 04.71.23.41.46 F 04.71.23.46.34
Closed beginning of Nov–end March. **Secure parking. TV. Disabled access.**

Since it stands above the viaduct built by Eiffel (yes, the same man who built the Eiffel Tower), the hotel is where you'll get the best view of the lake and the viaduct. It's a large building with bright roomy bedrooms. Doubles 150F, 220F and 250F. Excellent facilities include a heated swimming pool and tennis courts in wonderful surroundings. An ideal base for fishing, windsurfing and long walks. The restaurant offers set meals at 70F, 100F (a choice of sautéd veal with ceps, *coq au vin* or trout with bacon), 135F and 180F. Specialities include a *gratinée* of scallops, beef fillet with morels, grilled *confit* of duck with ceps, fried trout with bacon and hazelnuts, *chiffonnade* with warm Cantal cheese and frog's legs *provençal*.

NEUVÉGLISE 15260 (21KM SW)

🏠 🍽 HÔTEL-RESTAURANT L'AUBERGE DU PONT DE LANAU**

pont de Lanau; take the D921.
☎ 04.71.23.57.76 F 04.71.23.53.84
Closed beginning of Jan–end of Feb. **Secure parking. TV.**

Jean-Michel Cornut and his wife have made a delightful hotel and restaurant out of a beautifully restored renovated coaching inn. The fine gourmet cooking draws inspiration from traditional Auvergne cuisine and the set meals, ranging in price from 80F to 280F offer excellent interpretations of local dishes such as tripe on a bed of lentils, a *millefeuille* of *bleu d'Auvergne* (a local blue cheese), roast duck with a sauce made from wine lees, and escalope of *foie gras* with ceps. Original dishes are also available, including an excellent *alicots de canard* (stewed duck wings and giblets) with garlic. The wines are of the same high standard as the food, with ones from the Auvergne featuring large and some Boudes aged in oak barrels. The superb dining room has a large stone fireplace and Madame Cornut will give you a warm welcome. Unobtrusive service. The rooms come with bath and are quiet and warm since the wallcovering is quite thick. Terrace and large shady garden.

SAINT-GERVAIS-D'AUVERGNE 63390

🏠 🍽 HÔTEL-RESTAURANT CASTEL HÔTEL 1904**

rue du Castel.
☎ 04.73.85.70.42 F 04.73.85.84.39
Closed Nov 15–Easter. **Secure parking. TV.**

This house used to belong to Monsieur de Maintenon (the husband of one of Louis XIV's mistress), then to the monks of Cluny. If you want a genuine taste the simple pleasures of days gone by, this is the place to come. The restaurant offters two different kinds of *formule*. There's a traditional one, with prices starting at 75F, which is based on local traditional produce (not available Sunday lunchtimes), and a gourmet one, where Jean-Luc Mouty, who trained with Robuchon, shows what he can do. It's hardly surprising then that his fine cooking helps you rediscover tastes and flavours you thought had gone for ever. Try the *pavé* of zander with cider, *fondant* of cabbage with stewed young rabbit, *cromesquis* of veal sweetbreads (fried and battered) or the tomato salad with fresh chanterelles, which was sheer delight. Set meals 115–175F. The hotel is roomy and very quiet, and the refurbished and well-equipped rooms are very affordable. We took a special liking to room no.1 but they all have a nice rustic touch – it's rather like staying at your granny's. Expect to pay 295–325F for a double with shower/wc or bath.

CAFÉ TALLEYRAND

lieu-dit Talleyrand-Saint-Gervais; it's 3km away going towards the dam.
☎ 04.73.85.78.47
Closed Tuesday and Thursday evenings. **Car park.**

This remote farm beside the road leading to the dam is one of our all-time favourites in the region. You can order the tasty 60F *menu du jour* any lunchtime or evening in the small dining room or you could have some of their own delicious *charcuterie* or an omelette made with eggs from their own chickens. If you want to sample some of Marie's fabulous specialities though – potato cake, stuffed rabbit or game (in season) – you'll have to give her a call the night before to place your order. Marie is so nice you wish she was your granny.

SAINT-MARTIN-SOUS-VIGOUROUX 5230

10% LE RELAIS DE LA FORGE*

Centre; take the D990 – it's west of Pierrefort.
☎ 04.71.23.36.90 F➔ 04.71.23.92.48
Closed Wednesday evenings out of season. **Car park.**

A simple little country hotel cum restaurant that's very welcoming. The restaurant has a very substantial *menu du jour* for 70F which comes with a selection of, *charcuterie*, farm-bred quail, *truffade* (potato cake with *Cantal* cheese), salad, cheese, icecream and coffee. They'll welcome you like one of the family. The large dining room is a bit kitsch. Inglenook fireplace with two big seats. There are about ten clean simple rooms with washing facilities for 180F.

SAINT-NECTAIRE 63710

10% RELAIS MERCURE – HÔTEL DES BAINS ROMAINS***

☎ 04.73.88.57.00 F➔ 04.73.88.57.02
Secure parking. TV. Canal+. Disabled access.

Service noon–2.30pm and 7–10pm. This impressive building was turned into a hotel when spas were all the rage in Saint-Nectaire. Although we're not known for singing the praises of hotel chains, this is a delightful complex offering excellent value for money. Bedrooms are bright and very well equipped. Doubles 380F with shower/wc or bath. Facilities include an indoor pool with jacuzzi, outdoor pool, sauna, fitness machines, billiard room and piano bar. Staff are warm and friendly. The restaurant has been tastefully refurbished in neo-classical style. Set meals 110–165F. Special dietary needs can be met. À la carte there's *coq au vin*, mutton tripe, trout *en papillote*, fillet of duck with Cantal (a local cheese) or zander with a *fondue* of leeks.

SAINT-POURÇAIN-SUR-SIOULE 03500

10% HÔTEL-RESTAURANT LE CHÊNE VERT**

35 bd Ledru-Rollin (Centre).
☎ 04.70.45.40.6 F➔ 04.70.45.68.50
Closed Sunday evenings and Mondays out of season, and in January. **Car park. TV.**

Service 12.15–1.30pm and 7.30–9pm. The chances of missing out on *Le Chêne Vert* when you're in Saint-Pourçain are very slim indeed. It's a good conventional establishment with excellent facilities and quite reasonable prices. Pleasant bedrooms with fresh décor. Doubles 170F with shower (these are rather simple), 280F with shower/wc and 400F with bath (a bit on the expensive side). Good traditional cooking with lots of game in season. Set meals 95 (except Sundays)–205F.

SAINT-URCIZE 15110

10% *HÔTEL-RESTAURANT REMISE*

East; take the D12 then the D112.
☎ 04.71.23.20.02
Secure parking.

The owners of this place, Fred Remise and his wife, are both very nice people (and no, just because he's called Fred doesn't mean he's English). It's your typical good country inn that's popular with young and old alike and where anglers and fishers rub shoulders with cyclists and footballers. The wonderful home cooking is based on whatever the market has to offer and the dishes on offer might include *aligot*, (potato cakes made with *Aligot* cheese) nettle soup, and trout. There are no set meals or à la carte here – just the owner's suggestions. Expect to spend about 75F. Children's menu 45F. Jeannette, Fred's wife, makes dandelion jam from an old recipe. Since so many anglers stay here, they make up picnic baskets for the day for 45F. You've Fred to thank for that idea! He can probably tell you anything you want to know about the region from local history to the best walks and places to visit. If you want, he'll put in a good word for you with the old folk who know about the history of Saint-Urcize. The welcome is so friendly and the atmosphere so pleasant here you almost feel embarrassed about staying for such a short time. Doubles 130F with basin, 200F with shower/wc.

SALERS 15140

10% ☗ |●| HÔTEL DU BEFFROI**

rue du Beffroi (Centre); it's in the old part of town.
☎ 04.71.40.70.11 F➔ 04.71.40.70.16
Closed Nov–April. **Secure parking**. **TV**.

This old building, which was renovated not too long ago, looks onto a very busy pedestrian street. It has ten bedrooms with shower or bath. Doubles 220F and 230F. The cheaper ones are on the second floor – small and well laid out attic rooms with a rooftop view. The restaurant does hearty regional set meals for 65F (not Sundays), 75F, 95F and 132F featuring dishes like *truffade* (potato cake with *Cantal* cheese), *potée* (thick soup), *pounti* (a mixture of bacon and Swiss chard), and Salers beef. One of the good things about this place is the fact that it's too small for groups. Good friendly atmosphere. Half-board available.

|●| LES TEMPLIERS

rue du Couvent; take the D680 or the D22; it's in the walled part of the town.
☎ 04.71.40.71.35
Closed Mondays Nov–March, evenings up to April, and mid-Nov–mid-FebXXX clashes with first element.

Service noon–2pm and 7–9pm. The large comfy dining room on the first floor. has tablecloths and napkins made of real cloth. The restaurant has a good reputation even though the town's very touristy. It has set meals at 68F (mutton tripe, *truffade* and *pounti*), 95F (very good this – local ham and a choice of mutton tripe or Salers beef), 100F, 140F and 170F. A la carte, there's rib of beef for two at 160F or the local *fondue* at 55F per person (this has to be ordered in advance). They have a good selection of wines, with prices starting at 49F for a Côtes-d'Auvergne, 55F for a Châteaugay and 62F for a Saint-Pourçain-la-Ficelle.

|●| LE DRAC

place Tyssandiers-d'Escous (Centre).
☎ 04.71.40.72.12

Open every day. Service until 2am in summer. This early 16th century building is in the nicest part of this medieval town which has been well preserved but swarms with tourists at the height of the season. During the first half of the century what's now the restaurant was a cellar where they used to mature the local cheese, *Salers* (which is something like *Cantal*). The restaurant's been in the family for nine generations and they make you feel very welcome. Old stonework and exposed beams. Good regional 70F set meal plus the day's special, pizzas, salads and icecreams. They specialize in foreign beers. It's also a tearoom and a *crêperie*. A rather trendy place that's very popular in summer, but the staff are friendly and the service is quick.

FALGOUX (LE) 15380 (16KM NE)

☗ |●| HÔTEL-RESTAURANT L'ÉTERLOU**

Centre; take the D680 or the D37 – it's to the east of Salers.
☎ 04.71.69.51.14 F➔ 04.71.69.53.26
Closed Dec 1–22. **TV**. **Disabled access**.

It's got a good location halfway between Salers and Puy-Mary. The building is beautiful, traditional and very welcoming. The restaurant serves up hearty portions of tasty dishes. Set meals at prices ranging from 70F to 175F give pride of place to Auvergne specialities (the veal sweetbreads with morels are great).. Bedrooms are clean and pleasant. Doubles 210F with basin, 240F and 350F with bath. Half-board from 225F per person. Nice staff.

SAUGUES 43170

10% ☗ |●| LA TERRASSE**

cours Gervais (Centre).
☎ 04.71.77.83.10 F➔ 04.71.77.63.79
Closed Mondays (out of season) and January.
Secure parking. **TV**.

Service 12.15–2pm and 7.30–9.30pm. The numerous chapels dotted about the countryside make this a beautiful region to explore. And this is a very good place, friendly and with a nice owner. Doubles have been refurbished and cost 290–350F with shower/wc or bath. If you're looking for somewhere to eat, the brasserie serves classic dishes. Alternatively, the restaurant is a bit fancier and has specialities such as *fondant* of char with a lobster sauce or lamb fillet *en croûte* with rosemary. Set meals 60F (weekdays) – 160F.

PONT-D'ALLEYRAS 43580 (15KM SE)

10% ⌂ |●| HÔTEL-RESTAURANT DU HAUT-ALLIER**

How to get there: take the D33.
☎ 04.71.57.57.63 ➨ 04.71.57.57.99
Closed Sundays out of season, Mondays, and Dec–Feb. **TV. Disabled access.**

Service 12.30–2pm and 7.45–9pm. A delightful hotel cum restaurant in a little village in the valley of Haut-Allier. You'll get a warm welcome. The building was renovated recently and has a large restaurant with classical décor. The food is fairly elaborate and there's a wide choice of dishes in the set meals, which range in price from 120F to 200F. The *civet* of mussels and the young rabbit with herbs are both excellent. Try too the *blanquette* with Charroux mustard. If you're looking for something simpler, try the 65F *menu du jour* that's meant for people in a hurry. It comes with generous portions and is available at the bar or on the terrace. Wine is inexpensive – a nicely chilled Viognier is 70F for example. Doubles 235F with shower/wc and 260F with bath.

SAUVESSANGES 63840

10% ⌂ |●| HÔTEL-RESTAURANT ROURE**

Centre.
☎ 04.73.95.94.22 ➨ 04.73.95.33.96
Closed Mondays out of season and January. **Car park.**

A country hotel cum restaurant in the heart of the Forez mountains that's worth a visit for its reasonably priced gourmet dishes. Everything's home-made here, from the *terrines* to the pastries and cakes. They serve vegetables grown in their own garden (in season) and the mushrooms are picked locally. The modern restaurant, spacious and very bright, has a view of the Forez mountains. Set meals 65–155F. Bedrooms 120F with basin and 195F with shower/wc. Half-board is compulsory in August.

SAUXILLANGES 63490

10% ⌂ |●| HÔTEL-RESTAURANT CHALUT

rue des Fossés.
☎ 04.73.96.80.71 ➨ 04.73.96.87.25
Closed Sunday evenings, Mondays, Jan 25–Feb 15, and Sept 6–20. **Secure parking.**

Service noon–1.30pm and 7–9pm. Christine Chalut will welcome you with open arms to this charming inn decorated in delicate pastel shades. Her brother François's creative cooking, which is based on local produce and old family dishes like the superb potato "sausages", is sheer delight. But he doesn't limit himself to his own interpretation of regional specialities. He also has a talent for fish and we really liked the *choucroute* of fish and the langoustine ravioli with a herb sauce. The desserts aren't bad either and there is the most incredible set meal that consists of nothing but desserts (150F). There's a good 58F *menu du jour* on weekdays and the set meals at 98F, 130F, 165F and 190F are excellent. The bedrooms look as if they're from another era but they're very clean. Doubles with shower 155F.

SALLÈDES 63270 (16KM NW)

|●| L'AUBERGE DE LA REINE MARGOT

How to get there: take the D255, then the D14.
☎ 04.73.69.00.16
Closed Tuesday evenings, Wednesdays, and Jan 10–March 1.

The inn is named after the rather scandalous Queen Margot (you may remember that Isabelle Adjani played her in a film a few years ago) and is opposite the church where her remains are said to have lain. Owners Sylvie and Thierry Paris have set up two dining rooms on the first floor, one for fast and regional set meals (95–105F), and the other, more intimate, for a slightly more gourmet style of cooking (set meals 148–240F). Try the wonderful *rissoles* of snails with a nettle sauce, the char with lemon butter, the veal kidneys and sweetbreads with mustard seeds, Salers beef with morels, and the excellent *terrine* of *foie gras* which is simply superb. In short, a very appealing place – and you'll get a delightful welcome from Sylvie.

THIERS 63300

|●| RESTAURANT LE COUTELIER

4 place du Palais.

☎ 04.73.80.79.59
Closed Monday evenings (except July–Sept), Tuesdays, three weeks in June, and the second fortnight in December.

Service noon–2pm and 7–10pm. A "coutelier" is a person who makes or sells cutlery so it's logical to find a restaurant of that name in the town that's the centre of France's cutlery industry – especially when the restaurant is housed in a former cutler's workshop. There's a collection of genuine old cutlery decorating the walls, including a beautiful set of knives, and you begin to wonder if you've come to a restaurant or a museum. But it would be a pity to deprive yourself of good classic dishes that include Puy lentils with bacon, sausage stuffed with cabbage, mutton tripe and *coq au vin*. Set meals 69–135F, and for 78F you can have *truffade* (potato cake with *Cantal* cheese), ham, salad and dessert.

PESCHADOIRES 63920 (4KM)

I●I RESTAURANT LA FERME DES TROIS CANARDS

lieu-dit Biton; take the N89, then the D212 and head for Maringues – turn left at the sign and you'll find the restaurant 300m further along.
☎ 04.73.51.06.70
Closed Sunday evenings. **Car park**.

Service noon–2pm and 7–9pm. This has to be the most delightful place in the area. It's a beautifully renovated one-storey farmhouse in the heart of the countryside and only a stone's throw from the motorway exit. The cheapest set meal at 125F is perfect in terms of both cooking and presentation. The snails with bacon and the stewed oxtail that we had were both superb, the cheese was matured to perfection, and the desserts (made to order) were light and delicate. Staff are friendly and hard-working.

TOURNEMIRE 15310

☗ I●I AUBERGE DE TOURNEMIRE

rue principale; take the D60, the D160 and the D260 – you'll find it about 20km north of Aurillac.
☎ 04.71.47.61.28
Closed January.

Service noon–1.30pm and 7.30–8.30pm. This is a nice little inn in one of Cantal's most delightful villages. It stands on a hill, so you'll have a beautiful view of the valley at sunset. The five simple bedrooms (180–270F not including breakfast) are all very well kept and one or two have lovely sloping ceilings. The restaurant offers good cooking and set meals at 80F (*pounti* and black pudding with a *fondue* of onions), 110F, and 150F – this is for the gourmet and comes with *foie gras,* medallion of sole with morels, and lamb kebabs with a fish *coulis.* Half-board from 200F per person. By reservation only out of season.

VICHY 03200

10% ☗ HÔTEL DE LONDRES**

7 bd de Russie (Centre).
☎ 04.70.98.28.27 F➜ 04.70.98.29.37
Closed Oct 16–March 25. **TV**.

The *Hôtel de Londres* is an old luxury hotel which, like the town itself, has the charm of a bygone era. It deserves a footnote in the history books since Resistance leader Jean Moulin (who was later executed) organized a secret meeting here in 1941 and the hotel was eventually requisitioned by the Militia in 1943. Nowadays it's a decent place to spend the night. Rooms are well looked after and doubles range in price from 130F with washing facilities to 230F with bath. Good view from number 14 and 15.

10% ☗ I●I HÔTEL DU RHÔNE**

8 rue de Paris (Centre).
☎ 04.70.97.73.00 F➜ 04.70.97.48.25
Closed All Saints' Day–Easter. **Secure parking**. **TV**. **Disabled access**.

The owner is quite a character and will cheerfully announce that he deliberately hasn't installed a lift so as to give his guests a bit of exercise! We liked the old-fashioned cosy décor. The rooms are clean and simple – go for one overlooking the delightful patio with its hydrangeas in full flower. Doubles 150F with shower and 250F with shower/wc or bath. Set meals 59F (weekdays) – 185F The cooking is in the hands of the owner's wife, who lovingly prepares simple dishes like *Maroilles* tart (a strong cheese), sea bass with sorrel, *andouillette* in the local style, and strips of duck in orange sauce. No use coming here if you're on a diet!

10% ☗ HÔTEL DE NAPLES**

22 rue de Paris (Centre).
☎ 04.70.97.91.33 F➜ 04.70.97.91.28
Car park. **TV**. **Canal+**.

The hotel, in the most famous street in town, isn't luxurious but it has been spruced up. The pretty and well equipped rooms come with satellite TV and mini-bar. Doubles from 150F with basin/wc to 200F with bath. There's a pretty garden that's full of flowers in summer. Cordial welcome. Ask for a room overlooking the garden – the street's rather busy. Full board (about 450F for two) and half-board (350F for two) available by arrangement with three nearby restaurants.

10% ☗ ARVERNA HÔTEL**

12 rue Desbrest (Centre).
☎ 04.70.31.31.19 F➔ 04.70.97.86.43
Closed Dec 20–Jan 5. **Secure parking**. **TV**. **Canal+**.

Proprietor Robert Pérol spent many years travelling the world and stayed in a fair number of hotels. Now he's put all his likes and dislikes into practice in his own place. Friendly welcome with a personal touch. The bedrooms have been attractively decorated and numbers 101, 108 and 201 are particularly spacious and quiet. Prices start at 200F for a double with shower/wc. Full and half-board in conjunction with nearby restaurants.

10% ☗ I●I MIDLAND HÔTEL – RESTAURANT LE DERBY'S**

2-4 rue de l'Intendance (North).
☎ 04.70.97.48.48 F➔ 04.70.31.31.89
Closed Jan 1–April 23 and Oct 9–Dec 31. **Car park**. **TV**.

Service noon–2pm and 7–8.30pm. With its slightly shabby air – at least as far as the façade is concerned – and a foyer that's a bit of a mixture, this establishment is full of personality and warmth. We liked it. Whether you go for a room with modern décor or something older, they're all quiet and comfortable. The restaurant offers a wide range of dishes served up in generous portions. Set meals 85–155F. Two *formules* at 69F including drink. Try the Charolais steak flavoured with local wine, the breast of chicken in a blackcurrant sauce, or the escalope of steamed zander with lumpfish roe.

10% ☗ I●I LE PAVILLON D'ENGHIEN***

32 rue Callou.
☎ 04.70.98.33.30 F➔ 04.70.31.67.82
Closed Dec 22–Feb 1; restaurant closed Sunday evenings and Mondays. **Secure parking**. **TV**.

Service noon–2pm and 7.30–9.30pm. Recently renovated, it offers some of the best value for money that you'll find in an establishment of this calibre. The bedrooms are spacious, soundproofed and they've all got something different, particularly numbers 17, 18, 19 and 33. Doubles from 325F (200F Oct 15–Feb 15). Staff are courteous and helpful. The restaurant offers pleasant meals based on seasonal produce. Set meals 69F (weekday lunchtimes only), 100F and 120F. For a mere 100F, we got a *marbré* of young rabbit with herbs, escalope of salmon in a Saint-Pourçain sauce, cheese, and a rather good dessert. Nice swimming pool.

I●I RESTAURANT DE L'HÔTEL PLAZA

9 rue du Parc (Centre).
☎ 04.70.98.62.93
Secure parking.

Prices in this enormous restaurant, centrally located and built in the town's heyday, are surprisingly good. It offers three quite decent *formules* – meat or fish plus salad and dessert – at prices ranging from 50F to 60F and set meals (larger and with bigger portions) at 110F and 150F, the latter including an apéritif and wine. Try the salmon with Puy lentils, the oven-baked rack of lamb or the sole *meunière*. Smiling staff and good service. Delightful décor that seems to belong to another era. The bedrooms don't come cheap – 440F for a double.

I●I L'AUTRE SOURCE

10 rue du Casino (Centre).
☎ 04.70.59.85.68
Closed Sundays and Mondays.

Right in the centre, just behind the casino, this is probably the nicest and brightest little restaurant in the area – a welcome contrast to Vichy's rather dreary image. The atmosphere is relaxed and cheerful. It serves inexpensive (35F) salads and sandwiches made mostly from local produce, and the cheese platter contains some unusual varieties. It's also a wine bar and Patrice will gladly introduce you to the local wines and to a number of vintages personally chosen by him. You can buy wine by the glass for a very reasonable price. The opening hours are flexible to ensure maximum customer satisfaction. Last orders 12.30–1am.

I●I LA BRASSERIE DU CASINO

4 rue du Casino (Centre).
☎ 04.70.98.23.06 F➔ 04.70.98.53.17
Closed Tuesday evenings, Wednesdays, the first week in March, and all of November. **Car park**.

Service noon–1.30pm and 7.30–10pm. This has definitely got more character than any other restaurant in vichy. Big pre-war brasseries have a certain charm and this one, built in 1920 and now a listed building, is no exception. The walls are covered in photos of the many stars who used to come here after performing at the nearby opera house. Typical bourgeois brasserie cooking for middle-class people. The *à la carte* menu has a long list of classic dishes and balanced set meals are also available at 85F (weekdays), 99F and 145F.

I●I L'AMANDIER

7 av. de Gramont; it's near the station, at the corner of rue de Paris.
☎ 04.70.31.93.82
Closed Mondays, Tuesday lunchtimes, the last week in September, and the first week in October.

Stéphane Sabot has created a little corner of Provence here and his dining room is reminiscent of the sun, cicadas and the Mediterranean. The cooking too draws its inspiration from the south with dishes like salt cod with cherry tomatoes, ravioli stuffed with snails and goat's cheese, and poached chicken with Swiss chard. Not only does the chef insist on the freshest of produce and come up with some inspired combinations, he also uses old-fashioned vegetables with considerable success, making a meal here a delightful experience. Reasonably priced set meals (90–190F).

I●I LE PIQUENCHAGNE

69 rue de Paris.
☎ 04.70.98.63.45
Closed Tuesday evenings, Wednesdays, during the February school holidays, and for a fortnight late July–early Aug.

Service noon–2pm and 7 -10pm. If you need to be reassured that traditional cooking is alive and well, come here. It's a bit of a surprise in a spa town to come across dishes of the kind produced by chef Daniel Vincent – invigorating, prepared in classic fashion and honed to perfection. There's panfried fillet of bream, roast rabbit with coriander and cumin, fillet of sole with a mustard sauce, and *croustillant* of local lamb with a garlic sauce. It will all get the taste buds going but it won't do the waistline any good. (You'll have to decide for yourself what's more important.). Set meals 90F, 130F and 150F. The service and the welcome you get from Madame Vincent are as pleasant and traditional as the cooking.

I●I L'ENVOLÉE

44 av. E.-Gilbert.
☎ 04.70.32.85.15
Closed Tuesdays and Wednesday lunchtimes.

Service noon -2pm and 7.30–10pm. It's well away from the centre and the usual tourist haunts and has some surprises in store. Staff are pleasant and the service is good but the best thing about the restaurant is the wonderful cooking bursting with fresh flavours. The chef tends to stick to classical dishes but who can blame him when he produces things like *rillettes* of young rabbit, monkfish with Chinese flavourings, house smoked cod with shallot butter, free range chicken with garlic *confit*, chicory icecream, and a marvellous *croquant* of gingerbread. The dining room is decorated in shades of pink. Set meals 130–195F. Not exactly cheap but good value for money.

BELLERIVE-SUR-ALLIER 03700 (2KM SW)

☗ LA RIGON

route de Serbannes.
☎ 04.70.59.86.46 F➜ 04.70.59.94.77
Closed Sundays out of season, December and January.
Car park. **TV**. **Disabled access**.

It was a real pleasure coming across this place – a little haven of peace and quiet set in extensive grounds up in the Bellerives hills above Vichy and just five minutes from the town centre. You'll get the best of both worlds here – the excellent service and type of hours you'd expect from a hotel and the charm of a good quality guest house. It's a beautiful building with its own grounds and the well decorated country style bedrooms are all special in their own little way. Prices start at 270F out of season (330F in summer) for a double with shower/wc. Hearty breakfast 36F. Brilliant swimming pool in a large 1900s conservatory. Very friendly staff.

ABREST 03200 (3KM S)

10% ☗ I●I La Colombière*

route de Thiers; take the D906.
☎ 04.70.98.69.15 F➜ 04.70.31.50.89
Closed Mondays, Sunday evenings (out of season), and mid Jan–mid Feb. **Car park**. **TV**.

Service noon–1.30pm and 7.15–9pm. A delightful restaurant in an old dovecote high above the Allier and with a superb view of it. The cooking is imaginative and varied, with set meals from 95F (weekdays). There's one featuring good regional specialities while if your taste runs more to gourmet dishes you should go for the ones at 120F and 280F. Delicious home-made desserts, just like the bread that is baked on the premises. Four charming bedrooms, roomy and bright. Doubles 220F with shower/wc, 280F with bath. The "yellow" and "green" ones have a lovely view of the Allier.

CUSSET 03300 (3KM E)

LE BRAYAUD

64 av. de Vichy; you'll see it as you come into Cusset from Vichy.
☎ 04.70.98.52.43
Closed Wednesday evenings, Saturday lunchtimes, and one week at the beginning of September.

Service 11.45–2.30pm and 8pm–3am. This is where you come if you want to make a night of it in Vichy. More importantly though, it's the best place for meat round about here. The Charolais rib of beef weighs close to 400g and the skirt 300g. No talk of mad cow disease here! Expect to pay 90–98F for rib of beef depending on how it's cooked. A very hearty 85F set meal is available 8–10.30pm and offers a good variety of salads, a meat dish, cheese, and dessert. Enough to satisfy even the biggest apppetites. Friendly staff.

MAYET-DE-MONTAGNE (LE) 03250 (23KM SE)

LA VIEILLE AUBERGE

9 place de l'Église; take the D62.
☎ 04.70.59.34.01
Closed Monday evenings in season, Wednesdays out of season, the last three weeks in January, and the second fortnight in September.

Time seems to have stopped in this old inn in a wonderful little village deep in the mountains. The décor consists of stone, wood and posters. They serve traditional dishes like salads, duck *confit* and *coq au vin* and wonderful home-made desserts. The 55F set meal (weekdays) comes with a selection of cold meats, and there are others at 65F, 92F, 135F. À la carte also available. Once again we've found a place that perfectly describes the meaning of "rustic" and we liked it a lot

LAVOINE 03250 (30KM SE)

AUBERGE CHEZ LILOU

Le Fau; take the D49.
☎ 04.70.59.37.49
Car park.

Up in the mountains at an altitude of 1,000m, *Chez Lilou* has an extremely good reputation in these parts judging by the crowds that come on Sundays, and we fell in love with it. It's extremely simple, unpretentious and uses fresh farm produce in the local dishes that are all made on the premises. They do a 55F set meal during the week while at the weekend 75F buys you three courses, cheese, and dessert. Try their superb version of potato pie, the farmed trout (the fish farm's at the same kind of altitude as the inn), and the delicious fruit tarts (especially the bilberry one!). You'll be treated like one of the family. You'll definitely have to reserve because it's popular and is usually fully booked. There's one slight drawback – it's rather noisy so no candle-lit dinners for two.

VIC-SUR-CÈRE 15800

AUBERGE DES TROIS CHEMINS

Salvanhac; it's 2km from the centre of Vic-sur-Cère.
☎ 04.71.47.50.74
Car park.

A friendly traditional little inn – ideal for the evening or a few days. You'll find it in the upper part of town well away from the crowds that come to take the waters. The dining room has exposed beams and there's a roaring log fire as soon as there's a nip in the air. The cooking is hearty and regional and the dishes lovingly prepared. At lunchtimes, there's a day special for 39F and a set meal for 57.90F (including drink). Generous portions. Evening set meals are 99F, 103F, 135F and 160F. Specialities include *confit* of chicken, *coq au vin*, breast of duck, and mutton tripe. The wines are very reasonable – we even came across a half-litre with an alcohol content of 10.5% for 10F! The bedrooms (215F and 235F) are very simple but well looked after. The wallpaper can be a bit dreary so pick your room carefully. Half-board for a stay of three days or more.

VIEILLEVIE 15120

10% HÔTEL LA TERRASSE**

rue principale; take the D141.
☎ 04.71.49.94.00 Fax 04.71.49.92.23
Closed mid Nov–end March.

Service noon–2pm and 7.30–9pm. This is a pleasant hotel situated between the 11th century château and the river. (And if you collect facts and figures, it's at a lower altitude – 200m – than any other hotel in Cantal.) Expect to pay 290F July 11–Aug 25, 250F in mid season, and 220F out of season for one of the comfortable rooms. It has a shaded terrace, beautiful swimming pool, garden and tennis courts. Good cooking with set meals at 56F, 80F, 115F, 125F and 138F. Specialities are trout with bacon, pig's trotters and veal sweetbreads *en crépine*, fillets of roast chard, and duck breast with green peppercorns.

VITRAC 15220

10% L'AUBERGE DE LA TOMETTE**

centre
☎ 04.71.64.70.94 F 04.71.64.77.11
Closed beginning of Jan–end of March. **Car park**. **TV**. **Disabled access**.

This is a delightful village inn 25km south of Aurillac. The hotel part, set in a large flower-filled garden overlooking the countryside, is very pleasant and has comfortable bedrooms (250–320F). If you're booking ahead ask for one in the older part of the building. A few duplexes are available for families. The cosy rustic dining room offers good hearty food and a good choice of set meals with prices starting at 68F and 100F (that one offers traditional local dishes). For 125F you get *crépinette* of pig's trotters or fillet of sea bass with a *coulis* of peppers, and for 200F gourmet dishes like *foie gras*, *croustade* of veal sweetbreads *à la crémaillère* and *confit* of duck with ceps. Their speciality is fillet of trout with hazelnuts. Madame Chausi is friendly and helpful.

YSSINGEAUX 43200

10% AUBERGE AU CREUX DES PIERRES

Fougères; take the D152 towards Queyrière and it's 5km south of Yssingeaux.
☎ 04.71.59.06.81
Open Friday evenings, Saturdays and Sundays except in February, and every day July–mid Sept (except that the restaurant is closed on Tuesdays). **Car park**.

This is a delightful – the building's been superbly renovated, and the garden is wonderful. We enjoyed the simple home cooking – freshly prepared starters, leg of lamb and *gratin*, cheese, and tasty home-made fruit tarts – and were particularly impressed with the two delightful ladies who own the place. Set meals 85F and 65F (this one is quite light and is only available weekday lunchtimes). They have a few nice rooms. Doubles with shower/wc 180F – they don't charge for the mountain view. Peace and quiet guaranteed. Ten-bed dormitory for hill-walkers at 50F per night. Mountain bikes can be hired.

10% LE BOURBON**

5 place de la Victoire (Centre).
☎ 04.71.59.06.54 F 04.71.59.00.7
Closed Sunday evenings, Mondays (except in July and August), January, and June 25–July 6.
Car park. **TV**. **Canal+**.

The hotel's been refurbished and may have lost some of its character in the process. Doubles 290–360F. The handsome dining room decorated in "English-garden style". The kitchen serves up regional dishes that have been rethought and made considerably lighter. There are set meals ranging in price from 95F (not available Sundays) to 290F to suit all tastes and pockets. They, like the à la carte menu, change every three months, which is a very good sign. You'll find names of the local suppliers listed beside the dishes. Nice little touches like a list of the coffees available. A reliable and first-rate establishment.

Bourgogne

21 Côte-d'Or

58 Nièvre

71 Saône-et-Loire

89 Yonne

ANCY-LE-FRANC 89160

HOSTELLERIE DU CENTRE**

How to get there: it's 100m from the château.
☎ 03.86.75.15.11 F 03.86.75.14.13.
Closed Dec 20–Jan 5. **Secure parking**. **TV**. **Canal+**. **Disabled access**.

The hotel, which stands in the main street, is old but is refurbished on a regular basis. First impressions are that it's a bit high class but the atmosphere is easy-going.The cosy, restful bedrooms are decorated in pastel tones. Prices start at 265F for a double with shower/wc. One with lots of facilities – minibar, bathrobe and so on – will cost you 365F. The restaurant – the larger of the two dining rooms is prettier – offers traditional local dishes like snails, veal kidneys in a wine sauce, and ham in a Chablis sauce. Set meals are as varied as the portions are generous, and prices range from 78F (weekday lunchtimes) to 268F. There's a terrace for when the sun shines, and a heated indoor swimming pool. The type of hotel you wish were common in this part of Burgundy.

ARNAY-LE-DUC 21230

HÔTEL LE CLAIR DE LUNE

4 rue du Four (Centre).
☎ 03.80.90.15.50 F 03.80.90.04.64
Secure parking. **TV**.

The Poinsot family have more than one trick up their sleeve. Already running "Chez Camille", a restaurant with a few plush bedrooms upstairs, they now own a pretty little hotel in the small neighbouring street. It's very basic offering bright, modern and attractive accommodation at 180F. What's more, they offer dinner, bed & breakfast where you eat in the restaurant's conservatory, flower-filled all year round. Price: 280F per person or 420F for two. Gourmets might be tempted by the very reasonably priced "gourmet half-board" (590F for two). Children under eleven eat and sleep for free.

CHEZ CAMILLE

1 place Édouard-Herriot (Centre).
☎ 03.80.90.01.38
Car park.

This authentic, old-fashioned inn with the blue shutters, situated at the foot of the old town, is reminiscent of a scene from an operetta. Waitresses in flowery dresses enter the lounge, serving aperitifs with choux pastries and cheese and home-made ham sprinkled with chopped parsley, before leading you off to the conservatory which has been converted into a dining room. Here you can sit as though in a theatre and watch the amazing ballet of sous-chefs and kitchen staff, which is being performed on a kind of stage raised up behind a large window – on one side you've got the pastry kitchen, on the other a tangled web of branches. The whole scene is enacted beneath a glass roof in a room full of pot plants and wicker armchairs. If you choose the 80F set meal offering dishes like *terrine* and *bœuf bourguignon*, you might feel a bit out of place beside the local families treating themselves to 180–495F set meals, but it will be an experience. Terrific wines and a cellar worth visiting. Take a look round, just for the pleasure of it.

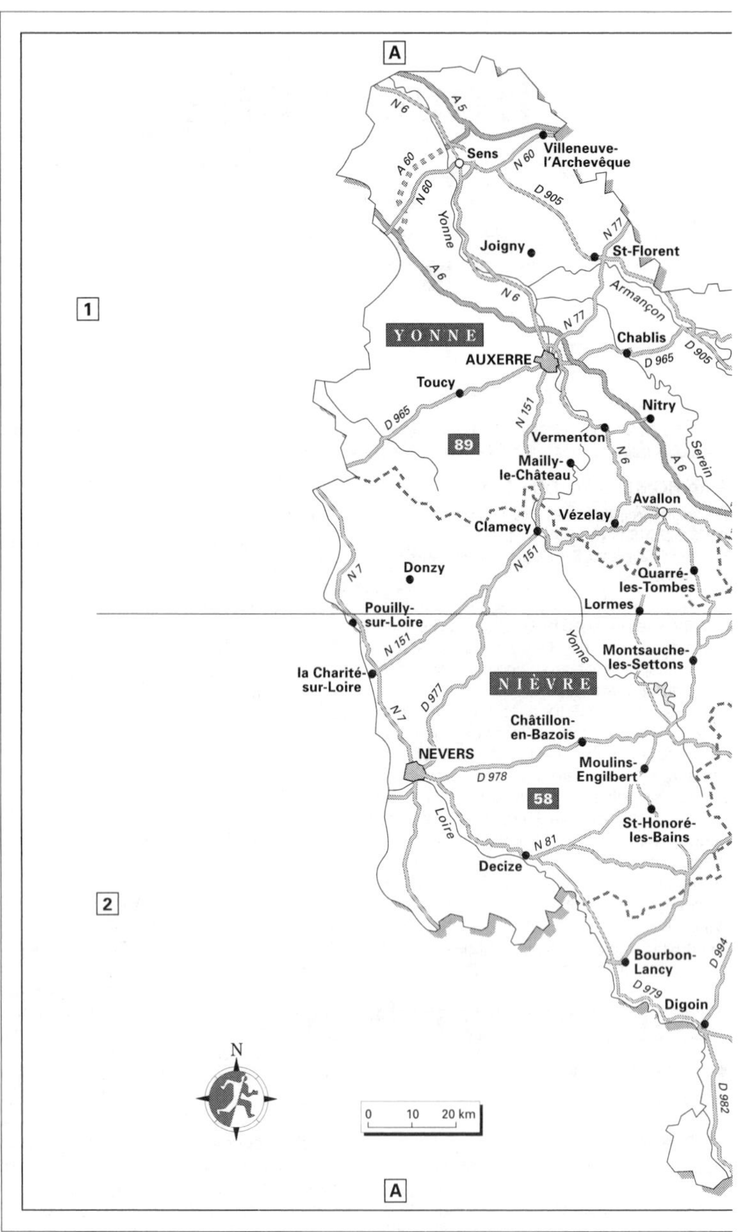
A
1
2
A 5
N 6
A 60
N 60
Sens
N 60
Villeneuve-
l'Archevêque
D 905
Yonne
Joigny
N 77
St-Florent
A 6
N 6
Armançon
N 77
YONNE
Chablis
D 965
D 905
AUXERRE
Toucy
D 965
N 151
Nitry
89
Vermenton
N 6
Serein
A 6
Mailly-
le-Château
Avallon
Vézelay
Clamecy
N 151
Quarré-
les-Tombes
N 7
Donzy
Lormes
Pouilly-
sur-Loire
N 151
Yonne
Montsauche-
les-Settons
la Charité-
sur-Loire
NIÈVRE
D 977
N 7
Châtillon-
en-Bazois
NEVERS
Moulins-
Engilbert
D 978
58
Loire
St-Honoré-
les-Bains
N 81
Decize
Bourbon-
Lancy
D 994
D 979
Digoin
D 982
N
0
10
20 km
A

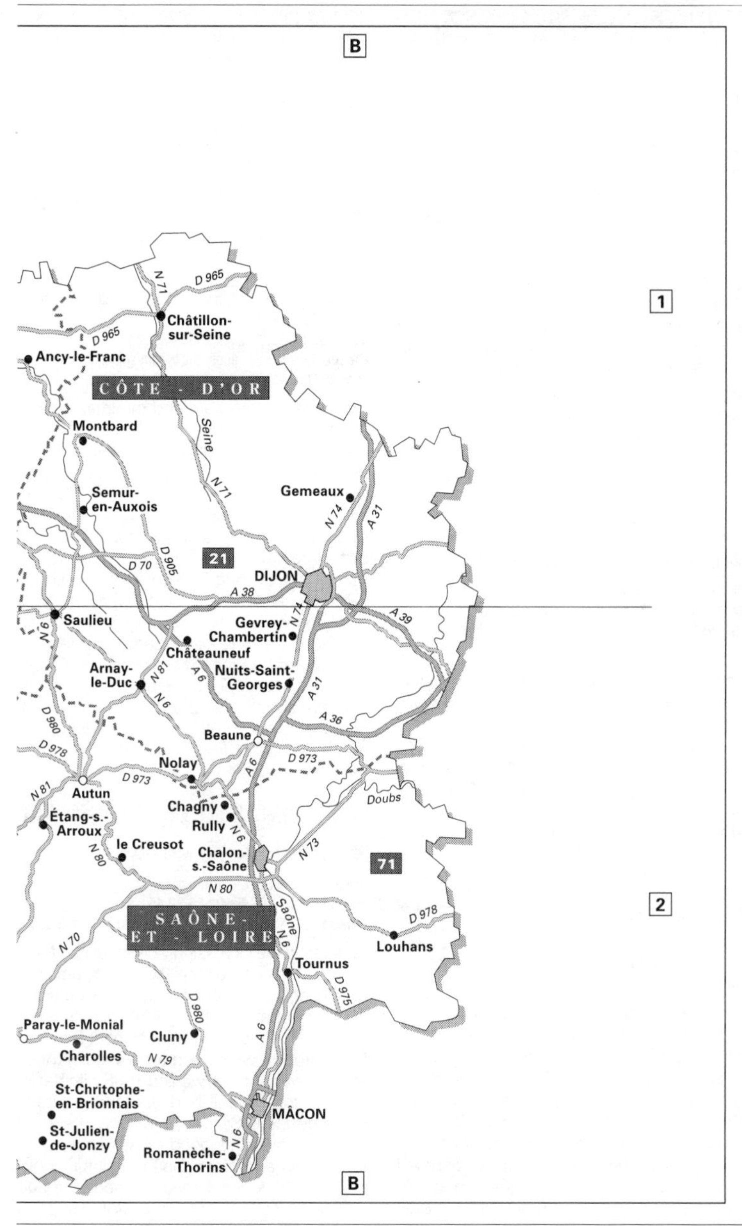
B
1
2
Châtillon-sur-Seine
Ancy-le-Franc
CÔTE - D'OR
Montbard
Semur-en-Auxois
Gemeaux
21
DIJON
Saulieu
Gevrey-Chambertin
Châteauneuf
Arnay-le-Duc
Nuits-Saint-Georges
Beaune
Nolay
Autun
Chagny
Rully
Étang-s.-Arroux
le Creusot
Chalon-s.-Saône
71
SAÔNE-ET-LOIRE
Louhans
Tournus
Paray-le-Monial
Charolles
Cluny
St-Chritophe-en-Brionnais
St-Julien-de-Jonzy
MÂCON
Romanèche-Thorins
Seine
Saône
Doubs
N 71
D 965
D 905
D 70
A 38
N 74
A 31
A 39
A 6
N 81
N 6
A 36
D 980
D 978
D 973
N 80
N 73
N 70
D 975
N 79

AUTUN 71400

HÔTEL-RESTAURANT DE LA TÊTE NOIRE**

1–3 rue de l'Arquebuse (Centre)
☎ 03.85.86.59.99 F 03.85.86.33.90.
Closed Dec 15–Jan 5. **Secure parking**. **TV**. **Canal+**.

The imposing frontage could do with some work but inside this comfortable hotel gets prettier every year. The rooms are charming and work is in hand to repair the ravages of time. Doubles 150F with washing facilities, 270F with shower/wc, and 320F with bath. Good cooking, with a starter, main course and dessert for 59F. There are set meals at 79.99F (ham on the bone in a port sauce or stew of ox cheek), 120F (fish soup and a choice of semi-salted duck with cabbage or fillet of zander with basil) and 150F (sea bass flambéd with Pernod or free-range chicken with morels). The 148F set meal features local specialities. Wine is available by the glass and the carafe. Friendly reception.

RESTAURANT CHATEAUBRIAND

14 rue Jeannin (Centre).
☎ 03.85.52.21.58
Closed Sunday evenings, Mondays, and a fortnight in Jan and July.

Centrally positioned behind the town hall, this is a reliable establishment offering wonderful, quality cooking year in year out. Classical dining room and good reception. The owner's little daughter fills the place with laughter and youth. Set meals 68–198F. Tender meat specialities such as fillet, rack of lamb, *andouillette*, and frogs' legs in the style of Provence. They also do excellent fish soup.

RESTAURANT LE CHALET BLEU

3 rue Jeannin (Centre).
☎ 03.85.86.27.30.
Closed Monday evenings, Tuesdays.

Even if the outside's nothing to write home about (no way does it look like a chalet!), you need have no fears about eating here. Philippe Bouché, who trained in the kitchens of the Elysée Palace, offers set meals from 85F (except Saturday evenings, Sundays and public holidays) to 245F. The cooking is imaginative – there are dishes like panfried zander with *andouille* coated in finely chopped garlic, stew of monkfish, mussels and crayfish tails, breast of guinea fowl with duck *foie gras* accompanied by snails with smoked bacon, and medallions of lamb with a sweet pepper sauce – and the helpings are generous. A wonderful dessert menu at no extra cost, offering such delights as crystallized oranges panfried with saffron and served on chocolate puff pastry and a *gratin* of tropical fruit with passion fruit *sabayon*. Not to be missed.

UCHON 71190 (12KM SE)

10% AUBERGE LA CROIX MESSIRE JEAN

La Croix Messire Jean; it's on the D275, 1km from the village of Uchon.
☎ 03.85.54.42.06 F 03.85.54.32.23
Closed Tuesday evenings and Wednesdays out of season. **Car park**.

Ideal base for walkers and mountain bikers planning to tackle one of the splendid routes on one of the highest mountains in the département (684m). It's a friendly inn offering basic, but perfectly adequate bedrooms. Expect to pay 120F per person–170F for a double. Tasteful, rustic décor and prices to suit all pockets. Remember there are lots of guests in July–Aug and on good weekends between seasons. The signpost at Uchon is highly effective. If you love peace and quiet, this won't be your scene. Large, shaded terrace where you can enjoy the 50F four o'clock snacklet or the exceptionally reasonably priced little set meals. They do a 60F *menu du jour* and others at 85F, 105F, 115F and 125F. Fried frogs' legs 52F. Mountain bike hire available.

SAINT-LÉGER-SOUS-BEUVRAY 71990 (20KM W)

10% HÔTEL DU MORVAN

place de la Mairie (Centre).
☎ 03.85.82.51.06 F 03.85.82.45.07
Closed out of season, Tuesdays and mid Nov–mid Jan.

Situated in the increasingly depopulated Morvan, this little village hotel faces up to adversity by keeping its prices reasonable, by making the comfort an well-being of its guests a priority. A good base for climbing mont Beuvray. Six bedrooms with a wonderful country touch at 240F with shower/wc and 160F with basin. Perfect for limited budgets and walkers. Madame Els O'Sullivan, the life and soul of the place, owes her good sense of hospitality to her Irish ancestors. Good, regional cooking, the 50F Morvan-style afternoon tea and set meals at 65F, 89F and 125F. Here's a peek at what's in store – *tariettes* of chicken, *confit* of breast of duck, *pavé* of beef in pastry, *gratin* of snails, *noix* of scallops with wild mushrooms, omelettes and various salad dishes. Children's set meal 40F.

ANOST 71550 (22KM NW)

10% HÔTEL VILLAGE FORTIN**

Centre; take the D978, then the D2.
☎ 03.85.82.71.11 Fax 03.85.82.79.62

This hotel, which lies in the nature reserve of Morvan, has an interesting history. The owner's a really friendly guy who explored all the jungles, deserts and oceans of the world before returning to his native land. He then played a vital role in giving a new lease of life to a village which, like so many others, is threatened by decay and depopulation, by setting up this little hotel with its ancillary operations of pub, restaurant and traveller's lodge. It's basic, clean and inexpensive, and no two rooms are the same. Tourists and walkers enjoy meeting for a drink in the friendly ground floor pub – a little oasis of conviviality in the middle of the Morvan tundra. The result is a kind of link, understanding even, between travellers and villagers. Doubles with bath from 220F.

LA GALVACHE

Grand rue.
☎ 03.85.82.70.88

A wonderful little village restaurant, run by the owner of the *Village Fortin*, offering terrific regional cooking served up in generous helpings. Their 65F *menu du jour* is amazing value for money. You can sample dishes like *terrine*, *escalope* of salmon with a leek fondue, delicious American-style crayfish, tasty Charolais steak, or *croustade* of veal sweetbreads with morels, etc. And to finish off with, some soft cream cheese of course. Other set meals at 85F, 125F and 155F.

DETTEY 71190 (28KM S)

10% RELAIS DE DETTEY

Centre; take the D994, then the D224.
☎ 03.85.54.57.19
Closed Monday evenings, one week at the start of Nov, and a fortnight in Jan. **TV**.

Situated in one of the smallest villages of the Saône and Loire, and at the top of one of the highest "mountains", this inn is a must. It's competing with the *Marissou* in the Cantal for the title of smallest hotel in the world. They've only one bedroom! But you'll be coming to experience the charm of the village and the inn and the delicious regional cooking. Cosy, low-ceilinged dining room with two enormous exposed beams and a big fireplace. You'll get a friendly reception from Daniel and Monique. He's in charge of the dining room and she takes care of the cooking. Local families come for a slap-up meal on Sundays. Everything's so tasty and served in such generous helpings, but they don't have an enormous choice, so you won't get into a state deciding what to pick. They do *andouillette à la ficelle* or frogs' legs with Aligoté (95F set meal), a terrific local dish and tender *pavé* of Charolais with the cream of spicy *époisse* cheese (130F). The 160F set meal varies – *profiterolle* of warm goat's cheese and Red Sea bream Provence-style, *gratin* of snails, trout Burgundy-style, lamb with basil or *cassolette* of fish etc. Affordable wines from 70F, Côtes du Rhône 78F, Beaujolais 95Fand a thoughtful selection priced 100–200F. On fine days you can eat on the terrace in the shade of the church while the horses frolic opposite. At bedtime there's a big studio with its own entrance – almost like a two-roomed flat with its bedroom and a lounge that sleeps two extra people. Large bathroom and really nice décor. Doubles 250F and 90F for each extra guest. Reservation compulsory, but that goes without saying.

AUXERRE 89000

10% HÔTEL NORMANDIE**

41 bd Vauban (West).
☎ 03.86.52.57.80 Fax 03.86.51.54.33.
Secure parking. TV. Canal+. Disabled access.

Sitting in a small garden, this fine large bourgeois house dates from the beginning of the century. The sign pays tribute to the famous French liner and and if you've ever been on a luxury transatlantic cruise then you'll recognise something of the atmosphere here in this elegant though slightly dated hotel with its uniformed night watchman and the distinguished looking Brits reading the Times over breakfast. The stylishly furnished rooms are very comfortable and extremely well looked after. Prices range from 250F for a double with shower/wc to 360F for a larger room with bath. Efficient and inexpensive room service is at your disposal should you want to dine in your room. A gym, sauna and billiard room are also at your disposal.

LE PARC DES MARÉCHAUX***

6 av. Foch (West).

☎ 03.86.51.43.77 ⊫ 03.86.51.31.72
Secure parking. TV. Canal+. Disabled access.

An air of calm, luxuriousness and sheer self-indulgence surrounds this large establishment that dates from the time of Napoleon III. You'll get an outstanding welcome and Madame Hervé's legendary good humour is contagious. She is a devotee of Napoleon Bonaparte and while all the bedrooms are called after a Marshal of France, Napoleon's Marshals are in the majority. The rooms are all different and decorated in "unobtrusive good taste" to quote the hotel brochure (which doesn't exaggerate). Doubles from 350F. If it's fine, have breakfast outside among hundred year old trees. The hotel also sometimes hosts concerts in the grounds. There's a cosy bar with a Victorian moulded ceiling. Room service isn't too expensive. This is the loveliest hotel in Auxerre. It also offers a special weekend package for 520F with all sorts of opportunities for interesting trips.

|●| LE JARDIN GOURMAND

56 bd Vauban; it's in the pedestrian precinct, 50m from the carrefour de Paris.
☎ 03.86.51.53.52
Closed Tuesdays, Wednesdays (Feb 17–March 11), and Sept 1–16. **Car park. Disabled access.**

The chef here is an artist and frequently makes a sketch of what his dishes look like. (He can also talk at great length about what he's found in the market.) His cooking is very inventive and maybe a bit over the top sometimes but if everything were just so in the décor and the cooking of this large bourgeois establishment, we might not like it quite as much. The service is impeccable and the dining room staff will gladly guide you through the à la carte menu that changes according to the whim of the chef and from season to season. Reckon on paying about 250F for a full meal featuring dishes like vegetables in lemon flavoured aspic with shellfish, fricassee of crayfish in a cider-based sauce, smoked free-range guinea fowl, sautéd veal with peanuts, and icecream in flavours such as aniseed and gingerbread. The set meals too offer an ideal introduction to what is truly imaginative cooking. For 140F, you can have a quite astonishing meal consisting of, for example, chicken and pistachio *terrine*, sautéd lamb with peppermint and haricot beans, and verbena icecream in plum brandy . Other set meals 195F, 230F and 270F. They have a small selection of Burgundies at about 100F a bottle. The dining room is cosy and there's a nice terrace for when the sun shines. You'd be well advised to reserve in advance.

CHEVANNES 89240 (8KM SW)

|●| LA CHAMAILLE

La Barbotière – 4 route de Boiloup; from Auxerre, follow the signs for Nevers-Bourgnes then take the D1.
☎ 03.86.41.24.80
Closed Mondays, Tuesdays, Jan 12–Feb 7, Sept 7–15 and Dec 23–25. **Car park.**

An excellent restaurant and wonderful scenery within minutes of Auxerre – what more could you ask for? It's housed in an old mill with a wonderful smell of furniture polish, a fire is lit as soon as there's a nip in the air, and "bucolic" is the word that springs to mind when you first see the little stream that meanders through the garden and the ducks splashing about in it. The cooking is conventional but shows considerable skill and the ingredients are first rate. The 165F set meal (available lunchtimes and evenings every day except public holidays) consists of, for example, a stew of oysters and winkles, braised rabbit with rosemary, cheese, and a caramelized mousse. The *menu carte* at 265F comes with *terrine* of *foie gras*, sautéd veal kidneys in a Chablis sauce, and a wonderful combination of chocolate and orange for dessert. And there's another set meal at 338F, if you feel like pushing the boat out. Wine is available by the glass at prices that won't have you wincing.

MONTIGNY-LA-RESLE 89230 (12KM NE)

10% ☗ |●| HÔTEL-RESTAURANT LE SOLEIL D'OR**

How to get there: on the N77.
☎ 03.86.41.81.21 ⊫ 03.86.41.86.88
Secure parking. TV. Disabled access.

The hotel and restaurant are housed in old farmhouses that have been renovated throughout. The rather pretty bedrooms all come with shower/wc or bath and all cost 305F for two people. The kitchen turns out classical dishes that are consistent in quality and sometimes show a touch of imagination. Set meals 98F (available every day) and 128–325F. Try the panfried foie gras with fruit or the calf sweetbreads in Chablis. Wine by the glass is rather expensive.

VINCELOTTES 89290 (14KM SE)

☗ |●| AUBERGE LES TILLEULS

12 quai de l'Yonne.

☎ 03.86.42.22.13 ➡ 03.86.42.23.51
Closed Wednesday evenings and Thursdays out of season, and Dec 18–Feb 18. **TV**.

Located in a rather pretty part of the world, this is a small inn with five very simple but pleasant rooms overlooking a narrow road that skirts the Yonne and that doesn't get much traffic at night Doubles with shower about 300F, with bath about 400F. Even when the weather is dismal you can't help feeling cheerful sitting in the restaurant that's full of flowers and paintings. If the weather's fine, you can sit on the shady waterside terrace. The cooking, like the owner, has considerable character. The chef's reputation is growing fast and prices are a bit steep (and wine will push the bill up even more). Set meals 140F (not available Saturdays, Sunday lunchtimes or public holidays), 230 and 300F.

AVALLON 89200

10% ☗ DAK'HÔTEL**

119 rue de Lyon – Étang des Minimes (South-East); it's on the edge of town, going towards Dijon.
☎ 03.86.31.63.20 ➡ 03.86.34.25.28
Secure parking. **TV**. **Canal+**. **Disabled access**.

Entirely new hotel, with all mod cons. The warmth of the reception makes up for the lack of it in the building. Lots of little extras that make all the difference, such as tea or coffee, a magazine, a chocolate on your pillow – and at no extra cost. No restaurant but if you arrive late or don't want to go out, you can have a meal on a tray for 70F. Doubles from 300F.

|●| RELAIS DES GOURMETS

47 rue de Paris; it's 200m from the main square.
☎ 03.86.34.18.90
Closed Sunday evenings and Mondays (Nov 1–May 1).

This used to be the *Hotel de Paris* in the days when Avallon was still a staging post and, unlike its contemporaries which have gone to rack and ruin, has found a new lease of life. Granted, it's no longer a hotel but you can have a good meal in a good-humoured and colourful atmosphere. Set meals 82F (served every day except Easter Sunday)) and 128–300F. The chef prepares fish with as much skill as he does the meat from neighbouring Charolais herds.

L'ISLE-SUR-SEREIN 89440 (15KM NE)

10% ☗ |●| AUBERGE DU POT D'ÉTAIN

24 rue Bouchardat.
☎ 03.86.33.88.10 ➡ 03.86.33.90.93
Closed Sunday evenings (except June–Sept), Mondays, February, and the third week in October. **Car park**. **TV**.

This charming and tiny country inn is one of the best places in the region to eat. The chef trained with some of the big names and his wonderful cooking is a mixture of the traditional and the modern – try the eggs poached in red wine, the ovenbaked *andouillette* in Chablis or the preserved shallots in white wine. We have fond memories of the rascasse with five spices that featured on the 158F set meal along with the smoked salmon cannelloni with celery. There's a *menu du jour* at 98F (not available Sundays), and other set meals range in price from 146F to 298F. They have the most fantastic cellar and the wine list has about 300 names on it. They have nine pleasant rooms, ranging in price from 220F for a double with shower/wc to 420F for a small suite. We liked the ones at the back of the flower-filled courtyard which are quieter.

BEAUNE 21200

10% ☗ |●| HÔTEL CENTRAL***

2 rue Victor-Millot (Centre).
☎ 03.80.24.77.24 ➡ 03.80.22.30.40
Car park. **TV**.

A hotel worthy of its name. Everyone, from trendy motorcyclists to fun-loving couples, loves the cosy facilities of the spacious bedrooms. Prices 250–410F. The cooking (which might look a bit austere, but isn't) also enjoys a good reputation. The owner digs into his book of magic spells, unearthing 17th and 18th century dishes which he interprets in his own way.You can treat yourself to milk soup of fennel accompanied by a large prawn roasted with pepper, *ravioles* of langoustine with ginger or tart *à l'ancienne*, all available in the 125F set meal. Gorgeous, and there's plenty to choose from.

10% ☗ HÔTEL GRILLON

21 route de Seurre (East).
☎ 03.80.22.44.25 ➡ 03.80.24.94.89

Why do people make do with chain hotels, when you can wake up to the sound of chirping birds in a place oozing charm, and fall into bed after a visit to the wine cellar? The rooms have style. Expect to spend 258F with shower and 298F with bath. In the summer, you can eat your breakfast in the garden, or on the terrace of this old family house. There's a restaurant, "Le Verger", in the park opposite (see below).

10% LE HOME**

138 route de Dijon (North); it's on the outskirts of Beaune, heading towards Dijon.
☎ 03.80.22.16.43 F 03.80.24.90.74
Secure parking. TV. Disabled access.

Tucked away at the bottom of a garden, this old Burgundian house swathed in Virginia creeper makes a very pleasant place to stop. The décor may raise a few eyebrows or provoke a few winces on occasions but the welcome is as charming as the location. Two annexes have bedrooms from which you can step straight out into the garden. You should eckon on paying 325–370F for a double. Ideal place for relaxing. Breakfast, visually appealing and good, is 35F.

AU BON ACCUEIL

La Montagne; take the D970, turn right, and at the Beaune exit go towards La Montagne.
☎ 03.80.22.08.80
Closed Monday and Tuesday evenings, Wednesdays, the last two weeks in Aug, Dec 20–start Jan, and two weeks at the end of Feb. **Car park.**

This is more like a reserve than a restaurant! Although the town centre's often more popular with tourists than locals, here at *La Montagne* you'll only come across the local people. They make a pilgrimage here on Sundays – arriving with all their relatives, their cousin who's a nun, brother who's a wine grower, nephew who's a soldier and their cousins from Paris – and treat themselves to a *terrine* of crudités and pâté (as much as they can manage!), while enjoying the magnificent panoramic view. For several decades now, roast beef has taken pride of place. Followed by a cheese platter and home-made tart, you'll pay no more than 100F. The same menu costs 85F weekdays. Lovers of snails and *pavé* of beef with morels will be thrilled with the 110F set meal . Typical local reception and wonderful terrace.

RESTAURANT "LES TONTONS"

22 faubourg Madeleine.
☎ 03.80.24.19.64
Closed Sundays and Monday lunchtimes.

This restaurant was opened by a couple of tearaways who've calmed down a bit now as they've got older. One of them has left to work further afield, while the other's discovered a passion for cooking. His wife "Pépita", a local from Beaune who looks as if she's stepped out of an operetta, is responsible for the atmosphere. She doesn't go over the top or get too much for the wine buffs who deliberately come here for a good time. The 89F "Bourgogne et Humeurs du jour" set meal is the perfect pick-you-up on dull days. Unless you'd prefer the 68F "L'instant présent". You won't be able to keep away once you've sampled *madeleine* of freshwater crayfish, breast of duck with spices, or *gigotin* of lamb *en croûte* in the 135F set meal.

RESTAURANT "LE P'TIT PARADIS"

25 rue Paradis (Centre).
☎ 03.80.24.91.00
Closed Monday evenings and Tuesdays.

The road to paradise was more like the road to hell, used by travellers lost between the l'Hôtel Dieu and the Musée du Vin. But then a brilliant little gem of a restaurant, painted in colours as fresh as the cooking, opened its doors just opposite the Musée du Vin. Very reasonable prices. And Jean-Marie Daloz is worthy of his title of youngest chef in Beaune. Sample the salad of skate with grapefruit, fillets of red mullet with basil and roast pear *à la confiture de lait*. Expect to spend 150–200F à la carte. We just loved the 69F *menu du jour* offering *marbré* of salmon and tuna, *émincé* of chicken with tarragon, and soft white cheese or dessert. Other set meals at 89F and 150F. Choice of wines at equally good prices

RESTAURANT "LE VERGER"

21 route de Seurre (East).
☎ 03.80.24.28.05
Closed Wednesdays and Thursday lunchtimes.

Opposite the hotel owned by the Grillon family, the architecture of this wonderful restaurant would seem pretty daring in the eyes of your average local. The smiling, rosy-cheeked owner is slowly building up a reputation with the help of her husband, in this region famous for its poached eggs and *bœuf bourguignon*. Forget about the 90F *petit menu*, and leave the one at 130F to lovers of local dishes. Sample the light aromatic cooking in the 115F set meal, offering warm black pudding with spicy apples, cheek of young pig with grapes and fine semolina, and grapefruit-flavoured *crème brûlée*. Let the expert on the Gevrey-Chambertin vineyards, or her husband, choose a wine to suit your taste. They also do a 210F *menu parfumé*. Enjoy the terrace in summer.

RESTAURANT LA CIBOULETTE

69 rue de Lorraine (Centre); it's in the old part of town, opposite the theatre.
☎ 03.80.24.70.72

Closed Monday evenings, Tuesdays, three weeks in February and two weeks in August.

The renovated premises are small and the décor restrained. Two set meals at good prices (91F and 125F) bring in the tourists and also the locals, which is reassuring. On the menu: *émincé* of calf's feet in vinaigrette, poached eggs in a red wine sauce, and beefsteak with *époisses* (a local cheese). An ideal spot to gather your strength for that tour of the Hospices or of the city's numerous wine cellars! Friendly atmosphere.

LE BENATON

25 faubourg Bretonnière; it's five minutes from the town centre, heading towards Autun.
☎ 03.80.22.00.26
Closed all day Wednesday and Thursday lunchtimes.

The cooking here is of the traditional local variety but don't think that means it's dull. Try the snail ravioli, the superb stew of ox cheeks or the boned pigeon in a style that was reminiscent of Morocco's *pastilla.* The 105F set meal, based on what the market has to offfer, is a model of its kind and the 155F one is rightly described as a bargain. Other set meals 195F and 230F. The wines aren't bad either but they don't come cheap – still, you didn't come to this part of the world to scrimp and scrape, did you? An ideal place to stop before carrying on to Pommard or Santenay.

LEVERNOIS 21200 (4KM SE)

LE PARC**

How to get there: take the D970 in the direction of Verdun-sur-le-Doubs then turn left.
☎ 03.80.22.22.51 ⮕ 03.80.24.21.19
Closed Dec 1–Jan 15. **Car park**. **TV**. **Disabled access**.

It's advisable to book. An old house that has become a charming hotel. There are trees a hundred years old in the grounds and a great many birds. The ideal spot to be lazy or energetic. The nearby tennis court, golf course and pool mean you can exhaust yourself to your heart's content should you feel so inclined. If it's excitement you're after, how about one of the balloon trips available in the area? In the evening, you can sit in the bar with a glass in your hand and chat about your day with your fellow guests. The bedrooms are really delightful – they're all different and they all have character. Doubles 245F (with shower/wc) and 295F (with bath).

POMMARD 21630 (4KM S)

10% HÔTEL "CAFÉ DU PONT"**

Centre.
☎ 03.80.22.03.41 ⮕ 03.80.24.14.19
TV.

In this wine-growing region where good establishments are few and far between and tourist traps the common thing, here's a pretty little hotel with cheerful, comfy bedrooms that retain a certain newness (250F and 300F). Treat yourself to some Pommard at the bar or on the terrace before starting on the set meals (or have a bottle alongside, why not indeed!) Dishes such as *terrine* or *palette* of pork (68F), or snails, *andouillette* or *coq au vin*, cheese or dessert (88F). There's a wine cellar downstairs for those who like to take away interesting souvenirs.

BOUZE-LÈS-BEAUNE 21200 (7KM NW)

LA BOUZEROTTE

How to get there: on the D970.
☎ 03.80.26.01.37
Closed Monday evenings and Tuesdays. **Car park**.

A real country inn, ten minutes from the centre of Beaune, with real Burgundians, real Burgundy accents, and real Burgundy cooking. Real flowers (so unusual nowadays you have to mention the fact!) decorate the old wooden tables, there is an old-fashioned sideboard and a fireplace, where a fire burns in cold weather. More to the point, they also have good wines from small local vineyards which Christine, who used to be a wine waiter, will immediately recommend. Good set meal of the day 89F. Even better is the 158F set meal with things like *salade de compotée de queue de bœuf* (oxtail that has been cooked until it practically forms a purée then served up in a salad), *poulet de Bresse* in a cream sauce, cheese matured in marc, and home-made tart. Sit out on the terrace in fine weather.

LADOIX-SERRIGNY 21550 (7KM NE)

LES COQUINES

N74 – Buisson.
☎ 03.80.26.43.58
Closed Wednesday evenings and Thursdays. **Car park**.

On one side of this old house there's an old storeroom and on the other large windows offer views of the surrounding countryside. They know what cooking and looking after guests is all about here. Stick to one of the set meals and you won't spend a fortune on food and wine. The one at 155F (salad with a spicy dressing and home-made *coq au vin*) seems specially designed for travellers who appreciate good food.

BOURBON-LANCY 71140

LE GRAND HÔTEL***

parc thermal.
☎ 03.85.89.08.87 F 03.85.89.25.45
Closed end October–end March. **Car park. TV. Disabled access.**

If you suffer from rheumatism or cardio-vascular disease, this is the ideal place to get your health back, since there's a covered walkway between the hotel and the hydro. If your health is fine but you get sentimental about old spa towns that look a bit shabby and down at heel, this is the place for you too. It's just the way you imagine a hotel in a spa town to be – showy and oversized. Lots of elderly people playing petanque in the extensive grounds. The rooms are clean, the bathrooms enormous, and the prices reasonable. Doubles 168F with washing facilities, 240F and 247F with shower/wc, and 261F and 278F with bath. Breakfast 32F. The restaurant offers set meals ranging in price from 90F to 165F. Classical dishes, not a wide choice of wine. For those who get all nostalgic for the days of *Last Year in Marienbad*.

CHABLIS 89800

10% HOSTELLERIE DES CLOS***

rue Jules-Rathier.
☎ 03.86.42.10.63 F 03.86.42.17.11
Closed Wednesdays and Thursday lunchtimes Oct 1–April 30, and Dec 20–Jan 10. **Car park. TV. Canal+. Disabled access.**

You wouldn't dare step inside some restaurants because of the waiters in tails, the tinkling chandeliers and the jewellery that makes Madame look like a Christmas tree. In this hostelry though, housed in a former hospital and chapel, even the illuminated gardens are delightful, the waiters don't take themselves too seriously, and Madame's laugh puts you at ease. Since her husband uses only the finest ingredients and his best known dishes are all subtly flavoured with Chablis, you'd be well advised to take your credit card with you – the cheapest set meal is 175F. If you're eating à la carte, choose just a main course – something like the pan-fried zander in a Chablis sauce – and a dessert (they won't hold it against you) and you'll get away with 250–300F, which will also cover a half-litre of Chablis. Lovely rooms from 288F.

LE VIEUX MOULIN

18 rue des Moulins (South-East).
☎ 03.86.42.47.30
Closed Dec 25 and Jan 1. **Car park.**

A lot of water – that of the Serein river – has flowed under the bridge since this restaurant started up in a house that used to belong to a wine-growing family. In the large dining room made from local stone, the unperturbable new owners continue to serve the kind of traditional local meals that are a real tonic – local ham, local *andouillette* with mustard seed, *andouillette terrine*, *navarin* of duckling in ratafia, and Chablis mousse with a *coulis* of soft fruit – and at quite reasonable prices too. The 98F set meal is available every day.

LIGNY-LE-CHÂTEL 89144 (15KM NW)

RELAIS SAINT-VINCENT**

14 Grande-Rue (Centre).
☎ 03.86.47.53.38 F 03.86.47.54.16
Secure parking. TV. Disabled access.

This is not to be missed! The village and the street seem to have stepped out of another age but you'll find all mod cons in this ancient (12th century) half-timbered house, which has been tastefully converted by the welcoming owners. Doubles 295F with shower/wc, 380F with bath. Set meals 80–165F, the cheapest being available every day. The walls are as substantial as the cooking (try the kidneys flamed with marc de Bourgogne). You can sit out on in the quiet flowery courtyard.

RESTAURANT LA MARMITE BOURGUIGNONNE

25 rue du Carrouge (Centre).
☎ 03.86.47.43.74
Closed Tuesday evenings, Wednesdays and Aug 22–Sept 10. **Car park.**

Even if there are a few weird-looking types in the bar and in the dining room, this is a good little restaurant offering typical cooking served without fuss and with local wines to enliven the atmosphere. You'll have a good time and it won't make a hole in your wallet. Set meal (including wine) 52F on weekdays.

Others from 65F to 140F. Dishes on offer include ham *à la Chablisienne* and snails.

CHAGNY 71150

10% AUBERGE LA MUSARDIÈRE**

30 route de Chalon; it's 500m from the town centre, heading toward Chalon.
☎ 03.85.87.04.97 F 03.85.87.20.51
Closed all day Monday Oct 1–April 30, Monday lunchtimes May 1–Sept 30, Sunday evenings Nov 1–April 1, and Dec–mid Jan. **Car park**. **TV**.

Situated in a quiet neighbourhood, the inn has a garden, a beautiful terrace and lovely rooms that have just been redecorated. Moreover, the cooking is decent, the dishes are well put together and prices are extremely reasonable, so it's easy to see why we chose it. Set meals 61F, 85F, 100F, 110F, 133F, 154F and 195F. The à la carte menu includes roast honeyed breast of duck, poached eggs in a red wine sauce, medallions of panfried monkfish, and panfried veal kidneys in a mustard sauce. Doubles 195F with basin/wc, 225F with shower/wc or bath. Friendly and informal welcome.

CHASSEY-LE-CAMP 71150 (5KM SW)

AUBERGE DU CAMP ROMAIN**

How to get there: take the D974 in the direction of Santenay then turn left – you'll find the inn just down the hill from the remains of a Roman camp.
☎ 03.85.87.09.91 F 03.85.87.11.51
Closed Jan 1–20. **Secure parking**. **TV**. **Disabled access**.

Advisable to book. The inn overlooks a lush green valley and you'd think you were in the mountains. Beneath the terrace are a tennis court, a crazy-golf course, a heated pool (with a barbecue and other activities in summer) and even a helipad! The inn is enormous and has 44 rooms and a wide range of prices. You'll pay 300F for a room with shower/wc, 370F for one with bath, 410F for a duplex, and 470F for a suite. Rooms in the annexe are 330F and 390F. Half-board is available if you're staying three days or more and prices start at 290F per person. The 120F set meal available weekday lunchtimes offers good value for money. Other set meals 157F, 207F and 241F. Specialities include lasagne of frogs' legs, poached eggs in a red wine sauce with snails, *carpaccio* of beef with onion rings, and monkfish *meunière* on a bed of green lentils and smoked bacon. Opportunities for hiking and biking, while the less actively inclined can play billiards. It's like the Club Med in miniature with its indoor pool, sauna, steam bath and jacuzzi. Nice place for a weekend of sport or just doing nothing but not ideal for lovers.

CHALON-SUR-SAÔNE 71100

10% HÔTEL CLARINE**

35 place de Beaune (Centre).
☎ 03.85.48.70.43 F 03.85.48.71.18
Secure parking. **TV**. **Canal+**.

Large hotel in a renovated old house. Accommodation is available in the main building or in the two annexes, the more recent one of which overlooks an inner courtyard and is quieter. We were taken with the few rooms that had parquet floors, open fireplaces and old furniture. Doubles with cable TV 260–285F. For keep-fit fans there's a sauna, a solarium and a gym.

10% HÔTEL SAINT-JEAN**

24 quai Gambetta (South).
☎ 03.85.48.45.65 F 03.85.93.62.69
TV. **Disabled access**.

Booking advisable. If you have to spend a night in Chalon, don't miss the *Saint-Jean*, the only hotel actually on the riverbank (and away from the traffic!). It used to be a mansion and has been tastefully decorated by a former restaurateur who gave up cooking in favour of hotel-keeping (an art that is all too often underestimated). Friendly and professional staff. A quiet, clean and welcoming establishment with magnificent views, where everything pleases and the prices are reasonable. You feel there should be a preservation order on the handsome staircase in imitation marble that dates from the turn of the century. The large bedrooms are decorated in fresh-looking colours.

RESTAURANT RIPERT

31 rue Saint-Georges (Centre).
☎ 03.85.48.89.20
Closed Sundays and Mondays, one week in January, one week at Easter, and Aug 1–21.

Alain Ripert offers four set meals at 75F, 100F, 140F and 160F every day. The cooking is simple and constantly changes depending on what is available at the market. The dining room is small with a few touches reminiscent of a 50s bistro (adverts, enamel signs) and fills up rapidly with locals (which is a good sign). Main courses include escalope of veal sweetbreads with ceps, stew of monkfish with saffron, house duck *confit,* and fillets of sea bass, and we can recommend desserts like the warm *gratin* of raspberries, the *nougat* with blackcurrant sauce, and the hot apple tart. Children's menu 45F. Unusually for this part of the world, some good wines are available in carafes

RESTAURANT DU MARCHÉ

7 place Saint-Vincent (South-East); it's in the market square, very close to the cathedral.
☎ 03.85.48.62.00
Closed Sunday evenings, Mondays and the second fortnight in August.

This is a rustic looking restaurant that serves three generous set meals at 85F, 105F and 160F. Specialities include pigeon *confit* with *choucroute*, fillets of sole with a fruit and cider sauce, and frogs' legs with buckwheat pancakes. Lots of choice, regardless of the size of your appetite! If you're not hungry, you can have just a main course or a salad. Wine comes from tiny local vineyards.

RESTAURANT CHEZ JULES

11 rue de Strasbourg (South-East); it's on île Saint-Laurent.
☎ 03.85.48.08.34
Closed Saturday lunchtimes, Sundays, two weeks in February and Aug 1–15.

This small restaurant, located in a quiet neighbourhood, is popular with the locals, and the salmon pink walls, beams, copper pots, paintings and old sideboard add to the cosy atmosphere. It offers a good variety of set meals (88F, 145F and 175F) and a wide range of main dishes such as veal kidneys and sweetbreads with a morel sauce, fillet of lamb with preserved garlic, veal sweetbreads and *foie gras*, and rabbit charlotte with mustard seeds. Good wine list, and wine is available by the glass and the carafe. A post-prandial stroll along the embankment will be called for.

LE GOURMAND

13 rue de Strasbourg (South-East); it's on the île Saint-Laurent.
☎ 03.85.93.64.61
Closed Monday evenings and Tuesdays, three weeks in August, and a fortnight in Jan or Feb.

Everything in this establishment is either yellow, beige or golden, and that includes the owner's clothes (at least the day we passed by!) Always friendly and smiling. Tastefully stylish décor and atmosphere. Richly decorated, but definitely not posh or over the top. Lots of regulars as everyone seems to know each other. Faultless presentation, particularly refined cooking, and combinations of tasty herbs make for very successful sauces. Fish cooked to perfection. Their 99F set meal is better than most. Sample salad of *foie gras* and smoked breast of duck in the 138F set meal. Another at 175F. Good choice à la carte such as *gratin* of crawfish with fresh pasta, *pavé* of zander with tails of freshwater crayfish, roast turbot on a bed of ratatouille, veal kidneys with a salt-flavoured crust and saddle of rabbit *en crépine* with savory (bitter herb) sauce.

CHATENOY-LE-ROYAL 71880 (4KM W)

AUBERGE DES ALOUETTES

1 route de Givry; take the Givry exit on the D69.
☎ 03.85.48.32.15
Closed Tuesday evenings, Wednesdays, during the February school holidays, and the second fortnight in July.

Its country location notwithstanding, this place has already attracted a loyal following. People come here for a breath of fresh air, wedding breakfasts, first communions and so on. It has fine old parquet flooring and some good pieces of furniture with the patina of age on them, and fresh flowers decorate the rooms. This is genuine country style and nothing is overdone. The cooking too is authentic and Jean-François Madon offers his guests things like extremely good snails, coq au vin, coddled eggs with lobster and morels, lobster stew with a shellfish sauce, chicken with preserved garlic, and *crêpes soufflées* with lemon and an apricot sauce. Substantial 90F set meal available every day; other set meals 120F, 165F and 260F.

BUXY 71390 (15KM SE)

AUX ANNÉES VINS

place du Carcabot (Centre); take the N81 and the D981.
☎ 03.85.92.15.76
Closed Tuesdays and Wednesday lunchtimes.

A delightful young couple have just taken over this old restaurant and renovated it. Frédéric does the cooking while Christelle looks after the front of house. You can eat in the smart dining room or, in summer, on the terrace that, overlooks the street (and is a bit noisy). Three mouth-watering set meals at 95F, 145F, 190F and 260F. We plumped for the 120F "discovery" set meal which came with *terrine* of ceps and *coulibiac* of salmon. The à la carte menu includes *foie gras pot au feu*, salad of veal sweetbreads and crayfish, pig's trotters, braised veal sweetbreads with grapes, and turbot stuffed with a hazelnut *mousseline*. If you like wine, you can indulge yourself here because you won't get ripped off. Whites, including Chardonnay, Montagny *premier cru* and Aligoté (55–80F a bottle), take pride of place but there are also some good red Burgundies with an excellent Pinot Noir (65–80F a bottle). A fair number of half-bottles are also available at 40–50F. There's a small tasting room on the ground floor with reasonable prices.

CHAROLLES 71120

10% HÔTEL-RESTAURANT LE LION D'OR**

6 rue de Champagny.
☎ 03.85.24.08.28 F 03.85.88.30.96
Closed Sunday evenings and Mondays (except in July , August, and September). **Secure parking. TV.**

This is a former 17th century coaching inn and stands on the banks of a small river. Large rooms, with doubles 135–260F. Our favourites were numbers 23 and 25, which had a view of the river. Top-notch restaurant with good regional cooking. The meat is exceptional, of course – this is Charolais country after all! Set meals 80F (except Sundays and publc holidays), 120F and 250F. Swimming pool.

HÔTEL-RESTAURANT DE LA POSTE***

2 av de la Libération (Centre).
☎ 03.85.24.11.32 F 03.85.24.05.74
TV.

This is a very important establishment in Charolais, run by Daniel Doucet, the famous ambassador of Burgundy gastronomy. His cooking has been delighting tastebuds for many years now and is still as fresh and tasty as ever. Richly decorated dining room, faultless and particularly attentive service, but definitely not affected. You'll get great advice on wine to suit your taste and choice of dishes. What a festival of aromas and flavours! Don't miss out on the sirloin of rib steak with Guérande salt, served on a hot plate. Absolutely delicious! You can sample dishes such as *truffe* of potatoes with snails in garlic sauce, *cassolette* of scallops with a leek fondue, *croustillant* of veal sweetbreads with morels and chanterelle mushrooms. Magnificent cheese platter and desserts. Set meals at 120F (except Sunday lunchtimes), 180F and 280F. Eat out under the maple trees and virginia creeper in the lovely interior garden on fine days. Comfy bedrooms at 350F.

BEAUBERY 71220 (12KM SE)

AUBERGE DE BEAUBERY

La Gare; take the N79 from Charolles or Mâcon, then the D79.
☎ 03.85.24.84.74
Closed Wednesday evenings.

Little inns like this, offering a complete meal with wine and coffee for 58F, are nowadays few and far between. Basic, home-made cooking, lovingly created and served in generous portions. The kind of dining room we expected with prints, kitschy old clock, full of regulars and local travelling salesmen. You can get a sandwich, local ham, omelette and soft white cheese for 55F. Other set meals offering frogs' legs (80F), Charolais steak or *salmis* of guinea fowl with mushrooms, bacon and potatoes (88F) and excellent *coq au vin* (98F). Expect to spend a maximum of 100–120F on Sunday's à la carte.

CHÂTEAUNEUF 21320

10% HOSTELLERIE DU CHÂTEAU**

How to get there: take the Pouilly-en-Auxois exit off the A6.
☎ 03.80.49.22.00 F 03.80.49.21.27.
Closed Monday evenings and Tuesdays (except out of season) and end Nov–Feb 10. **Disabled access**.

Almost all the 12th and 14th century houses in this picturesque village have been bought as holiday homes by outsiders. Standing in the shadow of a 12th century castle, the hotel may look medieval but it's comfortable and makes for a quiet and pleasant stay. It would be nice if the welcome was a bit warmer, the à la carte menu a bit simpler and the atmosphere a bit less stick-in-the-mud. However ... Have the 140F set meal (the others are 170F and 220F) and make the most of your bedroom (270–430F) and the view of the valley.

LE GRILL DU CASTEL

☎ 03.80.49.26.82
Closed Mondays out of season.

Facing the *Hostellerie* and the château, this is the place for people who love old stone buildings, meat that is simply but succulently grilled over a wood fire, salads and local wine. In summer, don't bother about the two parasols on the lawn – the real terrace is in the courtyard, away from prying eyes (this is Burgundy, where they value their privacy!). The 90F set meal (there is another at 130F) consists of *jambon persillé*, beef *bourguignon*, cream cheese and homemade tart. Congenial welcome.

VANDENESSE-EN-AUXOIS 21320 (5KM W)

RESTAURANT DE L'AUXOIS

How to get there: it's very close to Châteauneuf-en-Auxois and stands on the banks of the canal.
☎ 03.80.49.22.36
Closed Mondays and Dec 20–Jan 20. **Car park**.

The entire village has taken on a new lease of life with the re-opening of the grocery store and this restaurant, run by Walloons, which gives a little spice to the local style of cooking. The 105F set meal consisted of tripe in white wine, half a ham knuckle in a mustard sauce served on a bed of lentils, cream cheese and tart. The garden is superb in summer and there's an old-fashioned dining room for those grey days. Other set meals 75F (weekdays), and 120F–190F.

CHÂTILLON-EN-BAZOIS 58110

10% HÔTEL DE FRANCE**

29 rue du Docteur-Duret (Centre).
☎ 03.86.84.13.10 ➡ 03.86.84.14.32
Closed Sunday evenings out of season and Dec 23–Jan 15. **Car park**. **TV**.

Set back a little way from the road, this is an imposing building with heavy wooden shutters and exposed stonework that has been well repointed. Inside, there's a large fireplace, copper pots, beams and rustic furniture. Good old-fashioned cooking – sweetbreads, calf's head, snails etc – to go with the décor. Set meal at 58F is available weekdays and there's a large choice of carafe wines that won't make a hole in your wallet.

SAINTE-PÉREUSE 58110 (13KM E)

AUBERGE DE LA MADONETTE

Centre; from Châtillon-en-Bazois, take the D978 and follow the signs for Château-Chinon, turning left 8km from Châtillon-en-Bazois.
☎ 03.86.84.45.37
Closed Wednesdays and Dec 20–Feb 15. **Car park**.

Marie-Madeleine Grobost, who started off her professional life looking after disabled children, made a new career for herself in later years when she decided to take up the restaurant business. Armed with the necessary qualifications, she transformed this big house which is now decorated in gingham throughout and has a magnificent terraced garden with a stunning view of the Morvan foothills. She offers tasty country cooking and dishes like calf's head à l'ancienne, pan-fried lamb with parsley and garlic, and pan-fried sweetbreads on rosés (a type of mushroom). Set meals 66F (weekdays) to 240F.

CHÂTILLON-SUR-SEINE 21400

10% SYLVIA HÔTEL**

9 av. de la Gare.
☎ 03.80.91.02.44 ➡ 03.80.91.47.77
Secure parking. **TV**. **Disabled access**.

The former owners turned an enormous old middle-class family home set amidst parkland into a delightful hotel, naming it after their daughter Sylvia (who, as children do, grew up and moved away). The present owners love the place and do everything they can to make you love it too. Cosy rooms, table d'hôte dinners, wonderful breakfasts. Doubles with shower/wc 240F, with bath 280F. Set meals 60F and 80F.

LE BOURG-À-MONT

27 rue du Bourg-à-Mont; it's a bit away from the centre, in the old town, opposite the old courthouse and near the museum of archeology.
☎ 03.80.91.04.33
Closed Mondays and Sunday evenings out of season.

This is a pleasant surprise in a quiet little town known for the 5th century BC vessel unearthed at Vix and now housed in the museum here. The house, decorated with old adverts, original paintings and bright colours belonged to a grandmother who apparently had a bit of money. Log fires in winter. In summer, the windows overlooking a little flower garden are thrown wide open and you can even have lunch or dinner there (reservations are essential since there is a limited number of places). It all makes you feel pretty pleased with life, particularly since the cooking alone would be worth the trip! Set lunch 58F. Other set meals 80F, 95F, 125F and 160F. The best dishes are the *terrine* of local trout, the roast rabbit with prune stuffing, and what they call *bœuf Bourg à Mont*, which is a spicy version of beef bourguignon.

MONTLIOT-ET-COURCELLES 21400 (3.5KM N)

CHEZ FLORENTIN

How to get there: on the N71 – it's on the outskirts of the village.
☎ 03.80.91.09.70

Closed Mondays and Sunday evenings, except on public holidays.

You can go in through the bar, where the lorry drivers eat, without getting in the way. In the large dining room, used for banquets and christenings, the crowds that you'd expect on high days and holidays are an everyday occurrence, the local accents and laughter of the evening contrasting with the business lunch atmosphere of a few hours earlier. The reception is still friendly and the prices are unbeatable since the 65F set meal (along the lines of melon and ham, *blanquette de veau* and tart) is available at lunchtime and in the evening, and the other set meals cost 106F and 128F.

CLAMECY 58500

RESTAURANT L'ANGÉLUS

11 place Saint-Jean; it's opposite the beautiful Romanesque collegiate church.
☎ 03.86.27.23.25
Car park.

The restaurant is in one of the prettiest half-timbered houses in the town, which has been well restored and where Madame Chapuis apparently invented that famous sausage the *andouillette*. You can eat in the cosy, welcoming dining room, decorated in pale tones, or on the pretty terrace that faces the collegiate church. Delicious cooking based on what's available at the market. They do set meals at 95F, 150F and 250F and also a fast set lunch at 55F.

RESTAURANT LA GRENOUILLÈRE

6 rue Jean-Jaurès.
☎ 03.86.27.31.78
Closed Sunday evenings, Mondays, and Sept 1–15.

Pleasant surroundings and friendly welcome in this congenial little bistro-style restaurant. Wonderful specialities from the south-west of the country such as *cassoulet*, duck breast and duck *confit*, and frogs' legs *Provencal*. Set meals are 59F (weekday lunchtime), 98F, 148F and 190F.

RESTAURANT AU BON ACCUEIL

3 route d'Auxerre.
☎ 03.86.27.91.67
Closed evenings Oct-May (except Saturdays), Sunday and Wednesday evenings in summer, two weeks in March, and November.

A restaurant that lives up to its name even though it is right by the road. François Langlois cares about his customers and serves them dishes that change as the mood takes him, things like flan of snails, beef fillet with *foie gras* and red burgundy or saddle of young rabbit stuffed with gingerbread and served with a blackcurrant sauce. The cosy dining room – air-conditioned in summer on the quiet banks of the Yonne has a fine view of the collegiate church. Attentive service and a delightful welcome from Madame Langlois. Set meals 90F, 130F, 160F and 220F. It's not very big so it's a good idea to book in advance.

CLUNY 71250

10% HÔTEL DU COMMERCE*

8 place du Commerce (Centre).
☎ 03.85.59.03.09 F 03.85.59.00.87

In this expensive town, it's a good thing to have a small, well-maintained and central hotel that offers basic, clean accommodation at reasonable prices. Wonderfully friendly reception to boot. Bedrooms priced 100F, 130F, 150F, 195F and 220F.

HÔTEL SAINT-ODILON**

rue Belle-Croix; it's a ten-minute walk from the centre of town going toward Tournus, on the D15 beside the racecourse.
☎ 03.85.59.25.00 F 03.85.59.06.18
Closed Dec 20–Jan 5. **Secure parking**. **TV**. **Canal+**. **Disabled access**.

Surrounded by fields full of grazing Charolais cattle, this is a modern establishment but one that's in sympathy with its surroundings. It's low and squat, has a square courtyard and two wings and is generally reminiscent of the local farms. A nice place to stay – it has all modern facilities, the colour schemes are pleasant, and you'll get a friendly welcome from Monsieur and Madame Berry. Rooms with phone, TV, Canal+ and satellite channels are 280F (breakfast extra), which is pretty good value for money.

BERZÉ-LA-VILLE 71960 (10KM SE)

RELAIS DU MÂCONNAIS

La Croix-Blanche (North-West); take the N79 from Mâcon and Cluny, then the scenic D17.
☎ 03.85.36.60.72 F 03.85.36.65.47
Closed Mondays out of season and Jan. **TV**.

Some might say that the *Relais du Mâconnais* is too stylish for this guidebook or the décor too conventional. Others, however, think the good 135F set meal deserves a mention, that the hushed atmosphere will be to many people's liking and that the well spaced-out table arrangement means that you won't overhear the usual stories about families or inheritances or business not being what it used to be. Faultless cooking with a very personal touch. The small *tartare* of beetroot is so original, it deserves to be upgraded from appetizer to a starter. Dishes based on local produce and fine flavours. Sample cutlet of farm-bred milk calf and *gratin* of vegetables, back of roast John Dory with *barigoule* (a type of mushroom), red mullet stuffed with liver *en cocotte,* roast pigeon with garlic puree and sautéd with mushrooms. If portions had been just a little more generous, things would've been great. Good dessert trolley. They also do a good 230F set meal. About ten comfy bedrooms priced 330F.

BLANOT 71250 (10KM NE)

10% ⌂ |●| HÔTEL-RESTAURANT L'ÉTAPE*

Centre.
☎ 03.85.50.03.63

A small village inn, run by a young and very friendly Franco-British couple. Passers-by receive the best possible local hospitality. They've five clean, basic bedrooms with shower/basin (wc on the landing) at 180F and 250F, or 150F with basin only. Regional cooking in the restaurant served up in generous helpings. Popular with local workmen and especially woodcutters. *Formule* at 48F offers raw ham, omelette and fresh goat's cheese. Set meals (70F and 98F) serve *pavé* of beef, veal liver or chicken breast with morels. Our watchword is: long live small country hotels. They've definitely got our support! By the way, don't forget to pop into the wooden toy store next door and the potter's further up the hill.

10% |●| AUBERGE DU MONT SAINT-ROMAIN

Mont St-Romain.
☎ 03.85.33.28.93
Closed Tuesday evenings out of season.

One of our favourite inns, right up in one of the peaks of the Saône-et-Loire, with one of the most beautiful panoramic terraces there is. Great reception. Dishes given professional, loving attention. Day in day out a very nice young couple bear the brunt of scorching winds in summer and snowdrifts in winter to cater to the culinary needs of walkers, horseriders and nature lovers. Hearty portions based on regional dishes using fresh produce. Set meals at 66F, 79F, 85F, 110F and 149F offer good value for money. À la carte you can sample dishes like *mousseline* of fish with a herb sauce, frogs' legs Provence-style, salad of small snails, fillet of zander, and breast of duck. Well-chosen wines at exceptionally reasonable prices; for example, a jug will cost 17F and a bottle of red Mâcon 65F. There will soon be an "open veranda" so that they won't have to worry any longer about sunshades flying away. Horserides to help the digestion and a travel lodge for those who can't bear to leave. What more could you ask for?

CREUSOT (LE) 71200

|●| LE RESTAURANT

rue des Abattoirs (South).
☎ 03.85.56.32.33
Closed Sunday evenings and two weeks in Aug.

What is this place doing here amongst the abattoirs, a dark and deserted area in the evenings? The answer's simple – it's a firefly in the night for drivers who've lost their way. So standing apart from the rest of the town is not such as daft idea, and you won't regret having ended up here. Warm reception, nicely informal and everyone recognizes familiar faces. Bright, pleasant dining room, painted in fresh colours, has a tall appearance on account of its mezzanine. A few interesting paintings. The rest is elegantly bare and the zinc counter provide a smooth transitional point between tradition and innovation. Well-designed cooking, aiming to preserve the taste of good produce by cleverly combining herbs and other flavours. Set meals at 65F, 95F and 129F. Dishes such as *terrine* of eels in onion jelly (deliveries permitting), *tournedos* of salmon and cod, chicken soup, farm-bred pigeon, breast of duck with wild thyme and country-style lamb. Excellent selection of wines to suit all budgets – red Mâcon from 69F and a lovely 95F Givry François Lumpp. Those with lots of money might be interested in some high quality Burgundy wines at reduced prices. It's advisable to book in the evenings. This little establishment is going places.

|●| LE BISTROT DE LA GRIMPETTE.

16 rue de la Chaise (Centre).
☎ 03.85.80.42.00
Closed Sundays and the week of August 15.

Exactly halfway up the stairway connecting the upper and lower portions of the town, this is an inexpensive restaurant serving genuine Lyons specialities. The décor is wine red (Beaujolais of course!). Nothing's missing, not even the aromas of hot sausage, coddled eggs with morels, and salt pork with lentils. Attentive service and friendly welcome. The basic set meal is 75F and the portions are generous, so it's well worth the climb. Other set meals 89F and 98F. Warm salad of calf's feet, flank of beef *maquignon*, and salad of red mullet are just a few of the goodies on the à la carte menu.

TORCY 71210 (3KM S)

LE VIEUX SAULE

route du Creusot (South).
☎ 03.85.55.09.53
Closed Sunday evenings and Mondays.

Le Vieux Saule is one of the best restaurants in the region, located in a very old country inn at Torcy, on the outskirts of Creusot. Excellent welcome and brilliant décor. Good 100F set meal and others at 140F (local), 170F and 230F. Their cooking's particularly tasty – *foie gras* of duck with truffles, *mille-feuille* of lamb and apples, and stew of lobster covered in pastry, delicious *souris* of lamb (and nicely presented to boot!). Desserts along the same lines.

LE BREUIL 71670 (4KM E)

10% LE MOULIN ROUGE***

route de Montcoy (East).
☎ 03.85.55.14.11 F 03.85.55.53.37
Closed Friday evenings, Saturday lunchtimes, Sunday evenings and a fortnight at Christmas. **Car park**. **TV**.

A particularly friendly hotel complex situated outside the town with a little park, heated swimming pool and with the countryside right nearby. Peace and quiet guaranteed. Their cooking has enjoyed a good reputation for many years now. They've got about forty comfy bedrooms at 200–280F per person and 250–320F for a double. Cosy, rustic décor and tasteful copperware. Good provincial hospitality. The chef learnt his trade at the Côte d'Or in Saulieu alongside Alexandre Dumaine, perfected his skills at Maxim's in Paris and hung about the Royale as cook to a pasha. Set meals at 100F, 140F, 160F, 180F and a 200F *menu plaisir*. They even do a 130F local set meal. Let's see what's on offer à la carte – *effeuillé* of salt cod with green cabbage, back of zander with *choucroute*, *tournedos* of rabbit with palm hearts and braised celery, and *suprême* of chicken with morels in a cream sauce. Often accompanied by tasty little fritters.

DECIZE 58300

L'AGRICULTURE**

20 route de Moulins.
☎ 03.86.25.05.38 F 03.86.77.16.52
Closed Sunday evenings and Oct 1–20. **Car park**. **TV**.

It's worth stopping at this rather plain looking roadside hotel for its comfortable rooms (doubles 230–260F). Ask for one overlooking the garden. A very simple but substantial meal costs 70F and something a bit fancier 95F. The dining room is large and bright and the little bunch of seasonal flowers on each table is a delightful touch.

RESTAURANT LA GRIGNOTTE

57 av. du 14-Juillet (North).
☎ 03.86.25.26.20
Closed Sundays and Wednesday evenings.

An unpretentious restaurant situated (unfortunately) next to a busy road, but the dining room is a lovely bright room. A substantial set meal of, for example, mixed salad, meat with shallots, cheese, and home-made apple tart costs 65F. Other set meals are 99F and 140F. Excellent value for money.

DIGOIN 71160

10% LES DILIGENCES**

14 rue Nationale (Centre); it's in a pedestrianized street in the centre of town.
☎ 03.85.53.06.31 F 03.85.88.92.43
Closed Monday evenings and Tuesdays (except in July and August), June 20–28 and Nov 21–Dec 13.
Secure parking. **TV**.

A long time ago, in the 17th century, travellers arriving in the town by mail coach or boat stayed at this inn. Its past splendours have recently been restored and the exposed stonework, beams, polished furniture and gleaming copper that give it a country-chic look make it worth the trip. Prices are not too bad: the two cheapest set meals (98F and 140F) offer a generous portion of duck breast with sour cherries or *andouillette* and lobster bisque . You'll find à la carte dishes like fillet of Charolais beef with five different types of pepper, fricassee of ceps *à la bordelaise* (sautéd in oil with shallots and parsley), grilled sea bass with fennel, and monkfish steak with fresh pasta a bit expensive. Six tastefully furnished and decorated rooms at

270F overlook the quiet banks of the Loire. There's a duplex which is more like a flat than a hotel room and you'll have your own private spa in the immense and well-equipped bathroom. We recommend rooms number 6, 8 and 11, which are large and have a good view. Reservations advisable.

NEUZY 71160 (3KM NE)

LE MERLE BLANC***

36 route de Gueugnon-Autun; get the D994 going towards Autun.
☎ 03.85.53.17.13 F 03.85.88.91.71
Closed Sunday evenings and Monday lunchtimes Oct–end of April. **Car park. TV. Disabled access.**

The hotel is set back from the road and has doubles with shower/wc for 180F, with bath 250F. Substantial set meals at 80F (not available Sundays), 110F, 150F and 230F offer dishes such as panfried duck *foie gras* with apples or ceps (depending on the season), sirloin of Charolais beef with Roquefort, warm gratin of raspberries, and apple and walnut crumble. Half-board 290F for one, 370F for two. Friendly, efficient staff.

DIJON 21000

SEE MAP OVERLEAF

10% HÔTEL LE CHAMBELLAN**

92 rue Vannerie. **MAP C2-1**
☎ 03.80.67.12.67 F 03.80.38.00.39
TV.

If you like the splendours of yesteryear combined with all mod cons, you'll love the *Chambellan*, an old building and a delightfully old-fashioned establishment with extremely reasonable prices. Doubles with shower or bath start at 220F. They've all got character but go for one overlooking the 17th century courtyard.

HÔTEL LE JACQUEMART**

32 rue Verrerie. **MAP B1-3**
☎ 03.80.73.39.74 F 03.80.73.20.99
TV.

Book ahead to avoid disappointment. A lovely hotel, with lots of regulars, including sales reps and, during the season, opera singers. The rooms are quiet and comfortable and all have cable TV. An ideal spot for a well-earned rest after touring the old part of Dijon. Doubles 180–340F.

HÔTEL DU PALAIS

23 rue du Palais. **MAP B2**
☎ 03.80.67.16.26 F 03.80.65.12.16
TV.

Ideally situated in front of the public library – which is worth a visit even if you haven't come to Dijon to read the sort of books that it holds – and in front of the Law Courts – let's hope that that's not the reason for your coming to Dijon either!. It may be in the centre of the old town, but it's totally quiet. Clean, welcoming bedrooms at 200–280F. Just a pity the soundproofing's not up to much. Beautiful breakfast room.

10% HÔTEL AU MONTCHAPET**

26-28 rue Jacques-Cellerier. **MAP A1-4**
☎ 03.80.53.95.00 F 03.80.58.26.87
Car park.

A quiet hotel in a quiet neighbourhood. The warmth of the welcome you'll get from the new owners, and their kindness, have attracted a loyal following. People know they can ask where to find an all-night chemist, the best Chinese restaurant in town or the best *jambon persillé*. The hotel has dropped ceilings, reproduction antiques in the foyer, and a TV room cum lounge. The rooms (210–275F) are clean and almost pretty. Everything is simple and good, like the breakfasts.

HÔTEL VICTOR HUGO**

23 rue des Fleurs. **MAP A1-5**
☎ 03.80.43.63.45
Secure parking. TV.

The *Victor Hugo*, located in Dijon's middle-class neighbourhood, isn't the kind of place you come to to let your hair down, the atmosphere being ever so slightly staid. But the Brits love it – everything is as clean as a whistle and you could hear a pin drop in the corridors and in the twenty or so comfortable and welcoming rooms in this large establishment. Doubles with shower 230F, with bath 270F.

HÔTEL DES ALLÉES**

27 cours Général-de-Gaulle. **MAP B3-6**
☎ 03.80.66.57.50 F 03.80.36.24.81
Car park. TV. Disabled access.

Small modern hotel on a posh tree-lined avenue leading to the parc de la Colombière. The garden is full of birds and you can be sure of peace and quiet. Doubles with shower/wc 260F. Dogs welcome at no extra charge. So are children (joke) – mind you, that's only to be expected (joke again) since this used to be a maternity hospital and a number of well-known locals were born here. NB: they close the doors at 11pm, so remember to ask for the entryphone code.

|●| LE RAPIDO

102 rue Berbisey. **MAP A2-10**
☎ 03.80.30.95.55.
Closed Sundays.

Hervé's the guy in charge at *Le Rapido*. You'll find a happy bunch of people here who spill out onto the terrace in summer. Good, simple bistro cooking with occasional exotic touches, offering dishes such as *colombo* of chicken and fillets of red mullet served with oregano-flavoured ratatouille. But you could quite happily make do with a savoury tart and grilled *andouillette*, washed down with one of the owner's nice little bottles of wine. Expect to spend about 100–120F. Open till late.

|●| RESTAURANT LE BISTINGO

13 passage Darcy. **MAP A1-11**
☎ 03.80.30.61.38
Closed Sundays, Mondays and in August.

The *Bistingo*, half-pub, half-restaurant, serves substantial portions of inexpensive dishes and you'll pay 45–65F for things like salmon with lemon butter, skate with capers, and *andouillette*. It has lots of regulars but it's a friendly place where it's easy to get into conversation with the locals. The owner is a colourful character reminiscent of Figaro of opera fame and the friendly waiter uses the familiar *tu* with everybody. In the evening, you'll be served the delicious steak tartare almost automatically.

|●| LE PASSÉ SIMPLE

18 rue Pasteur. **MAP B2-13**
☎ 03.80.67.22.00
Closed Saturday lunchtimes and Sundays.

An authentic bistro decorated in old-fashioned style with cosy décor and informal service – the owner and his customers are on first name terms with each other. Some of the tasty dishes available in the 98F *formule carte* are as traditional as can be. Sample the warm sausage with apples cooked in oil, chicken with vinegar, *andouille* with mustard, and soft white herb-flavoured cheese or a good old *clafoutis.* At lunchtimes they do a good 58F *petit menu.* Join your friends for a drink at the bar, then settle down on the little terrace and stretch your legs out in the sun. For the indecisive amongst us, there's also a 72F set meal to choose from. So, what are you waiting for.

|●| MADE IN ITALIA

47 rue Jeannin. **MAP C2-17**
☎ 03.80.65.48.00
Closed Saturday lunchtimes and Sundays.

For several years now, Dijon has become very passionate about all things Italian. Verdi's operas have taken over the Grand Théâtre, and "authentic" restaurants have been popping up between pizzerias. And what advantage does this establishment have? The answer's simple – atmosphere! Customers have fun, there's laughter, the sound of happy voices, people blow kisses to the owner. They don't care for fancy dishes, prefering to sit and chat about the good old days over a plate of pasta and a bottle of Chianti. Lunchtime *formules* at 45F and 59F. Set meals offer dishes like *carpaccio*, spaghetti carbonara and *coupe amaréna* (77F), and *noix* of scallops with gorganzola cream sauce, sole with parsley and mild garlic, cheese and Italian desserts (107F). This is your chance to experience the up and coming district in town.

|●| LE SIMPATICO

30 rue Berbisey. **MAP B2-12**
☎ 03.80.30.53.33
Closed Sundays and three weeks in August.

Rue Berbisey, which has long welcomed all sorts and all cultures (the only street in the city to do so), rarely sees the sun, which is blocked out by the high walls of the private houses and former brothels. However, you'll find lots of sunshine in the pasta, ricotta ravioli, and carpaccio that chef Francesco serves up. Set meals 65F and 85F at lunchtime. Prices in the evening are a good bit steeper (115–185F) and the atmosphere isn't as good.

|●| COUM CHEZ EUX

68 rue Jean-Jacques Rousseau. **MAP B1-15**
☎ 03.80.73.56.87
Closed Sundays.

"You have to see it to believe it!" The establishment's motto perfectly matches the owner's personality. If you like his sense of humour – sometimes heavier than his cooking – then you'll simply fall in love with this place. Beams provide support for the enormous cauldrons, they've wooden tables decorated with checked polished tiles and you'll get a cheerful reception from an adorable owner. They do two *formules.* One at 85F and another at 115F based on the dish of the day – ham with lentils (Mondays), local soup

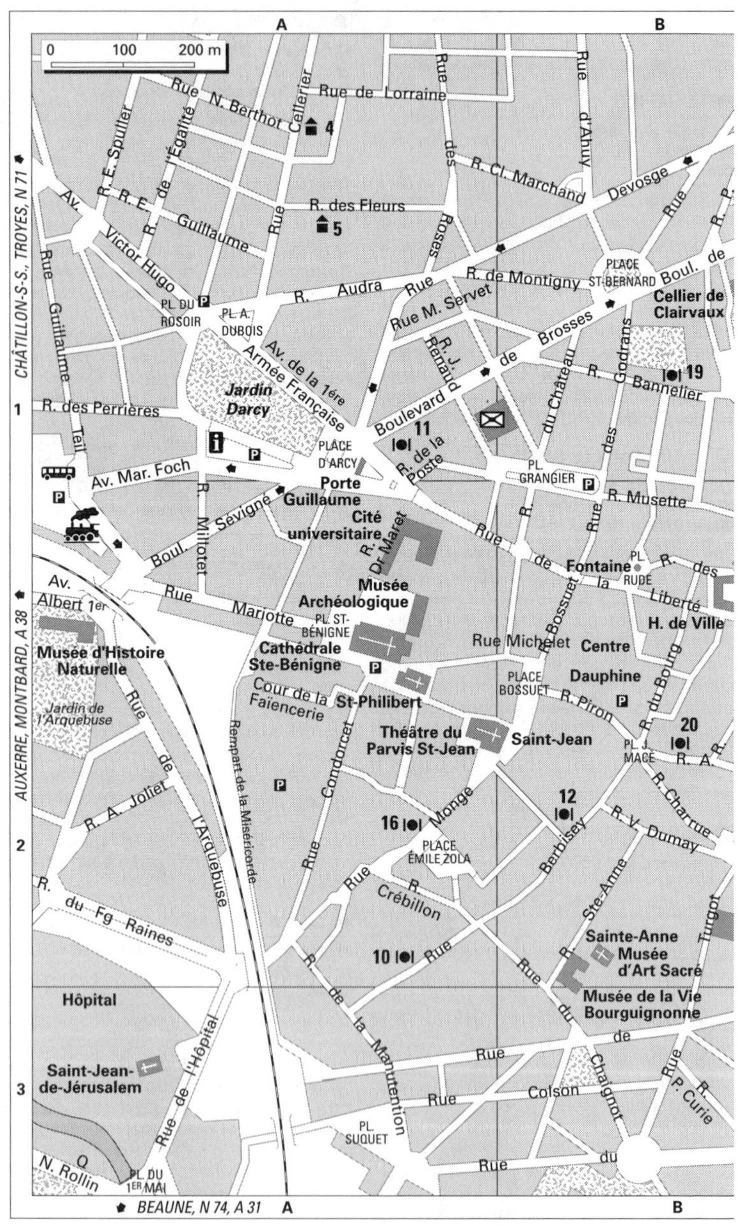

0 100 200 m
A
B
1
2
3
CHÂTILLON-S-S., TROYES, N 71
AUXERRE, MONTBARD, A 38
BEAUNE, N 74, A 31
Rue N. Berthot
Rue de Lorraine
Rue Cellerier
4
5
R. des Fleurs
Rue des Roses
Rue d'Ahuy
R. Cl. Marchand
Devosge
R. E. Spuller
R. de l'Égalité
R. E. Guillaume
Av. Victor Hugo
Rue Guillaume
R. Audra
Rue M. Servet
R. de Montigny
PLACE ST-BERNARD
Boul. de Brosses
Cellier de Clairvaux
PL. DU ROSOIR
PL. A. DUBOIS
Av. de la 1ére Armée Française
R. J. Renaud
Rue du Château
R. Bannelier
19
Jardin Darcy
R. des Perrières
Boulevard
11
R. de la Poste
PLACE D'ARCY
Teil
Av. Mar. Foch
PL. GRANGIER
R. Musette
Porte Guillaume
Cité universitaire
R. Dr Maret
R. Millotet
Boul. Sévigné
Rue de la Fontaine
Rue des Godrans
Rue Bossuet
PL. RUDE
R. de la Liberté
Av. Albert 1er
Rue Mariotte
Musée Archéologique
PL. ST-BÉNIGNE
Cathédrale Ste-Bénigne
Rue Michelet
Centre Dauphine
H. de Ville
Musée d'Histoire Naturelle
Jardin de l'Arquebuse
Cour de la Faïencerie
St-Philibert
PLACE BOSSUET
R. Piron
R. du Bourg
Théâtre du Parvis St-Jean
Saint-Jean
20
PL. J. MACÉ
R. A.
Rue de l'Arquebuse
R. A. Joliet
Rempart de la Miséricorde
Rue Condorcet
Monge
16
12
R. Charrue
R. V. Dumay
Berbisey
PLACE ÉMILE ZOLA
R. du Fg Raines
Rue
R. Crébillon
Ste-Anne
Turgot
10
Rue
Sainte-Anne Musée d'Art Sacré
Musée de la Vie Bourguignonne
R. de la Manutention
Rue du
Hôpital
Rue de l'Hôpital
Saint-Jean-de-Jérusalem
Rue de Colson
Chaignot
Rue P. Curie
Rue
PL. SUQUET
Rue du
Q. N. Rollin
PL. DU 1ER MAI

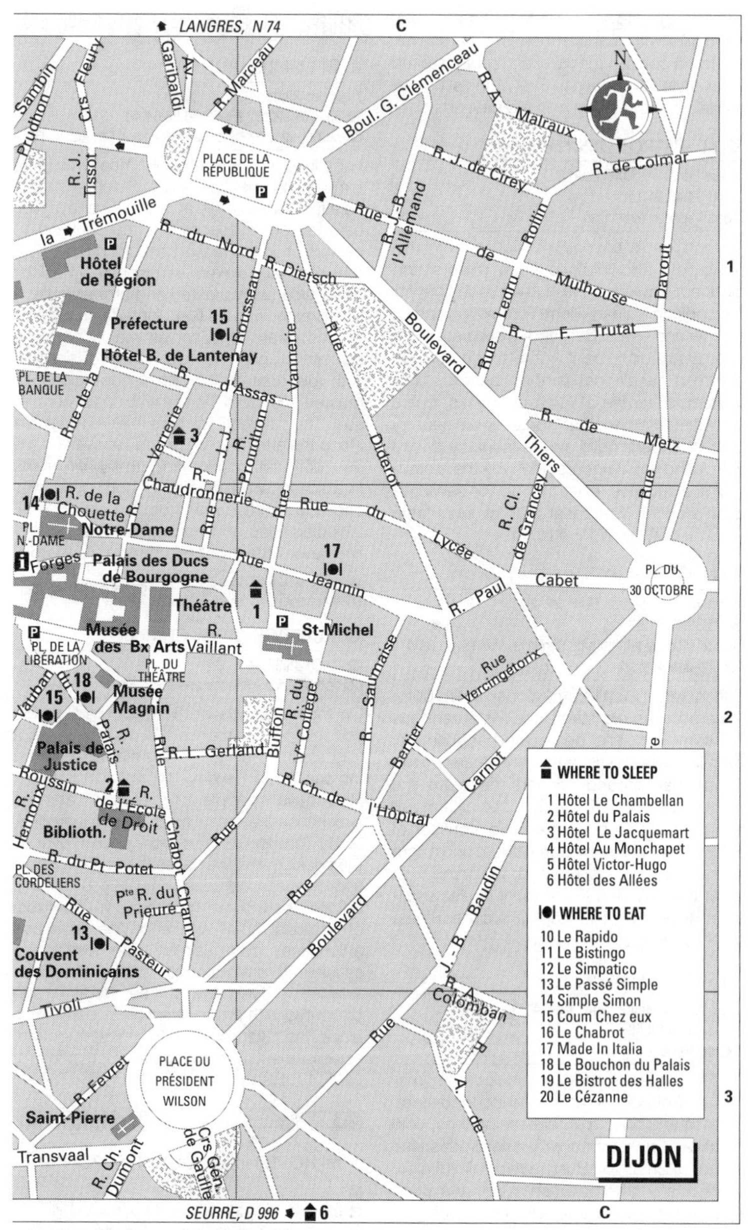
LANGRES, N 74
C
DIJON
PLACE DE LA RÉPUBLIQUE
Hôtel de Région
Préfecture
Hôtel B. de Lantenay
PL. DE LA BANQUE
Notre-Dame
PL. N.-DAME
Palais des Ducs de Bourgogne
Théâtre
St-Michel
Musée des Bx Arts
PL. DE LA LIBÉRATION
PL. DU THÉÂTRE
Musée Magnin
Palais de Justice
Biblioth.
PL. DES CORDELIERS
Couvent des Dominicains
PLACE DU PRÉSIDENT WILSON
Saint-Pierre
PL. DU 30 OCTOBRE
SEURRE, D 996
C
1
2
3
WHERE TO SLEEP
1 Hôtel Le Chambellan
2 Hôtel du Palais
3 Hôtel Le Jacquemart
4 Hôtel Au Monchapet
5 Hôtel Victor-Hugo
6 Hôtel des Allées
WHERE TO EAT
10 Le Rapido
11 Le Bistingo
12 Le Simpatico
13 Le Passé Simple
14 Simple Simon
15 Coum Chez eux
16 Le Chabrot
17 Made In Italia
18 Le Bouchon du Palais
19 Le Bistrot des Halles
20 Le Cézanne

(Tuesdays), stew of pork (Wednesdays), *andouille* with haricot beans (Thursdays), beef with sea salt (Fridays) and rabbit sautéd local style (Saturdays). Everything's home-made, from the starters to the desserts.

|●| LE BISTROT DES HALLES

10 rue Bannelier. **MAP B1-19**
☎ 03.80.49.94.15
Closed Sunday evenings.

Anyone who's anyone in Dijon eats in this old-style bistro with its large mirrors and gingham napkins. The man responsible for the cooking is Jean-Pierre Billoux, a wonderful chef and one of Burgundy's six great masters. Every dish, be it home-made *pâté en croûte à l'ancienne*, *jambon persillé*, pig's trotters, or *terrine* of lamb and leeks, bears his mark. Add to that some good country dishes, superb grills and reasonably priced wines and you'll understand why the restaurant is a success, even though the service is a bit uptight. Set meal 97F at lunchtime. Reckon on 150–200F à la carte.

|●| LE CÉZANNE

40 rue Amiral-Roussin. **MAP B2-20**
☎ 03.80.58.91.92
Closed Monday lunchtimes, Sundays, Aug 15–31, and Dec 22–Jan 4.

Lunch served until 2pm, dinner until 10pm. Located in an old street, the restaurant has old stonework and beams and an intimate, even impressionistic, atmosphere. Jazz plays in the background, flowers decorate the tables and there are happy faces all around. The 140F set meal, for example, consists of salmon *tian*, fish stew with saffron, and a light and colourful dessert, all of it served with great serenity. A 99F set meal is also available. Reckon on 180–250F à la carte. Pleasant little terrace.

|●| SIMPLE SIMON

4 rue de la Chouette. **MAP B2-14**
☎ 03.80.50.03.52
Closed Mondays.

This is an ideal spot for a snack in the timeless surroundings of the antique district. Cheese and onion pie, cheese scones, cold meat, and desserts are on offer in this little corner of Britain on Burgundian soil. Ideal for a break any time between 10am and 7pm. Also one of the few places in Dijon where you can get breakfast on a Sunday. Reckon on about 100F a head. Very pleasant staff.

HAUTEVILLE-LES-DIJON 21121 (8KM NW)

⌂ |●| LA MUSARDE**

7 rue des Riottes.
☎ 03.80.56.22.82 F➜ 03.80.56.64.40
Closed Sunday evenings and Mondays. **Car park. TV.**

For a long time, this establishment was more famous as a meeting place for people having an affair than as a restaurant. Nowadays, you have to reserve, especially at the weekend, to be sure of a table in this peaceful place where the informal, relaxed atmosphere is at the same time sophisticated and professional. A true Breton, with his feet planted firmly on the ground, Marc Ogé serves mainly fish and seafood dishes. Sample *terrine* of shellfish with *foie gras* and *confit* of aubergines, or roasted trout from the sea with *coulis* of mussels. The crowds flock here and you'll understand the attraction once you set eyes on the 99–205F set meals, and the *petit menu* (weekdays) which is ideal for both executives and your average man from the street (105F including wine and coffee). Nice terrace for fine days. Attractive bedrooms at 220–285F.

PRENOIS 21370 (12KM NE)

|●| AUBERGE DE LA CHARME

☎ 03.80.35.32.84
Closed Monday evenings and Tuesdays.

On the other side of the main road, before you reach the airfield of Darois, you'll see a little street leading to the village of Prenois, famous in its heyday for its racing circuit. Nowadays, people come from afar to experience the creations of the local prodigy, David Zuddas. You'll be more bowled over by the cooking and the prices than by the décor and the service (best to let you know!). Sample the 98F set meal serving appetizers of scallops, small *terrine* of *foie gras* and artichokes, roast salmon with lentils and sausage from Morteau (the chef was born in Arbois!). Everything's seasoned and presented with a rare attention to detail. This place has taken over as the most important establishment in these parts. Set meals at 130F, 175F and 245F.

VAL SUZON 21121 (15KM NE)

⌂ |●| HOSTELLERIE DU VAL SUZON***

N71.
☎ 03.80.35.60.15 F➜ 03.80.35.61.36
Closed Sunday evenings and Mondays (Nov–March). **Car park. TV.**

A peaceful, comfy establishment serving good food that sticks to its principles. You'll find it only fifteen minutes from Dijon, nestling in the hollow of the valley, in the heart of magnificent parkland and gardens. Whether you stumble across it during the hunting season, in the middle of winter or on a beautiful summer's evening, you're bound to fall under the spell of this place. The owner's kept a country feel to her welcome and still offers some countrified dishes, while at the same time catering for the tastes of passing Parisians and other "foreigners". Bedrooms costing 420–650F are situated above the restaurant and in the chalet. Peaceful and comfy, although the décor's sometimes a bit too much. Yves Perreau has been a chef for twenty years now. He still has fond memories of the Far East and likes to use spices and flavours, but his cooking remains fundamentally true to tradition. Set meals at 130–270F. Ideal for a romantic weekend for two. Wonderful terrace.

DONZY 58220

LE GRAND MONARQUE**

10 rue de l'Étape.
☎ 03.86.39.35.44 F→ 03.86.39.37.09
Closed Sunday evenings and Mondays.
Secure parking. **TV**.

This is a delightful village, with a number of 15th century half-timbered buildings. You'll find the hotel in the centre – it's the old stone house practically next door to the Romanesque church. It offers a combination of rustic charm and all mod cons and has a warm, friendly and tastefully decorated interior. Have a look at the fountain underneath the spiral staircase. Doubles with shower/wc 245F, with bath/wc 285F. Set meals 80–200F. The specialities are *croquets* (crisp almond biscuits) made to an ancient family recipe and home-made chocolates.

DUN-LES-PLACES 58230

LE CHALET DU MONTAL

How to get there: it's 1.5km north-east of the village.
☎ 03.86.84.62.77
Closed Monday evenings and Tuesdays out of season, and Jan 15–Feb 15. **Secure parking**.

Here's a genuine chalet perched above a river in wild surroundings worthy of *Twin Peaks*. It has lots of plants, a bar, an enormous central fireplace, and it's popular with the campers from round about. The cooking is simple but a lot of care goes into the preparation of dishes like *émincé* of Charolais beef, fillet of rascasse with peppers, and iced raspberry soufflé. Set meals 90–180F. There are four rooms if you suddenly get the urge to spend the night. They're a bit basic but will only set you back 120F.

ÉTANG-SUR-ARROUX 71190

10% HOSTELLERIE DU GOURMET**

45 route de Toulon.
☎ 03.85.82.20.88
Closed Sunday evenings), Mondays (out of season), and in January.

Rather clichéd in the classical tradition, with overtones of long banquets and family meals in the country. The welcome and the service uphold that tradition and neither can be faulted. It's grown a bit shabby over the years but the cooking is bang up to date. Set meals 75F (not available Sundays), 98F, 150F and 180F. Offerings à la carte include poached eggs in a red wine sauce, snails served various ways, braised guinea fowl with lentils and *poule au pot*. In keeping with the meditative atmosphere of the area (there are Buddhist monks nearby), there are a few very simple but well kept rooms at 150F with washing facilities, 165F with shower/wc and 210F with bath.

GÉMEAUX 21120

RESTAURANT TEJERINA

rue de la Liberté; it's near the old covered market.
☎ 03.80.95.01.51
Closed Sunday evenings, Mondays, the first fortnight in January, the last week in July and the first in August.
Car park.

Éric Tejerina, feeling totally lost in the desert of north Dijon, was still a boy when he decided to take over the family bistro in this village which has been quiet – a little too quiet perhaps – since the construction of the A31 between Troyes and Dijon. He and his mother – she does the serving – have pulled off quite a coup. The old stone house has been brought back to life and his light and aromatic cooking costs no more than it used to, with set meals at 60F (weekday lunchtimes) and from 80F to 148F. His great classics – snail ravioli with parsley, langoustine lasagne, and duck breast stuffed with *foie gras* – are available à la carte. Reckon on paying about 200F.

GEVREY-CHAMBERTIN 21220

10% ☗ |●| AUX VENDANGES DE BOURGOGNE

47 route de Beuane.
☎ 03.80.34.30.24 F➔ 03.80.58.55.44
Closed Sunday evenings out of season. **Car park. TV.**

Hiding among the big establishments, cellars and prices, what a lovely surprise to come across a old-fashioned hotel-cum-restaurant with checked tablecloths, old photos, friendly service and good local specialities served in hearty portions at reasonable prices. Sample dishes such as snails with garlic-flavoured sauce, *gibelotte* of rabbit, *coq au vin* and bread and butter pudding. Wine can be bought by the glass – we liked this – Aligoté de Bouzeron 94 (13F) and Gevrey-Chambertin 92 (18F). Set meals at 69F and 99F. Interior terrace. Very basic accommodation 190F.

JOIGNY 89300

10% ☗ |●| LE PARIS-NICE**

rond-point de la Résistance.
☎ 03.86.62.06.72 F➔ 03.86.62.44.33
Closed Sunday evenings, Mondays and in January. **Secure parking. TV.**

It had its hour of glory in the days when you had to take the N6 to get to the Côte d'Azur. Nowadays it's a simple but adequate establishment with rooms that are fairly basic but well looked after. A word of warning though – despite the detour, the rooms that look onto the street are a bit noisy, so go for the ones on the other side. Doubles with shower/wc 200F, with bath 230F. The very decent restaurant offers good value for money with set meals at 80F, 110F and 200F that feature simple traditional dishes like snails, calf's head, black pudding with apples, *pot au feu,* and ox cheeks.

10% ☗ |●| LE RIVE GAUCHE***

rue du Port-au-Bois; it's on the banks of the Yonne, very close to the old town.
☎ 03.86.91.46.66 F➔ 03.86.91.46.93
Car park.TV. Canal+.

Like all the greats in the food business, the Lorains could feel that things were changing so they built a modern hotel – it looks like one of a chain – opposite their famous *Côte Saint-Jacques* (which isn't listed here, so don't bother looking). The new establishment is welcoming and has very good-looking comfortable and functional rooms (doubles with bath 250–360F), a pool, tennis court, a flower-filled garden and terraces, and a dining room where the décor and the food both reflect today's tastes. The cooking is bistro style, with set meals 98–200F.

CELLE-SAINT-CYR (LA) 89116 (8KM W)

10% ☗ |●| AUBERGE DE LA FONTAINE AUX MUSES**

How to get there: when you leave the motorway, head for Joigny on the D943; after 3km, turn left when you come to the village of La Motte – the inn is 3km further on.
☎ 03.86.73.40.22 F➔ 03.86.73.48.66
Closed Mondays. **Car park. TV. Disabled access.**

The inn nestles among Burgundy's rolling hills and looks like a country house that's been redecorated by Parisians with good taste. The front is covered in Virgina creeper, the rooms are as rustic as you could wish (prices start at 345F!) and the cooking reminds you that you're in Burgundy. Dishes include casserole of snails, beef *bourguignon* simmered over a wood fire, and beef grilled in the dining room fireplace. Set meals are 115F (lunchtimes Wednesday–Friday) and 180F. Reckon on 200–250F à la carte. Since all the Langevin family are musicians (father Claude composed the European anthem!), don't be surprised if there are other musicians around at the weekend and a jam session results. Tennis court and heated swimming pool.

VILLEVALLIER 89330 (9KM NE)

10% ☗ |●| LE PAVILLON BLEU**

31 rue de la République.
☎ 03.86.91.12.17 F➔ 03.86.91.17.74
Closed Sunday evenings and Monday lunchtimes Oct–May and in January. **Secure parking. TV.**

The *Pavillon Bleu* is worth the trip, if only for the warmth of the welcome. What's more, it has some of the best prices in the region. Granted, the rooms are small but they are charming and comfortable. Doubles 195F with shower/wc or bath. The home cooking is served up in generous portions. The cheapest set meal is 65F (except Sundays). Other set meals 105F–205F.

LORMES 58140

☗ |●| HÔTEL PERREAU**

8 route d'Avallon (Centre).

☎ 03.86.22.53.21 F➔ 03.86.22.82.15
Closed Sunday evenings and Mondays out of season and in January. **Car park**. **TV**.

This is an imposing establishment that has been well renovated and could accommodate a regiment of backpackers. The restaurant is very pretty and rustic looking with a large fireplace and superb ceiling. The cooking is equally refined – try the fillet of zander in a mint infusion. Several set meals (72F, 85F, 120F and 160F). Rooms are spacious – the ones overlooking the garden have been renovated – and prices start at 260F.

VAUCLAIX 58140 (8KM S)

HÔTEL DE LA POSTE**

Centre.
☎ 03.86.22.71.38 F➔ 03.86.22.76.00
Car park. **TV**. **Disabled access**.

Located in deepest darkest Morvan, this is a well-known and friendly hotel. It's been in the Desbruères family for generations and they're constantly doing it up and introducing innovations to please the traveller. The low-key rooms are big but cosy (doubles from 205F), the dining room has big round tables and is decorated in warm tones, and there's a large swimming pool in the garden. The whole place exudes a feeling of quietness and sheer self-indulgence. The cooking alone is worth the trip. The two page menu offers traditional dishes such as beef fillet with morels and innovative ones like braised cabbage with *foie gras* and apples in honey sauce. Five set meals (70F, 98F, 158F, 195F and 250F).

LOUHANS 71500

10% HOSTELLERIE DU CHEVAL ROUGE**

5 rue d'Alsace.
☎ 03.85.75.21.42 F➔ 03.85.75.44.48
Closed Mondays and Tuesday lunchtimes (except in July and August), Jan 2–15, and one week in June. **Secure parking**. **TV**.

The archetypal good big country inn. Comfortable rooms 160F with basin, 260F with shower/wc and 290F with bath. A further 14 rooms will soon be available in an annexe. Set meals 80F (not available Sundays), 100F, 120F (that one comes with cod steak in a red wine sauce), 135F, 165F and 220F. Children's menu 40F. À la carte dishes include snails in puff pastry, zander, veal sweetbreads, and *poulet de Bresse*. Our only criticism was the uneven quality of service.

10% LE MOULIN DE BOURGCHÂTEAU**

route de Châlon; from the centre of town take the D978 and turn right before the Citroën sign.
☎ 03.85.75.37.12 F➔ 03.85.75.45.11
Closed Sundays Oct–Easter, Monday lunchtimes, and Dec 20–Jan 15. **Car park**. **TV**. **Disabled access**.

If you get the urge to do something romantic, then try this old mill built in 1778 on the banks of the Seille, a tributary of the Saône. The location is superb and the rooms are very cosy. We fell for the one in the attic but the second floor rooms – numbers 1 to 7 – have a stunning bird's eye view of the river. Doubles 250–300F. Very filling breakfast 45F. The restaurant, which overlooks the river, offers refined cooking and set meals at 100F, 160F and 210F. The cheapest of those comes with a choice of strips of duck flavoured with curry or beef fillet and represents excellent value for money. The à la carte menu changes regularly – when we were there, it included duck breast with pears and fillet of zander in a Pinot sauce. The ideal spot for a weekend away with that very special person.

RESTAURANT LA COTRIADE

4 rue d'Alsace.
☎ 03.85.75.19.91
Closed Tuesdays and Thursday evenings (except out of season), July 1–7, and Nov 15–30. **Car park**.

If you're the kind of person who has trouble making up your mind, you'll find eating at the *Cotriade* quite an agonizing experience. There are a number of set meals to choose from, all at reasonable prices – 68F (except Sundays), 105F (salmon tartare and a choice of rack of lamb or *poulet de Bresse*), 140F (fish and shellfish dishes), 160F and 198F. Freshness is all-important here and the ingredients for the monkfish with seaweed, the *cotriade* (stew of white fish with mussels, potatoes and cream), the fish soup and the sole with sorrel come straight from Brittany. Children's menu 45F. Wine prices are reasonable – a carafe of Côtes-du-Rhône, for example, will cost you 45F. A word of advice: don't hesitate to speak up if you get forgotten by the waiters between one course and the next – it has been known to happen.

SAVIGNY-SUR-SEILLE 71440 (11KM W)

10% AUBERGE LA RIVIÈRE

Tiellay.
☎ 03.85.74.99.03
Closed Wednesdays, a fortnight in Oct, and mid

Jan–mid Feb.

This adorable inn, right in the heart of the countryside, on the banks of the Seille, was once home to a ferryman. The attractive wooden framework has a certain charm. You'll get a good reception. Their cooking enjoys an excellent reputation. The owner is a fishing fanatic and catches his own produce, so freshness is guaranteed. Set meals at 88F, 138F and a lovely little à la carte. Try chicken with morels or baked in a salt crust and served with a cream sauce, *gâteau de foies de volaille* (pounded chicken livers with *foie gras*), *suprême* of freshwater crayfish, snails, salads, not forgetting of course the whitebait. Don't miss out on the silurid house-style (if it's on the menu), the monster fish of these fresh waters. *Pocheuse* (freshwater fish stew with garlic and white wine) made to order. Attractive desserts, mouthwatering iced nougat! There's a dreamlike terrace for fine days, with a lawn going down to the waters.

BEAUREPAIRE-EN-BRESSE 71580 (14KM E)

AUBERGE LA CROIX BLANCHE**

Centre; take the N78 in the direction of Lons-le-Saunier.
☎ 03.85.74.13.22 F➜ 03.85.74.13.25
Closed Sunday evenings and Mondays Sept 30–June 15 and Nov 15–Dec 10. **Secure parking. TV.**

You can be sure of a country atmosphere in this genuine 17th century staging post which has been sympathetically renovated. It's impossible to resist the first-rate free-range chicken and *poulet de Bresse* prepared in different ways at different times of the year by chef Gilles Poulet. Day's special 70F. Set meals are 87F (not available Sundays), 120F (local specialities), 147F, 198F and 200F, the latter consisting solely of fish. If you'd rather go à la carte, you can choose from dishes like panfried turbot with a cider sauce, rabbit with spinach, breast of *poulet de Bresse* with *foie gras*, and monkfish with garlic. All main courses change six times a year to reflect what the market has to offer. The hotel is at the back, fortunately hidden among the trees. It dates from the 70s but you forget that once you're in your room and you'll get a good night's sleep as long as you don't have noisy neighbours (the partitions are a bit thin). Wonderful breakfast (40F) is served on the veranda. Doubles with shower or bath 210F and 245F.

SAILLENARD 71580 (20KM NW)

10% AUBERGE LE MOULIN DE SAUVAGETTE

How to get there: take the D87 to Saillenard then go towards Bletterans – it's 3km from Saillenard and well signposted.
☎ 03.85.74.17.58 F➜ 03.85.74.17.58

For lovers of rustic retreats, for lovers pure and simple, here in the Burgundy borders is the ultimate place to hide away and to taste the delights of deepest darkest Bresse. It's an old mill in the heart of the countryside, attractively converted and decorated. Wonderful bedrooms furnished in old style at 250F. We were particularly fond of the "miller's room", but each has its own personal charm. You'll get a very friendly reception and sample excellent regional cooking served in a beautiful, rustic dining room. Dishes based on the seasons and what the market has to offer. Sample local *terrine,* free-range chicken, fillet of zander with hazelnuts, and *soufflé* of pike. Set meal at 110F. We'd definitely come back.

MÂCON 71000

10% HÔTEL D'EUROPE ET D'ANGLETERRE**

92 quai Jean-Jaurès (North-East).
☎ 03.85.38.27.94 F➜ 03.85.39.22.54
Closed Dec 24–Feb 2. **Secure parking. TV.**

This riverside hotel's a bit dated now but it's got character and still has some charm. Memories of its heyday linger on in the original staircase and the size of the rooms. You'll get a nice welcome from the owner. You don't need to worry about the N6 being so near – the rooms are sound-proofed. Doubles from 120F with basin to 260F with bath; rooms to sleep four and five are 295F and 355F respectively. Rooms 1 and 6 are quite stylish. Breakfast is free for one child under 10 per family.

10% HÔTEL DE GENÈVE**

1 rue Bigonnet (Centre).
☎ 03.85.38.18.10 F➜ 03.85.38.22.32
Secure parking. TV. Canal+.

It's fairly central and pretty conventional. Don't be put off by the dark and dreary corridors – the rooms are perfectly adequate and quite large. Doubles range in price from 239F (with basin/wc) to 350F (with bath). Ask for one of the rooms overlooking the courtyard, which are quieter. There's a rather rustic restaurant on one side and a brasserie on the other. Prices are reasonable, with set meals at 69F and 98F. Reckon on 120F à la carte. Small pleasant garden in summer. Paying car park (35F).

☗ GRAND HÔTEL DE BOURGOGNE**

6 rue Victor-Hugo (Centre).
☎ 03.85.38.36.57 📠 03.85.38.65.92
Secure parking. TV. Canal+. Disabled access.

Lovely hotel on a shady flower-filled square a stone's throw from the pedestrian precinct. Delightful interior with a foyer that's straight out of a Chabrol film. Rooms are done in pastel shades and have just been refurbished. Lots of twists and turns, half-landings and nooks and crannies. Doubles with shower/wc 328F, with bath 344–385F.

I●I LA VIGNE ET LES VINS (SCOUBIDOU)

42 rue Joseph-Dufour (Centre).
☎ 03.85.38.53.72
Closed Sunday lunchtimes and Mondays.

It's often hard to get a table in this local, rather ordinary-looking little restaurant, because the best meat and the most generous portions in Mâcon can be found here. The owner is a real meat buff. Their sirloin steak literally melts in your mouth. If you like, you can have it served with mouthwatering sauces and crispy French fries. There's a pretty good choice – fillet, cutlets of lamb, Châteaubriand, oriental kebabs, and on Wednesdays they do couscous. Large first floor dining room for groups having a night out.

I●I MAISON MÂCONNAISE DES VINS

484 av. de-Lattre-de-Tassigny (North); it's on the riverbank, as you come into town from the direction of Chalon-sur-Saône.
☎ 03.85.38.36.70
Closed May 1 and at Christmas. Open every other day 8am–9pm. **Car park.**

You'll find a great many wines from Chalon and of course Mâcon under one roof here. You can buy by the bottle or plastic container and food is available too so the fumes don't go to your head. Lots of regional specialities – beef bourguignon, cold salt pork – and omelettes, salads, tarts and so on are on offer for about 65F à la carte (there are no set meals). Just the thing to eat on the riverside terrace with a Saint-Véran, Pouilly-Fuissé, Rully or Givry – you'll be spoilt for choice. You can have your tipple by the bottle (from 60F) or the glass (12F).

I●I LE POISSON D'OR

allée du Parc port de plaisance (North); it's on the river bank, 1km from the centre of town.
☎ 03.85.38.00.88
Closed Tuesday evenings and Wednesdays and during the Christmas and February school holidays.
Car park. Disabled access.

Do you feel you have the soul of an artist? Then come and contemplate the reflections in the water and the shady river banks from the large picture windows of this rather plush but not starchy establishment. Set meals 88F (served every day), 96F, 118F and 145F. Regional specialities include rabbit with prunes and onion marmalade, fillet of zander with a chervil sauce, frogs' legs, and roast rack of lamb *à la provençale*, a cheese plate, and *crêpe bourguignonne* with pears and a *coulis* of soft fruit. Of course, this being quite a posh restaurant, it has thick white tablecloths, enormous bouquets of cut flowers and an extremely attentive staff. There are other set meals at 170F and 210F for those with a bit more money than the rest of us.

I●I RESTAURANT LE ROCHER DE CANCALE

393 quai Jean-Jaurès (Centre).
☎ 03.85.38.07.50
Closed Sunday evenings and Mondays (except on public holidays).

An 18th century house facing the river provides a refined and elegant setting for this restaurant. You'll love the 98F set meal (118F with wine), which is not just the kind of loss-leader all too often found in slightly upmarket restaurants. It's good, the helpings are large and you won't still be hungry after fresh cod with tomato and basil butter or panfried fillet of carp with a red Mâcon sauce. If you feel like pushing the boat out, there are four other set meals at 135F, 160F, 200F and 220F. The house specialities include warm flan of *foie gras*, snails with garlic butter, lobster stew, monkfish with basil, *poulet de Bresse* with a cream and morel sauce, and sturgeon stew. À la carte is rather expensive. They care about the little things here – the bread rolls, for example, are made on the premises.

I●I L'AMANDIER

74 rue Dufour (Centre).
☎ 03.85.39.82.00
Closed Sunday evenings and Mondays.

The regulars might stick to the house speciality of salad of pig's trotters that they know and love so well, but Florent Segain often varies his 98F set meal (not available public holidays) according to what's available at the market. Married to an Italian and a lover of all things Italian, he makes a wonderful tiramisu for dessert. It's easy to find the restaurant since it's blue – the outside is blue, the flowers are blue and the plates are blue. The fabrics used in the comfortable and rather plush dining room on the other hand are yellow . Other set meals130F, 150F, 170F, 195F, 280F and 340F. The à la carte menu offers many delights, including fillet of red mullet with olives, oven-roasted pigeon, snails in a red wine sauce, and *gratin* of crayfish tails.

RESTAURANT PIERRE

7 rue Duffour (Centre).
☎ 03.85.38.14.23
Closed several days end June and the beginning of July, also Feb holidays.

How did a Michelin star find its way into this guidebook? Well, it's the chance to sample very refined cooking for less than 200F, that's why. Wonderful setting for candlelit dinners. Dry stone walls, candelabras, fresh flowers, and a beautiful arch separating the dining rooms. Just one little complaint, the reception's a touch affected, and the service is rather prim and proper, if they think you're a peasant. That's what happens when you get an extra star. But enough of all this, let's see what's for eating. Good produce, skilfully prepared, wonderful festival of flavours, faultless fish dishes, excellent *foie gras*, and mouth-watering desserts. Students with grant cheques can afford almost all of these treats thanks to the wide range of set meals (105F, 140F, 170F, 205F and 275F). Here's a peek at some of the star dishes available ˆ la carte (depending on the season of course) – fillets of red mullet, *gratin* of tails of shelled freshwater crayfish with garlic-flavoured cream sauce, *quenelles* and black mushrooms with a shellfish *coulis*. The wines are, as you'd expect, along the same lines.

SANCÉ 71000 (3KM N)

10% LA VIEILLE FERME**

RN6 motorway exit Mâcon North.
☎ 03.85.40.95.15 03.85.40.95.16
Car park. TV.

A small hotel complex has been created from this former farm, which has been tastefully redecorated. Particularly well positioned on the banks of the Saône, surrounded by real cornfields and real cows, anglers and cyclists peacefully riding along the towpath. The modern part, resembling a motel, is not particularly attractive (especially at the front), but the bedrooms (250F) are spacious, pleasant and most overlook the Saône and the countryside. You'll hardly notice the high speed train! Lovely dining room with rustic décor and old-fashioned furniture. On fine days the terrace is everyone's favourite place to be. Their cooking's in keeping with the atmosphere and perfectly affordable. Set meals at 65F, 85F, 110F, 140F and 160F. Fairly standard à la carte menu, but dishes are executed with a professional touch – stew of young rabbit, free-range chicken with cream sauce, veal sweetbreads with morels, sautéd frogs' legs, breast of guinea fowl stuffed with ceps. Beautiful swimming pool in summer with a generous lunchtime buffet. Reception was a touch cold, but that's our one and only complaint.

CRÈCHES-SUR-SAÔNE 71680 (8KM S)

10% CHÂTEAU DE LA BARGE**

Centre.
☎ 03.85.37.12.04 03.85.37.17.18
Closed Saturdays and Sundays Nov 1–Easter, Oct 24–Nov 2, and Dec 19–Jan 4. **Car park. TV.**

If you ever think it would be nice to see how the other half lives occasionally, here's the place to do it. This enormous house, covered in Virginia creeper, dates from 1679 and has hundred-year old trees in its peaceful grounds. Quite a friendly welcome. Agatha Christie would have felt quite at home here with the rather shabby wallpaper and furniture, the large rooms, and the sound of birdsong. Doubles range in price from 250F with shower to 320F with bath and TV. They also have a few rooms with just basin for 120F. Rooms number 18–29 are particularly large. You'll find the same atmosphere and the same style in the restaurant which offers tasty simple cooking that allows the food – *terrine* of pike and tarragon, duck leg in a cider sauce, veal sweetbreads and morels in puff pastry, sautéd snails in a cream sauce, and medallions of lamb with bacon and gingerbread – to speak for itself and doesn't go in for pointless complications. Set meals 98F (available every day), 170F and 215F. The terrace is really nice.

MILLY-LAMARTINE 71960 (10KM W)

CHEZ KACK

Place de l'Église (Centre).
☎ 03.85.36.63.72

Closed Sunday evenings and Mondays. Out of season, closed evenings except weekends.

A lovely little village restaurant in the shade of a beautiful church and Lamartine's house. Enjoy some good local cooking. You'll find yourself sitting cheek by jowl with local workers and tourists in the traditional dining room. They put several tables outside in front of the church on fine days. *Menu du jour* 49F. À la carte you can have dishes like oven-baked *andouillette,* rib steak, warm sausage, veal kidneys in a cream sauce, and *tablier de sapeur* (slab of ox tripe coated with egg and breadcrumbs). Good wine selection. Jugs are 13–26F, Mâcon rouge and Régnié 65F, and Pouilly-fuissé 97F.

SAINT-VÉRAND 71570 (13KM S)

L'AUBERGE DE SAINT-VÉRAN*

How to get there: leave the A6 at exit 29.
☎ 03.85.37.16.50 F➔ 03.85.37.49.27
Closed Mondays and Tuesday lunchtimes out of season. **Car park**. **TV**.

This is the kind of inn you dream about finding in Beaujolais country – a beautiful stone house with a terrace and garden in a traditional village surrounded by vineyards and with a stream nearby. The hotel is simple, clean and very comfortable and the restaurant offers regional cooking. Set meals 105–220F, with inexpensive local wines (which is unusual so we thought we should mention it). The à la carte menu includes stew of *andouillette* in a white wine (they use Saint-Véran) sauce, monkfish in Pouilly, and *ballotine* of free-range chicken stuffed with morels. Rooms with shower/wc 260F, family rooms 300F.

BOURGVILAIN 71520 (18KM W)

AUBERGE LAROCHETTE

Centre; take the N79 from Mâcon, then the D22; or the D980 from Cluny then the D22.
☎ 03.85.50.81.73
Closed Sunday evenings, Mondays, and mid Feb–mid March.

This is a traditional, good, spacious village inn. Cosy dining room decorated in country style. Paintings in the style of Millet on the walls. You'll hear the tick tock of the old clock, sounding right on the hour. The cooking is just as spot-on – cream sauce served with delicious mushrooms and *gratin* of vegetables. Monsieur Bonin is a professional who adds his own little personal touch. What's more, portions are generous and Madame's very attentive. Their 115F set meal is remarkable value for money, but a fellow diner was perfectly content with the one at 75F. You might not be able to finish the one at 160F. À la carte you can sample dishes such as *tartare* of fish, *paupiette* of salmon with bacon, free-range chicken with cream sauce, tasty Charolais steak, *gâteau* of liver with *coulis* of crab and morels. Your chance to sample some of France's best gourmet cooking, which has many fine days ahead.

LA PIERRE SAUVAGE

col des Enceints; take the N79 then the D45 to Pierreclos, and follow the signs for col des Enceintes.
☎ 03.85.35.70.03
Closed Tuesday evenings and Wednesdays (except in July and August); Oct 1–Easter open weekends only. **Car park**.

Service until 9.30pm (10pm in summer). It really is advisable to book for there aren't many tables. It was love at first sight as far as we were concerned for this attractive restaurant, which stands at an altitude of 529m at the top of the pass. Fifteen years ago or so, it was a ruin but now it's a delightful place to stop at for a while. The décor is rustic (naturally) with some modern touches. Of course, if that was all the restaurant had to offer, it wouldn't be enough. But it's not, for the cooking is wonderful – trust the locals, they've been coming here for years. The cheapest set meal is 105F (it comes with a glass of Mâcon), with others at 125F and 170F. Children's meal 60F. Don't miss specialities like snails with mushrooms, vanilla scented guinea fowl with fresh figs, chicken with seasonal fruit, and pigeon with peaches. Snacks, raw ham and *terrines* are available any time. Nice welcome and friendly service. You'll be treated as a regular and everyone likes that. The terrace is superb in summer.

MAILLY-LE-CHÂTEAU 89660

10% LE CASTEL**

place de l'Église.
☎ 03.86.81.43.06 F➔ 03.86.81.49.26
Closed Wednesdays and Nov 15–March 15. **Car park**. **Disabled access**.

This solid late 19th century building with its courtyard and lime trees stands in a village square that is so true to the clichéd image – there's the town hall and over there's the church – it's almost comic. Both the hotel and the restaurant offer good value for money. Half-board is compulsory. Some of the rooms are a bit dreary but refurbishment is an ongoing process. Ask to see several (if possible) before making up your mind. At the moment we would recommend numbers 1, 6, 9 and 10. Doubles 320F with shower/wc, 330F with bath. Cheapest set meal 75F (except Sundays); others 100–170F.

MONTBARD 21500

LA MIRABELLE

Saint-Rémy-les Montbard; as you leave the town, go towards Forges de Buffon and it's 2km along.
☎ 03.80.92.40.69
Closed Tuesdays. **Car park**.

What joy to come across this little village restaurant in this desert of the north Côte d'Or. Blue and yellow décor and tablecloths, and prices that won't make you see red. The menu's on the slate. You can choose house *terrine* with figs, sautéd pork like your grandmother used to make it and iced nougat for 98F. Wine is their speciality, served by the glass by a real wine buff who's opened a shop next door. They've about 400 kinds of *appellations* and foreign wines waiting to be uncorked! Reception's very friendly indeed. Another set meal at 148F. A good place to stop off at, only 10km from the abbey of Fontenay.

MOULINS-ENGILBERT 58290

10% AU BON LABOUREUR**

place Boucaumont (Centre).
☎ 03.86.84.20.55 Fax 03.86.84.35.52
Closed Jan 15–30. **Car park. TV**.

The owner, despite her age, continues to welcome guests to this large building in the village square. She can't quite remember how many set meals she offers, but then neither can we. You can eat there quite cheaply and the food is plentiful, simple and carefully prepared. Set meals, with prices starting at 65F, offer a fine salmon escalope with sorrel, a few Charolais beef specialities and an enormous *nougat glacé*. Local wine starts at 8.50F(!) for a small carafe. Rooms are available – doubles with shower 250F, with bath 270F – so you can make the most of this beautiful village.

MOUX-EN-MORVAN 58230

10% HÔTEL-RESTAURANT BEAU SITE*

How to get there: by the D121.
☎ 03.86.76.11.75 Fax 03.86.76.15.84
Closed Sundays and Monday evenings Nov 15–March 20, and end Dec–Feb 10. **Secure parking**.

Here's another establishment that lives up to its name. The hotel and restaurant are in separate buildings (it's just five minutes on foot) but they both have nice views. Rooms (from only 140F) are large but very simple. The restaurant is bright and pleasant and the service attentive. Set meals 65F (more than adequate), 102F, 145F and 180F.

NEVERS 58000

HÔTEL BEAUSÉJOUR*

5 bis rue Saint-Gildard; it's opposite the shrine of St Bernadette.
☎ 03.86.61.20.84 Fax 03.86.59.15.37
Secure parking. TV.

The rooms are well sound-proofed (or quiet if they overlook the garden). They're rather functional – one bed, one table, one chair – but remarkably well looked after. A plus for TV fans – 17 channels and a TV dinner on request! Double with shower/wc from 190F.

RESTAURANT AUX CHŒURS DE BACCHUS

25 av. du Général-de-Gaulle (Centre).
☎ 03.86.36.72.70
Closed Saturday lunchtimes, Sundays, Aug 2–20, and during the Christmas holidays.

This delightful restaurant has a lovely dining room with old photos on the wall, a climbing vine and pretty porcelain dishes. The cheapest set meal is 126F, a three-course gourmet meal that includes a glass of wine, carefully chosen by the owner, with each course. The same goes for the set meals at 179F and 283F (119F and 183F respectively without wine). One speciality you should try is the *profiteroles* of calf sweetbreads with a sauce of spices and preserved figs. Attentive and charming staff. It really does make you want to sing the praises of Bacchus.

LA COUR SAINT-ÉTIENNE

33 rue Saint-Étienne (Centre); it's behind the church of Saint-Étienne.
☎ 03.86.36.74.57
Closed Sunday evenings, Mondays, Jan 7–21, and Aug 1–20.

Don't be fooled by its size or lack of ostentation and luxury – this is one of the best restaurants in the town and it offers great cooking at modest prices. Set meals from

85F with main courses like tuna in meat juices or *crépinette* of young rabbit roasted with sage. Dishes change regularly with the seasons. Wine isn't expensive either. Given all that, it's definitely a good idea to book.

|●| LE PUITS SAINT-PIERRE

21 rue Mirangron (Centre); it's close to the church of Saint-Pierre.
☎ 03.86.59.28.88
Closed Sunday evenings, Mondays, 1 week in February, and the first fortnight in July.

The restaurant, in a building several storeys high, stands in a prettty square. You'll see the well as you come in. The excellent cooking tends towards the classical and everything is home-made, right down to the bread rolls that are served with a generous hand. There are set meals from 90F and a few highly original specialities such as a *mille-tuiles* of calf sweetbreads and *foie gras* in aged vinegar or a *croquant* of dried fruit preserved in alcohol. It's heaven on earth.

|●| RESTAURANT JEAN-MICHEL COURON

21 rue Saint-Étienne (Centre); it's near the church of Saint-Étienne.
☎ 03.86.61.19.28
Closed Sunday evenings, Mondays, and three weeks late July–early Aug.

This is a delightful establishment with three small dining rooms. The first two are warm, quiet and inviting. The third is a magnificent 14th century chapel with lancet windows and a stone fireplace and you really should try for a table here. Chef Jean-Michel Couron serves up all the traditional local dishes but has pruned them of their excesses – the snails with sorrel and fresh herbs, for example, were light and springlike. Each dish stimulated the taste buds and was a preparation for the next. The halibut fillet in a dressing made of truffles, carrots and fresh herbs was sheer delight, and the 109F *menu d'appel* was appealing indeed. As for the prices – other establishments please copy! The best restaurant in town and, with prices like this, reservations are essential at the weekend.

MARZY 58000 (5KM W)

■ |●| LE VAL DE LOIRE*

Corcelles.
☎ 03.86.38.86.21
Car park. Disabled access.

Set among trees, this is a quiet hotel with a warm, family atmosphere. The pretty dining room has a large terrace where you can have fish from the Loire, frogs' legs or one of two very large set meals. For 60F you'll get home-made *terrine*, escalope in a cream sauce, cheese, and dessert. The more expensive one (120F) offers two starters (one of which is half a dozen snails), a Charolais ribsteak, cheese, and dessert. Doubles with basin/wc from 120F, with bath up to 160F. Its bucolic setting and moderate prices make this rather an unusual establishment.

NITRY 89310

|●| AUBERGE LA BEURSAUDIÈRE

chemin de Ronde.
☎ 03.86.33.62.51
Car park.

This superb Morvan building with its medieval-style dovecote is primarily a stopping place for holiday-makers heading for the south of France and, to be honest, they've overdone the local colour a bit with waitresses in traditional costume. A large terrace, extremely well laid out, means you can eat outdoors. But be careful, in summer it's HOT and you could take a real beating from the sun – and from the prices too. Since the 85F *formule* consists of just an hors d'œuvre and a main course, the cheapest "real" meal costs 165F. The style of cooking is regional and dishes like quenelles of pike with mussels, the eternal poached eggs in a red wine sauce, beef stew, and raviolis stuffed with snails and a cheese sauce (made from *Epoisses*) are meant for big appetites.

NOYERS-SUR-SEREIN 89310 (10KM NE)

■ |●| HÔTEL DE LA VIEILLE TOUR

place du Grenier-à-Sel (Centre).
☎ 03.86.82.87.69 F→ 03.86.82.66.04
Open Easter–Nov 1.

This beautiful 17th century house swathed in Virginia creeper houses an art gallery as well as very simple but pleasant rooms – 250F with shower/wc, 300F with bath. The atmosphere is relaxed and the setting warm and restful – more like a guest house than a hotel. The Dutch owner will share with you her joy of living and also her dinner table for 75F. The home cooking, sometimes with a touch of the exotic, uses herbs and vegetables from the garden. It's an astonishing place – it and the town make you feel you've stepped back in time.

NOLAY 21340

|●| RESTAURANT LE BURGONDE

35 rue de la République; Nolay lies between Beaune and Autun.
☎ 03.80.21.71.25
Closed Monday and Sunday evenings, the first fortnight in January, and June 20–30.

The restaurant is housed in what used to be a large store. The plate glass windows are still there and behind them lies a dining room — very provincial and middle-class looking with houseplants, an old wooden floor and masses of charm. The other dining room is a conservatory which still has its original glass roof. The atmosphere is friendly, warm and quiet. They have a wide range of set meals all the way up to 278F. Don't panic — take a good look at what the 98F set meal has to offer or go for the set meal of local specialities. It's a bit pretentious but very good and for 125F you get a choice of *rillette* of perch and gingerbread or panfried snails with garlic and poached eggs in red wine sauce followed by either ox cheek or chicken in a mustard sauce, cheese, and pears in wine. Pleasant staff and reasonably priced wine.

EVELLE 21340 (5KM N)

|●| L'AUBERGE DU VIEUX PRESSOIR

How to get there: after La Rochepot, take the route des coteaux in the direction of Orches and Saint-Romain.
☎ 03.80.21.82.16
Closed Wednesdays in the off season and Jan 1–15.

As you survey the two packed dining rooms of this old-style inn that used to be a village bistro, you wonder how all those people managed to find their way here. Mind you, the views alone that you get on the way up would make this bright and cheerful restaurant worth the climb. For 135F, you'll have a choice of poached eggs in a red wine sauce or a good house *terrine*, followed by either panfried calf's liver or beef with a shallot sauce, and local cheese and dessert. And while the 98F set meal won't send you into raptures, it's quite ample.

NUITS-SAINT-GEORGES 21700

☗ |●| HÔTEL-RESTAURANT DES CULTIVATEURS

On the N74 (South); as you leave the town, go towards Beaune, and it's opposite the **Car park**.
☎ 03.80.61.10.41
Closed Sunday evenings.

We might as well warn you straight off, this isn't the last word in luxury. It's criminal that this well-known little town doesn't have a friendly hotel-retaurant with a view of the vineyards. At least here you'll find cheerful faces at the bar and a smiling owner, stop-over accommodation from 240F, a little terrace and set meals at 70F, 94F and 97F. Wine growers who come here bringing their bottles of lovely wine just adore it.

VILLARS-FONTAINE 21700 (5KM W)

|●| AUBERGE DU COTEAU

(Centre)
☎ 03.80.61.10.50
Closed Tuesday evenings and Wednesdays. **Car park**.

Families come to this authentic country inn to sample dishes such as house *terrine*, grills (gently cooked over wood just as we like them!), *coq au vin*, and snails. Enough to satisfy the stomach and cheer the heart, especially when accompanied by a bottle of wine from the Hautes Côtes, after a trip round the vineyard. They've got fireplaces, little gingham tablecloths and old-fashioned prices. Set meals at 60F (lunchtimes), 72F, 105F and 115F. The ideal stopping point after a afternoon spent exploring the countryside, famous for its goats, soft fruit, craftsmen, hills, ruined castles and unusual museums.

VOUGEOT 21640 (10KM S)

10% ☗ HÔTEL DE LA PERRIÈRE

18 rue du Vieux-Château.
☎ 03.80.62.80.49 Fax 03.80.62.83.65
Car park.

You wouldn't expect to find an insignificant-looking little hotel like this in a village famous world over for the wine festivals organized by the Clos Vougeot brotherhood. Insignificant on the outside it may be but inside it's another story. It's lovely, quiet, comfortable, the rooms have a view of the château (ask for number 6 or 7), and there's a wine bar. The hotel almost deserves a round of applause, if only for not treating anyone who arrives with guidebook in hand like a tourist. Rooms 320–370F.

AUVILLARS-SUR-SAÔNE 21250 (15KM E)

|●| AUBERGE DE L'ABBAYE

Route de Seurre.
☎ 03.80.26.97.37

Closed Tuesday evenings and Wednesday evenings. **Car park**.

You mustn't miss out on this place after your visit to the abbaye de Citeaux. One kilometre from the village, this inn, like the abbey, is also a place of inner contemplation, where you sit before dishes rich in succulent flavours and a great chef's inventiveness at almost set meal prices. Other set meals at 145F and 210F. You can also sit in the bistro corner, which is as pretty as a picture, and have the 72F *menu du jour* – chicken liver *terrine*, pork fillet with apples and bread and butter pudding, say. Nice little terrace too.

PARAY-LE-MONIAL 71600

10% GRAND HÔTEL DE LA BASILIQUE**

18 rue de la Visitation (Centre); it's 100m from the basilica, opposite the chapel of the Visitation.
☎ 03.85.81.11.13 F 03.85.88.83.70
Closed Nov–mid-March. **Secure parking**. **TV**. **Disabled access**.

The hotel has a wide range of rooms from 240F to 300F. You'll get a good view of the basilica at sunset from the third floor if your room faces south. The restaurant offers regional style cooking with set meals 72–220F and specialities like *brunoise* of top quality Charolais beef, braised sole, and poached eggs in a red wine sauce. Half-board (215F) is compulsory July 24–Aug 15. You may come face to face with St Marguerite as you leave the bar on the ground floor, but you're not seeing things – there's a religious gift shop just next door. A delightful hotel but mind your p's and q's so as not to offend any of the people on pilgrimage. The hotel's a favourite haunt of theirs – and one of ours too.

10% HÔTEL TERMINUS

27 av. de la Gare (North).
☎ 03.85.81.59.31 F 03.85.81.38.31
Secure parking. **TV**.

Don't be misled or put off by the austere frontage of this large and extremely well renovated hotel. You'll get a warm welcome and the attention to detail will be obvious the minute you cross the threshold. Bedrooms are spacious and have been redecorated throughout with co-ordinating flower-patterned fabrics. Bathrooms are rather special, a bit futuristic and a mixture of wood, perspex, and high pressure water jets. Doubles from 290F (310F with bath). Brasserie style meals can be provided.

POUILLY-SUR-LOIRE 58150

LE RELAIS FLEURI

42 av. de la Tuillerie; it's 500m south-east of the centre, opposite the wine cellars.
☎ 03.86.39.12.99 F 03.86.39.14.15
Closed Sunday evenings and Mondays Oct–Easter and Jan 15–Feb 15. **Secure parking**. **TV**.

We could tell you that you'll receive a warm welcome in this establishment, that there are flowers everywhere, that it has some fine rustic furniture and so forth, but you really ought to see for yourself. Ask for one of the large rooms with a view of the Loire. Doubles with shower start at 195F. Sample the inspired local cooking in the form of a *civet* of duckling in red Sancerre or calf's head *ravigote*. They do set meals at 105F, 150F and 250F (for the big spenders!) with meat and fish.

HÔTEL-RESTAURANT L'ESPÉRANCE**

17 rue René-Couard.
☎ 03.86.39.07.69 F 03.86.39.09.51
Closed Monday evenings and Tuesdays. Restaurant closed Sept 24–March 1. **Secure parking**. **TV**.

A restaurant-cum-hotel that cares about its reputation. It only has three rooms but they're large, attractive, and extremely comfortable (270F). Set meals range in price from 78F to 158F and include dishes like house *terrine*, *timbale* of scallops, trout with almonds, chicken legs flambéd in whisky, leg of duck with green peppercorns, and roast quail with baby onions flambéd in cognac. A great place where you can sample Pouilly-sur-Loire and Pouilly Fumé. Charming welcome.

RESTAURANT CHEZ MÉMÈRE

72 rue Waldeck-Rousseau.
☎ 03.86.39.02.43
Closed Sunday evenings and Mondays.

A roadside restaurant with large windows that isn't much to look at from the outside. Inside, however, there's a pleasant rustic style dining room with a family atmosphere and an old dear who really knows how to cook! She turns out some great dishes, based primarily on local produce. Set meals at 60F, 90F, 110F and 130F.

QUARRÉ-LES-TOMBES 89630

AUBERGE DE L'ÂTRE

Les Lavaults; take the N6 then the D10, in the direction of lac des Settons.

☎ 03.86.32.20.79 F➜ 03.86.32.28.25
Closed Tuesday evenings and Wednesdays out of season, Nov 25– Dec 10, and Feb 1–March 10.
Secure parking. TV. Disabled access.

The sight of this inn will reassure the traveller lost in the depths of Morvan, especially on a rather cool night when the mist is beginning to form. The first room looks something like an old-fashioned bistro, while the décor in the restaurant proper is rustic but warm. The chef loves to experiment with the plants and mushrooms of Morvan and create new dishes like roast carp with a purée of chervil garnished with chanterelles, and sea bass with wild mushrooms. This is perhaps one of the most beautiful restaurants in the region at prices that are still affordable. Set meals 145F (except Sundays)–295F. They have seven pleasant rooms if you fall in love with the place. You'll also have to be feeling pretty flush – doubles 450F with shower/wc, 550F with bath.

BRIZARDS (LES) 89630 (6KM SE)

10% ☗ |●| AUBERGE DES BRIZARDS**

How to get there: take the D55 and follow the arrows.
☎ 03.86.32.20.12 F➜ 03.86.32.27.40
Car park. TV. Disabled access.

What could be more romantic than this charming inn in magnificent surroundings? Nestling deep in the woods and completely isolated, it seems like something out of a fairy story. Doubles 220–950F (!), the latter being an absolutely delightful cottage which is warm in winter (when a wood fire is provided) and cool in summer (thanks to its old stone walls). The restaurant has set meals at 100F (except Sundays), 160F and 300F, all served with a smile in a bright spacious room that now looks nothing like the one where grandma Odette received her customers amidst *terrines* and storage jars. The pork *tourte* and the homemade black pudding (the genuine article) with apples are both a must.

ROMANECHE-THORINS 71720

☗ |●| LA MAISON BLANCHE**

RN6 (Centre); it's south of Mâcon, on the border of Rhône.
☎ 03.85.35.50.53 F➜ 03.85.35.21.22
Closed Sunday evenings, Mondays and Jan.

Situated at the side of a very busy road, this establishment might not look like the kind of place that would make you want to stop. But that would be a mistake. You get fantastic regional cooking, prepared in a heart-warmingly professional style. OK, the décor and atmosphere are hardly backpacker's style (rather on the conventional side), but the service is attentive and it's what's on your plate that matters. Set meals at 90F, 125F and 155F. You can get lobster in three different ways for 220F. Some gems from the à la carte menu – *terrine* of mallard, home-made *foie gras*, ox cheek in aspic, *gratin* of *andouillette* with Beaujolais, home-made *coq au vin* (one of the best we've ever tasted!), *suprême* of zander with lobster *coulis*, panfried fillet steak with morels, and stew of hare. They've a few comfy bedrooms, but, alas, half-board's compulsory and some rooms overlook the street. There's a swimming pool.

RULLY 71150

☗ |●| LE VENDANGEROT**

place Sainte-Marie (Centre).
☎ 03.85.87.20.09 F➜ 03.85.91.27.18
Closed Wednesdays (except in July and August) and during the February school holidays.
Secure parking. TV.

This carefully renovated large establishment, surrounded by flowers and greenery, stands in the square of a picturesque wine-making village. In memory of its previous incarnation, it has retained the old *Hôtel du Commerce* sign. Excellent staff. Armand does the cooking and his signature dishes include puff pastry filled with snails, fillet of zander in a red wine butter sauce, and *coq au vin* made with white wine. They do set meals at 88F (weekdays), 146F, 165F and 215F and these include things like oxtail stew with vegetables and morels, crayfish tails in a wine sauce (they use a white Rully), veal sweetbreads and morels in a red wine sauce, and grain-fed pigeon with a truffle-flavoured sauce. The main produce here is wine, so why not try a glass of Rully at 18F as an aperitif? Rooms from 150F with washing facilities, 250F with shower and 280F with bath. The rooms have heavy shutters and the village is quiet, so this is an ideal place to escape from the stress of town life.

SAINT-CHRISTOPHE-EN-BRIONNAIS 71800

|●| BAR-RESTAURANT DU MIDI

Grand-Rue (Centre).
☎ 03.85.25.87.06
Closed Mondays and Jan.

For several years now, on Thursdays (fair day), Liliane and Bernard Degueurce have been providing hearty meals for horse dealers and delighted customers from the early hour of 6am. They crowd into the big dining room-cum-canteen on the other side of the bar and kitchen, to sample calf's head, streaky bacon or tasty stew. What a lot of good meat there is here! Things are much quieter weekdays. Main course and cheese (including a quarter litre of red wine and coffee) 55F, tripe and cheese 45F, and delicious siroin steak 70F. All washed down with a decent 45F Côte-du-Rhône and a 60F Saint-Véran.

CAFÉ DE LA PLACE (JARRIER)

le bourg (Centre).
☎ 03.85.25.81.58
Closed evenings.

Saint-Christophe-en-Brionnais is home to the largest weekly Charolais cattle market, held during the hours of darkness from Wednesday night to Thursday morning and it means you can eat ribsteak between 5 and 9 o'clock in the morning in the company of dealers and breeders and in the kind of atmosphere you won't get anywhere else. Here they'll do you a terrific Charolais rib-steak, so-so chips and cheese for 55F or a *pot-au-feu* that's out of this world, chips and cheese for 45F; calf's head and tripe are also available. Great nosh, great family atmosphere and friendly staff. Very substantial "working man"'s set meal for 55F (wine and coffee included) available the rest of the time.

SAINT-FLORENTIN 89600

LES TILLEULS**

3 rue Descourtive (Centre).
☎ 03.86.35.09.09 Fax 03.86.35.36.90
Restaurant **closed** Sunday evenings, Mondays, and Feb 11–March 4. **Car park**. **TV**.

It's centrally located but in a quiet street, and the pretty terrace surrounded by an equally pretty garden means you can have a quiet lunch under the trees and forget the stress of daily life. Set meals 85–140F. Staff are rather reserved. Rooms are comfortable and well equipped and start at 270F for a double.

NEUVY-SAUTOUR 89570 (7KM NE)

RESTAURANT LE DAUPHIN

route de Troyes.
☎ 03.86.56.30.01
Closed Sunday evenings and, out of season, Mondays (except for public holidays). **Secure parking**.

The chef decided we should all succumb to temptation and indulge in the sin of gluttony, so he devised some little marvels that would bring about the downfall of a saint, including panfried scallops with a butter sauce and fresh pasta, "*surprise*" of snails, whelks and other molluscs, and *crème brûlée* with poppy seeds. If you like bistro style food, they do a 70F *formule* (every day except Sunday). Failing that, there are set meals at 85F (lunchtimes only), 100F, 145F and 195F. Friendly staff.

SAINT-HONORÉ-LES-BAINS 58360

AUBERGE DU PRÉ FLEURI**

22 av. Jean-Mermoz (Centre); it's next to the thermal baths and opposite the campsite.
☎ 03.86.30.74.96 Fax 03.86.30.64.61
Closed Sunday evenings and Mondays Nov–March and during the February school holidays. **Car park**. **TV**.

No, you're not in somebody's home, this pretty house in the middle of a small tree-filled estate really is a hotel! There are just nine rooms, all tastefully decorated, with doubles from 350F. The restaurant, housed in a separate building nestling among the trees, has large plate glass windows, lots of flowers, and an intimate atmosphere. Three set meals are available at 92F, 135F and 185F – the leg of duck with berries is excellent.

SAINT-JULIEN-DE-JONZY 71110

HÔTEL-RESTAURANT-BOUCHERIE PONT BERNARD**

le bourg; it's 8km south of Saint-Christophe-en-Brionnais – from Paray-le-Monial, take the D34 and the D20.
☎ 03.85.84.01.95 Fax 03.85.84.14.61
Closed Monday evenings and during the February school holidays. **Car park**.

Right in the heart of Charolais country, 30km north of Roanne, this lovely little hotel cum restaurant doesn't do things by halves. There's no question here of taking themselves for the Troisgros brothers; they're happy sticking to what they know and Monsieur Pont is as much a butcher as he is a cook. The meat is of superb quality, portions are generous and the home cooking is simple but tasty. Set meals 78F, 105F (a choice of *coq au vin* or bream fillets with sorrel) 143F, and 173F (*terrine* of monkfish cheeks, duck fillet with peaches, grilled leg of lamb with thyme). Great desserts. They also do a *menu du jour* consisting of starter, main course and cheese or dessert for 55F at lunchtime on weekdays. Simple and comfortable hotel with rooms from 215F a night. Kind and congenial hosts.

SAULIEU 21210

LA BORNE IMPÉRIALE**

14–16 rue d'Argentine (Centre).
☎ 03.80.64.19.76
Closed Tuesday evenings, Wednesdays and Nov 15–Dec 15. **Secure parking**.

Gourmets come from all over the world to eat in this, one of the few remaining good old-fashioned inns in Burgundy. Refurbished from top to bottom (or practically) after fire broke out. Seven bedrooms (190–290F), the best of which have an attractive view of the garden. Beautiful dining room with terrace for fine days.The 95F set meal offers melon and grapefruit salad with mint, braised ham with red wine and dessert. Other set meals at 120F (local dishes), 136F and 160F.

10% LA VIEILLE AUBERGE

15 rue Grillot (South).
☎ 03.80.64.13.74
Closed Tuesday evenings and Wednedays. **Car park**.

You could drive past a dozen times without noticing it. In Saulieu's heyday, when everyone used the N6 to travel down south, this inn tucked away at a bend in the road would see all the beautiful people, and the not so beautiful, pass by. But just like the old town, this old inn fell into disfavour. Until the emergence of a new generation of restaurateurs, the Loiseau generation, put Saulieu back on the tourist map. Two young people decided it was worth a risk and took over. Set meals at 70F, 85F, 120F, 130F and 165F. Treat yourself to *terrine* of Charolais, *marbré* of rabbit, or roast zander with red wine. They've got a charming dining room and an attractive hidden terrace. Rooms 210F.

SEMUR-EN-AUXOIS 21140

HÔTEL DES CYMAISES**

7 rue du Renaudot (Centre).
☎ 03.80.97.21.44 F 03.80.97.18.23
Closed mid-Feb–early March and late Oct–mid Nov. **Secure parking. TV. Disabled access**.

In the very heart of the medieval city, just behind Porte Sauvigny, there's a beautiful 18th century building which has adapted extremely well to life as a 20th century hotel (which can't be said for all such buildings). You come and go as you please with whoever you like, breakfast is served under the pergola, and it's cool, clean and comfortable. Nicely furnished rooms from 300F. Friendly welcome from the owners' daughter.

RESTAURANT DES MINIMES

39 rue Vaux; it's 500m from the town centre.
☎ 03.80.97.26.86
Closed Tuesday evenings, Wednesdays and late Nov–beginning of Dec.

This former neighbourhood bistro near the ramparts is now a must for tourists in search of the soul, the voice and the cooking of Semur. It's decorated in as bucolic a fashion as any shepherd could wish for and the atmosphere is pretty laid-back. There are set meals at 61F (weekday lunchtimes) and 91F The proprietress loves good wine and repartee and she isn't impressed by local politicians or bad payers You can have two different wines with poached eggs in a red wine sauce salmon *à l'unilatéral* (cooked by being grilled on just one side), puff pastry with a filling of *époisses* cheese or the extremely good house ribsteak. Reckon on 150F à la carte.

LE CALIBRESSAN

16 rue Feveret
☎ 03.80.97.32.40
Closed Sunday evenings and Mondays.

"Local cooking with a Californian touch". That's the motto here. An attractive, little restaurant combining authentic rustic styles – exposed beams, bricks, flowers and little curtains – with the vitality and exoticism of the New World, represented by Madame, a Californian born and bred, at reception, and by certain sauces and side dishes, from the fantastic buffet starters to the *suprême* of chicken and shark steak. Good set meals at 78F (weekday lunchtimes), 98F, 112F and 165F. Relaxed atmosphere and music to match.

PONT-ET-MASSÈNE 21141 (3KM S)

10% HÔTEL DU LAC**

10 rue du lac.
☎ 03.80.97.11.11 F 03.80.97.29.25
Closed Sunday evenings, Mondays out of season, and Dec 20–Jan 10. **Secure parking. TV**.

You'll find this large 50s building just down from the lake. It has a few very pleasant rooms and some fairly antiquated ones at prices ranging from 265F to 310F. The restaurant offers a family atmosphere and regional cooking of the kind that used to gladden the hearts of Sunday lunchers years ago. Choose from dishes like *jambon persillé* made with local ham, ham in a cream sauce, chicken fricassee with mushrooms, *coq au vin*, and calf's head in a spicy vinaigrette. Set meals 87F (weekdays), 100F, 125F and 155F. And for wine, try the local Blanc de l'Auxois, which is very drinkable and deserves to be better known. There's a terrace with an arbour for fine summer days.

SENS 89100

RESTAURANT LE SOLEIL LEVANT

51 rue Émile-Zola (South-West); it's a stone's throw from the station.
☎ 03.86.65.71.82
Closed Sunday evenings and Wednesday evenings.

Here's a restaurant that's very classical in style, in terms of both décor and menu. It's known for its fish dishes, particularly salmon with sorrel, but even if you don't like seafood, you'll be well catered for – the calf sweetbread vol-au-vents went down particularly well. And everybody can indulge in one of the house desserts, which are sheer heaven. You'll pay all of 65F for the cheapest set meal (except Sundays) and it's incredibly good. Other set meals 93F and 155F.

VILLEROY 89100 (7KM SW)

10% RELAIS DE VILLEROY**

route de Nemours.
☎ 03.86.88.81.77 F→ 03.86.88.84.04
Closed Sunday evenings Nov 15–April 30, and Dec 20–Jan 30. **Car park. TV.**

This very smart-looking establishment is one of the nicest places in the area. The owners are trying, with considerable success, to create a family homy atmosphere and to offer good food and a warm welcome. The restaurant (which smells wonderfully of furniture polish, by the way) is well known to gourmets. There's a lot of fish on the menu and home-made pastries that melt in the mouth. Set meals 145F–260F. The prices in the bistro next door are much more affordable (there's an 80F formule, for example) but unfortunately it's closed Saturday evenings and Sunday lunchtimes. The bedrooms, with their flowered wallpaper and antique furniture, are in keeping with the rest of the establishment. Double glazing means you don't have to worry about traffic noise. Doubles start at 195F with shower/wc. There's a terrace and a veranda at the back for use in summer.

PONT-SUR-YONNE 89140 (12KM NW)

RESTAURANT LE TIRE-BOUCHON

26 rue Carnot.
☎ 03.86.67.16.54
Closed Monday evenings, Tuesdays, and Wednesday evenings.

This little restaurant has panoramic views of the river (and of the road!) from the glassed-in veranda on the upper of its two levels. If the view doesn't tempt you to linger over your meal, they have a 60F *formule* (available every day). Failing that, there are set meals at 85F (starter, main course with vegetables of your choice, and home-made after-dinner sweets) and 100F (the same three courses plus cheese). Traditional Burgundy dishes and a few more modern ones are also available.

TOUCY 89130

10% LE LION D'OR

37 rue Lucile-Cormier (Centre).
☎ 03.86.44.00.76
Closed Sunday evenings, Mondays, and Dec 1–20.
Secure parking.

This was one of the places in the Yonne that we fell in love with. It's an old hotel with a magnificent wooden staircase, everything smells of beeswax, and the rooms are simple but cosy and meticulously clean. Doubles start at 170F. The dining room, which is as delightful as its hostess, offers regional specialities such as ham cooked in Chablis, fish *en croûte* with sorrel, and (in season) roast wild boar in a peppery sauce. The cheapest set meal is 85F.

TOURNUS 71700

10% HÔTEL DE SAÔNE**

Rive Gauche (Centre).
☎ 03.85.51.20.65 F→ 03.85.51.05.45
Closed Mondays and Oct–March. **Car park. Disabled access.**

Great location on the river bank. There's no traffic so you can be sure of peace and quiet. It has rooms to suit all pockets – 190F, 210F, 240F and 310F. The restaurant offers good regional cooking and set meals at 75F (available every day), 125F (frogs' legs and a choice of sirloin or free-range chicken with a morel sauce), and 185F. If you feel like some fish, they have *petite friture* (whitebait is the closest equivalent), fillets of sole in a white wine sauce, and zander in a cream and white wine sauce. The terrace, which is very pleasant in summer, overlooks the houses down by the water and the abbey. Have a post-prandial stroll along the velvety green banks of the Saône.

10% HÔTEL-RESTAURANT AUX TERRASSES**

18 av. du 23 Janvier (South).
☎ 03.85.51.01.74 ➡ 03.85.51.09.99
Closed Sunday evenings, Mondays and Jan. **TV**.

This enormous roadside inn, probably a former coaching inn, is one of the best establishments in town, and nobody will tell you any different. The lounge separates two large, richly decorated dining rooms. Reception's a bit on the chic side, but the atmosphere's not particularly affected and the service is attentive. Set meals at 98F, and 120F (good value for money) going up to 240F. À la carte – *méli-mélo* of fish and scallops, breast of duck with peaches, *mille-feuille* of salmon with a chive sauce, *nage* of monkfish and scallops with saffron. They do an excellent fish soup. Comfortable rooms 300F.

10% HÔTEL LE SAUVAGE***

place du Champ de Mars (Centre).
☎ 03.85.51.14.45 ➡ 03.85.32.10.27
TV.

It's not hard to spot the façade covered with virginia creeper, a little set back from the main road. For many years now, this good old establishment has been ticking over quietly. Pleasant rooms from 360F. They do a good range of set meals. Choose from 84F, 98F, 120F serving *coq au vin* or fillet of duck with blackcurrants, 158F or 200F offering gourmet dishes. À la carte you can get *quenelles* of pike with a shellfish sauce, rack of lamb with garlic breadcrumbs, tart of zander with oyster mushrooms, or *lasagne* of snails. Wines start at afforable prices – 63F for a red Mâcon and 89F for St Véran.

BRANCION 71700 (14KM W)

AUBERGE DU VIEUX BRANCION

Centre; follow the D14 from Tournus and Comartin.
☎ 03.85.51.03.83
Closed Nov–Feb.

This little inn, situated in an adorable old village, offers pleasant rooms, some of which could even be described as charming. The village is practically a pedestrianized zone, so peace and quiet is guaranteed. Three bedrooms can be found in the inn itself and three others in a very old building alongside. Couples enjoying a romantic weekend or a honeymoon (or both!) will love the bright, spacious 300F one with bathroom on the first floor. The two at 250F with exposed beams, on the floor above, share the same bathroom. Suitable for families or friends travelling in groups. Choose from the 48F local dish and set meals at 68F (country-style) and 110F. Mâcon rouge 66 F.

PRAYES 71460 (20KM W)

10% AUBERGE DU GRISON

Centre; from Tournus take the D14 towards Chapaize, and it's near Chissey-les-Mâcon.
☎ 03.85.50.18.31
Closed Tuesdays except July–Aug.

This tiny little village in one of our favourite regions of the Saône and Loire is wonderfully friendly and pastoral. And you've got the charming village inn run by smiling, friendly Martine, offering nine bedrooms at 200F and the prospect of a very pleasant stay. Colourful, smart, cosy, some with exposed beams, but no two the same. Lovely dining room with wooden décor serving excellent regional cooking. Snacks available at all hours. Large salad selection, 43F cold meat and cheese special, thick local *crêpes, andouille* cooked in white wine, and Charolais steak with mushrooms. Wallet-friendly prices. Set meals at 65F, 85F, 98F and 110F available lunchtimes and evenings. Small shaded terrace. Wouldn't it be nice to come across an inn like this in every French hamlet?

VERMENTON 89270

AUBERGE L'ESPÉRANCE

3 rue du Général-de-Gaulle (Centre).
☎ 03.86.81.50.42
Closed Sunday evenings (except in July–August), Mondays, and Jan 1–Feb 5.

However glum you're feeling, the mere mention of this inn's name – "espérance" means hope – should perk you up. You'll get a delightful welcome, and the kitchen turns out some wonderful dishes, including the house *foie gras*, veal *à la morvandelle*, snails and eggs in a red wine sauce, and ostrich in a red wine vinegar sauce. Set meals 86–250F. Since we all keep on hoping for better days, the place has been redecorated throughout. They've even spared a thought for the younger generation by providing a children's play area, and for senior citizens, who will find the air conditioning brings blessed relief in summer.

ACCOLAY 89460 (3KM W)

10% HOSTELLERIE DE LA FONTAINE**

16 rue de Reigny.
☎ 03.86.81.54.02 F 03.86.81.52.78
Closed Sunday evenings and Mondays mid Nov–early March and in January. **Car park**.

A beautiful traditional Burgundy house in a nice little village in the Cure valley. On fine evenings you can relax in the garden while feasting on salad of snails with a mustard dressing, *quenelles* of pike, monkfish with preserved lemons, duck in a sauce made with ratafia (a type of liqueur), or puff pastry with a filling of *Chaource* (a soft and creamy cheese). Set meals 95F, 130F, 155F and 230F. You can then sleep it off in one of the quiet bedrooms (220–300F) described as "sweet" but very pleasant all the same. Good breakfast (32F). Winter has its attractions too, when the small cellar is pressed into service so that guests can enjoy traditional local dishes (95F, including cheese and dessert) and treat themselves to some Aligoté or Pinot Noir.

VÉZELAY 89450

10% AUBERGE DE JEUNESSE**

route de l'Étang (South-West).
☎ 03.86.33.24.18
Car park. **Disabled access**.

OK, it's on the outskirts of the village and doesn't have a view of the basilica but the scenery is superb, and what the hostel lacks in charm it makes up for in the warmth of the welcome. You'll pay 51F a night for accommodation in rooms that sleep 4–6 or a dormitory with 10 beds It's very well cared for and has a kitchen for hostellers' use and a large common room.

10% LE COMPOSTELLE**

place du Champ-de-Foire.
☎ 03.86.33.28.63 F 03.86.33.34.34
Closed in January and the first week in February. **TV**.

Some of our readers may not know that Vézelay was one of the assembly points for people making the pilgrimage to Santiago de Compostella. That fact is commemorated in the name given to this pretty house, which has reverted to the inn it once was at the turn of the century. The service is first rate and the modern bedrooms are well equipped and have views of the countryside or the garden (260–360F for a family room).

HÔTEL DE LA POSTE ET DU LION D'OR***

place du Champ-de-Foire.
☎ 03.86.33.21.23 F 03.86.32.30.92
Closed Nov 12–March 23; restaurant closed Mondays and Tuesday lunchtimes. **Secure parking**. **TV**. **Disabled access**.

This former coaching inn, a superb building covered in ivy, is an extremely pleasant place to stay. Rooms are well kept and tastefully decorated and overlook the basilica on one side and the valley on the other. If you want a view of the valley, ask for room number 11, 17, 34, 40 or 42. Doubles start at 330F. The cheapest set meal available in the restaurant, which has a beautiful terrace, is 118F. The rather expensive à la carte menu is a mixture of classical and regional dishes such as poached eggs in a red wine sauce, snails, rack of lamb with sage, roast pigeon, and (in season) fricassee of chanterelles and ceps.

RESTAURANT LE BOUGAINVILLE

26 rue Saint-Étienne.
☎ 03.86.33.27.57
Closed Tuesdays evenings and Wednesdays , and Dec 1–Feb 1.

This restaurant, housed in a beautiful old building overflowing with flowers, is very reasonable – a pleasant surprise in a town where low prices are as rare as hen's teeth. Traditional local dishes – poached eggs in a red wine sauce and ham on the bone *à la morvandelle* – are the stars of the cheapest set meal (79F, served every day). There are others at 98F, 128F and 180F. The dining room with its magnificent old fireplace makes a pleasant setting for your meal.

SAINT-PÈRE-SOUS-VÉZELAY 89450 (2KM S)

10% À LA RENOMMÉE**

route d'Avallon; it's on the D957, at the foot of Vézelay hill.
☎ 03.86.33.21.34 F 03.86.33.34.17
Closed Tuesdays Nov 11–Feb 28. **Secure parking**. **TV**. **Disabled access**.

The hotel acts as tobacconist's and newsagent's, hence the relaxed atmosphere. In the old part of the building, a double with basin/wc costs 170F, with bath 240F. The modern annexe is quieter and more comfortable and doubles there range in price from 260F to 320F with bath. The more expensive ones have a little balcony with a view over the countryside and the church of Saint Pierre. The small brasserie that's open in season is fine if you're stuck for anywhere else to eat.

FONTETTE 89450 (5KM E)

10% HÔTEL LES AQUARELLES**

How to get there: it's 5km from Vézelay on the D957, going in the direction of Avallon.
☎ 03.86.33.34.35 F 03.86.33.29.82
Closed Jan 1–March 15. **Car park**. **Disabled access**.

Set back from the road in the quiet Vézelay countryside, this former farmhouse is a cross between a hotel and a bed and breakfast. The house is full of character and has 10 lovely bedrooms (260–280F) to offer ramblers or backpackers who like a warm welcome, comfortable beds, views of the countryside, and good simple cooking. Francis Basseporte will let you taste his red and white burgundies while his wife prepares a plateful of good regional produce or a Charolais sirloin for 80-100F.

PONTAUBERT 89200 (10KM NE)

10% LES FLEURS**

route de Vézelay; take the D957.
☎ 03.86.34.13.81 F 03.86.34.23.32
Closed Wednesdays, Thursday lunchtimes out of season, and Dec 10–Jan 30. **Car park**. **TV**.

This beautiful and delightful hotel, a large white building sitting in the middle of a garden overflowing with flowers, has been carefully decorated by its owners. The dining roomi is wainscotted, and comfortable and pretty bedrooms with bath are available for 260–300F. The restaurant doesn't put a foot wrong, the prices are reasonable – the cheapest set meal is 90F – and there are lots of specialities such as cockerel *à la façon des ducs* and *pavé de Pontaubert*.

LE MOULIN DES TEMPLIERS**

vallée du Cousin; coming from Vézelay, turn right as soon as you pass the bridge and follow the arrows.
☎ 03.86.34.10.80
Closed Oct 31–March 15. **Car park**.

This large ochre-coloured waterside hotel deep in the country has oodles of charm, a big garden, and pleasant rooms 270F with shower/wc, 320–380F with bath).

BRETAGNE

22 Côtes-d'Armor

29 Finistère

35 Ille-et-Vilaine

56 Morbihan

AURAY 56400

RESTAURANT L'ÉGLANTINE

place Saint-Sauveur, Saint-Goustan, port d'Auray.
☎ 02.97.56.46.55
Closed Wednesdays (except July–Aug).

Well-presented traditional cuisine. Try the fish *choucroute*, grilled almond oysters, braised fillet of turbot in rosemary or seafood stew. Set meals for 75F (lunchtimes), 105F, 135F and 170F. The Saint-Goustan district is quite chic and distinguished but comfortable all the same. The restaurant walls are adorned with pictures of leaders of the army of Jean Chouan, who led an uprising in support of the monarchy during the French Revolution.

SAINTE-ANNE-D'AURAY 56400 (6KM N)

10% HÔTEL DE LA CROIX-BLANCHE**

25 rue de Vannes (East).
☎ 02.97.57.64.44 F 02.97.57.50.60
Closed Sunday evenings and Mondays off season and also in February. **Car park**. **Canal+**.

The meeting place for pilgrims and fervent admirers of Anne, the patron saint of the Bretons. An elegant establishment but not excessively so. Comfortable rooms for 200–350F, all with telephone. Rooms number 10–26 face the garden. Tempting set meals in the restaurant from 89F.

BELZ 56550 (12KM W)

LE RELAIS DE KERGOU*

route d'Auray.
☎ 02.97.55.35.61 F 02.97.55.27.69
Closed Sunday evenings (off season), Mondays, the second week of November and during the winter school holidays. **Car park**. **TV**.

Offers a pleasant retreat from the busier resorts. Of the eleven rooms, four face the garden (numbers 2, 10, 11 and 12). Costs range from 155–320F. Two dining rooms: one with old beams and fireplace and the other on a veranda opening onto the garden. The owner/chef always offers a choice of fish dishes and prime cuts of meat. Set meals at 65F, 90F and 125F.

BANGOR 56360

CRÊPERIE DES QUATRE CHEMINS

How to get there: it's at the crossroads of the two main roads on Belle-Ile.
☎ 02.97.31.42.13
Closed Wednesdays and from All Saints' Day to Dec 20. **Car park**.

Open from noon to midnight. This isolated establishment serves some of the best *crêpes* on the island. Hearty, delectable and cooked to perfection. Humorous menus and jovial atmosphere. Brightly decorated, complete with a small children's play area (McDonald's style). Discreet jazz or blues in the background and cheerful, friendly service. *Crêpe complète* (savoury) 32F.

BÉNODET 29950

HÔTEL L'HERMITAGE

11 rue Laënnec (Centre); it's 300m from the beach, part way up the hill overlooking the town centre.

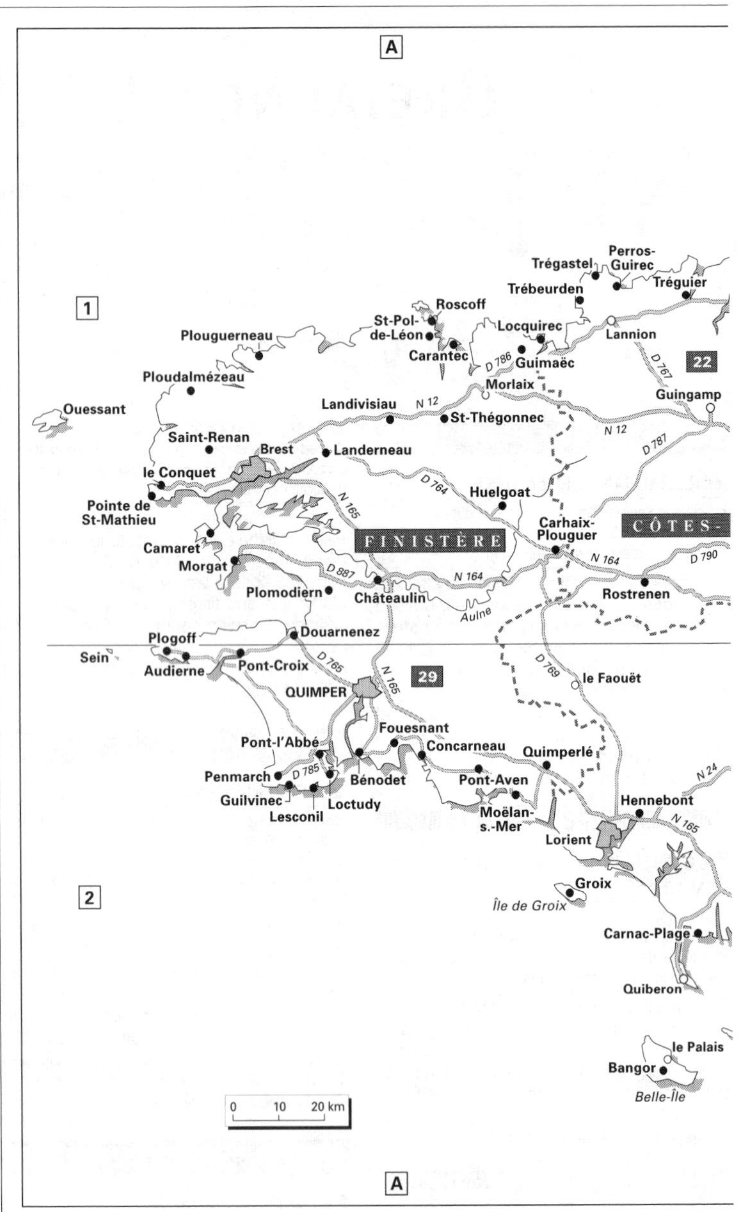
A
1
2
Trégastel
Perros-Guirec
Trébeurden
Tréguier
Roscoff
St-Pol-de-Léon
Locquirec
Lannion
Plouguerneau
Carantec
Guimaëc
D 786
D 767
22
Ploudalmézeau
Morlaix
Guingamp
Ouessant
Landivisiau
N 12
St-Thégonnec
N 12
Saint-Renan
Brest
Landerneau
D 787
le Conquet
D 764
Pointe de St-Mathieu
N 165
Huelgoat
Carhaix-Plouguer
FINISTÈRE
CÔTES-
Camaret
N 164
D 790
Morgat
D 887
N 164
Rostrenen
Plomodiern
Châteaulin
Aulne
Plogoff
Douarnenez
Sein
Audierne
Pont-Croix
D 765
N 165
29
D 769
le Faouët
QUIMPER
Fouesnant
Pont-l'Abbé
Concarneau
Quimperlé
Penmarch
D 785
Bénodet
Pont-Aven
N 24
Guilvinec
Loctudy
Hennebont
Lesconil
Moëlan-s.-Mer
N 165
Lorient
Groix
Île de Groix
Carnac-Plage
Quiberon
le Palais
Bangor
Belle-Île
0 10 20 km
A

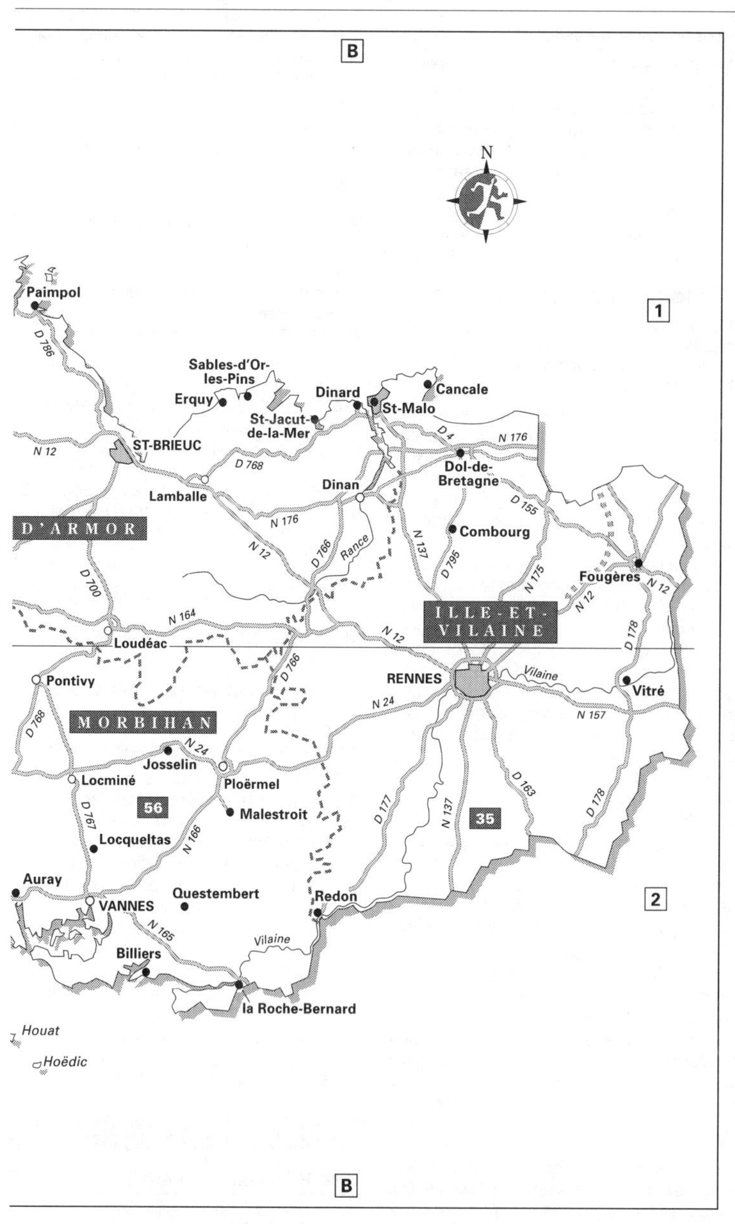
B
N
1
Paimpol
D 786
Sables-d'Or-les-Pins
Erquy
Dinard
St-Malo
Cancale
St-Jacut-de-la-Mer
N 12
ST-BRIEUC
D 768
D 4
N 176
Dol-de-Bretagne
Lamballe
Dinan
D 155
D'ARMOR
N 176
Combourg
N 12
D 766
Rance
N 137
D 795
D 700
N 175
Fougères
N 12
N 12
ILLE-ET-VILAINE
N 164
N 12
Loudéac
D 178
D 766
Pontivy
RENNES
Vilaine
Vitré
N 24
N 157
D 768
MORBIHAN
N 24
Josselin
Locminé
Ploërmel
D 163
56
Malestroit
D 767
D 177
N 137
35
D 178
Locqueltas
N 166
Auray
Questembert
Redon
2
VANNES
N 165
Vilaine
Billiers
la Roche-Bernard
Houat
Hoëdic
B

☎ 02.98.57.00.37
Closed Oct–May 15. **Car park**.

Madame Nader Le Moigne is very diligent in the upkeep of this large, white house with blue shutters which is surrounded by a garden full of hydrangeas. The interior is also blue and white, the colours of the open sea. This is a really lovely place at very reasonable prices. The rooms are plain but pleasant and cost 170–270F. Breakfast is 30F. Studio apartments can be rented by the week in a neighbouring building at reasonable prices.

10% 🏠 |●| HÔTEL LES BAINS DE MER**

11 rue de Kerguelen.
☎ 02.98.57.03.41 F➔ 02.98.57.11.07
Closed mid-November to mid-March.
Secure parking. **TV**. **Canal+**.

This hotel, situated in a famous, well-off seaside resort, has been completely refurbished. It now has every comfort and is quite luxurious. Spoil yourself with full board (and see how time flies on holiday! Very friendly welcome. If the weather is cloudy, dive into the swimming pool or try a relaxing sauna. Lovely double rooms with shower/wc from 250F. Excellent cuisine. Choose from two places to eat: the "Domino" open until 11pm (midnight in summer), with its speedy *formule* every lunchtime for 60F (a grilled dish or pizza, dessert and coffee). Mixed salads, pasta, pizzas and a selection of grilled dishes also served. Children's meal for 35F. Alternatively there is the restaurant which has set meals for 75, 90 and 150F. Half-board in July and August is highly advisable.

|●| FERME DU LETTY

quartier du Letty; it's 1km from the town centre, well signposted.
☎ 02.98.57.01.27
Closed Wednesdays (but only Wednesday lunchtimes in July and Aug), Thursday lunchtimes and end Nov–mid-Feb.

This restaurant has Michelin stars. The very reasonable prices of the first two set meals made it easy to review. The superbly restored building is full of Breton delights: exposed beams, large fireplace, stone walls, sumptuous furniture and ostentatious service from an army of waiters in bow ties. There's a lot of rushing about in all directions – but with little effect on the actual speed of the service! There's no requirement to wear a tie (especially in summer!) but the customers are only a tad less smartly done up than the staff. But enough of the pomp and ceremony, let's talk food. Without a doubt this is wonderful cuisine, with some inspired dishes. Set meals for 98F and 155F (with salmon with bacon and buckwheat butter and shoulder of lamb *confit* with dried fruit). There are other set meals for 193F, 290F, 390F and even 490F!. À la carte you will find roast monkfish with *vinaigre d'aigriade*, sole and mussel broth *à l'orange*, roast pigeon stuffed with giblets and mushrooms and sardines in nine herbs. Incredible desserts.

|●| RESTAURANT LA FORGE D'ANTAN

Pen Ar Valannec.
☎ 02.98.54.84.00.
Closed Monday and Tuesday lunchtimes in July and August, Mondays and Sunday evenings off season and during school holidays in February. **Car park**.

Right out in the country. Friendly welcome. Superb rustic décor. Imaginative – and expensive – seasonal cuisine. Atmosphere and clientele quite stylish. Set meals for 110F (Tuesday to Friday), 155F, 170F and 240F. À la carte: monkfish tails with morels, tuna tartare, veal kidneys in spices, young rabbit *gratinée*, turbot *à la fouesnantaise*, panfried prawns in champagne etc. Children's meal for 75F.

COMBRIT 29121 (5.5 KM W)

10% 🏠 |●| HÔTEL-RESTAURANT SAINTE-MARINE*

19 rue Bac; it's in the charming little port of Sainte-Marine opposite Bénodet.
☎ 02.98.56.34.79 F➔ 02.98.51.94.09
Closed Wednesdays from October to Easter and in November. **TV**.

A venue loved by seafarers from far and wide as well as novelists and film-makers. The wonderful dining room is decorated in a nautical style and has a magnificent view of the Odet river and pont de Cornouaille. Terrace. Doubles for 290F. Set meals for 100F, 149F and 195F. Plate of shellfish 120F. Seafood platter 340F for two people. À la carte: marinated scallops with seaweed, panfried sole *au caviar d'aubergines*, fresh braised cod, pork fillet with leeks, smoked salmon in seafood tartare. Half-board is strongly advised in the high season (from 250F per person). An excellent hostelry.

BILLIERS 56190

🏠 |●| HÔTEL-RESTAURANT LES GLYCINES

How to get there: it's in the village square.
☎ 02.97.41.64.63
Closed Mondays out of season.

The flowering wisteria hanging down over the front of this lovely country hotel provides an enchanting scene. The unpretentious bar is very welcoming to the traveller and the restaurant exercises a seductive charm over food lovers with its beautifully presented cuisine. What more could you want? Very decent rooms for 150–185F. Cheapest set meal 55F (weekday lunchtimes), or pay a bit more for an excellent set meal at 87F. Gastronomic delights abound in the 190F set meal. Impeccable service.

BREST 29200

10% HÔTEL ASTORIA**

9 rue Traverse (Centre).
☎ 02.98.80.19.10 F 02.98.80.52.41
Closed Dec 19–Jan 5. **TV**. **Canal+**.

A hotel similar to many others in Brest, but giving rare value for money. Around 220F for a double with shower/wc. Bright and cheerful decoration. The rooms facing the street are double-glazed, but choose one the rear (they're quieter). An excellent hotel both for its position (a stone's throw from the harbour) and the genuine welcome. In July and August the Brest *jeudis* are just 7 minutes walk away. This hotel really does the profession proud. Bravo!

RELAIS MERCURE***

2 rue Yves-Collet (Centre).
☎ 02.98.80.31.80 F 02.98.46.52.98
TV. **Canal+**.

Very centrally located, this three-star hotel excels both for its elegant décor and for the comfort of its rooms. The hotel foyer has retained its superb 1940s architecture. Rooms with every comfort for 300–500F with individualized bathrooms. A minor drawback is the rather gloomy breakfast room. Pleasant, competent staff. The best in Brest in its category.

CRÊPERIE MODERNE

34 rue d'Algésiras (Centre).
☎ 02.98.44.44.36
Closed Sundays. **Disabled access**.

Unexceptional setting, but the *crêpes* are delicious. This establishment goes back long way (it was founded in 1922. Open all year round from 11.30am–10pm. There is a 20% reduction from 2–6pm (except in July and August). *Crêpes* with butter for 12F or with scallops for 44F. Service can be a bit rushed in the high season.

AMOUR DE POMME DE TERRE

23 rue des Halles (Centre).
☎ 02.98.43.48.51
Disabled access.

Open at lunchtimes and in the evening until 11pm. A restaurant which is completely original in Brest (and indeed in Finistère): it is entirely dedicated to (potatoes. Needless to say, the owner is a potato fanatic. Only one type of potato is used, the "samba" (developed just five years ago), which is well-known for its baking properties. Friendly setting and walls displaying the proprietor's mission statement and posters extolling the virtue of the Incas' wonderful invention (worth a read!). Many different methods of cooking the noble tuber are offered: with Roquefort, goat's cheese, *plancoetin*, etc (good home-produced ingredients). Some dishes are curiously named, such as the "energy profile" and "queen of the fields". Try the *goémonier* – potatoes with smoked Molène sausage, Côtes-d'Armor sausage and bacon. Thursday lunchtimes have stew *au kig-har-farz*. Excellent home-made desserts (no (not made from potatoes!)

MA PETITE FOLIE

plage du Moulin Blanc (port de plaisance de Brest); coming from Quimper, it's on the left after the Elorn bridge.
☎ 02.98.42.44.42
Closed Sundays, Aug 10–24 and 2 weeks at the end Dec/beginning of Jan.

This place is on its way to becoming the best fish restaurant in Brest. It's not often that we've enjoyed being taken for a ride so much. Why? Well, the restaurant is in fact a superb, sturdy old Mauritanian fishing boat which landed hundreds of tons of crayfish on the coast of Mauritania between 1952 and 1992 and which has now taken a well-earned retirement from the sea and started a new and quieter life. It's been renovated and amazingly well transformed into a retaurant, retaining all the charm of a valiant seafaring vessel. The owner and his wife give you a very warm welcome and provide a culinary experience not to be missed. The food could not be fresher. If the hostess, with a secretive air (looking around to check that she is not being overheard), whispers the offer of a fish which is not on the menu into your ear (along the lines of "I've a fresh mullet going spare"), accept without hesitation! Your faith will be more than repaid. Cuisine with finesse. Good set meal for 110F, or order from the menu. Fish dishes for 78–130F. There are some real gems, including scallop and veal *terrine*, crab *rillettes*, excellent oysters, fillet of pollack in a butter sauce, grilled fish *cotriade* (soup), fillet of John Dory with dill flavoured butter and fennel, etc. Booking very strongly advised (virtually compulsory at weekends!). Remember that the food is not mass-produced. Service is generally slow in the evenings, which does have the benefit of allowing plenty of time to savour your meal. And the bill doesn't rock the boat!

GUILERS 29820 (5KM NW)

CRÊPERIE BLÉ NOIR

bois de Keroual; from Brest head towards Penfeld – the restaurant is near the Parc des Expositions.
☎ 02.98.07.57.40

Hidden away in the greenery next to a small lake, this crêperie is located in an old mill and is an ideal relaxing stop-off. Delicious *crêpes* in a modern setting. Friendly service and plenty of scope for a walk after the meal in the wonderful countryside. Set meals 56–79F. Children's meal for 19F. Among the specialities are *crêpe suzette* with lime and smoked salmon *galette*.

CAMARET 29570

LA VOILERIE

7 quai Toudouze.
☎ 02.98.27.99.55
Closed Wednesdays and Sundays off season and for the month of February. **Car park**. **Disabled access**.

Considered one of Camaret's most serious restaurants. Consistent quality, friendly welcome, but slow service. Large, pleasant dining room. *Formules* include fish of the day for 50F, *moules frites* for 48F, decent set meal for 65F, *Terre-Mer* for 100F (with *far tiède* in cider, guinea-fowl with oyster mushrooms). Seafood set meal for 135F (oysters and prawns) and other set meal for 160F including scallop *aumônière* with baby vegetables. A la carte try the delicious grilled sea bream in *sauce Marie-Jeanne*.

CANCALE 35260

10% HÔTEL-RESTAURANT LE GRAND LARGE

4 quai Jacques-Cartier; it is among the first houses at the southern end of the harbour.
☎ 02.99.89.82.90 Fax 02.99.89.79.03
Restaurant closed in January. **Car park**. **TV**.

A pretty little hotel in an old ivy-covered building. Very warm welcome. Flower-filled terrace looking out to sea. Rooms from 200F. Uncomplicated restaurant. Set meal for 75F.

10% HÔTEL-RESTAURANT L'ALIDADE**

8 place du Calvaire (Centre).
☎ 02.99.89.61.48
Restaurant closed Wednesdays. **TV**.

A small family hotel with sea views. The lively cafés nearby give the ground floor a good atmosphere. Rooms with every comfort for 295F.

10% HÔTEL LE CHATELLIER**

route de Saint-Malo; it's 1km from Cancale on the Saint-Malo road (D355).
☎ 02.99.89.81.84 Fax 02.99.89.61.69
Car park. **TV**.

Small, pretty hotel in a converted farmhouse. Cosy rooms 300–330F. Hearty breakfasts. Very genuine welcome and family atmosphere.

LE NARVAL

20 quai Gambetta (Centre).
☎ 02.99.89.63.12

Legendary. Still a sure bet. Charming little dining room adorned with maritime bric-a-brac. Set meals for 70F, 88F and 128F.

RESTAURANT LE SAINT-CAST

route de la Corniche; it's 5 minutes' walk from the town centre.
☎ 02.99.89.66.08
Closed Tuesdays and Wednesdays (off season only).

This is a delicious place, delicious in all senses of the word, with a set meal for 100F (lunchtimes and weekday evenings) which is of remarkable quality and balance. Situated in an elegant building away from the town centre and overlooking the sea, this is an ideal place to spend a delightful evening and to try some very fresh seafood expertly but simply cooked. Other set meals cost 150F and 200F and are in the same vein.

CARANTEC 29660

LA CAMBUSE – LE CABESTAN

☎ 02.98.67.08.92.
Closed Monday evenings and Tuesdays Nov 3–Dec 15, Tuesdays in July and August.

Located by the harbour. Here are two restaurants in one: La Cambuse and Le Cabestan. Which one you choose depends on your mood. The chef is the same for both but the serving staff and atmospheres are very different. La Cambuse is part brasserie, part pub. The atmosphere in summer is lively, even raucous, and some weekends overwhelming. A popular meeting place for young people with rock and Irish music at full blast. A mixture of locals and fun-loving holiday-makers of all nationalities drawn by the atmosphere and the reputation of the cuisine. Consistent and stimulating with generous servings at reasonable prices. A dozen oysters for 66F, *ceviche de fario* in lime juice for 65F, sausage *des monts d'Arrée ail nouveau*, lamb curry in coconut milk, *fario de Camaret* with sorrel, etc. Next door at La Cabestan the atmosphere is quieter, even hushed. Proper tablecloths, quiet clients, lovers who want to whisper sweet nothings over a pan of scallops and prawns with thyme and a part-smoked sea bream with a red butter sauce. Set meals for 110F, 175F and 240F.

CARNAC 56340

10% HÔTEL LE RÂTELIER**

4 chemin Douët.
☎ 02.97.52.05.04 Fax 02.97.52.76.11
Closed Tuesday evenings and Wednesdays from end Sept–end March. **Car park. TV.**

A charming little hotel in an attractive house smothered in ivy, tucked away in an alley in the town centre. Well-kept rooms for 230-280F depending on the time of year; half-board (compulsory in July and August) 590F for two, a tempting offer considering the quality of the food. Try the excellent set meal for 90F, probably the best of its kind around: oysters, of course, gurnard with fresh vegetables and mussels (or you can try the stuffed clams), followed by a chocolate dessert with liquorice sauce. The set meal for 135F features a much sought-after seafood stew. All this in an old-style French setting which is both comfortable and charming. The owner serves you impeccably.

HÔTEL LANN-ROZ**

36 rue de la Poste.
☎ 02.97.52.10.48 Fax 02.97.52.29.93
Closed Mondays (except during school holidays).
Car park. TV.

Booking advisable in the season. This hotel is always full of flowers, indeed the owner displays an almost irrational penchant for flowers. Stylish, comfortable rooms for 380–400F. Half-board is obligatory in summer (320–340F per person). Excellent food accompanied by the resident singing parrot. The cheapest set meal is 95F for weekday lunchtimes. Other set meals for 120F and 185F. Pollack in chive sauce, sole with prawns, panfried bass with asparagus sauce, *crêpes* filled with apples and rhubarb and served with a hot butterscotch sauce. Separate villa adjoining the hotel with a double room with shower/wc from 250F. Also a suite for 5 or 6 persons.

LA CÔTE DE BŒUF

Kermario; it's near the Kermario standing stones.
☎ 02.97.52.02.80
Closed Mondays (except July and August) and Jan 15–Feb 15. **Car park.**

The owners' son, Pierre, fresh out of hotel school, has decided to transform the family restaurant into a temple of gastronomic delight. So why not try the rare subtlety of the dishes offered. For 110F you are assured an uplifting experience. Even the *formule* at 75F (weekday lunchtimes) will cheer you up. To give you an idea: sea bream *galette à la tomate confite*, egg casserole with scallops (winter). Does this leave you cold?

CHÂTEAULIN 29150

LOPEREC 29590 (12 KM NE)

L'AUBERGE BRETONNE

5 place de l'Église (Centre); take the D770 and then the D121 after Pont-de-Buis-lès-Quimerch.
☎ 02.98.81.11.11
Closed Mondays.

An archetypal, adorable village inn which is hidden away in the deepest countryside. Fortunately for the proprietors, their reputation has spread by word of mouth and has induced extraordinary client loyalty. So you too should discover the elegant yet welcoming Breton décor of this establishment. Exquisitely chosen furniture and objets d'art. The dining room faces the flower-filled garden. The cuisine lives up to the friendly welcome provided by Marie and Jean Avan who run their business in a friendly but serious way. Gloriously fresh fish and seafood as well as local produce and succulent meat dishes. Remarkably reasonable prices. Set meals for 68F, 120F (with two starters), 148F and 190F. Excellent wine list (some exceptional Bordeaux!). Consider reserving (especially for Sunday lunch). One more compliment and this would be a rave review!

COMBOURG 35270

HÔTEL DU LAC**

2 place Chateaubriand.
☎ 02.99.73.05.65 F 02.99.73.23.34
Closed Friday and Sunday evening off season and for the month of November. **Secure parking**. **TV**. **Canal+**.

"It is in Combourg wood that I became what I am," wrote Chateaubriand in his epic *Mémoires d'outre-tombe*. This is a book to get to know by heart before stopping off at the village where Chateaubriand grew up. "Each evening I would go to the lake..." A tranquil charm, just a little old-fashioned. On one side there is the château and on the other the lake which was so dear to Chateaubriand. Very well-kept rooms but drab décor, from 200–358F depending on the view. The restaurant offers set meals from 62–154F.

RESTAURANT L'ÉCRIVAIN

place Saint-Gilduin; it's opposite the church.
☎ 02.99.73.01.61
Closed Monday evenings to Thursday off season, Thursdays in season and from mid-February to mid-March. **Car park**. **Disabled access**.

This friendly restaurant with its sophisticated cuisine was opened by an amiable young couple, who had previously worked in some of the best restaurants in the area. Its reputation is growing. The prices are astonishingly low considering the inventiveness and the flavours presented to you (roast sirloin with *foie gras* sauce, panfried prawns with courgette spaghetti). The set meals cost 75 and 110F. A place to visit again and again. The name of the restaurant is 'The Writer' and (appropriately enough) you can also buy illustrated books here.

HÉDÉ 35630 (15 KM SW)

RESTAURANT LE GENTY HOME

vallée de Hédé; take the D795 towards Tinténiac and it's 500m outside Hédé.
☎ 02.99.45.46.07
Closed Tuesday evenings, Wednesdays and during the February school holidays.

How can one fail to fall for this charming, flower-bedecked hostelry?. The young chef is brimming over with talent and has already attracted a following of food lovers. Continuous embellishment and improvement are his watchwords. An excellent chef, his set meals will satisfy the most demanding of foodies. Cheapest set meal 65F (weekday lunchtimes) (delicious. Other set meals for 88F, 125F and above.

CONCARNEAU 29110

HÔTEL-RESTAURANT LES OCÉANIDES

3 and 10 rue du Lin (Centre); it's near the harbour.
☎ 02.98.97.08.61 F 02.98.97.09.13
Closed Sunday evenings in May and June and Sundays from October to April. **TV**.

This establishment, known by the locals for generations as *La Crêpe d'or* has held on to its family atmosphere. Yvonne and family make you feel at home at the bar and will tell you about the region and its traditions and may even serenade you! This place is a must during the *Filets bleus* festival. Set meals for 50F (weekday lunchtimes), 70F, 105F (with two starters), 120F and 160F. Seafood platter for two people for 280F. From the menu: beef in pastry with onion marmalade, monkfish in pepper *coulis,* scallop brochettes *à la crème*, duck *aiguillettes aux baies roses*, fricassee of snails in watercress sauce. Children's meals. As for the accommodation, the prices are equally attractive with doubles at 185–270F. Half-board is an enticing 204–242F depending on the room and the time of year. Ten more rooms have recently been made available opposite the main building at *Petites Océanides*. A good hotel.

10% HÔTEL DE FRANCE ET D'EUROPE**

9 av. de la Gare (Centre).
☎ 02.98.97.00.64 F 02.98.50.76.66
Closed Saturday evenings, Nov 15–March 15 and Dec 20–Jan 3. **Secure parking**. **TV**.

Well positioned in the centre of town, this renovated hotel offers pleasant, comfortable rooms. Modern, colourful surroundings. Excellent sound insulation, telephones, alarm clocks. Enjoy a drink on the terrace. All this plus a cheerful welcome, a professional attitude and excellent information services. Newly refurbished double rooms for 270–320F (quality bed linen).

LES REMPARTS

31 rue Théophile-Louarn.
☎ 02.98.50.65.66
Closed Mondays out of season and mid-November to mid-February.

One of Concarneau's best *crêperies*. Located inside the town walls (in a quiet alley). The welcome and the freshness of the ingredients are unrivalled! The front of the building is a riot of flowers and there is a terrace on which to enjoy the delicious *crêpes*. Try the *Glénan* (cockles *and seaweed*) and the oyster mushroom *et lantins de chêne*, others worth tasting are the *Bergère*, *Paysanne* and *Nordique*. High quality seafood. Good selection of salads and ice cream.

|●| RESTAURANT LE PENFRET

40 rue Vauban; it's inside the town walls.
☎ 02.98.50.70.55
Closed Thursdays off season and Nov 1– March 31 (except for school holidays).

Open lunchtimes and in the evening until 10.30pm. This *restaurant-crêperie* is located in the busiest tourist street in Concarneau. You may legitimately ask: "Why is this restaurant included in the guide?" The answer is simply that it breaks with the usual tradition of most tourist places (in Brittany and elsewhere). Here, the clients are respected!. Good food is guaranteed and served with efficiency and courtesy. The ingredients are fresh, the portions generous and there is a dish for all tastes and all pockets from the simplest butter *crêpe* at 10F to a seafood platter for 165F. The proprietors are local and buy their produce from suppliers they went to school with. What is more the setting is pleasant (attractive crockery, wood panelling, a large stone fireplace, tasteful tablecloths and paintings. A wide choice of set meals and an extensive menu, the mainstay of which are wheat and buckwheat *crêpes*. Some specialities: *la Forestière* (*lardons*, mushrooms, *béchamel*) for 28F, *la Flibustière* (salmon, cream, chives) for 38F and *la Bretonne* (home-made *compote* flambéd with Lambig (cider brandy). You can also get home-made fish soup and a dozen oysters for 65F, *assiette Amiral* for 75F and fish of the day, 48F. Also chicken fricassee with apples and cider, beef kebabs etc. Set meals at 60F, 80F and 100F. Children's meal for 40F. Nearby is *La Porte-au-Vin*, same owners, same menu.

|●| RESTAURANT CHEZ ARMANDE

15 [bis] av. du Docteur-Nicolas; it's opposite the marina.
☎ 02.98.97.00.76
Closed Tuesday evenings, Wednesdays (with summer) and Dec 20–Jan 20. **Car park**.

One of the best reasonably priced restaurants in Concarneau. The dining area has lovely panelling and pleasant furniture and a fish-tank brimming with shellfish. Excellent fish and seafood straight from the harbour, which is just a stone's throw away. The cheapest set meal (91F) is only served during the week. There are other set meals at 129F (medallion of monkfish *à l'andouille (*a type of sausage (or *blanquette* of hake *à l'orange*) and 188F. À la carte: duck breast with prunes and spices, fillet of beef *au cabécou (*a type of cheese), scallops with saffron, grilled oysters etc. Very good dessert trolley. Don't overlook the *cotriade* (fish soup), the five-fish dish and the house special which is famous with Concarneau. You would come back just for that!

CONQUET (LE) 29217

10% ⌂ |●| LE RELAIS DU VIEUX PORT

1 quai Drellach.
☎ 02.98.89.15.91

In times gone by this old harbour inn provided simple rooms and a restaurant. After substantial alterations it is now a hotel which has thoughtfully upgraded its facilities. Imagine the homely charm of a guesthouse combined with the practicalities of a modern hotel. Friendly atmosphere. Undressed floors and white walls gently brightened up with blue stencilling. Very good quality beds. Three rooms with a view of the estuary. Rooms with shower/wc for 200F, 250F and 320F. These are really excellent prices for the quality of room offered. Each room bears the name of a Breton island. Avoid *Bannalec* (the cheapest) as it is the smallest and the shower is cramped. There's nothing run-of-the-mill about the breakfast room (a refectory-style table is laden with the offerings of white and brown bread and home-made jam. Breakfast is incredibly hearty and only 30F! The whole scene makes you want to grab your paintbrush and dash off a still life. Run by a family who know what a welcome is and how to make you feel at home. An catholic collection of books scattered here and there (a book by Satre was even being used as a doorstop! A fitting use for an author who strived for practicality… The restaurant is a large recently built room with a fine fireplace as its centrepiece. Local painters are often exhibited here. Good selection of *crêpes* (a savoury *complète* for 25F), fried mussels for 45F, children's meal 45F. A good wine cellar. There is live music on Wednesday evenings in summer. This hotel is at the forefront in the provision of services for tourists. Impressive (especially the bedrooms! One of the best establishments reviewed.

DINAN 22100

⌂ |●| AUBERGE DE JEUNESSE MOULIN DU MEEN

vallée de la Fontaine-des-Eaux (North-East); it's not far from the harbour.
☎ 02.96.39.10.83 F→ 02.96.39.10.62

This youth hostel is situated in an old windmill in a lovely wooded area. A night in an eight-bedded dormitory costs 49F. The washing facilities are a bit basic. Meals from 49F. Breakfast 19F. You can also camp for 26F, explore the surrounding countryside and take a course in photography.

10% HOSTELLERIE DU VIEUX SAINT-SAUVEUR

19 place Saint-Sauveur (Centre); it's in the old town.
☎ 02.96.85.30.20
TV.

Ideally located in the charming, quiet place Saint-Sauveur. This is one of the oldest buildings in Dinan and has four delightful, comfortable rooms (with shower/wc), three of which are at an unbeatable price of 180F. The other room is slightly more expensive (200–250F) but is actually a mini-suite with a TV room. The only drawback is that the bar downstairs does not shut until 1am. An excellent hotel if this doesn't bother you.

10% HÔTEL DE LA PORTE SAINT-MALO**

35 rue Saint-Malo (North).
☎ 02.96.39.19.76 F→ 02.96.39.50.67
Closed Wednesday afternoons. **Car park**. **TV**. **Disabled access**.

Outside the town walls, in a quiet area close to Saint-Malo harbour but just five minutes from the town centre. A charming, uncomplicated hotel which offers clean, spacious rooms from 180F (with basin) to 290F (with bath). Every room has a telephone. Welcoming proprietors. A good hotel.

10% HÔTEL LES ALLEUX**

route de Ploubalay (North); it's on the D2.
☎ 02.96.85.16.10 F→ 02.96.85.11.40
Car park. **TV**. **Canal+**. **Disabled access**.

A modern hotel without great charm, but it is surrounded by greenery. A good stopover on the Saint-Malo-Dinard road. The friendly welcome compensates for the uninspiring cuisine. The cheapest set meal is 68F for a buffet of starters, *coq au vin* and dessert. Doubles 280F with bath.

CRÊPERIE DES ARTISANS

6 rue du Petit-Fort (Centre); it's under the Jerzual gate.
☎ 02.96.39.44.10
Closed Mondays from mid-October to the end of March.

A beautiful old building in a rustic setting in one of the most charming streets of the old town. The relaxing atmosphere of this *crêperie* is largely due to the young, friendly staff. Excellent traditional *crêpes,* cider from the barrel and *lait ribot fermier* in vast quantities. The express set meal is unbeatable at 42F (a *galette complète ((*and two butter and sugar *crêpes* with lemon). Other set meals are also good value for money. All this and enjoyable music and, in summer, a large wooden table out in the street. Undoubtedly one of the best *crêperies* in the region!

RESTAURANT LA COURTINE

6 rue de la Croix.
☎ 02.96.39.74.41
Closed Tuesdays out of season.

This restaurant has genuine English feel to it (and a genuine warm welcome from the English hostess. The service is excellent and there is obviously a talented chef in the kitchen: duck with cherries and scallops with garlic and almonds. Set meals for 62F (weekday lunchtimes), 85F, 105F and 140F.

LE JACOBIN

11 rue Haute-Voie; it's in the old town.
☎ 02.96.39.25.66
Closed Tuesdays Oct–Easter.

This little restaurant is gaining increasing recognition for its consistency and quality (especially among the more discerning Brits). The décor is rustic and traditional. The chef/proprietor tempts you with classical cuisine, simple but pleasing, always using ingredients which are in season. Really tasty fish and sauces. The cheapest set meal costs 78F, but also there is the "pick of the market" set meal for 98F (tried and recommended) or a set meal at 135F (2 starters). Enticing wines of the month for around 60F.

LE BISTROT DU VIADUC

22 rue du Lion-d'Or; take the road to Rennes and the restaurant is on the left at the bend just after the viaduct.
☎ 02.96.85.95.00
Closed Mondays, Saturday lunchtimes and Dec 20–Jan 15.

Incredible location (one of the best views of the Rance valley. Moreover the restaurant has a pleasant interior (flowers and pastel shades, kitchen oven in the dining room) and delicious local cuisine. A fine menu including freshly home-made *foie gras* (90F), pig's trotters *ménagère* (55F) or the celebrated marrow bone dish (cheap at 40F). A good selection of affordable wines. There is a set meal on weekday lunchtimes for 85F. Apart from that everything is à la carte (budget for 200F with wine). Booking is essential.

PLÉLAN-LE-PETIT 22980 (13 KM W)

LE RELAIS DE LA BLANCHE-HERMINE

lieu-dit Lourmel; take the N176.
☎ 02.96.27.62.19
Closed Tuesdays.

This restaurant has a good reputation in the region and is housed in a long roadside building, made from local stone. The dining room is spacious, pleasant and lively. Cheapest set meal 75F (not served Sunday lunchtimes). Pay 148F and get the full monty: a dozen oysters, lamb cutlets or salmon escalope etc, cheese and dessert. Excellent meat dishes à la carte too, including spit-roasted suckling pig.

DINARD 35800

HÔTEL-RESTAURANT DU PARC**

20 av. Edouard-VII (Centre); it's very close to the town centre and only 5 minutes' walk from the sea.
☎ 02.99.46.11.39 Fax 02.99.88.10.58
Closed in October. **TV**.

A small family hotel typical of Dinard. Rooms for 140–230F (250F in season). Good honest value for money. Ask for a room at the back of the building where it is very quiet. Despite the hotel's name, there is no park or garden, but there is a stylish, congenial restaurant with set meals for 60F, 82F and 97F.

HÔTEL DE LA PAIX*

6 place de la République (Centre); it's 2 minutes' walk from l'Écluse beach and the casino.
☎ 02.99.46.10.38 Fax 02.99.46.77.82
Closed Nov 15–Feb 15. **Car park**. **TV**.

This hotel's central location, attractive prices and straightforward, kind welcome have made it a leader in its category. Completely renovated and very well kept. Most of the rooms face the rear (so they're quiet), prices from 200F (with shower) to 250F (with bath). Two rooms have facilities for a couple with a child. Set meals for 59F, 79F and 99F. A lovely, inexpensive hotel for a few days holiday.

10% HÔTEL LES MOUETTES

64 av. George-V; it's 50m from the Yacht Club.
☎ 02.99.46.10.64 Fax 02.99.16.02.49
Closed Nov 12–March 1.

A pleasant family hotel with 10 rooms. A very warm welcome. Charming cosy rooms for 210–230F. Friendly, uncomplicated and inexpensive.

RESTAURANT LA PRÉSIDENCE

29 bd Wilson (Centre); it's opposite the casino.
☎ 02.99.46.44.27
Closed Mondays and Sunday evenings, for two weeks in February and the first two weeks of December.

The emerald green façade of this hotel dates back to the early twentieth century and provides a contrast to the salmon-coloured interior. Appropriately salmon, skate and all the other good fish in the sea are the specialities of this restaurant which we recommend more for a quiet meal for two than for a big blow-out with a group of friends. Quite elegant surroundings and scrupulously prepared seafood. Cheapest set meal 90F, other set meals 130F and 155F.

RESTAURANT L'ESCALE ÀCORTO

12 av. George-V (East).
☎ 02.99.46.78.57
Closed lunchtimes and Monday evenings except for school holidays.

The proximity of the sea and the character of owner Corto Maltese give this lively little restaurant its own personality and account for its popularity with the young locals. It is also known as *restaurant des Marins*. Be welcomed by barman Dod while Marie toils in the kitchen to produce seafood salad, oysters, salmon tartare and various other fish dishes. There are no set meals, everything is à la carte, but about 150F should buy you a good, healthy meal. Seafood platter available (order the day before). A great nautical ambience. This restaurant is only open in the evenings as Corto likes to take a siesta on the beach in the middle of the day.

DOL-DE-BRETAGNE 35120

10% GRAND HÔTEL DE LA GARE*

21 av. A.-Briand (South-West).
☎ 02.99.48.00.44
Closed Mondays Oct–April. **Secure parking**.

A small, plain and unpretentious hotel. Rooms for 140–195F. Good, spacious restaurant cheerfully decorated in an antique style in shades of old pink. Set meals for 72–149F.

10% HÔTEL DE BRETAGNE**

17 place Chateaubriand (Centre).

☎ 02.99.48.02.03 📠 02.99.48.25.75
Closed in October; restaurant closed Saturdays from mid-November to the end of March. **Secure parking. TV. Disabled access.**

Well-kept hotel on an uninspiring square facing a small car park. Good welcome. Family atmosphere and rather quiet out of season. Double rooms from 190F (with basin) to 300F (with bath). Inexpensive restaurant with set meals 60–155F. Traditional decent food.

10% RESTAURANT DE LA BRESCHE-ARTHUR

36 bd Deminiac.
☎ 02.99.48.01.44 📠 02.99.48.16.32
Closed Sundays and Mondays (except July and Aug) and in February. **Car park. TV. Disabled access.**

Excellent food although a little sparing. Among the best in the region. Cheapest set menu 78F, other set meals for 135F and 195F. Lovely dining area. Astonishing value for money. The chef is a star and really brings out the natural flavours of the food (really worth a detour. Rooms are also available at 160–280F.

DOUARNENEZ 29100

10% HÔTEL DE FRANCE – LE DOYEN**

4 rue Jean-Jaurès.
☎ 02.98.92.00.02 📠 02.98.92.27.05
Restaurant closed Sunday evenings and Mondays except in July and August, and closed for the second week of January. **TV.**

This hotel and restaurant is in the town centre. Rooms for 280F. Take care as some of the rooms in the main building need refurbishing. Go for the rooms in the annexe which are quieter and newer. Set meals for 98F, 130F, 168F and 225F.

10% HOSTELLERIE LE CLOS DE VALLOMBREUSE***

7 rue Estienne-d'Orves (Centre).
☎ 02.98.92.63.64 📠 02.98.92.84.98
Car park. TV.

An attractive building from the turn of the century which is very close to the church and overlooks the sea. Allow 330F for rooms facing the garden and 450F for those with a sea view. Charming welcome, incredibly clean. The food is in harmony with the surroundings: fillet of pollack with orange butter, excellent seafood stew.

CRÊPERIE AU GOÛTER BRETON

36 rue Jean-Jaurès (Centre).
☎ 02.98.92.02.74
Closed Mondays and Sundays in winter except during school holidays. **Disabled access.**

Open from noon to 10pm in the summer. Full of character. The trendy proprietor gets around town by Harley-Davidson or Cadillac. The restaurant sign is painted by a child and inside the décor is very Breton. But the sound of Breton bagpipes has been replaced by jazz and rock music. Set meals of *crêpes* for 45F, 63F and 87F. There is also a traditional menu and the *crêpe* of the day. Specialities include *crêpes* with hot cheese or leek and *béchamel*, as well as *crêpes* with names such as "*moscovite*", "*les champs*", "*l'etable*", "*la mer*" etc. Children's menu. Flower-filled terrace to the rear.

RESTAURANT LE TRISTAN

25 [bis] rue du Rosmeur; it's in the street above the harbour.
☎ 02.98.92.20.17
Closed Wednesdays and Sunday evenings off season.

Open until 9pm. This restaurant is named after the mythological character Tristan, which seems apt for a place at the very extremity of France and Europe. Agreeable dining area enhanced by paintings. Well known for its cuisine, fresh ingredients and extra courses. There is a seafood platter for two people at 320F. Set meals for 98F, 138F and 198F. À la carte: monkfish with green peppercorns, scallops *à la bretonne*, hake with *rouille* sauce. Wines at affordable prices. Booking recommended.

ERQUY 22430

HÔTEL BEAUSÉJOUR**

21 rue de la Corniche.
☎ 02.96.72.30.39 📠 02.96.72.16.30
Restaurant closed Sunday evenings and Mondays Oct–May. **Car park. TV. Disabled access.**

Small, traditional holiday hotel with a friendly greeting. Located in a quiet street. Very well-kept rooms from 220–300F with shower/wc. Restaurant moderately priced. Set meals for 78F and 128F: mussels in cream, snails, salmon with sorrel, fisherman's *choucroute*, scallop brochettes etc.

RESTAURANT LE NELUMBO

5 rue de l'Église.
☎ 02.96.72.31.31

Closed Wednesdays and Sundays except during school holidays. **Car park**.

Recently redecorated. A kind welcome and good food make this a pleasant eating spot. Set meals from 55F (lunchtimes) to 148F. Fillet of sole *à l'anis*, monkfish *gigot* roasted in olive oil, langoustine tails *gratinées* etc. A lot of fish dishes.

RESTAURANT LE RELAIS SAINT-AUBIN

Saint-Aubin; it's 3km from Erquy-bourg, signposted from the main road (D34).
☎ 02.96.72.13.22
Closed Mondays and Tuesday lunchtimes off season and during the February holidays. **Car park**.

A characterful old house in a hamlet surrounded by a large garden. Complete peace in this idyllic pastoral location. A delightful dining room, or eat on the terrace in summer. Set meals for 78F (weekdays) to 175F. Meat and fish grilled on a wood fire, fricassee of mussels with bacon, monkfish in cider, scallops and much more.In a word, a place for all pockets and all appetites.

RESTAURANT L'ESCURIAL

bd de la Mer; it's next to the tourist office.
☎ 02.96.72.31.56
Closed Sunday evenings and Mondays.

One of the best known restaurants in the region. View the open sea from the dining area from comfortable green and white leather armchairs. Cheapest set meal 98F and others up to 200F. Seafood is a speciality of course: mussels *aumônière à la badiane*, fricassee of scallops and prawns, panfried *Saint-Pierre au foie gras*.

FOUESNANT 29170

10% HÔTEL À L'ORÉE DU BOIS**

4 rue de Kergoadig.
☎ 02.98.56.00.06 F 02.98.56.14.17
Secure parking. **TV**.

Small, traditional family hotel, completely renovated. Genuine welcome from the owners. Charming rooms at reasonable prices: 150F (with basin/wc), 240F (with shower/wc) and 270F (with bath and sea view). What more could you want? There are also triple rooms (280–300F) and quadruples (300–320F). There is a 20F fee for using the garage. Walking trails start just nearby. The beach is 3 minutes by car.

FOUGÈRES 35300

10% BALZAC HÔTEL**

15 rue Nationale (Centre).
☎ 02.99.99.42.46 F 02.99.99.65.43
TV. **Disabled access**.

Charming little hotel located in the most beautiful pedestrian street in the heart of the old town, where all the buildings are listed. Very quiet and very professionally run. Rooms for 200–220F (with shower/wc) and 230–270F (with bath). A great offer for off-season weekends: stay one night get a second night free (providing you have breakfast at the hotel: 29F). Valid for Friday, Saturday and Sunday nights.

RESTAURANT LE BUFFET

53 [bis] rue Nationale (Centre).
☎ 02.99.94.35.76
Closed Wednesday evenings and Sundays.

Clean, fresh dining area. Exhibition of photos and paintings. A decent set meal for 59F including wine. Other set meals for 90F and 130F.

GROIX (ILE DE) 56590

AUBERGE DE JEUNESSE DU FORT DU MÉNÉ

fort du Méné (East); take the coastal path leading to pointe de la Croix.
☎ 02.97.86.81.38 F 02.97.86.52.43
Closed Oct 15–April 1. **Car park**. **Disabled access**.

Open from 9am to noon and 6–8pm. This sixty-bed youth hostel has an exceptional location by the sea. Some dormitories are actually within the old fortifications. A romantic historical place – but basic. Beach at the foot of the cliffs. 40F per night and 19F for breakfast. Camping allowed. Tent hire.

GUILVINEC 29115

PENMARCH 29760 (5KM NE)

LE DORIS

port de Kerity, pointe de Penmarch.
☎ 02.98.58.60.92 F 02.98.58.58.16
Closed from All Saints' Day to Easter.

Situated on the quayside in this lovely little port, this place has become something of an institution. It has a really local feel and has served good seafood and fresh fish for many years. Run by a real fishing family who know what it is all about! Tradition reigns here. Pleasant rooms for 190F for two (breakfast included). Fish straight from the sea: scallop brochettes, poached turbot with a butter sauce, medallions of monkfish *cancalaise*. Excellent meat dishes too: escalope of lamb with herbs, duck breast with spicy wine sauce etc. Set meals for 65F, 95F, 140F (with two starters), 200F and 300F. Lively bar and you're guaranteed to meet some interesting characters. A good place to go.

SAINT-JEAN-TROLIMON 29120 (5KM N)

LE REFUGE

Centre.
☎ 02.98.82.01.34
Closed every evening. **Secure parking**.

This large stone building in the centre of the village has a bar where the locals gather together noisily. At the back is a restaurant with a dining area the size of a ballroom. Every lunchtime (except Sundays) the ritual is the same. Dozens of tasty starters (including hot starters) are arranged on the long tables in a beautifully presented buffet. Then you have the dish of the day, cheese, dessert, wine and coffee, and for 55F you'll have one of the best set meals available. The hospitality of the staff is a bonus. Sundays boast an "even better" meal for 100F.

GUINGAMP 22200

10% HÔTEL D'ARMOR**

44 bd Clemenceau (East); it's 50m from the station.
☎ 02.96.43.76.16 F 02.96.43.89.62.
Car park. TV. Canal+. Disabled access.

Recent, modern (satellite TV) and pleasant. Attractive rooms for 260–310F with shower/wc or bath. Rooms with numbers ending in 7 or 8 face the pretty garden. Friendly welcome.

RESTAURANT LA ROSERAIE

parc Styvel; 1km from the town centre on the Tréguier road, the restaurant is signposted on the right.
☎ 02.96.21.06.35
Closed Mondays off season. **Car park**.

Open 7–11pm. An attractive building set in its own garden like a cherry on a cake. This restaurant has one of the most delightful settings that there is. The dining areas are also pleasant and the food tasty, grills and seafood occupying the place of honour. Treat yourself to a feast! Reckon on 100–150F. Reservation highly recommended.

HENNEBONT 56700

10% HÔTEL-RESTAURANT DU CENTRE

44 rue du Maréchal-Joffre (Centre).
☎ 02.97.36.21.44 F 02.97.36.44.77
Closed Sunday evenings, Monday evenings and Wednesday evenings off season, for one week in February and a week around All Saints' Day.

A likeable young couple have taken over this grand old hotel and given it a new lease of life without sacrificing its simple provincial charm. The retro façade is crumbling under the geraniums. The charm of the hostess and the hotel's excellent value for money guarantee your contentment. Doubles from 150F (shower on the landing) to 190F (with shower, wc on the landing). Set meals from 75F (except Sundays), 98F, 120F and 135F, quietly and honestly good, indeed very good for fish and seafood. One of the best restaurants in the town.

HUELGOAT 29690

HÔTEL DU LAC**

9 rue du Général-de-Gaulle (Centre).
☎ 02.98.99.71.14 F 02.98.99.70.91
Closed Nov. **Car park. TV. Canal+.**

This hotel has just been entirely renovated (double glazing, Canal+). Rooms with a shower and wc are still reasonable at 220–290F. New dining room, but we far prefer the steakhouse next door with wood panelling and a crackling fire. Good meat dishes (grilled bacon, 42F) and pizza (around 50F). Dish of the day including a vegetarian course and a home-made dessert. Set meals for 70F, 95F, 110F and 150F. Half-board from 260F. Friendly. A good establishment.

SCRIGNAC 29216 (17.5KM NE)

RESTAURANT HÉNAFF

le bourg.
☎ 02.98.78.20.08
Closed each evening.

No sign, just the word "Restaurant" written up on the side of this big white building with blue shutters. Arrive early – by 12.30pm it's full. Climb up the steps to the dining room and experience a warm welcome and friendly atmosphere. There is no menu, you just enjoy the abundant meal of the day. First a creamy aromatic soup, then two starters, followed by the dish of the day (here's hoping you make it as far as the home-made tripe!), cheese, dessert and coffee. The litre of red wine holds pride of place on the table. All this for 60F. Sunday lunchtime sees a more elaborate meal for 80F and a seafood set meal for 120F.

JOSSELIN 56120

10% HÔTEL DE FRANCE**

place Notre-Dame (Centre).
☎ 02.97.22.23.06 F→ 02.97.22.35.78
Closed Sunday evenings and Mondays off season. **TV**.

Superb location opposite the basilica. Bright well-kept rooms for 260–280F. Half-board for 249F per person. Good traditional restaurant with the cheapest set meal costing 81F. In short (decent value for money in a place where things are done well.

LANDERNEAU 29220

L'AMANDIER**

55 rue de Brest.
☎ 02.98.85.10.89 F→ :02.98.85.34.14
Closed Sunday evenings and restaurant closed Mondays. **TV**.

On the Brest road, 500m from the town centre, this hotel offers remarkable value for money. Very elegant interior without being over-fussy. Attractive paintings and decoration and refined furniture. The rooms are particularly pleasant and offer superior comfort. Doubles for 230–280F, dinner, bed and breakfast for 310F. The local, traditional cuisine has a good reputation and there are some delightful new dishes. At lunchtimes during the week the dish of the day is 55F (with a starter 85F, with a dessert 80F). There are set meals for 105F (curried seafood *gratin*, *roulade* of roasted pig's trotters and pork knuckle or guinea-fowl with buttered cabbage) and 135F (two starters, nine oysters or a plate of stuffed mussels and clams, seafood *mouclade*, *croustade* of queen scallops in a butter sauce). Also a set meal for 170F. Excellent desserts (*gourmandise* with almond milk and red fruit, pear *tulipe* with chocolate, iced Grand Marnier soufflé etc).

ROCHE-MAURICE (LA) 29800 (4 KM NE)

AUBERGE DU VIEUX CHÂTEAU

4 Grand-Place.
☎ 02.98.20.40.52
Car park.

This fine inn, located on the square of a peaceful village near a lovely Breton church and in the shadow of a ruined eleventh century château, offers without doubt the best value for money in the whole of the Landerneau region. Astonishing set meals for 58F (weekday lunchtimes), 72F, 90F, 112F and 152F (with two starters) and 195F including half a crayfish. Children's meal for 42F. Fish specialities include *blanquette* of monkfish with saffron and other seafood dishes. Here you will find, cheek by jowl, farm labourers and travelling salesmen, executives and employees.

SIZUN 29450 (17KM SE)

HÔTEL-RESTAURANT DES VOYAGEURS**

2 rue de l'Argoat.
☎ 02.98.68.80.35 F→ 02.98.24.11.49
Closed Sept 5–28; restaurant closed Saturday evenings and Sundays Oct–Easter. **Secure parking TV**. **Disabled access**.

This small provincial hotel is plain but decent. Fully renovated rooms 180–260F. Good set meals for 72F (weekdays), 74F, 100F and 120F. Home-made *terrines* and cakes. Half-board for 190–250F per day. The hotel faces a pretty square and is next door to a marvellous church with an impressive porch.

LANDIVISIAU 29400

RESTAURANT LE TERMINUS

94 av. Foch (North-East).
☎ 02.98.68.02.00
Closed Sunday evenings. **Car park**. **TV**.

One of the best roadside restaurants in Finistère. Its impressive set meal for 60F is highly spoken of for miles around and comprises two starters (including seafood), main course with as many vegetables as you can eat, salad, cheese, dessert, coffee and... a bottle of red wine! Unbeatable. The number of lorries parked outside is evidence of its successful formula. Otherwise there is the adjoining restaurant with traditional set meals for 80F and 110F and a seafood platter for 120F. Some double rooms for 220F with shower and wc.

LANNION 22300

10% AUBERGE DE JEUNESSE LES KORRIGANS

6 rue du 73e-Territorial; it's very close to the station.

☎ 02.96.37.91.28 ➡ 02.96.37.02.06
Disabled access.

This youth hostel has been recently renovated and attractively decorated. Expect a warm welcome and no curfew. Accommodation comprises two and four-person rooms (each with bathroom) and a fully equipped kitchen. The youth hostel organises many artistic activities (various cultural exhibitions throughout the year) and outdoor events (bird-watching rambles) and provides extensive information on the local area. Truly one of the most dynamic youth hostels that we have encountered. In addition, a 5% discount is offered to the readers of this guide. The cost per night is 74F including breakfast. The mythical creatures from which the hostel takes its name, *Les Korrigans*, are gnomes who come out at night to protect, or disturb, one's sleep.

.|●| RESTAURANT LE SERPOLET

1 rue Félix-Le Dantec; it's behind the tourist office.
☎ 02.96.46.50.23
Closed Mondays and Sunday evenings.

Refined cuisine in a medieval setting. Set meals from 82–192F. The set meal for 102F gives you 8 hot oysters or hot salmon *terrine*, Breton duck *confit* or fillet of sole stuffed with pine kernels, raisins and orange, plus cheese and dessert. Good value for money.

|●| LA VILLE BLANCHE

route de Tréguier; it's 6km along on the Tréguier road, by Rospez.
☎ 02.96.37.04.28
Closed Sunday evenings (except July and August) and Mondays.

The chefs are two brothers who have returned to their homeland and now provide food fit for a king. Take them up on their offer to show you their aromatic herb garden. Cheapest set meal 105F (except at weekends), other set meals at 190F and above. Specialities: chicken *marbré au foie gras* with green asparagus, monkfish *au coulis de galatées*, Brie roasted with rhubarb and a wonderful pear *sabayon* with wine and liquorice ice-cream.

LOCQUIREC 29241

⌂ |●| HÔTEL LES SABLES BLANCS

15 rue des Sables-Blancs.
☎ 02.98.67.42.07 ➡ 02.98.79.33.25
Closed Wednesdays and Oct–end March except during the All Saints' Day holiday. **Secure parking**.

Small hotel and *crêperie*, tucked away in the dunes facing Lannion bay. Wild, magnificent setting and a warm welcome. Decent rooms with shower/wc for 250F. Choose room number 2, 3, 4, 5 or 8 (superb sea views). *Crêperie* and salad bar on a veranda looking out over the sea. Set meals from 60F. Mussels *au chouchen*, excellent *crêpes andouille* (a type of sausage). Oysters served at any time. Children's menu 40F.

LOCTUDY 29750

10% ⌂ HÔTEL DE BRETAGNE**

19 rue du Port.
☎ 02.98.87.40.21
Car park.

This charming hotel will give you a warm welcome. The owners have carried out exquisite renovation work on this old building, successfully providing excellent comfort while preserving the building's character and refreshing charm. Spruce rooms, all with shower, wc and telephone from 260F (a little cheaper in the low season). An extra bed can be provided for 50F. Breakfast for 35F per person. There is an attractive fixed price for two people for a weekend until May. Food for residents from 65–80F (off season only). Walkers and cyclists welcome. Without doubt some of the best accommodation in south Finistère.

|●| RELAIS DE LODONNEC

3 rue des Tulipes, plage de Lodonnec; it's 2km south of Loctudy.
☎ 02.98.87.55.34
Closed Mondays and from mid-January to mid-February.

This former fisherman's house, made of granite and just 20m from the beach, is home to one of the up-and-coming restaurants in the region. Reservation is advised at weekends. Pleasant ambience with pine and exposed beams. Attentive service and meticulous traditional cuisine. There are good set meals for 65F (lunchtimes and during the week), 98F (with 8 oysters) and 145F with a large seafood platter, *gratinée de fario saumoné* or fillets of mullet in a sea urchin sauce. There are also set meals for 200F and 215F. À la carte: seafood platter for 135F, grilled bass with basil for 100F, scallop *rosace* in two sauces. The wine list has some affordable bottles: Côtes-du-Rhône 55F and Touraine 70F.

LORIENT 56100

AUBERGE DE JEUNESSE

41 rue Victor-Schœlcher (South-West).
☎ 02.97.37.11.65 ➡ 02.97.87.95.49
Closed Dec 22– Jan 31. **Car park**. **Disabled access**.

Open from 8.30–10am and 5.30–10pm. On the banks of the beautiful lake of Ter. Reserve beds in advance in summer. This relatively new hostel has many comforts (kitchen, TV room, table football, table tennis etc) and costs 50F per night or 70F including breakfast. Rooms with 2–5 beds, camping in the summer. Set meal for 50F, but only if you book in advance.

10% HÔTEL-RESTAURANT GABRIEL**

45 av. de la Perrière (South); it's on the main road from the fishing port of Keroman.
☎ 02.97.37.60.76 ➡ 02.97.37.50.45
Closed Sundays Oct–end June. **TV**.

Small, uncomplicated hotel and restaurant, cheap and friendly. Modern, very clean doubles for 120–180F (10F extra for a TV). Set meal 50F including wine, served lunchtimes and evenings.

10% HÔTEL DU SQUARE*

5 place Jules-Ferry (Centre).
☎ 02.97.21.06.36
TV.

Small hotel with no restaurant (this does have the great advantage of having breakfast served in your room for just 25F, excellent!). Modest and quiet, next to Jules-Ferry gardens. Comfortable doubles 120–180F.

10% HÔTEL VICTOR HUGO**

36 rue Lazare-Carnot (South-East); it's close to the ferry terminal for île de Groix.
☎ 02.97.21.16.24 ➡ 02.97.84.95.13
Secure parking. **TV**. **Canal+**.

Warm welcome from the cheerful hostess. Clean rooms with every comfort. Doubles 160–260F. Buffet-style breakfast for 35F.

RESTAURANT LE PIC

2 bd du Maréchal-Franchet-d'Esperey (North); it's near the post office.
☎ 02.97.21.18.29
Closed Saturday lunchtimes and Sundays.
Disabled access.

A pleasant spot with its Parisian bistro décor and terrace for sunny days. Cheapest set meal 70F and others for 95F, 150F and 195F, offering, among other courses, braised beef with carrots, fresh cod in garlic mayonnaise etc. Unsophisticated food, but tasty. In addition the proprietor, Pierre Le Bourhis, is a wine connoisseur and was voted best wine waiter in Brittany in 1986. His cellar is doubtless worth a look!

LE CAFÉ LEFFE

port de plaisance.
☎ 02.97.21.21.30

If you want to find the picturesque and charming side of Lorient, look no further than the marina. And this establishment is ideally located to look out over the racing yachts and cruisers. Brasserie-style atmosphere and service. The cheapest set meal at 78F is more than adequate or there is a great seafood platter for 116F which truly amazed us: periwinkles, prawns, shrimps, oysters (slurp!), clams, cockles and spider crab to shell at your leisure (lovely! Taste and freshness assured, excellent portions too.

RESTAURANT LE JARDIN GOURMAND

46 rue Jules-Simon (North-West); it's near the train station.
☎ 02.97.64.17.24
Closed Sundays, and Monday evenings in winter.

You are strongly advised to book. Outside, underneath the trellis, or in the dining room which has an airy, elegant atmosphere, you are served with delicious dishes based on local seasonal produce, always well prepared and with that added ingredient (creativity. Shellfish stew with haricot beans and basil, aubergine tart with soft-boiled egg, braised hake with confit of tomato and thyme,, monkfish *feuillantine* with herbs etc. Courteous service from the host (while his wife slaves away in the kitchen) and very reasonable prices. Set meals only served at lunchtimes during the week for 90F and 140F. Otherwise allow about 220F for an excellent meal including wine. Our favourite restaurant in Lorient without doubt.

PORT-LOUIS 56290 (20KM S)

10% HÔTEL-RESTAURANT DU COMMERCE**

1 place du Marché (Centre).
☎ 02.97.82.46.05 ➡ 02.97.82.11.02
Closed Sunday evenings and Mondays off season and in Jan. **TV**. **Canal+**. **Disabled access**.

A quiet, comfortable hotel in the centre of town. Rooms 170–350F. The cheapest set meal in the week is 68F, other set meals for up to 270F. Good set meal of local ingredients for 100F or discover a wider range of dishes in the set meal for 178F. Lovely little tree-lined square out front and small orchard to the rear.

MALESTROIT 56140

RESTAURANT LE CANOTIER

place du Docteur-Queinnec.
☎ 02.97.75.08.69
Closed Sunday evenings and Mondays.

Good value for money at this restaurant on two levels which offers set meals for 70–200F: *émincé* of salmon on hot toast, monkfish *à la marmite*, fricassee of tripe *à la malestroyenne*, seafood. The best restaurant in the town. Easy parking at the market square.

CHAPELLE-CARO (LA) 56460 (8KM N)

LE PETIT KERIQUEL**

1 place de l'Église (Centre).
☎ 02.97.74.82.44 F➜ 02.97.74.82.44
Closed Sunday evenings and Mondays off season, during the February school holidays and Oct 1–21.
Secure parking. **TV**.

This pretty, rebuilt hotel has 8 decent, inexpensive rooms mostly facing the church. It is *Logis de France* listed and has a convivial atmosphere, completely unstuffy, in fact youthful and relaxed due to the spirited and relatively young hosts. Hearty welcome and traditional, fresh, generous food in the restaurant. Allow 170–225F for a room and 60F (except Sundays) to 170F for the set meals. Recommended.

MOLAC 56230 (13KM S)

10% HÔTEL-RESTAURANT À LA BONNE TABLE

place de l'Église.
☎ 02.97.45.71.88 F➜ 02.97.45.75.26
Closed Friday evenings off season.

An old coaching house (dating back to 1683) on place de l'Église. Set meal of the day during the week is 55F (a great West Indian meal on Tuesdays and couscous on Thursdays). There are other set meals for 105–148F. Cheerful popular atmosphere, plentiful traditional cuisine on well laid-out tables. The locals know that you can really do yourself proud here. Satisfactory, plain but clean rooms are available above the restaurant or in an annexe (quieter). Good beds. Very cheap: 105F (with washing facilities) and 140F (shower/wc).

MORGAT 29160

10% HÔTEL LA VILLE D'YS**

quai Kador.
☎ 02.98.27.06.49 F➜ 02.98.26.21.88
Closed Oct–end of March. **Car park**.

A quite exceptional location. Bright, cheerful rooms for 225–345F, some opening onto the terrace. Some cute attic rooms (wc shared with adjoining room). Half-board is compulsory in July to mid-September at 245F per person. Good restaurant with cheapest set meal 80F (evenings) and specialities of fish in sauce. Other set meals are 110F (with oysters), 155F (with seafood platter and fish soup), 190F (with turbot *suprême* or scallops and prawn in puff pastry with a cream sauce). À la carte: scallops *à la provençale*, grilled turbot with a butter sauce, escalope of braised monkfish with seaweed, etc. A real treat. Breakfast (36F) served in the dining room until 9.30am.

MORLAIX 29600

10% AUBERGE DE JEUNESSE

3 route de Paris (South).
☎ 02.98.88.13.63 F➜ 02.98.88.81.82

Youth hostel, accommodation in dormitories at 45F per night. Half-board available for groups of 10 or more for 111F.

HÔTEL-RESTAURANT SAINT-MÉLAINE

75 rue Ange-de-Guernisac (Centre); it's close to the viaduct on the harbourside.
☎ 02.98.88.08.79
Closed Sundays, two weeks in May and Dec 20–Jan 2.

Small family hotel in a quiet street. Plain rooms in which the furnishings are sometimes mismatched with the old-fashioned décor, but in general well maintained. Prices 140–175F (difficult to find cheaper. Very friendly host offering traditional cuisine. Set meal 58F (every day) including a good buffet of starters. Other set meal for 80F. Half-board 165F per person.

10% HÔTEL DU PORT**

3 quai de Léon (North); it's 400m from the viaduct on the quayside.
☎ 02.98.88.07.54
TV. **Canal+**.

Fresh, pleasant rooms with shower, wc, bath, telephone for 190–210F. View of the harbour. Very warm welcome, excellent value for money.

|●| LE BAINS-DOUCHES

45 allée du Paon-Ben; it's opposite the law courts.
☎ 02.98.63.83.83
Closed Saturdays and Sunday lunchtimes.

One of the most original restaurants in the town. Not to be missed for the walkways, tiles and ornate glass of its old public baths. Its turn-of-the-century atmosphere has been carefully preserved. The friendly Celtic/Parisian ambience is the setting for decent bistro food at very reasonable prices. Start with a dozen *carantecoises* oysters for 40F or fresh anchovies marinated *à l'orientale*, followed by *noisettes* of stuffed lamb at 66F, peppered duck steak for 75F or fricassee of rabbit in cider with gingerbread for 69F. Good desserts: coconut pear *gratin*, caramelized apples in puff pastry, etc. Lunchtime *formules* for 59F (except Sundays), 75F and 125F. Children's meal 39F.

|●| LA MARÉE BLEUE

3 rampe Saint-Mélaine (Centre).
☎ 02.98.63.24.21
Closed Sunday evenings and Mondays off season.

Restaurant with a good reputation which specializes in fish and seafood. Refined cuisine and a cheerful, genuine greeting. Elegant surroundings, wood and stone on two levels. On our visit we had beautifully fresh prawns and seafood as well as very tender meat. Set meals at 75F (weekdays), 98F (extraordinary value for money), 155F and 220F. Children's meal 48F.

|●| RESTAURANT BROCÉLIANDE

5 rue des Bouchers (South-East).
☎ 02.98.88.73.78
Closed Tuesdays. **Disabled access.**

This little restaurant in a pleasant district is something special. It's only open in the evenings. The charming décor harks back to a traditional provincial style and the music and furniture evokes the ambiguous atmosphere of the works of Proust. Comfortable. Good cuisine. Try the *filet mignon à la compote de rhubarbe* or honey butter stuffed mussels. Set meals 90–160F. Friendly welcome.

PAIMPOL 22500

⌂ |●| AUBERGE DE JEUNESSE

château de Kerraoul (West); it's 2km from the station.
☎ 02.96.20.83.60 F 02.96.20.96.46
Car park.

A pleasant youth hostel set in a large comfortable building which looks like a manor house. 46F per night. Half-board 114F, full board 163F. Camping allowed. The warden, Guy Cloarec, alias Monsieur Sea Kayak, organises excellent courses (in the art of using the sea kayak of course).

⌂ |●| LE REPAIRE DE KERROC'H***

29 quai Morand; it's at the marina.
☎ 02.96.20.50.13 F 02.96.22.07.46
Closed Jan 15–end Feb. Restaurant closed Tuesdays and Wednesday lunchtimes off season.
TV. Canal+. Disabled access.

This St-Malo-style building dates back to 1793 and was built by a pirate who served under Napoleon. It has 12 spacious and scrupulously clean rooms for 290–580F. Elegant dining room in shades of green where you can treat yourself to some oldrecipes revisited (including spiced honeyed roast duck, scallop specialities and delicious desserts. Set meals from 115F including wine.

|●| CRÊPERIE-RESTAURANT MOREL

11 place du Martray.
☎ 02.96.20.86.34
Closed Sundays out of season and mid-November to mid-December.

A genuine Breton *crêperie*, you'll love it. Massive dining area with all the charms of a welcoming tavern. Efficient, smiling service and a lively clientele of regulars. Delicious *galettes*, such as *à l'andouille de Guémené* (a type of sausage). For an aperitif, try *Menhir*, a genuinely local *pommeau*. A *crêpe complète* (savoury) is 31F and the day's special 45F.

PALAIS (LE) 56360

⌂ |●| AUBERGE DE JEUNESSE

Haute-Boulogne.
☎ 02.97.31.81.33 F 02.97.31.58.38
Closed Oct. **Car park. Disabled access.**

Be warned that this youth hostel in Belle-Île is such good value that you should book in advance. 100 beds. Reading and TV rooms. Café, communal meals or cook-your-own. 49F per night per person, breakfast 20F and meals 50F. The warden, Loïc, puts all his energies and skills into running the hostel and the benefits are clear! The hostel is well known for its courses in rambling, horse riding and kite-flying.

HÔTEL LA FRÉGATE

quai de l'Acadie; it's opposite the ferry terminal.
☎ 02.97.31.54.16
Closed Nov 1–March 31.

Charming little hotel. Cosy and pleasantly furnished. Excellent value for money and cheery greeting. Most of the rooms look out onto the harbour, 120–170F with basin or 230F with shower/wc.

SAUZON 56360 (8KM NW)

LE ROZ-AVEL

rue du Lieutenant-Riou.
☎ 02.97.31.61.48
Closed Wednesdays out of season and Nov 12–Feb 10, although open for 10 days at Christmas.

An elegant venue in Sauzon and without doubt the best restaurant on the island. Exquisite cuisine. The à la carte menu is quite expensive but the cheapest set meal at 100F provides excellent value for money (salmon tartare, mixed fish dish or local lamb). À la carte: a good Belle-Île *cotriade* (fish soup), skate wing cooked in foil and a really special island lamb *roulade* withchervil. Atmosphere and service to match the excellence of the food.

PERROS-GUIREC 22700

10% LES VIOLETTES*

19 rue du Calvaire (Centre).
☎ 02.96.23.21.33 F 02.93.23.10.08
Restaurant closed Saturdays and Sundays Oct 1–April 15 (except during school holidays). **TV**. **Canal+**.

A delightful Norman house which looks like an olde-worlde boarding house. Flowering plants adorn the cosy interior and compliment the excellent welcome. Well-kept, upgraded rooms 150–215F depending on the facilities and time of year. Half-board 185–230F. The restaurant has set meals of all kinds from basic (53F) to gourmet.

CRÊPERIE HAMON

36 rue de la Salle; it's in a steep little street opposite the marina **Car park**.
☎ 02.96.23.28.82
Closed Mondays and Fridays (except during school holidays).

Open only for one sitting in the evening at 7.15pm. Reservation essential. A secret little hideaway (apart from the fact that its reputation is known for miles around!) which is worth a visit as much for its rustic setting and good atmosphere as for the spectacle of the host flinging the *crêpes* to the waitress to catch before they are served. And boy, do they taste good!

PLOËRMEL 56800

10% HÔTEL-RESTAURANT SAINT-MARC**

1 place Saint-Marc (West).
☎ 02.97.74.00.01 F 02.97.74.05.64
Closed Sunday afternoons in winter. **TV**. **Canal+**.

Not many trains call at the neighbouring station anymore. Well-kept rooms for 135–210F. The bar of this hotel is a popular local meeting place but the establishment is also known for its very stylish restaurant, generally regarded as the best in Ploërmel. The 95F set meal offers mussel flan with butter, fillet of hake in sorrel sauce, cheese or goat's cheese salad, dessert trolley. Cheapest set meal 69F.

10% HÔTEL LE COBH**

10 rue des Forges (Centre).
☎ 02.97.74.00.49 F 02.97.74.07.36
Car park. **TV**.

The reputation of this hotel with its bright yellow façade is totally justified. Soak up the comfortable, tasteful Irish atmosphere. Good British furniture and spacious rooms for 140–260F. A truly royal suite is available for 285F which comprises a vast sitting room/bedroom, bathroom and another bedroom. There is a lodge in the garden which sleeps 6 (350F). Good restaurant with set meal of local ingredients for 88F and other set meals for 95F, 135F and 165F. Weekday lunchtimes there is a set meal for 55F and a very popular *formule* at the bar for 45F. We recommend the tray meal served in your room (65F).

PLOGOFF 29770

10% HÔTEL-RESTAURANT KERMOOR**

plage du Loch, route de la Pointe du Raz; it's between Plogoff and Audierne.
☎ 02.98.70.62.06 F 02.98.70.32.69
Restaurant closed Sunday evenings and Monday lunchtimes mid-October to Easter (except for school holidays). **Car park**. **TV**.

A recently renovated hotel which is traditional and comfortable and just a few hundred metres from the beach. Set well back from the road but with sea views. Good range of prices for double rooms: 170F (with basin/wc), 250F (with shower/wc) and 298F (with bath). Beds can be separated off from the rest of the room. Overnight stay with evening meal 180F and 280F or half-board 281–352F per person. The dining room has panoramic views. The hosts are very welcoming and in the kitchen Philippe Cassegrain is a master chef. Set meals for 80F, 98F (with a dozen stuffed shellfish), 120F (a more varied set meal), 160F, 198F (duck *foie gras* and sole *à la moelle*) and 265F. Some à la carte specialities: fricassee of prawns, mixed fish withspices, marinated pork *filet mignon au lard* and iced nougat with pecan nuts. Breakfast a bit on the spartan side, however.

10% HÔTEL DE LA BAIE DES TRÉPASSÉS**

bord de mer (Centre); it's 3km from pointe du Raz and pointe du Van.
☎ 02.98.70.61.34 F→ 02.98.70.35.20
Closed Jan 5–Feb 10. **Car park**.

Large, prosperous-looking hotel. Exceptional location in a wild setting with a broad beach just in front. Doubles 178–280F. Half-board compulsory from July 10–Aug 20. Large dining room serving set meals for 102F (half a dozen oysters), 145F (two starters), 190F, 240F and 285F. Specialities of scallop brochettes, grilled prawns in cream sauce, baked Alaska. Children's meal 42F.

PLOUDALMÉZEAU 29830

LA SALAMANDRE

place du Général-de-Gaulle (Centre).
☎ 02.98.48.14.00
Closed Wednesdays off season and mid-November to mid-December.

Here the art of *crêpe* making is passed from father to son, and the son of this establishment must have been christened in a vat of *crêpe* mixture! Both he and his wife are carrying on the tradition. This *crêperie* is pleasant and bright. Children are welcome and the *crêpes* tasty. Try one with scallops and baby vegetables (31F). Around 70F for a full meal.

PLOUGUERNEAU 29880

LE CASTEL AC'H**

plage de Lilia.
☎ 02.98.04.70.11 F→ 02.98.04.58.43
Car park. **TV**. **Disabled access**.

Excellently situated on Lilia beach, this modern hotel offers rooms for 170–280F. Allow 270F for a double with shower/wc. Half-board is 260–310F per day per person depending on the room's facilities. The restaurant offers good cuisine based on seafood (highly appropriate considering how close the hotel is to the sea). The cheapest set meal is 87F, then there are others for 118F, 175F and 210F (with seafood platter). The dish of the day is 64F weekday lunchtimes (drink included). À la carte: house fish soup, skate in a butter sauce, roast monkfish in cider, salmon *au gros sel de Guérande* and many more. A good spot for those who want to stay at the end of the world and not far from one of the most beautiful lighthouses in Brittany, the île Vierge lighthouse. But don't worry, its light won't keep you awake. A place for those who love the sea (and fish!).

RESTAURANT TROUZ AR MOR

Le Correjou; it's north of Plouguerneau, near Correjou beach, 2km from the town centre, towards Saint-Michel.
☎ 02.98.04.71.61
Closed Monday evenings out of season (except for public holidays). **Car park**.

On the outside, a totally typical *le Finistère* building with a terrace for fine weather. Inside the décor is traditional but thoughtful, the service is discreet and the local cuisine is abundant and of a high quality (very good value for money. All the set meals comprise seafood and fish. The day's special is 48F. Set meals cost 69F (76F on Sundays), 124F (with oysters and roast leg of duckling with cranberry juice or turbot steak) and 166F. Specialities include a dozen oysters for 66F, duck breast with pears in a Bordeaux sauce and poached fillet of pollack. Seafood stew on request for 148F. Children's meal 53F.

PONT-AVEN 29930

CRÊPERIE LE TALISMAN

4 rue Paul-Sérusier; it's on the way into the town on the Riec road.
☎ 02.98.06.02.58
Closed Sunday lunchtimes off season, Mondays all year round and 2 weeks mid-October.

We had a hard time finding a good restaurant with reasonable prices in this beautiful but very touristy, village. But the *crêpes* and side dishes lovingly concocted by Marie-Françoise in this *crêperie* are very satisfying (hardly surprising as the recipes have been handed down from grandmother to granddaughter! The location is a charmingly renovated old house with a lovely terrace facing the quiet garden. Three *crêpes* will set you back 50–60F. The house's special *crêpes* include the *Talisman* (ham, chipolatas, merguez sausage, smoked sausage, garlic, anchovies etc.), the "seafood" and the "Roquefort and nuts". Also flambéed potato *galette*, omelettes, salads and ice cream.

RIEC-SUR-BELON 29340 (4.5KM SE)

RESTAURANT CHEZ ANGÈLE

route de Rosbras; it's 900m from Rosbras and 5km southwest of Riec.
☎ 02.98.06.92.07
Closed Tuesdays (except during holidays) and in the week from mid-November to the end of January.
Car park. Disabled access.

Home-made *crêpes* and excellent cider. Enter the restaurant by the Ty Couz bar which is run by the proprietor's husband, a retired sailor. Warm interior of wood and stone in a lovely cottage dating back to the Revolution. Have a look at the strange *dolvouettes*, enormous tables with a special drawer for holding large loaves of bread. Reckon on something like 70F for a meal.

RESTAURANT CHEZ JACKY

port de Belon; it's 4km south of Riec.
☎ 02.98.06.90.32
Closed Mondays and Oct–end March.

Large house set in a lovely spot in an adorable little port tucked away on the Belon river. Excellent seafood, naturally, straight from the crab and shellfish tanks next to the dining room. So fresh! This is the ideal place to try the delights of Breton seafood even if the prices are a little on the expensive side and the atmosphere is inevitably touristy. Cheapest set meal 95F, served every day. Gourmet set meals for 160F and 360F. Seafood platter 200F per person, a dozen Belon oysters 78F, skate in butter, fresh salmon, scallops *à la bretonne*, *moules marinière* etc. Recommended venue for a pleasant spring or summer evening.

TRÉGUNC 29910 (6KM SW)

10% HÔTEL-RESTAURANT LE MENHIR

17 rue de Concarneau.
☎ 02.98.97.62.35 F 02.98.50.26.68
Closed Wednesday evenings Oct–May. **Car park.**

Cathy and Patrice Blomet took over this business a few years ago and have quickly built up a good reputation. Their welcome is cheerful and sincere. In addition the cuisine is refined, which is hardly surprising considering that Patrice has worked with some top chefs. His creations have a touch of the inspirational about them. They are tasty, aromatic, traditional and imaginative all at the same time. Pleasant dining room and a clientele of delighted regulars (just take a look at the visitor's book!). Set meal 65F at lunchtime. A very good set meal is available for 90F with *cotriade du Menhir* (fish soup) or roast cod *pavé à l'unilatérale* or duck *confit*. Other set meals for 125F and 165F. A dozen very fresh oysters for 60F. Also consider the fillet of bass *à la vanille*, panfried scallops with leeks, raw sardines *papillon au gros sel*, roast breast of duckling withspices, etc. For an overnight stay, decent rooms 150–260F.

PONT-CROIX 29790

HÔTEL-RESTAURANT TY-EVAN**

18 rue du Docteur-Neis (Centre); it's next to the town hall.
☎ 02.98.70.58.58 F 02.98.70.53.38
Closed Feb.

Pont-Croix is a delightful little cathedral town full of character and gentle charms. Pause to admire the magnificent cathedral portal. It is a good stopping-off point away from the sea (if the crashing of the waves becomes too much). This hotel on the quiet main square offers good rooms for 240–260F. Warm welcome and honest food. Set meals 75F, 115F and 180F. Half-board 235F per person.

PONTIVY 56300

HÔTEL-RESTAURANT ROBIC*

2 rue Jean-Jaurès.
☎ 02.97.25.11.80 F 02.97.25.74.10
Closed Sunday evenings from All Saints' Day to Easter.
Car park.

This hotel is plain but good. Set meals from 52F (58F Sundays) to 138F. Chef Louis offers *saucissonnade*, veal *au pineau et aux poires* and Breton cake. Cider by the pitcher or try the house aperitif, known as *apérobic*. Rooms are also available, doubles 155–250F (with TV), but the road is very busy and noisy. Choose room 3 or 29 which have recently been redecorated and face the rear.

QUIBERON 56170

HÔTEL AU VIEUX LOGIS*

rue des Goélettes; it's 2km to the north of town in Saint-Julien.
☎ 02.97.50.12.20

Opposite the lovely little chapel of Saint-Julien. This peaceful hotel is full of character and surrounded by flowers. The rooms are a little old-fashioned (but have good beds), but the old stone walls and the attractive, shady terrace are very pleasant. Doubles 175–225F. Set meals from 65F. All in all, an irresistible hotel!

CRÊPERIE-RESTAURANT DU VIEUX PORT

42-44 rue Surcouf; it's above the old harbour of Port-Haliguen.
☎ 02.97.50.01.56
Closed mid-November to mid-February. **Car park.**

As you sit in the shade of the trees in the garden and observe the fascinating ballet performed by the waiting staff, you will have no regrets that Jean-Marc Bonnel gave up the theatre to bring his grandmother's restaurant back to life. This is a superb spot. Park your car by the harbour and stroll up an alley to the restaurant. Far from the bustle of holiday-makers, feast on excellent *crêpes*, seafood *galette*, lobster *à l'armoricaine* or local dishes from recipes discovered by Jean-Marc in his grandmother's books and included in the set meal for 68F or à la carte.

LA CHAUMINE**

36 place du Manémeur; it's in the village of Manémeur.
☎ 02.97.50.17.67
Closed Sunday evenings and Mondays (except June 15–Sept 15) and Nov 15–Dec 15. **Car park. Disabled access.**

Surrounded by fishermen's cottages, this restaurant is set in an adorable little spot. Arrive in time for an aperitif at the bar and join the fishermen and locals sipping a Muscadet – a million miles from the stress and traffic jams of city life. The menu is unfussy and the set meals have no frills, just good, honest ingredients: mussels, prawns, fish. The chef will sometimes serve *tête de veau* for aficionados. Cheapest set meal 80F, then 140–260F.

RESTAURANT LA CRIÉE

11 quai de l'Océan.
☎ 02.97.30.53.09
Closed Sunday evenings (except July–Aug), Mondays (but only for lunchtimes in July–Aug) and the month of January.

One of the best seafood and fish specialists of the peninsula. Good value for money and service at the double with a smile. Set meal 89F.

SAINT-PIERRE-QUIBERON 56510 (5KM N)

HÔTEL DE BRETAGNE**

37 rue du Général-de-Gaulle.
☎ 02.97.30.91.47 F➔ 02.97.30.89.78
Closed Nov 15–Easter. **TV.**

This pleasing, traditional hotel is just 50m from the pretty beach of Saint-Pierre. Bright, well-kept rooms for 230F (with shower and telephone) in the low season. Prices rise in July–Aug when half-board is compulsory (310F per person). Friendly welcome.

QUIMPER 29000

10% LA TOUR D'AUVERGNE**

13 rue des Réguaires (Centre).
☎ 02.98.95.08.70 F➔ 02.98.95.17.31
Restaurant closed Saturday lunchtimes Oct 1–July 15 and Sundays until April 30 and Dec 17–Jan 9.
Secure parking. TV. Disabled access.

This hotel is located in the town centre and has been entirely renovated. Doubles 300–550F. Plush and traditional. Set meals for 120F, 155F, 198F and 250F. Children's meal for 72F. Some specialities: sole with spring vegetables in a seaweed and butter sauce, shellfish *taboulé* in vinaigrette with crispy vegetables, *Cézanne* fruit palette and seasonal sorbets.

LA CAMBUSE

11 rue Le Déan (Centre).
☎ 02.98.53.06.06
Closed Mondays and Sunday lunchtimes.

This friendly *crêpe* and *tarte* establishment is located by the station but is not far from the town centre. Original colourful décor in the style of a ship's cabin. Varnished wood, port-holes, maritime bric-a-brac (so you can voyage into a sea of culinary delights. Try the delicious home-made *tartes* which are a little out of the ordinary: aubergines and *saint-marcellin*; nuts, asparagus and brie; vegetables, cheese and meat. A great selection of wheat and buckwheat *crêpes* and some appetizing mixed salads. Recent additions to the menu are fried mussels and kebabs. Reasonable prices however. Take-aways available.

CRÊPERIE DU SALLÉ

6 rue du Sallé (Centre).
☎ 02.98.95.95.80
Closed Sundays, Mondays off season, three and a half weeks in Nov–Dec and 10 days in May–June.

Located in a half-timbered old building in the heart of the old town. This is the most touristy area but this *crêperie* has maintained a the quality of its welcome as if it were tucked away in the depths of the Breton hills. In theory it closes around 10pm, but you are always greeted with a smile and as the proprietor says: "As long as the lights are still on...!". Pleasant, rustic surroundings for delicious *crêpes*. Home-made pâté carefully and skilfully made with only the freshest of ingredients. Attentive service. The house special *crêpes* include *paysanne*, hot goat's cheese, scallop *provençale*, *forestière*, candied orange zest etc.

CRÊPERIE LA KRAMPOUZERIE

place au Beurre (Centre).
☎ 02.98.95.13.08
Closed Sundays and Mondays except during school holidays.

Good traditional *crêperie* where all the *crêpes* are made from organic buckwheat flour. *Crêpe complète* (savoury) for 22F. Other specialities: scallops with *emincé* of leek (33F), *crêpe aux algues d'Ouessant*. Fresh, clean venue. You can sit outside on the square.

CRÊPERIE AU VIEUX QUIMPER

20 rue Verdelet (Centre).
☎ 02.98.95.31.34
Closed Tuesdays, Sunday lunchtimes (except July–Aug) and the second fortnight of May.

This *crêperie* has a long-standing reputation. The small dining room with Breton furniture and exposed stonework fills up very quickly. Good-natured, family atmosphere: all and sundry gorge themselves on good *crêpes* accompanied by cider and *gros lait*. Try the *crêpe* with a filling of mushrooms and cream (24F) or a scallop *crêpe* (42F). Excellent eating place. Booking strongly advised.

LE CLOS DE LA TOURBIE

43 rue Elie-Fréron (Centre); take the road going uphill from the cathedral.
☎ 02.98.95.45.03
Closed Wednesdays and Saturday lunchtimes.

Chef Didier le Madec studied at some famous establishments and worked in London, Jersey and Ireland before returning home to open this lovely restaurant next to the cathedral. The setting is elegant, sober yet warm (restful shades of orange and mahogany, fresh flowers and leafy plants. A charming welcome. The quiet atmosphere encourages concentration on the particularly conscientious cuisine, full of generosity and inspiration. Set meal for 74F and superb set meals for 90F and 140F and a special meal for 180F for special occasions. Only fresh ingredients are used and the menu changes with the seasons to include revived classics such as stewed pig's trotters with oysters, braised veal sweetbreads with truffles or oyster mushrooms, roast lamb, stuffed pigeon, guinea-fowl *aux choux*, spiced duck fricassee and fisherman's hot pot. There are also wonderful inventions such as oyster and scallop *hure,* spatchcock pigeon with ceps and so on. Very good desserts. Our favourites were the red fruit *millefeuille*, strawberry shortbread and three-chocolate fondant. The wine list was short but offered a good choice in each category.

ERGUÉ-GABÉRIC 29500 (5KM E)

10% HÔTEL-RESTAURANT À L'ORÉE DU BOIS*

Odet; from the junction of the N165 and the Coray road, head towards Odet-Lestonan.
☎ 02.98.59.53.81 F 02.98.59.58.83
Restaurant closed Fridays, Saturdays and Sunday evenings (except for residents). **Car park. TV.**

Small neo-Breton establishment with the benefit of a small quiet garden and space for parking. Rooms 190–240F, half-board 210–250F. New beds recently installed. Set meal 50F lunchtimes (except Sundays). Other set meals 66F, 86F, 125F and 210F. Seafood specialities, medallion of monkfish *au Kig-Sal* and *au médoc*, scallop *cassolette au riesling*. Children's meal 48F.

PLUGUFFAN 29700 (6KM W)

10% LA COUDRAIE**

impasse du Stade.
☎ 02.98.94.03.69 F 02.98.94.08.42
Closed Saturdays and Sundays off season, one week in November and two weeks in February. **Car park. TV.**

Superb granite-built Breton house, surrounded by a well-kept garden. A nice spot to stay and relax if the sun comes out. The 11 rooms are well furnished and you could easily find yourself making new friends in the comfortable, British-style lounge. Choose room 3, 4 or 11 (more spacious). Doubles for 240F (with shower/wc) and 260F (bath).

PLONÉOUR-LANVERN 29720 (18KM SW)

10% HÔTEL-RESTAURANT DES VOYAGEURS**

Centre; it's behind the church.
☎ 02.98.87.61.35 F 02.98.82.62.82
Closed Friday evenings and Saturday lunchtimes and in November. **Secure parking**. **TV**.

Friendly, traditional village hotel. Affable welcome, very good cuisine and moderate prices. Pleasant rooms for 250F (breakfast extra). Choose room 4, 5 or 9 (more spacious). Set meals for 69F (lunchtimes), 99–130F (with seafood platter, skate with sherry vinegar or the chef's *coq au vin*, cheese and dessert). Also meals for 175F (with scallop kebabs or veal chop with morels), 225F (with two starters) and 270F (with seafood platter). Also special fish soup, Breton lobster in the chef's style, duck breast withcherries and port etc.

QUIMPERLÉ 29300

LE BISTRO DE LA TOUR

2 rue Dom-Morice; it's in the lower part of the town, opposite Sainte-Croix church.
☎ 02.98.39.29.58
Closed Saturday lunchtimes and Sunday evenings.

Beautifully furnished (which is hardly surprising as this establishment also deals in antique furniture. Traditional cuisine prepared by the very friendly host who is a great connoisseur of wine and who, appropriately enough, looks rather like Bacchus, the god of wine. Specialities include fresh fish of the day (Breton salmon, bass, sole etc) hot and cold scallops, panfried prawns *à la façon de ma grand-mère,* peppers stuffed with cod, tuna tournedos, oxtail *compotée,* lamb *roulade* withaubergine, cold *escabèche* of Breton sardines. Set meals 70F (weekday lunchtimes), 99F, 140F and 195F.

REDON 35600

HÔTEL LE FRANCE**

30 rue Du Guesclin (Centre).
☎ 02.99.71.06.11 F 02.99.72.17.92
Closed Dec 24–Jan 5. **Car park**. **TV**.

Unremarkable, modern but comfortable hotel located in the picturesque harbour district. Basically just a place to sleep. Rooms 150F (with shower/wc) to 270F (bath).

CRÊPERIE L'AKENE

10 rue du Jeu-de-Paume; it's near the old harbour.
☎ 02.99.71.25.15
Closed Tuesdays and Wednesdays.

Good quality, inexpensive food in a pleasant setting. *Crêpe complète* (savoury) 22F, *crêpe* with sugar 9F and mixed salads from 28–38F.

RENNES 35000

SEE MAP OVERLEAF

AUBERGE DE JEUNESSE

10-12 canal Saint-Martin; take bus number 2, 20 or 22 from the station. Off map **A1-1**
☎ 02.99.33.22.33 F 02.99.59.06.21
Car park. **Disabled access**.

This youth hostel is housed in a lovely building. Friendly welcome. Youth hostel membership is compulsory. Sheets and breakfast are included in overnight stays for 82–130F. Approximately one hundred beds in rooms of three or four. Café. Laundry. It's also a stopping-off point for boats.

10% HÔTEL DE LÉON*

15 rue de Léon; it's in the station area.
☎ 02.99.30.55.28 F 02.99.36.59.11
Closed July 20–Aug 15. **Secure parking**.

Small hotel set back from the road. Quiet. Attractive pre-war furniture. Rooms 135–190F, good value.

HÔTEL DE LA TOUR D'AUVERGNE

20 bd de la Tour-d'Auvergne. **MAP A2-8**
☎ 02.99.30.84.16
TV.

Plain but spotless rooms, with or without shower, 140–190F. A bargain! The kind of family hotel to dream about if your budget is limited. Every room has a telephone and the hostess is very friendly. A good hotel. Parking in the street.

HÔTEL D'ANGLETERRE*

19 rue du Maréchal-Joffre. **MAP B2-3**
☎ 02.99.79.38.61 F 02.99.79.43.85
Closed Sunday afternoons. **TV**.

Small, well-kept hotel. Friendly. Good value for money. Traditional, spacious rooms for 145–210F.

HÔTEL LANJUINAIS**

11 rue Lanjuinais. **MAP A2-6**
☎ 02.99.79.02.03 F 02.99.79.03.97
Car park. **TV**. **Canal+**.

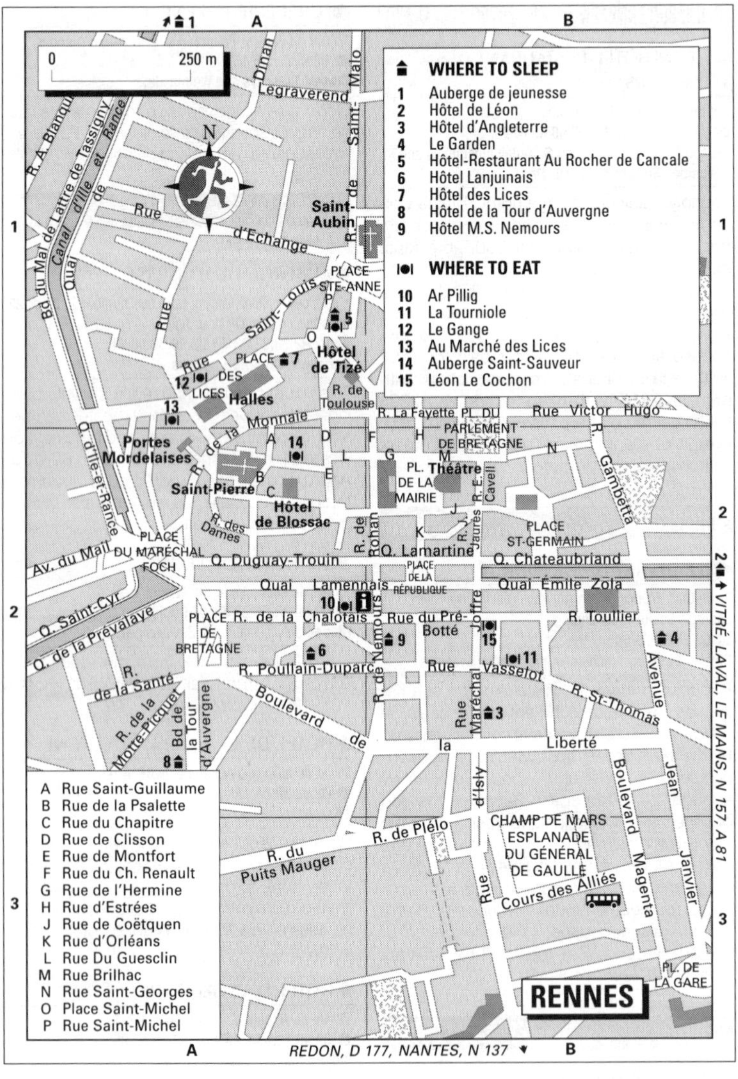
WHERE TO SLEEP
1 Auberge de jeunesse
2 Hôtel de Léon
3 Hôtel d'Angleterre
4 Le Garden
5 Hôtel-Restaurant Au Rocher de Cancale
6 Hôtel Lanjuinais
7 Hôtel des Lices
8 Hôtel de la Tour d'Auvergne
9 Hôtel M.S. Nemours
WHERE TO EAT
10 Ar Pillig
11 La Tourniole
12 Le Gange
13 Au Marché des Lices
14 Auberge Saint-Sauveur
15 Léon Le Cochon
A Rue Saint-Guillaume
B Rue de la Psalette
C Rue du Chapitre
D Rue de Clisson
E Rue de Montfort
F Rue du Ch. Renault
G Rue de l'Hermine
H Rue d'Estrées
J Rue de Coëtquen
K Rue d'Orléans
L Rue Du Guesclin
M Rue Brilhac
N Rue Saint-Georges
O Place Saint-Michel
P Rue Saint-Michel
0 250 m
Legraverend
Dinan
Rue de Saint-Malo
Saint-Aubin
Rue d'Echange
R. A. Blanqui
Bd du Mail de Lattre de Tassigny
Canal d'Ille et Rance
Quai
PLACE STE-ANNE
Rue Saint-Louis
PLACE DES LICES
Halles
Hôtel de Tizé
R. de Toulouse
Rue de la Monnaie
Portes Mordelaises
Saint-Pierre
Hôtel de Blossac
R. des Dames
R. La Fayette
PL. DU PARLEMENT DE BRETAGNE
Rue Victor Hugo
R. Gambetta
PL. DE LA MAIRIE
Théâtre
R. E. Cavell
R. J. Jaurès
PLACE ST-GERMAIN
R. de Rohan
Q. Lamartine
Q. Chateaubriand
Q. d'Ile-et-Rance
PLACE DU MARÉCHAL FOCH
Av. du Mail
Q. Duguay-Trouin
Quai Lamennais
PLACE DE LA RÉPUBLIQUE
Quai Émile Zola
Q. Saint-Cyr
Q. de la Prévalaye
PLACE DE BRETAGNE
R. de la Chalotais
Rue du Pré-Botté
R. Toullier
R. de Nemours
Joffre
R. Poullain-Duparc
Rue Vasselot
R. St-Thomas
Avenue Jean Janvier
R. de la Santé
R. de la Motte-Picquet
Bd de la Tour d'Auvergne
Boulevard de la Liberté
Rue Maréchal
d'Isly
Boulevard Magenta
R. de Plélo
R. du Puits Mauger
CHAMP DE MARS ESPLANADE DU GÉNÉRAL DE GAULLE
Cours des Alliés
Rue
PL. DE LA GARE
RENNES
VITRÉ, LAVAL, LE MANS, N 157, A 81
REDON, D 177, NANTES, N 137

Situated in a small street facing quai Lamennais. Renovated hotel offering a warm welcome. The rooms are adequate and comfortable, doubles 260–280F. Special bargains for off-season weekends.

☗ HÔTEL DES LICES**

7 place des Lices. **MAP A1-7**
☎ 02.99.79.14.81 ⮕ 02.99.79.35.44
Car park. TV. Canal+.

On one of the most beautiful squares in the old town. Completely modernized hotel: pleasant rooms with balconies and good general facilities. The upper floors have a good view out over the rooftops. Doubles 275–295F. Room number 532 is very spacious.

☗ |●| HÔTEL-RESTAURANT AU ROCHER DE CANCALE**

10 rue Saint-Michel. **MAP A1-5**
☎ 02.99.79.20.83
Closed Saturdays and Sundays and for 2 weeks in August. **TV.**

You couldn't dream of a better location (in a famous medieval street full of bars, right at the heart of the action. This is one of the liveliest streets in the town and so naturally one of the noisiest. The hotel has been renovated and the four very stylish and comfortable rooms cost 280F. Good restaurant on the ground floor. Set meals for 85–130F.

10% ☗ HÔTEL DE NEMOURS**

5 rue de Nemours. **MAP B2-9**
☎ 02.99.78.26.26 ⮕ 02.99.78.25.40
Car park. TV.

The proprietor, a collector of sailing memorabilia, and his charming wife have made their hotel feel very homely. The comfortable atmosphere is well appreciated by nautical types who will find a lot of talking points. Doubles 285–315F (with shower/wc) and 355–410F (bath).

☗ LE GARDEN**

3 rue Duhamel. **MAP B2-4**
☎ 02.99.65.45.06 ⮕ 02.99.65.02.62
Car park. TV. Canal+.

Charming, tasteful hotel, between the station and the old town. Café decorated in apple green and small internal garden. Friendly welcome. Very nice, individualized rooms, from 170F (single with basin) to 300F (double with shower/wc or bath).

|●| CRÊPERIE AR PILLIG

10 rue d'Argentré. **MAP B2-10**
☎ 02.99.79.53.89.
Closed Sundays.

The surroundings alone are worth a visit! The walls and ceiling have astonishing panelling representing Celtic legends of the forest. Good, honest, inexpensive *crêpes*: *complète* (savoury) 25F. The speciality is the *"Ar Pillig"* with apples in butter and blackcurrant *coulis* 22F.

|●| RESTAURANT LE GANGE

34 place des Lices. **MAP A1-12**
☎ 02.99.30.18.37
Closed Sunday lunchtimes.

Booking is advisable at weekends. This Indian restaurant is superbly fitted out and offers a cheerful welcome and meticulous service. The set meal during the week at 52F gives you an introduction to the delights of this carefully prepared cuisine. Set meals in the evenings are 85F and 110F. Punjabi chicken with basmati rice 55F.

|●| RESTAURANT LA TOURNIOLE

37 rue Vasselot. **MAP B2-11**
☎ 02.99.79.05.91
Closed Sundays and Mondays and for a week in winter and three weeks in summer.

This is a good, quiet little restaurant which offers genuine quality, inventive cuisine and attentive service. Very satisfying set meal for 64F (lunchtimes only) plus others at 80F, 115F and 140F. Quick *formule* for 54F. Medallions of lamb (from the leg) in mulled wine, salmon tartare and aubergine caviar are available depending on what is fresh in the market. Highly recommended.

|●| AU MARCHÉ DES LICES

3 place du Bas-des-Lices. **MAP A1-13**
☎ 02.99.30.42.95
Closed Sundays and the last two weeks of August.
Car park. Disabled access.

Relaxed and friendly atmosphere. Dish of the day 40F at lunchtimes (except Saturdays), mixed salads for around 30F and *galette complète* (savoury) for 26F. Good cider. Reckon on 65F for a meal. Open fire in the winter. Atmospheric.

|●| LÉON LE COCHON

1 rue du Maréchal-Joffre. **MAP B2-15**
☎ 02.99.79.37.54

The thinking behind this restaurant is both modern and noble. The result is a refined, authentic restaurant, a not an easy feat to achieve. Sample local dishes prepared without pretension or fuss. Lots of wood, bits of trees, walls hung with chili peppers, windows full of plants. At lunchtime the dish of the day is 42F and the *formule* 69F. Choosing à la carte in the evening will set you back around 180F including a good wine.

|●| AUBERGE SAINT-SAUVEUR

6 rue Saint-Sauveur. **MAP A2-14**
☎ 02.99.79.32.56
Closed Saturday lunchtimes and Sundays.

Located in a sixteenth century canon's house behind St-Pierre cathedral, this restaurant has an intimate, warm, sophisticated atmosphere. Set meals for 107F and 162F give you quality traditional cuisine. Among the dishes of the day at 55F are honeyed duck *aiguillette* and fillet of pollack withsorrel. At lunchtimes, the excellent quick *formule* come at 78F. Good place to bring your girlfriend or an old chum.

ROCHE-BERNARD (LA) 56130

⌂ |●| LES DEUX MAGOTS**

3 place du Bouffay (West).
☎ 02.99.90.60.75 F➔ 02.99.90.87.87
Closed Sunday evenings and Mondays (but in season Mondays only) and Dec 20–Jan 15. **TV**.

This comfortable hotel has a lovely façade with arched windows and 15 pleasantly furnished rooms. Prices 280–320F. Set meals from 80F (except Sunday lunchtimes). Other set meals 130 to (wait for it) 320F! Seafood predominates but don't overlook the veal sweetbreads with morels. Nice wine list. The bar has an impressive collection of miniature bottles of aperitifs, cognac, whisky etc. Friendly welcome.

ROSCOFF 29680

10% ⌂ HÔTEL LES TAMARIS**

49 rue Édouard-Corbière.
☎ 02.98.61.22.99 F➔ :02.98.69.74.36
Closed from the start of Oct–March 31. **TV**. **Disabled access**.

Well situated. This welcoming hotel looks out to île de Batz but is separated from the sea by the coast road. Bright, comfortable rooms; those with a sea view cost 330F. Sunsets over île de Batz all summer. Doubles from 260F (with shower/wc). No restaurant, but some of the best hospitality in Finistère.

⌂ |●| LES CHARDONS BLEUS**

4 rue Amiral-Réveillère.
☎ 02.98.69.72.03 F➔ 02.98.61.27.86.
Closed Thursdays except in July–Aug and Sunday evenings in winter, as well as for February. **TV**.

Up there with places offering some of the best value for money in the town. Good atmosphere. Set meals for 90F, 140F (stuffed clams, turbot *ballottine* stuffed with lobster) and 190F (3 courses). À la carte: *rouelle* of monkfish in cider, leg of lamb in port, seafood *choucroute*, scallops in a butter sauce. Also seafood platter for 190F. Comfortable rooms at reasonable prices: doubles 260–290F, triples 350F.

|●| L'ÉCUME DES JOURS

quai d'Auxerre.
☎ 02.98.61.22.83
Closed Wednesdays and Saturday lunchtimes out of season.

Set in a fine granite building (formerly probably a ship owner's house). A restaurant which is fast gaining an excellent reputation. Comfortable, warm, intimate interior with a large fireplace. Some inspirational dishes by the chef who combines local produce and seafood into some extraordinary offerings. The special lunch during the week is 55F (one course + wine + coffee). Set meals for 80F, 115F (with 10 oysters, fillet of pollack in red pepper sauce or sautéed pork withspices), 170F, 190F and 230F. There are some wonderful à la carte dishes: roasted queen scallop with smoked duck breast, warm oysters, smoked salmon *portefeuille*, braised emperor fillet with fresh vegetable *julienne*, etc.

BATZ (ILE DE) 29253 (5KM NW)

10% ⌂ |●| AUBERGE DE JEUNESSE.

How to get there: a ferry crosses every half hour in summer from Roscoff to Creach-ar-Bolloc'h. Last sailing 8pm.
☎ 02.98.61.77.69 F➔ 02.98.61.78.85
Closed Oct 1–March 31.

Excellent location; this youth hostel is very popular in the high season. Groups must reserve. Sailing courses July 1–Aug 31. Also sea kayaking, interesting environment, lots of old sailing paraphernalia. Life is governed by the ebb and flow of the tides! Around 49F per night and 49F per meal. Breakfast 19F.

ROSTRENEN 22110

⌂ |●| HÔTEL HENRI IV**

lieu-dit Kerbanel (South-West); it's on the N164 heading towards Carhaix, 800m from the town.
☎ 02.96.29.15.17 F➔ 02.96.29.26.67

Closed 3 weeks at Christmas; restaurant closed Sunday evenings. **Car park. TV. Disabled access.**

A modern hotel without much charm, but one of few in the area and also good value for money. Really comfortable rooms 180–230F, recently refurbished. Cheapest menu 68F with quite a good choice. Other set meals for 110–230F with, for example, scallops, guinea-fowl, plate of cheese and dessert. Seafood a speciality.

GOUAREC 22570 (10.5KM E)

10% HÔTEL DU BLAVET**

N164.
☎ 02.96.24.90.03 F 02.96.24.84.85
Hotel closed Christmas and February. Restaurant closed Sunday evenings and Mondays off season. **Car park. TV.**

Large stone-built house beside the river Blavet with the relaxed character of deepest Brittany. Big mahogany wardrobes, views of the Blavet and pleasant dining room. The chef/proprietor offers set meals for 82F (weekdays) to 300F. Good traditional cuisine like your grandmother used to make. Rooms 160–260F. Enjoy a sauna for a 45F supplement. Families who stay in room number 6 (with four-poster bed 350F) for more than one night are entitled to a drive in a vintage car (a 1929 Citroën) with the proprietor!

CARNOËT 22160 (30KM NW)

LES FOUS ANGLAIS

"Pen ar Vern"; it's 1km before the village on the D97 (coming from Callac).
☎ 02.96.21.52.32
Closed Thursdays and 2 weeks in January.

Hidden away in the Breton countryside, this is a lovely restaurant set in an charming old building. But why the name *Les Fous Anglais* (The Crazy English)? We asked the friendly owners, a couple from the English side of the Channel. "Do you know of anyone else crazy enough to open a restaurant in a place like this?" came the reply. It is true that only well-informed tourists make it to this fascinating corner of the Arrée hills. So why not discover this restful establishment with its original cuisine and family atmosphere. The walls are adorned with Celtic pictures and cultural posters. Set meals 48–125F and a good à la carte selection. Wood fire grilled dishes are a speciality. Also appetizing starters, moussaka, spaghetti, kebabs, *friture d'éperlans,* steaks and vegetarian courses. The desserts are tasty and home-made and children's meals are available. Theme nights (West Indian, Irish, Indian) on request. Terrace and adventure playground. All in all a place not to be missed. It is advisable to make a reservation at weekends and in high season. *Gîtes* available from 1998.

SABLES-D'OR-LES-PINS 22240

10% HÔTEL DES PINS**

allée des Acacias (Centre); it's 400m from the beach.
☎ 02.96.41.42.20 F 02.96.41.59.02
Closed Nov 11–end March.

Friendly little hotel, really well maintained. A warm welcome from the proprietors. Rooms 200F (with shower) and 260F (with shower/wc). Half-board advised in the peak season, 268–305F per person. Cheapest set meal 78F. Miniature golf and garden.

FRÉHEL 22240 (5KM E)

HÔTEL LE FANAL**

lieu-dit Besnard ☎ 02.96.41.43.19; take the road to Cap-Fréhel and on arrival turn right towards Plévenon – the hotel is on the left after 1.5km.
☎ 02.96.41.43.19
Closed Oct–March. **Car park.**

Rather delightful modern-style chalet reminiscent of Scandinavia, perfectly in keeping with the barren landscape out front leading down to the sea. Impeccable cleanliness and surroundings that could be a Bergman set. Satie playing in the lounge. Regulars come to recharge their batteries. Comfortable rooms 240–320F (TV banished). Rooms 6–9 are more spacious than the others.

SAINT-BRIEUC 22000

10% AUBERGE DE JEUNESSE – MANOIR DE LA VILLE-GUYOMARD

Les Villages (West).
☎ 02.96.78.70.70 F 02.96.78.27.47
Car park. Disabled access.

Youth hostel located in a superb fifteenth century Breton manor. Rooms with 1–4 beds. Around 60F per night (or 55F for those under 26 years old). Mountain bike hire.

10% HÔTEL-RESTAURANT LE DUGUESCLIN**

2 place Duguesclin; it's in the pedestrian area.
☎ 02.96.33.11.58 F 02.96.52.01.18
TV. Disabled access.

This centrally-located hotel has been completely refurbished. Bright, comfortable rooms without any nasty surprises. Double with shower/wc 240F. Set meals in the restaurant for 88–140F. A complimentary *kir* on presentation of this guide.

10% HÔTEL DU CHAMP DE MARS**

13 rue du Général-Leclerc.
☎ 02.96.33.60.99 F 02.96.33.60.05
Closed between Christmas and New Year.
TV. Disabled access.

This agreeable, well-kept, two-star hotel is also quite cheap: 250–300F for a double. Friendly owners at your service.

RESTAURANT LE SYMPATIC

9 bd Carnot; it's behind the train station.
☎ 02.96.94.04.76
Closed Saturday lunchtimes and Sundays and for the first 3 weeks of August.

Open until 11pm. A happy combination of a good atmosphere and good food grilled over a fire of vine shoots. A warm ambience; friendly, efficient service; large servings with side vegetables; quality ingredients; inexpensive: what more could you want? Set meals for 65F, 80F, 95F and 125F or à la carte.

AUX PESKED

59 rue du Légué; it's 2km north of the town centre.
☎ 02.96.33.34.65
Closed Sunday evenings and Mondays, the first two weeks of August and during the Christmas holidays.

The gastronomic reputation of this restaurant keeps growing and it is highly regarded in Sant-Brieuc. Hardly surprising considering the modern setting, which is sober and elegant, with superb views of the Légué valley from the terrace, and the delightful light dishes such as bass *à l'andouille de Guéméné, purée à l'ancienne*, brill with vanilla, lime, ginger and artichokes, pork knuckle *aux parfums d'andouille*, apples *gratin* in honey and cider, etc. Cheapest set meal 115F on a weekday (135F at the weekend), but we recommend the surprise set meal for 170F (2 starters, main course, dessert, appetizer etc.). Good wine list.

SAINT-JACUT-DE-LA-MER 22750

RESTAURANT LA PRESQU'ÎLE

164 Grande-Rue (North).
☎ 02.96.27.76.47
Closed Mondays off season and for 2 weeks in February.

A lovely little place, quiet and welcoming. The owner, Jacky, has sailed the oceans of the world. He cooks excellent fish: grilled sole with almond and hazelnut, turbot in lime juice, salmon with sorrel etc. Good meat dishes too, if you prefer. Set meals 95–135F. Reservation recommended 48 hours in advance in winter as Jacky only cooks the freshest of fish.

SAINT-MALO 35400

10% HÔTEL LE CROISEUR**

2 place de la Poissonnerie (Centre).
☎ 02.99.40.80.40 F 02.99.56.83.76

Although this hotel has no particular charm and is not especially cheap, it is very conveniently situated within the town walls. Small, functional rooms 220–270F.

10% HÔTEL DU LOUVRE**

2 rue des Marins (Centre).
☎ 02.99.40.86.62 F 02.99.40.86.93
Closed end Nov–start March except during the February school holidays and at Christmas. **TV.**

Although it has an impressive 44 rooms this is still a family hotel with a certain charm. Friendly with very comfortable rooms for 250–350F. Triples available and even a suite for 7 people at 700F. Rooms 17, 26 and 35 face the courtyard and are more spacious. The beds are not too new though.

HÔTEL DE L'UNIVERS**

place Chateaubriand; it's near the château, inside the town walls.
☎ 02.99.40.89.52 F 02.99.40.07.27
Restaurant closed on Wednesdays. **Car park. TV. Canal+.**

Lunch served noon–2pm, dinner 7–10pm. Next door to the legendary *Bar de l'Univers* this hotel has a splendid history and is one of Saint Malo's most stylish, full of retro charm. Good atmosphere and comfortable rooms, newly refurbished but with a gentle old-fashioned character, 270–310F. Rooms for 3 and 4 available. This hotel is unique and has a certain indefinable *je ne sais quoi*.

10% HÔTEL LA RANCE**

15 quai Sébastopol, Port Solidor, Saint-Servan (South).
☎ 02.99.81.78.63 F 02.99.81.44.80
Car park. TV.

Small, quiet hotel with 11 rooms. View of the harbour from the more expensive rooms. Family atmosphere, decorated with nautical paraphernalia. Not very spacious but provided with every comfort and set out with taste. Prices from 360F to 495F in season. Very filling breakfast for 47F. Parking in the street.

|●| CRÊPERIE LA BRIGANTINE

13 rue de Dinan; it's inside the town walls.
☎ 02.99.56.82.82
Closed Tuesday evenings, Wednesdays (except during school holidays) and mid-January to mid-February.

Snug, welcoming *crêperie*. Pictures of old sailing ships on the walls. Good *crêpes* at reasonable prices: sugar *crêpe* 9F, *complète* (savoury) 28F. Set meal for 58F or 28F for students.

|●| ENTRE DEUX VERRES

1 rue Broussais (Centre).
☎ 02.99.40.01.46
Closed Wednesday.

Good heavens! A wine bar! Not that usual in the land of cider. *Gratins, terrines* and *tartines* grace the plates and well-chosen wines of all regions fill the glasses. Lots of tasty dishes to try while you let your eyes wander over the walls which are covered by regular displays of canvasses by local artists. *Gratins* for around 40F.

|●| RESTAURANT BORGNEFESSE

10 rue du Puits-aux-Braies; it's inside the town walls.
☎ 02.99.40.05.05
Closed Monday lunchtimes, Saturday lunchtimes and Sundays.

Reservation recommended. A restaurant with a pirate theme. The larger-than-life host, poet and seafarer, is legendary in Saint-Malo and at the drop of a hat will regale you with tales of pirates and derring-do. He's bound to tell you the story about a pirate who got shot in the backside.. Good local country cuisine based on seafood. A warm welcome guaranteed. Set meals for 83F, 106F and 156F. *Formule* 62F lunchtimes.

|●| CRÊPERIE-SNACK SAINTE-BARBE

14 rue Sainte-Barbe.
☎ 02.99.40.98.11

Open every day until 10pm in summer and depending on the level of business in the off season. Serious, fresh, hearty cuisine in one of the most touristy districts. A very warm welcome. Try the delicately scented mussels when in season. Quite reasonable prices and thirst-quenching cider.

|●| RESTAURANT CHEZ GILLES

2 rue de la Pie-qui-Boit (Centre).
☎ 02.99.40.97.25
Closed Wednesdays off season, Wednesday afternoons July–Aug and Nov 25–Dec 10.

Seafood straight from the sea, lovingly cooked and served in a cosy, comfortable environment – the dining room has a certain intimacy. Set meal for 72F served at lunchtimes (except Sundays) and for 89F which gives you an insight into the owner/chef's skills in the kitchen. Fish cooked to perfection; excellent, aromatic sauces. Further set meals for 130F and 180F.

PARAMÉ 35400 (2.5KM E)

10% HÔTEL LES CHARMETTES*

64 bd Hébert; it's near Sillon beach.
☎ 02.99.56.07.31 F 02.99.56.85.96
Closed Jan. **Car park. TV.**

A sweet little hotel. Faces the sea, 50m from Sillon beach. Twenty decent rooms for 150–320F. This hotel is actually two houses, one behind the other, of which only the second has rooms with sea views. Decent prices for rooms with no view but rather expensive with a sea view, considering that the establishment is relatively modest.

10% HÔTEL LES COURLIS**

9 rue des Bains-Rochebonne; it's 100m from Rochebonne beach.
☎ 02.99.56.00.15 F 02.99.56.68.63
Closed Nov 20–Dec 20. **Car park. TV.**

Small hotel situated in a pretty turn-of-the-century house with retro charm. Simple, stylish rooms. Doubles 230–300F.

SAINT-POL-DE-LÉON 29250

|●| LE PASSIFLORE

How to get there: it's near the station.
☎ 02.98.69.00.52
Closed Sunday evenings. **TV.**

A friendly hotel. Traditional, unpretentious and offering pleasant rooms for 180F, 215F and 245F. The genuine welcome must be mentioned as well as the excellent restaurant, *Les Routiers*, on the ground floor. Don't be surprised if this place is full to bursting at lunchtimes. Set meals at 53F (very popular) with a plate of starters, 100F with a dozen oysters and 150F with 2 starters. Lobster for two 300F. Seafood platter, 280F for two (on request).

LA POMME D'API

49 rue Verderel; it's in a street at right angles to rue Général-Leclerc.
☎ 02.98.69.04.36
Closed Tuesday evenings, Wednesdays off season, the third week of November and during the February holidays.

Set in a lovely stone building dating back to the sixteenth century, this restaurant is full of real Breton charm. Stone and wood interior. Beautiful stone fireplace. Here you can sample some excellent food (according to word of mouth it is the best in town). Set meals for 68F (weekday lunchtimes), 98F (with 6 oysters or crab *terrine* flavoured with gin, honeyed leg of duck), 139F (with fricassee of artichoke heads and scallops, escalope of Breton salmon) and also 225F. Specialities include bass *pavé cuit en vapeur d'algues*, *blanquette* of sole fillet *au chouchen*, roast lamb *pavé*, etc.

SAINT-THÉGONNEC 29410

AUBERGE DE SAINT-THÉGONNEC***

6 place de la Mairie.
☎ 02.98.79.61.18 Fax 02.98.62.71.10
Closed Sunday evenings and Mondays from mid-September to mid-June, and for the Christmas holidays. **Private Car park. TV. Disabled access.**

Elegant, sophisticated surroundings, but not an oppressive atmosphere. Impeccable service. If you eat à la carte expect to pay around 250F. However chef Alain Le Coz sensibly offers a delicious set meal for 100F (during the week, drinks extra) which, among other things, includes a chicken liver *terrine* with Armagnac, fillet of pollack with aubergines and fresh tomato *coulis*. Other set meals cost 130F with a three fish *blanquette* and dessert (carafe of wine included) and 180F or there is the gourmet set meal for 220F (includes extra course) with scallop *terrine* and fillet of sole with tomato *concassé*; braised veal steak with morels; melon, strawberry and almond gateau. À la carte: veal sweetbreads *aumônière* in mustard with oyster mushrooms, turbot with slivers of cucumber and a lobster *coulis*, orange *terrine* with mint and Muscatel. Children's meal for 70F. In short, recommended as one of the best restaurants in Finistère. Also 3 lovely rooms with every comfort from 350F, with breakfast served in the comfortable lounge. The stuff that dreams are made of.

RESTAURANT DU COMMERCE

1 rue de Paris.
☎ 02.98.79.61.07
Closed Saturdays, Sundays and the first 3 weeks of August.

Roadside restaurant only open at lunchtime. Friendly welcome. Good, generous portions at low prices. For 56F you get soup, starter, dish of the day, cheese and dessert (the menu states that a drink is include for "workers" but not for those "passing through"!). Specialities include stew, *choucroute*, *Kig-ha-Farz* and couscous. Breakfasts available for 20F. Pleasant dining area with dry-stone walls. Lively atmosphere.

CRÊPERIE STEREDENN

6 rue de la Gare (Centre).
☎ 02.98.79.43.34
Closed Mondays April 1 to mid-June; Mondays and Tuesdays Oct–April and in January. **Disabled access**.

The proprietors Christine and Alain offer a friendly greeting. Wood fire. A choice of 150 good but inexpensive *crêpes*. Our favourites were the "Picardy" (leek sauce), the "Indian" (*béchamel*, onions, mushrooms and curry), the "Douarnenez" sardines and green peppercorns), the "Saint-Thégonnec" (onions, tomatoes, cheese, ham and curry) and the "Druid" (marmalade, almonds, Grand Marnier). Set meals for 59F, 61F and 66F with which you can drink cider brewed on the premises. Disabled access to the dining room.

SARZEAU 56370

AUBERGE DE KERSTÉPHANIE

route du Roaliguen.
☎ 02.97.41.72.41
Closed Tuesday evenings and Wednesdays off season. During the season closed Monday lunchtimes.

In all respects one of the best restaurants in the region of Morbihan. Elegant setting and service, but not uncomfortable, and virtuoso cuisine from the chef/owner Jean-Paul Jego (ably supported by his wife). For example the 125F set meal includes an appetiser, excellent seafood *brioche*, *granité*, chicken *suprême* with tarragon sauce which is genuinely supreme, and to finish an exquisite dessert of honey sabayon with apples and nougat ice cream. The cheapest set meal is 95F (except at weekends) and others are 155F, 175F and 195F. There is also an excellent à la carte menu. Absolutely fabulous – good food like this is available elsewhere, of course – but at these prices?

TRÉBEURDEN 22560

AUBERGE DE JEUNESSE**

60 la Corniche Goas-Treiz, lieu-dit Toëno (North); it's 2km north of town, in the hills but very close to the sea.
☎ 02.96.23.52.22 ➡ 02.96.15.44.34
Car park.

This recently renovated youth hostel is a modern building which is somewhat out of keeping with the landscape, but it is in one of the best hostel locations in Brittany. Overnight stays are 49F per person and breakfast is 20F. The cheapest set meal is 49F. Camping allowed. Activities: local ecological site, diving etc.

10% HÔTEL-RESTAURANT KER AN NOD**

rue de Pors-Termen (Centre); it's opposite île Millau.
☎ 02.96.23.50.21 ➡ 02.96.23.63.30
Closed Dec–mid-Feb. **TV**.

Charming, quiet hotel run by a very friendly young couple, Catherine and Gildas. Of the 20 rooms, 14 face the sea. Set very close to a vast beach. Rooms 250F (low season, facing the hills) to 350F (July–Aug, facing the sea). Comfortable and bright (picture windows extra). The restaurant is also very nice, offering fish and seafood. Set meals for 85F (with mussels, fish and dessert) to 165F.

TRÉGASTEL 22730

10% HÔTEL-RESTAURANT DE LA CORNICHE**

38 rue Charles-Le-Goffic (Centre); it's in the town centre, not far from the beaches.
☎ 02.96.23.88.15 ➡ 02.96.23.47.89
Closed Sunday evenings and Mondays (except for school holidays) and in January. **Car park**. **TV**.

A welcoming proprietor. Doubles for 280F (with shower) and 320F (with bath) in the summer and 200–250F off season. Cheerful décor that puts you in a good mood. Also does food: cheapest set meal 55F weekdays, next set meal 80F. Half-board 250F.

TRÉGUIER 22220

HÔTEL LES ROCHES DOUVRES**

17 rue Marcelin-Berthelot.
☎ 02.96.92.27.27
Closed Oct. **Car park**. **TV**. **Canal+**. **Disabled access**.

A completely new two-star hotel. Quiet, located on a small hill overlooking the sea. Flawless, comfortable rooms each with bathroom, 250F (290F in July–Aug). Breakfast 30F.

LA POISSONNERIE DU TRÉGOR

2 rue Renan (Centre); it's behind the cathedral.
☎ 02.96.92.30.27

Tastings from June–Oct. An original and welcoming establishment. Jean-Pierre Moulinet serves you with fish and seafood which you can taste above his shop (tasting room open June–Oct). Crab mayonnaise 55F, mussels 30F and selection platter for 110F. Of course you can buy produce to take away as above all this is a fishmonger's (much reduced prices).

VANNES 56000

HÔTEL LE BRETAGNE**

36, rue du Mené (Centre); it's 50m from the prison gates.
☎ 02.97.47.20.21
TV.

A little retro charm. Quiet rooms, some facing the town walls. Uncomplicated, courteous welcome. Doubles 180F with shower/wc or 230F with bath. Thoughtful concession to those on a tight budget – a room for 110F! Good value for money. Often full.

HÔTEL-RESTAURANT LE RELAIS DE LUSCANEN**

zone commerciale de Luscanen – N165, route d'Auray (West).
☎ 02.97.63.15.77 ➡ 02.97.63.30.45
Closed Saturday evenings, Sundays, Ascension Day weekend and 2 weeks in August. **Car park**. **TV**. **Canal+**.

A real roadside restaurant. The set meal at 54F (as much wine, bread and butter as you want) includes a choice from 2 starters and 3 main courses, cheese AND dessert. 23 rooms. Doubles with shower/wc for 180F.

HÔTEL LE MARINA**

place Gambetta (Centre).
☎ 02.97.47.22.81 ➡ 02.97.47.00.34
TV.

This hotel is above *L'Océan* bar in the drinking area around place Gambetta. Pretty rooms, most of which have been recently refurbished, with views of the harbour and town walls. Comfortable. TV. Ideal if you like to be at the centre of things. Doubles 180–300F.

|●| LE COMMODORE

3 rue Pasteur; it's behind the post office.
☎ 02.97.46.42.62
Closed Sundays and Monday lunchtimes.

Despite being poorly located in a quiet district with little passing trade, this restaurant has built up a steady clientele as a result of its attractive setting and excellent service and cuisine. The nautical decoration is simple, elegant and warm. And there are plenty of delights from the kitchen: fresh ingredients and generous, well-worked recipes. Try the *gravlax* (salmon marinated *à l'aneth*, 62F) or mullet in foil (96F) for a treat. Accompanied by honest, but inexpensive, wines. *Formule* 49F and cheapest set meal 59F for weekday lunchtimes. Other set meals 69–145F.

|●| RESTAURANT ARNAUD LORGEOUX – LE PAVÉ DES HALLES

17 rue des Halles (Centre).
☎ 02.97.47.15.96
Closed Mondays (except July–Sept), Sunday evenings and Jan 2–Feb 12.

This cosy, traditional restaurant occupies two floors of a characterful fourteenth century house in the pedestrian area in the centre of the town. The young owner/chef is full of talent and ambition and has succeeded in attracting a clientele of informed gourmets. His cheapest set meal for 88F (until 8.30pm) makes best use of simple ingredients. The set meal for 129F is really excellent (oyster *pomponettes tièdes en petite ange*, followed by *croustillant* of roast pigeon, cheese and coconut milk blancmange with grated coconut). The menu changes regularly in accordance with what the market has to offer.

SAINT-AVÉ 56890 (4KM N)

☗ LE MOULIN DE LESNÉHUÉ**

route de Monterblanc.
☎ 02.97.60.77.77 ➡ 02.97.60.78.39
Closed Dec 15–Jan 15. **Car park**.

An authentic water mill, with intact machinery, has been converted into a very pleasant hotel with simple good taste. Twelve rooms have shower, wc and telephone for 260F, or pay 280F for a room with a bath (200F Oct–end March). Peace and quiet is guaranteed even though you are only 30 minutes from the popular tourist areas.

|●| LE PRESSOIR

7 rue de l'Hôpital.
☎ 02.97.60.87.63
Closed Sunday evenings, Mondays, the first 2 weeks of March, the first week of July and the first 2 weeks of October. **Car park**.

Exceptional surroundings and comfort, a warm welcome and gastronomic delights in this attractive house located outside the town. Quite simply the best restaurant in the district. *Galette* of mullet with potato and rosemary, panfried sausage *au foie gras*, buckwheat tagliatelle, etc. The cheapest set meal is 130F (only on weekday lunchtimes) – worth going out of your way to try it. Other set meals for 200–400F.

LOCQUELTAS 56390 (6KM N)

10% ☗ |●| HÔTEL LA VOLTIGE**

8 rte de Vannes (North); take the Locminé road towards the airport.
☎ 02.97.60.72.06 ➡ 02.97.44.63.01
Closed 2 weeks in February and 2 weeks in October. Restaurant closed Mondays. **Car park**. **TV**.

A dozen well thought-out rooms for 210–285F, redecorated and impeccably clean. Check out the rooms for 3 or 4 people which have a mezzanine. Great! Half-board 215–250F, attractive because of the rather good traditional food. Cheapest set meal 72F. Garden.

ARRADON 56610 (8KM SW)

☗ |●| HÔTEL-RESTAURANT LE STIVELL***

rue Plessis-d'Arradon; take the D101.
☎ 02.97.44.03.15 ➡ 02.97.44.78.90
Restaurant closed Sunday evenings and Mondays off season, the first week in January and Nov 15–Dec 15. **Car park**. **TV**.

Located in one of the prettiest parts of the coast of Morbihan. Tennis courts nearby. Comfortable double rooms for 260–375F. Set meals 55F (weekday lunchtimes) to 235F. The chef is inspired by the sea – highly appropriate for Brittany. Seafood *choucroute*, warm oysters in champagne, etc. Ideal for those who like the serenity of the sea without having to stray too far from Vannes.

LARMOR-BADEN 56870 (19KM SW)

10% ☗ |●| HÔTEL DU CENTRE**

3 route de Vannes.
☎ 02.97.57.04.68 ➡ 02.97.57.20.94
Car park. **TV**.

Kept by the same family for three generations. The kind of hotel that has proved its worth over the years. Over a dozen rooms 210–280F and set meals 76–180F. Appetising menu: salad of chicken wings and ginger, seafood *choucroute* and pear in puff pastry with butterscotch sauce.

VITRÉ 35500

10% HÔTEL DU CHÂTEAU**

5 rue Rallon (Centre).
☎ 02.99.74.58.59 F 02.99.75.35.47
Secure parking. **TV**.

Quiet street. View of the château from the second floor up. Well-kept rooms, provincial atmosphere, 155–245F. Friendly welcome.

10% HÔTEL LE MINOTEL**

47 rue Poterie (Centre).
☎ 02.99.75.11.11 F 02.99.75.81.26

This rebuilt hotel in the old town fits in well with the prevailing style and offers modern comforts (although a bit too run-of-the-mill). Green and tartan décor in the manner of a golf clubhouse. Doubles 280–320F depending on size. Good welcome.

AUBERGE SAINT-LOUIS

31 rue Notre-Dame (Centre).
☎ 02.99.75.28.28
Closed Mondays and Sunday evenings.

Set in a fifteenth century house, this inn has a good reputation. The wood panelling in the dining room creates a sophisticated yet family-style atmosphere. The young proprietor offers appetisers with all the set meals. The feast then continues with a good selection of grilled meats and superb fish, accompanied by well-crafted sauces. Proper tablecloths and serviettes. Cheapest set meals 69F (weekdays), others at 89F, 115F and 135F.

CENTRE

18 Cher

28 Eure-et-Loir

36 Indre

37 Indre-et-Loire

41 Loir-et-Cher

45 Loiret

AMBOISE 37400

10% ☗ |●| HÔTEL-RESTAURANT DU LION D'OR**

17 quai Charles-Guinot (Centre); it faces the Loire and is near the château.
☎ 02.47.57.00.23 F➔ 02.47.23.22.49
Closed Sunday evenings and Mondays Nov 1–April 1, and Nov 15–Dec 15. **Secure parking** (pay-as-you-use garage).

Lunch served noon–2pm and dinner 7–9pm. The hotel has a few rooms overlooking the river. The standard of housekeeping is a bit uneven, so ask to see the room beforehand if possible. Doubles from 200F – prices are higher in season. Half-board is available. The dining room, decorated in olde worlde French style, is known for its cooking and offers set meals ranging in price from 86–193F. A typical set meal might consist of snails with mushrooms, lamb with port, salmon scollops with nettles, cheese and dessert. Nice brasserie set meal for 68F.

|●| RESTAURANT L'ÉPICERIE

46 place Michel-Debré (Centre); it's opposite the château **Car park**.
☎ 02.47.57.08.94
Closed Monday evenings and Tuesdays (except June 15–Sept 15). **Car park**.

Lunch served noon–2pm and dinner 7–10pm. A magnificent looking half-timbered building the colour of a good claret. Its specialities are fricassee of veal sweetbreads and kidneys, salmon with sorrel, duck in a wine sauce, and homemade *foie gras*. The cheapest set meal is 68F (not available Saturday evenings, Sundays and certain evenings in summer); others start at 110F. The one at 185F includes apéritif, wine and coffee. Service is sometimes a bit slow but the food is worth the wait.

POCÉ-SUR-CISSE 37530 (3KM N)

|●| CAVES DE LA CROIX VERTE

20 route d'Amboise; on the D431 from Amboise.
☎ 02.47.57.03.65 F➔ :02.47.57.03.65
Closed Monday and Tuesday evenings mid-Sept–May, and Sunday evenings. **Car park**.

This place will help you forget all the times you've been ripped off just because you're a tourist. You'll get a pleasant welcome from Émmanuelle, who'll give you all the time you need to decide which of the set meals – they range in price from 55F (weekdays) to 150F– you're going to have. This former wine cellar offers first-rate home cooking and simple dishes of the kind that need long slow cooking – things like *terrine* of goat's cheese curds with artichokes and horseradish salad and panfried plaice with a flan of potatoes and *beurre blanc*.

BLÉRÉ 37150 (10KM S)

☗ |●| HÔTEL-RESTAURANT LE CHEVAL BLANC**

place de l'Église (Centre).
☎ 02.47.30.30.14 F➔ 02.47.23.52.80
Closed Sunday evenings and Mondays (except in July and August), and in January. **Secure parking**. **TV**.

This is a delightful hotel housed in a 17th century building. Rooms are prettily arranged and prices start at 300F for a double with shower/wc. However, it's known primarily for

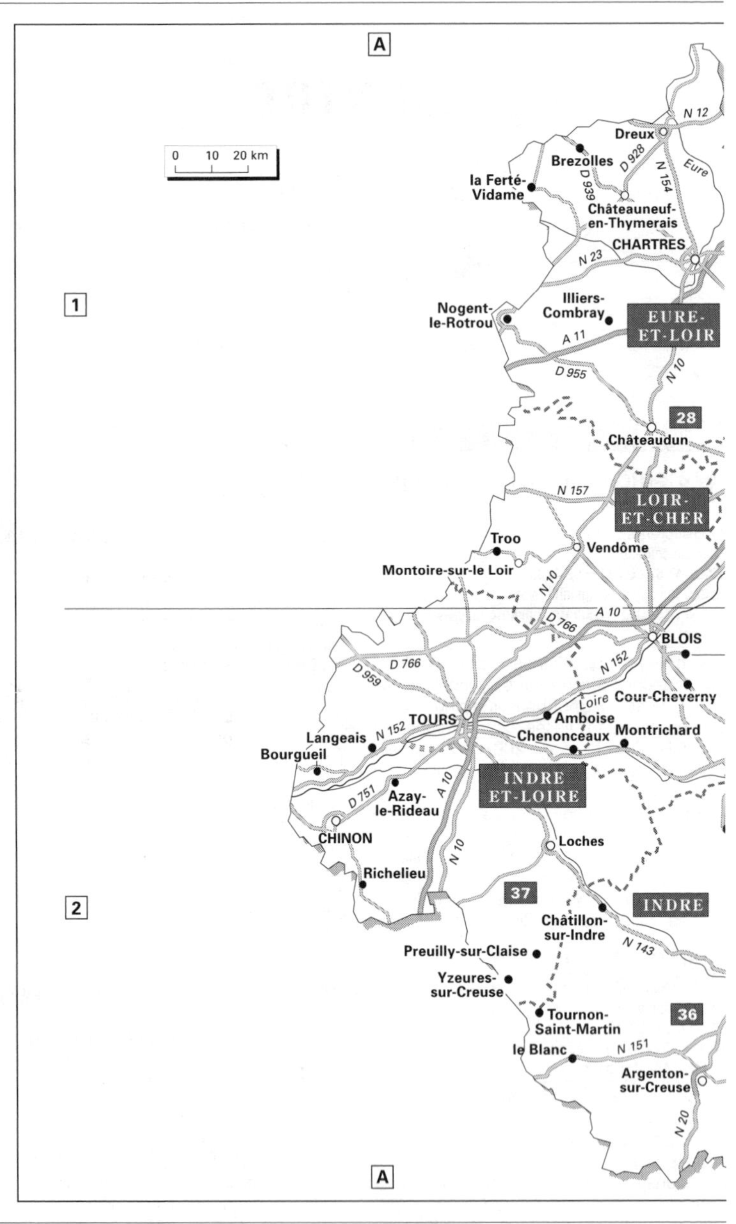
A
0 10 20 km
1
2
Dreux
N 12
Brezolles
D 928
N 154
Eure
la Ferté-
Vidame
D 939
Châteauneuf-
en-Thymerais
CHARTRES
N 23
Nogent-
le-Rotrou
Illiers-
Combray
EURE-
ET-LOIR
A 11
D 955
N 10
28
Châteaudun
N 157
LOIR-
ET-CHER
Troo
Vendôme
Montoire-sur-le Loir
N 10
A 10
D 766
BLOIS
D 766
D 959
N 152
Loire
Cour-Cheverny
TOURS
Amboise
Langeais
N 152
Chenonceaux
Montrichard
Bourgueil
INDRE
ET-LOIRE
D 751
Azay-
le-Rideau
A 10
CHINON
N 10
Loches
Richelieu
37
INDRE
Châtillon-
sur-Indre
N 143
Preuilly-sur-Claise
Yzeures-
sur-Creuse
Tournon-
Saint-Martin
36
le Blanc
N 151
Argenton-
sur-Creuse
N 20
A

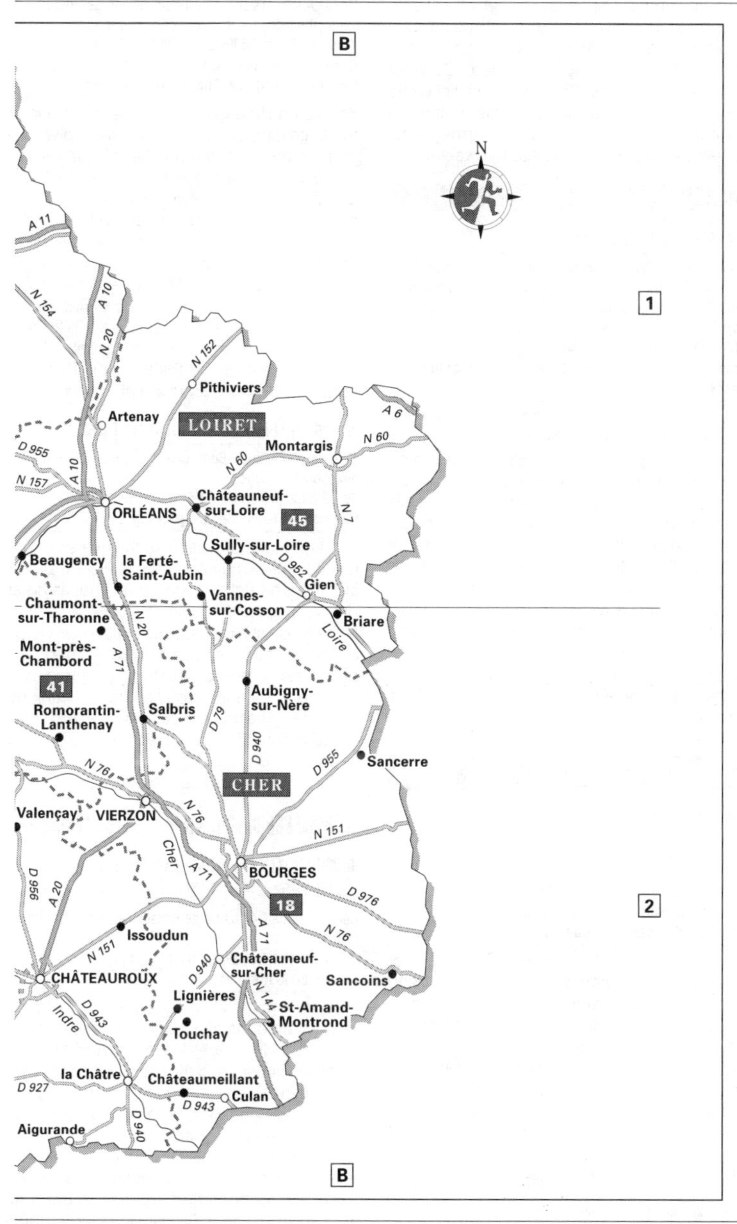
B
N
1
A 11
N 154
A 10
N 20
N 152
Pithiviers
Artenay
LOIRET
A 6
N 60
Montargis
D 955
N 60
A 10
N 157
Châteauneuf-
sur-Loire
ORLÉANS
45
N 7
Sully-sur-Loire
D 952
Beaugency
la Ferté-
Saint-Aubin
Gien
Vannes-
sur-Cosson
Chaumont-
sur-Tharonne
Briare
N 20
Loire
Mont-près-
Chambord
A 71
41
Aubigny-
sur-Nère
Romorantin-
Lanthenay
Salbris
D 79
D 940
D 955
Sancerre
N 76
CHER
Valençay
VIERZON
N 76
N 151
Cher
D 956
A 20
A 71
BOURGES
D 976
18
N 76
A 71
Issoudun
N 151
D 940
Châteauneuf-
sur-Cher
CHÂTEAUROUX
Sancoins
Lignières
Indre
D 943
N 144
St-Amand-
Montrond
Touchay
la Châtre
Châteaumeillant
D 927
D 943
Culan
D 940
Aigurande
2
B

the cooking of Michel Blériot, which is fresh, light and inventive. The 95F set meal (available weekdays only) represents some of the best value for money in the area. Gourmet set meals 200F and 270F. The wine list offers good regional wines and the restaurant has a superb collection of vintage Armagnacs. Reservations are essential at the weekend.

CANGEY 37530 (12KM N)

LE FLEURAY**

Route Dame Marie; if you're coming from Amboise, take the N152 in the direction of Blois, then turn left and take the D74 as far as Cangey.
☎ 02.47.56.09.25 F➔ 02.47.56.93.97
Closed during the school holidays (except in summer); restaurant closed lunchtimes. **Car park**. **Disabled access**.

This 19th century manorhouse, surrounded by greenery, is a cross between a hotel and a guest house. Hazel and Peter Newington have called all eleven of their prettily decorated rooms after flowers – "Capucine" (nasturtium) and "Perce-Neige" (snowdrop) are bigger than the others – and doubles start at 315F. The pleasant dining room offers gourmet cooking, with set meals from 125F. You must have a reservation. The Newingtons have shown that it is possible to be simple and welcoming, even in an area as touristy as Amboise, and to prove it, their customers come from all four corners of the globe.

ARGENTON-SUR-CREUSE 36200

10% HÔTEL-RESTAURANT DE LA GARE ET TERMINUS**

7 rue de la Gare (North).
☎ 02.54.01.10.81 F➔ 02.54.24.02.54
Closed Mondays and the second and third week in January. **Car park**. **TV**. **Canal+**.

After a trip to the Musée de la Chemiserie or a tour of the churches of Saint-Sauveur and Saint-Benoît, it's rather pleasant to sit down to a meal of zander and salmon with oyster mushrooms followed by a *feuilleté* of pears with chocolate sauce. This is what good regional cooking is all about. The cheapest set meal is 80F and there are others at 120F and 170F. The hotel is simple and has decent facilities. Rooms 115–280F. Numbers 4 and 10 overlook the courtyard.

10% HÔTEL-RESTAURANT LE CHEVAL NOIR**

27 rue Auclert-Descottes (Centre) How to get there: follow the signs for Gargilesse-Dampierre.
☎ 02.54.24.00.06 F➔ 02.54.24.11.22
Closed Sunday evenings out of season.
Secure parking. **TV**. **Canal+**. **Disabled access**.

You can quite easily imagine Balzac sitting in this large dining room with the polished wooden floor and ordering a salad of skate *vinaigrette* with tomato and lemon, panfried veal *piccata* with seasonal vegetables, and cherry *clafoutis*. Ask to be seated at the front of the dining room – there's a table at the back reserved for large groups and it can be quite noisy there. Set meals 90F (weekdays), 130F, 160F et 240F. Children's menu 50F. Rooms are quiet and comfortable – numbers 23, 26 and 29 have just been renovated. Doubles 250F (with shower/wc) and 280F (bath). There's a terrace in the inner courtyard of the hotel.

10% MANOIR DE BOISVILLERS**

11 rue du Moulin-de-Bord (Centre); by the N20 in the direction of Limoges.
☎ 02.54.24.13.88 F➔ 02.54.24.27.83
Closed Dec 1–15. **Secure parking**. **TV**.

The first stone of what was the riverside residence of the Chevalier de Boisvillers was laid in 1759. This uncommon country house hotel deserves more than two stars: the reception is the kind usually associated with much larger hotels, the décor is elegant, the fitted carpet muffles every sound, the little lounge next to the bar is friendly, you can have a drink by the pool in the grounds, and peace and quiet are all around. Doubles are 300–380F, which is not bad considering the facilities. People even come from abroad to stay here.

GARGILESSE-DAMPIERRE 36190 (13KM SE)

HÔTEL-RESTAURANT DES ARTISTES*

Centre; by the D48 as far as Badecon-le-Pin, then the D40.
☎ 02.54.47.84.05 F➔ 02.54.47.72.41
Closed Sunday evenings out of season.

When you get to Gargilesse-Dampierre, you'll see a sign to the effect that this is one of the most beautiful villages in France. And it is! The setting is superb and the village has been well preserved. It's easy to understand why novelist George Sand described "this garden created by Nature on both sides of the Creuse" as being Berry's oasis. If you're an admirer of hers, then this place is a must. It was renovated not too long ago and has doubles at 160F (with basin), 200F (with shower/wc) and 220F (with bath). The restaurant goes in for traditional dishes along the lines of rabbit *terrine* and veal kidneys. Set meals 75F, 105F and 165F. Children's menu 45F.

RESTAURANT CHEZ BERNADETTE

centre.
☎ 02.54.47.84.16
Closed Tuesday evenings out of season.

It's not much to look at – the local caff is the first thing that springs to mind, actually – and it's hard to imagine that you can eat well here and at no great cost. And yet people come from miles around for Bernadette's cooking, even though they never know quite what they'll be eating. Sometimes it's game (venison or boar in season) and often it's fish (sole, monkfish, salmon), but it's always a surprise because there's no menu and what Bernadette cooks depends on what she finds at the market. The bill in any case won't come to much. On weekdays, there's a "working man's" set meal at 50F and on Sundays a "middle-class" one at 80F.

AUBIGNY-SUR-NÈRE 18700

HÔTEL-RESTAURANT LA CHAUMIÈRE**

1 av. du Parc-des-Sports (North).
☎ 02.48.58.04.01 Fax 02.48.58.10.31
Closed Sunday evenings (except in July and August) and Monday lunchtimes. **Secure parking**. **TV**.

A very comfortable establishment with a thatched roof. The decoration of the rooms is up to standard, as is the reception. Small doubles 225F (with shower/wc or bath). The cheapest weekday set meal is 90F. Prices are decidedly more expensive at the weekend, when the cheapest set meal is 140F! Berry is known for its witches and if you're interested in them and their history, there's a museum of witchcraft with activities and all that sort of thing. You'll find the museum at Blancafort, a few kilometres from Aubigny-sur-Nère. Paying car park 20 F.

ARGENT-SUR-SAULDRE 18410 (10KM N)

LE RELAIS DU COR D'ARGENT

39 rue Nationale; it's set back from the D940, coming from Aubigny-sur-Nère.
☎ 02.48.73.63.49 Fax 02.48.73.37.55
Closed Tuesday evenings and Wednesdays (except in July and August), and mid-Feb to mid-March. **TV**.

Country-chic interior, with hunting memorabilia on the walls, a few copper pots, stuffed partridges and pheasants, and country flowers on the tables. The delicious smells wafting from Laurent Lafon's kitchen hint at the gastronomic delights to come, all of them typical Berry dishes – duck *confit*, *terrine* of venison, braised pig's cheeks with sauces that, as tradition demands, are perfection itself. Set meals from 78F. It's well worth spending the night in one of the seven tastefully renovated rooms that combine the charm of highly polished old-fashioned furniture and the comfort of modern bedding. Doubles 190–270F.

OIZON 18700 (10KM SE)

RESTAURANT LE BIEN ALLER

Les Naudins; by the D89 and follow the arrows you'll start to see 1km from the château de la Verrerie.
☎ 02.48.58.03.92.
Closed Wednesdays, two weeks in February, and two weeks in September. **Car park**.

Lunch served noon–1.30pm and dinner 7–9pm. Depending on the season, you'll be offered lamb stew with tarragon, pork fillet with lemon, seafood *choucroute*, fresh duck *foie gras*, snails, and apple strudel. Diners eat in relaxed surroundings in this former grocer's shop, choosing to sit either in the bar by the fireplace or in the small dining room. The menu, like the paintings displayed on the walls, changes regularly. The cheapest set meal is 68F (weekdays) and there are others at 98F and 138F, not exactly prices that will break the bank. A restaurant with style run by Dany et Jean who are in love.. with the business.

VAILLY-SUR-SAULDRE 18260 (17KM E)

LE LIÈVRE GOURMAND

14 Grand-Rue; by the D923 in the direction of Sancerre.
☎ 02.48.73.80.23
Closed Sunday evenings, Mondays, and mid-Jan–mid-Feb.

This old Berry house belongs to Australian William Page, whose cooking makes inspired use of spices – close your eyes and imagine poached leg of semi-cured duck with Szechuan peppercorns and salad of smoked red chicory, oven-baked lamb with spinach and green pepper flan, warm white chocolate, rum and coffee tart, and warm passion fruit soufflé. The specialities are so delicious, not to say poetic, that we'd like to give you the entire menu, but what's on offer changes with the season. Set meals 90F, 140F and 185F. Mr Page has some of his native Australia's vintages in the cellar. Be adventurous and try this restaurant – it's one of a kind.

AZAY-LE-RIDEAU 37190

10% HÔTEL DE BIENCOURT**

7 rue Balzac (Centre); it's in the pedestrian street leading to the château.
☎ 02.47.45.20.75 F 02.47.45.91.73
Closed Nov 15–March 1.
Car park. TV. Disabled access.

The inn is in a beautiful Tours house dating from the 18th century. It has a small patio with flowers at the back and 16 comfortable rooms decorated in country or Directoire style. Peace and quiet and beautiful surroundings guaranteed. Good value for money, with doubles at 210F (with shower), 270F with shower/wc (no TV), and 330F (with bath).

HÔTEL-RESTAURANT LE GRAND MONARQUE**

3 place de la République (Centre).
☎ 02.47.45.40.08 F 02.47.45.46.25
Closed Dec 15–Jan 31; restaurant closed Sunday evenings and Mondays Feb 1–March 25 and Nov 1–Dec 15. **Secure parking. TV.**

Service noon–2.30pm and in the evening till 9.30pm. A superb old house, swathed in Virginia creeper and built round a shady courtyard garden that has been turned into a terrace where you can relax and have a drink or a meal in summer. The comfortable bedrooms – 26 in all – start at 320F in high season (ie from mid-June). Cosy décor and lots of character - some of the rooms have exposed beams. Note that half-board from 360F a person is compulsory at weekends and during school holidays.

RESTAURANT L'AIGLE D'OR

10 av. Adélaïde-Richer; head for Langeais.
☎ 02.47.45.24.58 F 02.47.45.90.18
Closed Sunday evenings and Wednesdays, Tuesday evenings out of season, the February school holidays, the first week in September, and Dec 10–20.

Lunch served noon–2pm and dinner 7.30–9pm. Elegant surroundings and attentive service. Meals served in the garden in summer. Set meal weekday lunchtimes 95F. The à la carte menu changes frequently but always has one or two classics like langoustine salad with *foie gras*, *blanquette* of zander, and beef fillet in Chinon. Other set meals 145–270F. The wine list is educational, with maps showing where the numerous wines come from. A very good restaurant.

BEAUGENCY 45190

10% HOSTELLERIE DE L'ÉCU DE BRETAGNE**

place du Martroi (Centre).
☎ 02.38.44.67.60 F 02.38.44.68.07
Closed Mondays Sept 30–April 1 and Sunday evenings.
Secure parking. TV.

Despite the heraldic shields on the wall, the hotel, with an atmosphere reminiscent of a Chabrol film, has no connection with Brittany but derives its name from the Bertons who own the building and whose family has been here since the 15th century, so they're not exactly newcomers! Bedrooms (200–365F) are decorated in soft pastels and are being refurbished. Ask for a room in the hotel (an old coaching inn) rather than in the annex across the way. The restaurant is pricy, but the quality is good. Set meals range in price from 95F (not available Sundays) to 210F.

HÔTEL DE LA SOLOGNE**

6 place Saint-Firmin (Centre).
☎ 02.38.44.50.27 F 02.38.44.90.19
Closed weekends in January and Dec 20–Jan 6.
Car park. TV. Canal+.

The hotel is located in a delightful little square which has an 11th century keep towering over it. This is the historic heart of the town – rue de l'Évêché, which leads into the square, dates from the Middle Ages – and the hotel's handsome stone façade, festooned with geraniums, doesn't look out of place. Quiet well-equipped rooms. Doubles are 230–270F (with shower/wc) and 300–330F (with bath). The hotel is quite delightful. There's a little lounge with ceiling beams and fireplace, a balcony overlooking a flower-filled courtyard, and a conservatory where an enormous philodendron has pride of place. And you won't be able to fault the reception you get either.

AU VIEUX FOURNEAU

12 rue de la Cordonnerie (Centre); it's in the street that starts at the town hall and goes down toward the river.
☎ 02.38.46.40.56 F 02.38.46.40.56
Closed Sunday evenings, Mondays, and Nov 2–23.

The restaurant boasts two large, uncluttered and bright dining rooms where the inevitable old kitchen range has pride of place and also a rather gifted young chef who is livening up the traditional cooking of the area. The cheapest set meal (95F) offers *rémoulade* of endives with olives and cubed *rillons*, a casserole of three different kinds of fish, and a dessert of apples sprinkled with brown sugar that has been caramelized under the grill. Simple but very good and prettily presented. Other set meals 125F, 155F and 185F. Delightful staff.

BLANC (LE) 36300

10% ☗ |●| DOMAINE DE L'ÉTAPE***

route de Bélâbre; drive 5km along the D10 in the direction of Bélâbre.
☎ 02.54.37.18.02 ➡ 02.54.37.75.59
Car park. TV. Disabled access.

Lunch served noon–2pm and dinner 7.30–9.30pm. This magnificent estate, which dates from the last century, is a magical place. It has close to 500 acres of grounds, a lake that covers more than 40 acres, and 35 fully equipped rooms, each decorated in a different style. If there are two of you, you can have a room either in the 19th century château (290F), the more modern lodge (350F) or the rustic farm over by the stables (210F). You can ride over the entire estate (50F an hour) or go fishing for carp, zander and pike in the lake and have your catch cooked in the evening. Great, eh? Set meals 100F and 190F. Children's menu 65F.

☗ HÔTEL DU THÉÂTRE**

2 bis av. Gambetta (Centre).
☎ 02.54.37.68.69 ➡ 02.54.28.03.95
TV.

The tourist office and the town hall are both a stone's throw away from this little hotel, which is right in the centre of town. The rooms are clean, all have bath, and are soundproof to boot. Even so, since the street is extremely busy in summer – it's an alternative route to Paris – ask not to be on that side. Doubles 240F and 250F.

|●| CRÊPERIE DU VIEUX FOUR

16 quai Aubépin; it's on the banks of the Creuse, in the upper part of the city.
☎ 02.54.28.51.28.
Closed Mondays Oct–May.

Lunch served noon–2pm and dinner 7–10pm. The restaurant is an old potter's house that's been nicely converted. The kiln still stands in the flower-filled courtyard where you can have your meal weather permitting. All sorts of *crêpes* are available, with the 34F *crêpe au Pouligny* (a local cheese) and the 35F dessert *crêpe du Blanc* (cherries and two scoops of icecream made with cherries that have been soaked in maraschino) being popular choices. If you're one of those strange people who don't like *crêpes*, you could go ˆ la carte and have a salad with *lardons* and a poached egg (20F), steak and chips (51F) or an omelette – plain (17F) or Berry-style with onions and potatoes (34F). A relaxing place to stop for a meal when you're on the road.

|●| LA FLAMBÉE

22 rue des Gaudières (Centre).
☎ 02.54.37.01.43
Closed Sunday lunchtimes.

A very simple restaurant that's full to overflowing at lunchtime, the attraction being a substantial and inexpensive day's special – something like rabbit *chasseur* and salad topped with melted cheese for 42F, for example. They also have a big selection of very decent pizzas – Sophia Loren at 39F, for example, comes with tomato, cheese, ham and egg – spaghetti with butter (20F), spag bol (39F) and a fast set meal (not available weekends) for 68F that gets you a starter, the day's special, cheese and dessert. There's a terrace in the courtyard for sunny days. Other set meals 105F and 115F.

LINGÉ 36220 (16KM N)

☗ |●| AUBERGE DE LA GABRIÈRE**

La Gabrière; take the D975 in the direction of Azay-le-Ferron then turn onto the D6; when you get to Lingé, follow the signs for La Gabrière and you'll find the inn across from the lake.
☎ 02.54.37.80.97 ➡ 02.54.37.70.66
Disabled access.

The inn, ideally located for birdwatchers (the lake is a bird sanctuary), is also well known locally for its cooking and is always crowded winter and summer alike. Sit on the terrace and treat yourself to the 89F set meal of *terrine*, pig's cheek in a red Valençay or fillets of perch with chive sauce followed by cheese and dessert before setting off to explore. There are several other set meals, including one at 60F (weekdays only) and another at 130F (very substantial). À la carte there's fillet of carp *paysanne* (49F) and fricassee of frog's legs *provençale* (45F). The inn has a number of rooms, some of which overlook the lake. Doubles with shower/wc 195F.

BLOIS 41000

☗ AUBERGE DE JEUNESSE*

18 rue de l'Hôtel-Pasquier; take a number 4 bus in the direction of Les Grouëts and get off at the "Église" stop.

☎ 02.54.78.27.21
Closed 10am–6pm daily and mid-Nov–March.
Car park.

The hostel has 48 beds in two dormitories (one for men, one for women) and charges 61F for the first night (sheets included) and 44F for each night thereafter. Breakfast 19F. A kitchen is available for cooking your meals.

10% HÔTEL ANNE DE BRETAGNE**

31 av. Jean-Laigret; it's 300m from the château and the city centre.
☎ 02.54.78.05.38 Fax 02.54.74.37.79
Closed Feb 21–March 21. **Car park**. **TV**.

A stylish hotel with a welcoming atmosphere and a quiet bar for people who need to talk. It has 29 slightly noisy but pleasant rooms at prices ranging from 210F to 375F (shower or bath and phone).

10% HÔTEL LE SAVOIE**

6 rue Ducoux (North-West); it's in the street across from the station.
☎ 02.54.74.32.21 Fax 02.54.74.29.58.
TV. **Canal+**.

This is a nice little hotel – the atmosphere is reminiscent of a guest house – away from the hustle and bustle of the tourist area. Rooms are clean and bright and doubles start at 230F. Reckon on 280F for one with bath. Buffet-style breakfast 30F. Advisable to book. You'll get a very nice welcome.

RESTAURANT CÔTÉ SEL CÔTÉ COUR

5 rue du Grenier-à-Sel; it's in the old part of the city.
☎ 02.54.56.17.18.
Closed Monday lunchtimes and Sundays.

The restaurant is housed in a converted sculptor's studio in the part of Blois where the craftsmen attached to the court lived. With place Vauvert and its 15th century barn on one side and the second-hand shops on the other (this is where the terrace is), the entire neighbourhood provides inspiration for local artists and is a bargain-hunter's paradise. You can buy anything here, from an original painting to a set of fish knives. The food is always faultlessly presented but it's not really anything special. There's rollmops (48F), warm goat's cheese salad (35F) and duck specialities, and they do set meals at 68F and 90F (fish *terrine*, chilli con carne, cheese, dessert, and a glass of wine).

RESTAURANT LA GARBURE

36 rue Saint-Lubin (South-West); it's in the old part of the city, between the market place and the stairs leading to the château.
☎ 02.54.74.32.89.
Closed Wednesday and Saturday lunchtimes.

This restaurant, housed in a Louis XV building has two dining rooms. The main one has exposed beams while the tiny second one in the cellar is now used only for groups, unfortunately. Whichever one you end up in, you'll be treated to delicious specialities from the south-west of the country, things like breast of fattened duck *au torchon*, duck *confit* with potatoes and truffles and of course the hearty traditional soup called *garbure*, which they make here with cabbage, swedes, carrots, Toulouse sausage, wingtips, and drumsticks. Set meals 79F (weekdays) and 89F.

RESTAURANT LES BANQUETTES ROUGES

16 rue des Trois-Marchands; it's in the heart of the old city.
☎ 02.54.78.74.92.
Closed Sunday lunchtimes.

Service from noon and 7–11pm. A friendly little restaurant that takes its name from its red bench seats – it must be quite a squash sometimes, for there are always lots of regulars, winter and summer alike. Even tourists who drop in to ask for a glass of water or to use the loos are met with a smile. The food is traditional and beautifully presented. The cheapest set meal (not available Saturday evenings) is 89F. It changes every day but always consists of starter, main course, and dessert. There's another set meal at 130F and they also have some very handsome fish dishes à la carte. One of our favourite places in the area.

LE BISTROT DU CUISINIER

20 quai Villebois-Mareuil; it faces the Loire, 50m from pont Gabriel (also known as the Vieux Pont).
☎ 02.54.78.06.70 Fax 02.54.74.81.75
Disabled access.

Lunch served noon–3pm and dinner 7–11pm. You'll get a wonderful view of the city here and very good value for money in the large and unpretentious dining room. Set meals 94F and 132F. The cooking is full of flavour and you'll be served generous portions by the cook himself who comments on the dishes and is quite happy to pass on his secrets. His specialities include *andouillette* in puff pastry with a mustard and pepper sauce, fillet of perch in a cep sauce, braised ox cheek *parmentier*, and veal kidneys with green cabbage. The wine list is full of the best the Loire has to offer. Once a month or so, the proprietor introduces his customers to the cooking of other countries and other regions of France by offering them, in addition to their usual fare, traditional dishes from places like Poland, Russia, Italy, Louisiana, Spain and Provence.

|●| AU BOUCHON LYONNAIS

25 rue des Violettes (Centre); head for place Louis XII.
☎ 02.54.74.12.87
Closed Mondays, Sundays, and January.

Lunch served noon–2pm and dinner 5–10pm. Blois has everything, even a genuine traditional Lyon bistro with specialities like warm *saucisson*, salad *lyonnais* with warm lentils, eye of ribsteak in a Beaujolais sauce, calf's head, and grilled salmon escalope at prices that are really very reasonable given the quality and quantity. The cheapest set meal is 115F. Moreover, the setting is a superb Louis XII house and there's a terrace for sunny days. What more could you ask for?

|●| AU RENDEZ-VOUS DES PÊCHEURS

27 rue Foix; follow the château moat or take the RN152 along the north bank of the Loire.
☎ 02.54.74.67.48 ➡ 02.54.74.47.67
Closed Monday lunchtimes (all day if it's a public holiday), Sundays, one week in February, and three weeks in August. **Car park**.

If you don't like fish, just keep going. If you do, you'll love this great little bistro. You won't be doing it anything but justice if you decide to push the boat out (excuse the pun) and have the one and only set meal at 145F. It changes every week but just to give you an idea of the delights in store, we had asparagus and langoustines, panfried bream with some *escabèche* to give it a bit of a kick, and a dark chocolate *fondant*. And when it comes to choosing a wine to wash it down with, take the chef's advice. He knows what he's talking about.

MOLINEUF 41190 (9KM W)

|●| RESTAURANT DE LA POSTE

11, av. de Blois; take the D766 in the direction of Angers.
☎ 02.54.70.03.25 ➡ 02.54.70.12.46
Closed Wednesdays, Sunday evenings, and February.

Lunch served noon–2pm and dinner 7.30–9.30pm. You must stop at this little restaurant on the outskirts of Molineuf and treat yourself to some of the delicious creations of chef Thierry Poidras. There's cold crab soufflé, fillet of beef in a Chinon sauce, breast of chicken topped with *millefeuille* of leeks and shrimp, and boned young rabbit. Set meals are 89F (this one comes with cheese or dessert and isn't available on Sundays), 115F (cheese and dessert), 139F and 165F. Attentive service. An extremely good restaurant.

CANDÉ-SUR-BEUVRON 41120 (15KM SW)

10% 🏠 |●| LA CAILLÈRE**

36 route des Montils (South; take the D173 along the south bank of the Loire.
☎ 02.54.44.03.08 ➡ 02.54.44.00.95
Closed Wednesdays and January and February.
Car park. TV. Disabled access.

This is a delightful hotel cum restaurant housed in a sympathetically converted 18th century farmhouse. It has 14 rooms in all and doubles with shower/wc start at 330F. Some are wholly accessible to the disabled. The restaurant is well-known locally for its cooking and it's advisable to book. There are a number of good set meals on offer, ranging in price from 92F (not available weekends or public holidays) to 278F. Specialities, which vary with the season, are calf sweetbreads with a sauce of morels and *crème fraîche*, pigeon in a garlic sauce, sautéd sea bass with shrimp butter, frogs, and snails in a chive sauce. And if that doesn't make your mouth water then nothing will! Half-board 398F per person per day. In summer, meals are served in the very pleasant garden.

CHITENAY 41120 (15KM S)

🏠 |●| L'AUBERGE DU CENTRE**

place de l'Église (Centre); take the D956 as far as Cellettes and then the D38.
☎ 02.54.70.42.11 ➡ 02.54.70.35.03
Closed Sunday evenings and Mondays out of season and Feb 18–March 4. **Secure parking. TV. Disabled access.**

The classical frontage gives no hint of the very handsome interior or of the haven of peace and quiet to be found in the pleasant garden. Completely refurbished rooms have sophisticated décor and are well equipped. Doubles 335–395F. The restaurant has set meals at 108F (not available Saturday evenings, Sundays or public holidays), 146F and more. The specialities – they include guinea fowl with morels, game in season, *tartare* of sea bass and tuna with dill and fennel, and snails in puff pastry – are good. And you'll get a friendly welcome to boot.

CHAUMONT-SUR-LOIRE 41150 (18KM SW)

|●| RESTAURANT LA CHANCELIÈRE

1 rue de Bellevue; it faces the Loire very near the château.

☎ 02.54.20.96.95 ➡ 02.54.33.91.71
Closed Wednesday evenings and Thursdays in summer, three weeks from November 12, and Jan 15–Feb 8.
Disabled access.

Lunch served noon–2pm and dinner 7–9pm. This restaurant's reputation continues to grow. It has two dining rooms, one decorated in restrained country fashion, the other tending more towards the pretty. The style of the cooking is fresh and the flavours are delicate. The chef, who trained in the kitchens of Barriers and the Troisgros brothers offers dishes such as halibut with a lobster *coulis*, zander with *beurre blanc*, and a house terrine of *foie gras*. The meat is tender and the desserts first rate. Excellent value for money. The cheapest set meal is 79F (not available Sundays), followed by one at 118F. If you plump for the one at 152F or 200F, you're in for a feast. Staff can't do enough for you and service comes with a smile.

BOURGES 18000

SEE MAP OVERLEAF

☗ |●| HÔTEL-RESTAURANT LE CARNOT*

53 av. Carnot. Off map **C3-1**
☎ 02.48.67.08.94
Closed Saturdays and Sunday mornings.

Pleasant quiet rooms, with doubles 100–150F. Meals can be provided (55–65F) in the brasserie. Full board 180F. Good place if you're stuck and working to a budget.

10% ☗ L'AGRICULTURE**

18 bd de Juranville and 15 rue du Prinal; it's opposite the île d'Or stadium. **MAP A2-3**
☎ 02.48.70.40.84 ➡ 02.48.65.50.58
Secure parking. **TV**.

You'll get a very warm welcome indeed from Mme Maigret (but remember, she's heard all the jokes before!) and if you bring up the subject of animals she'll tell you about the farm she dreams of having in Sologne. Luckily for us she hasn't found the ideal spot yet and still gets a lot of pleasure out of looking after her guests. If you arrive by car, enter by the door opposite the car park. Rooms are quiet and pretty and have been completely refurbished. Doubles 160–280F. Numbers 15–19 go for 250F and they're air conditioned and have exposed beams. Everything has a price though – they're on the top floor! Bedsits available for rent.

10% ☗ HÔTEL LES TILLEULS**

7 place de la Pyrotechnie. Off map **C3-2**
☎ 02.48.20.49.04 ➡ 02.48.50.61.73
Closed Dec 24–Jan 3. **Car park**. **TV**. **Canal+**.
Disabled access.

It may be a bit away from the centre but it'll suit you very well if you're tired or if you and your partner are desperate for some peace and quiet. It has a beautiful garden and pretty rooms with bath. Doubles 270F. The minibars in the rooms are well stocked up but if you need physical exercise in order to wind down, you can work out in the gym or hire a mountain bike.

|●| LE COMPTOIR DE PARIS

1 rue Édouard-Vaillant. **MAP B2-15**
☎ 02.48.24.17.16
Car park.

Lunch served 11.30–2pm and dinner 6.30–10pm. You honestly can't miss this place – just look for the bright red frontage among all those wonderful mediaeval houses in the prettiest square in Bourges! The décor's a bit more subdued inside, being all wood. You'll find a friendly atmosphere and lots of animated conversation going on too. The people who embody all that's lively and creative about Bourges can be found here tucking into an *andouillette à l'ancienne*. Decent simple meals start at 59F. We preferred the downstairs dining room, which we thought was cosier.

|●| RESTAURANT LA COURCILLIÈRE

rue de Babylone; head for avenue Marx-Dormoy and look for a narrow street off to the right. Off map **C1-19**
☎ 02.48.24.41.91.
Closed Tuesday evenings, Wednesdays, and during the February school holidays. **Car park**. **Disabled access**.

An air of magic and mystery seems to surround this restaurant deep in the marshes on the banks of the Yèvre. The food consists of regional specialities all lovingly prepared by Denis Julien and there are set meals at 89F and 125F with excellent house *terrines* and ling fillets with mint from the garden. The place has been renovated throughout and the décor – handsome wooden furniture, small aviary, lots of flowers and so on – is very pleasing. Have your meal on the terrace overlooking the quiet Yèvre and enjoy the waterlilies. Everything's genuine here, from Annie's smile to the local accent of the gardeners, and you feel so relaxed that you lose all sense of time.

|●| LE SOUFFLÉ CHAUD

41 bd de Strasbourg; it's at the end of the street, behind the cathedral. **MAP C3-22**
☎ 02.48.20.06.80
Closed Mondays, Sunday evenings, three weeks in February, and two weeks in August.

Alban Mestre has used natural wood and soft pastels in his restaurant, and given it a large conservatory and a trompe l'œil garden. The result can probably best be described as elegant and low-key, words that could also be applied to Mestre himself. His specialities are fillet of duck and leg *confit* (the duck in question is a *mulard*, a cross bred specifically for *foie gras* and *confit*), plaice fillets with mushrooms *en paupiette*, and warm soufflés (try one with seasonal fruit and raspberry liqueur, which is just bursting with flavour). There's a set meal at 90F (not available Saturday evenings or Sundays) and *menus-carte* at 120F and 148F (with cheese). This is cooking of a very high level at very affordable prices.

|●| RESTAURANT LE JARDIN GOURMAND

15 bis av. Ernest-Renan; follow the signs for Nevers until you get to carrefour Malus. Off map **C3-20**
☎ 02.48.21.35.91
Closed Sunday evenings, Mondays, two weeks in July, and mid-Dec–mid-Jan. **Car park. Disabled access.**

Lunch served noon–1.45pm and dinner 7.30–9.30pm. This is a very pleasant restaurant with something of a reputation among local gourmets who come for a good meal in delightful surroundings. The dining room has handsome woodwork, lots of flowers and watercolours on the walls. Staff are pleasant, the service is unobtrusive and the cooking shows the same refinement as the décor. Specialities are roast *confit* leg of young rabbit, topside of veal *en paupiette* with langoustines, stuffed sea bass with citrus fruit, and game in season. Set meal 95F. You can eat in the garden, weather permitting. Another good restaurant in Bourges.

|●| RESTAURANT PHILIPPE LARMAT

62 bis bd Gambetta. **MAP A1-21**
☎ 02.48.70.79.00
Closed Sunday evenings, Mondays, and Aug 16–Sept 2.

The restaurant has become a must for local gourmets. It's the kind of place that says "Relax, enjoy yourself and let us take care of everything". Tables are spaced quite far apart and as you're escorted to yours, your every footstep will be muffled by the thick carpet. The 140F set meal represents excellent value for money but if you can't afford that the one at 95F (not available Friday evenings or weekends) is equally enjoyable. We were impressed with a few of the specialities served at the bar, including zander in a wine sauce with shallots, pigeon *en crépine*, and red gurnard in a sharp sauce. This is a well-known and stylish restaurant but it's not stiff and starchy.

ALLOGNY 18110 (18KM NW)

|●| RESTAURANT LE CHABUR

route de Mehun-sur-Yèvre; take the D944 in the direction of direction Neuvy-sur-Barangeon.
☎ 02.48.64.00.41 F→ 02.48.64.04.87
Closed Wednesdays, two weeks in January, and three weeks in September. **Car park.**

Service noon–10pm. This inn, deep in the forest, is a pretty nice place. The witches of Berry, who're supposed to have had their meetings around here, must have left some good vibrations behind them. Marie-Jo and Gérard serve good snacks, warm goat's cheese salads and cheese dishes like cream cheese with herbs and cream. Generous portions. Set meals (lunchtime only) 49F, 62F and 78F; Sundays 78F and 103F. It's à la carte only in the evening.

BOURGUEIL 37140

10% ⌂ |●| L'ÉCU DE FRANCE

9 rue de Tours (Centre); it's near the abbey.
☎ 02.47.97.70.18
Closed Sunday evenings and Mondays out of season, early June, one week in mid-October, and the Christmas and New Year holidays. **Secure parking.**

The inn, a handsome building that dates from 1637, is simple, comfortable and welcoming. It has nine rooms with shower/wc for 200F. The restaurant offers good local cooking, set meals at 55F (the cheapest, and available weekday lunchtimes only) and 78–180F, and dishes like *tarte tourangelle* (with a mixture of haricot and French beans), *rillons de Touraine*, *coq au vin* or one of the restaurant's fish specialities. And of course they have Saint-Nicolas-de-Bourgueil in carafe.

|●| RESTAURANT L'AUBERGE LA LANDE

Follow the signs for the cave touristique.
☎ 02.47.97.92.41
Closed Mondays, Sunday evenings, and January.
Car park.

The restaurant, in a very pleasant old bourgeois house, is a bit outside the village. If you're looking for good honest traditional cooking with no pretentions to be something it's not, then this is the place for you. Dishes include a warm salad of skate and potatoes, *coq au vin* (the wine being a Bourgueil) and eel stew. Set meals 50–145F. There are regular promotions of AOC Bourgueils at special prices.

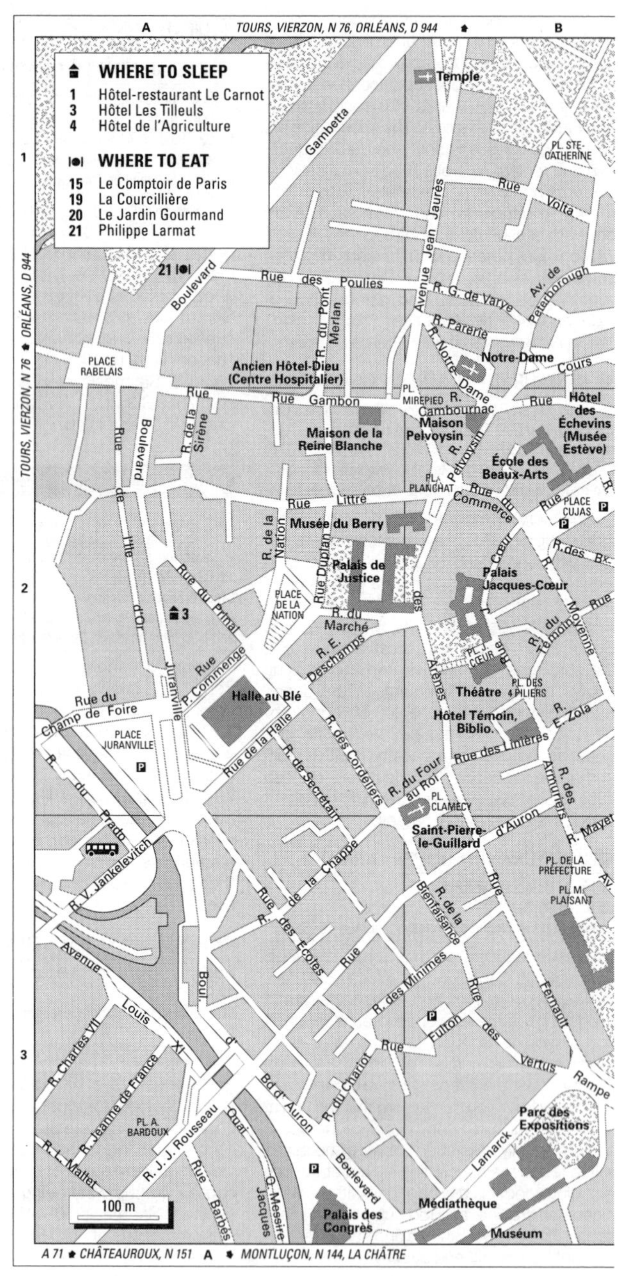
WHERE TO SLEEP
1 Hôtel-restaurant Le Carnot
3 Hôtel Les Tilleuls
4 Hôtel de l'Agriculture
WHERE TO EAT
15 Le Comptoir de Paris
19 La Courcillière
20 Le Jardin Gourmand
21 Philippe Larmat
TOURS, VIERZON, N 76, ORLÉANS, D 944
A 71 CHÂTEAUROUX, N 151
MONTLUÇON, N 144, LA CHÂTRE
Temple
PL. STE-CATHERINE
Rue Volta
Gambetta
Avenue Jean Jaurès
Av. de Peterborough
Rue des Poulies
R. du Pont Merlan
R. G. de Varye
R. Parerie
R. Notre-Dame
Notre-Dame
Cours
PLACE RABELAIS
Ancien Hôtel-Dieu (Centre Hospitalier)
Rue Gambon
PL. MIREPIED
R. Cambournac
Hôtel des Échevins (Musée Estève)
Maison Pelvoysin
Maison de la Reine Blanche
R. de la Sirène
Rue de l'Île d'Or
Boulevard Juranville
École des Beaux-Arts
R. Pelvoysin
PL. PLANCHAT
Rue Littré
Rue du Commerce
PLACE CUJAS
Musée du Berry
R. de la Nation
Rue Duplan
Palais de Justice
R. des Bx-
Palais Jacques-Cœur
Rue Jacques-Cœur
PLACE DE LA NATION
Rue du Prinal
R. du Marché
R. E. Deschamps
Rue des Arènes
R. du Guichet
PL. J. CŒUR
Rue Moyenne
R. du Témoin
Rue P. Commenge
Halle au Blé
Théâtre
PL. DES 4 PILIERS
Rue du Champ de Foire
PLACE JURANVILLE
Hôtel Témoin, Biblio.
R. E. Zola
Rue des Linières
Rue de la Halle
R. des Cordeliers
R. de Secrétain
R. du Four au Roi
R. des Armuriers
PL. CLAMECY
Saint-Pierre-le-Guillard
Rue d'Auron
R. Mayet
R. du Prado
R. V. Jankelevitch
PL. DE LA PRÉFECTURE
PL. M. PLAISANT
Rue de la Chappe
R. des Écoles
R. de la Bienfaisance
Rue des Minimes
Rue des Vertus
Rue Fernault
Avenue Louis XI
Boul. d'Auron
R. Charles VII
Rue Fulton
R. du Chariot
Rampe
R. Jeanne de France
Bd d'Auron
Parc des Expositions
PL. A. BARDOUX
R. J. J. Rousseau
Quai
Lamarck
R. L. Mallet
Rue Barbès
G. Messire Jacques
Boulevard
Médiathèque
100 m
Palais des Congrès
Muséum

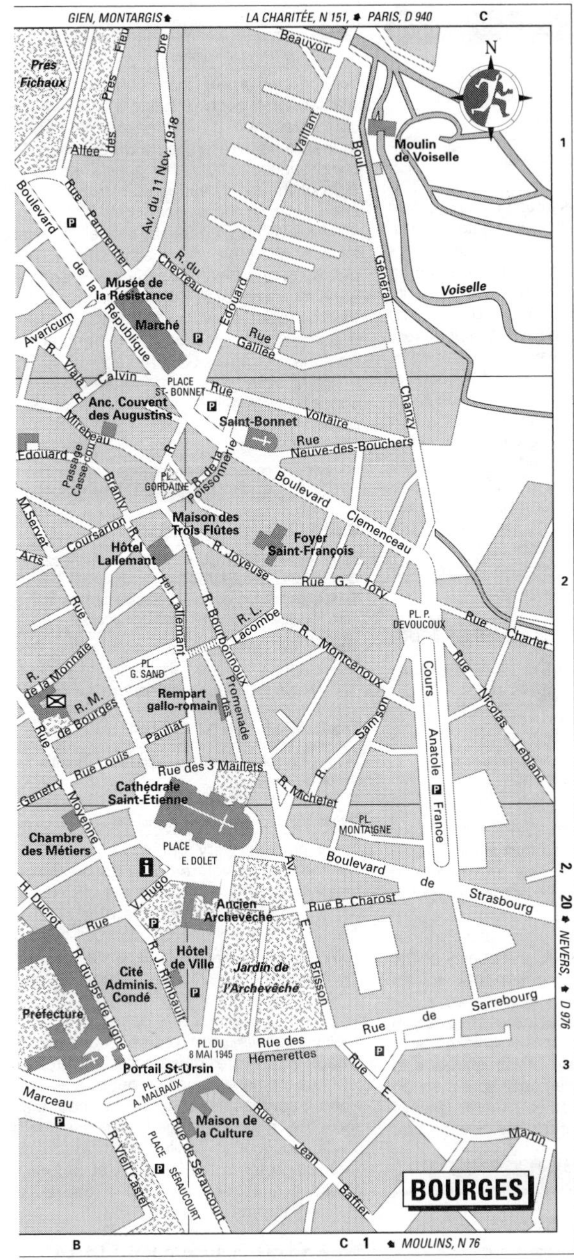
GIEN, MONTARGIS
LA CHARITÉE, N 151, PARIS, D 940
C
Prés Fichaux
Moulin de Voiselle
Voiselle
Musée de la Résistance
Marché
Rue Galilée
PLACE ST-BONNET
Anc. Couvent des Augustins
Saint-Bonnet
Rue Neuve-des-Bouchers
Boulevard Clemenceau
PL. GORDAINE
Maison des Trois Flûtes
Hôtel Lallemant
Foyer Saint-François
Rue G. Tory
PL. P. DEVOUCOUX
Rue Charlet
Cours Anatole France
Rue Nicolas Leblanc
PL. G. SAND
Rempart gallo-romain
Rue des 3 Maillets
Cathédrale Saint-Étienne
R. Michelet
PL. MONTAIGNE
Chambre des Métiers
PLACE E. DOLET
Boulevard de Strasbourg
Ancien Archevêché
Rue B. Charost
Hôtel de Ville
Cité Adminis. Condé
Jardin de l'Archevêché
Préfecture
Rue de Sarrebourg
PL. DU 8 MAI 1945
Rue des Hémerettes
Portail St-Ursin
PL. A. MALRAUX
Maison de la Culture
PLACE SÉRAUCOURT
Rue de Séraucourt
Rue Jean Baffier
BOURGES
B
C 1 MOULINS, N 76
1
2
3
2, 20 NEVERS, D 976

BREZOLLES 28270

10% ☗ |●| LE RELAIS DE BREZOLLES**

4 rue Berg-op Zoom; it's on the outskirts of town, heading in the direction of Chartres.
☎ 02.37.48.20.84 F➔ 02.37.48.28.46
Closed Friday evenings and in August.
Secure parking. TV.

When you first see this large pink and brown inn – it looks like a Black Forest gâteau – with its window boxes overflowing with flowers you might wonder if you've taken a wrong turning somewhere and ended up in Bavaria. The surroundings will soon put paid to that idea but there's no need to be disappointed. The proprietors' friendly welcome, the comfortable rooms (200F and 230F), some of which have been refurbished, the décor of the restaurant and the range of set meals (77–185) on offer will make you want to stay. If you decide to go à la carte, you'll find the menu is full of interesting meat, fish and vegetable dishes. The restaurant's specialities – *émincé* of scallops and monkfish with berries, *aiguillettes* of goose, snails in a Chablis sauce, and warm stewed apples with butterscotch – are very affordable.

MONTIGNY-SUR-AVRE 28270 (5KM NW)

☗ |●| HÔTEL-RESTAURANT MOULIN DES PLANCHES**

it's 10km from Brezolles on the D102.
☎ 02.37.48.25.97 F➔ 02.37.48.35.63
Closed Sunday evenings, Mondays, and January.
Car park. TV. Disabled access.

On the banks of the Avre, surrounded by woods and fields, there stands an old flour mill that has been turned into a very simple and very handsome inn by an ex-farming couple. It may be a hotel but you'll get the kind of welcome you associate more with a guest house (that's a compliment in our book). Revel in the quiet, the quality of the light, the delightful comfortable rooms (300–625F), and the food. They do a set meal at 98F (little pies that are as crisp as you could hope for, escalope of chicken with wheatgerm, and *terrine* of citrus fruit) and another at 150F. You can have your meal on the terrace in fine weather – there's always plenty of space there and in the dining room.

BRIARE 45250

|●| RESTAURANT LE BORD'EAU

27 rue de la Liberté; it's in the main street.
☎ 02.38.31.22.29
Closed Wednesdays year-round; Dec–March, open evenings by reservation only.

With a name like that, you couldn't be blamed for expecting to find a lovely waterside terrace with a cool breeze. Unfortunately, there's no terrace and no water either! But the proprietress treats her guests like members of the family and is so nice that you'll soon get over the disappointment. And the fish specialities prepared by Michel – braised salmon, sea bass with shallots, perch fillets *persillade* and bream in a Sancerre sauce – are a reminder (even if the location isn't) that this is a region of rivers and canals. The food is good, simple, and served up in generous portions. Set meals 95F, 145 and 180F. The pleasant dining room is decorated in pastel shades. It's small, though, so it's best to book.

CHARTRES 28000

☗ AUBERGE DE JEUNESSE

23 av. Neigre (North-East); it's quite far from the centre.
☎ 02.37.34.27.64 F➔ 02.37.35.75.85
Closed the last two weeks in December and the first week in January. **Car park. Disabled access.**

The hostel has 68 beds and charges 65F. Breakfast is included in the price. Sheets 17F. Meals (50F) available for groups only.

10% ☗ |●| LE CHÊNE FLEURI

14 rue de la Porte-Morard (South-East); it's near the church of Saint-Pierre.
☎ 02.37.35.25.70.
Closed Mondays and mid-Sept–mid-Oct.

A nice hotel in a very pretty part of town and just the place if you're on a budget. Unfortunately it's often full, so it's a good idea to book. It has 14 clean simple rooms, all of them redecorated recently, at prices ranging from 140F to 240F. The cheapest set meal in the restaurant is 98F and there are two othes at 140F and 195F. À la carte, there's fricassee of scallops *à la nage*, fish with a shellfish *coulis*, and braised calf sweetbreads with oyster mushrooms. The retaurant has theme evenings on public holidays, when it serves dishes from other countries and other regions (things like mussels and chips, couscous, paella, and *cassoulet*). Ideal place for something to eat before a pleasant nighttime stroll along the Eure. Pleasant terrace.

10% ☗ |●| HÔTEL-RESTAURANT DE LA

POSTE**

3 rue du Général-Kœnig (Centre); it's near place des Épars, 100m from the pedestrian precinct and 400m from the cathedral.
☎ 02.37.21.04.27 F 02.37.36.42.17
Secure parking. **TV**. **Canal+**.

A very practical place to stay, given its excellent location. It's not exactly a bundle of laughs, but you'll get a good night's sleep and your car will be safe in the garage (for which you'll pay 30F). Rooms 305F with shower/wc, 330F with bath. The restaurant does set meals at 85F, 110F and 180F.

LE CAVEAU DE LA CATHÉDRALE

12 rue au Lait; it's very near the cathedral, as its name implies.
☎ 02.37.34.91.64
Closed Tuesday evenings and Wednesdays.

People come here for the 12th century vault as much as they do the incredibly low prices. Don't make life difficult for yourself at lunchtime – go for the 62F *formule*, which comes with starter, main course, dessert and a glass of wine. There's an 89F *formule* in the evening. The restaurant specializes in *miche* (a large round loaf) stuffed with things like chicken and shrimp, kidneys in port, and beef Stroganoff.

LE PICHET

19 rue du Cheval-Blanc; it's 20m from the cathedral.
☎ 02.37.21.08.35 F 02.37.36.24.79
Closed Tuesday evenings out of season and Wednesdays.

A friendly bistro that offers good honest unpretentious cooking – things like calf's head *vinaigrettte* and *poule au pot* – and wine in small carafes. Ideal if you like to keep things simple and would rather save your mental energy for a tour of the cathedral. There's eggnog for dessert.. *Formules* at 69F, 90F and 130F.

LE DIX DE PYTHAGORE

2 rue de la Porte-Cendreuse; it's behind the cathedral.
☎ 02.37.36.02.38
Closed Sunday evenings, Mondays, and July 15–31.

Good old-fashioned classics – beef steak with truffles, salmon *à la Dugléré*, escalope of *foie gras* with grapes – are served up in the basement under the watchful eye of the proprietress. The service and the prices are the reasons this place is so popular. Set meals range in price from 75F (lunchtimes) to 142F. Reckon on 200–220F à la carte.

AU P'TIT MORARD

25 rue de la Porte-Morard.
☎ 02.37.34.15.89
Closed Sunday evenings, Mondays, and two weeks in February and August.

The lower end of town, where the good burghers of Chartres would never have set foot a quarter of a century ago, is now the liveliest, the friendliest, the greenest and, with its doors, mills and updated cafés, the loveliest part of town. You feel good here, indoors and out, on those evenings when the streets are full of cheerful crowds. Set meals 80F, 99F and 140F.

RESTAURANT LE SAINT-HILAIRE

11 rue du Pont-Saint-Hilaire; it's between place Saint-Pierre and pont Saint-Hilaire.
☎ 02.37.30.97.57 F 02.37.30.97.57
Closed Saturday lunchtimes, Sundays, two weeks in August, and Dec 24–Jan 7.

Lunch served noon–2pm and dinner 7–9.30pm. You can't possibly go to Chartres and not eat in this delightful little restaurant, where you'll get a friendly welcome, efficient service and good food. Five generations of Benoît Pasquier's family have been born and bred in the Beauce and he makes a point of showing off local produce to its best advantage. Try the partridge *pâté*, the sauté of thyme-fed rabbit served with garden peas or the panfried escalope of *foie gras* with Beauce lentils. Set meals 95F, 145F and 190F. Good selection of wines at reasonable prices.

CHÂTEAUDUN 28200

10% LE SAINT-LOUIS**

41 rue de la République (East).
☎ 02.37.45.00.01 F 02.37.45.16.09
Secure parking. **TV**.

Ben Maamar has pulled off quite a feat in the space of a few years. Not only has he transformed a ruin into a decent and comfortable hotel (doubles 260F with shower/wc or bath) where you'll get a nice welcome, he has opened alongside the traditional restaurant (set meals 90F, 130F and 195F) a brasserie that attracts the great and the good of Châteaudun, especially in summer when the piano bar gets going outdoors. Mussels, salads, grills – the restaurant has something for everyone at prices from 60F to 100F. What more could you want?

I●I LA LICORNE**

6 place du 18-Octobre (Centre); it's in the main square.
☎ 02.37.45.32.32
Closed Tuesday evenings, Wednesdays, and Dec 15–Jan 15.

The dining room, long and narrow and decorated in salmon pink, offers good bourgeois cooking and dishes like panfried skirt of beef with shallots, chicken in mushroom sauce, and duck breast with orange and honey. It's a pity that the welcome and the service aren't always of the same standard as the cooking. Set meals 70F, 88F, 125F and 180F.

I●I AUX TROIS PASTOUREAUX**

31 rue André-Gillet (South); it's between place du 18-Octobre and espace Malraux.
☎ 02.37.45.74.40 ➨ 02.37.66.00.32
Closed Sunday evenings and Mondays (unless it's a public holiday) and Dec 23–5 Jan.

The dining room is green, the tables are restrained, and the service is low-key. And though the name of the restaurant might have led you to assume otherwise, the staff does not consist of three shepherds in traditional costume.There's a wide variety of à la carte dishes to choose from – petit-gris snails with oyster mushrooms and Szechuan peppercorns, roast pigeon stuffed with wheatgerm and lemon juice, veal kidneys in a Côteaux-du-Layon sauce, and so on – and the cooking is fairly sophisticated. Set meals 79F (weekday lunchtimes), 102F, 116F, 148F, 165F and 220 F!

CHÂTEAUMEILLANT 18370

10% ☗ I●I HÔTEL-RESTAURANT LE PIET À TERRE**

21 rue du Château (Centre).
☎ 02.48.61.41.74
Closed February, and Sunday evenings and Mondays Oct–early March. **Car park**. **TV**. **Canal+**.

Don't try to sneak off without paying your bill and watch your alcohol intake – the police station's right next door. This wonderful restaurant has blue shutters perhaps as a silent tribute to the boys in blue. The décor in the dining room consists of exposed beams and pastel shades and there's always a good fire going on cold winter days. Thierry Finet loves cooking and resents every minute he has to be away from his kitchen. Even the bread and rolls and so on are made on the premises. The cheapest set meal is a bargain. For 98F, you'll get starter, main course (which reflects the mood of the chef and what the market has to offer that particular day), and either the cheese platter or *fromage frais* or the day's dessert. There's another at 160F that consists of five courses. By the way, the vegetables and herbs come from grandfather Piet's kitchen garden. The bedrooms have all been called after flowers. Facilities vary and consequently so do the prices: 260–350F.

CHÂTEAUNEUF-SUR-LOIRE 45110

☗ HÔTEL DU JET D'EAU**

80 Grande-Rue (Centre).
☎ 02.38.58.62.91 ➨ 02.38.46.24.43
Car park. **TV**.

We were quite taken with the quiet bedrooms overlooking the inner courtyard, the spick-and-span look of the ones that have been refurbished, and the brand new bed linen. Doubles 120F with washing facilities, 250F with bath. We fell in love with the breakfast room and the fantastic Cona coffee machines and appreciated the welcome we got from owner Bernard Ferry. If you stay more than a day or two he'll get the horse-drawn carriage out and take you for a ride along the banks of the Loire.

10% ☗ I●I L'AUBERGE DU PORT

83 Grande-Rue-du-Port (South); it faces the bridge across the Loire.
☎ 02.38.58.43.07 ➨ 02.38.58.98.31
Closed Wednesdays and in December.

An unpretentious little inn, with a nice family atmosphere. It's in a good location with the river being so close by and the boules players bring a touch of the south to the little square across the way. The hotel only has four bedrooms and, though they're not luxurious, they're well looked after. Doubles 175F with shower (wc in the corridor). They all overlook the river. The kitchen too, judging by the decent eel stew and zander in *beurre blanc* we had. Set meals 82F (weekdays), 138F and 185F. The little terrace is a bit noisy because of the traffic.

COMBREUX 45530 (13KM N)

10% ☗ I●I L'AUBERGE DE COMBREUX**

35 route du Gâtinais; take the D10 then the D9; it's on the outskirts of the village.
☎ 02.38.46.89.89 ➨ 02.38.59.36.19
Closed mid-Dec–mid-Jan. **Car park**. **TV**. **Canal+**.

You can see why Chris Gangloff, who's been a model and a photographer in her time, decided to give it all up in favour of this 19th century coaching inn swathed in ivy and Virginia creeper. She's turned it into an inn – ever so slightly chic of course, given her background, but very very pleasant. There's a cosy little sitting room with an open fire and a spot on country style dining room with a veranda overlooking a flower-filled garden. In fine weather you can sit outside. Set meals from 95F (weekdays) to 210F, featuring things like house *terrines*, game in season and warm fruit tarts. Bedrooms, whether they're in the main building or in one of the little annexes nestling among the trees are delightful, with flower-sprigged wallpaper, beams, and large wardrobes. They range in price from 325F (with shower/wc) to 495F (with jacuzzi). Half-board, which is compulsory at weekends and May–Oct, comes at 405F per person per day. You can hire a bike to explore the nearby Orléans forest and there's a tennis court and a heated swimming pool too. One of the best hotels we've come across.

CHÂTEAUROUX 36000

HÔTEL-RESTAURANT DE LA GARE**

5 place de la Gare (Centre).
☎ 02.54.22.77.80 Fax 02.54.22.83.72
Car park. **TV**. **Canal+**.

Get off the train, cross the street and you're there – ideal if you've spent hours travelling. Rooms are large and the bathrooms and wcs are well looked after. Doubles 200F (with shower/wc) and 230F (with bath). The food in the restaurant is merely passable. Set meals 50F (in the brasserie, lunchtimes only), 75F, 98F and 135F. Small pool. Free parking.

10% HÔTEL LA BOULE D'OR**

18 rue Bourdillon (Centre); it's near the tourist information office and the church of Saint-André.
☎ 02.54.60.24.24 Fax 02.54.27.98.01
Closed Saturdays out of season.

It's beginning to show signs of age but would do for a night even though the floor creaks a lot (the people in the room downstairs might wish the room upstairs was empty). Rooms 135F (with basin), 235F (with shower/wc) and 255F (with bath). Friendly welcome. Paying car park 30F.

10% HÔTEL BONNET**

14 rue du Marché; it's not far from the town hall.
☎ 02.54.22.13.54 Fax 02.54.07.56.78
Closed Sunday afternoons. **Secure parking**. **TV**. **Disabled access**.

The rooms are clean, comfortable and well looked after. The managers are extremely nice and they do a wonderful breakfast. Doubles 160F (with basin, no TV) and 220F (with shower/wc). There's a car park (10F a night) across the way. From the beginning of November until Easter they have a package that will save you 20–50F a room.

HÔTEL LE BOISCHAUT**

135 av. de La Châtre (South-East).
☎ 02.54.22.22.34 Fax 02.54.22.64.89
Closed Dec 31 and Jan 1. **Secure parking**. **TV**. **Disabled access**.

If you're a big Gérard Depardieu fan, you'll know that he comes from around here. In fact, his old house is not too far away (it's opposite the Jean-Moulin school to be exact). The hotel has large comfortable doubles at 198F (with shower/wc) and 240F (with bath). Unfortunately, it's a bit far out: it'll take you 20 minutes to walk into the centre of town. There's no restaurant but it does have a bar and you can have a meal on a tray (something hot plus cheese and dessert). Free lock-up parking for two-wheelers.

10% ÉLYSÉE HÔTEL***

2 rue de la République (Centre).
☎ 02.54.22.33.66 Fax 02.54.07.34.34
Closed Sundays unless you have a reservation. **TV**. **Canal+**.

This excellent little hotel right in the centre of town has pleasant and very clean rooms. The proprietress is extremely nice and full of energy. She does a good breakfast with homemade jam and cake. You'll get a key so you can come and go as please in the evening. Rooms 290–300F.

10% LE MANOIR DU COLOMBIER***

232 rue de Chatellerault (South-West); at the Châteauroux exit, take the D925 in the direction of Châtellerault.
☎ 02.54.29.30.01 Fax 02.54.27.70.90
Restaurant closed Sunday evenings, Mondays, and during the February school holidays. **Car park**. **TV**. **Canal+**.

This is a handsome bourgeois house standing in its own grounds on the outskirts of town on the road to Brenne. The décor in the bedrooms is very fresh and quietly elegant. Doubles 370F with shower/wc and 410–500F with bath. There's no better hotel in Châteauroux and the restaurant isn't bad either. Set meals 100F (not available Sundays), 155F, 245F and 300F.

|●| RESTAURANT LA CIBOULETTE

42 rue Grande (Centre).
☎ 02.54.27.66.28
Closed Sundays, Mondays, public holidays, one week in January, two at Easter, and three in July–Aug.

This is about the only place to eat in Châteauroux, which is a bit of a desert as far as good restaurants are concerned. Anybody who's anybody in town eats here. It has a pleasant décor, friendly service and set meals that have been carefully thought out. The 95F set meal offers eggs poached in red wine and served with a shallot sauce (this is a local speciality) and sautéd chicken with mushrooms, while the next one up comes with a platter of rather good farmhouse cheeses. Other set meals cost 115F (155F with wine) and 195F (245F with wine). Maurice, the proprietor has a very British sense of humour. About 12 wines are available by the glass and they also have a few organic wines.

|●| LE LAVOIR DE LA FONDS CHARLES

26 route du Château-Raoul (Centre); it's in the old part of town.
☎ 02.54.27.11.16
Closed Mondays and Sunday evenings.

This waterside restaurant – the Indre almost flows past its front door – used to be a café and is still the type of place where everyone feels at ease. People come mainly for the delightful setting (reservations are essential at the height of summer if you want to sit on the terrace) but the uncomplicated style of cooking also contributes to the relaxed atmosphere. Set meals 95F, 125F and 195F.

DÉOLS 36130 (2KM N)

|●| L'ESCALE VILLAGE

on the N20.
☎ 02.54.22.03.77

Look around the dining room here and you'll find a good cross-section of the population of the département tucking into a platter of seafood (145F), sole *meunière* (92F), flank of beef with shallots (55F) or maybe just some *moules marinière* (46F) washed down with some draught beer or a drop of white Reuilly or Valençay. It's a favourite with long-distance lorry drivers and they prefer to eat in the brasserie, where they can watch TV. Since it's open round the clock, it's not unusual after midnight to bump into artists who're passing through or sports celebrities (the owner's a cycling buff) exercising their right elbow. A lively place where feelings sometimes run high.

LEVROUX 36110 (21KM NW)

10% ♠ |●| HÔTEL-RESTAURANT DE LA CLOCHE**

3 rue Nationale; get there by the D956.
☎ 02.54.35.70.43 F 02.54.35.67.43
Closed Monday evenings, Tuesdays, and February.
Car park. TV.

This place has been handed down from father to son since 1895 and even today resembles a friendly village inn. In other words, you'll get an extremely warm welcome and good traditional cooking along the lines of monkfish cheeks with a langoustine *coulis* or fricassee of calf sweetbreads and kidneys in a mustard sauce. Set meals 68–240F. Children's menu 45F. Rooms with shower/wc 260F.

|●| RESTAURANT RELAIS SAINT JEAN

34 rue Nationale; it's near place de la Collégiale-de-Saint-Sylvain.
☎ 02.54.35.81.56 F 02.54.35.36.09
Closed Wednesday evenings and Sunday evenings.

Lunch served noon–2pm and dinner 7.30–10pm. The département of Indre has a number of good restaurants and this former coaching inn is one of them. Its owner and chef studied with Vergé and his skill, the quality of the ingredients and the charming welcome you'll get from his wife, not to mention a pleasant dining room and the fact that some tables give you a view of the chef beavering away in his spotless kitchen, all ensure that eating here will be a pleasant experience. In summer, sit on the terrace and admire the dramatic sunset over the collegiate church of Saint-Sylvain. Cheapest set meal is 85F (not available Sundays or public holidays), with others at 120F, 175F and 205F. There's also an impressive children's menu at 65F, which includes a drink. Specialities include scallop ravioli with a cep sauce and *émincé* of pigeon *confit* with young garlic. Everything is cooked just right and is full of flavour. We were bowled over. If you like cider, try the one from the Auge (45F) and you can dispense with an apéritif.

BUZANÇAIS 36500 (25KM NW)

10% ♠ |●| HÔTEL-RESTAURANT L'HERMITAGE**

route d'Argy-Écueille; take the N143 then follow the signs for Argy.
☎ 02.54.84.03.90 F 02.54.02.13.19

Closed Sunday evenings and Mondays (this does not apply to the hotel in July and August), the first fortnight in January, and Sept 13–22. **Secure parking**. **TV**.

Lunch served noon–1.30pm and dinner 7.15–9pm. If you like peace and quiet you'll love this place. The hotel, covered in Virginia creeper, overlooks a broad expanse of greenery on the banks of the Indre. There's a big kitchen garden and a really nice terrace. Bedrooms in the main building have been carefully decorated and have a view of the grounds. The ones in the annex have been redecorated but are not quite as attractive and overlook the courtyard. Comfortable doubles 290–340F. Set meals 88–230F (the cheapest is not available on Sundays). The cooking is fairly sophisticated and there are specialities from Berry and the Landes and lots of fish dishes.

CHÂTILLON-SUR-INDRE 36700

L'AUBERGE DE LA TOUR**

2 route du Blanc.
☎ 02.54.38.72.17 Fax 02.54.38.74.85
Closed Mondays Oct–end May. **Secure parking**. **TV**.

A lovely 17th century house that's been well renovated and is full of flowers. In summer, people eat on the terrace rather than in the rustic dining room with its fireplace and exposed beams. The chef's specialities include salmon in a Sauvignon-based sauce, beef fillet in a Chinon-based sauce, and andouille à la ficelle. Set meals 55F, 80F, 95F, 120F, 170F and 220F. Children's menu 50F. Rooms have been updated in terms of décor and facilities. Doubles from 140F (with shower) to 260F (with bath).

MÉZIÈRES-EN-BRENNE 36290 (20KM S)

HÔTEL-RESTAURANT AU BŒUF COURONNÉ**

9 place Charles-de-Gaulle; on the D43.
☎ 02.54.38.04.39 Fax 02.54.38.02.84
Closed Sunday evenings, Mondays, the first fortnight in January, the fourth week in June, and the first fortnight in October. **TV**.

This former coaching inn deep in the marshy Brenne has a porch that dates from the middle of the 16th century. Try the *boudin* of carp, the frog's legs, the whitebait, or the shin of veal in a Pouligny-Saint-Pierre sauce. The dining room's a little old-fashioned and a bit on the chilly side. Set meals range in price from 70F (not available Sundays) to 245F. Children's menu 40F (the child must be less than 8). Doubles with shower/wc 220F (no TV) and 230F.

CHÂTRE (LA) 36400

10% HÔTEL NOTRE-DAME**

4 place Notre-Dame (South).
☎ 02.54.48.01.14 Fax 02.54.48.31.14
Secure parking. **TV**. **Disabled access**.

La Châtre's a very quiet town and it must be nice to live here. The hotel is a 15th century building with a flower-filled balcony and the bedrooms, which are large (particularly numbers 30, 32 and 34) well laid-out, and decorated in shades of beige, fit in perfectly. It overlooks a little square where only the birds make the occasional noise. Doubles 250F (with shower/wc) and 270F and up (with bath). It has a terrace and a private garden and you can try your hand at boules. We need more hotels like this.

LE JARDIN DE LA POSTE

10 rue Basse-du-Mouhet (Centre).
☎ 02.54.48.05.62
Closed Mondays and Sunday evenings.

Notwithstanding the claims made for it, this is not one of the great restaurants. It is good though and the chef is a fairly consistent practitioner of his art so you can be pretty sure there'll be no nasty surprises in store. The 105F set meal of starter, main course (the traditional Berry dish of chicken in a red wine sauce thickened with blood, say, or *andouillette* in Sauvignon or calf sweetbreads in a port sauce), and cheese or dessert is pretty good value. Other set meals 165 and 250F.

NOHANT-VIC 36400 (6KM NW)

L'AUBERGE DE LA PETITE FADETTE**

place du Château; on the D943.
☎ 02.54.31.01.48 Fax 02.54.31.10.19
Car park. **TV**.

This beautiful building covered in Virginia creeper has been in the family for three generations. Novelist George Sand spent the greater part of her life in Nohant and her visitors included Flaubert, Balzac and Delacroix. The name of the inn commemorates one of her most famous stories for children. The bedrooms are very prettily decorated in shades of green. Doubles with shower from 295F. The dining room has hunting trophies and tapestries hung on the walls. Set meals from 80F.

PONDERON (LE) 36230 (8KM W)

|●| LE RELAIS DE LA CÔTE

How to get there: take the D927 in the direction of Neuvy-Saint-Sépulcre.
☎ 02.54.31.30.82.
Closed Mondays.

A good restaurant that manages to please the locals, long-distance lorry drivers and travelling salesmen all at once. A mere 60F gets you three starters, main course, cheese and dessert. When we were there we had cauliflower *vinaigrette*, two slices of salami and one of melon followed by two slices of stuffed shoulder of lamb in a port sauce, a bit of goat's cheese and a sizeable helping of *Paris-Brest* (a choux pastry ring filled with almonds and butter cream) from the dessert trolley, which had a pretty good choice and included Black Forest gâteau and *clafoutis*. Very simple décor and a nice grandmotherly type of waitress.

SAINT-CHARTIER 36400 (8.5KM N)

10% ⌂ |●| HÔTEL-RESTAURANT LA VALLÉE BLEUE***

route de Verneuil.
☎ 02.54.31.01.91 ⊳ 02.54.34.04.48
Closed Sunday evenings and Mondays Oct–end April. **Car park**. **TV**.

This part of France is George Sand country and her doctor used to live in this house. The people who converted it have done a wonderful job and retained all of its character. Harmony reigns throughout – in the dining rooms, the lounge and the bedrooms. It all makes for a pleasurable stay, particularly since the restaurant is pretty good too. Set meals 100F (weekday lunchtimes), 135F, 210F and 275F. You'll be spoiled for choice. The à la carte menu offers a vegetarian plate, carp with a lentil and star anis sauce, and a *pot-au-feu* of quail with local oyster mushrooms. Children's menu 70F. There are two terraces and a swimming pool in the 9 acres of grounds. Very comfortable rooms 350–590F.

LYS-SAINT-GEORGES 36230 (23KM NW)

|●| LA FORGE

How to get there: take the D927 in the direction of Neuvy-Saint-Sépulcre and then the D74. It's opposite the château.
☎ 02.54.30.81.68
Closed Mondays year round and Tuesdays Sept–June inclusive.

Lunch served noon–2pm and dinner 7.30–9.30pm. This rather good inn is the only commercial enterprise in a village of 180 inhabitants. It has handsome beams, pictures by local artists, an open fire in winter and a terrace with a pergola in summer where you can enjoy the peace and quiet and listen to the birds. The proprietress is friendly and very witty and her husband prepares tasty classic dishes with clearly defined flavours. The 65F cheapest set meal (weekdays) won't leave you feeling hungry and neither will the next one up (98F). It's a touch more sophisticated and is popular with the regulars on a Sunday, who tuck into dishes like salad of mussels and shrimp and braised duckling in a honey sauce. Other set meals 145F, 185F and 235F. Children's menu 48F.

CHAUMONT-SUR-THARONNE 41600

|●| RESTAURANT LA GRENOUILLÈRE

route de La Ferté-Saint-Aubin; when you get to the Chaumont exit, follow the signs for La Ferté-Saint-Aubin.
☎ 02.54.88.50.71 ⊳ 02.54.88.53.49
Closed Monday evenings and Tuesdays (except in July and August). **Car park**.

Lunch served noon–2pm and dinner 7–9.30pm. An old house deep in the forest that's been converted into a luxurious country inn with a wild life park where peacocks and golden pheasants shimmer in the sunlight. You take your meals in a glassed-in terrace opposite a pond that's home to carp, moorhens, swans and 40 species of wild duck!. Set meals 100F (weekdays only), 150F and 180F. These are very good and offer dishes like duck fillet with peppercorns, *terrine* of *pot-au-feu*, boned quail stuffed with *foie gras* and scallops with chanterelle mushrooms. Other set meals are much more expensive. After your meal, take a stroll down to the bottom of the garden and have a look at the aviaries and their occupants – golden pheasants from Tibet and Nepal. This is one for your address book.

CHENONCEAUX 37150

|●| RESTAURANT AU GÂTEAU BRETON

16 rue du Docteur-Bretonneau (Centre); it's in the main street.
☎ 02.47.23.90.14 ⊳ 02.47.23.92.57

Closed Tuesday evenings, Wednesday evenings, and Christmas–New Year's Day.

Large terrace for summer and a small dining room for winter. They offer several set meals starting at 57F which are good value for money and incredibly cheap for such a touristy area. For a mere 78F you'll get a starter, main course, cheese and dessert – and 1/4 litre of wine too!. The 102F set meal comes with two main courses, one of them salmon. The restaurant's specialities are chicken *à la tourangelle* (with mixed French and haricot beans) and roast guinea fowl, which is delicious and served up in generous portions. Children's menu 45F. Nice welcome.

CIVRAY-DE-TOURAINE 37150 (1KM W)

L'HOSTELLERIE DU CHÂTEAU DE L'ISLE**.

☎ 02.47.23.80.09 F➜ 02.47.23.82.91
Closed Nov 15–Dec 26. Restaurant closed Sunday evenings and Monday lunchtimes (unless you're a guest). **Car park**.

Lunch served noon–2pm and dinner 7.30–9pm. The staff do everything they can to make you feel at home in this beautiful 18th century house near the Cher. It has 10 comfortable rooms with shower/wc or bath ranging in price from 280F to 500F. Chef Sylvain Liboureau prepares first-rate dishes based on what the market has to offer. The restaurant is extremely pleasant and has two dining rooms, both with an open fireplace. Set meals 98F (weekdays), 148F and 205F. Boat trips on the Cher can be arranged. Half-board (350F a person) is compulsory in season. Weather permitting, you can eat on the terrace and then go for a stroll in the grounds and admire the hundred year old trees. One for the address book.

CHINON 37500

10% GRAND HÔTEL DE LA BOULE D'OR**

66 quai Jeanne-d'Arc (Centre).
☎ 02.47.93.03.13 F➜ 02.47.93.24.25
Closed Sunday evenings out of season and mid Dec–end Jan; restaurant closed Mondays. **TV**.

Rooms in this former coaching inn range in price from 210F to 330F and come with washing facilities, shower or bath, with or without wc, and with a view of the courtyard or the embankment. The restaurant offers excellent traditional and regional cooking and in fine weather meals are served in a lovely shady internal courtyard. The cheapest set meal is 98F (lunchtimes) and there's an interesting one at 160F. The speciality is of course *coq au vin*, the wine being Chinon. Half-board from 300F per person.

10% HÔTEL DIDEROT**

4 rue Buffon; it's away from the centre, 100m from place Jeanne-d'Arc.
☎ 02.47.93.18.87 F➜ 02.47.93.37.10.
Car park. TV. Disabled access.

Come through the big gate and at the other end of the courtyard you'll see a very handsome 18th century house covered in ivy and Virginia creeper. It's more like a guest house than a hotel and you'll be welcomed like one of the family. There are 28 very cosy rooms, no two of them the same. Numbers 22–25 are very cosy. Prices 280–395F. Wonderful jam at breakfast time. Car park closes at 10.30pm.

10% HÔTEL DE FRANCE-RESTAURANT À L'OSTÉRIA**

47-49 place du Général-de-Gaulle; it's in the heart of the old town.
☎ 02.47.93.33.91 F➜ 02.47.98.37.03
Closed Feb 23–March 9 and the second fortnight in November. **Secure parking. TV.**

Lunch served 12.30–2pm and dinner 7.30–10pm. The rooms in this beautiful 16th century building are comfortable and some overlook the château and place de la Fontaine. Doubles with shower or bath 320–390F. Prices are lower out of season (ie Oct–end March). The communal areas are very pleasant and there are several seating areas. There's a Mediterranean garden in the inner courtyard with banana, orange, lemon and bay trees lending a touch of the exotic. The restaurant offers Italian specialities.

L'ORANGERIE

79 bis rue Voltaire; the street runs parallel to quai Charles-VII, so take rue Parmentier on the left.
☎ 02.47.98.42.00 F➜ 02.47.93.92.50
Closed Sunday evenings and Wednesdays in the low season.

The restaurant is full of pleasant surprises. To start with, the large dining room is carved out of tufa (a soft porous rock), the last remnant of an ancient abbey, and has raspberry coloured tablecloths and a bright green carpet. Don't worry, you'll soon get used to it. Then there's the inventive cooking. The set meals (95–220F) offer dishes such as langoustines *en papillote* with *foie gras* and a delicious chocolate soufflé (and they're not stingy with the portions). And last but not least there's the simple and pleasant welcome. Our only criticism – and it's a small one – is that the noise from the kitchens can be heard in the dining room.

L'OCÉANIC

13 rue Rabelais (Centre); take rue Rabelais from place Charles-de-Gaulle.
☎ 02.47.93.44.55
Closed Mondays and in January.

Whoever decorated this lovely old house has got lots of taste – they even went so far as to have the waiters' waistcoats match the tablecloths. There's a small terrace outside. Lots of regulars and they're rather chic. The welcome's a bit on the chilly side. The restaurant's known for its cooking (primarily its fish dishes) which it describes as a spectacle played out against a different backdrop every day. So sit back and enjoy the show. Set meals from 98F.

AVOINE 37420 (5KM N)

10% HÔTEL LA GIRAUDIÈRE-RESTAURANT LE PETIT PIGEONNIER**

Beaumont-en-Véron; take the D749 in the direction of Beaumont and after about 4km turn left at domaine de la Giraudière – the restaurant is 800m further on.
☎ 02.47.58.40.36 ➡ 02.47.58.46.06
Restaurant closed in January and weekday lunchtimes except by reservation. **Car park**. **TV**.

Service 7.30–10pm. You can be sure of peace and quiet in this welcoming country house hotel that's off the beaten track. The attractive 17th century manor house has 25 recently renovated rooms all with phone and shower or bath. Doubles 200–590F. The 16th century dovecote is worth a look. The restaurant (tel: 02.47.58.98.96) offers very good gourmet cooking at affordable prices. Its specialities are leg of duck and dried pears in Chinon. Cheapest set meal 98F. Half-board starts at 280F.

COUR-CHEVERNY 41700

10% HÔTEL-RESTAURANT DES TROIS MARCHANDS**

rue Nationale (Centre); it's in the main street next to the church.
☎ 02.54.79.96.44 ➡ 02.54.79.25.60
Closed Mondays and Feb 2–March 12. **Car park**. **TV**.

Lunch served noon–2pm and dinner 7.30–9.30pm. The one or two exposed beams in the frontage give a touch of local charm to this good village inn. It has 36 rooms, some of which overlook the garden. Doubles 190–360F. A word of warning though – the rooms in the annex across the way are not great and nor is the welcome. It's well known locally for its cooking. Cheapest set meal is 115F, with prices rising thereafter to 185–315F. Half-board 210–320F a person.

RESTAURANT LE POUSSE-RAPIÈRE

rue Nationale (Centre); it's opposite the road that leads to the château.
☎ 02.54.79.94.23 ➡ 02.54.79.27.67
Closed Mondays, Sunday evenings, and Dec 15–Jan 5.
Disabled access.

Lunch served noon–2pm and dinner 7–9.30pm. You'll get a friendly welcome in this comfortable restaurant. You can have traditional Gascon dishes like *foie gras* and *confit* or go for something a bit more original – fillet of rascasse with oysters say, or zander with chanterelles, salmon with raisins, or game in season. Set meals 80–180F.

DREUX 28100

10% HÔTEL LE BEFFROI**

12 place Métézeau (Centre).
☎ 02.37.50.02.03 ➡ 02.37.42.07.69
TV.

Dreux isn't exactly a great place for a holiday but this is a decent enough place to spend the night. There's an underground garage in the square next door and the bedrooms are bright, quiet, and comfortable and overlook the river or the square. Rooms 285–350F (for 3).

AUX QUATRE VENTS

18 place Métézeau (Centre).
☎ 02.37.50.03.24
Closed evenings except Saturdays and during the summer.

We liked the slightly retro look of this bistro and the great value buffet *formule*. If you take the 100F set meal, you can go back as often as you like to the table of hors d'œuvres, which include salmon, shellfish, wonderful *charcuterie*, *crudités* and so on and follow that with a main course like rack of veal *à l'ancienne* or roast chicken and dessert. There's another set meal at 130F. Weather permitting, you can eat on the terrace.

FERTÉ-SAINT-AUBIN (LA) 45240

I●I L'AUBERGE DES CHASSEURS

34 rue des Poulies; it's one of the streets behind the tourist information office.
☎ 02.38.76.66.95
Closed Monday evenings and Tuesdays.

This used to be an inn that catered specifically to hunters, and the name stuck, as did some of the traditions. In other words, you'll get a warm welcome and in season you'll be served game in front of the impressive fireplace where a fire is lit as soon as there's a nip in the air. The food is good, simple and served up in generous portions. Set meals 65F, 98F and 145F. One departure from tradition – well, tradition in this part of the world – is the *formule* offering mussels, chips and beer for 55F.

MARCILLY-EN-VILLETTE 45240 (8KM NE)

10% ⌂ I●I AUBERGE DE LA CROIX BLANCHE*

118 place de l'ƒglise; by the N20 and then the D921.
☎ 02.38.76.10.14 ➧ 02.38.76.10.67
Closed Fridays and the second fortnight in August.
Car park.

Lunch served noon–2.30pm and dinner 7.30–9pm. When this inn opened in the 17th century, the then proprietor put up a sign to the effect that they served food and wine and also cut hair. The sign's still there, and they're still serving food (though they've stopped cutting hair). The cheapest set meal – eaten in the bar, where you can buy a newspaper – is 60F and it's best to book. If you opt for the pleasant dining room, you'll get good-natured service and traditional dishes prepared by a skilled chef. Set meals change almost every day and the chef is uncompromising when it comes to the quality of his raw ingredients. We'd love to go back if only for the desserts and maybe for the extremely simple but pleasant rooms overlooking the timelessly beautiful place de l'église. Set meals 88–170F. Rooms 160F with basin and 220F with shower.

FERTÉ-VIDAME (LA) 28340

I●I LA TRIGALLE*

How to get there: if you're coming from Verneuil, it's on the outskirts of the village on the right at a crossroads.
☎ 02.37.37.51.75 ➧ 02.37.37.51.75
Closed Mondays and Sunday evenings except on public holidays, and Feb 1–15. **Car park**.

It's a pleasure to find a good restaurant like this with inventive cooking and delicious meals like leg of rabbit *confit* with *aïoli*, beef stew *percheronne*, calf sweetbreads in maple syrup and *fromagée*, a regional speciality. Set meals 78F (weekdays), 99F, 115F and 130F, all of them good and served up in generous portions. Not many people know that Saint-Simon, the famous 18th century diarist who chronicled events at the court of Louis XIV, had a château here. It's in ruins now but it's worth a visit – the grounds are enormous.

GIEN 45500

⌂ SANHÔTEL**

21 quai de Sully; it's on the south bank, opposite the château.
☎ 02.38.67.61.46 ➧ 02.38.67.13.01
Car park. **TV**. **Canal+**. **Disabled access**.

We've included this fairly run-of-the-mill 2-star hotel on the banks of the Loire because of its prices, which are unbeatable (a double with bath costs 180F), and for its unobstructed views of the town, huddled at the foot of the château. Since life is full of swings and roundabouts, the rooms that don't have a view and overlook the garden are quieter. Nice welcome. The restaurant in the hotel is a separate entity and is rather expensive.

I●I RESTAURANT LE RÉGENCY

6 quai Lenoir; it faces the Loire, near the bridge.
☎ 02.38.67.04.96
Closed Sunday evenings, Mondays, and the first fortnight in January.

The restaurant specializes in fish from the Loire and simple local cooking. Dishes are carefully prepared and prices are reasonable. The cheapest set meal at 90F consists of chicken liver salad with raspberry vinegar and old-fashioned *blanquette de veau*, while the one at 145F comes with local terrine and fillet of zander with sorrel. The terrace faces the river – and the road. Nothing's perfect, is it?

ILLIERS-COMBRAY 28120

I●I LE FLORENT

13 place du Marché; it's near the church.
☎ 02.37.24.10.43 ➧ 02.37.24.11.78
Closed Sunday evenings and Mondays, except on public holidays. **Disabled access**.

An elegant restaurant but it's not pretentious and they don't flog the Proust connection to death. The little dining rooms are delightful and Hervé Priolet is an excellent and imaginative chef. He offers a tempting set meal at 105F (not available Sunday lunchtimes), another at 155F which has quite a following, and a third – named after Marcel Proust, which is memorable – at 185F. The dining room is full of ruddy-cheeked customers talking and eating at the same time.

BROU 28160 (13KM SW)

RESTAURANT DU STADE

1 rue du Mail (Centre).
☎ 02.37.47.01.39
Closed Wednesday evenings, Thursdays, the first fortnight in January, the second fortnight in June, the first week in July and the last week in December.

Regulars rave about it. They don't by any means live up to the stereotypical image of the "man with a beret and a baguette under his arm" but they like the very simple cooking and family atmosphere of this unpretentious restaurant. The cheapest set meal is 92F with as many hors-d'œuvre as you like, five main courses (complete with vegetables) to choose from, cheese platter and the house dessert of your choice. Treat yourself to the one at 130F or 150F if you're out with friends or the in-laws.

ISSOUDUN 36100

10% HÔTEL-RESTAURANT DE LA GARE**

7 bd Pierre-Favreau.
☎ 02.54.21.11.59 F→ 02.54.21.73.01
Closed Sundays, the first week in August, and Oct 23–Jan 14. **TV**.

It's worth stopping in Issoudun, with its connections with the French monarchy, so you can stroll through the narrow streets with their old houses and monuments, all that remains of its past glory. The hotel isn't fancy but it's clean (even though the stair carpet is very worn). Doubles with shower/wc 180F. Half-board from 190F. You'll get a very nice welcome. Set meals 62F (lunchtimes), 75F, 85F, 98F and 108F. The town centre is a five minute walk away.

10% HÔTEL DE FRANCE – RESTAURANT LES TROIS ROIS**

3 rue Pierre-Brossolette (Centre).
☎ 02.54.21.00.65 F→ 02.54.21.50.61
Closed Tuesdays, Sunday evenings, two weeks at the end of September, and two at the end of March.
Secure parking. **TV**.

The rooms, renovated throughout recently, are large and spotlessly clean. All have bath and TV. Doubles 280F. The dining room is comfortable and quite stylish, with superb mirrors, fleur-de-lys wallpaper, and woodwork that has the patina of age. You'll get an exuberant welcome from the proprietress, a very efficient lady who keeps an eye on everything. The cooking is conventional but you won't be disappointed. Set meals 90F (weekdays) 110F, 130F and 160F. The one at 110F – *émincé* of smoked salmon with olive oil and lemon juice, breast of duck with blackcurrants, sauté potatoes and Berry lentils, cheese, and dessert – is fairly substantial. In fine weather, sit out on the flower-filled terrace overlooking the courtyard.

HÔTEL-RESTAURANT LA COGNETTE***

2 bd Stalingrad; take the N151, go into the town centre and it's near the big market place.
☎ 02.54.21.21.83 F→ 02.54.03.13.03
Closed three weeks in January, Sunday evenings, and Mondays (except on public holidays and during the summer months). **TV**. **Disabled access**.

Lunch served noon–2pm and dinner 7.30–10pm. The inn's origins go back to the 19th century. Balzac gives a very accurate description of it in *La Rabouilleuse* (not one of his best-known novels). It was run by a couple called Cognet or Cognette and she was a very good cook, hence the name of the inn. The dining room is a mixture of Empire, Restoration and Louis-Philippe, which Balzac would like. He'd also like the arrangements of ornaments, wallhangings and pictures which look as if they've just happened but have in fact been carefully arranged. The restaurant is said to be one of the best in the département and the kitchens are in the hands of Alain Nonnet and his son-in-law Jean-Jacques Daumy. Set meals 155F, 320F, 395F et 495F. The formal atmosphere will make the solitary diner uncomfortable. The hotel, by contrast, is perfect in all respects. The rooms are comfortable and the bathroom comes complete with dressing gown and hairdrier. Each room has its own little terrace and if the weather's fine, you can have breakfast amid by the scent of roses. It thoroughly deserves the three stars.

LE PILE OU FACE

rue Danielle-Casanova (Centre).
☎ 02.54.03.14.91
Closed Sunday evenings and Mondays.

Lunch served noon–1.30pm and dinner 7–9pm. Whether you choose to eat in the conventional dining room or out on the more pleasant covered terrace, the menu is the same. Set meals 70F (weekday lunchtimes), 100F, 130F, 170F and 200F. Children aren't forgotten – they've got their own menu that costs a mere 45F. Specialities include *cassolette berrichonne*, veal kidneys with Pinot Gris, and zander with herbs.

DIOU 36260 (12KM N)

L'AUBERGEADE

route d'Issoudun; by the D918, heading for Vierzon.
☎ 02.54.49.22.28
Closed Wednesday and Sunday evenings.

Service until 2.15pm and 9.15pm. A warm welcome, a terrace, a pleasant and comfortable dining room (even though the tables are closer together than they are outside) and beautifully simple cooking – that's what you'll get in this restaurant. The 95F gives you a choice of starters (how about a salad of warm goat's cheese and walnut oil?), a main course (*quenelles* of pike with a basil flavoured white butter sauce or oven-baked *andouillette* with a *coulis* of ceps and Swiss chard), mature cheese or the house dessert of the day. Other set meals 145F and 195F.

BRIVES 36100 (13KM S)

RESTAURANT LE CÉSAR

Centre; take the D918; it's beside the church.
☎ 02.54.49.04.43.
Closed Monday evenings except in October and November, the first week in January, and the first fortnight in August.

The inn, near the church (almost invisible behind the trees) and the old Roman embankment, is still the hub of village life. Weary travellers who stop here will offer up a silent prayer of thanks for the simple tasty dishes prepared by the proprietress, particularly the 55F set meal. At the week-end, you'll have to order ahead of time if you want the set meal at 100F (house *terrine*, calf's head *vinaigrette*, *coq au vin* with potatoes, salad, cheese and dessert), 120F or 145F. On Sunday evenings, after a day's fishing you can have as much of the house *terrine* as you can eat plus a ham omelette, cheese and dessert for 56F.

LANGEAIS 37130

10% L'HÔTELLERIE DE LA DUCHESSE ANNE**

10 route de Tours (Centre).
☎ 02.47.96.82.03 F 02.47.96.68.60
Closed Sunday evenings, Mondays, during the February school holidays, and Nov 15–1 Dec. **Secure parking**. **TV**.

This is a friendly inn with a delightful garden at the back and 15 rooms – all different – with shower or bath. Doubles 230–294F, the most expensive having shower/wc. The décor's a bit old-fashioned but people come primarily for the cooking that's traditional and at the same time creative and altogether pretty good. They have good local wines and set meals ranging in price from 68F (weekdays) to 190F. Half-board is compulsory in July and August and costs 260F per double room.

LOCHES 37600

HÔTEL-RESTAURANT DE FRANCE**

6 rue Picois (Centre).
☎ 02.47.59.00.32 F 02.47.59.28.66
Closed Sunday evenings and Mondays except in July and August, and mid-Jan–mid-Feb. **Secure parking**. **TV**.

Lunch served noon–2pm and dinner 7–9pm. This used to be a coaching inn and has a flower-filled inner courtyard. Rooms are pleasant and rather plush, some with mezzanine floor; 230F with shower/wc, 350F with bath. The restaurant offers cooking that's sophisticated and inventive and the service is unobtrusive. Set meals are 85F (weekdays, with a choice of cheese or dessert) and 110–250F. The langoustines and courgettes in puff pastry was memorable. Half-board is from 245F per person and is compulsory from Easter to the end of September.

HÔTEL-RESTAURANT GEORGE SAND***

39 rue Quintefol (Centre).
☎ 02.47.59.39.74 F 02.47.91.55.75
Car park. **TV**.

The hotel stands on the banks of the Indre, in a very pretty building that dates from the 15th century. Rooms have all been soundproofed and are decorated in good taste. Doubles with shower/wc start at 270F, with prices going up to 650F for the largest ones with a view of the river. The restaurant, with a pleasant waterside terrace, serves up delicate and sophisticated dishes. Set meals range in price from 100F (not available Sundays) to 240F, with a special gourmet one of Touraine specialities at 290F. They bake their own bread. Very nice welcome. Half-board is 370–650F per person and is compulsory in summer.

|●| LA GERBE D'OR

22 rue Balzac.
☎ 02.47.59.06.38
Closed Monday evenings, Tuesdays and February.

With a very pleasant terrace and a vine-covered trellis to keep you cool, this is a great place for eating outdoors. Claude will soon make you feel at home. The cooking is regional in style and they also have fairly substantial salads – or you could opt for the very good 100F *formule*, which includes wine and coffee.

BEAULIEU-LÈS-LOCHES 37600 (1KM E)

⌂ HÔTEL DE BEAULIEU - RESTAURANT L'ESTAMINET**

3 rue Foulques-Nerra - place de l'Abbaye; take the D760 in the direction of Valençay. It's opposite the church.
☎ 02.47.91.60.80
Closed Oct–Easter. Restaurant closed Mondays.

Service until 2pm in the afternoon and 10pm in the evening. The hotel is housed in a very handsome typically Touraine building that dates from the 16th century and has nine country-style bedrooms laid out around a beautiful inner courtyard. Prices start at 195F for a double with shower/wc. The proprietors' son has a traditional little café just next door called *L'Estaminet* (tel.: 02.47.59.35.47) where you can have steak and chips, an omelette, ox tripe or *andouillette* and some good local wine.

CHANCEAUX-PRÈS-LOCHES 37600 (6KM NW)

|●| RESTAURANT LA BELLE ÉPOQUE

Centre.
☎ 02.47.59.38.16
Closed Mondays and the second fortnight in September. **Disabled access**.

The village is tiny and quite delightful. It has a remarkable chapel, a château, a basic country gîte and a pond, all tucked away in a wooded valley and as romantic as you could hope for. The white-painted inn feels very cosy inside, with its pink walls, piano and open fire. Its Iranian proprietor organizes painting exhibitions in summer. The restaurant offers simple regional dishes and the cooking is fairly decent. Set meals 68F, 85F and 125F. *Assiette gourmande* 95 F. Regional wine list.

MONTARGIS 45200

10% ⌂ GRAND HÔTEL DE FRANCE**

54 place de la République (Centre).
☎ 02.38.98.01.18 F➜ 02.38.85.79.30
Secure parking. **TV**.

This slightly old-fashioned but charming hotel reminiscent of a coaching inn overlooks a leafy square on one side and one of the famous Montargis canals on the other. It has a handsome inner courtyard whose stone walls are covered in vines. It has rooms of all kinds, all well looked after, at prices ranging from 120F for one with washing facilities to 240F with bath. If you can't bear the psychedelic wallpaper in your room, you don't have to put up with it – ask for one of the refurbished rooms. The proprietress is very nice. The hotel doesn't have a restaurant but it does have a bar with a terrace that's pleasant in fine weather. The bar's called the *d'Artagnan* by the way and the fresco of – guess what? – is worth a quick glance.

10% ⌂ HÔTEL LE BON GÎTE*

21 bd du Chinchon (Centre).
☎ 02.38.85.31.01 F➜ 02.38.93.28.06
Secure parking. **TV**. **Disabled access**.

Try this place if you want to get a good night's sleep at a reasonable price. It doesn't look like much from the outside but it's clean and quiet. It has a few simple rooms on the upper floors laid out around an inner courtyard – a bit like a motel, so fairly uninspiring. Doubles 150F with basin and bidet, 170F with shower/wc and 240F with bath and TV. The owners, who're Spanish and very nice, have been her for more than 30 years. Let them know if you'll be arriving after 8pm.

|●| RESTAURANT LES PETITS OIGNONS

81 bis av. du Général-de-Gaulle; it's in the same general area as the train station.
☎ 02.38.93.97.49
Closed Sunday evenings, Mondays, and the first three weeks in August. **Car park**. **Disabled access**.

The décor is ever so slightly modern and we liked the pale colours and uncluttered look. What we really fell for though was the garden and the terrace, where you can be sure of privacy and peace and quiet. Before you sit down, sneak a look at what's going on inside the kitchen (they even encourage you to). The cooking and the raw ingredients are first-rate, and we particularly liked the fillet of zander in a cream and saffron sauce (they still produce saffron hereabouts). You'll get a cheerful welcome and impeccable service. You might be excused for thinking that all of this would cost a pretty penny, but not a bit of it – set meals are 69–180F. And the proprietor is talking about opening an annex that would be more of a bistro. We can't wait!.

RESTAURANT L'ILE AUX CANARDS

10 rue du Loing (Centre).
☎ 02.38.98.44.22 F➜ 02.38.93.34.29
Closed Sunday evenings except on public holiday weekends.

Lunch served noon–2pm and dinner 7.15–10pm. You'll find this restaurant down by the water's edge. It has two small cosy dining rooms and its welcoming young chef offers all sorts of wonderful dishes based on duck (hardly surprising when you consider the restaurant's name). So it would seem illogical not to go for the 172F "duck" set meal of profiteroles of *foie gras* with verjuice-flavoured butter, *fondant* of panfried *foie gras* with gingerbread and apple sauce, *aiguillettes* of duck with honey and mustard, *tournedos Rossini* of duck with morels, and *suprême* of panfried *foie gras* with langoustines and coriander. We also liked the 135F set meal, which includes wine. The cheapest set meal is 99F and there's also a very nice children's menu at 60F. Attentive service.

MONT-PRÈS-CHAMBORD 41250

HÔTEL-RESTAURANT LE SAINT-FLORENT**

Centre; take the D33 to Huisseau then the D72. It's 8km from the château of Cheverny.
☎ 02.54.70.81.00 F➜ 02.54.70.78.53
Closed January; restaurant closed Monday lunchtimes. **Secure parking**. **TV**. **Disabled access**.

A spick-and-span hotel, complete with sauna, right in the heart of château country that has bright cheerful rooms at fair prices. Doubles with shower or bath 200–275F. The restaurant has a number of set meals starting at 82F (weekdays). Try the pig's trotter stuffed with *foie gras* (its speciality) or the fillet of pike with a Cheverny flavoured *mousseline.* Nice welcome.

MONTRICHARD 41400

10% HÔTEL DE LA CROIX-BLANCHE**

64 rue Nationale (Centre).
☎ 02.54.32.30.87 F➜ 02.54.32.48.06
Closed Nov–end March. **Secure parking**. **TV**.

The hotel, an old coaching inn near the keep, has been refurbished throughout. It's friendly, spotlessly clean and, while the rooms don't get much light, they're comfortable. All have bath and phone and a few have a view of the Cher. Doubles 275F. There's no restaurant but the proprietor also owns the more expensive *Hôtel Bellevue* where the cooking is good.

CRÊPERIE DU DONJON

17 rue du Pont; it's near the keep.
☎ 02.54.32.22.35
Closed Sunday lunchtimes and Mondays.

Tremendous *crêpes* (about 35F) – wash them down with one of the restaurant's carefully selected ciders that bring out the real buckwheat flavour. We opted for the one called Popeye, which was bursting with chopped spinach, but the country and Auvergne varieties sounded good too. Excellent value for money and the service couldn't be faulted.

FAVEROLLES-SUR-CHER 41400 (1.5KM S)

RESTAURANT LE GRILL DU PASSEUR

pont de Montrichard.
☎ 02.54.32.06.80

Lunch served noon–2.30pm and dinner 7–10.30pm. If you're feeling peckish, head for this little restaurant on the Cher. You might find the owner a bit off-putting but the rib steak will put you in a forgiving mood. Kitschy décor. From the window you'll have a view of the keep, which is lit up at night. Try one of the local wines with that rib steak, by the way. You'll get away with about 150F.

PONTLEVOY 41400 (7KM N)

HÔTEL-RESTAURANT DE L'ÉCOLE**

12 route de Montrichard (Centre); it's on the main road coming from Montrichard.
☎ 02.54.32.50.30 F➜ 02.54.32.33.58
Closed Tuesdays and February. **Car park**. **TV**.

After your tour of the imposing thousand year old abbey, stop at this delightful little hotel which has 11 comfortable rooms with shower/wc or bath and phone (260–400F). The cooking is very traditional but sophisticated and nicely presented. They do several set meals, including one at 155F with *quenelles* of pike and langoustines, salmon with crayfish tails or fillet of turbot. In fine weather, you can eat under the pergola in the garden. Excellent service.

OISLY 41700 (16KM NE)

RESTAURANT LE SAINT-VINCENT

Centre; take the D764 as far as Pontlevoy then turn right onto the D30.

☎ 02.54.79.50.04
Closed Sunday evenings, Mondays, evenings of public holidays, one week in spring, and two weeks at the end of October.

Lunch served noon–1.30pm and dinner 7–9pm. This is quite an exceptional restaurant. It doesn't look like much – the sign is pretty ordinary and you might think this was just another restaurant in just another village square. But you'll change your mind as soon as you step inside. The décor gives a feeling of freshness, the tables aren't close together, and the linen and cultery and so on are rustic but not too much so. The menu is varied, full of tempting and original dishes, including *terrine* of lobster and haddock with *crème fleurette* (which resembles whipping cream) sharpened with lemon juice, citronée, sautéd sea bass with fennel and coriander, guinea fowl in mulled wine and a meringue covered *terrine* of dark chocolate and candied fruits with a cinammon sauce that's to die for. But the chef is so creative he's probably invented other culinary delights by the time you read this. Set meals 98F (weekdays), 145F and 185F.

NOGENT-LE-ROTROU 28400

10% HÔTEL L'ELDORADO**

2 place du 11-Août (Centre).
☎ 02.37.52.01.78
Car park. TV.

A well-kept hotel in a large square. Some of the rooms are fairly small but they're all well looked after. The nice helpful owner is always ready for a chat and can give you some good tips about what to do and see while you're here. Doubles 130F with basin and 250F with shower/wc. A hearty breakfast is 20F.

ORLÉANS 45000

HÔTEL-RESTAURANT L'ÉTOILE D'OR

25-27 place du Vieux-Marché (South); it's between the river and place du Martroi.
☎ 02.38.53.49.20
Closed Sundays, August, and one week at the end of December.

It's very centrally located but the square is quiet. A very old half-timbered building, with stairs that twist and turn, run by a nice lady who works hard keeping the rooms clean. Rates are of the pre-war variety – a double with basin is 95F and one with bath (the most expensive) is 160F! The restaurant too is very simple and inexpensive, with set meals from 68F. One of the cheapest hotels in town.

HÔTEL DE PARIS

29 faubourg Bannier (North).
☎ 02.38.53.39.58
Closed Saturday lunchtimes and Sundays except by reservation.

You'll get a nice and very laid-back welcome. The rooms – from 108F with basin to 160F with bath – are simple but pleasant and a lick of paint and new wallpaper have made them look almost spruce. Your fellow guests will range from American students to workmen travelling to some job or other. There's a bistro on the ground floor that's popular with the locals and where you can have the day's special for 40F at lunchtime.

10% HÔTEL SAINT-MARTIN**

52 bd Alexandre-Martin (Centre); turn left as you come out of the train station and make for the theatre.
☎ 02.38.62.47.47 F 02.38.81.13.28
Closed Dec 23–Jan 2. **TV.**

A little hotel with a nice family atmosphere. Given that it's so near the station, it's surprising that the rooms – they overlook a tiny flower-filled courtyard – are so quiet. Prices start at 145F for a double with washing facilities, but no TV, and go up to 240F for one with shower/wc and TV with Canal+.

10% HÔTEL CENTRAL**

6 rue d'Avignon (Centre); it's 50m from rue Royale.
☎ 02.38.53.93.00 F 02.38.77.23.85
Car park. TV.

This nice provincial hotel has rooms with old-fashioned furniture at prices to suit all pockets: 158F with washing facilities, 173F with basin/wc, 236F with shower/wc and TV. The most luxurious is number 17 with its wainscoting and view of the courtyard. If it's already gone, ask for one that doesn't overlook the street. The hotel is VERY centrally located – the name couldn't be more apt.

10% HÔTEL MARGUERITE**

14 place du Vieux-Marché (Centre); it's 50m from rue Royale, near the main post office.
☎ 02.38.53.74.32 F 02.38.53.31.56
TV. Disabled access.

This is the kind of place that makes our day. It's a handsome building, delightfully old-fashioned, and offers its guests comfortable rooms, reasonable prices, and the type of welcome you associate with a 3-star hotel. As soon as you meet the jovial proprietor –

you'll find him manning the reception desk on the first floor – you'll realize what a nice helpful chap he is. The hotel has 25 large comfortable and well looked after rooms that range in price from 170F (with basin, no TV) to 250F (with bath).

☗ JACKOTEL**

18 cloître Saint-Aignan (South-East); follow quai du Châtelet in the direction of Montargis and turn before you get to the bridge.
☎ 02.38.54.48.48 F➔ 02.38.77.17.59
Secure parking. TV. Disabled access.

A nice hotel, recently built, with a flower-filled courtyard. The rooms, comfortable and well cared for, are worthy of a 3-star establishment. Doubles 290F with bath and phone. The parrots in the reception area don't talk by the way – in fact they don't even breathe. You'll have to make do with the real birds outside. Their twittering is about the only sound you'll hear from the lovely little square in the shadow of the church of Saint-Aignan. A good hotel.

I●I RESTAURANT LA CHANCELLERIE

27 place du Martroi (Centre); it's opposite the statue of Joan of Arc.
☎ 02.38.53.57.54 F➔ 02.38.77.09.92
Closed Sundays and two weeks in February.

Service until midnight. Stage coaches once left from the 18th century building that now houses the most famous brasserie in Orléans. It's almost an institution, in fact, and its customers include local worthies, businessmen and students. The terrace is always pretty lively in summer. The cooking is pretty decent and there's a wide range of dishes to suit all pockets. Lots of good wines are available by the glass – one of the owners was voted best wine waiter in France. If you're in a hurry, try one of the *formules* consisting of a main course plus a glass of wine. Prices start at 55F. They also do set meals at 125F, 140F and 145F. If you go à la carte, you'll be faced with a pretty hefty bill.

I●I RESTAURANT LA TÊTE DE L'ART

13 cloître Saint-Pierre-Empont (Centre); it's in a narrow little street between the Protestant church and the cathedral.
☎ 02.38.54.14.39
Closed Mondays and Sundays.

The restaurant is in a little square totally cut off from the hustle and bustle of the town, so you can have your meal in peace and quiet. And you can choose to eat on the terrace or in the pink dining room with its splendid collection of hats. The proprietress is extremely nice to her young customers who come for the relaxed atmosphere as well as the decent cooking and the generous portions. They stick to the old faithfuls here – no experimenting. The chef knows what he's doing (he's been doing it for forty years after all). Set meals 57F (weekday lunchtimes) and 95F (veal sweetbreads, kidneys, *coq au vin*, calf's head *ravigote*). We rather liked the semi-cured shin of veal on a bed of warm apples. Nice décor, friendly welcome and good value for money.

I●I RESTAURANT LES FAGOTS

32 rue du Poirier (Centre); it's near the covered market.
☎ 02.38.62.22.79 F➔ 02.38.77.99.87
Closed Mondays, Sundays, the first week in January, and the second fortnight in August. **Disabled access**.

As soon as you're over the threshold, you realize that this place has a very special atmosphere. In one corner, two people clearly in love are having a romantic dinner, in another a group of actors are deep in discussion with their director and, over there, two or three regulars are joking with the owner who's busy in the kitchen. The focus for all this activity is the big fireplace in the middle of the dining room with its old posters and enamel and china coffee pots. The restaurant specializes in chargrilling and thick steaks of donkey meat (the latter has to be ordered one day in advance). Set meals 65F (lunchtimes) and 85F. Friendly welcome and service. Given the atmosphere, we'd be tempted to classify it as a place for dinner but the terrace on a sunny day makes it a nice place for lunch too.

I●I RESTAURANT DON QUICHOTTE

165 rue de Bourgogne (Centre).
☎ 02.38.62.36.57
Closed Tuesdays, Wednesday lunchtimes, two weeks in February, and three in July.

Service noon–2.15pm and 7pm–12.30am. A Spanish restaurant with hams hanging from the ceiling to cure. The atmosphere is relaxed and if you like garlic, you'll love the cooking here. The locals are also fond of the paella (81F per person). Jug of sangria is 51F. There are no set meals but you can eat till very late, just like in Spain.

I●I RESTAURANT DES PLANTES

44 rue Tudelle (South-West); it's on the south bank.
☎ 02.38.56.65.55 F➔ 02.38.51.33.27
Closed Saturday lunchtimes, Sundays, Monday evenings, May 1–8, July 27–Aug 18, and one week at Christmas.

Proprietor Dominique Boisgard describes himself as a restaurant owner and wine waiter, so naturally this restaurant, a stone's throw from the local botanic gardens, has a superb cellar, with everything in it having been carefully and skilfully chosen. Put yourself in Dominique's hands and let him guide you in your choice of Loire wine. The cooking is good and a touch sophisticated and the dishes that emerge from the kitchen reflect what the market has to offer. There might be *terrine* of *foie gras* with Muscat, say, or veal kidneys flambéd in Cognac and flavoured with vanilla, panfried zander in a thyme-flavoured sauce, and a *chaud-froid gratin* of orange. Set meals 99F (weekdays), 138F, 158F, 205F and 225F. Last but not least, the welcome and service are friendly and courteous.

|●| LA PETITE MARMITE

178 rue de Bourgogne (Centre); it's near the préfecture.
☎ 02.38.54.23.83 F➔ 02.38.54.41.81

If you want to eat in what is one of the best restaurants in a street that's got more restaurants than any other in Orléans, you'll have to book. Traditional local dishes are what's on offer in the pretty rustic dining room and they do two set meals, one at 118F and one at 146F. The first one (which in theory is not available after 9pm) includes things like goat's chese pâté and rabbit in honey à l'orléanaise and the second comes with the house foie gras. We particularly liked the zander and salmon duo. A la carte there's confit of duck with wild mushrooms, casserole of calf kidneys in sherry vinegar, coq au vin, and tripe. Nice proprietress who spoils her customers.

|●| RESTAURANT LA P'TITE PORTE

28 rue de la Poterne (Centre); it's in the little street that cuts through the middle of rue de Bourgogne.
☎ 02.38.62.28.00
Closed Sundays, Mondays, one week in May, and the first three weeks in August.

This used to be one of those streets where the police had to go around in twos (at least!). The restaurant is housed in a 16th century shop and we were very taken with the long narrow dining room with its ochre walls, second-hand furniture, and house plants. Whoever's in the kitchen believes in keeping things simple and the menu offers a few good meat dishes, mussels with chips and so on. The day's specials chalked up on the board show a bit more imagination though. Best of all, the young owners are big fans of good wine produced by small local vineyards. Their cellar contains some rarer wines and, while they may lean towards those from the Loire, they also have wines from other regions, including the Jura and Côtes-du-Rhône. There are no set meals but you're unlikely to have to spend more than 120F à la carte satisfying your hunger.

MEUNG-SUR-LOIRE 45130 (20KM SW)

|●| RESTAURANT L'OLIVIER

15-17 rue du Général-de-Gaulle; on RN152.
☎ 02.38.45.13.41
Closed Sunday evenings and Tuesday evenings out of season. **Disabled access.**

Lunch served noon–2pm and dinner 7–9.30pm. The little terrace will help you forget that the restaurant's right next to the motorway. The dining room is lovely and the service attentive and unobtrusive. The chef shows considerable flair and imagination when it comes to fish – try the zander in Chinon, sea bass with wild mushrooms or stew of monkfish cheeks in cream. Set meals 75F, 89F, 135F and 175F. The wine list is short but has some incredible finds. By the way, if you like white wine from the Loire, the Cheverny is superb.

PREUILLY-SUR-CLAISE 37290

10% ☗ |●| AUBERGE SAINT-NICOLAS

6 Grande-Rue (Centre).
☎ 02.47.94.50.80. F➔ 02.47.94.41.77
Closed Sunday evenings and Mondays (except in July and August) and mid-Sept–beginning of Oct.
Secure private parking. **TV.**

Lunch served 11.30am–2pm and dinner 7.15–9pm. This hotel near the abbey has nine fully-equipped rooms all of which have been completely refurbished and are decorated in yellow. Doubles with shower/wc start at 180F. Pleasant welcome and good value for money. The dining room's a bit gloomy. Regional cooking, with set meals 68F (weekdays) and 120–210F.

PETIT-PRESSIGNY (LE) 37350 (9KM N)

|●| RESTAURANT LA PROMENADE

11 rue du Savoureulx; take the D41 in the direction of Loches then the D50.
☎ 02.47.94.93.52 F➔ 02.47.91.06.03
Closed Sunday evenings, Mondays, Jan 5–18, and Sept 21–Oct 6.

There used to be an inn here and the dining room has been turned into two pretty contemporary-looking rooms, full of soft lines and flower motifs. Jacky Dallais, who trained under Robuchon, is genuinely creative and his cooking shows integrity, hard work, attention to detail and imagination. He has not been resting on his laurels and the menu changes constantly. You don't have to be a millionaire to experience what he has to offer since the prices are incredibly reasonable. The 140F set meal (available weekdays) is excellent value for money, consisting of dishes like cream of pumpkin soup with hazelnuts, lemon chicken with crayfish butter, and cocoa sorbet with butterscotch. Other set meals 200–380F. Delightful welcome from the proprietress and efficient service overseen by the head waiter, who is also a wine waiter of some considerable skill. They don't demand that you wear a dinner jacket or even a tie, so relax. Reservations essential at the weekend.

RICHELIEU 37120

LES MOUSQUETAIRES

4 av. du Colonel-Goulier (Centre); it's two minutes from the town centre.
☎ 02.47.58.15.17
Closed Tuesdays until 8pm. **TV**. **Disabled access**.

An unpretentious but comfortable little hotel outside the old ramparts that has five double rooms leading straight out into the garden. Prices start at 155F for shower/wc rising to 225F for a room that sleeps four. You can have a TV if you want one (15F supplement). Nice welcome. The bill will come as a pleasant surprise. There's a small bar.

ROMORANTIN-LANTHENAY 41200

10% HÔTEL-RESTAURANT LE COLOMBIER**

18 place du Vieux-Marché; it's 150m from the town hall.
☎ 02.54.76.12.76 ➡ 02.54.76.39.40
Closed mid-Feb–mid-March. Restaurant closed Saturdays (except if there's a public holiday).
Secure parking. **TV**.

Lunch served noon–2pm and dinner 7–9pm. Rooms are comfortable and come with direct phone. Ask for one overlooking the courtyard. Doubles 240F with shower/wc, 270F with bath. Pleasant garden. The restaurant offers regional cooking and carefully prepared dishes, that change with the seasons – *chartreuse* of rabbit and duck *foie gras* with horn of plenty mushrooms, bream with a Bourgueil sauce, and panfried veal with morels, for example. Set meals 100F (starter, main course, cheese and dessert) and 175F. It has a good reputation.

HÔTEL-RESTAURANT-AUBERGE LE LANTHENAY**

rue Notre-Dame-du-Lieu; leave Romorantin by the Paris road, go past the Leclerc market and it's on the left.
☎ 02.54.76.09.19 ➡ 02.54.76.72.91
Closed Sunday evenings, Mondays, July 15–30, and Dec 22–Jan 10. **Car park**. **TV**. **Disabled access**.

Lunch served 12.15–2pm and dinner 7.30–9pm. The restaurant has two large dining rooms with classic low-key décor and caters for a wide range of customers who all have a taste for the simple things in life. The cooking is wonderful and the service impeccable. Cheapest set meal is 105F (not available Sundays or public holidays). The restaurant specializes in fish but also does *persillé* of veal with herbs, lamb stew, and pigeon in a red wine sauce. Comfortable bedrooms 245–300F. The ones in the west wing overlook the garden – ask for one of those.

SAINT-AMAND-MONTROND 18200

10% HÔTEL-RESTAURANT LE NOIRLAC**

215 route de Bourges (North-West); it's on the N144, 5km from the tollbooth on the A71 and 700m from the bypass on the N144.
☎ 02.48.96.80.80 ➡ 02.48.96.63.88
Closed for one week after Christmas. Restaurant closed Sunday evenings Nov–Easter. **Car park**. **TV**. **Canal+**. **Disabled access**.

Ideally situated for motorists even though visually it's not particularly appealing and looks like one of a chain. It's ultra modern and has a pool, tennis courts and putting green. Have a look round the back! The rooms (320F) are super comfortable and practical – there are even two specially designed for the disabled. Bravo! Efficient staff in both the hotel and the restaurant. The cheapest set meal (95F). is substantial and it's available every day of the week. The restaurant's specialities are fricassee of snails and *goujonnettes* of sole with mushrooms. Quite lively in summer. The Cistercian abbey of Noirlac, founded by St Bernard in 1150, is 2.5km away.

RESTAURANT LE SAINT-JEAN

1 rue de l'Hôtel-Dieu.
☎ 02.48.96.39.82
Closed Sunday evenings and Monday.

If you've been to the lovely Saint-Vic museum, think about coming here for a meal – it's worth it. It has a cosy country-style dining room complete with flowers, beams and old wooden floor. Chef Philippe Perrichon prepares a quite incredible set meal for 85F – chicken liver *terrine*, ling fillets with shellfish, cheese and *nougatine glacée*. That's the best value for money you'll find in town so there's no point in just turning up at the weekend – BOOK!

ORVAL 18200 (2KM W)

HÔTEL-RESTAURANT DU PONT DU CHER*

2 av. de la Gare; on the D925.
☎ 02.48.96.00.51 F 02.48.96.49.26
Closed Sunday evenings and Mondays (public holidays excepted). **Car park**.

Lunch served noon–2pm and dinner 7.30–9pm. A pleasant country-style inn with geraniums at the windows. A glassed-in terrace gives you a view of the Cher. The cooking is traditional and the chef a professional. He does a particularly good duck in orange sauce. Cheapest set meal 70F. The hotel is quiet and comfortable. Doubles 145–180F.

BRUÈRE-ALLICHAMPS 18200 (9KM NW)

AUBERGE DE L'ABBAYE DE NOIRLAC

How to get there: at Saint-Amand, take the N144 in the direction of Bourges; 4km further on, turn onto the Noirlac road; it's opposite the abbey.
☎ 02.48.96.22.58.
Closed Wednesdays and Jan 8–Feb 10.

The inn has two dining rooms. The first is for bistro-style food and during the summer months you can tuck into a sandwich, an omelette or a plate of *charcuterie* at prices starting from 25F. The second is for those who take their food a little more seriously and has a red quarry-tiled floor, beams, and exposed stonework. Chef Pascal Verdier is better at cooking meat than fish and we recommend the duck breast with panfried *foie gras* and the young rabbit with horn of plenty mushrooms. Prices are reasonable – the cheapest set meal at 95F includes cheese and dessert.

TOUCHAY 18160 (26KM W)

AUBERGE DES SEPT SŒURS

Centre; take the D300, then the D925 in the direction of Lignières, then the D3.
☎ 02.48.60.06.77
Closed Sunday evenings, Mondays (except in July and August), 10 days at the end of February, and 10 at the end of September. Out of season, the restaurant is open to hotel guests, except on Satuday evenings.

Lunch served noon–2pm and dinner 7.30–9pm. A good inn run by two sisters. It has large bay windows and rustic beams. Wonderful smells greet you as you walk through the door. The 57F *menu du jour* (weekday lunchtimes) gives you generous servings of fish *terrine*, *bœuf bourguignon* and floating islands. The 92F set meal is a bit fancier. Efficient service. You'll have to book for Sunday lunch.

SALBRIS 41300

10% DOMAINE DE VALAUDRAN***

route de Romorantin; it's at the Salbris exit, on the right as you head for Romorantin.
☎ 02.54.97.20.00 F 02.54.97.12.22
Closed January and February. **Car park**. **TV**. **Canal+**. **Disabled access**.

Lunch served noon–2pm and dinner 7–10pm. A magnificent 19th century mansion that stands proudly at the end of an avenue of trees. The sophisticated décor is like something out of a glossy magazine, the bedrooms are the last word in comfort and there's a heated outdoor swimming pool. The dining room is bathed in light and tantalizing smells come from the kitchens of chef Christophe Cosme, who trained under Bernard Loiseau and hasn't forgotten any of the great man's teaching. How much does all this luxury cost? Set meals – the menu changes every day – start at 120F (weekdays) and the least expensive double room is 385F. You'll get a particularly pleasant welcome.

NOUAN-LE-FUZELIER 41600 (12KM N)

LE DAHU

14 rue Henri-Chapron; take the N20 in the direction of La Ferté-Saint-Aubin.
☎ 02.54.88.72.88. F same.
Closed Tuesday evenings and Wednesdays (except in July and August) and Feb 20–March 20. **Car park**.

Lunch served noon–2pm and dinner 7.15–9.15pm. Marie-Thérèse and Jean-Luc Germain have created an incredible garden for their restaurant, a farmhouse surrounded by greenery in an otherwise rather dreary suburb. Outside it has hundred year old beams, while the cosy interior manages to be both rustic and elegant. Set meals 95F (not available Saturday evenings or Sundays, unfortunately), 125F, 158F (with cheese), 190F and 240F. The delights to emerge from the kitchen include *consommé* of garden peas and mint, guinea fowl with cider vinegar and honey, crayfish tails with coriander, and pear *fondant.*

SAINT-VIÂTRE 41210 (20KM NW)

AUBERGE DE LA CHICHONE**

place de l'Église; by the N20 and then the D93.
☎ 02.54.88.91.33 F 02.54.96.18.06
Closed Tuesday evenings, Wednesdays, and March. **TV**.

Lunch served noon–2.30pm and dinner 7.30–10pm.22h. If you're here in summer, book a table in the garden like a good many other people do. Inside, you'll find your typical Sologne farmhouse, hunting memorabilia, rustic décor as interpreted by the middle classes, and beams that have the patina of age. The cooking is that of the immediate area and dishes like salmon *à l'unilatérale* (cooked on one side only) and duck *confit* with apples are a success. Set meals range in price from 89F (not available Sundays) to 199F. Don't order that last one unless you've been out hiking all day – the one at 149F is pretty substantial as it is! Doubles 290F with shower/wc, 320F with bath. Ask for room number 1, 5 or 6 if you want to see traditional local décor. There's a 14th century church – the scene of many pilgrimages – just across from the inn and the beautiful *route des étangs* starts here. Don't forget your camera!

SANCERRE 18300

LE SAINT-MARTIN**

10 rue Saint-Martin (Centre); it's between the ramparts and Nouvelle-Place.
☎ 02.48.54.21.11 F 02.48.54.39.55
Closed beginning Nov–end March. **Car park**. **TV**. **Disabled access**.

There's nothing like a night in the *Saint-Martin* to make you feel full of the joys of life next day. The frontage is modern and perhaps a little stark. Inside, the rooms are large and fairly soundproof and the beds are comfortable. Prices for a fully equipped double range from 205F to 280F. The restaurant has set meals at 65F (not available Sundays or public holidays), 90F and 120F, featuring dishes like a salad of *crottin de Chavignol* (the famous goat's cheese) and a calf's head *ravigote* that will help you (almost) forget the light fixtures and false marble in the decidedly old-fashioned dining room. If you're a wine lover, ask at reception (a mini tourist information office) for details of how to get to the vineyards of Saint-Andelain, Pouilly-sur-Loire and Chaudoux. Or if you're more health-conscious, you can ask at the same place for a voucher entitling you to use the pool of a neighbouring establishment.

RESTAURANT LA POMME D'OR

place de la Mairie (Centre). If you're coming from Sancerre, follow the signs for the town hall.
☎ 02.48.54.13.30
Closed Mondays (Monday evenings only Oct–April) and Wednesday evenings.

An elegant restaurant in the old part of town. The cooking is basically traditional – though, to suit modern tastes, it's not as heavy – with some pleasant rustic touches. Try the saddle of rabbit with early vegetables, the roast zander in Sancerre, the veal kidneys in thyme flavoured juices, or the young pigeon with spices). The cheapest set meal is 78F (available lunchtimes except Sundays) and is excellent value for money. There are others at 128F, 178F and 218F. Proprietor Didier Turpin, a wine waiter who's mad about wine, has a wonderful selection, including some venerable Pouilly-Fumés, at good prices.

SAINT-SATUR 18300 (3KM NE)

10% HÔTEL-RESTAURANT LE LAURIER**

29 rue du Commerce; by the D955.
☎ 02.48.54.17.20 F 02.48.54.04.54
Closed Sunday evenings and Mondays (except in July and August), the first fortnight in March, and the second fortnight in November. **TV**.

After buying yourself a few bottles of a good Sancerre, carry on to Saint-Satur, which is not too far away. You'll find this place, swathed in Virginia creeper, 100m from a handsome abbey. The dining room, with its copperware, exposed beams and old wooden furniture, has clearly been decorated by someone with a taste for authenticity. You'll pay 110F for a double room with basin and 230F for a larger room with bath, prices that are truly reasonable for this very touristy area. The restaurant offers good regional cooking and set meals at 80F (weekdays) 100F, 140F and 190F. Its specialities are poached eggs in a wine saucecalf's head and tongue in two different sauces, zander with chive butter, and game in season.

|●| AU BORD DE LOIRE

2 quai de la Loire; from Sancerre, take the D955 in the direction of Cosne-Gien. Cross Saint-Satur and Saint-Thibault until you come to the bridge on the outskirts of the village.
☎ 02.48.54.12.15
Closed Monday evenings, Tuesdays, two weeks in February, and two in November.

A pleasantly rustic place this, with a pergola, wooden tables, and large windows overlooking the terrace and garden that stretch right to the water's edge. The owner is a Gascon and sometimes the set meals reflect that fact with one or two Gascon specialities. Set meals are 78F (not available Sunday lunchtimes) – 98F with cheese – 115F, 150F, 180F and 250F and offer things like pike in mustard, rabbit in a Sauvignon sauce, and the typically Berry dish of *veau au vin* (veal in a wine sauce).

CHAVIGNOL 18300 (5KM W)

|●| RESTAURANT LA CÔTE DES MONTS DAMNÉS

le bourg; from Sancerre, take the D955 in the direction of Cosne/Gien and then the D183.
☎ 02.48.54.01.72 F➜ 02.48.54.14.24
Closed Sunday evenings, Mondays, and February.

Lunch served 12.15–1.30pm and dinner 7.30–9.30pm. A rustic inn with beams, patterned fabrics, and a cosy, almost romantic, atmosphere. Local produce plays the starring role in robust dishes with very distinct flavours, things like tagliatelli with crottin (a fairly strong goat's cheese), saddle of lamb stuffed with veal kidneys, and a very good salmon with a sauce made from wine lees. The wine list is full of bargains from all parts of France. Nice staff. The 98F set meal give good value for money.

SANCOINS 18600

☗ |●| HÔTEL-RESTAURANT LE COMMERCE*

place de la Libération; it's in the square opposite the church.
☎ 02.48.76.20.61
Closed Fridays, Sundays in winter, and the third week in November. **Private Car park. TV.**

This place has been a must since the turn of the century. Cheerful Madame Jeannot will supply you with an omelette or a plate of *charcuterie* at any hour of the day or night. Set meals 51–210F. The walls are covered in Virginia creeper and the only sound you might perhaps hear in your room will be Mass from the church across the way. Doubles 145–230F.

☗ HÔTEL DU PARC**

8 rue Marguerite-Audoux.
☎ 02.48.74.56.60 F➜ 02.48.74.61.30
Closed Jan 1–15. **Secure parking.**

It looks like a château and it's got lots of class and extensive grounds. The rooms are lovely, with their Baroqu-style mirrors and red or blue velvet bedspreads, and they are quiet. Pleasant welcome. Doubles 175–270F.

GUERCHE-SUR-L'AUBOIS (LA) 18150 (15KM N)

☗ |●| RESTAURANT LE BERRY**

12 rue Jean-Jaurès (or route de Sancoins); by the D976.
☎ 02.48.74.00.41 F➜ 02.48.74.19.96.
Closed Friday evenings and Sundays out of season and Dec 20–Jan 4. **Secure parking. TV. Disabled access.**

Lunch served noon–1.30pm and dinner 7.30–9pm. This is a very nice inn that's full every day of the week. As its name indicates, it specializes in Berry dishes. A word of advice: make a reservation if you want to try the *andouillette* in Sancerre and all those sauces that go so well with fish and game. Set meals 75–190F. Just about every variation on the internal combustion engine seems to use this road – luckily the rooms are quiet. Doubles 300F with shower, 340F with bath.

SULLY-SUR-LOIRE 45600

10% ☗ |●| HÔTEL-RESTAURANT DE LA POSTE**

11 rue du Faubourg-Saint-Germain (Centre).
☎ 02.38.36.26.22 F➜ 02.38.36.39.35
Secure parking. TV. Canal+.

Lunch served noon–2pm and dinner 7–9pm. Some of the rooms in this former coaching inn have a view of the Loire. In others, you'll have to make do with the TV. Doubles range in price from 175F (with washing facilities) to 300F (with bath). The cheapest set meal is 96 F and may have crab cakes with sorrel or fillet of perch as its main course. Other set meals 105–210F. This place is a bit of an institution in Sully. And the large cage full of parrots in the courtyard is almost as well known.

SAINT-BENOÎT-SUR-LOIRE 45730 (8KM NW)

10% ☗ HÔTEL DU LABRADOR**

7 place de l'Abbaye; it's opposite the basilica.

☎ 02.38.35.74.38 ➡ 02.38.35.72.99
Closed in January. **Secure parking**. **TV**. **Disabled access**.

You'll find the hotel in a quiet little square that almost lends itself to meditation (must be something to do with the abbey being so close!). The hotel's rather nice, with old-fashioned rooms (180F for a double with basin). The rooms in the somewhat more modern annex are more comfortable and tastefully decorated. Some have exposed beams, others – numbers 4 and 7 for example – have a nice view of the abbey or the surrounding countryside. Doubles with shower or bath 310–335F. There's a tea room with a very pleasant terrace.

TOURNON-SAINT-MARTIN 36220

10% AUBERGE DU CAPUCIN GOURMAND**

7 bis route du Blanc -
8 rue du Bel-Air (Centre).
☎ 02.54.37.66.85 ➡ 02.54.37.87.54
Closed Sunday evenings and Mondays out of season, one week in October, and the month of February.
Secure parking.

Lunch served noon–2.30pm and dinner 7.30–9pm. The inn has a very large and pleasant front garden filled with flowers and that's where you eat, weather permitting. Friendly welcome and service. We had nothing but nice things to say about the 80F set meal which, when we were there, consisted of a country salad with Berri lentils *vinaigrette*, walnuts, and homemade *rillons*, followed by sautéd rabbit with sage from the garden and a choice of Pouligny goat's cheese or baked apple with angelica. Other set meals 100F, 120F, 160F and 195F. Bedrooms are spotless. Double with bath 270F.

TOURS 37000

SEE MAP OVERLEAF

10% HÔTEL SAINT-ÉLOI*

79 bd Béranger. **MAP A2-2**
☎ 02.47.37.67.34 ➡ 02.47.39.34.67
TV.

A little garden with a superb magnolia tree shields the hotel from the worst of the traffic noise. It's a small place run by a young couple and it's clean, quiet, simple and friendly. Rooms come with washing facilities or shower/wc. Doubles 140–180F. Street parking in front of or behind the hotel.

10% HÔTEL LE LYS D'OR*

21-23 rue de la Vendée. **MAP C2-9**
☎ 02.47.05.33.45 ➡ 02.47.64.19.00

It's ideally located and very quiet. Prices start at 120F for a double with washing facilities, rising to 185F for one with shower/wc. The country-style décor is pleasant enough. Rooms overlooking the garden are brighter. Friendly welcome.

10% HÔTEL-RESTAURANT MODERNE**

1-3 rue Victor-Laloux. **MAP C2-3**
☎ 02.47.05.32.81 ➡ 02.47.05.71.50
Closed Dec 22–Jan 28. Restaurant closed Saturday lunchtimes and Sundays. **Car park**. **TV**.

The hotel, a fine-looking building in the traditional Touraine style, is located in a quiet neighbourhood and has doubles – one or two of them attic rooms – at prices ranging from 179F to 330F. We loved the hushed atmosphere and also the proprietor's tasty rustic style of cooking. Set meals at 75F and 95F feature things like salad with *rillons* and *andouillette vouvrillonne*. (sausage cooked in Vouvray, a white wine from the Loire). Half-board available from 260F per person. There's a paying car park close by.

10% HÔTEL BALZAC**

47 rue de la Scellerie. **MAP C1-5**
☎ 02.47.05.40.87 ➡ 02.47.20.82.30
TV. **Canal+**.

A friendly, rather plush and very centrally located hotel with 18 rooms, 15 with shower or bath and 3 with basin. Doubles 220–300F. Numbers 15, 18 and 21 are particularly large and quiet. In fine weather, you can have a drink or breakfast on the nice internal terrace. If you don't want to miss your favourite TV programme, you can order a meal on a tray (no later than 7pm). Special rates for the Touraine golf course.

10% HÔTEL GAMBETTA**

7 rue Gambetta. **MAP B2-4**
☎ 02.47.05.08.35 ➡ 02.47.05.58.59
Car park. **TV**.

An extremely handsome 18th century town house with a long narrow garden in the central courtyard, which most of the rooms overlook. The Swiss proprietor trained and then taught at the hotel school in Lausanne and cares a lot about standards. Lots of different levels, crooked walls, and the colour schemes combine to create a charming interior. There are 39 rooms and while some of

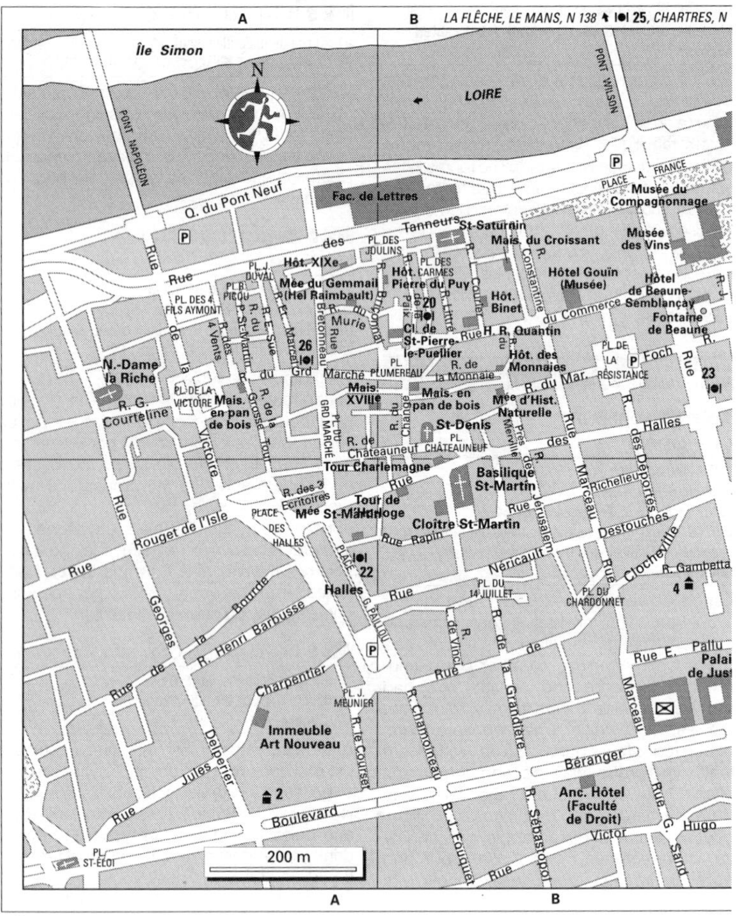
LA FLÈCHE, LE MANS, N 138 25, CHARTRES, N
Île Simon
LOIRE
PONT NAPOLÉON
PONT WILSON
Q. du Pont Neuf
Fac. de Lettres
PLACE A. FRANCE
Musée du Compagnonnage
St-Saturnin
Mais. du Croissant
Musée des Vins
Hôtel Gouïn (Musée)
Hôtel de Beaune-Semblançay
Fontaine de Beaune
Hôt. XIXe
Mée du Gemmail (Hel Raimbault)
Hôt. Pierre du Puy
Hôt. Binet
Cl. de St-Pierre-le-Puellier
H. R. Quantin
Hôt. des Monnaies
N.-Dame la Riche
Mais. XVIIIe
Mais. en pan de bois
Mée d'Hist. Naturelle
St-Denis
Basilique St-Martin
Tour Charlemagne
Tour de l'Horloge
Mée St-Martin
Cloître St-Martin
Halles
Immeuble Art Nouveau
Anc. Hôtel (Faculté de Droit)
Palais de Justice
200 m
A
B

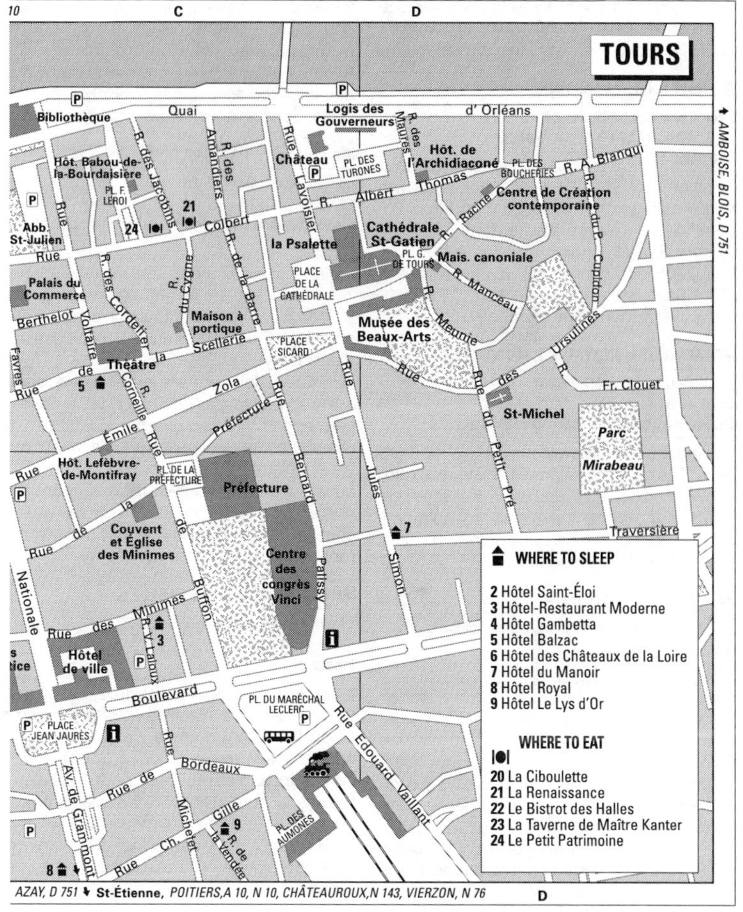
TOURS
Bibliothèque
Quai d' Orléans
Logis des Gouverneurs
Château
PL. DES TURONES
Hôt. de l'Archidiaconé
PL. DES BOUCHERIES
Hôt. Babou-de-la-Bourdaisière
PL. F. LEROI
Centre de Création contemporaine
Abb. St-Julien
Cathédrale St-Gatien
la Psalette
PL. G. DE TOURS
Mais. canoniale
PLACE DE LA CATHÉDRALE
Palais du Commerce
Maison à portique
Musée des Beaux-Arts
PLACE SICARD
Théâtre
St-Michel
Parc Mirabeau
Hôt. Lefèbvre-de-Montifray
PL. DE LA PRÉFECTURE
Préfecture
Couvent et Église des Minimes
Centre des congrès Vinci
Hôtel de ville
PL. DU MARÉCHAL LECLERC
PLACE JEAN JAURÈS
PL. DES AUMONES
AMBOISE, BLOIS, D 751
AZAY, D 751 St-Étienne, POITIERS, A 10, N 10, CHÂTEAUROUX, N 143, VIERZON, N 76
WHERE TO SLEEP
2 Hôtel Saint-Éloi
3 Hôtel-Restaurant Moderne
4 Hôtel Gambetta
5 Hôtel Balzac
6 Hôtel des Châteaux de la Loire
7 Hôtel du Manoir
8 Hôtel Royal
9 Hôtel Le Lys d'Or
WHERE TO EAT
20 La Ciboulette
21 La Renaissance
22 Le Bistrot des Halles
23 La Taverne de Maître Kanter
24 Le Petit Patrimoine

them may not be very large they're all quiet and comfortable. Doubles with shower/wc 265F. New bed linen. Very friendly welcome.

HÔTEL DU MANOIR**

2 rue Traversière. **MAP D2-7**
☎ 02.47.05.37.37 ➡ 02.47.05.16.00
Car park. TV.

This hotel, located in a quiet street, is a town house dating from the last century. It has 20 tastefully refurbished rooms done in pastel colours and with English-style furniture. Doubles 270F with shower/wc, 290F with bath. The attic rooms are very pleasant. Nice welcome. Very good value for money.

10% HÔTEL ROYAL CLARINE***

65 av. de Grammont. **MAP C2-8**
☎ 02.47.64.71.78 ➡ 02.47.05.84.62
Secure parking. TV. Canal+. Disabled access.

You'll get a friendly welcome in this modern hotel. The bedrooms and the dining room are furnished in Louis XV and Louis XVI style but they're not over the top. It's all very comfortable. All 50 rooms have bath, satellite TV and phone. Doubles from 350F.

L'ATELIER GOURMAND

37 rue Étienne-Marcel; it's in the old part of town, very near place Plumereau.
☎ 02.47.38.59.87

Lunch served noon–2pm and dinner 7–11.30pm. The two remarkable men who own this place – chef Fabrice and brother David who looks after the dining room – are doing great things with the local style of cooking. Try the fresh goat's cheese with green peppers (35F), lamb chops in a garlic sauce (55 F), and apple *confit* with prunes (35 F). The wine cellar contains the best vintages from their native Val-de-Loire (80–135F). The little 15th century dining room has been redecorated and hung with paintings by contemporary local artists. *Formule* 49F at lunchtime, 94F in the evening. Terrace.

RESTAURANT LA CIBOULETTE

25 rue de la Paix. **MAP B1-20**
☎ 02.47.61.57.28 ➡ 02.47.61.71.62
Closed Sundays and Monday lunchtimes.
Disabled access.

The restaurant is very pleasantly situated with a terrace overlooking the Saint-Pierre-Le Puellier garden and the handsome country-style dining room has exposed beams and a stone fireplace. They do a 68F set meal weekday lunchtimes. Other set meals – 98F and 140F – feature dishes like a salad of warm gizzards, *croustillant* of whiting with tomato butter, and red mullet with baby vegetables. Touraine wines available by the glass. Service is a bit slow.

LE PETIT PATRIMOINE

58 rue Colbert. **MAP C1-24**
☎ 02.47.66.05.81
Closed Sundays out of season and for the month of November.

Lunch served noon–2pm and dinner 7–10pm. There are lots of restaurants in rue Colbert but if you want to sample local dishes, this is the place to come. They have set meals ranging in price from 70F to 135F, all with wonderful regional specialities like *tourte aux rillons*, *andouillette à la Vouvrillonne*, (sausage in Vouvray, one of the white Loire wines), *matelote* of veal (veal stew with red wine, onions and mushrooms), and pike in *beurre blanc*. If you've still got room for dessert, try the pears in wine or the goat's cheese with blackberry jelly. Small dining room with exposed beams.

LE BISTROT DES HALLES

31 place Gaston-Paillhou. **MAP A2-22**
☎ 02.47.61.54.93
Closes at 11pm.

If you like old-fashioned bistros, you'll love this. The service is faultless but that doesn't mean the atmosphere is starchy. Regional specialities – *rillons, rillettes bouillabaisse* (fish soup) and so on – have pride of place in the menu here. The 95F *formule* is pretty decent, as are the set meals at 75F and 150F (which includes wine). Reckon on 110F à la carte. Good selection of Loire wines.

RESTAURANT LA RENAISSANCE

64 rue Colbert; take rue Nationale. **MAP C1-21**
☎ 02.47.66.63.25
Closed Mondays, Sunday evenings in winter, and the month of December.

You'll get a warm welcome in this restaurant, with its country-style dining room and padded chairs. The traditional cooking is first-rate and set meals start at 75F. If you take the one at 120F, you'll get scallops in a cream and lemon juice sauce followed by *andouillette* or another meat dish, cheese, and a good homemade dessert. The fruit tarts – cherry, apple, pear, grape or plum, depending on the season – are wonderful.

|●| LATAVERNE DE MAÎTRE KANTER

48 rue Nationale. **MAP B1-23**
☎ 02.47.05.66.84

Service noon–midnight. You'll feel at home immediately in this enormous tavern cum brasserie. Apart from anything else, the staff are nice and really look after you. You can have *choucroute* washed down with a good drop of beer or one of the seafood specialities which include a fairly hefty "fisherman's platter" of oysters, shrimp, langoustines, mussels, clams, winkles and whelks. Reckon on paying about 120F for a good meal. Definitely one for the address book!

|●| RESTAURANT CHARLES BARRIER**

101 av. de la Tranchée; it's on the other side of the Loire, in the street that's a continuation of pont Wilson. Off map **B1-25**
☎ 02.47.54.20.39 ➡ 02.47.41.80.95
Closed Sunday evenings. **Car park. Disabled access.**

Lunch served noon–2.30pm and dinner 7–9.30pm. If you're really into gourmet food, this is the place to indulge yourself. The cooking is traditional, of course, but it's an absolute joy. The setting – the dining room looks onto a garden – and the quality of the service will only add to your pleasure and give you a memorable time. Set meals start at 150F and 230F and go all the way up to 540F (for the seriously rich, that one). Roast langoustines, a stew of Loire eels in a prune and Chinon sauce, and pig's trotters stuffed with lamb sweetbreads and truffles are just a few of the delights on offer.

VOUVRAY 37210 (8KM NE)

⌂ |●| HÔTEL-RESTAURANT L'AUBERGE DU GRAND VATEL**

8 rue Brûlé (Centre); take the N152 and follow the north bank of the Loire – when you get to Vouvray, turn left after Hardouin the caterer's.
☎ 02.47.52.70.32 ➡ 02.47.52.74.52
Closed Sunday evenings out of season, Mondays, the first fortnight in March, and the first fortnight in December. **Secure parking. Disabled access.**

Bernard Copin's restaurant is one of the most famous in the area. He uses nothing but the freshest of local ingredients and serves up dishes like house *foie gras* (which is delicious), shrimp in orange butter, *beuchelle tourangelle* (veal sweetbreads and kidneys with morels and truffles in a cream sauce) and medallions of lamb with pecan nuts. The wine list naturally features wonderful old Vouvrays. The 230F set meal will give you a great deal of pleasure, and there are others starting at 98F (weekdays). Doubles 240–270F with bath.

MONNAIE 37380 (14KM NE)

|●| RESTAURANT AU SOLEIL LEVANT**

53 rue Nationale (Centre); on the N10 north of Tours.
☎ 02.47.56.10.34
Closed Mondays, Sunday evenings, the second fortnight in January, and the first in August.

Lunch served noon–2pm and dinner 7–9.15pm. This has to be one of the best gourmet restaurants in the area. Sophisticated décor. Seasonal produce and imagination combine to produce dishes that bear no resemblance to the usual things served up as regional specialities. However hungry you are and however much (or little) money you have to spend, there's a set meal to suit you. These range in price from 100F to 220F and offer lots and lots of good things, including braised sole with chives and *croustillant* of pig's trotters with a truffle sauce.

TROO 41800

|●| LE PETIT RELAIS

place du château; on the D917 – it's opposite the collegiate church.
☎ 02.54.72.57.92
Closed Monday lunchtimes.

Service from 12.30pm and 7.30pm. This little restaurant in the old part of the village is an absolute must – we fell in love with it. Maryse, the owner, is in a class all by herself. She's the one who lovingly prepares the tasty meals and then brings them to your table. And while she's serving you, she'll keep up a cheerful conversation, telling some story or commenting on the food – *rillons* of rabbit in Vouvray, perch in Cheverny, saddle of rabbit *à l'ancienne*, *andouillette* in Jasnières wine, and chicken cooked in Anjou wine. Reckon on about 150F à la carte. Maryse also does a day's special at lunchtime for 50F. For all we know, she's probably bottle-washer as well as head cook.

VALENÇAY 36600

⌂ HÔTEL DU LION D'OR**

place de la Halle; it's very near the château de Valençay.
☎ 02.54.00.00.87 ➡ 02.54.00.09.20
Restaurant closed Mondays and in January and February.
Secure parking. TV. Disabled access.

The hotel is opposite the pretty old building that used to house the town's corn exchange and, with its wooden balconies overlooking an inner courtyard and a handsome terrace shaded by an enormous wisteria, looks the way inns used to look. Talleyrand bought it when he was Napoleon's foreign minister so as to have somewhere to receive visiting foreign dignitaries. Unfortunately, the cooking is fairly heavy and difficult to digest, not quite what you'd expect in these romantic surroundings. Set meals 68F, 95F and 145F. Doubles with shower/wc or bath 250F or 260F.

CHABRIS 36210 (14KM NE)

10% HÔTEL DE LA PLAGE**

42 rue du Pont (Centre); take the D4 – it's between Valençay and Romorantin.
☎ 02.54.40.02.24 F 02.54.40.08.59
Closed Mondays and Dec 22–Feb 10. **TV**.

Lunch served noon–2pm and dinner 7.30–9pm. A nice little restaurant and a good place to stop for a meal and a rest. They do a 95F *formule* based on a main course and set meals at 140F (fricassee of wild mushrooms and snails, and fillet of *merval* in Reuilly), 180F and 220F. The wine list features mainly wines from Touraine, Val de Loire and the valley of the Cher. There's a conservatory with a fountain where you can eat in fine weather. Doubles with shower/wc from 194F.

VANNES-SUR-COSSON 45510

RESTAURANT LE VIEUX RELAIS

route d'Isdes.
☎ 02.38.58.04.14.
Closed Mondays and Sunday evenings. **Car park**.

Granted, this magnificent house doesn't look as if it was built last year but it's quite a shock to find out that it dates from 1462 (and some of the beams are even older) and that it's been an inn of one kind or another since 1515. If only the walls of what is one of the six oldest inns in France could speak, they would have thousands of stories to tell. Why are there marks of a sword on the staircase, for example? The cooking lives up to the magnificent surroundings and if you time it right you might get a chance to sample the chef's *foie gras*. Apart from that, he uses only seasonal ingredients. There's game naturally, considering the part of the world we're in, but everything from the scallops in a langoustine sauce to the *crème brûlée* is out of this world. Set meals 98F (weekdays), 145F and 195F. Reservations are essential.

VENDÔME 41100

HÔTEL-RESTAURANT L'AUBERGE DE LA MADELEINE

place de la Madeleine (Centre); head in the direction of Blois.
☎ 02.54.77.20.79 F 02.54.80.00.02
Restaurant closed Wednesdays and during the February school holidays. **Car park**. **TV**.

Lunch served noon–1.45pm and dinner 7.30–9pm. An unpretentious and charmingly old-fashioned place. Rooms 210F with shower/wc, 260F with bath. Numbers 7 and 8 are the largest. Good plain cooking with set meals 82–215F. The one at 135F was particularly nice, with calf's head, rabbit with mushrooms, cheese and dessert. Friendly welcome.

GRAND HÔTEL SAINT-GEORGES

14 rue Poterie (Centre); it's in the old part of town, 50m from porte Saint-Georges.
☎ 02.54.77.25.42 F 02.54.80.22.57
TV.

An extremely handsome hotel dating from the turn of the century, looking vaguely like the traditional kind of house you'd see in Normandy. The foyer and dining room are luxurious but the prices are quite affordable. A word of warning: the rooms vary in terms of desirability (some of them are very damp) so ask to have a look first. Doubles 245–270F. Staff in both the hotel and the restaurant are very professional in their approach. The restaurant's pretty expensive, with set meals at 95F and 150F (the latter includes home-smoked white fish or salmon). Fresh *foie gras*. And there's a wonderful *compote* of figs for dessert.

LE VIEUX MOULIN

21-23 rue du Change (Centre); it's in a pedestrian street between parc Ronsard and the jetty.
☎ 02.54.72.29.10

A brasserie that's been recently renovated. All that remains of the old mill is a reproduction wheel. Attentive service and decent cooking. It's not really anything special but it's in a pleasant setting and it's the only place in town with a terrace right on the river. And the prices are good – starters and desserts 30F, daily specials 55F à la carte. Specialities include *choucroute royale* (with champagne), calf's head, and zander with lemon butter.

|●| RESTAURANT LE PARIS

1 rue Darreau (North); go up faubourg Chartrain and it's after the train station.
☎ 02.54.77.02.71 F➜ 02.54.73.17.71
Closed Mondays, Tuesday evenings, Sunday evenings, and July 25–Aug 4.

This is an excellent gourmet restaurant with a charming proprietress, impeccable service, and an inspired chef, whose sauces are particularly good. Try the chicken livers with a shellfish sauce, the calf's head *ravigote* (in a spicy *vinaigrette*), which is served at just the right temperature, the succulent veal with Roquefort, casserole of gizzards with asparagus tips, pigeon done in the local style or the veal kidneys. Don't forget to order a good local wine like the Bourgueil Domaine Lalande. Cheapest set meal 89F; others 139F, 172F and 199F.

SAINT-OUEN 41100 (2KM N)

|●| LA VALLÉE

34 rue Barré-de-Saint-Venant. From Vendôme, take the D92 and head for Paris and Saint-Ouen.
☎ 02.54.77.29.93 F➜ 02.54.73.16.96
Closed Mondays and Sunday evenings (except public holidays), Jan 13–Feb 4, and two weeks in September.

Lunch served noon–2pm and dinner 7.30–9pm (9.30 Saturdays). Don't waste any time over the uninspiring exterior – go in, your tastebuds will thank you for it. Even the cheapest set meal (89F, not available Saturday evenings or Sundays) is a delight, consisting of, for example, seafood casserole and pike with leeks followed by cheese and dessert. Other set meals – 140F, 160F and up – offer things like salad of langoustine tails, snails with walnuts, and medallions of monkfish with cuttlefish. The cooking is sophisticated and the dishes are beautifully presented. Courteous welcome.

VIERZON 18100

|●| RESTAURANT LA GRANGE DES ÉPINETTES

40 rue des Épinettes (North-East).
☎ 02.48.71.68.81 F➜ same.
Closed Sunday and Monday evenings.
Secure parking.

Lunch served noon–2pm and dinner 7–9.30pm. This well-known restaurant is housed in a traditional style building covered in Virginia creeper and the dining room, with its antique furniture, is tucked away at the bottom of a flower-filled garden. The cheapest set meal (65F, including wine and coffee) is pretty conventional but good and the meat is as tender as you could wish. The other set meals at 100F and 170F are a bit more elaborate. The main courses in the set meals – flambéd veal sweetbreads with chanterelle mushrooms, asparagus in puff pastry with a chervil sauce, and roast rabbit with garlic *confit* – also feature on the à la carte menu. Attentive friendly service.

MÉREAU 18120 (11KM S)

☗ HÔTEL LE SOLOGNE***

route de Châteauroux; don't go as far as Méreau – take the D918 in the direction of Châteauroux and you'll come to it a bit after the sign for the Vierzon-sud exit.
☎ 02.48.75.15.20 F➜ 02.48.75.83.21
Secure parking. TV. Disabled access.

If Louis XIII had been the kind of person to stay at a hotel, he would have chosen this place to relax in after one of his hunting trips in the area. The rooms are quiet and full of character. Whether your taste in décor runs to Louis XIII, Louis XVI or modern, there's a room for you. Doubles 180–280F. A very pleasant place, made even more so by the friendliness of the proprietress.

|●| LE SOLOGNE

Le Pré Gaudré - 13 route de Châteauroux; don't go as far as Méreau – take the D918 in the direction of Châteauroux and you'll come to it a bit after the sign for the Vierzon-sud exit.
☎ 02.48.71.01.89
Closed during the February and Christmas school holidays. **Secure parking**.

A pretty red brick one-storey building with half-timbering on the edge of a small pond with an imposing weeping willow. Weather permitting, you can eat on the terrace. Delightful staff, nice atmosphere and gourmet cooking (150F).

VOUZERON 18330 (14KM NE)

☗ |●| LE RELAIS DE VOUZERON***

place de l'Église (Centre); take the D926 in the direction of the forest of Vierzon and when you come to the Étoile roundabout turn right onto the D104 and continue for a further 6km.
☎ 02.48.51.61.38 F➜ 02.48.51.63.71
Closed Mondays, Tuesdays, Jan 1–15, one week in September, and Dec 15–31.

Lunch served noon–1.15pm and dinner 7–9pm. More than 12,000 acres of forest (which is still accessible) protect Vouzeron from the polluted air of Vierzon. Watch out for animals on the road at night. The rooms in this former coaching inn, covered in Virginia creeper, are cosy and comfortable, have pretty fabrics, and smell of polish. Prices are 180–300F. Offerings from the young chef include quails in a port and honey sauce, smoked salmon in a Sancerre sauce, and all sorts of marinated salmon dishes served with aquavit, Scandinavia's answer to vodka. Set meals 90F, 130F and 170F.

NANÇAY 18330 (18KM NE)

|●| LE RELAIS DE SOLOGNE

2 rue Salbris.
☎ 02.48.51.82.26 F 02.48.51.10.70
Closed Tuesday evenings, Wednesdays, Feb 15–March 1, and Sept 1–15.

Alain Fournier, who wrote *Le Grand Meaulnes*, spent his childhood in this little village. The house, with flowers all around, positively asks you to go up and push open the door. Owner Alain Bonnot, renowned for his sauces, is unbeatable when it comes to game and other regional produce. His specialities are *poulet en barbouille* (*coq au vin* in other words) and salmon with sorrel sauce. You can eat either in the elegant dining room, decorated mainly in royal blue, or on the terrace. Set meals 72F (weekdays), 100F and 152F.

YZEURES-SUR-CREUSE 37290

10% ⌂ |●| HÔTEL-RESTAURANT LA PROMENADE***

1 place du 11-Novembre (Centre); on the D104.
☎ 02.47.91.49.00 F 02.47.94.46.12
Closed Tuesday lunchtimes and mid-Jan–mid-Feb.
Car park. TV.

A very handsome building dating from the 18th century, this used to be a coaching inn. It has 15 rooms decorated in restrained country style, with colours like pale green, grey and dark red. Doubles with bath 280F. There's a small sitting room with a piano on the mezzanine. Proprietress Madame Bussereau does the cooking, using what the market has to offer to prepare delicious dishes like pigeon fillets with mild spices and zander with citrus fruit and shredded chicory. And she bakes her own bread. The set meals, which range in price from 95F (not available Sundays) to 295F, are a bit on the expensive side but worth it. A good restaurant.

Champagne-Ardennes

08 Ardennes

10 Aube

51 Marne

52 Haute-Marne

AIX-EN-OTHE 10160

10% ☗ |●| AUBERGE DE LA SCIERIE***

3 rte de Druisy, lieu-dit «La Vove»; it's 1.5km from Aix-en-Othe on the D374, direction Ervy-le-Chatel.
☎ 03.25.46.71.26 ➡ 03.25.46.65.69
Closed Monday evenings, Tuesdays, Oct 16–April 14, Dec 20–end of Jan. **TV**.

If you're looking for a classy place and a bit of peace and quiet near the Aube, then stay at this very charming hotel-restaurant, which is actually an old 17th century mill. There are about 15 stylish rooms at 398F a night for 2. For the same price you can always rent one of two delightful little apartments with kitchen, bathroom and sitting room. The establishment is surrounded by a garden, which is great in the summer for dining outside. There is also a little wooden bridge where you can stop and gaze at the old mill wheel. Set meals 83F (lunchtimes only except Sundays and public holidays), 135F and 245F.

BAR-SUR-AUBE 10200

☗ HÔTEL SAINT-PIERRE

5 rue Saint-Pierre(Centre).
☎ 03.25.27.13.58
Closed Sundays. **Car park**

A simple, nice, well-kept family hotel. Just opposite the church of Saint Pierre (worth a visit for its wooden gallery and gravestones) which can be seen from rooms 8, 9, and 10. Every morning the church bells ring out at 7am! Doubles 85F (with basin), 100F (with shower) and 130F (with shower/wc). No restaurant, but there is a bar. A nice place at very reasonable prices.

|●| UN P'TIT CREUX

place du Corps-de-Garde (Centre); enter by 24 rue Nationale.
☎ 03.25.27.37.75
Closed Mondays except July 15–Aug 31.

This bright, friendly *crêperie* is in a modern shopping centre in what used to be the centre of Bar. It's ideal for whenever you fancy a quick bite to eat. Set meal at 69F, mainly *crêpes* and pizzas. Rather unusual mixture of Italy and Brittany. There's also a number of other set meals based mostly on *galettes* from 56–95F. Great in summer when you can sit outside on the terrace in the sun.

|●| LA TOQUE BARALBINE

18 rue Nationale.
☎ 03.25.27.20.34
Closed Mondays.

The owner of this place worked for years in lots of different restaurants on the Côte d'Azur before deciding to come back to his roots and open his very own gourmet restaurant here. After just a few months he quickly won a loyal following amongst the locals. Sophisticated cooking in very pleasant surroundings. Prices vary from 69F for the *formule* of main course and dessert (weekday lunchtimes only) to 280F for the *menu dégustation*. Friendly, unpretentious welcome.

ARSONVAL 10200 (6KM NW)

10% ☗ |●| HOSTELLERIE LA CHAUMIÈRE

How to get there: take the N19 in the direction of

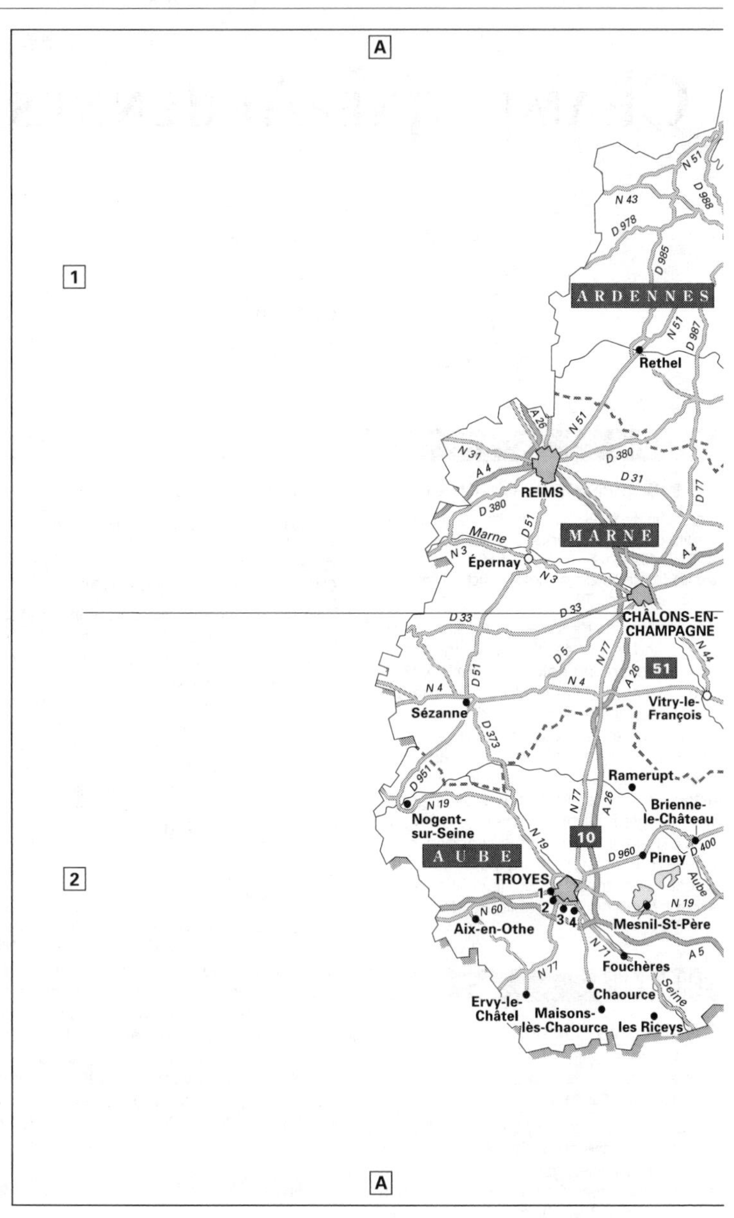

A
1
2
ARDENNES
MARNE
AUBE
N 51
D 988
N 43
D 978
D 985
D 987
Rethel
A 26
N 31
A 4
D 380
D 31
D 77
REIMS
D 51
Marne
N 3
Épernay
CHÂLONS-EN-CHAMPAGNE
D 33
N 44
51
D 5
N 77
N 4
Sézanne
Vitry-le-François
D 373
Ramerupt
D 951
N 19
Nogent-sur-Seine
Brienne-le-Château
10
D 960
Piney
D 400
Aube
TROYES
1
2
3
4
N 60
Aix-en-Othe
Mesnil-St-Père
N 71
Fouchères
A 5
Chaource
Seine
Ervy-le-Châtel
Maisons-lès-Chaource
les Riceys

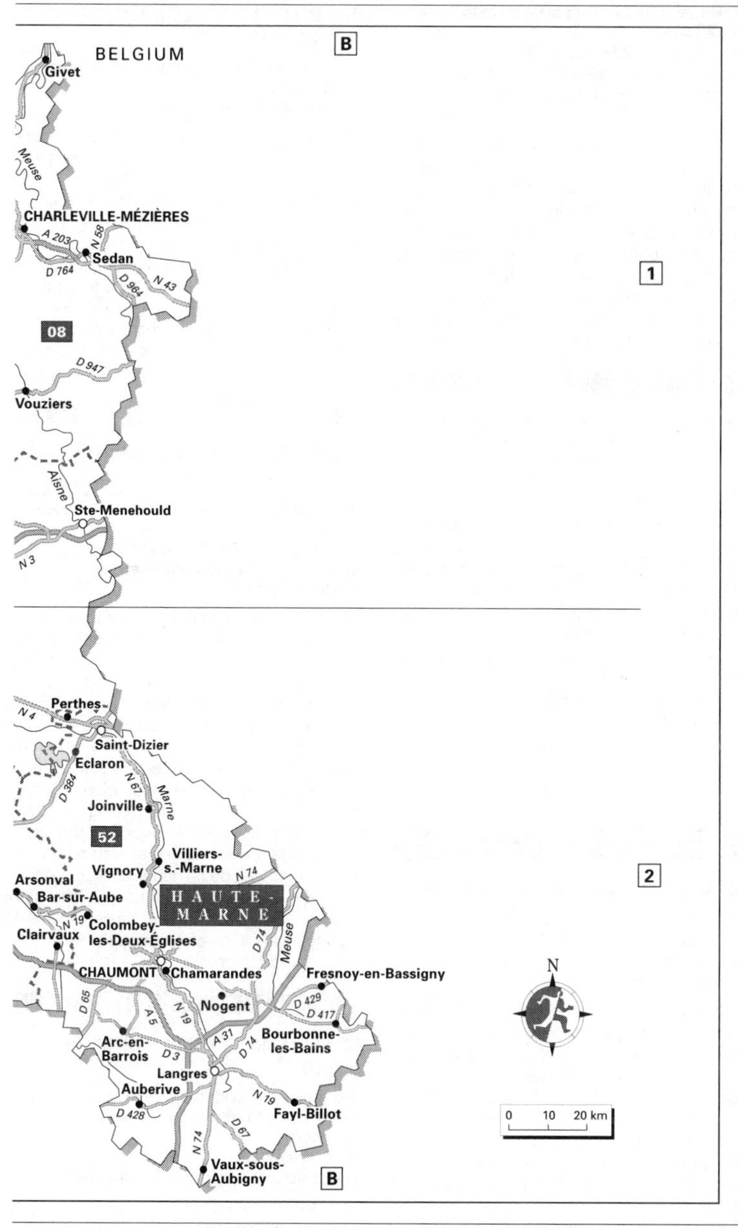

B
BELGIUM
Givet
Meuse
CHARLEVILLE-MÉZIÈRES
A 203
N 58
Sedan
D 764
D 964
N 43
1
08
D 947
Vouziers
Aisne
Ste-Menehould
N 3
Perthes
N 4
Saint-Dizier
Eclaron
D 384
N 67
Marne
Joinville
52
Villiers-
s.-Marne
Vignory
N 74
Arsonval
Bar-sur-Aube
HAUTE-
MARNE
N 19
Colombey-
les-Deux-Églises
Clairvaux
D 74
Meuse
2
CHAUMONT
Chamarandes
Fresnoy-en-Bassigny
N
D 65
A 5
N 19
Nogent
D 429
D 417
A 31
D 74
Bourbonne-
les-Bains
Arc-en-
Barrois
D 3
Langres
Auberive
N 19
D 428
Fayl-Billot
0 10 20 km
N 74
D 67
Vaux-sous-
Aubigny
B

Vendeuvre or Troyes and it's on the left on the outskirts of the village.
☎ 03.25.27.91.02 F 03.25.27.90.26
Closed Sunday evenings and Mondays (except in summer and on public holidays). **Car park**. **TV**.

This old village inn has a very good restaurant, 3 rooms, and a beautiful garden. Carefully prepared, generous meals. Weekday set meal 85F. Other set meals 100–195F. Charming, provincial décor. One room at 180F with shower and wc on the landing, 2 at 250F with shower or bath and wc. Ask for room number 1, which overlooks the garden. Good, friendly welcome. Well-kept family house, which has plans to expand in Spring 1998 with the opening of 9 new rooms in a converted barn.

CLAIRVAUX-SUR-AUBE 10310 (14KM SE)

HÔTEL-RESTAURANT DE L'ABBAYE*

How to get there: crossroads of D12 and D396.
☎ 03.25.27.80.12 F 03.25.27.75.79
Secure parking. **TV**.

You are no longer in Champagne here but have already crossed into the vast forests of Burgundy. In the woods of Clairvaux in the 12th century, Saint Bernard established the first Cistercian abbey, which today is a prison with high walls and watchtowers. The hotel is just opposite. Some may find this sinister, but it's ideal for those who enjoy metaphysical debate. Room number 17 has a view of this rather strange building. 150F for a double with basin, 230F with bath and wc. Very peaceful at night. Cheapest set meal 66F (weekdays), then from 77–125F.

BOURBONNE LES-BAINS 52400

HÔTEL-RESTAURANT D'ORFEUIL**

29 rue d'Orfeuil (South-West); 80m from the spas.
☎ 03.25.90.05.71 F 03.25.84.46.25
Closed end Oct–end March. **Car park**. **TV**.
Disabled access.

A lovely 18th century house unspoilt by time, set in hillside surroundings with a leafy garden and a very pleasant pool. Very tasteful décor inside, with antique family furniture, carpets and fireplaces. It's one of the rare friendly Bourbonne hotels and it's also good value for money: 220–250F for double with shower in the new annexe – the old part is reserved for people taking the waters. Ask for a room with a balcony and a view overlooking the park. Informal restaurant with set meals 60–160F. Very healthy breakfasts!

10% LES ARMOISES (HÔTEL LE JEANNE D'ARC)***

12 rue de l'Amiral Pierre (Centre); it's in the main street.
☎ 03.25.90.46.00
Car park. **Closed** Nov 25–March 1.

This is the only gourmet restaurant around here. The rooms are not exactly oozing with charm and they're a bit expensive, in our opinion, but the restaurant is quite good: we recommend the fricassee of snails in Coiffy wine or the pan-fried *foie-gras aux pommes fruits*. Set meals 89–150F. A word of warning – since the customers are here to take the waters and there's very little to do in town after 8pm anyway, the kitchens close at 8.30! There's definitely a lack of young people around here!

ENFONVELLE 52400 (10KM SE)

10% HÔTEL-RESTAURANT LE MOULIN DE L'ACHAT**

How to get there: take the D417 towards Fresnes-sur-Apance.
☎ 03.25.90.09.54 F 03.25.90.21.82
Closed Jan 1–March 10. **Secure parking**.
Disabled access.

This place is right in the heart of the country, far away from everything apart from an old mill, a stream and horses grazing in the meadow. A few rooms open out onto either the countryside or the swimming pool (from 260F for a double with shower/wc). There's a country-style restaurant: main courses 98–145F. The young owner, Christian Arends built a runway for the small planes which bring the tourists in, before turning his attention to a gym. He loves exploring this wonderful region and will advise you to do the same whether it be on horse-back, on mountain bike, by canoe or by barge. (The half-board package includes all these activities). Hearty meals. One of the best places to stay in the *département*.

FRESNOY-EN-BASSIGNY 52400 (12.5KM NW)

RESTAURANT DU LAC DE MORIMOND

How to get there: on the D139, 2.5km after Fresnoy-en-Bassigny, take the little road on the right (direction lac de Morimond).
☎ 03.25.90.80.86
Closed end Sept–Easter. **Car park**. **Disabled access**.

The little lake is tucked away here in the midst of forests where fishermen come in the middle of the night to do a spot of carp fishing! This is the ideal place to sit on the terrace and enjoy some freshly caught fried fish or a nice fillet steak with mushrooms. The choice on the menu is great. Expect to pay about 120F for a full meal. Very warm welcome. Lovely dining room with a welcoming fireplace.

FAYL-BILLOT 52500 (27KM SW)

HÔTEL-RESTAURANT LE CHEVAL BLANC**

2 place de la Barre.
☎ 03.25.88.61.44
Closed Sunday evenings and Mondays.
Secure parking.

The front of this hotel is covered with vines. The rooms are enormous and even the very busy wallpaper doesn't make them look any smaller. Expect to pay 220F for a double with shower or bath and telephone. Meticulously prepared food with dishes based primarily on local produce, fillet of zander with a saffron sauce, *aiguillettes* of duck with *chanterelles,* calf sweetbreads with morels. Set meals 67–160F. Very friendly welcome. Ask for the quieter rooms which look out onto the garden.

BRIENNE-LE-CHÂTEAU 10500

HÔTEL DE LA CROIX-BLANCHE

7 av. Pasteur; it's just next to the post office.
☎ 03.25.92.80.27. F :03.25.92.98.57
Closed Sunday evenings and from mid Sep–mid Oct.
Car park. **TV**.

Brienne! It was here that Napoleon first acquired his fighting skills before he rampaged through Europe. After visiting the museum, we ordered *truite meunière* (trout sautéd in butter and served with parsley and lemon juice) which was served by an elegant waiter in a striped waistcoat. First-class, filling, traditional cuisine for 70F a head. A few rooms: 190F for a double with shower and wc on the landing. 20 minutes from the forest of Orient and its artificial lake.

CHÂLONS-EN-CHAMPAGNE 51000

10% AUBERGE DE JEUNESSE

6 rue Kellermann (North-East)).
☎ 03.26.68.13.56
Car park
Open July–Aug.

Service 7.30am–10am and 5.30pm–10pm. Next to a large leafy square. As in most youth hostels you'll need to bring your own duvet. 40F a night per person. Breakfast 18F. Hire of sheets 16F. Kitchen available for own use.

HÔTEL-RESTAURANT JEAN-PAUL SOUPLY

8 faubourg Saint-Antoine (North West); 500m from the town centre, opposite hostel for young workers.
☎ 03.26.68.18.91 F 03.26.21.76.47
Closed Sundays and Aug. **Car park**

Family hotel, where everyone chips in. Grandma is at the bar, and the son is both chef and owner. He prepares quite nice traditional food, which is just right to fill you up. You can either go for the set meal at 65F or at 98F but avoid the one at 160F, because for that price you could find a much better place in town. Two room prices 120F and 140F. Half-board available all year from 180F.

HÔTEL PASTEUR**

46 rue Pasteur (East); it's about 600m from the church of Notre-Dame-en-Vaux.
☎ 03.26.68.10.00 F 03.26.21.51.09
Car park. **TV**. **Canal+**. **Disabled access**.

Part of the hotel used to be a convent, which is where the superb staircase came from. Ask for a room at the back: it gets the sun and it's quiet. From 150F for a double with shower (no TV), 210F with shower, wc and telephone.

10% HÔTEL DE LA CITÉ**

12 rue de la Charrière (North-East); take rue J.-J. Rousseau, then turn right after la place des Ursulines.
☎ 03.26.64.31.20
Closed Sunday afternoons. **Secure parking**.
Disabled access.

This is a peaceful place very much like a family home. Businessmen, sales reps and students can be found staying here. A warm welcome will always be given by the owners who don't stint on looking after their hotel. It's not exactly luxurious but it's clean. A few rooms look out onto the tiled roofs of the neighbourhood and the garden, where the owners have put out tables and chairs so their guests can enjoy breakfast outdoors (weather permitting) or just relax with a good book. It's provincial and peaceful. Room number 1 is bright, spacious, and has an enormous bathroom. Expect to pay 170F for a room with a shower, and 220F for a room with a bath. Also a pool table and TV room. Decent breakfast.

HÔTEL DU POT D'ÉTAIN**

18 place de la République (Centre).
☎ 03.26.68.09.09 F 03.26.68.58.18
Secure parking. **TV**. **Canal+**.

This impressive 15th century house has been successfully renovated by a family of bakers. Double rooms with shower/wc and telephone 290F, with bath 310F. One pleasant, single room available. Room number 102 has a view of the square, which is lively both day and night. There is a choice of 6 family-size rooms (for 4) at 400F. Mr. Georges, a retired baker, makes the croissants, tarts and puddings himself. The menu varies from day to day. If you want to make the most of your time here, we advise you to leave your car at the hotel and have a look round Châlons on foot.

HÔTEL LE RENARD**

24 pl. de la République (Centre).
☎ 03.26.68.03.78 ➡ 03.26.64.50.07
TV. Canal+.

The very futuristic décor of this establishment certainly won't be to everyone's liking, especially considering the fact that the 35 rooms available here all have the bed positioned right in the middle of the room. Doubles 335F, triples 450F. The restaurant terrace, which opens out onto the square, is naturally very popular and the food is pretty decent as well.

LE PRÉ SAINT-ALBIN

2 bis rue de l'Abbé Lambert.
☎ 03.26.70.20.26
Closed Sunday evenings and Mondays.

This magnificent establishment dates back to 1850 and still has all of its original glory: stained-glass windows, ornamental ceilings etc. It really does have a kind of quiet elegance about it and seems to attract people of the same kind. Tourists are fascinated by the architectural, almost aristocratic, splendour of the place, as are French holiday-makers, who like to come from their own bourgeois residences bringing their friends along, almost as if they were showing them what they aspire to. Everyone has their own reason for coming here. We liked it primarily because it's an incredible example of 14th century architecture, but also for the fact that when you're sitting on the terrace on a beautiful summer's evening, practically all alone in a wonderfully serene atmosphere, with anything you could wish for at the click of your fingers, you really do feel as if you're sitting down to have dinner in your own home. OK, maybe it is just a fantasy but we're all allowed to dream! In such a setting the set meal at 130F really is a gift. *Parfait* of crab with turmeric, marinated salmon with 4 spices, pan-fried *dorade* with fresh tomatoes and *reblochon* cheese, fricassee of quail *en rustique*, gazpacho of fresh fruit with mint, peach crumble. The choice of food is good and the experienced chef really does well in trying to please both those who like a bit of originality and guests who prefer traditional cuisine. The service is very attentive but be prepared for the bill (about 220F – wine included). Other set meals 170F and 223F, and there's also a bistro separate from the main restaurant, where you can get a *formule* at 95F, with cold buffet of starters, main course and dessert.

CHEPY 51240 (7KM SE)

COMME CHEZ SOI

49 rte Nationale; from Châlons, take the N44 in the direction of Vitry-le-François.
☎ 03.26.67.50.21
Closed in the evening on Sundays and Mondays, a fortnight in Feb and 8 days in Aug.

Both the setting and the cooking are classically provincial. A number of set meals, 60F (weekdays), 108F, 140F and 180F. Go for the regional set meal based on local produce: salad of *andouillette* and apples, braised trout with juniper berries, platter of regional cheeses and sorbet with *Marc de Champagne*. You can also get a set meal where the choice varies from steak and chips to more extravagant dishes such as a very special combination of potatoes and scallops. Friendly welcome.

CHAOURCE 10210

10% HÔTEL-RESTAURANT LES FONTAINES

1 rue des Fontaines; D443.
☎ 03.25.40.00.85 ➡ 03.25.40.01.80
Closed Monday evenings, Tuesdays, Jan 2–20, 1st week in Aug. **Car park**

Food which really sums up the regional tastes of Champagne and Burgundy. First-class set meal 75F (weekdays): traditional country *terrine,* braised ham with Chablis sauce, cheese and dessert trolley. Other set meals 119F, 129F, 169F: poached eggs in a red wine sauce, salmon escalope in champagne, local *choucroute* with *l'andouillette de Troyes* etc. A few rooms: 150F for a double with shower, wc and telephone. Half-board compulsory at weekends.

MAISONS-LÈS-CHAOURCE 10210 (6KM SOUTH)

10% HÔTEL-RESTAURANT AUX MAISONS**

How to get there: take the D34.

☎ 03.25.70.07.19 ➡ 03.25.70.07.75
Car park. **TV**. **Disabled access**.

A large, well-kept family hotel in a little village south of Aube, the region famous for Chaource cheese. Doubles 220F (with shower/wc), and 250F (with bath). Rooms number 11 and 12 overlook the garden and the swimming pool. A few rooms have been recently refurbished. The hotel also has 2 more basic rooms (with basin only) at 160F. As for food, the landlady, Monique Enfert, helped by her son, concocts exquisite, generous regional dishes. Set meals 60F, 100F, 130F and 160F. The service is a bit slow. A real haven of peace, which attracts locals, tourists, and sales reps alike. Nearby, there's a museum of dolls in a *fromagerie*.

RICEYS (LES) 10340 (22KM SE)

HÔTEL-RESTAURANT LE MAGNY**

route de Tonnerre; take the D17, then at the Ricey-Haut exit, it's on the D453 (route de Tonnerre).
☎ 03.25.29.38.39 ➡ 03.25.29.11.72
Closed Tuesday evenings, Wednesdays, end Jan–end Feb. **Car park**. **TV**.

Les Riceys has not only got three churches but it's also the only village in France that produces 3 AOCs, one of them a famous rosé. The wine is used in a number of dishes on the menu here, veal kidneys, for example. Set meal 70F. Peaceful rooms, good value for money: 220F for a double (with shower/wc and telephone), 240F (with bath). And if the hotel's garden isn't enough for you there's a park nearby, designed by Le Nôtre, which you really should visit.

CHARLEVILLE-MÉZIÈRES 08000

10% HÔTEL DE PARIS**

24 av. G.-Corneau (South-East); it's opposite the station sqaure.
☎ 03.24.33.34.38 ➡ 03.24.59.11.21
Closed 1st week in Jan. **Secure parking**. **TV**. **Canal+**.

This is still our favourite hotel in the town where Rimbaud was born (his statue is near the station). The owner and her cat(!) are really very friendly and welcoming. The rooms have been recently refurbished in a very classic fashion. The ones on the street side are soundproof, and the ones overlooking the inner courtyard couldn't be quieter. Prices range from 275F for a room with bath, also 3 family rooms at 400F. Small breakfast buffet 35F.

RESTAURANT LE DAMIER

7 rue Bayard (South); when coming into Mézières on the av. d'Arches, take the 2nd road on the right after the Meuse bridge.
☎ 03.24.37.76.89
Closed Saturday lunchtimes, Sundays, and Monday evenings in July and Aug.

This is quite a unique restaurant in that it's run by an association which tries to give young jobless people an opportunity (so be patient if the service is sometimes a bit below what you would normally expect). With a 37F dish of the day and a set meal at 55F, this is the ideal place to come for lunch. The restaurant is bright with a chequered floor. The food is simple but worth a go. On Friday and Saturday evenings the prices go up a bit (set meal with regional cuisine 95F and 150F) and the food is slightly more sophisticated: *feuilleté du Carolo*, beef with juniper berries, trout with a scallop sauce. Game in season. Children's set meal 38F.

BALARD RESTO

10 rue de Tivoli (South); from place Ducale, take rue de la République (pedestrian precinct), then go straight onto the cours A.-Briand and it's in the first street on the right.
☎ 03.24.33.60.06
Closed Sundays, Monday lunchtimes and Aug.

This unusual restaurant is named after one of the stops on the Paris métro and it lives up to its name pretty well: tiled murals, old wooden benches, and old train doors. The food is relatively simple, just perfect for lunch or a meal with friends. The dishes are small, to fit in with the Parisian style: tripe, marrowbone, calf's head, eggs in a red wine sauce. Good summer salads. And every day of the week has its own special dish, for example, Monday it's bacon salad, Tuesday it's *cacasse à cul nu* (a potato and bacon stew), Wednesday *cassoulet,* Thursday *pot-au-feu,* and Friday mussels and chips. Little jugs of wine. Dish of the day 48F. Expect to pay about 120F for a full meal à la carte. Pretty cool place to be.

RESTAURANT LE PANIER DE CANCALE

7 bis,] rue d'Aubilly; from place Ducale take rue du Moulin towards the Meuse and it's the first street on the right.
☎ 03.24.59.31.28
Closed Sunday and Monday evenings.

This little restaurant is tucked away in a lovely old building in a square that is the spitting image of Place des Vosges in Paris. It does reasonable food at excellent prices. Dishes are predominantly based on local produce and whatever is in season, but the regional food is usually pretty good. Friendly welcome. Intimate little dining area (probably what we'd class as an 'evening restaurant'). Set meal 100F (available at lunchtime and in the evening seven days a week) or 140F (with a glass of wine to accompany each dish). Also a fish menu at 160F (a little reminder of Cancale and Brittany?). Good wine list.

CHAUMONT 52000

HÔTEL-RESTAURANT LE RELAIS

20 faubourg de la Maladière (North-East); 1km from the centre of Chaumont, on the Nancy road (D417), just after the canal de la Marne à la Saône, known here as "port de Chaumont".
☎ 03.25.03.02.84
Closed Sunday evenings, Mondays, 2 weeks in Jan and 2 weeks in July. **TV**.

A former coaching inn on the outskirts of Chaumont, this is an unpretentious place by the roadside and on the banks of the canal linking the Marne and the Saône. It is is quite peaceful (rooms number 6 and 7 are particularly quiet) and the prices are reasonable. There are 7 rooms, 250F for a double with bath. Cheapest set meal is 60F weekdays, then 80–150F. Carefully prepared gourmet cuisine, most of which is seafood (kebabs) and fish (salmon escalope). Friendly welcome.

10% HÔTEL-RESTAURANT DES REMPARTS**

72 rue de Verdun (Centre); it's a 1 minute walk from the station (gare SNCF) beside the city walls.
☎ 03.25.32.64.40 F :03.25.32.51.70
Public car park opposite hotel. **TV**. **Disabled access**.

This place offers the best value for money in Chaumont. The rooms, decorated with posters from the Chaumont Arts Festival, are clean and fairly soundproof. Doubles 250–290F. We recommend you stay in the annexe, which is relatively new and more spacious. Rooms number 20 and 22 are particularly nice. First-class, imaginative cooking, set meals at 59F and from 87–230F, with a few specialities, such as salmon in Pinot Noir and veal sweetbreads in puff pastry with morels.

10% HÔTEL DE FRANCE***

25 rue Toupot-de-Beveaux (Centre); it's just beside the town hall.
☎ 03.25.03.01.11 F 03.25.32.35.80
Car park. **TV**. **Disabled access**.

This is a brand-new hotel right in the town centre, the kind of chic place to go in Chaumont. The rooms are impeccable, and are all decorated to a different country theme. You'll get a great welcome and it's very comfortable. TV and private telephone in each room. Also a Tex-Mex restaurant. Main courses à la carte are about 100F. Rooms 350–590F.

RESTAURANT FLOX

16 rue Victor-Mariotte (Centre).
☎ 03.25.32.67.22
Closed Saturdays and Sundays. Open 10am–6pm.

This charming, quite exotic-looking place, which often houses exhibitions, is and ideal place for lunch. It has a terrace looking out onto a quiet pedestrian street, which is lovely when the sun's out. Dish of the day 48F or set meal at 60F with starter, main course, cheese or house dessert and a glass of wine. The tricky part comes when you have to choose your coffee – Florence, the owner, will help you to decide from the 7 different types on offer. If you really want to stay up all night in Chaumont, why not try them all!

CHAMARANDES 52000 (2KM SE)

10% HÔTEL-RESTAURANT AU RENDEZ-VOUS DES AMIS**

4 place du Tilleul (South East).
☎ 03.25.32.20.20 F 03.25.02.60.90
Closed Aug 1–20, Dec 20–Jan 5, restaurant closed Friday nights and Saturdays. **Car park**. **TV**. **Canal+**.

This is a real country inn in a little village on the River Marne. The old church and school still stand alongside the river and if you look just past the park, you'll be able to make out the manor house. The charm and peacefulness of the place, along with the friendly welcome you'll get, makes it a great stop-over point. Doubles (which have been tastefully renovated) 230F (with washing facilities), 290F (with shower/wc or bath). In the restaurant you'll rub shoulders with hunters, fishermen, businessmen and travellers. Set meals 80F (weekdays)–250F, which, in the summer, are served outside on a lovely terrace shaded by an ancient lime tree. The cooking is creative – why not try the *foie gras* of duck and monkfish.

VIGNORY 52320 (20KM NORTH)

10% HÔTEL-RESTAURANT LE RELAIS VERDOYANT**

rue de la Gare; take the N67, then follow signs to Vignory station.

☎ 03.25.02.44.49 ➡ 03.25.01.96.89
Closed Sunday evenings, Monday lunchtimes (Monday evenings also Dec–April), Nov. **Secure parking. TV. Disabled access**

In the early 1900s this house was built for travellers who used the station at Vignory. Today the railway is no longer quite as busy, but the hotel and its garden have remained just as elegant as they were back in those days. Small, stylish rooms (210F for a double with shower/wc), which are as charming now as they look in the old photos of the hotel in the reception area. Traditional cuisine at good prices: set meal 65F (except Sundays and public holidays), then 82–135F.

ARC-EN-BARROIS 52210 (25KM SW)

10% HÔTEL-RESTAURANT DU PARC

1 place Moreau.
☎ 03.25.02.53.07 ➡ 03.25.02.42.84
Closed Sunday evenings, Mondays out of season, Feb 1–March 1. **Car park. TV.**

In a tiny village, opposite a castle, surrounded by forests full of game, you'll find this little inn tucked away in what used to be a hunting lodge. You'll get a friendly welcome here and the prices are reasonable: 270F with bath. Hearty food based on local produce. Set meals 100F (weekdays)–250F: venison and wild boar in season. Half-board 235F per person. Fishing, hunting, golf and mountain-bike hire all available here, all of which kind of makes you want to come back in the autumn.

COLOMBEY-LES-DEUX-ÉGLISES 52330

L'AUBERGE DE LA MONTAGNE**

rue d'Argentolles.
☎ 03.25.01.51.69 ➡ 03.25.01.53.20
Closed Monday evenings and Tuesdays out of season, mid Jan–mid Feb. **Car park. TV.**

This is a really good place in a little village, right beside a leafy meadow, and 200m from the cemetery where General de Gaulle is buried. The owner, Gérard Natali, was born here, and was one of the 12 young men who carried the coffin of France's liberator in 1970. Today people from all over the world come to stay here, from the former King of Yemen to the Japanese ambassador, from quarry-owners from Brittany to French colonials from Pondicherry. First-class hearty meals 120F weekdays, 160F at weekends. The rooms are really peaceful and charming, 240F (with shower)–270F (with bath).

ÉCLARON 52290

L'HÔTELLERIE DU MOULIN**

3 rue du Moulin.
☎ 03.25.04.17.76 ➡ 03.25.55.67.01
Closed Sunday evenings, Monday lunchtimes (sometimes evenings too in winter), 3 weeks mid Jan–start of Feb, 1 week end Sep–start of Oct. **Car park. TV.**

This pretty timber-framed house has a romantic lakeside setting 9km south-west of Saint-Dizier. There are five delightful rooms and our favourite, room 3, has a view of the mill race and the trees. It's very peaceful and the prices are reasonable: 240F for a double with shower/wc, telephone and TV. The young owner will offer you the choice of three good set meals, 80F (weekdays), 100F and 138F. You've got to try the house smoked salmon, the duck breast with blackberries and the fillet of halibut in champagne. Éclaron is definitely worth a visit.

ÉPERNAY 51200

HÔTEL DE CHAMPAGNE***

30 rue Eugène-Mercier (Centre); A26.
☎ 03.26.53.10.60 ➡ 03.26.51.94.63
Closed 1st fortnight in Jan. **Car park. TV.**

This is undoubtedly the best hotel in the town centre. It's modern and comfortable, and has double glazing. Room prices vary from 310F with shower to 450F with bath. About 10 rooms are going to be fitted with air-conditioning and their prices vary from 450F with shower to 550F with bath. Self-service breakfast buffet 55F.

LA GRILLADE

16 rue de Reims; it's near the station.
☎ 03.26.55.44.22
Closed Saturday lunchtimes and Sundays (except public holidays).

This place is more commonly known as 'Chez Blanche', after the owner. It's famous for its barbecue cooking: sardines, bass with fennel, T-bone steak, *andouillettes* etc. Everything is cooked on the barbecue until it's ready to be served up usually to a full house. You'll appreciate the pretty flower-filled garden and the shady terrace in summer. Set meals 80F, 100F and 170F. Wine by the glass from 12–15F. For dessert, the banana flambée, also done on the barbecue, is a real hit, and deservedly so.

EPERNAY-GAMBETTA 51200 (1KM)

|●| CHEZ MAX

13 av. A. Thevenet; it's in the direction of Dizy.
☎ 03.26.55.23.59
Closed Sunday evenings, Mondays and Jan 6–20.

This is a popular restaurant with a great reputation which has been going for about 27 years You must try it. Weekday set meal 66F (main course 45F) with a choice of 5 starters (muzzle of pork in spicey vinaigrette, *crudités*), 3 main courses (braised pork, fillet of *rascasse* in *bouillabaisse* sauce, veal stew), salads or cheeses and dessert. There is another set meal at 91F (main course 57F), which is a bit more fancy. The set meals do change quite regularly and, in addition, there's a special set meal at 150F, which is quite popular at the weekends.

SAINT-IMOGES 51200 (6KM N)

|●| MAISON DU VIGNERON

N 51; it's on the road to Reims.
☎ 03.26.52.88.00
Closed Sunday evenings and Wednesdays.

The wine-growers who gave their name to this place may not actually run it but they're definitely the principal shareholders and have put in a competent management team. You really can't fault the welcome, the service or the food here. All the dishes look great and have been carefully prepared by chef. There are a number of set meals on offer: 125F, 175F and 225F. The 125F set meal gives you melon salad, smoked duck and avocado, braised veal with fresh herbs, cheese platter and *crème brûlée* with almonds. That should give you something of an idea of what the chef is capable of! The rustic-style décor is maybe a bit over the top but we're sure you'll put up with it.

MONTMORT 51270 (18KM SW)

⌂ |●| HÔTEL-RESTAURANT LE CHEVAL BLANC**

rue de la Libération.
☎ 03.26.59.10.03 ⊳ 03.26.59.15.88
Closed Friday evenings Nov–March. **Secure parking**. **TV**.

A beautiful, 16th century brick castle is the focal point of this village, tucked away in the countryside, south of the vineyards of the region. This traditional inn offers a first-class set meal at 80F (weekdays) and it has a great wine and champagne list. There's a friendly, rather old-fashioned environment. Ask for a room which looks out onto the countryside. 240F for a double with shower/wc, 280F with bath.

ERVY-LE-CHATEL 10130

|●| AUBERGE DE LA VALLÉE DE L'ARMANCE –

How to get there: from the centre of the village take the D374 in the direction of Aix-en-Othe and it's opposite the station.
☎ 03.25.70.66.36
Closed Sunday, Tuesday and Wednesday evenings.
Car park.

You don't get into the restaurant through the bar, but round the back. Part of it has been converted from an old cowshed (you can still see an old wooden manger) and the whole rustic feel to the place is reinforced by the old bread shovels and forks hanging on the wall. Good regional food (you've got to try the *gratin d'andouillette*). Set meals 80F, 125F and 145F.

GIVET 08600

10% ⌂ |●| HÔTEL-RESTAURANT DU NORD*

27 rue Thiers (North).
☎ 03.24.42.01.78 ⊳ 03.24.40.46.79
Closed Fridays and Jan. **Car park.TV**.
Disabled access.

This is a small place which certainly won't break the bank. Although centrally located, the street it's in is quite quiet. Rooms above the restaurant or in an annexe opposite. They're basic and you've got to like psychedelic wallpaper! Doubles 140F (with washing facilities)–210F (with shower and wc). Unpretentious bar-restaurant with classic food and a slighty old-fashioned atmosphere. Set meals at 62F, 90F and 140F.

10% ⌂ HÔTEL LE VAL SAINT-HILAIRE**

7 quai des Fours (South); coming from Charleville it's on the left as you enter Givet.
☎ 03.24.42.38.50 ⊳ 03.24.42.07.36
Closed Dec 20–Jan 5. **Car park**. **TV**.
Disabled access.

This is a large 18th century blue stone house, which used to be the headquarters of a local printing works. The rooms are tastefully decorated in a contemporary fashion and are very pleasant. All are equipped with a shower/wc or bath: 345F for 2 people. The rooms which look out onto the street (and which have a view of the Meuse) have got double glazing (the ones on the ground floor are triple-glazed) but if you'd prefer you can always ask for a room at the back. At the moment the hotel doesn't have a restaurant but there is a bar with a terrace on the quay where the yachtsmen come in to dock. The owners, who still give the best welcome in town, will be only too happy to tell you about all the walks you can do in the area. Start by visiting la vallée de la Meuse, it's absolutely superb!

AUBRIVES 08320 (5KM SW)

HÔTEL-RESTAURANT DEBETTE**

2 place Louis-Debette; take the N51, direction Charleville.
☎ 03.24.41.64.72 F 03.24.41.10.31
Closed Sunday evenings (except public holidays), Monday lunchtimes, Jan 27–Feb 10. **Car park**. **TV**. **Disabled access**.

This place used to be a bit stuffy but since two young brothers have taken over it's become much more relaxed in terms of service and the welcome you'll get. The rooms (which are either in the house or in an annexe on the other side of a peaceful village square) are really comfortable and most of them have been refurbished, although the décor is not exactly sparkling with originality: 260F for a double with shower/wc or bath.The dining room is a bit on the fancy side and has huge bay windows which open out onto the garden.The young chef produces great classic dishes, like veal kidneys with scallops, and regional specialities such as ham of Ardennes or wild boar in season. Set meals 75F weekdays then 110F (mostly local food), 160F, 200F and 250F.

JOINVILLE 52300

HÔTEL-RESTAURANT DE LA POSTE**

place de la Grève; leaving the town, take the route de Saint-Dizier, it's near a shady **car park**.
☎ 03.25.94.12.63 F 03.25.94.36.23
Closed Sunday evenings in winter, and Jan 10–Feb 10. **Secure parking**. **TV**.

Yes, it is a hotel but the real reason to visit is to taste all the chef's delicious specialities: *emincé* of monkfish with baby vegetables, *poussin* with morels, trout *sire de Joinville*. Great set meal which is remarkable value for money during the week. For 80F: starter, meat or fish, cheese and dessert, which all in all is a pretty good deal! Impeccable service. Other set meals at 132F and 180F (210F on Sundays). Comfortable, peaceful rooms 200F–300F with double glazing, shower/wc or bath.

LE SOLEIL D'OR***

9 rue des Capucins(Centre); it's just beside the church of Notre-Dame.
☎ 03.25.94.15.66 F 03.25.94.39.02
Closed Sunday evenings, Mondays, 1st week in Aug, and 4th week in Feb. **TV**.

This hotel will be a real hit with those who love cosy rooms with dressed stone walls. It's spacious, light, and is the best value for money in town. Rooms 200–400F. The dining room, with its arches and wooden beams, has a warm atmosphere. Chef's specialities: quail of Dombes with cinnamon, pan-fried scallops with a saffron sauce. The prices are quite high, 190F–295F for the 2 gourmet set meals, but there is also a basic set meal on offer for 100F.

LANGRES 52200

L'AUBERGE DES VOILIERS**

lac de la Liez (East); it's 4km from Langres, on the route de Vesoul.
☎ 03.25.87.05.74 F 03.25.87.24.22
Closed Sunday evenings, Mondays (except May 1–Oct 1), Feb 1–March 15. **Car park**. **TV**. **Disabled access**.

Don't divulge the whereabouts of the Voiliers to just anyone, because in our opinion it's the best place in Langres. It's in lovely surroundings near to a peaceful lake. The prices are fair, you'll get a wonderful welcome and the food is great. Double rooms 220F with shower/wc and telephone. For 250F, room 4 has a balcony with a view of the lake and numbers 8 and 11 look out onto the countryside and over to the walled city of Langres on the far-off plateau. Set meal 80F (100F on Sundays), then 140–200F, Children's meals 45F. How could you forget their fillet of pike with nettles, the *nougat glacé* with fresh fruit, all in this little haven of tranquillity?

HÔTEL-RESTAURANT GRAND HÔTEL DE L'EUROPE**

23-25 rue Diderot (Centre).
☎ 03.25.87.10.88 F 03.25.87.60.65
Closed Sunday evenings and Monday lunchtimes. **Secure parking**. **TV**. **Canal+**.

This is the type of hotel you would expect to find in the olden days, where in the evening you would have mingled with the likes of duchesses, British scholars and Swiss novelists! Not only is this hotel quite unique but it's also provincial, friendly and very reasonable. It has the charm of pre-revolutionary France with its 17th century wood panelling, its squeaking floorboards and huge blue-shuttered rooms. Doubles 260F with shower and 290F with bath. The annexe at the back is definitely more peaceful. There's a great restaurant which reflects the whole image of the hotel: set meal 78F (weekdays), then at 110F, 120F, 150F and 220F. Local specialities at decent prices. 25F charge for use of the private car park.

LE CHEVAL BLANC**

4 rue de l'Estres (Centre); it's in the street at right angles to rue Diderot.
☎ 03.25.87.07.00 ➧ 03.25.87.23.13
Restaurant closed Tuesday evenings and Wednesday lunchtimes. **TV**.

Le Cheval Blanc is part of an old abbey from the Middle Ages and it's a real charmer, with its gothic arches in each room, a terrace looking onto a little church, its walls of dressed stone and exposed beams on every floor. The rooms are as peaceful as a monastic cell would have been! The décor is simple yet refined, just like the wonderful platter of gastronomical delights on offer in the restaurant. Set meals 110–200F. The most charming place in Langres – and it's also good value for money.

BANANAS

52 rue Diderot (Centre); it's on the main street.
☎ 03.25.87.42.96
Closed Sundays.

You get a real fuss made over you here. Country music, sparkling décor, red and white checked tablecloths, and a buffalo's head hanging on the wall. The atmosphere is great, just like the service and everything on the menu: tacos, enchiladas, chilli con carne, burgers and steaks. All you need is a cowboy hat and you're in a John Wayne movie! Evenings are usually very busy. An average meal will set you back about 100F.

VAUX-SOUS-AUBIGNY 52190 (25KM S)

AUBERGE DES TROIS PROVINCES

How to get there: N74.
rue de Verdun.
☎ 03.25.88.31.98
Closed Sunday evenings, Mondays and Feb 1–15. **Car park**.

Time seems to have stood still in this little village inn with its wonderful paved stone floor and its impressive fireplace. The décor goes well with the food here, cuisine based on local produce but with a sparkle of originality. Good set meal at 95F: home-made country *terrine*, old-fashioned casserole of guinea fowl, cheese platter with *cancoillote* and pears poached in wine. The chef hasn't forgotten that not long ago he was running the kitchen of a top restaurant. The wine list contains one or two curiosities.

AUBERIVE 52160 (27KM SW)

HÔTEL-RESTAURANT DU LION D'OR

How to get there: D428.
☎ 03.25.84.82.49 ➧ 03.42.79.80.92
Closed Tuesdays and mid Nov–start of April. **Car park. Disabled access**.

This adorable little country hotel is set right beside a 12th century Cistercian abbey in the midst of a forest in a peaceful little village. The Aube, which is really nothing more than a big stream, runs past the grounds of the house. The 8 rooms are all different and tastefully decorated. 300F for a double in season. The cooking here is based primarily on local produce: snails, rabbit *à la Dijonnais*. and you can dine at one of the tables around the fireplace. Cheapest set meal 65F. Prices are lower in spring and in autumn.

MESNIL-SAINT-PÈRE 10140

HÔTEL-RESTAURANT AUBERGE DU LAC***

How to get there: It's just as you get to the village coming from Troyes on the N19.
☎ 03.25.41.27.16 ➧ 03.25.41.57.59
Closed Mondays and the last 2 Sunday evenings in Sep. **Car park. TV**.

This is a pretty timber-framed house near to the lake in the forest of Orient – the ideal place for a romantic weekend. Fully-furnished rooms at 330F (with shower)–350F (with bath). You're guaranteed a good night's sleep here. The restaurant, Au vieux Pressoir, is really charming and the chef's cooking is, without a doubt, excellent, but the prices are quite high: cheapest set meal 130F (lunchtimes only), and others at 170F, 228F, 255F and 295F. Gourmet menu 310F. Rather expensive.

NOGENT 52800

10% HÔTEL DU COMMERCE**

pl. Charles-de-Gaulle (Centre).
☎ 03.25.31.81.14
Restaurant closed Sunday evenings Nov 1–Easter.
TV. **Canal+**.

A town like this, which makes cutlery, really ought to have a decent place to eat and this reasonably priced place fits the bill. Doubles from 175F, clean, well-kept and pleasant. The reception area is large and welcoming, as is the restaurant with its exposed beams and 18th century-style décor. Set meals are of generous proportions and well thought out. Prices between 100–140F. Try snail soup with a red wine sauce or fillet of duck with honey and spices.The ideal place to stay if you're visiting the cutlery museum.

NOGENT-SUR-SEINE 10400

HÔTEL-RESTAURANT BEAU RIVAGE**

20 rue Villiers-aux-Choux (North); follow signs to the swimming pool (la piscine) and the campsite; it's about 1km from place de l'Église.
☎ 03.25.39.84.22 F 03.25.39.18.32
Closed Mondays, Sunday evenings and one fortnight in Feb. **TV**.

This is a friendly, peaceful place with a beautiful garden beside the Seine. There are a few pleasant rooms at 280–290F for a double with shower/wc or bath. Breakfast 35F. All the rooms have been recently refurbished. Ask for rooms number 1, 2, 4 or 5 all of which have a view of the Seine, the trees, the countryside and, off in the distance, the outline of a nuclear power station, which seems to be apologizing for its very existence. Anyway, don't let it put you off coming here. Cheapest set meal at 82F. The owner has a weakness for herbs – he uses a lot of them in the kitchen – and he smokes his own salmon. Our favourite place in Nogent.

PERTHES 52100

HÔTEL-RESTAURANT LA CIGOGNE GOURMANDE

rue de l'Europe.
☎ 03.25.56.40.29 F 03.25.06.22.81
Closed Sunday evenings. **Car park. TV**.

Though this rather chic restaurant on the old RN4 caters for formal businessmen's lunches and fancy golden wedding parties, it also does an 80F set meal during the week that's a real godsend for travellers! Fine food goes hand in hand with meticulous service. We recommend the *chausson de foie gras* with sesame seeds and the *pomme glacée* with liquorice. The hotel has an annexe 200m away – you'll find 6 lovely rooms (180F with shower, no wc, 260F and 275F with bath and mini-bar) tucked away nicely in a little house near the church.

LE PARIS-STRASBOURG

rue de l'Europe (Centre); it's the first restaurant you come to after leaving the RN4.
☎ 03.25.56.40.64
Closed Sunday evenings and Mondays.

A great place to come if you love fine food and are willing to fork out that little bit extra for it. It's very cosy, the welcome and service are both impeccable, the presentation of food is superb and it's excellent value for money considering the quality you get. It's a bit of a favourite with businessmen during the week and tourists and locals tend to come at the weekend. We loved the salmon salad with snails and white grapes, and the wonderful breast of duck with apple sauce – and what comes with it in the way of vegetables etc is equally well-prepared. This is without a doubt the best place to come for good food east of Haute-Marne.

PINEY 10220

10% LE TARDONE**

1 pl. de la Halle; from Troyes, follow signs to Nancy, then Brienne-le-Château on the D960.
☎ 03.25.46.30.35 F 03.25.46.36.49
Closed Sunday evenings from Oct 1–Mar 31.
Secure parking. **TV**.

Near to the regional nature park in the forest of Orient, this huge half-timbered building houses a bar, a restaurant and a hotel. Half of the rooms can be found in a recently converted annexe. Cosy, stylish rooms, impeccably clean, all with bathroom and wc. 220F for a double with shower, 240F with bath. Prices include use of the very pleasant and quiet hotel pool. Peaceful and relaxing setting. For the not so extravagant, there are other more basic rooms available in the other building (with washing facilities, shower on the landing) from 160F a night for two. Set meals in the restaurant 59F (lunchtimes only), then 88F, 100F, 135F and 170F.

RAMERUPT 10240

RESTAURANT LE VAL D'AUBE

rue Cour-Première; leave Troyes on the N77 (direction Châlons-en-Champagne) and at Massonville take the D99.
☎ 03.25.37.39.45
Closed Tuesdays.

After enjoying great success cooking for the diplomats of Quai-d'Orsay, the young chef here, Hervé, decided to come back and join his family in this bar-restaurant in the country. He whips up decent traditional food: set meal 60F (weekdays) and 150F (weekends). His specializes in fish – the River Aube, remember, flows through a charming valley just nearby.

REIMS 51100

SEE MAP OVERLEAF

10% HÔTEL LINGUET

14 rue Linguet. **MAP B1-1**
☎ 03.26.47.31.89
Closed Sundays and week commencing Aug 15.

Situated in a paved street lined with town houses (one being the Pavillon de Muire, built around 1565, owned by the Veuve Cliquot-Ponsardin family). Originally Hôtel Linguet was a bourgeois town house. You can still sense a little *je ne sais quoi* of the place's history in the air, which sets it apart from other hotels in the city. In fact, you almost feel as if you're staying in somebody's home. Well looked after by M and Mme Fournier, this hotel has a peaceful, zen-like atmosphere and welcomes guests who appreciate these qualities almost as much as its no-smoking policy. The rooms are large and pleasant and prices are affordable: 135F for a double with bath (115F with basin), wc in the hall. There are also a few small rooms with basin on the third floor at 95F with shower on the landing (small charge). These rooms are good for students who come to study at Reims.

10% CENTRE INTERNATIONAL DE SÉJOURS ET DE RENCONTRES

parc Léo-Lagrange, allée Polonceau; take bus B or N (Colin stop), or H (Ch.-de-Gaulle stop). **MAP A3-2**
☎ 03.26.40.52.60 F 03.26.47.35.70
Closed Dec 22–Jan 4. **Car park**.

Not far from the town centre, in the peaceful surroundings of a park. 73 beds in rooms for 1, 2 or 3. 134F for a double with basin, 170F with bath. Breakfast 12F. Meal 58F. Fully equipped kitchen available.

10% AZUR HÔTEL**

9 rue des Écrevées. **MAP B1-6**
☎ 03.26.47.43.39 F 03.26.88.57.19
Secure parking. TV. Disabled access.

In a quiet and central street, this unobtrusive hotel with its rather English charm, its red carpet, and hushed atmosphere, is worth a stop-over. Great welcome and the rooms are neat and tidy. Doubles 175F (with washing facilities), 200F (with shower and wc), and 260F (with bath). Numbers 17, 27, 37, 12, and 22 are brighter than the others. A stone's throw from the Henry IV bar and the rather chic bistro Au comptoir. 10 minutes' walk from lively place d'Erlon.

AUX BONS AMIS

13 rue Gosset. **MAP B1-17**
☎ 03.26.07.39.76. F :03.26.07.73.06
Restaurant closed Friday evenings, Saturdays and Sundays.

This popular restaurant is always crammed full, especially at lunchtimes, when lots of businessmen and workers can be seen here, along with a number of local pensioners. Its success is due to the excellent value for money of the set meal on offer at 65F: each day you get a choice of 2 starters, 3 main courses, cheeses, dessert and a drink. The dishes are real classics: ox tongue with rice, *blanquette de veau* (a type of veal stew), sautéd veal etc and you get good-sized portions. Good, quick service guaranteed by the friendly waitresses. (They've all got a name badge on so it's more personal.) They don't stand still for a minute! Les Bons Amis is a very basic hotel, but it is clean. Doubles 190F (singles 110F), with shower on each floor. All rooms have a TV. Breakfast 25F. Half-board 200F per person.

10% HÔTEL LE SAINT-MAURICE*

90 rue Gambetta. **MAP C3-3**
☎ 03.26.85.09.10 F 03.26.85.83.20
TV.

Even though it has a large plateglass window at the front, the hotel looks as if it belongs in Spain or Portugal. Most of the rooms open onto a peaceful little courtyard where guests like to sit in the open air. The atmosphere is warm and friendly. Quite a few regulars have got 'their room', reminiscent of the days of guest houses. There are a number of single rooms available which aren't quite as nice as the others, but good for those on a budget: 2 with shower (wc on landing and no TV) 149F, and 7 with shower/wc and TV 165F. Rooms for 3 with shower 230F and doubles with bath 210F for 230F.

☗ ARDENN HÔTEL**

6 rue Caqué. **MAP A2-4**
☎ 03.26.47.42.38 ⮕ 03.26.86.82.44
Car park. TV. Canal+. Disabled access.

The place to stay if you don't want to fork out too much and still stay in the town centre. The hotel has been renovated but has awful kitsch décor. A favourite with artists appearing at the nearby theatres. Doubles with shower 220F and with bath 260F. The fact that there seems to be a constant change in the management of the place doesn't work in its favour but things are starting to settle down now, or at least we hope so. Let us know what you think.

10% ☗ HÔTEL LE BARON**

85 rue de Vesle. **MAP B2-9**
☎ 03.26.47.46.24
TV.

Don't let the name mislead you, there's nothing aristocratic about this place. The hotel has recently been totally renovated and the rooms are now furnished with all mod cons. Situated 300m from the cathedral and a stride away from la place d'Erlon. Le Baron is worth a look. Doubles 250F (with twin beds 260F), triples 290F. Rooms number 16, 17, 22 and 23 look out onto the street, the others are at the back.

10% ☗ |●| HÔTEL-RESTAURANT COTTAGE HÔTEL**

8 av. Georges-Pompidou (South); from the centre, follow direction Val-de-Murigny, take the av. de Champagne, then place des Combattants-d'AFN, av. Pompidou and it's 200m on your right. Off **map C4-7**
☎ 03.26.36.34.34 ⮕ 03.26.49.99.77
Restaurant closed Sunday evenings. **Car park. TV. Canal+. Disabled access.**

This place is perfect if you're looking for somewhere quiet, as opposed to being right in the town centre. Prices for the rooms are reasonable: 250F for a double with shower/wc and telephone. In the restaurant the 70F set meal served at lunchtimes and in the evenings (not at weekends) is really decent. There are other set meals 105F and 150F, children's meal 42F. Warm, professional welcome.

10% ☗ |●| HÔTEL-RESTAURANT LE BON MOINE**

14 rue des Capucins. **MAP B2-8**
☎ 03.26.47.33.64 ⮕ 03.26.40.43.87
Closed Sundays Sep–June, restaurant closed every Sunday. **Car park. TV.**

This place, a bit like a station hotel, has seen a fair bit of wear and tear over the years but it keeps going. It's comfortable but it just doesn't have much character and it's right in the town centre, a stone's throw from the place d'Erlon. Doubles with shower and separate wc 260F, rooms for three 330F, and for four 380F. Readers of this guide will get a 10% reduction. Take advantage of the amazing prices in the restaurant: day's special 39F, set meal of the day 59F (it changes every 3 weeks). However, the more expensive set meals at 80F, 100F and 150F are not such good value for money.

10% ☗ HÔTEL CRYSTAL**

86 place Drouet-d'Erlon. **MAP A1-5**
☎ 03.26.88.44.44 ⮕ 03.26.47.49.28
TV. Canal+.

There are 2 good reasons to stay here: its location, near to the liveliest square in Reims, and the fact that the place itself is nice and quiet. Inside, the hotel is bursting with history and a few impressive relics of the past remain, unspoilt by time (the lift, for example). Ah, if only the walls could talk! The rooms, which have been completely refurbished, are comfortable, and the bathrooms are very modern. Prices range from 260F for a double with shower to 350F with bath. There's also a pretty little courtyard where (weather permitting) you can have your breakfast outside.

|●| RESTAURANT LE CHAMOIS

45 rue des Capucins. **MAP B3-16**
☎ 03.26.88.69.75
Closed Wednesdays and Sunday lunchtimes.

Weary of the lowlands? Well try this rather intimate, unhassled restaurant where the food draws its inspiration from Alpine pastures and mountain peaks. On the menu there is *fondues savoyardes, raclettes valaisanne* or *vaudoise.* Traditional set meals are available 45–59F (weekday lunchtimes only) and 75F (weekday lunchtimes and evenings). A lot of readers have complained about the misleading information on the board outside, it would be good if they could put it right once and for all because the standard of service and food here are tremendous.

|●| BAR-RESTAURANT HENRI IV

29 rue Henri-IV. **MAP B1-15**
☎ 03.26.47.56.22
Closed Dec 20–Jan 20.

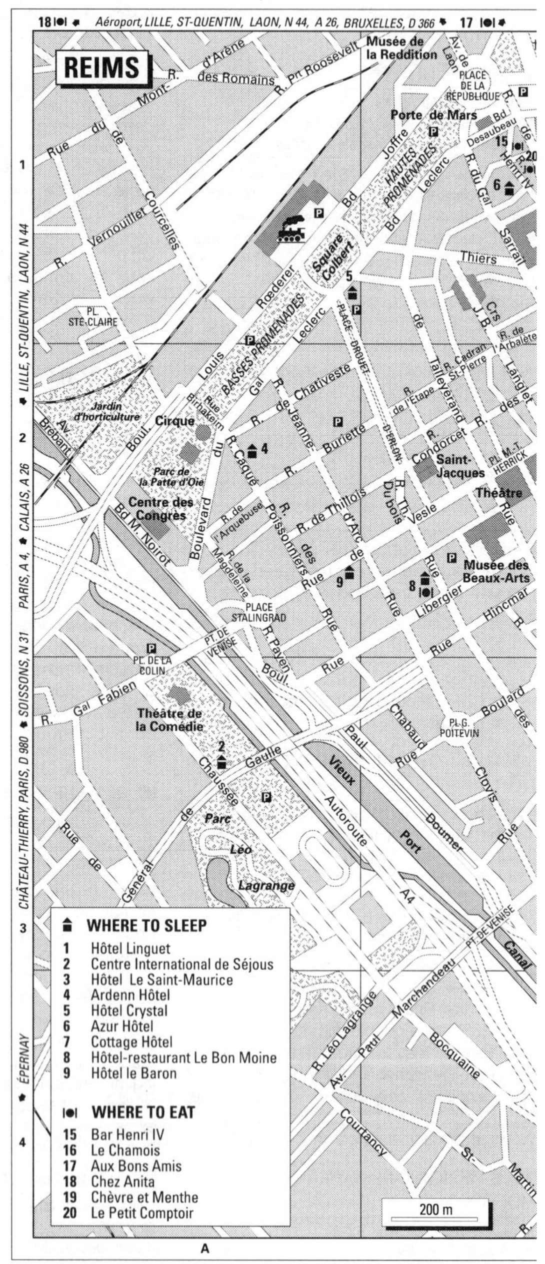
18 Aéroport, LILLE, ST-QUENTIN, LAON, N 44, A 26, BRUXELLES, D 366 17
REIMS
LILLE, ST-QUENTIN, LAON, N 44 CALAIS, A 26 PARIS, A 4, SOISSONS, N 31 CHÂTEAU-THIERRY, PARIS, D 980 ÉPERNAY
Musée de la Reddition
PLACE DE LA RÉPUBLIQUE
Porte de Mars
HAUTES PROMENADES
Square Colbert
BASSES PROMENADES
PLACE DROUET D'ERLON
PL. STE-CLAIRE
Jardin d'horticulture
Cirque
Parc de la Patte d'Oie
Centre des Congrès
Saint-Jacques
PL. M.-T. HERRICK
Théâtre
Musée des Beaux-Arts
PLACE STALINGRAD
PL. DE LA COLIN
Théâtre de la Comédie
PL. G. POITEVIN
Parc Léo Lagrange
Vieux Port
Canal
Autoroute A4
200 m
WHERE TO SLEEP
1 Hôtel Linguet
2 Centre International de Séjous
3 Hôtel Le Saint-Maurice
4 Ardenn Hôtel
5 Hôtel Crystal
6 Azur Hôtel
7 Cottage Hôtel
8 Hôtel-restaurant Le Bon Moine
9 Hôtel le Baron
WHERE TO EAT
15 Bar Henri IV
16 Le Chamois
17 Aux Bons Amis
18 Chez Anita
19 Chèvre et Menthe
20 Le Petit Comptoir

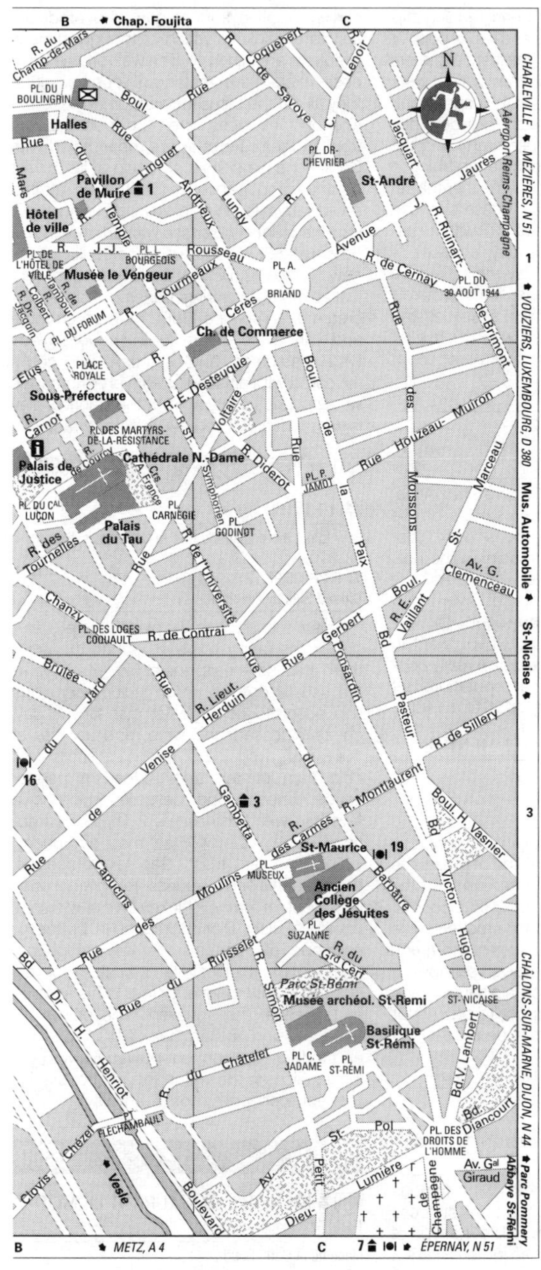

Jeannette Champion has been running this great little café for 19 years and it's as popular now as it ever was. At 7am the first customers of the day arrive, people on their way to work having a quick black coffee at the counter and a bit of a chat before they start their day, then at midday the lunchtime rush starts and the place is crammed with people grabbing a quick snack. You get a choice of either the set meal at 52F, main course, dessert, and a quarter litre of wine, or one at 62F with a platter of *crudités*, dish of the day, cheeses or dessert. The dish of the day varies but it's always something pretty safe, like shepherd's pie, roast veal and vegetables, sausages and haricot beans. On Saturdays, when it's market day, you're guaranteed a lively atmosphere.

|●| CHEZ ANITA

37 rue Ernest Renan. **MAP A1-18**
☎ 03.26.40.16.20
Closed Sunday evenings.

If you like Italian food you'll adore Chez Anita. There's everything you could ask for on the menu, from oven-baked pizza (with your choice of topping) to pasta galore. The portions are generous and very filling. As with certain medication, beware of over-indulgence as it could make you slightly drowsy! So don't come here for lunch if you want to stay active for the rest of the day. A really popular place with a good local reputation. Set meals 68F (lunchtimes only), 95F and 140F.

|●| RESTAURANT CHÈVRE ET MENTHE

63 rue du Barbâtre. **MAP C3-19**
☎ 03.26.05.17.03
Closed Sundays, Mondays and Aug.

For years this place has had an excellent reputation and that gives you a kind of guarantee that you won't be disappointed. Behind the painted windows you'll find 2 little rooms. The nicer one is reserved for smokers. The food sounds modest enough on the menu but is actually very impressive: salmon *en papillote, aiguillettes* of duck in a sauce made from *bleu d'Auvergne.* Expect to pay about 80F for a meal; drink not included.

|●| RESTAURANT AU PETIT COMPTOIR

17 rue de Mars. **MAP B1-20**
☎ 03.26.40.58.58
Closed Saturday lunchtimes, Sundays, Jan 1–11, Aug 10–26.

Fabrice Maillot has worked with famous chefs in the past and is having great success with this bistro, which is more like the type of place you'd find in Lyons than in Paris. He's a clever, creative sort of guy who produces first-rate cooking which, although it looks simple, is anything but. The well-off, the business execs, the restaurant connoisseurs, they all get the same longing, greedy expression on their faces when the food is put in front of them. For starters, bean salad with Cantal cheese (49F), carpaccio of lamb with houmus and pancetta (64F), then stuffed squid with salad in an olive oil dressing (89F), pan-fried fillet of *rascasse* with artichokes *à la bargoule* (88F) and pot-roasted duckling with new turnips (220F) for 2. The desserts are just as mouth-watering: peach milkshake, ice cream *à la verveine* (38F), rhubarb crumble and vanilla ice cream (39F), *nougat glacé* with pistachios and spices, kiwi coulis flavoured with aniseed (36F). Very impressive wine list (the selection from the Rhône valley is wonderful). Around 230F. With terrace.

VAL DE VESLE 51360 (18KM E)

|●| L'ÉTRIER

How to get there: take the N44 to Courmelais, then the D8.
☎ 03.26.03.92.12
Closed Sunday evenings.

This is a friendly, homely place where everyone in the family chips in. During the week there are 2 set meals, one at 57F which workers usually opt for, which includes *crudités* and assorted cold meats, dish of the day, cheese, dessert and wine, and another at 100F with a choice of *terrine,* 6 snails or a cold ham platter, sirloin steak in pepper sauce, cheese and dessert, which is a favourite with businessmen. The big attraction though is the 140F set meal on Sunday, which is a real feast. See for yourselves: house apéritif and savouries, *foie gras* of duck with toast, or *terrine* (chicken liver or venison), choice of fish: fillet of zander in butter, or escalope of fresh salmon in champagne, choice of meat: gigot of lamb or steak, or veal kidneys in champagne, or fillet of duck, salad and cheese, then dessert. The only thing that's missing is the glass of brandy at the end to finish it all off, but nowadays with the local police on the watch for any trouble, it's probably best not to bother anyway.

RETHEL 08300

10% ⌂ |●| HÔTEL-RESTAURANT LE MODERNE**

place de la Gare (South).

☎ 03.24.38.44.54 ➡ 03.24.38.37.84
Car park. TV. Canal+.

For forty years this place has been a real favourite with travellers passing through the large town of Rethel, the birthplace of France's dear Louis Hachette (famous publisher). Situated opposite the peaceful station, the rooms have been recently renovated but there are still remains of the old retro style in some which fit in with the overall look of the place. Well-equipped doubles 200F (with shower/wc) and 220F (with bath). Decent set meal 89F and à la carte you'll get the Moderne 'classics': grilled white pudding (the local speciality), calf's head with *sauce gribiche*. ...

HÔTEL-RESTAURANT LE CHAMPAGNE**

bd de la 2e-DI (West); it's opposite the Aisne.
☎ 03.24.38.03.28 ➡ 03.24.38.37.70
Car park. TV. Canal+. Disabled access.

Originally this was meant to be a residential building but it's now a hotel with shops above it, which consequently means it's not exactly oozing charm. However, the rooms are nice and clean and it's good value for money: 210F for a double with shower/wc or bath. Room 126 has a lovely view of the river.There are 2 restaurants: a cafeteria (eat there more for the prices than the surroundings: 50–60F for a meal) and a more expensive place with good traditional cuisine (local white pudding, calf sweetbreads, zander with ginger). Set meals 80F (weekday lunchtimes), 102F and 155F.

PAUVRES 08310 (15KM SE)

RESTAURANT AU CHEVAL BLANC

How to get there: its on the D946 just as you get to the village.
☎ 03.24.30.38.95
Closed Monday evenings and August. **Car park.**

You often see places with quite strange names in this area, like Mon Idée (My Idea) or Pauvres (Poor), this particular village. Well, Pauvres has certainly 'enriched' itself with this little gem of a place. Two famous French poets, Rimbaud and Verlaine, who were often seen hanging about this area, perhaps made this one of their stop-over spots. There is a sign outside which talks of parking your horse or yourself outside. Today you're more likely to see vans or commercial vehicles. At lunchtime workers from all walks of life come here for the set meal of the day at 65F (a litre of red wine included). Family cooking, good, hearty portions served with a smile. If only they could improve the desserts a bit we'd be entirely happy. At the weekend families come in for the more regional set meals from 80–160F (*tourte* of white pudding etc).

SIGNY-L'ABBAYE 08460 (23KM NORTH)

10% AUBERGE DE L'ABBAYE**

place Aristide-Briand; take the D985.
☎ 03.24.52.81.27 ➡ 03.24.53.71.72
Closed Wednesday evenings, Thursdays, and Jan–Feb.
Car park. TV.

This lovely inn, which has been in the same family since the times of the Revolution, can be found in the heart of a small picturesque market town on the edge of a huge forest. You'll get a warm welcome here and there's a nice family atmosphere. The rooms are all different, stylish and done up quite regularly. We've got a bit of a soft spot for room 9 which has it's own little sitting room Doubles with basin from 220F, with shower/wc 300F. With the fire crackling away and the country-style dining rooms, you're in an ideal environment to enjoy the home cooking based on food grown in the area. Set meals 75F and 140F during the week and 150F for Sunday lunch. The excellent beef comes from the Lefebvres' own cattle (they're still farmers) and the rhubarb for the rhubarb tart comes from their own garden. Yes, this type of place still exists even as we approach the end of the century. France still has these superb little spots waiting to be discovered, places like this little niche in the Ardennnes with its undulating woodlands and amazing fortified churches.

SAINTE-MENEHOULD 51800

HÔTEL-RESTAURANT DE LA POSTE**

54 av. Victor-Hugo (East).
☎ 03.26.60.80.16 ➡ 03.26.60.97.37
Closed Sunday evenings and January. **Car park. TV.**

An unassuming place not far from the station. The rooms are a bit old-fashioned but they're comfortable: all doubles with showers/wc and telephone from 200F. Rooms 7, 8, and 9 at the back are quieter and 9 is the largest. Set meals in the restaurant from 58F with, naturally, the local favourite, pig's trotters *à la Sainte-Ménehould*. Very friendly new owners.

☗ |●| HÔTEL-RESTAURANT LE CHEVAL ROUGE**

1 rue Chanzy (Centre).
☎ 03.26.60.81.04 F➔ 03.26.60.93.11
Closed Mondays out of season and Nov 17–Dec 8.

The excellent weekly set meal at 60F is reason enough in itself to stop over here. Judge for yourself. *Rillettes* of sardines with onion marmalade or cucumber gazpacho, followed by sautéd gizzards *basquaises* or fillet of cod with dill, and for dessert, *clafoutis* of rhubarb. For 60F most people would be happy with crudités to start, steak and chips, and a crème caramel. The set meal at 90F is just as imaginative (lamb with pineapple chutney in a curry sauce, pan-fried chicken *à la chinoise*, rack of lamb *dijonnais*). There are two other generous set meals at 150F and 210F. On the à la carte menu you'll find the local speciality, pig's trotters. According to real connoisseurs, the chef really is quite something. Comfortable rooms 240F–260F for a double with shower. (270F with bath, 1 available for 4 people).

|●| L'AUBERGE DU SOLEIL D'OR*

place de l'Hôtel-de-Ville (Centre).
☎ 03.26.60.82.49

The owner of this place, Yvan de Singly, a spry 70 year old, has two passions in life: his pedalo and pig's trotters. As regards the former, he does in fact hold the record for crossing the Channel on a pedalo! And the latter, well, it's a bit of a speciality around here. Taste it and believe! The trotters are wrapped in a cloth, simmered for 48 hours in an aromatic stock, kept in a cold room for 6 hours and then served covered in batter with apple sauce on the side. A real world exclusive. His inn is like an 18th century museum: crockery, saucepans, copperware, old furniture. Louis XVI would have spent his last night here before fleeing to Varennes in 1792. Expect to pay about 180F for a meal. The only thing that could be improved is the welcome, which can be rather on the gruff side.

FLORENT-EN-ARGONNE 51800 (7.5KM EAST)

10% ☗ HÔTEL LE JABLOIRE***

How to get there: on the D85.
☎ 03.26.60.82.03 F➔ 03.26.60.85.45
Closed Sunday evenings (out of season) and Feb.
Car park. **TV**. **Disabled access**.

The hotel stands on the same quiet square as the church. A splendid 19th century bourgeois house, it was a wedding gift from a cooper to his son. Barrel-making was at one time the livelihood of the village, and just above the front door of the hotel there's a carving which the owner, Yves Oudet, will gladly tell you all about. The rooms are peaceful, bright and uncluttered, all with shower/wc or bath, 250–380F for a double. A charming place.

|●| AUBERGE LA MENYÈRE

10 rue Basse; take the D85 (a very pretty route) to the village, it's about 100m from the church.
☎ 03.26.60.93.70
Closed Sunday evenings, Mondays, Feb 15–March 1, Aug 19–Sep 10.

This secluded half-timbered 16th century inn is in a little village in the heart of the beautiful forest of Argonne, which was an important place during World War 1. As soon as you step inside you're transported back in time and feel as if you're about to meet Louis XVI or the famous writer Victor Hugo on the stairs. Without a doubt this is one of the most beautiful inns on the Marne. Good set meal (drink included) at 65F (lunchtimes Tues–Friday). Game and mushrooms in autumn. Another set meal available at 140F.

SEDAN 08200

10% ☗ |●| LE RELAIS**

rue Gaston-Sauvage (South-west); Leaving Sedan, follow signs to Charleville-Mézières.
☎ 03.24.27.04.41 F➔ 03.24.29.71.16
Car park. **TV**. **Canal+**.

A huge brick building with quite a bit of character. It was once a soap factory. Today it's our favourite hotel in Sedan. Primarily for the friendly welcome you always get. Next, for the peaceful rooms (although you're still in town, there's a real country feel to the place) and for the good value for money: double with washing facilities 180F, 250F with shower/wc, 280F with bath. Rooms 31 and 32 have got more of a personal touch and look out onto the garden. We also like the rooms in the adjoining annexe. In the huge restaurant, set meals are served at 68F (7 days, lunch and dinner), 95F and 130F. Traditional cuisine with a choice of regional dishes (Ardennes pâté and the famous *cacasse à cul nu,* a stew of potatoes, onions, bacon and beef).

☗ |●| LE SAINT-MICHEL*

3 rue Saint-Michel (Centre).
☎ 03.24.29.04.61 F➔ 03.24.29.32.67
Closed July 22–Aug 19, restaurant closed Sunday evenings. **Secure parking**. **TV**. **Canal+**.

This place is in an ideal spot in a quiet, little street in the old town (1000 years old, in fact!), just beside the high walls of the castle (the largest in Europe apparently). The rooms are decent and they all have shower/wc or bath: 245F for a double. The restaurant is pretty traditional: set meal at 65F (lunchtimes and evenings except on Sundays), others available 100–165F. They do a few local specialities, like sautéd wild boar. Half-board 245F per person per night. However, the service could be a bit more attentive. 5% discount on presentation of this guidebook.

|●| RESTAURANT LA DÉESSE

35 av. du Général-Margueritte(North-West); go in the direction of Saint-Menges/Floing, it's about 200m after the Dijonval (Museum of Industry) on the right.
☎ 03.24.29.11.52
Closed evenings, Feb and Aug.

This little bar-restaurant is always full of regulars so grab a table somewhere whenever you get the chance! The atmosphere is warm, friendly and definitely informal. Good set meal (weekday lunchtimes) 67F. Fresh produce is used for everything here (including desserts) and there's not a microwave in sight. It's authentic and simple. What more could you ask! The service is informal but efficient and the owner always goes round and chats to all her customers to make sure everything's all right. The weekend set meal at 98F caters more for families. Children's meal 35F. This is by far the best value for money in Sedan, and has been for years!

BAZEILLES 08140 (4KM SE)

10% ⌂ |●| AUBERGE DU PORT**

route de Rémilly (South-East); from Bazeilles take the D129 towards Rémilly for about 1km.
☎ 03.24.27.13.89 F➜ 03.24.29.35.58
Closed Friday evenings, Saturday lunchtimes, Sunday evenings, Aug 16–31, Dec 20–Jan 15. **Car park**. **TV**. **Canal+**.

This pretty white house stands at the end of a little port (well, a mooring berth actually!) on the River Meuse. There's a kind of colonial atmosphere to the place with the garden and the surrounding meadows giving it a certain charm. It's a bit posh but nothing too heavy. The bedrooms are in a separate building; the ones looking out over the river get more light. We admit we've got a bit of a soft spot for room number 18, which is all in blue and very romantic (but with twin beds unfortunately). But the other rooms have got a bit of character about them too, 305F for a double with shower or bath. There's an excellent set meal at 98F (lunchtimes and evenings except Sundays) and others at 142F, 165F, 185F etc. The presentation of the food is great and quite imaginative: herb-covered veal sweetbreads *en crépinette*, medallions of pork in a ginger-sauce. The fish isn't that bad either: *rillettes* of salmon with spices, roast monkfish with artichokes and ginger. Game in season. Shaded terrace for summer months.

RÉMILLY-AILLICOURT 08450 (6KM SE)

⌂ |●| HÔTEL-RESTAURANT LA SAPINIÈRE**

How to get there: take the D6, direction Raucourt Vouziers.
☎ 03.24.26.75.22 F➜ 03.24.26.75.19
Restaurant closed Mondays, hotel closed 1st 3 weeks of Jan and 1 week in Aug. **Car park**. **TV**.

This is a traditional country hotel-restaurant which used to be an old coaching inn. The rooms look out onto the garden, so they are nice and quiet. Most of them are clean and spruce (some are a touch old-fashioned) and all are comfortable. Doubles 265F with shower/wc, 280F with bath. The restaurant has a big room which is often used for wedding parties and the like. Set meals start at 90F (except Sundays and public holidays), then are 130F, 160F and 200F. Traditional cuisine using local produce, which sometimes has a nice original touch: Ardennes ham with fresh fruit, grilled lamb chops, sautéd oyster mushrooms in mixed herbs. Game in season and summer salads (60–120F, except Sundays). Pleasant terrace.

CARIGNAN 08110 (20KM SE)

|●| RESTAURANT LA GOURMANDIÈRE

19 av. de Blagny.
☎ 03.24.22.20.99
Closed Mondays.

The rather fancy dining room here sets the tone of this elegant bourgeois residence. But there's still a very homely atmosphere about the place. The female chef is talented and daring with it, mixing local produce with foreign spices (*chiffonnade* of Ardennes ham sprinkled with garam masala). The food on the menu comes from all over so, go on, be adventurous: *assiette landaise au confit,* leg of duck, dried breast of duck, quail confit, pan-fried sirloin with oyster mushrooms and Chaource cheese, *pissaladière* of fillet steak with sesame seeds. Set meal 68F (weekday lunchtimes; choice of 2 starters, 2 main courses and dessert), then at 115F, 165F and 210F. Lovely terrace in the garden for sunny days.

SÉZANNE 51120

HÔTEL-RESTAURANT LE RELAIS CHAMPENOIS** –

157 rue Notre-Dame; on leaving Sézanne, go in the direction of Troyes.
☎ 03.26.80.58.03 F➜ 03.26.81.35.32
Closed Friday evenings and Sunday evenings out of season, and Dec 20–Jan 3. **Secure parking**. **TV**. **Canal+**. **Disabled access**.

You've now entered the real champagne country. This is a friendly old inn with lovely renovated rooms – 230F (with shower)–295F (with bath). Monsieur Fourmi is chef here and he prepares superb food inspired by local produce – for example, the *cassolette de ris de veau à la fine de la Marne*, or rib steak in a red wine sauce. Set meals 100F, 130F, 160F and 220F. This place is renowned for its quality of service and the great welcome you get. For 20 years now, everyone who has been coming to Sézanne has sung the praises of Monsieur and Madame Fourmi. Excellent reputation.

HÔTEL-RESTAURANT DE LA CROIX D'OR**

53 rue Notre-Dame; it's a stone's throw from the centre on the Troyes road.
☎ 03.26.80.61.10 F➜ :03.26.80.65.20
Closed Jan 3–18. **Secure parking**. **TV**. **Disabled access**.

Gun dogs and birds of prey watch over the car park of this hotel. Attractive rooms (240F with washing facilities, 300F for a double with shower). The set meals at 60F (lunch and dinner, Sunday included) and 79F are both ideal for the traveller on a budget. The others at 120F, 135F and 185F are in the hands of the chef (who seems to change a bit too often for our liking). As the saying goes, "When in doubt, don't". Make sure you remember that!

TROYES 10000

10% HÔTEL DES COMTES DE CHAMPAGNE**

54-56 rue de la Monnaie (Centre); it's in an old street between the town hall and the station, 300m from the church of Saint-Jean.
☎ 03.25.73.11.70 F➜ 03.25.73.06.02
Secure parking. **TV**.

A 12th century building, which served as a bank to the counts of Champagne in their heyday. Good prices for a 2-star hotel, which has been recently refurbished by new owners: doubles 120F (with basin but no TV), 270F (with bath). Thick walls, wood panelling from the times of Louis XIV, a distinct feeling of the past, a little peaceful garden. Rooms. 1, 14, 15, 19, 24 and 27 are spacious and quiet. Garage: 25F. Excellent welcome. Very good place.

10% HÔTEL ARLEQUIN**

50 rue de Turenne (Centre); it's near to the church of Saint Pantaléon.
☎ 03.25.83.12.70 F➜ 03.25.83.12.99
TV.

Unfortunately it doesn't have the charm of the old timber-framed houses in the area, but l'Arlequin is a brightly coloured, friendly hotel. Friendliness seems to be the motto around here and you'll get a very warm welcome from the landlord, who takes a real pride in looking after his guests. About twenty spacious, bright rooms at reasonable prices: 195F for a double wih shower, 230F with bath. Basically, when you don't know where to stay in Troyes, this is the answer. Another bonus: a loyalty card with your seventh night free. A good deal for those who are staying slightly longer or who are regular visitors to the town.

10% HÔTEL DE TROYES**

168 av. du Général-Leclerc (North-West); from the gare SNCF follow signs for 'Paris par Provins', turn right after the railway bridge.
☎ 03.25.71.23.45 F➜ 03.25.79.12.14
Secure parking. **TV**. **Canal+**. **Disabled access**.

For those who prefer somewhere a bit away from the town centre. Immaculate rooms 260–330F with shower/wc, decorated in a contemporary style. You'll get a charming welcome. Breakfast buffet 36F. There's no restaurant but the owner will gladly tell you of other good places to eat nearby. Guests are mainly people on business, so room prices tend to drop at weekends.

HÔTEL LE CHANT DES OISEAUX***

20 rue Linard Gonthier (Centre); it's near to the cathedral of Saint Pierre and the Museum of Modern Art.
☎ 03.25.80.58.50 F➜ 03.25.80.98.34
Secure parking. **TV**. **Canal+**. **Disabled access**.

In a cobbled street, lined with half-timbered

houses, you'll find this 3-star hotel, which dates back to the 15th century. There are 12 rooms and a private courtyard, lovely in the summer for breakfast. Most of the rooms vary in price from 450F up to 550F for a double. But the prices can soar up to 790F if you want the very best: two enormous suites, both with rather elegant names, 'La suite médiévale' and 'Les Bengalis', with exposed beams, armchairs, wing chairs. This is the ideal place for folk who are coming to Troyes for a special occasion or for a couple in search of a spot for a romantic break. A bewitchingly delightful place, as long as you've braced yourself for the cost

LE COIN DE LA PIERRE

34 rue Viardin (Centre).
☎ 03.25.73.58.44
Closed Sundays

This is an old half-timbered house on a street corner. The first thing you see when you go into this place is a little courtyard and a spiral staircase. The huge room with its fireplace is very welcoming and is the perfect setting to try out the special kinds of cheese you get here (*raclettes, pierrades etc*) Great variety of salads 40–47F. A place for those who are bored with *andouillettes.* Nice atmosphere and regular customers.

RESTAURANT AU CHEVAL DE 3

31 rue de la Cité (Centre); it's between the hospital and the cathedral of Saint-Pierre.
☎ 03.25.80.58.23
Closed in the evening on Sundays, Tuesdays and Wednesdays.

This is an unobtrusive little restaurant not far from the pedestrian precinct. Good, regional specialities which are meticulously prepared: *andouillette de Troyes,* salad with Chaource cheese. Set meals with a starter 59F weekdays, or 85F with starter, main course, cheeses and dessert. Other set meals 100F, 114F, 144F. The welcome is of the same high quality as the cooking.

LE JARDIN GOURMAND

31 rue Paillot de Montabert (Centre); it's near the town hall.
☎ 03.25.73.36.13
Closed Sundays and Monday lunchtimes.

This stylish and intimate little restaurant is right in the heart of old Troyes. It's got its own pretty courtyard, which is heated and sheltered in the winter and which looks out onto a timber-framed 16th century wall that the owner has restored. Excellent welcome. Set meal at 70F (lunchtimes) or 100F. But what really makes this place stand out is its speciality: home-made *andouillettes*, cooked in 6 different ways. This is a must for *andouillette* lovers and also one of our favourite spots in Troyes.

RESTAURANT LE CAFÉ DE PARIS

63 rue du Général-de-Gaulle (Centre); it's right next to the church of la Madeleine.
☎ 03.25.73.08.30
Closed Sunday evenings, Mondays and the 1st 3 weeks of August.

A good place at average prices. Set meals at 112F, 159F and 198F. The chef doesn't go too overboard (fricassee of snails with oyster mushrooms, house *foie-gras* of duck, roast kidneys of veal flavoured with Szechuan pepper), but it's all very good and the atmosphere is warm and friendly. It's popular with the locals both for lunch and in the evening for a nice candlelit dinner for two. A place that has something for everyone.

SAINTE-SAVINE 10300 (2.5KM WEST)

10% MOTEL SAVINIEN**

87 rue La Fontaine; from Troyes centre take the N60 (direction Paris par Sens), travel for at least 2km then turn right.
☎ 03.25.79.24.90 F 03.25.78.04.61
Restaurant closed Sunday evenings and Monday lunchtimes. **Car park**. **TV**. **Disabled access**.

This hotel looks as if it could be part of a chain but it isn't. It's quite popular with travelling salesmen. There's a swimming pool, a sauna and a massage parlour all available to guests. The rooms are pretty standard with not a lot of character, and all have some kind of view. You can get to the ones on the first floor by using an outside staicase, the type you see in American-style motels. Attractive prices considering the quality of service provided: 220F for doubles with shower/wc. Breakfast: 32F. Cheapest set meal 69F, then 80F–175F. Very warm welcome.

BRÉVIANDES 10450 (5KM SE)

10% HÔTEL-RESTAURANT LE PAN DE BOIS**

35 av. du Général-Leclerc; coming from Troyes centre, in the direction of Dijon, it's just to the left of the N71 before the intersection on the south-bound bypass.
☎ 03.25.75.02.31 F 03.25.49.67.84
Hotel closed Sunday evenings, restaurant closed Mondays and Sunday evenings. **Secure parking**. **TV**. **Disabled access**.

A fairly new, very well-designed establishment with all the facilities you would expect from one of a chain, but it's housed in a modern building that attempts to fit in with its surroundings. The rooms at the back looking out onto a row of trees are the most peaceful. Decent prices: 280F for a double with bath and telephone. The restaurant is just next door in the same type of building. Cheapest set meal 88F. Specialities: barbecued meats and steaks. Good local wines. Very pleasant terrace, which is lovely in the summer.

SAINT-ANDRÉ-LES-VERGERS 10120 (5KM SW)

10% MOTEL LES ÉPINGLIERS**

180 rte d'Auxerre; take the N77, in the direction of Auxerre and it's less than 1km after the Saint-André roundabout.
☎ 03.25.75.05.99 F 03.25.75.32.22
Car park. **TV**. **Canal+**. **Disabled access**.

This is a modern hotel with about 15 rooms (shower or bath, TV, Canal+, telephone, alarm service). Each one looks out onto a little bit of the garden. 220F for doubles. Breakfast buffet 30F. There isn't a restaurant here but there's one next door, and the landlord is not at all hesitant to recommend other good places.

LA GENTILHOMMIÈRE

180 rte d'Auxerre.
☎ 03.25.49.35.64
Closed Sunday evenings and Wednesdays. **Car park**.

From the outside you wouldn't think much of this place but it's actually rather nice. The atmosphere, service and food are all pretty sophisticated: we enjoyed our mussel soup flavoured with saffron, with Mozart on in the background. The delicious food seems to be a real hit with businessmen and locals. The chef's *andouillette,* chopped into small pieces with melted Chaource cheese on top, is an absolute must. Set meals at 100F, 130F and 200F.

ROSIÈRES-PRÈS-TROYES 10430 (7KM SOUTH)

AUBERGE DE JEUNESSE

chemin de Sainte-Scholastique (South-West); take bus 6 from la Place des Halles (behind the town hall) to the terminus.
☎ 03.25.82.00.65 F 03.25.72.93.78
Car park

The hostel stands on the site of a 12th century priory, where the moated remains of a chapel and a parlour are still visible. Although the hostel bulidings are modern, they don't spoil the charm of the place: 5 acres of grounds, huge gardens, trees. and all well away from the noise of the town. 104 beds in rooms for 6 with a shared bathroom. 65F per person for the first night, 50F from then on. Kitchen available for own use or meal 50F (reservation essential).

FOUCHÈRES 10260 (23KM SE)

L'AUVERGNE DE LA SEINE

How to get there: on the N71 it's between Troyes and Bar-sur-Seine.
☎ 03.25.40.71.11
Closed Tuesday evenings all year round and Wednesdays out of season. **Car park**.

This is a delightful restaurant beside the Seine which looks as though it should be in Normandy – remember, you're still in Champagne! The huge bay windows in the restaurant open out onto the river so you can soak up the atmosphere of the beautiful surroundings whatever the season. This relaxing setting complements the wonderful, inventive cuisine: flan with thick and creamy Chaource cheese, rabbit with baby vegetables, seafood specialities made from locally caught fish. Set meals at 65F (weekday lunchtimes), 110F and 160F. A stylish restaurant where you'll find a very warm welcome in absolutely beautiful surroundings.

VILLIERS-SUR-MARNE 52320

10% LA SOURCE BLEUE

Lieu-dit La Source Bleue (East); it's 1km east of Villiers s/Marne.
☎ 03.25.94.70.35
Closed Sunday evenings and Mondays. **Car park**. **TV**. **Canal+**.

In the heart of the countryside beside a river, this little place owned by a young couple is ideal for people who love the outdoors. It has a warm atmosphere and, although simple, is well looked after. The service is tremendous and the menu quite reasonably priced. We recommend the tartare of trout, the fillet of duck with red berries, and the exquisite desserts. There is a basic set meal at 65F but on average a meal will cost you around 150F. There are 2 lovely, country-style rooms available on reservation (250F weekdays, 300F weekends). The ponds that supply the restaurant with trout are worth a look – they've got a hidden spring.

VITRY-LE-FRANÇOIS 51300

10% HÔTEL-RESTAURANT DE LA CLOCHE

34 rue Aristide Briand (Centre).
☎ 03.26.74.03.84
Restaurant closed Sunday evenings out of season and from Jan 2–20

The town may at first appear somewhat lifeless (it was almost completely destroyed during the Second World War), but ignore your first impressions and whatever you may hear the natives say about it! It's basically a peaceful provincial town where you'll generally get a friendly welcome, Mme Sautet at the Hôtel de la Cloche being the perfect example. Everything is impeccable, whether it be the napkins in the restaurant, the sheets, the bedrooms, or the bathroom towels. You'll also get a good night's sleep. Jaques Sautet is the long-standing chef there who really knows what he's doing, and specializes in good traditional French food. His pâtisseries are loved by all. A number of set meals at 110F, 130F, 195F and 280F. Children's set meal 69F. Just next to the hotel you'll find a butcher's shop owned by Brelest, famous for its black puddings, *andouillettes* (a must for barbecues), garlic sausages, and brawn (fantastic in sandwiches).

10% HÔTEL-RESTAURANT DE LA POSTE***

place Royer-Collard(Centre); it's behind the Notre-Dame cathedral.
☎ 03.26.74.02.65 F 03.26.74.54.71
Closed Sundays and Dec 21–Jan 6. **Secure parking**. **TV**. **Disabled access**.

We recommend this place as just somewhere to stay, as the restaurant is quite expensive. Cheapest set meal is 98F, the others are 130F, 160F and 220F with seafood being the main speciality. Doubles with shower/wc and telephone from 280F (240F with shower and wc on landing), 340F with bath, family rooms for 3, 380F, suites with bath 620F. If your room doesn't have a jacuzzi, you can always relax in the sauna or solarium. There's a great choice of beer and whiskies in the bar The hotel looks out onto a quiet street, and you"ll be able to park quite easily. Warm welcome.

10% HÔTEL-RESTAURANT LE BON SÉJOUR*

faubourg Léon-Bourgeois (East); leave Vitry and go in the direction of Nancy – it's about 500m from the centre in a turning on the left.
☎ 03.26.74.02.36 F 03.26.73.44.21
Closed Friday evenings, Saturdays, the 2nd fortnight in Aug, and Christmas holidays. **Car park**. **TV**.

This is a small, very basic hotel but it's well looked after and clean. The rooms are in a rather drab-looking annexe and look out onto a quiet tree-lined street. Doubles with shower 240F (wc on landing). Set meal 59F (weekdays), then 93F, day's special 40F. À la carte also available. A fair number of sales reps. It's got the kind of atmosphere you'd get in a provincial bistro.

RESTAURANT L'ASIE

54 rue de la Tour (Centre).
☎ 03.26.72.13.87
Closed Mondays and Aug 11–Sep 3.

This highly popular restaurant, which has been run by Chinese Cambodians for 11 years now, is full every night. The reasons for this are not hard to find: the place is always exceptionally clean, you always get a really warm welcome and the food is consistently good. They specialize in Chinese and Thai food. Lunchtime set meal 56F. Evenings à la carte only. Expect to pay about 100F (with wine). Air-conditioned.

VITRY-EN-PERTHOIS 51300 (4KM NE)

AUBERGE DE LA PAVOISE

(Centre); on the D382, direction Givry-en-Argonne.
☎ 03.26.74.59.00
Closed every day except Saturday evenings, Sunday lunchtimes and public holidays.

This is what you would call your stereotypical country inn. The restaurant is in what used to be the cowshed belonging to the family farm. The fixed set meal at 105F (drink not included) offers you a great choice of dishes – for starters, salad of *gésiers* with snails, a savoury *soufflé* of chicken, or *velouté* of mushrooms; main courses include leg of duck with mirabelle plums, or guinea fowl with grapes. And finally, for dessert, charlotte, tarts or *bavarois,* which are a hit with young and old alike. Wines from Burgundy, Aligoté, Morgon, Regnié and more. All at reasonable prices.

CHÂTELRAOULD 51300 (8KM SW)

LA PETITE AUBERGE

(Centre); D2, in the direction of Chaumont.
☎ 03.26.72.84.15

The architecture of this pretty inn is a bit like that of farms you see in Normandy, but in fact, it belongs to the region of Der. Although the inside isn't quite as pretty as the outside, it's still pleasant, with a cosy atmosphere. In the main room there's a *baby-foot*, and in the corner a jukebox, which is never used (well, never at lunchtimes at least). The landlord looks after the bar, while his friendly wife cooks and serves meals. Good set meal during the week 48F (59F with wine and coffee). Weekend special meals 85F. Definitely good value for money A few basic rooms but still very well looked after. Doubles 105F (singles 90F). Breakfast 19F.

ARRIGNY 51290 (18KM SE)

CAFÉ-TABAC «CHEZ HENRI»

(Centre); on the D13, direction Éclaron.
☎ 03.26.72.61.95
Closed Monday evenings; the restaurant closed Sundays.

A typical village café where all you need to complete the picture are a couple of groups of men sitting around playing belote (a popular French card game). Anyway, the snack bar gets its fair share of customers every day from workers to travellers to sales reps to tourists. The set meal at 58F (coffee included) is a bit of a winner, typical starters – cold meats, *crudités* etc, the daily house specialities, *blanquette* of veal, beef *bourguignon*, steak and new potatoes, *coq au vin.* and a choice of either ice cream or fruit for dessert. Yet another place that MacDonald's just can't compete with!

SAINTE-MARIE-DU-LAC 51290 (20KM SE)

L'AUBERGE LA BOCAGÈRE

Les Grandes Côtes; take the D384 to Éclaron, then the D24 to Blaise-sous-Hauteville, then the D60. The hotel is beside the Der lake.
☎ 03.26.72.37.40
Closed Sunday evenings, Mondays, and Dec 15–March 1. **Car park**.

This peaceful and charming old farm is surrounded by wooden buildings and a garden which leads you right into the countryside. The bedrooms are simple yet pleasant, from 200F for a double with shower/wc. The place is run by a real character, Roger Kielen, whose kind of unaffected welcome makes you feel as if you're staying with friends. His wife, Françoise, is just the same and adopts a real homely approach to cooking. Set meals during the week 120F, 160F at weekends (wine included in both cases). This is a really nice, out-of-the-ordinary sort of place, but be warned: the service can be a bit inconsistent.

LE CYCLODER

2 rue de l'Église; take the D13 to Larzicourt, then the D57 to Blaize, then the D60.
☎ 03.26.72.37.05
Closed Sep–April except weekends in March, Oct and Nov.

A lovely *crêperie* where you can get great quality *galettes* (12–30F) and *crêpes* (10–23F) along with a friendly welcome. You can also hire bikes by the hour (25F), for a half-day (48F) or for a full day (70F). Visit the model village not too far away with its typical old Champagne buildings of wattle and daub.

GIFFAUMONT-CHAMPAUBERT 51290 (26KM SE)

10% HÔTEL-RESTAURANT LE CHEVAL BLANC**

21 rue du Lac; D384, then the D153.
☎ 03.26.72.62.65 F→ 03.26.73.96.97
Restaurant closed Sunday evenings, Mondays and 3 weeks in Sep. **Car park**. **TV**.

This is an adorable village with lots of half-timbered houses. The new young owner of Le Cheval Blanc, Thierry Gérardin, has really gone full speed ahead with this place. The rooms are modern and vary in price: 280F with shower and with bath 280–300F. Big renovation projects are planned for this year (they're going to work on the entrance hall and the prefabricated buildings outside), which will only add to the already fantastic look of the place. Sit outside on the terrace to dine but stick with the 115F set meal because the chef sometimes tries to be a bit too ambitious. The Der lake, the biggest artificial lake in Europe (1000 acres), and also the site of a big national bird reserve, is just beside the hotel. While you're here you should also try to visit some of the magnificent timber-framed churches of the region, like the church of Châtillon-sur-Broué, only a few kilometres from the Cheval Blanc.

RESTAURANT LA GRANGE AUX ABEILLES

4 rue du Grand-Der; on the D13 towards Arrigny, 500m from the village of Giffaumont.
☎ 03.26.72.61.97

Closed Tuesdays (except in July and Aug), Nov 15–end Feb.
Car park. **Disabled access**.

Just 5 minutes from the lake of Der-Chantecoq you'll come across this little timber-framed inn, a style typical of the Der region. Unfortunately, however, you don't get a view of the water from the dining room. Set meals start at 82F. We prefer the crêperie-brasserie, which is good for families. After your meal the kids can go off and find out all about bees and the secret of honey in an exhibition thought up by the owner, Michel Fagot. For mini-golf fans, there's a course of about 4800 square metres nearby, but be warned – it's quite popular.

VOUZIERS 08400

ARGONNE HÔTEL**

rte de Reims (West); leaving the town in the direction of Châlons s/Rethel, the hotel is opposite the first roundabout.
☎ 03.24.71.42.14 Fax 03.24.71.83.69
Restaurant closed Sunday evenings. **Car park**. **TV**.

This is a modern building in the commercial part of town. It's not exactly oozing charm but you will get an impeccable welcome and the rooms are great value for money. 195F for double with shower/wc or bath. Set meals 88F and 155F. Very classic cuisine with occasional exotic touches – rabbit with cream and thyme, pork fillet *à l'indienne*. Ideal for a stop-over.

Corse

20 Corse

AJACCIO 20000

10% HÔTEL MARENGO**

2 rue Marengo (West); it's near the casino and the beaches, on the route des îles Sanguinaires.
☎ 04.95.21.43.66 F 04.95.21.51.26
Closed Dec 15–March 15. **Car park. TV.**

This is a lovely little place hidden at the end of a cul-de-sac. A few of the rooms look out on to a peaceful flower-filled courtyard. Warm welcome. Double rooms 230F with shower (280F in peak season) and 250F with shower/wc (330F in peak season). It's basic but well looked after and has good facilities (telephone, TV and double-glazing).

10% HÔTEL FESCH***

7 rue Fesch (Centre).
☎ 04.95.51.62.62 F 04.95.21.83.36
Closed Dec 20–Jan 5.

Central and well-kept. The prices will vary depending on the facilities of each room and whether it's peak season or not. Double rooms range in price from 280F with shower/wc out of season to 395F with bath/wc in July and August. Mini-bar and satellite TV, a true 3-star hotel. And if you want a balcony on the top floor, it's 50F extra. Professional service.

LE PIANO

13 bd du Roi-Jérôme (Centre).
☎ 04.95.51.23.81
Closed Sundays.

Service until 11pm. Year in year out, this elegant yet informal restaurant continues to give a consistently good level of service. Set meals 60F (fish soup, calamari), 105F and 140F.

RESTAURANT DA MAMMA

passage Guingette (Centre); it's in a steep little street that runs from cours Napoléon to rue Fesch.
☎ 04.95.21.39.44
Closed Sundays in winter, and Sunday and Monday lunchtimes in summer.

This restaurant with its pleasant terrace is tucked away in a little street. Fast, efficient service and great food to go along with it. Set meals 65F, 95F and 140F (the latter includes young goat). The substantial 95F set meal offers *terrine* of pork liver and herb sausages with salad and fresh mushrooms, roasted quail with olives served with courgette fritters, and a tasty slice of chocolate cake. Don't forget the house wine at 35F which is so good it positively sits up and begs to be drunk. No complaints.

L'AQUARIUM

2 rue des Halles (Centre); it's in the old town, between Campinchi square and rue Fesch.
☎ 04.95.21.11.21
Closed Mondays except in July and August, and Jan 20–end of Feb.

If you like seafood, you'll love this place. Everything's fresh and the chef really knows what he's doing. What more could you ask for?. The 100F set meal offers whitebait that tastes so fresh it might have jumped straight out of the sea, a pair of plump, rosy-fleshed red mullet in fennel (absolutely delicious), and a crème caramel that is just out of this world. We had a digestif on the house (we don't know if this happens automatically – maybe they just liked the look of us!) Other set meals

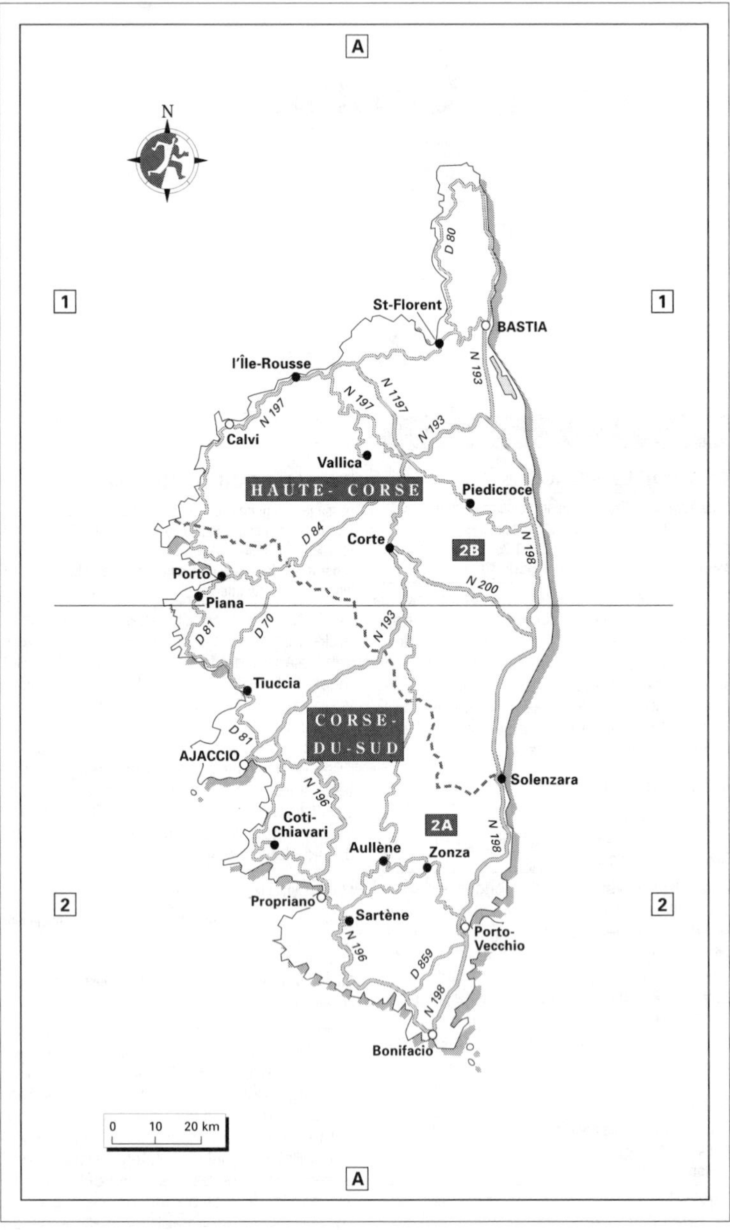

A
N
1
1
St-Florent
BASTIA
D 80
N 193
l'Île-Rousse
N 197
N 197
N 1197
N 193
Calvi
Vallica
HAUTE- CORSE
Piedicroce
D 84
Corte
2B
N 198
Porto
N 200
Piana
D 81
D 70
N 193
Tiuccia
CORSE-
DU-SUD
D 81
AJACCIO
Solenzara
N 196
Coti-
Chiavari
2A
N 198
Aullène
Zonza
2
2
Propriano
Sartène
Porto-
Vecchio
N 196
D 859
N 198
Bonifacio
0
10
20 km
A

70F, 110F and 150F. Good service. This is the real thing.

A CASA

21 av. Noël-Franchini (North); it's 2km north – go along the coast towards the airport and turn left at the end of boulevard Charles-Bonaparte.
☎ 04.95.22.34.78
Closed Saturday and Sunday lunchtimes July 1–Sept 15 and Sundays the rest of the year.

This restaurant is in a rather gloomy area a bit out of the centre, but it's well known among the people of Ajaccio for its originality. There are about 10 tables set out on the patio/balcony surrounded by plants, flowers and parasols. You'll be served satisfying, hearty, simple food. Set meals are 76F (lunchtimes) and 110F, then there's the gourmet South-West menu (the owner, Marie-Jo, comes from that beautiful region). Franck, her Corsican husband, takes charge of the drinks. He's got some very good Sartène and a Muscat that's out of this world. But that's not all. Franck is a professional magician and has set up his own stage with sequined curtains, a platform and so on. So, on Friday and Saturday evenings, it's magic-time, with illusions, conjuring and amazing tricks that'll leave you flabbergasted.

RESTAURANT DE FRANCE

59 rue Fesch (Centre).
☎ 04.95.21.11.00
Closed Sundays and in November.

This is one of the few good places with affordable prices on this touristy street. You have the choice of delicious Corsican dishes or French classics, all meticulously prepared and served on beautiful plates. The *brocciu* (a mild sheep's milk cheese) omelette is a must. The cheapest set meal at 95F (except Sundays) is remarkable value for money, and there's another one at 130F. Warm atmosphere.

BASTELICACCIA 20129 (13KM E)

M'HÔTEL L'ORANGERAIE**

☎ 04.95.20.00.09 F 04.95.20.09.24
Car park. TV. Disabled access.

The hotel bungalows are surrounded by Mediterranean plants like arbutus, palm trees and orange trees – the most amazing and most beautiful garden we've ever seen in Corsica. You can hire studios here for 2 or 4 people by the night or the week (200–320F out of season and 350–430F in July and August). They're not that new but they're well equipped and have good bedding, thermal insulation, hair-drier, kitchen, terrace and barbecue. There's a small swimming pool. Remember to book in advance since it's often full.

PILA-CANALE 20123 (30KM SE)

LE 20 123

☎ 04.95.24.20.80
Closed Wednesday lunchtimes and mid Oct–start of April.

Who'd run a restaurant in this completely out-of-the-way little village where you hardly ever see a tourist? The road's beautiful but it's long, full of twists and turns and generally hard going, but if you do take the trouble to come, you won't be disappointed – in our opinion, it's one of the best restaurants on the island. For 155F you get a wonderful set meal that gives you a choice of three main courses and three desserts and comes with first-rate *charcuterie*, a beautiful salad platter, tender roast pork with chestnuts (for example), delicious cheese, succulent *fiadone* (cheese and orange flan), and a liqueur. Authentic Corsican cuisine which is hearty yet subtle. To go with it, have the reasonably priced house wine. Friendly service. Gorgeous shaded terrace. Be warned – they don't accept credit cards.

AULLÈNE 20116

10% HÔTEL-RESTAURANT DE LA POSTE*

Centre.
☎ 04.95.78.61.21
Closed Oct 1–April 30.

They were still using stage-coaches when this very pleasant stone inn looking out over the mountains was built. Decent rooms from 240F for a double with shower/wc on the landing. Very good set meals from 95F. You must try the wild boar (in season) and the house *charcuterie*. The owner, Jeannot Benedetti, has explored every nook and cranny of the region and he'll lend you the little guide books he's written.

BASTIA 20200

10% HÔTEL-RESTAURANT LES VOYAGEURS**

5 av. du Maréchal-Sébastiani (Centre); it's 100m from the station.
☎ 04.95.31.29.31 F 04.95.31.53.33
TV.

People who love traditional cuisine have been coming here for more than 80 years. It's a family business and their motto is good quality at reasonable prices. They have three set meals (75F, 90F and 120F) and whether you have one of those or go à la carte, you'll get typical Corsican dishes and fish specialities, which you can enjoy whilst sitting on the terrace with its view of the impressive Pigno mountains. Warm welcome and good service. Above the restaurant there's a quiet little hotel with recently renovated rooms. Doubles 200–400F with air-conditioning and TV.

10% HÔTEL CENTRAL**

3 rue Miot (Centre).
☎ 04.95.31.71.12 F 04.95.31.82.40
TV.

Centrally located as its name implies. It has clean, comfortable rooms with fan, telephone, and TV at sensible prices, which vary depending on the season. Doubles 230–280F with shower/wc, 250–300F with shower/wc and a little flower-filled balcony (great for breakfast outside), and 250–320F with bath. There are a few at 200F with shower only, perfect for those on a budget. Good welcome.

RESTAURANT A CASARELLA

6 rue Sainte-Croix (South); it's in the citadel near the old Genoese governors' palace.
☎ 04.95.32.02.32
Closed Saturday lunchtimes and Sundays.

The inventive chef prepares good authentic Corsican dishes that are full of local flavour. We sat at a table on the terrace, with the old port down below, and had a feast. We loved everything, from the *casgiate* (a fromage frais fritter baked in the oven), the prawns in puff pastry and the rolled joint of topside of veal with herbs (excellent!) to the curious *storzapretti* (a kind of stodgy cake that the people here used to serve the parish priest on a Sunday) and the wonderful *fiadone* (cheese and orange flan). There are no set meals but the prices aren't too bad (expect to pay about 160F, wine included). A good place but the only thing we would fault is the service. This wasn't particularly outstanding or attentive when we were there last.

SAN-MARTINO-DI-LOTA 20200 (9KM NW)

HÔTEL-RESTAURANT DE LA CORNICHE**

☎ 04.95.31.40.98 F 04.95.32.37.69
Closed Sunday evenings and Mondays Oct–March, and in January. **Secure parking**. **TV**.

This place is like an eyrie, perched high up above everything. You can't escape the absolutely stunning view, whether you're on the terrace shaded by plane trees or in one of the rooms. Clinging to the eastern side of Cap Corse, the inn is surrounded by a vast amphitheatre of mountains tumbling down to the distant sea. Very good welcome and pleasant swimming pool. Excellent Corsican home cooking, with dishes like ravioli with cream cheese and herbs, rabbit *terrine*, breast of duck with coriander and honey, and a delicious selection of *charcuterie* from their own pigs. In winter they have wild boar and pigeon with olives. Set meals are 130F and 220F which is reasonable considering the quality on offer. And after all that it would seem a shame not to stay the night. Our favourite is room number 1 with its terrace and great panoramic view. Doubles 300–370F and 360–450F with bath.

BONIFACIO 20169

10% HÔTEL LES ÉTRANGERS*

av Sylvère-Bohn; it's 300m from the port (but hidden beneath a cliff) at the side of the road from Ajaccio.
☎ 04.95.73.01.09 F 04.95.73.16.97
Closed Nov 15–April 1. **Car park**. **TV**.

Despite the uninspiring décor, it's not too bad considering it's only got one star. It's definitely one of the few hotels in town where the prices are OK. Doubles 220–390F depending on the season, breakfast included. The windows have been made pretty soundproof so you don't get any of the noise from the roads. Friendly owner. Lockup for motorbikes.

L'ARCHIVOLTO

rue de l'Archivolto; it's at the top end of town, on a little square near the church.
☎ 04.95.73.17.58
Closed Sunday lunchtimes and Oct 1–Easter.

An antique shop serves as the setting for this unique restaurant where you can eat on the terrace or in the shade of the arcades. The food on the menu depends on what happens to be good in the market and whatever the chef wants to create – aubergine *gratin,* lamb with a creamy garlic sauce, summer *gratin* and an excellent apple crumble. Really first-class. No set meals. Expect to pay about 130F à la carte.

CALVI 20260

HÔTEL-RESTAURANT BVJ CORSOTEL

av. de la République.
☎ 04.95.65.14.15 F 04.95.65.33.72
Closed Nov 1–end of March. **Car park**.

This is a really nice hotel for young people in an old building overlooking the port of Calvi. The rooms accommodate 2–8 people and they're all very clean. The bathrooms are spotless. 120F per night per person, breakfast included (served buffet style, with as much orange juice, fruit, coffee, and milk as you want). Lockup for motorbikes. Evening meal at 60F is self-service. No need to book, but it does get very busy in summer. Surprisingly enough, it's the only hotel of its kind for young people in Corsica.

HÔTEL LES ARBOUSIERS**

route de Pietra-Maggiore (South); go about 800m in the direction of Bastia, then at the start of the pine forest which runs alongside the beach turn right and follow the arrows.
☎ 04.95.65.04.47 F 04.95.65.26.14
Closed start of Oct–start of May. **Secure parking**.

In Calvi it's best to go out of town if you want find somewhere to stay. If you're looking for a bit of breathing space then this the place to come. It's an attractive big house with pink walls and an old wooden staircase leading up to the bedrooms. The décor isn't spectacular but it's very clean and there are lots of pleasant little terraces overlooking the courtyard. Ask for a room facing south, they get the most sun. The prices are reasonable for Calvi. Doubles with bath 200–230F (300F July 20–Sept 1). Good welcome. Only five minutes walk to the beach.

HÔTEL LE BELVÉDÈRE*

av. de l'Uruguay (Centre); it's opposite the war memorial near the citadel.
☎ 04.95.65.01.25 F 04.95.65.43.51
TV.

Bright clean rooms with shower/wc, a few of which have a sea view. Laid-back atmosphere. Prices vary depending on the season and on demand (200–300F) but they're still pretty good. Be warned – they don't accept credit cards.

10% RÉSIDENCE LES ALOÈS**

quartier Donatéo (East); from the centre, take avenue Santa-Maria and keep going straight on.
☎ 04.95.65.01.46 F 04.95.65.01.67
Closed Oct–April. **Car park**. **TV**.

Built in the 60s, it has a great location above Calvi and you get a panoramic view of the bay, the citadel and the hinterland over to Monte Cinto! The surroundings are peaceful and flowery, the décor in the foyer is a bit kitsch but elegant. Refurbished, well-looked after rooms with TV, telephone and balcony. Prices range from 250F for a room with a view of the garden in mid-season to 350F for one with a sea view in July and August. Attentive staff.

LE CALELLU

quai Landry; it's by the harbour.
☎ 04.95.65.22.18
Closed Mondays out of season and Nov–April.

This is the fish restaurant to end all fish restaurants and you can have a set meal (fish of course!) for 95F. You can be sure that everything's fresh. Fast, efficient and friendly service and good value for money. And on top of this, it's got a great location. Pretty good all round then, but you really should book. Sylvester Stallone was turned away one evening because he hadn't booked!

LAVATOGGIO 20225 (15KM E)

LA FERME-AUBERGE CHEZ EDGARD

How to get there: drive 10km along the road to L'Ile-Rousse and take the D71 after Lumio.
☎ 04.95.61.70.75
Closed Oct–April and lunchtimes. **Car park**

This is a great place to have dinner. Owner Edgard Santelli has character and panache and so does his inventive cuisine. He, his wife and brother Rudolphe (who's also the mayor) will make you feel at home. Try the Corsican soup, the cream cheese fritters, or the roast leg of lamb, all served up in generous portions. Set meal 160F. Part of the Corsican holiday farm scheme.

CORTE 20250

10% HÔTEL DE LA POSTE*

2 place du Duc-de-Padoue (Centre).
☎ 04.95.46.01.37
Closed Nov–May. **Car park**. **Disabled access**.

An old hotel on a square with lots of shade. It has simple rooms at the back at very reasonable prices. Doubles 190F with basin, 230F with shower/wc. Good if you're on a budget and want somewhere central.

L'OLIVERAIE

lieu-dit Perru; from the town centre head for the university and keep on going when you come to the junction with the main road – the restaurant is 150m further on on the left
☎ 04.95.46.06.32
Closed Monday evenings in winter.

This very good restaurant is on the outskirts of town and there's lots of greenery around. Madame Mattei uses local produce to prepare tasty dishes like *buglidicce* (fromage frais fritters), herb tart, squid stuffed with *brocciu* (mild sheep milk's cheese) and for dessert, hazelnut and ground chestnut tart, the house speciality. Generous helpings. Popular with students and lecturers from the neighbouring campus. Set meals 65F, 95F and 140F.

U MUSEU

rampe Ribanelle; head for place du Poilu near the citadel.
☎ 04.95.61.08.36

A nice restaurant where you'll get good food and a hearty meal without paying a fortune. Very pleasant terrace. Set meals 75F (main course plus dessert) and 89F, offering dishes like herb tart, wild boar stew, and *délice* of chestnuts (truly delicious). They have jugs of AOC wine that go down a treat.

COTI-CHIAVARI 20138

HÔTEL-RESTAURANT LE BELVÉDÈRE

How to get there: it's on the left of the Acqua Doria road before you get to the village.
☎ 04.95.27.10.32
Restaurant closed in the evenings in winter. **Car park**. **Disabled access**.

A long, low and fairly modern building that stands in solitary splendour overlooking the bay of Ajaccio. You'll get one of the best views of the island here from the large circular terrace. The lovely owner, Caroline, makes a real fuss of all her guests. We loved the home cooking and dishes like Corsican soup, cannelloni stuffed with *brocciu* (a mild sheep's milk cheese), and lamb with local herbs, all served up in generous portions. Set meal 85F. The impeccable rooms (260F) all come with shower/wc and a sea view. Half-board 480F for two people. Very reasonable prices which, unusually for Corsica, are the same all year round. You don't get all the cost and razzmatazz of the coast either. A friendly place, this is the real thing. Be warned – they don't accept credit cards.

ILE-ROUSSE (L') 20220

10% HÔTEL SPLENDID**

av. Comte-Valéry (Centre).
☎ 04.95.60.00.24 Fax 04.95.60.04.57
Closed Nov 1–end of March. **Car park**

Not quite in the centre, this tall building, which has a colonial air about it, stands in a garden with palm trees and a mini-swimming pool. Refurbished rooms, some with TV. The ones at the far end have a lovely view of the sea. Doubles with shower/wc 250–360F depending on the time of year. Good welcome. Half-board possible (expect to pay 70F extra per person). The beach is just nearby.

LOZARI 20226 (10KM E)

10% AUBERGE A TESA

How to get there: from the Lozari beach take the little country road that goes to the Codole dam and the inn's about 3km further on.
☎ 04.95.60.09.55
Car park

This fairly new inn with olive-green shutters has seven pretty and cheerful rooms for its guests to choose from. Whether you go for the green, the pink or the blue, they cost 250F out of season and 300F in July and August (breakfast is included in the price). The owner, Marylène will give you a great welcome. As for the food, well, the cook, Marité, deserves a round of applause! Although we don't get to see her, she comes up with some incredibly tasty Corsican dishes. An incredibly good set meal of salad made with produce from their own garden, chicken in honey or salmon and *broccio terrine*, and chestnut ice-cream plus apéritif, wine and coffee, will cost you all of 160F. Advisable to book. In our opinion, it's one of the best restaurants in Corsica.

OLMI-CAPELLA 20259 (13KM SE)

LA TORNADIA

How to get there: it's about 2km from Olmi-Capella if you're going towards Pioggiola in Balagne.
☎ 04.95.61.90.93
Closed mid-Nov–mid March.

You might want to fast for a couple of days before eating here, because there's an enormous meal waiting for you! Whether you choose to sit out under the chestnut trees or in the wooden dining room, the wonderful dishes just keep on coming. There's roast lamb with local herbs, pasta (made from chestnut flour), strong cheeses, and even stronger brandy! Expect to pay 100–160F. Warm, friendly welcome. Very good place.

SPELONCATO 20226 (14.5KM SE)

10% A SPELUNCA**

place de l'Église; it's south of L'Ile-Rousse on a very windy road.
☎ 04.95.61.50.38 F 04.95.61.53.14
Closed Oct 1–April 30.

At last, a hotel with a bit of charm, in a village with a lot of character. Perched on a hill and a stone's throw from the church, this tall building with its pink walls and little tower used to be the summer residence of Cardinal Savelli, Secretary of State to Pope Pius IX. It was built as a palace in 1856 and you can almost picture yourself having intimate conversations with Napoleon. It has a number of spacious rooms arranged around a superb staircase. Doubles with shower/wc or bath 270F (attic rooms overlooking the street) and 330F (with a view of the valley). Very courteous, friendly welcome. Great value for money. If you're looking for the real Corsica, you'll find it here. Gérard Depardieu stayed here at the start of his career.

PIANA 20115

HÔTEL CONTINENTAL*

route d'Ajaccio; it's on the outskirts of town.
☎ 04.95.27.83.12
Closed Oct 1–March 31. **Secure parking**

An old building that looks something like a coaching inn. It's a bit retro, but very clean and delightfully old-fashioned. We liked the garden full of pine trees and apricot trees, the rooms with their undressed wooden floors, the big old-fashioned shutters, and the thick walls. Doubles 190F (no private facilities). The ones in the annexe (260F) are more comfortable and have shower/wc but not so much character. No credit cards.

PIEDICROCE 20229

10% HÔTEL-RESTAURANT LE REFUGE**

☎ 04.95.35.82.65 F 04.95.35.84.42
Closed mid-Oct–end Nov.

Like the other houses in the village, the inn is built against the southern slope of a mountain. This is the greenest part of Corsica because of all the chestnut trees, and the rooms that overlook the valley have a beautiful view of mountains, woods and little hillside villages. Doubles 230F with basin and bidet, 250F with shower/wc (looking out onto the street) and 280F (with a view of the valley). Half-board from 500F for 2 people. This is a real family business, with Madame Raffali doing the cooking and son Jean-Jean looking after the dining room. He knows the area like the back of his hand, so he'll be able to tell you about some great walks you can go on. Meals from 95F with starter, main course and dessert. Everything is authentically Corsican, particularly the *charcuterie*, which comes from their own pigs.

PORTO 20150

10% HÔTEL BELLA VISTA*

route de Calvi; it's on the hilltops of Porto.
☎ 04.95.26.11.08 F 04.95.26.15.18
Closed mid Oct–mid April. **Secure parking**.

This is a cute little pink stone house with white balconies. It's quiet and well looked after by a really nice couple. From the rooms you get a view of the mountain and a bit of the sea. They cost 190F with shower, 210F with shower, balcony and sea view, and 220F with bath, balcony and view. They also have lovely studios at 240F. Expect to pay 50F extra in peak season. Half-board (compulsory in August) is 500F for two people, which is not bad when you consider the quality of the food. Set meals 90F, 130F and 180F. The specialities – veal, suckling pig and *charcuterie* – come from their own farm.

PORTO-VECCHIO 20137

HÔTEL PANORAMA*

12 rue Jean-Nicoli (North); it's a bit beyond the old town.
☎ 04.95.70.07.96
Closed Oct–May. **Car park**.

This little family hotel is the cheapest place in town (Porto-Vecchio is incredibly expensive in summer). Basic doubles 220–310F with basin or shower/wc. Book in advance.

10% ☗ |●| LE SAN GIOVANNI**

route d'Arca; it's about 5km west – take the D659 south of Porto-Vecchio and the hotel is about 3km further.
☎ 04.95.70.22.25 F 04.95.70.20.11
Closed Nov–March. **Car park**. **TV**. **Disabled access**.

It's in the hinterland and there's lots of greenery around. Excellent facilities such as a heated swimming pool, jacuzzi, sauna, tennis court, and bicycle hire. Warm, friendly welcome. Pretty rooms overlook the grounds, which are full of flowers, trees and croaking frogs. Doubles 300–400F (depending on the season). The air-conditioned dining room serves authentic home cooking. Set meal 120F. Half-board (380F per person) is compulsory in August.

|●| L'ANTIGU

51 rue Borgo; it's at the top end of the town.
☎ 04.95.70.39.33
Closed Sunday evenings and mid Jan–Easter.

Whether you're sitting in the dining room or out on the terrace you'll get a bird's eye view of the bay of Porto-Vecchio. The food is excellent and served up in generous portions. There's herb tart, grilled pork, and aubergines stuffed with *brocciu* (a mild sheep's milk cheese). Or you might like to try their speciality, an excellent spit-roasted suckling pig. The prices aren't that bad either. You can have a starter plus main course or main course plus dessert for 70F at lunchtime (which makes a decent-sized meal), and there are set meals at 90F and 136F.

PROPRIANO 20110

|●| RESTAURANT L'HIPPOCAMPE

rue Jean-Paul-Pandolfi (South)
☎ 04.95.76.11.01
Closed Sundays out of season, and end of Sept–Easter.

Antoine, whose nickname is "the American", loves the sea and really fresh fish. So what you get in the evening is what Antoine happens to have caught in the morning in the Gulf of Valinco. Very good food served in warm, simple surroundings. Set meal 98F. Quite cheap à la carte. Without a doubt this place is the best value for money in town. Efficient, friendly service.

SAINT-FLORENT 20217

10% ☗ HÔTEL MAXIME**

Centre; it's in a quiet little street off place des Portes.
☎ 04.95.37.05.30 F 04.95.37.13.07
Car park. **TV**.

This is a new hotel, very clean and good value for money considering its location. Rooms come with mini-bar and terrace (some overlook the Poggio river, where you can arrange to moor your boat.) Doubles 250–360F depending on facilities (shower or bath) and the time of year.

|●| IND'E LUCIA (CHEZ LUCIE)

place Doria (Centre)
☎ 04.95.37.04.15

Rustic surroundings and typical Corsican cooking in a restaurant that's open year-round. The 100F set meal offers *terrine* of wild boar, rabbit, and cheese, and you can have a jug of an AOC wine for 20F. Great place. Friendly service.

SARTÈNE 20100

☗ HÔTEL LE JARDIN DES ORANGERS

route de Propriano (South-West); it's about 800m from the old part of Sartène.
☎ 04.95.77.02.72
Closed Oct 15–March 30. **Secure parking**. **Disabled access**.

All the aromas and flavours of the Mediterranean can be found in Jean Rossi's garden, which has orange trees, fig trees, pineapple trees, grapefruit trees, pomegranate trees, and lemon trees. Proprietor Jean Rossi, a retired farmer and now a DIY fanatic and that rare thing, an aesthete, has rooms at 200F with basin and 270F with shower and studios to hire on a nightly or weekly basis (June 15–Sept 15). In the evening you can sit in the garden with its antique statues and enjoy a glass of home-made vin d'orange and look over at Sartène. Swimming pool with great panoramic view.

SOLENZARA 20145

10% ☗ HÔTEL LA SOLENZARA**

Centre; it's just before you leave town in the direction of Bastia.
☎ 04.95.57.42.18 F 04.95.57.46.84
Closed out of season (except by reservation). **Car park**. **TV**. **Disabled access**.

This charming 200 year old hotel used to be the home of what we might call the squire of Solenzara. The rooms are huge, have high ceilings, and are simply but tastefully decorated. The bedrooms are cool in summer, and all have a new bathroom, TV and telephone. There are other more conventional rooms in the new part of the establishment. Big garden with palm trees and a magnificent swimming pool. Easy access to both the port and the beach. Prices are reasonable for a place with a bit of character like this. Doubles 250–420F with shower and 270–450F with bath depending on the season.

TIUCCIA 20111

10% HÔTEL-RESTAURANT BON ACCUEIL - CHEZ TOTO

Centre.
☎ 04.95.52.21.01 F 04.95.52.21.01
Secure parking. Disabled access.

This hotel isn't sign-posted very well and relies on its regulars. There are about 10 rooms (with shower) which are clean and quite cheap: 180F, who could say fairer than that? Half-board is compulsory May–Sept and, with prices starting at 400F for two, just as reasonable. Weekly rates are possible mid-season. Traditional cooking of the kind you find in the mountains. And the inn, with its dark wood, checked tablecloths and the fireplace where they roast young pig is typical of inland Corsica. Set meal 85F. Wine very reasonable – you'll get a half jug for 19F and a vintage Borgo for 45F. Superb beach 200m away.

VALLICA 20259

RESTAURANT U PIATTU SPARTU

How to get there: go up to Belgodère, then follow the superb D963 in the direction of Olmi-Cappella; 3km before you get there, take the little road on the left that goes to Vallica; it's about 100m after the church
☎ 04.95.61.92.76
Closed Monday–Friday in winter; Sunday evenings and Mondays March–Sept.

Far from the madding crowds and all the summer frenzy. This restaurant, owned by Daniel Luiggi, overlooks one of the most beautiful landscapes in Haute Balagne. Knock at the door and Daniel will answer and take you into a large and tastefully decorated room that has either jazz or classical music playing in the background. The food's always based on produce from the garden and while there are lots of Corsican dishes, there are other things too – Daniel takes a real pleasure in cooking and trying out new recipes. The result is perfection every time. The 130F set meal comes with everything (except the jug of wine, which was delicious). A place to come if you're a real foodie. You'll have to book in advance.

ZONZA 20124

HÔTEL-RESTAURANT L'AIGLON

rue Principale
☎ 04.95.78.67.79 F 04.95.78.63.62
Restaurant closed Mondays out of season.

This hotel and restaurant has been in the same family since the turn of the century and is owned at the moment by the lovely Colomba and her friendly young brother. The hotel is full of the colours, scents and floral patterns of Provence and has delightful rooms at 260F with shower and 280F with bath. Half-board (260–270F) is compulsory in season. The restaurant serves dishes like leg of pork with a fig sauce, spinach *gratin* with *brocciu* (a mild sheep's milk cheese), bacon and hazelnuts, *figatelli* (pork liver and herb sausages), and *polenta* (made with chestnut flour). The cake made with chestnut flour is a must as are drinks like Muscat Noir and fennel liqueur. Set meals 105F and 155F. A good place.

QUENZA 20122 (8KM NW)

10% AUBERGE SOLE E MONTI**

Centre; get there on the D420, in the direction of Aullène.
☎ 04.95.78.62.53 F 04.95.78.63.88
Closed end of Oct–start of March. **Car park. TV.**

This friendly inn has been in the hands of Félicien Balesi for 25 years, a bon vivant who knows how to make his guests feel at home. The regulars tend to gather round the fireplace in the sitting room and have many a lovely evening after a delicious meal inspired by old Corsican recipes. There's just one set meal (150F) and the portions are very generous. Pleasant well-equipped rooms. Half-board is compulsory and costs 350F per person (400F in peak season). The ideal spot to marvel at the beauty of the Corsican mountains.

LEVIE 20170 (9.5KM S)

FERME-AUBERGE A PIGNATA

route du Pianu (North-West); from Levie, drive 3km along the Sainte-Lucie-de-Tallano road then turn right towards Cucuruzzu; 2km further on, take the road on the left and then the second gate on the left.
☎ 04.95.78.41.90
By reservation only and closed in Nov. **Car park**

A very unobtrusive inn with no signposts, no arrows showing the way, nothing. So, basically, you either have to know it's there or stumble over it by accident. Once you're inside though, the hospitality is tremendous. According to the locals the authentic Corsican specialities you get here are the best in the region. These include cannelloni with *brocciu* (a mild sheep's milk cheese), stuffed aubergines, and braised wild boar. There's n\o à la carte but the 160F set meal is excellent and the portions are large. A great place.

FRANCHE-COMTÉ

25 Doubs

39 Jura

70 Haute-Saône

90 Territoire de Belfort

ARBOIS 39600

HÔTEL LE MÉPHISTO

33 place Faramand (South).
☎ 03.84.66.06.49
Closed on Mondays (except in July/August). **Car park.**

There's nothing diabolic about the place – quite the contrary! Warm, informal welcome in the ground-floor bistro with billiards table. 7 bright, spacious double rooms with rustic furniture on the upper floors. 132F (with basin) to 170F (with shower/wc). 260F for a room sleeping 3.

10% HÔTEL DES MESSAGERIES**

2 rue de Courcelles (Centre).
☎ 03.84.66.13.43 Fax 03.84.37.41.09
Closed Dec and Jan. **Secure parking. TV.**

You'll always get a warm reception at this comfy hotel with its pleasant, family atmosphere. Popular with foreign travellers passing through, which adds a nice international touch. Prices vary depending on facilities. Bedrooms from 187F with shower (wc on the landing) to 310F with bath.

RESTAURANT LA CUISANCE

62 place Faramand (South).
☎ 03.84.37.40.74
Closed Tuesday and Wednesday evenings and all January.

La Cuisance is the name of the little river which runs through Arbois and this lively village restaurant with particularly welcoming proprietors has been named after it. In summer you can eat on the terrace overlooking the river. Set meals start at 40F (weekday lunchtimes), which includes a starter, main course, cheese course and dessert. The other set meals are at 50F, 70F and 100F. Children's menu 35F.

ARC-ET-SENANS 25610

10% HÔTEL-RESTAURANT DE HOOP

36 Grande-Rue (South-West).
☎ 03.81.57.44.80
Closed Nov 1–April 30. **Secure parking.**

The owner (a Dutchman who found himself out of a job as a geologist when the colony of Surinam was granted independence) ended up more or less by chance in this picturesque stone house at the entrance to the Saline Royale. The atmosphere's a touch bohemian – our Dutchman's a pianist when the mood takes him. The dining room is somewhere between a 50s country inn and a colonial café straight out of the pages of Somerset Maugham. Magical leafy terrace. The food is uncomplicated but disorientating. For example, have a go at the "plat riche" – meat with rice, fried egg, banana, salad, coconut etc. Set meals at 90F, 110F and 150. The rooms are very basic but regularly freshened up. Doubles from 250F with shower and wc (but without TV, you have the choice), 270F with bath. Several rooms look out onto a garden, behind which you can make out the Saline.

ROSET-FLUANS 25410 (21KM N)

HÔTEL-RESTAURANT DE LA BERGE

How to get there: it's 8km from Saint-Vit heading towards the grottes d'Osselle, then 800m past the caves along the Doubs.

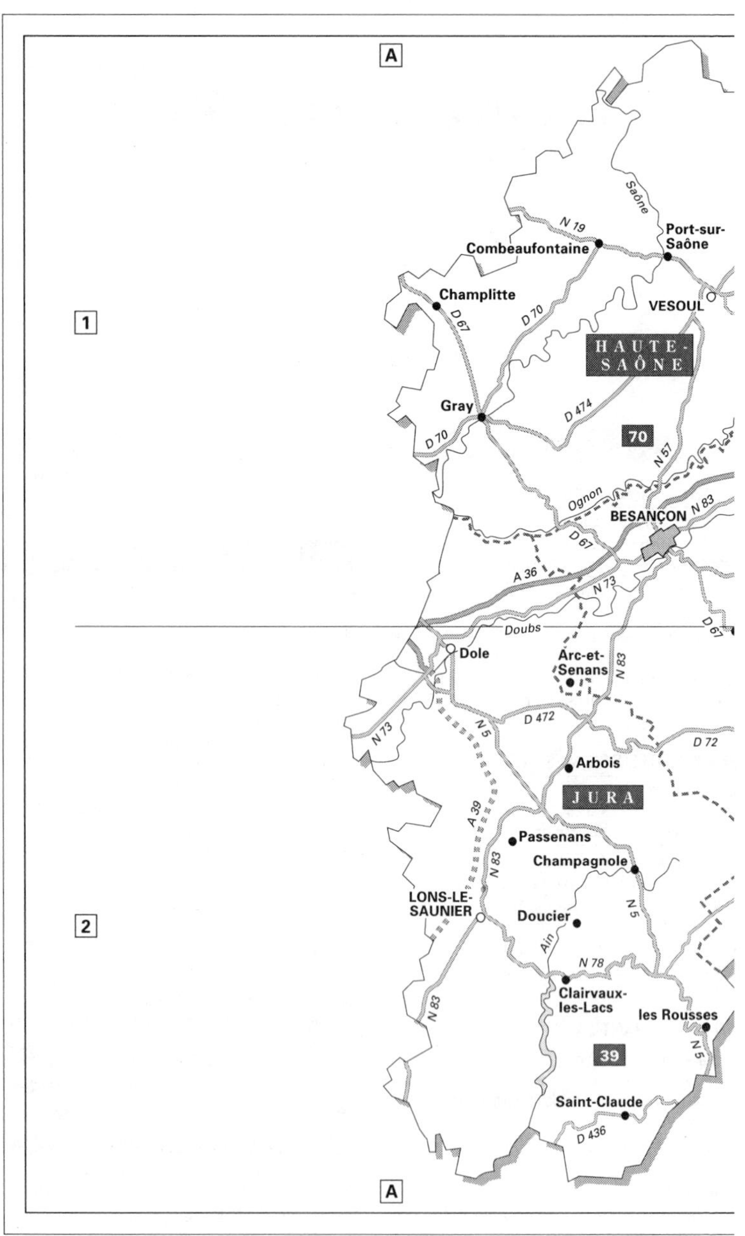
A
1
2
Saône
N 19
Port-sur-Saône
Combeaufontaine
Champlitte
D 67
D 70
VESOUL
HAUTE-SAÔNE
Gray
D 474
D 70
70
N 57
Ognon
BESANÇON
N 83
D 67
A 36
N 73
Doubs
D 67
Dole
Arc-et-Senans
N 83
N 73
N 5
D 472
D 72
Arbois
JURA
A 39
Passenans
N 83
Champagnole
LONS-LE-SAUNIER
Doucier
N 5
Ain
N 78
Clairvaux-les-Lacs
les Rousses
N 83
N 5
39
Saint-Claude
D 436
A

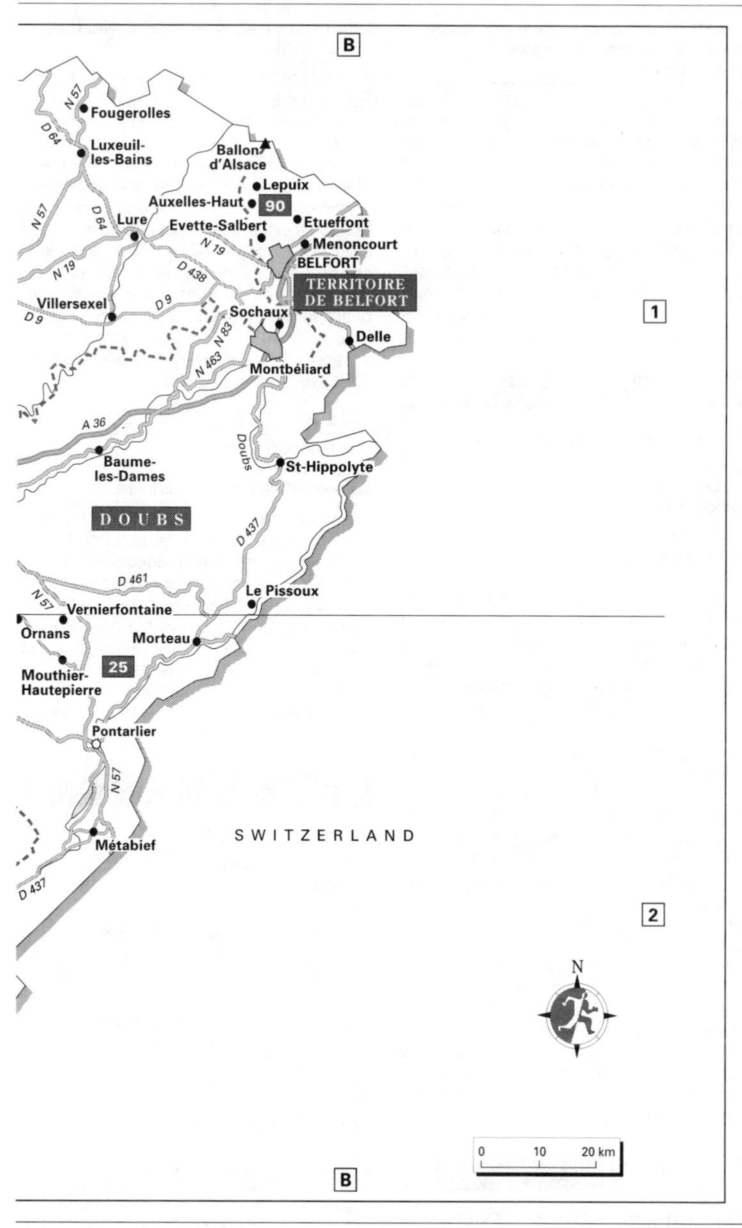
B
Fougerolles
N 57
D 64
Luxeuil-les-Bains
Ballon d'Alsace
Lepuix
Auxelles-Haut
90
N 57
D 64
Lure
Evette-Salbert
Etueffont
Menoncourt
N 19
BELFORT
N 19
D 438
TERRITOIRE DE BELFORT
Villersexel
D 9
D 9
Sochaux
1
N 83
Delle
N 463
Montbéliard
A 36
Doubs
St-Hippolyte
Baume-les-Dames
DOUBS
D 437
D 461
Le Pissoux
N 57
Vernierfontaine
Ornans
Morteau
Mouthier-Hautepierre
25
Pontarlier
N 57
Métabief
SWITZERLAND
D 437
2
N
0
10
20 km
B

☎ 03.81.63.61.74
Closed Mondays–Wednesdays March–May, Mondays in June and Sept 10–March 15. **Car park**. **Disabled access**.

Without doubt a unique location in France. The proprietor's first love is fishing and breeding frogs (which he uses in his own dishes). At the edge of the Doubs not far from the grottes d'Osselle, the establishment – which looks like the sort of place where you might expect to find open-air dancing – offers pike mousse for 32F, small deep fried white fish (the speciality) for 52F, the obligatory *"pauchouse"* (regional bouillabaisse made using fish from the river) for 94F and, of course, fresh frogs (only in season) at 55F a dozen.

AUXELLES-HAUT 90200

AUBERGE LE COIN DE LA STOLLE

It's by the church.
☎ 03.84.29.07.92
Closed Mondays.

A wonderful inn, situated in one of the most picturesque regional villages, offering cosy, white wood bedrooms painted in fresh colours. Impeccable washing and toilet facilities. Unbeatable prices – 150F per person and 185F based on two sharing, including breakfast! Reservation advisable as there's limited accommodation. Reception is wonderfully simple and friendly. Locals from Belfort are particularly fond of this place, crowding onto the terrace in summer. They do a dish of the day, and set meals at 79F and 90F serving dishes such as chicken with Riesling, fried carp, breast of chicken stuffed with mushrooms, and venison stew. The *repas marquère*, a local speciality, consists of home-made tart, potatoes cooked in white wine, and cheese, and the 55F *assiette franc-comtoise* is made from Morteau sausage, warm *cancoillotte* (mixture of ripe Metton cheese, butter, garlic and white wine) and cheese. Specialities like pork dishes and 80F *Baeckeoffe* (a stew of beef, mutton and pork, marinated in local wine, with potatoes and onions) made to order mid Oct–mid Dec. You'll sometimes be entertained by Claude on the accordion and Geneviève at the piano, so musical evenings are lively and cosy.

BAUME-LES-DAMES 25110

⌂ |●| RESTAURANT LE CHARLESTON

10 rue des Armuriers (Centre).
☎ 03.81.84.24.07
Closed Sunday evenings and Mondays March 15–30 and Nov 15–30.

The decor's not particularly reminiscent of the Belle Époque. As for the cooking, it consists of strictly orthodox regional dishes. In the 90F set meal you can sample dishes such as Morteau sausage with *cancoillotte* (mixture of Metton cheese, butter, garlic and white wine) or chicken cooked in Chardonay. For about ten francs extra you can have some more creative dishes. Set meals at 130F and 180F, and an à la carte menu offering stew of snails with oyster mushrooms, roast zander with poached sausage from Morteau and gentian-flavoured sauce. Friendly reception and impeccable service. They do a 60F small set meal weekday lunchtimes.

10% ⌂ HÔTEL CENTRAL**

3 rue Courvoisier (Centre).
☎ 03.81.84.09.64
Car park. **TV**. **Closed** Sundays Oct–April.

In a central position (the name gives it away!), or to be more exact, in the heart of the old town. Several interesting aspects of this 16th century building remain, such as the elegant façade and spiral staircase in the turret. Bedrooms may be very basic, but are perfectly pleasant. You'll get absolute peace and quiet if you choose one of those overlooking the courtyard. Expect to pay 200F for a double with shower/wc and 220F with bath. Warm welcome. No restaurant.

BELFORT 90000

10% ⌂ NOUVEL HÔTEL*

56 faubourg de France (Centre).
☎ 03.84.28.28.78
TV.

Right in the town centre in a pedestrianized street. On a value for money reckoning certainly about the best in town. Double rooms with basin 120F, with shower 140F, with shower/wc 210F and with bath 240F. All the rooms are impeccable and the proprietor is always ready to be of service. Free breakfast for under 12s.

10% ⌂ AU RELAIS D'ALSACE

5 av. de la Laurencie (North-East).
☎ 03.84.22.15.55 F→ 03.84.28.70.48

A cosy and colourful place that matches the personalities of Franco-Algerian couple Kim and Georges. Basic, clean bedrooms without any particular charm. But what matters here is the friendly reception, the mass of information about the town and region covering the walls, and most of all, Kim's good breakfast and infectious cheerfulness. Travellers will fall in love with this lovely place, the kind that is, unfortunately, few and far between nowadays. Bedrooms at 150F per person and 200F for a double. Breakfast with real fruit juice 28F.

HÔTEL VAUBAN

4 rue du Magasin (Centre).
☎ 03.84.21.59.37 F 03.84.21.41.67
TV.

Artists will love this well-maintained little hotel in a peaceful district just a stone's throw from the old town. The owner has covered the walls with his paintings, adding freshness and a party atmosphere. Pleasant bedrooms, some opening onto the lovely garden. On fine days, you can eat your breakfast beside the little waterlily pond as you listen to the sound of chirping birds. Good welcome. Rooms 260F, breakfast extra.

10% HÔTEL-RESTAURANT LE SAINT-CHRISTOPHE**

place d'Armes (Centre).
☎ 03.84.55.88.88 F 03.84.54.08.77
Closed over New Year. Restaurant closed Sundays. **TV**.

This dynamic establishment, always looking to improve itself, is situated in the heart of the attractively renovated old town. The main building has comfortable and spacious rooms – at 315F – with shower/wc and a view of the famous lion. The nearby annexe guarantees peace and quiet and offers impeccable rooms with the same level of comfort for 265F. The restaurant has a reasonable set meal for 63F (weekday lunchtimes). In the summer there is a lovely cold buffet on the terrace in the square where you can eat as much as you like for 80F. Other set meals 100–185F.

10% GRAND HÔTEL DU TONNEAU D'OR***

1 rue Reiset (Centre).
☎ 03.84.58.57.56 F 03.84.58.57.50
TV.

The foyer is reminiscent of a luxury hotel with its elaborate ceiling and grand staircase. Atmosphere and turn-of-the-century charm. Magnificent stained glass windows and a lounge with a listed dome. Spacious and exceptionally comfortable bedrooms 440–680F. Modern, tasteful décor. This small luxury establishment is full of character and absolutely wonderful! The piano bar is quite sophisticated.

AUX CRÊPES D'ANTAN

13 rue du Quai.
☎ 03.84.22.82.54

Fresh, cosy, attractive and decorated in shades of blue, grey and yellow. This good, little establishment not only serves excellent *crêpes*, but is open every day till late, offering a wide choice of dishes. Sample sweet or black wheat *crêpes* with various fillings – morels, *complète forestière* (mushrooms, bacon and potatoes), in the style of Vosges or Bigouden to name but a few. They also do salads, flank of beef, calf's head and there's always a dish of the day. Reasonable prices and a friendly welcome.

LA GRANDE FONTAINE

place de la Grande-Fontaine (Centre).
☎ 03.84.22.45.38
Closed Sunday evenings and Mondays.

You'll come across this pleasant dining room in the heart of the old town. Here's the perfect opportunity to sample some creative new cooking, brimming with mouthwatering flavours, based on fresh market produce. Their *souris* of lamb is of remarkably high quality. Intriguing combinations of herbs are used in many dishes so your tastebuds are in for a treat. We wonder if the chef, like Jean-Jacques Rousseau before him, gathers the herbs himself on the banks of the aptly named Savoureuse. They do excellent desserts and a good 150F set meal. And at lunctimes all this expertise can be yours in the 58F *menu du jour*. Reservations compulsory in the evenings. When the weather's fine they put a few tables out in the street. Just one little drawback: half bottles are very expensive and you can't buy wine by the glass.

L'AUBERGE DES TROIS CHÊNES

29 rue de Soissons (North-West).
☎ 03.84.22.19.45
Closed Monday to Thursday evenings and also Aug 10–31 and Dec 25–Jan 2. **Car park**.

Outside the town. A good and friendly little inn which serves a decent lunch for 60F (weekdays). Otherwise a set meal for 120F. At the weekend fish, fondue and other specialities, creating a friendly atmosphere.

I●I LE MOLIÈRE

6 rue de l'Étuve (Centre).
☎ 03.84.21.86.38
Closed Tuesday evenings, Wednesdays, the last week in Aug, a fortnight in Sept and the Easter holidays.

You'll come across this establishment on an attractive tree-lined square, surrounded by spruce façades and the sandstone which is typical of the Vosges. Try to forget about the plastic chairs, if you can, and soak up the charm and the excellence of the food. Only fresh produce here! The owner makes a little trip to Mulhouse every morning to get his fish. Cooking is a true festival of flavours based on the seasons and on blends of seasonal flavour. The à la carte choice is almost overwhelmingly huge (that old Freudian principle, to choose is to eliminate!) Set meals to suit every pocket: 100F except Sundays and public holidays, 148F, 158F, 189F, 200F and 215F. A few jewels in the crown: *pannequet* of snails flambéd with aniseed, lamb cutlet and *foie gras* with port and shallots, veal sweetbreads with sorrel-flavoured cream sauce and sautéed morels, fillet of zander with snails and bacon cubes, stew of large prawns and veal sweetbreads with garlic-flavoured cream sauce – to name but a few. Delicious desserts. The wine list is pretty impressive, and you're bound to be able to pick out a good little vintage for around 80F. Although the custom of drinking brandy at the end of the meal is going out of fashion, they've got a brilliant selection.

DANJOUTIN 90400 (3KM)

I●I LA TAVERNE DU BOUCHER

52 rue du Doc. E. Jacquot; it's 3km to the south-east.
☎ 03.84.28.47.11
Closed Sunday evenings, Monday lunchtimes, and either July or Aug.

It begins like a Racinian drama and ends as a gastronomic celebration. Once upon a time there was a butcher who was forced to hang up his apron because of the competition from nearby supermarkets. Never one to give up hope, he transformed his butcher's shop into a restaurant specializing in meat and offal. And there lies his success. His wide variety of meat dishes continued to delight his customers. Mouthwatering meat, superb sauces, and exquisite combinations, all of which bring "real food" back into its own. Try the tripe salad, *terrines* along the same lines, house *coq au vin*, testicles in a mustard sauce, *pierrade* (where you cook the ingredients yourself on a hot stone), and *gratin dauphinois*. We could sing forever the praises of these sensory delights. Of course, menu choice depends on deliveries. Freshness guaranteed. And we must mention the cosy, dry stone dining area stretching over two floors, a whirlpool of bright colours, old furniture, pretty knick-knacks and plates, unusual objects, and a fish pond. What's more, the reception you receive from the owner and his wife is as wonderful as the cooking.

PHAFFANS 90150 (7KM NE)

I●I L'AUBERGE DE PHAFFANS

10 rue de la Mairie; take the N83 then turn right onto the D46 towards Denney and Phaffans.
☎ 03.84.29.80.97
Closed Mondays, Wednesdays and Saturday lunchtimes, July 1–17and Dec 23–Jan 15. **Car park**.

The influence of neighbouring Alsace is felt in this quaint little village inn. House speciality: frogs' legs, guaranteed fresh all year round thanks to regular arrivals from Vendée. The same goes for the farmed eels served from April to December. The obligatory morel mushrooms *en croûte*, escalope in cream sauce and cooked ham from young wild boar are also served. Set meals at 95F and 118F. Children's meal 39.50F.

CHAUX 90330 (10KM N)

I●I RESTAURANT L'AUBERGE DE LA VAIVRE

36 Grande-Rue; take the Ballon d'Alsace road (D465).
☎ 03.84.27.10.61
Closed evenings, Saturday lunchtimes and from mid July–mid August. **Car park**.

This inn on the road leading up into the Vosges is run by women and has been attractively decorated by the mother and daughter of the family. Time is taken to prepare the food in the traditional way, for example fillet of zander with dill and conserve of duck in cider. Daily special (generous helping) and homemade dessert 68F during the week. Fresh trout (caught to order!) 55F. Attractive set meals 90–180F and fine wine list nicely presented.

BESANÇON 25000

SEE MAP OPPOSITE

10% ⌂ I●I AUBERGE DE LA MALATE*

chemin de la Malate; it's 10 minutes from the centre heading in the Lausanne direction; after the Porte taillé,

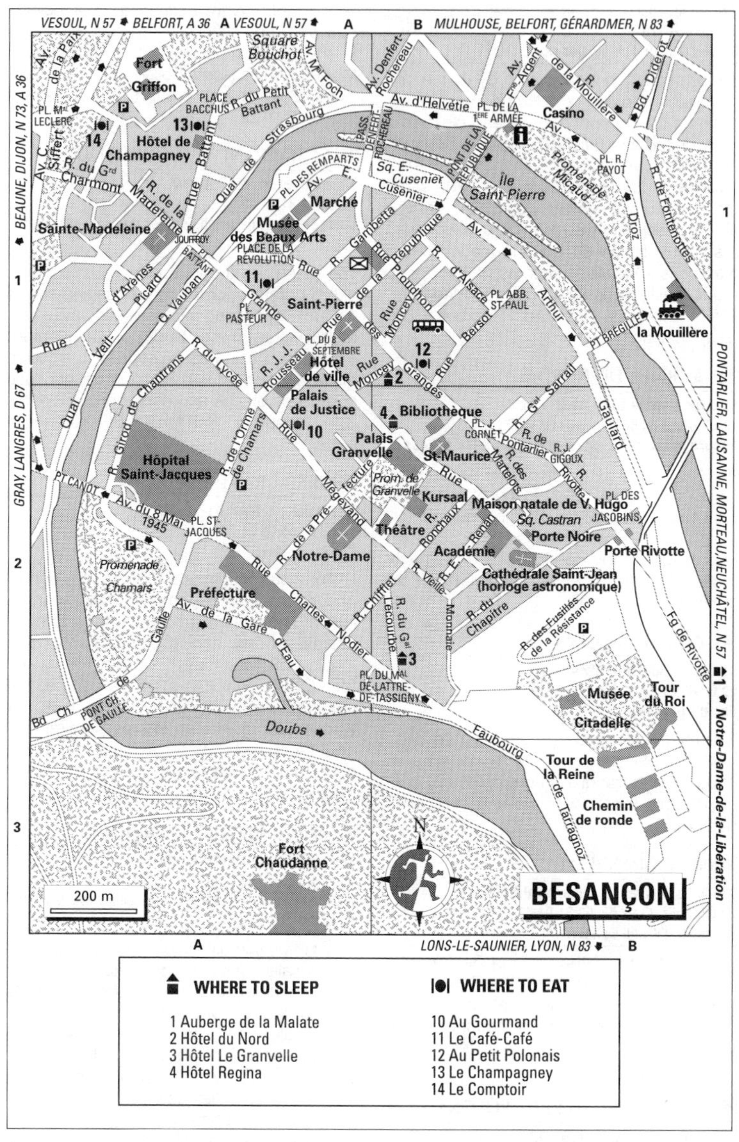
VESOUL, N 57
BELFORT, A 36
A VESOUL, N 57
A
B MULHOUSE, BELFORT, GÉRARDMER, N 83
BEAUNE, DIJON, N 73, A 36
GRAY, LANGRES, D 67
PONTARLIER, LAUSANNE, MORTEAU, NEUCHÂTEL, N 57
1 Notre-Dame-de-la-Libération
LONS-LE-SAUNIER, LYON, N 83
1
2
3
Square Bouchot
Av. Mal Foch
Av. Denfert-Rochereau
Fort Griffon
PL. Mal LECLERC
PLACE BACCHUS
R. du Petit Battant
Av. d'Helvétie
PL. DE LA 1ÈRE ARMÉE
Casino
R. de la Mouillère
Bd. Diderot
Av. Fts Argent
13
14
Hôtel de Champagney
Av. C. Siffert
R. du Grd Charmont
R. de la Madeleine
Rue Battant
Quai de Strasbourg
PASS. DENFERT-ROCHEREAU
PONT DE LA RÉPUBLIQUE
Sq. E. Cusenier
Cusenier
Île Saint-Pierre
Promenade Micaud
PL. R. PAYOT
R. de Fontenottes
Droz
PL. DES REMPARTS
Marché
Musée des Beaux Arts
PLACE DE LA RÉVOLUTION
Sainte-Madeleine
PL. JOUFFROY
PL. BATTANT
R. Gambetta
Rue de la République
R. Proudhon
R. d'Alsace
Av. Arthur
11
R. d'Arènes
Picard
Q. Vauban
Grande Rue
PL. PASTEUR
Saint-Pierre
Rue Moncey
PL. ABB. ST-PAUL
Bersot
la Mouillère
PT BRÉGILLE
Rue
Quai Veil-Picard
R. du Lycée
R. J. J. Rousseau
PL. DU 8 SEPTEMBRE
Hôtel de ville
Rue des Granges
12
2
R. Gal Sarrail
Gaulard
R. Girod de Chantrans
Palais de Justice
10
4
Bibliothèque
PL. J. CORNET
R. de Pontarlier
R. J. GIGOUX
Hôpital Saint-Jacques
R. de l'Orme de Chamars
Palais Granvelle
St-Maurice
R. des Martelots
R. Rivotte
PT CANOT
Av. du 8 Mai 1945
PL. ST-JACQUES
Rue Mégevand
Rue de la Préfecture
Prom. de Granvelle
Kursaal
Rue Ronchaux
Maison natale de V. Hugo
PL. DES JACOBINS
Sq. Castran
Porte Noire
Théâtre
R. E. Renan
Académie
Porte Rivotte
Promenade Chamars
R. de la Préfecture
Notre-Dame
Cathédrale Saint-Jean (horloge astronomique)
Rue Vieille
Préfecture
Av. de la Gare d'Eau
Rue Charles Nodier
R. Chiffret
R. du Gal Lecourbe
Monnaie
R. du Chapitre
R. des Fusillés de la Résistance
Fg de Rivotte
3
de Gaulle
PL. DU Mal DE-LATTRE-DE-TASSIGNY
Musée
Tour du Roi
Citadelle
Bd Ch. de Gaulle
PONT CH. DE GAULLE
Doubs
Faubourg de Tarragnoz
Tour de la Reine
Chemin de ronde
Fort Chaudanne
N
200 m
BESANÇON
A
B
WHERE TO SLEEP
1 Auberge de la Malate
2 Hôtel du Nord
3 Hôtel Le Granvelle
4 Hôtel Regina
WHERE TO EAT
10 Au Gourmand
11 Le Café-Café
12 Au Petit Polonais
13 Le Champagney
14 Le Comptoir

turn left towards Chalèze-Arcier. Off map **B2-1**
☎ 03.81.82.15.16
Closed Dec 19–Feb 10. **Car park. TV**.

This charming inn, renovated by its friendly, young proprietors, is located outside the town on the edge of a forest and close to a river. Peace and quiet guaranteed. Comfortable rooms with shower, telephone and toilet facilities on the same floor 170F. The same standard but with private wc 200F. It is advisable to reserve at the restaurant which offers a set meal for 53–67F during the week and numerous specialities such as fillet of perch, morel mushrooms *en croûte* and fried carp. Other set meals 110F and 140F, but a little disappointing.

10% HÔTEL DU NORD**

8-10 rue Moncey. **MAP B1-2**
☎ 03.81.81.34.56 F 03.81.81.85.96
Secure parking. TV with **Canal+. Disabled access**.

A pleasant city centre hotel run by real professionals always ready to be of service to their guests. The décor could be more cheerful but the 44 rooms are comfortable and kept in impeccable condition. Good value for money. Double room with shower/wc from 195F, with bath 310F.

10% HÔTEL REGINA**

91 Grande-Rue. **MAP B2-4**
☎ 03.81.81.50.22 F 03.81.81.60.20
Secure parking. TV.

Charming, quiet and comfortable hotel overlooking a pleasant inner courtyard. A haven of peace and tranquility right in the city centre. Double rooms with wc and shower or bath 235F.

10% LE GRANVELLE**

13 rue du Général-Lecourbe. **MAP B2-3**
☎ 03.81.81.33.92 F 03.81.81.31.77
Car park. TV with **Canal+**.

In a quiet part of the city not far from the citadel. Comfortable hotel in a house with character, creating a relaxing atmosphere. All the rooms look out onto an attractive paved courtyard. Double rooms with wc/shower 250F; with bath 270F.

RESTAURANT AU PETIT POLONAIS

81 rue des Granges. **MAP B1-12**
☎ 03.81.81.23.67
Closed Saturday evenings and Sundays.

About the best value for money in the city. A real institution owned and run by a pleasant but sometimes almost excessively chatty lady. For 68F try the *boîte chaude*: a regional *Edel de Ceron* cheese in spruce bark melted in the oven in its box and served with Morteau sausage and boiled potatoes – delicious! Daily special around 40F. Other set meals 58–120F.

RESTAURANT AU GOURMAND

5 rue Mégevand. **MAP A2-10**
☎ 03.81.81.40.56
Closed on Saturdays and Sundays and end July–end August.

The menu alone could nearly fill this guide: grilled potatoes, omelettes, eggs and salads with mind-boggling names like la Javanaise, Metro Goldwyn etc. Unpretentious "home-made" food using fresh produce. Ideal for a quick lunch – that is if there's room because collections of jugs and cats monopolize this little restaurant. Set meal 58F, 100F à la carte.

RESTAURANT LE CHAMPAGNEY

37 rue Battant. **MAP A1-13**
☎ 03.81.81.05.71
Closed Sundays.

Historic surroundings – the old 16th century hôtel de Champagney, recently and intelligently renovated to house apartments, offices, shops and this restaurant. Set meals 65F (weekdays), very regional, and 85–163F. Speciality menu at somewhat higher prices – average 130F for a meal. For winter a room with an impressive fireplace and for summer a terrace in the paved courtyard overlooked by dainty balconies made of painted wood.

RESTAURANT LE COMPTOIR

12 rue Richebourg. **MAP A1-14**
☎ 03.81.83.59.09
Closed Monday, Tuesday, and Wednesday evenings and Sundays.

You'll often find exhibitions in this wonderful, stone-walled dining room where the décor is quietly reminiscent of the 60/70s. You feel as though you've been invited round to a friend's place and she happens to be a pretty fantastic cook! So we're talking home cooking and restaurant food all in one, cooking that gives a new lease of life to dishes that you thought had no surprise left in store – skirt of beef with shallots or *blanquette*. Regulars adore the lunchtime *menu du jour* including coffee at 73F, including coffee, which goes up to 130F in the evenings offering, for example, *noix* of scallops in the style of Arbois, and rib steak with morels. Expect to pay about 100F à la carte. Natural, charming service. In a nutshell, this is a good, little establishment.

|●| RESTAURANT LE CAFÉ-CAFÉ

5 bis rue Luc Breton. **MAP A1-11**
☎ 03.81.81.15.24
Closed evenings and Sundays.

Discreet, very discreet. Hidden at the back of a little courtyard, the only way of spotting the entrance to Le Café-Café is the slate on which the day's offerings have been chalked up. Dishes around the 50F mark are never short of imagination or a touch of the exotic. Reservation compulsory in this lovely, pocket-sized little dining room, full of bric-a-brac. For approximately 60F you'll get a good meal (*jurassienne* - with bacon, onions and sorrel) farmhouse-style or à la Franche-Comté. Charming welcome. Our favourite lunchtime restaurant.

CHALEZEULE 25220 (2.5KM E)

☗ HÔTEL DES TROIS ILES**

rue des Vergers; follow the signs for Belfort then Chalezeule.
☎ 03.81.61.00.66 F 03.81.61.73.09
Closed Dec 20 –Jan 5. **Car park**. **TV** with **Canal+**.

Not far from the town centre in beautiful countryside, this recently built hotel belonging to the Relais du Silence chain offers a welcome, a charm and peace and quiet which are second to none. Double rooms with shower/wc 260F, with bath 280F.

CHAMPAGNOLE 39300

☗ |●| HÔTEL-RESTAURANT DE LA LONDAINE**

31 rue du Général-Leclerc (Centre).
☎ 03.84.52.06.69 F 03.84.52.55.30
Restaurant closed on Sundays. **Car park**.
TV with **Canal+**.

Unaffected and friendly welcome in this hotel which is reasonably quiet despite its location on a busy road. Double rooms with basin/wc (no TV) from 120F. Other rooms with shower 200F. The restaurant, run by the son of the family, is just nearby. Good brasserie-style set meal for 70F, day's special 42F.

10% ☗ |●| GRAND HÔTEL RIPOTOT**

54 rue du Maréchal-Foch (Centre).
☎ 03.84.52.15.45 F 03.84.52.09.11
Closed Nov 15–April 1. **Secure parking**. **TV**.
Disabled access.

And it is big, the Ripotot family's hotel. In an old building right in the town centre. 60 rooms with country-style furniture and varying degrees of comfort depending on the price. The hotel has belonged to the same family for 200 years, which brings a certain professionalism. Prices range from 160F for one person (with shower on the landing) to 260F. There are also four family rooms with shower at 310F (children under 8 stay for free). Large attractive garden with tennis court behind the hotel.

|●| PIZZERIA BIG-BEN

2 av. de la République (Centre).
☎ 03.84.52.08.95
Closed on Mondays and Sept 15–Oct 15.

It may be a pizzeria but not just any old pizzeria. "Night rock pizza" only open in the evenings. The *Big-Ben* has to be unique. The proprietor used to sing in a heavy metal band and words cannot describe the décor. The recent installation of a hanging model railway adds the finishing touch. Pizzas 40–58F and set meal 78F with – you've guessed it – a pizza as the main course. A polite notice at the entrance states that fuddy-duddies are not allowed but groups of bikers are accepted at weekend lunchtimes subject to reservation.

FONCINE-LE-HAUT 39460 (24.5KM SW)

10% ☗ |●| LE GRAND CHALET

Val Foncine: it's 2km from the village on the Grande Traversée du Jura route; take the N5 towards Saint-Laurent-en-Grandaux then the D127.
☎ 03.84.51.95.51 F 03.84.51.93.58
Closed Oct 26–Dec 13. **TV**.

16km from the Swiss border, this large, relatively modern establishment looks like a large chalet, making the name quite apt! Large, comfortable rooms with bathroom and direct-dial telephone 380F. Apartments sleeping 4 with balcony 630F. Special welcome for children (kid's club for 3–10 year-olds) and recommended for families. Children under 10 stay free and 10–16 year-olds get a 50% reduction. Half board 330–415F per person. The restaurant offers local specialities. Numerous activities – swimming pool, sauna, Turkish bath, billiards room, mountain biking, etc and is an ideal base for walking.

CHAMPLITTE 70600

10% ☗ |●| HÔTEL-RESTAURANT HENRI IV**

rue du Bourg (Centre).
☎ 03.84.67.66.81 Fax 03.84.67.80.65
Closed Monday evenings and Tuesdays November–March. **Secure parking**. **TV**.

The buildings date back to medieval times but the impressive spiral staircase leading up to the rooms is from the time of the *Vert galant*. This comfortable hotel is run by a Swiss couple and has spacious, impeccably kept rooms with beautiful antique furniture. 150F (with shower) to 220F (with wc and shower or bath). The restaurant with its traditional décor offers professional service and good simple home or regional cooking. Set meals (5 in all) start at 80F during the week.

10% HÔTEL-RESTAURANT DU DONJON**

46 rue de la République (Centre).
☎ 03.84.67.66.95 Fax 03.84.67.81.06
Restaurant closed Friday evenings out of season.
Car park. **TV**.

A "young" welcome, the only medieval element being the vaulted cellar which is used as the dining room. Reasonable set meal for 68F during the week. Other set meals 100–200F. The rooms have no great charm but are comfortable enough. Double rooms (with shower) 150F and (with wc and shower or bath) 200–220F.

L'AUBERGE FRANC-COMTOISE

allée Sainfoin (Centre).
☎ 03.84.67.61.25
Closed November/December.

Good restaurant opposite the castle with a pleasant terrace for the summer. Some regional specialities and Champlitte wine. Set meals 85–192F. Business lunch 50F (including starter, main course, cheese course, dessert and drink!) and daily specials in the ground-floor bistro. If you liked the wine go to the cellars of the Groupement viticole chanitois for some wine-tasting. Extremely warm welcome and special surprise for our readers.

PIÉMONT 70800 (5KM N)

10% HÔTEL-RESTAURANT LE GAULOIS

route de Langres; it's on the D67.
☎ 03.84.67.68.38 Fax 03.84.67.62.12
Closed Wednesday evenings and in October. **Car park**. **TV**.

A good place to stop off at. By the main road and a bit in the style of a roadside café. (Except that this establishment also has tea dances on Sunday afternoons for the region's older residents!). During the week set meal for 55F with starter, main course with French fries/rice and/or vegetables, cheese course, dessert and a quarter litre of wine. Other good set meals with generous portions at 75F, 95F and 145F. Upstairs double rooms with shower/wc 170F.

CHAUX-NEUVE 25240

AUBERGE DU GRAND-GÎT**

rue des Chaumelles.
☎ 03.81.69.25.75 Fax 03.81.69.15.44
Closed Sunday evenings and Mondays (except school holidays), also April 10–24 and Oct 24–Nov 4. **Car park**. **Disabled access**.

Some way out of the village, so peace and quiet are guaranteed. Recently built, yet typically regional, with a sloping roof and wooden façade. Excellent weclome. Only eight bedrooms, but they're rustic and cosy. Expect to pay 240F for a double with shower/wc and telephone. You'll get a lovely view of the surrounding countryside from numbers 1 and 7. Number 6, with its mezzanine, can sleep five guests. There's also stop-over accommodation for walkers, two rooms with six beds. They do a 70F weekday *menu du jour* and a 85F regional set meal offering, for example, ham Arbois-style or pink trout sautéed in butter and served with parsley and lemon juice. The ideal place for sporty types and nature lovers. The owner, a skiing instructor and uplands guide, knows the myriad local long-distance footpaths and cross-country skiing routes like the back of his hand.

CLAIRVAUX-LES-LACS 39130

HÔTEL-RESTAURANT LA RAILLETTE

50 rue Neuve (Centre).
☎ 03.84.25.82.21
Closed on Wednesdays out of season.

A small village restaurant with a friendly atmosphere were you can get a reasonable meal at lunchtime and during the week for 60F. The 85F set meal offers warm cheese mousse on a bed of salad. For late diners or people passing through, 9 very basic rooms from 150F for a double (with basin). Half-board 175F.

PONT-DE-POITTE 39130 (5KM W)

HÔTEL-RESTAURANT DE L'AIN**

Centre.

☎ 03.84.48.30.16 F→ 03.84.48.36.95
Closed Sundays, Mondays (except in July/August) and January. **Secure parking. TV**.

Warm welcome and very professional service in this establishment where the staff make a point of keeping the guests happy. The restaurant has a good reputation and serves fine regional specialities such as Bresse poultry with morel mushrooms, pike mousse and freshwater crayfish (in season). Set meals from 80F (except at weekends). The hotel has about ten rooms from 240F for a double (with shower/wc). Preferably ask for one which looks out onto the back with a view over the Ain. Pleasant breakfast terrace.

DELLE 90100

|●| RESTAURANT LE GALOPIN

29 Grand-Rue (Centre).
☎ 03.84.36.17.52
Closed Saturday lunchtimes and Sundays.

This is where local lovers of the good life (and sometimes their Swiss neighbours) meet. People gather in the restaurant cellar, which is over 100 years old, to celebrate the potato which constitutes the main component of dishes. There are trendy spuds with smoked salmon and a shallot sauce for 74F and other cheaper, more popular and more regional versions, for example with Morteau sausage and *à la cancoillotte*. Good, inexpensive and the proprietor is very friendly.

DOLE 39100

⌂ |●| AUBERGE DE JEUNESSE LE SAINT-JEAN

place Jean-XXIII (South-West); it's behind the very modern church of Saint-Jean.
☎ 03.84.82.36.74 F→ 03.84.79.17.69
Car park.

As a member of the FUAJ, this hostel for young workers offers 70 beds. You'll need a card, but they are sold on the spot. 64F/night for a single room and 40F for a meal; half-board 121F.

⌂ |●| HÔTEL DU VOYAGEUR**

av. Aristide Briant.
☎ 03.84.72.18.73

Although the station is only 200m off, the presence of the railway does not make itself felt in the rooms and you don't feel as though you're sleeping with a goods train. The double glazing does an excellent job. Bedrooms are spotless and seem to have been refurbished from top to toe. The basic décor's the only hiccup, but as uncle Jimmy would say, Rome wasn't built in a day, so let's wait and see. Anyhow, prices are reasonable – 130F with washing faciities and 160F with shower/wc – so travelling salesmen and tourists on limited budgets will be more than happy. You can even get a main course, cheese and dessert for 55F, or a full set meal for 68F. If you're not keen on sleeping and dining in the same establishment, you'll find *Le Terminus*, a smart restaurant further down the road at number 22, offers a good 68F set meal, and one at 48F serving poached sausage from Morteau, potatoes in a cream sauce and home-made dessert.

|●| CHEZ COCO

34 rue des Vieilles Boucheries (Centre).
☎ 03.84.79.10.78
Closed evenings and Sundays.

"Home-made cooking" it says at the top of the fairly basic menu. In a corner, the rows of sporting cups and photos of the town's junior teams will catch your eye. Coco, the manager, holds the fort behind his zinc counter, only popping out to take orders and serve the food. The 65F set meal is a model example, offering crudités, cutlet of Provençal pork or fillet of fish cooked in white wine, and dishes are served with three different vegetables, cheese and dessert. Coco's a good-humoured guy, chatting with his customers, and providing a typical southern French, unrushed service. He does a 65F couscous *formule* on a Saturday, accompanied by cheese and dessert.

|●| RESTAURANT LA ROMANÉE

13 rue des Vieilles-Boucheries (Centre).
☎ 03.84.79.19.05
Closed on Wednesdays (except in July/Aug).

Easy to get there – it's close to the cathedral. In beautiful rooms with carved stone vaulting which used to be butcher's shops, the chef, Patrick Franchini, offers authentic and imaginative cooking inspired by the Jura region. You will enjoy the Tortelet trout in Château Chalon or the slices of duck with Jura honey. The menu is not cheap but the range of set meals which starts at 70F is reasonable enough (despite rather stingy dessert portions). Good choice of Jura wines.

|●| LE BEC FIN

67 rue Pasteur (Centre).
☎ 03.84.82.43.43
Closed Mondays and Tuesdays.

What you most appreciate to start with is the owner's smiling and effusive welcome. She's lovely. Then the bright, well-set dining room filled with beautiful bouquets of flowers, overlooking the very romantic canal des Tanneurs. The two other rooms in the old medieval cellars, although not unappealing, they lack the light and character of the one with the view. We decided on the 85F set meal which seemed to have won the vote of passers-by. Thick soup of morels with *quenelles* of pike, *saucisson* of chicken with bacon and stewed leeks, *fondant* of dark chocolate and pears with vanilla confit – no complaints whatsoever! Other set meals at 105F (130F with a half bottle of wine), 150F and 190F. Children's set meal 50F. Service is a bit awkward, but attentive. Young parents aren't forgotten – they even have a high chair. And another important detail, seats are comfy and support your back, a rare find nowadays.

SAMPANS 39100 (3KM NW)

10% ☗ |●| LE CHALET DU MONT-ROLAND**

North; take the N5; before Monnières turn right towards mont Roland.
☎ 03.84.72.04.55 ➡ 03.84.82.14.97
Secure parking. **TV**. **Disabled access**.

At the top of mont Roland there is a large chalet with rooms offering a superb open view over the Chaux Forest. You can see mont Blanc on a clear day. Very friendly. The proprietor gives a warm welcome to the gypsies who sometimes camp in the area and allows them to fetch water – an attitude sufficiently rare to be commended. Double rooms 220–240F (with shower) and 280–320F (with bath). Good regional fare. Set meals start at 72F (lunchtime). Other set meals 80F and 108F. Children's meal 46F.

CHAUSSIN 39120 (20KM S)

10% ☗ |●| HÔTEL-RESTAURANT CHEZ BACH**

4 place de l'Ancienne-Gare; take the N73, then the D468 at La Borde.
☎ 03.84.81.80.38 ➡ 03.84.81.83.80
Closed Fridays and Sunday evenings. **Car park**. **TV** with **Canal+**. **Disabled access**.

Well worth a little detour. The establishment is an excellent stop for fine cuisine. Several set meals, offering forest snail soup, old-style fresh frogs and fillet of zander in *vin jaune*. Set meals start at 85F during the week. The rooms are comfortable and similar to those of large chain hotels. Double room from 200F.

DOUCIER 39130

☗ |●| HÔTEL ROUX - RESTAURANT "LE COMTOIS"

Centre.
☎ 03.84.25.71.21
Closed Friday evenings and Wednesdays out of season, also Dec 1–Jan 31. **TV**.

This establishment, like the young and friendly innkeeper, oozes personality and ideas. First of all, we'd like to congratulate him for his amazing wine list featuring the best regional varieties and comprehensive explanations alongside. It stands out from many fellow establishments in Jura, often lacking in that department, which is a pity for such a famous wine-growing region. We were also impressed by the dining room, fresh and pleasant on account of its successful combination of stonework, beams, well designed lighting and brightly coloured tablecloths. An essential little country touch is provided by the solid brick fireplace and the old, typically local sideboard. Not forgetting the brasserie/bistro-style cooking served up in generous portions – although perhaps somewhat lacking in that little creative touch to put it on the same footing as the wine. Set meals at 60F (weekday lunchtimes), 99F and 138F. Perfect service. The functional bedrooms could be brightened up by a few judiciously chosen knick-knacks. Doubles 295F including breakfast. Half-board from 228F per person.

ETUEFFONT 90170

|●| AUBERGE AUX TROIS BONHEURS

Centre; take the D23 from Valdoie and it's north of Belfort.
☎ 03.84.54.71.31
Closed Mondays.

The Inn of the Three Happinesses. We could easily add a fourth – travelling here through all these flower-filled villages to get here! It's a very popular restaurant around these parts, a rustic town house with brick and dry stone walls, on account of its hearty, tasty cooking served in generous portions. You'll come across big happy families, and groups of pensioners out to enjoy themselves, savouring dishes such as fantastic home-made head cheese, fried carp or zander (in a heat-proof dish!), chanterelle mushrooms, their special *planchette des Trois Bonheurs* and *tartiflette*. Children's set meal 35F. Seafood stew available à la carte. Open all day Sunday serving good home-made desserts, bilberry tarts and the like. Friendly reception and efficient service to boot!

EVETTE-SALBERT 90350

10% CENTRE D'HÉBERGEMENT DU LAC

lac de Malsaucy; leave Belfort by Valdoise, then take the D24.
☎ 03.84.29.21.84 F→ 03.84.29.14.71
Closed Nov–Feb. Phone beforehand.

This hostel serves the leisure complex on the lake of Malsaucy. Open to all. It's like a lovely big youth hostel with very pleasant and smartly kept rooms. Outside washing and toilet facilities are impeccably clean. 75F per person, 85F with breakfast. School parties and other groups often stay there so it's best to telephone in advance. Rooms with 2 or 4 beds. Possibility of half-board 145F, full board 195F. All sorts of watersport activities nearby.

AUBERGE DU LAC

lac de Malsaucy.
☎ 03.84.29.14.10
Closed Monday evenings and Tuesdays, as well as the last 2 weeks in October and the first 2 weeks in January.

This is a big pink-coloured house where you'll get a typical Franche-Comté welcome and good regional food. There's a large and pleasant dining room where the tables are well spaced out. And you also have the opportunity of settling down to a nice meal out on the terrace with the beautiful lake of Malsaucy in the background. Varied selection of dishes available. First of all, on the regional set meal at 80F we have *parmentier* (a kind of shepherd's pie), cream of lentil soup, *terrine* of oysters and mussels sprinkled with coriander, prawn kebabs etc. Or you could go à la carte with pan-fried fillet of red mullet with basil, trout with morels, honey-glazed breast of duck etc. Gourmet set meal 160F (with mushroom tart and *foie gras*). Good wines at affordable prices: Cairanne 65F, Bourgeuil 80F, or you can order them by the carafe. And if it starts to drizzle you can still have a good view of the whole lake from the comfort of the dining room

FOUGEROLLES 70220

RESTAURANT RESTOP

route de Plombières; it's just over a mile from the centre, joining the N57.
☎ 03.84.49.12.02
Closed on Sunday evenings. **Car park. Disabled access.**

A strange establishment this old haberdasher's shop near the main road. The proprietors, who have long since passed retirement age, offer a very decent set meal for 50F, but you should really try the *Gandeuillot* – a local sausage which is a cross between an *andouillette* and a saveloy and is served with sautéed potatoes(40F). It's good and very filling. Cherry fritters in season, home-made *cancoillotte* and delicious local apple juice.

FOURNET-BLANCHEROCHE 25140

10% HÔTEL-RESTAURANT LA MARAUDE**

How to get there: follow the sign posts from the D464 between Fournet-Blancheroche and Charquemont.
☎ 03.81.44.09.60 F→ 03.81.44.09.13
Car park.

This is an old 17th century farm, a bit remote, as places like this often are in Haut-Doubs. You're guaranteed peace and quiet right in the heart of nature! Even though the interior was completely transmogrified a few years ago, the place has still managed to retain a lot of its charm. A nice young couple who, like us, fell in love with the place as soon as they clapped eyes on it, have just moved in. There are 7 pretty rooms, with wooden décor all over, all at the same price: 350F for a double with shower/wc. Little sitting room with an old fireplace (where they used to smoke the salt meat), sauna, billiard room, tennis court. In the cosy dining room, you'll be served regional cuisine (*cassolette* of snails with Savagnin, fricassee of farmhouse chicken Franche-Comté-style, duo of sausage with Morteau and Montbéliard). Non-regional cuisine also available. *Menu du jour* (weekday lunchtimes) 70F. Other set meals 90F, 130F and 160F.

GRAY 70100

AUBERGE DE JEUNESSE

2 rue André-Maginot (North-East).
☎ 03.84.64.82.60 F→ 03.84.65.16.23
Car park.

This hostel for young workers sets aside a number of rooms for members of the FUAJ. Modern building with many amenities, in particular mountain bike hire and launderette. Several single/twin rooms with breakfast for 82F. For families 6 fully equipped studio apartments with kitchen, shower and wc for 100F. Meal at the self-service restaurant 52F.

10% HÔTEL-RESTAURANT LE BELLEVUE**

1 av. Carnot (Centre)
☎ 03.84.64.53.50 Fax 03.84.64.53.69
Closed on Saturdays and Sunday evenings out of season and in December (except for the self-service restaurant). **Secure parking**. **TV** with **Canal+**.

In the lower part of the town near the Saône. Ask for the rooms overlooking the park at the back which are considerably less noisy. Very basic double rooms with basin 165F; 205F with wc and shower or bath. The restaurant with river views offers set meals at 72F during the week and then at 115F and 195F. Self-service restaurant open every day in the same establishment.

RESTAURANT DU CRATÔ

65 Grande-Rue (Centre).
☎ 03.84.65.11.75
Closed lunchtimes in August.

A small restaurant in a sloping lane in the old part of Gray. Some restaurateurs use the choice of menus offered as an excuse for their high prices, but *Cratô* offers 10 starters and 6 main courses with a cheese course and dessert for 90–150F. Daily special with main course and cheese course or dessert 75F. Here fine food doesn't mean excessive prices. Clientele largely in suits and ties – business lunch. More trendy in the evening.

AUBIGNEY 70140 (10KM S)

AUBERGE DU VIEUX MOULIN**

Centre; take the D475 towards Pesmes then the D280.
☎ 03.84.31.61.61 Fax 03.84.31.62.38
Closed Sunday evenings and Mondays out of season and mid November–beginning March. **Car park**. **TV**.

At the point where Burgundy meets Franche-Comté, a little lost between Besançon and Gray, between fields and forests, between the river and ponds with freshwater crayfish. This old mill has for years been a meeting place for those who adore being pampered. The Mirbey ladies, cooks through the generations from mother to daughter, have transformed their family home into a welcoming inn (7 lovely little rooms at 385F) where *cancoillotte* and pâté are served with home-made jams for breakfast and where, with the small set meals at 100F, 150F, 200F and 250F, you can treat yourself to young rabbit or chicken with freshwater crayfish. Set lunch during the week 65F (daily special plus dessert). Adorable little terrace looking onto the park.

CHARENTENAY 70130 (30KM NE)

AUBERGE PARIS

How to get there: from Gray, take the D13 to Vellexon then the D256.
☎ 03.84.78.40.10
Car park. **Disabled access**.

A truly extraordinary establishment, without doubt the only restaurant in France where swallows nest up in the ceiling beams and chickens come to peck about in the dining room. Located next to a canal, this little inn is run by a proprietor who puts on a grumpy act so as to be able to concentrate on offering better service. There is no menu, either à la carte or table d'hôte. Meals are only served to order and on reservation which means that the food couldn't be fresher. The chef's speciality is *pauchoise*, a bouillabaisse made using river fish and freshwater crayfish in season. You can also try the delicious stuffed pigeon and lots of regional specialities washed down with Champlitte wine. Reckon on paying 80–120F for a meal. It is possible to stay in one of the gîtes or at the campsite which are all run by the proprietor of this establishment.

LEPUIX 90200

LE SAUT DE LA TRUITE**

Malvaux; take the D465
☎ 03.84.29.32.64 Fax 03.84.29.57.42
Closed Fridays and in December/January.
Secure parking. **TV**.

A superb establishment on a hairpin bend on the road leading up to the ballon d'Alsace. This comfortable hotel, located in a forest clearing, is pleasant in summer when the sound of the nearby waterfall is truly melodious. Lovely little rooms; 250F for a double with shower/wc. Freshly caught trout every day from the pond below the hotel and a fine selection of regional specialities such as bilberry tart. Set meals 90–175F.

LA CHAUMIÈRE

Ballon d'Alsace; take the D465, and it's just before you reach the summit.

☎ 03.84.29.31.66
Closed weekdays out of season.

Gourmet mountain dwellers will receive a friendly welcome at this thatched cottage on the slopes of Ballon d'Alsace. Tasteful rustic décor and large wooden tables. The owner, who used to work in country house hotels, has returned to his serf's cottage – but is still lord and master in the kitchen. He knows how to blend typical menus from the three adjoining regions – Lorraine, Franche-Comté and Alsace – and come up with a range of dishes to suit all pockets. The adventurous among you will love the 55F "youkaï-di" walker's platter, served at any time of day, and consisting of Luxeuil ham, smoky bacon from Lorraine, a quarter litre of Edelzwicker and home-made tart. They also do a 70F set meal. À la carte you can have *salade des douaniers*, *parmetière* of smoked salmon, local knuckle of beef, cheese platter (Münster fermier, Bangkas and Comté), delicious bilberry tart and sorbet. As soon as the sun comes out, zoom, everyone heads for the terrace.

LES ERRUES-MENONCOURT 90150

10% 🏠 |●| LA POMME D'ARGENT

13 rue de la Noye.
☎ 03.84.27.63.69
Closed Wednesdays and the 2nd and 3rd weeks in Nov.

In a big building off the beaten track, this place is yet another great find. Fresh, sophisticated cuisine in true traditional style. Isabelle Pontal is the chef here who concocts ambitious dishes that never strike a false note. Try the famous Vauban set meal at 98F where old recipes are revamped (delicious soup with poached fruit in wine and spices). Good choice of set meals: 48F at lunchtimes (except weekends and public holidays), 95F, 156F. À la carte, we noted boned rabbit *à la provençale*, and many regional delicacies (different kinds of sausage: *Montbéliard, Morteau, lion de Belfort*). The terrace is lovely when the sun decides to come out. 4 basic clean rooms available at very reasonable prices: 150F for 2 (180F with twin beds). All with shower-basin, but wc is on the landing.

LONS-LE-SAUNIER 39000

🏠 |●| HÔTEL-RESTAURANT TERMINUS**

37 av. Aristide Briand (Centre).
☎ 03.84.24.41.83 F 03.84.26.68.07
Closed Sundays and Christmas–New Year. **Car park**. **TV**. **Canal+**.

A well-established place that's gradually starting to fade as the years go by, just like the number of trains that pass through the neighbouring station. Luckily a change of ownership – although it stayed within the same family – put a stop to the process of decay. A massive renovation project has started for the entire establishment. The relatively large rooms have all been modernized and painted white so they look a lot lighter. They do the job, we'll say that (big coat and hat stand where you can hang up all your things), and could have looked even better if the décor had been a bit more deluxe, but you'll still get a good night's sleep here. Doubles with shower/wc 350F. The ones at the back are quieter.

|●| RESTAURANT GRAND CAFÉ DU THÉÂTRE

2 rue Jean-Jaurès (Centre).
☎ 03.84.24.49.30
Car park.

One of the few lively places in Lons-le-Saunier after 10 at night. The establishment has been taken over by a friendly young couple who offer their clientele the opportunity of watching sport on a large screen courtesy of Eurosport (muted so as not to disturb diners). The menu includes generous salads at 40F and 54F and the substantial Jura escalope for 64F.Pleasant and very large terrace where you can drink until late at night on fine days.

|●| BISTROT DES MARRONNIERS

22 rue de Vallière (Centre).
☎ 03.84.43.06.04
Closed Saturdays and Sundays.

A good place if you're a bit peckish in the evening. The type of place where tripe casserole, marrowbone and chicken/turkey supremes with chanterelle mushrooms are served. Jura wines by the jug. Reckon on paying about 100F à la carte.

CHILLE 39570 (1.5KM E)

10% 🏠 |●| HÔTEL-RESTAURANT PARENTHÈSE**

How to get there: head for Besançon on the bypass, then go just under a mile on the D157; the establishment is signposted.
☎ 03.84.47.55.44 F 03.84.24.92.13
Restaurant closed Monday lunchtimes, Sunday evenings and in February during the school holidays.
Secure parking. **TV**. **Disabled access**.

In a small village close to the major road arteries, this beautiful 18th century residence has been converted into a comfortable hotel and restaurant by its very friendly and welcoming proprietor. Located in the middle of a 7.5 acre park, the hotel has around 20 rooms which are tastefully decorated and named after painters. Reckon on paying 280–350F for a double room with wc and shower or bath. The restaurant offers a set meal at 80F during the week. A 3-star annexe – *Le Thélème* – has just been built. Doubles 650F.

BAUME-LES-MESSIEURS 39210 (20KM NE)

RESTAURANT DES GROTTES

How to get there: take the N83.; at Saint-Germain-lès-Arlay take the D120 to Voiteur then the D70
☎ 03.84.44.61.59
Closed Wednesdays in April, May, June and September, Oct 15–April 15 and every evening. **Car park**.

The location has something magical about it and reminds you of Marienbad's spa hotels. Opposite a marvellously frothy waterfall at the bottom of the Baumes-les-Messieurs natural amphitheatre. The tranquility of this restaurant is in sharp contrast to the masses of tourists at the nearby caves. Several set meals (lunchtimes only) at 80–140F offer Franche-Comté specialities. In summer you can also eat a plate of meats or cheeses washed down with a glass of Jura wine on the terrace for 50F.

LURE 70200

10% HÔTEL-RESTAURANT LE PONT DE L'OGNON*

4 route de la Saline (South-East); on the way out of Lure in the Belfort direction, turn right onto the D18 towards l'Isle-sur-le-Doubs
☎ 03.84.30.25.05 F 03.84.30.02.07
Closed Wednesday evenings (out of season). **Car park**.

The proprietor isn't always very attentive but the food is the best value for money in Lure. Set meals start at 60F during the week and there are many other set meals at 83–255F offering, for example, fried carp and stone-baked pizzas. Some basic rooms with basin at 145F and 130F for 2.

RONCHAMP 70250 (13KM E)

HÔTEL-RESTAURANT CARRER**

Le Rhien (Centre); take the N19 then turn left as you enter Le Rhien at the foot of Bourlement hill and the famous chapel designed by Le Corbusier
☎ 03.84.20.62.32 F 03.84.63.57.08
Car park. TV with **Canal+. Disabled access.**

People come from far and wide to eat in this restaurant located at the bottom of a valley which was once mining country. The family cooking is both traditional and inventive. Besides the usual Franche-Comté specialities, the à la carte menu offers salad of langoustine and scallops or slices of duck with lemons and grapes. Daily set meal 55F (weekdays) and 5 set meals at 80–210F. Rooms with basin/wc 155F and with bath 210F. Mountain bike hire.

CHAMPAGNEY 70290 (15KM E)

10% HÔTEL-RESTAURANT DU COMMERCE**

4 av. du Général-Brosset; take the N19 and then the D4.
☎ 03.84.23.13.24 F 03.84.23.24.33
Closed Mondays out of season and Feb 1–15.
Secure parking. TV.

A traditional establishment at the edge of a pleasant park, run by a lady who likes to look after her clientele of regulars. Double rooms with shower/wc 200–250F. More basic rooms with basin 160F. The restaurant offers simple home cooking and Franche-Comté specialities. Set meals during the week start at 70F.

LUXEUIL-LES-BAINS 70300

10% HÔTEL DE LORRAINE

14 rue Jean-Jaurès (Centre).
☎ 03.84.93.70.24
Secure parking. Canal+.

It's called *Hôtel de Lorraine* but the proprietor is Portuguese and lived near Boston in the United States for 10 years with her husband. They did up this little hotel themselves. Double rooms with basin 95F. Rooms sleeping 4 110F. The shared bathroom and toilet facilities could do with a facelift. Family atmosphere and warm welcome.

HÔTEL-RESTAURANT DE FRANCE**

6 rue Georges-Clemenceau.
☎ 03.84.40.13.90 F 03.84.40.33.12
Restaurant closed Sunday evenings. **Car park. TV.**

A quiet hotel with twenty or so rooms in an oasis of greenery. Double rooms 200F (with basin/wc) and 270F (with bath). The restaurant offers set meals at 70F (traditional), 120F (regional) and 170F (gourmet – large helpings). Warm welcome.

10% ☗ |●| HÔTEL-RESTAURANT BEAU SITE***

18 rue Georges-Moulimard.
☎ 03.84.40.14.67 F➜ 03.84.40.50.25
Closed Friday evenings and Sunday evenings in winter.
Car park. **TV** with **Canal+**.

Don't hesitate to ask the proprietors for information about the area. They can tell you about anything from walks and water cures to fishing and mountain biking. Close to the casino and the baths, this comfortable family establishment offers double rooms with shower/wc in the main building or the adjacent annexe at 320–340F. Gourmet cuisine in the restaurant or, in summer, on the terrace, with set meals starting at 85F. Bargain weekend spa package. Discounts for those who can show a copy of this guide.

SAINT-SAUVEUR 70300 (1KM SE)

10% ☗ |●| HÔTEL-RESTAURANT CHEZ MAXIM

10 av. Georges-Clemenceau (Centre).
☎ 03.84.40.02.91 F➜ 03.84.93.65.45
Closed Sunday evenings and in February.
Secure parking.

An unpretentious bar and restaurant close to Luxeuil-les-Bains' chic hotels. Very generous daily set meal 52F (except Sundays). Real family cooking — on the dessert menu there's a home-made raisin semolina instead of the traditional two scoops of ice-cream. Menus more elaborate on Sunday lunchtimes but prices still reasonable at 80F and 110F.

MÉTABIEF 25370

10% ☗ |●| HÔTEL-RESTAURANT L'ÉTOILE DES NEIGES**

4 rue du Village (North).
☎ 03.81.49.11.21 F➜ 03.81.49.26.91
Closed May 30–June 15 and Nov 15–Dec 15.
Secure parking. **TV**.

A modern building set a little way apart from the station above a small river. Double rooms 210 with shower/wc and 225F with bath/wc.

LES LONGEVILLES MONT D'OR 25370 (4KM SW)

☗ |●| HÔTEL-RESTAURANT LES SAPINS**

☎ 03.81.49.90.90
Closed April and Oct 1–Dec 15. **Car park**.

In the centre of a little village, which, although part of the Métabief resort, hasn't lost any of its authenticity. Pleasant rooms (those on the 2nd floor have sloping ceilings) that are some of the best value for money in the area. Doubles 180F with shower, 195F with shower/wc. The *menu du jour* (75F), served at both lunchtimes and in the evenings during the week is worth a try. Home-made regional cooking: *franc-comtoise* salad, cheese flan, undercut of beef and *gratin dauphinois*. Another set meal at 90F. A genuinely friendly welcome.

JOUGNE 25370 (5KM E)

☗ |●| HÔTEL-RESTAURANT DE LA COURONNE*

place de l'Église (Centre); take the D9 and the N57 then head for the Swiss border
☎ 03.81.49.10.50 F➜ 03.81.49.19.77
Closed over the All Saints' Day holiday and in November. **Car park**. **Disabled access**.

The hotel is set well away from the main road which cuts through Jougne and the only thing to disturb the peace and quiet is the sound of bells from the neighbouring church! Of the renovated rooms at 230F with shower/wc, numbers 23, 12, 14 and 16 offer a wonderful view plunging down into the magnificent and too little known Jougnenaz valley. Lovely garden. Set meals start at 90F. Specialities: fillet of duck with bilberries, fillet of trout and morel mushrooms and *petit-gris* en croûte.

MONTBÉLIARD 25200

10% ☗ |●| HÔTEL-RESTAURANT L'AUBERGE MON REPOS*

8 rue des Grands-Jardins (North-East).
☎ 03.81.94.52.67
Restaurant closed Saturday lunchtimes and Sundays.
Secure parking. **TV**. **Disabled access**.

The name of the quiet street running past the hotel means large garden and is appropriate here. No modern furniture for the rooms, which have just been tastefully renovated. Double rooms 160F (with wc) and 210F (with shower/wc). Very courteous welcome. This former parsonage is a real paradise! Reduction on presentation of this guide.

10% ☗ |●| HÔTEL DE LA BALANCE***

40 rue de Belfort (Centre); it's in the old part of town.
☎ 03.81.96.77.41 F➜ 03.81.91.47.16

Restaurant closed Saturday lunchtime. **Car park**. **TV**. **Canal+**. **Disabled access**.

Like a lot of the other buildings in the old town, this 16th century house is quite colourful: dusky pink façade and yellow-ochre for the elegant dining room. Antique furniture and a solid wooden staircase add to the charm of this place, which definitely bellies the rather sad and dull grey image people tend to have of the town. The rooms are stylish with all the mod cons, all with shower/wc or bath from 290F for a double. For any of our readers who are interested in history, Field Marshal De Lattre de Tassigny stayed in 1944. Buffet-style breakfast: 35F. Very classic set meals from 100F. Cosy piano bar.

RESTAURANT DU CHÂTEAU

4 rue du Château (Centre).
☎ 03.81.94.93.06
Closed Sundays except holidays.

A small establishment where during weekday lunchtimes you can treat yourself to fresh produce bought at the local markets. The proprietor is rightly proud of his boneless fried carp at 70F. (If you like bones it's FF65!) Set meals from 68F (weekdays) or 130F. Good wine list.

AUDINCOURT 25400 (3.5KM S)

HÔTEL DES TILLEULS**

51 av. Foch.
☎ 03.81.30.77.00 F 03.81.30.57.20
TV. **Canal+**. **Disabled access**.

In a quiet street – don't be misled by the "avenue" in the address. Excellent welcome. The rooms are equipped with all the mod cons (fridge, power shower, hair dryer) and are decorated in a contemporary style, plain but still cosy. They're all dotted about in the main building or in little annexes around the garden and the lovely heated swimming pool. Doubles with shower/wc or bath 280F, 310F for an executive suite, 350F for a room with a jacuzzi. There's no restaurant but you can get meals in the evening: main courses around 40F.

MORTEAU 25500

10% HÔTEL DES MONTAGNARDS**

7 [bis] place Carnot (Centre).
☎ 03.81.67.08.86 F 03.81.67.14.57
Closed Sundays (out of season) and during the week of July 14. **Secure parking**. **TV**. **Disabled access**.

This small, friendly hotel in the centre of the village, but looking out onto the surrounding countryside, has 18 comfortable panelled rooms done out in pastel shades. Doubles 185F (with washing facilities), 230F (with shower/wc) and 265F (with bath).

RESTAURANT L'ÉPOQUE

18 rue de la Louhière (North); it's just outside the centre, on the road to Besançon.
☎ 03.81.67.33.44
Closed Wednesday evenings and Sundays (except public holidays). **Car park**.

A restaurant that's quite happy the way it is. Both the welcome and the service are friendly without being over the top. There are two dining rooms with a bistro sort of feel to them, and you instantly feel right at home. Tasty food, that's inventive to just the right degree but which always includes regional produce: sausage *de Morteau* (of which the owner is a real fan) in red wine, *poulet de Bresse* in *vin jaune* (yellow wine from this region) and morels. Set meals 85–160F. The one at 98F has mousse of duck in port, salad with scallops in blackcurrant vinegar, *feuillantine* (small light pastry) of fillet mignon with mushrooms, bacon and potatoes, or fillet of stuffed lemon sole *à la Dieppoise* (poached in white wine with mussels, shrimps, mushrooms and cream). All pretty impressive (as is the owner's moustache, a local character who has a robot made to look just like him!). Selection of whiskies.

MONTLEBON 25500 (2KM SE)

HÔTEL-RESTAURANT BELLEVUE*

2 rue de Bellevue; it's just under a mile from the centre taking the D437 then the D48.
☎ 03.81.67.00.05 F 03.81.67.04.74
Closed Sunday evenings, Monday lunchtimes out of season and Dec 18–Jan 15. **Car park**.

This restaurant, from where you have a marvellous view over the Morteau valley, is aptly named. Regional cuisine on all the menus, from 55F (weekdays) to 150F. Trout meunière (coated in flour and fried in butter) with French fries 44F. Rooms good value at 150F (with basin) to 210F (with shower/wc).

ORNANS 25290

HÔTEL DE FRANCE***

51 rue Pierre Vernier (Centre)
☎ 03.81.62.24.44 F 03.81.62.12.03
Closed Sunday evenings and Mondays (outside school holidays), as well as Dec 20–Feb 1. **Secure parking**. **TV**.

A good traditional family hotel like you'd find in the good old days (well, given its name, that comes as no surprise) but it is quite well-to-do. There's a reasonable brasserie set meal (main course plus dessert) for 75F in the bar. As for the restaurant (with it's staunch classical décor) there are set meals from 110F (flan with ham Franche-Comté-style and blue trout with a lemon sauce)–300F. The rooms have an up-market rustic feel to them. A few of them look out on to the famous Grand Pont (which actually isn't that big) but the road outside is quite noisy. You'll get more peace and quiet in one of the rooms at the back. Doubles 280F with shower/wc (but no TV) and from 380F with TV and mini-bar. Private fishing.

VERNIERFONTAINE 25580 (17KM E)

10% L'AUBERGE PAYSANNE

18 rue du Stade (Centre).
☎ 03.81.60.05.21 Fax 03.81.60.05.21
Closed Thursdays; November–March closed Mondays–Fridays and during the school holidays. **Car park**.

Off the beaten track, this country inn is a real Aladdin's cave, containing all the treasures Franche-Comté has to offer. The decoration in the restaurant is certainly a little over the top but the traditional cuisine is excellent and the helpings generous. Country casserole (potato, bacon, eggs, onion, sausage and salad) 120F for 2. Unbeatable! Burgundy and Savoy fondues, attractive set meals for 78F, 95F and 125F. Some comfortable double rooms 180F with shower/wc. Hearty breakfasts with meats, cheese and yoghurt 60F. An excellent establishment.

PASSENANS 39230

10% HÔTEL-RESTAURANT L'AUBERGE DU ROSTAING

How to get there: take the N83 towards Lons-le Saunier then turn left onto the D101 after Tramelans
☎ 03.84.85.23.70 Fax 03.84.44.66.87
Closed Monday lunchtime to Tuesday lunchtime (out of season) and in January/December.

You couldn't imagine a more charming place than this little country inn run by a friendly and very green Swiss couple. This old Jura house seems almost embedded in the greenery of the vines which climb along the slope. The rooms are basic, spacious and rustic in style. 132F (with basin) to 248F (with shower/wc).

PONTARLIER 25300

10% HÔTEL-RESTAURANT SAINT-PIERRE*

3 place Saint-Pierre (Centre).
☎ 03.81.46.50.80 Fax 03.81.46.87.80
TV. **Closed** Sundays and Mondays (out of season).

This place sits on a square in the centre of a little district that's almost a village in its own right. Nearly all of the rooms look out on to the porte Saint-Pierre, the town's landmark, a rather over-the-top *arc de triomphe*. Double rooms with shower/wc that aren't exactly huge but they are stylish and good value for money: 180–220F (depending on the season). For those of you on a budget, there are slightly more old-fashioned rooms – a touch of faded grandeur – rooms with only a basin (shower/wc on the landing) at 150F and a few family rooms too (240F for 3). As for the restaurant, it serves decent traditional food: dish of the day 42F, set meal 75F. And one of the sunniest terraces in town, a perfect place to have your aperitif

10% HÔTEL-RESTAURANT DE MORTEAU**

26 rue Jeanne-d'Arc (Centre).
☎ 03.81.39.14.83 Fax 03.81.39.75.07
Closed every day 3–6pm, on Sundays and 1 week in March, 1 week in June, 2 weeks in September and 1 week in October. **Secure parking**. **TV**.

A huge building with a sloping roof and, on the side, a door which used to open onto a barn. An old house completely renovated. Best value for money in town. Doubles 170F (with washing facilities) and 210F (with wc/shower and telephone). The food is excellent with set meals starting from 68F.

GRANGETTES (LES) 25160 (12KM S)

HÔTEL-RESTAURANT BON REPOS**

How to get there: it's on the far side of the lac de Saint-Point taking the D437 then, after Oye-et-Pallet, the D129.
☎ 03.81.69.62.95
Closed Tuesday evenings, Wednesdays out of season and end October–Dec 20. **Car park**. **TV**.

A large Franche-Comté building overlooking the lake. Traditional inn atmosphere. White tablecoths and attentive welcome. Plateful of home-made meats 48F. Numerous set meals 67–164F with fine fish specialities. Comfortable rooms in good condition. 170F for a double room with basin; 220F with shared shower and toilet facilities but with a view of the lake.

OUHANS 25520 (17KM NW)

10% HÔTEL-RESTAURANT DES SOURCES DE LA LOUE*

13 Grande-Rue (Centre); take the N57 then at Saint-Gorgon-Main turn left onto the D41
☎ 03.81.69.90.06 F 03.81.69.93.17
Closed Oct 20–Nov 5 and Dec 20–Feb 1. **Car park. TV.**

This village inn is a fine establishment in wonderful countryside. For 75F (except Sundays) you can try the chef's salad with dried home-smoked meat, *gratinette* (potatoes au gratin with Morteau sausage) and a home-made dessert. Other set meals 90–195F. Pleasant rooms in pastel colours 200F (with shower/wc) and 220F (with bath).

RENÉDALE 25520 (19KM W)

AUBERGE DU MOINE

Grange-Carrée; it's 400m from the Belvédère du Moine.
☎ 03.81.69.91.22
Closed Monday evenings and Dec 20–March 15.

A very fine establishment. Wise to reserve. The monk (who gave his name to the place) must have loved peace and solitude. But it no longer exists. The natural surroundings though are still as beautiful. Small paths lined with trees and ample wood for the winter. Open grassland and dense forests. A silence punctuated only by the music of cowbells. On Sundays the dining room (a former stable renovated and covered with attractive pine wainscotting) is full of local people, regulars who have long known of this fine establishment. The lady who runs the place, Danielle, has kept the secrets of the (regional) family cuisine which she learnt from her parents. Set meals start at 65F (except Sundays). We found the generous 135F set meal delightful. When leaving, don't miss the view of the Loue valley from the Belvédère du Moine.

PORT-SUR-SAÔNE 70170

HÔTEL-RESTAURANT DE LA PAIX

3 rue Jean-Bogé (Centre).
☎ 03.84.91.52.80 F 03.84.91.61.21
Closed Sunday evenings out of season and in January. **Car park.**

The hotel is in an old 16th-century priory but unfortunately the decoration hasn't taken this into account, even though the proprietor makes an effort to renovate the rooms in turn. Double rooms 150F (with basin) and 180F (with shower/wc). The restaurant offers a set meal at 56F during the week. Other set meals 82–190F.

RESTAURANT LA MARINE

15 rue de la Fontaine.
☎ 03.84.91.51.00
Closed Wednesdays in winter.

A genuine *guinguette* (café with dancing, often in the open) where people travelling along the canal simply need to tie up their boats to come and have something to eat in this pleasant establishment. The proprietor, Philippe Noë, doesn't wait for floods of customers to treat you. The set meals at 75–150F change every week with numerous fish and game specialities in season. Advisable to book.

COMBEAUFONTAINE 70120 (12KM W)

HÔTEL-RESTAURANT LE BALCON**

Centre; take the N19.
☎ 03.84.92.11.13 F 03.84.92.15.89
Closed Sunday evenings, Mondays, June 29-July 8 and Dec 26–Jan 12. **Secure parking.**

In this former coaching inn covered in ivy and flowers Gérard Gauthier gives an unpretentious welcome to touring cyclists, canoeists and businessmen travelling from Paris to Basle. Doubles 250F (with shower/wc) and 380F (with bath and TV). The (rather exclusive) restaurant lowers its prices a little in the summer to make its cuisine more accessible (65F set meal served at lunchtimes). Gourmet menus 145–360F.

ROUSSES (LES) 39220

HÔTEL DU VILLAGE*

344 rue Pasteur (Centre).
☎ 03.84.34.12.75
Closed in June and November. **Secure parking.**

This 10-room hotel has been completely renovated. Large double rooms, all with wc and shower or bath 260–310F. Small suite sleeping 4–5 on the 2nd floor.

RESTAURANT LES P'LOSSES

South-West; take the N5.
☎ 03.84.60.06.68
Closed Monday and Wednesday lunchtimes (except during school holidays).

The welcome may have been a little on the reserved side but this small matter is soon forgotten when you get to your table and find food from all over the world on offer, including chicken/turkey escalope with *comté* cheese, Chinese fondue and Berber prawns. Reasonable set meal 65F (weekday lunchtimes). Other set meals at 90F, 120F, 155F and 195F. Children's set meal 45F.

BIEF-DE-LA-CHAILLE (LE) 39220 (2KM S)

AUBERGE DE JEUNESSE

South-West; take the N5 towards Gex then turn right onto a minor road 400m after the Rousses exit
☎ 03.84.60.02.80 ➡ 03.84.60.09.67
Closed April 20–May 16 and Sept 30–Dec 20 (except for groups). **Car park**.

FUAJ card compulsory. This small building right out in the country used to house a factory that polished spectacle lenses, harnassing the power of Le Bief-de-la-Chaille's river. 50F per person in dormitories with 4 to 6 beds. Meals available on request. In winter full board package (from 1,280F) for cross-country skiers.

SAINT-CLAUDE 39200

10% HÔTEL DE LA POSTE**

1 rue Reybert (Centre).
☎ 03.84.45.52.34
TV.

The most central hotel in town. Most of the rooms have two double beds, ideal for a couple with 2 kids. Rooms with shower 250F, with both beds occupied (185F for 2) and those with bath, 275F with both beds occupied (215F if you just use one double bed). The hotel also has a few rooms with showers just outside on the landing (145F for a double). Ask for one of the rooms that look out on to the place du 9 avril 1944 – they're much lighter. Breakfast 27F. With the post office just next door, this is the ideal time to write all those postcards you promised all your aunties and cousins, and quite frankly, there ain't much else to do here at night anyway.

LE LACUZON

5 rue Victor Hugo (Centre).
☎ 03.84.45.06.51
Closed Sunday evenings and Mondays, as well as 2 weeks in May.

This town is definitely lacking in nice friendly restaurants that don't take themselves too seriously. So this one here deserves all the praise it gets. It's not fancy but it serves good traditional food and you'll be welcomed by a friendly face. The set meal at 55F, with its platter of *hors-d'oeuvres*, braised beef and dessert, seems to come straight out of a good old-fashioned cookery book. The one at 96F with *terrine* of chicken liver or *quenelles* of pike with a *nantua* sauce (with fresh crayfish tails), *poulet de Bresse* with tarragon or sirloin of grilled beef, cheese and dessert, seems to come straight out of a book on "How to prepare feasts and banquets". At the end of the day, you'll get the feeling that you've certainly had your money's worth. A good sign, we reckon.

10% HÔTEL-RESTAURANT LE PRÉ FILLET**

Les Molunes; take the D436 towards the col de la Faucille then the D292.
☎ 03.84.41.62.89 ➡ 03.84.41.64.75
Closed Oct 14–Dec 1; restaurant closed Sunday evenings. **Secure parking**.

We particularly recommend this establishment to our gourmet friends with large appetites. Reservations recommended. This mountain restaurant with large bay windows looking out onto the high mountain pastures or snow (depending on the season) offers value for money to compare with the best in the region. From the wonderful dish of cold meats to the large cheese plate via the succulent dish of the day, you will spoil yourself with the 85F set meal. Not only that but the wine list has wines from all over France at unbeatable prices. For those not wanting to drive on after eating, double rooms with wc and shower or bath are available at 250F.

LE COLLÈGE

Les Molunes; take the D436 in the direction of Septmoncel, then the D25 in the direction of Moussières.
☎ 03.84.41.61.09
Closed Monday evenings and Tuesdays.

On the spot where there used to be a bakery/grocer's shop right in the heart of the hamlet of Molunes (don't even bother attempting to look for the church, there isn't one), 1250m up, Le Collège is famous throughout Haut-Jura. It can seat up to 64 people and there's often a fight to get in there at the weekend. You'll understand why as soon as you see the first course. Not only does it taste good but it looks good too. First class set meal at 52F, served during the week: a lovely delicatessen platter, followed by the dish of the day (sautéed veal served with rice, braised chicory and spinach, on the day of our visit), cheese and dessert. The one at 78F is just as good (we've got fond memories of the veal with mushrooms and the chocolate fondant with pears). Other set meals at 95F, 116F and 144F. Great wine list. Rather nice country-style décor.

MOIRANS-EN-MONTAGNE 39260 (21KM NW)

|●| LE REGARDOIR

Belvédère de Moirans-en-Montagne; yake the D436 in the direction of Dortan-Oyonnax, then the D470 in the direction of Lavans-les-St-Claude.
☎ 03.84.42.01.15
Closed Monday evenings and Tuesdays (except June 15–Aug 30), as well as Oct 10–April 10.

The exceptional panoramic view you get from here is reason enough in itself to stop and have a bite to eat in this *franc-comtoise guingette* (café with dancing, often outdoors). Open your eyes wide and take in the awe-inspiring view over the lake of Vouglans just below and the surrounding countryside. At sunset, the light takes on a quite special quality (that's the time to take your aperitif outside!). The staff are young and friendly, the menu's pretty straightforward, but it's all good stuff. We especially recommend the whitebait and the oven-baked pizzas (in summer only). It's always pretty full both at lunchtimes and in the evenings. Expect to pay 100–130F. *Formule* at 65F (75F in summer).

SAINT-HIPPOLYTE 25190

10% ☗ |●| AUBERGE DE MORICEMAISON

route du Dessoubre – Valoreille (South-West); head for the Dessoubre valley on the D39 for about 11km.
☎ 03.81.64.01.72
Closed Wednesdays mid September–mid May.
Car park.

Meeting place for anglers. If you want to do a bit of fishing, the proprietor will be happy to cook your catch for you. Simple and warm welcome in this former farm which has 6 rooms with basin (155F) looking out over the river. Good daily set meal for 55F during the week. Other set meals 90F, 130F and 185F. Trout in *vin jaune* and fried trout à la carte.

GOUMOIS 25470 (20KM SE)

10% ☗ |●| AUBERGE LE MOULIN DU PLAIN**

☎ 03.81.44.41.99 F➜ 03.81.44.45.70
Closed November–February inclusive. **Car park**.

Meeting place for anglers. Magnificent surroundings at the bottom of the valley. This inn, set up a few years ago by a family of farmers, is today a thriving business. 22 very comfortable double rooms – all with wc and shower or bath at 266–306F. In the restaurant set meals start at 95F (except Sundays). Other set meals 124F, 130F, 175F and 195F with numerous regional specialities. Advisable to book.

VESOUL 70000

☗ AUBERGE DE JEUNESSE

zone de Loisirs, lac de Vesoul-Vaivre (North-West); it's opposite the industrial estate.
☎ 03.84.76.48.55 F➜ 03.84.75.74.93
Car park.

Access 8am–9pm. FUAJ card compulsory (sold at the hostel). By the lake. 18 little chalets made of stained wood with 4 beds, a table with stools and cupboards: 47F per person per night. In the centre a large, modern building containing the toilet facilities, showers and two kitchens. Food available at the adjacent *Bar de la Plage*.

10% ☗ HÔTEL DU LION**

4 place de la République (Centre).
☎ 03.84.76.54.44 F➜ 03.84.75.23.31
Closed Saturday evenings in January, Aug 7–16 August and Dec 26–Jan 3. **Car park**. **TV** with **Canal+**. **Disabled access**.

Warm welcome and the feeling that good service and comfort are guaranteed in this family hotel in the town centre. Spacious rooms with modern furniture 230F with shower/wc and 255F with bath.

VILLERSEXEL 70110

10% ☗ |●| HÔTEL-RESTAURANT DU COMMERCE**

1 place du 13-Septembre (Centre).
☎ 03.84.20.50.50 F➜ 03.84.20.59.57
Closed Sunday evenings, Jan 1–15 and Oct 6–12.
Secure parking. **TV**.

Enjoyable evening barbecue on the terrace in summer where you can treat yourself for 25–80F. The restaurant offers local cuisine. Do try the home-smoked ham on the bone or the various options with fresh trout. 60F set meal during the week. Other set meals 85–240F. Rooms with every possible comfort 220F.

Ile-de-France

75 Paris
77 Seine et Marne
78 Yvelines
91 Essonne
92 Hauts-de-Seine
93 Seine-Saint-Denis
94 Val-de-Marne
95 Val-d'Oise

ANGERVILLE 91670

10% ⌂ |●| HÔTEL DE FRANCE***

2 place du Marché (Centre).
☎ 01.69.95.11.30 ➡ 01.64.95.39.59
Car park. TV.

This beautiful old inn which has links with the French monarchy has been restored time and time again since 1715 without losing an ounce of its character. With its old beams, fireplace, conservatory, drawing room and traditional cooking, it has that comfortable life style we associate with a bygone age – which is something of a compliment in this part of the world. Doubles with shower or bath 420F. Set meals at 100F (weekdays) and 140F offer things like cream of watercress soup (this is the region for watercress) and *salade mérévilloise*. Reckon on paying about 220F à la carte.

AUVERS-SUR-OISE 95430

|●| LE CORDEVILLE

18 rue du Rajon.
☎ 01.30.36.81.66

This is the town that attracted so many Impressionist painters. The restaurant, right in the centre, offers home cooking and the helpings are generous. The proprietress, a very nice lady, puts the cooking pot on the table to add to the convivial atmosphere generated by her varied clientele of workmen, holiday makers and regulars. Set meals 60F and 85F. There's not much choice of wine and they don't take Visa.

|●| LE VERRE PLACIDE

20 rue du Général-de-Gaulle; it's opposite the train station.
☎ 01.34.48.02.11

Good set meals available at 90F (not Sundays) and 120F. Paintings are often on exhibition in the restaurant.

|●| AUBERGE RAVOUX

8 rue de la Sansonne; it's in the same square as the town hall.
☎ 01.30.36.60.60
Closed Sunday evenings and Monday evenings.

The inn (now a historic monument) is famous because Van Gogh died while staying here in 1890 and the dining room is decorated in a style that recalls that era. The cooking is traditional with a spice of originality. The set meals (145F for two courses and 185F for three) offer dishes like young rabbit on a bed of lentils, *terrine de campagne*, leg of lamb *Ravoux* – which apparently needs to cook for seven hours – and grilled tuna with *sauce vierge*.

BARBIZON 77630

10% ⌂ |●| LES ALOUETTES**

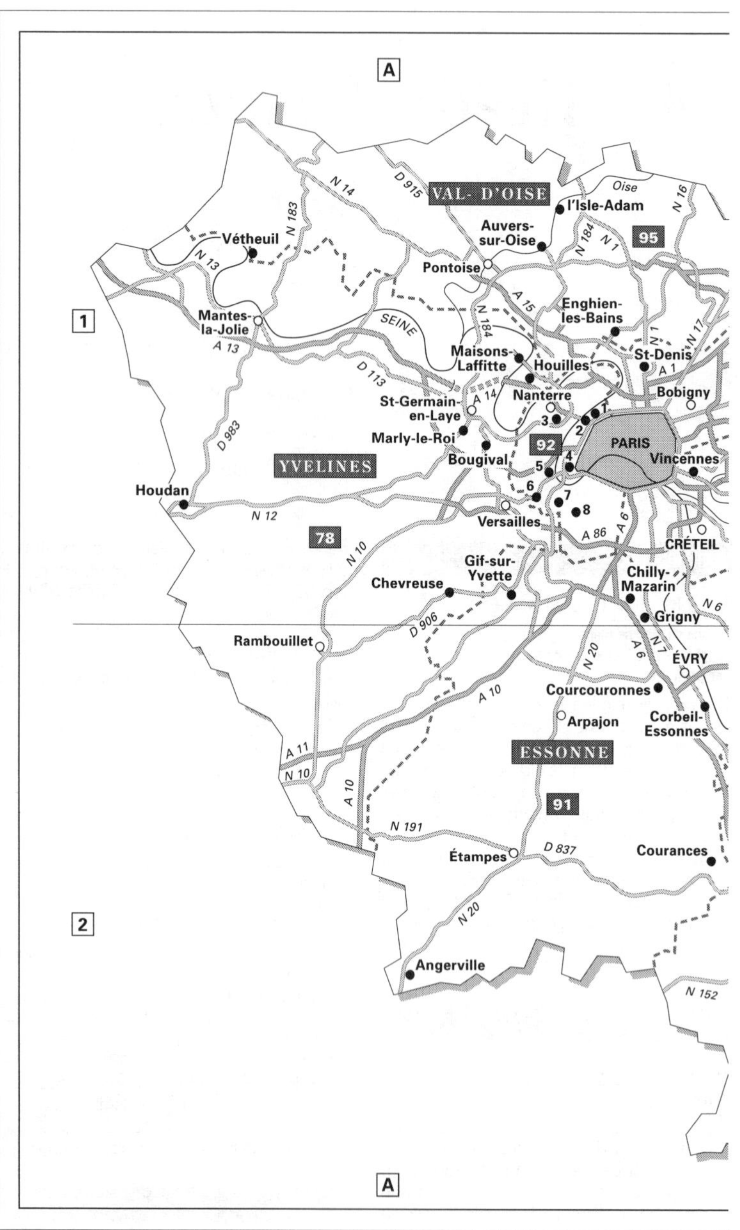
A
1
2
VAL- D'OISE
95
YVELINES
78
92
ESSONNE
91
PARIS
Vétheuil
Mantes-la-Jolie
Pontoise
Auvers-sur-Oise
l'Isle-Adam
Enghien-les-Bains
St-Denis
Bobigny
Maisons-Laffitte
Houilles
Nanterre
St-Germain-en-Laye
Marly-le-Roi
Bougival
Vincennes
Houdan
Versailles
CRÉTEIL
Chevreuse
Gif-sur-Yvette
Chilly-Mazarin
Grigny
Rambouillet
ÉVRY
Courcouronnes
Arpajon
Corbeil-Essonnes
Étampes
Courances
Angerville
Oise
SEINE
N 14
D 915
N 183
N 13
N 16
N 184
N 1
A 15
A 13
D 113
A 14
N 17
A 1
D 983
N 12
N 10
A 86
A 6
N 6
D 906
N 20
N 7
A 10
A 11
N 191
D 837
N 152
1
2
3
4
5
6
7
8

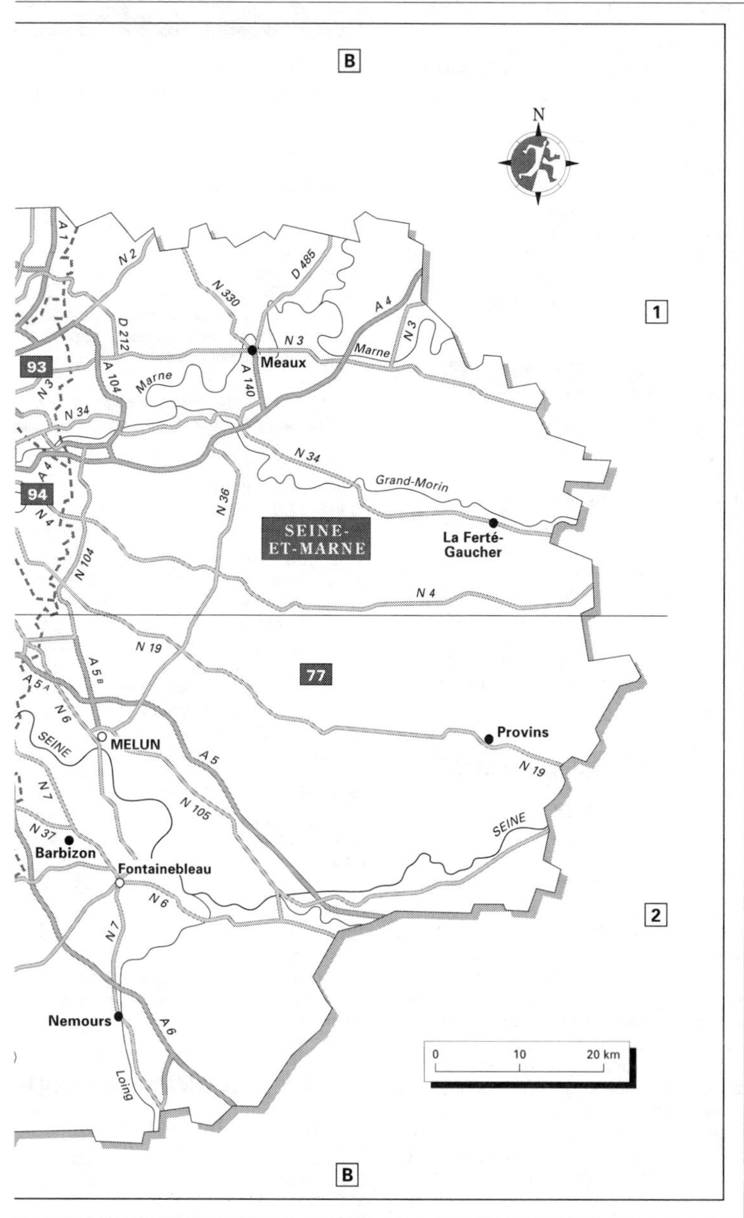
B
N
1
A 1
N 2
N 330
D 485
A 4
N 3
D 212
N 3
Marne
Meaux
93
A 104
Marne
A 140
N 3
N 34
N 34
Grand-Morin
A 4
94
N 4
N 36
SEINE-
ET-MARNE
La Ferté-
Gaucher
N 104
N 4
N 19
A 5B
77
A 5A
N 6
SEINE
MELUN
A 5
Provins
N 19
N 7
N 105
SEINE
N 37
Barbizon
Fontainebleau
N 6
2
N 7
Nemours
A 6
Loing
0
10
20 km
B

4 rue Antoine-Barye; it's 500m along the street that runs at right angles to rue Grande.
☎ 01.60.66.41.98 F➔ 01.60.66.20.69
Closed Sunday evenings out of season. **Car park. TV.**

This rather chic inn sits in its own grounds and has lots of trees and a garden. The décor is rustic. Doubles 250F with shower and 350F with bath – there are also two suites at 500F and 550F. Some of the rooms can be noisy. They do a set meal at 160F, and the house specialities include panfried fresh *foie gras* of Landes duck served with fruit and roast rabbit *aux saveurs provençales*. There's a tennis court and woods close by.

BOUGIVAL 78380

|●| LE CHALET SAVOYARD

102 rue du Maréchal-Joffre (Centre).
☎ 01.30.82.71.46
Closed Sundays, Mondays, and in August.

The restaurant has a welcoming rustic-look dining room with exposed beams and specializes in *raclette* and fondue. They have a good *formule* at lunchtime during the week – choose one of the house specialities (80–128F) for your main course and you'll get 1/4 litre of wine, dessert (icecream or floating islands) and coffee thrown in. Reckon on paying about 150F à la carte.

BRAY-ET-LÛ 95710

10% ⌂ |●| LE FAISAN DORÉ

12 route de Vernon.
☎ 01.34.67.71.68
Closed Sunday evenings, Mondays and mid Aug–early Sept. **TV.**

The front of the building is swathed in Virginia creeper and geraniums and petunias tumble from the balconies. Homy atmosphere, maybe just a bit too pretty. In summer, the terrace is better than the flowery parasols. Two set meals at 128F (starter, main course, cheese and dessert) and 160F (pepper steak, snails, and a light fruit *charlotte*). A la carte, reckon on 80F for a main course such as fricassee of veal sweetbreads with morels or veal chops Normandy style. Good value for money and attentive service. Basic rooms. Doubles 150F (wc in the corridor) and 180F (with shower). Free coffee if you can show them a copy of this guidebook.

CHAVILLE 92370

|●| RESTAURANT LE MAGLOIRE

2049 av. Roger-Salengro (North-East); it's on the N10, near place du Général Leclerc.
☎ 01.47.50.40.32
Closed Sunday evenings, Mondays, and July 1–Aug 18.

A place with lots of provincial charm and a rustic dining room overlooking a garden at the back. It's very pleasant in summer. They have an 85F set meal that comes with large helpings of good food and others at 180F and 230F. The à la carte menu offers a variety of dishes, including snails in puff pastry and fricassee of calf sweetbreads and flank. Reckon on 180F à la carte.

CHEVREUSE 78460

|●| AUBERGE DU MOULIN

56 rue de la Porte-de-Paris.
☎ 01.30.52.16.45
Closed Monday evenings, Tuesdays, and in September.

What you'll find here is a rustic setting, a pretty dining room where a fire is lit as soon as there's a chill in the air, and a pleasant terrace in summer. It's all rather attractive, particularly at lunchtime during the week, when they do a set meal for 90F. Like everywhere else in the Paris area, it's more expensive at the weekend and the cost of a set meal goes up to 140F. Good traditional cooking and the dishes are carefully prepared.

|●| RESTAURANT NORMAND

31 rue de Rambouillet (South).
☎ 01.30.52.09.93
Closed Sunday evenings and Monday lunchtimes.

The restaurant offers home cooking and a family atmosphere in its welcoming dining room with exposed beams. The garden, which has lots of flowers and trees and is enclosed by hedges, is pleasant in summer. Prices are less than the local average, with set meals 98–198F. Reckon on paying 170F à la carte.

SAINT-RÉMY-LÈS-CHEVREUSE 78470 (3KM E)

⌂ |●| HÔTEL-RESTAURANT AU BORD DU LAC

2 rue de la Digue.
☎ 01.30.52.00.43 F➔ 01.30.47.14.84
Closed Sunday evenings, Wednesdays (except for lunch in summer), and mid-Jan–mid-Feb. **Car park. TV.**

This is a little corner of paradise. It's a rare treat in the Paris area to open your window in the early hours and find yourself gazing down at a sleepy lake. And lunch on the terrace in a similarly idyllic setting should put the finishing touches to your sense of wellbeing. Doubles with bath 320F. Set meals are 108F (weekdays), 135F and 165F. Reckon on 200F à la carte. A great place.

CHILLY-MAZARIN 91380

THYM ET BASILIC

97 rue de Gravigny.
☎ 01.69.10.92.75
Closed Sunday evenings, Mondays, and in August.

The yellow and blue dining room serves typical Provençal food and dishes like *bouillabaisse*, langoustine, prawns, pasta with lobster, and panfried *foie gras* are well presented and smell wonderful (one would hope so, given the restaurant's name!). There's a 78F *formule* at lunchtime centring around a traditional dish such as *blanquette de veau* (veal stew), and they also do great set meals for 98F and 138F.

CLAMART 92140

À LA BRÈCHE DU BOIS

7 place Jules-Hunebelle (South-West); it's opposite the Hunebelle stadium.
☎ 01.46.42.29.06 F 01.46.42.25.99
Car park.

This family hotel, which overlooks a little square, is unpretentious, clean, and quiet. It's handy for both the centre of town and Meudon forest and has rooms to suit all budgets. Doubles 140F with basin, 250F with bath. Not bad at all, but we can't say as much for the welcome.

RESTAURANT LA COSSE DES PETITS POIS

158 av. Victor-Hugo (North-East); it's a little bit outside the centre of town, 300m from the train station.
☎ 01.46.38.97.60
Closed Saturday lunchtimes, Sundays, and Aug 10–24.

There are a few round tables set up in a small pleasant dining room with a fireplace. Attentive service. Somebody in the kitchen has considerable flair. There's a good set meal at 145F. Other set meals at 195F and 260F. Reckon on paying 180–250F à la carte. House specialities include smoked Norwegian salmon on a bed of *crème de caviar*. Quite expensive but not a rip-off, considering the quality of the food and the work that goes into it.

CORBEIL-ESSONNES 91100

L'ERMITAGE*

137 bd de Fontainebleau (South); take the N7.
☎ 01.64.96.29.42 F 01.60.88.48.82
Restaurant closed Saturday evenings, Sundays, and in August.

This small establishment is very clean and well-kept and guests get a friendly welcome. Rooms are simple but perfectly adequate. Doubles 120F with basin, 160F with shower and 200F with bath. Set meals 55F and 100F.

COUDRAY-MONTCEAUX (LE) 91830 (3KM S)

RESTAURANT LA RENOMMÉE

110 berges de la Seine; it's opposite the station.
☎ 01.64.93.81.09
Closed Tuesday evenings, Wednesdays, and in October.

The setting's very restful. There's a terrace facing the Seine and on fine days you can watch the fishermen in their boats gliding along the water. The dining room's cosy and not the least bit stiff or starchy so you can relax here too. The 95F set meal (not available Sundays) offers warm sausage in puff pastry with a port sauce and roast salmon with a green olive sauce. Other set meals are available at 145F, 175F and 185F. Careful though, for if you have a bottle of wine the bill soon mounts up. People come here mainly for a change of scene. Service is affable.

COURANCES 91490

AUBERGE ARC-EN-CIEL

6 place de la République (Centre).
☎ 01.64.98.41.66
Closed Tuesday evenings and Wednesdays.

Wouldn't it be nice if all villages were like this and gave you the opportunity to tour a magnificent château, take a walk in the grounds, and then have lunch – or dinner – in one of the inns on the leafy main square that the regulars often seem to keep to themselves. This particular inn has an old-fashioned dining room, a bar, waitresses who never seem to have heard of off days or sore feet, and simple, good and inexpensive cooking. Set meals 95F and 150F (this is the gourmet one). Lovely sheltered terrace where you can sit in fine weather.

COURCOURONNES 91080

|●| LE CANAL

31 rue du Pont-Amar; it's 5km south of Ris-Orangis.
☎ 01.60.78.34.72
Closed Sundays. **Disabled access**.

It's a bit of a concrete jungle around here, but this restaurant provides a gleam of hope in what is otherwise a pretty depressing area. It's an odd little place (it's a piano bar at the weekend) but the décor and the service are just fine. The owner does the cooking and it's robust and colourful – try the duo of bream and salmon with chives, for example. There are set meals at 74F, 110F, 149F and 159F, and the pigs' trotters are as good as anything the big names can come up with.

ENGHIEN-LES-BAINS 95880

☗ VILLA MARIE-LOUISE**

49 rue de Malleville.
☎ 01.39.64.82.21 ➡ 01.39.34.87.76
Car park. **TV**.

This is a fine-looking hotel. It's not too far from the lake and there are masses of flowers in the garden in summer. The rooms are simple and comfortable, and doubles cost 250F with shower/wc and 290F with bath. This is the only place to stay in in Enghien, where it's well-nigh impossible to find a hotel room that doesn't cost an arm and a leg.

BOUFFÉMONT 95570 (11KM NE)

|●| CÔTÉ SUD – "LA FERME"

16 rue de la République; from Enghien, take the N328 to Eaubonne, then the N309 to Domont and the D44.
☎ 01.39.35.15.84
Closed Sunday evenings and Monday evenings.
Car park.

The restaurant is in the depths of the country, in what used to be a farm belonging to Baron Empain. There's a field of apple trees and maize nearby and a windy road leading to Bouffémont and you go from Greek columns to the onions and garlic of Provence – hardly your ordinary restaurant setting. Three set meals are available at 95F, 115F and 160F and the latter offers house *foie gras* of duck, kangaroo steak with two sorts of peppercorns or ostrich meat Stroganoff, farmhouse goat's cheese, and dessert. All the produce comes from small producers, and freshness and authenticity are the restaurant's watchwords. The bread is home-made using organic flour. Free apéritif on presentation of your copy of this book.

ÉTAMPES 91150

☗ HÔTEL DE L'EUROPE À L'ESCARGOT**

71 rue Saint-Jacques (North); it's near the motorway entrance for the leisure complex.
☎ 01.64.94.02.96
Closed June 20–July 30. Private **car park**. **TV**.

You'll get a very warm welcome in this small, clean and very well-kept hotel with well-equipped and comfortable rooms. Prices are extremely reasonable – doubles 150F with shower/wc, 170F with bath.

|●| LE SAINT-CHRISTOPHE

28 rue de la République (Centre).
☎ 01.64.94.69.99
Closed Wednesdays, Sunday evenings, and in August.

If you ask the owner what his speciality is, he'll tell you it's dried cod. Traditional Portuguese cooking has star billing here and though the décor's pretty awful – tiles and plastic flowers – you can eat for less than 100F (and there's a set meal for 60F!).

|●| RESTAURANT LES PILIERS**

2 place Saint-Gilles (Centre).
☎ 01.64.94.04.52
Closed Tuesday evenings and Wednesdays.

If you're keen on architecture as well as good food then you're in luck. The restaurant is 30m from the church of Saint Gilles in the oldest house in the town, which dates from the 12th century. Enter through the arcade. The staff are very pleasant and a lot of care goes into the cooking. The cheapest set meal (90F) is good and it's available every day. Other set meals 125F and 178F. Rather expensive, granted, but worth every penny. And the place does have a bit of class!

FERTÉ-GAUCHER (LA) 77320

10% ☗ |●| LE BOIS FRAIS**

32 av. des Alliés (Centre).
☎ 01.64.20.27.24 ➡ 01.64.20.38.39
Secure parking. **Closed** Mondays.

The hotel is a fine 18th century building and has large, bright and restful rooms (doubles 200–300F and there's one lovely single at 105F). The décor is a mix of British chintz and Provençal prints and it actually works.

There's a cottage style garden at the back where you can have breakfast or just sit and dream. Hilary's cooking is light and balanced and the desserts are tasty. Set meals are available at 100F – 1/4 litre of wine and coffee included – 120F and 155F. Husband Alain, who is a cultivated man and built like a rugby player, has a good selection of wines and will gladly tell you all about the region. Ask him where to go for a stroll and what you should see. All in all, a first-rate establishment and really nice owners.

10% ☗ |●| HÔTEL DU SAUVAGE**

27 rue de Paris (Centre).
☎ 01.64.04.00.19 F➔ 01.64.20.32.95
Restaurant closed on Wednesdays. **Secure parking. TV.**

This is a very old inn – the "ladies" who worked there in the late 16th century received a lot of gentlemen callers. The Teinturier family, who've been innkeepers here for six generations, have other kinds of delight to offer their guests nowadays. If you have one of the set meals, which range in price from 85F to 195F, you'll get generous helpings of traditional local dishes. Try the wonderful coddled eggs in a Brie sauce, the beef fillet in Brie or a rather curious dessert of pears with a Roquefort sauce and *nougat glacé* with honey. The fish is good too. The hotel has wood panelling in the corridors and well-kept rooms at 280F.

FONTAINEBLEAU 77300

☗ LE RICHELIEU**

4 rue Richelieu; it's a stone's throw from the palace.
☎ 01.64.22.26.46 F➔ 01.64.23.40.17
Secure parking. TV. Canal+.
This is the least expensive hotel in town and it's clean and quiet. Rooms are 220F (with shower) – 310F (with bath).
|●| Le Caveau des Ducs
24 rue de Ferrare (Centre) .
☎ 01.64.22.05.05

Your first reaction might be that you've unwittingly wandered into the palace – vaulted cellars dating from the 17th century, chandeliers and a décor reminiscent of the olden days. This is a very good restaurant, popular with the town's respectable middle-class. It offers fine classical cooking, service to match, and set meals at 105F (except Saturday evenings), 175F and 240F. If you feel like treating yourself, the one at 185F (lunchtime), which includes aperitif, wine and coffee, is worth trying. Some of the dishes – the duck breast in cider vinegar, for example, or the hot apple tart flambéd in Calvados – are reminiscent of the type of thing you'd find in Normandy.

BOIS-LE-ROI 77590 (4KM NE)

10% ☗ LE PAVILLON ROYAL***

40 av. du Général-Galliéni; it's a stone's throw from the train station.
☎ 01.64.10.41.00 F➔ 01.64.10.41.10
Car park. TV. Disabled access.

A new building, very neo-classical in style, low-key, and not aesthetically displeasing. Quiet, spacious and impeccably clean rooms cost 295F. Very romantic pool and separate games room. And the manageress says they prefer to charge two-star prices for three-star service, which is good, since we prefer that too! Warm welcome.

VULAINES-SUR-SEINE 77870 (7KM E)

|●| LE PETIT CÈDRE

17 voie de la Liberté; on the D210, follow the directions for Vulaines-centre and you'll find it at the first roundabout.
☎ 01.64.23.93.85
Closed Tuesday evenings and Wednesdays.

The restaurant is set back from the river and depends on its regulars for survival – we found it totally by chance just because we got lost. It offers a typical old-fashioned bistro décor (there's a superb 1930s bar), a warm welcome and home cooking from a woman who loves to cook. Meals are available à la carte only, with starters around 35F, main courses 50F and desserts 30F. The menu also includes one or two Greek specialities (the owner is Greek). Some of the dishes – the tarragon-flavoured *terrine* of three types of meat, for example, and the *crème brûlée* that's famous throughout the area – show a masterly hand. There are some good wines at acceptable prices. One other thing: nobody will turn up their nose if you have just a starter or a main course and that's not so common nowadays.

MONTIGNY-SUR-LOING 77690 (10KM S)

☗ |●| HÔTEL DE LA VANNE ROUGE**

rue de l'Abreuvoir; take the D148.
☎ 01.64.78.52.49 F➔ 01.64.78.52.49
Closed Sunday evenings and Mondays (Mondays only in June, July and August) and Jan 15–Feb 20. **Car park. TV.**

Situated on the banks of the Loing, this big handsome establishment has nine quiet pleasant rooms, all of them with a view of the river. Doubles 270–300. There's a large sunny terrace and you can eat with your feet practically in the water, lulled by the sound of the waterfalls alongside an old mill. They do two impeccable set meals at 98F (weekdays only) and 165F that offer dishes like fillet of zander and veal sweetbreads with morels.

CHARTRETTES 77590 (11KM)

RESTAURANT LE CHALET

37 rue Foch; take the D39.
☎ 01.60.69.65.34
Closed Wednesdays, during the February school holidays, the second fortnight in August, and the first week in September. **Car park**.

This is the last quiet village on the banks of the Seine before you reach Melun. The atmosphere in the restaurant is lively and the simple cooking is of the hearty stew variety. Substantial set meals are 68F (not available Saturday evenings and Sundays), 110F and 155F. The calf's head vinaigrette (quite fashionable these days) and the *terrine* of duck are wildly popular. It's best to reserve.

GIF-SUR-YVETTE 91190

LE BŒUF À SIX PATTES

D 128 Chemin du Moulon; take the Centre universitaire exit off the N118.
☎ 01.60.19.29.60
Car park. Disabled access.

Follow that cow! You might get a crick in the neck from looking up at the one Slavik has hanging up in this restaurant, which specializes in meat dishes. They're first-rate and served with good chips and you'd ask for a second helping if only you weren't so full up. Good set meals at 59F, 78F and 129F. Terrace.

GRIGNY 91350

CHÂTEAU DU CLOTAY***

8 rue du Port; it's on the shores of lake Viry-Châtillon.
☎ 01.69.25.89.98 Fax 01.62.25.80.22
Closed Sunday evenings. **Secure parking. TV. Canal+.**

You'll forget the row upon row of buildings that are such a blot on the landscape when, just two minutes after leaving the autoroute du Sud, you find this delightful late 17th century château on the shores of a lake. It has very stylish and quiet rooms at 390F, a pool in the grounds and a superb restaurant with set meals from 150F (fish, rib of beef, and so on) that are very good value for money.

HAUTE-ISLE 95780

LE LAPIN SAVANT***

36 route de la Vallée; it's near La Roche-Guyon
☎ 01.34.78.13.43
Closed Wednesday evenings and Thursdays.
Secure parking.

A half-timbered house with exposed beams. You'd find it hard to miss the inn, given that it's festooned in geraniums and other flowers. Very close to Normandy. Twelve bedrooms decorated in rustic style. Prices 270–330F. For a twin room reckon on 370–380F. If you fancy yourself as something of a gourmet, there are two set meals at 135F and 165F. The casserole of young rabbit, the crawfish in puff pastry and the scallops are delicious.

HOUDAN 78550

10% HÔTEL DE LA GARE

5 bd de la Gare; it's opposite the train station.
☎ 01.30.59.60.53
Closed Sunday evenings. **Car park.**

Trains are few and far between so you can be sure of a good night's sleep in this clean and simple hotel where you'll get a friendly welcome. A room with bidet and basin is 140F. The cheapest set meal is 56F (weekday lunchtimes only), going up to 75F at weekends. Very provincial dining room.

RESTAURANT DE LA POSTE

9 Grande-Rue (Centre).
☎ 01.30.59.66.36
Closed evenings and Sundays.

Lots of local shopkeepers have lunch here – the décor's rustic, the atmosphere's good, and there are lots of traditional and cold dishes on the menu. They do a 52F *formule*, which gives you hors d'œuvres from the buffet, the day's special, cheese and dessert. Reckon on paying about 70F à la carte.

HOUILLES 78800

LE GAMBETTA

41 rue Gambetta.
☎ 01.39.68.52.12

Closed Sunday evenings, Mondays, Wednesday evenings, and in August.

The area round the station is depressing and less than salubrious and yet that's where you'll find this delightful restaurant, a veritable oasis of good taste. It has two spacious and prettily decorated dining rooms where you can totally forget the outside world. They have a 120F *formule* of main course plus dessert at lunchtime and a *menu-carte* at 140F. We started with pancakes of salmon marinated in dill, accompanied by aubergine puree, which was not bad at all. Then we tried the delicious slightly honeyed ostrich breast with berries and white pepper. It wasn't ostrich in fact but emu, which is much smaller – 50 kg as opposed to 120 – and has more tender flesh. The ostrich comes from Africa, of course, while the emu is Australian. (Well you might as well know something about what you're eating!) To finish, we had a tasty chocolate *marquise* with custard. Conscientious service. In short, a pleasant surprise in a part of the world where you'd least expect it.

ISLE-ADAM (L') 95290

LE CABOUILLET**

5 quai de l'Oise; it's after Cabouillet bridge, on the right coming from the station.
☎ 01.34.69.00.90 F 01.34.69.33.88
Closed Sunday evenings and Mondays. **TV**.

This large country-style establishment is fairly plush inside, with old masters on the walls and a beautiful wooden staircase. It has five prettily decorated rooms ranging in price from 320F to 340F. It also has what is undeniably the best restaurant in Isle-Adam but you'll have break open your piggy bank to eat here. Set meals are 155Fand 195F, and on weekdays they also have a 125F *formule* (this is served on the terrace). The cooking is refined and tasty, with dishes like *foie gras* cooked three different ways, fried eel with a herb salad, *gratin* of sole with morels and pigeon with ceps. Very bucolic.

AU RELAIS FLEURI

61 rue Saint-Lazare.
☎ 01.34.69.01.85
Closed Monday evenings and Tuesdays, and Aug 6–31.

The décor is of the classic kind – blue fabric on the walls and matching curtains etc. We liked the courteous welcome we got from the Roland brothers and we also liked their use of fresh ingredients, the sophisticated style of cooking and the fact that dishes change with the season. The cheapest set meal is 155F, for which you'll get a starter, main course, cheese, salad, dessert! Good value for money in a town where a meal out is still a bit of an expensive proposition. Lovers of good food who're looking to indulge themselves might care to go à la carte and choose from dishes like *aiguillettes* of zander with leeks and *lardons confits*, roast saddle of lamb with rosemary flavoured gravy and superb desserts. There's also a enormous shady terrace where you can digest your food in pleasant surroundings

JOUY-LE-COMTE 95620 (4KM NW)

L'EDEN GOURMAND

28 rue du Maréchal-Joffre; it's opposite the church.
☎ 01.34.69.68.68
Closed Sunday evenings and Mondays.

They do nothing but fish here and it's all mouthwatering stuff. Try the seafood *pot au feu* or the cabbage stuffed with shellfish. Set meals 100F (weekday lunchtimes) and 175F.

MAISONS-LAFITTE 78600

10% AU PUR-SANG*

2 av. de la Pelouse; once you've passed the Maisons-Lafitte bridge, turn right and skirt the race course until you come to the roundabout. Avenue de la Pelouse starts to the right of the roundabout.
☎ 01.39.62.03.21 F 01.34.93.48.69
Closed Sundays, three weeks in August, and a fortnight at the end of the year. **Car park**. **TV**. **Canal+**.

This thoroughly provincial looking hotel cum restaurant sits in a dead end at the far end of the race course. Simple rooms with shower 200F. You can eat your 70F set meal (which will be something along the lines of herring fillets, steak and homemade chips, and crème caramel) in a rustic dining room or outside on the terrace. À la carte only on race days.

MARLY-LE-ROI 78160

LE RALLYE*

29 Grande-Rue (Centre).
☎ 01.39.58.47.29
The restaurant is closed in the evenings, on Sundays and in August. **Car park**. **TV**.

You'll get a friendly reception and there's a good atmosphere at the bar. The place is clean and has doubles that range in price from 140F with shower (wc on the landing) to 200F with shower/wc and TV. They do a set meal at 69F – as many hors d'œuvres as you can eat and home-made dessert.

CAFÉ ROSA

23 Grande-Rue (Centre).
☎ 01.39.16.10.70
Closed Monday lunchtimes, Tuesday lunchtimes, and Monday evenings out of season.

A small Mexican restaurant that successfully carries off the spaghetti Western posters on pink walls, the Wild West saloon chairs, the ceiling fan and the obligatory cacti. They do a good chilli for 54F. It's a bit expensive sometimes, but you can get away with 110F à la carte and during the week there's an 80F set meal at lunchtime that includes 1/4 litre of wine.

LE FOU DU ROI

6 bis Grande-Rue.
☎ 01.39.58.80.20
Closed Saturday lunchtimes and Sundays

A little restaurant with bright simple décor. There are just two set meals on offer. The lunchtime one (95F) is very good and includes 1/4 litre of wine (or drink of your choice) and coffee. The evening one (145F) is a gourmet meal of, for example, coddled eggs with truffles, monkfish or veal sweetbreads, and chocolate *parfait*. It doesn't include drink. Check the blackboard for what's on offer – it all depends on what the chef picks up in the market. Classic well balanced dishes, fresh produce, courteous service, decent prices, and a full stomach – that's what makes a good restaurant. One of our favourites in the département. The dining room's small, so it's advisable to book in advance.

MEAUX 77100

10% ACOSTEL**

How to get there: take the N3 in the direction of Châlons-sur-Marne and the hotel is on the right just before you cross the bridge and arrive in Tilport.
☎ 01.64.33.28.58 F 01.64.33.28.25
Secure parking. **TV**.

Don't be put off by the bare concrete when you first arrive – you're at the back of the hotel. The front is much more appealing – you step straight out of the front door onto a lawn and the banks of the Marne, which is quite beautiful around here. Clean and well-equipped rooms on the ground floor 245–270F.

LA TAVERNE MELDOISE

8 rue Jean-Jaurès.
☎ 01.64.34.08.46
Closed Sunday evenings.

This inn, which specializes in seafood and the cooking of Alsace, has an enormous country-style dining room and a flower filled garden. On weekdays, there's a quite acceptable 85F *formule* of starter and main course, both of them substantial. They also do a 168F set meal that includes cheese and dessert. The *choucroute* à la carte is absolutely enormous. There's a Bavarian evening every three months. A good restaurant.

MEUDON-LA-FORÊT 92360

RESTAURANT LA MARE AUX CANARDS

carrefour de la Mare-Adam (North-West); at the Meudon-Chaville exit on the N118, take the first on the left at the radio mast then head in the direction of Mare Adam.
☎ 01.46.32.07.16
Closed Sunday evenings, Mondays, the last week in August, and the first two weeks in September.

It's fairly isolated and not easy to find but then good restaurants rarely are! This is just the place for lunch after a long walk in the woods of Meudon on a sunny or misty day. The big family dining room is quite convivial, and there are ducks roasting on a spit in a handsome fireplace. You'll be welcomed in the right way and the service is fast. The terrace is very pleasant in fine weather. They have a 67F *formule* of starter plus a quarter of chicken but apart from that there are no set meals. Reckon on paying about 160F a head à la carte.

NEMOURS 77140

10% HÔTEL-RESTAURANT LES ROCHES**

1-3 av. Léopold-Pelletier; it's not far from the Rochers Gréau and the pool.
☎ 01.64.28.01.43 F 01.64.28.04.27
Closed Sunday evenings; restaurant closed Sunday evenings and Monday lunchtimes. **Secure parking**. **TV**. **Disabled access**.

Here's a restaurant that gives remarkable value for money – you're guaranteed a splendid meal from start to finish. The décor and service are both first rate. So shovel down the house *terrine* then give way to temptation and have the three sorts of fish with excellent baby vegetables. The wines are good too, there's lots of variety on the cheese platter, and the pastries are heavenly. The *menu du jour* (available weekdays) is 90F and there are four other set meals ranging in price from 155F to 280F. Quiet comfortable, recently renovated rooms 180–230F.

PARIS 75000

SEE MAP ON PAGE 312

1st Arrondissement

BVJ CENTRE INTERNATIONAL

20 rue Jean-Jacques-Rousseau; M° Louvre or Palais-Royal.
☎ 01.53.00.90.90 Fax 01.53.00.90.91

A total of 200 beds in rooms for one to eight people. Open to everyone between the ages of 6 and 35. You'll pay 120F a head, which includes breakfast. Sheets and blankets are free. 60F per meal. They won't ask to see a membership card of any kind but if you're carrying a "Jeunes" or FYITHO card, you'll get a reduction of 10%. It's a good idea to book two or three days in advance. If you haven't, turn up or phone between 9 and 9.30 in the morning to find out what they've got available. Open 24 hours a day. If it's full, the same organization runs a similar kind of hotel in the Latin Quarter. Check-out 9am.

HÔTEL HENRI IV

25 place Dauphine; M° Pont-Neuf, Saint-Michel or Cité.
☎ 01.43.54.44.53

Reservations are necessary in this small and charmingly old-fashioned but recently renovated hotel overlooking one of the prettiest squares in Paris. A total of 21 rooms. Singles 130F, doubles 160–200F and 250F if you want a shower plus a view of the square, triples with shower 260F and 285F. The shower in the corridor costs 15F but breakfast is free. Comfort is not high on the list of priorities (old furniture and flowered wallpaper). You really should book. They don't take credit cards.

HÔTEL DE LA VALLÉE*

84 rue Saint-Denis; M° Les Halles, Rambuteau or Châtelet.
☎ 01.42.36.46.99 Fax 01.42.36.16.66

Right in the heart of the Halles so you couldn't find a more central location if you tried (though all those sex shops may not be to everyone's taste), and it's pretty decent for the price. Rooms overlooking the street are 203F with basin, 253F with shower, and 283F with shower/wc. The shower in the corridor costs 15F. The rooms with a view of the courtyard (there aren't many of them, unfortunately) are quieter – if you can't get one of those, ask for one on the upper floors. Frankly, it'd be hard to find anything cheaper in the area. They take credit cards but not cheques and rooms have to be paid for in advance.

HÔTEL DE LILLE**

8 rue du Pélican; M° Palais-Royal, Louvre or Pyramides.
☎ 01.42.33.33.42

The hotel's in a quiet street that's seen a lot of history in its time. In the 14th century it was called rue du Poil-au-Con, which could be translated euphemistically as Pussy St, because of the brothels there. The more respectable of their neighbours ended up calling it rue Pélican (which caused much less of a sensation on their visiting cards). It's small – only 14 rooms – a bit romantic and slightly old-fashioned, but well looked after by a nice family. Rooms number 1, 4, 7 and 10 are very gloomy. Doubles 230F with basin, 280F with shower. They don't serve breakfast but they do have a drinks machine. Ideal if you're on a budget.

10% HÔTEL DU PALAIS*

2 quai de la Mégisserie; M° Châtelet.
☎ 01.42.36.98.25 Fax 01.42.21.41.67

The rooms, which are double-glazed, have a superb view of the Seine, the Conciergerie and Notre Dame cathedral. The higher up you are the quieter it is, but the rooms are pretty basic (so cheaper). On the 5th floor all you can see is sky, but if you stand on a chair you can get a glimpse of the Châtelet. Doubles cost 236F without a shower, 320F with shower, and 350–380F with shower/wc or bath. Readers of this guidebook will receive a reduction of 15% Jan 1–March 31. Professional welcome. People come here because of the view and the location. It's a pity the carpets are so worn and the lift shaft is showing its age. On the whole though, it's fairly clean.

10% HÔTEL DU CYGNE**

3 rue du Cygne (Centre); M° Étienne Marcel or RER Châtelet -Les Halles.

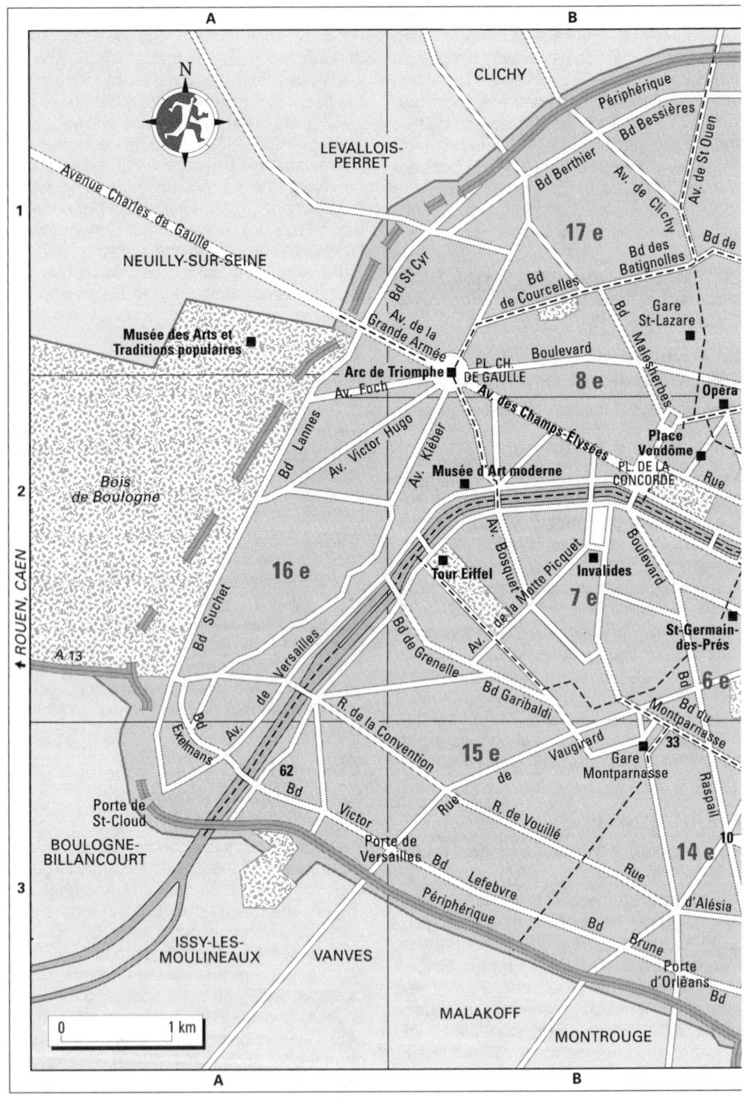
A
B
1
2
3
ROUEN, CAEN
A 13
N
CLICHY
LEVALLOIS-PERRET
NEUILLY-SUR-SEINE
Avenue Charles de Gaulle
Périphérique
Bd Bessières
Bd Berthier
Av. de St Ouen
Av. de Clichy
17 e
Bd des Batignolles
Bd de
Bd St Cyr
Bd de Courcelles
Av. de la Grande Armée
Gare St-Lazare
Bd Malesherbes
Musée des Arts et Traditions populaires
Arc de Triomphe
PL. CH. DE GAULLE
Boulevard
8 e
Av. Foch
Opéra
Av. des Champs-Élysées
Bd Lannes
Av. Victor Hugo
Av. Kléber
Place Vendôme
Musée d'Art moderne
PL. DE LA CONCORDE
Rue
Bois de Boulogne
16 e
Av. Bosquet
Tour Eiffel
Av. de la Motte Picquet
Invalides
Boulevard
7 e
St-Germain-des-Prés
Bd Suchet
Av. de Versailles
Bd de Grenelle
Bd Garibaldi
6 e
Bd Montparnasse
Bd du Montparnasse
Bd Exelmans
R. de la Convention
15 e
Vaugirard
33
Gare Montparnasse
62
Bd Victor
Rue de
R. de Vouillé
Raspail
Porte de St-Cloud
BOULOGNE-BILLANCOURT
Porte de Versailles
Bd Lefebvre
10
14 e
Rue d'Alésia
Périphérique
Bd Brune
Porte d'Orléans
Bd
ISSY-LES-MOULINEAUX
VANVES
MALAKOFF
MONTROUGE
0
1 km

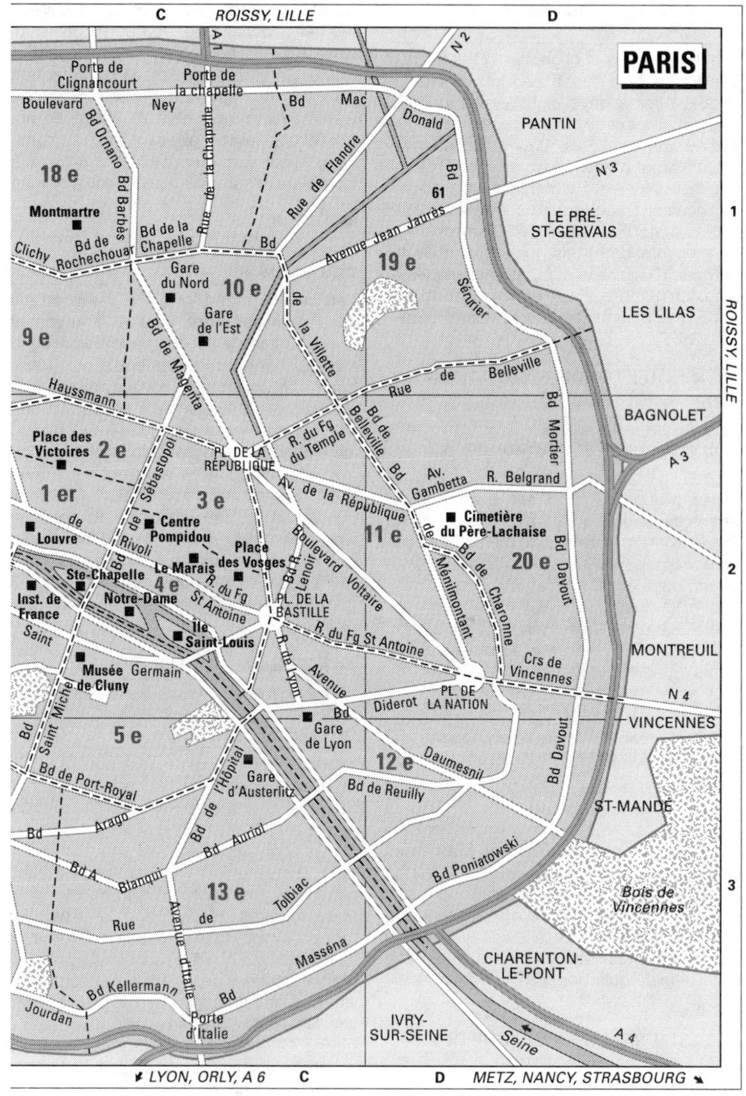
PARIS
ROISSY, LILLE
C
D
1
2
3
Porte de Clignancourt
Porte de la chapelle
Boulevard
Ney
Bd Mac Donald
Bd Ornano
Bd Barbès
Rue de la Chapelle
Rue de Flandre
18 e
Montmartre
Bd de Rochechouart
Clichy
Bd de la Chapelle
Bd 61 Sérurier
Avenue Jean Jaurès
19 e
PANTIN
N 2
N 3
LE PRÉ-ST-GERVAIS
LES LILAS
ROISSY, LILLE
BAGNOLET
A 3
Gare du Nord
10 e
Gare de l'Est
9 e
Bd de Magenta
Bd de la Villette
Rue de Belleville
Haussmann
Place des Victoires
2 e
PL. DE LA RÉPUBLIQUE
R. du Fg du Temple
Bd de Belleville
Bd Mortier
1 er
3 e
Bd Sébastopol
Av. de la République
Av. Gambetta
R. Belgrand
Louvre
Rivoli
Centre Pompidou
Le Marais
Place des Vosges
Boulevard Voltaire
Bd R. Lenoir
11 e
Cimetière du Père-Lachaise
Bd de Ménilmontant
Bd de Charonne
20 e
Bd Davout
Ste-Chapelle
4 e
Notre-Dame
Inst. de France
Ile Saint-Louis
R. du Fg St Antoine
PL. DE LA BASTILLE
MONTREUIL
Saint Germain
Musée de Cluny
R. de Lyon
Avenue Daumesnil
Crs de Vincennes
PL. DE LA NATION
N 4
Diderot
VINCENNES
Bd Saint Michel
5 e
Gare de Lyon
Gare d'Austerlitz
12 e
Bd de l'Hôpital
Bd de Port-Royal
Bd de Reuilly
ST-MANDÉ
Bd Arago
Bd A. Blanqui
Bd Auriol
Bd Poniatowski
13 e
Bois de Vincennes
Rue de Tolbiac
Avenue d'Italie
Masséna
CHARENTON-LE-PONT
Bd Kellermann
Jourdan
Porte d'Italie
IVRY-SUR-SEINE
Seine
A 4
A 1
LYON, ORLY, A 6
METZ, NANCY, STRASBOURG

☎ 01.42.60.14.16 ➡ 01.42.21.37.02
TV.

A hotel with lots of character in the heart of Les Halles in a street with lots of clothes shops. After a day's sight-seeing in Paris, relax in the pretty sitting room that's furnished with antiques. Well-equipped bedrooms. Most of them have satellite TV, safe, and hair-dryer – not to mention exposed ceiling beams. Doubles with shower/wc 420F, with bath 450F (360F and 390F respectively on presentation of this guide book). Go for number 16 which is decorated in shades or plum or number 35, a pretty suite at only 430F on presentation of this guide. Breakfast: 35F.

10% ☗ HÔTEL LONDRES SAINT-HONORÉ**

13 rue Saint-Roch; M° Tuileries.
☎ 01.42.60.15.62 ➡ 01.42.60.16.00
TV.

Here's a delightful hotel with a warm family atmosphere in an area that is not known for its friendliness. Comfortable rooms with flowered wallpaper all come with bath or shower/wc, double glazing, satellite TV, and minibar. Doubles 490–550F. Go for one overlooking rue Saint-Roch – they're quieter. Breakfast 35F. There are a number of car parks round about the hotel.

10% ☗ HÔTEL AGORA**

7 rue de la Cossonnerie; M° Les Halles or Châtelet.
☎ 01.42.33.46.02 ➡ 01.42.33.80.99
TV.

The street dates back to the 12th century and owes its name to the "cossons" or second-hand dealers who had their businesses here. The hotel has been well renovated in modern colours and has a small and tastefully laid-out foyer. Rooms are pleasant and unfussy. Doubles with shower or bath/wc 550–655F, breakfast 40F. It's a great little hotel – fairly quiet for this lively neighbourhood.

|●| RESTAURANT À LA CLOCHE DES HALLES

28 rue Coquillière; M° Louvre or Les Halles
☎ 01.42.36.93.89
Closed Saturday evenings, Sundays, public holidays, and two weeks in August.

Service until about 9pm. No false beams or farm tools hanging on the walls, just a bell over the entrance, which used to sound the opening and closing of the market (in the days when there was a market here). When the bell (cloche) rang, you could gather up what was left – hence the word "clochard" or tramp. Serge Lesage bottles the wine from his own little vineyard himself. For food, there's *charcuterie*, ham on the bone and farm cheese. A very pleasant place for something to eat at good prices. Reckon on 60F for a plate of something and a glass of wine.

|●| HIGUMA

32 [bis] rue Sainte-Anne; M° Pyramides.
☎ 01.47.03.38.59

Service 11.30am–10pm. This is a good little Japanese restaurant, a sort of upmarket works canteen where the people working for the Japanese companies in the neighbourhood turn up in droves for a quick but substantial meal. Various clear soups (40–46F) which won't leave you still feeling hungry, large helpings of sautéd noodles (48F) and a few goodies such as excellent fried ravioli (32F). Perfect set meal at 63F. Sit at the counter so you can admire the deftness with which the Japanese chefs knead the noodles or toss the vegetables in enormous woks. Don't count on getting a smile or even a look from them – at these prices you can't complain!

|●| RESTAURANT LA FRESQUE

100 rue Rambuteau; M° Étienne-Marcel or Les Halles.
☎ 01.42.33.17.56
Closed Sunday lunchtimes.

Service until midnight. This convivial little restaurant, housed in what used to be a shop that sold snails, is the kind of place where you're almost sitting in your neighbour's lap. It's fashionable, yet friendly and cosmopolitan and the atmosphere is laid-back. It's also extremely good-looking, with its old white tiles, coloured frescos, and long wooden tables. If you take the quick *formule* at lunchtime you'll get a substantial meal of starter, carefully prepared main course, 1/4 litre of wine and coffee for 65F. Long may it last! No set meals in the evening – reckon on paying 120F à la carte. Every day there are good starters, three or four traditional dishes as the main course, each with an original touch, and one vegetarian dish, which is unusual.

|●| CITÉ SAINT-HONORÉ

154 rue Saint-Honoré; M° Palais-Royal or Louvre.
☎ 01.42.60.62.01
Open every day.

Service at lunchtime and in the evening until 11pm. The small rustic-looking dining room is full to bursting point at lunchtime because of the robust 70F set meal (wine included). Upstairs there are two other rooms which are a bit more airy. At lunchtime, they do the type of dishes your Mum makes (if your Mum can cook!), while if you like the cooking of the south-west there are a few specialities from that region in the evening 85F set meal which offers things like good hors d'œuvres, veal chops with ceps, home-made cassoulet *au confit*, duck with prunes, *confits*, and home-made tart *fondante*. Reckon on 150F à la carte.

RESTAURANT FOUJITA

41 rue Saint-Roch; M° Pyramides or Tuileries.
☎ 01.42.61.42.93

Lunch served until 2pm and dinner until 10pm. One of the best reasonably-priced sushi bars in Paris. They do very substantial set meals at lunchtime for around 70F – there's sushi, *sashimi* (raw fish) and *natto* (bowl of rice with a topping of raw fish). Unfortunately, it's extremely small and smells of fish a bit. It's always full (which is a good sign) so try to get there early. There's also a much larger sister restaurant called *Foujita 2* at 7 rue du 29 juillet (which runs parallel to rue Saint-Roch), tel: 01.49.26.07.70.

RESTAURANT AU RENDEZ-VOUS DES CAMIONNEURS

72 quai des Orfèvres; M° Cité or Pont-Neuf.
☎ 01.43.54.88.74

Service at lunchtime and in the evening until 11.30. Reservations advisable. Very popular with people who work locally because of its good home cooking, and lawyers, police officers, journalists, tourists and gays all squeeze into the dining room together to chat in extremely relaxed surroundings. The bill won't ruin your day – set meals 78F (weekdays lunchtime), 98F and 128F. Day's special 60F. Reckon on paying 170F à la carte.

CA D'ORO

54 rue de l'Arbre-Sec; M° Louvre.
☎ 01.40.20.97.79
Closed Sundays and Aug 5–17.

Service until 11pm. This welcoming and unobtrusive little restaurant doesn't have ideas above its station and sticks to what it does best. Go through a tiny room and down a narrow corridor and you'll come to another room decorated – in low-key fashion – with scenes of Venice, the chef's home town. Treat yourself to *bruschetta* (a slice of toast rubbed with garlic and covered with olive oil, basil and tomato) for 30F or grilled peppers with basil (50F) before turning your attention to the pasta – there's spaghetti Elizabeth Taylor (tomatoes, olive oil and basil) at 55F, *penne disperata* (garlic, anchovies, capers and olive oil) at 60F, home-made ravioli at 55F or, for two, an excellent risotto (ceps or seafood) at 130F. Reckon on paying 130–160F with a little wine. The lunchtime *menu complet* at 80F (wine not included) is very good.

CAFÉ VÉRY

jardin des Tuileries; M° Tuileries.
☎ 01.47.03.94.84

Service until 11pm. Perfect place for a bite to eat on the terrace after an exhausting trip round the Louvre. Sit back, relax, and have another read of your guidebook before setting off to explore this historic neighbourhood. Tables are hard to come by on sunny days. Reckon on about 90F.

RESTAURANT LESCURE

7 rue de Mondovi; M° Concorde.
☎ 01.42.60.18.91
Closed Saturday evenings, Sundays, and usually in August.

Service at lunchtime and in the evening. Regulars get a warmer welcome than other people do in what is a very good restaurant considering that it's in the financial district. It's quite surprising to find chicken with rice or a beef *bourguignon* for less than 56F in this part of Paris. And the chicken dish is very substantial! The cooking may be bourgeois but the prices aren't – the 100F set meal offers real starters (delicious mackerel), generous helpings of the main dish (fried breaded haddock), a choice of cheese or dessert, and a half bottle of wine. There's even a chicken croquette at 27.50F! Even the three-piece suit types come here at lunchtime. The dining room's country style décor may not strike you as quite the genuine article but that's not important. In the evening, they sit people at the big communal table at the back of the room, which helps create a relaxed atmosphere. And, in summer, tables on the terrace go like hot cakes.

RESTAURANT L'ÉPI D'OR

25 rue Jean-Jacques-Rousseau; M° Louvre or Palais-Royal.

☎ 01.42.36.38.12
Closed Saturday lunchtimes, Sundays and in August.

Service at lunchtime and in the evening until 11.30pm. Delightful old-style bistro – the kind of place that used to be so common around les Halles – full of antique everyday objects. The 105F set meal offers fillets of herring, beef salad, rib steak in a wine, tarragon and shallot sauce, and *andouillette* in an Aligoté wine sauce. If you'd rather go à la carte, there's house steak tartare (92F), fish stew (90F), and a small ham *à la lyonnaise* for two people (205F). Reckon on paying about 200F. Before eating, have a stroll through passage Véro-Dadat which is almost next door to the restaurant.

|●| RESTAURANT AUX TONNEAUX DES HALLES

28 rue Montorgueil; M° Étienne-Marcel
☎ 01.42.33.36.19
Closed Sundays.

Service 7am–11pm. You might think that the market porters had never left, judging by this good-natured bistro. Inside, there have been no concessions to modernism for once and they haven't turned it into an imitation old-fashioned bistro either. The old fresco that has developed a patina over the years is still there at the back, as are the three doors leading to the phone booth, the loo and the kitchen. The barrels outside set the tone. Most of the customers are regulars. The boss used to be a regular winner of the waiters' race, as the trophies above the bar indicate, but he's barred from taking part now because he was too good. The menu isn't very long for meat reigns supreme here, particularly the ribsteak – a substantial piece of superb beef – in a wine, tarragon and shallot sauce (68F). Wash it down with some Beaujolais or a Loire wine. Reckon on 130F à la carte.

|●| WILLI'S WINE BAR

13 rue des Petits-Champs; M° Palais-Royal.
☎ 01.42.61.05.09
Closed Sundays.

The kitchen is open 11am–11pm and the bar until midnight. This is the chic type of wine bar. It's tastefully decorated, the wood gives it a cosy feel, the lighting's perfect, and there are big round tables for large groups of friends and pretty posters on the walls. *Willi's* is a magnet for British businessmen in Paris, lovers of good wine, Stock Exchange yuppies, and the lovely ladies from Place des Victoires. The food consists of a few elaborate dishes and original salads whose primary purpose is to act as a foil for the tremendous Côtes du Rhone, of which the owner is a great connoisseur. However, you'll also find Spanish, Californian and Italian wines on offer. A lot of wines are available by the glass. Excellent cheeses. Reckon on 100F for a wine tasting and 195F for a meal: *menu-carte* 145F(weekdays lunchtime), 180F (in the evening).

|●| RESTAURANT LA POULE AU POT

9 rue Vauviliers; M° Louvre or Les Halles.
☎ 01.42.36.32.96
Closed Mondays.

Service 7pm–6am. If you're around les Halles at 2 o'clock in the morning and suddenly feel peckish, make a beeline for this place. The long room is decorated with posters and copper pots, retro lighting that give the place a certain intimacy and a pleasant brasserie atmosphere. The service is well-mannered which is not always the case in this neighbourhood and the menu offers some oldies but goodies such as *pot-au-feu*, ribsteak with marrowbone and of course the *poule au pot* the restaurant is called after. Set meal at 160F. Reckon on paying about 230F. It's always crowded when things like the good home show are on.

|●| RESTAURANT PHARAMOND

24 rue de la Grande-Truanderie; M° Étienne-Marcel.
☎ 01.42.33.06.72
Closed Sundays and Monday lunchtimes.

Kitchen closes at 10.45pm. Advisable to book. More than 150 years ago, a man from Caen in Normandy arrived in the big city with a delicious recipe for tripe the way his Mum made it. That was the beginning of a dominance which has lasted to the present day. The restaurant is pure 1900s (and is a listed monument of course) – superb ceramics, painted beams, engraved and enamelled mirrors, and a funny narrow winding staircase leading to the private rooms upstairs that have seen many famous people come and go, not least the French President. One or two things have been added to the menu since 1850. As well as *tripe à la mode de Caen* (which is tripe cooked with pig's trotters and cider), there's grilled rib of beef served with marrowbone, duckling in lemon sauce, scallops in cider, cod with couscous spices, and so on. Main courses. Set meals 200F and 310F (drink included); main courses à la carte 85–145F, and you should reckon on about 280F in all – a bit expensive for a style of cooking that seems to be resting on its laurels. Customers at lunch time are mainly businessmen and middle-class provincials. Service is in the grand style. They also do tripe to take away.

2nd Arrondissement

10% ☗ HÔTEL SAINTE-MARIE*

6 rue de la Ville-Neuve; M° Bonne-Nouvelle.
☎ 01.42.33.21.61 ➡ 01.42.33.29.24
Secure parking. TV.

This is a pretty little hotel in a quiet street, very close to the fashionable shopping area of the Grands Boulevards. It has 20 or so very well looked after rooms.If you take one of the two attic rooms, mind you don't bang your head – the ceilings really are low. Doubles without shower 206F, with shower 281F; triples with shower/wc 392F. Breakfast 20F.

☗ TIQUETONNE HÔTEL*

6 rue Tiquetonne; M° Étienne-Marcel or Réaumur-Sébastopol.
☎ 01.42.36.94.58 ➡ 01.42.36.02.94
Closed in August.

Enjoy the quietness and beauty of the pedestrianized streets as you make your way to this one-star hotel. They care more about the impression their guests make than they do about the money they bring in, so it's no good trying to make a reservation for friends – the proprietress will want to see them first. The rooms are very well looked after (but the décor is less than appealing), they're quiet and some are larger than others. The ones on the first two floors have double-glazing and are quieter. Double with shower/wc 246F. Breakfast 25F.

10% ☗ HÔTEL BONNE NOUVELLE**

17 rue Beauregard; M° Bonne Nouvelle or Strasbourg-Saint-Denis.
☎ 01.45.08.42.42 ➡ 01.40.26.05.81
TV.

This pleasant little hotel, situated in a street that's very quiet even though it's not far from the fashionable shopping area of the Grands Boulevards, makes you feel you've wandered into the pages of *The Old Curiosity Shop*. In the breakfast room a stuffed cobra stares glassily across the room at the model of a covered wagon and the skin of some reptile that you most certainly would not like to run into. And as you head for the lift, you'll pass old maps of Paris. The rooms, all different and a subtle mix of the old and new (bath, wc, TV, direct phone and hair dryers), are sheer delight; number 26 is rather dark and you open the skylight in the bathroom with a system of counterweights. There's one suite for 610F or thereabouts (ideal for four), which has a splendid view of the Pompidou Centre, the Montparnasse tower, and the rooftops of Paris stretching to the horizon. Doubles range in price from 330F with basin to 390F with bath. Breakfast 30F (35F if you want it in your room).

☗ HÔTEL VIVIENNE**

40 rue Vivienne; M° Rue-Montmartre, Richelieu-Drouot or Bourse.
☎ 01.42.33.13.26 ➡ 01.40.41.98.19

Most of the hotel's neighbours are shops specializing in coins and medals. It's very close to the *Hard Rock Café*, *Musée Grevin* (the wax museum), and *Théâtre des Variétés* (the music hall), and there are countless lanes and narrow streets to explore. Warm and informal welcome. The rooms, which have been recently refurbished, are bright, clean, comfortable and quiet. If you're on the fifth or sixth floor you'll have a nice view. A few rooms have a balcony. Doubles 350F with shower, 430F with shower/wc, and 450–495F with bath. Breakfast 40F.

☗ GRAND HÔTEL BESANÇON***

56 rue de Montorgueil; M°Étienne Marcel or RER Châtelet-les Halles.
☎ 01.42.36.41.08 ➡ 01.45.08.08.79
TV. Disabled access

A new, clean and pretty hotel, squeezed between a bar-restaurant and a drugstore in a lively pedestrian street in the Réaumur area, a stone's throw from Les Halles. The Louis-Phillipe style furniture and the marble reception area add to the charm of this elegant hotel. Doubles with shower 560–590F, with bath 620–680F. Breakfast 40F (free on your first morning on presentation of this guide). A few of the rooms (number 12 for example) have a very nice little sitting area.

10% ☗ HÔTEL FRANCE D'ANTIN***

22 rue d'Antin; M° 4-Septembre or Opéra, RER Auber.
☎ 01.47.42.19.12 ➡ 01.47.42.11.55

This very pleasant three-star hotel located 100m from the Opéra Garnier and the Louvre, is classy and at the same time congenial, with a décor that includes wall hangings, a player piano, beige and dark green marble and chairs in the lobby, and, in the public rooms in the basement, exposed stonework and vaulted ceilings. The 30 rooms are pretty and equipped with the usual minibars, satellite TV etc; all are air-conditioned for those who can't stand the heat of a Paris summer. About 700F for a double. Breakfast 40F.

|●| RESTAURANT CHEZ DANIE

5 rue de Louvois; M° Richelieu-Drouot.
☎ 01.42.96.64.05
Closed evenings, Saturdays and Sundays.

This tiny restaurant a stone's throw from the *Bibliothèque nationale* is a bargain. *Bœuf ficelle*, goulash, and sautéd pork *à la flamande* are some of the main dishes on offer and they change every day. All the desserts are homemade. Offering as it does such great value for money, *Chez Danie* really stands out in an area full of mediocre and expensive sandwich shops. You can have a full meal for 54F.

|●| BAR-RESTAURANT LES VARIÉTÉS

12 passage des Panoramas; M° Rue-Montmartre
☎ 01.42.36.98.09
Closed Saturdays, Sundays, and in August.

Service at lunchtime and until 10pm (or maybe 11 – it depends). Forget the fast food outlets of the Grands Boulevards. Just five minutes away, in one of the area's most delightful narrow streets, is this old-fashioned Paris café. It's popular with people who work nearby who come for the owner's cooking rather than his jokes (which tend to fall flat). For about 85F at lunchtime and not much more in the evening you can eat before or after the theatre in an establishment that gives you a glimpse of what Paris used to be like. Day's special 48F.

|●| RESTAURANT LE CAFÉ DES THÉÂTRES

17 rue de Choiseul; M° 4-Septembre.
☎ 01.42.65.77.40
Closed Saturday lunchtimes and Sundays.

Lunch served noon–2.30pm and dinner 7–11.30pm. The whereabouts of this restaurant – halfway between the Opéra and the Stock Exchange – seems to be a matter of some secrecy. It's the kind of eating establishment that leads a double life – at lunchtime, Stock Exchange operators and whizz kids come for the 108F set meal, while in the evening it's full of theatre goers and opera lovers having a late supper. This chocolate box of a restaurant is a little affected but the cooking has its attractions. And the *carte-menu* (143F all in) spares you any unpleasant surprises. The perfectly adequate classics – *millefeuille* of sea bass and salmon, mullet in a vanilla sauce, chocolate profiteroles – are what make the difference. The chef may not be a genius but he – or she – gives a good solid workmanlike performance.

3rd arrondissement

10% ⌂ HÔTEL DU VIEUX SAULE**

6 rue de Picardie; M° République or Temple.
☎ 01.42.72.01.14 ➡ 01.40.27.88.21
Secure parking. TV.

This quiet elegant hotel with window boxes and a tiny flower garden is a stone's throw from lively rue de Bretagne. Modern and very comfortable doubles with shower/wc 380–480 or bath 480–510F. Avoid the one on the ground floor with bars at the windows! All rooms come with hair dryer, trouser press, telephone, safe, and cable TV (26 channels), and there's a free sauna. Pleasant staff. Breakfast (45F) is served buffet-style in a 16th century vaulted cellar.

|●| RESTAURANT L'ALISIER

26 rue de Montmorency; M° Arts-et-Métiers.
☎ 01.42.72.31.04
Closed Saturdays, Sundays, and in August.

You'll be delighted with this comfortable and elegant Paris bistro, especially since the food lives up to the décor. The suggestions include goat's cheese ravioli, *foie gras* with a sauce made from duck stock, and caramelized breast of veal with cumin and honey. And for dessert, try the mocha *millefeuille* with an iced cofee and liquorice sauce. The chef studied with Passard and Kéréver among others before taking over the kitchen here. They do a businessman's set meal at lunchtime for 180F, which includes wine and coffee and changes every week.

4th arrondissement

10% ⌂ |●| HÔTEL M.I.J.E. LE FAUCONNIER

11 rue Fauconnier; M° Saint-Paul.
☎ 01.42.74.23.45 ➡ 01.40.27.81.64

A superbly renovated 17th century town house with an imposing entrance in the form of a carved wooden door. Inside there are big old linen closets, massive chests, long rustic tables, and a magnificent staircase with a wrought iron banister. In summer, you can have breakfast on the patio. Rooms sleep 4-8. Basin and shower in the rooms, wc in the corridor. For prices, see *M.I.J.E. Maubuisson* below.

10% HÔTEL M.I.J.E. FOURCY

6 rue de Fourcy; M° Saint-Paul.
☎ 01.42.74.23.45 F 01.40.27.81.64

The hotel is a 17th century town house prettily situated between Place des Vosges and île Saint-Louis. The renovators have done a magnificent job and the building now houses clean-living youngsters who are quite surprised to find themselves living in this palace. There's a small garden at the corner of rue Charlemagne and the two buildings are linked by medieval-looking wooden bridges. Reckon on about 125F a night per person (breakfast included) in rooms with basin and shower (wc in the corridor) that sleep 4-8. Set meal 52F, formule of dish of the day plus drink and coffee 40F. Dining room.

10% HÔTEL M.I.J.E. MAUBUISSON

12 rue des Barres; M° Saint-Paul or Pont-Marie.
☎ 01.42.74.23.45 F 01.40.27.81.64

The hotel – a magnificent medieval building with an overhanging upper storey, half-timbering, stepped gables and so on – is in a quiet street with a view of the church. It's tastefully decorated inside with Gothic style doors and old heavy furniture. Rooms with shower that sleep four cost 125F a head with breakfast.

GRAND HÔTEL DU LOIRET*

8 rue des Mauvais-Garçons; M° Hôtel-de-Ville.
☎ 01.48.87.77.00 F 01.48.04.96.56

There's nothing grand about this place but the name. The rooms are fairly small and you should go for one that's been refurbished (the ones that haven't been are pretty depressing). They're all clean, though. Doubles with shower 220F. New doubles 300F and triples 400F (with bath, hair dryer and TV). Breakfast 30F.

HÔTEL ANDRÉA**

3 rue Saint-Bon; M° Châtelet or Hôtel-de-Ville.
☎ 01.42.78.43.93
TV.

The hotel, housed in a building that dates from the last century, is in a quiet street very close to the incredibly noisy rue de Rivoli. Rooms are decent and all have a phone and a TV. Doubles with basin 240F, with shower/wc 320–350F. Double-glazing.. Breakfast 30F.

GRAND HÔTEL JEANNE D'ARC**

3 rue de Jarente; M° Saint-Paul, Chemin-Vert or Bastille; RER Châtelet.
☎ 01.48.87.62.11 F 01.48.87.37.31
TV.

You couldn't find a better location than this quiet neighbourhood – you won't hear a sound – near beautiful place Sainte-Catherine. The hotel is well kept and quite delightful – it's stylishly decorated in blues and salmon pinks, has murals in the lounges and dining rooms, and the banisters, furniture and even the door numbers can all be described as decorative. The enormous mirror in the foyer which was made by a local artist is worth a look. A cot can be provided on request. Pets welcome. All of the rooms have been refurbished and have shower/wc or bath, phone and cable TV. Doubles range in price from 305 (with cot if necessary) to 490F, triples 530F, and rooms that sleep four 590F. Extra bed 75F. Breakfast 35F. It's essential to book.

HÔTEL SÉVIGNÉ**

2 rue Mahler; M° Saint-Paul or Bastille.
☎ 01.42.72.76.17 F 01.42.78.58.26

A reasonably priced and very well-kept hotel in a fairly quiet street in the heart of the Marais. Singles 335F, doubles 355F with shower, 360F with bath.

HÔTEL DU 7E ART**

20 rue Saint-Paul; M° Saint-Paul or Sully-Morland.
☎ 01.42.77.04.03 F 01.42.77.69.10
TV.

A fairly friendly hotel that's well looked after. The staircase is black, the walls are white, and the rooms are decorated with photomontages and posters for films made in the 40s, 50s and 60s. Film fans like the idea and it gives the rooms character. Doubles with shower or bath, TV (25 French and foreign channels) and so on 410–470F. Little suites with sloping roofs 600–650F. Breakfast 45F. There's a bar on the ground floor. Unusual display case with plaster figures of Ray Charles, Mickey Mouse, Donald Duck, Laurel and Hardy and so on.

HÔTEL DE LA PLACE DES VOSGES**

12 rue de Birague; M° Saint-Paul or Bastille.
☎ 01.42.72.60.46 F 01.42.72.02.64
TV.

The hotel is in the posh street leading from place des Vosges to the Pavillon du Roi and has 16 not very large but quiet and comfortable rooms. The furniture's not great but the place is impeccably clean. Doubles with bath/wc 475–490F, singles with shower 330F. Breakfast 30F. Rather a chilly welcome.

HÔTEL SAINT-LOUIS***

75 rue Saint-Louis-en-l'Île; M° Pont-Marie.
☎ 01.46.34.04.80 F→ 01.46.34.02.13.
Car park. TV. Disabled access.

Elegant middle-class establishment with antique furniture as befits the neighbourhood. Rooms are not very large but they're comfortable at 695–795F with shower/wc or bath. Breakfast 49F.

RESTAURANT LE PETIT GAVROCHE

15 rue Sainte-Croix-de-la-Bretonnerie; M° Saint-Paul or Hôtel-de-Ville.
☎ 01.48.87.74.26
Closed Saturday lunchtimes and Sundays. Open evenings only in August.

Last orders 11.30pm. A good restaurant that's been around for more than 15 years and is very popular with the locals. There's still the same nice atmosphere here – you feel at ease standing in the crowd at the bar. There are two screamingly funny and supposedly educational pictures on the wall depicting the evils of the demon drink, while above the tin-topped bar there's a drawing – a genuine one – by Poulbot, a French artist who went in for rather sentimental drawings of street urchins. They do dishes like escalope *normande*, veal chop with warm goat's cheese,mixed grill and sirloin steak with Roquefort cheese and whatever's available that particular day is chalked up on the blackboard. There's a substantial set meal for 45F at lunchtime and 48F in the evening (wine extra). If you're not all that hungry, the house salad will be more than ample – they believe in filling your plate here. It may not be haute cuisine but it's good nosh that fills your belly and doesn't empty your wallet. Upstairs is quieter.

RESTAURANT LA THÉIÈRE DANS LES NUAGES

14 rue Cloche-Perce; M° Saint-Paul.
☎ 01.42.71.96.11
Closed Sundays and in August.

A tiny restaurant offering authentic home cooking Guadeloupe style. The *accras* are light and spicy, the stuffed crab is succulent, and the Caribbean black pudding is very good. The main courses – fish cooked in its own juices, kid, *marmite créole* (smoked pork, kidney beans and flour dumplings) – show equal attention to detail and the desserts – coconut flan and coffee bush (coffee icecream, cold coffee, rum, fruit juice, spices and whipped cream) – are tempting. Good set meals range in price from 45F (lunchtimes only) to 108F. A few tables are set outside in fine weather.

RESTAURANT PICCOLO TEATRO

6 rue des Écouffes; M° Saint-Paul.
☎ 01.42.72.17.79
Closed Mondays and in August.

Service until 11pm. If you want excellent vegetarian food in pleasant surroundings, look no further. The décor consists of small wooden tables that promote togetherness, soft lights, and a few exposed beams. People who eat "rabbit food" aren't pale and sad and they certainly don't lack a sense of humour, judging by the names given to dishes such as a "caviar" of carrots, baby onions and coriander or warm goat's cheese. These are rather good – there's poetry on the plates as well as on the menu. They also do good *gratins* and a very substantial vegetarian plate. Our only criticisms are that the *tarte Tatin* was not what it should have been and the service was a bit slow. Reckon on paying 80F maximum à la carte. Set meals available at 48F at lunchtime.

RESTAURANT AU RENDEZ-VOUS DES AMIS

10 rue Sainte-Croix-de-la-Bretonnerie; M° Saint-Paul or Hôtel-de-Ville.
☎ 01.42.72.05.99
Closed lunchtimes, Sundays, Mondays, and September.

Open till 1am. This family restaurant has a warm atmosphere – friends gather here – and relaxed service and the proprietress is lovely. This is as refreshing a place as *Le Petit Gavroche* just along the street. It offers good traditional cooking and fresh salads and does a set meal at lunchtime for 60F. Reckon on paying about 90–120F à la carte. The restaurant is popular with local artists and has exhibitions of paintings and photographs.

RESTAURANT LE PETIT PICARD

42 rue Sainte-Croix-de-la-Bretonnerie; M° Rambuteau.
☎ 01.42.78.54.03
Closed Saturday and Sunday lunchtimes and all day Monday.

On weekdays, the restaurant is full at lunchtime because of the 64F *formule* (starter, main course, dessert and 1/4 litre of wine), undeniably one of the best bargains to be had in the neighbourhood. You can choose from seven starters (*crudités*, herring and potato salad and so on), five main courses (including ham in a Madeira sauce with green beans, panfried trout, chicken and rice), and five desserts. You'll get a decent and substantial meal and good service. The evening *formule* at 84F isn't much more elaborate and means you don't have to break open your piggy bank. A fairly hetero clientele at lunchtime but gays seem to predominate in the evening – you have been warned!

|●| RESTAURANT LE TEMPS DES CERISES

31 rue de la Cerisaie; M° Bastille or Sully-Morland.
☎ 01.42.72.08.63
Closed Saturdays, Sundays, and in August. No restaurant in the evening but you can get a drink until 8pm.

This picturesque low-ceilinged late 18th century building used to house the office of the Celestine convent's bursar but has been a bistro since 1900. They shot the Farah Fawcett film *Beate Klarsfeld's Story* here. The décor looks familiar right away – zinc top to the bar, marble-topped tables and imitation leather banquettes – and the day's menu is written up on a blackboard. That, plus the photos of Paris in the old days, the cheerful atmosphere, and the good-natured customers are reminders of what a Paris bistro used to be. They do a good set meal and it's unbeatable value at 68F – in other words, get there at 12 o'clock on the dot if you want a table.

|●| RESTAURANT L'ENOTECA

25 rue Charles-V; M° Saint-Paul.
☎ 01.42.78.91.44
Closed one week in August and one week between Christmas and New Year's Day.

Open 7 days a week till 2am. This wine bar, which specializes in Italian wines, almost qualifies as a must. It's full every evening and attracts a very Parisian clientele – it's not unusual to spot faces of the "I'm sure I've seen him/her on telly" variety. The décor is fairly Spartan but typically Marais – exposed beams, old stonework. The famous, the not so famous and the downright obscure come here to sample the wide range of Italian wines (the ones available by the glass change every week, which means you can travel north to south tasting the whites of Trentino and Sicily or the reds of Piedmont and Basilicata) and nibble on *antipasti misti* (60F), *crostini* with Parma ham and mozzarella (60F) or fresh pasta with beef stew, chicken livers and tomatoes (65F). Worth mentioning if only for its curiosity value is the dried horsemeat in olive oil and lemon juice (75F). Reckon on paying about 170–250F. A 75F *formule* of starter plus pasta and a glass of wine is available at lunchtime.

|●| RESTAURANT LES FOUS DE L'ILE

33 rue des Deux-Ponts; M° Pont-Marie.
☎ 01.43.25.76.67
Closed Mondays.

Service noon–11pm. This is primarily a restaurant, but it also does teas in the afternoon. There's a nice set meal at lunchtime for 75F but we've always preferred their sweet things to their savoury. In the evening, reckon on 140F à la carte. Sunday brunch (3 *formules* 100–140F). Live music – jazz, blues etc – every second Tuesday from 10pm.

|●| RESTAURANT BARACANE

38 rue des Tournelles; M° Bastille.
☎ 01.42.71.43.33
Closed Saturday lunchtimes and Sundays.

Lunch noon–2.30pm and dinner 7pm–midnight. *L'Oulette* may have moved to Bercy and *Baracane* opened up in its place but we haven't lost by it, especially since this tiny bistro is a kind of offshoot of *L'Oulette*. The word has spread and you have to fight for a table at both lunch and dinner, when the hordes descend. And how right they are. The 125F set meal (wine included) offers tremendous value for money and is available at lunchtime and in the evening. At lunchtime they also do a *formule* at 82F and there's another at 215F that starts with an apéritif and ends with coffee, taking in wine along the way. The cooking of the south-west – and of Gascony in particular – predominates, with dishes like a superb salad of duck hearts and gizzards, strips of veal braised in Cahors wine, tasty grilled breast of duck and a *croustillant* of apples in aged plum brandy, all of it washed down with excellent wines from the south-west, including a very fine Madiran (55F for 1/3 of a litre or 15F a glass). Prices like these are quite incredible, even if à la carte is rather expensive (reckon on 200F). Success hasn't had any effect on the service, which is attentive and pleasant.

|●| RESTAURANT AU BOURGUIGNON DU MARAIS

52 rue François-Miron (Centre); M° Saint-Paul or Hôtel de Ville.

☎ 01.48.87.15.40
Closed Sundays, public holidays, mid-July–mid & Aug.

Service 10.30am–10.30pm. Jacques and Christine Bavard who run this very cosy wine-tasting establishment come from a wine-making background in Burgundy. The tables are quite far apart so you won't feel you're sitting in your neighbour's lap. You may be lunching and dining with the very best of Marais society – journalists, designers and so on – but the atmosphere is still relaxed (Jacques runs a bistro, not a fashionable restaurant). Some dishes such as steak tartare (90F for 180 grams), duck *confit* (75F) and *andouillette* in an Aligoté wine sauce are always on the menu. Daily specials – a bit more expensive at about 110F – are chalked up on the blackboard. A good economic suggestion is to have the house *jambon persillé* (48F) followed by a platter of seven types of mature cheese with toast (70F). As far as liquid refreshment is concerned, wine is available by the glass, including a red burgundy from Féry-Meunier and a '92 Volnay "premier cru" from Henri Boillot. One more thing in its favour is that the tradition of "corkage" still holds good here. You can choose a 92 Jayer Gilles Hauts Côtes de Beaune from the cellar and have it with your meal for a mark-up of just 35F. The average price for a bottle is about 200F, but it depends on which vintage you go for.

RESTAURANT LE GRIZZLI

7 rue Saint-Martin; M° Hôtel de Ville or Châtelet.
☎ 01.48.87.77.56
Closed Sundays.

An oldie but goodie. The fact that Bernard Arény is now in charge of the kitchen is a guarantee of professionalism in matters culinary, something frequently lacking in this particular neighbourhood. Reckon on paying about 170F à la carte or there's a set meal at lunchtime for 115F and in the evening for 155F. We can recommend the *daube* of duck, the rabbit with raisins, the squid in its own ink, the *cassoulet*, and the beef and lamb cooked on a hot stone, the latter specialities of the Pyrenees where Bernard Arény comes from. There are wines to gladden the heart of any wine-lover – the Côtes du Marmandais, for example, served in a small carafe.

RESTAURANT À L'ESCALE

1 rue des Deux-Ponts; M° Pont-Marie.
2 quai d'Orléans
☎ 01.43.54.94.23
Closed evenings and Wednesdays, and in August.

In this rather pleasant restaurant (which gets the sun on the side facing the Seine), people up from the provinces who've been doing the stint between Notre Dame and Ile Saint-Louis will find all the comfort they need in the day's special (60F) lovingly prepared by Madame Tardieu, who's a second mother to her customers. *Pot-au-feu*, roast farm-bred veal, *coq au vin*, and grills are all good and can be accompanied by a glass of wine from Irancy or Touraine or somewhere else, all selected by Mr Tardieu who is quite a connoisseur. Unlike other establishments in the area, they don't get their icecreams and sorbets from *Berthillon* but from *chez Pascal* in the 16th arrondissement, whose reputation is growing and who makes the most wonderful sorbets.

BRASSERIE DE L'ILE-SAINT-LOUIS

55 quai de Bourbon; M° Pont-Marie.
☎ 01.43.54.02.59
Closed Wednesdays and in August.

Nonstop service noon–1am (6pm–1am Thursdays). Nothing's changed here for several decades, not even the waiters who've worked here for 25 years on average and are as enthusiastic and good-humoured as ever. The stuffed stork still lords it over the bar and an old clock from the Vosges ticks away to itself as customers who sit cheek by jowl with each other tuck into a plate of *choucroute* that's as good as Mum's. When there's a rugby match on, fans gather here in the evening for a beer. And household names in France like rock singer Renaud and politicians Roland Dumas and Lionel Jospin drop in quite regularly and even Grace Jones has been here. Naturally the star of the menu is the wonderful *choucroute* but they also do haddock and, as a starter, Welsh rarebit. With a decent wine from Alsace to wash it down with, reckon on about 160F. Or you could just have a *fines herbes* omelette as you gaze at the Seine and the back of Notre Dame. There's no place like it.

5th arrondissement

YOUNG AND HAPPY HOSTEL

80 rue Mouffetard; M° Censier-Daubenton or Monge.
☎ 01.45.35.09.53 ℻ 01.47.07.22.24

No access 2–8am. You can either book by letter (sending a night's deposit) or come along in person between 8am and 11am. It can accommodate 70 people in basic rooms (which now have phone) with 2, 3 or 4 bunk beds for 97F a head (75F in winter) including shower. Bathrooms and wcs have been redone but they're not always well looked after. Coin-operated phones in the hall, cold drinks machine, TV. Various nationalities, relaxed atmosphere and lots of fun – it's like a holiday camp. Ideal for young people and if you like to feel you're part of the neighbourhood. The street is quite noisy – be warned. You can eat in the nearby university refectory for 10F.

HÔTEL MARIGNAN*

13, rue du Sommerard; M° Maubert-Mutualité.
☎ 01.43.54.63.81

Reservations accepted unless you want a single room. Backpackers from the four corners of the globe have been coming here for more than 30 years now. Paul has taken over from his parents and keeps up the old tradition of a friendly welcome. Rooms come with or without shower and sleep two, three or four people. Moderate prices. For two people 300F, for three from 380 and for four or five you can have a family room with shower or bath from 460F to 600F (you can try negotiating this one). Breakfast is included in the price of the room. Washer, drier and iron available. There's even a kitchen with a fridge and microwave and a dining room where you can eat. You'll get a really friendly welcome and lots of tips about Paris etc. They don't take bookings for single rooms – if that's what you want, turn up about 10am.

HÔTEL ESMERALDA**

4 rue Saint-Julien-le-Pauvre; M° Saint-Michel.
☎ 01.43.54.19.20 F 01.40.51.00.68

This small (19 rooms) hotel is decorated like a doll's house. The building dates from the 17th century and the staircase is a listed monument. Ideal for honeymooners as long as they don't mind about the pretty dated furniture and the fact that the place looks a bit like a second-hand shop. Doubles with shower/wc 320F, with bath (plus a partial view of Notre Dame and Square Viviani) 420–490F. The bathrooms, especially the baths, are old-fashioned and still aren't very clean. It has some rooms for "students" overlooking the courtyard (160F a head). Breakfast is 40F. If you're a fan of *Mary Poppins* and/or love black and white photography, with a bit of luck you'll run into the bird lady near the square. Grab the opportunity to take some great pictures of her in her "coat" of pigeons.

FAMILIA HÔTEL

11 rue des Écoles; M° Jussieu, Maubert-Mutualité or Cardinal-Lemoine.
☎ 01.43.54.55.27 F 01.43.29.61.77
TV.

This is a comfortable pleasant hotel where you'll be welcomed in a manner that is both friendly and efficient. Doubles 380–440F with shower/wc, 440–520F with bath/wc. Cable TV. Breakfast 32F Go for one of the rooms on the 5th and 6th floors, which have views of Notre Dame and the rooftops of Paris. Artist Gérald Pritchard of the Beaux Arts (or art school) has personalized some of them by painting Notre Dame, Ile de la Cité and Pont-Neuf on the walls in burnt sienna. The flowery fitted carpet is soft and there's a genuine late 18th/early 19th century bookcase in the refurbished foyer.

LES DEGRÉS DE NOTRE-DAME

10 rue des Grands-Degrés; M° Maubert-Mutualité, RER Saint-Michel.
☎ 01.55.42.88.88 F same
TV.

Lovely little hotel with ten rather large rooms, some of which have a view of Notre Dame. And since you can't have everything, they're a bit noisier than the ones with no view that overlook the lane. All rooms have bath, TV, minibar and wc and range in price from 460F to 560F. Room number 501, which can sleep three or four, costs 560F plus 130F per occupant (breakfast included). It's on the fifth floor though, and there's no lift!. Very pleasant and a really good location in this historic neighbourhood which, curiously, tourists don't seem to know about. The welcome is pretty so-so, but that's no great deal. Book well in advance. It has a restaurant with set meals 67–145F.

10% HÔTEL DE LA SORBONNE**

6 rue Victor-Cousin; M° Saint-Michel or Cluny-Sorbonne.
☎ 01.43.54.58.08 F 01.40.51.05.18
TV.

This small pleasant hotel is located right in the student quarter and consequently at the centre of things. Entry under the arch. Doubles with shower/wc from 430F, with bath 470F, with twin beds 460F – very reasonable considering that it's quiet and well kept, the reception is pleasant, and there's a phone, TV and hair dryer in every room. Highest prices are for the largest rooms with marble bathroom. Breakfast 35F.

HÔTEL DES GRANDES ÉCOLES**

75 rue du Cardinal-Lemoine; M° Cardinal-Lemoine or Monge.
☎ 01.43.26.79.23 F 01.43.25.28.15
Car park.

Book well in advance, since this is a favourite with Americans who love Paris. The hotel, situated in a private lane just round the corner from place de la Contrescarpe, is actually a house, one of charm and character, with a small paved courtyard and a leafy garden – you'll think you're in the countryside rather than the city. The owner and her daughter have long been welcoming tourists from all around the world with a smile. Rooms, 51 in all on either side of the lane, are carefully looked after and tastefully arranged. They come with shower/wc or bath and range in price from 490F to 620F. In fine weather you can have tea in the garden even if you're not staying at the hotel.

I●I RESTAURANT TASHI-DELEK

4 rue des Fossés-Saint-Jacques; M° Luxembourg.
☎ 01.43.26.55.55
Closed Sundays and in August.

Service at lunchtime and in the evening until 11.00. A must! The people who run this, the first Tibetan restaurant to open its doors in Paris, have been here since the Chinese invaded their country. The Tibetan décor is restrained and the menu consists of regional dishes from U-Tsang, Kham and Amdo – do try a few in order to familiarize yourself with Tibetan cooking. How about *momok* (beef ravioli), *chabale* (stuffed pancakes), *baktsa markou* (pasta balls with melted butter and goat's cheese) and, if you're feeling brave, tea with salted butter? Reckon on paying about 90F for this taste of the exotic. Set meals 52F (lunch) and 64F (dinner).

I●I FOYER DU VIETNAM

80 rue Monge; M° Monge.
☎ 01.45.35.32.54
Closed Sundays.

Service till 10pm. This restaurant seems to have some connection with the Union of Vietnamese Workers in France. As you come through the door there's a poster of Uncle Ho with a child and on the left in a little space opposite the kitchen there's a TV that's supposed to keep the regulars amused but is an endless source of delight for the waiter. Visually, the place is nothing to write home about but the family style cooking makes no concessions to Western tastes and remains resolutely Vietnamese. They do an excellent and wonderfully tasty pork soup for 33F (the small serving is very substantial) and delicious steamed ravioli for 28F. The other dishes – fish simmered in a spicy sauce (31F), pork kebabs (38F), and Hanoi soup (33F) – are of the same calibre. There are a few interesting specialities at the weekend such as rice soup with tripe (which alternates with duck soup) or grilled *gambas* (large prawns) with vermicelli (52F). Set meals 56F and 67F.

I●I RESTAURANT LE VOLCAN

10 rue Thouin; M° Monge or Cardinal-Lemoine.
☎ 01.46.33.38.33
Closed Mondays.

Service until 11.30pm. This reliable restaurant has been around for a good many years but has never lost its popular appeal or become stiff and starchy. Main courses around 60F. Set meals (57F served until 8pm, 85F and 139F) all consist of starter, main course and dessert and, surprisingly, are also available in the evening – note, however, that liquid refreshment is included only at lunchtime. The cooking is French with a few nods in the direction of Greece (they do a good moussaka). Congratulations if you manage to spend more than 100F!

I●I RESTAURANT PERRAUDIN

157 rue Saint-Jacques; M° Luxembourg.
☎ 01.46.33.15.75
Closed Saturday lunchtimes, Sundays, Monday lunchtimes, and the second fortnight in August.

Service until 10.15 pm. A stone's throw from the Panthéon and the Luxembourg Gardens, there's a little bistro that offers traditional cooking and where dishes of the kind familiar to your grandparents are restored to their rightful place on the menu. It's unpretentious and unshowy and a favourite with students from the Sorbonne and publishers (including the people who work on the French language edition of this guide), who come for onion tart, *quiche lorraine*, leg of lamb with potatoes *Dauphinoise*, duck *confit*, beef *bourguignon* or rack of lamb with herbs. Set meal 63F. Reckon on 110F à la carte. In summer you can eat in a small interior courtyard.

I●I RESTAURANT AU BISTROT DE LA SORBONNE

4 rue Thoullier; M° Luxembourg or Saint-Michel.
☎ 01.43.54.41.49
Closed Sundays.

Service until 11pm. The restaurant consists of two little rooms that are full to bursting point at lunchtime and in the evening – blame the students from the place across the road. The 80F set meal at lunchtime gives you a starter, the day's special (something like chicken in a cream sauce) and cheese or dessert. The 95F evening set meal is worth the trip – fresh hors d'œuvres or goat's cheese on Poilâne bread with a green salad, a wonderful pepper steak with potatoes and panfried mushrooms or the famous *délice de la Sorbonne*, which is a meal in itself with chicken, shoulder ham, potatoes, cheese and then fresh fruit salad. In short, a good restaurant. If you were to dig a bit deeper, you could wash your meal down with an extremely good Saint-Nicolas-de-Bourgueil at 99F.

I●I RESTAURANT LE PORT DU SALUT

163 [bis] rue Saint-Jacques; M° Luxembourg.
☎ 01.46.33.63.21
Closed Sunday evenings and Mondays.

Lunch served noon–2.30pm and dinner 7–10.30pm. If *Perraudin* (see above) is full, this is the next best thing. Lovely setting with heavy beams, a tiny staircase, a piano and paintings of country scenes. All the famous French singers (too many to name) have passed this way. The 67F set meal is available every day. They also do an extremely good *formule* at 94F, which consists of starter and main course or main course and dessert, and gets you, for example, a casserole of mussels or warm goat's cheese salad followed by either veal stew or roast salmon with a *beurre blanc* sauce. Other set meals are 120F and 160F (only the lunchtime one includes dessert). All in all, a very pleasant restaurant with an intimate atmosphere, cloth napkins and attentive service. Large cellar for groups.

I●I RESTAURANT HAN LIM

6 rue Blainville; M° Monge.
☎ 01.43.54.62.74
Closed Mondays and in August.

This part of town is full of pleasant surprises. Right in the heart of Paris and surrounded by souvlaki joints, this is an excellent Korean restaurant that offers a lunchtime set meal for 73F. They also do a Korean barbecue for 100F, which is ridiculously cheap for the exotic thrill of a style of cooking that is totally new to you. Very good chargrilled meat and delectable garlic chicken. After your meal, why not knock back a pint at *Connolly's Corner*, the latest Irish pub in Paris?

I●I RESTAURANT SAVANNAH CAFÉ

27 rue Descartes; M° Cardinal-Lemoine.
☎ 01.43.29.45.77
Closed Sundays and Monday lunchtimes.

If you absolutely must have dinner in the Contrescarpe-Mouffetard area, our advice is to come here. Richard the owner, who is of Lebanese origin, will welcome you with that very particular Oriental politeness that it would be nice to come across more often in French restaurants. As befits a citizen of the world, Richard doesn't stick to the cooking of just one country. He offers tabbouleh, hummus, seviche, pumpkin with nutmeg, chicken with toasted almonds, aubergines with basil, milk-fed lamb with pistachio and pine nuts, chilli con carne, fruit and vegetable curry (with cardamom, coconut and chutney) and so on and so on. We can recommend the *crème de lait* for dessert. Set meals 75F (lunchtime), and 134F. If you'd rather go à la carte, reckon on paying about 135–145F.

I●I RESTAURANT PEMATHANG

13 rue de la Montagne-Sainte-Geneviève; M° Maubert-Mutualité.
☎ 01.43.54.34.34
Closed Sundays, Monday lunchtimes, and in August.

Lunch served noon–2.30pm and dinner 7–11pm. The Latin Quarter is still a magnet for the various ethnic groups in the French capital. Take this restaurant, for example, which has stepped straight off the high plateaus of Tibet. The cooking, which involves a lot of steaming, is full of delicate and subtle flavours – it's just as good as that of south-east Asia and deserves to be better known. While the dishes couldn't be anything but Tibetan, they do seem to give a nod in the direction of India, China and Japan all at once. At lunch time, students from the Sorbonne and white collar workers broaden their horizons by eating *sha momok* (which might remind you of dim sum), *then thouk* (home-made noodles in clear soup) and *pemathan* (meat balls in a sweet and sour sauce with sautéd vegetables). You'll be served with typical Oriental courtesy. *Formule* 79F. They also do a set meal for 115F, which enables you to sample the various Tibetan specialities.

I●I RESTAURANT LA VIEILLE GRILLE

1 rue du Puits-de-l'Ermite; M° Monge or Censier-Daubenton.
☎ 01.47.07.99.66
Closed Saturday lunchtimes and Sundays.

The grille at the door of this old building is two or three hundred years old and has been lovingly repainted time and time again. The ground floor, by the way, is run independently of the restaurant. It's home to the oldest dinner theatre in Paris, established in 1960 by Maurice Alezra who still runs it. Singer Jacques Higelin and actresses Claire Nadeau and Bulle Ogier all got their start there and jazz musicians Don Cherry, Barney Willen and Gato Barbieri have done gigs. The little restaurant on the first floor is one of the most delightful in Paris, with a warm and convivial atmosphere. In winter they serve dishes like Cantal cheese in flaky pastry accompanied by cumin flavoured potato croquettes, an extremely good breast of duck with thyme butter, lamb sweetbreads and kidneys, and tender Charolais beef. There's a speciality every day, often something like old-fashioned *blanquette de veau* (veal stew) or rabbit with ceps. *Formules* at 115F and 180F (which includes 1/4 litre of wine); 150F à la carte.

RESTAURANT AU JARDIN DES PÂTES

4 rue Lacépède; M° Jussieur or Monge.
☎ 01.43.31.50.71
Closed Mondays.

Lunch served noon–2.30pm and dinner 7–11pm. They serve nothing but pasta (home-made from organic flour) here and word of mouth alone has brought the customers in in droves. It offers real value for money, since you can have a substantial meal for 100F. Our favourite was the buckwheat pasts with chicken livers, sesame butter and prunes, but the rice pasta with sautéd vegetables, ginger and tofu was good too. There's another branch at 33 boulevard Arago in the 13th arrondissement (tel: 01.45.35.93.67).

RESTAURANT LE LANGUEDOC

64 bd de Port-Royal; M° Gobelins or Port-Royal.
☎ 01.47.07.24.47
Closed Tuesdays, Wednesdays, 4 weeks in August, and 2 weeks during the Christmas holidays.

Last orders 10pm. A favourite of several proofreaders who work in the companies round about. They have a reputation for knowing a lot about food so that tells you something about the restaurant. They specialize in the dishes of the south-west and the cooking is excellent. The service is reminiscent of the kind you'd get in a country restaurant, even if the proprietress is sometimes a bit on the curt side. If you order herring, for example, they'll bring the entire dish to your table. The duck *confit* with potatoes and truffles is the star turn but meat puts up a spirited performance too. Rouergue wine washes it all down quite superbly. The white and red Gaillac from the proprietor's own vineyard isn't bad either. Set meal 105F; 100–150 à la carte.

LE MAUZAC

7 rue de l'Abbé-de-l'Épée; RER Luxembourg.
☎ 01.46.33.75.22

Service 6.30am–9pm (11pm Thursdays and Fridays). With its rare pieces of 50s furniture (tables and zinc bar) and a few curiosities like a pilaster from a temple and a pillar disguised as a sturdy tree, this bistro is an endless source of amusement for the group of artists who are regulars here, particularly in the evening. The wines, it has to be said, are rich and fruity (there are 35 to choose from, at 12–19F a glass) and the daily specials prepared by Laurent, the young chef, are particularly good. These include lamb stew with baby vegetables, free-range chicken in tarragon vinegar, spelt (a kind of wheat) with mushrooms, and grilled scorpion fish with mashed potatoes flavoured with garlic and olive oil. What's on the menu depends on what proprietor Jean-Michel brings back from the market. Main courses are available Thursdays and Fridays. The rest of the week, it's just plates of *charcuterie* and cheese (available until 10pm). Reckon on 120F at lunchtime and 150F in the evening. Prompt service from Christine, the lady of the house, and her smiling waitress.

RESTAURANT LE BUISSON ARDENT

25 rue de Jussieu; M° Jussieu.
☎ 01.43.54.93.02
Closed Saturdays, Sundays, and three weeks in August.

Service at lunchtime and in the evening till 10pm. Best to book. This is one of our favourite restaurants, full of all the good smells of traditional French cooking. It's the kind of place you'd miss if it ever closed down. The décor is pleasant if conventional, and the atmosphere a little formal. They do an excellent set meal for 140F in the evenings consisting of starter, wonderful duck *confit* with garlic potatoes, cheese (or salad) and dessert (the charlotte and the chocolate cake are both yummy!). À la carte dishes include calf sweetbreads in cream and duck breast with pepper.

RESTAURANT LE BALZAR

49 rue des Écoles; M° Cluny-la-Sorbonne-Odéon.
☎ 01.43.54.13.67
Closed 4 weeks in August.

Service until midnight. This fairly plush brasserie is a very pleasant place for supper after the theatre or the cinema. it has the same kind of décor (artificial leather banquettes, large mirrors, and waiters in white aprons) and atmosphere as *Lipp* but slightly lower prices. It's extremely popular at lunchtime with people from nearby publishing houses. It has a very pleasant long narrow glassed-in terrace and in winter you can people-watch in the warmth. The house specialities are rabbit *terrine* (45F), skate in melted butter (110F) and *choucroute* (87F). Good food of the classic variety – expensive but it's being there that matters. A meal à la carte will set you back about 200F.

I●I RESTAURANT L'ATLAS

10-12 bd Saint-Germain; M° Maubert-Mutualité.
☎ 01.46.33.86.98

If you've been looking round the *Institut du monde arabe*, prolong the experience by eating food prepared by a man whom many people believe to be one of Arab cooking's best ambassadors in Paris. Benjamin El Jaziri, who has worked with some of the big names, has remained faithful to the cooking of his native Morocco but has made it a little less heavy on the fat and sugar. If you want proof, try his incredibly light couscous served with meat and vegetables that are above reproach or one of his superb tagines – there are 16 to choose from. Apart from these classics, you can feast on grilled *gambas* (large prawns) with paprika, lamb with leaves of the mallow plant, baked bream Moroccan style or, in season, partridge with mint and lemon. Warm welcome and attentive service. Reckon on paying 200F.

6th arrondissement

☗ ASSOCIATION DES ÉTUDIANTS PROTESTANTS DE PARIS

46 rue de Vaugirard; M° Luxembourg, Mabillon or Saint-Sulpice.
☎ 01.46.33.23.30 ⊫ 01.46.34.27.09
Open year round. Reception staffed weekdays 8.45am–noon and 3–7pm, Saturdays 8.45am–noon and 6–8pm, Sundays and public holidays 10am–noon.

Large building open to students aged 18-26. 10F registration fee plus 150F deposit. It's run by a friendly association that manages about 40 beds in dormitories for 4-6 people (77F for a bed). Breakfast is included in the price and you get free access to the gardens. Doubles with basin (88F per person) are available July–Sept only. It's old-fashioned and that's what makes it so delightful. That being said, they've repainted the corridors (which, to be honest, needed it). The rooms, especially the ones at the top, have a view of Saint-Sulpice and the Luxembourg Gardens. A common room, TV room and games room help residents have an enjoyable stay. If you're staying longer than about a month, they'll charge you a monthly rate of 1,400–1,600F for a double and 1,600–1,900 for a single. A bed in a dormitory costs more but it's to stop people taking up permanent residence!

10% ☗ DELHY'S HÔTEL*

22 rue de l'Hirondelle; M° Saint-Michel.
☎ 01.43.26.58.25 ⊫ 01.43.26.51.06
TV.

This small hotel, typically Parisian, is situated in a lane that has to be one of the capital's best kept secrets – no bad thing, since it means peace and quiet. In the 16th century it and number 20 formed a town house that François I gave to his favourite Anne de Pisseleu, the Duchess of Étampes, so expect to find exposed stonework and a few beams. Simply furnished rooms. Reckon on paying about 250F or 300F for a room with basin, 380F with shower. Not the cheapest in the neighbourhood but definitely the most central.

☗ HÔTEL DE NESLE

7 rue de Nesle; M° Odéon.
☎ 01.43.54.62.41

A word of warning: they don't take reservations so it's best to get there before 10am. This hotel, in a quiet street that has seen a lot of history, is one of the last remnants of the great hippy era. Most of the guests are Anglo-Saxon, and American accents mingle with Madame's North African one. She and her son shower affection on her guests and reign over their little kingdom with infinite good humour. It has to be said that "chaotic" rather than "organized" best describes things here – but there's a definite sense of people enjoying themselves. There are 20 rooms in all and they're simple, clean, well cared for and individually decorated. Doubles range in price from 250F for one with basin overlooking the street to 350F for one with shower and a view of the garden. There are wcs on each floor. Breakfast 25F. The shower is rather awe-inspiring and there's even a little hamam (or steam bath) in room number 4!. There's a little courtyard garden where you can have a quiet read but it's not always open.

10% ☗ HÔTEL DES ACADÉMIES*

15 rue de la Grande-Chaumière; M° Vavin.
☎ 01.43.26.66.44 ⊫ 01.43.26.03.72

Small family hotel in a quiet street, with an atmosphere that's slightly reminiscent of the

50s. Doubles 285F with shower, 325–340 with shower/wc. They have a few singles with basin at 210F but you'll have to book these a very long time in advance.

HÔTEL-CAFÉ-BAR STANISLAS**

5 rue du Montparnasse; M° Montparnasse-Bienvenue or Notre-Dame-des-Champs.
☎ 01.45.48.37.05 F 01.45.44.54.43
TV.

The street is quite quiet and the décor pleasant – the lovely foyer looks like a theatre. You can hear from the foyer what's going on in the bar – during term time it might be the sound of a guitar or the voices of youngsters from the school next door, who're on good terms with the manager. Each room is named after a painter and the number is in the shape of a palette in varnished terracotta. Doubles with telephone, shower/wc, hair dryer and TV 350–380F. Breakfast 32F.

GRAND HÔTEL DES BALCONS**

3 rue Casimir-Delavigne; M° Odéon.
☎ 01.46.34.78.50 F 01.46.34.06.27
TV.

You'd be hard pressed to find another place in the Latin Quarter that offers such value for money. Doubles 450–500 with shower/wc or bath. Breakfast – served buffet style and you can eat as much as you like – is 50F (and free if it's your birthday!). The hotel, with the exception of the functional bedrooms, is done up in Art Deco style. This is where the reps who sell the French version of this guidebook stay. And everyone gets a warm welcome. They don't accept Diner's or American Express.

10% HÔTEL DES CANETTES**

17 rue des Canettes; M° Saint-Germain-des Prés or Mabillon.
☎ 01.46.33.12.67 F 01.44.07.07.37
TV.

This establishment, located in a very busy street, looks old but, curiously enough, the décor is very colourful and hi tech. The rooms overlooking the street are brighter and don't have double glazing while the ones overlooking the courtyard are quieter but darker. Doubles with shower/wc 490F. Only two rooms don't have TV.Breakfast 40F. Readers of this guidebook get a 10% reduction in July and August and Nov–Feb.

HÔTEL DE LA LOUISIANE

60 rue de Seine; M° Mabillon or Saint-Germain-des-Prés.
☎ 01.43.29.59.30 F 01.46.34.23.87

Great location – one of Paris's most colourful markets is held just outside the hotel. This is an enormous complex of 70 small rooms that are comfortable but not much else. You get the feeling you're walking into a bank – after you've rung the bell the door is opened by somebody inside pushing a button and there are cameras in the upstairs corridors and monitors at reception. Not exactly full of warmth and vitality is it? No TV in any of the rooms. It's expensive for what it is but in view of its size, you might have more chance of finding a room there – mind you, that's about the only thing it's got going for it. Impersonal doubles with bath and double-glazing 500–610F (depending on the season), breakfast included. They don't take cheques.

HÔTEL DU LYS**

23 rue Serpente; M° Saint-Michel or Odéon.
☎ 01.43.26.97.57 F 01.44.07.34.90
TV.

This pleasant hotel situated in a quiet street has a nice family atmosphere. Cable TV, individual safes, hair dryer, they've thought of everything. And you'll get a great welcome – that's the icing on the cake. The rooms at the front are the best. Number 9 for example looks out onto the couryard and has a brightly coloured bedspread that tones in nicely with the wallpaper. Doubles with bath/wc or shower/wc (breakfast included) 500F. Unfortunately they don't accept credit cards.

HÔTEL DES MARRONNIERS***

21 rue Jacob; M° Saint-Germain-des-Prés or Mabillon.
☎ 01.43.25.30.60 F 01.40.46.83.56
TV

Book well in advance. We loved this place, which is tucked away at the back of a courtyard and is absolutely delightful. It has a little garden at the back and there's a veranda where you take your meals. Ask for a room overlooking the bell tower of the church of Saint-Germain. Prices start at 520F for one person, 715F for two, and 1,040F for three. Rooms are air-conditioned and have satellite TV.

RESTAURANT NOUVELLE COURONNE THAÏ

17 rue Jules-Chaplain; M° Vavin.
☎ 01.43.54.29.88
Closed Sunday lunchtimes and Mondays.

An excellent Thai restaurant in a secluded street. Someone has taken a lot of trouble over the setting, with its soft colours, subdued tones, and tables spaced well apart. Fish soup with coconut milk (delicately flavoured), casserole of seafood, lacquered chicken with lemon grass, spicy duck sautéd with bamboo shoots and pork spareribs are just some of the wonderful things listed on a very tempting menu, which also includes lots of Chinese dishes and some steamed specialities. The wine prices are very reasonable – you can have 1/4 litre of red for 12F or a Côtes du Rhone for 48F. Thai and Chinese beer. In short, remarkable value for money, delightful setting, charming welcome, efficient service and delicious food. Set meals 45F (lunchtime) and 69F (evening). There's also a special set meal for 2 at 98F. À la carte 120F or so.

I●I RESTAURANT L'ASSIGNAT

7 rue Guénégaud; M° Odéon.
☎ 01.43.54.87.68
Closed Sundays and in July.

Service at the bar 7.30am–8.30pm, in the restaurant noon–3.30pm. Who would have thought you'd find a quiet little neighbourhood restaurant in this crowded narrow street where there's hardly enough pavement to walk on? It's a haven for art dealers who're tired of having to fork out 200F for lunch, for the people who work at the Mint, and for art students, who learn all about that wonderful pre-war method of payment, tick. They eat what they want, write down in a book what they've had, and settle up at the end of the month. The restaurant is lively and cramped and provides simple food, the kind that sticks to your ribs. The owner's mother, who's been doing the cooking for a very long time, seems delighted with her lot. Main courses 40–45F, daily special 35F, and set meal 60F (70F with wine). The bill won't come to more than 75F.

I●I RESTAURANT OSTERIA DEL PASSEPARTOUT

20 rue de l'Hirondelle; M° Saint-Michel.
☎ 01.46.34.14.54
Closed Saturday lunchtimes, Sundays and two weeks in August. **Secure parking**.

Service at lunchtime and in the evening until 11pm. Refined, inventive and careful Italian cooking, that uses the freshest of fresh ingredients. They do pasta mostly, with great sauces – the ricotta and spinach ravioli was absolutely yummy and the meat cannelloni, the tagliatelle with ceps and the duck with balsamic vinear were out of this world. The starters were a bit on the small side, unfortunately, but the main course restored the balance. The curious might want to try *piato tris*, which is three kinds of pasta. Good cheese, delicious desserts. Set meals 65F and 70F (lunchtime), 86F and 130F (evening).

I●I RESTAURANT AUX TROIS CANETTES

18 rue des Canettes; M° Saint-Germain-des-Prés or Mabillon.
☎ 01.43.26.29.62
Closed Saturday lunchtimes and Sundays.

Service till about 11pm. Antonio, a dyed-in-the-wool Neapolitan, has been here since the 60s. The restaurant has changed very little in that time and in fact probably hasn't changed much at all since it opened its doors in the '20s. The building dates back to the 19th century and was originally a wine warehouse. The décor of seas and volcanos on the ground floor is meant to evoke Antonio's home town. The very handsome room upstairs is good for large groups. Antonio has remained faithful to the culinary tradition of his homeland. Try the salad of black chick-peas (25F), the sardines marinated in coarse salt (25F), the onions *à la sicilienne* or the aubergines in olive oil (both 70F), the seafood linguini (78F), the *saltimbocca San Daniele* (85F) or just have the whitebait, all of which put up a good show on the restaurant's behalf. Reckon on about 150F à la carte; set meal 75F. In June when the poetry fair is held in Place Saint-Sulpice, the restaurant awards an international literary prize.

I●I RESTAURANT LE PROCOPE

13 rue de l'Ancienne-Comédie; M° Odéon.
☎ 01.40.46.79.00

Non-stop service 11am–1am. This is the oldest café in Paris. In 1686, an Italian called Francesco Procopio dei Cotelli came to Paris and opened a café, introducing the then unknown beverage of coffee. The café was situated close to the Comédie Française and soon gathered a clientele of writers and artists. In the 18th century it was a meeting place for the *philosophes* (those who supported the ideas of the Enlightenment), and Diderot's famous Encyclopaedia had its beginnings in a conversation between him and d'Alembert, and Beaumarchais of *Figaro* fame waited there to hear the verdict on his plays at the Odéon. During the French Revolution, Danton, Marat and Camille Desmoulins to mention but a few met here. More recently, it was a haunt of Musset, Sand, Balzac, Huysmans, Verlaine and many other famous names. It's still a meeting place for intellectuals and, incredibly, its prices are still reasonable. Hats off for offering a set meal – starter, main course and dessert – for 106F! The cooking may not be extraordinary but the main thing is to say you've been here! They do two other set meals – the 123F one is available from 11pm, and for 178F you'll get oysters, fresh salmon in a champagne sauce, and dessert. Reckon on 200F à la carte. Reasonably priced wine list.

|●| RESTAURANT DES BEAUX-ARTS

11 rue Bonaparte; M° Saint-Germain-des-Prés.
☎ 01.43.26.92.64

Service at lunchtime and in the evening till 10.45pm, even on public holidays. This restaurant has long been the place to come to if you want an inexpensive and substantial meal – even the local preppies have been known to turn up some evenings. The dark frescos on the walls were painted by teachers and students from the Paris School of Art. Service is very fast – too fast maybe. Waitresses are firm about not serving you if you arrive too late at night. Set meal 79F (starter, day's special and dessert), wine included! À la carte also available but everybody plumps for the set meal. In winter, they serve a *pot au feu* with marrowbone which is legendary, but you can enjoy robust dishes like beef *bourguignon*, *coq au vin*, rabbit in a mustard sauce, *blanquette de veau* (veal stew), *pot au feu* and black pudding with apples year-round. Good selection of grilled dishes. And if it's your lucky day, you'll find their famous "grandmother's chicken" on the menu (wine sauce, mushrooms and cubes of bacon). Reckon on 110F à la carte. A good restaurant.

|●| BOUILLON RACINE

3 rue Racine; M° Cluny-Sorbonne or Odéon.
☎ 01.44.32.15.60

Just when we'd given up all hope of seeing anything but fast food joints and clothes shops in the Latin Quarter, a decent restaurant has come on the scene. Made a comeback might be a better description actually, since it made its first appearance at the beginning of the century as the *Bouillon Camille Chartier*. After lots of ups and downs it ended up as a civil service canteen. Luckily, it had been given listed building status so the interior was still there, though rather dilapidated. It was taken over by Belgian investors and this magnificent Art Nouveau establishment took on a new lease of life and its earlier elegance has been restored. It's all there – bevelled mirrors, milk glass, stained glass, marble mosaics, and gold leaf lettering. Beer plays a large part in the cooking, paying tribute to Belgium and its national drink. There's also beer to drink, including famous Trappist names like Rochefort, Chimay and Orval. Set meals 88F (drink included) and 159F. There's brown sugar tart and spiced buns at teatime (3–6pm) and you can have a jug of *café Liégois* (iced coffee and icecream) at any time.

|●| RESTAURANT INDONESIA

12 rue de Vaugirard; M° Odéon or Luxembourg.
☎ 01.43.25.70.22

Last orders 10.30pm, 11pm Fridays and Saturdays. Best to reserve in the evenings. This is the only Indonesian restaurant in Paris to be set up as a workers' co-operative. The food is good and the reception friendly. Several set meals (89–129F) in the shape of the *rijsttafel*, consisting of a whole series of dishes from Java, Sumatra, Bali and Celebes, including *rendang* (meat in coconut milk) and *balado ikan* (fish in spicy tomato sauce). The more expensive set meals offer a wider range of dishes. The menu tells you everything you ever wanted to know about rice. Great curries and mutton satay.

|●| NOURA

121 bd du Montparnasse; M° Vavin.
☎ 01.43.20.19.19

Less sophisticated than its counterpart on the Right Bank but it has something its sister restaurant doesn't – a small garden where you can eat outside in summer. Lebanese specialities are much in evidence on the menu and you're spoiled for choice. Cleverly constructed *formules assiettes* (with photos) help you make up your mind quickly if you don't know anything about Lebanese cooking – choose from a large or small plate of hors d'œuvres, mixed *charwarma*, and meat and chickpea *charwarma*. There are also two set meals at 97F and 149F. Be adventurous and try the *jellab* (dates in syrup with pine nuts) or the Lebanese beer. This is primarily a brasserie where you can have a very quick meal.

|●| L'ÉPI DUPIN

11 rue Dupin; M° Sèvres-Babylon.
☎ 01.42.22.64.56
Closed Saturdays and Sundays.

Service until 11pm. François Pasteau, who trained under Kérever and Faugeron, is a happy man as you can tell from his beaming smile. Why? – because his restaurant is full at lunchtime and in the evening and his satisfied customers leave nothing on their plates but the pattern. There's no denying you get value for your money – there's a *menu-carte* for 153F (wine extra) and a lunchtime *formule* for 97F. The menu reflects what's been available at Rungis that day and you get a choice of 6 starters, 8 main courses and 6 desserts every day. Dishes that don't come up to scratch are rare indeed and we congratulated ourselves on our choice of rabbit turnovers with aubegines, scallops with lemons and pears, and apples in puff pastry with a mascarpone sorbet. Sheer delight from start to finish. Pleasant and efficient service.

|●| LA RÔTISSERIE D'EN FACE

2 rue Christine; M° Odéon.
☎ 01.43.26.40.98
Closed Saturday lunchtimes and Sundays.

Lunch served noon–2pm and dinner 7.30–11pm (11.30pm Fridays and Saturdays). Top chef Jacques Cagna, whose flagship restaurant is a stone's throw away, has every reason to be pleased with himself. This particular place is a smash hit and in a few years he's made it one of the Left Bank's institutions. Try the free-range chicken with old-fashioned mashed potatoes or duck breast with honey and spices served with tomatoes and new potatoes. It's very good on the whole but there were a few hiccups when we were there, probably because of the large turnover of staff. The wine list isn't very tempting and the noise level from other tables rather high. Set meals 100–159F at lunchtime and 210F in the evening (reckon on 250F with wine).

|●| LA BAUTA

129 bd du Montparnasse; M° Vavin.
☎ 01.43.22.52.35
Closed Saturday mornings and Sundays, and Aug 10–20.

The décor may take its inspiration from Venice (there's a superb collection of masks on the walls) but the menu covers the whole of Italy. The beautiful people who eat here haven't got it wrong, for everything is remarkably fresh and cooked with finesse. The perfectly *al dente* pasta comes with a number of sauces – there's langoustine and rosemary, for example, cinammon, squid ink and scallops. Set meal 105F (lunchtimes). The 200F evening set meal; reckon on 250F à la carte.

|●| RESTAURANT AUX CHARPENTIERS

10 rue Mabillon; M° Mabillon or Saint-Germain-des-Prés.
☎ 01.43.26.30.05

Service at lunchtime and till 11pm in the evening. A good restaurant. It used to be the headquarters of the guild of master carpenters and the décor reflects that past, with a superb counter, scale models, souvenirs and old photos. The guild museum is through the wall but the restaurant's owner, an expert on the guild's history, is as tight lipped as if this was the Middle Ages when secrecy was essential. The atmosphere is what you'd get if you crossed a bistro with a conservative elegant restaurant. Good traditional bourgeois dishes. Each day has its own particular main course: veal Marengo (with tomatoes, garlic and mushrooms) on Monday, beef *à la mode* (simmered in wine with vegetables and herbs) and carrots on Tuesday, salt pork and lentils on Wednesday, *pot au feu* and vegetbles on Thursday etc. Daily specials around 75F. If you go à la carte, reckon on a minimum of 180F – main courses start at 80F and starters are expensive. They do a *formule* at 120F (that includes 1/4 litre of wine) at lunchtimes and 153F in the evenings.

|●| RESTAURANT LE MACHON D'HENRI

8 rue Guisarde; M° Saint-Germain-des-Prés.
☎ 01.43.29.08.70

Service till 11.30pm. Good wine bar serving rich food and generous helpings of classical dishes. The pork, whichever way it comes, is excellent, particularly the Corrèze sausage. Beef and carrots, *andouillettes* in cream, duck breast, calf's liver, kidneys, and *gratins* are also available. There's a wonderful fresco on the wall and the waiter's witty repartee is a bonus. Reckon on 150F or thereabouts for a full meal.

7th arrondissement

10% ☗ HÔTEL EIFFEL RIVE GAUCHE**

6 rue du Gros-Caillou; M° École-Militaire.
☎ 01.45.51.24.56 ➡ 01.45.51.11.77
TV.

Renovated in 1986, this little hotel in a quiet street meets all your criteria if you appreciate the discreet charm of the bourgeoisie. It has four floors linked by elegant walkways that encircle a pretty patio leading to a little conservatory with a sliding roof. Shades of ochre and dusky pink predominate in the décor. With a bit of imagination you might think you were in Andalusia! But if you're in room number 317, 321, 426 or 422 on the top floor (we can recommend these) and you crane your neck a bit, you can see the Eiffel Tower. Thirteen of the rooms look out onto the patio. Expect to pay 250–460F for a double, buffet breakfast 40F. All rooms have TV (15 channels). Alr-conditioning. Friendly welcome. Best to book.

10% ☗ HÔTEL DU PALAIS BOURBON**

49 rue de Bourgogne; M° Varenne, Chambre-des-Députés or Invalides.
☎ 01.44.11.30.70 F 01.45.55.20.21
TV.

You'll get a courteous reception from the family who've owned the hotel for decades. There's a pretty little room near reception with high ceilings and exposed beams. Rooms are reasonable and very clean. Some of them are enormous – one of the advantages of an old building – but that doesn't mean comfort has been overlooked. Facilities include renovated bathrooms, double glazing, minibar, TV (you can get CNN), Internet acces, and a special socket for your fax or modem. Prices are very reasonable for the area: doubles with shower (no TV) 330F, with shower/wc and TV 405F, and with bath/wc and TV 580F. There are also rooms that sleep four or five for 740F. All prices include breakfast.

10% ☗ GRAND HÔTEL LÉVÊQUE*

29 rue Cler; M° École-Militaire or Latour-Maubourg.
☎ 01.47.05.49.15 F 01.45.50.49.36
TV.

This is a well-known hotel, of course, so book ahead. The Eiffel Tower is just round the corner but it might well be overtaken in popularity by the very picturesque rue Cler market – the rooms overlooking the street go like hot cakes. You really feel you're part of the neighbourhood in this highly commendable hotel that charges reasonable prices. Doubles with shower/wc 335–380F, triples with shower 480F. Breakfast 30F. Even if the décor is eminently forgettable, the rooms are clean and reasonably comfortable. Jovial reception.

☗ HÔTEL-RÉSIDENCE ORSAY**

93 rue de Lille; M° Assemblée-Nationale or Solferino; RER Musée-d'Orsay.
☎ 01.47.05.05.27 F 01.47.05.29.48
Closed in August. **TV**.

This used to be a private town house and has a superb façade with statues. Faultless reception. Pleasant doubles with TV and double glazing on the first floor with shower 360F, with bath 450F – probably the best value for money in the 7th arrondissement. Breakfast 40F, free if you stay at least one week.

10% ☗ HÔTEL LE PAVILLON**

54 rue Saint-Dominique; M° Invalides.
☎ 01.45.51.42.87 F 01.45.51.32.79
TV.

A quiet little hotel set back from the street. A former convent with a pretty frontage and interesting architecture, it has retained its almost provincial charm. A little oasis, with lots of flowers. It has 18 unfussy and comfortable rooms – the one that used to be the Mother Superior's is the most sought after. Rooms with shower/wc and TV go for 460F and there are three doubles with bath and TV for 575F. Don't let them give you one of the rooms in the basement – they're incredibly depressing. Breakfast 41F.

☗ HÔTEL MUGUET**

11 rue Chevert; M° École Militaire or Latour-Maubourg.
☎ 01.47.05.05.93 F 01.45.50.25.37
TV. Canal+. Disabled access.

The hotel, located in a very quiet street that doesn't get much traffic, is spanking clean since it's been completely refurbished. Doubles 480F with shower, 510F with twin beds and triple 670F. All rooms have satellite TV. Breakfast 45F.

☗ HÔTEL BERSOLY'S SAINT-GERMAIN***

28 rue de Lille; M° Rue-du-Bac.
☎ 01.42.60.73.79 F 01.49.27.05.55
Closed in August. **Car park. TV. Disabled access.**

This definitely falls into the chic category for users of this guidebook but it's absolutely gorgeous. It used to be a private town house and has been renovated throughout. It's located right in the heart of historic Paris and not far from the right kind of shops if you're an antique-lover. Granted, the rooms are small but they're impeccable and awfully pretty. They're all called after a famous painter and have an appropriate reproduction on their walls, which gives them a touch of originality. Hushed atmosphere, exposed beams and period furniture all add to that sense of nostalgia you find in places that have a past and you begin to think Victor Hugo got it right when he said objects have a soul. To get down to practical matters, a double with shower/wc will cost you 600–650F, with bath 700–750F. All rooms have cable TV. Quite delightful welcome.

HÔTEL DU QUAI VOLTAIRE**

19 quai Voltaire; M° Rue du Bac.
☎ 01.42.61.50.91 ➨ 01.42.61.62.26

A 2-star hotel in a magnificent location on the banks of the Seine, opposite the second-hand book sellers' stalls and the Louvre, and near the Musée d'Orsay. Built in the 19th century, a number of famous people have stayed here, including Wagner, Baudelaire, Oscar Wilde and Pissarro. Doubles with bath and shower 620–690F. TV on request (40F). Breakfast 45F.

HÔTEL LENOX***

9 rue de l'Université; M° Saint-Germain-des-Prés or Rue-du-Bac.
☎ 01.42.96.10.95 ➨ 01.42.61.52.83
TV.

Sophisticated décor and a charming distinguished retro feel. The rooms on the fifth floor have sloping ceilings. Doubles with shower/wc 650F. Expect to pay about 700F with bath. For any lottery winners out there, there's a superb duplex suite complete with sitting room for 1,500F. The pleasant intimate bar with its Art Deco décor is open 5pm–2am. It tends to fill up with photographers, stylists and models whenever there's a fashion show on at the nearby Carré du Louvre, so book well in advance.

CHEZ GERMAINE

30 rue Pierre-Leroux; M° Duroc.
☎ 01.42.73.28.34
Closed Saturday evenings, Sundays, and in August.

The little dining room is simple and clean, the atmosphere a bit provincial, the welcome really nice. The restaurant gets its custom from people who work in the area, workmen in dungarees, people on a pension, and lovers. Given that this is the Left Bank, the 65F set meal is excellent value for money. The creamed salt cod is great – try it – and the ox tripe is tasty. Sautéd rabbit with mushrooms, *coq au vin*, cod fillets with *aïoli*, and pork *colombo* are also available, and there's home-made *clafoutis* for dessert. You can have a carafe of fairly decent Bordeaux – neither pretentious nor harsh – for 18F.

RESTAURANT LE ROUPEYRAC

62 rue de Bellechasse; M° Solférino.
☎ 01.45.51.33.42

Closed Saturday evenings, Sundays, public holidays, and usually in August. This is the kind of place you used to be able to find in Paris – the good little neighbourhood restaurant that never changes. There's no flimflam here, no fancy décor meant to take your mind off the fact that what you're eating came off a production line. Mr and Mrs Fau, both of them born and bred in Aveyron, have been running the restaurant for the past 23 years, calling it after a locality not far from Durenque in Aveyron. They offer their customers country style cooking and dishes like mutton stew (70F) or oxtail *pot au feu* (75F), or there's a 78F set meal with mushrooms *à la grecque*, lamb's brains coated in flour and fried, and chocolate pudding. They also do a "boarder's" set meal for the many clerks who work locally. Service is efficient and attentive.

RESTAURANT LE BABYLONE

13 rue de Babylone; M° Sèvres-Babylone.
☎ 01.45.48.72.13

Closed evenings, Sundays, public holidays, and in August. The large dining room is delightfully old-fashioned and the cooking is good. Set meal 90F, including drink. Main dishes 48–52F. You'll get away with a maximum of 90F.

THOUMIEUX

79 rue Saint-Dominique; M° Latour-Maubourg.
☎ 01.47.05.49.75 ➨ 01.47.05.36.96

Service noon–3.30pm, 6.30pm–midnight, Sundays noon–midnight. This delightful large brasserie founded in 1923 has been in the hands of Françoise Thoumieux and Jean Balassert since 1976. If it's a lively atmosphere and inexpensive food you want, this is the place you've been dreaming about. We particularly liked the house *cassoulet* with duck *confit* (95F), the cep omelette (90F) and the duck breast with blackcurrants (98F). There's a set meal for 150F consisting of specialities from the Corrèze – salad of grilled duck breast, maize flour dumplings, *cabécou* (goat's cheese) and 1/4 litre of Corrèze wine.

AU BON ACCUEIL

14 rue de Montessuy; M° Alma-Marceau.
☎ 01.47.05.16.11
Closed Saturday lunchtimes and Sundays and Christmas.

Service until 11pm. It might make you snigger to come across in the very aristocratic 7th arrondissement a restaurant with a name reminiscent of a motorway inn promising all the delights of the countryside but bite back your sarcastic remarks. You'll soon realize that the name means what it says and the cooking is equally genuine. Quality produce means everything to Jacques Lacipière, innkeeper and epicure. Almost every day, rain, hail or shine, he can be found prowling round Rungis to buy the best of whatever there is for his kitchen. The outcome of this painstaking search is there on the menu for all to see. Depending on what he's found, there might be sole *meunière* (125F), calf's liver *persillade* (118F) or braised brill with morels (125F). His finds also feature on a remarkable 120F *menu-carte* (with a drop of wine it'll come to 170F). We had oysters in aspic with creamed shallots and fricassee of lamb sweetbreads with sautéd mushrooms and celery, which were followed by a cod steak with seasonings and a superb ribsteak. The desserts – a warm apple and pear crumble and vanilla profiteroles with warm chocolate sauce – were astonishingly good. (The starters and desserts for the set meal cost 38F à la carte.) About 250F à la carte. You get a magnificent view of the Eiffel Tower – a few hundred metres away – from the terrace in the evening.

|●| RESTAURANT LE P'TIT TROQUET

28 rue de l'Exposition; M° École-Militaire.
☎ 01.47.05.80.39
ClosedSundays, Mondays and the first two weeks in August, between Christmas and New Year's Day.

This place does a good job of winning people over, looking as it does like a traditional inexpensive restaurant full of the type of things you associate with the old style bistro (percolators, siphons, coffee pots and an antique zinc counter). As if that weren't enough, Patrick Veyssière also offers an attractive 149F set meal based on what was available at the market. Depending on the luck he's had, you could choose as a starter scrambled eggs with haddock or *terrine* of beef and chicken livers, for your main course fricassee of rabbit with mushrooms and savory, lamb, free-range guinea fowl or skate wing in a caper sauce, and for dessert iced coffee cream or *pain perdu* (French toast) and butterscotch icecream. It's good and well presented and there's service to match. If you've got relatives up from the country or friends visiting from abroad, this is an ideal place for lunch or dinner after a trip to the Eiffel Tower.

|●| L'ŒILLADE

10 rue Saint-Simon; M° Rue-du-Bac.
☎ 01.42.22.01.60
Closed Saturday lunchtimes, Sundays, and public holidays.

Service at lunchtime and in the evening 7.30–11pm. Both dining rooms are always crowded. Chef Jean-Louis Huclin who likes his food and eats enough for four, likes to feed his customers as well as he does himself, so his 158F set meal regularly offers substantial dishes that will satisfy you even if you've got a bottomless pit for a stomach. There's stuffed cabbage, braised calf sweetbreads with morels, fricassee of chicken with *foie gras* and whole garlic cloves, stewed ox cheeks, tripe *à la mode de Caen* and so on. Reckon on about 210F à la carte. Service comes with a smile.

|●| RESTAURANT LE BASILIC

2 rue Casimir-Périer; M° Solferino or Invalides.
☎ 01.44.18.94.64

Lunch served noon–2.30pm and dinner 7.30pm–midnight. Anybody who's anybody in the 7th arrondissement comes to this comfortable brasserie with its welcoming terrace across the way from the church of St Clotilde. The leg of lamb roasted in a salt crust, the sole *meunière* and other classics of bourgeois cooking delight customers who tend quite conservative in their eating habits. About 200F. It's not really the place for our average reader but it's relaxing after a long walk through the streets of this neighbourhood with its fine architectural features.

8th arrondissement

☗ HÔTEL WILSON*

10 rue de Stockholm; M° Saint-Lazare.
☎ 01.45.22.10.85

Book ahead because it's often full. There's nothing special to recommend it, but it is close to Saint Lazare train station. There's no lift so you have to be fit to get to the 5th floor, where the rooms are bright and have a bird's eye view of the neighbourhood. Very simple, clean and functional. Doubles with shower 260F (breakfast included), 230F without shower and 245F with shower but no wc. An affordable one-star establishment.

☗ HÔTEL DES CHAMPS-ÉLYSÉES**

2 rue d'Artois; M∞ Saint-Philippe-du-Roule or Franklin-Roosevelt.
☎ 01.43.59.11.42 F➜ 01.45.61.00.61
TV. Canal+.

A clean, welcoming and comfortable 2-star hotel away from the brouhaha of the Champs Élysées. It has 36 large soundproof rooms, all of them different. Doubles with shower/wc, direct phone, minibar, safe, hair dryer and cable 465F; if you want a bath too, you'll pay 540F. You have breakfast (42F) in a pretty little room with a vaulted ceiling. in July or August and you'll get 10% off the price of a room if you show this guide. You'll need to book a long time in advance since it's often full.

|●| RESTAURANT CHEZ LÉON

5 rue de l'Isly; M° Saint-Lazare.
☎ 01.43.87.42.77
Closed Sundays and in August.

Lunch served noon–3pm and dinner 7–10pm. The "Relais routier" sign is intriguing. We're a stone's throw away from the Saint Lazare railway station after all, not the N7 motorway. But the sign's for real – it IS a relais routier. It's all there – the set meal, the little old ladies in white aprons, the transparent plastic on top of the tablecloths to keep them clean, the hole-in-the-floor loos, the '50s black and canary yellow formica fridges, the hors d'œuvres (20F), the daily specials of beef with pasta and tomato sauce (60F) or roast beef with mashed potatoes and cauliflower (60F) and the 1/4 litre of plonk. All that's missing is the big guy with the brilliantined hair standing at the bar having a drink and smoking a fag. This, the only relais routier in Paris, owes its sign to the road transport organization which had its headquarters across the road once upon a time and regarded *Léon* as a second home. There's a reason for everything!

|●| LE SINGE D'EAU

28 rue de Moscou; M° Liège or Place-de-Clochy.
☎ 01.43.87.72.73
Closed Sundays and in August.

Service at lunchtime and in the evening till 11pm. A real Tibetan restaurant that opened its doors in 1992, the Year of the Monkey according to the Chinese calendar, hence the name. Tashi Lhamo looks after the kitchen while Kusang is in charge of the dining room. They had a restaurant in Khatmandu for a long time and have managed to recreate the atmosphere of the Roof of the World. There's the authentic décor to start with – no kitschy folk motifs, just beautiful carpets on the bench style seats. The multicoloured frieze running round the room was inspired by the temples and there's a beautiful fresco at the back of the room. The authentic Tibetan cooking is simple and unsophisticated, just as it is in Tibet and other mountainous regions, but it's tasty and the portions are substantial. That goes particularly for the soup – the *thintuk* of beef and black radishes, for example, is delicious. Tibet's national dish *momos* (similar to dim sum) is of course available as are a few traditional dishes like *dhre gnos* (stir-fried beef and celery) and *lugsha goptse* (mutton curry with shallots). The traditional liquid accompaniment is tea with butter but there is a wine list. Set meal 65F (lunchtime). Reckon on 100F à la carte. The amiable reception comes free.

9th arrondissement

⌂ WOODSTOCK HOSTEL

48 rue Rodier; M° Anvers.
☎ 01.48.78.87.76 ➡ same
Closed 11.30am–5pm (but there's a 24 hour telephone service for reservations) and at night the doors close at 2am.

A hotel for students on a budget (mostly Americans). Rooms have bunk beds. You can sit on the little patio only until 9.45pm – the neighbours complained about the noise!. Say hello to Lilly, the cow that sits in reception. No breakfast but as much coffee as you want. You'll pay 75F June 1–March 31 and 81F the rest of the year. Expect to pay 10F extra for a double room.

⌂ HÔTEL DES TROIS POUSSINS

15 rue Clauzel; M° Saint-Georges.
☎ 01.53.32.81.81 ➡ 01.53.32.81.82
TV. Disabled access.

A good location at the foot of the Butte. The hotel is quite quiet, very friendly, and has just been refurbished throughout. It now has a lift. If you're a night owl, the "in" bars are just around the corner. Little patio at the back. Prices are pretty good, considering it's just about to become a two-star. Doubles with washing facilities 190F, with shower/wc or bath, TV, phone and hair dryer 290F. Some rooms come with kitchenette. Shower in the corridor (15F). Large breakfast 38F.

⌂ HÔTEL DES ARTS**

7 cité Bergère; M° Rue-Montmartre et Cadet.
☎ 01.42.46.73.30 ➡ 01.48.00.94.42
Car park. TV. Canal+.

A 2-star hotel with a pretty pastel pink façade in a rather nice passageway where you'll be spoiled for choice when it comes to hotels – this is the cheapest of them though. Friendly welcome. The rooms are tiny but decent, clean and quiet, away from the hustle and bustle of Montmartre. Doubles with shower/wc 360F, with bath 390F. The stairway is decorated with old showbills – well, it's not called Hôtel des Arts for nothing! Solitary souls among you can even practise your conversational skills on the handsome grey parrot in reception. Breakfast (30F) is free your first morning on presentation of this guide.

10% HÔTEL DES CROISÉS**

63 rue Saint-Lazare; M° Trinité.
☎ 01.48.74.78.24 Fax 01.49.95.04.43
TV.

You really ought to book because there are people who've been coming here for years – you'll soon see why! It's in a marvellous location but deserves a visit on looks alone. There's a superb reception area with old wood panelling and fitted carpet that you sink into and the lift that gets you upstairs is very retro with its wood interior and wrought iron grilles. You'll rave about the rooms, which are sheer magic. They're as large as you could hope for and they have style – period furniture and marble fireplaces and some have Art Deco woodowrk. The '50s style bathrooms – some of them enormous – aren't bad either. If you're looking for the latest mod cons you'll be disappointed, but everything is impeccably clean. All rooms have TV. There are no twin rooms. The doubles with bath at 450F are better than the ones with shower at 400F. Breakfast is 35F and you can have it in your room. There are only 26 rooms and it's very popular with business people so, as we said, it's best to reserve. This is a super 2-star with reasonable prices and you'll be bowled over by it. Almost enough to make you wish you were visiting the city and not living here.

HÔTEL CHOPIN**

46 passage Jouffroy; M° Richelieu-Drouot.
☎ 01.47.70.58.10 Fax 01.42.47.00.70
TV.

A 19th century town house at the end of a passageway a stone's throw from the Grands Boulevards. Picturesque and very quiet. The façade dates back to 1850 and is really worth a closer look for the old woodwork and the big window through which you can see the receptionist, who's almost hidden behind his desk. You really feel like you've stepped into another era here! The Musée Grévin is just nearby. The rooms are really quite pretty. The view over the rooftops is reminiscent of Impressionist paintings, especially at sunset. Doubles with shower or bath 450F or 490F. We recommend the rooms on the fourth floor (numbers 409–413) – they're very nice and get lots of light. Try to avoid the ones overlooking the courtyard as you'll get a great view of a massive wall. Buffet breakfast 38F. No problem about coming in late at night, the main door is always open

10% HÔTEL DE LA TOUR D'AUVERGNE***

10 rue de la Tour d'Auvergne; M° Cadet.
☎ 01.48.78.61.60 Fax 01.49.95.99.00
TV.

A pretty 3-star hotel that looks out onto a quiet street. The rooms (all with four-poster beds) naturally come with all the mod cons like bath or shower, TV, and hair dryer, and are spacious and elegantly decorated. Licensed bar and room service 24 hours. Double rooms 500–700F. The breakfast – yoghurt, corn-flakes, *pain au chocolat* etc – is especially good. It costs 55F.

LYCÉE 43

43 av. Trudaine; M° Anvers or Gare-du-Nord.
☎ 01.48.78.43.25
Closed Saturday evenings, Sundays, and in August.

This used to be a favourite haunt of chauffeurs and apparently even served coachmen in the early years of the century. But that was before it started to attract the all-in wrestlers fighting at the Élysée-Montmartre in the '50s. Mr Tachot, who used to work at Les Halles as a butcher, has owned the restaurant since 1969. He does the cooking while his very nice wife looks after the customers. The passing tourist en route to or from Montmartre gets the same kind of friendly welcome as the "villagers" or locals, who are still pretty much in evidence. The simplicity of the décor is a triviality when set against the substantial 70F set meal (there's another at 100F), the cat purring on top of the radiator and the family atmosphere. No snobs please.

HARD ROCK CAFÉ

14 bd Montmartre; M° Richelieu-Drouot or Rue-Montmartre.
☎ 01.42.46.10.00
Closed Christmas Day.

Service 11.30am–2am. If you get nostalgic about the good old days of rock and roll, then a trip to the temple dedicated to your gods is a must. They're all there complete with guitars, gold records and even their stage costumes or favourite clothes (Jim Morrison's leather jacket, for example). This is where the young and the not so young come in search of their share of the American dream. It's not a good place for a confidential chat – the rock music is deafening – but the American cooking is reasonable. You'll get a real hamburger for 60–95F, while the specialities are barbecued dishes (around 90F) and *fajitas*, and the strawberry cheesecake (52F) is great. They do a set meal for 79F during the week. There's another dining room upstairs. It's also a bar, but tables are hard to come by. The café has had a few run-ins with the authorities in the past because of the "mad cow disease" paranoia sweeping the country.

RESTAURANT CHARTIER

7 rue du Faubourg-Montmartre; M° Rue-Montmartre.
☎ 01.47.70.86.29

Closes 10pm. No reservations. When you come in through the heavy revolving door, you'll find yourself in an enormous 19th century restaurant that still looks the way it did then. In fact, it's a listed building. Get there quickly before they do some kind of renovation work on it. There are only two or three like it and this is the best of the lot. Bursting at the seams with regulars, little old ladies who live in the neighbourhood, students, artists down on their luck, and tourists. You can be sure of passable food (although it's not always as hot as it might be) for less than 86F. If you're interested in a few statistics, it can seat 350, has 16 waiters, and serves 1,300 meals a day!

RESTAURANT AU PETIT RICHE

25 rue Le Pelletier; M° Richelieu-Drouot.
☎ 01.47.70.68.68
Closed Sundays.

Service until 12.15am. The restaurant opened in 1880 and with its Edwardian-style private rooms evokes an atmosphere of excellent suppers, lady friends, carriages, and corsets. You feel like part of an illustration from a history book when you eat here. A "gourmand" 160F(lunchtime only) set meal offers several starters, main courses and desserts to choose from. The main dishes on offer when we were there were poached haddock in a sweet and sour sauce, boiled beef, and tuna with green peppercorns. A la carte is a lot more expensive (about 180F). A place with atmosphere. The restaurant and the theatres roundabout have established a close working relationship and got together to offer a theatre-dinner *formule*.

BISTROT DES DEUX THÉÂTRES

18 rue Blanche; M° Trinité.
☎ 01.45.26.41.43

Closes at 12.30am. This place is a must for nightowls and theatre goers in the Pigalle area. With its spick and span British chic AND its one and only set meal (169F), which offers authentic unpretentious food, it doesn't exactly blend into its surroundings. The starters – homemade lobster ravioli with a sauce made from the coral and fresh asparagus in puff pastry with chervil butter – are out of this world, the kitchen doesn't put a foot wrong when it comes to meat and fish, and there are desserts to match. Apéritif, coffee and wine included. And if you really want to stay up all night, *Le Dépanneur* in rue Fontaine is open round the clock.

CHEZ CATHERINE

65 rue de Provence; M° Chaussée-d'Antin.
☎ 01.45.26.72.88
Closed weekends and Monday evenings.

Service until 11pm. This venerable and good-looking bistro, which used to be the *Poitou*, has changed beyond all recognition since it was taken over a bit more than a year ago. Then, the food was hopeless and the wine list hit new heights – or depths – in mediocrity. Now, dishes are cooked to perfection, ingredients are treated with respect, and the cellar is full of astonishingly good wine. Catherine's father is a famous chef and she has inherited his talent. The *terrine* of lamb and mint (45F) is a minor masterpiece, the sausage *vigneron* and potatoes in oil as good as it is in Beaujolais, the bass with spices (80F) does delightful things to the tastebuds, and the grilled breast of Gers duck (90F) does the south-west proud. Husband Frédéric, who used to be in advertising, is a wine-lover and gives his cellar lots of tender loving care. In addition to a few wines served by the glass or carafe such as a Domaine Richaud Cairanne or a Domaine Colombier Coteaux de l'Ardèche, you'll find Robert Michel's Cornas, Clos Milan's Coteaux d'Aix les Baux de Provence and the superb Clos Rougeard Saumur-Champigny, all at very reasonable prices. Good food, good wine, unobtrusive service with a smile – what more could you ask?

10th arrondissement

HÔTEL VICQ D'AZIR

21 rue Vicq d'Azir; M° Colonel-Fabien.
☎ 01.42.08.06.70

Open 8am–10pm. A simple hotel with 70 rooms for people on a budget. The rooms look out onto a lovely little internal courtyard filled with shrubs. You pay on arrival and are given your own key to get in. Rooms with basin 100F for 1, 115F for 2; with shower 135F for 1, 170F for 2. No breakfast. It's not exactly the height of luxury but at those prices you can't expect the Ritz.

☗ HÔTEL MODERNE DU TEMPLE

3 rue d'Aix; M° République or Goncourt.
☎ 01.42.08.09.04 F 01.42.41.72.17

The archetypal "pleasant surprise" kind of hotel. It's between the lock of the Saint-Martin canal and the steep section of Faubourg-du-Temple, in a narrow street where the colours of the houses are reminiscent of little fishing ports baking under the sun. The hotel belongs to a friendly Slovak who, after rather modest beginnings in 1989, now has 43 rooms, all with at least the same standard of comfort you'd find in the nearby youth hostel. Very simple little bar. Doubles range in price from 140F and 180F with washing facilities to 240F with shower/wc. Room number 29 is especially nice. Direct telephone in each room. Breakfast 23F.

10% ☗ NEW HOTEL**

40 rue Saint-Quentin; M° Gare-de-l'Est.
☎ 01.48.78.04.83 F 01.40.82.91.22

The area around train stations has never really been the most inspiring of places and we're not going to pretend that this place is any better than any other cheap hotel but it's quiet, a fact that's definitely worth mentioning. The rooms are perfectly acceptable with everything you'd expect from a 2 -star hotel, from TV to the essential hair dryer (well, most rooms have them). And somebody with a sense of humour has converted the cellar into three little vaulted dining rooms decorated in medieval style and with a little fountain in a niche where you can have a hearty breakfast of croissants, *brioches*, cornflakes, orange juice and so on. If you turn right when you leave the hotel, there's a terrace at the end of a short street where you can watch the trains coming in and out of Gare de l'Est and get a magnificent view of Paris. Doubles 335F with shower, 450F with bath. A few rooms have air-conditioning and cost 510F. Breakfast included in price.

10% ☗ NORD-EST HÔTEL **

12 rue des Petits-Hôtels; M° Gare-du-Nord or Gare-de-l'Est.
☎ 01.47.70.07.18 F 01.42.46.73.50
Secure parking. TV.

You'll need to book a long time in advance if you want to stay in this lovely little hotel (well, when you think what the street's called it's hard to be anything else isn't it?) in a quiet street halfway between the two stations. It has oak panelling on the walls, clean functional rooms, and pink-tiled bathrooms. Doubles with shower/wc and TV 370F, with bath 400F. You might be able to talk them into reducing their rates if you're there out of season. Breakfast 30F. The private car park's expensive at 90F a day.

10% ☗ HÔTEL-RÉSIDENCE MAGENTA**

35 rue Yves-Toudic; M° Gare-du-Nord or Gare-de-l'Est. République or Jacques-Bonsergent.
☎ 01.42.40.17.72 F 01.42.02.59.66

Advisable to book one week in advance. This hotel, in a quiet street between République and the Saint-Martin canal, is a real bargain. We were taken with the rooms on the sixth floor with their panelled ceilings and exposed beams. If the weather's fine, have breakfast on the pretty little patio. Rooms have cable TV and direct phone. Doubles with shower/wc 380F–400F. Three people will pay 450F and four 530F. Breakfast 40F. The owners are pleasant and helpful and smile a lot. You'll pay 65F a day to park.

|●| RESTAURANT DE BOURGOGNE

26 rue des Vinaigriers; M° Jacques-Bonsergent or République.
☎ 01.46.07.07.91
Closed Saturday evenings, Sundays, public holidays, the last week in July, and the first two in August.

Service at lunchtime and in the evening until 11pm. This little neighbourhood restaurant, a stone's throw from the *Hôtel du Nord* and the romantic Saint-Martin canal with its Venetian bridge, hasn't changed a bit over the past few years. Ordinary people come here. Owner Maurice, a friend of ours, takes full advantage of his cooking to judge by his waistline. Very inexpensive set meals at 65F (evenings), drink extra, and 60F (lunchtimes). The house wine costs 33F and a Cotes de Provence 50F. What more could you ask for?

|●| QUAI N° 3

3 rue de Nancy; M° Jacques-Bonsergent.
☎ 01.42.08.03.00
Closed Sunday evenings and Mondays, the last week in August and the 1st 2 weeks in Sept.

Despite being decorated to look like a station platform, this restaurant is for lovers of good food rather than train enthusiasts. Gérard, who does the cooking, takes his inspiration from traditional French dishes but sometimes he uses spices from India, China and the

Caribbean to expose his customers to new culinary experiences. Meat and fish couldn't be in better hands and his sauces are sublime. Christophe looks after the front of the house and an extremely attentive host he is. A must. Lunchtime set meal 69F. Reckon on paying 140F in the evening.

|●| LA VIGNE SAINT-LAURENT

2 rue Saint-Laurent; M° Gare-de-l'Est.
☎ 01.42.05.98.20
Closed Saturdays, Sundays, three weeks in August, and one week at the end of the year.

Service till 2.30pm and 7–10.30pm. If you've got a train to catch or you're seeing somebody off, don't just dive into the nearest brasserie. Come to this little wine bar instead – it's only a couple of minutes walk from the station. Inside it's long and narrow with a lovely spiral staircase and is altogether a very pleasant place. The owners are two exceedingly polite chaps with mustaches and they do the cooking. Daily specials like) are put together with care. But if you just want something to nibble on they also do plates of *charcuterie*, and their cheese is superb (Saint-Marcellin matured *à la lyonnaise*, for example, or Arôme de Lyon matured in marc). Their many wines, including Viognier d'Ardèche, Coteaux-du- Lyonnais, Mondeuse-de-Savoie and Cairanne, are available by the glass or the bottle. About 130F for a meal.

|●| LE PHÉNIX CAFÉ

4 rue du Faubourg-Poissonnière; M° Bonne Nouvelle.
☎ 01.47.70.35.40
Closed Saturdays, Sundays, and in August.

Service until 11.30pm. All bistros should be like this. It has everything you're looking for – an old zinc bar with high stools and big round mirrors on the walls. Pleasant atmosphere and nice reception. There's no set meal or menu. Instead, everything's written up on slates hung at strategic locations round the walls. They have a wide range of salads (gizzard or *foie gras*, for example) and sandwiches – try the Phénix, a distinctly superior *croque monsieur*. Main courses 54–65F, wine by the glass 17F and 20F. Reckon on 120F for a meal. Good restaurant with good vibes.

|●| RESTAURANT FLO

7 cour des Petites-Écuries; M° Château-d'Eau.
☎ 01.47.70.13.59
Closed at Christmas.

Open every day till 1.30am. One of THE places for *choucroute*. Herr Floederer's old brasserie which dates from 1886 doesn't look a day older than when it opened. Actors appearing at the nearby theatres – Sarah Bernhardt for example, when she was at the Renaissance – had food delivered to them in their dressing rooms. Superb 1900 décor with stained glass windows between the rooms, richly decorated ceilings, leather banquettes, lights, and brass hatstands. They do seafood platters (206F), a terrific *choucroute* for two, escalope of *foie gras* with apples and grapes, and sole *meunière* (coated in bread-crumbs and fried in butter), Prices are reasonable when you consider the setting. There's a set meal for 123F at lunchtime and 128F in the evening (after 10pm) consisting of main course plus starter or dessert, drink included. There's another evening set meal at 169F. About 220F à la carte. Flo's customers are young and not so young Parisians and lots and lots of tourists. The atmosphere is always cheerful.

|●| RESTAURANT JULIEN

16 rue du Faubourg-Saint-Denis; M° Strasbourg-Saint-Denis.
☎ 01.47.70.12.06
Closed at Christmas.

Service every day till 1.30am. Another cheap restaurant – one of the oldest in Paris – given a makeover by the talented Monsieur Bücher. The same old ingredients continue to work their magic: the dazzling Art Nouveau interior, service that's as fast as it's efficient, and skilfully prepared dishes. Specialities include salad of duck *foie gras* and morels, warm *foie gras* with lentils, and a substantial goose *cassoulet*. Customers are mainly showbiz types. Set meals 123F and 169F at lunchtime, 128F and 183F after 10pm. Reckon on paying about 180F à la carte.

|●| RESTAURANT BAALBECK

16 rue de Mazagran; M° Bonne-Nouvelle.
☎ 01.47.70.70.02
Closed Sundays.

Service at lunchtime and in the evening until midnight (1am Fridays and Saturdays). A couple of pointers on how to have a successful time here: one, you absolutely positively MUST book and two, come in the evening. This Lebanese restaurant has some of the best Middle Eastern cooking in Paris. If there are four of you, have the special *mezze* at 595F and you'll get 18 different kinds of hors d'œuvre. Things really begin to hot up after 9.30, when the belly dancers make their appearance – they're the genuine article by the way. Reckon on 120–140F with wine, not to mention the tip for the dancers Don't run away with the idea that a couple of banknotes will buy you extra time though. One of our favourite restaurants in Paris.

CHEZ MICHEL

10 rue de Belzunce; M° Gare-du-Nord.
☎ 01.44.53.06.20
Closed Sundays and Mondays.

Service until 11pm. The countless people who for one reason or another choose to stay in one of the many hotels near the station will be delighted to know that they can now eat in the area as well as sleep there. Thierry Breton's restaurant resembles a little farm and it and his skills as a chef (He trained at the Ritz and the Crillon) stick out like a sore thumb in a part of the city where greasy spoons abound. He offers a set meal for 160F and what you get for your money is sheer magic – first-rate cooking and first-rate ingredients. The *terrine* of *andouille* with peppercorns and shortbread biscuits made with slightly salted butter (his *terrines* are out of this world) or the guinea fowl ravioli with a sauce made of ceps and crushed walnuts are so incredibly good you'll have to loosen your belt to make room for the *kig ha fong* of pig cheeks and pork fat, the *pain perdu* of Breton sardines or the roast scallops in herb butter and served with baby endives caramelized in orange juice. Desserts like *Paris Brest* (a choux pastry ring with almonds and buttercream) or warm *kouign amann* (traditional Breton yeast cake) are worth every single calorie. With a name like Breton, Thierry could hardly turn his back on the cooking of his native Brittany – and he doesn't!

11th arrondissement

HÔTEL DE VIENNE*

43 rue de Malte; M° Oberkampf or République.
☎ 01.48.05.44.42
Closed in August.

A clean, simple and well-cared for one-star hotel. It's pleasant inside though the wallpaper's a bit tacky. Reasonable prices. Doubles with basin 160F, with shower 220F. Breakfast 30F. Good location in a quiet street close to Place de la République. It would be nice if they smiled occasionally. No credit cards.

10% HÔTEL NOTRE-DAME**

51 rue de Malte; M° République or Oberkampf.
☎ 01.47.00.78.76 ➡ 01.43.55.32.31
TV.

Best to book. A well-kept 2-star hotel in a good location. Everything is grey, down to the business cards and the cat!. Rooms, refurbished recently and redecorated with taste, are well equipped with direct phones and clock-radios, and colour TV. The ones on the street side get more light. Singles with basin or shower 200–240F, doubles with shower/wc or bath 290–370F. Breakfast (35F) is served until 9.30am. They don't take cheques.

HÔTEL MONDIA**

22 rue du Grand-Prieuré; M° République.
☎ 01.47.00.93.44 ➡ 01.43.38.66.14
TV. **Canal+**.

This hotel in a quiet little street is a good base if you're doing the sights on foot – Belleville, Ménilmontant and the Bastille are not too far away and the Marais-Les Halles area is just round the corner. A family-run hotel that's very well cared for, it has comfortable rooms with full bathroom (shower or bath), hair dryer, safe, direct telephone and so on. Doubles from 320F. Prices are negotiable depending on the length of your stay. Breakfast 30F. Readers of this guidebook will get a 10% reduction, except when the World Cup's on.

10% HÔTEL BEAUSÉJOUR**

71 av. Parmentier; M° Parmentier or Oberkampf.
☎ 01.47.00.38.16 ➡ 01.43.55.47.89
TV.

A hotel with 31 rooms on six floors (don't worry, theres a lift!). They all have bath or shower, double-glazing, TV and direct telephone. There's a little bar in the reception area that's open 24 hours and you can also get room service. There's a little kitchen you can use if you don't want to put a strain on your food budget by always eating out. Rooms 320F for 1 person, 380F for 2, 480F for 3, and 550F for 4. Charming welcome and the icing on the cake is the fact that you'll get a 25–30% reduction on presentation of this guide book. All credit cards welcome.

10% HÔTEL DAVAL**

21 rue Daval; M° Bastille.
☎ 01.47.00.51.23 ➡ 01.40.21.80.26
TV. **Canal+**.

A nice 2-star hotel with modern décor and facilities (TV, double-glazing, and mini-safe) in the heart of the lively Bastille neighbourhood, near the bars of rue de Lappe and rue de la Roquette. Double rooms with shower 390F, breakfast – better than average – 45F. You'll get 10% discount on presentation of this guide. Don't be frightened of the Alsatian, he doesn't bite!

|●| NEW NIOULLAVILLE

32 rue de l'Orillon; M° Belleville.
☎ 01.40.21.96.18

Service until 1am. This immense restaurant, which can seat 500, has been given a whole new look. The kitchen has been renovated throughout, the ceiling and lighting in the dining rooms have been altered, and air conditioning has been put in. The dim sum (20–28F) trolley does its rounds from table to table until 11pm. Other delights are Cantonese or Szechuan specialities like duck smoked over jasmine – then there are the tofu dishes, the noodles, the soups and the roasts, and Cambodian dishes, not to mention the ones from Vietnam and Thailand. We had a memorable lacquered duck (the skin served with rice pancakes, the meat stir fried with vegetables or noodles, and clear soup) for 4 at 260F, the kind of thing that's good to share. There are a dozen or so high chairs available – French restaurants please copy – so parents can eat out with their children. Great atmosphere. Several set meals (48F, 58F, 68F and 78F) available at lunchtime only. Another, at 38F, is described as being for women and consists of plain salad, an assortment of dim sum and boiled rice.

|●| SUDS

55 rue de Charonne; M° Ledru-Rollin.
☎ 01.43.14.06.36
Closed Saturday lunchtimes.

"The south" is the restaurant's speciality, and not just the south of France either. Your choice of food and drink will also take you on a culinary tour of Spain, Portugal and Latin America. This is the place for you if you have a taste for the exotic. Try the *foie gras* with sweet potato (68F), the duck breast with a *tagine* of potatoes with garlic and saffron (88F) that comes with three "latino" sauces, one of them spicy or the *assiettes catalanes* (45F). The cod served in three ways (65F) and the mutton stew (68F) would make a hefty snack at lunchtime and in the evening respectively. Great Latin American music in the background.

|●| LES CINQ POINTS CARDINAUX

14 rue Jean-Macé; M° Faidherbe-Chaligny or Charonne.
☎ 01.43.71.47.22
Closed Saturdays, Sundays, and in August.

Service until 10pm. When the restaurant had to move because renovation work was starting at its old address, the proprietors headed a bit further east to this quiet spot in the 11th arrondissement. The address may have changed but the same spirit prevails and you can eat here (in Madame's words) "with no worries/without being ripped off whether you're middle-class or a tramp, a labourer or an intellectual. Old tools belonging to local craftsmen hang from the ceiling. The atmosphere is relaxed and the cooking unpretentious. You can eat very well here for 58F (wine included) at lunchtime; dinner costs 63F or 99F.

|●| RESTAURANT À L'AMI PIERRE

5 rue de la Main-d'Or; M° Ledru-Rollin.
☎ 01.47.00.17.35
Closed Sundays and Mondays.

Service until midnight. Marie-Jo's been in the Bastille area for more than 30 years now, the past 10 of them in this restaurant, which used to be the waiting room of the local bonesetter. She's a very relaxed sort and treats her clients like friends. The atmosphere can get a bit heated some evenings if the rugby fans tangle with the regulars – arty types like film-makers and designers. You can have a glass or two of wine (Pouilly, Cahors or Quincy, for example) and stoke up on a plate of *charcuterie* (50F) or the 60F day's special (substantial servings of things like beef *bourguignon*, *pot au feu*, ox tail, or creamed salt cod) for the long night ahead – which can go on until dawn sometimes!

|●| RESTAURANT LE ROYAL BELLEVILLE

19 rue Louis-Bonnet; M° Belleville.
☎ 01.43.38.22.72

Service 11am–2am. An immense restaurant housed in what used to be a department store, this is more like a works canteen than anything else and it's so ugly it's almost beautiful. The cooking however is perfectly adequate and the food perfectly fresh. The menu is as long as your arm and it's hard to single out any one dish, except maybe the crispy intestines which you don't come across every day. It's always busy but the service, while not friendly, is very good. Uninspiring set meal 66F. About 100F à la carte but you can get away with less.

|●| RESTAURANT CHEZ JUSTINE

96 rue Oberkampf; M° Saint-Maur or Ménilmontant.
☎ 01.43.57.44.03
Closed Monday lunchtimes, Sundays, and August.

Service until 11.00pm. A restaurant to warm the hearts of all those with big appetites and not much money. Justine is no Scrooge and for 90F you can help yourself to as many hors d'œuvres as you like from the buffet, follow that up with a meat dish of your choice, dessert, and wine from the barrel. You can pig out to your heart's content for 145F, which gets you two starters, a wide choice of main courses, and generous helpings of dessert. Rustic décor, log fire, and a clientele that's half working class, half intellectual.

CEFALU

43 av. Philippe-Auguste; M° Nation.
☎ 01.43.71.29.34
Closed Saturday lunchtimes, Sundays, and two weeks in August.

This Sicilian restaurant is one of the best ambassadors for regional Italian cooking in Paris and yet very few people know about it. Mr Cala comes from Mussomeli (famous for its impregnable fortress) and the skill with which he cooks does his homeland proud. He offers Sicilian *antipasti* (60F), wonderful spaghetti with fresh sardines, currants, wild fennel and pine nuts (65F), a superb sole with aubergine caviar (90F), and spaghetti Sicilian style – ie with garlic, tomatoes, aubergine, capers, anchovies, olives, basil and oregano (55F). For dessert, try the *cannolo* at 35F, a Sicilian treat traditionally served on Sundays. It's something like a brandy snap filled with fresh ricotta, candied fruit and chocolate, usually accompanied by a glass of Marsala. Pretty décor in the naïf style and very, very clean. They do an 89F *formule* (not available Friday evenings or Saturdays) and a *menu dégustation* at 180F.

LE CLOWN BAR

114 rue Amelot; M° Filles-du-Calvaire.
☎ 01.43.55.87.35
Closed Sundays lunchtime and the week of the 15th August.

Service until midnight. This wine bar is a listed building and is really easy on the eye. There's a frieze running round the walls depicting 15 or so clowns while the ceiling has a clown and a Pierrot sharing an umbrella. The daily special is reasonably priced and you won't feel you've been made to pay for the handsome surroundings. Starters 30–55F. Day's special 68–75F.

RESTAURANT CHEZ PAUL

13 rue de Charonne; M° Bastille or Ledru-Rollin.
☎ 01.47.00.34.57

Service at lunchtime and in the evening until half past midnight. Good location at the corner of rue Lappe and rue Charonne. The décor consists of rather faded mirrors (probably from seeing so many customers come and go), a few familiar objects such as old siphons, and rather curious flooring (the tiles seem to lose interest in Cubism about halfway and they all go off and do their own thing). At lunchtime there's a fair sprinkling of well-to-do youngsters and three-piece suits while in the evening it's rather more chic. It's all home cooking here, and hearty dishes like roast rabbit with goat's cheese and mint, boiled beef with vegetables in winter, calf's head with *sauce gribiche* (spicy vinaigrette), and *gratin dauphinois* are served up in generous portions. Reckon on 180F à la carte, not including wine. Tables outside on the pavement in good weather.

LE VILLARET

13 rue Ternaux; M° Parmentier.
☎ 01.43.57.75.56
Closed lunchtimes, Sundays, two weeks in May, all of August, and ten days at Christmas and New Year.

Service until 1am. Michel Picquart has left the restaurant and we won't see him behind the bar again joking with the customers. Joel, who used to be responsible for the dining room, and the 25 year old chef Olivier Gaslain have taken over the reins. What's on the menu still depends on what's available at Rungis (Olivier used to go with Michel on his sorties there), the prices haven't changed and neither has the restaurant's remedy for whatever ails you – a wine from the list that is still Michel's responsibility. They have lots of the great vintages at reasonable prices. Depending on what day it is and what the chef has been able to find at Rungis, you'll be served as a starter scallops and thyme *en papillote* (baked in paper), fricassee of ceps with garlic and flat parsley or great fat stalks of green asparagus followed by medallions of monkfish with a sauce made from small crabs, calf's liver in Banyuls vinegar or a terrific sirloin steak with shallots and a *gratin* of Jerusalem artichokes. One of the best restaurants in Paris for dinner. Reckon on paying about 160F.

12th arrondissement

HÔTEL DES TROIS GARES**

1 rue Jules-César; M° Gare-de-Lyon.
☎ 01.43.43.01.70 Fax 01.43.41.36.58
TV.

Good location in a quiet street between the Gare de Lyon, the Gare d'Austerlitz and Bastille-Plaisance. The foyer is decidedly modern and the rooms – functional, with minimalist décor – are too. Doubles with washbasin 230F, with shower/wc, TV and direct telephone 300–330F, with bath 350–420F. Breakfast is free if you can show them a copy of this guide! Very nice owner.

10% ☗ LUX HÔTEL**

8 av. de Corbéra; M° Reuilly-Diderot or Gare-de-Lyon.
☎ 01.43.43.42.84 F 01.43.43.14.45

The past still hangs in the air in the little TV room with its embroidered armchairs and the old-fashioned mural. The antiquated lift with its black grilles adds to the old-fashioned charm of this 2-star hotel with its misleading air of a boarding house. Doubles with shower/wc or bath, TV and wc 250–350F. Breakfast 27F. Some rooms have cooking facilities for people planning a longer stay, and prices are negotiable.

☗ MARCEAU**

13 rue Jules-César; M° Gare-de-Lyon or Bastille
☎ 01.43.43.11.65 F 01.43.41.67.70
Closed July 20–Aug 20. **TV**.

We don't know if General Marceau (he led the troops who, in 1793, put down the insurrections in the Vendée against the Revolutionary government) ever slept here. But the fact that the hotel and the general share a name has given the proprietor a good excuse for proudly putting on display in the reception area a page (bought at auction) in the General's handwriting. The rooms aren't bad and some are quite well décorated with co-ordinating fabric and wall lights and wood panelling in the same shades of grey. The rooms overlooking the courtyard don't have a great view but you can't have everything. Other rooms have what they call a Swedish shower – if you've never had one, make the most of this opportunity. Doubles 280F, 300F, 355F and 375F with shower or bath. Breakfast 35F.

☗ NOUVEL HÔTEL**

24 av. Bel Air; M° Nation.
☎ 01.43.43.01.81 F 01.43.44.64.13
TV.

A stone's throw from place de la Nation, so very handy for buses, the metro or the RER. The street couldn't be quieter and all the rooms have double-glazing too. It's as clean as a whistle, and has a delightful garden – most of the rooms look onto it – where you can sit and relax in the shade of a medlar tree. Rustic décor but excellent facilities. Doubles with shower 375F, with bath, 405F. Single rooms 355–375F. Connecting rooms for families 605F for 3 and 670F for 4. Breakfast 40F.

10% ☗ HÔTEL SAPHIR**

35 rue de Cîteaux; M° Faidherbe-Chaligny, Reuilly-Diderot or Gare de Lyon.
☎ 01.43.07.77.28 F 01.43.46.67.45
TV.

A stone's throw from faubourg Saint-Antoine. Well-equipped rooms, decorated in pink, blue, green, or beige (take your pick!). Doubles with shower/wc or bath, TV, mini-bar and direct telephone 470F. Rooms for that sleep three or four are 615F. Breakfast (35F) is free on presentation of this guide and is served in a wonderful vaulted cellar. And yet another little treat for our readers – you'll get a 10% reduction in peak season, 20% in low season.

|●| AU PAYS DE VANNES

34 [bis] rue de Wattignies; M° Michel-Bizot.
☎ 01.43.07.87.42
Closed evenings and Sundays.

If you're looking for a good local café, look no further. There's a large Breton flag on the wall, so you can assume that the proprietors are from Brittany and proud of the fact. It's busy, which is hardly surprising when you consider the reasonably priced 56.50F set meal (drink included) and the choice of dishes you get for your main course. How about sautéd pork with salsify, roast guinea fowl with shredded leeks, chicken with rice, or breast of veal stuffed with braised celery hearts? A starter (along the lines of egg mayonnaise) and dessert (home-made *crème caramel*) are included. A good simple traditional French meal of the kind that is becoming increasingly rare in Paris and the best value for money in the arrondissement. There's another set meal at 105F. Whole families turn up at lunchtime on Saturdays to stuff themselves on oysters that have come straight from Normandy. Friendly and down to earth reception and service.

|●| CAPPADOCE

12 rue de Capri; M° Michel-Bizot or Daumesnil.
☎ 01.43.46.17.20
Closed Sundays and three weeks in August.

Turkish hospitality, kindness and unobtrusiveness are the hallmarks of this establishment and they, together with fairly elaborate cooking, have helped spread its reputation far beyond the neighbourhood. The cheese roll and the aubergine caviar are exquisite and very Oriental while the *pides* (Turkish pizzas), the grills and the kebabs will give your tastebuds a real treat. It's obvious why the restaurant is a success and it's best to book ahead for dinner. There are three well thought out set meals available: vegetarian at 70F, slimmer's at 80F and gourmet at 125F. Don't overlook the home-made desserts – the pumpkin in syrup is extraordinary, a bit like quince paste.

PIZZÉRIA PALMA

38 av. Ledru-Rollin; M° Gare-de-Lyon.
☎ 01.43.43.90.78
Closed Sundays and in August.

Service noon–2pm and 7–10pm. The proprietors of this family-owned trattoria very close to the Gare de Lyon come from Lucca in Tuscany and their establishment is just like the ones you find in small towns in Italy. You can tell that by the number of Italian railway workers who eat here when they're in Paris. Don't expect great culinary flights of fancy but Mamma makes good pasta and the cannelloni is delicious. Husband Angelo makes decent pizzas with all the usual panache. Set meal (73F) offers *crudités*, rabbit *alla toscana*, lamb chops *alla Milanese* or squid casserole, and dessert.

LES ZYGOMATES

7 rue de Capri; M° Michel-Bizot or Daumesnil.
☎ 01.40.19.93.04
Closed Saturday lunchtimes, Sundays, and August.

Service noon–2pm and 7.30–10.30pm. It's advisable to book – honestly, how on earth do people think they can keep a good restaurant to themselves if they tell their friends about it? Nothing has changed here since the turn of the century. The trompe l'œil décor, the varnished wood, the marble and the hunting scenes that were there when this was a butcher's shop are still there. Best of all, the prices are reasonable – there's a set meal for 75F and the 130F *formule-carte* is incredibly good, offering house duck and pistachio nut *terrine*, cod with pears and basil, and *gratin* of fruits in Maraschino liqueur. Considering the quality of the cooking and what they charge, this is more like a philanthropic undertaking than a restaurant.

DAME TARTINE

59 rue de Lyon; M° Bastille.
☎ 01.44.68.96.95

Food served noon–11pm. French children sing a song called "Au pays de dame Tartine". Well, this restaurant's dame Tartine is a nice young lady, very modern in her outlook, who makes hot and cold snacks and if you've been good you can munch on one while chatting away to your friends. We had a slight preference for the cold variety – things like poached egg and shrimps with basil, beef marinated in herbs, taramasalata, and avocado and tomatoes – but the one with Comté cheese and green peppercorns is just the thing in winter. Prices 15-40F. Interesting selection of wines by the glass. It's 200m from the Opéra Bastille, so would be a good place for a snack before the curtain goes up.

RESTAURANT SQUARE TROUSSEAU

1 rue Antoine-Vollon; M° Ledru-Rollin.
☎ 01.43.43.06.00

Two layers of curtains – net and red velvet – shield you from curious eyes in this restaurant that in style and atmosphere resembles a 1900 bistro. Relax and enjoy the elegant surroundings – a superb antique zinc bar, mosaic flooring, red artificial leather banquettes, and mouldings on the ceiling. The day's specials and set meal are chalked up on blackboards. At lunchtimes only there's a set meal of starter, main course, dessert and coffee for 100F. Good home cooking but it's a bit elaborate. The à la carte menu changes every month according to the season and what's available at the market. The presentation is pretty and the wine list has been put together well – not the usual run of the mill stuff. Customers are elegant but relaxed. Sunday brunch 90F. Reckon on 200F à la carte. Children's menu 60F. A very good restaurant with a fair number of regulars. Terrace in summer.

RESTAURANT À LA BICHE AU BOIS

45 av. Ledru-Rollin; M° Gare-de-Lyon or Ledru-Rollin.
☎ 01.43.43.34.38
Closed Saturdays, Sundays, mid July–mid Aug, and Christmas week.

Service at lunchtime and in the evening until 10pm. You'd be well advised to book. If you like the old style of restaurant that does traditional bourgeois dishes then this is the place for you. It even has the right kind of delightfully old-fashioned décor – colour prints and amateurish paintings of woods in autumn, a Louis XIV style clock, artificial flowers, and artificial leather banquettes. This little restaurant gives some of the best value for money in Paris in the shape of its set meals at 105F and 120F. Depending on what day it is you'll get *foie gras* with salad, fillet of beef with a cep sauce, fillet of salmon with wild mushrooms, *coq au vin* (which comes to the table in the dish it was cooked in so you can help yourself to the succulent morsels that have absorbed all the flavours of a well reduced sauce), or game in season – haunch of venison say, or venison *terrine*, pheasant casserole, or wild duck with fruit of the forest. Home-made pastries and reasonably priced wines. This is an excellent restaurant for less than 150F.

13th arrondissement

HÔTEL TOLBIAC

122 rue de Tolbiac; M° Tolbiac or Place-d'Italie.
☎ 01.44.24.25.54 Fax 01.45.85.43.47
TV.

An enormous hotel with 47 rooms just five minutes from place d'Italie. Just the thing if you're on a budget. Doubles with basin and TV 160F, with shower/wc and TV 202F, breakfast 15–25F. Pleasant reception and the rooms are clean. Rue de Tolbiac is quite noisy but a number of the rooms are fitted with double glazing

10% HÔTEL STHRAU*

1 rue Sthrau; M° Nationale, Tolbiac or Porte d'Ivry.
☎ 01.45.83.20.35 Fax 01.44.24.91.21
TV.

A basic but clean little hotel five minutes from the *Bibliothèque François Mitterand* that's ideal if you're on a tight budget. Doubles with basin 170F, with shower 205F and with bath 256F. A single room costs only 130F. Breakfast 25F (free on your first morning on presentation of this guide). TV is 15F extra and an additional bed is 50F.

10% RÉSIDENCE LES GOBELINS**

9 rue des Gobelins; M° Gobelins; bus number 27, 47, 83 and 91.
☎ 01.47.07.26.90 Fax:01.43.31.44.05
TV.

As you can see, the hotel couldn't be more accessible if it tried! It's also quiet and great value for money. Proprietress Jennifer Poirier, a lovely woman, has lovely rooms with bath 395–425F (all have Canal+). You can sit outside in the little garden on spring evenings. Breakfast 37F. A brief history lesson: rue des Gobelins follows the same route as the street that was here in the Middle Ages, and the château belonging to Blanche of Castile, wife of Louis VIII and mother of Louis IX, is just round the corner.

10% RÉSIDENCE HÔTELIÈRE LE VERT GALANT*** –

41-43 rue Croulebarbe; M° Gobelins ou Corvisart.
☎ 01.44.08.83.50 Fax 01.44.08.83.69
Car park. TV. Disabled access.

This establishment, set back a little from the road, has about 15 superb newly renovated rooms, and a garden and lawn. It's quiet and rather charming. Doubles from 400F with shower, 450F with bath. Studio 500F. Breakfast 40F.

10% HÔTEL SAINT-CHARLES***

6 rue de l'Espérance; M° Corvisart.
☎ 01.45.89.56.54 Fax 01.45.88.56.17
TV. Disabled access.

In the heart of one of our favourite parts of Paris, la Butte aux Cailles. Absolutely impeccable rooms with shower, bath and TV. If you want a view of the church of Sainte-Anne and the south Paris then opt for one of the rooms on the upper floors. Little patio garden. Expect to pay about 500F for a double room with shower, 620F with bath. The prices are maybe a bit steep, but it's worth it.

NANG-LAN

1 av. de Choisy; M° Porte-de-Choisy.
☎ 01.45.84.58.07
Closed Mondays.

Set meals (weekday lunchtimes only) 55F and 75F. There may not be anything particularly original about the décor but the cooking – classic Vietnamese – is good. On the other hand, don't go overboard and order dishes that are too specialized. There's probably not much demand for these and freshness can't always be guaranteed. Go for simple things like *ph* (pronounced phew), the traditional soup, the *bo bun* or a kebab. And if you've never tasted sticky rice, now's the time to try. The size of the bill will depend on how hungry you are – reckon on 70–120F.

RESTAURANT LE TEMPS DES CERISES

18 rue de la Butte-aux-Cailles; M° Corvisart.
☎ 01.45.89.69.48
Closed Saturday lunchtimes and Sundays.

Lunch served noon-2pm and dinner 7.30-11.45pm. This a workers' co-operative whose fame has spread beyond the Butte aux Cailles and it can get quite crowded. It has the kind of relaxed atmosphere you get in a local bistro, and the waiters treat everybody with the same informality. The wine list is chalked up on a large blackboard. Set meals for 56F (lunchtime) and 60F (evening) and there's also a 118F *formule*. The restaurant is one of the pillars of the community and is a must. That being said, the cooking has become set in its ways and has been trundling along in the same old rut for a good few years now, give or take the odd blip (of both the pleasant and unpleasant variety). So, a few ups and downs as regards quality but there's always a warm welcome for good hearty dishes like pears with Roquefort and sautéd leg of lamb. Egalitarian prices.

|●| RESTAURANT L'ESPÉRANCE

9 rue de l'Espérance; M° Place-d'Italie or Corvisart.
☎ 01.45.80.22.55
Closed Sundays and in August.

Service at lunchtime and in the evening until 11pm. Friendly welcome. Unpretentious neighbourhood restaurant where the locals come for good food. They do a few specialities and these come in generous portions – couscous with merguez is 40–71F, for example. You won't find better. Set meal 55.50F.

|●| À LA BOUILLABAISSE, CHEZ KERYADO

32 rue Regnault; M° Porte-d'Ivry.
☎ 01.45.83.87.58
Closed Monday evenings, Sundays, and the second fortnight in August.

Located on the fringes of the 13th arrondissement and Bercy, this is a wonderful fish restaurant that has just been taken over by a young couple. Bistro-type décor. The *bouillabaisse* is excellent (and Lord knows it's easier to find a needle in a haystack than it is to find a decent *bouillabaisse* in Paris). Dishes are cooked to order and prices are not too bad considering. Set meal at lunchtime (weekdays only) 59F, 110F and 150F. Reckon on 150F à la carte but the quality of the meal justifies the size of the bill. A good place for reminiscing with friends about your last holiday meal together. If you don't want fish, there's a choice of grilled dishes and the meat is very tender.

|●| RESTAURANT BIDA SAIGON

44 av. d'Ivry; M° Porte-d'Ivry.
☎ 01.45.84.04.85

A large works canteen of a place that you'll find tucked away at the end of a corridor running at right angles to the galerie d'Oslo (near the terrasse des Olympiades exit). Friendly welcome. The menu consists of the standard 20 or so savoury dishes. The soups (*phô* and Saigon soup) come in large or small bowls (36–42F) and the helpings are generous. The spring rolls are crisp and the steamed rice cake is.. steamed rice cake. Pork spare ribs, grilled chicken with lemon grass, and rice with pork and stuffed crab will cost you 35–38F. Desserts are 14–17F. Try the white beans with sticky rice or the lotus seeds with seaweed and longans (which are a bit like lychees) – weird, but not unpleasant. It's not licensed except for beer, but naturally they also have fizzy drinks, fresh fruit juice and tea.

|●| RESTAURANT LA TOURAINE

39 rue Croulebarbe; M° Corvisart or Les Gobelins.
☎ 01.47.07.69.35
Closed Sundays.

Service at lunchtime and in the evening until 10.30pm. It's best to book, especially if you want a table on the terrace. It's really quiet in the evening. Delightful reception. Two large rooms with rustic – but not too rustic – décor. Lovely country cooking, with dishes like calf's sweetbreads with morels, zander with *beurre blanc*, and crayfish *à la tourangelle*. Substantial set meal 135F and, if you're not too hungry, the one at 69F, all in, is more than adequate. Free kir if you can produce this guide. And if you fancy a stroll to help with the digestive process, there's a little garden on the other side of the street. What more do you want?

|●| VIÊT-NAM MILLÉNAIRE

11 rue Philibert-Lucot; M° Maison-Blanche.
☎ 01.45.85.78.44
Closed Mondays and the second fortnight in August.

Cute little restaurant with tables far enough apart for you to whisper sweet nothings in somebody's ear without the other diners being able to hear every single word. Refined style of cooking in the best Vietnamese tradition. Try the Vietnamese fondu, the beef kebabs, the duck with banana flowers or the casserole of "beautifully moist fish from the delta", which is terrific. Set meal 90F (lunchtimes only). Reckon on about 100F à la carte. The quiet setting and attentive service justify the prices, which are slightly higher than average for the area.

|●| LE BISTRO DU VIADUC

12 rue Tolbiac; M° Chevaleret.
☎ 01.45.83.74.66
Closed Sundays and three weeks in August.

Léo Malet, who set one of his Nestor Burma stories under the nearby bridge, might have dropped into this bistro, which used to be a workingman's café called *Chez Mammy*. The proles have been replaced by white-collar workers and the cooking has become a touch more elaborate. The 95F set meal (drink included) won't make you think you're being taken for a ride and the one at 158F offers some noble dishes – langoustines with poached egg and tarragon vinegar, for example, or sole *meunière*. Good cooking, classical in style and none the worse for that.

L'ANACRÉON

53 bd Saint-Marcel; M° Les Gobelins.
☎ 01.43.31.71.18
Closed Sundays and Mondays, in August, and one week in winter.

Situated in a rather dreary street, this is a restaurant to cheer the hearts of local gourmets. The impeccable 180F set meal was devised by a chef who trained at *Prunier* and *La Tour d'Argent* and is a combination of country produce and great skill in preparation. It offers a choice of rabbit terrine with *foie gras* and vegetables or scrambled eggs with tomatoes and peppers followed by either veal kidneys in a mustard sauce or cod with endives and, for dessert, a *parfait* with custard. There's talent here and it shows. Extremely good service and a wine list that matches the cooking. Set lunchtime meal 125F.

CHEZ PAUL

22 rue de la Butte-aux-Cailles; M° Place-d'Italie or Corvisart.
☎ 01.45.89.22.11
Closed during the Christmas and New Year holidays.

Service at lunchtime and in the evening until midnight. New-style bistro that has been successfully grafted onto the Butte. Pleasant, low-key setting decorated with fleshy leaved plants. Excellent bistro cooking and friendly welcome. The proprietor has a sly sense of humour and has had some fun ideas (like digging up apéritifs from the Neanderthal age). The menu is quite extensive, offering dishes such as oxtail *terrine*, *coq au vin*, stewed beef in a wine sauce, roast suckling pig with sage, and home-made braised tripe. Wine is reasonably priced – you can have a Brouilly for 60F, for example, or a Château Ventenac for 75F. Desserts are delicious. There's always one or two daily specials on the traditional slate. Reckon on paying 150–200F.

14th arrondissement

HÔTEL FLORIDOR*

28 place Denfert-Rochereau; M° Denfert-Rochereau.
☎ 01.43.21.35.53 F 01.43.27.65.81
TV.

A nice little hotel. There's still an air of the past hanging around in the shape of the ancient lift with its swing doors. The rooms (all with double-glazing) are cute, with pretty wallpaper. Doubles with basin 195F, with shower/wc 259F, with bath 278F. Breakfast 25F. Good place if you're on a tight budget.

HÔTEL DU PARC MONTSOURIS**

4 rue du Parc-Montsouris; M° Porte-d'Orléans; RER Cité-Universitaire.
☎ 01.45.89.09.72 F 01.45.80.92.72
TV.

You'll appreciate the peace and quiet of this delightful street, just 10m from the park. The hotel, recently renovated, is resolutely modern and functional. Doubles with shower, TV and telephone from 320F, 380F with bath. Reckon on 430F for three people. Breakfast 30F.

HÔTEL DU ROND-POINT**

144 rue de la Tombe-Issoire; M° Porte-d'Orléans; bus number 28, 38 or 68.
☎ 01.45.40.67.95
TV.

The best thing about this hotel – a lot of reps use it – is its location: It's opposite the teaching hospital and is a stone's throw from Cité universitaire. An added advantage for anyone coming in from Orly is that the airport bus stops just outside (the name of the stop is Tombe-Issoire-Jourdan). The décor is pretty ordinary. The rooms couldn't be described as large (about nine square metres) but they all have TV and come with shower or bath. If you produce this guide, a double with shower or bath will cost you 310F, with bath 350F. Breakfast 35F. Friendly welcome.

HÔTEL DE GRANVILLE**

29 rue Deparcieux; M° Denfert-Rochereau or Gaîté.
☎ 01.43.22.29.57 F 01.43.27.22.02
TV.

A small 2-star hotel that has been well maintained. The cul-de-sac is extremely quiet and the rooms that overlook it are perhaps more interesting than the ones that don't. Doubles 380F with bathroom, TV and telephone. Breakfast (30F) offert July and August.

☗ HÔTEL DES BAINS*

33 rue Delambre; M° Vavin or Edgar-Quinet.
☎ 01.43.20.85.27 ➡ 01.42.79.82.78
Secure parking. TV. Canal+.

How to feel years younger in the middle of Paris! There's no denying that this 1-star hotel has character, despite the rather restrained façade. The rooms have been tastefully decorated and even the bedspreads and shades for the wall lights have been carefully chosen to blend in with the colour scheme. Doubles with shower/wc and TV (11 channels, including Canal+) 395F. One particularly nice thing about the hotel is that it puts luxury within everyone's reach. There are suites at 468F for 2, 530F for a un couple with child, 580F with 2 children and 630F with 3 children, in a separate building in the courtyard, which are ideal for families since they have two bedrooms and a bath. They're also very quiet and comfortable. Breakfast 46F. We really liked this place and it's not expensive considering what you get. Credit cards not accepted. Private car park 68F a day.

☗ HÔTEL DAGUERRE**

94 rue Daguerre; M° Gaité.
☎ 01.43.22.43.54 ➡ 01.43.20.66.84
TV. Disabled access.

If you have champagne tastes but beer income this is just the place for you! It may be only a 2-star establishment but it's treated itself to a facelift of the kind usually reserved for the great ones of the hotel world. The marble, the statue, the trompe l'œil painting, the co-ordinated fabrics, the exposed beams in the dining room, and the romantic patio all combine to create the illusion of a much more glamorous era. And the rooms haven't been forgotten – they're all equipped with safe, mini-bar, and cable TV, and everything is clean and shiny. There are even one or two rooms specially equipped for the disabled. The warm friendly welcome comes at no extra charge. And talking of money, the rates really are incredibly reasonable considering the level of service. Doubles with shower or bath about 430F, suites for foure people 550F. Breakfast (either buffet style or served in your room) 38F.

☗ HÔTEL DELAMBRE***

35 rue Delambre; M° Edgar-Quinet or Vavin.
☎ 01.43.20.66.31 ➡ 01.45.38.91.76
TV. Disabled access.

This hotel, which prides itself on having had André Breton, the founder of surrealism, as one of its guests, has just re-opened its doors after months of renovation work,. Double rooms 440–490F with bath or shower. Buffet breakfast 38F. Very reasonable prices for a hotel in this category.

☗ HÔTEL ISTRIA**

29 rue Campagne-Première; M° Raspail.
☎ 01.43.20.91.82 ➡ 01.43.22.48.45
TV.

A delightful hotel full of literary associations, not to say liaisons. It was here that Elsa Triolet and Aragon used to come and that Raymond Radiguet was unfaithful to Cocteau with a woman. Nancy Cunard used to slip out of the *Plaza* and meet her lovers here. And lots of famous names have stayed in the in the hotel at one time or another, including German poet Rainer Maria Rilke and American photographer Man Ray. So you'll be in illustrious company. The recently renovated rooms are large and well equipped with TV, safe, and hair dryer. You'll pay 495–590FR. If you're staying for two consecutive nights you'll get a 10% reduction if you show them this guidebook. Breakfast 40F.

|●| RESTAURANT AU RENDEZ-VOUS DES CAMIONNEURS

34 rue des Plantes; M° Alésia.
☎ 01.45.40.43.36
Closed Saturdays, Sundays, public holidays, and August.

Service at lunchtime and in the evening until 9.30pm. There aren't many tables so you almost have to book. Despite the name, there are very, very few cloth caps or overalls to be seen – lunchtime customers tend to be people who work in the area and there are a few artists in the evening. Set meal 75F, day's special about 50F. Rib of beef with marrowbone and the house *canard confit* à la carte. Rarely more than 120F and it's hard to see how you could do better.

|●| AUX PRODUITS DU SUD-OUEST

21-23 rue d'Odessa; M° Edgar-Quinet.
☎ 01.43.20.34.07
Closed Sundays, Mondays, and August.

Lunch served noon–2.30pm and dinner 7–10pm (11pm Fridays and Saturdays). This restaurant cum shop sells home-made preserves and conserves from the south-west and the prices are unbeatable. You won't get great gourmet cooking but you will get decent country fare like a plate of *charcuterie* (40F) or *terrine* of rabbit or wild boar (15F). If you're not very hungry, you could just have a serving of *cassoulet* with goose *confit* (52F), pigeons in a red wine sauce (48F) or duck *confit* served with baked sliced potatoes and truffles (75F). For dessert there's a terrific apple and (of course) Armagnac tart to round off a lunch that is, on the whole, very decent for the area.

|●| RESTAURANT LE CHÂTEAU POIVRE

145 rue du Château; M° Pernety.
☎ 01.43.22.03.68
Closed Sundays, the week of 15 August, and Christmas week.

Service till 10.30pm. A quiet neighbourhood restaurant that's popular with the locals. Dishes like osso buco with fresh pasta and leg of lamb with herbs are prepared by the bearded proprietor. The service is extremely pleasant, which is becoming more and more unusual these days. Excellent set meal 89F, à la carte about 180F.

|●| RESTAURANT LA COUPOLE

102 bd du Montparnasse; M° Vavin.
☎ 01.43.20.14.20

Breakfast served 7.30-10.30am, last orders for brasserie 2am. One of the last remaining dinosaurs in Montparnasse, this aircraft hangar of a restaurant is the largest in France in terms of square feet. Artists have been coming here since it opened its doors in 1927 – people like Chagall, Man Ray, and Josephine Baker complete with lion cub. It was here that Aragon met Elsa Triolet . La Coupole has had a facelift/taken on a new lease of life since 1988. The bar has been restored to its original location in the middle of the room and the pillars are the green they used to be. The restaurant can now accommodate 450 diners. The dance hall too has been preserved and you can trip the light fantastic in the early afternoon (tea dance) and in the evening at weekends. Set meal 89F at lunchtime (not available Sundays), 123F and 169F. Reckon on a minimum of 200F a head à la carte. It looks a bit better than it used to but it's more expensive too!

|●| RESTAURANT LE VIN DES RUES

21 rue Boulard; M° Denfert-Rochereau or Mouton-Duvernet.
☎ 01.43.22.19.78
Closed Sundays, Mondays, a week in February, and early Aug–early Sept.

Service from 1pm; Wednesdays and Fridays from 9pm, reservations only; bar 10am-8pm. The premises used to house an old Auvergne café and the proprietor hasn't touched the décor. Excellent cooking in the Lyons style with two or three very substantial day's specials that change every day. For starters there's a house Beaujolais *terrine* (28F) or *saladier lyonnais* (36F). Regional cheeses and home-made desserts. Wines and the day's menu are chalked up on a blackboard (which also tells you what saint's day it is and gives you a thought for the day). It has to be said that the customers are of two minds about the welcome they get – some say the proprietor is surly, others that he cultivates that image in imitation of the stereotypical bistro owner of old films (some customers like that sort of thing). One thing's for sure, though – you'll take your time over your meal here whether you like it or not. The only time the proprietor's been known to lose his temper was when somebody asked if they could be in and out in 20 minutes since they were in a hurry! Reckon on an average of 150–180F for a meal à la carte.

|●| LE RESTAURANT BLEU

46 rue Didot; M° Plaisance or Pernety.
☎ 01.45.43.70.56
Closed Saturday lunchtimes, Sundays and Mondays.

A quiet old bistro in the heart of working-class Paris that's worth a visit if only for the wonderfully old-fashioned décor. It was taken over recently by Christian Simon, an excellent chef who used to work at *Bertie's*. The 160F *menu-carte* that changes with the season pays homage to all the good things that come out of the Aveyron and, depending on what month it is, you'll be served game, mushrooms or soft fruit. The basket of Rouergue *cochonailles* (all sorts of goodies made from the noble pig) is a very good place to start, as is the *terrine* of mushrooms, leeks and *foie gras*. Then move on to the *truffade* (a dish from the Auvergne, a sort of pancake made with cheese and potatoes), stuffed tripe, or grilled fresh scallops with a parsley sauce. For dessert, try the pineapple and lemongrass *chaud-froid* or the iced apricot parfait. Christian Simon doesn't ignore the other regions of France or indeed other parts of the world if there's something particularly good available at Rungis. Fish is the big star on the menu, as both a starter and main course, on Fridays. Interesting lunchtime set meal 95F.

|●| L'AMUSE-BOUCHE

186 rue du Château; M° Mouton-Duvernet.
☎ 01.43.35.31.61
Closed Saturday lunchtimes, Sundays, and three weeks in August.

Gilles Lambert, formerly of *Cagna* and the *Miraville*, is a consummate artist in the kitchen. And if you want proof, try his *menu-carte* at 168F, with its starter of superb langoustine ravioli with tarragon or *mousseline* of pike with saffron mussels and main course of peppered tuna steak with a honey and soya sauce, cod risotto or *croustillant* of rabbit. The dessert of *croustillant* with lime mousse is to die for. Lunchtime set meal 138F.

LA RÉGALADE

49 av. Jean-Moulin; M° Alésia or Porte-d'Orléans.
☎ 01.45.45.68.58
Closed Saturday lunchtimes, Sundays, and Mondays.

Service at lunchtime and in the evening until midnight. This is a gem of a place, with a décor that's both low-key and refined and a chef who is quite simply inspired. Y. Camdeborde, the gentleman in question, puts as much warmth and enthusiasm into his recipes and his choice of vegetables as he does into his conversations with customers after their meal. Service is efficient and unobtrusive. The *menu-carte* at 170F (wine extra) offers as a starter a basket of *charcutailles* supplied by Camdeborde senior, who has a charcuterie in Pau. Try the silky smooth pumpkin soup, the delicate kidneys with preserved shallots, the heavenly smelling roast pigeon with bacon, the scallops with shredded celery, the braised cheek of suckling pig with caramelized cabbage, the fillet of sea bass with fennel – the list of wonderful things just goes on and on. Don't forget to have a look at the wine list, which is astonishing and all at giveaway prices. So far, success hasn't altered any of the remarkable qualities of this very special restaurant. Reservations essential – book at least five days ahead.

15th arrondissement

LE NAINVILLE HÔTEL

53 rue de l'Église; M° Félix-Faure.
☎ 01.45.57.35.80 ➡ 01.45.54.83.00
Closed 1–7pm Saturdays and Sundays and mid-July–end August. **TV**.

An unobtrusive little hotel, that brings back memories of silent films. It has a retro café on the ground floor, a genial proprietor and old-fashioned (in the nicest sense of the word) bedrooms. It's incredible to find a place like this in a neighbourhood that's in the grip of real estate fever. Clean and cheerful inside. Go for a room – number 40, for example – that has a view over square Violet but avoid number 1, which is very dark. Doubles 205F with basin, 290F with shower and 360F with shower/wc. Breakfast 37F. A very good hotel.

10% HÔTEL AMIRAL**

90 rue de l'Amiral-Roussin; M° Vaugirard.
☎ 01.48.28.53.89 ➡ 01.45.33.26.94
TV. Disabled access.

You'll be impressed with this hotel neatly tucked away behind the town hall. The staff are attentive, the rooms nice and the prices reasonable. Doubles with washing facilities 245–250F, with shower/wc and TV 330F–390F. Breakfast 34F (with orange juice). Rooms 7, 25, 26 and 31 all have balconies and a view of the Eiffel Tower. And if you're heading for an exhibition at the porte de Versailles, it's only a 15 minute walk away. Readers of this guidebook get a 10% reduction in July and August.

PACIFIC HÔTEL**

11 rue Fondary; M° Emile-Zola or Dupleix.
☎ 01.45.75.20.49 ➡ 01.45.77.70.73
TV.

This is a lovely little hotel, mainly because of the smiling welcome you get from the receptionist, the freshly decorated foyer, and the simplicity of the functional rooms. It's clean and well maintained. Doubles with basin 260F, with shower and TV 318F, with shower or bath, wc and TV 362F. Breakfast 32F.

10% DUPLEIX HÔTEL**

4 rue de Lourmel; M° Dupleix.
☎ 01.45.79.30.12 ➡ 01.40.59.84.90
TV.

We found it rather refreshing, coming from the 7th arrondissement and the Eiffel Tower, to be plunged so abruptly into the hustle and bustle of this very busy street. Ask for a room on the top floor. Number 19 is blue throughout and number 18 red. Doubles (all with shower/wc and double glazing) 290–320F. Breakfast (30F) can be served in your room if you wish. Clean, family-owned and handy if you're stuck for accommodation. Minibar and satellite TV.

10% HÔTEL DE L'AVRE**

21 rue de l'Avre; M° La Motte-Picquet-Grenelle.
☎ 01.45.75.31.03 ➡ 01.45.75.63.26
TV. Canal+. Disabled access.

The hotel is located in a quiet narrow street and, if you're a movie buff, the *Kinopanorama*'s not far. A lovely hotel with prices that are fairly reasonable for Paris. Doubles

360F–380F with shower/wc and phone, 400F–420F with bath. Of the renovated rooms decorated in blue or yellow our favourites were numbers 22 and 28, which overlook the garden. One of our recommendations for the neighbourhood, the only drawback being that it's difficult to park in the street. But there are two car parks just minutes away.

10% HÔTEL LE FONDARY**

30 rue Fondary; M° Émile-Zola.
☎ 01.45.75.14.75 ➡ 01.45.75.84.42
TV. Canal+.

Good location in a quiet street in one of the nicest parts of the 15th arrondissement. Modern décor. Pretty patio with a well completely filled in with plants. Prices are quite high but not excessively so for a 2-star – 385F for a double with shower and direct phone, TV with Canal + and mini-bar, 405F with bath. Breakfast (38F) is served in a tiny courtyard in summer. Quiet at night. No restaurant.

10% CARLADEZ CAMBRONNE**

3 pl. du Général-Beuret; M° Vaugirard.
☎ 01.47.34.07.12 ➡ 01.40.65.95.68
TV. Canal+.

If you're wondering about the name, Carladez is a region in Auvergne where the first owners came from. A charming hotel in a little square with a pretty fountain in a busy shopping area. All the rooms are soundproof and come with mini-bar, TV (with Canal+ and satellite), hair dryer and, of course, direct telephone. Doubles with shower 400F, with bath 435F. Breakfast: 36F.

RESTAURANT CHEZ FOONG

32 rue de Frémicourt; M° Cambronne.
☎ 01.45.67.36.99
Closed Sundays and the first fortnight in August.

You'll get a good introduction to Malaysian cusine in a series of mild and spicy Malaysian dishes skilfully prepared by Mr Foong, a Malay Chinese from Kuala Lumpur who is a past master in the art of using spices. The lesson might begin with a salad of shrimp and fresh mango in a subtle and delicate sauce or with beef curry using the restaurant's own blend of spices, continue with mixed satay (the restaurant's speciality) or fish wrapped in a banana leaf and grilled, and end with sweet potato balls or a Malaysian pancake stuffed with coconut. About 105F. Set meals 56, 78 and 85F.

RESTAURANT AUX ARTISTES

63 rue Falguière; M° Falguière or Pasteur.
☎ 01.43.22.05.39
Closed Saturday lunchtimes, Sundays and the week of 15 August.

Service until 12.30am. This restaurant is really something. We ate here 12 years ago and the cost of the set meal has hardly budged! The atmosphere and the décor haven't changed and there are coloured frescoes throughout. The customers are a mixed bunch. Students, teenagers from the housing estates who've come into the city centre to see a bit of life, professionals, a few artists (Modigliani came here in his time too), and some of the older generation with thinning hair and thickening a bit around the waist all tuck in in a noisy and lively atmosphere. You'll have to wait a fair bit for a table on weekend evenings at peak hours but the bar serves a mean kir. Set meal 76F (drink extra). Hors d'œuvres are substantial and you can have a steak in no less than four different ways. There's a surprise in store for you if you have the dessert poetically entitled "Young Girl's Dream". At lunchtime, there's a *formule* (either starter, main course and chips or salad, or main course and dessert) for 56F.

LE BISTROT D'ANDRÉ

232 rue Saint-Charles; M° Balard.
☎ 01.45.57.89.14
Closed Sunday.

Before the Citroen car plant vanished, there were lots of bistros hereabouts. This is one of the few survivors in an area that now seems to be living in the year 2000. It's been updated to cater to today's tastes by the people from the *Perraudin* in the 5th arrondissement and they've brought the place back to life. Pre-war prices for family dishes with appeal such as leg of lamb with *gratin dauphinois*, beef bourguignon, *andouillette* in a mustard sauce and *canard confit*. We're very proud of ourselves for having discovered a decent restaurant in an area where there's not much to speak of. Set meal 59F at lunchtime (except Sundays). It's à la carte in the evenings and reckon on a bit over 100F for starter, main course, dessert and drinks. Wine-lovers please note: there's a tasting of wines from very small vineyards every month.

RESTAURANT TY BREIZ

52 bd de Vaugirard; M° Montparnasse-Bienvenue.
☎ 01.43.20.83.72
Closed Sundays and in August.

Lunch served noon–3pm, dinner 7–10.30pm. A little bit out of the way compared with other restaurants that siphon off most of the audiences from shows in the neighbourhood, which probably explains why this pancake place still has a pleasant family atmosphere. It's ideal for children who get a particularly warm welcome. Very good *galettes*, especially the *savoyarde* (cheese and potato) at 44F. Even the simple double butter one is great, as long as you're not worried about your cholesterol level of course. The dessert galettes (about 40F) aren't bad either – try the chocolate and orange, *martiquinaise* or *normande*. Excellent value for money and the place is as clean as a whistle. A nice little extra is that they'll give you a free kir on presentation of this guide.

LE GARIBALDI

58 bd Garibaldi; M° Sèvres-Lecourbe.
☎ 01.45.67.15.61
Closed evenings, weekends and in August.

This is what used to be termed a workingman's caff, though nowadays white collar workers are much more in evidence. It's almost compulsory to have the *museau vinaigrette* or *crudités* as a starter. The 68F set meal features sautéd lamb with flageolet beans, beef bourguignon and *blanquette de veau*. Service is friendly and there are still a few traces of the past, such as the beautiful counter at the door and a 1900 ceiling, in the very simple décor. Every weekend Madame Deleu the proprietor goes back to her native Pas de Calais for vegetables, salt pork, smoked sausage and other delicacies to feed her customers. Free-range chicken regularly features on the menu and, every Friday, roast beef and mashed potatoes (homemade). Ten out ten for effort!

RESTAURANT LA PETITE AUBERGE

13, rue du Hameau; M° Porte-de-Versailles.
☎ 01.45.32.75.71
Closed weekends in summer and August 1–26.

Service until 10pm. This is the "headquarters" of supporters of the Racing rugby team and consequently sees lots of emotional highs and lows. If you prefer après ski to après match, avoid this place like the plague on match days. Good plain cooking with daily specials like salt pork *à la potée*, sautéd lamb with haricot beans, *blanquette de veau*, pork spareribs with lentils and roast chicken with herbs ranging in price from 49F to 72F. And 1/4 litre of Muscadet or of vin de pays at 14F won't make much difference to the bill of approximately 100F. When the agricultural show's on (the Porte de Versailles is close by), the restaurant is full of bluff farmers and you get to hear a whole range of interesting accents.

RESTAURANT L'AGAPE

281 rue Lecourbe; M° Convention.
☎ 01.45.58.19.29
Closed Saturday lunchtimes, Sundays and three weeks in August

Service until 10.30pm. Marc Lamic shows no signs of burning out. His *menu-carte* at 120F, which changes with the seasons, shows his head is still buzzing with ideas. You can kick off with chicken *paupiette* or a *confit* of duck in a savoury puff pastry case and follow that with lamb and aubergine or cheek of suckling pig in a beer sauce accompanied by red cabbage. Dessert is banana and candied oranges en papillote with a coffee sauce or prune ravioli with *creme caramel* and preserved ginger. Diners are fairly squeezed in so scratch this off the list of possible locations for a romantic dinner for two. Bland décor.

PHILIPPE DETOURBE

8 rue Nicolas-Charlet; M° Pasteur.
☎ 01.42.19.08.59
Closed Saturday lunchtimes and Sundays.

Service until 11pm. Philippe Detourbe is one of a group of young chefs who have realized that haute cuisine has to be rethought in times of crisis. He has forgotten the two toques Gault Millau gave him when he was at *Napoléon* in the 8th arrondissement and the kind of dishes that cost a king's ransom. Instead, he now offers a 198F *menu-dégustation* that he has to sweat blood over every day. Judging by his broad grin, the crowded dining room (you'll have to book several days ahead) and the pleasure we derived from the meal we had there, he's onto a sure thing. The five offerings on the *menu-dégustation*, which followed hot on each other's heels, amply demonstrated the chef's talent, a combination of skill and creativity. We had chicken wings and grilled foie gras on celery *remoulade*, langoustine tempura with curly green cabbage, monkfish with a fondu of fennel and tomatoes in foaming coriander scented butter, lamb fillet with sage, green beans and mushrooms, and a *moelleux* of chocolate and pistachio nuts with verbena ice cream. At lunchtime, there's a 160F *menu-carte* that comes with two starters, two main courses of your choice (there's always a fish or meat dish) and either cheese or two desserts of your choice. Fairly conventional décor. With wine, reckon on 240F.

RESTAURANT LE CLOS MORILLONS

50 rue des Morillons; M° Porte-de-Vanves.
☎ 01.48.28.04.37
Closed Saturday lunchtimes, Sundays and Aug 8–22.

Service till 11pm. Chef Philippe Delacourcelle has spent a long time in Asia. He still has a taste for spices and for sweet and sour combinations and East meets West here in a perfectly orchestrated and sometimes brilliant performance. As far as we were concerned, the 165F set meal was a star turn: warm calf's brains with cabbage and roast peanut vinaigrette, *parmentier* of smoked duck in China tea and baked pear with dried fruit and Marsala. Sheer bliss. The *menu-carte* at 250F is similarly inspired. Among the many bottles priced at 100F was the Vouvray by Champalou and the Anjou by Richou, both of them excellent winemakers. Colonial décor.

16th arrondissement

HÔTEL VILLA D'AUTEUIL**

28 rue Poussin; M° Porte-d'Auteuil.
☎ 01.42.88.30.37 Fax 01.45.20.74.70
TV.

Its location in the classy part of the 16th arrondissement says just about all there is to say. Don't be put off by the fact that this establishment has only two stars, compared with the number conferred on other hotels in the neighbourhood. The bedrooms are spotless, they all come with bath, and you'll get excellent value for money. And the staff can't do enough for you. The rooms at the back are quieter. Doubles 330F. Breakfast 30F.

10% AU PALAIS DE CHAILLOT**

35 av. Raymond-Poincaré; M° Trocadéro.
☎ 01.53.70.09.09 Fax 01.53.70.09.08
TV.

This is a delightful 28-room hotel run by two brothers who are just starting out in the business. It has been fully renovated and is fresh and clean looking. The rooms are done out in yellow with co-ordinating curtains in red or blue. All have satellite TV, phone and hairdryer. Breakfast is served buffet style in a bright little room on the ground floor (or you can have it in your room). There are a few singles with shower/wc (and the beds are a decent size) at 450F; doubles with shower/wc 520F, with bath 580F. Breakfast is 39F. A 2-star hotel that is easily worth three and thoroughly deserves our support.

RESTAURANT LA FERME DES GOURMETS

82 rue Boileau; M° Exelmans.
☎ 01.46.47.87.19
Closed Sundays

Lunch served noon–2pm and dinner 7–10.00pm. Advisable to book. This place may not look much like a farm but it's definitely meant for gourmets and it's brought some life to the neighbourhood. For 82F you'll get duck *confit*, baked loin of pork and pig's trotters with garlic and truffles or cassoulet *confit* with 1/4 litre of wine thrown in. If you decide to go à la carte, there's a half-cooked whole foie gras, which is excellent, wild boar with figs or rabbit with rosemary and olives. Try the *confit*, gizzard and salsify tart too.

TANT QU'IL Y AURA DES HOMMES

1 rue Jean-Bologne; M° La Muette.
☎ 01.45.27.76.64
Closed Sundays and Mondays, and August.

Service until 11pm. The name used to belong to a shop on rue Cherche-Midi that sold designer objects and chic men's fashion and when owner Jacques Dereux decided to go into the restaurant business instead, he kept the name. He specializes in regional cooking, which he describes as coming from the countryside and the gardens between Aveyron and Toulon. Raw vegetables with *anchoïade à la Carqueyranne* (40F), *salaisons de montagne* (50F) and leeks (38F) followed by *coq au vin* (the wine in question being Marcillac) and ceps, sausage and potato cake (80F), or a vegetarian plate (70F) gladden the hearts of the customers, who come from the Paris and New York rag trade. Lots of good little wines for less than 90F. Reckon on paying about 150F à la carte.

RESTAURANT LE PETIT RÉTRO

5 rue Mesnil; M° Victor-Hugo.
☎ 01.44.05.06.05
Closed Saturday lunchtimes and Sundays.

Service until 11pm. Superb décor with an aerial theme in the first dining room, coloured tiles and ceiling light fixtures dating from around the turn of the century. The bistro style cooking is terrific and everything else shrinks into unimportance. There's no set meal but the dishes on offer are simple and tasty, like poached eggs with pureed chorizo (40F), terrine of oxtail with shallots (44F), salmon ravioli with leeks and curry, and a crunchy black pudding with apples (88F). The desserts are to die for – try the brioche covered in honey and roasted in the oven then served with gingerbread icecream (42F) or the *nougat glacé* with dried fruit served with vanilla flavoured *crème brûlée* (40F). The wine list isn't very long but it offers several *crus* by the glass, Morgon, Touraine and Côtes du Rhône.

RESTAURANT DU MUSÉE DU VIN – CAVEAU DES ÉCHANSONS

5-7 square Charles-Dickens-rue des Eaux; M° Passy.
☎ 01.45.25.63.26
Closed Mondays and during the Christmas and New Year holidays.

Service noon–6pm. The first thing that strikes you about this place is the setting – 16th century vaulted cellars. The kind of dishes they go for are the kind that need long slow cooking, which is a bit unusual for a museum. As well as the house specialities, they offer daily specials at 72F (chicken breast with morels, perch fillets in a Muscadet sauce and sautéd lamb with almonds and honey, for example). The 109F set meal consists of a starter and the daily special. If you have the 175F set meal you'll get a starter, a main dish, the cheese of the month, salad, and a glass of three different wines. Since the restaurant is located in the cellars of the wine museum, you won't need us to tell you that the wines on offer are chosen very carefully. The last time we were there, 15 different *crus* were available including Bordeaux (27–48F a glass), Burgundy (26–37F a glass), Beaujolais, Saumur, Champigny, Madiran, whites and rosés 11–48F a glass.

17th arrondissement

HÔTEL PALMA**

46 rue Brunel; M° Porte-Maillot.
☎ 01.45.74.74.51 F 01.45.74.40.90
TV.

A stone's throw from the convention centre and the Air France terminal. The hotel is well-kept, has an attractive frontage and foyer and offers a degree of comfort for a reasonable price. Service is polite and efficient. Rooms 390–410F. It's a pity about the slightly tacky furniture and flowery wallpaper. Breakfast is 35F and you can have it in your room. The attic rooms on the 6th floor (which an American guidebook has spoken highly of) are – understandably – extremely popular so it's best to book.

10% HÔTEL PRONY**

103 bis av. de Villiers; M° Pereire.
☎ 01.42.27.55.55 F 01.43.80.06.97
TV.

Although this hotel is part of a chain it's still got character. Readers of this guide can have a doubles with bath or shower for 440F (that includes breakfast, which can be served in your room up until midday). Singles 385F. Extra bed 100F, no charge for children under 12. Room service, satellite TV, double-glazing. Room number 32 is huge – ideal for families with one or two kids. An excellent hotel a stone's throw from place Pereire and five minutes from Porte Maillot.

HÔTEL CHAMPERRET-HELIOPOLIS**

13 reu d'Heliopolis; M° Porte de Champerret.
☎ 01.47.64.92.56 F 01.47.64.50.44
Car park. **TV**. **Disabled access**.

A very quiet hotel with pretty wooden balconies and a delightful patio where you can have breakfast when the weather's nice. Most of the rooms look out onto it. The place is absolutely spotless, you'll get a very friendly welcome, and you have everything you could want – TV, telephone, hair dryer – to make your stay a pleasant one. Doubles with bath or shower 450–495F. The three night package is a good deal at 1,000F. Breakfast 38F. If you're there during the week you'll get a 10% discount if you can show them this guidebook.

10% HÔTEL MONCEAU-ÉTOILE***

64 rue de Lévis; M° Villiers.
☎ 01.42.27.33.10 F 01.42.27.59.58
TV.

As soon as you clap eyes on the well-kept foyer with its floral decorations, you feel that the owners know what they're about, an impression that's borne out by the polite and smiling welcome you receive at reception. Everything is spotless and the rooms look very spruce. Foreigners prefer the ones in the attic that get the sun, while family groups go for no 46 (it's divided in two by a partition, so parents get some peace and quiet) and businessmen in Paris for a conference like numbers 27 and 37, which overlook the courtyard and are very quiet. All rooms come with TV, minibar and hair dryer. Singles 600F with shower, doubles 650F with shower or bath. And you'll get a 50% – yes 50%! – reduction if you can show them a copy of this guidebook. So you'll pay only 325F for a double in a 3-star hotel. Breakfast 35F. The hotel is located in a busy shopping street, Parc Monceau is just round the corner and the Champs-Élysées is three metro stations away. A fax, photocopier and Minitel are available at no extra charge.

|●| RESTAURANT SHAH JAHAN

4 rue Gauthey; M° Brochant.
☎ 01.42.63.44.06

The décor of the Pakistani restaurant is like something out of a Barbara Cartland novel – heavy draperies and paste mirrors – and the background music is soft and haunting. We went à la carte, choosing shish kebab (30F), lamb roghan josh (52F) and *kara mutton* (52F), which is a very spicy mutton curry. That was accompanied by a cheese nan (18F) and basmati rice with saffron (22F) and to drink we had lassi flavoured with cumin and cardamom. Service couldn't have been nicer. Set meals 49F (lunchtime), 115F and 130F (drink included).

|●| L'ÉTOILE VERTE

13 rue Brey; M° Charles-de-Gaulle-Étoile.
☎ 01.43.80.69.34

Service until 11pm. The restaurant took its name not from the square just five minutes away but from the green star that Esperanto speakers use as their emblem (they used to have meetings on the first floor). It was redecorated just twoyears ago and though it hasn't lost its patina of age (it has been in business since 1947) it looks fresh and pleasant. Set meals 74F (until 9pm), 100F and 145F.

|●| RESTAURANT LA TÊTE DE GOINFRE

16 rue Jacquemont; M° La Fourche.
☎ 01.42.29.89.80
Closed Sundays. **Secure parking**.

The atmosphere is that of a country bistro (complete with checked napkins) and the menu is dominated by pork in one form or another. The waitresses bustle around under the eagle eye of the proprietor, whose moustache makes him a Georges Brassens lookalike. The cooking is simple and the portions are generous. You could start with the egg mayonnaise (29F) or the *"bricole du goinfre"* (42F), which is a meal in itself – sausage, country ham that has as much fat as you want, headcheese etc etc. To follow, there's *andouillette* (72F) of course or farmhouse black pudding (68F). You won't find any signs of pretentiousness here – nothing but robust, hearty dishes like beefsteak, veal escalope Normande (ie with cream, Calvados and apples) and skirt of beef with shallots and sauté potatoes. If you've still got room after all that, you have to try one of the home-made fruit tarts (the filling depends on what season it is) and the *tarte Tatin* (on which the establishment built its reputation) is a must. Reservations essential.

|●| RESTAURANT LE VERRE BOUTEILLE

85 av. des Ternes; M° Porte-Maillot.
☎ 01.45.74.01.02
Closed Dec 24–25.

Service noon–3pm and 7pm–5am. *Le Verre Bouteille* was named wine bar of the month by one of the 1997 issues of a famous food and drink magazine. It's open until dawn and night owls can stoke up on robust main meals or very, very large salads – the one called "the yellow dwarf" (80F) consists of *Comté* (a type of cheese), chicken, raisins and curry sauce (there's nothing racist about the name by the way – nain jaune is the name of one of the old card games on the walls). To drink, there's wine from all over France and all over the world; about 30 are available by the glass. Things can be fairly lively on weekend nights by the time 4am strikes.

|●| GRAINDORGE

15 rue de l'Arc-de-Triomphe; M° Charles-de-Gaulle-Étoile.
☎ 01.47.54.00.28
Closed Sundays.

Service until 10.30pm. Bernard Broux, who was Alain Dutournier's number two at the *Carré des Feuillants* is an inspired chef. He uses his expertise to the greater glory of his native Flanders, re-interpreting his culinary heritage. From his 188F set meal you can choose creamy beer soup, *carbonnade* of ox cheeks with juniper berries and red cabbage stewed with vinegar, apples and sugar or roast Scotch salmon with Ardennes ham, boiled cabbage with butter, farmhouse *Maroilles* supplied by Philippe Olivier of Boulogne or a dark chocolate *fondant* and spiced buns in a chicory and coffee sauce. If you go à la carte, you can still have a taste of Flanders – try the *waterzooi* of scallops and shellfish with shrimp (130F) or the panfried scallops served on a bed of chicory (or endive if you prefer) that has been stewed in white beer. All the produce is as fresh as it can be and dishes are cooked to order. Forget the wine list and stick to beer from the northern regions – any one of the many varieties available goes perfectly with the food. Set meal 165F at lunchtime. Reckon on 230F à la carte.

|●| LE BISTROT DU XVIIE

108 av. de Villiers; M° Pereire.
☎ 01.47.63.32.77

Service until 11pm. If business is booming, it's all down to the 169F *formule* that gives you the lot – aperitif, starter, main course, dessert, wine and coffee. Seventh heaven for people who think life's complicated enough as it is without having to make decisions about what to eat and who also love neat little packages. The dishes on offer include lobster ravioli with asparagus tips, tuna steak with braised celery, rabbit in an olive and tomato sauce, panfried fillet of sea bass with a shellfish sauce, and lemon soufflé. The décor – reminiscent of a bourgeois flat – adds a note of reassurance.

18th arrondissement

IDÉAL HÔTEL

3 rue des Trois-Frères; M° Pigalle or Abbesses.
☎ 01.46.06.63.63 F→ 01.42.64.97.01

Fine looking building in dressed stone. Good location and functional. It's a bit noisy and the beds aren't the most comfortable we've ever slept in but it's a good hotel and the prices won't break the bank. Doubles with washing facilities 190F, with shower 250F. Jacques Brel lived here when he was just starting out on his singing-songwriting career.

HÔTEL BOUQUET DE MONTMARTRE**

1 rue Durantin; M° Abbesses.
☎ 01.46.06.87.54 F→ 01.46.06.09.09

Conventional hotel that has been taken over by a young couple and refurbished throughout. The rooms are decent though they're small and don't have a wc. Double-glazing. Doubles with shower or bath 360F. Pleasant, excellent location, good reception. Breakfast 30F.

HÔTEL PRIMA LEPIC**

29 rue Lepic; M° Blanche.
☎ 01.46.06.44.64 F→ 01.46.06.66.11
TV.

This is the ideal place to start off on a stroll through the neighbourhood. The impasse Marie-Blanche, which we're rather fond of, is close by. There's a trompe l'œil of an English garden in the foyer, giving it a bright fresh atmosphere, an impression heightened by the garden furniture. Rooms, which look like something out of Homes and Gardens, are unfussy and well looked after. Doubles 380–420F with shower or bath. Avoid room numbers 11 and 17, which are very dark. Breakfast is usually 40F but you'll pay only 10F if you can show them a copy of this guidebook.

TIMHÔTEL**

11 rue Ravignan (pl. Émile-Goudeau); M° Abbessess or Blanche.
☎ 01.42.55.74.79 F→ 01.42.55.71.01
TV.

This is a beautiful hotel, recently renovated and located in a wonderfully romantic square. Doubles with shower or bath 550F. Each floor is dedicated to a painter: going from the ground flor to the fifth you have a choice of Toulouse-Lautrec, Utrillo, Dali, Picasso, Renoir et Matisse. All rooms have a direct phone and TV. Breakfast 49F. Rooms on the upper floors – ie the fourth onwards – have a view of the square or the city. Number 412 is especially nice. Great place for lovers as long as they're not short of a bob or two.

RESTAURANT SONIA

8 rue Letort; M° Jules-Joffrin.
☎ 01.42.57.23.17
Closed Sunday lunchtimes.

We hummed and hawed quite a bit before deciding to include this place in our listings since it's often impossible to get a table – the pink and crimson dining room only seats 25. Friendly reception. Tasty main courses 49F and 79F at lunchtime. Everything is delicately spiced and cooked just right, from the nan to the chicken Madras and chicken Vindaloo not to mention the lamb khorma and the aubergine bhartha. The flavours of India are all there as your tastebuds will tell you. Great set meal for 99F.

LA MAZURKA

3 rue André-del-Sarte; M° Château-Rouge or Anvers.
☎ 01.42.62.32.95
Closed Wednesdays.

Marek is Polish but this corner of Montmartre has been home for the past 10 years and more. He brought with him a suitcase, a guitar, a beaming smile and, best of all, the secret of some great dishes like *flambé* sausages, home-made ravioli, pork spareribs gipsy style, *bigos* (Poland's answer to *choucroute*), beef Stroganoff, *borscht* (the famous beetroot soup) and *blinis* (or pancakes) with all kinds of fillings, including taramasalata, smoked eel and smoked salmon. Set meals 79F (lunchtime only) and 115F (lunchtime and evening). Reckon on paying about 150F à la carte, though it all depends on your liquid intake – 25cl (half a pint or so) of vodka will cost you 130F and twice that amount 220F. If Marek feels in good form, he'll take out his guitar and sing and you'll feel as if you're in Warsaw or Gdansk. And if the pepper vodka really starts to flow, you'll swear you saw the rather clichéd paintings dance the mazurka!

RESTAURANT LE MOULIN À VINS

6 rue Burq; M° Abbesses.
☎ 01.42.52.81.27
Closed Sundays and Mondays, also three weeks in August.

Service 6pm–2am Tuesday to Saturday and 11am–3pm Wednesday and Thursday. An authentic wine bar at the foot of the Butte, which doesn't try to take people for a ride with its carefully prepared bistro dishes – things like *andouillette*, *bœuf mode*, *coq au vin*, and *civet de porc vigneronne* - and plates of *charcuterie* or cheese that are sheer heaven. Food is always better for a little wine of course and wine is Dany Bertin-Denis' first love. Thanks to his tender loving care, you can enjoy the best that the small winegrowers in Touraine, Corsica and elsewhere have to offer. Selecting wines isn't the only thing he's good at – he has been known to burst into song with some of the more heartrending ditties from the repertoire of Edith Piaf and other popular singers of the time.

RESTAURANT MARIE-LOUISE

52 rue Championnet; M° Simplon.
☎ 01.46.06.86.55
Closed Sundays, Mondays, public holidays and in August.

Last orders 930pm. You'd do well to book – this is a terrific restaurant and there are only nine others like it in the whole of Paris! When you walk through the door your first impression is that you've stepped into some typically French bourgeois family dining room with brass and copper so highly polished you can see your face in it. The cooking is traditional in style and the portions are enormous. The hors d'œuvres are great and there's a wide choice of main dishes – veal kidneys in Madeira sauce, chicken done in the house style, veal chops *grand'-mère* and *bœuf ficelle* – in what is a very appealing menu. If sea bass should happen to be on the menu when you're there then go for it. The quality of the cooking hasn't changed in years and it seems set to continue that way for a long time to come. And the prices are reasonable. The 130F set meal (starter, main course and dessert) is available at lunchtime and in the evening. Reckon on about 200F à la carte.

TAKA

1 rue Véron; M° Pigalle or Abbesses.
☎ 01.42.23.74.16
Closed Sundays, public holidays and mid July–mid Aug.

Dinner only served 7.30–10.30pm. Tiny little Japanese restaurant tucked away in a dark and narrow street at the foot of the Butte. Be warned – it's often full to bursting point, so it's best to book. Mr Taka is a lovely chap and can't do enough for you. Authentic Japanese cooking that is perfectly executed and the quality of which never wavers. All of the great Japanese dishes that those in the know love so well are available – sushi, sashimi and kebabs. Reckon on about 150F a head with a large Japanese beer. Set meal 110F. When it's time to tot up the bill, Mr Taka prefers an abacus to a calculator.

19th arrondissement

HÔTEL RHIN ET DANUBE**

3 place Rhin-et-Danube; M° Danube.
☎ 01.42.45.10.13 ➡ 01.42.06.88.82
TV.

The Buttes-Chaumont and the parc de la Villette are a couple of minutes away and if peace and quiet is important to you, you'll like this hotel, which has lots of provincial charm and located in a neighbourhood that seems somehow to have got lost. Quite a few famous names have stayed here – Alain Delon for one when he was shooting a film in the square. Reasonable welcome. You'll be pleasantly surprised to find that the hotel doesn't have bedrooms in the traditional sense of the word. What you'll get is a fairly decent sized bedsit with a bathroom, sleeping area and a kitchenette with all the necessary equipment – there's even enough dishes for four people. TV. Not at all expensive – singles 250F, doubles 300F, triples 350F and, for four people, 400F. A good way of keeping costs down. The welcome wasn't all that it might have been but the new manager who's only just taken over seems a bit more pleasant than his predecessor.

AUX ARTS ET SCIENCES RÉUNIS

161 av. Jean-Jaurès; M° Ourcq.
☎ 01.42.40.53.18
Closed Sundays.

Lunch served 11.30am–2pm and dinner 7–9pm. As you might guess from the compasses and set square that appear on the frontage, this is where the people who work at the headquarters of the carpenters guild eat. Go past the room with the bar, and you'll find an extremely attractive room with a parquet floor, mouldings, and lots of photos of guild members on the walls. The food, like the atmosphere, is provincial in style – things like escalopes, trout and grills. The 60F set meal is good, the helpings are generous and wine is included. Daily special 41F.

|●| AU RENDEZ-VOUS DE LA MARINE

14 quai de la Loire; M° Jaurès.
☎ 01.42.49.33.40
Closed Sundays and Mondays.

Service at lunchtime and in the evening until 9.45pm. Reservations highly advisable – it's often full. Delightful bistro where Marcel Carné, the famous film director, once shot a film. They put flowers on the tables, scatter a few nautical souvenirs around, put up photos of film stars and suddenly it's the in place to be. Noisy, especially at lunchtime and on the two Saturday evenings in the month (winter only) when a talented female singer out-Piaffs Piaff. The lady's not around in summer but as a consolation tables are set out on the terrace and you'll have a view of the canal. Food is reasonably priced and the helpings are generous, though the cooking is nothing special. Available items include the house chicken liver *terrine* (36F), mushrooms *à la provençale* (58F), the chef's special prawns (69F), scallops *à la provençale*(72F), and duck breast with green peppercorns. If you want paella, you'll have to order it the night before. Very good apple tart flambéd with Calvados. A la carte only – reckon on 110–140F.

|●| LE PAVILLON PUEBLA

parc des Buttes-Chaumont; M° Buttes-Chaumont.
☎ 01.42.08.92.62
Closed Sundays and Mondays.

If it's your fifth wedding anniversary, you've just won the lottery, and you've decided to celebrate in style then this is just the place for you. It stands in the middle of Paris's most beautiful park, the setting is bourgeois, with peach the predominant colour, there are fresh flowers, and the terrace is just out of this world – the kind of place you dream about when the weather starts to improve. You'll be received with style, but no bowing and scraping. The cooking is first-rate and chef Christian Verges will offer you delights like squid *à la catalane*, lobster stew with Banyuls, *pinata* (braised fish), and oyster ravioli with a curry sauce. The desserts are quite simply to die for. It's expensive – in fact it's very expensive if you go à la carte and have wine too – but a 180F set meal is available consisting of, for example, anchovies in a flaky pastry case, *bouillinade* (an upmarket sort of *bouillabaisse*), and chocolate *tuiles*. It's absolutely terrific and comes complete with nibbles, home-made rolls etcetera, etcetera. There's also a 240F set meal.

20th arrondissement

⌂ TAMARIS HÔTEL*

14 rue des Maraîchers; M° Porte-Vincennes or Maraîchers.
☎ 01.43.72.85.48 F 01.43.56.81.75
TV.

Reservations advisable. Very well looked after little hotel with prices of the kind you might be charged in the depths of the country. Judge for yourself – doubles with basin 165F, with shower 194F, with shower/wc 240F; rooms for 3 at 310F. We recommend room number 16 with a double and a single bed (190F for three). The rooms are small and pretty and have flowered wallpaper. Breakfast is 25F. TV in the lounge. It's a bit old-fashioned, a bit "Paris the way it used to be", and altogether delightful – and you'll get a warm welcome too. What more could you ask for?

⌂ HÔTEL PYRÉNÉES GAMBETTA**

12 av. du Père-Lachaise; M° Gambetta.
☎ 01.47.97.76.57 F 01.47.97.17.61
TV. Canal+.

A pleasant 2-star hotel in a quiet street leading to the Père-Lachaise cemetery. The rooms are perfectly adequate, with large beds tucked into alcoves and all come with TV and minibar. Doubles with shower/wc 300–375F. Breakfast is 35F and you can have it in your room. Delightful welcome. A good little hotel, quiet and cosy, in a pleasant neighbourhood that's not overrun with tourists.

|●| RESTAURANT ARISTOTE

4 rue de la Réunion; M° Maraîchers or Buzenval.
☎ 01.43.70.42.91
Closed Sundays and two weeks in August.

Service at lunchtime and till 11.30pm in the evening. This little Greek restaurant may not be much to look at but you won't have to remember to go to the bank before eating here. It offers generous helpings of Greek and Turkish specialities and service with a smile. Set lunchtime meal (the main dish changes every day) is 51F. It's à la carte in the evening, so reckon on 90–110F. The locals who come here know when they're on to a good thing and tuck into conventional but tasty hors d'œuvres and *pacha kebab* (leg of lamb on the bone) or *hunkar beyendy* (rack of lamb with aubergine), not to mention the warm bread it comes with. Background music, pleasant setting and good atmosphere.

|●| CHEZ IDA

64 rue des Pyrénées; M° Maraîchers or a number 26 bus.
☎ 01.43.70.77.86
Closed Friday evenings and Saturdays and in August.

Time seems to have stood still in this little restaurant since the first Italian immigrants arrived in the neighbourhood in the first half of the 20th century. You have to go through the kitchen to get to the toilets, which will give you a good opportunity to see how clean things are and to say hello to Ida, who makes delicious fresh pasta every day the same way her mother did. The dining room is small but there's no mistaking this is an Italian restaurant: the menu is long and the quality never wavers. As well as pasta and ravioli, Ida serves up a mean beef in balsamic vinegar, *fritto misto*, cutlets with gorgonzola and polenta, AND that elusive creature a home-made tiramisu. Set meals 60F at lunchtime and 89F and 150F in the evening. Terrific wine list.

|●| RESTAURANT PASCALINE

49 rue Pixérécourt; M° Place-des-Fêtes.
☎ 01.44.62.22.80
Closed Monday evenings and weekends, and the last three weeks of August.

This is a very nice restaurant that serves large helpings of good food for reasonable prices. Pleasant dining room with a large fresco and a sunny terrace where you can laze the afternoon away. Set meal 65F at lunchtime. Reckon on 110F in the evening if you've sampled any of the interesting wines by the glass.

|●| AU RENDEZ-VOUS DES AMIS

10 av. du Père-Lachaise; M° Gambetta.
☎ 01.47.97.72.16
Closed evenings, Sundays and July 14–Aug 15.

This is the kind of welcome we like. Madame, who is always full of life and good-humoured (how on earth does she do it?), is on first name terms with all her regulars and welcomes new customers with open arms. Home-style cooking is the order of the day and that's her husband's province. He uses only fresh ingredients and locals, reps, tradesmen and office workers flock here for things like his duck breast in honey. The place has just been redecorated in wood, formica and rather gaudy green leatherette – OK, it may not be to your taste but so what? If you're on a business trip and missing home or you get an attack of the blues and feel nobody loves you or even if you've just been visiting Père Lachaise cemetery, you'll find the atmosphere here warm, friendly and welcoming. Set meal 65F, a teeny bit more à la carte.

|●| RESTAURANT CHEZ JEAN

38 rue Boyer; M° Gambetta or Ménilmontant.
☎ 01.47.97.44.58
Closed Saturday lunchtimes, Sundays and the week of August 15.

Service until about 11pm. The eponymous Jean says his is the best restaurant in the street – the fact that it's the ONLY restaurant in the street doesn't detract from his claim. He used to be a journalist but then he decided a few years ago he'd rather own a restaurant and now he's master of all he surveys from his post behind the bar. If he wrote as well as he cooks, we'd willingly gobble down his books too. What he provides is home cooking in the best French tradition with a few added touches of his own. The atmosphere is that mixture of working class and trendy so typical of the neighbourhood. It's always pleasant and there's an accordeon player and singer on Fridays and Saturdays. The 66F set meal at lunchtime is served by Patricia, who always makes her presence felt. In the evening, the *menus du jour* is 92F and there's another set meal at 112F. Reckon on 130–150F (depending on how much you drink).

|●| LE CAFÉ NOIR

15 rue Saint-Blaise; M° Porte-de-Bagnolet or Alexandre-Dumas.
☎ 01.40.09.75.80
Closed Sundays, three weeks in August and between Christmas and New Year's Day.

Service 7pm–midnight. This was a dispensary at the turn of the century but there's not much sign of its medical past since the objects the proprietors collect so avidly tend to be coffee pots, hats, enamel signs and posters. It all makes for a pleasing décor. The present owners took over the restaurant in 1991 and they serve up generous portions of good food – dishes such as duck breast in lavender honey and thyme, *foie gras à la guérandaise*, fillets of sea bass with roast fennel, and boned saddle of rabbit with wild herbs. And you can indulge in a cigar afterwards – the bar sells single Havanas. A place like this is all that's needed to breathe life into the area, which can hardly be described as one of the successes of modern architecture. About 120F.

NEUILLY-SUR-SEINE 92200 (0.5KM NW)

10% ☗ HÔTEL CHARLEMAGNE**

1 rue Charcot (West); M° Pont-de-Neuilly; it's 50m from the metro station.
☎ 01.46.24.27.63 ⮕ 01.46.37.11.56
TV. Canal+. Disabled access.

Pleasant reception. Comfortable modern rooms. Doubles with mini-bar, direct phone and shower 395F, with bath 440F, which is reasonable for Neuilly, where everything is expensive. The street is quiet in the evening and at night. Ideal for anyone with an appointment at *La Défense* the next day but who doesn't want to spend the night there. And, for joggers, the Bois de Boulogne is not far away.

|●| LE CHALET

14 rue du Commandant-Pilot (South-East); M° Porte-Maillot; it's 300m from porte Maillot.
☎ 01.46.24.03.11
Closed Sundays.

A Swiss chalet for those who didn't get away on a skiing holiday last year. Nothing's been missed out – there's the snow (well, in photos), there's the wainscotting and there are the skis here, there and everywhere. At lunchtime there's a superfast *formule* at 63F and a set meal at 79F. In winter, they offer what they call a Savoy dinner with a fairly large fondue for 140F or a Mont-Blanc set meal for 155F. In summer, there's a super *formule* at 120F, which consists of a starter, half a lobster and fresh pasta, dessert and wine. Really pleasant. Children's set meal 50F. Our favourite place in Neuilly.

|●| RESTAURANT FOC LY

79 av. Charles-de-Gaulle (South-East); M° Sablons.
☎ 01.46.24.43.36
Closed Mondays July 15–Aug 15. **Car park**.

You can't miss it – it's got a pagoda roof and two lions guarding the entrance. This is undoubtedly one of the best Asian restaurants in the area, as the signatures of the great and the good in the foyer testify. A very refined and varied style of cooking. Extremely polite service. Set meal 99F (weekdays lunchtime). About 180F à la carte.

|●| LE BISTROT D'À CÔTÉ

4 rue Boutard; M° Pont de Neuilly.
☎ 01.47.45.34.55

One of the annexes belonging to the famous Michel Rostang. Bistro-style décor and a handsome collection of coffee grinders. The service is attentive but relaxed. At lunchtimes, there's a *formule* at 129F, 148F (main course plus starter or dessert) and 189F. Your meal might consist of potato cakes and fresh goat's cheese with olive *tapenade*, then pan-fried fillet of duckling with asparagus and risotto and, to finish, *crème au chocolat à l'ancienne*. The food's very good of course but the prices are a bit high.

BOULOGNE-BILLANCOURT 92100 (1KM SW)

10% ☗ LE QUERCY

251 bd Jean-Jaurès (South-East); M° Marcel-Sembat.
☎ 01.46.21.33.46 ⮕ 01.46.21.72.21
TV.

Modern facilities and furnishings of the kind you get in a chain hotel. Rooms, some of which have recently been renovated, are clean and perfectly adequate but wholly devoid of charm. Doubles with basin 140F (showers in the corridor 10F), with shower/wc 220–270 (TV). One of the least expensive hotels in the areas. You can rent by the month or the week. If you want breakfast, you'll have to order it the night before.

KRESTAURANT LA MARMITE

54 ter av. Édouard-Vaillant (East); M° Porte-de-Saint-Cloud or Marcel-Sembat; it's 300m from porte de Saint-Cloud.
☎ 01.46.08.06.12
Closed Sundays, public holidays and in August.

Inoffensive modern décor of square pillars and large mirror tiles. Traditional brasserie cooking of the mixed kebab and grilled salmon variety. Fresh fish daily. A very simple *formule* (starter, main course and cheese or dessert) is 68F. Set meals 88F and 145F (drink included). About 170F à la carte.

|●| RESTAURANT LA TONNELLE DE BACCHUS

120 av. Jean-Baptiste-Clément (North-West); M° Boulogne-Pont-de-Saint-Cloud; it's 20m from the métro.
☎ 01.46.04.43.98
Closed Saturdays, Sundays and Christmas to New Year's Day.

Pretty, comfortable dining room with a little upright piano that Valérie plays occasionally. You can eat outside on the pavement in summer. The bourgeois-style cooking is fairly expensive but of good quality. There's a *formule* (main course plus starter or dessert) for 115F, a set meal for145F, and you'll pay about 200F à la carte. Try the breast of duck with honey sauce, the fillet steak with green peppercorn sauce or the coddled eggs with *foie gras*. Excellent wine list.

LEVALLOIS-PERRET 92300 (1KM NW)

HÔTEL DU GLOBE

36 rue Louis Rouquier; M° Louise Michel.
☎ 01.47.57.29.39
This is a clean and unpretentious little family hotel in a fairly busy street. The rooms are small and have double glazing but no wc. Doubles 160F with basin (use of shower 20F) and 210F with shower in room. Average welcome.

LE PETIT POUCET

4 rond-point Claude-Monet (West); it's on the île de la Jatte, at the east end of the road that goes right round the island, just where it bends.
☎ 01.47.38.61.85

There's been a restaurant of some kind here for almost a hundred years. At the beginning of the century, working class men looking for a bit of fun used to bring their sweethearts here for a drink and a bite to eat in what was then just a drinking place in the country. The *Petit Poucet* became one of the island's fashionable restaurants in the early 80s and in 1991 was given a facelift to make it look cosy (there's a lot of wood, which makes for a warm atmosphere). It has three lovely terraces, the one on the banks of the river attracting lots of the beautiful people (in relaxed mode) as soon as the sun comes out. There's a *formule* at 110F (starter or dessert plus main course) or a *menu complet* at 180F (wine included). A mere 400F for two. Good classical French cooking and fast, efficient service. Best to book.

NANTERRE 92000 (1KM NW)

LE GRISON

39 rue Henri Barbusse; RER Nanterre-ville, then take bd du Couchant towards the centre of town
☎ 01.47.25.92.99
Closed Mondays.

Everything about this place, from the food to the rustic décor with the old skis at the front door, makes you feel you're in Savoy. Regional specialities include *tartiflette* and *raclette* of course but they also have *crêpes* and *galettes* from 14F, and the 129F Savoy regional set meal consists of salad, *pierrade* (where you cook the ingredients yourself on a hot stone), and dessert. They have a cabaret singer on Wednesdays and Thursdays.

HÔTEL SAINT-JEAN

24-26-33 av. de Rueil (West);RER Nanterre-ville.
☎ 01.47.24.19.20 F→ 01.47.24.17.65

The hotel is situated a little away from the centre in a very quiet neighbourhood. No two rooms are the same but they are all clean and more than adequate. Doubles from 145F with shower/wc to 230F. Friendly welcome.

RESTAURANT LE COIN TRANQUILLE

8-10 rue du Docteur-Foucault (Centre).
☎ 01.47.21.11.80
Closed Christmas to New Year's Day; restaurant also closed Sunday evenings.

Large dining room. Traditional cooking. Very good prices – the 64F (weekdays only)set meal for example includes 1/4 litre of wine. Other set meals are 120F and 158F or you can have mussels and chips with a glass of white wine for 55F. Best to reserve. Basic rooms with shower/wc 180–220F.

SAINT-CLOUD 92210 (1KM W)

10% HÔTEL MAGENTA*

1 place Magenta (North); it's closer to the park than it is to the centre of town.
☎ 01.46.02.90.18 F→ 01.47.71.28.53
TV.

Saint-Cloud only has three hotels and this is by far the cheapest, so it's probably best to book. Congenial reception. Rooms are small but all have direct phone and mini-bar. Doubles with shower/wc 240F and 270F, which includes breakfast.

VINCENNES 94300 (15KM SE)

RISTORANTE ALESSANDRO

51 rue de Fontenay; it's beside the town hall.
☎ 01.49.57.05.30
Closed Sundays and the first three weeks in August.

The regulars have been coming here for a very long time now and they've stopped counting the number of specialities that are so lovingly and expertly prepared by the chef and his wife. And since there's no reason why the people of Vincennes should be the only ones to enjoy themselves, here are the names of a few for you to drool over – spaghetti with langoustines, tagliatelli with scallops, and that wonderful combination of veal, Parma ham and sage, saltimbocca *alla romana*. They are all delicious. You'll soon realize that the restaurant's success lies in the little extra something the chef adds to everything — a herb here, a spice there or a totally unexpected flavour that comes from whatever it was he deglazed the pan with. It would be criminal to ignore the antipasti — there's artichokes, dried tomatoes, olives, preserved onions and fantastic *charcuterie*. And of course, for the diehard pizza fanatic, there's the real McCoy. Set meals 58F, 129F and 198F. Reservations essential. If you want to repeat the experience at home, trot along to *La Cucina Italiana* at 184 rue de Fontenay, Vincennes (tel 01.43.74.74.85) where you'll find the best of Italy — *charcuterie*, cheese, wine, olive oil and pasta. Once you've been there, the world divides into two groups: those who live near enough to drop in regularly and everybody else. Pity we're in the second category!

PROVINS 77160

LA BOUDINIÈRE DES MARAIS

17 rue Hugues-le-Grand (Centre); it's at the lower end of town.
☎ 01.60.67.64.89
Closed Sunday evenings and Mondays, and the last three weeks in August.

Incredible but true — everything here is made on the premises, even the smoked salmon! This is a place known to the locals and well-informed sales reps. For 65F you can get a well-cooked and substantial lunch on weekdays and there are other unbeatable set meals at 115F and 175F. Traditional French cooking — as the humorous fresco of Gargantua makes plain. Service and décor are both simple and genuine. It's high time we kicked fast food out of France and chef Prigent is going the right way about it. He deserves our support.

AUBERGE DE LA GRANGE**

3 rue Saint-Jean; it's in the upper part of town, just opposite the barn.
☎ 01.64.08.96.77
Closed Tuesday evenings and Wednesdays.

The restaurant consists of two small dining rooms with fireplaces in an old house that has been restored. Set meals are 98F, which comes with cheese — Brie of course — and dessert, and 170F, the latter being the gourmet meal.

RAMBOUILLET 78120

HÔTEL SAINT-CHARLES**

15 rue de Groussay (North-West); from the town hall, follow the road that runs along the park for about 1km.
☎ 01.34.83.06.34 Fax 01.30.46.26.84
Car park. TV.

A functional hotel not far from the centre. Most of the rooms are fairly spacious and they're all kept in mint condition. Rooms 280F, 30F extra per person for breakfast.

RESTAURANT LA POSTE

101 rue du Général-de-Gaulle (Centre).
☎ 01.34.83.03.01
Closed Sunday evenings, Mondays and during Christmas and New Year holidays.

If you want to eat in one of the best restaurants in town we strongly urge you to book. The dining room is extremely pretty, service is efficient and friendly, and the cooking is light and refined, with dishes like salmon escalope with sorrel, chicken fricassee with langoustines, and medallions of lamb cooked like venison. Set meals 103F (except Sunday lunchtimes), 146F and 190F. The restaurant has its own *foie gras*. Weekday lunchtimes, they also have a 74F formule of starter plus main course or main course plus dessert.

LE CHEVAL ROUGE

78 rue du Général-de-Gaulle (Centre); it's near the sous-préfecture.
☎ 01.30.88.80.61
Closed Tuesdays, Sunday evenings, and mid July–mid Aug

The sophisticated cuisine and attentive service justify its good reputation. Dishes include the house duck *foie gras*, asparagus parcels with smoked salmon, rack of lamb with thyme, and chicken with morels. For dessert, they have excellent fruit tarts. Set meals 130F and 175F; à la carte also available. There's a brasserie under the same roof with two more affordable set meals at 75F and 105F as well as dishes à la carte. There's fillet of beef, veal kidneys in port, tripe, lasagne and so on.

SAINT-GERMAIN-EN-LAYE 78100

10% LE HAVRE*

92 rue L_on-D_soyer (North-West).
☎ 01.34.51.41.05 Fax 01.34.51.41.05
TV.

The hotel, a couple of minutes from the town centre, is often full so it's best to book, especially in winter. Neat rooms recently refurbished with shower/wc 240F. Pleasant reception. Avoid rooms overlooking the street since they're a bit noisy. We preferred the other side, which overlooks the cemetery.. Definitely quieter!

RESTAURANT LE COLLIGNON

7 rue Collignon (Centre).
☎ 01.34.51.48.56
Closed Mondays.

Situated in a traffic-free zone. The pleasant inn-style dining room is on the first floor. There's a decidedly cool terrace for sunny days. The restaurant specializes in fish and the main courses are fairly substantial. *Formule* at 68F available weekdays at lunchtime. Varied set meal 140F.

RESTAURANT LE PETIT LYONNAIS

11 rue Saint-Pierre (Centre).
☎ 01.39.21.02.05
Closed Saturday lunchtimes and Sundays (except public holidays).

This is something along the lines of the traditional inexpensive restaurant you'd find in Lyons except it's a bit more refined. It has a very pretty small dining room, there are flowers on the tables and the chairs are comfortable. Everything is light and airy and since the cooking is of the kind you'd find in Lyons, you'll eat well. *Formule* at 71F available weekdays at lunchtime. Set meal 134F.

RESTAURANT LA FEUILLANTINE

10 rue des Louviers (Centre).
☎ 01.34.51.04.24

Located in a narrow pedestrianized street. Rather cosy inside and tastefully decorated. Careful service. No set meals but there is an original *formule* at 130F which allows you to choose for yourself what you'll have. The restaurant has its own *foie gras*. At lunchtimes there's a 75F *formule* (glass of wine, main course, coffee) and an 85F one (starter plus main course or main course plus dessert)..

SURESNES 92150

LES JARDINS DE CAMILLE

70 av. Franklin Roosevelt; from porte Maillot, take bus number 244 to pont de Suresnes.
☎ 01.45.06.22.66
Closed Sunday evenings.

This big house stands high above Paris on the side of Mont Valérien and you get a fabulous view of La Défense and the whole of the city. Beautiful terrace for sunny days. Care has been taken with the décor and service. They have a single *formule* at 160F which comes with starter, main course and dessert. A la carte, they have lots of Burgundy dishes. The helpings are generous but the food isn't particularly special. If we go back, it'll be for the view!

VERSAILLES 78000

HOME SAINT-LOUIS**

28 rue Saint-Louis (Centre).
☎ 01.39.50.23.55 F 01.30.21.62.45
TV. **Canal+**.

This is a quiet, comfortable and well-looked after hotel not far from the rather nice neighbourhood of Saint-Louis. Doubles with shower 220F, with shower/wc 265F, with bath 295F. Very good value for money.

10% PARIS HÔTEL**

14 av. de Paris.
☎ 01.39.50.56.00 F 01.39.50.21.83
TV. **Canal+**. **Disabled access**.

The reception could not be faulted in this hotel, which is 100m from place d'Armes. You get a friendly handshake from the proprietor when you come down for breakfast. Doubles 300–380F. We preferred the former, which overlook the tiny interior courtyard.

10% HÔTEL DU CHEVAL ROUGE**

18 rue André-Chénier (Centre).
☎ 01.39.50.03.03 F 01.39.50.61.27
Secure parking. **TV**.

This is a delightful, comfortable and extremely well located hotel. Doubles with shower 320F, with bath 370F, which is not too bad for a town where prices go up and up and up, especially in the neighbourhood of the château. The hotel is also a tea room. The private car park is an asset in this part of town.

RESTAURANT AU PETIT MARQUIS

6 rue André-Chénier (Centre).
☎ 01.39.50.14.18
Closed Sundays, Mondays, the last week in February and the first three weeks in July.

It's hardly surprising that the restaurant does a roaring trade with prices like 62F (lunchtime), 80F and 130F. Best of all, it's not just cheap, it's good. The cooking is in the bourgeois style and the local wines are affordable. The service is amiable and efficient service, the setting is pleasant, and there's a terrace overlooking the market square. Specialities put in an appearance in the evening and dishes such as casserole of scallops *à la provençale* and sea bass in flaky pastry with a *fondue* of leeks have customers coming back again and again.

RESTAURANT CHEZ LAZARE

18 rue de Satory (West).
☎ 01.39.50.41.45

There are copper pots and pans on the walls, cauldrons hang from the beams and the dining room is heated by the grill where meat and fish is being cooked. Live South-American music in the evening. Set meal 65F (lunchtimes only). Reckon on 150F à la carte. Service until 1am.

RESTAURANT LE BALTIKA

6 rue des Deux-Portes (Centre).
☎ 01.39.50.21.53
Closed Mondays.

In a narrow pedestrianized street in one of the oldest parts of town between the château and the covered market. The service is efficient and silent – ideal for a romantic dinner. Start with the tagliatelle with *foie gras* then go on to a good breast of duck with *gratin dauphinois* and, to finish, give way to temptation and have the chocolate profiteroles (to hell with the diet!). Set meals 85F and 125F, à la carte 160F. If you're above average height, watch out for the staircase – it's lethal! Terrace in summer.

RESTAURANT À LA FERME

3 rue du Maréchal-Joffre (South-East).
☎ 01.39.53.10.81

Closed Mondays and Tuesday lunchtimes. You really would think you were in a farmhouse. There are old farm tools hanging on the walls, old ceiling beams and little tables with flowery cloths – everything to remind you of countryside. The establishment specializes in fish dishes and grills. It offers an interesting *formule* at 87F (except Saturday evenings and Sundays) and a good set meal at 117F. 130F à la carte. Very amiable service.

LA CUISINE BOURGEOISE

10 bd du roi (Centre).
☎ 01.39.53.11.38
Closed Saturday evenings, Sundays and a fortnight in August.

It really lives up to its name. The very cosy dining room, decorated in shades of green, serves tasty classic French dishes and very good wine. Set meal 110F (lunchtimes), 168F and 190F (this one has four courses). Every second Monday of the month they have a special wine evening, where you get a glass of wine with each course (250F).

VIROFLAY 78220 (8KM SE)

RESTAURANT DOUCE FRANCE

42 av. du Général-Leclerc.
☎ 01.30.24.33.61
Closed Sunday evenings.

A tiny little dining room with an enormous naïf drawing and a stone wall. The service comes with a smile and the cooking is very decent. South-west dishes are a speciality and include a house *confit* of duck, ribsteak with Roquefort and fillet of beef in *Béarnaise* sauce. Set meals 70F, 100F and 130F.

Languedoc-Roussillon

11 Aude

30 Gard

34 Hérault

48 Lozère

66 Pyrénées-Orientales

AGDE 34300

10% HÔTEL BON REPOS*

15 rue Rabelais (Centre); it's 200m from the centre, going towards Béziers.
☎ 04.67.94.16.26
Secure parking.

Endless renovation projects have been taking place since this cheerful couple took over some time ago. Large, flower-filled terraces put you in the mood for a breath of fresh air. It has a rather interesting past. Now a simple and delightful little hotel, *Bon Repos* was once a brothel, which was turned into a police station in 1946. Bedrooms from 150F with shower to 225F with bath (only one of these). One of our favourite little places.

10% LES ARCADES*

16 rue Louis-Bages (Centre).
☎ 04.67.94.21.64

A former convent at the far end of a flower-filled courtyard. It has very basic rooms, the biggest of which is number 3, overlooking the Hérault. Doubles 170F with basin/bidet to 230F with shower/wc. Generally old-fashioned, but perfectly adequate, and the owner makes you feel genuinely welcome.

HÔTEL LE DONJON**

place Jean-Jaurès (Centre).
☎ 04.67.94.12.32 F 04.67.94.34.54
Closed Christmas–New Year's Day. **Secure parking**. **TV**.

Le Donjon is an old stone establishment next door, so to speak, to the very old cathedral of Saint-Étienne, and stands unobtrusively on a pleasant square that buzzes with excitement in summer. Bedrooms are comfy, refurbished, exceptionally well-maintained – and yet still good value for money. Doubles 250–320F with shower/wc or bath. Easy-going atmosphere.

HÔTEL-RESTAURANT LA TAMARISSIÈRE***

lieu-dit La Tamarissière (South-West); go along quai Commandant-Réveille, then follow the D32 for 5km.
☎ 04.67.94.20.87 F 04.67.21.38.40
Closed Jan 2–March 15; restaurant closed Mondays (Monday lunchtimes in season), and Sunday evenings. **Car park**. **TV**.

Long gone is the canal-side bistro popular in our parents' day. Nowadays, *La Tamarissière* is one of the most famous hotels in the region, nestling in a rose garden surrounded by a pine wood. Stylish modern bedrooms 350–550F depending on position and time of year. The wonderful cooking, brimming with Mediterranean flavours, successfully combines tradition and style. Choose from dishes such as salad of scallops with truffles sprinkled with parmesan, *navarin* of lobster with baby vegetables and casseroled veal sweetbreads slightly flavoured with mustard. Set meals 155F, 225F, 300F and 360F. If this seems rather expensive, just remember that Nicolas Albano is one of the top-class chefs. Easy-going atmosphere, fresh décor and swimming pool.

CHEZ BÉBERT, LOU PESCADOU

18 rue Chassefière (Centre).
☎ 04.67.21.17.10
Closed Dec–Feb (except school holidays).

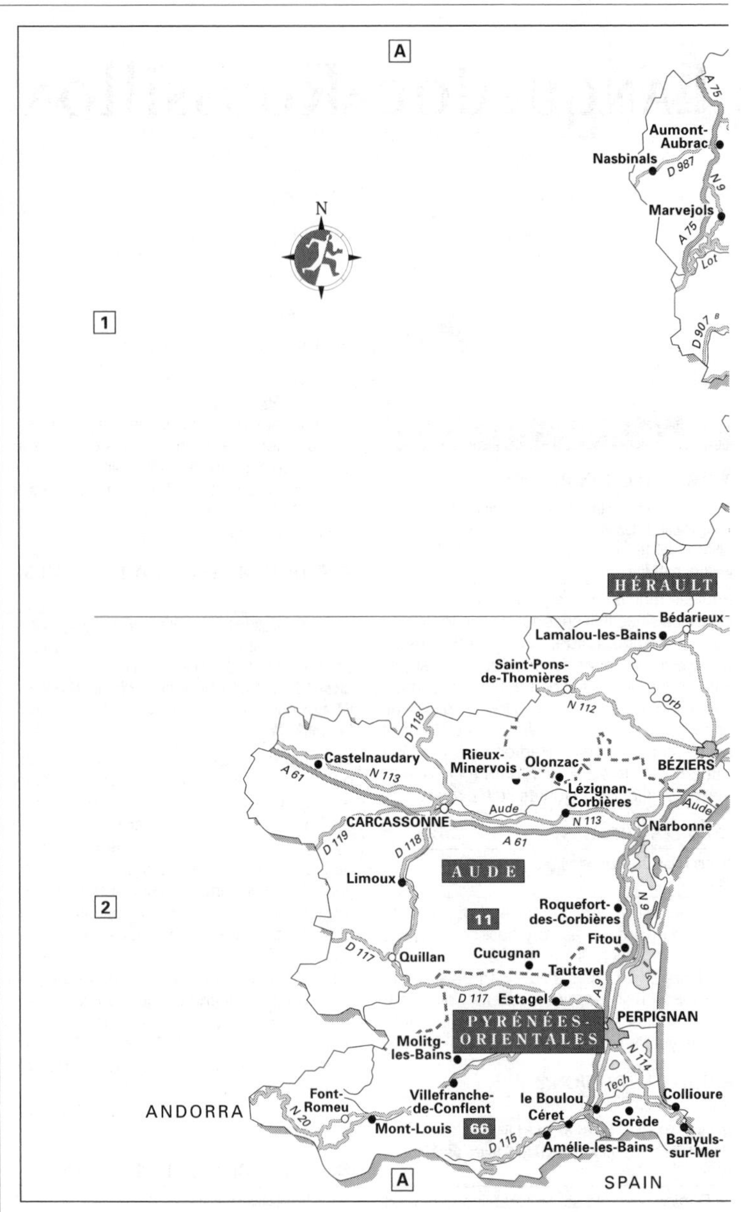
A
N
1
Aumont-Aubrac
Nasbinals
D 987
N 9
Marvejols
A 75
Lot
D 907
HÉRAULT
Bédarieux
Lamalou-les-Bains
Saint-Pons-de-Thomières
N 112
Orb
D 118
Castelnaudary
A 61
N 113
Rieux-Minervois
Olonzac
BÉZIERS
Lézignan-Corbières
Aude
CARCASSONNE
N 113
Narbonne
A 61
D 119
D 118
AUDE
Limoux
2
Roquefort-des-Corbières
N 9
11
Fitou
D 117
Quillan
Cucugnan
Tautavel
A 9
D 117
Estagel
PYRÉNÉES-ORIENTALES
PERPIGNAN
Molitg-les-Bains
N 114
Tech
Villefranche-de-Conflent
Font-Romeu
ANDORRA
N 20
Mont-Louis
66
le Boulou
Céret
Collioure
Sorède
D 115
Amélie-les-Bains
Banyuls-sur-Mer
SPAIN

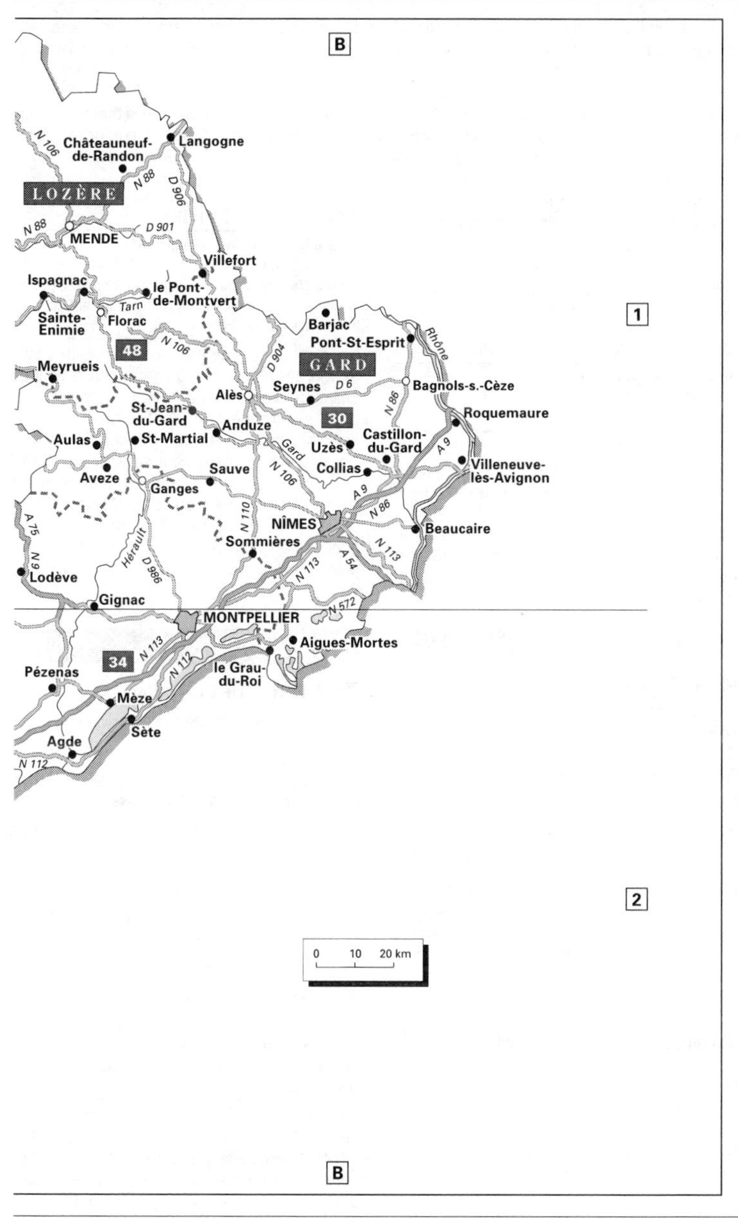
B
1
2
B
LOZÈRE
GARD
48
30
34
Châteauneuf-de-Randon
Langogne
MENDE
Villefort
Ispagnac
le Pont-de-Montvert
Sainte-Enimie
Florac
Tarn
Meyrueis
Barjac
Pont-St-Esprit
Rhône
Bagnols-s.-Cèze
Seynes
Alès
St-Jean-du-Gard
Anduze
St-Martial
Aulas
Aveze
Ganges
Sauve
Uzès
Castillon-du-Gard
Collias
Roquemaure
Villeneuve-lès-Avignon
Gard
NÎMES
Beaucaire
Sommières
Lodève
Gignac
Hérault
MONTPELLIER
Aigues-Mortes
le Grau-du-Roi
Pézenas
Mèze
Sète
Agde
N 106
N 88
D 906
D 901
D 904
D 6
N 86
A 9
A 75
N 9
N 110
D 986
N 113
A 54
N 572
N 112
0
10
20 km

Dinner served 8pm July 15–end Aug. Simplicity is the key word here. A bare room with long tables and wooden benches, where you soon get round to exchanging toasts with your neighbours, especially on summer evenings. Terrific 75F set meal offering hearty fish soup, *plâtrée* of mussels with tomato sauce and big slices of courgette, and pâté (just in case you're still peckish), lemon sole, cheese and an enormous dessert. Come on, you can fit in a little more! Gourmets will raise their eyebrows of course (mainly regarding the pâté) while others will wonder how to fit it all in. The rest of us of will think this is a great place. No payment by credit card.

RESTAURANT LA CASA PÉPÉ

29 rue Jean-Roger (Centre).
☎ 04.67.21.17.67
Closed Mondays out of season.

Everyone's crazy about this little rustic establishment situated at the back of a courtyard in the old town. What a brilliant atmosphere! And so cosy with its exposed beams and arbours. Set meals 80–130F and à la carte. Specialities such as turbot stuffed with scallops and fish soup have to be ordered ahead of time. Advisable to book.

LE GRAU D'AGDE 34300 (5KM S)

10% L'ÉPHÈBE*

12 quai du Commandant-Méric; it's on the north bank of the Hérault.
☎ 04.67.21.49.88
Closed Dec, Jan and Feb. **TV**.

A little hotel within 100m of the beach, overlooking the Hérault and the pretty port of Grau-d'Agde. Simple, perfectly adequate bedrooms with TV cost 160–220F depending on facilities and position. Dearer in July (190–270F) and even more so in August (270–310F). However, they do an interesting deal out of season – doubles 850F for a five-night stay, including breakfast. The owner's very easy-going.

MARSEILLAN 34340 (7KM NE)

LE JARDIN DU NARIS

24 bd Pasteur; take the D51.
☎ 04.67.77.30.07
Closed Monday evenings and Tuesdays out of season, and February.

This place, run by young, exceptionally friendly people, would have been described as "a bit hippy" in the 60s. You can eat in the conservatory surrounded by flowers and trees. They do simple traditional dishes like monkfish in the local style, breast of duck with bilberries, and mussels cooked in a rich white sauce. Set meals 69F, 98F, 138F and 165F. You'll find pencils on the tables if you're having trouble checking the bill, or feel like a spot of doodling (they keep a collection of their guests' drawings!).

LA TABLE D'ÉMILIE

8 place Carnot (Centre); take the D51.
☎ 04.67.77.63.59
Closed Monday lunchtimes in season, Wednesdays out of season, three weeks mid Nov–beginning of Dec, and the February school holidays.

Located near the covered market, this little restaurant has a dining room with a vaulted ceiling and a patio garden for use in summer that's a strange combination of rustic and sophisticated styles. *La Table d'Émilie* is a good gourmet restaurant serving traditional and creative dishes – a mirror image of the décor. The 95F set meal, based on local produce, offers *carpaccio* of salmon and either scallops and prawns or fillet of beef with *foie gras*. More expensive ones 170F, 230F and 270F.

AIGUES-MORTES 30220

10% HÔTEL DES CROISADES**

2 rue du Port (West); it's just outside the city walls, near the canal.
☎ 04.66.53.67.85 Fax 04.66.53.72.95
Closed Jan 15–Feb 15 and Nov 15–Dec 15.
Secure parking. **TV**. **Disabled access**.

A fairly new hotel with a hushed atmosphere run by some of the friendliest folk around. Air-conditioned doubles 240F with shower and 260F with bath. English and German channels (for TV fans!) and a delightful garden to boot. Represents the best value for money in town.

RESTAURANT LES ENGANETTES

12 rue Marceau; it's in the centre of town.
☎ 04.66.53.69.11
Closed Tuesdays and Wednesday evenings out of season. **Disabled access**.

You'll receive a friendly welcome even if you arrive at 2pm on an October day! The little interior terrace is an extension of the two tastefully decorated dining rooms. It's shaded and full of pot plants, with fans to keep you cool in summer. Good regional cooking, including delicious *gardianne de taureau* (beef – or bull rather – that's been marinated and then made into a stew), fish stew with *aïoli*, and *anchoïade* and great desserts. For 100F you'll get a full and very hearty set meal. Excellent reception.

RESTAURANT LE GALION

24 rue Pasteur (Centre)
☎ 04.66.53.86.41
Closed Mondays out of season.

Pleasant décor of stonework and exposed beams. How about trying something hearty and tasty like the home-made *Galion* salad? They also do *pierrade du pescadou* (fillets of sea bream and sea bass, which you cook yourself on a stone, served with three different sauces and an excellent little potato *gratin*) and various meat dishes. You'll get good advice from the owner, a charming young man and the bill won't come to much. Set meals 79F, 99F, 150F and à la carte. Nice welcome.

ALÈS 30100

10% HÔTEL DURAND**

3 bd Anatole-France; it's in a quiet street that starts opposite place de la Gare.
☎ 04.66.86.28.94
Secure parking. TV.

Monsieur and Madame Dumas, who used to run a dairy in La Grand-Combe, have branched out into the hotel business and taken over this rather neglected establishment. Renovations have added more warmth and character. Clean simple bedrooms. Doubles 180F and 190F with shower/wc. Friendly, attentive reception.

LE JARDIN D'ALÈS

92 av. d'Alsace (North); go towards Aubenas.
☎ 04.66.86.38.82
Closed Thursday evenings, Friday lunchtimes and July.
Car park.

The tourists still haven't discovered this place, which is all the more reason for us to recommend it. The dining room, decorated with great taste by the owners, offers fine cooking in the style of various regions of France and set meals 68–155F. They do pâté *en croûte cévenol*, veal stew *à la lyonnaise*, stuffed mussels *à la sétoise* (with brandy, tomato and garlic), mullet *à la marseillaise*, (baked with cheese, tomato and saffron) and chicken breast *à la périgourdine* (with truffles). You'll get a good reception here. Tiny and rather noisy terrace.

SAINT-HILAIRE-DE-BRETHMAS 30560 (5KM SE)

10% HÔTEL L'ÉCUSSON**

route de Nîmes (South-East); take the RN 106.
☎ 04.66.30.10.52 ➡ 04.66.56.92.48
Closed Dec 20–Jan 20. **Car park. TV.**
Disabled access.

A large, white building with shutters, offering good value for a two-star hotel. Doubles 200F and 250F with bathroom and telephone, exquisitely decorated in the style of Louis XVI. Nice little garden with lots of shade and a swimming pool and very friendly owner. Simple cooking and set meals from 80F (weekdays). The neighbourhood's rather unattractive – pity!

SEYNES 30580 (18KM E)

10% LA FARIGOULETTE**

Le bourg; take the D6 from Alès.
☎ 04.66.83.70.56 ➡ 00.66.83.72.80
Car park. TV. Disabled access.

People come from far afield to sample the pâtés, *terrines*, sausage, casseroles and *confits*. The owner and his family also run a *charcuterie* in the hamlet of Le Bourg. Everything's home-made – great! – and prices are reasonable. Set meals 70–160F. Beautifully simple, rustic dining room. Eleven, perfectly adequate bedrooms with doubles 230F. You might fancy a good long walk through the *garrigue*, along the footpaths leading to Mont Bouquet (631m high), to help work off your dinner before heading upstairs. An unfussy country establishment with a garden and swimming pool. We love it!

AMÉLIE-LES-BAINS 66110

10% LE CASTEL-ÉMERAUDE**

Petite Provence, route de la Corniche (South-East); cross the town and go towards the leisure centre (centre sportif Espace Méditerranée).
☎ 04.68.39.02.8. ➡ 04.68.39.03.09
Closed Jan and Dec. **Car park. TV. Disabled access.**

A very quiet inn on the banks of the river, surrounded by greenery. It's a big white building and looks a bit like a castle because of the two turrets but the inside is decorated in modern style. Doubles 240F with shower/wc and 360F with bath and terrace. Set meals 85F, 115F, 195F and a 100F Catalonian one guaranteed to delight holidaymakers looking for regional cooking. Those taking the waters get the benefit of a 25% reduction.

ANDUZE 30140

10% ☗ |●| LA RÉGALIÈRE**

1435 route de Saint-Jean-du-Gard (North).
☎ 04.66.61.81.93 ➡ 04.66.61.85.94
Closed Dec–Feb; restaurant closed Wenesday lunchtimes (except July–Aug). **Car park**. **TV**.

La Régalière is a very old, master craftman's house situated in vast parkland with twelve fully-equipped bedrooms and a swimming pool (covered and heated out of season!). Doubles 270–310F. Peace and quiet in a little green haven. You can eat on the shaded terrace in summer. House specialities include slivers of duck with honey and gentian liqueur, stew *languedocien en croûte*, creamed salt cod *gratiné* with *croutons à la tapenade*, and pan-fried duck *foie gras* with white chestnuts and grapes. Set meals 90F (starter, main course, plus dessert)–205F. Limited choice out of season.

|●| LE MOULIN DE CORBÈS

Corbès; take the route de Saint-Jean du Gard.
☎ 04.66.61.61.83
Closed Sunday evenings and Mondays out of season, January and February. **Car park**.

This isn't any old restaurant and you'll realize that straight away. Everything combines to create the atmosphere – a well-kept courtyard, steep staircase and even the crunch of the gravel under your feet. The stylish décor in the yellow, sun-filled dining room is complemented by the flower arrangements on the tables. The choice of dishes varies with the season but they're always simple, mouthwatering, and full of delicate flavours and pleasant combinations. Try the *fromage frais* ravioli with herb stock, slivers of duckling with lavender honey and preserved ginger, beef *pot au feu*, fillet of pan-fried beef with mulled wine. Then of course there's the must-haves – *terrine* of liver and cutlet of pan-fried liver. Set meals 148F, 180F and 320F. Ten bedrooms still at the planning stage.

AUMONT-AUBRAC 48130

10% ☗ |●| GRAND HÔTEL PROUHÈZE***

2 rue du Languedoc.
☎ 04.66.42.80.07 ➡ 04.66.42.87.78
Closed Sunday evenings and Mondays (except July–Aug) and Nov–Palm Sunday (beginning of April). **TV**.

If you're taking the A75 across the Lozère, cut off at Aumont-Aubrac so as not to miss this place. Guy Prouhèze's cooking is so wonderfully creative and professional, you won't regret stopping by. His subtle dishes bring out the full flavour of salmon, asparagus, mushrooms and other fresh produce in a way that's sheer magic! Excellent cellar full of good vintage wines and fantastic *vins de table*. Enormous, flower-filled dining room decorated in country style. Set meals 130F (weekday lunchtimes), 200F, 290F and 370F. If these prices look a bit scary, why not pop into *Le Compostelle* next door, offering two simpler but very good set meals at 80F and 100F. It's actually part of the same establishment and has the same chef. Comfy, attractive doubles 390–550F (and an absolutely faultless one at 290F).

FAU-DE-PEYRE 48130 (10KM NW)

10% ☗ |●| HÔTEL-RESTAURANT BOUCHARINC-TICHIT, DEL FAOU**

How to get there: take the D50 from Aumont-Aubral.
☎ 04.66.31.11.00 ➡ 04.66.31.30.00
Closed Sunday evenings out of season and Jan. **TV**.

"Faôu" is the regional word for "tree", and this inn in the old village of Aubrac is surrounded by them. The inn has terrific home cooking at very good prices. Very hearty set meals 58–110F. People actually queue up to sample the frogs' legs, trout with bacon and *manouls* (lamb tripe). Friendly, very natural owners. There's a modern building nearby housing faultless bedrooms with TV and all mod cons. Doubles 220–260F and half-board from 220F per person. One of best establishments in Aubrac – you'll leave with a real sense of well-being!

AVÈZE 30120

10% ☗ |●| L'AUBERGE COCAGNE**

place du Château.
☎ 04.67.81.02.70 ➡ :04.67.81.07.67
Closed Dec 20–March 1. **Car park**. **Disabled access**.

This inn is in the shadow of the château once owned by the Marquis of Montcalm, who died in Quebec fighting the British under General Wolf in 1759. In the south of France "cocagne" means "luck", and this country inn, shielded by a clump of trees, couldn't have been more aptly named. It's a thick-walled, 400-year-old building with red shutters and simple cosy bedrooms. The friendly couple in charge, Monsieur and Madame Welker, were travellers in their heyday and organize exhibitions in season. Hearty home cooking using organic produce provided by local farmers to create typical Cévennes dishes. Prices are reasonable, with set meals 68–170F. Eat out on the terrace in summer. Doubles 160F with basin, 210F with shower/wc and 245F with bath. Half-board (215F) compulsory mid July–mid Aug.

AULAS 30120 (6KM NW)

10% ☗ |●| HÔTEL-RESTAURANT LE MAS QUAYROL**

How to get there: take the D48 towards Espérou-Mont Aigoual, cross Aulas, turn left (it's signposted), then go uphill for about 1km.
☎ 04.67.81.12.38 ➡ 04.67.81.23.84
Closed Jan 1–Friday before Easter. **Car park. TV.**

Not an easy place to get to, but worth the effort. Perched on the side of the mountain, *Le Mas Quayrol* offers an extraordinary view of the valley of Arre. Unique setting, complete peace and quiet and the unmistakable scent of the Cévennes. Built in small stages, in keeping with local architecture, over a period of twenty years from a very old *mas* (house or farm typical of the south). Swimming pool and sixteen comfortable rustic bedrooms 280–540F. Lovely selection of set meals (95–235F) offering specialities such as *galette* of potatoes with *confit* of snails, braised trout with pistachio nuts and *cartagène* (a mixture of grape juice and *marc*), roast lamb *en croûte*, and *feuillantine* of raspberries. The ideal spot, between the gorges of the Tarn and the summits of Aigoual (1567m), for travellers with a bit of money and a taste for mysticism.

SAINT-MARTIAL 30440 (24KM NE)

10% ☗ |●| HÔTEL-RESTAURANT LA TERRASSE

le bourg; take the D999 across Le Vigan, then the D11 and the D20.
☎ 04.67.81.33.11 ➡ 04.67.81.33.87

Good living and good food go hand in hand at this mountainside inn. Dominique, the larger-than-life owner, is only too willing to boast about the beauty spots in her beautiful Cévennes, such as the 12th century Romanesque church, the pride and joy of the village. She's got a few perfectly adequate bedrooms, but people come here primarily for the local cooking. When we were there, the cheapest set meal (84F) offered tart *forestière* (with mushrooms, bacon and potatoes), roast guinea fowl with cider and apples, a platter of farmhouse cheeses, and home-made peach tart. For 171F you get an extra course and amazing specialities like *millefeuille* of onions with an olive oil *sabayon*. This place was a brilliant find!

BANYULS-SUR-MER 66650

10% |●| LA LITTURIME, HÔTEL DES ELMES***

plage des Elmes; go towards Port-Vendres.
☎ 04.68.88.03.12

This seafront establishment is one of Roussillon's best gourmet restaurants. After a long period working in Portugal, Jean-Marie Patrouix returned with a selection of local recipes and skilfully adapted them to his own style. Superb fish and seafood, terrific desserts and a wonderful list of regional wines. Set meals 100F, 160F, 180F and 240F. Expect to pay about 300F ˆ la carte. Bedrooms, decorated in an unmistakably modern style, can't be faulted. They've got about thirty, two of them with disabled facilities, and doubles cost 300–500F in season. There's a nature reserve nearby, so scuba-diving fans will be in their element.

BARJAC 30430

10% ☗ |●| HÔTEL-RESTAURANT LE MAS DU TERME***

route de Bagnols-sur-Cèze; it's 3km from the village, out in the vineyards.
☎ 04.66.24.56.31 ➡ 04.66.24.58.54
Closed Jan–Feb. **Car park. TV. Disabled access.**

This former silkworm farm dates from the 18th century and Monsieur and Madame Marron have refurbished it, the vaulted lounge, the internal courtyard, and the twenty-three quiet and attractive bedrooms in tasteful local style. Doubles with all mod cons 330–450F. Gourmet cooking. The set meals (95–280F) offer local specialities such as *foie gras* of duck *au torchon*, *rascasse*, roast rack of milk-fed lamb with thyme, and lavender-flavoured *crème brûlée.*not bad at all! The swimming pool's a welcome sight in warm weather. Yes, things are pretty expensive here, but you'll really enjoy your stay.

BÉZIERS 34500

☗ HÔTEL LUX**

3 rue des Petits-Champs.
☎ 04.67.28.48.05 ➡ 04.67.49.97.73
Secure parking. TV. Disabled access.

The name's got nothing to do with luxury or face soap, and everything to do with the Latin word for light. A quiet little hotel with clean simple bedrooms that are bathed in sunlight during the summer months. Nice welcome and reasonable prices. Doubles 130F (with basin, no TV)–220F (with bath and telephone). Ideal if you're on a budget.

HÔTEL LE CONFORT

3 rue Étienne-Marcel (Centre); it's 20m from allées Paul-Riquet.
☎ 04.46.76.23.98
TV.

"Cheap comfy accommodation in the town centre" – an eyecatching advertisement! And *Hôtel Le Confort* is, in fact, pretty reasonably priced. Clean, functional, and perfectly adequate bedrooms 149F with shower/wc and 169F with TV. Expect to pay more during the *feria* (festival). Smiling welcome and good value for money.

10% LE CHAMP-DE-MARS**

17 rue de Metz (Centre); it's near place du 14-Juillet.
☎ 04.67.28.35.53 Fax 04.67.28.61.42
Secure parking. **TV**.

Situated in a very quiet street, this little hotel with the geranium-covered façade has been renovated from top to bottom. The meticulous bedrooms overlook the garden. Doubles 160–230F. The best value for money in Béziers. The cheerful owner will tell you all about the town.

LE CAVEAU DES HALLES

13 pl. Pierre Sémard; it's beside the covered market.
☎ 04.67.28.47.87
Closed Sundays and in the evenings (except Fridays).

Run by two young women, this little hotel, decorated in Provençale style and filled with assorted furniture, doubles as a clothes shop and a place for sampling regional wines. Pleasant surroundings for a spot of lunch at very reasonable prices. Good, tasty, straightforward cooking and dishes that vary according to what's available at the market. You'll be offered something along the lines of asparagus tart, roast chicken with carrots and goat's cheese with honey. *Menu du jour* 67F, dish of the day less than 50F. And they've got some very good wines. Treat yourself to some Saint-Jean-du-Minervois, one of the best Muscats ever. Credit cards not accepted.

CHA-U-KAO

23 rue des Anciens-Combattants (Centre); it's opposite the old post office.
☎ 04.67.28.69.21
Closed Monday and Saturday lunchtimes, Sundays, and a fortnight in February.

This simple, bright restaurant with its pleasant terrace has a large group of regulars. With its friendly reception and cosy atmosphere, it feels almost like an eighties style remake of a Pagnol movie. Typical local cooking, brimming with Mediterranean flavours. There's whelks with *aïoli* (garlic-flavoured mayonnaise), mussels stuffed with spaghetti, and breast of duck with figs. And in season, the chef cooks asparagus better than anyone we know. Set meal 70F.

LE BISTROT DES HALLES

place de la Madeleine (Centre); it's in the quartier des Halles – go towards the Madeleine underground **car park**.
☎ 04.67.28.30.46
Closed Sundays and Mondays. Private **car park**. **Disabled access**.

Lively place with Parisian bistro décor. Set meals 74–124F available lunchtimes and evenings. Good variety of authentic – lots of seafood and shellfish, *carpaccio*, pig's trotters, *pot-au-feu* and *choucroute* (in winter). In summer you can sit out on the delightful terrace in the square.

LE CRÉMIER

6 av. Alphonse-Mas (Centre).
☎ 04.67.49.23.40
Closed Sundays and Monday lunchtimes; in July and August, closed Sundays and lunchtimes.

The first restaurant of its kind, one that doubles as a dairy and cheese shop. It's a case of cheese, cheese and more cheese, and Roquefort, Rocamadour and Pélardon, to name but a few, are all used in the cooking. It's one of the few places around these parts that serves a good *raclette* (melted cheese and jacket potatoes) and a proper *fondue savoyarde*. Set meals 85F and 120F. They do an absolutely incredible dinner plus show for 150F every last Monday in the month. Friendly, fun-filled atmosphere guaranteed.

LES ANTIQUAIRES

4 rue Bagatelle (Centre); it's at the foot of allées Paul-Riquet.
☎ 04.67.49.31.10
Closed Mondays, lunchtimes (except Sundays), and August.

If you're looking for something cosy and intimate, this tiny restaurant could be just what you're after. It's decorated with cherubs, old adverts and movie posters, and the cooking is wonderful. There's a large and very tasty salad of *Pélardon* (soft white goat's cheese with a nutty flavour) with strawberries and thin slices of apple, fillet of sea bass cooked to perfection, a big cheese platter and magnificent *crème brûlée.* And all for 91F! Another set meal at 140F. Good wines at reasonable prices and courteous service. It's not very big and it's very popular, so it's a good idea to book.

LE CAFÉ DES LOUIS

plan Saint-Nazaire.
☎ 04.67.49.93.13
Closed Saturday and Sunday lunchtimes.

Situated beside the cathedral, *Le Café des Louis* offers hearty traditional dishes, which can be enjoyed on the patio-cum-garden or in the pleasant vaulted dining room. We tried the dish of the day, a brilliant rack of lamb (45F). There's also a 75F *formule* or you can expect to pay 100F à la carte. The helpings are large and they have some good specialities, including *pot au feu*, cuttlefish *à la plancha* (which you cook yourself on a hot stone), and *anchoïade*. Friendly and efficient service.

L'AMBASSADE

22 bd de Verdun (Centre); it's opposite the railway station.
☎ 04.67.76.06.24
Closed Sundays and Monday evenings.

L'Ambassade, with its retro light fittings and faded *trompe-l'œil* paintings, is nicely old-fashioned, with touches all of its own like squeaky chairs and a rose stuck in the neck of an empty bottle of Abel Lepitre champagne. They're planning on changing the décor in the near future, but we care more about what's in front of us and it must be said that Patrick Olry is a good chef. You only have to try his "découverte" set meal at 155F, offering grilled scallops and oysters with leeks, followed by *pavé* of zander *à l'écaille.* Dishes to die for! The cheese is out of this world and so are the desserts. The waiters are dressed in black double-breasted suits but the atmosphere wasn't excessively formal and they offer excellent advice on their selection of wines. In a nutshell, everything at *l'Ambassade* met with our approval (even the bill!). Other set meals 115F and 220F. The menu changes depending on what the market has to offer and they use only high-quality seasonal produce.

LE JARDIN

37 av. Jean-Moulin (North); it's near the sous-préfecture.
☎ 04.67.36.41.31
Closed Mondays, Sundays, the first week in January, during the February school holidays, and the first fortnight in July.

The Santuré brothers have firmly established their reputation in this part of the world. Jean-Luc, whose talent is very much in evidence, serves up tasty dishes based on fresh market produce. Try the breast and legs of roast pigeon with thyme, the salmon with cooking salt and chives, oysters gratinéd in their shells, or the different kinds of *foie gras* of duck. Francis acts as wine waiter and has unearthed some particularly good wines. He'll advise you as to which are available by the glass. Set meals 115F (weekday lunchtimes), 130F (except Saturday evenings, Sundays and public holidays), 185F, 225F and 295F. The last two are sheer heaven if you have wine with them but that'll push the price up to 325F and 405F.

NISSAN-LEZ-ENSERUNE 34440 (11KM SW)

10% HÔTEL RÉSIDENCE**

35 av. de la Cave.
☎ 04.67.37.00.63 F 04.67.37.68.63
Closed Nov 1–30. **Secure parking**. **Canal+**.

A beautiful, white building, typically provincial, that oozes old-fashioned charm. Situated in a big village in the hinterland of Béziers, it's a good place for just one night or a week. Relaxed, informal and flower-filled. Several bedrooms have been recently added in the annexe at the foot of the garden. Doubles 250–280F. We were won over by the reception and the peaceful atmosphere. Restaurant, for the sole use of hotel guests, serves a 98F set meal.

ESPONDEILHAN 34290 (12KM N)

CHÂTEAU DE CABREROLLES***.

☎ 04.67.39.21.79 F 04.67.39.21.05
Car park. **TV**.

Situated in delightful flower-filled parkland, here's a 19th century castle that looks like an Italian villa. You've got all mod cons here. Doubles 320–480F, no two the same, suites 450F, and studio flats with small kitchen 320–380F. Beautiful swimming pool.

MAGALAS 34480 (22KM N)

LA BOUCHERIE

pl. de l'Église; take the D909, route de Bédarieux, then turn right about 20km further on.

☎ 04.67.36.20.82
Closed Sundays, Mondays, and during the November and February school holidays.

There's nothing out of the ordinary about a butcher's shop you might say. Ah yes, but this one doubles as a restaurant, and a good one at that. It has two dining rooms (they're a bit kitsch and look as if they've been decorated with stock from a second-hand shop) with brightly-coloured tablecloths and an attractive terrace on a typical village square. There's a 52F *menu du jour* (weekday lunchtimes) and two other set meals at 85F and 130F. You're in for a treat here – *tapas* from the market, selection of cold meat, stews, steak tartare that's made in front of you, and delicious *carpaccio*. If you like tripe, you'll love the way they do it here. Blues or jazz plays in the background and, to set it all off, there are some good wines. Definitely advisable to book.

CARCASSONNE 11000

AUBERGE DE JEUNESSE

rue du Vicomte-Trencavel (Centre); it's in the medieval part of town.
☎ 04.68.25.23.16 F→ 04.68.71.14.84
Closed Dec–Jan.

Doors open 8am–noon and 5–11pm out of season (7am–1am in season). Advisable to book in writing. This is an attractive and well-maintained youth hostel in the historic part of town. And it's not often we're so complimentary! Card holders only. Accommodation for 120 based on two–six sharing. 70F per night including breakfast. Sheet hire 14F. They do a 49F set meal for groups only. Common room with fireplace, kitchen, TV room and conservatory. Friendly staff and multicultural atmosphere.

HÔTEL TERMINUS**

2 av. du Maréchal-Joffre (North); it's near the station.
☎ 04.68.25.25.00 F→ 04.68.72.53.09
Closed Dec–Feb. **Secure parking**. **TV**.
Disabled access.

Various films have been shot in this enormous modern luxury hotel with a winter garden. It's worth seeing for the foyer alone, with its 30s revolving door, mouldings, double staircase, old tiling and gleaming bar. It has about 100 rooms at what are amazing prices considering the luxurious décor. However, some of them have lost their charm as a result of over-zealous renovation work. Doubles from 290F with shower/wc and 315F with bath. Couples could reserve no.7, nicknamed "The Bridal Suite", with their eyes closed. It's absolutely magnificent – as spacious as a government minister's office, stylish furniture, beautiful windows and all modern-day comforts. Amazing bathroom with two basins, and an old-fashioned bathtub. This little jewel costs only 450F! Hushed and rather conventional, typical country hotel atmosphere in other words. Buffet breakfast 38F. Prices in the restaurant are a bit steep for what is rather ordinary cooking. Paying car park 35F per night.

HÔTEL DU DONJON***

2 rue du Comte-Roger (South); it's in the heart of the medieval part of town.
☎ 04.68.71.08.80 F→ 04.68.25.06.60
Restaurant closed Sunday evenings end Oct–end March.
Car park. **TV**. **Canal+**. **Disabled access**.

You'll get the works here! Medieval building, magnificent beams, unusual staircase, bourgeois luxury, all mod cons, double glazing, air-conditioning, bar, lounges, garden etc etc etc. But these things come at a price – in this case 390F with shower and 490F with bath and air-conditioning. Buffet breakfast 53F. Very popular with Americans.

L'ESCALIER

23 bd Omer-Sarrant (Centre).
☎ 04.68.25.65.66

Service until 1am. People probably come for the décor first and the food second. It's not easy to describe the dining room, where the décor makes references to Ancient Greece, Mexico, America, and the cinema. It's easy to like it though, with its warm colour scheme, old film posters and background music. The cooking is mainly Mexican but they also do some Greek dishes. The *fajitas* and the chilli are worth a try. Another speciality is seafood *plancha* (a plate of squid, mussels, langoustine, prawns and crab on a bed of tagliatelle) for 110F. Set meal 60F weekday lunchtimes. Expect to pay about 80F à la carte. You'll get a cheerful reception. The toilets are absolutely amazing, so don't leave without a quick visit.

AUBERGE L'ŒIL

32 rue de Lorraine; it's behind the law courts.
☎ 04.68.25.64.81
Closed Saturday lunchtimes and Sundays (except for groups).

Situated in a little street in the "new" town, this small and tastefully decorated inn is worth seeing. For more than twenty years,

Christophe Cazaban has been using unseasoned oak (very important this) to grill his breast of duck, local sausage, beef cutlets and fish. Six hearty set meals offering three courses – 68F (lunchtimes) and 90–125F. You'll get a friendly welcome. Ideal for meat and fish lovers.

|●| RESTAURANT LA DIVINE COMÉDIE

29 bd Jean-Jaurès (Centre); it's opposite the law courts.
☎ 04.68.72.30.36.
Closed Sundays and two or three weeks at Christmas.

This place gives very good value for money and is popular with people who live and work locally. Enormous portions of excellent meat 71–78F. Specialities include *cassoulet* with *confit* of duck, *cassoulet carcassonais* (with mutton), thin slivers of duck with honey and apples, *blanquette* of lamb and *daube languedocienne*, baked cod with hard-boiled eggs, potatoes and tomatoes, and every kind of pizza under the sun. Waiters are polite and efficient. A good unpretentious restaurant, ideal for a quick bite to eat.

|●| L'AUBERGE DE DAME CARCAS

3, place du Château (South-East); it's in the medieval part of town.
☎ 04.68.71.23.23.
Closed Mondays and Tuesday lunchtimes out of season, and mid Jan–mid Feb.

There's plenty of room for everybody so take your pick from the terrace, the upstairs dining room or the old vaulted cellar. Rustic, carefully designed décor. The kitchen opens onto the dining room and a bell chimes as a way of saying thanks. Given that the quality is so high and this is a very touristy district, you could almost describe the set meals and dishes as cheap. They do a good 85F regional set meal, splendid chargrilled dishes, such as suckling pig with honey (absolutely terrific!), *crépinette* of pork in orange sauce and house *cassoulet*. And when the chefs sit down to eat after an evening's work they talk about food, which has to be a good sign. They even bake their own bread while you're having your meal. Regional wines at very reasonable prices. We're still pretty amazed we came across this inn among the tourist traps in the old town.

|●| RESTAURANT CHEZ FRED

86 rue Albert-Tomey and 31 bd Omer-Sarrant (Centre); it's opposite the botanic gardens.
☎ 04.68.72.02.23

An adorable brand-new establishment with a hushed atmosphere. The décor's pleasing and in good taste, with rattan armchairs and walls that are the colour of wine and plums. Frédéric Coste's cooking is modern and full of integrity, and a set meal might consist of *foie gras*, fricassee of lamb with thyme or breast of duck with caramelized pears, and for dessert, two kinds of chocolate *charlotte* or *croustillant* of apples with Armagnac and sorbet. Set meals 88F (weekday lunchtimes), 135F and 172F. A discreet place for bashful lovers.

|●| L'ÉCURIE

1 rue d'Alembert (Bd Barbès) (Centre).
☎ 04.68.72.04.04
Closed Sunday evenings.

Without a doubt *L'Écurie*, housed in an 18th century stable, is the most amusing and most original restaurant in Carcassonne! The décor's exceptionally tasteful and based on an equestrian theme. It might feel a bit like a private club but not to worry, the owner will soon put you at your ease. The cooking's good and while they do serve *cassoulet*, it's fish that features most prominently here, with dishes like roast cod with herbs and fresh goat's cheese, fillet of sea bream with asparagus, and salmon with apricots and polenta. Set meals 110F (weekday lunchtimes), 130F, 165F and 260F.

TRÈBES 11800 (7KM E)

|●| AUBERGE DU MOULIN

écluse de Trèbes.
☎ 04.68.78.83.00
Closed Thursdays all year round and Wednesdays Nov–March. **Car park**.

What a brilliant location! This very old lock-keeper's house is on the banks of the canal du Midi and the delightful terrace stretches right down to the water. You can eat the house *cassoulet* out here and get into conversation with the people on the river cruise barges. Friendly, good-humoured atmosphere and smiling reception. Good 75F set meal offering starter, main course, and cheese or dessert. Others 115F and 130F. Our favourite place on the banks of the canal du Midi (and there are quite a few).

PEZENS 11170 (11KM W)

|●| AUBERGE DU MOULIN D'ALZAU

How to get there: from Pezens take the route de Toulouse, and 3km along turn left onto a shaded little road.
☎ 04.68.24.97.38
Closed Mondays and Sunday evenings.

A word of warning: reservations are practically compulsory. What a pity there's no accommodation, for this old mill complete with waterwheel is a delightful spot. Enormous dining room with inn-style décor. Set meals at 75F, 100F and 160F, offering good, hearty portions. The house speciality is trout *au bleu*. It's an ideal place for a romantic dinner for two not far from Carcassonne.

CASTELNAUDARY 11400

GRAND HÔTEL FOURCADE**

14 rue des Carmes (Centre).
☎ 04.68.23.02.08 F 04.68.94.10.67
Closed Sunday evenings, Mondays Sept 15–April 15, and the last three weeks in January. **Secure parking. TV.**

The restaurant in this cosy old hotel full of knick-knacks is very popular in these parts. The cheapest set meal (80F) is pretty good – local sausage, *cassoulet* with *confit* of goose and dessert. For 130F you get the lot – *charcuterie*, duck liver or salad of lentils with gizzards, *cassoulet* with *confit* of goose, cheese salad and dessert. You'll need lots of money if you're going à la carte. Bedrooms are rather bare but then they're not expensive. Doubles 110F and 120F with basin. You'll find a much higher standard of comfort in the ones with shower/wc or bath (190F). Something for everyone! Reception's a bit abrupt to begin with, but perfectly charming thereafter.

VILLEPINTE 11150 (12KM SE)

10% AUX DEUX ACACIAS*

N113; take the N113 towards Carcassonne.
☎ 04.68.94.24.67 F 04.68.94.21.28
Secure parking. TV.

Cassoulet is sacred in Castelnaudary, and like any religion there's an area of common belief and a great many points that give rise to heated debate. We came across one of the best *cassoulets* we've ever had here. *Aux Deux Acacias* has been around for some time and lots of people share our opinion. Set meals only 69–105F. Warm friendly welcome and pleasant service. If you feel like a bit of a lie-down after your meal, they've got a few inexpensive, refurbished bedrooms. Doubles 150F with washing facilities and 170F with shower/wc.

CASTILLON-DU-GARD 30210

L'AMPHITRYON

place du 8-Mai-1945; it's opposite the town hall.
☎ 04.66.37.05.04.
Closed Wednesdays, one week in November and one week in February.

Calling all gourmets! Here's something to delight you – an old dining room with exposed stonework serving typical Provençal cooking. They do *foie gras* and veal sweetbreads in a port sauce, monkfish with pesto and a rosemary-flavoured sauce, and fillet of beef with olives. Set meals 95F (weekday lunchtimes), and 150–310F. The fountain brightens up the interior courtyard – you can sit out here on the terrace in summer and listen to the gentle splashing sound.

CÉRET 66400

HÔTEL-RESTAURANT VIDAL*

4 place du 4-Septembre (Centre); it's between the town hall and place Picasso.
☎ 04.68.87.00.85 F 04.68.87.62.33
Closed Saturday evenings (except holidays) and mid Oct–mid Nov.

This former bishop's residence, which dates from 1735, is listed as a historical monument and is quite delightful, with its handsome, sculpted façade. Renovations were carried out on the hotel a few years ago. The owner is friendly and the prices are very good for the area – 135F with basin/bidet and doubles 200F with shower/wc. There's only one room with bath (also 200F) and you'll have to book far ahead. Set meals 78–150F. Lots of cherry dishes à la carte (the cherry is the town's emblem), including duck with cherries and pan-fried *foie gras* with a cherry and wine sauce. The terrace is a welcome sight and you can relax out here in the evening.

LES FEUILLANTS

1 bd Lafayette.
☎ 04.68.87.37.88
Closed Sunday evenings and Mondays out of season.

Chef Didier Banyuls is held in high esteem by gourmets in this part of the world, and deserves his star rating just as much as our praise. His wonderful cooking, which changes with the seasons, is largely based on the wide range of Catalan produce, but he's no chauvinist and can cook the dishes of other regions and countries if necessary. The superb dining room with its high ceiling, mouldings and old parquet floor will put you in the right mood to enjoy the food. *Menu terroir* 260F (360F with a selection of regional wines). Expect to spend about 500F à la carte. The wine list is pretty remarkable, complementing the good food. Next door, the *Bistrot des Feuillants* offers a 130F set meal that's excellent value for money. We had pan-fried cuttlefish with a chickpea sauce, fricassee of chicken wing tips, squid and snails, cheese, and strawberry baba. If you want to stay, they've got three comfy bedrooms with stylish décor (400F) and one suite (750F).

REYNES 66400 (6KM W)

LE CHAT QUI RIT

La Cabanasse de Reynes; take the D115 towards Amélie-les-Bains.
☎ 04.68.87.02.22
Closed Monday lunchtimes in summer, Sunday evenings and Mondays out of season, and January.

We were drawn by the sign with the unusual name and the teak terrace shaded by parasols (we don't miss a thing!). As soon as we'd stepped inside, we knew we'd made the right decision. Perfectly delightful, with its exotic furniture and warm colours. Paintings, photos and drawings of cats are dotted about. A very stylish place, well liked by the locals. Set meals 68–158F, to suit all appetites, and a superb children's set meal.

CHÂTEAUNEUF-DE-RANDON 48170

10% HÔTEL DE LA POSTE**

How to get there: take the N88 and it's beside the Mausolée du Guesclin.
☎ 04.66.47.90.05 F 04.66.47.91.41
Closed Friday evenings, Saturday lunchtimes and Christmas–New Year's Day. **Secure parking**. **TV**. **Disabled access**.

This establishment may well be by the main road, but you don't have to worry about the traffic. Most bedrooms overlook the countryside, and what's more they've just been refurbished from top to bottom. Modern, spick-and-span doubles 250F with shower/wc, 260F with bath. The restaurant, housed in an old barn, has lost none of its rustic charm. José Laurens does the cooking and prepares tasty traditional dishes like *terrine* of pig cheeks, stew of snails with ceps, and fillet of guinea fowl. *Formule* 48F and set meals 98–160F.

COLLIOURE 66190

10% HOSTELLERIE DES TEMPLIERS**

quai de l'Amirauté (Centre); it's opposite the château.
☎ 04.68.98.31.10 F 04.68.98.01.24
Hotel closed one week in November and in January; restaurant closed Sunday evenings and Mondays Oct–April. **TV**.

The hotel's often full, so book well ahead to be sure of a room in the main building. Avoid the annexes. If you're planning on coming to Collioure, people who know and love the town will tell you to stay here. The present owner's father welcomed many painters and sculptors, offering board and lodging (like a lord) in return for paintings or drawings. Matisse, Maillol, Dali, Picasso and Dufy are some of those famous guests we'd like to have entertained ourselves. As a result, there are more than 2,000 original works of art on display all over the hotel – on the ceiling and stairs, in the corridors, the boat-shaped bar and, of course, on the bedroom walls. Unfortunately, some of the most precious ones (including a number of Picassos) were stolen a few years ago. Nowadays, you'll be made to feel just as welcome in this unusual "museum", which is light years away from being a showy luxury hotel. And prices have remained reasonable. Doubles 250–355F with shower/wc or bath depending on the season. Ask for number 30, as it's really rather good. Every room has its own special charm and most are absolutely superb, with their painted wooden beds, rustic chairs and colourful paintings. Restaurant specializes in fish dishes.

HÔTEL CASA PAÏRAL***

impasse des Palmiers (Centre); it's beside place du 8 Mai.
☎ 04.68.82.05.81 F 04.68.82.52.10
Closed start Nov–end March. **TV**.

A little palace in the kind of setting you dream of. There's a fountain on a patio with masses of greenery, a Hollywood-style swimming pool, a cosy lounge and absolute peace and quiet. High-class luxury in a little corner of paradise. Comfy spacious bedrooms with period furniture. Prices start at 340F for a double with shower (out of season), rising to 740F for the most attractive. Reservations are taken a long time in advance, especially for summer months. Professional staff. A reliable establishment.

CUCUGNAN 11350

10% AUBERGE DU VIGNERON**

2 rue Achille-Mir (Centre).
☎ 04.68.45.03.00 F→ 04.68.45.03.08
Closed Sunday evenings (out of season), Mondays and mid Dec–mid Feb. **Car park. TV.**

Cucugnan was immortalised by Alphonse Daudet, the great 19th century humourist, who wrote about its parish priest (although he apparently plagiarized the work of an obscure local author called Achille Mir). The townsfolk named a theatre after him. The *Auberge du Vigneron,* situated just across the way, is a perfectly adorable inn, offering rustic bedrooms with exposed stonework. Doubles 240F with shower/wc. There's a beautiful restaurant downstairs, in what used to be the wine grower's cellar, with barrels as big as the fireplace. Set meals 85–185F. Try the breast of duck with cherries, the fricassee of crayfish, or the duckling with apples. Nothing particularly special, but the dishes are cooked with lots of flair and the reception is just charming.

ESTAGEL 66310

10% HÔTEL-RESTAURANT LES GRAVES**

9 bd Jean-Jaurès (Centre); it's in place du village.
☎ 04.68.29.00.84 F→ 04.68.29.47.04
Secure parking. TV. Canal+.

If you don't know much about Graves (the area and the wine), this is the place to come to. François Susplugas makes his own wine – Cabernet, Merlot, Syrah, Viognier – which you can discover over dinner. At perfectly reasonable prices, why not go ahead and treat yourself. A bottle of Cabernet-Sauvignon is about 38F, Côtes du Roussillon-Villages 48F, Chardonnay 42F, and Viognier is the dearest at 65F. Make the most of your stay and try out the cooking – local hearty, invigorating and reasonably priced dishes such as *anchoïade,* house *tapenade* (anchovy paste with capers, olives and tuna fish) and *bolos de picolat* (small meatballs). Set meal 65F. You might as well go the whole hog and stay the night – the bedrooms in the hotel are just as delightful as those in the annexe. They all have red hexagonal floor tiles and eiderdowns, and some have a fireplace. Doubles 220–270F with shower. Reception and service very welcoming. So, why not spend the night?

FITOU 11510

LA CAVE D'AGNÈS

How to get there: it's at the top end of the village.
☎ 04.68.45.75.91
Closed Wednesdays and Oct 1–April 1. **Car park.**

Tasteful, simple, rustic décor in this very popular place, which used to be a wine cellar. You'll receive a delightful welcome from a Scotswoman. The cooking's good and the portions generous. Set meals from 110F. Great buffet of starters and local *charcuterie*, lobster, fillet of beef with Fitou and some very good wines.

FLORAC 48400

10% GRAND HÔTEL DU PARC**

47 av. Jean-Monestier (Centre).
☎ 04.66.45.03.05 F→ 04.66.45.11.81
Closed Dec 1–March 15; restaurant closed Mondays out of season. **Car park. TV. Canal+.**
Disabled access.

Without a doubt, this is the oldest and biggest hotel in the region. It's a large building in very pleasant parkland, reminiscent of spa hotels. But it's really like a delightful family guest house where people of all ages can rub shoulders quite amicably. A total of sixty bedrooms offering a good standard of comfort and priced 170–260F. On the other hand, the cooking's pretty ordinary. Set meals 88–185F.

LA SOURCE DU PÊCHER

How to get there: it's in the centre of town.
☎ 04.66.45.03.01
Closed end Nov–Easter.

Ideally situated on the river bank in the heart of the old town, *La Source du Pêcher* is pleasing to the eye and to the ear. From the terrace, there's a picture postcard view of sloping gables, intricate roof patterns and old architecture against a backdrop of tall green mountains while in front of you are some beautiful trees an ivy-covered façade and the sound of running water. The attentive young proprietor (who also acts as waiter) will bring you good local dishes such as nettle soup, warm *Pélardon* (goat's cheese) with Cévennes honey, and tripe made to an old recipe. Selection of mature house cheese at excellent prices. 89F *menu du jour* at lunchtimes, other set meals 118F and 168F. An above-average establishment.

SALLE-PRUNET (LA) 48400 (2KM S)

10% L'AUBERGE CÉVENOLE–CHEZ ANNIE ET SERGE

How to get there: take the route d'Alès.
☎ 04.66.45.11.80
Closed Sunday evenings and Mondays out of season (except public holidays) and mid Nov–start Feb.
Car park. **TV**.

An old building made of local stone nestling deep in the Mimente valley. Take your meals on the terrace in summer, and huddle round the fire in winter. Robert Louis Stevenson would have felt quite at home in this nice country inn. You feel as if you're eating in the family dining room. Set meals 85–160F. The 115F one is pretty hearty, offering local cold meats, *Pélardon* (warm goat's cheese on a bed of lettuce) and *Roquefort* salad. One of the house specialities is cushion of veal with a cep sauce. Accommodation also available – doubles 190F (wc on the landing) to 250F (shower/wc). Pleasant bedrooms and very well-maintained. Our favourite place in Florac. Advisable to book as it's very popular.

COCURÈS 48400 (5KM N)

LA LOZERETTE**

How to get there: take the D998.
☎ 04.66.45.06.04 F→ 04.66.45.12.93
Closed Tuesdays (except July–Aug) and All Saints' Day–Easter. **Secure parking**. **TV**. **Canal+**.
Disabled access.

This is a family business in a quiet little village on the picturesque road up to Mont Lozère. It's run primarily by the womenfolk. The granny, Eugénie, once owned an inn herself. Nowadays, Pierrette Agulhon's in charge, serving an 80F set meal of local specialities, and others at 105F (wonderful), 160F, 190F and 250F. They're all designed to introduce you to Pierrette's speciality, the best Languedoc wines. Yes, she's also a wine waitress! Take her advice on the best wine to accompany *panade* of cod with mild garlic, snail ravioli with nettles, or calf's feet with juniper berries. A successful combination of imagination, good taste and magnificent flavours. Bedrooms are as stylish as the dining room – floral, pastel-coloured and decorated with a keen eye for detail. Expect to pay 285F with shower/wc and 390F with bath. Breakfast is good.

GARDE (LA) 48200

10% LE ROCHER BLANC**

Centre; it's 1km from exit 32 on the A75 (the first in Lozère coming from the north); go along the main street.
☎ 04.66.31.90.90 F→ 04.66.31.93.67
Restaurant closed beginning of Nov–Easter. **Car park**. **TV**.

A good place to stop. The hotel has clean, quiet and fairly spacious bedrooms. Expect to pay 230F with shower/wc – 280F with bath. Swimming pool. Set meals 85–195F (the 92F one has regional specialities). Margeride is a wild and beautiful part of the country and the hotel is only 3km from the museum of Albaret-Sainte-Marie, the smallest in France.

CHAULHAC 48140 (10KM N)

LA MAISON D'ELISA

☎ 04.66.31.93.32
Closed one week in August and one week in February.

A pretty flower-filled village in the middle of nowhere. You've got to be adventurous to leave Lille and its coal tips behind to settle down here under the Mediterranean sun, surrounded by rivers and woodland. These Northerners did it, and are now running a cosy, unassuming inn. Decent, nicely presented 70F set meal (including wine and coffee) varies daily. Madame's touch and Monsieur's smiling service are always on show. *Truffade* and terrific *aligot* made to order.

GIGNAC 34150

LE BRASIER

9 bd de l'Esplanade.
☎ 04.67.57.57.12
Closed Jan.

A simple establishment in a big lively village. Delightful cooking, based mainly on local dishes, served in a pleasant, vaulted dining room. You'll see breast of duck and different meats cooking on the fireplace at the back. It's cosy, full of flowers and run by an energetic woman. Try the calf's head with spicy vinaigrette, crayfish *à l'armoricaine*, pork in a curry sauce or one of the tasty grills.

GRAU-DU-ROI (LE) 30240

LES ACACIAS**

21 rue de l'Égalité (South); it's in the old village, on the south bank, 300m from the centre.

☎ 04.66.51.40.86
Closed Mondays out of season and Oct 1–March 30.
Disabled access.

Les Acacias is an absolutely delightful establishment situated in a very touristy Camargue seaside resort. The décor in the bedrooms combines rustic and Provençal styles. Doubles 171F with basin, 220F with shower/wc and 250F with bath. In the high season 197F, 244F and 290F respectively. Try for one of the old rooms in the annexe as they're more comfy, although not as individual. Take your meals in the dining room or on the terrace under the shade of a plane tree. They have a terrific speciality – *rouille* of octopus. Or how about *bouillabaisse*, stuffed squid, *bourride* or fish soup? Everything's from the sea! Set meal 98F. Pleasant garden and a delightful welcome. Half-board (250F) compulsory in high season.

L'OUSTAU CAMARGUEN***

3 route des Marines; at Port-Camargue, follow the signs for plages sud.
☎ 04.66.51.51.65 F 04.66.53.06.65
Closed mid Oct–mid March. **Car park**. **TV**.

The décor at *L'Oustau Camarguen* is a combination of local and Spanish styles, with a few Provençal touches. Hushed atmosphere and masses of charm, even though it's fairly new. Away from the lively goings-on in town, and especially delightful in summer with the swimming pool and garden. Doubles 390–525F depending on the season. Good hearty meals in the evenings. Tuna and monkfish specialities. Set meals 95–167F. Absolutely perfect, considering the setting, facilities and friendly reception.

ISPAGNAC 48320

10% HÔTEL-RESTAURANT SAURY

le bourg.
☎ 04.66.44.21.14

They don't make them like this any more. Lace curtains, small rustic dining room and delightful cooking. Set meals 55F, 75F and 90F. This last one offers asparagus, *blanquette* of kid, cheese and dessert. Simple cheap rooms 175F with shower, 195F with shower/wc and 225F with bath.

LE LYS

Molines; it's 2km from Ispagnac by the D907 bis.
☎ 04.66.44.23.56
Closed Oct–April.

Le Lys is an old building with a rather unassuming façade, so we weren't quite sure what to expect. And we were nicely surprised! Everything's white and the contemporary paintings and sculptures inject a modern note. You might be a bit put out by the striking contrast, but that feeling soon disappears when you see the menu. The cooking is simple but the chef comes up with some interesting combinations. Vegetables are grown in the garden and someone goes mushroom picking in the morning. Set meals 95–160F feature dishes such as poached knuckle of beef cooked in stock and walnut cake with warm chocolate sauce. The good-natured owner has every right to be proud of his restaurant-cum-tearoom-cum-gallery.

LAMALOU-LES-BAINS 34240

LE COMMERCE*

av. Charcot (Centre).
☎ 04.67.95.63.14
Disabled access.

Le Commerce is an old, slightly old-fashioned, family-run establishment, and the bearded owner makes you feel most welcome. Spick-and-span, even if the interior's a touch dated. Doubles 100–165F with basin, shower or bath. Restaurant open exclusively for guests in the evenings. Amazing 53F set meal and 40F daily special serving things like stuffed quail. It's pleasant out on the terrace.

10% HÔTEL-RESTAURANT BELLEVILLE**

1 av. Charcot (Centre).
☎ 04.67.95.57.00 F 04.67.95.64.18
Secure parking. **TV**. **Canal+**. **Disabled access**.

No nasty surprises at this good provincial hotel. It's spacious and offers a good standard of comfort, and doubles cost 130–265F. If you fancy a marble bathroom with jacuzzi (as in number 317), expect to pay 290F. Many bedrooms overlook the garden. Rustic restaurant, serving set meals 82–190F, and local dishes such as seafood stew, thin slivers of duck with Muscatel, and monkfish stew with brandy, garlic and tomatoes. For those in a hurry (there's always someone), they do a 54F *menu-express* on the veranda. An excellent place.

BÉDARIEUX 34600 (8KM NE)

10% HÔTEL DELTA

1 rue de Clairac; it's on the street that runs at right

angles to avenue Jean-Jaurès.
☎ 04.67.23.21.19
TV.

A lovely young couple have converted this little clinic into a hotel. It may have no stars, but the bedrooms are clean and spacious. Fresh, unusual décor, with amusing Egyptian symbols and Chinese fans dotted about. Prices are reasonable. Doubles 140F with basin/bidet–190F with shower/wc and TV. If you're not one for getting up with the birds, try to avoid the rooms overlooking the avenue. This is a nice little place.

10% LE CENTRAL*

3 place aux Herbes (Centre); take the D908.
☎ 04.67.95.06.76
Closed Saturdays (out of season), one week at the end of June and a fortnight in October. **TV**.

Here's a country house with an attractive ivy-covered façade, overlooking the Orb. The dining room's rather dark and old-fashioned. Adequate accommodation. Doubles 150F with basin–195F with bath. Some have TV. Set meals 58–140F offering some good home-made and regional dishes – breast of duck *à l'orange, estoffat languedocien* (a type of stew) and *tarte vigneronne*.

LANGOGNE 48300

DOMAINE DE BARRES***

route de Mende.
☎ 04.66.69.71.00 ⮕ 04.66.69.71.29
Closed Sunday evenings, Mondays and mid Nov–mid March. **Car park**. **TV**. **Disabled access**.

It's hard not to sing the praises of this 18th century manor house. *Domaine de Barres* might seem just like another of France's many enormous historical buildings, but once you're inside you can't remain indifferent. They've refurbished the place from top to bottom, entrusting the job to Jean-Michel Wilmotte, François Mitterrand's favourite decorator. And the result is a stylish pared-down décor with lots of wood and simple colour schemes. The bedrooms are as uncluttered as in any Japanese home – ideal if you're into Zen Buddhism. But if you didn't sleep all that well, there's always the swimming pool, jacuzzi and sauna. And we think the cooking's just as impressive – *terrine* of leeks with fresh goat's cheese, pan-fried duck *foie gras*, braised pig's cheeks, mashed potatoes with diced *foie gras*, and pear roasted with barley (it's like rice pudding). And the prices? Doubles 420–520F and set meals 140–320F. Not exactly cheap, but pretty good for a dream come true.

LÉZIGNAN-CORBIÈRES 11200

HÔTEL-RESTAURANT LE TASSIGNY**

rond-point de-Lattre-de-Tassigny; take av. des Corbières towards the A9.
☎ 04.68.27.11.51 ⮕ 04.68.27.67.31
Restaurant closed Sunday evenings and the second week in October. **Secure parking**. **TV**.
Disabled access.

If you don't want to spend a fortune, here's a great place for an overnight stay. Ordinary on the outside, but cosy on the inside. The locals come primarily for the restaurant. Set meals 74F (except Sundays), 110F and 130F. Hearty specialities served up by Pierre, a cheerful and pleasantly plump chef. Spotlessly clean bedrooms. Doubles with bath 240F.

FABREZAN 11200 (9KM SW)

10% LE CLOS DES SOUQUETS

av. de Lagrasse; Tke the D611 towards Lagrasse.
☎ 04.68.43.52.61 ⮕ 04.68.43.56.76
Closed Sunday evenings and Nov 2–April 1. **Car park**. **TV**.

There may only be five bedrooms, but it's a little jewel, so why not treat yourself. The Julien family spend the winter in the Carribean, as we can see from the exotic touches in the bedrooms (280–420F) and in the dishes served round one of the two (yes, two!) swimming pools. We could get used to this kind of luxury. Terrific 100F set meal (southern-style salad, good home-made pizza, and cream cheese with honey). If you want to sample the *colombo* of lamb, go for the one at 145F. They also do very good *carpaccio* of fish and meat, but best of all is the grilled fish of the day.

HOMPS 11200 (10KM N)

AUBERGE DE L'ARBOUSIER

route de Carcassonne.
☎ 04.68.91.11.24 ⮕ 04.68.91.12.61
Closed Feb 15–March 15 and three weeks in November. **Car park**. **TV**.

The Canal du Midi is situated just alongside *L'Arbousier* whose décor's a combination of old stonework, exposed beams and modern art. It's a lovely spot, with a shaded terrace in summer and quiet comfy bedrooms and feels almost like a bed and breakfast. Doubles 210–250F with bath. The kitchen prepares classics like breast of duck with honey and pine nuts and fillets of mullet with oil from Bize. Set meals 80–205F.

|●| RESTAURANT LES TONNELIERS

port du Canal du Midi.
☎ 04.68.91.14.04
Closed Jan–Feb. **Car park**. **Disabled access**.

You'll also find the beautiful Canal du Midi running through this village. *Les Tonneliers,* only ten metres from the inn reviewed above, offers good food in rustic surroundings, but doesn't have the view. What does that matter though, when the canal is so close. If you listen very carefully, you can almost hear it. Four set meals, 78F, 98F, 120F and 180F, offering several specialities like *cassoulet* with *confit* of duck, and marinated salmon with two kinds of lemon. Lots of tourists come to see the canal in the evenings. As soon as summer appears, you can sit out in the attractive garden or on the shaded terrace.

LIMOUX 11300

10% ⌂ |●| GRAND HÔTEL MODERNE ET PIGEON***

place du Général-Leclerc (Centre); it's beside the post office.
☎ 04.68.31.00.25 F 04.68.31.12.43
Closed Dec 5–Jan 15; restaurant closed Mondays and Saturday lunchtimes. **Secure parking**. **TV**.

Before they converted this magnificent building into a hotel at the start of the century, it was a convent, then a townhouse and then a bank. Take a look at the frescoes on the wall above the beautiful staircase. Comfy and very well maintained. They've also kept the simple style we're particularly fond of. Lovely doubles 320F with shower/wc–400F with bath (520F with twin beds). Sophisticated décor and hushed atmosphere in the dining room. Cheapest set meal 150F. The 215F one is absolutely delicious and consists of *terrine* of langoustine with *coulis* of lobster, braised duck in sparkling white wine – this is the house speciality and you must try it – cheese platter and dessert. You could just have a glass of sparkling white wine in the cellar where the pool players hang out. In any case, say hi to André from us!

LODÈVE 34700

10% ⌂ |●| LA CROIX BLANCHE**

6 av. de Funel.
☎ 04.67.44.10.87 F 04.67.44.38.33
Closed Dec 1–April 1; restaurant closed Friday lunchtimes. **Secure parking**. **TV**.

The first thing to catch your eye will be the impressive collection of copper saucepans and bowls. We got a good feeling about this place right from the outset. You can easily picture generations of sales reps and businessmen stopping by to enjoy the local hospitality. Simple cheap accommodation. Doubles 130F with basin and 210F with shower/wc or bath. Time seems to have stood still in the dining room. Conventional décor, a bit bourgeois and ever so slightly rustic. Simple cooking and generous portions. Set meals 70–160F.

⌂ |●| HÔTEL-RESTAURANT DE LA PAIX**

11 bd Montalanque.
☎ 04.67.44.07.46 F 04.67.44.30.47
Closed Jan–mid March, and Sunday evenings and Mondays out of season. **TV**.

The same family have been running this place since 1887. It has recently been refurbished and offers clean comfortable rooms overlooking the mountains and the Lergue. Doubles 240F with bath. Half-board compulsory during summer months (230F per person). The hearty cooking isn't particularly creative but it's good. Set meals 75–150F. The house speciality is fresh salmon cooked with the skin on and served with lemon-flavoured butter. Mmm, yummy!

|●| LE PETIT SOMMELIER

3 place de la République; it's beside the tourist office.
☎ 04.67.44.05.39
Closed Mondays and Thursday evenings (except July 1–Sept 30).

A nice informal little place with simple bistro décor and tasty cooking. They do dishes such as breast of duck with apples and warm mussels in a red wine sauce. Set meals 75F and 98F. Pleasant terrace. You'll get a warm friendly welcome. It's not surprising that all the locals hang out here.

MANDAGOUT 30120

⌂ |●| AUBERGE DE LA BORIE

How to get there: take the D170; 9km along, turn right towards Mandagout, pass the village, continue towards

Saint-André-de-Majencoules, then follow a sloping street on the left for 250m.
☎ 04.67.81.06.03 F 04.67.81.86.79
Closed Jan–Feb. **Car park**. **Disabled access**.

An old Cévennes building, situated on a sunny mountainside, with a swimming pool and reasonable prices. The views are breathtaking and peace and quiet are guaranteed. The owners, Elisabeth and Jean-François Roche (a Breton from Rennes), make you feel most welcome. About ten nicely appointed bedrooms with old stone walls. Doubles 125–260F with basin or shower/wc. Try for number 8, 9 or 10 which are down in the ancient vaulted cellars and are wonderfully cool in summer. Home cooking based exclusively on local produce. Set meals 70–140F. Half-board (compulsory July–Aug) from 185F.

MENDE 48000

HÔTEL GTM-RESTAURANT LA CAILLE**

2 rue d'Aigues-Passes; it's in the old town.
☎ 04.66.65.01.39

La Caille is on the ground floor and the accommodation on the floor above. It's very hard to miss Monsieur Saleil's establishment – there's a large sign and a terrace at the crossroads, but this is definitely not a tourist trap. Decent well-maintained bedrooms 230F with shower and 280F with bath. Popular with sales reps who're perfectly used to the owner's slightly curt reception. Good brasserie cooking. 70F *menu du jour*, and other set meals from 110F.

10% HÔTEL-RESTAURANT DU PONT-ROUPT***

2 av. du 11-Novembre (East).
☎ 04.66.65.01.43 F 04.66.65.22.96
Restaurant closed Sunday evenings, Mondays and three weeks Feb–March. **Secure parking**. **TV**.

This large building that stands on the banks of the Lot on the edge of town, is a delightful hotel. Modern, low-key décor. Bedrooms are comfortable. Doubles 240–360F (you'll pay an extra 40F in July and August) and suites 510F. Pretty indoor swimming pool. The owner belongs to this family's fourth generation of chefs. Generous servings of traditional or more refined dishes. The *aligot* and quail with *foie gras* are wonderful. 89F *menu du jour* (includes wine and coffee), other set meals 120F, 148F and 185F.

LE MAZEL

25 rue du Collège (Centre).
☎ 04.66.65.05.33
Closed Monday evenings, Tuesdays, ten days late November, and Feb 20–March 15.

One of the few modern buildings in the town centre of Mende. Although the setting's not ideal, the tastefully refurbished dining room will soon take your mind off this tiny disadvantage. Jean-Paul Brun uses first-rate produce in fine flavoursome dishes such as *terrine* of morels and *confit* of duck. Set meals 79F, 100F, 120F and 157F. Popular for business lunches. Represents the best value for money in town.

CHABRITS 48000 (5KM W)

LA SAFRANIÈRE

How to get there: take the N88, go across the Roupt bridge, then straight ahead.
☎ 04.66.49.31.54
Closed Sunday evenings, Mondays and March.

Opened only very recently, this is the gourmet restaurant that's been missing in Mende and its surrounding district. Bright elegant dining room in a very old and attractively refurbished building. Cooking is light and delicate and makes clever use of herbs, spices and seasonings like basil, tarragon, cumin, saffron and coconut. We sampled the 135F set meal and it was absolutely wonderful. We had snail ravioli, fillet of duckling with a sweet-and-sour sauce and pinenuts, a decent cheese platter and a perfect *crême brûlée*. *Menus du jour* 95F (weekday lunchtimes), others 190F (meat and fish) and 230F (chef's choice).

PALHERS 48100 (28.5KM W)

LE MOULIN DE CHAZE

route de Mende; take the N88, then the108 towards Marvejols.
☎ 04.66.32.36.07
Closed Mondays (except public holidays) and two weeks in October. **Car park**.

You could easily imagine yourself in Italy, eating out on the terrace of this white stone building on a summer's day. Wrought-iron armchairs and tables. Inside, the stonework, beams, and wallhangings make for a comfortable setting. Pleasant cooking, brimming with fresh flavours. Not particularly creative, but no nasty surprises. Set meals 110F, 130F, 160F and 220F. Reception couldn't be faulted.

MEYRUEIS 48150

HÔTEL DE LA JONTE*

How to get there: Follow the D996 and the gorges of La Jonte.
☎ 05.65.62.60.52 F 05.65.62.61.62
Closed December, January and February. **TV**.
Disabled access.

A large establishment run by Monsieur Vergely, it's well known for its good cooking and the warmth of its welcome. It has two dining rooms, and one is more touristy than the other. Head for the one used by workers and reps – the cooking's better and the prices are reasonable (set meals 57–155F). Very well maintained bedrooms (160F and 180F) above the restaurant and in the annexe overlooking the river (the more expensive ones have TV and a view of the river). Small swimming pool, to boot! Cheap and very good.

10% HÔTEL FAMILY**

rue de la Barrière (Centre).
☎ 04.66.45.60.02 F 04.66.45.66.54
Closed Nov 1–end March. **Secure parking**. **TV**.
Disabled access.

A large building standing by the stream that runs through the village. Freshly painted façade and simple well-maintained bedrooms (230F with shower/wc and 250F with bath). The top-floor ones are our favourites. Traditional cooking at reasonable prices. Set meals 75–120F. There's a pleasant garden with a swimming pool opposite the hotel but you'll have to cross a little wooden bridge to get to it. Friendly reception.

HÔTEL DU MONT AIGOUAL**

rue de la Barrière.
☎ 04.66.45.65.61 F 04.66.45.64.25
Closed start Nov–end March. **Car park**. **TV**.

If things seem a bit ordinary at first glance, not to worry. You've Stella Robert's charming welcome, a beautiful swimming pool round the back, an enormous garden and comfortable, tastefully refurbished bedrooms to set your mind at rest. Doubles 260–320F with shower or bath. Daniel Lagrange is in the kitchens and prepares authentic and tasty traditional meals using local produce. Set meals 95F and 140F. Try the *confidou* (beef stewed in red wine), leg of lamb and the apple *galette* with Roquefort. One of the very good restaurants around these parts, offering consistent quality and reasonable prices.

MÈZE 34140

LE PESCADOU

33 bd du Port; go towards the harbour.
☎ 04.67.43.81.72
Closed Tuesday evenings, Wednesdays and Jan.

Le Pescadou is very popular with the locals. Engravings of boats and pot plants give a fresh relaxing feel to this spacious dining room. There's also a pretty terrace on the harbour. Set meals 74F, 99F, 148F and 185F. They do oysters, mussels, snails, and lots of fish dishes.

MOLITG-LES-BAINS 66500

10% HÔTEL-RESTAURANT LE SAINT-JOSEPH*

How to get there: it's opposite the spa and the tourist office.
☎ 04.68.05.02.11 F 04.68.05.05.23
Closed Nov–end March.

No showy details or false modesty here. Annie Raynal's hotel and restaurant, nestling in green parkland, is open to everyone. She's natural and friendly, so her guests won't be strangers for long. You may not get luxury bedrooms, but no two are the same and all have been decorated and refurbished by Annie herself. Good taste and lots of little details make for a really charming place. Doubles 160F with basin–175F with shower. The restaurant's decorated in simple style with Catalonian colours. We got *escalibade* of peppers, stew of duck with pine nuts and *crème catalane* for 80F. Menu changes daily.

MONT-LOUIS 66210

HÔTEL-RESTAURANT LOU ROUBAL-LOU

rue des Écoles-Laïques (Centre); it's on the ramparts, opposite the local primary school.
☎ 04.68.04.23.26 F 04.68.04.14.09
Closed May, Oct and Nov. **Car park**. **TV**.

The kind of family guest house we like – rustic, comfy, delightful, and full of charm and personality. You'll be greeted by Christiane Duval and receive a very warm welcome from the entire family. Christiane calls everyone "dear" and you can practically feel the heat of the sun when she talks about the Pyrenees. You'll feel perfectly at home, whether you're tucked up in a cosy bed in one of the attractive little rooms

(160F with basin and 230–320F with bath) or sitting in the tastefully decorated restaurant. Pierre's crazy about the mountainside and his fresh authentic cooking is, without a doubt, among the best in the region. Set meals 125–195F. Specialities – thin slivers of game with ceps (he collects them himself, marvellous!), boar stew, duck with fruit and honey sauce, and *boles de Picolat* (meatballs Catalan style) to name but a few. If you're planning to come in winter, don't miss out on the *ollada* (a hearty country soup) or the *hachis* (something like a shepherd's pie). And there are delicious mushrooms all year round, which brings us to the name of the hotel. *Rouballou* is a mushroom found in the moss, under little fir trees. Cheap, good and friendly. Readers of this guide will get a 10% reduction if they stay for a minimum of two days with half-board (excludes the February school holidays and July–Aug).

MONTPELLIER 34000

SEE MAP OVERLEAF

AUBERGE DE JEUNESSE

rue des Écoles-Laïques; bus no. 2, 5, 14 or 16 from the station and get off at Ursulines. **MAP B1-1**
☎ 04.67.60.32.22 Fax 04.67.60.32.30
Closed Christmas holidays.

Doors open 8am–midnight. No curfew. Accommodation for eighty-nine. They've got nineteen dormitories based on two–ten sharing. First night 82F, and 65F thereafter (includes breakfast and sheets). A well-kept place. Free lockers. In the summer you can eat on a pleasant shaded terrace. Meals available in the evenings. Bar (open 6pm–midnight) has table football and pool table. Members only.

HÔTEL LES FAUVETTES*

8 rue Bonnard. **MAP A1-2**
☎ 04.67.63.17.60
Closed the last weeks of July and December, and the first week in August.

We think *Les Fauvettes* is the best hotel in its class in Montpellier. A small establishment in a quiet street, run by a friendly couple, it's the cheapest in town. Bedrooms may be basic, but they're quiet (they look onto the interior courtyard) and clean. Breakfast on the veranda. Popular with all ages in summer. And the prices? Unbeatable value! Doubles 120F with basin/bidet, and more comfy ones 160F with shower, 180F with shower/wc and 200F with bath.

10% HÔTEL DES ÉTUVES

24 rue des Étuves. **MAP B3-4**
☎ 04.67.60.78.19

It may not offer high-class luxury, but this hotel is good, clean and friendly. The reasonable prices will appeal – 150F with shower/wc and 185F with bath. Not bad value for money and only a stone's throw from place de la Comédie.

HÔTEL VERDUN-COLISÉE**

33 rue de Verdun. **MAP C3-6**
☎ 04.67.58.42.63 Fax 04.67.58.98.27
TV.

It overlooks a lively, but not particularly noisy street. Decent, recently refurbished bedrooms in all price ranges – 150F with basin–270F with bath. Good reception.

10% HÔTEL FLORIDE**

1 rue François-Perrier. **MAP D3-5**
☎ 04.67.65.73.30 Fax 04.67.22.10.83
TV. **Canal+**.

Situated in a quiet street only a few steps from the new district of Antigone. You'll receive a warm welcome from Roland and Fabienne. Bedrooms 150F with basin – 230F with bath. We think the best ones overlook the flower-filled terrace. Good 15F breakfast for users of this guidebook – the owner's been one himself since day one.

10% HÔTEL DES TOURISTES

10 rue Baudin. **MAP C2-3**
☎ 04.67.58.42.37 Fax 04.67.92.61.37

Hôtel des Touristes, situated only 30m from place de la Comédie, offers bright clean bedrooms. They may be basic, but they're good value for money. Doubles 155F with shower (wc on the landing).

10% HÔTEL DE LA COMÉDIE**

1 bis rue Baudin. **MAP C2-8**
☎ 04.67.58.43.64 Fax 04.67.58.58.43
TV. **Canal+**.

You'd be hard pushed to find a more centrally located hotel. It's good, quiet and offers clean, refurbished and welcoming bedrooms. Friendly owner. Doubles 275–305F with shower/wc, satellite TV and air-conditioning. Free accommodation for children under sixteen and free breakfast for those under twelve and readers of this guidebook.

10% LES ARCEAUX**

33–35 bd des Arceaux; it's behind promenade du

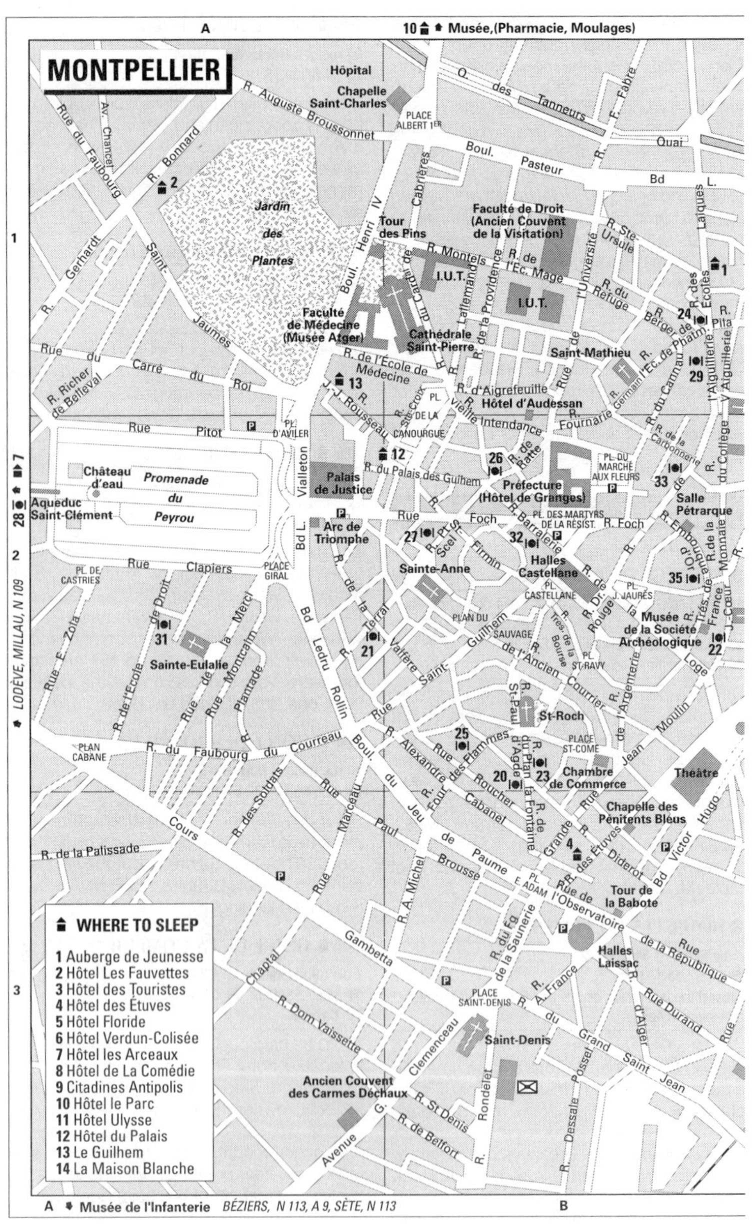
MONTPELLIER
A
10 Musée,(Pharmacie, Moulages)
Hôpital
Chapelle Saint-Charles
PLACE ALBERT 1ER
R. Auguste Broussonnet
Q. des Tanneurs
R. F. Fabre
Quai
Boul. Pasteur
Bd L.
Laiques
Rue du Faubourg
Av. Chancel
R. Bonnard
2
Jardin des Plantes
Boul. Henri IV
Cabrières
Tour des Pins
Faculté de Droit (Ancien Couvent de la Visitation)
R. Ste-Ursule
R. de l'Université
1
R. Gerhardt
Saint-Jaumes
R. Montels
I.U.T.
R. du Cardinal
R. Lallemand
R. de la Providence
R. de l'Ec. Mage
R. du Refuge
R. des Écoles
Faculté de Médecine (Musée Atger)
Cathédrale Saint-Pierre
R. de l'École de Médecine
13
Saint-Mathieu
R. Berger
R. de l'Ec. de Pharm.
R. Pila
24
29
R. l'Aiguillerie
V. Aiguillerie
Rue du Carré du Roi
R. Richer de Belleval
J.-J. Rousseau
R. d'Aigrefeuille
PL. ST-CROIX
R. Vieille Intendance
Hôtel d'Audessan
PL. DE LA CANOURGUE
R. Fournarié
R. Germain
R. du Cannau
R. de la Carbonnerie
R. du Collège
Rue Pitot
PL. D'AVILER
12
R. du Palais des Guilhem
26
R. de la Ratte
PL. DU MARCHÉ AUX FLEURS
33
Château d'eau
Promenade du Peyrou
Aqueduc Saint-Clément
Vialleton
Palais de Justice
Préfecture (Hôtel de Granges)
Salle Pétrarque
28
Bd L.
Arc de Triomphe
Rue Foch
PL. DES MARTYRS DE LA RÉSIST.
R. Foch
27
R. St-Firmin
32
R. Barralerie
R. Embouque d'Or
R. de la Monnaie
2
Rue Clapiers
PL. DE CASTRIES
PLACE GIRAL
Sainte-Anne
Halles Castellane
PL. CASTELLANE
35
PL. J. JAURÈS
R. Trés. de France
R. J.-Cœur
R. de la Terral
PLAN DU SAUVAGE
R. Guilhem
R. Dr. Rouge
Musée de la Société Archéologique
22
R. de l'Ancien Courrier
R. Trés. de la Bourse
PL. ST-RAVY
Loge
LODÈVE, MILLAU, N 109
Rue E. Zola
R. de Droit
31
Sainte-Eulalie
R. de la Merci
Rue Montcalm
R. Plantade
Bd Ledru Rollin
21
R. Valfère
Saint-
R. de l'Argenterie
Rue Jean Moulin
R. St-Paul
St-Roch
R. de l'Ecole
Rue de la Merci
25
Rue des Flammes
R. d'Agde
R. du Plan la Fontaine
PLACE ST-COME
PLAN CABANE
R. du Faubourg du Courreau
Boul. du Jeu de Paume
R. Alexandre Cabanel
Rue Roucher
20
23
Chambre de Commerce
Théatre
3
Chapelle des Pénitents Bleus
Rue Marceau
R. des Soldats
R. Four
R. de la Fontaine
Grande Rue
R. des Étuves
R. Diderot
Bd Victor Hugo
Cours Gambetta
R. de la Palissade
4
Brousse
PL. E. ADAM
Rue de l'Observatoire
Tour de la Babote
Rue Paul
R. A. Michel
Rue de la République
WHERE TO SLEEP
1 Auberge de Jeunesse
2 Hôtel Les Fauvettes
3 Hôtel des Touristes
4 Hôtel des Étuves
5 Hôtel Floride
6 Hôtel Verdun-Colisée
7 Hôtel les Arceaux
8 Hôtel de La Comédie
9 Citadines Antipolis
10 Hôtel le Parc
11 Hôtel Ulysse
12 Hôtel du Palais
13 Le Guilhem
14 La Maison Blanche
R. du Fg de la Saunerie
Halles Laissac
Chaptal
R. Dom Vaissette
PLACE SAINT-DENIS
R. A. France
R. du Grand Saint Jean
Rue Durand
R. d'Alger
Saint-Denis
Clemenceau
Ancien Couvent des Carmes Déchaux
R. St Denis
R. de Belfort
Avenue G.
R. Rondelet
R. Possel
R. Dessalle
A
Musée de l'Infanterie
BÉZIERS, N 113, A 9, SÈTE, N 113
B

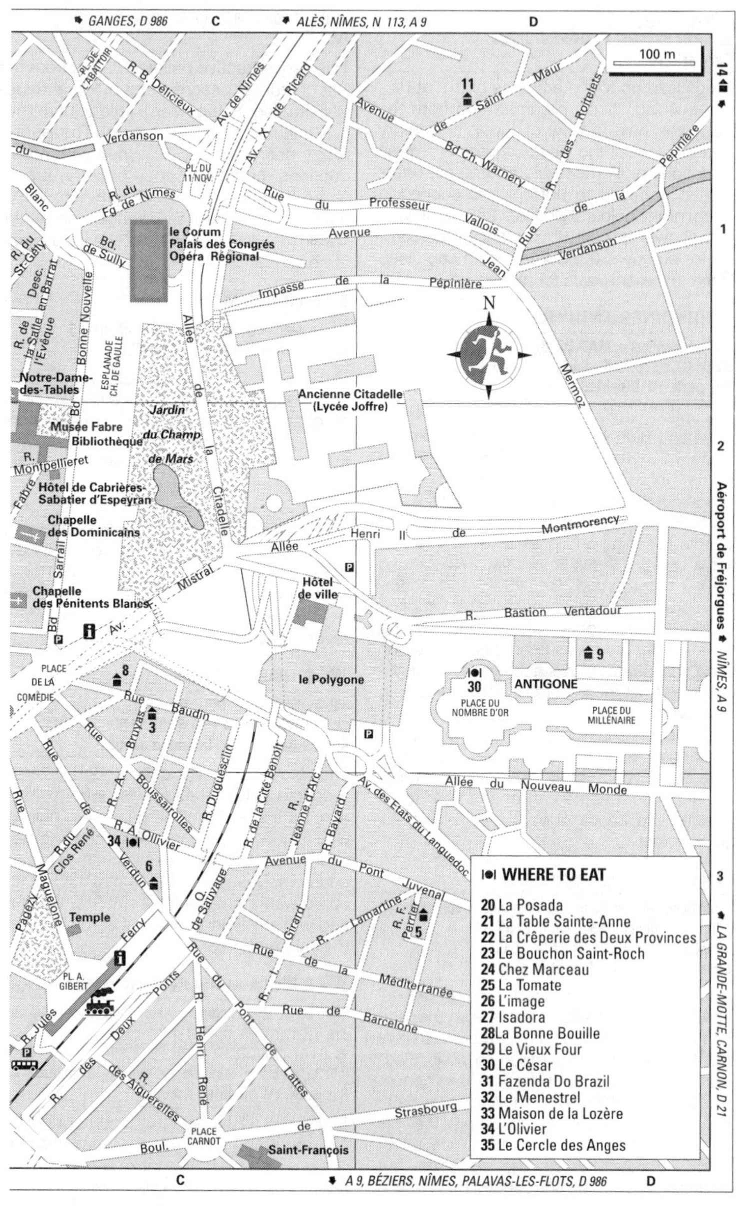

GANGES, D 986
ALÈS, NÎMES, N 113, A 9
C
D
100 m
14
1
2
3
Aéroport de Fréjorgues
NÎMES, A 9
LA GRANDE-MOTTE, CARNON, D 21
A 9, BÉZIERS, NÎMES, PALAVAS-LES-FLOTS, D 986
le Corum
Palais des Congrès
Opéra Régional
Ancienne Citadelle
(Lycée Joffre)
Jardin
du Champ
de Mars
Notre-Dame-des-Tables
Musée Fabre
Bibliothèque
Hôtel de Cabrières-Sabatier d'Espeyran
Chapelle des Dominicains
Chapelle des Pénitents Blancs
Hôtel de ville
le Polygone
ANTIGONE
PLACE DU NOMBRE D'OR
PLACE DU MILLÉNAIRE
PLACE DE LA COMÉDIE
Temple
PL. A. GIBERT
PLACE CARNOT
Saint-François
ESPLANADE CH. DE GAULLE
PL. DU 11 NOV.
PL. DE L'ABATTOIR
Verdanson
Avenue de Saint Maur
Bd Ch. Warnery
Rue des Roitelets
Rue de la Pépinière
Rue du Professeur Vallois
Avenue Jean Mermoz
Impasse de la Pépinière
Allée de la Citadelle
Allée Henri II de Montmorency
R. Bastion Ventadour
Allée du Nouveau Monde
Av. des États du Languedoc
Avenue du Pont Juvénal
Rue de la Méditerranée
Rue de Barcelone
Boul. de Strasbourg
Rue du Pont de Lattes
R. Henri René
R. des Aiguerelles
R. des Deux Ponts
R. Jules Ferry
Q. de Sauvage
R. de la Cité Benoît
R. Jeanne d'Arc
R. Bayard
R. Lamartine
R. F. Perrier
R. Girard
R. Duguesclin
Rue Boussairolles
R. A. Ollivier
Rue Baudin
Rue Bruyas
Rue Verdun
R. du Clos René
Rue Maguelone
Pagézy
Av. Mistral
Bd Sarrail
Bd Bonne Nouvelle
Bd de Sully
R. du Fg de Nîmes
Av. de Nîmes
Av. X. de Ricard
R. B. Délicieux
R. de la Salle l'Évêque
Desc. en Barrat
R. du St-Gély
R. Montpellieret
Fabre
11
9
8
3
6
5
30
34
WHERE TO EAT
20 La Posada
21 La Table Sainte-Anne
22 La Crêperie des Deux Provinces
23 Le Bouchon Saint-Roch
24 Chez Marceau
25 La Tomate
26 L'image
27 Isadora
28La Bonne Bouille
29 Le Vieux Four
30 Le César
31 Fazenda Do Brazil
32 Le Menestrel
33 Maison de la Lozère
34 L'Olivier
35 Le Cercle des Anges

Peyrou. Off map **A2-7**
☎ 04.67.92.03.03 F 04.67.92.05.09
Car park. TV.

Steps lead up to the entrance of this attractive building. It has a garden and from the back you have a view of the 17th century aqueduct near the Peyrou gardens. Homy atmosphere. Comfortable bedrooms, refurbished from top to bottom and painted in fresh, pretty colours. Doubles 265–315F with wc, shower or bath. If you fancy a balcony, try for number 302. Some rooms can sleep three. Excellent value for money.

CITADINES ANTIPOLIS**

588 bd d'Antigone. **MAP D2-9**
☎ 04.67.20.70.70 F 04.67.64.54.64
Car park. TV. Disabled access.

Reception staffed 7.30am–9.30pm weekdays and 8am–noon and 2–8pm weekends and public holidays. Only 300m from place de la Comédie, this establishment in the modern part of town has studios and flats for rent. Hotel services such as change of sheets, cleaning and breakfast are available for a charge. Small studio flat 270F, studio 320F, two-roomed flat 430F and three-roomed 570F. Cheaper prices after your first week. Deposit of 1,000F. required. And here's a big plus – you can save money on food, as guests have access to the fully-equipped kitchen. All in all, taking into account the two-star standard of comfort – it's functional if not particularly charming, spacious, clean and has facilities such as TV – you'll get your money's worth. Unlike traditional hotels, people can phone your room directly and knock at your door – just like back home!

10% HÔTEL LE PARC**

8 rue Achille-Bège; it's on the other side of Verdanson, 300m from the cathedral. Off map **B1-10**
☎ 04.67.41.16.49 F 04.67.54.10.05
Secure parking. TV. Disabled access.

A delightful hotel housed in a traditional Languedoc building that dates from the 18th century. Friendly welcome. There's a very quiet garden and flower-filled terraces. Bedrooms are clean, comfy and air-conditioned. Doubles 295–340F (with shower/wc or bath, mini-bar and telephone). Just a pity that the garden doubles as a car park – you might fancy breakfast out in the open air, but chances are you'll be surrounded by vehicles.

HÔTEL DU PALAIS**

3 rue du Palais-des-Guilhem. **MAP B2-12**
☎ 04.67.60.47.38 F 04.67.60.40.23
TV.

This very attractive building dating from the last century is peaceful and quiet, and ideally situated, being near a little square only five minutes from the centre. The bright, pretty bedrooms are furnished with reproductions, creating a cosy country atmosphere. Doubles 310–370F with shower or bath, mini-bar and air-conditioning. Great breakfast. A very good hotel with a homy atmosphere.

LE GUILHEM***

18 rue Jean-Jacques-Rousseau. **MAP A1-13**
☎ 04.67.52.90.90 F 04.67.60.67.67
TV.

This establishment is tucked away in a delightful little street. The bedrooms overlook a mysterious garden worthy of a Gothic romance, and you'll also have a view of the cathedral off in the distance. You'll be able to hear the bells but don't worry, they won't keep you awake. Tastefully refurbished from top to bottom. You'll feel really comfortable in the terrific bedrooms. Doubles 330F with shower/wc, 380F with bath and up to 650F for the biggest. Delightful reception from Monsieur and Madame Charpentier.

10% HÔTEL ULYSSE**

338 av. Saint-Maur. **MAP D1-11**
☎ 04.67.02.02.30 F 04.67.02.16.50
Secure parking. TV. Disabled access.

The hotel, in a quiet neighbourhood, is run by a couple of hospitable Swiss who love the sun. It's a long, Mediterranean-style building with a modern, yet cosy, décor and is impeccably clean. Different colour schemes in each bedroom. Doubles (all have bath) 330F; a few come with a small kitchen (350F). Wooden and wrought-iron furniture. Oh, by the way, the car park's free!

10% LA MAISON LANCHE***

1796 av. de la Pompignane; it's on the corner of 46 rue des Salaisons. Off map **D1-14**
☎ 04.67.79.60.25 F 04.67.79.53.39
Restaurant closed Sundays and Monday lunchtimes.
Car park. TV. Disabled access.

Situated in a little park that's got a preservation order on it because the trees are hundreds of years old, this looks like a southern mansion and Scarlett O'Hara would have felt quite at home. Spacious up-to-date bedrooms, decorated in shades of grey and the carpet's the sort your feet sink into. Lots of famous people have stayed here, including Rostropovich, Alain Delon and Johnny Halliday. It's quiet and they can get away from their adoring fans. You'll pay 350–480F for a taste of the Scarlett O'Hara way of life.

LA POSADA

20 rue du Petit Saint-Jean. **MAP B2-20**
☎ 04.67.66.21.25

This new establishment has been a roaring success. Seasonal produce, tried and tested home cooking (chips cut by hand) and hearty portions make it stand out from other budget hotels. *Menu express* 48F (starter, main course, plus dessert), others 65F and 84F. Pretty terrace on the little square, and small crowded dining room. Advisable to book.

LA TOMATE

6 rue du Four-des-Flammes. **MAP B2-25**
☎ 04.67.60.49.38
Closed Sundays and Mondays.

The locals have been coming to these little panelled dining rooms (there are three of them) for donkey's years now, either for the 50F *menu du jour* that offers things such as cold meat, chicken *à la diable* (in a spicy sauce) and strawberry tart, or for the specialities (in particular, the mussels with white haricot beans and aubergines and the seafood *crêpe*). Other set meals 57F (fish soup and *cassoulet)* and 70F (quail *à la vigneronne*). Cheap regional wines – only 6F for a quarter litre!

LE BOUCHON SAINT-ROCH

rue du Pan-d'Agde. **MAP B2-23**
☎ 04.67.60.94.18
Closed Sunday lunchtimes.

We liked this place a lot. It's in a quiet street, has a little terrace, and offers good home cooking that's served by the owner's smiling daughter. Four set meals (50–120F) are available both lunchtimes and evenings. Tasty dishes like salad of *Pélardon* (goat's milk cheese), seafood *cassoulet* and pan-fried scallops.

LA TABLE SAINTE-ANNE

20 rue Terral. **MAP A2-21**
☎ 04.67.60.45.35
Closed Saturday and Sunday lunchtimes and Monday evenings.

Here's a delightful little restaurant offering a 50F lunchtime set meal that includes a quarter litre of wine. The evening set meals (65F, 80F and 110F) are more elaborate. The décor is simple and rustic and you'll get a friendly welcome. First-rate cooking, with classics like tuna steaks and snails with *tapenade* and tomatoes *confit*

CHEZ MARCEAU

7 place de la Chapelle-Neuve. **MAP B1-24**
☎ 04.67.66.08.09
Closed Sundays in winter and Sunday lunchtimes in summer.

Chez Marceau, part bistro, part restaurant, stands on a beautiful little square shaded by plane trees and is the perfect place for a spot of lunch outdoors. It offers good simple cooking and generous portions. It's cheap but sometimes the standards slip. The 59F set meal (lunchtimes) is very satisfying. Set meals 89F and 109F in the evenings. They do a lovely breast of duck *à l'orange* and lots of fresh fish dishes.

RESTAURANT L'IMAGE

6 rue du Puits-des-Esquilles. **MAP B2-26**
☎ 04.67.60.47.79
Closed Sundays.

This is one of the local hang-outs. If you're claustrophobic, head for the little dining room upstairs. Décor consists of old local stonework and lots of beautiful posters. The simple dishes are brimming with Mediterranean flavours and the portions are generous. Set meals 59F (before 8pm) and 69–129F. They have a few specialities including *fondues* of various kinds and *pierrades* (where you cook the ingredients yourself on a hot stone). Musical evenings.

LA CRÊPERIE DES DEUX PROVINCES

7 rue Jacques-Cœur. **MAP B2-22**
☎ 04.67.60.68.10
Closed Sundays, Christmas and New Year's Day. Open 11.45–2.15pm and 6.45–midnight; Saturdays non-stop 11.45am–midnight.

Friendly, attentive waiters serve good hearty salads and *crêpes.* There's a big choice, with about 160 different *crêpes.* Prices are very good. Salad 25–50F, buckwheat *galette* 30–55F and *galette* with sweet filling 12–50F. A salad or a *crêpe* followed by a dessert is more than enough for lunch. It feels a bit like a canteen.

ISADORA

6 rue du Petit-Scel. **MAP B2-27**
☎ 04.67.66.25.23
Closed Saturday lunchtimes, Sundays, and Monday lunchtimes and Sundays in July and August.

Here's another wonderful 13th century vaulted dining room down in the cellars – this time the décor's Art Deco. Fine cooking. They have delicious seafood, and you'll be served by your host, a man who knows how to look after his customers. Set meals 80F, 120F and 250F. Everyone in Montpellier loves the place.

LE CÉSAR

pl. du Nombre d'Or, Antigone. **MAP D2-30**
☎ 04.67.65.31.76
Closed Saturdays.

Service until 10.30pm. A good brasserie offering a good 118F regional set meal with *fondants* of chicken or capon as a starter, followed by fresh cod with *aïoli* or *gardiane de toro* (beef that's been marinated and then made into a stew) and home-made dessert. The 90F set meal is simpler. Some local clubs have meetings here. The enormous terrace overlooks place du Nombre d'Or. A good restaurant.

LA BONNE BOUILLE

6 bd des Arceaux. **MAP A2-28**
☎ 04.67.52.94.27
Closed Saturday lunchtimes and Sundays.

This place with the enormous, brightly coloured murals offers a wide range of fish dishes. At lunchtimes, choose between the *formule TGV* (55F), offering fish, dessert and a quarter litre of wine, or the *formule grill* (75F). They also do a good 90F set meal with, for example, scallops in puff pastry, followed by a seafood *cassoulet* which goes down very nicely. Come on a Tuesday evening if you fancy a bit of musical entertainment.

LE MÉNESTRE

2 impasse Perrier. **MAP B2-32**
☎ 04.67.60.62.51
Closed Sundays and Mondays.

Booking is essential. Housed in a former corn exchange, the restaurant has a sumptuous vaulted dining room. It's rather chic and clearly the kind of place that expects you to conform. There are lace tablecloths on the tables and all the large fireplace needs is a labrador to complete the scene. There's a 78F *formule* at lunchtimes (starter plus main course or main course plus dessert). Set meals 90F and 140F. Good traditional bourgeois cooking. They do guinea fowl stuffed with gingerbread, *terrine* of pork with onion marmalade, and an excellent *bouillabaisse en gelée*. And the desserts are superb.

LE VIEUX FOUR

59 rue de l'Aiguillerie. **MAP B1-29**
☎ 04.67.60.55.95
Closed lunchtimes.

Service until approximately 11.30pm. Perpetual students will love this place. The décor hasn't changed for donkey's years. Candles create a cosy atmosphere. Wooden tables and counters. Expect to pay 60–80F for one of the very tasty grills. A meal will cost about 130F. Just one small disadvantage – the chips aren't made on the premises.

FAZENDA DO BRASIL

5 rue de l'École-de-Droit. **MAP A2-31**
☎ 04.67.92.90.91
Closed Saturday lunchtimes and Sundays.

We felt as if we really were in Brazil, particularly when the food arrived. Their speciality is *churrascos* – chargrilled meat served with as much *cassava*, *feijaos* (Brazilian black beans), onions and fried plantains as you can manage. No matter the size of your appetite or your wallet, there's a *formule* to suit you. There are five in all. For 90F you can have pork that's been marinated in lime juice, for 93F rump steak, for 95F four meat dishes, for 115F six meat dishes, and for 155F nine meat dishes. We found the service rather slow (meat is cooked as you go along, so side dishes tend to go cold). They have some good Argentinian and Chilean wines and the best piña colada we've ever come across. Simple colourful décor.

LE CERCLE DES ANGES

3 rue Collot. **MAP B2-35**
☎ 04.67.66.35.13
Closed Sundays and Monday lunchtimes.

The décor's a bit disconcerting. You can eat either in the enormous high-ceilinged dining rooms or, if the weather's fine, on the terrace. The fish and meat dishes are good and skilfully prepared. Try, for example, the breasts of quail with a *duxelle* of ceps, veal sweetbreads and *foie gras* all cooked in filo pastry with Madeira-enriched veal stock. You can get a satisfying meal for 110F at lunchtimes. Evening set meals (225F and 300F) consist of appetizer, starter, fish, *trou normand* (a glass of Calvados to help the digestive process), meat, salad, cheese and dessert!

MAISON DE LA LOZÈRE

27 rue de l'Aiguillerie. **MAP B2-33**
☎ 04.67.66.36.10
Closed Sundays, Monday lunchtimes, and three weeks in August.

Service 12.15–2pm and 8–10pm. This restaurant and its little sister in Paris are both meant to be showcases for Lozère and its produce and cooking, and a wonderful job they do too. You can almost hear the mushrooms growing, the torrents gushing and the wolves howling! First-rate cooking. The superb vaulted dining room in the basement serves a 125F set meal at lunchtimes that comes with – wait for it – a salad of goat's cheese from the C_vennes, trout fillets with basil sauce, *aligot* and a magnificent cheese platter. And in the evenings, you'll be more than happy with the 190F set meal. The place doubles as a first rate grocer's and there's plenty of produce to take away. Good choice of carefully chosen Languedoc wines.

L'OLIVIER

12 rue Aristide-Ollivier. **MAP C3-34**
☎ 04.67.92.86.28
Closed Sundays, Mondays, public holidays, and in August.

Modern, bourgeois and rather *nouveau riche* décor. The cooking is of the very finest and popular with local gourmets. Fish is prepared as skilfully as meat and the *millefeuille* of sardines with baby vegetables, the *croustillant* of pig's trotters with *foie gras*, and the fillet of lamb *en croûte* with thyme are all excellent. Delicate sauces, good presentation and efficient service. Set meals 160F and 198F. *L'Olivier* is faultless and your taste buds are in for an experience they won't forget.

MAUGUIO 34130 (10KM E)

LE PATIO

impasse Molière (Centre); take the D24; it's in a cul de sac off Grand-Rue.
☎ 04.67.29.63.90
Closed lunchtimes except Sundays.

A little restaurant housed in a former wine cellar. The décor is a bit kitsch – the furniture in the dining room looks as if it came from a second-hand shop. The grill takes centre stage and is used for cooking breast of duck, Mediterranean prawns and the like. They do an excellent *gardiane* (marinated beef stewed in onions, tomatoes, garlic, olives and red wine). Sit out on the courtyard terrace in summer. No set meals, but you can eat for about 100F.

LAURET 34270 (30KM N)

10% L'AUBERGE DU CÈDRE

domaine de Cazeneuve; take the D17 towards Quissac.
☎ 04.67.59.02.02 F 04.67.59.03.44
Restaurant closed lunchtimes Monday–Friday inclusive. **Car park**.

A former vineyard has been converted into a very attractive hotel and restaurant with self-catering cottages, a camp site and a swimming pool. For 150F you can have either what they call the hiker's platter – sausage, *terrine* with juniper berries, *coppa* and *chorizo* – or a succulent *croustillant* of salmon with figs and honey. They have a wide range of good Mediterranean wines, which are also available by the glass. Simple but perfectly adequate bedrooms decorated in soothing colours that sleep two, three or four cost 95F per person, including breakfast (120F during school holidays). The bedlinen is in good condition and bathrooms are on the landing. Self-catering cottages 80–105F per person depending on the time of year. Campsite (no facilities) 35F per adult. A nice place that comes highly recommended by one of our German readers who described it as being very attractive and not at all expensive and praised the courtesy of the owners and the quality of the food. All in all, she said, a little corner of paradise!

NARBONNE 11100

10% WILL'S HÔTEL**

23 av. Pierre-Sémard (Centre); it's in the street opposite the station.
☎ 04.68.90.44.50 F 04.68.32.26.28
Closed Dec 25–Jan 2. **TV**.

This bourgeois-style building has been converted into a hotel. You'll get a good feeling as soon as you set eyes on the beautiful façade, an impression reinforced by the owner's friendly reception. Bedrooms may not have much character, but they're clean, refurbished and decorated in pastel shades. Reasonable prices. Doubles 180F with basin and TV, 200F with basin/wc and TV, 220F with shower/wc and TV, and 250F with bath and TV.

10% HÔTEL LE LION D'OR**

39 av. Pierre-Sémard (South-East); it's opposite the station.
☎ 04.68.32.06.92 F 04.68.65.51.13
Closed Sundays out of season and Oct 15–April 1.

This small two-star hotel has lots of atmosphere and quite a history, since it's been run by the same family since 1936. Doubles 210F with bath. The owner, a wine waitress, presides over a lot of wine-tastings, so let her introduce you to some wonderful and reasonably priced wines from this and other parts of the country. If you're a wine buff, do have a chat with her – she knows everything there is to know about the local wines. Wine is served by the glass. Just one small drawback – the façade is an absolutely revolting shade of green.

10% LA DORADE**

44 rue Jean-Jaurès (Centre).
☎ 04.68.32.65.95 F 04.68.65.81.62
Car park. TV.

A superb pink building located in the historic district and overlooking the canal, this was the town's first hostelry, built in 1648. Louis Bonaparte (Napoleon's brother) slept here, as did the Queens of Spain and Holland, and a prince or too. Bedrooms are very spacious and well-equipped. Doubles with bath are 250F, a reasonable price for a two-star hotel. The restaurant's not so bad either. The very handsome dining room serves regional specialities (mainly fish and seafood dishes) and good set meals at reasonable prices (the cheapest is 85F). All the same, we found the welcome a bit offhand. And as for the drink machines in the corridors – good idea, but not particularly attractive.

LE PETIT COMPTOIR

4 bd du Maréchal-Joffre (Centre).
☎ 04.68.42.30.35
Closed Sundays and Mondays June 1–15 and Sept 1–15.

It's probably a good idea to book, since this restaurant-cum-bistro has become fashionable on account of its attractive décor and its cheerful owner, who always chooses his produce with care. Set meals 98F, 128F and 168F. Take one of those and you might be offered fillet of sea bream with a lasagne of courgettes and aubergines or saddle of stuffed rabbit. Mind you, the chef is very keen on improvising and varies his set meals depending on deliveries. We like it a lot.

NASBINALS 48260

10% HÔTEL-RESTAURANT LA ROUTE D'ARGENT*

route d'Argent; it's the big building beside the church and the village car park.
☎ 04.66.32.50.03 F 04.66.32.56.77
Car park. TV. Disabled access.

Everybody knows this place and it's something of an institution. It's owned by Pierre Bastide (who's a mine of information about the area) but you'll more than likely be greeted at reception (in a corner of the bar) by one of his sons, Bernard or Daniel. Guests always get a warm and friendly welcome here. The chef's portions are some of the most generous we've seen. He does trout with almonds, stuffed cabbage, *truffade* (potato cake with cheese) and, of course, *aligot* made to Bastide senior's special recipe. Set meals 60–150F. Doubles 190F (with basin)–280F (with shower/wc or bath). Breakfast is served at the bar and you're bound to bump into the local policeman, parish priest or postman – it seems as if everybody in Nasbinals comes here. For those of you who prefer more stylish establishments, they've opened a three-star hotel (prices roughly the same) just outside the town. It's called *Le Bastide* of course!

NÎMES 30000

SEE MAP OVERLEAF

10% AUBERGE DE JEUNESSE**

chemin de la Cigale; it's 2km from the town centre up among the hills round Nîmes; take a number 2 bus from the railway station in the direction of Alès and it's about a 20 minute ride. Off map **A1-1**
☎ 04.66.23.25.04 F 04.66.23.84.27
Car park.

It's not easy to find. But once you get to this hostel standing in its own grounds and with lots of trees to provide welcome shade, you'll agree that finding it was worth the effort. Best to reserve in summer. Doors are 24 hours in summer and 7.30am–11pm in winter (you'll need the code to get in after that and since it changes often for security reasons, always check before going out). Dormitories sleep six, eight or fourteen. Expect to pay approximately 67F per night including breakfast. Evenings meals 17–52F. You can camp under the olive trees if you like. Mountain bikes 50F for the day if you want to get to town or Pont-du-Gard. A minibus will pick you up at the station after 7.30pm (minimum of three passengers).

10% HÔTEL LE LISITA**

2 bis bd des Arènes. **MAP B2-3**
☎ 04.66.67.66.20 F 04.66.76.22.30
TV.

You'd be hard pushed to find a hotel with a better location – it's just opposite the Roman arena. The owner, Michel Cailar, has a passion for bulls and all things Spanish. He's the one responsible for the interior decorating – furniture from Languedoc, fabric from Provence and unpainted doors. The charm's starting to fade, but he's already refurbished half of the bedrooms and the rest will follow. The hotel's popular with visiting bullfighters who always ask for number 19 or 28 on account of the Spanish theme and the iron beds. You might catch sight of one of them heading off to the arena in their suit of lights. We liked it here. Doubles 200F with shower–300F with bath.

10% HÔTEL ROYAL***

3 bd Alphonse-Daudet. **MAP B1-4**
☎ 04.66.67.28.36 F 04.66.21.68.97
Restaurant closed Sundays. **Secure parking**. **TV**.

The hotel's Art Deco interior incorporates a lot of owner Anne-Véronique Maurel's own ideas. Guests include visiting actors, musicians and bullfighters' assistants and they all get a warm welcome. The rooms have a lot of character and most of them look onto the quiet pedestrian place d'Assas with its weird and wonderful fountain. The ceiling fans by the way are not purely decorative – you'll need them if you're here in summer. Fans on the ceilings are not a luxury in Nîmes. We liked rooms number 2 and 18. The hotel has recently been refurbished, using a combination of old stonework, modern art, fitted carpets and polished wooden floorboards, giving the place even more personality and charm. A good hotel with all mod cons for 220–480F. *La Bodeguita*, which is new, offers Mediterranean specialities with *tapas* from 14F.

HÔTEL CLARINE-PLAZZA **

10 rue Roussy. **MAP C2-5**
☎ 04.66.76.16.20 F 04.66.67.65.99
Secure parking. **TV**. **Canal+**.

The hotel, an old Nîmes house in a quiet street, opened in 1988. Part of the building has been renovated. Owner Bernard Viallet will make you feel welcome. They've got twenty-eight air-conditioned bedrooms with shower or bath and telephone at prices ranging from 265F to 345F. Each floor has a different colour scheme (blue, pink, beige) and the corridors are decorated with posters advertising bullfights and opera performances. Rooms on the fourth floor (415F) have very attractive little terraces and a view of the old tiled rooftops. One for the address book.

RESTAURANT LA TRUYE QUI FILHE

9 rue Fresque. **MAP B2-11**
☎ 04.66.21.76.33
Closed evenings, Sundays, and in August.
Disabled access.

A self-service restaurant with a beautiful 14th century vaulted ceiling. And it may be a self-service but there's nothing cold or clinical about it – the exact opposite, in fact, and it even has a lovely patio. Jean-Pierre Hermenegilde offers a 47F *plateau* (hot main course and dessert) featuring local dishes such as *rouille du pêcheur* (fish soup with a spicy mayonnaise) and *brandade* (creamed salt cod) in puff pastry. Set meal 52F. This was a well known inn as far back as 1400.

LE VINTAGE CAFÉ

7 rue de Bernis. **MAP B2-17**
☎ 04.66.21.04.45
Closed Saturday lunchtimes, Sundays, and Monday lunchtimes.

To Monsieur Salvador, the restaurant business is all about healthy eating so it's highly unlikely your stomach will give you problems after eating here – quite the reverse in fact. The dishes, full of flavour, reflect what the market has to offer. Regional wines are served by the glass. The lunchtime *formule* changes daily. When we were there we had *mesclun* (mixed green salad) with serrano ham, fresh cod with olive oil and a sweet pepper sauce, and figs *confit* with vanilla ice-cream, all for 78F. Choose from the 132F *menu-carte* in the evenings. Cosy atmosphere since it can only seat twenty, but that means you'll have to book.

RESTAURANT NICOLAS

1 rue Poise. **MAP C2-13**
☎ 04.66.67.50.47
Closed Mondays (except public holidays), July 1–15 and Christmas–New Year's Day.

The large dining room has stone walls and is well laid out. The locals like to eat here with friends and we don't blame them since we have particularly fond memories of the *anchoïade provençale*, the monkfish stew, the *terrine* of chicken livers, the *gardiane* (stew), the warm mussels, the creamed salt cod in puff pastry, and the house desserts like *clafoutis*. Set meals 70–140F.

AU FLAN COCO

31 rue Mûrier-d'Espagne. **MAP B1-10**
☎ 04.66.21.84.81
Closed evenings (except Saturdays and by reservation), Sundays, and the last two weeks in Aug.

Michel Pépin, a friendly sort with a moustache and a caterer by profession, runs this unusual

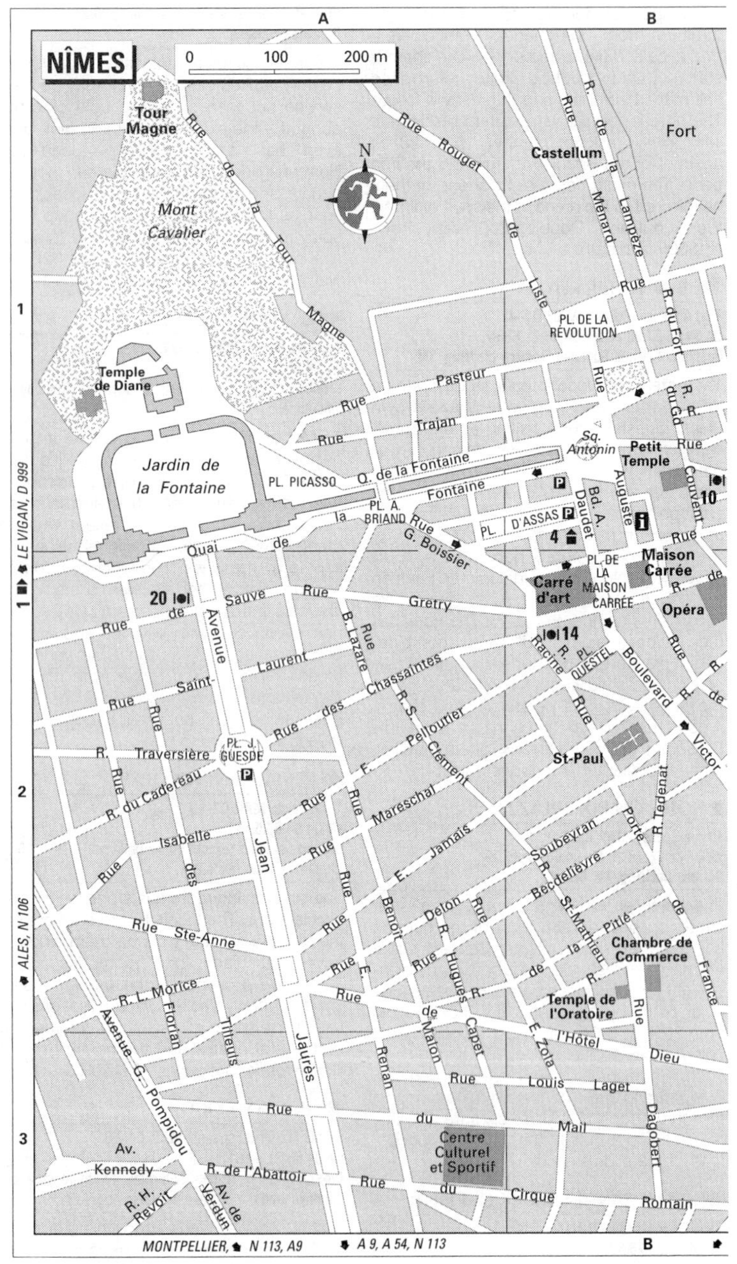
NÎMES
0 100 200 m
A
B
1
2
3
Tour Magne
Mont Cavalier
Rue de la Tour Magne
Rue Rouget de Lisle
Castellum
R. de la Lampèze
Rue Ménard
Fort
PL. DE LA RÉVOLUTION
R. du Fort
Temple de Diane
Rue Pasteur
Rue Trajan
Jardin de la Fontaine
PL. PICASSO
Q. de la Fontaine
PL. A. BRIAND
Rue G. Boissier
Sq. Antonin
Petit Temple
Rue Auguste
R. du Gd Couvent
10
Bd. A. Daudet
PL. D'ASSAS
4
Maison Carrée
Carré d'art
PL. DE LA MAISON CARRÉE
Opéra
Quai de la Fontaine
20
Rue de Sauve
Rue Gretry
Rue B. Lazare
14
R. Racine
PL. QUESTEL
Boulevard Victor Hugo
Avenue Jean Jaurès
Rue Saint-Laurent
Rue des Chassaintes
R. S. Clément
Rue F. Pelloutier
PL. J. GUESDE
R. Traversière
Rue St-Paul
R. du Cadereau
Rue Isabelle
Rue des
Rue Mareschal
Rue E. Jamais
R. Tedenat
Porte de France
Rue Soubeyran
R. Bedelièvre
R. St-Mathieu
Rue de la Pitié
Rue Benoit
Rue Delon
R. Hugues Capet
Rue Ste-Anne
Chambre de Commerce
Temple de l'Oratoire
R. L. Morice
Florian
Tilleuls
Rue E. Renan
Rue de Maison
E. Zola
Rue de l'Hôtel Dieu
Avenue G. Pompidou
Rue Louis Laget
Rue du Mail
Dagobert
Centre Culturel et Sportif
Av. Kennedy
R. de l'Abattoir
Rue du Cirque Romain
R. H. Revoil
Av. de Verdun
LE VIGAN, D 999
ALES, N 106
MONTPELLIER, N 113, A9
A 9, A 54, N 113

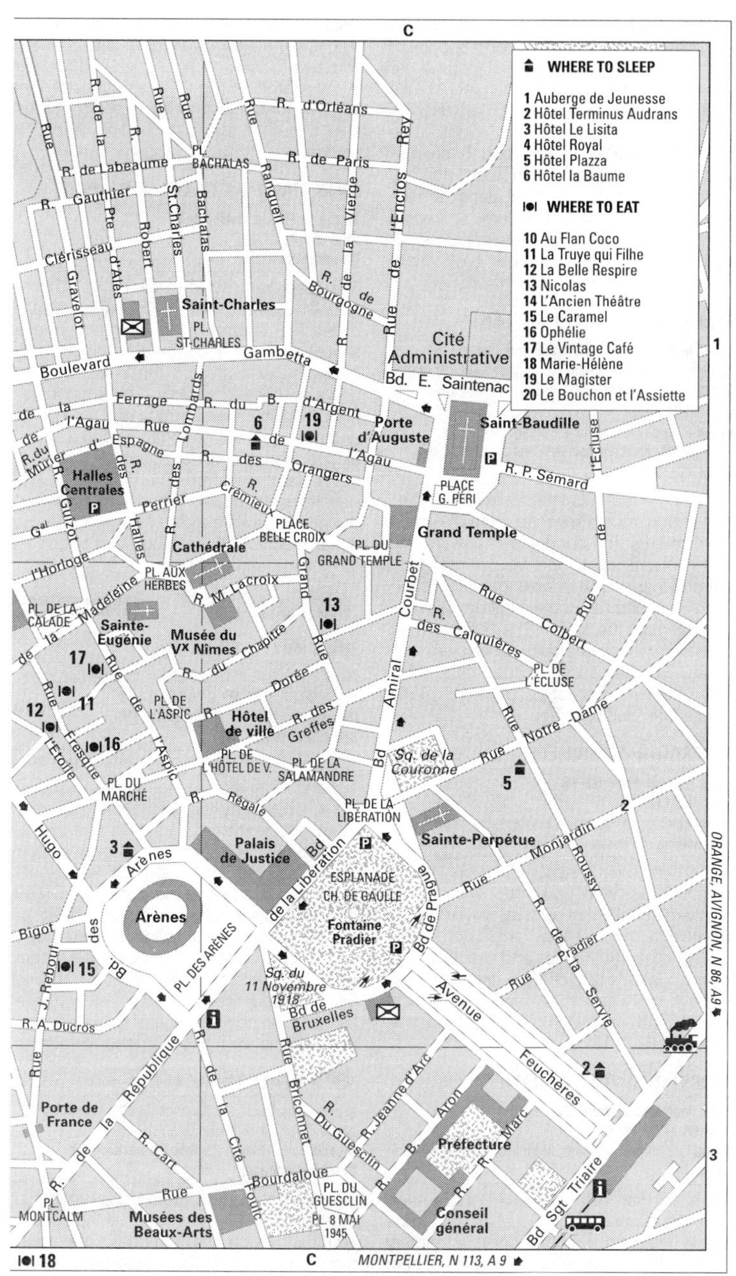
WHERE TO SLEEP
1 Auberge de Jeunesse
2 Hôtel Terminus Audrans
3 Hôtel Le Lisita
4 Hôtel Royal
5 Hôtel Plazza
6 Hôtel la Baume
WHERE TO EAT
10 Au Flan Coco
11 La Truye qui Filhe
12 La Belle Respire
13 Nicolas
14 L'Ancien Théâtre
15 Le Caramel
16 Ophélie
17 Le Vintage Café
18 Marie-Hélène
19 Le Magister
20 Le Bouchon et l'Assiette
Saint-Charles
Cité Administrative
Porte d'Auguste
Saint-Baudille
Halles Centrales
Grand Temple
Cathédrale
Sainte-Eugénie
Musée du Vx Nîmes
Hôtel de ville
Sq. de la Couronne
Palais de Justice
Sainte-Perpétue
Arènes
ESPLANADE CH. DE GAULLE
Fontaine Pradier
Sq. du 11 Novembre 1918
Porte de France
Préfecture
Conseil général
Musées des Beaux-Arts
ORANGE, AVIGNON, N 86, A9
MONTPELLIER, N 113, A 9

and delightful little restaurant. The two attractive dining rooms are decorated in shades of green and the tables have granite tops. Sit out on the beautiful terrace when summer comes along. Imaginative main courses vary daily, as does the 79F set meal, which might come with potato pie, creamed salt cod, or chicken leg stuffed with prawns. Expect to pay 110–120F à la carte for a meal along the lines of a large mixed salad, pork curry, and apple crumble with *crème fraîche*. Fresh produce is one of the rules here and prices are reasonable. Ideal for a spot of lunch in summer.

RESTAURANT MARIE-HÉLÈNE

733 av. Maréchal-Juin (North-West); it's beside the Chambre des Métiers on the Montpellier road. Off map **B3-18**
☎ 04.66.84.13.02
Closed Saturday lunchtimes, Sundays, evenings Mondays–Wednesdays inclusive, and two weeks in August.

Everything about this little restaurant brings back memories of Provence, from the warm bright colours, the bouquets of flowers and the table settings to the tall smiling dark-haired owner and the cooking (mainly char-grilled meat and fish cooked in front of you) – all redolent of the south. The 90F set meal offers several choices such as chicken with morels, creamed salt cod and home-made *crème catalane*. Expect to spend 120–130F à la carte (excluding wine).

RESTAURANT OPHÉLIE

35 rue Fresque. **MAP B2-16**
☎ 04.66.21.00.19
Closed lunchtimes, Mondays, Sundays, two weeks at the beginning of February, and Aug 14–Sept 1.

Take a stroll round nearby place du Marché and you'll soon work up an appetite. The tiny courtyard is delightful at dusk when Patricia Talbot lights the candles. People come here for Ophélie's authentic and fresh-tasting cooking. Take your pick from *gratin* of mussels with curry sauce, pan-fried *foie gras* in Muscat and roast lamb. Expect to pay approximately 140F a head.

RESTAURANT LE CARAMEL MOU

15 rue Jean-Reboul. **MAP B2-15**
☎ 04.66.21.27.08
Closed lunchtimes, Sundays, Mondays, Tuesdays, and in August.

Here's another restaurant with lots of originality. The décor is as individual as Jacqueline Bonafé (also known as Bobo), a primary teacher who works miracles in the kitchen. She comes up with hearty mouth-watering dishes like a stew of *rascasse* (a type of fish) with pesto, *carpaccio* of breast of duck, and lamb with olives and Chinese cabbage. And what's more, the wine list is pretty impressive. Expect to spend about 150F each. No set meals.

RESTAURANT LA BELLE RESPIRE

12 rue de l'Étoile. **MAP B2-12**
☎ 04.66.21.27.21
Closed Wednesdays.

The restaurant, which opened in 1979, is housed in what, until 1966, was a brothel called the *Bagatelle*. Something of its past lingers on in the décor though, including the barley sugar columns, the bull's-eye windows and the front door. The small dining room, which can seat thirty-one, has yellow and pink walls, wooden tables and a kind of alcove. Very friendly atmosphere and you'll get a warm welcome. The delightful owner describes the food as "good home cooking". Expect to pay around 150F à la carte. Set meals start at 75F. You should sit out on the terrace in summer.

SAINT-GILLES 30800 (19KM SE)

10% LE COURS**

10 av. François-Griffeuille (Centre); take the D42.
☎ 04.66.87.31.93 F 04.66.87.31.83
Closed Dec 20–Feb 25. **Car park. TV. Disabled access.**

You'll receive a friendly welcome in this large white building standing in the shade of plane trees. It has thirty-four bedrooms, thirteen of them air-conditioned. The décor is a bit 70s-ish. Doubles 240–290F with shower or bath. If you take half-board at 240F you'll get a very good deal, since the restaurant already offers excellent value for money. There are lots of set meals, ranging in price from 50F to 145F and offering dishes like squid *provençale* with *rouille* (a spicy mayonnaise), *gardiane de taureau* (a type of stew), grilled fish, and the house *terrine* of chicken livers. If you're in the area, this is a good restaurant.

10% HÔTEL HÉRACLÉE**

quai du Canal, port de plaisance (South); take the D42.
☎ 04.66.87.44.10 F 04.66.87.13.65
Closed Jan 1–March 23. **Secure parking. TV. Disabled access.**

This light coloured building is a remarkably pretty and friendly hotel. It faces the canal so you can watch the launches, the horse-drawn barges and the house-boats gliding up and down. It's a pity about the metal monstrosity on the other bank. Twenty-one tastefully decorated bedrooms. If you fancy a terrace overlooking the canal or the garden, try for number 322 or 323. Rooms range in price from 260F to 330F, but they're worth every penny – and besides, it's very peaceful. The owner was a garage mechanic before he took over the hotel. Given his talents as a host (and interior decorator), the garage business's loss is our gain.

OLONZAC 34210

RESTAURANT DU MINERVOIS

av. d'Homps.
☎ 04.64.91.20.73
Closed Sunday evenings and Saturdays (except in July and August), and evenings mid Oct–mid April.

Do come, if only to look at the enormous pink and pale green dining room with its neon lighting and the waiters dressed in red jackets and black trousers. Mind you, the cooking and the traditional local dishes are very good too!. The chef/proprietor's know-how and his skilful use of seasonings is obvious even in the cheapest 60F set meal (house *terrine* and a perfect omelette *aux fines herbes*). Other set meals 100F, 129F, 150F and 250F (this one is so good it will bring tears to your eyes). The wine list has a particularly good selection of regional wines at good prices. A restaurant that's consistently good and deserves the nice things people say about it.

SIRAN 34210 (10KM NW)

10% LA VILLA D'ÉLÉIS***

av. du Château; it's in the village.
☎ 04.68.91.55.98 F 04.68.91.48.34
Closed Sunday evenings and Mondays Oct–April and during the February school holidays. **Car park**. **TV**. **Disabled access**.

Phone before you arrive, out of season. This is the kind of place where you feel at peace with yourself and the world. You'll be delighted with the welcome you get from from Marie-Hélène and bowled over by the cooking of Bernard Lafuente, which is full of the warmth and sunshine of the south. It was not long before this talented young chef became a favourite with both the critics and the general public. The spacious bedrooms are superb. Doubles 350–550F, suites 600F and 650F. You can get a 10–20% reduction out of season. The restaurant has a 125F *formule* (main course plus dessert and coffee) and set meals at 155F, 230F (meat and fish) and 360F (five courses and a different wine with each!). Don't miss out on the starter of the vegetables from the *poule au pot* that are topped with gratinéd goat's cheese or the truly excellent cod with saffron. On top of that, your hosts organise musical evenings in summer (piano and flute recital – that type of thing), and walks to help you learn about the wildlife and history of the area.

PERPIGNAN 66000

AUBERGE DE JEUNESSE**

allée Marc-Pierre, parc de la Pépinière (Centre); it's half way between the coach and railway stations, behind the police station.
☎ 04.68.34.63.32 F 04.68.51.16.02
Car park.

Doors open 7–10am and 6–11pm, but you can usually drop your luggage off between 10am–6pm. Reservation essential in summer and you must have a hostelling card (sold on the premises). 70F per night including breakfast (as much as you can eat!) Sheet hire 19F. Meals can be taken on the beautiful terrace. A pleasant rather noisy hostel run by a very nice woman. Guests have use of the kitchen.

10% AVENIR HÔTEL*

11 rue de l'Avenir.
☎ 04.68.34.20.30
Secure parking.

Reception closed Sunday afternoons. This is the kind of hotel we like. It's in a quiet street not far from the station, you'll get a warm welcome, the rooms are simple but well cared for, and the prices are reasonable. Sales reps, American students on holiday, trainees on work placements. they all love the homy atmosphere and the sunny terrace on the first floor, where you can eat your breakfast (23F) and spend the whole afternoon lazing and reading and enjoying the peace and quiet. Single rooms 90F with basin and shower on the landing. Doubles 120F, 140F and 160F. Room number 18 has a little terrace, and number 19 is the best family room ever, with a bed and bunk beds. An extra bed can be provided for numbers 12, 22 and 32. And here's a little bonus – there's a private garage in the next street!

10% HÔTEL LE MAILLOL**

14 impasse des Cardeurs (Centre); it's between place de la Loge and the cathedral of Saint-Jean in place Gambetta.

☎ 04.68.51.10.20 ➡ 04.68.51.20.29
Secure parking. TV.

An excellent location in the heart of the old town. This nice little two-star hotel is housed in a rather pleasant 17th century building. Friendly owners. Bedrooms have been refurbished from top to bottom. Doubles 190–230F. Rooms with cot 250F.

10% HÔTEL DE LA POSTE ET DE LA PERDRIX**

6 rue Fabriques-Nabot (Centre); it's beside the tour du Castillet.
☎ 04.68.34.42.53. ➡ :04.68.34.58.20
Closed Jan 26–March 4. **TV.**

A beautiful hotel, full of character, that opened its doors in 1832. We were captivated by the old sign, the marble foyer and the gleaming old staircase. Take some time to admire the period stained-glass windows. The pleasantly old-fashioned bedrooms are well cared for and reasonably priced – 240F with shower (no TV), 260F with bath – but they could do with a lick of paint. We liked the accommodation but weren't so impressed with the restaurant.

PARK HÔTEL***

18 bd Jean-Bourrat (North-East); it's opposite square Bir-Hakeim, on the broad street that leads to route de Canet-plage.
☎ 04.68.35.14.14. ➡ 04.68.35.48.18
Restaurant closed Sundays. **Secure parking. TV. Canal+. Disabled access.**

Luxury at a reasonable price, that's what you'll find in this ordinary-looking modern hotel. The bedrooms, decorated in Spanish Renaissance style, are air-conditioned and have every facility you could think of and then some. Doubles 280F with shower, 320–480F with bath. If you're not in the mood for dining out, you could probably make do with the restaurant, but stick to the 150F set meal and the special seafood menu. The tourist office is a two minute walk away in square Bir-Hakeim and you can get to the town centre in five minutes.

10% HÔTEL-RESTAURANT VILLA DUFLOT

109 av. Victor-Dalbiez (Sud); make for the Perpignan south tollbooth then go towards Argelès and it's two minutes away.
☎ 04.68.56.67.67 ➡ 04.68.56.54.05
Car park. TV. Canal+. Disabled access.

You'll be delighted with the comfy, tastefully furnished bedrooms and the carefully prepared breakfast. Try for a room overlooking the swimming pool if you want a good view. This is a good place to stop if you're heading for Spain on the A9 from le Perthuis. On the other hand, if you're planning to stay in Perpignan, try for a hotel in the centre since the surroundings of this one (an industrial estate) aren't particularly enthralling. Luxury for 590–790F. The restaurant tends towards the modern style of cooking but also has traditional local dishes. Nice selection of Roussillon wines. Weekend set meal 200F. Expect to pay about 200F à la carte. The hotel's lit up in the evenings, giving it a special atmosphere.

LE SUD

12 rue Louis-Bausil (Centre); take rue ƒlie-Delcros from the Palais des Congrès then rue Rabelais on the left. Rue Louis-Bausil is a continuation of rue Rabelais.
☎ 04.68.34.55.71
Closed Oct–end of Feb, Mondays in March, April, and the second fortnight in September.

Once you get here, you'll want to stay forever and enjoy the good life. It looks like a hacienda and it's a marvellous combination of Provence, Mexico, the Middle East, Greece and Catalonia. The patio's overflowing with sweet-smelling trees, particularly winter jasmines. We recommend anything that's been grilled – salad of grilled squid, chicken kebabs (the chicken is marinated with ginger, lemon and chillis), or the breast of duck *à la plancha* (cooked on a hot stone). Children's set meal 35F. Expect to spend 150F. Smiling waitresses, hushed intimate atmosphere and lots of regulars. You'll find it in the gipsy neighbourhood of Perpignan, which could do with being renovated (but certainly not destroyed, because there are some beautiful buildings, even if they are in a bad way).

PÉZENAS 34120

LA POMME D'AMOUR

2 bis rue Albert-Paul-Allies (Centre); it's a few steps from the tourist office.
☎ 04.67.98.08.40
Closed Mondays and Tuesday evenings (except in summer).

This is a very pleasant little restaurant housed in an old stone building in the picturesque old part of town. Good simple cooking and traditional local dishes. They have a few specialities, such as mussels in a cream sauce, salmon with saffron, and tiramisu. Set meals 79F and 108F. You'll get a friendly welcome.

TOURBES 34120 (3KM W)

10% LA MAISON

9 av. de la Gare.
☎ 04.67.98.86.95
Closed Wednesdays out of season. **TV**.

La Maison offers several bright attractive bedrooms. Doubles 200F with shower/wc and TV. The country-style restaurant serves spit-roasted goat, grilled salmon, and mutton tripe and sheep's trotters. Good satisfying set meals 75F, 100F and 160F (with fish and meat). Paintings by the owner's mother – colourful and full of life, like the hotel – line the walls.

PONT-DE-MONTVERT (LE) 48220

LA TRUITE ENCHANTÉE (CENTRE).

☎ 04.66.45.80.03
Closed mid Dec–beginning of March, weekends in March, and mid Nov–mid Dec. **Secure parking**.

It's advisable to book if you want to spend the night or eat in this hotel. Situated at the side of the road running through the village, it's a nice family place with a total of eight bedrooms, looked after by Corinne and Edgard. The prices are reasonable; 125F with basin, 145F with shower (wc on the landing). Rooms are fairly basic but they're bright, clean and spacious. Good, hearty, regional cooking, served in the dining room next to the kitchen. Set meals 70–140F (gourmet).

MASMEJEAN 48220 (7KM E)

10% CHEZ DÉDET

How to get there: take the D998 from Pont de Montvert towards Saint-Maurice-de-Ventalon, then turn left towards Masméjean.
☎ 04.66.45.81.51

The food here is out of this world. It's a real country restaurant in an old farm building with enormous beams, walls made out of great slabs of stone and a hearth you could roast an ox in. They use produce from the family farm (pigs, sheep and poultry), local suppliers (snails, trout and mushrooms) and, in season, wild boar and hare that have been shot nearby. The portions are enormous and you probably won't be able to finish the 115F set meal consisting of three kinds of local *charcuterie*, stuffed duck's neck in salad (wonderful), snails with herbs (wonderful again!), *trou cévenol* (a glass of something to help the digestion), meat of the day (delicious fillet of pork, for example) plus vegetables, platter of local cheese (as much as you like) and dessert (absolutely perfect *crème caramel,* made with freshly-laid eggs). Other set meals 65F and 85F. This is the real McCoy – it serves authentic local dishes and real pork and does so with a smile. Just remember that credit cards aren't accepted and booking's advisable, especially in winter.

VIALAS 48220 (18KM E)

10% HOSTELLERIE CHANTOISEAU

Centre.
☎ 04.66.41.00.02 F 04.66.41.04.34
Closed Nov 1--Easter. **Car park**. **TV**.

You'll get authentic local cuisine in this former coaching inn, where the décor is a pleasant combination of chic and rustic. Patrick Pagès knows and loves this part of the world, its wild valleys, its mushrooms and chestnut trees and its fish and game. Try the *moche* (pork sausage with cabbage, potatoes and prunes, the *saucisse d'herbes* (herb sausage), the *pompétou* of trout or the *coupétade.* Or follow our example and go for the 200F set meal that comes with fresh vegetables and all sorts of pork based dishes, followed by a calf's head that was delectable. One of the best wine cellars in the region. Other set meals 100F, 300F and 400F. Doubles 300F, 400F and 450F. This gourmet restaurant is a must!

PONT-SAINT-ESPRIT 30130

AUBERGE PROVENÇALE**

route de Bagnols-sur-Cèze (South); take the N86 as you leave the village.
☎ 04.66.39.08.79 F 04.66.39.14.28
Closed Dec 24–Jan 2 inclusive. **Car park**.

It doesn't look like much from the outside but don't let that put you off – you'll be glad you came in. It's been run by the same family for more than thirty years and they cheerfully welcome travellers, long-distance lorry drivers, families and the local worthies alike. The two large air-conditioned dining rooms serve up large portions of good honest traditional food of a kind we don't often come across these days. The cheapest set meal (60F) sets the tone, offering *charcuterie*, *crudités* (raw vegetables), a choice between dish of the day plus vegetables or other accompaniment, trout and omelette, seasonal vegetables, cheese platter, and fresh fruit or icecream. Gigondas and Tavel served by the glass (10F). Fifteen bedrooms with bath all overlooking a peaceful courtyard. Half-board 180F per person.

RIEUX-MINERVOIS 11160

10% LOGIS DE MERINVILLE**

av. Georges-Clemenceau (Centre).
☎ 04.68.78.12.49 F 04.68.78.12.49
Closed Tuesday evenings and Wednesdays (except in July and August), February, and Nov 10–Dec 10.

As soon as you step inside this 19th century building, you'll feel as if you've stepped into the pages of a thriller. It's not surprising then that Pierre Morin, the owner and a big fan of Frédéric Dard, has devoted a whole room to San Antonio and he'll be more than happy to show off his little museum. (San Antonio, by the way, is a fictional detective and it's impossible to describe the books in a few lines. He's a James Bond character but people read the books for the humour and Dard's incredible way with language, which is impossible to translate.) Bedrooms with 30s furniture have a nice old-fashioned air. Doubles 170F (with basin)–250F (with bath). The conventional restaurant fits in with the general atmosphere of the place and offers breast of duck *vigneron*, fricassee of frogs' legs with garlic, guinea fowl in a Minervois wine sauce, and the house whole *foie gras*. Set meals 68–180F.

CAUNES-MINERVOIS 11160 (8KM NW)

10% HÔTEL-RESTAURANT D'ALIBERT**

place de la Mairie (Centre); take the D11 for 6km, then turn right onto the D620 in the direction of Caunes for 2.5km.
☎ 04.68.78.00.54
Closed Sunday evenings (out of season), Mondays. and Dec 23–March 1. **Secure parking**.

Tucked away in the narrow streets of a tiny village, this place is something straight out of *Romeo and Juliet*, and you'll find yourself travelling back in time and space to 16th century Florence. Monsieur and Madame Guiraud have been lovingly looking after this little jewel for quite some time. Although there are only seven bedrooms, each one's delightful and well-maintained. Expect to pay 200F with basin–350F with bath. All we need to complete the scene are the sounds of the marketplace and horses' hoofs on the cobblestones. The restaurant is just as impressive. It's rather stylish, rustic in the best sense of the word, and the fire is lit when there's a chill in the air. It serves traditional local dishes and while there are no great surprises in store, they're authentic and prepared with considerable skill. Set meals from 75F. You'll forget all about your problems, escape from the stress of daily life, and leave feeling revitalized.

ROQUEFORT-DES-CORBIÈRES 11540

LE LÉZARD BLEU

☎ 04.68.48.51.11
Closed Oct–April.

Keep an eye open for the signs with the picture of a lizard and you'll soon find this restaurant with the blue door. Inside, the walls are white and hung with modern paintings. The food, most of it related to duck in some way, is lovingly prepared by the owner, a friendly woman who's full of life. There's *foie gras*, *tagine* (a Moroccan stew), breast of duck, and duck *à l'orange*. Set meals 90F and 120F (desserts are a bit small for the price). Advisable to book.

SAINT-JEAN-DU-GARD 30270

10% INTER HÔTEL L'ORONGE**

103 Grand-Rue (Centre).
☎ 04.66.85.30.34 F 04.66.85.39.73
Closed Sunday evenings and Mondays out of season, and Jan–March. **Secure parking**. **TV**. **Canal+**.

It's hardly surprising that the stonework shows the passage of time. In the 16th century it was a coaching inn on the route Royale from Nîmes to Florac and remained one until 1920. If you've read Robert Louis Stevenson's Travels with a Donkey, you might be interested to know that this was where he ended his trip through the Cévennes after reluctantly selling Modestine (the donkey). Bedrooms decorated in old style with doubles 160F with basin–300F with bath/wc. The air-conditioned restaurant serves set meals at 60F, 100F, 150F and 230F.

SAINTE-ÉNIMIE 48210

LES 2 SOURCES

How to get there: it's in the centre, near the bridge.
☎ 04.66.48.53.87 F 04.66.48.57.69
Closed Nov 1–Easter.

Standing as it does on the banks of the Tarn (the terrace and bedrooms all overlook the river) this inn has the best location of all in what is the most touristy little town in Lozère. Classic cooking with no nasty surprises. The 79F set meal comes with dishes like *terrine forestière* with ceps, leg of lamb, cheese plus dessert. They also do a 58F *formule* (starter plus main course or main course plus dessert), and other set meals at 125F, 180F and 250F. There are four or five clean, cool and quiet rooms with shower/wc at 195F – good value for money.

SAINT-CHÉLY-DU-TARN 48210 (7KM SW)

10% ☗ |●| L'AUBERGE DE LA CASCADE*

How to get there: it's 5km from Sainte-Énimie in the gorges of the Tarn going towards Millau. Enquire at the restaurant on the left as you arrive in the village.
☎ 04.66.48.52.82 ➡ 04.66.48.52.45
Closed Oct 15–mid March. **Car park**. **TV**.
Disabled access.

They offer good value for money and it's advisable to book. Comfy, brand-new bedrooms situated in an annexe in the village. Doubles 180F with shower and 260F with bath. Swimming pool on the terrace overlooking the Tarn. You can get a pretty good meal here and lots of regional specialities. And what's more, prices are reasonable. Set meals 71–150F. We liked the one at 79F, which came with two starters, mutton tripe and a good home-made dessert.

SAUVE 30610

|●| RESTAURANT LE MICOCOULIER

3 place Jean-Astruc (Centre).
☎ 04.66.77.57.61
Closed lunchtimes July–Aug (except Sundays and public holidays) and Nov 1–Easter. **Car park**.

An unusual and very nice little restaurant perched on a clifftop in the medieval village. The pretty dining room and the terrace both have a soothing effect and the terrace is the kind of place where you can happily stay up till all hours of the night putting the world to rights. Alain has collected various recipes during his trips and tinkered with them until he's satisfied with his version of things like goulash, *tajine* (Moroccan stew), curry, and a number of Turkish and Mexican dishes. He's a bit of a historian, a bit of a sociologist and he could talk forever about cooking. He's as passionate about that as he was about directing (his first line of work). His American wife is in charge of the pastries and her chocolate cake, lemon tart and *crème caramel* are irresistible. Set meals 89F, 120F and 160F. One of our favourite places in this part of the world.

SÈTE 34200

☗ |●| LE P'TIT MOUSSE*

rue de Provence (West); it's in the area known as La Corniche.
☎ 04.67.53.10.66
Closed Oct 15–March 15. **Car park**.

A small bright ochre-coloured building situated in a quiet little street, very close to the sea. Bedrooms are clean but quite small. Doubles 145–190F and a room that sleeps four (two double beds) is an incredibly cheap 250F. Half-board 175F by arrangement with the restaurant downstairs, which has set meals at 75F and 98F. Simple cooking and homy atmosphere.

10% ☗ LE BOSPHORE*

La Corniche; go towards the coast road (la Corniche) and you'll see it behind the casino, at the roundabout.
☎ 04.67.53.05.53
Car park.

An attractive, unobtrusive villa dating from the turn of the century perched up on the coast road. It has a quiet garden and is only 300m from the beach. Prices range from 150F out of season for a room with shower (wc on the landing) and a view of the garden to 350F for the prettiest room in August (it's large, has been renovated throughout and has a large bathroom and sea view). Unfortunately, the sea view takes in the unlovely concrete of the sea wall. Cheaper by the week. Optional half-board approximately 90F extra per person per day. Guests have exclusive use of the restaurant. Relaxing atmosphere and excellent reception.

☗ |●| HÔTEL LA CONGA**

plage de la Corniche (South-West).
☎ 04.67.53.02.57 ➡ 04.67.51.40.01
Car park. **TV**.

Ideally situated just a few yards from the beach, this is another concrete shoebox in an area that's full of them. But the bedrooms are clean and rather pleasant. Prices are fairly good. Doubles 160–360F with shower or bath, depending on facilities and the time of year. The restaurant, *La Table de Jean*, is worth a visit. Mediterranean cooking with a sprinkling of good local specialities. There's shellfish, fresh fish, grills and a wonderful *bouillabaisse* (which you'll have to order in advance). Set meals 68F, 98F, 140F and 190F.

10% ⌂ LE GRAND HÔTEL***

17 quai de Lattre-de-Tassigny (Centre).
☎ 04.67.74.71.77 F➔ 04.67.74.29.27
Secure parking. **TV**. **Canal+**.

This is truly a grand hotel! Built in the 1880s, it hasn't lost any of its character. It's large, has period furniture and there's a magnificent patio with a metal-framed glass roof to keep out the bad weather. Bedrooms 195–410F, depending on facilities and the season. Expect to pay more for a flat or suite. Faultless service. Paying car park 40F.

10% ⌂ |●| LES TERRASSES DU LIDO***

rond-point de l'Europe–La Corniche (West).
☎ 04.67.51.39.60 F➔ 04.67.51.28.90
Closed Sunday evenings and Mondays out of season, a fortnight in February, and a fortnight in November.
Secure parking. **TV**. **Disabled access**.

It's advisable to book, as there are only nine bedrooms. Owners Michel and Colette Guironnet run the place with considerable skill and have lots of good taste. Everything's just right, from the décor in the bedrooms, lounge and dining room to the friendly welcome and the creative cooking. That's Colette's responsibility and she particularly likes to serve fish, shellfish, *bouillabaisse*, poached oysters on a purée of saffron-flavoured courgettes, and lobster lasagne with ceps. You can get a slap-up meal and you'll feel qute at home. So what are the prices like? Doubles with bath 280–450F, depending on the time of year. Half-board (300–380F per person) is compulsory in July and August. Set meals 140F, 200F and 300F. And there's even a swimming pool. One of the best in its category.

|●| LE RESTO DU MUSÉE

Musée Imaginaire de la Sardine 2 rue Alsace-Lorraine (Centre).
☎ 04.67.74.91.75
Closed Mondays, Tuesdays and Wednesdays.

In this funny and unusual little museum, sardines are given special treatment. They're cooked in every possible fashion – deep-fried, pan-fried, flambéd, breadcrumbed, stuffed, to mention just a few – and served with all kinds of sauce. If you like sardines, you'll be in seventh heaven! Eat out on the patio or in the little blue and white dining room. The 35F platter gives you sardines in five different ways and the 50F one is even better. Accompanied, of course, by a few glasses of Picpoul (a white wine). Musical entertainment Friday evenings 20F supplement.

|●| LA GOGUETTE

30 rue Révolution (Centre).
☎ 04.67.53.34.36
Closed Tuesday evenings and Saturday lunchtimes out of season.

In a little street a bit off the beaten tourist track you'll find this good-humoured local restaurant. It has naive, colourful, Art Nouveau décor, a tiny terrace, a tiny dining room, and a tiny mezzanine floor. Simple and cheap home cooking, with the day's special at 35F, set meals from 50F, and mussels and chips to take away 35F. Portions are generous and you'll get fast efficient service from an attractive woman. Lively cheerful atmosphere – popular with young and old alike. Book ahead as it's always crowded.

|●| LA PATELLE – CHEMIN DES QUILLES

La Corniche (West).
☎ 04.67.53.07.36
Closed Saturday lunchtimes, during the February school holidays, and Christmas–New Year's Day.

People have been coming here for donkey's years on account of the relaxed atmosphere, friendliness and spacious dining room. Unpretentious cooking with a sprinkling of local colour and fast, efficient service. Set meal 68F. The day's special – gratinéd mussels, squid, grilled fish or scallops – costs all of 35F and changes daily.

|●| RESTAURANT THE MARCEL

5 rue Lazare-Carnot (Centre); it's in a little street overlooking the canal.
☎ 04.67.74.20.89
Closed Sundays.

Service until 11pm, midnight Fridays and Saturdays. This isn't one of your tourist traps. Rather, it sees itself as having a part to play in the city's cultural life, and contemporary works of art line the walls of the enormous dining room (the proprietor also owns the art gallery next door). We felt completely relaxed here – plenty of room and no pressure. You can take all the time in the world to savour the good food. Expect to spend 150–200F. We recommend the grilled cuttlefish with *aïoli* (garlic-flavoured mayonnaise), washed down with some Picpoul (a white wine). They do a 75F *formule* at lunchtimes.

I●I LA PANNE

môle Saint-Louis (South-East).
☎ 04.67.74.49.50
Closed Sunday evenings and Mondays in winter, and ten days in October.

La Panne, moored at the jetty, belongs to the local yacht and water sports club and is in fact a restaurant. Stylish décor and tasty cooking (mainly fish and shellfish). It's very pleasant to be tossed about a bit in rough weather as you tuck into oysters, *gratin* of mussels with leeks or good grilled sea bass. Set meals (80F and 110F) and à la carte. Musical entertainment (French songs) twice a month.

I●I LA MARINE

29 quai Général-Durand (Centre).
☎ 04.67.74.30.03
Closed Tuesdays out of season and Tuesday mornings in July and August.

You can eat on the terrace with its view of the harbour and the trawler fleet or in the pretty dining room. Authentic traditional local cooking. They do an 85F *menu du jour* both at lunchtime and In the evening (served until 1pm and 8pm respectively), and the 120F set meal of *panaché* of shellfish, *bouillabaisse* and dessert is excellent. You'll pay a bit more à la carte.

I●I LA CORNICHE

pl. Édouard-Herriot; it's opposite the casino.
☎ 04.67.53.03.30
Closed Wednesdays out of season, Monday lunchtimes in July and August, and mid Jan–mid Feb.

With its big blue neon sign and its air of being on the lookout for tourists, you might think *La Corniche* looked a bit dodgy, but you couldn't be more wrong. It's a good establishment serving well-balanced local specialities prepared the way they ought to be. The 97F set meal offers fish soup to die for, authentic monkfish *sétoise* (with brandy, tomato and garlic) and a decent *crème brûlée.* Hearty, tasty and not too expensive. The 148F set meal comes with a shellfish platter, the chef's fish stew, cheese and dessert.

I●I RESTAURANT LA PALANGROTTE

quai de la Marine–rampe Paul-Valéry (Centre).
☎ 04.67.74.80.35
Closed Sunday evenings and Mondays except in July and August. **Car park**.

La Palangrotte has been Sète's gourmet restaurant for more than twenty years and is something of an institution. The dining room, bright and stylish, looks like an updated Venice palazzo. Owner/chef Alain Géminiani prepares fish in the traditional local way (with brandy, tomato and garlic) and his turbot *sétoise* is quite a revelation. Or how about *confit* of salmon with olive oil, *clafoutis* of mussels or stew of monkfish tails? They're all delicious. Set meals 120F (except Saturday evenings and Sundays) and 160–300F.

BOUZIGUES 34140 (15KM N)

I●I CHEZ LA TCHÈPE

av. Louis-Tudesq.
☎ 04.67.78.33.19
Open every day.

The little terrace with its plastic tables and chairs is often chock-a-block and pretty hard to miss. There are lots of places where everything comes straight from producer to consumer, but this one offers the best value for money. For example, you can get two dozen oysters, a dozen mussels, one *violet* (a small sea creature from the Mediterranean; the inside, which is eaten raw, looks like scrambled eggs), two warm *tielles* (a small squid soufflé with tomato sauce, a local speciality) and a bottle of white wine for 112F. Now we know what attracts the crowds! There are no set meals – you just choose what you want from the display. Sit-down or takeaway, and service at all hours of the day. They don't take credit cards.

I●I LES JARDINS DE LA MER

av. Louis-Tudesq.
☎ 04.67.78.33.23
Closed Thursdays, a few days at the end of September, and in January.

A pretty restaurant near an oyster farm. The shaded terrace is decorated with large white netting and an incredible number of shells. Sit back and enjoy the *gratin* of mussels with leeks that comes with the 95F set meal. The 135F set meal is bigger. They do seafood platters too, of course, or perhaps you'd prefer something from the grill (they use old vinestock as fuel).

SOMMIÈRES 30250

⌂ I●I AUBERGE DU PONT ROMAIN***

2 rue Émile-Jamais; As you leave the village take route de Junas and it's 300m from the Roman bridge.
☎ 04.66.80.00.58 F→ 04.66.80.31.52
Closed Jan 15–March 15 and in November; restaurant closed Wednesdays (except May–Sept). **Car park**. **TV**. **Disabled access**.

A gigantic place topped with a chimney stack, this has been a wool mill, a carpet mill, a silk farm, a distillery and a dye factory in its time. Nowadays, it's a pretty chic three-star hotel with prices that are still affordable. Doubles 250–450F. Some are designed for the disabled. Once you've set eyes on the shaded flower-filled terrace and swimming pool, you'll feel like lazing about all afternoon. The restaurant is expensive but the food is good. Cheapest set meal 125F.

SORÈDE 66690

LA SALAMANDRE

3 route de Larroque.
☎ 04.68.89.26.67
Closed Sunday evenings, Mondays, and mid Jan–mid March.

Even though the dining room is small, it's not particularly cosy. Still, the food really is worth trying. The fine cooking is full of originality and the menu is a combination of the familiar (regional gourmet dishes) and the not-so-familiar. Dishes like sea bream with lime accompanied by a *galette* of chickpeas and leg of lamb with *aïoli* (garlic-flavoured mayonnaise) are full of flavour. Set meals 85F (weekday lunchtimes) and 120F. Children's set meal 46F.

TAUTAVEL 66720

LE PETIT GRIS

Route d'Estagel; As you leave the village, go in the direction of Estagel.
☎ 04.68.29.03.23
Closed Mondays, evenings Nov–April, and two weeks in January. **Car park**.

A large restaurant with bay windows overlooking the rocky hillsides covered with vines. You've got to try the terrific *cargolade* (snails cooked over charcoal) cooked by the chef (the father) in the fireplace, where he also grills meat and breast of duck. The dining room is simply decorated and full of light. Set meals 68F, 107F and 160F. Not many people manage to finish the hearty portions of *estouffade* of snails, grilled quail with garlic, Catalonian sausage or *parillade* of fish. Excellent *crème catalane*. The son-in-law takes care of the starters, fish and desserts, father does the grilling, and mother and daughter wait on the tables. We love this family-run establishment!

UZÈS 30700

HÔTEL-RESTAURANT LA TAVERNE**

4-9 rue Xavier-Sigalon (Centre); it's in the street where the cinemas are.
☎ 04.66.22.47.08 Fax 04.66.22.45.90
TV.

The pleasant garden in the small courtyard provides a quiet setting for your meal (except when it's overrun by groups). Owner Gérard Hampartzoumian knows the town like the back of his hand and so is a good source of information. Good tasty cooking and set meals at 82F, 98F and 140F. They do *confit*, breast of duck, *cassoulet* (though strictly speaking this is not *cassoulet* country), and excellent scrambled eggs with truffles. The hotel is simple, quiet and well looked after. Bedrooms 220F with basin/wc–320F with bath.

HÔTEL SAINT-GÉNIÈS**

quartier Saint-Géniès, route de Saint-Ambroix (South-West)
☎ 04.66.22.29.99 Fax 04.66.03.14.89
Closed in January, and Nov 15–Dec 15. **Car park**.

This district is a kind of housing estate and very quiet in the evenings. Madame Tedeschi's husband, a contractor, built the hotel and the stone walls are so thick you won't hear a sound. Seventeen tastefully decorated bedrooms. Numbers 10, 11 and 12 are cosier and have sloping ceilings. Doubles with bath start at 230F. Meals can be arranged for hotel guests. Beautiful swimming pool.

HÔTEL D'ENTRAIGUES***

8 rue de la Calade (East); it's opposite the former bishop's palace and the cathedral of Saint-Théodorit.
☎ 04.66.22.32.68 Fax 04.66.22.57.01
Secure parking. **TV**. **Disabled access**.

A stylish establishment with a swimming pool, this is a 15th century town house that was restored in the 17th century and renovated in 1982. It combines charm with class and has twenty-nine air-conditioned bedrooms and flats furnished in classic style. You'll pay 290F out of season. Some rooms have a private terrace. Walk across a little footbridge to get to the restaurant *Les Jardins de Castille* (see below).

RESTAURANT LES JARDINS DE CASTILLE

place de l'Évêché–rue de la Calade (East).
☎ 04.66.22.32.68

It doesn't fall into the category of greasy spoon, soup kitchen or ideal place for hard-up travellers – in other words, it's not the type of place we're used to! – but we liked it a lot. The dining room is really chic and someone in the kitchen has amazing culinary skills. Set meals 110F, 165F, 190F and 250F. Try the *croustillant* of pieces of chicken and rabbit with steamed green cabbage, poached flank of beef with a wine sauce, and *aïoli* (garlic-flavoured mayonnasie) with shellfish. You can eat in the dining room overlooking the square or on the roof terrace.

COLLIAS 30210 (10KM SE)

10% LE CASTELLAS***

Grand'Rue (Centre); from Uzès take the D981 then the D3.
☎ 04.66.22.88.88 ➨ 04.66.22.84.28
Closed Jan 1–March 1. **Car park**. **TV**.

We recommend the hotel more than the restaurant, where the prices are a bit steep and the food a bit too sophisticated. *Le Castellas* is an old Provençal house that's been perfectly restored. It has seventeen bedrooms, all individually decorated in styles ranging from Art Deco to the 70s and contemporary. One of the rooms even has the bathroom in the middle of the floor. A perfectly charming reception combined with evident good taste helps make this a haven of peace and quiet and the prices seem almost reasonable (410–590F, breakfast 60F). Perfect for exploring Uzès, Pont-du-Gard and the green gorges of Gardon.

VALCEBOLLIÈRE 66340

AUBERGE LES ÉCUREUILS***

How to get there: take the N116 and the D30 from bourg Madame.
☎ 04.68.04.52.03 ➨ 04.68.04.52.34
Car park. **TV**.

We can recommend this cosy inn of wood and stone deep in the heart of Cerdagne, near the Spanish border. The cooking's pretty impressive too. Étienne Laffitte's creativity blossoms when he sets foot in the kitchen, serving up hearty portions of dishes based on local produce. Set meals 132F, 152F and 252F. Half-board 310F. Comfy bedrooms with marble bathrooms 350F. Gym, sauna and pool tables. Beautiful walks up the mountain (altitude of 2,500m) that dominates the hotel, and downhill skiing in winter.

VILLEFORT 48800

10% HÔTEL-RESTAURANT BALME**

place du Portalet (Centre).
☎ 04.66.46.80.14 ➨ 04.66.46.85.26
Secure parking. **TV**. **Closed** Sunday evenings and Mondays (out of season), and Nov 15–Feb 1.

A good and well-known hotel that's been around for quite some time. It's reminiscent of a spa hotel – same type of comfort, same English atmosphere. The food is excellent, a cuisine combination of local dishes and specialities from the Far East, especially Thailand, where chef Michel Gomy spends time every year. Set meals 120F and 270F. The à la carte menu changes often so we can't say what you'll find when you get there. To give you an idea though, when we were there we particularly liked the farm-bred lamb with pesto and the *nems* (small spring rolls) stuffed with pig's head. The kitchen opens onto the dining room so you can see what's going on. Since Micheline is a qualified wine waiter, they've got a magnificent cellar. The meals are the best value for money in the region. Doubles 185F with basin, 220F with basin/wc, 285F with shower/wc, and 315F with bath.

HÔTEL-RESTAURANT DU LAC**

lac de Villefort (Nord); take the D906 for 1.5km and it's a white building all by itself on the left beside the lake.
☎ 04.66.46.81.20 ➨ 04.66.46.90.95
Closed end Nov–March 15. **Car park**.

The bedrooms and the dining room all have a view of the lake and in summer you can swim in it. Reasonably priced accommodation, considering the excellent location. Doubles 250F with shower/wc, 350F with bath. The 85F set meal features regional specialities like cep tart followed by stew of suckling pig or veal stew. It's very popular in high season, so we can't promise peace and quiet.

VILLEFRANCHE-DE-CONFLENT 66500

AUBERGE SAINT-PAUL

7 pl. de l'Église; it's in the town centre.
☎ 04.68.96.30.95
Closed Mondays Easter–Oct, Tuesdays Oct–Easter, and in January.

The skill with which Patricia Gomez cooks, her imaginative combinations and top quality ingredients combine to produce some memorable meals and dishes such as roast squid with aubergine caviar and a *coulis* of sweet peppers, pan-fried young cod with Szechuan pepper served with tomatoes *confit* and olives, *julienne* of chicory with caramelized pineapple, *pastilla* of seasonal fruit, and butterscotch, honey and lemon icecream. Set meals 130F, 220F, 280F, 340F and à la carte. Brilliant wines selected by Charly Gomez. One of the best restaurants in the district. Beautiful terrace.

VILLENEUVE-LÈS-AVIGNON 30400

FOYER INTERNATIONAL YMCA

7 bis chemin de la Justice (South-West); if you're coming from Avignon, take avenue du Général-Leclerc when you get to pont du Royaume – this goes up into the area known as Bellevue aux Angles and chemin de la Justice is about 300m along on the left.
☎ 04.90.25.46.20 F➜ 04.90.25.30.64
Closed Christmas week. **Car park**.

A large building that looks like the hospital it once was. It has a total of 130 beds in dormitories that sleep two or three people (150F) or four (200F). The cost per person will be 90–110F (including breakfast). Half-board 150F, full board 185F. Swimming pool, bar, and a wonderful view of Avignon, the Rhône and île de la Barthelasse. A really nice hostel, especially in season when lots of youngsters liven the place up. Wild atmosphere during the festival. Groups can get meals for 65F.

10% HÔTEL DE L'ATELIER**

5 rue de la Foire (Centre).
☎ 04.90.25.01.84 F➜ 04.90.25.80.06
Closed beginning of Nov–Dec. **Secure parking**. **TV**.

A 16th century building offering nineteen bedrooms all with phone and antique furniture. It's quiet, comfortable and quite delightful and you'll get a very warm welcome. Doubles with shower or bath 220–450F, depending on the season. Breakfast (36F) is served in the dining room or on the flower-filled patio (if you want it in your room, you'll pay 40F). Rooftop terrace. Very good value for money so it's advisable to book in season.

RESTAURANT LA CALÈCHE

35 rue de la République; take the main street and you'll find it between the Chartreuse and the village square.
☎ 04.90.25.02.54
Closed Thursday evenings, Sundays, and in November.

The terrace and the patio are very pleasant during the summer months. The restaurant also has two pretty dining rooms decorated in warm colours. The walls are covered in posters and reproductions and, as you might guess from looking at them, the owner has a soft spot for Toulouse-Lautrec. Simple cooking, decent food, and specialities from Lyon and Provence. Set meals 69F, 98F and 119F. Friendly service.

RESTAURANT FABRICE

3 bd Pasteur (Nord); it's at the top end of Villeneuve.
☎ 04.90.25.52.79
Closed Sunday evenings and Mondays. **Car park**.

Fabrice, who comes from Avignon, has worked in some of France's best restaurants and now at the age of 30 has his own place. Have an apéritif on the terrace under the pergola or eat in the dining room with its model boats, fishing nets and colonial style décor. Everything's been carefully planned and even the smallest detail shows a sense of style. Fabrice cooks with passion and his dishes are full of flavour. There's bream with spring vegetables, sardines *en croûte* with rosemary, fillets of red mullet, and the most wonderful chocolate mousse served with a strawberry *coulis*. In summer the fish are barbecued in the garden. Attentive service.

RESTAURANT LA MAISON

1 rue Montée-du-Fort-Saint-André (Centre); it's behind the town hall, overlooking place Jean-Jaurès.
☎ 04.90.25.20.81
Closed Tuesday evenings, Wednesdays and Saturday lunchtimes. **Car park**.

A good restaurant. It's rather cute and the décor shows touches of originality like the lace curtains and the collection of pottery. Simple cooking and generous portions. You can get a good meal for 120F and the ceiling fans provide some relief in summer. Absolutely delightful service.

ROQUEMAURE 30150 (11KM N)

10% LE CLÉMENT V**

route de Nîmes (South-West); take the D980.
☎ 04.66.82.67.58 F➜ 04.66.82.84.66
Closed during the February and November school holidays, and Saturdays and Sundays out of season (except by reservation). **Secure parking**. **TV**.

A very nice place in a medieval village that doesn't see many tourists. You'll be welcomed by the friendly proprietress. The hotel has a total of nineteen bedrooms with bath. Doubles 270F and half-board from 230F. The restaurant is for the sole use of guests. The hotel has lots of facilities including a swimming pool, gym and fitness centre. It makes an ideal base for exploring Provence and visiting the summer festivals in Orange and Avignon. A good hotel offering value for money, it's already quite popular.

VINÇA 66320

LA PETITE AUBERGE

74 av. du Général de Gaulle.
☎ 04.68.05.81.47
Closed Wednesdays and Sunday evenings.

Tiny place offering simple cooking and generous portions. You'll get no nasty surprises with the 85F set meal offering a bufffet of hors-d'œuvres or cooked ham, then Catalan-style pan-fried sausage with tomatoes or fillet of red mullet *à la romaine* or dish of the day. We chose the dish of the day, which turned out to be an extremely plump stuffed quail with fresh peas. And to round it all off, house custard tart (which slips down very easily, we might add!). There's also a 65F set meal with main course plus starter or dessert The 148F *menu catalan* is full of character. Take your pick from dishes that include scrambled eggs with anchovies, *escalivade*, pig's trotters with snails, and veal cutlet with haricot beans. The dessert of *crème catalane* was worthy of its name.

Limousin

19 Corrèze

23 Creuse

87 Haute-Vienne

ARNAC-POMPADOUR 19230

10% AUBERGE DE LA MANDRIE**

route de la Nouailles; 5km from Pompadour on the D7 going towards Payzac and Périgueux.
☎ 05.55.73.37.14 F 05.55.73.67.13
Secure parking. **TV**. **Disabled access**.

This place, not very far from the Cité du cheval and the mediaeval village of Ségur-le-Château, has all the features of a holiday club – parkland, little chalets dotted around a fabulous heated pool, and a play area for children. Bedrooms are all on the same level and have a tiny terrace, telephone, and shower or bath. The décor could be a little cosier, and some of the bed linen is rather worn but it's an excellent establishment in spite of these little drawbacks. The owners take pride in their work and you'll get a warm welcome. The regional cooking is particularly nice and the way in which it is prepared occasionally gives it that bit extra. Try the île flottante of pike with crayfish coulis, for example, or the roasted monkfish in cider. Set meals are 66F (not available Sunday lunchtimes), 95F, 105F, 135F and 180F. You can eat in the dining room or on the enormous terrace off it.

VIGEOIS 19410 (16km E)

HÔTEL-RESTAURANT LES SEMAILLES

le bourg; take the D17 and then, once you're in Vigeois, the D3 in the direction of Uzerche or exit 45 on the A20.
☎ 05.55.98.93.69
Closed Sunday evenings and Mondays out of season, and Dec–March. **TV**.

Lunch served noon–1.30pm and dinner 7–9pm. Inside this large house with its façade covered in Virginia creeper you'll find a stone-walled dining room decorated in tapestries – and the food matches the elegant bourgeois surroundings. The cheapest set meal is 70F but be a devil and treat yourself to the one at 120F. You'll get the house *terrine* with onions *confit*, then duck or *pavé* of the wonderful Limousin beef, and finish with a delicious dessert. There are other set meals all the way up to 220F. Wine is served by the glass. We appreciated the unobtrusive and efficient service but were less enamoured of the rooms, which seemed to lack the easy-going charm of the dining room. Still, they're comfortable, well-kept and adequately equipped and worth the 200–250F. Renovations are being talked of.

AUBUSSON 23200

LE LION D'OR**

place du Général-d'Espagne (Centre).
☎ 05.55.66.13.88 F 05.55.66.84.73
Closed Sunday evenings out of season.

A good conventional provincial inn. Although the prices aren't extortionate, they're a bit high, just as they are everywhere else in the centre and south of Creuse. Bedrooms are comfortable and well-kept and doubles with shower/wc cost 270F. Courteous reception. Classical cooking. A la carte only.

HÔTEL DE FRANCE**

6 rue des Déportés (Centre).
☎ 05.55.66.10.22 F 05.55.66.88.64

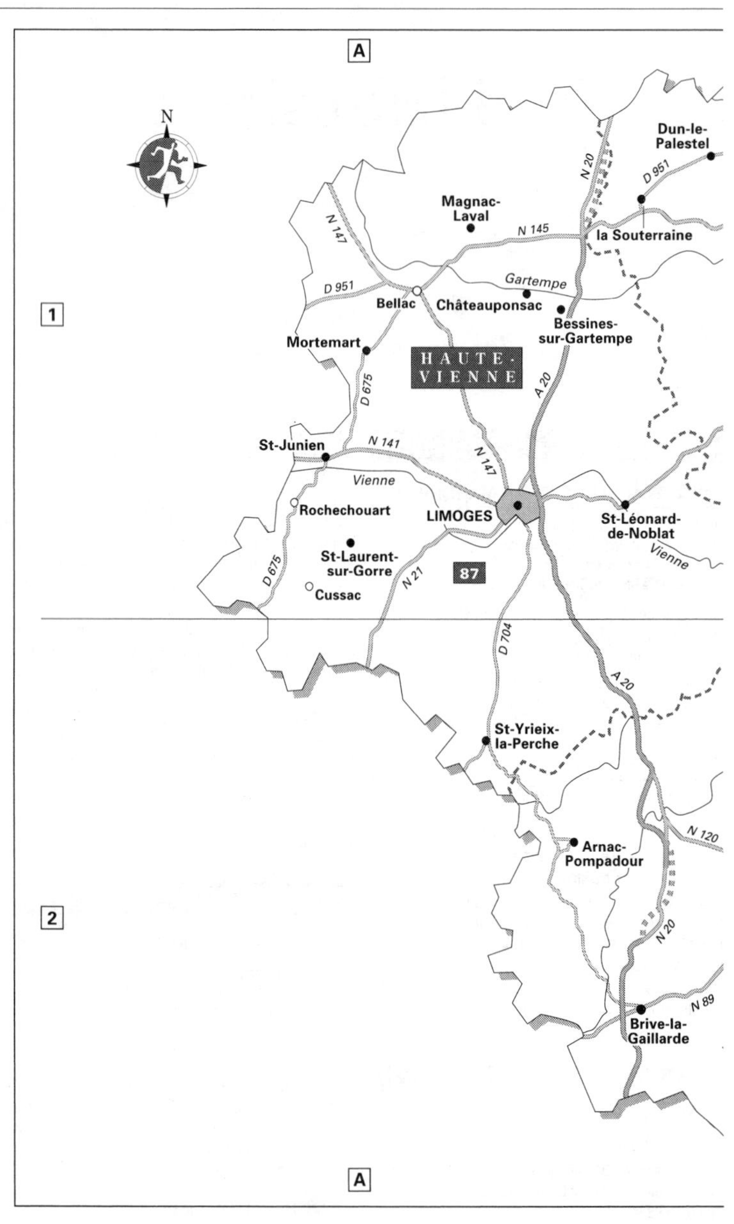
A
1
2
N
Dun-le-Palestel
D 951
N 20
Magnac-Laval
N 147
N 145
la Souterraine
D 951
Gartempe
Bellac
Châteauponsac
Bessines-sur-Gartempe
Mortemart
HAUTE-VIENNE
A 20
D 675
St-Junien
N 141
N 147
Vienne
Rochechouart
LIMOGES
St-Léonard-de-Noblat
St-Laurent-sur-Gorre
Vienne
D 675
N 21
87
Cussac
D 704
A 20
St-Yrieix-la-Perche
N 120
Arnac-Pompadour
N 20
N 89
Brive-la-Gaillarde
A

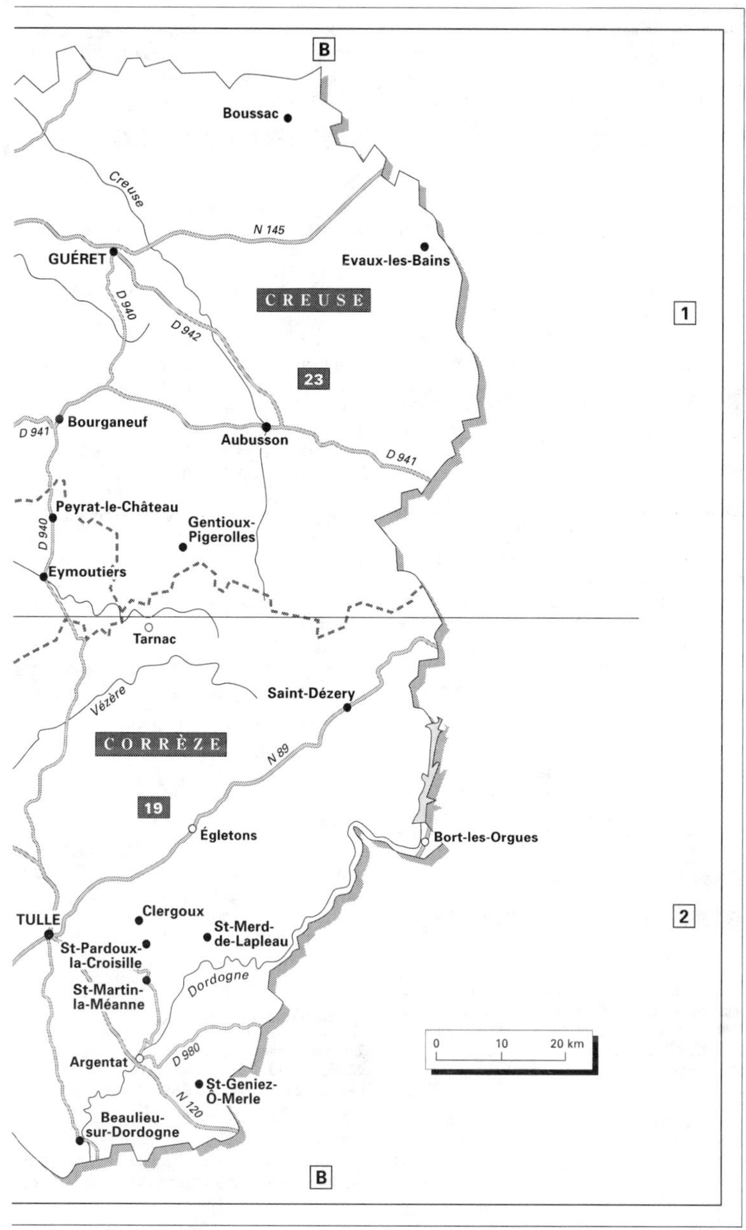
B
Boussac
Creuse
N 145
GUÉRET
Evaux-les-Bains
CREUSE
1
D 940
D 942
23
Bourganeuf
D 941
Aubusson
D 941
Peyrat-le-Château
Gentioux-
Pigerolles
D 940
Eymoutiers
Tarnac
Vézère
Saint-Dézery
CORRÈZE
N 89
19
Égletons
Bort-les-Orgues
TULLE
Clergoux
St-Merd-
de-Lapleau
2
St-Pardoux-
la-Croisille
Dordogne
St-Martin-
la-Méanne
0
10
20 km
Argentat
D 980
St-Geniez-
Ô-Merle
N 120
Beaulieu-
sur-Dordogne
B

Closed Sunday evenings out of season, Mondays, and January. **Secure parking. TV.**

Gérard Fanton has been here since 1994, and it's become Aubusson's most delightful establishment since extensive renovations were carried out in the style of the *Hôtel de Thaurion* in Saint-Hilaire-le Château which he also owns. Bedrooms are pleasant and very well-equipped and doubles cost from 300F. Give the ones overlooking the busy street a miss. The cooking is influenced by Fanton, who also makes regular appearances in the kitchen. There's a *menu du jour* at 92F, an attractive set meal of regional specialities at 140F, and two others at 200F and 270F. Make the most of the good summer days by having breakfast in the conservatory.

BLESSAC 23200 (4km NW)

LE RELAIS DES FORÊTS*

route d'Aubusson.
☎ 05.55.66.15.10 Fax 05.55.83.87.91
Closed Friday evenings, Sunday evenings out of season, and Feb 15–March 15. **Car park. TV.**

This is the only reasonably priced establishment in the area round Aubusson. and if you like generous portions of simple home cooking then this is the place to come to. The cheapest set meal comes in at 62F, followed by a 100F offering a balanced meal of regional dishes – a decent potato pie and a very tasty ribsteak (the famous Limousin beef). More elaborate ones are also available. You'll be welcomed like one of the family. The decor is rather kitsch. Bedrooms are clean, a bit out-of-date and you might find some of the flowery wallpaper rather overpowering after a while. Doubles are 155F with basin/wc (there's a shower down the corridor), 235F with shower/wc and 280F if you want a TV in your room.

NOUAILLE (LA) 23500 (22km SW)

LE RELAIS DES LAC

le bourg; from Aubusson, head in the direction of Ussel; once you've passed Felletin turn right towards Gentioux (D992) then 8km on turn right again onto the D26. It's 2km from there.
☎ 00.55.66.00.34

This is a rural bistro cum restaurant where the owner – who is also the cook and waitress – lovingly prepares her 60F *menu du jour*. And very good it is too, with country dishes that you only find at the back of beyond nowadays, things like a selection of *cochonnailles* (pork based products), stuffed home-grown marrow with good rice on the side, nice smelly cheese, and a *charlotte* of soft fruit (blackcurrants, blackberries and redcurrants when we were there). You'll be quite happy to devour the whole lot and wash it down with some of the litre of red wine that'll be put on the table.

SAINT-MARC-À-LOUBAUD 23460 (24km SW)

RESTAURANT LES MILLE SOURCES

le bourg; take the N141 towards Limoges, then the D7 towards Royère, left at Vallières in the direction of Saint-Yrieix, and follow the signs for Saint-Marc-à-Loubaud.
☎ 05.55.66.03.69
Closed Mondays Jan–April inclusive. **Car park.**

It's certainly a good idea to book because we're not the only ones to have fallen in love with this place, which you'll find in an out-of-the-way village north of the Millevaches plateau! It's a bit expensive but a must if you should find yourself in this part of the world, for the quality of the cooking is quite astonishing. Philippe Coutisson is a great chef, and those who've had the chance to taste his duck *à la ficelle* won't say any different. Specialities are chargrilled duck and leg of lamb. Set meals 135F and up. And to round it all off you'll get a warm welcome, the décor is delightful and the garden is full of flowers tended with loving care!

BEAULIEU-SUR-DORDOGNE 19120

AUBERGE DE JEUNESSE LA RIVIERA LIMOUSINE

place du Monturu; it's on the banks of the Dordogne.
☎ 05.55.91.13.82 Fax 05.55.91.26.06
Closed Oct 1–April 1. **Car park.**

This big old building opposite the Chapelle des Pénitents is rather nice. About thirty people can stay here at any one time with four or more sharing a room. There's a nice feel to the place even if it is a bit disorganized. You have to order meals if you want them. Breakfast will cost you 20F.

HÔTEL LE TURENNE**

1 bd Saint-Rodolphe-de-Turenne.
☎ 05.55.91.10.16 Fax 05.55.91.22.42
Closed Sunday evenings and Mondays out of season, and Dec–Feb inclusive. **Car park. TV.**

Located in the pretty town of Beaulieu, this is one of our favourite places in Corrèze. It's an ancient 12th century building that's been elegantly transformed into a delightful hotel cum restaurant. The dining room archways open onto a terrace and shady garden and the walls of the turret-topped building are covered in creepers. You've to climb up a stone staircase in order to reach the spacious bedrooms, no two of which are the same. They've all been renovated, are carefully and tastefully furnished and have bath, satellite TV and phone. A few have period fireplaces. Doubles less than 300F for two people. And the restaurant wasn't a disappointment – quite the reverse, in fact. Pascal Cavé has devised the menu with loving care and even in the 95F lunchtime set meal it's clear that he has taken pains to ensure that the various dishes complement each other. The cooking is inventive, they bake their own (very good) bread, and come up with unforgettable desserts like the three kinds of *crème brulée* flavoured with vanilla, walnuts, and liquorice If you can afford it, pay the supplement which entitles you to the *croustillant* of *foie gras* with ceps. There are two other set meals at 135F and 195F. A bit on the dear side, granted, but you get what you pay for. Professional service with a smile.

BOURGANEUF 23400

AUBERGE DE L'ATRE

17 av. Turgot.
☎ 05.55.64.10.10 F 05.55.64.08.99
Closed Sunday evenings and Monday evenings out of season. **Car park**.

This is a conventional inn with a menu consisting mainly of reasonably priced seafood – things like mussels *gratin*, panfried scallops *provençale*, lobster salad, and sea bass and vanilla *en papillote*. Local meat too has a starring role – the steaks are juicy and the ribsteak with *fourme d'Ambert* (a blue cheese from Auvergne) is wonderful. Set meals cost 60F, 80F, 95F and 135F – they change with the seasons and the mood of the chef! You'll be received courteously and with a smile. Rooms are very basic and come in at 155–185F.

SAINT-HILAIRE-LE-CHÂTEAU 23250 (15km NE)

10% HÔTEL DU THAURION**

10 Grand-Rue; take the D941.
☎ 05.55.64.50.12 F 05.55.64.90.92
Closed Wednesdays and Thursday lunchtimes (except in July and August) and Jan–Feb. **Car park. TV**.

Judging by the evidence, Gérard Fanton, owner of this pleasantly restored coaching inn, is the chef by whom all other chefs in the Creuze are judged. The 92F *menu du jour*, built up round what the market has to offer, is reasonably priced but it might not satisfy anyone who's really hungry. The more expensive 160F set meal of regional specialities in which Fanton shows what he can do is quite simply superb – an appetizer of *fondue creusoise, terrine* of liver, potatoes, chestnuts and red currants in vinegar, *pâté creusois* with potatoes in cream and seasonal salad, cabbage stuffed with oxtail and *foie gras* and, to finish off, a selection of local cheese and rhubarb flan. There are various other appealing set meals from 220F up. Gérard's wife, Marie-Christine, will give you a very warm welcome. Pretty bedrooms 220–350F.

BOUSSAC 23600

CENTRAL HÔTEL**

rue du 11-Novembre; it's very near Grand-Place.
☎ 05.55.65.00.11 F 05.55.65.84.15
Closed Dec 15–Jan 15. Restaurant closed Friday evenings and Saturdays in winter. **Car park. TV**.

This quiet and conventional hotel is struggling to find its feet in the current economic climate. Doubles are 180F with shower/wc, 220F with Minitel (practical if you need information but the bill can soon mount up – don't get carried away). The restaurant offers generous portions of traditional cooking. Pleasant set meals 80–160F.

CAFÉ DE LA PLACE

4 place de l'Hôtel-de-Ville (Centre).
☎ 05.55.65.02.70
Closed Sundays in June and Christmas Day. **Car park**.

Paulette Roger's a grandmotherly figure, brimming over with warmth and generosity. The only available set meal costs all of 60F, which gets you starter, two main courses and dessert – you're given a choice of five or six different things and you write down your own order, which might read something like melon, seafood, meat *en paupiette* and potatoes, and pear tart. Good value for money, even if the home cooking is a bit rich and heavy.

BRIVE-LA-GAILLARDE 19100

AUBERGE DE JEUNESSE

56 av. du Maréchal-Bugeaud - parc Monjauze; it's beside the public swimmimg pool.
☎ 05.55.24.34.00 F 05.55.84.82.80
Open all year. **Car park**.

This bourgeois building, only five minutes from the town centre, houses the hostel's reception, which is manned 8am–11pm, but not noon – 6pm at weekends. Dormitories are the only accommodation available and if you want a room for two, three or four people, you'll be put in the long recently-built annex (where the rooms have bunkbeds more often than not). Some have balconies and they're all very clean as is the communal shower room and the sheets you can hire for 16F. You can use the pool next door at reduced rates, there's table tennis, a TV room, storage for your bike, and you're allowed into the kitchen at any time of the day or night. You have to have a member's card but you can easily buy one from Dominique, the smiling red-haired receptionist. It'll cost you 70F if you're under 26, otherwise it's 100F. Dominique will even organize minibus tours round Corrèze. Expect to pay 50F a night per person, 19F for breakfast and 48F for a meal (which groups especially will have to book).

HÔTEL-RESTAURANT DE CORRÈZE

3 rue de Corrèze; it's in the centre of town.
☎ 05.55.24.14.07
Closed Sundays and for one week at the end of September.

You certainly won't discover a more typical hotel – at least not one as nice! Mme Rivière (Mimi to her friends) is the friendly owner of this bar cum hotel. They don't make dining rooms like this anymore. This is where the regulars come for their lunchtime drink and the buzz of excited chatter can be heard as they tuck into their 65F *menu du jour* (including wine) which is served at lunchtime and in the evening. Two other set meals – 120F and 150F – are aimed more specifically at tourists and if you want to try one of these it's probably a good idea to call ahead and say so. You'll get the chance to sample simple home-made cooking based on locally grown produce. A basic room with basin will cost you all of 75F (100F for half-board). There's a shower/wc on the landing. It's a good idea to book because there are only six rooms and just four in summer since Mme Rivière keeps two for her children.

RESTAURANT LA CRÉMAILLÈRE**

53 av. de Paris; it's in the centre of town.
☎ 05.55.74.32.47 F 05.55.17.91.83
Closed Sunday evenings and Mondays. **TV**.

Service from 12.30 and from 7.30pm. To the locals, *La Crémaillère* is known as Charlou's place. A writer as well as a restaurant owner, Charlou Reynal's one of key characters in Corrèze, a Marcel Pagnol type figure who can be found browsing round Brive-la-Gaillarde's market place. His cooking is traditional and draws on a wide variety of local produce. Set meals range in price from 100F to 220F. The first one centred round a *mique* (a type of bread called a brioche cooked in cabbage water and served up with cold meat and it was our favourite. It's a pity that the service isn't quite up to the standard of the bourgeois dining room with its well-planted courtyard which is perfectly charming. There are nine comfy bedrooms at 250F but they're a bit lacking in character.

RESTAURANT LE RUTHÈNE

2 rue Jean-Maistre.
☎ 05.55.23.08.66
Closed Sundays.

Service from 11.30am and 6.30pm.You'll receive a pleasant welcome here at La Ruthène where the proprietress is also the cook and a rather good one at that! She's not interested in culinary revolutions, and continues to serve tasty traditional and regional dishes and a few Roquefort cheese specialities. The dining room combines a country atmosphere with a touch of exoticism, although it could be a touch warmer. It's better at lunchtime than in the evening as the first set meal only costs 47F. If you prefer, there are various other choices priced 64–145F.

LE BOULEVARD

8 bd Jules-Ferry; it's near the main post office and the Thiers car park.
☎ 05.55.23.07.13
Closed Sunday evenings, Mondays, one week in June, two in October, and one during the Christmas/New Year holidays.

Lunch served noon–2pm and dinner 7.30–10pm (at least). As you might expect, the restaurant is in the boulevard surrounding the old town. However, it might not catch your eye right off since it's tucked away behind a terrace planted with tall sturdy chestnut trees. We can recommend it if the weather's fine. The downstairs dining room with the comfy chairs is rather lacking in character in spite of its big glass windows and roof. However, the complete opposite can be said of some of the specialities like *tourrin* (a type of garlic soup), which is served in seemingly unlimited quantities.The set meals – 60F, 85F, 135F and 260F – are a bit pedestrian but there aren't any unpleasant surprises and the desserts are wonderful. Polite staff.

CHEZ FRANCIS

61 av. de Paris.
☎ 05.55.74.41.72
Closed Sundays, Feb19–March 1 and Aug 7–23.

Service until 1.30pm at lunchtime and 10.00pm in the evening. This is one of our favourite restaurants in Gaillarde – and we don't seem to be the only ones to feel that way judging by the flattering remarks scribbled on the walls and the favourable reviews in other guidebooks. So it would definitely be a good idea to reserve a table at this delightful brasserie style restaurant which is full of objects collected from pre-war bistros (unfortunately we don't know which war!) You might wish the staff smiled a bit more but by the time you get to dessert you'll be just as happy as all the other customers! Francis can be found in the kitchen furiously whipping up dishes. He provides imaginative cooking and dishes that are well-made and very nicely presented with the first set meal coming in at 85F.The cooking is well thought out and the dishes are perfectly executed and nicely presented. We especially liked the chicken dishes but if you've enough money why not have one of the lobsters from the tank?

MALEMORT-SUR-CORRÈZE 19360 (3km NE)

10% AUBERGE DES VIEUX CHÊNES**

31 av. Honoré-de-Balzac - N121.
☎ 05.55.24.13.55 F→ 05.55.24.56.82
Closed Sundays. **Secure parking**. **TV**. **Canal+**.

This roadside cafe cum tobacconist's cum hotel cum restaurant isn't very appealing at first sight – but that's only until you find out what's on offer. Even the cheapest set meal (67F) gives you a chance to experience inventive country style cooking with a hint of the exotic – things like zander in *sauce vigneronne*, poached bone marrow, and thin slivers of duck breast with mustard can be enjoyed in a bright dining room which could be a touch warmer, as could the bedrooms. They've been refurbished, have all the modern facilities and are a bit like the ones you'd find in a chain hotel, except they cost less (250F for a double). Still, you'll get a very good welcome. This is a hotel that fully deserves its place in this guidebook.

DONZENAC 19270 (10km N)

RESTAURANT LE PÉRIGORD - HÔTEL LA GAMADE

le bourg; take the D920.
☎ 05.55.85.72.34 F→ 05.55.85.71.07

We really prefer to eat at the bar here even although there's a rather elegant dining room and a tiny terrace at the side of the road facing the village. Under Madame Salesse's stern but benevolent gaze the regulars come to the bar for a drink or two and something to eat while the pretty waitresses happily go about their work. There's a *menu du jour* at 70F, but we recommend the next one up, the 100F "terroir" set meal. More expensive ones are also available, but whatever you do don't leave without trying the duck in some form or other. Our favourite was the smoked breast, but it's a matter of taste. The hotel's located in a Virginia-creeper covered building just 50m away. It's been renovated throughout (and done with taste, which is not always the case) and has nine bedrooms, all of them different and all of them delightful. Doubles cost 240F with shower/wc or 290F for a big bathroom and a terrace with a view of the village. This is a good place to come.

SAINT-VIANCE 19240 (12km N)

10% L'AUBERGE DES PRÉS DE LA VÉZÈRE

le bourg; take the D901 then the D148.
☎ 05.55.84.00.50 F→ 05.55.84.25.36
Closed Sunday evenings, Monday lunchtimes and Oct 15–May 1. **Private car park**. **TV**. **Canal+**.

Lunch served noon – 2pm, dinner 7.30 – 9pm. This large hotel, like the church with the wonderful shrine, stands on the outskirts of town. It's shaded by maple and chestnut trees and, as you might guess from its name, there's a meadow between it and the Vézère river. There are eleven spacious and pretty bedrooms decorated in pastel shades and fully equipped. Doubles 250–350F. The restaurant has a good reputation and has a 88F set meal on offer at lunchtime. In the evening there are *menu cartes* at 125–150F offering a tempting *confit en parmentier*. As a matter of interest, you might like to know that it's run by the same owner as the prestigious *Hôtel de Castel-Novel* just a few steps away where Colette used to stay.

TURENNE 19500 (14km W)

LA MAISON DES CHANOINES

Route de l'église; take the D38 then the D150.
☎ 05.55.85.93.43
Closed Tuesday evenings and Wednesdays (except in July and August), and Nov 12–end of Feb.

Lunch served noon–1.30pm and dinner 7.30–8.30pm (9pm in summer). Turenne is a beautiful town and this hotel, with its Gothic style door, is quite delightful. You'll find it at the start of the lane that leads up to the church and the chateau. You've the choice of two dining areas (one with an vaulted ceiling) or you can eat under the arbour on the lovely terrace. There are several lunchtime set meals starting from 100F, not forgetting of course the duck specials (*grillons* – bits of meat left over from making *confit* – and breast). Although you won't get particularly large portions, the cooking's rather imaginative and the dishes are nicely presented. There are also three comfortable and stylish bedrooms costing 300–370F but they always go very quickly. You'll get a lovely welcome with a smile.

AUBAZINE 19190 (15km NE)

HÔTEL-CAFÉ-RESTAURANT DE LA TOUR**

place de l'Église; take the N89.
☎ 05.55.25.71.17 F 05.55.84.61.83
Closed Monday lunchtimes out of season, Sunday evenings, and two weeks in January. **TV**.

The *Hôtel de la Tour*, situated in the heart of the village just across from the abbey church, has more than one surprise up its sleeve. First of all, it's a good cheap little hotel overlooking the abbey and its double bedrooms (150F with shower/wc on the landing) are kept absolutely ship-shape just like your mother's back home. There are more expensive ones too with a separate bath and wc costing 280F, but the most impressive has definitely got to be the duplex (400F) in the tower – it's got a circular room and a terrace with a view of the abbey! The chef's worked in several major Parisian establishments learning how to prepare simple healthy dishes. Try the pan-fried *foie gras* with raspberry vinegar while admiring the gorgeous fireplaces in the two dining rooms. Set meals at 85F (not Sunday lunchtimes), 115F and 145F. Friendly welcome.

MEYSSAC 19500 (23km SE)

10% LE RELAIS DU QUERCY

av. du Quercy (Centre).
☎ 05.55.25.40.31 F 05.55.25.36.22.
Closed Nov 15–30. **TV**.

Lunch served noon–3.30pm and dinner 5–11pm. This village is made from the red sandstone that put its neighbour, Collonges, on the map. *Le Relais du Quercy* is a large bourgeois building which has a stylish dining area and a terrace with a pool directly below. Set meals start at 70F (lunchtimes only) going up to 80F for an omelette with ceps. Duck takes pride of place of course, but alongside classical dishes you'll find more inventive ones like chilli *à l'aiguillette*. The friendly easy-going team of people that work here know that little things count. They also have well-equipped rooms for 190–300F. The most expensive one overlooks the pool and is reminiscent of what you'd find in a holiday club.

CHÂTEAUPONSAC 87290

HÔTEL-RESTAURANT DU CENTRE*

place Mazurier; take the D1 and you'll find it just opposite the tourist office.
☎ 05.55.76.50.19
Closed Sundays except in July and August.

This popular unassuming hotel (with restaurant/bar) offers clean cheap rooms. Doubles range from 120F (bathroom and toilet in the corridor) to 180F (with shower/wc). They do a 68F *menu du jour* (weekday lunchtimes only) which includes cheese and dessert and goes down very nicely indeed. A good hotel for the kind of standard it offers.

BESSINES-SUR-GARTEMPE 87250 (9km E)

MANOIR HENRI IV**

La Croix du Breuil; take the N20 or from Limoges take the A20 and exit 24.
☎ 05.55.76.00.56 F 05.55.76.14.14
Closed Sunday evenings and Mondays Oct 1–May 1.
Car park. **TV**.

Lunch served 12.15–2pm and dinner 7.30–9pm. The tower of this 16th century manor set back from the road can be seen for miles around. Henri IV used to stay here on his hunting expeditions. There's still a good deal of history attached to the place – what with the stonework, panelling and the huge mantelpiece in the dining room. Bedrooms are clean and comfortable with rustic furniture. Doubles with shower/wc 230F, with bath 280F. The set meals are a touch on the dear side at 115F (this one not served on public holidays), 185F and 265F but the cooking is refined and the portions are generous. Dishes such as pan-fried *foie gras* and grilled Limousin steak with chestnuts are available. The atmosphere's rather hushed. It seems to have a feel of olden-day France.

ROUSSAC 87140 (11km SW)

LA FONTAINE SAINT-MARTIAL

le bourg; by the D771.
☎ 05.55.60.27.42
Open every day in July and August, but closed Wednesday evenings the rest of the year.

This is a very attractive brand new bar cum restaurant which also serves as a grocer's and tobacconist's. It's run by Marc Foussat, the modest young proprietor/chef who's doing a marvellous job. Seated in the little spick-and-span dining room beside the bar or on the terrace you can sample the 55F *menu du jour* (weekday lunchtimes) which includes cheese, dessert, wine and coffee. The 75F set meal, offering dishes like salad of gizzards, ling with hollandaise sauce, cheese, and home-made raspberry charlotte, really is something to write home about! And for 95F you can treat yourself to a dozen snails, a *roulade* of plaice with smoked salmon and the like. You'll find some pretty decent and inexpensive bottles on the short wine list. Having expressed our surprise at finding such classical cooking and such professional (and friendly) service in an establishment that has to wear so many hats, we learned that Marc has just graduated from hotel school (and that he has a passion for football but that's another story!) His bar is the meeting place for local football fans and things really heat up on Saturday and Sunday nights! People like this kind of place – one that helps to breathe some life back into the countryside. Keep up the good work Marco!

CLERGOUX 19320

HÔTEL CHAMMARD*

le bourg; at Roche-Canillac get back onto the D18 then take the D978 in the direction of Tulle.
☎ 05.55.27.76.04
Closed Nov–April1. **Car park**. **Disabled access**.

This is what hotels used to be like in the old days, with a lovely aroma of beeswax and home-made jam. Berthe is a delightful woman who'll welcome you into her home where the *cantou*, the inglenook fireplace, has pride of place. Doubles (150F with shower) are very well-kept and most look onto the garden and the back.

CUSSAC 87150

RESTAURANT CHEZ DENISE

le bourg.
☎ 05.55.70.94.84
Disabled access.

Located in the centre of town this cheerful hotel cum restaurant is also a cafe and tobacconist's. Denise, the owner, lovingly prepares generous portions of very reasonably-priced food, the kind that's only really found in this kind of area and even then you'll have to search high and low! There's a rural feel to this simple and friendly place where the locals gather to play cards. The "working man's set meal" comes in at the unbeatable price of 55F, and for that we got prime quality *tournedos*! There's another set meal at 90F offering specialities such as veal sweetbreads with Madeira sauce, cep omelette and fabulous fruit tarts. Rooms with shower/wc 130–180F.

DORAT (LE) 87210

HÔTEL DE BORDEAUX

39 place Charles-de-Gaulle.
☎ 05.55.60.76.88
Restaurant closed Sunday evenings, the last week in September and the first three weeks in January

Lunch served noon–2pm and dinner 7.30–8.30pm. This place fairly ticks along – the atmosphere's altogether provincial and you get service with a smile. The rooms – 155F with basin, 220F with shower/wc – are presentable but showing signs of age. The restaurant offers decent cooking and traditional dishes and does set meals at 68F, 98F, 125F and 185F. In short, a reliable establishment. It may not send you into ecstasies but it won't give you any nasty surprises either.

DUN-LE-PALESTEL 23800

10% HÔTEL-RESTAURANT JOLY**

square Fernand-Riollet: it's opposite the church.
☎ 05.55.89.00.23 F 05.55.89.15.89
Closed Sunday evenings, Monday lunchtimes, three weeks in March, and three in October. **TV**. **Disabled access**.

In this very typically French country hotel you'll find quiet well-kept rooms for 220F. Go for one in the recently built annex as they're spick-and-span and more comfortable. And the large country-style dining room offers faultless traditional cooking and service to match. We particularly liked the fabulous duck *rillettes*, zander with baby vegetables (lightly sugared carrots in particular), and *terrine* of carp with crayfish sauce (the chef's speciality). The cheapest set meal is 78F (not available Sundays) and the others at 96–186F are within everyone's means. Moreover, the owners will quite willingly organize bike trips for a day or more that are very easy going. This is a reliable and satisfactory sort of place.

CELLE-DUNOISE (LA) 23800 (10km NE)

☗ I●I HOSTELLERIE PASCAUD**

le bourg: follow the signs for Aigurande, then turn right on to the D15; when you reach the town it's on the right hand side of the main street once you've crossed the Creuse.
☎ 05.55.89.10.66
Closed two weeks in January and the second fortnight in October; restaurant closed Mondays out of season.

The restaurant's not up to much (set meals 60–80F), but the ten bedrooms – pretty, clean and bright – make this one of the best hotels in the region, particularly since six of them overlook the valley of the the Creuse, at its most placid here. Rates are extremely reasonable, with doubles 140–180F. You'll get a genuinely nice welcome. The café which doubles as a restaurant serves as a meeting place for the dwindling number of local youngsters who come here to chat about football and fishing trips. A really nice place.

CROZANT 23160 (11.5km NW)

I●I RESTAURANT L'AUBERGE DE LA VALLÉE

How to get there: on the D913; it's not far from Lake Chambon.
☎ 05.55.89.80.03
Closed Monday evenings, Tuesdays (except in July and August), and in January.

The cooking here is first-rate and they serve up fish, seafood, pigeon and ceps in ways that will set your mouth watering. The dining room staff are in local costume and the dishes sometimes come to the table under those dome-like covers called cloches. They do four set meals, starting at 76F (not available Sundays) and going up to 230F, and à la carte is also available. Staff are rather inconsistent – sometimes they'll tell you they're fully booked when the restaurant is in fact empty but on the other hand you do sometimes get the warmest possible welcome!

ÉVAUX-LES-BAINS 23110

10% ☗ I●I GRAND HÔTEL**

les thermes: it's down the hill from the town centre beside the spa.
☎ 05.55.65.50.01 F➜ 05.55.65.59.16
Closed Oct 20–April 1. **Car park. TV.**

Like these old buildings from the 1900s that possess an old-fashioned charm, the *Grand Hôtel* with its high ceilings and wide red-carpeted corridors has made it through the years right to the end of the century and is full of old-age pensioners here to take the waters. So amongst all these old buddies you'll realize how lucky you are to be young and make a point of enjoying the relaxed atmosphere. Large and well-heated rooms, a bell to attract the attendant's attention, total peace and quiet, and very friendly staff. These old folks are definitely well-cared for! Doubles 230F with basin/wc, 300F with shower/wc. Try for one of the ones that've been done up recently as they're impeccable!

FONTANIÈRES 23110 (8km S)

I●I LE DAMIER

le bourg; go along the D996 towards Auzances and it's on the left hand side of the road.
☎ 05.55.82.35.91.
Closed Monday evenings and Tuesdays.

Lunch served noon–2pm and dinner 7.30 - 9pm. It's not often that you find a pretty little inn like this in this part of the world – the kind that has a quiet and stylish atmosphere, with music playing in the background and serves light well-made dishes. The cheapest set meal served at lunchtime is 62F followed by the regional one at 98F that offers house *terrine* of duck with pistachio nuts, grilled beef with *beurre vigneron*, local cheeses and warm apple tart. There are other set meals available and also à la carte.Not bad at all.

EYMOUTIERS 87120

I●I LE PRÉ L'ANNEAU

pont de Nedde; follow the signs for Nedde-Felletin from the town centre then turn left after the bridge.

☎ 05.55.69.12.77
Closed Sunday evenings, Mondays and Dec 20–Jan 20.
Car park.

You'll eat very well here and it won't cost you an arm and a leg. The dining room and the staff are both very pleasant. And in the summer you can sit on the terrace and watch the Vienne flowing quietly by. You need have no fears about the cooking – it's creative, refined and served up in generous portions. We had a delicious melon and salmon *clafoutis,* a lamb curry that was unusual but very tasty, and *crêpe bérangère*, a house speciality that we won't forget for a long time! Set meals at 80F, 105F, 140F and 170F. Trust the chef's suggestions and the advice about wine, which is good and reasonably priced.

AUGNE 87120 (9km NW)

10% ⌂ |●| LE RANCH DES LACS

lieu-dit Vervialle: take the D14 towards Bujaleuf, pass through Chassat, then at the next junction instead of going in the direction of Augne go left towards Négrignas, and just before the small group of houses take the little road on the left going to Vervialle.
☎05.55.69.15.66 ➡ 05.55.69.59.52
Open all year round but best to telephone out of season.

Le Ranch des Lacs is run by a lovely Belgian couple and it's both original and attractive. This used to be a riding school and the equestrian atmosphere's definitely still in evidence. It's located right in the heart of the countryside and the décor consists of lots of wood and old saddles. From the veranda you'll get a view of Vienne – green, wooded, unspoiled, and not a house in sight. *Le Ranch des Lacs* is nowadays a cross between a hotel and a hostel with bar and restaurant. You've a choice of about thirty Belgian beers at the bar, and in the restaurant there are various set meals priced 75–195F offering tasty special Belgian dishes such as the *coffret du boulanger* (a loaf filled with scrambled eggs flavoured with herbs), *coucou de Malines* (chicken breast stuffed with a mixture of chicory, mustard and cream), veal cutlet *gaumaise* (with Gouda!) or, as long as you've ordered them ahead of time, as many helpings of mussels and chips as you like. If you want accommodation, Françoise and Jules Lahaye have two doubles with bath at 180F, and four very basic rooms for overnight stays at 65F a head – these contain three or four beds and have communal washing facilities. And it's worth mentioning that children are particularly welcome. There's a play area for them, Playmobile figures, Lego and, best of all, ponies that they can pet and feed and even ride round the village on (under parental supervision) free of charge. This is a really fabulous place. Long live the Belgians!

GENTIOUX-PIGEROLLES 23340

|●| LA FERME DE NAUTAS

Pigerolles; take the D982, the D35 then the D26.
☎ 05.55.67.90.68

We simply fell in love with the genuine country cooking based on first-rate produce. It's worth the trip just to see François Chatoux himself. He's a former engineer who's turned his hand to farming, and is so into the idea of hospitality that he even organized a trip to Ireland so the local farmers could see for themselves what the word meant. His wife works in the kitchen serving up generous helpings of the kind of tasty regional dishes we dream of! Things like potato pie, cep tarts and prime quality meat. The veal we tasted was the best we'd had for a very long time. The duck and lamb, reared on the premises too, are of the same high quality. The set meal at 100F is definitely a must! Guest rooms are also available at 160F with basin and 220Fwith shower/wc.

GUÉRET 23000

10% ⌂ |●| HÔTEL DE POMMEIL

75 rue de Pommeil.
☎ 05.55.52.38.54
Closed Mondays out of season, Monday mornings and Sunday afternoons in season, and June 14–July 2.
Car park.

A very simple but clean hotel with good prices. Doubles cost 115F with basin and 190F with shower/wc. They have a *menu du jour* at 62F and 96F offering veal escalope with a mushroom and cream sauce, and scallops with saffron. Even though they have two extra rooms now that still makes only nine so you'd be advised to book ahead Friendly welcome and atmosphere.

|●| LE PUB ROCHEFORT

6 place Rochefort (Centre).
☎ 05.55.52.61.02
Closed Sundays and the first fortnight in July.

Service noon–3pm and 7pm–3am. Situated in the heart of Guéret in the pedestrian precinct, *Le Pub Rochefort* is without a shadow of a doubt one of the best things in the town with its warm intimate atmosphere and beams and stonework from days gone by. Although the cooking isn't typically regional, it's good, simple, and served up in generous portions. Staff are pleasant and mild-mannered. The *menu du jour* costs 70F or if you'd rather go à la carte prices are reasonable and there's a good choice. You'd be well advised to book in advance because it's very popular.

SAINTE-FEYRE 23000 (7km SE)

RESTAURANT LES TOURISTES

place de la Mairie; take the D942.
☎ 05.55.80.00.07
Closed Tuesday evenings and Wednesdays out of season. **Car park**. **Disabled access**.

Service noon–2pm and 7.30–9pm. In this restaurant on the outskirts of Guéret, you can sample generous portions of Michel Roux's tasty classic local cooking which is in keeping with the quiet atmosphere and decorative surroundings. The cheapest set meal is absolutely delicious – you'll just love the house *rillettes* of goose and the half chicken *à la diable*. Set meals 89–215F. Good local meat and the chef's skills with fish are evident in a number of excellent dishes.

JOUILLAT 23220 (14km NE)

L'AUBERGE DU CHÂTEAU

How to get there: follow Route de la Châtre, then turn right when you get to Villevaleix and it's beside the church.
☎ 05.55.41.88.43 ℻ 05.55.41.88.44
Closed Oct 1–15.

If you're thinking that this is one of the usual olde worlde inns you often find when there's a château in the neighbourhood, then you're very far from the truth. In actual fact, *L'Auberge du Château* is one of those establishments that are helping to preserve social life in the depopulated countryside. Inside there's a rustic dining room and round the back a terrific patio. You've the choice between the *menu du jour* and a large platter of regional specialities – both are in the 50F range, which is brilliant! You'll find the locals at the bar with their glasses of red wine talking in the local dialect about fields, cows and tumbles in the hay. Think about booking in advance all the same, because places like this are slowly dying out and this particular small inn is popular with the locals.

SOUS-PARSAT 23150 (30km SE)

RESTAURANT L'AUBERGE DE CAMILLE

How to get there: once you've reached Ahun, take the D13 in the direction of Pontarion; 7.5km further on turn off onto the small road on the right.
☎ 05.55.66.97.97
Closed Sunday evenings, Mondays, and in Jan.

The attractive and friendly *Auberge de Camille,* named after the previous owner, can be found in a wonderful little village full of flowers and stone buildings. The style of cooking fits in nicely with the natural surroundings. Set meals at 60F (weekday lunchtimes) and 85F, 95F, 120F, 140F and 160F. Several specialities, all of them very tasty, are available à la carte, including *salade campagnarde* and beef *forestière*. The dessert trolley is worth sampling too. The terrace in summer and the fireplace in winter add further life to the décor. Friendly service, and it's worth noting that this is a favourite with local celebrity Nathalie Baye, one of France's best-known actresses!

LIMOGES 87000

SEE MAP OVERLEAF

10% HÔTEL DES BEAUX-ARTS*

28 bd Victor-Hugo. **MAP A2-1**
☎ 05.55.79.42.20 ℻ 05.55.79.29.13
Car park. **TV**. **Canal+**.

This hotel is centrally located just a few steps from the law courts but is rather noisy. There are big boulevards on either side and the sound of running water from adjoining rooms can be heard through the walls. The bedrooms, which have satellite TV, are rather nice. They're clean, spacious, decorated in dark blue and have pretty rustic tables. There are others – not as nice, not as big and not much cheaper. Ask for a quick look round before you take your pick. The owner's a rather pleasant character but standards slip when he's not there. Doubles 175–205F.

10% HÔTEL ORLÉANS LION D'OR**

9-11 cours Jourdan; it's only a couple of minutes from the station. **MAP B1-2**
☎ 05.55.77.49.71 ℻ 05.55.77.33.41
Closed between Christmas and New Year's Day. **TV**.

Although the foyer's a bit old-fashioned and the welcome's a bit characterless, the renovated rooms are bright and comfortable. Doubles with shower/wc (no TV) 220F, with bath 270F with bath. Watch out when choosing your room because a few are still waiting to be refurbished and are rather out-dated as well. Avoid these.

HÔTEL-RESTAURANT L'ALBATROS**

av. du Golf (South); follow the signs for Toulouse.
☎ 05.55.06.00.00 F 05.55.06.23.49
Closed Jan 1, May 1 and at Christmas; restaurant closed Sunday evenings. **Car park**. **TV**. **Canal+**.**Disabled access**.

Although this place is not exactly oozing with charm, about half of the bedrooms look onto the beautiful turf belonging to the local golf course. A well-kept and comfortable hotel where you'll get a friendly welcome from the owner. It's a bit expensive though – doubles start at 312F. Try out the bright restaurant in flower filled surroundings which also has a view of the golf course. Set meals 72–122F.

10% LE RICHELIEU***

40 av. Baudin; it's 300m from the town hall on the right hand side of the avenue going towards Périgueux. **MAP B3-3**
☎ 05.55.34.22.82 F 05.55.32.48.73
Secure parking. **TV**. **Canal+**. **Disabled access**.

24-hour service. This is a three star hotel which thoroughly deserves such an honour. The doubles at 360F are pretty, modern, comfortable, and come with big bathrooms. And the rooms at 405F and 450F are even better! Breakfast is 48F – expensive but it's a pretty substantial meal. Super-attentive staff.

RESTAURANT CHEZ COLETTE

place de la Motte; it's in the covered market. **MAP A2-10**
☎ 05.55.33.73.85
Closed Sundays.

Service lunchtime only. This little place serves traditional food in the lively area of the covered market. The cooking is simple – needless to say, it's based on what the market has to offer – and portions are generous. Colette will give you a lovely welcome and it's easy to get into conversation with your fellow diners. Cheapest set meal 45F. This is a must if you come to Limoges.

AU PETIT-AURÉLIEN

43 rue de la Boucherie; it's in the picturesque area of la Boucherie. **MAP A3-22**
☎ 05.55.32.92.87
Closed Sundays and Mondays Oct–April.

This newly opened *crêperie* is run by two young women who you'd swear came from Brittany. If you're looking for the best *galettes* in Limousin this is where to come. The *complète* costs 35F, the version with scallops 45F and don't dismiss the potato and *andouille* one at 35F. Portions are generous and come with a side salad, so you'll find that you only have room for the plainest *crêpe* (butter and sugar) for dessert. All in all it should cost you 50–60F and that includes cider. The savoury tarts and home-made cakes are also a big success. During the summer you can sit on the terrace which looks onto a charming old square that's been spruced up – you would never dream it was there since it's at the back of the restaurant. This place really is a delight.

RESTAURANT LE SANCERRE

18 rue Montmailler; it's only a few metres from place Denis-Dussoubs. **MAP A1-12**
☎ 05.55.77.71.95 F 05.55.77.71.95
Closed Saturday lunchtimes and Sundays.

Service noon–2pm and 7- 10.30pm. This restaurant has been popular for a long time because it has something to suit everybody, regardless of how much they can afford and how hungry they are. At lunchtimes there's a set meal at 47F and others going up to 125F. The décor's a bit of a mixture and the atmosphere is lively. They do *boudineaux* with chestnuts and their *foie gras* is excellent ... with a little drop of Sancerre!

LE GEYRACOIS

15 bd Georges-Perrin. **MAP B2-13**
☎ 05.55.32.58.51
Closed Sundays and public holidays.

Service 11.45am–2pm and 6.45–10.30pm. Granted the garish red and white cafeteria style décor may not be everyone's cup of tea, but you can eat well here and the prices are good. Without making a song and dance about it, this is one of the few restaurants in Limoges to serve local meat – tournedos, rib steaks and fillets that are succulent and just as juicy as you could wish. This comes as a bit of a surprise when you consider that the bulk of local production – top quality and theoretically free from mad cow disease – ends up in Rungis (the Paris meat market) and the big restaurants. Starters and desserts are served buffet-style and feature a wonderful *terrine* made by the owner and pastries by his wife. Set meals at 54F, 65F and 93F.

RESTAURANT CHEZ MARIE

11 rue des Allois; it's very close to the pretty place de la Cité.
☎ 05.55.32.91.90
Closed Wednesdays.
Disabled access.

The setting's simple and a bit bare looking,

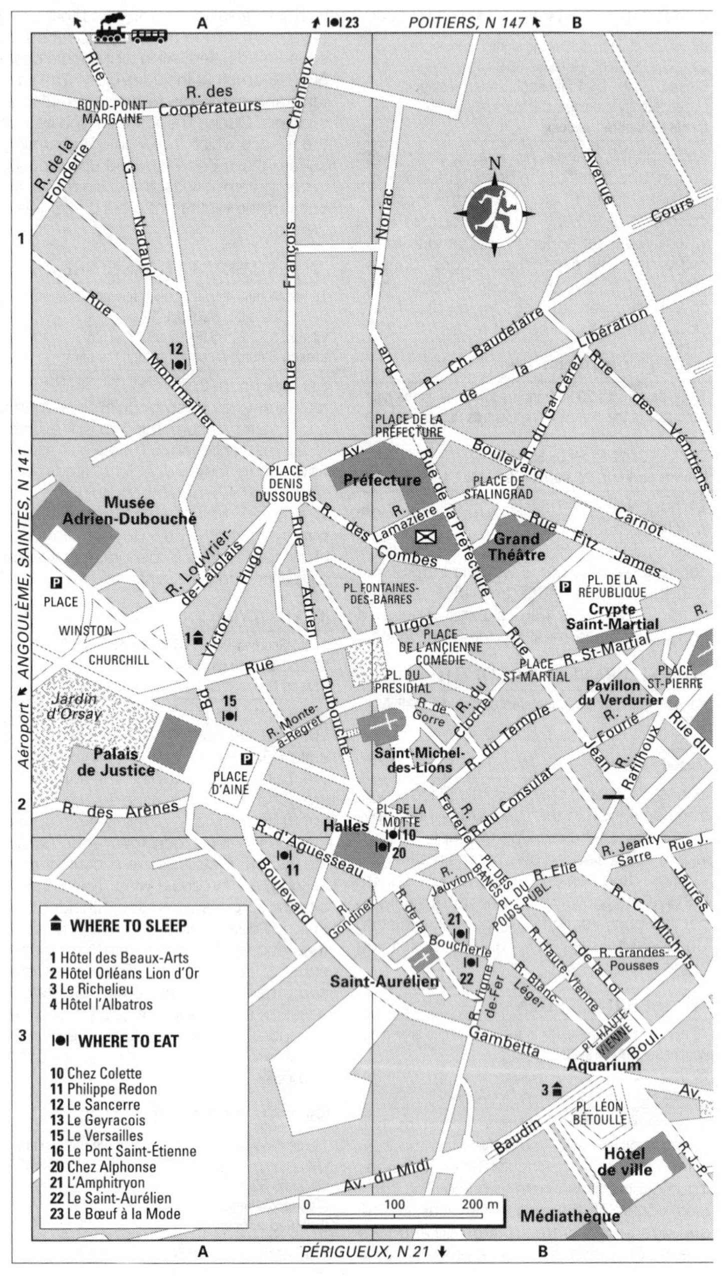

WHERE TO SLEEP

1 Hôtel des Beaux-Arts
2 Hôtel Orléans Lion d'Or
3 Le Richelieu
4 Hôtel l'Albatros

WHERE TO EAT

10 Chez Colette
11 Philippe Redon
12 Le Sancerre
13 Le Geyracois
15 Le Versailles
16 Le Pont Saint-Étienne
20 Chez Alphonse
21 L'Amphitryon
22 Le Saint-Aurélien
23 Le Bœuf à la Mode

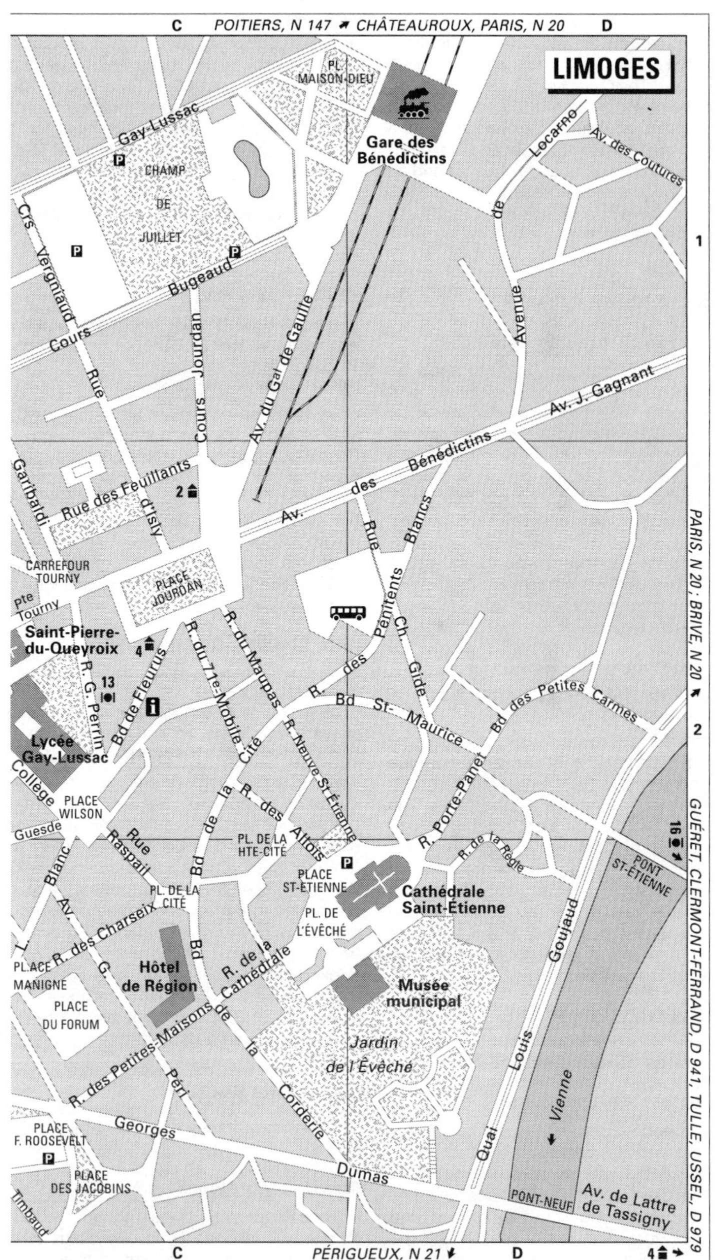
C
POITIERS, N 147 ↗ CHÂTEAUROUX, PARIS, N 20
D
LIMOGES
PL. MAISON-DIEU
Gare des Bénédictins
Gay-Lussac
CHAMP DE JUILLET
Locarno
Av. des Coutures
de
Avenue
1
Crs Vergniaud
Cours Bugeaud
Rue
Cours Jourdan
Av. du Gal de Gaulle
Av. J. Gagnant
Av. des Bénédictins
Garibaldi
Rue des Feuillants
d'Isly
2
Rue
Blancs
CARREFOUR TOURNY
Pte Tourny
PLACE JOURDAN
R. du Maupas
R. du 71e Mobile
Pénitents
Ch. Gide
Saint-Pierre-du-Queyroix
4
13
R. G. Perrin
Bd de Fleurus
R. des
Bd St-Maurice
Bd des Petites Carmes
2
Lycée Gay-Lussac
Collège
PLACE WILSON
Guesde
R. Neuve St-Étienne
Cité
R. des Allois
Bd de la
R. Porte-Panet
R. de la Règle
16
PONT ST-ÉTIENNE
Rue Raspail
PL. DE LA HTE-CITÉ
PLACE ST-ÉTIENNE
Cathédrale Saint-Étienne
Blanc
Av.
PL. DE LA CITÉ
PL. DE L'ÉVÊCHÉ
Goujaud
L.
G.
R. des Charseix
PLACE MANIGNE
Hôtel de Région
Bd
R. de la Cathédrale
Musée municipal
PLACE DU FORUM
R. des Petites-Maisons
de la Corderie
Jardin de l'Évêché
Louis
Vienne
Péri
Georges
Quai
PLACE F. ROOSEVELT
PLACE DES JACOBINS
Dumas
PONT-NEUF
Av. de Lattre de Tassigny
Timbaud
PARIS, N 20 : BRIVE, N 20 ↗
GUÉRET, CLERMONT-FERRAND, D 941, TULLE, USSEL, D 979
C
PÉRIGUEUX, N 21 ↓
D
4 →

with only a bar, a few tables and a tiny garden/terrace. But the welcome you get from Marie will make up for this as will her cooking and prices! The cheapest set meal is 55F. We tried the next one up at 85F which offered fresh marinated salmon that was spot on, a nicely prepared fillet of zander and baby vegetables, a selection of good cheeses and an excellent home-made dessert. In a nutshell, this is an extra special little restaurant that's as big-hearted as they come.

|●| LE PARIS

7 place Denis-Dussoubs. **MAP A2-17**
☎ 05.55.77.48.31
Open every day but no cooked meals on Sundays.

Here's another *brasserie* and yet again an absolute must. It's run professionally and competently. The proprietor also owns *Le Saint-Martial* across the street, a real brasserie with great beer. The tables look onto beautiful Place Dussoubs and people come here to sample the specialities – *boudin façon houblonnier* (35F), tripe in beer (45F) and mussels and chips served with a half litre of Saint-Martial (65F). We can recommend the mussels *à l'ostendaise* with sour cream and bleu d'Auvergne cheese, sheer heaven with a Limoges white beer.

|●| RESTAURANT LE VERSAILLES

20 place d'Aine. **MAP A2-15**
☎ 05.55.34.13.39
Closed May 1.

This brasserie gets a lot of custom from the law courts across the street and has been in business now for quite a long while. The locals know they won't get any unpleasant surprises here, just first-rate classical cooking and dishes like eggs poached in Cahors wine, sausages in Muscadet, skate with capers and a delicious rib of beef with bone marrow. Set meals at 60F, 75F and 129F. The dining room is fully air-conditioned and the paintings are for sale.

|●| LE PONT SAINT-ÉTIENNE

8 place de Compostelle; it's on the south bank of the Vienne, just ten minutes from the centre of town. **MAP C2-16**
☎ 05.55.30.52.54 ⊞ 05.55.30.56.07

Service noon–2pm and 7–10pm (11pm at the weekend). It's beautifully situated on the banks of the Vienne and has a stylish upstairs dining room and a terrace for sunny days. The cooking is rather refined and changes according to the season and the chef's fancies. Portions are generous. Although the choice is rather limited, meals are well-balanced and the ingredients always fresh. Wines have been selected with care and cost 60–100F a bottle. The 98F *formule* – starter plus main course or main course plus dessert – makes for a good lunch. The next set meals come in at 125F and 150F. At lunchtime, they do a 70F *formule d'assiettes.* There are two variations on the theme and both give you starter, main course and dessert. Quick informal service.

|●| CHEZ ALPHONSE

5 place de la Motte; it's behind the wholesale fruit and vegetable market. **MAP A2-20**
☎ 05.55.34.34.14
Closed Sundays and public holidays.

Chez Alphonse looks like a bistro, the trendy kind of bistro. It's the in place these days. People come here to be seen but they also come for the calf's head and feet prepared according to Alphonse's secret recipe and the ox's cheek just like your grandmother made it.They do just one set meal at lunchtime and it costs 89F. Expect to pay 130F à la carte. Pleasant service and lots of of atmosphere.

|●| RESTAURANT L'AMPHITRYON

26 rue de la Boucherie; it's between the law courts and the town hall. **MAP A3-21**
☎ 05.55.33.36.39 ⊞ 05.55.32.98.50
Closed Sundays, Monday lunchtimes, during the February school holidays, and two weeks in August.

You'll find the restaurant across from the delightful chapel of Saint-Aurélien (the patron saint of butchers). It's reliable, never disappoints, and is consistently good in terms of both service and food and drink. We had absolutely no complaints about the house *foie gras*, the *tagine* of pigeon and dates or the *roulé* of langoustine and fresh tomatoes, which were all nicely cooked and original without being over the top. They do a lunchtime set meal on weekdays at 85F but what people really come here for is a good dinner (set meals 140–190F).

|●| PHILIPPE REDON

3 rue d'Aguesseau; it's beside the covered market. **MAP A2-11**
☎ 05.55.34.66.22
Closed Sundays and Monday lunchtimes.

Philippe Redon's one of the big boys now with his elegantly designed dining room, pretty patio and sophisticated cuisine. He's got their ambition, financial means and his light imaginative cooking is definitely worth sampling. He does three set meals at lunchtime – 110F, 150F and 190F. We weren't too keen on the huge bay windows. You feel like a goldfish in a bowl because the passers-by have a tendency to stop and stare in at the people treating themselves to dinner. It could do with being a bit more cosy.

LE BŒUF À LA MODE

60 rue François-Chénieux. **MAP A1-23**
☎ 05.55.77.73.95
Closed Saturday lunchtimes and Sundays.

Service noon–2pm and 7pm–12.30am. Here's a new idea – a restaurant in a butcher's shop! And with the emphasis on the butcher's because Claude Lebraud is proud of the fact that he's a master butcher. You really are dealing with someone who knows his trade, from buying the product to preparing it. Dishes include sirloin of beef in cider, *épigramme* of lamb (cooked on one side only) with honey and spices, and chateaubriand with bone marrow. Pleasant décor and white tablecloths. A la carte. Expect to pay 150F per person.

FEYTIAT 87220 (4km E)

10% LE MAS CERISE**

14 av. Frédéric-Legrand; take the route d'Eymoutiers then turn right towards Feytiat.
☎ 05.55.00.26.28 F 05.55.00.23.87
Closed Dec 15–Jan 15; restaurant closed Oct–April and Saturday lunchtimes, Sunday evenings and Mondays the rest of the year. **Car park**. **TV**. **Canal+**.

The area hasn't got much character – all those straight rows of recently-built houses make it look like an estate – but *Le Mas Cerise* offers comfortable well-kept rooms at 245F for a double with shower/wc. Good reception. The restaurant's satisfactory although it's a bit expensive with the cheapest set meal at 120F. There's also a terrace and a swimming pool.

AIXE-SUR-VIENNE 87700 (13km SW)

AUBERGE DES DEUX PONTS

2 av. du Général de Gaulle; take the N21.
☎ 05.55.70.10.22 F 05.55.70.24.74
Closed Sunday evenings and Monday evenings (except July–Aug).

This restaurant on the banks of the Vienne is first rate. The décor is country style with lots of flowers, yellow and navy blue reminiscent of the sea. It's not surprising then to discover lots of seafood in the menu. Apart from that they do good charcoal-grilled steaks, duck breast with a Roquefort-based sauce, and grilled sea bream. Prices are reasonable, with set meals ranging in price from 65F to 200F.

SAINT-GENCE 87510 (13km NW)

LE MOULIN DE CHEVILLOU

☎ 05.55.75.86.13 F 05.55.75.86.13
How to get there: take the route de Bellac (N147), turn left towards Nieul and Saint-Genec is only 3km away. Go through the village and turn right 300m further on. It's signposted.
Closed Mondays to Thursdays Oct–March.

Service noon–2pm and 7–9pm. The *Moulin de Chevaillou* gives you a little taste of paradise. It's tucked away in a little valley beside the Glane, and is first and foremost a park with donkeys, goats, ponies, pheasants and doves. Children can play on the swings and the chute while the dads fish for trout. Then enjoy a pancake and some cider as you are lulled by the splashing sound of the watermill. There's also a good restaurant here. The cheapest set meal is 98F but because we're greedy we went for the 126F one which comes with starter, fish, meat, cheese and dessert. It was a real treat. We had perch with sweet and sour sauce and medaillons of lamb with fresh vegetables and a nice little inexpensive Sancerre. Service is efficient and staff are delightful. You're advised to book in advance as this is one of those secluded places everyone knows about. They're not daft in these parts!

SAINT-PRIEST-TAURION 87480 (13km NE)

LE RELAIS DU TAURION**

2 chemin des Contamines
☎ 05.55.39.70.14 F 05.55.39.70.14
Closed Sunday evenings, Mondays and the last two weeks in December. **Car park**. **TV**.

Service noon–2pm and 7.30–9pm. This is a beautiful ivy-covered master craftsman's house dating back to the start of the century. The surrounding parkland's a nice spot for a stroll. Comfortable, well-kept bedrooms 250F with shower/wc. There's a restaurant too, but it's a bit on the expensive side. The cheapest set meal is 100F (not available on Sundays), and the two others cost 140F and 190F. We remember the place more for its charm, bedrooms and excellent location.

AMBAZAC 87240 (17km N)

10% HÔTEL DE FRANCE*

place de l'Église (Centre); take the N20 then the D914 – it's at the main roundabout.
☎ 05.55.56.61.51 ➡ 05.55.56.61.51
Closed Dec 20–Jan 15; restaurant closed Sundays Nov–April. **TV**.

You'll receive a good welcome at this cheap, pleasant hotel cum restaurant cum bar that, with its garden, is not at all unpleasant. The doubles have out-dated furniture with no two pieces the same but they're clean and cost 150–160F. The cheapest set meal is 60F and half-board is 190F. We didn't try the restaurant – write and let us know what you think of it.

ROYÈRES 87400 (18km E)

10% HÔTEL BEAU SITE**

hameau de Brignac; take the N141 towards Saint-Léonard-de-Noblat, then turn left onto the D124.
☎ 05.55.56.00.56 ➡ 05.55.56.31.17
Restaurant closed Friday evenings, Saturday lunchtimes out of season, and Dec 28–April 1. **Car park**. **TV**.

This place won't let you down. You'll get good facilities in peaceful country surroundings. Comfortable bedrooms – no two are the same – decorated with Madame's delightful ornamental hand-painted designs. Doubles cost 280–330F. There's a nice garden and – a big plus – a wonderful heated pool. The restaurant offers a number of regional specialities such as *fricassée* of snails with ceps, Limousin beef, fillet of zander with chestnuts and a marvellous chestnut *charlotte*. The cheapest set meal – 85F – is excellent and there are others available up to 220F. The service is first-rate.

THOURON 87140 (22km NW)

LA POMME DE PIN

hameau de la Tricherie; take the N147, then right onto the D7.
☎ 05.55.53.43.43 ➡ 05.55.53.35.33
Closed Mondays and Tuesday lunchtimes. **Car park**. **TV**. **Disabled access**.

This chalet brings a touch of the mountainside to the Limousin forest. It's made from stone and wood, and can be found out in the wilds near an expanse of water. The nicely-presented dishes and charcoal grills will fill you with delight, and there's a remarkable list of excellent wines. Set meals 95–175F. Doubles are very comfy and cost 280F with shower and 330F with bath. This is one of the best places in Haute-Vienne.

MAGNAC-LAVAL 87190

LA FERME DU LOGIS

How to get there: go as far as Magnac-Laval, and when you get to the centre turn right in the direction of Bellac; the restaurant's 2km along on the left hand side.
☎ 05.55.68.57.23 ➡ 05.55.68.52.80
Closed Sunday evenings and Mondays except in July and August, at Christmas, and during the February school holidays.

Service noon–2pm and 7–9pm. You might just take a fancy to this place with its pleasant rustic dining room, full of flowers just like the terrace which is beautiful in summer. Other factors in its favour are the friendly staff and tasty local dishes served up in portions that are as generous as you could wish. It specializes in beef and venison, which come from the family farm. The cheapest set meal is 75F but we recommend the next one up at 115F, which is good and substantial. Wines are also very good.

MORTEMART 87330

HÔTEL LE RELAIS*

☎ 05.55.68.12.09 ➡ 05.55.68.12.09
Closed Tuesday evenings (except July 14–Aug 31), Wednesdays, and during the February school holidays.

Service noon–2pm and 7.30–9pm. This is one of the most beautiful villages in France and you might well describe *Le Relais* as the jewel in its crown. It's a pleasant and very attractive country inn that blends in perfectly with the setting. There are a few pretty rooms available for 280F (toilet is on the landing) and a stylish stone-walled dining room. Attentive service. Your tastebuds will relish the variety of flavours in dishes such as salad of artichokes with home-made vanilla-flavoured *foie gras*, fillet of quail with raspberries, and *gratin* of wild strawberries. Set meals 92F (except Sundays), 125F, 195F, 248F and there's also à la carte.

CIEUX 87520 (13km SE)

10% AUBERGE LA SOURCE**

av. du Lac; take the D5 as far as Blond, then turn right in the direction of Cieux.
☎ 05.55.03.33.23 ➡ 05.55.03.26.88
Closed Sunday evenings and Mondays out of season. **Car park**. **TV**. **Canal+**. **Disabled access**.

This former post house has recently been renovated and commands a marvellous view of the lake, the wooded countryside and the hills. The owner's an experienced hotel manager who's just returned to the area after thirty years of hard work in Paris and elsewhere. He knows what he's doing and makes a success of whatever he undertakes – just like his wife! Bedrooms are faultless (there's a lot of refurbishing been going on) and cost 350F with shower/wc April–October and 250F the rest of the year. The restaurant's cheapest set meal is 80F and consists of starter, main course, cheese, dessert, and coffee (only available weekdays) then prices vary 80–120F. They use fresh produce in their local dishes which are served in airy surroundings. Efficient service.

PEYRAT-LE-CHÂTEAU 87470

10% ☗ |●| AUBERGE DU BOIS DE L'ÉTANG**

38 av. de la Tour; take the D940 in the direction of Bourganeuf.
☎ 05.55.69.40.19 ➨ 05.55.69.42.93
Closed Sunday evenings and Mondays Nov–March and Dec 20–Jan 20. **Car park. TV.**

Situated in a wonderful peaceful area, just a few kilometres from Vassivière lake. You'll get a very warm welcome from Patricia and Serge Merle. Decent bedrooms, with doubles ranging in price from 150F to 280F depending on facilities and where the room is located. Go for one in the annexe as they've all been done up and are much quieter. They'll cost you 240–280F. The restaurant's very nice indeed and does set meals at 75F (that's until 1.30pm), 120F, 150F and 195F offering things like fresh salmon *tartare*, casserole of lobster tails, and *vacherin* of soft fruit.

10% ☗ |●| LE BELLERIVE**

29 av. de la Tour
☎ 05.55.69.40.67 ➨ 05.55.69.47.96
Closed mid Nov–April, and Sunday evenings and Mondays out of season.
Secure parking. TV.

The establishment owes its name to its location on the shores of Lake Peyrat. The friendly owner will go to any lengths to please his customers. Delightful bedrooms available with shower/wc or bath costing 230F and up. The good regional cooking is popular with the locals. Set meals cost 69F weekday lunchtimes and 95–245F.

AUPHELLE 87470 (8km E)

10% ☗ |●| LE GOLF DU LIMOUSIN**

How to get there: take the D13 towards Vassivière then the D222 as far as the lake.
☎ 05.55.69.41.34 ➨ 05.55.69.49.16
Closed Nov–April. **Car park. TV.**

Located only 200m from the manmade beach, this is one of the few hotels that almost overlook Vassivière lake. You wouldn't exactly describe the place as charming, but the bedrooms are clean and very comfy (doubles cost 221–278F). The traditional dining room can get rather crowded since lots of people come here for the country cooking and dishes like the absolutely delightful house *terrine*, mutton tripe and cheese platter. Set meals cost 84–155F. There are tennis courts and a crazy golf course across the way.

SAINT-DÉZERY 19200

10% ☗ |●| LES GRAVADES

le bourg
☎ 05.55.72.21.53 ➨ 05.55.72.82.49
Restaurant closed Friday evenings, Saturdays, and during the Christmas holidays. **Car park. TV.**

Service noon–2pm and 7.30–9.30pm. If you want a change from the classical stone house type of hotel that plays on its authenticity, here's a place that dares to be different. It's a huge building combining wood and concrete in a bold 70s style. The outcome's very successful and blends well with the surrounding countryside. The bedrooms which are at the back and overlook the swimming pool don't seem to suffer from the traffic on the nearby N89. They're bright, spacious, well-designed and have good facilities. Expect to pay 270F for a double. Although the dining room's well-lit, it could be a little warmer. However, it's not that big a deal because the smiles and good-natured personalities of Monsieur Fraysse (nicknamed "Monmon") and his son will warm your heart. Monmon's a former butcher and used to be Jacques Chirac's official cook when he was just an MP in Ussel. His cooking is traditional and reflects who he is and where he comes from. Set meals are 95F, 130F, 180F. The "President's set meal" costs 120F and offers calf's head and a stew of pig's trotters and oxtail. Monmon has the ability to come up with excellent dishes that suit everyone's pocket. He's one of the local characters and a charming man with it – when he has a minute to spare it's always a pleasure to have a little chat with him while eating your *brioches* at breakfast time.

SAINT-GENIEZ-Ô-MERLE 19220

LA VIEILLE AUBERGE

Soult
☎ 05.55.28.20.60.
Closed Saturday lunchtimes and in January. **Car park**.

La Vieille Auberge, a little inn with an adjoining riding farm, can be found in the south of Corrèze a short distance from the famous Merle towers. There's a big stove crackling away in the wooden-floored rustic dining room. The owner's really nice and is just as skilled on horseback as in the kitchen. You can sample the good quality regional dishes from the 87F and 145F set meals. We recommend the stuffed cauliflower, the *feuilleté* of perch and the duck breast with raspberry vinegar. And to work it all off, you can go horse-riding in Xaintrie (we advise you to check out the arrangements at least the night before), go mountainbiking or take a dip in the tiny pool. Young couples on the lookout for a place to hold their wedding reception should take note of the beautiful converted barn available for hire.

SAINT-JUNIEN 87200

10% LE RENDEZ-VOUS DES CHASSEURS**

lieu-dit Pont-à-la-Planche; take the Saint-Junien exit and you'll find it on the right hand side of the route de Bellac.
☎ 05.55.02.19.73 ⊳ 05.55.02.06.98
Closed one week at the start of August, two weeks in November, and from Christmas to New Year's Day; restaurant closed Fridays and Sunday evenings.
Car park. **TV**.

The restaurant has a good reputation. The cheapest set meal comes in at 72F but is not available Sundays, and the wonderful gourmet one costs 150F. Specialities include home-bred wild young boar and venison. The dining room's decorated in the style of olden-day France and in the summer you can enjoy sitting on the terrace. Bedrooms are well-kept just like the rest of the place. Doubles cost 200F with shower and TV.

LE RELAIS DE COMODOLIAC**

22 av. Sadi-Carnot
☎ 05.55.02.27.26 ⊳ 05.55.02.68.79
Closed Sunday evenings and Nov 1–Feb 28.
Car park. **TV**.

A very good restaurant where the standard of cooking makes up for the prices, which are a bit high for the area. The dining room is impersonal and lacking in character, which comes from trying too hard to create something new and up to date. However Georges Ferres, the owner, is absolutely delightful. If he takes a shine to you, you'll find yourself with lots of useful information and he might even take you round the local tourist attractions – you see he's awfully fond of his Haute-Vienne. Set meals 97–265F. Specialities include *terrine* of pork liver served with onion marmalade, ceps (in season) and local meat. Rooms are comfortable and modern – 270F for one overlooking the street and 310F for a view of the garden.

LE LANDAIS

6 bd de la République (Centre); take the outer boulevard.
☎ 05.55.02.12.07 ⊳ 05.55.02.90.95
Closed Tuesdays and the second fortnight in September.

Service noon–2pm and 7.30–9pm. As soon as you cross the threshold, you know you're going to eat well here. It's hardly surprising you should feel that way since owner Suzy, has brought a touch of the Landes to this part of Haute-Vienne. The restaurant, which adjoins the bar, is full of flowers and pot plants. You'll feel quite at home, which is just as well since you'll be here for a while. You'll be full and then some after things like *terrine* of quail with juniper berries, fillet of goose and salmi of woodpigeon. Set meals start at 60F (not Sundays), going up to 85F – we tried this one and it was faultless – and more. Suzy's very sweet and an attentive hostess.

LE DOMAINE DU BOIS AU BŒUF

lieu-dit Le Bois au Bœuf; go towards Rochechouart, cross the bridge over the river Vienne, then take the second on the left after the bridge and you'll find it about 7km further on.
☎ 05.55.02.43.19
Closed Mondays.

The restaurant is housed in former stables that have been tastefully renovated. The building itself is particularly elegant – large doorway, creamy-coloured walls and arched windows with red brickwork against a cream background. It would be hard to find a more pleasant country setting. The pleasing dining room is large and quiet. There's a terrace and swimming pool round the back and the most wonderful view – a scene of perfect harmony with the long meadow sloping down towards you framed by thickets, clumps of trees and dark woods. Definitely a beauty spot! We thought it would be nice to have our lunch there opposite the meadow – and the most exciting event of the day was when three donkeys went past. When we told the smiling waiter just how happy this place made us, he said he felt the same about working here. Some people just have it made! We tried the 79F set meal (not available weekends) and had no complaints – everything was good. There's also one at 119F, which offers smoked salmon and langoustines and veal sweetbreads. There's also a tearoom during the summer serving inexpensive chargrills and salads. It was a beautiful sunny day and we would've quite happily tried out the pool and had a doze in the hammock but unfortunately we'd other places to check out. We'll be back, though!.

SAINT-AUVENT 87310 (14km S)

AUBERGE DE LA VALLÉE DE LA GORRE

place de l'Église; on the D58.
☎ 05.55.00.01.27 Fax 05.55.00.01.27
Closed Sunday evenings, Monday evenings, the first week in January, and the first week in September.

A lovely little inn in a lovely village. The dishes are devised and prepared by Hervé Sutre, the creative young chef, and are very reasonably priced. He does set meals at prices ranging from 70F to 220F, offering dishes such as *terrine* of ox's cheek with crisp vegetables, *parillade* with *aïoli*, and a banana and chocolate dessert flavoured with rum. There's a pleasant covered terrace for sunny days. If you're planning to go for the weekend it'd be a good idea to book ahead.

SAINT-LAURENT-SUR-GORRE 87310

10% HÔTEL LE SAINT-LAURENT

place du Champ-de-Foire; take the N2, then turn left onto the D21.
☎ 05.55.00.03.96
Closed Saturdays (except in summer), during the February school holidays, two weeks at the end of September, and two weeks in October.
Secure parking.

This hotel which looks nothing special from the outside used to be the village police station. It has country style bedrooms costing 160F with shower/wc. A small river runs through the extensive grounds which are fairly wild and there's a play area for children. In a corner of the flower-filled restaurant there's a stove from the Jura Mountains – take your time to enjoy the house *terrines*, meat with ceps and the great veal stew in a white sauce. They do a "working man's" set meal at 55F (weekday lunchtimes) and others from 85F.

SAINT-LÉONARD-DE-NOBLAT 87400

LE GAY-LUSSAC

18 bd Victor-Hugo; it's in the old part of the town, about 30m from Place de la République.
☎ 05.55.56.98.45
Closed Tuesdays except June–Aug.
Free car park 20m away.

Service noon–2pm and 7–10pm (11pm in season). This informal restaurant, which has been tastefully renovated throughout, offers traditional home cooking and dishes that change with the season. The cheapest set meal, consisting of house *terrine* and goose *cassoulet* is 85F. The others are 95F and up but the prices won't break the bank. Dishes available include salad of gizzards, a duo of tournedos and salmon, fish *cassolette* or local beef. A la carte, reckon on paying 150F for a good dinner, including wine. Look out for the 60F *menu du jour* served at weekday lunchtimes – it's excellent value and you'll get a starter, main course, cheese, dessert and a quarter litre of red wine. However it's difficult to get a table as the prices are so reasonable. Staff are attentive and not at all snooty.

CHÂTENET-EN-DOGNON (LE) 87400 (10km N)

10% LE CHALET DU LAC**

Pont-du-Dognon
☎ 05.55.57.10.53 Fax 05.55.57.11.46
Restaurant closed Sunday evenings and in January.
Secure parking.

If you'd like a little treat without breaking the bank, then you've come to the right place. You can practise various water sports here on the lake that this impressive establishment is named for. Bedrooms are comfortable and range in price from 250F to 350F depending on their location – the ones overlooking the lake are more expensive – and although very classical the food's very pleasant. Set meals come in at 95–230F offering dishes like *pavé* of Limousin beef with bone marrow, lobster salad, seafood *choucroute*, and *gâteau creusois* with custard. There's even a health and fitness studio with sauna for those who want to boost their energy.

SAINT-MARTIN-LA-MÉANNE 19320

HÔTEL LES VOYAGEURS**

place de la Mairie
☎ 05.55.29.11.53 F 05.55.29.27.70
Closed Jan 3–31. **Secure parking. TV.**

This village house typical of the region has been turned into a family inn with lots of character and you'll feel quite at home here. Local produce figures largely in the cooking, of course, and the restaurant offers dishes such as warm escalope of *foie gras*, fillet of char and veal escalope with morels. There are four set meals available at prices ranging from 85F to 200F. Our favourite was the one at 100F, where the main course was duck and bilberries. Some of the bedlinen is worn, which detracted slightly from the rooms, but apart from that they're really nice and affordable. Doubles 235–305F depending on the facilities available; half-board 240–280F per person.

SAINT-MERD-DE-LAPLEAU 19320

10% HÔTEL-RESTAURANT FABRY

pont du Chambon; it's 8km from Saint-Merd-De-Lapleau via the CD13.
☎ 05.55.27.88.39 F 05.55.27.83.19
Closed mid-Nov to mid-Dec.

This large establishment on the banks of the Dordogne is heaven on earth for fishermen. There are lots of fish dishes à la carte and in the set meals which start at 78F (weekdays only) and then rise to 100–200F. Try the zander in *beurre blanc* or the pike with sauce *Nantua*. All eight bedrooms are comfortable and rather pretty, and five have a view of the river. Prices are 235–265F although at the height of the season you've no choice but to pay half-board (250F a person). That said, keen walkers like this place for the friendly welcome and magnificent setting. Talking of things to do, you can go out in a "gadare" (a small flat-bottomed boat) or, for a more sombre experience, take a walk to the cave used as a hideout by members of the Resistance until it was raided by the Vichy police.

SAINT-PARDOUX-LA-CROISILLE 19320

HÔTEL-RESTAURANT BEAU SITE***

How to get there: take the D131.
☎ 05.55.27.79.44 F 05.55.27.69.52
Closed Oct 1–April 30. **Car park.**

Service 12.15–1.30pm and 7.30–9pm. Situated in lovely peaceful suroundings – hence the name – this complex has a large garden, fishing pond, swimming pool and tennis courts. There are mountain bikes for hire and you can join in one of the organized trips. The country style cooking is fine but sometimes sounds better than it tastes, so stick to the old faithfuls like *foie gras*, char or zander to avoid disappointment. They do four set meals, starting at 99F (not available Sundays) and rising to 135–230F – a bit expensive. Bedrooms are 250–320F, depending on the standard of comfort and facilities. They're well looked after and the terraced ones have been renovated, but they're a bit lacking in charm. We could criticize the establishment for getting so many groups (especially out of season) but it's got the space and the owners have a living to make. It's a place for people who like sporty holidays coupled with good food and comfortable surroundings. Half-board costs 240–308F per person.

SAINT-YRIEIX-LA-PERCHE 87500

10% HOSTEL DE LA TOUR BLANCHE**

74 bd de l'Hôtel-de-Ville
☎ 05.55.75.18.17 F 05.55.08.23.11
Closed Feb 14–March 14 and Sundays Oct 1–April 15 (except public holidays). **Car park. TV.**

The recently refurbished bedrooms are pleasant enough. – the attic ones are a bit cramped but comfy all the same. Doubles cost 250F with shower/wc and TV. You won't be disappointed by the restaurant! The first of the two dining rooms – classical and bourgeois in style – offers stew of young wild boar with horn of plenty mushrooms (during the hunting season), house Limousine tripe and snails stuffed with *lardons* of goose and set meals at 81F and 102F. The other dining room's more like a snack bar and has terrific posters of New York at night. The style of cooking's simpler but still pleasant and you'll get big helpings. They do great salads in the 30–40F price range. If you want something a bit more substantial you'll pay about 10F more.

RESTAURANT LE PLAN D'EAU

How to get there: it's on the outskirts of town; head for the campsite.
☎ 05.55.75.96.84
Closed Tuesday evenings and Wednesdays out of season and in January. **Car park.**

This is a very nice little restaurant with a view of the Arfeuille lake. Proprietor Jean Maitraud always has time for a chat with his guests and prepares special set meals for important dates like Mother's Day and Father's Day. On less festive occasions he does set meals ranging in price from 50F (weekdays only) to 130F. Traditional cooking. You should also try the bistro – it's a nice place to stop on a hot afternoon.

À LA BONNE CAVE

(Centre); it's near the church.
☎ 05.55.75.02.12 F 55.75.02.12
Closed Sunday evenings and Mondays except in July and August.

This is an old stone building with a pleasant flowered-filled restaurant decorated in pastel shades. The cooking is simple and good, prices are reasonable, and there are a few surprises in store. The service comes with a smile and there you have it – a good restaurant with an atmosphere to match. Set meals 60F (not available Sundays) and 70–128F, with dishes like snail *profiteroles,* veal *tourtière* with ceps, and apple *croustade* with butterscotch sauce. And, of course, they have some good bottles of wine!

COUSSAC-BONNEVAL 87500 (11km E)

10% LES VOYAGEURS**

place de l'Église; take the D901.
☎ 05.55.75.20.24 F 05.55.75.28.90
Closed Sunday evenings, Mondays out of season, and in January. **Car park. TV. Canal+.**

This is a good hotel cum restaurant. It has nine clean comfortable bedrooms at 250F and five of them look onto the garden so you've a good chance of getting a nice view. You'll have a feast trying out the traditional cooking which is based on *foie gras*, veal sweetbreads, ceps and *confits.* Set meals range in price from 70F (weekdays) to 180F. And as a bonus, proprietor Henri Robert (nicknamed Riri), the VIP of the Limousine hotel and restaurant business, knows a lot about the chateau of Coussac and is always delighted to pass on his knowledge.

JANAILHAC 87800 (15km N)

RESTAURANT LA FORGE

le bourg; if you take the route de Limoges you'll find the village of Janailhac set back from the road on the right hand side.
☎ 05.55.00.70.32
Closed Wednesdays.

"Really nice" seems to sum this place up. In what was once a forge – there's an enormous pair of bellows hanging up in the dining room – Nathalie happily serves up grills and specialities prepared by the young cook, Alain, who always comes across in person to check that you're enjoying your meal before returning to the kitchen to keep an eye on things. And it's all very good, from the huge fillets and rib steaks cooked over charcoal and the home-made fruit tarts to the seasonal vegetables and the *faisselle du village*. The 68F *formule* (main dish and dessert) and the 120F set meal are both worth the money. If you get the chance, sample the ham *cul-noir* which "melts in your mouth and smells of hazelnuts" to quote the proprietor – and he's right. Tearoom style food available in the afternoon. This is the kind of place that's a bit remote, but is definitely worth the trip.

SERRE-DE-MESTES (LA) 19200

BAR-RESTAURANT LA CRÉMAILLÈRE

le bourg; take the D982.
☎ 05.55.72.34.74
Closed Mondays, the last week in June and the first week in August. **Car park.**

You have to go through the bar to get to the restaurant – and the first thing you notice is the owner's friendly smile. The dining room's rather dinky with its red-checked tablecloths and panelled walls. Set meals – 60F (weekdays) 80F, 110F, 130F and 150F – are largely based on local produce. The cooking's simple and the portions are large. Apart from the *confits* and *foie gras* we can recommend the meat (Limousin of course). Terrific home-made fruit tart for dessert. All in all, you might not think much of this place from the outside but you'll certainly get your money's worth. Attentive service.

VALIERGUES 19200 (3km S)

LES MOULINS DE VALIERGUES

Betines Betines; take the D982 and then the D125.
☎ 05.55.72.81.31
Closed Mondays out of season, the first two weeks in January, and Sept 8–15. **Car park.**

Philippe went to hotel school in Dijon and has just come back to his native Corrèze after spending several years as a wine waiter beside Lake Geneva. He started up his delightful country restaurant in this beautiful and harsh region with his wife Nadine – and it's been a success. You'll be welcomed in professional fashion – and with a smile – and get the chance to sample some creative cooking. Most of Philippe's ingredients are produced locally or picked by him in the surrounding woods – and since the main ingredients change with the seasons we can't really recommend any one dish. Just choose whatever takes your fancy because it's all good – and don't forget to leave room for the scrumptious desserts! Set meals start at 110F. The stylish dining room's delightful but is dwarfed by the huge mantelpiece. This is one of favourite beauty spots in the Haute-Corrèze – if you're making a visit to the nearby mill, you shouldn't miss it

MARGERIDES 19200 (12km SE)

HÔTEL DU PUY-BLANC

le bourg: take the D979 and the D45.
☎ 05.55.94.80.00
Closed Mondays and for three weeks in October.
Car park.

Time seems to have stopped in this little roadside hotel cum restaurant that's also a bar and grocer's shop – the furniture dates from the '40s, the plates have its name on the back the way they used to, and the *menu du jour*, consisting of three courses, cheese, dessert, wine and coffee costs only 75F. Home cooking with nothing fancy. The hotel is actually more like a family guest house. Rooms are very basic but very well-kept and doubles cost 140F with basin/wc – there's a shower and wc on the landing. Nice welcome.

MEYMAC 19250 (17km W)

CHEZ FRANÇOISE

rue Fontaine-du-Rat (Centre)
☎ 05.55.95.10.63
Closed Sundays out of season.

Service noon–2pm and from 7.30pm. This mouthwatering old grocer's shop is run by Madame Françoise Bleu and has more than one trick up its sleeve. First of all there's the grocery itself where you can buy a whole lot of very tempting regional products, some of which are made on the premises. Then there's the adjoining restaurant, where you can sample Françoise's *mounassous* (grated potatoes) and *farcedures* (*gratin* of Swiss chard). The rustic dining room is very pleasant and offers set meals at 85F (weekday lunchtimes) going up to 150F and more in the evening and on Sundays. Granted, it's a bit on the dear side but the superb cheese platter alone is worth it. The beautiful town of Meymac has good relations with the region of le Bordelais, which is why the wine list is as long as a PhD thesis. The quality's good and there's something to suit every budget. There are three exceptionally comfortable guest rooms upstairs and you'll receive a wonderful welcome. Highly recommended.

SOUTERRAINE (LA) 23300

HÔTEL MODERNE

11 place de la Gare (Centre)
☎ 05.55.63.02.33
Closed Sundays and the second fortnight in August.

This hotel doesn't exactly live up to its name as the standard of comfort is rather basic, but it's fine if you're on a budget. The hotel bar definitely deserves its name because it's easy to make new acquaintances here. The prices are along the same lines – a room will cost you about 110F, half-board's 140F and set meals 55F.

10% JADIS ET GOURMAND

21 rue de Lavaud (Centre)
☎ 05.55.63.80.36
Closed Sunday evenings and Mondays. **Car park.**

If you want to sample cooking based on fresh market produce that's a cross between original ideas and traditional recipes that have been adapted to modern lifestyles, this is the place to come. The cosy dining rooms are done in brown and beige and have porcelain plates and real serviettes. They have good Limousin beef, mouthwatering duck breast served with cherry vinegar, and cheese at the peak of perfection before rounding it all off with one of the special home-made desserts. There's no denying that this is a restaurant worthy of the name Set meals 95–165F. Service until 9.30pm, which is a bit unusual for this region. You'll receive a warm welcome from Philippe, who also has a few cheap and simple rooms available for 120F that would be fine if you were stuck for accommodation.

10% HÔTEL-RESTAURANT JINJAUD

4 route de Limoges (Centre)
☎ 05.55.63.02.53 Fax 05.55.63.02.53.

Service noon–2pm and 7.30–9pm. This is the friendliest little restaurant in the area run by a mother and daughter team. Try the first-rate home cooking based solely on fresh produce – especially the potato pie which has to be ordered the night before and the lovely Limousin meat dishes. Set meals cost 60F on weekdays and 75F. Rooms, ranging in price from 150F to 250F, are very simple but each one is different. Go for the double with shower looking onto the back. We loved this unassuming little place for its warm welcome and freshly prepared dishes.

SAINT-ÉTIENNE-DE-FURSAC 23290 (12km S)

HÔTEL NOUGIER**

How to get there: take the D1 in the direction of Fursac.
☎ 05.55.63.60.56 F 05.55.63.65.47
Closed Sunday evenings, Mondays (except for lunch in season), and Dec 1–March 1. **Secure parking**. **TV**.

This is a very appealing country inn with twelve comfy bedrooms. Doubles with bath at 300F. And there's also a pretty terrace. The elegant dining room serves local dishes updated for modern tastes – things like gizzards *confit* and smoked fillets of goose with sherry vinegar, salad of scallops and pan-fried *langoustine* with *foie gras*, grilled lamb medaillons and kidneys, and *croustillant* of pig's trotters. Set meals 70F (Mon–Sat lunchtimes only), 102F, 155F, 215F. A la carte also available.

TARNAC 19170

10% HÔTEL DES VOYAGEURS

le bourg
☎ 05.55.95.5312 F 05.55.95.40.07
Closed Sunday evenings and Mondays out of season, Dec 20–Jan 10, and one week in February.

This large stone house, kept in wonderful condition by M. and Mme Deschamps, can be found right in the heart of the village beside the church and the two commemorative oak trees. Madame Deschamps, a delightful woman, who can't do enough for you, is in charge of the dining room while her husband puts his culinary skills to very good use in the kitchen. He uses only fresh produce – fish, Limousin beef, mushrooms in season and so on. Set meals cost 85F, 130F and 160F, and à la carte is also available at very reasonable prices. The bedrooms large bright bedrooms upstairs are very pleasant and two people will pay 255F on average. Both the hotel and the restaurant offer excellent value for money.

TULLE 19000

10% HÔTEL DU BON ACCUEIL*

10 rue Canton
☎ 05.55.26.70.57
Closed Saturday evenings (except July–Aug), Sunday evenings, one week during the Feb holidays, one week at Easter and one at Christmas. **TV**.

This is a very good hotel cum restaurant centrally located on the left bank. It's in a quiet little street and definitely suits its name – behind the facade and very old arched windows are several cosy dining rooms serving excellent *confits*, potato pies and cep omelettes in season. Set meals cost 78–160F, and we're sure that the 105F one offering two starters will satisfy even the most demanding palates. The bedrooms, with flowery curtains, are quite large and very well-kept – definitely worth more than their one-star status. Doubles cost 160–180F with shower and/or wc.

10% HÔTEL-RESTAURANT DE LA GARE**

25 av. Winston-Churchill; it's opposite the station
☎ 05.55.20.04.04 F 05.55.20.15.87
Closed one week in February and the first fortnight in September. **Car park**. **TV**.

A very classical hotel housing a restaurant that's been completely refurbished. The locals seem to appreciate the generous portions and set meals at 88F (not available Sundays), 99F and 140F – we recommend the *coq au vin* and the veal sweetbreads with morels. The hotel can be proud of its comfortable and soundproof bedrooms, ranging in price from 180F to 250F if you want a fully-equipped bathroom. Breakfast costs 36F.

LA TOQUE BLANCHE

28 rue Jean-Jaurès - place Martial-Brigouleix (Centre)
☎ 05.55.26.75.41 F 05.55.20.93.95
Closed Sundays, Mondays, two weeks in Jan–Feb and the first week in July. **TV**.

Lunch served noon–2pm and dinner 7–9.30pm. We went to check out the restaurant and came back enthusing about the hotel. That doesn't mean the restaurant wasn't up to scratch – quite the reverse. It's one of the big places in town and always delivers on its promises. The welcome's not as stiff and middle-class as the dining room and customers might lead you to expect and you can eat extremely well. The 135F regional set meal changes each month to reflect what's in season and there's a *menu-carte* at 115F for main course plus dessert or 150F if you also want a starter (although you have to pay a supplement for certain dishes). Generous portions of well-made classical dishes that are very nicely presented – try the *pot-au-feu* of salt cod, medallions of lamb stuffed with basil and the delicious *crème brûlée*. Wine is served by the glass. And on top of that, if you've 170F to spare you can spend the night in one of the spacious rather pretty rooms with bathroom, wc, TV and phone. Breakfast will cost you 30F. All in all, you'll get very good value for money here.

HÔTEL LIMOUZI***

16 quai de la République (Centre)
☎ 05.55.26.42.00 F 05.55.27.30.31
Secure parking. **TV**. **Canal+**.

Don't worry, we're not going to start talking about what a hard life we inspectors have! But if like us you happen to arrive in Tulle in the small hours of the morning without a booking you'll be very glad to discover the *Limouzi*. It means you won't have to spend the night in your car (particularly fortunate if you've come by bike) or have to resort to any of the nearby hotel chains. Although this comparatively modern building on the banks of the Corrèze isn't overendowed with charm, it does have comfy well-equipped rooms on offer with doubles costing 310–345F. The buffet syle breakfast costs 37F – the *pains au chocolat* are great. There are two restaurants – an inexpensive steakhouse, and a more stylish but rather uninspiring establishment with a *menu carte* at 139F.

LE CANTOU

route de Lavergne; take the N89 and it's at the exit for Tulle going towards Ussel – follow the signposts on left.
☎ 05.55.26.67.74
Closed Sundays. **Car park**.

"Cantou" is the local word for an enormous inglenook fireplace and you'll find one in this aptly named restaurant, which is the nicest eating place for travellers in the area. You'll receive a very warm welcome from the owner as he prepares simple dishes – served up in generous portions – on top of the *cantou*'s stove. The cheapest set meal is 55F and includes cheese, dessert and wine, although fancier ones are available at 75F, 95F (with *foie gras* and *confit*) and 125F (with cep omelette in season). There's also an impressive array of *charcuterie* and a handsome cheese board. The dining room's pleasant and there are a few tables in the sun. This has got to be our favourite place in Tulle.

SAINTE-FORTUNADE 19490 (10km S)

LE MOULIN DE LACHAUD.

How to get there: it's not that easy to find even though there are a few arrows. Take the D940 as far as Ste-Fortunade then the D1 in the direction of Cornil; 4km further on, move onto the D94 towards Chastang, Beynat and Aubazin. It's 2km from there.
☎ 05.55.27.30.95
Closed Sunday evenings and Mondays.

Service noon–2pm and 7–9.15pm. We've given you very precise directions because we really took a liking to this old mill out in the country. The owners are a delightful young couple from Burgundy and Madame's smile brings a touch of warmth to the dining room which, despite the large fireplace, is not all that warm. Her husband works wonders in the kitchen, producing inventive dishes that suit all budgets. The cheapest set meal (built round the dish of the day) comes in at 85F and there are three others at 125F, 175F and 230F. He derives his inspiration from local produce and local dishes, which he redefines in his own way, and *émincés* are his speciality. Try the braised veal spareribs with rosemary and whatever you do don't miss out on dessert. And then to work off all that food, how about a nice stroll round the lake (the terrace has a lovely view of this by the way) or you can even try catching some fish for dinner.

LAGARDE-ENVAL 19150 (11km S)

LE CENTRAL**

☎ 05.55.27.16.12 F 05.55.27.31.85
Closed Mondays out of season and in September. **Car park**. **TV**. **Disabled access**.

Service noon–1.30pm and in the evening. This large house, which is swathed in Virginia creeper, has been in the same family for four generations now. It's across from the church and the pretty manorhouse which are rather overshadowed by the more modern buildings. And as there's no point in changing a winning combination, you'll be able to sample the same regional and gourmet dishes as before – cep omelette, *confit* and *farcidur* (vegetable dumplings) – in the same rustic dining room. Set meals cost 70F (not available Sundays), 100F and 150F. Very clean and comfortable bedrooms range in price from 140F to 220F depending on the bathroom facilities. Plenty of leisure facilities available nearby. We like this unassuming establishment a lot and the staff make sure you enjoy your stay – it is after all recommended by your favourite guide book!

GIMEL-LES-CASCADES 19800 (12km NE)

HÔTEL-RESTAURANT MAURIANGES-MONTEIL

It's by the station; take the RN89.

☎ 05.55.21.28.88
Restaurant closed Saturdays and Sundays out of season.

Service noon–1.30pm and 7.30–9pm. Everyone (including us) will tell you that you'll be served like a prince here even if you've got nothing to say for yourself. That's because it's a guest house and everybody gets the same set meal (appetizer, starter, main dish, cheese and dessert). You'll leave feeling satisfied and you won't have broken the bank as the set meal costs only 75F (120F on Sundays). The home cooking, which uses fresh produce and comes in generous portions, seems to be a hit with the workers whom the friendly owner is quite happy to serve. There are a few very inexpensive (110F) basic rooms with basin available in the same building as the restaurant . If you'd rather have something a bit more comfortable, go for one in the annex (135–175F). There's a private lake where hotel guests can take a dip. One for the address book.

L'HOSTELLERIE DE LA VALLÉE**

le bourg
☎ 05.55.21.40.60 F 05.55.21.38.74
Closed Nov 1–March 31. **TV**.

If you're thinking of coming here in summer, you'd best to book ahead because of the crowds that come to see the Gimel waterfalls. The sun-filled dining room overlooking the gorge makes this a delightful place to stop. Classical set meals available from 105F. Doubles are small but pleasant and come with shower or bath (from 240F). The welcome you'll receive depends on how the staff are feeling!

SEILHAC 19700 (15.5 km NW)

HÔTEL-RESTAURANT LA DÉSIRADE

le bourg; take the N120.
☎ 05.55.27.04.17
Closed Monday evenings out of season.

Despite its roadside location, we really liked this unassuming little hotel cum restaurant as much for the warm welcome from the owner as for the wooden dining room floor. Set meals come in at 52–75F, and you won't find any fancy stuff here, just Limousin steak, pizza (why not?) and lovely mixed salads. There's no denying the old-fashioned charm of the bedrooms even if it isn't immediately obvious. Doubles 100–140F depending on facilities. You might not want to spend five weeks of your holiday here, but it's good if you're on a tight budget and looking for decent accommodation.

QUATRE-ROUTES-D'ALBUSSAC 19380 (16km S)

10% HÔTEL ROCHE DE VIC**

How to get there: it's at the junction of the N121 and the D940, 26km from Brive.
☎ 05.55.28.15.87 F 05.55.28.01.09
Closed Mondays out of season and in January and February.
Secure parking. **TV**. **Disabled access**.

Service noon–2pm and 7–9pm. This village with the funny name has two establishments, both at a crossroads. We liked this large stone building that looks like a 50s style manorhouse only marginally better. The bedrooms (most of which face the back), the extensive grounds, the play area and the swimming pool don't seem to suffer too much from the noise of passing traffic. Most have been done up and come in at 160F with basin and 220F with bath. They could've been a bit prettier but they do represent good value for money. The restaurant offers a large choice of regional dishes, even in the set meals which cost 70F (not available Sundays) 85F, 110F, 140F, 150F and 160F. Note that you'll have to take half-board–240F per person – if you come in August. Having said that though, the wooden-floored dining room is very pleasant.

CORREZE 19800 (22km NE)

10% L'AUBERGE DE LA TRADITION

av. de la Gare; take the N120 and the D23, or the N89 and the D26.
☎ 05.55.21.30.26
Closed Sunday and Monday evenings and one week in January.

On May 7 1995, this big village house became famous because Jacques Chirac had lunch here (the chateau of Bity, his holiday home, is just next door). And just to remind those of you who might've forgotten – that very evening he was elected president. The following summer hordes of Chirac devotees arrived here to share a calf's head in memory of the day that proved so historic for the "big man" as he's called by his friends in these parts. The craze is dying out for obvious reasons. However, you can still sample one of the best calf's heads in the region here à la carte if you give at least one night's notice – you'll get the whole thing and you can just about eat as much as you like. If you didn't book, there's always the hearty local cooking to fall back on. Set meals 90–145F. Bedrooms – 180F for two people – are very well looked after and equipped, and you get to them by a beautiful polished staircase. The dining room could be a touch warmer but the owner and the regulars in the bar cum betting shop are so friendly that it doesn't matter.

CHAMBOULIVE 19450 (24km N)

10% ⌂ |●| L'AUBERGE DE LA VÉZÈRE

pont de Vernéjoux (East); take the D26.
☎ 05.55.73.06.94 **Car park.**

This is a charming little country inn on the riverbank where locals come to fish. It would be a good idea to book in high season. There are only seven bedrooms upstairs but they're all in the attic and all perfectly delightful. They come with shower/wc and cost 190F for two people. On the ground floor there's a friendly dimly lit bar with a *cantou* or enormous fireplace as its focal point, and a sunlit dining room decorated with a frieze of ducks which overlooks the river. Talking of duck, it features quite prominently in the 90F and 130F set meals – or there's an extremely good *confit* of pigeon. You'll get a very cheerful welcome from the proprietress, and once you've had your meal you can go for a quiet stroll along the banks of the beautiful Vézère.

LORRAINE

54 Meurthe-et-Moselle

55 Meuse

57 Moselle

88 Vosges

ABRESCHVILLER 57560

LE DONON

57 rue Pierre-Marie (Centre).
☎ 03.87.03.74.90 F 03.87.03.78.64
Closed Tuesdays. **Car park**.

This is a small family hotel, ideal for keen walkers with lots of woods and footpaths in the vicinity. There are six clean, simple rooms at prices ranging from 190F (with basin) to 230F (with bath). TV available on payment of a 20F supplement. The food is uncomplicated, invigorating, and served up in generous portions. The *choucroute* is great. Set meals 90F, 115F and 145F. If, like Madame, you're mad about jigsaws, you'll have a friend for life.

SAINT-QUIRIN 57560 (5KM SW)

L'HOSTELLERIE DU PRIEURÉ

163 rue du Général-de-Gaulle.
☎ 03.87.08.66.52 F 03.87.08.66.49
Closed Wednesdays and in February. **Car park**. **Disabled access**.

The church never had much time for the humbler kind of dwelling, particularly in the 18th century, hence the imposing nature of this red sandstone priory, now a restaurant. The previous occupants would definitely have approved of the cooking and of dishes such as stew of young wild boar, *quenelles de brochet* and grilled duck *foie gras* with Calvados. Prices are reasonable, with set meals 98–240F. The dining room is decorated in salmon pink and the décor generally is fairly plush. One of the area's better restaurants.

TURQUESTEIN-BLANCRUPT 57560 (15KM S)

10% HÔTEL-RESTAURANT LE KIBOKI**

route du Donon.
☎ 03.87.08.60.65 F 03.87.08.65.26
Closed Tuesdays and Wednesday lunchtimes out of season, in February and in November. **Car park**. **TV**. **Disabled access**.

There are places where you suddenly get an irresistible urge to do something crazy and the *Kiboki* is an ideal spot for a weekend – or longer – with your significant other. You'll fall in love with the hotel, the quietness, and the greenery that surrounds you on all sides. Cosy rooms with four-poster beds and country-style décor and furniture start at 400F. The Schmitts will all extend a very warm welcome. Sophisticated cooking, superb dining room. Set meals 100F, 140F and 199F. Half-board 450F. And as if that weren't enough, you can also make use of the grounds and the pool. This has to be our secret, OK?

LUTZELBOURG 57820 (24KM NE)

LES VOSGES**

149 rue Ackermann (Centre).
☎ 03.87.25.30.09 F 03.87.25.42.22
Closed Fridays until 5pm (except in July and August), Jan 15–Feb 3 and Nov 12–30. **Secure parking**. **TV**.

Home to several craftsmen, this is a delightful village in a beautiful part of the world and it would be a pity to pass it by. The long-established family hotel, with its antique furniture and lace bedspreads, has lost none of its charm over the years. Large doubles with basin/wc from 180F, with shower/wc 250F

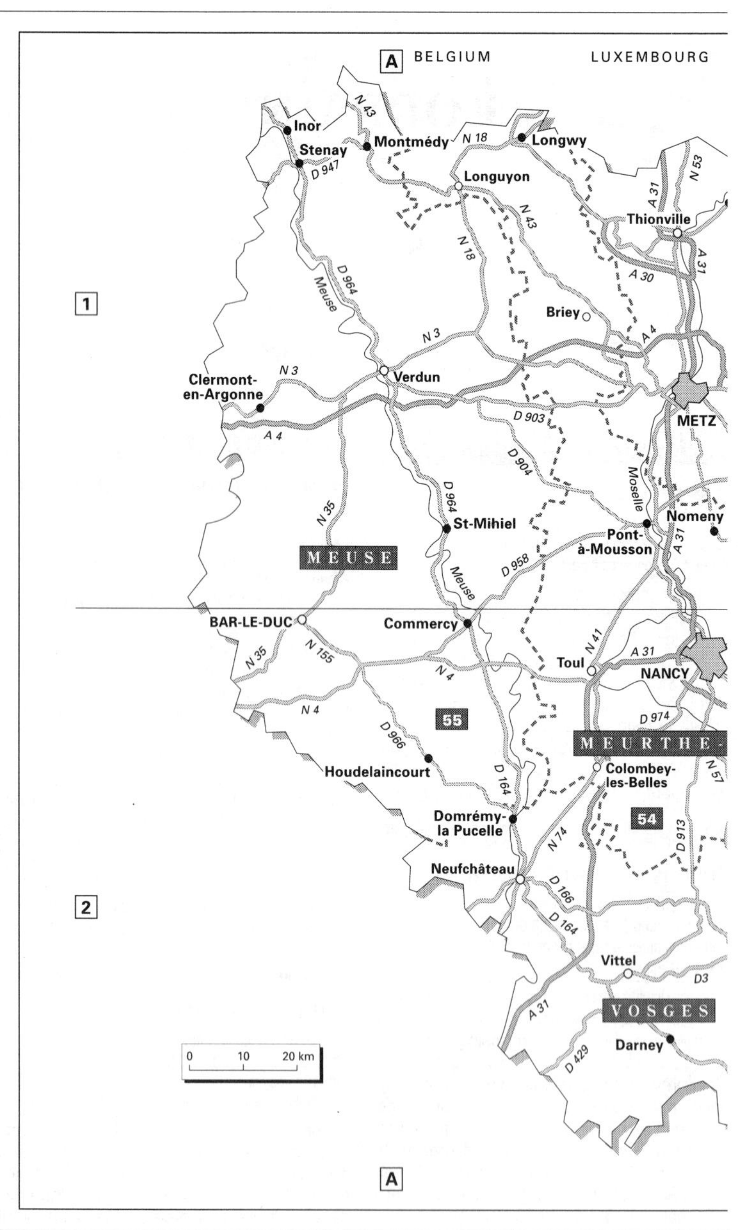
A
BELGIUM
LUXEMBOURG
1
2
Inor
Stenay
D 947
N 43
Montmédy
N 18
Longwy
Longuyon
N 53
A 31
Thionville
N 43
N 18
A 30
Meuse
D 964
Briey
N 3
A 4
Clermont-
en-Argonne
N 3
Verdun
METZ
A 4
D 903
D 904
Moselle
N 35
D 964
St-Mihiel
Nomeny
Pont-
à-Mousson
A 31
MEUSE
Meuse
D 958
BAR-LE-DUC
Commercy
N 155
N 35
N 41
A 31
Toul
NANCY
N 4
N 4
55
D 974
D 966
MEURTHE-
Houdelaincourt
Colombey-
les-Belles
N 57
D 164
54
Domrémy-
la Pucelle
D 913
N 74
Neufchâteau
D 166
D 164
Vittel
D3
A 31
VOSGES
Darney
D 429
0
10
20 km

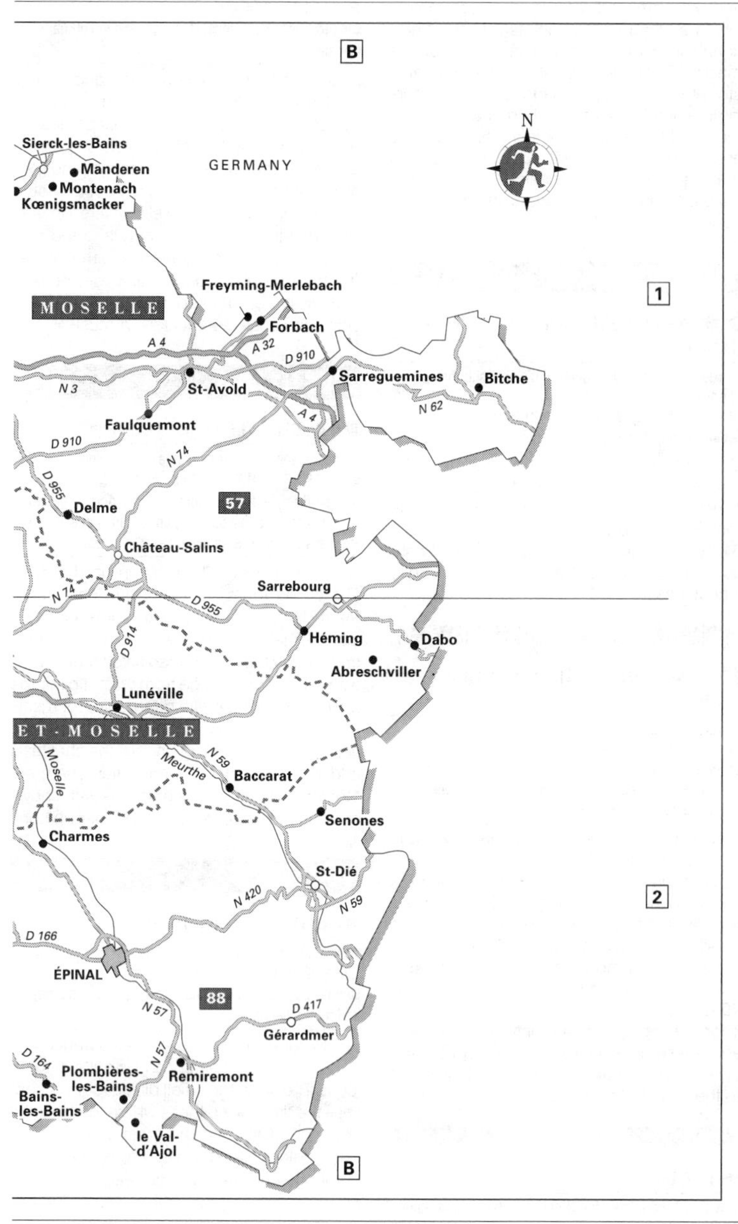
B
N
Sierck-les-Bains
Manderen
Montenach
Kœnigsmacker
GERMANY
MOSELLE
Freyming-Merlebach
Forbach
1
A 4
A 32
D 910
Sarreguemines
Bitche
N 3
St-Avold
N 62
A 4
Faulquemont
D 910
N 74
D 955
57
Delme
Château-Salins
Sarrebourg
N 74
D 955
Héming
Dabo
D 914
Abreschviller
Lunéville
ET-MOSELLE
Moselle
N 59
Meurthe
Baccarat
Senones
Charmes
St-Dié
N 420
N 59
2
D 166
ÉPINAL
88
N 57
D 417
Gérardmer
D 164
N 57
Plombières-
les-Bains
Remiremont
Bains-
les-Bains
le Val-
d'Ajol
B

and with bath 280F. At meal-times, silver cutlery is a fitting accompaniment to the traditional style of cooking. The cheapest set meal is 80F (weekdays only). There's a treat in store for you if you manage to get here during the hunting season, when pheasant with the small yellow plums known as mirabelles and young wild boar with berries appear on the menu. Other set meals 95–190F. Free covered parking for readers of this guidebook.

BACCARAT 54120

HÔTEL-RESTAURANT LA RENAISSANCE**

31 rue des Cristalleries (Centre); it's opposite the glassworks.
☎ 03.83.75.11.31 F 03.83.75.21.09
Closed Friday evenings.

Good place to stay if you want to tour the Baccarat museum and bring back a very expensive souvenir of your trip. Adequate rooms with shower/wc from 260F, with bath 310F. Conventional cooking with no surprises. Prices range from 62F (weekday lunchtimes) to 130F

AZERAILLES 54122 (5KM NW)

10% HÔTEL-RESTAURANT DE LA GARE*

15 rue de la Gare.
☎ 03.83.75.15.17 F 03.83.75.28.67
Closed Sunday evenings, Mondays, mid-Jan to the first week in Feb, the second week in July, and between Christmas and New Year. **Car park**. **TV**.

Lunch served noon–2pm and dinner 7–9pm. Not so long ago, *Chez la Marie* was where you dropped in for a drink and maybe a quick snack. Marie has taken up gardening as well now and the bistro's a restaurant offering good traditional cooking and dishes such as roast rack of lamb flavoured with thyme and terrine of quail with *foie gras*. Set meals 80–180F. The attic has been converted into bedrooms, but there are only seven of them and reservations are essential. Cosy country-style décor and atmosphere. You'll wake up to the sound of birdsong.

BERTRICHAMPS 54120 (5KM E)

L'ÉCURIE

How to get there: take the N59 in the direction of Saint-Dié, and when you get to Bertrichamps turn right (don't cross the rail line).
☎ 03.83.71.43.14.
Closed Sunday evenings, Mondays, and in February.
Car park.

Lunch served 11.45am–2pm and dinner 7.30–9.45pm. After driving along a road that leads nowhere else, you'll be disappointed if you were hoping to find room in this particular stable. You can eat here though, and it's a pleasurable experience. Lovely country-style dining room, with white walls covered in farm implements. The food is tasty and the portions are more than generous with goodies like the house *foie gras*, duck with berries, *croustillant* of smoked ham in honey and cider, and cheese pancakes. A must!

BAINS-LES-BAINS 88240

10% HÔTEL DE LA POSTE**

11 rue de Verdun (Centre); it's next to the spa.
☎ 03.29.36.31.01 F 03.29.30.44.22
Closed Dec 16–Jan 15. From mid-Oct–April 1, the hotel is closed and the restaurant open for lunch only, Mondays and Saturdays excepted. **TV**. **Canal+**.

This is the best establishment in the area. The dining room is elegant and chef Jean-Pierre Lutin comes up with some pleasant dishes that are extremely tasty and quite original. Try the sweetbread salad that comes with a *vinaigrette* made from walnut oil or the *aiguillettes* of duck with *ratatouille*. Set meals range in price from 75F to 166F and change almost daily depending on how the chef feels and what the market has to offer. There are 18 pleasant and well-kept rooms with shower or bath. Full board 251–318F per person.

BAR-LE-DUC 55000

RESTAURANT DE LA TOUR

15 rue du Baile (East).
☎ 03.29.76.14.08
Closed Saturday lunchtimes, Sundays, public holidays and mid-July–mid-Aug.

The building that houses the restaurant dates back to the 16th century and is quite magnificent. The fire in the small dining room is kept lit all the time, since that's where they grill the black puddings and the great *andouillettes*. The cooking, like the setting, is simple but authentic and there are no false pretences. *Formules* at 85F and 120F. A word of warning: dinner is served only until 8pm so you'll have to be prepared to eat early.

BITCHE 57230

10% ☗ |●| HÔTEL-RESTAURANT DE LA GARE

2 av. Trumelet-Faber.
☎ 03.87.96.00.14 F→ same.
Closed Saturdays, Sundays, public holidays and during the Christmas holidays. **Car park.**

Lunch served noon–2pm and dinner 7–8.30pm. This is the only cheap hotel in town. The rooms are fairly rudimentary but very clean and the atmosphere is friendly, so reservations are essential. Doubles with basin from 110F, showers and wc in the corridor. If you're planning on eating here you'd better not be allergic to plants and flowers because the dining room is full of them. Unpretentious country style cooking. Only one set meal (48.50F).

☗ |●| L'AUBERGE DE STRASBOURG**

24 rue Teyssier (Centre).
☎ 03.87.96.00.44 F→ 03.87.06.10.60
Closed Sunday evenings, Mondays and Jan 2–16.
Secure parking. TV

This is a lovely place, with coffered ceilings, country style décor, and naïf paintings on the walls. The cooking's pretty good too – try the *foie gras* with the small yellow plums known as *mirabelles*, the *marbré* of chicken, or the calf's sweetbreads and kidneys with oyster mushrooms. The prices are a bit high but they're justified. Set meals 75F (weekdays), 110F and 165F. In the evening, the brasserie menu is a bit more affordable. They have a few simple pretty and comfortable rooms from 190F (with basin) to 290F (with shower/wc and TV).

|●| L'AUBERGE DE LA TOUR

3 rue de la Gare; close to the citadel built by Vauban.
☎ 03.87.96.29.25
Closed Monday evenings, Tuesdays and in February.
Car park.

The Edwardian décor in this chic restaurant almost makes you feel embarrassed that you're not wearing tails. Hushed atmosphere. The cheapest set meal is 70F (weekday lunchtimes only), rising to 110–240F. There are some interesting combinations, like the medallions of monkfish with apples and cider and roast lamb fillet with peppers. Rather chilly welcome.

CHARMES 88130

☗ |●| HÔTEL-RESTAURANT VAUDOIS**

4 rue des Capucins (Centre).
☎ 03.29.38.02.40 F→ 03.29.38.01.58
Closed Sunday evenings and Mondays. **Car park. TV.**

The name of the town probably gives rise to lots of puns, but this place really is charming. The well-kept and rather elegant rooms range in price from 185F (overlooking the street) to 275F (overlooking the courtyard) with bath. Even the most demanding palate will be satisfied with the cooking, and great care is taken over dishes such as the *turban* of trout, leeks and Pinot Noir and zander with very special mashed potatoes. Set meals available at 98F (weekdays), 102F, 130F, 178F and 268F. Attentive service in the pretty dining room that on Sundays is full of local families.

CLERMONT-EN-ARGONNE 55120

☗ |●| HÔTEL-RESTAURANT BELLEVUE**

Centre.
☎ 03.29.87.41.02 F→ 03.29.88.46.01
Closed Sunday evenings out of season.
Secure parking. TV.

Lunch served noon–3pm and dinner 7–9pm. Don't go by first impressions. The outside may look a bit shabby and the décor in the first dining room isn't in the best of taste but the second dining room, a 1923 Art Deco creation, is a work of art. The cooking is simple and portions are generous. There's game in season, when they serve dishes like *navarin* of wild boar with fricassee of wild mushrooms. Set meals 75–170F. Seven bedrooms, ranging in price from 250F (with shower/wc) to 280F (with bath). Peace and quiet are guaranteed. Even the road doesn't see much traffic.

FUTEAU 55120 (10KM SW)

☗ |●| HÔTEL-RESTAURANT L'ORÉE DU BOI**

How to get there: via the N3; when you get to Islettes, turn right onto the D2 and it's on the left, 500m past Futeau.
☎ 03.29.88.28.41 F→ 03.29.88.24.52
Closed Sunday evenings and Tuesdays (out of season), in January, and during the autumn school holidays.
Car park. TV. Disabled access.

As you might have guessed from the name, there's a wood not very far away. This large establishment in the depths of the countryside is a haven of peace and quiet and you'll sleep well. The seven bedrooms (355–390F) are large, quiet, well-equipped and decorated with lovely fabrics and lots of flowers. It has a reputation locally for being a good restaurant too. Set meals are 120F (weekdays), 165F, 230F et 270F – not exactly rock-bottom prices but they're justified. Try the roast pig's ear and stuffed trotters or the local pigeon with coriander. Madame's two passions in life are cheese and wine so you'll find it impossible to say no to either. The cheese is superb and there are some pleasant surprises on the wine list. Friendly and enthusiastic staff. Not surprisingly, we fell in love with this lovely bit of Argonne.

COMMERCY 55200

HÔTEL DE PARIS**

9 place de la Gare (Centre).
☎ 03.29.91.01.36 ➡ 03.29.92.01.17
Closed Christmas–New Year's Day. **Car park. TV.**

Good value for money, our only quibbles being that the mattress was not super comfortable and there were a few too many trains for a really good night's sleep. Doubles from 185F with basin/wc, 205F with bath. Cheapest set meal 55F.

CONTREXÉVILLE 88140

10% HÔTEL LA LORRAINE*

122 av. du Roi-Stanislas (Centre); it's near the train station.
☎ 03.29.08.04.24
Closed mid-Oct–late March. **Car park.**

Don't worry about losing your beauty sleep, the trains don't run at night. This is a big pleasant old place that feels like the kind of guest house you thought you'd never see again except in a Chabrol film or a Maigret story. Wonderful welcome. The cooking is traditional and special diets can be catered for. Set meals start at 60F, rising to 75F, 95F, 110F (this one features Lorraine specialities), and 135F. Doubles 140–170F with basin/wc, 200F with shower/wc. Half-board 200–290F. Full board 500F for two.

10% HÔTEL-RESTAURANT DU PARC**

334 rue du Shah de Perse (Centre).
☎ 03.29.08.52.41 ➡ 03.29.08.54.75
Closed Sunday evenings and Mondays (out of season).
TV. Canal+.

Two young couples in their mid twenties decided to give this old establishment a new lease of life. Nothing outstanding on first appearances. The dining room still looks pretty traditional. But the set meal at 75F (weekday lunchtimes) gives you a good idea of the fresh, creative dishes on offer in all the other set meals at 95F, 130F, 160F and 255F: fillet steak of tuna with a Champagne sauce, breast of duck with spices, *minute* of trout with a creamy citrus fruit sauce.. As for the hotel, the rooms are pretty modest and have all been renovated bit by bit. Doubles with basin/wc 150F, with shower/wc 250F (not all of them have a TV), with bath 300F. Half-board 250–400F per person and per day.

10% HÔTEL DES SOURCES**

rue Ziwer-Pacha.
☎ 03.29.08.04.48 ➡ 03.29.08.63.01
Closed Oct–April. **Disabled access.**

An elegant building, very close to the lovely esplanade with its coloured fountains. Madame is very nice and the rooms are comfortable and have been decorated with care. There are a few attic rooms with basin for 145F, and doubles with shower are 255F, with bath 285F. The restaurant's not bad at all, with set meals from 100F. A good place to recharge your batteries.

HÔTEL DE LA SOUVERAINE***

parc thermal (Centre).
☎ 03.29.08.09.59 ➡ 03.29.08.16.39
Car park. TV.

Lovely 3-star hotel surrounded by trees. It's very cosy though the atmosphere's on the starchy side. Still, it makes a nice change to stay somewhere a bit fancy. And the passage of time doesn't seem to have any effect on anything. Comfortable rooms with basin/wc 280F, with shower/wc 321F, with bath 338F.

DABO 57850

RESTAURANT AUX CHASSEURS

2 place de l'Église.
☎ 03.87.07.48.42
Closed Wednesdays (except in July and August).
Car park. Disabled access.

The restaurant is centrally located and you'll find shops nearby selling good quality and original local produce and handicrafts. There's also a crystal showroom and a brandy museum where you can sample the goods. You may find people a bit stand-offish at first but they'll soon loosen up – it just takes a bit of time (and money!). Set meals are quite good and inexpensive (45–120F) and portions are generous. Excellent value for money. Specialities are flambéd tarts and game (in season). Not wholly typical of Moselle but not of Alsace either – somewhere between the two.

|●| RESTAURANT ZOLLSTOCK

11 route Zollstock, La Hoube; it's 6km from Dabo-village on the D45.
☎ 03.87.08.80.65 F➜ 03.87.08.86.41
Closed Mondays and during the Christmas/New Year holidays.

Lunch served noon–2.30pm and dinner 7–9.30pm. The restaurant stands in the middle of a wonderful pine forest and, since it doesn't get much by way of passing trade, most of the customers are regulars. We really liked it. Set meals (55–115F) offer simple but tasty specialities including some terrific venison in season. It's small, extremely pleasant and has a warm family atmosphere.

DARNEY 88260

10% ⌂ |●| HÔTEL-RESTAURANT DE LA GARE

How to get there: it's in the general area of the station, 1.5km from the centre, going towards Bains-les-Bains.
☎ 03.29.09.41.43
Car park.

Lovely little hotel miles from anywhere (the nearby station's been closed down) on the road through the forest of Darney. You can be sure of peace and quiet in what is a very pleasant little corner of rural France. Clean, simple and comfortable rooms with shower/wc cost 180F. Set meals are available at 68F and 94F. The cooking is traditional with things like *pieds-paquets* (sheep's tripe and trotters), *confit* of pig liver, stuffed mutton tripe, and melted Munster cheese with potato salad; and the helpings are generous. It won't do much for the diet but gosh it's good!

DELME 57590

⌂ |●| HÔTEL-RESTAURANT À LA XIIE BORNE*

6 place de la République (Centre).
☎ 03.87.01.30.18 F➜ 03.87.01.38.39
Secure parking. **TV**.

Lunch served till 2pm and dinner till 9.45pm. The Romans called Delme Adduodecimum and it was the first stop on the road between Metz and Strasbourg. There was an encampment at the 12th *borne* (what we would call a milestone) which later became the site of the village. If you're interested in that kind of thing, the distance between *bornes* was the equivalent of one Gaulish league or 2,222m and if you do your sums you'll see that Delme is 27km from Metz. We like to think that the encampment lives on in this hotel. It has clean and simple rooms from 152F (with basin) to 204F (with shower). Good cooking, popular with the locals. Set meals 56F (weekdays only), 92F, 152F and 234F. If you like calf's head then you'll love the way they do it here with two sauces. The welcome is unpretentious and friendly, just like the place.

DOMRÉMY-LA-PUCELLE 88630

⌂ HÔTEL JEANNE D'ARC

1 rue Principale (Centre).
☎ 03.29.06.96.06
Closed mid-Nov–late March. **Secure parking**.

A simple little hotel in a simple little village where life seems to revolve around the local saint. Rooms (160F) are clean and quiet. Pleasant staff.

AUTREVILLE 88300 (14KM NE)

10% ⌂ |●| HÔTEL RELAIS ROSE**

24 rue de Neufchâteau (East); take the N74.
☎ 03.83.52.04.98 F➜ 03.83.52.06.03
Secure parking. **TV**. **Canal+**. **Disabled access**.

This is a really lovely spot and you might well be tempted to spend a couple of nights here – if you like the back of beyond, that is. Eighteen pleasant and reasonably priced rooms with rustic furniture, beams and canopied beds. Doubles with basin 160F, rising to 250–400F, depending on facilities. Set meals come in at 100F, 130F and 165F. You'll find lots of specialities from the south-west on the menu, which is only to be expected, since Madame comes from Ariège. Also available, depending on the season and how Madame feels, are *tourte aux grenouilles*, snails and scallops in flaky pastry, and pheasant with red cabbage. The dining room is magnificient. Good wine list.

ÉPINAL 88000

⌂ HÔTEL DU COMMERCE*

13 place des Vosges (Centre).
☎ 03.29.34.21.65 F➜ 03.29.31.07.46
Secure parking. **TV**.

This is a very simple hotel in the town's lively main square. There's a café on the ground floor with a large terrace for when the sun shines. Clean and on the whole pleasant, unless you're looking for absolute peace and quiet. Doubles 120F with basin, 190F with shower or bath.

AZUR HÔTEL**

54 quai des Bons-Enfants (Centre).
☎ 03.29.64.05.25 F 03.29.64.00.40
TV. **Canal+**.

The hotel is located in a shopping area and has a view of the millrace that once brought water to the large mills here and is now used for canoeing and kayaking. You'll get a very friendly welcome. All rooms have a phone. Doubles with basin (shower and wc in the corridor) from 140F, with shower/wc 215F, with bath 260F. There's no restaurant.

ARIANE HÔTEL**

12 av. du Général-de-Gaulle; it's opposite the train station.
☎ 03.29.82.10.74 F 03.29.35.35.14
Closed Dec 22–Jan 2. **Secure parking**. **TV**. **Canal+**.

A delightful hotel in the way that hotels in the provinces so often are. We liked it a lot. It's clean, renovated throughout, and totally soundproof (just as well, given how noisy the area is). Doubles 290F with shower/wc, 315F with bath, Nice welcome. Free parking if you can show them this guidebook.

RESTAURANT LES FINES HERBES

15 rue La Maix (Centre); it's near place des Vosges.
☎ 03.29.31.46.70
Closed Sunday evenings and Mondays.

Jean-Louis and Cathie spent nine years in Africa before settling here. The cooking is quite refined and the service attentive. Modern, streamlined décor. Friendly welcome and an intimate atmosphere that's ideal for lovers. Prices are reasonable, with set meals at 68F (weekdays only), 95F and 145F that change every month. Specializes in fish.

RESTAURANT LE PINAUDRÉ

10 av. du Général-de-Gaulle (West); it's opposite the train station.
☎ 03.29.82.45.29
Closed Saturday lunchtimes and Sundays.

It would be quite easy – and a great pity – to walk right past this restaurant. Our friends in Épinal come here quite a lot for the good traditional cooking with a few modern touches. There are set meals at 70F (weekdays only), 88F, 98F, 110F and 150F and they're all fairly substantial. We particularly liked the scallops in vermouth and the pike in vin gris (which is a bit like rosé). The décor's a touch old-fashioned.

RESTAURANT LA TOUPINE

18 rue du Gal-Leclerc (Centre).
%03.29.34.60.11
Closed Sundays.

As the attempt to set up a Lyonnais café in this town was rather short-lived this place has now been transformed into a traditional restaurant. Tiny little dining room (bordering on the cramped) with paintings by local artists on the walls. Charming welcome and service. Good menu with dishes from 65F (if you're happy with one course)– 115F (if you go for starter, main course and dessert). Oysters and seafood in season. Wine list with lots of Bordeaux (also served by the glass).

CHAUMOUSEY 88390 (10KM W)

LE CALMOSIEN

37 rue d'Épinal; take the N460 in the direction of Darney.
☎ 03.29.66.80.77
Closed Sunday evenings.

This is a beautiful building and its elegant décor and dark colours make it look like the inside of a jewel box. It offers classic cooking of the kind that pleases the eye as well as the palate. The set meals, ranging in price from 115F to 215F reflect the changing seasons and what's available at the market. The pan-fried *foie gras* is a must, while the panfried turbot with mussels, green asparagus, orange zest and *sauce maltaise* and the veal steak with tea and star anise both offer an intriguing combination of flavours. They also have a fantastic *menu dégustation* at 290F and a great wine list with a few pleasant surprises. Since it has such an excellent reputation locally, it's best to book.

FAULQUEMONT 57380

HÔTEL CHÂTELAIN**

place Monroë (Centre).
☎ 03.87.90.70.80 F 03.87.90.74.78
Car park. **TV**. **Disabled access**.

It looks less than appealing from the outside but inside you'll find 25 comfortable rooms, 250F with shower/wc, laid out round a wonderful flower-filled conservatory. Everything about it is new and it does lack that lived-in feeling, but we liked the owner's enthusiasm.

FORBACH 57600

HÔTEL LE PIGEON BLANC

42 rue Nationale.
☎ 03.87.85.23.05
Closed Sundays. **Car park**.

For some inexplicable reason, there's no mention of this hotel anywhere, not even in the listings put out by the tourist office. And yet it's rather good, particularly the annexe. Doubles with basin 90F, with shower/wc 160F. The latter are very big and quiet. The only drawback is that you have to be out of your room by 10am. No restaurant.

10% HÔTEL DE LA POSTE**

57 rue Nationale (Centre).
☎ 03.87.85.08.80 Fax 03.87.85.91.91
Secure parking. **TV**. **Canal+**.

This is the oldest hotel in Forbach and has been putting people up for nearly a century. Rooms have been fully renovated and are decorated in blue, yellow or pink depending which floor they're on. Doubles with shower/wc or bath 250F. It's set back from the street so you'll get a good night's sleep whichever side you're on. Staff are friendly and unobtrusive.

OETING 57600 (2KM S)

RESTAURANT À L'ÉTANG

386 rue de Forbach.
☎ 03.87.87.33.85.
Closed Tuesday evenings, Wednesdays, and mid-July–early Aug. **Car park**.

Lunch served noon–2pm and dinner 7–10pm. The restaurant is in a big, rather pleasant house with country-style décor and a little pond out front. Good food. The cheapest set meal (60F) is a bit uninspiring but the others, starting at 95F and going up to 210F (tthat's the gastronomic one) offer quite incredible dishes like carp fillet with sorrel, *presskopf à l'ancienne* (brawn with shallots and gherkins in a Riesling flavoured aspic), frog's legs in Riesling and *pot-au-feu* of fish with horseradish sauce.

FREYMING-MERLEBACH 57800

HÔTEL-RESTAURANT AU CAVEAU DE LA BIÈRE

2 rue du 5-Décembre.
☎ 03.87.81.33.45 Fax 03.87.04.95.95
Closed Saturdays and Sunday evenings. **Car park**.

This used to be the industrial heartland of the Moselle but the blast furnaces have gone and things have changed. A few regulars sip their beer at a bar laden with hard-boiled eggs and packets of pretzels. This is your typical businessmen's hotel and generations of them have spent the night here. Rooms are clean and functional – 150F with basin/wc, 180F with shower and 250F with bath. Simple traditional cooking offers dishes like quiche lorraine and *choucroute* (Alsace is just down the road) and tripe in Riesling. Wash it all down with a glass of Amos, one of the last beers still being brewed in the region. Set meals 58–190F.

GÉRARDMER 88400

HÔTEL GÉRARD D'ALSACE**

14 rue du 152e- R.I.; it's 150m from the lake.
☎ 03.29.63.02.38 Fax:03.29.60.85.21
Closed Nov–mid-Dec. **Secure parking**. **TV**.

Large house in the traditional Vosges style that's been redecorated throughout. Rooms are clean and simple, with doubles 170–235F. Nice young proprietor.

10% HÔTEL DE PARIS**

3 rue de la Gare (Centre).
☎ 03.29.63.10.66 Fax 03.29.63.16.47
Closed the second fortnight in Oct. **TV**. **Canal+**.

A very simple little hotel with reasonable prices located in the town's busiest street. Rooms have recently been redecorated. Doubles from 170F with basin to 230F with shower/wc. Brasserie on the ground floor. The hotel's often full at the weekend so make sure of your room by sending a deposit.

10% RESTAURANT L'AUBERGADE - HÔTEL VIRY***

place des Déportés; it's 200m from the lake and the centre of town.
☎ 03.29.63.02.41 Fax 03.29.63.14.03
Restaurant closed Fridays. **Car park**. **TV**.

This is one of the best known hotels in Gérardmer and it's often full despite being a bit expensive (320F for a room with a shower). The restaurant on the other hand is really good and quite reasonable, not to say cheap, given the quality of the cooking. There are some very good specialities like a small ham in Riesling, *coq à la double crème* and *choucroute* (Alsace isn't all that far away). Day's special 46F. The 78F set meal offers nothing exceptional but there are lots of goodies à la carte – raw mountain ham (52F), fried lake fish (65F), trout (66F) and so on. There's a covered terrace which is very pleasant in summer. Courteous staff.

LES RIVES DU LAC

Centre; it's by the lake, near the landing stages.
☎ 03.29.63.04.29
Closed Oct 31–Feb 1.

Being on the shores of the most famous lake in the Vosges, the restaurant, as you might suspect, is full of tourists. Not only is the food good, simple though the cooking may be, but the prices are extremely reasonable, despite the location and the dream of a terrace. Cheapest set meal is 75F. The service is slow but you come here to relax. Do the tourist thing and try the great *fumé vosgien* (pork butt with potatoes and *fromage frais*).

HÔTEL-RESTAURANT CHÂLET DU LAC**

97 chem. de la droite du lac (West); it's beside the lake, 1km from the town centre on the D147 in the direction of Épinal.
☎ 03.29.63.38.76 F 03.29.60.91.63
Closed Fridays (out of season and outside school holidays) and in October. **Car park. TV.**

Gérardmer might claim to be the modern capital of fantasy films, but this place is more like common-or-garden "Monsieur Hulot's holiday in the Vosges". Cute wooden chalet overlooking the lake and the road (but at least the road is not too close). Friendly welcome. Even though the rooms have been renovated they've kept a certain special something about them (antique furniture) and they've all got a really nice retro feel to them. All the rooms have bath or shower, a balcony overlooking the lake, and they're all the same price: 300F for a double. There's an annexe in another chalet a few metres away on the edge of the forest. As for the restaurant, the food is traditional with regional influences. 6 set meals 90–130F. Lovely garden.

LE BISTROT DE LA PERLE

32 rue Charles-de-Gaulle(Centre).
☎ 03.29.60.86.24
Closed Wednesdays out of season.

This place used to be a butcher's shop and its pretty façade has remained untouched. It has *charcuterie*, tripe, salt pork with lentils, *andouillette* and, à la carte, mussels with chips and seafood from the Belle Marée, the good local seafood restaurant that this place is an annexe of. Light pleasant dining room, friendly service, no-fuss food. The 85F *formule* (main course plus dessert and either a glass of wine, a beer or a half bottle of mineral water) changes nearly every day. Expect to pay at least 100F à la carte.

THOLY (LE) 88530 (11KM W)

10% L'AUBERGE AU PIED DE LA CASCADE*

How to get there: take the D11 as far as Tholy and carry on for another 5km until you get to the Tendon waterfall.
☎ 03.29.33.21.18 F 03.29.33.29.42
Closed Wednesdays (except during school holidays) and Nov 11–Christmas. **Car park. TV. Disabled access.**

People who know the area wouldn't dream of staying anywhere else. Picture a typical old Vosges inn (recently renovated) in the depths of the country close to a forest and the famous Tendon falls. But its attractions extend beyond the setting, the terrace and the lovely hundred-year old dining room, because for years it's been serving the best trout in the area, caught fresh every day in the nearby pool. That's all the regulars – and there are lots of them – come for. The quiet hotel is tiny so it's often full. It's really cheap but something needs to be done about the meals that come with half-board. Doubles 150–310F, cheapest set meal 100F.

BRESSE (LA) 88250 (13KM SE)

10% HÔTEL-RESTAURANT LE CHEVREUIL BLANC**

3 rue Paul Claudel (North-West); it's as you leave the resort in the direction of Gérardmer.
☎ 03.29.25.41.08 F 03.29.25.65.34
Restaurant closed Sunday evenings (outside school holidays). **TV.**

This is a totally new place for Bresse. Granted it certainly doesn't look much from the outside, but once you're inside and the lovely Maria Pia greets you with a friendly smile, you'll be hooked. And that's before you try the food! It's sophisticated without being pretentious and, though there are lots of local dishes (the Val d'Anjou *andouillette* is an absolute must), the chef does other things too. He likes cooking fish, for example, and offers *rillettes* of salmon, fish stew and so on. Set meals 79F (except Saturday evenings and Sunday lunchtimes), then 88F, 98F, 135F, 180F and 198F. The hotel is very small with only nine classic rooms, all with shower or bath, wc and telephone: 270F for doubles (250F on the second floor). Half-board from 245F per day per person (special rates for children). If you're wondering about the photos of Gene Vincent and Buddy Holly, the owner is a fan of 50s rock'n'roll.

VALTIN (LE) 88230 (13KM NE)

AUBERGE DU VAL JOLI**

12 bis le Village (Centre); take the Gérardmer exit in the direction of Saint Dié and then turn right and head for Colmar; when you get to Xonrupt, turn left and take the little mountain road towards Le Valtin.
☎ 03.29.60.91.37 Fax:03.29.60.81.73
Closed Sunday evenings, Mondays out of season, and Nov 15–Dec 15. **Car park**. **TV**.

This is one of our best finds, located in one of the prettiest villages in the area. You'll soon unwind in the peace and quiet and there are some wonderful walks to be had in the pine-covered mountains all around. The real old-fashioned kind of inn with a tiled floor, heavy beams, and a tiled stove. And the atmosphere is still warm and friendly even though they now have a second, very modern dining room with enormous windows in addition to the delightfully rustic one on the first floor with the wonderful ceiling. The original very simple rooms are still there, but there are also four new ones (numbers 17–20), modern, smart and with balconies that look out onto the mountains. Doubles 100F with basin, 270F with shower/wc, 380F with bath (these are the new ones). Half-board, which is compulsory during the school holidays, costs 348–610F for two. Good cooking and traditional local dishes, as you can tell from the names given to the set meals at 60F (available at lunchtime and in the evening except Sundays), 70F, 97F and 120F. There's *pâté lorrain* (a sort of pie with a filling of pork mince), trout *au bleu* with a butter sauce, smoked trout with a sorrel sauce, *blanc de sautret* (chicken in a cream and Riesling sauce), *choucroute garnie*, Munster (a fairly strong cheese), and bilberry tart. On Sundays, set meals cost 120F, 145F, 185F and 230F.

XONRUPT-LONGEMER 88400 (15KM NE)

10% HÔTEL LE COLLET-RESTAURANT LAPÔTRE***

How to get there: on the D417, after Xonrupt, in the direction of col de la Schlucht Munster.
☎ 03.29.60.09.57 F 03.29.60.08.77
Restaurant closed Wednesdays (outside school holidays) and mid Nov–mid Dec. **Car park**. **TV**.

This is a big traditional chalet at an altitude of 1,100m on the way up to the col of the Schlucht. Great location right in the heart of the Vosges mountain nature reserve near the cross-country ski trails and the ski lifts, and just a few kilometres from the Route des Crêtes. Lots of local colour in the pretty bedrooms. Doubles with shower/wc or bath start at 390F (290F outside school holidays). The nicest one have a balcony with a view of the forest. There's a luxurious feel to the place but it's not showy – like the welcome you'll get, it's simple yet special. Generous buffet breakfast for 50F. Very good regional cuisine revamped by a young chef bursting with ideas and enthusiasm. Try the leg of duck *confit* with a light *choucroute* or the pork fillet coated with spices and served with potato *galettes*. And we hope the kind of prices they charge catch on. The 68F *formule* (weekday lunchtimes) offers cottage pie (they use *andouillette* though, and not mince!) plus a glass of wine or beer. If you go for the 88F lunchtime set meal, you'll get *bibelaskas* (fresh cheese flavoured with horseradish and herbs), *lewerknepfla* (*quenelles* of liver), and poached trout. Other set meals 118–158F. The wine list features a lot of wines from the Alsace region (with a few little gems) but other regions aren't forgotten.

HÉMING 57830

10% L'AUBERGE ALSACIENNE**

17 rue de Strasbourg.
☎ 03.87.25.00.10 F 03.87.25.95.27
Closed Saturdays and mid-Dec–mid Jan. **Car park**. **TV**. **Disabled access**.

If you've never eaten good *choucroute* and happen to find yourself in the neighbourhood then a visit to this establishment is a must. The 95F Alsace set meal – *choucroute royale* with ham and two types of sausage (*viennoise* and *lorraine*) followed by Munster cheese with Mirabelle liqueur – will have you drooling at the mouth. If you're addicted and want to make sure your next fix isn't too far away, they have comfortable rooms at prices ranging from 200F (with basin, no TV) to 260F (with bath).

HOUDELAINCOURT 55130

10% L'AUBERGE DU PÈRE LOUIS**.

☎ 03.29.89.64.14 F 03.29.89.78.84
Closed Sunday evenings, Mondays and during the February school holidays. **Car park**.

Service till 2pm and 9pm. For people who like good food, this is one of THE places to stop at in Meuse. The cooking is innovative and full of flavour, with dishes like plaice in a red wine and butter sauce, oven-baked ceps, and *ragoût* of calf's feet. As if that wasn't enough to make your mouth water, they also do an *escalope* of calf sweetbreads and Meuse truffles. Set meals 7–250F. If (understandably) you don't want to leave, they have seven quiet and pleasant rooms with shower/wc at 190F.

INOR 55700

HÔTEL-RESTAURANT LE FAISAN DORÉ**

☎ 03.29.80.35.45 F 03.29.80.37.92
Closed Friday lunchtime from Oct 1–Mar 1. **Car park**. **TV**.

This is one of those places that are very popular with hunters during the hunting season. In other words, they do you a very good meal, with dishes like omelette ardennaise, fillet of beef with ceps and, of course, game. Set meals 68–180F. The hotel is very decent and has doubles with bath from 200F. Peace and quiet guaranteed.

KOENIGSMACKER 57110

HÔTEL-RESTAURANT LA LORRAINE**

1 rue de l'Église.
☎ 03.82.55.01.44 F 03.82.50.19.84
Closed Sunday evenings in autumn and winter and the first fortnight in January. **Car park**. **TV**. **Canal+**.

Big middle-class establishment in a little town on the fringes of la Lorraine. You can picture all the local worthies sitting down to a traditional Sunday lunch with their families here. Good cooking. The two cheapest set meals, the *menu du jour* at 60F and the *menu lorrain* at 85F are reasonably priced, but the others are considerably more expensive (135–190F), which is a pity. Rooms 235F with shower/wc, 280F with bath.

GAVISSE 57570 (5KM NE)

RESTAURANT LE MEGACÉROS

19 place Jeanne-d'Arc (Centre).
☎ 03.82.55.45.87 F 03.82.55.42.24
Closed Sunday evenings, Mondays, and Christmas to New Year's Day. **Car park**. **Disabled access**.

Called after an extinct ancestor of the deer it may be but there's nothing prehistoric or fossilized about this restaurant. Quite the reverse in fact, it's very innovative in its subtle combination of ingredients and comes up with dishes like *foie gras* with cardamom, fricassee of frogs and black pasta with garlic butter, and kebabs of oysters (the chicken meat, not the mollusc) with vegetable ribbons that are unusual and maybe even a bit bizarre at times. Set meals 86F, 150F and 200F. Madame Seiler is a considerate hostess. We were rather underwhelmed by the décor but at least that left us free to concentrate on the food.

RODEMACK 57570 (8KM NW)

RESTAURANT LA MAISON DES BAILLIS

46 place des Baillis.
☎ 03.82.51.24.25 F 03.82.51.24.62
Closed lunchtime Monday to Friday Jan 15–early April, Mondays and Tuesdays the rest of the year, plus during the February school holidays, Nov 1, and Dec 24–Jan 15. **Car park**.

The first lords of Rodemack settled in this village in the 12th century. Three hundred or so years later, the Austrians confiscated the estate without so much as a by your leave. The building that houses the restaurant was built in the 16th century but the new occupants were bored to tears so far away from the Viennese court and soon packed their bags, leaving a bailiff in charge of their property. The village still has a mediaeval look as does the restaurant, which really is a magnificent historic building. Good food. Set meals 90–150F.

LONGWY 54400

HÔTEL DU NORD**

place Darche.
☎ 03.82.23.40.81 F 03.82.23.17.73
Car parking. **TV**. **Canal+**.

Most towns in France have a bar cum hotel like this. This one possibly stands out because of its location in lovely Place d'Armes right in the heart of the upper town. The rooms, 280F with bath, are modern (and not always to our taste), clean and quiet. The town's been in the doldrums for a while but people still smile.

COSNES ET ROMAIN 54400 (5KM W)

LE TRAIN BLEU.

How to get there: from Longwy-Haut, take the N18 in

the direction of Longuyon and after 4km turn right towards Cosnes-et-Romain.
☎ 03.82.23.98.09
Closed Mondays and Saturday lunchtimes.

The restaurant is made up of two railway carriages. The décor's rather plush and the atmosphere hallowed. It's very popular at weekends which is not surprising, given the quality of the cooking in dishes such as casserole of calf sweetbreads and chanterelles and sole fillets with a smoked salmon stuffing. There's something here for everybody and every budget. Set meals range in price from 78F (lunchtimes, except Sunday) to 230F.

AUBERGE DES TROIS CANARDS.

☎ 03.82.24.35.36. Fax 03.82.25.66.40.
Closed Mondays, Sunday evenings, Aug 20–Sept 10, and during the February school holidays. **Car park**.

Service from noon and 7.30pm. The Virginia creeper that smothers the house has covered up the sign (and brought down the walls too for all we know), so you'll have to keep an eye open or you'll go right past. The country-like atmosphere extends to the kitchen, which turns out dishes like calf's head *à l'ancienne*, leg of duck *Henri IV*, and quails with mirabelle plums for the set meals at 88F (lunchtimes) 115F, 136F and 208F. And you won't leave the table hungry.

LUNÉVILLE 54300

HÔTEL DES PAGES***

5 quai des Petits-Bosquets; it's opposite the château, on the other side of the river.
☎ 03.83.74.11.42 Fax 03.83.73.46.63
Secure parking. **TV**.

Hotels don't come any quieter than this one, which is set back from a road that doesn't see much traffic at the best of times. It's modern and comfortable. No great surprises but then it's not expensive. Doubles with bath 250F. You can have dinner next door at *Au Petit Comptoir*, which serves good wholesome cooking. Set meal 98F (except weekends and public holidays). A la carte is a bit expensive in the evenings.

RESTAURANT LE TROGLODYTE**

35 rue des Bosquets.
☎ 03.83.73.06.01 Fax 03.83.73.80.20.
Closed Mondays, Saturday lunchtimes, and Aug 1–15.

The décor is meant to be prehistoric and comes complete with wall paintings. Apparently the customers like it. The cooking centres on *pierrades* (where you cook the ingredients yourself on a hot stone), fondues and slightly fancier dishes like calf sweetbreads with asparagus and medallions of ostrich meat. Set meals 68F (lunchtimes) and 98F.

MARIE LESZCZYNSKA

30 rue de Lorraine (Centre); it's behind the château.
☎ 03.83.73.11.85
Closed Sunday evenings and Mondays.

The wife of King Louis XV, after whom the restaurant is named, couldn't possibly have eaten here but she would definitely have approved of the excellent cooking and dishes like scallops in vermouth, lamb *tournedos* with garlic, and snails in puff pastry with lardons and vin gris (a wine similar to rosé). The little orange and green dining room is a bit chilly but the warmth of the welcome makes up for it. There's a pleasant terrace in a pedestrianized street for when the sun shines.

MANDEREN 57480

LE RELAIS DU CHÂTEAU MENSBERG**

15 rue du Château.
☎ 03.82.83.73.16 Fax 03.82.83.23.37
Closed Jan 1–4. **Car park**. **TV**. **Disabled access**.

The château of Mensberg, built in the 7th century and rebuilt in the 15th with the help of the devil, according to legend, looms over this little inn. It has 15 or so comfortable and pretty rooms, each one a real little love nest. There's an extremely handsome dining room on the ground floor where you can sample a number of carefully prepared specialities that change with the seasons. The prices are a bit high but they're quite justified. The warmth of the welcome made us even more eager to stay. Doubles with shower/wc 300F. Set meals 78–300F.

METZ 57000

SEE MAP OVERLEAF

HÔTEL-RESTAURANT LUTÈCE*

11 rue de Paris. **MAP A1-1**
☎ 03.87.30.27.25
Restaurant closed Saturdays, Sundays, public holidays, and Dec 20–Jan 5. **Secure parking**. **TV**.

A modest but well-kept establishment. The owners care about the little things that help make a room pleasant – flowers, curtains in

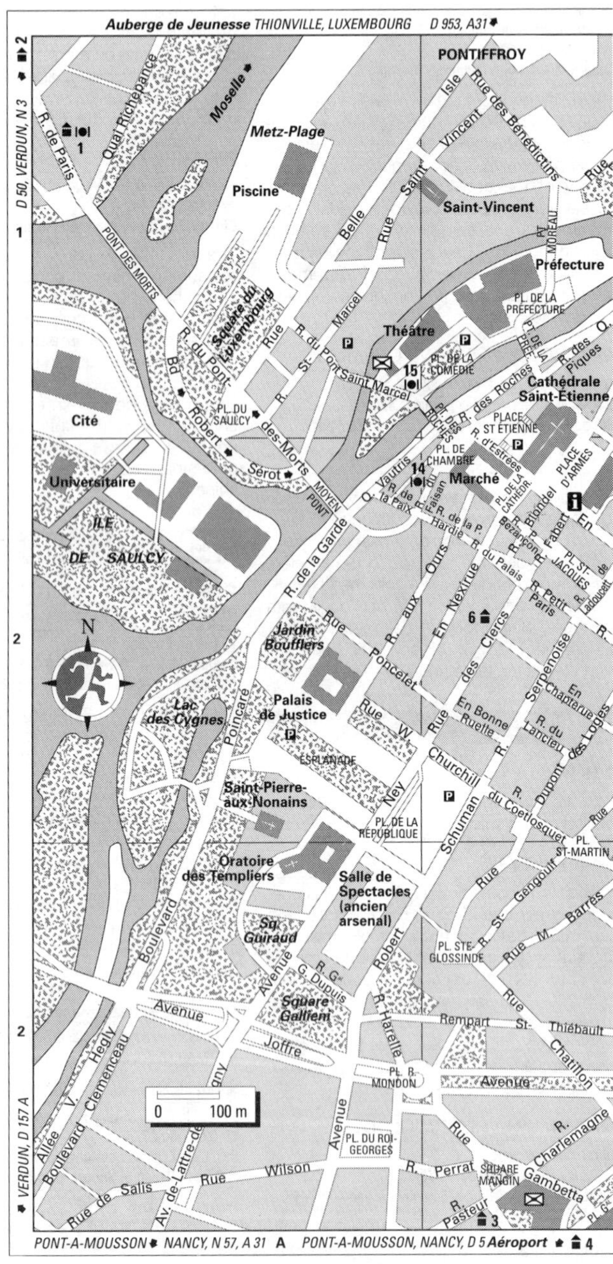
Auberge de Jeunesse THIONVILLE, LUXEMBOURG D 953, A31
D 50, VERDUN, N 3
VERDUN, D 157 A
PONT-A-MOUSSON NANCY, N 57, A 31 A PONT-A-MOUSSON, NANCY, D 5 Aéroport 4
PONTIFFROY
Moselle
Metz-Plage
Piscine
Saint-Vincent
Préfecture
PL. DE LA PREFECTURE
Théâtre
PL. DE LA COMEDIE
Cathédrale Saint-Etienne
PLACE ST ETIENNE
PLACE D'ARMES
Marché
PL. DE CHAMBRE
Square du Luxembourg
PL. DU SAULCY
Cité
Universitaire
ILE DE SAULCY
MOYEN PONT
PONT DES MORTS
Jardin Boufflers
Palais de Justice
ESPLANADE
Lac des Cygnes
Saint-Pierre-aux-Nonains
PL. DE LA RÉPUBLIQUE
Oratoire des Templiers
Salle de Spectacles (ancien arsenal)
Sq. Guiraud
Square Gallieni
PL. STE-GLOSSINDE
PL. ST-MARTIN
PL. ST-JACQUES
PL. R. MONDON
PL. DU ROI-GEORGES
SQUARE MANGIN
N
0 100 m
1
2
Quai Richepance
R. de Paris
Belle Isle
Rue Saint Vincent
Rue des Bénédictins
Rue St. Marcel
R. du Pont Saint Marcel
Bd Robert Sérot
R. du Pont des Morts
R. de la Garde
R. des Roches
R. des Piques
R. d'Estrées
R. Vautris
R. de la Paix
R. du Faisan
R. de la Hardie
R. du Palais
R. aux Ours
En Nexirue
R. des Clercs
Serpenoise
En Chaplerue
R. du Lancieu
R. Dupont des Loges
En Bonne Ruelle
Rue Poncelet
Rue W. Churchill
Ney
R. Schuman
R. du Coëtlosquet
Rue St. Gengoulf
Rue M. Barrès
Rue Châtillon
Boulevard Poincaré
R. G. Dupuis
Robert
R. Harelle
Rempart St- Thiébault
Avenue Joffre
Avenue
Allée V. Hegly
Boulevard Clemenceau
Av. de Lattre-de-Tassigny
Rue Wilson
Rue de Salis
R. Perrat
R. Pasteur
R. Charlemagne
Rue Gambetta
R. Fabert
R. Blondel
R. Petit Paris
R. Bezançon
PL. MOREAU
1
6
14
15
3

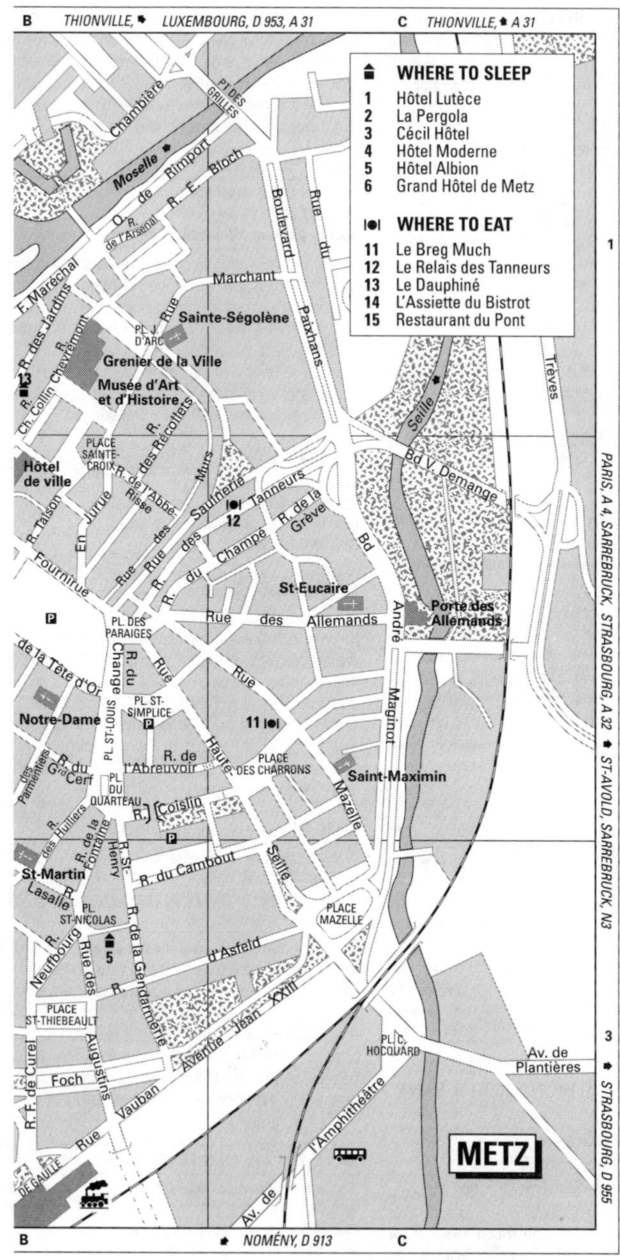
B
THIONVILLE, LUXEMBOURG, D 953, A 31
C
THIONVILLE, A 31
WHERE TO SLEEP
1 Hôtel Lutèce
2 La Pergola
3 Cécil Hôtel
4 Hôtel Moderne
5 Hôtel Albion
6 Grand Hôtel de Metz
WHERE TO EAT
11 Le Breg Much
12 Le Relais des Tanneurs
13 Le Dauphiné
14 L'Assiette du Bistrot
15 Restaurant du Pont
Moselle
Sainte-Ségolène
Grenier de la Ville
Musée d'Art et d'Histoire
Hôtel de ville
St-Eucaire
Porte des Allemands
Notre-Dame
Saint-Maximin
St-Martin
PLACE SAINTE-CROIX
PL. DES PARAIGES
PL. ST-SIMPLICE
PLACE DES CHARRONS
PL. DU QUARTEAU
PL. ST-NICOLAS
PLACE MAZELLE
PLACE ST-THIEBEAULT
PL. C. HOCQUARD
Rue des Allemands
Bd André Maginot
Av. de Plantières
Avenue Jean XXIII
R. du Cambout
PARIS, A 4, SARREBRUCK, STRASBOURG, A 32
ST-AVOLD, SARREBRUCK, N3
STRASBOURG, D 955
METZ
B
NOMÉNY, D 913
C

the same fabric as the bedcover and so on. Doubles 145F with basin, 235F with bath. Even though all the rooms are double glazed, go for one at the back. Set meals 52–73F.

HÔTEL LA PERGOLA**

13 route de Plappeville. **MAP A1-2**
☎ 03.87.32.52.94 F 03.87.31.41.60
Car park. TV.

It would be the easiest thing in the world to walk right past this place, and it would be a great pity if you did. Once you've seen the wonderful garden which is cut off from the outside world and been woken by birdsong, you'll understand why we love it so much. The bedrooms are all different, have brass beds and period furniture, and just ooze charm. Some of the bathrooms are as big as the rooms. Doubles are 190–250F. Ask for one overlooking the garden. Afternoon tea is served under the trees.

CECIL HÔTEL**

14 rue Pasteur. **MAP B3-3**
☎ 03.87.66.66.13 F 03.87.56.96.02
Closed Christmas–New Year's Day. **Secure parking. TV. Disabled access.**

The hotel is housed in a handsome turn of the century building near the station. Prices for modern and well-equipped but slightly impersonal rooms are pretty good, with doubles from 195F (with shower) to 290F (with bath). You'll get a good deal if there are four of you, since a room with two double beds costs 290F.

10% HÔTEL MODERNE**

1 rue Lafayette. **MAP B3-4**
☎ 03.87.66.57.33 F 03.87.55.98.59
Private car park. TV.

Rooms are modern and functional but still feel quite cosy. The quietest ones are at the back. They all cost somewhere in the region of 240F, so ones with two double beds – no. 7, for example – can work out extremely cheap. The owner, a very nice woman, eats in the Irish pub next door, which does a set meal for 70F, wine included.

10% HÔTEL ALBION - RESTAURANT DU PÈRE POTOT**

8 rue du Père-Potot. **MAP B3-5**
☎ 03.87.36.55.56 F 03.87.36.39.80
Secure parking. TV. Canal+. Disabled access.

Lunch served noon–2pm and dinner 7–10pm. It's centrally located but looks a bit out of place in this particular neighbourhood, its guests being primarily reps and respectable tourists. The rooms, with phone and mini-bar, are all alike but not unpleasant. Doubles 295F. Buffet-style breakfast 35F. Lots of the rooms, like number 105, overlook the inner courtyard of an old abbey.

GRAND HÔTEL DE METZ**

3 rue des Clercs. **MAP B2-6**
☎ 03.87.36.16.33 F 03.87.74.17.04
Secure parking. TV. Disabled access.

If they ever decide to remake Truffaut's Antoine Doisnel films, this hotel would make an ideal location. It's in a pedestrianized street in the old part of town, has an ultramodern entrance, and a superb staircase. Rooms, decorated in pastels and flower-patterned fabrics, are laid out round an inner courtyard. Clean and comfortable doubles 355F with shower/wc.

RESTAURANT LE BREG MUCH

51 rue Mazelle. **MAP C2-11**
☎ 03.87.74.39.79
Closed Sunday evenings and Mondays.
Disabled access.

A great many people in Metz eat here on a regular basis and it's not hard to see why. There's a pleasant dining room and a terrace for when the sun shines, you'll get a friendly welcome and, last but not least, the cooking's good. They do set meals at 58F (lunchtimes), 115F and 155F which change with the seasons. The produce couldn't be fresher and the chef turns out simple yet imaginative dishes. A great place for lovers who love good food.

RESTAURANT LE DAUPHINÉ

8 rue du Chanoine-Collin. **MAP B1-13**
☎ 03.87.36.03.04
Closed evenings (except Fridays and Saturdays) and for three weeks in August.

An unpretentious restaurant cum tearoom with exposed beams and paintings of people doing the kind of jobs that no longer exist. Service is a bit casual. The 69F country set meal comes with the inevitable roast potatoes and cream cheese with herbs. There are others at 75F (not available Sundays), 100F and 150F. The cooking is simple and the portions are generous.

LE RELAIS DES TANNEURS

2 bis rue des Tanneurs. **MAP C2-12**
☎ 03.87.75.49.09
Closed Sundays (unless you've booked) and the first three weeks in August.

The street's become rather dull since the tanners left, but the owner of this restaurant and her cooking won us over. Set meals 67F, 113F (*croustade* of mussels and veal escalope with morels), 133F et 165F. Lots of regulars make for a family atmosphere.

RESTAURANT L'ASSIETTE DU BISTROT

9 rue du Faisan. **MAP B2-14**
☎ 03.87.37.06.44 Fax 03.87.32.44.23
Closed Sundays and Monday lunchtimes.

Lunch served noon–2pm and dinner 7–9.30pm. A 30s bistro that seems to be very popular with men in suits, which doesn't leave much room for the rest of us. They're right, mind you, the cooking is terrific and the prices are reasonable. There are three *menus-carte* (88F, 128F and 160F, wine and coffee included) and they offer dishes like *pot-au-feu* of calf's head, *navarin* of lamb with turnips, and *charlotte* of guinea fowl with morels. The service is quite classy, just like the restaurant.

RESTAURANT DU PONT-SAINT-MARCEL

1 rue du Pont-Saint-Marcel. **MAP A1-15**
☎ 03.87.30.12.29
Car park. **Disabled access**.

This 17th century building houses an original and first-rate restaurant with a terrific location on the banks of the Moselle and there's not another like it in Metz. It's as if everything conspires to lure you into commiting the sin of gluttony. The regional cooking here ranges from suckling pig in aspic to eel *en matelote* in a Côtes de Toul wine sauce. There's a flower-filled terrace, the restaurant is decorated with frescos depicting life in the city in days gone by, and the dining room staff are dressed in period costume. This part of Metz has been done up and in the evening the street lights will make you feel you've been transported back through time. The cheapest set meal is 98F and you'll pay 168F for the "Taste of Lorraine" meal. As if that weren't enough, the wine list is full of Moselle and Lorraine wines. So what are you waiting for?

SAINT-JULIEN-LÈS-METZ 57070 (3KM NE)

RESTAURANT DU FORT SAINT-JULIEN

route de Thionville; it's in the restored part of the fort.
☎ 03.87.75.71.16
Closed Sunday evenings and Wednesdays. **Car park**.

The town has changed hands several times since 1870, being now French, now German. You'll be welcomed by Coco, the owner's mynah bird and he (the bird, not the owner) might favour you with his version of The Marseillaise or Bridge over the River Kwai. The place is decorated to resemble a cave, the atmosphere is relaxed and you can pig out with your friends. There's a set meal for four at 180F that includes kir, a bottle of wine and coffee. They serve the kind of food that sticks to your ribs – black pudding, quiche lorraine, flambéd quails and *choucroute* with Riesling.

WOIPPY 57140 (4KM N)

L'AUBERGE BELLES FONTAINES

51 route de Thionville.
☎ 03.87.31.99.46 Fax 03.87.31.98.87
Closed Sundays in winter and two weeks in August.
Car park.

You'll find a restful atmosphere in this inn a few minutes from the centre of Metz. It's decorated in classical fashion in the same shades of green as the trees outside. Customers are mainly regulars. Substantial set meals 59–150F. Attentive service. Terrace.

MONTENACH 57480

10% HÔTEL-RESTAURANT AU VAL SIERCKOIS

3 place de la Mairie.
☎ 03.82.83.85.20 Fax 03.82.83.61.91
Closed Monday evenings, Tuesdays and July 14–31.
Car park.

Lunch served noon–2pm and dinner 7–9.30 pm. Surrounded by the valleys and woods of northern Moselle, this delightful little inn near the Luxembourg and German borders is the ideal place to recharge your batteries. There are long walks to be had, you'll waken to the sound of birdsong, and meet with simplicity and sheer niceness wherever you go. The cooking is unpretentious. There's a set meal of Lorraine specialities at 75F or if you're feeling hungry there are other set meals at 90F, 130F and up. We remember the haunch of venison *Grand Veneur* with pleasure. If you want to stay longer, they have seven pretty rooms, two of them fairly new (with bath and TV), from 175F to 265F.

L'AUBERGE DE LA KLAUSS

1 rue de Kirschnaumen.
☎ 03.82.83.72.38 Fax 03.82.83.73.00
Closed Mondays and Dec 24–Jan 5. **Car park**.
Disabled access.

Anyone who loves good food should know about this place, where they carry on the tradition of good quality cooking using ingredients that are prepared on the spot. You can eat in one of four dining rooms, two of which have their own particular theme (clocks and hunting respectively). Wine buffs will be particularly taken with the cellar. The cheapest set meal at 130F is simple and based on Lorraine specialities, while the one at 170F is considerably more substantial. The chef's speciality is pan-fried homemade *foie gras* which he serves warm with apples, Calvados and acacia honey. The owner believes in keeping it all in the family – he has a farm where he rears 100 pigs and 4,000 ducks and the game comes from the nearby forests. After your meal you can even visit the farm and buy a few homemade goodies. You'll get a very warm welcome.

MONTMÉDY 55600

HÔTEL-RESTAURANT LE MÂDY**

8 place Raymond-Poincaré; it's in the main square.
☎ 03.29.80.10.87 F 03.29.80.02.40
Closed Sunday evenings and Mondays (except on public holidays) and in January. **Secure parking**. **TV**.

The hotel has extremely comfortable rooms starting at 250F. The restaurant serves generous helpings of good regional dishes, with a few specialities such as knuckle of pork with Mirabelle plums and trout *montmédienne*. Cheapest set meal 72F (not Sundays). Everything about the place – décor, cooking, welcome and background music – could be described as classic(al). Don't forget to visit the citadel.

NANCY 54000

SEE MAP OPPOSITE

GROUPE DES ÉTUDIANTS CATHOLIQUES

35 cours Léopold. **MAP A2-1**
☎ 03.83.32.30.87 F 03.83.30.60.76
Closed in August. **Disabled access**.

You'll need to book. Rooms with basin 80F a day, breakfast included. Showers and wc in the corridor. The university refectory is across the street. Cheap accommodation for travellers who miss their student days.

10% HÔTEL CARNOT**

2 cours Léopold. **MAP A2-2**
☎ 03.83.36.59.58 F 03.83.37.00.19
TV. **Disabled access**.

Don't go by the rather dismal exterior or by the very 70s foyer – this is a very pleasant hotel for an overnight stay. Doubles range in price from 130F with basin/wc to 260F with bath. Number 25 and number 34 (both with bath) are bigger, brighter and are at the back. A word of warning: a fair is held in the square in April so do ask for a room at the back then.

10% HÔTEL DE GUISE**

18 rue de Guise. **MAP A1-3**
☎ 03.83.32.24.68 F 03.83.35.75.63
Closed Aug 9–24 and Dec 20–Jan 2. **Car park**. **TV**.

This hotel in the heart of the old part of Nancy used to be the residence of the countess of Bressey. It's very atmospheric and will make you think of *The Three Musketeers* and other novels by Dumas. There's a magnificent monumental 18th century staircase leading to the rooms, which are simple but clean. Doubles with basin 130F and up, with bath 275F. We rather liked *2bis*, which had a lovely fireplace. Great value for money.

10% HÔTEL LE JEAN-JAURÈS**

14 bd Jean-Jaurès. **MAP A3-4**
☎ 03.83.27.74.14 F 03.83.90.20.94
Secure parking. **TV**. **Canal+**.

We liked the slightly old-fashioned atmosphere created by the mouldings and tapestries demanded by its previous incarnation as a master craftsman's house. Needless to say it was impossible to open the windows at the front. There's a quiet garden at the back. Doubles with basin/wc 150F, with shower/wc 190–230F. Nice welcome from the young and energetic owner who really cares about the comfort of his guests.

10% HÔTEL POINCARÉ**

81 rue Raymond-Poincaré. **MAP A2-6**
☎ 03.83.40.25.99 F 03.83.27.22.43
Secure parking. **TV**.

This hotel definitely offers some of the best value in the city. Rooms are 160F with basin/wc and 200F with shower. They have a good deal at weekends: spend Friday and Saturday night and you'll get Sunday night free. Don't think that because the rooms are so cheap you'll have to sacrifice a degree of comfort – you won't. Family atmosphere – mind you don't step on the toy motor cars belonging to the owners' little boy.

10% GRAND HÔTEL DE LA POSTE**

56 place Monseigneur-Ruch. **MAP B2-5**

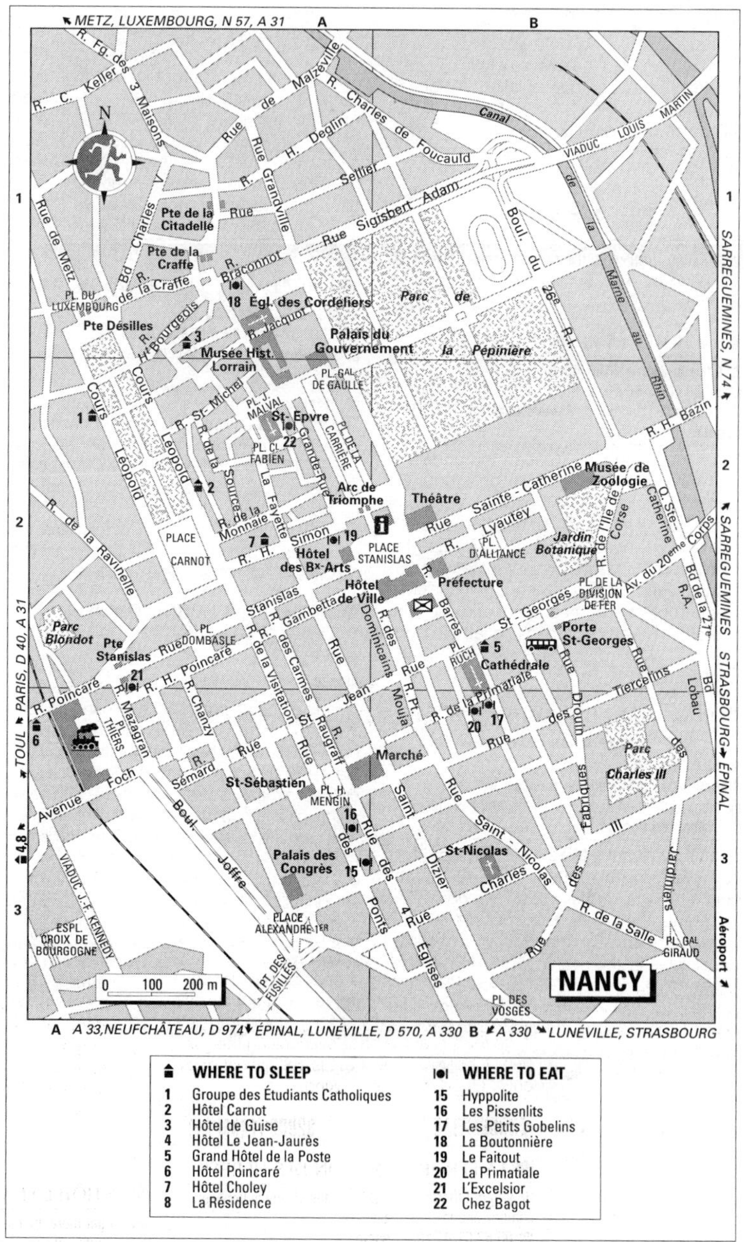

	WHERE TO SLEEP		WHERE TO EAT
1	Groupe des Étudiants Catholiques	15	Hyppolite
2	Hôtel Carnot	16	Les Pissenlits
3	Hôtel de Guise	17	Les Petits Gobelins
4	Hôtel Le Jean-Jaurès	18	La Boutonnière
5	Grand Hôtel de la Poste	19	Le Faitout
6	Hôtel Poincaré	20	La Primatiale
7	Hôtel Choley	21	L'Excelsior
8	La Résidence	22	Chez Bagot

☎ 03.83.32.11.52 ➡ 03.83.37.58.74
TV.

Don't worry about the ever so slightly shabby outside of this baroque building. Inside it's been refurbished from top to bottom. It has 44 rooms on three floors and they all have plain simple and tasteful wallpaper and a mixture of old and new furniture. Doubles with shower 165F, with shower/wc 185F, with bath 220F. Extremely good value for money when you consider that Place Stanislas is only a stone's throw away and you'll be wakened by the cathedral bells. Wonderful welcome.

10% ⌂ HÔTEL LA RÉSIDENCE***

30 bd Jean-Jaurès. **MAP A3-8**
☎ 03.83.40.33.56 ➡ 03.83.90.16.28
Closed Dec 31 and Jan 1. **Secure parking** (25F). **TV**. **Canal+**.

The minute you step through the door and are welcomed not by a receptionist but by a station master, you'll realize there's someone around who's mad keen on trains. The hotel's been cleverly decorated and is quite delightful in its way. You'll be reminded at every turn of the owner's hobby – there are magazines on the subject scattered about and even the bedrooms haven't escaped unscathed. Doubles with shower/wc 290F, with bath 340F. All aboard!

|●| RESTAURANT HYPPOLITE

47 rue des Ponts. **MAP A3-15**
☎ 03.83.32.97.92
Closed Saturday lunchtimes, Sundays, Monday evenings, July 15–Aug 15, Christmas, and New Year's Day. **Disabled access**.

Book if you want a table for Friday or Saturday night in this rather nice restaurant opposite the *Hôtel des Finances*. At lunchtime, they have daily specials 40–55F with the accompaniment of your choice. Specialities in the evening include *raclette*, six kinds of *pierrade* (where you cook the ingredients yourself on a hot stone) ranging in price from 70F to 100F, and eight fondues at around 60F. The décor's uninspiring but the important thing is that the servings are generous.

|●| LES PETITS GOBELINS

18 rue de la Primatiale. **MAP B2-17**
☎ 03.83.35.49.03
Closed Sundays and the first week in January.

A delightful little restaurant in a lovely building with a parquet floor, an assortment of furniture and collectables, paintings and photos of Lorraine artists on the walls, all of them for sale. Try the crunchy *millefeuille* of smoked salmon, the fillet of turbot with orange or (in winter) the baked Alaska with sour cherries. At lunchtime there's a 60F *formule* consisting of a main course and a dessert of your choice from the 98F set meal, and a 75F set meal built around what the market has to offer that particular day. Other set meals 148F and 220F. Welcome and service both lacking in confidence.

|●| CHEZ BAGOT – LE CHARDON BLEU

45 Grande-Rue. **MAP A2-22**
☎ 03.83.37.42.43 ➡ 03.83.35.78.38
Closed Sunday evenings, Mondays, and Aug 20–Sept 10.

It's a fair way from the shores of Brittany to the streets of Nancy but Patrick Bagot hasn't forgotten his homeland, for he offers his customers fish and shellfish that taste of the ocean alongside quail in white pudding and *jambonnettes* of chicken stuffed with *foie gras*. The elegant restaurant is bathed in light and the décor has a maritime feel to it. Set meals 75F (weekday lunchtimes), 125F and 190F.

|●| RESTAURANT LA BOUTONNIÈRE

4 rue Braconnot. **MAP A1-18**
☎ 03.83.36.51.45
Closed Sundays and Mondays.

Lunch served noon–1.30pm and dinner 7.30–10.30pm. The restaurant's biggest seller since 1976 has been the rib steak *boutonnière* and, as you might have guessed, it specializes in meat. Bistro-style décor, with naive paintings and humorous drawings on the wall (the owner's quite witty too). They do a set meal for 82F that offers a choice of five starters and five main courses – a model of its kind in terms of value for money. You'll get an apéritif on the house if you can show them this guide. There's a very quiet terrace in an inner courtyard.

|●| LE FAITOUT

7 rue Gustave-Simon. **MAP A2-19**
☎ 03.83.35.36.52
Closed for one week at the beginning of January.

A couple of minutes from the musée des Beaux-Arts (which you must visit) and Place Stanislas, *Le Faitout* is located in a pretty street well off the tourist beaten track. The red, black and white décor makes it look rather austere but we were quite won over by the jovial welcome we got from the proprietress. The cooking is simple, portions are generous and there are always a few surprises in store. Our personal hit parade included *terrine* of trout with cucumber, leg of lamb in a herb crust, and the seafood *pot au feu*. Set meals 85F, 105F and 125F. If you like all things Lorraine, there's a set meal of regional specialities that includes the most wonderful *pâté*. In the summer, there's a vegetarian set meal at 85F.

RESTAURANT LA PRIMATIALE

14 rue de la Primatiale. **MAP B2-20**
☎ 03.83.30.44.03.
How to get there: it's two minutes from place Stanislas. If you're coming from rue Saint-Jean, walk down the side of the cathedral.
Closed Saturday lunchtimes, Sundays and public holidays.

Lunch served 11.45am–1.30pm and dinner 7.15–9.30pm (10.30pm in summer). The restaurant is in a pedestrianized street well off the tourist beaten track. It's modern and trendy just like the décor and tends to be a bit clinical. However, the cooking is innovative and full of flavour and you can linger over dishes like *aumônière* of lamb sweetbreads with horn of plenty mushrooms, breast of goose with blueberries and salad of calf's brains with cumin seeds. Set meals 90F, 128F and 150F.

LES PISSENLITS

25 bis rue des Ponts. **MAP A3-16**
☎ 03.83.37.43.97 Fax 03.83.35.72.49
Closed Sundays and Mondays.

Lunch served 11.45am–2.15pm and dinner 7.15–10.30pm. *Les Pissenlits* is an offshoot of the nearby *La Table des Mengin*, one of the best restaurants in the region, so it's got everything going for it. The décor in the large dining room, with its marble tables and handsome dresser showing off a collection of Longwy porcelain, is part bistro, part junk shop. The expertise of the better-known establishment is evident in the traditional cooking and tables are understandably hard to come by. They do the most wonderful *baeckehoffe* (beef, mutton and pork stew) for 78F, oxtail with *spätzele* for 65F and a memorable calf's head *gribiche* for 60F. The daily special costs 48F. Danièle Mengin, one of France's best wine waiters, is responsible for a quite exceptional cellar and there is always a specially chosen selection of great little wines available by the glass.

RESTAURANT L'EXCELSIOR

50 rue Henri-Poincaré. **MAP A2-21**
☎ 03.83.35.24.57 Fax 03.83.35.18.48
Closed Christmas Eve evening.

This has become such an institution in Nancy that people refer to it as the *Excel*. You really have to see this historic monument with its Art Nouveau décor, the work of the greatest names of the School of Nancy, including walnut furniture by Majorelle and stained glass by Gruber who were the equal of the Viennese masters or Tiffany on the other side of the Atlantic. If you want to know more about the School of Nancy, have a look at Majorelle's villa and the musée des Beaux-Arts, which is full of first-rate examples of the work of Gallé, Daum and Prouvé. You'd better stoke up here first though before setting off. Both cooking and service are in the best brasserie style. Set meals 112F (in summer) and 153F. Don't miss the pigeon pie or the *choucroute paysanne*. After 10pm they do a late night set meal for 103F (wine included). Customers are a bit on the glamourous side but not stand-offish. This is a very good restaurant.

VILLERS-LÈS-NANCY 54600 (4KM SE)

10% AUBERGE DE JEUNESSE - CHÂTEAU DE RÉMICOURT-NANCY

149 rue de Vandœuvre.
How to get there: from the A33 or the N74, Nancy-Sud-Ouest-Brabois exit; from the centre of town, follow the arrows for Brabois-Rémicourt.
☎ 03.83.27.73.67. Fax 03.83.41.41.35
Closed Christmas–New Year's Day. **Car park**.

Access 9am–10pm, Sundays 8–9.30am and 5–10pm. Access to rooms from 5.30pm. A very high-class youth hostel this – the château of Rémicourt sits in about 20 acres of its own grounds. Ideal for nature lovers on a tight budget – 90F a night including sheets and breakfast the next day. Meals start at 45F. Perfect for getting to Nancy's botanic gardens which is home to more than 10,000 species of plants.

NEUFCHÂTEAU 88300

LE RIALTO**

67 rue de France (Centre).
☎ 03.29.06.09.40 Fax 03.29.06.06.63
Closed Sundays out of season. **Secure parking**. **TV**.

You'll get a pleasant welcome from the young proprietors of this old hotel in the centre of town. It's been fully renovated and rooms are clean. The ones overlooking the river are particularly nice. Doubles 230F with shower/wc. Nice terrace for when the sun shines.

|●| RESTAURANT LE ROMAIN

74 av. Kennedy (West); as you leave town, head in the direction of Chaumont
%03.29.06.18.80
Closed Sunday evenings and Mondays. **Car park**.

With a name like this you'd be excused for thinking it was a pizzeria. Well, it isn't, and the only thing even remotely Italian about it is the décor, which makes a few vague references to Ancient Rome! The young chef (who often comes out from his kitchen to chat to the customers) shows considerable panache in his cooking of traditional dishes. Everything is cooked for just the right amount of time and the flavours are spot on – you'll feel that you're tasting the old standards like pig's trotters with potatoes and mushrooms, pan-fried zander with creamy garlic sauce, and saddle of rabbit with mirabelle plums for the first time. Set meals 75F (lunchtimes) and 115F, with, for example, *terrine* of guinea fowl with onion marmalade, fillet of *rascasse* with fennelseeds or a simple yet excellent flank of beef with shallots, lovely cheese platter and great desserts. Charming welcome and service. You can sit on the terrace in summer but it's a bit close to the road and you're aware of the traffic, despite the thick hedge. Great wine list with a few wines available to try by the glass.

NOMENY 54610

|●| AUBERGE DU BOL D'AIR

2 route l'Éply.
☎ 03.83.31.36.35
Closed Sunday evenings, Mondays, the second fortnight in July, and the second fortnight in November. **Car park**.

Grounds, trees, a simple little building and nice people in a village that has perhaps seen better days – shades of *Little House on the Prairie*. Good honest cooking in the shape of dishes like grilled *andouillette* with Pinot Noir, osso buco, and calf's head *ravigote*. Set meals from 70F (lunchtimes) to 200F.

PLOMBIÈRES-LES-BAINS 88370

☗ |●| HÔTEL DE LA POSTE - DE FRANCE

14 rue de l'Hôtel-de-Ville (Centre).
☎ 03.29.66.01.10 F➔ 03.29.66.00.84
Closed Oct 10–April 30. **Secure parking**.

The atmosphere is relaxed, the rooms adequate and the prices reasonable. What more is there to say? Give the rooms overlooking the busy street a miss. Prices start at 100F for a double with basin, and 140F with shower. You can rent a TV. The 75F *menu curiste* consists of starter, main course, cheese and dessert. The cooking's light and the guests are elderly – this is a spa after all!

10% ☗ |●| HÔTEL DE LA FONTAINE STANISLAS**

Fontaine Stanislas - Granges de Plombières; it's 4km north of Plombières on the route d'Épinal via Xertigny.
☎ 03.29.66.01.53 F➔ 03.29.30.04.31
Closed Oct 15–March 31. **Secure parking**. **TV**.

This place overlooking the valley has been in the same family for four generations and you'll get a warm welcome from the present owners. Peace and quiet are guaranteed and you can walk in the forest or relax in the shady garden. Doubles from 190F with shower. You can get the lot – sitting room, balcony and bath – for 320F. Half-board 230–330F per person. The cheapest set meal at 92F comes with *flamiche*, trout *meunière*, cheese and dessert. Other house specialities are medallions of lamb *provençale*, snails with ceps and kirsch soufflé. All in all, definitely worth the trip.

PONT-À-MOUSSON 54700

10% ☗ HÔTEL BAGATELLE***

47-49 rue Gambetta; you'll find it as you enter the town from the east.
☎ 03.83.81.03.64 F➔ 03.83.81.12.63
Closed at Christmas and on New Year's Day.
Secure parking. **TV**. **Canal+**.

The *Bagatelle* stands out from the average kind of hotel in the area. The rooms are modern and tastefully laid out and prices – 275–370 with bath – are reasonable given the facilities.

BLÉNOD-LÈS-PONT-À-MOUSSON 54700 (3KM SW)

|●| AUBERGE DES THOMAS

100 av. Victor-Claude; it's 3km from Pont-à-Mousson on the N57.
☎ 03.83.81.07.72 F➔ 03.83.82.34.94
Closed Sunday evenings, Mondays, Wednesday evenings, during the February school holidays, and three weeks in August.

Lunch served noon–1.30pm and dinner 7–9pm. This nice little hotel with its blue country-style décor complemented by pale wooden furniture soon makes you forget the rather grim surroundings (there are factories across the way). They take pains to get the balance of flavours right in the food. And they take as much care over the lawn! You'll be offered snails with nettles, calf sweetbreads with preserved oranges and green cabbage, and an incredibly good country *andouillette*. Set meals 100F, 165F and 250F. Customers are mainly businessmen, so the atmosphere and service are businesslike.

REMIREMONT 88200

HÔTEL DU CHEVAL DE BRONZE**

59 rue Charles-de-Gaulle (Centre).
☎ 03.29.62.52.24 F→ 03.29.62.34.90
Secure parking. **TV**. **Canal+**.

The name of this establishment makes a nice change after all those white horse inns we've reviewed. It's a former coaching inn and has retained a lot of its charm. The entrance is in the arcade in the centre of town. You'll get a pleasant welcome and the rooms are clean and quiet. Doubles with basin and bidet 150F, with shower 200F, with bath 295F.

RESTAURANT LE CLOS HEURTEBISE

13 chemin des Capucins (South); if you're coming from the centre of town, go down rue Charles-de-Gaulle – once you're past the big crossroads turn right into the steep street and follow the arrows.
☎ 03.29.62.08.04
Closed Sunday evenings. **Car park**.

This is a rather posh and extremely good restaurant on the edge of a wood up in the hills that circle the town. The décor is classic provincial, the service is impeccable, and the menu is mouthwatering. The cheapest set meal is 90F (not available Saturday evenings or Sundays). The one at 145F is well worth the trip offering as it does, for example, pan-fried duck *foie gras* with bilberries, succulent roast pigeon, a handsome cheese platter and, to finish, something wickedly delicious from the dessert trolley. Connoisseurs will drool over the wine list. Undeniably the best restaurant in town.

SAINT-AVOLD 57500

10% HÔTEL-RESTAURANT DE PARIS

45 rue Hirschauer.
☎ 03.87.92.19.52 F→ 03.87.92.94.32
Closed Monday mornings. **Car park**. **TV**.

In the 16th century, the building belonged to the counts of Créhange who, being Protestant, weren't exactly popular at the time. So that they could practice their faith, they built a small chapel right at the back of the inner courtyard. That courtyard is now the restaurant's dining room and the proprietor has just finished restoring the chapel. You have to see it, if only for the sculpted keystones. The restaurant's not much to write home about but the hotel is very pleasant. Rooms are decent, clean and quiet. The décor's a touch old-fashioned. Doubles with basin/wc (no TV) 225F, with shower 180–225F, with shower/wc 270F.

SAINT-DIÉ 88100

10% HÔTEL DES VOSGES ET DU COMMERCE**

53-57 rue Thiers (Centre).
☎ 03.29.56.16.21 F→ 03.29.55.48.71
Secure parking. **TV**. **Canal+**. **Disabled access**.

A welcoming and well-looked after hotel with 30 rooms. Standards of comfort – and consequently prices – vary. There are rooms at 160F (shower and wc in the passage), at 230–260F with shower and wc and at 240–280F with bathroom. Open 24 hours (night porter). No restaurant. Car park and garage are free if you can show them a copy of this guidebook.

HÔTEL DE FRANCE**

1 rue Dauphine (Centre).
☎ 03.29.56.32.61 F→ 03.29.56.01.09
Secure parking. **TV**. **Canal+**.

All of the rooms in this centrally located hotel have shower or bath and mini-bar. Doubles 240–260F, depending on location. The friendly proprietor will give you the entry-phone code if you're planning on being out late.

LE BAR AMÉRICAIN

place du Marché (Centre).
☎ 03.29.56.28.69
Closed Sundays and end July–end Aug.
Disabled access.

More of a bar than a restaurant, and it's a bit heavy on the American décor. The atmosphere on a Saturday afternoon after the market's closed is terrific. They do only one set meal for which you'll pay 52F – not much for a substantial and fairly decent meal.

|●| RESTAURANT EUROPE

41 rue des Trois-Villes (North-West).
☎ 03.29.56.32.03
Closed Sunday evenings, Mondays, and the first three weeks in August.

The restaurant is decorated fairly conventionally in shades of blue. Nice owner, who offers traditional French cooking, grills and a few Eastern European dishes, including goulash. The food's good and there are meals to suit all pockets. They do set meals at 65F, 89F, 108F and 132F and daily specials from 43F.

|●| RESTAURANT LE PETIT CHANTILLY

rue du 11-Novembre (Centre).
☎ 03.29.56.15.43.
Closed Saturdays, two weeks during the February school holidays and three weeks in August. **Car park**. **Disabled access**.

The dining room is large and fairly elegant, and the cooking good and reasonably priced. The cheapest set meal is 95F and offers dishes such as *quenelles* of pike and skate with chervil. There's another one at 155F.

PETITE FOSSE (LA) 88490 (17KM NE)

⌂ |●| AUBERGE DU SPITZEMBERG**

2 Au Spitzemberg; head in the direction of Strasbourg and take the Provenchères-sur-Fave exit; turn right, then cross La Petite Fosse as far as the col d'Hermampaire; turn left and the inn's 1km further on.
☎ 03.29.51.20.46 ➡ 03.29.51.10.12
Closed Tuesdays, Nov 15–Dec 15, and Jan 6–29.
Secure parking.

A lovely inn in the depths of the Vosges forest where you can relax, enjoy the peace and quiet and tour the area. The bedrooms are comfortable and the dining room extremely pleasant. They go in for traditional cooking here and you should try the trout in a white Alsace wine and the Munster cheese flambéd in marc or in cumin flavoured alcohol. Doubles, all with phone, cost 250–330F with shower/wc or bath. The cheapest set meal is 82F (weekdays only). Half-board here works out fairly cheaply – you'll pay from 230F a head for a minimum of three nights, which is probably worth bearing in mind. And you can play clock golf in the garden at the front of the hotel. It will cost you 30F a night to use the garage.

SAINT-MIHIEL 55300

10% ⌂ |●| HÔTEL-RESTAURANT RIVE GAUCHE**

place de la Gare.
☎ 03.29.89.15.83 ➡ 03.29.89.15.35
Car park. **TV**. **Canal+**. **Disabled access**.

Lunch served 11.30am–3pm and dinner 6.30–11pm. The old station's been restored – they've made a wonderful job of it – and found a new role in life now the trains have stopped. Rooms are very comfortable, with shower/wc or bath, cable TV, and phone. There's a children's play area outside. It's quite expensive – doubles come in at 235F – but worth it and the atmosphere's very nice. The restaurant has good traditional cooking and the portions are fairly generous (which can't be said for other places in town). Set meals 60–148F.

HEUDICOURT-SOUS-LES-CÔTES 55210 (16KM NE)

10% ⌂ |●| HÔTEL-RESTAURANT DU LAC DE MADINE**.

☎ 03.29.89.34.80. ➡ 03.29.89.39.20
Closed Mondays Sept–May, and in January.
Secure parking. **TV**. **Disabled access**.

This is very popular with tourists and it gets very busy as soon as the good weather arrives. Inflation has inevitably had some impact but you still get good value for money. Large pleasant rooms with shower or bath, several with a balcony or patio, are 240–300F. The cheapest set meal is 80F, and the others range from 120F to 200F. The welcome could be better.

VIGNEULLES-LÈS-HATTONCHÂTEL 55210 (17KM NE)

⌂ |●| L'AUBERGE LORRAINE

50 rue Poincaré; take the D901
☎ 03.29.89.58.00
Closed Wednesdays (except in summer) and in February.

The inn is situated in the Lorraine regional park north of lac de Madine. It has five bedrooms, all renovated, and doubles with shower (wc in the corridor) are 150F. Extremely clean. This is definitely the best value for money in the area. There's one slight drawback though: if you're the early to bed type you may find the noise from the bar on the ground floor a problem. Set meals 59F, 69F and 98F. The owner may cultivate an image of detesting hard work and caring only about having a good time but he'll make you a calf's head or a *boeuf bourguignon* that you'll remember for a long time. You'll need to book.

NONSARD 55210 (23KM E)

LES ESSARTS.

☎ 03.29.89.32.40
Closed every evening except Saturday (unless you have a reservation) Oct–April, Saturday lunchtimes and Sunday evenings Dec–Jan, and the week between Christmas and New Year's Day.

Service until 11pm during the season. Having lost weight horse-riding, mountain-biking or sailboarding, it's sheer delight to put it back on here. Nothing has changed since Brigitte Corre took over this little inn, and the terrace and the green and peach dining room are as delightful as ever. In summer, there are lots of substantial salads for 50F. If you want more than a salad there are set meals at 65F (weekdays only) and at 110F. The fact that it's open so late means you can make the most of the lake.

SARREBOURG 57400

10% HÔTEL DE FRANCE**

3 av. de France (Centre).
☎ 03.87.03.21.47 ➡ 03.87.23.93.57
Secure parking. TV.

This is a big hotel with 50 rooms that are well-kept even if lacking in charm. Rooms with basin start at 150F and go up to 275F with shower/wc and 295F with bath. Rather cool welcome. The restaurant (belonging to the same family) is just next door.

RESTAURANT L'AMI FRITZ

76 Grand-Rue (Centre).
☎ 03.87.03.10.40
Closed Wednesdays, two weeks in February, and two weeks in October.

A good restaurant popular with local worthies, small businessmen and Germans. The house specialities are fillet of zander *à l'Alsacienne, choucroute, presskopf* (a type of brawn), tripe with Riesling, and calf's head with two sauces. Set meals to suit all pockets: 59F (weekday lunchtimes), 80F, 110F, 115F, 125F, 130F and 185F. The emphasis is on quantity.

L'AUBERGE DU ZOO

24 rue Saint-Martin (North-East); head in the direction of the motorway, cross the railway bridge at the Sarrebourg, then follow the arrows.
☎ 03.87.03.10.16 ➡ 03.87.23.99.44
Closed Monday evenings, Tuesdays, and Dec 20–Jan 10. **Car park.**

Lunch served noon–2pm and dinner 7–11pm. A pretty spot, particularly since the zoo has gone! The restaurant has a long history, as you'll discover when you get there. It serves good food at decent prices, with set meals 89–170F and Lorraine specialities that seem to go down well. The décor is fairly conventional and the dining rooms are too big, which doesn't make for an intimate atmosphere, but it's still pleasant. It's a bar in the evening too.

TROISFONTAINES 57870 (8KM SE)

RESTAURANT DU SAPIN VERT

64 rue des Vosges; it's very out of the way but well signposted.
☎ 03.87.25.50.30 ➡ 03.87.25.61.84
Closed Sunday evenings and Mondays. **Car park.**

The restaurant lies at the end of a road bordering a dark mysterious forest. Your tastebuds are in for a treat, with salmon smoked over wood shavings from deciduous trees, *civet* of wild boar, *feuilleté* of quail with calf sweetbreads, and *glace de truffes* being just a few of the items featured in the set meals at 64F (the *menu du jour*), 108F, 156F, 182F and 235F (all in). The cooking is sophisticated and innovative and the staff pleasant. The dining room is tiny and the restaurant has a loyal following, so it's best to book. Take a stroll while you're there, it's beautiful countryside.

SARREGUEMINES 57200

10% HÔTEL TERMINUS**

7 av. de la Gare (South-East).
☎ 03.87.98.55.46 ➡ 03.87.98.66.92
TV. Canal+. Disabled access.

This centrally located hotel has an arrangement with the nearby *Restaurant Laroche* to provide meals for reps and people on half and full board. You'll be welcomed in the same way as you would be in a more upmarket place. Doubles with basin/wc (no TV) 150F, with shower/wc 250F.

10% HÔTEL AUX DEUX ÉTOILES**

4 rue des Généraux-Cremer (Centre).
☎ 03.87.98.46.32
TV.

The name's no longer a misnomer now the hotel finally has its two-star rating. It has 20 reasonably priced rooms, with doubles at 200F (with basin), 240F (with shower) and 260F (with bath).

HÔTEL-RESTAURANT L'UNION**

28 rue Alexandre-de-Geiger; if you're coming from the centre of town, cross the river, take rue du Maréchal-Foch then turn left.
☎ 03.87.95.28.42 F 03.87.98.25.21
Closed Saturday lunchtimes, Sundays, and the Christmas and New Year holidays. **Secure parking**. **TV**. **Canal+**.

Sarreguemines is the earthenware capital of France, and if you like earthenware you'll love the dining room here, which has some extremely fine pieces. The food's decent too, with set meals 75–140F. The owners are friendly and very obliging and you'll pay about 300F for a comfortable room with shower/wc or bath. Give the ones overlooking the busy street a miss.

RESTAURANT LA BONNE SOURCE

24 av. de la Gare (Sud-Est).
☎ 03.87.98.03.79
Closed Sunday evenings, Mondays, and July 15–Aug 15. **Car park**.

They do good Alsace and Lorraine specialities here – things like *flammenküche* (bacon, cream and onion flan) and *knepfle* (a kind of fritter) with bacon and cream. Friendly welcome, pleasant atmosphere. Set meals at 67F (weekday lunchtimes), 77F and 92F offer excellent value for money. Traditional style décor with local earthenware, woodwork, and checked tablecloths and napkins.

RESTAURANT LAROCHE

3 place de la Gare (South-East).
☎ 03.87.98.03.23 F 03.87.95.75.71
Closed Friday evenings, Saturdays, July 6–27, and Dec 21–Jan 4. **Disabled access**.

There are two dining rooms – which one you're seated in depends on whether you want to eat in a hurry or not. The day's special (weekday lunchtimes) is 37F and there are set meals ranging in price from 80F to 200F. Dishes are nicely presented. You'll get a cordial welcome and extremely good value.

SENONES 88210

HÔTEL-RESTAURANT AU BON GÎTE**

3 place Vaultrin (Centre).
☎ 03.29.57.92.46 F 03.29.57.93.92
Closed Sunday evenings, during the February school holidays, the last week in July, and in August. **Car park**. **TV**.

You'd be well advised to book if you want to stay in this lovely old house that's been renovated throughout. Monsieur and Madame Thomas, the owners, are very welcoming. They have about ten very comfortable rooms with direct-dial telephones. Doubles range in price from 225F to 300F. The restaurant, which is very busy at the weekend, offers good regional cooking that also shows a bit of imagination. Set meals 58F (weekday lunchtimes), 90F, 125F and 160F.

LA SALLE DES GARDES

7 place Clemenceau (Centre).
☎ 03.29.57.60.06
Closed evenings, Thursdays, three weeks in June, and one week at Christmas. **Car park**. **Disabled access**.

This renovated bar cum restaurant is very popular with the local youngsters. The cooking, like the owner, is pleasant and straightforward, with a *menu du jour* at only 55F and meat dishes, grilled over an open fire, about 60F. The waiter is darts champion of France!

STENAY 55700

HÔTEL-RESTAURANT LE COMMERCE**

rue Aristide-Briand.
☎ 03.29.80.30.62 F 03.29.80.61.77
Closed Friday evenings and Sunday evenings in winter. **TV**. **Canal+**.

The hotel has been renovated throughout and offers cheerful comfortable rooms at prices ranging from 240F (with shower) to 450F (with bath). The restaurant serves simple and substantial set meals (75–250F). If you're interested in beer, there's a museum just down the street that will tell you everything you ever wanted to know about the subject.

THIONVILLE 57100

HÔTEL LE PROGRÈS*

18 rue Jemappes (Centre).
☎ 03.82.53.85.47
Closed Sundays. **Secure parking**. **TV**.

The hotel is in very good condition, the rooms have recently been refurbished, and the bed linen is quite good. Prices are reasonable – doubles with shower/wc 120–180F. A TV set is available on payment of a 20F supplement. It's quiet and there's a big car park at the back. Ideal if you're on a tight budget.

10% ☗ |●| HÔTEL-RESTAURANT DES AMIS**

40 av. du Comte-de-Bertier; leave the motorway by exit 40 and it's the fourth set of lights on the right.
☎ 03.82.53.22.18 F➔ 03.82.54.32.40
Closed Sundays until 5pm. **Car park**. **TV**.

A large establishment covered in Virginia creeper and geraniums. The name says it all – the proprietress is always ready for a chat and will treat you like a regular. The hotel is extremely clean and doubles with shower/wc or bath are 230–260F. The 60F country meal is a real treat – *crudités*, smoked country ham, house *terrine*, garlic sausage, *fuseau lorrain*, roast potatoes, and cream cheese with herbs. Our favourite place in Thionville.

☗ |●| HÔTEL-RESTAURANT LE LIBERTÉ**

69 bd Foch (Centre).
☎ 03.82.54.33.44 F➔ 03.82.54.34.80
Restaurant closed Sunday evenings. **TV**. **Canal+**. **Disabled access**.

Lunch served noon–2.30pm and dinner 7–10pm. With all that glass around, it's reminiscent of the United States but this is hardly New York since the building's only five storeys high. Rooms are attractive, modern and well-equipped and come with shower or bath. Doubles cost 300F but if you stay Friday to Sunday the price drops to 270F. Nice welcome.

HOMBOURG-BUDANGE 57920 (15KM SE)

|●| L'AUBERGE DU ROI ARTHUR

48 rue Principale; head in the direction of Bouzonville.
☎ 03.82.83.97.15 F➔ 03.82.83.54.04
Closed Sunday evenings, Monday evenings, and late August.

Lunch served noon–2.30pm and dinner 6–10pm. No, the Quest for the Holy Grail didn't lead King Arthur to Moselle. The truth is much more prosaic – the new owners merely decided that the old name of *Chez Arthur* was a bit lacking in pizzazz. The table may not be round but they serve good country-style cooking in a pleasant dining room. Set meal is 51F (available weekdays). The day we were there they had a terrific *andouillette*. There's also a set meal of Lorraine specialities at 59F. They get a lot of people coming back again and again, which is a good sign.

TOUL 54200

10% ☗ LA VILLA LORRAINE**

15 rue Gambetta (Centre).
☎ 03.83.43.08.95 F➔ 03.83.64.63.64
Secure parking. **TV**

The hotel is housed in a beautiful building and definitely offers the best value for money in the town. Pleasant welcome. The rooms overlooking the lane don't get much natural light. Doubles 120F with basin/wc, 220F with bath. There's a restaurant across the way.

10% ☗ HÔTEL DE L'EUROPE**

35 av. Victor-Hugo (Centre).
☎ 03.83.43.00.10 F➔ 03.83.63.27.67
Closed during Christmas and New Year holidays. **Secure parking**. **TV**. **Canal+**.

Handy for the station. The clean and pleasant rooms have 30s style furniture (as does the rest of the hotel) and range in price from 150F (with basin) to 220F (with bath). Rather stiff welcome.

|●| RESTAURANT LE CHAUDRON LORRAIN

place des Cordeliers (Centre).
☎ 03.83.64.10.94
Closed Christmas–New Year's Day. **Disabled access**.

This little restaurant located in a narrow street has a wide range of first-rate dishes. Specialities include *fondue des leucques* (chicken breast, fish and vin gris) and stuffed pig's tail. Set meals 59F (weekdays), 79F and 119F. The pleasantness of the surroundings – there's a lot of wood – adds to the natural warmth of the jovial proprietor.

LUCEY 54200 (9KM NW)

|●| L'AUBERGE DU PRESSOIR

rue des Pachenottes; take the D908.
☎ 03.83.63.81.91
Closed Sunday evenings and Mondays. **Car park**. **Disabled access**.

Lunch served noon–2pm and dinner 7–9pm. Lots of people in the area know and like the inn, so it's essential to book at the weekend and in summer. It's housed in what used to be the village station and there's a genuine antique winepress in the courtyard. The cooking is regional and offers a wide range of dishes and a number of specialities, including calf's sweetbreads, stuffed trout, and *tartare de langoustines* wrapped in smoked salmon. Set meals 75F, 100F, 130F and 155F.

VAL-D'AJOL (LE) 88340

HÔTEL-RESTAURANT LA RÉSIDENCE***

5 rue des Mousses (Centre).
☎ 03.29.30.68.52 Fax 03.29.66.53.00
Closed Nov 17–Dec 15. **Car park. TV.**

This handsome 19th century master craftsman's house has been transformed over the years by two generations of the same family (the third is waiting in the wings) and is now a very pleasant establishment. There are lots of nooks and crannies to explore on your way to the comfortable, cosy and quiet bedrooms, all with shower or bath, that range in price from 230F to 400F. As well as the main building there are two 3-star annexes. We were ready to fall in love with the place and being woken by the early morning sun that set the extensive grounds ablaze tipped us over the edge – that plus the pool and the tennis court and, more than anything, the great kindness of Madame Bongeot. The cooking was on a par with the hotel. Set meals start at 65F and go all the way up to 290F (you'd better be in training for that one). They also do an excellent set meal of regional specialities for 175F. Impeccable service.

VERDUN 55100

10% HÔTEL MONTAULBAIN**

4 rue de la Vieille-Prison (Centre).
☎ 03.29.86.00.47 Fax:03.29.84.75.70
TV.

Narrow streets, traffic jams and a one-way system make this place difficult to get to by car. The owner assured us that the rules didn't apply to his guests! Once you get there you'll find he has ten quiet comfortable rooms with phone. Prices 150–210F. Pleasant welcome and atmosphere.

HÔTEL LE SAINT-PAUL**

12 place Saint-Paul (North).
☎ 03.29.86.02.16 Fax 03.29.86.02.16
Closed Dec 12–Jan 12. **Secure parking.**

Your fellow guests will include tourists interested in war graves, veterans and history buffs. The well-situated hotel offers moderate prices, a good standard of comfort, peace and quiet, and a pleasant family atmosphere. You'll find that the restaurant serves good traditional dishes and you might as well eat here, given what the other restaurants in town are like. Rooms 165–260F and set meals 90–180F. For half-board, reckon on paying 120F a head in addition to the price of the room.

RESTAURANT LE PICOTIN

38 av. Joffre (East).
☎ 03.29.84.53.45
Closed Sunday evenings. **Disabled access.**

If you like peace eat in the dining room, since the terrace is fairly noisy. The décor inside is very attractive and has a surprising Anglo-American touch. Good quality cooking, with set meals 58–165F. Try the 1900 tournedos and the medley of fish with fresh pasta. The 120F set meal offers good value.

GLORIEUX 55100 (2KM W)

RESTAURANT LE BRASERO

13 rue de Blâmont (Nord-Ouest).
☎ 03.29.86.34.29.
Closed Mondays. **Disabled access.**

It may seem strange to find Savoy specialities in this part of the world but you have to have lived through a Verdun winter to properly appreciate a *fondue des Aravis* or a *braserade*. Generous portions of such dishes are served up in a cosy atmosphere for about 80F. The kind of restaurant that seems made for the short dark cold days of winter. There's a garden with a terrace for the long days of summer.

HAUDAINVILLE 55100 (5KM SE)

RESTAURANT LE CLOS LORRAIN

11 rue de Verdun.
☎ 03.29.84.74.63
Closed Wednesdays. **Disabled access.**

Lunch served noon–2pm and dinner 7–9pm. We fell in love with this restaurant. It has lots of regulars and that helps create a warm and friendly atmosphere. Like us, they come for the location, the trees and the flowers as much as for the food. Portions are generous and the prices very reasonable. Set meals 60F (weekdays), 120F and 155F. The grilled zander with dill, the rack of Périgord lamb and the duck breast with morels are worth the trip. A good restaurant.

VACHERAUVILLE 55100 (8.5KM N)

LE RELAIS

How to get there: by the D964.
☎ 03.29.84.51.74 Fax 03.29.84.51.74
Closed evenings and Saturdays. **Disabled access.**

Here's a little village restaurant of the kind you wish you came across more often. It offers simple cooking and generous portions. The 78F set meal, for example, consists of an enormous buffet of hors-d'œuvres, a few main courses to choose from (if you like calf's head you'll love the way they do it here) and cheese or dessert. On Sundays there are set meals at 98F and 138F.

MARRE 55100 (15KM NW)

HÔTEL-RESTAURANT LE VILLAGE GAULOIS

How to get there: from Verdun, take the D38 in the direction of Varennes.
☎ 03.29.85.03.45 F 03.29.85.00.09
Car park. Disabled access.

Once upon a time a baker from Moselle who was passionately interested in those "indomitable Gauls" turned his back on breadmaking and built this village. The restaurant is delightful. The dining room has lots of wood and stonework and there's a shady terrace courtesy of some oak trees. The cooking is traditional and you'll find lots of Lorraine specialities, including grilled pig's ears, suckling pig and veal's tongue with snails. Set meals 90–190F. The rooms – 250F with shower/wc or bath – are as rustic and genuine as the cooking. Unlike Asterix and the other villagers, you can sleep sound in your beds – there's no bard constantly breaking into song here.

SOMMEDIEUE 55320 (15.5KM SE)

LE RELAIS DES ÉPICHÉES

rue du Grand-Pont; take the D964 as far as Dieue then turn left onto the D159.
☎ 03.29.87.61.36 F 03.29.85.76.38
Closed Dec 15–Jan 8. **Secure parking. TV.**

Lunch served noon–2.30pm and dinner 7.30–10pm. A good restaurant in a peaceful village. The cooking is simple and the dishes are traditional. As you tuck into an excellent calf's liver with shallots you might come to appreciate the false beams. Set meals 65–150F. Rooms are clean and overlook a stream; 160F with basin, 220F with shower/wc or bath.

ÉTAIN 55400 (20KM NE)

HÔTEL-RESTAURANT LA SIRÈNE**

22 rue Prud'homme-Navette.
☎ 03.29.87.10.32 F 03.29.87.17.65
Closed Mondays out of season and late Dec–early Feb. **Secure parking. TV.**

Apparently, Napoleon III dined here after the battle of Gravelotte in 1870. It's an extremely handsome bourgeois house, decorated in country style and full of flowers and antiques. You'll get a pleasant welcome, the atmosphere is hushed and the customers are well-to-do. When we were there there were lots of groups of over 60s. Rooms are quite comfortable but go for one at the back because the street gets quite a lot of traffic. Doubles 150F with basin and bidet, 190F with shower/wc. Half-board (a minimum of three days) starts at 180F a head. Set meals 67–250F, with dishes like salmon with tarragon, ham with peaches, and *foie gras*. There are even two tennis courts if you're in the mood for some exercise or just feel you need to work off some calories!

SENON 55230 (29.5KM NE)

LA TOURTIÈRE

place Eugène-Antoine; take the N3 as far as Étain and then the N18; you'll find it on a narrow road on the left.
☎ 03.29.85.98.30
Closed Mon–Wed Nov 15–1 April (unless you have a reservation) and one week in September. **Car park.**

If you enjoy good food then this restaurant in a delightful little village must feature in your itinerary. Marie-Laure and Serge Moreau are delightful hosts and will have your tastebuds tingling with delightful and original dishes such as a pike and sorrel tart, a *feuilleté* of *foie gras* with local truffles and a flan of wild mushrooms with *petits gris* snails and a garlic sauce. And prices are very reasonable, with hearty set meals at 100F (weekdays), 155F, 190F and 250F. Your meal in the lovely country-style dining room will be punctuated by the sound of bells from the nearby church.

VITTEL 88800

10% HÔTEL LES OISEAUX

54 rue de Sugène (Centre).
☎ 03.29.08.61.93
Car park. TV.

This is not so much a hotel as a pretty little private house, a touch old-fashioned, that's been turned into a B&B by an extremely nice lady. Rooms with basin 140F, with bath 260F. It's quiet and pleasant, perfect if you need an inexpensive rest cure.

HÔTEL-RESTAURANT LA CHAUMIÈRE

196 rue Jeanne-d'Arc (Centre).
☎ 03.29.08.02.87
Closed Sundays in winter. **Car park**.

A tiny hotel cum bar cum restaurant which is nothing much to look at. But the proprietress is delightful, the chef (who's been in the business for 30 years) cares about what he's doing, and the impression you get of people enjoying themselves makes a nice change from the health farm atmosphere that pervades the rest of the town. Rooms are very simple but clean. Doubles with basin 180F. Set meals 60F, 85F and 170F.

HÔTEL DE L'ORÉE DU BOIS**

L'Orée du Bois (West); leave town by the D18 in the direction of Contrexéville – the hotel is 4km to the north, opposite the race course.
☎ 03.29.08.88.88 Fax 03.29.08.01.61
Closed Sunday evenings, and Nov–early March.
Secure parking. **TV**. **Canal+**. **Disabled access**.

A modern hotel that specializes in getting its guests back into shape. It's quiet, the rooms are comfortable, and you'll get a friendly welcome. Reckon on paying 270F for a double with bath. Prices in the restaurant are affordable, and they have set meals 66–180F. These change with the seasons but there are a few constants like grilled salmon *à l'unilatéral* (grilled on one side only), *grenadines* of veal and pork, and the house duck *foie gras*. There's a gym and a tennis court to help you work it all off. Free parking.

Midi-Pyrénées

09 Ariège

12 Aveyron

31 Haute-Garonne

32 Gers

46 Lot

65 Hautes-Pyrénées

81 Tarn

82 Tarn-et-Garonne

AIGNAN 32290

10% LE VIEUX LOGIS

rue des Arts; it's behind the town hall.
☎ 05.62.09.23.55 F➜ 05.62.09.23.55
Closed Sunday evenings. **TV**.

Service at lunchtime and from 7.30pm. If it hadn't been for the two ladies in straw hats standing arguing at the corner, we might never have noticed this establishment a stone's throw from the main square in the mediaeval part of town. There is such a thing as being too unobtrusive! Fun curtains, antiques and flowers tempt you in, as do the set meals at 52F, 85F (soup, salad, shrimp *à la provençale*, lamb kebabs and dessert) and 95F (soup, country ham, *confit* of duck and dessert). Terrace. Rooms with TV 200F!

ALBI 81000

AUBERGE DE JEUNESSE - MJC

13 rue de la République (Centre).
☎ 05.63.54.53.65 F➜ 05.63.54.61.55

Doors open 6pm–9pm (8pm–9pm Saturdays, Sundays and public holidays). Restaurant closed Saturday evenings, Sundays and public holidays. Lovely big house. You'll need to show your FUAJ card. 30F a night and you need a sheet, it'll cost you 15F. Breakfast (12F) is served 7.30–9.30am. There's a set meal for 91F at lunchtime and 38F in the evening. Package of evening meal plus bed plus breakfast the next morning costs 72F. If you're coming back late at night, ask for the door entry code.

10% LA RÉGENCE**

27 av. Maréchal-Joffre (South).
☎ 05.63.54.01.42 F➜ 05.63.54.80.48
Secure parking. TV.

The type of hotel that makes you think of a guesthouse. It's quiet, friendly, and has a nice garden at the back. Décor's a bit kitsch (flowery wallpaper). Doubles with basin/wc 120F, with shower or bath 195–210F. Good value for money.

10% HÔTEL GEORGE V**

29 av. Maréchal-Joffre (South).
☎ 05.63.54.24.16 F➜ 05.63.49.90.78
TV. Disabled access.

Judging by the carving of the staff and serpents on the fine oak door, the building must once have belonged to an apothecary. The old bourgeois house is now a hotel with large, bright and tastefully decorated rooms at extremely reasonable prices. Three of the rooms are 160F, one is 220F and five are 240F — incredible value for money considering how comfortable and charming it all is. The welcome couldn't have been nicer either. So all in all, Monique and André are doing a good job. There's a pretty garden where you

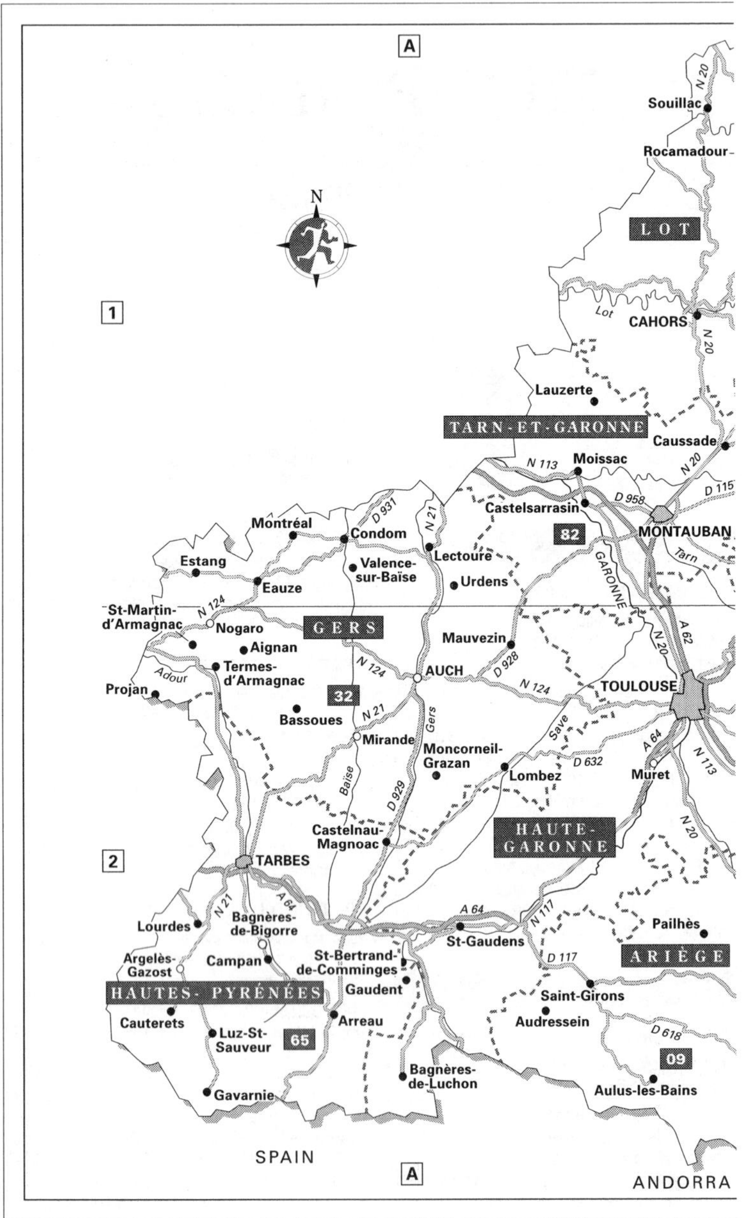
A
N
1
2
Souillac
Rocamadour
LOT
Lot
CAHORS
N 20
Lauzerte
TARN-ET-GARONNE
Caussade
N 113
Moissac
N 20
D 115
D 958
Castelsarrasin
MONTAUBAN
82
Tarn
GARONNE
D 931
Montréal
Condom
N 21
Lectoure
Estang
Valence-sur-Baïse
Eauze
Urdens
St-Martin-d'Armagnac
N 124
Nogaro
GERS
Aignan
Mauvezin
A 62
N 20
Termes-d'Armagnac
N 124
AUCH
D 928
N 124
TOULOUSE
Adour
Projan
32
Bassoues
N 21
Gers
Save
Mirande
Moncorneil-Grazan
A 64
D 632
Lombez
Muret
N 113
Baïse
D 929
Castelnau-Magnoac
HAUTE-GARONNE
N 20
TARBES
A 64
N 21
A 64
Lourdes
Bagnères-de-Bigorre
St-Gaudens
N 117
Pailhès
Argelès-Gazost
Campan
St-Bertrand-de-Comminges
D 117
ARIÈGE
HAUTES-PYRÉNÉES
Gaudent
Saint-Girons
Cauterets
Arreau
Audressein
Luz-St-Sauveur
65
D 618
09
Bagnères-de-Luchon
Gavarnie
Aulus-les-Bains
SPAIN
ANDORRA

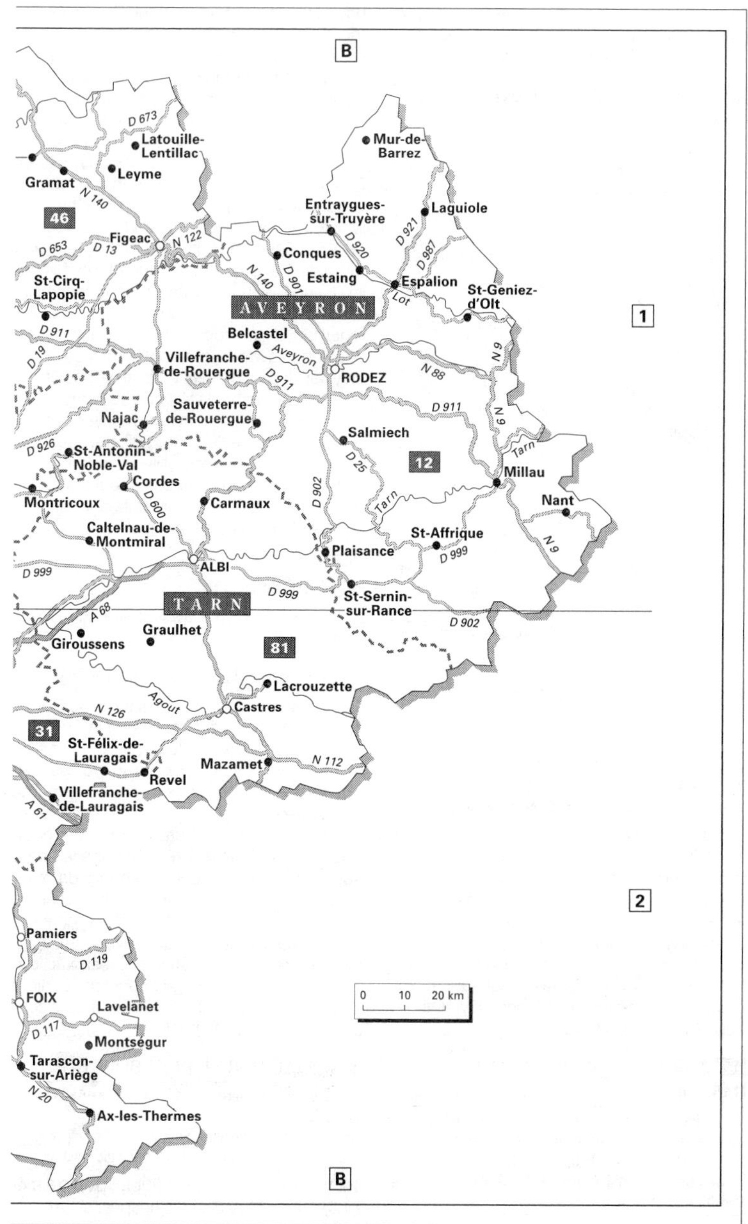
B
D 673
Latouille-Lentillac
Leyme
Gramat
N 140
46
Figeac
N 122
D 653
D 13
St-Cirq-Lapopie
D 911
D 19
Mur-de-Barrez
Entraygues-sur-Truyère
Laguiole
D 920
D 921
D 987
Conques
Estaing
N 140
D 901
Espalion
Lot
St-Geniez-d'Olt
AVEYRON
1
Belcastel
Aveyron
Villefranche-de-Rouergue
D 911
RODEZ
N 88
N 9
D 911
Sauveterre-de-Rouergue
Najac
Salmiech
D 926
St-Antonin-Noble-Val
D 25
12
Tarn
Millau
Cordes
Montricoux
D 600
Carmaux
D 902
Tarn
Nant
Caltelnau-de-Montmiral
St-Affrique
N 9
Plaisance
D 999
ALBI
D 999
D 999
St-Sernin-sur-Rance
TARN
A 68
D 902
Graulhet
Giroussens
81
Lacrouzette
Agout
N 126
Castres
31
St-Félix-de-Lauragais
Mazamet
N 112
Revel
Villefranche-de-Lauragais
A 61
2
Pamiers
D 119
0 10 20 km
FOIX
Lavelanet
D 117
Montségur
Tarascon-sur-Ariège
N 20
Ax-les-Thermes
B

can have your substantial breakfast (28F). A word of warning: it's often full, especially during motor races such as the Albi Grand Prix.

10% 🏠 |●| HÔTEL-RESTAURANT LE RELAIS GASCON - AUBERGE LANDAISE**

3 rue Balzac.
☎ 05.63.54.26.51 F➜ 05.63.49.74.89
Closed Sundays. **Car park. TV.**

An elegant but friendly setting where you can sample good regional cooking without going bankrupt. Set meals from 70F (weekdays only) to 180F. You'll get a bigger choice for 150F — gizzards, breast of duck, *salade gasconne* and *confit*. We enjoyed the chef's speciality, chicken breast stuffed with warm duck *foie gras*. Rooms are also available at reasonable prices. Well-kept doubles 200–220F with bath, where you can sleep off your meal.

🏠 HÔTEL SAINT-CLAIR**

8 rue Saint-Clair (Centre).
☎ 05.63.54.25.66 F➜ 05.63.47.27.58
Closed in January. **Secure parking. TV.**

A pretty 2-star hotel in the old part of town that's been recently renovated and is well loked after. Doubles with shower/wc 225F, with bath 310F (these are bigger and brighter). Nice owner.

🏠 |●| HÔTEL-RESTAURANT DU VIEIL-ALBY**

25 rue Henri-de-Toulouse-Lautrec (Centre).
☎ 05.63.54.14.69 F➜ 05.63.54.96.75
Restaurant closed Sunday evenings and Mondays, Jan 12–Feb 3, and Jun 22–July 6. **Secure parking. TV.**

Lunch served noon–2pm, dinner 7.30–9.30pm. Simple but very well maintained, this is one of the cheapest hotels in this part of town. Rooms with shower/wc 245F, with bath 265F. Note that half-board is practically compulsory in July and August. The owner's very nice and even-tempered but animals aren't allowed. Cheapest set meal 70F (weekday lunchtimes only). Others 120–250F. Food is excellent.

10% 🏠 |●| HÔTEL MERCURE ALBI BASTIDES***

41 rue Porta (Centre); it's on the left after the bridge over the Tarn in the direction of Paris-Carmaux.
☎ 05.63.47.66.66 F➜ 05.63.46.18.40
Closed Dec 22–Jan 2. **Car park. TV. Canal+. Disabled access.**

Lunch served noon–2pm, dinner 7.30–10.30pm. This former 18th century red brick mill on the banks of the Tarn opposite the cathedral has been converted into a luxury hotel. It has recently been renovated to suit the "technologically bang up to date businessman" type of client but its façade and enormous porch have been retained. You pay for your comfort of course (the rooms are a bit impersonal as you'd expect from a chain but they're air-conditioned and extremely well-equipped) as well as the view, which is probably the finest in Albi. Doubles 460–530F depending on the time of year and the view. We liked the restaurant too. Michelin, Gault-Millau and other food guides have already given it stars and chef's hats and regarded it as above average and we've decided to award it our golden backpack. It's only fair because the fine classical cooking is wonderful — especially when it's sampled on the terrace, with its view of the river and the old town. Set meals 100–160F, the cheapest being altogether acceptable. Wonderful wine list with rock-bottom prices (the restaurant's own réserve Mercure). Amiable and efficient service. A good establishment for its category and type.

|●| LE TOURNESOL

rue de l'Ort en Salvy; it's in a side street leading to place du Vigan.
☎ 05.63.38.38.14
Closed Mondays, Sundays and a fortnight in May.

Lunch served noon–2pm, dinner 7–9.30pm. This is THE vegetarian restaurant in Tarn, and a very good one it is, offering delightful meals at reasonable prices. The dining room is simply decorated and has air conditioning. The dishes on offer are very tasty. There's vegetarian *pâté* (26F), *assiette Tournesol* (a good selection of items with lots of variety, about 48F) and wonderful cakes like grandmother used to make (26F). To drink, there's apple juice and organic beer (15F). The clientèle is predominantly female (80% we were told); they looked unsophisticated, serious and intellectual, as if vegetarianism required thought, committment — and probably concern for your figure.

|●| RESTAURANT LE PETIT-BOUCHON

77 rue de la Croix-Verte.
☎ 05.63.54.11.75
Closed Saturday evenings, Sundays, public holidays, Aug 1–15 and during the school Christmas holidays.

Lunch served 11.30–2.30pm and dinner 7.30–10pm. Very clean. Cheapest set meal is 55F (weekdays only) and consists of a starter, daily special of your choice depending on what was available at the market (duck *confit*, stuffed mutton tripe, *cassoulet*, sirloin, *coq à la bière* etc) and dessert. Others at 65F and 105F. Fast, rather brusque service. Specializes in cocktails. A good restaurant along the lines of a Paris bistro. Good regional wine list.

LE GÉOPOLY

13 bis place de l'Archevêché (Centre).
☎ 05.63.49.74.67
Closed for two weeks in January.

Here's a restaurant that offers you the world on a plate, with dishes from Peru, France, Italy, the West Indies, Greece, the United States, China, the Seychelles, Réunion and Mexico. Well, maybe not the whole world – they don't do couscous. The styles of cooking all seem to be rather similar but it's an original idea and allows you to try something a bit different. We really liked the Peruvian *ceviche*, a mixture of scallops, shrimps and halibut flavoured with coriander (53F). Starters 35–50F, main courses 40–70F and desserts about 29F. *Assiette-repas* 55F. Unfortunately, being located in a square that is so popular with the tourists and the locals means it's often bursting at the seams, the staff are rushed off their feet and tend to be a bit short, and you sometimes have to wait rather a long time.

LA VIGUIÈRE D'ALBY

7 rue Toulouse-Lautrec.
☎ 05.63.54.76.44 Fax same
Closed Tuesdays and Dec 24–Jan 15.

Service 11am–10pm. You'll find an original *formule* that's typical of the area in this restaurant. It offers a choice of casseroles ranging in price from 12F to 20F and you really must try some of them as César gets stuck into your shoes. You choose from a list called *lou tastou*, which in the local dialect means something like tastes or samples. We had the local delicacy *al fecche sec* (dried pig's liver, radishes and artichokes), black pudding with *sauce pauvre homme*, sardines *à l'escabèche* (a southern classic) and great snails *à la gaillacoise*. The cooking is authentic and of the stick-to-your-ribs variety. It's also quite cheap, since you can get away with 65F or 75F with wine (there are some good Gaillacs). The restaurant also has a 140F set meal consisting of *salade paysanne*, three selections from *lou tastou*, duck *confit* and dessert. If your luck's in, you'll get to taste the *boudin de canard*, which has a powerful and concentrated flavour of duck. You can eat your meal on a pleasant patio to the sound of turtledoves while César moves on to your trouser leg. B-minus for the rather apathetic service from the owner. Life's surely not that bad, Madame, that you can't summon up the occasional smile! By the way, César is the resident tortoise . . .

MARSSAC 81150 (8KM SW)

LA TAVERNE

Centre, Castelnau-de-Lévis; from Albi, take the D600 and after 4km turn left onto the D1 – Castelnau is 3km further.
☎ 05.63.60.90.16 Fax 05.63.60.96.73
Closed Mondays, Sunday evenings (in winter), the last week in September and the first three in October.

This is heaven on earth for all lovers of good food. We took the 164F set meal. How about this: raw marinated salmon in salad with a *rillette* of salmon and herbs (there's salmon and there's salmon, and this was succulent), red mullet that couldn't have been fresher (and there wasn't a single bone left in it) served with a *mousseline* of prawns and then roast duck stuffed with raspberries that had us searching for superlatives. Dessert was out of this world too. As for the wine! – the list is extensive and included a terrific Buzet. You can enjoy your meal either in the air-conditioned dining room with its country-style décor or on the terrace. There are two other set meals at 115F (the chef's suggestion – trust him) and 245F (a *menu-surprise* consisting of four main courses and dessert, which must be really something!). The service matches the food. In short, one of the best restaurants in the region.

ARREAU 65240

HÔTEL D'ANGLETERRE**

route de Luchon (South).
☎ 05.62.98.63.30 Fax 05.62.98.69.66
Closed Mondays May 20–June 30 and Sept 15–30; Christmas–Easter, open weekends and during school holidays only. **Car park. TV.**

Lunch served 12.30–2pm and dinner 7.30–9pm. Located in a large village with mountains all around, this classic luxury hotel used to be a coaching inn. It also offers good regional cooking. Comfortable doubles 290–320F. Set meals 70–190F. They really prefer you to take half-board. Prices vary depending on what your choice of set meal is. Courses in hang-gliding, rafting and hydrospeeding. Long bicycle rides in the vallée d'Aure and the vallée du Louron. Covered cycle racks.

AUCH 32000

|●| RESTAURANT CLAUDE LAFFITTE

38 rue Dessoles (Centre).
☎ 05.62.05.04.80 Fax05.62.61.86.85
Closed Sunday evenings and Mondays (but not Monday lunchtimes in July and August). **Disabled access**.

The town's busiest street is home to one of its most famous restaurants. This is the big boy of Gascon cooking we're talking about, the temple of *charcuterie* – quality guaranteed, of course, since they have a shop next door. There's a décor and an atmosphère to match – colourful, cheerful and very Gascon! The menu's as long as your arm, so if you eat like a bird go somewhere else. For 75F on weekdays you'll get the day's special and dessert, while 140F (except on Saturdays, Sundays and public holidays), gets you either *charcuterie*, grilled pork and dessert or goose soup and grilled breast of goose or *cassoulet*. À la carte is incredibly expensive.

|●| RESTAURANT LE BAR DU IXE

2 place de la Libération (Centre).
☎ 05.62.61.71.99 Fax05.62.61.71.81
Secure parking in **private car park**. **TV**. **Canal+**.
Closed Jan 2–3.

Service noon till midnight. This little dining room in the great Daguin's basement has classical décor and a pleasant atmosphere. Customers are mainly businessmen in a hurry or people like you and me who want to sample the cooking of a legendary restaurant without having to ask for a bank loan. And you will indeed get Daguin quality for only 185F. What you eat here is made using the same techniques, the same fresh produce and the same tremendous baby vegetables as the main restaurant. Try the half duck breast with Madiran, the grilled rib of beef or the goose leg *confit*. There's also a set meal at 99.50F. Reception was a bit offhand.

MONTAUT-LES-CRÉNEAUX 32810 (10KM E)

|●| LE PAPILLON.

How to get there: it's on the N21, 6km from the centre of town, in the direction of Agen.
☎ 05.62.65.51.29. Fax: 05.62.65.54.33
Closed Wednesdays and the first fortnight in September. **Car park**. **Disabled access**.

Lunch served noon–2pm and dinner 7.30–9.30pm. This is the latest addition to Auch's good restaurants and its dismal surroundings really ought to be scheduled for immediate development. We might wish things were different but the important thing is to forget all about it and concentrate instead on a superb breast of duck with cherry sauce or a *fricassée* of sweetbreads with langoustines. Since you're not paying for the décor, prices are still affordable. Good set meal weekday lunchtimes is 74F. For 140F you'll get *terrine paysanne au foie gras* and leg of duck in a sweet and sour sauce.

AUDRESSEIN 09800

⌂ |●| L'Auberge d'Audressein*

route de Luchon; it's12km from Saint-Girons, at the mouth of the vallée du Biros.
☎ 05.61.96.11.80 F➜ 05.61.96.82.96
Closed Nov 15–Feb 15.

This inn, housed in a 19th century forge with sturdy stone walls, is one of the best we've ever come across. The renovated dining room has lost nothing of its warmth and the terrace overlooking the stream now has a roof. The cooking is still some of the best in Ariège and prices are extremely reasonable. The cheapest set meal is 80F, while 115F gets you *ravioles* of duck breast and garlic, *confit* and onion marmalade. The 149F set meal is wonderful: duck *foie gras*, salmon steak with sorrel sauce, scallops in puff pastry, *émincé* of duck. There's also a gourmet menu at 250F. And as always there's the famous panfried *foie gras* with hippocras sauce. Pleasant doubles 110–230F.

AULUS-LES-BAINS 09140

10% ⌂ |●| HÔTEL DE FRANCE**

rue Principale (Centre).
☎ 05.61.96.00.90 F➜ 05.61.96.03.29
Closed Nov–Dec. **Secure parking** in **private car park**.

Service at lunchtime until 3pm and in the evening until 9pm. A quiet charmingly old-fashioned country hotel where you'll get a warm welcome. Reasonable rooms 160Fand 200F (with bath and telephone). Good home cooking served up in the dining room, with set meals 58–150F. If you'd rather go à la carte, there's grilled duck breast, duck *confit*, trout with almonds and so on. Half-board at 190F a person is very cheap. There's a garden on the edge of a mountain stream.

10% 🏠 |●| HOSTELLERIE DE LA TERRASSE***

rue Principale (Centre).
☎ 05.61.96.00.98
Closed end Oct–early May. **Car park**. **TV**. **Canal+**.

Lunch served 12.30–1.30pm and dinner 7.30–8.30pm. Delightful establishment furnished with antiques. Rooms – all with shower or bath – 200–280F. Half-board (compulsory in July and August) 250–280F per person. Good cooking, pleasant dining room. Try the local dish of veal's head *en tortue* with bacon stuffing and potato cake. Set meals come in at 80F (duck leg *confit à l'ancienne* or grilled lamb), 135F (salmon and *foie gras en papillote*) and 160F (duck *foie gras* in a pie or monkfish kebabs). Children's menu. Waterside terrace.

AX-LES-THERMES 09110

10% 🏠 |●| LE GRILLON**

rue Saint-Udaut (South-East).
☎ 05.61.64.31.64 📠 05.61.64.25.48
Restaurant closed Tuesday evenings, Wednesdays (except during school holidays) and end Oct–early Dec.
Car park. **TV**.

Lovely mountain lodge type of hotel very close to the centre. Proprietors Nanette and Philippe are a nice go-ahead young couple who know the area well and can organize hikes or snowshoeing expeditions in winter. Comfortable rooms ranging in price from 195F to 250F for a double with bath. You can have half-board or full board and hiking or skiing packages are also available. The cooking is excellent and there's a subtle combination of sweet and savoury in dishes such as the house duck *confit* with a cider-flavoured *caramel*, salmon with vanilla, and *croustillant* of duck with mountain honey. Set meals 95–155F. Stop by if you're in the neighbourhood.

BAGNÈRES-DE-BIGORRE 65200

🏠 |●| HÔTEL PARADOR**

12 av. du Maréchal-Joffre.
☎ 05.62.91.05.43 📠 05.62.91.00.93
Closed the second fortnight in November. **TV**. **Canal+**.

Trains don't stop any more at Bagnères, and the old station hotel has undergone a transformation. The rooms are smart, modern and functional. Doubles 220–320F. Out of season, there's a package available that will give you the room and breakfast for two for 250F a night. The restaurant *El Meson* offers Spanish dishes such as *parillada* and prawns as well as traditional French ones. Set meals 60–120F. The proprietor is mad about golf and organizes golfing weeks or weekends at the hotel.

MONTGAILLARD 65200 (7KM NW)

🏠 |●| HÔTEL-RESTAURANT MONTGAILLARD*

How to get there: take the D935 in the direction of Tarbes.
☎ 05.62.91.50.73
Closed Mondays and every lunchtime in August.
Secure parking. **Disabled access**.

A very pleasant little hotel where you'll get a warm welcome. Quiet, since it's well away from the road. There are about ten reasonable rooms. Doubles with shower 180F. Great cooking, with set meals 48–120F. Local dishes such as *garbure* (a hearty vegetable soup) and duck *confit* with ceps are available.

BAGNÈRES-DE-LUCHON 31110

🏠 |●| GRAND HÔTEL DES BAINS**

75 allées d'Étigny (Centre).
☎ 05.61.79.00.58 📠 05.61.79.18.18
Closed Nov–Dec 20. **Car park**. **TV**.

Lunch served noon–1pm, dinner 7–11pm. Fine example of early 20th century architecture. Comfortable. Doubles 175F with basin/wc, 255F with shower/wc and 280F with bath. Lots of the rooms are enormous with period furniture and have their own charm. Others are more modern. There are three restaurants — the pizzeria isn't great.

10% 🏠 |●| L'AUBERGE DE CASTEL-VIELH

route de Superbagnères (South).
☎ 05.61.79.36.79 📠 same
Open Fridays, Saturdays and Sundays only Nov–Feb. Open every day during the school holidays and April–Oct. **Car park**. **TV**.

Lunch served noon–2pm, dinner 8–10pm. This is another pretty house in the style typical of the region. It stands alone on a lush green knoll, has a large garden and pleasant terrace, and is famed for its cooking. Set meals are 115F and 175F, while à la carte there's prawns with *mousserons* (a type of mushroom), *croustillant* of calf sweetbreads with stewed leeks, fricassée of frogs with a parsley sauce, and the wonderful *pancrémat*, a local delicacy based on *foie gras*. Accommodation also available. Doubles from 250F with shower/wc. Very nice staff.

LE PAILHET

12 av. du Maréchal-Foch (West).
☎ 05.61.79.09.60
Closed Mondays (except public holidays), July 1–Oct 15 and Nov 15–Dec 15. **Car park**.

Behind the trellised vines is a little dining room that's always packed out with regulars. Without any fuss you'll be served generous quantities of good honest regional cooking, dishes like *civet* of lamb, guinea fowl with olives, stuffed pig's trotters and, of course, the local specialities *pétéram* (a stew of sheep's trotters and tripe) and *pistaches aux haricots du Comminges* (braised leg of mutton with white haricot beans). Set meals 74F and 105F.

MONTAUBAN-DE-LUCHON 31110 (2KM E)

10% LES CASCADES*

How to get there: head for the church of Montauban and then follow the signs for the Herran forest road.
☎ 05.61.79.83.09 Fax same
Closed Nov–March 31. **Car park**. **TV**.

It really is advisable to book, for this is an exceptional establishment. It clings to the mountainside in the middle of an enormous park and you have to leave your car at the bottom and walk up – but you'll enjoy the scenery and you can be sure of peace and quiet once you get there. You eat outside in summer and the views over the valley are superb. Wonderful traditional cooking and of course they have *pétéram* (stew of sheep's trotters and tripe) and *pistache* (braised leg of mutton with white haricot beans). They also do a wonderful top rump of beef with ceps, duck breast with goat's cheese, casserole of pigeon in two types of Muscat. Set meals 100F and 120F (weekdays), 170F (Sundays). Warm and comfortable atmosphere in the dining room. A few rooms are available. Doubles with shower/wc are 230F. Breakfast is expensive.

BASSOUES 32320

HOSTELLERIE DU DONJON*

Centre.
☎ 05.62.70.90.04
Restaurant closed Saturday lunchtimes (and Saturday evenings in winter) and January. **Car park**.

Lunch served noon–1.30pm, dinner 7.30–8.30pm. Bassoues is a delightful 12th century fortified town that faces the Pyrenees and this is a delightful little hotel. It has eight pretty rooms, all of them nicely furnished. Doubles with shower or bath 125–225F. Full board 175–225F a person, which is great value for money. Half-board 150–200F. The cheapest set meal will cost you all of 59F for which you'll get soup, *crudités*, starter, main course and dessert; other set meals are 90F, 95F (drumsticks of duck *confit*), 125F (roast quail, grilled lamb, duck *confit*) and 195F (*foie gras* and grilled breast of fattened duck). Nice welcome. The energetic proprietors have established a reputation both at home and abroad. Madame is responsible for the wonderful cooking while her husband deals with reception, always injecting a note of humour into the proceedings. The cool quiet terrace is very pleasant when the sun's beating down.

BELCASTEL 12390

10% HÔTEL-RESTAURANT DU VIEUX PONT.

☎ 05.65.64.52.29 Fax 05.65.64.44.32
Closed Sunday evenings and Mondays out of season, January and February.

Lunch served noon–2pm, dinner 8–9pm. Sisters Michèle and Nicole Fagegaltier have turned their much-loved childhood home, near the castle in this delightful village, into an admirable establishment with some of the best cooking in the area, proving that tradition and creativity do not necessarily make strange bedfellows. They use old family recipes, drawing on their own expertise to update them. You'll drool over the combination of local produce and flavours from a bygone age in dishes like asparagus ravioli, fried sweetbreads with capers, pigeon breast fried in bacon fat and for dessert a chocolate box filled with melted plain chocolate and crunchy puffed rice. It's not cheap of course – set meals are 135–330F. You get to the hotel on the opposite side of the river by crossing the little 15th century bridge. The accommodation is as good as the cooking – the rooms are bright and well looked after and full of the little things that make all the difference. Doubles 400F (shower/wc) and 420F (bath). Welcome and service both outstanding.

CAHORS 46000

10% AUBERGE DE JEUNESSE

20 rue Frédéric Suisse.
☎ 05.65.53.97.02 Fax 05.65.35.95.92

This is a nice youth hostel with a large terrace only five minutes from the station. Holders of FUAJ cards pay 48F per night, 19F for breakfast and 19F for sheet hire – those without 55F, 20F and 20F. Meals (49F) served 7.15pm weekdays only.

HÔTEL-RESTAURANT A L'ESCARGOT

5 bld Gambetta.
☎ 05.65.35.07.66
Closed May 20–June 10 and Nov 15–Dec 10. **TV**.

Don't worry if things look pretty uninteresting from the outside – the owners have put all their energies into an ongoing refurbishment of the bedrooms. The quality is superb. We can say without a doubt that the beds are amazingly comfortable. The restaurant opens onto the street, while the eight bedrooms are located in a very peaceful annexe nearby. Each one is wonderfully decorated with made-to-measure furniture and matching curtains. Beautiful view of the church or private gardens. Bedrooms 207–326F. We've a soft spot for number 9 (sleeping two or three guests) with its mezzanine and marvellous window. Hearty, buffet style breakfast 32F. You'll get good value for money in the restaurant. Set meals 56–155F, serving tasty snails of course. Non-smokers are not forgotten about – there's a dining room especially for them. Chess games every Friday evening. Informal and very friendly reception. It's advisable to book accommodation. And if you're a bonsai enthusiast, you'll be pleased to know that the owner is very fond of her bonsai trees.

HÔTEL DE FRANCE***

252 av. Jean-Jaurès (Centre).
☎ 05.65.35.16.76 F 05.65.22.01.08
Closed for two weeks at the end of December.
Secure parking. **TV**. **Canal+**.

Plain, modern and functional architecture. The hotel has 80 very comfortable rooms with shower/wc or bath. Doubles 220–350. The ones overlooking the courtyard are quieter so ask for one of those. They all have a direct phone and a mini-bar and some have air-conditioning. There's no restaurant but the buffet-style breakfast (40F) is terrific.

10% LE GRAND HÔTEL TERMINUS***

5 av. Charles-Freycinet (West).
☎ 05.65.35.24.50 F 05.65.22.06.40
Restaurant closed Sunday evenings and Mondays.
Secure parking. **TV**. **Canal+**. **Disabled access**.

This is a delightful hotel dating from the turn of the century. It has recently been renovated throughout but care has ben taken to preserve one or two reminders of its long history such as the very old plaque that reads "Recommended by Nagel" (an early guidebook). Friendly welcome. Rooms are large and all have a phone. Doubles with bath and wc quite expensive at 460F.

RESTAURANT LE TROQUET DES HALLES

55 rue Saint-Maurice (Centre).
☎ 05.65.22.15.81
Closed Sundays. **Disabled access**.

The working man's caff that we all know and love. Market porters, stallholders, locals in social categories C and D, the less well-off, and tourists irresistibly drawn to friendly eating places have been coming here for more than half a century to fill up on the robust home cooking at pre-war – maybe even pre-world war I – prices. For 38F you get soup and the day's special, for 45F a starter plus main course or main course plus dessert, and for 55F soup or *charcuterie*, the day's special, cheese or dessert, and 1/4 litre of red wine. Incredible value for money. Lunch served until 3pm.

RESTAURANT DE LA BOURSE

7 pl. de la Bourse.
☎ 05.65.35.17.78
Closed Sundays.

Here's a friendly bar-cum-restaurant serving fresh, tasty dishes at perfectly reasonable prices. Set meals 55F, 75F and 85F. Dish of the day 35F. Specialities such as *salade gourmet* (lettuce, warm gizzards, pine kernels and tomatoes) and *salade cabécou*. They do an excellent breast of duck with pepper. A real quality place to suit all pockets with bright, attractive décor and good music. Bedrooms from 110F in the annexe some distance off, but they won't appeal to everyone.

LA PLANCHA

24 pl. Champollion.
☎ 05.65.35.15.35
Closed Sundays.

Here's a very informal bar-cum-restaurant specializing in tapas down near the quays. Paintings reminiscent of Dali are dotted around the walls – see what you make of them for yourself. Various tapas dishes available at reasonable prices, 60F for a selection. Themes nights such as couscous on Thursdays and paella on Fridays. Dish of the day 42F with a peach-flavoured liqueur to boot. We liked the warm, youthful atmosphere of this unpretentious place. Night owls will appreciate the late service up till 11.30pm. You can always sip a liqueur at the bar if you're not quite ready to hit the sack.

RESTAURANT L'ARAPAGOUS

153 rue Saint-Urcisse.
☎ 05.65.35.65.69
Closed Saturday lunchtimes and Mondays.

A beautiful, 14th century building with exposed beams and roughly-cut red stonework. Black and white photos to remind us of Quercy's rustic past. You'll find the owner in front of the monumental fireplace, keeping an eye on the meat and fish. Try the fillet of Rossini beef, salad of gizzards or truffle omelette. The *moelleux* of chocolate takes pride of place when it comes to desserts. Set meals 65F (weekdays), 85F and 190F. Good wine cellar to boot.

RESTAURANT LE RENDEZ-VOUS

49 rue Clément-Marot.
☎ 05.65.22.65.10
Closed Sunday lunchtimes in season and Mondays out of season.

This is an up-and-coming restaurant locally and reservations are almost essential if you want to sample simple dishes full of flavour and originality. Try the *foie gras* ravioli, for example, or the crispy zander with baby vegetables or, for dessert, the apple tart with caramel sauce. Set meals 72F (weekday lunchtimes only) and 105F.

PRADINES 46090 (3KM NW)

LE CLOS GRAND**

Laberaudie.
☎ 05.65.35.04.39 F→ 05.65.22.56.69
Closed Sunday evenings and Mondays (Monday lunchtimes only in July and August). **Car park. TV.**

Lovely inn with a big lush garden and a swimming pool. Rooms are very pleasant and comfortable, ranging in price from 250F (with shower) to 300F (with bath). The rooms in the annex have views of the fields. The restaurant has a very good reputation and the set meals at 83F (weekdays) and 105–230F offer regional dishes like *pastis quercynois* and stuffed duck breast and fish – seafood casserole, for example. The attractive dining room has country-style décor and a big open fireplace. Staff are very jolly.

SAINT-HENRI 46000 (5KM N)

RESTAURANT LA GARENNE

How to get there: by the N20 in the direction of Souillac.
☎ 05.65.35.40.67
Closed Tuesday evenings and Wednesdays (except mid-July–end Aug) and during the February school holidays. **Car park.**

The restaurant, in a large private house, is decorated wonderfully well to look like a country inn. Reception was polite without being over the top. The cooking is full of flair and imagination. There are set meals at 90F and 150F but if you reall want to appreciate the chef's originality then go for one of the others – for 190F for example you can choose between rack of lamb with unpeeled cloves of garlic, *gourmandise* of duck, scrambled eggs with truffles, fillet of sole in a truffle-scented *velouté* sauce served with fresh pasta and so on. An excellent restaurant in a beautiful part of Quercy.

CAMPAN 65710

RESTAURANT L'ISARD

Le Chiroulet; it's at the far end of the very pretty vallée de l'Esponne.
☎ 05.62.91.72.56
Closed Dec 15–Feb 1.

This is a tiny hamlet with a few mountain style houses, a wonderful setting for the restaurant which gives its clients an above average welcome and serves generous helpings of traditional peasant dishes like *garbure* (hearty vegetable soup), quails in aspic stuffed with duck livers, ceps *à la persillade*, *confit*, and wood pigeon in a red wine sauce. Prices are extremely reasonable, with set meals 70–185F. Three bedrooms with basin are available at 145F. Half-board offers really good value for money, with prices starting at 230F per day per person. Walk off your meal with a stroll round lac Bleu and feast your eyes on the scenery.

CARMAUX 81400

RESTAURANT LA MOUETTE

4 place Jean-Jaurès.
☎ 05.63.36.79.90 Fax05.63.76.40.76
Closed Sunday and Monday evenings and 10 days in February.

Lunch served noon–2pm and dinner 7–9pm.This restaurant, with its original and modern décor, is without question the best place to eat in Carmaux. The cheapest set meal is 57F (lunchtimes only). There are a number of others, including one at 140F (for which you get two starters, main course, cheese and dessert), and a *menu-surprise*. at 260F.You have to order this specially but it comes with – wait for it – six courses, a platter of local cheeses, and two desserts!

CASTELNAU-DE-MONTMIRAL 81140

10% AUBERGE DES ARCADES.

It's in the main square.
☎ 05.63.33.20.88

Doubles with shower or bath 180–200F. Lovely rooms – there are some really nice ones just under the eaves (ask for number 6) or overlooking the square. Half-board 240F. There's a simple and hearty *menu du jour* at 62F or you could opt for the 95F set meal and have roquefort salad, stew of wild boar (the house speciality), cheese, and dessert. If you go for the 115F or the 130F set meal, you'll get duck *confit*, and if you really want to push the boat out and spend more than that, you can.

CASTELSARRASIN 82100

10% HÔTEL MARCEILLAC**

54 rue de l'Égalité.
☎ 05.63.32.30.10 F 05.62.32.39.52
Secure parking in **private car park**. **TV**.

There's a big surprise in store for you when you walk into this seemingly ordinary hotel and close out the noise of the street. The rooms overlook a small interior courtyard with a glass roof and the reception area is in a kind of glass cage. The light and airy architecture and the pale colours on the walls make the hotel look as if it belonged in a spa town. When you find out that it was built at the turn of the century specifically as a hotel, you realize just how very different it is from a hotel that's a converted house. And it stands out from everything else in the région. The rooms – numbers 1 and 6 have just been refurbished – are all delightful and though the furniture may be as old as the hotel it has been well cared for. Doubles with shower/wc 195–215F (with or without TV), with bath 220–260F. Delightful welcome.

CASTRES 81100

10% HÔTEL RIVIÈRE**

10 quai Tourcaudière (Centre).
☎ 05.63.59.04.53 F 05.63.59.61.97
How to get there: it's on the banks of the Agout, opposite the old tanners' houses.
Secure parking. **TV**.

Service 7.30–10pm. The reproductions of Impressionist paintings on just about every vertical surface and the congenial staff give a pleasant feel to the hotel. Rooms are clean and pretty and prices are reasonable – 120F with basin and 220F with shower/wc and TV. Give the rooms overlooking the embankment a miss – they tend to be noisy. You can have a meal on a tray for 80F.

10% HÔTEL DE L'EUROPE***

5 rue Victor-Hugo (Centre).
☎ 05.63.59.00.33 F 05.63.59.21.38
TV. **Canal+**.

This glorious 17th century house, discovered and restored by a group of young people with a passion for art, architecture and decorating, must for a time have looked more like several artists' studios than a hotel in the making. But the transformation is complete and the hotel is a delight (once you're past the flower-filled patio that is, which is still a bit of a mess). Each bedroom is better than the next, a subtle mix of glass and warm brick, splendid beams and design furniture, dressed stone and modern bathrooms. You get to choose whichever one best suits your own personal fantasy, which is a great idea. Prices range from 180F to 250F depending on the time of year. All have a spanking new bathroom, phone and minibar and in some bathrooms, the tub is actually up a few steps (check out rooms 106, 110, 111, 118, 119 and 126). Evening meals – 75F with wine (weekdays only) – are served either at the bar or in your room. An extremely good hotel.

10% HÔTEL RENAISSANCE***

17 rue Victor-Hugo (Centre).
☎ 05.63.59.30.42 F 05.63.72.11.57
TV.

Alain Escaudemaison used to roam the world in his days as a TV cameraman but now he's staying put and has renovated this enormous 17th century building with its vaults, arches, nooks and crannies and old beams. The hotel is in the heart of the old town and you'll get a good night's sleep in the large rooms that Alain's wife has done a great job of decorating. Prices range from 290F for a double with bath to 600F for the suite. If you want to keep up with what's happening in the world, you can pick up CNN, the all-news channel, and Eurosport. Table d'hôte for residents in the evening (you'll need to order ahead) costs 78F. Good home cooking featuring local dishes. And if you want a bit of exercise, the hotel does golf weekends. Breakfast is free on presentation of this guidebook.

|●| LA TOUR D'EMPARE

18 rue d'Empare; it's in the street behind the old tanners' houses on the river bank.
☎ 05.63.35.19.43
Closed Saturday lunchtimes, Mondays, and Aug 15–Sept 10.

Superb architecture. Semicircular dining rooms, round tables and white tablecloths provide an elegant setting for your meal. The cheapest set meal is 70F but you might want to think about treating yourself to one of the others at 100F, 125F and 145F. We opted to spend 100F, and as well as cheese and dessert we got the house *terrine* (just the way we like it) followed by *aiguillettes* of duck with raspberries that was sensational. The dishes were nicely presented and the service was attentive.

|●| RESTAURANT LA MANDRAGORE

1 rue Malpas (Centre).
☎ 05.63.59.51.27
Closed Sundays and Monday lunchtimes.

This is a fairly new restaurant which has quickly become fashionable because of its futuristic designer décor and the meticulous cooking. The cheapest set meal at 75F consists of starter, main course and dessert, each course being accompanied by a glass of selected wine. The 130F set meal looked rather tempting — warm salad of skate with herbs, duck breast in wine, cheese plate, and *millefeuille* of seasonal fruit. The 160F *menu surprise* consisted of five courses. The wine list is as long as your arm, which is hardly surprising when you learn that the proprietor used to work at *Le Grand Écuyer* and was chosen as the best Belgian wine waiter. But don't worry, he'll choose something good just for you and it won't cost an arm and a leg.

SORÈZE 81540 (25KM SW)

|●| LE TOURNESOL

rue du Maquis.
☎ 05.63.74.11.10
Closed Tuesdays (except in August) and two weeks in January.

This is a wonderful place, full of regulars, gourmets and people who like their food "the way Mum used to make it". Madame David is the only person in the kitchen and she does all her own peeling, chopping and cooking. And if it's the right time of year she uses her day off to go mushroom hunting, bringing back baskets full of ceps and morels for her customers, lots of whom apparently drool at the thought of them just fried and sprinkled with parsley. The *daubes*, *blanquettes* and other dishes that need long slow simmering are out of this world. She makes a great *cassoulet* and if you take the trouble to phone in advance she'll make the necessary arrangements and it'll taste even better. Cheapest set meal is 65F, with others at 95F, 150F and 220F. Children's menu 45F.

CAUSSADE 82300

10% ⌂ |●| HÔTEL LARROQUE**

av. de la Gare (North-West).
☎ 05.63.65.11.77 F 05.63.65.12.04
Closed Dec 21–Jan 15. Restaurant closed Saturday lunchtimes and Sunday evenings out of season.
Secure parking in **private car park**. **TV**. **Canal+**.

A very old family-run business that goes back five generations and has a solid reputation. Guests and atmosphere are both rather elegant and the décor's a bit plush. Big swimming pool, garden and solarium — very pleasant. Doubles from 200F; if you want one with period furniture it'll be about 220F. The kitchen has taken regional dishes, updated them, added a touch of brio and come up with dishes like corn biscuits with *petits-gris* snails and parsley-scented oil, poached eggs in a red wine sauce (the red wine in this case being Coteaux du Quercy), rabbit in a sauce made from Jerusalem artichokes, duck *en daube* with grapes and maize flour cakes and, for dessert, sorbet and *croquant à la lavande de Saint-Antonin.* Set meals 70F, 95F, 120F and 170F.

CAUTERETS 65110

10% ⌂ |●| HÔTEL DU LION D'OR**

12 rue Richelieu (Centre).
☎ 05.62.92.52.87 F 05.62.92.03.67
Closed Oct 1–Dec 20.

The oldest hotel still in business in the spa town is a family affair managed by sisters

Bernadette and Rose-Marie. It's gradually being renovated with almost compulsive attention to details like the percolator for the bar and the wall lights in the bedrooms. These are very cosy and a double with shower or bath will set you back 225–340F. A TV will be provided if you want one. Good home cooking is served in a pleasantly old-fashioned dining room, which is still waiting its turn to be renovated. Half-board from 220F.

CONDOM 32100

10% ☗ HÔTEL LE LOGIS DES CORDELIERS**

rue de la Paix; it's near the bandstand, heading towards Agen.
☎ 05.62.28.03.68 F 05.62.68.29.03
Closed in January. **Secure parking** in **private car park**. **TV**.

This is definitely one of the best hotels in the area if you want to stop for a couple of nights somewhere. It's an extremely handsome place with a garden and a swimming pool, there isn't a sound, and the owners bend over backwards to make their guests happy. The rooms are large and very comfortable. Doubles with bath overlooking the street (which is very quiet) are 260F and those overlooking the garden and pool 370F.

10% ☗ |●| HÔTEL DES TROIS LYS***

38 rue Gambetta; it's in the heart of the old town.
☎ 05.62.28.33.33 F 05.62.28.41.85
Closed in February. **Secure parking**. **TV**.

This is a wonderful building dating from the 18th century. The furniture and the decoration are both in the best of taste, courtesy of owners who've got class, a sense of humour, and aren't too bad at public relations either. Treat yourself to a double room (380–560F). Once you've tried out the pool and tasted the great breakfast (42F) and the evening table d'hôte (for hotel guests Sunday and Monday evenings only and you have to book), you won't mind the fact that your wallet is distinctly lighter than when you arrived.

|●| MOULIN DU PETIT GASCON

route d'Eauze; it's on the outskirts of town, on the river bank facing the stadium.
☎ 05.62.28.28.42
Closed Mondays (except in July and August) and Dec–March.

Lunch served noon–1.30pm (2pm in summer), dinner 7.30–9.30pm (10pm in summer). A very special place that makes you think it was built just so it could be used as a film set. The lock has been renovated, the river bank is made for strolling, the terrace is the kind you dream about, and there's greenery on all sides. The cooking is light which makes a refreshing change after all those heavy country dishes. Prices are reasonable, with a 90 F set meal at lunchtime (weekdays only) consisting of starter, main course and dessert. If you go for one of the others at 115F et 140F you shouldn't be disappointed. And if the river beckons, Madame can tell you all about the surprise cruises that are available.

|●| L'ORIGAN

4 rue du Cadeo; it's on the way to the church, opposite the school.
☎ 05.62.68.24.84
Closed Sundays, Mondays (except in July and August), and end Sept–mid-October.

It's hard to miss this friendly rustic-looking restaurant with its fine stone walls and colourful proprietors. It deserves better than to be called a pizzeria, a term that's much abused these days. There's no set meal but the menu is full of Italian sunshine and for 100F you can tuck into antipasti and a generous helping of osso bucco. You might even want to try a pizza – it's the real McCoy.

CONQUES 12320

☗ RÉSIDENCE DADON

rue Émile-Roudié; it's opposite the abbey.
☎ 05.65.72.82.98

This local authority hostel for pilgrims, students at the Centre européen d'art roman, hikers and so on offers incredible value for money. Rooms in the 16th century hospice are simple and clean, have shower/wc, sleep 2–8 and cost 115F a night per person. You'll need to bring your own towels but sheets are included in the price. It's quite something to wake up in one of the rooms overlooking the bell towers of the abbey. Half-board available at 145F a day, full board 180F.

☗ |●| AUBERGE SAINT-JACQUES**

rue Principale (Centre).
☎ 05.65.72.86.36 F 05.65.72.82.47
Closed Mondays out of season and in January.
Secure parking. **Disabled access**.

The one hotel in Conques that everyone can afford and gives good value for money. Staff are pleasant and the rooms are clean. Doubles 175–300F – some are ideal for lovers!

The restaurant serves good country cooking. The 85F set meal consists of *tourte*, stuffed tripe, cheese and dessert while 170F gets you *foie gras*, duck *confit*, cheese and dessert.

GRAND-VABRE 12320 (5.5KM N)

CHEZ MARIE

How to get there: by the D901.
☎ 05.65.69.84.55
Closed Tuesday evenings and three weeks in January.

Lunch served noon–2pm, dinner 7–9pm. As you come to this tiny village in the depths of Aveyron, you get the feeling that something good is about to happen — and you won't be far wrong as far as the inn is concerned. The country-style décor is simple and the covered terrace means you can eat outdoors. Staff are amiable and the service is attentive. With good traditional food made from good quality produce, full of calories, you'll be offered things like sweetbreads with ceps, chicken with chanterelles, and roast kid with sorrel. Nothing too adventurous since Madame prefers to stick with the tried and trusted, but what she does she does well and we liked it a lot. We weren't the only ones so it's best to book. Set meals 78–125F.

SAINT-CYPRIEN-SUR-DOURDOU 12320 (7KM S)

10% L'AUBERGE DE DOURDOU*

route de Rodez; take the rather nice road that follows the river and the gorges.
☎ 05.65.69.83.20
Closed in winter. **Secure parking** in **private car park**.

A good country inn — if only there were more like it. Lots of regulars. Very friendly welcome. Rooms are clean and more than adequate. They range in price from 200F (with shower/wc) to 215F (with bath) and you can choose to have a view of the village or the valley. A good little hotel if you're looking for somewhere cheap to stay near Conques.

CORDES 81170

10% HOSTELLERIE DU PARC**

Les Cabannes.
☎ 05.63.56.02.59 F 05.63.56.18.03
Closed Sunday evenings and Mondays out of season. **Secure parking** in **private car park**. **TV**.

Lunch served noon–2.15pm, dinner 7.30–9.30pm. Large stone house overlooking an old park and garden, with a large dining room decorated in country house fashion. Speedy service. Set meals 90F (except Sunday lunchtimes), 130F, 160F, 189F and 220F. Chef Claude Izard is quite a character. He chairs an enormous number of associations and has appointed himself the champion of authentic local French cooking. He offers a few specialities that hit the spot — rabbit with cabbage and *petits-gris* snails with fresh *foie gras* or *à la tarnaise*. Accommodation is available in the shape of simple and quite comfortable rooms at 270F and 300F — worth it for the sheer pleasure of just being here.

EAUZE 32800

AUBERGE DU GUINLET*

route de Castelnau-d'Auzan; take the D43.
☎ 05.62.09.85.99 F 05.62.09.84.50
Closed Fridays. **Car park**. **TV**. **Disabled access**.

Everything you need for a good holiday in the country. Doubles in the hotel with shower/wc and direct phone are 240F or if you prefer self-catering there are waterside bungalows to rent 1km from the inn. Good facilities. 1,800F a week out of season, 2,000F in season. Fairly basic campsite also available. The restaurant has set meals at 60F (wine included), 78F (two courses plus soup), 98F (soup, ham, snails and *aiguillettes*) and 145F (*foie gras* and *aiguillettes* of duck). Lots of things to do, with tennis courts, a nice pool and a well-known 18-hole golf course in extremely pleasant surroundings.

ENTRAYGUES-SUR-TRUYÈRE 12140

10% HÔTEL DU LION D'OR**

Tour de Ville (Centre); it's in the main street.
☎ 05.65.44.50.01 Fax05.65.44.53.43
Secure parking in **private car park**. **TV**. **Disabled access**.

This is a large stone building with 50 nice rooms. Doubles 250F with shower and 290F with bath. Good traditional food along the lines of stuffed cabbage, stuffed tripe, trout and so on. Set meals 70F, 98F 135F, and 170F. Pleasant garden where you can swim in the pool or play tennis or crazy golf. In fact, relaxation seems to be the name of the game here. There's also a sauna and a gym.

10% LA TRUYÈRE**

60 av. du Pont-de-la-Truyère (North-East); it's near the Gothic bridge.
☎ 05.65.44.51.10 F 05.65.44.57.78
Closed Mondays and mid-Nov–late March.

Secure parking in **private car park**.
Disabled access.

Lunch served 12.30–1.45pm, dinner 7.30–8.45pm. Nice inn with a garden in pleasant surroundings. It has 25 doubles with bath at prices ranging from 220F to 285F – try for one with a view of the river and the valley. The cooking's good too and there are set meals at 70F, 100F, 130F et 200F offering things like *marbré* of chicken in a sauce made from chives, *rillettes* of trout with smoked salmon, kidneys in Madeira sauce, cheese and dessert. Some of the à la carte dishes are worth trying – sweetbread and cep pie, for example, or monkfish and salmon with allspice or fillet of beef with peaches. A good little family restaurant.

ESTAING 12190

10% HÔTEL-RESTAURANT AUX ARMES D'ESTAING**

quai du Lot.
☎ 05.65.44.70.02 F 05.65.44.74.54
Closed Jan 2–30 and two weeks in November.
Secure parking in **private car park**.

Traditional and delightfully provincial tourist hotel. More than adequate rooms with basin in the main building come in at 160F. Rooms in the annex, which have been nicely renovated, are 225F. Great value for money. Very pleasant dining room. The service can be a bit slow, especially if there are a couple of groups in, but the cooking's good. It tends towards the classical but there are one or two pleasant surprises in store. The chef's repertoire includes salad of lamb's sweetbreads with chanterelle mushrooms, monkfish with star anise and vanilla, duck breast with soft fruit, and fillet of veal with *foie gras*. *Aligot* (mashed potatoes with cheese and garlic) has to be ordered ahead of time. Set meals 65F, 90F, 110F and 155F

10% AUBERGE SAINT-FLEURET*

rue François-d'Estaing.
☎ 05.65.44.01.44 F 05.65.44.72.19
Closed Jan–Feb, and Wednesdays and Thursdays in winter.

Lunch served noon –1.30pm, dinner 7.30–9pm. It used to be nothing to write home about from the outside but the last we heard, renovation work was planned for the winter of 1997. And the inside has everything the outside lacks. The rooms have been renovated and the ones overlooking the garden are particularly pleasant. Doubles are 190F with basin/wc and 230F with shower/wc or bath. The dining room, decorated in blue chintz, is cosy and the cooking is of the classical and traditional variety, offering dishes like old-fashioned cabbage soup, stuffed snails, chicken leg *confit* with onions, rabbit cooked in a haybox and duck breast with mint. If you're puritanical about overindulgence, this is no place for you!. Prices are very reasonable, with set meals ranging from 60F to 175F and half-board at 215F a head. Our only criticism is that the reception was a bit offhand. But that'll probably sort itself out.

ESTANG 32240

10% HÔTEL-RESTAURANT DU COMMERCE

Centre; it's in the centre of the village, near the arena.
☎ 05.62.09.63.41 F 05.62.09.64.22

Lunch served noon–1.30pm and dinner (by reservation only) 8–9pm. This venerable establishment has had a facelift. The rooms have been renovated throughout and are ideal if you want to spend just one night (220F) or take half-board (255F). It's a temple of regional cooking and offers trout stuffed with ceps, warm *foie gras* with fruit, and leg of fattened duck in Madiran wine. Dive into the set meals at 70F and 120F, or treat yourself by going à la carte and, for 120F or so, indulging in a *portefeuille royal* (duck breast stuffed with *foie gras* and ceps) or similar delights. Colourful décor and friendly welcome.

FIGEAC 46100

10% HÔTEL DES BAINS

1 rue du Grifful.
☎ 05.65.34.10.89 F 05.65.14.00.65
TV.

Situated on the banks of the Célé, these former public baths have been converted into a twenty-one bedroomed hotel. Ten of them offer a beautiful view of the Célé. Expect to pay 150F with washing facilities (170F in high season) and 220–300F with shower. The owners refurbish a few rooms every year. Breakfast 33F in the dining room or 38F in your room. Friendly reception. Tourists on cycling holidays are most welcome.

HÔTEL CHAMPOLLION**

3 place Champollion (Centre).
☎ 05.65.34.04.37
TV.

The Champollion commemorated in the hotel's name was a famous Egyptologist in the first half of the 19th century. (He gave his name to the square as well and the house he was born in isn't too far away.) There's a bar on the ground floor and you'll find the entrance to the hotel in the street to the left. This is a pleasant and comfortable establishment with an impressive wooden staircase. Rooms were renovated recently and all have bath, cable TV, wonderful pine floors and there's something a bit Japanese about them – very pleasant. Doubles 250F. Friendly welcome.

RESTAURANT LA CUISINE DU MARCHÉ

15 rue Clermont.
☎ 05.65.50.18.55

An establishment that stands out from all the others. The cooking's just as tasty, but so much lighter, and the open-plan kitchen allows you to watch the chefs at work. Their fish dishes are as wonderfully fresh as the local produce served on the side. The market produce on offer definitely justifies the restaurant's name! Sample the *dôme* of soft fruits, one of their highly refined desserts. Set meals 65F (lunchtimes) - 220F, and a high quality wine cellar. Joël Centeno, the guy in charge, acts more like a foreman than an owner, and is responsible for creating the delightfully convivial atmosphere. Over a period of twenty years, he's held various positions in French restaurants abroad and has developed his own ideas. He personally takes care of the reception and service, with his wife and an energetic, attentive waitress at his side. They may not have been open very long, but everyone's talking about them already. Without a doubt, this is our favourite place in town. Advisable to book.

LA PUCE À L'OREILLE**

5 rue Saint-Thomas (Centre); it's in the heart of the old town.
☎ 05.65.34.33.08
Closed Mondays (except in July and August).

The restaurant's a pretty 15th century house in a narrow and picturesque side street. It has a quiet, pleasant dining room and the cooking has a great reputation. The cheapest set meal is 85F (not available Sundays or public holidays) and consists of warm Cabecou cheese in puff pastry with honey, roast quail with juniper berries and cheese or dessert. There are two set meals at 130F that change with the seasons – you might get a *millefeuille* of leeks, Roquefort cheese and walnuts, duck breast kebabs with orange butter and brown sugar *crème brûlée*.There are three other set meals at 150F, 170F and 250F, and a children's menu for 50F. Reckon on about 90F à la carte for things like sweetbread *minute* and calf's foot with ceps or thick-sliced calf's liver with aromatic herb butter. Good idea to book.

FOIX 09000

HÔTEL AUDOYE-LONS***

6 place G.-Duthil (Centre).
☎ 05.61.65.52.44 Fax 05.61.02.68.18
Closed Saturdays out of season and Dec 20–Jan 15.
TV. Canal+. Disabled access.

Lunch served noon–2pm, dinner 7.30–9.15pm. Your classic country town hotel with 40 rooms, all but two of which have shower/wc. Comfortable doubles from 180F (with basin) to 290F (with bath). Set meals 75F (buffet and *cassoulet*), 95F, 110F and 125F. À la carte is a bit more expensive. Half-board 240F.

SAINT-PIERRE-DE-RIVIÈRE 09000 (5KM W)

HÔTEL-RESTAURANT LA BARGUILLÈRE**

Centre; take the D17.
☎ 05.61.65.14.02
Closed Wednesdays and Nov–end of Feb.

Lunch served noon–2pm, dinner 7.30–9.30pm. Pleasant little village hotel with a nice garden. Doubles with bath 220F. Known for its good cooking. Cosy dining room. Set meals from 70F (cheese, dessert, wine and coffee included) are served at the bar. Children's menu 40F. Local dishes like trout with chives and shrimp are 75F. Great specialities include *mouclade* (the Pyrenees might not be quite the right region for this Charente speciality but that's where the chef comes from), *confit*, *aiguillettes* of duck with ceps, and tripe. There's also a "country" set meal that features local produce for 130F.

GAUDENT 65370

10% HÔTEL-RESTAURANT LA CHAPELLE D'ALBRET

How to get there: by the D26 and the D925.
☎ 05.62.99.21.13 Fax 05.62.99.23.69

Closed Mondays and the first week in January.
Car park. **TV**.

The establishment was built fairly recently but it fits in well with its surroundings, including the 12th century chapel that gave it its name. You'll find cows grazing under your balcony. Pleasant bedrooms on two levels. Doubles with shower or bath 220F. Proprietor Michel Castet, who does the cooking, was born in the valley and skilfully reworks traditional recipes like *roussolle* (chicken stuffing) and *parcellous* (stuffed cabbage in a sauce made from morels). Set meals 70–137F.

GAVARNIE 65120

LA CHAUMIÈRE

How to get there: it's 500m from the village, one of the last houses by the river.
☎ 05.62.92.48.08
Closed Nov 15–Dec 22. **Secure parking**.

You'll have an unobstructed view so do stop and admire it. Even though it's regarded primarily as an eating place, accommodation is available in the shape of two very simple but very well-cared for rooms. Doubles with shower 170F. The restaurant serves *crêpes*, omelettes, snacks, a few local specialities and afternoon tea. The cheapest set meal is about 55F but is only available during the holidays.

10% COMPOSTELLE HÔTEL**

rue de l'Église (South).
☎ 05.62.92.49.43
Closed Nov 12–Christmas holidays. **Car park**.
Disabled access.

Sylvie et Yvan (keen hikers and big fans of *Velvet Underground*) knocked about the world a fair bit before taking over this pleasant little family hotel. Rooms are called after Alpine flowers — edelweiss, columbine and the like — and almost all of them overlook the corrie. Doubles 205–280F. Yvan knows the area well and can organize walks.

GIROUSSENS 81500

10% HÔTEL-RESTAURANT L'ÉCHAUGUETTE

Centre.
☎ 05.63.41.63.65 Fax 05.63.41.63.13
Closed Sunday evenings, Mondays (except July–Sept), Feb 1–21, and Sept 1530.

Just in case you were wondering, an *échauguette* is a corner turret on a house — in this particular case a 13th century house in wonderful surroundings. There are five rooms with bath (270F) and a wide range of set meals from 60F (lunchtimes) to 260F. Pierrette Canonica is well-known in the area for her exquisite and refined cooking and you will be warmly welcomed by her husband, Claude, who knows everything there is to know about the history of the village and the region.

SAINT-SULPICE 81370 (9KM W)

AUBERGE DE LA POINTE

How to get there: take the N88 or exit 6 on the A68.
☎ 05.63.41.80.14 Fax05.63.41.90.24
Closed Tuesday evenings and Wednesdays, except in summer. **Car park**.

This is one of the leading contenders in the local good food league. The dining rooms are enormous but convivial and well-laid out, and there's a shady terrace by the river. It offers a number of set meals ranging in price from 65F to 190F with dishes like *croustillant* of calf's foot, saddle of rabbit with braised cabbage and raspberry soufflé.

GRAMAT 46500

10% LE RELAIS DES GOURMANDS**

2 av. de la Gare.
☎ 05.65.38.83.92 Fax 05.65.38.70.99
Closed Sunday evenings and Monday lunchtimes (except in July and August). **Car park**. **TV**.

An enormous private house (in immaculate condition) with a swimming pool and flower garden. Bright modern and functional rooms 270–420F, all with bath and direct phone. You'll get a polite and attentive welcome from Susy. She's actually British but you'd swear she was born here like husband Gérard. The love they both have for this part of the world is reflected in the cooking, which offers *millefeuille* of salmon with a sauce made from peppers, duck hearts *en brochette,* calf's head and tongue in *sauce gribiche*, *cassoulet* and so on. The cheapest set meal is 85F (weekdays only) and it's terrific. Others 95F–225F. Wash it all down with one of the inexpensive local wines.

GRAULHET 81300

LA RIGAUDIÉ

route de Saint-Julien-du-Puy (East); it's 2km from the centre of town.

☎ 05.63.34.50.07
Closed Saturday and Sunday evenings, the last week in December and the whole of August.

Mature parklands form a wonderful setting for an enormous air-conditioned dining room with a magnificent ceiling, where the cooking is excellent and the service professional. There are set meals at 77.50F (weekday lunchtimes), 114.50F and 145F. Spoil yourself and have an apéritif (the sweet white Gaillac) and the 145F fish menu. You'll start off with an appetizer and move on to a shrimp tart with cress sauce. After that, give the sole a miss in favour of the tremendous cod with *tapenade*. Cod's often regarded as a prettty ordinary fish but when it's as fresh as can be and is skilfully prepared — as here — it's up there with the best of them. To do it justice, choose a slightly sparkling Gaillac (70F or so), which will go equally well with desserts like the *gâteau meringué*. The cheese platter that precedes dessert is excellent. This is professional cooking and it makes for a wonderful experience.

LACROUZETTE 81210

L'AUBERGE DE CRÉMAUSSEL

How to get there: from Castres, take the D622 in the direction of Lacaune; after 5km, you'll come to Lafontas; carry on for another 2km then turn left in the direction of Lacrouzette-Rochers du Sidobre; when you get to the D30 4km further on, turn left and then right after 2km (still in the direction of Rochers du Sidobre). The inn is clearly marked.
☎ 05.63.50.61.33
Closed Wednesdays and for the months of January and February. **Car park**.

You should book. Five very clean rooms with pastel walls and wooden flooring 180F. Breakfast 25F. Friendly country-style restaurant with a solid reputation. The dining room has a stone wall and a fine fireplace. Very good Roquefort salad. The restaurant's specialities — cheese soup in winter and shrimp in summer — have to be ordered ahead of time. Set meals 90F and 130F; à la carte prices are reasonable (reckon on 120F). Finish off with the local pastry known as *croustade*, which is sheer heaven for 10F. An extremely good restaurant.

LAGUIOLE 12210

10% HÔTEL RÉGIS***

place de la Patte-d'Oie.
☎ 05.65.44.30.05 Fax 05.65.48.46.44
Closed Nov 11–Dec 20. **Car park. TV. Canal+**.

Lunch served noon–2pm, dinner 7.30–9pm. This is one of the oldest hotels in Laguiole and has become quite an institution. There's been a lot of refurbishment and as a result the rooms are comfortable but a little clinical. Doubles 185–220F (with shower/wc) and 250–330F (with bath). Good traditional cooking. Set meals 86F (Roquefort *feuilleté*, stuffed tripe, *aligot*, cheese and dessert) and 132F (salad of smoked goose and goose liver or *croustade* of snails followed by duck *confit* or tournedos and *aligot*.) A good place to stay in the area.

10% GRAND HÔTEL AUGUY***

2 allée de l'Amicale.
☎ 05.65.44.31.11 Fax 05.65.51.50.81
Closed Sunday evenings and Mondays (except during school holidays), June 11–18 and Nov 22–Jan 8.
Secure parking. TV. Disabled access.

This is an establishment with a good solid reputation. Rooms are pleasant, well-cared for and well equipped. Doubles 240F (with shower/wc) and 250–350F (with bath). The rather nice dining room is bright and while the décor might be a bit garish, who cares? The important thing is what's on your plates, and the cooking here is first-rate. It's as if having one of France's best chefs in the neighbourhood has got everybody straining to do better. And we're not complaining! Traditional local dishes hold their own in an extensive menu and it's all quite mouth-watering. Set meals 120F (not available Sundays), 145F, 170F and 280F offer delights like a *galette* of pig's trotters in meat stock with ceps and potato cake, stuffed tripe, grilled rib of beef with *aligot*, medallions of hare with juniper berries or salmon trout in a sauce made from Laguiole cheese. Indulge yourself and have one of the wonderful desserts. Words can't describe the *craquelin* of bitter almonds and strawberry compote we had. Half-board 240–280F per person in July and August. Welcome and service both very pleasant. Delightful staff who smile a lot. All in all, an extremely good restaurant.

CASSUÉJOULS 12210 (10KM NW)

CHEZ COLETTE

How to get there: from Laguiole, head in the direction of Saint-Flour and it's the first road on the left.
☎ 05.65.44.33.71
Closed whenever Colette needs a break.

Reservations essential. It always does the heart good to get lost on the back roads, especially when at the end of the day you come across places like this little country bistro. Colette has a talent for making you fall in love with the region, first by talking to you about it with such passion and warmth, secondly by serving you a few simple invigorating meals that every self-respecting grandmother in the region knows how to make. Colette's grandmother probably had a few more tricks up her sleeve and she's passed them on to her grand-daughter. The setting couldn't be simpler and the atmosphere is relaxed and friendly — for once, you won't feel like a fish out of water surrounded by regulars. You'll soon see why customers keep coming back — for 75F we were entitled to melon, a flan of oyster mushrooms, sausage with *aligot*, cheese and dessert. Beat that! If you don't have much of an appetite, you need only pay 55F to eat extremely well. In short, the kind of place we all dream of finding.

LATOUILLE-LENTILLAC 46400

RESTAURANT GAILLARD

le bourg.
☎ 05.65.38.10.25
Closed Nov.

This traditional restaurant enjoys an excellent reputation. The locals treat themselves regularly to fresh trout and tasty local dishes. Go on, try the mushrooms or the local lamb. Terrific desserts. Set meals 75–160F. We appreciated the really warm welcome.

LAUZERTE 82110

HÔTEL DU QUERCY

faubourg d'Auriac.
☎ 05.63.94.66.36 Fax: 05.63.95.73.21
Closed three weeks in October; restaurant closed Sunday evenings and Mondays out of season.
Car park.

Service at lunchtime and from 7.30pm. Simplicity and thoughtfulness are the words that spring to mind when describing this establishment and the welcome that the Bacou family, with father Frédéric at the head, give their guests. The rooms are simple, clean and inexpensive (from 170F with shower/wc and 200F with bath). The cooking is sophisticated, the portions are generous and you'll get incredible value for money. There's an exceedingly good set meal for 110F that consists of a *sabayon* of fish and shellfish, a wonderful leek fondue in a vermouth sauce, and panfried Barbary duck in a honey and whisky sauce. Other set meals are 140F, 170F and 230F, the cheapest available being 58F (weekday lunchtimes). This is the kind of establishment that will keep on surprising you. Doesn't take credit cards unfortunately.

DURFORT-LACAPELETTE 82390 (9KM S)

10% HÔTEL-RESTAURANT AUBE NOUVELLE

How to get there: on the D2, coming from Lauzerte, and the inn's on the left just before you actually get to the village.
☎ 05.63.04.50.33 Fax 05.63.04.57.55
Closed during the Christmas and New Year holidays.
Secure parking in private **car park**.

Marc de Smet's family moved to Quercy from Belgium in 1955 and he has now taken over the business from his parents. It's an idyllic spot. There are fields all around and a lovely terrace and garden. Clean and well-looked after rooms 160–270F. Numbers 4 and 14 are small but they've been completely refurbished. Substantial set meals range in price from 60F (weekday lunchtimes) to 190F. The cooking is regional in flavour, with a few Belgian dishes — mussels in cream, rabbit *à la flamande* , shellfish *waterzooi*, and sea bass in a sauce made from cream and one of those famous Belgian beers to remind you of Marc's origins. He tells his guests that just because it's not costing them a fortune doesn't mean that they're going to get half-empty plates. A really nice place, this.

LECTOURE 32700

10% HÔTEL DE BASTARD**

rue Lagrange (North).
☎ 05.62.68.82.44 Fax 05.62.68.76.81
Secure parking. **TV**.

Marvellous hotel with oodles of charm, ideal for honeymooners or those still in the first throes of passion. The building is a fine example of 18th century architecture and whoever chose the furniture and décor has got taste. Pleasant welcome and incredible value for money. Doubles 230–350F, half-board 260–360F per person per day. There's also a big terrace, gardens and a swimming pool with views of the surrounding countryside — everything you ever dreamed of in fact. The place is well-known for its cooking.

The 85F set meal, for example, is quite exceptional and available every day, if you ask nicely. Naturally, à la carte is a bit pricey. Children's menu is 48F.

LEYME 46120

HÔTEL-RESTAURANT LESCURE**

rte de St-Céré.
☎ 05.65.38.90.07

Situated in the little village of Leyme, here's the kind of hotel-cum-restaurant oozing with character that we like. It's been looked after by the same family for more than fifty years now, offering comfy accommodation at reasonable prices. Doubles 150–265F with shower/wc. A few, such as number 23, could do with a lick of paint. Breakfast 30F. Prices for half-board start at 210F. The big dining room, opening onto a pond, offers tasty, well put together, regional dishes. How about trying the terrific salted and smoked wild boar with local mushrooms? Set meals from 60F (weekdays) – 160F, 7F for a quarter of table wine. Selection of wines available. Carefully designed décor – have a good look at the Picasso print (the real thing!) alongside the Matisse reproductions. You've guessed it, the owner's got a passion for modern art, and an amazing personality to boot.

LOMBEZ 32220

HÔTEL LE RELAIS DE LA VALLÉE**

bd des Pyrénées.
☎ 05.62.62.35.10 F 05.62.62.55.05
Restaurant closed Wednesdays. **Car park. TV. Disabled access.**

It's not easy finding a good little place that's not too expensive in *foie gras* land, but here's a nice village hotel in an old house that's been renovated throughout. Warm welcome, family atmosphere and pleasantly understated. Rooms are inexpensive — a double with shower/wc will cost you 230F. If you can get it, go for one at the back overlooking the garden. Cheapest set meal is 68F (weekdays only). Good regional cooking.

ENDOUFIELLE 32600 (14KM NE)

LA FERME DE MANON DES HERBES

How to get there: on the D634 – the village is between Lombez and Isle-Jourdain.
☎ 05.62.07.97.19 F same.
Secure parking.

A modern-day smallholding, with Dad in the kitchen and his daughter looking after the dining room. There are straw-bottomed chairs, flowers and candles on the tables, bunches of dried flowers hanging from the beams, and a big open fireplace against a backdrop of antique furniture, old mirrors and elderly customers. It all gives you a very pleasant feeling of having stepped back in time. Appealing set meal at 125F offers *salade gersoise* as a starter followed by tasty duck legs *confit*, and a fresh and colourful homemade dessert. Other set meals cost 165F and 275F if you get the urge to splash out.

LOURDES 65100

10% HÔTEL MAJESTIC**

9 av. Maransin (Centre); it's a ten minute walk from the shrines, at the corner of the avenue and a cul-de-sac (you can park there).
☎ 05.62.94.27.23 F 05.62.94.64.91
Closed Oct 15–April 15. **TV. Disabled access.**

Service at lunchtime and from 7.30pm. There are masses of hotels in Lourdes but we chose this one because it gives you decent value for money. Doubles with shower/wc 240F, with bath 260F. Simple home cooking along the lines of duck necks stuffed with *foie gras* and veal escalope with morels. Set meals 50F, 120F et 150F. You can sit outside on the terrace when the weather's fine.

10% TAVERNE DE BIGORRE – HÔTEL D'ALBRET**

21 place du Champs-Commun (Centre); it's opposite the covered market, where Lourdes starts to look like a normal town.
☎ 05.62.94.75.00 F 05.62.94.78.45
Closed Nov 17–Dec 22 and Jan 5–Feb 7. Restaurant is also closed Mondays out of season. **TV.**

Lunch served noon–1.45pm, dinner 7–9pm. Comfortable rooms, recently renovated. Doubles 184–270F. Cordial welcome. The restaurant offers traditional cooking with some regional touches. Set meals 67–198F. The one at 91F — *garbure* with *manchons* of duck or catch of the day and dessert — was our favourite.

ADÉ 65100 (6KM N)

10% HÔTEL LE VIRGINIA****

How to get there: by the N21 – it's just at the Adé exit, on the route nationale going towards Tarbes.
☎ 05.62.94.66.18 F 05.62.94.61.32

Secure parking in private **car park**. **TV**. **Canal+**. **Disabled access**.

This is one of our favourite places in the region around Lourdes. The 44-room hotel consists of a main building and little bungalows scattered throughout the quiet and pretty grounds. Doubles with bath 260–300F. Cheapest set meal is 95F. Careful cooking focussing on regional dishes like salmon, trout, duck breast, sweetbreads and so on.

ARGELÈS-GAZOST 65400 (12KM S)

HOSTELLERIE LE RELAIS**

25 rue du Maréchal-Foch (Centre).
☎ 05.62.97.01.27 F➔ 05.62.97.90.00
Closed Nov–Feb. **Car park**. **TV**.

Quite a plush hotel with lovely rooms ranging in price from 200F to 265F. The cooking is excellent, the dining room pleasant and the set meals are particularly good. For 75F (except Sunday lunchtimes), you can have duck drumsticks *confit* or the day's special. There's a *menu-carte* at 120F et 158F with a choice of six starters, six meat dishes — or the day's special (things like *foie gras* with cabbage, rabbit *confit* or duck with cherries) — and six desserts. If you decide to splash out, 175F will get you prawns *provençale* and duck *foie gras* with apples and berries or you can have the 220F gourmet meal. Service until 9pm.

10% LE SOLEIL LEVANT**

17 av. des Pyrénées.
☎ 05.62.97.08.68 F➔ 05.62.97.04.60
Closed in January. **Car park**. **TV**.

Rather an uninspiring spa town hotel standing in its own grounds. There's a large terrace and you can be sure of peace and quiet. Rooms have been renovated throughout. Doubles 220–250F. Half-board available. The hotel is well-known for its cooking. There's a relaxed atmosphere in the large dining room, which is quiet and restful (as we said, you can be sure of peace and quiet). Set meals 60F, 78F, 130F, 150F and 160F. The one at 60F offers chicken livers in puff pastry with asparagus, trout in a white wine and cream sauce or skate *au beurre noir* and dessert — not bad, eh? Children's menu 40F.

10% HÔTEL LES CIMES**

place Ourout.
☎ 05.62.97.00.10 F➔ 05.62.97.10.19
Closed mid-Nov–mid-Dec. **Car park**. **TV**.

Very fine-looking hotel with a garden and swimming pool. The proprietor's a congenial type. Quiet rooms with country style décor. Doubles with shower/wc 290F. Cheapest set meal (72F) consists of warm goat's cheese salad, main course and dessert. Other set meals at 95F, 130F and 180F offer things like trout, *aiguillettes* of duck in vinegar, langoustines with *foie gras*, and sautéd duck in a Madiran wine sauce. Half-board from 260F per person per day is compulsory from June to September.

SALLES-ARGELÈS 65400 (12KM S)

LA CHÂTAIGNERAIE

☎ 05.62.97.17.84.
Closed Mondays and all of January. **Car park**.

Bookings are essential if you want to eat in the lovely dining room of this old farm. You can order your meal by telephone ahead of time. If you asked for your meat — duck breast, mutton chops, duckling etc — to be grilled, it'll be done in front of you. Prices vary. Cheapest set meal is 100F. Service comes with a smile. There's a rather nice terrace for summer days. Good restaurant.

ARCIZANS-AVANT 65400 (14KM S)

10% AUBERGE LE CABALIROS**

How to get there: on the N21 and the D13 – it's less than 2km from Argelès.
☎ 05.62.97.04.31 F➔ 05.62.97.91.48
Closed Wednesdays out of season and in October and November. **Car park**. **TV**.

A nice inn with a terrace facing the valley in a delightful and very quiet village. Cordial welcome. The rooms have been refurbished from top to bottom — there are a few really nice attic ones — and all have a direct phone and shower/wc or bath. Doubles from 260F. Half-board is extremely reasonable. Traditional regional cooking with set meals at 90F, 110F, 150F and 170F (with *foie gras*, this one). Children's menu 45F. A la carte is really good too — you can have *garbure bigourdane* (the real McCoy) with *confits* and stuffed neck if you order it ahead of time.

LUZ-SAINT-SAUVEUR 65120

10% AUBERGE DE JEUNESSE – GÎTE D'ÉTAPE LES CASCADES

Centre; it's near the GR10 and 150m from the church.
☎ 05.62.92.94.14.
Car park.

Lunch served noon–2pm, dinner 7–10pm (11pm in summer). You'll get a very nice welcome from the particularly dynamic young people who run the place. Pleasant rooms to sleep four, six or eight cost 55F a head and there are four double rooms for the same price. Half-board 125F a person. Wonderful big common room. Good cooking, and you'll get soup, starter, main course, salad and dessert for about 55F. In the evening there are things like paella, *garbure*, and grills. Very friendly atmosphere and they can tell you all you want to know about hiking in the area.

VISCOS 65120 (4KM NW)

10% AUBERGE DE VISCOS**

route d'Argelès-Gazost.
☎ 05.62.92.91.13 F 05.62.92.93.75
Car park. TV. Disabled access.

Lunch served noon–2pm, dinner 7–9.30pm. A wonderful inn in a picturesque village clinging to the mountainside. Lovely rooms, some with a view over the valley. Doubles with shower/wc 220F. Very comfortable self-catering accommodation also available. Delightful dining room is the setting for some excellent cooking. Set meals 85–220F. If you go à la carte, reckon on paying about 180F. The dishes on offer include *blanquette* of monkfish with baby onions and vegetable ribbons, fillet of beef *en croûte*, grilled saddle of lamb with ceps, casseroled pigeon, *gratin* of wild strawberries, and pies flambéd with Armagnac. In season, there's venison stew and *daube* of ceps (caps of young ceps with finely chopped shallots and ham in white wine). It's quiet, it's delightful, it has a garden, and the welcome cannot be faulted – in short, the inn is ideal for honeymooners. We're almost sorry we've given you the address – it's bound to be full the next time we want to go back.

MAUVEZIN 32120

LA RAPIÈRE

2 rue des Justices; take the first right as you leave the village heading for Montauban.
☎ 05.62.06.80.08 F same.
Closed Tuesday evenings, Wednesdays, two weeks in June, and two weeks in October.

This is one of the last restaurants where you can get authentic Gers cuisine. The style of cooking here owes nothing to anybody and everything to tradition – the 110F set meal, for example, consists of garlic-flavoured tourin (a soup made from onions and milk), stuffed duck's neck, confit and a homemade pastry The owner is grouchy but lovable and he has a devoted wife (she looks after the dining room) and charmingly self-conscious waitresses. Other tempting set meals 160F et 190F. There's a pleasant terrace and you can sit outside, weather permitting.

MAZAMET 81200

10% LE JOURDON**

7 av. Albert Rouvière (Centre).
☎ 05.63.61.56.93 F 05.63.61.83.38
Closed Sundays. **TV.**

What we liked most about this place was the food The hearty and tasty 95F *menu du jour* offers cream of vegetable soup, salad of red mullet *à l'escabèche*, rabbit with sweet peppers and polenta, cheese and dessert. Other set meals are 70F, 130F and 150F, and the day's special is about 40F. The wine comes in small carafes and goes down very nicely. The restaurant is well-known locally and popular with workers of all kinds. The atmosphere may be very relaxed but the service and the setting are both well up to scratch. Our only complaint is that there's not much elbow room. The same has to be said about the bedrooms (from 200F with shower, 240F with bath), which are, however, clean and have air-conditioning. Half-board 200–250F.

LES COMTES D'HAUTPOUL**

3 av. Charles-Sabatié.
☎ 05.63.61.98.14 F 05.63.98.95.76
Closed Sunday evenings and Saturdays in winter.
Secure parking in **private car park. TV.**

Lunch served noon–2pm, dinner 7.30–10pm. About 40 fairly modern rooms with shower/wc or bath. Reckon on 230F for a double with shower/wc or bath. The enormous and very bright dining room offers four set meals. The one at 100F is appetizing and there's a wide range of main courses including a substantial homemade *cassoulet*. For 150F, you'll get a starter and two main courses. Good and very reasonably priced Gaillacs.

CAUCALIÈRES 81200 (6KM NW)

RESTAURANT LE VIEUX LARDICOU

☎ 05.63.61.38.69
Closed lunchtimes, Tuesdays, and the first week of September. **Car park.**

Service from 7.30pm. You'll have to book! This is a wonderful stone house (it's been renovated) that's a bit off the beaten track. The little sitting room where you eat has lots of wood and kidskin tablecloths. You'll get a friendly and relaxed welcome from the chef, who settled here 20 years ago with his family. If your luck's in, he'll show you his albums and fun sculptures (he collects scrap metal and welds it together, coming up with weird things like a shortsighted duck that'll have you in fits of laughter). He's also a great cook, specializing in cheese. There's goat cheese grilled with bacon, cheese kebabs with a mustard sauce, warm Camembert with raisins, and *croustade aux pommes*. Reckon on 150F for that little lot together with an apéritif and some local wine. We fell in love with the place.

MILLAU 12100

☗ AUBERGE DE JEUNESSE

26 rue Lucien-Costes (North-East).
☎ 05.65.60.15.95 F➔ 05.65.60.50.59
Closed weekends Oct–April. **Car park**.

Reception 9am–noon and 2–6pm. Book eight days ahead, especially in summer. Open all year round. The youth hostel is In the local *Foyer des Jeunes Travailleurs*, a large modern building. Single or double rooms at 70F a person. You must be able to show your HI card. Sheets included. No curfew. Cafeteria and kitchen if you want to cook. Pleasant garden and friendly welcome.

☗ GRAND HÔTEL DE PARIS ET DE LA POSTE**

10 av. Alfred-Merle (North-West).
☎ 05.65.60.00.52
Closed Dec 15–March 15. **Car park**. **TV**.

A conventional and unpretentious hotel with decent rooms. Doubles 140F with basin (no TV), 200–270F with shower/wc, and 270F with bath. Very friendly welcome — they'll roll out the red carpet for you.

10% ☗ I●I INTERNATIONAL HÔTEL-RESTAURANT***

1 place de la Tiné (Centre).
☎ 05.65.59.29.00 F➔ 05.65.59.29.01
Restaurant closed Sunday evenings, Mondays, and out of season. **Secure parking** in **private car park**. **TV**. **Canal+**. **Disabled access**.

It looks for all the world like one of a chain and it's hard to credit that it's come down through three generations of the Pomarède family. The rather plush restaurant has an excellent reputation. The dishes are fairly elaborate. There are set meals at 125F (very good value for money) and 150–325F. À la carte, there's *civet* of duck, *boudin* of salmon and curry, and bream with stewed cuttlefish. Pleasant sitting room with panoramic views. The soundproof bedrooms are modern, tastefully decorated and have air-conditioning. There are lots of them — 110 to be exact — so you've got more chance of finding a vacancy in the high season. Prices are very reasonable for an establishment of this calibre — doubles with shower/wc (no TV) 258F, and 391–438F with bath and mini-bar.

☗ I●I HÔTEL-RESTAURANT LE CÉVENOL**

115 rue du Rajol (South); it's 500m from the centre of town.
☎ 05.65.60.74.44 F➔ 05.65.60.85.99
Closed Monday lunchtimes (except Easter Monday and Whit Monday), Friday lunchtimes in summer, Sundays, and Dec–late Feb. **Car park**. **TV**. **Disabled access**.

Pleasant modern establishment. Doubles with all mod cons from 308F. Cheapest set meal 97F. The restaurant has an extremely pleasant terrace. The cooking is good, and there are classics like trout stuffed with herbs, snail ravioli in a garlic flavoured sauce, and *crépinettes* of pig's trotters in a red wine sauce. We liked it because it was quiet (despite there being a busy road nearby) and gave us a friendly welcome.

I●I RESTAURANT LA LOCOMOTIVE

33 av. Gambetta (North-East).
☎ 05.65.61.19.93
Closed Sundays (except in summer).

Service until 1am during the week (3am Fridays and Saturdays). Various snacks, sandwiches, salads, squid fritters and so on. Main courses 25–50F, cheapest set meal 50F. Congenial setting and atmosphere. Young clientèle. Live music – rock, jazz, blues etc – every Saturday about 9pm and in summer twice a week or more. One of the liveliest places in Millau.

I●I RESTAURANT CHEZ CAPION

3 rue J.-F. Alméras; it's a stone's throw from boulevard de la République, near the town hall.
☎ 05.65.60.00.91 Fax: 05.65.60.42.13
Closed Wednesdays out of season and at the beginning of July for annual holiday

Lunch served noon–2pm, dinner 7–9.30pm. A great favourite with the locals who often come here for a blow-out, tucking into dishes based largely on local produce. The dining room is bright, the décor conventional and a touch old-fashioned (and none the worse for that). Prices are very reasonable, given the quality of the cooking. The daily special is 48F and set meals are available at 65F (weekday lunchtimes) which includes wine and coffee, 88F, 124F and 178F. If you go à la carte, there's a warm salad of quail in aspic, noisettes of lamb with a *fondue* of garlic and fillet of beef with morels. Friendly welcome.

AUBERGE OCCITANE

15 rue Peyrollerie (Centre).
☎ 05.65.60.45.54
Closed Sundays (except in July and August) and the second fortnight in March.

The restaurant is in an extremely old house. Given the restaurant's name, it's hardly surprising that the menu's in both French and langue d'oc (the local dialect). The 67F set meal offers *navarin de mouton* (a kind of lamb stew) and onion tart, cheese or dessert, while the one at 98F has *salade du berger*, *aligot*, a choice of duck breast, fillet of mutton or the famous Aubrac beef, cheese and dessert. Excellent regional specialities include cabbage with spelt (kind of wheat), beef stewed in red wine and trout fillets with a sauce made from nettles. Great *aligot* – treat yourself for 40F.

AGUESSAC 12520 (7KM N)

HÔTEL-RESTAURANT LE RASCALAT**

How to get there: it's just after Aguessac, which is on the N9.
☎ 05.65.59.80.43 F 05.65.59.73.90
Closed in January and February. **Car park**. **TV**. **Disabled access**.

A pleasant and comfortable family-run hotel set back from the road. Nice owners. Simple rooms to suit all budgets: 130F with basin, 280F with shower/wc and 350F with bath. The dining room is pretty and has a big open fireplace that comes into its own as soon as there's a nip in the air. Set meals are 95F and 160F, and the food is great. Try the spitroasted leg of lamb, the veal steak with morels, and the flambéd pigeon. In fine weather, enjoy the pleasant terrace and the garden. Half-board compulsory in July and August.

MOISSAC 82200

HÔTEL AU CHAPON FIN**

place des Récollets; it's in the market square, very close to the old part of town.
☎ 05.63.04.04.22 F 05.63.04.58.44
Secure parking. **TV**.

Conventional hotel with about 30 clean and pleasant rooms from 250F with shower/wc. Rooms with bath start at 260F and go all the way up to 600F for society types who want to entertain in the sitting room (leather upholstery!) of their little flat. The restaurant's prices are a bit steep with set meals 95F, 135F and 160F.

MONCORNEIL-GRAZAN 32260

RESTAURANT L'AUBERGE D'ASTARAC

How to get there: it's in a quiet village between Masseube and Simorre.
☎ 05.62.65.48.81
Closed Mondays, Sunday evenings out of season, and Dec 15–Jan 15

Lunch served noon–1.30pm, dinner 7.30–9pm. This is a modern-day inn, miles away from the busy highways, owned by two exceptional people who will let you share their simple lifestyle for a few hours. It has an old bar, a welcoming dining room and a wonderful flower-filled terrace a stone's throw from the kitchen garden. Christian Termote, who loves herbs and is very fond of this part of the world, taught himself to cook and has little if any help in the kitchen. Try the garden salad with roast herbs, the ox cheek with ceps and an orange and Madiran wine sauce or the monkfish and *foie gras* kebabs in an oyster sauce. There are a number of set meals: a fast one at 88F (lunchtimes only), one called "Garden" at 128F, and one consisting of fish and seafood at 158F. But Christian's wife, who looks after the dining room, won't be upset if you decide on the *menu terroir* at 198F.

MONTAUBAN 82000

10% HÔTEL DU COMMERCE*

9 place Franklin-Roosevelt (Centre); it's in the cathedral square.
☎ 05.63.66.31.32 F 05.63.03.18.46
Secure parking. **TV**.

Reception staffed 7am–11pm, but not 12.30–4.30pm on Sundays or public holidays. Traditional little country hotel with a slightly old-fashioned air about it, which is really nice. The ground floor is lovely with fine walnut and mahogany furniture. Bedrooms have all been renovated. Doubles with shower/wc 169–260F, with bath 199–290F. There's no restaurant.

HÔTEL-RESTAURANT DU MIDI**

12 rue Notre-Dame (Centre); it's in the cathedral square.
☎ 05.63.63.17.23 F 05.63.66.43.66
Closed 1 May.
Secure parking. TV. Canal+. Disabled access.

This is the most popular hotel in the centre of town and it offers good value for money. Comfortable rooms with bath and direct phone are 250–380F. American-style bar. The restaurant is well-known and the cooking is good. The dining room, with its handsome glass wall and potted plants is attractive and has a touch of real sophistication about it. Set meals range in price from 79F (a more than adequate meal) to 210F, where fish predominates. Good-looking hors d'œuvres are served buffet style. À la carte is more expensive of course. There's the famous steak tartare (enormous helpings), *aiguillettes* of duck with pinenuts, rack of lamb with *foie gras*, veal chop with morels, *civet* of monkfish and leeks, *confit d'oie* with sorrel and so on. Needless to say, the wine list is excellent. You'll even find tucked away in a corner a good Lavilledieu at 40F (I kid you not), a dry Gaillac at 50F and a Fronton Château-Cahuzac at 60F.

10% HÔTEL D'ORSAY – LA CUISINE D'ALAIN**

31 rue Roger-Salengro (South); it's opposite the station.
☎ 05.63.66.06.66 F 05.63.66.19.39
Closed Sundays, Monday lunchtimes, the middle two weeks in August, and during the Christmas holidays.
Secure parking. TV.

A pretty 2-star hotel with a garden and comfortable and pleasant rooms. Doubles with shower 250F, with bath 380F. The restaurant (rather plush décor) is one of the best in town and offers some imaginative cooking. The 120F set meal consists of the day's special, wine and coffee, and for 180F you'll get salmon and herb tartare, *émincé* of duck with honey and gingerbread, and a pastry from the trolley. There's also a *menu dégustation* at 280F consisting of seven courses. If you prefer à la carte, the kitchen can provide you with the local version of *cassoulet*, seafood lasagne, mussels with chives and grilled pepper *julienne*, and a plate of of *foie gras* done in three different ways (lightly cooked, cooked, cooked and salted). Delicious pastries and a fabulous dessert trolley. Specialities served on the flower-filled terrace in summer.

LE SAMPA

21 and 21 bis rue des Carmes (Centre).
☎ 05.63.20.36.46
Closed Sundays and public holidays.

The décor may have been inspired by Santa Fé but the cooking is 100% French – omelette, grilled meat – and regional to boot since they offer duck breast with ceps and a house *confit*. No set meals but you can have the day's special for 45F, and salads are 40–50F and meat dishes 50–85F. It's all good stuff and the helpings are absolutely enormous. The welcome and service were congenial if a bit trendy. The warm and friendly atmosphere at the bar in the evenings spreads to the dining room.

RESTAURANT LE CLOS DE PALISSE

52 rue de Palisse (West); it's very close to the centre of town; if you head in the direction of Castelsarrasin, it's the sixth on the right after the old bridge.
☎ 05.63.63.07.18
Closed Mondays. **Car park. Disabled access.**

The cheapest set meal (available weekday lunchtimes only) is 67F and quite acceptable, offering for example, duck *fritons* (the bits of meat left over from making *confit*) grilled steak (cooked in the modern fireplace that sits in the middle of the dining room) and a good *croustade aux pommes*. The cooking is traditional and regional dishes such as duck breast *bordelaise* and lightly cooked *foie gras* also feature regularly. There are other set meals at 90F, 135F and 170F, and also a children's menu. The quiet terrace is rather pleasant in summer.

RESTAURANT LE VENTADOUR

23 quai Villebourbon (West); it's on the other side of the river, opposite the Ingres museum.
☎ 05.63.63.34.58
Closed Sundays, Mondays, and the first fortnight in August.

The restaurant has become incredibly popular with the locals since being taken over. And rightly so – the vaulted brick dining room has been decorated like the inside of a castle and looks as if it's been used to film some TV drama set in the Middle Ages. The restaurant gets flooded whenever the Tarn overflows its banks but on the other hand it's always cool however hot it is outside. This is cooking at its most refined and the service is first-rate, but even so the prices are extremely reasonable. Judge for yourself – the 90F *menu saveur*, for example, offers grilled goat's cheese with mushrooms and tomatoes and duck drumsticks *confit* with shallot-flavoured butter, while the 115F *menu détente* consists of a salad of stuffed duck necks and gizzards followed by pan-fried salmon with *lardons* and raspberry vinegar. There are other set meals at 140F and 190F.

|●| RESTAURANT LE RABELAIS

13 rue de l'Hôtel-de-Ville (Centre); it's practically next door to the town hall, 50m from the Ingres museum.
☎ 05.63.63.21.09
Closed Sundays.

Service at lunchtime and from 8pm. If you plan on eating here on a Friday or Saturday evening, you'd better book. The large brick vaulted dining room makes a pleasant setting for good regional cooking, with dishes like *galinail de Montauban*, *daube de bœuf*, *cassoulet au confit*, duck breast with peaches and the restaurant's speciality duck *pot-au-feu*. Reckon on 120F à la carte. Warm welcome.

MONTRÉAL 32250

⌂ |●| HÔTEL DE LA GARE

route d'Eauze (South).
☎ 05.62.29.43.37 F 05.62.29.49.82
Closed Thursday evenings and Fridays out of season, Fridays in July and August, three weeks in January, and two weeks at the end of October. **Disabled access**.

This actually used to be the local station (it closed in 1968). The décor hasn't been changed and you'll feel as if you're eating in a railway museum. It's all there – the station clock, the till in the ticket office, the posters, the board showing what train's due next and a collection of traditional tools. Good regional cooking with set meals at 68F (weekdays, public holidays excepted), 98F (*salade gasconne* and duck *confit*) and 160F (*garbure*, *salmis* of guinea fowl and duck heart kebabs). There's nothing much to say about the five rooms except that they're dirt cheap (190F), but if you have a liking for peace and quiet and the unusual, ask for the lamp room (it's in the garden).

MONTRICOUX 82800

⌂ |●| LE RELAIS DU POSTILLON*

How to get there: it's 800m from the village at the junction of the D115 and the D694..
☎ 05.63.67.23.58 F 05.63.67.27.68
Closed three weeks in January, Friday evenings and Saturday lunchtimes Oct–May, and Nov 15–30.
Car park.

Service at lunchtime and from 8pm. Pleasant inn with good regional cooking. The rooms aren't particularly attractive but they're very well looked after. Doubles with shower from 125F. Cosy dining room where you can sample some wonderful house specialities. Set meals range in price from 90F (not available Sundays) to 200F. À la carte, there's salmon and sorrel in puff pastry, zander with saffron, salad of sorrel and grilled red mullet, tripe, and chicken with morels. There's a pleasant shady terrace and a garden for you to enjoy in fine weather.

MONTSÉGUR 09300

⌂ HÔTEL COUQUET

81 rue Principale.
☎ 05.61.01.10.28

It's a bit old-fashioned but well-kept and everything about it is reminiscent of France at its most French. The rooms – a few have brass beds – are about 150F. The biggest, with bath, is very pretty and is nicely furnished but the (private) wc is not in the room. Breakfast is 30F.

⌂ |●| HÔTEL-RESTAURANT COSTES**

52 rue Principale.
☎ 05.61.01.10.24 F 05.61.03.06.28
Closed Mondays out of season and Nov 15–mid-Feb.

The outside of the building is swathed in Virginia creeper. There are ten or so decent and reasonably priced rooms in the hotel, and a double with shower/wc will cost you 210F. The restaurant is very good and has set meals ranging in price from 79F to 175F. The house specialities are *civet* of wild boar, duck breast with figs, game *pâtés*, and duck *confit* with chanterelle mushrooms. Pleasant terrace and garden.

MUR-DE-BARREZ 12600

10% ⌂ |●| AUBERGE DU BARREZ**

av. du Carladez; it's on the edge of the village.
☎ 05.65.66.00.76 F 05.65.66.07.98
Restaurant closed Sunday evenings Jan 1–Easter and Nov 15–Dec 31, and Mondays Jan 1–June 30 and Sept 6–Dec 31, public holidays excepted. **Secure parking** in **private car park**. **TV**. **Disabled access**.

The inn is just this side of Aveyron's border with Cantal, in the former fiefdom of the princes of Monaco (at least here they didn't have to cope with the press). It's a modern building and may look a bit disconcerting at first sight, but there's no need to worry. Hotel chains aren't exactly numerous in this neck of the woods, and while proprietor Christian Gaudel doesn't think modern is a dirty word he also has a great deal of respect for tradition, which is alive and well hereabouts. Rooms are clean, comfortable, well-equipped and they all have a view of the surrounding countryside. Doubles 260–410F with shower/wc or bath. The cooking too is first-rate and there are lots of great finds on the menu – *pavé* with langoustine tails, rabbit stuffed with herbs, and stuffed tripe. Christian offers set meals at 65F (weekdays), 100F, 128F and 195F. You may get rather a dour welcome at first, but things soon loosen up.

NAJAC 12270

L'OUSTAL DEL BARRY**

place du Bourg.
☎ 05.65.29.74.32 ➡ 05.65.29.75.32
Closed Nov–March. Restaurant closed Monday lunchtimes in April, May, June and October.
Secure parking. **TV**. **Canal+**. **Disabled access**.

Najac, with its houses strung out on a rocky outcrop, is still one of the most delightful villages in Aveyron. Apart from being a tourist attraction, it also has this lovely inn, where you'll receive a nice welcome. The décor is plush but pleasantly so and the rooms, done in country chic style, are very elegant. Doubles with basin/wc (no TV) 210F, with shower/wc 300F, with bath up to 350F. The cooking is based largely on regional dishes and uses a lot of fresh and seasonal produce. The end result is a medley of colour and authentic flavours. There are set meals at 95F (weekday lunchtimes), 130F, 205F and 250F and depending on what time of year it is you might be offered chicken in cabbage, ox cheek in red wine, sweetbreads with ceps or a memorable *astet najacois* (roast pork with a stuffing of fillet steak, parsley and garlic). And then there are the desserts – mouth-watering creations like the pear and almond tart and the honey icecream. The wine list is quite superb.

10% LE BELLE RIVE**

le Roc du Pont (North-West).
☎ 05.65.29.73.90 ➡ 05.65.29.76.88
Closed Nov 1–end March. Open during winter months for seminars. **Secure parking** in **private car park**. **TV**. **Disabled access**.

This is a pleasant hotel that sits in green and leafy surroundings at a bend in the river. The swimming pool and tennis court give it something of a family holiday centre, which is not unpleasant. Rooms are bright and pleasant, and there are doubles at 245F (with shower/wc) and 280F (with bath). The cooking's good and the house specialities are duck breast with morels, fillets of zander with shrimp, *croustillant* of gizzards *confit*, *astet najacois* (roast pork with a stuffing of fillet steak parsley and garlic), and *aligot* made with Laguiole cheese. There are set meals at 75F, 100F, 150F et 200F and you can eat outside (weather permitting, of course).

L'AUBERGE DE COURNAILLE

How to get there: take the D39, go past the Frégère bridge and head in the direction of Mazerolles; turn left 3km further on onto the narrow road (the sign's easy to miss).
☎ 05.65.29.71.39
Closed lunchtimes (except in July and August), Sunday evenings, Mondays, and the last week of August. Beginning Nov–March, open Friday and Saturday evenings and Sunday lunchtimes only. **Car park**.

Once you get here, you'll be captivated by just how unspoilt and beautiful it all is. The stone house might belong to an artist looking for the solitude he needs in order to create. Alain Marciano-Prechner is an experienced chef and also an artist – some of his pictures are on display in the dining room. His artistic nature is evident in his cooking too, for he takes pains to compose each dish as if it were a canvas and he's so good at it that you're reluctant to destroy his creation. But it would be a pity not to because you'll get a lot of pleasure out of his cooking. The dishes are simple and the ingredients are absolutely first-rate. The menu changes with the seasons and reflects what's available in the market. If you get the chance to taste his crab soup, jump at it. The most astonishing thing about this restaurant though, is the prices – the set meals come in at 110F–165F, which is incredible value for money. And they know how to treat their customers. You'll be welcomed and served with lots of smiles. We fell in love with the place of course.

NANT 12230

10% HÔTEL DES VOYAGEURS*

place Saint-Jacques.
☎ 05.65.62.26.88 ➡ 05.65.62.15.64
Closed Sunday evenings and Mondays (except in July and August), and Jan–Feb. **Car park**.

The lovely little town of Nant makes an ideal base for hikers, and this pleasant hotel provides good bed and board. The rooms are quite acceptable and there's a simple and fresh look to the décor. Doubles 115F with basin, 145F with shower and 185F with shower/wc. The restaurant has a pretty terrace (smothered in wisteria in summer) and serves plain, honest food. There are set meals at 80F, 110F and 170F, offering things like crayfish (in season), trout with lemon butter, stuffed cabbage, *émincé* of rabbit *en papillote*; and a wide choice of homemade desserts. Pleasant welcome and service.

SAINT-JEAN-DU-BRUEL 12230 (7KM E)

HÔTEL-RESTAURANT DU MIDI-PAPILLON**

☎ 05.65.62.26.04 F 05.65.62.12.97
Closed Nov 11–Easter Sunday. **Secure parking**.

The hotel welcomed its first guests to this village in the depths of Aveyron back in 1850 and has been run by four generations of the Papillon family. The rooms are exceptionally pleasant, particularly those overlooking the Dourbie, and have recently been redecorated. Prices are very reasonable. Doubles with basin/wc 130F, 183F with shower/wc and 197–335F with bath. There's a nice swimming pool by the house. In the restaurant, proprietor Jean-Michel makes a point of using only fresh produce and he also grows his own fruit and vegetables, rears his own chickens and gathers his own mushrooms, the end result being food full of authentic flavours that delight the tastebuds. The other senses aren't forgotten: the dining room is decorated with flowers and overlooks the river. The pretty terrace is pleasant but often full. The cheapest set meal (not available Sunday lunchtimes) is 74F and very acceptable. There are others ranging in price from 115F to 208F (you have to be in training for that one). If you want to go à la carte, there's an enormous number of things to choose from, including duck *confit*, ceps *à la persillade*, duck leg with olives and Puy lentils, cabbage with a lobster stuffing, casserole of whole pigeon, and panfried local crayfish (in season). Keep a bit of room for one of the marvellous desserts – we've got a weakness for the warm chocolate tart. Staff are pleasant and the service is unobtrusive and efficient. It really is best to book. We need to take care of restaurants like this.They're becoming an endangered species.

PAILHÈS 09130

HÔTEL PONS

☎ 05.61.60.12.30
Closed Tuesday evenings (except in July and August), Wednesdays, the fourth week in June, and Oct 20–Nov 10. **Secure parking**.

This pleasant little village hotel has equally pleasant rooms from 130F to 200F. Set meals 55–150F. Good value for money.

PLAISANCE 12550

LES MAGNOLIAS**

Centre.
☎ 05.65.99.77.34 F 05.65.99.70.57
Closed March. **Car park**. **TV**.

Located in a pretty village, this is one of the most secluded hotels in all of Aveyron. The lovely and ancient house, parts of which date back to the 14th and 17th centuries, once belonged to the family of the poet Paul Valéry and it's easy to understand how you could become a poet living here. Outside, the building is swathed in Virginia creeper and there are three-hundred year old magnolia trees in the garden. Inside, it's magnificently decorated, has enormous fireplaces, and is furnished with antiques. Everything conspires to create a restful and serene atmosphere throughout and Marie-France is a kind and considerate host. The country-style décor in each of the six rooms is different, they all come with bath and TV, and they range in price from 250F to 320F (incredibly good value for money). We liked number 5, which overlooks the garden, and number 10, which is bigger than the others and has a mezzanine. As if that weren't enough, the food's good too, and the dining room's gorgeous. There are set meals at 68F (not available Sundays), 120F, 148F and 195F and out-of-this-world specialities like *croquant* of snails with truffle juices, *émincé* of duck with honey, and thick beef steak panfried with ginger and Roquefort cheese. If you want a room in season, you'll have to book at least two months in advance.

PROJAN 32400

10% LE CHÂTEAU DE PROJAN

How to get there: on the road connecting Saint-Mont with the N134.
☎ 05.62.09.46.21 F 05.62.09.44.08
Closed Wednesdays and Easter–Nov 15.
Secure parking.

It really is a château and it stands alone on a hill that dominates the surrounding countryside. The family who've owned it since 1986 have transformed the place, letting in light and colour and introducing some examples of contemporary art in all its various forms. You'll find something to surprise or delight you round every corner, and the prices are a surprise too (a pleasant one), ranging from 200F (wc and bath in the corridor) to 480F (with bath and wc). Take a morning stroll in the woods and you may well come across some deer. You can have dinner, but you'll have to book.

REVEL 31250

10% ☗ |●| HÔTEL-RESTAURANT DU MIDI**

34 bd Gambetta (North-West).
☎ 05.61.83.50.50 F➔ 05.61.83.34.74
Restaurant closed Nov 12–Dec 1, and Sunday evenings November to Easter. **Secure parking. TV.**

Lunch served noon –2pm, dinner 7.30–9.15pm. Pleasant inn with smart rooms ranging in price from 220F to 400F (with bath) and a restaurant that is popular with the locals. There's a nice dining room, divided up by little screens, and in summer you can eat outside in the garden. The 90F set meal (available weekdays only) consists of starter, *cassoulet du Lauragais* with homemade duck *confit* or the day's special, and dessert. Other set meals 120F and 180F. À la carte, there's a salad of lentils and stuffed duck neck, escalope of *foie gras* with apples and grapes, pot-roasted pigeon with preserved garlic *en chemise*, and stuffed pig's trotter *en crépinette* with a piquant sauce piquante. The wine list has some decent stuff – Corbières, Gaillac and Bordeaux – at decent prices.

ROCAMADOUR 46500

10% ☗ |●| HÔTEL-RESTAURANT LE LION D'OR

Cité médiévale.
☎ 05.65.33.62.04 F➔ 05.65.33.72.54
Closed All Saints' day–Easter.

A traditional hotel-cum-restaurant situated in the heart of Rocamadour. Comfy bedrooms representing reasonable value for money. Expect to pay 180–260F per night. Recent renovation work has shown respect for the character of the place. Set meals 58F, 70F, 85F, 120F, 140F, 160F and 200F. Specialities such as *confit* of duck and garnish, and truffle omelette deserve a mention. Brilliant desserts, one of which is iced walnut gateau with custard.

☗ |●| HÔTEL DU GLOBE*

Cité médiévale.
☎ 05.65.33.67.73
Closed early Dec–mid-March. **Car park.**

This is one of the cheapest hotels in town. You'll get a friendly reception and the rooms are clean and pleasant. Doubles with shower/wc from 190F. There are also rooms that sleep three (240F) and four (270F). What more could you want? Some of the rooms with a view of the cliff face may be slightly claustrophobic but they're nice and cool in summer. Mind you, it's also fairly noisy in summer, but you can't have everything. The snack bar on the ground floor is reasonable and it offers a set meal at 60F and omelettes, *crêpes* and so on.

10% ☗ |●| HÔTEL-RESTAURANT LES VIEILLES TOURS**

Lafage (West); drive 2.5km along the D673 in the direction of Payrac.
☎ 05.65.33.68.01 F➔ 05.65.33.68.59
Closed Nov 12–March 22; restaurant open at lunchtime on Sundays and public holidays. **Car park. TV. Disabled access.**

A splendid 13th century manor house that has been carefully restored by the proprietor, with the bonus of a beautiful garden and a swimming pool. The rooms are large and extremely pretty and each is furnished in a different style. All have phone and bath and prices vary (according to size) from 210F to 460F. TV set available on request. The restaurant concentrates on regional cooking with dishes like duck *foie gras*, duck leg with a stuffing of black pudding, and *gratin* of mushrooms with Cantal cheese. The cheapest set meal will cost you 115F and there is also a *menu-carte* at 175F. It's a good idea to book. In summer, the proprietor can organize hikes or bike rides in the neighbourhood.

10% ☗ |●| HÔTEL-RESTAURANT BEAU SITE***

Cité médiévale.
☎ 05.65.33.63.08 F➔ 05.65.33.65.23
TV.

The *Beau Site* is very appropriately named. Situated in the heart of Rocamadour, certain bedrooms have a breathtaking view of the abbey perched on the hill. This hotel-cum-restaurant boasts high quality facilities — just a pity that the prices are only within the range of our better-heeled readers. Expect to pay 300–650F for a well-kept, attractively decorated bedroom. The restaurant provides the perfect opportunity for a little gastronomic self-indulgence. Tasty, refined, aromatic dishes served in a beautiful, flower-filled dining room. Smiling waiters, unassuming and competent, a welcome change from the affected service you get in other places of this standard. An excellent establishment in its category.

MEYRONNE 46200 (14KM N)

10% HÔTEL-RESTAURANT LA TERRASSE**

How to get there: by the D673 and the D15.
☎ 05.65.32.21.60 F 05.65.32.26.93
Closed end Oct–beginning April. **TV**.

Meyronne is a lovely little village up in the hills and this establishment was at one time the summer residence of the bishops of Tulle. The building is full of charm and character – stonework, beams, turrets, ivy, the lot – and though it may look like a castle, the prices are reasonable. Comfortable rooms furnished with taste and character cost 260F in the hotel and 400F in the castle. They're also cool in summer, which is a considerable plus in this part of the world. The terrace overlooks the valley, which is particularly pretty in spring, and all in all this is an ideal place if you want to live like a king for a couple of days. The restaurant isn't bad either, with set meals at prices ranging from 70F to 270F. It specializes in regional dishes like *tourtière* of fresh duck *foie gras* on a bed of duck (!) and the portions are generous. The 135F set meal consisting of a starter and two courses offers good value for money.

CARENNAC 46110 (25.5KM NE)

HOSTELLERIE FÉNELON**

rue Principale.
☎ 05.65.10.96.46 F 05.65.10.94.86
Closed Fridays out of season, Saturday lunchtimes and Jan 6–March 10. **Car park**. **TV**.

This is a conventional hotel with very decent rooms furnished in country style. Doubles with shower or bath 300F. Half-board is compulsory in season. Good cooking. The 92F set meal gives you a choice of old-fashioned chicken fricassee or trout stuffed with crayfish. For 160F, you'll get *tourte verte* with oyster mushrooms and tomato *coulis* and roast quail on a bed of green cabbage, and for 200F, *salade quercynoise* and oven-roasted duck breast with orange sauce. The pleasant dining room overlooks a garden and in summer meals are served on the terrace. Service at lunchtime and in the evening until 9pm.

10% AUBERGE DU VIEUX QUERCY**

Centre.
☎ 05.65.10.96.59 F 05.65.10.94.05
Closed Mondays out of season and Nov 15–March 15. **Secure parking**. **TV**.

Handsome tourist complex – hotels, gardens and swimming pool – built around an old coaching inn. The setting is of course idyllic. The main building has character and you can have a room there or in one of the annexes around the pool. Pleasant doubles from 310F. Half-board from 300F is compulsory in July and August. The dining room has views of the garden and a forest of patina'd rooftops. It offers four set meals at prices ranging from 90F to 190F, with specialities like *aiguillette* of duck breast with green peppercorns, duck *confit* with lemon juice, truffle omelette and *cabécou* (a type of goat's or sheep's milk cheese). À la carte, there's terrine of duck *foie gras*, *pastis quercynois* and saddle of veal with kidneys done in the local style. For dessert, don't miss the house speciality of icecream with fruit soaked in old plum brandy.

RODEZ 12000

10% HÔTEL DU CLOCHER**

4 rue Séguy (Centre); it's very close to the cathedral.
☎ 05.65.68.10.16 F 05.65.68.64.27
TV.

A nice little family hotel in a converted town house in the centre of town. Built in the 17th century, it has a superb Louis XIV staircase and 24 clean and pleasant bedrooms. Doubles cost 140F (basin, no TV), 170F (shower), 220F (shower/wc) and 240F (bath). You'll get a friendly welcome. A very good hotel.

10% HÔTEL DE LA TOUR-MAJE***

bd Gally (Centre).
☎ 05.65.68.34.68 F 05.65.68.27.56
Car park. **TV**. **Canal+**. **Disabled access**.

This is your classic hotel. It's quiet, comfortable, pleasant and modern but incorporates the 14th century tour Maje, a remnant of the old ramparts. Doubles 340–390F. There's a piano bar in the evenings. No restaurant.

|●| RESTAURANT WILLY'S

3 rue de la Viarague; it's near the church of Saint-Amans.
☎ 05.65.68.17.34
Closed Sundays and Mondays.

Lunch served noon–1.45pm, dinner 7.45–9.30pm. A friendly restaurant that specializes in regional cooking based on quality produce but gives its dishes touch of originality and exoticism. Try the cod with rosabella potatoes, for example, or the salmon steak with bilberries. There are set meals at 70F (lunchtime only) and 110F. The restaurant is painted blue outside while the dining room is done in warm colours. You'll be welcomed without any fuss and the atmosphere is fairly informal and relaxed.

|●| RESTAURANT LA TAVERNE

23 rue de l'Embergue (Centre); it's in the square behind the cathedral.
☎ 05.65.42.14.51 Fax same.
Closed Sundays, public holidays, the first week in May, and the first week in October.

An unpretentious restaurant where you'll get a friendly welcome. In the vaulted basement dining room you'll be served traditional and regional food – ribsteak with Roquefort cheese, duck breast, *aligot* and so on, and there's also *houcroute*, fondue, *tripoux* and raclette in winter. Wonderful homemade tarts. Very reasonable prices. They have an 88F *menu carte* with a choice of nine starters and nine main courses. There's a terrace at the back, overlooking the garden.

|●| RESTAURANT GOÛTS ET COULEURS

38 rue de Bonald (Centre); it's in one of the streets leading to place de la Cité.
☎ 05.65.42.75.10 Fax05.65.78.11.20
Closed Sundays, Mondays, three weeks Jan–Feb, and one week in September.

Service until 9.30pm. It's advisable to book. The restaurant is decorated in pastel shades, the chef's paintings hang on the wall and the atmosphere is cosy, ideal for a romantic tête-à-tête, especially if you both care about good food as well as each other, for the cooking is truly inspired and the dishes full of imagination. The 95F set meal, which changes with the seasons, is available weekday lunchtimes only. If you decide on the one at 130F, you'll get excellent value for your money – *croustillant* of Cabécou cheese with crushed black olives, breast of lamb with a prune stuffing served with a herb vinaigrette, *fondant* of Bleu des Causses (a blue cheese) with juniper berries, and poached pears with fresh ginger. For 180F, you can have *crème de morue* with chopped tomatoes, *combavas* (a kind of tropical fruit) and fresh chilis followed by *parmentier* of lamb's tongue *confit* or panfried calf's liver stuffed with grilled cabbage. Great hors-d'œuvre and desserts – try the warm banana and coconut tart, the plain chocolate "pyramid" or the really yummy white mousse with orange and caramel. There's also a *menu surprise* at either 220F or 270F (depending on what's available at the market). In fine weather, enjoy the quiet little terrace at the back.

ONET-LE-CHÂTEAU 12850 (5KM N)

⌂ |●| SALOON GUEST RANCH

10 route Sainte-Radegonde; take the N140 in the direction of Valady and then the D568.
☎ 05.65.42.47.46 Fax 05.65.78.32.36
Closed lunchtimes to non-residents.

Alain Tournier has created a corner of the American Wild West in about 350 acres with horses and a saloon that's better than the real thing. His passion for authenticity extends to the smallest details – the mahogany furniture, the red fabric on the walls and ceiling, the carpets and the photos. If you share Alain's hobby, it'll make you think of the *Rosie O'Grady* at Disneyworld in Orlando. Meat figures large on the menu, of course, and it's some of the best in the area: there are thick ribsteaks, spare ribs and chargrilled rib of beef. Set meals with more than generous helpings range in price from 100F to 160F. Rooms are spacious and the décor is western – luxury version. Doubles are 300F (shower/wc) and 350F (bath). The staff are friendly and considerate. You can ride or take part in any of the other many activities available. Reservations are essential.

SALLES-LA SOURCE 12330 (10KM NW)

|●| RESTAURANT DE LA CASCADE

☎ 05.65.67.29.08
Closed Wednesday evenings out of season.

The small dining room is decorated in shades of pink and has a wonderful view of the surrounding valleys. The fast set meal at 55F (not available Sundays) is OK but nothing to write home about. The 75F set meal though is unbeatable when it comes to hearty local dishes. If you feel like treating yourself, and can order three days in advance you can have *charcuteries maison*, terrific stuffed cabbage, kid stew in a white sauce and *aligot* (naturally), all washed down with a Marcillac of course. If you want to work up an appetite, the Musée du Rouergue which is practically next door is well worth a visit.

SAINT-AFFRIQUE 12400

10% ⌂ |●| HÔTEL MODERNE**

54 rue Alphonse-Pezet; it's beside the disused train station.
☎ 05.65.49.20.44 F 05.65.49.36.55
Closed Dec 20–Jan 20. **Secure parking** in **private Car park**. **TV**. **Canal+**.

Lunch served noon–2pm, dinner 7.30–9.30pm. This is a fairly dull part of the town and a bit away from the centre, but it's quiet. Rooms are clean and acceptable and range in price from 250F with shower/wc to 320F with bath. There are also a few larger ones at 390F. The bar is out of this world. As for the atmosphere – well, it's what you used to find in hotels years ago. In all other respects though, this place has moved with the times. Local dishes may feature on the menu, for example, but they've been re-worked with a lot of imagination and such good cooking is rare in this town. There's pig's trotters and pork knuckle *en poivrade*, braised lamb and a few good specialities featuring Roquefort (which is only to be expected in this part of the world). Set meals 90–270F.

SAINT-ANTONIN-NOBLE-VAL 82140

10% ⌂ |●| HÔTEL DES THERMES**

bd des Thermes; if you're coming from the gorges, it's after the bridge on the left..
☎ 05.63.30.61.08. F 05.63.68.26.23.
Closed Thursdays out of season. **TV**.

The two best things about this hotel which was taken over by a young couple a few years ago are its waterside location and its prices. Rooms are decorated in a style that reminds you of a chain and can only just be described as comfortable. So the planned renovation is good news. Doubles with bath 180–210F. Some have a view of the river and the Anglars cliff face. The restaurant offers set meals at prices ranging from 59F (weekdays only) to 180F. The service is a bit slow but then it isn't a fast food outlet.

SAINT-BERTRAND-DE-COMMINGES 31510

10% ⌂ |●| HÔTEL-RESTAURANT DU COMMINGES**

place de la Cathédrale.
☎ 05.61.88.31.43 F 05.61.94.98.22
Closed Dec 1–31, except week-ends. **Car park**.

Lunch served noon–2pm, dinner 7.30–9pm. A quite delightful old family home, swathed in ivy and wisteria. Nice welcome. Small courtyard garden. Large rooms with period furniture. Doubles with basin 160F, with shower/wc 230F, and with bath 270F. The cheapest set meal is 80F (weekdays). Salads and homemade pastries are served on the little terrace opposite the cathedral. Worth noting for future reference if you're ever in the neighbourhood.

10% ⌂ |●| L'OPPIDUM**

rue de la Poste; it's a stone's throw from the cathedral.
☎ 05.61.88.33.50 F 05.61.95.94.04
Closed Wednesdays Oct–May and Nov 15–Dec 15. **TV**. **Disabled access**.

Small pretty hotel with comfortable rooms at 280F (shower/wc) and 280F (bath). Cheapest set meal is 85F (weekdays), with prices then rising to 105–160F. Children's menu 50F. Tea room. Bikes can be borrowed free of charge if you want to tour this wonderful area.

VALCABRÈRE 31510 (1.5KM E)

|●| LE LUGDUNUM

How to get there: after Valcabrère, join the N25, turn right and it's 400m further on.
☎ 05.61.95.88.22 F 05.61.95.01.45
Closed Sunday evenings and Mondays out of season. **Car park**.

Lunch served noon–2pm, dinner 7.30–9pm. A modern restaurant that looks a bit like a Roman villa. The terrace overlooks the maize fields and has a fantastic view of Saint-Bertrand. This is really unusual and has to be a first for France. Renzo Pedrazzini comes from these parts but his family originally came from Lombardy and he serves up not only traditional local dishes but also dishes from Ancient Rome. There's Hypotrima salad, Parthian lamb, Numidian chicken and Basilicata sausages. And with them he now serves a marvellous wine. He mixes honey and vinegar, doesn't use either tomatoes or lemons, because they were unknown at the time, and gets his spices from a local herbalist. He regards himself as an apprentice of Apicius, who wrote a recipe book about 2,000 years ago (the Roman Empire's answer to Paul Bocuse). If you feel like embarking on a culinary voyage through time, the "ancient world" set meal of forgotten flavours unearthed by Renzo costs around 180F. It's quite a strange feeling to know you're eating dishes that were served to Julius Caesar and Pompey.

SAINT-CIRQ-LAPOPIE 46330

RESTAURANT L'ATELIER

le bourg.
☎ 05.65.31.22.34

Situated right at the top of the hill on the left, here's an old building full of character. Drawings by passing friends cover the walls. Warm, cosy atmosphere so you'll feel quite at home. Hearty cooking will delight gourmets and your average traveller alike. Set meals 60–140F. Never-ending courses – we liked this! Excellent value for money. We'll quite happily return to this establishment – it really has a soul.

TOUR DE FAURE 46330 (3KM W)

10% HÔTEL LES GABARRES

le bourg; take the D662 towards Figeac.
☎ 05.65.30.24.57 F 05.65.30.25.85
Car park. TV.

The architecture may not be up to much, but the excellent reception and the bedrooms – bright, clean and spacious – more than make up for this. Half of them overlook the hotel's swimming pool. Great view of the valley. Bedrooms 247F with shower/wc or bath out of season going up to 278F in high season. Hearty buffet breakfast 37F. If you're stopping over for the night, expect to pay 300F. The couple in charge will happily tell you about the various walks around these parts. Half-board available with the *Chez Loulou* restaurant.

RESTAURANT CHEZ LOULOU

le bourg.
☎ 05.65.30.23.02
Closed Sundays out of season.

This establishment is popular with the locals. There's usually a good-humoured atmosphere. Set meals 75F and 160F, serving hearty cooking at reasonable prices.

SAINT-FÉLIX-LAURAGAIS 31540

AUBERGE DU POIDS PUBLIC***

faubourg Saint-Roch (West).
☎ 05.61.83.00.20 F 05.61.83.86.21
Closed Sunday evenings out of season and the month of January. **Secure parking. TV.**

Lunch served noon–1.30pm, dinner 7.30–9.30pm. Delightful rooms with views of the Lauragais hills. Doubles cost 260–310F with shower/wc or bath and direct phone. Half-board can be arranged. The large dining room has a marble floor and fine exposed stonework and, as in your room, you'll get panoramic views of the countryside. The atmosphere, needless to say, is a bit posh. The cooking is quite inventive. Several set meals are available. When we were there, for example, the one at 140 consisted of creamy pumpkin soup, chicken *pot-au-feu*, and *gâteau au fromage blanc*. For 210F, you'll get panfried turbot with sesame seeds, lamb cutlets *en crépine* with a tarragon sauce, kiwi fruit in puff pastry with a kiwi *coulis* and strawberry sorbet. And there's a super-duper version at 320F consisting of five specialities. You'll find comparative unknowns as well as the great vintages on the wine list. The terrace is extremely pleasant in summer.

SAINT-GAUDENS 31800

RESTAURANT DE L'ABATTOIR

boulevard Leconte-de-Lisle (South).
☎ 05.61.89.70.29
How to get there.
Closed Sundays and Dec 24–Jan 1. **Car park**

This is one of the best restaurants in the region as far as we're concerned. Nowhere else will you get meat that's as fresh, as tender and as downright delicious. Christian Gillet's idea of fun used to be criss-crossing deserts on his motor bike, but now he's settled down, and has decided he wants to be as close as possible to his source of supply. He's at the nearby abattoirs every morning at dawn choosing his own cuts of meat and then proceeds (still in the early hours of the morning) to feed the ravening hordes of dealers in from the country to sell their animals. The fact that the dining room is so crowded has to be a good sign. Try the sirloin, the flank of beef or the rib of beef with bone marrow. The grilled Arbas black pudding is good too, and Christian also does real Moroccan couscous (but you'll have to order it specially). You'll fork out somewhere in the region of 70–140F for a substantial meal, which is hardly the end of the world. The large dining room is bright and pleasant and the atmosphere is better described as hearty than intimate.

SAINT-GENIEZ-D'OLT 12130

HÔTEL DE LA POSTE**

3 place Charles-de-Gaulle.
☎ 05.65.47.43.30 F 05.65.47.42.75
Secure parking in **private car park**. **TV**.

A traditional village inn with a modern annex. The old part is furnished with superb antiques and is comfortable and cosy. The rooms are pleasant – numbers 7 and 8 are particularly nice – and cost from 200F with shower/wc and 285F with bath. It's well-known for its cooking and offers set meals 65F (Sundays excepted), 89F and 145F. Tasty regional dishes – lamb sweetbreads with ceps, rabbit terrine with oyster mushrooms, trout, veal chop with Roquefort and walnuts, duck *confit* and *tripoux* – are available à la carte at reasonable prices. Meals are served in the annex on the other side of the street and there's a very pleasant terrace among the trees or under the veranda on the first floor. Half-board (compulsory Aug 1–20) costs 285–330F a head.

SAINTE-EULALIE-D'OLT 12130 (3KM W)

10% AU MOULIN D'ALEXANDRE**

Centre.
☎ 05.65.47.45.85
Closed Sunday evenings in winter. **Car park**.

This has to be one of the most delightful country inns in the area. As its name implies, it's an old water mill and the 17th century building has been renovated by Monsieur Alexandre. The setting's idyllic and very restful. Pleasant welcome. The rooms are pretty and range from 240F (with shower/wc) to 260F (with bath). The cooking's good and the prices are reasonable. There are two set meals at 65F (not available Sundays or public holidays), 90F and 130F (with cheese and dessert) or you can go à la carte. The restaurant specializes in regional dishes like *tripoux* (homemade and wonderful), stuffed ceps, chanterelle omelette and stuffed breast of veal. The strawberry *mille-feuille* they do in season is quite something. Half-board costs 290F a head (480F for two) and is compulsory May–Sept. Boats and mountain bikes are available if you feel like some exercise.

SAINT-GIRONS 09200

HÔTEL MIROUZE**

19 av. Gallieni (South); it's two minutes from the centre of town, heading towards Aulus-les-Bains.
☎ 05.61.66.12.77 F 05.61.04.81.59
Closed Sunday evenings (Oct–April apart from school holidays), Mondays (restaurant only), and Dec 22–Jan 31. **Car park**. **TV**.

Nice, informal reception. The rooms are well looked after and reasonably priced, with doubles from 160F (with basin) to 250F. If you want peace and quiet, ask for one overlooking the garden. The restaurant serves honest regional dishes and set meals range in price from 69F to 140F. Customers are mainly salesmen and regulars.

10% HÔTEL-RESTAURANT LA CLAIRIÈRE**

av. de la Résistance (South-West); it's on the outskirts of town in the direction of Seix-Massat.
☎ 05.61.66.66.66 F 05.61.66.70.72
Secure parking in private **car park**. **TV**. **Canal+**. **Disabled access**.

Lunch served noon–2pm, dinner 7.30–10pm. The building is set back from the road and screened by trees, so it's quiet. Really nice reception. The modern architecture gives it a light and airy feeling and there's a lot of wood about. The wood carvings scattered throughout are quite remarkable. The rooms – doubles go for 220F – are pleasant and comfortable. The cooking is refined and the chef is creative. There are set meals at 85F–105F (panfried liver *au caramel*, duck ravioli with chanterelles or grilled duck breast with pink peppercorns) and 140F. One of our favourite places in Ariège.

SAINT-MARTIN-D'ARMAGNAC 32110

AUBERGE DU BERGERAYRE

☎ 05.62.09.08.72 F 05.62.09.09.74
Closed Wednesdays. **Car park**. **TV**. **Disabled access**.

Service at lunchtime and from 7.30pm. A wonderful inn deep in the countryside, complete with garden and swimming pool, where you can be sure of peace and quiet. Extremely comfortable rooms, all on one level, are 300F with shower/wc (no TV) and 400F with bath. The restaurant has a very good reputation in the area. The décor gives the dining room a warm friendly feeling and the reception couldn't be better. Set meals come at 80F, 120F, 160F, 170F and 200F. Try the braised knuckle of veal, the *poule au pot* or the three kinds of *foie gras* and finish off with the unforgettable *pastis gascon* flambéd with Armagnac.

SAINT-SERNIN-SUR-RANCE 12380

10% ☗ |●| HÔTEL CARAYON**

place du Fort; it's on the D999 between Albi and Millau.
☎ 05.65.98.19.19 F➔ 05.65.99.69.26
Closed Sunday evenings and Mondays out of season.
Secure parking in private **car park**. **TV**.

This place is an institution in Aveyron. Everyone you meet will tell you about it, which is hardly surprising since its name has long been synonymous with quality. The comfortable rooms – 199–389F – come with shower/wc or bath and some have a balcony overlooking the grounds and the surrounding countryside. It's also famous for its cooking and there are a total of seven set meals on offer, ranging in price from 75F (not available Sunday lunchtimes) to 300F. In between, in terms of price, are a couple of "theme" set meals – one at 169F built around goose and one at 179F that focuses on mutton. And there are some goodies à la carte too – lamb sweetbread with garlic and parsley, goose heart kebabs, cep omelette, pigeon cooked in the local way, and a few tempting desserts. If the weather's good, you can sit on the terrace with its panoramic views or swim in one of the two pools. You can also play tennis and clock golf, have a sauna or take a pedal boat on the river, all free of charge for hotel guests. The atmosphere's reminiscent of a holiday club.

SALMIECH 12120

10% ☗ |●| HÔTEL DU CÉOR*

☎ 05.65.46.70.13 F➔ same.
Closed Mondays out of season and in January and February.

Service at lunchtime and from 7.30pm. This little country hotel, a 19th century coaching inn, offers terrific value for money. It has thirty or so pleasant rooms, with doubles 125–175 F. Reckon on 166–218F a head for half-board. The pretty dining room is done up in country style and the inn is well-known for its cooking based on local produce. There are set meals at 80F, 98F, 129F – particularly attractive and offering crayfish in season – and 195F. This one is quite sensational, with homemade *foie gras*, ceps, walnut salad, breast of duck grilled over a type of vine shoot that gives the meat a special flavour all of its own, local cheese and, for dessert, *coupe glacée du Céor*. À la carte there's the house *confit de foie gras*, crayfish in the chef's special sauce, a *gratin* of lake perch and Champagne, and a number of chargrilled specialities. Other attractions include a shady terrace with a panoramic view of the village and a very welcoming owner. Well worth a visit.

SAUVETERRE-DE-ROUERGUE 12800

☗ |●| LA GRAPPE D'OR

How to get there: it's a stone's throw from Place des Arcades.
☎ 05.65.72.00.62.
Closed Wednesday evenings out of season.

A small village hotel that's very well looked after and has doubles with shower/wc at 160F. The restaurant offers simple and robust country cooking, with a set meal of the day at 65F, one based on local produce at 80F and a "celebration" one at 95F. The *tripoux* is great, and so is the chicken and duck *confit*. The garden is very nice and the setting alone is worth stopping for.

☗ |●| LE SÉNÉCHAL***

How to get there: head north, away from the fortifications.
☎ 05.65.71.29.00 F➔ 05.65.71.29.09
Closed Mondays and Tuesday lunchtimes (except in July and August) and Jan 2–March 2. **Car park**. **TV**. **Disabled access**.

You'll find all sorts of landscapes in Aveyron and Sauveterre, one of the finest fortified villages in the region, has some of the best bits. Local boy Michel Truchon loves this place and its hawthorns with a passion and he'll send you off to explore so you can work up an appetite. Local history isn't all he knows a lot about – he's got a good grasp of cooking too. He cares about quality produce and creates – the man's an artist so that's the only word for it – some wonderful dishes. The end result is cooking that is sophisticated, subtle and mouthwatering. He offers set meals at 150F, 230F and 330F and a *menu dégustation* at 450F. Treat yourself to *tournedos* of pig's trotters in balsamic vinegar, pigeon *en salmis* in a Cahors wine sauce, rabbit with fresh herbs and unforgettable desserts like the silky smooth chocolate and praline *quenelles*. The rooms are quite magnificent with their terra cotta floors and designer décor. Doubles from 550F in season, 450F out of season. The service is impeccable yet unpretentious and friendly. A star in the making.

SOUILLAC 46200

10% ⌂ |●| GRAND HÔTEL***

1 allée Verninac (Centre).
☎ 05.65.32.78.30 F 05.65.32.66.34
Closed Wednesdays and Nov–March. **Secure parking**. **TV**. **Canal+**.

This family hotel is run by relatives of Roger Couderc, the popular rugby correspondent. Comfortable rooms, some of them overlooking an atrium, come in at 190–290F – a double with shower/wc, for example, is 270F. There's also a solarium and a nice terrace with panoramic views. The restaurant, classical in style with an understated décor, has a good reputation for typical local dishes. The cheapest set meal is 75F and there are also three featuring regional specialities at 105F, 130F and 240F. Some of the house specialities feature truffles and it also does fresh duck *foie gras* with verjuice and apples and fricassee of gizzards with mushrooms. A trompe l'œil mural forms the backdrop for a shady terrace, which is pleasant in summer.

10% ⌂ |●| LA VIEILLE AUBERGE***

1 rue de la Recège (Centre).
☎ 05.65.32.79.43 F 05.65.32.65.19
Closed Sunday evenings and Mondays Nov 1–April 1. **Secure parking**. **TV**. **Canal+**.

You can't get much more modern than the hotel side of this operation. All the rooms (doubles from 300F in season) come with shower or bath, satellite TV and video, and there's also a gym, sauna, solarium and heated swimming pool. When it comes to food, however, owner Robert Véril is a staunch traditionalist and serves his guests local dishes made from local produce: Cabécou cheese coated with walnuts, for example, braised calf's head with rosemary, and *galette* of cabbage with duck *confit*. He has even unearthed some well-nigh forgotten dishes such as *vermicelle quercynois* (garlic and egg soup). The cheapest set meal, at 100F, gives a good indication of what he's capable of, and there are two *menus-carte* at 150F and 200F (these change every two months). The wine list leans rather heavily towards Cahors and other wines from the south-west.

TARASCON-SUR-ARIÈGE 09400

10% ⌂ HÔTEL CONFORT**

3 quai Armand-Sylvestre (Centre).
☎ 05.61.05.61.90 F 05.61.05.57.79
Car park. **TV**.

It's situated right in the centre of town, but its waterside location means it's quiet. Really nice welcome. Rooms 150–260F. Numbers 7 and 10 are large and overlook the river. Tea room.

10% ⌂ |●| HOSTELLERIE DE LA POSTE**

av. Victor-Pilhes.
☎ 05.61.05.60.41 F 05.61.05.70.59
TV. **Canal+**.

Comfortable doubles cost 160F (with basin and bidet) and 250–280F (with shower or bath). The dining room is decorated in country style and has a terrace overlooking the garden. You may want to try the *plat du terroir* (*azinat*, the local cabbage soup) at 80F. Alternatively, there are set meals at 65F and 95F that offer a choice of *azinat*, *confit* or *cassoulet au confit* plus cheese and *croustade*. If you feel like pushing the boat out there's another set meal at 185F or à la carte there's oven roasted kid with ceps for 120F and mixed grill for 110F. A good restaurant.

TARBES 65000

10% ⌂ |●| AUBERGE DE JEUNESSE

88 av. Alsace-Lorraine; it's 2km from the station.
☎ 05.62.38.91.20 F 05.62.37.69.81
Car park. **Disabled access**.

Lunch served noon–1pm (noon–12.30pm on Saturdays), dinner 7–7.30pm. 50F a night each. Meal 40F. Pleasant garden and climbing wall.

10% ⌂ |●| HÔTEL-RESTAURANT DE L'ISARD**

70 av. du Maréchal-Joffre (North); it's fairly close to the station.
☎ 05.62.93.06.69
Closed Sunday evenings. **TV**.

A tiny hotel with eight pleasant rooms. Doubles with shower/wc or bath 150–200F. The restaurant, is independent of the hotel and with five set meals to choose from nobody needs to worry about their budget. If you go for the 68F, 79F or 99F one (that comes with two starters), you'll get fish soup with either salmon mayonnaise or veal chop with orange sauce or rib steak, while 160F gets you a salad of marinated fish, a *gratin* of monkfish and mushrooms, and scallops *provençal*. If you go à la carte, you'll pay a bit more for things like fresh liver with lemon and trout with fennel. There's a terrace full of greenery that's extremely pretty in summer. Full marks for the first-rate cooking and welcome.

10% ☗ HÔTEL DE L'AVENUE**

78-80 av. Bertrand-Barère; it's 50m from the station.
☎ 05.62.93.06.36
Car park. **TV**. **Disabled access**.

This is a quiet little hotel despite its location. The décor in the rooms is a bit bland but they're good value for money – you'll pay 155F for a double with shower/wc. The ones overlooking the little internal courtyard are the quietest. Family atmosphere. The present owner's father may have retired but he is still often to be found welcoming the guests, which he does with considerable warmth.

|●| RESTAURANT L'ÉTOILE

2 place du Foirail (West).
☎ 05.62.44.87.53
Closed Sundays and public holidays. **Car park**.

Resembles the kind of bistro you'd find in Saint-Germain-des-Pré in Paris. Laid-back atmosphere and customers a bit on the trendy side. Decent classic cooking (salads and meat dishes mainly). Portions are generous. Ideal for a quick bite. Set meals 49F (lunchtimes only), 75F and 100F; à la carte also available. Nice terrace for when the sun shines.

JUILLAN 65290 (5KM SW)

☗ |●| L'ARAGON**

2 ter route de Lourdes.
☎ 05.62.32.07.07 F➜ 05.62.32.92.50
Closed Sunday evenings and during the February school holidays. **Car park**. **TV**. **Canal+**.

Lovely doubles 250F with shower/wc, 280F with bath. The dining room's rather plush, the service is impeccable, and the cooking enjoys quite a reputation, and rightly so, for it's outstanding. The cheapest set meal is 98F, with prices thereafter ranging from 180F to 260F. The menu changes five or six times a year, proof that the chef is not lacking in ideas. If you'd rather go à la carte, there's quail salad, zander with roast potatoes cooked in duck fat, and a range of desserts.

TERMES-D'ARMAGNAC 32400

☗ |●| RELAIS DE LA TOUR**

Centre.
☎ 05.62.69.22.77 F➜ 05.62.69.23.99
Closed Sunday evenings, Mondays and in February.
Car park. **TV**.

A conventional little hotel that's very well looked after. Cordial welcome and pleasant rooms – doubles with shower/wc and direct phone start at 230F. The ones at the back have a view of the tower. You'll find it has good regional cooking. The cheapest set meal comes in at 65F and there are others from 90F to 180F. The one at 110F has salad of gizzards *confit* and duck *confit*.

TOULOUSE 31000

SEE MAP OVERLEAF

☗ HÔTEL ANATOLE-FRANCE*

46 place Anatole-France. **MAP B2-2**
☎ 05.61.23.19.96
Car park. **TV**.

You'll get a very friendly welcome in this hotel, which offers terrific value for money. The reception desk is on the first floor. All rooms have a direct phone and are exceptionally clean. Doubles cost 145F with shower (135F if there's no TV) and 155F with bath. The lively café on the ground floor is popular with students.

☗ HÔTEL DU GRAND BALCON*

8 rue Romiguières. **MAP C2-3**
☎ 05.61.21.48.08 F➜ 05.61.21.59.98
Closed for three weeks in August and Christmas week.
TV.

This hotel has a place in the history of the French airmail service, for pilots spent their last night here before taking off for Alicante, Africa or South America. Saint-Exupéry, for example, had room 32. The hotel has hardly changed at all since and there are lots of photos recalling those heady days. The Misses Marquès ran the hotel for 50 years and Monsieur Brousse, who took over from them, has been here 38. Not what you would describe as a quick turnover! Doubles range from 120F with basin to 200F with bath. Rooms on the street side are noisy.

10% ☗ HÔTEL DES ARTS*

rue des Arts – 1 bis rue Cantegril. **MAP C2-4**
☎ 05.61.23.36.21 F➜ 05.61.12.22.37

The hotel is very centrally located in a picturesque neighbourhood. The rooms are quite pleasant once you get there – the place is a warren of corridors and internal courtyards. Doubles with basin/wc 120–135F, with shower/wc 135–170F.

10% ☗ HÔTEL TRIANON WILSON***

7 rue Lafaille. **MAP D1-8**
☎ 05.61.62.74.74 F➜ 05.61.99.15.44
Closed during the Christmas and New Year holidays.
Car park. **TV**.

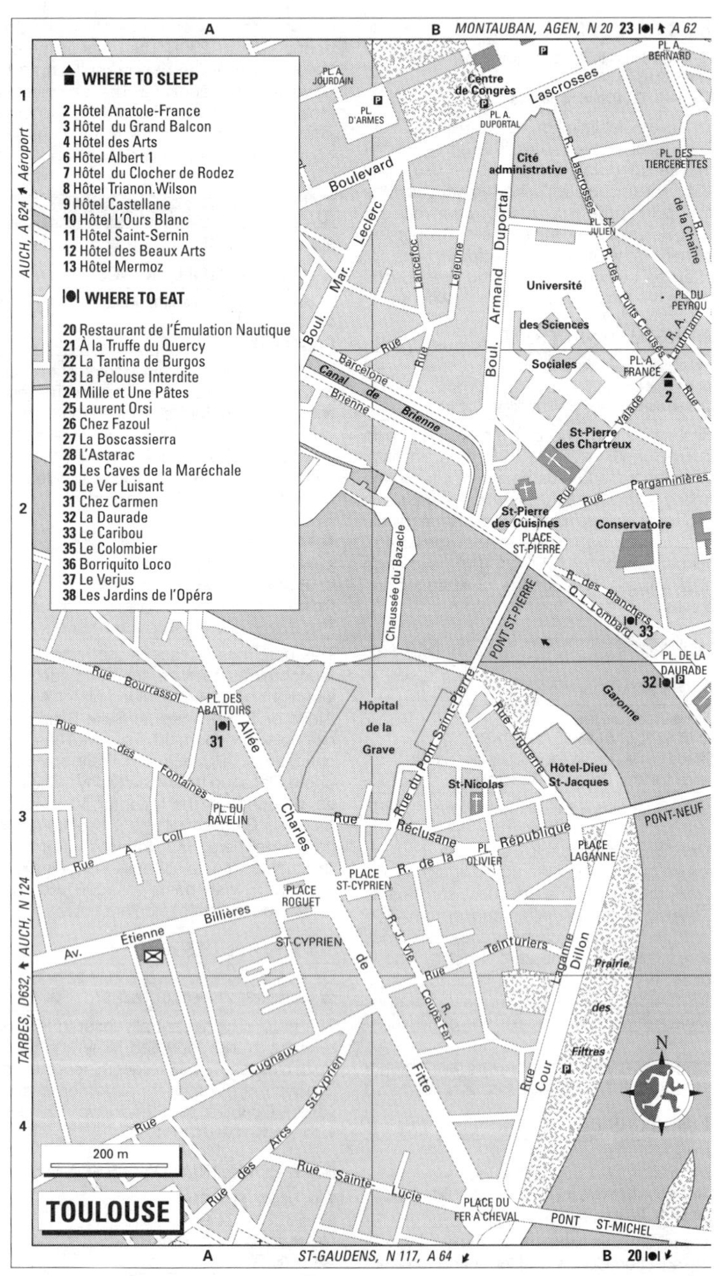
WHERE TO SLEEP
2 Hôtel Anatole-France
3 Hôtel du Grand Balcon
4 Hôtel des Arts
6 Hôtel Albert 1
7 Hôtel du Clocher de Rodez
8 Hôtel Trianon.Wilson
9 Hôtel Castellane
10 Hôtel L'Ours Blanc
11 Hôtel Saint-Sernin
12 Hôtel des Beaux Arts
13 Hôtel Mermoz
WHERE TO EAT
20 Restaurant de l'Émulation Nautique
21 À la Truffe du Quercy
22 La Tantina de Burgos
23 La Pelouse Interdite
24 Mille et Une Pâtes
25 Laurent Orsi
26 Chez Fazoul
27 La Boscassierra
28 L'Astarac
29 Les Caves de la Maréchale
30 Le Ver Luisant
31 Chez Carmen
32 La Daurade
33 Le Caribou
35 Le Colombier
36 Borriquito Loco
37 Le Verjus
38 Les Jardins de l'Opéra
MONTAUBAN, AGEN, N 20
A 62
AUCH, A 624 Aéroport
TARBES, D632, AUCH, N 124
ST-GAUDENS, N 117, A 64
Centre de Congrès
Cité administrative
Université des Sciences Sociales
St-Pierre des Chartreux
St-Pierre des Cuisines
Conservatoire
Hôpital de la Grave
St-Nicolas
Hôtel-Dieu St-Jacques
Garonne
Canal de Brienne
Prairie des Filtres
PONT ST-PIERRE
PONT-NEUF
PONT ST-MICHEL
PLACE ST-PIERRE
PLACE ST-CYPRIEN
PLACE ROGUET
PLACE LAGANNE
PLACE DU FER A CHEVAL
ST-CYPRIEN
200 m
TOULOUSE

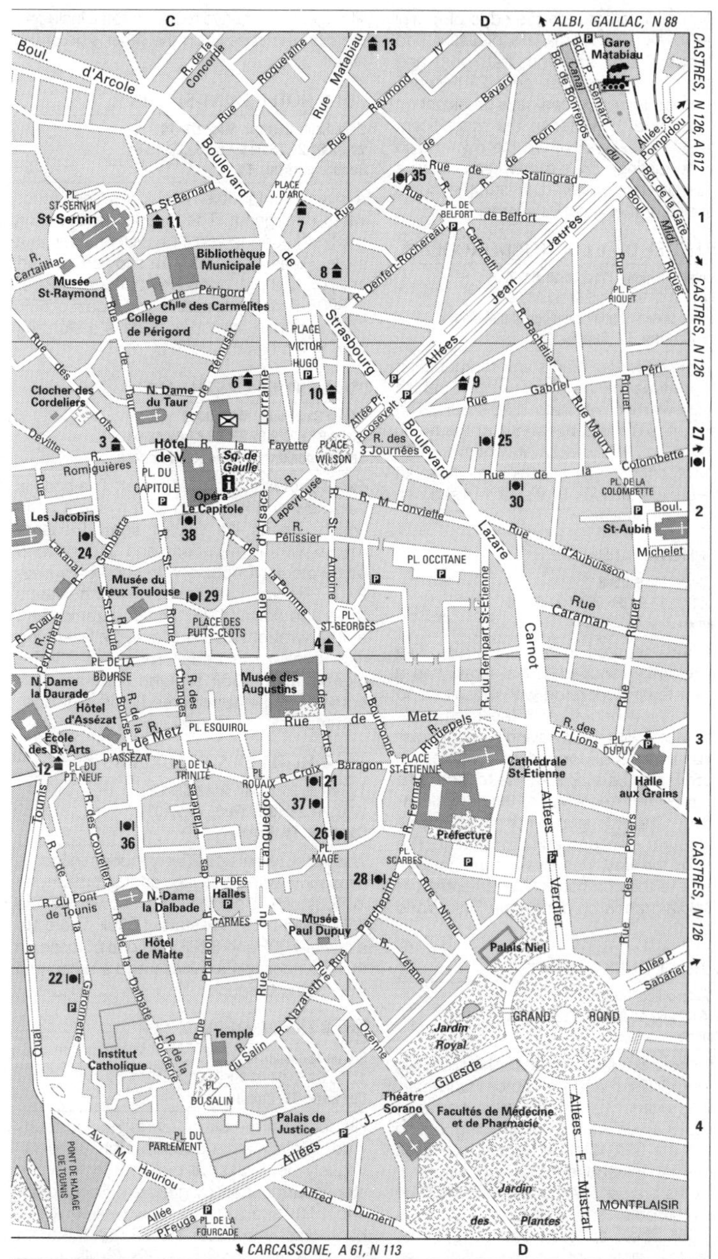

C
D
ALBI, GAILLAC, N 88
CASTRES, N 126, A 612
CASTRES, N 126
CASTRES, N 126
CARCASSONE, A 61, N 113
Gare Matabiau
St-Sernin
Bibliothèque Municipale
Musée St-Raymond
Collège de Périgord
Clocher des Cordeliers
N. Dame du Taur
Hôtel de V.
Sq. de Gaulle
Opéra Le Capitole
Les Jacobins
Musée du Vieux Toulouse
N.-Dame la Daurade
Hôtel d'Assézat
École des Bx-Arts
Musée des Augustins
Cathédrale St-Étienne
Halle aux Grains
Préfecture
N.-Dame la Dalbade
Hôtel de Malte
Musée Paul Dupuy
Palais Niel
Jardin Royal
Temple
Institut Catholique
Théâtre Sorano
Facultés de Médecine et de Pharmacie
Palais de Justice
Jardin des Plantes
St-Aubin
GRAND ROND
MONTPLAISIR
PONT DE HALAGE DE TOUNIS
PLACE VICTOR HUGO
PLACE WILSON
PL. DU CAPITOLE
PL. OCCITANE
PL. ST-GEORGES
PLACE DES PUITS-CLOTS
PL. DE LA BOURSE
PL. ESQUIROL
PLACE ST-ÉTIENNE
PL. DUPUY
PL. DE LA TRINITÉ
PL. ROUAIX
PL. MAGE
PL. SCARBES
PL. DES CARMES
PL. DU SALIN
PL. DU PARLEMENT
PL. DE LA FOURCADE
PL. DU PT. NEUF
PL. D'ASSÉZAT
PL. ST-SERNIN
PLACE J. D'ARC
PL. DE BELFORT
PL. F. RIQUET
PL. DE LA COLOMBETTE
Boulevard de Strasbourg
Boulevard Lazare Carnot
Allées Jean Jaurès
Allées Verdier
Allées F. Mistral
Allées J. Guesde
Boul. d'Arcole
Rue de Metz
Rue d'Alsace-Lorraine
Rue du Languedoc
Quai de Tounis
Rue de Bayard
Rue de Stalingrad
Rue Caraman
Rue Riquet
Canal du Midi
Boul. de la Gare
Av. M. Hauriou
Allée P. Feuga
Alfred Duméril
1
2
3
4

A delightful little hotel on the edge of a mini China Town. The rooms are pleasant and comfortable, all come with bathroom and satellite TV, and doubles cost 240F maximum. In summer, you can have breakfast on the patio and in winter in the magnificent vaulted wine cellars, where the owner also has wine tastings. He's rather keen on wine as you may have gathered. In fact, the rooms are all called after great vineyards!

HÔTEL DU CLOCHER DE RODEZ**

14-15 place Jeanne-d'Arc. **MAP C1-7**
☎ 05.61.62.42.92 F 05.61.62.68.99
Restaurant closed Sunday evenings and Mondays.
Secure parking. TV. Canal+.

Soft pastels, house plants and reproduction Greek statues make up the décor. Doubles with shower/wc or bath 250–330F. The restaurant is run independently of the hotel. Set meals at 79F (weekday lunchtimes); 98F and 140F offer dishes like chicken liver salad and a choice of duck breast or braised sea bass *à la provençale*.

10% HÔTEL ALBERT-IER**

8 rue Rivals. **MAP C2-6**
☎ 05.61.21.17.91 F 05.61.21.09.64
TV. Canal+.

The hotel, situated in a quiet street, has been recently renovated. It's small, has a pleasant foyer decorated with mosaics and the local pink bricks, and the rooms are comfortable, with most having air-conditioning. You'll pay 200F for one with shower/wc and 250F with bath. Prices rise to 235F and 280F in winter. Anne-Marie, the very pleasant owner, never lets up in her efforts to give the hotel its own particular character. The name, by the way, was given to the hotel as a tribute to the commitment and heroism of the Belgian monarch during the First World War.

HÔTEL L'OURS BLANC**

2 rue Victor-Hugo. **MAP C2-10**
☎ 05.61.21.62.40 F 05.61.23.62.34
TV. Canal+.

You'll find this place between the place du Président Wilson and the Victor Hugo market, in a district full of middle-of-the-range hotels. It's a beautiful, round building, dating back to the 30s, offering excellent facilities such as TV, telephone and air-conditioning. Bedrooms are very well equipped, although the bathrooms are pretty tiny. Doubles 260–290F. They've modernized the foyer, but they've thankfully kept the very old wooden lift cage. Seventy-five rooms in total, including those in the annexe on the other side of the street.

10% HÔTEL SAINT-SERNIN**

2 rue Saint-Bernard. **MAP C1-11**
☎ 05.61.21.73.08 F 05.61.22.49.61
Secure parking. TV.

A lovely comfortable hotel that's been renovated throughout. The reception desk is on the first floor and you'll be welcomed with a smile. Pleasant rooms with shower/wc start at 270F and with bath, direct phone mini-bar at 300F. Extra beds available at a cost of 50F. The rooms on the top floor have a stunning view of the basilica.

10% HÔTEL CASTELLANE**

17 rue Castellane. **MAP D2-9**
☎ 05.61.62.18.82 F 05.61.62.58.04
Secure parking. TV. Disabled access.

Excellent location, quiet street. The hotel is very new and has been built round a patio which means it's full of light. Pleasant rooms with all mod cons and decorated in pale colours. Doubles with shower or bath 270F. Room number 331, which sleeps three and costs 300F has a mezzanine and a little wrought iron balcony. Self-catering also possible in bedsit rooms at 250F a night. Parking 35F a night. Pleasant welcome from the aptly named Monsieur Bonhomme.

10% HÔTEL DES BEAUX-ARTS ****

1 place du Pont-Neuf. **MAP C3-12**
☎ 05.61.23.40.50 F 05.61.22.02.27
Car park. TV. Canal+.

This hotel, with its decidedly modern décor, is a favourite with politicians and actors staying in Toulouse. Doubles with shower/wc are 450F; with bath they start at 550F. There are a few at 700F and 800F, and one of these on the top floor has a terrace and a wonderful view of the Garonne.

10% HÔTEL MERMOZ***

50 rue Matabiau. **MAP D1-13**
☎ 05.61.63.04.04 F 05.61.63.15.34
Car park. TV. Canal+.

Hidden from the street by an interior courtyard, we're rather fond of this modern, vaguely neo-classical building (look at the steps) surrounded by greenery. They've got about fifty spacious and very well equipped bedrooms. The décor's based on the them of the airmail service — 30s furniture and aeroplane wallpaper designs. Doubles 465F, buffet breakfast 50F and paying garage. Special promotion in summer and at weekends – 445F including breakfast and garage.

|●| LA TANTINA DE BURGOS

27 av. de la Garonnette. **MAP C3-22**
☎ 05.61.55.59.29
Closed Saturday lunchtimes, Sundays and Mondays.

Service noon–2pm and till 12.30am. One of the musts in Toulouse. Ten years ago it was definitely a fringe establishment but nowadays it's very much an institution. though it's still pretty cool and the atmosphere's a bit bohemian. The terrace is very pleasant in fine weather while inside the large dining room is lively and you can sit at large tables or have some tapas at the bar. The place being such a success, they've opened a second, smaller, dining room. They serve a mixture of French and Spanish dishes at very reasonable prices, including *chicano* (chicken) at 41F, paella at 69F, squid, sea bass *tourte*, prawns and *empenadas*. There's a 54F set meal at lunchtime but it's à la carte only in the evening, so reckon on about 120F.

|●| À LA TRUFFE DU QUERCY

17 rue Croix-Baragnon. **MAP C3-21**
☎ 05.61.53.34.24
Closed Sundays and public holidays.

Renovated country-style setting and a relaxed family atmosphere. It has good traditional cooking, a respect for which has been handed down from father to son for the past 70 years. Set meals 55–125F. If you go à la carte, reckon on paying about 120F for the house *cassoulet au confit* or one of the Spanish specialities.

|●| RESTAURANT MILLE ET UNE PÂTES

1 bis rue Mirepoix. **MAP C3-24**
☎ 05.61.21.97.83.
Closed Sundays.

Service at lunchtime and till 9.30pm in the evening. What people come here for mainly is a quick pasta fix and there's an enormous choice - tagliatelli with smoked salmon, green tagliatelli with red mullet, black ravioli filled with monkfish (squid ink is what gives the ravioli its black colour) and lasagne with Roquefort, to name but a few. They also do good salads and have inexpensive local wines. You should try one of the strange desserts - soft fruit lasagne, for example. Main courses range in price from 33F to 70F and there are set meals at 59F (lunchtimes only) and 95F, the latter offering apéritif, starter, the day's special, dessert and coffee. There's another branch in Place du Peyrou and that one has a terrace.

|●| RESTAURANT DE L'ÉMULATION NAUTIQUE

allée Alfred Mayssonière. **MAP B4-20**
☎ 05.61.25.34.95
Closed Saturday lunchtimes and Sunday evenings.

The island of Ramier, on the Garonne and just south of the town centre, is devoted to sport. You'll come across the stadium and the town's two sailing clubs, *Le Rowing* and *L'Émulation Nautique*. Both have restaurants, but we took a liking to this one, welcoming non-club members, with its beautiful terrace under the plane trees looking out over the water. Set meals 59F and 65F weekdays. À la carte at the weekends offering dishes for about 70F. Sample the fantastic and enormous grills such as roast beef and *souris* of whole lamb, or one of the tasty salads. This is a wonderful place in summertime. *Le Rowing* is slightly more stylish and slightly more expensive.

|●| LA DAURADE

Moored at quai de la Daurade. **MAP B3-32.**
☎ 05.61.22.10.33
Closed Saturday lunchtimes and Sundays except May–Sept.

Since renovations were carried out with the help of the town hall, this boat has found its home base and its calling – it's become a pretty stylish, air-conditioned restaurant with a terrace-deck overlooking the water. Young people in sailor costumes serve tasty dishes based on market and local produce with a modern, Hispanic feel – for example, *confit*, *pavé* of cod with olives and green peppers, and *fondant* of chocolate. The setting and quality of cooking justify the prices, which are quite reasonable all the same. Set meals 60F weekday lunchtimes, 98F and up to 155F at the weekend. Main courses round about 100F. However, being a trendy place is no excuse for unfriendly reception or incompetent service. You can get a more simple meal on the quay at the *Terrasses de la Daurade*, a café-cum-ice-cream shop on the little square in front of the boat. It's open every sunny day 11.30am–7pm and does good salads. Don't forget to take a look round the church of Notre-Dame, on the square, with the unusual Black Virgin in her dress who watches over brides-to-be.

|●| RESTAURANT CHEZ FAZOUL

2 rue Tolosane. **MAP C3-26**
☎ 05.61.53.72.09
Closed Sundays. **Disabled access**.

This restaurant has been serving good food for some considerable time and has a lovely and rather elegant 17th century dining room with brickwork, antiques and discreet lighting. The cheapest set meal (weekday lunchtimes only) costs 62F, including wine and service, with a buffet of hors d'œuvres. There are others at 96F,125F, 130F and 163F which offer good local produce cooked in good traditional fashion. If you show your copy of this guidebook, you'll get some free homemade sangria.

|●| LA BOSCASSIERA

1 rue Saint-Paul. Off map **D2-27**
☎ 05.61.20.34.11.
Closed Saturdays, Sundays and Mondays and June 15–Sept 15. **Disabled access**.

Nicolas comes down from his hideaway in the Ariège to look after the restaurant from autumn to spring. The dining room is enormous – but then it would be, since this where the first French jet plane was designed. Nicolas' cooking features dishes from all over the region (*confit*, *fricandeaux* of duck), makes a bow in the direction of the Pyrenees (*garbure*) and gives star billing to fish (Baltic herrings and an outstanding *cassoulet* of cod). There's a 65F set meal at lunchtime and in the evening service continues until midnight. Reckon on 80–90F à la carte.

|●| RESTAURANT L'ASTARAC

21 rue Perchepinte. **MAP D3-28**
☎ 05.61.53.11.15
Closed Saturday lunchtimes, Sundays and mid-July–mid-Aug.

Service at lunchtime and in the evening until 10pm. This excellent restaurant tucked away in a back street in the old part of town offers Gascon style-cooking. The dining room has a high ceiling, elegant, understated décor, exposed beams and walls of red brick ornamented with a few pictures. You'll get a pleasant welcome, the atmosphere is intimate and there are banquettes of the kind that you sink into, perfect for romantic dinners. The cheapest set meal is 65F, available weekday lunchtimes only, rising to 105F and 160F. For 105F, you'll be offered dishes such as salad of duck legs with *foie gras* or *paupiettes* of chicken with a cep cream sauce, and for 160F two types of *foie gras*, tournedos of duck with a cep sauce or *poêlée gasconne*. You'll find some reasonably priced wines like Fronton and Côtes-de-Saint-Mont.

|●| RESTAURANT LES CAVES DE LA MARÉCHALE

3 rue Jules-Chalande. **MAP C2-29**
☎ 05.61.23.89.88
Closed Sundays and Monday lunchtimes.

The restaurant is housed in the converted cellar of a 17th century library which makes a wonderful setting for the reproduction statues and the elegant furniture. There are flowers and soft lighting and the restaurant is cool on a hot summer's day. At lunchtime they do a great "all you can eat" buffet of main course, dessert, wine and coffee for only 76F. The hors-d'œuvre are fairly elaborate and couldn't be any fresher. But you must be there early since it gets very crowded. In the evening there are set meals at 110F and 145F. Main courses – warm *foie gras* with potato puffs, fresh tagliatelli with marinated salmon, seafood stew with saffron etc – are about 90F. The Corbières and Fitou are reasonably priced. A good reliable restaurant.

|●| RESTAURANT LE VER LUISANT

41 rue de la Colombette. **MAP D2-30**
☎ 05.61.63.06.73
Closed Saturday lunchtimes, Sundays, two weeks in July, the week beginning Aug 15, and one week at Christmas.

The restaurant is popular with theatre people, artists and charmingly eccentric intellectuals – Bohemian in other words, but all in the best of taste. The cooking is of the classical kind and portions are generous. The meat is excellent and somebody seems to have just the right touch. In summer, there's grilled duck, salads, kebabs and so on and in winter they produce hearty dishes like *daube* or salt pork with lentils. Reckon on paying 80–150F. Day's special 30F. Great atmosphère, and there's a nice bar just as you come in where you can have an apéritif.

|●| RESTAURANT BORRIQUITO LOCO

25 rue des Paradoux. **MAP C3-36**
☎ 05.61.25.34.54

Service until 11.30pm. Bullfighting seems to have provided the inspiration for the dining room with its banquettes the colour of blood and ochre walls. Spanish specialities are available only à la carte, while the day's specials are chalked up on the blackboard. It does a good *ceviche*, fish cooked over coals and paella, and has Spanish wines. Prices are reasonable at about 100F. You can have tapas at the bar from 7pm on, while you're waiting for the flamenco to start.

|●| LE PELOUSE INTERDITE (BAR LE SUCCURSAL)

72 av. des États-Unis. **MAP B1-23**
☎ 05.61.47.30.40
Closed Oct–April and when it's raining.

Take care! Unusual places are like roses – they don't last for long. But we're really pleased to have found this place – and wish it a long life. The mother of one of the young partners used to have a working man's bar with an adjoining garden, set back from the long avenue where all the car dealers are. She lent them her licence and the plot of land, so they could make their romantic notion of a secret open-air restaurant a reality. It's a cross between a monastery, an open-air cafe and a surburban dream. The corners of this extraordinary garden are candle-lit and there's a sitting room with large armchairs, table football (even hammocks and beds!). Plain, inexpensive cooking. Salads and grills, 85F set meal and 45F dishes. Here are a few tips – you must reserve (it's a popular place even though it's not signposted), ring the bell and wait. Then everything will go to plan, even if things have slightly changed from what we've described above. Success has given them wings and and new ideas – unless they've headed off to pastures new. A place to keep an eye on!

|●| CHEZ CARMEN – RESTAURANT DES ABATTOIRS

97 allée Charles-de-Fitte. **MAP A3-31**
☎ 05.61.42.04.95
Closed Sundays and in August.

The abattoirs have gone, but the meat is as good as ever in this bistro decorated with still lifes. Smiling staff provide efficient service under the watchful eye of the proprietor. He's Carmen by the way – José-Antoine Carmen, to be precise! The 92F set meal consists of a starter, meat dish and dessert. À la carte, there are grilled dishes for about 80F. Great steak tartare. There are a few tables outside in summer.

|●| RESTAURANT LE CARIBOU

9 rue des Blanchers. **MAP B2-33**
☎ 05.61.22.93.78
Closed Sundays and Aug 1–20. **Disabled access.**

Dinner from 8pm. This is the place for you if you want to sample the delights of Québec in a log cabin setting. Exceptional welcome. The 98F set meal offers corn fritters with honey, scrambled eggs with smoked salmon, beef *tourtière* and maple syrup icecream. For 128F there's pâté, bison steak and the intriguing Huron *sagamite* (a mixture of trout, lamb, beef, kidney beans, corn and smoked pork), which needs twelve hours cooking time! Canadian beer, beaver and bison steak are available throughout the year. You'll get an apéritif on the house if you can show them this guidebook.

|●| LAURENT ORSI

13 rue de l'Industrie. **MAP D2-25**
☎ 05.61.62.97.43
Closed Sundays.

This establishment should mean something to gourmets from Lyons, as it's named after one of their famous chefs. And this Orsi, his brother, has successfully mastered the art of this region's specialities without turning his back on his roots. Apart from the set meals at 100F, 125F and 145F, based mainly on dishes from Lyons such as *tablier de sapeur* (slab of ox tripe coated with egg and breadcrumbs), pig's trotters, brains, he does a 165F set meal devoted to Gascony cooking, offering one of the best *cassoulets* in town. Middle-class customers don't appear to bother about the "Belle Époque Brasserie" décor, which is rather cold, just like the air-conditioning which works a touch too well, or the oilcloths and cellulose napkins that seem out of place. They're perfectly happy with the quality of the cooking and the quick service provided by very attractive waitresses.

|●| LE COLOMBIER

14 rue de Bayard. **MAP D1-35**
☎ 05.61.62.40.05
Closed Saturday lunchtimes, Sundays and in August.

People come here for the restaurant's famous *cassoulet,* the recipe for which has been lodged with a notary. It's been enjoyed by several generations of locals under the knowing gaze of Gargantua who graces the right hand side of an elegant dining room that is a pleasing combination of brick and wood. You can have it à la carte for 125F but it also appears in the 155F, 175F and 260F set meals, alongside other regional specialities such as salad of *lardons* with *confit* gizzards, medallion of duck *foie gras au torchon*, and *croustade* of apples in Armagnac. The cheapest set meal costs 100F. Grills and fish are also available à la carte.

|●| RESTAURANT LE VERJUS

7 rue Tolosane. **MAP C3-37**
☎ 05.61.52.06.93
Closed Sundays, Mondays, and mid-July–end of Aug.

Dinner is served 8–11pm. You'll get a nice welcome in this very simple restaurant with its marble tables and the occasional picture here and there. It's popular with bookshop owners and publishers for its lack of pretentiousness and good bistro cooking. Try the tripe with ginger and red wine, the squid *bonne femme*, the beef with Guinness, the veal tongue with a green sauce, the *ceviche* of rascasse, the pork *Aveiro* or the *gratin* of Collioure anchovies – the list goes on and on. The day's special depends on what's best at the market. Reckon on paying 160F for starter, main course, dessert, and wine. There are some very good wines from small vineyards (with those in the south of France making a particularly strong showing) at 60–110F a bottle.

|●| LES JARDINS DE L'OPÉRA

1 place du Capitole. **MAP C3-38**
☎ 05.61.23.07.76
Closed Sundays and three weeks in August.

The cooking here is refined and inventive and has long since made a name for itself. A la carte is very, very expensive, but you might want to treat yourself to the 295F set meal. Judge for yourself just how mouth-watering it is: *tartare* of salmon and special oysters served with blinis and cream flavoured with lemon juice and chives, bream with a *fondue* of potatoes and onions, and a *feuillantine* of chocolate with chocolate leaves. The décor falls into the de-luxe category and looks even better at night than during the day. There are some good wines and they're reasonably priced, given the quality of the food. Staff are very attentive.

URDENS 32500

|●| L'AUBERGE PAYSANNE

place de l'Église.
☎ 05.62.06.25.57
Closed Mondays in summer and Monday, Tuesday and Wednesday evenings out of season. **Car park**.

Urdens is a lovely village and very peaceful, and it's extremely pleasant to sit outside in fine weather. The inn is famous for its cooking. There are set meals at 65F (which includes wine but is available weekdays only) and 105–200F. We can recommend the grilled dishes, the snails with ceps and the *daube gasconne*. It has lost some of the charm it used to have but it's still quite good.

VALENCE-SUR-BAÏSE 32310

10% ⌂ |●| LA FERME DE FLARAN**

route de Condom; take the D930; it's on the outskirts of the village.
☎ 05.62.28.58.22 F➔ 05.62.28.56.89
Closed in January; restaurant closed Mondays (except in July and August) and Sunday evenings. **Car park. TV.**

Lunch served noon–1.30pm, dinner 7.30–9.30pm. A farmhouse once stood just a few hundred metres from the glorious abbey of Flaran. It's now been converted into an inn and is coming to life in the hands of a young couple with lots of good ideas, one of which is to make the hotel part of the operation – 15 rooms at 280F – and even more comfortable and welcoming than it already is. In the restaurant you'll find a rustic décor, local dishes – fricassee of sole with ceps, panfried *foie gras*, aniseed-flavoured *parfait glacé* – and set meals ranging in price from 95F to 180F.

VILLEFRANCHE-DE-LAURAGAIS 31290

10% ⌂ |●| HÔTEL DE FRANCE**

106 rue de la République (Centre).
☎ 05.61.81.62.17 F➔ 05.61.81.66.04
Closed mid-Jan–early Feb and July. **Car park. TV.**

Villefranche-de-Lauragais is one of the capitals of *cassoulet* (made with goose and duck hereabouts) and they do a very good one here as you'll discover if you take even the cheapest (67F) set meal. The inn, which dates from the 19th century, provides a warm welcome and has old style rooms (185F for a double with shower/wc). The ones at the back are quieter.

VILLEFRANCHE-DE-ROUERGUE 12200

10% ⌂ |●| HÔTEL-RESTAURANT BELLEVUE*

5 av. du Ségala (South); it's just behind the station.
☎ 05.65.45.23.17
Closed Tuesday evenings and Wednesdays in season, January and February. **Secure parking**.

It's nothing much to look at and is a bit shabby inside but never judge a book by its cover, for you'd miss out on some seriously good food if you passed it by. The cooking is excellent and uses fresh local produce. The prices are very reasonable given the quality, with set meals at 85F, 130F, 180F and 230F. Depending on how the chef feels that particular day, you might have *foie gras* and spinach *en papillote*, lamb sweetbreads with paprika, or red mullet with beef bone marrow. The hotel is clean, simple and unpretentious with doubles at 170F (shower/wc) and 190F (bath). The ones overlooking the street are a bit noisy.

HÔTEL DE L'UNIVERS**

place de la République (Centre); it's on the north bank of the Aveyron, on the other side of the tourist office.
☎ 05.65.45.15.63 F→ 05.65.45.02.21
Restaurant closed Friday evenings, Saturdays out of season (except before a public holiday), two weeks in January, one week in June, and one week in November.
Secure parking. **TV**. **Canal+**. **Disabled access**.

A fine-looking building, conventional and maybe a touch middle-class in atmosphere. Rooms are clean and have recently been renovated. Doubles with shower/wc are 185–295F, with bath 245–350F. The nicest ones overlook the river. The cooking is simple, with dishes like *tripoux*, calf's head *ravigote*, duck legs, and medallions of lamb *en chevreuil*. Set meals start at 75F (lunchtimes only) and then range from 85F to 245F. Granted, there were no big disappointments but it was all rather predictable.

LE RELAIS DE FARROU***

Farrou (North); head for Saint-Rémy, 3km away in the direction of Figeac.
☎ 05.65.45.18.11 F→ 05.65.45.32.59
Restaurant closed Sunday evenings and Mondays out of season, Feb 19–March 6, and Oct 22–Nov 6.
Secure parking in private car park. **TV**. **Canal+**. **Disabled access**.

This is either a large establishment or a small complex – take your pick! One thing you can be sure of though is that it's been designed with the tourist very much in mind. There's a park, a pool, a Turkish bath, and a hot tub. The reception was nothing to write home about unfortunately. The rooms are comfortable, some of them are air-conditioned, and they and cost 280–455F. The restaurant is a bit showy in a provincial kind of way but the cooking has a good reputation. They do a rather tempting *menu du terroir* for 124F, and other set meals range from 164F to 222F. Weekday lunchtimes they do an 85F *formule* of starter plus main course or main course plus dessert. Specialities include a duo of warm and cold *foie gras* with truffle juices, roast monkfish with prunes, and *grenadin* of veal with fresh *tomme* (a type of cheese).

RESTAURANT DE LA HALLE – CHEZ PINTO

place A.-de-Morlhon (Centre); it's near the cathedral.
☎ 05.65.45.07.74

This is one of the few remaining examples of that almost extinct breed, the workman's caff (which ought to go on the endangered species list). You'll get a cordial welcome and be served substantial helpings of home cooking. There's a *menu pensionnaire* at 40F and a *menu passage* at 55F. How cheap can you get?

LE BEL ISLE – CHEZ JACQUES

36, rue Belle-Isle (Centre).
☎ 05.65.45.10.35.

The owner is a big man in these parts and we'll long remember him as one of the jolliest people we met! The décor is pre-1914 but the welcome was very friendly and the atmosphere pretty laid-back. In the large dining room, we found locals, miscellaneous poets, a few alcoholic anarchists and some lost tourists rubbing shoulders quite happily with each other, all delighted to pay no more than 55F for a hearty meal (wine included). For 100F, you'll get soup, local ham, snails, duck *confit*, cheese and dessert. Just in case you were peckish, you understand!

L'ASSIETTE GOURMANDE

place A.-Lescure (Centre); it's beside the cathedral.
☎ 00.65.45.25.95
Closed Sundays, Tuesdays and Wednesday evenings out of season. **Car park**.

The décor's fairly clichéd (beams and copperware) but the cooking's good. Set meals 74–150F, with a robust *menu rouergat* at 100F. They grill a lot of things in an open fireplace using oak from the "causse" or chalk plateau (it can't be anything else apparently). The terrace is nice in summer.

MONTEILS 12200 (115KM S)

RESTAURANT LE CLOS GOURMAND

☎ 05.65.29.63.15 F→ 05.65.29.64.98

Reservations only Oct–March and reservations advisable the rest of the year. You'll get a friendly welcome from Anne-Marie Lavergne, who's very well known for the excellent regional specialities she serves her guests in what was once "the big house" on the edge of the village. There are set meals at 65F and 100F with the day's special, and an extremely good regional one for 100F consisting of salad of stuffed duck's neck and walnuts, trout with *lardons*, beef with Roquefort cheese and dessert. If you go for the *étape gourmande* (160F), you'll get salad *aveyronnaise*, terrine of *foie gras*, and *émincé de confit* with sorrel. Good traditional cooking.

Nord-Pas-de-Calais

59 Nord

62 Pas-de-Calais

ARRAS 62000

AUBERGE DE JEUNESSE

59 Grand-Place (Centre).
☎ 03.21.22.70.02 Fax 03.21.07.46.15
Open 7.30am–12.30pm and 5–11pm (winter 10pm), Feb 1–Nov 30.

Holders of the FUAJ card (you can buy it at the hostel) can spend the night in this hostel on Arras' austere but magnificent Grand-Place for 45F. One twin room only; other rooms have 3-7 beds (54 in total). Showers and wc on each floor, and your own locker. Meals for groups only but kitchen available. Public car park with free facilities for cycles.

CAFÉ-HÔTEL DU BEFFROI

28 place de la Vacquerie (Centre); it's behind the bell-tower.
☎ 03.21.23.13.78 Fax:03.21.23.03.08
Closed Sundays and the first two weeks in August.

At the end of a block of typically Flemish houses. There's a typical little bistro with a clientèle of regulars on the ground floor and above this (be warned, the stairs are steep) there are very basic (basin only; shower and wc on the landing) but charming and well-kept rooms at reasonable prices. Doubles 170F. Choose one overlooking the square (number 10, for example, which has a sloping ceiling) and you'll have a perfect view of the Golden Lion of Artois perched on top of the 75m bell-tower. Excellent little establishment.

10% HÔTEL DES TROIS LUPPARS**

49 Grand-Place (Centre); take the bypass from the Lille/Paris direction.
☎ 03.21.07.41.41 Fax 03.21.24.24.80
Secure parking. **TV**.

On one side of the huge cobbled main square (without doubt one of the finest in northern France). A listed building which is pure Gothic (15th century) and houses a most charming hotel. There's even a sauna (but you have to pay 25F to use it). The décor of the rooms may be a touch modern given the surroundings but they're very comfortable. All with shower/bath and good value for money at 250–290F for a double. The owner, Viviane de Troy, is the perfect hostess. And her husband, who has one of the finest collections of wine in France, will happily show you round his 16th century wine cellar, close to the hotel, where old vintages and quite exceptional wines quietly mature.

RESTAURANT CHEZ ANNIE

14 rue Paul-Doumer (Centre); it's 200m behind the bell-tower.
☎ 03.21.23.13.51
Closed weekday evenings and Sundays (except by reservation).

Entertaining little restaurant, rather like a brasserie in miniature with a staircase which is of almost monumental proportions given its location. Climb the flight of stairs and sit on the mezzanine floor, a strategic point from which to surreptitiously observe the regulars propping up the bar. Good home cooking served at lunchtimes only. Generous set meal 65F; daily special 41F. Special set meals in honour of public holidays. Good, unpretentious little establishment.

RESTAURANT LA RAPIÈRE

44 Grand-Place (Centre).

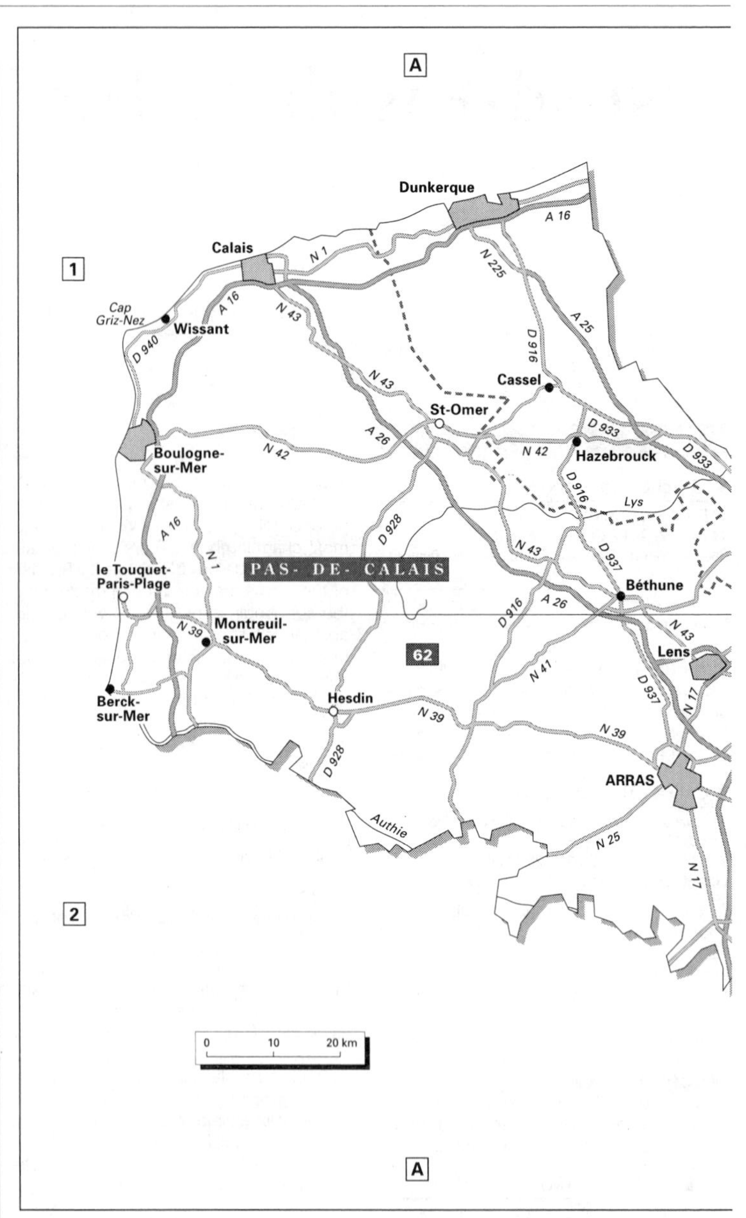
A
1
2
Dunkerque
Calais
Cap
Griz-Nez
Wissant
Cassel
St-Omer
Hazebrouck
Boulogne-
sur-Mer
Lys
PAS- DE- CALAIS
le Touquet-
Paris-Plage
Béthune
Montreuil-
sur-Mer
62
Lens
Berck-
sur-Mer
Hesdin
ARRAS
Authie
A 16
N 1
N 225
A 25
N 43
D 940
D 916
A 26
D 933
N 42
D 928
D 937
N 39
N 41
N 17
N 25
0
10
20 km
A

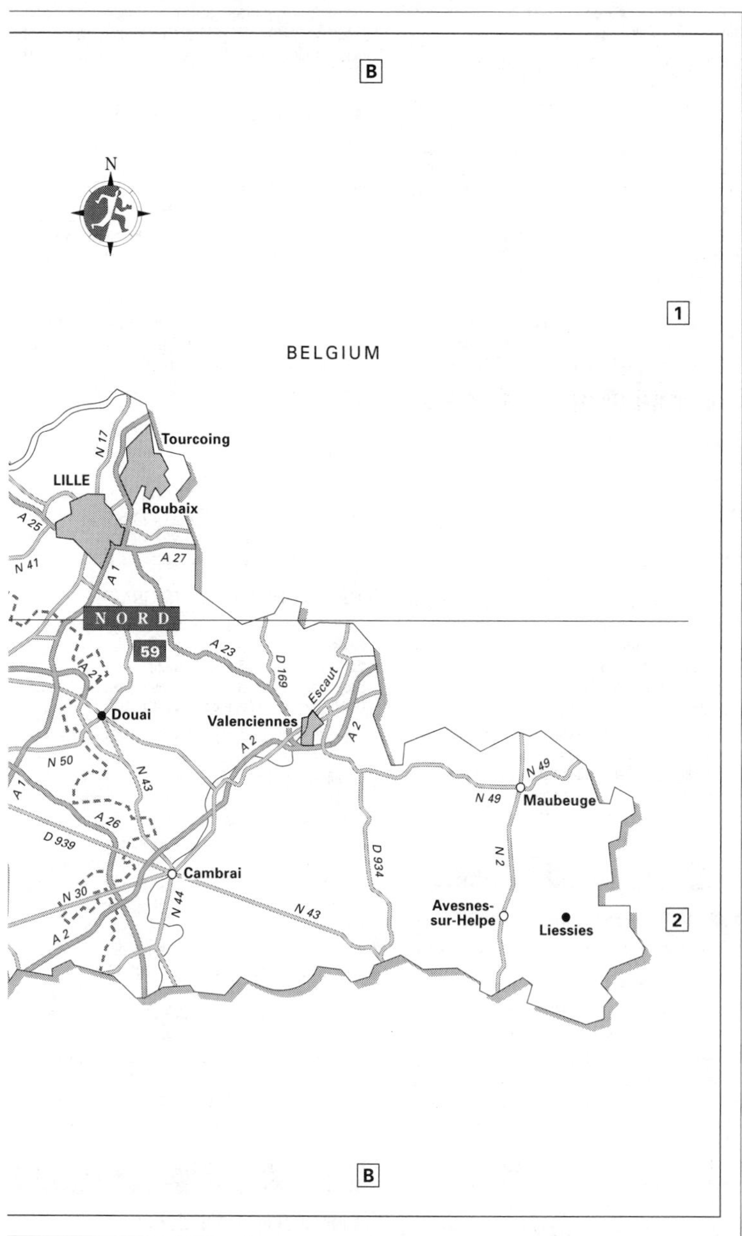
B
N
1
BELGIUM
Tourcoing
N 17
LILLE
Roubaix
A 25
N 41
A 27
A 1
NORD
59
A 23
D 169
A 21
Escaut
Douai
Valenciennes
A 2
A 2
N 50
N 43
N 49
N 49
Maubeuge
A 1
A 26
D 939
D 934
N 2
Cambrai
N 30
N 44
N 43
Avesnes-
sur-Helpe
Liessies
2
A 2
B

☎ 03.21.55.09.92 F➜ 03.21.22.24.29
Closed Sunday evenings.

Nestling under the sandstone arcades of one of the 155 houses around the main square (that square again!). A restaurant with wonderfully rustic décor above a vaulted 17th century cellar (make sure you're eating on expenses if you venture down there). A lot of effort is put into the traditional cuisine without going over the top. Dishes include salmon *en papillote* and fillet of beef with Roquefort. Some local specialities (Maroilles cheese flan for example) and the regional set meal at 115F is worth trying. Other set meals 82F (not on public holidays), 130F and 170F. Customers are a bit on the trendy side although the restaurant itself isn't.

SAINT-NICOLAS-LES-ARRAS 62223 (5KM N)

LA BELLE ÉTOILE**

ZA Les Alouettes; head for Lens – the ZA Les Alouettes is near the motorway.
☎ 03.21.58.59.00 F➜ 03.21.48.86.49
Restaurant closed Sunday evenings. **Car park**. **TV**. **Canal+**.

It's in the middle of an industrial estate so the surroundings aren't great but at the end of the day it's not too much of a problem since you're reasonably close to the centre. A bit like a motel. The rooms are comfortable and a little bit different with their cane bedheads. Doubles 275F (special offers at the weekend as the hotel is mainly used by business people). Meals also available — traditional cuisine and regional specialities (Maroilles cheese flan flambéd in Pommeau for example). Set meals 70F (weekdays) to 150F. Warm welcome.

BERCK-SUR-MER 62600

HÔTEL-RESTAURANT LE VOLTAIRE

29 av. du Général-de-Gaulle (Centre); it's opposite the casino.
☎ 03.21.84.43.13 F➜ 03.21.84.61.72
Closed Tuesdays out of season and Oct. **TV**.

Lunch served noon–2pm, dinner 7.30–10pm. The renovated rooms (they're not all done yet though) are impeccable, spacious (at least 20m² guaranteed — bring your tape measure!) and have excellent soundproofing. The décor is practical and modern. Doubles with shower 270F. Good breakfast buffet 27F. Warm and friendly welcome with a young feel and the same goes for the bar on the ground floor which specializes in beers. Apart from a few reasonable local specialities such as *ficelle picarde* (stuffed pancake), Welsh rarebit and charcoal-grilled beef though, we were not overly impressed by the food.

HÔTEL-RESTAURANT LES FLOTS BLEUS

17 rue du Calvaire (Centre).
☎ 03.21.09.03.42 F➜ 03.21.84.75.24
Closed Nov 15–Feb 15. **TV**. **Disabled access**.

The small, mossy garden has almost too many flowers and you can ask to eat there when the weather is fine. Inside, the style is rustic Normandy with exposed wood. No view of the blue waters the establishment is named after but the influence of the sea is reflected in the food — the 98F set meal has a whelk and prawn platter and fillet of *rascasse* (scorpion fish) braised with leeks. If you have an aversion to fishbones, the menu includes a number of meats grilled in the magnificent fireplace. Other set meals 130–175F. Welcome courteous without being overly formal. The rooms lack character. Doubles with shower or bath and wc 280F (230F out of season).

10% HÔTEL DU LITTORAL**

36 av. Marianne-Toute-Seule (Centre); it's opposite the tourist information centre
☎ 03.21.09.07.76 F➜ 03.21.09.57.38
Reservation recommended in winter. Restaurant closed Oct 1–Mar 30. **Secure parking**. **TV**.

The closest hotel to the sea in Berck. It's a sixties slab of concrete with little charm (unless you like that kind of thing). Customers are quiet and on the elderly side — they've been coming here for decades. Monsieur and Madame Devoucoux, the friendly proprietors who can't bring themselves to retire have been here that long too. The rooms are a shade old-fashioned but they're comfortable and reasonably priced for the area. Doubles with shower/wc 230F, with bath 240F. Given the type of place this is, half-board (from 270F per person) is advisable in season. Otherwise set meals (very traditional) at 65F, 95F and 120F. Oh, and we nearly forgot, ask for a room with a sea view (this includes part of the car park) and, if possible, with a balcony to breathe in Berck's sea air – which apparently contains more iodine than anywhere else in France.

BÉTHUNE 62400

HÔTEL DU VIEUX BEFFROI**

48 Grand-Place (Centre).

☎ 03.21.68.15.00 ➡ 03.21.56.66.32
Car park. TV. Disabled access.

This is a solidly built hotel with turrets and gables opposite the 14th century bell-tower whose bells make a nice sound to wake up to (in the morning – they don't ring at night!). A large hotel so don't count on receiving a special welcome. Old-fashioned rooms, some not short on charm. Hopefully, the forthcoming renovations will not make them too much alike. Doubles with shower or bath from 230F. Meals are served in a lively brasserie atmosphere. Set meals 75F, 110F, 120F and 180F. Dishes include *carpaccio* of beef with herbs, breast of roast duck with currants and salmon steak in an infusion of chicory.

RESTAURANT LA TAVERNE

1 place de la République (Centre).
☎ 03.21.56.80.80 ➡ 03.21.65.77.00
Closed Saturday lunchtimes.

A very traditional, unpretentious brasserie restaurant, and one of the best places in town. Set meals 70F (weekdays), 98F and 150F. The à la carte menu is quite varied and there are two main specialities: various kinds of sauerkraut (42–102F) and seafood, in particular an excellent and substantial fisherman's platter (75F). Customers are locals and on the elderly side.

BOULOGNE-SUR-MER 62200

10% AUBERGE DE JEUNESSE

place Rouget-de-l'Isle (South); it's opposite the station.
☎ 03.21.80.14.50 ➡ 03.21.80.45.62
Open 7.30–1am. **Car park. Disabled access.**

Handy location if you're travelling by train. Very comfortable youth hostel. 80F/night including breakfast and sheets. Rooms have three beds and a shower/wc. Bar and restaurant. Main course only 28F; full meal from 49F. Special dishes (fish and seafood) on request. Small kitchen area. The FUAJ hostelling card (compulsory and sold at the hostel) entitles holders to a whole host of reductions in Boulogne (cinema, shows, watersports etc). A friendly and lively hostel.

10% HÔTEL FAIDHERBE**

12 rue Faidherbe (Centre)
☎ 03.21.31.60.93 ➡ 03.21.87.01.14
TV. Canal+. Disabled access.

Good location near the harbour although this part of town was rebuilt after the war and lacks charm. Warm welcome. If the weather's fine Victor, the resident myna bird, might even say something just for you. Small, luxurious Victorian-style lounge – all right if you like that kind of thing. The individually decorated rooms (number 201 has to be the best), are comfortable but the bathrooms generally could do with a bit of a face lift. Doubles with washing facilities 160F, with shower/wc 250F, with bath 300F.

10% HÔTEL ALEXANDRA**

93 rue Thiers (Centre).
☎ 03.21.30.52.22 ➡ 03.21.30.20.03
Closed Jan 2–20. **Car park. TV.**

A small, unremarkable hotel in a street which manages to escape the worst of the town centre's heavy traffic. Warm and friendly welcome. Rooms are a shade on the old-fashioned side but comfortable. Doubles with shower/wc 230F, with bath 280F. Reservation recommended in high season and on public holidays.

L'ESTAMINET DU CHÂTEAU

2 rue du Château (East); it's in the old town opposite the basilica of Notre-Dame.
☎ 03.21.91.49.66 ➡ 03.21.31.92.96
Closed Thursdays.

In this picturesque street in the upper part of the town (with a very well preserved group of fortified 13th century buildings) where there's a whole string of often disappointing restaurants, the *Estaminet* is still a good bet. Tourists and locals alike come to this cosy little restaurant where traditions are respected. Accordion music hasn't as yet given way to techno and regulars still tend to prop up the bar. No complaints as far as the food is concerned. Set meals are reasonably priced, starting at 65F (available every day) and progressing to 95F, 125F and 165F. The specialities, which include monkfish kebabs, skate, monkfish stew, poached cod and langoustines, conjure up the smell of the sea.

RESTAURANT LE DOYEN

11 rue du Doyen (Centre); it's in a small street running at right angles to place Dalton.
☎ 03.21.30.13.08
Closed Wednesday evenings and Sundays.

This adorable little restaurant is THE place for fish and seafood in Boulogne, which is after all a fishing town, even though the "typical charm" of the centre might have you thinking otherwise. A few examples trawled from the reasonably priced set meals (70F weekdays, 92F and 130F) which, of course, change according to what is landed are: three-fish platter with prawn sauce, *endives au gratin* with smoked salmon, mussels in Muscadet, and grilled turbot steak with fennel. As a counterbalance to the fish, the menu also includes some meat dishes, such as veal escalope in cream sauce and pork fillet in curry sauce. And there are tempting desserts like chocolate tart, baked Alaska and *crème brûlée* with orange. Charming welcome.

PORTEL (LE) 62480 (4.5KM SW)

LE PORTELOIS

42 quai Dugay-Trouin; take the D119 and at Portel follow the signs to the beach.
☎ 03.21.31.44.60 F 03.21.31.34.83
Closed Sunday evenings, Mondays (except in July and August), and during October.

A real seaside restaurant with a panoramic view over the sea – you won't be able to take your eyes off it – interrupted only by the remains of a fort left there by Napoleon. And of course, the food's influenced by the sea too. They have no fewer than than 22 specialities with mussels (around 60F for a main course à la carte) cooked, for example, in traditional, Flemish, Pekinese(!) or Hungarian(!!) style. There's no shortage of fish dishes either – try the fish casserole in the 103F regional set meal or the fisherman's set meal at 158F. Set meals start at 69F during the week.

HESDIN-L'ABBÉ 62360 (9KM SE)

RESTAURANT L'AUBERGE DU MANOIR

How to get there: on the N1.
☎ 03.21.83.27.74
Closed Mondays, Jan 2–10, and mid July–mid Aug.
Car park.

Behind the unremarkable façade of this roadside establishment (don't be misled by the reference to a manor in its name) lies a neo-rustic restaurant (1.60m high fireplace with bellows and copperware) which, despite somewhat ill-assorted items of décor (such as reproductions of contemporary paintings and a display of rare bottles), has a certain measure of refinement. This extends to the choice of tableware, which, from the cutlery to the plates, is quite amazing. And what exactly is served on these plates? Food which allows itself a number of variations on a classic theme at relatively low prices. Chef Christophe Lefebvre specializes in duck (*confit*, duck breast and *foie gras*), but the set meals change every day depending on his mood. The lowest priced set meal (85F) – which in other establishments is often only a last resort – is excellent. Good wines are served by the glass and selected to accompany each dish perfectly (the chef was twice voted best wine waiter in Languedoc-Roussillon). A good restaurant.

WAST (LE) 62142 (15KM E)

HOSTELLERIE DU CHÂTEAU DES TOURELLES**

D127; take the N42 (towards Saint-Omer) then the D127 to Le Wast.
☎ 03.21.33.34.78 F 03.21.87.59.57
Car park. **TV**. **Disabled access**.

You'll see the hotel - a very elegant 19th century family mansion hidden behind a small park - as you enter the village. Behind the hotel there's a more modern annexe next to some tennis courts. Stay in the superb rooms of the 'château' with their Louis-Philippe furniture and small balconies. If your funds won't stretch to that, go for an attic room with a great sloping ceiling. All rooms come with bath. Doubles 280–350F. If you're staying for a number of days (the hotel is right in the middle of a regional park), opt for half-board (250F per person). Set meals start at 85F but this is just for hotel guests and the 160F set meal is really for business lunches. The next price up, at 220F, is expensive even for a double bill of duck and goose *foie gras* and fried fillet of beef with morel mushrooms. Wonderful welcome.

CALAIS 62100

10% HÔTEL WINDSOR**

2 rue du Commandant-Bonningue (North-East); head for the harbour – it's off place d'Armes.
☎ 03.21.34.59.40 F 03.21.97.68.59
Secure parking. **TV**. **Canal+**.

In a quiet part of town, not far from the marina. The atmosphere makes you think you're on the other side of the Channel. If you like English cooking this is the place for you! The welcome from the British proprietor who loves French literature, in particular works by the Flemish Marguerite Yourcenar, is both warm and low-key. Attractive rooms (number 14 is our favourite) from 160F for a double with basin, 200F with shower and 275F with bath.

10% HÔTEL PACIFIC**

40 rue du Duc-de-Guise (North); head towards the cathedral of Notre-Dame.

☎ 03.21.34.50.24 ➡ 03.21.97.58.02
Secure parking. **TV**.

A centrally located but quiet small family hotel. The new proprietors are making a start on renovation work. One good point is that they started with the bedding – which is brand new. Good value for money for Calais (doubles with shower 185F and with bath and telephone from 250F). Given the presence of the ferry, they, like just about every other hotel in town, have family rooms that sleep up to four people. Warm welcome; helpful and chatty service. The lounge and bar have a very retro look about them.

10% ⌂ LE RICHELIEU**

17 rue Richelieu (North); it's opposite the park of the same name.
☎ 03.21.34.61.60 ➡ 03.21.85.89.28
Closed at Christmas and on New Year's Day.
Secure parking. **TV**.

Bright, comfortable and quite pleasant rooms. Doubles with shower or bath 254F. The rooms on the third floor have a small balcony right opposite the huge and very lush Richelieu park. Ideal to give your eyes a rest from the profusion of neon signs in the adjacent streets. Complete relaxation is no problem; the welcome is low-key (perhaps too much so), the street is quiet and the classical statues of the museum of fine art make ideal neighbours.

|●| RESTAURANT L'IMPRÉVU

26 rue des Thermes (North-East); head for the harbour – it's off place d'Armes.
☎ 03.21.96.01.26
Closed Sunday evenings and Monday lunchtimes.

Not as "unexpected" as the person who named the restaurant "*L'Imprévu*" would like to think. Sparse décor, pleasant and knowledgeable staff and traditional cuisine. Forget the *moules marinière* and *crème caramel* and let yourself be tempted by specialities such as scallops *à la flamande* (poached in white wine with onions and mushrooms), and slices of duck with raspberries. Low prices with set meals at 54F (every day), 80F and 130F. Paella evenings on Friday if you book.

|●| RESTAURANT LE TEMPLIER

51 plage de Calais (North); along the beach, exit 14 off the A16.
☎ 03.21.97.57.09 ➡ 03.21.82.42.46
Closed Mondays (except in July/August) and end December. **Car park**.

All-day service. A nice little seaside bar/restaurant for once. Even though the basic set menu at 65F isn't very inspiring, the food isn't too bad. So pay a few francs more for the other set meals (80F, 105F and 150F) or try something from the à la carte menu (sole with herbs and white wine or the classic but tasty grilled beef with shallots). It gets a lot of regulars as you might expect. You'll have to book if you want to sit in the little wainscotted room overlooking the sea - with a bit of luck (and good eyesight!) you might be able to see the white cliffs of Dover. If not, you can watch the endless toing-and-froing of the cross-Channel ferries.

|●| RESTAURANT LE SAINT-CHARLES

47 place d'Armes (North); it's right in the centre of Calais-Nord.
☎ 03.21.96.02.96 ➡ 03.21.96.81.31
Closed Sunday evenings and Tuesdays. **Car park**.

The quintessential popular restaurant. Always busy (sometimes the service suffers as a result) and a host of set meals for every budget (59–185F). They do a number of seafood specialities - monkfish in cider, scallops and monkfish *à la nage* - and have some good meat dishes with as many chips as you can eat.

|●| RESTAURANT LA GOULUE GRILL

26 rue de la Mer (North); it's after the bell-tower on the right under the arcades.
☎ 03.21.96.16.52
Closed for one week at Christmas.

Retro décor with mirrors and velvet seats. The grilled meats are cooked in the fireplace in the corner under the watchful eye of the customers. You get a good piece of grilled steak in pepper sauce on the 72F set menu – but no dessert. Ah well, you can't have it all!

CAMBRAI 59400

⌂ HÔTEL DE FRANCE*

37 rue de Lille; it's 100m to the left of the station as you stand facing it.
☎ 03.27.81.38.80 ➡ 03.27.78.13.88
TV. **Closed** 5–27 Aug.

Typical station hotel. It's neat and tidy, quaintly old-fashioned (the postcards on sale at the reception desk are of 1950s vintage), and — surprisingly — quiet. That goes even for the rooms overlooking the tracks, since few trains run here at night. Doubles with basin 140F, with shower/wc 190F and with bath 210F. Low-key welcome.

10% ⌂ |●| LE MOUTON BLANC***

33 rue d'Alsace-Lorraine; it's 200m from the station, in

the street opposite it.
☎ 03.27.81.30.16 ➡ 03.27.81.83.54
Restaurant closed Sunday evenings, Mondays, and the first week in August. **Secure parking**. **TV**.

To start with, a Mouton Blanc (White Sheep) makes a nice change from the hundreds of Lions d'Or (Golden Lions) you see around France! Also, this solidly built 19th century middle-class residence has a great deal of charm. It may be a 3-star establishment but it has managed to keep a truly family atmosphere. The rooms reflect a certain opulence without going over the top. Doubles with shower/wc 260–300F, with bath 300–400F. In the large, half-timbered restaurant set meals start at 100F for which you get warm *andouillette* salad with creamy mustard dressing, chicken supreme and dessert. Other set meals 155F and 225F. The type of establishment which has a certain air of quality about it and some good French cooking.

|●| LE RESTO DU BEFFROI

4 rue du 11-Novembre; follow the avenue opposite the town hall then take the second right.
☎ 03.27.81.50.10
Closed Saturday lunchtimes, Sundays, during the February school holidays, and the last three weeks in August.

A rather unusual restaurant tucked away in a little street behind the main square (Grand-Place). The style of the décor is a mixture of traditional bistro and inn (with fragments of mirror stuck to the pink and black walls). Much of the menu originates from the south-west, which is understandable given that chef Yves Galan bred ducks before becoming a chef (nearly 30 years ago). For example, the 100F set meal offers duck breast, and *cassoulet* with *confit*. The real south-west accent is, to be honest, somewhat lacking in the cooking – you still feel as though you're in Cambrai – but the atmosphere is friendly and the daily lunchtime special (45F) is more than reasonable. Free house kir on presentation of this year's guide.

CASSEL 59670

|●| LA TAVERNE FLAMANDE

34 Grand-Place; it's opposite the town hall.
☎ 03.28.42.42.59 ➡ 03.28.40.51.84
Closed Tuesday evenings and Wednesdays.

Lunch served from 12pm, dinner from 7pm. This establishment's name (which translates as The Flemish Tavern) seems to underline the impression you get that the treaty of Nijmegen, signed in 1678 to mark the definitive annexation to France of this part of Flanders known as *Flandre maritime* hasn't really been taken on board yet. So what better place to go for an authentic Flemish set meal at 99F! Try Flemish *croustillons*, chicken casserole Ghent style (chicken in a home-made bechamel-type sauce), Flemish apple tart sprinkled with brown sugar or crêpes flambéd in Houlle. Three other set meals at 89F, 99F and 138F. It goes without saying of course that you should sit on the veranda which, perched on the slopes of Mount Cassel, overlooks the plane of Flanders and offers a panorama which apparently has already delighted the Romantic poet Lamartine, not to mention Charles X.

|●| ESTAMINET T'KASTEEL HOF

8 rue Saint-Nicolas; it's opposite the mill.
☎ 03.28.40.59.29 ➡ 03.28.42.43.23
Closed Mondays, Tuesdays, Wednesday and Thursday evenings (out of season), and Mondays June–Aug.
Car park.

The highest tavern in French Flanders at a mere 175.90m! It's at the top of Mount Cassel which, according to legend, originated from a clod of earth left by the local giants, Reuze Papa and Reuze Maman. Locals will also tell you that from the terrace you can see five kingdoms: France, Belgium, Holland, England and, if you raise your eyes, the kingdom of heaven. A wonderful little place with a tiny bar, just a few tables, wooden chairs which scrape on the floor, a fireplace, and baskets hanging from the beams. As you might have suspected, this tavern is just too typical not to be a reconstruction. From the starters — various kinds of soup with endives or cœur casselois (pork mince, cubes of smoked bacon and apples on a puff pastry base) — to the more familiar main courses (casserole or the famous potjevfleisch - veal, chicken and rabbit pâté - that Lamartine loved) and cheeses such as zermezeelois or mont-des-cats, the fare here is 100% Flemish. That goes for the mineral water too which comes from Saint-Amand. And the wine? What wine? This is hop country and it would hardly be an exaggeration to claim that the list of traditional beers offered by T'Kasteel Hof would be enough to fill this guide on its own! Reckon on paying about 100F for a meal, but you could settle for one of the typical and filling local 'planches' or platters with pâtés from Houtland (the wooded country which dominates Cassel) or cheeses.

BOESCHEPE 59299 (15KM E)

AUBERGE DU VERT MONT**

route du Mont-Noir; take the D948 towards Steenvoorde then the N348 to the Belgian border, and finally the D10 towards Bailleul.
☎ 03.28.49.41.26 ➡ 03.28.49.48.58
Car park. TV. Disabled access.

Ducks splash about in the pond, goats and sheep bleat – we're out in the country and this hotel cum restaurant tries to remember that it used to be one of the farms dotted about over the Flanders hills. Now though it's a small tourist complex with games for children, tennis courts etc. The rooms are adorable if you like pink. Reckon on paying 250F for a double with shower or bath. The welcome is friendly with a young feel. The restaurant, with its beams (very much in evidence) covered in flowers, offers a range of tried and tested regional dishes such as fish casserole, Hoegarden-style scallops and *pot-jevfleisch* (veal, chicken and rabbit pâté) Set meals at 85F, 135F and 165F and a large selection of Belgian and French beers. On the subject of beer, don't miss the hopfield next to the inn. The Flanders hills are one of the few places in France where they can still be seen.

DOUAI 59500

HÔTEL LE CHAMBORD**

3509 route de Tournai; it's in Frais-Marais, 4km from the centre on the D917.
☎ 03.27.97.72.77 ➡ 03.27.99.35.14
Closed Sunday evenings and Mondays; restaurant closed one week in Feb and two weeks in Aug.
Secure parking. TV.

This "suburb" of Douai has retained its village-like atmosphere but a main road runs past the hotel so don't take a room on that side of the building. Comfortable and quite attractive rooms at reasonable prices for the area (strangely, hotels are rather expensive in Douai). Doubles with bath 240F. Meals also available. Set meals from 92F (weekdays) to 190F.

RESTAURANT AU TURBOTIN

9 rue de la Massue (Centre); it's near the Scarpe River, opposite the law courts.
☎ 03.27.87.04.16
Closed Saturday lunchtimes, Sunday evenings, Mondays, the last week in February, and in August.

With its fish-tank enjoying pride of place, *Au Turbotin* is a real fish and seafood restaurant which does not, however, neglect local farm produce. Dishes include turbot with *Maroilles* (a rather strong local cheese) and asparagus *millefeuille*. The basic set meal at 91F (weekdays) also offers a combination of produce of the land and sea with fish soup or chicken liver salad and salmon with sorrel or Toulouse sausage. Other set meals 147F, 186F and 255F. With first-class, tasty food, chic yet low-key surroundings, courteous and refined service and customers who don't have to watch the pennies, it's one of the town's class establishments – but you feel at ease and, more important, you eat well.

DUNKERQUE 59240

10% TRIANON HÔTEL**

20 rue de la Colline (North-East); from the centre follow the signs to the beach; the hotel is then signposted.
☎ 03.28.63.39.15 ➡ 03.28.63.34.57
Secure parking. TV.

It's surrounded by the turn of the century picturesque seaside villas typical of this part of the coast, which was developed in 1865 by a man called Gaspard Malo. A quiet area for the retired who take their siestas behind the bow windows of their little houses. The hotel is not without charm. The rooms are pleasant, as is the tiny indoor garden next to which you breakfast. Very reasonable prices (doubles with washing facilities 195F, with shower/wc 215F and with bath 250F). One small quibble — the welcome leaves a little to be desired. No restaurant.

HÔTEL-RESTAURANT L'HIRONDELLE**

46-48 av. Faidherbe (North-East); from the centre head towards the beach; then you'll see it signposted.
☎ 03.28.63.17.65 ➡ 03.28.66.15.43
Restaurant closed Sunday evenings, Monday lunchtimes, Feb 14–28, and Aug 16–Sept 5.
Secure parking. TV. Canal+. Disabled access.

Lunch served 12–14.15pm, dinner 7.30–9.45pm. In Malo-les-Bains right next to a lovely little square (pity about the vast amounts of traffic around) and not far from the sea. Faultless establishment with modern décor throughout. The huge staircase makes the reception area look like a transatlantic liner. Modern and functional rooms (two adjectives which you will doubtless have seen elsewhere in this guide), all with shower or bath. Doubles from 312F. Welcome very by the book but friendly. The restaurant offers no surprises. Set meals 65F (weekdays), 90F, and 125F.

|●| RESTAURANT LE PLAISANCE

3 rue de la Poudrière (North); from place du Minck go past the docks then turn left into quai de la Citadelle and take the second on the right.
☎ 03.28.66.89.20
Closed Saturday lunchtimes and Sundays.

Lunch served 11.30am–2.30pm, dinner 6.45–10.30pm (11pm at weekends). A small, low-key establishment tucked away behind the fish stalls on the harbour. A few photos of sailing ships adorn the otherwise plain, whitewashed walls, reminding you yet again that you're by the sea. The waiter serves the courses of the 78F *menu du jour* (quite simply wonderful) as if he were on stage. The 125F set meal takes you to Flanders with Maroilles cheese pie, Minck casserole, *crème brûlée* with chicory or *tarte au sucre* (a bit like treacle tart and very very sweet). Once a month the already warm ambiance steps up a gear with a theme evening when *Le Plaisance* heads, for example, for the West Indies and the punch flows freely. An establishment worth getting to know and that's what this guide is all about isn't it?

|●| RESTAURANT LE PÉCHÉ MIGNON

11 place du Casino.
☎ 03.28.66.14.44 📠 same
Car park. **Closed** Saturday lunchtimes, Sunday evenings and Mondays.

Lunch served 12–2pm, dinner 7–10pm. This restaurant looks a bit on the posh side with its comfy seats and pastel shades, but if you've lost all your savings at the casino opposite, the lunchtime set meal (weekdays only) doesn't cost a fortune at 75F (including wine). Other set meals 125F, 170F and 200F. Traditional cooking with dishes like smoked salmon *terrine*, rabbit in creamy mustard sauce, cheek of beef and oxtail à la flamande and a tempting sweet trolley, all served up in generous portions When the weather's fine you can sit out on the small terrace in the garden - which makes up for not having a view of the sea.

|●| RESTAURANT-BRASSERIE LE FIGARO

2 place Paul-Asseman (North); it's 100m from the beach.
☎ 03.28.63.22.70 📠 same

This restaurant may be a little way from the seafront (although if you sit near the bay windows you can see the sea on the horizon), but this is more of an advantage than a disadvantage. The welcome is courteous, the dining room comfortable and the service attentive (not always the case at the nearby restaurants, strung out along the seafront – far from it), but the prices are typical of a seaside establishment with set meals at 85F, 120F (including aperitif, coffee and unlimited wine), 164F and 185F.

|●| RESTAURANT LE PETIT SAINT-ÉLOI

6 rue Thévenet
☎ 03.28.66.52.41
Closed Sundays and two weeks in August.

With a motorbike sitting in the window and a bar made from a converted church pulpit, the décor of this old bistro is rather eclectic. Daily specials, dishes that are permanent features, Flemish specialities, and good little wines served by the glass or jug. The restaurant's two dining rooms (one of them on the upper floor with a view of the church of Saint-Éloi) are always packed. Lots of regulars (who must be friends, given the atmosphere) and relaxed service. Daily special 42F. Otherwise reckon on paying 100F for a full meal. Good place to have lunch.

BERGUES 59380 (10KM SE)

🏠 |●| HÔTEL-RESTAURANT AU TONNELIER**

4 rue du Mont-de-Piété
☎ 03.28.68.70.05 📠 03.28.68.21.87
Closed the first fortnight in January and the second fortnight in August; restaurant closed Fridays.
Secure parking. **TV**.

This attractive inn with its yellow-orange brickwork is situated at the heart of the medieval village opposite a superb 17th century building, the Mont-de-Piété, which has been restored and converted into a museum. It's so quiet that it seems a shame to wake the charming old lady taking a siesta in the lounge (at 11am) to ask for a room. The welcome is nevertheless very warm. Doubles with basin (no TV) 190F, with shower/wc and cable TV (no less than 22 channels) 315–345F. We confess a weakness for the rooms looking out onto the lovely little paved courtyard, which are of course quieter and also get more light. The good plain home cooking doesn't seem out of place in the opulent surroundings of this restaurant (there's nothing like a Regency dining room). There are a number of regional specialities, including a terrific *potjevfleisch* (this mixture of veal, rabbit and chicken in aspic cooked in white wine and vinegar is impossible to pronounce but tastes wonderful). Set meals 98F (except Sunday lunchtimes),108F and 145F (128F and 165F Sunday lunchtimes).

HAZEBROUCK 59190

10% HÔTEL LE GAMBRINUS**

2 rue Nationale (Centre); it's between the main square and the station.
☎ 03.28.41.98.79 F 03.28.43.11.06
Car park. **TV**.

If you want to stay the night in Hazebrouck it's either your car or *Le Gambrinus*, the only hotel in town. So why, you ask yourselves, are we recommending a place you could have found all on your own? On the one hand because the fresh and simple decoration of this solidly built 19th century house shows good taste which no-one could object to; the rooms are pleasant and all have a bath (doubles 290F). On the other hand, and more importantly, because Francis Delaere and his wife are the kind of hoteliers you wish a few more people in their profession would take as an example. Here there's no need to look up the meaning of the word "welcome" in a dictionary!

RESTAURANT LE CENTRE

48 Grand-Place (Centre).
☎ 03.28.48.03.62
Closed Tuesday evenings. **Car park**.

The seats are comfortable (although the flowery material is a bit over the top) and the à la carte menu has something for everyone (as many mussels and chips as you can eat, salads and crêpes, pizzas etc). But for preference choose one of the reasonable regional specialties - Welsh rarebit, herring and warm apples, *carbonnade flamande* (beef and onions braised in beer) or classic but good dishes such as scallops and fillet of beef with morels and leg of duck with oyster mushrooms. Set meals range in price from 65F (lunchtimes only) to 175F, with one featuring regional specialities at 110F. Friendly welcome and service (yes, it's that word friendly again!).

RESTAURANT LA TAVERNE

61 Grand-Place (Centre).
☎ 03.28.41.63.09
Closed Sunday evenings and Mondays, one week in February and three weeks late July/early August.
Car park.

Except on Saturdays when it's *choucroute* night, everything in this convivial restaurant is of Flanders origin — Maroilles cheese and leek quiche, juniper and apple tart, *pot-jevfleisch*, rabbit, chicken and bacon *terrine*, and *carbonnade flamande* (beef braised in beer - they use Trois-Monts). The generous portions are served with a smile. Theme nights on certain days of the week (mussels and chips on Fridays, home-made Welsh rarebit on Sundays etc). Set meals at 95F (except Sunday evenings) and 145F. Reckon on paying about 100F à la carte.

MOTTE-AU-BOIS (LA) 59190 (5KM S)

AUBERGE DE LA FORÊT**

(Centre); it's 5 mins from Hazebrouck on the D946 heading towards Merville.
☎ 03.28.48.08.78 F 03.28.40.77.76
Closed Sunday evenings (and lunchtimes Dec 26–Jan 16), Mondays, and at Christmas. **Car park**. **TV**.

Lunch served 12–2pm, dinner 7.30–9pm. This hunting lodge, which dates from the fifties and is almost buried under foliage, is situated in the heart of a village deep in the vast Nieppe forest. The panelled rooms are simple but pleasant, in particular those with latticed windows opening onto lovely little gardens. Doubles with shower or bath 210–320F. It goes without saying that the restaurant is rustic in style. It offers some regional specialities but also a great deal of exceptionally inventive cooking (sometimes too much so!), which justifies the rather high prices. Set meals start at 135F on weekdays. Good wine list (the cellar is one of the best in the region). Customers are a bit on the posh side and the welcome could be warmer.

HESDIN 62140

10% HÔTEL DES FLANDRES**

20-22 rue d'Arras (Centre)
☎ 03.21.86.80.21 F 03.21.86.28.01
Closed July 5–15 and Dec 20–Jan 8. **Secure parking**. **TV**.

A little town with nothing out of the ordinary (although in the Middle Ages "les Merveilles d'Hesdin", a gigantic theme park ahead of its time, was the talk of the neighbourhood) and the kind of hotel you'd expect to find there. Family atmosphere and standard but comfortable rooms (doubles with shower/wc or bath 290F). The restaurant serves traditional local dishes like its big speciality, chicken in beer. Set meals range in price from 92F (weekdays) to 132F, 168F and 194F.

SAULCHOY 62870 (22.5KM SW)

LE VAL D'AUTHIE

How to get there: take the scenic route along the D928 (towards Abbeville) then turn right onto the D119 which runs along the River Authie.
☎ 03.21.90.30.20
Closed Thursdays out of season and the first week in September.

A good old friendly little country inn with character in the heart of one of those little Artois villages which the novelist Bernanos, who came from the area, described as being "full of the sound of rustling leaves and running water". The set meals offer "good plain home cooking prepared by the proprietor". You'll only find tried and tested recipes here (*vol au vent, coq au vin,* duck breast and leg of lamb) – and that's just fine. Set meals 80F (weekdays), 125F and 150F (including drinks). In season you can (for 250F) eat copious amounts of game dishes such as hare casserole, wild boar stew, venison in cream sauce, pheasant in port etc If you want to check that there are indeed otters hiding along the banks of the Authie, the inn offers attractive rooms (230F for 2 including breakfast) and a *gîte* sleeping 4–6 (700F at weekends).

LENS 62300

RESTAURANT LA DÉCOUVERTE

11 rue des Déportés; it's not far from the coach station.
☎ 03.21.42.70.00
Closed Sundays, Mondays and Tuesdays.

A quiet little restaurant tucked away in a small street without much traffic. Given the huge size of the place, the partitions decorated with flowers are a good idea. The (somewhat elderly) clientèle are amazed still to find a calf's head which is so good. The menu also includes pigs' trotter in vinaigrette, *rillettes* (potted pork and goose meat), liver *meunier* (coated in flour and fried in breadcrumbs) and grilled kidneys for the basic set meal at 69F and pigs' trotters coated in breadcrumbs for the 92F one. As one reader put it, "It's hard luck if you're a vegetarian". If you opt for *"réserve maison",* you'll only be charged for what you drink from the bottle.

BULLY-LES-MINES 62160 (5KM W)

10% L'ENFANT DU PAYS

152 rue de la Gare.
☎ 03.21.29.12.33.
Restaurant closed Sunday evenings. **TV**.

Well-known in the area for serving generous helpings of straightforward authentic dishes made with fresh produce. If you're really hungry, go for the *estouffade* of veal sweetbreads in port or the sautéd chicken in beer. And even if you feel you can't manage another mouthful, you'll find the cheese irresistible. Set meals 62–135F. Large dining room with a pleasant atmosphere and service to match. The bedrooms have all been redecorated and have TV and everything. Rock-bottom prices. Doubles 85F (!) with basin and TV (shower and wc in the corridor), 140F with bath, wc, TV and phone.

LIESSIES 59740

LE CHÂTEAU DE LA MOTTE**

How to get there: take the D133 towards the lac du Val-Joly.
☎ 03.27.61.81.94 F 03.27.61.83.57
Closed Sunday, Monday and Tuesday evenings out of season and Dec 23–Jan 31. Lunch served from 12.30pm, dinner from 7.30pm. **Car park**. **TV**.

This region may be thought of by many as being flat and bleak, but here in the Avesnois, on the contrary, the countryside is bright, lush and undulating The grounds of this hotel and restaurant, which back onto the Bois-l'Abbé national forest, invite you to get back to nature. *Le Château de la Motte* (formerly a place of retreat for the monks at the abbey of Liessies built in 1725) isn't bad either with its slate-topped pink brick walls which are reflected in the waters of the adjacent lake. The rooms offer total peace and quiet (it's guaranteed — the monks liked silence). Doubles with basin from 190F. In the restaurant set meals start at 98F (except Sundays) for which you can enjoy dishes such as *galantine* of sea troutwith a creamy pepper sauce and lamb with thyme followed by cheese and dessert. There's another set meal at 185F which includes a cider cocktail, wine and coffee. On Sundays only the 190F gourmet set meal is served.

LILLE 59000

SEE MAP OVERLEAF

10% LE SAINT-NICOLAS*

11 bis rue Nicolas-Leblanc; M° République. **MAP C3-2**
☎ 03.20.57.73.26
Access until 10pm. **Closed** Sundays 12.30–8pm.

Separated from the centre by the vast place de la République and its underground station, which looks like an ancient amphitheatre, this is the kind of little hotel where life is quiet. The furniture has been around for a while (but the beds are still comfortable) and the rooms are terribly old-fashioned (but still not without charm). Doubles with basin 140F, with shower 170F and with bath 180F (in all cases the toilets are on the landing). The whole of the rear part of the building is quiet. Low-key welcome. Pass for night owls. Several (paying) car parks nearby (Préfecture, Philippe-le-Bon etc). And the palais des Beaux-Arts is right on your doorstep.

10% HÔTEL DES VOYAGEURS*

10 place de la Gare and 28 rue du Priez. **MAP D2-1**
☎ 03.20.06.43.14

Reservation recommended. A well-kept, recently renovated hotel which remains one of the least expensive in Lille. Friendly and low-key welcome. Clientèle of regulars and travellers of all nationalities. Wonderful lift from days gone by ("and not once in 25 years has it broken down!" we were told). The proprietor has furnished the hotel with items acquired at auctions and the rooms think they are still in the 40s and 50s (which gives them their charm). Doubles 150F (with basin and wc or shower but no wc) and 170F (with shower/wc). All rooms have a telephone. Very substantial breakfast (18F!) served in a small family lounge.

10% LE BRUEGHEL* *

5 parvis Saint-Maurice. **MAP C2-5**
☎ 03.20.06.06.69 F 03.20.63.25.27
Secure parking. TV. Canal+. Disabled access.

A hotel with personality and – better still – with a soul. The decoration shows excellent taste. Trinkets and antique furniture (objets trouvés) are dotted about to fill every nook and cranny of this enormous brick building under the church of Saint-Maurice. Even the lift has charm! Double rooms to suit every pocket at 180F (basin), 290–345F (shower/wc) and 370–470F (with bath). The rooms at the rear are very pleasant and quiet. The welcome couldn't be better — the staff love their work (and the night porter almost has his own fan club!). Meeting place for actors appearing in shows in Lille and one of our favourite establishments in the region.

10% HÔTEL DE FRANCE**

10 rue de Béthune; M° Rihour. **MAP C2-4**
☎ 03.20.57.14.78 F 03.20.57.06.01
TV. Open all night.

The hotel is right in the centre — close to the Grand-Place in the area where all the cinemas are — so it's well situated, too much so in fact: the street is fairly busy at night and only the rooms on the first floor are soundproofed. It lacks charm but there's nothing really to find fault with. Reckon on paying 150F for a double with basin, 255F with shower/wc and 265F with bath and direct-dial telephone. Very friendly welcome. At breakfast it's impossible to escape the gigantic fresco in praise of Nord-Pas-de-Calais painted by a former night porter, a student at the art school. Let's hope that he has moved on to other things.

10% LE GRAND HÔTEL**

51 rue Faidherbe. **MAP C2-6**
☎ 03.20.06.31.57 F 03.20.06.24.44
Closed the first three weeks in August.
TV.

Comfortable hotel. The recently renovated rooms are attractively decorated and the welcome is particularly warm. Doubles with shower/wc from 280F, with bath 310F. A few family rooms (sleeping 3 and 4). Breakfast free at weekends.

HÔTEL FLANDRE-ANGLETERRE**

13 place de la Gare. **MAP D2-3**
☎ 03.20.06.04.12 F 03.20.06.37.76
Car park. TV with **Canal+.**

With a name which translates literally as "Flanders-England Hotel", you might have expected to be "treated" to British hospitality. Wrong. The welcome here couldn't be better and is more what you would expect to find in a traditional French family hotel. Unfussy, well soundproofed rooms with quite modern décor, all with nice bathrooms. Doubles 340F. Mainly business clientèle so the prices drop at the weekend if you stay at least two nights. A hotel where you quickly forget that you're opposite the station in a part of town which, despite its proximity to Euralille, has nothing much going on.

HÔTEL DE LA PAIX**

46 bis rue de Paris. **MAP C2-7**
☎ 03.20.54.63.93 F 03.20.63.98.97
TV with **Canal+. Disabled access.**

Past the grand reception area (and a welcome which couldn't be better), a superb 18th century staircase (it would really be a pity to use the lift) takes you up to tastefully furnished and spacious rooms. Doubles with shower/wc 360F, with bath 390F. The proprietor gave up painting for the hotel business but it has remained a passion. She has devoted each room to paintings by a different contemporary artist — they're only prints

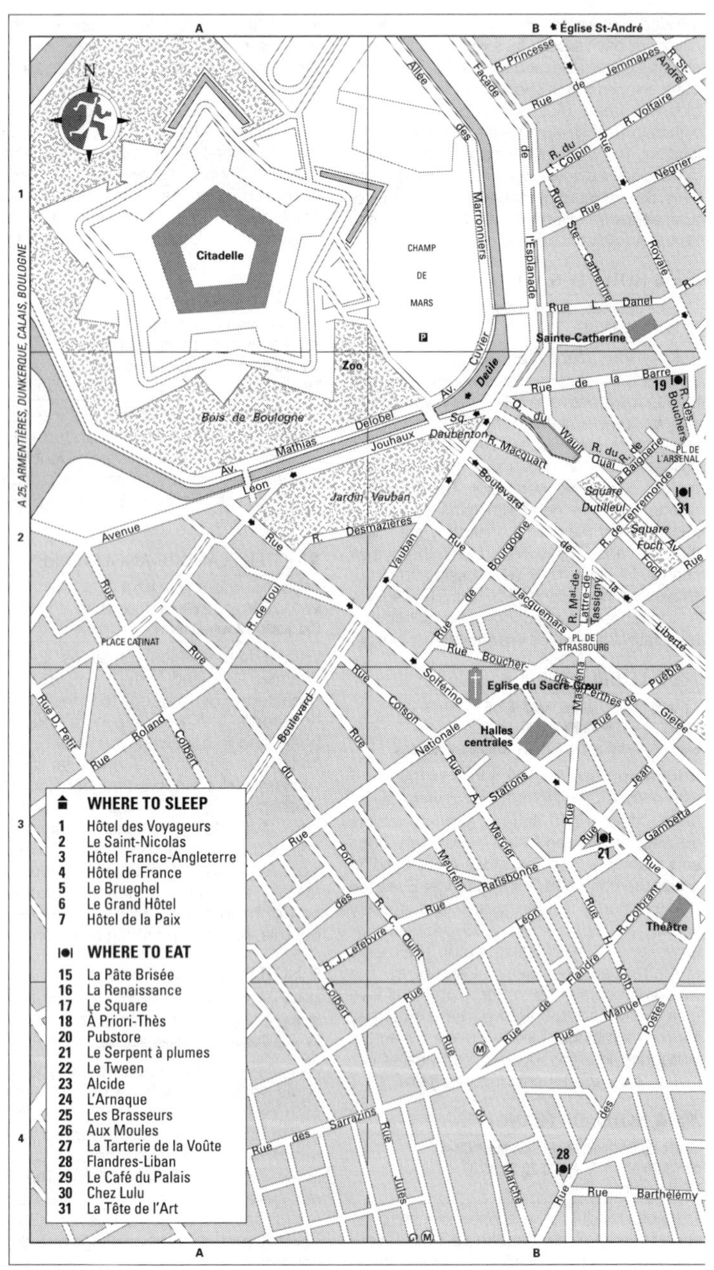
WHERE TO SLEEP
1 Hôtel des Voyageurs
2 Le Saint-Nicolas
3 Hôtel France-Angleterre
4 Hôtel de France
5 Le Brueghel
6 Le Grand Hôtel
7 Hôtel de la Paix
WHERE TO EAT
15 La Pâte Brisée
16 La Renaissance
17 Le Square
18 À Priori-Thès
20 Pubstore
21 Le Serpent à plumes
22 Le Tween
23 Alcide
24 L'Arnaque
25 Les Brasseurs
26 Aux Moules
27 La Tarterie de la Voûte
28 Flandres-Liban
29 Le Café du Palais
30 Chez Lulu
31 La Tête de l'Art
Citadelle
CHAMP DE MARS
Zoo
Bois de Boulogne
Jardin Vauban
Sainte-Catherine
Eglise du Sacré-Cœur
Halles centrales
Théâtre
Église St-André
PLACE CATINAT
PL. DE STRASBOURG
PL. DE L'ARSENAL
Square Dutilleul
Square Foch
A 25, ARMENTIÈRES, DUNKERQUE, CALAIS, BOULOGNE

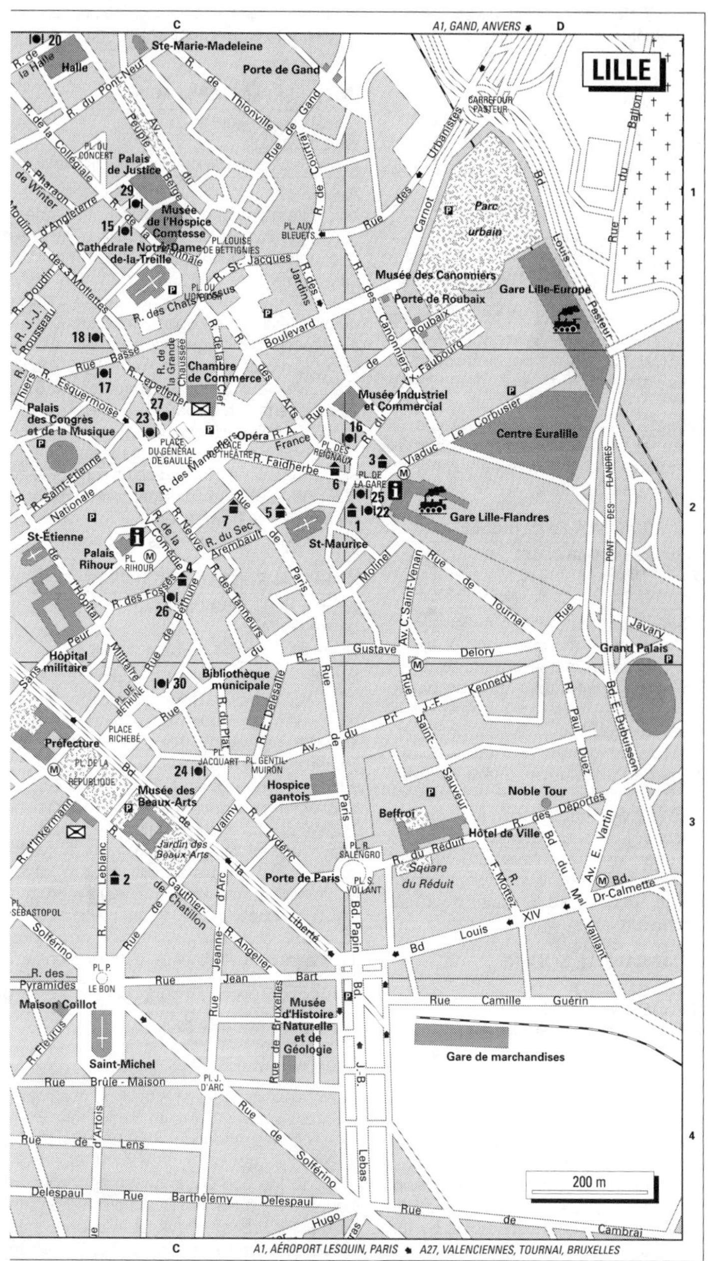
LILLE
A1, GAND, ANVERS
A1, AÉROPORT LESQUIN, PARIS
A27, VALENCIENNES, TOURNAI, BRUXELLES
Ste-Marie-Madeleine
Porte de Gand
Halle
Palais de Justice
Musée de l'Hospice Comtesse
Cathédrale Notre-Dame de-la-Treille
Musée des Canonniers
Porte de Roubaix
Gare Lille-Europe
Parc urbain
Chambre de Commerce
Musée Industriel et Commercial
Centre Euralille
Palais des Congrès et de la Musique
Opéra
Gare Lille-Flandres
St-Étienne
Palais Rihour
St-Maurice
Grand Palais
Hôpital militaire
Bibliothèque municipale
Préfecture
Musée des Beaux-Arts
Jardin des Beaux-Arts
Hospice gantois
Beffroi
Hôtel de Ville
Noble Tour
Square du Réduit
Porte de Paris
Maison Coillot
Saint-Michel
Musée d'Histoire Naturelle et de Géologie
Gare de marchandises
200 m

(how many hotel owners do you know who'd put up a Magritte in their rooms?), but it adds to the charm of the place. We fell in love with number 12 with its terrace and garden (yes, right in the town centre).

|●| RESTAURANT LA RENAISSANCE

29 place des Reignaux. **MAP C2-16**
☎ 03.20.06.17.56
Closed Sunday, Monday and Tuesday evenings and July 15–Aug 15.

A no-nonsense restaurant for broke young travellers and others. Don't go by the restaurant's outward appearance – inside is where it's at! Rustic décor, excellent family cooking and a number of regional specialities such as chicory Flemish style, *potjevfleisch* and Maroilles cheese tart and home-made desserts. Good *formule* at 43.50F (lunchtimes) which includes a daily special and a starter or dessert. Set meals 53.50F (not wonderful) and 69F (very varied choice). Excellent value for money.

|●| RESTAURANT LA PÂTE BRISÉE

65 rue de la Monnaie. **MAP C1-15**
☎ 03.20.74.29.00 ➡ 03.20.13.80.47
Lunch served 11.45am–2.15pm, dinner 7–10.30pm.

Even though the competition is fierce, this restaurant remains the specialist for sweet and savoury tarts (roquefort tart, Maroilles cheese, *tarte tatin* etc), regional baked cheese dishes (try the region's *tartiflette* with potatoes, cubes of bacon, braised onion and melted Maroilles cheese) and mixed salads. Various *formules* (including drinks) are available at 45F, 68F, 75F and 81F. Very reasonable prices given that the food is good and the portions generous. Packed at lunchtime so it's a good idea to get here early. Relaxed atmosphere with mostly students. Exceptional rustic décor. Also functions as a tearoom from 3pm.

|●| RESTAURANT LE SQUARE

52 rue Basse. **MAP C2-17**
☎ 03.20.74.16.17 ➡ 03.20.93.21.49
Closed Sundays, Monday evenings and Aug 1–22.

The décor is rustic but not overly so. The welcome and service are friendly, making the restaurant the type of place where friends meet. *Menu complet* (lunchtimes) 55F. À la carte you get warm or cold salads and generous portions of other reasonable dishes, some of them local and always in season. *Formule* well worth the money – good little wines are offered with most dishes, by the glass so you can try several. There is even a set meal at 125F (including wine of course) if you want to experiment without breaking the bank.

|●| LE SERPENT À PLUMES

180 rue Solférino. **MAP B3-21**
☎ 03.20.30.66.28
Closed Saturday and Sunday lunchtimes and Mondays.

A restaurant which has lost all trace of the north. Its name and décor are South American, as are the items on the menu – such as guacamole and chili con carne. The food here comes from far and wide which is the way the restaurant likes it (and this guide doesn't mind either). From Africa, *Le Serpent à Plumes* has brought back a *maffé* of beef with peanut butter and from the West Indies a shark *colombo* but the origin of the fried camembert with bilberries remains something of a poser... Mostly young people come here and it's a bit trendy. Set meals 65F and 85F at lunchtime. Reckon on paying between 90F and 120F à la carte depending on how hungry – or how greedy – you are (the chocolate banana cream is quite something).

|●| RESTAURANT LE PUBSTORE

44 rue de la Halle. **MAP C1-20**
☎ 03.20.55.10.31
Closed Sundays, public holidays and in August.

Lunch served 12–1.30pm, dinner 7.30–10.30pm.The building's façade with its multitude of very "pop" metal cylinders makes it hard to believe that this is a restaurant. The impression continues inside where, with the subdued lighting and candles (even at lunchtime!), you could be in a 70s nightclub. The menu is full of puns. Thank goodness then that, incomprehensible witticisms notwithstanding, the place is actually worth a visit for its atmosphere, its décor and (yes) for the food which it dishes up in kingsize helpings. *Formule* 65F at lunchtime. Reckon on paying 120F à la carte. An unusual establishment.

|●| RESTAURANT LES BRASSEURS

22 place de la Gare. **MAP D2-25**
☎ 03.20.06.46.25
Closed Aug 4–7.

Beer lovers, here at last is the kind of authentic brasserie you'd like to think there were more of! This wonderful drink as old as time (beer originated in Egypt where it was dedicated to the god Osiris before appearing in Gaul in the 1st century BC) is brewed on site by master brewer M. Varlet in superb vats which you can't miss. You'll find it hard to choose between the amber-coloured beer made with grilled malt, the Saint-Sauveur and the opalescent blanche de Lille – that's unless you decide on a beer cocktail (whether the purists like it or not). For those not set on having a liquid lunch, we recommend the *flammenküches* from 26–45F which you eat with your fingers (it's allowed here), the grilled shin on a bed of sauerkraut or the hopfield-style black pudding. Friendly atmosphere and attractive decoration.

I●I A PRIORI-THÉS

10 rue Masurel. **MAP C1-18**
☎ 03.20.31.54.89 F➜ 03.20.13.81.58
Closed Mondays, Tuesday to Friday evenings and Saturday lunchtimes; annual holidays July 15–Aug 31.

Service 3–6.30pm. There are just a few tables crammed into this little place. Wonderful selection of teas (a hundred or so!). If you like the teapot, you can buy it and, surprisingly, that goes for all the items of décor too (they'll cost you from a few hundred to a few thousand francs)! You'll need quite a bit of time for the delicious home-made desserts. And a different type of music takes centre stage each day (jazz, opera, classical... Marlene Dietrich!). *Formule* 45F. Regular theme evenings, for example: the splendours of French baroque music or a fancy dress evening with a champagne buffet. An establishment with atmosphere, a bit on the posh side, of course, but so pleasant.

I●I RESTAURANT AUX MOULES

34 rue de Béthune. **MAP C2-26**
☎ 03.20.57.12.46 F➜ 03.20.12.90.92

Service noon–midnight. This brasserie is famous for being the record-holder for the largest pile of mussel shells outside its door on the day of the Lille fair. The menu offers (as we're sure you've already guessed) mussels (a dozen or more specialities at 43–61F, from good old mussels and chips to mussel stew with leek fondue) and good regional specialities (Flemish-style charcoal-grilled beef, Welsh rarebit, rabbit in *Kriek* beer, tart sprinkled with brown sugar etc), all washed down (it goes without saying) with one of a wide selection of beers. 30s décor, friendly and efficient service, lively atmosphere and a little on the noisy side – the typical brasserie which is fast becoming an institution. Lunchtime *formule* 69F.

I●I RESTAURANT LE TWEEN

32 place de la Gare. **MAP D2-22**
☎ 03.20.31.16.21
Closed evenings, Saturdays, Sundays and for one month in July/August.

Idyllic surroundings the colour of snow and salmon with Greek-style columns and capitals. The elegant service must be praised. The food is of high quality and regional specialities such as *potje vlesch* pâté in onion preserve, Maroilles-style T-bone steak, cod in mature beer and ale pie are given particular emphasis. Set meals 105F, 128F (including wine and coffee) and 148F.

I●I BRASSERIE ALCIDE

5 rue des Débris-Saint-Étienne. **MAP C2-23**
☎ 03.20.12.06.95 F➜ 03.20.55.93.83
Closed at Christmas.

The discreet charm of the bourgeois brasserie. The waiters stand in a line decked out in their uniforms and there's an oak bar with mirrors etc. Mature clientèle who behave themselves. The type of establishment where you wouldn't be surprised to find yourself sitting next to the film director Claude Chabrol. The *formule* at 83F offers a choice between *moules marinière*, three regional dishes (including a very good charcoal-grilled beef) and three beers. Otherwise set meals from 127F for typical brasserie cuisine (of course).

I●I RESTAURANT LA TARTERIE DE LA VOÛTE

4 rue des Débris-Saint-Étienne. **MAP C2-27**
☎ 03.20.42.12.16 F➜ 03.20.55.93.83
Closed Sundays and Monday evenings.

As its name (literally: the archway tartery restaurant) implies, this little restaurant nestling under an arcade close to the Grand-Place offers sweet and savoury tarts and salads and doesn't neglect local cuisine. Dishes include Maroilles cheese quiche (delicious), the local-style pie and chicory Flemish style. The desserts hold their own and there's a wonderful double chocolate tart. Reckon on paying 80F for a full meal. Young, preppy clientèle.

I●I CHEZ LULU

8 rue d'Amiens. **MAP C3-30**
☎ 03.20.12.92.86
Closed evenings except Sundays.

The first thing to mention about *Chez Lulu*, a tiny bar/restaurant/shop is the guy who owns it – Lulu. He's a former surfer and informal is hardly the word. One Lulu is all it takes to create an atmosphere. The décor of the little place aims to recreate a mythical fifties America, as does the cooking with hamburgers and spare ribs. The daily specials though (around 50F) are very good and original, for example salt-cured sirloin with potato cakes and duck breast with bilberries. For dessert you absolutely have to try Aunt Selma's cheesecake (if you can find a seat – *Chez Lulu* is often packed). Reckon on paying 80–90F if you're happy with just a main course and a dessert, 100–110F if you have a larger appetite. A great place for lunch.

|●| RESTAURANT L'ARNAQUE

11 place Jacquart. **MAP C3-24**
☎ 03.20.54.68.02
Closed Saturdays, Sundays and in August. Service 12–2.30pm.

This simple little restaurant with its lively atmosphere and warm welcome is in a part of town which manages to escape the tourist hordes. The cooking – like the décor – doesn't go in for fancy touches and is very French. Good-quality meat (fried steak with shallots for example) and vegetables (such as *flageolets* and puréed carrots). Described like that it may sound a bit like canteen fare, but it's fresh, tastes good and comes at set meal prices. Daily specials start at 40F and a full meal will cost you about 90F. There's just one puzzle – translated literally the place is called "The Rip-Off Restaurant", so where's the rip-off?

|●| RESTAURANT LE CAFÉ DU PALAIS

4 rue du Palais-de-Justice. **MAP C1-29**
☎ 03.20.74.53.47
Closed Saturday lunchtimes and Sundays.

Lunch served noon–2pm, dinner 8–10pm (11pm Thursdays to Saturdays).This restaurant looks like a bistro from the turn of the century and is a meeting place for trendy young executives, lawyers and the quieter sort of student. A grand-looking and friendly restaurant where generous starters and traditional main courses (such as duck preserve, *andouillette* and Flemish-style charcoal-grilled beef) are served at reasonable prices. Reckon on paying about 90F for a full meal.

|●| RESTAURANT FLANDRES-LIBAN

125-127 rue des Postes. **MAP B4-28**
☎ 03.20.54.89.92

Lebanese restaurant on the edge of Wazemmes (the latest "in" part of Lille). The décor, with its delicate panels of carved wood, fountains and hangings, doesn't go overboard on local colour. Very good *mezzé*. Waiters whose polite demeanour never falters come to explain the secrets of the 20 specialities (hummus, *chawarma, kefta* in kebabs, cucumber yoghurt etc) and above all (always useful for the novice) how to eat them. Other typical dishes include three flavours of chicken kebab and *kebbé* (beef and ground wheat). Set meals start at 95F. Reckon on paying 80–100F à la carte – reasonable prices for what is definitely the best Lebanese restaurant in and around Lille.

|●| LA TÊTE DE L'ART

10 rue de l'Arc. **MAP B2-31**
☎ 03.20.54.68.89 **F➜** same
Closed Sundays, evenings (except Fridays and Saturdays) and three weeks in Aug.

Lunch served 12–2pm, dinner 7.30–10.45pm. An quiet little restaurant in a quiet little street. A nice place to eat - but take the trouble to reserve all the same. There's just one set meal at 132F (including as much wine as you like) but it's excellent. An unbelievably wide variety of giblets and regional dishes – mussels cooked in olive oil with white wine *à la provençale*, Maroilles cheese *craquant* with thinly sliced endives, salmon *rillettes* with chives or mullet cake with aniseed butter followed by pigs' kidneys in mustard or *andouillette* in Meaux mustard then cheese and dessert.

VILLENEUVE-D'ASCQ 59650 (8KM SE)

|●| RESTAURANT DU BOURBONNAIS

68 chaussée de l'Hôtel-de-Ville (Centre).
☎ 03.20.05.42.59 **F➜** 03.20.05.42.59
Closed Sundays and 2 weeks in August.

The décor (an odd assortment of items such as a red brick wall, paintings by local artists, a collection of wirelesses belonging to the proprietor and a rustic dresser) does what it can to make you forget that you're right in the middle of a new town singularly devoid of character. Set meals start at 69F (weekday lunchtimes) then go to 81F (largely regional; when we were there you could have Maroilles cheese tart and salmon *paupiette* in a white butter sauce, charcoal-grilled beef or fillet of sea bream *à la Duglard*) and 109F, smile included. Brilliant. See you soon!

|●| RESTAURANT LES CHARMILLES

98 av. de Flandre (North).
☎ 03.20.72.40.30
Car park. Closed Sunday and Monday evenings.

Very spacious and yet ideal for intimate meals for two. Decorated in pale green and olive, reminding you of the arbours after which the restaurant is named. The great originality of this restaurant is its culinary creativity. The menu includes dishes such as smoked salmon turnover, slices of duck breast in honey and Auvergne-style pears au gratin. The regional set meal at 100F takes us back to Flanders with leek quiche, *potjevfleisch* or Comines *andouillette* with juniper berries followed by a type of *crème caramel* sprinkled with brown sugar. Three other set meals from 69F (except Sundays) to 160F. Our only quibble is that the polite and formal welcome is lacking in spontaneity. Otherwise everything is fine.

MAUBEUGE 59600

10% ☗ HÔTEL DE LA POSTE*

15 rue Henri-Durre (Centre).
☎ 03.27.64.65.34 F→ 03.27.62.34.79
Car park. TV.

Very friendly little hotel in a quiet street close to the centre. The renovated rooms are quite pleasant and very good value for money. From 135F for a double with basin to 170F with bath (wc on the landing). The proprietors, M and Mme Pérou, are tireless travellers. There are superb photographs from their travels on the walls of some of the rooms and of the breakfast room. What better way to start the day than deciding what to have on your bread beneath a picture of the Machu Picchu?

10% ☗ |●| LE GRAND HÔTEL-RESTAURANT DE PARIS**

1 porte de Paris; it's near the station.
☎ 03.27.64.63.16 F→ 03.27.65.05.76
Secure parking. TV. Canal+. Disabled access.

The *Restaurant de Paris* is the best place to eat in the area and the place for family meals and business lunches. Local produce, fish and seafood. Set meals 70–245F. The hotel rooms really do need the forthcoming renovation.

MONTREUIL-SUR-MER 62170

☗ AUBERGE DE JEUNESSE

citadelle de Montreuil (Centre); it's 400m from the station and 200m from the centre.
☎ 03.21.06.10.83
Access 9.30am–12pm and 2–6pm. **Closes** at 10pm and Oct 1–Feb 1.

No membership card required. The main attraction of the hostel (which has just the basic comforts) is its location within the 16th century citadel, a few feet from the town walls. 45 beds available in 3 large rooms and 2 smaller ones with 6 beds. 40F/night for individuals, 35F for groups. Sheets provided free of charge. There's a kitchen where you can cook your own food.

☗ |●| LE DARNÉTAL

place Darnétal (Centre).
☎ 03.21.06.04.87 F→ 03.21.86.64.67
Closed Monday evenings, Tuesdays and the first week in July. **Car park.**

On a lovely little square in the old town. A traditional hotel which has been there for over a century. The restaurant boasts a collection of treasures which any antique shop owner could easily make a living off for years. Having admired them all, we tried, among other things, the brill cooked in a *court-bouillon*, the lobster in pastis and the warm oysters in champagne. Set meals 95 (except Saturday evenings and Sundays), 140F and 190F. The 4 spacious and rather bare rooms are in late 19th century bourgeois style. Ask to see them – they're all very different. Of course, there's no telephone or television, but that's fine! Doubles 220–300F.

☗ |●| HÔTEL-RESTAURANT DES REMPARTS**

place du Général-de-Gaulle (Centre).
☎ 03.21.06.08.65 F→ 03.21.81.20.45
Closed Sunday evenings, Wednesdays, 10 days at the end of June, 10 days at the end of September and a fortnight over Christmas and New Year. **Car park. TV. Disabled access.**

An attractive building in immaculate white, very neat behind its blue shutters. The restaurant is just as charming and has an air of luxury without being ostentatious. Pleasant staff. Good food with the emphasis on fish and seafood even though Montreuil has long since ceased to be on the sea. Dishes include sole profiteroles in garlic and cream sauce and scallop casserole. The chef, M. Merlin, lives up to his name, conjuring up simply magical desserts! Set meals at 79F (available every day), 98F and 160F. The hotel has 6 large, bright rooms from 260–330F for a double with shower/wc. One of them has a little terrace but it doesn't have a view of the ramparts in the establishment's name!

MADELAINE-SOUS-MONTREUIL (LA) 62170 (5KM W)

|●| AUBERGE DU VIEUX LOGIS

place de la Mairie; take the D139 or the D917 – it's right under the walls.
☎ 03.21.06.10.92
Closed Sunday evenings, Mondays and 2–3 weeks in February. Lunch served 12–2.30pm, dinner 7–9.30pm.

A real country inn, in one of those quiet little villages where time stands still. Traditional dishes (such as home-made casserole with goose dripping, veal kidneys *Vieux Logis* and excellent grilled beef) and other more original ones (*carpaccio* of raw fish for example). Set meals 100F, 130F and 170F. Very rustic décor. Unaffected and very nice staff. When the weather is fine you can eat out on the terrace.

ROUBAIX 59100

10% ☗ HÔTEL DU CENTRE*

1 rue Pierre-Motte (Centre).
☎ 03.20.73.26.34 ⮕ 03.20.73.26.69
Closes at 10pm but night owls needn't worry — there's an entrance code. **TV**.

A small hotel which is being reborn thanks to friendly new proprietors. Frankly, there is still work to be done, but the rooms which have already been renovated are pleasant and spacious (quieter on the courtyard side but the view isn't great). Understandably, the prices have gone up a little. Doubles with washing facilities 150F, with shower/wc or bath from 180F.

☗ |●| LE COQ HARDI**

1 place de la Gare (North); it's opposite the station.
☎ 03.20.70.82.06 ⮕ 03.20.24.42.61
Closed Friday and Sunday evenings, the week of July 14 and the week of Aug 15. **Secure parking**. **TV**.

The rooms lack charm (oh, this ubiquitous carpeting on the walls!) but are good value for money. Doubles with shower or bath 195F (and only 160F at weekends). Family atmosphere and the restaurant offers family cooking. Set meals from 60F (available every day). Full and half-board available for stays of more than 3 days.

SAINT-OMER 62500

10% ☗ |●| LES FRANGINS**

5 rue Carnot (Centre).
☎ 03.21.38.12.47 ⮕ 03.21.98.72.72
Restaurant closed at Christmas and on New Year's Day.
Secure parking. **TV**. **Canal+**. **Disabled access**.

Yann and Olivier, the *frangins* (brothers) after whom this hotel cum restaurant is named, know how to welcome guests (professionally but warmly) and also how to create a convivial atmosphere. The house speciality is *pierrade* (there's one on the 79F set meal), a dish which it is much more fun to eat if you're in a group. *Pierrades* with beef, chicken, salmon or gamba. Brasserie or restaurant *formule* (the latter is a little more up-market) to suit all pockets. *Formule* at 42F (main course and drink available weekday lunchtimes), otherwise set meals at 61F, 79F and 135F (dishes include home-made liver pâté, chicken escalope in cream sauce and hake pâté with garlic mayonnaise). Rooms modern throughout and, frankly, a little gloomy; doubles with shower or bath 250–340F.

☗ |●| HÔTEL SAINT-LOUIS - RESTAURANT LE FLAUBERT**

25 rue d'Arras (Centre).
☎ 03.21.38.35.21 ⮕ 03.21.38.57.26
Lunch served noon–2pm, dinner 7–11pm.
Secure parking. **TV**. **Canal+**. **Disabled access**.

A hotel which has been around for at least 70 years. Don't worry, it has been renovated (and attractively too). Quiet and comfortable rooms; doubles with shower/wc from 273F. Friendly retro-style bar. The restaurant goes for the dual approach with a brasserie menu at the *Petit Flo* (would the author of Madame Bovary have appreciated this affectionate nickname?) and more elaborate, up-market cuisine at the *Flaubert*. There are a number of specialities such as knuckle of ham with green pepper and sea bass with saffron. Set meals 75F (except weekends), 95F, 125F and 165F.

|●| AUBERGE DU BACHELIN

12 bd de Strasbourg (North-East).
☎ 03.21.38.42.77
Closed Sunday evenings and Mondays.

Classical décor complemented by a fine collection of old coffee grinders. Friendly atmosphere. The proprietor has a sense of humour, which is a big plus! Set meals start at 77F and then go to 133F and 180F. Home-made *couscous* every Friday. Pleasant and efficient service. A good little place to eat.

BLENDECQUES 62575 (4KM SE)

10% ☗ |●| LE SAINT-SÉBASTIEN**

2 Grand-Place (Centre); take exit 4 off the A26.
☎ 03.21.38.13.05 F➔ 03.21.39.77.85
Closed Saturday lunchtimes and Sunday evenings. Lunch served noon–2pm and 7.30–10pm. **TV**.

A square and a church. Solid stone walls. Direct and friendly staff. A number of pleasant, comfortable rooms (doubles with shower or bath 245F) and a nice rustic restaurant. Set meals start at 77F (dishes such as salad with *andouille* and chicken fricassee with vinegar); two other set meals at 120F and 160F. Offal-based meals JG(calf's head in herb and shallot sauce) and other pork dishes (stuffed pigs' trotters), an ale pie for a touch of local colour and delicious desserts to finish things off nicely. In the good little country hotel tradition.

TOUQUET (LE) 62520

HÔTEL MODERNE**

41 rue Jean-Monnet (Centre); it's behind the market place.
☎ 03.21.05.15.33 F➔ 03.21.05.41.60
Closed Nov 15–Feb. **Car park**. **TV**.

The prices are reasonable for Le Touquet. Doubles with basin from 200F, with shower/wc 280F and with bath 330F. The main thing about this establishment is that it's one of the few places to offer half-board (compulsory in July/August), from 250F per person. Full board also available. New proprietor.

HÔTEL LE CHALET**

15 rue de la Paix (Centre).
☎ 03.21.05.87.65 F➔ 03.21.05.47.49
Closed Jan 1–15.

The rooms are spick and span and the prices more than reasonable for Le Touquet. Doubles with basin 180F, with shower 290F and with shower/wc 310F. Some are grouped around a small patio. If you want TV and a sea view (you can see it from the balcony at the end of the street if you look to the left!), reckon on paying a bit more. Goodness knows though who decided to call this charming little hotel a chalet!

10% HÔTEL LE NOUVEAU CADDY**

130 rue de Metz (Centre); it's opposite the indoor market and 150m from the beach.
☎ 03.21.05.83.95 F➔ 03.21.05.85.23
Closed Nov 15–Dec 20 and Jan 5–Feb 15. **TV**. **Disabled access**.

This hotel has just been completely renovated (hence the "nouveau" in its name which, in this case, is fully justified). Right from the reception area and the adorable breakfast room, everything shows good taste. Each floor has its own predominating colour symbolizing a season. There's green for spring and we're sure you'll discover the rest for yourselves given that there are four floors and, fortunately, a lift. Pleasant and comfortable rooms, all with bath. Doubles 250–290F. Studios (with kitchenettes) also available from 285–325F. The proprietor started out taking in paying guests, hence the very warm welcome. Our favourite place to stay in Le Touquet.

10% HÔTEL LES EMBRUNS**

89 rue de Paris (Centre).
☎ 03.21.05.87.61 F➔ 03.21.05.85.09
TV. **Disabled access**.

Closed Jan 15–28. Quietly situated, set back from the road and not far from the sea. Warm welcome. The former *Nouvel Hôtel* (frankly, it no longer had anything *"nouvel"* about it) has just changed its name and is under new management. The simple, comfortable rooms ought to develop some character as a result. Doubles with shower 250–290F, with bath 290–310F. Rooms sleeping 3 and 4.

RESTAURANT LE SALADIN

72 rue de Londres (Centre)
☎ 03.21.05.15.56
Closed Tuesdays (except public holidays) Nov–April.

Salad bar which has kept its good reputation in Le Touquet despite a recent change of management. There are always lots of people in this pleasant restaurant, the walls of which are painted in a flowery, pastoral style. Salads and more salads, warm or cold, in numerous and sometimes surprising combinations. Some other dishes such as duck breast with peaches. The prices though are Le Touquet ones (50–85F for a salad).

RESTAURANT AU DIAMANT ROSE

110 rue de Paris (Centre).
☎ 03.21.05.38.10 F➔ 03.21.05.89.75
Closed Tuesday evenings (except in July/August), Wednesdays and Dec 20–Feb 1.

Lunch served noon–2.15pm, dinner 7–9.30pm (10pm on Saturdays). With its pastel pink façade, a restaurant which attracts a clientele of regulars and quiet holidaymakers. Lunchtime special 59F every day (except Sundays and holidays). Set meals 91F and 132F with dishes such as crab *au gratin*, grilled gambas in garlic butter and marinated salmon escalope. Seafood (to order), but also a wide variety of meats.

Good wine list. If you ask her nicely, the proprietress will show you her pink (imitation) diamond after which the restaurant is named.

AUBERGE L'ARLEQUIN

91 rue de Paris.
☎ 03.21.05.39.11 Fax 03.21.06.13.06
Closed Wednesdays May 1–end Sept, Wednesdays and Thursdays from Oct–end April and Dec 22–Jan 31.

The classic small restaurant. The food is plain and incorporates products of both land and sea with dishes such as monkfish casserole, lamb casserole, salmon in cream sauce with sorrel, rabbit in mustard sauce and *coq au vin*. Well-balanced basic set meal 85F (weekdays). Other set meals 90F and 130F.

RESTAURANT LA FLAMBÉE

117 rue de Metz (Centre); it's between the post office and the indoor market.
☎ 03.21.05.71.82
Closed Mondays except during the school holidays, a fortnight in June, a fortnight in Nov and a fortnight in Jan.

To look at the menu in this wainscotted restaurant, you would think you were in the mountains, but not all fondues come from the Savoie with cheese. The 95F set meal brings us quickly back to the côte d'Opale with dishes such as oysters, fish soup, whelks, mussels in white wine and fillet of hake *au gratin*. Another set meal at 145F. Reckon on paying 150F à la carte. A good, friendly little restaurant to take refuge in if a cool breeze whips up by the sea.

RESTAURANT PERARD

67 rue de Metz (Centre); it's near the post office.
☎ 03.21.05.13.33 Fax 03.21.05.62.32
Closed in January.

A flashy neon sign in the shape of a fish leaves you in no doubt as to the specialities at the *Perard*, a very lively restaurant with a fishmonger's next door. The place is worth going out of your way for just for the very 50s atmosphere and the irresistibly kitsch décor. It may be a bit pricey but you really can't come to Le Touquet and not try the *Perard*'s fish soup, especially since you can have as much of it as you like if you go for the 95F basic set meal (followed by fillets of mullet and a dessert). Another neon sign (just as flashy) warns you not to buy the *Restaurant Perard* fish soup or else the whole of France will be wanting some. If you don't go for the soup, a whole range of products of the sea are also served here, for example this region's variation on *bouillabaisse* ("no bones guaranteed") and seafood platter. A major disadvantage is that credit cards aren't accepted.

SAINT-JOSSE 62170 (7KM SE)

LE RELAIS DE SAINT-JOSSE

Grand-Place; follow the D143 for 5km, then take the D144 – it's near the church.
☎ 03.21.94.61.75 Fax 03.21.94.98.03
Closed evenings and Saturdays mid October–mid March, Mondays and Jan 15–Feb 15.

A village with flowers everywhere. The adorable little square has everything — post office, church, town hall and *Le Relais*, well turned-out with its geraniums hanging at the windows. In the bistro you wouldn't be surprised to see the lanky postman from the Tati film *Jour de fête*. From first thing in the morning Étienne Delmer, the proprietor who's a butcher's son, offers a menu which includes an excellent rabbit pâté, scrambled eggs, cold meats in aspic, a wonderful *pâté de campagne*, smoked fish and, in winter, a nice calf's head. Those who prefer to eat at conventional mealtimes will be just as enthusiastic about the restaurant. Set meals 75F (weekdays) and 98–150F. À la carte also available.

TOURCOING 59200

RESTAURANT LE RUSTIQUE

206 rue de l'Yser (North); from the town centre follow rue de Gand for 3km – this leads into rue de l'Yser.
☎ 03.20.94.44.62
Closed Mondays, evenings except by reservation and Aug 15–31. **Car park**.

Lunch served noon–3pm, dinner 7.30–9.30pm. The surroundings reflect the "Rustique" in the restaurant's name to a certain extent — wood burns in the fireplace and copper pans hang from the walls — but the service and food are rather more refined. Dishes include duck breast with honey and lime and *carpaccio* of salmon with herb salad. A number of regional specialities. Gourmet food at reasonable prices. Set meals start at 69F (weekdays) and there are others at 118F, 148F and 170F. You can eat on the terrace when the weather is fine and there's a large park nearby for a postprandial stroll.

HALLUIN 59250 (10KM N)

10% AUBERGE DU MANOIR**

70 rue Marthe-Nollet.
☎ 03.20.23.81.60 Fax 03.20.23.91.96
Restaurant closed Sundays. **Car park**. **TV**.

Lunch served 11am–3pm, dinner 7.30–11pm. Beware of the confusion which this establishment's name (literally The Manor Inn) might cause; in fact it's opposite the station but the street is a quiet one. The rooms are well laid out and not lacking in charm. Doubles 240F with shower/wc, mini-bar and telephone; 260F with bath. You get to them via a staircase lined with paintings of female nudes and a religious picture from Thailand – a strange combination! The local bar and restaurant and the prices are rather high, all things considered. Set meals start at 78.50F (weekdays) and there are others at 91F, 112F and 145F. Meat specialities (except Fridays when it's fish of course).

RESTAURANT LA CLÉ DES CHAMPS

273 rue de Lille (South).
☎ 03.20.37.34.34 F 03.20.46.10.32
Closed evenings (except Fridays and Saturdays) and in August. **Car park**.

The welcome – a shade old-fashioned – and the restaurant – rustic in style yet reflecting a degree of wealth – are well-suited to this solidly built bourgeois residence. The proprietor will love to tell you the history of the carved wooden fresco decorating one of the walls. Good food at reasonable prices. Set meals 75F (weekdays) and 140F. A number of classics including a good rabbit *à la Gueuze* and duck breast with morello cherries. Very good home-made desserts. Interesting (and pretty mind-blowing) wine list and beer cellar. A good place to eat.

VALENCIENNES 59300

LES ARCADES**

19 rue Saint-Jacques (North-East); it's between the station and the town hall.
☎ 03.27.30.16.59 F 03.27.30.31.34
Closed two weeks in Aug. **Car park**. **TV**. **Canal+**.

Friendly little hotel with simple but comfortable rooms. Ideal if you're on a limited budget with doubles at 119F (basin) and 185–192F (shower/wc). The restaurant under the arcades (at last, the arcades!) is pleasant and the menu has a bias towards the sea (dishes include fisherman's casserole with leeks and fisherman's pie). Set meals 79F, 118F and 160F.

LE BRISTOL**

2 av. de-Lattre-de-Tassigny (North); it's near the station.
☎ 03.27.46.58.88 F 03.27.47.34.39
TV. **Canal+**. **Disabled access**.

This hotel hasn't much originality but is quiet and clean. Pleasant staff with ready smiles. Bright and spacious rooms, some overlooking a courtyard and others the street (fortunately you don't hear the trains whistling!). Doubles with basin 200F, with shower/wc or bath 250F.

10% HÔTEL NOTRE-DAME**

1 place de l'Abbé-Thellier-de-Poncheville (Centre); it's opposite the basilica of Notre-Dame.
☎ 03.27.42.30.00 F 03.27.45.12.68
Car park. **TV**. **Canal+**. **Disabled access**.

This charming little hotel, housed in a former convent, has been fully renovated. The interior decoration shows exquisite taste. Chic but not flashy. Doubles with shower or bath and wc 310–330F. Also some rooms with shower at 250F. Number 36 on the ground floor, which looks out onto the indoor garden, is superb. Pleasant staff always ready with a smile. Paying car park.

RESTAURANT AU VIEUX SAINT-NICOLAS

72 rue de Paris (North); it's near the conservatoire.
☎ 03.27.30.14.93 F 03.27.30.14.93
Closed Monday evenings and the first 3 weeks in August.

The décor is fresh, clean and modern but warm. A statue of a bishop (no, it isn't the old St. Nicholas who gives the restaurant its name) stands looking thoughtfully at prints of works by Klee and Kandinsky. With dishes such as coddled egg with Maroilles cheese, chicken in beer and leg of duck in gin, you don't sit looking thoughtfully at your plate for too long. The food is simple but tasty and uses fresh produce; the service is charming and the atmosphere peaceful. Set meals 71F (weekdays), 95F, 105F, 142F and 165F. An unpretentious little place which we really like.

RESTAURANT LA TOURTIÈRE

34 rue E.-Macarez (East); it's a little way out of the town centre, near the tax office.
☎ 03.27.29.42.42
Closed Monday evenings and Saturday lunchtimes. **Car park**.

Out of the town centre, between a commercial area and allotments. The food is a mixture of regional dishes and Italian specialities (and sometimes the two are combined in dishes such as macaroni with Maroilles cheese). As you would expect then, the à la carte menu includes pizzas and pasta dishes, leek and onion quiches etc. To keep to the north/south divide there's an Italian set meal at 88F and a regional one (egg with Maroilles cheese, Avesnois veal and *tarte à la cassonade*). Generous portions (no good if you have a small appetite). Relaxed and lively atmosphere. A typical popular restaurant.

SEBOURG 59990 (10KM E)

HÔTEL-RESTAURANT AU JARDIN FLEURI**

23 rue du Moulin; take the Curgies exit off the A2, then the D250.
☎ 03.27.26.53.31 F 03.27.26.50.08
Restaurant closed Wednesdays, Sunday evenings and on public holidays. **Car park. TV.**

This hotel cum restaurant is named after a flower garden and it does indeed have such a garden, full of flowers. This has a little stream running through it which you cross by a wooden bridge — a deliciously pastoral place! The windows of the (charming) rooms all open out onto a little corner of nature (the flower garden or the adjacent meadows). Reasonably priced at 260F for a double with bath. Breakfast veranda (looking out onto the flowers in the garden) and, for fine days, a terrace (in the flower garden). When it rains (something which does happen occasionally in the north), you repair to the amazingly rustic restaurant inside. The tablecloths are well ironed (not surprising given the amazing collection of irons here) and the food is good. To book a table call 03 27 26 53 44. The menu is based almost exclusively on local produce. Numerous Avesnois specialities such as smoked tongue with *foie gras*, veal *à la crème de Jenlain*, Maroilles cheese fondue and *crème brûlée*. Afterwards take a post-prandial stroll in the flower garden where you'll find rare and classified species! Set meals 95F, 155F and 245F. A good place to find a bit of nature, 10 minutes from Valenciennes.

WISSANT 62179

10% HÔTEL DE LA PLAGE

place Édouard-Houssin.
☎ 03.21.35.91.87 F 03.21.85.48.10
Secure parking.

An old hotel not without charm. There's a wooden terrace by the side of a pond with a mill which has been turned into a little local history museum. Ask for a room on this side of the hotel (if the ducks don't disturb you!). Then there's the unaffected and friendly staff and the fifty or so rooms dotted randomly, it would seem, along a labyrinth of corridors. The renovated rooms are plain but pleasant (all no-smoking); doubles with shower or bath 265–295F. Family rooms (450F for 4, 525F for 5 in 4 beds) and special prices for windsurfers (Wissant boasts one of the best-known spots for windsurfing on the côte d'Opale). Large, traditional restaurant (tel 03 21 82 78 32). Fish and seafood and a good cellar of Bordeaux wines. Set meals 90F and 150F, daily special 45F.

HÔTEL-RESTAURANT LE VIVIER**

place de l'Église.
☎ 03.21.35.93.61 F 03.21.82.10.99
Restaurant closed Tuesdays and Wednesdays; closed Jan 10–mid February. **Secure parking. TV. Disabled access.**

Lunch served 11.30am–3.30pm, dinner 6.30–10.30pm. In front of the restaurant there's a "*flobart*" (a typical local fishing boat), announcing that this is a seafood restaurant. Set meals 89–189F. The little rooms above the restaurant are great but they're even better in the recently built annexe further along the Boulogne road — from their balconies or terraces there's a wonderful view of Cap Gris-Nez on the edge of the Wissant bay and, on a fine day, the English coast. Doubles with shower from 220F, with bath 250F.

ESCALLES-CAP BLANC-NEZ 62179 (5.5KM NW)

HÔTEL-RESTAURANT À L'ESCALE**

rue de la Mer; take the D940.
☎ 03.21.85.25.00 F 03.21.35.44.22
Closed Jan 4–Feb 4. **Car park. TV. Disabled access.**

In the heart of a tiny village, nestling in an ideal spot at the foot of the magnificent chalk cliffs of the cap Blanc-Nez. Attractive rooms behind the ivy-covered façade. Doubles with washing facilities 200F, with shower/wc 275F and with bath 315F. You cross the tiny road leading to the beach (and its thousands of fossils) to reach the big restaurant, where there's always lots going on. One strange feature is the ceiling which looks like the upside-down hull of a boat. The cooking makes skilful use of seafood (dishes include fisherman's stew and seafood platter) and local farm produce. From the good 80F set meal (available every day), for example, we remember an excellent Licques chicken dish. A whole range of other set meals at 100–150F. To book a table call 03.21.85.25.09. Mini tennis court and mountain bike hire.

BASSE-NORMANDIE

14 Calvados

50 Manche

61 Orne

AIGLE (L') 61300

|●| AUBERGE SAINT-MICHEL

Saint-Michel-Thubœuf.
How to get there: take the N26 and you'll find it 4.5km from Aigle.
☎ 02.33.24.20.12 F➔ 02.33.34.96.62
Closed Wednesday evenings, Thursdays, the first three weeks in January, and Sept 10–22. **Car park**. **Disabled access**.

Lunch served noon–2pm, dinner 7–9.30pm. One of the friendliest country inns you could possibly come across, and it's quiet despite being so close to the road. Unassuming, friendly staff provide excellent service with a smile. The cosy little dining rooms are full of character and offer traditional local dishes such as pig's trotters with mustard, delicious veal kidneys with Calvados, fillet of duck with Pommeau, and, for lovers of good food in search of the real thing, fresh cream cheese. Set meals 90F (also served Sundays) and 110–175F.

FERTÉ-FRÊNEL (LA) 61550 (14KM NW)

10% ☗ |●| HÔTEL DU PARADIS**

Grande-Rue.
☎ 02.33.34.81.33 F➔ 02.33.84.97.52
Closed Mondays, three weeks in February, and two weeks in October. **Car park**. **TV**. **Canal+**.

This is a pretty and pretty good little village inn – it could hardly be anything else with a name like that – with a homely, friendly atmosphere. Our favourite bedroom, and the most romantic one, was number 16 on the second floor, with its delightful bathroom and little windows. You can hear the street noises during the day but it's very quiet in the evening. The restaurant serves generous portions of lovingly prepared traditional local dishes like duck thighs with cider, guinea fowl with apples, and sole flambéd with Calvados. It's a very pleasant place to spend a summer or autumn evening, alone or in company. It doesn't really matter when you come or who you come with, you'll always feel at home. Set meals 55F (not available Saturday evenings or Sundays), 75F, 100F, 138F, 184F and 230F. Doubles 170F with basin, 240F with shower/wc or bath.

ALENÇON 61000

10% ☗ HÔTEL DE PARIS*

26 rue Denis-Papin; it's opposite the station.
☎ 02.33.29.01.64 F➔ 02.33.29.44.87
Car park. **TV**. **Canal+**.

This is the cheapest place in town, with very simple and very clean rooms – 110F and 130F with basin and telephone, doubles 180F with shower/wc. No fewer than seven of the rooms are available at this price. They all have double glazing so peace and quiet are guaranteed. Informal, good-natured staff and lots of regulars in the little bar.

10% ☗ |●| HÔTEL DE L'INDUSTRIE**

20 place du Général-de-Gaulle (East).
☎ 02.33.27.19.30 F➔ 02.33.28.49.56
Car park. **TV**. **Canal+**.

Lunch served noon–2pm, dinner 7–9.30pm. You'll find *Hôtel de l'Industrie* in one of the busiest parts of town. To be sure of a bit of peace and quiet try for a room at the back.

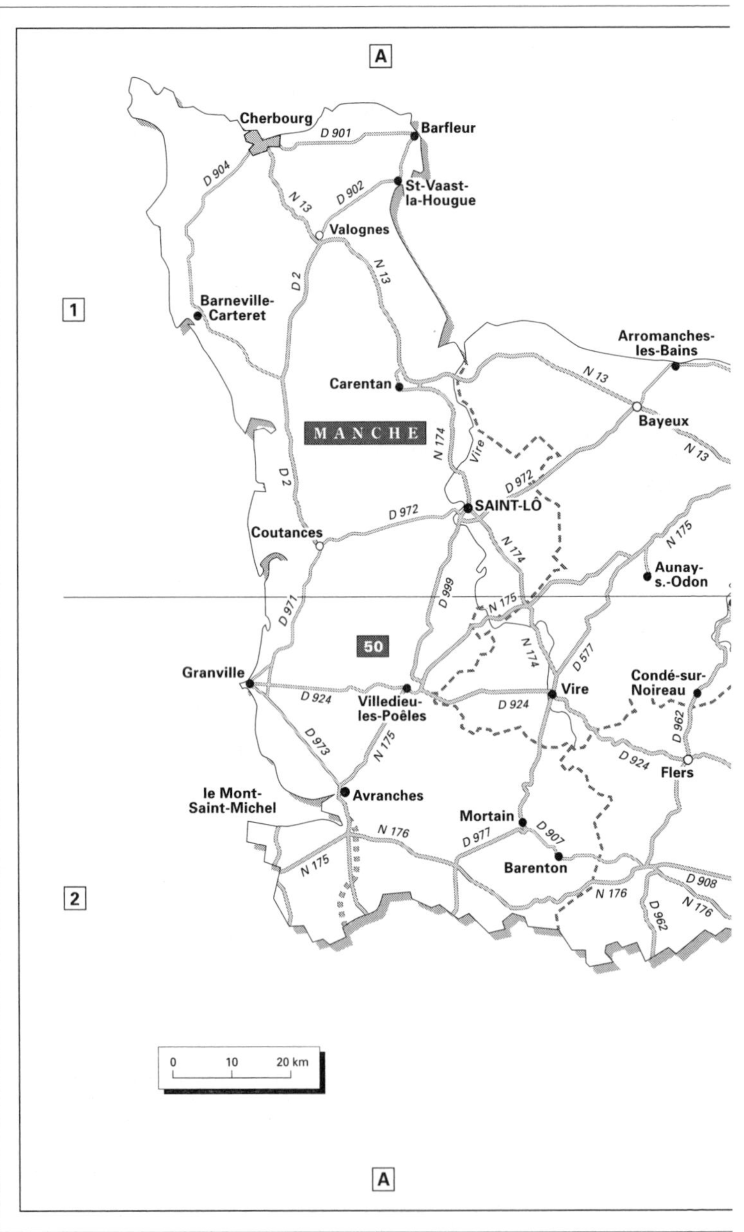
A
Cherbourg
D 901
Barfleur
D 904
D 902
St-Vaast-
la-Hougue
N 13
Valognes
D 2
N 13
1
Barneville-
Carteret
Arromanches-
les-Bains
N 13
Carentan
Bayeux
MANCHE
N 174
Vire
N 13
D 2
D 972
SAINT-LÔ
D 972
Coutances
N 175
N 174
Aunay-
s.-Odon
D 999
D 971
N 175
50
N 174
D 577
Granville
Condé-sur-
Noireau
Vire
D 924
Villedieu-
les-Poêles
D 924
D 962
D 973
N 175
D 924
Flers
le Mont-
Saint-Michel
Avranches
Mortain
N 176
D 907
D 977
Barenton
N 175
D 908
N 176
2
N 176
D 962
0
10
20 km
A

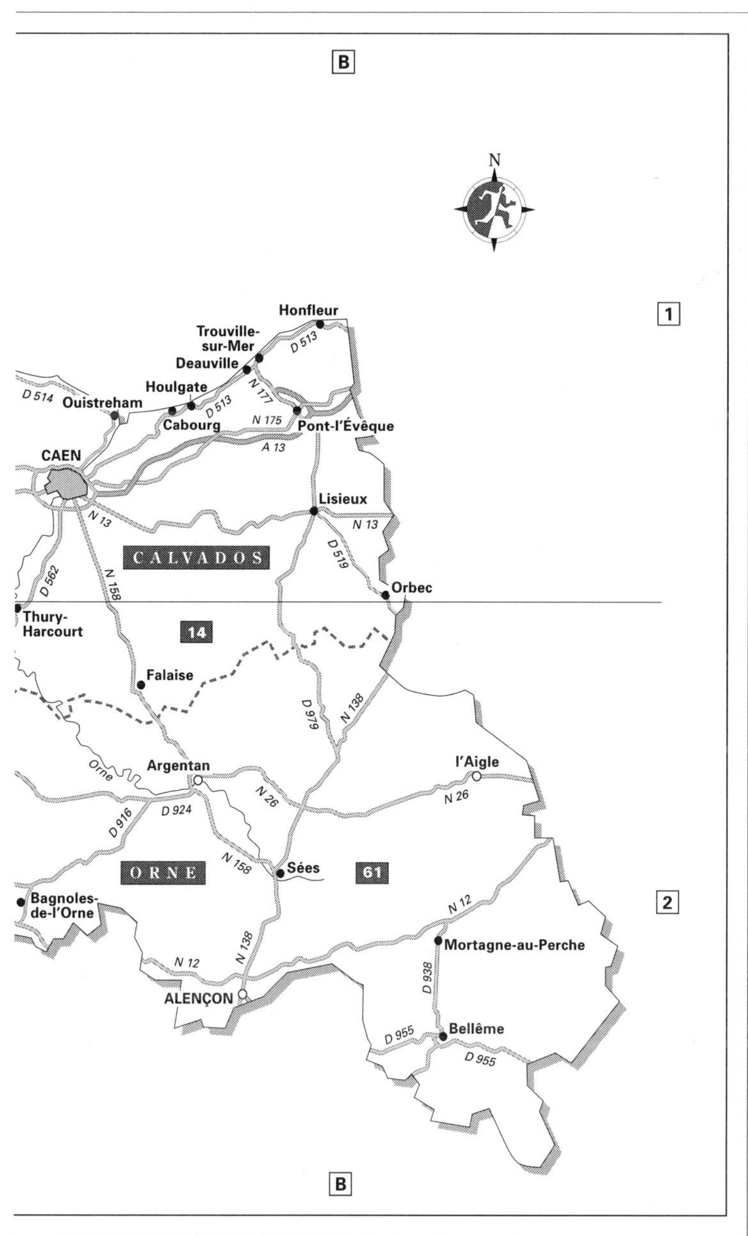

B
N
1
Honfleur
Trouville-sur-Mer
Deauville
Houlgate
D 514
Ouistreham
Cabourg
D 513
N 177
N 175
Pont-l'Évêque
A 13
CAEN
Lisieux
N 13
CALVADOS
D 519
Orbec
D 562
N 158
Thury-Harcourt
14
Falaise
D 979
N 138
Orne
Argentan
l'Aigle
N 26
D 924
D 916
N 158
Sées
61
ORNE
Bagnoles-de-l'Orne
N 12
Mortagne-au-Perche
2
D 938
ALENÇON
Bellême
D 955
B

The bedrooms aren't luxurious but they're well looked after and have a nice 50s touch which goes very well with the atmosphere of this post-war building. Doubles 200F with shower/wc. The cooking ranges from good traditional local dishes such as escalope of local beef to brasserie type dishes such as *choucroute* (imported from Alsace!), steak tartare and calf's head. There's a huge dining room but if there's a group of you, why not treat yourselves to the private room. Set meals 65F (every day), 72F (excellent), 110F and 160F. People keep on coming back, whch is hardly surprising when you consider the warm and homely atmosphere. Marc Lomitz (a keen golfer) and his wife Nicole go to great lengths to please their customers. Even the pet labrador's welcoming!

10% ☗ |●| LE GRAND SAINT-MICHEL**

7 rue du Temple; it's not far from the law courts and the corn exchange (Halle des Blés).
☎ 02.33.26.04.77 F➜ 02.33.26.71.82
Closed Sunday evenings, Mondays, the February school holidays, and mid July–mid Aug. **Car park**. **TV**.

Lunch served noon–2pm, dinner 7–10pm. A handsome stone building with apple-green shutters situated in a very quiet street in the old part of town. Inside, it's everything a hotel in the provinces should be. It has a large friendly dining room where the tables are attractively set out and the cooking is good. The chef's a big fan of flambéd dishes, so why not try one of his specialities such as veal kidneys flambéd with vermouth and mustard, escalope of *foie gras* flambéd with port, or flambéd fillet of beef *vieille mode*. You'll get a decent set meal for 95F (available every day), and there are others at 120F, 130F and 175F. Comfy renovated bedrooms although some bits of the décor — the garden chairs and imitation half-timbering, for example — are slightly out of keeping with the general style of the building. Doubles 260F with shower or bath. Ideal if you want somewhere quiet for those looking for some peaceful accommodation in the centre of town.

|●| RESTAURANT LES GLYCINES

32 rue Sainte-Blaise.
☎ 02.33.26.41.51
Closed Sunday evenings, two weeks in February or March, the first week in September, and one week at Christmas.

The décor and the façade are rather stylish but the prices are reasonable considering the quality of the cooking. The chef has successfully created his own version of traditional local dishes. Try the escalope of monkfish with Pommeau, warm oysters with seasoning, ox cheek with chocolate, fillet of ostrich with pink peppercorns and a kiwi sauce or *saucisson* of oxtail and pig's trotters. Set meals 69F (weekday lunchtimes), 78F, 98F, 130F and 175F. Perfect for lunch or dinner. At the first signs of summer you can eat out in the very pleasant garden. Efficient staff and the coffee's particularly good.

|●| RESTAURANT AU JARDIN GOURMAND

14 rue de Sarthe.
☎ 02.33.32.22.56
Closed Sunday evenings and Mondays. **Car park**.

Lunch served noon–1.30pm, dinner 7.30–9.30pm. You'll find this delightful restaurant in one of the oldest streets in town. We weren't exactly over the moon about the new façade but the three little dining rooms are as stylish as ever. The cooking's very creative and often up-dated. The young chef has considerable talent — give him the simplest of products (but they must be fresh and in season) and he'll work wonders. Try his mussels with spinach beet (similar to Swiss chard), his escalope of salmon with winkles, or his *terrine* of red mullet with a sauce of black olives. Cheapest set meal 70F, others 95F and 135F.

ARGENTAN 61200

10% ☗ |●| HÔTEL DU DONJON*

1 place de l'Hôtel-de-Ville (Centre).
☎ 02.33.67.03.76
Car park. **TV**.

The name — "donjon" means keep — is the only medieval thing about it. The rooms are simple, clean, and very reasonably priced for the area. Doubles 120F with basin/bidet (no TV) and 170F with shower/wc and telephone. It has a brasserie with one set meal at 50F. Just the place for the kind of people who read this guidebook.

|●| RESTAURANT D'ARGENTAN

22 rue du Beigle.
☎ 02.33.36.19.38
Closed Sundays and one week in February.

Lunch served noon–2pm, dinner 7–10pm. The three cosy little dining rooms buzz with activity. If things get a bit hectic in the dining room, the cook comes out to give a hand, leaving the *bœuf mode* (beef simmered in wine with vegetables and herbs) to take care of itself. Everything is as fresh as it can be (when they say "fish of the day" they mean it). Local and traditional dishes such as Camembert salad, fillet of duck with cider, and veal sweetbreads with Pommeau. The desserts are wonderful. The cheapest set meal (70F) is available every day and excellent value for money. Other set meals 85 -143F. A good little place.

ARROMANCHES-LES-BAINS 14117

10% ☗ |●| HÔTEL-RESTAURANT DE LA MARINE**

quai du Canada.
☎ 02.31.22.34.19 F 02.31.22.98.80
Closed Nov 15–Feb 15. **Car park**. **TV**.

Lunch served noon–2.30pm, dinner 7–9.30pm. From the large bay windows you can see the sea and the beach dotted with the remains of the pontoons used in the D-Day landings. Seafood dishes feature largely here. The quality of the set meals (88–150F) could be much better. The clean comfortable bedrooms offer much better value for money. Doubles 200F with basin, 300F with shower/wc and 350F with bath.

AUNAY-SUR-ODON 14260

10% ☗ |●| HÔTEL-RESTAURANT SAINT-MICHEL*

6-8 rue de Caen (Centre).
☎ 02.31.77.63.16 F 02.31.77.05.83
Closed Sunday evenings and Mondays (except in July and August), and in January.

Lunch served noon–2pm, dinner 7–9.30pm. This large hotel in a village that suffered badly during the D-Day bombings may not look great from the outside. Inside though, it's pleasant eating in the modern dining room decorated in warm vibrant colours that contrast with the classical and traditional cooking. The chef uses all the good things that Normandy has to offer and prepares dishes like *profiteroles* of scallops with onion marmalade, roast rack of lamb with garlic, *coq au vin* and *andouille* (a type of sausage) with cider flavoured butter. The 55F set meal (weekday lunchtimes) is very simple. Others 75F, 115F, 150F, 200F and 250F. Basic satisfactory bedrooms — 150F with basin/wc, 190F with shower, and 230F with shower/wc. A very good establishment.

10% ☗ |●| LA MAISON BOCAINE

Les Vingt-Becs, route d'Aunay – Campandré Valcangrain
How to get there: take the D6 from Thury-Harcourt towards Aunay-sur-Odon, and it's 7km away on a little road on the right.
☎ 02.31.77.74.42
Closed Sunday evenings (except in July and August) and weekdays Nov 1–Easter. **Car park**.
Disabled access.

Lunch served 12.15–1.30pm, dinner 7.30–9pm. It may not be particularly well-known but it's worth a visit for two reasons. First, it's the perfect introduction to the rolling hills, architecture, traditional interiors and produce of Normandy. Second, you'll have the opportunity to sample the imaginative cooking of the two Patricks, whose specialities include *croustillant* of sole with *Neufchâtel* cheese, *crémêt d'andouille* with cider, duck *pot au feu*, and iced soufflé with Benedictine. Wide range of set meals 75–160F. Portions are generous — very few people manage to clear their plate! Friendly, efficient service. Doubles 280F with shower/wc (includes breakfast). Half-board 560F for two.

AVRANCHES 50300

☗ |●| HÔTEL DE LA CROIX D'OR**

83 rue de la Constitution (North).
☎ 02.33.58.04.88 F 02.33.58.06.95
Closed Dec 1–March 1. **Car park**. **TV**.

This quite delightful 17th century coaching inn, beside the monument to General Patton, has a superb garden with a stone basin and an old cider press. It's like a museum inside, with its mellow stones, beams, enormous fireplace, and walls decorated with copper, pewter and earthenware. Doubles 150–380F depending on facilities and size. In the very attractive dining room there are flowers on the tables and the service is impeccable. Set meals 75F (lunchtimes only), 110F (fish flan with a watercress sauce and the house *terrine* with hazelnuts), 170F and 200F (warm oysters with apples, monkfish and sweet pepper kebabs, pork fillet with thyme). This has got to be the chicest place in town.

|●| LE LITTRÉ

place de la Mairie.
☎ 02.33.58.01.66

The façade might be rather ordinary but this is one of the nicest restaurants around with a absolutely beautiful dining room. No nasty surprises here – you could order the dish of the day with your eyes shut! Good traditional cooking along the lines of Sunday lunch at Mum's. Set meals 78–120F. Good desserts, including apple *clafoutis* and *pavé au chocolat*.

DUCEY 50220 (10KM SE)

10% AUBERGE DE LA SÉLUNE**

2 rue Saint-Germain; take the N176 then the Ducey exit and you'll find it on the left just before you get to the bridge.
☎ 02.33.48.53.62 F 02.33.48.90.30
Closed Mondays Oct 1–March 1, Nov 23–Dec 14, and two weeks in February. **Car park**. **TV**.

Lunch served noon–2pm, dinner 7–9pm. This enormous inn on the old Mont-Saint-Michel road used to be an old people's home. The comfortable and attractive bedrooms are individually decorated. Expect to pay 250–280F for a double. A lucky few will get a view of the garden that borders on the slow-moving Sélune, one of the best trout and salmon rivers in France. If you've brought your rod, the hotel can provide facilities and information. Very carefully prepared set meals 80F, 125F, 160F and 200F and specialities such as *paupiettes* of salmon with perry, house trout *soufflé*, stuffed saddle of rabbit with cider vinegar, and fillet of sole with Vermouth. Friendly staff.

BAGNOLES-DE-L'ORNE 61140

10% HÔTEL LES CAPUCINES**

36 bd Lemeunier-de-La-Raillère.
☎ 02.33.37.82.59 F 02.33.38.91.38
Closed mid Oct–end March. **Car park**. **TV**.

A beautiful old building in the part of town known for its Belle Époque (what we would call Edwardian) villas. Cheerful helpful staff – not at all snooty. Yves Ahyee, a native of Togo, simply fell in love with the place and you can see why. He and his wife (she's from Normandy) have given it a bit of a facelift. The bedrooms are simple but pleasant and some have a balcony with a view of the garden. But the best thing about them is they're incredibly quiet. Reasonable prices – 100F for a single with basin and 200F for a double with shower or bath. The set meals (65F and 120F) vary depending on the season and the mood of the chef (ie Yves). You'll often get fish dishes like trout soufflé, and local specialities such as ham in a sauce. A hotel with a retro feel to it where you'll find a mixture of artists and people who've come for treatment at the spa.

10% MANOIR DU LYS***

route de Juvigny-sous-Andaine; take the D235 and it's 3km from Bagnoles.
☎ 02.33.37.80.69 F 02.33.30.05.80
Closed Sunday evenings and Mondays Nov 1–Easter, and Jan 6–Feb 10. **TV**. **Canal+**. **Disabled access**. **Secure parking** in **private car park**.

This delightful manor deep in the Andaines forest used to be a hunting inn belonging to a fervent royalist. You'll hear cuckoos in the springtime and often catch sight of deer straying into the garden, after the orchard fruit. Bright bedrooms, tastefully decorated, some with a balcony overlooking the garden. Doubles 300–400F with shower/wc, 300–780F with bath. The staff and the cooking are as wonderful as the setting. The restaurant uses fresh local produce and comes up with flavours you thought had gone forever. There's *andouille* tart, *croquant* of Camembert with apples, oyster *paupiettes*, roast kid with shallot sauce and goat's cheese *gnocchi*, thick grilled steak, and tiny diced vegetables with oysters and Camembert. Heavenly desserts – *pain perdu* with local honey and cinammon ice-cream, *croustillant* of pear, strawberries with black pepper. Cheapest set meal 140F, others 195F upwards. Ideal for a romantic weekend with the man or woman of your life. What does money matter when you're in love?

TESSÉ-LA-MADELEINE 61440 (1.5KM SW)

10% HÔTEL-RESTAURANT LE CELTIC**

14 bd Albert-Christophe; you'll find it as you come into the village from Bagnoles.
☎ 02.33.37.92.11
Closed Christmas–mid February. **TV**.

The young owners, Michèle and Erick Alirol, inherited the "bar-tabac" sign which is totally out of keeping with a building that looks like the kind of hotel you'd find in a spa town. The pleasant bedrooms all come with bath and telephone. Doubles from 240F. Set meals 60F (weekday lunchtimes), 76F, 98F, 120F and 160F. Good plain cooking using fresh local and seasonal produce. A rustic dining room that's just right, friendly staff and service with a smile.

FERTÉ-MACÉ (LA) 61600 (7KM NE)

10% HÔTEL-RESTAURANT LE CÉLESTE**

6 rue de la Victoire (Centre); it's a few steps from the church of Notre-Dame and the tourist office.
☎ 02.33.37.22.33 F➜ 02.33.38.12.25
Closed Sunday evenings, Mondays, ten days in January, and ten in October. **Car park**. **TV**.

Lunch served 12.15–2pm, dinner 7.30–9.30pm. It's in a pedestrian street so it's quiet in the evening. Most of the bedrooms have been refurbished. Doubles 105F with basin and 170–225F with shower/wc or bath. The cheapest set meal is 68F and comes with some local dishes. The à la carte menu and the other set meals (90–250F) offer lots of fish dishes and, of course, the ubiquitous tripe done in the local style. At the first signs of summer you can eat out on the terrace. A good place that's well known locally.

CHAPELLE-D'ANDAINE (LA) 61140 (9KM SW)

10% ⌂ |●| HÔTEL-RESTAURANT LE CHEVAL BLANC**

8 rue de la Gare.
☎ 02.33.38.11.88
Closed Sunday evenings. **Car park**.

Lunch served noon–2pm, dinner 7–9pm. At last! — someone who's not scared of serving hard-boiled eggs and, an even greater achievement, who's managed to win over a large number of English guests to snails and tripe. Louis Féret is a cheerful sociable sort who could talk forever about Houlme (where he was born) and the superb 1790s scales decorating the hotel foyer and who is so fond of his slippers he can't bear to take them off even when serving! Nowadays, however, he's thinking of retiring. We'll really miss him but he's set a good example and we're sure the place will be as delightful, cheery and unpretentious as ever when his daughter and son-in-law take over. You'll waken to the sound of church bells or a rooster crowing in one of the gardens. Our favourite room is number 9 which has two windows. Numbers 4 and 5 overlook the garden while number 10, basic but very nice, has a view of a cherry and a hazel tree. Bedrooms 160F with basin and up to 240F with bath. In the restaurant we enjoyed the turkey escalope *à la normande* and the turbot with mussels. The *terrine* and *foie gras* really are home-made, and the coffee doesn't come out of a horrible little percolator but is filtered the way it was in the good old days. Set meals 55F (weekday lunchtimes), 90F, 145F and 220F.

RÂNES 61150 (20KM NE)

10% ⌂ |●| HÔTEL SAINT-PIERRE**

6 rue de la Libération.
☎ 02.33.39.75.14 F➜ 02.33.35.49.23
Restaurant closed Friday evenings out of season.
Secure parking. **TV**. **Canal+**.

Service 2–9pm. We really liked this place for its very friendly staff, excellent cooking and reasonable prices. It's a stone building and inside you'll find deep settees, a contemporary blue and pink dining room, paintings, cabinets, and diplomas for the best tripe in France. The restaurant serves traditional local dishes and the house specialities are tripe (home-made of course!), perfect roast chicken, bœuf ficelle (beef tied with string, roasted and then dropped into stock) with a Camembert sauce, trout normande, and frog's legs. Set meals 75F (weekdays) and 105F. Pleasant bedrooms, some with those enormous old wardrobes you find in Normandy. Doubles from 225F with shower/wc. Ask for one overlooking the courtyard because you'll get absolute peace and quiet. Cheerful, helpful owner.

BARENTON 50720

|●| RESTAURANT LE RELAIS DU PARC

place du Général-de-Gaulle (West).
☎ 02.33.59.51.38
Closed Mondays and Dec 20–Jan 15. Open in the evenings by reservation only.

The owner looks rather like a Viking and has a twinkle in his eye. If you arrive early you'll hear him giving the kitchen staff their orders in a cheerful voice. You're in good hands here and you'll enjoy your meal in the dining room with its fireplace and old clock. Set meals 66F, 100F and 148F. In the very good 66F one, he makes imaginative use of local produce in dishes such as fricassee of chicken with cider vinegar. Lots of the dishes feature apples — this is Normandy after all!.

BARFLEUR 50760

10% ⌂ |●| LE MODERNE

1 place du Général-de-Gaulle; it's in front of the post office.
☎ 02.33.23.12.44 F➜ 02.33.23.91.58
Closed Tuesdays (March 15–June 30 and Oct–end Jan), Wednesdays (Oct–end Jan), and Feb 1–March 15.

Lunch served noon–1.45pm, dinner 7–8.45pm. Barfleur is one of the most beautiful villages on the Nomandy coast and has a delightful little harbour. This is a colourful and very pretty place with lots of flowers. The clean simple bedrooms (there are no sea views) are 150F with basin/wc and 220F with bath. Half-board compulsory. Dishes are prepared with great care. Set meal at 85F Mondays–Fridays. Others 105–187F with dishes such as fish *choucroute* with a butter sauce and scallop kebabs. The owner smokes his own salmon and duck breast and the bread and puff pastry are also home-made. Marvellous desserts — warm flambéd apple tarts, raspberry *feuillantine*, and *gratin* of soft fruit. The place has a charm that's hard to put into words but we like it a lot. It's a pity the staff aren't always as nice as you'd like.

LE CONQUÉRANT**

16-18 rue Saint-Thomas-Becket.
☎ 02.33.54.00.82 F➔ 02.33.54.65.25
Closed Nov 15–March 15. Restaurant closed evenings unless you're staying at the hotel. **Car park**. **TV**.

This handsome 17th century building has a large and very pleasant French-style garden at the back and comfortable double bedrooms ranging in price from 200F with washing facilities to 310F with shower/wc or bath. The best ones overlook the garden (sorry, no sea views). Breakfast 30–60F. You can expect to pay 80–130F for a meal in the stylish dining room (it also serves crêpes).

BARNEVILLE-CARTERET 50270

10% L'HERMITAGE**

promenade Abbé-Lebouteiller.
☎ 02.33.04.96.29 F➔ 02.33.04.78.87
Closed Sunday evenings, Mondays, Jan 10–25, and Nov 15–Dec 29. **Car park**. **TV**.

Lunch served noon–2pm, dinner 7–9pm. You'll get a view of the sea and the little fishing port whether you sit inside or out on the terrace. The place speciaizes in seafood and the very hearty 90F set meal offers a starter of *moules marinière* then either skate *à la crème* or grilled *andouillette*. For 125F you'll get a large seafood platter for starters followed by, say, monkfish *à l'américaine*. If there are two of you, how about sharing an enormous seafood platter with sea snails, winkles, prawns, oysters and crab for 200F or all that plus lobster for 400F? Chargrilled fish and meat. They have a few pleasant bedrooms. Doubles 200F with shower/wc, 290F for one overlooking the harbour.

10% LES ISLES**

9 bd Maritime; it's beside Barneville beach.
☎ 02.33.04.90.76 F➔ 02.33.94.53.83
Closed Mondays out of season and Nov 30–Feb 15. **Car park**. **TV**.

A large white building with a garden, facing the sea. Doubles 205F (with basin and a view of the quiet garden), 290F (with shower/wc) and 325F (with bath and a view of the English Channel and the Channel Islands off in the distance). Half-board (305F per person) compulsory in July and August. They serve good food and dishes such as fillet of roast duck *en croûte,* gratinéd oysters with curry, salmon steak with three different seasonings, and seafood stew. Set meals 68F (weekdays), 95F and 135F. Children's set meal 45F. A smile or two and everything would have been perfect.

HÔTEL DE LA MARINE***

11 rue de Paris.
☎ 02.33.53.83.31 F➔ 02.33.53.39.60
Closed Sunday evenings and Mondays in February, March and October. **Car park**. **TV**.

Lunch served 12.30–1.30pm, dinner 7.30–9.30pm. You'll get wonderful views from this large white building overlooking the harbour. Some bedrooms have a balcony and others a tiny terrace. Stylish fresh décor. Doubles 398–560F. However, the hotel's known more for its restaurant. It's difficult to give a really accurate description of the cooking, which is sophisticated, imaginative and very elaborate all at the same time. The elegant dining room with its rather chic atmosphere is popular with the Brits. The efficient Monsieur and Madame Cesne make sure the place runs smoothly and that the service is everything it should be. Their son Laurent is the chef and he has put together a superb 138F set meal (available up to 9pm). The 200F one is sheer perfection and offers oysters *en nage* with gherkins, plaice with honey and thyme, and *galette croustillante* of tripe. For 250F you get an extra course. *Menu dégustation* 400F. À la carte is very expensive.

BAYEUX 14400

10% HÔTEL-RESTAURANT NOTRE-DAME*

44 rue des Cuisiniers (Centre); it's only a few steps from the cathedral.
☎ 02.31.92.87.24 F➔ 02.31.92.67.11
Closed Nov 15–Dec 15; restaurant closed Sunday evenings and Mondays Nov–Easter. **TV**.

It's friendly, well looked after, and has a homely atmosphere. Fancy cooking served up in generous portions. Set meals 65F (lunchtimes only), 90F (seafood *timbale* and fricassee of rabbit with cider for example), and 125F (regional specialities). Doubles 150F with washing facilities, 240F with shower/wc, 260F with bath. Half-board 190–240F per person (compulsory in July and August).

10% HÔTEL D'ARGOUGES

21 rue Saint-Patrice (Centre).
☎ 02.31.92.88.86 ➡ 02.31.92.69.16
Car park. **TV**.

If money is no object and/or you love beautiful buildings, head for this delightful hotel right in the centre. It's a town house built in the 18th century for the Argouges family and it's at the far end of a large courtyard, so it's quiet. There's a big garden with trees at the back – an ideal spot for breakfast if the sun's out. Superb dining room. Bedrooms 200–420F (all with shower/wc or bath).

LA TABLE DU TERROIR

42 rue Saint-Jean (Centre).
☎ 02.31.92.05.53 ➡ 02.31.92.05.53
Closed Oct 15–Nov 15 and Sunday evenings May 1–Oct 15.

Lunch served 11.30–3pm, dinner 6.30–10pm. Louis Bisson, a butcher by training, was eager to get back to his first love while at the same time sharing his passion for cooking. The "back shop" is a beautiful dining room with unusual stone décor and a few tables. These are soon covered with house *terrines*, rib of beef (160F for two), grilled flank of beef (55F), skirt (55F) or tripe (40F). No matter how hungry you are, one of the three pretty decent set meals (55F, 95F and 135F) should fit the bill. Customers are often regulars but it's a friendly little place with a smile for everyone be it the American tourist who's come to see the Bayeux tapestry, the hairdresser from across the street or the civil servant wanting a spot of lunch.

RESTAURANT LE PRINTANIER

2 rue des Bouchers.
☎ 02.31.92.03.01 ➡ 02.31.92.03.01
Closed Sundays, Monday lunchtimes (except public holidays), during the February school holidays, and the last week in December. **Car park**.

Service noon–9.15pm. The décor in the dining room is a bit tacky, not to say in bad taste, with vast quantities of artificial vine leaves and bunches of grapes dangling from the old beams and the ceiling. All the same, the cooking's pretty good and the chips that come with the braised ham with cider and other dishes are terrific. If you like your food, you'll want to try the chocolate *charlotte* with custard. Cheapest set meal 59F, others 72F and 108F. Attentive service.

LE PETIT BISTROT

2 rue Bienvenue (Centre); it's beside the cathedral.
☎ 02.31.51.85.40
Closed Sundays.

This is a genuine little bistro, a bit chic but very pleasant. You'll find the owner behind the counter. She knows what she wants and might seem a bit brusque until you've broken the ice and then she can't do enough for you. Her husband's cooking is fresh-tasting and flavoursome and he uses local produce to create dishes that are more than the sum of their parts. The veal sweetbreads with hazelnut butter is a model of its kind, as is the artichoke flan with foie gras. Set meals at 95F and 165F that change with the seasons. A very good Bayeux restaurant.

PORT-EN-BESSIN-HUPPAIN 14520 (9KM N)

RESTAURANT LE VIEUX PÊCHEUR

5 place de la Fontaine; it's near the marina and the fishing port.
☎ 02.31.21.71.27
Closed Sunday evenings and Mondays out of season, and Dec 20–Jan 31.

You'll get good value for money in this restaurant with the panelled ceiling that makes it look something like a boat. Stylish décor and smiling staff. Cheapest set meal 75F, others 98F, 125F and 150F. The à la carte menu has some quite imaginative fish dishes, including monkfish in a vanilla-flavoured sauce and scallops on a bed of seaweed.

COLOMBIERS-SUR-SEULLES 14480 (14KM E)

CHÂTEAU DU BAFFY**

How to get there: it's 10km from the landing beaches.
☎ 02.31.08.04.57. ➡ 02.31.08.08.29.
Restaurant closed Sunday evenings and Mondays mid-Nov–Feb (except school holidays). **Car park**. **Disabled access**.

Lunch served from noon, dinner from 7pm. This pretty château, which dates from the Age of Enlightenment and has a river running through its beautiful garden, is a lovely romantic spot. The bedrooms are comfortable but rather expensive, with prices starting at 390F (includes breakfast). Set meals 95–235F. The restaurant can do both home cooking and the more sophisticated kind. We enjoyed the *grenadin* of veal, the stuffed duck leg, and the seafood stew in a langoustine stock. And if you feel you need some exercise, there's a gym, tennis courts, mountain biking, archery and horse riding. This is where we'd choose to stay in the area if we decided to splash out.

CRÉPON 14480 (15KM E)

10% ⌂ |●| LA FERME DE LA RANÇONNIÈRE**

route d'Arromanches; take the D12 towards Cruelly –14km on, turn left onto the D65.
☎ 02.31.22.21.73 F 02.31.22.98.39
Car park. **TV**.

Lunch served noon–2pm, dinner 7–9.30pm. The inn, which is in a quiet little village on the road leading to the landing beaches, is housed in a fortified farmhouse that goes all the way back to the 13th century. Great décor. The bedrooms, all different, are tastefully furnished in traditional style. Some look onto a large garden. If you're looking for peace and quiet, you'll get lots of it here. Doubles 295–380F with shower/wc and 335 -380F with bath. We suggest you take half-board at the weekend, which costs 310–360F per person. Set meals 60–280F but the restaurant isn't up to much.

BELLÊME 61130

⌂ |●| LE RELAIS SAINT-LOUIS**

1 bd Bansard-des-Bois (Centre).
☎ 02.33.73.12.21 F 02.33.83.71.19
Closed Sunday evenings, Mondays, and ten days in October. **Car park**.

This is the good old-fashioned kind of inn. It's a long white pillared building on the old ramparts of this tiny village. The large dining room with its fireplace and waiters in bow ties is terribly old-fashioned but rather pleasant. The chef, Ghislaine, prepares classic dishes based on local recipes. Set meals 98F (weekdays), 120F and 138F and specialities like *foie gras* from Normandy and the famous black pudding from Perche. Bedrooms are tastefully decorated. Some overlook the trees in the gardens at the back of the inn. Doubles 250-300F with shower/wc or bath. An ideal base for exploring this beautiful region famous for its hills and forests and for meeting the mushroom pickers who come from all over France in September to try their luck in the magnificent forest of Bellême.

CABOURG 14390

10% ⌂ HÔTEL LE COTTAGE**

24 av. du Général-Leclerc.
☎ 02.31.91.65.61 F 02.31.28.78.82
Car park. **TV**. **Canal+**.

We fell in love with this delightful hotel, a traditional Normandy house with a pretty flower-filled garden. It may be at the side of the road but the bedrooms are quiet — thank heavens for double glazing! But that's just one of the good things about the hotel. You'll get a very warm welcome from the owner, who'll greet you like an old friend, and the bedrooms are charming and cosy with their Laura Ashley type décor. Doubles 320F with shower/wc and 390 with bath. Facilities include a billiard room, sauna and sunbed. Honestly, you'd think it rained all the time in Normandy!

⌂ LE BEAURIVAGE**

allée du Château (West); it's 800m from the centre of Cabourg on the route du Hôme.
☎ 02.31.24.08.08 F 02.31.91.19.46
Closed Nov 15–Dec 15. **Car park**. **TV**.
Disabled access.

This large ochre-coloured building is right beside the sea, which is a definite plus. The décor and the clean bedrooms are more than adequate but this is Cabourg and you're at the seaside so it's not cheap. Doubles 370F with shower/wc (breakfast included) and from 380F with bath.

|●| L'ANGE BLEU

4 av. du Commandant-Bertaux-Levillain.
☎ 02.31.91.07.33
Closed Thursdays.

Lunch served noon–3pm, dinner 6.30–10pm. There's a very maritime feel to this place, right down to the food. Cheapest set meal 64F (not available Sundays). There are lots of fish dishes in the other set meals (89–199F) and it's worth coming for the sole meunière or stuffed crab alone. The décor — lots of trinkets and Greek style statues — is maybe a bit affected. In the evening there's a pianist to help set the mood for candle-lit dinners for two. Good service and staff.

DIVES-SUR-MER 14160 (2KM S)

|●| RESTAURANT CHEZ LE BOUGNAT

29 rue Gaston-Manneville.
☎ 02.31.91.06.13
Closed in the evenings (except Fridays and Saturdays) and Tuesdays in season.

This excellent restaurant is one of our favourites on the coast. The owner, Fred, is a cheerful lively sort and the place runs like clockwork. The food is excellent, simple local dishes made from fresh produce and first-rate ingredients. Fred used to be a butcher and meat is served up in various forms, from steak tartare to *pot au feu* and *épigramme* of lamb (small thin slices off the breast that are grilled or sautéed). It's worth paying a visit to try his calf's head. The décor is really something – both floors are filled with metro signs, 50s advertising posters and furniture, trinkets and knick-knacks picked up on Fred's frequent visits to secondhand shops. The 79F set meal comes with starter, main dish, cheese AND dessert! À la carte also available. The best value for money in this part of the world so it would be advisable to book.

CAEN 14000

SEE MAP OVERLEAF

AUBERGE DE JEUNESSE

68 rue Eustache-Restout. Off map **C4-1**
☎ 02.31.52.19.96 ➡ 02.31.84.29.49
Closed Oct 1–June 1. **Car park.**

Doors open 7–11am and 5–10pm. Four-bedded rooms with shower and small kitchen. Several rooms also available for couples. 62F for everyone. Breakfast 10F. Good atmosphere. Organized outings and sports activities.

10% HÔTEL SAINT-ÉTIENNE*

2 rue de l'Académie. **MAP A2-3**
☎ 02.31.86.35.82 ➡ 02.31.85.57.69
TV.

Situated in a quiet little street this hotel with lots of character pre-dates the French Revolution and has kept its original stonework and panelling. Doubles 130F with basin and 170–190F with shower/wc and telephone, and one rather pretty little single 100F. The cheapest hotel in Caen so it's often fully booked. Very friendly staff.

10% CENTRAL HÔTEL*

23 place Jean-Letellier. **MAP B2-2**
☎ 02.31.86.18.52 ➡ 02.31.86.88.11
TV.

Although the building with its uninspiring 60s style architecture is decidedly lacking in charm, the area's quiet and Monsieur and Madame Du Jardin are friendly and helpful. Bright attractive rooms at reasonable prices. Doubles 150F with shower (wc on the landing) and a view of the castle. These are five floors up though, and there's no lift. The less athletic among you may prefer to pay slightly more (190F) for a room with bath or shower/wc on one of the lower floors. Excellent hotel considering it's only got one star.

10% HÔTEL BERNIÈRES*

50 rue de Bernières. **MAP C2-5**
☎ 02.31.86.01.26 ➡ 02.31.86.51.76
TV.

24hr service. This hotel in a busy street might not seem like the ideal place for a good night's sleep but not to worry. We've checked it out and the double glazing keeps out unwelcome noise. The clean and well-kept bedrooms are rather attractively decorated, as is the rest of the hotel. Pastel shades and light-coloured wood. You'll get a cordial welcome from the proprietress, who does everything she can for her guests. You'll be very impressed with the 28F breakfast (good inexpensive breakfasts are rare enough to be worth mentioning). Doubles 140F with basin, 160F with basin/wc, 210F with shower/wc and 220F with bath. A one-star hotel that thoroughly deserves to be upgraded to two. Our favourite place to stay in Caen.

10% HÔTEL DES CORDELIERS**

4 rue des Cordeliers. **MAP B2-4**
☎ 02.31.86.37.15 ➡ 02.31.39.56.51
Closed Sunday afternoons. **TV.**

This 17th century town house just oozes charm. The recently renovated bedrooms overlook the pleasant patio or a narrow and rather pretty pedestrian street. Doubles from 140F with basin, 250F with shower/wc and 300F with bath. It doesn't have a restaurant but there's a bar in the large vaulted cellar.

RESTAURANT CHEZ MICHEL

24 rue Jean-Romain. **MAP B3-10**
☎ 02.31.86.16.59
Closed Saturday evenings, Sundays and public holidays.

Service until 9pm. Paul Bocuse it's not (that's obvious from the word go) but it's very very good of its kind. Just ask the regular lunchtime crowd (who've been coming here for so long they even put their napkins in the rack before they leave) in the fairly basic dining room. Patrick and Chantal spent a fair

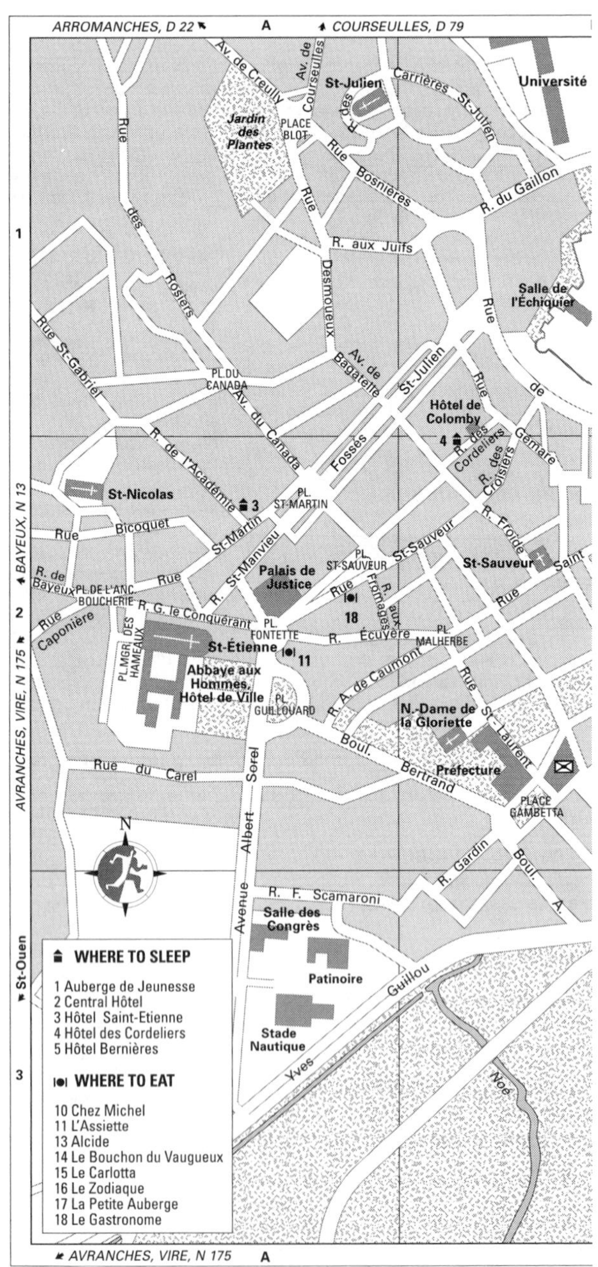
ARROMANCHES, D 22
A
COURSEULLES, D 79
1
2
3
BAYEUX, N 13
AVRANCHES, VIRE, N 175
St-Ouen
Av. de Creully
Av. de Courseulles
St-Julien
Carrières St-Julien
Université
Jardin des Plantes
PLACE BLOT
R. des
Rue Bosnières
R. du Gaillon
Rue des Rosiers
Rue Desmoueux
R. aux Juifs
Salle de l'Échiquier
Rue St-Gabriel
PL.DU CANADA
Av. du Canada
Av. de Bagatelle
St-Julien
Fossés
Hôtel de Colomby
R. des Cordeliers
R. des Croisiers
Gemare
R. de l'Académie
St-Nicolas
PL. ST-MARTIN
3
4
Rue Bicoquet
St-Martin
R. St-Manvieu
R. Froide
Palais de Justice
PL. ST-SAUVEUR
St-Sauveur
St-Sauveur
Saint
R. de Bayeux
PL.DE L'ANC. BOUCHERIE
R. G. le Conquérant
R. aux Fromages
18
Rue Caponière
PL. FONTETTE
R. Écuyère
PL. MALHERBE
PL.MGR. DES HAMEAUX
St-Étienne
11
Abbaye aux Hommes, Hôtel de Ville
PL. GUILLOUARD
R. A. de Caumont
N.-Dame de la Gloriette
Rue St-Laurent
Boul. Bertrand
Préfecture
Rue du Carel
Avenue Albert Sorel
PLACE GAMBETTA
N
R. Gardin
Boul. A.
R. F. Scamaroni
Salle des Congrès
Patinoire
Guillou
Yves
Stade Nautique
Noé
WHERE TO SLEEP
1 Auberge de Jeunesse
2 Central Hôtel
3 Hôtel Saint-Etienne
4 Hôtel des Cordeliers
5 Hôtel Bernières
WHERE TO EAT
10 Chez Michel
11 L'Assiette
13 Alcide
14 Le Bouchon du Vaugueux
15 Le Carlotta
16 Le Zodiaque
17 La Petite Auberge
18 Le Gastronome
AVRANCHES, VIRE, N 175
A

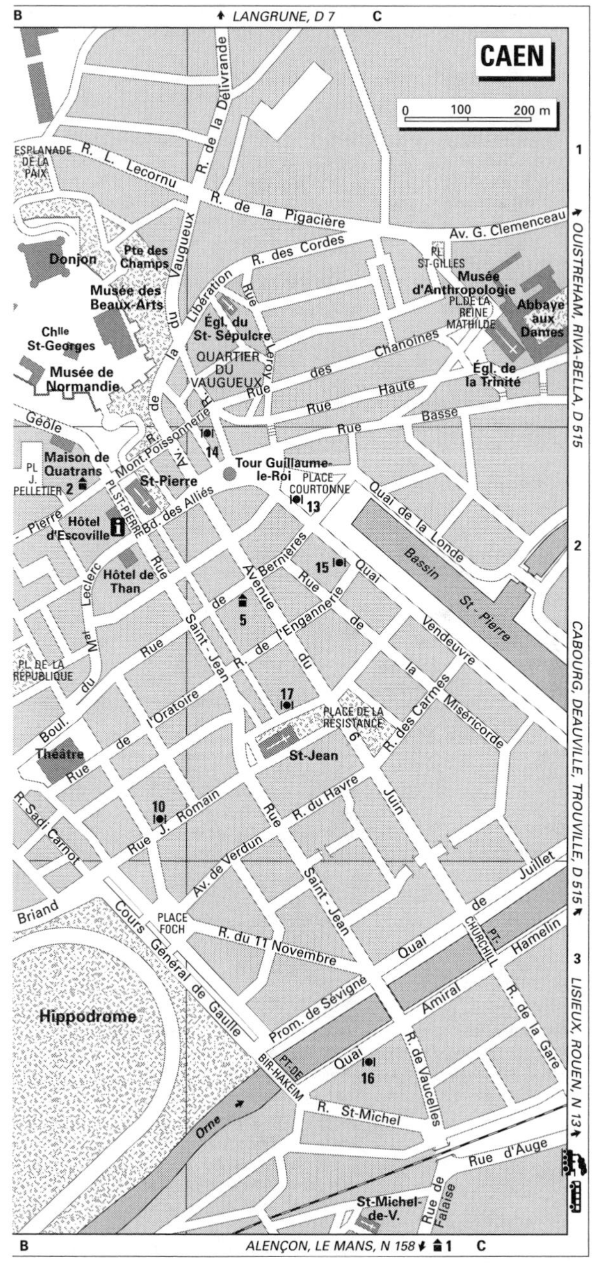
CAEN
LANGRUNE, D 7
0 100 200 m
ESPLANADE DE LA PAIX
R. L. Lecornu
R. de la Délivrande
R. de la Pigacière
Av. G. Clemenceau
OUISTREHAM, RIVA-BELLA, D 515
Donjon
Pte des Champs
Musée des Beaux-Arts
Chlle St-Georges
Musée de Normandie
R. des Cordes
Av. de la Libération
Rue Leroy
Égl. du St-Sépulcre
QUARTIER DU VAUGUEUX
PL. ST-GILLES
Musée d'Anthropologie
PL. DE LA REINE MATHILDE
Abbaye aux Dames
Rue des Chanoines
Égl. de la Trinité
Rue Haute
Rue Basse
Géôle
Maison de Quatrans
PL. J. PELLETIER
R. Mont. Poissonnerie
14
Tour Guillaume-le-Roi
PLACE COURTONNE
13
St-Pierre
PL. ST-PIERRE
Bd. des Alliés
Hôtel d'Escoville
Quai de la Londe
Bassin St-Pierre
Hôtel de Than
Rue Bernières
15
Rue de Bernières
Quai Vendeuvre
Avenue du 6 Juin
CABOURG, DEAUVILLE, TROUVILLE, D 515
5
Rue de l'Engannerie
PL. DE LA RÉPUBLIQUE
Boul. du Mal Leclerc
Rue Saint-Jean
Rue de l'Oratoire
17
PLACE DE LA RÉSISTANCE
R. des Carmes
Miséricorde
Théâtre
St-Jean
Rue de Sévigné
R. du Havre
10
Rue J. Romain
R. Sadi Carnot
Av. de Verdun
Rue Saint-Jean
Juillet
Briand
Cours Général de Gaulle
PLACE FOCH
R. du 11 Novembre
Quai de Juillet
PT. CHURCHILL
Quai Amiral Hamelin
R. de la Gare
LISIEUX, ROUEN, N 13
Hippodrome
Prom. de Sévigné
PT. DE BIR-HAKEIM
Quai
16
R. de Vaucelles
R. St-Michel
Orne
Rue d'Auge
St-Michel-de-V.
Rue de Falaise
ALENÇON, LE MANS, N 158 1
B
C
1
2
3

number of years in the restaurant business in Paris before the lure of the countryside, with its peace and quiet and quality of life, brought them here. Home cooking is what they provide and they serve up generous portions of simple dishes made with good fresh produce. You'll get astonishingly good value for money. There's a 50F set meal with a choice of eight starters, eight main dishes and eight desserts. We still remember the leeks *vinaigrette*, the liver and the fruit tarts.

|●| LE BOUCHON DU VAUGUEUX

12 rue du Graindorge. **MAP C2-14**
☎ 02.31.44.26.26
Closed Monday evenings, Sundays, the first three weeks in August, and Dec 23–Jan 5.

Lunch served 11.45am–2pm, dinner 6.45–11.30pm. In an area where restaurants do a thriving trade and the reputation that some of them have for good food is not always justified, this little place stands out. The dining room is decorated in warm dark colours, mainly red and black. You make your choice from the various suggestions chalked up on big blackboards. One of the enormous 46F salads — the "Normande" (*andouille*, potatoes, eggs and Camembert) is very good — would make an ideal lunch. If you're having something other than a salad, you can order a half portion at half the price. *Formule* 69F and set meal 89F. They do very tasty tripe with Calvados. Staff are really warm and friendly, just like the atmosphere. It's always very busy but that's only to be expected. We really do advise you to book.

|●| LA PETITE AUBERGE

17 rue des Équipes d'Urgence. **MAP C2-17**
☎ 02.31.86.43.30. ⊫ same
Closed Sundays, the first three weeks in September, and from the Sunday before Christmas to the first Monday after New Year.

The dining room is small and cosy but the décor (in our opinion) is pretty tasteless, with strips of brass on the ceiling, peach coloured walls, and brown carpet. But what does the décor matter if the food's good? And it's not bad at all. Hake, saddle of lamb with garlic, and tripe are typical dishes. *Formule du jour* 68F. *Menu-carte* 89F. Staff and service are unobtrusive and professional.

|●| RESTAURANT ALCIDE

1 place Courtonne. **MAP C2-13**
☎ 02.31.44.18.06 ⊫ 02.31.22.92.90
Closed Saturdays and Dec 20–31.

Although the décor's rather ordinary, the warm atmosphere makes up for it. There's no "nouvelle cuisine" here. Instead, there's good local cooking which is tasty and satisfying. If you order the house *terrine*, they'll give you such a large portion it will fill the entire plate. The pig's trotters, *coq au vin* and the terrific tripe *à la mode de Caen* reminded us of everything that was good about Normandy. If you want to try them too, have one of the three set meals (78F, 105F and 139F). One of the town's classics.

|●| RESTAURANT MAÎTRE CORBEAU

94 rue de Geôle.
☎ 02.31.86.33.97.
Closed Saturday lunchtimes and Sundays.

The décor is rather disconcerting – there's a cow on the ceiling – but you'll gather from the motley collection of adverts and packaging that cheese is the star attraction here. Specialities include cheese fondues (of course!) – you'll pay 74–84F – *tartiflette*, coddled eggs with cheese, and *escalopines* of Roquefort flambéd with Calvados. Set meals 88F and 120F. Informal and enthusiastic welcome and service. There's nowhere else like it in Calvados country.

|●| LE GASTRONOME

43 rue Saint-Sauveur. **MAP A2-18**
☎ 02.31.86.57.75 ⊫ 02.31.38.27.78
Closed Saturday lunchtimes, Sundays, and the first fortnight in August.

Lunch served noon–2pm, dinner 7.30–10pm. The dining room with its fairly low-key décor is quite chic. The cooking will please even the most demanding palates and Patrick Danet adds his own personal touch to classic and local ingredients to produce dishes like *croustillant* of tripe, spatchcock pigeon, and warm charlotte of *andouille*. Very decent set meals at 92F, 120F and 178F. The service is attentive, efficient and unobtrusive.

|●| LE CARLOTTA

16 quai Vendeuvre. **MAP C2-15**
☎ 02.31.86.68.99
Closed Sundays and two weeks in August.

Service until 11pm. The name makes it sound like a tacky pizza parlour and we weren't too sure what to expect but the white tablecloths, the waiters in white aprons, and the rather plush and quite tasteful décor soon put our minds at rest. It is in fact a brasserie and you'd have to go to Paris to find anything more typically Parisian.

The prices though, are nothing like the ones in Paris and you'll get first-rate cooking without having to spend a fortune. They do some good fish dishes (try the *galettes* of creamed salt cod) and the meat *is* succulent (the steak tartare is just about perfect). There's a good *formule* at 94F that's large enough to suit the biggest appetites and set meals at 105F, 118F (main course, dessert and wine) and 150F. Hearty portions and efficient service.

|●| RESTAURANT LE ZODIAQUE

15 quai Eugène-Meslin. **MAP C3-16**
☎ 02.31.84.46.31
Closed evenings Mondays–Wednesdays, Sundays, and August 1–15.

This cosy and recently redecorated restaurant (the signs of the zodiac feature prominently, of course) is famous for chargrilled meat, including rib steak, rib of beef, and breast of duck breast. Terrific home-made pastries for dessert. No set meals. Expect to pay about 100F à la carte.

BÉNOUVILLE 14970 (10KM NE)

⌂ |●| HÔTEL-RESTAURANT LA GLYCINE**

Centre; it's on the route d'Ouistreham.
☎ 02.31.44.61.94 F➔ 02.31.43.67.30
Closed Sunday evenings out of season and Feb 15–March 15. **Car park**. **TV**. **Disabled access**.

A beautiful stone building covered in wisteria, this place is ideal if you want to stop off somewhere before heading back to Great Britain. Refurbished bedrooms. Doubles 280F (in season) with shower/wc, telephone or bath. Good food, imaginative and carefully prepared. The young chef is in a class of his own when it comes to turbot or baby vegetables for the duck breast flavoured with five kinds of pepper. And you might like to try the local *foie gras*. Set meals 95F, 129F, 139F, 179F and 230F.

COLLEVILLE-MONTGOMERY 14880 (10KM N)

|●| RESTAURANT LA FERME SAINT-HUBERT

3 rue de la Mer; take the D515 and turn left 5km before you get to Ouistreham.
☎ 02.31.96.35.41
Closed Mondays (except in season), Sunday evenings, and Christmas holidays. **Car park**. **Disabled access**.

Lunch served noon–2.30pm, dinner 7.30–10pm. A large, typical Normandy house. You can have lunch in the cosy rustic dining room or in a bright conservatory. If you like good food, you'll love the *gratin* of mussels and the monkfish and salmon served with lobster *bisque*. Cheapest set meal 90F, others 148–255F.

NOYERS-BOCAGE 14210 (12KM SW)

⌂ |●| HÔTEL-RESTAURANT LE RELAIS NORMAND**

How to get there: take the D675 or the N175 and it's at the Noyers-Bocage exit.
☎ 02.31.77.97.37 F➔ 02.31.77.94.41
Closed Wednesdays, two weeks in January and in November. **Secure parking**. **TV**.

They can't do enough for you here. The proprietor/chef, who doesn't believe in breaking the rules, is particularly gifted when it comes to traditional local cooking. Three set meals 95–275F. À la carte you've got dishes like *chartreuse* of courgettes with salmon, duckling *à l'orange*, monkfish *portaise* (poached and served with cream sauce and scallops), and oysters poached in champagne. And how about trying the prize-winning dessert, the *Bonneau normand*? The attractive and fairly plush dining room is decorated in rustic style. Doubles 170–260F (with bath). It's very peaceful in this little out-of-the-way place.

SAINT-AUBIN-SUR-MER 14750 (16KM NW)

10% ⌂ |●| LE CLOS NORMAND "LES PIEDS DANS L'EAU"**

2 promenade Guynemer.
☎ 02.31.97.30.47 F➔ 02.31.96.46.23
Closed Nov 15–March 1. **Car park**. **TV**.

Lunch served noon–2.30pm, dinner 7.30–9.30pm. A lovely place that has a pretty garden and faces the sea. The atmosphere's rather reserved, practically British, although it has no connection whatsoever with things the English side of the Channel! The dining room doesn't let the rest of the place down. Set meals 69–270F. Lots of fish, seafood and a few nice dishes like quail with Pommeau and leg of duck marinated in cider. Clean and very well-kept bedrooms from 200F out of season to 340F in high season. The ones with a sea view are the nicest, of course. We really liked this place.

VILLERS-BOCAGE 14310 (26KM SW)

⌂ |●| AUBERGE LES TROIS ROIS**

2 place Jeanne-d'Arc.
☎ 02.31.77.00.32 F➔ 02.31.77.93.25

Closed Sunday evenings, Mondays, in January, and the last week in June. **Car park**. **TV**.

A white stone inn in the large village square. The restaurant is quite elegant if a bit showy. Good food, carefully prepared. Try the John Dory with fresh sorrel, the *crépinettes* of veal sweetbreads on a lettuce sauce, and the liqueur soufflé. And then of course there's the tripe – they've lost count of how many prizes it's won. Set meals 120F, 178F and 290F. The 14 recently renovated bedrooms are clean and well-kept. Numbers 12, 14, 18 and 19 have been refurbished recently. Doubles 200F with basin/wc, 300–380F with bath. Staff are a bit stiff.

CARENTAN 50500

HÔTEL DU COMMERCE ET DE LA GARE*

34 rue du Docteur-Caillard.
☎ 02.33.42.02.00
Closed for Christmas/New Year holidays. **Car park**. **TV**.

Beautiful ivy-covered façade. It was the restaurant we liked. The colour scheme and the old polished wooden floor create a restful atmosphere in the intimate, rather dark dining room. Very good home cooking. Set meals 69F, 99F and 149F. The one at 69F is pretty impressive and comes with Camembert in puff pastry, dogfish in a cream and white wine sauce, and *gâteau de riz* (which is like a fairly stiff rice pudding) with apples. Children's set meal 45F. The specialities are sautéd chicken with cider, kidneys prepared to a local recipe, skate wing with vanilla butter and Camembert quiche. The sign encouraging customers to tell the chef what they thought of the food is a nice touch. Doubles from 150F with basin and 200F with shower/wc.

MOITIERS-EN-BAUPTOIS (LES) 50360 (20KM NW)

KAUBERGE DU TERROIR DE L'OUVE

village Longuérac; it's 16km west of Sainte-Mère-Église.
☎ 02.33.21.16.26 ⊳ 02.33.41.83.61
Open Easter–end of Sept, by reservation only.

This lovely inn stands on the banks of the Ouve miles from anywhere, with just a few old farms, some horses frolicking about, and a line of trees at the water's edge for company. Romantic sunsets and a great welcome. The restaurant has attractive décor, a warm atmosphere wonderful local cooking, and good set meals at prices that won't break the bank. Judge for yourself – for 70F, you can have as much *terrine* as you want and a stew with creamed potatoes, for 90F smoked ham with cider (90F), and for 120F *salade Caroline* and duck with potatoes (120F). If you want to work up an appetite or work off what you've just had, you could rent one of the small boats, take a trip down the Douve or in the better weather go walking in the woods and marshes round about.

CHERBOURG 50100

10% HÔTEL DE LA RENAISSANCE**

4 rue de l'Église (Centre).
☎ 02.33.43.23.90 ⊳ 02.33.43.96.10
Car park. **TV**.

Great location in front of the wonderful church of Sainte-Trinité, and all the bedrooms overlook the harbour. Doubles 140F with basin, 220–300F with shower/wc. Madame's very artistic (she used to paint china) so you won't be too surprised to find that the bedrooms, which are very comfortable, are as pretty as can be – they're all decorated with reference to a specific flower. The colour of the façade, (sugared almonds spring to mind) is bound to please the aesthetes amongst us. Edith smiles a lot and goes to great lengths to please her guests. This is our favourite hotel in Cherbourg. There's no restaurant unfortunately but the breakfast's very substantial (30F).

10% HÔTEL DE LA CROIX DE MALTE**

5 rue des Halles (Centre); it's near the harbour, the theatre and the casino.
☎ 02.33.43.19.16 ⊳ 02.33.43.65.66
Car park. **TV**. **Disabled access**.

The hotel has been entirely refurbished and the quiet rooms are very spruce and extremely comfy. You'll get a very warm welcome from the owners. Doubles 180–280F with bath, direct telephone and TV. If booking in advance, ask for room number 3, 8 or 15 as they're the biggest. Users of this guidebook will get a 10% reduction (except July 15–Sept 15). Excellent value for money.

AU GRENIER

5 [bis] rue des Moulins; it's just after place de la Révolution, near the covered market and the church of Sainte-Trinité.
☎ 02.33.93.09.04

A good little restaurant, very cosy, in a pretty little square right in the heart of town. The terrace is an absolute delight in summer. The owner's a former gourmet cook, which explains the quality of the food. The 62F set meal is a real winner – melon with port, brill with a Roquefort sauce and a pretty decent dessert plus a quarter litre of red wine (and not just any old wine – Byzance!). You can also get wonderful mixed salads, crêpes with unusual fillings and meat and fish *pierrades* (you cook the ingredients yourself on a hot stone).

LE FAITOUT

25 rue Tour-Carrée; it's 150m from the town hall.
☎ 02.33.04.25.04
Closed Sundays, Monday lunchtimes, and two weeks at Christmas.

In the evening it's better to book ahead since it has a lot of regulars and is always busy – it's consistently good and the prices are very reasonable. There's a relaxed atmosphere in the pleasant dining room in the basement. Good traditional cooking. A starter of a dozen freshly caught oysters costs 55F. The day's special also costs 55F and for that you'll get a generous helping of something like duck braised in cider, calf's head *gribiche* (with a cold *vinaigrette* with mayonnaise, capers, gherkins and herbs), *andouillette* with Calvados, or grilled salmon. *Pot au feu* 75F. Bottle of cider 35F. Don't think you can't eat here if you're on a budget – they've got *moules marinière* or *à l'escabèche* (marinated and served cold) for 35F, and mussels in a cream sauce for 40F.

OMONVILLE-LA-PETITE 50440 (20KM NW)

10% LA FOSSARDIÈRE

hameau de la Fosse.
How to get there: take the coast road, the D45.
☎ 02.33.52.19.83
Closed Nov 15–March 15. **Car park.**
Disabled access.

A lovely little flower-filled hamlet in the rolling countryside of the Cotentin, only 500m from the sea, straddling a stream. A warm welcome from owner Gilles Fossard will get things off to a good start and you'll feel like one of the chosen few. And once you've discovered the comfortable bedrooms, the tiny sauna, the whirlpool bath, and the reasonable prices you'll be hooked! Doubles 270–380F.

AUDERVILLE 50440 (28KM NW)

RESTAURANT L'AUBERGE DE GOURY

port de Goury.
How to get there: take the D901.
☎ 02.33.52.77.01 Fax 02.33.08.14.37
Closed two weeks in February and during the Christmas holidays. **Car park.**

Lunch served noon–3pm, dinner 7–9pm. It feels like the ends of the earth, out here at the very tip of La Hague. Enormous windows overlook the sea so whatever the weather – bright and sunny or blowing a gale – you'll have a ringside seat. There are lots of appreciative comments in the visitors' book from stars of stage and screen. And the owner's a real extrovert (the kind of personality we like) so it's hardly surprising he gets lots of customers in high season. The restaurant specializes in chargrilling fish and the lobster enjoys a particularly good reputation. Set meals 85F, 135F (this comes with two main courses such as seafood platter, monkfish with leeks in puff pastry, and grilled leg of lamb) and 280F (this is absolutely enormous and comes with lobster). If you like good food you'll really get your money's worth here.

FLAMANVILLE 50340 (28KM SW)

10% HÔTEL BEL AIR**

le bourg; take the D4 and it's 300m from the château..
☎ 02.33.04.48.00 Fax 02.33.04.49.56
Closed for a fortnight in winter. **Car park. TV.**

A very attractive hotel in the heart of the countryside and very close to the magnificent headland of Flamanville. The friendly welcome and atmosphere will soon have you feeling at home. Extremely quiet. Rooms are comfortable and have a certain charm. You can have one overlooking the fields or the pretty garden. The doubles in the annexe (small, lovely and as cosy as you could wish for) are 215F. The ones in the main building are 270F with shower/wc and 290F with bath. You'll have to make up your own mind of course but we could stay here for ever!

SAINT-GERMAIN-DES-VAUX 50440 (29KM NW)

RESTAURANT AU MOULIN À VENT

Hameau Danneville; take the D901 and when you get to the Saint-Germain-des-Vaux exit, head for Port-Racine.
☎ 02.33.52.75.20 Fax 02.33.52.22.57
Closed Saturday lunchtimes, Sunday evenings, and Mondays (except holiday weekends and public holidays).
Car park.

Lunch served noon–2pm, dinner 7.30–9pm. You're strongly advised to book. A temple of gastronomy that stands high above the bay beside the remains of an old mill. The large pleasant dining room, decorated in soft colours, overlooks a little garden full of exotic plants like yuccas and miniature palm trees and the cove of Saint-Martin. Superb cooking. The food is prepared with great care and what you eat depends on what was available at the market (the kitchen uses nothing but the freshest of produce). There's a 100F set meal (weekdays) that comes with eight oysters and is incredibly good value for money. Expect to pay a little bit more à la carte for duck breast with sage, roast pigeon, grilled mullet fillets, salmon steak *à l'unilatérale* (cooked on one side only) and lobster stew with fresh pasta. Reckon on 200F for a complete meal. Children's set meal 42F.

CONDÉ-SUR-NOIREAU 14110

10% HÔTEL-RESTAURANT DU CERF**

18 rue du Chêne; head in the direction of Aunay-sur-Odon and it's 500m from the centre.
☎ 02.31.69.40.55 Fax 02.31.69.78.29
Closed Sunday evenings and the November school holidays. **Car park**. **TV**.

Lunch served noon–2pm, dinner 7.30–9.15pm. This country hotel may have been around for rather a long time but it certainly knows how to move with the times. You'll be greeted like a friend by Madame Malgrey, a very nice lady who also happens to be the vice-president of the local tourist office and knows Suisse normande like the back of her hand. Her husband is in charge in the kitchen and his speciality is traditional local cooking. The 67F set meal (not available weekends or public holidays) is fairly uninspiring but the others (90F–170F) are much better. The *andouillette* and the beef *à la ficelle* are especially good. Ask for room number 6, 8, 9 or 10, all of which overlook the garden. Doubles 214F with shower/wc and 224F with bath.

COUTANCES 50200

RELAIS DU VIADUC

25 av. de Verdun (South); it's beside the service station at the Coutances exit on the Granville road.
☎ 02.33.45.02.68 Fax 02.33.45.69.86
Closed Friday evenings and Saturdays out of season, and the second fortnight in February. **Car park**. **TV**.

Rooms are basic but pleasant. Doubles 150F with basin and 200F with bath. Half-board 190F per person. Numbers 4, 6 and 8 have a pretty view of the upper part of town and the towers of the cathedral. The restaurant is really a good quality roadside café. Set meals 55F (weekdays), 75F, 98F, 135F and 180F. They get full marks for effort when it comes to dishes like duck *foie gras*, sea bass steak with star anise, and fillet of scabbard fish with a ginger sauce. The 75F set meal offers pâté *en croûte* made to the chef's special recipe and calf's liver with baby onions. Children's set meal.

RESTAURANT NOTRE-DAME

rue d'Harcourt; it's in the centre of town beside place Saint-Nicolas.
☎ 02.33.45.00.67
Closed Sundays (except in summer).

One of the few restaurants in town that's open Sunday lunchtimes in season. Don't be misled by the look of the place and the hushed atmosphere — the prices are very reasonable. Staff are welcoming and the food is good. Cheapest set meal 60F, others 85F, 125F and 160F, children's 40F. Specialities include breast of duck with Pommeau and two kinds of fish in Sauvignon. The *crêpes* and *galettes* are panfried in the old way and the owner has a selection of organic wines.

MONTMARTIN-SUR-MER 50590 (10KM SW)

HÔTELLERIE DU BON VIEUX TEMPS**

7 rue Pierre-des-Touches (Centre); it's opposite the post office.
☎ 02.33.47.54.44 Fax 02.33.46.27.12
Closed Sunday evenings out of season. **Car park**. **TV**.

Lunch served noon–1.30pm, dinner 7.30–9pm. This inn certainly lives up to its name. We're rather fond of the panelling in the spacious dining room and the paintings, as we are of the good country cooking with its use of cream and cider. They do grilled lobster (you'll have to order in advance), warm *andouille* with a Pommeau sauce, and fillet of salmon stuffed with poached oysters and served with a Benedictine sauce. Cheapest set meal 62F (not available Saturday evenings, Sundays or public holidays). Others 100F, 150F and 200F. Children's set meal 45F. Doubles 150F with basin, 240F with shower/wc and 270F with bath. Everything is very well looked. And the sea's just over a mile away.

REGNÉVILLE-SUR-MER 50590 (10KM SW)

LE JULES GOMMÈS

le bourg; take the D20 towards Granville, then 7km further on the D49 towards Regnéville.
☎ 02.33.45.32.04
Closed Tuesdays and Wednesdays except in July and August.

When you arrive in Regnéville by the splendid D49, the sea's straight ahead and on your right, just before you reach the water's edge, is this place. It's part restaurant, part crêperie and part Irish pub and is the cosiest place we've come across in la Manche. First-class décor, beautiful furniture and walls covered in rather nice watercolours of the region's beauty spots. The young owners are as nice as can be, you've a magnificent view of the sea, and the food's good too. Terrific *crêpes* and *galettes*, especially the hearty 33F "Jules Gommès" and the crêpe flambéd with Calvados. At 59F, 91F and 144F, the set meals are very affordable – and good. And if you want to make make some new friends you won't go far wrong with the pub.

SAVIGNY 50210 (10KM E)

LA VOISINIÈRE

rue des Hêtres; it's signposted from route Saint-Lô-Coutances — take the D52 or the D380.
☎ 02.33.07.60.32 F➜ 02.33.46.25.28
Closed Tuesday evenings, Wednesdays (except in July and August), and the second fortnight in October.
Car park. **TV**.

Reservations only Sunday lunchtimes. A large building right out in the country. It oozes charm and the large garden has some superb Brazilian plants, including gunneras (the things that look like huge sticks of rhubarb). Just five bedrooms (doubles 240F) but they're all attractive and nicely furnished in traditional style. The cooking's very well known around these parts. Set meals 79F, 98F (a choice of escalope of salmon with leek fondue or fricassee of guinea fowl with mushrooms as your main course), 120F, 142F and 218F. Delicious specialities include panfried langoustine flavoured with orange, fricassee of guinea fowl with grapes and juniper berries, and skate with capers. The meat is tender, the fish is delicious, and the seafood wonderful. Not to mention the desserts! Children's set meal 50F.

MESNILBUS (LE) 50490 (12KM NE)

10% AUBERGE DES BONNES GENS

le bourg; go to Saint-Sauveur-Lendelin and then take the D53.
☎ 02.33.07.66.85
Closed Sunday evenings and Mondays out of season.
Car park.

A good little village inn with beautiful countryside all around. Four pleasant bedrooms 140F with shower. It has a big rustic dining room (of course) that serves up generous portions of traditional local dishes – they're not stingy with the cream here and would seem never to have heard of cholesterol. Prices to suit every pocket. Set meals 50F (weekday lunchtimes), 89F (fish soup, local ham with cider or tripe, cheese and ice-cream), 125F and 148F. Specialities include veal sweetbreads with Pommeau, warm oysters *au gratin* with cider, monkfish stew, and fillet of bass cooked in red wine.

TRELLY 50660 (13KM S)

VERTE CAMPAGNE**

hameau Chevalier; take the D7 or the D971, south of Coutances.
☎ 02.33.47.65.33 F➜ 02.33.47.38.03
Closed Sunday evenings and Mondays out of season, Monday lunchtimes in season, Jan 15–30, and Dec 1–8.
Car park.

Lunch served 12.30–1.30pm, dinner 7.30–9pm. Probably best to book ahead. A magnificent building with traditional architecture and swathed in ivy in a tiny village deep in the countryside. Wonderful surroundings and lovely interior with enormous beams, stone walls and lots of beautiful, decorative objects on display. The staff aren't over friendly but the cooking's some of the very best we've ever tried. Set meals 140F, 185F, 230F and 350F. Of course, you pay more à la carte but who dares to mention money here? There's roast pigeon with spices, roast langoustine with creamed salt cod, red mullet and artichokes in a warm vinaigrette, ox cheek with *foie gras* and, for dessert, *moelleux* of chocolate. Good choice of wine at very reasonable prices. Very pleasant doubles 220–380F. One of our favourite places in la Manche.

DEAUVILLE 14800

10% LE PATIO**

180 av. de la République (Centre); it's near the racecourse.
☎ 02.31.88.25.07 F➜ 02.31.88.00.81
TV. **Disabled access**.

The bedrooms in this large white hotel are their old charming selves again now that the refurbishment is complete and in fact the whole place is pretty comfortable now. You can get a room overlooking the shaded flower-filled patio from which the hotel took its name. Prices are reasonable for Deauville. Doubles from 270F with shower (wc on the landing) to 400F with bath, TV and phone. There's no chance of piling on the pounds here as they don't have a restaurant, but there's a gym if you want to get into shape.

HÔTEL DES SPORTS**

27 rue Gambetta; it's behind the covered fish market.
☎ 02.31.88.22.67
Closed Sundays out of season. **TV**.

It's above a popular café. Two of the twelve bedrooms have a balcony. Doubles 210–340F. Out of season you can get a 20% reduction (except at weekends). Slightly less busy than other two star hotels.

10% HÔTEL LE CHANTILLY**

120 av. de la République (Centre); it's 500m from the train station.
☎ 02.31.88.79.75 F 02.31.88.41.29
Closed the second and third weeks in January. **TV**.

Reception staffed 8am–10.30pm. It would be advisable to book. This hotel has been renovated throughout and has all the comforts you could wish for. It also radiates a certain charm. Doubles 295F with shower/wc or bath (335F in high season) – prices like these are few and far between in Deauville. You'll get a nice welcome from the friendly and chatty proprietress.

FALAISE 14700

10% HÔTEL-RESTAURANT DE LA POSTE**

38 rue Georges-Clemenceau.
☎ 02.31.90.13.14 F 02.31.90.01.81
Closed Sunday evenings, Mondays, and Dec 20–Jan 20. **Secure parking**. **TV**. **Canal+**.

Lunch served noon–2pm, dinner 7–9pm. This is a very pleasant inn in a small town that, to be honest, doesn't have much else to recommend it. It's the kind of place where you feel at ease and the owners care as much about the quality of the food as they do about the comfort of their guests. Nicely decorated in pale colours. Don't worry if you bump into the occasional gendarme – it's the food they've come for (French policeman don't eat just anywhere you know!). The chef is very fond of local ingredients. He comes up with simple traditional dishes like calf's head *ravigote* (in a spicy *vinaigrette*), sautéd veal kidneys with morels, tripe kebabs, and monkfish *à la normande*. Set meals 85F, 128F, 175F and 240F. Bedrooms – well cared for and with double glazing – 200F with basin/wc, 280F with shower/wc and 360F with bath. Efficient staff and service with a smile.

LA FINE FOURCHETTE

52 rue Georges-Clemenceau.
☎ 02.31.90.08.59
Closed Tuesday evenings, Wednesday evenings out of season, and Feb 8–27.

The restaurant has been modernized but the cooking hasn't changed – it's as good as ever. The colours in the dining room will raise your spirits however tired and hungry you are and you'll thoroughly enjoy the fricassee of chicken wing tips, the *croustillants* of calf's feet, the leg of duck with acacia honey, and the veal sweetbreads with peach sauce. Set meals 85F, 130F, 170F and 190F. Efficient service and genuinely friendly staff.

PONT-D'OUILLY 14690 (18KM W)

10% HÔTEL DU COMMERCE**

rue de Falaise (Centre).
☎ 02.31.69.80.16 F 02.31.69.78.08
Closed Sunday evenings and Mondays (except June–Sept), three weeks in January,and the first week in October. **Car park**. **TV**.

Lunch served noon–2pm, dinner 7–9pm. A hotel with a garden and a bright traditional style restaurant surrounded by the pastures and cosy little farms of Suisse normande. You'll realize straight away that the staff here are genuinely friendly. The roast chicken in the 65F set is definitely free-range. The chef's specialities include braised veal medallions and salmon with a cider and butter sauce. If you go for the 160F set meal, do consider paying the 50F supplement so you can try the crawfish flambéd with Calvados – the chef's particularly proud of it. The bedrooms, especially the ones overlooking the garden, are quiet. Doubles 200F with washing facilities and 250F with shower/wc or bath.

10% AUBERGE SAINT-CHRISTOPHE**

How to get there: take the D511 towards Pont-d'Ouilly for 17km then the D23 in the direction of Thury-Harcourt.
☎ 02.31.69.81.23. F 02.31.69.26.58
Closed Sunday evenings, Mondays, mid Feb–mid March, and during the November school holidays. **Car park**. **TV**.

An inn in the heart of Suisse normande that knows what hospitality is all about. The Virginia creeper scrambling over the front and the pretty décor give the place its undeniable charm. When summer comes along you can eat out in the lush flower-filled garden. The chef serves up traditional dishes of course, but with a special little twist that makes all the difference. Try the *pithiviers* of salmon with a butter sauce, the free-range chicken with cider (very tasty!) or the *ficelle* of beef with a Camembert sauce. No matter how hungry you are, one of the set meals (95–210F) is bound to suit. Staff are welcoming and attentive. Pretty little bedrooms overlooking the garden. Doubles 280F with shower/wc or bath. One of our favourite places in the area.

FLERS 61100

☗ HÔTEL OASIS**

3 [bis] rue de Paris (Centre).
☎ 02.33.64.95.80 F 02.33.65.97.76
Car park. TV. Canal+.

It doesn't have the charm you expect from a country inn, but then the town was destroyed in the Second World War and had to be rebuilt. But behind the very ordinary exterior there's a little haven of peace and quiet right in the centre of town centre. And you'll get a rather nice welcome. The décor's a bit kitsch but the bedrooms are comfy, well-kept and good value for money. Doubles 130–250F with shower or bath and satellite TV. 15F supplement for use of the garage.

|●| RESTAURANT AU BOUT DE LA RUE

60 rue de la Gare (South-West).
☎ 02.33.65.31.53 F 02.33.65.46.81
Closed Sundays and public holidays (except Christmas and Mother's Day).

Lunch served noon–2pm, dinner 7.30–10pm. The jazzy retro décor — a motley collection of trinkets, old record players and the like — is actually quite successful. Attentive service and the staff make you feel welcome. The cooking's fairly imaginative and the dishes on offer include raw salmon marinated in spices and herbs, shredded Belgian endives in a curry sauce, ravioli stuffed with snails and served with a cream sauce, fish soup with chillis, cod steak with slivers of chorizo, and a steak tartare that makes the Japanese customers forget all about sushi. The desserts are equally creative — there's strawberries and kiwi fruit in puff pastry with apple sauce (they use Granny Smiths), and waffles with bilberry purée and whipped cream. Superb 150F *menu-carte*. The 75F *formule* consists of starter plus main course, while for 99.50F you also get dessert. Good selection of wines at reasonable prices. Interesting choice of coffee from Costa Rica, Ethiopia and Colombia. Air-conditioned.

|●| AUBERGE DES VIEILLES PIERRES

Le Buisson Corblin; take the Argentan road and it's 3km from the centre.
☎ 02.33.65.06.96 F 02.33.65.80.72
Closed Sunday evenings, Mondays, during the February school holidays, and Aug 3–25. **Car park. Disabled access.**

One of the best restaurants in Suisse normande and it's got lots of surprises in store! The attractive dining room has a nice light décor and pretty little tables. The young owners give an informal natural feel to the place. And there must be an undiscovered genius working his magic in the kitchen because the cooking is superb and the dishes are skilfully prepared. The chef's got a special liking for fish. It's hard to find fault with the 78F set meal (not available Saturday evenings and Sundays) — salt cod with leeks and braised guinea fowl with cabbage. The other set meals (112–205F) are just as good. To sum up, we were completely won over by the talented young people who've injected new life into an old restaurant and brought it bang up to date.

FERRIÈRE-AUX-ÉTANGS (LA) 61450 (10KM S)

|●| AUBERGE DE LA MINE

Le Gué-Plat; take the D18, then the route de Domfront (D21) and turn left 1.5km further.
☎ 02.33.66.91.10 F 02.33.96.01.90
Closed Tuesday evenings, Wednesdays, at the beginning of January, and the beginning of September. **Car park.**

There are still lots of things around to remind you that this used to be a mining area. This large ivy-covered brick house, for example, was apparently once the miners' canteen. But times have changed and this delightful little place with its stylish décor is now a rather chic restaurant. Intimate, and ideal for a night out. The chef is very artistic — his dishes are as good to look at as they are to eat. Try the fricassee of langoustine served in a buckwheat crêpe, the veal sweetbreads with a Saint-Fouin sauce, and the caramelized apple on a sponge base. Cheapest set meal 90F (except weekends), others 125F, 140F, 165F and 230F. Cheerful, friendly staff.

GRANVILLE 50400

10% LE MICHELET**

5 rue Jules-Michelet.
☎ 02.33.50.06.55 F 02.33.50.12.25
Car park. TV.

Near the sea, a few steps from the casino and the sea-water therapy centre, this little hotel with an attractive white façade is just the kind of place we like. One of the nicest young couples you could possibly hope to meet will give you the kind of welcome you really ought to get more often. The bedrooms are simple but they're bright, very well kept, and all have a direct-dial telephone. Doubles 130F with basin and bidet, 220F with shower/wc, and 270–290F with bath. Breakfast 28F.

RESTAURANT LE PHARE

rue du Port.
☎ 02.33.50.12.94
Closed Tuesday evenings and Wednesdays out of season, and Dec 20–Jan 25. **Car park.**

Lunch served noon–2pm, dinner 7–9.30/10pm. You'll get a wonderful panoramic view of the fleet of fishing and sailing boats. Since the fish market is just yards away, you really couldn't expect the restaurant to specialize in anything but seafood. There's fillet of sea bream, pollack with butter sauce, and monkfish and cod with chive sauce. The medley of fish with a butter sauce more or less sums up the restaurant's philosophy of serving the freshest of produce at reasonable prices. Delicious seafood platter 184F. Set meals 68F (not available weekends), 85F, 115F, 138F, 210F and 340F. If you're hungry, in the mood for celebrating, and not too hard up, the 340F set meal comes with lobster. And if you don't have that kind of money, they also do a 45F fast *formule* of moules *marinière* and a jug of wine. All the desserts are home-made by the way. Children's set meal 42F.

L'ÉCHAUGUETTE

24 rue Saint-Jean.
☎ 02.33.50.51.87
Closed Thursdays except during school holidays, and for five weeks some time after November 11.

Lunch served noon–3pm, dinner 7pm–midnight. A pretty special little crêperie in the upper (or old) part of town among the maze of pretty little streets. The notice "Crêperie fine" just about sums it up. Even the very simple 12F crêpe with butter gives you a fairly good idea of the treats that lie ahead. Unobtrusive staff and a cosy atmosphere provide the perfect setting for sampling the house specialities, in particular the crêpes *gratinées* — try the one with scallops. Expect to spend less than 100F for a meal.

CHAMPEAUX 50530 (15KM S)

HÔTEL LES HERMELLES – RESTAURANT AU MARQUIS DE TOMBELAINE.

How to get there: take the D911 that runs along the coast.
☎ 02.33.61.85.94 F 02.33.61.21.52
Closed Tuesday evenings, Wednesdays, and in January.
Car park. TV. Disabled access.

A hotel on top of the Champeaux cliffs across from Cancale but on the Normandy coast and one of the most beautiful seascapes ever. Comfy double bedrooms 290F. The décor in the cosy dining room is a successful combination of stonework, panelling and beams. Good food. The chef's a disciple of Escoffier and does a wonderful sole soufflé, salt cod with warm *andouille*, and brill with winkles. Four set meals 98F, 155F, 230F and 350F. Children's set meal 50F. Half-board 280F per person.

HONFLEUR 14600

LA FERME DE LA GRANDE COUR**

Côte de Grâce; from place Sainte-Catherine take rue des Capucins, go up towards Côte de Grâce and then follow the arrows.
☎ 02.31.89.04.69 F 02.31.89.27.29
Car park. TV.

An old farmhouse (as you might have guessed from the name) in the heart of the countryside up above Honfleur. It's a really pleasant setting — orchards, horses, outdoor terrace — and very quiet. Bedrooms are quite large and regularly refurbished. They're done in pastel shades and flower patterns. Doubles 220F with shower/wc and 350–400F with bath. Half-board (520–700F for two) is compulsory at weekends and in season. The dining room's in an old barn that's been nicely converted. Simple well-made dishes, mainly seafood and fish. Set meals 105F, 180F and 230F.

10% HÔTEL DU DAUPHIN**

10 place Pierre-Berthelot (Centre); it's beside the church of Sainte-Catherine.
☎ 02.31.89.15.53 F 02.31.89.92.06
Closed in January. **TV.**

Reception staffed until 4pm. A little half-timbered hotel – the kind you often see in these parts. Try for a bedroom overlooking the church. Doubles 265F and 350F with shower/wc, 350F with bath and 600F for everything including a jacuzzi! The renovated rooms in the annexe are simpler and consequently cheaper. You'll be welcomed like one of the family.

10% ☗ |●| LES CASCADES*

17 place Thiers (Centre); it's just a few steps from the old harbour.
☎ 02.31.89.05.83 F 02.31.89.32.13
Closed Monday evenings and Tuesdays (except during the February school holidays, at Easter, and in July and August), and Nov 11–mid Feb. **TV**.

A rather basic hotel in a good location that's been run by the energetic Madame Cogen for the past 27 years. Cheapest double 200F with shower. Dinner compulsory in season. Set meals 80–185F. It's a pity the cooking doesn't quite come up to scratch. Seafood specialities. No reservations by phone.

☗ HÔTEL DES LOGES**

18 rue Brûlée (Centre).
☎ 02.31.89.38.26
TV.

This hotel has a slate-covered façade and is run by a lovely lady who'll make you feel at home. She's renovated it from top to bottom just the way she saw it one night in a dream and it's clear from the moment you step inside that here's somebody who loves decorating. You'll get lots of ideas for your own home, starting with the lovely candles on the mantelpiece beside the reception. The same spirit prevails in the bedrooms, which are decorated in warm colours and have been designed with comfort in mind. Of course, luxury doesn't come cheap but the prices aren't outrageous. Doubles 310–410F depending on the size. Charming welcome and unobtrusive staff.

☗ |●| HÔTEL LE BELVÉDÈRE**

36 rue Émile-Renouf (Centre).
☎ 02.31.89.08.13 F 02.31.89.51.40.
Car park.

We fell in love with the tiny garden of this beautiful hotel (formerly the house of a master craftsman) which offers peace and quiet and an escape from the crowded town centre and port in summer. About ten bedrooms 310–340F with shower or bath, all completely refurbished. Like all good hotels, it's often fully booked at the weekend. Set meals 98F, 138F, 198F and 280F. Specialities include seafood platter with vanilla, veal cutlets with Camembert, and John Dory with citrus fruit.

|●| RESTAURANT LE GAI LURON

20 pl. Sainte-Catherine
☎ 02.31.89.99.90
Closed Wednesday evenings and Thursdays.

This is not your typical Honfleur restaurant. Some people deplore its very existence but we love it. Sit out on the flower-filled terrace, weather permitting or in one of the pretty and very pleasant dining rooms. The friendly and helpful service is a good sign of what lies ahead as far as food is concerned. Granted, the repertoire's pretty standard but the produce is fresh and the preparation skilful and the end result is rather tasty. Lots of seafood and imaginative combinations like spinach salad with smoked salmon, skate with redcurrants, and haddock with cucumber and a chive sauce. Set meals 78F, 115 and 165F.

|●| LA TORTUE

36 rue de l'Homme-de-Bois (Centre); it's near the church of Sainte-Catherine.
☎ 02.31.89.04.93
Closed Tuesdays and mid Jan–mid Feb.

Service noon and 7pm. A friendly place that's well maintained. The staff will make you feel welcome. Mouthwatering set meals 99F, 135F and 178F. The cheapest one is excellent value for money especially since they've included the *trou normand* (a shot of Calvados halfway through the meal to aid the digestion). Panfried *foie gras* (very good), fillets of mullet à la *paysanne*, apples with butterscotch. A terrific place.

|●| AU P'TIT MAREYEUR

4 rue Haute (Centre).
☎ 02.31.98.84.23 F 02.31.89.99.32
Closed Monday evenings and Tuesdays.

Lunch served noon–2.30pm, dinner 7–9.30pm. The fine fish and seafood dishes in Nicolas Boyère's 120F *menu-carte* are full of flavour just the way we like them. He's an imaginative chef and 120F is a small price to pay for oysters simmered in a liquorice sauce, semi-salt cod with sea urchin flesh, and snails in puff pastry with *andouille*. Our favourite place in Honfleur.

HOULGATE 14510

☗ HOSTELLERIE NORMANDE**

11 rue E.-Deschanel (Centre).
☎ 02.31.28.77.77 F➜ 02.31.28.08.07
Disabled access.

This beautiful 19th century building covered in Virginia creeper is the oldest hotel in Houlgate and has been renovated throughout. The style is Baroque — the cherubs on the bedroom doors are rather flashy — but the rooms themselves are very comfy without being too expensive. Doubles 270–350F, depending on the time of the year. You'll get a nice welcome. Sit out in the lovely garden and enjoy a leisurely breakfast. You'll pay 89F for simple, satisfying dishes like calf's head and *andouille* wih mustard and there's another set meal at 129F.

SANTA CECILIA**

25 allées des Alliés.
☎ 02.31.28.71.71 F➜ 02.31.28.51.73
TV.

A pretty villa from the 1880s with the kind of atmosphere that evokes images of crinolines and turn-of-the-century swimming costumes. The 1900s dining room with its murals is a real work of art. You'll get a wonderful welcome from the owner (the perfect hostess!). Bedrooms are faultless, all different, and some have been furnished in traditional style. Doubles from 315F with shower/wc. An ideal place for a weekend break — or longer if you can afford it!

10% LE NORMAND

40 rue du Général-Leclerc (Centre).
☎ 02.31.24.81.81 F➜ 02.31.28.03.74
Closed Wednesdays and Thursdays out of season, December and January.

Service from noon and 7pm. A little restaurant that's good in every respect. The pleasant dining room is well set out and the copper pots and pans on the walls give the place a rustic charm — and they've got to be polished on a regular basis! Simple authentic dishes — stuffed mussels, sea snails, chicken, and fillet of duck in a Pommeau sauce — are prepared by the chef, who uses fresh produce from the market across the way. Set meals 75F, 98F, 130F and 160F. They also have rooms but we haven't tried these. doubles 190F with basin, 240F with shower/wc.

LISIEUX 14100

LA COUPE D'OR**

49 rue Pont-Mortain (Centre).
☎ 02.31.31.16.84 F➜ 02.31.31.35.60
Closed Friday evenings, Sunday evenings, and Jan 1–10 (except by reservation). **TV**.

A classic and well cared for hotel in the centre of a town that's often full of pilgrims. The bedrooms are clean and the hopelessly outdated 70s décor has a certain appeal. Lovely bathrooms. Doubles 280F with shower/wc or bath. Half-board, round about 250F, is compulsory for weekend stays of more than two nights. The cooking is fairly conventional and there are no surprises. Set meals 68F (weekday lunchtimes) and 88–180F offering classic Normandy dishes like John Dory with mussels, grilled lamb chops with herbs, seafood stew, and tripe *à la mode de Caen*.

10% HÔTEL DE LOURDES**

4 rue au Char (Centre).
☎ 02.31.31.19.48 F➜ 02.31.31.08.67
Car park. **TV**.

The bedrooms, all of which have TV, are simple but bright and well kept. Doubles 210–230F with shower/wc and 250F with bath. Rates drop by 10F in winter. Nice little hotel, popular with pilgrims.

10% AZUR HÔTEL***

15 rue au Char (Centre).
☎ 02.31.62.09.14 F➜ 02.31.62.16.06

A three-star hotel that's been refurbished from top to bottom and decorated in bright colours and flower patterns. Pleasant well-equipped bedrooms — they may lack the patina of age but you can't have everything. Nice staff. Doubles 300F with shower/wc, and 360–420F with bath. The breakfast room is very pretty.

AU VIEUX NORMAND

14 rue Henri-Chéron (Centre).
☎ 02.31.62.03.35
Closed Mondays except public holidays.

It's got everything — half-timbering, a cosy old dining room with a fireplace, and a wide range of appetizing dishes. The 56F set meal offers no fewer than seven starters and six main courses for you to choose from. The bacon omelette is tasty and the strawberry tart excellent. Other set meals 82F and 130F.The lunchtime *formule* at 46F offers a substantial helping of *pot au feu* or succulent ham in cider. Very quick service.

RESTAURANT AUX ACACIAS

13 rue de la Résistance (Centre).
☎ 02.31.62.10.95
Closed Sunday evenings, Mondays, two weeks in March, and the second fortnight in July. **Car park**.

Lunch served noon–2pm, dinner 7–9.30pm. It's hard to resist this good centrally located restaurant with its cosy, almost English décor — shades of soft green and cream, red and white gingham curtains, bunches of dried flowers and pretty trinkets — that looks as if it's straight out of a Laura Ashley catalogue. It's fresh, pleasant and imaginative, just like the cooking. Dishes like braised pigeon with a pepper and orange sauce, farmed rabbit *en crépine* or the ox cheek in wine-flavoured aspic cooked over a wood fire are an introduction to a world of new and sometimes disconcerting flavours. The desserts are a bit on the heavy side. Set meals range in price from 90F (not available weekends) to 280F. Efficient service with a smile.

MONT-SAINT-MICHEL (LE) 50170

10% HÔTEL DU GUESCLIN

Grande-Rue.
☎ 02.33.60.14.10 F 02.33.60.45.81

A well-maintained hotel that offers reasonable value for money when you consider the prices charged by its competitors. Comfortable and very clean doubles 250–420F. It has two dining rooms, take your pick. Downstairs you've got the brasserie with quick service and *formules express* at 50F and 60F. Upstairs you'll get a superb view of the bay, classic dishes and set meals 75–160F. Children's set meal 48F. Efficient service and pleasant staff (which is quite an achievement in these parts!).

BEAUVOIR 50170 (4KM S)

10% HÔTEL LE GUÉ DE BEAUVOIR*

route de Pontorson.
☎ 02.33.60.09.23
Closed Sept 30–Palm Sunday. **Car park**.

Most of the hotels in the area are pretty bland - but not this one. It's a handsome bourgeois-style building with lots of flowers standing in its own grounds next to the campsite of the same name. The bedrooms may be simple but they're very appealing (150–250F). Have breakfast (29F) in the pleasant conservatory.

PONTORSON 50170 (9KM S)

10% HÔTEL-RESTAURANT LE BRETAGNE**

59 rue Couesnon; take the D976 from the main street in the centre of town and go towards Rennes.
☎ 02.33.60.10.55 F 02.33.58.20.54
Closed Mondays and Jan 15–Feb 15. **Car park. TV**.

A wonderful welcome and friendly atmosphere await you in this 18th century coaching inn. The very pleasant bedrooms all have telephone and shower/wc or bath, Doubles 250–300F. Half-board 300F. You'll find a crowd of regulars in the restaurant, which has to be a good sign. The dishes are prepared with care and the chef uses only fresh ingredients. Set meals 70F (weekdays), 85F, 120F, 160F and 200F. Children's set meal 45F. Here, in no particular order, is a selection of what's available — *rillettes* of mackerel with a cucumber sauce, warm fish *terrine* with langoustine sauce, lamb sweetbreads and kidneys in a Bordeaux sauce, and warm goat's cheese with honey. All in all, you'll get very good value for money here.

SERVON 50170 (10KM SE)

10% AUBERGE DU TERROIR**

Centre; take the D107 — it's between Pontaubault and Pontorson.
☎ 02.33.60.17.92 F 02.33.60.35.26
Closed Wednesdays out of season and during the February school holidays. **Car park. TV**.

A lovely hotel in a quiet little village where you'll get lots of peace and quiet. It's been attractively refurbished by the friendly young owners, who've named the rooms after famous musicians and composers. In the old presbytery there are three nicely renovated rooms that range in price from 260F to 320F for the one that sleeps four, while the annexe has doubles with shower/wc at 240F. Pretty grounds with a tennis court. The pleasant dining room serves wonderful Périgord specialities like semi-cooked *foie gras* and breast of duck with honey and lots of fish dishes such as seafood stew and salmon with green cabbage. Set meals 84F, 120F, 165F and 240F.

CÉAUX 50220 (15KM E)

HÔTEL-RESTAURANT AU P'TIT QUINQUIN**

Les Forges; take the D275 in the direction of Avranches, then the D43 as far as the crossroads – from the village of Courtils, it's only another 2km.
☎ 02.33.70.97.20 F 02.33.70.97.42
Closed Sunday evenings, Mondays (except in season), Jan 7–Feb 15, and Nov 15–Dec 5. **Car park. TV**.

Lunch served noon–2pm, dinner 7–9.30pm. Far from the madding crowd. Doubles 155F with washing facilities, 225F with shower/wc and 235F with bath. Dinner, bed and breakfast 245F. Try for a room at the back since the ones overlooking the road are very noisy. The 72F set meal is good value for money, with dishes like fish *terrine* with two sauces and exquisite steamed pollack fillets with thyme. For 85F you'll get half a dozen six oysters or the chef's *terrine* with Cognac followed by salmon and pollack with a mild chilli sauce or fillet of salmon with a spinach sauce. Other set meals 96F, 130F and 169F.

MORTAGNE-AU-PERCHE 61400

10% HÔTEL DU TRIBUNAL**

4 place du Palais (Centre).
☎ 02.33.25.04.77 F 02.33.83.60.83
TV.

It's impossible not to fall for this handsome traditional Percheron house which dates back to the 13th century (some parts are 18th century). You'll almost believe you've travelled back in time, so rustic is the little square nearby. The hotel's façade doesn't seem to have changed since the end of the 19th century. Although it's been renovated throughout, the interior has lost nothing of its character even if it no longer has that well lived-in look. Doubles 260–280F. The rooms in the lovely annexe at the back are even quieter, come with bath, and overlook a tiny flower-filled courtyard. Yves Montand stayed here while they were shooting his last film *IP5*. Very good food. Set meals 85F, 100F, 125F and 170F. Try the *croustillant* of sausage, the trout with crayfish, the chicken fricassee with Camembert, or the langoustine omelette. A delightful place. It's a bit stylish of course but the warmth of the welcome will leave you in no doubt that this is still a friendly little village inn and you'll feel quite at home.

TOUROUVRE 61190 (15KM NE)

10% HÔTEL DE FRANCE**

19 rue du 13-Août-1944.
☎ 02.33.25.73.55 F 02.33.25.69.43
Closed Sunday evenings, Mondays, and one week at the end of December. **Car park**. **TV**. **Disabled access**.

Lunch served noon–2pm, dinner 7.30–9pm. The façade is uninspiring but this is a wonderful place. Proprietor Gilbert Feugueur, a charming young man who's passionate about this particular little corner of Perche, will be a very attentive host. His wife, Béatrice, gives added life and flavour to traditional Normandy cooking with dishes such as grilled sausage, trout with cider, veal chop with ceps and salad of skate with honey and raspberry vinegar. Set meals 70F (weekdays), 100F (perfection), and 130F; à la carte also available. The walls in the dining room are covered in old adverts on loan from the fascinating grocery museum next door. The wine list has a few good wines and they also have a wonderful selection of whiskies (one of Gilbert's passions!). There's dinner theatre once a month or so, with the actors moving backwards and forwards between the tables. There's also a *cave à chansons,* an idea that came from Quebec where so many local people emigrated to in the 17th century. Pleasant low-key bedrooms. The ones at the side or the back are quieter. Doubles 220F with shower and 275F with bath.

MORTAIN 50140

HÔTEL DE LA POSTE**

place des Arcades; it's a few steps from the famous waterfalls, opposite the collegiate church.
☎ 02.33.59.00.05 F 02.33.69.53.89
Closed Friday evenings, Saturdays, Sunday evenings, the first fortnight in February, and the second fortnight in October. **Car park**. **TV**. **Disabled access**.

It's an impressive granite building with bright refurbished bedrooms. Expect to pay 190–400F depending on facilities and location (you can have a view of the street or of the wonderful valley of Cance). Set meals 90F, 136F and 176F. À la carte you can get veal chop *manchoise*, fillet of brill with a cider flavoured *mousseline*, lobster salad with truffle vinaigrette and monkfish stew with Rhône valley wine.

ORBEC 14290

10% HÔTEL DE FRANCE**

152 rue Grande (Centre).
☎ 02.31.32.74.02 F 02.31.32.27.77
Closed Dec 20–Jan 25; restaurant closed Sunday evenings Sept–Easter. **Car park**. **TV**. **Canal+**. **Disabled access**.

A good little country hotel. When you set foot in the bar you'll really believe that time here stopped during the last century. And when there's a fire burning away in the magnificent fireplace, it really does feel as if you're experiencing the real France. Clean and more than adequate bedrooms to suit all tastes and pockets. Doubles 155F with washing facilities, 270F with shower/wc, 310F with bath and two suites for 420F. The owner's in charge of the cooking, which is plain and satisfying in accordance with local tradition. Try the salmon with a cream and white wine sauce, the trout *à l'orbecquoise* or the ox tongue with a spicy sauce. *Menu du jour* 70F, other set meals 90F, 122F and 170F.

OUISTREHAM-RIVA-BELLA 14150

10% ⌂ |●| HÔTEL-RESTAURANT LE NORMANDIE – LE CHALUT**

71 av. Michel-Cabieu.
☎ 02.31.97.19.57 F➜ 02.31.97.20.07
Closed Sunday evenings and Mondays Nov–March, and Dec 21–Jan 9. **Car park**. **TV**.

Lunch served 12.15–2pm, dinner 7.15–10pm. Two classic hotels facing each other near the harbour, both refurbished throughout and attractively decorated and both run by an energetic young couple, Arielle and Christian Maudouit. Doubles 250–320F all with shower/wc or bath and telephone. You can get wonderful food in the *Normandie*'s stylish restaurant but it tends to be rather expensive. Still, it's one of the best places to eat in the region. Set meals 88–340F. The other hotel has a salad bar which is very popular with the local youngsters who come for the *menu bistrot* and the Italian dishes. Good variety of set meals 35–76F.

|●| LE BRITANNIA

rue des Dunes; it's opposite the ferry.
☎ 02.31.96.88.26 F➜ 02.31.96.93.10
Closed Mondays (except Easter–mid October) and in January. **Car park**.

An unpretentious brasserie with rather faded décor. They don't pressure you to spend more than you want to.The cheapest set meal — perfectly decent — is 65F. The service comes with a smile, the wine is cheap. *Formules* 105F, 115F and 168F, and an appealing seafood platter for 90F. What more could you want? You'll get a delicious *zakouski* (selection of fish and vegetables) with your aperitif and it's almost as big as a starter. Champagne 35F. A very good little place.

|●| RESTAURANT LE MÉTROPOLITAIN**

1 route de Lion; it's near the post office.
☎ 02.31.97.18.61
Closed Monday evenings and Tuesdays Oct–April inclusive. **Car park**.

Parisians will feel right at home here since it's decorated to look like a 1930s metro! Local produce and seafood are cooked to perfection and attractively presented as you'll see from the cold whiting and crab soufflé, the fillet of mullet with saffron sauce, and the sole with chives. Set meals 90F, 147F and 192F.

PONT-L'ÉVÊQUE 14130

|●| RESTAURANT LA POMME D'OR

52 rue Saint-Michel (West).
☎ 02.31.64.01.98
Closed Tuesdays (except in summer), and Feb 15–28. **Car park**.

Service noon–9pm. This little bar cum restaurant with its old-fashioned dining room offers a surprisingly wide selection of fresh plain dishes — ten in fact. The chef is sociable — you won't find him hiding away in the kitchen. Try the salt pork with lentils, which you hardly ever get in restaurants nowadays, or tripe cooked in the local way. House desserts. Set meals 60F and 90F.

|●| AUBERGE DE LA TOUQUES

place de l'Église (Centre).
☎ 02.31.64.01.69
Closed Monday evenings and Tuesdays (except in August), Jan 2–25, and Dec 3–26. **Car park**. **Disabled access**.

Lunch served noon–2.30pm, dinner 7–9.30pm. A handsome building with typical Normandy architecture standing on the river bank near the village church. It's a good place for sampling all the classics of Normandy cooking. Veal chop *normande*, brill with apples, *boudin* of monkfish and lobster flan are just some of the dishes that await you. Set meals 78F, 105F and 170F. Attentive service from the pleasant waitresses.

DRUBEC 14130 (8KM W)

|●| LA HAIE TONDUE

take the D58 and it's 2km south of Beaumont-en-Auge at the N175 junction.
☎ 02.31.64.85.00
Closed Monday evenings (except public holidays and in August), Tuesdays (except public holidays), one week in February or March, one week at the start of October, and one week at Christmas. **Car park**.

This beautiful old house, covered in ivy, offers very good food at reasonable prices. The cheapest set meal (which will cost you a total of 115F) is just as good as the more expensive ones at 158F and more. In our humble opinion, this is the best value for money in the area. Pleasant décor, faultless service, good wine list and perfectly prepared dishes such as chicken with balsamic vinegar, *paupiettes* of sole with lettuce *coulis*, and fillets of duck with apricots. For your starter, how about trying the wonderful *compote* of rabbit with onion marmalade? Try not to be there when the coach parties roll in one after the other.

SAINT-LÔ 50000

10% ⌂ |●| L'AUBERGE NORMANDE

20 rue de Villedieu (Centre).
☎ 02.33.05.10.89 F➜ 02.33.05.37.26
Closed Mondays, Dec 22–Jan 12.

Élisa and Sylvain Maquaire, who completely refurbished the inn when they took it over, will make you feel very welcome. Sylvain takes particular care over the preparation of his dishes, and his repertoire includes ravioli with a filling of sea bass, marinated salmon *à la suédoise*, crab bisque, mussel soup with saffron and duck breast with honey and Pommeau. Cheapest set meal 58F (weekday lunchtimes). Others 82F, 120F and 168F. Doubles 139F with basin and 159F with shower/wc.

10% ⌂ ARMORIC HÔTEL*

15-17 rue de la Marne (North).
☎ 02.33.05.61.32 F➜ 02.33.05.12.68
Car park. TV. Canal+. Disabled access.

You'll get a very warm welcome in this quiet hotel and excellent value for money. The comfy bedrooms are tastefully decorated and all have phone and TV. Doubles 160F with basin and 230F with bath/wc. If you've had a tiring journey, you'll love numbers 16 and 21, both of which have a whirlpool bath (280F). Number 2 is ideal for newly weds and number 18 is bright and cheerful. One of our favourites in la Manche. Breakfast 25F.

|●| LE BISTROT

42 rue du Neufbourg; it's halfway between the town hall and the church of Sainte-Croix.
☎ 02.33.57.19.00
Closed Monday evenings and Sundays.

There's a good atmosphere here, the kind you often get in cosy bistros, and that may have something to do with the fact that this is where the fans of the Caen Football Club gather. It's a little restaurant that caters for customers who want a meal that has to be quick but good. You'll find lots of home cooking with dishes like shepherd's pie, calf's head *gribiche* (with mayonnaise, capers, gherkins and herbs) and *teurgoule* (a type of rice pudding). Dish of the day 39F, starter 30F. Choice of three *formules* — main dish and dessert (62F), starter and dessert (51F) or a very hearty *menu complet* (69F). Good value for money.

|●| LE PÉCHÉ MIGNON

84 rue du Maréchal-Juin (East); go towards Bayeux — it's well away from the town centre.
☎ 02.33.72.23.77 F➜ 02.33.72.27.58
Closed Mondays and Saturday lunchtimes.

Hushed atmosphere. The young chef has chosen to offer top-of-the-range gourmet food. Very attentive service — in fact it's almost obsequious. And the food is absolutely marvellous. Set meals 85F, 135F, 168F and 198F. Even the cheapest one is pretty impressive — fricassee of roasted sea snails with basil flavoured oil, fillet of hare with Madras curry, and sabayon of *apples* and cinnamon. Children's set meal 45F.

SAINT-PIERRE-DE-SEMILLY 50810 (9KM E)

|●| RESTAURANT LES GLYCINES

Le Calvaire; it's by the side of the D972.
☎ 02.33.05.02.40
Closed Sunday evenings, Mondays and February holidays.

Lunch served noon–2.30pm, dinner 7–9pm. A converted farmhouse with a dining room decorated in shades of green and salmon-pink. The tables are well spaced out. In summer you can eat in the wonderful walled garden. Chef Philippe Fouchard is good in the kitchen and offers refined and often creative dishes. Set meals 98F (except Sundays), 158F, 198F and 298F. It's a bit of an institution and the prices reflect that of course.

SAINT-VAAST-LA-HOUGUE 50550

⌂ |●| HÔTEL DE FRANCE – RESTAURANT LES FUCHSIAS**

20 rue du Maréchal-Foch; it's less than two minutes from the harbour.
☎ 02.33.54.42.26 F➜ 02.33.43.46.79
Closed Mondays out of season, Tuesday lunchtimes Nov–March inclusive, January and February.

Lunch served noon–2pm, dinner 7–9.15pm (7.30–9.45pm in summer). Our favourite place in the Cotentin. Bedrooms are very pretty and most overlook a little garden of Eden — the fuchsia is a hundred years old and grew in a particularly mild microclimate in the valley of Saire. Every year they have chamber music concerts in the garden in the last ten days of August. Doubles 155F with basin, from 280F with shower/wc, and 375–410F with bath. The most attractive rooms are in the garden – the one with the little suite (485F) stands out in particular. Half-board (225–365F per person) is compulsory in July and August. This is also one of the best restaurants in the eastern part of la Manche. The cheapest set meal is 82F (weekdays) and you'll get generous helpings of incredibly good things like very fresh *noisettes* of Saint-Vaast oysters followed by either *croustillant* of sea trout with a seaweed and butter sauce or fish *choucroute*, and apples in puff pastry with a Calvados flavoured sauce. Other set meals 125F, 175F, 205F and 265F. The children's 58F set meal is pretty special. The chef still gets produce from the family farm. Pretty trompe l'œil paintings in the conservatory.

SÉES 61500

10% ☗ THE GARDEN HÔTEL**

12 [bis] rue des Ardrillers; it's 400m from the cathedral.
☎ 02.33.27.98.27 ➡ 02.33.28.90.07
Car park. TV. Disabled access.

This ivy-covered hotel has quite a history. First it was an orphanage and then it became a hotel run by an Australian who has since gone back home. The present owners have held onto the Anglo-Saxon name. Things are remarkably quiet around here – the nuns in the convent next door don't throw wild parties every night of the week! And to return the favour, none of the bedrooms faces the convent. Instead, they all overlook a flower-filled garden dotted with trees. Basic bedrooms with a nice retro touch. Excellent value for money – doubles range in price from 160F with basin to 220F with bath. Staff are perfectly lovely. And there's an amusing collection of religious knick-knacks in keeping with the spiritual atmosphere. No restaurant.

10% ☗ |●| HÔTEL-RESTAURANT LE DAUPHIN**

31 place des Halles; it's in the heart of the old town, opposite the corn exchange.
☎ 02.33.27.80.07 ➡ 02.33.28.80.33
Closed Sunday evenings and Mondays out of season.
Car park. TV. Canal+.

A typical Normandy house (half-timbered of course). The Dauphin of France slept in a room with a four-poster bed in the gabled turret and if the two of you are in the mood for splashing out, it's yours for 500F. The other rooms – rustic and rather plush – aren't bad either. Doubles from 300F with shower/wc. Although there's a stylish feel to this place, it still generates a simple and genuinely homely atmosphere. It's got the best restaurant in town, no two ways about it. The kitchen produces great local dishes using only the freshest ingredients and without making the food unnecessarily complicated. There's *cassolette* of scallops and langoustine, fillet of local trout, escalope of brill with noodles and fillet of duck with cider. Wonderful desserts and an interesting selection of tea and coffee. When summer comes along you can sit out on the pretty little terrace next to the imposing corn exchange. On weekdays, the cheapest set meal is 80F (wine included).

THURY-HARCOURT 14220

☗ |●| HÔTEL DU VAL D'ORNE

9 route d'Aunay-sur-Odon.
☎ 02.31.79.70.81 ➡ 02.31.79.16.12
Closed Saturday lunchtimes in season, Friday evenings and Saturdays out of season, during the February school holidays and at Christmas. **Car park. TV**

Lunch served noon–2pm, dinner 7–9pm. Deep in the lush countryside of Suisse normande. It's clean and comforting, just like the surrounding countryside with its cows, hedges, hills and rivers. The rooms are basic but they've been totally refurbished. Doubles 130F with basin and 200F with shower/wc or bath. The dining room is decorated in rustic Normandy style, with naive paintings on the walls depicting scenes from country life. Cheapest set meal 52.50F (weekday lunchtimes). Others 72–151F.

TROUVILLE-SUR-MER 14360

10% ☗ LES SABLETTES**

15 rue Paul-Besson (Centre); it's not far from the casino.
☎ 02.31.88.10.66 ➡ 02.31.88.59.06
Closed in December (except weekends) and January.

Reception staffed 8am–10pm. Run by a charming lady, this place is as pretty as can be and could almost be described as a guest house. Very cosy atmosphere, comfortable lounge, old wooden staircase and very very clean. Low-key stylish doubles, ranging in price from 240F with basin/wc and TV to

360F with bath. Good value for money for Trouville.

10% ☗ |●| HÔTEL-RESTAURANT LE DOULT**

4 rue des Bains (Centre).
☎ 02.31.88.10.27 ➡ 02.31.88.33.79
Closed Mondays and mid Nov–mid Dec.

Lunch served noon–2pm, dinner 7–9.30pm. A little restaurant with fresh pleasant décor in the centre of Trouville. Set meals 98F, 125F, 165F and 210F and lots of good local dishes like warm langoustine salad with langoustine bisque, lamb's head, poached skate and mullet with pesto. It also has six clean well-kept bedrooms. Doubles 280–350F with shower/wc.

|●| LES VAPEURS

160 bd Fernand-Moureaux (Centre); it's beside the town hall, opposite the fish market.
☎ 02.31.88.15.24 ➡ 02.31.88.20.58.

Lunch served noon–1pm. This is undoubtedly the best known brasserie in Trouville. Although it opened its doors in 1927, it has more of a 50s atmosphere thanks to the neon signs that were added during that decade. All the American actors in Deauville for the film festival come here – Jack Nicholson's a regular – and since it's always full you can reasonably assume that success hasn't led to any decline in quality. You must try the house specialities – steamed local mussels and freshly cooked prawns. Everything is fresh since the fishing boats are only minutes away. The tripe's good too, especially with a nice little glass of Saumur. Don't worry about your lack of celebrity status – you'll get the same kind of welcome as Jack. It's difficult to give you an idea of prices as there are no set meals, but you can expect to pay 50–120F for a main course. You'll definitely have to book at the weekend – unless you decide to get the day off to a good start by arriving at 10am for a few oysters in Muscadet.

|●| RESTAURANT LES MOUETTES

11 rue des Bains (Centre).
☎ 02.31.98.06.97 ➡ 02.31.88.42.22

A fish restaurant in a busy little street with décor that's reminiscent of what you'd find in Parisian bistros. Pleasant welcome. You'll really enjoy the *gratin* of salmon and Chavignol (a mild goat's cheese) and the fish *pot au feu.* Set meals 68F and 129F (drink included in the latter).

|●| RESTAURANT LE CHALUTIER

3 rue de Verdun (Centre); it's opposite the fish market on a steep little street.
☎ 02.31.88.36.39
Closed Tuesday evenings and Wednesdays out of season, and Jan 15–Feb 15.

Trouville and Deauville are two completely different towns and this cosy little restaurant makes that point very nicely. The décor in all three of the tiny interlinked dining rooms has a maritime theme. Fish, seafood, and a few good regional specialities. Set meals 90–170F. It's advisable to book, especially in season.

|●| RESTAURANT LA PETITE AUBERGE

7 rue Carnot (Centre); it's in a little street that starts at place du Maréchal-Foch, in front of the casino.
☎ 02.31.88.11.07
Closed Tuesdays and Wednesdays out of season.

Lunch served noon–2.15pm, dinner 7–10pm. This restaurant could only be found in Normandy, given the style of cooking and the décor (which is rather pretty, with lots of plates and copper pots and pans on the walls). No à la carte menu. The set meals (123–259F) change with the season and, given the quality of the food, represent quite good value for money. We liked the braised *andouillette* with potatoes, the roast monkfish with local ham and the *pain perdu* (something like French toast) with soft fruit *sabayon*. Nice welcome and efficient service.

|●| BISTROT LES QUATRE CHATS

8 rue d'Orléans (Centre).
☎ 02.31.88.94.94
Closed Wednesdays and Thursdays out of season.

If you think it looks a bit out of place in this part of Trouville, then you're spot on! Anybody who's anybody in Paris comes here, and there's at least one famous face in the photo that adorns the business card of Serge and Muriel Salmon. Have a look at it and at the dining room with its little bistro tables and old rose décor. It's packed with books, postcards, photos and newspapers, and has a wonderful percolator sitting on the counter. The chef has spiced up the classical dishes by adding a few unexpected flavours. Lovers of traditional food will appreciate the leg of lamb *de 7-heures* (supposedly cooked for seven hours) but might not be so keen on the breast of duck with ginger. The *carbonnade flamande* (beef braised in beer), the lamb curry and the pig's trotters stuffed with *foie gras* are all worth trying too The home-made bread is a nice little touch. Expect to pay 150–200F.

VILLEDIEU-LES-POÊLES 50800

10% ⌂ |●| HÔTEL SAINT-PIERRE ET SAINT-MICHEL

12 place de la République (Centre).
☎ 02.33.61.00.11 F 02.33.61.06.52
Closed Friday evenings mid Nov–mid March, and in January. **Secure parking**. **TV**

Service from noon and 7pm. An attractive hotel full of character with a hushed and cosy atmosphere. All the bedrooms are comfortable and individually decorated. If you're looking for a quick bite to eat try the brasserie, which has a fast 82F set meal (weekdays). For the gourmets there's an elegant dining room offering set meals at 115F and 147F. Very refined traditional Normandy dishes including scallops with asparagus tips in a dill-flavoured sauce, *andouillette* with grain mustard, and ham on the bone with Pommeau. Doubles cost 250–280F in high season and 235–265F out of season. A very good place.

⌂ |●| LE FRUITIER**

place des Costils (Centre).
☎ 02.33.90.51.00 F 02.33.90.51.01
Closed Dec 20–Jan 2. **Car park**. **TV**. **Canal+**. **Disabled access**.

Lunch served noon–2pm, dinner 7–9pm. A modern hotel with very spacious and well laid out bedrooms. Doubles 260F with shower/wc and 280F with bath. The dining room has a lovely thick carpet and frescoes depicting country scenes. Set meals start at 83F. The one at 114F offers a fish crêpe in a gratinéd sauce and salmon *à l'unilatérale* (which means that the fish is grilled only on one side - don't worry though, it's thoroughly cooked). There are other set meals at 159F and 174F, a fast *formule* at 66F and a children's set meal at 45F.

GOUVETS 50420 (15KM NE)

|●| RESTAURANT LES BRUYÈRES

How to get there: take the N175 towards Caen.
☎ 02.33.51.69.82.
Closed Sundays. **Car park**. **Disabled access**.

A fairly modern roadside restaurant that doesn't look particularly appealing from the outside. But, as we keep telling you, don't judge by appearances. The staff make you feel welcome, there's a spring-like atmosphere and you get excellent value for money. Set meals are 68F, 98F and 140F, and there's also a very good fast *formule* (main course plus terrific dessert) for 80F. The main courses change every week depending on what the market has to offer. When we were there, for example, they had escalope of salmon with fresh pasta, rabbit *à la provençale* and lamb stew with baby vegetables. We particularly liked the pastries they had for dessert — wickedly good!

HAMBYE 50450 (20KM N)

10% ⌂ |●| AUBERGE DE L'ABBAYE D'HAMBYE**

route de l'Abbaye.
☎ 02.33.61.42.19 F 02.33.61.00.85
Closed Sunday evenings (except in July and August), Mondays (except public holidays), Feb 10–25, and the first fortnight in October. **Car park**. **TV**.

A quiet little hotel in leafy surroundings with pretty and comfortable bedrooms. Doubles 260–280F. The whole place is extremely well cared for. Moreover, Micheline and Jean Allain are wonderful hosts and provide delicious regional dishes such as Burgundy snails *à l'alsacienne*, fish soup, seafood platter, kebabs of local lamb grilled over a wood fire, and rack of lamb (for two). And the house crêpes are great. Set meals 98F, 158F, 188F and 248F.

VIRE 14500

⌂ |●| HÔTEL DE FRANCE**

4 rue d'Aignaux (Centre).
☎ 02.31.68.00.35 F 02.31.68.22.65
Closed Dec 20–Jan 10. **Car park**. **TV**. **Canal+**. **Disabled access**.

A large and fairly plush looking hotel, built from the local granite. Comfy refurbished bedrooms. Doubles range in price from 200F with shower/wc to 300F with bath. Try for one at the back as it'll be quieter and give you a marvellous view of the small wooded valleys. In the restaurant, the local *andouille*, made right here in Vire, is a must. There are six set meals (58–220F) offering dishes such as *savarin* of fish with a warm chive sauce, veal cutlet *archiduc* (with paprika and cream), veal sweetbreads, and tripe *à la mode de Caen*. The *Hôtel Saint-Pierre* on the other side of the square is run by the same people. It's cheaper but not as nice, and it's popular with groups. To be avoided.

SAINT-MARTIN-DE-TALLEVENDE 14500 (1KM W)

10% LE MARTILLY

6 place de Martilly.
☎ 02.31.68.05.26
Closed Mondays. **Car park**. **TV**.

A sweet little place with blue bedrooms that have been completely refurbished. And it's not expensive. Doubles 190F with shower (breakfast included), studio flats 330F. Friendly welcoming new owners who make sure everything runs smoothly. You can enjoy the terrace in summer.

HÔTEL-RESTAURANT LE RELAIS NORMAND

22 place de Martilly.
☎ 02.31.68.08.67
Closed Saturdays out of season. **TV**.

You can't miss this ivy covered building, a coaching inn built in the reign of Napoléon III, since there's a big old cart sitting just outside. Unfortunately they have just one double with bath (190F). The others come with basin (160F). The restaurant offers a better deal, with set meals at 52F, 80F (three courses) and 125F. The owner deals with the best local suppliers and his tripe is a world-beater, his *andouille* comes from Vire (naturally), and his cheese is the best there is. And the cider is some of Normandy's best. A splendid establishment. It's popular with the locals which is, needless to say, a good sign.

SAINT-GERMAIN-DE-TALLEVENDE 14500 (5KM S)

L'AUBERGE SAINT-GERMAIN

☎ 02.31.68.24.13
Closed Sunday evenings, Mondays and during the February school holidays. **Car park**.

Lunch served noon–2pm, dinner 7–10pm. An attractive inn standing in the square of this delightful village. It's made from the local granite that's so typical of the area. Cosy welcoming dining room with a fireplace and low beams. Quick service with a smile. The chef gives local dishes the starring role and offers things like braised ham with Pommeau, chicken fricassee with cider (the chicken is free range), and *andouillette* of sole. Set meals 75F (weekdays), 95F, 140F and 170F. In short, good local dishes that are well prepared and represent very good value for money. When summer comes along you can eat on the little terrace.

BÉNY-BOCAGE (LE) 14350 (14.5KM N)

10% LE CASTEL NORMAND**

How to get there: take the D577 towards Caen for 9km then left onto the D56 for 2km.
☎ 02.31.68.76.03 Fax 02.31.68.63.58
Closed Sunday evenings, Mondays, and in February. **Car park**. **TV**.

Lunch served 12.15–1.45pm, dinner 7.30–9.30pm. A lovely building with lots of character in a square near the handsome covered market. And though this isn't exactly the seaside, the owners have chosen to decorate entirely in blue. Refined décor that can only be described as chic. You eat at round tables, which may seem like a minor detail but in fact has a lot to do with the cosy atmosphere. The cooking evokes the same kind of reaction as the décor and is full of flavours that come as a bit of a surprise in this part of the world. The chef is as good as any in the country when it comes to combining ingredients. Dishes such as breast of duck with dried fruit, monkfish with bacon, fillet of beef with morels and crown roast of lamb with lemon thyme are worth trying. Set meals 85F (except weekends), 138F, 178F and 245F. If you want to stay, the rooms are in keeping with the rest of the establishment. Doubles 300F with shower/wc or bath. First-class service.

Haute-Normandie

27 Eure

76 Seine-Maritime

ANDELYS (LES) 27700

HÔTEL DE NORMANDIE**

1 rue Grande, Le Petit Andely.
☎ 02.32.54.10.52 F 02.32.54.25.84
Closed December; restaurant closed Wednesday evenings and Thursdays. **Car park**. **TV**.

Lunch served noon–2.30pm, dinner 8–9.30pm. Run by the same family for several decades, this large hotel, a traditional Normandy building, is the ideal place if you fancy an enjoyable weekend with lots of good food on the banks of the Seine. Set meals 105F (daily)–175F and à la carte. The chef's specialities include monkfish stew with Pommeau, salmon *boudin*, and a variation on the *trou normand* – this is usually a shot of Calvados served between courses to aid the digestion but here it comes in the form of a Calvados sorbet. You can laze about in the little garden for hours on end admiring the Seine. Doubles decorated in typical country style (200–300F). Friendly welcome.

HÔTEL DE LA CHAÎNE D'OR***

27 rue Grande, Le Petit Andely; it's on the banks of the Seine opposite the church.
☎ 02.32.54.00.31 F 02.32.54.05.68
Closed Sunday evenings, Mondays and January.
Car park. **TV**.

Service noon–2pm and 7.30–9.30pm. You'll get lots of peace and quiet in this long, low and solidly built hotel with a unique riverside location. Built in 1751, it gets its name from the chain that stretched from the riverbank to the nearby island, beyond which point tolls had to be paid. It was nicknamed the "Chaîne d'Or" because it brought in so much money. The hotel may be rather luxurious but the easy-going attitude of the staff makes you feel quite at home. Biggest doubles 510–740F. The ones overlooking the Seine are tastefully decorated and furnished whereas the others are more modern. The wonderful dining room has a view of the barges and a fire is lit when there's a nip in the air. And believe it or not, there's a signed photo of Ronald Reagan on the wall. One of the good restaurants in this part of the world.

BERNAY 27300

10% HÔTEL D'ANGLETERRE ET DU CHEVAL BLANC*

10 rue du Général-de-Gaulle (West); it's in the main street opposite the post office, near place Derou.
☎ 02.32.43.12.59 F 02.32.43.63.26
Secure parking. **TV**.

Service 11.45am–2.30pm and 7–10.30pm. They added the "Angleterre" after a visit from Edward VII in 1908. They had stabling for 300 horses in the courtyard at that time. The hotel, which has been run by the same family since 1926, is beginning to show its age though it still has lots of character, and the present owner is gradually trying to get all the bedrooms back into shape – a mammoth task, since there are so many of them. The ones with bath are the nicest (230F), especially number 23 which overlooks the garden of the music school next door. Madame does the cooking, using fresh produce to prepare classic dishes. Set meals 75F (except Sundays) to 180F.

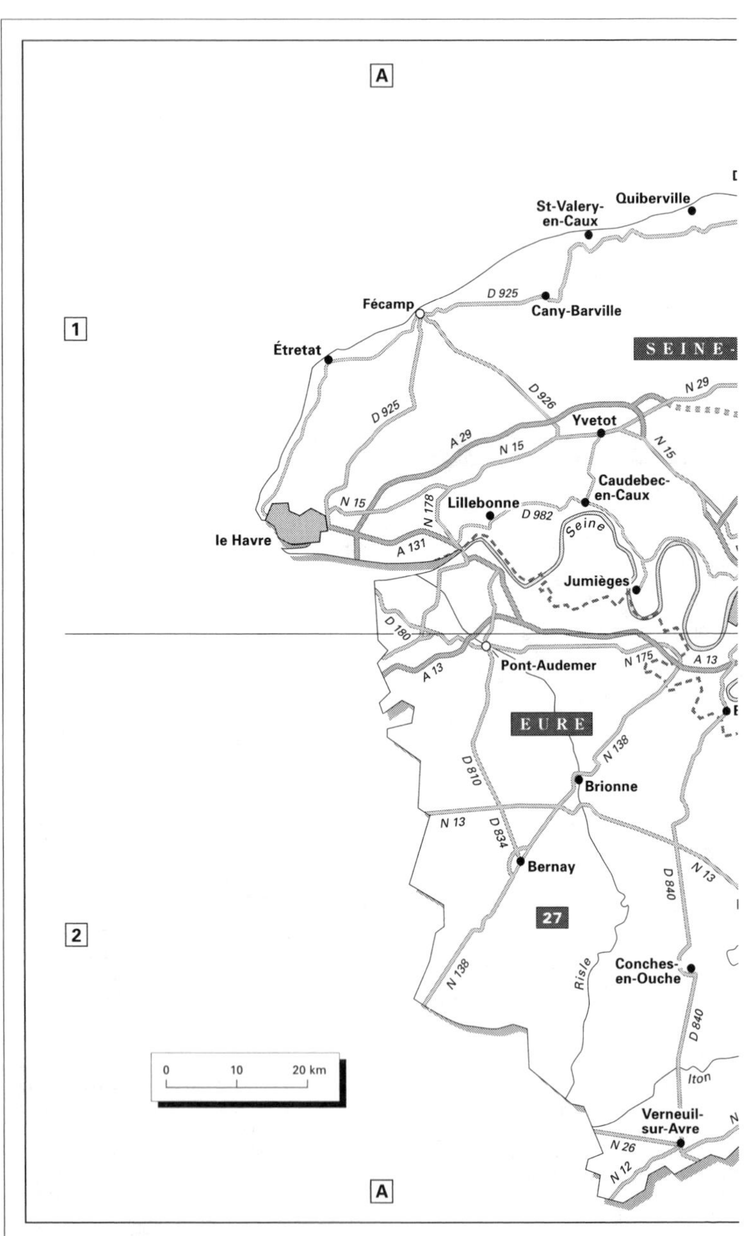
A
1
2
St-Valery-
en-Caux
Quiberville
D 925
Fécamp
Cany-Barville
Étretat
SEINE-
D 926
N 29
D 925
Yvetot
A 29
N 15
N 15
Caudebec-
en-Caux
N 15
N 178
Lillebonne
D 982
Seine
le Havre
A 131
Jumièges
D 180
Pont-Audemer
N 175
A 13
A 13
EURE
N 138
D 810
Brionne
N 13
D 834
Bernay
D 840
N 13
27
N 138
Risle
Conches-
en-Ouche
D 840
0
10
20 km
Iton
Verneuil-
sur-Avre
N 26
N 12
A

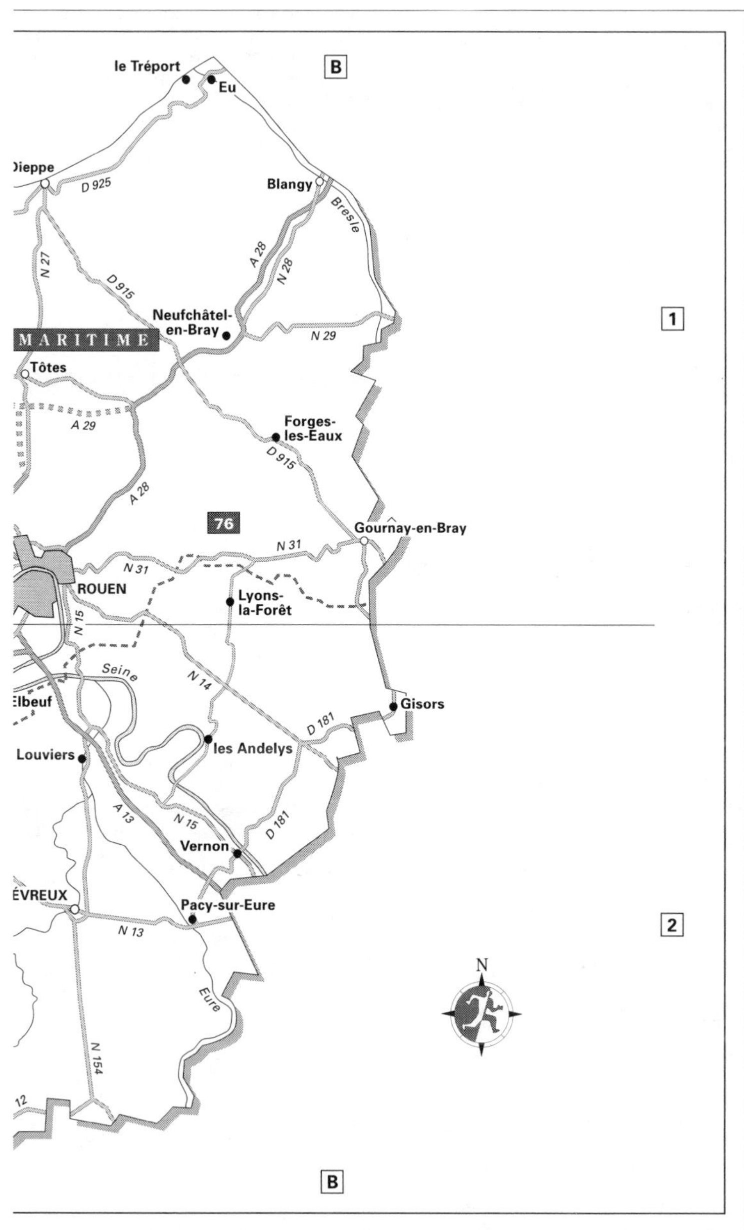
B
le Tréport
Eu
Dieppe
D 925
Blangy
Bresle
A 28
N 28
N 27
D 915
Neufchâtel-
en-Bray
N 29
1
MARITIME
Tôtes
A 29
Forges-
les-Eaux
D 915
A 28
76
Gournay-en-Bray
N 31
N 31
ROUEN
Lyons-
la-Forêt
N 15
Seine
N 14
Elbeuf
Gisors
D 181
les Andelys
Louviers
A 13
N 15
D 181
Vernon
ÉVREUX
Pacy-sur-Eure
N 13
2
N
Eure
N 154
12
B

10% ⌂ |●| LE LION D'OR**

48 rue du Général-de-Gaulle (Centre); it's in the main street.
☎ 02.32.43.12.06 ➡ 02.32.46.60.58
Restaurant closed Sunday evenings (in winter) and Monday lunchtimes. **Car park**. **TV**. **Canal+**. **Disabled access**.

A renovated former coaching inn. The low-key décor in the bedrooms is fairly unimaginative but it's all very clean and the staff make you feel welcome. Doubles 220F with shower/wc and 240F with bath. The restaurant (02.32.44.23.85), run by different people, offers set meals at 75F (except Sundays and holidays), 100F (good value), 135F and 165F. Specialities include fillet of trout with Camembert, panfried oyster mushrooms, and fish (which varies according to what has been landed at Cherbourg or Caen). In France each day of the year is named after a saint and the menu that's posted up outside will tell you just what saint's day it is.

|●| LA FERME D'ANTAN

27 rue Gabriel-Vallée (West); it's on the corner of rue Follope, the pedestrian street where all the secondhand shops are.
☎ 02.32.43.45.12
Closed Tuesday evenings, Wednesdays and Nov 1–15.

Service noon–2pm and 7–9pm. Warm, friendly atmosphere. The young owner looks after the cooking while her husband makes sure everything runs smoothly in the dining room and that their guests are well looked after. Light tasty cooking and set meals from 76F (except Sundays and public holidays). There are a number of things you really must try here and a good way of doing that is to have the 185F set meal, which consists of sautéd scallops with leeks, veal sweetbreads *à la normande*, cheese platter and dessert. If that's a bit too expensive for you, you can just have the starter and main course (or main course and dessert) for 112F. They've got a little terrace for use in summer.

SAINT-AUBIN-LE-VERTUEUX 27300 (4KM S)

⌂ |●| L'HOSTELLERIE DU MOULIN FOURET

☎ 02.32.43.19.95 ➡ 02.32.45.55.50
Closed Sunday evenings and Mondays. **Car park**.

It's advisable to book if you want to eat in this 16th century windmill that stands in spacious grounds on the banks of the Charentonne. François Deduit creates imaginative dishes and sauces using fresh and seasonal local produce. He offers very simple dishes alongside more elaborate ones and his specialities are panfried *andouille* (a type of sausage) with Camembert, *croustillant* of veal sweetbreads with a port-flavoured sauce, and turbot with a vermouth sauce on a bed of and a fennel. And for dessert? How about iced fondant of preserved ginger with dark chocolate flakes, *montgolfière* of fruit with wild strawberry liqueur, or apple surprise with cider-flavoured caramel? Top class service. Set meals 100F (available every day), 158F and 295F. You can go fly-fishing nearby and, if you'd like to stay, they have bedrooms for about 250F. We simply fell in love with the place.

SAINT-QUENTIN-DES-ISLES 27270 (4KM S)

|●| RESTAURANT LA POMMERAIE

N138.
☎ 02.32.45.28.88 ➡ 02.32.44.69.00
Closed Sunday evenings and Mondays.

Lunch served noon–2pm, dinner 7.30–9pm. A long low building with a neo-classical façade set back from the road. Stylish décor. The large dining room is both fresh and bright and has a view of the garden and ducks splashing about in the pond. The idea here is for guests to relax and forget about the stress brought on by driving. You'll be served warm appetizers as you wait for the 145F set meal. We especially liked the monkfish *risotto* with cider and saffron and the fruit *bavarois* that followed the cheese.

BRIONNE 27800

10% ⌂ |●| HÔTEL AQUILON**

9 route de Calleville; it's 500m from the centre – head for the keep.
☎ 02.32.44.81.49 ➡ 02.32.44.38.83
Car park. **TV**. **Disabled access**.

A large brick bourgeois-style building with a garden, up by the 11th century keep. Doubles 280F with shower/wc and 320F with bath. No two rooms are the same and there's a nice mini suite with sloping ceilings on the second floor. The ones with bath in the main building are lovely, especially number 3, which is very cheerful and has a view of the valley on one side and of the garden on the other. Homy atmosphere. On weekdays, they have a 90F set meal featuring regional dishes. If you're not staying in the hotel, you'll have to order this in advance.

☗ |●| HÔTEL-RESTAURANT L'AUBERGE DU VIEUX DONJON**

place Fremont-des-Essarts (Centre).
☎ 02.32.44.80.62 F 02.32.45.83.23
Closed Sunday evenings and Mondays out of season, and Oct 15–beginning of Nov. **Secure parking**. **TV**.

A large half-timbered inn that respects local tradition. Rooms overlook the garden and you can expect to pay 260F with shower/wc and 280F with bath. Have breakfast or pre-dinner drinks on the courtyard terrace. Cheapest set meal 76F. Others, more imaginative and also more substantial, 120F, 160F and 190F.

☗ |●| LE LOGIS**

1 place Saint-Denis.
☎ 02.32.44.81.73 F 02.32.45.10.92
Closed Monday lunchtimes, and Sunday and Monday evenings out of season. **Secure parking**. **TV**.

This modern hotel may look as if it belongs to a chain but it doesn't. You'll pay about 280F for a double with shower/wc and 350F with bath. Half-board (350F per person) is compulsory in season. Chef Alain Depoix has talent and imagination and his cooking is fresh and full of flavour. Set meals 95F and 140F (weekdays) and 180–350F. Set meals change four times a year to reflect the changing seasons.

BEC-HELLOUIN (LE) 27800 (5KM N)

|●| LE CANTERBURY

rue de Canterbury.
☎ 02.32.44.14.59. F same
Closed Tuesday evenings and Wednesdays.

It's just behind the village hall, which is the ugly building huddled between the village square and the entrance to the 1034 abbey. It's really rather pleasant sampling the house specialities – warm scallop salad, breast of duck with bitter cherries and *mousse de fleurs* with a fruit *coulis* – in the big dining room with its exposed beams and fireplace or on the flower-filled terrace. Set meals 80F (weekdays), 98F, 125F, 155F and 190F.

NEUBOURG (LE) 27110 (15KM SE)

|●| RESTAURANT CÔTÉ JARDIN

10 rue du Docteur-Couderc; take the D137 and it's very near place Aristide-Briand.
☎ 02.32.35.81.89
Closed Mondays and Sunday evenings.

Service noon–1.30pm and 7–9.30pm. The restaurant, decorated in soft colours, occupies two storeys of a private house and offers some of the most imaginative and inspired cooking in the département, using the freshest of produce. Set meals change twice a year. Here's a peek at what the 100F *formule* had to offer recently – sardines marinated in lime juice, turbot *à la fleur de bière,* fillet of lamb with juniper berries and a dessert of chocolate and Irish whisky. They also have a "wine of the month" giving you the chance to sample either some excellent regional wine from a less popular year or a great wine at a ridiculous price. Friendly welcome. Exhibition of national painters once or twice a year.

CANY-BARVILLE 76450

|●| L'AUBERGE DE FRANCE

73 rue du Général-de-Gaulle; it's in the main street, beside the bridge across the river Durdent.
☎ 02.35.97.80.10
Closed Sunday evenings, Tuesdays, ten days in February and two weeks in September.

Lunch served noon–2pm, dinner 7–9.15pm. A large white building that looks more like a café than a restaurant. The chef's creations such as fillet of plaice with langoustines, *grenadins* of veal with morels, and John Dory with peas change with the seasons. Set meals 78F (weekday lunchtimes and in the evenings until 8.30pm), 120F (two courses), 160F (three courses) and 172F. Superb wines.

CAUDEBEC-EN-CAUX 76490

10% ☗ |●| LE CHEVAL BLANC*

4 place René-Coty; from the town hall go towards Saint-Arnoult-Lillebonne and place René-Coty is just a few metres further along.
☎ 02.35.96.21.66 F 02.35.95.35.40
Closed three weeks from the end of January; restaurant closed Sunday evenings (unless the Monday is a public holiday). **Secure parking**. **TV**.

Friendly staff, tasty cooking and attractive décor. Doubles 180F (with basin/wc)–260F (with bath). Regional dishes like ox tripe *à la normande* and cod with *andouille*. Set meals 59F (weekday lunchtimes), 70F (not weekends or public holidays), and 100–160F. If you're coming for dinner, make sure you arrive before 9.30pm since the kitchens close early.

10% ☗ |●| HÔTEL-RESTAURANT LE NORMANDIE**

19 quai Guilbaud; it's a few steps from the town hall.
☎ 02.35.96.25.11 F 02.35.96.68.15

Closed February; restaurant closed Sunday evenings (except public holidays). **Car park**. **TV**. **Canal+**.

Lunch served noon–2.30pm, dinner 7–9.30pm. A comfortable welcoming post-war building with modern rooms that don't have much character. Doubles overlooking the Seine 254F (with shower/wc) and 360F (with bath). The ones without a river view are cheaper and quieter. Satellite channels for TV fans, but nothing on the box can compare with the sight of the Seine and the floodlit bridge. And the chef's in a class of his own when it comes to duck, which he prepares in a variety of ways – the pressed Rouen duck is great! He also does regional and fish dishes including *effilochée* of rabbit with Calvados and brill with cider. Set meals 59F (except Sundays and public holidays), 98F, 149F and 190F. There's miniature golf and a maritime museum just across the road.

SAINT-WANDRILLE-RANÇON 76490 (3KM E)

RESTAURANT LES DEUX COURONNES

How to get there: it's opposite the church.
☎ 02.35.96.11.44 F 02.35.56.56.23
Closed Sunday evenings and Mondays.

Lunch served noon–2pm, dinner 7.30–9.30pm. A 17th century inn just a few steps from the famous abbey. Gluttony is a sin but surely the monks will understand that it's impossible to withstand temptation when faced with *panaché* of kidneys, oysters, warm apple tart, apple *crêpes* and cinnamon icecream. Two set meals available until 9pm (two courses of your choice for 130F or three for 160F). Only ˆ la carte afterwards – expect to pay 200F.

VILLEQUIER 76490 (4.5KM SW)

HÔTEL DU GRAND SAPIN

quai de Seine; it's at the Villequier exit going towards Caudebec.
☎ 02.35.56.78.73 F 02.35.95.69.27
Closed Tuesday evenings and Wednesdays (except in July and August), during the February school holidays and the second fortnight in November. **Car park**. **TV**.

Service noon–2pm and 7.30–9.30pm. This is a magnificent traditional Normandy building on the banks of the Seine. And, surprise surprise, there's an enormous fir tree growing in the flower-filled garden. It has a large rustic dining room with wooden balconies and five doubles (250F) overlooking the Seine. This is a remarkably charming, friendly and cosy place. Essential to phone ahead and book. Set meals 65F (weekdays and Saturday lunchtimes) and 115–150F. You'll get excellent value for money here.

SAINTE-GERTRUDE 76490 (3KM N)

RESTAURANT AU RENDEZ-VOUS DES CHASSEURS

How to get there: it's opposite the church.
☎ 02.35.96.20.30
Closed Wednesdays (except public holidays), during the February school holidays, one week in September and at Christmas.

A quiet little restaurant nestling between the forest and the small village church, this is the kind of place we like. Hunters and travellers alike have been coming here for more than 150 years. Good regional cooking at prices to suit all pockets. Set meals 60–160F. You'll have to come back in winter to sample the game – the chef makes a delicious stew with pheasant, venison and hare.

CONCHES-EN-OUCHE 27190

BEAUBRAY 27190 (8KM S)

10% L'AUBERGE DE LA COMTESSE

2 rue de Villeneuve; take the D840 towards Breteuil then turn right.
☎ 02.32.67.27.26 F 02.32.67.20.52
Car park. **Disabled access**.

Service 12.15–1.45pm and 7.15–9.45pm. A lovely little Normandy house that once belonged to a countess. There are fields all around and the forest is very close by. Set meals 75F (weekdays), 100F, 165F and 220F. The house speciality (not available in summer months) is grilled suckling pig. It'll cost you 135F but that includes a cocktail and wine. In summer, how about trying one of the grills? They also do refined dishes that change with the seasons such as crab soufflé and salmon *coulibia* (ie wrapped in pastry). Swings and swimming pool in the garden to keep the kids amused. The refurbished, comfortable and very clean bedrooms (210F with shower/wc) overlook the fields. You'll get peace and quiet here and it's ideal for a weekend if you like being woken by birdsong.

DIEPPE 76200

AUBERGE DE JEUNESSE

48 rue Louis-Fromager (Sud-Ouest); it's quite far out of town so take a number 2 bus that's going to Val Druel

and get off at the Château-Michel stop.
☎ 02.35.84.85.73 ➡ 02.35.84.89.62
Closed Nov 15–Feb 15.

Reception open 8–10am and 5–10pm. Nice welcome in a part of the world that's not known for being friendly. Accommodation for forty-six. Expect to pay 67F per night (including breakfast) for a bed in the dormitory or in a room sleeping two, four or six. Free use of the kitchen if you fancy a spot of cooking.

10% TOURIST HÔTEL*

16 rue de la Halle-au-Blé (Centre).
☎ 02.35.06.10.10 ➡ 02.35.84.15.87
Closed three weeks in January. **TV**.

Although it's only a stone's throw from the beach, none of the rooms has a sea view. It's an ordinary-looking little place without any special charm but the prices are good and facilities reasonable. Bedrooms 160F with basin/wc, 190F with shower and 200–240F with shower/wc. Covered storage for bikes.

HÔTEL AU GRAND DUQUESNE*

15 place Saint-Jacques (Centre); it's in the street opposite the church of Saint-Jacques.
☎ 02.35.84.21.51 ➡ 02.35.84.29.83 T
TV. **Canal+**.

Lunch served noon–1.30pm, dinner 7–10.15pm. This hotel has been entirely refurbished in a tasteful modern style. Pretty fully-equipped bedrooms with bath and telephone (165–235F).

10% HÔTEL EPSOM**

11 bd de Verdun (Centre).
☎ 02.35.84.10.18 ➡ 02.35.40.03.00
TV.

Definitely the best seaside hotel in Dieppe. The bedrooms are comfortable and cosy, and most have a sea view. The décor's pretty ordinary except for the astonishing bar, which is full of light and as English as English can be with its big comfortable armchairs and a grand piano in the middle of the floor. Rooms all come with shower/wc or bath and you'll pay 295F for one with a sea view and 265F for one overlooking the courtyard. A very good hotel with a friendly team at reception.

À LA MARMITE DIEPPOISE

8 rue Saint-Jean (Centre); it's just a few steps from quai Duquesne.
☎ 02.35.84.24.26 ➡ 02.35.84.31.12
Closed Sunday evenings and Mondays.

Service noon–2.15pm and 7.15–9.30pm. A classic Dieppe restaurant. The brick walls are hung with copper dishes that are ever so slightly tacky but even if décor isn't its strong point it's been serving up good food for a great many years. If money's a bit tight, they do an 86F set meal (up to Saturday lunchtimes) featuring fish in a cream sauce. Their signature dish though is still the *marmite diéppoise* –monkfish, ling, brill, mussels and langoustines all cooked together in a casserole. The end result is full of flavour and absolutely wonderful! In fact all the dishes are just perfect – just a pity the prices aren't as easy to swallow.

POURVILLE-SUR-MER 76550 (4.5KM W)

L'HUÎTRIÈRE

rue du 19-Août; it's on the seafront, 4km west of Dieppe.
☎ 02.35.84.36.20 ➡ 02.35.84.38.09
Closed end Sept–Easter. **Car park**.

Service every day 10am–approximately 8pm. You'll find it on a big quiet beach in this peaceful little coastal village. Outmoded rather kitsch décor with maritime bric-a-brac that looks as if it's come from a junk shop. You'll eat off formica topped tables. They do all kinds of seafood – oysters, clams, winkles, house smoked salmon – and *crêpes*. Ground floor takeaway open all year round.

VARENGEVILLE-SUR-MER 76119 (8KM SW)

HÔTEL DE LA TERRASSE**

route de Vastérival (South); take the D75, go past Varengeville as far as Vastérival; it's a little beach with just one or two houses and the forest of Ailly in the background.
☎ 02.35.85.12.54 ➡ 02.35.85.11.70
Closed Oct 10–mid March. **Car park**.

A large turn of the century building that overlooks the sea and is surrounded by maritime pines. Half-board is compulsory but you shouldn't have any problem with that since the cooking's wonderful. Comfy bedrooms 260F with shower/wc and 285F with bath (includes meals). A really delightful place, ideal if you want peace and quiet and lots of fresh air. You can eat either on the terrace or in the bay-windowed dining room. They do mainly fish – sole *meunière*, *marmite dieppoise* (fish and shellfish stew) and seafood platters. Those who've come for a meal and nothing else can choose from the set meals at 85F (every day), 92F, 150F and 170F. Guests have use of the tennis court looking over the sea.

ELBEUF 76500

LE SQUARIUM*

25 rue Pierre-Brossolette (South-East); it's opposite the cinema.
☎ 02.35.81.10.52
Closed Sundays and August. **Car park**.

If you're planning on coming to this cosy little hotel cum bar it's advisable to book ahead. Bedrooms are well-maintained and quite spacious. Doubles 120F with basin and 160F with shower. You'll get your money's worth here.

10% LE PROGRÈS**

47 rue Henry (Centre); it's almost opposite the town hall.
☎ 02.35.78.42.67
Closed Sunday evenings. **Secure parking**. **TV**.

A quiet hotel with a very good location between the Seine and the shopping streets. Good prices. Doubles range in price from 160F with basin/wc to 200F with bath. There's a pleasant saloon-style *brasserie* offering set meals from 50F. Or if that's not your scene, how about trying the plain regional dishes in the dining room alongside – it's prettily decorated and more down-to-earth. Set meals 75F (available every day) and 105–195F (gourmet).

RESTAURANT LE JARDIN SAINT-LOUIS

24 rue Proudhon (Centre); it's in place de la République.
☎ 02.35.77.63.22 F 02.35.77.25.28
Closed Sundays. **Car park**.

You'll receive a friendly welcome in this restaurant that's well away from the busy roads (phew, fresh air at last!). Pleasant cooking and classics like *tartare* of salmon with fresh herbs, roast langoustine with lemon butter and braised beef marrow. Or you might like to try the local speciality of quail with leeks. Set meals 55F (weekdays), 79F and 130F.

SAINT-AUBIN-LÈS-ELBEUF 76410 (2KM N)

10% HÔTEL DU CHÂTEAU BLANC**

65 rue Jean-Jaurès; it's on the other side of the Seine – take the first street on the right after the bridge and you'll see it at the corner.
☎ 02.35.77.10.53 F 02.35.77.10.53
Car park. **TV**.

A large bourgeois-style building. It's rather noisy in the morning on account of the nearby main road but it has plenty of good points too, such as an enclosed garden which serves as a car park, a large pleasant lounge where you can sit and glance over the paper, and spacious, very well-maintained bedrooms. Expect to pay 190F with shower/wc and telephone. No restaurant but you can have something cold on a tray on request.

ÉTRETAT 76790

L'ESCALE**

place Foch (Centre); it's opposite the old market.
☎ 02.35.27.03.69 F 02.35.28.05.86
Car park. **TV**.

This completely refurbished hotel is as nice as can be. The panelled bedrooms are on the small side but pleasant and have shower/wc, telephone and TV. Expect to pay 160F (out of season)–290F (summer months). The lively ground floor restaurant cum brasserie has both simple food (mussels and chips, omelettes, salads, *crêpes* and the like) and more gourmet dishes. You can watch the goings-on in the square from the terrace.

10% HÔTEL LA RÉSIDENCE

4 bd René-Coty (Centre).
☎ 02.35.27.02.87 F 02.35.27.04.31
TV.

One of the most beautiful hotels in Normandy from the outside. It was built in Lisieux in the 14th century and moved to Étretat at the start of this century. The décor inside is a successful combination of different styles. Renovated bedrooms, no two the same, simply and tastefully decorated by the owner herself. Prices are reasonable all year round. Doubles 230–280F with shower/wc and 340–380F with bath. They also have a suite that sleeps six for 640F. You'll receive a friendly welcome and you can borrow the hotel's bikes to tour the area. All in all, there's plenty to make your stay in Étretat a pleasant one.

HÔTEL D'ANGLETERRE

35 av. George-V (Centre); it's 100m from the sea in the street that starts at the tourist office and goes towards Le Havre.
☎ 02.35.27.01.65 F 02.35.28.78.44

A clean, welcoming and reasonably priced hotel away from the touristy part of town – in other words, something of a find. Doubles 350F with shower/wc. Have breakfast in the pleasant lounge and if the fancy takes you, show off your talents on the piano (check with the owner first).

10% ⌂ |●| HÔTEL LE CORSAIRE**

rue du Général-Leclerc; it's on the seafront.
☎ 02.35.10.38.90 ➡ 02.35.28.89.74
TV.

Service noon–3pm and 7–approximately 9.30pm. One of the few hotels on the seafront. It's got a pretty red brick façade and a magnificent view of the famous cliffs. Modern bedrooms decorated in very different styles. Prices 275–490F depending on facilities (shower/wc or bath) and view (overlooking the sea or not). Some of the rooms with balcony and sea view have two double beds. Expect to pay 610F based on four sharing. Although they've got a restaurant, the service is so-so as is the cooking.

|●| CRÊPERIE DE LANN-BIHOUÉ

45 rue Notre-Dame (Centre); it's behind the town hall.
☎ 02.35.27.04.65
Closed Tuesdays and Wednesdays except during school holidays.

Here's a Breton *crêperie* housed in a typical and pleasant old Normandy inn. Cheap *crêpes* to suit every taste. If you're not very hungry, the 50F set meal (available weekdays) is the perfect answer – as long as you like *crêpes* that is.

|●| RESTAURANT LE GALION

bd René-Coty (Centre).
☎ 02.35.29.48.74 ➡ 02.35.29.74.48
Closed Wednesdays, Thursday lunchtimes, three weeks before Christmas and mid Jan–mid Feb.

There's no use denying it – this is the best restaurant in town. It has 17th century décor, an enormous fireplace, little tinted window panes, old beams, waitresses in uniform and high-class service. It's got a typically Normandy feel to it. Hushed atmosphere. The well-balanced 115F set meal of a velvety smooth fish soup and a skilfully prepared escalope of salmon with Muscadet is just perfect. Go for the 160F set meal if you like your food and the 230F one if you're feeling flush.

CRIQUETOT-L'ESNEVAL 76280 (8KM SE)

|●| LE PHÉNIX

rue du 8-Mai-1945; take the D39 and when you get to the village it's just to the right of the town hall.
☎ 02.35.27.24.96
Closed Sunday evenings and Mondays out of season.

Lunch served noon–2pm, dinner 7–9pm. An informal and unpretentious little bar cum restaurant with simple delicious dishes, lovingly put together using fresh ingredients. Everything's home-made, from the quiche and *terrine* to the *foie gras*. The 55F set meal (wine included) is unbeatable value for money and is served up to Saturday evening. The other set meals at 80F and 120F are along the same lines. A fantastic establishment that will certainly make a name for itself.

SAINT-JOUIN 76280 (11KM S)

|●| LE BELVÉDÈRE

How to get there: take the D940 towards the south, turn at Beaumesnil, and carry on as far as pointe de Saint-Jouin opposite cap d'Antifer.
☎ 02.35.20.13.76 ➡ 02.35.30.74.60
Closed Sunday evenings, Mondays, and three weeks Dec–Jan.

Service 12.30–1.30pm and 7.30–9pm. This restaurant seems totally out of place here. It looks like a blockhouse and stands out in the fields, overlooking the cliff and the port d'Antifer, Le Havre's oil port. Ideal for admiring the sea and watching the odd oil tanker calling in. They do lots of seafood and a few meat dishes for the diehard carnivores. Set meals 75F (available lunchtimes, evenings and even weekends!), 140F and 180F.

EU 76260

⌂ |●| CENTRE DES FONTAINES - AUBERGE DE JEUNESSE

rue des Fontaines.
☎ 02.35.86.05.03 ➡ 02.35.86.45.12
Closed Dec 20–Jan 4.

It's housed in what used to be the kitchens of the neighbouring castle. The reception desk is manned 5–10pm but you'll get a key so you can come and go as you please. It has bedrooms with basin or shower (wc on the landing) that sleep four, six and nine. Expect to pay 95F with a hostelling card (breakfast included) or 115F without. This is a bit steep when you consider that you can have the dormitory all to yourself for the same amount even if it's not full. Meals can be provided. If you take half-board, reckon on an extra 50F.

10% ⌂ |●| HÔTEL DE LA GARE**

20 place de la Gare.
☎ 02.35.86.16.64 ➡ 02.35.50.86.25
Closed the second fortnight in August; restaurant closed Sunday evenings and Aug 18–Sept 11. **Car park**. **TV**.

The station isn't there any more, but they haven't changed the name of the hotel. It's a beautiful master craftsman's house, full of light and very quiet. The restaurant is decorated in a very tasteful manner. The bedrooms, some pleasant and modern, others slightly old-fashioned, come with shower/wc and telephone. Doubles 280F and 300F. Half-board is compulsory at weekends from Easter onwards but 600F for two is a real bargain considering the high standard of cooking. Even if you aren't planning to stay the night, you must have a meal in the excellent restaurant. The cooking is modern but takes its inspiration from local culinary tradition. Set meals 90F (weekdays) and 135F (based on either meat or fish).

RESTAURANT DE LA POSTE

5 rue de la Poste (Centre).
☎ 02.35.86.10.78
Closed Sunday and Monday evenings (except in July and August). **Car park. Disabled access.**

A restaurant in a narrow street that feels a bit like a 1900s bistro with old photos, lace lampshades, dried flowers, and lots of space between the tables. Set meals 59F (weekday lunchtimes), 95F and 140F. Simple cooking using good produce.

ÉVREUX 27000

10% HÔTEL-RESTAURANT DE LA BICHE**

9 rue Joséphine, place Saint-Taurin (West).
☎ 02.32.38.66.00. Fax:02.32.33.54.05.
Closed August; restaurant closed Sunday evenings.
Car park. TV. Disabled access.

An amazing place on the edge of an extremely pretty square. It's built round an interior patio and the glassed-in reception desk, the cheerful mauve colours, the naive paintings on the walls and the gallery leading to the bedrooms give it a marvellous retro feel. Once the hunting lodge of François I, then the most sophisticated brothel in the country, it's now a good hotel and restaurant. Film-maker Louis Malle shot "Le Voleur" here. It's the complete opposite of an impersonal hotel chain: everything's special, including the owner with his friendly smile. Doubles 140F with basin, 230F with shower/wc and 260F with bath. You'll either get a view of place Saint-Taurin (very quiet in the evenings) or the river. In the restaurant, we were simply bowled over by the atmosphere, the cheerful welcome from the owner and the first-rate food. It's home cooking but the chef prepares imaginative dishes like marrow bones on toast and sautéd free-range chicken with cider and tarragon. Set meals 75F and 128F (the latter is particularly good).

10% HÔTEL DE FRANCE**

29 rue Saint-Thomas (Centre); it's behind the market square.
☎ 02.32.39.09.25 Fax 00.32.38.38.56
Restaurant closed Sunday evenings and Mondays.
Car park. TV. Canal+.

A little two star hotel with quiet, attractive and very comfortable rooms (270–340F with shower/wc or bath). Staff are exceptionally hospitable and the welcoming restaurant overlooks the river and the garden. The gourmet cooking, which is 4-star quality, is regarded as the best in town and yet, at 150F, the cheapest set meal is much less expensive than in similar restaurants. The *carte-menu* changes often. The chef's specialities include scallops *en papillotte* with seaweed, veal sweetbreads with a Camembert sauce, and roast pigeon with cabbage and bacon cubes.

RESTAURANT LA CROIX D'OR

3 rue Joséphine (West).
☎ 02.32.33.06.07

A very good restaurant offering fine food and dishes that are carefully and lovingly prepared by people of intelligence. You won't come across the pretentious tiny portions typical of nouvelle cuisine. Waiters dressed as sailors race between the tables that are often occupied by locals (always a good sign!). The chef gets his produce directly from the food markets at Rungis so dishes are as fresh as can be. Superb set meals 77F, 105F, 140f and 180F. A small 58F one (weekday lunchtimes) offers genuine surprises like *terrine* of half-cooked salmon with a *coulis* of tomatoes, olives and basil, and *millefeuille* of mullet and langoustine with a honey and citrus fruit sauce. But THE speciality has got to be the *bouillabaisse*.

GRAVIGNY 27930 (4KM N)

LE SAINT-NICOLAS

38 rue Aristide-Briand (Centre); take the D155 towards Louviers and it's on the right.
☎ 02.32.38.35.15 Fax 02.32.31.19.34
Closed Sunday evenings and the second fortnight in August.

Lunch served noon–2pm, dinner 7–10pm. A fairly unobtrusive place by the roadside. Inside, there are a number of lovely little dining rooms decorated in a low-key and sophisticated fashion. They've got intimate ones for candlelit dinners and large ones for lively groups. Chef Claude Sauvant makes a point of using only the best that the market has to offer. We treated ourselves to warm oysters, fricassee of scallops, pig's trotters (without the bones), and *gratinée* of soft fruits. Superb wine list.

JOUY-SUR-EURE 27120 (12KM E)

LE RELAIS DU GUESCLIN

place de l'Église.
☎ 02.32.36.62.75
Closed Wednesdays and two weeks in August.
Car park.

Service noon–2pm (dinner is by reservation only). A little Normandy inn with the church on one side and fields on the other. Peace and quiet are guaranteed and you can have lunch outside. They do a daily *formule* for 85F of capon salad plus the dish of the day. If that doesn't appeal, they have set meals at 150F and 180F. They specialize in everything that's good about Normandy cuisine – duck *terrine*, sole, trout, breast of duck, veal sweetbreads with morels and tripe. Good bottled cider.

CHAMBRAY 27120 (15KM NE)

RESTAURANT LE VOL AU VENT

1 place de la Mairie (Centre).
☎ 02.32.36.70.05
Closed Mondays, Tuesday lunchtimes, Sunday evenings, in August and during the Christmas/New Year holidays.

Service noon–2pm and 8–9.30pm. A little village house in the Eure valley. It has a very stylish dining room which you get to through a small lounge cum smoking room where they serve your apéritifs and coffee – a bit the way they do in Britain. The cooking is exquisite and full of subtle flavours. Set meals 160–700F(!). Specialities include (depending on the season) oysters, veal sweetbreads in puff pastry with wild mushrooms, and snails. For dessert, try the *millefeuille* of seasonal fruit. Wine is not cheap.

FÉCAMP 76400

10% LE MARTIN

18 place Saint-Étienne (Centre) .
☎ 02.35.28.23.82 F→ 02.35.28.61.21
Closed the first fortnight in March and the first fortnight in September; restaurant closed Sunday evenings and Mondays except public holidays. **TV**.

Lunch served noon–2pm, dinner 7–9.30pm. A good little restaurant that refuses to be a slave to fashion. You'll get typical Normandy and classic dishes prepared by a real chef and served in a rustic dining room with exposed beams. The 65F set meal (not available Saturday evenings, Sundays or public holidays) is incredibly good value for money. Three other set meals 90F, 110F and 145F. The basic rooms range in price from 140F to 180F – a godsend if you're on a budget.

HÔTEL DE LA MER**

89 bd Albert-Ier.
☎ 02.35.28.24.64 F→ 02.35.28.27.67
Closed for a fortnight during the February school holidays. **TV**.

This modern establishment may look rather unfriendly but it's an excellent hotel, and one of the few actually to face the sea. Comfy well-equipped rooms, some with balcony and sea view. Cheapest 180F with basin, 260F and 290F with shower/wc or bath. Nice homy atmosphere and pleasant owners.

HÔTEL D'ANGLETERRE**

93 rue de la Plage (Centre).
☎ 02.35.28.01.60 F→ 02.35.28.62.95
Closed Christmas. **Secure parking**. **TV**. **Canal+**.

Not one of the greats of the hotel world but it offers decent value for money for what it is and it's only a stone's throw from the beach. Doubles 200–300F with shower or bath.

HÔTEL DE LA PLAGE**

87 rue de la Plage (Centre).
☎ 02.35.29.76.51 F→ 02.35.28.68.30
TV. **Canal+**. **Disabled access**.

Here's a modern well-equipped hotel very close to the beach. Doubles 310F with shower/wc, 340F with bath, smaller ones 285F and 295F. Most have just been refurbished from top to bottom. No nasty surprises and a great location.

FERME DE LA CHAPELLE***

sente de la Chapelle; it's on the cliff of Amont – follow the signs for the chapelle Notre-Dame-du-Salut from the town centre.
☎ 02.35.29.12.19 F→ 02.35.29.78.01
Closed Dec 21–Jan 18. **Car park**. **TV**.
Disabled access.

In a fabulous position beside the chapel, this 16th century farm has been converted into a superb hotel complex. The attractive rooms, which don't have much character but are very comfortable, are laid out around the huge lawn and nice swimming pool. Expect to pay 300–450F with bath. Some have a mezzanine floor and can sleep up to five people. You can have something on a tray in the evening if you order in advance.

|●| LE VICOMTÉ

4 rue du Président-Coty; it's 50m from the port behind the palais Bénédictine.
☎ 02.35.28.47.63
Closed Wednesday evenings, Sundays, one week in August and Christmas.

Lunch served noon–1.30pm, dinner 7–9pm. A very welcoming and rather unusual bistro. Checked tablecloths, old newspaper articles on the walls and the owner with his moustache – you're a long way from the world of the trawlers down at the port. Décor's a successful combination of retro and country styles. There is just one set meal but it's different every day and offers regional cooking based on fresh produce. For 83F you'll get excellent value for money and impeccable service.

|●| LE MARITIME**

2 place Nicolas-Selles; it's just across from the marina.
☎ 02.35.28.21.71 ➡ 02.35.27.22.08
Closed Tuesdays Oct–March.

Lunch served noon–2.30pm, dinner 7–9.30pm (10pm in season). It looks like a liner – a luxury one – and it's been around for years. There's a maritime theme to the décor and they serve lots of fish and seafood. Set meals 78F (available every day) and 95–195F. Specialities are leg of duck with Pommeau, cod steak *gratiné* with *sabayon normand* (Fécamp used to be one of the biggest ports in France for cod), and of course shellfish from the tank. Takeaway.

SAINT-LÉONARD 76400 (2KM S)

⌂ |●| AUBERGE DE LA ROUGE**

route du Havre; take the D925.
☎ 02.35.28.07.59. Fax:02.35.28.70.55.
Closed Sunday evenings and Mondays.
Secure parking. TV. Disabled access.

This large and delightful inn has just celebrated its 100th birthday. The owner loves to share his passions for cooking and running (he does marathons) and guests are quite welcome to go for an early morning or evening run with him. What better way to work up an appetite! You can eat beside the fountain in the garden and listen to the birds. A high quality establishment with brilliant food and very classy to boot! Depending on the season they do great grilled sole in oyster stock, steamed turbot with basil and *aumônière* of frogs' legs. Set meals 105F (every day except Sunday lunchtimes), 195F and 280F. They also have a few comfortable bedrooms but these are a bit close to the road.

YPORT 76111 (8KM W)

⌂ |●| HÔTEL-RESTAURANT LA SIRÈNE**

7 bd Alexandre-Dumont; take the D940 and the D211.
☎ 02.35.27.31.87 ➡ 02.35.29.47.37
Closed Mondays Nov–Feb except during the school holidays. **Car park.**

A littel hotel cum restaurant overlooking the beach. You couldn't really call it charming but it's simple and pleasant. You'll get the best view of Yport from here. Very basic bedrooms 200F with shower/wc (some have a seaview). Breakfast 25F. The large second floor dining room offers simple cooking and regional specialities *moules marinière*, seafood, pollack,and ham *à la normande.* Set meals 75F (weekdays and Saturday lunchtimes), 98F, 110F and 140F.

FORGES-LES-EAUX 76440

⌂ LE CONTINENTAL***

110 av. des Sources; it's only yards from the casino.
☎ 02.32.89.50.50 ➡ 02.35.90.26.14
Car park. TV. Disabled access.

An impressive building that's been renovated throughout. It has the nicely old-fashioned atmosphere of the old casino hotels. Large foyer. Have breakfast on your balcony or simply pop out for a breath of fresh air. Fully equipped bedrooms 320F.

|●| RESTAURANT LA SOURCE

106 av. des Sources; turn right after the railway station before you reach the casino.
☎ 02.35.90.59.28
Closed Wednesday lunchtimes, evenings Mondays–Thursdays, three weeks at Easter and two weeks in October.

A fairly conventional restaurant but you won't get any nasty surprises. The cheapest set meal costs 58F (weekday lunchtimes) and comes with a quarter litre of wine and cheese. Other set meals 95F and 130F. To help the digestive process, take a walk through the casino grounds and have a drink of iron-rich water from the spring before you hit the road again.

VILLERS-HAUDRICOURT 76390 (19KM NE)

L'AUBERGE DE LA MARE-AUX-FÉES

How to get there: it's 19km along the D9 in the direction of Aumale.
☎ 02.35.93.41.79.
Closed Saturdays and Sundays (except by reservation) and in August.

An authentic country inn, simply and tastefully decorated, that offers traditional home cooking and a friendly atmosphere. If you have the 90F set meal (which includes cheese, dessert and wine) you'll eat at a country kitchen table beside roadworkers and locals. There's also a more conventional dining room.

GISORS 27140

HOSTELLERIE DES TROIS POISSONS

13 rue Cappeville (Centre).
☎ 02.32.55.01.09
Closed Monday evenings, Tuesdays and in June.
Car park.

This lovely half-timbered restaurant decorated in traditional style opens onto a huge terrace. Set meals 80F, 110F and 175F. Specialities are omelette with morels and rabbit in cider. If you're stuck for somewhere to stay, they have very basic rooms with washing facilities at 90F and 120F.

HAVRE (LE) 76600

SEE MAP OVERLEAF

10% HÔTEL JEANNE D'ARC*

91 rue Émile-Zola. **MAP B3-1**
☎ 02.35.21.67.27
Closed afternoons, Sundays, and public holidays. **TV**.

A cheap, simple hotel. The proprietress loves needlepoint and there are tapestries on every wall. Small well-kept rooms 149F with basin and 164F with shower. Guests can eat with the owners in the evening. Informal atmosphere.

HÔTEL LE MONACO

16 rue de Paris. **MAP B4-3**
☎ 02.35.42.21.01 F 02.35.42.01.01
Car park. **TV**. **Canal+**.

One of the nearest hotels to the ferry departure point. Generally well-maintained. Doubles from 165F with washing facilities and 210–260F with bath.

10% HÔTEL FOCH**

4 rue de Caligny. **MAP A3-4**
☎ 02.35.42.50.69 F 02.35.43.40.17
Secure parking. **TV**.

A very good two-star hotel half-way between the town centre and the seafront. You'll always get a smiling welcome from the owners. Nice bedrooms, all with bath, vary in size. It doesn't have a restaurant but you can get something on a tray for 85F. Buffet breakfast.

RESTAURANT LE CROCUS

67 rue Jules-Tellier. **MAP D2-10**
☎ 02.35.53.25.96 F 02.35.53.25.96
Closed evenings except Fridays and Saturdays.

Service noon–2.30pm. Other restaurants could learn a lot from this one. Plenty of good ideas such as free coffee, a free apéritif every Friday 13th, and an extraordinary set meal of starter, main course, cheese or salad, dessert and drink for only 57F (the smiles are free!) On Fridays and Saturdays you can have dinner and see a show for 100F, and on Sundays the 110F set meal comes with live music. The atmosphere's reminiscent of the Left Bank and the entertainment varies from plays to jazz to singing.

RESTAURANT LE TILBURY

39 rue Jean-de-La-Fontaine. **MAP C3-11**
☎ 02.35.21.23.50
Closed Saturday lunchtimes, Sunday evenings and Mondays.

The romantic and naive décor and the little booths that look like horse-drawn carriages get full marks for originality. Try the house specialities of snails in a *brioche*. Friendly staff and low prices. The cheapest set meal, served all day Tuesday to Friday, is 62F including coffee. Other evening set meals are 83F (with cheese and dessert) and 110F. Excellent value for money.

RESTAURANT LE LYONNAIS

7 rue de Bretagne. **MAP C3-12**
☎ 02.35.22.07.31
Closed Saturday lunchtimes and Sundays.

They've successfully recreated the atmosphere of a typical Lyon bistro. It's still got that new look but time will take care of that. It's all been calculated with an eye to effect, from the tablecloths and little bunches of flowers on the tables to the chequerboard floor tiles and the brick walls, but it works, just like the typical Lyon dishes. Try the *gâteau* of chicken livers with stewed fresh tomatoes, sausage with boiled potatoes, and warm upside-down apple tart. Set meals 70F

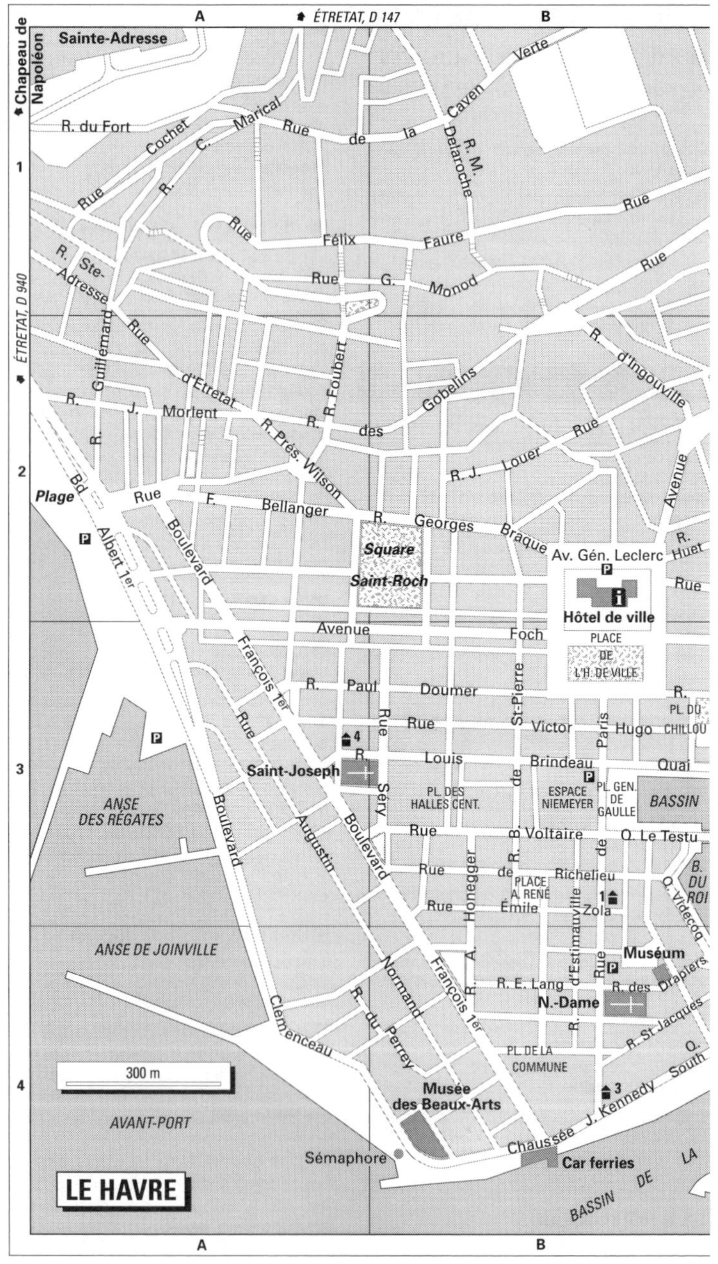
A
ÉTRETAT, D 147
B
Chapeau de Napoléon
Sainte-Adresse
R. du Fort
Rue Cochet
R. C. Marical
Rue de la Cavée Verte
R. M. Delaroche
Rue Félix Faure
Rue G. Monod
R. Ste-Adresse
Rue d'Etretat
R. Guillemard
R. J. Morlent
R. Foubert
R. des Gobelins
R. d'Ingouville
R. Prés. Wilson
R. J. Louer
Avenue
Bd Albert 1er
Plage
Rue F. Bellanger
R. Georges Braque
Boulevard François 1er
Square Saint-Roch
Av. Gén. Leclerc
R. Huet
Hôtel de ville
PLACE DE L'H. DE VILLE
Avenue Foch
R. Paul Doumer
Rue Victor Hugo
Rue de Paris
R. de St-Pierre
PL. DU CHILLOU
Rue Séry
R. Louis Brindeau
Quai
Saint-Joseph
PL. DES HALLES CENT.
ESPACE NIEMEYER
PL. GEN. DE GAULLE
BASSIN
ANSE DES RÉGATES
Rue Augustin Normand
Boulevard
R. B. Voltaire
Q. Le Testu
Rue de Richelieu
PLACE A. RENÉ
Rue Émile Zola
R. A. Honegger
R. d'Estimauville
B. DU ROI
Q. Videcoq
ANSE DE JOINVILLE
Muséum
R. E. Lang
R. des Drapiers
N.-Dame
R. St-Jacques
Q. Southampton
Clemenceau
R. du Perrey
PL. DE LA COMMUNE
300 m
Musée des Beaux-Arts
Chaussée J. Kennedy
AVANT-PORT
Sémaphore
Car ferries
BASSIN DE LA
LE HAVRE
ÉTRETAT, D 940
1
2
3
4

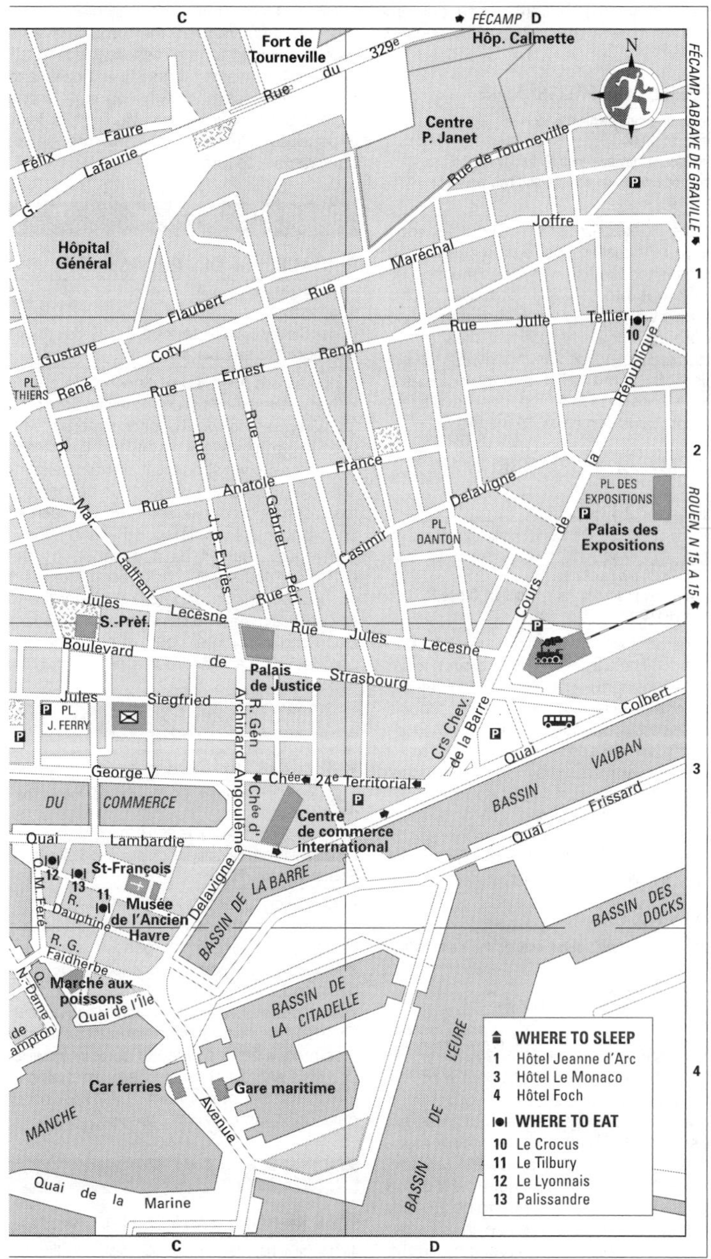
Fort de Tourneville
Hôp. Calmette
Centre P. Janet
Hôpital Général
Palais des Expositions
Palais de Justice
S.-Préf.
Centre de commerce international
St-François
Musée de l'Ancien Havre
Marché aux poissons
Car ferries
Gare maritime
FÉCAMP
FÉCAMP ABBAYE DE GRAVILLE
ROUEN, N 15, A 15
WHERE TO SLEEP
1 Hôtel Jeanne d'Arc
3 Hôtel Le Monaco
4 Hôtel Foch
WHERE TO EAT
10 Le Crocus
11 Le Tilbury
12 Le Lyonnais
13 Palissandre

(served every day), 98F (this one delivers what it promises) and 125F. Well chosen wines.

|●| RESTAURANT PALISSANDRE

33 rue de Bretagne. **MAP C3-13**
☎ 02.35.21.69.00
Closed Wednesday evenings, Saturday lunchtimes, Sundays, one week in February and two weeks in August.

It's in the oldest part of town. The dark wood gives you the feeling you're on a boat. Good classic dishes like fish with cider, mussels or, if you're not into seafood, *andouillette* or a meat dish with sauce (which shows the hand of a professional). The 85F set meal represents excellent value for money. Other set meals 118F and 149F (the latter includes a drink). And if you're in a rush, they have a fast set meal that is served in 20 minutes.

SAINTE-ADRESSE 76310 (2KM NW)

|●| LES TROIS PICS

promenade des Régates; it's at the northernmost end of the beach at Le Havre.
☎ 02.35.48.20.60. Fax:same.
Open every day in season 9am–midnight. **Closed** Mondays Feb–Sept.

It stands on the quay and looks like a liner in dry dock. The large wooden dining room offers a wonderful panoramic view of the mouth of the Seine and the maritime décor is imaginative without being over the top. From the ship's rail you can see Deauville 10 miles off in the distance. They do very decent brasserie cooking and offer two cheap set meals (69F and 95F) every day. Wine is rather expensive. Have a drink on the terrace in summer – when the lights come on across the way, it's like being at sea!

|●| YVES PAGE

7 place Clemenceau; it's at the northernmost end of the beach at Le Havre.
☎ 02.35.46.06.09
Closed Sunday evenings and Mondays.

You can be sure of getting good gourmet food in this unobtrusive looking restaurant. In the foyer there's a grand old sofa that has seen better days and that tells you straight away what the place is like – it's got a hushed atmosphere, its customers are mainly regulars, and the service is attentive but unfussy. From the dining room you'll get a view of the sea and any ships that happen to be around. There's a little terrace for use in summer (advisable to book). We can recommend the 130F set meal. That's not available on Sundays but if you're there then, you'll have no regrets if you go for the *menu-carte* at 158F, which offers warm langoustine *terrine* and *millefeuille* of salmon with cabbage and a juniper berry sauce. The wine list is fairly expensive. Take a stroll along the beach afterwards – so romantic!

JUMIÈGES 76480

⌂ |●| AUBERGE DES RUINES

place de la Mairie (Centre).
☎ 02.35.37.24.05
Closed Sunday evenings, Mondays, Dec 16–Jan 15, and one week in February. **Car park**.

Lunch served noon–2pm, dinner 7–9pm. This is the best restaurant in Jumièges and the food (primarily fish) is worthy of the monks who used to live opposite. It's a pity that the cheapest (or maybe we should say the least expensive!) set meal at the weekend is beyond the reach of a lot of people. Set meals 93F (served up to Saturday lunchtimes), 167F and 240F. If you regard yourself as a gourmet, try the *émincé* of snails with garlic, courgettes and *anchoïade* or the *tartare* of oysters and smoked salmon. The dining room has a fireplace and in summer you can eat under the pergola. Four basic bedrooms with basin 170F.

LILLEBONNE 76170

⌂ |●| HÔTEL DE FRANCE**

1 bis rue de la République (Centre); it's near the Roman theatre.
☎ 02.35.38.04.88 F→ 02.35.38.34.30
Restaurant closed Saturday lunchtimes and Sundays.
Secure parking. **TV**.

A charming unobtrusive hotel in lush surroundings offering an escape from traffic and everyday life. Simple, inexpensive and nicely decorated bedrooms. Doubles 130F with basin and 250F with bath. Traditional cooking with a touch of originality added by the chef. Try the potted cow's head and calf's feet in a mustard sauce or *émincé* of duck in a sweet and sour sauce of honey, sherry vinegar, and tomatoes. Set meals from 79F. The kind of quiet unpretentious place we like.

LOUVIERS 27400

10% ⌂ |●| HÔTEL LA HAYE-LE-COMTE***

4 route de la Haye-le-Comte (South-West); take the

D133 towards Neubourg and it's just at the Louviers exit.
☎ 02.32.40.00.40 F➔ 02.32.25.03.85
Closed Dec1–March 1; restaurant closed Mondays and Tuesday lunchtimes. **Car park**. **TV**. **Canal+**. **Disabled access**.

Service noon–1.30pm and 7–9pm. This delightful and reasonably priced hotel is housed in a little 16th century manor that stands in its own extensive grounds. The ideal base for an activity weekend because the people here are no strangers to the outdoor life and certainly don't mind the sight of muddy trainers after a spot of mountainbiking in the surrounding countryside. Doubles 270–490F with bath. 10% reduction for a stay of three nights or more. In the restaurant, the chef's specialities include *mousseline* of pike with a tarragon sauce and veal sweetbreads with Calvados and cream. Set meals 100F, 130F, 190F plus à la carte. You can play tennis, table tennis, pétanque, and croquet and there are mountain bikes for children and adults alike. You might be interested in taking a look at the records of of one of the oldest private telephone lines in France, which dates back to 1888.

LE PRÉ-SAINT-GERMAIN***

7 rue Saint-Germain (Centre); it's to the north-east of place Ernest-Thorel.
☎ 02.32.40.48.48 F➔ 02.32.50.75.60
Car park. **TV**. Restaurant closed Saturday lunchtimes and Sundays.

Built in the middle of what used to be an orchard, this neo-classical style hotel boasts all the facilities of a typical three-star establishment. It belongs to the Deniau family, as does the *Clos Normand* (see below). In other words, you can count on getting good food and a delightful welcome. Doubles from 390F. Cheapest set meal 110F.

RESTAURANT LE JARDIN DE BIGARD

39-41 rue du Quai; it's on the corner of rue du Coq.
☎ 02.32.40.02.45
Closed Wednesday evenings. **Car park**.

A centrally located and unpretentious restaurant with a bright airy dining room offering simple but carefully prepared dishes at reasonable prices. Set meals 60F (weekday lunchtimes) and 80–165F. Specialities include scallops with cider and escalope of salmon poached in white wine and served with a cream sauce.

LE CLOS NORMAND

rue de la Gare–chaussée du Vexin; it's to the north east of the town centre – cross the Eure by rue des Anciens-Combattants d'AFN and you're right there.
☎ 02.32.40.03.56 F➔ 02.32.40.61.24
Closed August.

Rustic décor (every single restaurant in the region seems to use the same decorator!) Set meals 70F (weekdays), 95F, 145F and 170F. If you take the 95F one, you'll have a choice of *suprême* of guinea fowl with leeks or skirt of beef with wild mushrooms followed by cheese or dessert. Fish specialities and dishes based on regional produce.

ACQUIGNY 27400 (5KM S)

LA CHAUMIÈRE

15 rue Aristide-Briand (Centre).
☎ 02.32.50.20.54
Closed Monday evenings and Tuesdays. **Car park**.

A really nice restaurant with rustic décor and a relaxed atmosphere. If it's chilly, they'll light a fire and grill the meat of your choice over it. No set meals but the à la carte prices are reasonable. They have a very good selection of wines which can be bought by the glass, including a Château de la Roulerie Côteaux-du-Layon that went very well with our veal liver flambéd with raspberry vinegar.

LÉRY 27690 (7KM NE)

LA FONTAINE SAINT-GABRIEL

2 place de l'Église.
☎ 02.32.59.09.39
Closed Sunday evenings and Mondays (except public holidays). **Car park**.

A delightful square with lots of trees, a pretty Romanesque church and the shaded banks of the Eure only a stone's throw away make an ideal setting for a restaurant with exquisite cooking. It serves mainly seafood and for 130F during the week you can enjoy a generous helping of either grilled seafood or something from the barbecue followed by cheese or dessert. They also have a 180F *menu-carte* and a 315F *menu dégustation*. They're all good so just choose one to suit your budget. And why not take a stroll along the river afterwards to help the digestive process?

PONT-DE-L'ARCHE 27340 (11KM N)

10% HÔTEL DE LA TOUR**

41 quai Foch (Centre); go left at the bridge that the N15 crosses and it's on the riverbank.
☎ 02.35.23.00.99 F➔ 02.35.23.46.22
Car park. **TV**.

The façade has been preserved so as not to spoil the pretty line of hotels along the quay, but the interior has been completely and expertly refurbished by the charming owners, Monsieur and Madame Helouard. Everything about it – the colours, the décor, the little details that make for a comfortable stay and of course the a really friendly welcome – give it a quality not normally found in a hotel in this category. If they're not fully booked, you'll get a tour of a few empty rooms so you can choose for yourself. All of the rooms are quiet, whether they overlook the ramparts and the church of Notre-Dame-des-Arts or the lush riverbank. There's a little patio garden at the back. You'll get a good deal at the weekend – 520F for two nights or from 280F for one night (excludes breakfast).

NEUFCHÂTEL-EN-BRAY 76270

10% LES AIRELLES**

2 passage Michu (Centre); it's opposite the church.
☎ 02.35.93.14.60 F 02.35.93.89.03
Closed three weeks at the end of the year. **Car park**. **TV**. **Canal+**.

Lunch served noon–2pm, dinner 7.30–9pm. You have to go through an archway to get to this large hotel, which is surrounded by greenery. It's very well looked after in every respect and the décor is visually generally very appealing. The bedrooms are fully equipped and impeccable, even if the décor here is rather unimaginative. Doubles from 220F. We've no complaints about the mouth-watering set meals (89–170F), offering traditional, almost conventional dishes. One of the specialities is the roast *Neufchâtel* (a type of cheese) with a caramel and pepper crust. There are a few tables on the covered terrace. A pleasant place with decent prices.

HOSTELLERIE DU GRAND CERF**

9 Grande-Rue-Fausse-Porte (Centre); go down the main street and it's after the church.
☎ 02.35.93.00.02 F 02.35.94.14.92
Secure parking. **TV**. **Canal+**.

Service noon–2.30pm and 7.30–9.15pm. You'll be spoiled rotten here and you'll have the waitress to answer to if you don't clear your plate! Classic décor and traditional and regional cooking. Cheapest set meal 66F (not available Sunday lunchtimes). How about trying the house marinated fresh mackerel (something you don't often see), the *crêpe* with Neufchâtel (a type of cheese) or the exquisite *marmite diéppoise* (stew of fish and shellfish). Very well maintained doubles range in price from 220F with shower/wc to 265F with bath. Half-board (it's not compulsory) from 210F per person based on two sharing.

PONT-AUDEMER 27500

AUBERGE DU VIEUX PUITS**

6 rue Notre-Dame-du-Pré (Centre).
☎ 02.32.41.01.48 F 02.32.42.37.28
Closed Mondays and Tuesdays (except summer) and Dec 22–Jan 31. **Car park**. **TV**. **Disabled access**.

A magnificent half-timbered 17th century building. It has only twelve bedrooms and people dining at the inn get priority. The rooms in the oldest part are cheaper and more typical of the region but the sound-proofing's not as good. Expect to pay 280F with shower (320F with shower/wc) and up to 430F with bath. Traditional refined Normandy cooking. You can eat either in the cosy dining room decorated with pretty earthenware and copperware or in a little sitting room that's more intimate. There's a delightful room on the first floor that can be hired for functions. The cheapest set meal is 198F and it's available only at lunchtime on weekdays (between October and March, however, it's also available at weekends unless it's a holiday weekend). Expect to pay 200–320F à la carte. Specialities include trout with champagne, duck with cherries, and apple tart. Set meals and the à la carte menu change frequently. We strongly advise you to take half-board.

RESTAURANT HASTING

10 rue des Cordeliers (Centre); from place Victor-Hugo take place Louis-Gillian then rue des Cordeliers.
☎ 02.32.42.89.68
Closed Wednesdays and February.

Lunch served noon–2.30pm, dinner 7–9.30pm. If it wasn't for the fact that it's right in the centre of town, we'd describe this place as the kind of little country restaurant we like! The little dining room has checked tablecloths and the kitchen serves up simple but effective dishes like oysters, fish soup, trout with almonds, and stuffed mussels. The sea, after all, is not too far away and the rivers around here are teeming with fish! Set meals 58F (every day), 75F and 90F (includes cheese and dessert). *Formule brasserie* available weekdays. You'll get a friendly reception.

CAMPIGNY 27500 (5KM SE)

10% RESTAURANT L'ANDRIEN - HÔTEL LE PETIT COQ AUX CHAMPS

La Pommeraie sud; it's 1km from the town centre.
☎ 02.32.41.04.19 ➡ 02.32.56.06.25
Closed Jan 5–25. **Car park. TV.**

Service 12.30–2.30pm and 7.30–9.30pm. The type of setting you dream about, deep in the Normandy countryside. The restaurant is welcoming and has a relaxed atmosphere even though it's fairly sophisticated, and the food is excellent. The 225F set meal includes drinks. Chef Jean-Marie Huard keeps coming up with new dishes that are a delight to both the palate and the eye. His speciality is *foie gras pot au feu* with crunchy cabbage – terrific, but it doesn't come cheap. They have accommodation too, if you can afford it!

BEUZEVILLE 27210 (14KM W)

AUBERGE DU COCHON D'OR**

place du Général-de-Gaulle; take the N175 towards Pont-l'Evèque.
☎ 02.32.57.70.46 ➡ 02.32.42.25.70
Closed Mondays and Dec 15–Jan 15. **Secure parking. TV.**

An inn that's been known for its cooking for twenty years. It specializes in regional dishes like eels stewed in cider, chicken *quenelles* with a Camembert sauce, and medallions of lamb in gravy. The large rustic dining room serves set meals at 85F (except Saturday evenings and Sundays), 114F (except Sunday lunchtimes) and all the way up to 240F. Doubles 205F with shower, 210F with shower/wc and 240F with bath. There's an annexe across the road with rooms 260–335F. It's a touch dearer here since you overlook the garden.

10% HÔTEL DE LA POSTE**

60 rue Constant-Fouché; it's opposite the town hall.
☎ 02.32.57.71.04 ➡ 02.32.42.11.01
Restaurant closed Wednesdays and Nov 15–March 15.
Car park. TV.

Lunch served noon–2pm, dinner 7–9pm. A large brick building right in the centre of this little town that was badly damaged during the Hundred Years War (which, as we all know of course, means sometime between 1337 and 1453). A former coaching inn dating back to 1844, it has a garden and terrace at the back. Bedrooms with shower or bath 250–330F. If you're there at the weekend, it's advisable to take half-board (270F). Set meals 79F (weekday lunchtimes), 99F (including cheese and dessert), 139F (very good) and 189F. Regional specialities, including *andouille* (a type of sausage) in various guises – the owner has a weakness for it (he also, by the way, cares passionately about his work). A friendly place just fifteen minutes from Honfleur where the hotels are expensive and often fully booked.

ROSAY-SUR-LIEURE 27790

10% HÔTEL LE CHÂTEAU DE ROSAY

How to get there: it's 5km south-west of Lyon-la-Forêt.
☎ 02.32.49.66.51 ➡ 02.32.49.70.77
Car park.

A magnificent building that dates back to 1611. Famous guests who've stayed here include Lulli, who composed music for the court of Louis XIV, Flaubert, who wrote *Madame Bovary* and, more recently, film director Claude Chabrol and his crew when they were shooting the film version of that same novel. Superb grounds with waterfalls, streams, moats and even a little swimming pool. The interior has been refurbished from top to bottom and decorated with copies of masterpieces (some of them quite good) by students from the art school in Rouen. Nineteen pretty rooms and, if you can afford it, four wonderful suites furnished with antiques and four-poster beds. Doubles with bath 450–670F. There are a few simpler rooms in the hunting lodge while the cheapest ones are at the far end of the grounds beside the little swimming pool. The lounges are stunning and there's a wonderful smell of beeswax polish.

ROUEN 76000

SEE MAP OVERLEAF

10% HÔTEL DE LA GARE*

3 bis rue Maladrerie (North). **MAP B1-2**
☎ 02.35.71.57.90 ➡ 02.35.71.57.90
Closed Sunday lunchtimes–Monday mornings. **TV.**

A friendly and inexpensive hotel with simple, clean and quiet rooms. Expect to pay 150F with basin and 170F with shower (based on two sharing). Family rooms with two double beds 280F.

10% HÔTEL BEAUSÉJOUR**

9 rue Pouchet. **MAP B1-5**
☎ 02.35.71.93.47 ➡ 02.35.98.01.24
Car park. TV. Disabled access.

A bit depressing but it has a delightful garden and a lounge bar. You'll get peace and quiet

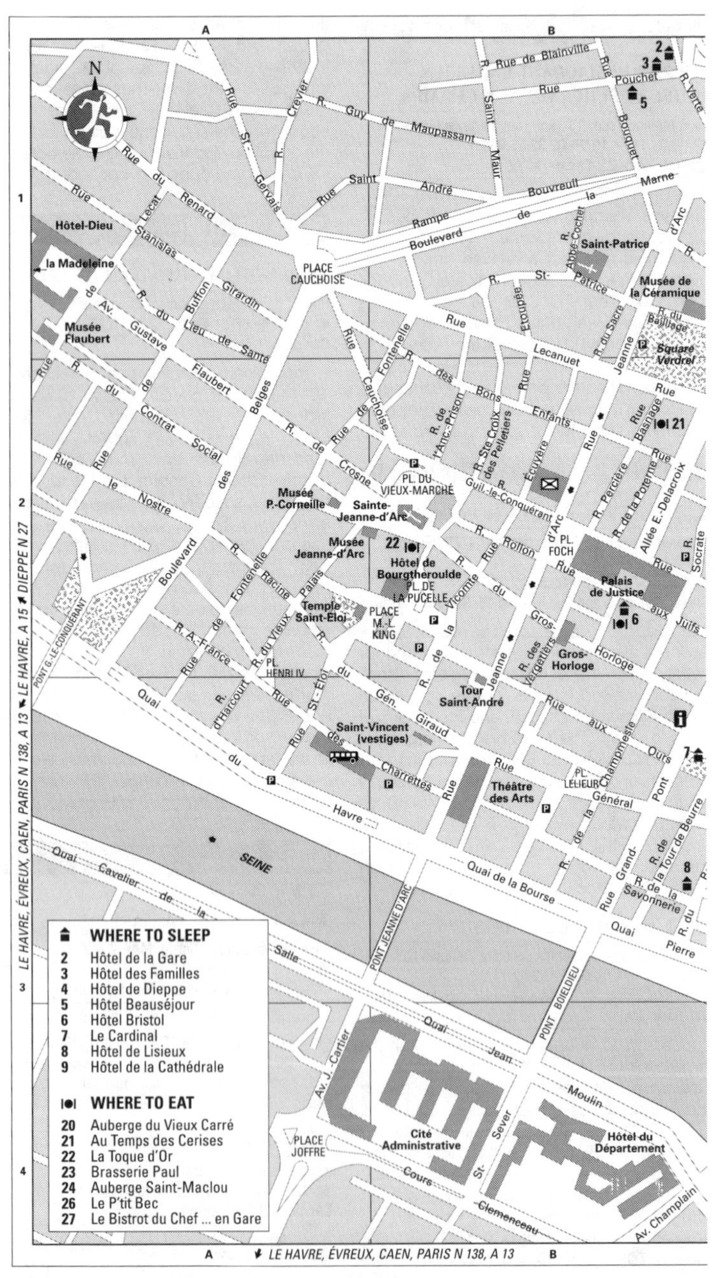

WHERE TO SLEEP
2 Hôtel de la Gare
3 Hôtel des Familles
4 Hôtel de Dieppe
5 Hôtel Beauséjour
6 Hôtel Bristol
7 Le Cardinal
8 Hôtel de Lisieux
9 Hôtel de la Cathédrale
WHERE TO EAT
20 Auberge du Vieux Carré
21 Au Temps des Cerises
22 La Toque d'Or
23 Brasserie Paul
24 Auberge Saint-Maclou
26 Le P'tit Bec
27 Le Bistrot du Chef ... en Gare
Hôtel-Dieu
la Madeleine
Musée Flaubert
PLACE CAUCHOISE
Saint-Patrice
Musée de la Céramique
Square Verdrel
Musée P.-Corneille
Sainte-Jeanne-d'Arc
PL. DU VIEUX-MARCHÉ
Musée Jeanne-d'Arc
Hôtel de Bourgtheroulde
PL. DE LA PUCELLE
PLACE M.-L. KING
Temple Saint-Éloi
PL. FOCH
Palais de Justice
Gros-Horloge
Tour Saint-André
Saint-Vincent (vestiges)
Théâtre des Arts
PL. LELIEUR
PL. HENRI IV
SEINE
PONT JEANNE D'ARC
PONT BOIELDIEU
PONT G.-LE-CONQUÉRANT
PLACE JOFFRE
Cité Administrative
Hôtel du Département
Quai du Havre
Quai de la Bourse
Quai Cavelier de la Salle
Quai Jean Moulin
Cours Clemenceau
Av. J. Cartier
Av. Champlain
LE HAVRE, ÉVREUX, CAEN, PARIS N 138, A 13
LE HAVRE, A 15
DIEPPE N 27

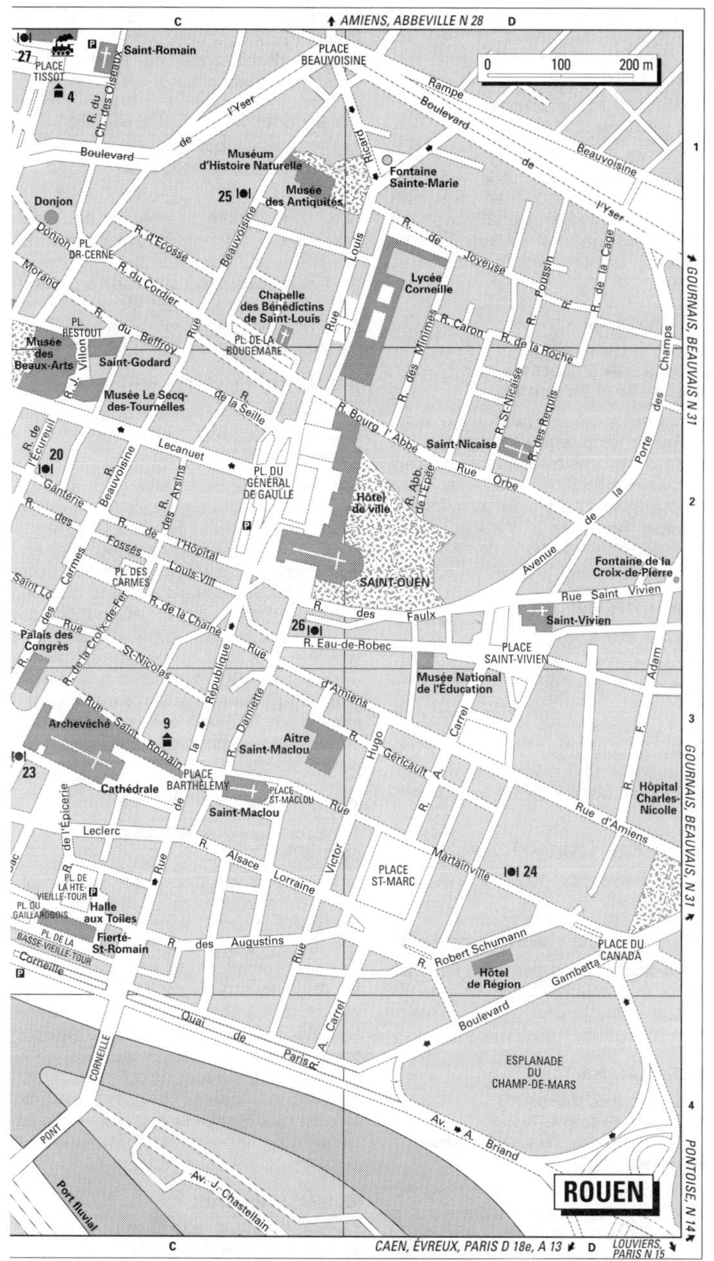
AMIENS, ABBEVILLE N 28
ROUEN
0 100 200 m
Saint-Romain
PLACE TISSOT
PLACE BEAUVOISINE
Muséum d'Histoire Naturelle
Musée des Antiquités
Fontaine Sainte-Marie
Donjon
Lycée Corneille
Chapelle des Bénédictins de Saint-Louis
PL. DE LA ROUGEMARE
Musée des Beaux-Arts
Saint-Godard
Musée Le Secq-des-Tournelles
Saint-Nicaise
PL. DU GÉNÉRAL DE GAULLE
Hôtel de ville
SAINT-OUEN
Fontaine de la Croix-de-Pierre
Saint-Vivien
PLACE SAINT-VIVIEN
Palais des Congrès
Musée National de l'Éducation
Archevêché
Cathédrale
PLACE BARTHÉLEMY
Aitre Saint-Maclou
PLACE ST-MACLOU
Saint-Maclou
Hôpital Charles-Nicolle
PLACE ST-MARC
Halle aux Toiles
Fierté-St-Romain
Hôtel de Région
PLACE DU CANADA
ESPLANADE DU CHAMP-DE-MARS
Port fluvial
GOURNAIS, BEAUVAIS N 31
PONTOISE, N 14
CAEN, ÉVREUX, PARIS D 18e, A 13
LOUVIERS, PARIS N 15

and the prices are good for a two-star hotel. Doubles 220F with shower/wc.

HÔTEL CÉLINE**

26 rue de Campulley; it's near the station.
☎ 02.35.71.95.23. Fax:02.35.89.53.71.

A large white bourgeois-style building in remarkably peaceful surroundings. Clean modern bedrooms decorated in pastel shades. Some of the ones on the top floor are particularly large but you'll find them a bit too hot at the height of summer. Good prices (215–250F).

HÔTEL ANDERSEN*

4 rue Pouchet; it's near the station.
☎ 02.35.71.88.51 F 02.35.07.54.65
Closed Dec 22–Jan 10. **Car park. TV.**

A very old building but a clean bright hotel that's been renovated throughout by Françoise, the proprietor. She offers doubles with shower/wc for 260F. It's more like a guest house than a hotel in atmosphere, since guests have use of the lounge and washing machine. In short, you'll feel at home.

10% HÔTEL BRISTOL

45 rue aux Juifs. **MAP B2-6**
☎ 02.35.71.54.21
Closed Sundays, evenings, and the first two weeks in August. **TV.**

Service 11.30am–3pm. A beautiful restored half-timbered building. Nine bedrooms. Expect to pay 250F for a double with bath and telephone. Small 49F set meal served weekdays.

10% HÔTEL DE LISIEUX**

4-6 rue de la Savonnerie; it's between the cathedral and the Seine. **MAP B3-8**
☎ 02.35.71.87.73 F 02.35.89.31.52
Closed Christmas–New Year's Day. **Secure parking. TV.**

This is a welcoming and well cared for hotel. Fully equipped doubles 280F (with shower/wc) 320F (with bath). Most have been renovated.

10% LE CARDINAL**

1 place de la Cathédrale. **MAP B3-7**
☎ 02.35.70.24.42 F 02.35.89.75.14
Closed Christmas/New Year. **Car park. TV. Canal+. Disabled access.**

It's got the best location in town. Almost every room overlooks the cathedral which is a splendid sight when floodlit in the evenings. The owner's perfectly charming and the rooms are extremely well maintained. Doubles 275F (with shower/wc) –360F (with a brand new bathroom). You'll definitely get your money's worth here.

10% HÔTEL DE LA CATHÉDRALE**

12 rue Saint-Romain. **MAP C3-9**
☎ 02.35.71.57.95 F 02.35.70.15.54
TV.

Service 7am–10pm. Situated in a pedestrian street that runs alongside the cathedral, a marvellous and delightful little hotel (one of the few in Rouen) laid out round a pleasant patio. Good location and it's quiet. Doubles 300F with shower/wc, 355F with bath. Just a pity that the reception is a bit curt.

HÔTEL DE DIEPPE***

place Bernard-Tissot. **MAP C1-4**
☎ 02.35.71.96.00. Fax:02.35.89.65.21.
TV. Canal+.

Service noon–2.30pm and 7.30–10pm. A large traditional hotel run by a family who've been in the business longer than anyone else in town. Stylish 30s décor and top notch service. Prices for the fully equipped rooms start at 510F but you can get a special weekend rate of 360F if you stay Friday and Saturday (or Saturday and Sunday). The restaurant's very well known for its speciality of pressed Rouen duck. Gourmet set meals start at 138F. If you like eating late, we can recommend the hotel bar which is open until 1am. Good grills and set meals at 98F and 128F served all week.

LA TOQUE D'OR

11 place du Vieux-Marché. **MAP B2-22**
☎ 02.35.71.46.29

Eat here and you'll be in the very square where the English burnt Joan of Arc at the stake. This attractive Normandy building has two dining rooms: a stylish one on the ground floor aimed at middle-class customers, and a large informal one upstairs with no table cloths for the younger generation. As you've probably guessed, we preferred the atmosphere upstairs. The cooking's just as good and the set meals, which start at a mere 58F (except Saturday evenings and Sunday lunchtimes) are cheaper, not to say terrific value. Pleasant medieval décor.

BRASSERIE PAUL

1 place de la Cathédrale. **MAP C3-23**
☎ 02.35.71.86.07 F 02.35.15.14.43

Lunch served 11.30–3pm, dinner 6.30–11pm. As it says at the top of the menu, this place has been serving copious helpings of food to the locals since 1911. Simone de Beauvoir was a regular and she was right to be. They do enormous fresh salads and main courses of the kind that need long slow cooking. *Formules* from 59F. We recommend the dish of the day which is unbeatable value for money at 39–49F. Chef Gaétan (there's a portrait of him in the dining room) is mellow, pleasantly plump and a Norman through and through. You can't leave without trying his great speciality – apple and Camembert turnover which is a real treat! Have dinner on the terrace on summer evenings and enjoy the view of the floodlit cathedral.

AU TEMPS DES CERISES

4-6 rue des Basnage. **MAP B2-21**
☎ 02.35.89.98.00
Closed Sundays and Monday lunchtimes.

You won't find another restaurant in Rouen that offers such a wide range of cheese dishes. Cheerful décor, kitsch colour scheme and funny knick-knacks connected with dairy farming. Don't miss the escalope of turkey with Camembert or treat yourself to the Normandy *fondue*. Local youngsters come for the imaginative yet simple food as much as for the low prices. Set meals 60F (lunchtimes only), 88F and 125F.

AUBERGE SAINT-MACLOU

224-226 rue Martainville. **MAP D3-24**
☎ 02.35.71.06.67
Closed Sunday evenings and Mondays.

Despite being in such a touristy street, this is not one of those over-rated tourist traps. It's a timber building with genuine rustic décor and a little terrace in summer. The kind of cooking that puts new life into you after an exhausting day doing the sights. They do a very decent 65F set meal at lunchtimes (includes wine and coffee!). Evening set meals 79F (served until 8.30pm on Saturdays in summer only), 99F, 129F and up.

LE P'TIT BEC

182 rue Eau-de-Robec. **MAP C2-26**
☎ 02.35.07.63.33
Closed Sundays and every evening except Fridays.

Service noon–3pm, and until 11pm on Fridays. Wonderful home cooking at lunchtime. It specializes in *gratins* and coddled eggs. Bright dining room and delightful service from the waitresses racing about to keep all the regulars happy. Advisable to book. There may only be one set meal (72F) but it's very well put together. In fine weather, sit out on the terrace that overlooks one of the prettiest streets in Rouen. Serves tea in the afternoons.

LE BISTROT DU CHEF... EN GARE

place Bernard-Tissot (North). **MAP C1-27**
☎ 02.35.71.48.66 F➜ 02.35.15.14.43
Closed Sundays, Monday evenings and August.

We've got well-known local chef Gilles Tournadre to thank for the fact that this station buffet, unlike so many others, serves excellent food. On the ground floor there's a beautiful Art Déco room that functions as a self-service cafeteria at mealtimes and offers terrific value for money. Upstairs there's a large, quieter room that's open at lunchtime (except on Saturdays and in July and August). Hushed atmosphere and regular customers. Cheapest set meal 75F. The 120F one (the price includes apéritif, wine and coffee) offers bistro specialities with a Normandy flavour and is hard to beat.

AUBERGE DU VIEUX CARRÉ

34 rue Ganterie (Centre). **MAP C2-20**
☎ 02.35.71.67.70 F➜ 02.35.98.56.21
Closed Sunday evenings and Mondays.

Lunch served noon–2pm, dinner 7–9pm. A truly delightful restaurant at the far end of a small paved courtyard. You've the choice of eating on the flower-filled patio or in the dining room with its pale wood furniture. The cooking is firmly based on traditional local dishes and livened up with some creative touches. Set meals 120F, 170F and 230F. À la carte you've got *soufflé* of three different kinds of fish, medallions of monkfish with an anchovy sauce, braised veal sweetbreads with acacia honey, and *andouillette* of Peking duck with Szechuan pepper. You're in for a treat!

DUCLAIR 76480 (16KM NW)

LES FALAISES

75 rue Jules-Ferry; turn right in front of the town hall.
☎ 02.35.37.79.17
Closed Mondays (except in season and on public holidays). **Car park. TV.**

Lunch served noon–2pm, dinner 7–9pm. A little 19th century building upstream from the village. Pleasant informal service. Bedrooms may be old-fashioned but they're clean and spacious. Expect to pay 125F (with basin), 250F (with shower/wc). They do classic regional cooking at reasonable prices and a nice 70F set meal is available every day.

RESTAURANT AU VAL DE SEINE

380 quai de la Libération; take the D982 – follow the river, and you'll see it just across from the ferry.
☎ 02.35.37.99.88
Closed Monday evenings and Tuesdays.

You'll be greeted by smiling staff at this place, which can probably provide you with the kind of food you're looking for since it's a café, a brasserie, a restaurant AND a tearoom. The neutral colours are fairly uninspiring but you've got a view of the Seine and the ferries. Panoramic dining room on the first floor and very reasonable prices. The set meals at 65F and 72F are particularly satisfying and there are another three for less than 108F. Dishes include warm salad of queen scallops, mussels with raspberry vinegar, John Dory with basil, and seafood platter. Attentive service. It's cheap and consistently good so it gets a lot of regulars.

CLÈRES 76690 (18,5KM N)

LE FLAMANT ROSE

place de la Halle; take the D27; turn off onto the D6 at Boulay.
☎ 02.35.33.22.47
Closed Monday evenings, Tuesdays and Oct 15–Nov 15.

Service noon–2pm. You're bound to feel a bit peckish after visiting the zoo and the antique car show and this place offers simple cooking, regional dishes and a few brasserie classics such as perch fillets and tripe with Calvados. Set meals 50F (lunchtimes only), 68F, 89F and up. Reservations compulsory in the evenings.

RY 76116 (20KM E)

RESTAURANT LE BOVARY

Grande-Rue.
☎ 02.35.23.61.46.
Closed Monday evenings and Tuesdays.

Flaubert went into raptures over the church, the covered market and even this restaurant with its cosy atmosphere and wonderful timber façade. But back then he probably didn't have so many set meals to choose from. Now you can have one for 60F (weekdays), 90F, 110F, 130F and 165F. There's something for everybody, no matter how low on funds you are or the size of your appetite. It's not often you get as good value for money as you do with the terrific 60F set meal. Staff are welcoming and the service hard to fault, which is rather amazing when you consider how little you're paying. In the evening, the 110F set meal is sheer delight and offers oysters, smoked salmon or snails in puff pastry. The main course will change with the seasons but is something along the lines of fillets of duck, *coq au vin* or scallops.

SAINT-VALÉRY-EN-CAUX 76460

HÔTEL-RESTAURANT LA MARINE

113 rue Saint-Léger (South-West); from the bridge pass the tourist office then take the first on the left.
☎ 02.35.97.05.09
Closed Fridays in winter and end Nov–start Feb.

Lunch served noon–2pm, dinner 7–9pm. You'll be made to feel very welcome in this quiet little family-run hotel and restaurant. Bedrooms 180–200F with shower/wc or bath and TV. There may be no fancy trimmings, but the facilities are perfectly adequate. Set meals 60F (weekdays), 90F, 120F and 150F served in two nicely old-fashioned little dining rooms. Regional specialities. Half-board 185F.

10% HÔTEL HENRI IV**

16 route du Havre (South-West); from the centre go towards Fécamp and Cany-Barville and you'll find the hotel several hundred metres along on the left.
☎ 02.35.97.19.62 F→ 02.35.57.10.01
TV. Disabled access.

Owner Michèle loves what she's doing and there's a cheerful atmosphere in this large, ivy-covered, brick building. Comfortable bedrooms range in price from 190F with basin to 290F with bath. The ones at the back are the quietest. Michèle's also very fond of flying and if you'd like a trip along the coast, she can arrange it with her friends at the flying club.

LE RESTAURANT DU PORT

18 quai d'Amont (Centre).
☎ 02.35.97.08.93 F→ 02.35.97.28.32
Closed Sundays and Mondays out of season.

As you might have guessed from the name, it's by the harbour and specializes in fish and seafood. It's the chicest place in town, elegant but not showy. A classy establishment in other words and the prices reflect that. Set meals 118F (simple and classic) and 198F (*cassoulet* of seafood and smoked salmon *terrine*. Seafood platter 158F. They also have a few choices for meat lovers. The service can't be faulted. Large windows offering a good view of the port.

SOTTEVILLE-SUR-MER 76740 (10KM E)

HÔTEL DES ROCHERS**

place de l'Église.
☎ 02.35.97.07.06
Closed Jan–Feb. **Disabled access**.

A big bourgeois-style building that was once the presbytery. The delightful garden's surrounded by a high wall. They have ten or so quiet and comfortable rooms with shower or bath (250–280F). A good hotel and the reception is excellent, so you're in a for a pleasant stay.

RESTAURANT LES EMBRUNS

place de l'Église; go towards Dieppe and turn left onto the D68 at Veules-les-Roses.
☎ 02.35.97.77.99
Closed Sunday evenings, Mondays, and Jan 20–Feb 10.

This former bar and tobacconist's has been transformed into a gourmet restaurant. Main courses range from 120F to 180F in the evening and starter, cheese and dessert are included in the price, while at lunchtime they start at 72F, with starter and dessert or coffee. Specialities range beyond the purely regional to include *noisettes* of lamb *à la provençale*, lobster with fresh basil, and chicken with morels.

SAINT-MARTIN-AUX-BUNEAUX 76540 (17KM W)

HÔTEL-RESTAURANT DE LA PLAGE

92 rue Joseph-Heuzé; take the D925 towards Fécamp and it's in the main street 50m from the beach.
☎ 02.35.27.40.77
Closed Sunday evenings and Wednesdays out of season, and in February, at Easter and during the Christmas school holidays.

You'll get a warm welcome from proprietors Monsieur and Madame Pierre in this handsome brick building with its wooden balconies and delightful turrets. It's very quiet and the cosy rooms are inexpensive, ranging in price from 170F with basin (private shower/wc on the landing) to 230F with bath. You don't often find such a good hotel on the coast with rates like these. The little dining room, a mixture of traditional and modern styles, hass been tastefully and lovingly decorated. Fine cooking (of a quality that's evident even in the starters) and dishes like warm oysters on a bed of lettuce (the house speciality), *civet* of winkles with cider and *coulis* of beetroot with apples. Set meals 88F (served every lunchtime and evening!), 135F and 158F.

RESTAURANT L'ESPÉRANCE

76 rue Joseph-Heuzé (Centre).
☎ 02.35.27.42.77

A charming little corner restaurant of brick and wood with a terrace and two rather English-looking dining rooms. The cooking resembles the traditional dishes your granny used to make. Very satisfying set meals 70–130F. The kind of country place we love. Drinks are a bit expensive though.

TRÉPORT (LE) 76470

10% HÔTEL DE CALAIS

1-5-11 rue de Paris.
☎ 02.35.86.07.46
Car park.

This former coaching inn, which has been perched above the harbour for close to two centuries now, has seen a fair bit of life and has welcomed people ranging from Victor Hugo to workers on their first paid holiday and American GIs. It's got a lot of character – as you'll realize after spending the night in one of the rooms with large windows, a little wooden table, flowery wallpaper, and lino. And you can't leave without seeing the breakfast room – it's got old engravings and photos of the area, a cosy atmosphere and a view of the harbour. The rooms, all different, are very basic. Some overlook the harbour, some don't – don't say we didn't warn you! Lovely reception and prices to match. Doubles 180–200F with basin (and period bidet) and 250–300F with shower/wc. There's a 30F supplement for TV. They've got furnished flats and rooms in the annexe but it's best to enquire about those for yourself since there are so many options it would take too long to list them all here.

LE RICHELIEU*

50 quai François-Ier; it's by the harbour.
☎ 02.35.86.26.55 F 02.35.86.09.60
Car park. **TV**.

A clean modern hotel near the beach with fully equipped bedrooms, some of which have a sea view. Doubles 280–350F. The restaurant, which serves fish and seafood, is decorated in 30s style with a 90s touch. The cheapest set meal on a weekday is 55F and includes cheese or dessert. Others 69–125F.

|●| MON P'TIT BAR

3-5 rue de la Rade (Centre).
☎ 02.35.86.28.78

The kind of authentic and unstuffy little place we like so much, and it makes a nice change from certain other places nearby which shall be nameless. It's not so much a conventional restaurant as a bar serving food all day and late into the night. People come for the dishes based on fresh market produce, the low prices and the friendly reception rather than the décor. Good seafood platters.

|●| LA MATELOTE

34 quai François-Ier (Centre).
☎ 02.35.86.01.13 F 02.35.86.17.02
Closed Christmas/New Year holidays.

Service 11.30–3pm and 6–10.30pm. Let's get one thing straight – the fish and seafood dishes are the only reasons for coming here because they're as fresh as can be. Navy blue and prawn pink are the predominant colours and the whole décor is pretty naive but ok. From the first-floor dining room you'll be able to watch the boats in the harbour and the waves breaking on the pier during a storm. They do dishes like sole *meunière*, grilled sea bream, *gratin* of mussels and fillets of brill. Set meals 79F (except weekends and public holidays) and 125–230F. Seafood platters 88F, 125F and up. Service may be rather affected but there's a wide choice on the menu and no nasty surprises.

CRIEL-SUR-MER 76910 (4.5KM SW)

⌂ |●| HOSTELLERIE DE LA VIEILLE FERME**

Mesnil-Val-Plage; take the scenic road along the cliffs and it's in the main street 300m from the beach.
☎ 02.35.86.72.18 F 02.35.86.12.67
Closed Sunday evenings out of season. **Car park**. **TV**. **Canal+**.

An enormous traditional Normandy building that has all the facilities a terrace, a large garden with a children's play area and a manicured lawn) plus cider presses and birds singing in the trees. Cosy rustic décor. Very comfortable bedrooms 340–460F. The set meals, which feature dishes like seafood *pot au feu*, lobster salad with asparagus tips and raspberry butter, and Grand Marnier soufflé, start at 109F and are served in a beautiful bourgeois-style dining room. The ideal place for a breath of fresh air and a spot of relaxation.

VERNEUIL-SUR-AVRE 27130

⌂ |●| HÔTEL LE SAUMON**

89 place de la Madeleine; it's on the same square as the church.
☎ 02.32.32.02.36 F 02.32.37.55.80
Closed Christmas–Jan 5. **TV**. **Canal+**.
Disabled access.

Lunch served noon–2pm, dinner 7.15–9pm. A good provincial hotel, very well looked after. To get to the bedrooms in the annexe, you have to pass the kitchens in the internal courtyard and they really do inspire confidence. Doubles from 210F with shower/wc and a view of the old city walls or the square and the magnificent church tower (these are the most expensive). Whichever way your room faces you'll get a good night's sleep. The restaurant is very good and serves dishes typical of this particular part of Normandy. There's salmon of course and lobster, seafood, veal sweetbreads, and leg of duck *à la normande*. Set meals 65F (weekdays), 85F, 155F and 260F. The hearty buffet breakfast certainly perked us up. A conventional hotel and restaurant that's been around for a long time and that you can rely on.

BÂLINES 27130 (2KM E)

10% ⌂ |●| MOULIN DE BALISNE**

N12.
☎ 02.32.32.03.48 F 02.32.60.11.22
Secure parking. **TV**.

Service noon–2.30pm and 7.30–10.30pm. Close to 30 acres of meadows, woods, ponds and rivers surround this place, making it the perfect place for lovers and for people who love peace and quiet. They've got eight comfortable and delightful rooms full of trinkets and souvenirs (400–450F) and two suites. Half-board advisable weekends and public holidays. The dining room's decorated with antique bric-a-brac and beautiful paintings and the cooking's as creative as it's tasty (even if they don't always know when to leave well enough alone). You can get lovely set meals from 100F. House specialities include artichoke hearts with fresh *foie gras*, *cassolette* of veal sweetbreads *à la normande* and *marquise* of smoked salmon. Wonderful terrace.

VERNON 27200

⌂ |●| HÔTEL D'ÉVREUX – RESTAURANT LE RELAIS NORMAND***

11 place d'Évreux (Centre).

☎ 02.32.21.16.12 F➔ 02.32.21.32.73
Restaurant closed Sunday evenings except Easter and Whitsun. **Secure parking**. **TV**.

Lunch served noon–2pm, dinner 7–9.30pm. A word of advice – it's a very good idea to book. A typical Normandy house from the outside but inside it looks as if it has stepped straight out of the Black Forest. The Austrian proprietress has created a cosy atmosphere by decorating it with things to remind her of home. There's a collection of beer tankards, a kitsch rustic bar and an impressive fireplace.The conservatory is open during the summer months. They've got a French chef who's particularly fond of good food. Try one of his specialities – rabbit in aspic, *saucisson* of pig's trotters with truffle sauce, or cod *Bovary*. Set meals 120F (except Sundays), 165F and 250F. The refurbished rooms (280–350F) are clean and quiet.

I●I LE RELAIS DES TOURELLES

Vernonnet–rue de la Chaussée (North-East); it's opposite Vernon on the other side of the Seine.
☎ 02.32.51.54.52 F➔ 02.32.21.63.66
Closed Mondays and Sunday evenings. **Car park**.

Louis IX of France came to this little village for the watercress. You too can sample the regional specialities (don't worry, they have more than watercress) in this cosy, charming little timbered restaurant. How about John Dory with *beure nantais* or warm oysters with a *fondue* of leeks? Set meals 99F (starter – as much as you can eat – main course, cheese and dessert) and 159F. À la carte also available. A good restaurant only 4km from Giverny but a world away from the hordes of tourists and their coaches.

GIVERNY 27620 (5KM E)

⌂ I●I HÔTEL LA MUSARDIÈRE**

123 rue Claude-Monet (Centre); it's just after the museum.
☎ 02.32.21.03.18 F➔ 02.32.21.60.00
Secure parking. **TV**.

A large bourgeois-style building with a veranda and a huge garden, not far from Monet's house. Expect to pay 300–400F for a double. Set meals 80F (weekdays), 145F and 220F. They've got a crêperie too.

I●I RESTAURANT LES NYMPHÉAS

rue Claude-Monet (Centre); it's across from the Monet museum.
☎ 02.32.21.20.31
Closed Mondays and Oct 31–April 1. **Car park**.

The ideal place if you've been to see Monet's house and gardens and want something to eat before heading off to the American museum. Marble tables give the place a bistro atmosphere. It has two terraces: one opposite the car park and the other (covered) on the other side. Courteous welcome. Everything's à la carte, with substantial main dishes ranging in price from 55F to 70F, various salads (40F and 50F or thereabouts), cheeseboard and icecream. Decorated with Toulouse-Lautrec posters!

I●I LES JARDINS DU GIVERNY

1 rue du Milieu (chemin du Roy); it's signposted – take the D5 from Vernon and it's on the left 1km after the petrol station.
☎ 02.32.21.60.80 F➔ 02.32.51.93.77
Closed Mondays, Sunday evenings, and February.
Car park.

Lunch served noon–3.30pm, brunch until 6pm. Not Monet's garden at Giverny but it's not lacking in charm – and Monet did eat here, as did the politicians Clémenceau and Aristide Briand and lots of other famous people. It's a typical Normandy building serving typical Normandy dishes in a Louis 16th dining rooml. You can still see the rings they used to tie their horses to. The set meals (120F, 170F and 230F) all come with a *trou normand* (usually a shot of Calvados served half-way through the meal to aid digestion but here it's a cider and Calvados sorbet). Excellent local specialities and fish dishes, some of the latter flavoured with seaweed. And alongside the set meal menu you'll find advice on which wine to choose. A very classy place.

FOURGES 27630 (15KM NE)

I●I LE MOULIN DE FOURGES

38 rue du Moulin; take the D5 towards Magny-en-Vexin and watch out for the signposts as you come into Fourges.
☎ 02.32.52.12.12 F➔ 02.32.52.92.56
Closed Mondays, Sundays evenings (except during summer) and Jan 2–Feb 12.

A former mill on the banks of the Epte, a beautiful fast-flowing river, that's worth visiting for the romantic setting alone. Decorated in soothing pastel colours. The shaded terrace is enjoyable in summer. Fine cuisine and set meals at 115F (except weekends), 155F, 225F and 295F. A bit of advice: stay well away at the weekend when the tour buses and cars fight over the parking spaces – as close to the mill as they can possibly get, of course! We wonder what Monet and the other Impressionists would have made of it all.

YVETOT 76190

|●| BRASSERIE DU CHEMIN DE FER

place de la Gare (North).
☎ 02.35.95.10.33
Closed Sundays.

Monique will serve up traditional dishes based on fresh produce at any time of day. The dish of the day (35F) will be something along the lines of escalope *normande*, mussel or crab tart, *pot au feu*, or veal stew *à la normande.* And as you'd expect there's plenty of home-made pastries. The ideal place to pop into while waiting for your train.

|●| RESTAURANT LA PERGOLA

52 av. Clemenceau (North-East); take the N15 and you'll see it as you come into Yvetot from Rouen.
☎ 02.35.95.08.13 F→ 02.35.95.00.25
Closed Monday evenings, Tuesdays and two weeks in July. **Car park**.

Service noon–3pm and 7–9.30pm. The best restaurant of its kind in town. The traditional décor, the hushed atmosphere and the first-rate cooking combine to make this a very pleasant place to eat. The 73F set meal (available lunchtimes and evenings) represents unbeatable value for money and offers dishes like mussels in a cider and cream sauce, calf's head with herbs, and warm *tarte Tatin* (a kind of upside down apple cake) with cream. The other set meals (110F, 160F and 175F) come with seafood specialities. They also have a 75F *formule* at lunchtime on weekdays which includes everything. Good wine list.

CROIX-MARE 76190 (5KM SE)

|●| AUBERGE DE LA FORGE

How to get there: take the N15 towards Rouen.
☎ 02.35.91.25.94
Closed Tuesday evenings and Wednesdays (except public holidays and the day before public holidays).
Car park.

Service noon–2pm and 7–9pm. A low-key country restaurant serving traditional regional dishes. Friendly professional service and an owner directing his dining room staff like some great master chef from the kitchens. Set meals 102F, 115F, 150F, 170F, 245F (for big eaters, this one) and 250F. There are lots of tasty treats in store such as leg of guinea fowl *confit* and *bavarois* of stuffed brocoli.

10% |●| AUBERGE DU VAL AU CESNE

How to get there: follow the D5 from Yvetot in the direction of Duclair for 3km.
☎ 02.35.56.63.06 F→ 02.35.56.92.78
Car park.

Lunch served noon–2pm, dinner 7–9pm. The farm animals frolicking outside this cosy old Normandy inn create a perfect pastoral setting – not just any old cows and sheep, mind you, since the proprietor has a strongly developed sense of the aesthetic, but mandarin ducks, pedigree black sheep, bantams and beautiful doves in an aviary. The excellent cooking and the unusual setting make the prices a bit less hard to swallow. You can eat outside in summer and the chickens will come and peck at the crumbs. Try the stuffed pigeon, the escalope of turkey made to a recipe devised by one of the old ladies in the area or the juicy steak. We didn't mind spending 150F for a set meal of starter, main course and dessert. Expect to pay at least 220F à la carte.

Pays-de-la-Loire

44 Loire-Atlantique

49 Maine-et-Loire

53 Mayenne

72 Sarthe

85 Vendée

AIGUILLON-SUR-MER (L') 85460

HÔTEL LES VOYAGEURS*

13 rue du Général-Leclerc (North).
☎ 02.51.56.40.90
Closed Mondays Oct 1–June 30, one week in March and one week in October

A very affordable hotel in a quiet neighbourhood. It's above a bar and offers 13 attractive little bedrooms. Doubles 140F with basin/bidet and 180F with shower/wc. You won't see many seaside hotels with prices like these! Warm welcome.

ANGERS 49000

SEE MAP ON PP.600–601

CENTRE D'HÉBERGEMENT DU LAC DE MAINE-AUBERGE DE JEUNESSE

49 av. du Lac-de-Maine; it's about 2km from the centre; take a number 6 or 16 bus towards Bouchemaine and get off at the "Lac du Maine" or "Perrusaie" stop. Off map **A3-1**
☎ 02.41.22.32.10 ➡ 02.41.22.32.11
Secure parking. **Disabled access**.

Accommodation for approximately 125. Rooms sleep one, two or four people. You'll pay 132F a night in a single room and 97F in a twin. Prices include breakfast. Membership card compulsory (15F) unless you have an FUAJ card. A few family rooms. Two meals will cost you 47F. Spacious and well equipped, with the added bonus of a park and a lake. Water sports and nature trails nearby.

10% HÔTEL DU CENTRE

12 rue Saint-Laud. **MAP B2-3**
☎ 02.41.87.45.07

This traditional little hotel may be a touch out-dated, but it's not depressing. A maze of staircases lead to the 15 or so bedrooms. They don't have much character but they're well looked after. Doubles 140F (wc on the landing) and 160F with shower/wc. Ground floor bar and terrace very popular with young people. Things can get a bit noisy in the evenings.

10% HÔTEL DU MANS*

34 bis bd Ayrault. **MAP B1-4**
☎ 02.41.87.49.63 ➡ 02.41.86.19.83
Closed Sundays and Aug 1–15. **Car park**. **TV**.

A small hotel without any special charm in an uninspiring part of town but you'll get an exceptionally warm welcome and it's very well cared for. Refurbished, attractive bedrooms in pale colours 185F with shower/wc. A few doubles with basin 170F (185F with basin/wc). Try for one of the quieter ones overlooking rue Choudieu.

L'AUBERGE BELLE RIVE

25 bis rue Haute-Reculée; from the centre, go past port de la Haute-Cha"ne, then follow the river. Off map **B1-6**
☎ 02.41.48.18.70
Closed Saturday lunchtimes, Sunday evenings and end of Jan–mid Feb. **Car park**. **TV**.

Although it's a bit out of the centre it's very popular with the locals, so you'd be well advised to book. A private house with an elegant dining room that sees lots of businessmen at lunchtime. Fairly chic clientele in the evenings. Good cooking. Set meals 95–235F. Specialities include *gigot* of monkfish with lobster, veal kidneys with two kinds of mus-

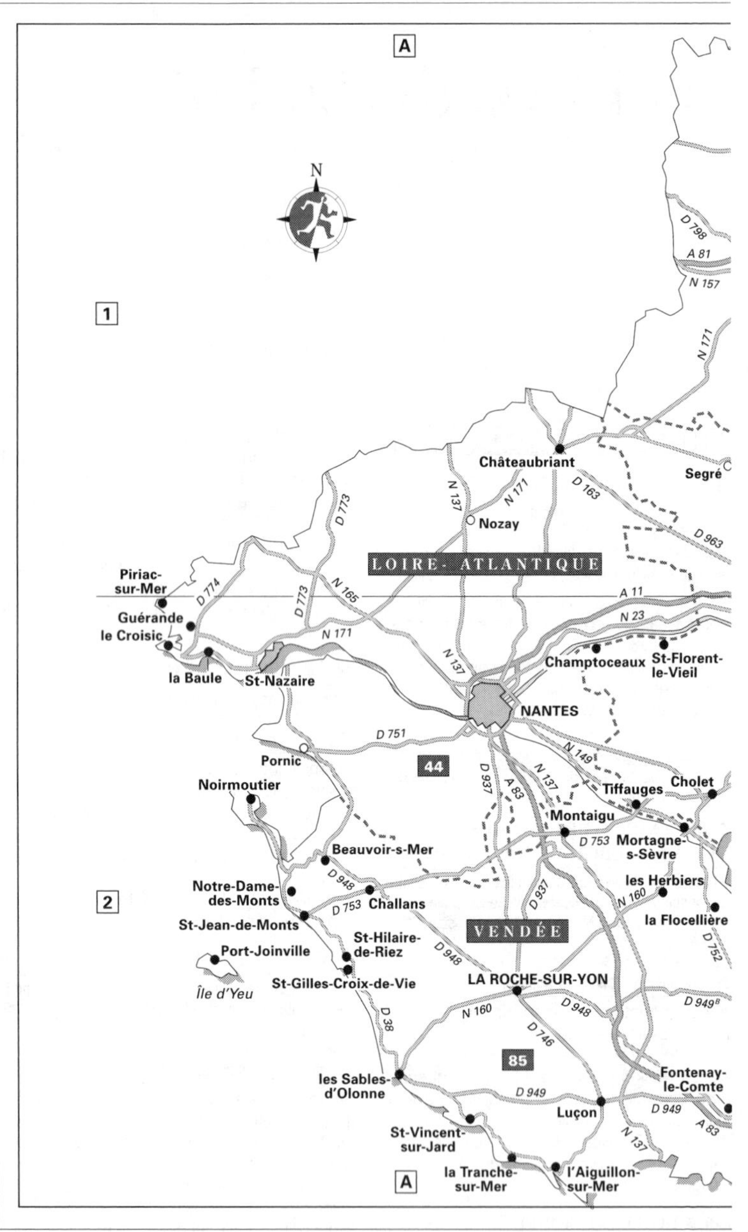
A
1
2
N
LOIRE-ATLANTIQUE
VENDÉE
44
85
Châteaubriant
Segré
Nozay
Piriac-sur-Mer
Guérande
le Croisic
la Baule
St-Nazaire
Champtoceaux
St-Florent-le-Vieil
NANTES
Pornic
Noirmoutier
Tiffauges
Cholet
Montaigu
Mortagne-s-Sèvre
Beauvoir-s-Mer
les Herbiers
Notre-Dame-des-Monts
Challans
la Flocellière
St-Jean-de-Monts
St-Hilaire-de-Riez
Port-Joinville
Île d'Yeu
St-Gilles-Croix-de-Vie
LA ROCHE-SUR-YON
les Sables-d'Olonne
Fontenay-le-Comte
Luçon
St-Vincent-sur-Jard
la Tranche-sur-Mer
l'Aiguillon-sur-Mer
D 798
A 81
N 157
N 171
D 163
D 963
N 137
D 773
D 774
N 165
A 11
N 23
D 751
D 937
A 83
N 149
D 753
D 948
N 160
D 752
D 949
D 949B
D 746
D 38

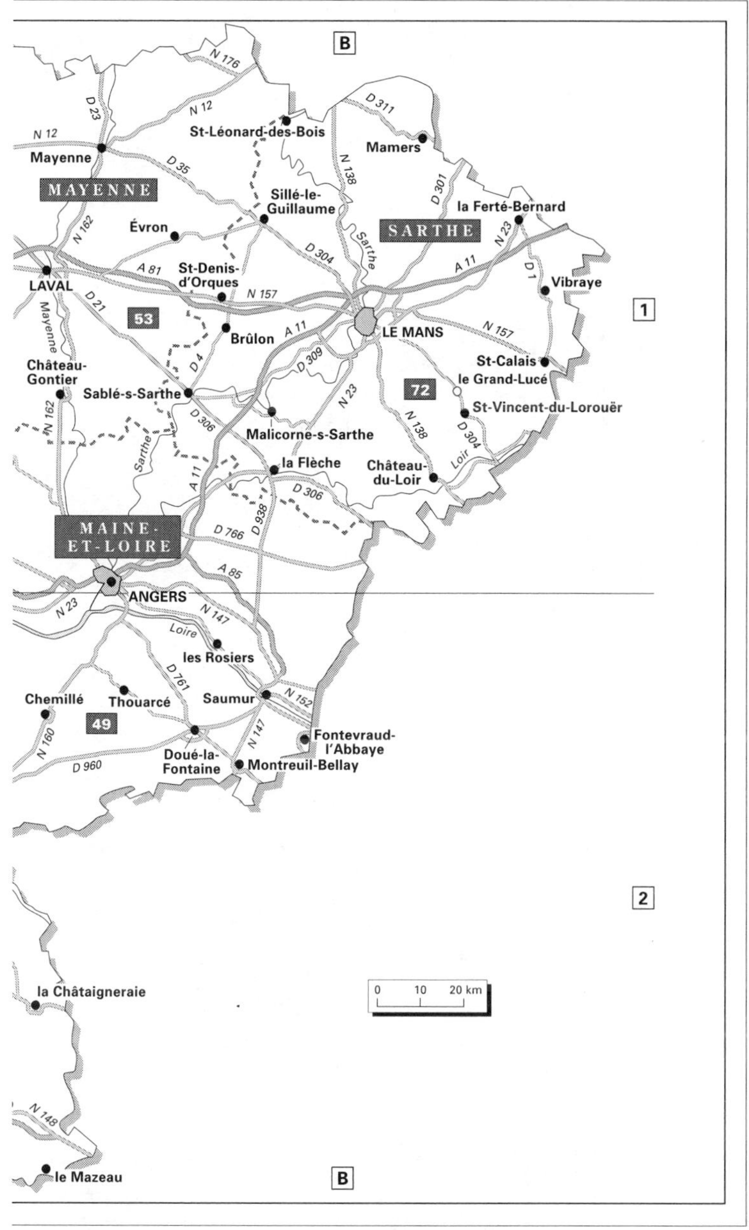
B
N 176
D 311
D 23
N 12
N 12
St-Léonard-des-Bois
Mamers
Mayenne
D 35
N 138
MAYENNE
Sillé-le-Guillaume
D 301
la Ferté-Bernard
N 162
Évron
SARTHE
N 23
D 304
Sarthe
A 81
St-Denis-d'Orques
A 11
D 1
LAVAL
Vibraye
D 21
N 157
Mayenne
53
1
Brûlon
A 11
LE MANS
N 157
D 309
Château-Gontier
St-Calais
D 4
le Grand-Lucé
72
Sablé-s-Sarthe
N 23
St-Vincent-du-Lorouër
N 162
D 306
N 138
D 304
Malicorne-s-Sarthe
Sarthe
Loir
la Flèche
Château-du-Loir
A 11
D 306
D 938
MAINE-ET-LOIRE
D 766
A 85
ANGERS
N 23
N 147
Loire
les Rosiers
D 761
Chemillé
Thouarcé
Saumur
N 152
49
N 160
N 147
Fontevraud-l'Abbaye
Doué-la-Fontaine
D 960
Montreuil-Bellay
2
la Châtaigneraie
0
10
20 km
N 148
le Mazeau
B

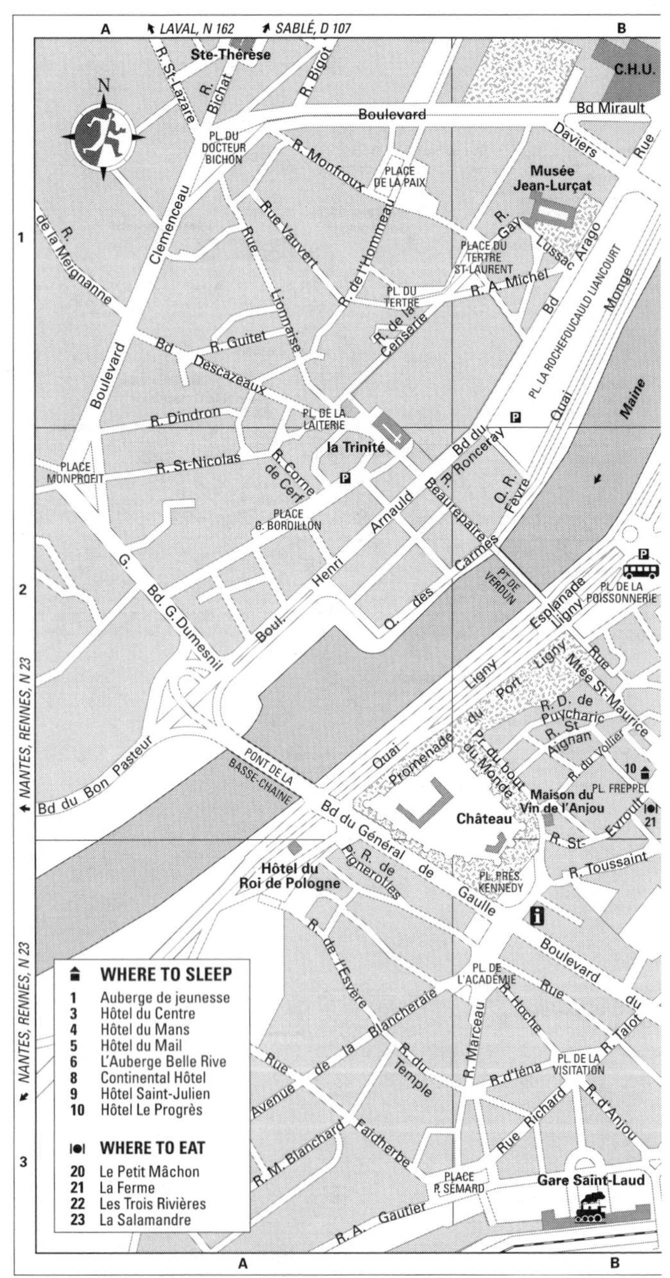
LAVAL, N 162
SABLÉ, D 107
NANTES, RENNES, N 23
Ste-Thérèse
C.H.U.
Boulevard
Bd Mirault
Musée Jean-Lurçat
la Trinité
Château
Maison du Vin de l'Anjou
Hôtel du Roi de Pologne
Gare Saint-Laud
Maine
PLACE DE LA PAIX
PL. DU DOCTEUR BICHON
PLACE DU TERTRE ST-LAURENT
PL. DU TERTRE
PL. DE LA LAITERIE
PLACE MONPROFIT
PLACE G. BORDILLON
PL. LA ROCHEFOUCAULD LIANCOURT
PT DE VERDUN
PL. DE LA POISSONNERIE
PONT DE LA BASSE-CHAINE
PL. FREPPEL
PL. PRÉS. KENNEDY
PL. DE L'ACADÉMIE
PL. DE LA VISITATION
PLACE P. SÉMARD
Bd du Bon Pasteur
Bd du Général de Gaulle
Boulevard Clemenceau
Bd G. Dumesnil
Bd Descazeaux
Bd Arago
Bd du Ronceray
Boul. Henri Arnauld
Quai Monge
Quai Ligny
Esplanade Ligny
Promenade du Port Ligny
Q. des Carmes
Q. R. Fèvre
R. Beaurepaire
R. Dindron
R. St-Nicolas
R. Corne de Cerf
R. Guitet
Rue Lionnaise
Rue Vauvert
R. de l'Hommeau
R. Monfroux
R. de la Censerie
R. A. Michel
R. Gay Lussac
R. de la Meignanne
R. St-Lazare
R. Bichat
R. Bigot
Rue Daviers
R. de Pignerolles
R. de l'Esvière
Rue de la Blancheraie
R. du Temple
R. Marceau
R. Hoche
R. d'Iéna
Rue Richard
R. d'Anjou
R. Talot
Boulevard du Roi René
Rue Faidherbe
Avenue
R. M. Blanchard
R. A. Gautier
R. Toussaint
R. St-Evroult
R. du Vollier
R. St Aignan
R. D. de Puycharic
Rue Mtée St-Maurice
Pl. du bout du Monde
WHERE TO SLEEP
1 Auberge de jeunesse
3 Hôtel du Centre
4 Hôtel du Mans
5 Hôtel du Mail
6 L'Auberge Belle Rive
8 Continental Hôtel
9 Hôtel Saint-Julien
10 Hôtel Le Progrès
WHERE TO EAT
20 Le Petit Mâchon
21 La Ferme
22 Les Trois Rivières
23 La Salamandre

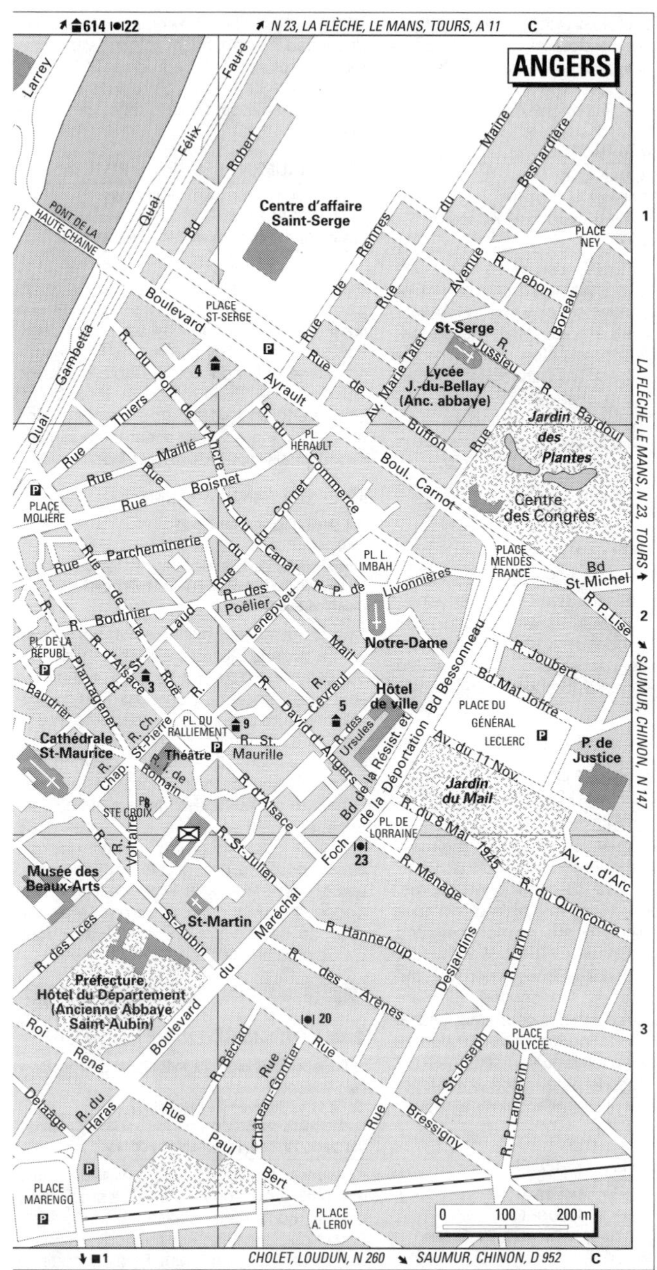
614 22
N 23, LA FLÈCHE, LE MANS, TOURS, A 11
C
ANGERS
1
2
3
LA FLÈCHE, LE MANS, N 23, TOURS
SAUMUR, CHINON, N 147
Centre d'affaire Saint-Serge
PONT DE LA HAUTE-CHAINE
PLACE ST-SERGE
PLACE NEY
St-Serge
Lycée J.-du-Bellay (Anc. abbaye)
Jardin des Plantes
Centre des Congrès
PL. HÉRAULT
PLACE MOLIÈRE
PL. L. IMBAH
PLACE MENDÈS FRANCE
Notre-Dame
Hôtel de ville
PLACE DU GÉNÉRAL LECLERC
P. de Justice
Jardin du Mail
PL. DE LA RÉPUBL.
PL. DU RALLIEMENT
Cathédrale St-Maurice
Théâtre
STE CROIX
PL. DE LORRAINE
Musée des Beaux-Arts
St-Martin
Prefecture, Hôtel du Département (Ancienne Abbaye Saint-Aubin)
PLACE DU LYCÉE
PLACE MARENGO
PLACE A. LEROY
0 100 200 m
Quai Félix Faure
Bd Robert
Larrey
Boulevard Ayrault
Quai Gambetta
R. du Pont de l'Ancre
Rue Thiers
Rue Maillé
Rue Boisnet
Rue Parcheminerie
R. du Commerce
R. du Cornet
R. du Canal
R. P. de Livonnières
Rue de Rennes
Rue de Buffon
Av. Marie Talet
Avenue du Maine
R. Besnardière
R. Lebon
Boreau
R. Jussieu
R. Bardoul
Boul. Carnot
Bd St-Michel
R. P. Lise
R. Joubert
Bd Mal Joffre
Av. du 11 Nov.
Bd Bessonneau
Bd de la Résist. et de la Déportation
Rue de la Roë
R. Bodinier
R. Laud
R. des Poëlier
Lenepveu
Mail
R. David d'Angers
R. Cevreul
R. des Ursules
R. d'Alsace
R. St-Aignan
Baudrier
Plantagenet
R. Ch. St-Pierre
R. St. Maurille
R. Chap.
R. de Romain
R. Voltaire
R. St-Julien
St-Aubin
R. des Lices
Boulevard du Maréchal Foch
R. du 8 Mai 1945
R. Ménage
R. du Quinconce
Av. J. d'Arc
R. Hanneloup
R. des Arènes
Desjardins
R. Tarin
R. St-Joseph
R. P. Langevin
Rue Bressigny
Rue Château-Gontier
R. Béclad
Rue Paul Bert
Roi René
Delaâge
R. du Haras
4
3
9
5
23
20
1
CHOLET, LOUDUN, N 260
SAUMUR, CHINON, D 952

tard, and fillet of sole with poached oysters. Perfectly adequate doubles 183F with bath (wc on the landing). On a fine day, you can eat on the romantic patio. The dining room has a view of the river. Rather chilly welcome.

HÔTEL DU MAIL**

8 rue des Ursules. **MAP C2-5**
☎ 02.41.88.56.22 F→ 02.41.86.91.20
Closed Sundays noon–6.30pm and public holidays.
Secure parking. **TV**.

A 17th century townhouse with a nice touch of olden-day France about it in a very quiet street. There's nowhere else like it in Angers and reservations are essential The atmosphere is both sophisticated and pleasingly conventional. Beautiful furniture. Refurbished bedrooms oozing charm 185F with shower/wc and 290F with bath. In fine weather, enjoy a buffet breakfast (31F) on the terrace in the shade of a hundred year old lime tree.

10% HÔTEL LE PROGRÈS**

26 rue Denis-Papin. **MAP B2-10**
☎ 02.41.88.10.14 F→ 02.41.87.82.93
TV. **Canal+**.

A comfy hotel offering good value for money. Bedrooms 270F with shower/wc and 280F with bath. The ones next to the lift are a bit noisy but cheaper at 200F. Understated décor and standard furniture. Very friendly reception.

10% HÔTEL SAINT-JULIEN**

9 place du Ralliement. **MAP C2-9**
☎ 02.41.88.41.62 F→ 02.41.20.95.19
Closed Sundays. **Car park**. **TV**.

You'd be hard pushed to find anything more central. It has about 30 comfortable and individually decorated air-conditioned rooms. Most have been nicely refurbished and have excellent bedlinen. Hushed atmosphere and nice welcome. Doubles 270–300F with bath. The most expensive ones overlook the square. Rooms on the second floor are smaller. The small interior courtyard is ideal for breakfast on a fine day. If you're hungry but don't feel like exerting yourself, there's a Mediterranean-style cafe in the hotel foyer offering an exceptional 89F set meal. Advisable to book.

10% CONTINENTAL HÔTEL**

12 rue Louis-de-Romain. **MAP B2-8**
☎ 02.41.86.94.94 F→ 02.41.86.96.60
Closed Sundays 12.30–4pm. **Car park**. **TV**. **Canal+**.
Disabled access.

Very good location. The communal areas are decorated in warm, bright colours. Very comfortable refurbished bedrooms 280F with shower/wc–300F with bath. Friendly welcome. Very pleasant little lounge and breakfast room.

RESTAURANT LES TROIS RIVIÈRES

62 promenade de Reculée. Off map **B1-22**
☎ 02.41.73.31.88
Closed Sunday evenings and Mondays. **Car park**.

You'll need some form of transport to get to this famous riverside restaurant with its panoramic dining room. It's full even on weekdays, so you'd be well advised to book. Fish specialities. Set meals at 57F (weekday lunchtime only and not available on public holidays), 79F (fillet of perch in a butter sauce) and up to 186F (*foie gras*, scallops and prawns in a vanilla scented sauce). An exceptionally friendly owner to boot.

RESTAURANT LA FERME

2-4 place Freppel. **MAP B2-21**
☎ 02.41.87.09.90
Closed Wednesdays, Sunday evenings, the fourth week in July, and the first week in August. **Car park**.
Disabled access.

One of the most popular restaurants in town with a large quiet terrace in the shadow of the cathedral. You can be sure of finding a seat here. People may only just have discovered it but it's been offering the same type of food for a fair number of years. The standard of service might slip when it's crowded, but everyone keeps their sense of humour. Expect to spend 50–60F for a main course. Set meals 71F (weekday lunchtimes), 89F and 175F. They specialize in poultry — *coq au vin*, *poule au pot*, escalope of *foie gras*, and breast of duck in wine lees (they use Cabernet Sauvignon) or *à l'orange*. A la carte you can have warm *rillons d'Anjou*, duck *choucroute* or calf's head.

AVRILLÉ 49240 (3KM NW)

HÔTEL-RESTAURANT LE CAVIER**

La Croix-Cadeau (North); it's on the Laval road, not far from the airport.
☎ 02.41.42.30.45 F→ 02.41.42.40.32
Restaurant closed Sundays and two weeks at Christmas.
Car park. **TV**. **Canal+**. **Disabled access**.

A very well known restaurant in a renovated mill that's typical of the area. The small, cosy dining rooms are pleasantly decorated. Rather chic clientele. Reservations essential. Set meals — melon with Pineau, gratinéd perch fillets or roast pork fillet with herbs, cheese and dessert, say — range in price from 107F to 173F. Expect to spend 180F à la carte for dishes like duck *foie gras*, zander with *beurre blanc*, *navarin* of veal sweetbreads with crayfish, and Cointreau soufflé and honey ice-cream. It also has 43 comfortable bedrooms located in the modern, functional and fairly soulless part of the establishment. Doubles 286–320F.

BOUCHEMAINE 49080 (11KM SW)

HÔTEL-RESTAURANT L'ANCRE DE MARINE*

la Pointe de Bouchemaine; take the D111.
☎ 02.41.77.14.46 F 02.41.77.25.71
Restaurant closed Sunday evenings and Mondays. **TV**.

A small, very quiet and quite delightful hotel in a tiny village that stands just where the Maine and the Loire meet. They've got about ten individually decorated rooms. Doubles range in price from 200F with basin to 320F with bath. Simple, pleasant décor. Very attractive rustic dining room. Good set meals 98F (weekdays), 165F and 230F — *terrine* of three kinds of fish, trout on a bed of leeks, pike with *beurre blanc*, escalope of salmon with sorrel, breast of duck with apples and bilberries, and fillet of beef with preserved ginger. The chef also works at *La Terrasse* (see below). You get the same food here but you pay a bit less.

RESTAURANT LA TERRASSE

la Pointe de Bouchemaine — place Ruzebouc.
☎ 02.41.77.11.96

The dining room offers one of the most wonderful panoramic views of the banks of the Loire. Ask for a table near the windows. Despite the soft colour scheme, the décor's rather austere and there's the slightest hint of a stuffy atmosphere. This is the kind of place grandmothers like to book for family celebrations. It's well known for its cooking and the sauces are heavenly. Set meals 98F (except Sundays), 175F, 225F and 280F. À la carte, you can expect to pay 90–130F for dishes like scallops with vermouth, eel *à la provençale*, *panaché* of fish, veal kidneys with ceps, and pork fillet with preserved ginger. The quality of service sometimes slips.

BÉHUARD 49170 (18KM SW)

RESTAURANT LE NOTRE-DAME

place de l'Église; follow the south bank of the Loire.
☎ 02.41.72.20.17
Closed evenings, Wednesdays and January. **Car park**.

A nice little restaurant in one of the most captivating villages in the Angers areas. The interior décor may be pretty ordinary, but the terrace in the square is really pleasant on a fine day. Pretty good cooking, and the restaurant's known particularly for its fish dishes. Set meals 90F (*moules marinière*, skate with *beurre noisette* nut-flavoured butter or one of the grills). 125F (one main course), and 170F (two courses) offering *friture* of eels, rack of veal *à l'angevine*, *assiette périgourdine*, zander with *beurre blanc*, breast of duck in cider and home-made *nougat glacé*. You can have a *crêpe* at any time. Pleasant and attentive staff.

RESTAURANT LES TONNELLES

rue Principale.
☎ 02.41.72.21.50
Closed Sunday evenings and Mondays March–Oct (except July–Aug), Sunday evenings–Thursday evenings in November, December, and two weeks in February. Annual holidays Jan 1–Feb 14. **Car park**.

The terrace is delightful in summer. Sit under the arbour and enjoy some of the wonderful food. Set meals 130F (weekday lunchtimes), 165F and 185F. *Menu dégustation* 245F (295F with wine). If you don't want to spend that much, you can have a glass of three different regional wines with the meal of your choice for an extra 50F. The à la carte menu changes often. Specialities include lots of fish dishes — roast zander with mild spices, *gratin* of crayfish, and *cotriade* (stew of white fish with mussels). Your tastebuds are in for a treat!

SAINT-GERMAIN-DES-PRÉS 49170 (23KM W)

LA CHAUFFETERIE*

How to get there: on the D15 (it's between Saint-Germain-des-Prés and Saint-Augustin-des-Bois) or the A11, Beaufreau-Chalonnes exit.
☎ 02.41.39.92.92
Closed Tuesdays and Wednesdays. **Car park**. **Disabled access**.

A little farmhouse deep in the country that was taken over by a Parisian couple a few years ago and offers a range of good simple cooking. Set meals 90–140F. Try the *daube* of duck in aspic, the pigeon stuffed with ceps or the zander with *beurre blanc*. You'll get very attentive service from the owner, a trained astrologist, while his wife does the cooking.

CHENILLÉ-CHANGÉ 49220 (31KM N)

10% ☗ |●| AUBERGE LA TABLE DU MEUNIER

How to get there: via the N162 north of Lion-d'Angers, then the D78.
☎ 02.41.95.10.98 ⊳ 02.41.95.10.52
Closed Monday evenings, Tuesdays and Wednesdays (except July–Aug), also start Feb–mid March.
Secure parking. Disabled access.

This is the kind of setting you dream about. There's a working water mill on the banks of a peaceful river and the village is full of flowers. The restaurant is very well known for its cooking and has a sheltered terrace and rustic, tastefully decorated dining room. Cheapest set meal 99F, others 129–239F. They offer dishes like *crème d'oignons* with *rillauds*, *paupiettes* of zander *belle angevine*, scallops flambéd with Calvados, smoked salmon *blinis* (small thick Russian pancake) with leeks, duck breast with apples and *beurre blanc*, and *nougat glacé* with a raspberry *coulis*. They have a few rooms if you want to do it all again the next day. Doubles 190F with shower/wc or bath.

BAULE (LA) 44500

10% ☗ HÔTEL MARINI**

22 av. Clemenceau (Centre); it's between the tourist office and the railway station.
☎ 02.40.60.23.29 ⊳ 02.40.11.16.98
Closed Nov 17–March 10. **Secure parking. TV.**

Recent renovation work has given this little hotel a pleasantly fresh and youthful appearance. As soon as you step inside you're hit by an overpowering smell of chlorine, but the comfortable and tastefully furnished rooms make up for it. Particularly good value for money, with doubles 240–320F (in high season). Run by two friends who know the true meaning of the words hospitality and service.

☗ |●| HÔTEL LUTÉTIA-RESTAURANT LE ROSSINI**

13 av. des Evens (South); it's near the town hall.
☎ 02.40.60.25.81 ⊳ 02.40.42.73.52
Closed Sunday evenings and Mondays out of season. **TV.**

A classic. The smiling owner and her husband's fresh, straightforward, good home cooking are a winning combination. Set meals 115–245F. It's had a facelift and though it may no longer be unpretentious, it's not pretentious either, which is a good sign. Bedrooms 300–450F out of season. Half-board at 350F is compulsory in July and August.

10% ☗ |●| HOSTELLERIE DU BOIS**

65 av. Lajarrige (Centre).
☎ 02.40.60.24.78 ⊳ 02.40.42.05.88
Closed Nov 1–Feb 15. **Car park. TV.**

It's set back from a very lively street, shaded by pine trees, and has a flower-filled garden. There are 15 bedrooms in all and they cost 380F (340F out of season). Half-board from 350F (295F out of season) per person per day. Set meals 85–175F. A delightful place, pleasantly cool, and full of flowers, pleasant aromas and souvenirs of Southeast Asia.

|●| RESTAURANT CHEZ L'ÉCAILLEUR

av. des Ibis; it's near the market.
☎ 02.40.60.87.94
Closed evenings and Mondays.

When the market closes, treat yourself to a dozen plump oysters from Brittany (92F), or clams with a half litre of Gros-Plant (52F) sitting at the bar in the relaxed atmosphere. Bliss!

|●| LA FERME DU GRAND CLOS

52 av. de Lattre-de-Tassigny; it's opposite the riding school.
☎ 02.40.60.03.30
Closed Tuesdays, Wednesdays and Thursdays out of season, March 3–26 and Sept 29–Oct 20.

The poshest *crêperie* in town, but don't let that put you off. Even if you don't stick your little finger out when you eat a *crêpe*, you'll be delighted with this little place. Maybe Marie-Antoinette should have said let them eat *crêpes*, not cake! Treat yourself to some real home cooking — it's better than you'll get in one of those tourist traps. Expect to pay 80–180F.

POULIGUEN (LE) 44510 (3KM W)

|●| RESTAURANT L'OPÉRA DE LA MER

promenade du port.
☎ 02.40.62.31.03
Closed Wednesdays and Thursdays out of season.
Car park.

Families strolling by the harbour stop under the trees to catch a glimpse of all the smiling and relaxed people involved in this particular opera performance. The style's more reminiscent of Mozart than Wagner. Fresh salads, nice fish soup and good oysters. The terrace is chock-a-block in summer. The cheapest set meal (100F) is pretty good or you might prefer the people's choice of mussels and chips at 50F. Expect to pay 180F à la carte.

PORNICHET 44380 (6KM E)

10% ☗ |●| HÔTEL-RESTAURANT LE RÉGENT**

150 bd des Océanides.
☎ 02.40.61.05.68 F➔ 02.40.61.25.53
Closed Mondays in winter, and Dec 15–Jan 15.
Secure parking. **TV**.

A family hotel facing the sea that's been updated to reflect the tastes of the 90s. It's bright and colourful and just needs to be a bit less stick-in-the-mud. But this is Pornichet where quiet mornings and happy families are the norm. Doubles 320–420F in summer, 245–365F out of season. Set meal 98F. In summer, set meals at 120F, 145F and 185F. It specializes in fish and seafood dishes as you've probably already guessed.

|●| RESTAURANT LA BRIGANTINE

How to get there: it's by the harbour.
☎ 02.40.61.03.58
Closed Tuesday evenings and Wednesdays (except during school holidays), and mid Nov–mid Feb. **Car park**.

La Brigantine is the only *crêperie* with a terrace overlooking the harbour. Pleasant décor and a log fire. Crêpes (from 42F) and kebabs à la carte and a few exotic dishes. Set meals 88–125F. A la carte is probably a better bet — expect to pay 100–150F. A welcome escape from all that dreary concrete.

BATZ-SUR-MER 44740 (8KM W)

|●| RESTAURANT LE DERWIN

rue du Golf; it's on the seafront between Batz and Le Pouliguen.
Closed Tuesdays (all year round), Wednesdays and Thurdays (except during the school holidays). **Car park**.

It's got lace curtains and is popular with the sailing fraternity — women with Hermès scarves tucked into the necks of their "sailor" jumpers and families all dressed in blue. They may not have a telephone or an electronic till (so no payment by credit card) but they're never short of custom. The ideal place for tucking into mussels, seafood and *crêpes*. Expect to pay 80–120F per person.

BEAUVOIR-SUR-MER 85230

☗ |●| LE RELAIS DES TOURISTES**

1 rue Gois (East).
☎ 02.51.68.70.19 F➔ 02.51.49.33.45
Secure parking. **TV**. **Canal+**. **Disabled access**.

You'll be given an unaffected welcome in this large hotel and shown proudly to your room. And they're right to be proud for it's really well cared for. It has pretty nice rooms, a heated indoor swimming pool, a sauna and a fitness room. Doubles range in price from 175F with basin (no TV) to 315F with bath. Try for one with shower as they're cheaper and give access to the pool. The rather good restaurant's on the other side of the street. Set meals 66–225F. Book a long time in advance as it's very popular with groups.

SAINT-GERVAIS 85230 (4KM SE)

|●| RESTAURANT LA PITCHOUNETTE

48 rue Bonne-Brise (West).
☎ 02.51.68.68.88
Closed Mondays out of season. **Car park**.
Disabled access.

Service noon–1.30pm and 7.30–9.30pm. A very attractive restaurant that's full of flowers and very welcoming! Gérard Thoumoux's cooking outshines the décor — sole stuffed with prawns, snails in puff pastry, and *aumonière* of crab. Go on, forget about the 50F set meal for once and treat yourself. The others range from 95F to 166F and the two in the middle are quite remarkable — and they come with a "douceur gervinoise" (a drop of something to aid the digestion) to boot!

BOUIN 85230 (8 KM NE)

10% ☗ |●| HÔTEL LE MARTINET**

1 place de la Croix-Blanche; it's beside the church.
☎ 02.51.49.08.94 F➔ 02.51.49.83.08
Hotel open all year round; restaurant open Easter–Sept or by reservation. **Secure parking**. **TV**.
Disabled access.

A large and beautiful 18th century house in traditional Vendée style. You have a choice of bedrooms — an old-fashioned type overlooking the square or one of the ones built near the swimming pool that give you direct access to the garden. Absolute peace and quiet — except when the church bells bring you back to the land of the living! Breakfast is served in the old dining room which smells delightfully of polish. In the evenings, they do a dozen oysters, followed by grilled sole with potatoes. It's a family business — the owner's an oyster farmer, the son's the chef and Françoise likes decorating. Together they've made it a little paradise. Pink and blue colour schemes and lots of wood. Bedrooms 275F with shower/wc and 330F with bath. Excellent set meal 100F.

RESTAURANT LE COURLIS

15 rue du Pays-de-Monts.
☎ 02.51.68.64.65
Closed Mondays, Wednesday evenings and Christmas–New Year's Day.

Service noon–1.30pm and 7–9.30pm. A white rather squat building, typical of the area. Spruce, flower-filled dining room decorated in soft greens. The cooking deserves all our attention — quail stuffed with sweet peppers, *chartreuse* of rabbit with mushrooms and a lentil *coulis*, warm oysters with winkles, and semi-wild duck with grapes. Mouthwatering! Set meals 83F, 114F, 164F and 205F.

BRULÔN 72350

10% HÔTEL-RESTAURANT LA BOULE D'OR

How to get there: it's in the main square.
☎ 02.43.95.60.40 Fax 02.43.95.07.78
Closed Saturday evenings, Sundays and two weeks in January. **TV**.

Nothing seems to have changed in this sturdy village house during the past three decades — not the owner, not the customers, not the atmosphere, and not even the aromas wafting from the plates as they're carried into the dining room. You can treat yourself without breaking the bank. Cheapest set meal 57F (78F Sundays). For 105F you can have half a dozen oysters, *rascasse* (a type of fish) with sorrel sauce, a delicious *noix* of rib steak, cheese platter and dessert. Clean, comfortable bedrooms 170F with shower/wc.

CHALLANS 85300

10% HÔTEL-RESTAURANT LE MARAIS**

rue de la Redoute et 16, place Charles-de-Gaulle (Centre).
☎ 02.51.93.15.13 Fax 02.51.49.44.96
Secure parking. TV. Canal+.

Service noon–2pm and 7–9.30pm. A family hotel in the centre of town that gets bigger and better all the time. Perfectly adequate but small rooms are 170F with shower/wc. Full board compulsory in summer. Conscientious chef. The food is a mixture of local poultry (fillet of duck with Mareuil wine and roast *poulet noir* with mustard) and fish and shellfish from the coast. Cheapest set meal 70F (very filling). Others 85–195F. You can eat in the brasserie for 40F.

10% HÔTEL DE L'ANTIQUITÉ

14 rue Galliéni (Centre).
☎ 02.51.68.02.84 Fax 02.51.35.55.74
Closed Christmas–New Year's Day, and Saturday evenings from Oct. **Car park. TV**.

A funny place but we're delighted to have discovered it. It might not seem like much to look at, but wait till you step inside. It could very well be called "The discreet charm of the bourgeoisie". Cosy atmosphere. Breakfast is served in a very kitsch orange dining room with rows of individual tables — it's like something out of a movie. Apart from that, the furniture is of fine quality — only to be expected since the proprietress is an antique dealer. Beautiful bedrooms, half of which have been renovated and are laid out round a wonderful swimming pool. Doubles 300–400F.

RESTAURANT LA COURONNE

4 rue de la Redoute.
☎ 02.51.49.11.33

This restaurant offers good food at affordable prices. You eat either in the panelled dining room with its old cart wheel or at the large counter with its impressive model of a boat. The 75F meal consists of fillets of duck with a sweet pepper sauce, fish wrapped in crisp pancakes, and a delicious banana concoction for dessert. Service with a smile, nicely presented food, and excellent value for money. Please sir, can we have some more?

RESTAURANT LA GITE DU TOURNE PIERRE

Route de Saint-Gilles; it's 3km by the D69, between Challans and Soullans.
☎ 02.51.68.14.78
Car park. Disabled access.

Lobster has pride of place here, alongside the home-made *foie gras*, duck *Rossini* (with truffles and *foie gras*), and fricassee of sole with mushrooms and *foie gras*. Set meals 125–330F. A piece of culinary theatre in which the service, faultless but unpretentious, plays an important role. A good place if you've got a healthy bank balance or you want to remember what the word "cooking" means.

CHAMPTOCEAUX 49270

10% HÔTEL-RESTAURANT LE CHAMPALUD**

promenade du Champalud; it's in the centre of town.
☎ 02.40.83.50.09 F 02.40.83.53.81
Closed January; restaurant closed Wednesdays out of season. **Car park**. **TV**. **Disabled access**.

If you fancy coming to this well-known restaurant in a charming village on the banks of the Loire, remember that reservations are almost compulsory. The *repas du jour* (weekday lunchtimes) costs 61F and includes cheese, dessert and wine. Set meals 79–189F. During the week they also have set meals at 99F and 149F featuring traditional local dishes, but these have to be ordered in advance. And set meals accompanied by specially selected wines start at 99F. If you want to go à la carte (prices are fairly steep), how about *délice* of salmon with two different sauces, tournedos *en croûte* or *terrine* with Muscadet? Pleasant doubles with shower from 230F. Pub, *brasserie*, mountain bike hire, tennis, sitting room with games like chess. And last (but not least), a little cellar boasting a fresco of Noah, the first wine grower. Friendly and very energetic owner and good value for money.

CHÂTAIGNERAIE (LA) 85120

10% L'AUBERGE DE LA TERRASSE**

7 rue de Beauregard (Centre).
☎ 02.51.69.68.68 F 02.51.52.67.98
Closed Saturday lunchtimes and Sunday evenings out of season, and during the Christmas holidays.
Car park. **TV**. **Canal+**. **Disabled access**.

A large and attractively renovated inn in the archetypal provincial French town. The owner makes a point of introducing his guests to local produce from the land and the sea. Try the *prefou* of eels with a langoustine *coulis*, *pot au feu* of skate cheeks, medallions of monkfish with lamb juices, and *viennoise* of sole with seaweed. Set meals range in price from 58F (weekday lunchtimes) to 135F and there's also a very good 165F *menu dégustation*. Bedrooms 265F with shower/wc. Half-board (265F) is compulsory at weekends June–end of Aug.

VOUVANT 85120 (12.5KM S)

10% HÔTEL-RESTAURANT L'AUBERGE DE MAÎTRE PANNETIER**

place du Corps-de-Garde (Centre); take the D938 towards Fontenay-le-Comte and change to the D30 at Alouette.
☎ 02.51.00.80.12 F 02.51.87.89.37
Closed Sunday evenings and Mondays out of season, during the February school holidays, and at the end of November. **TV**.

You won't have any trouble finding this inn in the centre of one of the most beautiful villages in France near the forest of Mervent. Nice welcome and good accommodation. Pleasant bedrooms with light wood furniture cost 210F with shower/wc and 270F with bath. Most important of all, the restaurant is good. The food of the upmarket rustic variety and chef Rémy Guignard works wonders in the kitchen. Try, for example, *pavé* of salmon, chicken and snail tart, *pavé* of turbot with asparagus, bass with morels, or *confit* of duck. Set meals range in price from 70F (weekdays except public holidays) to 220F. Superb vaulted dining room with stone walls, oil lamps on the tables with petrol lamps, and a fireplace for dull days.

CHÂTEAUBRIANT 44110

LE POÊLON D'OR

30 bis rue du 11-Novembre; it's two steps from the post office and the town hall.
☎ 02.40.81.43.33
Closed Sunday evenings, Mondays and the first two weeks in August.

The service is nicely formal and the customers are exceptionally well-behaved – until a glass or two livens things up, that is. The rustic décor reinforces the typically French feel to the place, but once the food arrives – the tender, succulent *chateaubriand* or the fillet of bass *en écailles* – you won't be able to concentrate on anything else. Ideal for gourmets who've been saving their pennies. Set meals 102–250F.

CHÂTEAU-DU-LOIR 72500

HÔTEL-RESTAURANT LE GRAND HÔTEL**

59 av. Aristide-Briand (Centre).
☎ 02.43.44.00.17 F 02.43.44.37.58
Car park. **TV**.

Nobody seems to know just how old this former coaching inn is. Rooms 170–250F. The food, from the *terrine* of young rabbit in aspic to the *marmite sarthoise* (a kind of stew of chicken, rabbit, ham and mushrooms), lives up to its reputation. They even serve the 95F set meal on Sundays.

VAAS 72420 (8KM SW)

10% HÔTEL-RESTAURANT LE VÉDAQUAIS**

Centre; take the D305 or the D30.
☎ 02.43.46.01.41 F 02.43.46.37.60
Closed Sunday evenings and Mondays. **Car park**. **TV**.

This used to be the local school before the town turned it into a good old-fashioned kind of village hotel. Ideal if you need cheering up. Daniel Beauvais is a very good chef who doesn't talk much and his wife Sylvie is a very good hostess who chats away quite happily. Set meals, ranging in price from 85F to 220F, are a real treat, fresh-tasting, straightforward, and brimming with creativity. For 150F you could try a *rillette* of zander with marinated eel, followed by a fish soup (they use freshwater fish) or leg of duck with pears, accompanied by two glasses of wine (from the Loire valley of course). And the menu promises one or two little treats to finish with. The rooms (250F) are just as pleasant.

MARÇON 72340 (8.5KM NE)

RESTAURANT L'HÔTEL DU BŒUF

21 place de l'Église (Centre); take the N138, then cut off onto the D305.
☎ 02.43.44.13.12
Closed Sunday evenings and Mondays (except July–Aug), and Jan 15–March 1.

People come here for food that's quite different from what they're used to. Creole dishes take pride of place in the set meals, which range from 75F (weekdays) to 200F. There's chicken with crayfish, prawn fricassee with coconut milk, and lamb *colombo* to name a few. Have some punch and a few fritters to start with and round things off with a house liqueur. You'll have a smile on your face in the middle of the afternoon — even if it starts to rain.

PONT-DE-BRAYE 72310 (14KM W)

10% HÔTEL-RESTAURANT LA PETITE AUBERGE

rue Principale (Centre); it's between La Chartre-sur-le-Loir and Bessé-sur-Braye.
☎ 02.43.44.45.08 F 02.43.44.18.57
Closed Monday evenings and Tuesdays (out of season). **Car park**.

We fell for this little inn covered in Virginia creeper — the welcome is very warm and friendly and the cooking truly inspired. Cheapest set meal 70F (except Saturday evenings and Sunday lunchtimes). For 125F you'll get superb value for money with dishes like fricassee of snails, *quenelle* of asparagus *mousseline*, pike with pink radishes, breast of duck with soft fruit and a sweet and sour sauce. There's another set meal at 183F. A little bit of advice, try the house speciality, *roulade* of chicken with fresh thyme. Three attractive bedrooms 150F with shower (wc on the landing).

RUILLÉ-SUR-LOIR 72340 (19KM NE)

HÔTEL-RESTAURANT SAINT PIERRE*

42 rue Nationale (Centre); take the D305 and it's 6km from La Chartre-sur-le-Loir.
☎ 02.43.44.44.36
Restaurant closed Sunday evenings.

We really liked this little village hotel with its unassuming façade and cosy, friendly atmosphere. There used to be so many places like this in villages throughout France in the 50s and 60s, but now Saint Pierre is one of the few left. The nice proprietress spoils all her customers and nobody around these parts can match her 49F worker's set meal. It's pretty impressive to see just how many plates of hors d'œuvres have been got ready for the rush. Bottle of red wine included in the price. The set meal goes up to 80F on Sundays and offers a choice of leg of lamb, duck leg with pepper or sirloin, salad, cheese platter and dessert. For 120F you can also get fish. A few simple, but perfectly adequate doubles 110F.

CHÂTEAU-GONTIER 53200

10% HÔTEL LE CERF**

31 rue Garnier (South).
☎ 02.43.07.25.13 F 02.43.07.02.90
Secure parking. **TV**. **Canal+**. **Disabled access**.

It's next to the cattle market in Château-Gontier and may not look like much, but you'll only pay 160–220F for a double with shower/wc or bath. Ask for one at the back, it'll be quieter.

RESTAURANT L'AQUARELLE

village de Pendu-en-Saint-Fort, route de Ménil (South); it's 400m from the centre; follow the road that runs along the north bank of the Mayenne, towards Sablé, and at the roundabout take the Ménil road.
☎ 02.43.70.15.44

Closed Mondays Oct–April, and Jan 15–31. **Car park**. **Disabled access**.

A bit outside town on the banks of the Mayenne, a hotel that will set you daydreaming. The terrace is beautiful on summer days. Panoramic dining room, air-conditioned in summer, offers a magnificent view of the river. Light, creative cooking and dishes like grilled silurid (a freshwater fish similar to burbot) with lime butter and a medley of lamb and langoustine with thyme. Set meals 80–180F.

AZÉ 53200 (2KM E)

LE PRIEURÉ

1 pl. de l'Église (Centre); take the D22.
☎ 02.43.70.31.16
Closed Mondays and Feb. **Car park**.

The cooking was surely never this good back in the 18th century nor the atmosphere as easy-going. The proprietress, a good business woman, knows how to treat her guests. The 108F set meal comes with a delicious *terrine* of young rabbit, tasty *coq au vin*, cheese and fruit tart. They use only fresh produce and the skill of the chef is evident even in the cheapest set meal at 78F. Others 148F and 208F. Dinner is served on the terrace in summer with its view of the grounds and the river. An enchanting place.

COUDRAY 53200 (7KM SE)

RESTAURANT L'AMPHITRYON

2 route de Daon (Centre); take the D22 and it's opposite the church.
☎ 02.43.70.46.46
Closed Tuesday evenings, Wednesdays (except lunchtimes July–Aug), February school holidays and the first week in July. **Disabled access**.

An inn on a corner looking like just another inn. We'd probably have passed it by and carried on our way but luckily the word's got around and people have been describing it as one of the most delightful places in the département for quite a few years now. There's something invigorating about both the cooking and the décor. The 92F set meal is light and colourful and offers *rillettes* of two types of salmon, fish *soufflé* with langoustine *coulis*, warm Camembert and seasonal fruit tarts. If you're pretty hungry, the 190F set meal isn't bad either – *aumonière* of *andouille*, fillet of zander and eel ravioli, free-range chicken with Pommeau, cheese pastry, and for dessert, something with apples. If you're looking for something in between, the 135F set meal changes often. On weekdays, they have a light set meal at 72F.

DAON 53200 (11.5KM SE)

HÔTEL-RESTAURANT À L'AUBERGE

Centre; take the D22.
☎ 02.43.06.91.14
Closed one week in February and one week in October.

A good country inn, specializing in fish and seafood dishes and popular with fishermen. During the week, they do a delightful 48F *menu complet* (58F at weekends). Other set meals 80F and 135F. Hearty seafood platter for two 170F. Basic bedrooms with basin (115F and 165F) suitable for a few nights stay. Half-board 140F per person.

BALLOTS 53350 (30KM NW)

RESTAURANT L'AUBERGE DU MOUILLOTIN

9 place de l'Église (Centre); take the D22, and it's 9.5km after Craon on the D25 going towards La Guerche-de-Bretagne.
☎ 02.43.06.61.81
Closed Tuesday evenings, Wednesdays, one week in February, and two weeks in August. **Disabled access**.

Every year on the night of April 30, round about midnight, the locals go from farm to farm asking for eggs so they can make a gigantic omelette. You might want to take part in this charming custom yourself if you're in the area then – the chances of coming across wild parties here are few and far between. This restaurant naturally has all kinds of omelettes, including with bone marrow, *foie gras* or snails. And they're mouthwatering! Other treats in store in the set meals ranging from 55F (weekdays) to 130F set meals. How do you fancy fillet of perch with cider or breast of duck with raspberries? Pretty dining room overlooking the garden.

CHEMILLÉ 49120

10% L'AUBERGE DE L'ARRIVÉE

15 place de la Gare.
☎ 02.41.30.60.31 Fax 02.41.30.78.45
Closed Sunday evenings Oct–May. **Secure parking**. **TV**.

A large private house. Half-board is compulsory in July and August, but the chef's pretty talented so we've no problems with that. Perfectly adequate doubles 160–265F with good bedlinen. The fairly plush dining room serves good regional food. The cheapest set meal (79F) offers starter, main course, and cheese or dessert. Other set meals 100–160F. À la carte there's *ballotine* of duck with *foie gras*, escalope of zander with tips of wild nettles, braised swordfish steak with herbs, prawn kebabs with lime and wild rice, and pork fillet with spices. Pleasant terrace filled with pot plants. Excellent reception.

CROISIC (LE) 44490

RESTAURANT LE BRETAGNE

11 quai de la Petite-Chambre.
☎ 02.40.23.00.51
Closed Sunday evenings and Mondays out of season, and Nov 15–Dec 15.

If it's one those days when you want your mum — or her cooking at least — this is the place to come. It's decorated in typical Breton style and run by Michèle Coïc and her family. The atmosphere will make your problems disappear, and the authentic local cooking (seafood and country dishes) will take care of the rest. Well worth 200F! Set meals (99–229F) change with the seasons. Very good wine list.

DOUÉ-LA-FONTAINE 49700

10% HÔTEL-RESTAURANT DE FRANCE**

place du Champ-de-Foire (Centre).
☎ 02.41.59.12.27 F 02.41.59.76.00
Closed Sunday evenings and Mondays except July–Aug, and Dec 20–Jan 20. **Car park**. **TV**.

The archetypal small town hotel. Perfectly adequate bedrooms from 230F with shower/wc. Standard décor in the dining room. Good traditional cooking. The set meals (120–230F) come with main courses like turbot with mustard seeds, fillet of duck with bilberries, and warm scallop and langoustine salad. Cheapest set meal (80F) is fairly typical. If you're here in the year 2000, the Jarnot family will be celebrating — they'll have been here 50 years by then.

LOURESSE 49700 (6KM N)

RESTAURANT LES CAVES DE LA GÉNÉVRAIE

13 rue du Musée – Rochemênier (Centre); take the D761 or the D69 the north of Doué-la-Fontaine.
☎ 02.41.59.34.22
Closed Mondays. **Car park**. **Disabled access**.

People took refuge down here during the wars of religion. The pleasant cosy dining room with lots of alcoves has been carved out of the rock — so of course it's cool on hot summer days. Friday and Saturday evenings and Sunday lunchtimes, they do *fouaces*. These are wheat *galettes* cooked in the oven or on ashes and stuffed with *rillettes* (cubed pork cooked in its own fat) or beans. They're the local speciality and together with hors-d'œuvres and Layon wines they'll cost you 115F. Reservations only.

ÉVRON 53600

HÔTEL-RESTAURANT BRASSERIE DE LA GARE**

Centre.
☎ 02.43.01.60.29 F 02.43.37.26.53
Restaurant closed Sundays. **TV**. **Canal+**.

It looks like something out of another age and you'd probably hesitate for quite a long time before deciding to try it out. Even if you're not crazy about station hotels or you didn't meet the love of your life on a train journey, you'll appreciate the exposed beams and the quiet and comfortable bedrooms (215F with shower and 242F with bath). Good regional cooking and generous portions. Your journey might start with the house *terrine* and take in a rib steak before ending with rhubarb tart. Set meals 79F (weekdays), 100F and 159F.

MEZANGERS 53600 (6KM N)

10% RELAIS DU GUÉ DE SELLE***

Route de Mayenne – D7.
☎ 02.43.91.20.00 F 02.43.91.20.10
Closed Sunday evenings and Mondays out of season, and in February. **Car park**. **TV**.

It used to be a farmhouse in the depths of the country with the forest at its back and a pond at the front but there's nothing of the farmhouse about the atmosphere now. It's been restored and turned into an inn and lovers of good food, walkers, young people who've just spent the afternoon windsurfing on the lake, and trainee priests on a spree are all equally welcome. Try the *terrine* of foie gras and fillet of zander with cider or the *escalope* of veal sweetbreads with honey. Great set meals 71F (weekdays) –185F. Absolute peace and quiet in the evenings. The pleasant, comfortable bedrooms — some of them duplexes — overlook the garden, the swimming pool or the countryside.

You'll pay 325–475F. Excellent for a spot of relaxation.

NEAU 53150 (6KM W)

10% ⌂ |●| HÔTEL-RESTAURANT LA CROIX VERTE**

2 rue d'Évron (Centre); from Évron, go towards Laval.
☎ 02.43.98.23.41 ➡ 02.43.98.25.39
Closed Sunday evenings and February school holidays. **Car park**. **TV**.

Your heart might well sink when you see this place at an uninteresting junction with its typical bed and breakfast façade and cheap and nasty parasols. But you'll be pleasantly surprised when you you step inside and you might be tempted to stay longer than you planned. It has superbly refurbished bedrooms (220F) and a nice bar, and the dining room, decorated with hilarious frescoes, has an à la carte menu full of tasty specialities. Try the duck *foie gras mayennais*, the fillet of trout with Pommeau or the delicious rib steak. When it's crowded, take the waitresses' advice – just sit back and relax. Set meals 65F (weekdays) –160F.

SAINTE-SUZANNE 53270 (7KM SE)

|●| RESTAURANT L'AUBERGE DE LA CITÉ

7 place Hubert-II (Centre); take the D7.
☎ 02.43.01.47.66
Closed Mondays, Tuesday evenings (except July–Aug), public holidays and January.

The proprietress is a very good cook and the fact that the restaurant is housed in a 14th century building probably inspired her passion for medieval cooking. The 150F *menu médiéval* is solely for groups who've booked. Anyway, people usually go for the *crêpes* and *galettes*. If those don't appeal, set meals 99–129F.

DEUX-EVAILLES 53150 (12KM NW)

|●| LA FENDERIE

Site de la Fenderie; get there via the D129 between Jublains and Montsurs.
☎ 02.43.90.00.95
Closed Mondays. **Car park**.

It stands in 40 acres of grounds with a fair amount of bird life during the week and lots of picnickers at the weekend. So get away from the crowds on fine Sundays by relaxing on the terrace opposite the pond. Treat yourself to the delightful 98F set meal that offers dishes like warm chicken and apple salad with cider vinegar, pike with *beurre blanc*, cheese and fruit tart. When skies are grey, enjoy the dining room with its fireplace, beams, the little tables with their attractive place settings, and the local dishes that change daily. Set meals 58–180F.

JUBLAINS 53160 (17KM NW)

|●| LA FERME DE MAUPOIRIER

Maupoirier; it's signposted between Deux-Évailles and Jublains.
☎ 02.43.04.52.75
Closed Sunday evenings, Mondays and Feb. **Car park**.

Some people find it a bit difficult to sit down and eat an animal whose relatives they've just seen frolicking around outside, so be advised that the set meals (77F, 98F, 125F and 160F) feature venison *terrine*, venison tongue and venison stew. Authentic cooking, completely refurbished décor, and very informal welcome. In any case, it's unusual enough to merit a visit in between the basilica at Evron and the Roman baths at Jublains. And the countryside is particularly beautiful and the roads are very quiet.

FERTÉ-BERNARD (LA) 72400

10% ⌂ |●| HÔTEL-RESTAURANT LA PERDRIX**

2 rue de Paris.
☎ 02.43.93.00.44 ➡ 02.43.93.74.95
Closed Monday evenings, Tuesdays and Feb 1–26. **Secure parking**. **TV**.

You can't come to Sarthe and not eat or stay here. It's as pleasing to the eye as it is to the palate and in the restaurant Serge Thibaut offers set meals at 105F (every day), 150F and 220F. Here's just a few of the dishes on offer — panfried duck *foie gras* with raspberries, fillet of roast zander cooked with the skin on, and *salmis* of pigeon with potato pancakes. The wine cellar boasts almost 600 vintage wines! Doubles 230F and 380F with shower/wc. Families might be interested in the attractively decorated duplex. Seven parking spaces in the garage. As is often the case, exceptional talent goes hand in hand with great modesty and outstanding hospitality.

|●| RESTAURANT LE RABELAIS

11 rue du Bourg-Neuf (Centre).
☎ 02.43.71.38.90
Closed Monday and Tuesday evenings.

It doesn't look like the kind of place to put you in the party mood but once you're inside you'll soon change your mind. It's like a dream – friendly customers, a good fire and a waitress who doesn't think she's made for better things. The cooking may not be particularly imaginative and the meat's not that tender but we had a soft spot for the kebabs. They may have specialities from Périgord on the menu, but people come here primarily for the grills and the fruit tarts. Set meals 49F (weekdays), 69F, 95F and 135F.

LE DAUPHIN

3 rue d'Huisne (Centre).
☎ 02.43.93.00.39
Closed Sunday evenings and Mondays.

A delightful restaurant in a historic building near porte Saint-Julien. It's popular with lovers and gourmets (not that these are mutually exclusive terms). Set meals at 95F (weekdays), 135F, 185F and 235F. The first is delicious and well-balanced and the second consists of *crème brûlée* with sea urchin corals and *concassé* tomatoes, guinea fowl with *moutarde de Meaux*, *feuilleté* of Fourme d'Albert cheese with pears and apricot *clafoutis*. OK, it might be a bit hushed but you can hardly expect a brasserie kind of atmosphere on top of what you're already getting.

SAINT-ULPHACE 72320 (14KM SE)

LE GRAND MONARQUE

Centre; it's right in the heart of the village.
☎ 02.43.93.27.27
Closed Friday and Saturday evenings, the end of August, and the beginning of September.

You'll find a good-natured atmosphere here at this old "Monarch", especially when the "loyal subjects" appear for a feast on certain Sunday afternoons and continue celebrating for quite some time. The 90F "Welcome" set meal lives up to its name, offering salad, country ham, veal cutlet and baby potatoes. The set meals at 130F, 165F and 220F come with good solid middle-class dishes like salad of *confit* of quail with *foie gras* and chanterelles and *blanquette* of lobster with baby vegetables and fresh pasta. It's reservations only on weekday evenings out of season.

MONTMIRAIL 72320 (15KM SE)

CRÊPERIE L'ANCIENNE FORGE

11bis place du Château.
☎ 02.43.71.49.14
Closed Mondays.

A pretty little restaurant. About one in three customers (well, the French ones anyway) ask if the château in the background, on the other side of the terrace, was the one they used for the film, "Les Visiteurs". Sorry to disappoint, but the cinema world doesn't seem interested – for the moment at least – in the historical significance of the Montmirail château. In the meantime, you can have a very good meal here for a reasonable 100F – *taboulé*, rib steak, and ice cream with strawberries. They do wonderful salads and *galettes*. Soft background music and friendly smiles.

FLÈCHE (LA) 72200

HÔTEL-RESTAURANT DU VERT GALANT**

70 Grande-Rue (Centre).
☎ 02.43.94.00.51 Fax 02.43.45.11.24
Restaurant closed Thursdays Sept–mid April, and mid Dec–mid Jan. **Car park**. **TV**.

An unusual hotel run by an unusual man. Monsieur Berger may not be altogether in his prime but – under the less enthusiastic gaze of his wife – he's still overflowing with new ideas for the hotel and the restaurant. Set meals 82F, 100F (*rillettes* and *poule au pot*), and 110F (half a dozen oysters and pike with *beurre blanc*). The owner gets the inspiration for his 155F and 180F *menus carte* from Escoffier – potted pig's head in jelly and *pot au feu* with three different kinds of meat. The bedrooms (285F) look as if they're from another age too. Americans love them, but don't let that put you off.

10% RELAIS CICERO

18 bd d'Alger (Centre); it's near place Thiers, two steps from the famous Prytanée.
☎ 02.43.94.14.14 Fax 02.43.45.98.96

A beautiful building dating from the 16th and 18th centuries, well away from the crowds and noise of the town. There's an English bar, a reading room, a comfortable breakfast room, an open fire, and hushed conversations. Bedrooms in this building are so stylish and comfortable, they're worth splashing out on (525F). But on the other side of the flower-filled garden is the actual hotel and you might fall for one of the cosy rooms there, particularly since they're cheaper (425F). Great breakfast. This place oozes charm – the discreet charm of the bourgeoisie, of course.

The most attractive place in Sarthe.

LE MOULIN DES QUATRE SAISONS

rue Galliéni (Centre).
☎ 02.43.45.12.12
Car park.

A great riverside location opposite the château des Carmes (which sounds more poetic than "town hall"). You might almost think you were on the banks of the Danube – the owner's accent, the country inn décor with flowers painted on the woodwork, the apple strudel for dessert, and the syrupy background music. Middle-class types sit indoors while the more laid-back sort head for the wonderful terrace. They all come for the atmosphere and Camille Constantin's tasty cooking. You'll get brilliant value for money with the 98F set meal of *pastilla* of ox tail with a small salad followed by salmon with fresh pasta. The "seasonal" set meals (125F and 165F) make your mouth water in anticipation, just as they should.

RESTAURANT LA FESSE D'ANGE

place du 8-Mai-1945 (Centre).
☎ 02.43.94.73.60
Closed Sunday evenings, Mondays, the third week in February, and Aug 1–21.

This establishment is one of the best in Sarthe with its bold modern décor and attractive logo. The delicious 105F set meal (not served Saturday evenings, Sundays or public holidays) consists of fish of the day or *suprême* of guinea fowl in a nettle sauce, cheese and magnificent desserts. And the 160F set meal (205F with both fish and meat) is sheer bliss. Dishes on offer include *escalopines* of warm *foie gras* with peppered pears, fillet of zander with Jasnières (a white wine that you must try at least once since this is where it comes from!), and warm raspberry soufflé.

VOUVRAY-SUR-LOIR 72500 (6KM E)

HÔTEL DU PORT GAUTIER

Le Port Gauthier; take the D61 from Marçon as far as Port Gauthier, then the D64.
☎ 02.43.79.44.62 F 02.43.44.66.03
Closed Sunday evenings and Mondays out of season.
Car park.

Just the idea of buying a disused railway station to live in is pretty impressive. And though we might have preferred something a little more authentic, this modern little hotel, built alongside and decorated in shades of green and raspberry is a pleasant place to stay. Bedrooms 220F and 240F. And the restaurant is nothing like the traditional station buffet. Delicious set meals 80F (*terrine*, sirloin in a mustard sauce, cheese and dessert), 115F (*tartare* of tomatoes, leg of rabbit with whole baked cloves of garlic), 150F and 180F (for customers travelling first class). Enjoyable and rather original.

BOUSSE 72270 (12KM N)

L'AUBERGE DE SAVOIE

Centre; take the D12, then the D102.
☎ 02.43.45.71.59
Closed Sunday evenings and Wednesdays.

A "Savoy inn" in a little village where you can get away from it all. It looks a bit out of place but what does that matter? The cheapest (55F) set meal, tasty and served up in generous portions, has quite a following. Settle down in the cool little dining room for the 92F set meal of *quenelles* of pike with crayfish sauce, a good *pavé* of beef with shallots, cheese and dessert. If you like fish, go for either the 148F or the 182F set meal – they offer dishes like sea bass, mullet on a bed of leeks and char with violets. Don't ask about typically Savoie dishes. The talented chef has a sense of humour, even going so far as to put sirloin of kangaroo on the menu – an animal not often seen in these parts.

LUCHÉ PRINGÉ 72800 (13KM E)

10% AUBERGE DU PORT-DES-ROCHES

Lieu dit "Le Port des Roches".
☎ 02.43.45.44.48. F 02.43.45.39.61
Closed Sunday evenings, Mondays and February.
Car park.

This inn's had a lot of ground to make up. Just take a peek at the flowery paper at the back of the cupboards and you'll see what a narrow escape you've had. It's now run by an energetic and hard-working young couple who're bringing it back to life. Brightly coloured bedrooms 240–300F. The dining room (not as bright) serves skilfully made dishes based on market produce. Very cosy atmosphere, typical country prices, and set meals 115–190F. How do you fancy *gratin* of goat's cheese gnocchi with beetroot sauce, poached char with walnuts, a platter of Loire cheese, *Paris Brest* (large choux pastry ring with almonds and butter cream) with preserved pineapple, and local wine all for 150F? Pretty impressive for the cheapest set meal! Great flower-filled terrace overlooks the river, as do some of the bedrooms.

FONTENAY-LE-COMTE 85200

10% ☗ |●| HÔTEL FONTARABIE - RESTAURANT LA GLYCINE**

67 rue de la République (Centre).
☎ 02.51.69.17.24 ➡ 02.51.51.02.73
Closed Dec 20–Jan 15. **Secure parking**. **TV**.
Disabled access.

A long time ago Spanish merchants used to travel to Fontenay from Fontarabie to sell their ponies in return for mules from Vendée. They stayed in this very coaching inn – hence the name – and it hasn't changed since. A handsome white stone building with a slate roof, it's just had a make-over, and the new décor is tasteful, if a touch too modern. Clean bedrooms with adequate facilities. Try to avoid the ones overlooking the street – they're smaller and noiser than the others. Doubles from 210F with shower/wc. The restaurant was named after the wonderful wisteria at the front door. They do good plain cooking and serve up generous portions of dishes like grilled *andouillette*, grilled calf's liver with bacon and a mouthwatering chocolate mousse. Set meals 44–119F. You'll get a cheerful reception from young, smiling staff.

PISSOTTE 85200 (4KM N)

|●| CRÊPERIE LE POMMIER

9 rue des Gélinières (Centre); take the D938.
☎ 02.51.69.08.06
Closed Mondays, two weeks in October and two weeks in winter. **Car park**. **Disabled access**.

An old building with green shutters, a garden a conservatory and an air of serenity. It's covered in wisteria and Virginia creeper (unusual in these parts) and stands next to an old wine storehouse. The type of place where you feel quite at home. They do *crêpes* served with a generous side dish. Try "Bretonne" (*andouillette*, apples and salad), "caprine" (goat's cheese and thyme) or "Syracuse" (smoked breast of duck, pan-fried apples and an orange sauce) together with a nice bottle of rosé made by brother Xavier, the wine grower – much better than cider. Expect to pay 25–40F for a crêpe.

MERVENT 85200 (11KM NE)

|●| CRÊPERIE DU CHÂTEAU DE LA CITARDIÈRE

Les Ouillères; take the D99 from Mervent.
☎ 02.51.00.27.04
Closed Wednesdays in season, and Saturdays, Sundays and public holidays out of season.

Imagine you're looking round a medieval castle, and lo and behold, you come across a *crêperie*! It's been renovated and smells deliciously of firewood and the most wonderful *crêpes*. Sit out on the terrace in summer, and enjoy the fresh air. Service is a bit slow, but it's well worth the wait. (Have a look at one of the many exhibitions in the other rooms). Wonderful local apple juice. Expect to spend 25–45F for a savoury *crêpe* and 15–45F for a sweet one.

VELLUIRE 85770 (11KM SW)

10% ☗ |●| L'AUBERGE DE LA RIVIÈRE**

How to get there: take the D938 as far as Nizeau, then the D68.
☎ 02.51.52.32.15 ➡ 02.51.52.37.42
Closed Sunday evenings and Mondays (out of season), and Jan 10–Feb 25. **Secure parking**. **TV**.
Disabled access.

Ideal if you're looking for peace and quiet, secretly have a hankering for luxury, and long for good cooking. Start from the centre and head towards the river and you'll soon be comfortably installed in the dining room with its yellow tablecloths, beams, pot plants, furniture and tapestries. The owner's quite something and so is his wife's cooking. Try the fresh salmon with sorrel, the langoustine in puff pastry, or the young pigeon with morels. Set meals 110F, 190F and 230F. The country-style bedrooms will enchant even the most hardened city dweller. Number 10 is the only one not to overlook the river, and numbers 7, 8, 12 and 14 have bigger beds. Perfect for those who like to take things easy.

MAILLEZAIS 85420 (15KM SE)

☗ HÔTEL SAINT-NICOLAS**

rue du Docteur-Daroux (Centre).
☎ 02.51.00.74.45 ➡ 02.51.87.29.10
Closed Nov 15–Feb 15. **Secure parking**. **TV**.

The young owner of this friendly, renovated, little hotel takes care of everything from the very simple rooms (220–330F) to the terrace with its tiny gardens on different levels. What's more, he even finds time to run the tourist office. You should have no worries about exploring the marshes since he knows the area like the back of his hand and will show you his own little walks. A very good hotel for a short stay.

FONTEVRAUD-L'ABBAYE 49590

HÔTEL-RESTAURANT LA CROIX BLANCHE**

7 place des Plantagenêts; it's beside the famous abbey.
☎ 02.41.51.71.11 F➔ 02.41.38.15.38
Closed mid Jan–mid Feb, and one week round about mid Nov. **Secure parking**. **TV**. **Disabled access**.

A delightful hotel with elegant local architecture. Nice welcome. They have 21 quiet bedrooms laid out round a flower-filled courtyard. Doubles from 305F with shower/wc or bath and direct telephone. Some have a fireplace. The restaurant is well known for its food. Pleasant dining room. The set meal at 126F offers salad of sausage with walnuts and apples, *salmis* of young guinea fowl with mushrooms, cheese and dessert. Vegetarian set meal 99F. For 175F or 215F (two main courses) you can have snail and mushroom fricassee, scallops with buttered red cabbage and celery with citrus butter, breast of duck with five different peppers, and baked Alaska.

GUÉRANDE 44350

ROC MARIA**

1 rue des Halles.
☎ 02.40.24.90.51 F➔ 02.40.62.13.03
Closed Nov 15–Dec 15. **TV**.

A beautiful, old-fashioned establishment that fits in well with the architectural style of the old town and is a bit out of the way of the summer crowds. They offer ten bedrooms on various floors. The ones in the attic were our favourites. Enjoy a *galette* and a drop of cider in the *crêperie* on the mezzanine floor. The atmosphere's nicely old-fashioned too. Expect to pay 60–100F.

HERBIERS (LES) 85500

10% HÔTEL-RESTAURANT LE RELAIS**

18 rue de Saumur (Centre).
☎ 02.51.91.01.64 F➔ 02.51.67.36.50
Closed Sunday evenings. **TV**. **Canal+**.

A very good hotel with a beautiful renovated façade. The 26 bedrooms are as luxurious as the dining room. Although it's by the roadside like lots of other hotels in the area, the double glazing is pretty effective. Choose between the traditional cooking of *La Brasserie* and the more gourmet cooking of *La Cotriarde*. You can have some Mareuil wine with the 58F set meal (not served Sundays) if the fancy takes you. They do other set meals which are just as hearty (78F, 89F, 98F, 130F and 200F). Doubles from 250F with shower/wc or bath.

HÔTEL-RESTAURANT DU CENTRE**

6 rue de l'Église (Centre).
☎ 02.51.67.01.75 F➔ 02.51.66.82.24
Closed Friday evenings, Saturdays out of season, the first fortnight in August, and Christmas holidays. **TV**.

It's the good hearty cooking that attracts the customers during the week. Low-key pleasant décor. Doubles 270F with shower/wc and 300F with bath. If you believe in using seasonal produce and like fresh fish then you'll love what the proprietor has to offer – tuna stew *minervois* (with olives and anchovies), *escabèche* of sardines *piémontaise*, and ox tongue with mushrooms. Set meals 70–170F. Dinner compulsory at the "Puy du Fou" show. You'll get a marvellous welcome. The Morillons love the area and can give you lots of tips on what to see and do.

SAINT-LAURENT-SUR-SÈVRE 85290 (20KM NE)

10% HÔTEL-RESTAURANT L'HERMITAGE**

2 rue de la Jouvence (Centre); take the D752 and it's on the river bank opposite the basilica.
☎ 02.51.67.83.03 F➔ 02.51.67.84.11
Closed Saturdays out of season, the February school holidays, and the first fortnight in August. **Car park**. **TV**.

A nice family inn with a terrace overlooking the river. The chef/proprietor gets up at the crack of dawn to pick what he needs from his kitchen garden and sometimes fishes for trout in the river. The dining room is like something out of a very old episode of "The Avengers", with its orange Knoll style seats and carpet that your feet sink into. The rooms are a bit kitschy too, with psychedelic green carpet (remember that kind of thing?), but very comfortable. Number 29 with its view of the river is particularly nice. Doubles 220–260F. Generous portions and set meals 80–95F.

LA FLOCELIÈRE 85700

CHÂTEAU DE LA FLOCELIÈRE

La Flocelière; follow the signposts from Saint-Michel.
☎ 02.51.57.22.03 F➔ 02.51.57.75.21
Car park.

Did someone say castle? How about a neo-gothic one? It's coming back to life having been bought a few years back by the Vignal family. When you consider the terrific, spacious bedrooms, 550F for two sharing a double doesn't seem too much to ask. Perfectly charming thanks to the little British touches in the décor. Guests have access to the large park, swimming pool and the ruins of the 13th century castle. Luxurious and very tasteful with it. You'll have to book a long time in advance. If you've got 6,000F and lots of relatives, you could rent the whole dungeon for a week (it's not all that expensive when you consider that it's big enough for three families).

LAVAL 53000

10% ⌂ MARIN HÔTEL**

100-102 av. Robert-Buron (North-East); it's opposite the train station.
☎ 02.43.53.09.68 F 02.43.56.95.35
Secure parking. TV. Disabled access.

This establishment belongs to the Inter-Hôtel chain. It's modern, functional, and has good soundproofing. Nice reception. Doubles 225–270F with shower/wc or bath. 10% reduction weekends. Ideal if you've just got off the TGV. There are lots of restaurants in the area if you can't be bothered going as far as the old town – but that would be a shame, as there's plenty going on.

|●| RESTAURANT LE COURT-BOUILLON

99 rue du Pont-de-Mayenne (Centre).
☎ 02.43.56.70.87
Closed Sundays July–mid Sept, Saturday lunchtimes and Sunday evenings the rest of the year.

A little restaurant in a quiet street in the centre of town. They do traditional dishes like calf's head, ox cheek *fondue*, and cod's tongue. Dish of the day and dessert for 55F. Substantial set meals 95F and 135F ideal for those with big appetites.

|●| L'ANTIQUAIRE

5 rue des Béliers (Centre); it's behind the cathedral.
☎ 02.43.53.66.76
Closed Wednesdays, Saturday lunchtimes and the last two weeks in July.

If you're the sort who'll settle for second best, in life and matters culinary, walk on by. They appreciate beauty here, good workmanship and good friends. Don't be taken in by the name, because the cooking is what counts here and it's just magnificent! The cheapest set meal is a bargain. For 98F you'll get salad of rabbit legs with *confit* of tomatoes and rosemary, hake with a Camembert sauce, fresh cream cheese, and tart of the day. The 129F set meal comes with the famous crayfish tail lasagne with local *andouille* and the 175F one is quite extraordinary. Head over to rue des Béliers as soon as you can!

|●| LA BRAISE

4 rue de la Trinité (Centre); it's in the old town, near the cathedral.
☎ 02.43.53.21.87
Closed Sundays and Mondays.

What a cute little place! You'll feel quite relaxed here among the old jugs, beautiful furniture, beams and red hexagonal floor tiles. Not to mention Annie's wonderful welcome and the simple authentic dishes that are so skilfully cooked over charcoal. Grilled fish and meat are the specialities, as you'll have guessed – monkfish kebabs, seafood kebabs and beef with a marrowbone sauce. With *terrine* as a starter and a home-made pastry for dessert, you'll end up paying 130–160F. Or you could have the 98F set meal or the dish of the day. If it's a nice day, sit on the terrace.

|●| RESTAURANT LE BISTRO DE PARIS

22 quai Jehan-Fouquet (Centre); it's on the banks of the Mayenne.
☎ 02.43.56.98.29
Closed Saturday lunchtimes, Sundays and two weeks in August.

Surprise surprise, this is still the best place in town! And also the most expensive, unless you choose the 135F *menu-carte* that offers wonderful dishes like *tarte de lisette* with herb sauce and a *minute* of tuna with capers and potatoes. Take the time to savour those before you succumb to the temptation of chocolate and butterscotch tart. Year in year out, Guy Lemercier comes up with creative ideas to delight his regulars, who get a good-natured but not effusive welcome. Nicely old-fashioned brasserie décor which sometimes looks like a hall of mirrors. *Menu dégustation* 245F. Good service and fine wines.

CHANGÉ 53810 (4KM N)

|●| LA TABLE RONDE

Place de la Mairie (Centre).
☎ 02.43.53.43.33
Closed Sunday evenings and Mondays. **Car park.**

Don't take the wrong door. Upstairs it's the restaurant (come here if you've got somebody you want to impress). What we like is the bistro downstairs, with its 30s décor, smiling waitresses and low prices. On a fine day, sit on the terrace with the town on one side and the park on the other to give you a little taste of the countryside. *Menu du jour* 75F. The 98F set meal (lunchtimes and evenings) offers dishes like two kinds of salmon, small seafood stew, and *sablé* of strawberries with lemon-flavoured cream. Skilfully prepared, rich in flavour, colourful – and not not necessarily fattening. Worth the effort of getting here.

LE GENEST SAINT ISLE 53940 (12KM W)

RESTAURANT LE SALVERT

route d'Olivet.
☎ 02.43.37.14.3
Closed Sunday evenings and Mondays. **Car park. Disabled access.**

Just ten minutes from Laval, by the étang d'Olivet. Come here in summer and sit on the terrace. Come in winter too and sit at the fireside. This isn't the place for a quick bite to eat, so try to avoid coming in shorts or boots. The 95F set meal offers *ballotine* of chicken and veal chop with lemon. If you can afford 145F, you'll get the *salad gourmande* of your dreams, followed for example by stuffed saddle of rabbit steamed, cheese platter and a wonderful selection of desserts. Their bread's home-made, just like everything else.

COSSÉ-LE-VIVIEN 53230 (18KM SW)

10% HÔTEL-RESTAURANT L'ÉTOILE**

2 rue de Nantes (Centre); take the N171.
☎ 02.43.98.81.31 F 02.43.98.96.64
Closed Sunday evenings, Mondays and in August. **Car park. TV. Disabled access.**

They have seven perfectly adequate bedrooms, but the décor's pretty tacky (and kitschy too). Doubles 155–220F with shower/wc or bath. Good middle-class style of cooking. Cheapest set meal 55F (weekdays). Others 77F and 110F offering dishes such as *fondant* of oxtails and *gratin* of pears with cinnamon, a change from the usual *tarte Tatin*. Give dessert a miss if you like but the Musée Robert Tatin, a stone's throw away, is a must.

VAIGES 53480 (22KM E)

HÔTEL DU COMMERCE***

Rue du Fief-aux-Moines (Centre).
☎ 02.43.90.50.07 F 02.43.90.57.40
Car park. TV. Canal+.

Since 1882, every generation of the Oger family has had one thing on their mind – making sure their guests sleep well and have plenty on their plates! And the reason the hotel is still in existence is that each generation has adapted to a changing clientele. So you can quite happily spend a night or two in one of the quiet bedrooms (300–360F) and an evening or two in the conservatory, which is where they serve good food based on local produce. The 149F set meal offers asparagus in puff pastry with *sauce maltaise* (*hollandaise* flavoured with the juice of blood oranges), leg of rabbit in cider, cheese, and apple tart. *Formule* 82F, set meals 98–250F.

ERNÉE 53500 (30KM NW)

LE GRAND CERF**

17-19 rue Aristide Briand (Centre).
☎ 02.43.05.13.09 F 02.43.05.02.90
Closed Sunday evenings and Mondays out of season, and the last two weeks in January. **Car park. TV.**

A good hotel known for its hospitality, facilities and restaurant in northern Mayenne, an area famous for its dolmens and standing stones. The atmosphere is fairly hushed in the restaurant and more relaxed in the bistro corner (the door from the street has been shut up but the proprietress hopes to open it again if business picks up). You can have the dish of the day (40F or 50F) in here if you don't fancy the dining room and its delicious 108F and 158F set meals. You're in for a real treat if you choose the first one – *salade gourmande* or potted ham *en persillade*, cod or *navarin* of lamb, and *blanc en neige* (a bit like floating islands) or stuffed *crêpe*. Beautiful bedrooms 195–248F. The perfect place to stop on the way to Mont St Michel.

SAULGES 53340 (34 KM SE)

10% HÔTEL-RESTAURANT L'ERMITAGE***

Centre; take the N157 and the D24, then turn left at Chéméré-le-Roi.
☎ 02.43.90.52.28 F 02.43.90.56.61
Closed Sunday evenings and Mondays Oct–mid April, and Feb. **Secure parking. TV. Disabled access.**

Despite its name, you'll find no monks' cells or meatless days at *L'Ermitage*! A modern hotel near a wonderful Merovingian church, it has bright, spacious and comfortable rooms overlooking the park, swimming pool and surrounding countryside. Expect to pay 340–450F. The restaurant's run by a father and son team who combine, in their own style, traditional and modern cooking. Try the scallops in Jasnières (a white wine), *suprême* of guinea fowl with a morel sauce, apple tarts and ice-cream with gingerbread. Choose from the wide selection of set meals (100–300F). Ideal if you want to eat a lot and explore the area. Plenty of nice walks nearby. Set meals 100–250F.

|●| GROTTES ET CANYON DE SAULGES

☎ 02.43.90.52.29
Closed Tuesdays out of season, and Jan.

At the start of the road leading to the famous caves. Whoever came up with the idea for this unusual restaurant didn't have to think very hard about a name for it. by countryside in the form of a canyon. The décor — reproductions of prehistoric frescoes and stone-shaped tables — will put you in the right frame of mind to try a 45F *pierrade* of fish or meat. You cook your own meal on a hot stone. Expect to pay 75–100F à la carte. Buffet starters.

LUÇON 85400

⌂ |●| HÔTEL-RESTAURANT DU CROISSANT*

place des Acacias (Centre).
☎ 02.51.56.11.15
Closed Sundays out of season and Oct.
Secure parking.

Since 1930, this establishment has remained true to the tradition of the French family-run hotel business, putting the emphasis on hospitality and good food rather than modern facilities and functionalism. A magic place with an astonishing foyer that's a mixture of brown and beige and has a reception desk dating back to the 40s. It's decorated in old-fashioned style and never seems to get any older. The enormous staircase creaks — but only ever so slightly. You'll feel quite at home in the very pleasant bedrooms. Doubles 130F with washing facilities, 200F with shower/wc and 220F with bath. Even the prices date from another era!. The designs on the plates may be starting to fade, but the cooking's as traditional and irresistible as ever, as is the extremely popular beef *bourguignon*. Set meals 62–110F. Unlike most hotels, they do an excellent breakfast. Let's hope they keep up the good work!

⌂ |●| HÔTEL-RESTAURANT LE BŒUF COURONNÉ**

55 route de La-Roche-sur-Yon (West).
☎ 02.51.56.11.32 F 02.51.56.98.25
Closed Sunday evenings and Mondays (except holiday weekends). **Car park**. **TV**. **Disabled access**.

This attractive establishment is unfortunately rather close to the road. The pergola almost groans under its weight of flowers in summer and there's a delightfully cosy lounge for cold days. Good cooking with no nasty surprises and several dining rooms. How about *grenadin* of veal with chanterelles, *paupiettes* of filets of sole with langoustines or breast of duck with peaches? Set meals 70–198F. It's a delight to watch them preparing the flambéd dishes. If you feel like a good night's sleep, they have four rather plush bedrooms. Expect to pay 250F with shower/wc and 260F with bath.

MALICORNE-SUR-SARTHE 72270

|●| RESTAURANT LA PETITE AUBERGE

5 place Du-Guesclin.
☎ 02.43.94.80.52
Closed Sunday evenings and Mondays (except June–Sept), evenings Tuesday–Thursday inclusive out of season, and Feb. **Car park**. **Disabled access**.

This place is on a riverbank and has a rather attractive terrace, where you can treat yourself to pike *terrine*, fillet of sea trout, cheese and dessert for a mere 84F. Set meals on Sundays are a bit more expensive (130–192F). and attract a bigger crowd. À la carte dishes change according to what's in season and deliveries of fish at the market. The elegant flower-filled dining room has a fireplace and is ideal for cloudy days.

MAMERS 72600

⌂ |●| HÔTEL-RESTAURANT LE DAUPHIN**

54 rue du Fort.
☎ 02.43.34.24.24
Closed Sunday evenings. **Secure parking**. **TV**.

Pay a visit to Mamers if you want to sample *rillettes* (cubed pork cooked in its own fat) at their best. *Le Dauphin* is a good, unpretentious little hotel with perfectly adequate bedrooms at 190F and 230F. Specialities such as omelette with *rillettes* and *marmite sarthoise*, available à la carte, are a must. Unless you'd prefer to have one of the very reasonable set meals ranging in price from 60F (weekdays) to 153F.

NEUCHÂTEL-EN-SAOSNOIS 72600 (9KM W)

RELAIS DES ÉTANGS DE GUIBERT.

☎ 02.43.97.15.38 F 02.43.97.66.42
Closed Mondays (except public holidays) and Oct–Easter. **Car park**.

It's at the edge of the forest of Perseigne, near the pond and comes to life as soon as the sun shows its face. It's pretty difficult to get a room at the weekends – lots of people come for the pleasant décor, the wonderful welcome, and the excellent value for money. Rooms are individually decorated (you can choose one with a sailing or hunting theme for example) and the prices (270–320F) won't shock you – quite the reverse. Have one of the simple set meals (85F, 130F and 180F) before setting off to explore one of the most beautiful areas in this part of France on horseback, by boat or on foot.

ROUPERROUX LE COQUET 72110 (18KM SE)

LE PETIT CAMPAGNARD

D301.
☎ 02.43.29.79.74
Closed Mondays. **Car park**.

A pretty little place that makes you want to stop. Lots of other have exactly the same idea, especially on a Sunday. The unbeatable 60F set meal offers *rillettes* (cubed pork cooked in its own fat), chicken with cider, cheese and dessert. You'll get a rather good deal for 96F, and for 130F you can try unusual dishes like venison flambéd with whisky or ostrich with pepper sauce. Each to his (or her) own taste!

FRESNAYE-SUR-CHÉDOUET (LA) 72600 (22KM NW)

10% L'AUBERGE SAINT-PAUL

How to get there: Take the D3 and the D234.
☎ 02.43.97.82.76 F 02.43.97.82.76
Closed Sunday evenings and Mondays (except public holidays). **Car park. Disabled access**.

A former stud farm far from the madding crowd – ideal if you like to eat in peace. If you feel like spending the night, they've four little bedrooms, as rustic as can be, at 225F and 230F. It's a pity they don't have the same timeless charm as the inn, which has a fireplace, red hexagonal floor tiles, attractively set little tables and very professional waitresses. Pascal Yenk's cooking reflects today's preference for food that is skilfully prepared and full of flavour and he offers dishes like – *suprême* of bass in a potato crust, medallions of lamb with *confit* of vegetables, and roast langoustine. Wonderful set meals 125F, 168F and 220F. To put the finishing touch to a perfect day, take a little stroll in the forest.

MANS (LE) 72000

AUBERGE DE JEUNESSE LE FLORE

23 rue Maupertuis (Centre); take the number 12 bus (destination Californie) and get off at Erpell.
☎ 02.43.81.27.55 F 02.43.81.06.10
Canal+. Disabled access.

FUAJ youth hostel card required. Most of the year 22 beds are available, but if you have a large family wait until July or August when there are 40 beds! Most rooms have 2 or 3 beds, one room has 4 beds and there is an apartment with 7 beds. Overnight stays cost 46–83F. Meals 29–36F.

HÔTEL LA POMMERAIE**

rue de l'Éventail (East); follow signs for Paris (N23) and turn into rue de Douce-Amie at auberge Bagatelle.
☎ 02.43.85.13.93
Car park. TV.

If you have been on the road for hours then this hotel will revive you – although close to the centre of the city (if travelling by car) the silence is unbroken in the large, flower-filled garden with majestic trees. Concentrate on the garden and enjoy the hospitality and feeling of luxury and might even be able to forgive the bland, post-war architecture. Rooms are 210F (with shower/wc) and 240F (with bath). The young hotelier who has breathed new life into these pleasant surroundings lets you view the rooms in peace. If only he would redecorate, your happiness would be guaranteed.

GREEN 7 HÔTEL

447 av. Georges Durand (East); it's on the way into Le Mans on the Tours road.
☎ 02.43.85.05.73 F 02.43.86.62.78
Car park. TV. Canal+.

Enjoy the restful, calm surroundings of this modernized hotel just 1.7km from the Le Mans 24 Hours Race Circuit and the Motor Museum. The restaurant is handy if you don't fancy a trek into the city centre and offers a quite remarkable breakfast buffet for 35F. A pleasing, practical location with garden and parking. Rooms 265–325F, set meals for 80–126F. Relaxed atmosphere.

HÔTEL CHATECLER

50 rue de la Pelouse (East).
☎ 02.43.24.58.53 ➡ 02.43.77.16.28
TV.

Just a short distance from the palais des Congrès, this hotel offers peace and comfort within easy reach of the old part of Le Mans. The welcome is sincere, the service competent, the parking easy and the breakfast, served in the conservatory, rather good. There is also a restaurant on the ground floor, but be warned that it does not compare to the rest of the establishment. Very decent rooms for a short stay, 335–395F.

L'ATLAS

80 bd de la Petite Vitesse (South-East).
☎ 02.43.61.03.16
Closed Monday and Saturday lunchtimes.

If you get stranded in Le Mans because forest fires have caused the cancellation of your train (it has happened!) then you will be delighted to find this Moroccan restaurant near the station, an area with little else of interest for the hungry tourist. The proprietor has done his country proud with both the cuisine on offer and the décor. Walk through the doors and find yourself in an Arabian palace. Very attentive, friendly service. Excellent *tajines* and very fresh Oriental pastries. The dream of North Africa is complete at weekends when shows are put on. Allow 110–150F to dine à la carte. Open until 11.30pm.

CRÊPERIE LE BLÉ EN HERBE

48 Grande-Rue (Centre).
☎ 02.43.28.39.00
Closed Sundays (from October to the end of February), Monday lunchtimes and between Christmas and New Year.

Although situated in a touristy area, this amiable *crêperie* is worth a visit. Dine in a vaulted cellar in the winter and out on the terrace in summer. Savoury *crêpe* for 30F, local cider 40F. Allow 60–65F for a full meal. Relaxed, affable service.

RESTAURANT "CHEZ JEAN"

9/11 rue Dorée (West).
☎ 02.43.28.22.96
Closed Sunday evenings and Mondays.

A typical brasserie in old Le Mans which is often full when its neighbours are decidedly empty – always a good sign. An unpretentious venue with serious cuisine which follows both seasons and fashions. Uncomplicated set meals based on market produce are offered (from 89F including wine and coffee) as well as traditional meals (set meals 184–240F). Satisfaction guaranteed with scrambled egg *vol au vents*, monkfish *blanquette* or *saucisson lyonnais*. Good house wines and pleasant terrace opening out onto place de l'Éperon.

LE NEZ ROUGE

107 Grande-Rue (North-West).
☎ 02.43.24.27.26
Closed Sundays and Monday lunchtimes.

Although this old-town restaurant is called "The Red Nose" don't expect to be entertained by clowns. This establishment likes to describe itself as a "gourmet restaurant" and is the place to come for a *Mongolfière* of mussels and cockles in a leek sauce, poached turbot in Champagne or fillets of *grenadier* (a salt water fish) in a butter and white wine sauce (they use Jasnières, the local white). Set meals 99F and 149F. For a more relaxed atmosphere try the same establishment's charming "gourmet *crêperie*" which is nearby in place du Hallai (set meals 75F and 90F).

LE FLAMBADOU

14 bis rue Saint-Flaceau (West).
☎ 02.43.24.88.38
Closed Sundays, a week at Easter and for a week around 15 August.

The owner/chef presents specialities from his native area of Landes and Perigord. The hotel is named after a "*flambadou*" – a ladle which was heated up over the fire and used to baste meat in times gone by. A rather sweet little dining room where you will receive a warm, hearty welcome. On sunny days sit out on the shady terrace. The à la carte main dishes are so generous that you may not be able to manage a dessert. The offerings include goose casserole *à la lotoise*, fricassee of duck and, for enthusiasts (like us), succulent calf's feet *à la mode de tante Alice*. A place to come for a good meal after a stroll around the medieval part of Le Mans. Highly recommended. Allow around 150F for a meal.

YVRÉ-L'ÉVÊQUE 72530 (5KM E)

10% HÔTEL-MOTEL PAPEA**

Bener; leave Le Mans on the N23 and follow signs to Papea.

☎ 02.43.89.64.09 ➡ 02.43.89.49.81
Car park. **TV**.

Near the abbey of Epau, this "hotel-motel" is set in lovely grounds and comprises some 20 comfortable chalets well separated from each other by bushes and trees. The cost is 200–275F for two people (breakfast extra). Ideal for those who like to stay in the country but also want to be very close to the city. You can hardly even hear the passing TGVs. Tray meals on request, 50F. Reductions for weekends, long stays and commercial travellers. A friendly welcome — the proprietors chat engagingly as they take you to your chalet "home" as wild rabbits follow inquisitively.

MULSANNE 72230 (8KM S)

HÔTEL-RESTAURANT ARBOR – AUBERGE DE MULSANNE**

route de Tours; 10 minutes from Le Mans, at the 24 Hours Race circuit.
☎ 02.43.39.18.90 ➡ 02.43.39.18.99
Restaurant closed Saturday lunchtimes and Sunday evenings. **Car park**. **TV**. **Disabled access**.

When the 24 Hours Race is on this hotel is the base for many of the teams and is understandably somewhat overwhelmed. If you are not interested in the race, come at other times of the year and discover the hotel's sauna and swimming pool. Impeccable rooms for 300F with bath. Set meals for 95F during the week (145F at the weekend), 185F, 235F and 370F.

SAINT-GERMAIN-SUR-SARTHE 72130 (9KM N)

RESTAURANT "LE SAINT-GERMAIN"

Lieu-dit "La Hutte"; take the N138 – it's at the crossroads.
☎ 02.43.97.53.06
Closed evenings Sunday, Monday and Tuesday.

It doesn't look like much from the outside but drivers speeding past on the main road between Mans and Alençon don't know what they're missing when they turn their nose up at this place. There's nowhere else like it. People smile and laugh and congratulate Madame on her flower arrangements and Monsieur on his sauces. We wish we could have taken some of our starter — rabbit *terrine* — home. For 97F, 112F or 148F (depending on your appetite and budget), you'll get the rabbit *terrine* plus a splendid *cassolette* of fish and/or grilled rib of beef *béarnaise*. Spend more (157F, 172F or 207F) and you can have a choice of *salade gourmande* or a dozen oysters, *gratin* of lobster and/or *fondant* of veal with morels. And if you're not all that hungry, they even do a 69F set meal of *terrine* and roast veal. France at its best.

FILLÉ-SUR-SARTHE 72210 (15.5 KM SW)

RESTAURANT LE BARRAGE

rue Principale.
☎ 02.43.87.14.40
Closed Sunday evenings and Wednesdays.

Good local reputation. Pleasant dining area and warm welcome. The highlight is the terrace at the rear which looks out directly onto the Sarthe river. A serene, rural setting in which to enjoy casseroled lamb's brains with mushrooms, duck's leg in Cassis (blackcurrant liqueur) or fillet of duck with oyster mushrooms. Set meals for 58F (except Sundays and public holidays), 85F and 148F. On Sundays the set meals are 98–148F. Consider reserving a table on the terrace as they are quickly taken!

DOMFRONT-EN-CHAMPAGNE 72240 (18KM NW)

RESTAURANT DU MIDI**

rue Principale; it's on the D304, heading towards Mayenne.
☎ 02.43.20.52.04
Closed evenings from Tuesday to Sunday (except Fridays and Saturdays). **Closed** for the month of February.

The dining room is comfortable although the surroundings are a little posh. Cuisine with an excellent reputation and attentive service. Good set meal for 79F (99F at the weekend) — beef with spices or stuffed and roasted duck's leg served with its own juices. The set meal for 147F includes a *gratin* of cockles and the 199F one escalope of sea trout in a Champagne sauce or fillet of veal with ginger. À la carte dishes include *foie gras* ravioli with a morel sauce, braised duck's leg with bilberries, and mullet with beef marrow and blackcurrant vinegar. Reasonable prices — and that also goes for some of the wines from a good list: a bottle of Touraine for 65F and a Côtes-du-Rhône for 80F.

BEAUMONT-SUR-SARTHE 72170 (25KM N)

HÔTEL-RESTAURANT DU CHEMIN DE FER**

place de la Gare; turn off the N138 onto the D26 towards Vivoin; the hotel is less than 1km from the town centre.

☎ 02.43.97.00.05 F 02.43.33.52.17
Secure parking. **TV**. **Closed** Friday and Sunday evenings, Mondays from November to April and during the November and February school holidays.

Any doubts on your choice of restaurant will be removed by the cheerful staff, the mouth-watering aromas coming from the kitchens and the sight of happy clients, both arriving and leaving. With the garden behind the house and the pastoral atmosphere in the large dining room you could almost be in the country. Treat yourself to the flambéd scallops in whisky, the *marmite sarthoise* (the local hotpot) or a good rib of beef. You could well be tempted to stay over in one of the fifteen pleasant rooms for 207–295F. Set meals 87F (weekdays), 120F, 140F, 175F and 200F. A good set meal of local dishes for 100F with duck *compote* and sautéd rabbit with mushrooms .... mmmm!

THORIGNÉ-SUR-DUÉ 72160 (28KM E)

10% HÔTEL-RESTAURANT SAINT-JACQUES**

place du Monument; take the N23 and D302.
☎ 02.43.89.95.50 F 02.43.76.58.42
Closed Mondays and in January. **Secure parking**. **TV**. **Disabled access**.

Comfort, courtesy and good food all come together in this traditional family hotel. Doubles for 320–400F. Garden. Set meals for 98F, 175F, 245F and 325F. Specialities include scallops with vanilla butter, warm salad of veal sweetbreads with *foie gras* and truffle vinegar, and braised chicken in cider. Children's meal for 68F.

MAYENNE 53100

10% L'AUBERGE DES TROIS ÉPIS

15 rue de la Madeleine; it's on the Laval road.
☎ 02.43.04.87.34 F 02.43.04.83.60
Hotel closed for the first two weeks of August. Restaurant closed Friday evenings and Saturday lunchtimes. **Car park**. **TV**.

Quiet, peaceful hotel in the style of years gone by. All double rooms are 170F with shower or bath but the wc is on the landing. In the restaurant Madame Petitpas serves Normandy dishes including *andouillette* in cider and trout. The cheapest set meal is 56F on weekdays; other set meals for 74F and 95F.

10% LE GRAND HÔTEL**

2 rue Ambroise de Loré (Centre); it faces the Mayenne river.
☎ 02.43.00.96.00 F 02.43.32.08.49
Closed Christmas week. **Car park**. **TV**.

If only the rest of the town could be renovated as well as this hotel where tourists arriving by car, bike and even boat are greeted with a cheery smile. Those lucky enough to stay in these well-appointed rooms for 175–460F experience a part Breton, part Norman cuisine in a quaint ambience and can round off the evening in the bar with a good whisky. The set meal for 120F offers dishes based on cider; there are other set meals for 89–148F.

10% HÔTEL LA TOUR DES ANGLAIS**

13 bis place Juhel (Centre).
☎ 02.43.04.34.56 F 02.43.32.13.84
Car park. **TV**. **Disabled access**.

Very close to Château de Mayenne. This hotel would be wonderful if all the rooms were the same as the one in the fortified tower with its dramatic view of the Mayenne river (270F per night)). The other rooms are comfortable, if more modern, with shower or bath, 200–240F. If you want some company, go down to the English-style bar with its billiard table and impressive wood beams.

FONTAINE-DANIEL 53100 (4KM SW)

RESTAURANT LA FORCE

Centre.
☎ 02.43.00.34.85
Closed Wednesdays and Sunday evenings.

A magical spot opposite a small lake. A setting so timeless that you could imagine it as a set in a classical TV series, where the locals all depended, from the day they were born until the day they died, on the local mill producing Mayenne cloth. Visit the mill and buy some cloth to take home before discovering this lovely restaurant on the main square which would not be out of place in a fairy tale. Dine out on the pretty terrace in the summer and enjoy excellent ingredients all year round. The set meal for 110F offers a tomato and queen scallop gazpacho, *blanquette* of cod *à la normande* and a selection of cheeses or prune *fondant*. Other excellent set meals for 160F and 190F. Special dishes, changed weekly, for 90F.

MOULAY 53100 (4KM S)

10% HÔTEL-RESTAURANT BEAU RIVAGE

How to get there: it's on the N162 between Mayenne and Moulay.

☎ 02.43.00.49.13 ➡ 02.43.04.43.69
Car park.

To find this lovely hotel-restaurant just follow the Mayenne river. It is a sight to behold, set on the river bank with faithful clients crowding the dining room and the terrace, which reaches down to the water. Make sure you reserve a table. Set meals for 70F (weekdays) to 172F. The set meal for 84F offers rabbit and prune *terrine*, calf's head *ravigote* (with a spicy vinaigrette) and *crème caramel*, and the 134F one *cassolette* of queen scallops, lacquered pork spareribs, cheese and *crème brûlée*. Three rooms available, 200–250F.

LA MARJOLAINE**

Le Bas Mont; it's on the way out of Moulay heading towards Laval.
☎ 02.43.00.48.42 ➡ 02.43.08.10.58
Closed Sunday evenings, Christmas and in February. **Car park. TV.**

If you would rather be carrying a rucksack than wearing a tie, then this place may not at first glance appeal to you, but it will gladden the hearts of people who love peaceful spots with gourmet food and don't mind dressing smartly if the circumstances demand it. The quality of the cuisine and freshness of the ingredients is exemplary. Set meals 95–240F. When available try the fresh fish for 95F, such as John Dory with a cardamom-scented sauce or sea bream with sorrel and panfried whelks. An up-and-coming restaurant. Twelve brand new rooms which, although comfortable, are not particularly cosy, 250–320F.

MONTREUIL-POULAY 53640 (12KM N)

L'AUBERGE CAMPAGNARDE

Le Presbytère.
☎ 02.43.32.07.11
Closed Sunday evenings, Wednesdays and Nov–Feb.

A kind welcome in a restaurant where the service is friendly without being overfamiliar. Aperitif and coffee served on the terrace even if the weather is not quite fine enough to warrant taking the whole meal outside. The set meal at 105F (or 125F with a fish course) offers an astonishing selection of good local food and grilled dishes. How about *terrine* of duck and Pommeau in winter or of baby vegetables in summer, a choice of pike in a wine and butter sauce or sea bream with chervil, and duck in cider in summer and goose in winter? Finish off with a strawberries and cream cake or *fondant glacé* with apples. Another good set meal for 90F. Be sure to reserve.

GORRON 53120 (22KM NW)

HÔTEL-RESTAURANT LE BRETAGNE**

41 rue de Bretagne (East); take the D12 to Saint-Georges-Buttavent and then the D5.
☎ 02.43.08.63.67 ➡ 02.43.08.01.15
Closed Sunday evenings and Mondays. **Car park. TV.**

A good village restaurant where you can get a hearty meal. Set meals 78–180F offering *mousseline* of zander with a crab sauce, shellfish casserole with vermouth and/or honey-glazed roast breast of duck with Perry. The décor doesn't merit a special mention, but the price of the rooms (230F) and the overall quality do!

VILLAINES-LA-JUHEL 53700 (28KM E)

L'HOSTELLERIE DE LA JUHEL*

27 rue Jules-Doitteau (Centre); take the D113.
☎ 02.43.03.23.24 ➡ 02.43.03.79.87
Closed Friday and Sunday evenings and for three weeks in February. **Car park. TV.**

The chef loves his work and invites his clientele to savour his culinary inspirations, such as his grilled meat dishes and guinea-fowl braised in cider. Excellent value for money. Set meal for 49F during the week and ample set meals based on local produce for 75–125F. Rooms available for 205F (with shower, wc and TV).

MAZEAU (LE) 85420

RESTAURANT L'AUBERGE MARAICHINE

☎ 02.51.52.90.20
Closed Sunday and Wednesday evenings (except on the eve of public holidays). **Car park.**

The owner of this unusual, old village bistro was certainly not concerned with what people would say when he painted it green, making it look like a leprechaun's house! With a mischievous look and a roguish bow tie, proprietor Bernard Diot serves up a slice of *farci poitevin* (a kind of stuffed cabbage), stuffed snails and ham with haricot beans in the 95F set meal, and frogs' legs or eels in the 115F set meal. The cheapest set meal (59F) offers a buffet of starters, dish of the day and dessert. If he has five minutes to spare he has a whole host of tales to tell over a little glass of something.

MONTREUIL-BELLAY 49260

10% HÔTEL-RESTAURANT SPLENDID'HÔTEL**

139 rue du Docteur-Gaudrez (Centre); it's close to the twelfth-century château.
☎ 02.41.53.10.00 Fax 02.41.52.45.17
Closed Sunday evenings off season. **Car park. TV. Disabled access.**

A place not to miss: the ambience is captivating and the owner hilarious. A place where you will soon be mixing with the locals. In short, a great place for a holiday. It has everything — the building comprises beautiful adjoining fifteenth and seventeenth century wings offering a wide range of rooms, including one for 180F (basin, TV, telephone) and others with shower/wc for 270F. In the mornings the only sound to be heard is the fountain, whereas in the evenings you can enjoy the lively bar. There is also a large function room for parties. Pleasant dining room with cuisine which is fresh, copious, gourmet and family all at the same time. Set meals 75–220F. The set meal for 175F for example offers *salade gourmande*, *assiette de Loire* or pike sausages and veal chop with morels or cockerel in Champigny (a type of red wine). The set meal for 220F includes fresh homemade *foie gras*. À la carte offerings include zander in a white wine and butter sauce, frogs *à la provençale*, perch fillets in a vermouth sauce, and breast of duck with onions. Half-board 270–370F. The swimming pool is covered in the winter and there is a jacuzzi, sauna and Turkish bath.

HÔTEL-RELAIS DU BELLAY**

96 rue Nationale (Centre); it's behind the château.
☎ 02.41.53.10.10 Fax 02.41.52.45.17
Closed Sunday evenings from October to Easter. **Secure parking. TV. Disabled access.**

Same owner as the *Splendid Hôtel* with a common reception. This hotel also has a relaxed, friendly welcome. Quieter than the *Splendid Hôtel*, but if you want a bit of life you could always eat at the *Splendid*. This hotel is made up of two old houses (a former school). Very comfortable, spacious rooms, completely renovated in the main building, from 270F for a double. Some look out onto the château and fortifications. Large, pleasant garden with swimming pool. You will leave in fine shape if you make use of the fitness room, sauna, Turkish bath and jacuzzi.

L'AUBERGE DES ISLES

How to get there: it's down from the château, beside the river.
☎ 02.41.52.30.63
Closed Sunday evenings and Mondays off season, and for the month of January. **Disabled access.**

The most beautiful terrace in the area; peaceful and rural on the river bank. Good, traditional food with generous helpings. Country salads and grilled dishes make up the cheapest set meal for 72F (except on Sundays). Other set meals for 109–169F. Fish specialities. Don't miss out on the fried eel. Relaxed atmosphere. Miniature golf, boats and pedalos available for a post-prandial excursion on the river Thouet.

MORTAGNE-SUR-SÈVRE 85290

10% HÔTEL-RESTAURANT DE FRANCE ET LA TAVERNE***

4 place du Docteur-Pichat.
☎ 02.51.65.03.37 Fax 02.51.65.27.83
Closed Saturdays (except June–Aug) and July 30–Aug 12. **Secure parking. TV. Canal+. Disabled access.**

There was a revolution in Mortagne in 1968... the *Hôtel de France*, first constructed in 1604, was renovated. Since then nothing more has changed. You can't miss this beautiful, noble building as you arrive in the main square — it's smothered in ivy. Endless corridors and odd little corners lead to plush, comfortable rooms. Doubles for 165F (with washing facilities, no TV), 290F (with shower and wc) and 350F (with bath and covered terrace). For food, you have a choice between the brasserie (*La Petite Auberge*) with traditional dishes, set meals 80–100F; or if you want to splash out there is *La Taverne* restaurant. This is a sumptuous dining room in subtle, warm tones, with refined décor, medieval furnishings, a collection of pewter pots on the chimney breast and flowers everywhere. Impeccable service. The food is a festival of delicate, surprising flavours. Poussin in vinegar and raspberry liqueur, duck *Grand Veneur* (in a peppery red wine and redcurrant sauce) etc. The prices are high, but if you want the best you have to pay. Set meals 163–320F. There's a swimming pool too, just to complete the picture!

NANTES 44000

SEE MAP OVERLEAF

AUBERGE DE JEUNESSE LA MANU

2 place de la Manu. Off map **D1-1**
☎ 02.40.29.29.20 ➡ 02.40.29.23.54
Closed Sept 15–June 27.

FUAJ membership required. This youth hostel is located in an old tobacco factory not far from the city centre. There are 62 beds in about 20 rooms; an overnight stay in a room with 2–4 beds costs 70F (breakfast included) and you can hire sheets for 16F. Single rooms cost 100F (sheets and breakfast included). Meals cost 49F but must be booked in advance. There is a bar in the evenings. The facilities include a laundry room, kitchen and showers. The hostel caters for a wide range of activities from an introduction to microlight flying to excursions to local vineyards.

10% HÔTEL DUCHESSE ANNE**

3–4 place de la Duchesse Anne. **MAP D2-8**
☎ 02.40.74.30.29 ➡ 02.40.74.60.20
Secure parking. TV. Canal+.

A real find — the finest (or one of the finest) hotels in Nantes is not the most expensive. Behind the château, this magnificent building, with its palatial style, has only been awarded two stars although most of the rooms deserve a much higher rating. The hotels has around 60 rooms divided into two categories. If you described those doubles for around 300F as very comfortable, those for around 400F are simply regal, with stone balconies looking out to the château, massive bathrooms and acres of space. The hotel is being renovated and when the work is finished it could be given a higher classification with a corresponding hike in prices. Phone to check.

10% HÔTEL SAINT-DANIEL*

4 rue du Bouffay. **MAP C2-2**
☎ 02.40.47.41.25 ➡ 02.51.72.03.99
TV.

A remarkable little hotel, clean and well-kept. Double for 140F (with shower) and 160F (with bath). The 19 rooms all have telephones and alarm clocks (TV optional extra for 20F). Some rooms face the pedestrian street, others the garden and the charming Sainte-Croix church in the Bouffay district.

HÔTEL FOURCROY*

11 rue Fourcroy. **MAP B3-3**
☎ 02.40.44.68.00
Secure parking. TV.

Plain but decent. Doubles from 169F (with shower/wc) to 210F (with bath). Quiet.

10% HÔTEL CHOLET**

10 rue Gresset. **MAP B3-4**
☎ 02.40.73.31.04 ➡ 02.40.73.78.82
TV. Canal+.

Excellent welcome and very clean, well-kept rooms. And this hotel is quiet thanks to that wonderful invention: double glazing. Some rooms actually used to be apartments in neighbouring buildings, so you may find yourself in a cosy attic room or a proper suite with two rooms and bathroom! From 225F (with shower/wc) to 245F (with bath). At weekends and public holidays doubles with shower/wc or bath for 195F.

10% HÔTEL AMIRAL**

26 bis rue Scribe. **MAP B2-5**
☎ 02.40.69.20.21 ➡ 02.40.73.98.13
Car park. Canal+.

This brand new chain hotel has everything a businessperson could want (double glazing, mini-bar etc). The pleasant rooms are 309F during the week but prices drop to 240F at the weekends. Friendly.

10% L'HÔTEL***

6 rue Henri-IV. **MAP D2-7**
☎ 02.40.29.30.31 ➡ 02.40.29.00.95
Secure parking. TV. Canal+. Disabled access.

A pleasant hotel, currently undergoing renovation, which doesn't take itself too seriously. The residents are mostly quiet business people who like to get up and out early — a warning to those who like a lie-in! A double room with bath is 400F. Some rooms open out onto the garden. A professional, cheerful attitude. Reductions available at weekends.

HÔTEL LA PEROUSE***

3 allée Duquesne. **MAP B2-6**
☎ 02.40.89.75.00 ➡ 02.40.89.76.00
Car park. TV. Canal+. Disabled access.

Advance warning: you will either instantly hate this hotel or you won't want to leave. This new hotel designed by the architects Barto and Barto is unique in Nantes, indeed in France. Constructed like a large block of white granite, heavy and compact. Its large windows look out to cours des Cinquante-Otages and the rooftops. Inside there is lots of wood, designer furniture, space and tranquillity. The atmosphere is lightened by the smiles of the receptionists, despite the stern attitude of the manageress. Rooms 440F. Not the place for you if you are nostalgic for the hotels of yesteryear — you won't get used to the shapes of the lamps, washbasins, chairs or windows.

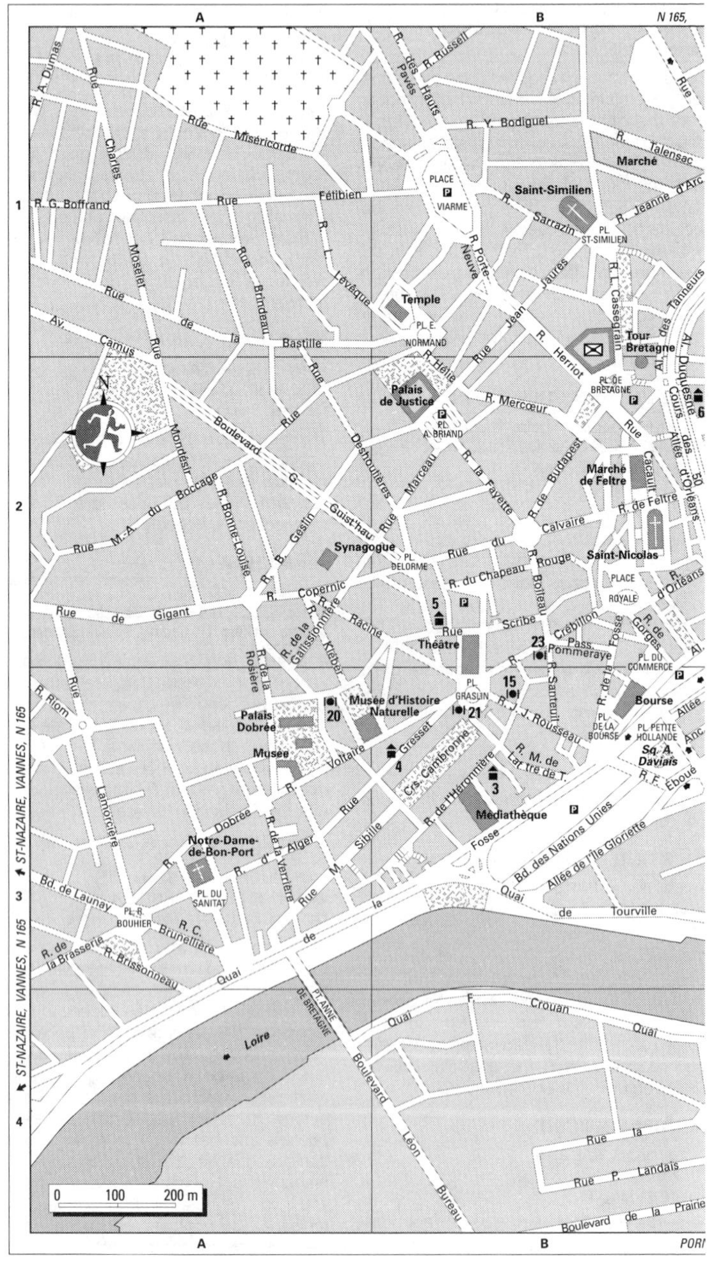
A
B
N 165,
1
2
3
4
R. A. Dumas
Rue Charles Monselet
Rue Miséricorde
R. des Pavés
R. Russell
R. des Hauts Pavés
R. Y. Bodiguel
R. Talensac
Marché
PLACE VIARME
Saint-Similien
R. Sarrazin
PL. ST-SIMILIEN
R. Jeanne d'Arc
R. G. Boffrand
Rue Félibien
R. L. Lévêque
Rue Brindeau
R. Porte-Neuve
Rue Jean Jaurès
R. L. Cassegrain
Al. des Tanneurs
Rue de la Bastille
Av. Camus
Temple
PL. E. NORMAND
R. Hélie
R. Herriot
Tour Bretagne
PL. DE BRETAGNE
Al. Duquesne
Cours des 50 Otages
Allée d'Orléans
Palais de Justice
PL. A. BRIAND
R. Mercœur
Rue Mondésir
Boulevard G. Guist'hau
Rue Deshoulières
R. Marceau
R. la Fayette
R. de Budapest
Marché de Feltre
Rue Cacault
R. de Feltre
Rue du Boccage
R. M.-A. du Boccage
R. Bonne-Louise
R. B. Gestin
Synagogue
PL. DELORME
Rue du Calvaire
R. Boileau
Rouge
Saint-Nicolas
PLACE ROYALE
R. d'Orléans
R. du Chapeau
R. Copernic
Rue de Gigant
R. de la Galissonnière
R. Kléber
Racine
5
Rue Scribe
R. Crébillon
Pass. Pommeraye
R. de la Fosse
R. de Gorges
Théâtre
23
PL. DU COMMERCE
Al.
R. de la Rosière
Rue Riom
PL. GRASLIN
15
R. Santeuil
Bourse
Palais Dobrée
20
Musée d'Histoire Naturelle
21
R. J.-J. Rousseau
PL. DE LA BOURSE
PL. PETITE HOLLANDE
Sq. A. Daviais
Allée
Musée
R. Voltaire
Gresset
4
Crs. Cambronne
R. M. de Lattre de T.
3
R. F. Éboué
Lamoricière
R. de l'Héronnière
Médiathèque
Bd. des Nations Unies
Allée de l'Île Gloriette
R. Dobrée
Notre-Dame-de-Bon-Port
R. d'Alger
R. de la Verrerie
Rue M. Sibille
Fosse
PL. DU SANITAT
Bd. de Launay
PL. R. BOUHIER
R. C. Brunellière
Quai de la Fosse
Quai de Tourville
R. de la Brasserie
R. Brissonneau
Quai
PT ANNE DE BRETAGNE
Loire
Quai F. Crouan
Boulevard Léon Bureau
Rue la
Rue P. Landais
Boulevard de la Prairie
0
100
200 m
ST-NAZAIRE, VANNES, N 165
ST-NAZAIRE, VANNES, N 165
PORI

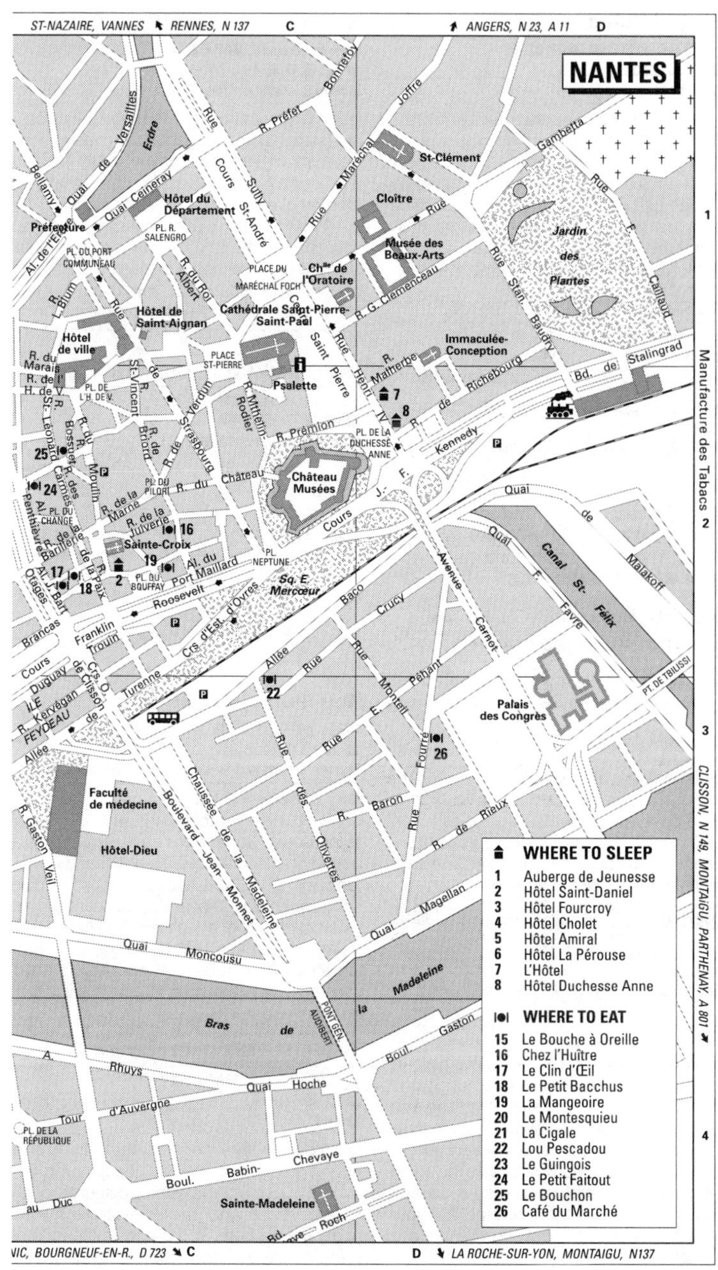
NANTES
ST-NAZAIRE, VANNES
RENNES, N 137
ANGERS, N 23, A 11
Manufacture des Tabacs
CLISSON, N 149, MONTAIGU, PARTHENAY, A 801
VIC, BOURGNEUF-EN-R., D 723
LA ROCHE-SUR-YON, MONTAIGU, N137
St-Clément
Cloître
Jardin des Plantes
Musée des Beaux-Arts
Hôtel du Département
Préfecture
Chlle de l'Oratoire
Cathédrale Saint-Pierre-Saint-Paul
Hôtel de Saint-Aignan
Hôtel de ville
Immaculée-Conception
Psalette
Château Musées
Sainte-Croix
Sq. E. Mercœur
Canal St-Félix
Palais des Congrès
Faculté de médecine
Hôtel-Dieu
Bras de la Madeleine
Sainte-Madeleine
WHERE TO SLEEP
1 Auberge de Jeunesse
2 Hôtel Saint-Daniel
3 Hôtel Fourcroy
4 Hôtel Cholet
5 Hôtel Amiral
6 Hôtel La Pérouse
7 L'Hôtel
8 Hôtel Duchesse Anne
WHERE TO EAT
15 Le Bouche à Oreille
16 Chez l'Huître
17 Le Clin d'Œil
18 Le Petit Bacchus
19 La Mangeoire
20 Le Montesquieu
21 La Cigale
22 Lou Pescadou
23 Le Guingois
24 Le Petit Faitout
25 Le Bouchon
26 Café du Marché

I●I CHEZ L'HUÎTRE

5 rue des Petites ƒcuries. **MAP C2-16**
☎ 02.51.82.02.02
Closed Sundays.

A small bistro between two Greek restaurants in the Bouffay district with rough walls covered with old metal signs. One of our favourites. Salmon and oysters prepared by the youthful proprietor. Try to find a place among the regulars when the "oyster aperitif" is served – 6 oysters and a glass of Muscadet for 30F. Live music on some evenings.

I●I RESTAURANT LE PETIT FAITOUT

2 rue Armand-Brossard. **MAP C2-24**
☎ 02.40.89.60.40
Closed Saturday lunchtimes, Sundays and in August.

Efficient staff and friendly host in this pleasing restaurant that only serves fresh and/or home-made food. Good set meals for 100–120F, traditional cuisine from southwest France including *foie gras*, grilled duck breast with ceps, *cassoulet* etc. Speedily served *formules* at lunchtime at low prices: 35F, 45F and 55F. The good, hearty food makes you forget the bland surroundings.

I●I RESTAURANT LA MANGEOIRE

16 rue des Petites-Écuries. **MAP C2-19**
☎ 02.40.48.70.83
Closed Mondays, Sundays, and for one week in January, May and September.

Cuisine that combines French tradition and creativity (casserole of snails, fish with saltwort, escalope of trout with mint) in surroundings laden with memorabilia. Family photos on the stone walls. A good selection of set meals for 82–142F and excellent desserts. Eat outside. The set meal at lunchtime costs 58F.

I●I RESTAURANT LE MONTESQUIEU

1 rue Montesquieu. **MAP A3-20**
☎ 02.40.73.06.69
Closed Friday evenings, Saturdays and Sundays in August.

Not the place to choose for a quiet snack. Here your plate is piled high and you have to shout to be heard. Allow 60F for lunch and 75F for an evening meal including wine and an aperitif. This local restaurant, with its typical checked tablecloths and crockery adorning the walls, has a regular clientele including local employees and students. A perfect venue if your wallet is nearly as empty as your stomach and you love salmon *rillettes* and tuna loaf with *aïoli*.

I●I RESTAURANT LE PETIT BACCHUS

5 rue Beauregard. **MAP C2-18**
☎ 02.40.47.50.46
Closed Sundays and Aug 1–20.

Does this restaurant get so busy for its pleasant bistro atmosphere or for the cheeky erotic photos from the 1920s on the walls? It couldn't just be for the amazing value-for-money food on offer, could it? Excellent set meals for 80–125F including stuffed mussels, marinated salmon, grilled steak *à la fleur de sel* or duck breast *à l'orange*, not to mention the tarts and cakes. The cheapest set meal is 60F (lunchtimes) and there is a set meal of local cuisine including zander in butter for 105F.

I●I RESTAURANT LE GUINGOIS

3 bis rue Santeuil. **MAP B2-23**
☎ 02.40.73.36.49
Closed Mondays and Sundays.

One of the hubs of social life in Nantes, open until midnight and offering good food from fresh market ingredients at decent prices. The welcome is not over-cheerful but then you don't come here for the welcome. The menu, or rather the blackboard, offers home cooking without fuss or flourish – monkfish skewers, squid fritters, fish *gratin* etc. Cheapest set meal 65F (lunchtimes) and 81–200F in the evenings.

I●I LE BOUCHE À OREILLE

14 rue Jean-Jacques-Rousseau. **MAP B3-15**
☎ 02.40.73.00.25
Closed Monday and Saturday lunchtimes and Sundays.

Very close to the Nantes Opera House, this bar with check tablecloths and old metal signs doesn't provide fancy cuisine, but is a gathering place for theatre-goers and sports fans for a few glasses of Beaujolais and some *quenelles*, *tabliers de sapeurs* (grilled ox tripe) and other appetisers. The décor is as heavy as your head will be feeling the morning after. Allow 100–120F per person in the evenings. At lunchtimes the set meal is 69F and main courses 60F.

I●I RESTAURANT LE CLIN D'ŒIL

15 rue Beauregard. **MAP C2-17**
☎ 02.40.47.72.37
Closed Sundays and Mondays.

Don't be put off by the tiny, gloomy dining area on the ground floor, go straight up to the first floor. This restaurant is worth a detour as much for the very bright, plastic décor as for the homy atmosphere. The quality of the food, a blend of local and more exotic offerings, is only equalled by the charming, good-hearted service. Set meals 69–89F, or main course and dessert for 48F (catering for the pockets and tastes of this restaurant's youthful clientele).

|●| LA CIGALE

4 place Graslin. **MAP B3-21**
☎ 02.51.84.94.94

The "in" restaurant in Nantes. The local high society comes here for supper after the theatre (which is just opposite) and visiting celebrities are often to be seen too. The cuisine isn't particularly brilliant and the slow service is a little tiresome, but you shouldn't miss the superb décor of this brasserie dating back to 1900. The painted ceilings, wood panelling and coloured ceramics formed the background for some scenes in the film "Lola". Not too expensive to dine (set meals from 75F) or if you want to avoid the mediocre cuisine, take breakfast (50F) or try the set meal on Sunday evenings based on oysters and white wine for 105F.

|●| RESTAURANT LE BOUCHON

7 rue Bossuet. **MAP C2-25**
☎ 02.40.20.08.44
Closed Saturday lunchtimes and Sundays.

In the quiet district around the town hall, this establishment styles itself "the best restaurant in rue Bossuet" and you can't argue with that. In fact it is the only one, apart from *Les Bouchoneries*, where you can get a light meal for a reasonable price. The trendy tapas bar format invites you to enjoy the surroundings while perched on a futuristic stool. The dining room is rather traditional with the half-timbering outside and extends out into a charming, shady courtyard. The service is laid-back and the cuisine fresh and inventive with a bias towards seafood. The cheapest set meal for 130F includes queen scallops, scallops and fish casserole with baby vegetables.

|●| LOU PESCADOU

8 allée Baco. **MAP C3-22**
☎ 02.40.35.29.50
Closed Saturday lunchtimes and Sundays.

It's a good idea to book since it's currently one of the best seafood restaurants around and gets pretty busy. The chef is a real culinary enthusiast and Muscadet aficionado, and between extravagant discussions disappears into the kitchen to cheerfully prepare the fish of the day delivered specially by a local fisherman. This is the ideal place to try something in a white wine and butter sauce, particularly the magnificent bass baked in a salt crust. Equally good are the skate, monkfish or, if you can afford it, lobster and crayfish from the tank. Set meals 100–320F. Expensive but worth it. Ask nicely and between courses you could try a few different vintages of Muscadet. If you need another reason for going, just try the appetisers.

|●| CAFÉ DU MARCHÉ

1 rue de Mayence. **MAP D3-26**
☎ 02.40.47.63.50
Closed evenings, Saturdays, Sundays and in August.

Near the new *Cité des Congrès* in a rapidly developing area, what a pleasure to find a real restaurant of regulars which nothing and no-one seems to be able to change. The same good home cooking has been served here for over 50 years, with three starters, a single main course (go on a Tuesday if you like calf's head), cheese and dessert. That plus a glass of red wine and you can cope with anything in the afternoon. The ladies who run this establishment pay attention to detail and provide proper napkins and tablecloths, in pink if you please. Set meal 110F.

CARQUEFOU 44470 (10KM N)

|●| RESTAURANT L'AUBERGE DU VIEUX GACHET

Le Gachet; take the Gachet road as far as the Erdre river – about 7km north of Nantes.
☎ 02.40.25.10.92
Closed Mondays, Sunday evenings, two weeks at the end of August and during the February holidays.
Car park.

An attractive old country inn with a terrace. The staff and surroundings are from times gone by and the inventive dishes are full of the best of France (salmon, mushrooms stuffed with crab, quail with *foie gras*). It's so lovely to be on the banks of the Erdre river. And very affordable prices too! There are four set meals, 90F (weekday lunchtimes) and 140–220F. You can walk here from Nantes, just follow the path along the Erdre for two hours. Gourmets should note the excellent appetisers and, if you like architecture, Château de la Gacherie is just opposite.

SAINT-FIACRE 44690 (18KM SE)

|●| LE FIACRE

1 rue d'Échirens; take the D59 towards Clisson.
☎ 02.40.54.83.92
Open evenings and at weekends on reservation.

If you decide to leave Nantes to visit the lovely Muscadet vineyards, your first stop should be here at this small country restaurant. Here you eat good food on unfussy, wooden tables for the amazing price of 57F. The restaurant is very well known locally and lovers of good wine and food come from far and wide to eat here. This village bistro becomes a gourmet venue in the evenings and weekends (reservations only) and offers some enticing set meals from 100F. If you have an interest in wine, corner the proprietor who has over 100 Muscadets in the cellar. He knows them all individually and can talk to you about them for hours. Better than any museum of wine.

MESSAN 44640 (20KM W)

LE TISONNIER

Centre; it's on the Saint Brévin-Painbœuf road (D723) on the way into Messan.
☎ 02.40.64.29.83
Closed the last two weeks of August and in December.

Not the sort of place you'd think of going to, this little village beside the Acheneau river. Although this restaurant is not much to look at you can eat well for 49F (sausage in Muscadet plus cheese or dessert and a quarter litre of wine). The set meals at 60F, 75F, 100F and 130F offer popular dishes which are a little more elaborate (a half cockerel, 8 oysters, sirloin). Retired people, who're no richer than anyone else, and workers come here for lunch. And they get a good deal in this restaurant-café which also serves as a tobacconist's and newsagent's. It would be hard to find better value for money and speedier service.

NOIRMOUTIER-EN-L'ILE 85330

HÔTEL-RESTAURANT LES CAPUCINES**

38 av. de la Victoire (North); it's on the bois de la Chaize road.
☎ 02.51.39.06.82 F 02.51.39.33.10
Closed Wednesdays off season and Nov 15–Feb 15.
Car park. TV. Disabled access.

This hotel has just been taken over by new proprietors Anne et Jean-Luc David. Their watchwords are continuity in quality and modernization. The wholesome food and comfortable rooms make it well worth a visit. Doubles for 210F with shower, 270F with shower/wc and 320F with bath (add on 100F in the summer). Set meals for 72–170F including stuffed snails *en robe*, local mussels, and salmon and turbot in a butter and saltwort sauce. Half-board (330F) is compulsory in summer at

10% HÔTEL ESPERANZA

10a rue du Grand Four; it's just behind the château.
☎ 02.51.39.12.07
Car park.

The new managers of this hotel share a passion for renovation. Shortly after arriving they had already renovated several apartments. The 27 rooms in the main hotel have yet to be touched, however, and they still have the old-fashioned charm of orange wallpaper with a peacock design and worn carpets. A room with shower costs 250F. The bathrooms are separated from the bedrooms by sliding doors; not pretty but effective. A charming spot with a delightful welcome. Quite affordable for Noirmoutier and thus often full. Make reservations well in advance.

LE CHÂTEAU DE PÉLAVÉ*

allée de Chaillot.
☎ 02.51.39.01.94 F 02.51.39.70.42
Closed in December. **Car park.**

This vast, recently renovated, nineteenth century house is set in lovely wooded grounds. The Victorian charm of the place is undiminished. Comfortable, spacious rooms for 260F with shower/wc. If you choose room number 4 or 8 you can take your breakfast out on the little terrace. Greenery, tranquillity and clean air guaranteed. Reserve well in advance and ask about the prices as they change with the seasons (as you would expect by the sea). Half-board compulsory in July and August for 270–375F per person.

HÔTEL-RESTAURANT LES DOUVES**

11 rue des Douves (Centre); it's opposite the château.
☎ 02.51.39.02.72 F 02.51.39.73.09
Closed in January. **Car park. TV.**

This plush building nestles below the château in a very peaceful spot. The fresh rooms have a flowery décor. Ideal for relaxing in the heart of the island's biggest town. In the summer double rooms are 390F with shower/wc and 422F with bath. The chef offers fine, succulent cuisine and dishes such as bass fillets *aux écailles de charlotte* and oyster *gratin*. Set meals for 99–184F served in a glorious, bright dining room or out on the terrace next to the swimming pool.

I●I RESTAURANT "IODE"

13 rue du Vieil Hôpital; it's just behind the château.
☎ 02.51.39.55.49
Open Easter–Nov 1 12.30–2.30pm and 7pm–2am.

There are lots of restaurants in the area but we were taken with this one mainly because of its décor and youthful ambience. You won't get gourmet cooking but the *foie gras* and breast of duck are particularly good (and inexpensive). The fish soup starter was a real treat for the taste buds. Eat by the fireplace in winter. Set meal for 65F. The fish is especially good. The perfect spot for travellers who like a relaxed restaurant with fast friendly service.

I●I AU VIEUX LOUP DE MER

97 av. Mourain (Centre); it's next to the church.
☎ 02.51.39.08.68
Closed Saturdays except during the holidays.

A simple restaurant with old-fashioned charm. The aromas from the kitchen really make your mouth water. The fish set in front of you comes directly from that day's auction. Large, whitewashed dining room with check tablecloths and a garden at the back. *Moules marinière*, salmon steak, seafood. The cheapest set meal offers hearty portions for 65F. Other slightly more elaborate set meals for 85–105F.

I●I RESTAURANT LA SALAMANDRE

9 rue du Robinet (Centre); it's just behind the château.
☎ 02.51.39.76.07
Closed Thursdays off season and from mid-November to mid-December.

This restaurant, located in a lovely building behind the château, isn't lacking in attractions. The carefully prepared food can be enjoyed in the dining room with its sloping ceiling and original décor or on the pleasant terrace in the quiet courtyard. Sardine kebabs with anchovy butter, red mullet *à la noirmoutaine*, *moules marinière*, salmon *terrine* with two sauces and much more. Set meals 75–190F.

I●I RESTAURANT CÔTÉ JARDIN

1 bis rue du Grand-Four (Centre).
☎ 02.51.39.03.02
Closed Sunday evenings, Mondays and Jan 15–Feb15. **Car park**.

You can't miss this creeper-covered building. The cuisine is entirely devoted to seafood and will really make your taste buds tingle. Hot oysters garnished with rice and tomatoes, skate wing with saltwort, scallop tart with fennel, clam and mussel flan – all this is included in the set meals for 91–189F. The elegant surroundings of stone walls and ceiling beams makes it a pleasure just to be here. Friendly welcome.

NOTRE-DAME-DE-MONTS 85690

⌂ I●I HÔTEL-RESTAURANT LE CENTRE**

1 rue de Saint-Jean-de-Monts.
☎ 02.51.58.83.05 F➔ 02.51.59.16.62
Closed in the evenings from November to mid-February, Mondays from November to March and for the months of December and January. **Car park**. **TV**. **Disabled access**.

This hotel is much better than its rather banal name suggests, but it is indeed centrally located. Clean, fresh rooms for 250–290F with shower/wc or bath. But be careful, the showers tend to flood. The restaurant deserves particular attention. The food offers flavours which are often astonishing and always subtle and sometimes reminds you of ones you'd forgotten. *Terrine* of eel and nettle, cuttlefish and smoked cod *gratin* on a bed of spinach, pig cheeks and pepper goulash, saddle of rabbit with oyster mushrooms, duckling casserole. Set meals (70–230F) are served in a stylish dining room. The welcome is a little impersonal, however.

⌂ HÔTEL DE LA PLAGE CIVEL

154 av. de la Mer.
☎ 02.51.58.83.03 F➔ 02.51.58.97.12
Closed Nov 1–April 1.

Even if it means being a bit extravagant, this place is worth it. If you want to look at the sea when you open the curtains in the morning and breathe in salt air in your room at any time, then this is the place for you. Of course it isn't cheap: allow 410F for a double room with shower in the summer (360F in the off season – makes you want to go in September!). But considering the quality of the location, the rooms and the kind welcome, this is more than reasonable. Ask for a room with a view. If you're lucky you'll get a terrace too!

PAULX 44270

I●I RESTAURANT LES VOYAGEURS

1 pl. de l'Église (Centre).
☎ 02.40.26.02.76
Closed Sunday evenings, Mondays, mid Aug–mid Sept, and two weeks in Feb.

What a cliché! Candlesticks, Maurice Chevalier, very old brandy, and very large bottles. It might seem out of our league, but if you give them a call and tell them your price range they might be able to sort something out (otherwise known as their *formule* "carte blanche"). Local businessmen congregate here at lunchtime, so it would be best to come in the evening to sample their tasty cooking. Cheapest set meal 98F weekdays and 125F weekends.

PIRIAC-SUR-MER 44420

10% HÔTEL-RESTAURANT DE LA POINTE

1 quai de Verdun (North); it's down by the sea wall.
☎ 02.40.23.50.04
Closed Wednesdays off season and from Nov 1–March 15. **Car park**.

A good hotel for a nice relaxed stay. Doubles with shower/wc for 240F. They're not very up to date but some have a view of the harbour and beach. The dining room has been redecorated in traditional bistro style. Although the cuisine makes no claims to being gourmet standard, the salads, fish and seafood are guaranteed to satisfy the hunger of those who have worked up a good appetite out in the sea air. Set meals 95F and 135F. Friendly welcome. Half-board (275F) is compulsory in July and August.

CRÈPERIE LACOMÈRE

18 rue de Kéroniau (Centre).
☎ 02.40.23.53.63
Only open at weekends during the off season. Also closed Nov 11–Christmas and Jan–Feb.

The menu is inspired by the owner's travels around the world. Main courses, usually based on what the market has to offer, cost 70–90F. Try Jean-Michel's fish *tajine* at 85F — it's so delicious that despite the huge portion you feel like asking for more. This restaurant is a little more inventive than the standard *crêperie* in the tourist areas. But be warned that there are only about 10 tables, so make sure you reserve.

PORNIC 44210

RESTAURANT L'ESTAMINET

8 rue Maréchal-Foch (Centre).
☎ 02.40.82.35.99
Closed Mondays and Sunday evenings from September to June and the first two weeks of February.

Judged by outward appearances, this restaurant in a busy street in Pornic is nothing out of the ordinary. But just taste the chef's fresh cuisine and experience his wife's lovely manner as she takes your order and brings you your food and you'll soon change your mind. A whole range of set meals for 83–175F and two *formules* (weekday lunchtimes) for 65 and 70F. Try the warm skate salad or the scallops *en papillote*.

RESTAURANT BEAU RIVAGE

plage de la Birochère.
☎ 02.40.82.03.08
Closed Sunday evenings and Mondays (off season), from Nov 16–23 and in January.

A beautiful spot, right over the beach. A friendly restaurant full of colour. As you admire the view from your table it is no surprise that the sea is the main influence on the thinking of chef Gérard Corchia who thoughtfully (a pleasant change!) crafts his excellent cuisine from seafood. Grilled bass in virgin olive oil, seafood medley etc. Allow around 200–250F unless you're happy with the good set meal at 125F (weekdays and Saturday lunchtimes only). The bistro has a cheaper (90F) *formule*.

PORT-JOINVILLE 85350

10% ATLANTIC HÔTEL***

quai Carnot (Centre).
☎ 02.51.58.38.80 Fax 02.51.58.35.92
Closed for 3 weeks in January. **Car park**. **TV**. **Disabled access**.

An entirely renovated hotel. Fifteen cute little rooms with every comfort, although a little unoriginal. Half the rooms face the fishing harbour, the focus of local activity, the other half look out over the village. Both outlooks are pleasant. The prices depend on the season and the view — 260F in the off season (view of the village) to 400F in summer (view of the harbour). Breakfast 35F — which doesn't change with the view.

10% HÔTEL-RESTAURANT FLUX HÔTEL**

27 rue Pierre-Henry (North).
☎ 02.51.58.36.25 Fax 02.51.59.44.57
Closed Nov 20–Jan 6. **Car park**. **TV**. **Disabled access**.

Away from the bustle of Port-Joinville, this hotel's peaceful grounds bordering the seashore make it a select location. Well-kept double rooms looking out to the garden for 330F. Room number 15 has just about everything: it is spacious, away from the main hotel, has a fireplace and rustic furniture — just like your granny's country house. The restaurant on the same site, *La Marée*, is run by different people, but you only realise this when it comes to paying the bill. The enormous dining room has a huge fireplace for winter evenings and a lovely terrace for dining outside beneath the shade of the trees in summer. Traditional cuisine which allows for the unexpected: fish don't always cooperate in being caught when you want them. One constant however is the creamy soups, a speciality of the house and the island. Set meals 88–180F. Smiling, friendly service.

LA CRÊPERIE BLEUE

quai Carnot (Centre).
☎ 02.51.58.71.95
Closed Mondays, in January and for two weeks in October.

Despite the colour of the dining room, this is not home to a family of Smurfs. A friendly place with polished wood tables, a bar with a nautical theme, pictures of ships on the walls and a terrace with a lovely overhead trellis for summer. This restaurant is run entirely by women, from kitchen to dining room. Pleasant, friendly welcome. Lots of different *crêpes* available, all filled with good, and sometimes surprising, ingredients. Generous portions guaranteed. Savoury *crêpes* 30–45F, sweet ones 15–30F. Tuck into one of these and you could easily imagine yourself in deepest Brittany

ROCHE-SUR-YON (LA) 85000

10% MARIE STUART HÔTEL**

86 bd Louis-Blanc (Centre); it's opposite the station.
☎ 02.51.37.02.24 F 02.51.37.86.37
Restaurant closed Saturday lunchtimes and Sunday evenings (except in season). **TV**.

Welcome to Scotland! This hotel is completely decorated in Scottish trappings. Tartans and the different clans' coats of arms adorn the walls and of course there is portrait of Mary, Queen of Scots. The rooms are rather chic and spacious, decorated with stylish furniture. Doubles from 289F with bath. The restaurant serves good, simple food — seafood hotpot, grilled sole etc. Set meals from 69F at the bar for a starter and main course; others 95–190F. If you fancy a wee dram, the bar has a selection of malts.

HÔTEL LE LOGIS DE LA COUPERIE

route de Cholet; 5 minutes from the town centre – take the main road to Cholet and then the D80.
☎ 02.51.37.21.19 F 02.51.47.71.08
Secure parking. TV.

Let's say this straight away — this is one of our favourite hotels in the Vendée region. Set in the middle of the countryside, tucked away in a mass of greenery where the tranquillity is almost palpable, this hotel is a stately old building dating back to the fourteenth century. Don't come here expecting a wild time but rather to enjoy the pleasures of a peaceful way of life. The atmosphere in this family home (which used to be a guest house) is a combination of refinement and simplicity. The corridors are full of knick-knacks and bookshelves. There are just seven cosy rooms, each named after a flower. The pastel decoration is in an English style and the look is completed by canopy beds and antique furniture. Doubles 298F with shower/wc or 338F with bath. The only sounds to wake you are the quacking of the ducks and the croaking of the frogs in the pond. Don't miss the lovingly prepared breakfast. A cordial welcome from a charming host.

SAINT-CHARLES RESTAURANT

38 rue du Président-de-Gaulle (Centre).
☎ 02.51.47.71.37
Closed Saturday lunchtimes, Sundays and Aug 1–15.

This restaurant has a strong jazz theme — photos of jazz stars and instruments adorn the walls and jazz plays softly in the background. Even the menu features jazz references. Against this good atmosphere the chef produces his cuisine in the same spirit. He offers a few pleasant surprises such as mussel profiteroles and country ham with spinach, inventive dishes like panfried rabbit with grapes and *foie gras,* an inspired combination of sole soufflé and oyster mushrooms, and traditional roast lamb with preserved garlic. The set meals (98–195) offer good value for money.

VENANSAULT 85190 (8KM NW)

HÔTEL-RESTAURANT LE MOULIN DE LA BERGERIE*

La Grolle; by the Landeronde road (N160).
☎ 02.51.40.36.94 F 02.51.40.39.00
Closed at weekends in winter unless a reservation is made. **Car park. TV. Disabled access.**

A pleasant, unpretentious stopover where you are received, lodged and served meals without any fuss. Rooms for 200F with shower/wc. The set meals (56–120F) change regularly, offering classic dishes that hold no surprises but are well made. The frogs' legs are excellent. They're planning on introducing a buffet of starters in 1998.

POIRÉ-SUR-VIE (LE) 85170 (13.5KM NW)

HÔTEL-RESTAURANT LE CENTRE**

19 place du Marché (Centre); take the D6.
☎ 02.51.31.81.20 F 02.51.31.88.21
Closed Friday and Sunday evenings off season.
Car park. **TV**. **Disabled access**.

This welcoming hostelry is right in the middle of the village. The rooms are comfortable and clean and there is a swimming pool which is ideal for the weary traveller. The restaurant offers simple authentic regional cooking and dishes like fillet of zander in a butter and white wine sauce, country ham *à la crème*, scallop ragout and much more, all for reasonable prices. Set meals 82–159F plus a basic set meal for 56F. Double rooms range in price from 168F with basin to 325F with bath.

MACHÉ 85190 (22KM)

RESTAURANT LE FOUGERAIS

How to get there: take the D948, and after Aizenay turn left after crossing the Vie river (signposted).
☎ 02.51.55.75.44
Closed Wednesdays off season. **Car park**.

A lovely building covered in ivy. The atmosphere in this old converted barn is quiet and cosy. Huge meals welcome the weary traveller. Well-made food served on simple tables. The chef adds a few vine stems to the open fire to add flavour to the eel and salmon dishes. Simple food served in hearty portions. A very good set meal for 98F with oysters, grilled salmon and dessert. Other, even more generous, set meals for 125–170F.

ROSIERS (LES) 49350

RESTAURANT AU P'TIT BAGNARD GOURMAND

4 rue de la Corderie (South-East); 400m from the town centre heading towards Saumur.
☎ 02.41.51.87.76
Closed Sunday evenings, Mondays and Jan 2–23.
Car park.

As soon as you arrive you start planning when you can come back again. Quite unusual surroundings. Local cuisine based on a single main course. One of the offerings is a traditional old dish called *cabérillon* of duck — drumsticks marinated in red wine for 24 hours and then slowly cooked in goose fat (it's something like *confit* only not so greasy). This is preceded by some delicious *charcuterie* or *foie gras* accompanied by a Coteaux-de-l'Aubance and fresh mushrooms from the riverside. The main course is served up with mouth-watering potatoes with butter. Leave room for one of the best chocolate mousses we've ever tasted. The chef really knows how to make his guests feel at home. If the moment is right, he'll accompany you on the piano. We were very enthusiastic about this restaurant — a genuinely pleasurable place. Lunchtime set meal 60F (except on Sundays) and other set meals for 98F, 115F and 150F (including wine). Excellent children's meal for 37F to initiate your little ones into French culinary delights.

RESTAURANT LA TOQUE BLANCHE*

How to get there: it's on the way out of the village towards Angers.
☎ 02.41.51.80.75
Closed Tuesday evenings and Wednesdays. **Car park**.

One of the region's up-and-coming restaurants. It is becoming increasingly necessary to reserve a table (compulsory for Sunday lunch!). Inventive cuisine served in an elegant, air-conditioned setting. Friendly too. Set meal for 99F including wine (weekday lunchtimes) and also for 179F and 206F (extra course), with home-smoked salmon, red mullet mousse with caviar sauce, liver *parfait* in port accompanied by a glass of Layon, langoustine tails sautéd with vanilla pods, poached chicken à l'*angevine*, sweet and sour duck leg and much more.

SABLES-D'OLONNE (LES) 85100

HÔTEL ANTOINE**

60 rue Napoléon (Centre).
☎ 02.51.95.08.36 F 02.51.23.92.78
Closed Nov 1–beginning of March. **Secure parking**. **TV**.

A delightful haven of peace right in the centre of the town, between the harbour and the beach. Proprietors Isabelle and Philippe Robin care for their hotel and are lovingly doing it up. Rooms 20 and 22 have recently been renovated and their work continues. This is a place in which to forget your stresses and to build up your strength. Quiet rooms, some of which look out over the garden, 260F with shower/wc (in the annex) or 300F with bath (in the main hotel). Prices are a little lower in the off season. Half-board, compulsory in July and August, starts at

230F per person but this is not a drawback as your host prepares some excellent food from fresh market produce.

HÔTEL LES HIRONDELLES**

44 rue des Corderies (Centre).
☎ 02.51.95.10.50 F 02.51.32.31.01
Closed from the start of October to the end of March. **Secure parking. TV.**

This hotel does not look very attractive from the outside, but appearances can be deceptive. The fresh, modern décor in the rooms makes you forget your first impressions and the kindness of the hostess completely wins you over. The hotel actually comprises two buildings. Some of the flowery rooms have balconies (ideal for breakfast). Double rooms for 280F with shower/wc. A place to eat and sleep really well. Set meals for 95–130F based on fish and seafood of course.

RESTAURANT LE CLIPPER

19 bis quai Guiné.
☎ 02.51.32.03.61
Closed Tues evenings, Wed, the last week of Nov and for two weeks in Feb. **Closed** Mon in July–Aug.

The sea, the sea. The owner of this restaurant has dedicated his establishment to the oceans. The setting includes a lot of wood, hurricane lamps and portholes to give the impression of an exotic cruise ship, and there's a lot of unusual fish dishes on offer. The subtle yet astonishing combinations include mullet fillets with liquorice, salmon tartar with a fresh goat's cheese sauce, and a *ragoût* of snails in a ginger-scented sauce. If you're feeling less adventurous, there's also sole *meunière*, bass baked in a salt crust and so on. A look at the prices (set meals 66–189F) explains why many locals come here regularly. The 90F set meal is particularly attractive. Considerate, attentive service.

RESTAURANT GEORGE V

20 rue George-V – La Chaume.
☎ 02.51.95.11.52
Closed Sunday evenings and Mondays.

The elegant dining room looks out to the harbour entrance. The bright, agreeably decorated surroundings do not distract from the excellent food. Chef Olivier Burban captains the ship admirably. Not surprisingly fish is the main ingredient, but it is imaginatively prepared. Unexpected flavours astonish in dishes such as the salad of squid fritters with walnut oil, the chef's hotpot and the *gâteau* of langoustines (something like fishcakes but of course made with something a lot more exotic!). It would be a crime if you didn't leave some room for the *pain perdu* (France's answer to bread and butter pudding) or the hot apple tart. And it's not even expensive! Set meals 75–158F.

AU CAPITAINE

5 quai Guiné.
☎ 02.51.95.18.10
Closed Wednesday evenings, Thursdays, for the month of February and for the first week in October.

Chic and clean, entering this restaurant is like going aboard a luxury ship. Views of the harbour from upstairs. The interior is bright and spacious. The décor displays good taste, as does the fine cooking. Salmon *terrine* with onion *confit* (a real treat), fresh *moules marinière*, monkfish, whiting. Simple but effective set meals 79F, 99F and 169F. A dependable restaurant to return to again and again.

SABLÉ-SUR-SARTHE 72300

10% L'HOSTELLERIE SAINT-MARTIN

3 rue Haute-Saint-Martin (Centre); it's on a small street leading off the town hall square.
☎ 02.43.95.00.03.
Closed Mondays

This hotel in the town centre benefits from the mild climate (the proof of which is a palm tree on the other side of the road). Agreeable rooms for 152–220F. The high-ceilinged dining room has an antiquated charm and lots of the things you associate with provincial hotels – a dresser, a Norman clock, heavy red velvet curtains and copper pots and pans. Fresh flowers adorn the tables and the parquet floor squeaks delightfully as you walk across it. Good traditional, local food with set meals from 95F and a local welcome too, with warm smiles for the regulars and those who have reserved (take the hint!).

HÔTEL-RESTAURANT L'ESCU DU ROY**

20 rue Léon-Legludic (Centre); it's opposite the church.
☎ 02.43.95.90.31 F 02.43.92.17.52
Closed Fridays from October to the end of February and Sunday evenings all year round. **Car park. TV.**

Small hotel with 10 rooms priced at 250–280F. The restaurant has a good reputation and offers a remarkable welcome. Comfortable surroundings and a pretty, stylish dining room (it makes a change from exposed beams). Traditional cuisine including a delicious hotpot. Set meals for 95F, 149F and 200F.

LES PALMIERS

54 Grande Rue (Centre).
☎ 02.43.95.03.82
Closed Tuesdays.

If you are touring the region this restaurant offers a change from *rillettes* and local hotpots (however good they are!). Here you will discover genuine Moroccan hospitality offered by a charming couple. Husband Abdou mans the kitchens while his French wife greets the guests. There is little passing trade in what is a pretty rundown street in the old part of town and the owners depend on the restaurant's reputation being spread by word of mouth. The two large dining rooms are smart and very well decorated, offering comfortable surroundings in which to enjoy the best of Moroccan cuisine. Large helpings of aromatic stews, vegetables and excellent meat. You'd almost think that the chef had been collecting his herbs from the slopes of the Atlas mountains. Superb *tajines* 69–75F, couscous with a selection of meats 69–100F and home-made pastries. The genuine welcome is an added bonus.

DUREIL 72270 (16KM E)

L'AUBERGE DES ACACIAS

Centre; take the D309 to Parcé-sur-Sarthe or the D23 to Malicorne, then turn down the small road that follows the Sarthe river.
☎ 02.43.95.34.03
Closed Sunday evenings, Mondays, for the month of February and for a week at the end of October.

It may not be smothered in Virginia creeper any more but it's still worth a visit. People come for fish, the house speciality. Try the zander in raspberry butter and monkfish in a vermouth sauce. Set meals cost 125–205F. The terrace is delightful and in winter you can snuggle up beside the cosy fireplace.

SAINT-CALAIS 72120

À SAINT-ANTOINE

8 pl. St-Antoine (North-East).
☎ 02.43.35.01.56
Closed Sunday evenings, Mondays and two weeks in April. **Car park**.

The Achard brothers caused quite a stir when it became known that they were going to take over the old bistro in place Saint-Antoine and turn it into a "real" restaurant. They served their apprenticeships as wine waiter and chef at Maxim's and Plaza Athénée respectively, two of Paris's top restaurants. The resulting establishment is unfussy; a place where local policemen, employees and business people meet at the bar before returning to their respective occupations. The small dining room soon fills up. The colourful and tasty cooking is evident even in the 98F set meal, which offers mackerel *timbale* with tomato *confit*, *panaché* of fish and cockles, fresh cream cheese, and tart. The cheapest (60F) set meal is brilliant – *terrine* of beef in aspic, sautéd veal, cheese, and dessert. Other set meal 160F. Good local wines at affordable prices too. Let's hope it lasts!

SAINT-GERVAIS-DE-VIC 72120 (4KM S)

LE SAINT-ÉLOI

1 rue Bertrand Guilmain; it's near the church.
☎ 02.43.35.19.56
Closed Sunday evenings and Monday lunchtimes off season.

The proprietors of this restaurant were previously pork butchers and did not have many free weekends – now they have none at all, as the word has spread and their dining rooms is full every Sunday with regulars clamouring for the set meals at 100F, 130F and 150F. The most expensive comes with three courses – a starter, a fish dish and breast of duck with green peppercorns. During the week 55F secures a buffet of starters, *blanquette* or *coq au vin*, cheese, tart, coffee and wine.

SAINT-DENIS-D'ORQUES 72350

L'AUBERGE DE LA GRANDE CHARNIE

rue Principale (Centre); it's on the N157 halfway between Laval and Le Mans.
☎ 02.43.88.43.12
Closed Sunday evenings, Mondays and during the school holidays in February. **Car park**.

In this exquisite dining room you will discover excellent local cuisine that won't lighten your wallet excessively. There is always a dish of the day (something along the lines of beef stew) for 45F. Set meals 78F (home-made *rillettes*), 98F (grilled flank of beef with shallots *confit*, local hotpot etc) or for 138F enjoy the *foie gras* prepared on the premises. Other set meals at 170–218F will suit the gourmet. À la carte offers duck fillet with bilberries and peach *confit* or saddle of lamb in tarragon sauce.

SAINT-FLORENT-LE-VIEIL 49410

L'HOSTELLERIE DE LA GABELLE**

12 quai de la Loire (Centre); it's at the foot of the suspension bridge.
☎ 02.41.72.50.19 F 02.41.72.54.38
Closed Nov 1–Dec 25. **Car park**. **TV**.

Plush dining room with a rather quiet atmosphere. The cheapest set meal in the week is 80F and there are others for 125–200F. Simple but enjoyable food — salmonin puff pastry, eels from the Loire, home-made foie gras, zander in a white wine and butter sauce. Double rooms for 250F with shower/wc or 270F with bath. The décor is somewhat bland and the staff are a little standoffish, but it is a well-located venue if you want to stop off by the Loire between Nantes and Angers.

INGRANDES-SUR-LOIRE 49123 (11KM NE)

10% HÔTEL-RESTAURANT LE LION D'OR**

place du Lion-d'Or; head towards Ingrandes-sur-Loire from the N23 or D751.
☎ 02.41.39.20.08 F 02.41.39.21.03
Closed Feb 4–18. **Secure parking**. **TV**.

This newly renovated establishment deserves a visit both for its restaurant and its accommodation. The rustic setting with dashes of colour forms a background for good traditional cuisine — fresh, generous and well presented. Set meals from 65F (served lunchtimes during the week and in the evenings for residents) and also for 85F, 105F and 135F. Or splash out 180F and savour *foie gras* with a glass of Coteaux de la Loire, fillet of zander with *hollandaise* sauce and a glass of white Anjou, cheese with a glass of red Anjou followed by a gourmet *panaché* with a glass of champagne. A good *blanquette* of scallops in puff pastry is also available. Comfortable rooms, entirely redecorated in fresh, tasteful colours from 200F with shower/wc.

SAINT-GILLES-CROIX-DE-VIE 85800

HÔTEL-RESTAURANT LES EMBRUNS**

16 bd de la Mer.
☎ 02.51.55.11.40 F 02.51.55.11.20
Closed Sunday evenings and Mondays off season, Jan 10–25 and Nov 15–30. **TV**.

This white-fronted hotel faces the ocean and has lovely rooms with bathrooms, spacious and bright, some with balconies facing the sea (although this puts the price up!). Doubles for 220–450F depending on the view. Enjoy the outlook over the sea in the cheerful, modern dining area decorated in pastel shades. This is a popular restaurant with the locals and is often full. There are a few tables on the terrace but needless to say it's more expensive to dine there. Chef Jean-Claude Patrone presents a menu based on seafood which offers no surprises but is more than satisfactory. The menu features risotto of oysters and veal sweetbreads, fillet of sole with cardamom and *piperade* with fresh squid. Set meals 90–280F.

LA CRÊPERIE

4 rue Gautté (Centre); it's opposite pont de la Concorde.
☎ 02.51.55.02.77
Closed Sunday lunchtimes and Mondays.

Classic *crêpes* — excellent and substantial. Not just any old eatery. Savoury *crêpes* 10–55F and sweet ones 10–35F. The most attractive feature however is the décor — worthy of a great designer. A harmonious combination of white stone walls, warm colours and wrought ironwork, all augmented by a touch of local colour in the form of fishing nets and seascapes.

COMMEQUIERS 85220 (12KM NE)

HÔTEL DE LA GARE

rue de la Morinière; take the D754.
☎ 02.51.54.80.38
Closed Mondays and January. **Car park**.

This pleasing station hotel was built at the turn of the century when the railways served even the smallest settlements in the most remote parts of France. The building's white exterior and green shutters give it a Victorian charm. It's a shame that there are no longer any trains, but equally it is a lot quieter and hotel residents now sleep peacefully. The prettily decorated rooms are agreeable, charming even. From 150–200F with washing facilities, shower or bath. The dining room is decorated in a bright colours, predominantly green, inducing an almost exotic atmosphere of early morning by the sea. Behind the scenes in the kitchen the chef slaves away to produce good, uncomplicated food in large portions that is really not over-expensive. Set meals, 70F and 98F (three courses). Grilled sardines, stuffed snails, leg of lamb with haricoat beans, roast duck etc. There's a small garden to relax in and a swimming pool for some exercise.

SAINT-HILAIRE-DE-RIEZ 85270

RESTAURANT LA BOURRINE DE RIEZ

221 av. de la Corniche.
☎ 02.51.55.01.83

Charming panelled walls adorned with copper pots. And, of course, a display of a multitude of diplomas and certificates from a whole host of culinary associations (included the slightly surreal "Sardine Association"). A place where you can eat well without spending too much. Ham with haricot beans, *émincé* of marinated salmon with fennel, scallop *croustillant* with mixed vegetables. For once the à la carte menu — you can eat well for 100F — is better priced than the set meals (75–145F).

SAINT-JEAN-DE-MONTS 85160

HÔTEL-RESTAURANT LE ROBINSON**

28 bd Leclerc (Centre).
☎ 02.51.59.20.20 ➡ 02.51.58.88.03
Closed Dec 10–Jan 25. **Car park. TV.**

This family business has become an unmissable tourist complex over the years (almost a holiday village). The original hotel has been changed greatly with many extensions and additions, but quality has been maintained. Double rooms are available for a wide range of prices depending on the facilities and the time of year, from 195–320F. Traditional, pleasant cuisine in the restaurant. Set meals for 70F (weekdays) to 180F. As usual for this part of the world, reserve well in advance.

10% HÔTEL LE RICHELIEU***

8 av. des Œillets (South-East).
☎ 02.51.58.06.78 ➡ 02.51.59.74.45
Closed Nov 15–April 1. **Car park. TV.**

The Norman architecture of this large comfortable house is quite surprising for this area. Set just back from the seafront (you can be there in two seconds flat!) with its own garden, it has eight very comfortable, tastefully decorated rooms. Doubles with bath 280F. Half-board compulsory in July–August for 290F per person. They'll treat you like one of the family and offer simple food and meals made from excellent ingredients. Stuffed clams, skate with saltwort, sole *paupiettes* with scallops. Set meals 98–295F.

RESTAURANT DES TROIS CHARRUES

Petit-Bois Verdon (North).
☎ 02.51.58.62.75
Closed Mondays off season. **Car park. Disabled access.**

You can't miss this thatched chalet. The pretty surrounding garden looks as if this is where the chef plants all his vegetables and herbs. Salmon with sorrel and scallops *à la crème* are to be found in the set meals at 70F (lunchtimes), 85F and 120F. But the star of the show is the amazing waitress — long may she continue!

SAINT-LÉONARD-DES-BOIS 72590

TOURING HÔTEL

How to get there: follow the "Alpes Mancelles" route.
☎ 02.43.31.44.44 ➡ 02.43.31.44.49
Car park. TV.

A good place to stay, near the Sarthe river which gives this region its name and in the heart of the hills known as "les Alpes Mancelles". Although the building is constructed from concrete, the atmosphere, hospitality, cuisine and swimming pool soon make you forget this. Thirty-five quiet, well-appointed rooms 440–475F They all come with a trouser press and a rubber duck in the bathroom, maybe because this is the only French hotel owned by the British company, Forestdale! Set meals 110F, 160F and 220F. Try the cheapest set meal, which offers plaice with mussels and *trompettes de la mort* (a type of mushroom) sandwiched between a starter of home-smoked salmon and dessert of chocolate cake.

SAINT-NAZAIRE 44600

10% KORALI HÔTEL**

place de la Gare (North).
☎ 02.40.01.89.89 ➡ 02.40.66.47.96
TV. Canal+. Disabled access.

The lack of pleasant hotels in Saint-Nazaire makes you appreciate this welcoming hotel all the more. With its modern comforts it makes an ideal stopover. Half-board is 298F per person. A big advantage if you have to get on your way early in the morning is that breakfast is served from 5am. Set meals for 85F and 120F.

10% HÔTEL DE TOURAINE*

4 av. de la République (Centre).
☎ 02.40.22.47.56 ➡ 02.40.22.55.05

To find a clean, new, pleasant room in Saint-Nazaire for 200F where you get a substantial breakfast in the garden (in good weather) for 26F and can also get a shirt ironed at no extra cost is sufficiently unusual to merit a mention. Excellent hospitality as you may have guessed! Another plus is the 25% reduction on room prices at weekends Oct 1–May 31.

RESTAURANT LE MODERNE

46 rue d'Anjou (Centre).
☎ 02.40.22.55.88
Closed Sunday evenings and Mondays.

As Saint-Nazaire is not known for its cuisine, you will appreciate the offerings and prices of this family restaurant all the more. Try the traditional seafood *choucroute* or fillet of zander with chanterelle mushrooms. Set meals for 60–198F.

SAINT-JOACHIM 44720 (2KM)

10% L'AUBERGE DU PARC, LA MARE AUX OISEAUX

162 île de Fédrun.
☎ 02.40.88.53.01 ➜ 02.40.91.67.44

The inhabitants of île de Fédrun, a proud people, have adopted Éric Guérin as their favourite chef. Still under 30 years old, this young man is full of ideas and puts a touch of inspiration onto the plates of his customers. His dishes all have lyrical — and lengthy — names. In rather more prosaic terms, he offers dishes like snails and cuttlefish with wild nettles (80F), lacquered zander (120F), and frogs on a bed of seaweed (90F). This chef seems able to produce offerings of a quality seemingly beyond his years. Eat well and be entertained at the same time. Four rooms under a reed-thatched roof which is in keeping with the local *Brièronne* atmosphere (350–380F).

SAINT-BREVIN-L'OCÉAN 44250 (12KM S)

HÔTEL-RESTAURANT ROSE MARIE**

1 allée des Embruns; it's near the beach, 2 minutes from the centre.
☎ 02.40.27.20.45 ➜ 02.40.39.14.66
Secure parking. TV.

Run by the last in the line of a family which has kept this unusual hotel since 1932. He's a bit of a character, has travelled around a bit and come back to play a bit of piano now and then.. You can taste the sea in the food, which is a real compliment here. Try the bass in a white wine and butter sauce or the scallops. The only fault is the disappointing selection of local wine. Jazz on the terrace at the weekends and lovely rooms for 250–270F. Full board in summer; 670F for two.

SAINT-VINCENT-DU-LOROUËR 72150

L'AUBERGE DE L'HERMITIÈRE

sources de l'Hermitière; it's 4.5km south of Saint-Vincent-du-Lorouër.
☎ 02.43.44.84.45
Closed Monday evenings, Tuesdays and from November 15 to the beginning of March.

One of the largest restaurants in the Sarthe region which nevertheless manages to maintain quality. A very good set meal is offered during the week for 90F, with an often sumptuous main course, accompanied by a salad and dessert. This brick and wood house is adorable, tucked away as it is on the river bank. The Queen Mother once honoured the restaurant with her presence, but she couldn't stay overnight as the planned hotel had not been started. By the time you arrive you may be able to stay a few nights to enjoy the tranquillity of this delightful spot. The set meal of local dishes for 155F includes courses worthy of mention such as the pork kidneys in cider (awarded a special prize by the National Academy of Cuisine) and a *sauté sarthois* (ham, chicken, and snails with *crème fraîche*) in Jasnières, the local white wine — mmm!

SAINT-VINCENT-SUR-JARD 85520

HÔTEL-RESTAURANT L'OCÉAN**

rue Georges-Clemenceau (West); it's next to musée Clémenceau.
☎ 02.51.33.40.45 ➜ 02.51.33.98.15
Closed Thursdays off season and from mid-November to mid-February. **Car park. TV. Disabled access.**

This pre-war hotel, located close to where Clemenceau used to come for his holidays, has continued to grow in reputation and hospitality. The rooms with flowery wallpaper do not have views of the sea but do look out onto a quiet garden. Half-board 230–390F per person. There are six set meals for 85–225F which should satisfy lovers of seafood. Double rooms range in price from 180F with shower to 340F with bath. There is also a swimming pool where you can have a dip even if you've just dropped in for a drink. Your hostess is adorable but a little deaf at times. She looks like somebody out of a Balzac novel.

SAUMUR 49400

HÔTEL LE CRISTAL**

10 place de la République (Centre).
☎ 02.41.51.09.54 F 02.41.51.12.14
Secure parking. **TV**.

A very good location next to the town hall. Comfortable rooms in soft tones, the more expensive ones with a view of the Loire. Four floors with no lift, but the staircase is listed. Doubles 195–280F (with shower/wc) and 340F (with bath). Competitive prices for four people. The breakfasts are very substantial and the hostess very friendly.

HÔTEL LE VOLNEY**

1 rue Volney (South); it's near the central post office.
☎ 02.41.51.25.41
Closed Dec 20–Jan 15. **TV**.

A very distinctive, charming hotel. Cosy rooms which are ideal for tired travellers to relax in. Rooms with shower, wc and phone for 220F. The hostess is truly amazing — so kind, helpful and knowledgeable about the local region. She can also keep you entertained with hundreds of interesting anecdotes about her life in the hotel trade. We didn't think that hotels like this existed any more. Highly recommended.

10% HÔTEL DE LONDRES**

48 rue d'Orléans (Centre).
☎ 02.41.51.23.98 F 02.41.51.12.63
Car park. **TV**. **Canal+**.

This well-kept hotel is in a good location. Although on a main street the sound insulation is very efficient. The friendly proprietor offers double rooms for 250F (with shower/wc) and 270F (with bath). Old-fashioned surroundings and wonderful main stair (dates back to 1850). Room number 28 is particularly good.

10% CENTRAL HÔTEL**

23 rue Daillé (Centre); from quai Carnot take rue Fidélité and it's the first on the left after rue Saint-Nicolas.
☎ 02.41.51.05.78 F 02.41.67.82.35
Car park. **TV**. **Canal+**.

Modern building, entirely renovated inside and out. The 27 rooms are spacious and all different, some with shower and wc for 270F. Pleasant, rather refined décor, internal arches and exposed beams which lend character to the place. Affable, welcoming host. Large room for four people gives excellent value for money.

10% HÔTEL-RESTAURANT ANNE D'ANJOU***

32-33 quai Mayaud (Centre); it's below the château, beside the Loire.
☎ 02.41.67.30.30 F 02.41.67.51.00
Closed Dec 23–Jan 4. **Secure parking**. **TV**.
Disabled access.

An elegant 18th century building, full of charm. Flower-filled internal courtyard. Superb listed internal staircase. Comfortable rooms with antique furniture. One room is Empire style for 680F, ideal for a special treat or honeymoon. Other rooms 350F (with shower/wc) and 530F (with bath). You are received very correctly. The restaurant has a good reputation and offers set meals from 120F (except Sundays) to 230F.

LA PIERRE CHAUDE

av. du Général-de-Gaulle; it's on île d'Offard, between the two bridges.
☎ 02.41.67.18.83
Closed Saturday lunchtimes and Sundays (except in July and August). **Disabled access**.

As the name of this restaurant implies (The Hot Stone) you are provided with a hot stone on which to cook a selection of meats at your table, accompanied with delicious sauces. Set meals for 63F (lunchtimes during the week), 82F and 110F.

RESTAURANT LES MÉNESTRELS

11-13 rue Raspail; it's next to the law courts.
☎ 02.41.67.71.10
Closed Sundays and Monday lunchtimes from October to June and on Sunday evenings only for the rest of the year. **Disabled access**.

Without doubt the best restaurant in the area. Rustic setting, original beams and exposed stonework. The chef deserves a Michelin award. His set meal is a real crescendo of tastes, offering combinations of fine and complex flavours. A gourmet experience to remember. Set meals from 98F (except Sundays). The specialities change regularly, but if you are lucky enough to be offered langoustine ravioli or veal sweetbreads with a cardamom-scented sauce, don't hesitate to accept. Excellent welcome.

RESTAURANT LE RELAIS

31 quai Mayaud; it's beside the Loire, near the château.
☎ 02.41.67.75.20
Closed Saturday lunchtimes, Sundays and in February.

A hushed atmosphere in this colourful setting, brightened by the stained-glass windows. Delicious fine cuisine. Set meals 100F (including a glass of wine), 120F and 180F or eat à la carte. Semi-cooked duck *foie gras*, *croustillant* of scallops, chicken breast with *foie gras*, zander in a red wine and butter sauce, chocolate *croquant*, etc.

|●| L'AUBERGE REINE DE SICILE**

71 rue Waldeck-Rousseau (North-East); it's on île d'Offard, between the two bridges.
☎ 02.41.67.30.48
Closed Mondays, Sunday evenings and in August.
Car park. Disabled access.

This restaurant, situated beside a charming medieval building, is away from the usual tourist circuit. A welcoming dining room. Specialities of grilled dishes (meat and fish) on a wood fire. Set meals 110F (fish *terrine* and rib of Charolais beef or grilled salmon), 130F (*moules marinière*, eels stewed in a wine sauce, hot pike *terrine*, lamb chop or *andouillette*), 160F (home-made *foie gras*, zander in a white wine and butter sauce, and duck *confit* or leg of lamb). A la carte dishes include monkfish *à l'américaine* and escalope of salmon. It's important to reserve. Very quiet. Warm welcome.

ROU-MARSON 49400 (6KM W)

|●| RESTAURANT LES CAVES DE MARSON

How to get there: leaving Saumur on the N147 heading towards Cholet, take the D960; it's signposted after 6km.
☎ 02.41.50.50.05.
Open June 15–Sept 15 except Sunday lunchtimes and Mondays. For the rest of the year open Friday and Saturday evenings and Sunday lunchtimes, except Dec 24–Jan 15. **Car park.**

In terms of restaurants set in wine producer's *caves* we consider this one to be the best as regards quality, price, conviviality and originality. After reading what we have to say you won't be surprised to hear that you have to book a table several days in advance in the high season. It's in a real cave and the dining room has a unique charm. The hospitality is without par. Try the proprietress's mouth-watering *fouées* — a kind of *galette* filled with beans, *rillettes*, goat's cheese or even *foie gras* (at extra cost). Food that Rabelais would have gone into paroxysms of delight about. As a starter you could try a flambéd tart with a glass of Coteaux-du-Layon. And to finish a salad and a delicious *gratin* of seasonal fruit. To go with it, have an excellent bottle of red Anjou. But what of cost? Talking money is almost indecent given the quality of the cooking and the atmosphere! But allow 120F or just 55F for the children's meal.

SILLÉ-LE-GUILLAUME 72140

10% 🏠 |●| LE BRETAGNE

1 pl. de la Croix d'Or (Centre).
☎ 02.43.20.10.10
Closed Sunday evenings and Mondays. **Car park.**

If you judged this hotel from the outside you would see a deteriorating family hotel and would hurry on. But once inside you will discover that the hotel has taken on a youthful countenance in terms of the welcome and the décor. Two of the locals have returned to their native area after having worked at famous establishments, and the restaurant they have opened offers fresh tasting and quite exciting dishes right through the range of set meals from 120F (leek terrine, walnut oil and *foie gras* salad, lightly smoked salmon, green lentils, cheese and lovely desserts) to 160F (*fondant* of ox tail, scorpion fish with lemon grass, cheese and a delicious *Paris-Brest*) and 180F. Welcoming rooms 190–210F.

THOUARCÉ 49380

|●| RESTAURANT LE RELAIS DE BONNEZEAUX**

Bonnezeaux; it's on the D24, about 1km from Thouarcé heading towards Angers.
☎ 02.41.54.08.33
Closed Mondays and Sunday evenings during the February school holidays and for the second two weeks of December. **Car park. Disabled access.**

This restaurant is housed in the old station built at the end of the nineteenth century but there's not much of the old atmosphere left. The dining room has a panoramic view which is an elegant setting for refined cuisine, fish in particular. Set meals 72F (weekday lunchtimes), 120F, 165F, 210F and 265F (gourmet). There are some delicious, original house specialities à la carte such as zander *suprême* in red Anjou wine, duck *foie gras* and *nougat glacé* with Cointreau. Shady terrace and playground for the children. The wine list includes amazing bottles of Coteaux-du-Layon — the 1899 vintage costs 3,500F, the 1949 is 1,800F and the 1954, 600F. Or you could just have a glass of the house red. . .

CHAMP-SUR-LAYON (LE) 49380 (6KM W)

L'AUBERGE DE LA CONTRÈCHE

How to get there: take the D125 from Champ-sur-Layon towards Rablay-sur-Layon.
☎ 02.41.78.48.18
Closed Mondays and for the months of February and September. **Car park. Disabled access.**

Reservation is highly recommended. A lovely auberge lost in the Layon hills. Very well appointed and spacious in a tasteful rustic style. All the food is rigorously prepared on the premises: *charcuterie*, cakes, fresh vegetables. The set meal at 105F offers very good value for money. Large portions. Delicious stuffed mushrooms to accompany the meat. Three charming rooms, with rustic décor costing from 250F for a double including breakfast (tasty home-made jam). Miniature golf to keep the fanatic quiet for a while.

TIFFAUGES 85130

HÔTEL LA BARBACANE**

2 place de l'Église.
☎ 02.51.65.75.59 F 02.51.65.71.91
Secure parking. TV. Canal+. Disabled access.

An astonishing place from all points of view. Firstly there is the amazing house, vital and welcoming with its garden full of cedars, magnolias, wisteria and roses. Then there is the swimming pool, the billiard room and the gentle, comfortable rooms looking out to the church or château. Not least there is also the proprietor Madame Bidan and her two and four-legged sons – she calls her dog "my son" on occasions. If you like her style and she takes to you, she will welcome you with open arms, even if you've never met before, and offer you drinks, cakes and even pizza. Rooms 290–310F with shower and 309–459F with bath. Mouth-watering breakfasts.

TRANCHE-SUR-MER (LA) 85360

RESTAURANT LE MILOUIN

99 av. Maurice-Samson.
☎ 02.51.27.49.49
Closed Mondays and Tuesdays off season and Nov 25–March 14.

You will feel at home in this restaurant's small blue and white dining room with exposed beams. There is also a terrace out the front for summer. They serve quick snacks as well as more substantial fare. Good set meals for 69–195F. Tasty regional cuisine. Monkfish *suprême* in a herb sauce, fish tartare, warm oysters in puff pastry and, for dessert, several types of home-made *crème brûlée*.

RESTAURANT LE NAUTILE

103 rue du Phare.
☎ 02.51.30.32.18
Closed Sunday evenings, Mondays, a week in October and a week in January.

This restaurant of anonymous architecture is hidden away in the residential part of La Tranche. The setting is a little characterless, except for the terrace, but Cyril Godard's fine, flavoursome cuisine is worth a visit. Stylish and good, although a little expensive. Salmon *aumônière* with saltwort, flambéd langoustine *cassolette*, and more. Set meals for 98–195F. One of the region's fashionable venues – a good sign!

VIBRAYE 72320

HÔTEL-RESTAURANT LE CHAPEAU ROUGE**

place de l'Hôtel-de-Ville.
☎ 02.43.93.60.02 F 02.43.71.52.18
Closed Sunday evenings, Mondays and Jan 15–31.
Car park. TV. Disabled access.

This hotel, covered in Virginia creeper, has a well-established reputation. Traditions have been preserved by the host and can be tasted in the meals he serves up – for example, authentic *tournedos Rossini*, good local meat dishes, fish fresh from La Rochelle and classic *crème caramel*. The dining room is full of hunting trophies. Set meals 80F (weekdays), 150F and 190F. À la carte offerings include home-made *terrine* of duck *confit* and *foie gras*, *paupiette* of John Dory with sorrel, monkfish *andouillette*, *ragoût* of langoustine tails etc. A very likeable hotel – a good atmosphere is guaranteed in the bar on market days, but quiet is guaranteed at night in the 16 rooms, five of which have a mini-bar. Doubles with shower/wc for 290F.

10% L'AUBERGE DE LA FORÊT

rue Gabriel Goussault (Centre).
☎ 02.43.93.60.07 F 02.43.71.20.36
Closed Sunday evenings and Mondays except for public holidays and in July and August. **Car park. TV.**

Although this hotel's name might lead you to think it was out in the middle of the forest, it is actually right in the town. But peace is guaranteed now that a new traffic system has left the centre of Vibraye so quiet that you can walk your dog without a lead. Comfortable rooms for 210–250F. Take your time in the restaurant over the set meal of good local dishes (100F), which offers as your main course the famous *marmite sarthoise* (a kind of local hotpot) carefully prepared with Jasnière, the local white wine. You'll start with *rillettes* tart and finish with the house dessert. The more elaborate set meals at 158F and 215F include hot oysters on a bed of leeks, roast duck in cream and cider, etc. Good professional work. Basic set meals 65F and 87F on weekdays.

Picardie

02 Aisne

60 Oise

80 Somme

ABBEVILLE 80100

🏠 |●| GRAZND HÔTEL DE LA GARE*

21 av. de la Gare.
☎ 03.22.24.04.09
Closed Friday evenings and Saturday lunchtimes Sept–April. **Secure parking**. **TV**.

A reasonably priced hotel, simple but pleasant. Clean well-kept bedrooms with doubles 140–195F. Try for a room overlooking the courtyard. The restaurant offers home cooking, regional specialities and tasty salads. Popular with working people and travellers. Set meals 60–130F, and prices for a half litre of wine start at 10F!.

ALBERT 80300

10% 🏠 |●| HÔTEL DE LA BASILIQUE**

3-5 rue Gambetta (Centre).
☎ 03.22.75.04.71 F➜ 03.22.75.10.47
Closed Saturday evenings and Sundays out of season, for two weeks in August, and at Christmas. **TV**.

The red-brick basilica in Albert with its *Virgin and Child* and stained-glass windows is worth a visit. The hotel is too but for different reasons – a friendly welcome, small comfortable bedrooms, and of course the good regional cooking. The 148F set meal offers dishes like home-made duck *pâté en croûte* and rabbit with prunes. Doubles cost 290F.

AMIENS 80000

SEE MAP ON P.648

🏠 HÔTEL VICTOR HUGO*

2 rue de l'Oratoire; it's beside the cathedral. **MAP C2-3**
☎ 03.22.91.57.91 F➜ 03.22.92.74.02
TV.

This is a small and very old establishment which has retained some of its original charm despite having been completely renovated (it now has double glazing). Some rooms are more comfortable than others, but they're all different. Those on the first floor have high ceilings. You might get one of the attic rooms – they're small but have the advantage of a romantic rooftop view. Doubles with shower/wc 195F.

10% 🏠 HÔTEL CENTRAL ET ANZAC**

17 rue Alexandre-Fatton; it's near the station. **MAP C2-1**
☎ 03.22.91.34.08 F➜ 03.22.91.36.02
Secure parking. **TV**. **Canal+**.

Ideally situated for travellers with lots of luggage who don't want far to go once they've struggled out of the station at Amiens! You'll get a very friendly welcome but chose your room very carefully. If you've enough energy left to climb several flights of stairs, take one of the recently renovated attic rooms. Definitely avoid those on the first floor. Expect to spend 205–255F for a basic standard of comfort.

🏠 HOTEL ALSACE-LORRAINE

18 rue de la Morlière; it's between the station and the river. **MAP C1-6**
☎ 03.22.91.35.71

Behind the enormous green door is a delightful little hotel with 13 predominantly green and white rooms. The welcome is as charming as the décor. Doubles 240–350F.

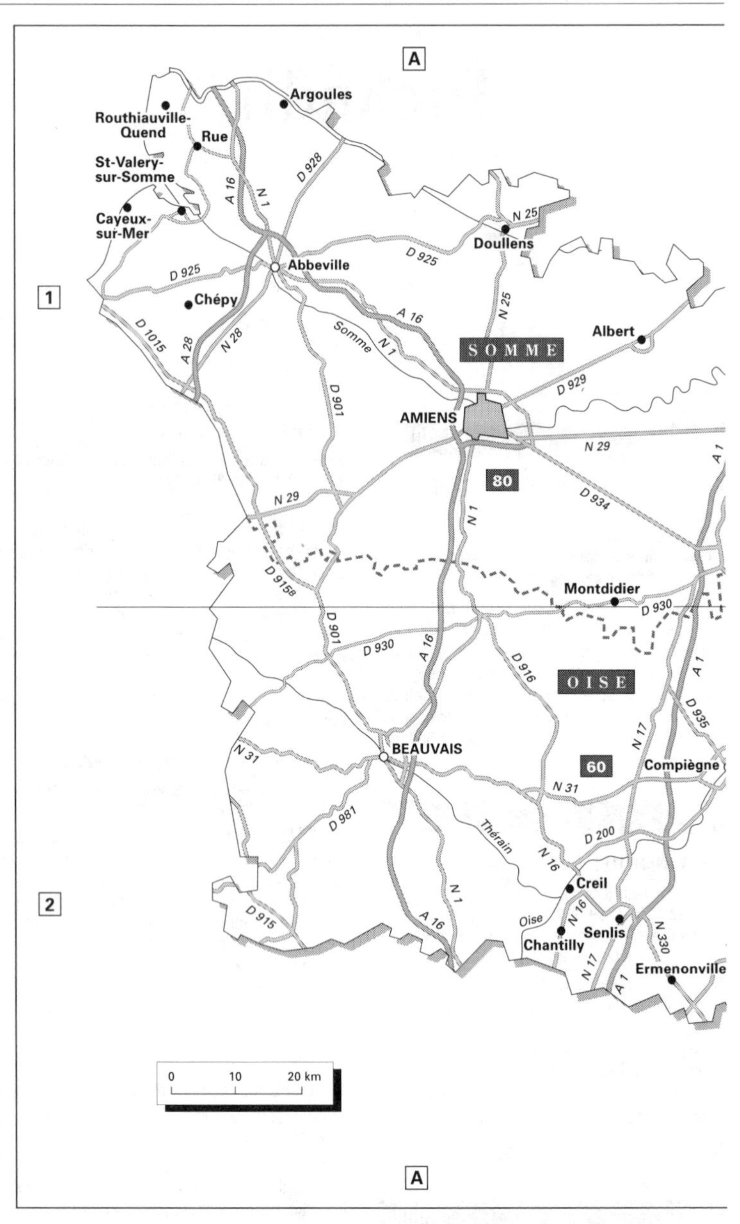
A
Argoules
Routhiauville-Quend
Rue
St-Valery-sur-Somme
Cayeux-sur-Mer
A 16
N 1
D 928
N 25
Doullens
D 925
Abbeville
D 925
1
Chépy
A 16
Somme
N 1
N 25
Albert
SOMME
D 1015
A 28
N 28
D 929
D 901
AMIENS
N 29
A 1
80
N 29
D 934
N 1
Montdidier
D 9158
D 930
D 901
D 930
A 16
D 916
OISE
A 1
D 935
N 17
N 31
BEAUVAIS
60
Compiègne
N 31
D 981
Thérain
D 200
N 16
Creil
2
N 1
N 16
Oise
Senlis
D 915
A 16
Chantilly
N 330
N 17
A 1
Ermenonville
0
10
20 km
A

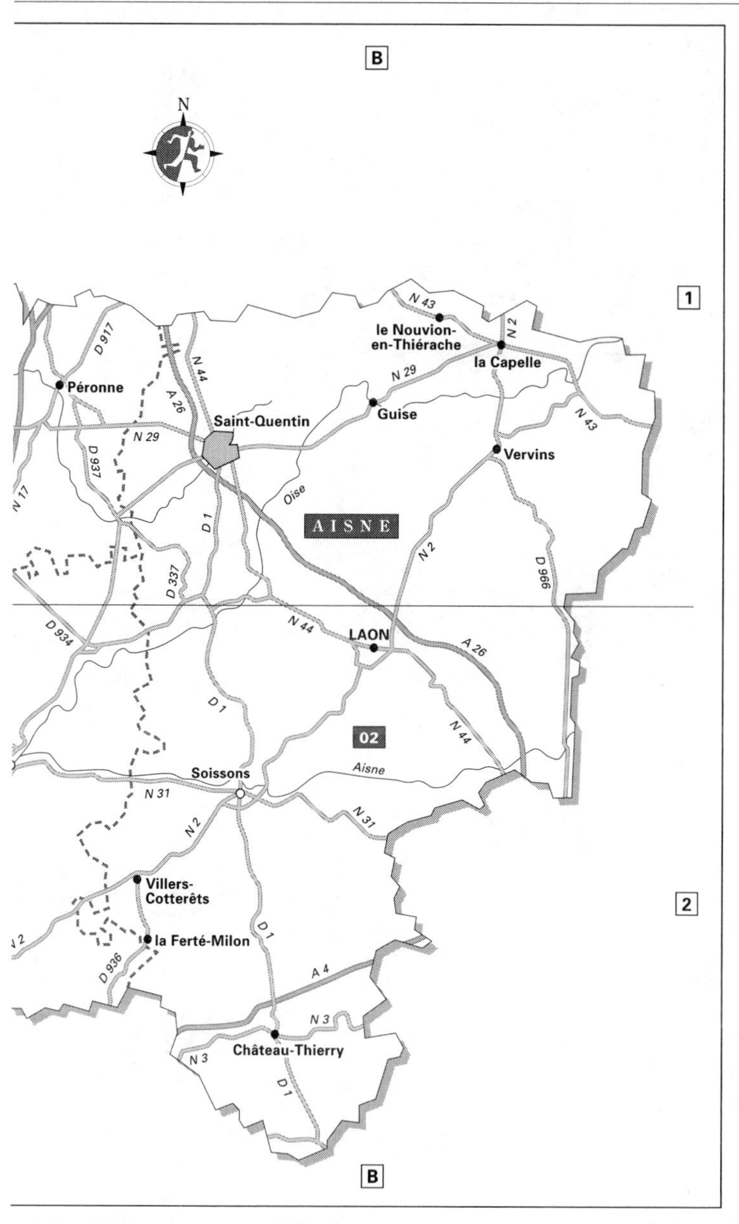
B
N
1
le Nouvion-en-Thiérache
la Capelle
Péronne
Guise
Saint-Quentin
Vervins
AISNE
LAON
02
Soissons
Aisne
Oise
Villers-Cotterêts
la Ferté-Milon
Château-Thierry
2
B
N 43
N 2
N 29
D 917
N 44
A 26
D 937
N 17
D 1
D 337
D 934
D 966
N 31
A 4
N 3
D 936

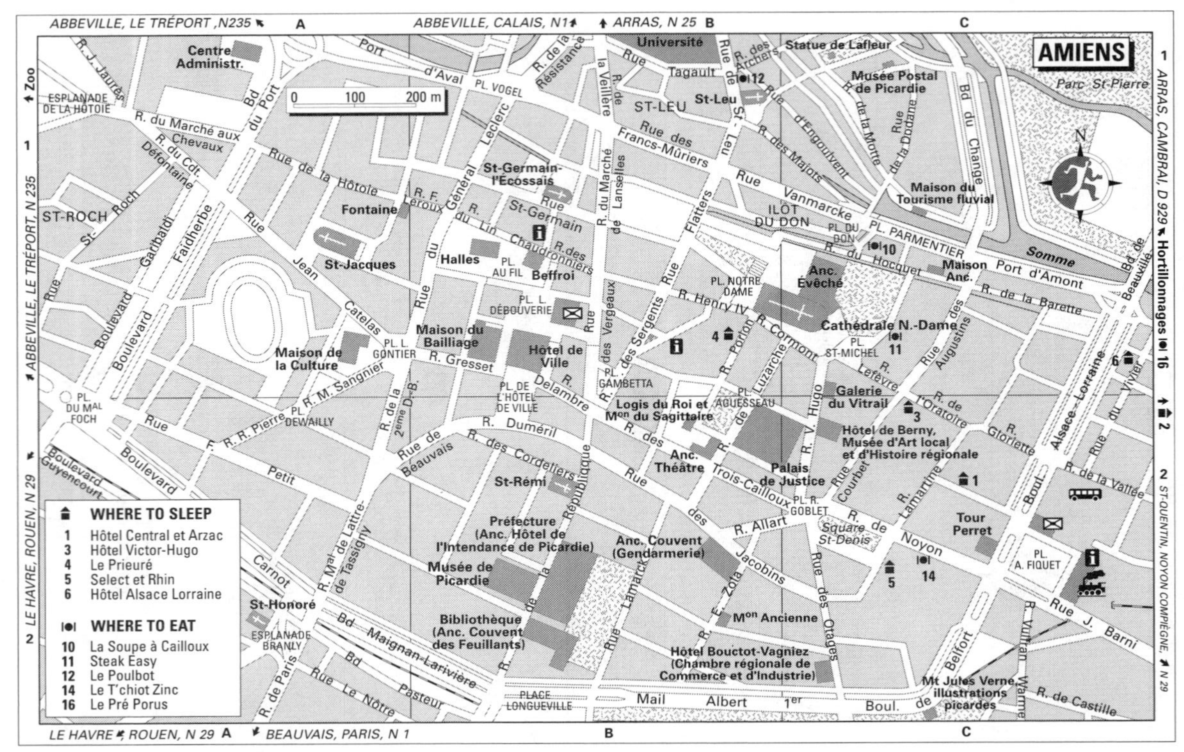
AMIENS
WHERE TO SLEEP
1 Hôtel Central et Arzac
3 Hôtel Victor-Hugo
4 Le Prieuré
5 Select et Rhin
6 Hôtel Alsace Lorraine
WHERE TO EAT
10 La Soupe à Cailloux
11 Steak Easy
12 Le Poulbot
14 Le T'chiot Zinc
16 Le Pré Porus
ABBEVILLE, LE TRÉPORT ,N235
ABBEVILLE, CALAIS, N1
ARRAS, N 25
ARRAS, CAMBRAI, D 929 Hortillonnages 16
ST-QUENTIN, NOYON COMPIÈGNE, N 29
LE HAVRE, ROUEN, N 29
BEAUVAIS, PARIS, N 1
ABBEVILLE, LE TRÉPORT, N 235
Zoo
0 100 200 m
Centre Administr.
Université
Statue de Lafleur
Musée Postal de Picardie
Maison du Tourisme fluvial
Parc St-Pierre
Somme
St-Leu
ST-LEU
St-Germain-l'Écossais
Fontaine
Halles
Beffroi
St-Jacques
ST-ROCH
ILÔT DU DON
Anc. Évêché
Maison Anc.
Cathédrale N.-Dame
Maison de la Culture
Maison du Bailliage
Hôtel de Ville
Logis du Roi et Mon du Sagittaire
Galerie du Vitrail
Hôtel de Berny, Musée d'Art local et d'Histoire régionale
Anc. Théâtre
Palais de Justice
St-Rémi
Préfecture (Anc. Hôtel de l'Intendance de Picardie)
Musée de Picardie
Anc. Couvent (Gendarmerie)
Mon Ancienne
Bibliothèque (Anc. Couvent des Feuillants)
Hôtel Bouctot-Vagniez (Chambre régionale de Commerce et d'Industrie)
Tour Perret
Mt Jules Verne illustrations picardes
St-Honoré
PL. A. FIQUET
PLACE LONGUEVILLE
Mail Albert 1er
Boul. de Belfort
Rue J. Barni
Rue des Otages
Rue de Noyon
Boul. Alsace-Lorraine

☗ |●| LE PRIEURÉ**

17 rue Porion; it's a stone's throw from the cathedral, on the way to the law courts. **MAP B1-4**
☎ 03.22.92.27.67 F➔ 03.22.92.46.16
Restaurant closed Sunday evenings and Mondays. **TV**.

Situated in a quiet, picturesque street, *Le Prieuré* has the charm of old buildings. Prices start at 260F for a room with shower/wc. You can sample the good plain regional cooking in the all-white dining room. Three set meals at 110F, 150F and 200F. A few more smiles wouldn't do any harm.

10% ☗ |●| SÉLECT ET RHIN**

69-71 place René-Goblet. **MAP C2-5**
☎ 03.22.91.32.16 F➔ 03.22.92.42.31
Car park. TV.

Located near a little square which is a haven from the hustle and bustle of the main shopping street, the hotel has large and well-equipped rooms. Doubles 270–340F. Traditional dishes and a very friendly welcome are to be had in the ground floor bistro, which has set meals at 81–190F.Popular in the evening with artists appearing at the local theatre.

|●| LA SOUPE À CAILLOUX

16 rue des Bondes; it's in the St Leu district between the cathedral and the Somme. **MAP C1-10**
☎ 03.22.91.92.70
Closed Mondays and during the Christmas/New Year holidays.

It's ideally situated and the terrace makes it very pleasant in summer, so it's often chock-a-block. The cook buys his produce at the nearby riverside market and prepares tasty regional dishes like ham and cheese pancake, chicken with a cheese sauce (*Maroilles*, which is quite strong), salad of gizzards *confit* , salmon with bacon, and mutton with prunes, almonds and sesame seeds. Set meals 67F (lunchtimes during the week) and 95F. Expect to pay a little bit more à la carte. It's very popular and often full.

|●| LE POULBOT

48 rue Saint-Leu. **MAP B1-12**
☎ 03.22.91.28.00
Closed Mondays and Sunday lunchtimes.

This small restaurant near the science faculty isn't much to look at from the outside. Inside though, there's a colourful and cosy little dining room decorated with puppets. Try the lovely 79F set meal that uses fresh and simple ingredients in dishes that change according to the season and the chef's moods. Other set meal at 120F.

|●| RESTAURANT STEAK EASY

18 rue Metz-l'Évêque; it's behind the cathedral. **MAP C1-11**
☎ 03.22.91.48.38
Closed at Christmas and on New Year's Day
Disabled access.

Service noon–1am. This former church hall has been completely transformed into a Tex-Mex restaurant where young trendies hang out. The unusual décor makes it worth a visit. There's a real 60s fridge attached to the wall and a life-size aeroplane in full flight. It's the best example of American cooking here in Picardy. Rock and blues play in the backgound. Informal, fast service. No set meals. Barbecue ribs (very generous helping) cost 65F, chilli 42F, salads start at 25F, and cheesecake is 20F.

|●| LE T'CHIOT ZINC

18 rue de Noyon; it's five minutes from the old town, on the way to the station. **MAP C2-14**
☎ 03.22.91.43.79
Closed Sundays and Monday lunchtimes.

This is one of our favourites on account of its art-deco style, cosy bistro setting, and first-rate cooking. We recommend the ham and cheese pancakes ,of course, but there's also a duck *terrine* made according to a traditional Amiens recipe. Another speciality is rabbit in aspic with oven-browned potatoes. They also do a 66F *formule express* lunchtimes and evenings and a *menu complet* at 92F (drink included).

|●| RESTAURANT LE PRÉ PORUS

95 rue Voyelle; if you're coming from Amiens, it's as you approach Camon, just before the bridge. **MAP C1-16**
☎ 03.22.46.25.03
Closed Mondays, Tuesday evenings, and Feb 15–March 15. **Car park. Disabled access**.

It's just a couple of steps (or strokes if you prefer) from the reclaimed marshland that is now vegetable fields and this has to be one of the loveliest settings for a restaurant. Set meals (lots of fish dishes) are 95F during the week and 180–230F at the weekend. The quality of the cooking is not always high enough to justify the difference in price.

DREUIL LES AMIENS 80730 (6KM NW)

|●| LE COTTAGE

385 bld Pasteur; take the RN235 in the direction of Picquigny.
☎ 03.22.54.10.98
Closed Sunday evenings, Mondays, and in August.

This is a good little restaurant, even though it is by the side of the motorway. The unpretentious dining room (it has exposed beams) serves sophisticated dishes. The 120F set meal, which is good value for money, offers snail ravioli in a garlic scented sauce, a choice of *gratin* of scallops with leeks or veal kidneys in a mustard sauce, and dessert. Other set meals 150F, 165F and 215F.

BELLOY-SUR-SOMME 80310 (8KM NW)

HOSTELLERIE DE BELLOY*

29 route Nationale.
☎ 03.22.51.41.05
Closed Mondays, the first week in January, and Aug 16–Sept 5.

The *Hostellerie de Bellroy* must be one of those fortunate inns that are never short of custom judging by the tables of regulars and cheerful faces. You'll get a very friendly welcome, generous portions and service that is unpretentious, just like the décor. The artificial flowers were the only thing that struck a false note. Set meals at 80F, 120F (terrine of goose confit with onion marmalade and home-made fruit tart), 160F, and 190F.

ARGOULES 80120

10% AUBERGE DU GROS TILLEUL**

place du Château; it's in the village square, opposite the 18th century castle.
☎ 03.22.29.91.00. ⊳ 03.22.23.91.64
Closed Mondays (except public holidays) and in May, July and August. **Car park**. **TV**. **Canal+**.

According to legend, the big lime tree was planted by Sully and that the French monarchy made use of its services as a branch of a Siennese bank. Because of the stories and also because of its delightful surroundings, the inn is in all the guide books. It has set meals to suit all pockets, from the 70F *formule express* (weekdays only) to the 195F gourmet meal. The cooking is rich but not very sophisticated - the price of success? It has a few well-equipped rooms at prices ranging from 290F to 495F. *gourmet's meal.*

BEAUVAIS 60000

10% NORMANDIE HÔTEL

20 rue de la Taillerie; it's just a few yards from place de l'Hôtel-de-Ville. (Centre)
☎ 03.44.45.07.61
Closed Monday evenings. **TV**.

Located in a quiet pedestrianized street in the centre of town, this establishment offers neat bedrooms at very reasonable prices – doubles are 115F (with basin, no TV) and 155F (basin/wc). In the restaurant the *menu du jour* comes in at 56F and there are three other set meals 80–170F. A very friendly welcome, even for people who are just passing by. Ideal if you're on foot.

HÔTEL DE LA POSTE*

19-21 rue Gambetta; it's between the post office and place Jeanne-Hachette. (Centre)
☎ 03.44.45.14.97 ⊳ 03.44.45.02.31
Closed Sundays. **Secure parking**. **TV**.

The small, bright bedrooms have been recently renovated and are very comfortable and well-equipped. Doubles with washing facilities cost 145–205F - there's a wc on the landing. A word of warning: breakfast isn't served on Sundays. The restaurant offers a good *formule brasserie* which is very popular, especially at lunchtimes when the cheapest set meal comes in at 55F. The daily special is nicely presented and changes frequently. The 79F set meal is excellent value for money.

10% HÔTEL LA RÉSIDENCE**

24 rue Louis-Borel (North).
☎ 03.44.48.30.98 ⊳ 03.44.45.09.42
Secure parking. **TV**. **Canal+**.

This hotel is located in a very quiet street – the silence seems to be broken only by the sound of passing bikes – in a residential area that's a fifteen minute walk from the town centre. You'll get a joky, good-natured welcome, a modern, well-equipped room, and good value for money. All that probably explains why this is one of our favourite hotels in Beauvais. Doubles from 190F.

RESTAURANT LE MARIGNAN

1 rue de Malherbe (Centre).
☎ 03.44.48.15.15
Closed Sunday evenings and Mondays (except on public holidays).

On the ground floor there's a typical bar cum brasserie where you can have a decent meal for 62F on weekdays. But in order to make full use of the eating facilities, you'd be better off going up to the first floor dining room. It's rather plush and has a reproduction of the battle of Marignan hanging on the wall. Here you can sample *flamiche* (leek tart) and other Picardy specialities or chicken fricassee with chanterelles, raspberry *gratin* with almonds, and *crème brulée* with caramelized sugar. Dishes vary and are well-made. The cheapest set meal, which comes in at 99F, is very tasty, and there's also one at 159F offering delicious home-made *terrine* of *foie gras*.

AUBERGE DES VIEUX MARAIS

186 rue Saint-Just-des-Marais.
☎ 03.44.48.04.12
Closed Saturday lunchtimes. **Disabled access**.

This cosy retro-style inn with rustic beams is one of the best known gourmet restaurants in Beauvais but it's a bit far from the town centre. You can have duck but the house speciality is fish. Set meals 150F (all in), 160F, 210F.... It doesn't come cheap, of course, but it is good quality.

MORTEFONTAINE-EN-THELLE 60570 (19KM S)

RESTAURANT LE BEC AU VENT

la Mare d'Ovillers; it's on the N1.
☎ 03.44.08.67.10
Closed Sunday evenings and Monday evenings.
Car park.

The dining room, which manages to be both rustic and mediaeval, offers regional dishes, fish and, of course, the house special – duck – in all its guises. Not a bit of the bird is wasted and whatever you want – be it *confit*, gizzards, breast or *foie. gras* – they've got it. If you're a fan, you won't be disappointed. Set meals range from 65F (which comes with 1/4 litre of wine) to 130F.

AGNETZ 60600 (20 KM S)

10% HÔTEL-RESTAURANT LE CLERMOTEL**

N31; take the RN31 in the direction of Clermont and leave the motorway by the Agnetz zone hôtelière exit.
☎ 03.44.50.09.90 Fax 03.44.50.13.00
Restaurant closed Dec 22–Jan 6. **Car park**. **TV**. **Canal+**. **Disabled access**.

This is a modern motel type establishment close to the beautiful forest of Hez. Well-equipped and very comfortable bedrooms are 310F. Go for the ones at the back that have direct access to the grounds, where there are tables and chairs ready and waiting for you. There's a garden and tennis court if you're in the mood for relaxing. You'll find the large bright dining room delightful. The modern cooking is good and goes down very nicely, although it's maybe not as nice as your mother used to make. A buffet option is available if you'd rather have that. Set meals at 93F, 125F and 149F.

AUBERGE DE GICOURT

old N31-Gicourt; head for Gicourt and take the Gicourt zone hôtelière exit.
☎ 03.44.50.00.31
Closed Sunday and Monday evenings, two weeks in February, and the first fortnight in August.

If you're planning to go at the weekend we strongly recommend that you book in advance as there are lots of regulars. Just the kind of pleasant inn we like, with very attentive service and a large variety of tasty, hearty dishes in the 108F set meal. There was nothing we didn't like, and the other set meal (155F) isn't bad either. The owner and chef, Jean-Marie, will always come over for a few words before you leave. Our favourite top-of-the-range eating place in the region.

CAPELLE (LA) 02260

10% HÔTEL-RESTAURANT DE LA THIÉRACHE**

16 av. du Général-de-Gaulle (North); it's on the main street near the town centre.
☎ 03.23.97.33.80 Fax 03.23.97.85.88
Restaurant closed Friday evenings in winter and Dec 24–Jan 3. **Secure parking TV**. **Canal+**.

Once you're inside, the traffic and exhaust fumes will seem far away. It's a large building set well back from the street and you can be sure of peace and quiet. The welcome could be a touch friendlier. Doubles 150–240F. The bedrooms have recently been done up.. Plain cooking. Set meals from 75F (weekdays) to 195F.

CAYEUX-SUR-MER 80410

CHEZ ADRIENNE

83 av. Paul Doumer; it's near the station.
☎ 03.22.26.60.22
Closed Wednesdays out of season.

Adrienne, who owns this Creole restaurant where hitchhikers, tourists and revellers rub shoulders over a drink, is funny with her Josiane Balasko type humour (as in the film "French Twist"). This is the kind of restaurant we like – it's out of the way, close to a railway station that'is only used now by the little tourist train, and full of house plants and friendly faces. The specialities are a mixture of Creole and regional dishes, with *colombo* of lamb and fish featuring alongside leg of salt-meadow lamb. Set meals 70F, 90F and 110F.

CHANTILLY 60500

10% AUBERGE DU LION D'OR

44 rue du Connétable (Centre); it's near the château.
☎ 03.44.57.03.19 F 03.44.57.92.31
Closed Wednesdays and Dec 23–Jan 16.

This is one of the few hotels in town that's still reasonably priced and it's best to book ahead since it only has seven rooms. They start at 150F and are comfortable but not luxurious. Toilets are on the landing. The modern meals served in the restaurant are fairly ordinary, but the mixed grills are tasty and go down very nicely. Set meals at 114F and 142F offer seafood *gratin*, scallops provençale, mussels in a cream sauce, stuffed snails, and veal escalope *à la normande.* If you're staying at the hotel, don't forget that the doors close about midnight or else you'll find yourself locked out! Service is uneven.

RÔTISSERIE DU CONNÉTABLE*

75 rue du Connétable.
☎ 03.44.57.02.91
Closed Tuesday evenings and Wednesdays.

This is a nice restaurant with an enormous rustic dining room, a fireplace and copper saucepans. It offers dishes such as lobster omelette, calf sweetbreads with morels, and fresh game in season. The cheapest set meal comes in at 100F (weekdays except public holidays). There are others at 145F and 190F and à la carte is also available.

RESTAURANT LE GOUTILLON

61 rue du Connétable.
☎ 03.44.58.01.00

As soon as you sit down, the waiter brings the blackboard across. Yes it's true – instead of a menu a huge blackboard is placed on the chair in front of you. It's an idea that's become very popular, so be prepared to wait. Old-style décor with exposed beams and stonework and walls covered with old posters. Nice starters cost round about 40F (snails are the house specialty) and main dishes such as duck breast, chicken fricassee in a curry sauce, and *andouillette* are 60–120F. At lunchtime, there's an 80F *formule* that includes wine. The atmosphere's laidback, the welcome's friendly and the owner's never too far away.

VINEUIL-SAINT-FIRMIN 60500 (4KM NE)

RESTAURANT LES GRANDS PRÉS

☎ 03.44.57.71.97
Closed Sunday evenings and Mondays (except in July and August) and Monday lunchtimes in July and August.
Car park.

This place is right out in the country, so you'll get the chance of some fresh air while sitting on the terrace or strolling in the garden. Reasonable traditional dishes like panfried lamb kidneys and sweetbreads with oyster mushrooms, and *nage de Saint Jacques* (poached scallops). Set meals 98Fand 152F. They also do a 190F *formule* which includes an apéritif, wine and coffee.

SAINT-LEU-D'ESSERENT 60340 (5.5KM NW)

HÔTEL DE L'OISE*

25 quai d'Amont (East); take the N16 then follow the D44.
☎ 03.44.56.60.24 F 03.44.56.05.11
Restaurant closed Friday evenings, Saturdays, Sunday evenings, and the first three weeks in August.
Car park. TV.

This is the type of place you dream about – a delightful little riverside hotel offering peace and quiet and hospitality within spitting distance (well, almost) of Paris. Refurbished doubles 260F with shower or bath. The restaurant, with its rustic décor andwainscoting, offers starter, main course, and cheese or dessert for 70F, and delightful specialities à la carte.

CHÂTEAU-THIERRY 02400

10% HÔTEL-RESTAURANT HEXAGONE**

50 av. d'Essômes; take the Paris road from the centre of town then follow the signs for Charly sur Marne.
☎ 03.23.83.69.69 F 03.23.83.64.17
Closed Sundays except for groups. **Car park. TV. Canal+. Disabled access**.

You'll get a warm welcome in this modern two-storey hotel, which has comfortable well-equipped doubles at 250F. The hearty 30F buffet-style breakfast – cereals, cheese, *charcuterie* and so on – is worth mentioning. The restaurant's cheapest set meal (80F) is perfectly adequate, and there are four others ranging in price from 98F to 170F. Good traditional home cooking. You'll be well looked after.

COMPIÈGNE 60200

HÔTEL DE FRANCE-RÔTISSERIE DU CHAT QUI TOURNE**

17 rue Eugène-Floquet (Centre).

☎ 03.44.40.02.74 F➔ 03.44.40.48.37
How to get there: it's beside an unusual building with grandiose Corinthian columns. **TV**.

It appears there once was a street entertainer who taught his cat to turn a spit – hence the name of the restaurant. Not many people know that ... Nowadays, the hotel provides a degree of comfort and style of cooking that are of 3-star standard. Set meals 135–250F. The bedrooms are all different. and decorated very tastefully. Doubles 165–380F (with bath). A delightful hotel for those who can afford it. Friendly and courteous welcome.

10% ☗ HÔTEL DE FLANDRE**

16 quai de la République (Centre).
☎ 03.44.83.24.40 F➔ 03.44.90.02.75
Closed during Christmas and New Year holidays.
Secure parking. **TV**. **Canal+**.

The building is enormous and classical in style. The hotel offers a good standard of comfort and has been redecorated in pastel shades. Expect to pay 270–290F for a double with shower/wc or bath. Rooms are spacious and the double glazing guarantees peace and quiet. Pleasant welcome.

|●| RESTAURANT LE BOUCHON

5 rue Saint-Martin (Centre).
☎ 03.44.40.05.32

This restaurant is situated in a charming little pedestrian street lined with half-timbered houses. You can have the day's special – *pot au feu*, say, or a stew of some kind – for 48F and a glass of first-rate wines (there are over seventy to choose from!) for about 25F. Though the idea's not original, they've developed it here. Country-style décor, pleasant atmosphere (the owner pulls everybody's leg) and regional cooking. The restaurant has regular wine-tasting sessions which include a meal and the chance to sample six diifferent kinds of wine. The owner's never short of ideas, and this is a restaurant where hospitality and personality go hand in hand. Bravo!

|●| BISTROT DE FLANDRE

2 rue d'Amiens (Centre).
☎ 03.44.83.26.35

Here's a bistro with all the features of a brasserie – spacious dining room, waiters in white aprons, and quick service. They have set meals at 88F and 135F (not available Sundays), while à la carte there are good specialities like veal sweetbreads with morels, the house tournedos and of course *foie gras* of duck. On Sundays the 88Fset meal goes up to 128F.

MEUX (LE) 60880 (10KM S)

|●| LA MAISON DU GOURMET**

1 rue de la République.
☎ 03.44.91.10.10
Closed Saturday lunchtimes and Sunday evenings.
Car park.

This is a new restaurant that'll soon make a name for itself. Mind you, the owner-chef isn't exactly new to this game – he spent seven years at Maxim's and then went on to the château of Raray. The 98F set meal alone makes it worth a visit. Terrine of veal sweetbreads with spring vegetables, fillet of sole with a red pepper *coulis*, and a warm soufflé with soft fruit are some of the specialities on offer. Another set meal comes in at 145F, and you'll also find a wide range of dishes à la carte. You'll be greeted and served in a friendly and efficient manner.

CREIL 60100

|●| LA PETITE ALSACE

8 place Charles-Brobeil (Centre); it's beside the railway station.
☎ 03.44.55.28.89
Closed Saturday lunchtimes, Sunday evenings, Mondays, and two weeks in August. **Car park**.

Not very typical of the region, but gosh it's good. Try the *choucroute* (prices start at 69F). It's good and satisfying and goes well with an Alsace wine or a cool beer. Set meals 85–185F. And to top it all off, you get served by waiters in traditional costume!

DOULLENS 80600

☗ |●| LE SULLY**

45 rue Jacques-Mossion (Centre); it's beside the railway station.
☎ 03.22.77.10.87
Closed Mondays and two weeks at the end of June. **TV**.

A fairly modern building, with seven rooms in all at 195F. They're very clean and well equipped but they don't have much character. Reception is at the foot of a majestic wrought iron staircase. The restaurant has good set meals at 59F, 89F and 159F and skilfully prepared regional specialities.

EPY 80210

⌂ |●| L'AUBERGE PICARDE**

pl. de la Gare; it's just opposite the Chépy-Valines station.
☎ 03.22.26.20.78 ➡ 03.22.26.33.34
Restaurant closed Saturday lunchtimes and Sunday evenings; hotel and restaurant closed Aug 15–25 and late December. **Car park**. **TV**.

It's big, it looks more like a motel than a hotel and it's got one of the best restaurants in the region. Set meals 125F, 153F, and 185F and seafood and regional specialities like zander with shrimp, scallops, and oysters with shallots. It can be crowded at the weekend so it's probably a good idea to book.

ERMENONVILLE 60950

10% ⌂ |●| AUBERGE DE LA CROIX D'OR**

2 rue Radziwill.
☎ 03.44.54.00.04 ➡ 03.44.45.05.44
Closed Mondays, and Dec 20–Jan 26. **Car park**. **TV**.

You probably go to Ermenonville for the château and the grounds. The *Auberge de la Croix d'Or* gives you another reason to visit. It's very rustic, has a really nice atmosphere, offers a high standard of comfort and first-rate food and it's quite a mixture of architectural styles. What more could you ask for?. Doubles 220F with shower/wc. Set meals 130 and 175F. There's a 95F weekday *formule* consisting of main course plus starter and dessert that puts less of a strain on the wallet.

FERTÉ-MILON (LA) 02460

10% ⌂ HÔTEL RACINE**

place du Port-au-Blé (Centre).
☎ 03.23.96.72.02 ➡ 03.23.96.72.37
Car park. **TV**.

This is a superb little hotel housed in a building that dates from the 17th century. It's not surprising that de la Fontaine (the man who wrote the fables) celebrated his marriage here. There are eight pleasant and tastefully decorated bedrooms, reasonably priced at 270F.The outside isn't bad either – there's a garden with a paved courtyard and a pretty corner turret on the banks of the Ourcq. The owners organize painting courses so it's time to dig out your paintbrush and easel! Pleasant welcome.

GUISE 02120

⌂ |●| HÔTEL-RESTAURANT CHAMPAGNE-PICARDIE**

41 rue André-Godin (Centre).
☎ 03.23.60.43.44
Closed early August and late December; restaurant closed Friday evenings and Sundays. **Secure parking**. **TV**.

This is a beautiful bourgeois building encircled by a little park and standing in the shadow of the château belonging to the duc de Guise (although according to our sources he no longer lives there). There are twelve comfortable bedrooms which are both spacious and bright. Doubles cost 240F. Service in the restaurant is pleasant and so is the food – hearty regional dishes that are not too expensive. The 60F *menu du jour* is very simple or there's a more elaborate one at 80F. If you go for the most expensive one at 140F, you'll get medallions of *foie gras*, sole *meunière*, and a choice of cheese and desserts. Courteous welcome.

LAON 02000

10% ⌂ HÔTEL LES CHEVALIERS**

3-5 rue Sérurier (Centre); it's in the middle of the mediaeval town between the cathedral and place de la Mairie.
☎ 03.23.27.17.50 ➡ 03.23.23.40.71
Closed Dec 15–Jan 5. **TV**.

Nicely decorated and functional bedrooms with low ceilings and exposed beams in a stylish old building – ideal for romantics! Ask for a room with a view of the countryside. There are sixteen bedrooms and the most basic ones are fairly inexpensive. Expect to pay 185–320F for two people which includes breakfast.

|●| RESTAURANT LE RÉTRO

18 bd de Lyon (Centre); it's in the lower part of town on the main street.
☎ 03.23.23.04.49
Closed Sunday lunchtimes (unless you have a reservation).

A nice place that's often full and is popular with travellers and workers at lunchtime. Owner Marie-Thérèse made a name for herself with the men who built the elevated railway as being the kind of person who doesn't stand on ceremony There's a wonderful set meal at 75F offering good, traditional cooking such as Maroilles tart, house *terrine*, calf's head *vinaigrette*, and *emincé* of chicken with basil. The décor's a bit kitsch, with house plants and artificial flowers all over the place.

|●| RESTAURANT LA PETITE AUBERGE

45 bd Brossolette (Centre); it's in the lower part of town, very near the station.
☎ 03.23.23.02.38
Closed Saturday lunchtimes and Sundays (except on public holidays). **Car park. Disabled access.**

This is the best gourmet restaurant in Laon. Rustic décor. The cooking is modern and the owner's son, Willy Marc Zorn, introduces a touch of originality to tasty dishes such as sea bass with peppercorns, *crème au lard*, and panfried veal sweetbreads in lager with a *fondue* of chicory. Pretty good but still on the expensive side – set meals 100F, 149F, 169F and 200F. There's a free glass of champagne for everyone with a copy of this guide book. If you can't afford those prices, try *Le Saint-Amour* (tel: 03.23.23.31.01) next door with its brasserie-style décor and magnificent fresco. It's owned by the same people and offers home-made country cooking and excellent Beaujolais. Set meals 59F, 75F and 89F.

MONTDIDIER 80500

10% ☗ |●| HÔTEL DE DIJON**

1 place du 10-Août; follow the signs for Beauvais.
☎ 03.22.78.01.35 ➡ 03.22.78.27.24
Restaurant closed Saturdays, Sunday evenings, the February school holidays, and Aug 1–15.
Secure parking. TV.

There's a rather crazy signposting system and you'll probably see a lot of the town before you finally arrive at your destination. The hotel's at a crossroads and has been renovated throughout. Bright, comfortable and colourful rooms range in price from 215F for the simplest ones to 280F for one with wc and TV). The restaurant specializes in meat dishes with a set meal at 82F.

|●| RESTAURANT LE PARMENTIER

11 rue Albert-Ier; it's opposite the post office.
☎ 03.22.78.15.10
Closed weekday evening (except by reservation), and the last three weeks in August.

Montdidier is the birthplace of Parmentier who did so much to popularize that all-purpose vegetable, the potato, which proved its worth in several famines So it would have been scandalous if the town had lacked a restaurant offering good home cooking. No need to worry though – *Le Parmentier* fills that niche very nicely. Cheerful staff serve up generous portions of reasonably priced dishes featuring fresh local produce and the restaurant has all it takes to become very popular with both locals and people just passing through. Set meals at 60F, 99F and 130F offer dishes like seafood salad and medallions of monkfish in a whisky sauce.

NOUVION-EN THIÉRACHE (LE) 02170

☗ |●| HÔTEL DE LA PAIX**

37 rue Vimont-Vicary (North-West).
☎ 03.23.97.04.55 ➡ 03.23.98.98.39
Closed Monday lunchtimes and Sunday evenings.
Secure parking. TV.

This is a good country hotel with friendly staff and a style of cooking that has broken away from the merely everyday. Regional dishes, seafood specialities, and tasty desserts will delight even the most fastidious. Set meals cost 90F (weekdays), 135F and 163F. The bedrooms (285F) are all very big and comfortable.

PÉRONNE 80200

10% ☗ |●| HOSTELLERIE DES REMPARTS**

23 rue Beaubois; it's 100m from the main street.
☎ 03.22.84.01.22 ➡ 03.22.84.31.96
Secure parking. TV.

This country inn, which is reminiscent of France in the post-war years, is as peaceful as the grounds and the street outside. The bedrooms (280–450F) are comfortable and elegant as is the dining room, which serves traditional local dishes. Prices start at 90F (includes a drink weekday lunchtimes). Other set meals 95F, 150F, 185F and 280F. One for the address book.

ROUTHIAUVILLE-QUEND 80120

☗ |●| AUBERGE DU FIACRE

Hameau de Routhiauville
☎ 03.22.23.47.30 ➡ 03.22.27.19.80
Closed Wednesday lunchtimes out of season and Jan 15–Feb 15. **Car park. TV. Disabled access.**

This pleasant half-timbered building has a good reputation locally for its cooking. The menu changes with the seasons and features fish and regional specialities. Set meals 100F (weekdays), 150F, 170F, and 220F. It has ten or so comfortable rooms (330F with shower/wc, 360F with bath) that overlook an attractive garden at the back of the main building.

RUE 80120

☗ |●| LE LION D'OR**

5 rue de la Barrière (Centre).
☎ 03.22.25.74.18 F➜ 03.22.25.66.63
Closed in December; restaurant closed Sunday evenings out of season. **Car park**. **TV**. **Canal+**.

This is a classic example of the kind of hotel we come across so often on our travels in France. It's an ideal place to spend the night, with its comfortable practical rooms at 300F and its restaurant from a bygone age where you can have *mouclade* (mussel stew) in season, oysters *gratiné* in vermouth, and braised pork in cider. Set meals 100–200F.

FAVIÈRES 80120 (6KM S)

|●| RESTAURANT LA CLÉ DES CHAMPS***

place des Frères-Caudron (Centre); take the D9 in the direction of Crotoy, then the D140.
☎ 03.22.27.88.00
Closed Sunday evenings, Mondays, in January, and the first week in September. **Car park**. **Disabled access**.

If you want to get away from it all, come to this well-known inn set among the salt-meadows. The specialities are local fish and dishes based on what the market has to offer. Set meals cost 86–195F.

SAINT-QUENTIN 02100

☗ |●| LE FLORENCE**

42 rue Émile-Zola (Centre).
☎ 03.23.64.22.22 F➜ 03.23.62.52.85
Restaurant closed Monday lunchtimes and Sundays.
Secure parking.**TV**. **Canal+**.

The hotel has been refurbished from top to bottom and the bedrooms are simple and clean, with doubles 135–225F. The restaurant specializes in good Italian dishes such as osso bucco, pizza and fresh pasta. There's a set meal at 95F. Expect to spend about 100F for a meal. Pleasant welcome.

10% ☗ HÔTEL DE FRANCE ET D'ANGLETERRE**

28 rue Émile-Zola (Centre); it's a few steps from the town hall.
☎ 03.23.62.13.10 F➜ 03.23.62.63.44
Secure parking. **TV**. **Canal+**.

It's very well situated, bedrooms are comfy and the reception is spot on. In a word, it's good value for money. Doubles cost 155–250F and the ones overlooking the courtyard are quieter. The owners are extremely nice and only too willing to point out the best places to eat in town. Although there's no restaurant, a few light meals are on offer.

☗ |●| HÔTEL-RESTAURANT DE GUISE*

93 rue de Guise (South-East); it's rather far from the town centre, on the way to La Capelle.
☎ 03.23.68.27.69
Secure parking. **TV**. **Disabled access**.

The rooms are clean, comfortable enough, and very reasonably priced. Doubles with shower 160F (206F with two double beds). They do a 55F *menu express* at lunchtime, which is just a bite to eat, but really specialize in couscous (60–75F) and paella (75F).

☗ |●| HÔTEL DE LA PAIX**

3 place du 8-Octobre (Centre).
☎ 03.23.62.77.62 F➜ 03.23.62.66.03
Secure parking. **TV**. **Canal+**.

A pleasantly updated establishment with impressive 1914 architecture. There are two restaurants on the ground floor. *Le Bresilien* serves traditional specialities although you wouldn't think so from its name, and a gourmet set meal at 160F (rather expensive). *Le Carnotzet* has specialities from Savoy. You can eat there till quite late on in the evening. If you're on a tight budget, both places do pizzas. Doubles with shower/wc 285F (260F Friday–Sunday evening), with bath 320F (300F Friday–Sunday evening).

|●| RESTAURANT LE GLACIER

28 place de l'Hôtel-de-Ville (Centre).
☎ 03.23.62.27.09
Closed Mondays and Sunday evenings. **Car park**.

Service up to 11pm. A small restaurant with a dining room upstairs. It's well-decorated – a fresco on the wall, checked tablecloths and milk glass lamps. The restaurant opens onto the pretty Place de l'Hôtel-de-ville and in summer you can enjoy sitting on the terrace. You can have an ice-cream but the house specialities are mussels *en cocotte,* steak tartar and *choucroute* with shin of beef or with fish (68–88F), all served on a hotplate. Day's special 42F. Set meals at 78F, 99F, 115F and 135F are good value for money.

SAINT-VALÉRY-SUR-SOMME 80230

HÔTEL DU PORT ET DES BAINS*

1 quai Blavet; it's in the lower part of town right on the mouth of the Somme.
☎ 03.22.60.80.09
Closed for two weeks in November.

A nice little place with an ivy-covered façade, situated in a town with lots of different architectural styles and varied landscapes. We recommend the seafood – after all, it is the region for it. A word of warning – both of the restaurant's dining rooms are very busy. Set meals 81–184F. Very basic doubles 180F, 150F with no shower.

10% LE RELAIS GUILLAUME DE NORMANDIE**

46 quai Romerel; : it's very close to the upper part of town along the sea front near the Porte Nevers.
☎ 03.22.60.82.36 F 03.22.60.81.82
Closed Tuesdays (except in July and August) and in December. **Secure parking**. **TV**. **Canal+**.

Our favourite place in the Somme. This tall and narrow manor house, which is a bit of an architectural mishmash and very oddly shaped, stands in a superb garden. It was built at the water's edge about 100 years ago by an English lord for his mistress. All of the bedrooms have been renovated and are remarkably comfortable. Doubles 290F with shower/wc, and 340F with bath. Ask for one with a sea view or, even better, room number 1, which has a delightful little terrace. Set meals (80–210F) featuring delicious regional specialities are served in the beautiful refurbished dining room. However, the welcome is rather impersonal.

CROTOY (LE) 80550 (6KM N)

LES TOURELLES

2–4 rue Pierre Guerlain .
☎ 03.22.27.16.33 F 03.22.27.11.45.
Closed three weeks in January. **TV**.

If there's a vacancy, jump at it! There are only 19 rooms in the hotel, and since they're booked weeks in advance you should thank your lucky stars that you came along at just the right time. The red brick building, surmounted by two turrets, stands by the Baie de la Somme and used to belong to Pierre Guerlain of perfume fame. Everything's just about perfect. The very attractive restaurant overlooks the garden and serves French and Belgian dishes (Set meals 90F, 130F, and 160F). The delightful bedrooms have wonderful views (our favourites were number 33 in the keep and no 14 which faces due south). Relax in the bar lounge, decorated in the Swedish style that's all the rage at the moment. There's a play room for children and the hotel even has a pair of binoculars you can borrow to watch the seals!. Doubles 260–315F. Pets are allowed and if you're there during the week, the third night of your stay is free. Places like this are few and far between!

CHEZ GÉRARD

22 rue Victor-Petit; it's near the beach.
☎ 03.22.27.04.50
Closed Tuesdays.

This is a funny, friendly and very reliable gourmet restaurant on the Picardy coast. You'll find proprietor Gérard surrounded by bric-a-brac, naive paintings and locals with good repartee and he'll entertain and cook for you at the same time. The appealing 98F set meal offers mussels prepared according to his own special recipe or marinated mackerel followed by rack of salt-meadow lamb or sole *meunière*. There's another one at 190F.

SENLIS 60300

10% HÔTEL DU NORD**

110 rue de la République (Centre); it's on the A1 and the N17.
☎ 03.44.53.01.16 F 03.44.53.60.60
Closed Sunday evenings and Mondays Oct–April. **Secure parking**. **TV**.

This little hotel is a bit noisy but the eighteen bedrooms are very well kept. Doubles 170–240F. Good cooking with a *formule express* at 75F, and a nice set meal at 95F that changes frequently. This year's specialities are *ballotine* of salmon, terrine of citrus fruit with a kiwi fruit *coulis*, chicken livers and *foie gras* in a port sauce, *quenelles* of leeks with herbs, monkfish *à la picarde* and *craquant* of orange and cinammon. Another set meal comes in at 150F. You'll get a charming welcome.

FONTAINE-CHAALIS 60300 (8KM SE)

L'AUBERGE DE FONTAINE**

22 Grande-Rue (Centre); take the D330 towards Nanteuil-le-Haudoin.
☎ 03.44.54.20.22 F 03.44.60.25.38
Closed Tuesdays Oct 1–March 31. **Disabled access**.

The inn, very well-known in the area, has recently changed hands. Dominique, the new owner, has even bigger plans for it and we were captivated by his enthusiasm. The cheapest set meal is 95F (weekdays only), and there are three others ranging in price from 135F to 240F. The chef's specialities include the house *foie gras* with lavender, fillets of perch with *tapenade*, calf's sweetbreads with chanterelles and *foie gras,* roast salmon with honey, and rack of lamb à *la provencale.* There are eight clean and comfortable rooms. Doubles 255F with shower/wc, 275F with bath. This establishment is worth watching. Do write and let us know what you think – it'll give us the chance to sit back and have a rest for a change!

SOISSONS 02200

LE CLOVIS*

7 rue Ernest-Ringuier (Centre); it's near the town hall gardens.
☎ 03.23.59.26.57
Secure parking. **Disabled access**.

This is a hotel that's neither outstandingly beautiful nor ugly but which does have a certain amount of style. The owner's very friendly and takes pleasure in advising his guests on places to go and things to see. There are only eight bedrooms and some have a view of the Aisne while others look onto a private courtyard where part of the old city walls still survive. Doubles cost 125F withwashing facilities, 175F with bath, and there's also a wc on the landing. No TV, thank goodness.

10% LE POT D'ÉTAIN

7 rue de Saint-Quentin (Centre).
☎ 03.23.53.27.39
Closed Sunday evenings.

Just a basic hotel without any particularly outstanding features. The bathrooms and wcs could do with a little sprucing up, but the bedrooms are spick-and-span. Ideal if you're on a tight budget or travel a lot. The restaurant's home cooking will revive your flagging strength if you've been out exploring Picardy. *Terrines* and desserts are homemade. Set meals 65F–140F. Doubles with washing facilities 130F, with bath 150F. Half-board 190F per person. A cheap hotel which has the advantage of being centrally located.

VERVINS 02140

10% LA TOUR DU ROY***

45 rue du Général-Leclerc (Centre).
☎ 03.23.98.00.11 F 03.23.98.00.72
Secure parking. **TV**. **Canal+**. **Disabled access**.

So you've finally got your hands on the money you inherited from auntie or you just want to impress the latest love of your life. You decide to go back to your roots and find out more about the history of France and enjoy the peace and quiet of countryside at the same time. And here you are in the tower where Henry of Navarre was crowned king of France, surrounded by mediaeval furniture, an atmosphere to match, and with a view of the Thierache down below. But it's the food you'll find particularly memorable and you'll drool over the calf's sweetbreads and frog's legs in puff pastry,, the suckling pig with a honey crust, and the almond *croustillant* with a fruit sauce. Set meals 98F (weekday lunchtimes)–350F. Bedrooms start at 350F and go up to 800F for the duplex in the donjon. Go for a room overlooking the countryside – the views are wonderful. Yes, we know it's expensive, but why not splash out just this once?

ÉTRÉAUPONT 02580 (10KM N)

10% LE CLOS DU MONTVINAGE ET L'AUBERGE DU VAL DE L'OISE**

8 rue Albert-Ledent (Centre); take the N2.
☎ 03.23.97.91.10 F 03.23.97.48.92
Closed Sunday evenings (the restaurant is also closed Monday lunchtimes), one week in February, and Aug 5–23. **Secure parking**. **TV**. **Disabled access**.

We fell in love with this place. It's an enormous 19th century building standing in its own quiet grounds that has a few leisure facilities (pool tables, tennis courts, and bike hire) and, best of all, spacious comfortable bedrooms. Doubles 340–450F. A charming welcome that's not overdone. If you cross the Thon to the restaurant run by the same family, you can enjoy sautéd scallops and lobster or calf's sweetbreads with ceps. Set meal prices range from 95F (this one includes a quarter litre of wine but is not available Saturdays or Sundays) to 195F (this comes with an apéritif, a half-bottle of Bordeaux and coffee). This is definitely our favourite place in Thierache!

VILLERS-COTTERÊTS 02600

HÔTEL LE RÉGENT***

26 rue du Général-Mangin (Centre).
☎ 03.23.96.01.46 F 03.23.96.37.57

Closed Sunday evenings Nov–March (except pulic holidays). **Secure parking**. **TV**.

There's a 16th century coaching inn behind the 18th century façade. The hotel is run by the charming and very distinguished Madame Thiebaut and has seventeen bedrooms, all different from each other. Some are even classifed as historic monuments! They range in price from 250F to 340F with shower or bath, and from 375F to 385F with a whirlpool bath. A charming little hotel offering excellent value for money.

L'ORTHOGRAPHE

63 rue du Général-Leclerc.
☎ 03.23.96.30.84
Closed Wednesdays and Sunday evenings.

Here's a restaurant that's starting to make a name for itself. The cheapest set meal (120F) is definitely enough to make your mouth water – scallops in a langoustine-based sauce, a mixture of duck liver and smoked breast, duck in cider, rabbit with tarragon and, to finish, a scrumptious white chocolate mousse. Two other set meals are available at 150F and 180F. They also do an 89F lunchtime *formule* (weekdays) offering you your choice of main course from the à la carte menu plus dessert. Service with a smile.

LONGPONT 02600 (11.5KM NE)

10% HÔTEL DE L'ABBAYE**

rue des Tourelles (Centre); take the N2 then branch off onto the D2.
☎ 03.23.96.02.44 F 03.23.96.02.44
Secure parking. **TV**.

Here's the inn of your dreams! It's on the edge of the forest of Retz, has an ivy covered façade and stone fireplaces. The rooms are a bit pricy but you'll get a hearty breakfast. Expect to pay 180–330F (for a double with bath). Ask for number 112 – it's one of the cheapest but the shower's in the corridor. Set meals are expensive but the cooking's decent. If you're planning to take a look round the magnificent abbey on the opposite side of the street, it's worth remembering that you can always pop in here to sample the mouthwatering pancakes. There's a slightly romantic feel to this place.

Poitou-Charentes

16 Charente

17 Charente-Maritime

79 Deux-Sèvres

86 Vienne

AIX (ILE D') 17123

10% HÔTEL-RESTAURANT LE NAPOLÉON**

rue Gourgaud (Centre); it's accessible only by boat.
☎ 05.46.84.66.02 F→ 05.46.84.69.70
Closed Nov 15–Dec 30 and Jan 5–30.

If you've come here looking for absolute peace and quiet you won't have any problems deciding where to stay — *Le Napoléon* is the only place open. It's comfortable and welcoming and has about 15 bedrooms. Three date from 1993 and the others, renovated in 1987, have also been up-dated. Doubles 360F with shower/wc and 390F with bath. Half-board (300F per person) compulsory July–Aug. Cheapest set meal 90F (summer months), others 110F and 160F. The seafood is local — it hasn't come hundreds of miles in a refrigerated lorry. There's storage for bikes (bikes can also be hired) but no cars are allowed on the island.

ANGOULÊME 16000

10% AUBERGE DE JEUNESSE

île de Bourgine (North).
☎ 05.45.92.45.80 F→ 05.45.95.90.71
Closed Dec 23–Jan 10. **Car park**. **Disabled access**.

Not far from the Houmeau district (the old port of Angoulême), or to be more precise on the île de Bourgine. Roomy, well-kept hostel, dynamic staff. It has a large riverside terrace and an enormous dining room that's homely, friendly and cosmopolitan. Lots of activities — disco, canoeing, mountainbiking, swimming and tennis to name but a few. There's a wonderful walk called the *Coulée verte* that you can take along the river Charente and when you get to the end there's a pool where you can have a dip. And last but not least, you'll get good cooking (prices start at only 48F) and pleasant accommodation. You'll pay 66F each in a room with six beds or 86F in a twin. Prices include breakfast. What more could you ask for?

10% LE GASTÉ

381 route de Bordeaux (South-West).
☎ 05.45.91.89.98 F→ 05.45.25.24.67
Closed Saturday and Sunday evenings, Aug 1–21, and Dec 23–Jan 7. **Secure parking**. **TV**.

An unobtrusive roadside hotel known for its hospitality and good food. Set meal at 64F. Clean simple refurbished bedrooms with shower/wc at prices that won't break the bank. Doubles 135F with washing facilities and 155F with shower/wc. Pleasant terrace. It's worth taking a walk round the ramparts.

LE CRAB**

27 rue Kléber-La Grand-Font (East); from the station go towards Libourne as far as the sports centre.
☎ 05.45.95.51.80 F→ 05.45.95.38.52
Closed Saturdays. **Car park**. **TV**. **Canal+**.

A cosy inn outside town — there may be a lively bar but you'll find it's quiet. The large dining room has just been refurbished. Good regional dishes such as breast of duck and braised crab with Pineau. Set meals 60F (lunchtimes), 78F and 160F. Bedrooms have also recently been updated. Doubles 140F with washing facilities and 240F with bath.

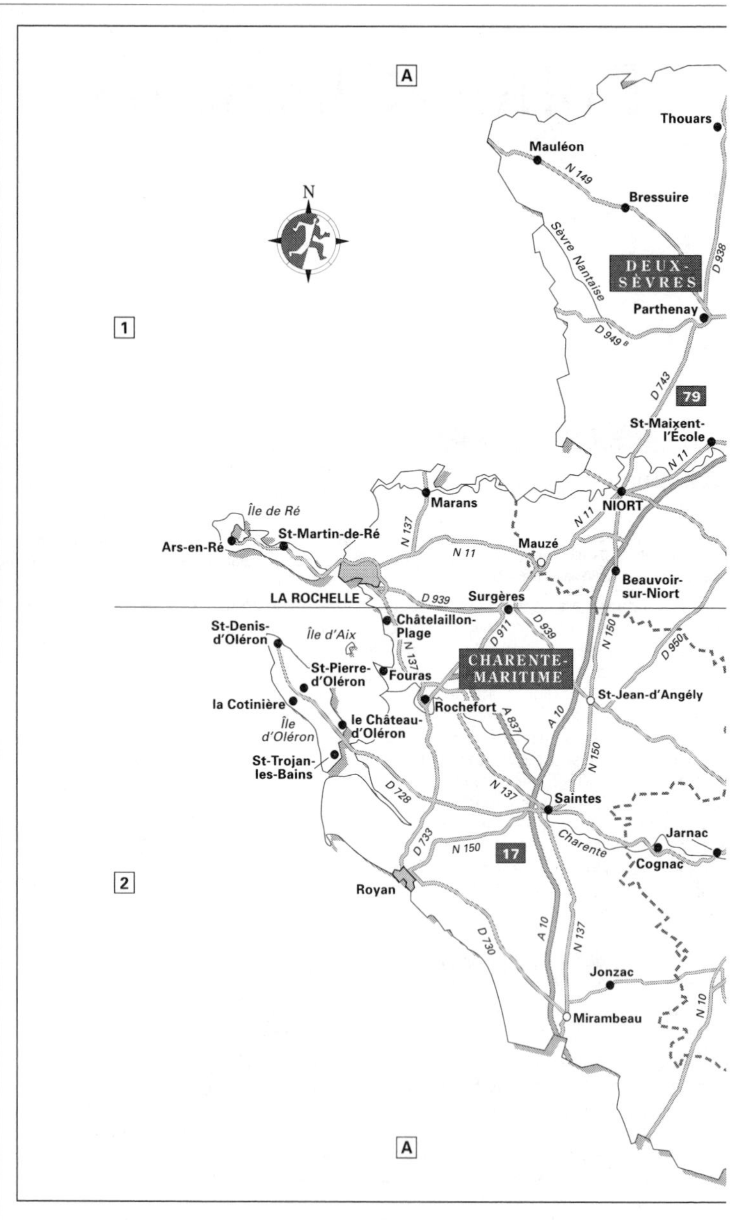
A
N
1
2
Thouars
Mauléon
N 149
Bressuire
Sèvre Nantaise
DEUX-SÈVRES
D 938
Parthenay
D 949 B
D 743
79
St-Maixent-l'École
N 11
Marans
NIORT
Île de Ré
St-Martin-de-Ré
N 137
Ars-en-Ré
N 11
Mauzé
N 11
Beauvoir-sur-Niort
LA ROCHELLE
D 939
Surgères
Châtelaillon-Plage
D 939
St-Denis-d'Oléron
Île d'Aix
D 911
N 150
D 950
N 137
CHARENTE-MARITIME
St-Pierre-d'Oléron
Fouras
la Cotinière
Rochefort
A 837
A 10
St-Jean-d'Angély
Île d'Oléron
le Château-d'Oléron
N 150
St-Trojan-les-Bains
D 728
N 137
Saintes
Charente
Jarnac
D 733
N 150
17
Cognac
Royan
D 730
A 10
N 137
Jonzac
N 10
Mirambeau
A

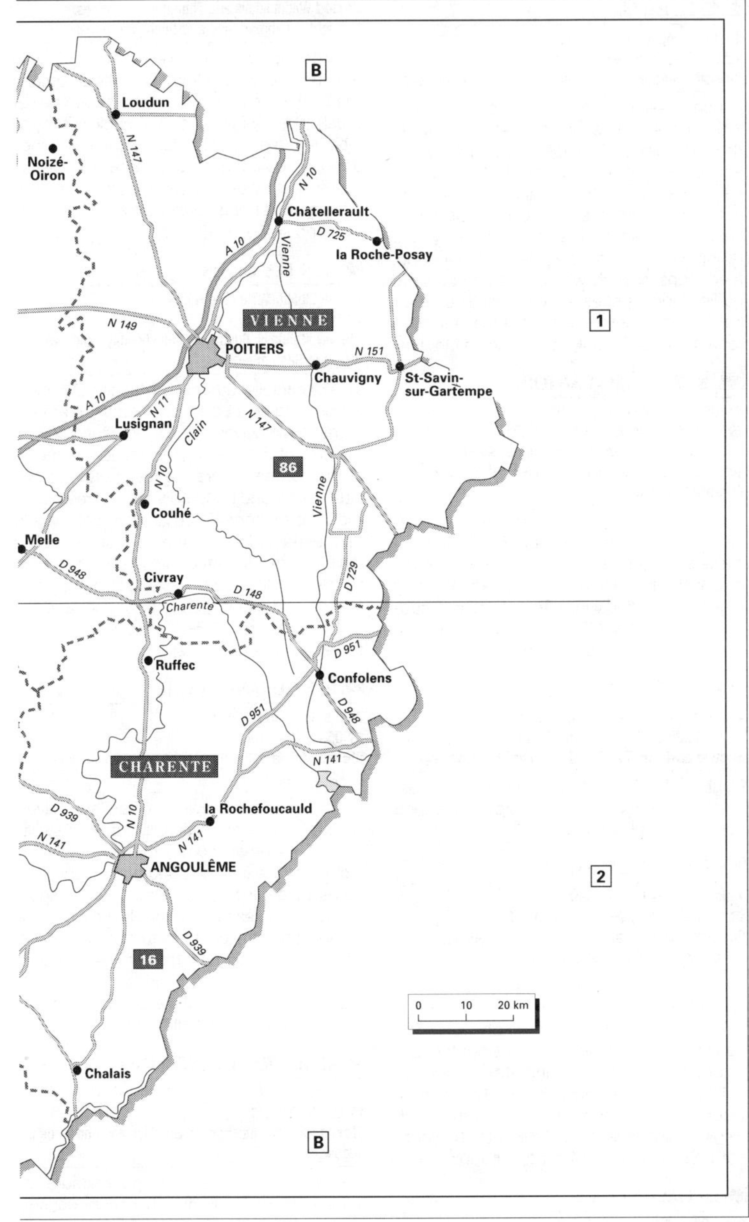
B
Loudun
N 147
Noizé-
Oiron
N 10
Châtellerault
D 725
la Roche-Posay
A 10
Vienne
VIENNE
1
N 149
POITIERS
N 151
Chauvigny
St-Savin-
sur-Gartempe
A 10
N 11
Lusignan
Clain
N 147
86
N 10
Couhé
Vienne
Melle
D 948
Civray
D 148
D 729
Charente
D 951
Ruffec
Confolens
D 951
D 948
N 141
CHARENTE
D 939
la Rochefoucauld
N 10
N 141
N 141
ANGOULÊME
2
D 939
16
0
10
20 km
Chalais
B

LE PALMA

4 rampe d'Aguesseau (Centre).
☎ 05.45.95.22.89 F➜ 05.45.94.26.66.
Closed Sundays and two weeks at the end of the year.

Lunch served 11.45am–2pm, dinner 7.30–9.45pm. This district, just next door to the old town of Angoulême, is more urban and paradoxically more old-fashioned. But *Le Palma*'s local cooking and the restaurant itself are worth the trip. *Cagouilles* (small snails) *à la charentaise*, casserole of young rabbit with lentils, *paupiette* of salt cod, medallions of lamb with thyme and *confit* of garlic. Good prices — cheapest set meal 64F. Friendly informal staff. Pleasant bedrooms. Doubles 160F with washing facilities.

10% LE SAINT-ANTOINE**

31 rue Saint-Antoine (North-West).
☎ 05.45.68.38.21 F➜ 05.45.69.10.31
Restaurant closed Saturday lunchtimes, Sunday evenings and at Christmas. **Car park**. **TV**. **Canal+**. **Disabled access**.

New and easy to get to. The terrace is pleasant and the dining room has a fireplace. Specialities such as escalope of warm duck *foie gras* with Pineau and melon, breast of young pigeon, and duck legs with buttered cabbage. Set meals 85F, 120F, 150F; à la carte also available. Doubles from 190F.

LE FLORE**

414 route de Bordeaux (South-West).
☎ 05.45.25.35.35 F➜ 05.45.25.34.69
Secure parking. **TV**. **Canal+**. **Closed** Sundays.

Doubles 195F with shower/wc or bath. Set meals 80F, 125F and 175F. Expect to spend about 160F à la carte.

10% HÔTEL DU PALAIS**

4 place Francis-Louvel (Centre).
☎ 05.45.92.54.11 F➜ 05.45.92.01.83
Restaurant closed Saturday evenings and Sundays. **Secure parking**. **TV**. **Canal+**.

It looks onto a pretty little square near the cathedral. The façade is one of the most beautiful of its kind in the south-west. The hotel has an old-fashioned style but the rustic and provincial décor and atmosphere are delightful and it deserves its good reputation. Courteous welcome. Doubles from 210F with washing facilities to 330F with shower or bath. Suites 330–370F for two people.

LE GASTRO-CAVE

3 rue Trois-Notre-Dame (Centre).
☎ 05.45.92.45.47
Closed Wednesdays and Thursday lunchtimes, a fortnight in February and a fortnight in October.

Service noon–2pm and 7–11pm. A little restaurant in the old town that offers some of the best value for money in the area. The set meals (60–125F) offer a wide choice. They all include a meat or fish dish and the helpings are generous. Classical cooking with dishes of the south-west featuring prominently. Terrific *cassoulet* and *confit* of duck. Quick service and smiling staff.

SUR LES QUAIS

24 rue Cloche-Verte (Centre).
☎ 05.45.95.18.06
Closed Mondays, Sundays, public holidays and two weeks in September.

This remarkably attractive 17th century building used to be a bookshop and there are still some bookshelves left. It's nice eating out in the cool of the evening — you've the choice of the garden, where the roses grow alongside the ivy and hundred year old trees, or in the conservatory. When autumn sets in you can retreat indoors to the cosy stone-walled dining room decorated with photos of actors. Good mixed salads, pasta, calf's liver with orange and green grapes or bacon, and the dish of the day (48–64F). Service with a smile. A very romantic spot.

RESTAURANT LA CITÉ

28 rue Saint-Roch (Centre).
☎ 05.45.92.42.69
Closed Mondays, Sundays, February school holidays, and Aug 1–15.

A smiling efficient owner, clean attractively set tables and exceptionally fresh fish specialities. In other words, the kind of family restaurant we like! Seafood platter, shellfish, home-made fish soup, home-made squid fritters and fricassee of mussels are just a few of the dishes the chef has to offer. In spite of his obvious passion for the sea, he also does grilled breast of duck and braised veal sweetbreads. Set meals 72F (except Saturdays), 98F (very good), 120F and 155F.

RESTAURANT LANE-XANG

29 rue de Genève.
☎ 05.45.38.43.11
Closed Saturday lunchtimes, Sundays and one week in August.

The town has a few foreign restaurants, some of them Asian, and this rather unusual Laotian one took us by surprise. Even Paris doesn't have many places like this! Pleasant décor with beautiful fabric on the walls. The *Lane-Xang* (the name means "a million elephants") offers dishes from various Asian countries but you've got to try the Laotian ones first — *tom yam* (spicy fish, prawn and chicken soup), steamed monkfish Laotian style, *lap* (steak tartare Laotian style) and *kaotom* (rice pudding with coconut milk and banana served in a banana leaf). If staff were a bit better organised and the portions a bit bigger, this little place would be a pretty good restaurant. Set meal 78F.

LA RUELLE

6 rue des Trois-Notre-Dame (Centre).
☎ 05.45.92.94.64
Closed Saturday lunchtimes, Sundays, one week in January, one week in February, one week in April and three weeks in August.

Gourmet travellers on the lookout for new experiences will find Véronique Dauphin's cooking gives them food for thought. During her extensive travels she has been to places such as Amsterdam, Réunion and Provence and she offers imaginative dishes that incorporate the different spices and flavours she encountered. Perfectly reasonable à la carte prices. The favourites have got to be *vinaigrette* of monkfish with spices, panfried veal sweetbreads with broad beans, and guinea fowl with walnuts and apple chutney. Very good set meals 170F (lunchtimes only, includes wine and coffee), 260F. Top of the range wine list at reasonable prices. Every day two wines can be bought by the glass.

GOND-PONTOUVRE (LE) 16160 (2KM N)

LA TRUITE SAUMONÉE

83 route de Vars.
☎ 05.45.68.77.67
Car park.

This nice old-fashioned inn serves traditional dishes that are decent but nothing to go into raptures over to country people (and that's not meant to be pejorative). You can sit in peaceful surroundings on the shaded terrace at the back and have one of the three set meals–65F (starter, main course and dessert), 125F or the gourmet one at 165F. Dishes are based on what the market has to offer and the meat comes straight from the Angoulême abattoir. The chef's specialities include panfried veal sweetbreads with morels, warm *foie gras* of duck with apples and chicken fricassee with chanterelle mushrooms. Staff are friendly and polite. Nine bedrooms, very basic with shower/wc, for people passing through. Try for number 2 overlooking the courtyard.

L'ENTRECÔTE

45 route de Paris.
☎ 05.45.68.04.52
Closed Saturday lunchtimes, Sundays and the week starting Aug 15. **Car park. Disabled access.**

Service noon–2pm and 8–9.30pm. The best meat restaurant in Angoulême is this cosy place that resembles a tavern. The main attraction's the enormous rib steak grilled over a woodfire. You might think 95F is a bit much but it's well worth the price — you'd probably have to go to Argentina to find the same quality. Not only do they show you your portion before cooking it (just in case you think it's too big) but they cook it exactly the way you want it. We also recommend the enormous rib of beef for families and those who haven't eaten for ages — absolutely wonderful. Smiling owners and perfect service. They'll give you two plates if you want to share a dessert. A pretty good restaurant.

PUYMOYEN 16400 (7KM S)

10% L'AUBERGE DES ROCHERS

How to get there: it's opposite the church.
☎ 05.45.61.25.77
Car park.

A country house ideal for holidaying with family or friends — basic, quiet and quite cheap. Set meals 60–120F. Doubles 100F with basin. Full board is 190F per person — a pretty good deal — and half-board 160F. Friendly staff. There's a lovely paper mill (*Le Moulin du Verger*) nearby, and high stone cliffs will attract rock climbers. And then there's the deer farm — the animals are left to roam about but, if you fancy a closer look, they'll come running when the farmer whistles.

CHAMPNIERS 16430 (9KM NE)

HÔTEL CLIMAT DE FRANCE**

N10.
☎ 05.45.68.03.22 F→ 05.45.69.07.67
Car park. TV. Canal+. Disabled access.

A well-designed hotel with a conservatory cum lounge looking onto the garden. Doubles from 290F. No eating facilities but there's a restaurant (*Le Feu de Bois*) nearby.

RESTAURANT LE FEU DE BOIS**

N10.
☎ 05.45.68.69.96

Car park. **Disabled access**.

Lunch served noon–2pm, dinner 7.30–10.15pm. Before you get onto the N10 take a little detour into the rolling wooded countryside between Champniers and Les Cloux and admire the traditional houses with their attractive tiled roofs. The restaurant is something else altogether. It has a large octagonal dining room and meat is grilled in the centre of the room over old vine roots. Regional specialities include grilled ham. Set meals 83F, 105F, 145F and 175F.

RESTAURANT LE LOGIS D'ARGENCE

La Chignolle.
☎ 05.45.69.99.93
Closed Sunday evenings and Mondays. **Car park**.

A traditional little inn with a terrace overlooking the small garden.The new owner, who arrived early in 1995, is very nice. Pleasant décor and imaginative, tasty dishes based on local produce. Try the scallops with *foie gras*. Set meals 85–160F.

MOUTHIERS-SUR-BOËME 16440 (13KM S)

CAFÉ-RESTAURANT DE LA GARE

place de la Gare.
☎ 05.45.67.94.24
Closed Sunday evenings. **Car park**.

Service 11.15am–3pm and 7–10pm. The valley of the Boëme is a must — the road behind the church will take you there. The beautiful dining room is another welcome sight — hospitable staff on hand and good cooking. The 60F set meal offers soup, starter, main course, cheese, dessert, coffee and a quarter litre of wine — not much room for improvement. Other set meals 85F, 95F, 110F and 130F.

CHAZELLES 16380 (20KM E)

RESTAURANT LES GROTTES DU QUEROY

☎ 05.45.23.53.85
Closed Wednesdays (except July-Aug). **Car park**. **Disabled access**.

You could very easily forget all about town life as you sit here on this large terrace, especially since there is evidence of prehistoric man only 50m away, in the form of caves that are 4,000–5,000 years old. They were discovered 100 years ago by a woman out looking for her dog. This is a good place for children and adults aliike. Have the trout *meunière* with almonds cooked *à la bretonne* — the fish is caught nearby. Set meals 72–155F. The *foie gras* is excellent.

VIBRAC 16120 (22KM W)

10% LES OMBRAGES**

route Claude-Bonnier.
☎ 05.45.97.32.33 Fax 05.45.97.32.05
Closed Sunday evenings and Mondays in winter.
Car park. **TV**.

Lunch served noon–2pm, dinner 7.30–9.30pm. In the 14th century the people of France spent a lot of time on the road and had enormous appetites. The abbey of Bassac, not far from Vibrac in the direction of Saint-Jacques-de-Compostelle, was a popular stopping place for travellers in the Middle Ages. Nowadays, this hotel cum restaurant with its shaded garden is keen on emphasizing the health aspect — outdoor pool, tennis courts and table tennis. Very pleasant setting, with lots of greenery around. There are two dining rooms, one in a conservatory overlooking the garden. Try the *croustade* of oysters. Set meals 70F (except weekends), 105–170F and à la carte. Bedrooms 270F with shower/wc and 300F with bath.

VILLEBOIS-LAVALETTE 16320 (28KM SE)

HÔTEL-RESTAURANT DU COMMERCE

How to get there: take the D939.
☎ 05.45.64.90.30
Closed Tuesday afternoons.

From this hillside village you'll get a wonderful view of the fields disappearing over the horizon, making you feel at one with nature. A simple set meal of starter, main course, cheese, dessert, coffee and a quarter litre of wine costs all of 55F (65F weekends). Other set meals 95–135F. Doubles 180F with shower/wc. You'll see something rather unexpected on the way to Angoulême — a life-size replica of a Versailles façade built on the edge of a forest using salvaged materials and sculptures from the real Versailles.

SAINT-GROUX 16230 (30KM N)

10% HÔTEL-RESTAURANT LES TROIS SAULES**

How to get there: take the N10 as far as Mansle then the D739 towards Aigre — it's about 3km from there.
☎ 05.45.20.31.40 Fax 05.45.22.73.81
Closed February school holidays and November.
Car park. **TV**. **Disabled access**.

The village, which stands at a bend in the river, was named after a hermit who lived in Angoumois in the 16th century. This is a cosy attractive inn with attentive staff. Try the scallops in Pineau, the sole with ceps, and the quail with *foie gras*. Set meals 60F (except Sundays), 85F, 130F, 165F and à la carte. Doubles 197F with shower/wc and 230F with bath. Half-board 200F.

ARS-EN-RÉ 17590

LE PARASOL**

route de Saint-Clément; it's as you leave Ars and head for Saint-Clément.
☎ 05.46.29.46.17 ➡ 05.46.29.05.09
Closed Nov 15–March 1. **Car park**. **TV**.
Disabled access.

A very good location away from traffic. The buildings, surrounded by pine forest, are on a human scale. Studio flats with kitchenette 410–450F depending on the season. Doubles from 365F (345F out of season). Half-board (320–385F). is compulsory June–September. Set meals 125–189F.

RESTAURANT LE CAFÉ DU COMMERCE

☎ 05.46.29.41.57
How to get there: it'sby the harbour.
Disabled access.

If you fancy a spot of lunch (or dinner) by the harbour, you'd be better off coming here than going to Saint-Martin. Toni and Pierre Ollivier have turned the *Café du Commerce* into a popular hangout for a large number of locals and Parisians who enjoy coming to Portes, Ars and Saint-Clément. There's so much to choose from, including crêpes, seafood, Tex-Mex specialities and bistro dishes. It may not be the finest cuisine (and the quality is tending to drop) but the prices are more than reasonable compared with other places on the island. Six medium oysters 41F, chilli 44.50F, *galette complète* 39.50F, grilled *andouillette* 57F, and cheeseburger 50.50F. Several children's meals at 39.50F. Wine sold by the glass. In the evening sit with a cocktail and watch the boats.

LE BISTROT DE BERNARD

1 quai de la Criée.
☎ 05.46.29.40.26 ➡ 05.46.29.28.99
Closed Monday evenings and Tuesdays out of season, and Jan 5–Feb 15.

The terrace makes an ideal place for discreet people-watching — you get a wonderful view from the harbour in summertime. If you don't like crowds but hate feeling shut in, you'll appreciate the fact that Bernard Frigière's dining room has large windows overlooking a garden. As you would expect, fish and seafood feature largely here and dishes vary depending on what the market has to offer — the one in Ars is held every day in season and is one of the islanders' favourites. Set meals 130F and 175F. Some wines are sold by the glass (15–20F), a good idea since it means you won't spend a fortune. Children's meal 50F.

SAINT-CLÉMENT-DES-BALEINES 17590 (4KM NW)

LE CHAT BOTTÉ**

place de l'Église.
☎ 05.46.29.21.93 ➡ 05.46.29.29.97
Closed Jan 5–Feb 6 and Dec 1 -15. **Car park**. **TV**.
Disabled access.

A charming peaceful hotel opposite the church that has bright rooms with lots of wood. Try for number 5 or 6 which are all wood. Have breakfast (43F for the traditional one or 60F for the energy-packed one) on the flower-filled patio before settling down to a spot of sunbathing away from the crowds on one of the loungers dotted about the large and beautiful garden. And to add to your enjoyment, the hotel has a small health complex with mineral baths, seaweed treatment and other facilities and two tennis courts. Doubles 340–380F with shower/wc and 360–580F with bath (out of season). Covered storage for bikes.

RESTAURANT LE CHAT BOTTÉ

2 rue de la Mairie.
☎ 05.46.29.42.09 ➡ 05.46.29.29.77
Closed Mondays out of season and Jan 8–Feb 15.
Car park.

Service 12.15–2pm and 7.30–9.30pm. Owner Daniel Massé, brother of Chantal and Géraldine, is regarded as one of the best chefs on the island. The cheapest set meal 125F (weekdays) is well put together. Some of the chef's specialities — bass *en croûte* and turbot with clams — feature in the 175F and 265F set meals. Large attractive dining room and a terrace that faces due south. Stylish service. Children's set meal 65F.

PORTES-EN-RÉ (LES) 17880 (10KM N)

RESTAURANT LE CHASSE-MARÉE

1 rue Jules-David.

☎ 05.46.29.52.03 ➡ 05.46.29.62.10
Closed Mondays and Tuesdays except during school holidays, and Nov 15–April 1.

Lunch served 12.30–2pm, dinner 7.30–10pm. A delightful and elegant restaurant in the island's most chic village. The walls are hung with a number of interesting paintings of the *Chasse-Marée* by various artists, an piano and a trombone sit in a corner, and a motley collection of second-hand objects complements the table layout. Several set meals (125, 165 and 250F). The customers are mainly Parisians who're regulars here. The 125F set meal was well planned and could not be faulted in terms of either flavour or presentation. The chef particularly recommends his fillets of raw marinated sardines, langoustine tails in puff pastry and bass *en croûte* with leeks.

BEAUVOIR-SUR-NIORT 79360

L'AUBERGE DES VOYAGEURS

41 place de l'Hôtel-de-Ville.
☎ 05.49.09.70.16 ➡ 05.49.09.65.78

Jean-Claude Batiot, the owner of this charming stone-walled village inn, proudly serves typical regional cuisine. You can't leave without sampling his snail fricassee, the recipe for which came from his grandmother (take snails whose shells are too brittle for them to be prepared in the normal way, cook them in stock and then sauté them with potatoes, mushrooms, garlic, parsley and shreds of country ham). *Gratin* of eels and a few other specialities are also available. Set meals 130–325F, cheapest 75F.

VILLIERS-EN-BOIS 79360 (10KM SE)

10% L'AUBERGE DES CÈDRES

☎ 05.49.76.79.53 ➡ :05.49.76.79.81
Closed Sunday evenings, Mondays and February.
Car park. **Disabled access**.

A very clean and unpretentious little restaurant on the edge of the forest of Chizé. Everyone makes their way here at Sunday lunchtime to try "the owner's cooking" — he emphasizes this point in case anyone should have doubts. Set meals 60F (except Sundays)– 178F. À la carte there's warm oysters in puff pastry with leeks, fricassee of eels with young garlic and escalope of salmon with fresh sorrel from the garden. They also have a few quiet rooms at 165F and 210F.

BRESSUIRE 79300

HÔTEL-RESTAURANT LA BOULE D'OR**

15 place Émile-Zola (South-West); it's near the station.
☎ 05.49.65.02.18 ➡ 05.49.74.11.19
Closed Sunday evenings, Monday lunchtimes, the first three weeks in January, and the first three weeks in August. Secure **car park**. **TV**. **Canal+**.

This establishment successfully combines good cooking (but there are no surprises) with a rather plush and comfortable interior. Cheapest set meal 67F. Doubles 230F with shower/wc. Four people can share for 280F. Warm welcome.

HÔTEL-RESTAURANT LA SAPINIÈRE**

route de Boismé (via boulevard de l'Europe) (South-East); 2.5km from the centre turn off the Bressuire south-east bypass and take the tiny road between the Niort and Parthenay roads and head for Boismé; it's 400m along on the left.
☎ 05.49.74.24.22 ➡ :05.49.65.80.38
Restaurant closed Sunday evenings.
Secure **car park**. **TV**. **Canal+**. **Disabled access**.

Service noon–2pm and 7.30–9pm. Deep in the country and with a great location next to a quiet lake. The customers are a bit more lively at the weekend, but between Monday and Friday it's heaven on earth for fishermen and people of a melancholy disposition. Doubles — some of them a bit dreary — start at 240F. Set meals 85F, 110F and 145F. Welcome can't be faulted.

CHALAIS 16210

LE RELAIS DU CHÂTEAU

château des Talleyrand.
☎ 05.45.98.23.58
Closed Tuesday evenings and Wednesdays (except in summer) and February school holidays. **Car park**.

This enormous 14th century castle dominates the valley of the Tude and the Vivonne rivers and offers a splendid view. You get to the restaurant by means of a drawbridge (it still works). Period décor and a vaulted ceiling make for a handsome dining room. The à la carte menu is a journey back in time. Give in to temptation and sample the various kinds of *foie gras*. Set meals 95F (even Sundays)– 210F. Children's 50F. Car park available for motorhomes.

CHARROUX 86250

HOSTELLERIE CHARLEMAGNE**

7 rue de Rochemeaux (Centre); it's beside the remains of the abbey, opposite the covered food market.
☎ 05.49.87.50.37
Closed Sunday evenings out of season. **Car park. TV.**

It's hard to imagine Charroux as a cultural and religious capital in the 11th century, when it had 40,000 inhabitants and a large abbey (one tower is about all that's left of it). The inn, built from the abbey's stones, takes us back in time to this rich period in history. The dining room's like something out of a cloak and dagger story. Tasty dishes such as ox cheek with cherries and bilberries, roast rack of lamb with herbs, and a selection of fresh and salt water fish with thyme. Doubles 155F with basin (no TV) and 185F with shower/wc. We've a special liking for number 8 with its bathroom of dressed stone. The prices are rather good too. Set meals 80F, 140F and 190F. Just a pity that the mood of the staff changes with the season.

CHÂTEAU-D'OLÉRON (LE) 17480

10% HÔTEL DE FRANCE**

11 rue du Maréchal-Foch (Centre).
☎ 05.46.47.60.07 Fax 05.46.75.21.55
Restaurant closed Sunday evenings, Mondays October–April, and Dec 24–Jan 20. **TV.**

Service noon–1.30pm and 7–9pm. A decent hotel if you want to spend some time in this historical village, which still has solid reminders of its military past in the form of a citadel and ramparts built by Vauban, Louis XIV's expert in fortifications. Doubles 240–280F with shower/wc or bath. Half-board (260–300F) is optional. Wonderful restaurant with set meals at 88F (weekdays), 148F and 195F. Children's set meal 55F.

BOURCEFRANC-LE-CHAPUS 17560 (7KM SE)

10% HÔTEL-RESTAURANT LE TERMINUS**

port du Chapus
☎ 05.46.85.02.42 Fax 05.46.85.32.39
Car park. TV.

Whether you're staying at the hotel or have come to try the restaurant, you'll get a lovely view of the harbour, Île d'Oléron and tiny Fort Louvois (you can look round it at low tide). Bedrooms 210F with shower and wc on the landing, 240F with bath. Set meals 80F, 110F, 130F and 160F. Mostly seafood dishes. Staff speak English, German, Italian and Spanish.

CAYENNE (LA) 17320 (15KM SE)

RESTAURANT LA VERTE OSTREA

port de La Cayenne.
☎ 05.46.85.36.00 Fax 05.46.85.20.13
Closed Mondays and Thursday evenings.

They have a most acceptable 65F set meal available weekday lunchtimes consisting of seven oysters, grilled sardines and fruit tart of the day. Other set meals 97F (oysters and *tarte Tatin*) and 144F (very filling). Specialities include *blanquette* of shark, eel with chopped parsley and garlic, sole in a salt crust, and seafood paella. The produce is always fresh, the portions are more than generous, and the prices are reasonable — three essential qualities for a good establishment. There's even a pleasant terrace looking out to sea.

RONCE-LES-BAINS 17390 (18.5KM S)

10% HÔTEL LE GRAND CHALET**

2 av. de la Cèpe (Centre).
☎ 05.46.36.06.41 Fax 05.46.36.38.87
Closed Tuesdays and Nov 15–Feb 15. **Car park.**

Ronce-les-Bains, near the forest of Coubre and the superb beaches of this part of the world, has that quiet charm of an old-fashioned seaside resort. Families are especially attracted by the relaxed atmosphere and the beautiful post-war villas surrounded by pine trees. *Le Grand Chalet,* down by the water, is known not only for its hospitality but also for its restaurant, *Le Brise-Lames.* We got to look round the impeccably clean kitchens. Madame Moinardeau's in charge of the cooking and she doesn't put a foot wrong. Set meals 69F and 89F (lunchtimes except Sundays), 130F, 185F (fish) and 230F (gourmet). Doubles with shower/wc or bath cost 200F if they're at the front. In season, you'll pay 290F for a sea view (290–335F out of season). Half-board 280–320F per person. Home-made bread and pastries. Terrace facing the sea.

CHÂTELAILLON-PLAGE 17340

10% HÔTEL LES GOÉLANDS*

69 bd de la Mer (Centre).
☎ 05.46.56.18.68
Closed end Sept–start April (except Easter weekend).

A clean basic seafront hotel with a few bedrooms facing the sea (sunlit in the afternoon). The beach is within easy reach just across the esplanade – two strides and you're there! What could be better? Doubles with bath/wc and sea view 180F (250F in season).

10% ☗ HÔTEL D'ORBIGNY**

47 bd de la République (North).
☎ 05.46.56.24.68 ➡ 05.46.30.04.82
Closed Nov 30–March 15. **Secure parking**. **TV**.

This large hotel 150m from the beach was a holiday home at the start of the century. It has a swimming pool – a great plus. The tide goes out a good kilometre at Châtellaillon so you'll be glad of the pool while you're waiting for high tide again. There's table tennis too, so you can indulge in a bit of sport before going for another dip. Try for a room on the first floor as they've all been refurbished. Doubles 230–280F with shower/wc.

CHÂTELLERAULT 86100

10% ☗ 🍽 LE CROISSANT**

15 av. J.F.-Kennedy (Centre).
☎ 05.49.21.01.77 ➡ 05.49.21.57.92
Restaurant closed Sunday evenings (except July-Aug), Mondays, and during Christmas week. **TV**.

Descartes used to live in this exceptionally quiet part of the world. *Le Croissant* is a sun-filled hotel cum restaurant and the light gives an old-fashioned country feel to the place – you can picture generations of families meeting here for Sunday lunch. Olive green imitation leather, salmon pink tablecloths, lots of pot plants and a wonderful aquarium full of tropical fish. Set meals 80F, 100F, 120F and 180F. Local dishes such as veal sweetbreads *à la rabelaisienne*, *tournedos* of duck in aspic made with aged Chinon and fillet of zander with tarragon. Perfectly delightful bedrooms. Doubles 210F with shower/wc and 240F with bath.

🍽 HOSTELLERIE NOTRE-DAME

8 place Notre-Dame.
☎ 05.49.21.05.85
Closed Sundays except by reservation (minimum of ten people) and Monday evenings Aug 15–30. **Car park**.

Lunch served noon–2pm, dinner 7–10pm. An unpretentious family inn on the banks of the Vienne with a bar, three dining rooms and a terrace. Good simple dishes and friendly staff. You can't leave without trying the snails that they breed themselves. The 53F set meal is available at lunchtime and in the evening. À la carte there's stuffed snails, fish soup, rare rib steak or beef flank with shallots.

BEAUMONT 86490 (14KM S)

🍽 RESTAURANT LA BOHÈME

la Tricherie; it's as you leave la Tricherie by the N10.
☎ 05.49.85.51.74.
Car park.

Owner Jacques, born in Paris in the 13th arrondissement to Armenian parents, was a tailor by trade and was made redundant in 1976. The inn is more than 600 years old and the enormous fireplace was all that remained intact when Jacques bought it. He restored it to its former self, incorporating vaulted ceilings and exposed stonework. He's such a big-hearted guy and so proud to be the owner. Traditional dishes and Armenian specialities (these have to be ordered in advance). Set meals 60F (weekdays), 75F, 95F and 130F. We're very fond of this place and its owners so even if you don't have time for a meal, have a drink in the bar.

DANGÉ-SAINT-ROMAIN 86220 (14KM N)

10% ☗ 🍽 LA CHAUMIÈRE

21 rue Saint-Romain.
☎ 05.49.86.40.38
Closed Sunday and Monday evenings, Christmas and February. **Car park**.

There's not much we can say about the décor except that it's flowery. But what does that matter? – people come here to eat and they certainly don't go away disappointed. Five set meals 80–260F. Francis Polo may only use simple ingredients but he has an expert hand and the end result is much greater than the sum of its parts. Lots of meat and poultry dishes such as chicken breast glazed with a red wine sauce. And don't miss out on the apple and orange *mille-feuille* for dessert – absolute heaven. The staff are friendly and the service is faultless. A good restaurant.

☗ 🍽 LE DAMIUS**

16 rue de la Gare.
☎ 05.49.86.40.28 ➡ 05.49.93.13.69
Closed Sunday evenings, Mondays and Dec 23–Jan 15. **Secure parking**. **TV**.

Lunch served noon–2pm, dinner 8–10pm. A little family-run hotel lovingly looked after by Michel and Martine Malbrant. The restaurant overlooks the terrace and there's a garden specially designed for kids. Good home cooking. Set meals 82–185F. Try the duck *rillettes*, the house *terrine*, and, if you're really feeling adventurous, the pig's trotters *Sainte-Menehould*. Doubles 270F with shower/wc, 300F with bath and 340F based on four sharing. The hotel is completely soundproof but light sleepers should note that the TGV line runs past the hotel. A good place for a short stay.

DISSAY 86130 (19KM SW)

10% ☗ |●| HÔTEL-RESTAURANT BINJAMIN**

N10.
☎ 05.49.52.42.37 F➜ 05.49.62.59.06
Closed Saturday lunchtimes, Sunday evenings, and Mondays. **Car park**. **TV**.

Service noon–1.45pm and 7.45–9.30pm. Unusual architecture — a not altogether successful combination of squares and circles. Attractive restaurant with green furniture, lots of flowers, and tables set with china and silverware. Subtle classical cooking. It's very popular with the middle classes who enjoy good regional cooking. Try the langoustine ravioli with saffron flavoured butter, zander with potatoes in a sauce made from veal juices, or small red mullet with *foie gras* butter. They have a wonderful wine list and an excellent selection of Bordeaux, Bourgogne and wines from the Loire. Set meals 110F (weekdays), 165F, 220F, 260F and ˆ la carte. The refurbished and soundproof bedrooms are all alike. Doubles from 280F with shower/wc.

|●| RESTAURANT LE CLOS FLEURI

474 rue de l'Église (North).
☎ 05.49.52.40.27 F➜ 05.49.62.37.29
Closed Sunday evenings. **Car park**.

With its turrets, skylight windows and loopholes at water level, the château of Dissay is like something out a fairytale. Cocteau could have used it as a set for his version of *Beauty and the Beast,* and if he had, the film crew would only have had to cross the street to this restaurant which is housed in one of the outbuildings. For 25 years now Jean Jack Berteau has been an ardent campaigner for traditional local cooking and produce, and who could blame him? His calf's head *gribiche* (in a spicy *vinaigrette*) is very popular as is the flank of beef with shallots and the *navarin* of lamb. Set meals 89F (weekdays), 132F, 182F and 198F. Good wine list featuring carefully selected local wines that are kept in a special cellar.

LEIGNÉ-LES-BOIS 86450 (19KM SE)

☗ |●| HÔTEL-RESTAURANT BERNARD GAUTIER

place de la Mairie (Centre).
☎ 05.49.86.53.82 F➜ 05.49.86.58.05
Closed Sunday evenings, Mondays, one week in February, and Nov 11–Dec 8. **Car park**.

The chances of finding somewhere as secluded as this place are very slim indeed. This part of northern Vienne is really off the beaten track and the hotel's not exactly welcoming so we were going to pass it by — what a mistake that would've been! Bernard Gautier's subtle combinations of flavours will delight your palate. There's cod with spices and herbs, *gâteau* of young rabbit with tartare sauce, *tartare* of fresh salmon, zander with a light *beurre blanc*, and *tournedos*. If you like *andouillette à la ficelle* then you're in for a real treat, and the *crème brûlée* is the best in Vienne. Set meals 68F (weekdays), 100F, 180F, 195F and 250F. Extremely generous portions. You'll probably feel like nodding off after such a feast, but don't worry about that because they have clean simple bedrooms where you'll get a good night's sleep. Doubles 150F with washing facilities. Good food, good hotel and a cheerful owner — you'd be hard pushed to find a better place.

CHAUVIGNY 86300

10% ☗ |●| HÔTEL-RESTAURANT LE LION D'OR**

8 rue du Marché (Centre).
☎ 05.49.46.30.28 F➜ 05.49.47.74.28
Closed Saturdays in winter and Dec 15–Jan 15.
Secure parking. **TV**. **Disabled access**.

Service noon–2pm and 7–9pm. A traditional middle-class hotel right in the heart of town next to the church. Bedrooms are well-equipped, modern and on the whole fairly conventional, just like the cooking. You'll find all the usual dishes — stuffed cabbage in the local style, rack of lamb with herbs, and veal sweetbreads with oyster mushrooms. Set meals 90F (weekdays), 100F, 140F and 175F. Doubles 270F with shower/wc and 280F with bath. The kind of hotel where people usually stop for just one night but you might be tempted to stay a bit longer so you can have a look round the town.

CIVRAY 86400

AUBERGE DU CHEVAL BLANC

5 rue du Temple.
☎ 05.49.87.48.08
Closed Sunday and Monday evenings.

A little inn at the far end of a courtyard full of flowers and trees. The gravel makes that nice crunchy sound under your feet. We like the restaurant but we're not as keen on the hotel. Very simple doubles 160F with bath. Generous portions of tasty dishes served by the very capable proprietress. Set meals 70F (weekdays)– 185F. Don't leave without trying the *compote* of rabbit with Pineau, *andouillette* of fish and rabbit with young garlic.This place definitely won us over. Why not try it for yourself?

COGNAC 16100

10% HÔTEL LA RÉSIDENCE**

25 av. Victor-Hugo (Centre).
☎ 05.45.32.16.09 F 05.45.35.34.65
Secure parking. **TV**.

This charming little hotel is only a few steps from the pedestrian precinct. It has been recently renovated and offers smart soundproof bedrooms decorated in soft colours. Very pleasant welcome and helpful staff. Bedrooms 200F with washing facilities, 260–290F with shower/wc and 320F with bath.

10% L'ÉTAPE**

2 av. d'Angoulême (Centre).
☎ 05.45.32.16.15 F 05.45.36.20.03
Closed Saturday lunchtimes, Sunday evenings and Dec 22–Jan 10. **Car park**. **TV**. **Canal+**.

Lunch served noon–2pm, dinner 7.30–10pm. Hennessy and Martell are two of the big names in Cognac. If you want to find out more about the brandy business, this hotel, a little bit out of town, will make a good base. Informal welcome and homely atmosphere. It has two dining rooms. The one on the ground floor resembles a brasserie and has a 57F *menu rapide,* and there's traditional dining room in the basement with slightly sophisticated set meals at 68F, 98F (every day) and 135F. Comfy bedrooms. Doubles 270F with shower or bath.

RESTAURANT LA BONNE GOULE

42 allée de la Corderie (Centre).
☎ 05.45.82.06.37 F 05.45.36.00.76
Closed Sundays. **Car park**.

Service noon–2pm and 7.30–10pm. The restaurant's mottos are on the wall for all to see – "You'll always get good food at the *La Bonne Goule*", "To eat well you've got to take your time". All the attractions of Charente can be found here – quiet cosy atmosphere, country-style décor with lots of character, wood, red tablecloths, racks suspended from the ceiling full of bunches of grapes and vine leaves (plastic, unfortunately). Good list of local wines. Dishes are all home-made and the portions are generous. Cheapest set meal 60F (every day). Others 85–140F and à la carte. Musical evenings Friday and Saturday.

LE NAUTILE

2 rue du Port (Centre).
☎ 05.45.82.68.56
Closed Sundays and Monday lunchtimes.

This has got to be the best place for fish in Cognac – you'll be spoiled for choice. The delightful dining room is elegant and quiet and the atmosphere is friendly. Good desserts. Set meals 60F (lunchtimes), 95–195F. Staff are attentive and service comes with a smile.

RESTAURANT LA BOÎTE À SEL

68 av. Victor-Hugo (South-East); take the Angoulême/Cognac road from the centre of town.
☎ 05.45.32.07.68 F 05.45.32.37.20
Closed Mondays and Dec 23–Jan 5.

Lunch served noon–2.30pm, dinner 7–10pm. Many people find themselves drawn to the two display cases containing top of the range wines. And there are plenty of them, given that there are 80,000 hectares of vineyards in this region. By the way, did you know that the amount of brandy that evaporates every year is the equivalent of 23 million bottles? — it's surprising we don't get drunk on the fumes. But don't worry, wine is sold by the glass so you needn't spend a fortune. Excellent local cooking. Set meals 75F, 135F, 170F, 205F and à la carte. Rather a chilly welcome.

SEGONZAC 16130 (14KM SE)

LA CAGOUILLARDE*

How to get there: take the D24 towards Barbezieux.
☎ 05.45.83.40.51
Closed Saturday lunchtimes and Sunday evenings.

People from Charente are known as "cagouillards" (or snails) because everything is done at a leisurely pace — even the brandy takes ten years to mature. That's how things are here too. Unusual décor combining rustic and modern styles. The dining room with the round marble garden tables leads to another room at the back which has a large fireplace used for vine stock grills. Relaxed atmosphere and jazz playing in the background. Try the stuffed snails and the grilled cutlets with walnut oil (60F). Good selection of Pineau. Set meals 75F, 115F, 145F and à la carte.

CONFOLENS 16500

10% ☗ |●| LA MÈRE MICHELET**

19 allées de Blossac.
☎ 05.45.84.04.11 F➜ 05.45.84.00.92
Car park. TV.

A dynamic family-run business. Try the Saint-Barthélemy veal sweetbreads and home-made pastries. Set meals 72F, 125F, 200F and à la carte. Bedrooms 135F with washing facilities, from 230F with shower/wc and 255F with bath. Half-board from 225F per person and full board from 285F.

10% ☗ |●| HÔTEL-RESTAURANT DE LA VIENNE**

rue de la Ferrandie.
☎ 05.45.84.09.24 F➜ 05.45.84.11.60
Closed Friday afternoons and Saturdays April–June 15, Friday afternoons, Saturdays and Sundays October–end March. **Car park. TV.**

People come from all over the world for the folklore festival held in the first fortnight of August. This beautiful hotel with a large waterfront terrace is in one of the narrow alleys in the old neighbourhood around the church of Sainte-Maxime. It has spacious country-style bedrooms and you'll get a nice welcome. Good and inexpensive food. Try the *terrine* of chicken livers with Pineau, *croustade* of ham or *mousseline* of pike with a crayfish sauce. Set meals 72–190F. Doubles 170F with washing facilities, 240F with shower/wc and 290F with bath.

|●| AUBERGE DE LA TOUR DE NESLE

3 rue de la Côte (Centre).
☎ 05.45.84.03.70

Service noon–2pm and 7–10pm. A wonderful hotel tucked behind the church in this delightful and historical little town. It's an attractively refurbished medieval building and everything shows that the owners care about the little things, love what they're doing and know how to entertain guests. We won't bother listing the dishes here as they often vary but you certainly won't be disappointed. The cooking is of a high standard and shows considerable imagination. Despite all that the prices are perfectly reasonable – there's a 100F set meal including coffee. And for 147F you get a choice of really wonderful dishes, the cheese is superb, and the desserts are mouthwatering. Undoubtedly one of the best restaurants in this neck of the woods.

COUHÉ 86700

☗ |●| HÔTEL-RESTAURANT LA PROMENADE

lieu-dit Valence; it's on the outskirts as you come into Couhé from Poitiers.
☎ 05.49.59.20.88
Closed Wednesdays, February and the November school holidays. **Secure parking. TV. Disabled access.**

Lunch served noon–2pm, dinner 7–9pm. The town dates from feudal times and this is a bit like a roadside café. Cosy atmosphere, friendly welcome and good value for money. Set meals 53F (except Sundays), 80F and 112F. Ideal if you want to treat yourself to a good meal without spending a fortune. Spacious well-equipped bedrooms suitable for large families cost 152F with shower/wc and 162F with bath.

10% ☗ |●| AUBERGE DU CHÊNE VERT

rue des Bons-Enfants (Centre).
☎ 05.49.59.20.42 F➜ 05.49.53.42.20
Closed Jan 2–12. **Secure parking. TV.**

Service noon–2.30pm and 7–9.30pm. A totally unpretentious little country inn. It's not really the same now it's been taken over by new owners but let's give their style of cooking time to settle down. At the moment the only distinctive feature is that you can get ostrich and buffalo meat (at a price!). Typically Poitou. Set meals 70F (weekday lunchtimes), 90F and 120F. Doubles 190F with shower or bath.

FONT-D'USSON (LA) 86350

10% ☗ |●| AUBERGE DE L'ÉCURIE**

Centre; at Lussac take the Poitiers exit and then the D727 towards Mazerolles and Bouresse; the restaurant is 3.5km further along, before you get to Usson-du-Poitou.
☎ 05.49.59.53.84 F➜ 05.49.58.04.50
Closed one week in October. **Car park. TV. Disabled access.**

Situated in the depths of the country and surrounded by meadows, these former stables have been very attractively refurbished in rustic style. Time seems to have stopped a long time ago. Ideal for a break in the sun. Peaceful atmosphere and friendly staff. They use good produce and offer simple dishes such as *bouillitures* of eels, lamb sweetbreads with cream sauce, frogs' legs and venison stew. Set meals 75F, 125F and 160F. Comfy double bedroooms 220F with shower/wc.

FOURAS 17450

10% ☗ |●| GRAND HÔTEL DES BAINS**

15 rue du Général-Brüncher (Centre); it's 50m from the Vauban fort and the sea.
☎ 05.46.84.03.44 ➡ 05.46.84.58.26
Secure parking. TV. Closed All Saints' Day–Easter.

If you want to get to the island of Aix then you have to go through Fouras. A nicely old-fashioned place between the fishing village and the seaside resort. It's an attractively refurbished former coaching inn a few steps from the beach, kept in tip-top condition and well equipped. The pretty courtyard garden is just as clean as the bedrooms and an ideal spot for breakfast. Rooms 250–330F with shower and 280–350F with bath, depending on the season.

10% ☗ HÔTEL LA ROSERAIE**

2 av. du Port-Nord (North-West); as you come into Fouras, follow the signs for port de la Fumée.
☎ 05.46.84.64.89
TV. Disabled access.

Monsieur and Madame Lacroix lavish lots of attention on their little hotel, which looks like a big detached house. The prices are perfectly reasonable for the area. Doubles from 210F (320F in season) with shower/wc. Bright clean bedrooms with good bedlinen, overlooking the sea or the garden. Dogs welcome. And unlikely as it may sound, the entrance hall looks like a Paris nightclub from the 50s! Friendly welcome.

SAINT-LAURENT-DE-LA-PRÉE 17450 (4KM E)

|●| RESTAURANT DE LA PLACE

place de l'Église.
☎ 05.46.84.52.18

Service noon–2pm and 7–9pm. It's the archetypal village bar and restaurant (the locals come to the bar for an aperitif and a game of billiards) and they serve a 60F set meal (weekday lunchtimes) that's guaranteed to please absolutely everyone. In the evening, there's an enormous 100F set meal of starter, fish, meat, cheese and dessert! (reservations only). It may feature dishes like *salade gourmande,* skate with *beurre noir,* eels wih parsley, *paupiettes* of veal with *sauce printanière,* salad of gizzards, lemon *tôt-fait* and fruit salad.

JARNAC 16200

|●| RESTAURANT DU CHÂTEAU

15 place du Château (Centre).
☎ 05.45.81.07.17 ➡ 05.45.35.35.71
Closed Sunday evenings, Mondays, Wednesday evenings, February school holidays and three weeks in August.

Lunch served noon–2pm, dinner 7.15–9pm. This is one of the best restaurants in the area, and the meals reflect the changing seasons and what's available at the market. Cosy setting. Specialities include seafood salad with citrus fruit, turbot with mustard, and *suprême* of roast chicken with honey and langoustines. Set meals 105F (lunchtimes), 155F, 225F and à la carte. The wine list is as impresive as the cooking and lists more than 100 Bordeaux!

ROUILLAC 16170 (16KM N)

10% ☗ |●| AUBERGE DES FINS BOIS

19 rue de Jarnac (West).
☎ 05.45.96.85.15 ➡ 05.45.96.82.97
Closed evenings in winter until Easter and one week in November. **Secure parking.**

Every building with a black roof has brandy stored in it — it's the evaporation process that has this strange effect on the roof. Everybody in this part of the world seems to derive their living from brandy – with the notable exception of this refurbished little hotel. It offers good value for money. Set meals 56F (every day), 80–128F (good duck *tournedos* with Pineau) and à la carte. Bedrooms 160F with washing facilities and 180F with shower/wc.

JONZAC 17500

☗ |●| LE CLUB**

8 place de l'Église (Centre).
☎ 05.46.48.02.27 ➡ 05.46.48.17.15
Closed two weeks after Christmas. **Secure parking. TV.**

A little hotel in the market square offering large, clean and well-equipped bedrooms that have been recently refurbished. Expect to pay 220F (with shower)–280F (with bath). Decent prices — probably the best value for money in town. It gets lots of regulars, so it's a good idea to book. Slightly formal but friendly welcome. Basic brasserie on the ground floor if you fancy a bite to eat.

LOUDUN 86200

HOSTELLERIE DE LA ROUE D'OR**

1 av. d'Anjou (North).
☎ 05.49.98.01.23 F 05.49.22.31.05
Closed Sunday evenings October–Easter.
Secure parking. TV. Disabled access.

A former coaching inn with slightly faded pink walls covered in Virginia creeper. It's at a crossroads so it can get a bit noisy. This is a place that's rich in history and full of memories. Staff are usually friendly (sometimes a touch offhand) and you'll find yourself in cosy surroundings reminiscent of former times. Simple regional dishes made with good produce, including house *foie gras,* duck *à l'orange* and calf's head. Not very imaginative perhaps but really good. Set meals 75F (weekdays)– 220F. The bedrooms don't show much imagination either though a few beams give some of them a bit of character. Doubles 280F with shower or bath.

LA REINE BLANCHE

6 place de la Bœuffeterie (Centre).
☎ 05.49.98.51.42
Closed Sunday evenings and Mondays.

All the local worthies seem to congregate in the panelled dining room of this handsome 15th century house. Whether it's for a business lunch, a family meal or a candle-lit dinner, the locals love this beautiful stylish dining room and the skilful cooking of a talented chef who's always on the lookout for new flavours. The *menus-cartes* at 140F, 180F and 210F – which are flawless and served up in generous portions — may be a bit too expensive for the average reader of this guidebook but they also do a perfectly adequate 98F set meal of *salade du pêcheu,* roast duck cutlet with mild spices, and dessert. The service is a bit over-formal but that's only to be expected.

LUSIGNAN 86600

LE CHAPEAU ROUGE**

1 rue Nationale.
☎ 05.49.43.31.10 F 05.49.43.31.20
Closed Sunday evenings, Mondays and January.
Car park. TV.

Lunch served noon–2pm, dinner 7.30–9.30pm. A former coaching inn dating from 1643 with a faded façade. The large fireplace which dominates the beautiful dining room is just made for story-telling sessions. Good cooking and lots of fish dishes such as risotto of dogfish *Degleré,* trout with almonds, veal sweetbreads with asparagus and local snails in a Sauvignon sauce. Set meals 80F, 130F and 200F. Pleasant well-equipped bedrooms. Expect to pay 220F with shower/wc and 260F with bath. It's a pity that the bar has suffered slightly at the hands of a decorator who didn't care about the building's character.

COULOMBIERS 86600 (8KM NE)

LE CENTRE POITOU**

39 route Nationale; take the N11 towards Poitiers.
☎ 05.49.60.90.15 F 05.49.50.05.84
Closed Sunday evenings, Mondays (October–June), and Jan 22–Feb 12. **Car park.**

Service noon–2.30pm and 7.30–9.30pm. A large establishment with lots of character. If you appreciate good food then this is the place of your dreams. Sophisticated dishes and subtle flavours mirror the personality of the proprietress, who does the cooking and looks after the dining room. Try the quail's eggs in a red wine sauce served with warm *foie gras*, the langoustine ravioli with a sea urchin sauce, or the veal sweetbread and morel tart. Set meals 99F, 185F and 390F. Lunchtime *formule* (48F) can be eaten under a delightful arbour that's unfortunately positioned right beside the road. Doubles from 260F with bath.

MARANS 17230

10% HÔTEL-RESTAURANT DES VOYAGEURS**

11 rue des Fours.
☎ 05.46.01.10.62 F 05.46.01.03.85
Closed Sunday evenings out of season, Mondays and January.

All the traffic coming from Nantes or Niort and going to La Rochelle or Bordeaux passes through Marans. Still, the town's not without character and if you like your grub you'll be more than satisfied with what you get there. For 120F, you can have a very substantial set meal of starter, fish course, meat course, cheese platter and dessert. And though there is a cheaper set meal at 90F, it's not for those watching their waistlines either. The décor is rustic in keeping with the style of cooking. Accommodation is available but we can only recommend it if you're stuck for somewhere to spend the night.

RESTAURANT LA PORTE VERTE

20 quai Foch (Centre).
☎ 05.46.01.09.45
Closed Wednesdays and February school holidays.

Service noon–2pm and 7–9pm. You'll have to go through two doors. The first opens onto a tiny garden with a view of the canal – it's rather pleasant to have dinner here after the sun's gone down. The second leads to the heart of this charming establishment. The dining rooms are decorated entirely in white, full of flowers, and cosy as can be. The largest has a magnificent fireplace and there's always a roaring fire in winter. The cheapest set meal (85F) gives you an idea of what's to come – sardines *en escabèche* or eggs in aspic with smoked ham, escalope of chicken with preserved lemon or fillet of plaice with *beurre blanc*, and for dessert a *petit pot de chocolat* with a crisp *tuile* biscuit. The 115F set meal comes with even more good things (we recommend the starter of rabbit and Muscadet *terrine*) and the 165F one offers oysters, a fish course, a meat course, cheese platter and dessert. The set meals come with excellent appetizers. The best thing of all about this magical place (run by chef/proprietor Didier Montéran and his wife, the two of whom used to own a hotel and restaurant in Winston-Salem, North Carolina) are the magnificent rooms and the enormous bathrooms. The price of 280F includes breakfast and is unbeatable value for money. A perfect place for an overnight stay.

MAULÉON 79700

HÔTEL-RESTAURANT L'EUROPE**

15 rue de l'Hôpital (Centre).
☎ 05.49.81.40.33 ➡ 05.49.81.62.47
Closed Mondays, the first week in January and two weeks in February. **Secure parking**. **TV**.

It's a hundred years old and still going strong! The combination of modern décor and Jacques Durand's generous portions of elaborate dishes have given this former coaching inn a new lease of life. Set meals 68–150F. Warm oysters with cider, turbot cooked in white wine and herbs, langoustine and salmon kebabs with a tarragon sauce, and young pigeon stuffed with sautéd ceps and morels. Old-fashioned bedrooms from 210F with shower/wc.

MELLE 79500

10% HÔTEL-RESTAURANT LES GLYCINES**

5 place René-Groussard (Centre).
☎ 05.49.27.01.11 ➡ 05.49.27.93.45
Closed Sunday evenings (except July–Aug). **TV**.

Service 12.15–2.30pm and 7.30–9.30pm. An impressive 12th century building, the hotel takes its name from the wisteria that covers it – though it's not as vigorous as it may once have been. Expect to pay 265F for a double with bath. Informal and relaxed welcome and service. The cooking is just a touch refined – panfried pigeons with langoustine salad, and traditional stewed eels. Set meals 78F, 92F, 100F, 125F, 145F and 185F. A good base for exploring an area that has an extraordinary Norman architectural heritage.

NIORT 79000

HÔTEL SAINT-JEAN*

21 av. Saint-Jean-d'Angély (Centre).
☎ 05.49.79.20.76
Secure parking.

A basic well maintained hotel a stone's throw from the centre of town. Doubles range in price from 100F with washing facilities to 165F with shower/wc and telephone. Delightful welcome. A few carved birds, the work of the owner, will keep you company at breakfast.

HÔTEL DU MOULIN**

27 rue de l'Espingole.
☎ 05.49.09.07.07 ➡ 05.49.09.19.40
Closed Christmas–New Year. **Car park**. **TV**. **Disabled access**.

This recently built hotel in the centre of town overlooks the river. Bedrooms are very comfy and all are equipped with bath, telephone and radio. Doubles 250–280F. Two are designed especially for the disabled and nine have a balcony overlooking the neighbouring gardens. Friendly welcome. This is where celebrities stay when appearing at the cultural centre on the other side of the river. If you're interested in finding out if anybody famous stayed in your room there's a list pinned up at reception.

10% ☗ LE GRAND HÔTEL***

32 av. de Paris (Centre).
☎ 05.49.24.22.21 F 05.49.24.42.41
Secure parking. TV. Canal+.

It's been refurbished and brought back to life by a couple who go to a great deal of trouble for their guests. The prices are really rather good considering the wonderful décor. Doubles 335–435F with bath. You can have breakfast in the courtyard garden. Here's a little tip — bedrooms ending in a 5, 6 or 7 overlook the garden.

|●| RESTAURANT LES QUATRE SAISONS

247 av. de La Rochelle (South).
☎ 05.49.79.41.06
Closed Sundays (except for reservations).

This restaurant offers decent traditional — and sometimes regional — cooking. Set meals 59F, 69F and 130F, the latter consisting of stuffed snails, eel stew with wine from Haut-Poitou, fillet of pork with Pineau des Charentes, goat's cheese and angelica soufflé.

|●| RESTAURANT LA CASE CRÉOLE

54 av. du 24-Février.
☎ 05.49.28.00.26
Closed Mondays and Sundays.

If you're spending some time in Niort, this restaurant will make a nice change. Take the 95F Caribbean set meal and try the rum with *accras* (spicy appetizers) followed by Creole *boudin* or *massalé* of pork from Réunion. You'll soon feel full of the joys of life again!

BESSINES 79000 (4KM SW)

☗ REIX HÔTEL**

av. de La Rochelle.
☎ 05.49.09.15.15 F 05.49.09.14.13
Closed between Christmas and New Year's Day.
Car park. TV. Disabled access.

A good place to spend the night en route to your holiday destination. The garden and pool are very pleasant prospects in summer. Bedrooms 280–300F with bath. Very decent.

MAGNÉ 79460 (7KM W)

|●| L'AUBERGE DU SEVREAU

24 rue du Marais-Poitevin; it's half-way between Niort and Coulon.
☎ 05.49.35.71.02
Closed Mondays (out of season).

If you take a quick glance at the menu (eggs in a red wine sauce, fricassee of snails) you might think you're in Burgundy, but once you've seen the river and sampled the traditional eel stew on the terrace you'll be in no doubt as to where you are. Set meals 57F (weekdays)–158F.

COULON 79510 (13KM W)

10% ☗ |●| HÔTEL-RESTAURANT LE CENTRAL

4 rue d'Autremont.
☎ 05.49.35.90.20 F 05.49.35.81.07
Closed Sunday evenings, Mondays, Jan 12–27 and Sept 27–Oct 8. **Car park.**

Lunch served noon–1pm, dinner 7.45–9pm. A must. Everything about it is so French, from the walls and chairs to and the cooking. There's fricassee of eels, local lamb, warm oysters with tips of wild nettles, duckling, and *crème brûlée* with angelica. The cheapest set meal is 98F and it's good. The others — 164F and 198F — are very substantial. Small rooms (210–235F) if you're stuck for somewhere to stay.

☗ HÔTEL AU MARAIS***

46-48 quai Louis-Tardy.
☎ 05.49.35.90.43 F 05.49.35.81.98
Closed Jan. **Car park. TV. Disabled access.**

A traditional riverside hotel. It exudes freshness and youthfulness and is somewhere to really relax between walks (which the owners can organize) in this area where you're never altogether sure where the ground stops and the water begins. Bright cheerful doubles 290–450F.

PARTHENAY 79200

10% ☗ |●| HÔTEL RENOTEL - RESTAURANT ROSALIA**

bd de l'Europe (East).
☎ 05.49.94.06.44 F 05.49.64.01.94
Closed Sundays mid-October–end March. **Car park. TV. Disabled access.**

Lunch served noon–2pm, dinner 7–9pm. A functional hotel surrounded by greenery on the Poitiers road. You won't get any surprises here. Bright bedrooms and the restaurant is very handy if you're not in the mood for heading back into town. Doubles 290F with shower/wc. Cheapest set meal 78F.

|●| RESTAURANT LE FIN GOURMET

28 rue Ganne (West).

☎ 05.49.64.04.53
Closed Sunday evenings, Mondays, two weeks in February and two weeks in September. **Car park**.

It only has room for fifty people and that's how the regulars like it. Set meals 60F, 85F, 110F, 130F and 170F. Not bad at all for oysters stuffed with hazelnuts, salmon with langoustine or any other dish based on fresh regional produce. Try the unusual banana soup.

POITIERS 86000

10% AUBERGE DE JEUNESSE

1 allée Roger-Tagault (South); take a number 3 bus outside the station in the direction of Pierre Loti and get off at "Cap Sud" – or drive towards Bordeaux and then turn right to Bellejouanne.
☎ 05.49.58.03.05 ➡ 05.49.37.25.85
Closed Dec 20–Jan 2. **Car park. Disabled access.**

Service 12.30pm and 8pm. Almost a quarter of Poitiers' inhabitants are students and the city boasts one of the biggest youth hostels in France. It's a veritable holiday camp. The grounds cover 8,000 square metres and you can take part in numerous activities like archery, football, and jogging or just laze about. Inside there's a jukebox, billiards and a large dining room. A swimming pool and the public library are just a few steps away. In other words, there's plenty to educate you and amuse you. Enjoy a good night's sleep in one of the cool bright rooms (three or four sharing). Accommodation 62F (you can even sleep in a teepee May–October). Meals 50F.

10% HÔTEL DE PARIS*

123 bd du Grand-Cerf (West).
☎ 05.49.58.39.37
Closed Mondays. **TV**.

Service noon–2pm and 7–10pm. This 60s hotel may be a bit out of date but it's a worthy representative of the old style of hotel. You'll be pampered by the owner and her employee, charming people, who know the area well. Perhaps a touch noisy but you can eat well for reasonable prices. Try the fricassee of small eels caught in the marsh or the veal kidneys with Armagnac. Set meals 75F, 92F, 125F and 190F. Doubles 148F with washing facillities (no TV) and 195F with shower/wc. Half-board 270F.

LE PLAT D'ÉTAIN**

7-9 rue du Plat-d'Étain (Centre).
☎ 05.49.41.04.80 ➡ 05.49.52.25.84
Closed Dec 20–Jan 13. **Secure parking. TV. Canal+.**

A former coaching inn in a tiny lane in the centre of town with a delightful neo-colonial décor that's a touch out of date. Quiet and pretty bedrooms with starched bedlinen. Each has a name. Doubles 145F with washing facilities, 225F with shower/wc and 295–350F with bath.

10% HÔTEL-RESTAURANT CITOTEL LE TERMINUS**

3 bd Pont-Achard (West).
☎ 05.49.62.92.30. ➡ 05.49.62.92.40.
Car park. TV. Canal+.

A large hotel cum brasserie lovingly run by a charming couple. The quiet bedrooms were refurbished recently — some are rustic, some with sloping ceilings are decorated in English fashion, and others are more modern. All have been soundproofed to keep out the noise of the station opposite. Doubles 260F with shower/wc and 290F with bath. The archetypal station hotel.

10% HÔTEL DU CHAPON FIN**

place du Maréchal-Leclerc (Centre).
☎ 05.49.88.02.97 ➡ 05.49.88.91.63
Closed Friday evenings in winter and Christmas school holidays. **Secure parking. TV. Canal+.**

It's to the right of the town hall. Warm welcome. Quiet spacious bedrooms, no two the same. Doubles 270F with shower/wc and 290F with bath.

10% LE CONTINENTAL**

2 bd Solférino (West); it's opposite the station.
☎ 05.49.37.93.93 ➡ 05.49.53.01.16
TV. Canal+. Disabled access.

Classic hotel with clean and well planned bedrooms. Ideal for an overnight stay in town. Prices vary. Doubles 295F with shower/wc or bath Mondays–Thursdays. Elsewhere, rates usually soar at the weekend but here you'll get a 10% reduction.

10% GRAND HÔTEL DE L'EUROPE**

39 rue Carnot (Centre).
☎ 05.49.88.12.00 ➡ 05.49.88.97.30
Secure parking. TV. Canal+. Disabled access.

Large and well designed bedrooms. Doubles from 330F with shower/wc or bath. A good base for exploring the town, one of the most fascinating in France from an architectural point of view.

10% LE GRAND HÔTEL***

28 rue Carnot (Centre).
☎ 05.46.60.90.60 ➡ 05.46.62.81.69
Secure parking. TV. Canal+.

A quiet and pretty decent hotel right in the heart of the city. The modern Art Deco décor gives the whole place a 30s look. Spacious and well equipped bedrooms. Doubles 430F with shower/wc and 490F with bath. Friendly welcome.

|●| RESTAURANT CHEZ FERNANDO

1 bis rue des Carmélites (Centre).
☎ 05.49.55.96.64
Closed Sundays and August.

This is just like one of those eating places you get in fishing ports, the kind of place everybody comes to. It's a mini Portugal — Portugese customers play cards under the benevolent eye of the owner and there's a little grocer's if they get homesick for certain foods. Interesting faces and a good atmosphere, especially on Friday evenings, when Fernando cooks his salt cod on live coals. Grills at lunchtime. There's something different every day in the 57F lunchtime set meal. À la carte in the evening.

|●| RESTAURANT LES BONS ENFANTS

11 bis rue Cloche-Perse (Centre).
☎ 05.49.41.49.82
Closed Sunday evenings, Mondays, Aug 1–15, and Christmas–New Year's Day. **Disabled access.**

Lunch served noon–2pm, dinner 7–10pm. The old walled city with its many 16th century buildings is the original centre of Poitiers. And it's this delightful area that's home to a doll's house of a restaurant, a place that looks as if it belongs in a fairy tale. The walls are decorated with angels and stars — maybe this is how somebody imagines heaven — and a large fresco of "Alice in Wonderland". And the food's good too, which isn't exactly a drawback. Set meals 66F, 111F and 145F. Try the house *foie gras*, the fish stew, the *confit* of duck, the meat cooked on a hot stone, and chocolate soufflé. Absolute bliss! If you're not very hungry, you can have the dish of the day plus dessert for 56F (lunchtimes only).

|●| LE POITEVIN

76 rue Carnot (Centre).
☎ 05.49.88.35.04 ➡ 05.49.52.88.05
Closed Sundays, Christmas–Jan 2, February school holidays and three weeks in July.

Service noon–2pm and 7–10pm. Quiet intimate atmosphere and criss-crossing beams. It's popular with businessmen at lunchtime and with lovers looking for some quiet time together, away from prying eyes, in the evening. No problem there — you've the choice of three little candlelit dining rooms. classic regional cooking and dishes such as roast kid cooked in local style and salt pork *farci poitevin* (stuffed with vegetables and herbs and cooked in stock). Set meals 90F (substantial) and 138–230F.

|●| RESTAURANT CHEZ CUL DE PAILLE

3 rue Théophraste-Renaudot (Centre).
☎ 05.49.41.07.35
Closed Sundays, public holidays and August.

Walls yellow with age, long wooden tables for eating side by side, strings of garlic and chilli peppers hanging from the beams, patient waiters — that just about sums up the décor and atmosphere. Authentic regional cooking and pork dishes ranging from brains cooked in red wine to the famous *farci poitevin*. Set meal 110F (weekdays only). Open till late but try to avoid ordering after 11pm because prices shoot up quite a lot.

|●| L'AQUARIUM

2 rue de la Croix-Blanche (Centre).
☎ 05.49.88.92.33
Closed Saturday lunchtimes, Sundays, Christmas–New Year's Day and August.

It's hard to describe *L'Aquarium* without using too many superlatives or embarrassing the owner. We loved everything about it — the understated stylish décor, the formal but not starchy atmosphere, and the tasty and imaginative food. They do mainly fish dishes — try the *gratin* of warm oysters with oyster mushrooms and the *pavé* of braised turbot with chicken livers. Reasonable prices. Set meals 99F and 149F. So we've just one piece of advice — pay a visit as soon as you can.

CROUTELLE 86240 (2KM S)

10% ⌂ MONDIAL HÔTEL**

La Berlanderie; take the N10.
☎ 05.49.55.44.00 ➡ 05.49.55.33.49
Car park. TV. Canal+. Disabled access.

The architecture is a mixture of Poitou and Louisiana — rather strange but pleasing to the eye. The horsehoe-shaped hotel is laid out round a glittering swimming pool that tempts you to jump in without so much as a second thought. Pleasant welcome. Self-contained bedrooms with full facilities. Doubles from 298F with bath.

SAINT-BENOÎT 86280 (2KM S)

⌂ |●| LE CHALET DE VENISE***

6 rue du Square (Centre); it's not far from the remains of

the Roman aqueduct.
☎ 05.49.88.45.07 ➡ 05.49.52.95.44
Restaurant closed Sunday evenings, Mondays, February school holidays and the first week in September.
Car park. TV. Disabled access.

This beautiful inn has just been refurbished and earned itself a star in the process. There's a garden at the back, trees with spreading branches and riverside fountains. It's a wonderful place to wake up in even when it's raining. Bright, uncluttered restaurant with a large window. Good food skilfully prepared by talented Serge Mautret, a chef who's always on the lookout for new flavours and interesting combinations. Try the tart of local snails with herb butter, casseroled veal chops with a cocoa and cinnamon sauce or fish in an aniseed-flavoured stock. Set meals 140F, 170F, 220F and 290F. Modern bedrooms 350F with terrace and shower or bath. One of those very chic places.

CHASSENEUIL-DU-POITOU 86360 (10KM NE)

HÔTEL DELTASUN**

Téléport 4-Futuroscope.
☎ 05.49.49.01.01 ➡ 05.49.49.01.10
Car park. TV. Disabled access.

Named after its delta-wing style of architecture. Some of you will love the décor and others will just hate it – the restaurant's a combination of pink and grey and the bedrooms are decorated in shades of grey. The rooms have excellent soundproofing, ten TV channels, hairdryer and trouser press – all very modern but then it is right next door to Futuroscope. Doubles 380F. The restaurant, which looks onto the swimming pool, offers regional cooking of a high standard. Set meals 95F, 145F and à la carte.

VIVONNE 86370 (14KM SW)

LE SAINT-GEORGES**

12 Grand-Rue; it's just beside the church.
☎ 05.49.89.01.89 ➡ 05.49.89.00. 22
Car park. TV. Canal+. Disabled access.

Service from 7.30pm. A brand new hotel in the centre of Vivonne. Naturally it's slightly lacking in character, but that's nothing the passing of time won't fix. There are 26 modern bedrooms with lots of facilities – trouser press, hairdryer and even Minitel if you're interested. Doubles 240F with shower/wc and 260F with bath. Breakfast 30F. The owner's extremely friendly and welcoming. Reservations are essential since it's so close to Futuroscope. Dinner is served to hotel residents every evening except Sunday (70F, wine included).

RESTAURANT HÉLIANTHE

59 Grand-Rue (Centre).
☎ 05.49.43.40.49 ➡ 05.49.89.01.74
Closed Mondays and Tuesdays (but not Tuesday evenings during school summer holidays).

There's a hint of the exotic here. The décor points to a mix of cultures – the owners have both Cambodian and French connections and souvenirs from their travels about the world are on display. Exotic odds and ends like statues of Buddha, musical instruments, vases and jugs purchased in distant lands. All you need is a little imagination and you'll be thousands of miles away. Good cooking as varied as the décor, full of amazing, unusual and sometimes disconcerting flavours. There's ox tongue with honey, salmon *crêpe* with a garlic sauce, turbot with coconut milk and seafood *terrine*. Set meals 55F and 65F (weekday lunchtimes), others 99F, 129F and 169F. You can take your coffee in the beautiful garden if you fancy being surrounded by banana trees and exotic fragrances.

RESTAURANT LA TREILLE

10 av. de Bordeaux (South).
☎ 05.49.43.41.13 ➡ 05.49.89.00.72
Closed Wednesdays in winter. **Car park.**

Lunch served noon–3pm, dinner 7–9pm. Napoleon decided to stop at this inn on his way to Spain. Panic broke out as staff tried to prepare a dinner fit for an emperor. In the end, all that he got was *farci poitevin* (a variation on stuffed cabbage) and it completely won him over. Napoleon eventually lost his throne but the inn survived down through the ages, as welcoming and well looked after as ever. Staff are friendly and attentive but the service is too slow. Good middle-class cooking rich in traditional flavours reminding us (as if we could forget) that gourmet is a French word. Set meals 77F (not available weekends), 115F (this includes the famous *farci poitevin*), 165F and 225F (for those with enormous appetites). Don't miss out on the lamb stew with haricot beans, the *compote* of duck or the sautéd kid with sorrel.

NEUVILLE-DE-POITOU 86170 (15KM NW)

10% L'OASIS**

2 rue Daniel-Ouvrard (Centre).
☎ 05.49.54.50.06 ➡ 05.49.51.03.46
Closed Sundays out of season. **Car park. TV.**

If the owner's not around, play a few notes on the piano near reception and he'll come rushing out to attend to you. The rooms are bright, spring-like and decorated in cool shades. Doubles 290F with shower/wc and breakfast. The restaurant, open in the evenings only, offers simple and unpretentious dishes. Set meals 85F and 100F. A good place not too far from Futuroscope.

|●| RESTAURANT SAINT-FORTUNAT

4 rue Bangoura-Moridé (Centre).
☎ 05.49.54.56.74
Closed Sunday evenings, Mondays, Aug 18–Sept 1, and Jan 5–26.

A rustic building with exposed stonework, a veranda, and a converted courtyard full of cherry trees. Faultess service even if the atmosphere's a bit solemn. The cooking is excellent, and dishes like langoustine salad with crystallized apples or *andouillette* of pig's trotters with *foie gras*, are a mixture of the simple and the sophisticated. Set meals 98F (every day), 125F, 170F and 220F (*menu dégustation*). The saint after whom the inn is called was an epicurean and would surely have approved of all this good food and the excellent regional wines like Garnay, Chardonnais, Saumur.

VOUILLÉ 86190 (17KM NW)

☗ |●| HÔTEL-RESTAURANT LE CHEVAL BLANC*

3 rue de la Barre (Centre); take the N149 towards Parthenay.
☎ 05.49.51.81.46 F 05.49.51.96.31
Car park. **TV**. **Canal+**.

Lunch served noon–2pm, dinner 7.30–9.30pm. Back in 507, a battle was fought here between the Franks and the Visigoths, which the Franks won hands down. Things are pretty peaceful nowadays in the village and in this waterside hotel. The whole family is involved in looking after their guests. The restaurant serves regional dishes like eels stewed in wine, duck breast with russet apples, and pike with *beurre blanc* and on the wine list you'll find wines from the Loire, Bordeaux and Burgundy. Good value for money but the service is a bit slow. Set meals 70–220F and à la carte. Doubles 140F with washing facilities and 220F with shower/wc.

☗ LE CLOVIS**

place François-Albert (Centre).
☎ 05.49.51.81.46 F 05.49.51.96.31
Car park. **TV**. **Canal+**. **Disabled access**.

Owned by the same family as the hotel and restaurant reviewed in the previous entry. If you're staying at the *Cheval Blanc*, this is where you'll come for breakfast. Modern pleasant bedrooms for those who like their comfort. Doubles from 250F with shower/wc and 270F with bath.

ROCHEFORT 17300

10% ☗ AUBERGE DE JEUNESSE

20 rue de la République (Centre); it's 1km from the station — go towards the town centre.
☎ 05.46.99.74.62 F 05.46.99.21.25
Closed Sept–June except by reservation.

Accommodation for 52 people. Bedrooms based on two, three, four or eight sharing. Room for the night 48F, sheet hire 17F and breakfast 20F. Set meals 28F (picnic style) and 45F. Half-board 113F.

10% ☗ HÔTEL ROCA FORTIS**

14 rue de la République (Centre).
☎ 05.46.99.26.32 F 05.46.87.49.48
Secure parking. **TV**.

Roca Fortis is Latin for Rochefort. The hotel, a former town house, is in a street full of beautiful old buildings. It's a delightful and peaceful place to stay, and the young manageress, who's not been here very long, makes all her guests feel quite at home. We recommend it. The rooms are individually decorated and have a view (particularly good from numbers 311, 415 and 417) of the very quiet garden that's full of colour and scent. If you fancy a spot of reading it's rather pleasant sitting out here in one of the armchairs. Doubles 160F with basin, 240F with shower/wc and 270F with bath.

10% ☗ |●| HÔTEL LE PARIS**

27-29 rue La Fayette (Centre).
☎ 05.46.99.33.11 F 05.46.99.77.34
Closed Christmas–Jan 15; restaurant closed Sundays.
TV. **Canal+**.

Service noon–2pm and 7.30–10pm. Centrally located and very functional, as well as having been refurbished throughout, this hotel might be just what you're looking for. Service with a smile and good croissants for breakfast (which is not something you get every day of the week). Cheapest double 220F (250F in season) with shower/wc. Half-board 520F based on two sharing (600F July–Aug). The modern décor in the dining room is uninspiring but the tables are set quite far apart and the prices are reasonable. The owner does the cooking and turns out dishes like duck *confit parmentier*, calf's mesentry (the membrane enclosing the intestines) *à l'ancienne*, scallops with lemon butter, and *croustillant* of banana. Set meals 125F, 165F, 195F and a 90F *formule* (main course and dessert chosen from the 125F set meal).

RESTAURANT LE GALION

38 rue Toufaire (Centre); it's opposite the musée de la Marine.
☎ 05.46.87.03.77 Fax 05.46.99.15.56

You can eat either in the conventional restaurant or the more modern self-service. Cheapest set meal 78F (weekdays), others 98–165F.

RESTAURANT LA MARGELLE

191 bd Pouzet (North-West); take the La Rochelle bypass, route La Rochelle/Royan.
☎ 05.46.99.96.77
Closed Wednesday evenings, Sundays and Aug 8–25.

André Cluzeau has come back home after a long time working in the best restaurants in London and he's proud of what he's learned. The restaurant is opposite the old Rochefort airfield (there are two planes in full view so it's pretty hard to miss). This former sauce chef offers a good 112F set meal of duck ravioli with mint sauce, a choice of duck fillet with haricot beans or fish fresh from the market, cheese and dessert. Tasty and attractively presented — the work of a professional. The rather gloomy décor in the dining room needs to be changed and the walls could do with a lick of paint. Set meals 85F (weekdays) and 182F.

RESTAURANT LE TOURNE-BROCHE

56 av.Charles-de-Gaulle (Centre); it's in one of the main streets in town.
☎ 05.46.99.20.19 Fax 05.46.99.72.06
Closed Sunday evenings, Mondays and the first three weeks in January.

Service noon–2pm and 7–10pm. Owner Jean Klein, a good-natured and very large gentleman, and his wife Dina were both born in Luxembourg. The large dining room is full of flowers and plants and decorated in pale colours. The 105F "bonne franquette" set meal is a real bargain and offers a series of carefully prepared dishes — *poutargue* with shallots, grilled leg of lamb with *mojettes* (a type of haricot bean) and chocolate mousse. The food's good, it's pleasing to the eye, you'll get high-quality service and, with a drop of wine you'll pay round about 200F — go on, spoil yourself. Other set meals 150–200F. Children's menu 40F.

BROUAGE 17320 (13KM SW)

RESTAURANT LE BROUAGE

rue du Québec (Centre).
☎ 05.46.85.03.06
Closed Mondays (April–Aug) and Nov–April (except weekends and public and school holidays).

Service from noon and 7.30. Brouage, a pretty fortified 17th century village deep in the marshes is a must. This is where the founder of Quebec, Samuel de Champlain, was born. After you've done the sights, come here for a meal — you'll be glad you did. For 99F you can get *mouclade* (mussels in a creamy sauce) or the house *terrine* (they'll bring the dish to your table but try not to get carried away — leave room for something else) followed by a choice of fricassee of eels (the best in the region) or stuffed tripe, cheese and dessert. It's good, well prepared, and the portions are generous. Portions are just as big in the 112F set meal.

ROCHEFOUCAULD (LA) 16110

10% LA VIEILLE AUBERGE DE LA CARPE D'OR***

13 faubourg de la Souche (Centre).
☎ 05.45.62.02.72 Fax 05.45.63.01.88
Secure parking. TV. Canal+. Disabled access.

Apparently you can rent rooms in the 11th century castle — but at around 1,000F a night, it's way out of our league! We prefer this quiet old inn, an attractively converted 16th century coaching inn in the centre of town. Hearty local dishes are on offer in the set meals, which range in price from 68F (lunchtimes and evenings except Sundays) to 180F. Bright bedrooms 170–295F.

CHASSENEUIL-SUR-BONNIEURE 16260 (11KM NE)

HÔTEL DE LA GARE*

9 rue de la Gare (Centre); take the D141.
☎ 05.45.39.50.36 Fax 05.45.39.64.03
Closed Mondays, Sunday evenings, Jan 1–15 and July 1–22. **Secure parking. TV.**

A good place for an overnight stay and it's very good value for money. In the restaurant, go for the specialities — panfried ham *à la charentaise,* fillet of trout with Pineau or steamed kidneys with Cognac. Several set meals from 62F. Doubles 150F with washing facilities and up to 240F with bath.

ROCHELLE (LA) 17000

SEE MAP OVERLEAF

10% ☗ |●| AUBERGE DE JEUNESSE

av. des Minimes (South); it's near the port of Minimes, quite a way from the historical centre of La Rochelle. Off map **C4-1**
☎ 05.46.44.43.11 ➡ 05.46.45.41.48
Closed Christmas/New Year holidays. **Canal+.**
Disabled access.

Not just a youth hostel, a *Centre international de séjour* (a kind of international holiday camp). It's modern, very big, gets a lot of guests and is a fairly lively place. It's dearer than your traditional youth hostel. You'll pay 75.50F per person (includes sheet hire and breakfast) and there's a 35F supplement for single rooms. Meals 48F, half-board 120F and full board 168F (compulsory for groups in July–Aug).

☗ |●| HÔTEL LE TRANSATLANTIQUE

av. des Minimes (South). Off map **C4-2**
☎ 05.46.45.04.47 ➡ 05.46.44.95.43
Closed weekends and school holidays; restaurant closed Mon. **Car park. TV. Disabled access.**

This is in fact a hotel school, and it has absolutely unbeatable prices. Doubles 150F with shower/wc–180F with bath, and you can choose your level of facilities (from one to four stars). Just one little disadvantage – there are only eight bedrooms so you'll have to book a long time in advance. Meals are prepared by the students. Lunch – either a 65F*formule rapide* or an 85F set meal – is served every day but they do dinner (130F) on Tuesdays and Fridays only The restaurant has sixty place settings and is booked up almost a month in advance (and that's just with the locals) so tourists might not get a look-in.

10% ☗ HÔTEL LE BORDEAUX*

43 rue Saint-Nicolas (Centre); it's near the old harbour and 500m from the station. **MAP C4-3**
☎ 05.46.41.31.22 ➡ 05.46.41.24.43
Closed Dec 23–Jan 10. **TV.**

This one-star hotel's for you if you're having trouble making ends meet. But don't worry, it's not a dump and perfectly adequate for a hotel of its kind. All of the rooms have recently been refurbished. The ones in the attic get a lot more light. Doubles 155–185F with basin (shower/wc on the landing) and 210–250F with shower/wc. 10% discount for students out of season. The owners make you feel welcome and are more than happy to help with travel information etc.

☗ |●| HÔTEL DU COMMERCE**

6-12 place de Verdun. **MAP C2-4**
☎ 05.46.41.08.22 ➡ 05.46.41.74.85
Closed three weeks in January; restaurant closed Friday evenings and Saturdays October–end February. **TV. Canal+.**

This beautiful 18th century building only two minutes from the historical town centre was turned into a hotel at the turn of the century. It has about sixty bedrooms catering for all tastes and all pockets. Doubles 165–320F in high season. Good deals Sept 15–April 30. Set meals 75–102F.

10% ☗ HÔTEL DE LA PAIX*

14 rue Gargoulleau (Centre). **MAP B3-5**
☎ 05.46.41.33.44 ➡ 05.46.50.51.28
TV.

This 18th century building, formerly a private home, is delightful as all old buildings are, but it is showing its age. Most of the bedrooms are very big and have high ceilings, as in all old houses. They're all different and some are decorated with bits and pieces. The family rooms, which sleep 4–5, are recommended. They come with shower or bath and cost 330–400F. The cheapest room is 170F with washing facilities and shower on the landing. If you fancy something a bit more comfortable, expect to pay 260F for one with shower/wc and 280F with bath. The young owners are very understanding as they themselves have travelled extensively with the French version of this guidebook in their back pocket. What's more, as they have children of their own, families are welcomed with open arms. Some rooms have TV and there's a little courtyard where you can store your bike.

10% ☗ HÔTEL LE ROCHELOIS**

66 bd Winston-Churchill (South); take rue Philippe-Vincent as you come to the old port from allée du Mail. Off map **A4-8**
☎ 05.46.43.34.34 ➡ 05.46.42.10.37
Secure parking. TV. Canal+. Disabled access.

If you're the sporty type and are in La Rochelle on a business trip, this is just the hotel for you. Guests have free use of the gym, jacuzzi, sauna, Turkish bath, tennis courts and swimming pool. Functional bedrooms. The ones on the first floor have a terrace. Rooms with bath and a sea view cost 280F out of season and 400F in season.

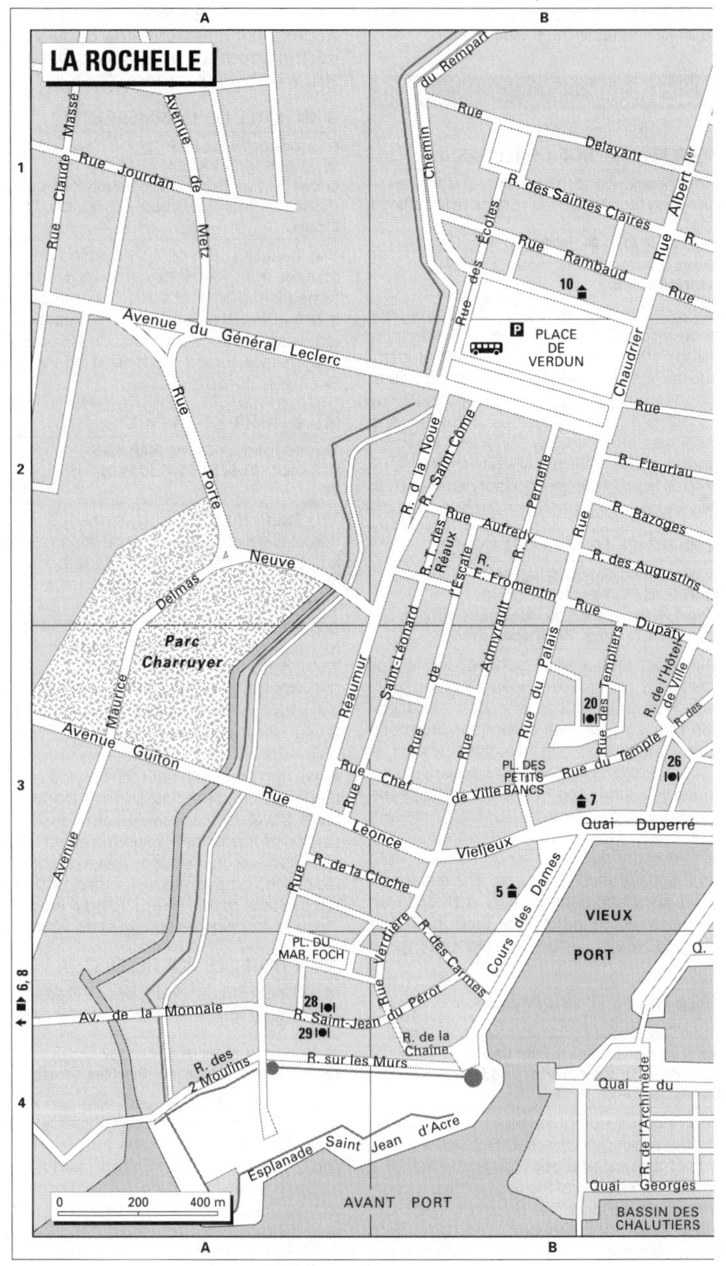
LA ROCHELLE
A
B
1
2
3
4
Rue Claude Massé
Avenue de Metz
Rue Jourdan
Chemin du Rempart
Rue Delayant
R. des Saintes Claires
Rue des Écoles
Rue Rambaud
Rue Albert Ier
10
PLACE DE VERDUN
Avenue du Général Leclerc
Rue Chaudrier
Rue Porte Neuve
R. d la Noue
R. Saint Côme
Rue Pernelle
R. Fleuriau
R. Bazoges
Rue Aufredy
R. des Augustins
R. E. Fromentin
Rue Dupaty
Delmas
Parc Charruyer
Avenue Maurice
Réaumur
Saint-Léonard
Rue de l'Escale
Rue Admyrault
Rue du Palais
Rue des Templiers
R. de l'Hôtel de Ville
20
26
Avenue Guiton
Rue Chef de Ville
PL. DES PETITS BANCS
Rue du Temple
7
Rue Léonce Vieljeux
Quai Duperré
R. de la Cloche
5
Cours des Dames
VIEUX PORT
PL. DU MAR. FOCH
Rue Verdière
R. des Carmes
28
29
Av. de la Monnaie
R. Saint-Jean du Pérot
R. de la Chaîne
R. des 2 Moulins
R. sur les Murs
Esplanade Saint Jean d'Acre
Quai du
R. de l'Archimède
Quai Georges
AVANT PORT
BASSIN DES CHALUTIERS
0 200 400 m
6, 8

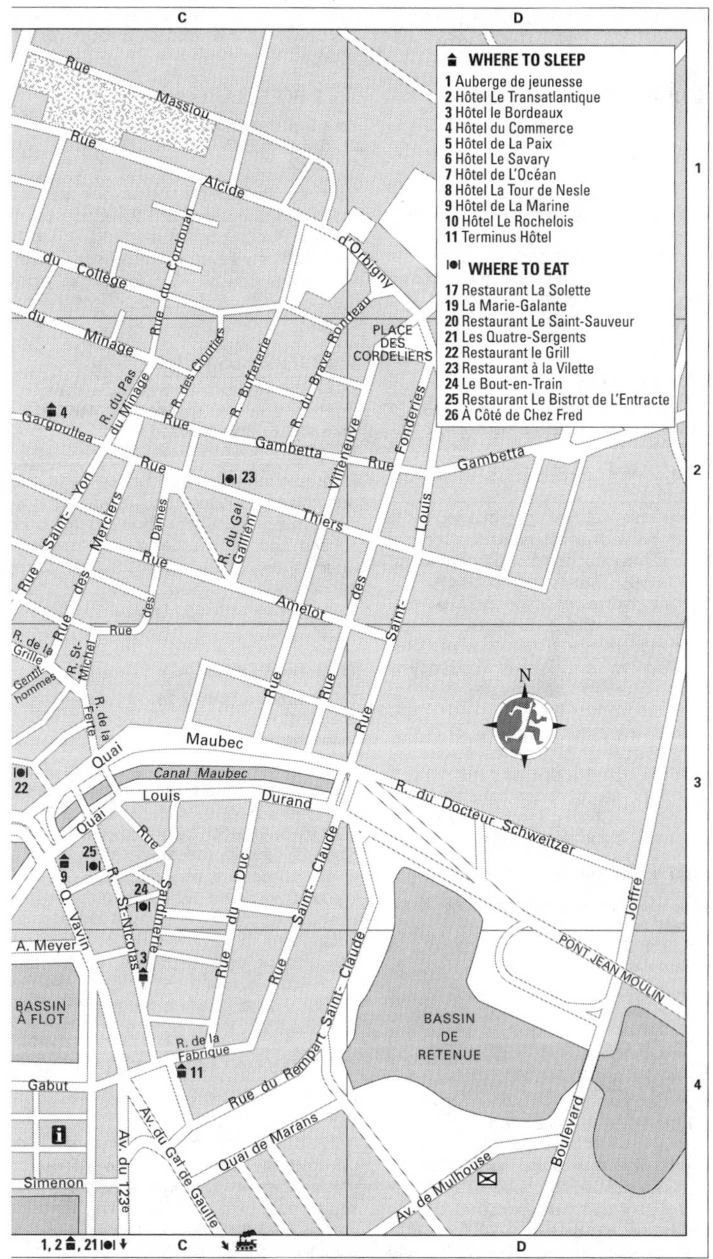
WHERE TO SLEEP
1 Auberge de jeunesse
2 Hôtel Le Transatlantique
3 Hôtel le Bordeaux
4 Hôtel du Commerce
5 Hôtel de La Paix
6 Hôtel Le Savary
7 Hôtel de L'Océan
8 Hôtel La Tour de Nesle
9 Hôtel de La Marine
10 Hôtel Le Rochelois
11 Terminus Hôtel
WHERE TO EAT
17 Restaurant La Solette
19 La Marie-Galante
20 Restaurant Le Saint-Sauveur
21 Les Quatre-Sergents
22 Restaurant le Grill
23 Restaurant à la Vilette
24 Le Bout-en-Train
25 Restaurant Le Bistrot de L'Entracte
26 À Côté de Chez Fred
PLACE DES CORDELIERS
Canal Maubec
BASSIN À FLOT
BASSIN DE RETENUE
PONT JEAN MOULIN
Rue Massiou
Rue Alcide d'Orbigny
Rue du Collège
Rue du Minage
Rue Gambetta
Rue Thiers
Rue Amelot
Quai Maubec
Quai Louis Durand
R. du Docteur Schweitzer
Rue du Rempart Saint-Claude
Quai de Marans
Av. de Mulhouse
Av. du Gal de Gaulle
Boulevard Joffre
1, 2, 21

Doubles with shower/wc but no view are 230F. Garage 20F (free of charge out of season).

10% ☗ HÔTEL DE L'OCÉAN**

36 cours des Dames (Centre); it's in the pedestrian precinct by the harbour. **MAP B3-7**
☎ 05.46.41.31.97 F➔ 05.46.41.51.12
TV.

It's ideally situated so you'll get the full effect of La Rochelle's lively night life from your bedroom window. Double glazing blocks out some of the noise which sometimes goes on into the early hours of the morning. Quieter rooms at the back. Doubles 350F with shower/wc and sea view.

☗ HÔTEL LE SAVARY**

2 bis rue Alsace-Lorraine (West); from the old port go up allée du Mail as far as parc Delmas then turn right. Off map **A4-6**
☎ 05.46.34.83.44. F➔ :05.46.43.83.44.
Car park. **TV**. **Canal+**.

This large white cube-shaped building in the heart of the residential area is a perfect example of how architects defined "modern" in the late 50s. Bedrooms are as clean as can be and, ladies will be pleased to learn, come equipped with a hairdryer – not a common occurrence in this type of hotel. They have a few family rooms with practical bunkbeds. The nicest rooms are in an old house at the back of the main building and overlook a very quiet garden full of plants. You can have breakfast there too. If you want to enjoy the night life down by the old port but you've no car, it's a ten minute walk to the Tour de la Chaîne. Doubles 220–280F with shower/wc and from 280F with bath.

☗ HÔTEL LA MARINE*

30 quai Duperré (Centre); it's on the wharfs opposite the old port. **MAP A4-9**
☎ 05.46.50.51.63
Closed Sunday afternoons and January.

You might not notice this tiny 12 room hotel straight away as it's huddled between two restaurants, *La Marine* and *Le Gavroche*. Pleasant spruce bedrooms. The ones overlooking the old port have a lovely view but the double glazing unfortunately does not drown out all the noise (the area round the hotel gets pretty busy in the evenings). Breakfast is served only in your room. TVs available for a 15F supplement. The cheapest double is 220F (with shower), while for a room with shower/wc prices range from 240F to 380F. Out of season prices are 190F and 210–290F respectively. Some rooms have a sea view. Madame Leleu will greet you with a smile.

10% ☗ HÔTEL LA TOUR DE NESLE**

2 quai Louis-Durand (South). Off map **A4-8**
☎ 05.46.41.05.86 F➔ 05.46.41.95.17
TV. **Canal+**.

Very well situated. Bedrooms look onto the old port or the canal and the église Saint-Sauveur. You're right in the touristy part of town and only seven minutes from the station. Bedrooms 220–420F. In summer, enjoy the roof terrace and its beautiful view of the town.

10% ☗ TERMINUS HÔTEL

place du Commandant-de-La-Motte-Rouge; it's very close to the tourist office and the station. **MAP C4-11**
☎ 05.46.50.69.69 F➔ 05.46.41.73.12
TV.

Quiet and individually decorated bedrooms with country-style furniture. It's just like staying at your grandmother's home in the country and prices are more than reasonable. Doubles range in price from 280F for one at the back with shower/wc to 350F for one at the front with bath (and brighter, prettier and larger too).

I●I LE BOUTE-EN-TRAIN

2 rue des Cloutiers. **MAP C3-24**
☎ 05.46.41.73.74
Closed Sundays.

Service noon–2pm and 7.15–9.30pm (10pm in summer). After a busy morning shopping with granny or your mother-in-law, this is an ideal place for lunch before doing something more cultural in the afternoon. The blue colour scheme is very pretty. Good plain home cooking and dishes along the lines of beef with carrots, salt pork with lentils, steak tartare, and rib steak with Roquefort. Prices vary with the ingredients used, but the dish of the day's round about 45F, starters 22–38F and specialities roughly 75F. Staff could be a little friendlier.

I●I RESTAURANT LA TERRASSE

26 rue des Templiers (Centre).
☎ 05.46.41.79.79

A little piece of America in La Rochelle! People obviously come here to have dinner on the terrace, which is in a very pretty little square and, best of all, well away from the crowds that flock to the town during the summer months. Modern/trendy décor –

which means shades of grey – TV permanently tuned to MTV and background music. The customers are young of course (nobody seems to be over 40), and the service is pretty informal. One good thing about it is that, unlike lots of American restaurants, it offers good and carefully prepared food. Excellent starters like seafood nachos and Mississippi shrimps, then you can attack the tasty chilli con carne or a Madison Burger made from real ground beef. Brunch Saturdays and Sundays. Set meals 49F and 140F.

LE SOLEIL BRILLE POUR TOUS

13 rue des Cloutiers; it's near the covered market.
☎ 05.46.41.11.42
Closed Sundays and Mondays.

Babeth, who does the cooking and looks after the dining room, prepares delicious macrobiotic dishes which vary according to the season and her mood. The 52F *formule* – starter and dish of the day accompanied by freshly cooked vegetables – is very good value. There's a small à la carte menu offering sweet and savoury *crêpes*, *galettes* and tarts, all under 40F. Mixed salads are the house speciality and make a very satisfying lunch. We particularly recommend the one called "lune'", which contains avocado, tomatoes, ricotta, lettuce, grated carrots and *toffinettes*. (We'll leave it to you to find out what these are.) Exceptionally fresh market produce, very tasty dishes, and extremely large portions. And if the sun happens to be out you couldn't ask for more.

LA MARIE-GALANTE

35 av. des Minimes (South-West). Off map **C4-21**
☎ 05.46.44.05.54
Closed Monday, Tuesday, Wednesday and Thursday evenings out of season.

Minimes, a tiny village, has four restaurants side by side in its old houses, so watch you don't mix them up. This particular one has a large terrace and looks like the kind of place you'd find by the beach. When the weather's good it's nicer to eat outdoors of course. They have a 65F *formule express* (except weekends and public holidays) that offers salad of the day, dish of the day and coffee, and a 78F set meal that gives you a choice of six oysters, fish soup, a platter of whelks or *moules marinière*, followed by flank of beef with shallots or fish of the day, then cheese or dessert.

RESTAURANT LE SAINT-SAUVEUR

24 rue Saint-Sauveur (Centre); it's opposite the cathedral Saint-Sauveur. **MAP B3-20**
☎ 05.46.41.18.16 F 05.46.41.63.87
Closed Sundays and Monday evenings (out of season) and February.

If you've been looking for somewhere with a homely atmosphere, this unobtrusive little restaurant is just the place for you. The owner's very attentive without being overbearing and the staff follow her lead. The food is authentic and served up in generous portions. There's mussels, marinated raw salmon, very fresh oysters, and a large variety of fish (monkfish with vermouth, eels with chopped parsley, skate with blackcurrant vinegar). Try the chef's specialities of sautéd langoustines, *bouillabaisse*, or the unusual but delicious bass stuffed with bananas. Set meals 68F, 98F (very good) and 128F.

LES QUATRE SERGENTS

49 rue Saint-Jean-du-Pérot; it's just a stone's throw from the old port. Off map **C4-21**
☎ 05.46.41.35.80 F 05.46.41.95.64
Closed Sunday evenings and Mondays.

A town house that dates back to 1842 and has a wonderful conservatory. There are elements of both brasserie and gourmet restaurant here. The dishes are sophisticated and the helpings are generous (such a rare combination that it's worth mentioning). Some of the dishes are quite imaginative – hake in white sauce with pistachio nuts and orange peel, monkfish and sweet pepper kebabs, breast of duck with honey and lime, and fillet of beef with morels. Set meals 80F (good value for money), 110F, 135F and 180F. Expect to pay 180F for a meal à la carte. Wine is served by the glass. Unobtrusive and professional service. We liked it a lot.

RESTAURANT TEATRO BETTINI

3 rue Thiers (Centre); it's beside the covered market.
☎ 05.46.41.07.03
Closed Sundays, Mondays and Sept 22–Oct 4.

Lunch served noon–2pm, dinner 7.30–11pm. You'll probably think La Rochelle is a bit far to come for a pizza. True enough, but when they're made the way they should be and are better than what some of those restaurants that supposedly specialize in seafood and fish turn out, it would be a crime to miss out. Pasta dishes above average. Large choice of Italian wines. Expect to pay about 90F. Children's set meal 38F.

RESTAURANT LA SOLETTE

11 place de la Fourche (South); it's not far from the old port but set back a bit (near quai Louis-Durand).

☎ 05.46.41.74.45
Closed Sundays out of season and January.

The area known as Saint-Nicolas used to be a part of town that respectable people avoided but now it's a pretty upper-class neighbourhood. This is where you'll find *La Solette,* which has a great location in a little square where a magnificent paulownia (tree) adds a touch of the south. You can sit out here on the terrace in summer. Reasonable prices – dishes of the day 48–68F, *formule* based on a single dish 95–130F and cheapest set meal 98F. Dishes reflect the changing seasons and what's available at the market.

RESTAURANT À LA VILLETTE

4 rue de la Forme (Centre); it's opposite the main market. **MAP C2-23**
☎ 05.46.41.27.03
Closed Sundays.

Service 7am–3pm. After your walk round the covered market, which is a must especially on Wednesdays and Saturdays when it spills onto the surrounding streets, this is the place to come for a snack. The Paris-born owner gets his meat from the butchers in the market. After a generous portion of herrings with potatoes cooked in oil, tuck into flank of beef with sauté potatoes or a mixed grill guaranteed to delight the dieheard carnivore, and wash it down with a drop of red. As simple as can be but very nicely presented. Expect to pay about 110F à la carte. Dish of the day from 55F.

RESTAURANT LE GRILL

10 rue du Port (Centre). **MAP C3-22**
☎ 05.46.41.95.90
Closed Saturday and Monday lunchtimes, Sunday lunchtimes (all day in winter), and school and public holidays.

A tiny place with very few tables and room for about ten people at the counter. This is where people come to treat themselves to delicious thick steaks, lovingly cooked on the grill. But lovers of seafood needn't feel left out, for the owner used to work at the wholesale fish market in La Rochelle and they'll have a choice of several dishes every day depending on what the market has to offer – grilled tuna and basmati rice *à la provençale,* little grilled cuttlefish, *tartare* of salmon. Customers are mainly regulars – and if they've got friends passing through, they'll bring them here. Wine served by the glass and nice house desserts. Expect to pay about 100F for a meal. Excellent value for money.

À CÔTÉ DE CHEZ FRED

rue Saint-Nicolas (South-East) **MAP B3-26**
☎ 05.46.41.65.76
Closed Sundays.

If you're wondering about Fred, he's the fishmonger next door to this seaside bistro. So at least we know where the fish comes from, which is no bad thing since it features so prominently on the menu. What's available depends on what's been caught, so it's hard to recommend any one special thing. Go for the simplest seasonal dishes. Informal staff make for a relaxed atmosphere. Main courses from 39F. Expect to pay about 140F for a good meal (not counting drink).

RESTAURANT LE BISTROT DE L'ENTRACTE

22 rue Saint-Jean-du-Pérot (South). **MAP C3-25**
☎ 05.46.50.62.60 Fax 05.46.41.99.45
Closed Sundays.

Service from noon and 7.30pm. The restaurant is run by Didier Cadio who used to work with La Rochelle's top chef so you're in good hands here. He offers just one set meal of main course and dessert at 145F. Dishes such as *gâteau* of langoustines with tarragon sauce, sole with almonds and pistachio nuts, *tournedos* of roast cod with buttered cabbage and *parmentier* of young duck are pleasing to both the eye and to the palate and have found considerable favour with his middle-class customers. Lots of choice. Good desserts and an impressive wine list.

AYTRÉ 17440 (3KM S)

RESTAURANT LES PLATANES*

29 av. du Commandant-Lysiak; from La Rochelle take the bypass towards Aytré.
☎ 05.46.44.29.91 Fax 05.46.31.06.90
Closed Sundays. **Car park. TV. Disabled access.**

Lunch served noon–2pm, dinner 7–9.30pm. The perfect example of a well-run restaurant offering simple food and exceptional value for money. Madame Lechat and her smiling waitresses effortlessly go about their work in the large country-style dining room. Workmen come from the Aytré industrial estate to polish off the 62F set meal which varies daily. These feasts sometimes start with skate wing with capers, then lamb stew with haricot beans followed by cheese or dessert with a quarter litre of red wine to boot! The 120F set meal is particularly hearty and attracts a large crowd in the evenings and at weekends. We had six oysters, cheek of monkfish with parsley vinaigrette, lamb stew, cheese platter and dessert (enormous slices of gâteau). Frankly, we couldn't find a thing wrong with this place.

LAUZIÈRES 17137 (7KM N)

BAR PORT LAUZIÈRES

port du Plomb; it's at the seafront opposite the île de Ré.
☎ 05.46.37.45.44
Closed Tuesdays (except July 14–Aug 15), and Sept–March. **Car park**.

If authenticity is important to you, you'll be taken by this fisherman's hut that's been converted into a bar cum restaurant. The bar's on one side and is popular with the local oyster farmers. On the other is the dining room which has a sea view and a cosy fireplace ideal for wintry evenings. As a bonus there's a delightful terrace in summer. The owner, an ex-diver, is quite happy to let things tick along gently. He offers mussels, langoustines, grilled sardines, six oysters (available even when there isn't an R in the month) and a fish platter (oysters, langoustine, prawns and sardines). Add a little wine and you're talking not much more than 100F for a meal.

CHARRON 17230 (16KM N)

RESTAURANT THEDDY-MOULES

72 rue du 14-Juillet; it's on the port road known as le Pave.
☎ 05.46.01.51.29 F→ 05.46.01.57.31
Closed Oct 1–April 30.

Charron's a quiet little village famous for its mussels and people come for just one reason — Theddy-Moules. Theddy, a mussel farmer, came up with the good idea of arranging a few tables in a kind of large shed and putting a terrace out front. Customers come for Theddy's mussels but he also serves oysters and other seafood and also local fish (sole or bass 55F, grilled sardines 38F). You can sit on the terrace facing the road and enjoy the simple pleasures of mussels "Spécial Theddy" (36F), an *assiette dégustation* of langoustine, oysters, whelks, winkles and prawns (58F) or a seafood platter (98F). Generous portions and exceptionally fresh.

ROCHE-POSAY (LA) 86270

HOSTELLERIE DU VAL DE CREUSE**

9 place de l'Église.
☎ 05.49.86.20.71
Closed Nov–end March. **Car park**. **TV**.
Disabled access.

Service noon–2pm and 7–9.30pm. This is the European capital of thermal dermatology. Once you've taken care of your skin, pop along to this old bourgeois-style building on the banks of the Creuse and give your stomach a treat. The terrace is surrounded by old city walls and a splendid fortified church, and the dining room alone is worth a visit for its romantic décor and dishes full of flavour. Try the breast of duck with raspberry vinegar, the *paupiettes* of sole with scallops or the pan-fried *foie gras* with grapes. Set meals 100F, 160F and 235F. Madame Lussier-Sabourin is a charming woman who keeps the place running like clockwork. Ask for a bedroom overlooking the Creuse and you'll wake up thinking you're on a boat. Doubles range in price from 250F for something quite simple up to 320F for one with bathroom and Louis XV furniture. There's no doubt about it — the staff here do their utmost to please their guests in the best tradition of hotel hospitality.

ROYAN 17200

10% HÔTEL LE PLAZZA**

17 rue Font-de-Cherves (Centre).
☎ 05.46.05.30.79
Closed Jan 1–March 1. **TV**.

Right in the centre of town and only 200m from the beach, *Le Plazza* is a typically French hotel run by friendly owners. We especially recommend the family rooms (which are more like suites) since they're enormous and you won't feel as if you're living on top of each other. Doubles 255F with shower/wc, 320F with bath and large terrace. Triples 330F out of season and 360F in season, and rooms that sleep four 385F out of season and 410F in season.

HÔTEL BELLE-VUE**

122 av. de Pontaillac (South-West).
☎ 05.46.39.06.75 F→ 05.46.39.44.92
Closed Nov 1–end Feb. **Car park**. **TV**.

As the name implies, the view is pretty good. You'll be welcomed by polite smiling staff when you arrive at this old guest house built in 1953. It has the appearance of a typical bourgeois house. There are antiques and flowers everywhere and some rooms have a terrace where you can sit and gaze at the sky and the sea. Attractions include the beach, crazy golf (for sensible souls) and the casino (for the more extravagant). Doubles with shower/wc 355F (overlooking the sea) and 305F (at the back). Smaller room also available with TV for 275F.

|●| RESTAURANT LE CHALET

6 bd de la Grandière (East); it's at the eastern end of the seafront, opposite the tourist office.
☎ 05.46.05.04.90
Closed Wednesdays (except July–Aug) and Jan 15–Feb 18.

Rustic décor, stylish service and good cooking – *Le Chalet* is a must. This is a restaurant that the locals themselves will recommend. The cheapest set meal is 100F and it's good (not available Sunday evenings or public holidays); others 150F, 220F and 280F. A few regional specialities such as *chaudrée* (conger eel and white fish stew) in the 145F set meal and lamb shank with haricot beans.

SAINT-GEORGES-DE-DIDONNE 17110 (4KM S)

⌂ |●| HÔTEL-RESTAURANT COLINETTE*

16 av. de la Grande-Plage (North-East).
☎ 05.46.05.15.75 F➔ 05.46.06.54.17
Hotel open all year round. Restaurant open every day April 1–Oct 1, weekends and holidays only Oct 1–March 31, annual closure Dec 15–Jan 15.

Colinette looks like a guest house out of a 50s or 60s movie, whereas its sister hotel which is slightly further away looks more like a bland 70s villa (but it does have the advantage that you can be more independent there). Very conventional bedrooms. Doubles 120–150F with basin, 150–200F with basin and shower/wc, and 200–260F with shower/wc. Half-board, which is compulsory in July and August, costs 190–250F per person depending on what type of room you're in. Set meals 55F (available every day), 69F, 85F, 92F, 117F and 155F. Children's set meal 37F.

⌂ HÔTEL LE SUZAC***

17–26 chemin du Fort-de-Suzac; it's on the road going towards Meschers.
☎ 05.46.06.26.46 F➔ 05.46.06.26.13
Closed Nov 1–March 15. **Car park**. **TV**.
Disabled access.

This hotel, whose architecture combines modern and old styles, stands on the cliffs and is reminiscent of those "beach" hotels we used to dream of back in the 60s. It's completely white – impossible to miss. Friendly staff, clean comfortable bedrooms, and a beautiful big beach on your doorstep. The rates are pretty good out of season – from 285F with no sea view – but extortionate in July and August (up to 690F), which is rather a shame.

SAINT-PALAIS-SUR-MER 17420 (6KM W)

⌂ LE FRIVOLE**

10 av. du Platin.
☎ 05.46.23.25.00 F➔ 05.46.23.20.25
Closed Oct–March.

A large bourgeois-style building dating back to the turn of the century. The stone walls and attractive garden give it character. Madame has very good taste – she decorated the eleven exquisite bedrooms herself and keeps them in tip-top condition. The regulars are mainly Germans and Swedes who know the place well and come year after year. No TV thank goodness – just peace and quiet. Prices range from 190F to 440F, depending on facilities and the time of year. What's more, the owner, a well-educated chap, can chat about literature, gastronomy and sometimes mysticism. Advisable to book.

⌂ |●| HÔTEL-RESTAURANT TÉTHYS**

60 av. de la Corniche (South-East).
☎ 05.46.23.33.61
Closed Sept 15–end May. **Car park**. **TV**.

Service 12.30–2pm and 7.30–9.30pm. The archetypal seaside hotel, and one with a great location. You'll get an unobstructed view from the dining room and from some of the pleasant bedrooms, which are quiet and quite big. Everything's spick-and-span and the beach is only 300m away. Half-board 315F per person in season, bedrooms 270–300F, and set meals 100F, 140F, 160F and 190F (children's 40F). There's also a terrace/garden where you can have a game of table tennis.

|●| LE PETIT POUCET

La Grande Côte.
☎ 05.46.23.20.48 F➔ 05.46.23.20.48
Closed Wednesdays.

This concrete 50s restaurant may be situated at a bend on the road to La Palmyre but don't let this put you off. It has a magnificent view of the Grande Côte beach and a bright pretty dining room serving delicious regional dishes. The 79F set meal offers a light and delicate *fondant* of three vegetables and mussels *à la rochelaise* (stuffed with herb butter and browned). Other set meals 109F and 169F. Gourmets will love the *mouclade* (mussels in creamy sauce with saffron, turmeric and white wine) and langoustines with Pineau from the à la carte menu. Unfussy service but staff are quick and attentive.

MESCHERS-SUR-GIRONDE 17132 (12KM S)

10% LES GROTTES DE MATATA**

bd de la Falaise.
☎ 05.46.02.70.02 F 05.46.02.78.00
Closed Nov–Feb.

A pleasant crêperie in the famous caves of Matata with a view of the estuary of the Gironde and a décor of wood and a wall with fossilized shells dating back to the Cretaceous period. Lots of celebrities have passed through here. You'll see signed photos of actors and singers including Johnny Halliday. There's a recently built hotel just above the caves offering a few bedrooms (300–350F) and a view of the spectactularly beautiful estuary.

MORNAC-SUR-SEUDRE 17113 (13KM N)

LE TAHITI

How to get there: it's opposite the harbour.
☎ 05.46.22.76.53
Closed Mondays and Dec 1–March 15.

Mornac is a charming village full of craftsmen and artists and is home to a beautiful 12th century church, so of course it has a number of so-called "gourmet" restaurants. *Le Tahiti* looks like a nice little traditional bar with its terrace facing the little harbour on the Seudre. The 69F set meal offers a starter of six small oysters with sausage, followed by grilled mullet with tarragon sauce, whitebait or grilled sardines, and for dessert the house fruit tart or fruit salad with Pineau. The 100F set meal is also good value for money.

PALMYRE (LA) 17570 (18KM NW)

HÔTEL LA CÔTE D'ARGENT**

4 av. de l'Océan (Centre).
☎ 05.46.22.40.07 F 05.46.23.66.04
Closed Nov 15–March 15. **Secure parking**. **TV**.
Disabled access.

A very well designed modern hotel. Most bedrooms have a good-sized balcony. Doubles 190–295F with shower/wc and 260–325F with bath. Prices depend on the time of year. Use of car park 40F per day. Sauna.

10% PALMYROTEL**

2 allée des Passereaux (Centre).
☎ 05.46.23.65.65 F 05.46.22.44.13
Closed Nov–March. **Car park**. **TV**. **Disabled access**.

Palmyrotel is next to the famous zoo. Surrounded by pine trees, it looks just like the kind of hotel you'd see in the Mediterranean. Well-kept extensive grounds, very clean functional bedrooms with balconies (lots of them get the sun), adventure playground for kids. The staff are fairly professional in their approach. Bedrooms all come with bath and cost 250–385F depending on the time of year. Triples 310–470F and rooms that sleep four 350–495F. No charge for children under 5. Half-board 250–315F per person. Set meals 99F (pretty good), 132F and 169F (fish dishes). Set meal for under 15s 58F, for under 10s 45F.

BOUTENAC-TOUVENT 17120 (28KM SE)

10% LE RELAIS DETOUVENT**

Centre.
☎ 05.46.94.13.06 F 05.46.94.10.40
Closed Sunday evenings and Mondays except in summer, and Dec 20–Jan 6. **Car park**. **TV**.
Disabled access.

Service from noon and 8pm. Well-kept refurbished bedrooms decorated in soft warm shades (240F with shower–260F with bath). The restaurant has a good reputation. Cheapest set meal 85F, others slightly dearer but skilfully prepared. Brilliant wine cellar. Extensive grounds with lots of trees.

RUFFEC 16700

LE MOULIN DE CONDAC

Condac; take the Confolens road.
☎ 05.45.31.04.97 F 05.45.31.29.74
Closed Monday, Tuesday, Wednesday and Thursday evenings in winter. **Car park**.

A welcoming restaurant in an attractively restored 18th century mill on the banks of the Charente. It offers good traditional local cooking. Cheapest set meal 70F (weekdays only) and gourmet set meals 98–190F (aperitif, wine and coffee included). Try the *gratin* of calf's head or the local lamb. Beautiful shaded terrace, pedalos and mini-golf. Our favourite place in this particular part of the world.

VERTEUIL-SUR-CHARENTE 16510 (6KM SE)

HÔTEL LA PALOMA*

rue Fontaine.

☎ 05.45.31.41.32
Closed Sunday evenings, Mondays and two weeks in February. **Car park**. **Disabled access**.

A beautiful village dominated by a majestic castle. *Hôtel La Paloma* is an inn with country furniture and a very pleasant open terrace. Do try the house cheese tart. Set meals 67F, 79F, 96F, 130F and 160F. Doubles 170F with shower and 225F with bath. Ask for room number 1 so you can try out the unusual bath. The quality of the service is uneven, which is a shame.

SAINT-DENIS-D'OLÉRON 17650

10% HÔTEL-RESTAURANT LE MOULIN DE LA GALETTE*

8 rue Ernest-Morisset (Centre); it's near the market square and the church.
☎ 05.46.47.88.04
Closed Oct–April 1. **Disabled access**.

Lunch served 12.30pm, dinner 7.30pm. It's worth traipsing from one end of the island to the other to get to this hotel, which makes a nice change from places that are so similar you can't tell them apart. An old Rococo style building, it's very striking and there's not another quite like it on the island! Staff are very welcoming – such signs of hospitality are few and far between nowadays. The assortment of mismatched objects might surprise – or perhaps unsettle – you. Doubles 265F with shower/wc. The owner takes a professional approach to cooking and uses only fresh produce. The result? Good set meals at 90F (flawless oysters and fish), 145F (enormous portions) and 165F. There are a few tables set out on the courtyard cum terrace opposite the market. Homely atmosphere.

SAINT-MAIXENT-L'ÉCOLE 79400

10% HÔTEL-RESTAURANT LE LOGIS SAINT-MARTIN***

chemin de Pissot (South-East); head for Niort and turn left at the last set of lights on the outskirts of Saint-Maixent.
☎ 05.49.05.58.68. F :05.49.76.19.93.
Restaurant open weekday lunchtimes and evenings; closed January. **Car park**. **TV**.

If you're only spending one night in Saint-Maixent here's your chance to splash out in a hotel housed in a large 17th century bourgeois-style building by the river. It stands in its own grounds and you're guaranteed peace and quiet just a couple of hundred yards from the town centre. Doubles 390F with shower/wc and 490F with bath. Set meals 80F (lunchtimes only). Others 150–260F offering mainly fish dishes. Despite the impressive surroundings the staff are very down-to-earth.

AIRIPT 79260 (10KM S)

L'AUBERGE DU PORT D'AIRIPT

How to get there: take the Niort road on leaving Saint-Maixent and when you get to La Crèche, head for Sainte-Neomaye and then Aiript.
☎ 05.49.25.58.81 F 05.49.05.33.49
Restaurant closed Sunday evenings and Mondays.
Car park.

Service noon–2pm and 8–10pm. This place has quiet corners for couples, a warm atmosphere for families nostalgic about the past, two large rooms for wedding receptions, and a Hollywood-style swimming pool in magnificent surroundings for everyone. Set meals 85F and 165F. Expect to pay 130–160F à la carte. Enjoy crêpes and grills by the pool in summer. Five bedrooms 215F with shower/wc or bath.

MOTHE-SAINT-HÉRAY (LA) 79800 (11KM SE)

10% HÔTEL-RESTAURANT LE CORNEILLE**

13 rue du Maréchal-Joffre (Centre); it's in the main street.
☎ 05.49.05.17.08 F 05.49.05.19.56
Restaurant closed Friday evenings, Sunday evenings out of season and Christmas/New Year holidays. **Car park**. **TV**.

Lunch served noon–2pm, dinner 7.30–9pm. Doctor Corneille, the last descendant of the famous tragedian, used to live in this very building. Nowadays it's a little family hotel that smells of old wood. An ideal base for exploring the region once you've done Futuroscope and before you head off to the marshes. Bedrooms from 200F. Good regional cooking. Cheapest set meal 65F, others 95–180F.

SAINT-MARTIN-DE-RÉ 17410

CAFÉ DE LA PAIX

11 quai Poithevinière.
☎ 05.46.09.20.55 F 05.46.09.03.41

There's a string of restaurants on the harbour of Saint-Martin and most of them offer the same type of food. Here though, they make an effort to pay as much attention to the décor and the atmosphere as they do to what they put on your plate. The dining room's small and the covered terrace isn't particularly big either so it's just as well they're open late into the night. Set meals 72–150F and a brasserie menu. The house specialities are *délice* of salmon with a langoustine *coulis*, *croquant* of scallops with baby vegetables, fisherman's stew, and *pierre-à-feu du boucher* and *du pêcheur* (an assortment of meat and fish respectively) and cost round about 130F.

COUARDE-SUR-MER (LA) 17670 (4KM SW)

HÔTEL-RESTAURANT LA SALICORNE

16 rue de l'Olivette (East); it's in the main street.
☎ 05.46.29.82.37 F 05.46.29.82.37
Closed All Saints' Day–Easter (except on public holidays).

A restaurant that's as much about meeting up with your friends as it is about eating. The dining room is long and narrow and attractively decorated. Set meals 90F (lunchtimes) and 130F. Forget about those though. If you want to experience the full range of Luc Dumond's skills, order à la carte. This means that you'll end up paying more than 100F a head, but this is the *l'île de Ré* after all! Doubles 180F with washing facilities.

RESTAURANT LA CABINE DE BAIN

How to get there: it's at the start of the pedestrian street.
Grande-Rue (Centre)
☎ 05.46.29.84.26
Closed Sunday evenings, Mondays, and weekdays in winter.

The man who owns this place also owns the fishmonger's next door and a fish stall at the covered market. He has an excellent reputation in town so if you like fish you need have no fears about coming here. The kitchen comes up with some sophisticated and imaginative dishes. For 39–55F, you can have raw bass with coriander, mussels in Pineau (of course!), raw salmon *à la japonaise* or *cassolette* of clams. Spend a bit more (76–99F) for grilled salmon with olives, *pavé* of meagre (a bit like sea bass) with orange butter, *Rossini de la mer,* and roast cod with basil. And if you feel like splashing out a bit, 130F gets you lobster stew. There are a few unusual round tables on the terrace. Service can be a bit on the slow side. Expect to pay about 170F à la carte.

FLOTTE (LA) 17630 (4KM SE)

RESTAURANT L'ÉCAILLER

3 quai de Sénac (Centre).
☎ 05.46.09.56.40
Closed Mondays out of season and All Saints' Day–Easter (except Christmas holidays).

Service from noon and 8pm. You could order a meal blindfold in *L'Écailler* because it's one of the most reliable restaurants on the island. It's an old 17th century building situated across from the port. It does nothing but fish and seafood and the chef uses extremely fresh quality produce. But you can't get all this for peanuts – expect to pay about 300F.

BOIS-PLAGE-EN-RÉ (LE) 17580 (5KM S)

HÔTEL-RESTAURANT L'OCÉAN**

172 rue Saint-Martin; it's 50m from the church.
☎ 05.46.09.23.07 F 05.46.09.05.40
Closed Jan 5–31. **Car park. TV.**

In a quiet street away from passing traffic. The magnificent flower-filled patio that's very typical of the island isn't its only asset. Staff make you feel welcome and the recently refurbished bedrooms are quiet. Have dinner on the patio and then you'll really feel you're on holiday. The 140F set meal offers a dozen local oysters, a choice of cuttlefish or duck *aiguillettes* with pink peppercorns, salad, cheese and dessert. Children's set meal 50F. Good selection of wines. Half-board 340–400F per person. Doubles 350–380F with shower/wc and 380–500F with bath. There's a place to leave your bike.

HÔTEL LES GOLLANDIÈRES**

av. de la Plage (Centre).
☎ 05.46.09.23.99 F 05.46.09.09.84
Closed start Nov–April 1. **Car park. TV.**
Disabled access.

A well designed hotel complex covering about two and a half acres and just 100m from the island's most popular beach. It's ideal if you like the holiday club concept. Everything runs smoothly under the watchful eye of its competent owner. The rooms are impeccable and the swimming pool is clean. Buffet breakfast – cheese, hard-boiled eggs, bread, croissants and jam – is 45F. Doubles 310–390F with shower/wc and 400–450F with bath. Prices vary depending on the time of year. Half-board (350–450F) is compulsory in season and at holiday weekends. Cheapest set meal 120F.

|●| LA BOUVETTE GRILL DE MER

Moulin de Morinand (North).
How to get there: take the bypass so as to avoid Saint-Martin-de-Ré, go left towards Le Bois-Plage and it's about 1km further along.
☎ 05.46.09.29.87
Closed Tuesdays and Wednesdays (out of season) and Dec–Jan.

Dinner and Sunday lunch only. Situated in magnificent surroundings, one of the island's most interesting restaurants is housed in a former garage that doesn't look like much from the outside. Olivier, the owner, serves seafood that tastes as if it's jumped straight out of the water and onto your plate. Suggestions are chalked up on the board – *salade terre-mer,* six oysters, *éclade* of mussels, langoustine fricassee, sardines, sole, salmon, grilled bass, stuffed crab and, for afters, warm goat's cheese, house fruit tarts, fresh pineapple and floating islands. The *salade Bouvette* (salmon, scallops and cuttlefish) will melt in your mouth, the *éclade* of mussels served in a frying pan on a bed of pine needles is delicious (the dash of raspberry vinegar's a good idea), and the stuffed crab is sheer bliss. You must try the fresh pineapple for dessert. If you want lobster from Brittany (160F per 300g) you'll have to order it in advance. *La Bouvette* provides what people want – a good atmosphere and good food – and is already pretty popular. It can only handle 40 people at a time and you'll have to book several days in advance in season.

|●| RESTAURANT AU PETIT BOIS

23 rue de l'Église (Centre).
☎ 05.46.09.37.21
Closed Monday evenings and Sundays out of season.

Jacqueline spent many years working in the catering trade in her home town of La Rochelle and opened this restaurant not too long ago. The fish is fresh and bought from her fishermen friends.The 92F set meal offering *moules marinière*, fish of the day (sole, plaice etc) and dessert is good value for money, as is the 130F one of starter, main course, cheese and dessert. We got locally grown potatoes with the sole *meunière* (something which doesn't happen everywhere). À la carte offerings include eel *persillé*, prawns *persillé*, and crab. "Le Royal" (70F), a white wine from the island is light and refreshing. Children's set meal 39.50F. Just one little disadvantage however – you sometimes have a bit of a wait for your food.

SAINTE-MARIE-DE-RÉ 17740 (10KM N)

10% ⌂ HÔTEL DU PEU-BRETON**

31 rue de la Cailletière; it's on the road that goes from Sainte-Marie towards La Noue.
☎ 05.46.30.23.55 F➔ 05.46.37.15.35
Closed October. **Car park. TV. Disabled access.**

A fairly modern hotel. The delightful swimming pool and the deckchairs look very inviting on a summer's day. Doubles from 300F with shower/wc and 350–400F with bath. Family rooms with shower/wc 370F (based on three sharing) and 420–460F (for four). Very nice buffet breakfast and there's a billiard table in the lounge if you feel like unwinding at the end of the day.

SAINT-PIERRE-D'OLÉRON 17310

⌂ LE SQUARE**

place des Anciens-Combattants (Centre).
☎ 05.46.47.00.35 F➔ 05.46.75.04.90
Closed Nov–Easter. **Car park. TV.**

An unpretentious hotel with good facilities – sauna and pool – and clean rooms with TV and direct telephone. Expect to pay 260F with shower, 280F with bath out of season (prices rise by 100F in July and August). Courteous welcome.

|●| LE MILLE PÂTES

place Gambetta (Centre).
☎ 05.46.47.33.44.
Closed Tuesday evenings and Wednesdays (except during school holidays) and January. Open every day in season.

Service until midnight. A good and inexpensive pizzeria with a terrace facing place Gambetta. Its specialities are seaweed ravioli, house pasta (including spaghetti, which is unusual) and large pizzas baked in a wood-fired oven. The 49F *formule* of dish of the day, a quarter litre of wine and coffee is just the thing if you're not too hungry and don't have much money to spend. Quick, friendly service.

|●| CHEZ FRANÇOIS

55 rue de la République (Centre).
☎ 05.46.47.29.44 F➔ 05.46.47.02.33
Closed Sunday evenings and Mondays out of season, and in December.

One of the best restaurants in town. In the 78F set meal you can get pâté of artichokes with smoked pork, fish of the day or a meat dish that changes when the set meal does, and a wonderful *crème caramel.* A well-balanced and pretty flawless meal. Other set meals up to 167F and an interesting à la carte menu.

COTINIÈRE (LA) 17310 (3KM S)

HÔTEL FACE AUX FLOTS**

24 rue du four (Centre).
☎ 05.46.47.10.05 F➜ 05.46.47.45.95.
Closed Nov 6–start Feb (except Christmas holidays). **TV**. **Disabled access**.

Service from 12.15pm and 7.15pm. A very well cared for hotel about 300m from the busy harbour area. As the name implies, you'll have a view of the sea. A smiling and efficent blond in her forties is in charge, and she takes her role as hostess very seriously and can be relied on to leave nothing to chance. The restaurant has a panoramic view, and there's a bar, a little garden and a swimming pool. Doubles with shower/wc 320F out of season and 320–450F in season and depending on which way the rooms face. Half-board, compulsory in July and August costs 350–420F based on two sharing. Set meals 100F, 148F and 195F.

CHÉRAY 17190 (5KM N)

RESTAURANT LE BREUIL

☎ 05.46.76.60.79
Closed Tuesdays–Friday evenings out of season.

Claude and Patrick have created a cosy atmosphere in this former farmhouse. Rustic dining rooms and good food. The 60F lunchtime *formule* offers starters from the buffet, plus the dish of the day and dessert. The cheapest set meal (90F) offers, for example, oysters, mullet with dill, cheese and dessert. À la carte, the stuffed oysters and the salmon stuffed with prawns and avocado have proved a big success.

SAINT-SAVIN-SUR-GARTEMPE 86310

10% HÔTEL DU MIDI**

N 151; it's a stone's throw from the church on the route du Blanc.
☎ 05.49.48.00.40
Closed Sunday evenings and Mondays (except in July and August). **Secure parking**. **TV**.

Service from noon and 7.30pm. People usually come to Saint-Savin to admire the superb 11th and 13th century frescoes in the abbey. This former coaching inn, run by a friendly couple, has been an inn since 1762. The owner, who collects firearms, offers a few good specialities like salmon and sorrel *terrine*, ham *à l'ancienne,* fillet of perch with *beurre blanc* and stuffed snails. Doubles 140F with washing facilities and 200–250F with shower/wc or bath. Set meals 70F, 90F, 130F and 150F. Excellent value for money.

LA GRANGE*

route d'Antigny; it's just a few steps from the famous Benedictine abbey.
☎ 05.49.48.07.06 F➜ 05.49.48.21.04
Closed Wednesdays. **Secure parking**.

An impressive barn with exposed stonework, a fireplace and solid wood. Yokes that oxen used to wear have been turned into light fixtures and there are old feeding racks on the walls. It specializes in fish and *terrines.* Set meals 60F (weekdays), 80F, 110F and 140F. Bright pleasant bedrooms 180F with shower and 250F with bath. It's advisable to check the price when booking.

SAINT-TROJAN-LES-BAINS 17370

10% LE COUREAU**

88 rue de la République (Centre).
☎ 05.46.76.05.53
Closed Mondays (except in June, July and Aug) and November. **TV**. **Disabled access**.

A hotel and bar in the main (pedestrian) street of a delightful village. Very friendly and down to earth atmosphere. Fourteen bedrooms – most are basic but perfectly adequate. 170F with well-kept bathrooms in the corridor. Rooms on the ground floor are dearer but also better equipped (TV, modern furniture, rather pretty décor, shower/wc). But what we really liked about it was the friendly and straightforward welcome we got from new owners Marie-Claire (who paints watercolours when she's in the mood) and Gervais, both of whom are pretty laid-back about things. You'll find people at the counter telling jokes and playing dice. In July and August, entertainment is provided (until midnight) in the form of concerts involving drums, banjos and clarinets. It may annoy the neighbours but is guaranteed to delight the night owls amongst the holidaymakers. Peace and quiet out of season. And last of all, you might like to know that Marie-Claire doesn't like grumpy folk so she'll very kindly give them the names of hotels (Novotel, Formule1 etc) they're better suited to.

☗ |●| HÔTEL-RESTAURANT L'ALBATROS**

11 bd du Docteur-Pineau (South-East); it's in the same neighbourhood as L'Embrun.
☎ 05.46.76.00.08 ➡ 05.46.76.03.58
Closed mid Nov–mid Feb. **Car park**. **TV**.
Disabled access.

You've got the beach on your doorstep and a magnificent view of the sea from the terrace. Have dinner as the sun goes down — it's a magic moment that will stay with you for a long time. Set meals 89F (simple but with the catch of the day — mullet or grilled sardines), 109F, 137F and 159F. Children's set meal 62F. The rooms, some of them in a bungalow at the back, aren't bright but they're comfortable. Doubles from 359F with shower/wc or bath. Half-board, compulsory June–Sept and during school holidays, is 359F per person.

GRAND-VILLAGE 17370 (3KM NW)

|●| LE RELAIS DES SALINES

port des Salines.
☎ 05.46.75.82.42 ➡ 05.46.45.21.55
Closed Oct–March.

A lovely setting beside the canals and a group of the brightly coloured huts — red, blue and green — that are so typical of the area. The restaurant appeals both to the eye and to the palate. The 58F set meal offers half a dozen oysters, panfried *céteaux* (it resembles sole) and a delicious *crème brûlée*. Brilliant specialities such as warm oysters with *beurre blanc*, langoustines flambéd with Pineau, fricassee of eels with garlic, and grilled bass. The secret of their success? Fresh produce, a passion for their work, a sure hand and reasonable prices. Terrific!

SAINTES 17100

10% ☗ |●| AUBERGE DE JEUNESSE***

2 place Geoffroy-Martel (Centre); it's near the Abbaye-aux-Dames.
☎ 05.46.92.14.92 ➡ 05.46.92.97.82
Closed mid Dec–mid Jan. **Disabled access**.

This youth hostel can accommodate 70. Two or four bedded rooms with basin, shower and wc 66F per night (includes breakfast but not sheets). Sheets for hire. Set meal 49F and half-board 117F per person. Very cheap and perfectly adequate. Rates reduced by 8–15% for groups.

10% ☗ HÔTEL BLEU NUIT**

1 rue Pasteur (West); go along cours National towards the A10.
☎ 05.46.93.01.72 ➡ 05.46.74.43.80
Closed Sunday evenings Oct 15–April 1.
Secure parking. **TV**. **Canal+**. **Disabled access**.

A pleasant hotel with particularly good prices. You'd be hard put to find better rates for a hotel that's been recently renovated (simply but with good taste) and isn't one of a chain or located in a business park. It stands at a pretty busy crossroads, but that's no problem thanks to the double glazing. Bedrooms 220–250F with shower/wc and fan. 20F supplement for pets. Secure car park 30F. The best value for money in Saintes.

10% ☗ HÔTEL DES MESSAGERIES**

rue des Messageries (Centre).
☎ 05.46.93.64.99 ➡ 05.46.92.14.34
Closed Christmas holidays. **Secure parking**. **TV**. **Canal+**.

A very quiet hotel even though it is right in the heart of Saintes. At least it's away from the busy main street. Recently refurbished and well cared for — highly recommended. Doubles 255–360F with shower/wc or bath. A few family rooms that sleep five. Plenty of foreign TV channels. There's even a laundry and an ironing board which is very convenient. Reductions for sales reps, but only if they're regulars.

10% ☗ HÔTEL LES BOSQUETS***

107 cours du Maréchal-Leclerc (West).
☎ 05.46.74.04.47 ➡ 05.46.74.27.89
Closed two weeks between Christmas and New Year.
Car park. **TV**. **Canal+**. **Disabled access**.

A comfortable hotel that's a bit like one of a chain but still has that little something. Bedrooms are spacious and well equipped and some look onto a pretty little garden. Expect to pay 285–305F depending on the position. They speak English, German, Spanish and Italian — and French of course!.

|●| RESTAURANT LA SARRAZINE

12 rue Saint-Michel; it's in the pedestrian precinct, just a few steps from the cathedral.
☎ 05.46.74.17.55
Closed Sundays (except July–Aug) and February.

The locals love this crêperie. *Galettes* are made with genuine buckwheat flour from Brittany (which is unfortunately not always the case). Try the plain salted butter one (14F) and you'll know exactly what we mean. "*La Forestière*" (cubes of bacon, smoked breast, mushrooms and *crème fraîche*) and "*l'Atlantique*" (scrambled eggs, smoked salmon, asparagus and *crème fraîche*) are two of the most popular specialities. And the *crêpes* are good too. The 54F set meal offers butter *galette*, *galette* with ham and Emmenthal and *crêpe* with jam. Go for the room at the back which has a beautiful stone fireplace (log fires in winter) and a conservatory — they open the roof on fine summer evenings.

LE PISTOU

3 place du Théâtre (Centre).
☎ 05.46.74.47.53 ➡ 05.46.94.14.29
Closed Sundays and Saturday lunchtimes in winter.

A centrally located restaurant with a fairly new owner. Monsieur Ranché takes a professional approach to his work, which he loves. His unpretentious cooking is based on fish and seafood (clams with pesto, medallions of monkfish and Mediterranean prawns with a langoustine *coulis*, and *gratinée* of seafood) and country classics like *grillons charentais* (*grillons* are the bits left over from cooking *confits*). Three set meals (79F, 105F and 135F) and there's always a fish of the day. Attentive unaffected service and relaxing décor.

LA CARAVELLE

5 quai de la République.
☎ 05.46.93.45.65.
Closed Sundays.

Lunch served noon–2pm, dinner 7–10pm.Two little flower-filled dining rooms decorated in pastel shades and facing the river. Pleasant service and decent traditional food. Brilliant 59F *formule* (weekday lunchtimes) offering dish of the day, wine and dessert. Set meals 70F, 88F and 108F. You won't be disappointed.

RESTAURANT LA CIBOULETTE

36 rue Pérat (Centre); go down cours National, cross the Charente, go along avenue Gambetta, then take the third street on your left after the bridge.
☎ 05.46.74.07.36 ➡ 05.46.94.14.54
Closed Saturday lunchtimes and Sundays.

The young chef who recently took over comes from Brest, so there's lots of fish and shellfish on offer. His successes include scallops with garlic and almonds, seafood platter, and salmon pancake *à la norvégienne*. And as we're in Charente-Maritime you also get several local specialities — fricassee of eels and *mouclade* — that are just as skilfully prepared. Home-made bread and desserts. Set meals 90F (except Sundays and public holidays), 130F, 149F, 169F and 180F (regional dishes). You really must taste the regional speciality known as *jonchée* (fresh unsalted cheese). Reasonably priced wine list (try the regional ones). Rustic décor.

RÉTAUD 17460 (12KM SW)

RESTAURANT LE SAINT-TROJEAN

Centre.
☎ 05.46.92.23.18
Closed Sunday evenings (out of season) and Mondays.

Service from noon and 7.30pm. An exceptional restaurant that's well worth the effort. We were surprised and delighted to find it but we're not quite sure how to word this review in case we're accused of being over the top. The décor's elegant and simple, staff are friendly and Monsieur Chapelle is a young and talented chef. The 58F set meal (lunchtimes) includes starter, main course, cheese or dessert, a jug of very acceptable wine and — are you ready for this? — as much mineral water as you want (a rare occurrence!). Other set meals 90F (this offers one of the best gizzard salads we've ever tasted) and 110F (this comes with two main courses — sturgeon steaks made to the chef's special recipe and pork fillet with four spices). And if you're really hungry, go for the 148F set meal. One of our most favourite restaurants ever on account of its excellent value for money, exceptionally fresh produce and the quality of the food. The restaurant was started as part of a local campaign to bring the village back to life. It's been a success and other places might like to follow their example — as long as they've a good cook on hand of course!

TAILLEBOURG 17350 (12KM N)

AUBERGE DES GLYCINES

How to get there: it's down by the river – take the Saint-Savinien road from Saintes.
☎ 05.46.91.81.40
Closed Wednesdays, February and October. **Car park**.

On the banks of the Charente, this inn is a godsend if you need to switch off for a while and have a quiet meal. Eat either in the flower-filled garden — cottage garden is the description that springs to mind — where the sun blazes down at lunchtime or on the shaded little terrace on the first floor. The silence is broken only by the sound of carp snapping at flies. Set meals 78F (except weekends and public holidays) and 100F offer traditional cooking. Good food and a change of scenery guaranteed. Pity the service is a bit on the casual side.

PONS 17800 (22.5KM S)

10% HÔTEL-RESTAURANT DE BORDEAUX**

1 av. Gambetta.
☎ 05.46.91.31.12 F➔ 05.46.91.22.25
Closed Sunday evenings Oct–April. **Secure parking. TV. Canal+.**

Service noon–2pm and 7.30–9.30pm (10pm in summer). The kind of little provincial hotel we like in the heart of Pons, an old town that isn't any less delightful for not being particularly well known. The young owner has made it both traditional and modern. Very tasteful low-key décor in the bedrooms, which are fully equipped. Doubles 260F with shower or bath. The restaurant offers good imaginative cooking by the owner (yes, him again!), a talented chef and passionate about his work. A few original dishes (they vary depending on the season) — langoustine and Parmesan *pastilla* (a kind of pie made with filo pastry), langoustine *gazpacho*, iced melon with Lillet (a type of apéritif) and soft fruit, medallions of lamb with a sauce made from preserved garlic, and saddle of rabbit with a *compote* of onions in Pineau. Cheapest set meal 90F. The regulars drop by in the morning for a chat with the owner over a quick coffee before heading off to work.

SURGÈRES 17700

10% ☗ |●| HÔTEL-RESTAURANT GAMBETTA*

49 rue Gambetta (North).
☎ 05.46.07.03.64 F➔ 05.46.07.37.32
Closed Sunday lunchtimes and Christmas–New Year's Day. **Car park. TV.**

Surgères is a crossroads and may be just the place to stop if you're coming from Niort, La Rochelle, Rochefort or Saint-Jean-d'Angély. The *Gambetta* is popular with sales reps and workers on placements and will suit you down to the ground. Clean standard bedrooms. The very simple 62F set meal means you won't go to bed hungry. There's another set meal at 100F and à la carte is also available. The proprietress comes from Beaujolais country and has Morgon, Régnié and Chénas at very decent prices. Doubles 180F with shower and 230F with shower/wc. Half-board round about 200F. Full board 210–280F.

THOUARS 79100

☗ |●| HÔTEL-RESTAURANT DU CHÂTEAU**

Saint-Jean-de-Thouars; from the centre of Thouars head for Parthenay-Niort, turn left as you leave town, and it's about 2km further on.
☎ 05.49.96.12.60 F➔ 05.49.96.34.02
Closed Sunday evenings. **Secure parking. TV. Canal+.**

Quiet surroundings, away from the road. Doubles 220–240F with bath. Some of the rooms (like the dining room) have a beautiful view of the old town and, of course, the château. Set meals start at 59F and go up to 187F. We strongly recommend half-board in season. A very typical establishment.

POMPOIS 79100 (4KM NW)

|●| RESTAURANT DU LOGIS DE POMPOIS

Sainte-Verge BP86(Centre); head for Argenton-Château and when you get to the hotel called L'Acacia turn right towards Saumur and then take the first left; it's pretty easy after that — just follow the arrows.
☎ 05.49.96.27.84 F➔ 05.49.96.13.97
Closed Sunday evenings, Mondays and Christmas–New Year's Day. **Car park.**

Service noon–1.30pm and 7.30–9pm. Magnificent surroundings. Once the setting for a wine business, it's now a large dining room with exposed beams and stonework very typical of Poitou. A remarkable place on account of the quality of the cooking and the welcome (not at all pretentious). Set meals 120F (weekday lunchtimes) - 240F. Try the salmon and langoustine tart.

VIGEANT (LE) 86150

|●| LA GRIMOLÉE

Port de Salles.
☎ 05.49.48.75.22
Closed Tuesday evenings, Wednesdays, two weeks in February and two weeks in November. **Car park.**

It's not very difficult to work out why the *Grimolée* is so popular. It stands in its own grounds with lots of greenery round, it's only a few metres from the river and a little bit further from the Val de Vienne motor racing circuit (you'll sometimes hear the cars zooming by). And there's more to come — the dining room is bathed in light and the cooking is fresh and inventive. You'll be delighted with dishes like scallops with lamb's lettuce, medallions of monkfish with a langoustine sauce, and ice cream *gratinée* with pineapple and *sauce créole.* Set meals range in price from 90F at lunchtime (drink included) to 235F. A pleasant place and it's best to book.

PROVENCE-ALPES-CÔTE d'AZUR

04 Alpes-de-Haute-Provence

05 Hautes-Alpes

06 Alpes-Maritimes

13 Bouches-du-Rhône

83 Var

84 Vaucluse

AIX-EN-PROVENCE 13100

SEE MAP ON P.702

CIRS (CENTRE INTERNATIONAL DE RENCONTRES ET DE SÉJOURS)

3 av. Marcel-Pagnol — Le Jas-de-Bouffan (West). Off map **A2-1**.
☎ 04.42.20.15.99 F 04.42.59.36.12
Closed Dec 20–Feb 1. **Car park. Disabled access.**

This youth hostel is located near the Vasarely Foundation, 2km from the town centre in a quiet district. One hundred beds in small dormitories. The first night costs 80F (including breakfast), subsequent nights 69F. Meals for 49F. Garden, tennis and adventure playground.

HÔTEL VIGOUROUX

27 rue Cardinale. **MAP B2-3**
☎ 04.42.38.26.42

This hotel is only open in the summer. During the rest of the year the rooms are rented out to students and teachers – although there are exceptions. Write in advance to book. The atmosphere is that of a large family house. Eleven rooms, some with shower/wc for 230F There is also an apartment. Reduced prices for long stays. Garden, but no dogs allowed.

HÔTEL LE PRIEURÉ**

route des Alpes; take the N96, route des Alpes, towards Manosque-Sisteron. Off map **B1-5**
☎ 04.42.21.05.23 F 04.42.21.60.56
Car park.

This former priory used to be the Archbishop's residence but some time ago it was converted into a 23-bedroom hotel. All the rooms look out onto picturesque Pavillon Lanfant park but unfortunately this ornate garden is not open to the public, so you'll just have to enjoy the view. The rooms are very pleasing to the eye too. A double with a bathroom is 298F with a double bed or 400F with twin beds. Breakfast is 39.50F served in your room or on the terrace. A lovely hotel. Proprietress Madame Le Hir greets you with a cheery smile.

10% HÔTEL CARDINAL**

24 rue Cardinale. **MAP B2-4**
☎ 04.42.38.32.30 F 04.42.26.39.05
TV.

An 18th century building in the heart of the quiet Marazin district. Superb rooms (antique furniture and panelling, prints on the wall, carpets, etc) each with telephone. Reasonably priced for Aix-en-Provence: 230–300F for a double. There are seven rooms in an annexe which are larger and have cooking facilities, 350F. One even has a little patio with a fountain. Not over-friendly however.

10% LES QUATRE DAUPHINS**

54 rue Roux-Alphéran. **MAP B2-6**
☎ 04.42.38.16.39 F 04.42.38.60.19
TV.

A quiet, charming hotel. It takes its name (The Four Dolphins) from the nearby fountain with its amazing, scale-covered dolphins. Small, tastefully furnished rooms spread haphazardly around the three floors of this comfortable house, each with telephone and mini-bar. A double with a shower is 360F, or

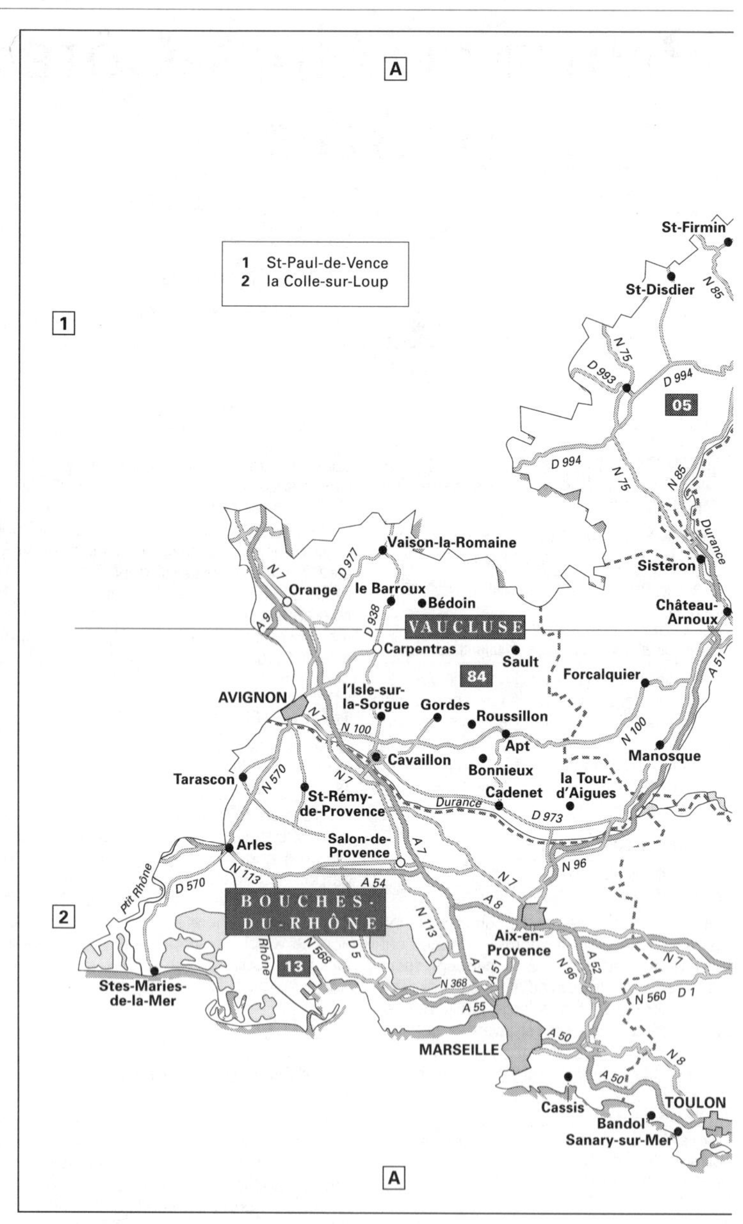

A
1 St-Paul-de-Vence
2 la Colle-sur-Loup
1
2
St-Firmin
St-Disdier
N 85
N 75
D 993
D 994
05
D 994
N 75
N 85
Durance
Sisteron
Château-Arnoux
Vaison-la-Romaine
N 7
D 977
Orange
le Barroux
Bédoin
A 9
D 938
VAUCLUSE
Carpentras
Sault
84
Forcalquier
A 51
AVIGNON
l'Isle-sur-la-Sorgue
Gordes
Roussillon
N 7
N 100
Apt
N 100
Manosque
Cavaillon
Bonnieux
Tarascon
N 570
N 7
la Tour-d'Aigues
Cadenet
St-Rémy-de-Provence
Durance
D 973
Arles
Salon-de-Provence
A 7
N 96
N 113
D 570
A 54
N 7
Ptit Rhône
A 8
BOUCHES-DU-RHÔNE
N 113
N 568
D 5
Rhône
13
Aix-en-Provence
N 96
A 52
N 7
Stes-Maries-de-la-Mer
A 7
A 51
N 368
N 560
D 1
A 55
A 50
MARSEILLE
N 8
A 50
Cassis
TOULON
Bandol
Sanary-sur-Mer
A

B
la Grave
Névache
Briançon
la Chapelle-en-Valgaudemar
Ristolas
Molines-en-Queyras
St-Véran
St-Crépin
Guillestre
HAUTES-ALPES
ITALY
1
Embrun
GAP
Barcelonnette
ALPES-DE-HAUTE-PROVEN
Allos
St-Étienne-de-Tinée
Auron
Col de Tende
ALPES-MARITIMES
St-Martin-Vésubie
St-Dalmas-de-Tende
la Brigue
Valberg
DIGNE-LES-BAINS
Annot
Massoins
Utelle
Breil-sur-Roya
Sospel
04
l'Escarène
Peille
06
Moustiers-Ste-Marie
Castellane
Thorenc
Èze
Menton
Vence
Monaco
Beaulieu-sur-Mer
St-Jean-Cap-Ferrat
Comps-sur-Artuby
Grasse
NICE
Fayence
Biot
Bargemon
Cagnes-sur-Mer
Mougins
Antibes
Villecroze
Draguignan
Cannes
VAR
Théoule-sur-Mer
2
Fréjus
St-Raphaël
Ste-Maxime
83
St-Tropez
Gassin
Bormes-les-Mimosas
Cavalaire-sur-Mer
le Lavandou
Hyères
Îles d'Hyères
0 10 20 km

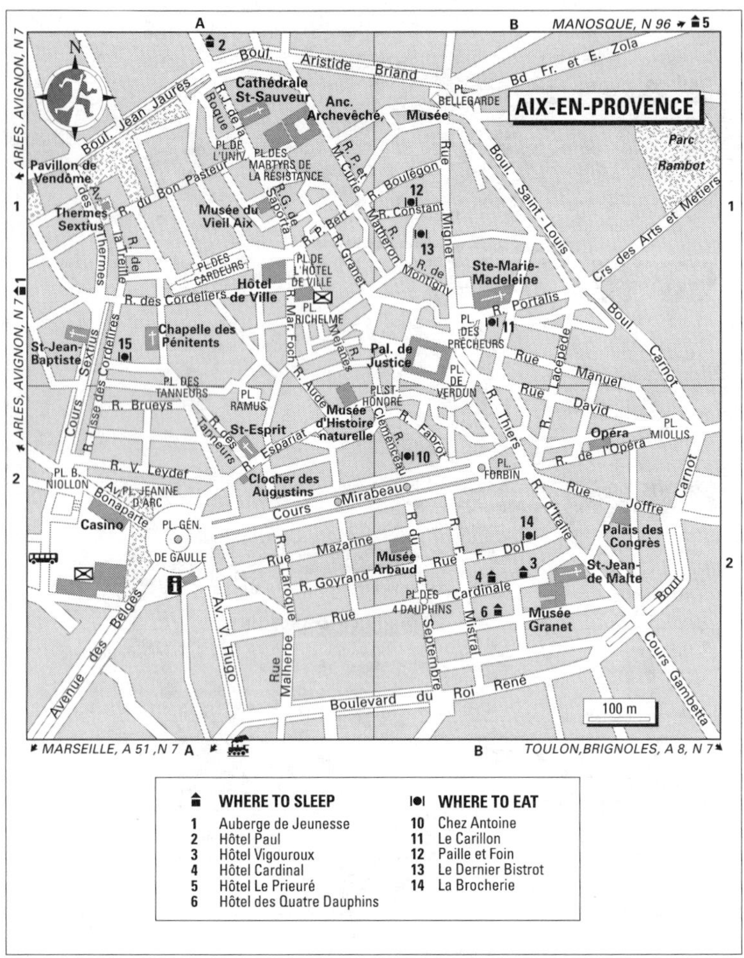
AIX-EN-PROVENCE
A
B
MANOSQUE, N 96 5
ARLES, AVIGNON, N 7
ARLES, AVIGNON, N 7 1
1
2
MARSEILLE, A 51 ,N 7
TOULON,BRIGNOLES, A 8, N 7
100 m
N
Boul. Aristide Briand
Bd Fr. et E. Zola
PL. BELLEGARDE
Boul. Jean Jaurès
Cathédrale St-Sauveur
Anc. Archevêché
Musée
Parc Rambot
Pavillon de Vendôme
R. J. de la Roque
PL. DE L'UNIV.
PL. DES MARTYRS DE LA RÉSISTANCE
R. P. et M. Curie
R. Boulégon
R. du Bon Pasteur
Boul. Saint-Louis
Crs des Arts et Métiers
Thermes Sextius
Musée du Vieil Aix
R. G. de Saporta
R. Constant
Rue Mignet
R. Matheron
R. P. Bert
R. Granet
R. de Montigny
Av. des Thermes
R. de la Treille
PL. DES CARDEURS
PL. DE L'HÔTEL DE VILLE
Hôtel de Ville
Ste-Marie-Madeleine
R. des Cordeliers
PL. RICHELME
R. Portalis
PL. DES PRÊCHEURS
Boul. Carnot
St-Jean-Baptiste
Chapelle des Pénitents
R. Mar. Foch
R. Méjanes
Pal. de Justice
Rue Manuel
Cours Sextius
R. Lisse des Cordeliers
PL. DES TANNEURS
PL. RAMUS
R. Aude
PL. ST-HONORÉ
PL. DE VERDUN
Rue David
R. Lacépède
R. Brueys
R. des Tanneurs
St-Esprit
R. Espariat
Musée d'Histoire naturelle
R. Clémenceau
R. Fabrot
R. Thiers
Opéra
R. de l'Opéra
PL. MIOLLIS
R. V. Leydet
PL. B. NIOLLON
Av. Bonaparte
PL. JEANNE D'ARC
Clocher des Augustins
Cours Mirabeau
PL. FORBIN
Rue Joffre
R. d'Italie
Casino
PL. GÉN. DE GAULLE
Rue Mazarine
Musée Arbaud
R. du 4 Septembre
R. F. Mistral
Rue F. Dol
Palais des Congrès
Rue Laroque
R. Goyrand
Rue Cardinale
St-Jean-de Malte
PL. DES 4 DAUPHINS
Musée Granet
Avenue des Belges
Av. V. Hugo
Rue Malherbe
Boul.
Cours Gambetta
Boulevard du Roi René
WHERE TO SLEEP
1 Auberge de Jeunesse
2 Hôtel Paul
3 Hôtel Vigouroux
4 Hôtel Cardinal
5 Hôtel Le Prieuré
6 Hôtel des Quatre Dauphins
WHERE TO EAT
10 Chez Antoine
11 Le Carillon
12 Paille et Foin
13 Le Dernier Bistrot
14 La Brocherie

380F with a bath. Lots of Provençal prints on the walls and charming painted wooden furniture.

|●| RESTAURANT LE CARILLON

10 rue Portalis. **MAP B1-11**
Closed Saturday evenings, Sundays and Aug.

The telephone never rings at this restaurant — there isn't one. So don't bother reserving, just turn up early and take a seat with the regulars, many of whom are retirees faithful to the home cooking on offer. Completely unpretentious, ideal for lunch. Set meals 55F and 75F.

|●| RESTAURANT PAILLE ET FOIN

14 rue Constantin. **MAP B1-12**
☎ 04.42.96.41.03
Closed Sunday lunchtimes.

Italian restaurant specializing in pasta. The menu changes with the seasons. Choose from a huge range of pasta including tagliatelle with rabbit or chicken and aubergine, *involtini di vitello* (think of beef olives made with veal), rigatoni with three cheeses and don't forget the *gratin....* of pasta of course! Set meals 56F (weekday lunchtimes), 85F and 100F. For à la carte allow around 100F.

|●| CHEZ ANTOINE

4 rue Georges Clemenceau. **MAP B2-10**
☎ 04.42.38.27.10
Closed Sundays and the first two weeks of January.

A hang-out for rich kids and students and also for musicians during the festival. Provençal and Italian cuisine but no set meals. Allow about 50–90F for dishes such as *gnocchi* with mushrooms, calf's liver *vénitien* (baked with bacon, mushrooms and shallots) and, of course, a wide range of pasta dishes. Open until midnight, but you may have to be patient and wait for a table in the small dining room or on the equally small terrace. Good atmosphere.

|●| LE DERNIER BISTROT

19 rue Épinaux. **MAP B1-13**
☎ 04.42.21.13.02
Closed Sundays, public holidays and lunchtimes from June to September.

An adorable little bistro that is well hidden away. On sunny days it timidly comes out onto its little terrace. Set meals 98F and 125F, the latter with a selection of starters. The food is a combination of traditional bistro and Provençal food — creamed salt cod in puff pastry, oven-roasted peppers, flank of beef *au gros sel* and oven-baked lamb. Pleasant background music. The rose-coloured walls are decorated with a collection of straw hats.

|●| RESTAURANT LA BROCHERIE

5 rue Fernand-Dol. **MAP B2-14**
☎ 04.42.38.33.21
Closed Sundays and August.

Pleasant, rustic atmosphere where chicken is roasted in the Renaissance fireplace. The spit-turning mechanism has been preserved, complete with antique weights and gearing. The service is friendly but a little slow. Try the bass grilled over the wood fire, the veal kidney brochettes or the monkfish with *herbes de Provence*. Traditional set meals for 106–132F. For something a little different try the *formule* with buffet and dessert of the day for 45F.

ALLOS 04260

10% ⌂ |●| HÔTEL-RESTAURANT LES GENTIANES*

Grand'rue.
☎ 04.92.83.03.50

This small inn is frequented by skiers in the winter and walkers in the summer. Friendly, family atmosphere. Cute rooms for 160F with basin and 180F with shower. Straightforward, hearty food with offerings such as rib steak with ceps and *tagliatelle carbonara* among others. Set meals 80F and 130F. *Crêpes* also served during the school holidays.

BEAUVEZER 04370 (13KM S)

10% ⌂ |●| HÔTEL LE BELLEVUE**

place du Village; it's on the D908 towards St André des Alpes.
☎ 04.92.83.51.60
Closed Nov–Dec. **Car park**.

A charming place to stop off between Provence and the Alps; the sea and the mountains. A haven of peace and tranquillity lies behind the ochre façade as well as renovated rooms tastefully decorated in warm colours and Provençal fabrics. Very comfortable. Doubles with shower, 215F, or with shower/wc, 230F. Consider asking for one of the six rooms that have views of the mountains. Sleep well and eat heartily. Set meals 70F (lunchtime including wine), 97F and 125F. Delicious aubergine and garlic tart, bass *en papillote*, cep ravioli, duck with olives, etc. A place you could really fall for.

ANNOT 04240

HÔTEL DE L'AVENUE**

av. de la Gare (South-East).
☎ 04.92.83.22.07 F 04.92.83.34.07
Closed Nov 4–April 1. **TV**.

The buildings in the region between Provence and the Alps are made to withstand severe winters but inside they are full of Provençal charm. This hotel boasts tastefully decorated, pleasant rooms. Some have a ceiling fan for when the weather is sultry. In the restaurant the rather impersonal décor contrasts sharply with the fine cuisine, full of subtlety and brimming with original combinations. Pure delight abounds in dishes such as prawn ravioli with tiny broad beans in butter, shin of veal with preserved garlic, ratatouille and aubergine lasagne and trout *meunière* with fennel seeds. Set meals 85F, 110F and 150F. Double rooms 220–260F with shower/wc or 240F with bath/wc. Note that half-board (240–280F) is compulsory in July and August. A fine hotel which combines simplicity, generosity and wonderful food.

ANTIBES 06600

LE RELAIS DU POSTILLON**

8 rue Championnet.
☎ 04.93.34.20.77 F 04.93.34.61.24
Restaurant closed Sunday evenings and in November.
TV.

This seventeenth century coaching inn is full of charm. The rooms have been renovated to reveal a lot of old stonework and a lift has even been installed. Professionally run and welcoming. A respectable hotel with rooms at 250–450F. Breakfast is a little expensive for what you get. The restaurant has good set meals for 98F, 148F and 255F (gourmet). We loved the sea urchin flan with saffron, the grilled fillet of scorpion fish, and rabbit leg *à la gueuze*. The terrace opens out onto the pretty place de la Résistance.

10% HÔTEL DE L'ÉTOILE**

2 av. Gambetta (Centre).
☎ 04.93.34.26.30 F 04.93.34.41.48
Secure parking. **TV**. **Canal+**.

The only hotel of its category to be located in the centre of Antibes. Although it is modern and comfortable, this hotel is more a stopping-off point than a place to base a holiday around. Spacious rooms with good sound insulation. Doubles 320F with shower/wc or bath. Friendly, but the requirement to pay for your room in advance is a little tiresome.

LE MAS DJOLIBA***

29 av. de Provence.
☎ 04.93.34.02.48 F 04.93.34.05.81
Car park.

A pretty Provençal house surrounded by greenery. Enjoy a comfortable stay in delightful rooms decorated in the local style. Doubles 400–630F. Half-board requested but not compulsory in the season for 370–475F per person. Relax in the swimming pool — why get crowded out on the beach? The hotel as a whole is relaxing in fact. The only hotel in its category to offer these facilities at these prices. It's a pity that the reception by the staff is a little cool.

RESTAURANT LE SAFRANIER

1 place du Safranier.
☎ 04.93.34.80.50
Closed Mondays off season and Mondays and Tuesday lunchtimes in July and August.

You may be surprised to find that places like this still exist on the Côte d'Azur. The terrace is covered with a trellis and you are greeted with a friendly welcome and good service. You get the impression of being in a small Provençal village, the tourists seem so far away. A haven of tranquillity. Set meal for 58F. Budget 100F for à la carte. Excellent fish soup and a superb bouillabaisse (this has to be ordered ahead of time). Grilled fish always available; sea bream, porgy, etc. Credit cards not accepted.

RESTAURANT CHEZ JULIETTE

18 rue Sade.
☎ 04.93.34.67.37
Closed Monday and Tuesday lunchtimes. **Car park**.

Charming atmosphere and friendly welcome in this restaurant located in a vaulted cellar. Wood-fired ovens. The set meal for 80F is recommended — good value for money. There is another set meal for 100F with rabbit *chasseur* or Provençal casserole with polenta. A good place to dine with a few friends.

JUAN-LES-PINS 06160 (2KM W)

HÔTEL DES TAMARIS*

37 rue Bricka.
☎ 04.93.61.20.03
Closed mid-October to the end of January.

Relaxed, pleasant atmosphere in this hotel which offers rooms for 170–300F off season. Half-board is compulsory in June, July and August at 240F. Pretty garden and upright piano in the dining room on which to practise your scales. Honest food – fairly inexpensive. Set meal 75F.

10% LA JABOTTE*

13 av. Max-Maurey, Cap d'Antibes.
☎ 04.93.61.45.89 F 04.93.61.07.04
Car park. Disabled access.

This hotel is excellent value for money. Really well kept rooms with shower or bath for 230–360F depending on the facilities and the time of year. We recommend the chalets looking out onto the terrace. Half-board is a competitive 250–310F. Friendly, relaxing and the advantage of the gentle pace of life in Cap d'Antibes.

LE PARISIANA*

16 av. de l'Estérel (Centre).
☎ 04.93.61.27.03 F 04.93.67.97.21
TV.

Central, clean, in a 1930s building. Doubles with shower/wc or bath for 285F (245F in the off season) and triples for 347F (287F in the off season). Reductions negotiable by the week. Enthusiastic, genuine welcome. Our favourite hotel in the centre of Juan-les-Pins. Avoid rooms facing the street, especially in summer, as the nightlife can get pretty raucous. But do you come to Juan-les-Pins to sleep at night?

10% HÔTEL SAINTE-VALÉRIE***

rue de l'Oratoire.
☎ 04.93.61.07.15 F 04.93.61.47.52
Car park. TV.

A quiet, stylish hotel which will delight. Set in a quiet part of Juan-les-Pins just a short distance from the pine woods and the sea. Pretty, shady garden full of trees where you can take refuge from the heat. Ideal hotel for lovers. Modern double rooms 300–840F, tastefully decorated. And there is a swimming pool to give that luxury hotel feel.

LE PERROQUET

Av. G.-Gallice (Centre).
☎ 04.93.61.02.20
Closed Nov–Dec.

Lovely dining area decorated in a relaxing Provençal style; pastel blue and salmon. Charming terrace facing the park. Set meals for 140–170F. The cheapest set meal has a good gazpacho and tasty ravioli with two sauces. Perfect food from starter to dessert and attentive service. Dispels the myth that you can't find a good restaurant in a tourist area.

APT 84400

HÔTEL-RESTAURANT LE PALAIS**

24 place Gabriel-Péri (Centre); it's opposite the town hall.
☎ 04.90.04.89.32
Restaurant closed Mondays and from October to March.

A relatively characterless hotel in a town which is rather lacking in accommodation. Doubles 150F with basin or 260F with bath. Fine if your budget is limited and you need to stop over in Apt. Set meals 69F, 89F and 119F.

DAME TARTINE

17 place du Septier (Centre); it's in the old town.
☎ 04.90.74.27.97
Closed Sundays and Mondays.

Open 10.30am–7pm. The old plane tree and gently trickling fountain in the square outside this restaurant give a pleasant sense of coolness. Against this setting you are offered food made up of salads and sweet and savoury tarts. The hostess, Marie, displays a larger-than-life conviviality and doesn't go in for gourmet cuisine. All her various tarts – *Maroilles* (a fairly strong cheese), spinach and Roquefort; lemon, apple, and coconut – cheesecakes, and fruit crumbles are fresh and home-made. Every lunchtime regulars crowd in to taste the daily delights. The menu changes regularly depending on the market, the season and Marie's whims. Reckon on 47F per course and 25F for dessert.

SAIGNON 84400 (4KM SE)

10% AUBERGE DE JEUNESSE REGAIN

How to get there: it's 2.5km beyond the village.
☎ 04.90.74.39.34
Closed Jan 10–Feb 15. **Car park.**

This youth hostel was founded in 1936. The warden, François Morenas, runs the hostel in an old Provençal house perched on top of the cliffs in a really beautiful spot. He used to be a travelling film projectionist and occasionally screens an old film from his collection to his guests. A keen walker and author of excellent tourist guides, he will also doubtless encourage you to venture out on a local ramble. Youth hostel membership is required. An overnight stay is 75F (breakfast included) and the evening meal is 60F (not compulsory). Half-board 135F.

ARLES 13200

AUBERGE DE JEUNESSE

20 av. Foch (South); 5 minutes from the town centre.
☎ 04.90.96.18.25 Fax 04.90.96.31.26
Closed Dec 18–Feb 5.

One hundred beds. The first night costs 77F and subsequent nights 65F, sheets and breakfast included. Meals for 48F.

10% HÔTEL CONSTANTIN**

59 bd de Craponne (South-West); in the road running parallel to boulevard Clemenceau.
☎ 04.90.96.04.05 Fax 04.90.96.84.07
Closed Nov 15–March 15 except during the Christmas holidays. **Secure parking. Disabled access.**

The rooms are plain and comfortable. Doubles from 130F with basin (but remember the extra 20F you have to pay each time you use the shower on the landing) to 270F. Pleasant lounge. Family atmosphere. The car park costs 30F.

10% HÔTEL GAUGUIN**

5 place Voltaire (North-East); it's between the station and the Roman amphitheatre.
☎ 04.90.96.14.35 Fax 04.90.18.98.87
Closed Jan 10–Feb 15 and Nov 15–Dec 20. **Car park.**

Although this concrete-built hotel is far from being an architectural masterpiece, its cleanliness and warm welcome make it a good place to stay. The rooms facing the square have balconies, which is a plus even if it can get a little noisy. Doubles 170–200F. A nice touch is the daily weather forecast posted at the foot of the stairs.

HÔTEL CALENDAL**

22 place Pomme (Centre); it's between the Roman arena and theatre.
☎ 04.90.96.11.89 Fax 04.90.96.05.84
Secure parking. TV. Disabled access.

Arles is the very heart of Provence where everything seems to be so vividly coloured — fabrics, vases, flowers. Arles also has strong associations with photography and in this hotel a display of photos adorns the staircase. A shady garden is a welcome refuge when the sun is too strong, and makes an ideal spot to relax and chat about the latest photography exhibition or bullfight (the Roman amphitheatre is very close) or simply just put the world to rights. Rooms 250–350F (with shower/wc or bath). Three rooms have a terrace and cost about 420F. Snacks and salads are served in the garden and there is a tea-room. The rooms are air-conditioned, which is a great advantage in the summer. One of our favourite hotels! The secure parking costs 40F.

10% GRAND HÔTEL NORD PINUS

place du Forum (Centre).
☎ 04.90.93.44.44 Fax 04.90.93.34.00
Secure parking. TV.

This hotel has a place in the folk memory of the people of Arles as the hub of its social life and in particular a meeting point for those involved in the world of bullfighting. It was opened in 1865 by Monsieur Pinus and the current owner, Anne, took over in 1989. Characters of almost mythical status have stayed here: Jean Cocteau, Winston Churchill, King Farouk, Scott Fitzgerald, Pablo Picasso and generations of matadors. The visits of the famous are celebrated by a display in a glass cabinet in the foyer. The décor is equally striking; luxurious without ostentation. Each room is decorated differently. A single room is around 770F and a double 836–990F. Breakfast 75F. Just the thing if you feel like going a little mad for once or if you're spending the night with someone special. Otherwise just have a meal in the restaurant or a drink in the bar with its display of a matador's "suit of lights" and bullfighting memorabilia and photos.

LE GRILLON

rond-point des Arènes; it's behind the Roman amphitheatre.
☎ 04.90.96.70.97
Closed Wednesdays and Jan 15–Feb 25.

This combined restaurant/brasserie/crêperie/ice cream parlour may not be much to look at but it doesn't half serve some good food. A very decent set meal for 81F (lunchtimes and evenings every day) with fish soup, fricassee of duck with mustard seeds, and cheese or dessert. Allow around 70F for a main course à la carte. Enormous salads 49F.

LE JARDIN DE MANON

14 av. des Alyscamps; it's a little way from the town centre, below boulevard des Lices, after the police station.
☎ 04.90.93.38.68
Closed Wednesdays off season.

This is a friendly restaurant. It has a small garden out the back but unfortunately it is also a focal point for mosquitoes in the evening! Set meal for 95F including onion *fondant* with red pepper *coulis*, vegetable *barigoule*, roast guinea-fowl *suprême* with potatoes and olives followed by some lovely desserts. Set meals also available for 135F and 170F including baked eggs with sea urchin corals and asparagus *millefeuille*. The set meal for weekday lunchtimes is 80F. Bon appétit!

BRASSERIE DE L'HÔTEL NORD PINUS

place du Forum (Centre).
☎ 04.90.93.44.44
Closed Tuesday evenings and Wednesdays off season and for the month of February.

Dine inside amid tasteful décor or out on place du Forum in the shade of a statue of a local dignitary. The food is very fresh and Provençal: aubergine *millefeuille*, salmon tartare. rack of lamb with garlic, raspberry *clafoutis* and more. You could find yourself seated next to film stars, fashion photographers or journalists from *Vogue* or *Harper's Bazaar*. A trendy venue indeed! And the cost? Set meals 120–160F or about 60F for the day's special.

AURON 06660

HÔTEL LAS DONNAS**

Grande-Place (Centre); it's next to the ice-rink.
☎ 04.93.23.00.03 F 04.93.23.07.37
Closed April 15–July 10, and Sept 1–Dec 19. **TV**.

This is a pleasant peaceful hotel high above the centre, 7km south of Saint-ƒtienne-de-Tin_e. Half-board 200–375F. It has 50 sunny rooms. Doubles 240–450F. Home cooking. The set meals (100F and 135F) offer beef fondue and *raclette* in winter, and *mousseline* of fish, *rillettes* of young rabbit and so on in summer. Expect to pay about 140F à la carte. Lovely glassed-in terrace.

AVIGNON 84000

SEE MAP OVERLEAF

HÔTEL INNOVA*

100 rue Joseph-Vernet. **MAP B3-2**
☎ 04.90.82.54.10 F 04.90.82.52.39
TV.

The friendly proprietor likes to describe his hotel as "plain, unpretentious but comfortable". Eleven rooms with telephones (with outside lines) for 130F with basin, 200F with shower/wc or 250F for 4 people with shower, wc and TV.

HÔTEL MIGNON*

12 rue Joseph-Vernet. **MAP B2-4**
☎ 04.90.82.17.30 F 04.90.85.78.46
TV.

The décor is a little busy, even baroque. But does this matter? The rooms are tastefully furnished with coffee tables and period armchairs (it's hard to say which period) and thick curtains. Double glazing and insulation keep the street noise out. Doubles 220F with shower/wc. No lift and three flights of stairs could be a problem. Each room has a telephone, TV with 21 channels in 5 languages and a whole host of other services you wouldn't expect in a one-star hotel. Well-kept and welcoming.

HÔTEL-RESTAURANT LE MAGNAN**

63 rue du Portail-Magnanen. **MAP C3-6**
☎ 04.90.86.36.51 F 04.90.85.48.90
Restaurant closed Saturdays, Sundays, Christmas, New Year and July and August. **Secure parking**. **TV**. **Canal+**.

This hotel is not particularly attractive but it is very close to the station. Its positive points are hidden inside – the patio is refreshing and quiet, just what the exhausted traveller needs, and the rooms are clean and provided with modern comforts. Doubles with shower/wc 250–345F in the season. Children under 12 stay free. Restaurant with moderate prices but not much to get excited about.

10% HÔTEL SAINT-ROCH**

9 rue Paul-Mérindol. **MAP A3-5**
☎ 04.90.82.18.63 F 04.90.82.78.30
Secure parking. **TV**. **Disabled access**.

The picturesque entrance hall with exposed stonework and antique floor tiles gives access to 15 decent-sized rooms where you will feel at home. Doubles 280–320F. Rooms for 3 or 4 also available for 350–450F with bath. Some rooms have air conditioning. There's also a large garden of about 600 square metres where you can have breakfast. All in all this is an excellent hotel in a city where it can be difficult to find a bed for the night when the festival's on.

10% HÔTEL BRISTOL***

44 cours Jean-Jaurès. **MAP B3-7**
☎ 04.90.82.21.21 F 04.90.86.22.72
Closed Feb 14–March 8. **Secure parking**. **TV**.

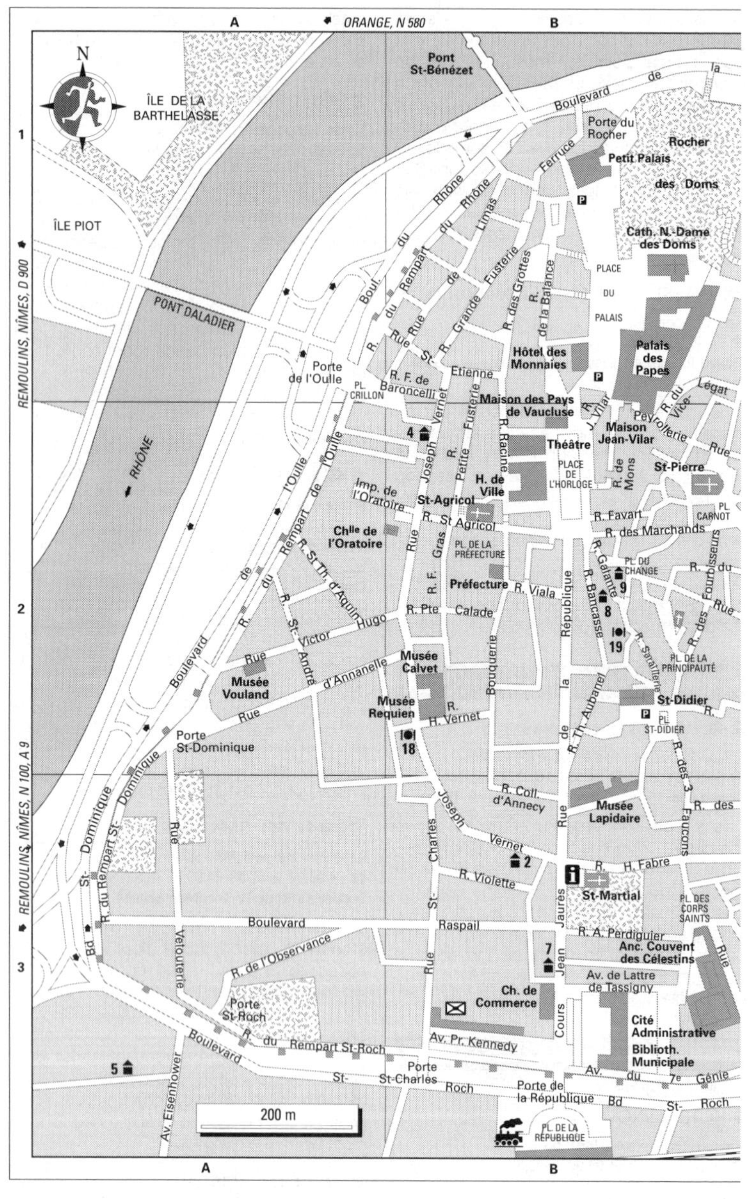
ORANGE, N 580
REMOULINS, NÎMES, D 900
REMOULINS, NÎMES, N 100, A 9
ÎLE DE LA BARTHELASSE
ÎLE PIOT
Pont St-Bénézet
PONT DALADIER
RHÔNE
Porte du Rocher
Rocher des Doms
Petit Palais
Cath. N.-Dame des Doms
PLACE DU PALAIS
Palais des Papes
Hôtel des Monnaies
Porte de l'Oulle
PL. CRILLON
Maison des Pays de Vaucluse
Maison Jean-Vilar
Théâtre
PLACE DE L'HORLOGE
H. de Ville
St-Agricol
St-Pierre
PL. CARNOT
Chlle de l'Oratoire
PL. DE LA PRÉFECTURE
Préfecture
PL. DU CHANGE
PL. DE LA PRINCIPAUTÉ
Musée Calvet
Musée Vouland
Musée Requien
St-Didier
PL. ST-DIDIER
Porte St-Dominique
Musée Lapidaire
St-Martial
PL. DES CORPS SAINTS
Anc. Couvent des Célestins
Porte St-Roch
Ch. de Commerce
Cité Administrative
Biblioth. Municipale
Porte St-Charles
Porte de la République
PL. DE LA RÉPUBLIQUE
200 m
Boulevard de la Ligne
Boul. du Rhône
R. du Rempart du Rhône
Rue de Limas
Rue Ferruce
R. de la Balance
R. des Grottes
Grande Fusterie
Rue St-Étienne
R. F. de Baroncelli
Rue Joseph Vernet
R. Petite Fusterie
R. Racine
Imp. de l'Oratoire
R. St Agricol
R. Favart
R. des Marchands
R. Peyrollerie
R. du Vice-Légat
R. de Mons
J. Vilar
Boulevard du Rempart de l'Oulle
R. St Th. d'Aquin
R. St-André
R. F. Gras
R. Viala
R. Pte Calade
Rue Victor Hugo
Rue d'Annanelle
R. H. Vernet
Rue Bouquerie
Rue de la République
R. Galante
R. Bancasse
R. Th. Aubanel
R. Saraillerie
R. des Fourbisseurs
R. des 3 Faucons
R. Coll. d'Annecy
R. H. Fabre
R. Violette
Rue St-Charles
Boulevard Raspail
Cours Jean Jaurès
R. A. Perdiguier
Av. de Lattre de Tassigny
Av. Pr. Kennedy
Av. du 7e Génie
Bd St-Roch
Boulevard St-Roch
R. du Rempart St-Roch
R. de l'Observance
Rue Velouterie
Av. Eisenhower
Bd St-Dominique
R. du Rempart St-Dominique
A
B
1
2
3
4
5
7
8
9
18
19

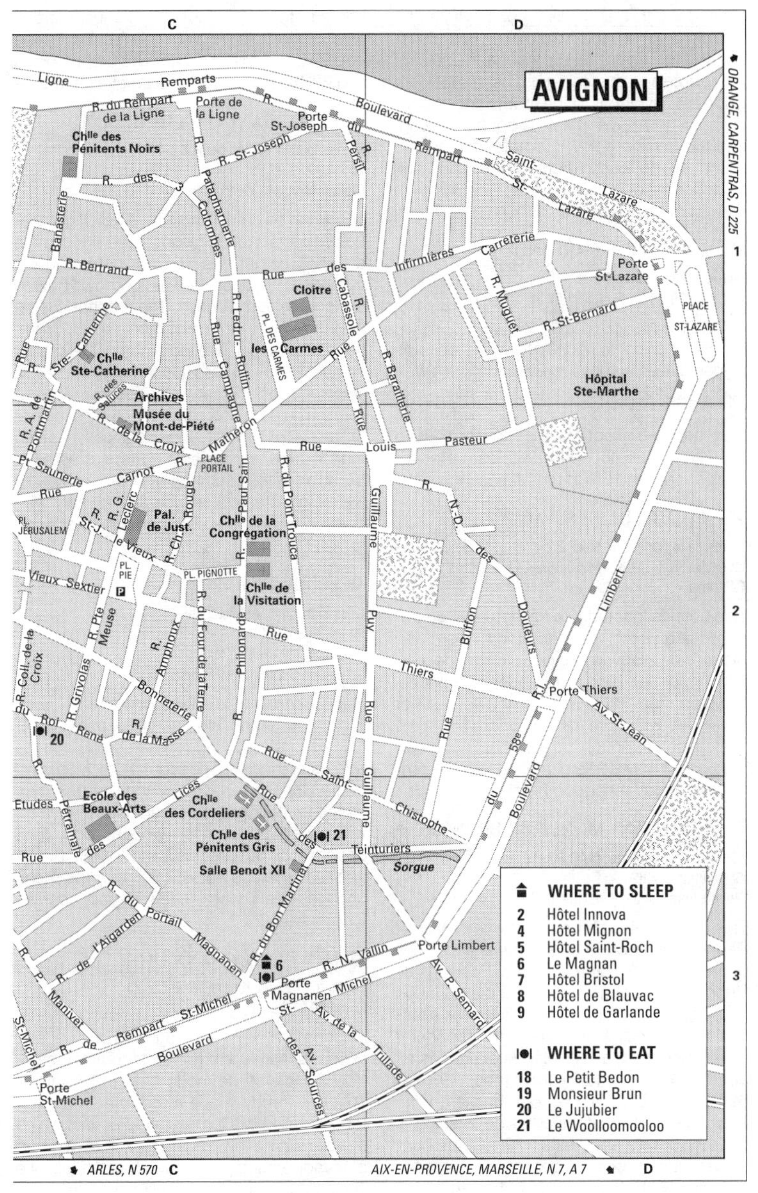
AVIGNON
C
D
1
2
3
ORANGE, CARPENTRAS, D 225
ARLES, N 570
AIX-EN-PROVENCE, MARSEILLE, N 7, A 7
Chlle des Pénitents Noirs
Cloitre
les Carmes
Chlle Ste-Catherine
Archives
Musée du Mont-de-Piété
Pal. de Just.
Chlle de la Congrégation
Chlle de la Visitation
Hôpital Ste-Marthe
Ecole des Beaux-Arts
Chlle des Cordeliers
Chlle des Pénitents Gris
Salle Benoit XII
Porte de la Ligne
Porte St-Joseph
Porte St-Lazare
PLACE ST-LAZARE
Porte Thiers
Porte Limbert
Porte Magnanen
Porte St-Michel
PLACE PORTAIL
PL. PIE
PL. PIGNOTTE
PL. JERUSALEM
Sorgue
20
21
6
WHERE TO SLEEP
2 Hôtel Innova
4 Hôtel Mignon
5 Hôtel Saint-Roch
6 Le Magnan
7 Hôtel Bristol
8 Hôtel de Blauvac
9 Hôtel de Garlande
WHERE TO EAT
18 Le Petit Bedon
19 Monsieur Brun
20 Le Jujubier
21 Le Woolloomooloo

A modern, rather stylish hotel where the friendly greeting and helpfulness is a pleasant change from the impersonal manner of other hotels in this category. Its facilities are tailored to Avignon: all the rooms are air-conditioned and have effective double glazing, and the garage below the hotel means you don't have to worry about your car and can get on and enjoy your visit. Doubles with shower or bath are 300–380F.

10% HÔTEL DE GARLANDE**

20 rue Galante. **MAP B2-9**
☎ 04.90.85.08.85 ⮕ 04.90.27.16.58
TV.

Proprietor Michèle Michelotte is the epitome of friendliness and has really made this a welcoming establishment, set in the shadow of the steeple of the church of Saint-Didier. Pleasant, well-kept rooms for 320F with shower/wc and 350–400F with bath. Reductions of around 15% in the off season.

10% HÔTEL DE BLAUVAC**

11 rue de la Bancasse. **MAP B2-8**
☎ 04.90.86.34.11 ⮕ 04.90.86.27.41
TV. Canal+.

This hotel is located in a seventeenth century building which was once the home of the Marquis de Blauvac and offers clean, decent, well-appointed rooms at reasonable prices. Doubles for 320F with shower/wc or 350–390F with bath (reduction of 15% in the off season). Although the views are not great, it is right in the middle of the old town. Attentive service. A very good hotel.

RESTAURANT MONSIEUR BRUN

23 rue de la Bancasse. **MAP B2-19**
☎ 04.90.27.08.62
Closed from Sunday evenings to Tuesday inclusive.

This restaurant is named after one of Marcel Pagnol's characters and you will find many posters of his films on the walls. Paintings by Dubout are also favoured here, even though he is not a local. The bright décor gives a festive atmosphere. Don't offend the proprietor by refusing the glass of Mâcon offered as an aperitif. Set meals 63F (lunchtimes), 79F and 89F comprising main course, dessert, wine and coffee. The set meal in the evening is more elaborate and costs 120F. Come hungry as the portions are generous. The menu changes with the seasons, but the host always serves a few *charcuterie* delights fresh from Lyons. Another house custom is the ringing of a little bell when the bill is presented "to thank those generous patrons who intend to leave a little something for the staff". Young, friendly staff. The proprietor, as you will have gathered, is a bit of a character!

RESTAURANT LE PETIT BEDON

70 rue Joseph-Vernet. **MAP B2-18**
☎ 04.90.82.33.98
Closed Mondays, Sundays and Aug 15–31.

You'll feel so comfortable here you'll get that back to the womb feeling! The welcoming atmosphere is due to the natural good humour of the host, who really knows how to put people at their ease. The emphasis is on having a good time and good food. Traditional Provençal fare dominates the menu. The set meals for 89F (lunchtimes) and 149F (evenings) include such classics as *crespéou vauclusien*, frog and chive pancake, shoulder of lamb *confit* with whole cloves of garlic, mutton tripe and sheep's trotters, *crépinette* of rabbit with rosemary, and more. Mouthwatering! Attentive service and friendly welcome. Surely this is enough to convince you to visit?

LE JUJUBIER

1 rue Pétramale. **MAP C2-20**
☎ 04.90.86.64.08
Closed in the evening (except during the festival), Saturdays, Sundays and in August.

This charming restaurant offers fresh Provençal cuisine full of sunshine in a delightfully decorated dining room in ochre shades with green beams. The proprietors, Marilyn et Marie-Christine, have revived recipes perfected by their grandmothers including lamb with spelt (a kind of wheat), cod *tian*, *papeton* of aubergines, and rabbit *bouillabaisse*. There is no set meal and the menu changes every week, offering main courses for around 50F.

LE WOOLLOOMOOLOO

16 bis rue des Teinturiers. **MAP C3-21**
☎ 04.90.85.28.44

Avignon has never rested on its cultural and historical laurels and this restaurant is a striking example of the modern side of Avignon. This is a trendy venue rather than a restaurant, installed in a former printworks of which there are still a few traces. It's run by a group of friendly young people and has the feel of a Terry Gilliam set. Untreated concrete walls, an old printing press, subdued lighting, candles and flower petals strewn over the tables and the floor. This is a place to visit more for the ambience than the cooking– the microwave rules here. But this is the end of the twentieth century and at least they're not hypocritical about it – the microwaves aren't hidden away. Anyway the food is rather good. The colours of Africa reign with chicken *yassa* and *tieb bou yap*. No set meals, eat à la carte for around 150F. A place to go with a few friends to put the world to rights until the early hours.

BANDOL 83150

10% ☗ |●| L'ERMITAGE**

résidence du Château (South-West); it's on the Château peninsula between the beach and the harbour.
☎ 04.94.29.31.60 F➔ 04.94.29.31.99
In July and August the restaurant is only open to residents. **Secure parking. TV. Disabled access.**

A decent, modern two-star hotel. Doubles with bath 250–430F in the season. Longer stays can be arranged. The set meal for 100F changes every day but is only available in the evenings. The owner is an inexhaustible source of information on local events.

10% ☗ |●| HÔTEL-RESTAURANT L'OASIS**

15 rue des Écoles (South-West); it's halfway between the harbour and the beach.
☎ 04.94.29.41.69 F➔ 04.94.29.80.01
Restaurant closed Sunday evenings and Nov–March.
Car park. TV. Disabled access.

This is a well-situated small hotel with a shady garden and terrace. Lovely rooms 285–330F with mini-bar and telephone. Avoid those facing the street. Half-board is compulsory mid June–mid Sept at 295F per person. The restaurant is quite uninspiring, however.

BARCELONNETTE 04400

10% ☗ |●| HÔTEL DU CHEVAL BLANC**

12 rue Grenette (Centre).
☎ 04.92.81.00.19 F➔ 04.92.81.15.39
Closed Sundays off season and Oct–Dec.
Secure parking. TV.

This hotel and restaurant has been in the Barneaud family for three generations (and the fourth is almost ready to make its contribution). There have been changes over the years; the stable is now home to mountain bikes rather than horses – the hotel is very popular among cycle tourists. The cooking has also evolved; packed meals are available as are special "sporty" breakfasts. Double rooms with shower, wc and television 280F. Set meals at 70F, 80F and 120F. Middle-class cooking based on game, fresh pasta and of course spinach pie and *andouillette*. Ask the proprietor to show you the accounts kept by his ancestors and menus from the end of the nineteenth century. They certainly knew how to eat in those days!

|●| LA MANGEOIRE GOURMANDE

place des 4 Vents.
☎ 04.92.81.01.61
Closed Mondays and Tuesdays off season, from the start of May to mid-June and Oct–Nov.

The seventeenth century vaulted dining room of this restaurant hosts the perfect marriage between the mountains and the sea. There is a warm, genuine welcome. The food is authentic, really tasty and full of surprises, treading the fine line between tradition and innovation. Witness the intricate ballet of the serving staff as they weave their way around the stoves æ the kitchens in a corner of the room can be seen by everybody in the dining room. The choreographer is Loïc Balanec, a young chef brimming over with talent, who has brought new life to this restaurant. He offers a delightful salad of veal sweetbreads, prawns in shellfish vinaigrette and *émincé* of pigeon *suprême* in hazelnut oil. For an explosion on the taste buds try the roast fillet of duck in curry sauce or the meltingly tender pork fillet with *gnocchi* and baby vegetables. This is a restaurant with a reputation, so you should book to be sure of getting a table. Set meals for 98F (lunchtimes), 148F, 198F and 280F.

SAUZE (LE) 04400 (1.5KM SW)

☗ |●| LA FERME DE LA RENTE

route de Super-Sauze; it's between Le Sauze and Super-Sauze at the bottom of a ski lift.
☎ 04.92.81.08.39
Car park.

A welcoming hotel, but phone to check when it is open. The ambience a little muted but relaxed. The small number of rooms means that you will get to know your fellow guests. Eight rooms, two of which have baths, the others with shower and wc on the landing. Doubles 280–320F. The rooms have been lovingly decorated and the dining room has the allure of a pleasant wine cellar. Traditional home cooking – lamb, fresh pasta, and so on. Set meal 85F. Allow about 100F à la carte. Why not try the house specialities of fondue and *raclette* (110–130F per person)?

Home-made desserts. A note of interest for film enthusiasts: Camus's "Les Chants du Monde" was filmed here, a fact of which the owner is very proud.

UVERNET-FOURS 04400 (4.5KM SW)

RESTAURANT LE PASSE MONTAGNE

How to get there: take the D902 towards Pra-Loup, and turn before the junction for col d'Allos.
☎ 04.92.81.08.58
Closed Tuesday evenings and Wednesdays and Nov 15–Dec 15. **Car park**.

The same warm atmosphere as a wooden chalet. Admire the mountains from the terrace. The menu has been written by a schoolchild on a piece of paper that has fallen out of a school satchel. The walls are decorated with poems and mementoes. The peaceful atmosphere is heightened in the winter by a roaring fire in the huge fireplace. The chef has rediscovered Provençal cooking from his grandmother's era and used his talent to adapt it to the present day. Fresh ewe's milk cheese with *cébettes*, stuffed baby vegetables as good as you'd get in Nice, *sanguin* tart (it's a kind of fungus that grows in pine woods), roast capon *à la crème*, mushroom *croûte*. Set meals 98–178F.

BARGEMON 83830

RESTAURANT LA TAVERNE

place Philippe-Chauvier (Centre).
☎ 04.94.76.62.19
Closed Sunday evenings and Mondays off season.

This charming old-fashioned restaurant is a must if you are anywhere near this amazing village clinging tenaciously to the hillside. Pleasant but stiff service. The cooking really is something to write home about and the talented young chef prepares ultra-traditional dishes that are really very good. Duck breast in *vin d'orange*, crayfish fricassee (in season), veal with morels, roast lamb with herbs and much more. Set meals 90F, 130F and 160F. The restaurant is packed out with local families at Sunday lunchtime.

BARROUX (LE) 84330

HÔTEL-RESTAURANT LES GÉRANIUMS**

place de la Croix.
☎ 04.90.62.41.08 F 04.90.62.56.48
Closed Jan 5–March 1. **Car park**.

A village hotel in a handsome white stone building that has been beautifully renovated. The terrace and some rooms have sweeping views of the surrounding countryside. A good night's sleep is guaranteed in this quiet spot where the only sound after dark is that of the cicadas. Traditional comfort without fuss. Doubles 240F with shower and wc and 270F with bath. Provençal cooking which is simple and traditional. No frills. Set meals range in price from 90F (except Sundays) to 250F. Specialities include quail pâté with onion marmalade, mutton tripe and sheep's trotters *à la provençale*, rabbit with savory, pigeon with apples, and saffron *crème brûlée*. Provence on a plate!

BEAULIEU-SUR-MER 06310

HÔTEL SELECT*

1 place du Général-de-Gaulle (Centre).
☎ 04.93.01.05.42 F 04.93.01.34.30
TV.

This is a very cosy hotel right in the middle of Beaulieu, as friendly as a family guest house from a sitcom. The best value for money in the town, especially if you can get a room facing the square, which is fairly quiet. Doubles 220F with basin/bidet, 250F with shower and 300F with shower or bath and wc. Room for 4 with shower/wc, 400F. The proprietor is genuinely friendly and helpful and can tell you a lot about the area. Stay six nights and get the seventh night free, not bad.

10% HÔTEL LE HAVRE BLEU**

29 bd Mar_chal-Joffre (North).
☎ 04.93.01.01.40 F 04.93.01.29.92
Car park. **TV**. **Disabled access**.

A turn-of-the-century hotel painted white with Matisse blue shutters, reminding you that the Mediterranean is not far away. Not close enough for there to be a sea view, however. Family atmosphere, quiet. Doubles 270F with shower/wc, 290F with a terrace and 310F with bath/wc and terrace. Simple, clean décor.

BÉDOIN 84410

10% HÔTEL LA GARANCE**

Sainte-Colombe; 3km from the village on the Mont Ventoux road.
☎ 04.90.12.81.00 F 04.90.65.93.05
Car park. **TV**. **Disabled access**.

The hotel takes its name from the French for madder, which was grown in the area and used as a red dye for clothing and specifically for the trousers of French soldiers in the First World War. The plant brought prosperity to the area for many years. The vivid colours of Provence are not forgotten in this captivating hotel where the pace of life is slower. You'll love the hotel's décor and tranquillity. Clean, stylish rooms. Doubles 250–285F with shower/wc or 295F with bath. The pleasant terrace looks out to Mont Ventoux and is ideal for a invigorating outdoor breakfast (36F) that includes homemade jam. You can cool off in the swimming pool too. Low-key welcome, but efficient, attentive service. No restaurant but half-board available with meals at the restaurant (La Colombe) opposite the hotel.

|●| RESTAURANT LA COLOMBE

Sainte-Colombe.
☎ 04.90.65.61.20
Closed Mon–Thurs end of Nov–end of March; closed Mon April–Nov. **Car park**.

Pleasant restaurant in Provençal colours. Relaxed atmosphere set in an enchanting location; this is the perfect antidote to stress. Congenial terrace for sunny weather — and there is plenty of that. The proprietor offers fresh, tasty food which will leave you with fond memories. This restaurant is always popular. Set meals for 90F and 135F. In winter they have venison steak with truffles, spit-roasted game and stews, and in summer aubergine and sweet pepper *terrine*, vegetable and basil soup, and kid stew. You'll get an enthusiastic welcome from the owner.

BIOT 06410

10% ☗ |●| CAFÉ-TABAC-HÔTEL-RESTAURANT DES ARCADES*

16 place des Arcades.
☎ 04.93.65.01.04 ➨ 04.93.65.01.05
Restaurant closed Mondays and from mid-November to mid-December. **TV**.

A charming family hotel high up in the village on a pretty square enclosed by colonnades. This is the place to meet friends and enjoy a good honest meal. The menu depends on the season and set meals are offered for 160F at lunchtimes and 180F in the evenings. Specialities include *aïoli*, *bourride*, etc. But the delight of this establishment is in the rooms — which are more like suites. They feature an outrageous mixture of the old (vast fireplaces, mosaic bathrooms, canopy beds) and the new — the owner is a modern art aficionado. The most expensive rooms are recommended (numbers 10, 11 and 12) as the memories they'll leave you with are priceless. You won't be disappointed by the other rooms however. Doubles are 360–460F. Take breakfast in the bistro and hear the latest village gossip.

|●| CAFÉ-RESTAURANT BRUN

44 impasse Saint-Sébastien (Centre); in the first dead-end street on the left on entering the old village.
☎ 04.93.65.04.83
Closed Saturday lunchtimes and Sundays.
Disabled access.

This place offers stiff competition to restaurants where the pastis flows — here beer is king. The atmosphere is very much like a Dutch pub. Old musical instruments hang from the ceiling and huge servings of Mediterranean and more exotic food (mainly Indonesian) are dished up. The chef is part Cypriot, part Scots and the owners English. The set meal on weekdays is 48F. Huge creative salads in summer for the same price. A full meal costs about 70F. A youthful, relaxed place.

|●| BISTROT DU JARRIER

28 passage de la Bourgade (Centre).
☎ 04.93.65.11.68
Closed Monday evenings and Tuesdays (except in summer). **Disabled access**.

This bistro is an offshoot of the well-known gourmet restaurant, L'Auberge du Jarrier and æ much to everyone's delight æ provides excellent service and high quality food at lower prices. Straightforward dishes, attractively presented: ox tail and *foie gras terrine*, an excellent gazpacho, salmon grilled with its skin on, rabbit *confit*, duck *confit*, etc. The many specials of the day are written up on a slate as in Parisian bistros. The wine list has been well put together. Set meal 135F. At lunchtime, there's an 80F *formule* that comes with main course, dessert and wine.

BONNIEUX 84480

☗ |●| HÔTEL CÉSAR**

place de la Liberté.
☎ 04.90.75.80.18 ➨ 04.90.75.99.35
Closed Thursdays and from Nov 1–March 1.

Although the front of this hotel looks fairly uninspiring, behind it lies a friendly hotel set in a charming Provençal village. The rooms are unoriginal but clean. A double with shower and basin (wc on the landing) is 200F but the rooms at 350F are much better and have a shower or bath, wc and a view of the valley. The well-run restaurant changes its offerings in accordance with the seasons. The cheapest set meal is around 100F (lunchtimes only) and there are others at 149F and 170F. Dishes on offer include goat's cheese *croustillant*, fricassee of snails, and stuffed rabbit *à la niçoise*. Everything is beautifully presented.

LE FOURNIL

5 place Carnot (Centre).
☎ 04.90.75.83.62
Closed Mondays, Tuesday lunchtimes and in November.

This establishment has a pleasant terrace right in the heart of the village next to the fountain. Very decent set meals for 90F (weekday lunchtimes), 119F and 165F. Good middle-class cooking with overtones of Provence and dishes like *galette* of pig's trotters, ravioli with a filling of lamb's brains, twice-cooked kid, roast milk-fed lamb, and *pot au feu* of new vegetables with basil.

BORMES-LES-MIMOSAS 83230

LA TERRASSE

19 place Gambetta; it's high up in the village.
☎ 04.94.71.15.22
Closed Nov–Dec.

A typical provincial hotel, with old-fashioned charm. Plain rooms which are well-kept and inexpensive. Half-board is around 205F per person in the peak season and during school holidays. Off season, doubles from 125F (with basin). Set meals 90–130F offering Provençal beef stew, fisherman's hotpot and other local dishes.

10% HÔTEL PARADIS**

62 impasse de Castellan (South); it's on the right as you go down from the village.
☎ 04.94.71.06.85
Closed Oct–end March. **Car park**.

This peaceful hotel is well off the tourist beaten track. The very nice owner has every right to be very proud of his lush garden. The hotel lives up to its name æ it really is like a little Garden of Eden. Clean, simple and pleasantly decorated rooms, some with a sea view. Doubles from 315F with a view of the village. An annexe has a pleasant suite that sleeps 5 for 510F per day. That makes it worth bringing the family!

BREIL-SUR-ROYA 06540

10% HÔTEL-RESTAURANT LE CASTEL DU ROY**

route de Tende.
☎ 04.93.04.43.66 F→ 04.93.04.91.83
Closed Nov 1–Feb 28. Restaurant closed Tuesday evenings off season. **Car park**. **TV**. **Disabled access**.

This excellent hotel is set in a pretty garden next to the river with a view of the mountains. The owner, Michel Huyghe, is passionate about his local region and its wildlife — the kind of hotel owner you would like to meet more often. His hotel is ideal for relaxing; it has a heated swimming pool, badminton, table tennis, mountain bikes (free), archery, etc. Stylish rooms for 310–340F in the off season and 370–410F in summer. Chef Marc Lantieri shows off his incredible talent and revamps traditional local dishes in things like smoked trout in olive and yoghurt sauce, fresh anchovy tart, rabbit *croustillant*, prawns in warm stock with red lentils, roast pigeon with pearl barley and caramelized fillets of sea bream with sesame seeds. Set meals 110F (except Sundays), 155F and 210F.

BRIANÇON 05100

10% HÔTEL DE PARIS**

41 av. du Général-de-Gaulle (East).
☎ 04.92.20.15.30 F→ 04.92.20.30.82
Secure parking. **TV**. **Disabled access**.

This modern hotel is very close to the station and has bright, clean rooms which look out to the mountains. Flowers brighten the dining room and lounge. The cheapest set meal is 49F. Double rooms with shower and wc from 190F.

10% LE CRISTOL**

6 route d'Italie (North-East); north of the upper town, 200m from the gate in the town walls, on the N94.
☎ 04.92.20.20.11 F→ 04.92.21.02.58
Car park. **TV**.

A traditional hotel with a warm welcome. The bright dining room is decorated with tapestries made by the proprietor, showing mythological figures including unicorns. Double rooms with shower/wc from 275F. Choose the rooms to the rear of the hotel — they catch the sun in the morning and give a good view of the Vauban fortifications. Half-board from 265F. Set meals for 70F, 89F and 115F. In co-operation with other restaurants in Briançon, this hotel offers a "Vauban" set meal.

The idea is to highlight the local culinary heritage, with different chefs in the town offering recipes dating back to the seventeenth century. If you have the 140F set meal for example, you can try quail *à la cendre* or herb *gratin*. A worthy initiative.

10% HÔTEL EDELWEISS**

32 av. de la République (Centre).
☎ 04.92.21.02.94 F 04.92.21.22.55
Closed Nov. **Car park. TV.**

This small hotel has the great advantage of being very near the magnificent Vauban fortress, opposite the town's administrative buildings and cultural centre. The rooms face east, with a lovely view of local woods, or west, overlooking the town. Clean and quiet. An excellent choice if you want a cosy family atmosphere. Double 290–330F (with bath).

LE PIED DE LA GARGOUILLE

64 Grande-Rue; it's in the old town opposite the municipal library.
☎ 04.92.20.12.95
Closed Wednesdays, Thursday lunchtimes off season and Oct 15–Nov 15.

The centrepiece of this restaurant is the fireplace at which the host busies himself, keeping an expert eye on the delicious grilled dishes. The walls are adorned with antique skis and snow shoes, a reminder of the harsh struggle for existence on the nearby mountain slopes. Expect an enthusiastic welcome. Eating à la carte is not too expensive. The sweet and savoury *tourtons* (pancakes) are excellent. Cheapest set meal 60F.

RESTAURANT LE PASSÉ SIMPLE**

3 rue Porte-Meane.
☎ 04.92.21.37.43

A popular restaurant with the locals. Antique photographs and dried flowers give the place a hushed, intimate atmosphere. The welcome is not unfriendly. Set meals 65F (lunchtimes), 78F, 98F, 118F. There's also a special 17th century gourmet set meal which is served twice a week and costs 140F. Try the saddle of lamb and the home-made desserts.

RESTAURANT LE RUSTIQUE

rue du Pont-d'Asfeld (Centre).
☎ 04.92.21.00.10
Closed Sundays and Mondays (except in high season); June 24–July 7 and Nov 20–Dec 10. **Disabled access.**

Not only is this restaurant attractively decorated in a pastoral style but it also offers cooking of a high standard. Chef Jean-Luc Libaud's specialities are cheese fondue with morels (135F) and fresh trout with all sorts of sauces. For a special treat try trout with apples flambéd in Calvados. If sweet and savoury sauces are not to your liking, the leek *coulis* and the garlic and Roquefort sauces are also excellent. Very generous salads. A main course à la carte is around 70F. Set meals for 97F and 135F. A friendly welcome — including an aperitif. What's more, Jean-Luc and his wife serve until 11pm! Genuine culinary know-how combined with excellent hospitality. In our opinion the best restaurant in town.

NÉVACHE 05100 (20KM N)

10% AUBERGE LA DÉCOUVERTE

Ville-Basse (Centre); from Briançon take the N94 and turn left along the D994.
☎ 04.92.21.18.25 F 04.92.21.37.95
Car park.

When you arrive at this large inn the proprietors, Isabelle et Jérôme, will open the doors wide and welcome you in. Located in the centre of the village of Névache at 1,600m, this very well-kept auberge is nearly a hundred years old and offers rooms from 194F, dormitories for 195F per night and small apartments from 1,500F a week. Reservation is recommended in the high season (summer and winter). Half-board from 220F per person. The set meal for 92F is prepared by Isabelle. In the winter Jérôme organises skiing courses and excursions for all abilities. A very good hotel which is a leading light in the local tourist trade.

BRIGUE (LA) 06430

LA CASSOLETTE

How to get there: it's in the street next to the river.
☎ 04.93.04.63.82
Closed Sunday evenings and Mondays except for public holidays.

This cute little restaurant (with chickens everywhere) offers home cooking and good service. The chef sometimes disappears next door to the butcher's for an extra steak or duck. Perhaps he also goes to the river over the road to fish out a fresh trout. Dish of the day 45F and set meals 75F, 95F, 135F, 155F and 175F. When we were there the cheapest meal consisted of *Brigasque* pie (leeks, potatoes and courgettes), rabbit *à la provençale* and dessert. The duck tournedos with *foie gras* is also worth trying. Not at all bad.

CAGNES SUR MER 06800

10% HÔTEL LE DERBY**

24 av. Germaine.
☎ 04.93.20.79.20 F 04.93.20.79.22
Car park.

Just 100m from the beach, this quiet, quaint hotel owes its name to the nearby racecourse. Clean, pleasant rooms for 260F with shower, 290F with shower/wc and 320F with bath/wc. Friendly hostess who loves to spoil her guests. If you want a bit of local colour then challenge the regulars to a game of petanque in the courtyard.

LE RENOIR

10 rue J.R. Giacosa.
☎ 04.93.22.59.58
Closed Sunday evenings, Mondays and Thursday evenings.

The entrance of this restaurant, just opposite the market, is not much to look at. But don't be surprised when you find a sumptuous dining room on the first floor, decorated in deep shades of red. The setting is as hearty and warm as the food. Dish of the day 60F, set meals 75F and 130F. And if you're agonising over whether to have the rabbit with pureed olives, the *sanguins* (a kind of fungus that grows in pine woods) with red peppers, the *daube* of ceps or the panfried escalope of salmon with artichokes, the very nice proprietress will help you make up your mind.

LE RESTAURANT DES PEINTRES

71 montée de la Bourgade.
☎ 04.93.20.83.08
Closed Monday lunchtimes and Dec 1–20.

Be prepared to build up a healthy appetite in the climb up to this restaurant, a rather stylish hideaway where the new chef prepares his dishes with only the finest ingredients. Elegant and restrained décor. Flavours blend wonderfully in the casseroles, ready to explode on the tongue — a veritable festival for the taste buds. Creamed salt cod with *tapenade*, braised tail of monkfish, casserole of stuffed pigeon *aux cinq perfums*, roast lamb with thyme, and polenta with mascarpone. Wonderful food masterfully prepared. The set meals are quite expensive at 190–310F, but worth it.

CANNES 06400

10% HÔTEL NATIONAL

8 rue du Maréchal-Joffre (Centre).
☎ 04.93.39.91.92 F 04.92.98.44.06
TV.

Centrally located, this hotel is 200m from both the beach and the station. A very well-kept hotel efficiently run by its British owners. A warm welcome and decent prices: doubles 150–200F with shower on the landing or 200–300F with shower. Choose a room facing the courtyard and remember you'd be well advised to book in advance.

LE CHANTECLAIR

12 rue Forville.
☎ 04.93.39.68.88 F 04.93.39.68.88
Closed Nov.

This hotel has clean, functional rooms, white walls, simple pine furniture and is ideally located 100m from the liveliest part of town. It is nonetheless perfectly quiet. Other benefits are the prices at 200–260F for a double (160–200F off season), the charming patio on which to have breakfast and the warm welcome from the host who is a helpful, chatty sort of guy. He may share stories with you about his career in the Air Force, or share with you his mysterious "crumbless" bread recipe (strange but true) — try some with your meal. Recommended as one of the best hotels in Cannes. Not all credit cards accepted.

10% TOURING HÔTEL**

11 rue Hoche.
☎ 04.93.38.34.40 F 04.93.38.73.34
TV.

This hotel is just off rue d'Antibes in a pedestrian area, which ensures peace and quiet. You'll love the pretty white façade. A gem of a hotel which is just a stone's throw from the Palais des festivals. Sweet little rooms, some with a balcony. Breakfast is served on a sunny terrace. Doubles 250F with shower, 300F with shower/wc and TV and 400F with bath and TV. Cheaper off season.

10% HÔTEL MOLIÈRE**

5-7 rue Molière (East).
☎ 04.93.38.16.16 F 04.93.68.29.57
Closed Nov 15–Dec 20. **TV. Disabled access**.

This hotel is actually two adjoining buildings, one from the nineteenth century with a pretty façade and the other modern. The two halves of the hotel are furnished in the appropriate style, traditional or modern. Really lovely rooms with shower or bath for 400–600F (15% reduction in the low season). Although the hotel is very close to the town centre and la Croisette (100m), the location is quiet and there is a large garden in which to enjoy your breakfast. Friendly welcome.

10% LE SPLENDID***

4-6 rue Félix Faure.
☎ 04.93.99.53.11 F 04.93.99.55.02
TV.

This street is home to a restaurant of the "Terminator" chain, where you can eat inferior food at high prices. But pause a moment and look above the restaurant and you will see a majestic turn-of-the-century façade resembling the palace de la Croisette. Behind this is one of the town's loveliest hotels. The Cagnat family run this hotel and will look after you in beautiful rooms with antique furnishings. Although expensive at 460–900F for a double, the price is justified. A charming hotel which is ideal for lovebirds making a romantic journey and who just want to spend lazy mornings relaxing in the height of luxury.

LE LION D'OR

45 bd de la République (North-East).
☎ 04.93.38.56.57
Closed Saturdays and Nov 15–Dec 15. **Car park**.

During World War II the set meal cost 5F and customers would queue right down the street. Nowadays the set meal is 67F and the dining area is still full of regulars, mostly elderly people and local office workers. The new owners haven't changed the traditions of this restaurant æ which hasn't closed its doors for over 60 years. Dependable, tasty food. Everything, even the cakes and pastries, is made on the premises. A speciality is *baeckaoffa* (stew of beef, mutton and pork), a dish from Alsace which was traditionally prepared by housewives and eaten on Mondays — wash day!

LE JARDIN

15 av. Isola.
☎ 04.93.38.17.85

This is one of the most popular restaurants among the locals in Cannes. It's a simple little place far from the tourist areas and the boisterous crowds of la Croisette. Granted the district is a little depressing, as is the bar you enter in order to get to the restaurant, where a TV mumbles and flickers in the corner. But pass through the bar and you come to a garden. In this delightful courtyard you can dine in peace on simple, tasty food like *daube provençale*, and breast of duck with green peppercorns. There's grilled fish aplenty too, including sole, sardines, bass, sea bream, and *pageot* (a type of sea bream). And the most surprising thing, apart from the hospitality, is the cost. Set meals for 69F and 110F. Say no more!

LE BOUCHON D'OBJECTIF

10 rue Constantine (East).
☎ 04.93.99.21.76
Closed Mondays.

A restaurant with a photographic theme. Each month a different photographer's work is displayed on the walls. Set meals 85F and 130F. Simple, original food. Snails in puff pastry with aniseed, grilled rack of lamb, rabbit *terrine* with grapes and pistachios, veal escalope in honey and grape juice, etc. Friendly service. Pretty terrace in a modern pedestrian area.

RESTAURANT AUX BONS ENFANTS

80 rue Meynadier (Centre).
Closed Saturday evenings (except in June and July), Sundays, Christmas, New Year's Day and in August.

No telephone. The regulars (often elderly) pop in during the morning to reserve a table while the vegetables, bought in the market across the road, are being peeled in the bright dining room. You'll get local dishes and home cooking, just as you would have done when the restaurant was in the hands of the current owner's mother. Fish soup, stuffed sardine fritters, goat's cheese *terrine* with tomato *confit*, rabbit with rosemary, *osso bucco*, *aïoli* (Fridays), veal *blanquette* and stuffed courgettes. Dishes like these speak from the heart. Set meal 92F. Good-natured greeting and service, just as it should be.

RESTAURANT AU BEC FIN

12 rue du 24-Août (Centre).
☎ 04.93.38.35.86
Closed Saturday evenings, Sundays and Dec 20–Jan 20. **Disabled access**.

This restaurant is often full — don't arrive too late! The cheapest set meal for 95F offers a staggering choice with nearly 20 starters and almost as many main courses. Mostly local cuisine (*daube provençal* beef, vegetable soup with basil, scorpion fish *à la pêcheur*, etc.) which will take your mind off the bland décor. Good daily specials. The set meal for 115F is also excellent value for money.

|●| LA PAPILLE

38 rue Georges-Clemenceau (Centre).
☎ 04.93.39.27.28
Closed Sunday evenings, Mondays, in January and lunchtimes in July and August.

We were delighted to discover this excellent restaurant. The tone is set by the smart little dining room with just ten tables. Old menus decorate the walls to emphasize the traditional cuisine. The women who run the restaurant give it a sense of tact and elegance. Only the freshest ingredients are used and the food plays on the twin themes of Provence and tradition. Exceptional *fûtins* of courgettes, warm oysters with baby vegetables, quail with figs, and stuffed baby vegetables. In addition there are well-chosen and reasonably-priced local wines and aperitifs (make sure you try *Chicouloun*, a liqueur distilled from local herbs). Finally, even the cheeses (a choice of mild or strong goat's cheese) and desserts are of the highest order. Set meals from 98F. Well done ladies!

|●| RESTAURANT LOU SOULEOU

16 bd Jean-Hibert (South-West).
☎ 04.93.39.85.55
Closed Mondays, Tuesdays and Wednesday evenings off season and in November.

This restaurant is located behind the old harbour in a district where few tourists go. The set meals are excellent value for money. For 125F tuck into *blanquette* of monkfish with mussels, fillet of sea bass with watercress (or the day's special) and a home-made pastry. Or you might be happy with just the *bourride du pêcheur* (fish soup) at 99F, which contains monkfish, prawns, mussels, garlic *croûtons*, and rouille (a spicy mayonnaise). There's also a gourmet set meal for 210F. Sip a kir, investigate the nautical memorabilia and admire the view of the Estérel hills.

|●| LA REINE PÉDAUQUE

place Frommer.
☎ 04.93.99.29.19

Opposite the Palais des festivals, this restaurant is on its way to becoming the most fashionable in Cannes with its neo-Italian, almost post-Renaissance, décor. Owner Philippe Dorange defines his establishment as a gourmet bistro, a description which is appropriate considering his culinary expertise. His cooking is fresh and full of subtle fragrances. The combinations are very skilful but he also pays a great deal of attention to preparation and seasoning. Naturally Mediterranean fish and Provençal ingredients play a major part in dishes that include panfried mullet in thyme, cod *aïoli* with new vegetables and delicious top rump of beef. The lunchtime *formule* at 100F is very good. Set meals for 150F, 200F and 250F. A trendy place to hang out.

GOLFE-JUAN 06220 (4KM NE)

10% ☗ HÔTEL CALIFORNIA*

222 av. de la Liberté (East); it's on the N7, 800m from the station, close to the sea.
☎ 04.93.63.78.63
Closed during the All Saints' Day holidays. **Car park**. **TV**.

This 1930s-style house is set back from the main road. You can imagine how it used to look when it stood all alone here, many years ago. The conversion into a hotel produced pretty double rooms for 130–260F off season and 180–310F in the summer. Studio apartments available.

VALLAURIS 06220 (6KM NE)

|●| LE MANUSCRIT

224 chemin Lintier (Centre).
☎ 04.93.64.56.56
Closed Mondays in the season and Sunday evenings, Mondays and Tuesdays off season.

A fine grey-stone building which used to be a perfume factory. You should go there as much for the exceptional surroundings as for the food. Whether you are seated in the dining room, where wonderful prints and canvasses are displayed, in the conservatory full of near-tropical flowers, or on the terrace under the hundred-year-old magnolia, you will have a great meal. Four set meals are available at 95F (weekdays), 120F, 175F and, for famished gourmets, 245F.They offer a wide range of dishes, including seafood *terrine*, panfried *andouillette* in Muscadet, and cod in a sea-urchin sauce. Affordable wines too.

|●| RESTAURANT LA TONNELLE

rue Hoche (Centre).
☎ 04.93.64.34.01
Closed Sundays and Monday evenings (except July and August). **Disabled access**.

Right in the centre of the town, just off the main street, satisfy your rumbling stomach with countless different types of pizza and fresh pasta as well as some good Provençal dishes. Ideal for lunch — sit under the trellis or in the cool dining room. Set meal 98F. Attentive staff.

|●| RESTAURANT LA GOUSSE D'AIL

11 av. de Grasse (Centre).
☎ 04.93.64.10.71
Closed Tuesdays, Monday evenings in winter and Nov 9–Dec 9. **Disabled access**.

Located just behind the church, this restaurant is a match for any in town. A cosy atmosphere (although avoid wearing shorts) where you can dine on fine, traditional dishes prepared from first-rate ingredients. Duck and grape *terrine*, vegetable soup with basil, duck with cherries, panfried beef fillet with morels, roast lamb with rosemary, stuffed pork trotters, etc. Set meals for 110F, 145F and 170F. Everything is well presented. Good service although the attitude is a little stuffy (no shorts allowed — but ties not required either) in plush surroundings. The upstairs dining room is air-conditioned. A well-established restaurant which consistently delivers the goods here in Picasso's town.

VALBONNE 06560 (11KM N)

|●| LA FONTAINE AUX VINS

3 rue Grande.
☎ 04.93.12.93.20
Closed Mondays.

This wine bar in the old part of Valbonne is a very convivial place to try a few tapas (10F) or better still a dish à la carte, 35–50F per main course. Worth trying are the veal *andouillette* and tomatoes stuffed with goat's cheese — so fresh you can almost hear the goat still bleating. Simple, warm service and surroundings and musical entertainment on Saturday nights with virtually a whole orchestra. Local wares also for sale. Congratulations to the atttractive young ladies who run this place — long may they continue!

|●| L'AUBERGE FLEURIE

1016 route de Cannes (South); coming from Cannes, it's 1km before arriving in Valbonne.
☎ 04.93.12.02.80
Closed Wednesdays and from mid-December to the end of January. **Car park**.

A very good restaurant in a very pretty, wisteria-covered building. Inside there are large mirrors. In these pleasant surroundings you will be served with a smile and a good set meal for 115F consisting of a starter (salad of salmon escalope or fish soup) and a delicious and substantial main course such as rabbit in mustard or pollack in red wine. Inventive, sunny dishes made from the best ingredients giving uncomplicated flavours. Other set meals 155F and 185F. The clientele includes a lot of regulars, which is always a good sign.

CARPENTRAS 84200

10% ☗ HÔTEL LE FIACRE**

153 rue Vigne (Centre).
☎ 04.90.63.03.15 F→ 04.90.60.49.73
Secure parking. TV. Canal+.

Located in a quiet street in the centre of town this 18th century convent was converted into a town house then a hotel some forty years ago. You go up a massive staircase to the rooms æ no two the same æ set out around a delightful patio. Allow about 290F for a double with shower/wc and 350F with bath. If you really want to spoil yourself there are two superb suites.

|●| RESTAURANT MARIJO

73 rue Raspail (Centre).
☎ 04.90.60.42.65
Closed Sunday evenings and for two weeks in January.

The interior of this restaurant is rather sweet, in an unfussy Provençal style. The two rustic dining rooms with exposed stonework are decorated in shades of plum, blue and white. Generous portions at reasonable prices. Set meals at 65F, 85F and 120F, usually offering good fish depending on what's on offer at the market, such as mullet with sea urchin coral for example. Don't forget the chicken with crayfish or the mutton tripe and sheep's trotters *à la marseillaise*. The house wine is a decent Ventoux, but in our opinion the quality of the food here deserves something chosen from the wine list to go with it.

|●| LE CANARD TOQUÉ

place de la Marotte; it's by the Monteux gate.
☎ 04.90.60.42.44

This restaurant is very original for Provence — the menu is almost entirely devoted to the cooking of southwest France, rich dishes served in generous portions. Superb truffle omelette, duck *au sang*, *coq au vin* and, on Thursdays, *cassoulet*. Rustic stone dining room in a converted stable. Pleasant, polite service. Set meals for 70F (except weekends and public holidays), 95F, 130F and 180F. The wine list is somewhat disappointing.

|●| LE VERT GALANT

12 rue de Clapies (Centre).
☎ 04.90.67.15.50

Closed Saturday lunchtimes and Sundays, 10 days in March and 3 weeks in August.

Jacques Mégean is the owner of this restaurant, which is without doubt the best in town. In a simple, almost austere, setting you are served tasty dishes made from excellent combinations of traditional ingredients such as herb *fondant* with snails and pine kernels, *aïgo* (garlic soup) with prawns, artichokes, and mangetout, and rabbit and broad bean stew. The truffle flavoured mash that comes with the duck is a work of art. As for the desserts, the selection is so overwhelming that we won't try to describe it — enjoy the surprise. The set meals offer excellent value for money: 138F (lunchtimes), 210F and 290F. In winter the fresh truffle set meal is 340F. Good value and excellent service.

MONTEUX 84170 (5KM SW)

10% LE SELECT HÔTEL***

24 bd de Carpentras.
☎ 04.90.66.27.91 F➔ 04.90.66.33.05
Closed Saturdays and Sundays off season and Dec 20–Jan 8. **Car park. TV.**

A really friendly, genuine welcome from the owners, a Dutch couple. Even if you don't want to stay the night, it's worth a visit for the food. The food is simple and original, fine and light. Excellent quality set meals for 95F, 120F, 140F and 170F. Enhance your meal with a locally bottled Côtes-du-Ventoux rosé. We won't say any more so as not to spoil your surprise in discovering food which we found delightful. In summer, eat outside on the terrace in the shade of the plane trees beside the swimming pool. If you decide to stay, doubles with bath start at 320F.

CASSIS 13260

AUBERGE DE JEUNESSE

La Fontasse; coming from Marseille by road, turn right after about 15km towards col de la Gardiole (3km of good road, 2km of gravel).
☎ 04.42.01.02.72

Open 8–10am and 5–11pm. A membership card is compulsory to stay in this youth hostel but you can join on the spot. Make sure you get there in the morning in July and August or else the no-vacancies sign may be upl (walkers and cyclists are never turned away though). Superbly situated in the Calanques hills, this is one of the most beautiful places to stay in Provence. The hostel is a charming Provençal house and an overnight stay in one of the 65 beds costs 47F. Kitchen facilities. The warden is very friendly and knows the surrounding area like the back of his hand. Bring your own food. Children under 7 not allowed. No family room.

LE CLOS DES ARÔMES

10 rue Paul-Mouton; it's 2 minutes from the town centre.
☎ 04.42.01.71.84 F➔ 04.42.01.31.76
Closed Monday, Tuesday and Wednesday lunchtimes except on public holidays. **Car park.**

This elegant restaurant is a short distance from the town centre and is finely decorated in the colours of Provence. Sample sophisticated dishes in the large, shady flower-filled courtyard. Set meals 110F and 170F. Specialities include fresh salmon with fennel seeds, baked sea bream, scorpion fish and lemon salad, *bouillabaisse* etc. This is a really peaceful retreat, far from the harbour and noise of the town. Ask for one of the 8 rooms at 300–480F.

HÔTEL LIAUTAUD**

How to get there: it's by the harbour.
☎ 04.42.01.75.37 F➔ 04.42.01.12.08
Closed Dec 1–Feb 1. **Secure parking. TV.**

Imagine Cassis at the end of the nineteenth century — a small fishing port with a solitary hotel facing the sea. This is that hotel. First opened in 1875 — but don't worry it has been repainted and the beds have been replaced since then. Allow 320–380F. A well-kept hotel with double glazing.

LE DAUPHIN

3 rue Séverin-Icard.
☎ 04.42.01.10.00
Closed Wednesdays, Thursday lunchtimes, the last three weeks of January and Nov 15–30.

Dozens of readers have written in to recommend this restaurant and with good reason — thank you! Set in a car-less street parallel to the harbour, peace and quiet reign. The bill won't make a hole in your pocket either. Good, simple set meals 65F, 79F and 95F. Specialities include fisherman's hotpot for 102F. A charming welcome.

CASTELLANE 04120

NOUVEL HÔTEL DU COMMERCE***

How to get there: it's in the village square.

☎ 04.92.83.61.00 F➜ 04.92.83.72.82
Closed from the start of November to the start of February. **Secure parking**. **TV**. **Canal+**. **Disabled access**.

Rooms look out onto the village square or the *roc*, a 184m cliff. Sandwiched between the post office and the town hall, this large hotel decorated in a kitsch Provençal style is popular with German visitors. Add on 20F to the price of each room in the high season and make sure you book in advance. Doubles 310–355F. Set meals 110F 160F and 230F. Care is taken over the dishes, which use mainly Provençal produce. Especially good are the gnocchi with asparagus and Parmesan, the roast milk-fed lamb with parsnips, the calf sweetbreads studded with truffles, the quail and chanterelle risotto, and the aromatic rabbit stew. A riot of flavours in a friendly atmosphere, although the service is little formal at times.

GARDE (LA) 04120 (3KM SE)

10% AUBERGE DU TEILLON**

rte Napoléon; it's on the N85 towards Grasse.
☎ 04.92.83.60.88 F➜ 04.92.83.74.08
Closed mid-October to the end of March.

On his journey back from Elba, Napoleon passed by but failed to stop at this lovely inn – a serious error. Don't repeat the mistake, make a point of discovering the cooking of Yves Lépine. Like a skilled orchestral conductor, he brings together Provençal ingredients to produce wonderful harmonies of flavours. It's hardly surprising that people come here from all along the coast at the weekend to satisfy their hungers. Cocooned in the rustic little dining room enjoy a set meal for 100F, 150F, 175F or 220F. The dishes on offer include smoked leg of lamb, duck *confit en parmentier*, scallop ravioli in truffle sauce, veal kidneyswith morels, roast pigeon with ceps, and a tasty rack of lamb *provençal*. Prolong the pleasure by taking a room for 180F with basin, 230F with shower or 260F with shower/wc. Rooms facing the main road can be noisy if you are planning a lazy morning. A simple, cordial welcome.

ROUGON 04120 (17KM SW)

10% AUBERGE DU POINT-SUBLIME**

How to get there: it's on the D952 at the entrance to the Verdon gorges.
☎ 04.92.83.60.35 F➜ 04.92.83.74.31
Closed Nov 5–April 1. **Car park**. **TV**. **Canal+**.

There are two small dining rooms on the veranda, one smoking and one no smoking. Both have check tablecloths, floor tiles, lots of leafy plants and miscellaneous souvenirs and photos of Verdon. There is quite a treat for your taste buds too. Set meals 91F, 103F, 130F and 192F. Fresh, local dishes including hare or boar casserole and mackerel *pâté* and regional classics such as trout, scrambled eggs with truffles, and *aïoli provençal*. The desserts are also worth a detour – fig *crème brûlée,* for example. And don't forget to try the local aperitifs made from oranges, walnuts, honey, blackberry and herbs (32F). Rooms are also available for 237–290F, peace and quiet guaranteed. Note that half-board is compulsory in summer. And don't forget to reserve in the high season.

PALUD-SUR-VERDON (LA) 04120 (25KM SW)

AUBERGE DE JEUNESSE

Le Trait d'Union (South).
☎ 04.92.77.38.72 F➜ 04.92.77.38.72
Closed Dec 1–end Feb. **Secure parking**.

This youth hostel is 1km from the centre of La Palud-sur-Verdon in a technicolor dream setting. You need an FUAJ card, but this can be purchased on the spot. A night in an 8-bed dormitory costs 67F including breakfast. Double room with basin, 80F per person (including breakfast). Camping is allowed in the garden (with use of the kitchen and washing facilities) for 28F. Completely isolated and completely quiet.

HÔTEL-RESTAURANT LE PROVENCE**

route La Maline; it's on the D23.
☎ 04.92.77.38.88 F➜ 04.92.77.31.05
Closed from November to Easter. **Car park**. **TV**. **Disabled access**.

This hotel is located just 100m from the main square in this village of 1,000 inhabitants and has unrestricted views of the route des Crêtes. Set meals for 75F, 85F, 100F and 110F. The specialities include trout, rabbit *à la provençale*, honeyed duck, warm quail salad and truffle omelette. Doubles for 220F with shower/wc and 260F with bath. Relaxing lounge with a billiard table. Baby-sitting service. Half-board is compulsory from mid-July to the end of August for 220–260F per person. Sip a cool drink on the terrace and savour the peace and quiet.

10% HÔTEL DES GORGES DU VERDON***

To get there: take the D952, the road north of the gorges.

☎ 04.92.77.38.26 📠 04.92.77.35.00
Closed mid-October to the end of March. **Car park**. **TV**.

This hotel is in the heart of the gorge district, set on a hillside facing the village and the surrounding countryside. A panoramic view – just like a film set. It makes you forget the hotel's somewhat gloomy modern architecture. The rooms are rather uninspiring, but well equipped, comfortable and clean. Doubles with shower 250F and with shower/wc or bath, 390F. Relax in the pool or tone yourself up on the tennis court. Very good food which features traditional Provençal dishes: *anchoïade*, artichokes *en barigoule* (stuffed with mushrooms and ham), braised beef *provençal*, mutton tripe and sheep's trotters etc. Set meals 120F and 165F. A conventional but pleasant hotel.

CAVAILLON 84300

HÔTEL BEL-AIR

62 rue Bel-Air (Centre).
☎ 04.90.78.11.75

An archetypal hotel for travellers on a tight budget who like an old-fashioned atmosphere where friendliness and good company are more important than comfort. Seven pleasant rooms, all simply decorated. Doubles with basin 170F or with shower and telephone 190F. Extra beds available for 60F. Each room has an information pack on Cavaillon and the surrounding area and a bowl of sweets – a thoughtful touch. Breakfast with fruit and home-made jam around the big communal table for 35F.

10% HÔTEL DU PARC**

183 place François-Tourel (West).
☎ 04.90.71.57.78 📠 04.90.76.10.35
Secure parking. **TV**. **Canal+**.

A very large old hotel opposite the Roman arch. Good hospitality and family atmosphere, but the building is beginning to show its age a bit. Choose a room facing the park at the side of the hotel and be woken by beautiful sound of birds singing. Doubles 240F with shower and wc, or 260F with bath. Sun lounge on a large, colonnaded terrace.

RESTAURANT LE PANTAGRUEL

5 place Philippe-de-Cabassole (Centre).
☎ 04.90.76.11.30
Closed Sundays and Monday lunchtimes.

An imposing building with a beautiful vaulted dining room and massive fireplace, where meat and fish are grilled. The bishops of Cavaillon used to reside here – they would have been horrified to know that the building later became a brothel. Set meals 95F, 125F and 155F. Tomato *crespéou*, hot *anchoïade*, lamb *à la ficelle*, monkfish *choucroute* and more. Don't miss the melon and strawberry soup in summer. A fine, comprehensive wine list.

LA CUISINE DU MARCHÉ

place Gambetta (Centre).
☎ 04.90.71.56.00
Closed Wednesdays, Saturday lunchtimes and Sunday evenings in winter and Saturday and Sunday lunchtimes in the summer.

The entrance of this restaurant is not much to look at, but climb the stairs and you will find a pleasant dining area unfussily decorated in shades of pastel green, ochre and pink. You have a view of the main square of Cavaillon as you dine. But the culinary offerings are more important than the setting. Chef Olivier Mahieu offers fresh dishes with a strong southern French accent. The result is worth stopping off for: scorpion fish *émincé* with artichoke, *brousse* (unsalted goat's cheese) with ceps, and mutton tripe and sheep's trotters *à la provençale*. Set meals 70F (lunchtimes), 87F, 110F and 140F. Dish of the day 50F. A restaurant with a growing reputation.

RESTAURANT FLEUR DE THYM

91 rue Jean-Jacques-Rousseau (Centre).
☎ 04.90.71.14.64
Closed Sundays and in July.

One of Cavaillon's rather chic restaurants. The pink façade conceals an attractive stone-vaulted cellar with a large fireplace. Those who absolutely insist on eating outside in the summer might find it a little cool, but they'd be wrong not to give it a try. Jean-Yves Benoît serves up original dishes prepared from good, fresh produce. The set meal is 148F and changes with the seasons. We enjoyed fricassee of artichokes with morels and asparagus, cod with winkles and rack of lamb with garlic *confit*. For dessert the rice pudding (with crystallized melon) is a masterpiece, just like your mum used to make. A treat which will take you back to your childhood.

CHAPELLE-EN-VALGAUDEMAR (LA) 05800

HÔTEL-RESTAURANT DU MONT-OLAN*

☎ 04.92.55.23.03

Closed from September 15 to the Easter holidays.
Secure parking.

Chalet-style hotel. The well-kept rooms all look out to the soaring peaks that dominate the village. Owners Monsieur and Madame Voltan serve up huge quantities of ravioli *au miel* and potato pie in a large dining room with a panoramic view of the fast-flowing Navette. Set meals 65F, 85F, 90F and 125F. An ideal place in which to build up your strength for an assault on the mountains. Doubles from 235F with shower and wc.

SAINT-FIRMIN 05800 (16KM SW)

10% HÔTEL-RESTAURANT LE VAL DES SOURCES*

Saint-Maurice-en-Valgaudemar; before the village of Le Roux cross the bridge to the right, then turn right again; the hotel is about 300m further.
☎ 04.92.55.23.75
Closed from All Saints' Day to Easter.

Some time ago, owner Claude and his wife decided to come back to this beautiful, wild valley and take over the family hotel. A dynamic duo, they have been steadily upgrading the facilities year by year and now offer rooms which are simple but comfortable (good beds). Reckon on 280F for a double with shower and wc. Mouth-watering food is also on offer, based mostly on local produce. The main courses are quite old-fashioned, such as "donkey's ears" (it's not what you're thinking but pastry filled with spinach and Chinese leaves and shaped to look like donkey's ears), ravioli *au miel* and *flozon* (potato pie with *lardons* and shallots) — a real taste of yesteryear. The cheapest set meal is 95F and there is another for 130F. Booking advisable for the restaurant. Half-board is compulsory in summer (from 210F per person). The hotel also has a garden and self-catering accommodation. Pony trekking for 300F (cold lunch included).

CHATEAU-ARNOUX 04160

AU GOÛT DU JOUR

RN 85.
☎ 04.92.64.48.48
Closed Sundays and Mondays off season and in January and February.

Don't get the wrong door or else you will find yourself eating very well but rather more expensively in the neighbouring upmarket bistro, the *Bonne Étape*. The atmosphere in *Au Goût du Jour* is more relaxed — friendly service and appetizing food against a background décor of fresh yellow and orange. *Formules* for 85F and 130F. The main courses are written up on a slate and change with the seasons and what the market has to offer. The owners were among the first to become passionate about regional cooking at a time when *nouvelle cuisine* was all the rage. Rediscover tastes and flavours rescued from oblivion. It's a delight to tuck into mussel and saffron soup or anchovies marinated in fennel. In addition there's tuna *en chartreuse* (braised with cabbage and bacon), stuffed breast of veal, duck leg with olives and delicious *tarte alsacienne* with strawberries. A lovely place to come with a few friends.

L'OUSTAOU DE LA FOUN

RN 85.
☎ 04.92.62.65.30
Closed Sunday evenings and Mondays

Discover food that balances fine ingredients with delicious flavours in a Provençal hacienda which although rather chic is not uncomfortable. Chef Gérald Jourdan proves that you don't have to be old to be expert. He experiments with new flavour combinations æ to the delight of the diner. And he certainly knows his stuff when it comes to the local culinary heritage; nobody is more knowledgeable than he when the conversation turns to food. Furthermore he has shown that he doesn't believe that the art of cooking should be the sole preserve of a few initiates — he organizes cookery courses. Enrol on one and you could return home with the secret of braised panfried calf's head served on a bed of potatoes and goat's cheese. Learn too how to concoct sardine and herb fritters, and rabbit and artichoke casserole with rosemary and juniper. Even if you don't want to learn how to cook dishes like these, come for the sole garnished with raw ham and rack of lamb with thyme. If you only have room for one dessert, go for the *cassant coulant*, a heavenly combination of dark chocolate, cherries and sorbet. Everything here is a labour of love. The dishes are very precise and the accompaniments well thought out, and the result – uncomplex, delicious food. Set meals for 110F, 145F, 165F and 198F.

COLLE SUR LOUP (LA) 06480

LE CLOS DU LOUP

rte de Grasse.

☎ 04.93.32.88.76
Closed Sunday evenings, Mondays, and mid-December to mid-January.

A charming little inn at the side of the road on the way in to La Colle. Restrained and sophisticated décor. Tasteful tablecloths and crockery aid the appreciation of well-prepared seasonal fare. Fish marinated in lime, ravioli *niçois*, scorpion fish *croustillant*, lamb with *herbes de Provence*, sautéd veal *à la provençale* etc. Simple, classic and really tasty. Set meals 99F (main course and dessert) and 159F (full meal).

COMPS-SUR-ARTUBY 83840

10% GRAND HÔTEL BAIN**

☎ 04.94.76.90.06 Fax 04.94.76.92.24
Secure parking. **TV**.

Closed Nov 11–Dec 25. This hotel has been in the Bain family since 1737 and is well known by hunters who stop by for pâté studded with local truffles, omelettes (with truffles in season) and goat's cheeses. And people come from far and wide at lunchtime for the rich hare stew, the *daube provençale*, and roast rack of lamb. Set meals 78F (every day), 128F and 190F. Pleasant rooms if you want to stay in this hotel which is a real local institution. Doubles 250F with shower/wc or 270F with bath.

DIGNE-LES-BAINS 04000

10% HÔTEL-RESTAURANT L'ORIGAN

6 rue Pied-de-Ville (Centre).
☎ 04.92.31.62.13
Closed Sundays and for one week in February (school holidays).

If you would prefer a culinary cure to taking the thermal waters in this spa town, then this restaurant is for you. Chef Philippe Cochet administers John Dory fillets with basil, a cold *aïoli* of cod and vegetables, mutton tripe and sheep's trotters, stuffed veal fillet and mullet with chives in his restaurant in the heart of the old town. Set meals 70F, 98F, 125F and 170F. Some fairly basic rooms from 100F (with basin) to 140F (with shower).

HÔTEL DU PETIT SAINT-JEAN*

14 cours des Arès (Centre).
☎ 04.92.31.30.04 Fax 04.92.31.30.04
Closed Dec 25–start Jan. **Secure parking**.

Most of us can recall holidays at our grandparents', eating lovingly prepared food and sleeping in a cosy bed in an old-fashioned room. This is the hotel to bring back all those memories, with the added bonus of the warmth of Provence. Positioned on the corner of place Charles-de-Gaulle, the hotel offers double rooms for 140F with basin, 190F with shower and 260F with bath. Your cheerful host serves up decent food in the restaurant on the first floor. Treat yourself to rabbit with onions, stew of suckling pig, *bœuf en daube* or *blanquette* of veal and on Fridays, *aïoli*. Set meals 57F, 65F, 82F and 135F. Half-board (from 210F) is compulsory in the high season.

HÔTEL CENTRAL**

26 bd Gassendi (Centre).
☎ 04.92.31.31.91 Fax 04.92.31.49.78
Car park. **TV**.

In Digne-les-Bains, a town of 16,000 inhabitants, a green neon sign shines out in the peaceful night advertising the presence of *Hôtel Central* on the main street, boulevard Gassendi. The entrance to this hotel is a little impersonal and at night you get in by using a magnetic card. Rooms with washing facilities for 150F, with shower 190F and with shower/wc 260–290F. Choose a room facing the pedestrian street rather than the boulevard which can be noisy early in the morning. Family suite for up to 6 with bath, shower and wc for 600F.

10% HÔTEL DU GRAND PARIS

19 bd Thiers.
☎ 04.92.31.11.15
Closed Sunday evenings and Mondays off season and Dec 20–Jan 5. **Car park**. **TV**.

This seventeenth century building used to be a convent. When the nuns moved out it was transformed into a stylish hotel. Don't be put off by the slightly formal welcome or you will miss out on some excellent food. Chef Jean-Jacques Ricaud prepares very traditional fare from tried and tested recipes. Good ingredients giving lovely flavours æ have a taste of the rabbit with spelt (a type of wheat), pigeon *en bécasse* (cooked undrawn), lamb *en croûte* or braised veal sweetbreads in an orange sauce. The cheapest set meal is good value for money at 150F. Lovely rooms, comfortable and tastefully decorated. Doubles 400–800F.

LA CHAUVINIÈRE

54 rue de l'Hubac (Centre).

☎ 04.92.31.40.03
Closed Sunday evenings, Mondays and the last Tuesday of the month.

One of the few restaurants in town where you can always depend on getting good value. The somewhat drab dining room is brightened up by pretty Provençal fabrics. The terrace is cool and pleasant and a good place to enjoy *blanquette* of lamb, saddle of rabbit stuffed with goat's cheese, ceps and snails in puff pastry, home-made *caillettes* (pork and vegetable faggots) with tomato *coulis* or monkfish *ragoût*. Set meals 70F (weekday lunchtimes), 100F and 150F.

DRAGUIGNAN 83300

|●| RESTAURANT LE BARON

42 Grand-Rue (Centre).
☎ 04.94.67.31.76
Closed Mondays.

The white stone frontage of this building looks rather grand. Once inside you feel you have made a mistake – the atmosphere is more like a doctor's surgery than a restaurant. But a restaurant it is and not a bad one either. The great French classics are what's on offer, including flambéd sea bream with fennel, duck with olives, and *coq au vin* (they use vin jaune). Set meals 65F, 98F and 140F.

|●| RESTAURANT LE TEMPS DES METS

35 rue Notre-Dame-du-Peuple (Centre).
☎ 04.94.68.86.89
Closed Sunday evenings and July 15–Aug 15.

Pass through the kitchen to the simply decorated dining room – no fuss or frills to distract from the food, which is prepared by a promising young chef. We particularly liked the clam *croustade à la provençale*, the scallops with garlic butter, the beef stew, and the scrambled eggs with ceps. Set meals 70F (weekdays) and 120F.

EMBRUN 05200

⌂ |●| HÔTEL NOTRE-DAME**

av. Général-Nicolas – route de Chalvet.
☎ 04.92.43.08.36 ➡ 04.92.43.58.41
Closed Sunday evenings and Mondays, except for school holidays, and for 2 weeks in January. **Car park. TV.**

Just 5 minutes walk from the centre of town, this hotel is a peaceful haven. There are no cars here – this family hotel is set at the far end of a large garden. After receiving a warm welcome you will be shown to extremely clean rooms with excellent beds. Reckon on 260F for a double. Good quality food based on local produce. The cheapest set meal is 99F and there are others for 129F and 169F. Half-board from 260F (compulsory during school holidays). Recommended.

10% ⌂ |●| HÔTEL DE LA MAIRIE**

place Barthelon (Centre).
☎ 04.92.43.20.65 ➡ 04.92.43.47.02
Closed Sunday evenings and Mondays in winter (except during school holidays) and Oct 1–Dec 1. **TV.**
Disabled access.

This hotel is a model of its type with a superb brasserie, quality food and competent, charming staff. A good sign: locals regularly visit this convivial place for a drink with friends or a traditional Sunday lunch. Among the specialities the sautéd prawns *à la provençale* and the duck *confit* are excellent. Set meals 92F and 120F. Reservation advisable. The walls display works by local artists throughout the year. Clean, bright rooms (from 270F for a double) – choose one which looks out onto the square. Half-board (from 260F), but not compulsory. A dependable hotel.

|●| LES PIEDS DANS LE PLAT

34 rue de la Liberté (South-West).
☎ 04.92.43.43.33
Closed Mondays, Tuesdays except for school holidays and from mid-October to the end of November.

This place is worth a visit not only for Madame Brun's beef *carpaccio* and leg of lamb with crayfish, but also for the exhibitions of painting and drawings. Perhaps your visit will coincide with the monthly music night (jazz, bossa nova). Set meals from 70F (lunchtimes) with truly wonderful sauces. A free tequila slammer on presentation of this guidebook.

CALÉYÈRE 05200 (3.5KM NW)

|●| RESTAURANT PASCAL

Caléyère (North-West); from Embrun take the winding Caléyère road.
☎ 04.92.43.00.69
Closed in September.

Don't come to this restaurant if you want a cosy meal for two æ this is a place to enjoy the friendly, family atmosphere. You'll get a welcoming handshake from the owner herself. There's just one set meal and for 65F you'll get a substantial meal based on fresh farm produce – vegetables, eggs, meat. The ambience is excellent and you won't leave feeling hungry.

SAINT-ANDRÉ-D'EMBRUN 05200 (6KM NE)

RESTAURANT LA GRANDE FERME

hameau Les Rauffes; it's on the Crévoux road.
☎ 04.92.43.09.99
Closed Mondays and Tuesday lunchtimes, and from the start of October to mid-December. **Car park**.

Owners Nicole and Thierry welcome you to their magnificent vaulted dining room which they themselves restored. This restaurant offers excellent traditional food and has a well-deserved reputation throughout the region. In addition to the set meal for 86F, the chef offers a vegetarian set meal at 68F and a set meal of local dishes, which we can particularly recommend for 120F. The baked eggs with Queyras blue cheese and pear *gratin à l'eau-de-vie des Hautes-Alpes* alone are worth the visit. Good selection of wine. Gîtes available.

ÈZE 06360

HERMITAGE DU COL D'ÈZE**

Grande Corniche (North); from Èze take the D46 and then the Grande Corniche; it's 500m on the left.
☎ 04.93.41.00.68 F 04.93.41.24.05
Closed Dec 15–Jan 15. Restaurant closed Mondays and Thursday lunchtimes and Oct 15–Feb 15.
Car park. **TV**.

If this hotel seems familiar, that may be because you have seen it in a Van Damme action film. But Monsieur and Madame Bérardi's hotel is more a place for relaxing than for action. The swimming pool is a welcome revitaliser for walkers' tired feet (the hotel is the start/finish point for many mountain walks). The air is also cooler at this altitude which is a relief from the heat of the coast. Doubles 170–310F with shower/wc or bath/wc. Splendid view of the southern Alps. The restaurant offers well-prepared food. Set meals 90–180F.

AUBERGE ÉRIC RIVOT**

basse Corniche.
☎ 04.93.01.51.46 F 04.93.01.58.40
Closed mid-November to mid-December.

Without this guide you would have passed right by this modest inn hidden away at a bend in the Basse Corniche road. And you would have missed an establishment of some renown – the culinary skills of Éric Rivot are worth stopping for. His training with a top chef left him with a mastery of the art of combining flavours and with a taste for high-quality ingredients. He uses his affinity with Provence to full effect to offer *terrine* of guinea-fowl with *foie gras*, tomatoes stuffed with snails, *paupiettes* of beef flank with oyster mushrooms, offal and sorrel vol au vents, rabbit hotpot with Provençal vegetables, etc. The set meals are very reasonably priced considering the quality: 120F, 165F and 205F. Rustic but rather posh dining room and pretty, sheltered terrace, although a little noisy. Nine clean, cheerfully decorated rooms with bath, wc and TV for 280F.

AUBERGE DES DEUX CORNICHES**

Èze-Village (North); 1km along the D46.
☎ 04.93.41.19.54 F 04.93.41.19.54
Closed start of November to mid-December. **Car park**. **TV**.

This hotel is above the village of Èze, at an altitude where you get a view of the sea from your room. The proprietor offers a charming welcome and the surroundings are peaceful and quiet, so no wonder that this hotel is often full in summer. Pleasant double rooms (some with balcony) but rather expensive at 330F. Half-board 310F per person (compulsory in July and August). Carefully prepared food.

FAYENCE 83440

10% LA SOUSTO

4 rue du Paty.
☎ 04.94.76.02.16

The very best of Provence. This attractive little hotel in the centre of the old village perched above the valley is run by Guy and Chantal, who left the city for a very different life here in Fayence. The rooms are pleasant enough, simply furnished, and give the impression that you are visiting a charming old aunt. Every room has a hotplate, fridge, sink and some also have a shower. Each room is individual and our favourite was number 5 with its sunny little terrace looking out over the valley. A great place to while away the afternoons. A fully equipped room for 2 or 4 costs 260–340F. Very well kept. Provence still has a few surprises hidden away.

FORCALQUIER 04300

10% HOSTELLERIE DES DEUX LIONS***

11 place Bourguet.
☎ 04.92.75.25.30 ➡ 04.92.75.06.41
Closed Sunday evenings and Mondays off season, Jan–Feb and mid-November to mid-December.
Secure parking. TV.

A rather stylish, comfortable hotel-restaurant æ places like this are becoming increasingly few and far between in France. This place must have seen countless receptions for weddings, baptisms and first communions. It has to be said that the food is good: ox tail with *foie gras* and leeks in aspic, pressed fish with saffron and cold crab soup, caramelized bass in a cep sauce, roast duckling *en faux canard à l'orange*, rabbit stuffed with *tapenade* and, to finish, morello cherry soup and Génépi (a herb-flavoured liqueur) sorbet. Set meals for 160F, 230F and 350F. Some beautiful rooms for 280F with shower/wc and 300–500F with bath.

LE LAPIN TANT PIS

place Vieille.
☎ 04.92.75.38.88
Closed Monday evenings and Tuesdays off season.

This restaurant is in the quaint little streets of the old town, just a minute's walk from the *co-cathédrale* (titled thus by Rome in the eleventh century to give it equal status with the bishop's palace in Sisteron). Go through the shop — you will want to make some purchases on the way out — and enter the dining room full of Provençal local colour. The sun is always shining under the vaulted roof. Hardly surprising then that the atmosphere is friendly and the place has a way of charming all its visitors. You will really feel at home in this cosy bistro. The food prepared by Gérard Vivès from ingredients fresh from the market doesn't disappoint. Cauliflower *terrine* and tomato *confite* with thyme, sardines marinated in balsamic vinegar, *taureau* en daube, ravioli with two cheeses and much more. Set meals 85F and 125F. In addition the host can offer some lovely, light, invigorating little wines. And don't hesitate to try the teas prepared from herbs from the garden.

LARDIERS 04230 (18KM N)

LE CAFÉ DE LA LAVANDE

How to get there: take the D950 towards Banon and at Notre Dame turn right onto the D12 towards Saumane.
☎ 04.92.73.31.52
Closed Mondays.

The village looks out to the Lure mountains. It's worth hurrying here to discover this country café of a type which is increasingly rare in France. Regulars drop in for a glass of white wine or *pastis* as an aperitif. They should do as you do and take the time to have a meal. Don't expect gourmet cuisine: the keyword is simplicity. Duck with cherries, lamb stew, creamed salt cod. Fresh and good. The dish of the day is 46F and the set meal 85F. The wine offered by the owner is sure to raise your spirits.

FRÉJUS 83600

10% AUBERGE DE JEUNESSE

chemin du Counillier (North-East); 2km from Fréjus old town.
☎ 04.94.53.18.75 ➡ 04.94.53.25.86
Car park.

A delightful youth hostel set in a seven hectare garden, 4.5km from the beach and just a short walk from Fréjus old town. Overnight stays in dormitories (67F including breakfast) or in rooms sleeping four with washing facilities and wc (82F including breakfast). Camping in the garden is allowed for 32F a night. Meals for 50F. A bus leaves every morning for the station and the beach. You must have a membership card (but this can be bought at the hostel).

10% HÔTEL-RESTAURANT LE RIVIERA*

90 rue Grisolle (Centre).
☎ 04.94.51.31.46
Closed Jan.

This is an uncomplicated one-star hotel run by a Danish lady. The décor is a little out of date but the hotel is well-kept. Doubles for 140F with basin or 200F with bath. The proprietor has abandoned her native Danish cooking in favour of authentic French dishes. Set meals 60F (including a quarter bottle of wine), 68F and 88F.

HÔTEL ARENA***

139 rue du Général-de-Gaulle (Centre).
☎ 04.94.17.09.40 ➡ 04.94.52.01.52
Closed Jan. **Car park. TV. Disabled access.**

This hotel is new and offers modern, comfortable double rooms for 350–600F with bath. Relaxed atmosphere, Provençal-style colourful décor and many plants. The central location means that you can have a relaxing dip in the swimming pool before going out to dinner. The food here is good in every respect but a little expensive. The cheapest set meal is 120F.

|●| RESTAURANT CHEZ VINCENT

19 rue Desaugiers (Centre).
☎ 04.94.53.89.89
Closed Wednesdays.

The entrance to this restaurant is difficult to miss as it is decked out with geraniums, petunias, pansies and fig plants. Inside, pastel décor and a thirteenth century vaulted ceiling, beneath which you can enjoy well thought-out dishes in a traditional regional style æ quail *confit* salad, sautéd chicken *à la provençale*, medallions of veal *à la provençale*, etc. Reasonable set meals for 75F, 95F and 145F.

|●| RESTAURANT LA ROMANA

155 bd de la Libération (South).
☎ 04.94.51.53.36
Closed Sunday evenings and Mondays.

A seafront restaurant offering very decent food – good portions but not expensive. Mostly Italian and Provençal dishes: pizza, fresh pasta, fish stew, beef stew *à la provençale* etc. Set meals 95F and 125F. In a tourist district like this where you can never be sure of what you're getting, this is a good find.

SAINT-RAPHAËL 83700 (3KM E)

|●| LA SARIETTE

rue de la Vieille-Église (Centre); it's near the town hall.
☎ 04.94.19.28.13
Closed Sunday evenings and Mondays.

This restaurant offers Provençal food and is run by incomers from the south-west of France who have not entirely left their culinary origins behind however. The owner is also the chef and serves up smoked salmon, *foie gras*, prawns, tomato and green salad and a dish of the day. Eat out under the plane trees in fine weather. All you need is the sound of cicadas to complete the relaxing scenario. Set meals 69–99F. Warm-hearted weclome from the owner.

GAP 05000

10% ⌂ UNIC HÔTEL*

La Placette, rue Jean-Eymar; it's near the tourist office.
☎ 04.92.51.05.96 F 04.92.51.94.11
Closed Sundays and the second week in September. **TV**.

Located in a quiet pedestrian area, this is a modest sort of hotel which it would be nice to come across more often in tourist towns. Clean, friendly, bright, and welcoming with a family atmosphere. And it won't make a hole in your pocket: 140F for a basic room to 195F with shower/wc. Rooms 1, 2, 5 and 10 are the best equipped.

⌂ |●| STATION GAP-BAYARD — CENTRE D'OXYGÉNATION

Grand Plateau-Bayard; head towards Grenoble on the N85 and after 7km turn right after the service station.
☎ 04.92.50.16.83 F 04.92.50.17.05
Closed mid-November to mid-December. **Car park**.

Set in huge grounds, this is a sports training centre surrounded by trees. Although it's primarily for sports people, stressed-out city dwellers and weary travellers can join the athletes in a meal. The set meal is 60F and half-board is 176F in rooms with two or three beds. A golf course (18 hole) is open in the summer and there are two magnificent exercise trails and 50km of cross-country skiing tracks.

10% ⌂ LA FERME BLANCHE***

route des Romettes (North-West); from the station take the col Bayard road, turn right onto the Romettes road and then left; the hotel is at the end of this road.
☎ 04.92.51.03.41 F 04.92.51.35.39
TV. **Canal+**.

This charming hotel is full of character. Set back from the main road, it has a sunny terrace where you can bask in the sun. Inside lovely furniture compliments the vaulted rooms. An old bank counter has been given a new lease of life in the bar. Open and welcoming, the owner is a mine of information on local walks and the cultural events of the village. Don't be surprised if you bump into a celebrity — actors often stop off here. Bright, comfortable rooms; doubles with shower/wc for around 270F. Breakfast is 38F and served until noon. Meals can be taken in the adjoining restaurant, *La Roseraie*. Cheapest set meal 130F. Half-board is not compulsory, even in peak season. A dependable establishment.

10% ⌂ |●| HÔTEL-RESTAURANT PORTE-COLOMBE**

4 place Frédéric-Euzières (West).
☎ 04.92.51.04.13 F 04.92.52.42.50
Restaurant closed Friday evenings and Saturdays (except in August and September), Jan 6–28 and April

27–May 16. **Secure parking**. **TV**.

A modern hotel with a comfortable interior. All the rooms are different shapes and differently decorated. Don't let the electric shutters and multi-channel TV distract you from the beautiful view of Gap and its cathedral. The rooms even have serving hatches so you don't have to bother getting dressed for breakfast. Chef Yves Reynaud presents fine food such as salmon *mousseline* with crab *coulis*, ravioli *en tourtons* and succulent desserts. The cheapest set meal is 85F. Double rooms 260F with shower/wc.

LE TOURTON DES ALPES

1 rue des Cordiers (North-East).
☎ 04.92.53.90.91

This restaurant has been successful for a long time and it must be said that it does serve the best *tourtons* in the Hautes-Alpes region. Accompanied by green salads and raw ham, the *tourtons* – or potato fritters – are excellent. If you're in a hurry just ask for a plate of *tourtons*. Of course the set meals (78F and 110F) include them too. This place is a real institution with the locals.

RESTAURANT LE PASTURIER

18 rue Pérolière (Centre).
☎ 04.92.53.69.29
Closed Sundays, the first week in January and the second fortnight of June.

Subtle décor with exposed beams and walls covered in salmon-coloured cloth. The quiet, intimate atmosphere is ideal for an intimate meal for two. The owners are lively and welcoming and chef Pascal Dorche changes the menu frequently. The lamb with truffle is really excellent, as are the desserts. Set meals for 110F, 160F and 260F. A main course à la carte costs around 100F. Pleasant terrace for the summer.

LAYE 05500 (11.5KM N)

RESTAURANT LA LAITERIE DU COL BAYARD

How to get there: take the N85 from Gap.
☎ 04.92.50.50.06
Closed Mondays (except in school holidays and on public holidays) and Nov 15–Dec 15. **Car park**.

Owner Monsieur Bertrand is a third generation farmer and really loves his cheese. He expresses his passion in the vast dining room by inviting you to view his little cheese museum and videos about cheese. The offerings include salads with a blue cheese or smoked ham sauce, *plateau champsaurin* (10 pieces for 68F), fondues, etc. Needless to say, a must for cheese-lovers. Reckon on 100F.

GASSIN 83580

HÔTEL BELLO-VISTO**

place des Barrys (East).
☎ 04.94.56.17.30 F 04.94.43.45.36
Restaurant closed Nov–Dec 25 and Jan 4–April.

An ideal place off season. This small, two-star hotel is excellently situated and has a terrace with a superb view of the bay of Saint-Tropez. Good, recently renovated rooms which are relatively cheap for this area. Doubles 250–380F. If you manage to get a room in July or August without booking first – buy a lottery ticket immediately. Provençal cuisine. Set meal 130F with delicious mussels in a rich white sauce.

RESTAURANT LE MICOCOULIER

place des Barrys (Centre).
☎ 04.94.56.14.01
Closed mid-October to Easter.

The ambience is dictated by the nautical décor in the dining room, but if the weather is good (often the case in this part of France!), dinner by candlelight on the terrace is genuinely enchanting. Views of the bay of Saint-Tropez and the hills as you feast on rabbit *barigoule* with pesto or grilled fish fresh from the sea. This dream is wholly achievable as the prices here don't live up to the area's reputation for being expensive. Set meals 110F (lunchtimes), 160F and 260F. Considerate, meticulous service.

GORDES 84220

LE PROVENÇAL

place du Château (Centre).
☎ 04.90.72.10.01 F 04.90.72.04.20
Closed Nov 15–Dec 15. **Secure parking**. **TV**.

A straightforward hotel with low prices which makes it rather attractive in this region. Eight very clean rooms with new bathroom fittings. Rooms 1 and 2 have lovely views of the château. Double rooms 220F with bath. Good, mostly Provençal, food without any great surprises. Set meals 98F and 120F. Many specialities of the day for around 65F.

AUBERGE DE CARCARILLE**

Les Gervais (South); it's 3km below Gordes on the D2.

☎ 04.90.72.02.63 ➡ 04.90.72.05.74
Closed Fridays off season and mid-November to the end of December. **TV**.

A welcoming, well-kept hotel even if the modern style lacks character. Set meals for 98F, 145F and 195F. Good food in the Provençal tradition: rabbit brawn with sage, crayfish *quenelles*, mutton tripe and sheep's trotters etc. Pleasant rooms – but not cheap, which is not really surprising in the heart of Luberon. Doubles 330–380F with shower and wc or bath.

LA MAYANELLE***

6 route de la Combe (Centre); it's on the hillside at the entrance to the village.
☎ 04.90.72.00.28 ➡ 04.90.72.06.99
Closed Jan 3–March 1. Restaurant closed Tuesdays and Wednesday evenings. **Car park. TV**.

This two-storey hotel offers wonderful views, especially from the garden and terrace where you can have breakfast. The dining area is in a stylish, whitewashed vaulted room. The lounge is a long room, also vaulted, with exposed stonework and a fireplace at one end, furnished with high-backed chairs upholstered in tapestry. Stained glass windows give an impressive, stately effect. There is no swimming pool so think about visiting in spring rather than summer. Doubles 400F with shower/wc or 500F with bath. The restaurant is a little expensive for the sort of dishes on offer. Readers of this guide get a 5% reduction.

10% LE MAS DE LA SÉNANCOLE***

hameau Imberts; 5km along the D2.
☎ 04.90.76.76.55 ➡ 04.90.76.70.44
Closed Jan–Feb. **Car park. TV. Disabled access.**

Although this is a completely new building, it has been built in the Provençal style and fits in well with the surroundings. The inside could do with a bit more character but is generally very welcoming. Provençal décor and exceptional comfort. Doubles 450–500F with shower/wc (add on 50% for air conditioning). Two superb apartments are available which, although a little more expensive are furnished with wrought-iron furniture and have conservatories and enormous bathrooms. Lovely garden with swimming pool. Especially pleasant when the sky is blue, as it often is in this region. No restaurant.

GOULT — 84220 (8KM SE)

LE CAFÉ DE LA POSTE

place de la Libération.
☎ 04.90.72.23.23
Closed evenings, Wednesdays and from the end of October to the start of April.

In this pretty village, in the shade of the trees, you will find the *Café de la Poste* which was one of the locations in the film *L'Été meurtrier*. Dine in a friendly atmosphere, although it is a bit touristy in summer. Good value for money. House specialities include rabbit *à la provençale*, vegetable *terrine*, *crespéou* and lemon chicken. The cheapest set meal is 66F, the dish of the day costs 55F and salads are 30–50F. Friendly welcome.

AUBERGE LE FIACRE

quartier Pied-Rousset; on the N100 heading towards Apt.
☎ 04.90.72.26.31
Closed Sunday evenings off season and Wednesdays. **Car park**.

An excellent restaurant, well-known to people who like this part of the world. Light, inventive Provençal cooking using local produce. The owners greet you with a kind, cheerful welcome. Mother and daughter wait on your table while the father is closeted in the kitchen, slaving away over the ovens. The vegetable soup with basil and lamb *tian* alone are worth the visit. Game in season. In summer dine outside under the lime trees to the sound of the cicadas. Set meals (110F and 160F) offer good value for money.

AUBERGE DE LA BARTAVELLE

rue du Cheval-Blanc (Centre).
☎ 04.90.72.33.72
Closed Wednesdays and Thursday lunchtimes (off season) and from mid-November to the start of February.

Once you cross the threshold of this restaurant you're in a microcosm of Provence. Ochre-coloured walls, Provençal fabrics and a relaxed, welcoming atmosphere. The food is so typically Provençal you can almost hear the chirrup of the cicadas; in fact it's the crackling of the fire over which the chef concocts tasty traditional dishes. Cod with crab *coulis*, spatchcock quail with *tapenade*, pigeon breast in honey and spices, panfried veal sweetbreads in an orange sauce. For dessert, don't miss the wonderful apple and cinnamon tart. Set meals 118F and 165F.

MURS — 84220 (8.5KM NE)

10% LE CRILLON

Centre.

☎ 04.90.72.60.31 ➡ 04.90.72.63.12
Closed Thursdays off season and for the month of November. **Car park**. **TV**.

A beautiful road leads through rural Luberon to this characterful village hidden away in the depths of the countryside. The hotel is named after Crillon the Brave, a companion in arms of Henri IV. Much better value for money than the hotel of the same name on place de la Concorde in Paris. Stylish doubles for 255–350F with bath and telephone. Set meals for 70F (weekdays), 100F and 125F. Some lovely dishes: tournedos with morels, truffle omelette, stew, hare and local game. The place for you if you long for the countryside and all that it stands for.

BEAUMETTES 84220 (9KM SE)

RESTAURANT LA REMISE

Centre.
☎ 04.90.72.23.05
Closed Tuesdays and Jan 15–Feb 15.
Disabled access.

The set meal for 75F is perhaps the best value in Luberon. Unpretentious and modest. The 125F set meal is obviously more elaborate: fish soup and bass with thyme. Other good house specials include escalope of salmon with sorrel, fillet of bass with tarragon, *émincé* of beef with ceps. Meals also served on the shady terrace. A good little restaurant.

GRASSE 06130

10% HÔTEL-PENSION LES PALMIERS*

17 av. Yves-Beaudoin (North-West).
☎ 04.93.36.07.24

You enter this small hotel by crossing a garden full of jasmine, reminding you that Grasse is the world capital of perfume!. Homely feel and a nice welcome. There are only 13 rooms, all of which are bright and spacious with shower and washing facilities. From 170–210F for a double even in season, a price which is unbeatable in this region. Half-board for around 180F per person per day. TV room on the ground floor. Book well in advance. Deposit required.

RESTAURANT LA GALERIE GOURMANDE

3, rue des Fabreries (Centre); it's in the old part of Grasse, near place aux Aires.
☎ 04.93.36.80.69
Closed Sunday evenings and Mondays in the off season.

Superb décor with arches and old stonework. In the summer food is served in the enclosed garden. Set meals for 89F and 125F with fish soup, onion tart, fillet of bass with green peppercorns, duck with spices and escalope of salmon with sorrel. Dish of the day 60F, which was delicious mullet in tarragon when we visited. Very pleasant in the evenings.

RESTAURANT PIERRE BALTUS

15 rue de la Fontette (Centre); it's in the old part of Grasse.
☎ 04.93.36.32.90
Closed Wednesday evenings, Saturday lunchtimes and from mid-February to mid-March. **Disabled access**.

It's often said that the food in Grasse is not brilliant, but the standards set by this restaurant prove otherwise. The chef, Pierre Baltus, practises his culinary skills in a tiny dining room (15 covers) decorated almost entirely in blue in a tiny street in the old town. If the chef can't get the fresh ingredients for a dish he doesn't cook it — that's how it should be! We tried the salmon *terrine* with asparagus, pan-fried prawns with aniseed flavoured butter, breast of duck with honey and raspberry vinegar and veal sweetbreads with morels (divine!). The set meals for 95–150F offer exceptional value for money. The à la carte dishes are perhaps even more mouth-watering. Good choice of wines. "Real" *bouillabaisse* on request. Needless to say, make a reservation or you'll be disappointed.

SPÉRACÈDES 06530 (10KM SW)

HÔTEL-RESTAURANT LA SOLEILLADE

3 rue des Orangers (Centre); 3km from Cabris heading towards Peymeinade.
☎ 04.93.60.58.46
Hotel closed for 6 weeks between the end of October and the start of December. Restaurant closed Sunday evenings, Mondays and Tuesdays (except for residents).

Two English women from Kent took over this hotel and lovingly run the place themselves (cooking, cleaning, decorating). Pretty rooms decorated in a blue and white maritime style. Doubles with washing facilities 190F. Shower on the landing. Half-board 225F per person. Breakfast is served on the terrace or in the dining room but isn't as good as it could be. The set meal for 135F offers a choice of at least 8 courses (3 starters, one main course and 4 desserts).

SAINT-VALLIER-DE-THIEY 06460 (12KM NW)

10% ☗ |●| HOSTELLERIE LE PRÉJOLY**

route Napoléon, place Rouguière (Centre).
☎ 04.93.42.60.86 ➡ 04.93.42.67.80
Closed Tuesdays (off season) and Dec 15–Jan 15. **TV**. **Canal+**.

A chic establishment but with at reasonable prices. A charming hotel with a large quiet garden, sauna and solarium. Rooms, most with a terrace, for 250–300F with shower/wc or bath. The restaurant is especially good. Previous diners have included the actors Charles Bronson and William Holden. Set meals for 96F, 165F and 195F. Artichoke *émincé* with *foie gras*, panfried scallops with a crayfish sauce, honeyed breast of duck, rib steak with a truffle scented sauce, rabbit stew, mutton tripe and sheep's trotters *à la provençale*, calf's tongue, etc. Good, traditional cuisine which sets greater store by good quality of the ingredients than any stylishness of preparation. But at least you know where you are with it. Half-board compulsory in summer.

GRAVE (LA) 05320

10% ☗ |●| L'EDELWEISS**

Centre.
☎ 04.76.79.90.93 ➡ 04.76.79.92.64

This establishment is worth noting. The owners organise the world-famous Mieje ski race each year on a piste that drops 2,150m. Relax on the terrace of this recently renovated building away from the traffic and study the summits of the 4,000m Alps through binoculars. A sauna and jacuzzi are now available for the exhausted athletic types. The clientele is international and sporty and a good atmosphere is assured in the evenings. The rooms are on the small side but clean (285F for a double with bath). The cheapest set meal is 95F. A place you are sure to like.

GUILLESTRE 05600

☗ |●| HÔTEL-RESTAURANT BARNIÈRES***

North.
☎ 04.92.45.04.87 ➡ 04.92.45.28.74
Closed Oct 15–Dec 20. **Car park. TV. Disabled access.**

Twenty years ago Monsieur Garcin owned a small bar and betting office in Guillestre. Today he owns this three-star hotel, the town's most prestigious establishment, complete with swimming pool, shady garden, tennis court, miniature golf, etc. It is comfortable and quiet, has splendid views, large, distinctive rooms with balconies and refined cooking — you are bound to like it here. After trying some of the house specialities, a visit to the weight-training room is wouldn't do any harm, followed by a sauna or dip in the jacuzzi. The only problem with this hotel is that you won't want to leave. Doubles with shower/wc are 300F. The cheapest set meal is 110F. Half-board is compulsory in the season; reckon on 350–380F.

☗ |●| LE CATINAT FLEURI**

La Longeagne (North); it's opposite the cinema.
☎ 04.92.45.07.62 ➡ 04.92.45.28.88
Car park. TV.

A traditional hotel and restaurant which has the advantage of being away from busy roads. Use of the swimming pool and tennis court is included in the price of a double room with shower/wc (330F). Half-board (not compulsory) from 320F. The cheapest set meal is 84F and there are others for 105F, 140F and 165F. Chalets are available or you can camp in the summer. A fee of 30F for using the secure garage.

|●| RESTAURANT LA CABANE DU PÊCHEUR

rte de Réotier (Centre).
☎ 04.92.45.21.21
Closed Tuesday evenings and Wednesdays except for school holidays.

In association with the fish farmers of Haute-Durance, this new restaurant offers trout with Queyras blue cheese, bacon or *crème fraîche*. Set meals for 78F (lunchtimes) or 98F. The à la carte prices are not excessive (around 60F for a main course). Friendly welcome. Jazz on Saturday evenings.

|●| RESTAURANT L'ÉPICURIEN

rue Sainte-Catherine (Centre).
☎ 04.92.45.20.02
Closed Monday evenings and Tuesdays, the first 2 weeks of June and Nov 15–Dec 15.

This restaurant, located in the heart of the old town with a pleasant vaulted dining room, is highly regarded by the locals. And this is no coincidence. Epicurus, the hedonistic Greek philosopher, is a very apt choice of name for this restaurant. The escalope of veal in Queyras blue cheese is delicious. You should also try the trout and salmon *terrine*, quails with bilberries and the local lamb with juniper berries. The chef's daily special is around 75F or a set meal of local dishes is 125F. Other set meals for 145–200F. A warm welcome and well-presented, high-quality food. And when food tastes as good as it looks, a meal becomes a feast! Reservation advisable. In our opinion the best restaurant in Guillestre.

SAINT-CRÉPIN 05600 (9KM N)

L'AMISTOUS

Centre.
☎ 04.92.45.25.30
Closed Mondays and Tuesdays off season, 10 days in January and for October.

The pizzas on offer here may make you think this is a restaurant just for tourists but the clientele includes a number of locals – and the pizzas are really good. Have the set meal at 75F and you are guaranteed to leave with a full stomach: inventive mixed salads in summer, veal sweetbreads *au goût des bois*, trout *au bleu* (cooked in boiling vinegar) – that alone makes the trip worthwhile – and chestnut charlottewith custard. The chef's speciality is a must – meat or shellfish grilled and flambéd in whisky or anis and accompanied by home-made sauces. Allow 120F (dessert included). A quite extensive wine list with an affordable wine for each region. They have unearthed a Côtes-du-Rhône for 48F or for 55F try the white Hautes-Alpes or Château-Cadillac.

HYÈRES 83400

HÔTEL DU SOLEIL**

rue du Rempart (North-East); it's very close to the Saint-Bernard gardens and villa de Noailles.
☎ 04.94.65.16.26 F➔ 04.94.35.40.40
TV.

A hotel absolutely engulfed by ivy in a very peaceful, dreamy spot next to the medieval town. The rooms in this old building are haphazardly furnished. Doubles from 180F with shower/wc to 390F with bath. A genuine welcome.

HÔTEL LES ORANGERS**

64 av. des Iles-d'Or (Centre).
☎ 04.94.65.07.01 F➔ 04.94.35.25.90
TV.

A straightforward, quiet family hotel which owes its name to the orange trees on the patio. This is where the marmalade at breakfast comes from – delicious! A sincere, warm-hearted welcome. Choose a room which looks out onto the pleasant courtyard. Doubles 225F with shower/wc and 255F with bath.

10% HOSTELLERIE PROVENÇALE LA QUÉBÉCOISE**

20 chemin de l'Amiral-Costebelle (South-West); coming off the motorway, turn right towards Costebelle at the roundabout, then straight on and follow the signs.
☎ 04.94.57.69.24 F➔ 04.94.38.78.27

The owner, from Quebec, left the -40∞C winters of Canada behind her some years ago for this Provençal hotel tucked away in the woods on a sunny hillside. You can understand why! Each room is different and all are attractive. Doubles 260F with basin or 380F with bath and terrace. Half-board is compulsory in July and August. Swimming pool. A very likeable hotel æ but which is starting to get expensive.

10% HÔTEL-RESTAURANT LES PINS D'ARGENT***

bd de la Marine; it's next to Saint-Pierre harbour.
☎ 04.94.57.63.60 F➔ 04.94.38.33.65
Closed Sunday evenings and Mondays in April, May and June. Restaurant closed Sept 28–April 10. **Car park**. **TV**.

Although this hotel is not really out in the wilds, you could make yourself believe that this is a corner of paradise. The turn-of-the-century building nestles beneath the shelter of palm trees, umbrella pines and other trees. Even though the town is extremely popular with tourists there are still some people in the hotel trade who realise that the reception given to guests is of paramount importance. This hotel is a real family affair and their warmth makes the place genuinely attractive. Pleasantly furnished, pretty rooms. Rooms 205 and 309 are especially nice. Doubles with bath for 320–530F depending on the time of year. The dining room is right next to the swimming pool and makes a pleasant place to eat. Fine cooking and dishes are prepared exclusively from fresh ingredients. The highlights are fish soup with *rouille* (a spicy sauce), sardines with *tapenade* and courgette *confit*, and local lamb chops. A special mention should be made of the house smoked salmon and a special prize given to the *nougat glacé* with chocolate and honey sauce. Set meals 100F, 150F and 180F. In fact the hotel as a whole deserves a prize.

|●| LE BISTROT DE MARIUS

1 place Massillon (Centre); it's in the old town.
☎ 04.94.35.88.38
Closed Tuesdays (off season).

This bistro is set on a charming square which you reach by climbing up a pretty street – handy for giving you an appetite. You won't be disappointed by this bistro where the host does his utmost to make his clients forget their day-to-day worries. Their aim is to empty your head of worries and fill your stomach. So forget everything – apart from eating. There's pike *quenelles* lyonnaises, old-fashioned wild boar stew (in season), *aïoli provençal*, and much more. Set meals for 90F, 140F and 190F. A very good bistro.

ISLE-SUR-LA-SORGUE (L') 84800

⌂ |●| LA SALADELLE

33 rue Carnot (Centre).
☎ 04.90.20.68.59 F 04.90.20.68.59
Closed Saturdays (except July and August), Sunday evenings and Dec 15–Jan 6.

Small, typical family *pension*. Friendly. Very simple rooms but clean. Half-board for around 170F. The set meal for 70F offers home cooking using fresh market produce.

|●| LE CARRÉ D'HERBES

13 av. des Quatre-Otages (Centre).
☎ 04.90.38.62.95
Closed Tuesday evenings Wednesdays and Dec 23–Jan 16.

An idyllic spot in this town which is quickly swamped by people as soon as the weather gets good. Dine in a pretty room with antique furniture and bric-a-brac (the town is renowned for its second-hand trade), on the terrace or in a converted aviary. Don't worry, the birds moved out ages ago. Set meal 130F. The food is full of freshness and original aromas. *Tartine de la bergère*, rabbit and olive stew, salad, fruit crumble. Attentive, helpful service.

LAVANDOU (LE) 83980

10% ⌂ |●| L'AUBERGE PROVENÇALE*

11 rue Patron Ravello (Centre).
☎ 04.94.71.00.44 F 04.94.15.02.25
Restaurant closed Tuesday and Wednesday lunchtimes.
Car park.

You can't get more Provençal than this. Superb, rustic décor. Large fireplace in the dining room. Enjoy typical food full of the flavours of the sea and Provence: mussel and crab soup, mullet *à l'escabèche*, grilled bass with thyme, baked rabbit with prunes. Set meals 98–240F. À la carte offerings include *bourride* (fish stew) and *aïoli* on Thursdays and Fridays. If you fancy staying over, pleasant double rooms are 170F with basin, 220F with shower, 250F with shower/wc and 300F with bath. A really friendly place. Get a free aperitif on presentation of this guide.

⌂ L'OUSTAOU**

20 av. du Général-de-Gaulle (Centre).
☎ 04.94.71.12.18 F 04.94.15.08.75
Secure parking. **TV**. **Disabled access**.

Right in the centre of town, just a stone's throw from the beaches, this hotel is charming and colourful and is certain to put you in a good mood. As soon as you walk through the wrought-iron gates you can abolish two adjectives from your vocabulary: conventional and characterless. The comfortable rooms and family setting make this ideal for a longer stay. Doubles 180F with basin and 280F with shower/wc. Attractive price reductions in the off season. A warm welcome.

10% ⌂ HÔTEL LE RABELAIS**

2 rue Rabelais (South-East).
☎ 04.94.71.00.56 F 04.94.71.82.55
Closed Nov 15–Dec 15. **Car park**. **TV**.
Disabled access.

A small hotel recently entirely redecorated, now with white walls and green shutters. Comfortable, pretty rooms. Doubles 230F (with basin) to 330F (with shower/wc and balcony looking over the harbour). This port is where Rabelais is reputed to have left his footprint on a rock while he was a medical student in Montpellier.

⌂ |●| HÔTEL-RESTAURANT BEAU SOLEIL**

Aiguebelle plage; it's 5km from the centre heading towards Fréjus.
☎ 04.94.05.84.55 F 04.94.05.70.89
Closed October to Easter. **Car park**. **Disabled access**.

A small hotel which, although a little eccentric, is quiet and far away from the noisiness of Lavandou on summer nights. The dynamic young owners offer a kind and considerate welcome to tourists. Simple, but very pleasant, well-kept rooms for 250F with shower/wc and 300F with bath, sea view and air conditioning. Half-board is compulsory in the high season at 350F per person. Set meals

98–185F with a very wide choice of local specialities. The *bourride* deserves a special mention.

RAYOL-CANADEL 83820 (13KM E)

MAURIN DES MAURES

av. du Touring-Club (Centre).
☎ 04.94.05.60.11

Here owner Dédé Del Monte paces up and down behind his bar like a croupier behind a gambling table. The locals, perched on their stools, exchange gossip and drink very strong pastis. The host welcomes his clients warmly as he shows them to the more formal setting of the "tourist's dining room" which looks out to sea. The fare includes omelettes, ham, mussels, grilled fish and *bouillabaisse*. An authentic restaurant in an area that tends to lose its true soul as the weather gets warmer. Set meals 68F (weekday lunchtimes), 110F and 140F.

L'ESCARÈNE 06440

HÔTEL LES TROIS VALLÉES***

Col du Turini.
☎ 04.93.91.57.21 ➡ 04.93.79.53.62
Car park. TV.

A gourmet's delight awaits inside this beautiful mountain chalet set at the summit of a pass legendary among rally drivers. The tranquillity and natural beauty of the mountains in the Mercantour national park and the excellent food are reason enough not to pass by. The dining area is a large room with rustic décor which, although somewhat outdated, is charming nonetheless. The local food is full of mountain goodness and very rich – perhaps the idea is to give the clients energy for the following day's walk. Salad of veal sweetbreads with raspberry vinegar, wild boar and hare *terrine*, tomato and basil tart, roast monkfish with spices, trout stuffed with *foie gras*, venison stew, venison steak with ceps, the list goes on and on. Set meals for 85F, 125F, 158F and 250F. Allow 320–550F for rooms in the low season (370–600F in summer). The rooms are a little cheaper in the annexe (*Les Chamois*) opposite the hotel.

MANOSQUE 04100

AUBERGE DE JEUNESSE

parc de la Rochette (North); it's 10 minutes' walk from the centre.
☎ 04.92.87.57.44 ➡ 04.92.72.43.91
Closed in January. **Car park.**

This is quite a modern place. You'll pay 66F for one night, breakfast included. Kitchen available for own use. Rooms with basin and 2–6 beds. Communal tents can accommodate about 20. Meals 50F. Half-board 112F. Swimming pool about 50m away.

10% HÔTEL PEYRACHE**

37 rue Jean-Jacques-Rousseau.
☎ 04.92.72.07.43
TV.

It's a stone's throw from Notre-Dame-de-Romigier with its Renaissance gate and its 12th century statue of the Black Virgin. They keep things simple here. The entrance, next to a clothes shop, isn't particularly prominent and you'll have to buzz on the intercom to get in. The rooms are clean, with pretty, flowery wallpaper and cost 220F and 250F. Breakfast is served in your room — there's no dining room!

RESTAURANT LE LUBÉRON

21 bis place Terreau.
☎ 04.92.72.03.09
Closed Sunday evenings, Mondays, and during the Christmas holidays

All the flavours of Provence, including olive oil and basil, can be found in the food here, even if the chef is a "Northern lad". He's got lots of imagination, as you can see in dishes like artichoke and truffle salad, and grilled pigeon with rosemary. Set meals 82F (weekdays), 140F, 165F, 200F and 300F. Tasteful rustic décor, terrace with a pergola.

MARSEILLE 13000

SEE MAP OVERLEAF

1st arrondissement

10% HÔTEL AZUR**

24 cours Franklin-Roosevelt; M° Réformés-Canabière.
MAP D1-2
☎ 04.91.42.74.38 ➡ 04.91.47.27.91
TV. Canal+.

A pleasant hotel with friendly owners in a steep and fairly quiet street lined with handsome buildings. The rooms have been renovated and most of them have air conditioning (20F extra). Doubles 250F with shower, 260F with bath. At the back, the nicest ones look out onto little gardens where there's a Christmas tree now several feet tall. If you're on a budget, they have a few basic rooms at 150F.

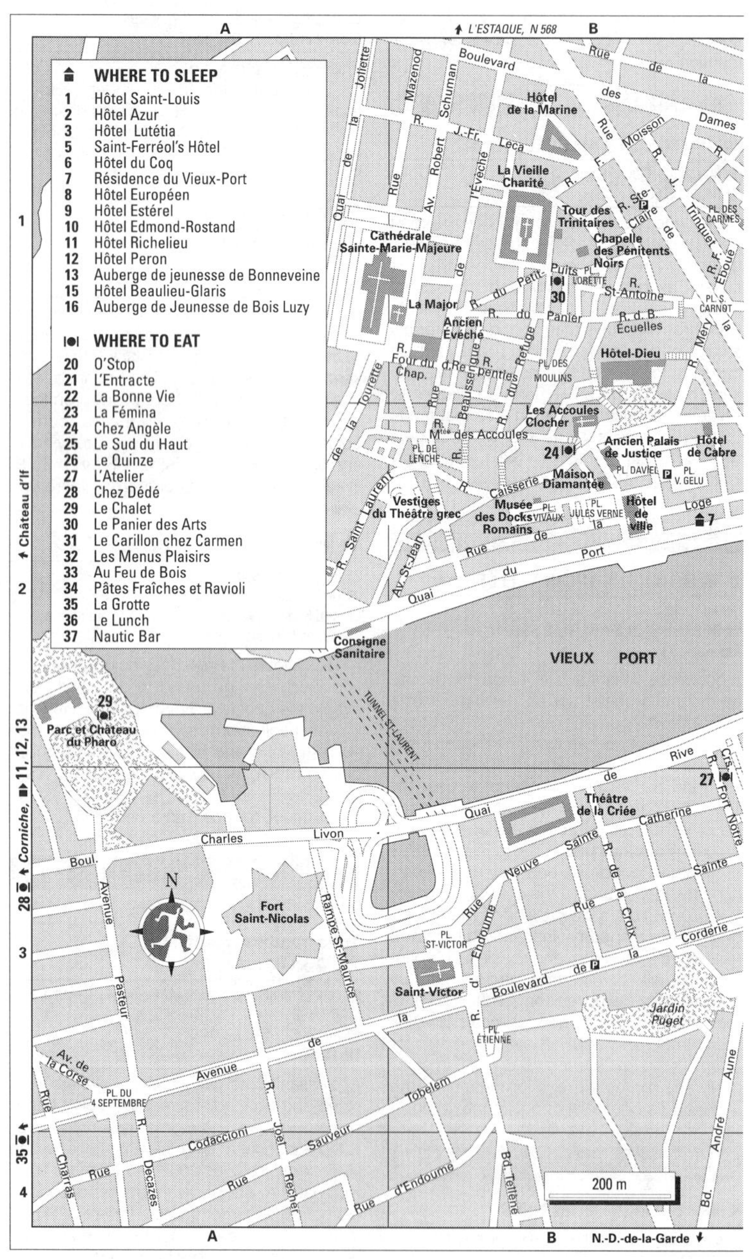
WHERE TO SLEEP
1 Hôtel Saint-Louis
2 Hôtel Azur
3 Hôtel Lutétia
5 Saint-Ferréol's Hôtel
6 Hôtel du Coq
7 Résidence du Vieux-Port
8 Hôtel Européen
9 Hôtel Estérel
10 Hôtel Edmond-Rostand
11 Hôtel Richelieu
12 Hôtel Peron
13 Auberge de jeunesse de Bonneveine
15 Hôtel Beaulieu-Glaris
16 Auberge de Jeunesse de Bois Luzy
WHERE TO EAT
20 O'Stop
21 L'Entracte
22 La Bonne Vie
23 La Fémina
24 Chez Angèle
25 Le Sud du Haut
26 Le Quinze
27 L'Atelier
28 Chez Dédé
29 Le Chalet
30 Le Panier des Arts
31 Le Carillon chez Carmen
32 Les Menus Plaisirs
33 Au Feu de Bois
34 Pâtes Fraîches et Ravioli
35 La Grotte
36 Le Lunch
37 Nautic Bar
L'ESTAQUE, N 568
Château d'If
Corniche, 11, 12, 13
28
35
N.-D.-de-la-Garde
Hôtel de la Marine
La Vieille Charité
Tour des Trinitaires
Chapelle des Pénitents Noirs
Cathédrale Sainte-Marie-Majeure
La Major
Ancien Evêché
Hôtel-Dieu
Les Accoules Clocher
Ancien Palais de Justice
Hôtel de Cabre
Maison Diamantée
Vestiges du Théâtre grec
Musée des Docks Romains
Hôtel de ville
Consigne Sanitaire
VIEUX PORT
TUNNEL ST-LAURENT
Parc et Château du Pharo
Théâtre de la Criée
Fort Saint-Nicolas
Saint-Victor
Jardin Puget
200 m

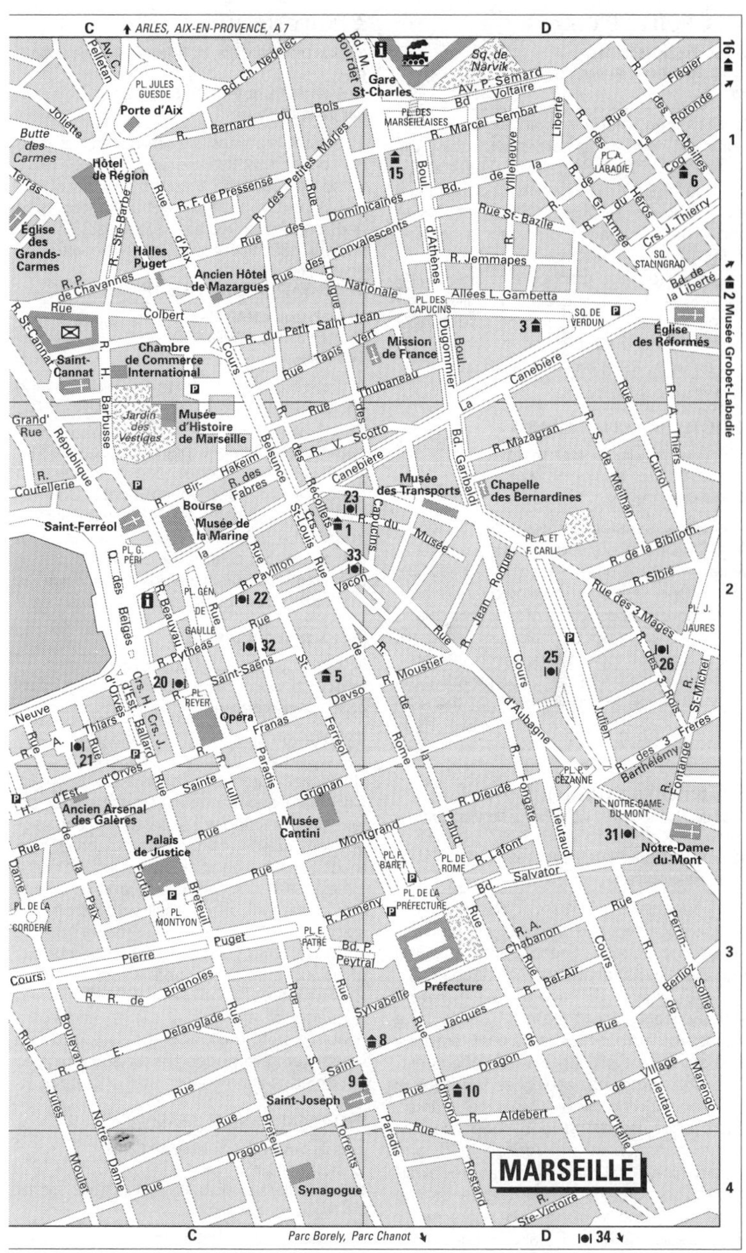
ARLES, AIX-EN-PROVENCE, A 7
Gare St-Charles
Sq. de Narvik
Porte d'Aix
PL. JULES GUESDE
Butte des Carmes
Hôtel de Région
Église des Grands-Carmes
Halles Puget
Ancien Hôtel de Mazargues
PL. DES MARSEILLAISES
PL. DES CAPUCINS
SQ. DE VERDUN
Église des Réformés
Mission de France
Saint-Cannat
Chambre de Commerce International
Jardin des Vestiges
Musée d'Histoire de Marseille
La Canebière
Musée des Transports
Chapelle des Bernardines
Bourse
Saint-Ferréol
Musée de la Marine
PL. G. PERI
PL. GÉN. DE GAULLE
PL. A. ET F. CARLI
PL. J. JAURES
Opéra
PL. REYER
PL. P. CÉZANNE
PL. NOTRE-DAME-DU-MONT
Notre-Dame-du-Mont
Ancien Arsenal des Galères
Palais de Justice
Musée Cantini
PL. P. BARET
PL. DE ROME
PL. DE LA PRÉFECTURE
PL. DE LA CORDERIE
PL. MONTYON
PL. E. PATRÉ
Préfecture
Saint-Joseph
Synagogue
MARSEILLE
Parc Borely, Parc Chanot
Musée Grobet-Labadié
C
D
1
2
3
4

10% HÔTEL DU COQ*

26 rue du Coq. **MAP D1-6**
☎ 04.91.62.61.29 F 04.91.64.02.05
TV

Our favourite hotel in the unpretentious category. You get an excellent welcome, the rooms have been attractively refurbished (they've kept the old floor tiles) and the prices are reasonable. Doubles 165 without shower and 195F with shower. Breakfast is included in the price. Despite the name of the hotel, you won't be disturbed by a cock crowing and the street is quiet, but if you like complete peace and quiet you'll be glad to hear that nearly all the rooms are at the back. If you arrive by train, they can even send a car for you.

HÔTEL BEAULIEU-GLARIS

1 place des Marseillaises. **MAP D1-15**
☎ 04.91.90.70.59 F 04.91.56.14.04
Closed Christmas–Jan 1. **TV**.

This place is a stone's throw from the enormous flight of stairs at Saint-Charles station, where you get a great view of the city. So it's pretty handy if you're travelling by train. It's a travelling salesman's type of hotel with bland décor and while not the height of luxury, it's clean and well looked after, even though it could do with a lick of paint. The rooms at the back are large and quiet and get the sun. Doubles 190–210F with shower/wc, triple 260F.

.10% HÔTEL SAINT-LOUIS**

2 rue des Récolettes; M° Vieux-Port or Noailles. **MAP C2-1**
☎ 04.91.54.02.74 F 04.91.33.78.59
TV. **Disabled access**.

An impressive building dating from Napoleonic times that has been well renovated on the outside. Friendly welcome and rather relaxed atmosphere. The huge reception area where you have breakfast is a bit shabby. Doubles with bath 200–220F. The rooms at the front have a balcony but they also get quite a bit of noise from the street. This isn't surprising, seeing as the hotel is right beside the lively Capucins market. There are a few good food shops nearby, including Armenian and African food, and several nice restaurants (some are reviewed later). The hotel has loyalty cards for the under 25s, and you can get some pretty good deals. Satellite TV and a garage for motorbikes. Travellers'cheques accepted.

HÔTEL LUTÉTIA**

38 allée Léon-Gambetta; M° Réformés-Canebière. **MAP D1-3**
☎ 04.91.50.81.78. F 04.91.50.23.52
Car park. **TV**. **Canal+**

This hotel, in a quiet little side street, has got a nice bright reception area and has been renovated (though we thought it wasn't very cosy).The rooms are simple but well equipped and very well looked after. Doubles 250F with shower, 280F with bath. Good welcome.

10% SAINT-FERRÉOL'S HÔTEL***

19 rue Pisançon. **MAP C2-5**
☎ 04.91.33.12.21 F 04.91.54.29.97
TV. **Canal+**.

A good location, close to the old port and shops like Galeries Lafayette and Virgin. The rooms, which are a bit glitzy-looking, are all named after famous painters such as Van Gogh, Picasso, Monet, and Cézanne and decorated with appropriate prints. Doubles 370–420F with bath, 440–480F with jacuzzi. You'll get a 10% discount on presentation of this guide. No charge for children under 4. Breakfast 40F (with fresh orange juice, just as the folder said!). Excellent welcome.

LA BONNE VIE

25 rue Pavillon; M° Noailles. **MAP C2-22**
☎ 04.91.54.89.88
Open weekday lunchtimes.

If you haven't got much time and you want to see as much of the city as possible, then this little snack bar that's close to the old port, La Canebière, and a number of museums is perfect. It's quick and not expensive. Meat, vegetables, salads. take your pick, say how much you want and pay by weight. We had a plate of salt cod with garlic and tomatoes that came with a meatball with herbs and spices for 20F and a slice of melon for 10F. Total: 30F. And you've got the added bonus of having a sit-down meal without wasting too much time (five minutes' waiting time and a quarter of an hour to eat – and not a minute more!). The bulk of the customers are women who've popped in for something to eat before getting on with their shopping.

RESTAURANT LE FEMINA

1 rue du Musée; M° Noailles. **MAP C2-23**
☎ 04.91.54.03.56
Closed Sunday lunchtimes, Monday lunchtimes, and the first two weeks in August.

You can eat till quite late in this huge restaurant with its high ceilings and naive frescoes depicting life in the Kabylia countryside. Naturally, the speciality here is *couscous* — plain (without meat, 35F), with meatballs (40F), with lamb kebabs (50F) and with grouper (85F). Try the *couscous* made with barley (from 65F), which is typical of the region. It's good for you and easy to digest.

PIZZERIA AU FEU DE BOIS

10 rue d'Aubagne; M° Noailles. **MAP C2-33**
☎ 04.91.54.33.96
Closed Sundays.

A pizzeria on two levels taken over by a former baker. It's not always had the same name but it's long been known for its outstanding oven-baked pizzas. A small one costs 50–65F and they come with a range of toppings including *royale* (mushrooms, garlic, sausage, and cheese), and *orientale* (pastrami, cream cheese, egg, and tomatoes). À la carte, there's *pieds-paquets* (mutton tripe cooked with sheep's trotters and tomatoes in white wine) for 60F and lasagne for 55F. Nothing unusual about the décor, regular customers, friendly service. If you're in a rush, you can always get a 1/4 pizza to take away from the counter outside.

O'STOP

16 rue Saint-Saens. **MAP C2-20**
☎ 04.91.33.85.34
Open 23 hours a day, 365 days a year (closed 7–8am).

Everyone knows about this great little snack bar. It attracts a wide range of customers, from ladies who lunch to the local working girls, and before a performance at the opera house you could quite easily bump into the odd singer or stage hand. The house specialities are meatballs (48F), pasta with basil (35F), and braised beef or chicken *provençale* (50F) and they're all pretty decent. The well prepared sandwiches aren't bad either. Good atmosphere in the small hours. A must in Marseilles.

LES MENUS PLAISIRS

1 rue Haxo; M° Vieux-Port-Hôtel-de-Ville. **MAP C2-32**
☎ 04.91.54.94.38
Closed evenings and weekends.

This is a very friendly and clean place with lots of nice old prints on the walls. Excellent value for money. The 62F set meal, which changes every day, offers a small salad of peas or feta and a choice of main courses like skate in a butter sauce, meat lasagne, and sautéd pork with kidney beans. The desserts are good too — try the fig tart with custard, the peaches in wine, or the apricot and strawberry tart. Starter and main course 52F, main course and dessert 55F, main course on its own 49F. Friendly welcome and service from the owner, who'll open in the evenings for groups of 15 or more.

L'ATELIER

18 place aux Huiles; M° Vieux-Port-Hôtel-de-Ville. **MAP B2-27**
☎ 04.91.33.55.00
Closed Saturday evenings, Sundays, and in August.

There are lots of bars and restaurants in the immediate vicinity but you've got to try this place. It belongs to a former pastry chef who's got an excellent reputation — everybody with a sweet tooth swears by his desserts! But before you get to those, have the regional speciality of stuffed baby vegetables (60F). It's light enough for you not to feel guilty about indulging in the *Castel* chocolate pudding (30F), the strawberry and raspberry icecream cake (30F) or the delicious *"Gritti"*, a pear and chocolate cake flavoured with bitter orange (30F). There are a few tables out on the terrace shaded by a nice lime tree. Expect to pay about 150F. There's a lunchtime *formule* (main course plus dessert and coffee) for 85F, and an evening one for 125F.

L'ENTRACTE

place Thiars; M° Vieux-Port-Hôtel-de-Ville. **MAP C2-21**
☎ 04.91.33.50.20
Closed Saturday lunchtimes and Sundays.

Great location. A wealthy businessman took over this place when it was going rapidly downhill. He's made it into a modern and bourgeois-style restaurant that's bright and airy and has a beautiful terrace where you can enjoy a nice meal without sitting in your neighbour's lap. In particular, he had the good sense to employ a young chef who had worked in a number of top restaurants. The result is fresh, well-blanced and visually appealing dishes like spinach canneloni, and lamb marinaded in honey and ginger. At lunchtime they do a 110F *formule* of main course plus dessert and a glass of wine and in the evening there's a set meal at 150F. The à la carte menu is small but everything is skilfully prepared and well presented.

2nd arrondissement

10% HÔTEL LA RÉSIDENCE DU VIEUX PORT ***

18 quai du Port; M° Vieux Port-Hôtel de Ville. **MAP B2-7**
☎ 04.91.91.91.22 F 04.91.56.60.88
TV. **Canal+**.

It's on the town hall side of the old port (and so has a view of Notre-Dame) and you can sit on your balcony and watch the boats. The rooms are up to three-star standard. They're large, full of light and pleasantly furnished. It's a pity that the bathrooms are a bit on the small side. Doubles 450F and a suite for 4 or 5 people 750F. A great family hotel, in an ideal spot to start off your sight-seeing. Friendly service and good breakfast. The "Bon week-end à Marseille" promotion allows you to spend Friday and Saturday there and pay for just one night.

|●| LE PANIER DES ARTS

3 rue du Petit-Puits; M° Vieux-Port-Hôtel-de-Ville. **MAP B1-30**
☎ 04.91.56.02.32
Closed Sundays and Saturday lunchtimes.

Good atmosphere and warm welcome in this restaurant, whose owner moved about a lot before deciding to settle in Marseilles. As a starter, why not share a *"panier des arts"* (95F for 2) — a basket full of fresh vegetables and lots of dips like taramasalata and *anchoïade* (anchovy and garlic paste) — and then move on to *pastilla* (a kind of Moroccan pie) of young rabbit with cinnamon (76F) or tuna fish with rosemary (76F). With a little wine, expect to pay about 150F. Good set meals at 70F (lunchtimes) and 98F. Pleasant bistro décor.

|●| RESTAURANT CHEZ ANGÈLE

50 rue Caisserie; M° Vieux-Port-Hôtel-de-Ville. **MAP B2-24**
☎ 04.91.90.63.35
Closed Saturday lunchtimes, Sunday lunchtimes (and evenings June–Sept), and in August.

One of the oldest pizzerias in town. You'll get a crisp and piping hot pizza straight from the antique oven (fuelled with firewood), that will really make your mouth water. The choice of toppings naturally includes mozzarella and anchovies but whatever you have, the smallest size (42–62F) will probably be quite large enough. Set meal 95F. Mixed clientele and trattoria-style décor for football fans, with pennants and other souvenirs singing the praises of OM, the local team. There's another great pizza place in the area, which is quite unusual in that it hasn't got a telephone, you can't book, and there's no menu, yet it's always full — *Étienne,* 2 rue Lorette, closed Sundays and mid July to end of August.

6th arrondissement

10% ⌂ HÔTEL ESTÉREL**

124–125 rue Paradis; M° Estrangin-Préfecture. **MAP D3-9**
☎ 04.91.37.13.90 ⮕ 04.91.81.47.01
TV. Canal+.

In a shopping street next to the massive church of St Joseph. Rooms in the main building and the annexe across the way are modern and functional for the most part and come with video, mini-bar and air conditioning (greatly appreciated in summer!). They fall into three categories and prices range from 180F to 283F according to size and plumbing arrangements. Breakfast is included in the price of the most expensive rooms. And as a bonus, you'll get a 15% reduction on presentation of this guide. Lots of little gestures like crisps and sweets for guests, and there's also a lovely sitting room with an aquarium and lots of old books. Overnight parking can be arranged.

⌂ HÔTEL EUROPÉEN**

115–117 rue Paradis; M° Estrangin-Préfecture. **MAP D3-8**
☎ 04.91.37.77.20 ⮕ 04.91.81.40.80
Secure parking. TV. Canal+.

A renovated hotel with air conditioning and good sound-proofing. It's fairly central — in the main shopping street — and run by a friendly young couple. Singles with basin 150F, and a pretty little suite in the attic that's furnished with antiques and sleeps four 350F. Doubles range in price from 200F for one with basin/wc to 280F with bath. If you can show them this guide though, you'll get the comfort of the latter for the price of the former — so your saving will almost pay for the book!

10% ⌂ |●| HÔTEL EDMOND ROSTAND**

31 rue Dragon (on the corner of rue Edmond Rostand); M° Estrangin-Préfecture. **MAP D3-10**
☎ 04.91.37.74.95 ⮕ 04.91.57.19.04
TV.

A family hotel, very well cared for, in a quiet little street. If you've seen *Cyrano de Bergerac* the film, you might be interested to know that the Edmond Rostand referred to in the hotel's name wrote the play and was born in a house not too far away from here. The rooms are bright and modern and all have bath and direct telephone. Doubles 250–290F, and rooms that sleep four 350F. (These are popular with families, sales reps, and executives.) Ask for a room with a view of the garden. Breakfast 30F with excellent home-made jam, and a nice little lunchtime set meal at 60F, with Italian specialities.

|●| RESTAURANT LE CARILLON-CHEZ CARMEN

26 place Notre-Dame-du-Mont; M° Cours-Julien. **MAP D3-31**
☎ 04.91.47.50.08
Closed Mondays and in August.

Service 7pm–4am.This is a female-dominated business! It may have moved from its old premises behind the opera house but the spirit of the place is just the same. All sorts of people on the nightshift, from labourers to working girls, come here for something to keep them going. You can either eat inside or on the terrace, and relish the pizzas and *calzone* cooked in the special oven by Carmen's daughter. Pizzas large enough for two start at 46F. The customers and the atmosphere vary, depending on what time of night (or early morning!) it is.

LE SUD DU HAUT

80 cours Julien; M° Noailles. **MAP D2-25**
☎ 04.91.92.66.64
Closed Sundays, Mondays, evenings Tuesday–Saturday, and lunchtimes Thursday–Saturday.

You could say that this restaurant was quite chic. Why? Well, certainly not because of the prices, which are very reasonable. At lunchtime, they have *formules* at 54F and 70F (this comes with a fish dish) and a set meal at 100F that includes a quarter-litre of wine. In the evening main courses range from 70F to 100F and the jugs of wine are certainly not expensive. No, when we say chic, we're referring more to the surroundings and just for the fact we like the place. The bric-a-brac – holiday souvenirs, bits and pieces picked up second-hand, different kinds of furniture and paintings that are for sale – goes well with the Afro-Cuban-Carribbean music playing in the background and there's a terrace where you can admire the wonderful fountain in Cours Julien. The service manages to be both attentive and relaxed. And last but certainly not least, the restaurant deserves the "chic" description because of the food. Old recipes are revamped here, with a touch of finesse being added to dishes like stuffed vegetables, chicken with basil, and rack of lamb with herbs. So to sum up, it's elegant, it's refined, and it's different. A super restaurant and one that we hope will take our advice to keep it simple.

LE QUINZE

15 rue des 3-Rois; M° Cours-Julien-Notre-Dame-du-Mont. **MAP D2-62**
☎ 04.91.92.00.52
Closed lunchtimes and December 24.

This street runs parallel to the famous *Cours Julien* and acts as a kind of overflow for it – it now has just as many restaurants. This particular one is lively, very laid-back and has a great atmosphere – elbows on the table, tall stories and jokes are all part and parcel of your evening. Despite its name, it's not rugby they talk about here when the question of sport comes up but the local football team, OM. Simple home cooking is what you'll get here and meat dishes like *daube* and good curries. Substantial set meals 89F and 109F. Owner Denise is quite a character and has just refurbished her restaurant.

7th arrondissement

10% LE RICHELIEU**

52 corniche Kennedy (West); take a number 83 bus from Vieux-Port, and get off at the Catalans stop. Off map **A3-11**
☎ 04.91.31.01.92 F 04.91.59.38.09
Secure parking.TV. Canal+.

This hotel is virtually on the water's edge, so it goes without saying that you should ask for a room with a balcony and a view of the Mediterranean (a few of them, number 31 in particular, have been prettily refurbished; the rooms that look out onto the street aren't as nice). Wonderful panoramic view of the islands of Frioul. There's a sunny terrace with a patch of shade where you can have breakfast. The lovely little beach of Catalans is a stone's throw away (but be warned, you've got to pay to use it). Doubles 180F with shower and sea view, 205F with shower/wc and 240–260F with bath. Triples 280F. There's a not-too-expensive Vietnamese restaurant with a terrace on the ground floor.

10% HÔTEL PERON**

119 corniche Kennedy (West); take a number 83 bus from Vieux Port and get off at the Corniche-Frégier stop. Off map **A3-12**
☎ 04.91.31.01.41 F 04.91.59.42.01
Closed July and August. **Secure parking. TV.**

First of all, the décor. In the 1950s, each room was allocated a country or a region of France and decorated with murals and dolls in traditional dress, and there are ceramic fish and sea creatures in the bathrooms. It's all irresistibly kitsch! Doubles with bath from 240F. Secondly, the location right beside the sea means you get a great view from the balconies. Although the rooms at the back don't have a view, they are quieter, as the road runs past the hotel. You'll get a cheerful welcome and attentive service. The atmosphere is nice and homely, just like the food served in the little restaurant, not to be confused with the *Peron* restaurant opposite. You'll have to book, by the way. Set meals from 80F. In short, we loved it, even though the bed linen is getting a bit old and the paintwork's a bit shabby. It definitely grows on you.

|●| LE CHALET

jardin du Pharo (West). **MAP A2-29**
☎ 04.91.52.80.11
Open March–Oct noon–6pm.

It's tucked away in the gardens of the palace built by Napoléon III for the Empress Eugénie and is more like an outdoor café than a chalet. Unpretentious cooking with main courses like cuttlefish *à l'armoricaine* (with onions and tomatoes), tuna *provençale,* and grilled ribsteak with chips for about 65F. Salads around 50F. In summer, when the sun blazes down, the shaded terrace gets a light sea breeze, which is very refreshing. There's a very good vantage point from which you can watch the goings-on in the old port. Lovely place for a quiet drink in the afternoon.

8th arrondissement

⌂ |●| AUBERGE DE JEUNESSE DE BONNEVEINE

47 av. Joseph-Vidal (impasse Bonfils) (South-West); M° Rond-Point-du-Prado; take a number 19 bus (Vidal-Collet stop) or a 44 (place Bonnefon).
☎ 04.91.73.21.81 F→ 04.91.73.97.23
Closed in January. **Car park. Disabled access.**

A modern youth hostel with a garden. It's in the process of being renovated and while it doesn't exactly ooze charm it's in a quiet area not far from the beach. They get 150 people through here every day according to the warden. We advise you to keep your things in the lockers (15F, no time limit) to avoid any unpleasant surprises. Doubles 119F a night with breakfast, visitor's tax, and sheets included. Only 68F per person in a dormitory for five. The curfew is normally 1am and you've got to have a hostel membership card. There's a little snack bar and, as long as you order in advance, you can have a meal for 49F.

|●| PÂTES FRAÎCHES ET RAVIOLIS

150 rue Jean-Mermoz, on the corner of rue Émile Sicard (South); M° Rond-Point-du-Prado.
☎ 04.91.76.18.85
Closed every evening, Sundays, public holidays, and the first three weeks in August.

You've got to go through the kitchen of this Italian restaurant if you want a table on the veranda, where all the windows open out onto a gravel courtyard. Marcel Pagnol, the famous author and film director used to come here (his studios were just nearby). As a starter, how about some Parma ham or a mozzarella kebab before trying one of the great pasta or ravioli dishes? Expect to pay 80–100F. It's in a very quiet middle-class area. Almost next door, the Grancafé (tel 04 91 22 70 84, open weekday lunchtimes) with its formule-buffet at 59F is worth a try too. Pleasant surroundings.

|●| CHEZ DÉDÉ

32 bd Bonne Brise; follow the corniche road to La Madrague, after Pointe-Rouge. It's signposted after the main road.
☎ 04.91.73.01.03
Closed Sunday evening to Wednesday evening in winter.

If the wind's right, body surfers will be in seventh heaven but since the restaurant's terrace juts out over the water, eating outside won't be a practical proposition. Opt instead for the dining room, which is decorated with unsophisticated and amusing model boats. The menu is simple — oven-baked pizzas of course, pasta, and grilled fish. As far as we know, it's one of the few places to serve grilled sardines (60F for 6). Delicious. Average prices for everything else.

|●| LA GROTTE

Calanque de Callelongue (South); M° Castellane and then a number 9 bus to La Madrague and a 20 to Callelongue.
☎ 04.91.73.17.79

Callelongue is the starting point for walkers who want to get to Cassis along the Calanques. It consists of a few cottages, a tiny port with the occasional boat, and *La Grotte*. At lunchtimes the terrace, shaded with an awning, is very popular with the people of Marseilles. The superb flower-filled patio gets too much sun at that time of day and they save it for dinner. Pizza is the favourite snack of the South and here, as in so many other places, it's the star of the show. By all means order it, for it's pretty decent. You can have grilled fish if you want, but it's more expensive of course! Don't forget your mosquito repellent since there are always a few around at night — but the customers still outnumber them. The place itself is really big and runs a bit like a computerized factory, but it's still pleasant. Be warned — they don't accept credit cards.

9th arrondissement

|●| LE NAUTIC BAR

calanque de Morgiou; M° Rond-Point-du-Prado and then

a number 23 bus and get off at the Morgiou-Beauvallon stop. You've still got a fair bit of a walk after that.
☎ 04.91.40.06.37

By reservation only in winter. Whatever the time of year, it's always better to phone and check. The locals refer to it as "chez Sylvie" and it's got a nice terrace that makes an ideal setting for a bit of seafood – some whitebait, say, for 55F or fish soup for 60F, or *girelles* (a fish found only in the Mediterranean) for 85F. Sip some chilled wine and enjoy the breeze off the sea and the wonderful surroundings. It's got everything you could want after a morning of swimming and diving. Be warned – the roads leading to the creeks are closed to unauthorized vehicles from June to September, a wise precaution when you consider the forest fires that raged through parts of Marseilles last summer. In any case, if you phone the restaurant beforehand, you might get permission as long as the restrictions don't get even tighter in the meantime.

LE LUNCH

calanque de Sormiou (West); M° Rond-Point-du-Prado, then a number 23 bus (La Cayolle stop) and the free shuttle service (7.30am–7pm).
☎ 04.91.25.05.37
Closed Oct 15–end of March.

Be warned: the access road is closed to cars and motorbikes June 23–Sept 8. However, if you book a table at the restaurant you can get in and park your car there (but there is a charge). But as we said before, the rules may get tougher because of the fires. Telephone and take the free shuttle instead. Going down towards the creek you get a magnificent view of the magical blue sea dotted with little spots of turquoise. All you have to do then is to sit down on the terrace with a little glass of kir and order the catch of the day, which could be sea bream or red mullet. Watch out – the cost of the fish depends on the weight, so your bill can mount up pretty quickly. Expect to pay about 200F. Good *bouillabaisse* – order it one day in advance.

12th arrondissement

AUBERGE DE JEUNESSE

château de Bois-Luzy allée des Primevères (East).
How to get there: it's in the area known as Montolivet; take a number 6 bus (get off at the Marius-Richard stop) or an 8 (Bois-Lusy stop).
☎ 04.91.49.06.18 Fax 04.91.40.06.18
Service 7.30am–noon and 5pm–11pm.
Secure parking.

The hostel, about 5km from the centre, is housed in a magnificent country house dating back to 1850 that stands in its own grounds and has a view of the stretch of water off Marseilles. You can pitch your tent. It's 50F for one person in a double room, 45F in a dormitory with 4–6 beds. Hire of sheets 16F, breakfast 18F and meal (you'll have to book) 43F. Kitchen available for own use. Wonderful entrance hall and other architectural features. There's a sports stadium with tennis courts practically next door.

MASSOINS 06710

10% AUBERGE DE MASSOINS

☎ 04.93.05.77.60 Fax same
Closed Sunday evenings and Mondays except in July and August. **Car park**.

The inn of your dreams in the village of your dreams. Hard to believe? Don't worry, we were sceptical at first too! But it does actually exist, so you've got to promise not to tell anyone about it, unless they'll really appreciate the great favour you're doing them. It's got masses of charm and the restaurant has huge plate glass windows that brings the countryside into the dining room. Set meals at 75F and 120F, featuring the cusine of Provence. Very pretty little rooms, newly decorated, are 170F with shower/wc and TV. And there's a swimming pool. Who said the Côte d'Azur was expensive? We strongly advise you to book, for the rooms at least.

MENTON 06500

AUBERGE DE JEUNESSE

plateau Saint-Michel (North).
How to get there: from the town hall follow the signs to the Saint-Michel campsite; go past the campsite and it's on the left.
☎ 04.93.35.93.14 Fax 04.93.35.93.07
Closed noon–5pm, and Dec 1–Feb 1. **Car park**.

You can walk to it but it's a bit of a hike – take the shuttle bus from the bus station instead. 68F a night with breakfast and shower (you've got to become a hostel member). The very generous dinner costs 51F and is served in a refectory with large windows that give you a wonderful view of Menton and the surrounding area. The warden, a pioneer of the hostel movement, is well known locally. And he keeps his hostel super clean. It has 80 beds in all, but you can't book by phone. It's a case of first come first served, so get there early!

HÔTEL NAPOLÉON***

29 porte de France baie de Garavan.
☎ 04.93.35.89.50 F➔ 04.93.35.49.22
TV.

A large building, with typically dreary 60s or 70s architecture, it doesn't look like much from the outside. But inside it's a different story. There are lots of references to Napoleon in the reception area. The rooms are spacious and comfortable and most of them have a terrace with a sea view. Doubles 450–600F. The restaurant is decent, even though it's a bit pricey, and meals are served by the swimming pool. Set meals 120F and 140F. Attentive, efficient service.

10% HÔTEL CHAMBORD***

6 av. Boyer.
☎ 04.93.35.94.19 F➔ 04.93.35.30.55
TV.

A friendly family hotel right in the main street in the centre of Menton. It's not unusual to meet people who've been coming here since it opened in 1976. The rooms are very spacious and really comfortable. They come with bath and TV and cost 470–680F, depending on the season. Breakfast and taxes included. All just a stone's throw from the sea and near a tennis club — don't forget your rackets!

A BRAÏJADE MÉRIDIOUNALE

66 rue Longue.
☎ 04.93.35.65.65
Closed lunchtimes in July and August.

People are generally enthusiastic in what they say on leaving this little restaurant in the old part of town — it's hard to find a dissatisfied customer. The rustic dining room has exposed stonework and behind the bar there's a big wood-burning oven that gives good flavour to the meat. You know exactly what you're getting here. The set meals include everything from aperitif to coffee — and possibly even a liqueur if you're good! Lunchtime *formule* 75F or set meals 105F, 145F and 185F. There's a lot of marinaded and grilled meat on the menu, like garlic chicken kebabs, but they also do the old regional favourites, like beef stew *niçoise* with ravioli. Everything is served in generous portions by nice, friendly staff. So at the end of your visit you too will be singing its praises!

LE PISTOU

2 rue du Fossan.
☎ 04.93.57.45.89
Closed Sunday evenings, Mondays, the first fortnight in December, and the first fortnight in June.

This used to be the kind of place that catered to the elderly gentlemen and young lads of Menton in search of new experiences. Today, you can get a decent meal of traditional Provence dishes at reasonable prices. The 80F set meal offers *soupe au pistou* (vegetable soup with pesto), rabbit *provençal* and dessert. The home-made ravioli is excellent. The house may have changed its type of business, but it still has the same varied clientèle.

RESTAURANT LE CHAUDRON

28 rue Saint-Michel.
☎ 04.93.35.90.25
Closed Mondays and Tuesday evenings out of season, and Nov 5–Dec 25.

A little family restaurant in the centre of town that serves authentic and fresh-tasting local dishes. Set meals 87F and 105F. The pleasant dining room is air-conditioned and there are a few tables set out on the terrace in the pedestrian street. How about courgette *mousse* with tomato *coulis* that any top chef could be proud of, followed by either *croquant* of fillet of sole with chanterelles or fillet of John Dory with baby vegetables and Roquefort? Friendly welcome.

ROQUEBRUNE-CAP-MARTIN 06190 (3KM S)

LES DEUX FRÈRES

In the village.
☎ 04.93.28.99.00 F➔ 04.93.28.99.10
Closed Thursdays and Friday lunchtimes. **Car park**.

This is one of our favourite places in the area. It stands on the outskirts of the village and is housed in a belvedere, so you get a marvellous view of the whole area. It's a sort of paradise on earth, the type of place that makes you glad to be alive and causes you to lose all sense of time. The view from rooms 1 and 2 is extraordinary — it makes you want to pick up a pen and become the next Hugo or Châteaubriand. The young Dutch owner has entirely renovated the house and redecorated throughout so now it's just as charming as the dining room. A perfect setting for food that's full of flavour, prepared with high-quality produce and not short on imagination. The dishes on offer include a cold mussel soup flavoured with *colombé*, chicken fricassee (they use *poulet de Bresse*) with citrus fruit, lamb steaks with preserved garlic, and minestrone of crabs and langoustines. Set meals 95F and 120F (wine included) at lunchtimes, 180F and 240F in the evenings. There are 10 rooms — one with a view of the mountain will cost you 385F, and a sea view 495F.

LE JARDIN DU CAP

230 av. Virginie Hériot.
☎ 04.93.57.26.71

You might have thought that a young chef from Lyons attempting to introduce *andouillette* or *saucisson chaud* in the area round Menton was courting disaster. And yet the melding of two cultures and two different kinds of food seems to have worked, and cep ravioli, *rascasse* (scorpion fish) with basil, and risotto sit quite happily alongside *andouillette* made entirely from calf's mesentery (the membrane enclosing the intestines) and veal kidneys in mustard. The à la carte features a greater number of typical Lyons dishes in winter, when people feel they need warming up. Set meals 110F, 165F and 180F. You can eat either in the tiny dining room or out on the terrace among the flowers and trees.

BEAUSOLEIL 06240 (8KM S)

HÔTEL DIANA**

17 bd du Général-Leclerc (Centre).
☎ 04.93.78.47.58 F 04.93.41.88.94
Car park. TV.

It's a bit more expensive than a hotel on the other side of the street would be (well naturally — this side is France, while the other is Monte Carlo). The green façade is quite Edwardian-looking and it's got a great view of. blocks of concrete. Doubles with basin/bidet 170F, with shower/wc and TV 280F, with bath and TV 350F. A wonderfully rickety lift takes you up to the rooms. Good welcome.

10% HÔTEL BOERI**

29 bd du Général-Leclerc (Centre).
☎ 04.93.78.38.10 F 04.93.41.90.95
TV. Canal+.

A pretty hotel with geraniums in the windows surrounded by palm trees and tucked away among the high rises of Monte Carlo's version of a housing estate. Very large double rooms decorated in a fairly restrained fashion. If you ask for room number 201, 202, 301 or 302, you'll have a fraction of a sea view. But keep that to yourselves. Doubles 230F with shower/wc, 395F with bath. In summer, prices rise to 260F and 475F respectively.

MOLINES-EN-QUEYRAS 05350

10% LA MAISON GAUDISSARD**

North; as you come into town turn left after the post office, and the hotel is 600m further on.
☎ 04.92.45.83.29 F 04.92.45.80.57
Closed April 14–June 14 and Sept 14–Dec 20.
Car park.

It was in 1969 that Bernard Gentil made his house into the first cross-country ski centre in France and it's been introducing new services and facilities ever since. In winter, they offer courses in cross-country skiing and other ski-related activities, including a trek to Queyras. In summer, it's hiking and paragliding that bring the crowds in. After a nice brisk walk, what better than to relax on the terrace high above the village where you get such a wonderful view of the mountains? The bar's worth a look, by the way — the wood it's made of is larch. The establishment also has a sitting room and a Finnish sauna. There's one set meal at 90F. Doubles with shower from 360F. Breakfast 32F. Half-board starts at 268F. *Gîtes* and flats are available.

MOUGINS 06250

RESTO DES ARTS

rue du Mal Foch.
☎ 04.93.75.60.03
Closed Mondays in season, and Sunday evenings and Mondays out of season.

Mougins is known to attract celebrities and millionaires but here's a restaurant that's well within the reach of the average reader of this guide. Denise does the cooking and prepares traditional tasty and simple dishes made to recipes handed down from her mother, and her mother before her. In fact, there have been about six generations of cooks in the family so you're in good hands! She does the shopping herself and is off every morning looking for the best ingredients for her *daube provençale, aïoli* (garlic mayonnaise), fish *pot-au-feu*, *stouffi* of lamb with *polenta*, and stuffed baby vegetables. And Grégory will serve you. He's a former hairdresser to the stars, but he's settled down in Mougins and still has the gift of the gab and a friendly laid-back nature. Set meals 65F (lunchtimes) and 100F. A perfect place.

MOUSTIERS SAINTE MARIE 04360

10% LE RELAIS

pl. du Couvert.
☎ 04.92.74.66.10 F 04.92.74.60.47
Closed Fridays out of season and Dec–March. **TV.**

Standing on the bank of the stream, right in the centre of the village, this is one of those inns that people flock to as soon as summer arrives. So it's advisable to book. Very pretty rooms 230F with washing facilities, 290F with shower/wc and 380F with bath. If you're a light sleeper, you might like to avoid the ones that look out onto the waterfall. The restaurant deserves a round of applause for its traditional dishes like *barigoule* of snails flavoured with aniseed, baked pork and vegetable faggot *provençal, pieds-paquets* (mutton tripe with sheep's trotters), *paqueton* of rabbit with goat's cheese and olives, red mullet *en chartreuse* (braised with cabbage), and trout poached in walnut liqueur. Three set meals at 98F, 148F and 198F. A slightly curt welcome.

AUBERGE DE LA FERME ROSE***

chemin Embourgues; it's a short walk from the town.
☎ 04.92.74.69.47 Fax 04.92.74.60.76
Closed beginning of Dec–mid March. **Car park**.

We wouldn't be the least bit surprised to hear that people from an interior design magazine were here just before us. This is a little gem of a place — a typical Provençal farmhouse — deep in the country and you expect traditional rustic décor. Not a bit of it! The owner is a real fan of the 50s and 60s and he's decorated the bar and the bedrooms with items from that era, including a jukebox, bistro tables, coat stands, and lots of bric-a-brac. The kitchen, where breakfast is prepared, is a perfect example of what the rest of the place looks like, and it could all very easily look a bit tacky. But everything fits in perfectly. The rooms are really quiet and the ones on the ground floor have a pretty terrace. Doubles 390F with shower but no TV. An ideal place for lovers who want to be alone. Just a tiny criticism about breakfast — it's a bit expensive at 48F.

LA TREILLE MUSCATE

pl. de l'Église.
☎ 04.92.74.64.31

A gourmet restaurant with a good reputation, but it's not cheap. The owner decided to go back to basics to discover the pleasure that cooking simple food gives him, but that doesn't mean that he skimps on flavour. A dinner in the moonlight on a beautiful terrace becomes a magical moment. At lunchtime, if the sun gets a bit too much, then perhaps you'd prefer to sit inside in the cool and delightful dining room that's full of amazing little knick-knacks. All they offer by way of set meals is a *menu-carte* at 160F. We had fish *terrine* with *aïoli* (garlic mayonnaise), veal kidneys with mustard, and a cherry, rhubarb and pear *clafoutis*. No nasty surprises on the wine list. There's a good selection of first-rate Côtes du Rhône or Côtes de Provence (red, white or rosé) for 100F.

MONTAGNAC MONTPEZAT 04730 (26KM S)

10% LE RELAIS DE LA LAVANDE

pl. du Village; take the D952 to Riez, then the D11 and the D111.
☎ 04.92.77.53.68

A very pretty little country inn that you might have missed if we hadn't told you about it. You're right in the heart of Provence here. The village has one little square, some plane trees, and one church. The hotel has seven simple but well-kept rooms, 120F with basin and 250F with bath. The warmth and simplicity of the hotel is reflected in the food. Treat yourself to a goat's cheese omelette, stew of suckling pig, sole *meunière*, or *pieds-paquets* (mutton tripe with sheep's trotters). Set meals 70F, 140F and 220F. The 140F one is enormous and comes with four courses plus cheese and dessert. We're lucky that there are still places like this in the out-of-the-way parts of France.

NICE 06000

SEE MAP OVERLEAF

AUBERGE DE JEUNESSE

route forestière du Mont-Alban; take a number 17 bus from the station, then a 14 on boulevard Jean-Jaurès; if you walk, it'll take 45 minutes. Off map **D3-1**
☎ 04.93.89.23.64 Fax 04.92.04.03.10
Secure parking.

It's often full and unfortunately you can't book in advance. Get there before 10am if you want a chance of getting in. From the hill you get a fantastic view of the city, the port and the baie des Anges. Now we see why travellers from all over the world come here! 66F for a bed, shower and breakfast included. Sheets 15F, dry cleaning 35F. Kitchen available for own use. Covered storage for bicycles. Good atmosphere in the evenings.

10% RELAIS INTERNATIONAL DE LA JEUNESSE CLAIRVALLON.

26 av. Scuderi, Cimiez; take a number 15 bus from the station and get off at the Scuderi stop. Off map **C1-2**
☎ 04.93.81.27.63 Fax 04.93.53.35.88
Canal+.

A villa that once belonged to a marchioness in a quiet neighbourhood. Superb grounds with a swimming pool. You'll pay 75F a night, breakfast included. In summer, eat on the delightful terrace in the shade of the olive trees. Set meal 60F!

10% ☗ HÔTEL LA BELLE MEUNIÈRE*

21 av. Durante. **MAP B3-3**
☎ 04.93.88.66.15
Closed in January and December. **Car park**.

You'll be met by the scent of pine trees, cypress trees and fig trees. It's a delightful hotel, very well kept and the extremely nice owner always has time for a chat. You can have a picnic in the garden. Doubles 160F with basin and 265F with shower/wc, breakfast included. If there are three or four of you, book the lovely big room with balcony for only 400F. Travellers from all over the world come here.

10% ☗ HÔTEL DU DANEMARK

3 av. des Baumettes.
☎ 04.93.62.48.46
Closed Sundays and Monday lunchtimes.

This is a lovely quiet ochre-coloured house, hidden behind a few pretty trees. The area is completely built-up but the owners were so nice that we fell in love with it. The rooms are simple, tastefully decorated and clean. Doubles 180F with shower and 200F with shower/wc. If you're good, you may even get to try one of the delicious tarts that the owner makes herself.

☗ |●| HÔTEL LES CAMÉLIAS**

3 rue Spitalieri. **MAP C3-5**
☎ 04.93.62.15.54 ➡ 04.93.80.42.96
Closed in November. **Car park. Disabled access**.

Madame Vimont-Beuve has had this hotel for 48 years, and some of her guests have been coming here since she opened. They all have their own favourite room and their own napkin ring! It's a haven of tranquillity with a little garden full of exotic plants right in the heart of Nice. Rooms 200F with washing facilities, 240F with shower and 360F with shower/wc. There's a bar in the foyer for pre-dinner drinks and a TV room and some books for any insomniacs among you. Car park 20F per day. Set meal 65F — the menu is posted in the lift. By the way, has the orange stool always been there?

10% ☗ HÔTEL AMARYLLIS**

3 rue Alsace Lorraine; It's near the station.
☎ 04.93.88.20.24 ➡ 04.93.87.13.25
Closed in November. **TV**.

As soon as you walk in, you start wondering whether you're in Nice or Manhattan, for the décor and the atmosphere remind you of those small and very simple hotels you find in New York. Luckily the prices are French. Doubles 280F with shower/wc and TV. A few rooms look out onto a quiet little courtyard. Friendly welcome and very helpful staff.

10% ☗ HÔTEL LOCARNO***

4 av. des Baumettes. **MAP A3-7**
☎ 04.93.96.28.00 ➡ 04.93.86.18.81
Secure parking. TV. Canal+.

It's a few minutes walk from the Promenade des Anglais and has 50 comfortable air-conditioned rooms that have been recently refurbished and come with all mod cons — 290–550F, with a few at 420F. We liked the slightly old-fashioned sitting rooms and billiard room. You have to book a space in the garage. Customers are often businessmen and sales reps. Very formal welcome.

10% ☗ HÔTEL SAINT-GOTHARD**

20 rue Paganini. **MAP B3-8**
☎ 04.93.88.13.41 ➡ 04.93.82.27.55
TV.Disabled access.

A hotel with a homy atmosphere just a stone's throw from the station. You'll get a very friendly welcome. It dates back to 1948, so they've had a fair bit of experience! About 60 well-equipped rooms. Doubles 300F with shower/wc, triples 340F. There's no restaurant but you can have half-board by arrangement with the place opposite (cheapest set meal 65F).

☗ HÔTEL DURANTE**

16 av. Durante; It's near the station.
☎ 04.93.88.84.40 ➡ 04.93.87.77.76
Closed in November. **Car park. TV**.

A hotel with a handsome trompe-l'œil façade at the bottom of a cul-de-sac. And for a moment you wonder what's in store for you inside — but the charming and tactful proprietress soon sets your mind at rest. It's very well managed and the rooms are clean and tastefully decorated. They look out onto a little garden and the shutters let in a nice little breeze on really hot days. Doubles 320–350F with shower/wc and 390–490F with bath/wc. The one word that could be used to describe this place is "peaceful".

10% ☗ HÔTEL L'OASIS***

23 rue Gounod. **MAP B3-9**
☎ 04.93.88.12.29 ➡ 04.93.16.14.40
Car park. TV. Canal+.

It's set back a little way from the road right in the middle of town, and really lives up to its

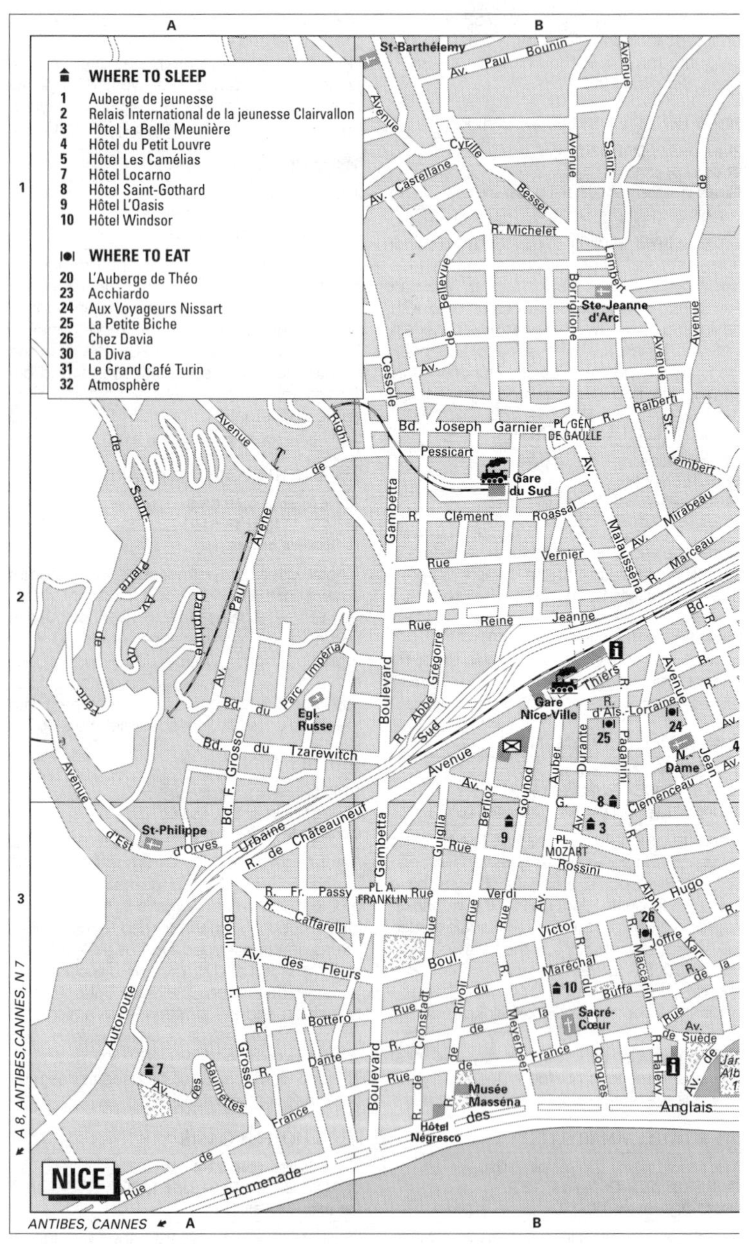
WHERE TO SLEEP
1 Auberge de jeunesse
2 Relais International de la jeunesse Clairvallon
3 Hôtel La Belle Meunière
4 Hôtel du Petit Louvre
5 Hôtel Les Camélias
7 Hôtel Locarno
8 Hôtel Saint-Gothard
9 Hôtel L'Oasis
10 Hôtel Windsor
WHERE TO EAT
20 L'Auberge de Théo
23 Acchiardo
24 Aux Voyageurs Nissart
25 La Petite Biche
26 Chez Davia
30 La Diva
31 Le Grand Café Turin
32 Atmosphère
NICE
St-Barthélemy
Gare du Sud
Gare Nice-Ville
Ste-Jeanne d'Arc
Egl. Russe
St-Philippe
N.-Dame
Sacré-Cœur
Musée Masséna
Hôtel Négresco
PL. GÉN. DE GAULLE
PL. MOZART
PL. A. FRANKLIN
Promenade des Anglais
A 8, ANTIBES, CANNES, N 7
ANTIBES, CANNES

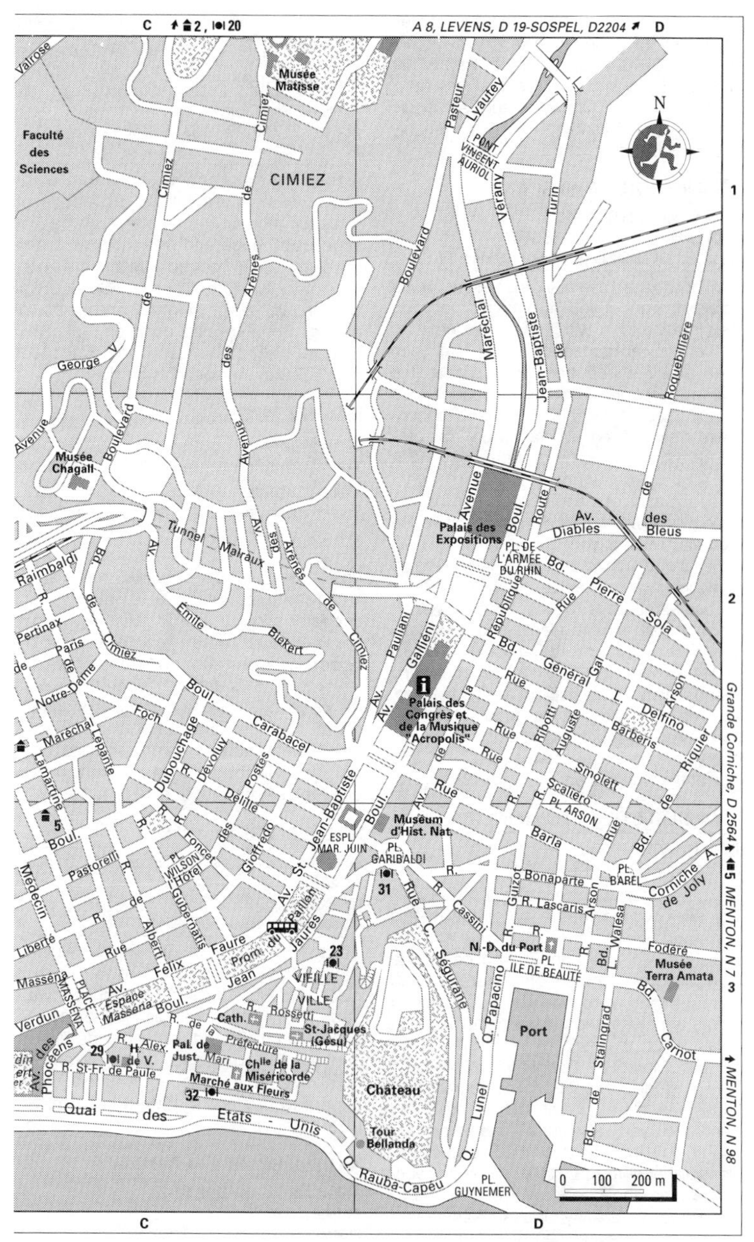
A 8, LEVENS, D 19-SOSPEL, D2204
Musée Matisse
Faculté des Sciences
CIMIEZ
PONT VINCENT AURIOL
Musée Chagall
Palais des Expositions
PL. DE L'ARMÉE DU RHIN
Palais des Congrès et de la Musique "Acropolis"
Muséum d'Hist. Nat.
ESPL. MAR. JUIN
PL. GARIBALDI
PL. ARSON
PL. BAREL
N.-D. du Port
PL. ILE DE BEAUTÉ
Musée Terra Amata
Port
VIEILLE VILLE
Cath.
St-Jacques (Gésu)
Pal. de Just.
Ch^lle de la Miséricorde
Marché aux Fleurs
Château
Tour Bellanda
PL. GUYNEMER
Quai des Etats-Unis
Q. Rauba-Capeu
PLACE MASSÉNA
Espace Masséna
PL. WILSON
Grande Corniche, D 2564
MENTON, N 7
MENTON, N 98
0 100 200 m

name. It's surrounded by a shaded garden and is very quiet. Comfortable rooms. Expect to pay 380–430F for a double. Paying car park. And you should know that this hotel once welcomed Chekhov and a certain Vladimir Ilyich Ulianov – more commonly known as Lenin!

10% HÔTEL WINDSOR***

11 rue Dalpozzo. **MAP B3-10**
☎ 04.93.88.59.35 F 04.93.88.94.57
Restaurant closed Sundays. **Secure parking**. **TV**.

This hotel is a dream. A marvellous world unfolds in front of you from the moment you step into the foyer with its Oriental furniture. In the tropical garden, bougainvillea, palm trees and bamboo trees surround a little swimming pool where a few people are lounging about listening to the birdsong. There are some real birds around – the others have been taped by contemporary musical artists. Contemporary art is important here, and each of the rooms has been decorated by a different artist. So having catered to the artistic side of your nature, the hotel then turns its attention to your physical well-being and guests can make use of the sauna, Turkish baths, massage rooms, and a relaxation room decorated with plants and Thai statuettes. Double rooms 400–750F. Half-board 320–495F per person. It's cheaper Nov 1–end March. The restaurant has no set meal and you can expect to pay about 140F for a good meal that is primarily southern in flavour. Afterwards, sit back, listen to the birds and look at the works of art!

10% HÔTEL DE LA FONTAINE***

49 rue de France.
☎ 04.93.88.30.38 F 04.93.88.98.11
TV.

The new owners took a gamble with this place and, luckily for them, it paid off. You could walk right past and not notice it since it's a bit insignificant, but once you've stayed there it's hard to forget. The good-looking rooms are clean and pleasant and you can breakfast on the patio to the sound of the fountain. Moreover, it's right in the centre of Nice, a stone's throw from the sea and the pedestrian street. What more could you want? Well, you'll also get a friendly welcome – it could almost be described as an example for other hotels to follow – from the very nice owner who'll bend over backwards to make sure you enjoy your stay. Both he and his staff are polite and friendly and totally natural. Rooms 450F with bath/wc and TV. Ask for one overlooking the courtyard. Three-star buffet breakfast 40F.

HÔTEL GRIMALDI***

15 rue Grimaldi (Centre).
☎ 04.93.87.73.61 F 04.93.88.30.05
TV.

A delightful hotel in a luxurious turn of the century building with tasteful modern décor. Cheerful, informal welcome and service. The large, comfortable and well-equipped rooms are decorated in fresh colours and have contemporary furniture. Doubles 600–800F, all with shower/wc or bath, TV and air-conditioning. Sorry to disappoint any fans, but despite the hotel's name you won't see Prince Rainier or any of his family.

CHEZ PIPO

13 rue Bavastro.
☎ 04.93.55.88.82
Open from 5pm only.

The dining room's a bit dark. From the outside, you can vaguely make out long wooden tables where everyone sits side by side. No class war here – people from all walks of life can be found sitting at the same table eating the local speciality *socca* (a thin flat cake made from chickpea flour). Those who know say that this place has the best *socca* in Nice (and therefore in the world!). It's definitely worth trying, as is the *pissaladière* (a kind of onion tart) and the Swiss chard pie. That's all you'll get here – well, the chef doesn't want to spread himself too thin. Everything costs 12F a portion. Why deny yourself the pleasure?

L'AUBERGE DE THÉO

52 av. Cap-de-Croix; it's in the Cimiez district. Off **map C1-20**
☎ 04.93.81.26.19
Closed Mondays and Aug 20–Sept 10.

Service until 11pm. An inn with a delightful patio in the hills around the town. It's reminiscent of Florence and the dishes have a strong Italian influence. Dish of the day 51F, chargrilled meat and fish with side dishes, and a good choice of tasty pizzas that hardly fit on the plates! A good place. Expect to pay about 120F à la carte. Set meal 130F.

RESTAURANT CHEZ DAVIA

11 [bis] rue Grimaldi. **MAP B3-26**
☎ 04.93.87.91.39
Closed Wednesdays and in November.
Disabled access.

A very pretty restaurant with checked tablecloths and a homy atmosphere (lots of family photos on the walls). Set meal 63F with risotto, *coq au vin* or escalope *milanaise,* and dessert. For 88F, we had fish soup, cheese soufflé, sautéd veal and dessert. You can get *bouillabaisse* (90F) and *paella* (65F) à la carte. Portions are generous and prices very reasonable, so it's hardly surprising that locals of all ages come here for a good night out with friends.

NISSA LA BELLA

6 rue Ste Reparate; it's in the old town.
☎ 04.93.62.10.20
Closed Tuesday, Wednesday and Sunday lunchtimes.

Whatever you have as a main course — baked rabbit with polenta, beef stew *provençal*, home-made ravioli, or stuffed baby vegetables — don't order anything else because we bet you'll have trouble enough finishing that. They serve traditional local dishes that are full of the flavours and aromas of Provence. Most of the handsome ochre dining room is open to the street, and it's got a relaxed feel to it. And you'll leave feeling full and a bit better than when you arrived. What more could you ask for (unless it's some information about the prices)? Around 65F for a main course.

RESTAURANT VOYAGEUR NISSART

19 rue d'Alsace-Lorraine. **MAP B2-24**
☎ 04.93.82.19.60
Closed the last fortnight in July.

Service 11.30am–2pm and 6.45pm–10pm. Good regional cuisine in a country-style setting. Two set meals at 65F and 95F. They offer pretty much the usual kind of thing but you get a lot of it. Here's your chance to try simple and well-made local dishes that are basic and well-made. The house specialities are grilled sardines, ravioli *niçois*, courgette tart, stuffed baby vegetables, peppers *à la provençale*, and *soupe au pistou* (soup with pesto).

RESTAURANT ACCHIARDO

38 rue Droite. **MAP C3-23**
☎ 04.93.85.51.16
Closed Saturday evenings, Sundays, and in August.

This place is really determined to cater to ordinary people rather than tourists. The surroundings are very informal — the big tables are covered with red oilcloths — and the atmosphere is cheery. The dish of the day (65F), always good, is something along the lines of tripe *à la niçoise* (not in summer), *soupe au pistou* (vegetable and pesto soup), *daube* or *ratatouille.* The ravioli (35F) is excellent and comes with bolognaise sauce, pesto or Gorgonzola. Very popular. They don't accept cheques or credit cards.

RESTAURANT LA PETITE BICHE

9 rue d'Alsace-Lorraine. **MAP B2-25**
☎ 04.93.87.30.70

A place for really classic dishes, slightly outside the touristy part of Nice. A lot of older inhabitants come here for the traditional Sunday lunch of roast leg of lamb. Set meals 66F and 84F with fillets of sole *Mornay* or rabbit in a mustard sauce.

LA CAVE

rue Francis Gallo; it's in the old part of Nice.
☎ 04.93.62.48.46
Closed Sundays and Monday lunchtimes.

We went twice but we have to admit we have no idea why it's called *La Cave* — we couldn't find a cellar anywhere! The décor in the little dining room is a bit on the chocolate box side but it's cosy. You can also eat on the little terrace amid all the old buildings of the city. The young chef is quite something and turns out dishes that are very pleasing to the eye and the palate. Try the courgettes with goat's cheese and basil, the fricassee of scampi *provençal,* the fillet of sea bream with a citrus fruit sauce or the fish *pot au feu*. He'll finish off the seduction plan with a chocolate and orange tart, a creamy chocolate pudding or a wonderful lemon tart. Weekday lunchtime set meals 70F, 90F, 125F and 170F. Let us know if you can help solve the mystery of the name.

LE GRAND CAFÉ TURIN

5 place Garibaldi. **MAP D3-31**
☎ 04.93.62.29.52
Closed June

Service 8am–10pm (5pm–11pm in July and August). This seafood restaurant is a bit of an institution in Nice. You can have fresh oysters any time of day, guaranteed! Expect to pay 85–110F for a seafood platter with oysters, prawns, whelks and so on (and sea urchins in season). The two dining rooms and the terrace are always full. You can even just have a drink! They don't accept cheques but they do accept credit cards.

RESTAURANT LA DIVA

4 rue de l'Opéra. **MAP C3-30**
☎ 04.93.85.96.15
Closed Mondays.

A pleasant restaurant that's good value for money. The fresh-tasting local dishes are well prepared. Set meals 90F (weekday lunchtimes), 125F and 160F. There are a few delicious specialities like seafood stew, ravioli stuffed with duck and ceps, fillet of *rascasse* (scorpion fish) with a sweet pepper sauce, spaghetti with scallops, and panfried calf sweetbreads. The kitchen is at the back of the room and is clearly run by professionals! The welcome could be a bit friendlier.

RESTAURANT ATMOSPHÈRE

36 cours Saleya. **MAP C3-32**
☎ 04.93.80.52.50

Philippe Joannides and Cédric Monzoni are two unrivalled chefs gifted with imagination and a sense of colour. They create seafood dishes that are both pleasing to the eye and the palate. Inside the tables too please the eye, set out under the false blue sky of the trompe l'œil ceiling and little retro lamps. The prices are surprisingly reasonable for such excellent food. 99–148F for a set meal. The many house specialities include *bouillabaisse* of course, seafood *paella, rascasse provençale*, monkfish with bacon, roast rack of lamb with rosemary, and oysters. One of the few pleasant restaurants to be found the length and breadth of Cours Saleya!

CAGNES 06800 (6KM SE)

LE VAL DUCHESSE**

11 rue de Paris.
☎ 04.92.13.40.00 ➡ 04.92.13.40.29
Secure parking. TV.

The neighbourhood is very quiet though a bit built-up. The hotel has a pleasant garden with palm trees, a swimming pool, table tennis and games for the kids. A decent hotel for a stay on the Côte d'Azur. It's friendly, you'll get a warm welcome and the décor is very "South of France". And it's not expensive either, with studios 175–210F (300–320F peak season) and suites 270–290F (430–450F peak season). The suites sleep four and come with bathroom and a terrace that faces due south.

VILLEFRANCHE-SUR-MER 06230 (7KM E)

10% HÔTEL RESTAURANT LE PROVENÇAL**

4 av. du Maréchal Joffre.
☎ 04.93.01.71.42 ➡ 04.93.76.96.00
Closed end of Oct–Christmas.

A pretty house with blue shutters and three towers that give the place a unique charm. Pleasant and clean rooms. We liked the ones on the second and third floors with a view of the garden and the sea. But they're very popular so remember to book well in advance. Doubles 200–350F with shower/wc and 400–420F with bath. Delightful patio where you can eat. They do a lunchtime *formule* of dish of the day plus dessert for 50F and a set meal for 125F. The *terrine* of suckling pig with pistachio nuts, the ravioli with pesto, the stew of dried cod *en stofficada* (with garlic, tomatoes, potatoes and olives), and the rabbit *provençal* flambéd in Marc de Bandol are all delicious.

HÔTEL-PENSION PATRICIA*

chem. des Pépinières, pont Saint-Jean.
☎ 04.93.01.06.70 ➡ same
Closed Sundays in winter and Nov 10–Dec 28.
Car park.

A delightful fresh-looking villa in typical Provence colours, down from the corniche. It has a flower garden and a superb view of the stretch of water off Villefranche. Doubles 245–320F depending on facilities. Half-board 205–266F. Room number 3 (290F) is super, with its long balcony and view of the bay. There are only 12 rooms so book well in advance if you're planning on being here at the height of the season. Friendly welcome. A few good set meals 78–115F, with fish being the speciality.

RESTAURANT LE NAUTIC

1 quai Courbet (South).
☎ 04.93.01.94.45
Closed Mondays and Friday lunchtimes in peak season, Monday and Sunday evenings out of season, and Nov 12–Dec 20.

One of the many harbourside restaurants and it's very pleasant. The 95F set meal is good value for money. And we're sure it'll come as no surprise that fish is on the menu here. There's grilled sea bream, red mullet with capers, sole *meunière*, very good grilled perch with fennel, and a terrific *bouillabaisse* at 130F. Get there early if you want a table on the terrace. It may be big, but it soon fills up.

RESTAURANT MICHEL'S

pl. Amélie Pollonnais.
☎ 04.93.76.73.24

The large terrace really comes into its own on a summer evening, of course. There are no set meals but the à la carte menu is full of wonderful dishes prepared with seasonal produce. This is definitely the in place at the moment and the atmosphere's pretty laid-back. The food — mainly fish and seafood — is good though and worth the trip. There's salad of octopus with basil, mackerel *terrine* with juniper berries, grilled sea bream, veal chop with an apple and Calvados purée, and strawberry cheesecake with custard. Expect to pay about 130F for a meal. Friendly attentive service.

ASPREMONT 06790 (16KM NW)

10% ☗ |●| HÔTEL-RESTAURANT LE RELAIS SAINT-JEAN*

60 route de Castagniers (Centre); from Nice take the D4.
☎ 04.93.08.00.66 F➜ 04.93.08.06.46
Closed Sunday evenings and Mondays out of season, in October, and in January. **Car park**.

OK, it's a few miles off the beaten track but it's worth the effort of getting there. Young Stéphane Viano is an excellent chef and he already has a loyal following of customers who come from Nice for the dishes he prepares from old recipes handed down from his grandmother — *gnocchi*, ravioli filled with Swiss chard, *soupe au pistou*, *borsotti* of Swiss chard with a Parmesan cheese sauce (a real treat!), fillet of trout with artichokes. And he does his own creations. Desserts are his speciality and it would be criminal to miss his *nougat glacé* with sour cherries and *coulis* of soft fruit or the excellent pear and chocolate cake. Set meals 75F (weekdays) and 98–210F. If you can afford it, don't hesitate to go for the two most expensive — that's the best way of appreciating the talent of a young man who has worked at some of the top restaurants on the Côte d'Azur. Excellent wine list. If you appreciate good food, you'll love this place. A few simple rooms are available, with doubles 190–220F. The terrace has a splendid view of the Cap d'Antibes.

ORANGE 84100

10% ☗ HÔTEL LE GLACIER**

46 cours Aristide-Briand (Centre).
☎ 04.90.34.02.01 F➜ 04.90.51.13.80
Closed Sundays Nov–Easter and Dec 23–Feb 1.
Secure parking. **TV**.

This is a very comfortable hotel and it's been well looked after by three generations of the Cunha family. All the rooms have shower/wc and direct phone. Doubles 280F with shower/wc. In our opinion, the best value for money in Orange. And the musicians in town for the festival often stay here.

10% ☗ HÔTEL ARÈNE***

place de Langes (Centre).
☎ 04.90.11.40.40 F➜ 04.90.11.40.45
Closed Nov 8–30. **Secure parking**. **TV**.

A quiet and quite delightful hotel in the heart of the pedestrian precinct. The air-conditioned rooms are decorated in a pretty style typical of Provence. A few of them have a terrace which is a very pleasant place to have breakfast, which comes with home-made jam and Provence specialities (44F). Doubles 340F with shower/wc and 440F with bath. It really is a pity there's no restaurant.

|●| RESTAURANT LE YACA

24 place Silvain (Centre).
☎ 04.90.34.70.03
Closed Tuesdays (except in summer), Wednesdays, and in November.

The exposed beams and stonework don't overwhelm the intimate and pleasant dining room with its pretty pictures on the walls and little vases of fresh flowers on each table. The 90F set meal offers a choice of about 10 starters, main courses and desserts. Other set meals at 55F, 65F and 125F. You've got to try the home-made chicken liver *terrine* with onion marmalade, the gratinéd leg of lamb with olive purée or the seafood casserole with saffron sauce.

|●| RESTAURANT LA ROSELIÈRE

4 rue du Renoyer (Centre).
☎ 04.90.34.50.42
Closed Wednesdays and in November.

The décor, heterogeneous and just a little way-out, consists of a motley collection of enamel signs from the 50s and 60s, drawings of cartoon characters, teddy bears and bits and pieces picked up in second hand shops or in the streets. If the weather's not good enough to eat outside, come inside and listen to the music, which ranges from Jacques Brel to Mahler. There's just one set meal (90F) at lunchtime and it comes with a choice of four starters, four main courses, and a few desserts. The banana tart is out of this world. It's hard to say just what's on offer, since Fred changes the menus each week depending on what's in season and what the market's got to offer. If the *terrine* of fresh goat's cheese is still there, go for it — it's delicious! The 90F set meal is also available in the evenings, as is one at 130F — same number of courses to choose from. Just to complete the picture, Fred's cellar is full of good inexpensive wines that she chose herself. And since Fred hates doing what everybody else does, your credit card will be of absolutely no use to you here.

PIOLENC 84420 (4KM N)

10% AUBERGE L'ORANGERIE

4 rue de l'Ormeau; take the N7.
☎ 04.90.29.59.88 F 04.90.29.67.74
Closed Mondays out of season and 10 days in November. **Car park. TV.**

A beautiful inn surrounded by trees. Gérard and his wife have been here for more than 10 years now, having decided to create the inn of their dreams after being in hotel after hotel all over the world. It's almost exactly the inn of our dreams too. It has six pleasant cosy rooms with rustic-style furniture. Doubles 280–350F with shower/wc or bath. We've got a soft spot for the one with a private terrace away from everything else. The whole house is decorated with copies of masterpieces that Gérard painted himself. And he's a talented guy at that. The restaurant offers set meals at 90F, 140F and 200F that feature dishes from all over the world. There's stuffed crab, *colombo* of fish, thin slices of kangaroo meat with ginger and orange, and some good traditional Provençal dishes too. Gérard's cellar, which has more than 350 different vintages, is unbelievable. This man means business! And to finish off the evening, his selection of whiskies is enough to make the greatest connoisseurs green with envy. And your stay can't be complete without a visit to the toilets — if that indeed is the right term for this small museum crowded with bric-a-brac and 10 sorts of scented toilet paper (and they're all different colours too!). If you haven't got the idea by now, we liked it a lot.

PEILLE 06440

BELVÉDÈRE HÔTEL

3 place Jean-Miol.
☎ 04.93.79.90.45
Closed Dec 1–24. **Disabled access.**

You have to book in writing. This hotel is run by the very friendly Madame Beauseigneur. She only has five simple rooms but they're clean and have a splendid view of the mountain. Doubles 180–220F. Expect to pay about 220–240F per person half-board. The restaurant is very good and you get a bird's eye view of the valley. Good set meals 88–155F. A few specialities like *osso bucco*, *gnocchi*, rabbit *chasseur*, ravioli stuffed with ricotta cheese. Food to share with friends!

RISTOLAS 05460

10% LE CHALET DE SÉGURE**

How to get there: take the road that goes up behind the church, then follow the signposts.
☎ 04.92.46.71.30 F 04.92.46.79.54
Closed Mondays, April 15–May 25, and Sept 25–Christmas. **Secure parking.**

This chalet up in the tree-covered mountains of Haut Queyras is the ideal place to come it you need to recharge your batteries. It's very well cared for by Pascale and Jean-Marie, who really love what they do. Jean-Marie will even give you the chance to go on one of his walks with him every Monday (in winter, you'll be on snow-shoes!). The décor in the restaurant changes with the seasons. In winter Pascale decorates the room with dolls dressed in traditional costume and in summer with examples of everything the perfect schoolkid needed for class in the early part of the 20th century. Most of the furniture was made by Jean-Marie. The hotel is full of flowers, plants and Pascale's collection of ABC books. The rooms (from 260F for a double) are bright and spacious. Half-board from 270F per person. Set meals at 75F, 95F, 125F and 140F. The honey-glazed breast of duck with spices is the chef's speciality.

ROUSSILLON 84220

RESTAURANT MINCKA'S

place de la Mairie (Centre).
☎ 04.90.05.66.22
Closed Thursdays and Nov–Easter (except during the Christmas and February school holidays).

In a part of the world where everything seems to be ochre, this very prettily decorated little restaurant is a good place to stop for a meal that's full of pleasant surprises for all the senses. Set meals at 90F and 110F. We thought the profiteroles of fresh goat's cheese with basil and the *taillerin* of chestnuts with chicken livers, were out of this world. And there's lots more where that came from!

SAINT-DALMAS-DE-TENDE 06430

10% LE TERMINUS**

rue des Martyrs de la Résistance.

☎ 04.93.04.96.96 F➔ 04.93.04.96.97
Closed mid Nov–Easter. **Car park**.

Le Terminus is run by a mother and daughter-in-law team. You'll get a friendly welcome and will immediately feel at ease in this old family home. The nights are cool (we're in the mountains now!) so sleeping's no problem and it will probably be the birds that waken you. Simple and very pretty double rooms 190–320F. Pleasant garden at the front and a pretty dining room where they do lavish meals for 150F. Lovely copper saucepans and antique plates hang on the wall. The food is all prepared by mother-in-law. And her ravioli is unforgettable.

SAINT-DISDIER 05250

10% ⌂ |●| AUBERGE LA NEYRETTE**

How to get there: it's where the Saint-Étienne-en-Dévoluy road meets the Veynes road.
☎ 04.92.58.81.17 F➔ 04.92.58.89.95
Closed Nov–mid Dec. **Secure parking**. **TV**.

An inn standing in solitary splendour at the bottom of a little valley. People come from all over to stay here as the little rooms are impeccable and the restaurant is very good. But, with twelve rooms reserved for guests who've come to enjoy the peace and quiet and the natural surroundings, it's a good idea to book in advance. Come and enjoy this old grain mill and have some trout (from the lake), the house *terrine*, the *tourtons* (a kind of pancake) and other specialities. Set meal 98F. Expect to pay about 300F for a double room with bath.

SAINT-JEAN-CAP-FERRAT 06230

⌂ HÔTEL LE CLAIR LOGIS**

12 av. Centrale (Centre); it's in the centre of the peninsula, on the corner of allée des Brises.
☎ 04.93.76.04.57 F➔ 04.93.76.11.85
Closed Jan 10–March 1 and Nov 15–Dec 15.
Car park. **TV**.

Book three weeks in advance in summer if you want to stay in this haven of peace and quiet with an exotic garden in a beautiful residential neighbourhood. We understand that General de Gaulle stayed here in 1952. All 18 rooms have a balcony or little terrace. The prices are quite high, but reasonable for the peninsula (a millionaires' haunt). They range from 400F with shower/wc to 650F with bath in peak season. A good hotel, ideal for a romantic weekend on the Côte d'Azur.

|●| RESTAURANT LE SKIPPER

port de plaisance (Centre).
☎ 04.93.76.01.00
Disabled access.

This is one of the best fish restaurants in the area. The atmosphere is that of a rather chic brasserie and it has a terrace from where you can watch the boats. The 95F set meal of fish soup, seafood casserole, and cheese or dessert offers unbeatable value. The one at 159F isn't such a good deal. Fast efficient service.

|●| LE SLOOP

How to get there: it's near the new harbour.
☎ 04.93.01.48.63
Closed Wednesdays out of season and Nov 15–Dec 15.

You'll be warmly welcomed to this restaurant with the pleasant terrace facing the harbour. The cooking is pretty sophisticated, which is only to be expected from a chef who used to work in a top restaurant. The 155F set meal is very appealing and excellent value for money. How about *quenelles* of sole with potatoes, grilled gilt-head bream, whole roast sea bass with tomatoes and basil or veal chop studded with truffles and served with its own juices? There's a whole string of fancy restaurants by the harbour – this is our favourite.

SAINT-MARTIN-VÉSUBIE 06450

10% ⌂ |●| HÔTEL-RESTAURANT LA BONNE AUBERGE**

allée de Verdun; turn left as you leave Saint-Martin and head for Colmiane and Boreon.
☎ 04.93.03.20.49 F➔ 04.93.03.20.69
Closed Nov 15–Feb 1. **TV**.

This beautiful stone hotel is comfortable and well-looked-after. Doubles 160F with washing facilities, 240F with shower/wc and 270F with bath/wc. Try to avoid the ones that look out onto the avenue, which is particularly busy at the weekend. Apparently the footballers from the Nice squad come here to rest, which is a good sign. Set meals 95F and 130F. The traditional food – *terrine* of mackerel *confit*, trout *meunière* (from the fish tank), lamb stew, duckling with olives, quail casserole, and so on – slips down very nicely. Pleasant terrace, surrounded by hedges.

SAINT-PAUL-DE-VENCE 06570

⌂ AUBERGE LE HAMEAU***

528 route de la Colle; it's 1km from the village on the

D7, route de la Colle.
☎ 04.93.32.80.24 F 04.93.32.55.75
Closed Jan 8–Feb 15, and Nov 16–Dec 22.
Secure parking.

It's got a garden and swimming pool and is surrounded by greenery. Superb view of the village of Saint-Paul. Comfortable air-conditioned rooms with nice furniture. Doubles with mini-bar 440–620F. They also have three suites at 720F. Ask for a room in the main building rather than the annexe, since they've got much more character. Ideal for couples who fancy splashing out a bit.

SAINT-RÉMY-DE-PROVENCE 13210

10% HÔTEL DE LA CAUME**

route de Cavaillon (East); it's 1.5km from the town centre, on the N99.
☎ 04.90.92.43.59 F 04.90.92.06.11
Secure parking. **TV**. **Disabled access**.

Ask for a room at the back, it'll be quieter. All rooms have telephone. Doubles 180–250F with shower/wc and 310F with bath. Pleasant garden and swimming pool. Pétanque, mountain-biking, table tennis and games for the kids. You can have picnics here.

LE CAFÉ DES ARTS**

30 bd Victor-Hugo (Centre).
☎ 04.90.92.08.50 F 04.90.92.55.09
Closed Tuesdays. **Car park**. **Disabled access**.

One of the oldest establishments in town, but neither Nostradamus (who was born here) nor Van Gogh (who spent some time in the town asylum) knew about it. It has a terrace and pergola where you can have an aperitif or the "Gargantua" breakfast at 70F. Inside there's a pretty dining room and a little garden. Set meals 110F, 120F and 140F. Salt cod with garlic mayonnaise and vegetables is served on Fridays. They also do *daube de "toro"* and squid with *rouille* (spicy mayonnaise with red pepper and garlic). Dish of the day 70F. They have a few rooms (200–350F) on the upper floors.

HÔTEL VILLE VERTE**

place de la République (Centre).
☎ 04.90.92.06.14 F 04.90.92.56.54
Restaurant closed Nov 1–March 15. **Secure parking**. **TV**. **Disabled access**.

Legend has it that Charles Gounod (who composed "Faust") wrote another of his operas here, and a plaque was put up in 1913 to commemorate the event. The hotel is only minutes from the centre and has prices to suit everybody. They range from 210F for a room with shower to 260F with shower/wc and balcony. Studios with kitchenette 1,500F a week, based on two people sharing (there's a charge of 150F for each additional person per week). Swimming pool, courtyard and pleasant terraces. The restaurant, which dates back to the 17th century, is popular with families. Set meals 95F and 155F. The service could do with a bit of tightening up.

10% LE CHEVAL BLANC**

6 av. Fauconnet (Centre).
☎ 04.90.92.09.28 F 04.90.92.69.05
Closed mid Nov–mid Dec and mid Jan–mid Feb.
Secure parking. **TV**. **Disabled access**.

It's worth putting your money on this particular horse, especially since it has a private car park with 15 spaces, a considerable asset in the centre of Saint-Rémy. Refurbished rooms come with shower/wc or bath and direct telephone. Doubles 250–300F. Lovely terrace and veranda. Garage: 30F.

HÔTEL DU SOLEIL**

35 av. Pasteur (South).
☎ 04.90.92.00.63 F 04.90.92.61.07
Closed mid Nov–mid March. **Secure parking**. **TV**.

The hotel is laid out round a large courtyard with lots of space – including space for those who need to park. Swimming pool, terrace and garden. All rooms have TV. A few of them aren't particularly spacious. Doubles 250–374F with shower/wc or bath. Mountain bikes available for hire.

XA

24 bd Mirabeau (Centre).
☎ 04.90.92.41.23
Closed Wednesdays.

This place is like a prettily decorated flat with bistro chairs, mirrors, and spotlights. Terrace. Set meal 140F. À la carte prices for main courses range from 70F to 100F. Good food, and dishes like *parfait* of chicken livers and onion marmalade, grilled sardines *à la sicilienne* (with pasta, cheese and pistachio nuts), and *mousseline* of *rascasse* (scorpion fish) – not to mention the *pannacotta* for dessert – show a touch of imagination. Needless to say, we had a bit of a feast!

BISTROT DES ALPILLES

15 bd Mirabeau (Centre).
☎ 04.90.92.09.17
Closed Sundays.

Open until 10pm. Efficient service in pleasant surroundings. The terrace is often packed so it's a good idea to book. The 75F set meal of starter, main course and dessert changes daily. The house speciality is fresh pasta, which comes with pesto, smoked salmon or ceps. Equally good is the leg of lamb *à la ficelle*.

RESTAURANT LA GOUSSE D'AIL

25 rue Carnot (Centre).
☎ 04.90.92.16.87
Closed Wednesdays in winter, and in February.

The restaurant is aptly named since a day without garlic in the South of France is like a day without sunshine! Intimate atmosphere and food that offers excellent value for money. Set meal 90F lunchtimes, *menu-carte* 170F evenings (they change each day). House specialities: *pavé* of bull with creamy garlic sauce, snails *à la provençale* and a few vegetarian dishes. Tuesday is *bouillabaisse* day. Great wine list. Jazz every Thursday.

LA MAISON JAUNE

15 rue Carnot (Centre).
☎ 04.90.92.56.14
Closed Mondays and Sunday evenings in winter, Mondays and Tuesday lunchtimes in summer, and in February.

Ready to push the boat out a bit for a touch of class? In a décor worthy of a glossy interior design magazine, you'll be served imaginative dishes at prices to suit everyone. They have a light lunch (weekday lunchtimes only and not on public holidays) of nibbles, chicken fricassee with fresh tomato *compote*, and kiwi soup for 120F, which includes a glass of wine and coffee. The other option is to pay 170F or 235F for a gourmet set meal. House specialities include sea trout tartare, roast pigeon in Baux and hot walnut tart, and there's a superb terrace where you can enjoy your meal.

GRAVESON 13690 (9KM NW)

HÔTEL DU MOULIN D'AURE**

quartier Cassoulen.
☎ 04.90.95.84.05 ➡ 04.90.95.73.84
Closed beginning of Nov–end of March. **Car park**.

A little haven surrounded by 8,000 square metres of grounds with pine trees and olive trees. The cicadas are singing, the swimming pool awaits, and the proprietress has a friendly face. Pleasant rooms 290F–340F. In July and August, you can eat by the pool if you really can't be bothered moving. Nice, lazy atmosphere.

SAINT-TROPEZ 83990

LOU CAGNARD**

18 av. Paul-Roussel (North).
☎ 04.94.97.04.24 ➡ 04.94.97.09.44
Closed Nov 4–Dec 20. **Car park**. **TV**

Large house in the typical style of Provence. Decent rooms 340F with shower/wc and 440F with bath. Pleasant terrace and flower garden. It would be better if you reserved a room that looks out onto the garden so you can get to sleep in summer. But, then again, who comes here to sleep?

RESTAURANT CÔTÉ JARDIN

1 rue des Tisserands (Centre).
☎ 04.94.97.26.41
Closed lunchtimes in season.

We like this restaurant, tucked away in a little alley. The décor is maybe a bit too much – the enormous chandelier in the dining room is rather overpowering – and would make a prima donna feel perfectly at home. The 155F *menu-carte* is rather good value for money, considering this is Saint-Tropez. Decent food with all the classic flavours. Fried cuttlefish, stuffed squid, mussels with saffron.

RESTAURANT-BAR LES GRANIERS

plage des Graniers (West).
☎ 04.94.97.38.50
Closed every evening and Oct 1–April 30. **Car park**.

In a nice area. The tables are outside, on a beach with parasols. The restaurant has a good reputation and there's no falling off in quality, even at the height of summer. Reasonably priced grills and fish (sea bream, red mullet, sole and so on). Dish of the day about 100F. Expect to pay about 180F à la carte. Local wines.

GARDE-FREINET (LA) 83680 (20KM W)

LA COLOMBE JOYEUSE

place Vieille (Centre).
☎ 04.94.43.65.24
Closed Tuesdays out of season, Tuesday lunchtimes June 15–Sept 15, and Nov 3–Jan 31.

We loved everything about this place – the warm tones of blue, yellow, pink and green used in the décor, its terrace in the heart of a village that couldn't be more typical of

Provence if it tried, and the food. David de Scheemaecker loves birds, particularly homing pigeons. He breeds them just outside the village. And it's around this love for pigeons that the restaurant menu has been created. Some people might think that's in bad taste or rather shocking but there isn't much we can do about that. Sheep farmers eat lamb, don't they? And the pigeons here are excellent, whether they come in a casserole, with honey, with orange or *à la normande* (with cream and a white wine sauce). And if you want a meal based entirely on pigeon, the *terrine* with onion marmalade is a must. As for the prices, well, they certainly won't take you to the cleaner's. Set meals at 89F and 125F. At lunchtimes there's a self-service buffet for 80F. Without a doubt, one of the best restaurants in the Var.

SAINT-VÉRAN 05350

10% 🏠 |●| AUBERGE-GÎTE D'ÉTAPE LE MONCHU**

La Chalp-Sainte-Agathe.
☎ 04.92.45.83.96 F 04.92.45.80.09
Closed May, Oct–Dec 20 (except for group reservations). **Car park**

At an altitude of 2,040m, this is the highest village in France. Nathalie and Philippe Babinet are used to welcoming groups to their inn. They've converted a big farmhouse into a *gîte* with all the comforts of a more than decent hotel. The cooking is traditional and meals are served in a very handsome dining room with a vaulted ceiling. Specialities include fondue, *tartiflette*, *raclette* (you'll have to order in advance). All the rooms are very bright and comfortable. Half-board, which is compulsory, costs 180–290F, depending on the number of people per room. Sauna, billiard room and table tennis.

SAINTE-MAXIME 83120

|●| RESTAURANT LA MAISON BLEUE

24 bis rue Paul-Bert (Centre); it's in the pedestrian precinct on the sea front.
☎ 04.94.96.51.92
Closed Tuesdays out of season, and Nov–Dec.

This is the sort of doll's house that every little girl dreams about. It's very tastefully decorated in blue (naturally), ochre and yellow, and the terrace with its comfortable and pretty bench seats is a lovely spot for a meal. Yes, in addition to everything else, the food's good! Fresh fish soup, ravioli with a sardine filling, stuffed mussels, sea bream with fennel *en papillote*. Set meals 95F and 135F. Very good place, but the service could do with a bit of tightening up.

|●| AUBERGE SANS SOUCI

34 rue Paul-Bert (Centre).
☎ 04.94.96.18.26
Closed Mondays out of season and Oct 30–Feb 10.

This inn is a great place to eat — the food is typical of Provençe, simple, tasty, and full of the flavours of the *garrigue*. In summer you can eat on the pleasant terrace in the town's "gourmet" street or, if there's a nip in the air, move into the cosy dining room. Sautéd veal *provençal*, tripe *à la niçoise* (with white wine, onions, carrots, and garlic), marinated sardine fillets, and *rillettes* of rabbit with rosemary all feature in the two set meals at 96F and 136F. A great meal will be had.

SAINTES-MARIES-DE-LA-MER 13460

🏠 |●| HÔTEL-RESTAURANT LE DELTA*

place Mireille (Centre); it's on the edge of the town, near the church and 200m from the beach.
☎ 04.90.97.81.12 F 04.90.97.72.85
Closed Jan 10–Feb 15. **TV**.

Good regional cuisine with specialities like *bourride* (a sort of fish stew with garlic mayonnaise), *bouillabaisse*, and salt cod with *aïoli*. Dish of the day 55F and set meals 70–155F. Double rooms 210F with shower. Covered terrace. Very touristy.

10% 🏠 |●| LE MIRAGE**

14 rue Camille-Pelletan (North-East); it's 200m from the beach.
☎ 04.90.97.80.43 F 04.90.97.72.22
Closed mid Oct–mid March. Restaurant open in the evenings. **Car park**. **Disabled access**.

A modern comfortable hotel with a white façade, this was actually a cinema from 1953 to 1963 and has a pretty sitting room on the first floor. Doubles 290F with shower/wc and direct telephone, 320F with bath. The terrace opens onto a little garden, where you can sometimes have a quiet picnic. The restaurant has set meals at 90F, 130F and 150F.

10% 🏠 HÔTEL LE BLEU MARINE**

av. du Docteur-Cambon.
☎ 04.90.97.77.00 F 04.90.97.76.00

Closed Nov–April, but open during the Christmas and New Year holidays. **TV**. **Disabled access**.

As you might have guessed from the name of this place, water isn't far away — the 26 rooms all face the swimming pool. Tasteful décor and friendly welcome. Rooms 350–370F. Breakfast 30F. There's a campsite nearby and it can be a bit noisy. In summer, light snacks and salads are served beside the pool.

RESTAURANT L'IMPÉRIAL

1 place des Impériaux (Centre).
☎ 04.90.97.81.84
Closed Tuesdays out of season and Nov 4–March 20.

The owner's certificates on the wall really say it all — first prize at hotel school, winner of the Cointreau Cup 1979 etc etc. And of course now he features in your favourite guidebook! For 130F, you'll have a (difficult) choice of sole with coconut or monkfish in a curry sauce, followed by salad and cheese or dessert. *Bouillabaisse* 175F. Plain tasteful décor. Little sheltered terrace.

SALON-DE-PROVENCE 13300

10% HÔTEL VENDÔME**

34 rue du Maréchal-Joffre (Centre).
☎ 04.90.56.01.96 Fax 04.90.56.48.78
Car park. **TV**. **Disabled access**.

We advise you to take one of the rooms that look onto the cool and delightful patio. The décor is pink and pistachio green; the bed linen is excellent. Huge bathrooms that are a little on the retro side. Rooms 245F with shower/wc and about 270F with bath. Attentive, slightly formal staff.

LA SALLE À MANGER

6 rue du Maréchal-Joffre (Centre).
☎ 04.90.56.28.01
Closed Sunday evenings, Mondays, Aug 8–24, and Dec 22–Jan 5.

A restaurant for megalomaniacs — the splendid rococo décor is absolutely palatial. The two *formules* (89F and 125F) consist of starter and main course. Specialities are oysters, casserole of stuffed cuttlefish, and lamb with *tapenade* (a thick paste of anchovies, capers, olives and tuna). Should we stop there? They have 40 desserts (about 39F), including lots of charlottes (chocolate and orange, pears and hot chocolate). A treat for your eyes and your palate, and a feast fit for a king — wash it all down with some of their good local wine.

RESTAURANT REGAIN

13 place Neuve.
☎ 04.90.56.11.04
Closed Sunday evenings and Mondays.

A small unobtrusive restaurant opposite the château. Terrace for when the weather's nice. The tasteful décor with pretty navy blue tablecloths makes a nice change from the neo-rustic look. Set meals 98F and 160F. The specialities have all got a touch of Provence about them, like the saddle of young rabbit with artichoke *coulis* or the lavender honey *nougatine* (a small iced cake). Every Friday Sept–May, you can have *aïoli* (salt cod with garlic mayonnaise), dessert, wine and coffee for 130F.

SANARY 83110

10% HÔTEL-RESTAURANT BON ABRI**

94 av. des Poilus.
☎ 04.94.74.02.81
Closed Mondays and Dec 1–Feb 28. **Car park**. **Disabled access**.

We've got a bit of a soft spot for this very simple but quite delightful hotel. Owners Monsieur and Madame Hamel have nine large, clean rooms with lots of nooks and crannies and full of little knick-knacks. The décor is slightly old-fashioned but it goes well with everything else. Doubles at 200F with basin and 240F with shower/wc. Half-board compulsory May 1–Sept 30. Good plain cooking, a bit like you'd get at home.

SAULT 84390

HOSTELLERIE DU VAL DE SAULT***

old chemin d'Aurel; it's 1.5km from the centre of the village — follow the signs.
☎ 04.90.64.01.41 Fax 04.90.64.12.74
Closed Nov 1–March 27. **Car park**. **TV**. **Disabled access**.

A landscape of many colours — the blue of the lavender, the yellow of the sun and the green of the forests — is the setting for this fairly new hotel and restaurant in a part of the world much loved by the writer Jean Giono. It's a haven of peace, the type of place you can spend a long time searching for and never find. It faces Mont Ventoux and has 11 spacious rooms, each with a little sitting area and terrace (ideal for breakfast). Doubles with bath 490F out of season (10% more in June and September, 25% more in July and August!). Not cheap, but it's good value for money. In the kitchen, Yves Gattechaut knows how to combine traditional ingredients and innovative flavours. His spelter (a type of wheat) *galette* with lamb offal and *compote* of shallots is a real treat, as is his fish soup with pesto and saffron, and his leg of lamb with bacon. Set meals 133F (lunchtimes) and 149–217F (evenings). And if you love truffles (known as black diamonds) and don't mind splashing out a bit, there's a wonderful set meal created around them. As good as anything any of the big names can come up with.

SISTERON 04200

10% 🏠 |●| LA CITADELLE**

126 rue Saunerie (Centre).
☎ 04.92.61.13.52 F➔ 04.92.61.06.39
Closed Mondays out of season and Oct–Nov. **Car park**. **TV**. **Disabled access**.

It may be a tourist haunt in summer but the food is still pretty good. Set meals 90F and 130F and dishes like guinea fowl *à l'ancienne*, courgette fritters, and the house *pieds paquets* (mutton tripe cooked with sheep's trotters). Not the type of place you'd expect to do pizzas – but they do. Rooms 180F with shower, 200F with shower/wc, and 275F if you want TV too. Don't forget to ask for a room with a view – the river's on one side and the citadel, with a backdrop of snow-topped mountains, is on the other.

10% 🏠 |●| GRAND HÔTEL DU COURS***

allée de Verdun.
☎ 04.92.61.00.50 F➔ 04.92.61.41.73
Secure parking. **TV**.

The chic hotel in town where you're almost guaranteed to get one of the 50 rooms on offer. Provincial atmosphere. Courteous welcome and attentive service. A word of advice – the rooms are all very clean but some are quieter than others. Avoid the ones that look out onto the main road, otherwise you might not get to sleep till late and be woken up early. Ask for one with a view of the château and the cathedral. Doubles 230–450F with shower/wc or bath. Expensive restaurant.

|●| LES BECS FINS

16 rue Saunerie.
☎ 04.92.61.12.04
Closed Wednesdays out of season.

A gourmet restaurant but one with a warm and friendly atmosphere. The professionalism is reflected in the set meals that are in the purest tradition of Provence – sautéd and flambéd frogs' legs, *pieds-paquets* (mutton tripe cooked with sheep's trotters), duck breast prepared in nine different ways and *Châteaubriand* in eight. Lamb chops also feature of course – this is after all the lamb capital of France. Set meals 80F, 110F, 160F, 199F and 250F.

MISON 04200 (11KM NW)

|●| L'IRIS DE SUSE

How to get there: take the N75 in the direction of Grenoble, turn off when you get to Mison-les-Armand and follow the arrows.
☎ 04.92.62.21.69
Closed Mondays, Sunday evenings, mid Nov–mid March, and Tuesdays in July and August.

If there was an examination for hotel and restaurant owners then Madame Matz would deserve an honourable mention for the way in which she receives her customers. She's attentive, friendly and always has a kind word for everyone. Her restaurant is a delightful little house on the edge of a village with a pergola and whitewashed walls hung with a few pictures and souvenirs. And the food – typically Provence dishes prepared by Jean-Pierre – is equally delightful. How about stuffed young rabbit, honey-glazed breast of duck, panfried leg of lamb with a creamy garlic sauce, scrambled eggs with truffles, and spelter (a type of wheat) pancakes. The prices are just up our street, with set meals at 98F and 115F. Definitely worth the effort of getting there. The name of the restaurant, by the way, is taken from the title of a book by Jean Giono, who came from these parts.

SOSPEL 06380

10% 🏠 |●| HÔTEL DES ÉTRANGERS**

7 bd de Verdun (East).
☎ 04.93.04.00.09 F➔ 04.93.04.12.31
Closed Nov 24–Feb 20. **Car park**. **TV**.

This place is run by Monsieur Domerego, who was born here and knows the area like the back of his hand. He has 35 comfortable rooms with shower/wc or bath (290–360F). The rooms look out onto the river and the little terraces onto the mountain. Garden, swimming pool (heated from April 1–Oct 30), sauna, and accommodation for walkers (75F a night). Good restaurant with set meals

75–145F and dishes like sturgeon with lavender-flavoured butter, quail with grapes, stuffed leg of rabbit, and *osso bucco à la niçoise*. One of the few places where you can taste grilled ostrich, bison and kangaroo meat. And with a little Australian wine to wash it all down, it's worth your while coming here.

RESTAURANT L'ESCARGOT D'OR

3 bd de Verdun (East).
☎ 04.93.04.00.43
Closed Fridays and end of Oct–end of Nov.

We really liked the pleasant terrace, which has a view of the river and the mountain. Good food with a few regional dishes. Set meals 68–149F. Specialities: goat's cheese cooked in olive oil, rabbit with mustard sauce, *daube provençale*, and duck breast flambéd in cognac.

TARASCON 13150

AUBERGE DE JEUNESSE

31 bd Gambetta (East).
☎ 04.90.91.04.08 F 04.90.91.54.17
Closed in January and February.

It's well looked after and has a friendly atmosphere. 46F a night. Breakfast 19F. Your first breakfast is compulsory, so you'll pay a total of 65F. After that it's up you. Kitchen available.

THÉOULE-SUR-MER 06590

AUBERGE DE JEUNESSE

route de la Véronèse; from the station, head for the area known as Le Trayas — it's about 2km.
☎ 04.93.75.40.23 F 04.93.75.43.45
Closed beginning of Jan–mid Feb. **Car park**. **Disabled access**.

If it's summer and you're planning on spending more than three nights here, then it's advisable to book in advance. You must have a youth hostel membership card. It's in a great location — you'll have a view of the sea and the Estérel — but it's not easy to get to. 64F a night, breakfast included. Meal 49F. Half-board at 115F a person is compulsory if you're staying for more than three nights in summer. You can camp in the garden, 27F a night. Courses in windsurfing and water-skiing.

THORENC 06750

10% HÔTEL DES VOYAGEURS**

av. Belvédère (East).
☎ 04.93.60.00.18 F 04.93.60.03.51
Closed Thursdays out of season and Nov 15–Feb 1.
Secure parking. **TV**.

A total of 12 very clean rooms for which you'll pay 180–300F. Half-board is compulsory in season and costs 250–300F per person per day. Good restaurant. Set meals 91–145F, along the lines of assorted *crudités,* calf's head *sauce ravigote* (with a spicy vinaigrette) or a meat dish (sautéd rabbit, for example), and cheese or dessert. Pleasant terrace and garden. View of the village.

TOULON 83000

10% HÔTEL LITTLE PALACE*

6–8 rue Berthelot (Centre).
☎ 04.94.92.26.62 F 04.94.89.13.77
Car park. **TV**.

Doubles 100F with basin (no TV), 130F with basin/wc, 180F with shower/wc and 200F with bath. Good if you're on a budget.

10% HÔTEL MOLIÈRE*

12 rue Molière (Centre).
☎ 04.94.92.78.35 F 04.94.62.85.82
Closed in January. **Car park**. **TV**.

A very simple little family hotel with unbeatable prices. The owners really know what they're doing in terms of the welcome they give and will do their very best to make sure you have a pleasant stay. Comfortable, clean and soundproof rooms. Doubles 110F with basin (no TV), 180F with shower/wc. Room numbers 18, 19 and 20 all have a great view of the water off Toulon. An excellent place of its kind.

10% HÔTEL LE JAURÈS*

11 rue Jean-Jaurès (Centre).
☎ 04.94.92.83.04 F 04.94.62.16.74
Car park. **TV**. **Canal+**.

A long-standing favourite with us and it really should have two stars. It's friendly, clean and offers some of the best value for money in town. Expect to pay about 150F for a double with shower/wc, and 170F with bath. The rooms overlooking the courtyard are quiet. Covered storage for bikes.

10% HÔTEL D'EUROPE**

7 rue de Chabannes (Centre); it's near the station.
☎ 04.94.92.37.44 F 04.94.62.37.50
TV.

The owner of this place, a former sailor, knows the town very well and if he's not in the middle of renovating one of the rooms, he'll gladly tell you a few stories about its past. Doubles range in price from 160F with shower/wc (number 28 has a balcony with a view of the sea and the mountain) to 310F with bath, in-house video, double-glazing, soundproofing and air conditioning. Mountain bikes (one per room) are available free of charge for the duration of your stay.

LES BARTAVELLES

28 rue Gimelli (Centre); it's behind place de la Liberté.
☎ 04.94.92.85.00
Closed Sundays, public holidays, one week at the beginning of February, and one week at the beginning of August.

A simple little restaurant that isn't exactly eye-catching. We would have walked past it if our friends from Toulon hadn't warmly recommended it. And we weren't disappointed. The food is simple, predominantly seafood. Set meal 68F and dish of the day 45F. Evening set meal 108F. What's on offer might include conger-eel soup with saffron, gratinéd mussels or gilt-head bream with local herbs but of course it depends on what's been caught. Friendly welcome from the proprietress.

RESTAURANT LE CELLIER

52 rue Jean-Jaurès (Centre).
☎ 04.94.92.64.35
Closed Saturdays and Sundays.

If you're looking for a bit of human warmth, then you need go no further. Odette's a real earth mother type and she'll offer you a choice of three set meals ranging in price from 80F to 160F and including dishes like mussels with shallots, red mullet in Côtes-de-Provence, and monkfish in cider. The décor is pretty kitsch – somebody doesn't have much taste – but that's half the appeal of this quiet little place.

RESTAURANT-GALERIE CAFÉ DES ARTS

9 bd E.-Pelletan (South).
☎ 04.94.41.65.43
Closed lunchtimes and Sundays.

Well off the tourist beaten track, in a little street in a residential area. It's popular with intellectuals and artists, who like the Bohemian atmosphere they find here. From the moment you walk in, you feel as if you're in an artist's garret (very clean and tidy, mind you). The walls are full of pictures by local painters that change week by week and season by season – a bit like the food. If the décor and the atmosphere (a bit trendy, it has to be said) are what make this place so appealing, it definitely doesn't hurt that the food is pretty good. There's a marked Italian and Provence influence. There are no set meals and you can expect to pay about 120F à la carte. The menu offers *mille-feuille* of *foie gras* with artichokes and chanterelle mushrooms, calf's liver with honey and lemon, sardines stuffed with goat's cheese and spinach, and *tagine* of lamb with almonds. You get rather a wary welcome if you're not a regular, but that too is part of its charm.

LE JARDIN DU SOMMELIER

20 allée Courbet; it's beside place d'Armes, behind the Arsenal.
☎ 04.94.62.03.27
Closed Saturday lunchtimes and Sundays.

What's more important to people who appreciate good food and wine – what's on the plate or what's in the glass? Christian and Ariane Scalisi know you can't have one without the other and their restaurant is full of great flavours, wonderful aromas and pretty colours. The yellow and blue colour scheme makes for a bright and sunny dining room. Mouth-watering smells waft off the plates and your first taste of the fresh tomato and aubergine tart, the *barigoule* of artichokes and medallions of monkfish, the roast sea bream and the gingerbread with vanilla icing makes you realise that if you care passionately about what you do then you'll achieve great things. Set meals 160–220F. Needless to say, you'll get a friendly welcome.

TOUR-D'AIGUES (LA) 84240

AUBERGE DE LA TOUR

51 rue Antoine-de-Très (Centre).
☎ 04.90.07.34.64
Closed Mondays.

A handsome and tastefully decorated dining room with a vaulted ceiling and made of white stone. The set meals (96F and 130F), feature fish and traditional Périgord dishes. We treated ourselves with meatballs *à la provençale, blanquette* (a kind of stew) of kid, and crayfish fricassee. A good restaurant with a friendly atmosphere – we like it a lot.

UTELLE 06450

10% LE BELLEVUE*

route de la Madone.

☎ 04.93.03.17.19 ➡ same
Restaurant closed Wednesdays out of season; hotel closed Oct–April. **Car park**.

Very simple but very good. Splendid view. Clean comfortable rooms from 200F. The restaurant has quite a good reputation. Reserve a table with a view in the rustic dining room. Set meals 70F (weekdays) and 90–150F (weekends). The chef's specialities are *pissaladière* (a type of onion tart), rabbit with herbs, home-made ravioli and *daube provençale*.

AUBERGERIE DEL CAMPO

rte d'Utelle.
☎ 04.93.03.13.12

As the road climbs steadily up towards Utelle, you're puzzled by the sight of a few cars parked under a tree at the side of the road. If you look down a bit, you'll see an old shepherd's house dating back to 1785 that's been lovingly restored. Sylvain Moreau is a passionate believer in local produce and settled here to spread the word. The rustic dining room with its handsome fireplace and olive wood floors and walls serves classic dishes like ravioli with a duck and cep filling, scallop fricassee with raspberry vinegar, and braised trout with tarragon, all made from top-quality produce. Lunchtime *formule* 65F and set meals 105F, 140F and 160F. In fine weather, enjoy the beautiful terrace that looks out over the Vésuble gorges. Friendly atmosphere. Dinner by reservation only.

VAISON-LA-ROMAINE 84110

10% HÔTEL BURRHUS**

1 place Montfort (Centre).
☎ 04.90.36.00.11 ➡ 04.90.36.39.05
Closed Sundays and mid Nov–mid Dec.
Secure parking. **TV**.

Good taste is evident everywhere you look in this hotel. The décor of the rooms is both refreshing and relaxing. Doubles 240–290F with shower/wc and from 290F with bath. Your choice from the dishes on the small à la carte menu will be served on the shaded terrace on the main square. The welcome can't be faulted. The hotel is named after the Swiss benefactor who in 1925 sponsored the first excavations of the town's Roman remains, and it holds regular showings of contemporary art.

10% L'HOSTELLERIE DU BEFFROI***

rue de l'Évêché (South).
☎ 04.90.36.04.71 ➡ 04.90.36.24.78
Hotel closed Feb 15–March 20 and Nov 11–Dec 20. Restaurant closed lunchtimes (except weekends) and Nov 1–April 1. **Secure parking**. **TV**.

Two authentic 16th and 17th century buildings. The hotel is superbly furnished and offers good facilities. Expect to pay about 450F for a double with shower/wc or 545–655F with bath. Set meals 98F (lunchtimes), 145F and 195F. The food is good — rabbit, hazelnut and tarragon *terrine*, lamb stew, leg of lamb spiked with garlic, *crème brûlée* with lavender. Salads served in the garden in summer. An exceptional place all round.

VALBERG 06710

CÔTÉ JARDIN

☎ 04.93.02.64.70

Ski resorts are not usually synonymous with gourmet food, but here's the exception to the rule. True, you can get *tartiflette, raclette* and fondue too but it would be a pity to stay with dishes that are more typical of Savoy than of Provence, particularly when the 89F and 120F set meals come with dishes that show just what the talented chef can do. There's *terrine* of zander and raw ham, ravioli stuffed with *foie gras* in a truffle sauce, stuffed baby vegetables, breast of pheasant with morels, house duck *confit*, and a fabulous *foie gras* casserole. Not only does the food taste good, but the presentation of the dishes is exceptional. The dining room faces the garden. Friendly service.

VENCE 06140

HÔTEL-RESTAURANT LA CLOSERIE DES GENÊTS*

4 impasse Maurel (Centre).
☎ 04.93.58.33.25
Closed Sunday evenings. **TV**.

This little hotel at the end of a cul-de-sac is really quiet despite being right in the centre. The prices aren't too bad. Doubles 240F with shower/wc and 280F with shower/wc, TV and twin beds. Nice restaurant that does fairly ordinary food. Set meals 85F (weekdays) and 120F.

AUBERGE DES SEIGNEURS**

place Frêne (Centre).
☎ 04.93.58.04.24 ➡ 04.93.24.08.01
Closed Nov 15–March 15.

This beautiful building, which dates back to the 15th century, is situated on the ramparts at the entrance to the old town. The rooms are all called after painters and we liked the Modigliani and Soutine suites for their mountain view and for the fact that they're more like suites than hotel rooms. And the prices are more than reasonable — two will pay 334–364F. No half-board, but why not treat yourself to a meal in the restaurant? Sophisticated, imaginative cooking and set meals at 170F (6 courses) and 240F. Warm welcome.

HÔTEL LA ROSERAIE**

14 av. H.-Giraux, route de Cousegoules (North-East); if you're coming from the town centre it's just before the Matisse chapel.
☎ 04.93.58.02.20 F→ 04.93.58.99.31
Secure parking. **TV**. **Disabled access**.

We really fell for this charming little hotel. Monsieur and Madame Ganier love what they do and will give you a warm welcome. All the rooms are individually decorated in Provence style and the furniture was bought second-hand locally. A few rooms have a view of the Baou (the hill just opposite), which features in a lot of Impressionist paintings. The attractively tiled bathrooms are amply supplied with bunches of lavender, bath salts, perfumed soap, and so on. Pretty garden and circular swimming pool, which is very pleasant in summer. Substantial balanced breakfast 55F served on a pleasant terrace. In short, it's so delightful that most of the guests come back year after year. Doubles 395–560F. That may seem a bit steep but, honestly, it's worth every penny. Book a long time in advance if you plan to come in the summer.

LE P'TIT PROVENÇAL

4 place Clémenceau.
☎ 04.93.58.50.64

A new restaurant in the centre of the old town with a relaxed informal atmosphere where you can sample extremely imaginative cooking that still manages to be typically Provençal. And you can eat on the terrace and watch what's going on around you — the old town is pretty lively. Set meals 85F and 135F and *formule* (dish of the day plus dessert) 60F. Stew of cheek of suckling pig, ravioli *à la bouillabaisse*, panfried *pangre* (it's a fish!), leg and shoulder of rabbit with *tapenade*, stuffed baby vegetables. We like this place.

VILLECROZE 83690

AUBERGE DES LAVANDES*

place du Général-de-Gaulle (Centre).
☎ 04.94.70.76.00 F→ 04.94.70.10.31
Closed Tuesday evenings and Wednesdays (except in July and August), and Oct 13–March 28. **Car park**.

A very pleasant little place with a light-hearted and informal atmosphere and a restaurant that's just as good as the hotel. The colour scheme in the dining room is in shades of lavender (naturally) and the décor is pleasant. There are a lot of regulars, which isn't surprising as the food is good, not expensive, and served up in generous portions. Terrace on the square shaded with plane trees. Lamb *à la provençale* and rabbit *à l'anchoïade*. Do try the local goat's cheese, which is delicious. Dish of the day 49F, set meal 69F, *menu du jour* 89F. Cute rooms 220F with shower and wc for two, and 250F with bath. A delightful little place — we're really fond of it.

Rhône-Alpes

01 Ain
07 Ardèche
26 Drôme
38 Isère
42 Loire
69 Rhône
73 Savoie
74 Haute-Savoie

AIX-LES-BAINS 73100

AUBERGE DE JEUNESSE

promenade du Sierroz (North-West); follow the signs from the centre of town or take a number 2 bus in the direction of Grand Port and get off at the "camping" stop.
☎ 04.79.88.32.88 ➡ 04.79.61.14.05
Closed in winter except during school holidays.
Car park. Disabled access.

Doors open 6–10pm. Surrounded by fields and near a little river that flows into the lake 200m further on, the youth hostel has some interesting architectural features, being a mixture of regional and contemporary styles. Rooms are on three different levels. They sleep four, have washing facilities, and cost 51F per person per night. Meals 49F. Half-board at 120F per person is compulsory if you're staying more than three days. If you're planning on being there between May and September, it's probably a good idea to book — good places are always very busy.

HÔTEL REINE VICTORIA

1 av. du Petit-Port (Centre).
☎ 04.79.35.10.07 ➡ 04.79.88.11.80

The customers in the ground floor bar are a bit of a mixture — not usually what you expect to find in a spa town. Upstairs there are nine simple but inexpensive rooms. Doubles 130F with basin. And the owner's a nice sort. One set meal 50F. Couscous a speciality.

10% HÔTEL-RESTAURANT AU PETIT VATEL**

11 rue du Temple (Centre).
☎ 04.79.35.04.80 ➡ 04.79.34.01.51
Secure parking. TV.

You'll find it in a quiet street in the centre of town, just next door to the Anglican church of St Swithin, which Queen Victoria attended when she stayed in Aix; it's a charmingly old-fashioned place and has rooms at the back (complete with balcony) that overlook a little garden whose walls are swathed in ivy. Prices range from 150F (in the low season) for a room with washing facilities to 250F (in the high season) for one with shower/wc; it's rather elegant but not offputting. Beautiful dining room with a pleasant atmosphere. Set meals 62–200F. The frogs' legs *à la provençale* and the trout are both worth trying.

HÔTEL-RESTAURANT CHEZ LA MÈRE MICHAUD**

82 bis rue de Genève (Centre).
☎ 04.79.35.06.03 ➡ 04.79.61.57.72
Closed Tuesdays and Dec 9–Jan 8. **TV.**

This place is typical of the kind of establishment you find deep in the provinces. It stands in a square with plane trees, which probably explains why it reminded us a little of Provence. It opened its doors a good century ago and it's called after the woman who first owned it; it's not just her name that lives on, it's the tradition

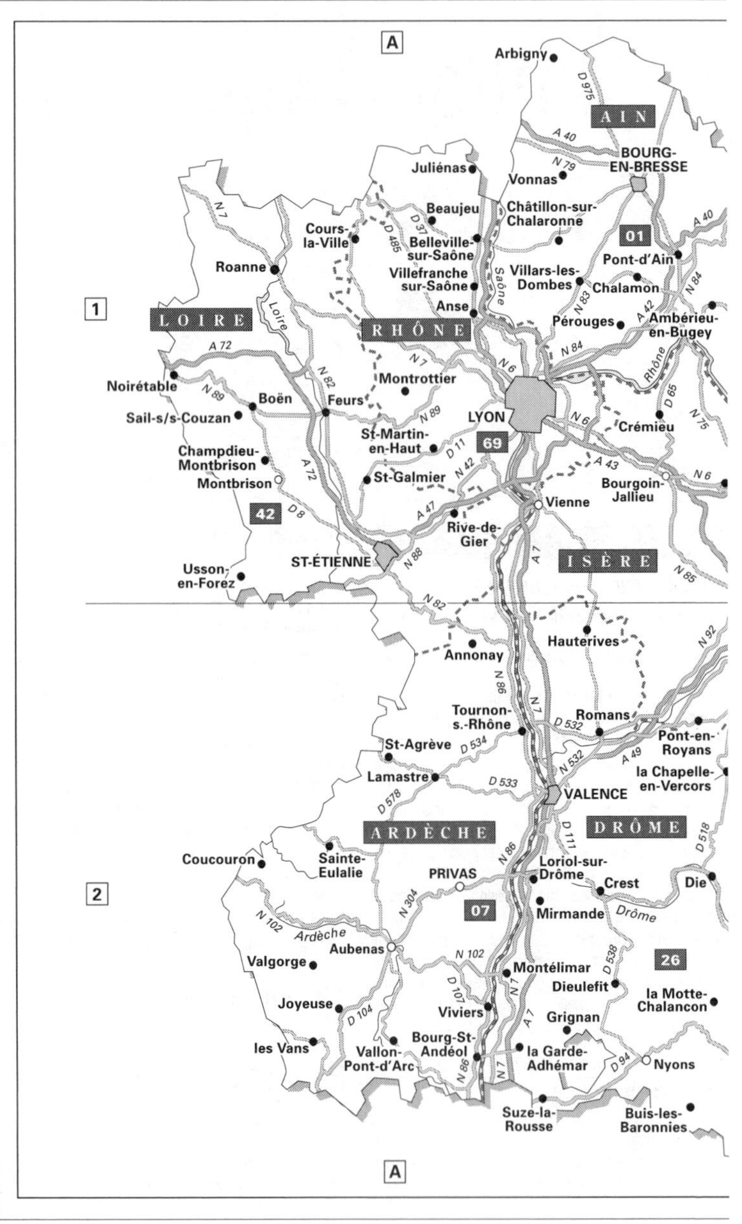
A
1
2
AIN
LOIRE
RHÔNE
ISÈRE
ARDÈCHE
DRÔME
01
69
42
07
26
Arbigny
BOURG-EN-BRESSE
Juliénas
Vonnas
Beaujeu
Châtillon-sur-Chalaronne
Cours-la-Ville
Belleville-sur-Saône
Villefranche sur-Saône
Villars-les-Dombes
Pont-d'Ain
Chalamon
Roanne
Anse
Pérouges
Ambérieu-en-Bugey
Noirétable
Boën
Feurs
Montrottier
Sail-s/s-Couzan
LYON
Crémieu
St-Martin-en-Haut
Champdieu-Montbrison
Montbrison
St-Galmier
Bourgoin-Jallieu
Vienne
Rive-de-Gier
ST-ÉTIENNE
Usson-en-Forez
Hauterives
Annonay
Tournon-s.-Rhône
Romans
Pont-en-Royans
St-Agrève
la Chapelle-en-Vercors
Lamastre
VALENCE
Coucouron
Sainte-Eulalie
PRIVAS
Loriol-sur-Drôme
Crest
Die
Mirmande
Aubenas
Valgorge
Montélimar
Dieulefit
la Motte-Chalancon
Joyeuse
Viviers
Grignan
les Vans
Vallon-Pont-d'Arc
Bourg-St-Andéol
la Garde-Adhémar
Nyons
Suze-la-Rousse
Buis-les-Baronnies
Saône
Loire
Rhône
Ardèche
Drôme
D 975
A 40
N 79
N 7
D 37
D 485
A 42
N 83
N 84
A 72
N 82
N 89
N 6
D 65
N 75
D 11
N 42
A 43
D 8
A 47
N 88
A 7
N 85
N 92
N 86
D 532
D 534
A 49
N 532
D 533
D 578
D 111
D 518
N 304
N 102
D 538
D 107
D 104
D 94

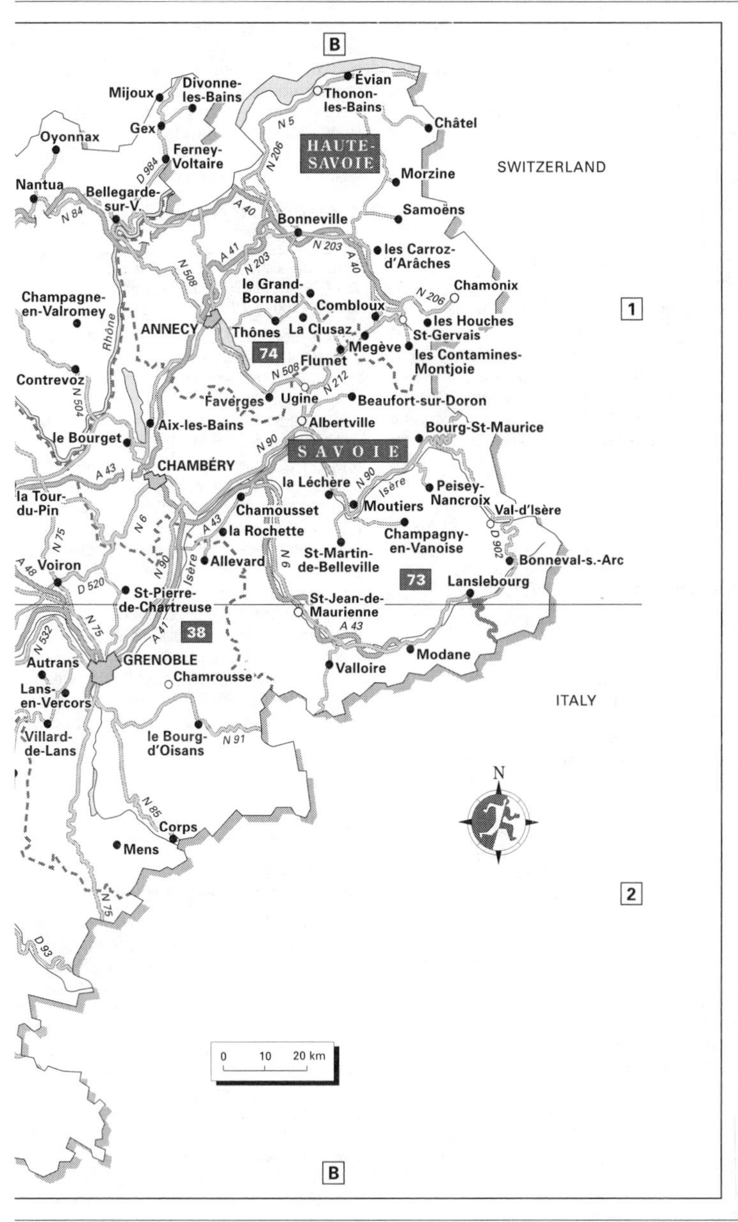
B
Évian
Thonon-les-Bains
Divonne-les-Bains
Mijoux
Gex
Oyonnax
Ferney-Voltaire
Châtel
HAUTE-SAVOIE
SWITZERLAND
Morzine
Nantua
Bellegarde-sur-V.
Samoëns
Bonneville
les Carroz-d'Arâches
Chamonix
le Grand-Bornand
Champagne-en-Valromey
Combloux
ANNECY
Thônes
La Clusaz
les Houches
St-Gervais
Megève
les Contamines-Montjoie
74
Flumet
Contrevoz
Faverges
Ugine
Beaufort-sur-Doron
Aix-les-Bains
Albertville
Bourg-St-Maurice
le Bourget
SAVOIE
CHAMBÉRY
la Léchère
Peisey-Nancroix
la Tour-du-Pin
Moutiers
Val-d'Isère
Chamousset
la Rochette
Champagny-en-Vanoise
St-Martin-de-Belleville
Bonneval-s.-Arc
Voiron
Allevard
73
Lanslebourg
St-Pierre-de-Chartreuse
St-Jean-de-Maurienne
38
GRENOBLE
Modane
Autrans
Chamrousse
Valloire
Lans-en-Vercors
ITALY
Villard-de-Lans
le Bourg-d'Oisans
N
Corps
Mens
1
2
0 10 20 km
B
N 5
N 206
D 984
A 40
N 84
A 41
N 203
N 508
Rhône
N 212
N 90
A 43
N 6
N 75
A 48
D 520
Isère
D 902
N 532
N 91
N 85
D 93

of good home cooking too. Day's special 40F, set meals 55–135F. Specialities are fondue, *tartiflette*, *gratin savoyard* (potatoes with cheese) and whitebait. If you want accommodation, young owners Stéphane and Florence (she's a great-granddaughter of Mère Michaud) have doubles from 140F (with basin) to 200F (with shower/wc). The rooms are well cared for but they're a bit old-fashioned.

10% ☗ |●| HÔTEL BROISIN*

10 ruelle du Revet (Centre).
☎ 04.79.35.06.15 F➜ 04.79.88.10.10
Closed Dec 1–end Feb. **TV**.

Service from 12.15pm and 7pm. This little hotel, recently renovated, stands in a quiet and picturesque street in the centre of town, with the spa and the park not too far away. Prices are extremely reasonable, starting at 150F for a double, 190F–200F with shower/wc. Of course, quite a few of the 50,000 people who come to Aix-les-Bains every year know about the hotel, so it's often full. Most of the time the guests are elderly and have been coming here for years. The restaurant does two set meals at 55F (evenings only) and 65F (lunchtimes only). The cooking is aimed primarily at residents and is not particularly inspiring.

☗ |●| HÔTEL-RESTAURANT L'ASSIETTE FLEURIE

1 bd Charcot (South-West); take the N201 in the direction of Tresserve-Chambéry and you'll find it on the outskirts of Aix.
☎ 04.79.88.00.01 F➜ 04.79.61.53.78
Closed Tuesday evenings (except in July and August), Wednesdays, and Nov 15–Jan 20. **Car park**.

Service until 1.30pm and 9.30 (and later) in the evening. A wooden chalet by the lake with a garden full of roses and geraniums and a few rooms upstairs. Doubles 180F with shower. A large family room in the attic can be rented by the week. The ground floor restaurant serves up generous portions of traditional dishes, home-made desserts, genuine regional specialities and fish. Set meals start at 65F. Families are particularly welcome – there's a sign up at the door to the effect that children are king here. They have their own menu (35F) and a play area out in the garden among the trees. One for the address book. What's more, the proprietress enjoys travelling on a shoestring too.

10% ☗ HÔTEL DU CASINO**

20 rue des Bains (Centre); it's near the spa.
☎ 04.79.35.06.28 F➜ 04.79.08.18.60
Closed beginning Nov–end March. **TV**.

This handsome 19th century bourgeois house has been in the same family for several generations. Rooms are spacious and decorated in pastel colours and flower-patterned fabrics. Doubles 225F with basin/wc (no TV), 240F with shower/wc, and 260F with bath. Reckon on paying 15% more in season. All prices include breakfast. Pleasant welcome. A good traditional hotel.

☗ |●| HÔTEL-RESTAURANT LE MANOIR***

37 rue Georges-Ier; it's behind the spa.
☎ 04.79.61.44.00 F➜ 04.79.35.67.67
Secure parking. **TV**.

Lunch served 12.15–1.30pm and dinner 7.30–9.30pm. Tucked away near the spa and surrounded by trees, this is the place to come if you're looking for somewhere where you'll feel comfortable – and maybe even cosseted – in a town that often seems a bit stiff and formal. The enormous house may be luxurious but it has a young and relaxed staff. You'll sleep soundly in the cosy and well-equipped rooms – the only sound to disturb your slumbers will be the dawn chorus. Doubles 295–595F with shower/wc or bath. The dining room's pretty classy and the food is very, very good. They do a lot of fish dishes but there's also medallions of veal in an almond-based sauce, ravioli stuffed with mushrooms and sardines, and lamb with tarragon. Still, at 135–245F, the set meals are a bit on the expensive side. There's a pool and a jacuzzi if total relaxation is what you're after. How could you not feel good after being here?

|●| CRÊPERIE LA QUIMPÉROISE

4 rue Albert-Ier (Centre); it's in the pedestrian precinct.
☎ 04.79.88.99.48
Closed Mondays Sept 30–beginning June.

Non-stop service till 10pm in winter, midnight in summer. The first thing to catch your eye is the Breton flag (the Savoie flag in on the other side – Catherine the owner, born and bred in Brittany, is a member of a club formed to promote links between the two regions). Inside though, the décor – fishing nets, shells, hulls of boats – is pure Quimper. You'd almost swear you could smell the sea. What you WILL smell are Catherine's wonderful crêpes. Nobody can make them the way she can. Ones made with wheat flour start at 13F, ones made with buckwheat flour at 26F, and there's a *kouingn-amamn* (a traditional rich yeast cake from Brittany) to die for. The food is good, which is why we recommend a Breton crêperie in the land of *tartiflette* and fondue.

|●| RESTAURANT LA POULE AU POT

20 rue des Bains (Centre).
☎ 04.79.35.01.19 ➡ 04.79.61.25.96
Closed Sunday lunchtimes and every lunchtime mid-Nov–mid-Feb.

Lunch served noon–2pm and dinner 7–10.30pm. The owner wanted to give his restaurant a 20s look – hence all the lithographs and sepia photos. The cooking here is traditional, full of flavour and quality ingredients. Set meals 60F (weekdays), 85F and 115F, with dishes like *tartiflette*, *fondue savoyarde* (potatoes and melted cheese), and of course *poule au pot*; it's a pedestrian street, so the terrace is pleasant in summer.

|●| RESTAURANT L'AUBERGE DU PONT ROUGE

151 av. du Grand-Port (North-West).
☎ 04.79.63.43.90
Closed Sunday evenings, Thursdays, and Dec 20–Jan 20.

Every time one of the regulars asks "How are things?", owner José says "Terrible", which is a bit hard to credit when you see just how many people there are in the little dining room with its fairly uninspiring modern décor. If the weather's fine, you can sit in the garden. If there's no room, José's wife will squeeze you in beside the bar. The cooking is traditional and the emphasis is on carefully chosen fresh produce that will give the maximum flavour. They do five set meals (65–165F) and lots of dishes from the southwest, including Charolais beefsteak with truffles, *confit* of duck, and perch fillets.

ALBERTVILLE 73200

10% ⌂ HÔTEL-RESTAURANT LE COSTAROCHE**

1 chemin Pierre-du-Roy (South); take the pont du Mirantin – it's near the medieval town of Conflans and the château in Costaroche.
☎ 04.79.32.02.02
Car park. TV.

Lunch served noon–1.30pm and dinner 7–9.30pm. This old and rather impersonal establishment (we wouldn't have noticed but for the fact that everyone had been telling us how nice the owners were) has doubles with bath from 255F. The very natural welcome we received was refreshing considering that even the hairdressers have become pretty snooty since Albertville hosted the Winter Olympics in 1992. Set meals 80F and 160F. The cooking is fairly ordinary. There's a garden with lots of trees. And the traffic on the two nearby roads isn't bad enough to keep you awake, honest.

|●| LE LIGISMOND

How to get there: it's in the medieval town of Conflans.
☎ 04.79.37.71.29. ➡ same.
Closed Mondays and Sunday evenings.

Book by phone in winter. You'll have to leave your car in the car park since Conflans is closed to traffic but the climb up to the village square will give you an appetite. And if you are hungry by the time you get there, no need to worry – the set meals are not only tasty, they're substantial too. The cooking is traditional, of course, with things like fondues and *diots* (vegetable and pork sausage preserved in oil and cooked in white wine) and one or two slightly more original dishes like fillet of zander in local Gamay or medallions of veal with tarragon. Set meals 78F, 95F, 128F and 168F. Cheapest set meal weekday lunchtimes is 68F. The dining room has exposed stonework and in summer there's a lovely terrace that overlooks the pretty museum.

MONTHION 73200 (8KM SW)

|●| LES SEIZE CLOCHERS

How to get there: on the D925, between Grignon and Notre-Dame-des-Millières, turn left onto the D64.
☎ 04.79.31.30.39
Closed Wednesdays and January. **Car park.**

Here's a restaurant that looks nothing like a restaurant. It stands on the outskirts of the village and has a superb view of at least 16 steeples in the Combe de Savoie. The cooking is traditional and local specialities – *diots* (vegetable and pork sausages) in white wine, *tartiflette*, fricassee of snails *à la savoyarde* (with cheese and potatoes) and chanterelles in puff pastry – play a starring role. And they do a very very cheap fondue at 55F! Set meals 87F (not available Sundays), 105F, 128F and 158F. A really nice little restaurant.

PLANCHERINE 73200 (11KM W)

10% |●| CHALET DES TRAPPEURS

Col de Tamié; from Albertville, follow the signs for Gilly-sur-Isère and then col de Tamié.
☎ 04.79.32.21.44
Closed Mondays. **Car park.**

The building, made of wood (and it does look very much like a trappers' chalet), stands in the middle of the Alpine meadows of the col de Tamié, where the monks from the abbey produce excellent cheese. The hunting trophies, antique furniture and the sheepskins by the fireplace inside are as appealing in winter as the striped deck chairs outside are in summer. It would be hard to find anything more typical of Savoie than this. The mouthwatering menu lists a number of authentic specialities like *navarin* (a type of stew) of lamb, black pudding, and rabbit stew with polenta. And then of course there's *tartiflette*, *raclette* (potatoes with melted cheese), *reblochonnade* and fondue – Savoie wouldn't be Savoie without those; it's a pity that the altitude has had an effect on the prices. Cheapest set meal (weekdays lunchtime) is 60F. Other set meals 85–150F. A la carte is expensive

ALLEVARD 38580

LA BONNE AUBERGE*

10 rue Laurent-Chataing.
☎ 04.76.97.53.04 F 04.76.45.84.62
Closed Sunday and Monday evenings out of season. **TV**.

The welcome you get in both the hotel and the restaurant couldn't be bettered. Bedrooms have a view of Brame-Farine. Doubles with washing facilities 130F, with shower/wc, TV and direct phone 190F. The country style restaurant has sardine ravioli in crayfish butter, duck with honey and bilberries and *tartiflette* of goat's cheese. Reckon on 65F for the cheapest – and very acceptable – set meal. They also do a *formule* of the day's special plus dessert for 50F.

GONCELIN 38570 (10KM S)

RESTAURANT LE CLOS DU CHÂTEAU

How to get there: on the D525 from Allevard.
☎ 04.76.71.72.04 F same
Closed Sunday evenings, Mondays, one week in February during the school holidays, and two weeks in August. **Car park**. **Disabled access**.

Lunch served noon–1.30pm and dinner 7.30–9pm. Imagine a traditional 13th century house up among the mountains of Chartreuse and Belledonne and there you have it; it's been brought back to life by its new owners, two extremely nice British people who would also – judging by the happy faces all around – appear to have brought more than a little joy to the lives of those fortunate customers who've known where to look for this out-of-the-ordinary restaurant (it's set back from the road and the grounds are so extensive you might very easily pass it by). Suzie Glayser acts as waitress in the dining room and on the terrace while husband Laurent prepares the air-dried duck with *tapenade* (anchovy paste with capers and olives), the cod steak, and the apple crumble that make up the 120F set meal. He's particularly good with fish and baby vegetables and the 165F set meal, built up around what the market has to offer, is a feast for the senses.

FERRIÈRE (LA) 38580 (17KM SE)

AUBERGE NEMOZ

Hameau La Martinette; take the D525 in the direction of Fond-de-France.
☎ 04.76.45.03.10 F 04.76.45.88.75
Closed Mon–Wed during term time and mid-Nov–mid-Dec. **Car park**.

A meal in this restaurant, located deep in the forest, in the valley of Haut-Breda (an area that very few people know about), will leave you in an extremely good mood and full of a sense of well-being. The old stonework and the young faces glow in the light of the fire that's always burning in the hearth for raclette and of the candles that are lit at nightfall. If you're not a big fan of fondue, *tartiflette* or other cooked cheese dishes, go for the 95F set meal of snail ravioli, trout *en papillote*, and fresh cream cheese or the one at 120F, which comes with sautéd lamb among other things. Lots of atmosphere.

AMBÉRIEU-EN-BUGEY 01500

HÔTEL TERMINUS ET DE LA GARE**

80 rue Roger-Salengro (South).
☎ 04.74.38.00.02 F 04.74.46.89.47
Car park. **TV**.

The station might have prompted Dali to declare it the most beautiful in the world. You'll get a nice family-type welcome from the Schaefers in this cosy little hotel in a bourgeois house. They have 18 clean, inexpensive and slightly old-fashioned rooms. Double with shower 150–300F, room that sleeps four 300F. Breakfast is so substantial it might keep you going until dinner time. The bar is popular with elderly locals.

ÉVOSGES 01230 (23KM NE)

10% L'AUBERGE CAMPAGNARDE**

(North-East); as you leave Saint-Rambert, head for Belley; 1km from town, take the D34.
☎ 04.74.38.55.55 F 04.74.38.55.62

Closed Tuesday evenings and Wednesdays Oct–March and three weeks in January. **Secure parking. TV.**

Service from noon and from 8pm. The road to Évosges, a little village on the plateau, winds its way through the vineyards of Bugey clinging to the hillside and offers some pretty good views. The inn seems to be the centre of village life – it's not just a hotel cum restaurant, it's also a bar and a play area for children. And it offers gourmet food in a cosy plush dining room. Although it uses the very best ingredients and the portions are substantial, the prices of the set meals reflect the quality of the cooking and start at 100F. Bedrooms are quiet and comfortable. Three-quarters of them have been refurbished. Doubles with shower/wc 280F. Pleasant garden. Very nice welcome.

PEZIÈRES-RESINAND (LES) 01110 (25KM NE)

LE BOOMERANG

How to get there: take the N504 to Saint-Rambert and then turn left onto the D34; it's signposted from the village of Oncieu.
☎ 04.74.35.58.60 F 04.74.38.58.32.
Closed Mondays and when the owner pops over to Australia to do some shopping!

A few scattered houses huddled in one of Bugey's isolated but of course superb valleys. A sign in the garden of one of the houses warns of the presence of kangaroos and no, it's not a joke. Brent Perkins, originally from Adelaide, really does have a kangaroo called Skippy. He (Brent, not Skippy) fell in love with this part of France (and with wife Rose-Marie, who comes from Bugey). This is hardly the Australian Outback but you'll get a genuine "barbie" and you can savour the equally genuine flavourings and sauces. Prices range from 105F for a vegetarian barbecue to 158F for the king-size. That gets you a green salad with a walnut oil dressing, steak with British and Australian sauces, eggs, cheese and dessert. The rest of the menu is a little closer to home, with things like fresh frog's legs (order ahead of time) and chicken in a cream sauce. The wine list too divides its favours equally between Australia and Bugey. A quite astonishing restaurant.

ANNECY 74000

SEE MAP OVERLEAF

AUBERGE DE JEUNESSE

4 route du Semnoz (South-East); it's 1km from the town centre on the D41 in the direction of Le Semnoz.
☎ 04.50.45.33.19 F 04.50.52.77.52
Secure parking.

Doors open 8am–noon and 2–10pm. A very new building that's a stone's throw from the forest of the Crêt du Maure and faces the lake and the mountains. You'll pay 70F a night (breakfast is included) for a bed in dormitories that sleep 4–5, with shower/basin. Meals 50F. Half-board 119F, full board 168F. You can use the kitchen 3–9pm.

CRYSTAL HÔTEL**

20 rue Louis-Chaumontet. **MAP A1-4**
☎ 04.50.57.33.90 F 04.50.67.86.43
Secure parking. TV.

If only all hotel owners were like this one!. He's mad about computers though so if you get him started you might find you've let yourself in for an all-night session. Apart from that, you can be sure of peace and quiet. You won't even hear any trains even though the station is so close. All the comforts of home in a place that looks like home. Doubles with shower/wc or bath 179–296F, depending on the time of year.

10% HÔTEL DU NORD**

24 rue Sommeiller. **MAP A2-7**
☎ 04.50.45.08.78 F 04.50.51.22.04
TV. Canal+.

Some people have been coming here for more than 60 years! The old lady's had a facelift recently but she still has some traces of her past glory, including the veranda. The rooms are done up in pastel shades and flower-patterned fabrics and look a bit feminine. Doubles with shower/wc from 238F out of season, 278–298F in July and August. Room number 47 has a splendid view of the old town. By the way, "Sommeiller" has got nothing to do with sleep (even though the hotel is very quiet) – it's the name of the engineer who masterminded the first tunnel through the Alps.

ALÉRY HÔTEL**

5 av. d'Aléry. **MAP A2-6**
☎ 04.50.45.24.75. F 04.50.51.26.90
Secure parking. TV. Canal+.

This is a hotel in the best French tradition. It offers a very nice welcome, comfort, and reasonable prices. The street is very busy during the day but you could hear a pin drop at night. We even managed to sleep with the window open. The rooms are pleasant and decorated in warm shades. Doubles 240–370F with shower or bath. Breakfast

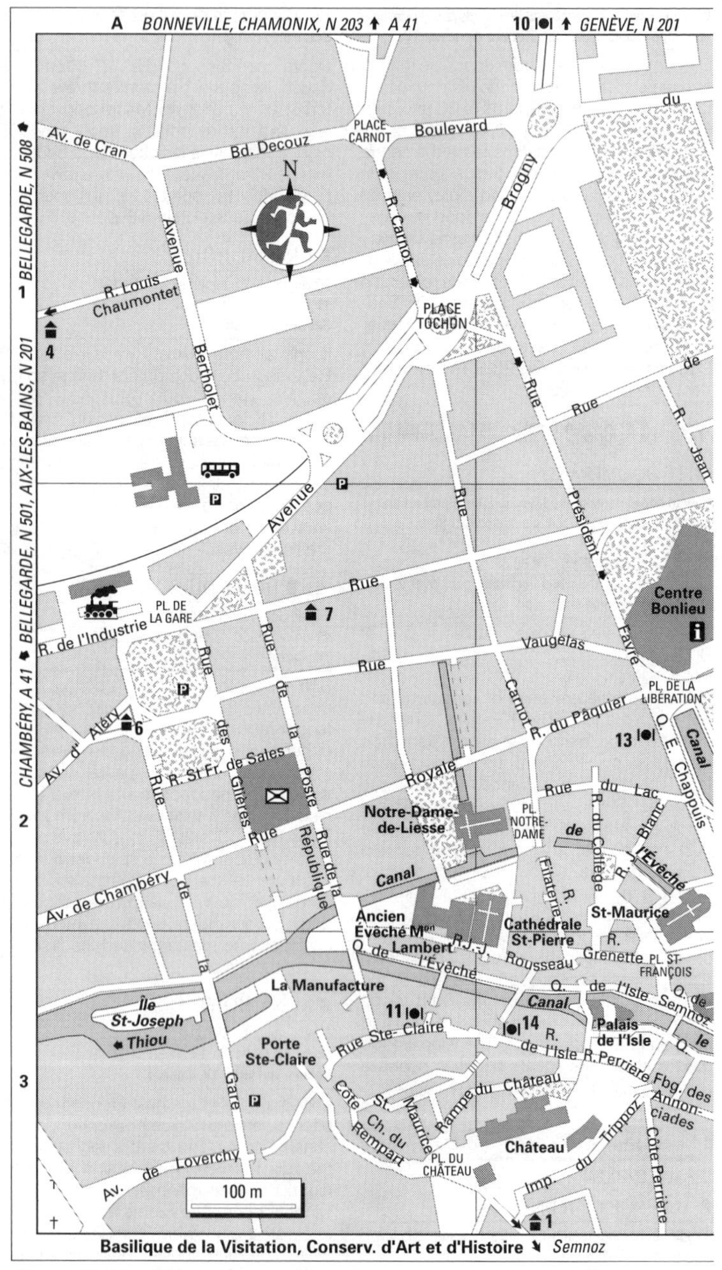
A BONNEVILLE, CHAMONIX, N 203 ↑ A 41
10 ↑ GENÈVE, N 201
BELLEGARDE, N 508
CHAMBÉRY, A 41 ← BELLEGARDE, N 501, AIX-LES-BAINS, N 201
Av. de Cran
Bd. Decouz
PLACE CARNOT
Boulevard du
Brogny
R. Carnot
Avenue Berthollet
R. Louis Chaumontet
PLACE TOCHON
Rue Président Favre
Rue de
R. Jean
Avenue
Rue
Rue Vaugelas
Centre Bonlieu
PL. DE LA GARE
R. de l'Industrie
Rue de la Poste
Rue des Glières
Rue Carnot
R. du Pâquier
PL. DE LA LIBÉRATION
Q. E. Chappuis
Canal
Av. d' Aléry
R. St Fr. de Sales
Rue Royale
Rue du Lac
R. du Collège
Blanc
Notre-Dame-de-Liesse
PL. NOTRE-DAME
de
R. Filaterie
R. de l'Évêché
Rue de la République
Av. de Chambéry
Canal
Ancien Évêché Mgr Lambert
Cathédrale St-Pierre
St-Maurice
R. J.-J. Rousseau
R. Grenette
PL. ST-FRANÇOIS
Q. de l'Évêché
La Manufacture
Q. de l'Isle
Semnoz
Q. de
Île St-Joseph
Thiou
Canal
Palais de l'Isle
Porte Ste-Claire
Rue Ste-Claire
R. de l'Isle
R. Perrière
Fbg. des Annonciades
Rue de la Gare
Côte St-Maurice
Ch. du Rempart
Rampe du Château
Château
Imp. du Trippoz
Côte Perrière
PL. DU CHÂTEAU
Av. de Loverchy
100 m
1
2
3
4
6
7
11
13
14
Basilique de la Visitation, Conserv. d'Art et d'Histoire ↘ Semnoz

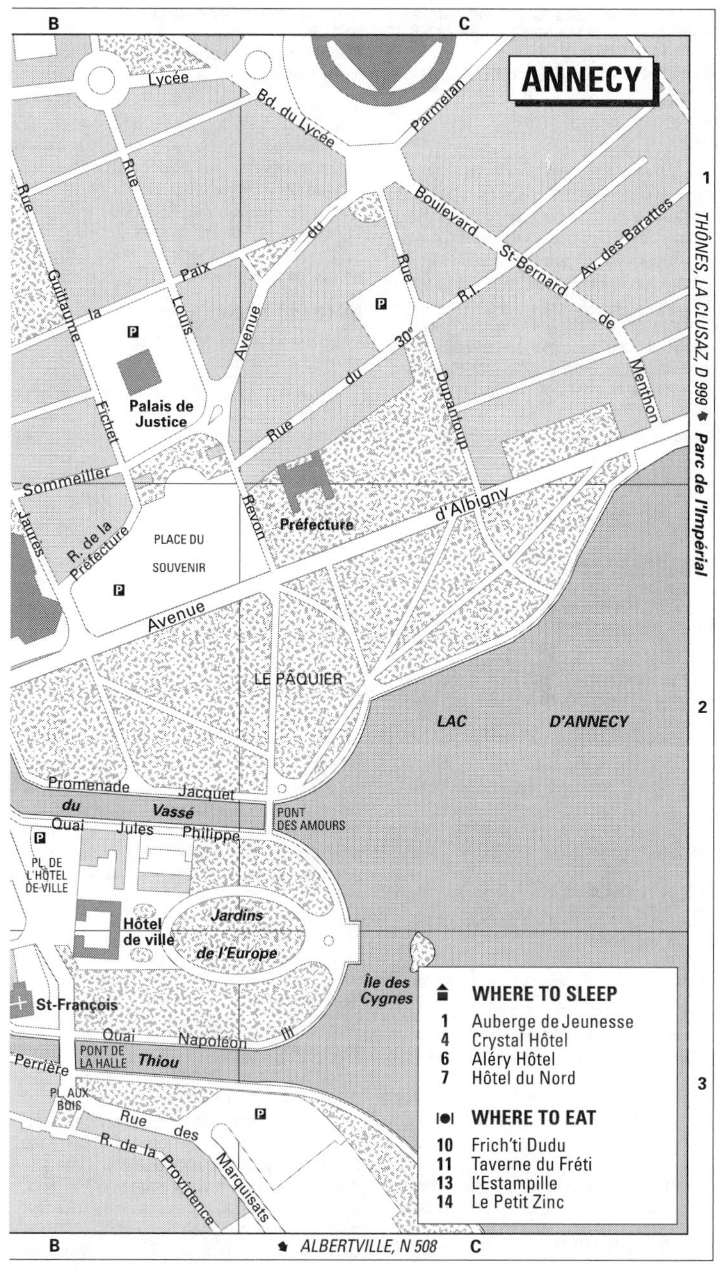
ANNECY
B
C
1
2
3
Lycée
Bd. du Lycée
Parmelan
Boulevard
St-Bernard
de
Menthon
Av. des Barattes
Rue
Guillaume
Fichet
Rue
Louis
Paix
la
Avenue
du
Rue
Rue
du
30e
R.I.
Dupanloup
Palais de Justice
Sommeiller
Jaurès
R. de la Préfecture
PLACE DU SOUVENIR
Revon
Préfecture
Avenue
d'Albigny
LE PÂQUIER
LAC
D'ANNECY
THÔNES, LA CLUSAZ, D 909 ➧ Parc de l'Impérial
Promenade
Jacquet
du
Vassé
PONT DES AMOURS
Quai
Jules
Philippe
PL. DE L'HÔTEL DE VILLE
Hôtel de ville
Jardins de l'Europe
Île des Cygnes
St-François
Quai
Napoléon
III
PONT DE LA HALLE
Thiou
Perrière
PL. AUX BOIS
Rue
des
R. de la Providence
Marquisats
➧ ALBERTVILLE, N 508
WHERE TO SLEEP
1 Auberge de Jeunesse
4 Crystal Hôtel
6 Aléry Hôtel
7 Hôtel du Nord
WHERE TO EAT
10 Frich'ti Dudu
11 Taverne du Fréti
13 L'Estampille
14 Le Petit Zinc

38F. A good place to stay halfway between the train station and the historic part of town.

HÔTEL DU PALAIS DE L'ISLE**

13 rue Perrière.
☎ 04.50.45.86.87 F➜ 04.50.51.87.15
TV. Canal+.

A stone's throw from the lake, in the heart of the old town, this is the place for you if you think a hotel should be cosy and comfortable. The welcome's a bit frosty, but overall there's a warm atmosphere to this place with its contemporary furniture and old walls and you'll have a great night's sleep. Well you will if you're lucky enough to get one of the rooms that look out onto the canal and the old palais de l'Isle. If you're on the side that looks out onto the pedestrian street, you'd better have the earplugs handy, particularly in summer. Or of course you too could party until the small hours (if you can't beat them, join them). The hotel is an architects's dream that needn't necessarily turn into a nightmare – forewarned is forearmed! Superb rooms 280–495F.

10% HÔTEL DE BONLIEU**

5 rue de Bonlieu; it's beside the Palais de Justice.
☎ 04.50.45.17.16 F➜ 04.50.45.11.48
TV. Canal+. Car park.

If you're looking for a bit of peace and quiet and all the mod cons rather than a trip down memory lane, then this is a good little place, targeted more at young business execs than carefree travellers. But you'll get a friendly welcome, it's near the lake and old Annecy, and the prices are fairly reasonable (rooms 290F and 330F, good breakfast buffet 38F). A place you can depend on, which is not as common as it used to be.

FRICH'TI DUDU

11 rue Louis-Armand (North); it's in the pedestrian precinct. Off map **B1-10**
☎ 04.50.09.97.65.
Closed evenings (except reservation) and week ends.

Service 11.45am–2pm. OK, it's not exactly the nicest part of town but this place does raise the tone a bit; it's really packed at lunchtime and it's hardly surprising — the prices are incredibly cheap and you're treated like royalty The cooking is simple but it doesn't cost much more to eat here than it does in a fast food joint. So make up your own mind. Various *formules* on offer, 44–55F. Full set meal which changes every day 55F.

TAVERNE DU FRÉTI

12 rue Sainte-Claire. **MAP A3-11**
☎ 04.50.51.29.52
Closed Mondays (except during the school holidays) and lunchtimes.

This is a good place for regional specialities even if it is fairly touristy. It offers quality (it's also a cheese shop with row and rows of raclette makers) and reasonable prices, with fondue 65–75F, *raclette* about 65F, *tartiflette* 65F, and potatoes with blue cheese or goat's cheese 65F. There's a pretty dining room upstairs if the weather's not good enough to sit out on the terrace.

LE PETIT ZINC

11 rue du Pont-Morens. **MAP B3-14**
☎ 04.50.51.12.93

This little restaurant is a welcome refuge when it's cold outside. The green and ochre, the wooden ceiling, and the little lamps with old-fashioned mats under them combine to create a feeling of warmth. All that's missing is a fireplace. The cooking is traditional and of course the portions are generous — if you're a compulsive calorie-counter, this is not the place for you!. Set meals 65F, 80F, 150F and 220F. Day's special 50F. What's cooking? Why, *tartiflette*, black pudding with apples, fondue, *diots* (pork and vegetable sausages) in white wine, and *frikacoffe* of course — this IS Savoie!

LE BISTRO D'ARNAUD

36 av. de Chambéry.
☎ 04.50.45.51.42
Closed Sundays and Monday lunchtimes.

It's away from the pedestrian area but that's no obstacle to people who love typical Lyons food all kinds. There's a nice warm atmosphere and you can get a real calf's head, *andouillette* or *quenelles* of pike - all pretty light stuff if you were brought up on cheese fondue and *tartiflette*. Decent prices (set meals 68F weekday lunchtimes and 108F). Good wine in jugs.

L'ESTAMPILLE

4 quai E.-Chappuis. **MAP B2-13**
☎ 04.50.45.21.16

Open Mon–Sat 10.30am–10.30pm. Everything here is for sale — food, wine, even the table you're eating off and the chair you're sitting on. If you like the lamp, you can take it home with you. Tables, vases, ornaments — it all has to go. So where are you? — you're in an antique shop cum restaurant (or maybe it's a restaurant cum antique shop). Whoever decorated the dining room has exquisite taste and has created a hushed and intimate atmosphere. And since they have a fairly quick turnover of stock, you'll never feel you're eating in the same place however often you come. The cooking is as impressive as the setting. They do a substantial *menu du jour* for 69F that's always good and will keep you going for the rest of the day. There's another at 89F if you are really and truly very very hungry. Tea served in the afternoon. You must try the *thé blanc*. Definitely our favourite place in Annecy.

SEVRIER 74320 (5KM S)

AUBERGE DU BESSARD

525 route d'Albertville; on the N508.
☎ 04.50.52.40.45
Closed Oct 21–March 19. **Car park**.

This establishment has been in the same family for about 50 years. If for some reason you're not feeling in a particularly good mood, the waterside terrace where you can practically paddle and eat at the same time will soon put you right. The restaurant specializes in fish dishes and things like fried lake fish (60F) and fillets of perch are always popular. The cheapest set meal is 95F (weekdays only) and consists of fish *terrine*, *féra* (a type of salmon particular to Savoie), and cheese or dessert. Do take the time to have a snooze after your meal or to go for a swim in the pure water of the lake.

SAINT-JORIOZ 74410 (9KM S)

10% HÔTEL AUBERGE DE LA COCHETTE*

lieu-dit "La Magne" à Saint-Eustache.
☎ 04.50.32.03.53 F➔ 04.50.32.02.70
Closed in January, February, and weekdays from the end of Oct–May. **Car park**.

You can't miss this place – just go to St Jorioz and follow the signs all the way up. You'll need a bit of patience but the magnificent view over the lake of Annecy, 6km away as the crow (or paraglider) flies will be ample reward. Owner J.-P Jonckhere loves paragliding — you can go up with him and land just behind the hotel. Moreover, he has nice rooms from 195F, and the food is good whether it's served on the terrace (sheer bliss!) or in the rustic dining room. Great set meals at 98F, 120F and 150F that make a nice change from the *raclettes, tartiflettes* and so on that you may enjoy at the time but suffer for later.

CHAPEIRY 74540 (11KM SW)

10% AUBERGE LA GRANGE À JULES**

How to get there: leave the A41 by the Rumilly exit and take the N201 in the direction of Annecy. After Alby, turn left towards Chapeiry and you'll find it after the bridge on the right.
☎ 04.50.68.15.07
Closed Sunday evenings and Mondays. **Car park**. **TV**.

We really like these little places at the back of beyond, and though the nearby motorway may be a reminder of a more commonplace world you'll be able to put it all behind you here. In summer, you can eat out in the garden surrounded by trees and flowers. In winter, the fireplace takes the chill out of the air. Set meals range in price from 75F (weekdays) to 230F and there are lots of good things to eat. The *navarin* of lamb (a kind of stew) was memorable. The rooms (200–250F with shower or bath) are large, with flower-pattterned fabrics and wallpaper. The whole place is decorated in a pretty country style.

DOUSSARD 74210 (12KM SE)

10% A L'AUBERGE

rte de Chevaline.
☎ 04.50.44.86.28
Car park.

A little village inn off the beaten track. It's an old house that's full of life at lunchtimes with people enjoying the 60F set meal. The owner is on her own in the dining room but she's a woman of character and even the burliest of her customers meekly accept any slight delay there may be in the service. The little terrace is rather nice in summer. Unpretentious regional cuisine that doesn't do too much damage to the old wallet (expect to pay 100–120F à la carte). Clean well equipped rooms 170F.

DUINGT 74410 (12KM SE)

HÔTEL-RESTAURANT DU LAC**

☎ 04.50.68.90.90 F➔ 04.50.68.50.18
Closed Oct–Feb (hotel), Oct–May (restaurant).
Car park. **TV**.

We've got a real soft spot for this place. It's quite far from the road so all you can see is the lake and all you can hear is the birds. The rooms have all been completely renovated and cost 295–380F. Very good buffet breakfast 40F. The restaurant is full of young people, the owners included. The colours are bright and fresh and you're guaranteed service with a smile. Even the "oldies" here are young! The female chef creates interesting inventive dishes with set meals at 130F, 175F and 220F, and she skilfully blends together different colours, flavours and textures. Try the *fera* (a type of salmon) from the lake with sesame vinaigrette or the *confit* of rabbit with mixed spices. Gorgeous terrace for sunny days.

GRUFFY 74540 (17.5KM SW)

10% AUX GORGES DU CHÉRAN**

pont de l'Abîme; take the N210 and 1km after Chaux turn onto the D5 – once you've passed Gruffy, it's a further 1.5km.
☎ 04.50.52.51.13 F 04.50.52.57.33
Closed Nov 15–March 15. **Secure parking. TV.**

You'll find this pleasant chalet, typical of the region, clinging to the cliff above the Chéran near the bridge which is aptly named — this is quite an abyss. Simple rooms, with doubles 250–320F. The restaurant has the usual local specialities. Set meals 79F, 100F and 128F; it's fairly touristy round here but so beautiful that we felt you should have the name of this place.

LESCHAUX 74320 (18KM S)

LES QUATRE VENTS

col de Leschaux; by the N508 which skirts lac d'Annecy and then the D912 in the direction of Col de Leschaux.
☎ 04.50.32.03.58
Closed Tuesdays (except during school holidays) and Nov 28 – Dec26.

We're rather pleased with ourselves for discovering, tucked away in the mountains, this little restaurant with its big fireplace, panelled dining room and gingham tablecloths and curtains. Everything's home-made from the freshest of local produce. Try the potatoes stuffed with snails and a Reblochon cheese sauce, the pigeon with morels or the frog's legs *à la savoyarde* (with cheese and potatoes). If you take the 65F set meal, you'll get starter plus main course plus dessert (the price goes up to 95F on Sundays but you also get cheese), while the 85F one comes with an assortment of mountain *charcuteries*, potato fritters, salad, and cheese or dessert.

SEMNOZ (LE) 74320 (18KM S)

HÔTEL SEMNOZ - ALPES 1704**

How to get there: by the D41.
☎ 04.50.01.23.17 F 04.50.64.53.05
Closed Sunday evenings out of season, end of Easter holidays–May 20, and Sept 30–Dec 20. **Car park.**

The history of this hotel, built by an Annecy architect in 1876 in the middle of the Alpine meadows at an altitude of 1,704m, would fill an entire page, as would the story of the man who bought it in 1951, mountain guide and ski champion Alfred Couttet. And it would take another page to describe the chalet and its rooms, each one "hand-made" by Alfred's son François, the warmth of the welcome extended by his wife Denise, the view of Mont Blanc, and the set meals of typical mountain dishes. Maybe you should just go and see for yourself. Doubles range in price from 170F (with basin) to 290F (with bath). Set meals 78F, 92F, 130F and 160F. Specialities are *croûte au fromage* (grilled cheese on a layer of puff pastry), strips of duck with bilberries, *féra* (a type of salmon) with orange, and tournedos with chanterelle mushrooms.

ANNONAY 07100

10% HÔTEL DU MIDI**

17 place des Cordeliers (Centre); it's in the lower part of town.
☎ 04.75.33.23.77 F 04.75.33.02.43
Secure parking. TV.

The hotel's in a good location on a very busy square; it's rather surprising to come across a sturdy building of the kind designed by Haussmann in this part of the world; it's rather plush inside with wide corridors, large rooms and carpets that you sink into. There are pictures and engravings of hot air balloons all over the place to remind you that the Montgolfier brothers who invented and ascended in the first hot air balloon were born in Annonay. By the way, the French for hot air balloon is "montgolfière". Doubles 170F (with basin), 230F (with shower/wc), and 270F (with bath).

RESTAURANT MARC ET CHRISTINE

29 av. Marc-Seguin; it's opposite the old station.
☎ 04.75.33.46.97 F 04.75.32.30.00
Closed Sunday evenings, Mondays, during the February school holidays, and Aug 17–Sept 1.

Lunch served noon–2pm and dinner 7.15–9.30pm. The restaurant's customers are mainly locals and they seem to appreciate the inventive cooking. Christine gives her guests a warm welcome and ushers them into a sitting room done in peachy tones. Have a look at the fresco on the wall which illustrates the fable of the fox and the crow (in which the fox flattered the crow's vanity and got him to drop a particularly tempting piece of cheese that the fox appropriates for himself). Marc does the cooking and prepares dishes that combine classic and local ingredients – there's a crayfish and onion soup or example, and Burgundy snails with pig's trotters. Reckon on 70F for main courses à la carte. Set meals 100–225F. Large selection of wines available by the glass. In summer, enjoy the pleasant garden. A reliable restaurant, because it's run by people who love what they're doing and love their own particular little corner of France.

SATILLIEU 07290 (14KM S)

10% ⌂ |●| HÔTEL-RESTAURANT SAPET

place de la Faurie; from Annonay, follow the signs first for the centre of town and then for Lalouvesc (D578A). You'll find it in the centre of the village.
☎ 04.75.34.95.42 F 04.75.69.91.13
Secure parking. TV.

Lunch served noon–2pm and dinner 7–9.30pm (8pm in winter). This place has an excellent reputation and it has to be said that the welcome was really nice and the cooking first-rate. One of the restaurant's specialities is *crique ardéchoise*, which consists of potatoes cakes (the potatoes having been grated first) sprinkled with garlic, onions and parsley. Set meals 60F (weekdays only), 89F, 110F and 145F. The recently renovated bedrooms are clean and comfortable. Doubles with shower/wc 230F in low season. Half-board starts at 190F but is not compulsory. If you want to go mountain biking or hiking, arrangements can be made. There's also an open air swimming pool in season.

ANSE 69480

|●| LE COLOMBIER

pont de Saint-Bernard; on the outskirts of town, head in the direction of Trévoux; it's just after the bridge.
☎ 04.74.67.04.68 F 04.74.67.20.30
Closed Sunday evenings and Mondays (except April 1–end Sept), and Nov 12–March 1. **Car park.**

Service from noon and 7pm. Boats glide up and down the Saône and busy waiters thread their way through tables of cheerful people in the dining room and out on the terrace tucking into plates of whitebait or frog's legs. Things haven't changed all that much from a hundred or so years ago when labourers and clerks brought their wives and girlfriends for a meal to a riverside café or "guinguette". People have been coming to this particular waterside restaurant for the past 15 years to eat well at reasonable prices. Set meals range in price from 90F (buffet of hors d'œuvres, whitebait, tart) to 220F. And if you like frog's legs, you'll love the 130F set meal.

ARBIGNY 01190

10% ⌂ |●| LE MOULIN DE LA BREVETTE**

How to get there: by the D37 then the D933 and take the little road off to the right between Arbigny and Pont-de-Vaux.
☎ 03.85.36.49.27 F 03.85.30.66.91
Car park. Disabled access.

The inn is housed in an old mill deep in the countryside. The wheel has gone but the river still flows quietly under the trees. The bedrooms are in a converted farmhouse. They're a bit impersonal for such a delightful spot but they're large, bright, comfortable and, of course, quiet. Doubles with shower/wc 250–350F. Numbers 15–19 and 29–32 have the best views. Nice, simple welcome. Cheapest set meal in the restaurant is 110F.

AUBENAS 07200

⌂ |●| HÔTEL DES NÉGOCIANTS*

place de l'Hôtel-de-Ville (Centre); it's in the old part of town opposite the château.
☎ 04.75.35.18.74
Closed Sundays out of season. **Car park. TV.**

You'll get a family atmosphere and home cooking here. To get to the bedrooms, which are pretty uninspiring and not always well soundproofed, you take an old stairway inside a keep. Prices start at 120F and you'll pay 210F for one with shower/wc. Good regional cooking is on offer in the restaurant, with dishes like *caillette* (baked pork and vegetable faggot) done local style, duck with olives, and shoulder of beef. Set meals 40F–103F. Customers tend to be locals.

⌂ |●| CHEZ JACQUES*

9 rue Béranger-de-la-Tour (Centre); it's near the town hall.
☎ 04.75.93.88.74 F 04.75.35.37.54

This very simple restaurant in a steep street in the old part of town offers home cooking and set meals at 65F, 95F (this one has regional specialities) and 120F. Jacques, who was born and bred in the Ardèche, can wax quite lyrical about goat's cheese if you get him started. Try the *caillette* (baked pork and vegetable faggot) and the house desserts. The rooms upstairs are well cared for and have recently been refurbished. Doubles 150F with basin, 240F with shower/wc.

LA PINÈDE**

route du camping Les Pins (North-West); it's 1km from the centre of town, by the D235.
☎ 04.75.35.25.88 ➡ 04.75.93.06.42.
Car park. **TV**. **Disabled access**.

It's probably a good idea to book in summer. A very pleasant location on the fringes of a residential neighbourhood up in the hills overlooking the town. You can be sure of peace and quiet and it's very easy to forget that the town is so near. Doubles from 270F with shower/wc. Note that half-board is compulsory in July and August. Prices start at 260F per person. The restaurant offers acceptable value for money, with set meals 85F, 110F and 170F. You'll get a panoramic view from around the swimming pool, the trees in the grounds provide shade, and there's a pine wood, a tennis court and a climbing wall nearby. A nice place.

RESTAURANT LE FOURNIL

34 rue du 4-Septembre.
☎ 04.75.93.58.68 ➡ 04.75.93.58.68
Closed Sunday evenings and Mondays (except in July and August), during the Christmas, February and November school holidays, and June 15–July 1.

This handsome 15th century building with its patio and its vaults is the ideal setting for sampling the exquisite dishes prepared by Michel Leynaud; it's a very stylish affair altogether, from the welcome you receive to the food. You must try the rabbit in aspic flavoured with old plum brandy or the *terrine* of artichokes with a tomato *coulis*. Main courses à la carte are about 150F. Set meals 98F, 150F, 180F and 260F. The wine list is fairly extensive. The décor in the second dining room could do with being brightened up.

ANTRAIGUES-SUR-VOLANE 07530 (14KM N)

LO PODELLO

How to get there: it's in the village square.
☎ 04.75.38.71.48.
Closed Thursdays, June and October. **Disabled access**.

Hélène is an excellent cook and offers her guests set meals at 95F, 120F and 160F all of which feature traditional old local dishes like *maouche* or *pouitrolle*, thrushes with chestnuts, monkfish *bouillabaisse*, local *cassoulet* and *bombine*. Order in advance. Traditional Ardèche furniture. And the countryside is superb.

SAINT-PONS 07580 (26KM E)

HOSTELLERIE GOURMANDE MÈRE BIQUETTE**

Les Allignols (North); leave the N102 before you get to Alba, turning left onto the D293. Carry on until you reach Saint-Pons, where you should start to see signs for the inn – it's 4km further.
☎ 04.75.36.72.61 ➡ 04.75.36.76.25
Closed Christmas Eve and Christmas Day.
Secure parking. **TV**.

Lunch served noon–2pm and dinner 7–9pm (9.30pm in summer). As the road twists and turns you'll catch sight of a number of signs with messages on them urging you not to give up. This old farmhouse has extensive grounds, a swimming pool, and a terrace with breathtaking views of the mountains. Not a sound breaks the silence. The country-style bedrooms are very handsome with lots of wood around. Beauty doesn't come cheap though — doubles range in price from 290F to 450F with shower/wc or bath. Set meals 100–250F. Half-board 270–350F per person for a minimum of 3 or 4 days, depending on the season. If you're taking full- or half-board, you can borrow a mountain bike.

AUTRANS 38880

10% LES TILLEULS**

La Côte (Centre); from the centre of town, take the Mortier tunnel road. After 150m, you'll see a steep narrow road on the right; the inn is at the top.
☎ 04.76.95.32.34 ➡ 04.76.95.31.58
Car park. **TV**.

Lunch served noon–1.30pm and dinner 7.30–8.30pm; it's clean and comfortable, has new carpets and wallpaper throughout, and offers you a wide range of accommodation to choose from. There are 8 rooms with basin (190–210F), 14 with shower/wc, and one with bath (prices for all of these range from 270F to 290F). There's a lounge with TV on the ground floor. The cheapest (78F) set meal in the restaurant is unpretentious and substantial. Other set meals 95–160F. Dishes include chicken with crayfish, trout with ravioli and *gratin à la crème*. A great place if you're looking for somewhere quiet.

LE MONTBRAND**

How to get there: take the Gève road 500m from the centre of the village and turn off onto the first road on

the left after the cemetery. The hotel is 200m along.
☎ 04.76.95.34.58 F➔ 04.76.95.72.71
Open Christmas–Easter, July and August; other times of the year by reservation only. **Car park**. **TV**.

Being a bit out of the village means it's quiet — there's nothing at the back but fields and woods. In winter, the cross country ski trails start practically at the front door. Relax in the cosy lounge with its wood panelling. You can have breakfast there too or it can be brought up to your room. There are two rooms with shower/wc and six with bath; all are 290F.

MÉAUDRE 38112 (6KM S)

10% AUBERGE DU FURON

How to get there: by the D106.
☎ 04.76.95.21.47 F➔ 04.76.95.24.71
Closed Sunday evenings and Mondays out of season and Nov 1–Dec 15. **Car park**. **TV**.

Lunch served noon–2pm and dinner 7–9pm. At the far end of the village, on the edge of the forest and very close to the ski trails, the inn is wonderfully well situated for both summer and winter activities. The proprietress gives her guests a warm welcome, the kitchen takes care over its preparation of regional dishes, and prices are reasonable. It only has a few bedrooms. They're rustic but comfortable and cost 255F (with bath). Set meals 80–170F. The 140F one — melon with walnut liqueur, chicken with crayfish and *gratin à la crème du Vercors* — got our vote.

BEAUFORT 73270

HOSTELLERIE DU DORON*

place de l'Église (South-East).
☎ 04.79.38.33.18 F➔ 04.79.38.30.96
Closed Friday evenings, Jan 3–Feb 3, April 19–28, and Nov 20–Dec 20. **Car park**.

Beaufort is a typical village. The inn, located in a quiet square, has clean, unfussy rooms. Doubles range in price from 180F (with basin) to 220F (with shower/wc). The cooking too is simple. Set meals 80–125F (one of them features regional dishes). The kitchen has a few specialities, notably herb sausages called *pormoniers*.

HÔTEL-RESTAURANT LE GRAND MONT**

place de l'Église (Centre); take the Albert-Beaufort road.
☎ 04.79.38.33.36 F➔ 04.79.38.39.07
Closed April 28–May 4 and in October. **TV**.

The owners come from around here so of course the menu in the restaurant features primarily regional dishes. For about 100F à la carte, you can have the famous *diots* (vegetable and pork sausages) in white wine together with *crozets* (a type of pasta) and a sauce made from *Beaufort*, the local cheese and (so they say) the best Gruyère that ever was. Set meals are 80F, 95F and 125F and they all contain *Beaufort* in some shape or form, whether it's in a tart, an omelette or a salad. Thirteen rooms have a few doubles with shower/wc and TV for 220F.

HAUTELUCE 73620 (11.5KM N)

AUBERGE D'HALTELOCE

How to get there: take the D925 in the direction of Albertville and after 3km turn right and take the D218 to Hauteluce.
☎ 04.79.38.83.54
Closed whenever the proprietor feels like it.

You might best describe this inn in a remote little village as a bit of a mixture. The music ranges in style from rock to soul to funk to jazz-fusion, while the food is very, very traditional and includes *tartiflette* and *diots* (vegetable and pork sausages) in white wine. And now everybody — young people, tourists, and the old men from the mountains — comes here for a drink, a meal or a game of cards. The young owner, who's mad about music (which you might have guessed from the piles of CDs on the bar) has already become something of a local celebrity. And your enjoyment will in no way be diminished by the very reasonable prices. They do an excellent day's special for 42F, a generous *assiette du montagnard* for 55F, a *menu du jour* for 69F and a *menu complet* for 115F. Needless to say, it's very busy so it's a good idea to book.

BEAUJEU 69430

HÔTEL-RESTAURANT ANNE DE BEAUJEU**

28 rue de la République.
☎ 04.74.04.87.58 F➔ 04.74.69.22.13
Closed Sunday evenings, Mondays, one week in August, and mid-Dec–mid-Jan. **Car park**. **TV**.

Lunch served noon–2pm and dinner 7.30–9pm. If you're wondering about the name of the hotel, Anne de Beaujeu was the daughter of Louis XI. She was around in the late 15th century and though this delightful hotel is old, it's not that old. It has a garden, a plush foyer, and an impressive dining room. The large bedrooms too have the charming country house look. Doubles 335F with shower/wc and 360F with bath. The restaurant serves classic dishes like *chartreuse* of pigeon (braised with cabbage) and monkfish in a white sauce. Prices of set meals (120–280F) are as steep as the hills round about.

|●| AUBERGE DU FÛT D'AVENAS

col du Fût d'Avenas; it's 9km out of town on the D136.
☎ 04.74.04.20.76 F➔ 04.74.69.90.76
Closed weekdays out of season.

There used to be a monastery here a long time ago and the inn, in its own inimitable fashion, is carrying on the monks' tradition of hospitality. The owners, who are cabinet-makers (and craftsmen as much as they are artists) concentrate on that during the winter months, only opening their doors at the weekend until the end of June. There's a lounge area with an open fire and the magnificent cellar is used to exhibit their work. In summer, it's open every day and you eat outside. For 76F, you can have what they call a *casse-croûte beaujolais* — raw ham, sausage, omelette, salad, goat's cheese and tart — at any time, but if you want the 96F country meal, you'll have to order it in advance.

BELLEGARDE-SUR-VALSERINE 01200

⌂ HÔTEL EUROPA**

19 rue Joseph-Bertola (Centre).
☎ 04.50.56.04.74 F➔ 04.50.48.19.11
Secure parking. TV.

The outside's not in the best of taste but at least you can see it a long way off. However, you won't be disappointed with what's inside. The double rooms are modern and all the same except that they're either pink or green, depending on which floor you're on. They're all the one price too — 250F. Very hospitable owners. You can have a meal as long as you order it in advance.

LANCRANS 01200 (3KM N)

10% ⌂ |●| LE SORGIA**

Grande-Rue (North-West); follow the signs for Col de la Faucille.
☎ 04.50.48.15.81 F➔ 04.50.48.44.72
Closed Sunday evenings, Mondays, and end Aug–Sept 20. **Secure parking. TV.**

A large chalet-type building. The restaurant is fairly ordinary, offering generous portions of simple dishes. Set meals 75F and 170F. The rooms are clean and very comfortable for the price. Doubles 215F with shower/wc and 235F with bath. Go for one overlooking the valley.

CHÂTILLON-EN-MICHAILLE 01200 (5KM NW)

10% ⌂ |●| AUBERGE DE LA FONTAINE**

Ochiaz (East); take the D101 in the direction of Vouvray, Seyssel. The inn's on the outskirts of Ochiaz, just after Vouvray.
☎ 04.50.56.57.23 F➔ 04.50.56.56.55
Closed Sunday evenings, Mondays, Jan 4–30, and June 9–17. **Secure parking.**

The spring in the inn's name is just by the roadside, in front of this pretty country house. The garden is particularly pleasant in fine weather. You'll be delighted with your welcome. The rooms are comfortable and quiet and you'll get a good night's sleep. Prices are reasonable — doubles 200F with shower/wc and 220F with bath. The restaurant is more expensive but quality doesn't come cheap. Set meals 98F (weekdays)–300F. This is a high-class establishment — you won't be disappointed.

BELLEVILLE 69220

|●| LE BUFFET DE LA GARE

place de la Gare.
☎ 04.74.66.07.36 F➔ 04.74.69.69.49.
Closed evenings (except by reservation), weekends, and August. **Car park.**

Stations are no longer the things dreams are made of so you'll probably think you're having an optical illusion when you see this cute little house all bright and shiny, full of flowers and house plants, with café curtains at the windows, and decorated with old posters, Art Deco light fixtures, and mirrors that don't look as if they've been turned out by the thousand. Proprietress Hélène Bessy always has a smile and a kind word for her customers. The 89F set meal is chalked up on the blackboard and might consist of leeks *vinaigrette*, stuffed tomatoes and courgettes, cheese and dessert. Her husband supplies the wine. Reservations necessary in the evening. But if you're there during the grape harvest, don't be surprised to find the place is still pretty busy at one o'clock in the morning.

SAINT-LAGER 69220 (6KM W)

|●| LE GOUTILLON

Centre; take the D37 in the direction of Beaujeu as far as Cercié then turn left.

☎ 04.74.66.82.69 ℻ 04.74.66.84.48
Closed Tuesday evenings, Wednesdays, and the November school holidays.

Lunch served noon–2pm and dinner 7.15–9pm. This is a very pretty restaurant located in the village square practically next door to the old weighbridge. In fine weather, the people on the terrace bring a bit of life to the square. If you're looking for a cosy refuge, this is ideal even on the dullest days since both the dining room and the proprietress are cheerful and friendly. Good set meals 85–184F. The one at 127F — rabbit stew and *andouillette* (a type of sausage) in Saint-Véran — just eases the others into second place. You might as well go on drinking Beaujolais-Villages — they've got a big selection.

QUINCIÉ-EN-BEAUJOLAIS 69430 (8.5KM W)

RESTAURANT LA VIGNE ET LES VINS

Centre; follow the signs for Beaujeu then turn left once you've passed Cercié.
☎ 04.74.04.32.40
Closed Tuesdays.

They don't go on serving for very long, so get there early! A typical little village clinging to the side of a hill, Quincié produces a Beaujolais-Villages that made our day. The restaurant, located in the square, doesn't look like much but it offers good home cooking. There's just one set meal but it changes every day and will set you back all of 60F. Doubles from 180F with basin. A traditional country restaurant that's a really nice place to stop.

RESTAURANT AU RAISIN BEAUJOLAIS

How to get there: it's on the Belleville-Beaujeu road.
☎ 04.74.04.32.79 ℻ 04.74.69.02.12
Closed evenings, Saturdays, and three weeks in August.

Service noon–3pm. Here's the archetypal unpretentious bistro — just the kind of place you want to come across at lunchtime in wine-growing country. The proprietor, a man who's never stuck for anything to say, looks after the dining room while his wife is busy in the kitchen preparing the kind of dish that needs long slow cooking. You'll be spoiled for choice when it comes to wine, with all that Beaujolais around. There's an enclosed and air-conditioned terrace, which is great in summer. Try the 100F set meal, which comes with snails in garlic butter and *andouillette* (a type of sausage) in Mâcon-Village.

AUBERGE DU PONT DES SAMSONS

Le Pont des Samsons; take the D37 in the direction of Beaujeu.
☎ 04.74.04.32.09
Closed Wednesday evenings and Thursdays. **Car park**.

Service until 2pm at lunchtime and 9pm in the evening. The junction makes an ideal location. The restaurant doesn't look like much from the outside but that's our only negative comment. The menu is mouthwatering, you'll get a pleasant welcome, the décor is nice, it's very clean, the service comes with a smile, the cooking is excellent of course, and the prices won't put you off your food (which might not actually be such a bad thing since the portions are so big). The 95F set meal offers salad *beaujolaise* and *andouillette* (a type of sausage). The next more expensive ones — 125F, 155F and 205F — tend more towards variations on local specialities. Attentive service from start to finish.

CHIROUBLES 69115 (11KM NW)

LA TERRASSE DU BEAUJOLAIS

How to get there: take the col du Truges in the direction of Avenas.
☎ 04.74.69.90.79
Closed evenings Sunday–Tuesday except week ends Nov 15–March 15. **Car park**.

Lunch served 11.30am–2pm and dinner 6.30–8.30pm. Even though the roads in Beaujolais country twist and turn, you can't miss this place. It looks so gorgeous that you're sure the bill is going to be astronomical and the food diabolical. How wrong can you be? The Rongeats are not the kind of people to let things go to their head and you'll get a cordial welcome, something that is pretty rare in these parts. A la carte they do good mixed salads, great *terrines* and the local *andouillette* (a type of sausage). If you're really hungry, try the 125F set meal, which includes dessert. If you feel like pushing the boat out (but remember, no-one's forcing you) there are other set meals at 150F and 190F.

ODENAS 69460 (12KM SW)

CHEZ JEAN-PIERRE

How to get there: head for Beaujeu and when you reach Cercié, turn left onto the D43.
☎ 04.74.03.40.55
Closed evenings and Dec 23–Jan 10.

Jean-Pierre Angoud, a mountain of a man with an enormous beard and a loud voice that can have quite an effect on children, may look intimidating but in fact he's a pussy cat. He loves it when people criticize Beaujolais Nouveaux which he despises and is quick to sing the praises of his Côtes-de-Brouilly, which he's ready to defend to the death; it's wonderful to be welcomed by him as he stands under the big plane tree outside his restaurant, and you finish up everything on your plate – *andouillette*, frog's legs or rib steak – because you don't want to upset him, and you drain your glass even if you don't think too much of his Côtes-de-Brouilly. To help the digestive process, join in a game of boules after you've eaten. Set meals 90–162F.

BOËN 42130

LE CUVAGE

La Goutte des Bois; it's 1km out of Boën going in the direction of Leigneux, on a narrow road overlooking the D8.

☎ 04.77.24.15.08

Closed Mondays and Tuesdays Oct 1–April 1.

Two of the greatest *bon viveurs* in the Saint-Étienne restaurant business have recently reappeared on the scene and bought this restaurant, the mere name of which must have drawn them like a magnet. Brothers Gilles and Patrick Pampagnain, enormous men with an enormous appetite for life, good food and good wine, have put together their set meals as if they were catering for themselves. For 78F, you get *charcuterie*, house *terrine* and *crudités* (as much as you can eat), followed by meat or fish, a selection of superb cheese, and dessert. On weekday lunchtimes, you can have the day's special, a choice of cheese or dessert, wine, and coffee for 65F. There's live music on Friday and Saturday evenings sometimes, in a room decorated to look like a pub. Sunday lunchtime, weather permitting, they serve spit-roasted suckling pig on the terrace.

SAIL-SOUS-COUZAN 42890 (6KM W)

LES SIRES DE SEMUR*

☎ 04.77.24.52.40

Closed Friday evenings, Saturday lunchtimes, Sunday evenings, and two weeks in July and August.
Car park. **TV**.

This place, on a village square dominated by the ruins of a medieval castle, is run by a very nice man from Burgundy and his wife and offers authentic cooking by a chef who is always on the lookout for new ideas. One of his greatest sources of inspiration is very old cookbooks and you must try his guinea fowl in puff pastry with a sauce made from a recipe by Apicius, the Roman gourmet. Set meals 85–225F. The restaurant's next to a spring, but you needn't worry about that being an indication of a dry house – the wine cellar is well stocked! The hotel, a decent 1-star, is being renovated. Rooms 165–215F (shower and wc in the corridor). You'll get a very nice welcome. The many reps who stay here enoy the homely atmosphere.

BONNEVAL-SUR-ARC 73480

10% HÔTEL LA BERGERIE**

How to get there: it's 100m from the tourist information office.

☎ 04.79.05.94.97 F 04.79.05.93.24

Closed May 1–June 15, Oct 15, and all of October, November and December. **Secure parking**. **TV**. **Canal+**.

A rather ugly but light and airy hotel in the middle of Vanoise park opposite the magnificent massif des Évettes. The cooking is typical of the Savoie and local produce features in dishes like *fondant* of salmon, cheese tart (made with Beaufort, one of the Savoie cheeses), *quenelles*, meat-filled ravioli and the local version of meat pasty, and strips of duck meat with morels. Good set meals 68–128F. Doubles with shower or bath 280–300F.

AUBERGE LE PRÉ CATIN

☎ 04.79.05.95.07 F 04.79.05.88.07

Closed Mondays, May 3–June 18, and Sept 25–Dec 19.
TV.

Lunch served noon–2pm and dinner 7–9pm. A lovely stone house with a roof made of "lauzes", which are flat stones weighing an average of 70kg. It was built only recently but it's in the style typical of the area and blends in well with the other buildings in this very pretty village. In any case, it offers real gourmet cooking that makes a pleasant change from the eternal *tartiflette* and *raclette*. The dining room has been tastefully decorated in pale shades and there's always a fire in winter (the windows are tiny so as not to lose any of the heat). It all makes for a very cosy and relaxing setting. They have quite a variety of set meals – which is probably bad news if you can never make up your mind – ranging in price from 68F (lunchtimes in winter) to 165F. There's one at 98F where all the dishes feature cheese, a vegetarian one at 125F, and one of local specialities at 143F. If none of that appeals, there's *poulet de Bresse* with *crozets* in a dry white Savoie wine, *diots* (pork and vegetable sausages) in wine, ravioli stuffed with snails and so on. Really, there's something to satisfy the most demanding palate. You'll get a friendly welcome from your delightful hosts Josiane and Daniel. As soon as the fine weather arrives, the terrace under the trees comes into its own; it's a pity it's so close to the road, but then if there wasn't any road how would you get here?

BONNEVILLE 74130

10% HÔTEL DE L'ARVE**

70 rue du Pont (Centre).
☎ 04.50.97.01.28 F 04.50.25.78.39
Closed Friday evenings and Saturdays (except in February and August) and in September.
Secure parking. TV.

A conventional provincial hotel where the owner plays cards with his mates in the evening. Doubles with shower/wc 240F. Ask for one at the back, where you'll overlook a little flower-filled patio and picturesque rue Brune. Set meals 77–195F. The simple traditional dishes are fairly conventional too but they're good — try the fricassee of scallops with ceps, veal kidneys with chanterelle mushrooms, panfried scallops caramelized in orange juice, langoustines with bacon or the breast of duck with quinces. Fast friendly service.

MONT-SAXONNEX 74130 (11KM SE)

HÔTEL-RESTAURANT LE JALOUVRE*

How to get there: take the N202 as far as Thuet and then the D286 which goes up towards Mont-Saxonnex.
☎ 04.50.96.90.67
Closed in May and Sept 15–beginning Dec.
Secure parking.

A simple welcoming little hotel; it's got a homely atmosphere and is disorganized in the nicest possible way. Typical Savoy — ie rustic — décor in the bedrooms, which are clean and well cared for. Doubles 170F with basin, 220F with shower/wc. The lime tree on the terrace provides welcome shade in hot weather. Simple cooking.

BOURG-D'OISANS (LE) 38520

LE FLORENTIN**

rue Thiers (Centre).
☎ 04.76.80.01.61 F 04.76.80.05.49
Closed Tuesdays in May, June and October and Nov 3–Dec 20. **Car park. TV.**

The Nevros have created a very homely atmosphere here and they'll be able to give you all sorts of good advice on things to do and see in the area. Clean and comfortable doubles 250F, with a 20% reduction in prices April–June and Sept–Oct. In the restaurant, take our advice and have the avocado stuffed with salmon mousse, the escalope of veal with herbs or the roast lamb. Cheapest set meal, available every day, is 108F.

GARDE (LA) 38520 (4KM N)

10% LES GORGES DE SARENNE

Centre; take the N91 then the D211.
☎ 04.76.80.07.85
Closed Tuesdays out of season. **Car park. TV.**

Service from noon and 7pm. There are 21 bends in the road up to Alpe-d'Huez and this restaurant deserves to be a rest stop on your own version of the Tour de France. You'll just have time for a quick glance at the gorges and the forest before you find yourself tucking into *raclette*, fondue or *gardette*, the restaurant's own variation on the fondue theme. Fast friendly service. The cheapest set meal — 69F — comes with a very good trout with an almond stuffing. Other set meals at 79F, 89F and 120F are very reasonable, something which can't be said for the nearby famous ski resort. They have a few rooms. Reckon on paying 350F for two sharing. The price includes breakfast and dinner (drink extra).

ORNON 38520 (7KM S)

RESTAURANT LE POTIRON

La Palud; take the D526 in the direction of La Mure.
☎ 04.76.80.63.27.
Closed Sunday evenings out of season. **Car park.**

The restaurant stands at a bend in the road. For 65F, it can do you what it calls a country snack — raw ham, bacon omelette and fresh cream cheese — at any time or you could just have soup, a salad or some terrine. If we recommend the 95F set meal, which comes with a plate of raw ham and the meat dish of the day, it's because it's served with vegetables prepared in Dany's own special way — you might get celery flan, courgette fritters with coriander, or what they call "donkey's ears", which are in fact vegetable turnovers. And do try the homemade walnut or gentian wine. If you're here in winter, it's a good idea to book in advance, otherwise you might find it's closed.

VENOSC 38520 (15.5KM SE)

10% LE LAUVITEL

La Danchère; take the N91 as far as Clapiers and then the D530. Before you get to Venosc, you'll see a little bridge on the right – it leads up to Danchère.
☎ 04.76.80.06.77 F 04.76.80.29.64
Open by reservation only Sept–Jan, April and May.
Car park.

Jocelyne Guerre spent ten years of her adult life in Nepal before coming back in 1994 on impulse to open this hotel near the hiking trails south of Lake Lauvitel. She's spent practically every day here since putting the place to rights. She has about 15 rooms, all with new bed linen. The views are superb and you can be sure of a good night's sleep. Half-board is 260F for a room with shower, 330F with bath. She likes to ring the changes as far as food is concerned and regulars have become quite used to following up their trout *meunière* (coated in flour and fried in butter) in a vermouth sauce with *dal bhat*. You'd have to go to Nepal to find a better version. Meals, which are 80–120F without wine, are served in the dining room or in the garden in summer. In winter, a shuttle bus will pick you up at Bourg-d'Oisans and you can get there by the Venosc-Les 2-Alpes cable car.

10% HÔTEL-RESTAURANT LES AMIS DE LA MONTAGNE*

Le Courtil; take the N91 then the D530.
☎ 04.76.11.10.00 F 04.76.80.20.56
Closed April 20–June 15 and Sept 8–Dec 20.

If you need anything at all while you're in Venosc, a real little mountain village 1,000m up, ask one of the Durdan clan. They run hotels and restaurants and give ski lessons, they know how to do everything and teach others to do it too. The older members of the family rent out furnished rooms, while the younger generation run shops, bothies/basic accommodation gîte, grocery stores, pizza parlours and so on. Most of their efforts, winter and summer alike, are focused on this hotel, which is sheer delight if you're keen on mountains (the real thing that is) and are looking for peace and quiet. Rooms 250–300F and half-board 240–320F per person. Great breakfast. The grill room, with lots of atmosphere, has appealing set meals at 100F and 146F. Do try the first, which comes with salad *dauphinoise*, *grenaillade* with Saint-Marcellin (a mild cheese) and fresh cream cheese with bilberries. The desserts look good and taste even better. The hotel has a pool, a Turkish bath and a sauna if you feel you have to do something about your calorie intake.

BOURG-EN-BRESSE 01000

HÔTEL RÉGINA**

6 rue Malivert (Centre).
☎ 04.74.23.12.81. F same
Secure parking. **TV**. **Canal+**. **Disabled access**.

The proprietress, a fine woman in every respect, is quite a character. For 20 years now she's been passionate about her hotel and her garden. The one is as pleasant as the other and you'll soon feel at home in the hotel. And it's cheap — doubles 190F or 195F — clean, and well cared for. We liked numbers 12, 14 (our favourite) and 16. An ideal place to stay if you're looking to spend a few days in the area.

HÔTEL-RESTAURANT DU MAIL**

46 av. du Mail (West); from the centre of town, follow the signs for Villefranche-sur-Saône.
☎ 04.74.21.00.26 F 04.74.21.29.55
Closed Sunday evenings, Mondays, July 14–Aug 5, and Dec 22–Jan 6. **Secure parking**. **TV**.

The rooms are comfortable, pretty, decorated in contemporary style and — a plus if you're here in summer — air-conditioned. Go for one overlooking the garden — despite the double glazing the station's a bit too close for comfort as far as the others are concerned. Good value for money. Doubles 180F with shower, 260F with bath. The restaurant's rather plush, with extremely comfortable chairs and sytlish service, and is popular with the locals. Cheapest set meal 105F, others 150–300F. Traditional local cooking with dishes like frog's legs, *poulet de Bresse* and an impressive dessert trolley. Nice terrace. A good professional restaurant with no surprises.

HÔTEL DE FRANCE***

19 place Bernard (Centre).
☎ 04.74.23.30.24 F 04.74.23.69.90.
Secure parking. **TV**.

The location might be slap bang in the middle of Bourg but the little square is delightful, almost like a village square. The hotel first opened its doors back in the middle of the last century and looks no older now than it did then. The foyer is almost luxurious and you'll feel reluctant to walk on the superb mosaic. The bedrooms are similarly impressive with their fireplaces (now purely ornamental, unfortunately) and rustic furniture. and come in a wide range of prices. Doubles 195F with washing facilities (no TV), 330F with shower/wc and 380F with bath. Some have been refurbished. The atmosphere is a bit upmarket of course but you'll get a nice welcome and staff are approachable. There's a hushed atmosphere in the bar, which is open till very, very late.

10% LES NÉGOCIANTS**

9 rue Charles-Robin (Centre); it's at the corner of 10 rue du 4-Septembre.
☎ 04.74.23.13.24 ➡ 04.74.23.71.61
Closed Saturdays and Sundays out of season. **TV**.

This 17th century coaching inn, a half-timbered building with a wooden balcony, fronts onto two streets. The country-style bedrooms – 260–280F (with bath) are quiet and come with shower or bath and direct phone. There's nothing much – good or bad – to say about the welcome but it's a quiet, charming, historic and handsome hotel and you could do worse than to spend the night here.

LA PETITE CROÛTE

9 rue Jules-Migonney; it's in the old part of town.
☎ 04.74.45.34.86
Closed Saturday lunchtimes, Sundays, and public holidays.

This is a fairly classy restaurant in the pedestrian precinct. The dining room is quite magnificent with stone walls, Provençal print tablecloths and subdued lighting. Set meals 85F–145F. A bit on the dear side but you'll get value for money. The cooking is first-rate, the portions are generous, and the house *terrines* are wonderful. And then there are lots of dishes of the kind we like, updated for modern tastes, including stuffed pig's ear with green peppercorns, panfried frog's legs with a parsley garnish, and *poulet de Bresse* with morels in a cream sauce. You'll see a whole range of ingredients here that you rarely see elsewhere. And if none of the above appeals, you can choose from the à la carte menu.

LA TABLE RONDE

126 bd de Brou (South-West); head for the church of Brou.
☎ 04.74.23.71.17
Closed Saturday lunchtimes, Sundays, and two weeks in August.

Lunch served noon–2.30pm and dinner 7.15–11pm. In the space of just a few years, this restaurant has become THE place to go to in Bourg. Take our advice and book, because the cosy dining room is small. Lots of big names have eaten here, including rock singer and film star Johnny Hallyday and actress Josiane Balasko (remember her opposite Gérard Depardieu in "Trop Belle pour Toi"?). If you think all those photos of famous people on the walls are in bad taste, keep your opinion to yourself or you'll upset the very nice proprietress. Chef Stéphane Arthur trained under Georges Blanc and his former teacher doesn't need to be ashamed of him. The cooking is a mixture of new and old, fairly rich, and full of taste and flavour. At 78–98F, the set meals are well within the reach of mere mortals and change every week according to how the chef feels and what the market has to offer. If breastbones of chicken are available, jump at the chance. À la carte is a bit more expensive but *poulet de Bresse* with crayfish isn't something you have every day now, is it? Courteous service.

RESTAURANT DE L'ÉGLISE DE BROU

162 boulevard de Brou (South-West); head for the church of Brou.
☎ 04.74.22.15.28
Closed Tuesdays, Wednesdays, June 15–July 15, and during the Christmas holidays.

Lunch served noon–2pm and dinner 7.30–9.30pm. As you might have guessed from the name, the restaurant is across the way from the famous and recently renovated church, which is fairly restrained as Gothic churches go. There's nothing flashy about the restaurant either. The décor is banal in the extreme but what matters here is the food on your plate. And what you'll get is good traditional regional cooking and things like frog's legs with a parsley garnish, *quenelles* of pike with crayfish tails, *poulet au vinaigre* (chicken with shallots, tomatoes, white wine, vinegar and cream), and a quarter of *poulet de Bresse* with a cream and morel sauce. The cheapest set meal is 85F and consists of starter, main course, and a choice of cheese or dessert. Other set meals 112–195F. Since the portions are on the generous side, a walk may be in order. How about the nearby monastery, the only one in France with three cloisters?

CEYZÉRIAT 01250 (8KM SE)

10% HÔTEL-RESTAURANT RELAIS DE LA TOUR**

1 rue Joseph-Bernier (Centre); on the D979.
☎ 04.74.30.01.87 ➡ 04.74.25.03.36

Closed Wednesdays and Sunday evenings out of season and Oct 15–Nov 10. **TV**.

This is your classic country hotel with its bar cum betting shop full of the usual customers. So it's a bit of a surprise, once you're past the reception desk and the lounge (which must have been modern in the 70s) to find rather plush country-style bedrooms that have a certain charm. Reckon on paying 220F for a double with bath. The dining room with its deep comfortable chairs and antique dresser is equally impressive. Traditional regional cooking that's decent enough. Set meals start at 75F.

MEILLONNAS 01370 (15KM NE)

|●| AUBERGE AU VIEUX MEILLONNAS

How to get there: take the N83 in the direction of first Lons-le-Saunier, then the A40 and last Meillonnas; or take the D979 in the direction of Oyonnax and turn off onto the D52.
☎ 04.74.51.34.46 F➜ same
Closed Wednesdays and during the February school holidays. **Car park**.

Lunch served noon–2pm and dinner 7–10pm. A little village inn in a pretty ochre-coloured stone house that's typical of this peaceful part of the world. Monsieur does the cooking while Madame looks after the front of house. In fine weather, eat in the delightful garden with its weeping willows, pine trees and — no, you're not seeing things, they ARE banana trees. Maybe there's a microclimate here. In any case, the cooking too is bright and sunny. There's raw ham, veal escalopes in lime juice, rabbit and rosemary in puff pastry, and medallions of monkfish with saffron. The presence on the menu of chicken with cream and morels and of frog's legs with a parsley garnish is a reminder that the restaurant is halfway between Bresse and the Jura. Wide range of good set meals from 65F (very acceptable but available weekday lunchtimes only) to 220F.

SAINT-LAURENT-SUR-SAÔNE 01750 (29KM W)

|●| LE SAINT-LAURENT

1 quai Bouchacourt (South-East).
☎ 03.85.39.29.19
Closed mid Nov–mid Dec.

Even if you don't get the table Mikhail Gorbachev and François Mitterand had when they dropped in unannounced in 1993, you might get one on the wonderful terrace that overlooks the placid Saône. You can safely leave the rest to Marc Drillien, a disciple of Georges Blanc (the region's leading chef), and we guarantee you'll be completely won over. What you'll get is first-class cooking in a very refined old-style bistro setting — a marriage made in heaven. Prices are extremely reasonable. The 98F set meal (available every day) is a real bargain, consisting of appetizer, warm sausage and lentils *vigneronne*, *blanquette* of pollack with herbs or traditional *blanquette de veau*, and cake with hot chocolate sauce. You can wash it all down with a small carafe (46 cl) of Mâcon Village at 47F. Other set meals 140F, 160F and 220F. And how about these dishes, chosen at random from the à la carte menu — venison stew with caramelized apples, oven-roasted pigeon, cod with buttered potatoes sprinkled with ginger, *andouillette* with shin of veal *parmentier*, and snail and mushroom ravioli. Best to book if you want to sample these delights. The town's lit up at night and you'll have a stunning view of it and the old bridge.

BOURGET-DU-LAC (LE) 73370

⌂ |●| HÔTEL DU LAC

bd du Lac (Centre).
☎ 04.79.25.00.10
Closed Wednesdays and Nov 20–March 15.
Car park. **Disabled access**.

The hotel, a pretty stone building that stands close to the water, has been in the same family for four generations. Very simple doubles with basin 180F. In summer, sit on the flower-filled terrace and watch the comings and goings at the lakeshore. Fish is, of course, much in evidence on the à la carte menu and in the set meals (100–165F). There's whitebait, for example, and lavaret (a fish something like salmon that's found in deep lakes). Half-board (220F per person) is compulsory in July and August.

10% ⌂ |●| HÔTEL-RESTAURANT LA CERISAIE**

618 route des Tournelles (North); 2.5km from Bourget, take the D42 in the direction of Les Catons.
☎ 04.79.25.01.29 F➜ 04.79.25.26.19
Closed Sunday evenings, Wednesdays out of season, the first week in January, and during the November school holidays. **Car park**. **TV**.

Lunch served 12.15–2pm and dinner 7.15–9pm. The hotel stands at the foot of the mountain known as Dent du Chat surrounded by fields planted with a few cherry trees. The proprietors are from Chamonix — Brigitte looks after the hotel side of things while husband Philippe does the cooking. All seven rooms are called after plants and four of them have a splendid view of the lake (which was a source of inspiration for Lamartine, one of France's great Romantic poets). Doubles 250F with shower/wc. The cheapest set meal is 98F. Try the fillets of *lavaret* (a fish like salmon) or the *Saint-Marcellin* (a mild cheese) *en chemise*. Fish dishes à la carte.

BOURDEAU 73370 (3KM N)

HÔTEL-RESTAURANT LA TERRASSE**

☎ 04.79.25.01.01 F➜ 04.79.25.09.97
Car park. TV.
Restaurant closed Oct 15–March 1. Hotel closed Sept 15–June 15. Both closed Mondays.

A delightful little village. The stone building that houses the hotel and restaurant stands on the steep wooded shore of the lake. Doubles with bath 280F. You can pick up an enormous number of TV channels but why you would want to watch TV when the dining room, the garden and the terrace all have such wonderful views? There's a wide choice of set meals, ranging in price from 98F (weekdays) to 240F, and a lot of fish dishes à la carte, including braised char in Chardonnay. Only to be expected of course since Bourdeau used to be a fishing village.

VIVIERS-DU-LAC 73420 (3KM E)

RESTAURANT LA MAISON DES PÊCHEURS

611 rive du Lac (East); follow the lakeshore in the direction of Aix-les-Bains.
☎ 04.79.54.41.29. F➜ same
Closed Tuesdays in winter.

If you wander into the garden of this waterside restaurant, you'll be met with the sight of brightly coloured fishing boats that have been hauled out of the water to dry. In the bar, fishermen compare the size of their catch over a drink while in the kitchen Titi is busy preparing the fish dishes that have been the mainstay of his restaurant's reputation over the past 15 years. There's fillets of perch or *lavaret* (which resembles salmon) frog's legs, trout, and whitebait. Cheapest set meal 90F (110F at weekends).

BOURG-SAINT-ANDÉOL 07700

HÔTEL-RESTAURANT LE PRIEURÉ**

quais du Rhône.
☎ 04.75.54.62.99 F➜ 04.75.54.63.73
Closed Saturday lunchtimes and Sunday evenings out of season, and Sundays in summer. **TV**.

The oldest part of this imposing building on the banks of the Rhône dates from the 12th century. We were drawn to it as much for its architecture as its bedrooms (all different), its lounges and the terrace overlooking the river. Doubles from 280F. Breakfast 38F. Half-board (340F) is not compulsory. Cheapest set meal 68F (not available evenings and Sundays), others 98–145F. One of the chef's specialities is fricassee of duck with a tarragon sauce. A well-run hotel.

BOURG-SAINT-MAURICE 73700

HÔTEL-RESTAURANT LA PETITE AUBERGE*

Le Reverset; it's 1km from the centre of town on the N90 in the direction of Moûtiers.
☎ 04.79.07.05.86 F➜ 04.79.07.26.51
Closed May. Restaurant closed Sunday evenings and Mondays. **Car park. Disabled access.**

Lunch served noon–2pm and dinner 7.30–9pm. Away from the motorway, this is a quiet little inn with unpretentious but comfortable rooms which cost 250F with shower or bath. The restaurant (tel 04.79.07.37.11), which is not part of the hotel, offers simple, pleasant food of consistent quality. Fast friendly service. Meals are served in the low-ceilinged dining room in winter, while in summer you can eat on the terrace with trees all around. Set meals 80F (weekdays), 118F and 128F. Specialities are *diots* (vegetable and pork sausages) in white wine, fondue, *tartiflette*, and *terrine* of duck livers.

SÉEZ 73700 (3KM E)

AUBERGE DE JEUNESSE LA VERDACHE

How to get there: from Séez, head in the direction of Tignes and after 2km take the narrow road opposite Longefoy.
☎ 04.79.41.01.93. F➜ 04.79.41.03.36
Closed Sept 30–Dec 19. **Car park.**

Best to book in advance. The youth hostel stands at the edge of the forest of Malgovert on the banks of the Petite Isère. Nearby is the river's big sister, the Isère, where the youth hostel organizes courses in kayaking and white water rafting. It caters primarily to course participants but will accommodate you if you're just passing through. The rooms, which have recently been renovated, sleep 2, 4 or 6 and cost 50F a night. As in most ski resorts, you'll have to reserve for a minimum of one week in winter. If the hostel's full, they can put you up in a tent for 32F a night. Meals — compulsory in season — are 50F. Half-board 155F in winter, 120F in summer.

10% ⌂ |●| RELAIS DES VILLARDS**

Villard-Dessus; it's 4km from the centre — take the N90 that goes up to the Petit-Saint-Bernard pass.
☎ 04.79.41.00.66 F➔ 04.79.41.08.13
Closed May and beginning Oct–Dec 20. **Car park**. **TV**.

Since Italy is only 20km or so away, this is our last stop before the border; it's a typical chalet, pleasant and expertly run by Madame Mérendet and has 10 pretty rooms with shower or bath at prices ranging from 240F to 320F. Traditional Savoie cooking with a capital T. ie *tartiflette*, *raclette* and so on. Set meals 75F and 150F. You can also try your hand at or take courses in sports like paragliding, riding, white water rafting and mountain-biking or there's an Olympic ski package at Les Arcs. Half-board 240–310F per person based on two sharing a double room.

|●| RESTAURANT L'OLYMPIQUE

rue de la Libération; take either the RN90 in the direction of Tignes-Val d'Isère or the Col du Pont Saint-Bernard.
☎ 04.79.41.01.52
Closed Wednesdays and June 15–July 2.

Lunch served noon–2pm and dinner 7.30–8.45pm. A very simple restaurant that was opened long before the Olympic Games by a local whose good humour is infectious. The 80F set meal at lunchtime is more than acceptable; it's à la carte in the evening and the menu is long and varied, with dishes like fillets of sole in a lemon sauce, veal kidneys in Madeira, and chicken with crayfish. At 58F, their fondue is one of the cheapest in the area, so cheap in fact that a customer once rang up to check they were using real cheese! People come here almost year round to eat, which is a bit unusual in this neck of the woods.

BUIS-LES-BARONNIES 26170

⌂ VVF CANTERELLE "CLOÎTRE DES DOMINICAINS"

rue de la Cour du Roi Dauphin (Centre).
☎ 04.75.28.06.77 F➔ 04.75.28.13.20

Reception staffed 9am–noon and 5pm–7pm. Housed in a restored Dominican in the centre of town. (In case you didn't know, the Dominicans were at the forefront of the Inquisition) This is definitely the best solution if you want to stay in the centre of town but not pay a fortune. Ask for a room that looks out onto the cloisters. Kitchenette, beds on a mezzanine floor, shower and you can store your bike in the courtyard. 240F for a studio.

|●| LE GRILL DU FOUR À PAIN

24 avenue Boissis d'Anglas (South West).
☎ 04.75.28.10.34
Closed Mondays, lunchtimes, and Nov 15–Dec 20.

A nice name for a nice little restaurant squeezed into one of the narrow streets in the centre of town. The service is pleasant and the sophisticated food good and inexpensive. The 58F set meal (out of season) offers *terrine* of vegetables and sautéd lamb d'agneau; while the 98F one comes with *terrine* of lamb served with *tabbouleh* (they use spelt, a kind of wheat that used to be much more common) and sautéd pork with *pistou* (France's answer to pesto). And if you opt for the 120F set meal, you probably won't be able to move for some considerable time afterwards! Wines are very reasonably priced too so it's well worth dropping in if you're in the neighbourhood.

PLAISIANS 26170 (8.5KM SE)

|●| AUBERGE DE LA CLUE

How to get there: take the D72 then the D526.
☎ 04.75.28.01.17
Closed weekdays out of season and Mondays April–Oct.
Car park. **Disabled access**.

The Truphémus family only have to stand at the window that looks on to the Ventoux to see the hordes of gourmets descending (which may not be the right word, given the climb that's involved) on them, especially at the weekend. What's the big attraction? — good food, large portions, and low prices. The two sons do the cooking, while their mother, who's got a terrific laugh and a great line in patter, looks after the dining room. To give you something to nibble on while you're waiting for your meal to arrive, she'll bring over an incredibly good terrine to your table and leave it there until your hors d'œuvres put in an appearance. And speaking of hors d'œuvres, the *caillette* (baked pork and vegetable faggot) with herbs is delicious. If you opt for the 120F set meal, you can have either home-made mutton tripe and sheep's trotters or kid stew as your main course. For dessert, try the quince sorbet with quince liqueur — it's out of this world.

MÉRINDOL-LES-OLIVIERS 26170 (9KM W)

10% ☗ |●| AUBERGE DE LA GLORIETTE

How to get there: on the D147.
☎ 04.75.28.71.08. Fax: 04.75.28.71.08
Closed Sunday evenings and Thursdays out of season, and Jan 5–Feb 10. **Car park**.

This is like something out of a Pagnol film. On your left there's a baker's where people come to bake their own bread and cakes, on your right an old-style restaurant and in between the two a wonderful terrace. Sit in the shade of an old plane tree, gaze at the hillsides planted with olive and apricot trees, let yourself be lulled by the sound of the water from the nearby spring and let your thoughts drift as you eat a hearty breakfast after a good night's sleep in one of the rooms tucked away at the back. All of this peace and quiet can be yours for 200–250F. If you're still there a few hours later lunch on some good savoury tarts, sausage with olives and a fruit tart straight from the oven. And if you still haven't managed to tear yourself away by dinner time, have the 95F set meal of terrine and guinea fowl or anything else that might catch your eye. Neat, eh?

CARROZ-D'ARÂCHES (LES) 74300

☗ |●| LES AIRELLES*

346 route des Moulins (Centre).
☎ 04.50.90.01.02 ⮩ 04.50.90.03.75
Closed in May. **Car park**.

A little hotel with a pleasant atmosphere and 10 rooms – 3 with basin and 7 with shower/wc. Doubles 230–350F. Full board and half-board 210–320F per person depending on the season. Set meals 90F, 95F and 140F. À la carte also available. Reckon on paying about 90F for specialities like *raclette*, fondue, *diots* (pork and vegetable sausages) in white wine, and pela (potatoes, onions and Reblochon cheese) – you'll have to order that in advance. Nice terrace.

CHALAMONT 01320

|●| RESTAURANT CLERC

Grande-rue.
☎ 04.74.61.70.30 ⮩ 04.74.61.75.00
Closed Monday evenings and Tuesdays. **Car park**.

Lunch served noon–2pm and dinner 7.30–9.30pm. The locals have known about this good restaurant for years. The menu tells you that they've specialized in frog's legs for three generations and the cooking is traditional. The chef, representing the third generation, is trying to introduce some changes but doing so very slowly so as not to upset the people who've been coming here since the year dot. In any case, the 135F set meal and the 195F "traditional" (we told you so!) one still offer local dishes – frog's legs sautéd in butter with herbs, salad of nuggets of fried carp (which they've been catching around here since the 12th century), salad of chicken livers and so on. Set meal (weekday lunchtimes) 86F.

CHAMBÉRY 73000

10% ☗ |●| HÔTEL-RESTAURANT AUX PERVENCHES**

Les Charmettes (South-East); from the centre of town head for vallon des Charmettes and the Jean-Jacques Rousseau museum.
☎ 04.79.33.34.26 ⮩ 04.79.60.02.52
Secure parking. **TV**.

Lunch served noon–2pm and dinner 7–9pm (later by reservation). In the late summer of 1736, Jean-Jacques Rousseau set up house with Madame de Warens in Les Charmettes, which he described as being near Chambéry and yet so isolated that it might have been a hundred leagues distant. If he was to come back to the valley now, he'd probably swap the place he stayed in then for this one. It has pleasant bedrooms (from 140F with basin to 190F with bath) and an excellent restaurant (set meals 95–160F with a good stew of scallops in a white sauce, sautéd frog's legs *à la provençale* and duck breast with mushrooms) and the owners fit the picture that Rousseau had of the people of Savoie – "pleasant and honest in their dealings with you.. the best and most sociable people I have ever met."

☗ HÔTEL DES VOYAGEURS

3 rue Doppet (Centre); it's not far from the musée des Beaux-Arts.
☎ 04.79.33.57.00
Closed Sundays 1.30–5.30pm.

You'll find the hotel in a quiet little street in the centre of town. It has the most wonderful bar that could well be part of the museum's collection. The bedrooms, very simple and very clean, are upstairs. Doubles 130F with basin, 150F with shower and wc in the corridor. You'll get a nice welcome from Rose, who comes from the island of Réunion in the Indian Ocean.

☗ LE LION D'OR**

1 av. de la Boisse (South-East); it's across from the station.
☎ 04.79.69.04.96 F➜ 04.79.96.93.20
Secure parking. TV. Disabled access.

The hotel has an impressive façade with lots of balconies and 40 rooms, most of them fairly large. They're also soundproof, which is a plus given the location. Doubles range in price from 165F with basin to 225F with shower/wc or bath. If you're an animal lover, the foyer and bar on the ground floor should appeal.

10% ☗ CITY HÔTEL**

9 rue Denfert-Rochereau (Centre); it's between carré Curial and the cathedral of Saint-François.
☎ 04.79.85.76.79 F➜ 04.79.85.86.11
Secure parking. TV. Canal+. Disabled access.

The hotel is very centrally located. Bedrooms are decorated in contemporary style, which is a bit surprising given that this is an 18th century building. Go for one at the back rather than one with a view of the theatre. They may be soundproof and the street below may be closed to traffic but it can still be fairly noisy with people leaving the theatre after a show and a tobacconist's that seems to be open till all hours. Doubles from 190F with basin to 290F with bath. A practical place to stay if you're just passing through.

10% ☗ |●| HÔTEL-RESTAURANT SAVOYARD**

35 place Monge (South-East); it's near carré Curial.
☎ 04.79.33.36.55 F➜ 04.79.85.25.70
Closed Sundays (except in the case of public holidays and group bookings). **Secure parking. TV. Disabled access.**

Lunch served noon–2pm and dinner 7–10.30pm. There are no surprises in store in this big friendly establishment with ten or so rooms and windowboxes full of geraniums. The rooms are soundproof and have been renovated throughout. Doubles with shower/wc 230–260F. In the restaurant, it's easy to see that the owner is descended from a long line of restaurateurs. He offers set meals at prices ranging from 75F to 200F that feature Savoie specialities and regional produce — only to be expected given the name of the place.

10% |●| RESTAURANT LA POTERNE

3 place Maché (Centre); head for the château.
☎ 04.79.96.23.70
Closed Monday evenings and Sundays. **Car park.**

Lunch served 11.30am–2pm and dinner 7–10.30pm. The restaurant has a little wooden balcony at the bottom of the porte Saint-Dominique stairway that goes up to the château and in fact the vaulted dining room is tucked into one of its buttresses. At lunchtime they do a set meal of the day's special plus cream cheese or dessert for 56F. Other set meals 67–128F. The cooking is simple but of a high standard, with dishes like braised chicken in Calvados and fillets of zander in orange sauce available à la carte.

|●| CAFÉ-RESTAURANT CHEZ CHABERT

41 rue Basse-du-Château (Centre); it's opposite the château.
☎ 04.79.33.20.35
Closed Sundays.

At lunchtime, a noisy cheerful crowd throngs into this bistro in a narrow street that was laid out in the Middle Ages. People with time to spare wait at the old oak counter, where Rémy lines up the glasses of white Savoie wines like Chignin or Apremont. These are to accompany the generous servings of traditional Savoie dishes like *diots* (pork and vegetable sausages) in white wine and veal escalopes with a cream and vermouth sauce. When he tells you what the damage is (which will be all of 64F for a full meal), you'll want to become a regular too.

|●| LA TABLE DE MARIE

193 rue Croix-d'Or (Centre).
☎ 04.79.85.99.76
Closed Sundays and Monday lunchtimes.

Here's how it all began. Marie decided to open a restaurant but she needed a chef and the ads and the interviews weren't any help in finding the pearl she was looking for. And then along came Pascal from the north of France and in two days it was all settled and Pascal had moved to the south-east. Since then, this dynamic duo have been working in partnership, with Marie looking after the customers and Pascal in the kitchen. His cooking is imaginative, constantly changing and yet he lets the food speak for itself. Marie will tell you that he's obsessive, a perfectionist and is constantly looking for new ideas and trying to improve on things. However you look at it, his cooking is wonderful, with dishes like a *tian* of salmon and *rascasse* (scorpion fish), kebabs of monkfish in a bacon and white wine sauce, and *crème brûlée* with orange peel. There's a friendly atmosphere in the tastefully decorated dining room. If you want lots of peace and quiet while you eat, try the little dining room in the old cellar. Alternatively, the terrace is so pleasant that you could linger there for hours putting the world to rights. And last but not least, it's cheap with the day's lunchtime special at 49F and set meals at 79F and 145F. The best restaurant we found in Chambéry.

L'HYPOTÉNUSE

141 carré Curial (Centre); follow the signs for carré Curial.
☎ 04.79.85.80.15 ➡ 04.79.85.80.18
Closed Saturday lunchtimes, Sundays, one week in January, and four in August.

The restaurant stands on an old barracks square. The décor, modern and in good taste (a rare occurrence!) can hold its own against the sophisticated and flavourful cooking of Hubert Bonnefoi as exemplified by the *brioché* of duck with mushrooms and parsley, the steamed sea bass with hazelnut oil, and the kid with morels. Set meals 88F (lunchtimes only) and 98–220F. In summer, sit out on the terrace in the middle of place d'Armes — ie the old parade ground. Don't worry — there won't be any square-bashing squaddies to disturb the peace.

RESTAURANT LA VANOISE

44 av. Pierre-Lanfrey; it's near the main post office.
☎ 04.79.69.02.78 ➡ 04.79.62.64.52
Car park. Disabled access.

Lunch served noon–2pm and dinner 7–10pm. As a tribute to Savoie, chef Philippe Lenain called his restaurant after the national park and the region of the Alps of the same name. He came here from Paris 15 years ago and his adopted home continues to provide inspiration for the regional set meals (140F) that change every two weeks. His menu contains almost as many fish as the local lakes do, with dishes featuring *féra* (a type of salmon), char, *pageot* (a type of sea bream), red mullet and so on. The cheapest set meal is 110F, which is reasonable when you consider that his sauces too are excellent. The wine list is impressive — it will be of interest to connoisseurs and won't overawe the amateur. You can sit out on the terrace in fine weather or the bang up-to-date pink dining room provides a welcome refuge on cloudy days. All in all, the restaurant is that enviable combination of tradition, innovation and quality. Advisable to book.

APREMONT 73190 (8KM SE)

RESTAURANT LE DEVIN

lieu-dit Au Devin; take the D201 and once you get to Apremont, follow the signs.
☎ 04.79.28.33.43
Closed Sunday evenings, Mondays, and Aug 20–Sept 10.

Service noon–3.30pm and 7pm–midnight. The restaurant, tucked away among the hills of Apremont wine country, offers a welcome break from fondue and *raclette*. Specialities include sausages and cabbage, *ravioles* (something like ravioli) and *farçon savoyard*, a dish that offers a subtle mix of sweet and sour in the form of potatoes baked with bacon, prunes, pears, raisins and eggs. The cheapest set meal (weekdays only) is 50F and provides a full country-style meal featuring an omelette of oyster mushrooms. Other set meals 70F, 86F, 90F and 105F.

SAINT-JEAN-D'ARVEY 73230 (8KM NE)

HÔTEL-RESTAURANT THERME*

How to get there: take the N512 and then the D912 in the direction of La Feclaz.
☎ 04.79.28.40.33 ➡ 04.79.28.46.63
Car park. TV.

The rooms, which have a view of the Bauges or the Chambéry valley, are simple. Doubles 140F with washing facilities. Rooms to sleep three 165F, to sleep four 180F. The very large terrace, planted with trees, also overlooks the valley. That's where meals are served in summer. Robust home cooking, with set meals at 85F (weekday lunchtimes only), 120F (Sundays), and 135–150F. Half-board 200F per person.

CHAMONIX 74400

HÔTEL DU FAUCIGNY**

118 place de l'Église (Centre); it's opposite the tourist information office.
☎ 04.50.53.01.17
Closed June 1–30 and Nov 6–Dec 10. **Car park.**

An unpretentious little hotel with a homely atmosphere in a quiet and rather depressing street. Choose your room carefully if you want a view of Mont Blanc — they're not all on that side. Clean doubles with a modest degree of comfort 320F with shower/wc. It doesn't have a restaurant but it does have a pleasant garden.

HÔTEL LA SAVOYARDE***

28 rue des Moussoux (North); it's beside the Brévent cable car station.
☎ 04.50.53.00.77 ➡ 04.50.55.86.82
Closed end of May–mid June and begining of December. **Car park. TV.**

A little chalet, facing Mont Blanc, that's been renovated and extended. It's quiet and covered with flowers. It has 14 rooms with all the mod cons, which justifies the price (around 500F or more depending on the season). The restaurant has very good food and the service is great. The 88F set meal is superb, and offers *Reblochon* (a mild local cheese) in puff pastry or chicory salad, escalope of sea trout with a creamy parsley sauce or the local version of cabbage soup, and cheese or pastry of the day. They also do a 120F set meal. Or if you'd rather go à la carte, then try the jacket potatoes or the *berthou chablaisien*.

ARGENTIÈRE 74400 (6KM NE)

|●| LA CRÉMERIE DU GLACIER

766 route de la Glacière; take the dirt road after the Lognan cable car; in winter take the chemin de la Rosière.
☎ 04.50.54.07.52
Closed mid-Sept–mid-Dec and mid-May–end June.
Car park.

This is where the people from Chamonix come when they want to get out of town. And it really takes them back to their roots. There's *farçon* (potatoes with milk, eggs, bacon, raisins and prunes, the traditional accompaniment to smoked ham or cured meat) for 98F with all the salad and dessert you can eat and on Fridays, if you order in advance, *farçon* with all sorts of pork products. The restaurant's specialities are fondue (55–70F) and all sorts of open cheese sandwiches (30–55F). Salads 20–38F.

LES HOUCHES 74310 (8KM W)

10% ☗ |●| HÔTEL PETER PAN

côté Chavans.
☎ 04.50.54.40.63
Closed Monday evenings, May and Oct 15–Dec 15.
Car park.

An evocative name and the type of hotel you dream about. It's difficult to get a table in the restaurant since the proprietress gives preference to hotel guests. Rooms 200–265F, half-board 250–270F. The restaurant has been in existence for 25 years and at lunchtime there's a substantial 145F *menu du jour* along the lines of tomato and mozarella salad, *croûte*, rabbit *chasseur*, cheese and dessert). In the evening, there's a lighter offering for 95F of home-made soup, calf's liver, and salad. Try this place before the owners are bought out, if only to get a taste of the way they live in the mountains, in a place where time seems to stand still. Superb view from the terrace of the mountains of the Mont Blanc range.

10% ☗ AUBERGE "LE MONTAGNY"

lieu-dit "Le Pont"; as you come into the village coming from Chamonix, it's 450m further along on the left.
☎ 04.50.54.57.37 ➡ 04.50.54.52.97
Car park. **TV**.

What a joy it is to find a place like this after all the standardised hotels that have made a fortune in the past few decades. We're tempted to describe it as old, even if inside there's nothing left of the farmhouse that it once was 100 years ago. It has eight rooms in all. They're quiet and spacious with lots of wood and the bathrooms are bright. Genuine, attentive welcome, and all the information you could ask for about walks in summer and skiing in winter. Incredibly quiet. All rooms 360F. Good breakfast 42F.

CHAMOUSSET 73390

10% ☗ |●| HÔTEL-RESTAURANT CHRISTIN**

La Lilette (centre); take the N90 from Albertville in the direction of Chambéry, and when you reach Pont-Royal, follow the signs for Chamousset.
☎ 04.79.36.42.06 ➡ 04.79.36.45.43
Closed Sunday evenings, Mondays, the last week in April, Sept 15–Oct 2, and Dec 23–Jan 2.
Secure parking. **TV**.

Lunch served noon–1.45pm and dinner 7.30–8.45pm. This is the perfect country inn, standing on a tiny square shaded by chestnut trees with a little river flowing nearby that you can hear but not see because the vegetation is so thick. Lots of people come for the tasty traditional cooking that is served up in generous portions in a pleasant dining room with enormous bay windows. Set meals range in price from 68F (not available Sunday) to 140F. The rooms are large but the buildings they're in are fairly ordinary. Prices start at 190F for a double with shower/wc. If only somebody would move the railway lines!

CHAMPAGNE-EN-VALROMEY 01260

10% ☗ |●| AUBERGE DU COL DE LA LÈBE*

How to get there: take the D8 and follow the signs for Col de la Lèbe.
☎ 04.79.87.64.54 ➡ 04.79.87.54.26
Closed Mondays and Tuesdays (restaurant closed

Monday evenings and Tuesdays in July and August), ten days at the end of June, and Nov 15–Dec 15.
Car park. TV. Canal+.

It's right out in the country, on the way up to the pass. The cosy dining room has lots of wood and house plants. The service is stylish but not in the least pretentious. The cooking is sophisticated and the dishes on offer include slices of duck meat stuffed with *foie gras* and rolled, fillet of beef *gourmandine*, zander with a chive sauce, and orange and chocolate *terrine*. Prices are still affordable, with set meals at 79F (weekdays), 89F, 120F, 148F and 196F. Since this is mountain country, you could also have something chargrilled – simple but good. Rooms are fairly modest but their old-fashioned air gives them a degree of style. You'll get lots of peace and quiet. Doubles 175F with shower, 230F with bath. You'll get a wonderful view of the valley below from the swimming pool.

PETIT-ABERGEMENT (LE) 01260 (15KM N)

10% LA SOUPIÈRE A DES OREILLES

How to get there: on the D31.
☎ 04.79.87.65.81 F 04.79.87.54.46
Closed Mondays (except during school holidays) and in November. **Car park.**

This is a substantial stone building in a quiet village 800m up in the quite wonderful vallée du Valromey; it's almost ten years since Claude Masclet left the French railway company and moved here with his wife Colette. Most of their customers have become friends, which is only to be expected since you so very quickly feel at home here. There's a nice homely atmosphere. The rooms are very very simple but pleasant and the only sound you'll hear is the bells from the little church next door. Doubles with shower/wc 190F. The rustic dining room serves up good home cooking using local ingredients (the raw ham is excellent). Regional specialities include *diots* (pork and vegetable sausages) hot sausage, fondues, and chicken in a sauce of cream and morels). They have a special one-night package for hikers at 180F. The terrace gets the full force of the sun; it's off the bar, where there's always an exhibition of paintings. Claude, who never seems to run out of energy, set up a painting festival, which is held every year at the beginning of August. If you're here in winter and you enjoy cross-country skiing, you'll be in your element. The women's biathlon winner at Albertville was born in the village. We liked this place a lot.

CHAMPAGNY-EN-VANOISE 73350

10% AUBERGE LE BOUQUETIN

Le Planay; head in the direction of Champagny-le-Haut.
☎ 04.79.55.0113. F 04.79.55.04.76
Closed Oct 15–Dec 15. **Secure parking. TV.**

The restaurant may be simple but the cooking makes the effort of getting here worthwhile. Their famous *menu surprise* is available every day for 150F. À la carte, reckon on paying 100–160F for *raclette*, *pierrade* (where your meal is cooked on a hot stone), fondue, *pela* (potatoes, onions and Reblochon cheese), or *croûte savoyarde* (ham on a layer of puff pastry with cheese sauce). The large terrace under the birch trees will give you a panoramic view of Courchevel. They also have rooms and flats that sleep 2–12 people to let on a daily or weekly basis. Lots of facilities.

CHAPELLE-EN-VERCORS (LA) 26420

HÔTEL DU NORD-CHEZ ROGER ET BRIGITTE

av. de Provence (Centre).
☎ 04.75.48.22.13
Closed Oct 10–Nov 10.

Best to book in summer. A wonderfully unobtrusive and simple place with eight unpretentious rooms. Reckon on paying 145F for a double with shower. The restaurant offers home cooking and regional specialities like *ravioles*, (a lot like ravioli), leg of lamb, and trout *meunière*. Set meals 65F (not available Sundays), 70F, 85F and 90F. Half-board 175F. If you don't manage to get a room with a mountain view, console yourself with a visit to the wonderful Draye Blanche caves.

SAINT-AGNAN-EN-VERCORS 26420 (4KM S)

10% AUBERGE MAGALI

D518; head in the direction of col du Rousset.
☎ 04.75.48.22.50
Closed Sunday evenings, Mondays, and Nov 20–Dec 14.
Car park.

Lunch served noon–2pm and dinner 7–9pm (and later). The inn, on the other side of the *grotte de la Luire*, stands by the side of a road that gets little traffic except in July and looks a bit forlorn. And yet this is one of the best restaurants on the Vercors plateau. The Guillemins came here from Toulon and still have their accent and a taste for the sunny cooking of the south. The 95F set meal offers the house *terrine*, guinea fowl, and cream cheese. Other set meals 148F and 240F. You can eat either on the terrace or in the dining room, where there's a fire all year round. The Guillemins also have nine very simple but extremely comfortable rooms with a view of the meadows and the mountain (280–400F with bath).

BOUVANTE 26190 (31KM W)

AUBERGE DU PIONNIER*

col du Pionnier; take the D178 and then the D199 in the direction of col de la Machine.
☎ 04.75.48.57.12 F 04.75.48.58.26
Closed Nov 1–Dec 20. **Secure parking**.

Depending on what state the roads are in, you may have to detour via the forest of Lente, which is actually quite relaxing. A few hairpin bends later, once you've passed col de la Portette, you should see signs for the inn. It has nine very simple rooms (155–250F) that look out onto the mountain, the pine trees, and the meadows where the animals of the forest frolic undisturbed. These Disney-like exteriors give way to Tex Avery-like scenes in the dining room, where hunters sit and talk about hunting and sex. The food is extremely simple. If you take the 80F set meal, the proprietress, an astonishing woman who's cook and waitress will bring you a substantial slice of *pâté*, salad, chicken in cream sauce and potatoes, and a piece of tart. If she takes a liking to you, the coffee's on the house.

CHÂTEL 74390

RESTAURANT L'ABREUVOIR - CHEZ GINETTE**

hameau de Vonnes; head for Switzerland and you'll find the restaurant 1km out of town, very near lac de Vonnes.
☎ 04.50.73.24.89
Car park.

You'll be welcomed by Ginette from behind the bar and she'll serve you local specialities such as *berthoud de la vallée d'Abondance*, which is a platter of cheeses from Abondance (in the Haute Savoie) and elsewhere that have been diced and marinated in white wine vinegar, Madeira and garlic. It then goes into the oven; it's absolutely delicious. If there's a bit of a celebration going on, Louky, who's a real comic, will pick up his accordion and lead you in a well-oiled singsong. They even come here from the Club Med at Avoriaz, which shows you how good it is. Set meals 80–140F. Reckon on about 160F à la carte. You'll get a great view of the mountain and the lake, which is lit up at night, from the garden. If you want to stay, they have doubles ranging in price from 260F to 280F in summer. In winter, it's full board only — 260–280F per person. Free sauna for residents.

10% HÔTEL-RESTAURANT LES FOUGÈRES**

route du Petit-Châtel (Centre).
☎ 04.50.73.21.06 F 04.50.73.38.34
Closed April 20–July 5 and Aug 24–Dec 18.
Secure parking.

The owners are nice young people and they've created a homely country atmosphere in their converted old farmhouse. They have 12 panelled bedrooms, all with shower/wc and recently renovated, from 240F. Half-board 200–275F, less for children. Buffet-style breakfast 48F. They have a delightful and very attractive dining room and the food's good and the service pleasant. Set meals 94F and 140F. Specialities are fondues, *tartiflettes*, and *croûte au fromage*. From the terrace you look due south and have a view of Super-Châtel.

10% L'ARC-EN-CIEL**

au Petit-Châtel (South); it's about 1km from the centre of town.
☎ 04.50.73.20.08 F 04.50.73.37.06
Closed May and June and Sept–Dec 20. **Car park**. **TV**.

This would be just another hotel if it wasn't for the terrific atmosphere created by Henri Gonon, winner of the 1987 European surfing championship — there are always lots of nice young people around. Rooms are large and have a wonderful view of the village and the valley. Doubles with shower/wc or bath 250–330F. Set meal 80F. If you'd rather go à la carte, the restaurant specializes in *fondue*, *raclette*, and *pierrade* (where your meal is cooked on a hot stone). There's a sauna so you can ease your aching muscles or you can relax in the TV room or on the terrace, where you'll get a clear view of the mountains and Super-Châtel.

10% HÔTEL-RESTAURANT LA PERDRIX BLANCHE**

Pré-de-la-Joux (Centre); It's 2.5km from the centre in the direction of le Linga, at the bottom of the cable lifts.
☎ 04.50.73.22.76 F 04.50.73.35.21
Closed mid-May–mid-June and mid-Sept–Nov 1.
Car park. **TV**.

This really delightful chalet, typical of Savoie, is right away from the resort, standing among fir trees at the foot of the ski runs. The rooms — clean, simple and cosy — have lace curtains at the windows and some have a balcony. Doubles 250F. The traditional local cooking — *tartiflette*, *berthoud* (oven-baked marinated cheese) and fondues — may not hold any surprises but the portions are substantial and just the thing after a day's skiing or hiking. The 130F set meal is for big appetites. Half-board 220–260F in summer, 260–360F in winter.

RESTAURANT LA BONNE MÉNAGÈRE

How to get there: it's one street north of the one the tourist information office is in.
☎ 04.50.73.24.45
Closed May and June, mid-Sept–Dec 20, and lunchtimes in summer.

A restaurant that's popular with the ski crowd. Beatrice will welcome you with a lovely smile while Daniel is in the kitchen. A woman's touch is evident in the décor of the two dining rooms, which have old enamel plaques, little bunches of dried flowers and lots of wood. Husband Daniel is in the kitchen, preparing starters like local *charcuterie* or large salads and main dishes like *berthoud* (marinated cheese that has been baked in the oven), fondues, and *croûte aux champignons* (mushrooms on a layer of puff pastry covered with cheese and then grilled). For dessert, try the pear sorbet with pear liqueur. The prices are fair and there's the kind of atmosphere that takes you back to the good old days; it's à la carte only — reckon on paying about 100–120F.

AUBERGE LA HAUTE BISE

Col de Bassachaux; it's 11km from the centre – head in the direction of Linga and go up to the top of the pass, where the road stops.
☎ 04.50.73.31.97
Closed Oct–May.

The inn, a typical Alpine chalet, is in the most wonderful location on a mountain top 1,863m up; it's a real bargain if you're badly in need of some calories and though the cooking may be simple, it's well worth the effort of getting there. *Berthoud* (cheese marinated in white wine, Madeira and garlic and then baked in the oven) is 56F, *tartiflette* 65F, and fondue 70F. Have a look at the walls, which are covered in quotations — each more educational than the last — along the lines of "A forest is like a woman, it is to be conquered, not raped".

CHAPELLE D'ABONDANCE (LA) 74360 (5.5KM W)

10% L'ENSOLEILLÉE**

rue Principale (Centre).
☎ 04.50.73.50.42 Fax 04.50.73.52.96
Closed April 15–end of May and end of Sep–Dec 15.
Car park. TV.

We get more (complimentary) letters about this than any other from our readers in the Haute-Savoie. This huge family house thoroughly deserves all the praise it gets from its regulars, who can't believe it hasn't featured in this guide book before. The rooms (260–450F) have fitted carpets, doilies, prints and traditional décor combined with modern facilities but what impressed us most was the welcome we got from the entire Trincaz family Madame and her husband look after the dining room and their guests while one son takes care of the bar and the *Carnotzet*, where all the fondue lovers gather, and the other is chef. He uses only the finest ingredients for everything, from the selection of various meats cooked on a hot stone (the local speciality) to the *cassolette* of calf's sweetbreads with a creamy mushroom sauce. The dining rooms are as welcoming as the waitresses and full of the sound of people enjoying themselves, so even when it's grey outside the sun is always shining here! Set meals 95–180F.

LES GENTIANETTES**

Centre.
☎ 04.50.73.56.46 Fax 04.50.73.56.39
Car park. TV. Canal+.

Ideal if you need to recharge your batteries. It feels new but the experience and professionalism of the owners are obvious the moment you step inside. It's in the centre of the village, away from the noise of the road and a stone's throw from the cross-country ski trails. It has 30 bright comfortable rooms, 265–380F half-board. The restaurant, decorated like a mountain chalet, serves sophisticated cuisine that's quite inventive for the region and comes as a a nice surprise for the residents and anyone stopping off for a bite to eat. Set meals at 138F and 158F offer dishes like a very good medley of fish with wild chives and escalope of veal with cheese and potatoes. Lovely walks in the surrounding area and pretty little indoor swimming pool.

CHÂTILLON-SUR-CHALARONNE 01400

10% HÔTEL-RESTAURANT DE LA TOUR**

place de la République (Centre).
☎ 04.74.55.05.12 ➡ 04.74.55.09.19
Closed Sunday evenings and Wednesdays.
Secure parking. TV.

This is a delightful place in a delightful well-preserved medieval town. You can't miss the hotel, with its exposed white stonework, half-timbering and pepper-pot turret. It was built in the 16th century (don't worry, it's been restored since!) and has a great deal of style. The inside's not bad either, with comfortable rooms that are good value for money. Doubles 160F with washing facilities, 280F with shower/wc, and 310F with bath. The restaurant's equally good, even if it is a bit expensive with set meals ranging in price from 110F (not available Sundays) to (gulp) 350F.

CORMORANCHE-SUR-SAÔNE 01290 (24KM NW)

10% ⌂ |●| HÔTEL-RESTAURANT CHEZ LA MÈRE MARTINET

How to get there: take the N6 in the direction of Villefranche as far as Crêches-sur-Saône and then the D51; alternatively, take the D51 from Saint-Laurent-sur-Saône.
☎ 03.85.36.20.40 ➡ 03.85.31.77.19
Closed the first fortnight in January. **Car park. TV.**

This is a nice little village inn. Madame Martinet senior still keeps a watchful eye on it, even though her son has taken over the management. They're quite happy not to venture beyond traditional dishes featuring local produce and what they do they do very well. There's breast of chicken in a cream sauce, fresh frog's legs garnished with a mixture of parsley and garlic, salad of lobster and chicken breastbones, duo of zander and carp with leeks, panfried calf's liver and sweetbreads with mushrooms and a stew of lake fish with baby vegetables. The cheapest set meal — 72F — offers warm sausage and whitebait. Other set meals 98–210F. In fine weather, you can sit out on the little terrace in the garden. They have a few very simple rooms — doubles 200F — and you'll get a very warm welcome.

ARS-SUR-FORMANS 01480 (32KM SW)

10% ⌂ |●| HÔTEL-RESTAURANT LA BONNE ÉTOILE**

Centre.
☎ 04.74.00.77.38 ➡ 04.74.08.10.18
Closed Tuesdays and Nov 15–Dec 15.
TV. Disabled access.

Best to book. Although the village is a place of pilgrimage — Jean-Marie Vianney, who was priest here for more than 40 years in the last century, was canonized after his death and made the patron saint of parish priests — it's not something you're very conscious of. Granted, the underground church is enormous and pretty ugly, but at least it's hidden from sight. This is the kind of hotel we like — the rooms are clean and comfortable, and it's got atmosphere. The proprietress hasn't thrown anything away for years and it's a bit like a second-hand shop. Doubles (only 10 in all) 220F with shower/wc.The restaurant is huge (it's got three dining rooms) and, as you would expect, very touristy. Set meals 70F (weekdays) to 130F.

CLUSAZ (LA) 74220

10% ⌂ |●| LES AIRELLES**

Centre.
☎ 04.50.02.40.51 ➡ 04.50.32.35.33
Car park. TV.

In the centre of the village in what might be a pedestrian precinct one day if all the businesses in the area agreed on it. It's a gorgeous little hotel that's been entirely renovated and has bright colourful rooms with all the mod cons. Expect to pay 288–420F in winter and 230–320F in summer, with free use of the jacuzzi, sauna and the swimming pool belonging to the relatives who own the hotel "Les Sapins" a bit further up (the prices there are higher). Genuine simple welcome, just like the food. Set meals 80F (weekday lunchtimes) –155F. All the regional specialities.

10% |●| LE CHALET DU LAC

Lac des Confins; just before you get to the lake, take the dirt road on the right.
☎ 04.50.02.53.26
Car park.

This is a family business and everybody does their bit to keep it running smoothly. Everything's simple and genuine. The menus feature Savoie specialities even if the owner, who spent some time working in Quebec, brought back with him a passion for all things Indian. Set meals (59–129F) offer old-style fricassee of suckling pig, *tartiflette*, sautéd chicken with three types of vinegar and, for people who like that sort of thing, a set meal built around a salad of *tomme blanche*. (This needs to be ordered a couple of days in advance.) Sunny terrace. The atmosphere is informal — it even gets a bit mad some evenings.

|●| RESTAURANT L'OURSON

pl. de l'Église (Centre).
☎ 04.50.02.49.80
Closed Sunday evenings, Mondays out of season, and end of April–beginning of June.

Vincent Lugrin does occasionally seem a bit like a bear with a sore head – maybe that's why he called his restaurant "The Bear Cub"? It's a pretty place on the first floor of a building right in the centre. The prices, like his cooking, are good enough to tempt any gourmet traveller. There's a nice set meal at 99F, while the 128F regional set meal offers warm goat's cheese salad, chicken supreme with herb-flavoured mustard, trio of house cheeses, *mousse glacée* with a herb-flavoured liqueur, 1/2 a bottle of local Gamay, coffee and *petits fours*. What more could you ask for? The chef has a weakness for vanilla so if you want to treat yourself go à la carte and try the bass flavoured with vanilla and the crème brûlée! If you don't do anything mad, you'll get away with 180–220F.

COMBLOUX 74920

10% ☗ |●| LES GRANITS*

1409 route de Sallanches; it's 1.5km from the centre on the Sallanches road.
☎ 04.50.58.64.46 ➡ 04.50.58.61.63
Closed mid April–mid June and mid Sept–mid Dec.
Car park. **Disabled access**.

This is the cheapest hotel in the area; it's a bit out of town and you'll have to rely on shuttle buses but you'll get a terrific view of Mont Blanc. It has 20 rooms in all, five of them in the new annexe. Doubles 220F with washing facilities and 270F with shower/wc or bath. Set meal 79F. Reckon on 228–258F per person for half-board (compulsory during school holidays). A family guest house type of place, with the owner doing the cooking and his wife running everything.

☗ |●| HÔTEL-RESTAURANT LE COIN SAVOYARD**

300 route de la Cry; it's opposite the church.
☎ 04.50.58.60.27 ➡ 04.50.58.64.44
Closed Mondays out of season, end April–June 1, and end Sept–beginning Nov. **Car park**. **TV**.

You'd be wise to book well in advance. This is a friendly and informal little place with 10 recently renovated rooms (some of them a bit noisy). Doubles 400F. You can have a drink or something light for dinner – a good omelette and salad say – in a traditional Savoie setting. Meals are à la carte only and specialities like fondue, *raclette* and *pierrade* (where your meal is cooked on a hot stone) are about 120F. The lovely sunny terrace is right opposite Mont Blanc.Once you've tried it, you'll want to come back time and time again; it's simple, not very expensive, and a nice place to spend some time.

CONTAMINES-MONTJOIE (LES) 74170

10% ☗ |●| LE MONT-JOLY*

La Chapelle.
☎ 04.50.47.00.17
Closed in October and November. **Car park**.

A pretty little hotel on the outskirts of town that makes you think of the gingerbread house in Hansel and Gretel. It even has lace curtains (are they edible too?) at the windows. Simple and pleasant doubles. Half-board 185F per person for two sharing a double with shower. Set meals 65F, 80F and 98F. Reckon on 150F. Specialities are fondue and *raclette*. There's a nice terrace surrounded by trees with a view of the mountains; it's friendly and quiet but it's 2km away from the ski slopes, which might be a bit too far for some people.

☗ LA CLEF DES CHAMPS*

route de la Frasse; it's above the village, in the street opposite the tourist office.
☎ 04.50.47.06.09
Closed April 28–June 15 and Sept 15–Dec 20.
Car park.

Reservations are compulsory in winter and advisable in summer if you want to stay in this old restored farmhouse that offers good value for money. Doubles with shower/wc 210F. Half-board – compulsory in winter – is 220F per person. Special rates for under 4s and under 8s. Restaurant open to residents on half-board only. Garden and view of the valley. Our kind of place.

10% ☗ |●| HÔTEL-RESTAURANT LE GAI SOLEIL**

BP4; it's above the church.
☎ 04.50.47.02.94 ➡ 04.50.47.18.43
Closed April 15–June 14 and Sept 18–Dec 20.
Car park.

This old wooden farmhouse, built in 1823, has been renovated several times; it's very well decorated and looked after like a much loved family home; it's the best hotel in the resort and you'll get a tremendous welcome. It has 19 handsome rooms, some with a mezzanine floor so that parents and children can all be in the one room and all with shower/wc or bath and direct phone at prices ranging from 300F to 430F. Half-board — 290–360F — is compulsory during the school holidays. Set meals 99F and 150F (that one's for people on half-board) offer cheese dishes like fondue during the week.

CONTREVOZ 01300

LA PLUMARDIÈRE

How to get there: on the N504.
☎ 04.79.81.82.54 Fax 04.79.81.80.17
Closed Mondays, Tuesdays (in winter), the last week in June, the first week in September, and end Dec–Feb. **Car park**.

We're always surprised to find such lovely restaurants in such small towns. This particular restaurant was a farmhouse a great many years ago and contains several reminders of that long-ago agricultural past, including a big fireplace and an enormous pair of blacksmith's bellows. The star attraction though is the terrace and you really ought to take the time to eat there. You'll be surrounded by fruit trees and only the occasional cyclist will break the silence. The cooking is excellent — sophisticated and elegant, a subtle mix of the traditional and "nouvelle cuisine". The *gâteau de foie blond* (pounded chicken livers mixed with *foie gras*, eggs and cream and then steamed) with a crayfish sauce will meet with your wholehearted approval. Set meals 98F (also available at the weekend) and 130–250F. You CAN have your cake and eat it too.

CORPS 38970

BOUSTIGUE HÔTEL**

route de la Salette.
☎ 04.76.30.01.03 F 04.76.30.04.04
Closed Oct 20–April 20. **Secure parking**. **TV**.

There are some funny signs of the road leading to Notre-Dame-de-la-Salette (a place of pilgrimage). "This way", "You're getting close", they urge you on. You would be hard pushed to find a better place to relax than this large hotel that stands all alone on a plateau 1,200m up and has a panoramic view of the village of Corps and lac du Sautet. It has lots of little seating areas, a sauna, a pool, facilities for you to practice your golf, and pleasant rooms ranging in price from 266F to 345F. While Monsieur Dumas senior looks after the fabric of the hotel, son Bernard is in the kitchen preparing Immoderately priced local traditional dishes. The two cheapest set meals are both appealing — the 92F one consists of rabbit *terrine*, stew of suckling pig and cheese, while the 120F one includes ravioli stuffed with sardines and chicken in raspberry vinegar.

COUCOURON 07470

10% HÔTEL-RESTAURANT AU CARREFOUR DES LACS**

☎ 04.66.46.12.70 F 04.66.46.16.42
Closed Dec 1–Feb 15. **Secure parking**. **TV**.

This is an attractive mountain inn that stands near a lake in the middle of the Ardèche plateau. Clean rooms 170F with shower/wc. Half-board is compulsory in season and costs 200F per person. The large handsome dining room offers good food prepared from fresh ingredients. Try the *charcuterie*, the good local cheeses, and the home-made desserts. Set meals 80F, 135F and 170F. They also have what they call a "working man's" set meal for 55F. The proprietress is unstuffy and very friendly.

COURS-LA-VILLE 69470

LE NOUVEL HÔTEL**

5 rue Georges-Clemenceau (Centre).
☎ 04.74.89.70.21 F 04.74.89.84.41
Closed Dec 25–Jan 3 and one week in Aug. **Secure parking**. **TV**. **Canal+**.

The friendly dining room offers good regional food at reasonable prices. Set meals 78F (not available on Sundays)–162F. The pretty rooms have white walls and brightly coloured duvet covers and cost 265F and up with bath and phone, 170F with basin (wc in the corridor). We wish we came across more places like this.

10% LE PAVILLON**

col du Pavillon; it's 3km from Cours-la-Ville on the D64 heading in the direction of Écharmeaux.
☎ 04.74.89.83.55 F 04.74.64.70.26
Closed Saturdays Nov–March and during the February school holidays. **Car park**. **TV**. **Canal+**. **Disabled access**.

Lunch served noon–2pm and dinner 7–9pm. Standing quite alone and surrounded by fir trees at an altitude of 755m, the hotel makes a good base for walkers. If you're not a keen walker it's also a good place to relax, even if the owners do seem to be the kind who go in for lots of physical activity. There are photographs on the walls of their many expeditions to Morocco, India and South Africa – there's even a certificate testifying that they've done the Great Wall of China. Modern comfortable rooms 330F with shower or bath. The pleasant restaurant has set meals that range in price from 78F (weekdays) to 270F and offer a variety of dishes such as crayfish flan with seafood and halibut and salmon in vermouth.

CRÉMIEU 38460

10% L'AUBERGE DE LA CHAITE**

cours Baron-Raverat.
☎ 04.74.90.76.63 F 04.74.90.88.08
Closed Sunday evenings, Mondays, Jan 2–31, and the third week in April. **Secure parking**. **TV**.

Lunch served noon–2pm and dinner 7.30–9pm. There's not another place like this in Cremieu – it's the best hotel and the best restaurant in town. The setting is medieval, and the rooms overlooking the garden are really lovely. Doubles with basin150F, with shower/wc 255F. The cooking is imaginative – Philippe Seroux has quite a reputation as a chef – and served with considerable style both in the dining room and on the terrace. Prices are very affordable – the cheapest set meal will cost you 70F – and you'll have a choice of things like fillet of salmon with mushrooms and fried chicken with a rum and ginger sauce.

HÔTEL DE LA POSTE

21 rue Porcherie; it's opposite the covered market.
☎ 04.74.90.71.41
Closed Wednesdays out of season, two weeks in February, and two in September.

Be advised: despite the name, there's no post office in the vicinity and this is NOT a hotel – or rather, it's not a hotel any more. The rooms are in such a state that the present owners have decided not to let them out, which shows that these are people with taste, for the rooms would have been totally out of keeping with the exceptionally pretty ground floor. There's a bistro there with a cosy old-fashioned atmosphere. Lots of old posters and young men in suits. Have the day's special or one of the set meals (68–158F) featuring fish and shellfish.

SAINT-HILAIRE-DE-BRENS 38460 (6KM SE)

AU BOIS JOLI

How to get there: if you're coming from Crémieu, you'll find it at the junction of the Morestel and Bourgoin-Jallieu roads.
☎ 04.74.92.81.82 F 04.74.92.93.27
Closed evenings, Mondays, the first 10 days in January, and Aug 25–Sept 25. **Car park**.

Service noon–1.30pm. This is the Vistalli family's famous restaurant with its garden and two large dining rooms that can accommodate about 100 people. Gérard and Alain Vistalli do the cooking and are carrying on the family tradition under the vigilant eye of their mother, who's quite a character. Try the frog's legs *provençale*, the chicken livers with crayfish sauce or the duck with orange sauce. Set meals 68F (not available Sundays), and 100–160F.

CREST 26400

LE KLÉBER**

6 rue Aristide-Dumont (Centre).
☎ 04.75.25.11.69 F 04.75.76.82.82
Closed Sunday evenings, Mondays, Jan 15–Feb 4, and Aug 18–Sept 2. **Secure parking**. **TV**.

Lunch served noon–1.30pm and dinner 8–9.30pm. A very smart looking little place. The restaurant is known for its gourmet food and specializes in fish and regional dishes. Tempting set meals range from 95F (weekdays) to 250F. They have a few rooms at very affordable prices. Doubles 180F with shower, 240F with shower/wc. Prettily decorated. The nicest place in town in our opinion.

LA TARTINE

10 rue Peysson (centre); it's near the church of Saint-Sauveur.
☎ 04.75.25.11.53
Closed Wednesday evenings out of season, Saturday lunchtimes and Sunday lunchtimes in season, two weeks in February, and two at the beginning of November.

Lunch served noon–2pm and dinner 7.30–9.30pm. The restaurant occupies the whole of the first floor of a very old house in this quiet little town of 7,500 inhabitants. There's a piano in the large high-ceilinged dining room and a jazz fan will often sit down and play something. He – or she! – might then be joined by a guitarist or saxophonist and before you know where you are you've got live music. As you might have guessed from this, the restaurant is popular with music lovers who can have one of the sandwiches devised by owner Véronique, the day's special, or something very simple grilled for 55F, 63F or 99F. A really nice place.

SAOU 26400 (14KM SE)

|●| L'OISEAU SUR SA BRANCHE

La Placette (Centre).
☎ 04.75.76.02.03
Closed Monday evenings and Tuesday evenings out of season. **Disabled access**.

The words of a song by Charles Trénet extolling the virtues of France are inscribed on the yellow and blue walls of this village restaurant which has been transformed by a restaurateur and poet who settled here after many years travelling around in the Congo and other countries. In summer, there's a buffet – available on the terrace too – which offers *pissaladière* (an open tart of onions, anchovies and olives), aubergine caviar, and beetroot puree for 95F. If that doesn't appeal, how about the one and only set meal (115F)? It includes a choice of medallions of monkfish or leg of rabbit with a herb stuffing, goat's cheese and a "plate of chocolate" that, like all the other courses, will have been put together like a picture, and is full of colour and texture. During the week, you can eat in the red and yellow bistro for 65F. Do the trunk and the globe on the counter mean the owner's getting ready to go off on his travels again?.

OMBLÈZE 26400 (29.5KM NE)

10% ⌂ |●| AUBERGE DU MOULIN DE LA PIPE

South-West; at Plan-de-Baix, take the D578 and you'll find it 5km further on.
☎ 04.75.76.42.05 ⊳ 04.75.76.42.60
Closed Mondays Sept–March. **Car park**. **Disabled access**.

This restored former inn lies at the far end of a valley, and there are gorges, a river, and waterfalls nearby. Young people from all over the département (and even further afield) flock to Omblèze for the climbing school, the rock, blues and reggae concerts, and this restaurant, which specializes in *pierrade* (where your meal is cooked on a hot stone) of meat or fish. Weekday prices start at 65F. Rooms and studio flats 170–350F. Half-board 155–250F. An ideal place if you need some country air but don't want to die of boredom. Owned and managed by a nice group of youngsters, there's not another place like it in the area.

DIE 26150

|●| LA FERME DES BATETS

quartier des Batets; as you approach the town, follow the signs for Chamaloc-col de Rousset.
☎ 04.75.22.11.45
Closed October, Sunday and Monday evenings and, in season, Monday lunchtimes. **Car park**.

If you've been for a walk in the Vercors and you're weary and footsore, this old farmhouse will be a welcome sight. Try the guineafowl or the lamb and wash it down with some local red wine; it's best when it's not busy because then you can enjoy the peace and admire your surroundings – a lovingly restored 300 year old cowshed. If they suggest Clairette de Die (a sparkling white wine) at dessert time, don't feel obliged just because you don't want to look like a tourist. Set meals from 92F.

PONTAIX 26150 (10KM W)

⌂ |●| L'EAU VIVE

D93.
☎ 04.75.21.22.40
Closed Wednesdays and Sunday evenings. **Car park**.

A good inexpensive hotel. It doesn't have any stars but it's very well cared for and has nine very simple rooms from 145F with basin and shower. The cooking's pretty decent too, with set meals starting at 75F. Try the trout in Clairette de Die, a white sparkling wine. A good place to stop on your way south; it's the type of nice, informal place our readers find appealing.

BARNAVE 26310 (13KM SE)

10% ⌂ |●| L'AUBERGERIE

Grande-Rue.
☎ 04.75.21.82.13
Restaurant closed Tuesdays in season and during the week in winter. **TV**.

You can pay 85F and tuck into a savoury pie and either guinea fowl in a cream sauce or rabbit in Clairette de Die (a white sparkling wine) in the large dining room, which is done up to look like an old stable. In the café upstairs, meanwhile, the widows of the village will be settling down to play cards. Rooms, tastefully and simply decorated, are in the outbuildings. Prices start at 180F.

LUC-EN-DIOIS 26310 (19KM SE)

⌂ |●| HÔTEL DU LEVANT**

route de Gap (Centre); take the N93.
☎ 04.75.21.33.30 ⊳ 04.75.21.31.42
Closed Nov 5–April 1. **Car park**.

This 17th century coaching inn is ideal if you want to stop somewhere in this part of the world. Comfortable rooms 160–250F. Go for one at the back, where you'll have a stunning view of rooftops and mountains – number 5 is particularly good in that respect. The rustic dining room, which has ornaments to spare, offers an 95F set meal of regional specialities. There's one drawback – half-board is practically compulsory in summer. There's an enormous garden with a pool – on the other side of the road!

DIEULEFIT 26220

AUBERGE LES BRISES

route de Nyons; it's 1.5km from the centre of town.
☎ 04.75.46.41.49
Closed Tuesday evenings and Wednesdays out of season.

Didier le Doujet and his wife swapped their native Brittany for the Drôme and the taste of the sea for that of the land. His restaurant has soon made a name for itself as offering good food and a friendly reception. Very appealing set meals at 110F and 140F. Eat on the shady terrace in summer or in the genuine imitation rustic dining room. If you're stuck for somewhere to stay, they have rooms at 160F. They're small though and far from luxurious – don't say we didn't warn you. Half-board 170F.

LA PÉNICHE

16 quai Roger-Morin; it's below the old part of town, near the river.
☎ 04.75.90.62.98
Closed Sunday evenings and Mondays out of season. **Car park**.

No, it's not a floating restaurant and it's not among the trees but on the other side of the road (the sign's not very visible). This is a simple, cheerful place, with a little terrace and a dining room decorated in cream and terracotta, like the local pottery. The cooking's cheerful and uncomplicated too and for 98F you can have things like *bavaroise* of fennel vinaigrette, guineafowl in Clairette de Die (a sparkling white wine), fresh cream cheese, and warm apple and cinammon tart. The day's special is 49F, and the 78F set meal represents exceptional value – and enjoyment – for money. Other set meal 128F.

FÉLINES-SUR-RIMANDOULE 26160 (12KM NW)

RESTAURANT CHEZ DENIS

How to get there: take the D540 then the D179.
☎ 04.75.90.16.73
Closed Tuesday evenings and Wednesdays out of season. **Car park**.

"Denis" is actually the present chef's father but he won't be offended if you assume that he is. He hasn't made any drastic changes since taking over from his father, quietly carrying on in the same way, and on Sundays and sunny days people flock to this handsome restaurant up in the hills. You'll eat in a relaxed atmosphere to the sound of running water and children's laughter and be more than happy to linger over your meal on the cool terrace. Set meals 100–210F.

DIVONNE-LES-BAINS 01220

LA TERRASSE FLEURIE**

315 rue Fontaine (Centre); it's very near the casino.
☎ 04.50.20.06.32 F 04.50.20.40.34
Closed end Oct–mid March. **TV**.

A very quiet and aptly named hotel. The modern rooms are quite nice. Doubles with direct phone 250–300F. Sliding scale rates if you take full or half-board. The restaurant offers simple inexpensive home cooking, with set meals at 81F (lunchtimes), 69F (evenings) and 91F (Sunday lunchtimes). For Divonne, this is excellent value for money.

LE DIVONA**

37 rue de Genève (Centre).
☎ 04.50.20.00.91 F 04.50.20.29.24
Secure parking. **TV**.

This centrally located hotel (don't worry, it's not right on the street) has been refurbished throughout (in a rather bland style). Prices are reasonable for the area – remember that Divonne is a spa town with a lake just down the road from Geneva. If you're stuck for somewhere to eat, the restaurant does pizza and pasta, with a set meal at 80F. Packages are available for people here to take the waters (21 days minimum). There's also a seven-day "get back into shape" package. The hotel has a sauna and a fitness room.

ÉVIAN 74500

10% AUBERGE DE JEUNESSE – CENTRE INTERNATIONAL DE SÉJOUR

av. de Neuvecelle (South-West); on the D21 in the direction of Abondance.
☎ 04.50.75.35.87 F 04.50.75.45.67
Car park. **Disabled access**.

Check in 8am–8pm. There's no bus service in winter. Two people sharing a room with shower/wc will pay 145F a night – expensive for a youth hostel. Modern buildings surrounded by greenery with a stunning view of the lake. Very friendly welcome.

10% HÔTEL CONTINENTAL**

65 rue Nationale (Centre).
☎ 04.50.75.37.54 F 04.50.75.31.11

Is it because the new owners of this hotel spend a lot of time in the USA that they've managed to turn it into a place that's full of life, where each room has its own personality, the furniture's not standard hotel issue, the atmosphere is genuinely friendly, and the little things matter? With a bit of luck you might find a scrap of the original wallpaper at the back of a cupboard so you can see what you've been lucky enough to miss! Courteous welcome and great prices, considering the charm of the place. Rooms 230–310F.

PUBLIER 74500 (3.5KM W)

10% HÔTEL-RESTAURANT LE CHABLAIS**

rue du Chablais.
☎ 04.50.75.28.06 F 04.50.74.67.32
Closed Sundays in winter and Dec 20–Jan 20.
Car park. **TV**. **Canal+**.

A clean, tidy and efficient hotel which would probably appeal to the Swiss on the other side of Lake Geneva. Half of the rooms have a good view of the Lake. Doubles 220F–280F. So sure is the proprietress (she's been here since 1968) that you won't find a speck of dirt anywhere, she'd let you into her kitchen to check out her pots and pans. Set meals 84F and 97–155F. It has a good reputation and decent prices – two good reasons for you to go some way out of Évian.

THOLLON-LES-MEMISES 74500 (10KM E)

10% HÔTEL BON SÉJOUR**

Centre.
☎ 04.50.70.92.65 F 04.50.70.95.72
Closed Nov 1–Dec 18. **Secure parking**. **TV**.

The Dupond family – mum, grandmother, daughter and her children – live together and work together. This is a real family hotel where everyone chips in, which is ideal in a family resort like this. The younger ones of the family would really like to refurbish the bedrooms which are getting on a bit now, but you'll sleep like a baby there (half-board compulsory 260–300F). As the mother adores antiques it goes without saying that the place is absolutely charming. Especially with the view and the garden. As for the restaurant you get good local food at reasonable prices. Set meals 85F, 110F, 125F at lunchtimes, and 100F, 115F and 130F in the evenings. The food is meticulously prepared and served with a smile, or at least that's what it says on the menu!

BERNEX 74500 (14KM SE)

RESTAURANT LE RELAIS DE LA CHEVRETTE

Trossy; get there on the D21 and the D52 – go through Bernex and head for Dent-d'Oche.
☎ 04.50.73.60.27
Closed Wednesdays (except during school holidays) and Nov 15–Dec 20. **Car park**.

Just outside the family ski resort of Bernex, you'll find a chalet with red and white wooden shutters that looks like something out of an operetta. The menu features typical local produce and the meat and ham are dried, salted and smoked in-house. Simple dishes like omelettes and bilberry tart are on offer and Savoie wines feature large on the wine list. There's an open fire in winter and in summer you can enjoy the garden and the stream that runs through it. Reckon on 100F for a substantial meal. Warm welcome.

10% RESTAURANT L'ÉCHELLE

How to get there: it's beside the church.
☎ 04.50.73.60.42
Closed Mondays and Tuesdays outside school holidays and Oct 1–Nov 15. **Car park**.

A restaurant where everyone takes time out to enjoy the finer things in life. If you see the chef having a drink and a laugh at the bar in the evening at around 8pm, don't worry, he's not running late. Oh no, he's just finishing off as the lunchtime guests are leaving! Pierre Mercier follows the cooking methods of his mother, "la Félicie", who used to feed all the mountain walkers, at the bottom of the slopes, at Saint-Michel and at many an evening do. Try the *Chapeaurade* (meat grilled on the *chapeau)* to share with friends. Set meal-menu 145F. Wine from the best of vineyards. Possibility of staying half-board 250–350F.

VACHERESSE 74360 (20KM SE)

AU PETIT CHEZ SOI

☎ 04.50.73.10.11
Car park.

A place from another time, another universe. Between Lake Geneva and the lively resorts above, this is an old house where the father is still making all the same old jokes, the mother still gets excited about the minister coming for tea, and the residents still sign the visitors book. Set meal 80F with whatever's going, everything included. Full board 206F(!) – the rooms also look like they're from another era, but you'll get just as good a nights sleep here as anywhere. The daughters come in to lend a hand and don't be surprised if you end up doing so as well.

FAVERGES 74210

|●| LA CARTE D'AUTREFOIS

25 rue Gambetta.
☎ 04.50.32.49.98
Closed Sunday evenings, Wednesdays, the first fortnight in July, and Christmas–New Year's Day.

You'll find Faverges just where Savoie becomes Haute-Savoie; it's a delightful spot and so is this little restaurant, which takes you back a fair number of years. It offers set meals at 80F, 120F and 155F and dishes such as *confit* of duck in a garlic sauce, veal kidneys flambéd in liqueur made from the little yellow plums known as *mirabelles*, and *nougat glacé* with a raspberry *coulis*. The cooking is pleasing and full of flavour and makes a nice change from the ubiquitous *tartiflettes* and fondues.

FERNEY-VOLTAIRE 01210

|●| RESTAURANT LE CHANTECLAIR

13 rue de Versoix (Centre).
☎ 04.50.40.79.55
Closed Sundays and Monday evenings.

This is a first-rate little restaurant offering gourmet food and it's very popular with the Swiss. At 95F, the lunchtime set meal is excellent value for money. We would be tempted to echo the great man himself and say that all was for the best in the best of all possible worlds if it wasn't for the fact that prices shoot up in the evening, with set meals at 105F, 200F, 260F and 300F! So if you're touring Voltaire country and fancy eating here, you know when to come!

FEURS 42110

|●| CHALET DE LA BOULE D'OR

42 route de Lyon (East); it's near the Feurs east exit.
☎ 04.77.26.20.68
Closed Sunday evenings, Mondays, and first two weeks in August.

Here's a gourmet restaurant that's eminently affordable – on weekdays at any rate. The cheapest set meal, at 93F, is pretty pleasant and is available until Saturday lunchtime. The other set meals are a bit more elaborate and go all the way up to 250F. Staff are attentive without being irritating, the food delicate and the wine list has been carefully put together, though prices are quite high. Everything's good, so go for whatever you like the sound of, whether it's the *marbré* of rabbit or the roast monkfish. The appetizers are full of subtle flavours and the desserts are out of this world. Pleasant dining room.

MARCLOPT 42210 (11KM S)

10% ⌂ |●| LE KHAN

☎ 04.77.54.58.40
How to get there: on the N82 in the direction of Montrond-les-Bains; alternatively, take autoroute A72, leave it via the Montbrison-Montrond exit and then take the D115 to Marclopt.
Closed Thursday evenings except in season. **Car park**.

This is the kind of inn we like and it's in a lovely little village. The décor is original, consisting of murals and stone dressed by the owner's son (that's what his company specializes in). The welcome you'll get from the proprietress couldn't be warmer and her cooking is fresh and original. Everything is home-made, from the marinated or smoked fish and the *foie gras* to the casserole of beef and marrowbone that simmers for hours on the edge of the stove. The 65F *menu du jour* has no choice of main course but you can have as much as you like of what there is while the 80F set meal gives you a choice. If you're keen on *foie gras*, they have a set meal offering as much of the stuff, both fresh and panfried, as you can eat for 70F – just make sure you order in advance. This was our favourite place in the area and if you want to stay longer, you can have a large country-style bedroom for 170F. There are only four of these delightful rooms and it's best to book – lots of people seem to agree with our very favourable verdict last year. For 25F you'll get a superb breakfast.

VIOLAY 42780 (22KM NE)

10% ⌂ |●| HÔTEL-RESTAURANT PERRIER**

place de l'Église; from Feurs, head for Balbigny and take the D1 in the direction of Tarare.

☎ 04.74.63.91.01 F➔ 04.74.63.91.77
Closed Saturday and Sunday evenings, and Jan–Feb.
Secure parking. TV.

You'll get a nice welcome from Jean-Luc Clot and his wife. The south-west of France frequently provides the inspiration for the cooking here. Prices are reasonable, especially on weekdays, with a 40–50F *formule* and set meals from 65F; the one at 85F represents extremely good value for money. The *confit* of duck and chicken and the crayfish *provençale* are particularly good. The hotel is well looked after and prices are very affordable — 150–220F for a pretty, feminine room; all rooms have bath. Violay is a lovely little mountain village and people come here for the cross-country skiing. And if you're bothered by the sound of bells, the church across the way is silent during the hours of darkness.

FLUMET 73590

10% ⌂ |●| HÔTEL-RESTAURANT LE PARC DES CÈDRES***

Centre.
☎ 04.79.31.72.37 F➔ 04.79.31.61.66
Closed mid April–beginning June and end Sept–Dec 20.
Secure parking. TV.

The Jond family have been in the hotel business for more than a hundred years in this resort not too far from Megève between col des Aravis and col des Saisies. The building is green on the outside while inside the dining room is pink. Some of the bedrooms are decorated in 70s style, others are a little more traditional. They've used lots of pastels and have created quite a cosy atmosphere. Doubles 250F with washing facilities, 275–350F with shower/wc or bath. In the restaurant, good quality produce makes for good cooking. Set meals at 85F, 103F, 130F and 160F offer things like oven baked veal kidneys flambéd in cognac, roast quail, and sautéd calf's liver. The terrace under the cedar trees is wonderful in summer.

SAINT-NICOLAS-LA-CHAPELLE 73590 (1.5KM SW)

⌂ |●| HÔTEL-RESTAURANT L'EAU VIVE**

Centre; take the N212 in the direction of Ugine and after 1km turn right towards Saint-Nicolas-la-Chapelle.
☎ 04.79.31.60.46 F➔ 04.79.31.79.76
Closed April 20–beginning May, June 1–20, and Oct 1–Dec 20. **Car park.**

The motto of this place is "Let food be your first medicine"; it's a superb little Savoie chalet tucked away in a delightful village and at first looks like just another hotel with a wooden balcony and geraniums in summer. But this is a health farm and offers reflexology, seaweed baths, steam baths with plant essences and something it calls polarizing energy equilibrium. The food's healthy too and everything's organic — no pesticides or chemicals; it's good for you — and good. They cater for vegetarians of course — cheese ravioli, and *galette paysanne* — but they also do traditional Savoie dishes like *diots* (vegetable and pork sausages cooked in wine). Set meals 80F (weekday lunchtimes) and 130F. The décor of the bedrooms reflects the relaxed "green" philosophy of the place. A three-day "get back in shape" package will cost you 1,600F. A quiet spot away from it all for a healthy meal or a longer stay to get you ready to face the world again. Two things you should be aware of though — it's non-smoking throughout and they don't take plastic (well, they wouldn't, would they?).

MANANT 73590 (3KM N)

|●| AU BON ACCUEIL

route des Aravis; take the D909 in the direction of col des Aravis.
☎ 04.79.32.92.60
Closed Wednesdays, May 15 – June 20, and Sept 15 –Oct 20.

This is the type of unpretentious café cum restaurant you dream of; it's housed in what used to be a slate quarry and offers simple traditional Savoie dishes like *diots* (pork and vegetable sausages) in white wine for 68F and *farcement* (potatoes baked with milk, eggs, raisins and prunes) for 78F (you'll have to order that the day before). Substantial set meals 55F and 68F. You'll get a friendly welcome from Pierre Chatellard, who's been here for donkey's years.

NOTRE-DAME-DE-BELLECOMBE 73590 (5KM S)

|●| LA FERME DE VICTORINE

Le Mont-Rond; take the N218 in the direction of Les Saisies and when you're 3km from Notre-Dame-de-Bellecombe, turn left towards Le Planay.
☎ 04.79.31.63.46 F➔ 04.79.31.79.91
Closed Sunday evenings and Mondays in spring and autumn, and Nov 15–Dec 15.

You realize this place has atmosphere the minute you step inside. The bay window in the bar looks onto the old stable, the dining room is as pretty as everything else in the restaurant and has a big fireplace for cold winter days. In summer, you can eat on the bright sunny terrace with its great view of the mountain. Set meals 115F, 149F and 198F. There are some good traditional Savoie dishes à la carte, including mushroom fondue (85F), leek and *tamié* (a local cheese) tart (89F), and *reblochonnade* (98F), and even the biggest appetites will be satisfied with the *farcement* (potatoes baked with eggs, milk, raisins and prunes) at 89F.

SAISIES (LES) 73620 (14KM S)

RESTAURANT LE CHAUDRON

Centre; take the D218; it's beside the police station.
☎ 04.79.38.92.76
Closed May–mid June and mid Sept–mid Dec.

Service from noon and from 7pm. Les Saisies was one of the sites of the 1992 Winter Olympics (you can still see the Olympic torch outside the tourist information office) and well-known skier Franck Piccard comes from around here (he can be spotted on the slopes or in the street occasionally). Even so, it's just another local ski resort and has nothing out of the ordinary to recommend it. But we liked this restaurant; it's got a very friendly atmosphere and the traditional décor is nice, though maybe they've tried a bit too hard to make it look authentic. Good local cooking — fondue, *reblochonnade* and *potence* — is what's on offer and the portions are substantial — just what you need after you've spent the entire day skiing or hiking. Reckon on 72–170F for a meal. A bit expensive but this IS a ski resort. Nice terrace where you can get a good view of Mont Blanc on a clear day.

GARDE-ADHÉMAR (LA) 26700

LOGIS DE L'ESCALIN

(North-West); leave the A7 by the Montélimar-Sud or Bollène exit and then head for Donzère. You'll find it 1.5km further along.
☎ 04.75.04.41.32 ➡ 04.75.04.40.05
Closed Sunday evenings, Mondays, and Jan 2–10.
Car park.

A little hotel clinging to a hillside and overlooking the Rhône Valley. The motorway's just over a mile away as the crow flies but it seems much, much further. The hotel, a handsome example of the local style of building, has six rooms and you'll pay 250F for one with shower/wc. Nice décor. The very pleasant garden provides shade and there's a swing for children. The cheapest set meal on weekdays costs 98F and for that you get salad, mutton tripe and sheep's trotters or some other local dish, fresh cream cheese, and a home-made dessert. Other set meals 148–278F. A good place for a weekend break or if you need somewhere to stop on the way south.

GEX 01170

10% HÔTEL-RESTAURANT DU PARC**

av. des Alpes (Centre).
☎ 04.50.41.50.18 ➡ 04.50.42.37.29
Closed Mondays, Sunday evenings, January, and 10 days at the end of September. **Car park**. **TV**.

Lunch served 12.30–2pm and dinner 7.30–9pm. The proprietress is mad about geraniums, roses and begonias and wins prizes in what we might call "Hotels in Bloom" competitions. Check out the certificates on the foyer walls. You'll be won over, as we were by this delightful and first-rate hotel, which has been owned by the same family for more than 70 years. Rooms 280F with shower/wc, 350F with bath. The food in the gourmet restaurant is excellent but unfortunately it's a bit expensive. Set meals 120–335F.

RESTAURANT L'ARLEQUIN

165 rue Charles-Harent; it's near the church.
☎ 04.50.41.61.69
Closed Tuesdays.

The décor is ever so slightly kitschy and reminiscent of a pizza parlour with its enormous commedia dell'arte fresco.The restaurant specializes in cheese dishes — *tartiflette*, fondue (made with "yellow wine" from Franche Comté), raclette, and the less well-known *malakoff* (deep-fried cheese balls). Reckon on 60–100F à la carte. Set meal featuring regional specialities 120F. The big wooden tables and benches make for a convivial atmosphere. Ideal on a winter evening.

CESSY 01170 (2KM SE)

MOTEL LA BERGERIE**

805 route Plaine (South).
☎ 04.50.41.41.75 ➡ 04.50.41.71.82
Closed over Christmas and on New Year's Day.
Car park. **TV**. **Disabled access**.

It's surrounded by fields and there's a disco next door (don't worry, you won't spend a sleepless night). The rooms are large and they all come with bath; it's far from luxurious but offers excellent value for money. Doubles 180F, triples 220F. They do a substantial breakfast for 30F, and it's served until noon (which is so unusual it deserves to be mentioned). So if you feel like a lie-in, go right ahead!

SEGNY 01170 (6KM SE)

LA BONNE AUBERGE**

rue du Vieux-Bourg (Centre); take the N5.
☎ 04.50.41.60.42 F 04.50.41.71.79
Closed Christmas–beginning March. **Secure parking**. **TV**.

The welcome, the comfort and the décor all combine to make this a pleasant place to stay. All those people who come back time and time again can't be wrong, can they? It has 13 rooms in all. Doubles with double bed 200F, with twin beds 225F. Unfortunately it doesn't have a restaurant.

CROZET 01170 (8KM SW)

LE BOIS JOLY*

route du Télécabine (South); take the D984 in the direction of Bellegarde then right onto the D89 as far as Crozet – the hotel is 500m from the cable car.
☎ 04.50.41.01.96 F 04.50.42.48.47
Closed Fridays, school holidays at Easter, and in October. **Car park**. **TV**.

A large establishment with a terrace that has a stunning view of the Alps and where you can eat in fine weather. The restaurant provides generous portions of regional dishes and has set meals at 80F, 100F, 140F and 160F. The bedrooms, like the dining room, are simple and rustic but come with the essentials. Doubles 178F with basin, 248F with bath. Sliding scale rates for people on half-board and full board.

COL DE LA FAUCILLE 01170 (11.5KM NW)

HÔTEL DE LA COURONNE***

(South-West); take the N5.
☎ 04.50.41.32.65 F 04.50.41.32.47
Closed Oct 15–Dec 15. **Car park**. **TV**.

Lunch served noon–2pm and dinner 7–9pm. At an altitude of more than 1,300m, le col de la Faucille is one of the leading tourist centres in the area and might even be described as the place where people from Geneva come to ski. The hotel is expensive but is extremely comfortable and quiet. Rooms – 340F – are very large and come with balcony and bath. Genial welcome. Pleasant garden. Use of the swimming pool can be arranged. The cosy restaurant offers sophisticated cooking and set meals at 110F and 200F.

GRAND-BORNAND (LE) 74450

10% HÔTEL-RESTAURANT LA CROIX SAINT-MAURICE**

Centre.
☎ 04.50.02.20.05 F 04.50.02.35.37
Closed in May, the first three weeks of June, and mid Sept–mid Dec; restaurant closed in summer.

Run by the same family for the past 30 years, this is a hotel for families in a ski resort. You'll find that the regulars come back every winter for what amounts to a family reunion. It has about 20 rooms overlooking the Aravis chain of mountains, some with a balcony or terrace. The prices will take you back almost 30 years – 250–295F in winter, 200–250F in summer. Half-board, at 220–330F, is strongly advised. The restaurant has good set meals at 87F (weekday lunchtimes) – this one changes every day and goes up to 120F on Sundays – 90F, 100F and 170F. Lots of regional specialities à la carte. The proprietress is delightful.

10% HÔTEL DE LA POINTE PERCÉE**

Centre; it's opposite the tourist information agency.
☎ 04.50.02.20.02 F 04.50.02.74.40
Closed mid May–mid June and mid Sept–mid Dec.
Car park. **TV**.

A big building with a welcoming atmosphere, it stands on the main square opposite the church and is called after the loveliest peak of the Aravis chain of mountains. Very friendly welcome. Nice rooms with direct phone and TV. Prices start at 250F for a double with basin and bidet and go up to 273F for shower/wc. Half-board 187–290F per person, 183–285F in winter. Classic Savoie dishes with no surprises are served in a dining room that's a bit traditional. Set meals 78F (weekday lunchtimes)–120F.

10% HÔTEL-RESTAURANT LES GLAÏEULS**

Centre; it's at the foot of the slopes, where the cable cars start from.
☎ 04.50.02.20.23 F 04.50.02.25.00
Closed mid April–mid June and mid Sept–mid Dec.
Car park. **TV**.

A very well cared for hotel. All 22 rooms have bath and phone and cost 290F. Half-board 250–340F, depending on which way the room faces. Good cooking. Set meals range in price from 90F to 230F and dishes include escalope of duck *foie gras* in wine and casserole of snails and mushrooms. There's a view of the Aravis chain of mountains from the sunny terrace and when the snow disappears it's soon replaced by masses of flowers.

HÔTEL LES CIMES

Le Chinaillon (Centre).
☎ 04.50.27.00.38 ➡ 04.50.27.08.46

A stone's throw from the village of Chinaillon and 100m from the pistes, this is a traveller's dream come true. The couple who had the idea of creating this lovely chalet - it has a great smell of wood and polish - really knew what they were doing when they converted an ordinary place above one of the 'chic' boutiques in the resort into a friendly place where you can listen to the silence before falling asleep under a cosy duvet. The prices (390–590F, depending on the season) are justified, especially since they include a superb breakfast. Unfortunately the couple don't have the time now to go on their travels, but we're delighted to have met them on ours.

LA FERME DE LORMAY

Vallée du Bouchet; 7km from the village, in the direction of the col des Annes, turn right when you get to the little chapel.
Closed Sep 10–Dec 15, and May 1–June 15, on reservation in winter.

They haven't had a sign up here for a long time so it stays nice and quiet, and remains just for those 'in the know'. There's a nice authentic atmosphere at this farmhouse belonging to Albert, a character who's often imitated, as is his food. In summer why not try the chicken with crayfish, the trout or the house *quenelles,* on the terrace of this old farm in its original state. Just sit back and enjoy! When it gets cold, you can warm yourself up near the fireplace where the desserts are laid out (tarts, clafoutis, etc.)but they won't be there for long! In winter there's more meat on the menu with pig, and bacon soup. Is your mouth watering yet? But the only snag is, you've got to meet with the owners approval. If not, they'll send you to another restaurant — that's the way they work. Expect to pay about 180–250F à la carte.

LE CHÂTILLON

How to get there: it's where the Rosey cable car comes in and the Lachat cable car leaves from.
☎ 04.50.27.02.76
Closed mid May–mid June and mid sept–mid Dec. **Secure parking**.

Stunning décor — traditional Savoie — and stunning views. If you're not very hungry, they have salads starting at 35F. If you're starving, better go for the *beugnets* — a kind of fritter made with grated potatoes, eggs and onions — and salad, And they have fondue and *raclette* of course and, less well known, *rucheti savoyard* (which also comes with salad). Set meals 80F and 120F. Reckon on about 100F à la carte. There's a very homely atmosphere about the place — hardly surprising when you consider that owner Gérard Missilier was actually born just a couple of doors away.

AU BON VIEUX TEMPS

Villavit.
☎ 04.50.02.32.38
Closed May 1–31, and Sept 30–Dec 15. **Car park**.

It IS like the good old days. This mountain chalet is ageless, full of warmth and history and smiling Raymond makes it his job to see that everything is done in accordance with tradition. He'll welcome you wearing his hat and nobody else can tell you the things about Grand-Bornand and the mountains that he can. The dining room is as rustic as rustic can be and has red and white waxed tablecloths. All that's missing is a cow or two! They serve up hefty portions of traditional dishes like *pela* (potatoes, onions and Reblochon cheese), flambéd tripe with cheese, smoked *diots* (vegetable and pork sausages) and fondue. And the bread is home-made. Set meals 129F.

GRENOBLE 38000

SEE MAP OVERLEAF

HÔTEL DE L'EUROPE**

22 place Grenette. **MAP C3-1**
☎ 04.76.46.16.94 ➡ same
TV. **Canal+**.

The hotel is right in the centre of Grenoble, where the first rays of sunshine bring out all the students, tourists and locals to sit on the terraces of their favourite cafés until all hours. Don't worry, it's sound-proof and noise won't be a problem. It has 46 rooms which are constantly being upgraded, it's comfortable, and the welcome will teach you more about

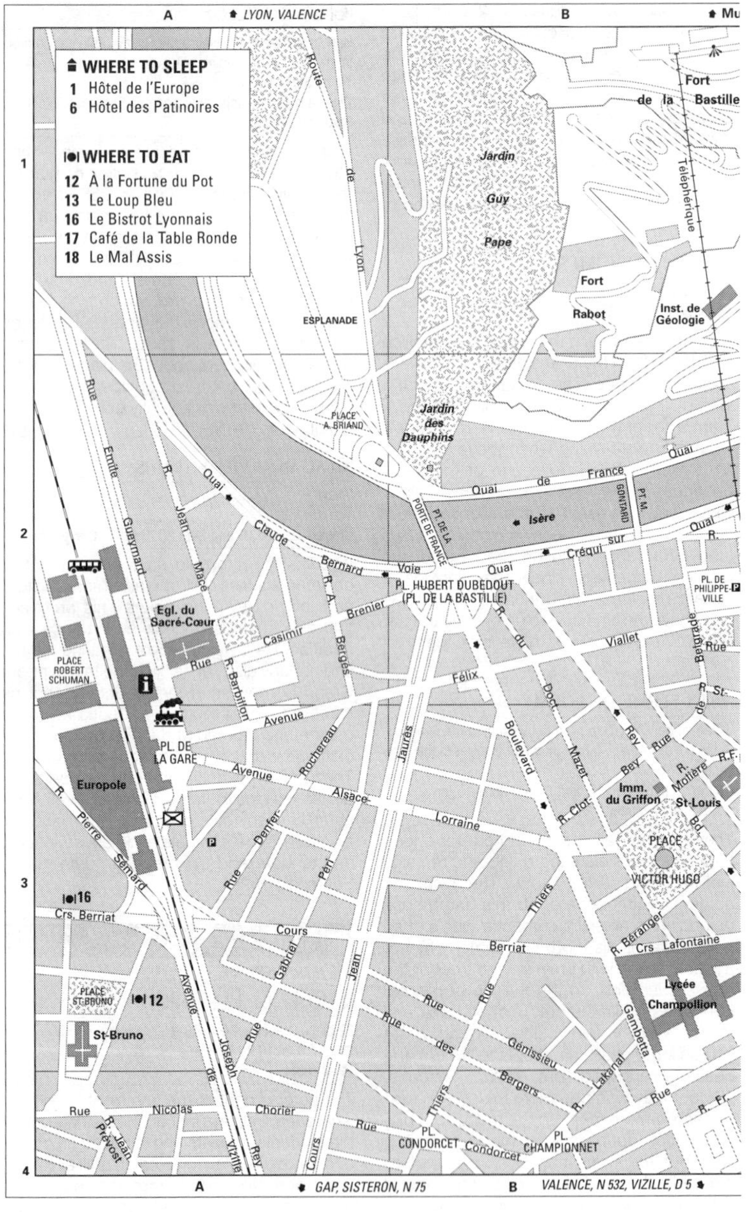

WHERE TO SLEEP
1 Hôtel de l'Europe
6 Hôtel des Patinoires
WHERE TO EAT
12 À la Fortune du Pot
13 Le Loup Bleu
16 Le Bistrot Lyonnais
17 Café de la Table Ronde
18 Le Mal Assis
LYON, VALENCE
GAP, SISTERON, N 75
VALENCE, N 532, VIZILLE, D 5
Fort de la Bastille
Téléphérique
Jardin Guy Pape
Fort Rabot
Inst. de Géologie
ESPLANADE
Route de Lyon
PLACE A. BRIAND
Jardin des Dauphins
Quai de France
Isère
PT. DE LA PORTE DE FRANCE
Quai Claude Bernard
Voie
Quai Créqui
PL. HUBERT DUBEDOUT (PL. DE LA BASTILLE)
PL. DE PHILIPPE-VILLE
Rue Emile Gueymard
R. Jean Macé
Egl. du Sacré-Cœur
Rue Casimir Brenier
R. A. Bergès
R. Barbillon
PLACE ROBERT SCHUMAN
Avenue Félix Viallet
PL. DE LA GARE
Europole
Avenue Alsace-Lorraine
R. Pierre Sémard
Rue Denfert-Rochereau
Péri
Jaurès
Boulevard
R. du Doct. Mazet
Rue Bayard
R. Molière
Imm. du Griffon
St-Louis
R. Clot-Bey
PLACE VICTOR HUGO
Thiers
Crs. Berriat
Cours Berriat
R. Béranger
Crs Lafontaine
Lycée Champollion
Gambetta
PLACE ST-BRUNO
St-Bruno
Avenue de Vizille
Joseph Rey
Rue Gabriel
Cours Jean Jaurès
Rue Génissieu
Rue des Bergers
R. Lakanal
Rue Nicolas Chorier
R. Jean Prévost
PL. CONDORCET
Rue Condorcet
PL. CHAMPIONNET

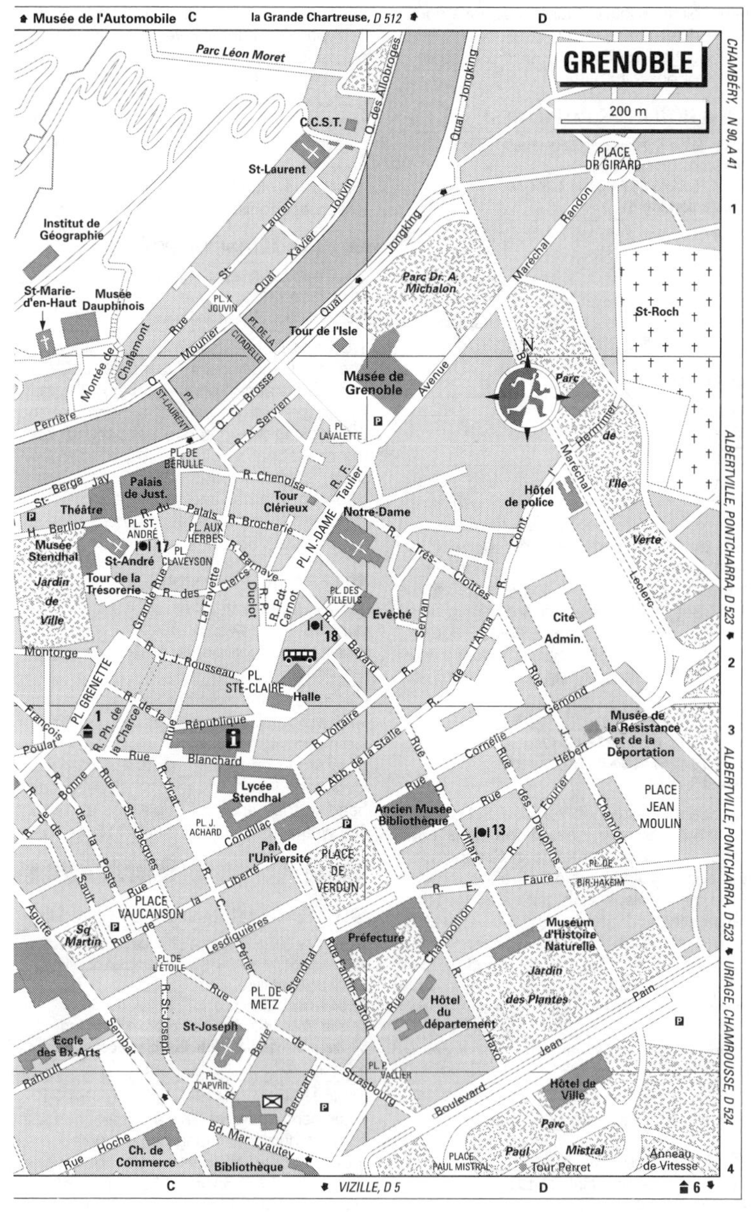

GRENOBLE
200 m
Musée de l'Automobile
la Grande Chartreuse, D 512
CHAMBÉRY, N 90, A 41
ALBERTVILLE, PONTCHARRA, D 523
ALBERTVILLE, PONTCHARRA, D 523
URIAGE, CHAMROUSSE, D 524
VIZILLE, D 5
Parc Léon Moret
C.C.S.T.
St-Laurent
Institut de Géographie
St-Marie-d'en-Haut
Musée Dauphinois
Tour de l'Isle
Parc Dr. A. Michalon
Musée de Grenoble
PLACE DR GIRARD
St-Roch
Palais de Just.
Théâtre
Musée Stendhal
St-André
Tour de la Trésorerie
Jardin de Ville
Tour Clérieux
Notre-Dame
Hôtel de police
Evêché
Cité Admin.
Halle
Musée de la Résistance et de la Déportation
PLACE JEAN MOULIN
Lycée Stendhal
Ancien Musée Bibliothèque
Pal. de l'Université
PLACE DE VERDUN
PLACE VAUCANSON
Sq Martin
Préfecture
Muséum d'Histoire Naturelle
Jardin des Plantes
Hôtel du département
St-Joseph
Ecole des Bx-Arts
Hôtel de Ville
Parc Paul Mistral
PLACE PAUL MISTRAL
Tour Perret
Anneau de Vitesse
Ch. de Commerce
Bibliothèque
Bd. Mar. Lyautey
Boulevard Jean Pain
PL. DE METZ
PL. DE L'ÉTOILE
PL. D'APVRIL
PL. P. VALLIER
PL. J. ACHARD
PL. GRENETTE
PL. STE-CLAIRE
PL. DES TILLEULS
PL. CLAVEYSON
PL. AUX HERBES
PL. ST-ANDRÉ
PL. DE BÉRULLE
PL. LAVALETTE
PL. N.-DAME
PL. X JOUVIN
PL. DE BIR-HAKEIM
17
18
13
1
6

Grenoble than lots of tourist brochures could. The prices are quite unusual for the area, ranging from 150F for a double with basin to 260F for one with bath.

10% HÔTEL DES PATINOIRES**

12 rue Marie-Chamoux; it's 500m south of the Palais des Sports. Off map **D4-6**
☎ 04.76.44.43.65 F➔ 04.76.44.44.77
Secure parking. TV.

It's a long way from the centre and it's not the easiest place in the world to find but it's got lots of charm and a serene comfortable atmosphere. A haven for people who don't want to be surrounded by tourists. Doubles with shower/wc 250F, with bath 275F.

LE MAL ASSIS

9 rue Bayard. **MAP C2-18**
☎ 04.76.54.75.93
Closed Mondays and Sundays.

Lunch served noon–2pm and dinner 7.30–10pm. Surrounded by antique shops and picture galleries, this is a favourite spot with the locals who know how to live. It has wood panelling and a fireplace. At lunchtime, there's just one *formule*. In the evening, the 128F set meal might offer something along the lines of *fondant* of vegetables, saddle of rabbit with *aïoli*, and plain chocolate *marquise*. Book, and get here early!

CAFÉ DE LA TABLE RONDE

7 place Saint-André. **MAP C2-17**
☎ 04.76.44.51.41 F➔ 04.76.51.14.83
Closed Sundays.

Service until midnight. You couldn't possibly be more centrally located than this café, which is now an institution in Grenoble; it's the second oldest café in France (only *Le Procope* in Paris is older), and tradition, hospitality and conviviality are its watchwords now as they were when it first opened in 1793. You can eat here too, even if food is not what it does best. So, in order to enjoy the passing show on the square from the terrace or admire the décor of the dining room, stick with the 70F *formule*, which comes with the day's special. You can see a real show while you eat upstairs "Au Grenier".

LE LOUP BLEU

7 rue Dominique-Villars. **MAP D3-13**
☎ 04.76.51.22.70
Closed Saturday lunchtimes, Sundays, public holidays, and the first fortnight in August.

Lunch served noon–2pm and dinner 8–10pm; it's unobtrusive, quiet inside and out, and everything is in good taste. The cooking and the service are both first-rate quality and the atmosphere has that certain something. The 68F set meal reflects the changing seasons. If you want a slightly more gourmet meal, go for the 105F or 190F set meal which offer traditional dishes and excellent meat and fish.

À LA FORTUNE DU POT

34 rue de l'Abbé-Grégoire. **MAP A3-12**
☎ 04.76.96.20.05
Closed Sunday, Monday and in August.

The Saint-Bruno street market is the liveliest and most traditional in Grenoble and you'll find the restaurant on the corner of the market square; it's got loads of atmosphere and the cooking is — naturally — based on what the market has to offer by way of fresh produce. There's all sorts of local gossip being traded at the bar and you'll be totally won over by the traditional atmosphere. One set meal only at 75F.

LE BISTROT LYONNAIS

168 cours Berriat. **MAP A3-16**
☎ 04.76.21.95.33 F➔ same
Closed Mondays, Sundays, Dec 23–Jan 5, May 2–11, and Aug 15–Sept 1.

OK, it's a bit far away but parking's no problem (which has to be something of a first for Grenoble), it's a pleasure being here (everybody smiles and the flower arrangements are lovely), and the food's good. Try the calf's head or the *boudin* of frog's legs and you'll see what we mean. Set meals 115–145F.

CORENC 38700 (10KM N)

CAFÉ-RESTAURANT DE LA CHAPELLE

12 route de Chartreuse; it's 15 minutes from the centre of Grenoble; take the D512 in the direction of Saint-Pierre-de-Chartreuse.
☎ 04.76.88.05.40
Closed Mondays (unless it's a public holiday) and Sunday evenings. **Car park. Disabled access.**

If you're here in summer, do what the locals do and head for the hills instead of sweltering in the centre of town. This unpretentious café cum restaurant has long had a reputation as a place where you could enjoy home cooking, a friendly atmosphere, and best of all a shady terrace. Set meals 66F, 90F and 130F. If you don't like *gratin dauphinois* or bilberry tart, pass on by.

URIAGE-LES-BAINS 38410 (10KM SE)

☎ |●| AUBERGE DU VERNON

Les Davids; when you get to Uriage, follow the signs for Chamrousse via col du Luitel.
☎ 04.76.89.10.56
Closed Oct–April (except by reservation). **Car park**.

Service until 9pm. The Girouds have been welcoming guests for the past 27 years and for 75F you can enjoy good home cooking served up in generous portions. If that doesn't appeal, ask for whatever takes your fancy and they'll see what they can do. Country cooking with morels and cream, and homemade desserts. Reckon on 120–200F. You won't be able to move for the next two days. Animals are not allowed, except on the terrace. They also have six tiny and very pretty rooms at prices ranging from 150F to 250F. Peace and quiet guaranteed.

|●| HÔTEL-RESTAURANT LES MÉSANGES**

How to get there: it's 1km along the Saint-Martin-d'Uriage road – turn right on the Bouloud road.
☎ 04.76.89.70.69 F➜ 04.76.89.56.97
Closed Oct 20–Easter (except weekends and school holidays). **Car park**. **TV**. **Canal+**.

Lunch served 12.30–2pm and dinner 7.30–9pm. The Prince family has owned this place since 1946 and it has a solid reputation. All the rooms have been refurbished and the loveliest ones, which have big balconies, have a view of the valley as far as Vizille. Doubles 250F with shower/wc, 295F with balcony and TV. In the restaurant, you don't need to have second thoughts about the 120F set meal based on traditional local dishes. If that doesn't appeal, there are other set meals ranging in price from 80F (not available on Sundays) to 230F, which have got lots of taste even if they're low in calories. Lovely walks nearby. Heated swimming pool.

GRIGNAN 26230

|●| LA PICCOLINA

How to get there: it's beneath the château, close to the town hall.
☎ 04.75.46.59.20
Closed Mondays and Dec 15–Jan 10.

A delightful little restaurant serving grills, good salads and tasty pizzas – one of those pizza places that are as good as some self-styled "gourmet" restaurants. Reckon on 80–120F a head.

HAUTERIVES 26390

|●| LE RELAIS**

place de l'Église (West).
☎ 04.75.68.81.12 F➜ 04.75.68.92.42
Closed Sunday evenings, Mondays (except in July and August), and February. **Secure parking**.

If you stop in Hauterives, it's probably to have a look at the fantastic structure built by the postman Ferdinand Cheval, using stones he collected during his rounds. Photos and engravings of the town's famous son decorate the walls of this impressive 19th century building with its thick sturdy walls and large country-style bedrooms with flowered wallpaper. Prices are very reasonable – doubles 150F with basin, 240F with shower/wc or bath. The restaurant offers regional set meals at prices ranging from 78F to 140F. Don't forget to toast the postman!

SAINT-MARTIN-D'AOÛT 26330 (9KM S)

10% |●| HÔTEL-RESTAURANT REY-PIEFERT

Centre; it's in the square.
☎ 04.75.68.63.12 F➜ 04.75.68.63.50
Closed Friday evenings, Saturdays (except for groups), and Sunday evenings (out of season); accommodation may be possible when the hotel is closed as long as you book. **Car park**.

This is an ideal place to stay if you're planning to spend a couple of days having a look at the countryside that would have been so familiar to Ferdinand Cheval, the postman who built that surreal structure in Hauterive. It has very simple rooms at prices ranging from 130F to 160F and they overlook the main square of this quiet little village where people still stop to watch cars go by. In the restaurant, your fellow diners will more than likely be hunters and other regulars. Treat yourself to the house *charcuterie*, ravioli stuffed with sardines, and stew of suckling pig or fillet of beef with morels, all of which you'll find in the set meals at 60F (weekday lunchtimes – evenings 68F), 80F, 100F and 130F.

JOYEUSE 07260

|●| HÔTEL DE L'EUROPE**

Centre; on the D104.
☎ 04.75.39.51.26 F➜ 04.75.39.59.00
Car park. **TV**. **Disabled access**.

Small refurbished bedrooms at decent prices. Doubles 160F with basin and 200F and up with shower/wc or bath. Large heated indoor pool and a pitch for boules. Half-board 210F per person. Prices in the restaurant/pizzeria are average, with a set meal at 58F. Overall, fair value for money for a place that's on the way to the gorges of the Ardèche and the Cévennes.

|●| RESTAURANT VALENTINA

place de la Peyre (Centre).
☎ 04.75.39.90.65
Closed Mondays (except in summer) and Nov 1–April 1.

Lunch served noon–2pm and dinner 7–11pm. This is the only restaurant in the old part of town and, since it's well away from traffic, the terrace overlooking a nice little square makes a pleasant place to sit. The owners are a nice Italian couple who are keen travellers — the light fixtures are made out baskets they bought on a trip to Guatemala. As far as the cooking is concerned, your tastebuds will be eternally grateful for you having introduced them to the flavours of pasta with pine nuts, ravioli with ceps, and tagliatelli with smoked salmon and a vodka sauce. Reckon on 70F or thereabouts for the *menu du jour.* They also do a 118F set meal. The home-made desserts are seriously good — try the *delizia*, made from chocolate, amaretti biscuits, and hazelnuts, or the tiramisu. Good Italian wines. A nice place.

SAINT-ALBAN-AURIOLLES 07120 (10KM SE)

☗ |●| HÔTEL DOUCE FRANCE**

(South-West); on the D208.
☎ 04.75.39.37.08 F 04.75.39.04.93
Car park. **Disabled access**.

It's advisable to book in summer if you want to stay in this reasonably priced hotel with a pool. In the main building, doubles with shower go for 250F. And half-board, starting at 230F, is a pretty good deal. Reckon on 280F for accommodation in the bungalows, which are better situated. Prices in the restaurant are very affordable, with set meals 65–200F. There are vineyards all around and the maternal grandparents of 19th century author Alphonse Daudet lived not too far away.

LA-MOTTE-CHALANCON 26470

|●| LES 3 DIABLES

47 bis Grand Rue (Centre).
☎ 04.75.27.21.33
Closed Wednesday evenings and in January.

It's small, friendly, informal and lively – and it has a lunchtime set meal for just 70F. The chef always takes time to ask his customers (with a note of anxiety in his voice) if they enjoyed their meal. He and his two daughters – one in the dining room, the other in the kitchen – will serve you some great little dishes, like flambéd *Picodon* (a rather strong goat's milk cheese) with fine herbs which will really have you licking your lips...They're not shy about using a bit of alcohol in their dishes especially in the home-made tarts, and we certainly didn't leave a crumb. See for yourself – if they carry on the way they're doing at the moment, you won't be disappointed. Other set meals 93F, 123F and 142F. Devilishly good!

JULIÉNAS 69840

10% ☗ |●| CHEZ LA ROSE**

(Centre).
☎ 04.74.04.41.20 F 04.74.04.49.29
Closed two weeks in February and Nov 15–Dec 15; restaurant closed Mondays and Tuesday lunchtimes.
Car park. **TV**.

Lunch served noon–2pm and dinner 7.15–9.30pm. Rose is no longer with us but her spirit lives on in the house and the regulars still talk about her with genuine affection. Two separate buildings house the comfortable country-style bedrooms. Doubles 200–290F with shower/wc, 240–320F with bath. The magnificent dining room is a fitting setting for the renowned regional cooking. The set meals are a bit expensive — prices range from 98F to 275F — but worth the money.

LAMASTRE 07270

|●| AUBERGE DU RETOURTOUR

(West); from Lamastre, head for Puy; the restaurant is on the right 2km further on — follow the arrows.
☎ 04.75.06.41.61 F 04.75.06.45.09
Closed end Oct–end March.

The inn offers traditional cooking and good value for money. The 89F set meal, for example, consists of four courses. Other set meals 120F and 175F. The chef's specialities include frog's legs and skate wing with green peppercorns. On the wine front, you can have a Côtes-du-Rhône for 50F. In summer, grilled dishes and pizzas are served on the terrace. There's a lake practically on the inn's doorstep and another interesting feature is the rockface at the back of the dining room. One more thing that makes this place special – if you're coming from the station, all you have to do is call and they'll lay on free transport.

CRESTET (LE) 07270 (8KM NE)

10% LA TERRASSE**

Centre; take the D534 in the direction of Tournon.
☎ 04.75.06.24.44 F 04.75.06.23.25
Closed Wednesdays in winter.
Secure parking. TV. Disabled access.

Service from noon and 7.30pm. There's an air of serenity about this classic hotel cum restaurant and you get the feeling that the people here know how to live well. Once a week, Danièle and Michel organize an outing for their customers that always ends with the traditional game of pétanque. The rooms are adequate. Doubles with basin 170F, with shower/wc from 230F. The set meals (60–160F) feature regional dishes. Don't forget to try the local goat's cheese called *picodon* – as its name suggests, it has a slightly piquant flavour. The dining room has a lovely view of the valley of the Doux and, in summer, the garden laid out round the pool is full of flowers and a rampant vine provides shade for the terrace.

LANS-EN-VERCORS 38250

HÔTEL-RESTAURANT LES ALLIÈRES

BP18; 4km on foot from the village.
☎ 04.76.95.90.90 F same
Closed in November.

Lunch served noon–3pm and dinner 7.30–9.30pm. The inn basks in the sun at the foot of the mountain known as Saint-Michel and it will take you exactly 20 minutes to walk up to it from the village. It has just what everyone needs, from something quick on the terrace for the hiker or crosscountry skier to a warm goat's cheese salad, *crosets* or *croûte au bleu*. Meals 85–140F. In the evening, treat yourself to *raclette* (100F) or *braserade* (135F) and if you're tired, they have a few rooms – half-board is 190F. So why not treat yourself to that brandy after all?

10% HÔTEL-RESTAURANT DE LA SOURCE**

Bouilly (South-West); head for Villard-de-Lans until you come to the tiny village of Bouilly.
☎ 04.76.95.42.52 F 04.76.95.41.29
Closed Sunday evenings and Mondays out of season (Sept–Jan inclusive and April–June inclusive), and Oct 15–Dec 1. **Car park. TV** (on request).

The pretty terrace overlooks parkland and you'll get a panoramic view of the mountains of Vercors, with pic Saint-Michel to the west and Grande Moucherolle to the east. Regional specialities are what's on offer and the set meals are very varied and the dishes well presented. What's more, you'll get a very nice welcome. Special rates for groups and coach parties (set meal 98F including wine and coffee). For individuals, there's a set meal at 90F. Half-board is compulsory in season and costs about 260F. Doubles 250F with shower/wc.

10% AUBERGE DE LA CROIX-PERRIN

col de la Croix-Perrin; from Lans-en-Vercors, head in the direction of Autrans; 4km further on, you'll come to col de la Croix-Perrin.
☎ 04.76.95.40.02 F same
Closed Wednesdays out of season and one week in December. **Car park.**

The old mountain hut, which lies deep in the forest at an altitude of 1,200m, has been modernized but has lost none of its charm – quite the reverse! The handsome wood-clad dining room with its panoramic views and old engravings, the traditional cooking and the hearty welcome combine to make the city seem far far away. The hotel's been renovated. Doubles 250F with shower/wc, set meal 88F. You'll feel you could climb a mountain.

LANSLEBOURG 73480

10% HÔTEL DE LA VIEILLE POSTE**

☎ 04.79.05.93.47 F 04.79.05.86.85
Closed mid April–mid May and Nov 1–Dec 20.
Secure parking. TV.

A large building, typically Savoyard in appearance, and the centre of downhill skiing in Val Cenis. The French national team are regulars here and medals and cups have overflowed the confines of the bar and are beginning to colonize the dining room. The set meals, at 70–110F, feature home cooking and traditional dishes. Bedrooms are modern and pleasant – they've been refurbished throughout – and prices start at 270F.

LÉCHÈRE (LA) 73260

RESTAURANT LA VIEILLE FORGE

Bellecombe.
☎ 04.79.24.17.97 F same

Closed lunchtimes and Tuesdays but open till 4am. **Car park**.

The restaurant used to be a blacksmith's shop and the former occupant seems to have left some of his things behind. The present occupant has introduced all sorts of instruments, from a piano to a balafon (an African instrument something like a xylophone) so that his customers can indulge in a jam session if the mood takes them. Tasty traditional cooking and set meals 65–150F. This is the type of place where you can party till dawn. Live music every Friday.

VALMOREL 73260 (18KM S)

RESTAURANT CHEZ ALBERT

Centre; head for Moutiers-Aigueblanche.
☎ 04.79.09.81.77
Closed beginning May–end June and mid Sept–mid Dec.

Yes, they serve pizzas but these aren't just any old pizzas. Rumour has it — and we quite agree — that these are the best in Valmorel. There's a whole range to choose from, and toppings include scallops, mushrooms and cheese (40–90F). They also have mixed salads and pasta dishes. If you go à la carte, reckon on about 80F or there are set meals for 68F, 73F and 96F. A good restaurant with a friendly atmosphere, just like the ski resort itself.

RESTAURANT LE SKI ROC

Centre; it's in a pedestrian street at the end of the main street.
☎ 04.79.09.83.17
Closed mid May–mid June and mid Sept–mid Dec.

Relax on one of the loungers on the terrace and look at the view as music plays in the background. Anybody who's anybody in Valmorel comes here — Denis and Valérie have turned it into one of the in places. Set meals 78F and 98F; à la carte, reckon on about 130F. They do a good fondue and *braserade* and we haven't tasted a better *raclette* made with Reblochon (a mild local cheese). Good value for money and friendly service.

LORIOL-SUR-DRÔME 26270

CAFÉ DES POMMIERS OU CHEZ LE RUGBYMAN

route du Pouzin; it's on the left-hand side of the road between Loriol and Le Pouzin.
☎ 04.75.63.80.75
Closed the second and third week in August.

You'll think somebody's having you on at first but as you cast your eyes over the number of people stuffing their faces you'll realize that the punters don't come here for gourmet food and picturesque surroundings (that's the last word that could be applied to the dining room). What they do come for is a good *cassoulet* or a rare breast of duck. Since the prices are incredibly cheap and you can get away with 60F (that includes a small carafe of local wine), it's hardly surprising the atmosphere is so cheerful; it's just off the motorway so why have a dreary sandwich in an equally dreary layby when you could eat here instead? Especially when there's a terrace.

LYON 69000

SEE MAP OVERLEAF

1st arrondissement

10% HÔTEL SAINT-VINCENT**

9 rue Pareille; M° Hôtel de Ville. **MAP B1-1**
☎ 04.78.27.22.56 Fax 04.78.30.92.87
TV.

The little street that the hotel's in leads to "La Fresque des Lyonnais", a wall with paintings of all the town's celebrities on it. The hotel, freshly repainted itself, is not lacking in charm, despite the rather cold breakfast room. All of the rooms are very well equipped and a few also have beautiful fire-places and are pleasantly furnished. Prices 220–300F depending on the sanitary arrangements. Excellent welcome guaranteed.

LA RANDONNÉE

4 rue Terme; M° Hôtel de Ville. **MAP C1-31**
☎ 04.78.27.86.81
Closed Sunday lunchtimes and Mondays.

At the bottom of a steep road that goes towards Croix Rousse, this is one of the least expensive restaurants in Lyons and is very popular with its young customers who can't rely on Daddy's Jaguar (and wallet) to get them everywhere in life. The very nice owners offer simple home cooking and typically Lyons dishes at very reasonable prices. Lunchtime main courses 25F and 35F, with one at 30F for vegetarians. In the evening, prices start at 35F and those with a bit more money in their pockets can splash out on the 68F set meal. Wines at giveaway prices. The hardest thing will be to find a table among all these youngsters squeezed into the two little dining rooms, one up and one down.

|●| RESTAURANT LA MEUNIÈRE

11 rue Neuve. M° Cordeliers. **MAP D2-21**
☎ 04.78.28.62.91
Closed Sundays, Mondays, and mid July–mid Aug.
Disabled access.

What you'll get here is a wonderful welcome, an abundance of good local dishes, a buffet of mouthwatering starters, and a friendly atmosphere; it's just the place whether you're a complete novice or a diehard fan when it comes to traditional Lyons food. Dishes include the old faithfuls *cochonnaille* (various parts of the pig), *tablier de sapeur* (ox tripe coated with egg and breadcrumbs before being grilled), and *andouillette* (a type of sausage). Have some Beaujolais or Côtes-du-Rhône to wash it down. Set meals 95F, 120F and 150F. Terrific.

|●| RESTAURANT LA ROMANÉE

19 rue Rivet; 800m from M° Croix-Paquet. **MAP B1-22**
☎ 04.72.00.80.87
Closed Saturday lunchtimes, Sunday evenings, Mondays, and in August.

Its reputation has not lessened over the years and Élisabeth Denis is still a fine cook. We loved the *foie gras*, the *terrine* of lamb with coriander and *tapenade*, the breast of duck with mushrooms and a truffle-scented sauce, and the stew of monkfish, mussels, shrimp and prawns that featured in the 155F set meal. And we were equally ecstatic over the selection of four home-made desserts. The impressive wine list runs to a total of 400 different wines. The restaurant has a maximum capacity of just 25 couverts and it's often fully booked several days in advance. So do book — and leave your car behind since parking can be a problem. One more thing — the dining room is a totally smoke-free zone. Set meals 98F, 155F and 195 F.

|●| RESTAURANT CHEZ GEORGES - AU P'TIT BOUCHON

8 rue du Garet. M° Hôtel-de-Ville-Louis-Pradel. **MAP D1-20**
☎ 04.78.28.30.46
Closed Saturdays and Sundays.

Set this down alongside an old Paris bistro and you wouldn't be able to tell them apart — same gingham napkins, same imitation leather bench seats, same mirrors on the wall, and same zinc-topped bar. The attentive but unobtrusive owner is on duty in the dining room while his wife is busy with the pots and pans in the pocket-handkerchief sized kitchen. The 115F "Lyon" set menu is well balanced and consists of pork sausage with lentils, grilled veal sausage, an astonishingly good Saint-Marcellin (a mild cheese from the Dauphiné) supplied by local cheese-merchant Alain Martinet, and a great apple tart. Reckon on paying 130F if you also have a half bottle of Côtes-du-Rhône. Set meal (lunchtimes) 84F.

|●| CAFÉ DES FÉDÉRATIONS

8 rue du Major-Martin – 8 rue Lyon-Terreaux. M° Hôtel-de-Ville. **MAP C2-23**
☎ 04.78.28.26.00
Closed Saturday lunchtimes, Sundays, and in August.

Raymond Fulchiron is keeping up the tradition of the "bouchon" (the local word for an eating establishment that specializes in sausages and wine) and that has earned him the gratitude of the locals, who regularly occupy the imitation leather banquettes that are as old as the frontage of the restaurant. The *tablier de sapeur* (ox tripe coated with egg and breadcrumbs before being grilled) and rabbit in mustard sauce together with some Morgon to wash it down will make all seem right with the world. Substantial helpings. Set meal 148F (118F at lunchtime).

|●| CHEZ HUGON

12 rue Pizay; M° Hôtel de Ville. **MAP D1-30**
☎ 04.78.28.10.94
Closed Saturdays, Sundays and Aug

An authentic and slightly old-fashioned Lyons "bouchon" in a narrow street not far from the town hall. We loved it. The dining room has only a few tables (they're covered with check tablecloths) and the owner makes sure everything's running smoothly from the bar. His wife prepares excellent Lyons specialities like sheep's trotters, black pudding, *museau* (muzzle of beef or pig), *tablier de sapeur* (ox tripe coated with egg and breadcrumbs, grilled, and served with garlic butter), *gâteau de foies de volaille* (chicken livers mixed with *foie gras*, eggs, and cream). Expect to pay 120–150F à la carte.

|●| LES MUSES

place de la Comédie; there's a lift beside the entrance to the opera house — take it to the 7th floor. **MAP D1-41**
☎ 04.72.00.45.58

Service until midnight. If you can't get a seat for the opera or ballet, this might be the next best thing. The long narrow dining room will give you a bird's eye view of what's going on down in the street. The décor is mainly black which is not such a bad idea since the eye is drawn to the large terrace overlooking the

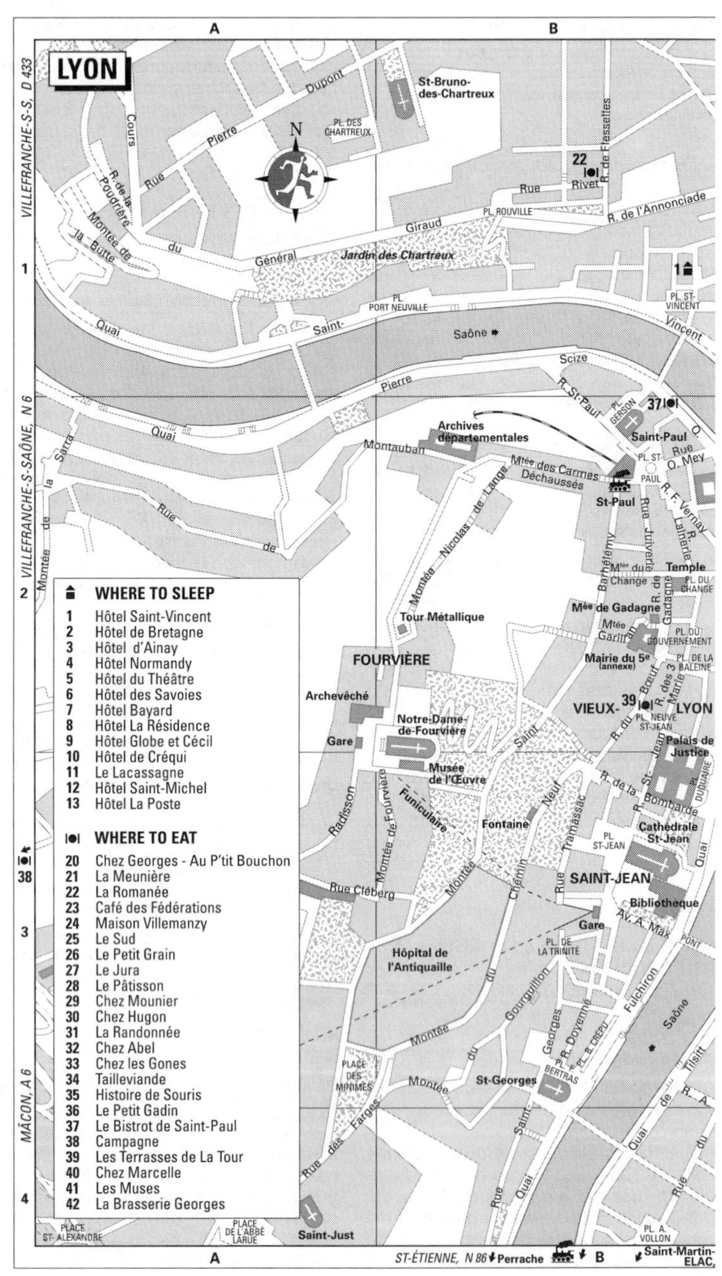
LYON
A
B
VILLEFRANCHE-S-S, D 433
VILLEFRANCHE-S-SAÔNE, N 6
MÂCON, A 6
St-Bruno-des-Chartreux
PL. DES CHARTREUX
Jardin des Chartreux
PL. ROUVILLE
R. de l'Annonciade
R. de Flesselles
Rue Rivet
Cours
Rue Pierre Dupont
R. de la Poudrière
Montée de la Butte
Quai Saint-Vincent
PL. PORT NEUVILLE
Saône
Quai Pierre Scize
PL. ST-VINCENT
R. St-Paul
PL. GERSON
Saint-Paul
Archives départementales
Montauban
Mtée des Carmes Déchaussés
St-Paul
Rue de la Sarra
Montée Nicolas de Lange
Rue Juiverie
R. Lainerie
R. F. Vernay
Temple
PL. DU CHANGE
Mtée du Change
Mée de Gadagne
Tour Métallique
FOURVIÈRE
Archevêché
Notre-Dame-de-Fourvière
Gare
Musée de l'Œuvre
Mairie du 5e (annexe)
PL. DU GOUVERNEMENT
PL. DE LA BALEINE
VIEUX-LYON
PL. NEUVE ST-JEAN
Palais de Justice
R. de la Bombarde
Cathédrale St-Jean
PL. ST-JEAN
SAINT-JEAN
Bibliothèque
Av. A. Max
Funiculaire
Fontaine
Rue Tramassac
Rue Cléberg
Montée de Fourvière
Radisson
Hôpital de l'Antiquaille
PL. DE LA TRINITÉ
Fulchiron
Montée du Gourguillon
PLACE DES MINIMES
St-Georges
Rue des Farges
Saint-Just
PLACE ST-ALEXANDRE
PLACE DE L'ABBÉ LARUE
PL. A. VOLLON
ST-ÉTIENNE, N 86
Perrache
Saint-Martin-ELAC
1
2
3
4
22
37
39
38
WHERE TO SLEEP
1 Hôtel Saint-Vincent
2 Hôtel de Bretagne
3 Hôtel d'Ainay
4 Hôtel Normandy
5 Hôtel du Théâtre
6 Hôtel des Savoies
7 Hôtel Bayard
8 Hôtel La Résidence
9 Hôtel Globe et Cécil
10 Hôtel de Créqui
11 Le Lacassagne
12 Hôtel Saint-Michel
13 Hôtel La Poste
WHERE TO EAT
20 Chez Georges - Au P'tit Bouchon
21 La Meunière
22 La Romanée
23 Café des Fédérations
24 Maison Villemanzy
25 Le Sud
26 Le Petit Grain
27 Le Jura
28 Le Pâtisson
29 Chez Mounier
30 Chez Hugon
31 La Randonnée
32 Chez Abel
33 Chez les Gones
34 Tailleviande
35 Histoire de Souris
36 Le Petit Gadin
37 Le Bistrot de Saint-Paul
38 Campagne
39 Les Terrasses de La Tour
40 Chez Marcelle
41 Les Muses
42 La Brasserie Georges

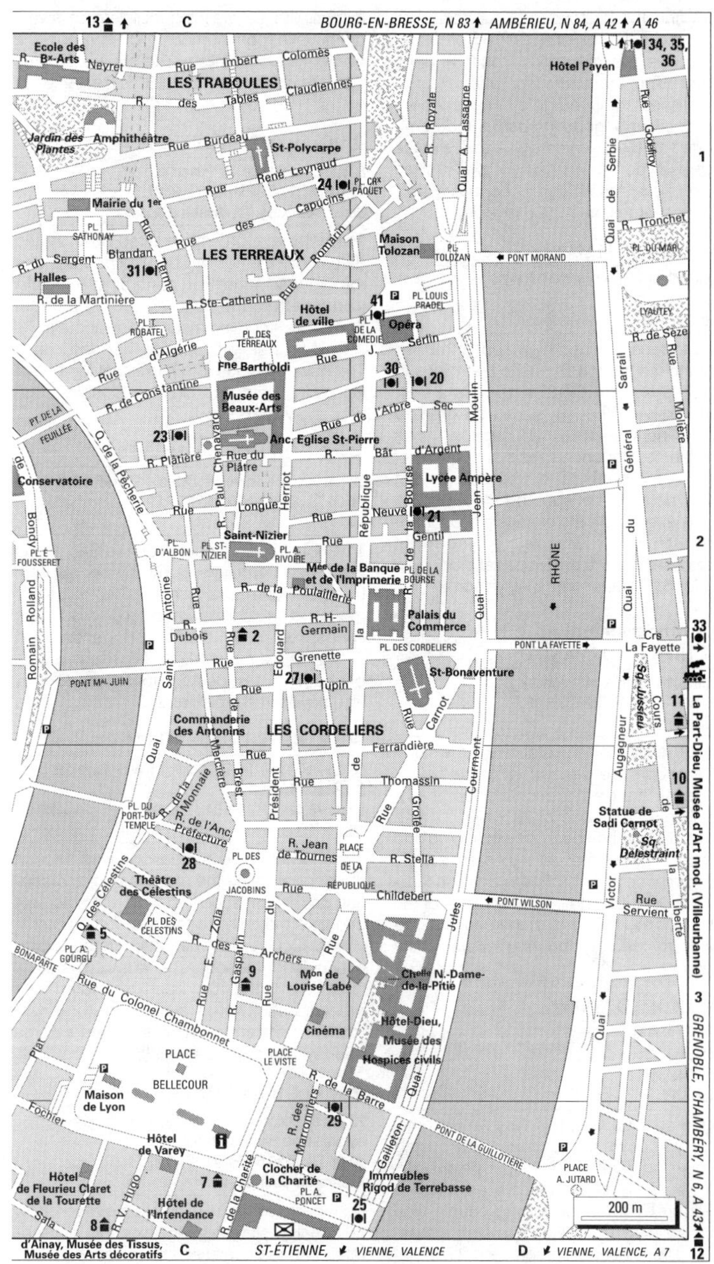
BOURG-EN-BRESSE, N 83
AMBÉRIEU, N 84, A 42 A 46
LES TRABOULES
LES TERREAUX
LES CORDELIERS
Hôtel de ville
Opéra
Musée des Beaux-Arts
Anc. Eglise St-Pierre
Lycée Ampère
Saint-Nizier
Mée de la Banque et de l'Imprimerie
Palais du Commerce
St-Bonaventure
Commanderie des Antonins
Théâtre des Célestins
Mon de Louise Labé
Chelle N.-Dame-de-la-Pitié
Hôtel-Dieu, Musée des Hospices civils
Cinéma
PLACE BELLECOUR
Maison de Lyon
Hôtel de Varey
Hôtel de Fleurieu Claret de la Tourette
Hôtel de l'Intendance
Clocher de la Charité
Immeubles Rigod de Terrebasse
Statue de Sadi Carnot
Hôtel Payen
Maison Tolozan
St-Polycarpe
Mairie du 1er
Amphithéâtre
Jardin des Plantes
Ecole des Bx-Arts
Halles
Conservatoire
RHÔNE
PONT MORAND
PONT LA FAYETTE
PONT WILSON
PONT DE LA GUILLOTIÈRE
PONT Mal JUIN
200 m
La Part-Dieu, Musée d'Art mod. (Villeurbanne)
GRENOBLE, CHAMBÉRY, N 6, A 43
ST-ÉTIENNE, VIENNE, VALENCE
VIENNE, VALENCE, A 7
d'Ainay, Musée des Tissus, Musée des Arts décoratifs

square and the belltowers of the town hall and to the colourful and skilfully prepared food that is the hallmark of chef Philippe Chavent. The *menu du jour* offers typical Lyons dishes but if you go à la carte there's an astonishingly good *croustillant* of lamb and dried apricots served with a sauce made from preserved lemons and coriander, or an amusing tuna "hamburger". *Formules* 90F, 120F (lunchtimes) and 150F (evenings).

MAISON VILLEMANZY

25 montée Saint-Sébastien. **MAP C1-24**
☎ 04.78.39.37.00
Closed Sundays and 3 weeks in Jan.

With a terrace perched high above the city, this authentic bourgeois house that clings to the slopes of Croix-Rousse is worth a visit; it's best to book though, since it's extremely popular. The kitchen is in the capable hands of Guillaume Mouchel, asssistant to one of the city's top chefs. The well thought out *menu carte* (125F) offers modern-day bistro food while reflecting the changing seasons. If you're watching your waistline, you might want to consider the day's special plus green salad for 68F. Handsome dining room.

2nd arrondissement

10% HÔTEL NORMANDY**

3 rue du Bélier (South); M° Perrache.
☎ 04.78.37.31.36 F 04.78.40.98.56
TV. Canal+.

It may be just beside the station (on the same side as cours de Verdun), but the hotel's called after that great French liner and has a painting of her on one of its walls. It's in a quiet street that has been smartened up and has about forty small but elegant rooms, ranging in price from 160F with washing facilities to 270F with bath. Reduced rates at the weekend. The double-glazing keeps out the noise from the neighbouring railway quite well.

10% HÔTEL D'AINAY*

14 rue des Remparts-d'Ainay (South). M° Ampère-Victor-Hugo.
☎ 04.78.42.43.42
Car park. TV.

If you're on a budget, this very simple hotel will suit you down to the ground; it's located in a quiet and rather delightful neighbourhood not far from the magnificent basilica and is run by a friendly young couple who work very hard to provide a restful atmosphere. The cheapest room — 170F — comes with just washing facilities but is very bright. Like room number 210 (shower/wc) it overlooks a very village-like square. Rooms with shower/wc or bath 230F. Reception is on the first floor.

HÔTEL DES SAVOIES**

80 rue de la Charité. M° Perrache.
☎ 04.78.37.66.94 F 04.72.40.27.84
Secure parking. TV. Disabled access.

The hotel is apparently a listed building and dates from the 40s or 50s. The frontage and the pretty wrought-iron handrail of the staircase are from the same period. Apart from that, there's nothing much to say about it; it's very staid but well looked after and clean. The private garage (35F), unusual for a hotel in the city centre, is a big plus. Doubles 250F with shower, 260F with bath.

10% HÔTEL DE BRETAGNE*

10 rue Dubois (Centre). M° Cordeliers. **MAP C2-2**
☎ 04.78.37.79.33 F 04.72.77.99.92
TV.

This hotel, half-way between the Saône and place des Cordeliers, is run by people from the Auvergne and offers good value for money. The rooms are clean, smart, and soundproof. Doubles with shower/wc 210–220F. Number 102 (270F) has two double beds and is ideal for four people. They also have three triples at 260F.

10% HÔTEL DU THÉÂTRE**

10 rue de Savoie. M° Bellecour; it's near place des Célestins. **MAP C3-5**
☎ 04.78.42.33.32 F 04.72.40.00.61
TV.

The show starts as soon as you walk through the door and see the staircase up to reception on the first floor. It looks like a stage set and sets the tone for the rest of the hotel. If you're lucky, you'll get one of the rooms overlooking the square — the view is stunning. The hotel has been renovated and redecorated. There's a nice little breakfast room and the atmosphere is relaxed. Rooms 265F with shower, 295F–335F with bath.

HÔTEL BAYARD**

23 place Bellecour. M° Bellecour; it's in the largest square in the city. **MAP C4-7**
☎ 04.78.37.39.64 F 04.72.40.95.51
Secure parking. TV.

No two rooms are alike and some have lots of personality. Number 2 for example is decorated in Directoire style with a canopied bed and a polished parquet floor just like Versailles — and it's got a great view of the square too. Number 5 has an enormous bathroom and number 15, which overlooks the courtyard, can sleep four. The little breakfast nook has a very country feel to it. Rooms 297 and 327F (the ones decorated in a specific style are 323–387F).

10% HÔTEL LA RÉSIDENCE***

18 rue Victor-Hugo. M° Bellecour or Ampère-Victor Hugo. **MAP C4-8**
☎ 04.78.42.63.28 F→ 04.78.42.85.76
TV. Canal+. Disabled access.

A bit old-fashioned but it's got all mod cons and it's not flashy — in other words, it's the kind of old-style place that gets handed down from father to son (or daughter) and where nothing ever changes; it's well situated in a busy and lively pedestrian street. Doubles 300F with shower/wc, 335F with bath.

10% HÔTEL GLOBE ET CÉCIL***

21 rue Gasparin. **MAP C3-9**
☎ 04.78.42.58.95 F→ 04.72.41.99.06
TV. Disabled access.

One of the best 3-stars in the city centre. Every room has its own particular character — some have handsome marble fireplaces and air-conditioning — and has been decorated in a style suitable to its size. The fabrics and the furniture have been carefully chosen. The rooms that overlook the street are brighter than the others. Some have a balcony. The service can't be faulted — your every wish is their command and they do it with a smile. An excellent hotel. Doubles 399–560F.

RESTAURANT CHEZ MOUNIER

3 rue des Marronniers. M° Bellecour. **MAP C4-29**
☎ 04.78.37.79.26
Closed Sunday evenings, Mondays and 3 weeks in Sept.

Lyons is famous for its puppets and the one in the window smiling at passers-by and inviting them in is Guignol, a nicer version of our Punch — for one thing, he doesn't beat up his wife!. The restaurant has two little dining rooms separated by a kind of corridor that gives you a bird's eye view of the wine cellar. There's a good atmosphere here and the regional cooking retains all of its character. The tarts they produce for dessert are pretty ordinary. Set meals 44F (weekday lunchtimes), 59F, 83F and 93F. Frankly, it's the best this very touristy street has to offer.

LE PETIT GRAIN

19 rue de la Charité (South). M° Ampère or Bellecour.
☎ 04.72.41.77.85
Closed Sundays and evenings after 8pm.

A simple little snack bar in an old milliner's shop near rue Auguste-Comte (the street with all the antique shops) that's prettily decorated with a scattering of objects picked up by the cheerful Vietnamese owner from street markets. For 40F, you can have a substantial *bo bun* (stir-fried beef and noodles), a delicious ham and orange salad, and the 45F day's special (which is often something Vietnamese or Chinese). For another 16F, you can also sample one of Olivier's terrific tarts — pear and chocolate, say, or apple and cinammon. While you're here, take a stroll — it's a nice neighbourhood.

LE PÂTISSON

17 rue du Port-du-Temple (Centre). M° Bellecour. **MAP C3-28**
☎ 04.72.41.81.71
Closed Friday evenings, Saturdays (open Saturday evenings Oct–March), Sundays, and the second fortnight in August.

Yves Perrin, owner of the only vegetarian restaurant in the city, worked in some good restaurants before deciding that, for health reasons, he should become a vegetarian. He's still proud of the diplomas he won in the old days though and has some of them on display. He hasn't lost any of his skill and his medallions of tofu with a julienne of saffron-flavoured vegetables and daily specials like millet and aubergines *provençale* bear all the hallmarks of a chef. Set meals 63F and 70F (lunchtimes), 70F, 90F and 110F (evenings). The décor's a bit bland — they'll need to have a think about it.

CHEZ ABEL

25 rue Guynemer (South). M° Ampère.
☎ 04.78.37.46.18
Closed Saturday lunchtimes, Sundays, and Aug 1–20.

This very old wainscoted restaurant a stone's throw from the Saône and 200m from the basilica looks like a folk museum — it's full of things, including hefty wooden tables and a very kitsch beer pump dating from 1925. House specialities include liver, calf's head, sausage in red wine, chicken with rice and *quenelles* of pike. Set meals 80F (lunchtimes) and 120F; à la carte, reckon on 150–170F.

LA BRASSERIE GEORGES

30 cours de Verdun; it's next to Perrache station.
☎ 04.72.56.54.54
Closed May 1.

This is where all the people come who don't go in for ostentation or who don't want to spend a lot of money ("you mustn't give the game away" says Madame Rinck with a smile). Her husband Didier comes from a big brewing family in Alsace and this enormous yet cosy old Art Deco brasserie with its cosmopolitan atmosphere is as authentic as they come. The food (not to mention the waiters) is authentic too and ranges from *saucisson brioché* (sausage in *brioche* dough with truffled *foie gras*) to *quenelles* of pike, taking in the inevitable *choucroute* along the way of course. Cheapest set meal is 85F. Reckon on 150–200F à la carte. "Could do better" say a few carping voices and so it could, but you don't get to see a place like this every day of the week.

LE SUD

11 place Antonin-Poncet (South). M° Bellecour. **MAP D4-25**
☎ 04.72.77.80.00
Car park.

Paul Bocuse, an ambassador for French cooking, cheerfully rides the waves of culinary fashion. With his previous venture *Le Nord* (18, rue Neuve, 04.72.10.69.69) he brought us the rotissoire. Here, as the name suggests, he has set out to capture the warmth and sunshine of the south in both the décor — the colour scheme is blue and yellow — and in the food, and dishes like roasted peppers and aubergine, *poulet de Bresse* cooked Moroccan style with preserved lemons, osso buco, risotto, and pizza with grilled vegetables are proving a hit. Set meal 105F (weekdays). Brasserie atmosphere. Big terrace on an uncluttered square.

LE JURA

25 rue Tupin (Centre). M° Cordeliers. **MAP C2-27**
☎ 04.78.42.20.57
Closed Saturdays and Sundays in summer, Sundays and Mondays in winter and July 20–Aug 20.

A period "bouchon" with globe-shaped lamps, a formica bar, and sawdust on the floor. There's *andouillette* (a type of sausage) in white wine, delicious chicken livers with *foie gras*, and a good *tablier de sapeur* (ox tripe coated with egg and breadcrumbs before being grilled). Reckon on paying 130F à la carte. Set meal 98F.

3rd arrondissement

10% LE LACASSAGNE***

245 av. Lacassagne (East). M° Grange-Blanche; it's a fair distance from the centre, near the hospitals and the town of Bron. Off map **D2-11**
☎ 04.78.54.09.12 Fax 04.72.36.99.23
Secure parking. TV. Disabled access.

It won't appeal to the tourists but it's ideally situated if you're in medicine or a related field since there are no fewer than five hospitals in the neighbourhood, plus the international training school for nurses. The rooms are pretty big and some overlook a garden. Nice welcome and reasonable prices. Doubles with bath 230–310F. Light meals (salad, *croque-monsieur*, cream cheese) can be provided for 55F.

10% HÔTEL DE CRÉQUI**

158 rue de Créqui (East). M° Guichard; it's not far from the TGV station. Off map **D3-10**
☎ 04.78.60.20.47 Fax 04.78.62.21.12
TV. Canal+.

A new and spanking clean hotel. The bedrooms are comfortable, cheerful — yellow walls and blue carpet — and of an adequate size (367F with bath). Lots of smiles from the staff but they're professional too and know their business. To get into the city centre, all you have to do is cross pont Wilson; it's about a 10 minute walk. Set meals from 50F.

CHEZ LES GONES

102 cours Lafayette. Off map **D2-33**
☎ 04.78.60.91.61
Closed Sundays and Mondays.

You'll find this welcoming "bouchon" in the covered market, with all the fish stalls on one side and vegetables on the other. Lyons takes on a whole new look from the little dining room where people stop off early in the morning for something to eat in the company of relaxed market traders. Set meal 75F. If you like oysters and shellfish, try a restaurant called *Merle*, which specializes in them (and is packed with locals on Sunday mornings). Why not do some shopping while you're here? Pick up a good *saucisson de Lyon* or some *rosette* (dry pork sausage eaten cold in slices) from Colette Sibilia or some Saint-Marcellin from Alain Martinet's cheese stall. You won't regret it.

4th arrondissement

10% HÔTEL DE LA POSTE

1 rue Victor Fort (North); M° Croix-Rousse. Off map **C1-13**
☎ 04.78.28.62.67

One of the least expensive hotels in town and certainly one of the nicest. It's located in the heart of the marvellous Croix-Rousse neighbourhood and housed in a working class block of flats and though it's not exactly oozing with charm, it's very well looked after. The lovely proprietress has a friendly smile for everybody, but only lets half of her twenty rooms, reserving the others for her regulars. So, it's up to you to become one. Rooms from 100F, then 135–180F (with shower).

|●| RESTAURANT HISTOIRE DE SOURIS

2 rue de Belfort or 36 quai Arloing (North). M° Croix-Rousse. Off map **D1-35**
☎ 04.78.30.51.40
Closed Saturday lunchtimes and Sundays.

Two very unpretentious restaurants where, in keeping with the village atmosphere of the neighbourhood, everyone knows everyone else and people exchange their news over steak tartare or fondue. The service is informal and the atmosphere friendly. Set meals 62F and 90F. Day's special 46F.

|●| LE PETIT GADIN

17 rue d'Austerlitz (North). M° Croix-Rousse. Off map **D1-36**
☎ 04.78.39.72.85
Closed Saturday lunchtimes, Sundays, Christmas–New Year's Day, and one week for the Assumption (August 15).

The artists and yuppies who've moved into the area really appreciate the restaurant's enormous garden, which is a forest of sun umbrellas in summer. If you want to have dinner, you'll have to book since it's very popular once the sun's gone down and it's a bit cooler. The large dining room, with its windows overlooking the garden (open wide to catch the breeze) and solid stone walls, is very pleasant. À la carte, there's *charlotte* of lamb and aubergines, queen scallops and haddock in puff pastry with a saffron sauce, duck with olives, and the catch of the day; it's all prepared with lots of TLC. Relaxed atmosphere and friendly waitress service. Set meal 118F. The 63F lunchtime *formule* (starter plus main course) is terrific value for money.

|●| TAILLEVIANDE

3 place des Tapis (North). M° Croix-Rousse. Off map **D1-34**
☎ 04.78.28.48.82
Closed Sunday evenings, Mondays and, usually, May.

Proprietor Yves Daguin is first and foremost a butcher and to get to the restaurant you'll have to go through his butcher's shop! Since he loves what he does and loves good meat he decided to bring it to people's attention in a very simple way. He's no cook so you choose your meat unadorned, with no sauce. For a starter, why not share a platter of lamb kidneys, sweetbreads and testicles (65F) or one of *saucisson de Lyon* (50F), before moving onto the meat you've selected for yourself or *andouillette beaujolaise* (a type of sausage cooked in Beaujolais) for 75F. To drink, there's a very good selection of reasonably priced wines from tiny vineyards around Beaujolais and Côtes-du-Rhône, much better than you'd find in a good many "bouchons". Set meals 72F, 90F and 135F. Reckon on about 150F à la carte. Big terrace in front of the butcher's shop.

5th arrondissement

|●| LE BISTROT DE SAINT-PAUL

2 quai de Bondy. **MAP B2-37**
☎ 04.78.28.63.19
Closed Sundays, public holidays and a few days around Aug 15.

If you're getting just the teeniest bit tired of Lyons specialities and feel like breast of duck or *cassoulet*, make a beeline for this bistro, where these and other authentic dishes from the south-west of France are lovingly prepared by Jean-Paul Labaste. The *confit* of duck with *pommes sarladaises* (baked sliced potatoes and truffles), the veal fillet with ceps and warm *foie gras*, and the cassoulet all burst with flavour. Set meals 67F (lunchtimes), 99F and 159F.

|●| CAMPAGNE

20 rue du Cardinal-Gerlier; take the Saint-Just funicular.
☎ 04.78.36.73.85

Anyone who's anyone in the city comes to this former boules pitch that's been converted into a fashionable *guinguette* (which is a place on the edge of town where you can dance and have drink, usually out of doors). There's an accordionist on hand on Tuesdays and Thursdays to entertain you as you sit under the trees, drink in hand, waiting for your meal. The starters and main courses come from various countries but they're all Mediterranean in flavour. There's tzatziki and hummus from Greece, *tapenade* and *anchoïade* from Provence, bulgur salad with herbs, *aïoli*, *keftedes* (Greek meatballs with herbs), stuffed vegetables, and eggs with sweet peppers. There's a chicken run at the back so don't be surprised if you hear a cock crowing. Reckon on 120–150F à la carte. Set meals 68F (lunchtimes) and 100F.

6th arrondissement

|●| CHEZ MARCELLE

71 cours Vitton (East). M° Massena.
☎ 04.78.89.51.07
Closed Saturdays, Sundays and Aug.

Marcelle is one of the last genuine "mères" (the name given to the old-fashioned style of woman cook) in the city. You don't come here for the décor (there isn't any) but for the food. The ritual is unchanging. First comes the selection of hors-d'œuvres — a whole series of salad bowls full of lentils, salad of fresh green beans (in season), wonderful *cervelas* (pork sausage), bacon, green peppers and so on. And it's a house rule that you don't ever say you can't eat any more. Next comes your choice of *tablier de sapeur* (ox tripe coated with egg and breadcrumbs before being grilled). — which is out of this world — calf's liver, or a thick slab of succulent meat. The orgy ends with a terrific *crème caramel*. Set meal (lunchtimes)150F. Reckon on about 200F *à la carte*.

7th arrondissement

10% HÔTEL SAINT-MICHEL*

64 rue Saint-Michel (South-East). M° Saxe-Gambetta.
☎ 04.78.72.48.84
Disabled access.

Reception closed noon–6pm. The hotel stands in a quiet street next to the church of Saint-Michel. Once you're inside, you'll find it quite dazzling. A 19th century town house, it still has some traces of its previous incarnation, including a very fine stair rail, a handsome light fixture in the lounge, and old woodwork here and there. The rooms are fairly bright, absolutely enormous, and furnished with the kind of heavy beds and wardrobes your grandmother had. It all makes a nice change from the usual run of the mill hotel. The bathroom is a bit of a do-it-yourself job (what a shower!) and the wcs are on the landing, but you can't have everything. Prices are good and the hotel is well looked after by a nice couple. Doubles 150–230F, depending on the size of the room. There's one with two double beds that can sleep four.

ÉCULLY 69130 (5KM NW)

RESTAURANT LE RELAIS

6 av. du Docteur-Terver (Centre); take the D77.
☎ 04.78.33.26.39
Closed Saturdays, Sunday evenings, Monday evenings, one week in February, and three weeks in August.

Lunch served noon–2pm and dinner 7–9pm. It's good to find an affordable restaurant in the centre of Écully, one that also gives you a nice welcome and where the cooking is very good and the décor pleasing. We hope you like our latest find. Set meals range in price from 78F (weekdays) to 176F. Classic dishes à la carte.

CHAPONOST 69630 (10KM SW)

RESTAURANT LE CROÛTON

27 bis av. Paul-Doumer (Centre); take the D50.
☎ 04.78.45.06.47
Closed Wednesdays and in August.

This little restaurant is making a reputation for itself and could become — if it isn't already — extremely popular with people who love good food. There are two dining rooms, one on each floor, and the décor is restful and in good taste. Lots of businessmen and families come here for the imaginative style of home cooking (which may sound like a contradicton in terms but isn't). Set meals range in price from 60F (weekdays) to 190F. À la carte also available. A wonderful restaurant.

ALBIGNY-SUR-SAÔNE 69250 (15KM N)

LE PÈRE RIGODON

31 quai Henri Barbusse.
☎ 04.72.08.84.88
Closed Oct–April.

A team who cut their collective teeth on several successful bars and night clubs have taken over this old café on the north bank of the Saône. The walls have been restored at some considerable expense and it's been fitted out with wonderful bistro-style furniture, enamelled plaques and collections of carafes and ash trays. As for food, you can either have a frog's legs set meal (98F) or a whitebait set meal (75F). There's room for improvement in both but they're pretty decent. What makes it so attractive is of course the marvellous gravel terrace that goes all the way down to the river. The colourful furniture and the accordionist who puts in an occasional appearance add to the cheery atmosphere. It does have one or two drawbacks – it's a bit too close to the D51, the young staff don't smile enough, and the whole place feels a bit artificial.

CHASSELAY 69380 (20KM N)

GUY LASSAUSAY

How to get there: take the A6
☎ 04.78.47.62.59
Closed Tuesday evenings, Wednesdays, one week in February, and three weeks in August.

After working under a number oftop chefs, Guy Lassausay decided to take over his family's restaurant in this fairly dull village and give it a new lease of life. His dishes are basically classical but he's added some modern touches to them and he is bound to make a name for himself in time. A great wine list with wines from all over the world, fast friendly service, and prices that are very reasonable for this type of restaurant makes this a great place to eat if you like gourmet food. Even the cheapest (160F) set meal gives you a good idea of the intelligent combination of ingredients. It's impossible to give you an example of what's on the menu as it changes all the time. But remember to leave room for the wonderful mature cheese and something from the delicious dessert trolley.

MEGÈVE 74120

10% HÔTEL CHALET DES OURS*

chemin des Roseaux (Centre).
☎ 04.50.21.57.40 F 04.50.93.05.73
Closed in May and November. **Car park**.

We still haven't got over the shock of finding such a little gem in the opulent surroundings of Megève. It's run by an Englishwoman who moved to France, bringing all her culture and refined ways with her. The panelled rooms are decorated in a low-key manner with vases of flowers, and the duvets make you want to snuggle down in bed. It's like a B&B. There's a room with a beautiful fireplace, where you can sit and read or watch TV. There's a small dining room in the basement. The food is simple, but there's a rather exotic Thai set meal for 80F. Doubles with shower/wc 280–380F. And there's a choice of five different kinds of tea for breakfast! We love this place.

MENS 38710

10% LA MEISOU DOU BOURG***

place du Breuil (Centre).
☎ 04.76.34.81.00 F 04.76.34.80.90
TV. **Disabled access**.

You wonder what on earth possessed the locals to scrape together the money for this funny place. It's never closed, and you can just walk in and wander round the bar, the sitting room, the terrace and the garden. So why are there hardly any people here, when it's so quiet and clean? Could it be the prices? 230–300F. Set meals 70F, 90F and 120F.

CHICHILIANNE 38930 (20KM W)

CHÂTEAU DE PASSIÈRES**

How to get there: take the D526 from Mens to Clelles, then the D7 to the foot of mont Aiguille.
☎ 04.76.34.45.48 F 04.76.34.46.25
Closed Sunday evenings and Mondays (out of season), and Nov 15–Dec 30. **Car park**. **TV**.

A 15th century château in a magnificent location in a village with an unforgettable name. The owner, by the way, is also the mayor. All the rooms are bang up to date in terms of comfort and the prices (240–370F) are the kind we like. What's nice about this place is the lounge, where you can sit and chat into the small hours, the bar, and the imaginative cooking served in the large dining room. Set meals at 95F (*compote* of duck and trout with walnuts), 135F (little turnovers studded with truffles on a creamy leek sauce – delicious – and salmon steak with dandelion honey), 180F and 220F. Museum in the grounds and a nice swimming pool.

SAINT-PAUL-LÈS-MONESTIER 38650 (23KM NW)

10% HÔTEL-RESTAURANT AU SANS SOUCI**

How to get there: on the D34 from Mens to Monestier; leave the village by the N75 and the hotel's 2km further on.
☎ 04.76.34.03.60 F 04.76.34.17.38
Closed Sunday evenings and Mondays out of season, and in January. **Secure parking**. **TV**.

Service noon–1.30pm and 7pm–8.30pm. You don't have to worry about a thing when you come to this place! Everything in this family hotel has been running smoothly here for years, in fact the place has just celebrated its 60th birthday. Lovely, comfortable rooms 275–280F. It's a stone's throw from Vercors regional park and surrounded by greenery. The restaurant is showing its age (but they shouldn't change anything!) and you'll feel great there, both before and especially after your meal. Set meals 89F (weekdays), 98F (goat's cheese tart with chives and braised trout from their pond), 120F, 135F and 170F (with char or lamb *en croûte* in garlic butter). Swimming pool, boules, and so on.

MIJOUX 01410

LES VUARNES**

rue Val-Mijoux (Centre).
☎ 04.50.41.32.13 F 04.50.41.32.18

Closed the third week in May and Nov 1–third week in Dec. **Car park**.

When you think of Mijoux, you think of peace and quiet, walks, nature, and, in winter, skiing. There's a relaxing atmosphere, which will help you unwind. Though the hotel has the outmoded uniformity of style characteristic of the 60s and 70s, there is a certain charm about it. The rooms are spacious, with bath, telephone, and balcony, so you can sit out in the sun. Doubles with bath from 265F. The dining room too is fairly anonymous but it serves good regional food – trout, escalopes with cream and morels – and isn't expensive. Set meals 65–150F. Half-board (from 260F) is compulsory during the February school holidays. Friendly welcome and service.

LÉLEX 01410 (8KM SW)

HÔTEL-RESTAURANT MONT JURA**

old route de Mijoux (Centre); take the D991.
☎ 04.50.20.90.53 F 04.50.20.95.20
Closed Tuesdays out of season.
Secure parking. Disabled access.

This large house is in a tiny village, and, although it doesn't have a lot of character and the country-style décor is pretty uninspiring, the warm reception you get from the family who own it makes up for it all. Hearty regional food at decent prices. Set meals 85F and 120F (this is the gourmet meal). Spacious rooms, which are simple but comfortable. Doubles 180F with washing facilities, 280F with shower or bath.

MIRMANDE 26270

RESTAURANT MARGOT

Centre; it's near the post office.
☎ 04.75.63.08.05
Closed Wednesdays and Dec–Jan.

This is a place for people who love traditional cooking. In summer you can go inside to cool off in the dining room which is tastefully decorated with paintings and old posters, or you can sit out on one of the benches on the terrace in the shade of the climbing vines. Set meals range in price from 75F (weekdays) to 135F. Choice of regional specialities à la carte. The restaurant, like the village (which is listed) is a mixture of stylishness and rustic simplicity.

CLIOUSCLAT 26270 (2KM N)

LA TREILLE MUSCATE**

How to get there: leave the autoroute du Soleil at Loriol-sur-Drôme and it's 6km further south.
☎ 04.75.63.13.10 F 04.75.63.10.79
Closed Wednesdays and in January.
Secure parking. TV. Canal+. Disabled access.

A large pretty house with green shutters and walls partially covered in ivy. Inside, the dining room is bright and roomy, with a fireplace in one corner and a few stylish tables. This part of the world is known for its bright sunshine and subtle aromas, and the food reflects that. It's bright and fresh and local produce is used in dishes like rabbit in puff pastry with broad beans and basil. Set meals 85F and 135F. Excellent value for money. You'll get a first-class welcome too. Rooms 300F with shower/wc and 300–550F with bath; it's ideal if you feel the need to escape the motorway for a while. And there's a charming village to explore too. Our favourite spot in Drôme.

MODANE 73500

10% HÔTEL-RESTAURANT LE PERCE NEIGE**

14 av. Jean-Jaurès (Centre); it's opposite the station.
☎ 04.79.05.00.50 F 04.79.05.12.92
Closed May 1–15 and mid Oct–start of Nov. **TV**.

The type of place you spend one night in since there's not much about the town that would tempt you to stay longer. The rooms are simple and the welcome could be described in the same way as the town — nondescript. Doubles 245F with shower/wc, 333F with bath. Good traditional food. Set meals 73–114F; it's all pretty soundproof, which is just as well, seeing as the hotel is on the main road and right opposite the railway line.

MONTBRISON 42600

10% HÔTEL-RESTAURANT DES VOYAGEURS

16 rue Simon-Boyer (Centre).
☎ 04.77.96.17.64
Closed 1 week at Christmas. **Car park. TV.**

A hotel in a little street in the centre of town; it's got a bit of old-fashioned charm, and that's what we like about it. The spacious rooms, with furniture from the 1930s and 40s, come with bath and cost 185–200F (breakfast included). The restaurant is pretty average.

LE GIL DE FRANCE

18 bis bd Lachèze; it's just beyond the centre.

☎ 04.77.58.06.16 ➡ 04.77.58.73.78
Car park. TV. Canal+.

Totally different, and not much more expensive, is this modern hotel on the outskirts of town in front of a big park. The rooms are bright and fresh with all mod cons (220–250F). The friendly young team who run the place will help you forget (we hope!) the slightly standardized feel to the place. Anyway, it's better than the hotels in the centre. Don't expect any miracles in the restaurant, which has about as much charm as a café in a motorway service station.

|●| RESTAURANT YVES THOLLOT

93 route de Lyon; take the D496.
☎ 04.77.96.10.40
Closed Mondays (or Tuesday if it's a public holiday on Monday), Sunday evenings, and three weeks from the end of July–mid Aug.

To tell you the truth, we don't like the dining room at all since it hasn't any atmosphere. Fortunately, though, once you've met the owner, cheerful and good-natured Yves Thollot, and sampled his cooking you'll forget all about the dining room. There are a number of set meals (95–290F) and they're all available at lunchtimes and in the evenings (a fact which is greatly appreciated). We recommend the fillet of swordfish (if it's still on the menu), the rack of lamb with garlic and, for dessert, butterscotch ice cream with hot chocolate sauce. Bliss!

|●| LE GOURMANDIN**

4 bis rue des Pénitents (Centre).
☎ 04.77.58.58.72
Closed Sunday evenings, Mondays, and three weeks between July and August.

Christian Bellot decided to open his restaurant (which richly deserves its two stars) in what used to be an old warehouse. The modern décor with its black ceiling won't be to everyone's taste and the restaurant's customers are primarily the middle classes and businessmen. Set meals 95F (except Saturday evenings and Sunday lunchtimes), 132F, 165F, 185F and 310F. Try the house *foie gras*, and marvel at the skilful way the meat and fish have been prepared. Attentive, professional service; it's a pity the wine is so expensive – and we wish they'd do something about those infuriating door chimes!

CHAMPDIEU 42600 (5KM)

|●| HOSTELLERIE DU PRIEURÉ

route de Boën; it's on the D8, outside the town centre.
☎ 04.77.58.31.21
Closed Thursdays (except public holidays) and three weeks in August. **Car park.**

This is a good place on the outer edges of the département and the owner is a real stickler for traditional cooking techniques. The cheapest set meal is 70F; of generous proportions but built around just one course, and served every day except Sunday and public holidays. Gourmet set meals 98–240F. You'll criticize it for being a bit pretentious and its roadside location (mind you, it isn't that close to the road), but you won't criticize the food. Affordable wine.

MONTÉLIMAR 26200

10% ⌂ HÔTEL PIERRE**

7 place des Clercs; it's near the church of Sainte-Croix in the old town, next to a little square.
(Centre).
☎ 04.75.01.33.16
Closed in February. **TV.**

A prettily renovated 16th century town house that looks like a little convent; it's got a porch, a corridor with candelabras, a paved courtyard, an ivy-covered terrace, and a staircase in dressed stone, and there's a striking atmosphere about the place that hits you as soon as you walk through the door: Very quiet. Low-key welcome. The 12 rooms (135–250F) are fairly ordinary compared with the rest of the place.

VALAURIE 26230 (19KM SE)

10% ⌂ |●| LA TABLE DE NICOLE

route de Grignan; take the N7, then the D133, in the direction of Grignan and Nyons (D541).
☎ 04.75.98.52.03 ➡ 04.75.98.58.45
Car park. TV. Canal+. Disabled access.

Nicole is a gorgon with a croaky voice — but she's lovely, really. This isn't the sort of restaurant to cater for men in suits or people who don't know how to relax. You can eat on the terrace or in the dining room which is decorated in old-fashioned colours. Set meals from 145F. Nicole will offer you a selection of about 15 starters – *terrines, tapenade (*a thick anchovy paste with capers, olives and tuna), different *crudités*, house *fois gras* and so on – each one tastier than the last. These will be followed by rabbit in a creamy garlic sauce or roast lamb with herbs, depending on how she feels. There are 10 quiet rooms with a view of the trees or the swiming pool (our favourites). They're very handsome and have antique furniture and Provençal fabrics. Prices 340–520F. You'll have to eat here in summer since half-board is compulsory, but that should be no hardship.

10% ☗ |●| DOMAINE LES MÉJEONNES

How to get there: on the D541 in the direction of Grauges Goutardes, a little after the road that goes towards Roussas.
☎ 04.75.98.60.60 ➡ 04.75.98.63.44
Closed Jan and Feb

If you want to see this recently renovated old farmhouse at its best then arrive in the mellow glow of late afternoon or in the evening when the floodlights illuminate the trellised vines and the old stones. Lovely spacious comfortable rooms (from 350F for a double) and good food that goes down very easily (even if the names of the dishes go on for ever). Set meals 95–195F. Courteous welcome. And when you see the swimming pool it might well be love at first sight.

MONTROTTIER 69770

10% ☗ |●| L'AUBERGE DES BLÉS D'OR**

La Curtillat – route de Saint-Julien-sur-Bibost; take the N89 and then the D7; once you've passed Saint-Bel, head for Bibost, then take the D246 and keep going until you're within 2km of Montrottier.
☎ 04.74.70.13.56 ➡ 04.74.70.13.56
Closed Tuesdays. **Car park**. **TV**. **Disabled access**.

This is a real country inn with lots of flowers standing on its own among the fields. It's run by two amazing women and they have to decide they like you before they'll let you have a meal or a room for the night. Hélène, the "chef", will go off to market for something to cook a meal with and this improvised meal will soon begin to look like a feast. For 120F you'll get salad, *terrine, rillettes* or warm mushroom tart, *coq au vin* or leg of lamb, and cream cheese. You can eat in a pretty room with wood panelling or on the terrace. The eight rooms (250F) are all charming, with their comfy double beds, little TV, bathroom (complete with dressing gown and facecloth!) and terrace, where you can sit and watch the sun go down behind the hill opposite, with the church of Montrottier all lit up. The next day, you won't want to leave!

MORZINE 74110

☗ |●| LES PRODAINS**

village des Prodains; it's at the foot of the Avoriaz cable-car.
☎ 04.50.79.25.26 ➡ 04.50.75.76.17
Closed April 20–June 20 and Sept 10–Dec 20.
Car park. **TV**.

The renovation of this place up in the mountains has turned it into a real gem. The balconies all have a fantastic view of the ski slopes. Doubles 220–300F. Set meals 48–175F. Expect to pay about 140F à la carte. There's a big choice of house desserts for those of you with a sweet tooth, including coconut and pineapple charlotte with raspberry sauce. They also offer a traditional set meal with *pierrade* (where you cook the ingredients yourself on a hot stone), fondue and *raclette*. Try the pan-fried scallops or the duck with pineapple. The owner has a mountain chalet, where he invites his guests to sample Savoy specialities and enjoy the sunshine. A really friendly family business, where father and son take charge of the cooking, and Mum makes sure everyone settles in nicely. Swimming pool for the summer.

☗ |●| HÔTEL LES LANS***

quartier des Prodains; it's 300m from the cable car that goes to Avoriaz.
☎ 04.50.79.00.90 ➡ 04.50.79.15.22

He was a ski instructor, she's mad about local history and culture. Today along with their two daughters, they've breathed life into this newly built big chalet that fits in with its surroundings of mountains and woods. The prices are unbeatable considering what you get – they charge 240–260F for half-board! Monsieur Mallurez happily takes care of the cooking, and once a week takes people on wildlife discovery trips, while Madame still does her guided tours. And it's free for children. The kind of place that hangs out the "no vacancies" sign when its competitors are empty.

☗ |●| HÔTEL-RESTAURANT LA KINKERNE

Les Prodains; it's the first restaurant on the right as you come into Morzine.
☎ 04.50.79.08.04
Closed beginning of May–mid June and mid Oct–mid Dec. **Secure parking**. **TV**.

Marthe, the owner, will explain to you that the oil lamps here were the ones that were used in the olden days. You'll get the cheapest fondue in town here, and also a gigantic omelette with morels and chanterelle mushrooms. If you're really hungry, there are also a number of set meals available, ranging in price from 65F to 155F. They're nothing outstanding but you do get big portions. Expect to pay about 130F à la carte. Specialities are

Chinese fondue, cheese fondue, beef fondue, *pierrade* (where you cook the ingredients yourself on a hot stone*), braserade.* They have a good selection of meat dishes toos. You get a great view of the Haut-Fort mountain range from the terrace. They have five double rooms with shower/wc at 290F.

|●| RESTAURANT-BAR LE CAFÉ CHAUD

rue de Joux-Plane; it's 100m from the ski school.
☎ 04.50.79.03.31
Closed in summer. **Car park**.

Service from 4pm (noon if the weather's bad). This is a very cosy place with a great atmosphere. You'll sit at old sewing-machine tables (minus the sewing-machines, of course!). The bar is really the HQ of the inn and the local community and is decorated – in complete contrast to the dining room – fairly exotically with bamboo, tortoiseshell, canoes, snakeskin and of course, Jojo, the cuddly toy monkey, who's a real favourite with the punters! It's very lively at night. Monsieur Morisseau, the owner, is very nice. They do salads, *andouillette,* fondue, warm *vacherin* (a mild and creamy Alpine cheese), *pela* and *raclette*. Good selection of meat and specialities like cheese fondue, potato fricassee, and *pierrade* (where you cook the ingredients yourself on a hot stone) of beef and duck. Lively fancy-dress evenings every week.

|●| RESTAURANT "LA GRANGETTE"

How to get there: it's near the Nyon cable car
☎ 04.50.79.05.76
Closed end of April–end of June and Sept–Christmas.

A little family business at the foot of the ski slopes, where you can enjoy a good meal in a friendly atmosphere. There's a good set meal at 58F with the dish of the day (something along the lines of beef *bourguignon*) and home-made tart for dessert. Other set meals 82F, 128F and 200F. When we tell you that the house speciality is frog's legs in a creamy sauce, you might feel like dropping in in either summer or winter. Good starting point for a number of walks.

|●| LA CHAMADE

Centre; it's near the tourist office.
☎ 04.50.79.13.91

This place is a bit of an institution around here and has taken on a new lease of life now that son Thierry has taken over in the kitchen and his wife in reception. Thierry likes pork and you've got to try it here, whether it be the *pâté* of pig's head or the *atriaux* (a type of patty) or the grilled suckling pig. The two dining rooms are a bit over the top. If they were a bit more simple then this would have to be our favourite spot in the area! Expect to pay 120–150F à la carte. The terrace is really great in summer.

MONTRIOND 74110 (6KM NE)

AUBERGE LA CHALANDE

Lieu-dit Ardent.
☎ 04.50.79.19.69
Closed Sep 20–Dec 20 and April 20–June 20.

Yet another place that seems to prefer staying out of the limelight. There are no signposts to help you find it between the lake of Montriond and Les Lindarets, but given the number of strangers who seem to find their way here the bush telegraph must be working pretty well. Gilles Lanvers runs this old chalet that used to belong to his mother and he hasn't changed the warm, rustic surroundings a bit. In the kitchen he turns out set meals at 70F, 120F and 150F and all that is required of you is a little patience before you are served with a truly excellent meal. If you opt for the cheapest set meal, you'll get cheese *croûte*, braised sausage with leeks and potato fritters, and bilberry tart. The more expensive set meals feature salmon and crayfish. Wonderful welcome. Remember to book!

MOÛTIERS 73600

10% ☗ HÔTEL DU COMMERCE*

13 av. de la Gare (centre); it's a stone's throw from the station.
☎ 04.79.24.26.37 F 04.79.24.26.37

For 20 years this little hotel has been hidden away behind the wisteria that covers the walls. Just look for the greenery, the front door is in there somewhere! Today, Hervé Martin is bringing it back to life with his nonstop DIY, refurbishing one room at a time. Doubles 160F with basin, 200F with bath. Good luck! Pets welcome.

10% ☗ |●| HÔTEL WELCOME'S **

33 av. Greyffié-de-Bellecombe.
☎ 04.79.24.00.48 F 04.79.22.99.96
Secure parking. TV. Disabled access.

During the Games, all the American television crews stayed here because it's the only hotel in Moûtiers with a lift. Sports journalists may be lazy but that's surely not the only reason. Comfortable doubles with bath 310F. And in the restaurant you've got a choice between the 'high-calorie' *formule* or the 'light' one of one course (*choucroute*, for example) plus cheese or dessert for 70F. Other set meals 120–250F. Half-board 285F per day per person. A nice gourmet treat for our journalist friends!

NANTUA 01130

RESTAURANT BELLE RIVE

23 route de la Cluse (North-West); take the N84 from Cluse and it's just before you get to Nantua.
☎ 04.74.75.16.60
Closed Tuesday evenings and Wednesdays (out of season). **Car park**.

It's right by the lake and very popular, so either book in advance or get there early if you want a spot on the pleasant veranda overlooking the lake. The cheapest set meal (66F) is pretty decent and the 87F one includes the famous *quenelles de Nantua*. You have to wait a full 15 minutes for them, but that's a good sign and they're worth it. Now if only they smiled a bit more and the service was a bit less rushed..

CHARIX 01130 (10KM S)

10% AUBERGE DU LAC GÉNIN

How to get there: take the N83 in the direction of Bellegarde, then turn off to the left on the D95.
☎ 04.74.75.52.50 Fax 04.74.75.51.15
Closed Sunday evenings, Mondays, and mid Oct–Dec 1. **Car park**. **TV**.

The setting alone, a magnificent lake in the beautiful unspoiled forests of Jura, makes the trip worthwhile. It's difficult to get there in winter, so make sure you bring the necessary equipment with you. The lakeside inn is friendly and welcoming. The country-style rooms all have direct phone. We've got a soft spot for number 5, which looks out over the lake. Reasonable prices. Doubles 140F with basin, 200F with shower and 250F with bath. The food is served up in generous portions in true Jura tradition. Set meals 62F, 90F and 110F. Fantastic value for money.

LALLEYRIAT 01130 (14KM E)

LES GENTIANES

How to get there: take the N84 (in the direction of Bellegarde) as far as Neyrolles and then the D55.
☎ 04.74.75.31.80
Closed Wednesdays, Sunday evenings, and the end of January.

With a sign that looks the way this one does, you'd naturally expect to find a few traditional mountain specialities in this lovely stone-walled village inn. Well, you won't! For one thing, the chef is from Paris originally and his wife is English. And though he does serve regional dishes, his cooking is also full of surprises. There's chicken *terrine* with apricots in Armagnac served with a mixed salad with an Armagnac *vinaigrette*, ham with almonds in a port sauce, salad of chicken livers with walnuts and a *vinaigrette* made with aged wine, grilled turkey escalope with a creamy mushroom sauce, and *bavarois* of fresh tomatoes with a creamy basil sauce. The second bit of good news is that the prices are great. Cheapest set meal 99F. Charming, natural welcome.

NOIRÉTABLE 42440

10% HÔTEL-RESTAURANT AU RENDEZ-VOUS DES CHASSEURS**

route de l'Hermitage (South-West); it's about 2km from the centre of the village (on the A72).
☎ 04.77.24.72.51 Fax 04.77.24.93.40
Closed Sunday evenings, Mondays out of season, ten days in the February school holidays, and three weeks Sept–Oct. **Car park**. **TV**.

The inns here used to be far from inviting but this one made us forget that the A72 is only 6km from the village. All you can see for miles around are the mountains of Forez and you get a great view of them from the dining room. Pretty countryside. The inn has 14 rooms ranging in price from 130F (with washing facilities) to 215F (with shower/wc or bath). Cheapest set meal 60F weekdays, other set meals 100–200F. All the flavours of Forez can be found in the dishes here, which include chicken with *Fourme de Montbrison* (a local blue cheese) and *parfait* of chicken liver with bilberries. A good place, even if you don't hunt.

LA GILBERNIE

How to get there: take the N89, about 1km from the town centre, in the direction of Chabreloche or the A75 motorway – it's about 5km from the Les Salles exit.
☎ 04.77.24.93.01
Closed Sunday evenings and Wednesdays.

Hélène, a former English teacher, hung up her rucksack a few years back and moved here along with her friend Mireille to start a farm holiday business. You'll sleep in dormitories and have great meals made with produce from the neighbouring farms.The specialities are lamb *boulangère* (braised with onions and potatoes) and free-range chicken with fresh garden vegetables and fruit from the orchard. Anyway, since you have to book, you could always ask what's on the evening menu before you decide to go. *Menu du jour* 60F and gourmet set meal (often based on goose) 85F. Drinks are extra, but not expensive, as they've got friends who have their own vineyards. One Saturday per month, they have a dinner-concert, all for 100F. The music varies from jazz, to vocals, to Irish ballads and the atmosphere is great. Warm welcome and pleasant dining room.

JURÉ 42430 (20KM NE)

AUBERGE LE MOULIN

How to get there: take the D53, and turn right onto the D86 before you get to Saint-Just-en-Chevalet.
☎ 04.77.62.55.24
Open 11.30am–8.30pm Saturdays, Sundays, and public holidays March–Nov and every day (except Mondays) in July and August. **Car park**.

What a shame that this little inn, housed in a mill, doesn't open its doors more often! The setting is idyllic and the little river that flows underneath powers the generator. The country-style set meals are delicious, offering excellent *terrines, rissoles*, free-range poultry, and home-made pastries that go down a treat with cider. Snack 60F, and set meals 70F, 80F and 100F. They prefer you to order in advance. Very affordable wines.

NYONS 26110

LA PICHOLINE***

promenade de la Perrière; it's on the hilltop as you come into the town.
☎ 04.75.26.06.21 Fax 04.75.26.40.72
Restaurant closed Monday evenings and Tuesdays (out of season). **Car park**. **TV**.

The décor in the foyer and the restaurant is a bit tacky, but the owners make a real fuss of their guests, usually elderly couples, who seem to like the food and the accommodation. An ideal place to spend the night up above the town. The rooms are big, light, and pleasant (280–375F). The restaurant is good, even though it's not exactly a bundle of laughs. The regional set meal at 125F should fill you up a treat. There's a swimming pool surrounded by olive trees.

LE PETIT CAVEAU

9 rue Victor Hugo; it's in the street at right angles to the Pavillon du tourisme.
☎ 04.75.26.20.21
Closed Sunday evenings and Mondays.

Muriel Cormont is a graduate of the Suze-La-Rousse wine university and her husband used to work for Robuchon. It was Muriel who had the bright idea of offering a *formule* at 69F where you can try three different types of wine that vary according to how she feels and what she's got in stock. You won't have any difficulty in recognising her, she's alway in the dining room and always has her apron on. Her husband is a very good chef. Try his leg of rabbit *confit* with thyme and olive oil, which incorporates all the good things to be found in this part of the world, or his scallops and fresh chanterelles sautéd with garlic and served with *tétragone* (a kind of spinach) – we hope you enjoy these as much as we did. So basically with these two experts in charge you're getting the best of both worlds at a reasonable price (110F and 170F).

MIRABEL-AUX-BARONNIES 26110 (7KM S)

LA COLOQUINTE

Av. de la Résistance; take the D538.
☎ 04.75.27.19.89
Closed Wednedays, Thursday lunchtimes, and in February.

The food is good and they use only fresh seasonal produce. When the sun's out, it's nice to sit on the lovely shaded patio. Set meals start at 90F weekdays but treat yourself to the one at 133F, which offers colourful dishes that are full of flavour such as vegetable caviar with a red pepper sauce, fillet of *rascasse* in rosemary, *fromage frais* and mocha cake with walnuts. And the 163F set meal is fit for a king!

ROUSSET-LES-VIGNES 26770 (9KM NW)

RESTAURANT AU CHARBONELON

rue Principale (South-West); take the D538.
☎ 04.75.27.91.61
Closed Mondays, Tuesdays, and Jan–Feb.

A little restaurant in one of the prettiest villages in this part of Drôme. It's got real character, a nice sign, and one cosy, warm dining room. The bread basket hangs from the ceiling and you help yourself from it, giving you something to nibble on while you decide whether to have the 88F or the 130F set meal. There's no menu since the owner prefers to let the market and the inspiration of the moment dictate what he serves his guests. We hope he never changes that approach. Remarkable value for money.

VINSOBRES 26110 (10KM SW)

10% |●| AUBERGE DU PETIT BISTROT

4 rue Sous-les-Barris; it's near the church.
☎ 04.75.27.61.90
Closed Wednesdays.

Art Deco posters, local dishes served with very good local wine, unusually friendly service, and prices that we certainly don't see every day. For 88F, you get hors d'œuvres, daube (a kind of stew), cheese, and strawberry charlotte. The most expensive set meal is 145F and comes with a truffle omelette. And if you like the village, then you'll be glad to hear that Claudette Dechomme has converted her old house in the square into two bedrooms and a studio (220F and 280F respectively). Given their size, their charm, and the fact that they're very peaceful, there should be a bit of a rush for them.

PIÉGON 26110 (11KM S)

10% ⌂ |●| AUBERGE DU PONTILLARD

(South); take the D938, then a little signposted road that winds in and out of the vineyards.
☎ 04.75.27.09.09 F 04.75.27.09.08
Closed every lunchtime, and Nov–Feb. **Car park**. **TV**.

Lost amid the olive trees and vine, with a view of Ventoux, this little inn is run by a former computer scientist who woke up one morning and realised he'd been promoted to the level of his own incompetence. The next day he and his wife decided they should take over the cooking at the family inn. So get here fast, because he's set himself a deadline for the restaurant business too – as soon as it stops being fun, he'll give it up. There's no silver cutlery and no crystal glasses but that won't prevent you enjoying a tasty rib steak with lots of side dishes. One set meal 130F. We really liked the tablecloths. They have a very impresssive selection of local wines (includng some of the great vintages) which are lovingly stored in a real cellar. Good welcome, simple rooms with flowered wallpaper, and hearty breakfasts. Doubles 268F with shower/wc.

OYONNAX 01100

⌂ NOUVEL HÔTEL**

31 rue René-Nicod (Centre).
☎ 04.74.77.28.11 F 04.74.77.03.71
Secure parking. **TV**. **Canal+**.

You might have reservations about staying in a place with a name like this, and very often you'd be right. This place though, despite the fact that it's clearly getting on a bit, is quite nice as you can see even in the reception area with its display of the plastics for which Oyonnax is famous. The rooms, which have recently been refurbished, are good value for money: Doubles 180F with shower, larger rooms with shower/wc or bath 230–260F. And all the little things they do for you here make a difference. You can have breakfast brought to your room, for example, at no extra charge.

10% ⌂ |●| HÔTEL-RESTAURANT BUFFARD**

place de l'Église; it's near the station.
☎ 04.74.77.86.01 F 04.74.73.77.68
Hotel always open. Restaurant closed Friday evenings, Saturdays, Sunday evenings, and two weeks in August.
Car park. **TV**. **Canal+**.

Service noon–2.30pm, 7.15pm–9.30pm. This hotel-restaurant has lived up to its excellent reputation for 100 years. It's like being at home or staying with an old auntie (who just happens to have satellite TV!). Rooms with antique furniture: 180F with washing facilities, 220–250F with shower, and 250–300F with bath. In the restaurant you'll get good home cooking and a generous helping of the dish of the day and coffee for 50F. Pay a bit more and you can have regional specialities like *quenelles Nantua*, *gratin* of crayfish tails, frog's legs, chicken with morels, *délice* of duck liver. Set meals 70F, 110F, 130F, and 180F.

PEISEY-NANCROIX 73210

⌂ |●| REFUGE DE ROSUEL – PORTES DU PARC DE LA VANOISE

☎ 04.79.07.94.03
Closed beginning of Oct–end of May. **Car park**.

You really feel like you're at the end of the world here. The restaurant — although the décor is quite modern — has a quite unique atmosphere, like a shelter in the middle of nowhere for walkers who've come across the Alps and strangers from all over – travellers in fact! Wonderful fireplace where you can thaw out. Set meals 70F and 85F. Dormitories for 8–24 people: 68F a night. Reductions for students and under 18s.

⌂ LE RELAIS DES TROIS STATIONS*

How to get there: it's before Vigogne, on the right.

☎ 04.79.07.93.09 ➡ 04.79.07.94.52
Closed beginning of Sept–mid Dec.

This is one of our finds; it's got a very nice atmosphere and Yvette and Michel are doing all they can to give their hotel character. They have 17 rooms, all with direct telephone. Doubles 200F with shower/wc or bath. Set meals at 58F, 90F, 110F. Fondue and *tartiflette* à la carte: Package deals for full board and use of ski-lifts in the winter. The terrace faces south.

L'ORMELUNE

☎ 04.79.07.93.32
Closed end of April–mid June and Nov 1–mid Dec.
Car park.

A small traditional restaurant in the heart of a charming old village, run by Béa and her team. Warm welcome. Everyone knows about the delicious *raclette* but they do other regional specialities too, including *tartiflette* (potatoes with onions, bacon and *Reblochon* cheese), fondue and rib steak. Good set meals 84F and 140F. Good value for money. Friendly atmosphere.

RESTAURANT CHEZ FÉLIX

Plan-Peisey; it's between Les Mélèzes and Val Landry.
☎ 04.79.07.92.41
Closed end of April–end of June, and Sept–mid Dec.
Car park.

You get a bird's-eye view of the Ponturin valley from this simple restaurant, where you'll pay 58F for *diots* (vegetable and pork sausages preserved in white wine), 58F for fondue, and 90F for *raclette.* The *crêpes* and the fresh raspberry juice are a must. Expect to pay about 110F à la carte. A nice place. Meals are served on the terrace at the first signs of summer. But when it comes to setting, we prefer the other restaurant (open in summer) housed in a chalet that dates back to 1885. You'll find it on the road to Rosuel park.

RESTAURANT L'ANCOLIE

How to get there: make for Landry and then Peisey-Nancroix.
☎ 04.79.07.93.20 ➡ 04.79.07.91.65
Closed Mondays (in winter), beginning of May–end of June, and beginning of Oct–beginning of Dec.

Service 12.30pm–1.30pm and 7.30pm–9pm. The building, tucked away behind a curtain of greenery, dates back to 1760 and is a real historic monument. The authentic rustic dining room has been tastefully decorated with lots of tools and dried-flower arrangements. Set meals 146F, 172F and 202F, all with inventive dishes such as *blanquette* of young goat, lamb chops with honey, rabbit stew with bilberries and *galettes* with *Reblochon* cheese and walnuts. Absolutely delicious! Pleasant terrace in a covered walkway which is a good place to shelter from the elements. Here, you get a history lesson and gourmet food in one stop!

PÉROUGES 01800

AUBERGE DU COQ

rue des Rondes (Centre).
☎ 04.74.61.05.47 ➡ 04.74.61.37.15
Closed Sunday evenings, Mondays, and in February.

Service noon–2pm and 7pm–9pm. The prices charged by most of the restaurants in this old medieval town, which is often overrun with tourists, are too high. This is one of the few affordable ones and has a set meal at 88F (except public holidays). Very decent food. Other set meals 115–217F. Period décor, but quite impersonal service.

MEXIMIEUX 01800 (2KM E)

10% HÔTEL-BAR DU LION D'OR**

16 place Vaugelas (Centre).
☎ 04.74.61.00.89 ➡ 04.74.61.43.80
Closed in November. **Secure parking**. **TV**.

This hotel and bar were entirely rebuilt after the war, a German soldier having destroyed it while trying to park his tank. Some people are just so clumsy! Excellent welcome. Big rooms, which are slightly old-fashioned, but not unpleasant by any means. The quiet ones are at the back. Doubles with bath 240F. No restaurant but the bar on the ground floor gets a lot of regulars. This is the place to come if you want to stay near the medieval village of Pérouges but don't want to have to fork out too much.

PONT-D'AIN 01160

RESTAURANT LE TERMINUS

71 rue Saint-Exupéry (North).
☎ 04.74.39.07.17
Closed Sunday evenings and Mondays. **Car park**.

Pretty little dining room, even if it is a bit cramped. Monsieur Berthiller puts a lot of effort into his cooking and he always gets good results. Friendly welcome and efficient service. Generous portions of regional food at decent prices. set meals 60F (starter and main course), 79F, 98F, 130F and 160F.

PONT-EN-ROYANS 38680

RESTAURANT LE GOURNIER

grottes de Choranche (North); 2km past the village, there's a road on the left that leads up to the caves and the restaurant.
☎ 04.76.36.09.88 F 04.76.36.11.91
Closed Nov 1–March 31.

Service at lunchtimes only. This restaurant, which has a wonderful panoramic view, looks right over the superb cirque de Choranche while the cliffs above are home to peregrine falcons. And the caves of Choranche down below are an unforgettable sight – there's nothing else like them in all Europe. You'll probably be on a high after seeing all these wonderful sights, so how about some food to calm you down? They do a nice set meal at 72F with ravioli and cream cheese and a typically regional one for 115F that which starts off with pork and vegetable faggot and salad. After dinner, why not take a look round Pont-en-Royans?

PRIVAS 07000

RESTAURANT ASTIC LA CALADE

7 av. de Chomérac (West).
☎ 04.75.64.25.88 F 04.75.64.15.30
Closed Saturdays, Sunday evenings, and Monday evenings.

Service noon–2.30pm and 7.15pm–10pm. A very central and rather chic looking restaurant that actually has quite reasonable prices. The dish of the day is 50F (lunchtimes), while the cheapest set meal is 88F and offers dishes like *rillettes* of tuna with avocado, marinated fresh salmon, breast of duck with raspberry vinegar, and monkfish kebab with smoked bacon. It attracts a lot of businessmen, especially at lunchtimes. Attentive service. Refreshing décor in pale pink tones, lovely chairs. There's an air-conditioned room for hot summer days. Quite a good restaurant.

ALISSAS 07210 (4KM SE)

RESTAURANT LOUS ESCLOS

quartier Rabagnol (South-East); it's by the side of the D2, which bypasses Alissas.
☎ 04.75.65.12.73
Closed Saturday lunchtimes, Sunday evenings, Mondays, the first three weeks in August, and Dec 22–Jan 5. **Car park**. **Disabled access**.

This is a rather stylish restaurant with quite reasonable prices ranging from 97F (weekdays) to 185F. The 97F set meal offers a choice of sautéd veal with olives or duck's leg *confit* with chestnuts for your main course. In the summer, the crickets will come and join you for your meal on the terrace, which looks out onto the *garrigue*. The relaxing setting alone is worth the trip. The dining room is air-conditioned and gives you a view of the countryside. For the linguists among you, *lous esclos* is the local dialect for 'clogs'.

SAINT-ÉTIENNE-DE-BOULOGNE 07200 (12KM W)

10% HÔTEL-RESTAURANT LE PANORAMIC-ESCRINET**

col de l'Escrinet; from Privas, take the N104 in the direction of col de l'Escrinet.
☎ 04.75.87.10.11 F 04.75.87.10.34
Closed Monday lunchtimes (except in summer) and Nov 15–March 15. **Secure parking**. **TV**.

Service noon–2pm and 7.30pm–9pm. Situated between Privas and Aubenas, this is a great place to stop. Not only do you get a terrific view of the valley of the Ardèche, you also get a chance to taste Guy Rojon's cooking. The rooms lead out onto a terrace that overlooks the magnificent grounds and the swimming pool. Prices start at 270F for a double with shower/wc. Half-board (from 320F) is compulsory in summer. The sunlit lounge room is full of green plants. Set meals 130F, 190F, 240F and 290F. Expect to pay around 100F for a main course à la carte. Specialities include sautéd kid, fillet steak with goat's cheese, and veal kidneys with langoustine tails. Delicious.

RIVE-DE-GIER 42800

RESTAURANT GEORGES PAQUET

Combeplaine.
☎ 04.77.75.02.18
Closed Monday lunchtimes, evenings (except Fridays and Saturdays), during the February school holidays, and July 14–Aug 14. **Car park**. **Disabled access**.

In this desolate area of factories and industrial wasteland, there's a restaurant between the motorway and the main road that serves good food. It's got a hushed atmosphere and is decorated in soft bright colours. The speciality here is fish and it comes in all shapes and sizes, accompanied by a pleasant sauce. They do a fast set meal at lunchtime for 70F and the 85F set meal, which offers a choice of three starters and three main courses, followed by cream cheese or dessert, and includes a drink, is very good value for money. The other set meals (125–220F, drink not included), are a bit expensive, in our opinion. If you've got a sweet tooth, you'll love the set meal of desserts they do on Friday evenings (by reservation).

SAINT-MARTIN-LA-PLAINE 42800 (8KM W)

LE FLAMANT ROSE

How to get there: take the D37, follow the signs to the "parc zoologique".
☎ 04 77 75 18 68.

The beautiful terrace is the only lovely thing about this big building that stands in front of a stretch of water opposite the zoo. Having said that though, the two dining rooms get lots of light, even if the one reserved for the excellent and substantial 60F lunchtime set meal hasn't had the same kind of treatment as the other, reserved for the more expensive set meals (105–240F). But forget this sectarianism. The food is pleasant and the chef takes a few risks, successfully combining sweet and savoury flavours. Very good desserts and home-made bread. Very warm welcome. The restaurant can give you a picnic meal (about 55F) to take with you if you're going to the zoo. It's quite good but a bit expensive at 45F with no reductions. It's open every day.

SAINTE-CROIX-EN-TAREZ 42800 (10KM E)

LE PRIEURÉ*

How to get there: take the D30.
☎ 04.77.20.20.09
Closed in February and Monday lunchtimes out of season. **TV**.

The road that leads up to this place runs along the Couzon and past the dam of the same name. Sainte-Croix, north of the Pilat park, is a wonderful sight. It is in fact the site of an old monastery which, despite its fortifications, was dismantled during the Revolution and turned into a village. Part of it is still open to the public (for further information phone 04 77 20 20 81). You'll get bed and board in the former guest quarters of the monastery. The hotel, a *Logis de France,* has only four rooms (240F for 2). They're simple but very well equipped. Peace and quiet – not to mention lots of fresh air – ae guaranteed. The restaurant offers satisfying traditional local dishes and set meals that start at 62F (for this you get *râpée* – potato pancake – and *charcuterie*). Other set meals 80F, 120F, 150F, and 200F. If you like tripe then the home-made stuff on the 80F set meal is a must. Everyone will admire the beautiful vaulted dining room wth its oak furniture. In summer, there's a little terrace on the village square Warm welcome. A delightful and beautiful place with lots of walks in the surrounding area.

ROANNE 42300

HÔTEL DE L'ANCRE

24 place du Maréchal-de-Lattre-de-Tassigny (Centre).
☎ 04.77.71.22.70

This modest hotel is in a lovely building of the kind you'd get in a seaside resort in the1930s, and it doesn't seem to have changed much since it was built. Even the ashtrays advertise brands that no longer exist. If you're nostalgic about the past, love old things and are looking for cheap accommodation, then this is the place for you! Rooms with furniture from the mid-twentieth century, 85–160F for 2 (depending on what you have by way of plumbing). The ladies and gentlemen who run the place are very nice and serve home cooking in a magnificent room with a parquet floor. Set meals 50–85F.

10% HÔTEL-RESTAURANT DE LA GRENETTE

12 place Maréchal-de Lattre-de-Tassigny (Centre).
☎ 04.77.71.25.59 F→ 04.77.71.29.69
TV.

Not far away from the hotel reviewed above, this little place has recently been taken over by a lovely couple who believe that the hotel industry in the town centre can compete with the awful standardized places you get in the outskirts. We agree. The rooms are basic but well looked after: 170–190F for 2, with wc on the landing. The restaurant is nothing special, but if you're stuck for somewhere to eat, they do a conventional *menu du jour* for 65F*; it's* advisable to phone ahead.

HÔTEL TERMINUS**

15 cours de la République (place de la Gare) (West); it's opposite the train station.
☎ 04.77.71.79.69 F→ 04.77.72.90.26
Secure parking. TV. Disabled access.

You get hotels like this everywhere and, like all the others, it's handy for the station. It's a good hotel of its kind, with about 50 rooms. Doubles with bath 200–270F. Ask for one overlooking the courtyard – they're quieter and it's one way of expressing your disapproval at the ugly way the windows at the front have been renovated.

TROISGROS

place de la Gare (also known as place Jean-Troisgros) (West).
☎ 04.77.71.66.97 F 04.77.70.39.77
Closed Tues evenings & Wed May–Oct; closed all day Tues & Wed rest of year. **Car park. TV. Canal+.**

You could go to any old restaurant or you could go to *Troisgros*; it's been an institution and a landmark in the world of French gastronomy for two generations and it's often thought of as being beyond the reach of the man on the street. Which it is, at weekends (book 2 months in advance) and in the evenings (à la carte only). However, there are a few ways you can tackle these obstacles and be able to say that you have actually eaten there. First, there's the buffet breakfast at 125F, which will make your early morning arrival in Roanne absolutely unforgettable. Next, there's the *Grand Dessert*, served 2–4pm (reservations only) and costing 120F (drink extra). This is an incredible array of sweets, cakes, and delicacies (the slices of dried pineapple are really something) and when you bite into one you'll get an explosion of flavour. Last is the bar, where you can have a drink with a selection of savoury nibbles, and then the set lunch at 300F. With a Côte-Roannaise and a coffee, you're looking at just over 700F for two. It is, of course, delicious, beautifully presented, and served with care. Mind you, so it should be when you consider the restaurant has a staff of about 40 and sometimes fewer than 15 customers! That said, the day we went (and we do apologise for telling you our life story), a waiter brought us the sweet trolley by mistake (not included in the 300F menu). A station waiter then gave him a discreet ticking-off and whipped the trolley away from under our noses – not quite the type of thing you expect from a top restaurant. There's also a hotel with rooms 700–1,850F (is that in your price range?) and another restaurant (see next).

LE CENTRAL

20 cours de la République; it's opposite the station.
☎ 04.77.67.72.72
Closed Monday lunchtimes and Sundays.

The Troisgros family has opened up this much more affordable annexe next door to their flagship restaurant. The designer's made it look like an old-fashioned grocery store, but it's just a bit too perfect to feel authentic. It has two dining rooms, an open kitchen, and a young staff and it's like being in a trendy restaurant in some European capital. As for prices, the *menu-carte* has starters at 40F, main courses at 80F and desserts at 30F. The wine is affordable and is served the way it is in a bistro (ie the bottle's opened). You could also say that the à la carte menu gives a little taste of the imagination that goes into the cooking next door at *Troisgros*. Unfortunately, there are no pleasant surprises and the creation of the dishes quite frankly lacks precision and finesse. It all seems a bit over-rated and light years away from the perfection of its neighbour. If you want to see what the *Troigros* world is actually like, we advise you to save your pennies and go for the real thing, instead of settling for second-best.

L'AVENTURE

24 rue Pierre-Despierre.
☎ 04.77.68.01.15
Closed Mondays, Sundays, the first three weeks in August and one week at Christmas.

A good restaurant away from the centre, in a little street not far from the Loire. The front of the building is green and looks like a bistro but inside there's a cosy restaurant decorated in pastel colours. The kitchen opens out into the dining room — it's not at all showy and adds to the friendly atmosphere of the place. Chef Jean-Luc Trambouze, a local boy, is a young man on the way up and his dishes are full of imagination and fresh ideas. If you ask Jean-Luc what his particular speciality is, he won't be able to tell you. The success of his cooking is a combined result of his dynamism in the kitchen and the strong flavours he uses. He does an excellent set meal at lunchtime for 95F, and other set meals range in price from 128F to 280F. Affordable wine list.

POUILLY-SOUS-CHARLIEU 42720 (14KM N)

AUBERGE DU CHÂTEAU DE TIGNY

How to get there: take the D487 – it's east of the village and is signposted.
☎ 04.77.60.09.55
Closed Monday evenings, Tuesdays, and Christmas–mid Jan.

This is undoubtedly one of our favourite spots in this part of the world. Marie Blin and Jacques Rivière were at one time market gardeners who supplied the top restaurants in the region and loved old buildings and good food. Then, one day, they decided to give it all up and instead set about restoring a magnificent little manor house and turning it into this delightful inn. (Jacques will be delighted to tell you the stories behind some of the stones.) The exceptional set meal at 105F with its wide choice and innovative, fresh cooking (and fresh fish) is the best value for money in the region. There's also a fast set meal at 70F (weekday lunchtimes) that consists of the dish of the day, salad, and dessert, and gourmet set meals at 103F, 150F and 190F. When the weather's nice, you have a choice of dining on the very pleasant terrace or in the cool interior of this country house. Marie will give you a charming welcome. The nearby river and lake make for a wonderful setting.

NOAILLY 42640 (15KM NW)

10% ☗ |●| CHÂTEAU DE LA MOTTE***

La Motte; take the N7 to Saint-Germain-Lespinasse, then the D4 towards Charlieu and the château's between Noailly and La Benisson-Dieu.
☎ 04.77.66.64.60 F➔ 04.77.66.64.38
Closed Sunday evenings and Mondays (except in July and August), and Jan–end of March.
Car park. **TV**. **Disabled access**.

Of course, this romantic château isn't really in our price range, but you might be tempted to splash out a bit when we tell you that the lovely rooms are decorated and furnished with such imagination and taste, that you can go horse riding with owner Sylvie Fayolle as your guide, and that there's a swimming pool in the grounds and a pergola down by the pond just made for a few quiet hours with a book. Expect to pay 450–800F, depending on the room (you only live once!) Discounts out of season, and reduced prices for a four-night stay. The restaurant is carrying on the tradition of local cuisine. The cheapest set meal – 95F – is excellent value for money but it's served only at lunchtime during the week.

ROCHETTE (LA) 73110

10% ☗ |●| LES CHÂTAIGNIERS

1 rue Maurice-Franck; take the Pontcharra exit on the Grenoble-Chambéry motorway and it's 200m from the town hall.
☎ 04.79.25.50.21 F➔ 04.79.25.79.97
Closed Wednesdays, Saturday lunchtimes, Mondays and Tuesdays out of season, evenings July–Aug, a week in September, a week in November, and Jan 1–20.
Car park.

To look at it, you would never think that this very respectable bourgeois establishment was in fact home to a lovely, yet absolutely crazy family. After a few visits you're no longer shocked to see the mother-in-law putting on a little performance for her guests, while the son-in-law, the cook/comedian, regales you with some of his own poetry (not always in the best of taste) as you enjoy a wonderful meal in a room that would make an second-hand dealer green with envy. For 120F, you can have sausage, *quenelles* of chicken, cream cheese, and a tart. And the last surprise is the bedroom, which is more like a full-size apartment, where you'll be made to feel like a long-lost cousin. Funny, fantastic, for 450F or more. Great, if you like that kind of thing.

ROMANS-SUR-ISÈRE 26100

10% ☗ |●| HÔTEL DES BALMES**

(North-West); follow the Tain road (the D532) for 2km, then turn right in the direction of Les Balmes.
☎ 04.75.02.29.52 F➔ 04.75.02.75.47
Closed Sunday evenings (out of season). Restaurant closed Monday lunchtimes. **Secure parking**. **TV**. **Canal+**.

It's advisable to book in summer as it gets very busy. Located in a sleepy little village, it has a swimming pool and 12 pretty rooms with bath and balcony. You'll pay 260–280F. The restaurant is well known locally – people even come from Grenoble. However, despite its name and the exotic décor — glass beads, loincloths, and shells — it doesn't do Tahitian food! Set meals 85F, 100F, 120F and 160F. A pleasant, welcoming place on the way to the Alps; comfort, and peace and quiet guaranteed.

|●| RESTAURANT LA CASSOLETTE

16 rue Rebatte (Centre); it's in a pedestrian precinct, near tour Jacquemart.
☎ 04.75.02.55.71 F➔ 04.75.02.55.71
Closed Sundays, Mondays, and end July–mid Aug

Service noon–2pm and 7pm–9.30pm. An intimate restaurant with two little dining rooms with arched ceilings housed in a charming 13th century building. Set meals range in price from 78F (lunchtimes) to 200F. It does lots of fish and its specialities are crayfish, *cassolette* of snails with hazelnuts, ravioli *à l'ancienne*, and fricassee of sole and lobster. Good wine list. If you're thinking about having lunch there on a Saturday, it's probably a good idea to book.

10% CAFÉ-THÉÂTRE-RESTAURANT LA CHARRETTE

15 place de l'Horloge (Centre); it's a stone's throw from tour Jacquemart.
☎ 04.75.02.04.25
Closed Sundays and public holidays.
Car park. **Disabled access**.

There's a sign outside to the effect that this isn't a restaurant, but it serves one reasonably priced meal that changes every day. You're invited to ask what's cooking or to just sit down and see what they bring you. They do home cooking at around 80F for a meal, 45F for the dish of the day. Instead of the usual ravioli you get everywhere else, try their sea bass *en papillote*. Informal and relaxed atmosphere with music in the background. Try to come one night when there's a show on. This place is a must.

GRANGES-LÈS-BEAUMONT 26600 (4KM W)

10% HÔTEL-RESTAURANT LES VIEILLES GRANGES**

How to get there: take the D532.
☎ 04.75.71.50.43 Fax 04.75.71.59.79
Closed Sunday evenings and Mondays.
Car park. **TV**. **Disabled access**.

A collection of old buildings overlooking the Isère and surrounded by fruit trees that have been renovated and turned into a hotel cum restaurant with a terrace under the lime trees. Comfortable rooms 240F–300F (the more expensive ones have a view of the river). Tasty food with a set meal at 90F, and 115–160F. Indulge yourself with the delicious *caillette* (pork and vegetable faggot). But it won't be as easy to choose a wine. Luckily, the staff are patient and helpful. Romantic, and the owners are discreet!

SAINT-AGRÈVE 07320

LE CLAIR LOGIS**

route du Cheylard (South-East); head for Le Cheylard; the hotel is past the junction of the road D120 and D21, 800m further on, opposite a lake.
☎ 04.75.30.13.24 Fax 04.75.30.22.05
Closed Oct 20–Dec 25. **Car park**.

We recommend that you book in advance since it's very popular. Monsieur and Madame Reynaud will give you a warm welcome. Comfortable doubles 180–220F with shower/wc. The hotel occupies almost all of a chalet and there's lots of wood, old tiled floors, a mountain atmosphere and a view of the plateau. Good local food, including *charcuterie* and fillets of suckling pig *à l'ardéchoise*. Set meals range in price from 65F (weekdays) to 95F. The guests have mostly come for the sports activities in the area, including walking, cross-country skiing and mountain-biking.

DOMAINE DE RILHAC**

lieu-dit Rilhac; from Saint-Agrève, follow the directions to Le Cheylard for about 1km; when you come to the fork in the road take the D21 and watch for the arrows.
☎ 04.75.30.20.20 Fax same
Closed Mondays and Tuesday evenings (except in July and August), and in February.
Car park. **TV**. **Disabled access**.

A 16th century farm that has been tastefully restored and is now a delightful hotel-restaurant with a lot of endearing qualities. It's in a unique location and faces mont Mézenc and mont Gerbier. With its dressed-stone façade, its blue shutters, the finely engraved wrought ironwork inside that goes so well with the ochre plaster and the exposed ceiling and wall beams, it's the type of place you dream about when you need to recharge your batteries. The doubles in the attic are 360F (be warned, there are only six). Breakfast (65F) is served until 10.30am, handy if you like a bit of a lie-in! Half-board (from 420F) isn't compulsory. There's a set meal at 115F (3 courses), served only at lunchtimes during the week. Other set meals 150F, 175F, 195F, 255F and 320F. The à la carte menu changes with the seasons and specialities include breast of duck with chestnuts and home-made *foie gras terrine*. A luxury hotel at affordable prices!

SAINT-ÉTIENNE 42000

BAR-HÔTEL SPLENDID

16 rue du Théâtre (Centre).
☎ 04.77.33.72.94

A huge ochre building with green balconies, centrally located. It must have had its moment of glory followed by years of decline before being taken over by the young woman who now owns it. The rooms don't have a lot of character but they're spacious and clean (110–160F with/without bathroom). The ones overlooking the street are bigger, but noisier of course, than those at the back. Good value for money.

☗ GRAND HÔTEL DES ARTS**

11 rue Gambetta (Centre).
☎ 04.77.32.42.11 ⊳ 04.77.34.06.72
Secure parking. TV.

Not far from the museum of old Saint Étienne, in a street off the Grand rue where the trams run, is this 2-star hotel that's excellent value for money. The rooms (150–300F) vary in price depending on the facilities, but they're all of an acceptable standard. Good welcome. Garage available.

10% ☗ HÔTEL LE CHEVAL NOIR**

11 rue François-Gillet (Centre).
☎ 04.77.33.41.72 ⊳ 04.77.37.79.19
Closed Aug 1–15. **Secure parking. TV. Canal+.**

This old hotel, which had lost a lot of its original splendour, was taken over by a couple of former bankers who completely renovated the place to give it — and them — a new lease of life; it's got a great many rooms and lots of them are now fairly well equipped. The prices are very moderate for a hotel in the centre of town and you'll pay 150–270F, depending on the facilities available (bathroom/washing facilities/TV). The most you'll pay at the weekend is 180F. During the week they offer a sliding scale tariff.

☗ HÔTEL LE BALADIN**

12 rue de la Ville (Centre); it's in a busy pedestrian precinct.
☎ 04.77.37.17.97 ⊳ 04.77.41.70.34
Closed the first three weeks in August. **TV. Canal+.**

It would be a good idea to book in advance since it fills up very quickly, especially during the theatre season - this is where actors appearing at the nearby *Comédie de Saint-Étienne* stay; it's a pleasant little hotel with 14 small rooms, all with shower or bath. Prices range from 200F for a single to 240F and 300F with bath. Snack bar on the ground floor.

10% ☗ HÔTEL TERMINUS DU FOREZ***

31 av. Denfert-Rochereau; it's opposite the Châteaucreux station, five minutes from the centre.
☎ 04.77.32.48.47 ⊳ 04.77.34.03.30
Secure parking. TV. Canal+.

Your classic big three-star hotel, with stylish décor, pleasant surroundings and modern facilities; it's a family hotel and makes a nice change from the chains on the outskirts. Doubles from 285F with shower. Friendly welcome and helpful staff. The restaurant is on the ground floor.

|●| RESTAURANT LA RISSOLÉE

23 rue Pointe-Cadet (Centre); it's just before you get to the pedestrian precinct.
☎ 04.77.33.58.47
Closed Saturday lunchtimes, Sundays, Monday lunchtimes, and in August.

It's still in the same street (one with lots of restaurants) but the new premises are a lot more suitable and have been well renovated. At last, we can have great mussels and chips cooked by Gilbert without the smell of the fat fryer in our nostrils all night. At lunchtimes, hearty *menu du jour* at 49F. Evening set meal with Belgian specialities 60F and 80F.

|●| LE CERCLE

15 place de l'Hôtel-de-Ville (Centre); it's opposite the town hall.
☎ 04.77.25.27.27
Closed Monday evenings, Sunday evenings, and the week of August 15.

Part of the former premises of the St Etienne bridge club on the first floor of a superb building opposite the town hall. The owners have fortunately kept the panelling and the gilding in one of the most beautiful rooms, which is pure Napoléon III style. It's a shame that they've covered the original parquet floor with wall-to-wall carpet. The restaurant seems to have set out to attract the local worthies but the prices are nevertheless very reasonable, with set meals from 88F (except Sundays and public holidays). It even does a 50F *formule* (main course plus dessert) at lunchtimes during the week. Other more expensive set meals 138F, 220F and 280F. Decent food, pleasantly presented and friendly service.

|●| LA FOURCHETTE GOURMANDE

10 rue Francis Garnier (Centre).
☎ 04.77.41.76.86
Closed Sunday lunchtimes.

We're not going to beat around the bush here – this is our favourite place. It used to be called *Le Petit Coq*, and this was where the the Saint-Étienne football team came to celebrate their victories back in '70s. Well, as the team slowly went downhill so did the restaurant and a new owner took over. Not only is he friendly and professional, this guy has also got taste — he hired a chef trained by Gagnaire, with tremendous results. Don't be intimidated by the slightly pretentious à la carte menu or be put off by the rather ordinary décor. For 80F, you can have aubergine cannelloni and chicken flavoured with vanilla or salmon. Other set meals 55F (lunchtimes), 100F, 130F and 170F. Even if the candle holders and fabric tablecloths create a more chic atmosphere in the evenings, you'll get the same high quality and meticulous presentation of food whatever tiem you come. Gourmet food at motorway service station prices.

LES CORNES D'AUROCH

18 rue Michel Servet (Centre).
☎ 04.77.33.34.31
Closed Saturday lunchtimes and Sundays.

A pretty bistro with typical Lyons dishes and specialities like *andouillette*, *tablier de sapeur* (ox tripe coated with egg and breadcrumbs, grilled and served with garlic butter) and brains. And if you fancy trying a little bit of everything, have the *assiette Gargantua*. They do set meals at 110F, 150F and 190F in the evenings and fish features quite a lot. At lunchtimes, the 75F set meal is a good deal since it includes a glass of wine and coffee. The owner is a bald, cheery man and his wife is friendly and eager to help. They don't encourage smoking. Mind you it's your cholesterol level you should be worried about after your meal rather than your lungs.

NOUVELLE

30 rue St-Jean (Centre).
☎ 04.77.32.32.60
Closed Sunday evenings and Mondays.

This is the in place in Saint-Étienne and it's right in the centre. It's got everything a gourmet restaurant should have, from the décor — a subtle grey with hints of beige — to the staff — young and very elegant — and the kind of menu you dream about. But it doesn't charge the kind of prices you usually get in places like these. At weekday lunchtimes, they have an 85F *menu du jour* (100F with a glass of wine and coffee) that gives you a chance to experience all of this. Other set meals 130F, 170F and much much more. The young chef loves to revamp "poor man's food" like *brandade de morue* (salt cod pounded with garlic, oil and cream) and comes up with new pasta dishes like ravioli stuffed with lamb and salmon lasagne. Portions are generous and it's all very imaginative, even if the sauces are a bit on the heavy side (at least they were in the 130F set meal). But we're just being picky now, it really is great. We advise you to book in advance.

RESTAURANT À LA BOUCHE PLEINE

8 place Chavanelle; it's near the fire station.
☎ 04.77.33.92.47
Closed lunchtimes, Sundays, Mondays, and Aug.

Reservations are essential because it's very popular. It's on the square where the wholesale market used to be before it was knocked down to make way for the bus station and it's the place where actors and other people who're around in the small hours congregate. Photos of all the regulars are stuck up on the walls of the cosy little dining room and you may well meet some of the people appearing at the theatre. Like them, when you've finished a meal lovingly prepared by Henriette, you'll try to find out the recipe for the *Diable au corps*, the explosive – and flambéd! – house cocktail. You'll get a really nice welcome from Marco. Cheapest set meal 115F, then 129F and 180F.

SAINT-GENEST-MALIFAUX 42660 (12KM S)

10% AUBERGE DE CAMPAGNE LA DILIGENCE

Le Château du Bois; take the N82 to Bicètre, then the D501 – the restaurant is 3km from the village.
☎ 04.77.39.04.99
Closed Mondays and Tuesdays (except in July and August), and Jan 1–Feb 10.

A very nice restaurant in a farmhouse that's part of a 13th century castle (which still has people living in it). It belongs to the nearby agricultural college of Saint-Genest. Good food and pleasant service, with seasonal set meals 80–100F. You can also have a snack for around 55F. The handsome dining room has a fireplace, and there's a terrace in the farm courtyard. If you'd like to stay, you'll pay 40F (breakfast is not included) for a bed in a dormitory for 4–8 people or you can camp in the grounds for next to nothing. The farm has got horses, so you can go riding if you want. Advisable to book.

RESTAURANT MONTMARTIN

18 rue du Velay; take the N82, then the D501 to Plafony.
☎ 04.77.51.21.25
Closed Wednesdays, one week in January, and one week in July. Open evenings, by reservation only, at 7.30pm sharp.

Located in one of the less attractive villages in this part of the world, this restaurant was opened in the post-war years by the grandmother of the present owners, who haven't changed a thing – the atmosphere is as warm and cosy as ever and the floorboards still squeak! They don't seem to have heard of *nouvelle cuisine*, and this is the place to come for rich food – morels, frog's legs and *quenelles* – served up in generous portions. The type of place that families keep on coming back to for Sunday lunch. Four set meals 74–150F.

SAINT-VICTOR-SUR-LOIRE 42230 (15KM W)

|●| LE CROQUE CERISE

Base Nautique de Saint-Victor.
☎ 04.77.90.07.54
Closed Monday evenings and Tuesday evenings.

A big building, not particularly elegant, but the dining rooms with their large windows and the terrace by the harbour are really pleasant. Simple food (whitebait, oven-baked pizza in the evenings) that's sometimes quite inventive (grapefruit *terrine*), and always meticulously prepared. Set meals with main course, dessert and coffee, 65F at lunchtimes, then from 90F (except Sunday lunchtimes and public holidays)–150F. A few hiccups in the décor (plastic plants) but definitely none in the food or the service. And at the end of the day, that's what counts.

SAINT-PAUL-EN-CORNILLON 42240 (17KM SW)

|●| LA CASCADE

How to get there: go in the direction of Firminy; take the D3 and then the D46 to the left before the bridge over the Loire.
☎ 04.77.35.70.02
Closed Mondays and Tuesdays.

It's down from the road that runs through the village and has a view of the river. The dining room is nothing special but it gets lots of light and there's a very pleasant terrace shaded by plane trees (which are dwarfed by an impressive sequoia). It's a pity that the car park is between the terrace and the river. The cheapest set meal (not available Sunday lunchtimes) is 78F and consists of a salad of *Montbrison* (quite a strong blue cheese from the Auvergne) and trout *meunière* (coated in breadcrumbs and fried in butter). Other set meals 107F, 142F and 195F. Friendly, efficient service.

BESSAT (LE) 42660 (18KM SE)

⌂ |●| HÔTEL LA FONDUE – RESTAURANT CHEZ LE PÈRE CHARLES**

Grande-Rue; on the D8; it's in the centre of the village.
☎ 04.77.20.40.09 F→ 04.77.20.45.20
Closed Dec 1–end Feb. **Secure parking**. **TV**.

A good restaurant at an altitude of 1,170m right in the middle of the Pilat regional park, where the people of Lyons and Saint-Étienne come for a bit of fresh air. Gourmets, get your knives and forks ready. For 73F any day but Sunday, you can have trout and, for dessert, various chocolates and home-made nibbles. Delicious, just like all the other set meals at 117F, 155F, 175F, 188F and 255F. Warm atmosphere. Doubles 165F with basin, 190F with shower/wc and 260F with bath. The ones with bath are bigger but if you go for one with shower/wc, you'll find they're concealed in a rather intriguing revolving cupboard.

|●| RESTAURANT LE PETIT CHEF

Grande-Rue; on the D8; if you're approaching the village from Saint-Étienne, it's the first restaurant on the right.
☎ 04.77.20.40.92
Closed Monday evenings (and sometimes Tuesday evenings).

It's advisable to book in summer, especially at the weekend. A nice little place with a friendly owner and a rather homely atmosphere. Country cooking and generous portions You've got to try the potato *galette* and the duck with bilberries. Set meals 59F, 60F, 85F and 125F.

|●| AUBERGE DE LA JASSERIE

La Jasserie; it's 6km out of Le Bessat at an altitude of 1,310m; follow the arrows from the village.
☎ 04.77.20.40.16

This old farmhouse, with its litle turret, is a bit of an institution around here. It's one of those simple, country inns where you sit at wooden tables and chairs in a huge old dining room. The only downside is that it's always busy and noisy at the weekends. You sometimes feel like you're being rushed but there's a great friendly atmosphere. Generous portions of traditional dishes made from local produce. Snacks 52F, and set meals from 78F; it's very near the cross-country ski trails and you can drop in for hot chocolate when the weather gets a bit too chilly for skiing. You can also go mountain-biking or paragliding, and if you can't face the thought of going back down at the end of a tiring day, you can have a bed in a pretty basic dormitory for 45F, which includes breakfast.

SAINT-CHRISTO-EN-JAREZ 42320 (23KM NE)

⌂ |●| HÔTEL-RESTAURANT BESSON – LES TOURISTES*

How to get there: go to Saint-Chamond, then take the D2 in the direction of Valfleury and col de la Gachet.
☎ 04.77.20.85.01
Closed Wednesdays (except in July and August) and three weeks end of Aug–beginning of Sept.
Secure parking.

Far away from the hustle and bustle of Saint-Étienne and Saint-Chamond is this little village of about 1,200 inhabitants at an altitude of 800m on the south side of the monts du Lyonnais. Lovely fresh air! The hotel, a pretty brick-red house, is a bit old-fashioned but it's quiet and you'll get lots of pure mountain air. Ask for a room with a view of the Pilat mountain range on the other side of the valley – superb! Doubles 180F with bathroom and toilet on the landing. Cheapest set meal 70F. The salami, which comes from the surrounding villages, is a must, as is the *gratin dauphinois* (which has to be ordered in advance). Light country-style meal 60F (evenings), with *charcuterie*, omelette, cream cheese and dessert. Other set meals 70F (lunchtimes), then 90–170F.

SAINT-MARCELLIN-EN-FOREZ 42680 (25KM NW)

|●| MANOIR DU COLOMBIER

9 rue Carles-de-Mazenod; you can either take the A172, and get off at the Andrézieux-Bouthéon exit, or take the D8 to Bonson, then the D498.
☎ 04.77.52.90.37
Closed Tuesday evenings and Wednesdays. **Car park**.

In a little village at the foot of the Forez mountains is this beautiful 16th century manor house, a rare vestige of the past, which luckily nobody has attempted to demolish. There are three slightly kitsch dining rooms, all decorated differently, and a wonderful courtyard where you can dine. The food is pleasant if not particularly sophisticated, and the portions are generous. The cheapest set meal (95F) is good. Others 135–265F. If you want to splash out a bit, treat yourself to the roast pigeon. Friendly welcome.

SAINT-SAUVEUR-EN-RUE 42220 (25KM S)

10% ⌂ |●| CHÂTEAU DE BOBIGNEUX

Bobigneux; take the N82 south to col du Grand-Bois, then the D22 for 11km and it's 2.5km from the village.
☎ 04.77.39.24.33 F 04.77.39.25.74
Closed Wednesdays and Jan–Feb. **Car park**.

After 18 years in Greenland (which is where all the souvenirs and the stuffed birds you see around the place came from), the owners decided to move here and take over this 16th century stone manor house just next to a farm belonging to the wife's brother. The farm provides them with all the fresh produce they need and the husband creates great food with it all. Country-style set meal 68F and family cooking 98–130F, depending on how many courses you have. Try the oyster mushrooms in puff pastry. The dining rooms have been pleasantly renovated, and the terrace and garden are both lovely. On the first floor there are six pretty, bright and spacious country-style rooms. They don't have TV or phone and cost 240F (breakfast included). A delightful and romantic place to stay, and the prices are reasonable. A lovely welcome, not the usual recital of trite phrases.

SAINT-GALMIER 42330

|●| LE BOUGAINVILLIER

Pré Château; it's near Coise and it's signposted from the Badoit spring.
☎ 04.77.54.03.31
Closed Mondays, Sunday evenings, during the February school holidays, and three weeks mid Aug–beginning of Sept. **Car park**.

A pretty building swathed in Virginia creeper in the rather stylish little town that's home to the famous Badoit mineral water. The restaurant has three dining areas, one of them a veranda overlooking a walled garden by the water's edge. Gérard Charbonnier is one of the most interesting young chefs in the area. He spent two years in a well-known restaurant where he was encouraged to be inventive. He still is although he has had to adapt to a style of cooking that is a bit more traditional – and more affordable too!. The only complaint we have about the cheapest (90F) set meal is that it isn't available at weekends. Other set meals 135–270F. Charming low-key welcome. Well worth the 15 minute drive from Saint-Étienne. After your meal, why not take a stroll to the nearby Badoit spring?. In the evenings, all the town people queue up there to get some of the wonderful mineral water — it's free for them!

VEAUCHE 42340 (6KM S)

⌂ |●| HÔTEL-RESTAURANT DE LA GARE

55 av. H.-Planchet; take the D12.
☎ 04.77.54.60.10 F 04.77.94.30.53
Closed Sunday evenings and public holiay evenings. **Secure parking**.

A good neighbourhood restaurant. They have a *menu du jour* for 48F (except on Saturday evenings, Sundays and public holidays) including a drink, and good set meals ranging in price from 69F to 250F. The one at 98F is particularly tempting and comes with a choice of *compotée* of pig's trotters or salmon flan, cheese, and a good selection of desserts. Pleasant conventional décor and a warm friendly welcome. The hotel has 10 basic rooms 115–165F, depending on their (relative) comfort. Bear it in mind if you're stuck for somewhere to stay, but the great view of the station and the factory is probably not quite what you're looking for.

ANDREZIEUX-BOUTHÉON 42160 (8KM S)

10% LES IRIS

32 rue Jean-Martouret; take the D12.
☎ 04.77.36.09.09 ➡ 04.77.36.09.00
Closed the first week in August; restaurant closed Sunday evenings, Tuesday and Wednesday evenings.
Car park. TV. Disabled access.

A handsome bourgeois-style residence with two elegant flights of steps on the outskirts of a rather industrial town, home to the airport of Saint-Éienne. The main building has been sympathetically restored. The bedrooms, ten in all, are on two levels and overlook the swimming pool and the garden with its gigantic cedar tree. They're functional but pleasant and they're all called after flowers. Two people will pay 410F. The restaurant serves conventional middle-class food and has décor to match. Set meals 110F (not available on Sundays) and 135–255F. Attentive but unobtrusive service. There's a bistro in the basement (the St Étienne equivalent of a Lyons café) which does a 74F set meal every day except Sundays. The atmosphere there is more laid-back than in the main restaurant, and you can even play darts or boules. We liked this place – not only is it delightful but it's great for a family holiday, a romantic weekend or a seminar.

CHAZELLES-SUR-LYON 42140 (10KM NE)

CHÂTEAU BLANCHARD**

36 route de Saint-Galmier; it's very near the hat museum.
☎ 04.77.54.28.88 ➡ 04.77.54.36.03
Closed Sunday evenings and Mondays, also the first two weeks in Jan. **Secure parking. TV.**

The town is the capital of the hat-making industry in France and this "castle", built in 1930, used to be the home of a hat-maker. It lay neglected for 40 years but has now been restored to its original splendour. We fell in love with the place. Outside, the garish frontage is decorated with friezes. Inside, the décor is a glorious jumble of neoclassical, modern and downright kitschy. Very well-equipped doubles 280F. Number 6 (360F) still has its original décor The restaurant fits into its surroundings very nicely. You'll get a warm welcome and classic, well presented dishes. Set meals 88F (weekdays), 120–245F. It specializes in fresh fish. You can eat on the terrace.

SAINT-JEAN-DE-MAURIENNE 73300

HÔTEL DES SPORTS*

10 rue Brun-Rollet.
☎ 04.79.64.02.40
Closed Sundays.

A recently renovated little hotel, where rugby seems to be the main topic of conversation at the bar. The rooms are well-looked-after and not expensive. Doubles 150F with shower and 180F with bath/wc. Why so cheap? Not as many people come to Saint-Jean as used to, says owner Michel Gaden, who breaks into a smile when he starts talking to you.

10% HÔTEL-RESTAURANT DU NORD**

place du Champ-de-Foire.
☎ 04.79.64.02.08 ➡ 04.79.59.91.31
Closed Sunday evenings and in October.
Car park. TV. Disabled access.

A former coaching inn flanked by a little tower. The restaurant, which has a vaulted ceiling, and the reception area are both in the former stables and they bear more traces of the past than the rooms do (although they're still very pleasant, with roughcast white walls). Doubles from 245F with shower/wc. Set meals 70–175F, with the inevitable local specialities but also a few good main courses such as guinea fowl with *Reblochon* (a mild cheese from Savoie) and a *chaud-froid* of smoked salmon.

JARRIER 73300 (7KM SW)

HÔTEL-RESTAURANT BELLEVUE*

How to get there: go towards the valley of Arvan, then follow the signs to the hotel on the D78.
☎ 04.79.64.31.03 ➡ 04.79.64.28.61
Car park.

Service from 12.30pm, then from 7.30pm. There must be hundreds of hotels In France called *Bellevue* (beautiful view) but this one definitely lives up to its name. Most of the rooms here have a superb view of the Maurienne valley, as does the restaurant, housed in a former barn. Denise Léard, the owner, always checks on the bar before going to the kitchen to prepare some of her traditional dishes. Set meals at 80F, 95F and 150F, all offering regional specialities. Half-board 190–220F, full board 220–250F. Doubles 140–210F with bath. This place is a must!

SAINT-MARTIN-DE-BELLEVILLE 73440

LE LACHENAL**

(Centre).
☎ 04.79.08.96.29 F 04.79.08.94.23
Closed mid April–end of June and Sept 1–Dec 20.

This place is like a lovely doll's house that you always dreamed of having as a child. Cosy rooms with flower-painted shutters and panelled walls. Doubles 270F with shower/wc. Simple dishes, prepared in a way that lets the food speak for itself, include fillet of beef (from the Salers breed of cattle) with mushrooms, fondue flavoured with kirsch, and frog's legs with a creamy sauce. Sounds appetising, doesn't it? Set meals 80F, 120F and 165F. And if you're not already tempted, another good reason to come here is the fact that the Lemattre family are wonderful hosts. In fact, it's so good that it's often full, so it's a good idea to book in advance.

CHEZ BIDOU

Quartier des Granges; it's 4km from the centre on the D117 going towards Ménuires.
☎ 04.79.08.97.12
Closed mid April–end of June, and mid Sept–mid Dec.

Good, friendly, and not too expensive. These are the three qualities we look for in a place, and we found all three here. The chalet looks as if it was built before the Flood and the tiny little vaulted dining room in the basement is light years removed from the tourist traps you see all over the place. There are no fancy frills in this place, just a genuine welcome and a plate full of tasty specialities. There's *raclette* (92F), *tartiflette* (75F), and two regional set meals at 92F and 192F. The first offers mountain *terrine*, *diots* (vegetable and pork sausages in white wine), *crozet* and *polenta* (maize meal porridge, with butter and grated cheese), cheese and dessert – and the second is even more substantial! Reservations are essential if you don't want a wasted journey.

LA BOUITTE

quartier Saint-Marcel; take the D117 towards Les Ménuires (about 2km).
☎ 04.79.08.96.77
Closed April 19–beginning of July and beginning of Sept–Dec 15. **Car park**.

Without a doubt, this is the best restaurant in the valley. They use simple ingredients and produce but they combine them in ways that result in astonishingly good dishes that are full of flavour. Try the snail flan with a nettle sauce, the sautéd frog's legs with ginger, calf's liver spinach or the rabbit tart with shallot marmalade. Give your taste buds a treat by having an unforgettable meal in the elegant country-style dining room. Everything is first-class – the service is faultless, the desserts are out of this world and there are lots of wonderful nibbles to have with your coffee. Set meals 98F (118F in winter), 180F and 270F. It's a bit expensive but it really is worth it for the wonderful cooking of René Meilleur.

SAINT-MARTIN-EN-HAUT 69850

RESTAURANT LES QUATRE SAISONS

place de l'Église (Centre).
☎ 04.78.48.69.12
Closed Tuesdays out of season and in February.

A hilltop village near the monts du Lyonnais with a surprising restaurant in its pretty square. The dining room has frescoes by a painter from Lyons, Michel Cornu, and the home cooking, served in generous portions, is proof that there are still people around who know how to make their customers happy. Friendly welcome. Set meals 95F, 130F and 168F. Or you could have a 60F set meal in the bar just next door.

AVEIZE 69610 (9KM NW)

HÔTEL-RESTAURANT RIVOLLIER

How to get there: take the D34.
☎ 04.74.26.01.08 F 04.74.26.01.90
Secure parking.

How on earth can a place this size survive in such a small village you'll ask yourself when you first get here. You'll know how when you leave, for you'll have had a first-class welcome and service and a superb meal in a pleasant airy dining room, all for a price that would kill off the competition, but seeing as there isn't any in the village, it's not a problem. Wonderful set meals (62F, 95F and 160F) and a wide selection of daily specials that change frequently. If you're stuck for accommodation, they also have eight rooms that don't claim to be anything other than basic put-me-ups for the passing traveller.

SAINT-PIERRE-DE-CHARTREUSE 38380

10% ☗ |●| L'AUBERGE DU CUCHERON

col du Cucheron (north); it's 3km north of the town centre, on the D512.
☎ 04.76.88.62.06 F 04.76.88.65.43
Closed Mondays except during the school holidays, Jan 5–17, and Oct 15–Dec 25. **Car park**.

Service noon–2pm and 7.30pm–9pm. Incredible – the kind of nice old inn you used to be able to find; it's got magnificent views, there are trees everywhere, and the proprietress is delightful. She has seven rooms (146–205F), which are always very popular with all the American tourists, because they look like ones you get in all the old films (that's French films, not American ones!). Half-board 228F. Set meals 95F (walnut salad, trout *meunière*) and 160F. You're only 20m from the ski slopes in winter and it's blissfully quiet in summer.

SAINTE-EULALIE 07510

10% ☗ |●| HÔTEL DU NORD**

How to get there: it's opposite the church.
☎ 04.75.38.80.09 F 04.75.38.85.50
Closed Wednesdays (except in July and August) and Nov 15–Feb 15. **Car park. Disabled access**.

The hotel has been given a new lease of life. Half of the rooms, the sitting room, and the façade have been completely refurbished, and two lounges (one with a veranda) have been created. They both have a magnificent view of the plain of the Loire (the source of the river is only 5km from here). Doubles from 230F with shower/wc. Half-board (minimum 3 days) starts at 235F. Set meals from 98F. The specialities on offer include trout soufflé with *beurre blanc* and pork stew in Ardèche wine. As for desserts, the *crème brûlée* with bilberries and raspberries is an absolute must! A great place with a long-standing reputation.

SAMOËNS 74340

10% ☗ |●| HÔTEL LES SEPT MONTS***

How to get there: it's 200m from the town centre.
☎ 04.50.34.40.58 F 04.50.34.13.89
Restaurant closed Oct–Nov and April–May. **Car park. TV**.

A rather modern chalet with lots of flowers on which the sun always seems to shine in the sun; it's a great place to enjoy life whether you're here in summer or winter. Warm atmosphere. The rooms come with all mod cons and a balcony. You'll pay 390F for the nicest ones. The restaurant has good traditional dishes served up in generous portions. Set meals 68–160F.

|●| LA FANDOLIEUSE

Centre.
☎ 04.50.34.98.28

Service summer and winter alike noon–2pm and 4.30pm–11pm. This is a pleasant little crêperie with wainscotted walls. If you come here you've got to try the *'soupe châtrée'* (80F) which is made with bread, local cheese and onions and is the kind of food that sticks to your ribs. It used to be the traditional dish the locals ate on Saint Christopher's Day. They do all sorts of fondues and crêpes with amazing names. These names come from an ancient local dialect that the old masons of the valley spoke among themselves. There are no set meals but you can eat for about 90F.

SUZE-LA-ROUSSE 26790

☗ HÔTEL LE COMTE**

route de Bollène (West); it's on the right, just as you leave town in the direction of Bollène.
☎ 04.75.04.85.38 F 04.75.04.85.37
Closed Jan 15–Feb 15. **Car park. TV. Disabled access**.

This is a big Provence farmhouse that's been wonderfully converted. Doubles 270F–300F. The nicest (and most expensive) rooms are in the tiny keep. Luxurious bathrooms and polished wood panelling. A few of the rooms have a terrace overlooking the neighbouring vineyards. In the evening, there's a *menu du jour* for residents. The very original wine university isn't very far away.

SAINT-RESTITUT 26130 (8KM NW)

|●| RESTAURANT LES BUISSES

South-East; leave Saint-Restitut by the Suze-la Rousse road, go past the statue of the Virgin Mary, and follow the D218.
☎ 04.75.04.96.50
Closed Saturday lunchtimes and Mondays out of season. **Secure parking**.

There's no à la carte or choice of set meals here, just one fixed price of 135F, lunchtimes and evenings. For that you get a choice of four starters (like deep-fried stuffed courgette flowers in a tomato and basil sauce), four main courses (grilled red mullet stuffed with fennel, say, or *tian* of aubergines and tomatoes with lamb), cheese and dessert. Good traditional food of the south, eaten on the terrace in front of this handsome traditional house, surrounded by a Provence-style garden. Cicadas in summer. One of our favourites.

THÔNES 74230

NOUVEL HÔTEL DU COMMERCE**

5 rue des Clefs (Centre).
☎ 04.50.02.13.66 F 04.50.32.16.24
Closed Sunday evenings, Mondays out of season, and in November. **Secure parking**. **TV**.

It smells like the country, you're beginning to see mountains, and the architecture is looking more and more typical of Savoy. And what a joy to wake up to a view of the forest. The rooms are colourful, sometimes a bit too much so, but you can easily put up with it. Doubles 230–302F, with shower or bath, and depending on the season. But the real star of the show here is the food. Chef Robert Bastard-Rosset prepares dishes like *millefeuille* of beef with onion marmalade, stuffed pigeon with cardamom. and one of the best *farcements* (potatoes baked with milk, eggs and prunes) in the region. Perfect service in the cosy dining room with lots of wood. The owner is very friendly and makes a real fuss of her guests. Set meals 73–350F. If you go for the 350F set meal all you'll want to do after a feast like that is go to bed. The only criticism we have is that the reception area has been refurbished in 70s style; it's ugly!

MANIGOD 74230 (6KM SE)

HÔTEL-RESTAURANT DE LA VIEILLE FERME**

col de Merdassier; from Thônes, take the D12, then the D16 towards Manigod, pass La Croix-Fry and head for the resort of L'Étale.
☎ 04.50.02.41.49
Closed Wednesdays except during the school holidays, in May, and Nov 1–Dec 15. **Car park**. **TV**.

A traditional Alpine chalet at the foot of the ski slopes. It's what you would expect from a typical mountain chalet and at the same time it's really cute. They have five pretty rooms at 250F with shower or bath. Set meals 90–120F with typical authentic food, just like the place. Charming service.

THONON-LES-BAINS 74200

RESTAURANT LE VICTORIA

5 place des Arts (Centre).
☎ 04.50.71.02.82
Closed Dec 23–Jan 15.

A pleasant dining room, the outside swathed in greenery so that passers-by can't see in. They do an impressive set meal for 110F with a choice of eight starters, seven main courses and lots of desserts. You've got a difficult choice to make, as everything is mouthwatering. There's another set meal at 160F. Lots of tasty fresh fish from the lake.

MARGENCEL 74200 (5KM SW)

10% HÔTEL-RESTAURANT LES CYGNES*

port de Séchex; when you get to Margencel, head for the port of Séchex on the D33.
☎ 04.50.72.63.10 F 04.50.72.68.22
Closed Tuedays out of season and Dec–Jan.
Car park. **TV**.

It's known locally as 'Chez Jules'. It's a real family business and since 1938 has specialized in fresh fish from the lake. You'll find fish in all their set meals – the 110F one has whitebait, the 145F one *féra* (a type of salmon), and the 165F one fillet of perch – and on the à la carte menu. Pleasant doubles, all with shower/wc, 280F. A hotel that's right beside the lake – guests who come by boat can tie up next to the car park!

ARMOY 74200 (6.5KM SE)

10% HÔTEL-RESTAURANT LE CHALET

L'Ermitage; D26.
☎ 04.50.71.08.11 F 04.50.71.33.88
Closed end of Sept–end of Feb. **Car park**.

A tiny village on the edge of the Thonon forest. The hotel stands at the top of a wooded slope high above the village and Lake Geneva. Lots of peace and quiet and a superb view from most of the rooms. Once you're here, you won't want to leave! Doubles 230–250F with shower/wc. If you're here in summer, ask for one of the little cabins in the garden, next to the swimming pool. Set meals 95–170F.

TOUR-DU-PIN (LA) 38110

10% HÔTEL DE FRANCE – RESTAURANT LE BEC FIN**

place du Champ-de-Mars (Centre).
☎ 04.74.97.00.08 F 04.74.97.36.47

Restaurant closed Sunday evenings.
Secure parking. **TV**.

Service from noon, then from 7pm. The rooms have been renovated throughout. Doubles 150F–210F (with bath). As for the food, they don't skimp on the care they take over the dishes or the size of the portions. For a mere 105F, you'll get snail salad and a choice of ravioli with sardine stuffing or calf's-head *pot au feu* – amazing!. Pleasant dining room.

SAINT-DIDIER-DE-LA-TOUR 38110 (4KM SE)

10% AUX BERGES DU LAC

chemin du Lac.
☎ 04.74.97.32.82 F 04.74.97.08.21
Closed in the evenings in winter (except weekends) and 10 days at Christmas. **Car park**.

Service noon–1.30pm, and 7pm–9.30pm. This place is so simple yet so pleasant you wonder why on earth there aren't more places like it in France, where you can sit and have something to eat and a bit of a giggle. Here you get laughter, music, and set meals that range in price from 45F (weekdays) to 149F. Great for a family treat on a Sunday.

VIGNIEU 38890 (10KM NW)

CHÂTEAU DE CHAPEAU CORNU***

How to get there: take the D16 in the direction of Saint-Chef.
☎ 04.74.27.79.00 F 04.74.92.49.31
Restaurant closed Sunday evenings, Dec 20–30 and Jan 1–5. **Car park**. **TV**.

A funny name for a funny place! If only the residents of this 13th century castle could see their home now — a restaurant and a three-star hotel with bright comfortable rooms with a mixture of antique furniture and contemporary art. Great prices, ranging from 200F for a room with basin, in the annexe to 380F for one with bath and a view of the valley. Meals are served in the vaulted dining rooms or on the terrace. The kitchen uses only local produce. Set meals range in price from 75F (weekday lunchtimes) to 335F (ravioli with snails, trout fillets *en papillote)*. Limited à la carte menu on Monday and Tuesday evenings.

SAINT-SAVIN 38300 (16.5KM NW)

RESTAURANT LE DEMPTÉZIEU

place du Château (North-West); take the N6 in the direction of Bourgoin-Jallieu, then the D143 on the right.
☎ 04.74.28.90.49 F 04.74.28.81.60
Closed Monday evenings, Tuesdays, and in January.
Car park.

This used to be an old village café and restaurant before being taken over by a young couple who love the business and care passionately about it. Madame looks after the dining room and her husband does the cooking. You can dine on the terrace in summer in the shadow of the château of Demptézieu. The food on offer is a bit of a change from the usual, with a few inventive dishes that shouldn't be missed, like roast duckling with oranges or trout soufflé with onion marmalade. Set meals range in price from 65F (weekday lunchtimes) to 180F. The latter is definitely for the gourmets and includes supreme of guinea fowl in a chervil sauce and snails with watercress butter. Definitely one for the address book.

TOURNON-SUR-RHÔNE 07300

10% HÔTEL AZALÉES**

6 av. de la Gare (South-West).
☎ 04.75.08.05.23 F 04.75.08.18.27
Closed Dec 25–Jan 2. **Secure parking**. **TV**. **Disabled access**.

Service noon–2pm and 7pm–9.30pm. The first nice thing about this place is that you can sit on the terrace and watch the steam train puffing its way through Haut-Vivarais en route to Lamastre. Secondly, the rooms are very pleasant and have all mod cons. Prices start at 230F. Ask for a room in the annexe, which is even quieter than the main building. Good food. Set meals 104F (mainly regional specialities) and 152F. The latter consists of a great many courses and thankfully comes with a trou ardéchois, a glass of something alcoholic halfway through to help the digestive process.

RESTAURANT AUX SABLETTES

187 route de Lamastre (West); go 3km along the Lamastre road, turn left, and it's opposite the Acacias campsite.
☎ 04.75.08.44.34
Closed Wednesdays (except in July and August).
Car park.

This restaurant and bar is a bit out of the way, but it's popular with the young locals and people from the nearby campsite. The décor doesn't have much character, but the menu is pretty good and pretty inventive too – they put beer in everything, including the desserts. How about some beer mousse or beer tart? The less adventurous among you will be happy with the ravioli, a delicious regional speciality. Set meals 60F, 80F and 130F.

RESTAURANT L'ESTRAGON

6 place Saint-Julien; it's opposite the church.
☎ 04.75.08.87.66
Closed Wednesdays (except in summer), in February, and during the Easter holidays.

This place is in a great location (a stone's throw from the Rhône and in the middle of the pedestrian precinct) and it offers good simple food at reasonable prices. Set meals 64F and 85–120F. The salads are large and the pan-fried fillet of *rascasse* (scorpion fish) with anchovy butter is delicious. Expect to pay about 130F for a main course à la carte. You can also get a '*pierre chaude*' set meal at 100F, consisting of salad, topside of veal or sirloin steak, cheese and dessert. Lithographs of Van Gogh, Gauguin and Picasso decorate the walls of the restaurant. Pity the welcome isn't warmer.

USSON-EN-FOREZ 42550

10% HÔTEL RIVAL*

rue Centrale (Centre).
☎ 04.77.50.63.65 F 04.77.50.67.62
Closed Mondays Oct–June. **Secure parking. TV.**

A typical good family hotel in a little village in the mountains of Forez with a restaurant serving large portions of traditional dishes. They do set meals at 68F (weekdays), 100F, and 135F and up, and these can be served on the terrace. The rooms are clean and affordable, even if they're a bit lacking in character. Doubles 140–250F, depending on the facilities. Very friendly proprietress.

CHAPELLE-EN-LA-FAYE (LA) 42380 (16KM NE)

AUBERGE DU MARAIS

How to get there: it's at the Saint-Bonnet-le-Château exit in the direction of Saint-Anthème; follow the D14 for 8km.
☎ 04.77.50.00.40
Closed Tuedays (except in July and August) and evenings (except Fridays, Saturdays and Sundays).
Car park.

This is one of our favourite places in the area. You'll get lots of peace and quiet and good fresh air. The talented young lady of the house makes a wide range of great vegetable and meat *terrines* and offers her interpretation of regional dishes. The savoury turnovers stuffed with kid are delicious. Set meals 80F and 110F, and there are barbecues on the terrace at weekends. You'll get a warm welcome in this old farmhouse, which has been pleasantly refurbished. There are paintings on the walls by artist friends of the owner. There's also a *gîte,* where you can stay the night for 105F, which includes evening meal and breakfast at the inn.

VALENCE 26000

10% AUBERGE DE JEUNESSE – CENTRE DE L'ÉPERVIÈRE**

chemin de l'Épervière (South-West); head for Montélimar and it's 2km from the town centre, between the Rhône and the A7.
☎ 04.75.42.32.00 F 04.75.56.20.67
Car park. TV. Disabled access.

This is a multipurpose building in the middle of a park on the riverbank. Dormitories with 3 or 6 beds for 54F and 41F. Expect to pay around 6–7F extra if you haven't got an IH card. Doubles with shower 220F. In the restaurant, set meals cost 85F or more. It has a cafeteria too. Pity it's so far from the town centre.

10% HÔTEL DE L'EUROPE**

15 av. Félix-Faure (Centre); it's near the tourist office and the station.
☎ 04.75.43.02.16 F 04.75.43.61.75
Closed Sundays 2pm–6pm.
Secure parking. TV. Canal+.

Valence isn't much of a holiday resort, but this is a good hotel with quite pleasant and quiet air-conditioned rooms at prices ranging from 230F with shower to 330F with bath; it's conveniently located and has been renovated throughout There are enough restaurants nearby to stop you going hungry and enough TV channels to make sure you go to bed happy.

RESTAURANT L'ÉPICERIE

18 place Bélat (Centre); it's beside the church of Saint-Jean.
☎ 04.75.42.74.46 F 04.75.42.10.87
Closed Saturday lunchtimes, Sundays, and Aug 4–20.
Disabled access.

Service noon–1.45pm and 7.30pm–9.45pm. One of the town centre's good restaurants, on the fringes of the pedestrian precinct. As the name implies, it used to be a grocery. The dining room is spacious, with thick stone walls. It has geat regional dishes, like *caillette* (pork and vegetable faggot), ravioli or lamb.

Set meals 99–300F. When the weather's nice, you can sit on the terrace on a little square opposite an old covered market. Friendly welcome.

10% ☗ |●| HÔTEL-RESTAURANT PIC

285 av. Victor Hugo (South);it's not far from the train station.
☎ 04.75.44.15.32
Closed Aug.

Despite the Relais & Châteaux sign the prices here are fairly reasonable, and you can have a main course plus dessert for 120F. (Do choose the right door though – the other place is incredibly expensive.) The dining room is small though so you really ought to reserve in autumn and winter when you can no longer sit out on the terrace. The hotel itself is inviting and comfy.

VALGORGE 07110

10% ☗ |●| HÔTEL LE TANARGUE**

Centre.
☎ 04.75.88.98.98 ⮕ 04.75.88.96.09
Closed Jan 3–March 15. **Car park**. **TV**. **Disabled access**.

The hotel, at an altitude of 500m, huddles at the foot of Mont Tanargue on the edge of the Ardèche. Large and pretty doubles 245–360F. Ask for one with a view of the valley since they get more light. The cheapest set meal – 90F – comes with starter, main course (very good quail), cheese and dessert. Every day except Sunday, they also have a 55F lunchtime *formule* of dish of the day plus dessert. The portions are generous. The dining room is vast and luxurious and has a giant pair of bellows hanging above the fireplace. You could quite happily stay in this cosy hotel for a lot longer. Half-board, which is not compulsory, starts at 275F.

VALLOIRE 73450

10% ☗ |●| HÔTEL CHRISTIANIA**

Centre.
☎ 04.79.59.00.57 ⮕ 04.79.59.00.06
Closed April 25–mid June and Sept 15–Dec 1.
Secure parking. **TV**.

Service 12.30pm–2pm, and 7.30pm–9pm. This place is something of an institution in Valloire and it's always pretty lively, as everyone seems to come here, ski instructors and skiers alike. The hotel has been recently renovated and looks nice from the outside with all the balconies. Rooms 180F with basin, 300F with shower/wc, and 320F with bath. There's a big dining room next to the bar and it serves home cooking and great traditional dishes like *diots* (vegetable and pork sausages in white wine), *tartiflette*, and fondues. Set meals 80–170F.

10% ☗ |●| LE RELAIS DU GALIBIER**

Les Verneys; it's 2km from the town centre, opposite the Verneys chairlift.
☎ 04.79.59.00.45 ⮕ 04.79.83.31.89
Closed April 10–June 20 and Sept 15–Dec 1.
Car park. **TV**.

Service from 12.30pm, then from 7.30pm. A traditional hotel at the foot of the ski slopes that's very popular with walkers and cyclists in summer. The rooms are clean and very decent and cost 300F with shower/wc, and 340F with bath. Traditional home cooking. Set meals 85–160F. In winter, the hotel is the HQ for the ski teams while they're training.

10% ☗ |●| HÔTEL LA SETAZ – RESTAURANT LE GASTILLEUR***

Centre.
☎ 04.79.59.01.03 ⮕ 04.79.59.00.63
Closed in May and Sept 20–Dec 20.
Secure parking. **TV**.

The outside is pretty uninspiring not to say ugly, but inside, this is a very classy hotel, admirably well run by Monique Villard. The rooms and the décor are modern. Doubles 330F with shower/wc and 480F with bath and balcony. Jacques Villard is the chef and he prepares the kind of dishes that take his French customers back to their childhood but adapts them to suit modern tastes. Our ideal set meal consisted of oxtail t*errine*, casseroled knuckle of veal with chanterelles, and warm chocolate tart. The service is flawless, and you'll get a pleasant welcome. In the summer, they often have barbecues in the garden. In the case of this place, definitely don't judge the book by its cover.

|●| L'ASILE DES FONDUES

Centre; it's near the church and the tourist office.
☎ 04.79.59.04.71
Closed out of season.

Service from noon, then from 7pm. In our opinion, this is the nicest restaurant in Valloire. It's in an old house with a charming country-style dining room that is possibly not as old as it's trying to look, but the welcome you get is so lovely that you feel you want to come back time and time again. As much *raclette* as you can eat 120F, *diots* (pork and vegetable sausages in white wine) 60F and ten or so different fondues 90F. A place we like very much.

VALLON-PONT-D'ARC 07150

LE MANOIR DU RAVEYRON**

rue du Raveyron (South-West); it's a stone's throw from the town centre, opposite the school.
☎ 04.75.88.03.59 Fax 04.75.37.11.12
Closed Oct 15–March 15.

Service 12.15pm–1.30pm and 7.15pm–9.15pm. There are about 15 rooms here. Doubles 210F with shower/wc, 280F with bath. Nice terrace and very pleasant garden. The restaurant does a good snail *terrine*, trout with leek *coulis*, and lots of other dishes featuring the herbs and flavours of the Ardèche. Regional set meal 72F (lunchtimes) and 98F (evenings) and others up to 218F.

RESTAURANT LE CHELSEA

bd Peschère-Alizon (Centre); it's in the main street.
☎ 04.75.88.01.40
Closed Nov–mid March.

Service noon–3pm, 6.30pm–11pm. At last, a trendy young restaurant Ardèche style. Pictures of Tintin and Milou and Harley Davidson motorbikes decorate the walls of the little dining room that leads out into the garden. Good salads around 40F (we liked the one called Chelsea, which had pasta, sweet peppers, basil, and *crème fraîche*). They also have some unusual beers. Expect to pay 60–90F à la carte. The 85F set meal changes every Friday.

LABASTIDE-DE-VIRAC 07150 (9KM S)

RESTAURANT LA PETITE AUBERGE

South-East; take the D579 in the direction of Barjac, then turn left onto a little road that leads to Aven-de-la-Forestière and Orgnac-l'Aven.
☎ 04.75.38.61.94
Closed end of Sept–Easter.

Service from noon, then from 7pm. This is an old country house with an handsome frontage looking over the *garrigue* and the vineyards. Fine cooking served up in generous portions. Set meals 60–180F. The cheapest set meal offers a choice of lamb and olive fricassee or duck drumsticks with orange followed by cheese and dessert. A relaxing place away from the hustle and bustle of the touristy Vallon-Pont-d'Arc.

VANS (LES) 07140

10% HÔTEL LES CÉVENNES

place Ollier (Centre); it's in the main square.
☎ 04.75.37.23.09
Closed Sunday evenings, Mondays, three weeks in February, and the first fortnight in October. **Car park.**

Service noon–2pm and then 7.30pm–9.30pm. From the minute you walk in here, you're aware of a very special atmosphere, of a sort of madness that seems to have infected the whole place. The décor is a real jumble, with flowers, knick-knacks, paintings, photos, documents which really could be the basis of a museum of Vans all jostling for space. It's impossible to say just what style the house is but you'll be glad you came here if only for the setting. You quickly forget about the only average facilities of the rooms. Doubles with shower/wc on the landing 160F. Ask for number 8. The restaurant serves generous portions of fresh tasting dishes like the speciality, home-made ravioli. Set meals 90F, 130F and 180F. Without a doubt, the most eccentric hotel in the Ardèche. Look out for the mobile made of old records near the car park.

10% LE CARMEL-ANCIEN COUVENT**

How to get there: it's next to the post office.
☎ 04.75.94.99.60 Fax 04.75.37.20.02
Hotel closed Jan 10–Feb 20, Nov 12–Dec 20.
Car park. TV. Disabled access.

There's an air of serenity and peacefulness about the place, which is hardly surprising since it used to be a convent and the outside remains totally unchanged. You'll get a warm welcome from owner Marc. He's a local history buff and takes his guests on a tour of the various rooms explaining the everyday life of the nuns. Keep an eye out for the confessional, now a telephone box! The rooms are as clean as can be, spacious and full of light. Expect to pay 300–380F for a double with shower/wc or bath, depending on the season. Breakfast (40F, and free for under 10's) is served until midday. The restaurant is only open in the evening and has set meals at 100F and 140F. A charming place, complete with swimming pool, that's worth a visit.

RESTAURANT LE GRANGOUSIER

rue Courte; it's opposite the church.
☎ 04.75.94.90.86
Closed Wednesdays and Sunday evenings (except in

July and August), and Dec 15–Feb 1.

Service noon–2pm and 7pm–9pm. This luxurious restaurant has a 95F set meal, as well as others at less affordable prices (130F, 145F, 230F) that will appeal to the gourmets among you. The cooking is imaginative and it's pretty decent value for money. The stuffed rabbit with Swiss chard and the chicken livers mixed with *foie gras,* eggs and cream and served with a nettle sauce lived up to our expectations. The dining room with its arched ceiling and its dressed stone is the perfect setting for these wonderful delicacies. As for the wine, the Merlot Domaine des Terriers is only 60F. A stylish place which is still accessible to those on a tighter budget. It's just a shame the staff aren't a bit more friendly!

VIENNE 38200

|●| RESTAURANT L'ESTANCOT

4 rue de la Table-Ronde (North).
☎ 04.74.85.12.09
Closed Sundays and Wednesday evenings.

It's in one of the most touristy little streets in Vienne, but this place just keeps on getting it right. Lots of flowers outside, and inside a beautiful long dining room. People come for the *criques* (potatoes, parsle, and eggs) and *paillassons* (potatoes) from 40F. Traditional set meals 72F and 98F, with a dish of the day at 42F served weekday lunchtimes.

ESTRABLIN 38780 (8KM SE)

10% ☗ LA GABETIÈRE***

How to get there: take the D502 and it's on the left after the crossroads that takes you to Estrablin.
☎ 04.74.58.01.31 F➜ 04.74.58.08.98
Car park. TV.

A good hotel and we like it. It's a lovely country manorhouse, where you feel you want to hide away forever. For pleasure. For luxury. For the beauty of the 16th century stones and the warm water in the swimming pool. If you get one of the pastel rooms with a view of the grounds (a miniature garden), you won't want to leave. Trust seems to be the motto around here. If you're thirsty, they'll tell you to help yourself from the bar and just let them know the next day what you had. Doubles with shower/wc or bath 260–350F. Unbelievable! They even have a suite in the tower that sleeps four for 460F.

VILLARD-DE-LANS 38250

10% ☗ VILLA PRIMEROSE**

147 av. des Bains.
☎ 04.76.95.13.17
Closed Nov–mid Dec. **Car park.**

Here's a place where you're really made to feel at home! A very beautiful old house with quiet rooms that look out onto the Gerbier mountain range. Expect to pay 140–250F for a room for 1–3 people, depending on the season and the facilities. There's a kitchen you can use on the landing. Breakfast 35F (buffet in season).

10% ☗ |●| À LA FERME DU BOIS BARBU**

How to get there: it's 3km from the centre in the direction of Bois-Barbu.
☎ 04.76.95.13.09 F➜ 04.76.94.10.65
Restaurant closed Wednesdays and Sunday evenings end of March–end of June. **Closed** last week of June and Oct–Nov. **Secure parking.**

A real mountain inn on the edge of a forest. Relax in a nice comfy armchair while Nadine, your hostess, plays the piano. Small rooms from 250F with shower/wc. Ideal for cross-country skiers since the trails are just nearby. As for the food, give in to the temptation of the trout *au bleu*, the home-made *caillettes* (pork and vegetable faggots) and the honey pastries. Set meals 80–150F.

10% ☗ HÔTEL LE DAUPHIN***

220 av. du Général-de-Gaulle; it's opposite the tourist office.
☎ 04.76.95.95.25 F➜ 04.76.95.56.33
Car park. TV.

A nice hotel with a homely atmosphere (or so the brochure says, and for once it's got it right!) up in the mountains. Grandads and teenagers alike will have a great time under the indulgent eye of the lady of the house, who makes a real fuss of all her guests. The rooms (300–350F) are all quiet and some of them have a view of the pine trees. Arrangements can be made for you to have half-board (275–298F) but no-one's going to force you into it, not even the owner!

CORRENÇON-EN-VERCORS 38250 (5.5KM S)

10% ☗ |●| HÔTEL LES CLARINES**

Centre.
☎ 04.76.95.81.81 F➜ 04.76.95.84.98
Closed Tuesdays (out of season), April 15–May 15, and Oct 5–Dec 15. **Car park. TV.**

Service to 2pm lunchtimes and 9pm evenings. As you would expect, after 50 years, this family hotel is showing signs of wear and tear. But the atmosphere is still great, even if the dining room does remind you of an old guesthouse. Good set meal 92F (where rabbit is usually on the menu). The ones at 125F and 160F are a bit out of the ordinary. If you don't fancy them, go for a fondue or a house *tartiflette*. Beautiful terrace and swimming pool in pleasant surroundings. Very comfortable rooms 250–480F.

ENGINS 38360 (14KM N)

10% LE GRILL CAMPAGNARD

route de Villard-de-Lans; take the D531.
☎ 04.76.94.49.03
Car park.

This former coaching inn at a bend in the road is a marvellous place if you're willing to play the game. There's no set meal and no prices. It all depends on the mood Harika's in and the dishes the chef has had time to prepare. Harika has managed to recreate that old-fashioned atmosphere, full of wonderful aromas, pots of jam and bottles of preserves. The crockery is all made out of terracotta and the wines have got character. As a starter, you might be given a succulent *fromage de tête* (brawn) followed by eggs *à la gitane* (Harika comes from Istanbul), a wonderful *gratin* and *clafoutis*. Expect to pay 100–190F. But remember to book!

RENCUREL 38680 (17KM NW)

10% HÔTEL PERAZZI**

How to get there: take the D531 to La Balme-de-Rencurel, then the routes des Écouges on the right.
☎ 04.76.38.97.68 F 04.76.38.98.99
Closed Nov 1–May 1. **Car park**. **TV**.

A traditional Vercors house, where the Perazzi kids grew up before it was their turn to run the hotel. Cosy atmosphere whether you're sitting next to the fireplace in winter or sitting out on the terrace in summer (which is a bit like the village square since everyone eventually passes by). Good old comfortable rooms 130–270F. The restaurant does a regional set meal of salad, trout, *gratin*, cream cheese, and dessert) for 85F, while for 110F and 150F you have a choice of starters from a buffet and the famous trout (plus baron of lamb with herbs if you've gone for the most expensive set meal). Swimming pool, sauna, fishing – what more could you want!

VILLARS-LES-DOMBES 01330

AUBERGE LES BICHONNIÈRES**

Ambérieux-en-Dombes; take the D904.
☎ 04.74.00.82.07 F 04.74.00.89.61
Closed Monday lunchtimes in season, Sunday evenings, Mondays Oct–June, and Christmas–New Year.
Car park.

The inn is just the right distance away from the road. The rooms look out on to the yard full of trees and flowers, so you're guaranteed a bit of peace and quiet. And, as a bonus, you can wake up to the sounds of little birds singing. Regional-style furniture and not bad taste in décor. Doubles 250–320F with shower/wc. When the weather's nice, you can sit out on the patio and dine. *Cassolette* of frog's legs with parsley, *foie gras* of duck with walnuts – you're right to feel tempted, it is as good as it sounds. Set meals at 98F, 130F, 185F and 250F. If the welcome was a bit more up to scratch, it really would be the ideal place to stay if you wanted to explore the superb, slightly mysterious region of Dombes, full of ponds, birds and fishermen.

RESTAURANT L'ÉCU DE FRANCE

rue du Commerce (Centre); it's on the main street, next to the church.
☎ 04.74.98.01.79 F 04.74.98.27.77
Closed Tuesday evenings, Wednesdays and Jan.

The bird sanctuary and the fact that it's pretty central in Dombes make Villars a popular tourist spot. As a result, the restaurants and the hotels there are slightly more expensive. But *L'Écu de France* is still affordable. The rustic dining room offers regional specialities including frog's legs, of course, and fillet of carp. Friendly welcome. Set meals 100–200F.

VILLEFRANCHE-SUR-SAÔNE 69400

AU VIEUX SAINT-PIERRE

16 place d'Oran; head for Mâcon as you leave town, take rue Roncevaux, and turn right towards the square.
☎ 04.74.68.34.94
Closed Sundays.

In the summer, it's a real treat to sit outside and have something to eat under the trees on the square, a stone's throw from the town centre. It would be a shame if the complaints of a few people who live nearby who don't like to see their town liven up a little actually forced this lovely place shut down. You can get set meals for 70F, 90F or 110F with good local produce, all meticulously prepared and served with a smile. Try the fillet of John Dory with the chef's special sauce. The inside of the restaurant is more conventional but it's still very pleasant.

L'ÉPICERIE

55 rue de Thizy (Centre).
☎ 04.74.62.04.04 F 04.74.68.86.60
Closed Sundays and August.

Service noon–2.30pm and 7.30pm–11.30pm. Although the location isn't particularly good, this bistro (in the style of a Lyons café), with its wooden tables and chairs, certainly knows how to satisfy your appetite and make you feel relaxed. The surroundings — an old grocery with its original tiled floors and atmosphere — are nice, and the set meals at 65F (lunchtimes), 89F (evenings) are quite good as well, featuring *terrine*, stuffed tomatoes, cream cheese, house dessert. There are lots of salads and Lyons-type specialities à la carte, as well there might be, but in season they also have seafood, for a bit of a change. If you're still in need of a pick-me-up, then there's a piano bar called *Nel's Pub* that's owned by the same people. Turn right on your way out.

LE JULIENAS

236 rue d'Anse; go back up the main street, near the town exit in the direction of Lyons.
☎ 04.74.09.16.55
Closed Saturday lunchtimes and Sundays, as well as 3 weeks in Aug, Christmas and Jan 1.

A modern bistro that's a bit too clean and well cared for, but it makes a change from the others around that have stopped trying or have let themselves go. On the 80F set meal, served weekday lunchtimes and evenings, you'll get good authentic traditional food like sausages, rack of pork with tarragon or *andouillette,* cream cheese, and dessert. The more expensive set meals, at 110F and 150F, are definitely worth trying, especially if someone else is paying. The wine list is full of temptation and the bill can soon mount up, even if you choose the Beaujolais.

LIERGUES 69400 (5KM SW)

AUBERGE DE LIERGUES

Centre; take the D35, in the direction of Tarare.
☎ 04.74.68.07.02 F 04.74.68.07.02
Closed Tuesday evenings, Wednesdays and the second fortnight in Aug.

Service noon–2pn and 7pm–8.30pm. The welcome you get here makes a nice change. The owner likes to have a good laugh and will insist on you having a glass of Beaujolais. How could you resist a place like this where there are more local wine-growers about than tourists (which is definitely not a bad thing!). There's a good set meal (65F) weekday lunchtimes with *terrine,* braised ham, cheese, and dessert. The others are 58F, 120F and 160F. There's lots of specialities typical of Lyons, but they also do game in season. Eat in the bistro with its wooden tables rather than in the dining room on the first floor with pink tablecloths.

MARCY-SUR-ANSE 69480 (10KM SW)

LE TÉLÉGRAPHE

How to get there: take the D39 (in the direction of Tarare), then the D70, turn right at the Lachassagne exit.
☎ 04.74.60.24.73
Closed Sunday evenings and Mondays. **Car park**.

Service from 12.15pm, then from 7.15pm. The 90F set meal is an absolute must, with the salad *beaujolais* and the rare skirt of Charolais beef, or you could go for the one at 120F. As a starter, try the *'bouquet de salade des pierres dorées'*. It's a kind of mixed salad that we love, with black pudding, *andouillette* and cheese. You could then order the duck with green peppercorns. Great desserts, beautiful terrace with lots of local colour. Even without going overboard on the Beaujolais you'll think that life is wonderful and the village and the signalling tower superb.

ALIX 69380 (13KM SW)

LE VIEUX MOULIN

How to get there: take the D39 and, before you get to the D38, turn left.
☎ 04.78.43.91.66 F 04.78.47.98.46
Closed Mondays, Tuesdays, Aug 16–start Sept.
Car park.

Service to 1.15pm, then to 9.15pm. Yet another mill that has your heart skipping a beat and makes you want to break into song! It's been converted into three little rooms full of cosy little corners for couples, and 'the barn' for families or large groups. People come from all over to try the frog's legs, the *andouillette* and the roast guinea fowl in the set meals from 110F to 175F, both of which will fill you up a treat. Afterwards you could have a game of bowls or relax on the terrace, listening to Annie Umhauer, the owner, who likes to talk about her problems (it's not that she's a moaner, she just likes to gossip!).

THEIZÉ 69620 (15KM W)

10% 🏠 |●| HÔTEL-RESTAURANT LE THEIZEROT*

Centre; take the D39, cross the D38 and go in the direction of Oingt.
☎ 04.74.71.22.26
Restaurant closed Monday evenings, Wednesdays and Sunday evenings. **Car park**.

A backpacker's paradise – they don't mind if you take your packed lunch out of your rucksack and tuck in. This is an old village café, where you really do feel at home. The young owners have even got one room set aside for kids, in case they want to have a nap. Adults pay about 110–120F. It's not the height of luxury by any means but it's ideal if you've gone one mile too far on your bike or walked through one vineyard too many. You'll get a warm welcome and it's not expensive. Set meals 70F (weekday lunchtimes)–125F. Regional set meal 95F.

SARCEY 69490 (17KM SW)

🏠 |●| LE CHATARD**

place du Bon-Coin; take the D39 to Pont-Nizy, then the D38; turn left after about 2km.
☎ 04.74.26.85.85 F➔ 04.74.26.89.99
Closed Jan 1–15. **Car park**. **TV**. **Canal+**.

This is a good hotel-restaurant, where you'll find tourists attracted by the swimming pool and the peacefulness of the place, as well as businessmen and local families attracted by the prices and the top-quality set meals. They're 85F for residents, 110F for the country meal with bacon salad and *blanquettte* of veal, 146F for the businessman's meal, and 186F for the regional meal. The rooms may be lacking in charm but they've got all mod cons. You'll pay 200–360F.

VAUX-EN-BEAUJOLAIS 69460 (17KM NW)

10% |●| AUBERGE DE CLOCHEMERLE

rue Gabriel-Chevallier; take the D43 in the direction of Odenas; at Saint-Étienne-des-Oullières, take a left turn, in the direction of Vaux.
☎ 04.74.03.20.16 F➔ 04.74.03.28.48
Closed Tuesdays, Wednesdays, 2 weeks in Feb and 2 weeks in Aug. **TV**. **Disabled access**.

This is the only village in France where people come from far and wide to see.. the street urinal. This place inspired Gabriel Chevallier to write his famous novel, and truly deserves to have an inn named after. For those on a budget, a *manchon* — cooked ham, omelette, cream cheese — is served daily. It costs 69F and includes a quarter litre of local Beaujolais and coffee. The *vigneron* set meal is 95F, and there are others up to 360F. Lovely shaded terrace for the summer.

VIVIERS 07220

|●| RESTAURANT CARPE DIEM

place de la Roubine; from the tourist office, take the street which leads down to the Rhône.
☎ 04.75.52.79.43
Closed Tuesdays out of season (except public holidays).

This gourmet restaurant is teeming with seafood specialities. The *millefeuille* of plaice with orange butter and the steamed cod with fresh herbs are both skilfully prepared by the chef. Main courses à la carte are around 100F. Weekday set meal 85F, others 125F, 160F and 210F. Good varied wine list. Courteous welcome. In summer, the huge plane trees and a nearby fountain provide welcome relief from the heat; it's a bit expensive but good.

VALVIGNÈRES 07400 (12KM W)

10% 🏠 |●| LA TOUR CASSÉE

How to get there: from Viviers, take the D107 to Saint-Thomé, then the D210 to Valvignères.
☎ 04.75.52.62.56
Closed Wednesday evenings and Thursdays (except July–Aug).

Service from noon, then from 7.30pm. Fabienne Le Moal welcomes you with open arms. The rooms are simple – they've only got a basin and the shower/wc are on the landing. But the prices are unbeatable (130F for a night) and the bedding is all top-quality. Breakfast only 25F! Half-board (not compulsory) 190F. The restaurant does good food. The lounge, with its old wooden chairs and tables, has a charming retro atmosphere to it. Set meals at 60F, 90F, 105F and 125F. We had a slight preference for the regional set meal since the chef's *bombine* (stew of pork, potatoes and carrots) is excellent. Good home-made desserts. In the summer, there's a lovely terrace. A good place, which is worth a visit both for the warm welcome you get and for the wonderful food.

VOIRON 38500

|●| RESTAURANT LE BOIS JOLI

la Tivollière; in the direction of Chambery, about 2km on, turn left.
☎ 04.76.05.22.25 F➜ 04.76.66.10.79
Closed Mondays out of season, Tuesdays, and the first three weeks in January. **Car park. Disabled access.**

Service noon–2pm and 7pm–9pm (10pm in the summer). Tasty, hearty cooking, which ranges from the traditional *gratin dauphinois* to the ubiquitous home-made chocolate mousse, but also includes more unusual dishes like kid with morels and veal kidneys with a madeira sauce. There is a veranda which is great to sit and relax on while you look out at the countryside. Set meals 55F (weekdays)–155F.

SAINT-NICOLAS-DE-MACHERIN 38500 (9KM N)

|●| LA PETITE BOUFFE

How to get there: take the D520, then the D49.
☎ 04.76.06.00.84 F➜ 04.76.55.35.40
Closed Mondays and Sept 15–May 20. **Car park.**

This is an authentic country restaurant, with a little bit of madness thrown in for good measure. Amuse yourself counting the 600 or so radios dotted about all over the place including the big dining room with its naive paintings and the swimming pool which is actually on the second floor (go up by lift!). You usually get popular dance music on in the background. Service with a smile. Great food, which is primarily based on regional produce with a few exotic touches here and there. The set meal at 96F offers succulent *marbré* of chicken and rabbit, lamb, cream cheese. There's also one at 118F.

CHARAVINES-LES-BAINS 38850 (13KM NW)

10% ⌂ |●| HÔTEL-RESTAURANT BEAU RIVAGE**

le bord du lac (West).
☎ 04.76.06.61.08 F➜ 04.76.06.66.58
Closed Sunday evenings, Mondays out of season, and Jan. **Secure parking. TV. Disabled access.**

Service noon–2pm and 7.30pm–9pm. In winter you get a panoramic view from the dining room and in summer a magnificent view from the terrace of the Paladru lake. The kids can even go in for a swim under the watchful eyes of Mum and Dad. The rooms are very pleasant and the hearty, no-frills food is good value for money. Cheapest set meal 80F. Doubles 260F (with shower/wc) and 280F (with bath).

MONTFERRAT 38620 (13KM N)

|●| AUBERGE FÉFETTE

Le Vernay (North); it's on the hilltops, about 4km from the lake.
☎ 04.76.32.40.46
Closed Tuesdays. **Car park.**

OK, so you don't get such a great view here, but what you can enjoy here is the intimacy of it all, despite the nearby presence of the local night club, *Roxane*. This is a place where you'll really feel at home and if you're staying at the hotel you'll get in free and receive an aperitif on the house. You've got to come here for dinner. The delicacy of the dishes makes up for the fact that you've no longer got a view of the lake and that the salad *bressane* and the escalope of *foie gras* of duck with raspberries are not exactly regional specialities - and at 70f, who cares? It really is a little paradise —the lovely cook, who has never forgotten her south-western roots and her husband out front, unruffled behind his bow tie. Great set meals at 110F (salad *landaise* — with goose fat, garlic, pine kernels - fillet of trout with watercress, house dessert) and at 150F (salad with scallops and pan-fried chanterelles and boned rack of lamb with thyme, for example.

VONNAS 01540

|●| L'ANCIENNE AUBERGE

place du Marché.
☎ 04.74.50.90.50 F➜ 04.74.50.08.80
Closed Jan 5–Feb 13.

Service to 2.30pm, then to 10pm. Vonnas is known as 'Blanc-City' — the name of the famous chef gets everywhere. The inn is opposite a little wooden romantic bridge, which crosses the Veyle, and you can still see a beautifully written inscription on the front from the days when it was *Café-restaurant Blanc aîné*. It's an old family inn, where Georges Blanc apparently first developed his amazing passion for cooking. It dates back to 1872, but has since been restored, so it still looks virtually the same. Georges Blanc may not be in the kitchen any more but he's definitely watching over the smooth running of the house, which is now the responsibility of Isabelle Blanc (it's staying in the family). There may not be quite the same kind of atmosphere or food that was around in the past but the set meals still pay homage to the restaurant's history. The recipes and produce used remains true to the region: country *terrine*, sautéd frog's legs, chicken livers mixed with *foie gras*, eggs, and cream, and *poulet de Bresse* with pilau rice. And the prices are reasonable, the cheapest set meal (weekdays only) is still less than 100F, and the set meal at 160F is simply amazing. Charming welcome and friendly service.

Index

A

B

C

N

O

P

Q

R

S